D1095547

The New International Dictionary of New Testament Theology

The New International Dictionary of

Volume 4: Indexes

New Testament Theology

Colin Brown
GENERAL EDITOR

Translated, with additions and revisions, from the German
THEOLOGISCHES BEGRIFFSLEXIKON
ZUM NEUEN TESTAMENT

Edited by Lothar Coenen, Erich Beyreuther *and* Hans Bietenhard
General Index Compiled by Norman Hillyer
Scripture Index and Index to Extrabiblical Literature Compiled by
David Townsley and Russell Bjork

ZondervanPublishingHouse
Grand Rapids, Michigan

A Division of HarperCollins*Publishers*

THE NEW INTERNATIONAL DICTIONARY OF NEW TESTAMENT THEOLOGY

Originally published in German under the title:
THEOLOGISHES BEGRIFFSLEXIKON ZUM NEUEN TESTAMENT

© 1967, 1969, 1971 by Theologisher Verlag Rolf Brockhaus, Wuppertal.
English Language edition volume 4 copyright © 1978, 1986, The Zondervan
Corporation, Grand Rapids, Michigan, U.S.A., and The Paternoster Press,
Ltd. Exeter, Devon, U.K.

Requests for information should be addressed to:
Zondervan Publishing House
Academic and Professional Books
Grand Rapids, Michigan 49530

Library of Congress Cataloging in Publication Data
Main entry under title:
    The new international dictionary of New Testament theology

    "Translated, with additions and revisions, from the German *Theologishes
Begriffslexikon zum Neuen Testament,* edited by Lothar Coenen, Erich
Beyreuther and Hans Bietenhard."
    "Companion volume: The new international dictionary of the Christian
Church."
    Includes bibliographical references and indexes.
    1. Bible   N.T.—Theology—Dictionaries.   2. Bible.
N.T.—Dictionaries.   I. Brown, Colin.
BS2397.N48   230'.03   75-38895

ISBN 0–310–33230–3 (vol. 4)

ISBN 0–310–33238–9 (4 volume set)

Printed in the United States of America

    94 95 96 / AM / 10 9 8

This edition is printed on acid-free paper and meets the American
National Standards Institute Z39.48 standard.

Contents

INTRODUCTION 7

SCRIPTURE INDEX 11

INDEX OF EXTRABIBLICAL LITERATURE 267

INDEX OF HEBREW AND ARAMAIC WORDS 323

INDEX OF GREEK WORDS 339

GENERAL INDEX 383

ERRATA 591

Introduction

The *Scripture Index* was intended from the outset to be as inclusive as possible. For that reason, the reader should not expect to find a substantive discussion of a given passage every time that passage is cited. Secondary citations can, however, lead the reader to discussions of related passages and provide many "fresh trails."

The *Index to Selected Extrabiblical Literature* also opens the way for the serious reader to benefit from the wealth of background and illustrative material so important to a proper understanding and appreciation of the New Testament. Used in conjunction with the *Scripture Index,* it can provide yet another way of cross-referencing related Scripture passages. Used alone, it facilitates the study of the extrabiblical literature in its own right.

In certain Old Testament passages, the verse numbers of the English versions differ from those of the Septuagint (LXX) and/or the Hebrew Masoretic text. An asterisk (*) following a reference indicates that such a numbering variation was noted in one or more of the articles citing the passage. The asterisks are included as a reminder to the reader that the pursuit of a given verse will be affected at these points, depending upon whether an English or an ancient language text is being consulted.

The preparation of the *Scripture Index* has brought to light a number of citation errors. The *Index* lists the corrected citations. A dagger (†) following an entry alerts the reader to check the Errata on pages 319–20, since on one or more of the pages given for that entry an incorrect reference will be found.

Scripture Index

Old Testament

Genesis

1–11	**Vol. 1:** 209
1	**Vol. 1:** 76, 211, 379, 383, 630 **Vol. 2:** 691, 889 **Vol. 3:** 851, 980, 1087, 1100, 1105
1:1 ff	**Vol. 2:** 564, 690 **Vol. 3:** 502
1:1–2:4a	**Vol. 1:** 522 **Vol. 3:** 1153
1:1–2:3	**Vol. 3:** 406
1:1	**Vol. 1:** 380 **Vol. 2:** 70, 190 **Vol. 3:** 1115
1:2	**Vol. 1:** 175, 180, 422 **Vol. 2:** 197, 205 **Vol. 3:** 691, 707, 983, 990, 1177
1:3 ff	**Vol. 2:** 491
1:3–5	**Vol. 1:** 379
1:3	**Vol. 2:** 494, 672, 834
1:4 f	**Vol. 1:** 422
1:5–2:2	**Vol. 2:** 887
1:5	**Vol. 1:** 272 **Vol. 2:** 887, 889
1:6 ff	**Vol. 1:** 523
1:6 f	**Vol. 2:** 613
1:6–8	**Vol. 3:** 1177
1:6	**Vol. 3:** 990
1:7	**Vol. 1:** 379, 523 **Vol. 3:** 984
1:8 f	**Vol. 1:** 272
1:8	**Vol. 2:** 189, 889
1:9 f	**Vol. 3:** 983
1:9	**Vol. 1:** 296, 515 **Vol. 2:** 720 **Vol. 3:** 983, 990
1:11 ff	**Vol. 3:** 524
1:11 f	**Vol. 2:** 502
1:11	**Vol. 1:** 389 **Vol. 2:** 211
1:13 f	**Vol. 2:** 889
1:14 ff	**Vol. 1:** 380 **Vol. 2:** 491
1:14 f	**Vol. 1:** 523
1:14	**Vol. 2:** 189 **Vol. 3:** 835
1:16	**Vol. 1:** 165 **Vol. 2:** 428, 491, 889 **Vol. 3:** 730, 734
1:17	**Vol. 1:** 523 **Vol. 2:** 430
1:18 f	**Vol. 2:** 889
1:18	**Vol. 1:** 165, 422 **Vol. 2:** 99
1:20	**Vol. 3:** 680
1:21	**Vol. 1:** 172, 670
1:22	**Vol. 1:** 211, 732 **Vol. 2:** 128
1:23	**Vol. 2:** 889
1:24 f	**Vol. 1:** 113
1:26 ff	**Vol. 2:** 576
1:26 f	**Vol. 2:** 160–161, 287 **Vol. 3:** 1056
1:26	**Vol. 1:** 522, 670 **Vol. 2:** 189, 287, 498, 502, 505, 564
1:26a	**Vol. 3:** 1056
1:27 f	**Vol. 2:** 576 **Vol. 3:** 1056
1:27	**Vol. 1:** 85, 87, 166, 380 **Vol. 2:** 563, 569–570, 579 **Vol. 3:** 181, 539, 980
1:27a	**Vol. 2:** 564
1:27b	**Vol. 3:** 1056
1:27c	**Vol. 1:** 383
1:28	**Vol. 1:** 180, 211, 288, 522, 560, 617, 732, 734 **Vol. 2:** 128, 564, 576
1:29 f	**Vol. 2:** 268
1:29	**Vol. 1:** 743 **Vol. 2:** 268
1:30	**Vol. 2:** 268
1:31	**Vol. 1:** 523 **Vol. 2:** 103, 889
2 f	**Vol. 1:** 84, 87 **Vol. 3:** 585
2	**Vol. 1:** 379, 383, 434 **Vol. 2:** 564, 761 **Vol. 3:** 980, 1063
2:1	**Vol. 1:** 522 **Vol. 2:** 189 **Vol. 3:** 410
2:2 f	**Vol. 3:** 255–256, 405, 1148
2:2–4a	**Vol. 2:** 889
2:2	**Vol. 2:** 690, 697 **Vol. 3:** 257, 410
2:3	**Vol. 1:** 211 **Vol. 3:** 94, 215
2:4	**Vol. 1:** 181–182, 678 **Vol. 2:** 70 **Vol. 3:** 656
2:4b–3:24	**Vol. 2:** 889
2:4b–25	**Vol. 1:** 522
2:4b	**Vol. 1:** 72 **Vol. 2:** 564, 889
2:5	**Vol. 1:** 743
2:6	**Vol. 1:** 585
2:7 ff	**Vol. 2:** 564
2:7	**Vol. 1:** 85, 520, 665 **Vol. 2:** 478, 564–565, 787 **Vol. 3:** 269, 680, 683–684, 703, 707, 915
2:8	**Vol. 2:** 761
2:9–17	**Vol. 2:** 482
2:9	**Vol. 1:** 389, 562 **Vol. 2:** 268
2:10 ff	**Vol. 2:** 689
2:10–14	**Vol. 2:** 761 **Vol. 3:** 986–988
2:10	**Vol. 1:** 165
2:11 f	**Vol. 2:** 95
2:11	**Vol. 2:** 720
2:13 f	**Vol. 3:** 215
2:15	**Vol. 1:** 522 **Vol. 3:** 1148
2:16 f	**Vol. 2:** 564
2:16	**Vol. 1:** 332 **Vol. 2:** 268 **Vol. 3:** 215
2:17	**Vol. 2:** 103, 272, 478, 889 **Vol. 3:** 578
2:18 ff	**Vol. 2:** 161, 540, 564
2:18–25	**Vol. 1:** 87 **Vol. 3:** 1056
2:18–24	**Vol. 2:** 576
2:18	**Vol. 1:** 385 **Vol. 2:** 103, 724 **Vol. 3:** 539, 542, 1056
2:18b	**Vol. 2:** 576

Genesis *(cont'd)*

2:19 f	**Vol. 2:** 649
2:19	**Vol. 1:** 272, 522
2:20	**Vol. 1:** 84
2:21 ff	**Vol. 2:** 160, 213 **Vol. 3:** 1056
2:21–24	**Vol. 3:** 1056
2:21	**Vol. 1:** 672
2:23 f	**Vol. 2:** 576
2:23	**Vol. 1:** 241, 672 **Vol. 2:** 395
2:24	**Vol. 2:** 349, 564, 570, 579, 722 **Vol. 3:** 181, 251, 329, 505, 534–535, 538–539, 1064, 1069–1070
2:25	**Vol. 3:** 563
3	**Vol. 1:** 78, 86–87, 434, 508–510 **Vol. 2:** 459, 478, 576, 761, 763 **Vol. 3:** 472, 578
3:1 ff	**Vol. 3:** 801
3:1	**Vol. 1:** 168, 510 **Vol. 2:** 616
3:2 f	**Vol. 2:** 271
3:3	**Vol. 3:** 860
3:4	**Vol. 2:** 116 **Vol. 3:** 892
3:5 f	**Vol. 2:** 103 **Vol. 3:** 186
3:5	**Vol. 1:** 76, 562, 565 **Vol. 2:** 99, 498, 729 **Vol. 3:** 892
3:6	**Vol. 2:** 272
3:7	**Vol. 1:** 85, 723 **Vol. 2:** 268, 395, 729 **Vol. 3:** 563
3:8	**Vol. 2:** 214–215 **Vol. 3:** 514, 846, 943
3:10	**Vol. 2:** 214–215 **Vol. 3:** 943
3:13	**Vol. 2:** 458
3:14 f	**Vol. 1:** 113, 168, 208
3:14	**Vol. 1:** 209 **Vol. 2:** 889
3:15	**Vol. 1:** 85, 241 **Vol. 2:** 132 **Vol. 3:** 522
3:16 ff	**Vol. 2:** 420
3:16	**Vol. 1:** 85, 187, 288 **Vol. 2:** 157, 446, 562
3:17 ff	**Vol. 3:** 256, 1148
3:17	**Vol. 1:** 84, 209, 285 **Vol. 2:** 173, 272, 423, 889
3:18	**Vol. 1:** 725–726, 743
3:19	**Vol. 1:** 433 **Vol. 2:** 478, 564 **Vol. 3:** 261, 915
3:20	**Vol. 1:** 87 **Vol. 2:** 649
3:21	**Vol. 1:** 84, 314, 316
3:22	**Vol. 1:** 562, 565 **Vol. 2:** 103 **Vol. 3:** 866
3:24	**Vol. 1:** 101, 280, 453 **Vol. 3:** 395, 866
4	**Vol. 3:** 82, 578
4:1	**Vol. 1:** 87, 343 **Vol. 2:** 395, 649
4:3 ff	**Vol. 3:** 421
4:3–10	**Vol. 3:** 434
4:3–8	**Vol. 3:** 942
4:3	**Vol. 3:** 421
4:4 f	**Vol. 3:** 425
4:4	**Vol. 2:** 41 **Vol. 3:** 425
4:5	**Vol. 1:** 585
4:6 f	**Vol. 3:** 421–422
4:7	**Vol. 1:** 76 **Vol. 3:** 351
4:8 ff	**Vol. 1:** 255
4:8 f	**Vol. 3:** 422
4:8	**Vol. 1:** 181, 429 **Vol. 3:** 430
4:9 ff	**Vol. 2:** 363
4:10 f	**Vol. 2:** 525
4:10	**Vol. 1:** 225, 410 **Vol. 3:** 393, 436, 1014
4:11 f	**Vol. 1:** 209
4:11	**Vol. 1:** 208–209
4:12	**Vol. 3:** 1148
4:13	**Vol. 2:** 138 **Vol. 3:** 574
4:14	**Vol. 2:** 887 **Vol. 3:** 614
4:15	**Vol. 2:** 572, 626, 690 **Vol. 3:** 93
4:16	**Vol. 1:** 321
4:17	**Vol. 1:** 343 **Vol. 2:** 802
4:19	**Vol. 3:** 747
4:22	**Vol. 2:** 97
4:23 f	**Vol. 3:** 578
4:23	**Vol. 2:** 173 **Vol. 3:** 1208
4:24	**Vol. 2:** 697, 770
4:25	**Vol. 1:** 84 **Vol. 3:** 522
4:26	**Vol. 1:** 272, 451 **Vol. 2:** 650
5	**Vol. 1:** 65, 208 **Vol. 2:** 576, 698 **Vol. 3:** 264, 653, 851
5:1 ff	**Vol. 2:** 287
5:1	**Vol. 1:** 181–182, 244 **Vol. 2:** 287 **Vol. 3:** 656
5:2–5	**Vol. 1:** 84
5:2	**Vol. 2:** 569 **Vol. 3:** 539, 1056
5:3	**Vol. 2:** 287
5:18	**Vol. 1:** 531
5:21–24	**Vol. 3:** 264, 266
5:22–24	**Vol. 3:** 615
5:22	**Vol. 2:** 815
5:24	**Vol. 2:** 191, 627, 815, 817 **Vol. 3:** 261–262, 558, 602–603
5:28 f	**Vol. 2:** 681
5:29	**Vol. 1:** 209 **Vol. 2:** 681 **Vol. 3:** 1148
6–9	**Vol. 3:** 578
6–8	**Vol. 3:** 983, 989
6:1 ff	**Vol. 2:** 213, 458 **Vol. 3:** 468, 579
6:1–8:22	**Vol. 3:** 203
6:1–6	**Vol. 1:** 102
6:1–4	**Vol. 1:** 451–452
6:1	**Vol. 1:** 164
6:2	**Vol. 1:** 537 **Vol. 2:** 161 **Vol. 3:** 636
6:3	**Vol. 1:** 679 **Vol. 2:** 478, 887 **Vol. 3:** 705, 828
6:4	**Vol. 3:** 636, 828
6:5	**Vol. 1:** 184, 732 **Vol. 3:** 578
6:6	**Vol. 2:** 103
6:7	**Vol. 2:** 189 **Vol. 3:** 1153
6:8	**Vol. 2:** 117, 681
6:9	**Vol. 1:** 182 **Vol. 2:** 60, 62, 681–682, 815
6:11 f	**Vol. 3:** 578
6:11–9:19	**Vol. 2:** 681
6:11	**Vol. 1:** 468
6:13	**Vol. 2:** 477
6:14	**Vol. 1:** 389
6:15*	**Vol. 2:** 199 **Vol. 3:** 851

Genesis (*cont'd*)

6:17 ff	**Vol. 1:** 672
6:17	**Vol. 3:** 991
6:18	**Vol. 1:** 366
6:19 f	**Vol. 2:** 569
6:22	**Vol. 1:** 332 **Vol. 2:** 682
7:1	**Vol. 2:** 36, 681
7:2 f	**Vol. 2:** 569
7:4 ff	**Vol. 2:** 689
7:4	**Vol. 1:** 420 **Vol. 2:** 696
7:9	**Vol. 2:** 569
7:11 f	**Vol. 3:** 982
7:11	**Vol. 1:** 523 **Vol. 2:** 189 **Vol. 3:** 983
7:11a	**Vol. 2:** 726
7:11b	**Vol. 2:** 726
7:15 f	**Vol. 2:** 569
7:23	**Vol. 1:** 471 **Vol. 3:** 248
8:1	**Vol. 3:** 232, 235, 239, 690
8:2	**Vol. 3:** 983
8:5	**Vol. 2:** 157, 720
8:6–12	**Vol. 1:** 173
8:6	**Vol. 2:** 696
8:7	**Vol. 1:** 515
8:9	**Vol. 3:** 255
8:13	**Vol. 3:** 310
8:20 ff	**Vol. 3:** 150, 425
8:20	**Vol. 1:** 172 **Vol. 3:** 33, 418
8:21 f	**Vol. 1:** 640 **Vol. 2:** 117
8:21	**Vol. 1:** 50, 162, 184, 673 **Vol. 3:** 125, 578, 600–601
8:22	**Vol. 2:** 887 **Vol. 3:** 255
9:1–7	**Vol. 2:** 682
9:1	**Vol. 1:** 734 **Vol. 2:** 128
9:2	**Vol. 1:** 113, 670
9:3	**Vol. 2:** 268
9:4 ff	**Vol. 3:** 159
9:4 f	**Vol. 3:** 680
9:4	**Vol. 1:** 221 **Vol. 2:** 309, 477 **Vol. 3:** 150, 158
9:5	**Vol. 1:** 113, 221–222 **Vol. 3:** 158
9:6	**Vol. 2:** 287, 525, 532, 854 **Vol. 3:** 94, 159
9:7	**Vol. 1:** 180 **Vol. 2:** 128
9:8 ff	**Vol. 1:** 366 **Vol. 2:** 626
9:8–17	**Vol. 2:** 681
9:9	**Vol. 1:** 367 **Vol. 3:** 522
9:11 f	**Vol. 1:** 672
9:12	**Vol. 1:** 366
9:13	**Vol. 3:** 1002
9:15 f	**Vol. 3:** 235
9:19	**Vol. 2:** 34
9:20 f	**Vol. 3:** 918
9:20–27	**Vol. 3:** 919
9:20	**Vol. 2:** 681
9:21	**Vol. 1:** 513
9:22	**Vol. 3:** 45
9:24	**Vol. 2:** 675
9:25	**Vol. 1:** 209
9:26	**Vol. 1:** 208
10	**Vol. 2:** 690, 697, 791
10:5	**Vol. 1:** 472
10:6	**Vol. 1:** 530
10:8–12	**Vol. 1:** 140
10:9	**Vol. 1:** 140
10:11 f	**Vol. 2:** 679, 802
10:11	**Vol. 2:** 679
10:12	**Vol. 2:** 679
10:13	**Vol. 1:** 530
10:19	**Vol. 3:** 93
11–12	**Vol. 2:** 117
11	**Vol. 2:** 791 **Vol. 3:** 578, 653, 782
11:1 ff	**Vol. 1:** 209 **Vol. 2:** 363
11:1–9	**Vol. 1:** 77, 140
11:4 ff	**Vol. 2:** 189
11:4 f	**Vol. 2:** 802
11:4	**Vol. 2:** 34, 157 **Vol. 3:** 787
11:5	**Vol. 2:** 190
11:7	**Vol. 2:** 173 **Vol. 3:** 1079
11:8	**Vol. 2:** 802
11:9	**Vol. 2:** 649
11:10 ff	**Vol. 1:** 208
11:10–30	**Vol. 3:** 851
11:10	**Vol. 1:** 182
11:27–25:11*	**Vol. 1:** 76
11:30	**Vol. 1:** 285
11:31 ff	**Vol. 3:** 241
11:31	**Vol. 2:** 584
11:32	**Vol. 3:** 464
12–50	**Vol. 1:** 65
12–36	**Vol. 1:** 207
12	**Vol. 1:** 210 **Vol. 3:** 464
12:1–8	**Vol. 2:** 180
12:1–3	**Vol. 1:** 53, 80–81, 208–209 **Vol. 3:** 69
12:1	**Vol. 1:** 208 **Vol. 3:** 569
12:2–3	**Vol. 1:** 209
12:2	**Vol. 1:** 209, 411 **Vol. 3:** 740
12:3	**Vol. 1:** 76, 416, 640–641, 695 **Vol. 2:** 794 **Vol. 3:** 69, 329, 491, 871, 1012, 1112
12:3b	**Vol. 1:** 209, 214
12:4 f	**Vol. 3:** 946
12:6 ff	**Vol. 3:** 418
12:6	**Vol. 3:** 786
12:7	**Vol. 2:** 317 **Vol. 3:** 464, 523
12:8	**Vol. 1:** 76, 531, 606 **Vol. 2:** 650 **Vol. 3:** 425, 811
12:10–13:1	**Vol. 1:** 531
12:10–20	**Vol. 1:** 80
12:10	**Vol. 1:** 691 **Vol. 2:** 265
12:13	**Vol. 1:** 255
12:14	**Vol. 2:** 103
12:15 ff	**Vol. 1:** 452
12:15	**Vol. 1:** 99, 165 **Vol. 3:** 816–817
12:16	**Vol. 1:** 415
12:18	**Vol. 3:** 45
13:2	**Vol. 2:** 841
13:3–4	**Vol. 1:** 531
13:3	**Vol. 3:** 811
13:4	**Vol. 1:** 272 **Vol. 3:** 425

Genesis *(cont'd)*

13:6	**Vol. 2:** 845
13:10	**Vol. 2:** 761 **Vol. 3:** 93
13:11	**Vol. 1:** 537
13:12 f	**Vol. 3:** 93
13:13	**Vol. 1:** 565
13:14–17	**Vol. 1:** 76
13:15	**Vol. 2:** 317, 431 **Vol. 3:** 740, 828
13:16	**Vol. 2:** 317
13:18	**Vol. 3:** 418
14	**Vol. 2:** 36 **Vol. 3:** 460, 959
14:3	**Vol. 3:** 983
14:4	**Vol. 1:** 606
14:8	**Vol. 3:** 93
14:10 ff	**Vol. 3:** 93
14:13	**Vol. 2:** 305
14:14	**Vol. 2:** 173
14:17 ff	**Vol. 3:** 41
14:17–20	**Vol. 2:** 694
14:18 ff	**Vol. 1:** 208, 619
14:18 f	**Vol. 2:** 199, 375
14:18–22	**Vol. 2:** 67
14:18–20	**Vol. 1:** 214 **Vol. 2:** 590–591
14:18	**Vol. 2:** 378, 592–593 **Vol. 3:** 36
14:19	**Vol. 1:** 380
14:20	**Vol. 2:** 591, 693 **Vol. 3:** 852
14:22	**Vol. 1:** 380 **Vol. 2:** 149
14:23	**Vol. 2:** 841
14:24	**Vol. 2:** 303
15	**Vol. 1:** 56, 210, 604 **Vol. 3:** 825
15:1	**Vol. 1:** 622 **Vol. 2:** 297 **Vol. 3:** 138, 140, 513, 626, 722, 1120
15:2 ff	**Vol. 1:** 76
15:2	**Vol. 1:** 506
15:4 ff	**Vol. 3:** 425
15:4	**Vol. 1:** 209
15:5	**Vol. 1:** 411, 732 **Vol. 3:** 522, 734
15:6	**Vol. 1:** 77–78, 596–597, 604 **Vol. 2:** 301 **Vol. 3:** 169, 362, 369–370, 490, 823–825, 1112, 1187
15:7	**Vol. 2:** 278
15:9 f	**Vol. 1:** 368
15:10	**Vol. 1:** 534 **Vol. 3:** 739
15:12–21	**Vol. 1:** 80
15:12	**Vol. 1:** 609
15:13 f	**Vol. 3:** 464
15:13–16	**Vol. 1:** 76, 367
15:13–14	**Vol. 1:** 531
15:13	**Vol. 1:** 684, 691 **Vol. 2:** 689
15:14	**Vol. 2:** 363, 425
15:15	**Vol. 1:** 433 **Vol. 2:** 148, 478, 777–778
15:16	**Vol. 1:** 734
15:17–21	**Vol. 2:** 317
15:17	**Vol. 1:** 655 **Vol. 2:** 485
15:18	**Vol. 1:** 76
16	**Vol. 1:** 531–532, 650 **Vol. 3:** 594
16:1 ff	**Vol. 2:** 576
16:1–16	**Vol. 1:** 81
16:1–14	**Vol. 1:** 80
16:1–6	**Vol. 3:** 1057
16:1–4	**Vol. 2:** 582
16:1 f	**Vol. 1:** 498 **Vol. 2:** 576
16:2	**Vol. 2:** 179
16:7–14	**Vol. 3:** 986
16:9	**Vol. 2:** 264
16:12	**Vol. 1:** 255
16:13	**Vol. 1:** 585 **Vol. 2:** 67
16:15	**Vol. 1:** 284 **Vol. 3:** 1014
17	**Vol. 1:** 76 **Vol. 3:** 69
17:1–14	**Vol. 1:** 308
17:1–13	**Vol. 3:** 594
17:1–8	**Vol. 2:** 317
17:1	**Vol. 2:** 67, 139, 278–279, 649–650, 815 **Vol. 3:** 729, 924
17:3	**Vol. 1:** 609
17:4 f	**Vol. 1:** 76
17:4	**Vol. 1:** 411
17:5	**Vol. 1:** 411, 477 **Vol. 2:** 649, 794
17:6	**Vol. 2:** 128
17:7 f	**Vol. 1:** 366 **Vol. 2:** 797
17:7	**Vol. 2:** 596 **Vol. 3:** 522–523, 740
17:8	**Vol. 1:** 691 **Vol. 3:** 522–523
17:9–14	**Vol. 1:** 159
17:10 ff	**Vol. 3:** 499
17:10–14	**Vol. 1:** 154
17:10	**Vol. 2:** 437
17:11 ff	**Vol. 1:** 672
17:11	**Vol. 2:** 626 **Vol. 3:** 499
17:12 f	**Vol. 3:** 608
17:12	**Vol. 1:** 308 **Vol. 2:** 692
17:14	**Vol. 1:** 308, 699 **Vol. 2:** 569
17:15	**Vol. 1:** 80
17:16	**Vol. 1:** 285
17:17–19	**Vol. 1:** 81
17:17	**Vol. 1:** 609 **Vol. 2:** 431, 435, 596, 627, 649
17:19	**Vol. 1:** 531 **Vol. 3:** 1067
17:20	**Vol. 2:** 128
17:23	**Vol. 2:** 569 **Vol. 3:** 835
17:26	**Vol. 3:** 835
17:27	**Vol. 3:** 594
18	**Vol. 1:** 101
18:1 ff	**Vol. 1:** 687, 706
18:1–15	**Vol. 1:** 76, 80
18:1	**Vol. 1:** 332 **Vol. 3:** 846
18:2	**Vol. 2:** 876
18:3	**Vol. 1:** 322, 690 **Vol. 3:** 528
18:4	**Vol. 1:** 153, 239
18:5	**Vol. 2:** 181
18:6	**Vol. 3:** 917
18:7	**Vol. 3:** 946
18:8	**Vol. 3:** 1012
18:10	**Vol. 1:** 209 **Vol. 3:** 835, 846
18:11–14	**Vol. 3:** 1067
18:11	**Vol. 1:** 194 **Vol. 2:** 627
18:12–15	**Vol. 1:** 81
18:12 f	**Vol. 2:** 430
18:12	**Vol. 1:** 504 **Vol. 2:** 431, 435, 513, 562, 649 **Vol. 3:** 1067

Genesis *(cont'd)*

18:14	**Vol. 2:** 627 **Vol. 3:** 835, 846, 1121
18:15	**Vol. 1:** 455 **Vol. 2:** 430
18:16–32	**Vol. 3:** 93
18:17	**Vol. 2:** 214 **Vol. 3:** 639
18:18	**Vol. 1:** 209, 411 **Vol. 2:** 596 **Vol. 3:** 329, 491, 523, 1112
18:19	**Vol. 3:** 937
18:21	**Vol. 3:** 513
18:22–23†	**Vol. 2:** 863
18:23–33	**Vol. 2:** 216
18:25	**Vol. 3:** 357
18:26	**Vol. 1:** 698 **Vol. 3:** 528
18:27	**Vol. 1:** 164
18:28 f	**Vol. 3:** 528
18:33	**Vol. 1:** 321
19	**Vol. 1:** 677 **Vol. 2:** 570, 767 **Vol. 3:** 455
19:1 ff	**Vol. 1:** 687
19:1	**Vol. 2:** 876
19:2 f	**Vol. 1:** 690
19:2	**Vol. 3:** 178
19:3	**Vol. 1:** 250
19:4 ff	**Vol. 1:** 194
19:4	**Vol. 2:** 796
19:7	**Vol. 1:** 255
19:8	**Vol. 2:** 395
19:9	**Vol. 1:** 687, 691
19:11	**Vol. 2:** 426 **Vol. 3:** 448
19:14	**Vol. 3:** 821
19:15	**Vol. 3:** 1169
19:16	**Vol. 3:** 204, 370, 716
19:17	**Vol. 1:** 493
19:19	**Vol. 3:** 354, 528, 748
19:21	**Vol. 2:** 622
19:24 f	**Vol. 3:** 93
19:24	**Vol. 1:** 655, 657 **Vol. 3:** 203
19:26	**Vol. 1:** 493 **Vol. 3:** 93, 240, 1058
19:28	**Vol. 3:** 93
19:29	**Vol. 3:** 204, 235, 370
19:30	**Vol. 3:** 380
19:31	**Vol. 2:** 675
19:32 ff	**Vol. 1:** 442
19:32–35	**Vol. 3:** 919
19:33	**Vol. 1:** 420
19:34 f	**Vol. 2:** 675
19:38†	**Vol. 2:** 675
20:1–17	**Vol. 1:** 80
20:1	**Vol. 1:** 691
20:3 ff	**Vol. 3:** 574, 720
20:3–7	**Vol. 2:** 576
20:3	**Vol. 1:** 420, 512 **Vol. 2:** 898 **Vol. 3:** 1065
20:6	**Vol. 3:** 860
20:7	**Vol. 1:** 76 **Vol. 2:** 862 **Vol. 3:** 77
20:12	**Vol. 2:** 628
20:13	**Vol. 1:** 76 **Vol. 3:** 354
20:16	**Vol. 1:** 415
20:18†	**Vol. 2:** 69

21:1 ff	**Vol. 2:** 627 **Vol. 3:** 846
21:1–7	**Vol. 1:** 80–81
21:1	**Vol. 1:** 189
21:2	**Vol. 1:** 284 **Vol. 3:** 1014, 1067
21:3	**Vol. 2:** 431 **Vol. 3:** 425
21:4	**Vol. 1:** 308
21:6	**Vol. 1:** 81 **Vol. 2:** 431
21:7	**Vol. 1:** 283
21:8–21	**Vol. 1:** 80–81
21:8	**Vol. 3:** 1153
21:9–12	**Vol. 1:** 284
21:9	**Vol. 1:** 81 **Vol. 3:** 1014
21:10 ff	**Vol. 3:** 490
21:10	**Vol. 1:** 453, 531
21:12	**Vol. 1:** 275 **Vol. 3:** 523
21:13	**Vol. 3:** 522
21:14	**Vol. 1:** 283
21:16	**Vol. 2:** 416
21:19	**Vol. 1:** 734 **Vol. 2:** 726
21:20 f	**Vol. 3:** 739
21:21	**Vol. 2:** 578 **Vol. 3:** 1069
21:22 ff	**Vol. 1:** 366
21:22	**Vol. 3:** 835
21:23	**Vol. 3:** 354, 739
21:25	**Vol. 2:** 140
21:33	**Vol. 2:** 67
22	**Vol. 1:** 604 **Vol. 2:** 411 **Vol. 3:** 425, 800
22:1 ff	**Vol. 2:** 543
22:1–19	**Vol. 1:** 81
22:1–14	**Vol. 3:** 370
22:1	**Vol. 1:** 76 **Vol. 3:** 799, 1120
22:2	**Vol. 2:** 76, 725, 819 **Vol. 3:** 421, 863, 946, 1009
22:3 f	**Vol. 3:** 786
22:3	**Vol. 1:** 389 **Vol. 3:** 543
22:5	**Vol. 1:** 283 **Vol. 2:** 876
22:8	**Vol. 3:** 513
22:9 f	**Vol. 3:** 418
22:9	**Vol. 3:** 418, 787
22:12	**Vol. 1:** 283 **Vol. 2:** 76, 725 **Vol. 3:** 643
22:13	**Vol. 3:** 421, 1179
22:16 f	**Vol. 1:** 214 **Vol. 2:** 771 **Vol. 3:** 202
22:16	**Vol. 2:** 76, 596, 725 **Vol. 3:** 643, 740, 1120
22:17	**Vol. 1:** 411, 732 **Vol. 2:** 596 **Vol. 3:** 523, 734
22:18	**Vol. 2:** 179 **Vol. 3:** 522, 1012
23	**Vol. 2:** 847 **Vol. 3:** 464
23:1–2	**Vol. 2:** 417
23:2	**Vol. 2:** 417, 422
23:3 ff	**Vol. 1:** 444
23:4	**Vol. 1:** 264, 684, 690–691 **Vol. 2:** 789
23:6	**Vol. 2:** 222 **Vol. 3:** 238–239
23:7	**Vol. 2:** 876
23:9	**Vol. 1:** 520 **Vol. 3:** 238–239, 380
23:11	**Vol. 2:** 173, 803
23:12	**Vol. 2:** 876
23:15	**Vol. 2:** 96

Genesis *(cont'd)*

23:16	**Vol. 2:** 173 **Vol. 3:** 146
23:20	**Vol. 1:** 664
24	**Vol. 3:** 608, 1072
24:2	**Vol. 2:** 149
24:3	**Vol. 2:** 190, 578 **Vol. 3:** 473
24:5	**Vol. 3:** 1016
24:7	**Vol. 2:** 317
24:9	**Vol. 1:** 207 **Vol. 2:** 148–149
24:10 f	**Vol. 3:** 1057
24:11–20	**Vol. 3:** 988
24:11–18	**Vol. 3:** 986
24:11	**Vol. 1:** 442
24:13	**Vol. 3:** 1072
24:14	**Vol. 3:** 117, 608, 1072
24:16	**Vol. 2:** 876 **Vol. 3:** 1072
24:23	**Vol. 2:** 879 **Vol. 3:** 178
24:25	**Vol. 1:** 743
24:26 f	**Vol. 2:** 864
24:26	**Vol. 2:** 876
24:27	**Vol. 2:** 478 **Vol. 3:** 354, 879
24:28	**Vol. 3:** 1069
24:32	**Vol. 1:** 743
24:34–36	**Vol. 1:** 208
24:35	**Vol. 3:** 608
24:38	**Vol. 3:** 871
24:40	**Vol. 2:** 815
24:43	**Vol. 2:** 87 **Vol. 3:** 1072
24:44	**Vol. 3:** 117
24:47	**Vol. 2:** 879
24:48	**Vol. 2:** 876
24:49	**Vol. 3:** 354, 879
24:52	**Vol. 2:** 876
24:53	**Vol. 2:** 41
24:55	**Vol. 3:** 1072
24:57	**Vol. 2:** 856, 879
24:58	**Vol. 1:** 272 **Vol. 3:** 1057
24:59 ff	**Vol. 2:** 584
24:60	**Vol. 1:** 207 **Vol. 2:** 578, 698 **Vol. 3:** 1055
24:62–67	**Vol. 1:** 81
24:63	**Vol. 2:** 864
24:66	**Vol. 1:** 574
25	**Vol. 1:** 557
25:1	**Vol. 3:** 841
25:6	**Vol. 2:** 576
25:7	**Vol. 2:** 478
25:8	**Vol. 1:** 264 **Vol. 2:** 478, 796
25:15	**Vol. 3:** 841
25:19–28	**Vol. 1:** 81
25:20	**Vol. 2:** 689
25:23	**Vol. 1:** 697 **Vol. 2:** 319, 587
25:24	**Vol. 1:** 734
25:25	**Vol. 1:** 667
25:26	**Vol. 1:** 241, 272 **Vol. 2:** 431
25:27–34	**Vol. 2:** 431
25:27	**Vol. 2:** 395 **Vol. 3:** 811
25:29–34	**Vol. 2:** 782, 847 **Vol. 3:** 869
25:30	**Vol. 1:** 205 **Vol. 2:** 269
26	**Vol. 1:** 210
26:3	**Vol. 1:** 214
26:4	**Vol. 3:** 734, 1012
26:5	**Vol. 3:** 354
26:10	**Vol. 2:** 720
26:11	**Vol. 2:** 142
26:12–13	**Vol. 1:** 81
26:21	**Vol. 2:** 363
26:24	**Vol. 1:** 209
26:25	**Vol. 3:** 418, 425
26:26 ff	**Vol. 1:** 366
26:27	**Vol. 2:** 879
26:29	**Vol. 1:** 81, 207, 565 **Vol. 2:** 777
26:30	**Vol. 2:** 521
26:31	**Vol. 2:** 777
26:34–36	**Vol. 1:** 209
26:35	**Vol. 3:** 691
27	**Vol. 1:** 81, 208, 617
27:1 ff	**Vol. 1:** 208
27:1	**Vol. 2:** 422 **Vol. 3:** 513
27:4 ff	**Vol. 2:** 547
27:4	**Vol. 1:** 207
27:5–17	**Vol. 2:** 317
27:12	**Vol. 1:** 461
27:13	**Vol. 1:** 285
27:16	**Vol. 1:** 241
27:17	**Vol. 2:** 862
27:27 ff	**Vol. 1:** 214
27:27–29	**Vol. 2:** 317
27:27	**Vol. 3:** 600
27:28	**Vol. 3:** 919
27:29	**Vol. 2:** 317, 876
27:30 ff	**Vol. 1:** 214
27:30–40	**Vol. 2:** 847
27:36	**Vol. 2:** 431
27:40	**Vol. 1:** 241 **Vol. 3:** 1161
27:41	**Vol. 3:** 720
27:44	**Vol. 1:** 108 **Vol. 2:** 720
27:45	**Vol. 2:** 720
28	**Vol. 1:** 557
28:3	**Vol. 1:** 293 **Vol. 2:** 67 **Vol. 3:** 729
28:10–22	**Vol. 2:** 778
28:10–17	**Vol. 2:** 317 **Vol. 3:** 630
28:11	**Vol. 1:** 314, 732 **Vol. 2:** 157 **Vol. 3:** 786
28:12 ff	**Vol. 1:** 511
28:12	**Vol. 1:** 140, 512 **Vol. 2:** 185–186, 194
28:13	**Vol. 2:** 278, 317
28:14	**Vol. 1:** 209, 411 **Vol. 2:** 317 **Vol. 3:** 1012
28:17	**Vol. 1:** 140 **Vol. 2:** 29
28:18	**Vol. 2:** 711
28:19	**Vol. 3:** 786
28:20–22	**Vol. 3:** 853
28:21	**Vol. 2:** 778
28:22	**Vol. 2:** 693 **Vol. 3:** 787, 852
29:1–4	**Vol. 3:** 986
29:2 ff	**Vol. 3:** 565
29:2–10	**Vol. 3:** 459
29:2	**Vol. 3:** 255

Genesis *(cont'd)*

29:3	**Vol. 3:** 147
29:6	**Vol. 2:** 170, 778
29:7	**Vol. 3:** 846
29:12 ff	**Vol. 1:** 255
29:13	**Vol. 1:** 574
29:14	**Vol. 1:** 672
29:15–30	**Vol. 2:** 431
29:15	**Vol. 2:** 41, 139 **Vol. 3:** 608
29:17	**Vol. 1:** 704 **Vol. 2:** 103 **Vol. 3:** 993
29:18	**Vol. 3:** 608
29:20	**Vol. 2:** 428
29:21–30:24	**Vol. 3:** 1055
29:21–30	**Vol. 2:** 576
29:22	**Vol. 2:** 576, 578
29:27	**Vol. 2:** 578
29:31 ff	**Vol. 2:** 649
29:31	**Vol. 1:** 555 **Vol. 2:** 726
29:32–35	**Vol. 1:** 272
29:33	**Vol. 1:** 555
29:34	**Vol. 2:** 466 **Vol. 3:** 835
29:35	**Vol. 1:** 61 **Vol. 2:** 305, 319
30:1 ff	**Vol. 1:** 498
30:1–13	**Vol. 3:** 1057
30:1–4	**Vol. 2:** 582
30:1 f	**Vol. 1:** 288
30:1	**Vol. 1:** 285
30:2	**Vol. 1:** 721
30:6–24	**Vol. 1:** 272
30:6	**Vol. 2:** 363
30:13	**Vol. 1:** 216 **Vol. 3:** 872
30:16	**Vol. 2:** 139
30:18	**Vol. 2:** 139 **Vol. 3:** 138
30:20	**Vol. 2:** 41
30:22	**Vol. 3:** 232–233, 246
30:23	**Vol. 3:** 340
30:25 ff	**Vol. 1:** 208
30:27	**Vol. 2:** 554
30:28	**Vol. 3:** 138
30:30	**Vol. 3:** 565
30:31	**Vol. 3:** 1153
30:32 f	**Vol. 3:** 138
30:33	**Vol. 3:** 377
30:36	**Vol. 2:** 687
30:38	**Vol. 2:** 412 **Vol. 3:** 988
30:39	**Vol. 1:** 186
30:41	**Vol. 3:** 835
30:43	**Vol. 2:** 841
31:1	**Vol. 2:** 49, 317
31:2	**Vol. 1:** 585 **Vol. 2:** 317
31:7	**Vol. 2:** 139 **Vol. 3:** 851
31:8a	**Vol. 3:** 138
31:8b	**Vol. 2:** 139
31:10–13	**Vol. 1:** 512
31:11	**Vol. 1:** 512
31:13	**Vol. 1:** 120, 181 **Vol. 2:** 67
31:14	**Vol. 2:** 303
31:15	**Vol. 1:** 684 **Vol. 3:** 823
31:16	**Vol. 2:** 841
31:18	**Vol. 2:** 845
31:19	**Vol. 2:** 284 **Vol. 3:** 377
31:23	**Vol. 2:** 805
31:25 ff	**Vol. 2:** 139
31:27	**Vol. 2:** 578 **Vol. 3:** 673
31:28	**Vol. 3:** 1156
31:30	**Vol. 1:** 456 **Vol. 2:** 317
31:34 f	**Vol. 2:** 284
31:35	**Vol. 3:** 528, 533
31:37	**Vol. 2:** 140–141
31:40	**Vol. 1:** 652
31:41	**Vol. 2:** 139
31:42	**Vol. 1:** 546, 622
31:44 ff	**Vol. 3:** 1041
31:44–50	**Vol. 1:** 366
31:44	**Vol. 3:** 1040
31:46 ff	**Vol. 3:** 1041
31:46	**Vol. 2:** 521
31:50	**Vol. 3:** 739
31:53	**Vol. 1:** 622
31:54	**Vol. 1:** 367 **Vol. 2:** 521 **Vol. 3:** 33, 422, 425
32:1 f*	**Vol. 1:** 101
32:4–6	**Vol. 3:** 1089
32:5	**Vol. 2:** 116
32:6	**Vol. 2:** 116, 318
32:7	**Vol. 1:** 534
32:8	**Vol. 2:** 796
32:9	**Vol. 1:** 181
32:10*	**Vol. 3:** 608, 879
32:11*	**Vol. 2:** 148 **Vol. 3:** 354
32:12	**Vol. 1:** 411
32:13	**Vol. 2:** 41
32:14 f	**Vol. 1:** 415
32:14	**Vol. 3:** 421
32:17*	**Vol. 1:** 665 **Vol. 3:** 564
32:18 f	**Vol. 2:** 41
32:18	**Vol. 1:** 332
32:19	**Vol. 3:** 421
32:20*	**Vol. 3:** 153–154
32:21 f	**Vol. 3:** 421
32:23 ff	**Vol. 1:** 108
32:23–33	**Vol. 3:** 986
32:24 ff	**Vol. 1:** 648
32:24 f	**Vol. 1:** 645
32:25 ff	**Vol. 1:** 108
32:25	**Vol. 3:** 860
32:28	**Vol. 1:** 61 **Vol. 2:** 305, 649
32:30 f	**Vol. 3:** 514
32:30	**Vol. 1:** 585 **Vol. 2:** 317
32:32	**Vol. 1:** 61
33:1–4	**Vol. 2:** 317
33:3	**Vol. 1:** 322 **Vol. 2:** 876
33:5	**Vol. 1:** 288 **Vol. 3:** 608
33:6 f	**Vol. 2:** 876
33:9 f	**Vol. 2:** 876
33:10	**Vol. 3:** 745
33:11	**Vol. 1:** 214 **Vol. 3:** 711
33:14	**Vol. 1:** 241, 322
33:15	**Vol. 2:** 796

Genesis *(cont'd)*

33:18	**Vol. 3:** 458
33:19	**Vol. 1:** 116 **Vol. 2:** 303, 318 **Vol. 3:** 458, 464
33:20	**Vol. 1:** 272 **Vol. 2:** 67, 796 **Vol. 3:** 418, 425
34	**Vol. 2:** 318, 675 **Vol. 3:** 455–456
34:2	**Vol. 2:** 260
34:3	**Vol. 2:** 87 **Vol. 3:** 1072
34:5	**Vol. 3:** 104
34:7	**Vol. 1:** 61
34:12	**Vol. 2:** 578 **Vol. 3:** 1057
34:13–17	**Vol. 1:** 309
34:15	**Vol. 2:** 501
34:21	**Vol. 2:** 593
34:22 f	**Vol. 2:** 501
34:23	**Vol. 2:** 837
34:25	**Vol. 3:** 747
34:29	**Vol. 3:** 590
34:30	**Vol. 2:** 683
35:1–7	**Vol. 3:** 418
35:6	**Vol. 2:** 796
35:7	**Vol. 2:** 67 **Vol. 3:** 318, 425
35:10	**Vol. 1:** 61
35:11	**Vol. 1:** 239, 293, 411 **Vol. 2:** 67, 128, 278 **Vol. 3:** 729
35:14	**Vol. 2:** 711 **Vol. 3:** 423
35:16–20	**Vol. 3:** 872
35:18	**Vol. 2:** 146 **Vol. 3:** 680
35:19	**Vol. 1:** 170
35:20	**Vol. 3:** 239
35:22	**Vol. 3:** 1074
35:23	**Vol. 3:** 872
35:25	**Vol. 1:** 663
35:27	**Vol. 1:** 691
35:29	**Vol. 2:** 318
36:6 f	**Vol. 2:** 845
36:6	**Vol. 3:** 680
36:40	**Vol. 3:** 871
37	**Vol. 1:** 531, 650 **Vol. 2:** 318
37:1–11	**Vol. 2:** 431
37:2 ff	**Vol. 1:** 555
37:2	**Vol. 1:** 182
37:4*	**Vol. 2:** 547
37:5–10	**Vol. 1:** 512
37:5	**Vol. 3:** 45
37:7	**Vol. 3:** 591
37:10	**Vol. 1:** 572
37:14	**Vol. 2:** 169, 778 **Vol. 3:** 513
37:15	**Vol. 1:** 104
37:16	**Vol. 3:** 531
37:17	**Vol. 3:** 1185
37:18	**Vol. 1:** 695
37:20	**Vol. 1:** 113, 565
37:22	**Vol. 2:** 854 **Vol. 3:** 1004
37:23	**Vol. 1:** 314
37:24	**Vol. 1:** 546
37:25	**Vol. 1:** 743 **Vol. 2:** 294
37:26	**Vol. 2:** 319 **Vol. 3:** 137, 159
37:27	**Vol. 1:** 672 **Vol. 2:** 319
37:31	**Vol. 1:** 449
37:33	**Vol. 3:** 601–602
37:34–35	**Vol. 2:** 417
37:34	**Vol. 1:** 239
37:35	**Vol. 1:** 569 **Vol. 3:** 1019
38	**Vol. 1:** 61 **Vol. 2:** 577 **Vol. 3:** 1062
38:6–30	**Vol. 1:** 499
38:6	**Vol. 2:** 578
38:8 ff	**Vol. 2:** 577
38:8	**Vol. 3:** 275, 279
38:11	**Vol. 2:** 584
38:15 f	**Vol. 2:** 582
38:15	**Vol. 1:** 498 **Vol. 2:** 212 **Vol. 3:** 821
38:17 ff	**Vol. 2:** 40
38:24	**Vol. 1:** 655 **Vol. 2:** 582 **Vol. 3:** 538
38:26	**Vol. 3:** 355
38:28	**Vol. 1:** 171
38:29	**Vol. 3:** 950
39–50	**Vol. 1:** 531
39:1	**Vol. 1:** 560
39:2 f	**Vol. 3:** 1030
39:4	**Vol. 2:** 815
39:6	**Vol. 2:** 103
39:14	**Vol. 1:** 410
39:21	**Vol. 2:** 117 **Vol. 3:** 1030
39:22	**Vol. 3:** 591
40:2	**Vol. 1:** 560
40:5 ff	**Vol. 1:** 512
40:8	**Vol. 1:** 512, 577
40:12 ff	**Vol. 2:** 687
40:15	**Vol. 2:** 305 **Vol. 3:** 377
40:16	**Vol. 3:** 351
40:18 f	**Vol. 1:** 393
40:19	**Vol. 1:** 113
40:20	**Vol. 1:** 165 **Vol. 2:** 687
40:23	**Vol. 3:** 232
41	**Vol. 3:** 50
41:1 ff	**Vol. 1:** 512
41:2	**Vol. 1:** 537, 672 **Vol. 2:** 103
41:4	**Vol. 1:** 537 **Vol. 3:** 279
41:5	**Vol. 2:** 185
41:7	**Vol. 3:** 279
41:8	**Vol. 1:** 574, 577 **Vol. 2:** 555 **Vol. 3:** 680, 691, 1027
41:9	**Vol. 3:** 239
41:12	**Vol. 1:** 577
41:13	**Vol. 3:** 147
41:16	**Vol. 2:** 778
41:21	**Vol. 1:** 164
41:24	**Vol. 1:** 574 **Vol. 2:** 555
41:28	**Vol. 3:** 569
41:31	**Vol. 2:** 395
41:35 ff	**Vol. 2:** 268
41:35	**Vol. 2:** 32
41:40–46	**Vol. 3:** 1030
41:40	**Vol. 2:** 612, 796
41:42	**Vol. 2:** 96 **Vol. 3:** 498
41:43	**Vol. 3:** 50
41:45	**Vol. 2:** 576, 649

Genesis *(cont'd)*

41:48	**Vol. 2:** 32
41:49	**Vol. 2:** 683
41:50 ff†	**Vol. 2:** 306
41:53 ff	**Vol. 2:** 265
41:56	**Vol. 1:** 268
41:57	**Vol. 1:** 267
42:1 ff	**Vol. 2:** 265
42:3	**Vol. 2:** 173
42:6–45:4	**Vol. 2:** 432
42:6	**Vol. 2:** 876
42:13	**Vol. 2:** 675
42:15	**Vol. 2:** 675
42:16	**Vol. 3:** 880
42:20	**Vol. 1:** 596 **Vol. 2:** 675
42:21 f	**Vol. 2:** 173
42:21	**Vol. 1:** 322
42:22	**Vol. 3:** 158
42:23	**Vol. 1:** 373, 580
42:24	**Vol. 1:** 322
42:25	**Vol. 1:** 734
42:27	**Vol. 1:** 743 **Vol. 3:** 177
42:28	**Vol. 1:** 527
42:34	**Vol. 1:** 268 **Vol. 2:** 675
43:3–10	**Vol. 2:** 319
43:11	**Vol. 2:** 294
43:14	**Vol. 2:** 116 **Vol. 3:** 729
43:20	**Vol. 2:** 860
43:23	**Vol. 2:** 777 **Vol. 3:** 157, 160
43:24	**Vol. 1:** 743
43:25 ff	**Vol. 2:** 521
43:27 f	**Vol. 2:** 170, 778
43:28	**Vol. 2:** 876
43:29	**Vol. 1:** 285
43:31	**Vol. 1:** 495
43:32	**Vol. 2:** 305
43:33	**Vol. 1:** 193, 527
44	**Vol. 2:** 675
44:4	**Vol. 3:** 377
44:5	**Vol. 2:** 554
44:14	**Vol. 1:** 609
44:15	**Vol. 2:** 554
44:16–34	**Vol. 2:** 319
44:16	**Vol. 3:** 355
44:18	**Vol. 2:** 860
44:20	**Vol. 1:** 255
44:33	**Vol. 3:** 228, 1179–1180
45:1	**Vol. 2:** 765
45:2	**Vol. 2:** 416
45:5 ff	**Vol. 3:** 720
45:5	**Vol. 1:** 532
45:6	**Vol. 3:** 525
45:7–8	**Vol. 1:** 531
45:7	**Vol. 1:** 532
45:9	**Vol. 3:** 224
45:14	**Vol. 1:** 609
45:16	**Vol. 2:** 357
45:17	**Vol. 1:** 743
45:20	**Vol. 2:** 845
46:1	**Vol. 3:** 425
46:2	**Vol. 3:** 513
46:3	**Vol. 1:** 411
46:4	**Vol. 2:** 60
46:27	**Vol. 2:** 690
46:29	**Vol. 1:** 609 **Vol. 2:** 416 **Vol. 3:** 1161
47:2	**Vol. 3:** 604
47:4	**Vol. 1:** 691
47:7–10	**Vol. 1:** 208
47:18	**Vol. 2:** 845
47:23	**Vol. 3:** 521
47:24	**Vol. 2:** 303
47:25	**Vol. 2:** 116 **Vol. 3:** 206
47:28	**Vol. 2:** 478
47:29	**Vol. 1:** 207 **Vol. 2:** 149
47:30	**Vol. 1:** 442
47:31	**Vol. 1:** 408 **Vol. 2:** 876 **Vol. 3:** 739
48:1 ff	**Vol. 1:** 207–208
48:1–6	**Vol. 2:** 318
48:3	**Vol. 2:** 67 **Vol. 3:** 729
48:7	**Vol. 1:** 170
48:8–49:27	**Vol. 2:** 318
48:10	**Vol. 1:** 207
48:12	**Vol. 2:** 876
48:13 ff	**Vol. 1:** 207
48:14	**Vol. 2:** 148
48:15 f	**Vol. 1:** 214
48:15	**Vol. 2:** 815 **Vol. 3:** 565
48:16	**Vol. 3:** 202
48:18	**Vol. 2:** 151
48:20	**Vol. 2:** 649
48:22	**Vol. 1:** 116 **Vol. 2:** 318 **Vol. 3:** 458
49	**Vol. 1:** 208 **Vol. 2:** 695 **Vol. 3:** 461
49:2	**Vol. 2:** 32
49:3	**Vol. 1:** 667
49:4	**Vol. 2:** 587
49:5 ff	**Vol. 3:** 33, 456
49:5	**Vol. 1:** 534
49:6	**Vol. 1:** 108, 230, 293 **Vol. 3:** 1016
49:7	**Vol. 1:** 108
49:8 ff	**Vol. 2:** 335
49:8–12	**Vol. 1:** 61 **Vol. 2:** 374 **Vol. 3:** 461
49:8	**Vol. 1:** 61 **Vol. 2:** 876 **Vol. 3:** 816
49:9 f	**Vol. 3:** 649, 652
49:9	**Vol. 1:** 118 **Vol. 3:** 650, 872
49:10	**Vol. 1:** 407 **Vol. 2:** 319, 791, 899 **Vol. 3:** 650
49:11	**Vol. 1:** 224 **Vol. 3:** 591, 919
49:12	**Vol. 1:** 204
49:14	**Vol. 3:** 255
49:15	**Vol. 3:** 255
49:16	**Vol. 1:** 61 **Vol. 2:** 796
49:17	**Vol. 1:** 241 **Vol. 3:** 872
49:18	**Vol. 2:** 239 **Vol. 3:** 228
49:23	**Vol. 3:** 346
49:24	**Vol. 2:** 104 **Vol. 3:** 381, 565
49:25	**Vol. 1:** 240, 523 **Vol. 2:** 67
49:27	**Vol. 3:** 604
49:28 ff	**Vol. 1:** 207
49:28	**Vol. 1:** 61

Genesis *(cont'd)*

49:29–33	**Vol. 3:** 464
49:30	**Vol. 3:** 239
49:33	**Vol. 2:** 796 **Vol. 3:** 255
50:1–13	**Vol. 2:** 318
50:1	**Vol. 2:** 416
50:2	**Vol. 1:** 120, 264 **Vol. 2:** 167, 305
50:3	**Vol. 1:** 264 **Vol. 2:** 422
50:4	**Vol. 2:** 116
50:5 ff	**Vol. 1:** 531
50:5	**Vol. 3:** 239
50:7	**Vol. 1:** 194 **Vol. 3:** 579
50:10 f	**Vol. 2:** 422
50:13	**Vol. 3:** 239, 464
50:17	**Vol. 1:** 698
50:20	**Vol. 1:** 531 **Vol. 2:** 100 **Vol. 3:** 234, 720
50:24	**Vol. 3:** 720
50:25	**Vol. 1:** 240, 531
50:26	**Vol. 1:** 264

Exodus

1–15	**Vol. 1:** 531 **Vol. 2:** 644
1:1	**Vol. 2:** 305
1:5	**Vol. 3:** 680
1:6	**Vol. 1:** 430 **Vol. 2:** 36
1:7	**Vol. 1:** 732 **Vol. 2:** 130
1:8	**Vol. 2:** 636, 670 **Vol. 3:** 275
1:11	**Vol. 2:** 635–636, 822
1:13 f	**Vol. 3:** 711
1:15–19	**Vol. 2:** 305
1:16 ff	**Vol. 2:** 569
1:16	**Vol. 2:** 636
1:18	**Vol. 1:** 272
1:20	**Vol. 1:** 732
1:22	**Vol. 2:** 569, 636, 796
2	**Vol. 2:** 216
2:1 f	**Vol. 3:** 33
2:1–10	**Vol. 2:** 636
2:1	**Vol. 2:** 636
2:2	**Vol. 2:** 569, 887
2:6	**Vol. 2:** 416
2:8	**Vol. 2:** 87 **Vol. 3:** 1071
2:9 ff	**Vol. 2:** 189
2:9	**Vol. 3:** 138
2:10	**Vol. 1:** 673 **Vol. 2:** 636
2:11–15	**Vol. 2:** 636 **Vol. 3:** 963
2:11–13	**Vol. 2:** 305
2:11	**Vol. 1:** 255
2:12	**Vol. 1:** 165 **Vol. 3:** 345
2:13	**Vol. 1:** 258
2:14	**Vol. 1:** 168 **Vol. 2:** 363, 489 **Vol. 3:** 199
2:15 f	**Vol. 2:** 635 **Vol. 3:** 459
2:15–22	**Vol. 3:** 459
2:15–21	**Vol. 3:** 986
2:15	**Vol. 1:** 691 **Vol. 3:** 531
2:16–22	**Vol. 2:** 636
2:16	**Vol. 3:** 564

2:17	**Vol. 3:** 201
2:18 ff	**Vol. 3:** 33
2:18–26	**Vol. 2:** 636
2:18	**Vol. 2:** 636
2:19	**Vol. 3:** 201
2:21	**Vol. 2:** 576, 578
2:22	**Vol. 1:** 691 **Vol. 2:** 636
2:23 ff	**Vol. 2:** 636
2:23	**Vol. 1:** 410
2:24 f†	**Vol. 3:** 69
2:24	**Vol. 2:** 423 **Vol. 3:** 235, 241
3	**Vol. 2:** 69, 651
3:1 ff	**Vol. 2:** 173 **Vol. 3:** 330, 1005
3:1–4:20	**Vol. 2:** 635
3:1–22	**Vol. 2:** 636
3:1 f	**Vol. 3:** 1014
3:1	**Vol. 2:** 636 **Vol. 3:** 33, 1013
3:2 f	**Vol. 1:** 655
3:2	**Vol. 1:** 656–657
3:3	**Vol. 3:** 513
3:4	**Vol. 1:** 273
3:5	**Vol. 1:** 239 **Vol. 2:** 53, 225 **Vol. 3:** 177, 179
3:6	**Vol. 2:** 91, 215, 318, 650 **Vol. 3:** 263–264, 464–465
3:7	**Vol. 2:** 175, 178, 796 **Vol. 3:** 514
3:8	**Vol. 1:** 683 **Vol. 3:** 1162
3:9	**Vol. 1:** 320 **Vol. 2:** 807
3:10 ff	**Vol. 2:** 68
3:10	**Vol. 2:** 796, 807
3:11	**Vol. 1:** 272
3:12	**Vol. 2:** 350, 626 **Vol. 3:** 464, 550
3:13 ff	**Vol. 2:** 68
3:13	**Vol. 2:** 650, 879
3:14 ff	**Vol. 1:** 383
3:14 f	**Vol. 1:** 56
3:14	**Vol. 2:** 68, 278, 513, 649–651 **Vol. 3:** 969
3:15 f	**Vol. 3:** 263
3:15	**Vol. 2:** 68, 318, 650 **Vol. 3:** 237
3:16	**Vol. 1:** 195 **Vol. 2:** 32 **Vol. 3:** 611
3:18	**Vol. 1:** 195 **Vol. 2:** 305, 687
3:19	**Vol. 3:** 717
3:21	**Vol. 1:** 546 **Vol. 2:** 117
3:22	**Vol. 2:** 96, 856
4 ff	**Vol. 2:** 154
4	**Vol. 2:** 627
4:1 ff	**Vol. 2:** 626
4:1–9	**Vol. 1:** 596 **Vol. 2:** 636
4:1	**Vol. 1:** 272
4:5	**Vol. 3:** 263
4:6	**Vol. 1:** 240
4:10 ff	**Vol. 3:** 730
4:10–17	**Vol. 2:** 636
4:10	**Vol. 1:** 272 **Vol. 2:** 860 **Vol. 3:** 1079
4:11	**Vol. 1:** 218, 428
4:12	**Vol. 2:** 68, 726
4:13–16	**Vol. 3:** 33
4:13	**Vol. 1:** 272, 475–476
4:14	**Vol. 1:** 108

Exodus *(cont'd)*

4:15   **Vol. 2:** 68, 635, 726
4:18   **Vol. 2:** 170
4:19   **Vol. 2:** 640   **Vol. 3:** 531
4:20   **Vol. 2:** 640
4:21   **Vol. 2:** 155   **Vol. 3:** 1185
4:22 f   **Vol. 2:** 68, 71   **Vol. 3:** 636
4:22   **Vol. 1:** 177, 288, 617, 667   **Vol. 2:** 715, 835   **Vol. 3:** 638
4:23   **Vol. 3:** 550, 1016
4:24 ff   **Vol. 1:** 108, 308, 451
4:24   **Vol. 1:** 108   **Vol. 3:** 794
4:27–31†   **Vol. 1:** 596   **Vol. 2:** 636
4:28   **Vol. 1:** 332
4:29   **Vol. 1:** 195   **Vol. 2:** 32
4:31   **Vol. 2:** 876   **Vol. 3:** 1162
5:1–23   **Vol. 2:** 636
5:1   **Vol. 2:** 796
5:2   **Vol. 1:** 273
5:5   **Vol. 3:** 255
5:6   **Vol. 3:** 478
5:9   **Vol. 1:** 277
5:21   **Vol. 3:** 1040
5:22 f   **Vol. 2:** 651
5:22   **Vol. 3:** 342
5:23   **Vol. 2:** 796   **Vol. 3:** 202
6:1–7:7   **Vol. 2:** 637
6:1   **Vol. 3:** 717
6:2 ff   **Vol. 3:** 729
6:2 f   **Vol. 2:** 68
6:2   **Vol. 2:** 649–650
6:3   **Vol. 2:** 67   **Vol. 3:** 316
6:4 f   **Vol. 1:** 366
6:4   **Vol. 1:** 691
6:5   **Vol. 2:** 423   **Vol. 3:** 235, 241
6:6   **Vol. 2:** 200   **Vol. 3:** 192, 201, 1162
6:7   **Vol. 1:** 368   **Vol. 2:** 395, 797   **Vol. 3:** 799, 813
6:8   **Vol. 3:** 235
6:12   **Vol. 2:** 173
6:14 ff   **Vol. 3:** 660
6:16   **Vol. 1:** 691
6:25   **Vol. 1:** 544
6:27   **Vol. 3:** 820
6:30   **Vol. 2:** 173
7 f   **Vol. 2:** 629
7–12   **Vol. 2:** 627
7   **Vol. 3:** 986
7:1   **Vol. 3:** 77
7:2   **Vol. 1:** 332
7:3   **Vol. 2:** 627
7:4   **Vol. 2:** 149
7:5   **Vol. 2:** 395
7:7   **Vol. 2:** 637
7:9–12   **Vol. 1:** 508
7:9   **Vol. 2:** 633
7:10 ff   **Vol. 2:** 219
7:11   **Vol. 2:** 554–555, 642
7:13   **Vol. 1:** 332   **Vol. 2:** 154

7:14 ff   **Vol. 3:** 984
7:14–25   **Vol. 3:** 987
7:14   **Vol. 1:** 261
7:16   **Vol. 2:** 796   **Vol. 3:** 550
7:17 ff   **Vol. 1:** 224
7:17   **Vol. 2:** 395
7:18   **Vol. 1:** 670
7:19–25   **Vol. 2:** 637
7:22   **Vol. 2:** 154, 555
7:23   **Vol. 3:** 125
8:1–14   **Vol. 2:** 637
8:1*   **Vol. 3:** 550
8:3   **Vol. 2:** 555   **Vol. 3:** 917
8:13   **Vol. 1:** 520
8:14 f   **Vol. 2:** 555
8:15   **Vol. 2:** 154
8:16–19   **Vol. 2:** 637
8:19   **Vol. 2:** 150
8:20–32   **Vol. 2:** 637
8:20*   **Vol. 3:** 550
9:1–7   **Vol. 2:** 637
9:1   **Vol. 3:** 550
9:2   **Vol. 3:** 1016
9:3   **Vol. 2:** 149
9:5   **Vol. 1:** 294
9:8–12   **Vol. 2:** 637
9:11   **Vol. 2:** 555
9:13–35   **Vol. 2:** 637
9:16   **Vol. 3:** 45, 48, 329, 490
9:18   **Vol. 1:** 380   **Vol. 3:** 846
9:22   **Vol. 2:** 211
9:24   **Vol. 1:** 655, 657
9:28   **Vol. 3:** 224
9:29   **Vol. 2:** 190
9:33   **Vol. 2:** 190
10   **Vol. 1:** 119
10:1–20   **Vol. 2:** 637
10:1 f   **Vol. 2:** 396   **Vol. 3:** 760
10:3 f   **Vol. 3:** 1016
10:3   **Vol. 3:** 550
10:4   **Vol. 3:** 846
10:5   **Vol. 1:** 729
10:7 f   **Vol. 3:** 550
10:12   **Vol. 1:** 189
10:13   **Vol. 2:** 628, 889   **Vol. 3:** 1001
10:15   **Vol. 3:** 248
10:17   **Vol. 2:** 863
10:19   **Vol. 2:** 628   **Vol. 3:** 248, 1001
10:21–29   **Vol. 2:** 637
10:22   **Vol. 1:** 422
10:23   **Vol. 2:** 586
10:24   **Vol. 3:** 550
10:26   **Vol. 3:** 550
10:27   **Vol. 3:** 1016
11:1–12:30   **Vol. 2:** 637
11:1   **Vol. 1:** 162   **Vol. 3:** 857
11:2   **Vol. 1:** 258
11:3   **Vol. 2:** 117
11:5   **Vol. 3:** 394
11:8   **Vol. 2:** 876

Exodus *(cont'd)*

11:9	**Vol. 2:** 350, 633
11:10	**Vol. 2:** 350
12	**Vol. 2:** 478
12:1 ff	**Vol. 1:** 295 **Vol. 3:** 69
12:1–28	**Vol. 2:** 637
12:1	**Vol. 3:** 1121
12:3 ff	**Vol. 1:** 617
12:3	**Vol. 1:** 294
12:4	**Vol. 2:** 683
12:5	**Vol. 1:** 632 **Vol. 2:** 410, 521, 569, 778 **Vol. 3:** 200, 435
12:6	**Vol. 1:** 292, 294 **Vol. 2:** 521
12:7	**Vol. 1:** 223 **Vol. 2:** 410
12:8 f	**Vol. 2:** 521
12:8	**Vol. 1:** 250, 654 **Vol. 2:** 522
12:11–14	**Vol. 1:** 632
12:11	**Vol. 1:** 250, 632 **Vol. 3:** 121, 1169
12:12 f	**Vol. 1:** 465 **Vol. 2:** 784
12:12	**Vol. 1:** 626
12:13	**Vol. 1:** 162, 223, 632 **Vol. 2:** 410, 626 **Vol. 3:** 159
12:14 ff	**Vol. 3:** 828
12:14–20	**Vol. 1:** 250 **Vol. 2:** 461
12:14	**Vol. 3:** 233, 237
12:15	**Vol. 1:** 699 **Vol. 2:** 461
12:16	**Vol. 1:** 272
12:17	**Vol. 1:** 626 **Vol. 2:** 784, 889
12:18	**Vol. 1:** 665
12:19	**Vol. 1:** 295 **Vol. 2:** 461, 716
12:21 ff	**Vol. 1:** 115
12:21–27	**Vol. 1:** 194
12:21–23	**Vol. 1:** 632
12:21	**Vol. 1:** 272, 632
12:22 f	**Vol. 1:** 221, 223
12:22	**Vol. 2:** 854
12:23–27	**Vol. 2:** 784
12:23	**Vol. 1:** 101, 465, 632 **Vol. 2:** 167, 410
12:24	**Vol. 2:** 134
12:25 f	**Vol. 3:** 550
12:26 f	**Vol. 1:** 617 **Vol. 3:** 777
12:26	**Vol. 1:** 288 **Vol. 2:** 522
12:27 f	**Vol. 2:** 876
12:27	**Vol. 1:** 632 **Vol. 2:** 876
12:31 ff	**Vol. 2:** 637
12:33	**Vol. 3:** 1169
12:34	**Vol. 1:** 250 **Vol. 2:** 461 **Vol. 3:** 917
12:36	**Vol. 2:** 117
12:37	**Vol. 2:** 698
12:38	**Vol. 1:** 252
12:39	**Vol. 1:** 250 **Vol. 2:** 461, 773, 784 **Vol. 3:** 227
12:42	**Vol. 2:** 132
12:43 ff	**Vol. 1:** 684
12:43–48	**Vol. 1:** 308
12:43	**Vol. 2:** 441
12:44	**Vol. 3:** 594, 608
12:45	**Vol. 1:** 691 **Vol. 2:** 139
12:46	**Vol. 1:** 240, 629 **Vol. 2:** 527
12:48	**Vol. 1:** 159, 308, 360
13:1–10	**Vol. 3:** 105, 487
13:2	**Vol. 1:** 474, 667 **Vol. 2:** 570, 729 **Vol. 3:** 430, 660
13:3–10	**Vol. 1:** 250 **Vol. 2:** 892
13:3	**Vol. 3:** 593, 717
13:4	**Vol. 2:** 675
13:5	**Vol. 1:** 683 **Vol. 3:** 550
13:7	**Vol. 2:** 716
13:8	**Vol. 3:** 233
13:9	**Vol. 2:** 136, 149, 440, 864 **Vol. 3:** 237, 717
13:10	**Vol. 3:** 846
13:11–16	**Vol. 3:** 105, 487
13:12	**Vol. 2:** 570, 729 **Vol. 3:** 430, 660
13:13	**Vol. 3:** 190, 192, 857
13:14 ff	**Vol. 1:** 617
13:14	**Vol. 3:** 593, 717
13:15	**Vol. 3:** 190, 192
13:16	**Vol. 1:** 254 **Vol. 2:** 136, 149 **Vol. 3:** 559, 717
13:17 f	**Vol. 2:** 637
13:17	**Vol. 1:** 356 **Vol. 3:** 937
13:19	**Vol. 1:** 531 **Vol. 2:** 637
13:21 f	**Vol. 2:** 491–492
13:21	**Vol. 1:** 420
13:22	**Vol. 1:** 655
14 f	**Vol. 3:** 989
14	**Vol. 2:** 627
14:4	**Vol. 2:** 395
14:6	**Vol. 3:** 1161
14:7	**Vol. 1:** 537
14:11	**Vol. 3:** 238
14:13	**Vol. 1:** 328 **Vol. 3:** 208, 828, 841
14:14	**Vol. 2:** 374
14:15–18	**Vol. 1:** 373
14:17 f	**Vol. 2:** 45
14:18	**Vol. 2:** 395
14:19	**Vol. 1:** 101
14:21	**Vol. 2:** 628 **Vol. 3:** 543
14:23	**Vol. 3:** 983
14:25	**Vol. 3:** 711
14:26 ff	**Vol. 3:** 147
14:27	**Vol. 3:** 560
14:28	**Vol. 3:** 983
14:30	**Vol. 3:** 201
14:31	**Vol. 1:** 598
15	**Vol. 1:** 513 **Vol. 3:** 960, 984
15:1 ff	**Vol. 3:** 69
15:1–18	**Vol. 1:** 245
15:1	**Vol. 1:** 598 **Vol. 3:** 672–674, 983
15:2	**Vol. 1:** 618 **Vol. 2:** 201 **Vol. 3:** 207
15:3	**Vol. 2:** 650
15:4 f	**Vol. 3:** 983
15:5	**Vol. 2:** 197
15:6	**Vol. 2:** 602
15:7	**Vol. 1:** 732
15:8	**Vol. 3:** 691, 988
15:9	**Vol. 2:** 805
15:10	**Vol. 3:** 983, 1001

Exodus *(cont'd)*

15:11	**Vol. 2:** 720 **Vol. 3:** 1153
15:13	**Vol. 1:** 570 **Vol. 2:** 602 **Vol. 3:** 192, 354, 794, 937
15:15	**Vol. 3:** 747
15:16	**Vol. 1:** 609 **Vol. 3:** 192
15:17	**Vol. 2:** 296 **Vol. 3:** 117, 350, 866
15:18	**Vol. 2:** 898 **Vol. 3:** 841
15:20 f	**Vol. 2:** 635
15:20	**Vol. 3:** 77, 1057
15:21	**Vol. 3:** 672, 983
15:22 ff	**Vol. 2:** 275
15:23	**Vol. 1:** 201–203 **Vol. 2:** 274, 637
15:24	**Vol. 2:** 836
15:25 f	**Vol. 3:** 354
15:25	**Vol. 3:** 799
15:26	**Vol. 1:** 230 **Vol. 2:** 167
15:27	**Vol. 1:** 252 **Vol. 2:** 637, 754 **Vol. 3:** 986
16 ff	**Vol. 3:** 427
16	**Vol. 1:** 252 **Vol. 2:** 637
16:1 ff	**Vol. 1:** 294–295
16:1	**Vol. 3:** 1013
16:2 ff	**Vol. 3:** 804
16:2 f	**Vol. 2:** 836
16:3 ff	**Vol. 2:** 265, 267
16:3	**Vol. 2:** 628
16:4	**Vol. 1:** 251 **Vol. 2:** 194, 218 **Vol. 3:** 799
16:6 f	**Vol. 2:** 395
16:6	**Vol. 2:** 395
16:7	**Vol. 2:** 45, 175
16:8	**Vol. 2:** 175
16:9	**Vol. 1:** 294, 322 **Vol. 2:** 175
16:10	**Vol. 2:** 45
16:12	**Vol. 2:** 175, 395
16:13–15	**Vol. 2:** 194
16:13	**Vol. 1:** 173 **Vol. 2:** 586 **Vol. 3:** 255
16:14	**Vol. 2:** 440, 586
16:15	**Vol. 1:** 252 **Vol. 2:** 871
16:16	**Vol. 2:** 158, 683
16:18	**Vol. 2:** 130–131 **Vol. 3:** 402
16:20	**Vol. 1:** 108, 202
16:23	**Vol. 1:** 626 **Vol. 2:** 130–131 **Vol. 3:** 94, 255–256
16:25	**Vol. 1:** 626 **Vol. 3:** 256
16:28	**Vol. 2:** 440 **Vol. 3:** 1016
16:29	**Vol. 3:** 940
16:31	**Vol. 1:** 459
16:32 ff	**Vol. 1:** 253
16:33 f	**Vol. 3:** 815
16:33	**Vol. 1:** 252
16:35	**Vol. 1:** 252, 519 **Vol. 2:** 303, 696 **Vol. 3:** 843
17	**Vol. 2:** 627 **Vol. 3:** 383
17:1 ff	**Vol. 2:** 274
17:1–7	**Vol. 2:** 637 **Vol. 3:** 459
17:1–6	**Vol. 3:** 382
17:2	**Vol. 3:** 799–801
17:3 ff	**Vol. 2:** 265
17:5 f	**Vol. 3:** 986, 988
17:5	**Vol. 1:** 195
17:6	**Vol. 2:** 276 **Vol. 3:** 381
17:7	**Vol. 1:** 203 **Vol. 3:** 346, 799–801
17:8 ff	**Vol. 3:** 33
17:8–16	**Vol. 2:** 331, 637
17:9 ff	**Vol. 3:** 208
17:9 f	**Vol. 3:** 1009
17:9	**Vol. 1:** 537
17:11	**Vol. 1:** 207
17:12	**Vol. 3:** 878
17:14	**Vol. 1:** 243, 471 **Vol. 2:** 639 **Vol. 3:** 236–237, 484
17:15	**Vol. 1:** 71 **Vol. 3:** 418
18:1	**Vol. 3:** 1013
18:3	**Vol. 2:** 720
18:5	**Vol. 3:** 1013
18:7	**Vol. 2:** 778, 876
18:8–11	**Vol. 2:** 396
18:9	**Vol. 2:** 99
18:11	**Vol. 2:** 425
18:12 ff	**Vol. 3:** 33
18:12	**Vol. 2:** 521
18:13 ff	**Vol. 1:** 195
18:13–14	**Vol. 3:** 588
18:13	**Vol. 1:** 195
18:16	**Vol. 1:** 503 **Vol. 2:** 440
18:17	**Vol. 3:** 351
18:20	**Vol. 1:** 59 **Vol. 2:** 440 **Vol. 3:** 938, 1041
18:21	**Vol. 3:** 29, 137, 880
18:22	**Vol. 3:** 846
18:23	**Vol. 2:** 778
18:24 ff	**Vol. 2:** 637
18:26	**Vol. 3:** 846, 1120
19–24	**Vol. 1:** 626 **Vol. 3:** 1013
19	**Vol. 2:** 640, 784–785 **Vol. 3:** 1005, 1013–1014
19:1–13	**Vol. 2:** 637
19:1	**Vol. 1:** 626 **Vol. 2:** 784 **Vol. 3:** 937
19:3 ff	**Vol. 3:** 799, 806
19:3	**Vol. 3:** 1013
19:4 ff	**Vol. 3:** 805
19:4	**Vol. 1:** 173
19:5 f	**Vol. 2:** 70, 790, 800 **Vol. 3:** 435
19:5	**Vol. 2:** 174, 297, 791, 838–840 **Vol. 3:** 190
19:6	**Vol. 2:** 380, 795 **Vol. 3:** 36–38, 1120
19:7	**Vol. 1:** 272
19:8	**Vol. 2:** 174 **Vol. 3:** 908
19:9 ff	**Vol. 1:** 108
19:9	**Vol. 3:** 1001
19:10 ff	**Vol. 2:** 225
19:10 f	**Vol. 3:** 117
19:10	**Vol. 3:** 101, 1013, 1041
19:11	**Vol. 3:** 1013
19:12 ff	**Vol. 1:** 656
19:12 f	**Vol. 3:** 557
19:12	**Vol. 1:** 430 **Vol. 3:** 860, 949

23

Exodus *(cont'd)*

19:13   **Vol. 3:** 191
19:14–20:17 **Vol. 2:** 637
19:14   **Vol. 3:** 1013
19:15   **Vol. 2:** 225   **Vol. 3:** 117
19:16–24 **Vol. 3:** 1013
19:16–19 **Vol. 2:** 784
19:16   **Vol. 3:** 112–113, 1013
19:17 f   **Vol. 1:** 195
19:18   **Vol. 1:** 655 **Vol. 2:** 190, 485 **Vol. 3:** 325, 557, 559
19:19   **Vol. 3:** 828
19:20   **Vol. 3:** 1013
19:21   **Vol. 3:** 126, 1041
19:22   **Vol. 3:** 166
19:23   **Vol. 3:** 1013
19:24   **Vol. 3:** 711
20   **Vol. 2:** 640 **Vol. 3:** 464, 1013–1014
20:1 ff   **Vol. 2:** 173
20:1–17 **Vol. 1:** 54 **Vol. 2:** 639
20:1   **Vol. 1:** 531 **Vol. 3:** 1102
20:2 ff   **Vol. 2:** 441
20:2 f   **Vol. 1:** 636
20:2   **Vol. 1:** 367, 716 **Vol. 2:** 68, 278, 797 **Vol. 3:** 1102, 1121
20:3–6   **Vol. 2:** 871 **Vol. 3:** 94
20:3 f   **Vol. 2:** 284
20:3   **Vol. 2:** 68
20:4   **Vol. 1:** 175, 518, 523 **Vol. 2:** 70, 287, 501 **Vol. 3:** 485
20:5   **Vol. 1:** 219, 555 **Vol. 2:** 68, 876 **Vol. 3:** 156, 550, 1166
20:6   **Vol. 2:** 541, 698
20:7   **Vol. 1:** 550 **Vol. 2:** 191, 449, 650, 652, 871 **Vol. 3:** 94, 342, 740
20:8–11 **Vol. 2:** 871 **Vol. 3:** 405–406
20:8   **Vol. 2:** 890 **Vol. 3:** 235
20:9 f   **Vol. 2:** 887 **Vol. 3:** 94, 1148
20:9   **Vol. 3:** 1153
20:10   **Vol. 1:** 115, 360, 688, 691 **Vol. 3:** 256, 406, 594, 608
20:11   **Vol. 2:** 889 **Vol. 3:** 255
20:12–17 **Vol. 2:** 871
20:12   **Vol. 1:** 115, 288, 336, 617, 619 **Vol. 2:** 43, 49, 640 **Vol. 3:** 95, 1057, 1069–1070
20:13   **Vol. 1:** 717 **Vol. 3:** 183
20:14   **Vol. 1:** 717 **Vol. 2:** 576, 580, 583 **Vol. 3:** 95, 183, 536
20:15 f **Vol. 3:** 70
20:15   **Vol. 1:** 717 **Vol. 3:** 377
20:16   **Vol. 1:** 717 **Vol. 2:** 471 **Vol. 3:** 1041
20:17   **Vol. 1:** 336, 456, 717 **Vol. 3:** 1057
20:18   **Vol. 2:** 485 **Vol. 3:** 1120
20:19   **Vol. 3:** 325
20:20   **Vol. 1:** 328 **Vol. 3:** 799–800
20:21   **Vol. 2:** 215
20:22–23:33 **Vol. 3:** 418, 484
20:22–23:20 **Vol. 2:** 635

20:22–23:19 **Vol. 2:** 822, 841 **Vol. 3:** 1103
20:22   **Vol. 3:** 256
20:23   **Vol. 1:** 115 **Vol. 2:** 96
20:24 ff **Vol. 3:** 418
20:24   **Vol. 2:** 649 **Vol. 3:** 233
20:25   **Vol. 1:** 203
21   **Vol. 1:** 115
21:1–23:33 **Vol. 2:** 637
21:1–23:19 **Vol. 2:** 441
21:1   **Vol. 3:** 354
21:2 ff   **Vol. 1:** 716 **Vol. 3:** 594
21:2–11 **Vol. 3:** 593
21:2   **Vol. 1:** 716 **Vol. 2:** 41, 96, 306, 822 **Vol. 3:** 593
21:4   **Vol. 3:** 594
21:5 f   **Vol. 3:** 594, 608
21:5   **Vol. 1:** 716
21:6   **Vol. 2:** 572 **Vol. 3:** 434, 594, 827
21:7–11 **Vol. 3:** 594
21:8   **Vol. 1:** 268 **Vol. 2:** 815
21:9   **Vol. 3:** 354
21:10   **Vol. 3:** 379
21:11   **Vol. 2:** 41 **Vol. 3:** 943
21:12   **Vol. 2:** 441 **Vol. 3:** 94
21:15 ff **Vol. 2:** 441
21:15   **Vol. 1:** 288, 617 **Vol. 3:** 94–95, 1069
21:16 f **Vol. 1:** 430
21:16   **Vol. 1:** 415 **Vol. 3:** 95, 377, 380, 593, 1070
21:17   **Vol. 1:** 617 **Vol. 3:** 95, 1069
21:18   **Vol. 2:** 586 **Vol. 3:** 346
21:20–27 **Vol. 3:** 594
21:20   **Vol. 1:** 162
21:21   **Vol. 3:** 608
21:22–25 **Vol. 3:** 94
21:22   **Vol. 2:** 96 **Vol. 3:** 963
21:23 ff **Vol. 2:** 96 **Vol. 3:** 94
21:23–25 **Vol. 3:** 1179
21:23   **Vol. 3:** 196, 680
21:24   **Vol. 3:** 183
21:26 f **Vol. 3:** 95, 594
21:27   **Vol. 1:** 716
21:30 f **Vol. 2:** 96
21:30   **Vol. 3:** 190, 192, 196
21:31   **Vol. 3:** 354
21:32   **Vol. 3:** 594
21:33 f **Vol. 3:** 95
21:33   **Vol. 1:** 609 **Vol. 2:** 726
22   **Vol. 1:** 115 **Vol. 3:** 134
22:1 f   **Vol. 3:** 377
22:1–4 **Vol. 2:** 96
22:1   **Vol. 3:** 95
22:2   **Vol. 2:** 142 **Vol. 3:** 594, 608
22:3   **Vol. 2:** 96 **Vol. 3:** 95
22:4   **Vol. 3:** 95
22:5 f   **Vol. 3:** 95
22:6   **Vol. 1:** 725 **Vol. 3:** 377
22:11–24 **Vol. 3:** 95
22:14* **Vol. 2:** 139 **Vol. 3:** 138
22:15 f **Vol. 3:** 1057

Exodus *(cont'd)*

22:16 f	**Vol. 3:** 95
22:16	**Vol. 2:** 578
22:17	**Vol. 2:** 554–555
22:18*	**Vol. 2:** 555 **Vol. 3:** 94
22:20 ff	**Vol. 1:** 410
22:20–23:9	**Vol. 1:** 717
22:20*	**Vol. 1:** 684 **Vol. 2:** 724 **Vol. 3:** 94
22:21 ff*	**Vol. 1:** 360
22:21–24	**Vol. 2:** 257
22:21	**Vol. 1:** 688, 691 **Vol. 2:** 822 **Vol. 3:** 1073
22:22 f	**Vol. 1:** 409 **Vol. 3:** 1074
22:22–27	**Vol. 2:** 822
22:22–24	**Vol. 2:** 738
22:23 f	**Vol. 1:** 109
22:24	**Vol. 2:** 820 **Vol. 3:** 1073
22:25	**Vol. 2:** 254, 856
22:27	**Vol. 1:** 415 **Vol. 3:** 342
22:27b	**Vol. 2:** 822
22:28*	**Vol. 3:** 40, 94, 97, 416
22:30 f	**Vol. 3:** 1103
23	**Vol. 1:** 531
23:1 ff	**Vol. 3:** 1103
23:1	**Vol. 2:** 173 **Vol. 3:** 1041, 1062
23:3–8	**Vol. 3:** 435
23:4 f	**Vol. 1:** 115 **Vol. 2:** 157
23:4	**Vol. 1:** 177, 553
23:6 ff	**Vol. 2:** 822
23:7 f	**Vol. 2:** 41
23:7	**Vol. 1:** 607 **Vol. 3:** 355–357
23:9	**Vol. 1:** 360, 688, 691 **Vol. 2:** 822
23:10 f	**Vol. 2:** 822 **Vol. 3:** 918
23:10	**Vol. 2:** 32
23:11	**Vol. 3:** 191
23:12	**Vol. 1:** 360 **Vol. 3:** 254–255, 405, 409, 594, 686
23:13	**Vol. 3:** 239
23:14 ff	**Vol. 3:** 835
23:14–17	**Vol. 1:** 626 **Vol. 2:** 463
23:14	**Vol. 2:** 687
23:15	**Vol. 2:** 675
23:16	**Vol. 2:** 783 **Vol. 3:** 852
23:17–21	**Vol. 1:** 280
23:17	**Vol. 2:** 562, 687 **Vol. 3:** 1055
23:18	**Vol. 3:** 159
23:19	**Vol. 3:** 415–416, 786, 852
23:20–23	**Vol. 1:** 101
23:20	**Vol. 3:** 117, 119
23:22	**Vol. 1:** 332, 554 **Vol. 2:** 800, 838 **Vol. 3:** 37
23:24 f	**Vol. 3:** 550
23:24	**Vol. 2:** 876
23:25	**Vol. 3:** 988
23:27	**Vol. 1:** 527
23:31	**Vol. 3:** 983
23:33	**Vol. 2:** 705
24	**Vol. 2:** 540, 637
24:1	**Vol. 1:** 195 **Vol. 2:** 754, 876
24:2	**Vol. 2:** 724
24:3 f	**Vol. 2:** 1103
24:3–8	**Vol. 2:** 533 **Vol. 3:** 425, 1103
24:3	**Vol. 3:** 354
24:4–8	**Vol. 1:** 373
24:4	**Vol. 2:** 639
24:5–8	**Vol. 1:** 222, 369
24:6 ff	**Vol. 1:** 115, 221
24:6	**Vol. 1:** 223
24:7 f	**Vol. 2:** 797
24:7	**Vol. 1:** 243, 245 **Vol. 2:** 173, 639
24:8 ff	**Vol. 1:** 369
24:8	**Vol. 1:** 223–225 **Vol. 2:** 525–526, 533, 854 **Vol. 3:** 28
24:9 ff	**Vol. 1:** 367, 585 **Vol. 2:** 190
24:9–16	**Vol. 3:** 863
24:9–11	**Vol. 2:** 191
24:9 f	**Vol. 2:** 796
24:9	**Vol. 3:** 1013
24:10	**Vol. 1:** 239
24:11	**Vol. 2:** 272, 521
24:12	**Vol. 1:** 485 **Vol. 3:** 484, 631
24:13	**Vol. 2:** 331
24:15 ff	**Vol. 2:** 48
24:15	**Vol. 2:** 212
24:16	**Vol. 1:** 630 **Vol. 3:** 1001, 1013
24:17	**Vol. 1:** 655 **Vol. 2:** 485
24:18	**Vol. 2:** 696 **Vol. 3:** 1013
25 ff	**Vol. 3:** 812
25–31	**Vol. 1:** 66 **Vol. 2:** 637 **Vol. 3:** 484
25:1	**Vol. 3:** 1105
25:2 f	**Vol. 3:** 415
25:2	**Vol. 3:** 821
25:6	**Vol. 2:** 711
25:8–9	**Vol. 3:** 813
25:8	**Vol. 3:** 190, 786
25:9*	**Vol. 1:** 380 **Vol. 2:** 189, 194 **Vol. 3:** 569
25:10 ff	**Vol. 1:** 389
25:10–22	**Vol. 3:** 812
25:11	**Vol. 2:** 95
25:13 ff	**Vol. 2:** 487
25:16	**Vol. 3:** 787, 815
25:17–22*	**Vol. 3:** 153, 156
25:17	**Vol. 3:** 164
25:18–22	**Vol. 3:** 163
25:21 f	**Vol. 3:** 787, 815
25:22	**Vol. 3:** 788
25:23–30	**Vol. 3:** 812
25:26	**Vol. 1:** 239
25:30	**Vol. 1:** 250, 586 **Vol. 3:** 423, 814
25:31 ff	**Vol. 2:** 485 **Vol. 3:** 814
25:31–40	**Vol. 3:** 812
25:31	**Vol. 2:** 95
25:40*	**Vol. 2:** 189 **Vol. 3:** 42, 569, 814, 904–905
26	**Vol. 3:** 851
26:1	**Vol. 1:** 280
26:15–29	**Vol. 3:** 795
26:26 f	**Vol. 2:** 303

Exodus *(cont'd)*

26:31–35   **Vol. 3:** 543
26:31   **Vol. 1:** 280   **Vol. 3:** 794
26:33 ff   **Vol. 3:** 794
26:33   **Vol. 3:** 786, 794
26:34   **Vol. 2:** 212
26:36 f   **Vol. 3:** 814
26:37   **Vol. 3:** 794
27:1–8   **Vol. 3:** 812
27:2   **Vol. 3:** 715
27:9–19   **Vol. 3:** 812
27:10–17   **Vol. 3:** 795
27:20   **Vol. 2:** 711
27:21   **Vol. 3:** 794, 828
28–39   **Vol. 3:** 551
28   **Vol. 3:** 35, 396
28:1   **Vol. 2:** 592
28:2 ff   **Vol. 2:** 226
28:3   **Vol. 1:** 735   **Vol. 3:** 1027
28:4   **Vol. 3:** 120–121
28:12   **Vol. 3:** 236
28:15 ff   **Vol. 3:** 966
28:15–21   **Vol. 1:** 205
28:17–20   **Vol. 3:** 396
28:18   **Vol. 3:** 395–396
28:21   **Vol. 3:** 397
28:29   **Vol. 3:** 236, 786
28:30   **Vol. 2:** 296
28:35   **Vol. 3:** 673, 786
28:36   **Vol. 3:** 500
28:38   **Vol. 2:** 232   **Vol. 3:** 38, 150
28:39*   **Vol. 3:** 120
28:40–43   **Vol. 1:** 204
28:40*   **Vol. 3:** 120
28:41   **Vol. 1:** 122   **Vol. 2:** 232   **Vol. 3:** 38
28:42   **Vol. 1:** 672
28:43   **Vol. 3:** 786
29:1–3   **Vol. 1:** 122
29:1   **Vol. 2:** 232   **Vol. 3:** 38, 200, 435, 924
29:2   **Vol. 2:** 711   **Vol. 3:** 36, 917
29:4   **Vol. 1:** 122   **Vol. 3:** 989, 1040
29:5 f   **Vol. 1:** 122
29:7   **Vol. 1:** 122   **Vol. 2:** 711
29:9   **Vol. 2:** 60   **Vol. 3:** 36, 120, 827
29:10 f   **Vol. 3:** 1040
29:10   **Vol. 3:** 169
29:12   **Vol. 1:** 223   **Vol. 3:** 418
29:14   **Vol. 3:** 965
29:16   **Vol. 1:** 221
29:17   **Vol. 1:** 230
29:18   **Vol. 3:** 601
29:19 ff   **Vol. 3:** 435
29:20   **Vol. 1:** 239
29:21   **Vol. 1:** 221, 224   **Vol. 2:** 232, 711   **Vol. 3:** 38
29:22   **Vol. 2:** 61
29:26   **Vol. 1:** 122   **Vol. 2:** 61, 303   **Vol. 3:** 424
29:27   **Vol. 3:** 424

29:29 f   **Vol. 2:** 34
29:29   **Vol. 1:** 122   **Vol. 2:** 60
29:30 f   **Vol. 1:** 221
29:30   **Vol. 3:** 786
29:31   **Vol. 3:** 787
29:33   **Vol. 1:** 684   **Vol. 2:** 742   **Vol. 3:** 152, 159
29:36   **Vol. 3:** 152
29:37   **Vol. 2:** 226   **Vol. 3:** 152
29:38   **Vol. 3:** 924
29:40   **Vol. 2:** 711   **Vol. 3:** 423, 917, 919
29:41   **Vol. 3:** 423
29:42   **Vol. 3:** 421
29:45 f†   **Vol. 1:** 272   **Vol. 3:** 799
29:45   **Vol. 2:** 797
29:46   **Vol. 2:** 395
29:49 ff   **Vol. 3:** 799
30:1–10   **Vol. 3:** 418, 436, 812
30:1–3   **Vol. 2:** 689
30:1   **Vol. 3:** 418
30:5   **Vol. 2:** 746
30:6   **Vol. 3:** 794
30:7   **Vol. 2:** 293–294
30:8   **Vol. 2:** 69, 293–294   **Vol. 3:** 860
30:9   **Vol. 3:** 422
30:10   **Vol. 2:** 716   **Vol. 3:** 152–153, 159, 418, 815
30:11–16   **Vol. 1:** 684   **Vol. 2:** 851   **Vol. 3:** 752, 853
30:12–16   **Vol. 3:** 154
30:12   **Vol. 3:** 190, 192, 196, 1179
30:13–16   **Vol. 3:** 190
30:13   **Vol. 2:** 379, 610   **Vol. 3:** 752
30:15 f   **Vol. 3:** 153
30:15   **Vol. 2:** 841
30:16   **Vol. 3:** 192, 236, 752
30:17 ff   **Vol. 1:** 153   **Vol. 3:** 989
30:17–21   **Vol. 3:** 812
30:18 ff   **Vol. 2:** 149
30:18   **Vol. 2:** 854
30:23   **Vol. 2:** 294
30:24 f   **Vol. 2:** 711
30:24   **Vol. 3:** 1002
30:25   **Vol. 1:** 121   **Vol. 3:** 1153
30:26   **Vol. 1:** 122
30:29   **Vol. 2:** 226
30:31   **Vol. 2:** 711
30:34–35   **Vol. 2:** 293
30:34   **Vol. 2:** 723
30:35   **Vol. 2:** 723   **Vol. 3:** 445
30:36   **Vol. 3:** 788
31:3   **Vol. 1:** 735   **Vol. 3:** 691, 1027
31:7   **Vol. 3:** 153, 156
31:11   **Vol. 2:** 711   **Vol. 3:** 786
31:12–18   **Vol. 1:** 626
31:12–17   **Vol. 3:** 405
31:13–17   **Vol. 3:** 94
31:13   **Vol. 2:** 396, 626
31:14   **Vol. 3:** 405, 407
31:15   **Vol. 2:** 890   **Vol. 3:** 255

Exodus (*cont'd*)

31:17	**Vol. 2:** 626 **Vol. 3:** 255, 406
31:18	**Vol. 3:** 255, 484, 1040
32	**Vol. 1:** 531 **Vol. 2:** 637 **Vol. 3:** 806, 1013
32:1 ff	**Vol. 3:** 33
32:1	**Vol. 1:** 293
32:4	**Vol. 2:** 95, 356 **Vol. 3:** 431
32:5	**Vol. 3:** 51
32:6	**Vol. 2:** 356 **Vol. 3:** 431
32:8	**Vol. 2:** 876 **Vol. 3:** 937
32:10	**Vol. 1:** 109
32:11 f	**Vol. 3:** 155
32:11–14	**Vol. 2:** 307, 863
32:11	**Vol. 2:** 860
32:12	**Vol. 1:** 109, 699 **Vol. 3:** 152, 157, 255
32:13	**Vol. 1:** 732 **Vol. 3:** 235, 608, 734, 828
32:14	**Vol. 1:** 109, 699 **Vol. 3:** 152, 155
32:15	**Vol. 2:** 303 **Vol. 3:** 1040
32:16	**Vol. 2:** 635 **Vol. 3:** 483–484, 488
32:17	**Vol. 2:** 331
32:19	**Vol. 1:** 108 **Vol. 2:** 637 **Vol. 3:** 1013
32:20	**Vol. 2:** 34
32:25 ff	**Vol. 3:** 33
32:26	**Vol. 1:** 322
32:27	**Vol. 1:** 429 **Vol. 2:** 96
32:28	**Vol. 2:** 698
32:30 ff	**Vol. 3:** 159
32:30	**Vol. 3:** 153–154
32:32 f	**Vol. 1:** 243, 471
32:32	**Vol. 2:** 307 **Vol. 3:** 484
32:34	**Vol. 1:** 189
33:7 ff	**Vol. 1:** 294
33:7–11	**Vol. 1:** 373 **Vol. 3:** 787
33:9 f	**Vol. 3:** 257
33:10	**Vol. 2:** 876
33:11	**Vol. 2:** 173, 331
33:12–23	**Vol. 2:** 637
33:12 f	**Vol. 3:** 641
33:12	**Vol. 2:** 117 **Vol. 3:** 316
33:13	**Vol. 2:** 117, 791 **Vol. 3:** 528
33:14 f	**Vol. 1:** 585
33:14	**Vol. 3:** 255
33:16	**Vol. 2:** 117
33:17–23	**Vol. 2:** 45 **Vol. 3:** 1013
33:17	**Vol. 2:** 117
33:18 ff	**Vol. 2:** 281, 478
33:18–34:35	**Vol. 2:** 48
33:18	**Vol. 2:** 45, 489 **Vol. 3:** 514, 890
33:19	**Vol. 2:** 68, 118, 597–598 **Vol. 3:** 912
33:20 ff	**Vol. 3:** 335
33:20	**Vol. 1:** 585 **Vol. 3:** 179, 514
33:21	**Vol. 3:** 381
33:23	**Vol. 3:** 179, 514
34	**Vol. 1:** 54, 366 **Vol. 3:** 418, 862, 882, 889–890
34:1 ff	**Vol. 3:** 1013
34:1–4	**Vol. 2:** 637
34:1	**Vol. 3:** 484, 1120

34:2 ff	**Vol. 3:** 806
34:2	**Vol. 3:** 117
34:4	**Vol. 2:** 185 **Vol. 3:** 484
34:5	**Vol. 1:** 474 **Vol. 3:** 1001
34:6 f	**Vol. 3:** 167
34:6	**Vol. 2:** 71, 119, 351, 769 **Vol. 3:** 879, 882, 889
34:7	**Vol. 2:** 351, 698 **Vol. 3:** 354
34:8	**Vol. 2:** 876
34:9	**Vol. 2:** 595
34:10–27	**Vol. 2:** 637
34:12	**Vol. 2:** 705
34:13	**Vol. 3:** 418
34:14	**Vol. 2:** 876
34:15 f	**Vol. 1:** 492
34:18 ff	**Vol. 3:** 835
34:18	**Vol. 1:** 626 **Vol. 2:** 675
34:20	**Vol. 3:** 190, 192
34:21	**Vol. 3:** 255–256, 405–407, 525
34:22–26	**Vol. 3:** 852
34:22 f	**Vol. 1:** 626
34:22	**Vol. 1:** 296 **Vol. 2:** 783
34:23	**Vol. 2:** 562
34:24	**Vol. 1:** 453
34:26	**Vol. 3:** 786
34:27 f	**Vol. 3:** 484, 1120
34:28–35	**Vol. 2:** 637
34:28†	**Vol. 1:** 612 **Vol. 2:** 640, 893 **Vol. 3:** 1087, 1102
34:29 ff	**Vol. 2:** 641
34:29–36	**Vol. 2:** 45
34:29–35	**Vol. 3:** 861, 864
34:29	**Vol. 3:** 631
34:30	**Vol. 1:** 195 **Vol. 2:** 46, 213
34:31 f	**Vol. 1:** 294
34:32	**Vol. 1:** 195, 332
34:33 ff	**Vol. 3:** 795
34:33–35	**Vol. 2:** 213
34:33	**Vol. 3:** 255
34:34–35	**Vol. 2:** 212
34:34	**Vol. 2:** 213
35–40	**Vol. 2:** 638
35–38	**Vol. 3:** 812
35:1–3	**Vol. 3:** 405
35:1	**Vol. 1:** 293–294
35:2	**Vol. 3:** 255–256
35:3	**Vol. 1:** 654 **Vol. 2:** 890 **Vol. 3:** 405
35:5 f	**Vol. 3:** 416
35:8	**Vol. 2:** 711
35:9	**Vol. 3:** 36
35:10	**Vol. 3:** 1027
35:12	**Vol. 3:** 153, 156, 794
35:13	**Vol. 1:** 586 **Vol. 3:** 423, 814
35:14 f	**Vol. 2:** 711
35:19	**Vol. 3:** 786
35:21 f	**Vol. 3:** 821
35:21	**Vol. 3:** 680
35:22	**Vol. 3:** 125, 497
35:25	**Vol. 3:** 1027
35:26	**Vol. 3:** 821, 1027

Exodus *(cont'd)*

35:28	**Vol. 2:** 711
35:30 ff	**Vol. 1:** 279
35:31–35	**Vol. 3:** 691
35:31	**Vol. 3:** 1027
35:33	**Vol. 3:** 1027, 1153
35:35	**Vol. 3:** 1027
36:1 f	**Vol. 3:** 1028
36:1	**Vol. 3:** 786, 1027
36:2	**Vol. 2:** 181 **Vol. 3:** 1027
36:3 ff	**Vol. 3:** 786
36:4	**Vol. 3:** 1027
36:6	**Vol. 3:** 51
36:7	**Vol. 3:** 728
36:8	**Vol. 3:** 1027
36:18*	**Vol. 3:** 395–396
36:26	**Vol. 3:** 811
36:35*	**Vol. 3:** 794
36:36*	**Vol. 3:** 794–795
36:37 f	**Vol. 3:** 814
36:37*	**Vol. 3:** 794
37:1 ff	**Vol. 3:** 788
37:6*	**Vol. 3:** 153
37:7 ff	**Vol. 3:** 163
37:7–9	**Vol. 1:** 280
37:8 f*	**Vol. 3:** 153
37:17 ff	**Vol. 3:** 814
37:17–24	**Vol. 3:** 812
37:25–28	**Vol. 3:** 812
37:29	**Vol. 2:** 711
37:37 f	**Vol. 2:** 711
38:1–7	**Vol. 3:** 812
38:2	**Vol. 2:** 97
38:5	**Vol. 2:** 97
38:6*	**Vol. 3:** 156
38:8 f*	**Vol. 3:** 156
38:8	**Vol. 3:** 812
38:9–20	**Vol. 3:** 812
38:18*	**Vol. 3:** 794
38:24 ff	**Vol. 3:** 752
38:24*	**Vol. 3:** 416
38:26	**Vol. 1:** 684 **Vol. 2:** 698 **Vol. 3:** 752
38:27*	**Vol. 3:** 786, 794
38:36 f	**Vol. 2:** 651
39:1	**Vol. 3:** 786
39:8 ff	**Vol. 3:** 966
39:10–13	**Vol. 3:** 396
39:19	**Vol. 3:** 36
39:20	**Vol. 1:** 122
39:27 ff	**Vol. 1:** 204
39:29*	**Vol. 3:** 120
39:30	**Vol. 3:** 483
39:36	**Vol. 1:** 586, 696 **Vol. 3:** 423, 814
39:38	**Vol. 2:** 711
39:40*	**Vol. 3:** 794
39:41	**Vol. 3:** 786
40–48	**Vol. 3:** 418
40:2 ff	**Vol. 3:** 1040
40:2	**Vol. 2:** 890
40:3	**Vol. 3:** 794, 1040
40:4	**Vol. 1:** 696
40:5	**Vol. 3:** 418, 794
40:9	**Vol. 1:** 121–122 **Vol. 2:** 711
40:10	**Vol. 1:** 122
40:13	**Vol. 1:** 122
40:15	**Vol. 1:** 120, 122 **Vol. 2:** 711 **Vol. 3:** 36, 828
40:20	**Vol. 3:** 787
40:21	**Vol. 3:** 543, 794
40:22–27	**Vol. 3:** 436
40:22	**Vol. 3:** 794
40:23	**Vol. 3:** 423
40:24	**Vol. 3:** 812
40:26	**Vol. 3:** 794
40:29–32	**Vol. 3:** 812
40:29	**Vol. 3:** 422
40:30 ff	**Vol. 3:** 989
40:34 f	**Vol. 1:** 735 **Vol. 2:** 45 **Vol. 3:** 257, 554
40:38	**Vol. 2:** 305

Leviticus

1–9	**Vol. 1:** 115
1–7	**Vol. 2:** 638
1:1	**Vol. 2:** 638
1:2 f	**Vol. 2:** 41 **Vol. 3:** 423
1:2	**Vol. 2:** 43, 305, 412
1:3	**Vol. 2:** 569 **Vol. 3:** 421, 572, 924
1:4 f	**Vol. 3:** 421
1:4	**Vol. 3:** 159, 421
1:5–10	**Vol. 3:** 421
1:5	**Vol. 1:** 223
1:6	**Vol. 1:** 162 **Vol. 3:** 421
1:7 ff	**Vol. 1:** 655
1:9 ff	**Vol. 3:** 421
1:9	**Vol. 3:** 421, 600–601
1:10	**Vol. 2:** 41, 569 **Vol. 3:** 421, 423, 924
1:11	**Vol. 1:** 223
1:13	**Vol. 3:** 421, 600
1:14 ff	**Vol. 1:** 172 **Vol. 3:** 421
1:14	**Vol. 2:** 41, 379, 610
1:17	**Vol. 3:** 421, 600
2	**Vol. 1:** 250
2:1–16	**Vol. 2:** 711
2:1	**Vol. 2:** 41 **Vol. 3:** 422–423
2:2	**Vol. 2:** 293 **Vol. 3:** 238, 423
2:3	**Vol. 2:** 272
2:4 ff	**Vol. 2:** 41
2:4	**Vol. 3:** 422, 917
2:5	**Vol. 1:** 249 **Vol. 3:** 422–423, 917
2:6	**Vol. 2:** 272
2:7	**Vol. 3:** 422
2:9 ff	**Vol. 2:** 272
2:9	**Vol. 3:** 238, 423
2:11 ff	**Vol. 3:** 422
2:11	**Vol. 2:** 461
2:12	**Vol. 3:** 415, 600
2:13	**Vol. 2:** 746 **Vol. 3:** 444–446

Leviticus *(cont'd)*

2:14 f	**Vol. 3:** 422
2:14	**Vol. 2:** 675
2:16	**Vol. 3:** 238, 423
3	**Vol. 3:** 422–423
3:1	**Vol. 2:** 569 **Vol. 3:** 423, 923–924
3:2	**Vol. 1:** 221 **Vol. 3:** 423
3:3 ff	**Vol. 3:** 423
3:5	**Vol. 1:** 655 **Vol. 3:** 423
3:6–17	**Vol. 3:** 423
3:6	**Vol. 2:** 569 **Vol. 3:** 923–924
3:7	**Vol. 3:** 423
3:9	**Vol. 3:** 924
3:13	**Vol. 3:** 423
3:16 f	**Vol. 3:** 159
3:17	**Vol. 1:** 221 **Vol. 3:** 158
4	**Vol. 3:** 419
4:2–21	**Vol. 3:** 420
4:2	**Vol. 3:** 420, 680
4:3	**Vol. 1:** 122 **Vol. 3:** 924
4:4 ff	**Vol. 3:** 1040
4:5 ff	**Vol. 3:** 419
4:5	**Vol. 2:** 60
4:6	**Vol. 3:** 786, 794
4:7	**Vol. 1:** 223 **Vol. 3:** 418, 436, 686, 715
4:11 f	**Vol. 3:** 419
4:12	**Vol. 3:** 965
4:13 ff	**Vol. 1:** 294
4:13	**Vol. 1:** 294–295 **Vol. 3:** 420
4:14	**Vol. 3:** 924
4:16 ff	**Vol. 3:** 419
4:17	**Vol. 3:** 794
4:18	**Vol. 1:** 223
4:20 ff	**Vol. 1:** 698
4:21	**Vol. 3:** 965
4:22 f	**Vol. 3:** 419
4:22	**Vol. 3:** 420
4:23	**Vol. 2:** 569
4:24	**Vol. 3:** 421
4:25	**Vol. 1:** 223 **Vol. 3:** 419
4:26	**Vol. 3:** 159
4:27 f	**Vol. 3:** 419
4:27	**Vol. 3:** 420
4:28	**Vol. 3:** 924
4:30	**Vol. 1:** 223
4:32	**Vol. 3:** 924
4:33	**Vol. 3:** 421
4:34	**Vol. 1:** 223
5:1–13	**Vol. 3:** 420
5:1	**Vol. 3:** 680
5:2	**Vol. 3:** 680
5:3–6	**Vol. 3:** 740
5:3	**Vol. 3:** 104
5:4	**Vol. 3:** 680
5:5 f	**Vol. 3:** 427
5:5	**Vol. 3:** 420
5:6 ff	**Vol. 1:** 698
5:6	**Vol. 3:** 420
5:7	**Vol. 3:** 421, 728
5:8	**Vol. 3:** 420
5:11 ff	**Vol. 3:** 422
5:11	**Vol. 2:** 293, 711 **Vol. 3:** 1164
5:12	**Vol. 3:** 238, 423
5:14–6:7	**Vol. 3:** 196
5:14	**Vol. 3:** 420
5:15	**Vol. 3:** 420, 680, 752, 924
5:16	**Vol. 3:** 155
5:17 ff	**Vol. 3:** 420
5:17	**Vol. 2:** 664 **Vol. 3:** 420
5:18	**Vol. 2:** 406 **Vol. 3:** 420, 924
5:19	**Vol. 3:** 420
5:24*	**Vol. 3:** 420
5:25*	**Vol. 3:** 924
6	**Vol. 2:** 440
6:1–7*	**Vol. 3:** 420
6:2–7	**Vol. 3:** 95
6:2–6	**Vol. 3:** 421
6:2 f*	**Vol. 2:** 471
6:4*	**Vol. 3:** 420, 601
6:5 f*	**Vol. 3:** 109
6:6*	**Vol. 3:** 420
6:7 f	**Vol. 3:** 422
6:8*	**Vol. 3:** 238, 421, 423
6:9 ff	**Vol. 1:** 655
6:9	**Vol. 3:** 787
6:12*	**Vol. 2:** 569
6:14	**Vol. 3:** 422
6:15*	**Vol. 2:** 440, 711
6:17	**Vol. 2:** 461
6:19 f	**Vol. 3:** 787
6:21	**Vol. 1:** 144 **Vol. 2:** 711 **Vol. 3:** 917
6:23	**Vol. 3:** 786, 1203
6:27	**Vol. 3:** 419
6:28	**Vol. 1:** 144 **Vol. 3:** 419, 914
6:29–30	**Vol. 1:** 612
6:29	**Vol. 3:** 419
6:30	**Vol. 3:** 419
6:37*	**Vol. 2:** 569
7:2	**Vol. 3:** 421, 917
7:8	**Vol. 3:** 421
7:9	**Vol. 3:** 422
7:10 ff	**Vol. 2:** 711
7:11–16	**Vol. 3:** 422–423
7:12–15*	**Vol. 3:** 816
7:12 f	**Vol. 3:** 423, 817
7:13	**Vol. 2:** 461
7:15 f	**Vol. 3:** 423
7:15*	**Vol. 2:** 41 **Vol. 3:** 423
7:18*	**Vol. 3:** 817, 823
7:19 f	**Vol. 3:** 104
7:23 ff	**Vol. 2:** 271
7:26 f	**Vol. 1:** 221 **Vol. 3:** 158
7:33*	**Vol. 2:** 303
7:34	**Vol. 3:** 424
7:37	**Vol. 3:** 422, 1203
7:38	**Vol. 3:** 423, 1013
8–9	**Vol. 2:** 638
8:2	**Vol. 2:** 711
8:3 ff	**Vol. 1:** 294

Leviticus *(cont'd)*

8:3	**Vol. 1:** 293
8:4	**Vol. 1:** 293
8:6	**Vol. 3:** 38
8:7	**Vol. 3:** 120
8:8	**Vol. 2:** 296
8:10	**Vol. 1:** 122 **Vol. 2:** 711
8:12	**Vol. 2:** 711
8:13	**Vol. 3:** 120
8:15	**Vol. 1:** 223 **Vol. 3:** 104
8:21	**Vol. 3:** 421
8:27	**Vol. 3:** 424
8:30	**Vol. 2:** 711 **Vol. 3:** 38
8:33	**Vol. 1:** 734
9:2 f	**Vol. 3:** 420, 924
9:2*	**Vol. 3:** 109, 171
9:3	**Vol. 2:** 410
9:4	**Vol. 2:** 711 **Vol. 3:** 423
9:5 ff	**Vol. 1:** 294
9:7 f	**Vol. 1:** 322
9:7	**Vol. 3:** 421
9:9	**Vol. 1:** 223 **Vol. 3:** 419
9:12	**Vol. 1:** 223 **Vol. 3:** 421
9:15	**Vol. 3:** 420
9:17	**Vol. 3:** 421
9:22 f	**Vol. 1:** 211
9:23 f	**Vol. 1:** 655 **Vol. 2:** 45
9:24	**Vol. 3:** 421
10	**Vol. 2:** 638
10:1–11	**Vol. 2:** 293
10:1	**Vol. 1:** 655, 684
10:2	**Vol. 1:** 655
10:3	**Vol. 1:** 295
10:4 f	**Vol. 3:** 965
10:6	**Vol. 1:** 294
10:7	**Vol. 2:** 711
10:9	**Vol. 3:** 919
10:14 f	**Vol. 3:** 424
10:17 f	**Vol. 3:** 159
10:17	**Vol. 3:** 151, 786
11–15	**Vol. 2:** 34 **Vol. 3:** 989
11	**Vol. 3:** 104
11:7	**Vol. 1:** 117
11:8	**Vol. 3:** 860
11:10	**Vol. 3:** 680
11:13–19	**Vol. 1:** 172
11:14 ff	**Vol. 2:** 501
11:18	**Vol. 1:** 172
11:20 ff	**Vol. 1:** 119
11:20 f	**Vol. 1:** 172
11:27	**Vol. 2:** 638
11:33	**Vol. 3:** 419
11:35	**Vol. 3:** 419, 914
11:36	**Vol. 1:** 296
11:44 f	**Vol. 2:** 307
11:45	**Vol. 1:** 531 **Vol. 2:** 797
12–15	**Vol. 3:** 419
12:1 ff	**Vol. 3:** 989
12:2–8	**Vol. 3:** 430, 790
12:2–5	**Vol. 3:** 1058
12:3	**Vol. 1:** 308, 672 **Vol. 2:** 437, 692 **Vol. 3:** 405
12:4	**Vol. 1:** 320 **Vol. 3:** 786
12:6 ff	**Vol. 1:** 172
12:6	**Vol. 3:** 421, 924
12:7	**Vol. 2:** 569 **Vol. 3:** 104
12:8	**Vol. 3:** 104, 421
13 f	**Vol. 1:** 241 **Vol. 2:** 167 **Vol. 3:** 997
13	**Vol. 1:** 151, 204 **Vol. 2:** 464–465
13:4	**Vol. 1:** 472 **Vol. 2:** 465
13:8	**Vol. 2:** 465
13:10 ff	**Vol. 2:** 169
13:13	**Vol. 2:** 465
13:17	**Vol. 3:** 104
13:18 ff	**Vol. 2:** 465
13:23	**Vol. 3:** 224
13:28	**Vol. 2:** 288
13:40 f	**Vol. 2:** 465
13:44	**Vol. 3:** 104
13:45	**Vol. 2:** 212, 464
13:46	**Vol. 3:** 534
13:47 ff	**Vol. 2:** 465
13:47	**Vol. 2:** 465
13:49	**Vol. 2:** 631 **Vol. 3:** 37, 569, 1043
13:52	**Vol. 1:** 655
13:59	**Vol. 2:** 465
14	**Vol. 1:** 151, 221 **Vol. 3:** 419
14:2–32	**Vol. 3:** 1043
14:2 f	**Vol. 2:** 464 **Vol. 3:** 37
14:5	**Vol. 3:** 914
14:6 f	**Vol. 1:** 225
14:8 f	**Vol. 3:** 989
14:10–32	**Vol. 3:** 420
14:10–29	**Vol. 2:** 711
14:10	**Vol. 2:** 410 **Vol. 3:** 422, 917, 924
14:13	**Vol. 3:** 421, 786–787
14:14	**Vol. 3:** 424
14:18	**Vol. 3:** 159
14:19	**Vol. 3:** 419, 421, 1203
14:20	**Vol. 3:** 421–422, 1196
14:21	**Vol. 3:** 422, 424
14:22	**Vol. 3:** 421
14:24	**Vol. 3:** 424
14:29	**Vol. 3:** 159
14:31	**Vol. 3:** 171, 421
14:34 ff	**Vol. 2:** 465
14:42	**Vol. 1:** 471
14:43	**Vol. 1:** 471
14:44	**Vol. 2:** 465
14:48	**Vol. 1:** 471
14:50	**Vol. 3:** 914
14:51	**Vol. 1:** 225
14:55	**Vol. 2:** 465
14:57	**Vol. 1:** 574
15	**Vol. 1:** 151, 683 **Vol. 3:** 989
15:2 f	**Vol. 1:** 672
15:2	**Vol. 3:** 104
15:11	**Vol. 1:** 233
15:12	**Vol. 3:** 419, 914

Leviticus *(cont'd)*

15:14 f   **Vol. 3:** 421
15:16 f   **Vol. 2:** 586
15:16   **Vol. 1:** 233   **Vol. 2:** 586   **Vol. 3:** 104, 522
15:17   **Vol. 2:** 586
15:18   **Vol. 2:** 586
15:19–31   **Vol. 3:** 1058
15:19–24   **Vol. 3:** 861
15:19   **Vol. 1:** 233   **Vol. 3:** 104, 861
15:21   **Vol. 2:** 587
15:23   **Vol. 2:** 587
15:24   **Vol. 2:** 587   **Vol. 3:** 95, 104, 861
15:25–30   **Vol. 3:** 861
15:25   **Vol. 2:** 890   **Vol. 3:** 104
15:26   **Vol. 2:** 587
15:29 f   **Vol. 3:** 421
15:32   **Vol. 2:** 586
16   **Vol. 1:** 114–115, 221, 223   **Vol. 2:** 151, 199, 598, 718   **Vol. 3:** 38, 41, 94, 104, 151, 156, 192, 198, 243, 366, 419, 433, 579, 788, 794, 812, 941, 947
16:2 f   **Vol. 3:** 786, 812
16:2   **Vol. 3:** 153, 156, 788, 794, 1001, 1040
16:4   **Vol. 1:** 151, 233   **Vol. 3:** 120, 989
16:5   **Vol. 3:** 420, 1203
16:6   **Vol. 1:** 151, 221
16:8   **Vol. 1:** 451   **Vol. 2:** 296
16:10   **Vol. 1:** 451   **Vol. 3:** 159, 1005
16:11–19   **Vol. 1:** 225
16:11   **Vol. 3:** 420
16:12 f   **Vol. 1:** 655   **Vol. 3:** 815
16:12–13   **Vol. 2:** 293–294
16:12   **Vol. 1:** 495   **Vol. 3:** 794
16:13 ff   **Vol. 3:** 153, 156
16:13   **Vol. 1:** 151
16:14 ff   **Vol. 3:** 161
16:14   **Vol. 2:** 690
16:15 ff   **Vol. 1:** 221
16:15   **Vol. 3:** 794, 815
16:16 f   **Vol. 3:** 786
16:16   **Vol. 1:** 380   **Vol. 3:** 153, 419, 574
16:17   **Vol. 2:** 29
16:19   **Vol. 2:** 690
16:20 ff   **Vol. 1:** 699   **Vol. 3:** 150
16:20   **Vol. 1:** 699
16:21 f   **Vol. 3:** 574, 1005
16:21   **Vol. 3:** 164
16:22   **Vol. 1:** 699
16:24   **Vol. 3:** 989
16:26   **Vol. 1:** 451, 698   **Vol. 3:** 989
16:27   **Vol. 3:** 159, 434, 723, 965, 1203
16:28   **Vol. 3:** 419, 989
16:29   **Vol. 1:** 612   **Vol. 2:** 260
16:30   **Vol. 3:** 104
16:31   **Vol. 1:** 495, 612   **Vol. 3:** 255
16:33   **Vol. 3:** 153
17–26   **Vol. 1:** 61   **Vol. 2:** 226
17   **Vol. 1:** 221

17:3 f   **Vol. 3:** 159, 423
17:4   **Vol. 3:** 159, 574, 680, 823
17:7   **Vol. 1:** 451, 551   **Vol. 3:** 200
17:8   **Vol. 1:** 221
17:9   **Vol. 3:** 574
17:10   **Vol. 1:** 221   **Vol. 3:** 158
17:11   **Vol. 1:** 221, 699   **Vol. 2:** 477   **Vol. 3:** 150–151, 158–159, 199, 423, 425, 680
17:12–15   **Vol. 1:** 684
17:12   **Vol. 3:** 158
17:13 f   **Vol. 1:** 226   **Vol. 3:** 422
17:13   **Vol. 1:** 172, 221
17:14   **Vol. 1:** 221   **Vol. 2:** 477   **Vol. 3:** 150, 158, 425, 680
17:15   **Vol. 1:** 221
17:16   **Vol. 3:** 420
18   **Vol. 3:** 538
18:4   **Vol. 2:** 134
18:5   **Vol. 1:** 417   **Vol. 2:** 363, 445, 479
18:6 ff   **Vol. 3:** 104, 310
18:6–18†   **Vol. 1:** 499   **Vol. 2:** 577   **Vol. 3:** 1195
18:6   **Vol. 1:** 673, 675
18:7–18   **Vol. 3:** 95
18:16   **Vol. 3:** 540
18:19–33   **Vol. 2:** 577
18:19   **Vol. 3:** 95, 861
18:20   **Vol. 2:** 576, 586–587   **Vol. 3:** 104, 536
18:21   **Vol. 2:** 375, 649   **Vol. 3:** 421
18:22   **Vol. 2:** 569–570, 587   **Vol. 3:** 95, 104
18:23   **Vol. 2:** 587   **Vol. 3:** 95
18:24–29   **Vol. 3:** 95
18:27 f   **Vol. 3:** 160
18:29   **Vol. 2:** 570   **Vol. 3:** 95, 538
19:2   **Vol. 2:** 226, 230, 307
19:3   **Vol. 1:** 622   **Vol. 3:** 95, 1055, 1057
19:5 ff   **Vol. 3:** 422
19:6   **Vol. 2:** 890
19:8   **Vol. 1:** 337   **Vol. 3:** 545
19:10   **Vol. 2:** 821   **Vol. 3:** 918
19:11   **Vol. 2:** 471   **Vol. 3:** 377
19:12   **Vol. 2:** 471   **Vol. 3:** 94, 183, 740
19:13 ff   **Vol. 3:** 576
19:13   **Vol. 2:** 139   **Vol. 3:** 95, 574, 601
19:14   **Vol. 1:** 218, 622   **Vol. 2:** 707
19:15   **Vol. 1:** 587
19:15a   **Vol. 2:** 451
19:16   **Vol. 2:** 449
19:17 f   **Vol. 1:** 255, 555
19:17   **Vol. 2:** 141
19:18   **Vol. 1:** 111, 257–259, 334, 555, 738   **Vol. 2:** 157, 177, 427, 540–541, 544, 716   **Vol. 3:** 97, 173, 183, 491, 542, 1064
19:19   **Vol. 2:** 441, 742   **Vol. 3:** 1160, 1164
19:20 ff   **Vol. 2:** 582
19:20   **Vol. 1:** 716   **Vol. 2:** 586   **Vol. 3:** 190, 192, 594
19:21   **Vol. 2:** 650
19:26   **Vol. 2:** 554–555   **Vol. 3:** 158

Leviticus *(cont'd)*

19:28	**Vol. 1:** 233 **Vol. 2:** 418, 573 **Vol. 3:** 455, 483, 498
19:29	**Vol. 1:** 499
19:30	**Vol. 3:** 786
19:31	**Vol. 1:** 450 **Vol. 2:** 554–555, 559
19:32	**Vol. 1:** 92, 622 **Vol. 2:** 49
19:33 f	**Vol. 1:** 258, 717
19:34	**Vol. 2:** 540–541
19:35	**Vol. 3:** 402, 1161
19:36	**Vol. 3:** 356, 1160
19:37	**Vol. 2:** 441
20:1–5	**Vol. 3:** 421
20:2 ff	**Vol. 3:** 418
20:2–5	**Vol. 3:** 95
20:2	**Vol. 1:** 655
20:3	**Vol. 1:** 463 **Vol. 3:** 786
20:4	**Vol. 3:** 786
20:5	**Vol. 1:** 463
20:6	**Vol. 1:** 463 **Vol. 2:** 554–555
20:7	**Vol. 2:** 226
20:9–27	**Vol. 2:** 142
20:9	**Vol. 3:** 95, 159, 1070
20:10	**Vol. 2:** 576, 582 **Vol. 3:** 95, 227, 536, 538
20:11 ff	**Vol. 3:** 159, 310
20:11–21	**Vol. 3:** 95
20:11 f	**Vol. 3:** 535
20:13	**Vol. 2:** 569–570, 587 **Vol. 3:** 95
20:14	**Vol. 1:** 655 **Vol. 2:** 96
20:15	**Vol. 3:** 95
20:16	**Vol. 3:** 159
20:18	**Vol. 3:** 95, 786
20:19 ff	**Vol. 2:** 577
20:19	**Vol. 1:** 673
20:21	**Vol. 2:** 576 **Vol. 3:** 540
20:22	**Vol. 2:** 363
20:23	**Vol. 3:** 786
20:24	**Vol. 1:** 683
20:26	**Vol. 2:** 307
20:27	**Vol. 2:** 554–555 **Vol. 3:** 94–95, 159, 786
21	**Vol. 2:** 34
21:1 ff	**Vol. 2:** 415
21:2 f	**Vol. 2:** 53
21:7	**Vol. 1:** 453 **Vol. 2:** 577, 592 **Vol. 3:** 95
21:8	**Vol. 3:** 445
21:9	**Vol. 1:** 655 **Vol. 2:** 96 **Vol. 3:** 95
21:10 ff	**Vol. 2:** 711 **Vol. 3:** 35
21:12	**Vol. 3:** 786
21:13 ff	**Vol. 1:** 619
21:13 f	**Vol. 2:** 577, 592
21:14	**Vol. 3:** 1074
21:17	**Vol. 3:** 424, 445
21:18 ff	**Vol. 1:** 219
21:18	**Vol. 1:** 219
21:20	**Vol. 1:** 520
21:21	**Vol. 2:** 53
21:22	**Vol. 3:** 424
21:23	**Vol. 2:** 53 **Vol. 3:** 786, 794
22:4	**Vol. 2:** 464, 586 **Vol. 3:** 522
22:10	**Vol. 1:** 684, 691 **Vol. 2:** 139, 742
22:11	**Vol. 3:** 594
22:12	**Vol. 3:** 416
22:14	**Vol. 2:** 406
22:17–25	**Vol. 3:** 200, 435
22:18 f	**Vol. 3:** 421
22:18	**Vol. 1:** 344, 534
22:19 ff	**Vol. 2:** 415
22:19–25	**Vol. 3:** 745
22:19	**Vol. 2:** 569 **Vol. 3:** 924
22:21	**Vol. 1:** 534 **Vol. 3:** 422, 924
22:22 f	**Vol. 3:** 1074
22:22	**Vol. 1:** 219
22:23 f	**Vol. 3:** 95
22:23	**Vol. 3:** 423
22:25	**Vol. 1:** 468
22:27	**Vol. 2:** 43
22:29	**Vol. 3:** 423
23	**Vol. 1:** 626
23:1–3	**Vol. 3:** 405, 407
23:2–37	**Vol. 1:** 272
23:3 ff	**Vol. 3:** 918
23:3	**Vol. 3:** 255
23:5	**Vol. 1:** 632
23:6–8	**Vol. 1:** 632
23:6	**Vol. 2:** 690
23:10 f	**Vol. 3:** 1200
23:10	**Vol. 3:** 415
23:12	**Vol. 3:** 421, 924
23:13	**Vol. 3:** 422–423, 919
23:14	**Vol. 2:** 43
23:15 ff	**Vol. 3:** 417
23:15–21	**Vol. 2:** 783
23:15	**Vol. 2:** 890 **Vol. 3:** 424
23:16 f	**Vol. 3:** 422
23:16	**Vol. 2:** 675
23:17	**Vol. 3:** 424
23:18	**Vol. 3:** 924
23:19	**Vol. 3:** 423
23:20	**Vol. 3:** 424
23:22	**Vol. 2:** 821
23:24	**Vol. 3:** 237, 255
23:26–32†	**Vol. 1:** 626
23:27–32	**Vol. 1:** 612
23:27 f	**Vol. 2:** 890 **Vol. 3:** 150, 153
23:27	**Vol. 1:** 495, 612
23:29	**Vol. 1:** 465
23:32	**Vol. 1:** 495, 612
23:34–36	**Vol. 3:** 1005
23:34	**Vol. 2:** 690 **Vol. 3:** 811
23:37	**Vol. 3:** 422–423
23:39–55	**Vol. 3:** 594
23:39	**Vol. 3:** 255
23:42 f	**Vol. 3:** 811, 1005
23:43	**Vol. 1:** 626 **Vol. 2:** 784
24:2	**Vol. 2:** 711
24:3	**Vol. 3:** 794

Leviticus *(cont'd)*

24:5–9	**Vol. 3:** 423
24:7 ff	**Vol. 3:** 792
24:7	**Vol. 2:** 293 **Vol. 3:** 238–239, 423
24:8 f	**Vol. 3:** 239
24:8	**Vol. 2:** 890 **Vol. 3:** 407
24:9	**Vol. 3:** 37, 814
24:10 ff	**Vol. 3:** 342–343
24:10–16	**Vol. 3:** 342
24:11–23	**Vol. 3:** 94
24:14	**Vol. 1:** 294 **Vol. 2:** 29
24:15 f	**Vol. 3:** 95
24:16	**Vol. 1:** 294 **Vol. 2:** 231, 449, 801 **Vol. 3:** 341
24:18	**Vol. 3:** 95
24:19 f	**Vol. 3:** 94
24:20	**Vol. 3:** 183
24:21	**Vol. 3:** 95
25	**Vol. 1:** 698 **Vol. 2:** 298 **Vol. 3:** 191
25:1	**Vol. 3:** 1013
25:3	**Vol. 2:** 32
25:4 f	**Vol. 3:** 255
25:6	**Vol. 1:** 691 **Vol. 2:** 139
25:8	**Vol. 3:** 255
25:9	**Vol. 2:** 890 **Vol. 3:** 150, 156, 873
25:18	**Vol. 3:** 354
25:20	**Vol. 2:** 32
25:22	**Vol. 2:** 713
25:23	**Vol. 1:** 640, 688, 691 **Vol. 3:** 190
25:24	**Vol. 3:** 190
25:25 ff	**Vol. 3:** 728
25:25	**Vol. 3:** 192
25:26	**Vol. 3:** 190
25:28	**Vol. 3:** 256
25:29	**Vol. 3:** 190, 193
25:30	**Vol. 1:** 664 **Vol. 3:** 192
25:31 f	**Vol. 3:** 190, 193
25:31	**Vol. 3:** 823
25:33	**Vol. 3:** 192
25:34	**Vol. 1:** 520
25:35 ff	**Vol. 1:** 690–691 **Vol. 3:** 593
25:35	**Vol. 2:** 540
25:36	**Vol. 2:** 254
25:37	**Vol. 3:** 190
25:38	**Vol. 1:** 531
25:39 ff	**Vol. 2:** 96
25:39–43	**Vol. 3:** 594
25:40	**Vol. 2:** 139
25:44 ff	**Vol. 3:** 593
25:47–55	**Vol. 3:** 594
25:48 f	**Vol. 3:** 190, 192
25:48	**Vol. 3:** 190, 193
25:49	**Vol. 1:** 673
25:50	**Vol. 2:** 139 **Vol. 3:** 191
25:51 f	**Vol. 3:** 190
25:53	**Vol. 2:** 139
25:54	**Vol. 3:** 192
25:55	**Vol. 3:** 190–191
26:1	**Vol. 2:** 876

26:2	**Vol. 1:** 622 **Vol. 3:** 786
26:4	**Vol. 3:** 835, 982, 1001
26:5	**Vol. 1:** 663 **Vol. 3:** 144
26:6	**Vol. 1:** 113 **Vol. 2:** 778
26:8	**Vol. 3:** 962
26:10	**Vol. 2:** 675
26:11 f	**Vol. 2:** 251 **Vol. 3:** 784, 800
26:12	**Vol. 1:** 368 **Vol. 2:** 797, 800 **Vol. 3:** 813, 944–945
26:13	**Vol. 2:** 735 **Vol. 3:** 1161
26:15 f	**Vol. 1:** 367
26:18	**Vol. 3:** 777
26:19	**Vol. 3:** 29–30
26:22	**Vol. 1:** 113
26:25	**Vol. 3:** 93
26:28	**Vol. 3:** 777
26:30	**Vol. 2:** 284
26:31	**Vol. 3:** 600
26:32	**Vol. 2:** 622
26:33	**Vol. 2:** 34
26:34–43	**Vol. 3:** 191
26:36	**Vol. 3:** 249
26:39	**Vol. 3:** 574
26:41	**Vol. 1:** 308
26:42	**Vol. 2:** 596 **Vol. 3:** 235
26:45	**Vol. 3:** 235
26:46	**Vol. 3:** 1013
27	**Vol. 1:** 698 **Vol. 3:** 420
27:3	**Vol. 2:** 569
27:5 ff	**Vol. 2:** 569
27:13	**Vol. 3:** 190, 192
27:15	**Vol. 3:** 190, 192
27:18	**Vol. 1:** 413
27:19 f	**Vol. 3:** 190, 192
27:19	**Vol. 1:** 267, 413
27:23	**Vol. 2:** 683 **Vol. 3:** 756, 823
27:27–31	**Vol. 3:** 192
27:29	**Vol. 1:** 414 **Vol. 3:** 192
27:30–33	**Vol. 2:** 693 **Vol. 3:** 1053
27:30–32	**Vol. 2:** 694 **Vol. 3:** 852
27:30	**Vol. 1:** 116
27:31	**Vol. 3:** 190
27:33	**Vol. 3:** 192

Numbers

1–4	**Vol. 1:** 189
1	**Vol. 2:** 638
1:2	**Vol. 1:** 165, 294 **Vol. 2:** 158
1:3*	**Vol. 2:** 569
1:4–49	**Vol. 2:** 695
1:16	**Vol. 2:** 698
1:21	**Vol. 1:** 190
1:23–46	**Vol. 2:** 698
1:23	**Vol. 1:** 190
1:25	**Vol. 1:** 190
1:44	**Vol. 1:** 189
1:49	**Vol. 2:** 683
2	**Vol. 2:** 638 **Vol. 3:** 397
2:2	**Vol. 3:** 871

Numbers *(cont'd)*

2:3	**Vol. 1:** 165, 665
2:4–32	**Vol. 2:** 698
2:4	**Vol. 1:** 189
2:5	**Vol. 1:** 165
2:7	**Vol. 1:** 165
2:25	**Vol. 3:** 872
3–4	**Vol. 2:** 789
3	**Vol. 2:** 638
3:1	**Vol. 3:** 1013
3:2	**Vol. 1:** 667
3:3	**Vol. 1:** 120 **Vol. 2:** 149
3:4	**Vol. 1:** 655
3:7	**Vol. 1:** 294
3:10	**Vol. 2:** 592 **Vol. 3:** 36, 418, 794, 860
3:26	**Vol. 3:** 794
3:28	**Vol. 3:** 786
3:31 f	**Vol. 3:** 786
3:38	**Vol. 3:** 786, 860
3:39	**Vol. 1:** 189
3:40	**Vol. 2:** 569
3:43	**Vol. 2:** 698
3:46–51	**Vol. 3:** 190
4	**Vol. 2:** 638
4:5	**Vol. 2:** 212 **Vol. 3:** 794, 1040
4:6	**Vol. 2:** 212
4:7	**Vol. 1:** 586 **Vol. 3:** 423
4:8	**Vol. 2:** 212
4:9	**Vol. 2:** 711
4:12	**Vol. 2:** 212 **Vol. 3:** 786
4:15 f	**Vol. 3:** 786
4:15	**Vol. 2:** 212–213, 226 **Vol. 3:** 786
4:16	**Vol. 2:** 711
4:18	**Vol. 2:** 803
4:20	**Vol. 2:** 212–213, 226 **Vol. 3:** 786
4:25 ff	**Vol. 3:** 1040
4:32	**Vol. 3:** 794
4:34	**Vol. 1:** 292
5	**Vol. 2:** 638
5:1 ff	**Vol. 1:** 151
5:2	**Vol. 2:** 464
5:5–8	**Vol. 3:** 196
5:6 ff	**Vol. 3:** 420
5:6 f	**Vol. 3:** 427
5:7 f	**Vol. 3:** 420
5:8	**Vol. 3:** 153, 155–156
5:9	**Vol. 3:** 416
5:11–31	**Vol. 1:** 98 **Vol. 2:** 583
5:11–28	**Vol. 3:** 740
5:12	**Vol. 3:** 583
5:13	**Vol. 1:** 343 **Vol. 2:** 586
5:14	**Vol. 3:** 691
5:15	**Vol. 2:** 41, 711 **Vol. 3:** 236, 239, 243, 422
5:16–28	**Vol. 3:** 208
5:17	**Vol. 2:** 226 **Vol. 3:** 914
5:18 f	**Vol. 2:** 140
5:18	**Vol. 3:** 236, 310, 422
5:19 f	**Vol. 3:** 583
5:19	**Vol. 1:** 98
5:20	**Vol. 2:** 587
5:22	**Vol. 1:** 97
5:23 f	**Vol. 2:** 140 **Vol. 3:** 484
5:25	**Vol. 3:** 422
5:26	**Vol. 3:** 238, 423
5:27	**Vol. 2:** 140
5:29	**Vol. 2:** 440 **Vol. 3:** 583
6	**Vol. 1:** 211 **Vol. 2:** 638
6:1 ff	**Vol. 2:** 225
6:1–21	**Vol. 3:** 431, 793
6:1–12	**Vol. 3:** 420
6:2–21	**Vol. 3:** 101
6:3	**Vol. 3:** 101, 919, 921
6:5	**Vol. 1:** 734 **Vol. 2:** 157
6:6	**Vol. 3:** 680
6:10 f	**Vol. 3:** 421
6:13	**Vol. 2:** 440
6:14 ff	**Vol. 3:** 420
6:14	**Vol. 2:** 41 **Vol. 3:** 421, 423, 923–924
6:15	**Vol. 2:** 711 **Vol. 3:** 422–423
6:17	**Vol. 3:** 423
6:18 f	**Vol. 3:** 422
6:20	**Vol. 3:** 424
6:21	**Vol. 2:** 41, 440
6:22 f	**Vol. 2:** 777
6:23 f	**Vol. 2:** 778
6:23	**Vol. 1:** 211
6:24 ff	**Vol. 2:** 649, 777
6:24–26	**Vol. 1:** 211 **Vol. 2:** 778
6:25 ff	**Vol. 1:** 585
6:25	**Vol. 3:** 318–319
6:27	**Vol. 1:** 211 **Vol. 2:** 649, 778
7	**Vol. 2:** 638
7:1	**Vol. 1:** 122
7:9	**Vol. 3:** 786
7:13 ff	**Vol. 3:** 422
7:13–79	**Vol. 2:** 711
7:25	**Vol. 2:** 43 **Vol. 3:** 155
7:69	**Vol. 3:** 924
7:88	**Vol. 3:** 924
7:89	**Vol. 1:** 280 **Vol. 3:** 153, 156
8	**Vol. 2:** 638
8:4	**Vol. 3:** 569
8:5–22	**Vol. 3:** 989
8:8	**Vol. 3:** 422
8:9	**Vol. 1:** 294–295
8:11	**Vol. 3:** 424, 1148
8:13	**Vol. 3:** 424
8:15	**Vol. 3:** 424
8:18	**Vol. 2:** 711
8:19	**Vol. 3:** 786
8:20	**Vol. 1:** 294
8:21	**Vol. 3:** 101, 424
8:24	**Vol. 3:** 1147
8:25	**Vol. 1:** 606
9:1–10:10	**Vol. 2:** 638
9:2	**Vol. 3:** 835, 846
9:3	**Vol. 2:** 441 **Vol. 3:** 835
9:7	**Vol. 3:** 835, 953

Numbers *(cont'd)*

9:9	**Vol. 1:** 115
9:10 f	**Vol. 2:** 528
9:12	**Vol. 2:** 527
9:13	**Vol. 1:** 699 **Vol. 3:** 835, 953
9:14	**Vol. 2:** 441
9:15	**Vol. 2:** 889
9:17 f	**Vol. 1:** 115
10:4	**Vol. 2:** 698
10:8	**Vol. 3:** 237
10:9	**Vol. 3:** 207, 239
10:10	**Vol. 2:** 890 **Vol. 3:** 237, 239, 873
10:11	**Vol. 2:** 638
10:15–27	**Vol. 2:** 695
10:21	**Vol. 3:** 786
10:29 ff	**Vol. 2:** 99
10:33	**Vol. 3:** 255
10:35 ff	**Vol. 3:** 960
10:35	**Vol. 1:** 555 **Vol. 2:** 34 **Vol. 3:** 279
10:36	**Vol. 2:** 698 **Vol. 3:** 255
11	**Vol. 1:** 252
11:1–3	**Vol. 2:** 638
11:1	**Vol. 1:** 655 **Vol. 2:** 117
11:4 ff	**Vol. 2:** 836 **Vol. 3:** 804
11:4–9	**Vol. 1:** 252 **Vol. 2:** 871
11:4	**Vol. 1:** 456
11:5	**Vol. 2:** 41 **Vol. 3:** 234
11:8	**Vol. 1:** 459 **Vol. 2:** 711 **Vol. 3:** 394
11:10–30	**Vol. 2:** 638 **Vol. 3:** 77
11:11 ff	**Vol. 3:** 342
11:11	**Vol. 3:** 528, 721
11:12 f	**Vol. 3:** 805
11:12	**Vol. 1:** 186, 240 **Vol. 3:** 878
11:16 ff	**Vol. 1:** 195
11:16	**Vol. 2:** 32, 696, 754 **Vol. 3:** 478
11:22	**Vol. 3:** 727
11:24–29	**Vol. 1:** 527
11:25–27	**Vol. 3:** 691
11:25 f	**Vol. 3:** 255
11:25	**Vol. 3:** 256
11:27 ff	**Vol. 2:** 331
11:28	**Vol. 1:** 485 **Vol. 2:** 222
11:29	**Vol. 3:** 78, 699
11:31 f	**Vol. 1:** 173
11:31	**Vol. 3:** 1001
11:32	**Vol. 2:** 32, 889
11:33 f	**Vol. 3:** 804
11:33	**Vol. 1:** 672
11:34 f	**Vol. 3:** 238
11:34	**Vol. 1:** 456
12:1–16	**Vol. 2:** 638
12:1	**Vol. 2:** 576, 578, 684
12:2	**Vol. 2:** 175
12:3	**Vol. 2:** 257
12:6	**Vol. 1:** 512 **Vol. 3:** 87
12:7 f	**Vol. 3:** 608
12:7	**Vol. 1:** 595–596 **Vol. 2:** 248–249
12:8	**Vol. 1:** 704 **Vol. 2:** 745, 756 **Vol. 3:** 345, 514
12:9	**Vol. 1:** 108
12:11 f	**Vol. 3:** 33
12:12	**Vol. 1:** 182 **Vol. 2:** 756
12:13	**Vol. 2:** 860
13 f	**Vol. 3:** 1005
13–14	**Vol. 2:** 638
13:2–15	**Vol. 2:** 695
13:8	**Vol. 2:** 331 **Vol. 3:** 208
13:16	**Vol. 3:** 208
13:18	**Vol. 3:** 713, 993
13:20*	**Vol. 2:** 767
13:24	**Vol. 1:** 723
13:26*	**Vol. 1:** 294 **Vol. 3:** 569
13:29	**Vol. 2:** 802 **Vol. 3:** 985
14	**Vol. 1:** 203
14:1 ff	**Vol. 1:** 294–295
14:1–35	**Vol. 3:** 434
14:2	**Vol. 2:** 666
14:3 f	**Vol. 2:** 180
14:5	**Vol. 1:** 295
14:6–9	**Vol. 2:** 331
14:7 ff	**Vol. 1:** 296
14:8	**Vol. 1:** 683 **Vol. 2:** 818
14:9	**Vol. 1:** 606–607, 622
14:11	**Vol. 2:** 627 **Vol. 3:** 342, 368
14:13–22	**Vol. 2:** 863
14:13	**Vol. 3:** 713
14:14	**Vol. 1:** 655
14:18	**Vol. 2:** 769
14:19	**Vol. 1:** 698 **Vol. 2:** 595 **Vol. 3:** 152, 157
14:20	**Vol. 1:** 165 **Vol. 3:** 157
14:21–23	**Vol. 3:** 742
14:21	**Vol. 1:** 735 **Vol. 2:** 229 **Vol. 3:** 740
14:22	**Vol. 3:** 514, 799–800
14:23	**Vol. 3:** 342
14:27	**Vol. 2:** 175
14:28	**Vol. 3:** 740
14:29	**Vol. 2:** 458
14:30–38	**Vol. 2:** 331
14:30	**Vol. 1:** 321
14:31	**Vol. 1:** 607
14:33	**Vol. 2:** 458 **Vol. 3:** 1195
14:34	**Vol. 3:** 804, 843
14:41	**Vol. 3:** 583
15:2	**Vol. 1:** 321
15:3	**Vol. 3:** 423, 601
15:4–9	**Vol. 2:** 711
15:4	**Vol. 3:** 422, 917
15:5	**Vol. 2:** 410 **Vol. 3:** 423
15:6	**Vol. 3:** 422
15:7	**Vol. 3:** 423, 919
15:9	**Vol. 3:** 422
15:10	**Vol. 3:** 423, 919
15:15 f	**Vol. 1:** 360
15:16	**Vol. 3:** 354
15:17 ff	**Vol. 3:** 416
15:17–21	**Vol. 3:** 416
15:20 f	**Vol. 3:** 415, 917
15:22–26	**Vol. 3:** 420

Numbers *(cont'd)*

15:22	**Vol. 1:** 294
15:24	**Vol. 3:** 423, 924
15:25 f	**Vol. 1:** 698
15:25	**Vol. 3:** 155
15:27–31	**Vol. 3:** 419
15:27	**Vol. 3:** 94
15:28	**Vol. 3:** 416
15:30 f	**Vol. 3:** 94, 342, 1206
15:30	**Vol. 1:** 360 **Vol. 3:** 29, 31
15:32–36	**Vol. 3:** 94–95, 405
15:32	**Vol. 2:** 890 **Vol. 3:** 407
15:35 f	**Vol. 1:** 294
15:35	**Vol. 2:** 29
15:37–41	**Vol. 2:** 174, 177, 864
15:39	**Vol. 3:** 233
16	**Vol. 2:** 638 **Vol. 3:** 1054
16:3	**Vol. 1:** 293
16:5	**Vol. 1:** 295, 537 **Vol. 2:** 395, 400 **Vol. 3:** 500
16:9	**Vol. 1:** 294
16:15	**Vol. 3:** 421
16:16	**Vol. 3:** 117
16:22	**Vol. 1:** 674 **Vol. 3:** 690
16:25	**Vol. 1:** 195
16:28	**Vol. 3:** 630, 645
16:30	**Vol. 3:** 342
16:33	**Vol. 1:** 293, 463
16:35	**Vol. 1:** 655 **Vol. 2:** 485
16:40*	**Vol. 1:** 292, 684 **Vol. 2:** 742 **Vol. 3:** 236
16:41–50	**Vol. 3:** 155
16:46 f	**Vol. 3:** 155
16:46	**Vol. 2:** 294 **Vol. 3:** 159
17	**Vol. 1:** 162 **Vol. 2:** 638
17:1 ff	**Vol. 3:** 484, 815
17:2*	**Vol. 2:** 34
17:5	**Vol. 3:** 236
17:7	**Vol. 1:** 293
17:10	**Vol. 1:** 408 **Vol. 3:** 815
17:12	**Vol. 1:** 295
18:1–7	**Vol. 2:** 34
18:1	**Vol. 2:** 592 **Vol. 3:** 36, 416, 786
18:2	**Vol. 3:** 415
18:3	**Vol. 2:** 34 **Vol. 3:** 786
18:5	**Vol. 3:** 786
18:7	**Vol. 3:** 36, 794
18:8	**Vol. 3:** 416
18:9	**Vol. 2:** 232 **Vol. 3:** 38, 420, 422
18:11	**Vol. 3:** 416
18:12	**Vol. 3:** 416
18:14	**Vol. 1:** 414
18:15	**Vol. 3:** 190, 192, 416
18:17	**Vol. 3:** 192
18:18	**Vol. 3:** 424
18:20–32	**Vol. 2:** 693
18:20–24	**Vol. 2:** 693
18:20	**Vol. 2:** 302
18:21 ff	**Vol. 2:** 693
18:21	**Vol. 2:** 466 **Vol. 3:** 853
18:22 ff	**Vol. 3:** 150
18:22	**Vol. 3:** 1206
18:23 f	**Vol. 2:** 298
18:24	**Vol. 2:** 466
18:26 ff	**Vol. 2:** 466
18:26	**Vol. 2:** 693
18:27	**Vol. 3:** 823
18:28	**Vol. 2:** 693 **Vol. 3:** 853
18:29 f	**Vol. 3:** 416
18:30	**Vol. 3:** 823
18:31	**Vol. 2:** 139
18:32	**Vol. 3:** 416
19	**Vol. 1:** 225 **Vol. 3:** 104
19:2	**Vol. 1:** 203, 205 **Vol. 3:** 924, 1161
19:4	**Vol. 1:** 221
19:8 ff	**Vol. 3:** 419
19:9	**Vol. 2:** 32
19:11 ff	**Vol. 1:** 151
19:11 f	**Vol. 3:** 989
19:11	**Vol. 3:** 860
19:12	**Vol. 3:** 101
19:13	**Vol. 1:** 151
19:14 f	**Vol. 3:** 104
19:14	**Vol. 3:** 811
19:15	**Vol. 2:** 726
19:16	**Vol. 1:** 444 **Vol. 3:** 238, 860
19:17	**Vol. 2:** 854
19:18 f	**Vol. 1:** 144
19:18	**Vol. 3:** 238
19:20	**Vol. 3:** 420, 786
19:21	**Vol. 3:** 419
20	**Vol. 3:** 383
20:1 ff	**Vol. 1:** 294–295
20:1–14	**Vol. 2:** 638
20:1–13	**Vol. 3:** 382
20:1–11	**Vol. 3:** 459
20:1	**Vol. 2:** 638
20:2–5	**Vol. 1:** 203
20:3	**Vol. 2:** 666 **Vol. 3:** 346
20:4	**Vol. 3:** 346
20:6	**Vol. 1:** 293
20:8	**Vol. 1:** 293 **Vol. 3:** 381
20:10 ff	**Vol. 3:** 342
20:11	**Vol. 2:** 276
20:12	**Vol. 2:** 638
20:13	**Vol. 3:** 346
20:16	**Vol. 1:** 410 **Vol. 3:** 1014
20:20	**Vol. 2:** 800
20:22–29	**Vol. 2:** 638
20:27	**Vol. 3:** 939
20:29	**Vol. 1:** 506
21	**Vol. 2:** 638
21:2 f	**Vol. 1:** 415
21:3	**Vol. 1:** 272, 413
21:4 ff	**Vol. 3:** 804
21:4–9	**Vol. 1:** 465 **Vol. 3:** 1005–1006
21:5	**Vol. 3:** 345
21:7	**Vol. 3:** 345
21:8 f	**Vol. 1:** 510

Numbers *(cont'd)*

21:9	**Vol. 1:** 390
21:14	**Vol. 1:** 243
21:16 ff	**Vol. 3:** 459
21:16	**Vol. 2:** 32
21:17	**Vol. 3:** 459, 672–673
21:21	**Vol. 1:** 194
21:22	**Vol. 1:** 520
21:23	**Vol. 2:** 32
21:27	**Vol. 3:** 119
21:29	**Vol. 3:** 590
21:35	**Vol. 3:** 248
22–24	**Vol. 1:** 208, 416 **Vol. 2:** 638 **Vol. 3:** 942, 1054
22	**Vol. 2:** 431
22:1–6	**Vol. 1:** 208
22:4	**Vol. 1:** 293
22:5	**Vol. 1:** 194
22:6–12	**Vol. 1:** 416
22:6	**Vol. 1:** 416
22:7	**Vol. 2:** 554
22:8	**Vol. 3:** 178
22:11	**Vol. 1:** 416
22:12	**Vol. 1:** 208
22:17	**Vol. 1:** 416
22:19	**Vol. 2:** 773
22:20	**Vol. 2:** 898
22:22	**Vol. 1:** 101 **Vol. 3:** 468
22:25	**Vol. 3:** 948
22:28	**Vol. 2:** 726
22:31	**Vol. 1:** 208 **Vol. 2:** 876 **Vol. 3:** 311, 312
22:32	**Vol. 3:** 468
22:38	**Vol. 1:** 208
23:1 f	**Vol. 3:** 418
23:1	**Vol. 3:** 117
23:3–5	**Vol. 1:** 208
23:4	**Vol. 3:** 418
23:5	**Vol. 3:** 1120
23:7–18	**Vol. 2:** 745
23:7–10	**Vol. 1:** 208
23:7	**Vol. 1:** 416 **Vol. 2:** 318
23:9	**Vol. 1:** 688, 694 **Vol. 2:** 307
23:10	**Vol. 2:** 318 **Vol. 3:** 355
23:14	**Vol. 3:** 418
23:16	**Vol. 3:** 1120
23:18–24	**Vol. 1:** 208
23:19	**Vol. 2:** 470 **Vol. 3:** 226, 613, 622
23:23	**Vol. 2:** 318, 554
23:27	**Vol. 2:** 815
23:29 f	**Vol. 3:** 418
23:29	**Vol. 3:** 117
24:1	**Vol. 2:** 103, 554
24:2	**Vol. 2:** 898 **Vol. 3:** 691
24:3–9	**Vol. 1:** 208
24:3	**Vol. 2:** 745
24:4	**Vol. 1:** 527 **Vol. 3:** 311, 1118
24:5 f	**Vol. 1:** 208
24:7	**Vol. 2:** 899 **Vol. 3:** 988
24:9	**Vol. 3:** 255
24:10	**Vol. 2:** 149
24:15–24	**Vol. 1:** 208
24:15	**Vol. 2:** 745
24:16	**Vol. 3:** 311, 1118
24:17	**Vol. 1:** 407 **Vol. 2:** 308, 313, 337, 495, 557, 596, 677 **Vol. 3:** 649–650, 652, 734, 736
24:18	**Vol. 1:** 554
24:20–23	**Vol. 2:** 745
25	**Vol. 2:** 638
25:1–18	**Vol. 2:** 699 **Vol. 3:** 154
25:1–3	**Vol. 2:** 677
25:1–2	**Vol. 2:** 677–678
25:1	**Vol. 3:** 1067
25:2	**Vol. 2:** 876
25:3	**Vol. 1:** 109 **Vol. 2:** 60
25:4	**Vol. 1:** 165 **Vol. 2:** 291
25:5	**Vol. 2:** 60
25:6–11	**Vol. 1:** 109
25:11	**Vol. 3:** 152, 155, 255, 1166
25:12	**Vol. 2:** 778
25:13	**Vol. 3:** 36, 159
26	**Vol. 2:** 638, 789
26:4–63	**Vol. 2:** 695
26:17	**Vol. 1:** 674
26:52–56	**Vol. 2:** 297
27	**Vol. 2:** 638
27:1 f	**Vol. 3:** 1057
27:1–11	**Vol. 3:** 662
27:6	**Vol. 3:** 1057
27:7*	**Vol. 3:** 351
27:11	**Vol. 1:** 673 **Vol. 3:** 354
27:15 ff	**Vol. 2:** 151
27:16	**Vol. 1:** 189, 677
27:17	**Vol. 1:** 191 **Vol. 2:** 412–413, 459
27:18	**Vol. 2:** 151, 331 **Vol. 3:** 691
27:21 ff	**Vol. 2:** 331
27:21	**Vol. 2:** 296
27:23	**Vol. 2:** 151
28 f	**Vol. 2:** 854
28	**Vol. 3:** 421–422
28:1 f	**Vol. 3:** 600
28:2	**Vol. 3:** 424
28:3	**Vol. 3:** 924
28:5 ff	**Vol. 3:** 422
28:5–18	**Vol. 2:** 711
28:7	**Vol. 3:** 208, 423, 786
28:8	**Vol. 3:** 423
28:9–29:39	**Vol. 1:** 626
28:9–24	**Vol. 3:** 423
28:9 f	**Vol. 3:** 37, 792
28:9	**Vol. 2:** 890 **Vol. 3:** 407, 924
28:11	**Vol. 3:** 924
28:13	**Vol. 3:** 421
28:14	**Vol. 3:** 423, 919
28:16	**Vol. 2:** 675
28:19	**Vol. 3:** 924
28:25	**Vol. 1:** 272
28:26–31	**Vol. 2:** 783

Numbers *(cont'd)*

28:26	**Vol. 2:** 675 **Vol. 3:** 422
28:27	**Vol. 3:** 924
28:31	**Vol. 3:** 423, 924
29	**Vol. 3:** 421–422
29:1–11	**Vol. 1:** 626
29:2	**Vol. 3:** 924
29:3–14	**Vol. 2:** 711
29:3	**Vol. 3:** 422
29:6–37	**Vol. 3:** 423
29:7	**Vol. 1:** 495, 612
29:8	**Vol. 3:** 924
29:9	**Vol. 3:** 422
29:11	**Vol. 3:** 153
29:13	**Vol. 3:** 924
29:14	**Vol. 3:** 422
29:17	**Vol. 3:** 924
29:20	**Vol. 3:** 924
29:23	**Vol. 3:** 924
29:26	**Vol. 3:** 924
29:29	**Vol. 3:** 924
29:32	**Vol. 3:** 924
29:36	**Vol. 3:** 924
29:39	**Vol. 3:** 422–423
30	**Vol. 3:** 1057
30:1 ff	**Vol. 2:** 43
30:1*	**Vol. 1:** 165
30:3–12	**Vol. 1:** 472
30:3 f	**Vol. 3:** 740
30:3	**Vol. 3:** 183
30:4*	**Vol. 3:** 224
30:5*	**Vol. 3:** 224
30:9*	**Vol. 3:** 224
30:12*	**Vol. 3:** 224
30:14	**Vol. 1:** 495
30:16†	**Vol. 3:** 354
31	**Vol. 2:** 638
31:1–54	**Vol. 3:** 155
31:2	**Vol. 3:** 93
31:3 ff	**Vol. 1:** 294
31:6	**Vol. 3:** 786
31:7 ff	**Vol. 3:** 593
31:7 f	**Vol. 1:** 429
31:9	**Vol. 3:** 590
31:12 ff	**Vol. 1:** 294
31:16	**Vol. 2:** 677
31:17 f	**Vol. 2:** 569
31:17	**Vol. 2:** 587
31:18	**Vol. 2:** 587
31:21	**Vol. 3:** 354
31:22 f	**Vol. 3:** 419
31:25–41	**Vol. 1:** 252
31:28	**Vol. 3:** 756
31:29	**Vol. 3:** 416
31:32–47	**Vol. 3:** 593
31:32	**Vol. 1:** 655
31:35	**Vol. 2:** 587
31:37–41	**Vol. 3:** 756
31:50	**Vol. 3:** 154, 498
31:54	**Vol. 3:** 236
32	**Vol. 2:** 638
32:2	**Vol. 1:** 294
32:4	**Vol. 1:** 294
32:10	**Vol. 1:** 109 **Vol. 2:** 889
32:18 f	**Vol. 2:** 298
32:23	**Vol. 3:** 574
32:33	**Vol. 3:** 748
32:39	**Vol. 1:** 463
33–36	**Vol. 2:** 638
33:2	**Vol. 2:** 639
33:8 f	**Vol. 1:** 202
33:9	**Vol. 3:** 986
33:10 f	**Vol. 3:** 983
33:16–36	**Vol. 3:** 1013
33:16 f	**Vol. 3:** 238
33:38	**Vol. 3:** 937
33:52	**Vol. 1:** 463
33:55	**Vol. 1:** 726 **Vol. 3:** 268
34:3	**Vol. 3:** 444
34:6	**Vol. 1:** 472
34:11	**Vol. 3:** 983
34:13–28	**Vol. 2:** 695
34:18–28	**Vol. 3:** 871
34:22–15	**Vol. 3:** 94
35	**Vol. 3:** 35
35:5	**Vol. 3:** 940
35:12	**Vol. 1:** 294
35:15	**Vol. 1:** 691
35:19	**Vol. 2:** 96 **Vol. 3:** 94, 159, 190
35:21	**Vol. 2:** 96 **Vol. 3:** 190
35:23	**Vol. 1:** 553
35:24	**Vol. 1:** 294 **Vol. 3:** 190
35:25	**Vol. 2:** 711 **Vol. 3:** 190
35:27	**Vol. 2:** 142 **Vol. 3:** 190
35:29	**Vol. 3:** 354
35:30	**Vol. 1:** 302 **Vol. 2:** 471, 686 **Vol. 3:** 1041
35:31 f	**Vol. 3:** 190, 192
35:31	**Vol. 3:** 94, 190
35:32	**Vol. 3:** 190
35:33	**Vol. 3:** 153–154, 159–160
36	**Vol. 3:** 1057
36:1–12	**Vol. 3:** 662
36:5–9	**Vol. 2:** 577
36:8	**Vol. 3:** 662
36:13	**Vol. 3:** 354

Deuteronomy

1–3	**Vol. 3:** 1103
1	**Vol. 3:** 1013
1:1–31:23	**Vol. 2:** 638
1:1	**Vol. 2:** 638, 830 **Vol. 3:** 1103
1:2	**Vol. 3:** 1013
1:3	**Vol. 1:** 332
1:5	**Vol. 1:** 164
1:8	**Vol. 1:** 77 **Vol. 2:** 367 **Vol. 3:** 522, 740
1:9 ff	**Vol. 1:** 195

Deuteronomy *(cont'd)*

1:9	**Vol. 3:** 836
1:10	**Vol. 3:** 734
1:12	**Vol. 1:** 712
1:13	**Vol. 3:** 1027
1:15	**Vol. 1:** 196 **Vol. 2:** 363 **Vol. 3:** 1027
1:16	**Vol. 3:** 836
1:17	**Vol. 1:** 587 **Vol. 2:** 363, 428 **Vol. 3:** 1120
1:18	**Vol. 3:** 836, 1103
1:19	**Vol. 3:** 946
1:21	**Vol. 1:** 622
1:25	**Vol. 1:** 721
1:26	**Vol. 1:** 589
1:29	**Vol. 1:** 622
1:31	**Vol. 1:** 617 **Vol. 3:** 805, 843
1:32	**Vol. 3:** 878
1:33	**Vol. 3:** 569, 946
1:34 f	**Vol. 3:** 740
1:34	**Vol. 3:** 742
1:35	**Vol. 2:** 36
1:38	**Vol. 3:** 208
1:39	**Vol. 1:** 565
1:43 – 45	**Vol. 2:** 864
1:43	**Vol. 2:** 175 **Vol. 3:** 583
2:4	**Vol. 1:** 255 **Vol. 2:** 90
2:5	**Vol. 2:** 369 **Vol. 3:** 464, 523
2:7	**Vol. 3:** 804, 1148
2:11	**Vol. 3:** 823
2:14	**Vol. 2:** 458 **Vol. 3:** 740
2:20	**Vol. 3:** 823
2:26	**Vol. 1:** 194
2:33 f	**Vol. 3:** 836
3:3	**Vol. 3:** 836
3:13	**Vol. 3:** 823
3:20	**Vol. 3:** 255 – 256
3:21	**Vol. 3:** 208
3:24	**Vol. 2:** 602 **Vol. 3:** 569
3:27	**Vol. 3:** 806
3:28	**Vol. 1:** 570 **Vol. 3:** 208
4:1	**Vol. 2:** 258 **Vol. 3:** 354, 760
4:2	**Vol. 3:** 1103
4:3	**Vol. 1:** 481
4:5 – 10	**Vol. 2:** 307
4:5 f	**Vol. 3:** 354
4:6	**Vol. 3:** 1027
4:7	**Vol. 2:** 53
4:8	**Vol. 3:** 354
4:9 – 24	**Vol. 3:** 485
4:10	**Vol. 1:** 293, 484 **Vol. 2:** 889 **Vol. 3:** 760, 1013, 1103
4:12	**Vol. 1:** 585, 655, 704
4:13	**Vol. 3:** 484, 1103
4:14	**Vol. 1:** 484 **Vol. 3:** 354, 760, 836
4:15	**Vol. 1:** 655 **Vol. 3:** 485
4:16 ff	**Vol. 2:** 501
4:16	**Vol. 2:** 287
4:17	**Vol. 1:** 172
4:18	**Vol. 1:** 670
4:19	**Vol. 1:** 522 **Vol. 2:** 189, 876 **Vol. 3:** 550, 731, 735
4:20	**Vol. 2:** 98, 797
4:21	**Vol. 3:** 740
4:24	**Vol. 1:** 655
4:25 ff	**Vol. 1:** 688
4:26	**Vol. 3:** 1041
4:27 ff	**Vol. 3:** 249
4:27	**Vol. 2:** 428, 791
4:28	**Vol. 3:** 550
4:29	**Vol. 3:** 531
4:30	**Vol. 1:** 354
4:31	**Vol. 3:** 740
4:32	**Vol. 1:** 379 **Vol. 2:** 194 **Vol. 3:** 1120
4:33	**Vol. 1:** 655
4:34	**Vol. 2:** 627 **Vol. 3:** 799
4:35	**Vol. 2:** 627
4:36	**Vol. 2:** 190 **Vol. 3:** 776, 1103, 1120
4:37	**Vol. 1:** 538
4:39	**Vol. 2:** 190
4:40	**Vol. 3:** 354
4:41	**Vol. 1:** 472
4:43	**Vol. 3:** 1009
4:45	**Vol. 3:** 354
5	**Vol. 3:** 1013
5:1	**Vol. 2:** 134, 173 **Vol. 3:** 354
5:2	**Vol. 3:** 1013
5:4	**Vol. 3:** 409
5:5 – 21	**Vol. 2:** 639
5:5	**Vol. 3:** 1103
5:6 ff	**Vol. 2:** 173
5:6 – 21	**Vol. 1:** 54
5:7 – 10	**Vol. 2:** 871
5:7 f	**Vol. 2:** 284
5:8	**Vol. 1:** 175
5:9	**Vol. 1:** 219, 555 **Vol. 2:** 876 **Vol. 3:** 156, 550
5:10	**Vol. 2:** 698
5:11 ff	**Vol. 3:** 94
5:11	**Vol. 2:** 871 **Vol. 3:** 342
5:12 – 15	**Vol. 2:** 871, 889 **Vol. 3:** 256, 406
5:13 f	**Vol. 3:** 1148
5:13	**Vol. 2:** 650
5:14	**Vol. 1:** 115 **Vol. 3:** 254, 594
5:15	**Vol. 2:** 890 **Vol. 3:** 232, 235
5:16 – 21	**Vol. 2:** 871
5:16 – 20	**Vol. 3:** 379
5:16	**Vol. 2:** 43, 478 **Vol. 3:** 95, 1057, 1070
5:17*	**Vol. 3:** 183, 1041
5:18	**Vol. 2:** 576, 580, 583 **Vol. 3:** 183, 536
5:19	**Vol. 3:** 377
5:21	**Vol. 1:** 336 **Vol. 3:** 1057
5:22	**Vol. 1:** 296 **Vol. 3:** 484
5:24	**Vol. 2:** 45
5:25*	**Vol. 3:** 351
5:28*	**Vol. 3:** 354, 760
5:33	**Vol. 3:** 255, 257
6 – 8	**Vol. 3:** 804 – 805
6	**Vol. 3:** 806
6:1 f	**Vol. 3:** 354

Deuteronomy *(cont'd)*

6:1	**Vol. 3:** 760
6:3	**Vol. 1:** 683 **Vol. 3:** 354
6:4 ff	**Vol. 2:** 173, 864
6:4–9	**Vol. 2:** 174, 177, 864 **Vol. 3:** 105, 1161
6:4 f	**Vol. 2:** 73, 720 **Vol. 3:** 806
6:4	**Vol. 2:** 720–721 **Vol. 3:** 173, 490, 694, 1103
6:5	**Vol. 1:** 259, 334, 456, 622 **Vol. 2:** 68, 177, 181, 427, 541, 544 **Vol. 3:** 131, 542, 685
6:6	**Vol. 3:** 484, 836, 1120
6:7	**Vol. 1:** 288, 617
6:8 f	**Vol. 3:** 484
6:8	**Vol. 2:** 136, 149, 864 **Vol. 3:** 484, 490, 559
6:9	**Vol. 3:** 483
6:10–12	**Vol. 1:** 484
6:10	**Vol. 1:** 77 **Vol. 3:** 740
6:11 f	**Vol. 2:** 272
6:13 ff	**Vol. 1:** 109
6:13	**Vol. 1:** 622 **Vol. 2:** 349, 724, 876, 893 **Vol. 3:** 550, 739, 806–807
6:16	**Vol. 2:** 893 **Vol. 3:** 790, 799–802, 805–806
6:17	**Vol. 3:** 354
6:18	**Vol. 2:** 103 **Vol. 3:** 740
6:20 ff	**Vol. 1:** 617 **Vol. 3:** 358
6:20	**Vol. 3:** 354
6:22	**Vol. 2:** 627
6:23	**Vol. 3:** 740
6:24	**Vol. 1:** 332 **Vol. 3:** 354
7:1 f	**Vol. 3:** 960
7:1	**Vol. 1:** 96 **Vol. 2:** 300
7:3 f	**Vol. 2:** 576
7:4	**Vol. 1:** 607 **Vol. 3:** 550
7:5	**Vol. 3:** 94, 418
7:6–11	**Vol. 2:** 541
7:6	**Vol. 2:** 226, 297, 791, 797, 800, 838, 840
7:7	**Vol. 1:** 538 **Vol. 2:** 307, 798
7:8	**Vol. 1:** 716 **Vol. 2:** 307 **Vol. 3:** 192–193, 717, 740
7:9–11	**Vol. 1:** 555
7:9	**Vol. 1:** 596 **Vol. 2:** 698–699
7:10	**Vol. 1:** 585
7:11	**Vol. 3:** 354
7:12	**Vol. 3:** 354, 740
7:13–16	**Vol. 1:** 209
7:13	**Vol. 1:** 721 **Vol. 2:** 711 **Vol. 3:** 919
7:15	**Vol. 1:** 555 **Vol. 3:** 999
7:16	**Vol. 3:** 550
7:18	**Vol. 3:** 232, 235, 238
7:19–24	**Vol. 3:** 960
7:19	**Vol. 2:** 627 **Vol. 3:** 717, 799
7:21	**Vol. 3:** 716–717
7:25	**Vol. 3:** 94
7:26	**Vol. 1:** 414
8	**Vol. 3:** 806
8:1–6	**Vol. 3:** 777
8:1	**Vol. 3:** 740
8:2 ff	**Vol. 3:** 804
8:2 f	**Vol. 2:** 871, 893
8:2	**Vol. 3:** 232, 799–800, 804, 937, 1005
8:3	**Vol. 1:** 250, 252 **Vol. 2:** 267–268, 479–480, 893 **Vol. 3:** 329, 805, 1120
8:4–9	**Vol. 3:** 487
8:4	**Vol. 2:** 714 **Vol. 3:** 805
8:5	**Vol. 1:** 617 **Vol. 3:** 776, 778
8:6	**Vol. 3:** 946
8:7	**Vol. 3:** 986, 988
8:8	**Vol. 1:** 723 **Vol. 3:** 806
8:9	**Vol. 2:** 822
8:10	**Vol. 2:** 272
8:11	**Vol. 3:** 354, 806
8:14 ff	**Vol. 3:** 805
8:14	**Vol. 3:** 806
8:15 f	**Vol. 2:** 893
8:15	**Vol. 1:** 510 **Vol. 3:** 988, 1005
8:16	**Vol. 3:** 799
8:17	**Vol. 1:** 484
8:18	**Vol. 3:** 232, 740
8:19	**Vol. 2:** 876 **Vol. 3:** 806
9:3	**Vol. 1:** 655
9:4–6	**Vol. 1:** 484
9:4 f	**Vol. 2:** 93
9:5	**Vol. 1:** 77 **Vol. 2:** 307 **Vol. 3:** 1104
9:7	**Vol. 3:** 232, 235
9:9	**Vol. 1:** 612
9:10	**Vol. 1:** 293, 295 **Vol. 3:** 484
9:14	**Vol. 1:** 471
9:16	**Vol. 3:** 806
9:18	**Vol. 3:** 804
9:19	**Vol. 1:** 318 **Vol. 2:** 893 **Vol. 3:** 324, 836
9:22	**Vol. 1:** 456 **Vol. 3:** 238, 799–800, 804
9:23 f	**Vol. 1:** 589
9:24	**Vol. 2:** 889
9:26–29	**Vol. 2:** 297, 863
9:26	**Vol. 2:** 602 **Vol. 3:** 192–193
9:27	**Vol. 1:** 77 **Vol. 3:** 235, 608
9:29	**Vol. 2:** 303, 602
10:1 ff	**Vol. 1:** 484
10:1–5	**Vol. 3:** 787
10:4	**Vol. 1:** 293 **Vol. 3:** 1103, 1120
10:8	**Vol. 1:** 474 **Vol. 2:** 649–650
10:9	**Vol. 1:** 636 **Vol. 2:** 297, 302–303 **Vol. 3:** 33
10:10	**Vol. 3:** 1019
10:12 f	**Vol. 2:** 42, 541 **Vol. 3:** 550
10:12	**Vol. 1:** 259 **Vol. 2:** 307, 856 **Vol. 3:** 946
10:13	**Vol. 3:** 354
10:14	**Vol. 2:** 189–190
10:16	**Vol. 1:** 154, 241, 308 **Vol. 2:** 184
10:17 f	**Vol. 1:** 622
10:17	**Vol. 1:** 587 **Vol. 2:** 41, 622 **Vol. 3:** 713

Deuteronomy *(cont'd)*

10:18   **Vol. 1:** 688   **Vol. 2:** 363, 737   **Vol. 3:** 1073–1074
10:20   **Vol. 2:** 349, 876   **Vol. 3:** 739
10:21   **Vol. 3:** 318
10:22   **Vol. 3:** 680, 734
11:1   **Vol. 3:** 354
11:2   **Vol. 1:** 484   **Vol. 2:** 425   **Vol. 3:** 513, 717, 777–778
11:3   **Vol. 3:** 1148
11:6   **Vol. 1:** 711
11:9   **Vol. 3:** 274
11:11   **Vol. 3:** 988
11:12   **Vol. 1:** 189
11:13 ff   **Vol. 3:** 1001
11:13–21   **Vol. 2:** 174, 177, 864   **Vol. 3:** 105, 487
11:13   **Vol. 3:** 550
11:14   **Vol. 2:** 711   **Vol. 3:** 846, 919
11:15   **Vol. 1:** 743
11:16   **Vol. 2:** 876
11:18   **Vol. 2:** 136, 149, 864   **Vol. 3:** 559
11:19   **Vol. 3:** 760
11:21   **Vol. 2:** 189
11:22   **Vol. 3:** 914
11:24   **Vol. 2:** 369
11:26 ff   **Vol. 3:** 805
11:26–29   **Vol. 1:** 416
11:26 f   **Vol. 3:** 938
11:29   **Vol. 1:** 210   **Vol. 3:** 1010
12–26   **Vol. 3:** 418
12   **Vol. 3:** 1103–1104
12:1 ff   **Vol. 3:** 806
12:2–9   **Vol. 3:** 1010
12:2   **Vol. 3:** 786
12:3   **Vol. 3:** 418
12:5–6   **Vol. 2:** 693
12:5   **Vol. 2:** 190, 803   **Vol. 3:** 786
12:6–19   **Vol. 2:** 693
12:6   **Vol. 3:** 416, 852
12:7   **Vol. 2:** 521
12:9   **Vol. 3:** 256
12:10   **Vol. 1:** 426, 663   **Vol. 3:** 255–257
12:11   **Vol. 1:** 272   **Vol. 2:** 41, 190, 650, 693   **Vol. 3:** 415, 852
12:12   **Vol. 2:** 297, 302–304   **Vol. 3:** 594
12:13   **Vol. 3:** 513
12:15–21   **Vol. 2:** 802
12:16   **Vol. 1:** 226   **Vol. 3:** 158
12:17–18   **Vol. 2:** 693
12:17   **Vol. 1:** 344   **Vol. 2:** 711   **Vol. 3:** 415, 852
12:18   **Vol. 3:** 594, 608, 805
12:19   **Vol. 3:** 841
12:20 f   **Vol. 1:** 456
12:20   **Vol. 3:** 680
12:21   **Vol. 2:** 190   **Vol. 3:** 680, 805
12:23   **Vol. 1:** 221, 226   **Vol. 2:** 477   **Vol. 3:** 151, 158, 425, 680
12:28   **Vol. 2:** 103   **Vol. 3:** 1103

12:31   **Vol. 1:** 655   **Vol. 3:** 421
13   **Vol. 1:** 433
13:1–5   **Vol. 2:** 96   **Vol. 3:** 95, 800, 806
13:1   **Vol. 2:** 350   **Vol. 3:** 1120
13:2 ff   **Vol. 2:** 629
13:2–6   **Vol. 1:** 512
13:3   **Vol. 3:** 680, 800
13:4*   **Vol. 1:** 492   **Vol. 3:** 799
13:5*   **Vol. 1:** 481   **Vol. 3:** 192–193
13:6 ff   **Vol. 1:** 556
13:6   **Vol. 1:** 240, 570   **Vol. 2:** 458, 498   **Vol. 3:** 83
13:7   **Vol. 1:** 518   **Vol. 2:** 53
13:9   **Vol. 1:** 196, 665
13:10–16   **Vol. 3:** 94
13:10   **Vol. 1:** 607   **Vol. 3:** 227
13:11   **Vol. 1:** 622
13:13   **Vol. 1:** 607
13:14   **Vol. 3:** 880
13:15   **Vol. 1:** 415   **Vol. 2:** 856
13:16*   **Vol. 1:** 413, 654   **Vol. 2:** 32   **Vol. 3:** 828
13:17   **Vol. 1:** 414
14:1 f   **Vol. 1:** 617
14:1   **Vol. 1:** 290   **Vol. 2:** 418, 782   **Vol. 3:** 638
14:2   **Vol. 1:** 538   **Vol. 2:** 226, 297, 797, 800, 838–840   **Vol. 3:** 200
14:4   **Vol. 2:** 271
14:8   **Vol. 1:** 672
14:11–20   **Vol. 1:** 172
14:17   **Vol. 1:** 172
14:19   **Vol. 1:** 172
14:21   **Vol. 1:** 684   **Vol. 2:** 226
14:22–29   **Vol. 3:** 852, 1053
14:22–27   **Vol. 2:** 693
14:22–23   **Vol. 2:** 211, 694
14:23 ff   **Vol. 3:** 805
14:23 f   **Vol. 1:** 272
14:23   **Vol. 1:** 484   **Vol. 2:** 650, 711, 803   **Vol. 3:** 786
14:25   **Vol. 3:** 786
14:27   **Vol. 2:** 302
14:28–29   **Vol. 2:** 693
14:28   **Vol. 2:** 737   **Vol. 3:** 852
14:29   **Vol. 2:** 737, 823   **Vol. 3:** 1074, 1148
15:1 ff   **Vol. 1:** 255
15:1–18   **Vol. 2:** 823
15:1–9   **Vol. 1:** 698
15:1 f   **Vol. 2:** 667
15:2–18   **Vol. 3:** 191
15:2   **Vol. 1:** 272, 698   **Vol. 2:** 666–667
15:3   **Vol. 1:** 546, 684
15:6   **Vol. 1:** 96, 165
15:9   **Vol. 2:** 667   **Vol. 3:** 1120
15:10   **Vol. 3:** 1120
15:12 ff   **Vol. 1:** 716   **Vol. 3:** 593
15:12 f   **Vol. 1:** 716
15:12   **Vol. 2:** 306   **Vol. 3:** 594
15:13 ff   **Vol. 1:** 716

Deuteronomy *(cont'd)*

15:15   **Vol. 3:** 190, 192–193, 232, 235, 1103
15:16 f   **Vol. 2:** 572   **Vol. 3:** 594, 608
15:17   **Vol. 3:** 594, 827
15:18   **Vol. 2:** 139
15:19–23   **Vol. 3:** 852
15:19   **Vol. 1:** 203   **Vol. 3:** 237
15:20   **Vol. 3:** 805
15:21   **Vol. 1:** 219   **Vol. 2:** 415
15:23   **Vol. 3:** 158
16:1 ff   **Vol. 1:** 626
16:1–16   **Vol. 1:** 626
16:1–8   **Vol. 1:** 632
16:1   **Vol. 1:** 632   **Vol. 2:** 675
16:2   **Vol. 1:** 272, 632   **Vol. 3:** 805
16:3 f   **Vol. 2:** 676, 716
16:3   **Vol. 2:** 461, 522   **Vol. 3:** 232
16:5–7   **Vol. 2:** 521
16:6 f   **Vol. 1:** 538
16:6   **Vol. 1:** 272   **Vol. 3:** 805
16:8   **Vol. 3:** 183
16:9–12   **Vol. 2:** 783
16:10   **Vol. 1:** 360   **Vol. 2:** 783
16:11   **Vol. 1:** 272   **Vol. 2:** 737   **Vol. 3:** 594, 805, 1074
16:12   **Vol. 1:** 332   **Vol. 3:** 232, 235
16:13–17   **Vol. 3:** 1005
16:13 f   **Vol. 1:** 360
16:14   **Vol. 2:** 737   **Vol. 3:** 594, 1074
16:16   **Vol. 3:** 155, 805, 813, 835
16:19   **Vol. 1:** 219, 587   **Vol. 2:** 41   **Vol. 3:** 1027
16:20   **Vol. 2:** 258, 806
16:21   **Vol. 3:** 865
17:1   **Vol. 3:** 1087
17:2–7   **Vol. 2:** 96   **Vol. 3:** 95
17:2–6   **Vol. 3:** 28
17:3   **Vol. 2:** 876   **Vol. 3:** 731
17:4   **Vol. 3:** 880
17:6 f   **Vol. 2:** 471   **Vol. 3:** 1041
17:6   **Vol. 2:** 686   **Vol. 3:** 1043, 1062
17:7   **Vol. 3:** 95, 227
17:8–12   **Vol. 3:** 94
17:8   **Vol. 1:** 241   **Vol. 3:** 33, 805
17:9   **Vol. 2:** 440
17:10   **Vol. 3:** 805
17:11 f   **Vol. 2:** 440
17:11   **Vol. 2:** 440
17:12   **Vol. 3:** 29
17:13   **Vol. 1:** 622   **Vol. 2:** 93, 527   **Vol. 3:** 83
17:15   **Vol. 1:** 472
17:17   **Vol. 2:** 576
17:18 ff   **Vol. 1:** 245
17:18   **Vol. 1:** 54, 243   **Vol. 2:** 34   **Vol. 3:** 478, 484
17:19   **Vol. 1:** 484   **Vol. 3:** 354, 1103
18   **Vol. 3:** 418
18:1 f   **Vol. 2:** 297
18:1   **Vol. 2:** 303, 466   **Vol. 3:** 433, 793

18:3   **Vol. 2:** 778
18:4   **Vol. 2:** 711   **Vol. 3:** 415, 919
18:5 f   **Vol. 1:** 538
18:5   **Vol. 1:** 474, 538   **Vol. 2:** 638   **Vol. 3:** 953
18:8   **Vol. 1:** 474   **Vol. 2:** 303
18:9 ff   **Vol. 2:** 189
18:9–14   **Vol. 2:** 296
18:9   **Vol. 2:** 791
18:10–14   **Vol. 2:** 555
18:10 f   **Vol. 2:** 555   **Vol. 3:** 94
18:10   **Vol. 1:** 655   **Vol. 2:** 555, 559   **Vol. 3:** 421
18:11   **Vol. 1:** 444, 450   **Vol. 2:** 206, 559
18:13   **Vol. 2:** 60
18:14   **Vol. 1:** 332
18:15 ff   **Vol. 1:** 66   **Vol. 2:** 337
18:15–18   **Vol. 3:** 80
18:15   **Vol. 1:** 465   **Vol. 2:** 638, 641   **Vol. 3:** 48, 83, 86, 460, 463–465, 624, 643, 696, 864, 1007
18:18 ff   **Vol. 2:** 651
18:18 f   **Vol. 1:** 465   **Vol. 3:** 696
18:18   **Vol. 2:** 641   **Vol. 3:** 48, 86, 460, 463–465
18:19   **Vol. 1:** 465
18:20 ff   **Vol. 3:** 94
18:20   **Vol. 2:** 93, 651   **Vol. 3:** 83
18:21 f   **Vol. 3:** 1104
18:22   **Vol. 2:** 93
19:6   **Vol. 1:** 318   **Vol. 2:** 181
19:10   **Vol. 2:** 142, 525, 854   **Vol. 3:** 159
19:13   **Vol. 3:** 159
19:15 ff   **Vol. 2:** 471   **Vol. 3:** 1041
19:15   **Vol. 1:** 83, 302   **Vol. 2:** 448, 686   **Vol. 3:** 226, 1041, 1043–1045, 1122
19:16 ff   **Vol. 3:** 1041
19:18   **Vol. 3:** 1041
19:19   **Vol. 3:** 95
19:21   **Vol. 3:** 94, 183
20:3   **Vol. 3:** 178
20:4   **Vol. 3:** 207
20:5   **Vol. 2:** 670, 673   **Vol. 3:** 478
20:7   **Vol. 2:** 562, 578
20:10 ff   **Vol. 2:** 802   **Vol. 3:** 593
20:10–20   **Vol. 2:** 699
20:10–14   **Vol. 3:** 593
20:11   **Vol. 2:** 179   **Vol. 3:** 528
20:16 ff   **Vol. 2:** 576
20:17†   **Vol. 1:** 415
20:18   **Vol. 3:** 760
20:19   **Vol. 3:** 951
21:1–9   **Vol. 3:** 94, 151, 154, 159
21:2   **Vol. 1:** 196
21:3   **Vol. 3:** 1161
21:6   **Vol. 2:** 149   **Vol. 3:** 990
21:8 f   **Vol. 3:** 159
21:8   **Vol. 3:** 150–151, 153, 157, 192
21:10 ff   **Vol. 2:** 576   **Vol. 3:** 590

Deuteronomy *(cont'd)*

21:10	**Vol. 3:** 593
21:13	**Vol. 3:** 1065
21:14	**Vol. 1:** 716 **Vol. 2:** 260, 562
21:15 ff	**Vol. 1:** 555, 667
21:17	**Vol. 2:** 317 **Vol. 3:** 266
21:18 ff	**Vol. 3:** 95
21:18	**Vol. 3:** 776
21:19	**Vol. 1:** 343
21:21	**Vol. 2:** 527 **Vol. 3:** 777
21:22 f	**Vol. 1:** 390, 393–394 **Vol. 2:** 96
21:22–23	**Vol. 1:** 265–266
21:23	**Vol. 1:** 233, 264–265, 389–390, 417, 509 **Vol. 2:** 445, 709 **Vol. 3:** 171, 1195
22:1	**Vol. 1:** 115 **Vol. 2:** 458
22:2 ff	**Vol. 3:** 227
22:4	**Vol. 1:** 115
22:9	**Vol. 3:** 918
22:10	**Vol. 1:** 115 **Vol. 2:** 742 **Vol. 3:** 1160
22:13 ff	**Vol. 1:** 555 **Vol. 2:** 562
22:13–21	**Vol. 1:** 505 **Vol. 3:** 1195
22:13–19	**Vol. 2:** 577
22:14	**Vol. 1:** 565 **Vol. 3:** 95
22:18 f	**Vol. 2:** 96
22:18	**Vol. 2:** 96
22:19	**Vol. 3:** 841
22:20 f	**Vol. 2:** 577
22:21	**Vol. 3:** 1024
22:22 ff	**Vol. 2:** 582
22:22–27	**Vol. 2:** 576
22:22 f	**Vol. 2:** 96 **Vol. 3:** 95
22:22	**Vol. 1:** 500, 505 **Vol. 3:** 536, 538, 1065
22:22b	**Vol. 2:** 583
22:23–27	**Vol. 3:** 95
22:23 f	**Vol. 3:** 1058
22:23	**Vol. 2:** 563
22:24	**Vol. 1:** 463
22:25 ff	**Vol. 2:** 577
22:25 f	**Vol. 3:** 1206
22:25	**Vol. 3:** 711
22:27	**Vol. 1:** 520
22:28 f	**Vol. 1:** 505 **Vol. 2:** 577, 582 **Vol. 3:** 95
22:28	**Vol. 3:** 711
22:29	**Vol. 2:** 96 **Vol. 3:** 841
23:1	**Vol. 1:** 560
23:2 ff	**Vol. 1:** 293
23:2	**Vol. 1:** 295
23:3 ff	**Vol. 1:** 295
23:3	**Vol. 1:** 295 **Vol. 3:** 828
23:4	**Vol. 1:** 295
23:5*	**Vol. 2:** 139 **Vol. 3:** 37
23:6*	**Vol. 2:** 778 **Vol. 3:** 828
23:9	**Vol. 1:** 295
23:10	**Vol. 3:** 1120
23:11 f	**Vol. 3:** 989
23:15 f	**Vol. 1:** 717 **Vol. 3:** 594
23:17 f	**Vol. 1:** 499
23:17	**Vol. 1:** 537 **Vol. 2:** 570
23:18 f	**Vol. 1:** 625
23:18	**Vol. 1:** 117
23:19 f	**Vol. 2:** 254
23:19*	**Vol. 2:** 139
23:21 ff	**Vol. 2:** 43
23:21	**Vol. 3:** 183
23:23	**Vol. 3:** 740
23:25	**Vol. 3:** 408
24:1 ff	**Vol. 1:** 505 **Vol. 3:** 189
24:1–14	**Vol. 3:** 660
24:1–4	**Vol. 1:** 500 **Vol. 2:** 576 **Vol. 3:** 172, 181, 183, 534–535, 538–539, 1057
24:1	**Vol. 1:** 243–244, 335, 505, 606 **Vol. 2:** 116 **Vol. 3:** 484, 538, 1065, 1195
24:3	**Vol. 1:** 243–244, 606 **Vol. 3:** 484
24:4	**Vol. 3:** 95
24:5	**Vol. 2:** 562, 578 **Vol. 3:** 1057
24:6	**Vol. 3:** 394
24:7	**Vol. 3:** 377, 380, 593–594
24:7a	**Vol. 2:** 565
24:8	**Vol. 3:** 45
24:9	**Vol. 3:** 235
24:10	**Vol. 2:** 666–667
24:13	**Vol. 3:** 358
24:14–22	**Vol. 2:** 823
24:14 f	**Vol. 2:** 257
24:14	**Vol. 1:** 688 **Vol. 2:** 139 **Vol. 3:** 379
24:15	**Vol. 1:** 410 **Vol. 2:** 139
24:16	**Vol. 2:** 139 **Vol. 3:** 1192
24:17–22	**Vol. 2:** 737
24:17	**Vol. 3:** 1073–1074
24:18	**Vol. 3:** 192–193, 232, 235, 1103, 1120
24:19 ff	**Vol. 3:** 1073–1074
24:20	**Vol. 3:** 232, 1120
24:21	**Vol. 3:** 918
24:22	**Vol. 3:** 232, 235, 1103, 1120
25:1–3	**Vol. 1:** 163 **Vol. 2:** 96
25:1	**Vol. 3:** 355
25:3	**Vol. 2:** 696
25:4	**Vol. 1:** 115, 737 **Vol. 2:** 446, 755 **Vol. 3:** 490–492
25:5 ff	**Vol. 2:** 691 **Vol. 3:** 1074
25:5–10†	**Vol. 1:** 499 **Vol. 2:** 576–577 **Vol. 3:** 95, 487, 1055
25:8	**Vol. 1:** 196
25:12†	**Vol. 2:** 96 **Vol. 3:** 448
25:14 f	**Vol. 3:** 402
25:15	**Vol. 3:** 356
25:17	**Vol. 3:** 235
25:19	**Vol. 3:** 255–256
26	**Vol. 1:** 367
26:1 ff	**Vol. 1:** 210
26:1–15	**Vol. 2:** 693 **Vol. 3:** 852
26:2	**Vol. 1:** 538 **Vol. 3:** 415
26:5–11	**Vol. 1:** 633
26:5	**Vol. 2:** 683
26:6	**Vol. 3:** 1148
26:9	**Vol. 1:** 683
26:10	**Vol. 2:** 876 **Vol. 3:** 415, 852

Deuteronomy *(cont'd)*

26:12–19   **Vol. 2:** 797
26:12–15   **Vol. 2:** 737
26:12 f   **Vol. 3:** 1073–1074
26:12   **Vol. 2:** 693, 823   **Vol. 3:** 852
26:15   **Vol. 2:** 190
26:16–19   **Vol. 2:** 797
26:16 f   **Vol. 3:** 354
26:18 f   **Vol. 2:** 226
26:18   **Vol. 2:** 297, 838, 840
26:19   **Vol. 2:** 226
27 ff   **Vol. 3:** 928
27   **Vol. 3:** 1103
27:2–8   **Vol. 2:** 639
27:3   **Vol. 3:** 483–484, 1103
27:4   **Vol. 1:** 67   **Vol. 2:** 878   **Vol. 3:** 451–452
27:5   **Vol. 3:** 418
27:7   **Vol. 3:** 422
27:8   **Vol. 3:** 483
27:9 f   **Vol. 3:** 33
27:10   **Vol. 3:** 354
27:12 f   **Vol. 3:** 1010
27:14–30:20 **Vol. 3:** 805
27:14–26   **Vol. 3:** 33
27:15 ff   **Vol. 1:** 416   **Vol. 3:** 1104
27:15–26   **Vol. 1:** 97–98
27:15   **Vol. 2:** 215, 287
27:18   **Vol. 1:** 218   **Vol. 2:** 458
27:19   **Vol. 2:** 737   **Vol. 3:** 70, 1073–1074
27:20–23   **Vol. 2:** 577
27:25   **Vol. 2:** 41   **Vol. 3:** 159
27:26   **Vol. 1:** 417   **Vol. 2:** 445   **Vol. 3:** 226, 491
28   **Vol. 1:** 208   **Vol. 3:** 135, 740
28:1–15   **Vol. 2:** 139
28:1–14   **Vol. 1:** 210   **Vol. 3:** 800, 804
28:1 f   **Vol. 1:** 210
28:1   **Vol. 2:** 174
28:3 ff   **Vol. 3:** 140
28:3–7   **Vol. 1:** 209
28:4–11   **Vol. 1:** 288
28:5   **Vol. 1:** 209
28:11   **Vol. 1:** 732
28:12   **Vol. 1:** 96   **Vol. 3:** 835
28:13   **Vol. 2:** 158
28:14   **Vol. 1:** 332   **Vol. 3:** 1103
28:15 ff   **Vol. 1:** 219
28:15–68   **Vol. 1:** 210   **Vol. 2:** 139
28:15 f   **Vol. 1:** 210
28:15   **Vol. 1:** 332   **Vol. 3:** 382, 1104, 1108
28:16 ff   **Vol. 1:** 416
28:20   **Vol. 1:** 463
28:21   **Vol. 2:** 349
28:25   **Vol. 1:** 685
28:26   **Vol. 1:** 264, 444
28:27   **Vol. 1:** 520
28:28 f   **Vol. 1:** 218
28:28   **Vol. 1:** 527

28:29   **Vol. 1:** 218   **Vol. 3:** 574
28:30   **Vol. 3:** 382, 1108
28:33   **Vol. 3:** 144
28:40   **Vol. 1:** 121   **Vol. 2:** 711
28:45   **Vol. 3:** 354
28:47   **Vol. 2:** 181
28:48   **Vol. 1:** 312
28:49   **Vol. 1:** 173   **Vol. 2:** 55, 444, 446
28:50   **Vol. 2:** 622
28:51†   **Vol. 2:** 711
28:53   **Vol. 2:** 807
28:55   **Vol. 2:** 807
28:56   **Vol. 2:** 735   **Vol. 3:** 799
28:57   **Vol. 2:** 807
28:58–64   **Vol. 2:** 798
28:58   **Vol. 1:** 243   **Vol. 2:** 639   **Vol. 3:** 1103, 1120
28:60   **Vol. 2:** 349
28:61   **Vol. 2:** 440, 639   **Vol. 3:** 999
28:62   **Vol. 3:** 249, 734
28:65   **Vol. 1:** 239   **Vol. 3:** 255
29:2*   **Vol. 2:** 627   **Vol. 3:** 799
29:4   **Vol. 2:** 174   **Vol. 3:** 805
29:5   **Vol. 2:** 714   **Vol. 3:** 804
29:12 ff   **Vol. 3:** 740
29:13   **Vol. 1:** 77
29:15   **Vol. 2:** 313
29:16*   **Vol. 2:** 284
29:17   **Vol. 3:** 687
29:18 ff   **Vol. 1:** 108
29:18   **Vol. 1:** 202   **Vol. 2:** 27, 782, 847   **Vol. 3:** 866
29:19 f   **Vol. 2:** 639
29:19*   **Vol. 2:** 237
29:20   **Vol. 2:** 440   **Vol. 3:** 152, 1166
29:22   **Vol. 1:** 109
29:23   **Vol. 3:** 93, 444, 560
29:25 ff   **Vol. 1:** 109
29:25*   **Vol. 2:** 876
29:26   **Vol. 2:** 639
29:28*   **Vol. 1:** 688   **Vol. 3:** 1103, 1154
29:29   **Vol. 2:** 215   **Vol. 3:** 828
30:1–20   **Vol. 2:** 478
30:1–19   **Vol. 1:** 416
30:3   **Vol. 2:** 32
30:4   **Vol. 1:** 518, 685   **Vol. 2:** 32, 35, 38, 917
30:6   **Vol. 1:** 154   **Vol. 2:** 786
30:7   **Vol. 1:** 555
30:9   **Vol. 3:** 787
30:10   **Vol. 2:** 440, 639   **Vol. 3:** 354
30:11–14   **Vol. 2:** 174
30:12–14   **Vol. 3:** 1122
30:12   **Vol. 2:** 189
30:14   **Vol. 1:** 484   **Vol. 2:** 441   **Vol. 3:** 1103
30:15 ff   **Vol. 3:** 938
30:15–20   **Vol. 2:** 297
30:15 f   **Vol. 3:** 938
30:15   **Vol. 1:** 434   **Vol. 2:** 99, 478   **Vol. 3:** 140
30:16   **Vol. 3:** 354

Deuteronomy *(cont'd)*

30:17 f	**Vol. 3:** 938
30:17	**Vol. 2:** 876
30:18	**Vol. 1:** 463
30:19	**Vol. 1:** 210 **Vol. 2:** 478, 481 **Vol. 3:** 740, 940
30:20	**Vol. 1:** 77
31:3 ff	**Vol. 3:** 208
31:3	**Vol. 2:** 331
31:4 ff	**Vol. 3:** 33
31:7	**Vol. 2:** 331
31:8	**Vol. 2:** 331
31:9	**Vol. 2:** 639 **Vol. 3:** 484
31:10	**Vol. 2:** 667 **Vol. 3:** 813
31:11	**Vol. 2:** 639
31:12 f	**Vol. 1:** 484
31:12	**Vol. 3:** 1103
31:14 f	**Vol. 2:** 331
31:16	**Vol. 3:** 273
31:17	**Vol. 1:** 562
31:19	**Vol. 3:** 484, 673, 760, 1041
31:20	**Vol. 1:** 367 **Vol. 3:** 342, 806
31:21 f	**Vol. 3:** 673
31:21	**Vol. 3:** 1041
31:22	**Vol. 3:** 760
31:23	**Vol. 2:** 331
31:24 ff	**Vol. 2:** 639 **Vol. 3:** 33
31:24	**Vol. 2:** 638
31:26	**Vol. 2:** 440
31:27	**Vol. 1:** 203
31:28	**Vol. 3:** 1041
31:30	**Vol. 3:** 668, 673
32	**Vol. 2:** 791 **Vol. 3:** 263
32:1–43	**Vol. 2:** 639
32:2 f	**Vol. 3:** 960
32:4	**Vol. 2:** 237
32:5 f	**Vol. 1:** 618
32:5	**Vol. 2:** 36
32:6	**Vol. 1:** 538, 617 **Vol. 2:** 71 **Vol. 3:** 1025, 1027
32:7	**Vol. 1:** 617 **Vol. 3:** 232, 828
32:8 f	**Vol. 2:** 297, 791
32:8	**Vol. 3:** 636
32:9	**Vol. 2:** 303
32:10 ff	**Vol. 3:** 805
32:11	**Vol. 1:** 173
32:12	**Vol. 2:** 724
32:13	**Vol. 3:** 382
32:14	**Vol. 1:** 224 **Vol. 3:** 919
32:15 ff	**Vol. 3:** 806
32:15	**Vol. 1:** 239, 607 **Vol. 2:** 705 **Vol. 3:** 218
32:16 f	**Vol. 2:** 284
32:16	**Vol. 1:** 684
32:17	**Vol. 1:** 451 **Vol. 2:** 286 **Vol. 3:** 806
32:18	**Vol. 1:** 186
32:20	**Vol. 2:** 36
32:21	**Vol. 1:** 112 **Vol. 2:** 176, 284, 490, 794, 880 **Vol. 3:** 131–132, 456, 461
32:22	**Vol. 1:** 661 **Vol. 3:** 1010
32:24	**Vol. 1:** 113 **Vol. 2:** 265
32:26	**Vol. 3:** 237, 255
32:28	**Vol. 3:** 1016
32:30	**Vol. 3:** 962
32:31	**Vol. 3:** 126
32:32	**Vol. 1:** 202 **Vol. 2:** 27 **Vol. 3:** 93
32:34	**Vol. 3:** 498, 673
32:35 f	**Vol. 2:** 230 **Vol. 3:** 28, 136
32:35	**Vol. 1:** 111 **Vol. 2:** 96, 157–158, 513 **Vol. 3:** 93, 97, 345
32:36	**Vol. 1:** 569 **Vol. 2:** 363–364
32:37 f	**Vol. 3:** 919
32:38	**Vol. 3:** 344
32:39 ff	**Vol. 2:** 279
32:39	**Vol. 2:** 279, 478–479 **Vol. 3:** 263
32:40	**Vol. 2:** 190
32:41 ff	**Vol. 3:** 154
32:41	**Vol. 3:** 93
32:43	**Vol. 2:** 96, 356, 799, 876 **Vol. 3:** 152
32:44	**Vol. 3:** 760
32:46 f	**Vol. 3:** 1118
32:46	**Vol. 1:** 617
32:47	**Vol. 2:** 479 **Vol. 3:** 1014, 1103–1104
33	**Vol. 1:** 208 **Vol. 2:** 638
33:1–29	**Vol. 2:** 639
33:1	**Vol. 3:** 77
33:2	**Vol. 2:** 190, 376, 735 **Vol. 3:** 318, 1013–1014
33:3	**Vol. 3:** 745
33:8 ff	**Vol. 3:** 33
33:8	**Vol. 2:** 237, 296 **Vol. 3:** 346, 799–800
33:9	**Vol. 2:** 395 **Vol. 3:** 1118
33:10	**Vol. 2:** 296, 467 **Vol. 3:** 33, 354, 421, 478
33:12	**Vol. 3:** 255, 873
33:13 f	**Vol. 3:** 845
33:13	**Vol. 1:** 523
33:16	**Vol. 3:** 845
33:17	**Vol. 3:** 212, 715
33:19	**Vol. 2:** 842 **Vol. 3:** 356
33:21	**Vol. 3:** 356, 372, 415
33:26	**Vol. 2:** 190
33:29	**Vol. 1:** 227 **Vol. 3:** 207
34	**Vol. 1:** 76 **Vol. 2:** 638
34:1–4	**Vol. 2:** 893 **Vol. 3:** 806, 1009
34:4	**Vol. 1:** 77 **Vol. 3:** 806
34:6	**Vol. 1:** 104 **Vol. 3:** 345
34:8	**Vol. 2:** 416 **Vol. 3:** 720
34:9	**Vol. 1:** 66, 735 **Vol. 2:** 151, 331
34:10 f	**Vol. 2:** 638
34:10	**Vol. 2:** 395 **Vol. 3:** 77
34:11	**Vol. 2:** 627

Joshua

1:1–17	**Vol. 2:** 639
1:1	**Vol. 3:** 208
1:2	**Vol. 1:** 430
1:3	**Vol. 2:** 369

Joshua *(cont'd)*

1:4	**Vol. 3:** 983
1:8	**Vol. 1:** 243 **Vol. 2:** 440
1:9	**Vol. 3:** 423
1:13	**Vol. 3:** 255–256, 423, 1103
1:15	**Vol. 3:** 255–256
1:16	**Vol. 1:** 127
2:1–21	**Vol. 3:** 369, 1067
2:1	**Vol. 3:** 1062
2:12	**Vol. 3:** 1153
2:14	**Vol. 3:** 423
2:18	**Vol. 2:** 303
2:19	**Vol. 2:** 142
2:20	**Vol. 3:** 311
3 f	**Vol. 3:** 788
3	**Vol. 2:** 627
3:3	**Vol. 1:** 492
3:5	**Vol. 3:** 1153
3:7	**Vol. 2:** 69, 639
3:12	**Vol. 1:** 475–476
3:13	**Vol. 3:** 255
3:16	**Vol. 3:** 991
4	**Vol. 3:** 656
4:2	**Vol. 1:** 475
4:6 f	**Vol. 3:** 233, 777
4:7	**Vol. 3:** 237, 316, 828
4:10 ff	**Vol. 2:** 639
4:12	**Vol. 1:** 332
4:21 ff	**Vol. 3:** 777
5:2–7	**Vol. 1:** 308
5:6	**Vol. 1:** 683
5:13 ff	**Vol. 1:** 101
5:14	**Vol. 2:** 189
5:15	**Vol. 2:** 225 **Vol. 3:** 177
6	**Vol. 1:** 208 **Vol. 2:** 627 **Vol. 3:** 788
6:1–8:29	**Vol. 3:** 960
6:1 ff	**Vol. 2:** 691
6:3	**Vol. 2:** 716
6:4–21	**Vol. 3:** 874
6:4–20	**Vol. 3:** 673
6:5	**Vol. 1:** 609
6:6	**Vol. 1:** 322 **Vol. 3:** 469
6:7	**Vol. 1:** 340
6:9	**Vol. 1:** 492
6:10	**Vol. 1:** 322
6:14	**Vol. 2:** 716
6:16	**Vol. 1:** 409
6:17–21	**Vol. 3:** 590
6:17	**Vol. 1:** 413
6:19	**Vol. 2:** 225, 830
6:20	**Vol. 1:** 609
6:21	**Vol. 1:** 415
6:22 f	**Vol. 3:** 590
6:22–25	**Vol. 3:** 1067
6:24	**Vol. 2:** 830 **Vol. 3:** 811
6:25	**Vol. 3:** 206
6:26	**Vol. 3:** 444
7	**Vol. 1:** 109 **Vol. 2:** 847 **Vol. 3:** 720
7:6	**Vol. 1:** 520 **Vol. 3:** 788
7:7	**Vol. 3:** 342
7:8	**Vol. 1:** 554
7:11	**Vol. 3:** 377, 583
7:12	**Vol. 1:** 413
7:13	**Vol. 2:** 797
7:14	**Vol. 3:** 569, 871
7:15	**Vol. 1:** 655
7:19	**Vol. 1:** 345
7:22	**Vol. 3:** 1185
7:25	**Vol. 1:** 264
8:1	**Vol. 3:** 812
8:3	**Vol. 3:** 713
8:6	**Vol. 2:** 636
8:12 ff	**Vol. 3:** 248
8:28	**Vol. 3:** 828
8:29	**Vol. 1:** 393–394
8:30 ff	**Vol. 3:** 787
8:30 f	**Vol. 3:** 418, 788
8:30–35	**Vol. 1:** 367 **Vol. 2:** 639
8:30	**Vol. 2:** 796
8:31–35	**Vol. 2:** 639
8:31*	**Vol. 2:** 440
8:32	**Vol. 3:** 483
8:33	**Vol. 3:** 1010
9:1	**Vol. 3:** 1008
9:4	**Vol. 1:** 412
9:5	**Vol. 2:** 714
9:9	**Vol. 1:** 531 **Vol. 2:** 655
9:11	**Vol. 3:** 608
9:13	**Vol. 2:** 670, 714
9:14 f	**Vol. 2:** 521
9:18 ff	**Vol. 1:** 294
9:18 f	**Vol. 2:** 797
9:23–27	**Vol. 3:** 593
9:24	**Vol. 2:** 639
10	**Vol. 2:** 324, 627–628
10:1–11:43	**Vol. 3:** 960
10:1	**Vol. 2:** 324, 590
10:6	**Vol. 3:** 178
10:11	**Vol. 3:** 1001
10:12	**Vol. 2:** 889
10:16	**Vol. 3:** 380
10:20	**Vol. 3:** 248
10:24	**Vol. 1:** 239, 241
10:26	**Vol. 1:** 390, 393
10:27	**Vol. 2:** 96
10:28 ff	**Vol. 1:** 413–414
10:28	**Vol. 2:** 477
10:30	**Vol. 3:** 1154
10:33	**Vol. 3:** 1154
10:37 f	**Vol. 3:** 1154
11:6	**Vol. 3:** 846
11:12–23	**Vol. 2:** 639
11:12	**Vol. 3:** 248
11:20	**Vol. 2:** 154
11:21	**Vol. 1:** 413
11:23	**Vol. 1:** 332 **Vol. 3:** 255
12:3	**Vol. 3:** 983
12:6	**Vol. 2:** 639
13–19	**Vol. 2:** 298

Joshua *(cont'd)*

13:8–33	**Vol. 2:** 639
13:14	**Vol. 2:** 297
13:19	**Vol. 2:** 297
13:22	**Vol. 2:** 554
13:23	**Vol. 1:** 241
13:27	**Vol. 1:** 472 **Vol. 2:** 303 **Vol. 3:** 983
14:1	**Vol. 2:** 300
14:2–11	**Vol. 2:** 639
14:4	**Vol. 2:** 303
14:7	**Vol. 3:** 594
14:10	**Vol. 3:** 1154
14:12	**Vol. 2:** 856
14:15	**Vol. 2:** 802
15	**Vol. 1:** 61
15:2	**Vol. 2:** 303
15:8	**Vol. 2:** 208
15:9	**Vol. 1:** 366 **Vol. 2:** 802
15:12	**Vol. 1:** 472
15:13	**Vol. 2:** 303, 802
15:15 f	**Vol. 2:** 802
15:18 f	**Vol. 2:** 584
15:21	**Vol. 1:** 665
17:2	**Vol. 2:** 569
17:4	**Vol. 2:** 298, 639
17:13	**Vol. 3:** 713
17:16	**Vol. 2:** 98
18:1 ff	**Vol. 3:** 426
18:1	**Vol. 1:** 293
18:3	**Vol. 3:** 178
18:5	**Vol. 1:** 534
18:7	**Vol. 2:** 639 **Vol. 3:** 36
18:8 f	**Vol. 3:** 484
18:9	**Vol. 1:** 243
18:16	**Vol. 2:** 208
18:19 f	**Vol. 2:** 303
18:20	**Vol. 1:** 472
19:1–22:21	**Vol. 2:** 695
19:15	**Vol. 1:** 170
19:26	**Vol. 3:** 983
19:47	**Vol. 2:** 773
20:2	**Vol. 2:** 639
20:3	**Vol. 3:** 190
20:4	**Vol. 1:** 195
20:5	**Vol. 3:** 190
20:7	**Vol. 2:** 305
21	**Vol. 2:** 34, 789 **Vol. 3:** 565
21:2	**Vol. 2:** 639
21:8	**Vol. 2:** 639
21:9	**Vol. 2:** 650
21:11	**Vol. 2:** 305
21:42	**Vol. 3:** 255
21:43 ff	**Vol. 2:** 297
21:43–45	**Vol. 3:** 69
21:44	**Vol. 3:** 256
21:45	**Vol. 1:** 609 **Vol. 3:** 1104
22	**Vol. 1:** 607
22:1–5	**Vol. 2:** 297
22:2–9	**Vol. 2:** 639
22:4	**Vol. 3:** 255
22:5	**Vol. 2:** 181 **Vol. 3:** 1153
22:10–34	**Vol. 3:** 418
22:10 f	**Vol. 3:** 418
22:12 ff	**Vol. 1:** 294
22:16 ff	**Vol. 1:** 606
22:16	**Vol. 3:** 418
22:19	**Vol. 2:** 296 **Vol. 3:** 418
22:21	**Vol. 2:** 698
22:23	**Vol. 3:** 418
22:24	**Vol. 2:** 91
22:26	**Vol. 3:** 418
22:27 f	**Vol. 3:** 1040
22:27	**Vol. 3:** 550
22:30	**Vol. 2:** 698
22:34	**Vol. 3:** 418
23:1	**Vol. 3:** 255
23:6	**Vol. 2:** 639
23:7	**Vol. 2:** 876
23:10	**Vol. 2:** 374 **Vol. 3:** 962
23:13	**Vol. 2:** 707 **Vol. 3:** 268
23:14	**Vol. 1:** 609 **Vol. 3:** 69, 938, 1104
23:15	**Vol. 3:** 1104
23:16	**Vol. 2:** 876
24	**Vol. 1:** 626 **Vol. 2:** 67, 306
24:1 ff	**Vol. 3:** 787
24:2	**Vol. 1:** 164 **Vol. 3:** 452
24:3	**Vol. 1:** 617
24:5	**Vol. 2:** 639
24:6	**Vol. 2:** 440
24:14–24	**Vol. 3:** 550
24:14	**Vol. 3:** 354, 882
24:15	**Vol. 1:** 537
24:15b	**Vol. 1:** 617
24:17	**Vol. 2:** 796
24:19–24	**Vol. 3:** 113
24:23	**Vol. 1:** 688 **Vol. 2:** 796
24:24†	**Vol. 1:** 367
24:25	**Vol. 1:** 245 **Vol. 2:** 441
24:26	**Vol. 3:** 786–787
24:27	**Vol. 3:** 1040
24:29	**Vol. 3:** 594, 608
24:31	**Vol. 3:** 550
24:32	**Vol. 3:** 459, 464

Judges

1:1–7	**Vol. 2:** 319
1:1	**Vol. 2:** 879
1:3	**Vol. 2:** 298
1:4	**Vol. 2:** 698
1:7	**Vol. 3:** 134
1:14	**Vol. 3:** 557
1:16	**Vol. 2:** 305, 639
1:17	**Vol. 1:** 413
1:19	**Vol. 2:** 98
1:20	**Vol. 2:** 639
1:24	**Vol. 3:** 569
1:27 ff	**Vol. 2:** 802
1:28	**Vol. 3:** 713

Judges *(cont'd)*

2:1 ff	**Vol. 1:** 716
2:1–5	**Vol. 3:** 425
2:1	**Vol. 1:** 531 **Vol. 3:** 788, 828
2:2	**Vol. 1:** 531 **Vol. 2:** 416, 876
2:3	**Vol. 2:** 707 **Vol. 3:** 1069
2:4	**Vol. 2:** 305
2:6 ff	**Vol. 3:** 135
2:6–3:6	**Vol. 3:** 578
2:7	**Vol. 2:** 395 **Vol. 3:** 595
2:9	**Vol. 2:** 298
2:10 f	**Vol. 2:** 396
2:11–22	**Vol. 3:** 1104
2:12 f	**Vol. 1:** 492
2:12	**Vol. 1:** 481 **Vol. 2:** 876
2:14	**Vol. 1:** 109 **Vol. 2:** 148, 367
2:16	**Vol. 3:** 218, 279
2:17	**Vol. 2:** 173, 876
2:18	**Vol. 1:** 356, 569 **Vol. 2:** 423 **Vol. 3:** 218, 279, 594
2:19	**Vol. 2:** 876
2:20	**Vol. 1:** 109
2:22	**Vol. 3:** 799–800
3:1–5	**Vol. 2:** 802
3:1	**Vol. 1:** 698 **Vol. 2:** 791 **Vol. 3:** 799–800
3:2	**Vol. 3:** 760
3:4 ff	**Vol. 3:** 800
3:4	**Vol. 2:** 639 **Vol. 3:** 799
3:9	**Vol. 1:** 409 **Vol. 2:** 363 **Vol. 3:** 218, 462
3:10	**Vol. 3:** 691
3:11	**Vol. 3:** 111
3:15–18	**Vol. 3:** 421
3:15	**Vol. 2:** 41, 363, 414 **Vol. 3:** 218, 462
3:17 f	**Vol. 2:** 41
3:25	**Vol. 2:** 730, 773 **Vol. 3:** 228
3:29	**Vol. 2:** 698 **Vol. 3:** 209
3:30	**Vol. 3:** 111
4:3	**Vol. 2:** 98
4:4	**Vol. 3:** 836, 1057
4:6–23	**Vol. 3:** 960
4:6–14	**Vol. 2:** 698
4:6	**Vol. 3:** 1057
4:10	**Vol. 1:** 239 **Vol. 2:** 139
4:11	**Vol. 2:** 639 **Vol. 3:** 255, 534
4:15	**Vol. 1:** 527
4:17 ff	**Vol. 1:** 687
4:17	**Vol. 2:** 777
4:19	**Vol. 2:** 726
4:23	**Vol. 2:** 260
5	**Vol. 1:** 245
5:1–31	**Vol. 3:** 1057
5:1	**Vol. 3:** 672–673
5:3	**Vol. 2:** 796 **Vol. 3:** 672
5:4 f	**Vol. 2:** 190 **Vol. 3:** 960, 1014
5:4	**Vol. 2:** 898 **Vol. 3:** 556
5:5	**Vol. 2:** 796 **Vol. 3:** 1010, 1013
5:7	**Vol. 3:** 1069
5:9	**Vol. 3:** 87
5:10	**Vol. 1:** 117 **Vol. 2:** 257
5:11	**Vol. 2:** 796 **Vol. 3:** 355–356
5:12	**Vol. 3:** 673
5:13	**Vol. 2:** 796
5:15	**Vol. 1:** 534
5:19	**Vol. 2:** 41 **Vol. 3:** 137
5:20	**Vol. 2:** 189 **Vol. 3:** 735, 1001
5:21	**Vol. 2:** 602
5:25	**Vol. 2:** 856
5:27	**Vol. 1:** 442
5:29	**Vol. 3:** 1027
5:30	**Vol. 3:** 593
5:31	**Vol. 2:** 602 **Vol. 3:** 730, 1068
6	**Vol. 2:** 627
6:2	**Vol. 2:** 139 **Vol. 3:** 1009
6:3	**Vol. 3:** 144
6:4	**Vol. 1:** 711
6:5	**Vol. 2:** 139 **Vol. 3:** 811
6:9	**Vol. 1:** 453 **Vol. 3:** 201
6:11–24	**Vol. 1:** 101
6:11–23	**Vol. 3:** 212
6:12	**Vol. 2:** 69
6:13	**Vol. 1:** 273 **Vol. 2:** 367
6:15 ff	**Vol. 2:** 260 **Vol. 3:** 962
6:15	**Vol. 2:** 428, 698 **Vol. 3:** 993
6:16 ff	**Vol. 2:** 626
6:17	**Vol. 2:** 626 **Vol. 3:** 528
6:18–21	**Vol. 3:** 422
6:18 f	**Vol. 3:** 155
6:18	**Vol. 3:** 421, 534
6:19	**Vol. 1:** 114 **Vol. 2:** 876
6:20	**Vol. 2:** 854 **Vol. 3:** 381, 816
6:21	**Vol. 1:** 655 **Vol. 3:** 381
6:22 f	**Vol. 1:** 585
6:22	**Vol. 3:** 514
6:23	**Vol. 1:** 622
6:24 ff	**Vol. 3:** 418, 425
6:24	**Vol. 2:** 777
6:25a	**Vol. 1:** 116
6:28a	**Vol. 1:** 116
6:33–7:25	**Vol. 3:** 960
6:34	**Vol. 1:** 739 **Vol. 3:** 691
6:36 ff	**Vol. 2:** 626
6:36 f	**Vol. 2:** 626
6:39	**Vol. 3:** 799
7	**Vol. 1:** 650
7:2	**Vol. 3:** 206
7:4	**Vol. 3:** 808
7:5	**Vol. 3:** 1079
7:7	**Vol. 3:** 206
7:10	**Vol. 1:** 283
7:13	**Vol. 1:** 574
7:15	**Vol. 1:** 574–575 **Vol. 2:** 876
7:16	**Vol. 2:** 485 **Vol. 3:** 874
7:18 ff	**Vol. 3:** 673
7:20 ff	**Vol. 3:** 874
7:20	**Vol. 2:** 485
7:22	**Vol. 2:** 374
7:25	**Vol. 3:** 590

Judges *(cont'd)*

8:1	**Vol. 2:** 363 **Vol. 3:** 820
8:3	**Vol. 1:** 165 **Vol. 3:** 255, 691
8:7	**Vol. 1:** 725 **Vol. 3:** 268
8:10	**Vol. 2:** 698
8:12	**Vol. 1:** 527 **Vol. 3:** 716
8:14	**Vol. 1:** 195, 283
8:16	**Vol. 1:** 195, 725
8:19	**Vol. 3:** 739, 1069
8:20	**Vol. 2:** 675
8:21	**Vol. 1:** 241
8:22	**Vol. 3:** 206
8:23	**Vol. 2:** 374
8:26	**Vol. 2:** 96
8:27	**Vol. 2:** 707
8:33	**Vol. 1:** 367
8:34	**Vol. 3:** 201–202
9:1–3	**Vol. 3:** 1069
9:2	**Vol. 1:** 195
9:3 f	**Vol. 1:** 492
9:4	**Vol. 1:** 367, 546 **Vol. 2:** 139
9:7	**Vol. 3:** 1009
9:8	**Vol. 1:** 121 **Vol. 3:** 866
9:9	**Vol. 1:** 698
9:10	**Vol. 1:** 723
9:11	**Vol. 1:** 698
9:12	**Vol. 1:** 165
9:13	**Vol. 1:** 698 **Vol. 3:** 919
9:15	**Vol. 1:** 121
9:16	**Vol. 2:** 61
9:17	**Vol. 3:** 201
9:19	**Vol. 2:** 61
9:23	**Vol. 3:** 720
9:26–41	**Vol. 2:** 521
9:27	**Vol. 3:** 673
9:30	**Vol. 1:** 108
9:34	**Vol. 1:** 165
9:36	**Vol. 3:** 554
9:37	**Vol. 1:** 523 **Vol. 2:** 554
9:45	**Vol. 3:** 444
9:46	**Vol. 1:** 367
9:50–54	**Vol. 2:** 431
9:53	**Vol. 3:** 394
9:54	**Vol. 1:** 283
10:1–5	**Vol. 2:** 363
10:4	**Vol. 1:** 117 **Vol. 2:** 257
10:6	**Vol. 3:** 1069
10:10	**Vol. 1:** 410
10:12 ff	**Vol. 3:** 207
10:16	**Vol. 1:** 262 **Vol. 2:** 815
10:18	**Vol. 1:** 164 **Vol. 2:** 158
11:3	**Vol. 1:** 546
11:5 ff	**Vol. 1:** 195
11:6	**Vol. 1:** 165
11:7	**Vol. 3:** 957
11:16	**Vol. 3:** 983
11:18	**Vol. 1:** 609
11:24	**Vol. 2:** 67
11:26	**Vol. 3:** 835
11:27	**Vol. 2:** 363 **Vol. 3:** 356
11:29	**Vol. 1:** 739 **Vol. 3:** 691
11:30–40	**Vol. 3:** 425
11:31	**Vol. 3:** 421
11:34	**Vol. 3:** 673, 1202
11:35	**Vol. 1:** 316 **Vol. 2:** 93
12:1	**Vol. 1:** 272
12:2 f	**Vol. 3:** 206
12:3	**Vol. 3:** 218
12:6	**Vol. 2:** 698
12:7–15	**Vol. 2:** 363
12:8–10	**Vol. 1:** 170
12:14	**Vol. 1:** 117 **Vol. 2:** 257
13:2	**Vol. 2:** 789
13:4	**Vol. 3:** 919, 921
13:5	**Vol. 1:** 203 **Vol. 3:** 206
13:6	**Vol. 3:** 318
13:7	**Vol. 2:** 225, 228–229 **Vol. 3:** 919, 921
13:8	**Vol. 2:** 863
13:11	**Vol. 3:** 946
13:14	**Vol. 3:** 919
13:15 f	**Vol. 3:** 711
13:16	**Vol. 3:** 422
13:17 f	**Vol. 1:** 101
13:19	**Vol. 3:** 381
13:20	**Vol. 1:** 655
13:21 f	**Vol. 3:** 212
14	**Vol. 2:** 584
14:1	**Vol. 2:** 576
14:4	**Vol. 3:** 835
14:6	**Vol. 3:** 691
14:8	**Vol. 1:** 610
14:11	**Vol. 2:** 578
14:12–20	**Vol. 2:** 745
14:12	**Vol. 2:** 578
14:15	**Vol. 2:** 458
14:18	**Vol. 2:** 745
14:19	**Vol. 1:** 739
14:20	**Vol. 1:** 258
15 f	**Vol. 1:** 171
15:1	**Vol. 1:** 189, 498
15:4	**Vol. 1:** 343 **Vol. 2:** 485
15:5	**Vol. 2:** 485
15:13 f	**Vol. 3:** 591
15:13	**Vol. 3:** 669
15:17	**Vol. 2:** 225
15:18 f	**Vol. 2:** 478
15:18	**Vol. 2:** 275, 416
15:19	**Vol. 3:** 686, 690, 694
16:3	**Vol. 3:** 951
16:5	**Vol. 2:** 458 **Vol. 3:** 713
16:7	**Vol. 3:** 993
16:8	**Vol. 1:** 120
16:11	**Vol. 3:** 993
16:17 ff	**Vol. 1:** 203
16:17	**Vol. 1:** 607 **Vol. 2:** 225, 228 **Vol. 3:** 993
16:19	**Vol. 1:** 607
16:20	**Vol. 1:** 607 **Vol. 2:** 395
16:23 ff	**Vol. 3:** 782

Judges *(cont'd)*

16:24	**Vol. 1:** 99 **Vol. 3:** 668, 816–817
16:26	**Vol. 3:** 255, 716
16:28	**Vol. 2:** 416 **Vol. 3:** 235
16:29	**Vol. 2:** 148
17	**Vol. 3:** 33
17:2	**Vol. 3:** 474
17:3	**Vol. 2:** 96, 225
17:5	**Vol. 3:** 33
17:7	**Vol. 1:** 170 **Vol. 3:** 33
17:8	**Vol. 3:** 1153
17:10	**Vol. 1:** 617 **Vol. 2:** 887 **Vol. 3:** 1161
17:13	**Vol. 2:** 466 **Vol. 3:** 33, 1161
18	**Vol. 3:** 33
18:2	**Vol. 3:** 255
18:4	**Vol. 2:** 139
18:5 f	**Vol. 3:** 33
18:5	**Vol. 2:** 856, 879
18:6	**Vol. 2:** 778
18:7	**Vol. 2:** 437
18:9	**Vol. 3:** 111
18:10	**Vol. 3:** 953
18:11	**Vol. 3:** 120
18:15	**Vol. 2:** 778
18:19	**Vol. 1:** 617
18:29	**Vol. 2:** 650
18:30	**Vol. 3:** 33, 872
18:31	**Vol. 3:** 426, 786
19:1	**Vol. 1:** 170 **Vol. 3:** 33
19:5	**Vol. 2:** 181
19:7	**Vol. 3:** 711
19:10 f	**Vol. 2:** 324
19:15 ff	**Vol. 2:** 521
19:16–30	**Vol. 3:** 872
19:19 f	**Vol. 3:** 953
19:19	**Vol. 1:** 743
19:20	**Vol. 2:** 777
19:22	**Vol. 1:** 687 **Vol. 2:** 511
19:23 f	**Vol. 3:** 1024
19:23	**Vol. 2:** 511
19:25	**Vol. 1:** 420
19:29	**Vol. 1:** 230
19:30	**Vol. 2:** 889
20:1	**Vol. 1:** 293
20:2–46	**Vol. 2:** 698
20:2	**Vol. 1:** 296
20:6	**Vol. 3:** 1024
20:10	**Vol. 3:** 1024
20:15 f	**Vol. 1:** 537
20:16	**Vol. 2:** 414, 690
20:23	**Vol. 2:** 416
20:26	**Vol. 1:** 612 **Vol. 2:** 60, 416 **Vol. 3:** 588
20:27	**Vol. 3:** 788
20:43	**Vol. 3:** 255–256
20:48	**Vol. 1:** 654
21	**Vol. 3:** 872
21:3	**Vol. 2:** 797
21:4	**Vol. 2:** 60
21:5	**Vol. 1:** 295
21:6	**Vol. 1:** 356
21:8	**Vol. 1:** 295
21:10	**Vol. 1:** 414
21:11 f	**Vol. 2:** 569
21:11	**Vol. 1:** 414 **Vol. 2:** 587
21:12 ff	**Vol. 3:** 426
21:12	**Vol. 2:** 587
21:22	**Vol. 2:** 363
21:23	**Vol. 3:** 601
21:24	**Vol. 3:** 943

Ruth

1–4	**Vol. 1:** 499
1:1	**Vol. 1:** 520
1:2	**Vol. 1:** 520
1:4	**Vol. 3:** 656
1:6	**Vol. 1:** 189 **Vol. 2:** 584
1:9	**Vol. 3:** 255
1:12	**Vol. 1:** 710, 712
1:13	**Vol. 1:** 202
1:14	**Vol. 1:** 481
1:19	**Vol. 3:** 112
1:20 f	**Vol. 3:** 729
1:20	**Vol. 1:** 201
1:22	**Vol. 1:** 170
2:2	**Vol. 1:** 520 **Vol. 2:** 116 **Vol. 3:** 1074
2:5 f	**Vol. 1:** 283
2:7	**Vol. 2:** 32 **Vol. 3:** 255
2:8	**Vol. 2:** 349
2:10	**Vol. 1:** 609 **Vol. 2:** 116, 876
2:12	**Vol. 2:** 139
2:13	**Vol. 2:** 116
2:14	**Vol. 1:** 250 **Vol. 3:** 846
2:16	**Vol. 1:** 572
2:20	**Vol. 3:** 191
2:21	**Vol. 2:** 60, 349 **Vol. 3:** 525
3:1	**Vol. 3:** 255
3:2	**Vol. 2:** 34
3:3	**Vol. 1:** 120 **Vol. 3:** 191
3:6 ff	**Vol. 2:** 578
3:6–18	**Vol. 3:** 1062
3:9	**Vol. 3:** 191, 555
3:10	**Vol. 1:** 492, 665 **Vol. 2:** 841
3:12	**Vol. 3:** 191
3:13	**Vol. 3:** 191
4	**Vol. 3:** 95
4:1 ff	**Vol. 2:** 363
4:1–13	**Vol. 2:** 577
4:1	**Vol. 3:** 191
4:3	**Vol. 3:** 191
4:4	**Vol. 3:** 191
4:5	**Vol. 3:** 191, 1057
4:6	**Vol. 3:** 190–191
4:7	**Vol. 3:** 166, 354
4:8	**Vol. 3:** 191
4:9 ff	**Vol. 3:** 1041
4:10	**Vol. 3:** 1057
4:11 f	**Vol. 2:** 578

Ruth (*cont'd*)

4:12	**Vol. 1:** 170
4:13 f	**Vol. 1:** 207
4:14	**Vol. 3:** 178, 191
4:16	**Vol. 1:** 240
4:18 ff	**Vol. 3:** 191, 652

1 Samuel

1 ff	**Vol. 3:** 782
1	**Vol. 2:** 478 **Vol. 3:** 1072
1:3 ff	**Vol. 3:** 426, 1055
1:3–8	**Vol. 3:** 1057
1:3 f	**Vol. 2:** 562 **Vol. 3:** 1058
1:3	**Vol. 2:** 185, 876 **Vol. 3:** 33, 787–788
1:4	**Vol. 1:** 288 **Vol. 2:** 226
1:6	**Vol. 3:** 1055
1:7	**Vol. 2:** 416 **Vol. 3:** 786
1:9 ff	**Vol. 3:** 1055
1:9	**Vol. 3:** 786
1:10 f	**Vol. 2:** 863
1:10	**Vol. 2:** 862
1:11	**Vol. 1:** 288 **Vol. 2:** 260–261 **Vol. 3:** 235
1:12	**Vol. 2:** 862
1:13	**Vol. 3:** 823
1:15	**Vol. 2:** 854
1:16	**Vol. 2:** 260
1:17	**Vol. 2:** 856
1:18	**Vol. 2:** 116 **Vol. 3:** 794
1:19	**Vol. 2:** 876
1:20	**Vol. 1:** 343 **Vol. 2:** 856
1:21	**Vol. 3:** 422
1:22	**Vol. 3:** 827
1:23	**Vol. 3:** 1104
1:25	**Vol. 3:** 1016
1:26 f	**Vol. 2:** 862
1:26	**Vol. 3:** 739
2	**Vol. 3:** 263, 1072
2:1 ff	**Vol. 3:** 1055
2:1–10	**Vol. 2:** 596 **Vol. 3:** 30
2:1	**Vol. 2:** 862 **Vol. 3:** 715
2:2	**Vol. 2:** 225
2:3*	**Vol. 1:** 332
2:5	**Vol. 2:** 265
2:6	**Vol. 3:** 263
2:7 ff	**Vol. 2:** 260
2:7	**Vol. 2:** 201, 262, 596, 841
2:8	**Vol. 1:** 523 **Vol. 2:** 614, 820 **Vol. 3:** 588
2:10	**Vol. 1:** 227 **Vol. 2:** 336, 596, 841–842 **Vol. 3:** 130, 715
2:12–17	**Vol. 3:** 426
2:13–16	**Vol. 3:** 422
2:13	**Vol. 1:** 672 **Vol. 3:** 354, 422
2:15	**Vol. 1:** 672
2:17*	**Vol. 1:** 74 **Vol. 3:** 421
2:19	**Vol. 3:** 1153
2:22	**Vol. 1:** 193
2:24	**Vol. 2:** 173
2:25	**Vol. 2:** 863
2:26	**Vol. 2:** 119
2:27 f	**Vol. 3:** 33
2:27	**Vol. 3:** 311
2:28	**Vol. 1:** 407, 538
2:29	**Vol. 3:** 415, 421, 424
2:30	**Vol. 2:** 797 **Vol. 3:** 828
2:31	**Vol. 1:** 320
2:33	**Vol. 1:** 729
2:35	**Vol. 2:** 181 **Vol. 3:** 162
2:36	**Vol. 2:** 876 **Vol. 3:** 36
3	**Vol. 1:** 511
3:1–4:1	**Vol. 3:** 311
3:1	**Vol. 3:** 311, 1091, 1120
3:2 ff	**Vol. 1:** 442
3:3	**Vol. 3:** 786, 788
3:4–10	**Vol. 1:** 273
3:7	**Vol. 3:** 311, 1091
3:8	**Vol. 3:** 1028
3:9 ff	**Vol. 3:** 311
3:9	**Vol. 1:** 442
3:13 f	**Vol. 3:** 574, 828
3:13	**Vol. 1:** 568 **Vol. 3:** 342
3:14	**Vol. 3:** 153, 155, 423, 740
3:15	**Vol. 2:** 726
3:16	**Vol. 1:** 177, 285
3:17	**Vol. 2:** 214–215
3:18	**Vol. 2:** 214
3:19	**Vol. 1:** 609
3:20	**Vol. 1:** 595–596
3:21	**Vol. 3:** 311–312
4	**Vol. 3:** 788
4:2	**Vol. 2:** 698
4:3 ff	**Vol. 3:** 426
4:3	**Vol. 1:** 195 **Vol. 3:** 207
4:4	**Vol. 1:** 280
4:6	**Vol. 2:** 305
4:7	**Vol. 3:** 1051
4:8	**Vol. 1:** 531 **Vol. 3:** 857
4:9	**Vol. 2:** 305
4:10	**Vol. 2:** 698
4:11	**Vol. 3:** 342
4:13	**Vol. 2:** 803
4:15	**Vol. 3:** 112
4:21 f	**Vol. 2:** 45
5 f	**Vol. 2:** 45
5:1–7:2	**Vol. 3:** 788
5:2	**Vol. 3:** 786
5:5	**Vol. 3:** 787
5:6	**Vol. 2:** 149
5:11	**Vol. 2:** 149
6:2	**Vol. 2:** 554
6:3 f	**Vol. 3:** 420, 856
6:6	**Vol. 1:** 531
6:7	**Vol. 3:** 1161
6:8	**Vol. 3:** 856
6:10	**Vol. 3:** 1161
6:11	**Vol. 2:** 287
6:14 f	**Vol. 3:** 426
6:14	**Vol. 1:** 562 **Vol. 3:** 208

1 Samuel *(cont'd)*

6:17	**Vol. 3:** 856
6:18	**Vol. 3:** 208
6:19 f	**Vol. 2:** 225
6:19	**Vol. 2:** 698
6:20	**Vol. 2:** 224
7:1	**Vol. 2:** 225 **Vol. 3:** 1010
7:2	**Vol. 2:** 305
7:5	**Vol. 2:** 862
7:6	**Vol. 2:** 854
7:9	**Vol. 3:** 421, 426
7:13	**Vol. 2:** 149, 260
7:17	**Vol. 3:** 426
8–12	**Vol. 2:** 374
8–11	**Vol. 2:** 335
8	**Vol. 1:** 109
8:1–22a	**Vol. 2:** 374
8:1–3	**Vol. 1:** 426
8:1	**Vol. 1:** 472
8:3	**Vol. 1:** 492 **Vol. 3:** 354, 747
8:4 ff	**Vol. 1:** 195
8:5–7	**Vol. 2:** 374
8:6	**Vol. 2:** 862
8:7	**Vol. 1:** 425 **Vol. 2:** 376
8:8	**Vol. 1:** 531 **Vol. 2:** 889
8:9	**Vol. 3:** 354
8:10–18	**Vol. 1:** 716 **Vol. 2:** 432
8:11 f	**Vol. 3:** 608
8:11	**Vol. 3:** 354
8:15	**Vol. 1:** 560 **Vol. 2:** 693 **Vol. 3:** 523
8:17	**Vol. 2:** 693
8:18	**Vol. 1:** 537–538
8:19	**Vol. 1:** 426
8:20	**Vol. 2:** 363
9–12	**Vol. 2:** 306
9:1 ff	**Vol. 2:** 336
9:1–10:16	**Vol. 2:** 374
9:1 f	**Vol. 3:** 872
9:6–20	**Vol. 3:** 77
9:6	**Vol. 2:** 898
9:9	**Vol. 2:** 879
9:11–24	**Vol. 3:** 426
9:12 ff	**Vol. 3:** 1010
9:15	**Vol. 3:** 311–312
9:16 f	**Vol. 2:** 797
9:16	**Vol. 1:** 121, 410 **Vol. 2:** 374
9:19	**Vol. 3:** 45
9:22 ff	**Vol. 2:** 521
9:22	**Vol. 1:** 665 **Vol. 3:** 794
9:24†	**Vol. 3:** 422, 1041
9:25†	**Vol. 3:** 1010
10:1 ff	**Vol. 2:** 626–627
10:1	**Vol. 1:** 121 **Vol. 2:** 711, 797
10:2	**Vol. 1:** 170 **Vol. 3:** 531, 560
10:4	**Vol. 3:** 416
10:5 ff	**Vol. 3:** 77
10:5 f	**Vol. 1:** 527 **Vol. 3:** 77
10:5	**Vol. 3:** 77, 426
10:6	**Vol. 3:** 77
10:8	**Vol. 3:** 426
10:10 ff	**Vol. 3:** 77
10:10	**Vol. 1:** 527
10:12	**Vol. 2:** 745
10:14	**Vol. 3:** 531
10:17–27	**Vol. 2:** 374
10:18	**Vol. 1:** 531
10:19	**Vol. 2:** 698 **Vol. 3:** 218
10:20 f	**Vol. 2:** 296
10:20	**Vol. 2:** 226
10:21	**Vol. 2:** 698 **Vol. 3:** 528
10:24	**Vol. 1:** 538
10:25	**Vol. 3:** 354, 484
10:26	**Vol. 3:** 860
10:27	**Vol. 1:** 415
11:1–11	**Vol. 2:** 374
11:1	**Vol. 1:** 366
11:3	**Vol. 3:** 206
11:5	**Vol. 1:** 574
11:6†	**Vol. 1:** 108, 527 **Vol. 3:** 691
11:7	**Vol. 1:** 492
11:11	**Vol. 1:** 165 **Vol. 2:** 34 **Vol. 3:** 846
11:13†	**Vol. 3:** 207
11:14 f	**Vol. 2:** 374
11:14	**Vol. 2:** 673
11:15	**Vol. 2:** 521 **Vol. 3:** 426
11:16	**Vol. 3:** 691
12:3 ff	**Vol. 3:** 1041
12:3	**Vol. 2:** 336 **Vol. 3:** 153, 192
12:5	**Vol. 2:** 336
12:6–25	**Vol. 3:** 1104
12:6	**Vol. 2:** 639
12:7	**Vol. 3:** 355–356
12:8	**Vol. 1:** 426 **Vol. 2:** 639
12:10	**Vol. 1:** 426
12:12	**Vol. 1:** 426 **Vol. 3:** 748
12:13	**Vol. 2:** 856
12:14 ff	**Vol. 1:** 426
12:14	**Vol. 3:** 113
12:17	**Vol. 2:** 856 **Vol. 3:** 513
12:19	**Vol. 2:** 862
12:22	**Vol. 2:** 257
12:23	**Vol. 2:** 862 **Vol. 3:** 771
12:24	**Vol. 2:** 181
13:3	**Vol. 2:** 305–306, 742
13:6	**Vol. 3:** 381
13:8	**Vol. 1:** 294 **Vol. 3:** 1040
13:9	**Vol. 3:** 426
13:11	**Vol. 1:** 294 **Vol. 2:** 34 **Vol. 3:** 1040
13:12	**Vol. 1:** 495 **Vol. 2:** 860
13:13	**Vol. 3:** 117, 828
13:14	**Vol. 2:** 797
13:19	**Vol. 2:** 98, 305–306
13:20	**Vol. 2:** 98
13:23	**Vol. 1:** 710
14:1	**Vol. 1:** 283
14:2 ff	**Vol. 3:** 150
14:3	**Vol. 3:** 426
14:4	**Vol. 1:** 711
14:6	**Vol. 2:** 428 **Vol. 3:** 962

2 Samuel *(cont'd)*

1:14	**Vol. 3:** 97
1:17 f	**Vol. 3:** 673
1:17–27	**Vol. 2:** 418
1:18	**Vol. 3:** 484, 760
1:21	**Vol. 3:** 416
1:22	**Vol. 3:** 159
1:23	**Vol. 3:** 716
1:26	**Vol. 2:** 355, 540
2–3	**Vol. 3:** 873
2:1	**Vol. 3:** 1089
2:2–5	**Vol. 3:** 1062
2:4 ff	**Vol. 2:** 336
2:4	**Vol. 1:** 61
2:5	**Vol. 2:** 596 **Vol. 3:** 263
2:6	**Vol. 3:** 1153–1154
2:10	**Vol. 1:** 492
2:13	**Vol. 3:** 1194
2:16	**Vol. 2:** 303
2:25 f	**Vol. 3:** 1009
2:32	**Vol. 1:** 170
3	**Vol. 1:** 366
3:1	**Vol. 3:** 994
3:2–5	**Vol. 2:** 576
3:9	**Vol. 2:** 612
3:12 f	**Vol. 1:** 366
3:13	**Vol. 3:** 1057
3:17	**Vol. 1:** 195
3:18	**Vol. 3:** 206, 608–609
3:21	**Vol. 1:** 366
3:24	**Vol. 2:** 777
3:27	**Vol. 3:** 1192
3:29	**Vol. 1:** 324
3:31–34	**Vol. 2:** 417
3:31	**Vol. 3:** 120
3:33 ff	**Vol. 2:** 418
3:39	**Vol. 3:** 134
4:1	**Vol. 3:** 178
4:2	**Vol. 3:** 823
4:3	**Vol. 1:** 690
4:4	**Vol. 2:** 414
4:6	**Vol. 3:** 209
4:8	**Vol. 3:** 531
4:9	**Vol. 3:** 192
4:10	**Vol. 2:** 108
5:1–12	**Vol. 1:** 121
5:1–5	**Vol. 1:** 61
5:1	**Vol. 1:** 241
5:2	**Vol. 2:** 797 **Vol. 3:** 565
5:3	**Vol. 1:** 195 **Vol. 2:** 336
5:6 ff	**Vol. 1:** 218 **Vol. 2:** 324, 335–336, 802
5:6–10	**Vol. 2:** 325 **Vol. 3:** 1010
5:6 f	**Vol. 2:** 186
5:6	**Vol. 2:** 415
5:8 f	**Vol. 2:** 415
5:8	**Vol. 3:** 860
5:9	**Vol. 1:** 272
5:10*	**Vol. 2:** 69
5:14	**Vol. 3:** 659
5:23	**Vol. 2:** 898
6	**Vol. 2:** 325 **Vol. 3:** 782, 788
6:1 ff	**Vol. 2:** 335–336
6:2	**Vol. 1:** 280 **Vol. 2:** 69, 325, 650
6:3	**Vol. 3:** 1010
6:5	**Vol. 3:** 673
6:7	**Vol. 1:** 108
6:11*	**Vol. 1:** 143
6:15 f	**Vol. 2:** 186
6:16 ff	**Vol. 3:** 426
6:16 f	**Vol. 3:** 1057
6:18	**Vol. 2:** 69, 649–651
6:21	**Vol. 1:** 538
7	**Vol. 1:** 122, 177 **Vol. 2:** 378 **Vol. 3:** 426, 828, 1092, 1104
7:1–11b	**Vol. 2:** 374
7:1	**Vol. 1:** 426
7:2	**Vol. 2:** 69 **Vol. 3:** 787
7:4	**Vol. 2:** 898 **Vol. 3:** 1090
7:5 f	**Vol. 2:** 247
7:5	**Vol. 3:** 946
7:6	**Vol. 2:** 889 **Vol. 3:** 794
7:8 ff	**Vol. 1:** 596
7:8*	**Vol. 2:** 69
7:9	**Vol. 1:** 209 **Vol. 3:** 636
7:10	**Vol. 1:** 277 **Vol. 3:** 866
7:11–14	**Vol. 3:** 650
7:11 f	**Vol. 2:** 247
7:11	**Vol. 1:** 426 **Vol. 3:** 254, 787
7:12 ff	**Vol. 3:** 509
7:12–17	**Vol. 3:** 787
7:12–16	**Vol. 1:** 366 **Vol. 3:** 636, 642, 648, 650, 652
7:12	**Vol. 2:** 614 **Vol. 3:** 117, 279, 639
7:13	**Vol. 2:** 612, 650
7:14 f	**Vol. 3:** 778
7:14	**Vol. 1:** 123, 178, 241, 615, 617 **Vol. 2:** 614 **Vol. 3:** 637, 639, 648–650
7:15	**Vol. 1:** 607
7:16	**Vol. 1:** 210, 596 **Vol. 2:** 247, 374, 614 **Vol. 3:** 786
7:18 f	**Vol. 2:** 247
7:18	**Vol. 3:** 588
7:21	**Vol. 3:** 314
7:23	**Vol. 2:** 425 **Vol. 3:** 192–193, 318
7:24	**Vol. 3:** 117
7:25 ff*	**Vol. 2:** 69
7:25–29	**Vol. 2:** 247
7:25	**Vol. 3:** 1104
7:26 f	**Vol. 2:** 69
7:27	**Vol. 2:** 862–863 **Vol. 3:** 311
7:29	**Vol. 1:** 207
8:2	**Vol. 3:** 421
8:6	**Vol. 3:** 207, 421
8:14	**Vol. 3:** 207
8:16–18	**Vol. 3:** 478
8:17	**Vol. 2:** 34 **Vol. 3:** 408, 478
9:3	**Vol. 2:** 414
9:6	**Vol. 2:** 876
9:7	**Vol. 2:** 521

2 Samuel *(cont'd)*

9:8	**Vol. 2:** 876	**Vol. 3:** 595, 608
9:13	**Vol. 2:** 415	
10:4	**Vol. 1:** 128	
10:5	**Vol. 2:** 49	
10:6	**Vol. 1:** 128	**Vol. 2:** 139, 698
10:12	**Vol. 2:** 563	**Vol. 3:** 718
10:17	**Vol. 2:** 32	
10:18	**Vol. 2:** 698	
10:19	**Vol. 3:** 608	
11–12	**Vol. 2:** 336	
11:2	**Vol. 2:** 103	
11:3	**Vol. 1:** 266	**Vol. 2:** 576
11:4	**Vol. 2:** 225	**Vol. 3:** 861
11:7	**Vol. 2:** 777–778	
11:13	**Vol. 2:** 586	
11:14 f	**Vol. 1:** 246	**Vol. 3:** 484
11:14	**Vol. 1:** 243	
11:23	**Vol. 3:** 716	
11:24	**Vol. 3:** 608	
12	**Vol. 3:** 1092	
12:1 ff	**Vol. 3:** 78	
12:1–4	**Vol. 2:** 747	
12:1 f	**Vol. 2:** 841	
12:1	**Vol. 2:** 820	
12:3	**Vol. 1:** 240	**Vol. 2:** 820, 822
12:4	**Vol. 1:** 687	**Vol. 2:** 820, 841
12:5	**Vol. 1:** 108	
12:7	**Vol. 3:** 201	
12:13	**Vol. 1:** 109	**Vol. 3:** 579
12:14	**Vol. 1:** 554	**Vol. 3:** 342
12:15 ff	**Vol. 3:** 997	
12:15	**Vol. 1:** 433	
12:16–23	**Vol. 1:** 612	
12:19	**Vol. 2:** 554	
12:20	**Vol. 1:** 120	**Vol. 2:** 876
12:23	**Vol. 3:** 946	
12:24 f	**Vol. 3:** 605	
12:28	**Vol. 2:** 649	
12:29	**Vol. 2:** 32	
12:30	**Vol. 1:** 405	
12:31	**Vol. 1:** 726	
13	**Vol. 1:** 555	**Vol. 2:** 478
13:1	**Vol. 2:** 103	
13:3	**Vol. 3:** 1027	
13:11	**Vol. 3:** 747	
13:12	**Vol. 2:** 260	
13:13	**Vol. 1:** 258	**Vol. 3:** 1024
13:14	**Vol. 1:** 331	
13:17	**Vol. 1:** 194	
13:19	**Vol. 2:** 157	**Vol. 3:** 94
13:25	**Vol. 3:** 711	
13:27	**Vol. 3:** 711	
13:35	**Vol. 2:** 898	
13:37	**Vol. 2:** 422	
14:2	**Vol. 1:** 120 **Vol. 2:** 711 **Vol. 3:** 480, 1027	
14:4	**Vol. 2:** 876	**Vol. 3:** 206
14:5–7	**Vol. 2:** 747	

14:7	**Vol. 3:** 94, 109	
14:9	**Vol. 2:** 612	
14:11	**Vol. 1:** 609	**Vol. 3:** 94
14:13 f	**Vol. 3:** 823	
14:14	**Vol. 1:** 433	**Vol. 3:** 820, 823–824
14:16	**Vol. 2:** 297	**Vol. 3:** 201
14:20 f	**Vol. 3:** 1120	
14:20	**Vol. 3:** 1027	
14:22	**Vol. 2:** 116, 876	
14:25	**Vol. 3:** 817	
14:26	**Vol. 3:** 752	
14:30	**Vol. 2:** 303	
14:33	**Vol. 2:** 876	
15:1–6	**Vol. 3:** 357	
15:4	**Vol. 2:** 363	**Vol. 3:** 355
15:5	**Vol. 2:** 876	
15:6	**Vol. 2:** 363	
15:7	**Vol. 2:** 60	
15:10	**Vol. 2:** 173	
15:13	**Vol. 3:** 45	
15:14	**Vol. 2:** 803	
15:15	**Vol. 1:** 534, 537	**Vol. 3:** 608
15:16	**Vol. 1:** 698	
15:24 ff	**Vol. 2:** 778	**Vol. 3:** 439
15:24–29	**Vol. 3:** 788	
15:25	**Vol. 2:** 117	
15:30	**Vol. 2:** 157	
15:32	**Vol. 2:** 876	
15:34	**Vol. 3:** 350	
16:1	**Vol. 3:** 919, 1161	
16:2	**Vol. 2:** 257	
16:4	**Vol. 2:** 876	
16:5–13	**Vol. 3:** 872	
16:8	**Vol. 3:** 134, 159	
16:10 ff	**Vol. 1:** 108	
16:10 f	**Vol. 1:** 698	
16:14	**Vol. 3:** 686	
16:20 ff	**Vol. 3:** 1074	
16:21	**Vol. 1:** 331	
16:23	**Vol. 1:** 665	
17:4	**Vol. 1:** 195	**Vol. 3:** 1120
17:8	**Vol. 3:** 178	
17:15	**Vol. 1:** 195	**Vol. 3:** 439
17:23	**Vol. 1:** 117, 433	
18:18	**Vol. 2:** 149, 590, 649 **Vol. 3:** 239	
18:20	**Vol. 2:** 108	
18:21	**Vol. 2:** 876–877	
18:22	**Vol. 2:** 108	
18:28 f	**Vol. 2:** 778	
18:28	**Vol. 2:** 170, 876	
18:31	**Vol. 2:** 363	**Vol. 3:** 356
19:1	**Vol. 2:** 422	**Vol. 3:** 1179
19:6 f	**Vol. 1:** 555	
19:6	**Vol. 3:** 209	
19:9	**Vol. 2:** 363	**Vol. 3:** 201
19:11	**Vol. 3:** 439	
19:12	**Vol. 1:** 195	
19:19	**Vol. 3:** 823	
19:20*	**Vol. 3:** 820, 823	
19:21 f	**Vol. 1:** 122	

2 Samuel *(cont'd)*

19:22	**Vol. 2:** 336
19:26	**Vol. 1:** 117
19:27*	**Vol. 2:** 415
19:29*	**Vol. 3:** 354
19:35*	**Vol. 2:** 395 **Vol. 3:** 672–673
19:39	**Vol. 1:** 537
19:44*	**Vol. 3:** 29, 823
20:2	**Vol. 2:** 349
20:3	**Vol. 1:** 698
20:8	**Vol. 3:** 1161
20:9	**Vol. 2:** 170
20:14	**Vol. 1:** 293
20:16	**Vol. 3:** 1027
20:19	**Vol. 3:** 1069
20:20	**Vol. 3:** 157, 160
20:22	**Vol. 3:** 1027
20:24	**Vol. 3:** 239
21:1–14	**Vol. 3:** 154
21:3 f	**Vol. 3:** 159
21:6	**Vol. 1:** 538
21:10	**Vol. 1:** 113 **Vol. 3:** 255
21:17	**Vol. 3:** 109
22:1	**Vol. 3:** 673
22:2	**Vol. 3:** 381, 673
22:3	**Vol. 3:** 715
22:5	**Vol. 2:** 621
22:6	**Vol. 3:** 180
22:7	**Vol. 3:** 786
22:8	**Vol. 2:** 189
22:9	**Vol. 1:** 657
22:11	**Vol. 1:** 280
22:15	**Vol. 3:** 1001
22:17	**Vol. 2:** 636
22:18	**Vol. 1:** 555 **Vol. 3:** 201
22:20	**Vol. 2:** 817
22:23	**Vol. 3:** 354
22:24	**Vol. 3:** 924
22:26	**Vol. 2:** 60
22:28	**Vol. 2:** 260, 262, 596, 821
22:29	**Vol. 2:** 485
22:31	**Vol. 3:** 924
22:32 ff	**Vol. 2:** 602
22:32	**Vol. 1:** 382
22:33	**Vol. 3:** 924
22:35	**Vol. 3:** 760
22:36	**Vol. 2:** 179
22:43	**Vol. 3:** 915
22:44	**Vol. 3:** 201
22:49	**Vol. 3:** 201
22:50	**Vol. 1:** 344 **Vol. 2:** 655 **Vol. 3:** 672
23:1 f	**Vol. 1:** 122
23:1	**Vol. 2:** 336 **Vol. 3:** 671
23:2	**Vol. 3:** 691
23:4	**Vol. 2:** 491
23:14	**Vol. 1:** 170
23:16 f	**Vol. 3:** 158
23:16	**Vol. 2:** 854
23:17	**Vol. 3:** 157
23:24	**Vol. 1:** 170
24	**Vol. 3:** 1092
24:1	**Vol. 1:** 108, 451, 562 **Vol. 3:** 468, 557
24:3	**Vol. 3:** 1016
24:4	**Vol. 3:** 152
24:9	**Vol. 2:** 698
24:10 ff	**Vol. 3:** 997
24:10	**Vol. 1:** 349 **Vol. 3:** 1025
24:11 ff	**Vol. 3:** 1089
24:12	**Vol. 1:** 537
24:13	**Vol. 2:** 265
24:14	**Vol. 1:** 609 **Vol. 2:** 598
24:15	**Vol. 2:** 698 **Vol. 3:** 846
24:16 f	**Vol. 1:** 101
24:16	**Vol. 1:** 109, 468
24:17–25	**Vol. 3:** 150
24:17	**Vol. 2:** 412 **Vol. 3:** 565
24:18–25	**Vol. 3:** 418, 787
24:20	**Vol. 2:** 876
24:24	**Vol. 2:** 41
24:25	**Vol. 3:** 421

1 Kings

1–11	**Vol. 3:** 606
1	**Vol. 3:** 605
1:8	**Vol. 3:** 78
1:11 ff	**Vol. 3:** 78
1:12	**Vol. 3:** 209
1:14	**Vol. 1:** 734
1:16	**Vol. 2:** 876
1:23	**Vol. 2:** 876
1:25	**Vol. 2:** 521
1:29	**Vol. 3:** 192
1:31	**Vol. 2:** 876
1:33 ff	**Vol. 1:** 122
1:33	**Vol. 2:** 711
1:36	**Vol. 1:** 98
1:39 f	**Vol. 3:** 673
1:39	**Vol. 1:** 121
1:41 ff	**Vol. 2:** 521
1:41	**Vol. 3:** 112
1:42	**Vol. 2:** 109
1:47	**Vol. 2:** 586, 876 **Vol. 3:** 636
1:48	**Vol. 2:** 797
1:53	**Vol. 2:** 876
2	**Vol. 3:** 605
2:2	**Vol. 3:** 938
2:3	**Vol. 2:** 639 **Vol. 3:** 354, 937
2:4	**Vol. 3:** 879, 1104
2:5	**Vol. 1:** 239 **Vol. 3:** 120, 159
2:6	**Vol. 3:** 1027
2:9	**Vol. 3:** 1027
2:12	**Vol. 2:** 376
2:13 ff	**Vol. 3:** 1074
2:13	**Vol. 2:** 876
2:19	**Vol. 2:** 146, 612 **Vol. 3:** 588
2:24	**Vol. 1:** 117
2:26	**Vol. 1:** 520
2:27	**Vol. 1:** 735 **Vol. 3:** 426, 1104

1 Kings *(cont'd)*

2:28	**Vol. 3:** 419
2:29†	**Vol. 1:** 559
2:31	**Vol. 3:** 159
2:32 ff	**Vol. 3:** 159
2:34	**Vol. 3:** 94
2:35	**Vol. 1:** 665 **Vol. 3:** 439
2:42*	**Vol. 3:** 1041
3:1	**Vol. 1:** 531 **Vol. 2:** 357 **Vol. 3:** 240, 605, 1027
3:2	**Vol. 2:** 650 **Vol. 3:** 426
3:4–15	**Vol. 1:** 511–512
3:4	**Vol. 3:** 1010
3:5–14	**Vol. 3:** 1029
3:6	**Vol. 3:** 879
3:7 ff	**Vol. 2:** 336
3:7	**Vol. 2:** 428
3:9	**Vol. 1:** 503 **Vol. 3:** 130–131, 606
3:11 ff	**Vol. 2:** 478
3:11	**Vol. 2:** 841 **Vol. 3:** 130
3:12	**Vol. 2:** 181 **Vol. 3:** 606, 1027
3:13	**Vol. 2:** 841
3:14	**Vol. 1:** 332 **Vol. 3:** 946
3:16–28	**Vol. 3:** 606, 1029
3:16	**Vol. 1:** 498
3:20	**Vol. 1:** 239–240
3:28	**Vol. 3:** 354
4:2 ff	**Vol. 3:** 33
4:3	**Vol. 3:** 239
4:6	**Vol. 2:** 254
4:7–19	**Vol. 3:** 605
4:16	**Vol. 3:** 815
4:20*	**Vol. 3:** 1028
4:25	**Vol. 1:** 724 **Vol. 3:** 256, 866
4:29–34	**Vol. 3:** 606
4:29*	**Vol. 1:** 670 **Vol. 2:** 181
5:9–14*	**Vol. 3:** 1028
5:9 f*	**Vol. 3:** 1027
5:9*	**Vol. 1:** 127 **Vol. 3:** 1027
5:10	**Vol. 3:** 787, 1028
5:11–16*	**Vol. 2:** 698
5:11*	**Vol. 3:** 1028–1029, 1033
5:12 f*	**Vol. 3:** 1029
5:12*	**Vol. 1:** 366 **Vol. 3:** 605, 673, 1029
5:13	**Vol. 3:** 1069
5:14*	**Vol. 3:** 1027, 1029
5:17	**Vol. 2:** 650
5:18*	**Vol. 3:** 254, 787
5:21*	**Vol. 3:** 1029
5:26*	**Vol. 2:** 777 **Vol. 3:** 1027
6 f	**Vol. 3:** 782
6–8	**Vol. 3:** 787
6–7	**Vol. 3:** 783
6	**Vol. 3:** 606
6:1	**Vol. 3:** 937
6:3	**Vol. 3:** 786
6:4	**Vol. 3:** 787
6:5	**Vol. 3:** 786, 948
6:12	**Vol. 3:** 933, 1104
6:15	**Vol. 1:** 389
6:23–28	**Vol. 1:** 280
6:33	**Vol. 3:** 786
6:36	**Vol. 3:** 787, 794
7–9	**Vol. 3:** 426
7:5	**Vol. 2:** 830
7:9 f*	**Vol. 1:** 661
7:12	**Vol. 3:** 787
7:13–47	**Vol. 2:** 97
7:13 f	**Vol. 3:** 787
7:14*	**Vol. 2:** 395
7:15–45	**Vol. 3:** 795
7:21	**Vol. 3:** 786
7:23–26	**Vol. 3:** 418, 787
7:38	**Vol. 1:** 742
7:48	**Vol. 1:** 586 **Vol. 3:** 423
7:50†	**Vol. 3:** 786
7:51	**Vol. 1:** 734
8	**Vol. 1:** 195, 531
8:1 ff	**Vol. 3:** 788
8:1	**Vol. 1:** 293 **Vol. 2:** 324
8:4	**Vol. 3:** 786, 812
8:5	**Vol. 3:** 426, 815
8:8	**Vol. 3:** 786
8:9	**Vol. 2:** 639 **Vol. 3:** 815
8:10 f	**Vol. 1:** 735 **Vol. 2:** 45 **Vol. 3:** 788
8:10	**Vol. 3:** 786
8:12–13	**Vol. 2:** 190
8:12	**Vol. 1:** 422 **Vol. 2:** 215
8:13	**Vol. 2:** 650
8:14 ff	**Vol. 2:** 650
8:14	**Vol. 1:** 210
8:15	**Vol. 1:** 735 **Vol. 3:** 1104
8:16 f	**Vol. 3:** 784
8:16	**Vol. 1:** 538
8:17	**Vol. 2:** 181
8:20	**Vol. 3:** 1104
8:22 ff	**Vol. 2:** 863
8:22	**Vol. 3:** 418, 787
8:24 ff	**Vol. 3:** 608
8:24	**Vol. 1:** 735 **Vol. 3:** 1104
8:25	**Vol. 3:** 946
8:26	**Vol. 1:** 596
8:27	**Vol. 2:** 189–190, 247 **Vol. 3:** 727
8:28 ff	**Vol. 2:** 336, 862
8:28 f	**Vol. 2:** 863
8:28	**Vol. 2:** 860
8:29	**Vol. 3:** 786
8:30	**Vol. 2:** 190, 860 **Vol. 3:** 157, 786
8:31 f	**Vol. 3:** 740
8:32	**Vol. 3:** 355, 357
8:33–47	**Vol. 2:** 860
8:33–36	**Vol. 1:** 345
8:33	**Vol. 2:** 862
8:34	**Vol. 3:** 157
8:35	**Vol. 2:** 260, 862 **Vol. 3:** 1001
8:36	**Vol. 3:** 157, 316
8:37 ff	**Vol. 2:** 265
8:38	**Vol. 2:** 860, 863
8:39	**Vol. 3:** 157, 533

1 Kings (*cont'd*)

8:41 ff	**Vol. 1:** 688
8:42	**Vol. 1:** 320 **Vol. 2:** 862
8:44	**Vol. 2:** 862
8:45	**Vol. 2:** 860, 863 **Vol. 3:** 354
8:46–53	**Vol. 3:** 1104
8:48	**Vol. 2:** 862
8:49	**Vol. 2:** 860, 863
8:50	**Vol. 3:** 157
8:51	**Vol. 2:** 297
8:52	**Vol. 2:** 860
8:53	**Vol. 2:** 297, 639 **Vol. 3:** 673
8:54	**Vol. 1:** 210 **Vol. 2:** 860, 862–863 **Vol. 3:** 418
8:56	**Vol. 2:** 357, 639 **Vol. 3:** 256, 1104
8:58	**Vol. 3:** 937
8:59	**Vol. 3:** 354
8:60	**Vol. 2:** 720
8:61	**Vol. 2:** 60, 593, 778
8:62–65	**Vol. 3:** 426
8:63	**Vol. 2:** 673
8:64	**Vol. 3:** 418, 787
8:65	**Vol. 1:** 293
8:66	**Vol. 2:** 357
9	**Vol. 3:** 828
9:3	**Vol. 2:** 860, 863
9:6–10	**Vol. 3:** 815
9:6–9	**Vol. 1:** 354
9:6	**Vol. 2:** 876
9:9	**Vol. 2:** 876
9:15–19	**Vol. 3:** 605
9:21	**Vol. 3:** 593
9:25	**Vol. 3:** 418, 787
9:26	**Vol. 3:** 983
9:27	**Vol. 3:** 593
10:1–13	**Vol. 2:** 680 **Vol. 3:** 606
10:1–10	**Vol. 2:** 381 **Vol. 3:** 1030
10:1–9	**Vol. 3:** 1029
10:1	**Vol. 2:** 745 **Vol. 3:** 799
10:7	**Vol. 3:** 1027
10:18 ff	**Vol. 2:** 612
10:18	**Vol. 2:** 96
10:21	**Vol. 2:** 96 **Vol. 3:** 823
10:22	**Vol. 3:** 606
10:23 f	**Vol. 3:** 1029
10:23	**Vol. 2:** 841
10:25–29	**Vol. 1:** 117
10:25	**Vol. 1:** 415 **Vol. 3:** 606
10:26	**Vol. 3:** 605
10:28–29	**Vol. 1:** 531
11:1 ff	**Vol. 1:** 492 **Vol. 2:** 791
11:1–11	**Vol. 2:** 576
11:1–10	**Vol. 3:** 606
11:2	**Vol. 2:** 349
11:4	**Vol. 1:** 688 **Vol. 2:** 60, 593, 778 **Vol. 3:** 835
11:5	**Vol. 2:** 67
11:11*	**Vol. 1:** 333
11:13	**Vol. 1:** 538
11:14	**Vol. 3:** 468
11:15	**Vol. 1:** 264
11:23	**Vol. 3:** 468
11:25	**Vol. 3:** 468
11:25b	**Vol. 3:** 468
11:27	**Vol. 3:** 950
11:29 ff	**Vol. 2:** 626
11:29	**Vol. 2:** 670
11:31	**Vol. 2:** 797
11:32	**Vol. 1:** 538
11:34	**Vol. 1:** 538
11:38	**Vol. 1:** 332
11:40	**Vol. 1:** 531
11:41	**Vol. 3:** 1120
12	**Vol. 1:** 61
12:1 ff	**Vol. 1:** 295 **Vol. 2:** 374
12:1–20	**Vol. 3:** 606
12:3 ff	**Vol. 1:** 293
12:3	**Vol. 1:** 295
12:4	**Vol. 3:** 752
12:6 ff	**Vol. 1:** 195
12:8	**Vol. 3:** 1016
12:9 ff	**Vol. 3:** 1161
12:10	**Vol. 1:** 239
12:11	**Vol. 1:** 510
12:14	**Vol. 1:** 510
12:15	**Vol. 3:** 1104
12:21	**Vol. 1:** 293 **Vol. 2:** 305
12:24	**Vol. 2:** 765 **Vol. 3:** 255, 1120
12:26 ff	**Vol. 2:** 325 **Vol. 3:** 33
12:27 f	**Vol. 3:** 426
12:27	**Vol. 2:** 325
12:28 ff	**Vol. 3:** 33, 104
12:28 f	**Vol. 3:** 872
12:28	**Vol. 2:** 325
12:32	**Vol. 1:** 474
13:1 ff	**Vol. 2:** 626
13:1–31	**Vol. 3:** 77
13:2 ff	**Vol. 3:** 426
13:3	**Vol. 2:** 633
13:4	**Vol. 1:** 515 **Vol. 3:** 999
13:5	**Vol. 2:** 633
13:6	**Vol. 2:** 860, 862
13:11	**Vol. 3:** 78
13:17*	**Vol. 1:** 332
13:20	**Vol. 3:** 254, 588
13:22	**Vol. 1:** 264
13:30	**Vol. 3:** 1051
14:2 ff	**Vol. 3:** 426
14:6	**Vol. 1:** 127
14:7	**Vol. 2:** 797
14:8	**Vol. 1:** 481 **Vol. 3:** 608, 946
14:9	**Vol. 1:** 233
14:11	**Vol. 2:** 859
14:16	**Vol. 2:** 116
14:21	**Vol. 1:** 538
14:24	**Vol. 2:** 791
14:25 ff	**Vol. 1:** 531
14:26	**Vol. 2:** 830 **Vol. 3:** 788
15:3	**Vol. 2:** 593, 778

1 Kings *(cont'd)*

15:14	**Vol. 2:** 778
15:18	**Vol. 2:** 830 **Vol. 3:** 788
15:29	**Vol. 3:** 1120
15:31	**Vol. 1:** 243
15:34	**Vol. 3:** 938
16:8	**Vol. 3:** 788
16:9	**Vol. 2:** 254
16:17	**Vol. 3:** 418
16:31	**Vol. 2:** 582, 876 **Vol. 3:** 1067
16:34	**Vol. 3:** 444
17–19	**Vol. 1:** 209
17 f	**Vol. 2:** 627
17	**Vol. 1:** 543 **Vol. 3:** 558
17:1–18:1	**Vol. 2:** 730
17:1	**Vol. 1:** 209, 474, 545 **Vol. 2:** 265, 688, 861 **Vol. 3:** 1091
17:2	**Vol. 3:** 1090, 1120
17:3 f	**Vol. 2:** 274
17:4 ff	**Vol. 1:** 173
17:4	**Vol. 2:** 688
17:7	**Vol. 1:** 515 **Vol. 3:** 786
17:8	**Vol. 3:** 1090, 1120
17:12–16	**Vol. 2:** 711
17:12	**Vol. 1:** 543
17:13	**Vol. 1:** 328
17:14	**Vol. 3:** 1001
17:17–24	**Vol. 2:** 433, 628, 630 **Vol. 3:** 1059, 1067
17:17–22	**Vol. 3:** 261
17:18–16	**Vol. 3:** 1062
17:18	**Vol. 3:** 78, 239
17:19	**Vol. 1:** 240, 442
17:21	**Vol. 1:** 272 **Vol. 2:** 167 **Vol. 3:** 680
17:24	**Vol. 3:** 880
18–22	**Vol. 3:** 1057
18	**Vol. 2:** 724 **Vol. 3:** 426
18:1	**Vol. 1:** 209 **Vol. 2:** 688, 861 **Vol. 3:** 1090, 1120
18:2 ff	**Vol. 2:** 274
18:2a	**Vol. 1:** 209
18:3 ff	**Vol. 3:** 608
18:3	**Vol. 2:** 254
18:4	**Vol. 2:** 582 **Vol. 3:** 988
18:12 ff	**Vol. 3:** 266
18:13	**Vol. 2:** 582 **Vol. 3:** 988
18:16 f	**Vol. 1:** 209
18:17	**Vol. 3:** 1091
18:19–40	**Vol. 3:** 77
18:19	**Vol. 1:** 589
18:24 ff	**Vol. 1:** 272
18:26	**Vol. 2:** 863
18:27	**Vol. 2:** 432
18:28	**Vol. 1:** 527 **Vol. 2:** 437, 573, 854
18:29	**Vol. 2:** 863
18:30 ff	**Vol. 3:** 426
18:31 f	**Vol. 3:** 418
18:36 ff	**Vol. 2:** 627
18:36	**Vol. 3:** 609, 1091
18:38	**Vol. 1:** 655 **Vol. 2:** 628 **Vol. 3:** 266, 421
18:39	**Vol. 1:** 610
18:40	**Vol. 3:** 209
18:41 ff	**Vol. 1:** 210
18:41–46	**Vol. 1:** 209
18:41–45	**Vol. 3:** 988
18:42	**Vol. 3:** 1009
18:44	**Vol. 3:** 1161
18:45	**Vol. 3:** 266
18:46	**Vol. 2:** 898 **Vol. 3:** 946
19	**Vol. 3:** 721
19:1–18	**Vol. 3:** 1013
19:1 f	**Vol. 2:** 582
19:2 ff	**Vol. 3:** 962
19:2	**Vol. 3:** 846
19:3 ff	**Vol. 3:** 1008
19:4–6	**Vol. 3:** 1005
19:8	**Vol. 2:** 893 **Vol. 3:** 804
19:10	**Vol. 1:** 545 **Vol. 2:** 724, 882 **Vol. 3:** 252, 426, 531, 1166
19:11 ff	**Vol. 2:** 281
19:11–18	**Vol. 3:** 1005
19:11–14	**Vol. 3:** 266
19:11 f	**Vol. 1:** 655
19:11	**Vol. 3:** 382, 707
19:12	**Vol. 1:** 280 **Vol. 3:** 1010, 1091
19:14	**Vol. 1:** 545 **Vol. 2:** 724 **Vol. 3:** 531, 1166
19:16 ff	**Vol. 3:** 97
19:16	**Vol. 2:** 337, 711
19:17	**Vol. 3:** 209
19:18	**Vol. 1:** 545 **Vol. 2:** 85, 690–691, 699, 859, 876 **Vol. 3:** 248, 252, 325, 436
19:19 ff	**Vol. 1:** 485
19:19	**Vol. 1:** 116 **Vol. 3:** 121, 1161
19:20 f	**Vol. 1:** 492–493
19:20	**Vol. 1:** 481
19:21	**Vol. 1:** 492 **Vol. 3:** 1161
20	**Vol. 3:** 960
20:6	**Vol. 3:** 533
20:7 f	**Vol. 1:** 195
20:7*	**Vol. 3:** 513
20:8*	**Vol. 3:** 497–498
20:9	**Vol. 1:** 127
20:11	**Vol. 1:** 227
20:13*	**Vol. 2:** 395–396, 800
20:20	**Vol. 1:** 268 **Vol. 3:** 209
20:28	**Vol. 2:** 395–396
20:33	**Vol. 2:** 554
20:34	**Vol. 1:** 366
20:39	**Vol. 3:** 593
20:41	**Vol. 2:** 573
20:42	**Vol. 1:** 414
21	**Vol. 1:** 640 **Vol. 3:** 1091
21:1	**Vol. 3:** 782
21:2*	**Vol. 3:** 166
21:5–25	**Vol. 2:** 582
21:6	**Vol. 3:** 846
21:7	**Vol. 2:** 181

1 Kings (cont'd)

21:8	**Vol. 1:** 195, 716 **Vol. 2:** 650
21:9 f	**Vol. 1:** 246
21:9*	**Vol. 1:** 165
21:10*	**Vol. 2:** 686 **Vol. 3:** 1041
21:11*	**Vol. 1:** 127, 165, 195, 716
21:12	**Vol. 2:** 158
21:13*	**Vol. 3:** 342, 1041
21:17 ff	**Vol. 3:** 1090
21:17–19	**Vol. 3:** 1091
21:19 ff	**Vol. 1:** 410
21:27	**Vol. 1:** 612, 672
21:29	**Vol. 2:** 117
22	**Vol. 3:** 960
22:2	**Vol. 2:** 663
22:8	**Vol. 1:** 555
22:10 f	**Vol. 3:** 1099
22:10	**Vol. 3:** 77
22:11	**Vol. 2:** 754 **Vol. 3:** 715
22:12	**Vol. 3:** 77
22:16	**Vol. 3:** 473
22:17	**Vol. 2:** 104, 413, 459
22:19 ff	**Vol. 2:** 190–191 **Vol. 3:** 474
22:19–23	**Vol. 3:** 720
22:19	**Vol. 2:** 189, 613–614 **Vol. 3:** 588
22:21 ff	**Vol. 2:** 458 **Vol. 3:** 693
22:21 f	**Vol. 3:** 692
22:24 ff	**Vol. 3:** 78
22:24	**Vol. 3:** 78
22:25	**Vol. 2:** 891
22:27 f	**Vol. 2:** 778
22:54	**Vol. 2:** 876

2 Kings

1	**Vol. 3:** 1091
1:2 f	**Vol. 3:** 469
1:2	**Vol. 2:** 67
1:3 f	**Vol. 1:** 101 **Vol. 3:** 1090–1091
1:3	**Vol. 1:** 273
1:8	**Vol. 3:** 121
1:9	**Vol. 1:** 273
1:10 ff	**Vol. 2:** 630
1:10	**Vol. 1:** 544, 655, 657
1:12	**Vol. 1:** 544, 654
2	**Vol. 3:** 558, 602
2:1 ff	**Vol. 3:** 78
2:1–15	**Vol. 3:** 266
2:1	**Vol. 3:** 78
2:2	**Vol. 3:** 265
2:3 ff	**Vol. 3:** 78
2:3	**Vol. 3:** 262
2:4	**Vol. 3:** 78
2:5	**Vol. 3:** 78, 262, 265
2:9–12	**Vol. 2:** 82
2:9 f	**Vol. 3:** 265
2:9	**Vol. 3:** 262, 691
2:11 f	**Vol. 3:** 602
2:11	**Vol. 1:** 655 **Vol. 2:** 189, 191 **Vol. 3:** 261, 266, 747
2:12	**Vol. 1:** 177, 617 **Vol. 3:** 602
2:13 f	**Vol. 1:** 116, 207 **Vol. 3:** 121
2:15	**Vol. 2:** 876 **Vol. 3:** 255, 266
2:16 ff	**Vol. 3:** 266
2:19–22	**Vol. 3:** 78, 444
2:23–25	**Vol. 3:** 78
2:24	**Vol. 2:** 651 **Vol. 3:** 584
3:13	**Vol. 3:** 1069
3:15	**Vol. 3:** 78, 673
3:21	**Vol. 3:** 120
3:22	**Vol. 1:** 205
3:27	**Vol. 3:** 421
4	**Vol. 3:** 558
4:1–7	**Vol. 3:** 78
4:1	**Vol. 2:** 96 **Vol. 3:** 594, 608
4:4	**Vol. 1:** 734
4:8–37	**Vol. 3:** 78
4:9	**Vol. 2:** 225
4:10	**Vol. 2:** 487
4:12	**Vol. 1:** 485
4:13 f	**Vol. 2:** 664
4:16 ff	**Vol. 3:** 846
4:16 f	**Vol. 3:** 846
4:17–37	**Vol. 2:** 433
4:18–37	**Vol. 2:** 628 **Vol. 3:** 78, 261
4:23	**Vol. 3:** 407
4:25–37	**Vol. 3:** 1067
4:29	**Vol. 1:** 207 **Vol. 3:** 120
4:32 ff	**Vol. 2:** 206
4:32–37	**Vol. 2:** 630 **Vol. 3:** 1059
4:33	**Vol. 2:** 862
4:34	**Vol. 2:** 167
4:37	**Vol. 2:** 876
4:38	**Vol. 3:** 78
4:42–44	**Vol. 3:** 1007
4:42	**Vol. 3:** 424
5	**Vol. 2:** 628
5:1 ff	**Vol. 2:** 464
5:1–19	**Vol. 3:** 986–987
5:1–14	**Vol. 3:** 78
5:1	**Vol. 2:** 622, 625
5:6	**Vol. 1:** 246
5:7	**Vol. 1:** 316 **Vol. 2:** 167
5:10	**Vol. 3:** 989
5:11–15	**Vol. 3:** 860
5:12	**Vol. 3:** 986
5:13 ff	**Vol. 2:** 167
5:13	**Vol. 1:** 617
5:14	**Vol. 1:** 144 **Vol. 3:** 989, 991
5:15	**Vol. 2:** 396
5:17	**Vol. 3:** 1161
5:18	**Vol. 2:** 876 **Vol. 3:** 152, 156, 255
5:23	**Vol. 3:** 711
5:25	**Vol. 1:** 474
5:27	**Vol. 2:** 349
6 f	**Vol. 2:** 627
6:1	**Vol. 3:** 78
6:3	**Vol. 2:** 257
6:5 ff	**Vol. 2:** 628
6:12	**Vol. 3:** 78

2 Kings *(cont'd)*

6:16   **Vol. 3:** 469
6:17 f   **Vol. 2:** 862
6:17   **Vol. 2:** 189, 729, 919
6:21   **Vol. 1:** 617
6:24 ff   **Vol. 1:** 210
6:26   **Vol. 3:** 206
6:31 ff   **Vol. 3:** 962
6:32   **Vol. 3:** 588
6:33   **Vol. 2:** 773
7:2   **Vol. 2:** 189   **Vol. 3:** 255
7:6   **Vol. 2:** 139
7:7–8   **Vol. 3:** 811
7:10   **Vol. 1:** 171
7:17   **Vol. 3:** 255
8:3   **Vol. 2:** 60
8:5   **Vol. 1:** 574
8:7–15   **Vol. 3:** 78
8:13   **Vol. 3:** 608
9   **Vol. 3:** 1092
9:3   **Vol. 1:** 121   **Vol. 2:** 711
9:6   **Vol. 1:** 121   **Vol. 2:** 711
9:7–37   **Vol. 2:** 582
9:7   **Vol. 3:** 93, 97, 608
9:11   **Vol. 1:** 527
9:13   **Vol. 2:** 379   **Vol. 3:** 873
9:18 ff   **Vol. 1:** 117
9:21   **Vol. 3:** 1161
9:22   **Vol. 2:** 554–555   **Vol. 3:** 1067
9:25   **Vol. 3:** 1161
9:30   **Vol. 3:** 1067
9:34   **Vol. 1:** 416
10:1–6   **Vol. 1:** 246
10:1   **Vol. 3:** 484
10:6   **Vol. 3:** 484
10:10–14   **Vol. 3:** 454
10:10   **Vol. 1:** 609   **Vol. 3:** 1104
10:11   **Vol. 3:** 33
10:19 ff   **Vol. 3:** 33
10:20   **Vol. 2:** 234   **Vol. 3:** 51
10:23   **Vol. 3:** 608
10:24   **Vol. 3:** 196, 209
10:30   **Vol. 2:** 117
10:31   **Vol. 2:** 440
11:1–12   **Vol. 3:** 33
11:4   **Vol. 1:** 366
11:12   **Vol. 1:** 122   **Vol. 2:** 711   **Vol. 3:** 636
11:14   **Vol. 3:** 673
11:18   **Vol. 2:** 287
11:19   **Vol. 1:** 122
12:4–16   **Vol. 3:** 426
12:10   **Vol. 2:** 830   **Vol. 3:** 478, 752
13   **Vol. 3:** 558
13:2   **Vol. 1:** 492
13:5   **Vol. 3:** 218, 462
13:7   **Vol. 3:** 266
13:14 ff   **Vol. 3:** 78
13:14–19   **Vol. 3:** 1099
13:14   **Vol. 1:** 617

13:17   **Vol. 2:** 726
13:20 f   **Vol. 3:** 261
13:23   **Vol. 1:** 366   **Vol. 2:** 117, 318
14:2   **Vol. 2:** 422
14:4   **Vol. 3:** 426
14:6   **Vol. 2:** 639   **Vol. 3:** 484
14:7   **Vol. 1:** 343
14:14   **Vol. 3:** 528
14:15 f   **Vol. 3:** 1120
14:16   **Vol. 1:** 442
14:22   **Vol. 1:** 442
14:26   **Vol. 2:** 117
14:29   **Vol. 1:** 442
15–17   **Vol. 1:** 52   **Vol. 2:** 306   **Vol. 3:** 94
15   **Vol. 3:** 267
15:4   **Vol. 3:** 426
15:5   **Vol. 3:** 860
15:7   **Vol. 1:** 442
15:11–36   **Vol. 3:** 1120
15:16   **Vol. 3:** 1166
15:22   **Vol. 1:** 442
15:30   **Vol. 3:** 208
15:35   **Vol. 3:** 426
15:38   **Vol. 1:** 442
16:3   **Vol. 1:** 655   **Vol. 2:** 208, 791
16:7 f   **Vol. 3:** 608
16:13 ff   **Vol. 3:** 426
16:13   **Vol. 3:** 423
16:15   **Vol. 3:** 421, 423
16:17   **Vol. 3:** 787–788
17   **Vol. 3:** 465
17:1   **Vol. 2:** 887   **Vol. 3:** 208
17:3   **Vol. 3:** 208
17:4   **Vol. 1:** 531   **Vol. 3:** 208
17:6   **Vol. 3:** 208
17:7 ff   **Vol. 3:** 1104
17:7–23   **Vol. 1:** 717   **Vol. 2:** 791
17:7   **Vol. 1:** 531
17:8   **Vol. 3:** 354
17:13 f   **Vol. 3:** 938
17:13   **Vol. 3:** 354, 1041
17:16   **Vol. 2:** 189, 876
17:17   **Vol. 1:** 268, 655   **Vol. 2:** 554–555
17:18   **Vol. 1:** 607
17:19 f   **Vol. 3:** 1104
17:19   **Vol. 3:** 354
17:20 f   **Vol. 3:** 460
17:23   **Vol. 3:** 594
17:24 ff   **Vol. 3:** 451
17:24   **Vol. 3:** 450
17:27 f   **Vol. 2:** 34
17:29   **Vol. 3:** 450
17:30   **Vol. 3:** 450
17:34   **Vol. 3:** 354
17:35 f   **Vol. 2:** 876
17:37   **Vol. 3:** 354
18 ff   **Vol. 2:** 325
18   **Vol. 3:** 267
18:1   **Vol. 3:** 208
18:3   **Vol. 1:** 559

2 Kings *(cont'd)*

18:4	**Vol. 1:** 509 **Vol. 2:** 639 **Vol. 3:** 426
18:6	**Vol. 2:** 349, 639
18:9 ff	**Vol. 1:** 67
18:9 f	**Vol. 3:** 208
18:12	**Vol. 2:** 639
18:13	**Vol. 3:** 866
18:14	**Vol. 2:** 96
18:15 f	**Vol. 3:** 782, 788
18:15	**Vol. 2:** 679
18:16	**Vol. 3:** 786, 878
18:17	**Vol. 3:** 115
18:18	**Vol. 2:** 254 **Vol. 3:** 232, 239
18:19	**Vol. 3:** 1089
18:21	**Vol. 1:** 531
18:22	**Vol. 2:** 876
18:29	**Vol. 3:** 1089
18:30–35	**Vol. 3:** 342
18:30	**Vol. 1:** 596
18:31	**Vol. 3:** 1089
18:32	**Vol. 3:** 201, 919
18:37	**Vol. 2:** 254 **Vol. 3:** 239
19:2	**Vol. 2:** 254 **Vol. 3:** 208
19:3	**Vol. 2:** 890
19:4	**Vol. 1:** 127 **Vol. 2:** 863 **Vol. 3:** 248, 341–342, 436
19:6	**Vol. 3:** 341–342
19:7	**Vol. 3:** 342
19:10–13	**Vol. 1:** 246
19:14	**Vol. 2:** 185
19:15†	**Vol. 1:** 280 **Vol. 2:** 724, 862–863
19:18	**Vol. 2:** 77
19:19	**Vol. 2:** 724
19:20	**Vol. 2:** 862
19:21	**Vol. 2:** 326
19:22	**Vol. 3:** 341–342
19:23	**Vol. 2:** 199 **Vol. 3:** 1009
19:26†	**Vol. 2:** 211
19:29	**Vol. 2:** 626
19:30	**Vol. 3:** 867
19:31	**Vol. 3:** 1166
19:35	**Vol. 1:** 444
19:36	**Vol. 2:** 679
19:37	**Vol. 2:** 876
20	**Vol. 2:** 628
20:1 ff	**Vol. 2:** 478
20:3	**Vol. 3:** 235, 943
20:5	**Vol. 2:** 863
20:7	**Vol. 2:** 167
20:8 ff	**Vol. 2:** 627
20:9 ff	**Vol. 3:** 554
20:9–11	**Vol. 3:** 846
20:12	**Vol. 1:** 246
20:13	**Vol. 2:** 357, 607
20:17	**Vol. 1:** 320
20:18	**Vol. 3:** 782, 786
21:3–6	**Vol. 2:** 555
21:3	**Vol. 2:** 189, 876 **Vol. 3:** 426
21:4	**Vol. 3:** 788
21:6	**Vol. 1:** 655 **Vol. 2:** 208, 554 **Vol. 3:** 94
21:8	**Vol. 1:** 333 **Vol. 2:** 639
21:10–15	**Vol. 1:** 717
21:13	**Vol. 3:** 402
21:14	**Vol. 2:** 297
21:16	**Vol. 2:** 525 **Vol. 3:** 94
21:21	**Vol. 2:** 876
22 f	**Vol. 1:** 55
22:1–23:30	**Vol. 3:** 783
22:3–13	**Vol. 3:** 478
22:4 ff	**Vol. 3:** 788
22:4	**Vol. 2:** 32 **Vol. 3:** 498
22:6	**Vol. 3:** 858
22:7	**Vol. 3:** 878
22:8	**Vol. 2:** 440
22:11	**Vol. 2:** 440
22:14–20	**Vol. 3:** 1057
22:16	**Vol. 3:** 786
22:17	**Vol. 3:** 109
22:19 f	**Vol. 1:** 717
22:20	**Vol. 2:** 32, 778 **Vol. 3:** 111
23–25	**Vol. 1:** 52, 61 **Vol. 3:** 94
23	**Vol. 2:** 306 **Vol. 3:** 783
23:1–12	**Vol. 3:** 788
23:1–3	**Vol. 2:** 797
23:3	**Vol. 3:** 354
23:4	**Vol. 3:** 786
23:5–9	**Vol. 2:** 34 **Vol. 3:** 426
23:5	**Vol. 3:** 731
23:10	**Vol. 2:** 208, 375 **Vol. 3:** 110, 421
23:11	**Vol. 3:** 266, 731, 796
23:12	**Vol. 3:** 787
23:13	**Vol. 3:** 1069
23:21–23	**Vol. 1:** 632 **Vol. 2:** 521
23:24 f	**Vol. 3:** 485
23:24	**Vol. 2:** 554–555
23:25 ff	**Vol. 1:** 717
23:25	**Vol. 1:** 354 **Vol. 2:** 639
23:27	**Vol. 1:** 607
23:33–34	**Vol. 1:** 531
23:33	**Vol. 2:** 96
23:34	**Vol. 2:** 649
24:3 f	**Vol. 3:** 156
24:11–21	**Vol. 1:** 686
24:13	**Vol. 3:** 782, 786
24:14 ff	**Vol. 1:** 686
25	**Vol. 3:** 959
25:4	**Vol. 3:** 948
25:7–30	**Vol. 3:** 1104
25:7	**Vol. 1:** 219
25:9	**Vol. 3:** 185, 788
25:10	**Vol. 3:** 178
25:12	**Vol. 3:** 918
25:13–17	**Vol. 3:** 185, 788
25:17	**Vol. 3:** 389
25:18	**Vol. 2:** 34
25:19	**Vol. 3:** 478
25:27–30	**Vol. 2:** 521
25:27	**Vol. 2:** 158

1 Chronicles

1:1	**Vol. 1:** 84
1:34	**Vol. 2:** 305 **Vol. 3:** 658
2:1 ff	**Vol. 3:** 652
2:21	**Vol. 2:** 578
2:24	**Vol. 3:** 1074
2:34 f	**Vol. 3:** 593
2:55	**Vol. 3:** 478
4:10	**Vol. 1:** 272
4:23	**Vol. 3:** 911
4:27	**Vol. 2:** 131
4:40	**Vol. 2:** 777 **Vol. 3:** 111
5:1	**Vol. 2:** 587
5:12	**Vol. 2:** 157
5:18	**Vol. 3:** 760
5:23	**Vol. 2:** 131
6:3	**Vol. 2:** 639
6:16–33	**Vol. 2:** 34
6:16*	**Vol. 3:** 256
6:31	**Vol. 3:** 673
6:49	**Vol. 2:** 639
6:54–81*	**Vol. 2:** 297
6:61–81†	**Vol. 2:** 695
7:2–40	**Vol. 2:** 698
7:5	**Vol. 2:** 683
7:22	**Vol. 2:** 422
8:6	**Vol. 1:** 165
8:28	**Vol. 1:** 165
9:21	**Vol. 3:** 1040
9:23	**Vol. 3:** 786
9:27	**Vol. 2:** 234, 730 **Vol. 3:** 786
9:29	**Vol. 2:** 293 **Vol. 3:** 786
9:32	**Vol. 1:** 586 **Vol. 3:** 117, 423, 814
10:13	**Vol. 2:** 554, 559
10:14	**Vol. 2:** 559
11–29	**Vol. 1:** 426
11:2	**Vol. 3:** 565
11:4 ff	**Vol. 2:** 324
11:4	**Vol. 2:** 324
11:19	**Vol. 3:** 157, 160
12:17	**Vol. 2:** 777
12:18	**Vol. 2:** 777
12:19	**Vol. 2:** 778
12:20–37	**Vol. 2:** 698
12:23	**Vol. 2:** 376
13:2	**Vol. 1:** 293
13:4	**Vol. 1:** 293
13:5	**Vol. 1:** 293
13:6	**Vol. 1:** 280
14:2	**Vol. 3:** 117
14:14	**Vol. 2:** 898
15:1	**Vol. 3:** 117
15:3	**Vol. 1:** 293
15:15	**Vol. 2:** 639
15:22	**Vol. 3:** 673
15:26	**Vol. 3:** 673
15:27	**Vol. 3:** 672–673
16:2	**Vol. 3:** 426
16:4	**Vol. 1:** 344 **Vol. 3:** 816
16:7	**Vol. 3:** 816, 817
16:9	**Vol. 1:** 574 **Vol. 3:** 668, 672–673
16:10	**Vol. 3:** 816
16:15	**Vol. 3:** 235, 828
16:23	**Vol. 3:** 672
16:24	**Vol. 1:** 574
16:25	**Vol. 1:** 622
16:26	**Vol. 2:** 285
16:28 f	**Vol. 1:** 227
16:29	**Vol. 2:** 876
16:33	**Vol. 3:** 865
16:34	**Vol. 2:** 100 **Vol. 3:** 828
16:35	**Vol. 3:** 218, 816
16:36	**Vol. 1:** 98–99 **Vol. 3:** 816, 828
16:39	**Vol. 3:** 812, 1010
16:40	**Vol. 3:** 426
16:41	**Vol. 1:** 537 **Vol. 3:** 816
16:42	**Vol. 3:** 673
17:5	**Vol. 3:** 794
17:7	**Vol. 2:** 69
17:10	**Vol. 2:** 260
17:11	**Vol. 3:** 117
17:13	**Vol. 1:** 617
17:19	**Vol. 2:** 425
17:21	**Vol. 3:** 192–193
17:23 ff	**Vol. 1:** 596
17:25	**Vol. 2:** 862
18:15–17	**Vol. 3:** 478
18:17	**Vol. 1:** 665
19:6 f	**Vol. 2:** 139
20:1	**Vol. 1:** 468
21	**Vol. 3:** 1092
21:1	**Vol. 1:** 562 **Vol. 3:** 468, 557
21:9	**Vol. 3:** 513
21:12–15	**Vol. 1:** 465
21:15	**Vol. 1:** 356
21:17	**Vol. 3:** 565
21:18–30	**Vol. 3:** 426
21:21	**Vol. 2:** 876
21:25	**Vol. 3:** 787
21:26	**Vol. 1:** 655
21:28 f	**Vol. 3:** 836
21:29	**Vol. 2:** 639 **Vol. 3:** 426, 1010
22:1	**Vol. 3:** 426
22:3	**Vol. 2:** 98 **Vol. 3:** 787
22:8	**Vol. 3:** 787
22:9	**Vol. 2:** 591, 778 **Vol. 3:** 111, 254–255
22:10	**Vol. 1:** 617
22:12	**Vol. 3:** 1027
22:13	**Vol. 2:** 639
22:15	**Vol. 3:** 1027
22:18	**Vol. 3:** 254
22:19	**Vol. 3:** 786
23:4	**Vol. 3:** 478
23:5	**Vol. 3:** 816
23:13 ff	**Vol. 2:** 639
23:23	**Vol. 3:** 255
23:25	**Vol. 2:** 778
23:28–31	**Vol. 3:** 426
23:29†	**Vol. 1:** 586 **Vol. 3:** 402, 423, 917

1 Chronicles *(cont'd)*

23:30	**Vol. 3:** 816
23:32	**Vol. 3:** 786, 1040
24	**Vol. 2:** 34
24:3 ff	**Vol. 1:** 534
24:3	**Vol. 1:** 190 **Vol. 2:** 34
24:5 f	**Vol. 2:** 296
24:6	**Vol. 3:** 478
24:7 ff	**Vol. 1:** 200
24:7	**Vol. 1:** 665
25:3	**Vol. 1:** 344 **Vol. 3:** 208
25:6	**Vol. 3:** 669
25:7	**Vol. 3:** 673, 760
25:8	**Vol. 1:** 485
25:9 ff	**Vol. 1:** 200
25:15	**Vol. 3:** 208
26:14	**Vol. 2:** 299
26:25	**Vol. 3:** 208
26:29	**Vol. 1:** 503
27:1 ff	**Vol. 1:** 534
27:20	**Vol. 3:** 208
27:23	**Vol. 3:** 734
27:24	**Vol. 1:** 243
27:32	**Vol. 3:** 478
27:33	**Vol. 1:** 665
28:1	**Vol. 1:** 293
28:2	**Vol. 3:** 255
28:4	**Vol. 1:** 534
28:5	**Vol. 2:** 612
28:6	**Vol. 1:** 534, 537, 617
28:9	**Vol. 2:** 778
28:10	**Vol. 1:** 534
28:11	**Vol. 3:** 153, 156, 782
28:12	**Vol. 3:** 794
28:13	**Vol. 3:** 550
28:16	**Vol. 1:** 250, 586
28:20	**Vol. 3:** 156
28:21	**Vol. 3:** 1027
29:3	**Vol. 2:** 817, 838
29:4	**Vol. 2:** 234 **Vol. 3:** 786
29:7	**Vol. 2:** 848
29:9	**Vol. 3:** 572
29:10	**Vol. 1:** 293
29:11 ff	**Vol. 2:** 869
29:11	**Vol. 1:** 227, 650 **Vol. 3:** 514
29:12 f	**Vol. 1:** 345
29:12	**Vol. 2:** 841 **Vol. 3:** 713
29:13	**Vol. 1:** 344 **Vol. 3:** 816
29:15	**Vol. 1:** 688, 691 **Vol. 2:** 773 **Vol. 3:** 555
29:17	**Vol. 3:** 572
29:18	**Vol. 1:** 617
29:20	**Vol. 2:** 859, 876
29:21	**Vol. 3:** 423
29:22	**Vol. 3:** 36, 439
29:23	**Vol. 2:** 612
29:28	**Vol. 2:** 841

2 Chronicles

1–9	**Vol. 3:** 606
1:3	**Vol. 2:** 639 **Vol. 3:** 1010
1:4	**Vol. 3:** 117
1:6	**Vol. 3:** 426
1:10 f	**Vol. 3:** 1027
1:11 f	**Vol. 2:** 841, 845
1:12	**Vol. 2:** 845
1:13	**Vol. 3:** 1010
2:2–18*	**Vol. 2:** 698
2:4	**Vol. 1:** 586
2:6 f*	**Vol. 3:** 1027
2:8 ff	**Vol. 3:** 919
2:11 ff*	**Vol. 3:** 1027
2:15	**Vol. 3:** 919
3–5	**Vol. 3:** 787
3–4	**Vol. 3:** 783
3:10–13	**Vol. 1:** 280
3:14	**Vol. 3:** 794
3:17	**Vol. 3:** 786
4:1	**Vol. 3:** 418, 787
4:7 f	**Vol. 3:** 786
4:9	**Vol. 3:** 787
4:19	**Vol. 1:** 586 **Vol. 3:** 423
4:22	**Vol. 3:** 786, 794
5	**Vol. 1:** 195
5:2	**Vol. 2:** 324
5:5	**Vol. 3:** 786, 1040
5:6	**Vol. 1:** 295 **Vol. 3:** 426
5:10	**Vol. 2:** 639
5:11	**Vol. 3:** 786
5:12	**Vol. 3:** 873
5:13	**Vol. 2:** 100 **Vol. 3:** 673, 816
5:14	**Vol. 1:** 735
5:27	**Vol. 3:** 316
6:3	**Vol. 1:** 295
6:6	**Vol. 2:** 878
6:12 f	**Vol. 2:** 149
6:13	**Vol. 2:** 234 **Vol. 3:** 786
6:16	**Vol. 2:** 440
6:19 ff	**Vol. 2:** 862
6:19 f	**Vol. 2:** 863
6:21	**Vol. 3:** 157
6:23	**Vol. 3:** 355
6:24–27	**Vol. 1:** 345
6:24	**Vol. 2:** 862
6:25	**Vol. 3:** 157
6:26	**Vol. 2:** 260, 862
6:27	**Vol. 3:** 157
6:29	**Vol. 2:** 863
6:30	**Vol. 3:** 152
6:32	**Vol. 2:** 862
6:34	**Vol. 1:** 538 **Vol. 2:** 862
6:35	**Vol. 2:** 863 **Vol. 3:** 354
6:36–39	**Vol. 3:** 207
6:38	**Vol. 1:** 538 **Vol. 2:** 803, 862
6:39	**Vol. 2:** 863 **Vol. 3:** 157
6:41	**Vol. 3:** 207, 255
6:42	**Vol. 3:** 235

2 Chronicles *(cont'd)*

7:1	**Vol. 1:** 655, 735 **Vol. 2:** 862 **Vol. 3:** 421
7:3	**Vol. 2:** 876 **Vol. 3:** 816
7:4–8	**Vol. 3:** 426
7:5	**Vol. 2:** 673
7:6	**Vol. 3:** 669, 673
7:8	**Vol. 3:** 836
7:12	**Vol. 2:** 863 **Vol. 3:** 422
7:13	**Vol. 1:** 119
7:14	**Vol. 2:** 862 **Vol. 3:** 157, 531
7:15	**Vol. 2:** 863
7:19	**Vol. 2:** 876
7:21	**Vol. 2:** 116
7:22	**Vol. 2:** 876
8:11	**Vol. 3:** 1058
8:12	**Vol. 3:** 782
8:13	**Vol. 2:** 639
8:14	**Vol. 3:** 816
8:16	**Vol. 2:** 60
8:18	**Vol. 3:** 593
9:1–12	**Vol. 2:** 381 **Vol. 3:** 1030
9:1	**Vol. 2:** 745 **Vol. 3:** 799
9:3	**Vol. 3:** 1027
9:5	**Vol. 3:** 1027
9:6 f	**Vol. 3:** 1027
9:12	**Vol. 3:** 593
9:20	**Vol. 3:** 823
9:21	**Vol. 1:** 743
9:22 f	**Vol. 3:** 1027
9:22	**Vol. 2:** 841
9:25	**Vol. 3:** 835
9:29	**Vol. 3:** 513
10:4	**Vol. 3:** 1161
10:6 ff	**Vol. 1:** 195
10:7	**Vol. 2:** 817
10:9 ff	**Vol. 3:** 1161
10:9–14	**Vol. 3:** 1161
10:11	**Vol. 1:** 510
10:14	**Vol. 1:** 510 **Vol. 2:** 675 **Vol. 3:** 1161
11:6	**Vol. 1:** 170
11:15	**Vol. 1:** 451, 551 **Vol. 2:** 285
11:16	**Vol. 3:** 531
11:17	**Vol. 2:** 376
12:12	**Vol. 1:** 109 **Vol. 2:** 60
12:13	**Vol. 1:** 538
13:4	**Vol. 3:** 1009
13:6	**Vol. 1:** 606
13:7	**Vol. 2:** 675
13:10 ff	**Vol. 3:** 426
13:11	**Vol. 1:** 586 **Vol. 3:** 423
13:14	**Vol. 3:** 673
14:2*	**Vol. 2:** 103, 199
14:5 f*	**Vol. 3:** 255
15:3	**Vol. 3:** 883
15:5	**Vol. 3:** 835
15:7	**Vol. 2:** 139 **Vol. 3:** 178
15:8	**Vol. 3:** 782
15:10–12	**Vol. 2:** 784
15:10	**Vol. 2:** 784
15:12	**Vol. 3:** 531
15:15	**Vol. 3:** 255
15:17	**Vol. 3:** 426
16:9	**Vol. 2:** 593
16:11	**Vol. 2:** 56
16:12	**Vol. 2:** 167
16:14	**Vol. 1:** 120 **Vol. 3:** 238
17	**Vol. 3:** 478
17:5	**Vol. 2:** 841
17:6	**Vol. 2:** 199
17:7 ff	**Vol. 3:** 761
17:7	**Vol. 3:** 760
17:9	**Vol. 3:** 760
17:14	**Vol. 2:** 684
18:1	**Vol. 2:** 841
18:4	**Vol. 3:** 531
18:7	**Vol. 3:** 531
18:10	**Vol. 2:** 754
19:2	**Vol. 1:** 108
19:7	**Vol. 2:** 622
19:10	**Vol. 3:** 354
20:3	**Vol. 1:** 612 **Vol. 3:** 51
20:4	**Vol. 2:** 32
20:5	**Vol. 1:** 293
20:6	**Vol. 2:** 149
20:7	**Vol. 1:** 77 **Vol. 3:** 369
20:8	**Vol. 3:** 786
20:14	**Vol. 1:** 293
20:15	**Vol. 2:** 800 **Vol. 3:** 962
20:18	**Vol. 2:** 876
20:19	**Vol. 3:** 816
20:21	**Vol. 3:** 816
20:22	**Vol. 1:** 344
20:28	**Vol. 3:** 673
20:30	**Vol. 3:** 255
20:33	**Vol. 3:** 426
20:34	**Vol. 2:** 56
21:8	**Vol. 1:** 606
21:10	**Vol. 1:** 606
21:12–15	**Vol. 1:** 246
23:12	**Vol. 3:** 816
23:13	**Vol. 3:** 668, 672, 817
23:18	**Vol. 2:** 440, 639 **Vol. 3:** 484, 673
24:5	**Vol. 2:** 32
24:6	**Vol. 2:** 639 **Vol. 3:** 752, 1040
24:8	**Vol. 1:** 143
24:9	**Vol. 2:** 639 **Vol. 3:** 51, 752
24:10 f	**Vol. 1:** 143
24:11	**Vol. 1:** 190 **Vol. 2:** 32, 131
24:12	**Vol. 2:** 139
24:13	**Vol. 3:** 478
24:14	**Vol. 3:** 426
24:17	**Vol. 2:** 876
24:18	**Vol. 2:** 284
24:20 ff	**Vol. 3:** 82
24:21	**Vol. 3:** 430
24:22	**Vol. 3:** 514
24:27	**Vol. 1:** 581 **Vol. 3:** 483
25:4	**Vol. 2:** 639

2 Chronicles *(cont'd)*

25:5	**Vol. 1:** 537
25:6	**Vol. 2:** 139
25:14	**Vol. 2:** 876
25:15	**Vol. 1:** 108 **Vol. 2:** 285
25:26	**Vol. 2:** 56
26:2	**Vol. 1:** 442
26:10	**Vol. 3:** 918
26:16	**Vol. 3:** 786
26:18	**Vol. 1:** 606 **Vol. 3:** 786
26:19	**Vol. 2:** 293
26:22	**Vol. 3:** 208
26:23	**Vol. 1:** 442
27:2	**Vol. 3:** 786
27:6	**Vol. 3:** 117
28:6	**Vol. 2:** 889
28:8 ff	**Vol. 3:** 593
28:15	**Vol. 1:** 120
28:18	**Vol. 3:** 426
28:19	**Vol. 1:** 606
28:22	**Vol. 1:** 606
29:5	**Vol. 3:** 786
29:6	**Vol. 1:** 606
29:7	**Vol. 3:** 109, 782, 786
29:17	**Vol. 3:** 782
29:18	**Vol. 1:** 586
29:19	**Vol. 3:** 117
29:21–35	**Vol. 3:** 426
29:21	**Vol. 3:** 786
29:23 f	**Vol. 1:** 221
29:24	**Vol. 3:** 152
29:27–28	**Vol. 3:** 873
29:27	**Vol. 3:** 673
29:28 ff	**Vol. 2:** 876
29:28	**Vol. 3:** 672
29:30	**Vol. 3:** 668
29:31	**Vol. 3:** 423
29:32	**Vol. 3:** 421
29:34	**Vol. 3:** 421
29:35	**Vol. 3:** 423
29:66	**Vol. 3:** 786
30:2 f	**Vol. 2:** 528
30:2	**Vol. 1:** 293, 295
30:4	**Vol. 1:** 293, 295 **Vol. 2:** 815
30:5	**Vol. 3:** 51
30:7	**Vol. 1:** 606
30:8	**Vol. 3:** 595
30:10	**Vol. 2:** 431
30:13	**Vol. 1:** 295 **Vol. 2:** 528
30:15	**Vol. 2:** 528
30:16	**Vol. 1:** 333 **Vol. 2:** 639
30:17	**Vol. 1:** 295
30:18 f	**Vol. 3:** 153
30:18	**Vol. 2:** 862 **Vol. 3:** 152, 154
30:19	**Vol. 3:** 101
30:27	**Vol. 1:** 320 **Vol. 2:** 863
31:1	**Vol. 3:** 418
31:2	**Vol. 1:** 344 **Vol. 3:** 816
31:5–12	**Vol. 2:** 693
31:5 f	**Vol. 3:** 853
31:5	**Vol. 2:** 131, 711 **Vol. 3:** 415
31:10	**Vol. 3:** 415
31:11	**Vol. 3:** 117
31:12	**Vol. 3:** 415
31:14	**Vol. 3:** 415
31:18	**Vol. 1:** 292
32	**Vol. 2:** 325
32:5	**Vol. 3:** 119
32:8	**Vol. 1:** 673, 679
32:12	**Vol. 2:** 876
32:13 ff	**Vol. 3:** 342
32:17	**Vol. 3:** 484
32:20	**Vol. 2:** 862 **Vol. 3:** 208
32:21	**Vol. 1:** 104, 320 **Vol. 3:** 342
32:22	**Vol. 3:** 255
32:24	**Vol. 2:** 633, 862
32:26	**Vol. 1:** 109
32:27	**Vol. 2:** 841
32:28	**Vol. 2:** 711
32:31	**Vol. 1:** 194, 373 **Vol. 2:** 633 **Vol. 3:** 799–800
32:32	**Vol. 3:** 208
33:3 f	**Vol. 3:** 426
33:3	**Vol. 2:** 876
33:6	**Vol. 2:** 208, 554–555
33:7	**Vol. 2:** 287
33:8	**Vol. 2:** 639 **Vol. 3:** 354
33:9	**Vol. 2:** 458
33:13	**Vol. 2:** 862
33:16	**Vol. 3:** 423
33:18 f	**Vol. 2:** 863
33:19	**Vol. 1:** 606
34:1–35:27	**Vol. 3:** 783
34:4	**Vol. 3:** 238
34:8–21	**Vol. 3:** 478
34:12	**Vol. 3:** 673
34:14	**Vol. 2:** 639
34:25	**Vol. 3:** 109
34:28	**Vol. 3:** 238
34:29*	**Vol. 2:** 32
35:3	**Vol. 3:** 788
35:4	**Vol. 3:** 117
35:5	**Vol. 3:** 786
35:6–14	**Vol. 3:** 426
35:6	**Vol. 2:** 639 **Vol. 3:** 117
35:12	**Vol. 2:** 639
35:13	**Vol. 1:** 654
35:14 f	**Vol. 3:** 117
35:16	**Vol. 3:** 117
35:25	**Vol. 3:** 673
36	**Vol. 1:** 52
36:13	**Vol. 1:** 354
36:21 f	**Vol. 1:** 735
36:21	**Vol. 1:** 734, 736 **Vol. 3:** 191
36:22 f	**Vol. 3:** 97
36:22	**Vol. 1:** 340 **Vol. 3:** 51
36:23	**Vol. 1:** 332

Ezra

1	Vol. 3: 788
1:1 ff	Vol. 3: 97
1:1–8	Vol. 3: 451
1:1	Vol. 3: 691
1:7*	Vol. 2: 284
2:6	Vol. 3: 208
2:19	Vol. 2: 773
2:21	Vol. 1: 170
2:36–39	Vol. 2: 466
2:40	Vol. 2: 466 Vol. 3: 208
2:63	Vol. 2: 296
2:69	Vol. 2: 848
3:2 f	Vol. 3: 788
3:2–7	Vol. 3: 427
3:2	Vol. 2: 639 Vol. 3: 484–485
3:5	Vol. 3: 421
3:6	Vol. 3: 786
3:8 ff	Vol. 3: 788
3:9	Vol. 2: 319
3:10	Vol. 3: 786, 873
3:12	Vol. 3: 788
4	Vol. 3: 451
4:1	Vol. 3: 873
4:7–6:12	Vol. 1: 246
4:7	Vol. 1: 580
4:8 f	Vol. 3: 478
4:8–6:18	Vol. 1: 51
4:12 f	Vol. 3: 350
4:12	Vol. 1: 606
4:14	Vol. 3: 444
4:15	Vol. 1: 606
4:16	Vol. 3: 350
4:17	Vol. 2: 431
4:19	Vol. 1: 606
5:3	Vol. 3: 350
5:9	Vol. 3: 350
5:11 f	Vol. 2: 190
5:11	Vol. 3: 350
5:12	Vol. 3: 177–178
6:2	Vol. 3: 236
6:3	Vol. 2: 199
6:5	Vol. 3: 782
6:9 f	Vol. 2: 190 Vol. 3: 427
6:11	Vol. 1: 393–394
6:14	Vol. 1: 196 Vol. 3: 350
6:17	Vol. 2: 683 Vol. 3: 427
6:18	Vol. 2: 639
7:6–26	Vol. 3: 485
7:6	Vol. 2: 149, 639 Vol. 3: 478–479
7:10	Vol. 1: 580 Vol. 3: 478, 760
7:11	Vol. 3: 479
7:12–26	Vol. 1: 51 Vol. 3: 479
7:12*	Vol. 2: 190, 441
7:14*	Vol. 2: 441
7:17	Vol. 3: 427
7:21*	Vol. 2: 190, 441 Vol. 3: 485
7:22	Vol. 3: 444
7:23	Vol. 2: 190
7:25*	Vol. 2: 441
7:26*	Vol. 2: 441
8:1 ff	Vol. 1: 196
8:15–20	Vol. 2: 466
8:20	Vol. 2: 311 Vol. 3: 593
8:21–23	Vol. 1: 612
8:21	Vol. 1: 612
8:22	Vol. 1: 109
8:23	Vol. 1: 612 Vol. 2: 864
8:35	Vol. 3: 427
9 f	Vol. 1: 688 Vol. 2: 576
9–10	Vol. 1: 505
9	Vol. 2: 174 Vol. 3: 658
9:1	Vol. 2: 60 Vol. 3: 534
9:2	Vol. 3: 654
9:3–4	Vol. 3: 588
9:8	Vol. 3: 250, 787
9:11	Vol. 2: 796
9:13	Vol. 3: 255
9:15	Vol. 3: 250, 357
10:1	Vol. 1: 293 Vol. 2: 862
10:3	Vol. 3: 485
10:8	Vol. 1: 295, 414
10:11*	Vol. 1: 344–345
10:12	Vol. 1: 295
10:14	Vol. 1: 196
10:19	Vol. 2: 149 Vol. 3: 420, 427
10:23	Vol. 2: 319

Nehemiah

1:2 f	Vol. 3: 250
1:4–11	Vol. 2: 863
1:4	Vol. 1: 612 Vol. 2: 862, 864
1:6	Vol. 2: 862–863
1:7 f	Vol. 2: 639
1:8	Vol. 3: 234
1:9	Vol. 1: 685
1:10	Vol. 3: 192–193
1:11	Vol. 2: 863
1:32*	Vol. 1: 332
2:2	Vol. 1: 565
2:3	Vol. 3: 239
2:4	Vol. 2: 862
2:5	Vol. 3: 239
2:6	Vol. 2: 898
2:8	Vol. 2: 761
2:19	Vol. 1: 606
3:3	Vol. 1: 670
3:5	Vol. 1: 241
3:7	Vol. 2: 612
3:30	Vol. 3: 796
4	Vol. 3: 451
4:5*	Vol. 3: 255
4:9*	Vol. 2: 862
4:10	Vol. 1: 520
4:15*	Vol. 2: 395
5:1–5	Vol. 3: 594
5:3	Vol. 1: 98
5:5	Vol. 2: 70, 96

Nehemiah *(cont'd)*

5:6	**Vol. 1:** 108
5:8	**Vol. 3:** 111
5:13	**Vol. 1:** 317 **Vol. 3:** 816
5:14 f	**Vol. 3:** 711
5:18	**Vol. 3:** 711
5:19	**Vol. 3:** 235
6:2	**Vol. 3:** 823
6:3	**Vol. 3:** 255
6:6	**Vol. 1:** 606 **Vol. 3:** 823
6:10	**Vol. 1:** 420
6:12	**Vol. 2:** 139
6:14	**Vol. 3:** 235
6:16	**Vol. 2:** 60
6:18	**Vol. 3:** 786
7:1	**Vol. 3:** 672
7:3	**Vol. 2:** 136
7:26	**Vol. 1:** 170
7:44	**Vol. 3:** 672
7:46	**Vol. 3:** 36, 672
7:63 f	**Vol. 1:** 619
7:65	**Vol. 2:** 296
7:70	**Vol. 2:** 848
7:73	**Vol. 3:** 672
8 ff	**Vol. 1:** 333
8	**Vol. 2:** 34, 307, 441 **Vol. 3:** 485
8:1–13:28	**Vol. 3:** 485
8:1	**Vol. 2:** 639 **Vol. 3:** 478
8:2	**Vol. 1:** 293, 295
8:3	**Vol. 2:** 440 **Vol. 3:** 846
8:4	**Vol. 2:** 369
8:5	**Vol. 2:** 726
8:6	**Vol. 1:** 98 **Vol. 2:** 876
8:8	**Vol. 1:** 245 **Vol. 3:** 760
8:9	**Vol. 2:** 422, 887
8:10	**Vol. 2:** 355
8:14	**Vol. 2:** 440, 639
8:17	**Vol. 1:** 295 **Vol. 2:** 331
9	**Vol. 2:** 174
9:1	**Vol. 1:** 612
9:2	**Vol. 3:** 534
9:3	**Vol. 2:** 876
9:6	**Vol. 2:** 876 **Vol. 3:** 983
9:9	**Vol. 1:** 531
9:10	**Vol. 2:** 627
9:11	**Vol. 2:** 197
9:12	**Vol. 2:** 491
9:14	**Vol. 2:** 639
9:15	**Vol. 3:** 382
9:16	**Vol. 3:** 29
9:17	**Vol. 3:** 240
9:18	**Vol. 1:** 531
9:21	**Vol. 2:** 714 **Vol. 3:** 804–805, 953
9:26	**Vol. 1:** 354, 606–607 **Vol. 3:** 1041
9:27	**Vol. 2:** 807 **Vol. 3:** 218
9:28	**Vol. 3:** 202, 254
9:29 f	**Vol. 3:** 1041
9:30	**Vol. 3:** 691
9:34	**Vol. 3:** 1041
10:1	**Vol. 3:** 498
10:3	**Vol. 3:** 415
10:24	**Vol. 3:** 208
10:28	**Vol. 3:** 672
10:29	**Vol. 2:** 639
10:31	**Vol. 1:** 267 **Vol. 3:** 191
10:32–39	**Vol. 3:** 853
10:32	**Vol. 3:** 407, 752
10:33–37	**Vol. 3:** 427
10:33	**Vol. 1:** 586
10:34	**Vol. 3:** 421, 423–424, 484, 841
10:35*	**Vol. 2:** 440
10:37 f	**Vol. 2:** 467, 693
10:37*	**Vol. 2:** 440, 693
10:38–39	**Vol. 2:** 693
10:38*	**Vol. 3:** 796
10:39*	**Vol. 3:** 672, 796
10:40*	**Vol. 3:** 416
11:3	**Vol. 1:** 165
11:9	**Vol. 1:** 190 **Vol. 2:** 319
11:14	**Vol. 1:** 190
11:16 f	**Vol. 1:** 165
11:17	**Vol. 2:** 863
11:22	**Vol. 1:** 190 **Vol. 3:** 672
12:8	**Vol. 2:** 319
12:24	**Vol. 3:** 77, 668–669, 816
12:27	**Vol. 1:** 344 **Vol. 3:** 673
12:28 f	**Vol. 3:** 672
12:36	**Vol. 2:** 319 **Vol. 3:** 77, 673, 816
12:37	**Vol. 3:** 816
12:42	**Vol. 1:** 190 **Vol. 3:** 672
12:44	**Vol. 2:** 303, 693 **Vol. 3:** 415, 796, 852
12:45 ff	**Vol. 3:** 672
12:46	**Vol. 1:** 665 **Vol. 3:** 669
12:47	**Vol. 2:** 303
13:1–10	**Vol. 1:** 688
13:1	**Vol. 2:** 639
13:2	**Vol. 2:** 139
13:4 f	**Vol. 3:** 796
13:4–9†	**Vol. 3:** 35, 788
13:5*	**Vol. 1:** 332 **Vol. 2:** 693 **Vol. 3:** 416, 427, 672
13:7	**Vol. 3:** 796
13:8 f	**Vol. 3:** 796
13:9	**Vol. 3:** 427
13:10	**Vol. 2:** 303 **Vol. 3:** 672
13:12	**Vol. 2:** 693 **Vol. 3:** 853
13:13	**Vol. 1:** 670 **Vol. 3:** 823
13:14	**Vol. 3:** 235
13:15–22	**Vol. 3:** 407
13:15	**Vol. 3:** 1041
13:17	**Vol. 1:** 716
13:19	**Vol. 1:** 283
13:20	**Vol. 2:** 716
13:21	**Vol. 3:** 1041
13:22	**Vol. 3:** 235
13:23 ff	**Vol. 1:** 505, 688
13:28†	**Vol. 3:** 35, 451
13:29	**Vol. 3:** 36, 235
13:31	**Vol. 3:** 235, 841

Esther

1:1 ff	**Vol. 1:** 512
1:1	**Vol. 2:** 807 **Vol. 3:** 823
1:4	**Vol. 2:** 841–842
1:6	**Vol. 3:** 588
1:7	**Vol. 2:** 96
1:8	**Vol. 2:** 254, 441 **Vol. 3:** 115
1:10	**Vol. 3:** 545
1:13	**Vol. 2:** 441
1:14	**Vol. 1:** 665 **Vol. 2:** 53
1:15	**Vol. 2:** 441
1:18	**Vol. 1:** 364
1:19	**Vol. 2:** 441 **Vol. 3:** 821
1:20	**Vol. 2:** 841
2:2	**Vol. 3:** 545, 1071
2:9	**Vol. 3:** 570
2:12	**Vol. 2:** 294
2:18	**Vol. 2:** 576
2:19	**Vol. 2:** 164 **Vol. 3:** 1071
2:22	**Vol. 2:** 488
2:23	**Vol. 3:** 232
3:2	**Vol. 2:** 876–877
3:4	**Vol. 2:** 895
3:5	**Vol. 2:** 876–877
3:8	**Vol. 2:** 441
3:9	**Vol. 1:** 330 **Vol. 3:** 796, 821
3:10	**Vol. 3:** 498
3:12	**Vol. 2:** 650 **Vol. 3:** 478
3:13	**Vol. 1:** 688 **Vol. 2:** 144 **Vol. 3:** 570, 711, 924
3:15	**Vol. 2:** 803
4:7	**Vol. 3:** 69
4:8	**Vol. 1:** 330
4:13	**Vol. 3:** 234
4:14	**Vol. 3:** 873
4:16	**Vol. 1:** 612 **Vol. 2:** 441
4:17	**Vol. 1:** 637 **Vol. 2:** 291, 876 **Vol. 3:** 29–30, 109, 669, 816
5:1	**Vol. 2:** 863
5:2	**Vol. 3:** 820
5:4	**Vol. 3:** 821
5:10	**Vol. 2:** 839
5:11	**Vol. 1:** 665 **Vol. 2:** 841–842
5:14	**Vol. 1:** 390, 393
6:1	**Vol. 3:** 236, 545, 766
6:3	**Vol. 2:** 116 **Vol. 3:** 545
6:4	**Vol. 1:** 393
6:5	**Vol. 3:** 545
6:9	**Vol. 3:** 51
6:10	**Vol. 2:** 164 **Vol. 3:** 585
6:11	**Vol. 3:** 51
6:12	**Vol. 2:** 839
7:4	**Vol. 3:** 468
7:5	**Vol. 1:** 364
7:7	**Vol. 3:** 279
7:8	**Vol. 3:** 588, 711
7:9 f	**Vol. 1:** 393
8:1	**Vol. 2:** 41 **Vol. 3:** 468, 846
8:3	**Vol. 2:** 860
8:5	**Vol. 2:** 116, 452 **Vol. 3:** 821
8:8	**Vol. 3:** 484, 498, 821
8:9	**Vol. 2:** 254 **Vol. 3:** 478
8:10	**Vol. 3:** 498
8:12	**Vol. 1:** 393 **Vol. 2:** 803
8:13	**Vol. 2:** 735, 876 **Vol. 3:** 29, 818
8:17	**Vol. 2:** 357
9:2	**Vol. 3:** 846
9:13 f	**Vol. 1:** 393
9:16 ff	**Vol. 3:** 254
9:17	**Vol. 3:** 255
9:22	**Vol. 2:** 576 **Vol. 3:** 254
9:23	**Vol. 3:** 484
9:27	**Vol. 2:** 357
9:28	**Vol. 3:** 237
10:1	**Vol. 3:** 756
10:3 ff	**Vol. 1:** 512
10:3†	**Vol. 2:** 842
10:3*	**Vol. 1:** 580

Job

1 f	**Vol. 1:** 83 **Vol. 2:** 191
1	**Vol. 1:** 111
1:1–2:10	**Vol. 3:** 720
1:1	**Vol. 1:** 704 **Vol. 2:** 139 **Vol. 3:** 355
1:3	**Vol. 1:** 188 **Vol. 3:** 1161
1:5	**Vol. 3:** 421, 425
1:6 ff	**Vol. 1:** 89 **Vol. 2:** 189–190
1:6	**Vol. 1:** 101, 474 **Vol. 3:** 636
1:7	**Vol. 3:** 943
1:8	**Vol. 1:** 704 **Vol. 2:** 144 **Vol. 3:** 355, 608
1:10	**Vol. 3:** 1148
1:11 f	**Vol. 3:** 801
1:11	**Vol. 3:** 342
1:12	**Vol. 3:** 474, 860
1:20	**Vol. 2:** 876
1:21 f	**Vol. 2:** 771, 775
1:21	**Vol. 3:** 821
1:22	**Vol. 3:** 1024
2	**Vol. 1:** 111
2:1	**Vol. 3:** 232, 636
2:2	**Vol. 3:** 943
2:3–10	**Vol. 1:** 467
2:3	**Vol. 2:** 144 **Vol. 3:** 608, 924
2:4	**Vol. 2:** 478
2:5	**Vol. 1:** 240 **Vol. 3:** 342
2:6 f	**Vol. 3:** 801
2:6	**Vol. 3:** 857
2:8	**Vol. 3:** 588
2:9	**Vol. 2:** 767 **Vol. 3:** 255, 342
2:10	**Vol. 2:** 771, 775 **Vol. 3:** 720, 1024–1025
2:11 f	**Vol. 1:** 89
2:11	**Vol. 3:** 908
3:1	**Vol. 2:** 727, 887
3:3	**Vol. 2:** 569
3:5	**Vol. 3:** 554
3:8	**Vol. 1:** 326, 523

Job (*cont'd*)

3:9	**Vol. 2:** 495, 773 **Vol. 3:** 735
3:11 f	**Vol. 2:** 478
3:12 – 19	**Vol. 3:** 270
3:12	**Vol. 1:** 240
3:13	**Vol. 3:** 254
3:16	**Vol. 1:** 182
3:17	**Vol. 2:** 93 **Vol. 3:** 254, 256
3:18	**Vol. 3:** 908
3:23	**Vol. 3:** 255
3:26	**Vol. 3:** 254
4:3	**Vol. 1:** 568, 570
4:4	**Vol. 3:** 994
4:5	**Vol. 3:** 1169
4:6	**Vol. 3:** 1024
4:7	**Vol. 3:** 103
4:8	**Vol. 3:** 522, 525 – 526
4:9	**Vol. 1:** 108 **Vol. 3:** 691
4:10	**Vol. 3:** 109
4:14	**Vol. 3:** 557
4:15	**Vol. 1:** 672
4:16	**Vol. 1:** 706 **Vol. 3:** 293
4:17	**Vol. 3:** 924
4:18	**Vol. 1:** 101
4:19	**Vol. 3:** 915
4:21	**Vol. 3:** 815, 1027
5:1	**Vol. 1:** 101
5:6 f	**Vol. 1:** 262
5:9	**Vol. 3:** 1153
5:11	**Vol. 2:** 261 – 262, 596, 771
5:12	**Vol. 1:** 412 **Vol. 3:** 166
5:13	**Vol. 2:** 616 **Vol. 3:** 747, 1027
5:14	**Vol. 2:** 498
5:17 f	**Vol. 1:** 562
5:17	**Vol. 2:** 141 **Vol. 3:** 717
5:18	**Vol. 2:** 149, 167
5:19	**Vol. 2:** 663
5:20	**Vol. 3:** 166, 201
5:21	**Vol. 3:** 859
5:24	**Vol. 2:** 778
5:25	**Vol. 3:** 846
5:26	**Vol. 3:** 835, 846
6:2	**Vol. 3:** 908, 1160
6:5	**Vol. 1:** 409, 520
6:6	**Vol. 3:** 444, 449
6:10	**Vol. 2:** 765, 773
6:11	**Vol. 2:** 773 **Vol. 3:** 680
6:15	**Vol. 2:** 53
6:19	**Vol. 2:** 93
6:24	**Vol. 3:** 721, 760
6:26	**Vol. 2:** 765
6:27	**Vol. 2:** 737
7:1	**Vol. 2:** 139, 475
7:2	**Vol. 2:** 139
7:3	**Vol. 1:** 420, 547 **Vol. 2:** 773
7:6	**Vol. 1:** 547
7:7 – 10	**Vol. 3:** 235, 261
7:11	**Vol. 2:** 663
7:12†	**Vol. 1:** 508 **Vol. 3:** 983
7:15	**Vol. 1:** 240 **Vol. 3:** 166
7:16	**Vol. 1:** 547 **Vol. 2:** 475
7:18	**Vol. 1:** 190 **Vol. 3:** 255
8:4 – 6	**Vol. 3:** 140
8:5	**Vol. 3:** 717
8:7	**Vol. 1:** 665 **Vol. 3:** 134
8:9	**Vol. 2:** 475
8:10	**Vol. 3:** 760, 1027
8:11	**Vol. 3:** 866
8:12	**Vol. 1:** 608 **Vol. 2:** 211, 261
8:13	**Vol. 2:** 93
8:15	**Vol. 2:** 773
8:19 f	**Vol. 2:** 93
8:21	**Vol. 2:** 261, 431
8:22	**Vol. 1:** 314 **Vol. 2:** 93
9:4	**Vol. 2:** 773 **Vol. 3:** 1027
9:5	**Vol. 2:** 714 **Vol. 3:** 1010
9:6	**Vol. 1:** 523, 661
9:7	**Vol. 3:** 498, 731, 735
9:8	**Vol. 2:** 724 **Vol. 3:** 943, 983
9:12 – 20	**Vol. 3:** 342
9:12	**Vol. 3:** 166
9:13	**Vol. 1:** 670
9:17 ff	**Vol. 2:** 167
9:20 f	**Vol. 2:** 93
9:20	**Vol. 3:** 924
9:23	**Vol. 3:** 355
9:25	**Vol. 1:** 326 **Vol. 3:** 821
9:31	**Vol. 1:** 479
9:32 f	**Vol. 3:** 721
9:33	**Vol. 1:** 373
9:34	**Vol. 3:** 166
10:2 f	**Vol. 2:** 93
10:2	**Vol. 3:** 760
10:3	**Vol. 2:** 735
10:4	**Vol. 1:** 679
10:7	**Vol. 2:** 93
10:8 – 9	**Vol. 3:** 915
10:11	**Vol. 1:** 672
10:15	**Vol. 2:** 49, 93
10:19	**Vol. 3:** 166, 238
10:20	**Vol. 2:** 428 **Vol. 3:** 254, 842
10:21 f	**Vol. 2:** 206
10:21	**Vol. 1:** 523 **Vol. 3:** 946
10:22	**Vol. 2:** 735
11:4	**Vol. 2:** 144 **Vol. 3:** 924
11:6	**Vol. 3:** 1027
11:8	**Vol. 2:** 197
11:9	**Vol. 3:** 402
11:11	**Vol. 3:** 1149
11:15	**Vol. 1:** 479
11:17	**Vol. 2:** 495
11:18	**Vol. 1:** 277 **Vol. 2:** 777
11:20	**Vol. 3:** 1027
12:2	**Vol. 3:** 1027
12:3	**Vol. 2:** 565
12:4	**Vol. 2:** 431 **Vol. 3:** 924
12:8	**Vol. 1:** 670
12:11	**Vol. 1:** 503 **Vol. 3:** 125
12:12 f	**Vol. 3:** 1027

Job *(cont'd)*

12:13	**Vol. 3:** 130
12:15	**Vol. 2:** 222
12:16†	**Vol. 2:** 458
12:19	**Vol. 2:** 596
12:20	**Vol. 3:** 166
12:22	**Vol. 1:** 423 **Vol. 2:** 197, 212 **Vol. 3:** 554
12:24 ff	**Vol. 2:** 206
12:24	**Vol. 3:** 166
12:25	**Vol. 2:** 491
13:3	**Vol. 3:** 1016
13:5	**Vol. 3:** 1027
13:10	**Vol. 1:** 503 **Vol. 2:** 622
13:11	**Vol. 1:** 609
13:12	**Vol. 3:** 236
13:13	**Vol. 3:** 255
13:22	**Vol. 1:** 272 **Vol. 2:** 766
13:23	**Vol. 3:** 760
13:24	**Vol. 2:** 215
13:25	**Vol. 1:** 743
13:28	**Vol. 2:** 714
14	**Vol. 2:** 565
14:1 ff	**Vol. 1:** 551
14:1	**Vol. 3:** 842
14:2	**Vol. 1:** 609 **Vol. 3:** 555
14:4	**Vol. 1:** 479
14:5	**Vol. 3:** 842
14:6	**Vol. 2:** 139
14:7 ff	**Vol. 3:** 866
14:7	**Vol. 3:** 866
14:9	**Vol. 1:** 503 **Vol. 3:** 599
14:12	**Vol. 1:** 442
14:13–22	**Vol. 2:** 206
14:13	**Vol. 3:** 238, 842
14:14	**Vol. 1:** 184 **Vol. 2:** 773, 890 **Vol. 3:** 261
14:15	**Vol. 3:** 1148
14:17	**Vol. 1:** 142 **Vol. 3:** 498–499
14:18	**Vol. 2:** 714
14:19	**Vol. 2:** 773
14:21 f	**Vol. 2:** 206
15:2–6	**Vol. 3:** 342
15:2	**Vol. 3:** 1027
15:5	**Vol. 1:** 503 **Vol. 3:** 1079
15:6	**Vol. 3:** 1041
15:7 f	**Vol. 2:** 761
15:8	**Vol. 3:** 1027
15:10	**Vol. 1:** 92
15:11	**Vol. 2:** 71
15:12	**Vol. 1:** 364
15:14	**Vol. 2:** 144 **Vol. 3:** 348, 924
15:15	**Vol. 1:** 101 **Vol. 2:** 144, 376 **Vol. 3:** 103, 924
15:18	**Vol. 3:** 1027
15:20	**Vol. 2:** 475
15:21	**Vol. 2:** 778 **Vol. 3:** 821
15:24	**Vol. 2:** 663
15:26 f	**Vol. 3:** 29
15:29	**Vol. 2:** 841 **Vol. 3:** 224
15:31	**Vol. 2:** 773
15:33	**Vol. 1:** 609
15:34	**Vol. 1:** 295 **Vol. 3:** 1040
16:2	**Vol. 1:** 89
16:9	**Vol. 2:** 421
16:11	**Vol. 3:** 574
16:15*	**Vol. 3:** 109, 715
16:16	**Vol. 3:** 554
16:18 ff	**Vol. 1:** 410
16:19	**Vol. 3:** 178, 704
16:20	**Vol. 3:** 1041
16:22	**Vol. 3:** 938, 946
17:1	**Vol. 3:** 691
17:6	**Vol. 2:** 431
17:8	**Vol. 2:** 622 **Vol. 3:** 355
17:9	**Vol. 2:** 149
17:13	**Vol. 2:** 773
18:5 f	**Vol. 2:** 491 **Vol. 3:** 109
18:8 ff	**Vol. 1:** 172
18:14	**Vol. 2:** 138
18:16	**Vol. 3:** 866
18:17	**Vol. 3:** 237
18:20	**Vol. 2:** 622, 890
19:2	**Vol. 2:** 221
19:3	**Vol. 3:** 345–346
19:6–21	**Vol. 3:** 342
19:7	**Vol. 2:** 431
19:8	**Vol. 1:** 422
19:10	**Vol. 3:** 866
19:16	**Vol. 2:** 860
19:21	**Vol. 3:** 860
19:24	**Vol. 2:** 98
19:25 ff	**Vol. 2:** 479
19:25–27	**Vol. 2:** 207
19:25 f	**Vol. 1:** 672 **Vol. 3:** 178, 261
19:25	**Vol. 1:** 433 **Vol. 2:** 479 **Vol. 3:** 178, 704
19:26	**Vol. 3:** 178
20:7	**Vol. 2:** 60 **Vol. 3:** 821
20:8	**Vol. 1:** 512 **Vol. 2:** 622 **Vol. 3:** 324
20:11	**Vol. 1:** 240
20:14	**Vol. 2:** 27
20:15	**Vol. 2:** 842
20:18	**Vol. 1:** 262 **Vol. 2:** 269, 842
20:20 ff	**Vol. 3:** 261
20:20	**Vol. 3:** 209
20:22	**Vol. 2:** 663 **Vol. 3:** 821
20:26	**Vol. 2:** 773 **Vol. 3:** 111
20:28	**Vol. 2:** 890
20:29	**Vol. 1:** 190 **Vol. 2:** 845
21:4	**Vol. 2:** 140
21:5	**Vol. 2:** 622
21:6	**Vol. 3:** 1169
21:7	**Vol. 2:** 714, 842
21:13	**Vol. 3:** 255
21:14	**Vol. 3:** 1016
21:15	**Vol. 3:** 137, 729
21:16	**Vol. 3:** 1149
21:17	**Vol. 3:** 109

Job *(cont'd)*

21:21	**Vol. 3:** 957
21:22	**Vol. 3:** 760, 1028
21:23	**Vol. 3:** 1024
21:32	**Vol. 2:** 137
21:33	**Vol. 1:** 321
21:34	**Vol. 1:** 547 **Vol. 3:** 255
22:2	**Vol. 3:** 760
22:3	**Vol. 2:** 144 **Vol. 3:** 924, 957
22:9	**Vol. 2:** 737 **Vol. 3:** 1074
22:12	**Vol. 3:** 29
22:16	**Vol. 1:** 343
22:19	**Vol. 2:** 430 **Vol. 3:** 924
22:21	**Vol. 2:** 773
22:26	**Vol. 2:** 735
22:28	**Vol. 2:** 491
22:29 f	**Vol. 3:** 209
22:29	**Vol. 2:** 202 **Vol. 3:** 29
22:30	**Vol. 3:** 201–202, 209
23:2	**Vol. 2:** 140
23:7	**Vol. 2:** 60
23:12	**Vol. 1:** 240
23:15	**Vol. 1:** 568
24:1	**Vol. 3:** 846
24:3	**Vol. 2:** 737
24:4	**Vol. 2:** 257
24:5	**Vol. 2:** 675
24:9	**Vol. 2:** 737
24:12	**Vol. 2:** 423
24:13	**Vol. 1:** 339
24:14	**Vol. 3:** 1149
24:15	**Vol. 1:** 694
24:16	**Vol. 3:** 498
24:17	**Vol. 3:** 554
24:20	**Vol. 3:** 240
24:21	**Vol. 3:** 1074
25:2	**Vol. 2:** 778
25:3	**Vol. 2:** 491
25:5	**Vol. 2:** 144 **Vol. 3:** 733, 924
26:2	**Vol. 1:** 464
26:3	**Vol. 3:** 1027
26:5	**Vol. 2:** 206
26:6	**Vol. 1:** 312, 463
26:7	**Vol. 1:** 523
26:11	**Vol. 1:** 523 **Vol. 2:** 189
26:12 f	**Vol. 1:** 508
26:12	**Vol. 3:** 255
27:2	**Vol. 1:** 202
27:5	**Vol. 3:** 166
27:6	**Vol. 3:** 1156
27:9	**Vol. 2:** 663
27:10	**Vol. 2:** 735
27:12	**Vol. 1:** 547
27:17	**Vol. 2:** 845
27:18	**Vol. 2:** 842
27:19	**Vol. 2:** 841
27:22	**Vol. 1:** 559
28	**Vol. 3:** 1029
28:1–11	**Vol. 2:** 97
28:1	**Vol. 2:** 96
28:3	**Vol. 3:** 554–555
28:4	**Vol. 3:** 994
28:8	**Vol. 3:** 30
28:9	**Vol. 3:** 1010
28:12 f	**Vol. 3:** 528
28:12	**Vol. 3:** 1027
28:14	**Vol. 2:** 197
28:15	**Vol. 3:** 166
28:18	**Vol. 3:** 1027
28:18a	**Vol. 3:** 394
28:18b	**Vol. 3:** 395
28:20	**Vol. 3:** 1027
28:22	**Vol. 1:** 463–464
28:25–28	**Vol. 3:** 641
28:25	**Vol. 3:** 402
28:28	**Vol. 3:** 1027–1028
29:3	**Vol. 2:** 485
29:7–8	**Vol. 3:** 588
29:10 f	**Vol. 1:** 216
29:10	**Vol. 2:** 349
29:12	**Vol. 2:** 821 **Vol. 3:** 209
29:14	**Vol. 1:** 314
29:15	**Vol. 1:** 218 **Vol. 2:** 415
29:18	**Vol. 3:** 842
29:20	**Vol. 2:** 49
29:21–25	**Vol. 2:** 49
29:24	**Vol. 2:** 430–431
30:1–12	**Vol. 2:** 49
30:1	**Vol. 1:** 568
30:3	**Vol. 3:** 953
30:4	**Vol. 2:** 49 **Vol. 3:** 1006
30:6	**Vol. 3:** 381, 383
30:8	**Vol. 2:** 49 **Vol. 3:** 109, 1024
30:15	**Vol. 3:** 207
30:16	**Vol. 2:** 890 **Vol. 3:** 680
30:17	**Vol. 1:** 240
30:18–23	**Vol. 3:** 342
30:21	**Vol. 1:** 652
30:23	**Vol. 3:** 261
30:25	**Vol. 2:** 423
30:26	**Vol. 1:** 422
30:27	**Vol. 2:** 890
30:30	**Vol. 1:** 652
30:31	**Vol. 2:** 416 **Vol. 3:** 720
31:1	**Vol. 3:** 448
31:2	**Vol. 3:** 729
31:6	**Vol. 3:** 1160
31:7*	**Vol. 2:** 663 **Vol. 3:** 860
31:12	**Vol. 1:** 655
31:15	**Vol. 3:** 594
31:22	**Vol. 2:** 730
31:25	**Vol. 2:** 842
31:28	**Vol. 3:** 823
31:30	**Vol. 2:** 856
31:32	**Vol. 1:** 687, 689
31:38	**Vol. 1:** 410 **Vol. 2:** 423
32:1	**Vol. 3:** 111
32:2 f	**Vol. 1:** 108
32:3	**Vol. 2:** 93

Job *(cont'd)*

32:4	**Vol. 2:** 773
32:6	**Vol. 3:** 111
32:7	**Vol. 3:** 1027
32:8	**Vol. 3:** 760
32:9	**Vol. 3:** 1028
32:13	**Vol. 3:** 1027
32:16	**Vol. 2:** 773
32:19	**Vol. 1:** 743
32:20	**Vol. 3:** 255
33:2	**Vol. 2:** 727
33:4	**Vol. 3:** 705, 760
33:5	**Vol. 2:** 773
33:9	**Vol. 2:** 144 **Vol. 3:** 924
33:10	**Vol. 2:** 144
33:11	**Vol. 1:** 389
33:14–18	**Vol. 1:** 511
33:16	**Vol. 2:** 212 **Vol. 3:** 125
33:17	**Vol. 3:** 201
33:19	**Vol. 2:** 586
33:21	**Vol. 3:** 570
33:22	**Vol. 1:** 101 **Vol. 3:** 355
33:23	**Vol. 2:** 144 **Vol. 3:** 125, 704
33:24	**Vol. 3:** 192
33:26	**Vol. 3:** 704
33:30	**Vol. 2:** 479, 492 **Vol. 3:** 816
33:31	**Vol. 3:** 1028
33:33	**Vol. 3:** 760, 1027
34:2	**Vol. 3:** 1027
34:5	**Vol. 3:** 166
34:8	**Vol. 1:** 641 **Vol. 2:** 93
34:10	**Vol. 2:** 93, 513
34:12	**Vol. 2:** 513
34:14 f	**Vol. 2:** 478
34:15	**Vol. 1:** 672
34:19	**Vol. 2:** 49
34:21 f	**Vol. 1:** 423
34:22	**Vol. 2:** 215
34:23 f	**Vol. 1:** 423
34:24	**Vol. 3:** 748
34:25	**Vol. 3:** 1149
34:26	**Vol. 3:** 109
34:27	**Vol. 3:** 354
34:29	**Vol. 2:** 370
34:30	**Vol. 2:** 468
34:32	**Vol. 3:** 760
34:34	**Vol. 3:** 1027
34:35 ff	**Vol. 3:** 342
34:37	**Vol. 3:** 823
35:3	**Vol. 3:** 137
35:12	**Vol. 3:** 29
35:14	**Vol. 3:** 816
35:15	**Vol. 3:** 585
36:2	**Vol. 3:** 224
36:9	**Vol. 3:** 585–586
36:12	**Vol. 1:** 568
36:13	**Vol. 1:** 108 **Vol. 2:** 468
36:15	**Vol. 2:** 257
36:18	**Vol. 1:** 108 **Vol. 3:** 192
36:19	**Vol. 2:** 663
36:22	**Vol. 3:** 716
36:23	**Vol. 3:** 1156
36:27	**Vol. 2:** 189
36:28	**Vol. 1:** 683 **Vol. 3:** 846
37:2	**Vol. 2:** 653
37:4	**Vol. 3:** 29–30
37:5	**Vol. 3:** 1001
37:7	**Vol. 3:** 498
37:8	**Vol. 2:** 586 **Vol. 3:** 111
37:9	**Vol. 2:** 189
37:14	**Vol. 1:** 568
37:15	**Vol. 1:** 387
37:16	**Vol. 1:** 503
37:19	**Vol. 3:** 760
37:24	**Vol. 3:** 1027
38–41	**Vol. 3:** 209
38:1–42:6	**Vol. 3:** 721
38:1	**Vol. 3:** 266, 514
38:2	**Vol. 3:** 342
38:4	**Vol. 1:** 387
38:5	**Vol. 3:** 402
38:7	**Vol. 1:** 101 **Vol. 3:** 636, 669, 816
38:8 ff	**Vol. 3:** 983
38:8–11	**Vol. 3:** 983
38:8	**Vol. 3:** 950
38:12	**Vol. 2:** 495
38:14	**Vol. 3:** 497
38:15	**Vol. 2:** 491 **Vol. 3:** 29
38:17	**Vol. 2:** 29
38:18	**Vol. 1:** 568
38:20	**Vol. 2:** 890
38:22 ff	**Vol. 3:** 846
38:22	**Vol. 2:** 189, 830
38:25 ff	**Vol. 2:** 274
38:25	**Vol. 1:** 683 **Vol. 3:** 117
38:27	**Vol. 1:** 743
38:28	**Vol. 1:** 177
38:30	**Vol. 1:** 683
38:31	**Vol. 3:** 950
38:32	**Vol. 3:** 835
38:36 f	**Vol. 3:** 1027
38:37	**Vol. 2:** 189
38:40	**Vol. 2:** 586
38:41	**Vol. 1:** 173, 409 **Vol. 3:** 117
39:1	**Vol. 3:** 835
39:2	**Vol. 3:** 177, 180
39:5	**Vol. 3:** 177
39:7	**Vol. 2:** 144
39:10	**Vol. 3:** 1161
39:17	**Vol. 3:** 1027
39:24–25	**Vol. 3:** 874
39:27–30	**Vol. 1:** 173
39:28	**Vol. 3:** 381
39:30	**Vol. 1:** 175
39:32*	**Vol. 2:** 468
40:2	**Vol. 3:** 342, 729
40:6 ff	**Vol. 2:** 432
40:7*	**Vol. 2:** 93
40:8	**Vol. 3:** 342

Job *(cont'd)*

40:11*	**Vol. 3:** 29
40:12*	**Vol. 3:** 29, 109
40:14*	**Vol. 1:** 344
40:15–24	**Vol. 3:** 1006
41	**Vol. 3:** 179
41:3*	**Vol. 2:** 773
41:9*	**Vol. 2:** 349, 495
41:10 ff	**Vol. 2:** 485
41:10*	**Vol. 2:** 485
41:15	**Vol. 2:** 349
41:16*	**Vol. 2:** 720
41:19	**Vol. 2:** 485
41:20*	**Vol. 3:** 557
41:21*	**Vol. 3:** 823
41:24*	**Vol. 3:** 823
42	**Vol. 3:** 209
42:4	**Vol. 3:** 760
42:6	**Vol. 1:** 356
42:7 ff	**Vol. 3:** 425
42:7 f	**Vol. 3:** 608
42:8	**Vol. 3:** 421
42:9	**Vol. 3:** 177
42:11	**Vol. 2:** 622
42:12	**Vol. 3:** 1161

Psalms

1	**Vol. 3:** 865, 938
1:1	**Vol. 1:** 216 **Vol. 2:** 93 **Vol. 3:** 938, 1016
1:2	**Vol. 1:** 245 **Vol. 3:** 866
1:3	**Vol. 1:** 389 **Vol. 3:** 835, 866–867
1:4 ff	**Vol. 2:** 93
1:5	**Vol. 1:** 292
1:6	**Vol. 1:** 254 **Vol. 2:** 395 **Vol. 3:** 929
2	**Vol. 1:** 123, 178–179, 408, 426 **Vol. 2:** 336, 644 **Vol. 3:** 639
2:1 f	**Vol. 1:** 168 **Vol. 2:** 793
2:1	**Vol. 2:** 799
2:2 f	**Vol. 3:** 611
2:2	**Vol. 2:** 378 **Vol. 3:** 1194
2:3	**Vol. 3:** 592, 1161
2:4	**Vol. 2:** 431–432 **Vol. 3:** 588
2:5	**Vol. 1:** 108
2:6 ff	**Vol. 2:** 79
2:6	**Vol. 2:** 225, 326
2:7	**Vol. 1:** 123, 177–179, 186, 288, 617, 668 **Vol. 2:** 336, 374, 543, 612, 819 **Vol. 3:** 637, 639, 641–644, 648, 698, 807, 863, 987
2:8 f	**Vol. 2:** 888
2:8	**Vol. 2:** 856 **Vol. 3:** 636, 638
2:9	**Vol. 1:** 111, 164, 407 **Vol. 2:** 98, 570 **Vol. 3:** 649, 911, 913
2:12	**Vol. 1:** 216
3:3	**Vol. 2:** 158
3:4*	**Vol. 2:** 175, 225, 863
3:7	**Vol. 3:** 207
3:8*	**Vol. 3:** 633

4	**Vol. 3:** 673
4:1	**Vol. 2:** 863
4:3	**Vol. 1:** 409
4:5	**Vol. 1:** 111
4:6	**Vol. 2:** 491 **Vol. 3:** 356, 569
4:8	**Vol. 2:** 724, 777–778
5:1*	**Vol. 1:** 230 **Vol. 2:** 175
5:2	**Vol. 2:** 862 **Vol. 3:** 1120
5:3*	**Vol. 1:** 474
5:5	**Vol. 1:** 555
5:6	**Vol. 2:** 471
5:7*	**Vol. 1:** 732 **Vol. 2:** 225, 876 **Vol. 3:** 783, 786
5:8 ff	**Vol. 1:** 554
5:8	**Vol. 1:** 553
5:9	**Vol. 1:** 265 **Vol. 2:** 726–727 **Vol. 3:** 937, 1079
5:10	**Vol. 2:** 93
5:11	**Vol. 1:** 227
5:12	**Vol. 2:** 818
6	**Vol. 3:** 669
6:1*	**Vol. 1:** 318, 373 **Vol. 2:** 141
6:2*	**Vol. 1:** 109 **Vol. 3:** 994
6:4	**Vol. 3:** 201, 207
6:5	**Vol. 1:** 433 **Vol. 2:** 206 **Vol. 3:** 233
6:6	**Vol. 3:** 237
6:7	**Vol. 1:** 420
6:8	**Vol. 1:** 606–607 **Vol. 3:** 1192
6:9	**Vol. 2:** 860, 863
6:10	**Vol. 3:** 562–563
7	**Vol. 3:** 672
7:1*	**Vol. 2:** 806 **Vol. 3:** 201
7:2*	**Vol. 3:** 201, 207
7:3*	**Vol. 3:** 602
7:4 f	**Vol. 3:** 1148
7:5*	**Vol. 2:** 806
7:7–11	**Vol. 3:** 357
7:7*	**Vol. 3:** 633
7:7b	**Vol. 2:** 614
7:9*	**Vol. 2:** 181 **Vol. 3:** 356
7:10	**Vol. 3:** 533, 966
7:11	**Vol. 2:** 71
7:12 ff	**Vol. 2:** 769
7:12	**Vol. 2:** 363
7:13	**Vol. 3:** 966
7:14	**Vol. 1:** 343
7:15	**Vol. 1:** 186 **Vol. 3:** 858
7:16*	**Vol. 3:** 574
7:17*	**Vol. 1:** 344 **Vol. 2:** 649
8	**Vol. 3:** 644
8:2*	**Vol. 1:** 281 **Vol. 3:** 350, 792, 817
8:3–8*	**Vol. 2:** 49
8:3	**Vol. 3:** 350, 733
8:4*	**Vol. 1:** 191 **Vol. 3:** 613, 1148
8:5–8*	**Vol. 2:** 51
8:5–7*	**Vol. 3:** 632
8:5 f	**Vol. 2:** 287
8:5*	**Vol. 1:** 406 **Vol. 2:** 502, 564
8:6–8*	**Vol. 3:** 632
8:6*	**Vol. 3:** 644

Psalms *(cont'd)*

8:7*	**Vol. 1:** 522 **Vol. 3:** 632, 1148
8:9*	**Vol. 1:** 670 **Vol. 2:** 502
9	**Vol. 2:** 257, 823
9:1*	**Vol. 1:** 345
9:2	**Vol. 2:** 622
9:3	**Vol. 3:** 994
9:4 f	**Vol. 3:** 93
9:4	**Vol. 2:** 326
9:5	**Vol. 1:** 572
9:6	**Vol. 3:** 828
9:7	**Vol. 2:** 60 **Vol. 3:** 117, 237
9:8*	**Vol. 1:** 519
9:11	**Vol. 2:** 326
9:12	**Vol. 2:** 820 **Vol. 3:** 159
9:13	**Vol. 1:** 555
9:14	**Vol. 2:** 353 **Vol. 3:** 816
9:16	**Vol. 1:** 343 **Vol. 3:** 673
9:18	**Vol. 2:** 773, 820
9:23*	**Vol. 2:** 93
9:28*	**Vol. 1:** 202, 416
9:34*	**Vol. 2:** 93
10	**Vol. 2:** 257, 823
10:1	**Vol. 1:** 607 **Vol. 2:** 215
10:2*	**Vol. 2:** 737 **Vol. 3:** 29, 820
10:3*	**Vol. 3:** 137, 816–817, 820
10:7	**Vol. 1:** 202, 262, 743
10:8*	**Vol. 2:** 215, 841
10:9*	**Vol. 2:** 821
10:14*	**Vol. 1:** 262 **Vol. 2:** 738 **Vol. 3:** 126
10:17 f*	**Vol. 2:** 260
10:18†	**Vol. 2:** 771
11:1*	**Vol. 3:** 1009
11:4	**Vol. 2:** 596 **Vol. 3:** 784, 786
11:6	**Vol. 2:** 735
12:1*	**Vol. 3:** 207
12:3 f	**Vol. 2:** 468
12:5*	**Vol. 2:** 735, 821
12:6	**Vol. 3:** 101
12:7*	**Vol. 2:** 36, 134
13:2	**Vol. 1:** 585
13:3	**Vol. 1:** 442, 553 **Vol. 2:** 854
13:4	**Vol. 1:** 416
13:5	**Vol. 2:** 355
13:6*	**Vol. 3:** 672
13:10	**Vol. 3:** 940, 1017
14:1*	**Vol. 2:** 430, 860 **Vol. 3:** 1024–1025
14:2	**Vol. 1:** 433 **Vol. 3:** 131–132, 532
14:3*	**Vol. 2:** 27
14:7	**Vol. 2:** 318, 327 **Vol. 3:** 203
15*	**Vol. 3:** 355, 367
15:1	**Vol. 1:** 691 **Vol. 2:** 225
15:2*	**Vol. 3:** 924, 1148
15:5	**Vol. 2:** 41, 302
15:8*	**Vol. 1:** 695
16	**Vol. 3:** 262, 297
16:2	**Vol. 2:** 100
16:3	**Vol. 2:** 227
16:4	**Vol. 3:** 423
16:5 f	**Vol. 2:** 297
16:5	**Vol. 2:** 479 **Vol. 3:** 208
16:6	**Vol. 1:** 609
16:8–11	**Vol. 2:** 356
16:8 f	**Vol. 3:** 491
16:8	**Vol. 1:** 695 **Vol. 3:** 559
16:9 ff	**Vol. 2:** 479
16:9	**Vol. 1:** 230 **Vol. 2:** 353 **Vol. 3:** 859, 1079
16:9c*	**Vol. 3:** 813
16:10*†	**Vol. 1:** 266, 470, 677, 695 **Vol. 2:** 186, 231, 238, 354, 919 **Vol. 3:** 262, 491, 651, 683, 1200
16:11*	**Vol. 2:** 355, 479 **Vol. 3:** 262, 314, 938, 940–941
17*	**Vol. 2:** 863
17:1–5*	**Vol. 3:** 356
17:1*	**Vol. 2:** 860, 863
17:3*	**Vol. 3:** 808
17:4*	**Vol. 3:** 583, 858
17:5*	**Vol. 3:** 350, 858
17:6 f	**Vol. 2:** 863
17:6*	**Vol. 2:** 175 **Vol. 3:** 858, 1120
17:8	**Vol. 2:** 134 **Vol. 3:** 554, 721, 805
17:10*	**Vol. 3:** 29
17:13*	**Vol. 2:** 199 **Vol. 3:** 201
17:14	**Vol. 1:** 698
17:15	**Vol. 1:** 743 **Vol. 3:** 106, 515
17:26*	**Vol. 2:** 116
17:44*	**Vol. 2:** 173
18	**Vol. 1:** 522 **Vol. 2:** 644 **Vol. 3:** 673, 966
18:1*	**Vol. 3:** 713
18:2	**Vol. 3:** 212, 715
18:3*	**Vol. 1:** 636 **Vol. 2:** 596 **Vol. 3:** 816
18:4 ff	**Vol. 3:** 180
18:5 ff	**Vol. 2:** 478
18:5*	**Vol. 1:** 519 **Vol. 3:** 986
18:6*	**Vol. 2:** 863 **Vol. 3:** 783, 786
18:7*	**Vol. 1:** 661 **Vol. 3:** 986
18:9 ff	**Vol. 1:** 422
18:10*	**Vol. 1:** 101, 280 **Vol. 2:** 190 **Vol. 3:** 1001
18:12*	**Vol. 3:** 514
18:15	**Vol. 1:** 661
18:17*	**Vol. 1:** 555 **Vol. 3:** 748, 983
18:18	**Vol. 2:** 889
18:19*	**Vol. 3:** 207, 1019
18:21 ff	**Vol. 3:** 1148
18:21*	**Vol. 3:** 938
18:22–24*	**Vol. 3:** 356
18:22*	**Vol. 3:** 354
18:23*	**Vol. 3:** 924
18:26*	**Vol. 2:** 705
18:27*	**Vol. 2:** 260 **Vol. 3:** 29
18:28	**Vol. 2:** 485
18:29*	**Vol. 3:** 201
18:30*	**Vol. 3:** 924
18:32*	**Vol. 3:** 121, 924
18:33*	**Vol. 3:** 350

Psalms *(cont'd)*

18:34*	**Vol. 3:** 760
18:35*	**Vol. 2:** 146 **Vol. 3:** 760
18:39*	**Vol. 3:** 121
18:46*	**Vol. 2:** 201
18:47	**Vol. 1:** 210
18:49*	**Vol. 1:** 344, 346 **Vol. 2:** 791 **Vol. 3:** 672
18:50	**Vol. 2:** 336
18:51*	**Vol. 3:** 828
19	**Vol. 2:** 355
19:1 ff	**Vol. 3:** 327, 331
19:1*	**Vol. 2:** 45, 175, 190 **Vol. 3:** 331
19:2*	**Vol. 3:** 45
19:4*	**Vol. 1:** 519 **Vol. 2:** 176 **Vol. 3:** 1118
19:5*	**Vol. 2:** 353 **Vol. 3:** 1120, 1122
19:6	**Vol. 2:** 175
19:7*	**Vol. 1:** 518 **Vol. 2:** 449 **Vol. 3:** 331, 924, 1028
19:8*	**Vol. 1:** 281 **Vol. 3:** 101, 354, 1033
19:9*	**Vol. 2:** 175 **Vol. 3:** 355
19:10*	**Vol. 3:** 358
19:11	**Vol. 3:** 595
19:12*	**Vol. 2:** 215 **Vol. 3:** 585–586
19:13*	**Vol. 3:** 595, 924
19:14*	**Vol. 3:** 178, 193
20:2	**Vol. 2:** 326, 889
20:3	**Vol. 3:** 421
20:4*	**Vol. 3:** 235
20:5	**Vol. 3:** 636
20:6*	**Vol. 1:** 734 **Vol. 2:** 225, 336
20:7	**Vol. 3:** 266
20:9*	**Vol. 2:** 890 **Vol. 3:** 207
21:1	**Vol. 2:** 353
21:2	**Vol. 3:** 636
21:3	**Vol. 3:** 636
21:4*	**Vol. 2:** 856 **Vol. 3:** 636
21:5*	**Vol. 1:** 409 **Vol. 3:** 828
21:11*	**Vol. 1:** 721 **Vol. 3:** 820
21:13*	**Vol. 3:** 672
21:22*	**Vol. 1:** 295
22	**Vol. 1:** 396 **Vol. 2:** 82, 263 **Vol. 3:** 202, 720
22:1*	**Vol. 1:** 411, 544, 615 **Vol. 3:** 585
22:2*	**Vol. 1:** 396 **Vol. 3:** 125
22:3*	**Vol. 3:** 817
22:4*	**Vol. 1:** 617 **Vol. 3:** 202
22:5*	**Vol. 3:** 209
22:6	**Vol. 2:** 272
22:7 f	**Vol. 1:** 396 **Vol. 2:** 82
22:8 f	**Vol. 3:** 287
22:8*	**Vol. 3:** 202, 209
22:9	**Vol. 1:** 396
22:10*	**Vol. 3:** 1071
22:13*	**Vol. 3:** 601
22:15*	**Vol. 2:** 349 **Vol. 3:** 491, 713, 914
22:17*	**Vol. 3:** 126
22:18*	**Vol. 2:** 64, 82, 296, 299 **Vol. 3:** 543, 670
22:19	**Vol. 1:** 396 **Vol. 2:** 299 **Vol. 3:** 287
22:20*	**Vol. 3:** 201
22:21*	**Vol. 3:** 203, 209
22:22*	**Vol. 1:** 255, 304, 396 **Vol. 2:** 82–83, 722 **Vol. 3:** 48, 207, 668, 670
22:23*	**Vol. 1:** 293 **Vol. 3:** 816
22:24	**Vol. 1:** 411
22:25*	**Vol. 3:** 817
22:26*	**Vol. 1:** 295, 411 **Vol. 2:** 181 **Vol. 3:** 816
22:27*	**Vol. 2:** 83, 876, 888
22:28 f*	**Vol. 3:** 233, 514–515
22:28	**Vol. 2:** 83
22:29*	**Vol. 2:** 876
22:30 f*	**Vol. 2:** 83 **Vol. 3:** 45
22:30	**Vol. 3:** 522
22:31*	**Vol. 3:** 357
23	**Vol. 2:** 104, 412, 479 **Vol. 3:** 565–566
23:1*	**Vol. 3:** 255, 804
23:3*	**Vol. 2:** 650 **Vol. 3:** 937
23:4*	**Vol. 1:** 422, 562 **Vol. 3:** 555
23:5	**Vol. 1:** 120 **Vol. 2:** 711 **Vol. 3:** 208
23:6	**Vol. 2:** 99, 247
24	**Vol. 2:** 186, 613
24:1	**Vol. 1:** 519, 691, 734 **Vol. 2:** 286, 375 **Vol. 3:** 853
24:2*	**Vol. 1:** 589 **Vol. 3:** 117, 983, 986, 990
24:3 ff*	**Vol. 3:** 355, 357
24:3 f	**Vol. 2:** 225 **Vol. 3:** 106
24:3	**Vol. 3:** 787
24:4	**Vol. 2:** 149
24:5*	**Vol. 3:** 218, 355
24:6	**Vol. 1:** 586 **Vol. 3:** 531
24:7 ff	**Vol. 2:** 44, 898
24:7	**Vol. 1:** 321
24:8*	**Vol. 3:** 716, 960
24:9	**Vol. 1:** 321
25:2	**Vol. 3:** 563
25:3*	**Vol. 2:** 773
25:4 f*	**Vol. 3:** 760
25:5*	**Vol. 2:** 773 **Vol. 3:** 218, 220
25:6 f*	**Vol. 3:** 234
25:6–9	**Vol. 2:** 364
25:6*	**Vol. 2:** 595, 598 **Vol. 3:** 235
25:7 f	**Vol. 2:** 105
25:8*	**Vol. 3:** 316
25:9*	**Vol. 2:** 257 **Vol. 3:** 760, 937
25:10*	**Vol. 3:** 879, 937
25:11*	**Vol. 1:** 698–699 **Vol. 3:** 152, 156
25:12	**Vol. 1:** 534
25:16 ff*	**Vol. 3:** 156
25:16	**Vol. 2:** 823
25:17*	**Vol. 2:** 663
25:18*	**Vol. 1:** 698 **Vol. 2:** 260, 263
25:20*	**Vol. 3:** 201
25:21*	**Vol. 2:** 773
25:22*	**Vol. 3:** 192–193
25:25	**Vol. 1:** 585
26:1–6*	**Vol. 3:** 356
26:1*	**Vol. 3:** 924

Psalms *(cont'd)*

26:2*   **Vol. 2:** 181   **Vol. 3:** 799–800, 808
26:3*   **Vol. 2:** 815
26:5   **Vol. 1:** 293, 555
26:6*   **Vol. 2:** 149   **Vol. 3:** 990
26:7*   **Vol. 2:** 622   **Vol. 3:** 816
26:8   **Vol. 2:** 45, 247
26:11*   **Vol. 3:** 192, 924
26:14*   **Vol. 2:** 563
27   **Vol. 1:** 622
27:1*   **Vol. 1:** 636   **Vol. 2:** 479, 491   **Vol. 3:** 218
27:2*   **Vol. 3:** 994
27:4*   **Vol. 1:** 189   **Vol. 2:** 247, 478, 856   **Vol. 3:** 782, 786, 991
27:5*   **Vol. 2:** 201, 215
27:6*   **Vol. 2:** 201   **Vol. 3:** 673
27:8 f   **Vol. 3:** 648
27:8   **Vol. 3:** 531
27:9*   **Vol. 1:** 109   **Vol. 3:** 218, 220
27:10*   **Vol. 3:** 748
27:11*   **Vol. 3:** 938
27:12*   **Vol. 3:** 680, 1041
27:14*   **Vol. 2:** 773
28:2*   **Vol. 2:** 149, 860   **Vol. 3:** 782
28:3   **Vol. 1:** 562
28:6 f   **Vol. 1:** 345
28:6*   **Vol. 1:** 210   **Vol. 2:** 860
28:8   **Vol. 2:** 336
28:9*   **Vol. 3:** 207, 565
29   **Vol. 3:** 1087, 1105
29:1   **Vol. 2:** 44   **Vol. 3:** 636
29:2   **Vol. 2:** 225
29:3 ff   **Vol. 3:** 1105
29:3 f*   **Vol. 3:** 113
29:3*   **Vol. 2:** 44, 876
29:4*   **Vol. 3:** 713
29:8*   **Vol. 2:** 650   **Vol. 3:** 113
29:9*   **Vol. 2:** 190   **Vol. 3:** 350, 783, 786
29:10 ff*   **Vol. 2:** 778
29:10 f*   **Vol. 2:** 778
29:10*   **Vol. 2:** 175, 190   **Vol. 3:** 588, 991
29:11*   **Vol. 3:** 713
30:1*   **Vol. 2:** 201
30:2 f*   **Vol. 3:** 262
30:3   **Vol. 2:** 167–168
30:4*   **Vol. 1:** 344   **Vol. 3:** 233, 238
30:5*   **Vol. 3:** 237
30:6   **Vol. 1:** 109
30:8   **Vol. 2:** 860
30:9*   **Vol. 1:** 433   **Vol. 2:** 206   **Vol. 3:** 45, 880
30:11*   **Vol. 2:** 357, 418   **Vol. 3:** 121, 262, 1192
30:12   **Vol. 1:** 230
30:20*   **Vol. 2:** 115
30:25*   **Vol. 2:** 563
31:1*   **Vol. 3:** 202
31:2   **Vol. 2:** 175
31:4 f   **Vol. 2:** 479

31:4*   **Vol. 1:** 725   **Vol. 3:** 381, 937
31:5*   **Vol. 2:** 212   **Vol. 3:** 192–193
31:6*   **Vol. 3:** 690
31:6a   **Vol. 1:** 554
31:7*   **Vol. 2:** 260, 353
31:8*   **Vol. 2:** 332
31:10*   **Vol. 3:** 713, 994
31:12   **Vol. 2:** 633
31:15*   **Vol. 2:** 806   **Vol. 3:** 835
31:16*   **Vol. 3:** 207, 318
31:17*   **Vol. 2:** 263
31:18*   **Vol. 3:** 29
31:19–20   **Vol. 2:** 215
31:19*   **Vol. 1:** 732   **Vol. 2:** 105
31:21*   **Vol. 1:** 210
31:22*   **Vol. 2:** 860
31:23*   **Vol. 3:** 29
31:24   **Vol. 3:** 718
32:1 ff*   **Vol. 2:** 168   **Vol. 3:** 997
32:1 f*   **Vol. 1:** 79, 216   **Vol. 3:** 169
32:1*   **Vol. 1:** 698, 702   **Vol. 3:** 192
32:2*   **Vol. 2:** 513   **Vol. 3:** 691, 823–824
32:3   **Vol. 2:** 714
32:5   **Vol. 1:** 698   **Vol. 2:** 212, 215
32:6*   **Vol. 2:** 237, 862   **Vol. 3:** 836, 991
32:11   **Vol. 1:** 227   **Vol. 2:** 353
32:16*   **Vol. 1:** 732
33   **Vol. 1:** 383, 523   **Vol. 3:** 1087
33:1*   **Vol. 2:** 668
33:2*   **Vol. 3:** 671
33:3*   **Vol. 2:** 670   **Vol. 3:** 673
33:4   **Vol. 3:** 1105, 1194
33:5*   **Vol. 2:** 364   **Vol. 3:** 357
33:6*   **Vol. 2:** 109, 190   **Vol. 3:** 690, 1105
33:7   **Vol. 2:** 189
33:8   **Vol. 1:** 519
33:9*   **Vol. 1:** 380   **Vol. 3:** 1105
33:10 f*   **Vol. 3:** 823, 1016
33:11*   **Vol. 3:** 224
33:12   **Vol. 1:** 636   **Vol. 2:** 297
33:13 ff   **Vol. 3:** 1105
33:15*   **Vol. 2:** 724
33:16 f*   **Vol. 3:** 206, 209
33:17   **Vol. 1:** 409
33:18 f*   **Vol. 3:** 202, 804
33:18   **Vol. 2:** 240
33:19*   **Vol. 2:** 478   **Vol. 3:** 201
33:20*   **Vol. 2:** 773
33:21   **Vol. 2:** 355
34   **Vol. 2:** 772
34:2*   **Vol. 2:** 257   **Vol. 3:** 816
34:3*   **Vol. 2:** 201–202
34:4*   **Vol. 2:** 735   **Vol. 3:** 201
34:5   **Vol. 1:** 520   **Vol. 2:** 270
34:7*   **Vol. 3:** 202
34:8*   **Vol. 1:** 216   **Vol. 2:** 269–270   **Vol. 3:** 513
34:9*   **Vol. 2:** 227
34:10*   **Vol. 2:** 99, 265, 270, 841   **Vol. 3:** 804, 953

Psalms *(cont'd)*

34:11*†   **Vol. 1:** 285   **Vol. 2:** 596, 735   **Vol. 3:** 760
34:12 ff*   **Vol. 1:** 562
34:13–17   **Vol. 2:** 270
34:13*   **Vol. 1:** 240   **Vol. 3:** 1079
34:14*   **Vol. 2:** 806   **Vol. 3:** 531, 1079
34:15*   **Vol. 1:** 230   **Vol. 2:** 778, 782   **Vol. 3:** 1153
34:16   **Vol. 2:** 178, 861   **Vol. 3:** 370
34:17*   **Vol. 2:** 860   **Vol. 3:** 201, 237
34:18*   **Vol. 2:** 260
34:19*   **Vol. 2:** 53, 807–808   **Vol. 3:** 201, 691
34:20   **Vol. 2:** 270
34:21   **Vol. 1:** 555
34:22*   **Vol. 3:** 192
35   **Vol. 2:** 823
35:3*   **Vol. 2:** 806
35:4*   **Vol. 3:** 531, 823
35:7   **Vol. 2:** 41
35:10*   **Vol. 2:** 822
35:11*   **Vol. 2:** 879   **Vol. 3:** 1041
35:13*   **Vol. 1:** 495, 612   **Vol. 2:** 863
35:14*   **Vol. 2:** 815
35:16*   **Vol. 2:** 421   **Vol. 3:** 799–800
35:18*   **Vol. 2:** 863   **Vol. 3:** 816
35:19   **Vol. 2:** 41, 448   **Vol. 3:** 329
35:20*   **Vol. 3:** 820
35:23   **Vol. 3:** 93
35:26   **Vol. 3:** 562–563
35:27*   **Vol. 2:** 353, 778
35:28*   **Vol. 3:** 817, 1079
36:1*   **Vol. 3:** 940
36:4*   **Vol. 3:** 820, 823
36:8 ff   **Vol. 2:** 479
36:8 f   **Vol. 3:** 805
36:9   **Vol. 2:** 478, 486, 492
36:10*   **Vol. 2:** 70, 772   **Vol. 3:** 987
36:11*   **Vol. 3:** 29
36:33*   **Vol. 2:** 370
37   **Vol. 2:** 841
37:2   **Vol. 1:** 743
37:3*   **Vol. 2:** 842
37:4*   **Vol. 1:** 240, 608
37:5*   **Vol. 3:** 938
37:8 f   **Vol. 1:** 108
37:8   **Vol. 2:** 423
37:9*   **Vol. 2:** 298, 773
37:11*   **Vol. 2:** 257–258, 778
37:12   **Vol. 2:** 421
37:13   **Vol. 2:** 431
37:14*   **Vol. 1:** 428   **Vol. 2:** 257, 824
37:16 f*   **Vol. 2:** 428
37:17   **Vol. 1:** 466
37:18*†   **Vol. 2:** 395   **Vol. 3:** 924
37:19*   **Vol. 1:** 743   **Vol. 2:** 890   **Vol. 3:** 804, 835–836
37:20*   **Vol. 1:** 554   **Vol. 2:** 201
37:22   **Vol. 2:** 298

37:28*   **Vol. 3:** 93, 924
37:29   **Vol. 2:** 298
37:30*   **Vol. 3:** 1027, 1079
37:32   **Vol. 3:** 126
37:34*   **Vol. 2:** 773
37:39*   **Vol. 2:** 807   **Vol. 3:** 836
38*   **Vol. 2:** 167   **Vol. 3:** 233, 239
38:1   **Vol. 1:** 318
38:3 ff*   **Vol. 2:** 168   **Vol. 3:** 997
38:3   **Vol. 2:** 777
38:5*   **Vol. 2:** 683   **Vol. 3:** 953, 1024
38:6*   **Vol. 1:** 711
38:8*   **Vol. 1:** 712   **Vol. 2:** 260
38:9   **Vol. 2:** 215, 421
38:10*   **Vol. 2:** 181
38:12*   **Vol. 1:** 690   **Vol. 2:** 175
38:18*   **Vol. 1:** 277
38:19   **Vol. 3:** 233
38:22*   **Vol. 2:** 260
39 f   **Vol. 2:** 168
39*   **Vol. 3:** 673
39:2   **Vol. 3:** 1176
39:3   **Vol. 1:** 318
39:4   **Vol. 3:** 953
39:6*   **Vol. 2:** 287
39:7*   **Vol. 2:** 773   **Vol. 3:** 1203
39:8*   **Vol. 3:** 201–202, 1024
39:9*   **Vol. 3:** 997, 1025
39:11*   **Vol. 1:** 162
39:12*   **Vol. 2:** 789, 860, 863   **Vol. 3:** 997
39:13†   **Vol. 1:** 686, 688, 690–691
40   **Vol. 3:** 783
40:1*   **Vol. 2:** 240, 773, 824, 860
40:3*   **Vol. 1:** 177   **Vol. 2:** 586, 670   **Vol. 3:** 669, 673
40:4*   **Vol. 2:** 471
40:5*   **Vol. 2:** 683   **Vol. 3:** 820
40:6 ff   **Vol. 2:** 818   **Vol. 3:** 433
40:6*   **Vol. 1:** 234   **Vol. 2:** 856   **Vol. 3:** 171, 350, 421
40:7 ff   **Vol. 3:** 1023
40:7 f   **Vol. 3:** 427
40:8*   **Vol. 3:** 1019
40:9*   **Vol. 2:** 109   **Vol. 3:** 357, 1154
40:10*   **Vol. 1:** 241   **Vol. 2:** 222   **Vol. 3:** 357
40:11*   **Vol. 2:** 595, 598
40:13*   **Vol. 2:** 817   **Vol. 3:** 201–202
40:14   **Vol. 3:** 563
40:15   **Vol. 3:** 562
40:17*   **Vol. 2:** 257, 823
41:1*   **Vol. 1:** 216
41:2*   **Vol. 3:** 209, 242
41:4*   **Vol. 3:** 997
41:5   **Vol. 2:** 168
41:7*   **Vol. 3:** 823, 908
41:8   **Vol. 2:** 554
41:9*   **Vol. 2:** 521   **Vol. 3:** 329, 491
41:10   **Vol. 2:** 650   **Vol. 3:** 1192
41:13   **Vol. 2:** 596
41:13*   **Vol. 1:** 98, 210

Psalms *(cont'd)*

42   **Vol. 3:** 236
42:2*   **Vol. 1:** 586   **Vol. 2:** 266   **Vol. 3:** 515
42:3   **Vol. 3:** 106
42:4*   **Vol. 2:** 247
42:5*   **Vol. 2:** 240   **Vol. 3:** 236
42:6*   **Vol. 3:** 683
42:7*   **Vol. 2:** 205
42:8*   **Vol. 2:** 863
43   **Vol. 1:** 544
43:1*   **Vol. 3:** 93, 201, 881
43:3   **Vol. 3:** 881
44:3*   **Vol. 2:** 491   **Vol. 3:** 206
44:4*   **Vol. 2:** 817
44:5*   **Vol. 1:** 332
44:6 f*   **Vol. 3:** 206
44:8*   **Vol. 3:** 816
44:15   **Vol. 2:** 212
44:16*   **Vol. 3:** 345
44:19*   **Vol. 2:** 260   **Vol. 3:** 555
44:22*   **Vol. 3:** 823
44:23   **Vol. 3:** 824
44:24   **Vol. 2:** 215
44:25 f*   **Vol. 2:** 260
44:26*   **Vol. 3:** 192
45   **Vol. 1:** 122   **Vol. 2:** 584–585
45:1*   **Vol. 2:** 602
45:2*   **Vol. 2:** 116
45:4*   **Vol. 2:** 257   **Vol. 3:** 881
45:5*   **Vol. 2:** 622
45:6 f   **Vol. 1:** 123
45:6–7   **Vol. 1:** 408
45:6   **Vol. 1:** 162, 164
45:7 f   **Vol. 1:** 122
45:7*   **Vol. 1:** 122, 239, 427   **Vol. 2:** 71, 354, 374, 448, 602, 711–712   **Vol. 3:** 365, 575, 648, 1061
45:8*   **Vol. 2:** 294
45:9*   **Vol. 2:** 146
45:11*   **Vol. 2:** 602
45:12*   **Vol. 2:** 841, 876
45:15*   **Vol. 3:** 782
45:17*   **Vol. 3:** 233
46   **Vol. 1:** 622   **Vol. 2:** 361, 613   **Vol. 3:** 783
46:3 f*   **Vol. 3:** 983
46:3*   **Vol. 3:** 112
46:4   **Vol. 2:** 803
46:6*   **Vol. 3:** 709
46:10*   **Vol. 2:** 396, 791
47:1*   **Vol. 2:** 149
47:2   **Vol. 2:** 375
47:3   **Vol. 2:** 375
47:5   **Vol. 2:** 644
47:8*   **Vol. 2:** 225, 375, 602
48*   **Vol. 3:** 673, 783, 1068
48:1   **Vol. 2:** 803
48:2   **Vol. 2:** 327, 803
48:5*   **Vol. 1:** 241

48:6   **Vol. 2:** 622
48:7   **Vol. 3:** 1001
48:8   **Vol. 2:** 803
48:9*   **Vol. 3:** 786
49*   **Vol. 2:** 207, 841   **Vol. 3:** 262
49:2*   **Vol. 1:** 519   **Vol. 2:** 841
49:3*   **Vol. 3:** 1027
49:4*   **Vol. 2:** 745
49:5*   **Vol. 2:** 890
49:6*   **Vol. 2:** 841
49:7 f*   **Vol. 3:** 174
49:7*†   **Vol. 3:** 192
49:8*   **Vol. 3:** 153, 192–193
49:10*   **Vol. 2:** 842   **Vol. 3:** 1024, 1027
49:11   **Vol. 2:** 649
49:12*   **Vol. 3:** 126
49:15*   **Vol. 2:** 491   **Vol. 3:** 174, 192, 262, 265
49:16*   **Vol. 2:** 479, 841
49:19   **Vol. 2:** 491
50   **Vol. 1:** 367   **Vol. 2:** 261   **Vol. 3:** 425, 783
50:1–6   **Vol. 2:** 363
50:2   **Vol. 2:** 735   **Vol. 3:** 514
50:3 f   **Vol. 1:** 320
50:3   **Vol. 1:** 655
50:5   **Vol. 2:** 237
50:7*   **Vol. 3:** 1041
50:8–15   **Vol. 3:** 424, 427
50:8*   **Vol. 3:** 316
50:9*   **Vol. 1:** 471
50:10*   **Vol. 1:** 240   **Vol. 3:** 853
50:12 f   **Vol. 3:** 422
50:13*   **Vol. 2:** 93
50:14   **Vol. 3:** 423–424
50:15   **Vol. 1:** 320
50:16*   **Vol. 3:** 354
50:17*   **Vol. 1:** 555   **Vol. 3:** 777
50:18*   **Vol. 2:** 303
50:20*   **Vol. 3:** 345–346, 1069
50:21   **Vol. 1:** 474
50:22*   **Vol. 3:** 601–602
50:23*   **Vol. 3:** 423, 569
51*   **Vol. 1:** 433   **Vol. 2:** 167   **Vol. 3:** 105, 579, 783
51:1*   **Vol. 1:** 732   **Vol. 2:** 595, 598
51:4 ff   **Vol. 2:** 472
51:4*   **Vol. 2:** 724   **Vol. 3:** 320, 355
51:6*   **Vol. 1:** 650   **Vol. 2:** 430   **Vol. 3:** 881, 1027
51:7*   **Vol. 1:** 144, 151, 204, 225
51:10*   **Vol. 1:** 184, 349, 379   **Vol. 2:** 181, 673   **Vol. 3:** 692
51:11*   **Vol. 2:** 227
51:12*   **Vol. 3:** 691, 694
51:13*   **Vol. 3:** 760
51:14*   **Vol. 3:** 201, 357
51:15*   **Vol. 3:** 45
51:16 ff*   **Vol. 2:** 817
51:16*   **Vol. 3:** 1079
51:17*   **Vol. 2:** 181, 260, 865   **Vol. 3:** 691

Psalms *(cont'd)*

51:18 f	**Vol. 3:** 427
51:19*	**Vol. 2:** 818 **Vol. 3:** 421
51:21*	**Vol. 3:** 356, 421
52:1	**Vol. 1:** 227
52:2*	**Vol. 3:** 823
52:3*	**Vol. 3:** 575
52:7*	**Vol. 2:** 841–842 **Vol. 3:** 203
52:8*	**Vol. 2:** 247, 711
52:9 f	**Vol. 2:** 237
52:9*	**Vol. 2:** 239, 772–773
53:1*	**Vol. 2:** 430 **Vol. 3:** 1024
53:2*	**Vol. 3:** 1025
53:5*	**Vol. 2:** 815
54*	**Vol. 3:** 669
54:1*	**Vol. 2:** 650 **Vol. 3:** 207
54:2*	**Vol. 2:** 863
54:3*	**Vol. 1:** 672, 696 **Vol. 2:** 363
54:6	**Vol. 1:** 427 **Vol. 2:** 650
55*	**Vol. 3:** 669
55:1*	**Vol. 2:** 860, 863
55:3	**Vol. 1:** 554
55:5*	**Vol. 1:** 609 **Vol. 3:** 710
55:6*	**Vol. 3:** 255
55:7*	**Vol. 1:** 241
55:13*	**Vol. 2:** 498
55:14*	**Vol. 2:** 479, 653
55:16†	**Vol. 1:** 409
55:17	**Vol. 1:** 575
55:18*	**Vol. 2:** 778 **Vol. 3:** 192
55:19*	**Vol. 3:** 166
55:21	**Vol. 2:** 711
55:22*	**Vol. 1:** 277–278
56:1*	**Vol. 1:** 589
56:3*	**Vol. 3:** 816
56:4	**Vol. 1:** 679
56:5*	**Vol. 3:** 820
56:6*	**Vol. 1:** 672 **Vol. 2:** 773
56:8*	**Vol. 1:** 243
56:10*	**Vol. 3:** 816
56:12	**Vol. 1:** 672 **Vol. 3:** 423
56:13*	**Vol. 1:** 416 **Vol. 2:** 302, 478, 492, 815 **Vol. 3:** 201
57:1*	**Vol. 1:** 174 **Vol. 3:** 554
57:2	**Vol. 3:** 805
57:3	**Vol. 3:** 879
57:4*	**Vol. 3:** 201
57:5*	**Vol. 2:** 201 **Vol. 3:** 1079
57:7*	**Vol. 3:** 117, 673
57:10	**Vol. 3:** 879
57:11*	**Vol. 2:** 201
58:3	**Vol. 2:** 471
58:5*	**Vol. 3:** 1028
58:6	**Vol. 2:** 554
58:7*	**Vol. 3:** 994
58:10*	**Vol. 3:** 93, 159
59:1*	**Vol. 3:** 192, 769
59:2*	**Vol. 3:** 207
59:3*	**Vol. 3:** 201

59:8	**Vol. 2:** 431
59:10*	**Vol. 3:** 569
59:12*	**Vol. 3:** 29
59:15	**Vol. 1:** 743
59:16*	**Vol. 3:** 673
59:17	**Vol. 2:** 889
60	**Vol. 3:** 233
60:3*	**Vol. 2:** 275 **Vol. 3:** 569, 919
60:5*	**Vol. 3:** 207
60:11*	**Vol. 3:** 207
61*	**Vol. 3:** 669
61:1*	**Vol. 2:** 860, 863
61:2*	**Vol. 2:** 201
61:5*	**Vol. 1:** 688, 691 **Vol. 2:** 863 **Vol. 3:** 805, 946
61:7	**Vol. 3:** 879
62:2*	**Vol. 3:** 218
62:3	**Vol. 3:** 950
62:5*	**Vol. 2:** 240, 773
62:6*	**Vol. 3:** 218
62:7	**Vol. 3:** 232, 381
62:9*	**Vol. 2:** 209 **Vol. 3:** 1160
62:10*	**Vol. 1:** 683 **Vol. 2:** 842
62:11*	**Vol. 2:** 716 **Vol. 3:** 716
62:12*	**Vol. 3:** 134, 167
63	**Vol. 3:** 236
63:1*	**Vol. 2:** 266, 305 **Vol. 3:** 680
63:2	**Vol. 1:** 672
63:3*	**Vol. 2:** 117, 479 **Vol. 3:** 816
63:5*	**Vol. 3:** 816
63:6*	**Vol. 2:** 197
63:8	**Vol. 3:** 805
63:9*	**Vol. 1:** 492 **Vol. 2:** 209
63:11*	**Vol. 3:** 574, 816
64:1*	**Vol. 2:** 863
64:4*	**Vol. 3:** 924
64:9*	**Vol. 3:** 45
64:10*	**Vol. 1:** 513 **Vol. 3:** 816
65	**Vol. 1:** 210, 523
65:1*	**Vol. 2:** 668 **Vol. 3:** 669
65:2*	**Vol. 2:** 863
65:3*	**Vol. 1:** 698–699 **Vol. 3:** 153–154, 156
65:4*	**Vol. 3:** 783, 786
65:5 ff	**Vol. 1:** 699
65:5–8*	**Vol. 3:** 207
65:5*	**Vol. 2:** 478 **Vol. 3:** 218, 357, 748
65:6*	**Vol. 3:** 117, 121, 1010
65:7	**Vol. 3:** 560
65:8*	**Vol. 3:** 983
65:9*	**Vol. 2:** 275, 841 **Vol. 3:** 117
65:10*	**Vol. 3:** 986
65:11*	**Vol. 2:** 105
65:13*	**Vol. 3:** 668
66:1*	**Vol. 3:** 671, 986
66:4*	**Vol. 2:** 876
66:5*	**Vol. 1:** 622
66:10*	**Vol. 3:** 808
66:12*	**Vol. 3:** 983
66:19 f*	**Vol. 2:** 863
66:20	**Vol. 1:** 210

Psalms *(cont'd)*

67*	**Vol. 2:** 261 **Vol. 3:** 669
67:1 f*	**Vol. 3:** 207
67:1*	**Vol. 3:** 318
67:2	**Vol. 3:** 221
67:3*	**Vol. 3:** 937
67:4*	**Vol. 1:** 519
67:5	**Vol. 2:** 363
67:13	**Vol. 2:** 69
67:18*	**Vol. 2:** 195
68:1*	**Vol. 1:** 555 **Vol. 2:** 34 **Vol. 3:** 671
68:3*	**Vol. 1:** 711
68:4–10	**Vol. 1:** 618
68:4*	**Vol. 2:** 190 **Vol. 3:** 673
68:5*	**Vol. 1:** 617–618 **Vol. 2:** 738 **Vol. 3:** 1073
68:6*	**Vol. 1:** 203
68:8 f*	**Vol. 3:** 565, 960
68:8	**Vol. 3:** 1013
68:9*	**Vol. 2:** 296 **Vol. 3:** 350, 1001
68:11*	**Vol. 2:** 109
68:13	**Vol. 2:** 313
68:14*	**Vol. 3:** 915
68:17 f	**Vol. 3:** 557
68:17*	**Vol. 3:** 786
68:18*	**Vol. 1:** 99 **Vol. 2:** 186, 209, 698 **Vol. 3:** 203, 494, 591
68:19*	**Vol. 1:** 210 **Vol. 2:** 199 **Vol. 3:** 87
68:20*	**Vol. 1:** 636 **Vol. 2:** 895
68:24–27*	**Vol. 1:** 245
68:24*	**Vol. 3:** 786
68:25*	**Vol. 2:** 87 **Vol. 3:** 1071
68:28 f*	**Vol. 3:** 783
68:28*	**Vol. 2:** 602 **Vol. 3:** 350
68:29*	**Vol. 3:** 786
68:30*	**Vol. 2:** 41 **Vol. 3:** 808
68:31 f*	**Vol. 2:** 294
68:32*	**Vol. 2:** 41 **Vol. 3:** 673
68:36*	**Vol. 2:** 258, 622–623, 625
69:1*	**Vol. 3:** 207
69:2 f*	**Vol. 3:** 986
69:2*	**Vol. 2:** 197 **Vol. 3:** 695
69:4–7	**Vol. 3:** 562–563
69:4	**Vol. 1:** 555 **Vol. 2:** 41
69:5*	**Vol. 2:** 215, 449 **Vol. 3:** 1024
69:6*	**Vol. 2:** 773, 797
69:8*	**Vol. 3:** 1069
69:9*	**Vol. 2:** 816, 828, 835 **Vol. 3:** 430, 770, 1013, 1166
69:10	**Vol. 1:** 612
69:12*	**Vol. 3:** 671
69:13*	**Vol. 2:** 863 **Vol. 3:** 879
69:14*	**Vol. 1:** 555 **Vol. 2:** 197 **Vol. 3:** 201, 207
69:15 f*	**Vol. 3:** 986
69:15	**Vol. 3:** 695
69:16*	**Vol. 2:** 595
69:18*	**Vol. 3:** 192
69:19 f	**Vol. 3:** 562–563
69:20*	**Vol. 2:** 773
69:21*	**Vol. 2:** 27–28, 267
69:22*	**Vol. 2:** 708
69:23	**Vol. 1:** 424
69:26	**Vol. 3:** 1008
69:27*	**Vol. 3:** 357
69:28 f*	**Vol. 2:** 824
69:28*	**Vol. 3:** 355
69:29*	**Vol. 2:** 823
69:30*	**Vol. 3:** 816
69:32 f*	**Vol. 2:** 824
69:34*	**Vol. 3:** 816
69:35	**Vol. 2:** 326
70*	**Vol. 3:** 233, 239
70:2	**Vol. 3:** 563
70:4	**Vol. 3:** 233
70:15–17*	**Vol. 3:** 233
70:16b*	**Vol. 3:** 233
71	**Vol. 2:** 261
71:2*	**Vol. 3:** 202, 207, 355
71:4*	**Vol. 3:** 201
71:5*	**Vol. 2:** 239, 773
71:6*	**Vol. 3:** 1071
71:7*	**Vol. 2:** 633 **Vol. 3:** 669, 716
71:8*	**Vol. 3:** 669
71:9	**Vol. 3:** 835
71:16*	**Vol. 2:** 211, 724
71:17*†	**Vol. 2:** 622 **Vol. 3:** 45, 760
71:18	**Vol. 1:** 193
71:20*	**Vol. 2:** 163, 205, 807 **Vol. 3:** 569
71:22	**Vol. 3:** 880
71:23*	**Vol. 3:** 192
71:24	**Vol. 3:** 357, 563
72	**Vol. 1:** 426 **Vol. 2:** 257 **Vol. 3:** 357
72:1 f	**Vol. 2:** 363
72:2	**Vol. 2:** 823 **Vol. 3:** 192
72:4*	**Vol. 2:** 820, 823 **Vol. 3:** 192, 206–207
72:5*	**Vol. 1:** 262 **Vol. 3:** 733
72:6*	**Vol. 3:** 461
72:7*	**Vol. 1:** 732 **Vol. 3:** 733
72:8*	**Vol. 1:** 519 **Vol. 2:** 888 **Vol. 3:** 985
72:10 f*	**Vol. 2:** 294, 888
72:10	**Vol. 2:** 41
72:11*	**Vol. 2:** 876
72:12 ff	**Vol. 2:** 823
72:12	**Vol. 2:** 820 **Vol. 3:** 192
72:13*	**Vol. 2:** 820, 822 **Vol. 3:** 192, 206
72:14*	**Vol. 3:** 158, 192–193
72:15*	**Vol. 2:** 96, 862
72:17*	**Vol. 3:** 224
72:18 f*	**Vol. 2:** 627
72:18*	**Vol. 1:** 210 **Vol. 2:** 596, 724 **Vol. 3:** 1024, 1153
72:19	**Vol. 1:** 98, 735
72:20*	**Vol. 3:** 669
72:22*	**Vol. 3:** 1024
73	**Vol. 1:** 211 **Vol. 2:** 479, 841 **Vol. 3:** 565, 938
73:1	**Vol. 3:** 659
73:2*	**Vol. 2:** 428

Psalms *(cont'd)*

73:3*	**Vol. 2:** 777–778
73:6*	**Vol. 3:** 29
73:11*	**Vol. 1:** 240
73:12*	**Vol. 2:** 842
73:13*	**Vol. 3:** 355, 358, 990
73:17	**Vol. 2:** 61
73:20*	**Vol. 1:** 512 **Vol. 2:** 287
73:21	**Vol. 2:** 167
73:23 ff*	**Vol. 1:** 433 **Vol. 2:** 207 **Vol. 3:** 727
73:23*	**Vol. 1:** 562
73:24*	**Vol. 2:** 191 **Vol. 3:** 262, 748, 1016
73:25 f	**Vol. 2:** 297
73:25	**Vol. 1:** 636
73:26*	**Vol. 1:** 673 **Vol. 2:** 181, 303, 479
74	**Vol. 2:** 416, 823
74:1*	**Vol. 1:** 164 **Vol. 2:** 412 **Vol. 3:** 565
74:2*	**Vol. 2:** 297 **Vol. 3:** 192, 234–235
74:3*	**Vol. 3:** 29, 786
74:8*	**Vol. 3:** 255
74:9	**Vol. 3:** 80
74:12*†	**Vol. 2:** 830 **Vol. 3:** 207
74:13 f*	**Vol. 1:** 508 **Vol. 3:** 983
74:14	**Vol. 1:** 523
74:15*	**Vol. 3:** 986, 988
74:16*	**Vol. 3:** 350
74:18*	**Vol. 1:** 381 **Vol. 3:** 234–235, 1025
74:21*	**Vol. 2:** 260 **Vol. 3:** 816
74:22*	**Vol. 3:** 93, 234–235, 1025
75	**Vol. 2:** 261
75:1	**Vol. 3:** 659
75:4*	**Vol. 2:** 202
75:5*	**Vol. 2:** 202
75:6	**Vol. 1:** 572
75:7*	**Vol. 2:** 202, 262
75:8*	**Vol. 2:** 275 **Vol. 3:** 919, 922
75:9	**Vol. 2:** 276
76*	**Vol. 3:** 669, 783
76:3	**Vol. 2:** 458, 592
76:5*	**Vol. 2:** 842
76:9*	**Vol. 3:** 207
77	**Vol. 3:** 236
77:1–11	**Vol. 2:** 863
77:2–11	**Vol. 3:** 236
77:3	**Vol. 2:** 889
77:4*	**Vol. 3:** 236
77:5*	**Vol. 3:** 820
77:9*	**Vol. 2:** 733
77:12 ff	**Vol. 3:** 236
77:13*	**Vol. 2:** 425
77:14*	**Vol. 2:** 724
77:15*	**Vol. 3:** 192
77:17*	**Vol. 3:** 983
77:18	**Vol. 3:** 1001
77:20*	**Vol. 1:** 683 **Vol. 2:** 412, 639 **Vol. 3:** 565, 937
77:22*	**Vol. 3:** 1212
77:32*	**Vol. 3:** 1212
77:37*	**Vol. 2:** 302
77:61 f*	**Vol. 3:** 590
77:62*	**Vol. 3:** 1187
78*	**Vol. 2:** 627 **Vol. 3:** 451, 578
78:2	**Vol. 1:** 377–378 **Vol. 2:** 217, 753
78:8*	**Vol. 3:** 691
78:9*	**Vol. 2:** 889
78:10*	**Vol. 2:** 134, 440 **Vol. 3:** 1016
78:11*	**Vol. 3:** 569
78:12*	**Vol. 1:** 240, 531
78:15 f*	**Vol. 3:** 382, 988
78:15*	**Vol. 3:** 1005
78:16*	**Vol. 3:** 986, 988
78:17*	**Vol. 3:** 1005
78:18 ff	**Vol. 3:** 804
78:18*	**Vol. 2:** 268, 856 **Vol. 3:** 799, 802
78:19 f*	**Vol. 3:** 117
78:19*	**Vol. 3:** 345, 1005
78:20*	**Vol. 1:** 673 **Vol. 3:** 117
78:21	**Vol. 1:** 109
78:24 f	**Vol. 1:** 252 **Vol. 2:** 871
78:26 ff	**Vol. 3:** 804
78:27	**Vol. 1:** 172, 673
78:30	**Vol. 2:** 268
78:35*	**Vol. 3:** 193
78:38*	**Vol. 1:** 109, 679, 698–699 **Vol. 3:** 153–154, 156
78:39*	**Vol. 1:** 673, 679 **Vol. 2:** 565 **Vol. 3:** 690
78:40 f*	**Vol. 3:** 800
78:40*	**Vol. 3:** 1005
78:41*	**Vol. 3:** 799
78:42*	**Vol. 2:** 889 **Vol. 3:** 192–193
78:43*	**Vol. 1:** 531 **Vol. 2:** 627
78:44*	**Vol. 3:** 986
78:49	**Vol. 1:** 101
78:51*	**Vol. 1:** 531 **Vol. 3:** 415
78:52 f	**Vol. 2:** 104, 412 **Vol. 3:** 565
78:52*	**Vol. 2:** 412 **Vol. 3:** 1005
78:56*	**Vol. 3:** 799
78:60	**Vol. 3:** 426
78:63*	**Vol. 2:** 422
78:67–72	**Vol. 3:** 461
78:71 f	**Vol. 3:** 565
79	**Vol. 2:** 416
79:1	**Vol. 2:** 296 **Vol. 3:** 786
79:2	**Vol. 2:** 237
79:5*	**Vol. 2:** 509
79:6	**Vol. 2:** 650, 854
79:8*	**Vol. 3:** 156, 234
79:9*	**Vol. 1:** 698–699 **Vol. 3:** 154, 161, 201–202, 218
79:10	**Vol. 3:** 93
79:13	**Vol. 3:** 565
79:14*	**Vol. 1:** 117, 520
79:15*	**Vol. 3:** 950
79:19*	**Vol. 3:** 202
80	**Vol. 2:** 416 **Vol. 3:** 233
80:1	**Vol. 1:** 280 **Vol. 2:** 412 **Vol. 3:** 565
80:2*	**Vol. 1:** 320 **Vol. 2:** 735
80:3*	**Vol. 3:** 318

Psalms *(cont'd)*

80:4*   **Vol. 2:** 863
80:5*   **Vol. 3:** 402
80:6   **Vol. 2:** 431
80:7*   **Vol. 3:** 318
80:8 ff*   **Vol. 2:** 248
80:8–19   **Vol. 2:** 747
80:8–15*   **Vol. 3:** 614
80:8–13*   **Vol. 3:** 918
80:8 f*   **Vol. 2:** 313   **Vol. 3:** 866
80:8   **Vol. 1:** 531
80:10 f*   **Vol. 3:** 867
80:14*   **Vol. 1:** 189
80:15*   **Vol. 3:** 350
80:17 f   **Vol. 3:** 614
80:19*   **Vol. 3:** 318
81:7*   **Vol. 2:** 215   **Vol. 3:** 808
81:9*   **Vol. 2:** 876
81:10   **Vol. 2:** 726
81:16*   **Vol. 1:** 743   **Vol. 3:** 382, 836
82   **Vol. 3:** 187–188
82:1 ff   **Vol. 3:** 629
82:1*   **Vol. 1:** 503   **Vol. 2:** 190, 591
82:2   **Vol. 2:** 591   **Vol. 3:** 187
82:3*   **Vol. 2:** 260, 820, 822   **Vol. 3:** 187, 355
82:4*   **Vol. 3:** 187, 201
82:5 ff*   **Vol. 2:** 260
82:5   **Vol. 3:** 187
82:6*   **Vol. 2:** 231, 448   **Vol. 3:** 186, 629, 636
82:8*   **Vol. 2:** 260
83:14*   **Vol. 3:** 1010
83:16–18   **Vol. 3:** 563
83:16   **Vol. 3:** 531
83:17   **Vol. 3:** 563
83:18*   **Vol. 2:** 724
83:24*   **Vol. 3:** 265
84:2*   **Vol. 2:** 181, 212
84:3*   **Vol. 1:** 173–174
84:4*   **Vol. 2:** 247   **Vol. 3:** 816
84:5   **Vol. 2:** 478
84:8*   **Vol. 2:** 863
84:9   **Vol. 2:** 336
84:10*   **Vol. 1:** 537   **Vol. 2:** 247, 698, 887   **Vol. 3:** 811
84:11*   **Vol. 2:** 99, 777   **Vol. 3:** 731
84:12*   **Vol. 1:** 216
85   **Vol. 3:** 356
85:2   **Vol. 1:** 698   **Vol. 2:** 212
85:3*   **Vol. 3:** 255
85:7*   **Vol. 3:** 207, 569
85:8*   **Vol. 2:** 237, 778
85:10   **Vol. 2:** 777   **Vol. 3:** 879
85:11*   **Vol. 3:** 938
85:12   **Vol. 1:** 598
85:13*   **Vol. 2:** 209
86*   **Vol. 2:** 863
86:1*   **Vol. 2:** 175, 820, 822–823
86:2*   **Vol. 2:** 336   **Vol. 3:** 595
86:4*   **Vol. 2:** 336   **Vol. 3:** 595, 680

86:5   **Vol. 2:** 257
86:6*   **Vol. 2:** 860, 863
86:7   **Vol. 2:** 890
86:9*   **Vol. 2:** 876
86:10*   **Vol. 2:** 622, 627, 724
86:11*   **Vol. 3:** 938
86:12 f*   **Vol. 3:** 262
86:13*   **Vol. 3:** 201–202
86:14*   **Vol. 1:** 696
86:15   **Vol. 2:** 769
86:16*   **Vol. 2:** 336   **Vol. 3:** 207, 595, 716
87:3   **Vol. 2:** 803
87:6*   **Vol. 2:** 209
88   **Vol. 2:** 167   **Vol. 3:** 262
88:2*   **Vol. 2:** 860, 863
88:3*   **Vol. 1:** 320   **Vol. 3:** 595
88:4 f   **Vol. 1:** 444
88:5*   **Vol. 1:** 433   **Vol. 2:** 206   **Vol. 3:** 262
88:6*   **Vol. 1:** 295, 422   **Vol. 3:** 555
88:7 f*   **Vol. 3:** 997
88:9*   **Vol. 3:** 559, 994
88:10 f*   **Vol. 3:** 262
88:10   **Vol. 1:** 444
88:11*   **Vol. 2:** 206   **Vol. 3:** 30
88:12   **Vol. 1:** 464
88:13*   **Vol. 2:** 863
88:14*   **Vol. 2:** 863
88:15 ff* **Vol. 3:** 997
88:48*   **Vol. 1:** 710–711
88:51 f*   **Vol. 2:** 835
89   **Vol. 3:** 356, 649–650
89:1*   **Vol. 3:** 673
89:2*   **Vol. 2:** 190   **Vol. 3:** 117
89:3 ff*   **Vol. 3:** 636
89:3*   **Vol. 3:** 594
89:4*   **Vol. 3:** 117, 522, 648
89:5–7   **Vol. 2:** 376
89:5*   **Vol. 1:** 101
89:6   **Vol. 1:** 293
89:7 ff   **Vol. 2:** 613
89:7*   **Vol. 1:** 101   **Vol. 2:** 498   **Vol. 3:** 636
89:9 f*   **Vol. 3:** 960
89:9*   **Vol. 3:** 153, 716
89:10   **Vol. 1:** 523   **Vol. 3:** 30
89:11*   **Vol. 3:** 29
89:12*   **Vol. 1:** 379   **Vol. 2:** 353
89:13*   **Vol. 2:** 201
89:14*   **Vol. 3:** 117
89:15   **Vol. 2:** 491
89:16 f   **Vol. 1:** 227
89:16*   **Vol. 2:** 201   **Vol. 3:** 355
89:17*   **Vol. 2:** 818
89:20*   **Vol. 2:** 227, 711
89:21*   **Vol. 2:** 149
89:24   **Vol. 2:** 650
89:26 f   **Vol. 2:** 336
89:26   **Vol. 1:** 617
89:27 ff   **Vol. 1:** 667
89:27 f*   **Vol. 3:** 636
89:27*   **Vol. 1:** 168   **Vol. 2:** 378

Psalms *(cont'd)*

89:29*	**Vol. 2:** 189
89:31*	**Vol. 3:** 354
89:36*	**Vol. 3:** 730, 1068
89:37*	**Vol. 1:** 99 **Vol. 3:** 350, 1041
89:38–45	**Vol. 2:** 644
89:38	**Vol. 1:** 99 **Vol. 2:** 336
89:39	**Vol. 1:** 405 **Vol. 2:** 336
89:47	**Vol. 1:** 379
89:48*	**Vol. 3:** 201, 235, 513
89:49*	**Vol. 3:** 209
89:50 f	**Vol. 2:** 835
89:51*	**Vol. 2:** 336 **Vol. 3:** 235
89:52*	**Vol. 1:** 98, 210
89:57*	**Vol. 3:** 166–167
90*	**Vol. 1:** 433 **Vol. 2:** 639, 863
90:1*	**Vol. 2:** 69, 71 **Vol. 3:** 841
90:2*	**Vol. 3:** 1010
90:3*	**Vol. 2:** 260, 263
90:4*	**Vol. 2:** 697–699, 701, 887
90:5	**Vol. 1:** 512
90:10	**Vol. 2:** 690
90:12*	**Vol. 3:** 1027
90:16*	**Vol. 3:** 1148
90:17*	**Vol. 2:** 485 **Vol. 3:** 1148
91	**Vol. 1:** 210 **Vol. 2:** 893
91:1 f	**Vol. 3:** 729
91:1	**Vol. 3:** 554
91:3*	**Vol. 3:** 201
91:4	**Vol. 1:** 174 **Vol. 3:** 797, 805
91:5	**Vol. 1:** 420 **Vol. 3:** 268
91:6	**Vol. 3:** 268
91:9	**Vol. 3:** 729
91:11 f*	**Vol. 2:** 705–706 **Vol. 3:** 790, 805
91:11*	**Vol. 1:** 332, 335
91:13	**Vol. 1:** 510 **Vol. 3:** 806
91:16*	**Vol. 1:** 433 **Vol. 3:** 207, 569
92	**Vol. 2:** 261, 263 **Vol. 3:** 407
92:2*	**Vol. 3:** 45
92:3*	**Vol. 3:** 673
92:4	**Vol. 2:** 353
92:5*	**Vol. 3:** 820
92:6*	**Vol. 3:** 1024
92:10	**Vol. 2:** 711
92:13*	**Vol. 2:** 247
93	**Vol. 2:** 613
93:1–4*	**Vol. 3:** 960
93:1	**Vol. 2:** 375
93:2*	**Vol. 3:** 117
93:4*	**Vol. 2:** 199
93:5*	**Vol. 2:** 669
93:21*	**Vol. 2:** 370
94:1*	**Vol. 2:** 735
94:2*	**Vol. 3:** 29
94:4	**Vol. 1:** 227
94:6	**Vol. 3:** 1074
94:8*†	**Vol. 3:** 1024–1025
94:9	**Vol. 2:** 175
94:10*†	**Vol. 3:** 760
94:11*	**Vol. 1:** 551 **Vol. 2:** 513 **Vol. 3:** 820
94:12*†	**Vol. 3:** 760
94:13*	**Vol. 2:** 890
94:14	**Vol. 2:** 799
94:20	**Vol. 1:** 262
94:22	**Vol. 2:** 71
95:1*	**Vol. 3:** 218
95:3 ff	**Vol. 2:** 375
95:3 f	**Vol. 2:** 898
95:4*	**Vol. 2:** 199 **Vol. 3:** 1010
95:6*	**Vol. 1:** 609 **Vol. 2:** 859, 876
95:7 f	**Vol. 1:** 372 **Vol. 3:** 227, 434
95:7–11*	**Vol. 1:** 203 **Vol. 2:** 775 **Vol. 3:** 937, 1005
95:7*	**Vol. 2:** 412, 891–892 **Vol. 3:** 565
95:8 ff*	**Vol. 2:** 627
95:8 f*	**Vol. 3:** 802
95:8*	**Vol. 1:** 203 **Vol. 2:** 155, 178, 889 **Vol. 3:** 799–800, 1005
95:9*	**Vol. 3:** 799, 808, 1148
95:10*	**Vol. 2:** 395, 459–460, 696
95:11*†	**Vol. 3:** 73, 256–257
96–99	**Vol. 2:** 613
96	**Vol. 2:** 109 **Vol. 3:** 671
96:1 ff	**Vol. 2:** 888
96:1*	**Vol. 3:** 673
96:2 ff	**Vol. 2:** 109
96:3–9	**Vol. 2:** 45
96:3	**Vol. 2:** 45
96:5	**Vol. 1:** 451
96:8	**Vol. 3:** 421
96:9 f	**Vol. 2:** 888
96:9*	**Vol. 2:** 876
96:10	**Vol. 2:** 375
96:11 ff	**Vol. 2:** 353
96:11	**Vol. 1:** 734 **Vol. 2:** 353, 355
96:13*	**Vol. 1:** 320, 519 **Vol. 3:** 865
97	**Vol. 3:** 356
97:1	**Vol. 2:** 355, 375
97:2 f	**Vol. 2:** 917
97:2	**Vol. 2:** 613 **Vol. 3:** 1001
97:4	**Vol. 2:** 836
97:7*	**Vol. 2:** 876
97:8	**Vol. 2:** 353
97:9*	**Vol. 2:** 201
97:10*	**Vol. 2:** 596 **Vol. 3:** 201
97:12*	**Vol. 3:** 233, 237–238
98:1*	**Vol. 3:** 673, 960
98:2 f*	**Vol. 3:** 311
98:3*	**Vol. 2:** 596 **Vol. 3:** 235
98:4*	**Vol. 3:** 673
98:7	**Vol. 1:** 519, 734
98:8*	**Vol. 3:** 986
98:9	**Vol. 1:** 320, 519
99:1	**Vol. 1:** 280 **Vol. 2:** 375, 613
99:2	**Vol. 2:** 326, 375
99:3	**Vol. 2:** 225
99:4	**Vol. 3:** 357
99:5*	**Vol. 2:** 201, 876
99:6	**Vol. 2:** 639

Psalms *(cont'd)*

99:8	**Vol. 3:** 93
99:9*	**Vol. 2:** 201, 876
100	**Vol. 3:** 423
100:2	**Vol. 1:** 320
100:3	**Vol. 2:** 412 **Vol. 3:** 565
100:4*	**Vol. 1:** 320, 344 **Vol. 3:** 669, 816
101:1*	**Vol. 3:** 673
101:2*	**Vol. 3:** 924
101:3*	**Vol. 1:** 696 **Vol. 2:** 349 **Vol. 3:** 583–584
101:5*	**Vol. 3:** 29, 345–346
101:6*	**Vol. 3:** 514, 924
101:7*	**Vol. 2:** 137 **Vol. 3:** 29
102*	**Vol. 2:** 257, 863
102:1*	**Vol. 2:** 863
102:2	**Vol. 1:** 320
102:3 f	**Vol. 2:** 890
102:3*	**Vol. 2:** 890
102:4*	**Vol. 1:** 743 **Vol. 2:** 211, 272 **Vol. 3:** 836
102:6 f	**Vol. 1:** 173
102:8*	**Vol. 3:** 816
102:9 f	**Vol. 2:** 272
102:11	**Vol. 1:** 743 **Vol. 2:** 211
102:12*	**Vol. 3:** 224
102:13*	**Vol. 3:** 237
102:14	**Vol. 1:** 520
102:15–20*	**Vol. 2:** 261
102:15 f	**Vol. 2:** 888
102:15*	**Vol. 2:** 817
102:17*	**Vol. 2:** 261, 863
102:18*	**Vol. 1:** 379 **Vol. 3:** 816
102:19*	**Vol. 2:** 225
102:20*	**Vol. 2:** 199 **Vol. 3:** 177
102:21 f	**Vol. 2:** 888
102:21*	**Vol. 2:** 602
102:25*	**Vol. 1:** 317
102:26*	**Vol. 2:** 714
102:27 f	**Vol. 2:** 69
103:1*	**Vol. 3:** 262
103:3 ff*	**Vol. 3:** 262
103:3*	**Vol. 2:** 167–168, 610 **Vol. 3:** 943, 997
103:4*	**Vol. 1:** 468 **Vol. 3:** 192–193
103:5*	**Vol. 1:** 173, 663
103:6 ff	**Vol. 2:** 364
103:6–13	**Vol. 1:** 109
103:6*	**Vol. 3:** 355, 357
103:7*	**Vol. 2:** 639 **Vol. 3:** 235, 1019
103:8 ff*	**Vol. 3:** 167
103:8*	**Vol. 2:** 71, 598, 769
103:11	**Vol. 1:** 622
103:13	**Vol. 1:** 617, 622 **Vol. 2:** 596
103:14 ff	**Vol. 1:** 551
103:14*	**Vol. 3:** 235
103:15	**Vol. 1:** 743
103:17 f	**Vol. 1:** 367
103:17	**Vol. 1:** 622 **Vol. 2:** 596
103:18*	**Vol. 1:** 332
103:19*	**Vol. 1:** 522 **Vol. 2:** 376 **Vol. 3:** 117
103:21*	**Vol. 3:** 1019
104–106	**Vol. 1:** 99
104	**Vol. 1:** 99, 383
104:2*	**Vol. 2:** 189, 491 **Vol. 3:** 1068
104:3 f	**Vol. 3:** 1001
104:3*	**Vol. 1:** 523 **Vol. 2:** 189–190, 917 **Vol. 3:** 984
104:4*	**Vol. 1:** 655 **Vol. 3:** 553, 690
104:5	**Vol. 1:** 523
104:6*	**Vol. 3:** 983
104:7*	**Vol. 3:** 113, 983, 1001
104:10 f*	**Vol. 3:** 865, 986
104:11*	**Vol. 3:** 109
104:12*	**Vol. 3:** 113, 813
104:13	**Vol. 1:** 743
104:14 f	**Vol. 2:** 357
104:15*	**Vol. 2:** 711 **Vol. 3:** 919
104:18*	**Vol. 3:** 381
104:19	**Vol. 3:** 835
104:20	**Vol. 1:** 422
104:21*	**Vol. 3:** 601
104:24 ff*	**Vol. 3:** 983
104:24*	**Vol. 1:** 381 **Vol. 3:** 1027
104:27 f	**Vol. 3:** 804
104:29 f	**Vol. 2:** 478
104:29*	**Vol. 1:** 84, 585, 670 **Vol. 3:** 690
104:30*	**Vol. 1:** 84, 379
104:32*	**Vol. 3:** 1010
104:33*	**Vol. 3:** 673
105	**Vol. 1:** 99 **Vol. 2:** 863
105:1–15	**Vol. 3:** 671
105:1–6	**Vol. 1:** 345
105:1–3	**Vol. 2:** 650
105:2*	**Vol. 1:** 574 **Vol. 3:** 673
105:3 f	**Vol. 3:** 531
105:3*	**Vol. 3:** 816
105:4*	**Vol. 1:** 586 **Vol. 3:** 716
105:6*	**Vol. 1:** 77 **Vol. 3:** 867
105:8*	**Vol. 2:** 596 **Vol. 3:** 235, 241
105:9	**Vol. 1:** 572
105:12	**Vol. 3:** 1212
105:15	**Vol. 2:** 835
105:16*	**Vol. 1:** 273
105:20*	**Vol. 3:** 177
105:21*	**Vol. 1:** 381, 472 **Vol. 3:** 1030
105:22*	**Vol. 3:** 1028, 1033
105:26	**Vol. 2:** 639
105:27*	**Vol. 2:** 627
105:28	**Vol. 1:** 422 **Vol. 2:** 60
105:33	**Vol. 3:** 865
105:36*	**Vol. 3:** 415
105:38*	**Vol. 3:** 937
105:40*	**Vol. 1:** 173 **Vol. 2:** 856
105:41*†	**Vol. 1:** 683 **Vol. 3:** 986
105:42*	**Vol. 3:** 235, 594
105:43	**Vol. 1:** 538
105:45*	**Vol. 3:** 354
106	**Vol. 1:** 99 **Vol. 2:** 863
106:3*	**Vol. 3:** 836

Psalms *(cont'd)*

106:4*	**Vol. 3:** 234
106:5*	**Vol. 1:** 189 **Vol. 3:** 816
106:6	**Vol. 1:** 409
106:7–12*	**Vol. 3:** 1005
106:7*	**Vol. 1:** 203, 531, 617 **Vol. 3:** 241
106:10*	**Vol. 2:** 596 **Vol. 3:** 192
106:12*	**Vol. 3:** 673, 816
106:13–33*	**Vol. 3:** 1005
106:13*	**Vol. 2:** 773
106:14*	**Vol. 3:** 799–800
106:16	**Vol. 2:** 231, 639
106:19*	**Vol. 2:** 876
106:21*	**Vol. 1:** 531 **Vol. 2:** 425
106:22*	**Vol. 2:** 622 **Vol. 3:** 318
106:23	**Vol. 2:** 639
106:26*	**Vol. 2:** 205
106:30*	**Vol. 3:** 152, 155
106:31*	**Vol. 3:** 357, 823
106:32	**Vol. 2:** 639
106:36*	**Vol. 2:** 707
106:37 f	**Vol. 3:** 806
106:37	**Vol. 1:** 451
106:38	**Vol. 2:** 525
106:44*	**Vol. 2:** 860 **Vol. 3:** 513
106:45*	**Vol. 1:** 356 **Vol. 2:** 596 **Vol. 3:** 235, 241
106:47*	**Vol. 1:** 344–345 **Vol. 3:** 207
106:48	**Vol. 1:** 98, 210 **Vol. 2:** 596
107*	**Vol. 2:** 261
107:1	**Vol. 1:** 345
107:2*	**Vol. 3:** 192
107:5	**Vol. 2:** 265
107:6*	**Vol. 2:** 663
107:8	**Vol. 1:** 345
107:9	**Vol. 1:** 743 **Vol. 2:** 266, 596
107:10 f	**Vol. 1:** 422
107:10	**Vol. 3:** 555
107:11*	**Vol. 1:** 345 **Vol. 3:** 1118
107:12*	**Vol. 3:** 994
107:13*	**Vol. 2:** 663
107:14	**Vol. 3:** 555, 592
107:15	**Vol. 1:** 345
107:17 ff*	**Vol. 3:** 997
107:17	**Vol. 1:** 345
107:18	**Vol. 2:** 29
107:19*	**Vol. 2:** 663
107:20*	**Vol. 3:** 209
107:21	**Vol. 1:** 345
107:22	**Vol. 3:** 423
107:27*	**Vol. 3:** 1027
107:28*	**Vol. 2:** 663
107:30*	**Vol. 3:** 1019
107:31	**Vol. 1:** 345
107:32*	**Vol. 2:** 201 **Vol. 3:** 816
107:33*	**Vol. 3:** 986–987
107:35*	**Vol. 3:** 992
107:36 ff	**Vol. 2:** 265
107:43*	**Vol. 3:** 1027
108:1*	**Vol. 3:** 117, 673
108:4	**Vol. 3:** 879
108:5*	**Vol. 2:** 201
108:6*	**Vol. 3:** 207
108:7*	**Vol. 2:** 370 **Vol. 3:** 786
108:10	**Vol. 2:** 742
108:14*	**Vol. 1:** 471
109:4*	**Vol. 2:** 863 **Vol. 3:** 40
109:6*	**Vol. 3:** 468
109:7*	**Vol. 2:** 863
109:8*	**Vol. 2:** 428 **Vol. 3:** 152, 747
109:9	**Vol. 2:** 737
109:10	**Vol. 2:** 737
109:14*	**Vol. 3:** 232, 240, 242
109:15*	**Vol. 3:** 237
109:18	**Vol. 2:** 711
109:19*	**Vol. 3:** 120
109:22	**Vol. 2:** 823
109:23	**Vol. 3:** 560
109:24*	**Vol. 1:** 612 **Vol. 3:** 994
109:26*	**Vol. 3:** 207
109:30*	**Vol. 3:** 816
109:31	**Vol. 1:** 474 **Vol. 2:** 820
110–118	**Vol. 1:** 99
110	**Vol. 1:** 99, 178, 426–427 **Vol. 2:** 336, 590, 644 **Vol. 3:** 41, 297
110:1 ff	**Vol. 3:** 643
110:1 f	**Vol. 1:** 554 **Vol. 3:** 648
110:1*	**Vol. 1:** 239, 477 **Vol. 2:** 80, 146–147, 194, 196, 199, 245, 374, 515, 614, 665 **Vol. 3:** 588, 614, 629, 638, 644, 651, 792
110:2	**Vol. 3:** 636
110:3*	**Vol. 1:** 177 **Vol. 2:** 495 **Vol. 3:** 269, 565
110:4*	**Vol. 1:** 356 **Vol. 2:** 448, 590–591 **Vol. 3:** 36, 41, 588, 742, 830
110:6	**Vol. 1:** 610
111:1	**Vol. 2:** 863
111:2	**Vol. 3:** 242
111:3*	**Vol. 3:** 224
111:4*	**Vol. 2:** 598, 771 **Vol. 3:** 237–238
111:5*	**Vol. 3:** 235
111:7*	**Vol. 1:** 332
111:8	**Vol. 3:** 882
111:9*	**Vol. 3:** 193
111:10*	**Vol. 1:** 165 **Vol. 3:** 130, 224, 1027–1028
112:3*	**Vol. 2:** 841 **Vol. 3:** 224
112:4	**Vol. 1:** 422 **Vol. 2:** 492, 834
112:6*	**Vol. 3:** 237
112:7*	**Vol. 3:** 117
112:9*	**Vol. 2:** 34, 821, 827 **Vol. 3:** 224
112:10	**Vol. 2:** 421
113:1*	**Vol. 2:** 740, 822 **Vol. 3:** 816
113:3*	**Vol. 3:** 816
113:5 ff	**Vol. 2:** 596
113:5–9*	**Vol. 2:** 261
113:5 f	**Vol. 2:** 190
113:9*	**Vol. 3:** 1055

Psalms *(cont'd)*

114–118	**Vol. 3:** 669
114:3*	**Vol. 1:** 419
114:8*	**Vol. 3:** 986, 992
115–118	**Vol. 2:** 522, 528
115	**Vol. 2:** 175
115:1	**Vol. 3:** 879
115:12–15	**Vol. 1:** 210
115:13*	**Vol. 2:** 428
115:15–17	**Vol. 2:** 189
115:15*	**Vol. 3:** 113
115:17*	**Vol. 1:** 444 **Vol. 2:** 206 **Vol. 3:** 816
116:1*	**Vol. 2:** 261, 472, 860
116:3*	**Vol. 1:** 433 **Vol. 3:** 180
116:6*	**Vol. 1:** 281 **Vol. 3:** 209
116:7*	**Vol. 3:** 255
116:8*	**Vol. 1:** 433 **Vol. 2:** 478 **Vol. 3:** 262
116:9*	**Vol. 2:** 815
116:10*	**Vol. 2:** 261
116:11	**Vol. 2:** 471
116:12–19	**Vol. 3:** 436
116:13*	**Vol. 2:** 275 **Vol. 3:** 208
116:15	**Vol. 3:** 158, 436
116:16	**Vol. 3:** 592
116:17	**Vol. 3:** 423
117:1*	**Vol. 2:** 513, 799 **Vol. 3:** 816–817
117:2*	**Vol. 3:** 224, 880
117:7*	**Vol. 1:** 597
117:8*	**Vol. 1:** 589
118*	**Vol. 2:** 479 **Vol. 3:** 669, 1040
118:1–4*	**Vol. 1:** 345 **Vol. 3:** 388
118:1	**Vol. 2:** 100
118:5 ff*	**Vol. 3:** 388
118:5–21*	**Vol. 3:** 388
118:7*	**Vol. 3:** 262
118:10 ff	**Vol. 2:** 650
118:10–21*	**Vol. 3:** 388
118:12*	**Vol. 3:** 109
118:14*	**Vol. 3:** 669
118:15 f	**Vol. 2:** 149
118:15	**Vol. 2:** 146
118:19 f*	**Vol. 3:** 388
118:20	**Vol. 2:** 31, 706
118:21	**Vol. 1:** 345
118:22 ff	**Vol. 2:** 313 **Vol. 3:** 809
118:22 f*	**Vol. 2:** 253 **Vol. 3:** 384
118:22*	**Vol. 1:** 74, 541 **Vol. 2:** 129, 159, 706 **Vol. 3:** 329, 382, 388–391, 393, 624
118:23*	**Vol. 2:** 622–623
118:24*	**Vol. 3:** 1068, 1153
118:25 f	**Vol. 1:** 323
118:25*	**Vol. 1:** 100 **Vol. 3:** 207
118:26 f*	**Vol. 3:** 388
118:26	**Vol. 1:** 100, 174, 213, 321 **Vol. 2:** 328, 379
118:27*	**Vol. 3:** 318, 418–419, 715
118:28 f*	**Vol. 3:** 388
118:28*	**Vol. 2:** 201
118:88*	**Vol. 3:** 1040
118:119*	**Vol. 3:** 1040
118:129*	**Vol. 3:** 1040
118:146*	**Vol. 3:** 1040
118:167 f*	**Vol. 3:** 1040
119*	**Vol. 2:** 261, 355, 439 **Vol. 3:** 938
119:1*	**Vol. 1:** 216 **Vol. 2:** 440 **Vol. 3:** 924, 946
119:5*	**Vol. 3:** 354
119:7 f*	**Vol. 1:** 484
119:8*	**Vol. 3:** 354
119:11	**Vol. 2:** 215
119:12*	**Vol. 1:** 210 **Vol. 3:** 354, 760
119:14*	**Vol. 2:** 355, 842
119:16*	**Vol. 3:** 354
119:17*†	**Vol. 3:** 595
119:18*	**Vol. 3:** 311
119:19	**Vol. 1:** 688, 691 **Vol. 2:** 215
119:20*	**Vol. 3:** 354
119:21*	**Vol. 3:** 29
119:23*	**Vol. 3:** 345, 354, 595
119:24*	**Vol. 3:** 354
119:26*	**Vol. 3:** 354, 760
119:27*	**Vol. 1:** 332 **Vol. 3:** 354
119:28*	**Vol. 1:** 658 **Vol. 3:** 680
119:29	**Vol. 1:** 607 **Vol. 3:** 575
119:30	**Vol. 1:** 534, 537
119:31	**Vol. 2:** 349
119:32*	**Vol. 1:** 254 **Vol. 3:** 946
119:33*	**Vol. 3:** 354
119:34*	**Vol. 2:** 440 **Vol. 3:** 131
119:36	**Vol. 1:** 137 **Vol. 3:** 137
119:38*	**Vol. 3:** 595
119:43	**Vol. 3:** 880
119:44*	**Vol. 2:** 440
119:48*	**Vol. 3:** 354
119:49*	**Vol. 3:** 234–235, 595
119:50	**Vol. 1:** 329, 569 **Vol. 2:** 263
119:51*	**Vol. 3:** 29
119:52*	**Vol. 3:** 236
119:54*	**Vol. 1:** 691 **Vol. 3:** 354
119:55*	**Vol. 3:** 236
119:56*	**Vol. 1:** 332 **Vol. 3:** 354
119:57*	**Vol. 1:** 332 **Vol. 2:** 303
119:59*	**Vol. 3:** 820
119:64*	**Vol. 3:** 354, 760
119:65*	**Vol. 3:** 595
119:66*	**Vol. 1:** 597 **Vol. 3:** 760
119:68*	**Vol. 3:** 354, 760
119:69*	**Vol. 3:** 29, 575
119:71*	**Vol. 1:** 484 **Vol. 3:** 354
119:73*	**Vol. 1:** 484 **Vol. 3:** 117, 131
119:75	**Vol. 3:** 357
119:76*	**Vol. 3:** 595
119:78*	**Vol. 3:** 29
119:79*	**Vol. 2:** 395
119:80*	**Vol. 3:** 354, 924
119:81*	**Vol. 3:** 207
119:83*	**Vol. 3:** 354
119:84*	**Vol. 3:** 595

Psalms *(cont'd)*

119:89   **Vol. 2:** 190
119:93 f*   **Vol. 3:** 354
119:93*   **Vol. 1:** 332
119:94*   **Vol. 3:** 207
119:95*   **Vol. 2:** 773
119:98*   **Vol. 3:** 1028, 1033
119:99*   **Vol. 3:** 760
119:101*   **Vol. 1:** 485   **Vol. 2:** 222
119:104   **Vol. 1:** 555   **Vol. 3:** 574–575
119:105*   **Vol. 2:** 492   **Vol. 3:** 882, 938
119:108*   **Vol. 3:** 760
119:112*   **Vol. 3:** 354
119:117 f* **Vol. 3:** 354
119:119*   **Vol. 3:** 823
119:121   **Vol. 3:** 574
119:122*   **Vol. 3:** 29, 595
119:124 f* **Vol. 3:** 595
119:124*   **Vol. 3:** 354, 760
119:125*   **Vol. 3:** 131
119:130   **Vol. 1:** 281
119:134*   **Vol. 3:** 192–193
119:135*   **Vol. 3:** 318, 354, 595, 760
119:139*   **Vol. 1:** 332
119:140*   **Vol. 3:** 595
119:141*   **Vol. 1:** 332   **Vol. 3:** 354
119:142   **Vol. 2:** 232   **Vol. 3:** 881–882, 892
119:143*   **Vol. 2:** 663   **Vol. 3:** 882
119:145*   **Vol. 3:** 354
119:154–169* **Vol. 3:** 1118
119:154*   **Vol. 3:** 192–193
119:155*   **Vol. 3:** 354
119:162   **Vol. 2:** 355
119:163   **Vol. 3:** 575
119:164*   **Vol. 3:** 816
119:165*   **Vol. 2:** 707, 778
119:169   **Vol. 2:** 53
119:170   **Vol. 1:** 320
119:171*   **Vol. 3:** 354, 669, 760
119:175*   **Vol. 3:** 816
119:176*   **Vol. 1:** 464   **Vol. 2:** 412,
            458–459   **Vol. 3:** 595
120:5   **Vol. 1:** 691
121   **Vol. 1:** 210
121:3   **Vol. 3:** 966
121:4   **Vol. 3:** 565
121:6*   **Vol. 3:** 733
121:8*   **Vol. 3:** 937
122:1   **Vol. 2:** 247
122:2*   **Vol. 3:** 595
122:5   **Vol. 2:** 612
122:6 ff*   **Vol. 2:** 778
123   **Vol. 2:** 737
123:4*   **Vol. 3:** 29
123:22*   **Vol. 2:** 511
124:4 f*   **Vol. 3:** 986
124:6   **Vol. 1:** 210
124:7   **Vol. 1:** 172
125:5*   **Vol. 2:** 778

126:1 f   **Vol. 2:** 433
126:1*   **Vol. 2:** 137
126:2*   **Vol. 2:** 353, 431   **Vol. 3:** 1079
126:4   **Vol. 3:** 560
126:5 f   **Vol. 2:** 825   **Vol. 3:** 144
126:5   **Vol. 2:** 353, 357   **Vol. 3:** 526
127:1   **Vol. 2:** 247
127:2   **Vol. 2:** 272
127:3 ff   **Vol. 1:** 288
127:3*   **Vol. 2:** 139   **Vol. 3:** 140
127:4   **Vol. 2:** 746
127:5   **Vol. 1:** 216
127:7 ff*   **Vol. 3:** 1057
128   **Vol. 1:** 210
128:3 ff   **Vol. 3:** 1057
128:3*   **Vol. 1:** 288   **Vol. 2:** 711   **Vol. 3:** 918
129:4 f*   **Vol. 3:** 355
129:8   **Vol. 1:** 210
130:1*   **Vol. 2:** 197
130:2*   **Vol. 2:** 860, 863
130:3   **Vol. 3:** 717
130:4   **Vol. 3:** 156
130:5 ff   **Vol. 2:** 772
130:5*   **Vol. 2:** 239, 773
130:7*†   **Vol. 3:** 193
130:8*   **Vol. 2:** 332, 447   **Vol. 3:** 192–193, 200
131*   **Vol. 2:** 161   **Vol. 3:** 727
131:1*   **Vol. 2:** 201
131:2*   **Vol. 2:** 201, 260–261
132   **Vol. 1:** 210
132:1*   **Vol. 3:** 235, 245
132:4*   **Vol. 3:** 255
132:5   **Vol. 2:** 319   **Vol. 3:** 465
132:7*   **Vol. 2:** 876
132:8*   **Vol. 3:** 255
132:10   **Vol. 2:** 336
132:11   **Vol. 3:** 648
132:12*   **Vol. 3:** 760, 960
132:14*   **Vol. 3:** 256
132:15   **Vol. 1:** 743   **Vol. 2:** 823
132:16*   **Vol. 1:** 314   **Vol. 3:** 207, 960
132:17   **Vol. 2:** 336, 596   **Vol. 3:** 715
132:18*   **Vol. 1:** 405, 554   **Vol. 3:** 960
134   **Vol. 1:** 99   **Vol. 3:** 673
135   **Vol. 1:** 99
135:1*   **Vol. 3:** 816
135:3*   **Vol. 3:** 816
135:4*   **Vol. 2:** 838, 840
135:7   **Vol. 2:** 189
135:9*   **Vol. 2:** 627
135:13*   **Vol. 3:** 237
135:14   **Vol. 1:** 569   **Vol. 2:** 800
135:15   **Vol. 3:** 560
135:17   **Vol. 2:** 175
135:21   **Vol. 2:** 326
136   **Vol. 1:** 523
136:4*   **Vol. 2:** 724
136:7*   **Vol. 2:** 724
136:8   **Vol. 2:** 53   **Vol. 3:** 859
136:12   **Vol. 3:** 717

Psalms *(cont'd)*

136:23*	**Vol. 2:** 261 **Vol. 3:** 235
137	**Vol. 2:** 325 **Vol. 3:** 236, 783
137:1 ff*	**Vol. 3:** 590
137:1*	**Vol. 3:** 236, 588, 986
137:3 f*	**Vol. 3:** 673
137:3*	**Vol. 3:** 668–669, 673
137:4*	**Vol. 3:** 673
137:6*	**Vol. 2:** 157, 349 **Vol. 3:** 236
137:7*	**Vol. 2:** 889 **Vol. 3:** 234
137:9	**Vol. 3:** 716
138:2*	**Vol. 2:** 876 **Vol. 3:** 783, 786
138:3*	**Vol. 1:** 695 **Vol. 2:** 889
138:5*	**Vol. 3:** 673
138:6*	**Vol. 2:** 261
138:8*	**Vol. 3:** 1148
138:15*	**Vol. 1:** 710, 712 **Vol. 2:** 209
139*	**Vol. 1:** 685
139:1*	**Vol. 3:** 808
139:2*	**Vol. 2:** 53 **Vol. 3:** 820
139:3*	**Vol. 3:** 514
139:5*	**Vol. 1:** 165
139:7–12	**Vol. 2:** 215
139:7*	**Vol. 3:** 514, 691
139:8*	**Vol. 1:** 433 **Vol. 2:** 206
139:10	**Vol. 2:** 146
139:11 f	**Vol. 1:** 422 **Vol. 2:** 491
139:13 ff	**Vol. 2:** 478
139:14*	**Vol. 3:** 680
139:15*	**Vol. 2:** 209, 215
139:16*	**Vol. 1:** 243 **Vol. 3:** 514
139:17*	**Vol. 2:** 49
139:19	**Vol. 3:** 583
139:20*	**Vol. 3:** 820
139:21 f	**Vol. 1:** 554–555
139:21	**Vol. 1:** 555
139:23*	**Vol. 3:** 808
140	**Vol. 2:** 823
140:1*	**Vol. 3:** 203
140:2*	**Vol. 3:** 823
140:3*	**Vol. 2:** 27–28 **Vol. 3:** 1079
140:4*	**Vol. 3:** 823, 1079
140:5*	**Vol. 3:** 29
140:6*	**Vol. 2:** 860
140:8	**Vol. 2:** 889
140:9*	**Vol. 3:** 820
140:10	**Vol. 2:** 157
140:12	**Vol. 3:** 93
141:2*	**Vol. 2:** 294, 863
141:3*	**Vol. 3:** 498
141:4	**Vol. 1:** 559
141:5*	**Vol. 2:** 141, 711, 818, 863
141:9*	**Vol. 2:** 707
141:10*	**Vol. 2:** 724
142*	**Vol. 2:** 863
142:2	**Vol. 2:** 854
142:5*	**Vol. 2:** 297, 303
142:6*	**Vol. 2:** 261
142:7*	**Vol. 2:** 478, 773
143:1*	**Vol. 2:** 860, 863 **Vol. 3:** 356
143:2*	**Vol. 2:** 336 **Vol. 3:** 355
143:3	**Vol. 1:** 444
143:4*	**Vol. 3:** 710
143:5*	**Vol. 3:** 236
143:6	**Vol. 2:** 266
143:10*	**Vol. 2:** 100 **Vol. 3:** 760, 1019
143:11*	**Vol. 1:** 700 **Vol. 3:** 355
143:14*	**Vol. 3:** 950
144:1*	**Vol. 3:** 760
144:3*	**Vol. 3:** 823
144:4	**Vol. 2:** 501 **Vol. 3:** 555
144:6	**Vol. 3:** 1001
144:7*	**Vol. 2:** 199
144:8	**Vol. 3:** 575
144:9*	**Vol. 2:** 670 **Vol. 3:** 673
144:10*	**Vol. 3:** 192, 207
144:11	**Vol. 3:** 575
144:12*	**Vol. 3:** 784
144:15	**Vol. 1:** 636
145 ff	**Vol. 1:** 99
145–150	**Vol. 1:** 99
145	**Vol. 3:** 233
145:2*	**Vol. 3:** 816
145:4*	**Vol. 3:** 816
145:5	**Vol. 1:** 574
145:6*	**Vol. 3:** 318
145:7*	**Vol. 3:** 238, 674
145:9*	**Vol. 2:** 773
145:11–13	**Vol. 2:** 376
145:15	**Vol. 3:** 804
145:16	**Vol. 2:** 149, 726
145:17*	**Vol. 2:** 237 **Vol. 3:** 937
145:18	**Vol. 2:** 53 **Vol. 3:** 882
145:19*	**Vol. 2:** 860
145:20	**Vol. 2:** 134
146	**Vol. 3:** 817
146:1 f*	**Vol. 3:** 816
146:2*	**Vol. 2:** 35
146:3*	**Vol. 3:** 206
146:4*	**Vol. 2:** 565 **Vol. 3:** 820
146:6*	**Vol. 3:** 983
146:7*	**Vol. 2:** 265, 364 **Vol. 3:** 177, 804
146:9*	**Vol. 2:** 71, 737–738 **Vol. 3:** 1073
147:1*	**Vol. 3:** 816
147:2	**Vol. 1:** 685
147:4*	**Vol. 2:** 649 **Vol. 3:** 947
147:5*	**Vol. 3:** 713
147:6	**Vol. 2:** 257, 596
147:7	**Vol. 1:** 344
147:8*	**Vol. 3:** 117, 1009
147:9	**Vol. 1:** 173
147:10*	**Vol. 3:** 817
147:11*	**Vol. 2:** 240, 817
147:12*	**Vol. 3:** 816
147:14	**Vol. 2:** 778
147:15 ff	**Vol. 3:** 1105
147:15–18	**Vol. 3:** 1116
147:15	**Vol. 3:** 1105
147:16	**Vol. 3:** 1105

Psalms (cont'd)

147:17	**Vol. 3:** 1105
147:18	**Vol. 1:** 683 **Vol. 3:** 1105
147:19*	**Vol. 3:** 354, 1106
148	**Vol. 1:** 523
148:1–4	**Vol. 3:** 816
148:1	**Vol. 1:** 99
148:3	**Vol. 3:** 735
148:4–6	**Vol. 2:** 189
148:4*	**Vol. 2:** 189 **Vol. 3:** 984
148:5	**Vol. 1:** 379 **Vol. 3:** 1105
148:7	**Vol. 1:** 508 **Vol. 3:** 816
148:8	**Vol. 3:** 1001, 1105
148:10	**Vol. 1:** 113, 172
148:12	**Vol. 3:** 816
148:13	**Vol. 2:** 724
148:14	**Vol. 2:** 202 **Vol. 3:** 669
148:15*	**Vol. 3:** 1118
149:1 ff	**Vol. 2:** 670
149:1	**Vol. 1:** 293 **Vol. 3:** 673
149:2	**Vol. 2:** 326
149:3	**Vol. 3:** 816
149:4	**Vol. 2:** 257, 817
149:9	**Vol. 3:** 484
150	**Vol. 2:** 263 **Vol. 3:** 817
150:1–6	**Vol. 3:** 816
150:1	**Vol. 3:** 786
150:2	**Vol. 1:** 732 **Vol. 2:** 425
150:3	**Vol. 3:** 112

Proverbs

1:1	**Vol. 2:** 745, 757 **Vol. 3:** 606
1:2	**Vol. 3:** 777, 1027
1:3	**Vol. 3:** 125
1:4	**Vol. 1:** 283, 412 **Vol. 2:** 391, 830 **Vol. 3:** 125
1:5 f	**Vol. 3:** 1027
1:5	**Vol. 1:** 194 **Vol. 3:** 1028
1:6	**Vol. 2:** 745
1:7	**Vol. 1:** 622 **Vol. 2:** 93, 391 **Vol. 3:** 130, 777, 1027–1028
1:9	**Vol. 2:** 116
1:10	**Vol. 2:** 93
1:12	**Vol. 2:** 206 **Vol. 3:** 238
1:14	**Vol. 1:** 142
1:18	**Vol. 3:** 159
1:19	**Vol. 2:** 93 **Vol. 3:** 137
1:20 ff	**Vol. 3:** 1029
1:20 f	**Vol. 2:** 735 **Vol. 3:** 1056, 1069
1:20	**Vol. 2:** 735 **Vol. 3:** 668, 1027
1:21	**Vol. 1:** 327 **Vol. 3:** 51
1:22	**Vol. 1:** 281, 555 **Vol. 2:** 93 **Vol. 3:** 29
1:23	**Vol. 3:** 760
1:24–31	**Vol. 2:** 840
1:26	**Vol. 1:** 320 **Vol. 2:** 431
1:27	**Vol. 2:** 621
1:29	**Vol. 1:** 555 **Vol. 3:** 1027
1:31	**Vol. 1:** 281 **Vol. 2:** 93
1:32	**Vol. 2:** 93

2:1 ff	**Vol. 3:** 130
2:2	**Vol. 3:** 1027
2:3 f	**Vol. 2:** 835
2:3	**Vol. 2:** 391 **Vol. 3:** 1027
2:4 ff	**Vol. 2:** 391
2:4 f	**Vol. 2:** 830
2:4	**Vol. 2:** 261 **Vol. 3:** 533
2:5	**Vol. 3:** 130
2:6	**Vol. 2:** 395 **Vol. 3:** 1027
2:8	**Vol. 3:** 354
2:9	**Vol. 3:** 130
2:10	**Vol. 3:** 821, 1027
2:11	**Vol. 3:** 125, 1016
2:12	**Vol. 3:** 938
2:15	**Vol. 1:** 729 **Vol. 3:** 1027
2:16 ff	**Vol. 2:** 583
2:17	**Vol. 2:** 578 **Vol. 3:** 769
2:18 f	**Vol. 2:** 479
2:18	**Vol. 3:** 1027
2:19	**Vol. 2:** 478
2:20	**Vol. 3:** 938
2:22	**Vol. 2:** 93
3:1 f	**Vol. 2:** 478
3:1	**Vol. 2:** 132
3:2	**Vol. 2:** 475, 479, 778
3:3	**Vol. 1:** 241 **Vol. 3:** 484, 880
3:4	**Vol. 1:** 695 **Vol. 2:** 103
3:5	**Vol. 3:** 1027
3:6	**Vol. 3:** 352
3:7	**Vol. 2:** 618
3:10	**Vol. 2:** 690
3:11 f	**Vol. 2:** 141–142, 230, 757 **Vol. 3:** 365, 778, 998
3:11	**Vol. 1:** 462 **Vol. 2:** 549 **Vol. 3:** 189, 776
3:12	**Vol. 1:** 163, 617, 639 **Vol. 2:** 141
3:13	**Vol. 1:** 216 **Vol. 3:** 1027
3:14	**Vol. 1:** 268
3:15	**Vol. 3:** 348
3:16–22	**Vol. 2:** 432
3:16	**Vol. 2:** 475, 478, 841
3:17	**Vol. 2:** 778 **Vol. 3:** 938
3:18	**Vol. 1:** 390, 663 **Vol. 2:** 479 **Vol. 3:** 866
3:19	**Vol. 2:** 616 **Vol. 3:** 117, 1027
3:20	**Vol. 1:** 683
3:21	**Vol. 3:** 125
3:23	**Vol. 2:** 777–778
3:25	**Vol. 2:** 93
3:32	**Vol. 3:** 355
3:33	**Vol. 2:** 93
3:34	**Vol. 2:** 117, 123, 261–262, 618, 757 **Vol. 3:** 29–31, 161
3:35	**Vol. 2:** 93 **Vol. 3:** 1027
4:1	**Vol. 1:** 283 **Vol. 3:** 125
4:2	**Vol. 2:** 41
4:3	**Vol. 2:** 179
4:4	**Vol. 2:** 479 **Vol. 3:** 760
4:5	**Vol. 3:** 1027
4:9	**Vol. 2:** 116

Proverbs (cont'd)

4:10	**Vol. 2:** 479 **Vol. 3:** 745
4:11	**Vol. 3:** 760, 938, 1027
4:18 f	**Vol. 2:** 492 **Vol. 3:** 938
4:18	**Vol. 2:** 486, 492 **Vol. 3:** 929
4:19	**Vol. 2:** 486, 491 **Vol. 3:** 929
4:22	**Vol. 2:** 479
4:23	**Vol. 3:** 813
4:26	**Vol. 3:** 351
5:1	**Vol. 3:** 1027
5:2	**Vol. 3:** 125
5:3	**Vol. 2:** 711
5:4	**Vol. 1:** 202 **Vol. 2:** 27
5:5	**Vol. 3:** 1024
5:6	**Vol. 2:** 479 **Vol. 3:** 938
5:11	**Vol. 1:** 673, 675 **Vol. 2:** 421
5:12 f	**Vol. 2:** 141
5:12	**Vol. 1:** 555
5:13	**Vol. 3:** 760, 766
5:15	**Vol. 3:** 813
5:18	**Vol. 2:** 578
5:19	**Vol. 2:** 116
5:20	**Vol. 1:** 239
6:1 ff	**Vol. 2:** 149
6:1	**Vol. 1:** 258
6:5	**Vol. 1:** 172
6:6–11	**Vol. 2:** 823
6:6	**Vol. 3:** 1028
6:8	**Vol. 2:** 93 **Vol. 3:** 1027
6:8b	**Vol. 2:** 456
6:9–10	**Vol. 2:** 432
6:12	**Vol. 3:** 1024, 1028
6:13	**Vol. 3:** 760
6:15	**Vol. 1:** 320
6:16 ff	**Vol. 1:** 555
6:17	**Vol. 3:** 29, 159, 355, 574, 1079
6:18	**Vol. 3:** 823
6:20–35	**Vol. 2:** 583
6:23	**Vol. 2:** 141, 479, 492
6:25	**Vol. 1:** 364, 650 **Vol. 3:** 192
6:27 ff	**Vol. 1:** 655
6:27–29	**Vol. 2:** 746
6:27	**Vol. 1:** 240
6:30	**Vol. 3:** 377
6:31	**Vol. 2:** 845 **Vol. 3:** 201
6:34	**Vol. 3:** 1166
6:35	**Vol. 2:** 583, 845 **Vol. 3:** 190, 192
7:4	**Vol. 3:** 1027
7:5–27	**Vol. 2:** 583
7:7	**Vol. 3:** 1024
7:9	**Vol. 3:** 111
7:14	**Vol. 3:** 422
7:16	**Vol. 1:** 531
7:17	**Vol. 2:** 587
8	**Vol. 2:** 279 **Vol. 3:** 1032
8:1 ff	**Vol. 3:** 1162
8:1–21	**Vol. 3:** 1029
8:1–3	**Vol. 3:** 1056, 1069
8:1	**Vol. 3:** 51, 1027
8:3	**Vol. 3:** 668
8:5	**Vol. 1:** 412
8:6	**Vol. 2:** 93 **Vol. 3:** 351
8:7	**Vol. 3:** 880
8:9	**Vol. 3:** 351
8:10	**Vol. 1:** 537 **Vol. 3:** 808
8:11 f	**Vol. 3:** 1027
8:12	**Vol. 3:** 125, 1016, 1027
8:13	**Vol. 3:** 29, 938
8:14	**Vol. 1:** 663 **Vol. 3:** 713
8:15	**Vol. 3:** 97
8:17	**Vol. 2:** 547 **Vol. 3:** 528
8:18 f	**Vol. 2:** 96
8:18	**Vol. 2:** 841, 845 **Vol. 3:** 1028
8:19	**Vol. 1:** 537
8:20	**Vol. 2:** 481 **Vol. 3:** 354, 933, 938
8:21	**Vol. 2:** 547, 845 **Vol. 3:** 1028
8:22–36	**Vol. 3:** 1116
8:22–31	**Vol. 3:** 1029
8:22–30	**Vol. 3:** 641
8:22	**Vol. 1:** 380, 668
8:23	**Vol. 1:** 476, 668 **Vol. 3:** 828
8:27 f	**Vol. 1:** 523
8:27	**Vol. 3:** 117
8:28	**Vol. 1:** 663
8:29	**Vol. 1:** 661 **Vol. 3:** 983
8:32 ff	**Vol. 3:** 1029
8:32–36	**Vol. 3:** 1028
8:33	**Vol. 3:** 777, 1027–1028
8:35	**Vol. 2:** 479
9:1 ff	**Vol. 3:** 1029
9:1	**Vol. 3:** 1027
9:2	**Vol. 3:** 911
9:3	**Vol. 3:** 51
9:4	**Vol. 3:** 1024
9:5	**Vol. 3:** 911, 1162
9:6*	**Vol. 2:** 481 **Vol. 3:** 1024
9:7 f	**Vol. 2:** 141
9:8 f	**Vol. 3:** 1027
9:9	**Vol. 3:** 1028
9:10	**Vol. 3:** 130, 1027–1028
9:11	**Vol. 2:** 479 **Vol. 3:** 842
9:16	**Vol. 3:** 1024
9:18	**Vol. 2:** 479 **Vol. 3:** 842
10:1	**Vol. 2:** 745 **Vol. 3:** 1024, 1027
10:2	**Vol. 2:** 830
10:4	**Vol. 2:** 841 **Vol. 3:** 545, 1024, 1028
10:7	**Vol. 3:** 109, 237–238
10:8 f	**Vol. 3:** 572
10:8	**Vol. 3:** 745, 1027
10:10	**Vol. 2:** 735, 782
10:11	**Vol. 3:** 987
10:12	**Vol. 1:** 555, 733 **Vol. 2:** 214
10:13	**Vol. 3:** 1027
10:14	**Vol. 3:** 1027
10:15	**Vol. 2:** 841
10:18	**Vol. 3:** 346, 1024
10:20 f	**Vol. 2:** 181
10:21	**Vol. 3:** 1142
10:22	**Vol. 2:** 841

Proverbs *(cont'd)*

10:23	**Vol. 2:** 431 **Vol. 3:** 1024, 1027, 1156
10:31	**Vol. 3:** 1027
10:32	**Vol. 2:** 116
11:1	**Vol. 2:** 261 **Vol. 3:** 1160
11:2	**Vol. 2:** 261 **Vol. 3:** 29, 1027
11:3	**Vol. 1:** 475 **Vol. 2:** 61 **Vol. 3:** 248
11:4	**Vol. 1:** 110 **Vol. 2:** 890
11:5 f	**Vol. 2:** 93
11:5	**Vol. 1:** 609 **Vol. 3:** 352, 924
11:6	**Vol. 3:** 351
11:7	**Vol. 2:** 239
11:8	**Vol. 1:** 314, 479
11:9	**Vol. 2:** 803
11:12	**Vol. 2:** 803 **Vol. 3:** 111
11:14	**Vol. 1:** 194
11:15	**Vol. 1:** 663
11:16	**Vol. 2:** 841 **Vol. 3:** 818
11:18	**Vol. 2:** 139 **Vol. 3:** 140, 1149
11:20	**Vol. 3:** 924
11:21	**Vol. 2:** 139 **Vol. 3:** 140, 747
11:22	**Vol. 2:** 746
11:25	**Vol. 3:** 572
11:27	**Vol. 2:** 116
11:28	**Vol. 1:** 609 **Vol. 2:** 841, 845
11:30	**Vol. 3:** 525, 866
11:31	**Vol. 3:** 140, 215, 370
12:1	**Vol. 2:** 391 **Vol. 3:** 721, 777, 1024
12:2	**Vol. 2:** 116
12:5	**Vol. 1:** 194 **Vol. 3:** 823
12:7	**Vol. 3:** 228
12:10	**Vol. 2:** 599
12:12	**Vol. 2:** 93
12:13	**Vol. 1:** 609
12:14	**Vol. 3:** 1142
12:15 f	**Vol. 3:** 1024
12:15	**Vol. 2:** 430, 481
12:16	**Vol. 1:** 108, 412
12:17–22	**Vol. 3:** 880
12:17	**Vol. 3:** 1041
12:18	**Vol. 3:** 1142
12:19	**Vol. 3:** 880, 1041
12:22	**Vol. 2:** 841
12:23	**Vol. 3:** 1024
12:25	**Vol. 2:** 158 **Vol. 3:** 1142
12:27	**Vol. 2:** 845
13:1	**Vol. 1:** 412 **Vol. 2:** 179 **Vol. 3:** 721
13:2	**Vol. 3:** 525
13:3	**Vol. 2:** 132
13:5	**Vol. 2:** 735
13:7	**Vol. 2:** 841–842
13:8	**Vol. 2:** 822, 841 **Vol. 3:** 190, 192
13:9	**Vol. 2:** 485, 492 **Vol. 3:** 109
13:10	**Vol. 3:** 29, 1028
13:11	**Vol. 2:** 93
13:12	**Vol. 3:** 866
13:13	**Vol. 1:** 622 **Vol. 3:** 1028
13:14	**Vol. 2:** 440 **Vol. 3:** 459, 987, 1027
13:15	**Vol. 1:** 254
13:16	**Vol. 3:** 1024
13:17	**Vol. 3:** 1028
13:19	**Vol. 2:** 93
13:20	**Vol. 3:** 1024, 1027–1028
13:22	**Vol. 2:** 842
13:24	**Vol. 3:** 776
14:1	**Vol. 3:** 1024, 1027
14:2	**Vol. 3:** 351
14:3	**Vol. 3:** 29, 1024, 1027
14:5	**Vol. 3:** 1041
14:6	**Vol. 3:** 528, 1027
14:7 f	**Vol. 3:** 1024
14:7	**Vol. 3:** 1028
14:8	**Vol. 3:** 125, 1027
14:9	**Vol. 3:** 1024
14:10	**Vol. 3:** 29
14:12	**Vol. 1:** 254 **Vol. 3:** 821
14:13	**Vol. 2:** 357, 420
14:14	**Vol. 3:** 125
14:15	**Vol. 1:** 357
14:16	**Vol. 3:** 1024, 1027
14:17	**Vol. 1:** 555
14:18	**Vol. 3:** 1024
14:20	**Vol. 2:** 822, 841
14:21	**Vol. 2:** 49, 257
14:23	**Vol. 1:** 277, 729
14:24	**Vol. 3:** 1024, 1027
14:25	**Vol. 3:** 1041
14:27	**Vol. 3:** 987
14:29	**Vol. 2:** 769 **Vol. 3:** 691, 1024
14:30	**Vol. 1:** 557 **Vol. 2:** 181
14:31	**Vol. 2:** 49, 823
14:32	**Vol. 2:** 237
14:33	**Vol. 3:** 1024, 1027
15:2	**Vol. 3:** 1024, 1027
15:4	**Vol. 1:** 735 **Vol. 3:** 866, 1079, 1142
15:5	**Vol. 3:** 1024
15:6	**Vol. 2:** 830
15:7	**Vol. 1:** 663 **Vol. 2:** 391 **Vol. 3:** 1024, 1027
15:8	**Vol. 3:** 427, 745
15:9	**Vol. 2:** 806
15:11	**Vol. 1:** 463–464
15:12	**Vol. 2:** 141 **Vol. 3:** 1027
15:14	**Vol. 3:** 351
15:15	**Vol. 2:** 890
15:19	**Vol. 1:** 725
15:20	**Vol. 3:** 1024, 1027
15:21	**Vol. 3:** 126
15:22	**Vol. 3:** 823
15:24	**Vol. 3:** 125
15:25	**Vol. 3:** 29, 1073
15:26	**Vol. 2:** 93 **Vol. 3:** 101, 823
15:28*	**Vol. 3:** 745, 1143
15:32	**Vol. 1:** 555
15:33*	**Vol. 2:** 260–261 **Vol. 3:** 776, 1027–1028
16:2	**Vol. 2:** 261
16:5	**Vol. 3:** 351
16:6	**Vol. 3:** 157, 880

Proverbs *(cont'd)*

16:7	**Vol. 3:** 745
16:9*	**Vol. 3:** 691, 823
16:11	**Vol. 3:** 1160
16:14	**Vol. 1:** 153–154, 1027
16:16	**Vol. 1:** 537 **Vol. 3:** 1027
16:17	**Vol. 2:** 132 **Vol. 3:** 745, 1028, 1033
16:18 f	**Vol. 3:** 29
16:19	**Vol. 2:** 261 **Vol. 3:** 29
16:21	**Vol. 3:** 1027
16:22	**Vol. 3:** 125, 987, 1024
16:23	**Vol. 3:** 125, 1027
16:25	**Vol. 2:** 481 **Vol. 3:** 351, 821
16:27	**Vol. 3:** 1024, 1143
16:28	**Vol. 3:** 1143
16:30	**Vol. 1:** 472 **Vol. 3:** 820, 823
16:31	**Vol. 1:** 227, 229
16:32	**Vol. 2:** 769 **Vol. 3:** 716
16:33	**Vol. 2:** 296, 299
17:1	**Vol. 1:** 459 **Vol. 2:** 777
17:2	**Vol. 2:** 303 **Vol. 3:** 1024
17:3	**Vol. 1:** 656 **Vol. 3:** 808
17:5	**Vol. 2:** 822
17:6	**Vol. 1:** 227
17:7	**Vol. 3:** 1024
17:8	**Vol. 2:** 139
17:10	**Vol. 1:** 572 **Vol. 3:** 1024
17:12	**Vol. 1:** 277 **Vol. 3:** 820, 1024
17:16	**Vol. 3:** 1024, 1027
17:17	**Vol. 2:** 663
17:18	**Vol. 3:** 1024
17:21	**Vol. 3:** 1024
17:23	**Vol. 3:** 354
17:24 f	**Vol. 3:** 1024
17:24	**Vol. 3:** 1028
17:28	**Vol. 3:** 126, 821, 823, 1027
18:2	**Vol. 3:** 957, 1024, 1027
18:4	**Vol. 2:** 197 **Vol. 3:** 459, 987
18:5	**Vol. 2:** 622
18:6 f	**Vol. 3:** 1024
18:7	**Vol. 3:** 1024
18:10 f	**Vol. 2:** 845
18:10	**Vol. 1:** 272 **Vol. 2:** 650
18:11	**Vol. 2:** 841
18:12	**Vol. 2:** 260
18:13	**Vol. 3:** 1024
18:15	**Vol. 3:** 125, 1027
18:18	**Vol. 1:** 472 **Vol. 2:** 296
18:21	**Vol. 3:** 1079, 1142
18:22	**Vol. 2:** 116, 261
19:3*	**Vol. 3:** 1024
19:4*	**Vol. 2:** 822, 842
19:6	**Vol. 2:** 164
19:7	**Vol. 1:** 555 **Vol. 2:** 822 **Vol. 3:** 125
19:10	**Vol. 3:** 29, 1024
19:11	**Vol. 2:** 769
19:12	**Vol. 2:** 421
19:13	**Vol. 2:** 139 **Vol. 3:** 1024
19:15	**Vol. 2:** 265
19:16	**Vol. 1:** 461 **Vol. 2:** 132, 134
19:17	**Vol. 2:** 822 **Vol. 3:** 134
19:18	**Vol. 3:** 29, 776
19:20	**Vol. 3:** 1028
19:21	**Vol. 3:** 823
19:22	**Vol. 2:** 822
19:24	**Vol. 2:** 432
19:25	**Vol. 2:** 141
19:28	**Vol. 3:** 354, 1024
19:29	**Vol. 3:** 1024
20:1	**Vol. 1:** 513 **Vol. 3:** 919, 1024, 1028
20:3†	**Vol. 3:** 346, 1024
20:7	**Vol. 3:** 924, 933
20:9	**Vol. 2:** 735 **Vol. 3:** 101
20:13	**Vol. 3:** 345
20:20	**Vol. 1:** 423 **Vol. 3:** 109
20:22	**Vol. 2:** 157, 773
20:23	**Vol. 3:** 1160
20:24	**Vol. 3:** 125
20:26	**Vol. 3:** 1027
20:28	**Vol. 3:** 354
20:29	**Vol. 1:** 522 **Vol. 3:** 1027
21:1	**Vol. 1:** 412
21:3	**Vol. 3:** 427
21:4	**Vol. 1:** 108 **Vol. 3:** 29
21:5	**Vol. 3:** 953
21:6	**Vol. 3:** 1147
21:8	**Vol. 3:** 101
21:9	**Vol. 1:** 641
21:11	**Vol. 3:** 745, 1027
21:13	**Vol. 3:** 950, 994
21:16	**Vol. 1:** 339 **Vol. 3:** 254
21:17	**Vol. 2:** 711, 842 **Vol. 3:** 919
21:18	**Vol. 1:** 479
21:20	**Vol. 2:** 711 **Vol. 3:** 1024, 1027
21:21	**Vol. 3:** 528
21:22	**Vol. 3:** 963, 1027
21:24	**Vol. 2:** 435 **Vol. 3:** 30
21:27	**Vol. 3:** 427
21:30	**Vol. 3:** 1027
22:1	**Vol. 2:** 841
22:2	**Vol. 2:** 822, 841
22:4	**Vol. 2:** 260, 841
22:5	**Vol. 1:** 726
22:7	**Vol. 2:** 822, 841
22:8	**Vol. 2:** 827 **Vol. 3:** 134, 522
22:9	**Vol. 2:** 49
22:11	**Vol. 3:** 924
22:14a	**Vol. 2:** 664
22:15	**Vol. 1:** 288 **Vol. 3:** 125
22:16	**Vol. 2:** 841
22:17–23:11	**Vol. 3:** 1028
22:17	**Vol. 3:** 1027, 1092
22:21	**Vol. 3:** 760, 880
22:22	**Vol. 2:** 257 **Vol. 3:** 994
22:24	**Vol. 3:** 1027
22:26	**Vol. 2:** 149
23:1	**Vol. 2:** 521
23:4	**Vol. 2:** 841 **Vol. 3:** 125
23:9	**Vol. 3:** 1024

Proverbs *(cont'd)*

23:10–11 **Vol. 2:** 738
23:11 **Vol. 3:** 192, 716
23:12 **Vol. 3:** 117
23:13 **Vol. 1:** 281   **Vol. 3:** 776
23:15 **Vol. 3:** 1028
23:17 **Vol. 1:** 622   **Vol. 2:** 240
23:18 **Vol. 1:** 606   **Vol. 2:** 240
23:19 **Vol. 3:** 125, 1028
23:20 f **Vol. 3:** 919
23:21 **Vol. 2:** 823
23:22 **Vol. 1:** 461, 617
23:23 **Vol. 3:** 777, 880
23:24 **Vol. 3:** 1027
23:25 **Vol. 2:** 357
23:29 **Vol. 3:** 1051
23:31 ff **Vol. 3:** 919
23:31 **Vol. 3:** 922
23:32 **Vol. 2:** 27
24:3 **Vol. 3:** 1027
24:4 **Vol. 2:** 842
24:5 f* **Vol. 3:** 557
24:5 **Vol. 2:** 616   **Vol. 3:** 1027
24:7 **Vol. 3:** 125, 823, 1027–1028
24:11 f **Vol. 2:** 157
24:12 **Vol. 3:** 167
24:14 **Vol. 3:** 1027
24:16 **Vol. 1:** 608, 610
24:17 f **Vol. 2:** 157
24:17 **Vol. 1:** 609   **Vol. 2:** 157
24:20 **Vol. 3:** 109
24:21 **Vol. 1:** 622
24:23* **Vol. 3:** 1027
24:26* **Vol. 3:** 1028
24:27 **Vol. 3:** 119
24:28* **Vol. 2:** 803
24:29 **Vol. 2:** 157   **Vol. 3:** 183
24:30* **Vol. 3:** 1024
25:1 **Vol. 2:** 745, 757
25:4 **Vol. 3:** 808
25:6 **Vol. 3:** 30
25:7 **Vol. 2:** 261–262
25:11–13 **Vol. 2:** 746
25:12 f **Vol. 1:** 657
25:12 **Vol. 3:** 1027
25:13 **Vol. 1:** 595
25:14 f **Vol. 3:** 402
25:14 **Vol. 1:** 227
25:15 **Vol. 1:** 240   **Vol. 2:** 769
25:16 **Vol. 3:** 728
25:18 **Vol. 3:** 1041
25:21 f **Vol. 2:** 268, 757   **Vol. 3:** 97, 183
25:21 **Vol. 2:** 157, 266
25:24 **Vol. 1:** 641   **Vol. 3:** 346
25:26 **Vol. 3:** 950–951
25:27 **Vol. 3:** 957
26:1 ff **Vol. 2:** 746
26:1 **Vol. 3:** 1024
26:2 **Vol. 1:** 173

26:3 **Vol. 1:** 511
26:4 f **Vol. 3:** 1024
26:4–11 **Vol. 3:** 1024
26:5 **Vol. 3:** 1027
26:7 **Vol. 2:** 745, 757
26:9 **Vol. 1:** 725   **Vol. 2:** 745
26:11 **Vol. 1:** 117   **Vol. 2:** 757
26:12 **Vol. 3:** 821, 1027
26:16 **Vol. 2:** 690   **Vol. 3:** 1027
26:18 **Vol. 3:** 799
26:20 f **Vol. 1:** 654
26:21 **Vol. 3:** 346
26:22 **Vol. 2:** 599
26:23 **Vol. 3:** 914
26:27 **Vol. 3:** 720
27:1 **Vol. 1:** 251
27:2 **Vol. 3:** 817
27:3 **Vol. 1:** 108   **Vol. 3:** 1024
27:4 **Vol. 1:** 108
27:9 **Vol. 2:** 711
27:11 **Vol. 3:** 1028
27:13 **Vol. 3:** 29
27:14 **Vol. 3:** 821
27:15 **Vol. 2:** 432   **Vol. 3:** 346
27:20 **Vol. 1:** 463   **Vol. 2:** 206
27:21 **Vol. 1:** 227, 656   **Vol. 3:** 808
27:22 **Vol. 3:** 1024
27:23 **Vol. 2:** 395
28:1 **Vol. 1:** 559
28:2 **Vol. 1:** 412
28:3 **Vol. 2:** 822
28:4 **Vol. 2:** 440
28:6 **Vol. 2:** 822, 841, 845
28:7 **Vol. 2:** 440
28:8 **Vol. 2:** 822, 842
28:9 **Vol. 2:** 440, 863
28:10 **Vol. 2:** 99
28:11 **Vol. 2:** 841, 845   **Vol. 3:** 1028
28:13 **Vol. 1:** 574
28:14 **Vol. 2:** 91, 155
28:15 **Vol. 2:** 421, 820, 822
28:16 **Vol. 3:** 137, 842
28:17 **Vol. 1:** 663   **Vol. 2:** 138   **Vol. 3:** 159
28:22 **Vol. 2:** 841
28:24 **Vol. 3:** 821
28:26 **Vol. 3:** 209, 1024, 1027
28:27 **Vol. 2:** 822
29:1 **Vol. 2:** 155
29:3 **Vol. 2:** 842   **Vol. 3:** 1027
29:5 **Vol. 3:** 119, 1143
29:6 **Vol. 2:** 357
29:7 **Vol. 2:** 820
29:8 f **Vol. 3:** 1028
29:8 **Vol. 1:** 108
29:10 **Vol. 1:** 555
29:11 **Vol. 3:** 1024, 1028
29:14 **Vol. 3:** 1040
29:15 **Vol. 2:** 141   **Vol. 3:** 1027
29:17 **Vol. 3:** 254, 776
29:18 **Vol. 1:** 574

Proverbs *(cont'd)*

29:20	**Vol. 3:** 1024
29:23	**Vol. 2:** 203, 260–261 **Vol. 3:** 29
29:24	**Vol. 1:** 555 **Vol. 3:** 739
29:25	**Vol. 3:** 218
29:26	**Vol. 2:** 164
30:2*	**Vol. 3:** 1024
30:3*	**Vol. 2:** 395 **Vol. 3:** 760, 1027
30:4	**Vol. 2:** 185
30:7–30	**Vol. 2:** 745
30:7*	**Vol. 2:** 856
30:8*	**Vol. 1:** 251, 597 **Vol. 2:** 841
30:9	**Vol. 3:** 377
30:15	**Vol. 3:** 727
30:17	**Vol. 1:** 175
30:19	**Vol. 2:** 87 **Vol. 3:** 1071
30:20	**Vol. 2:** 583
30:23	**Vol. 3:** 1065
30:24*	**Vol. 3:** 1027
30:26	**Vol. 3:** 381
30:27*	**Vol. 1:** 342, 409
30:28	**Vol. 3:** 786
30:30	**Vol. 3:** 713
30:33	**Vol. 1:** 108
31:1	**Vol. 3:** 325
31:3*	**Vol. 2:** 842
31:5*	**Vol. 3:** 1027
31:6–7	**Vol. 2:** 28
31:9	**Vol. 1:** 503 **Vol. 2:** 257
31:11	**Vol. 1:** 327
31:12	**Vol. 3:** 1147
31:14	**Vol. 2:** 475, 842
31:18	**Vol. 2:** 269, 485
31:20	**Vol. 2:** 257
31:26*	**Vol. 3:** 1028
31:28	**Vol. 2:** 841 **Vol. 3:** 816
31:29	**Vol. 2:** 842
31:30 f	**Vol. 3:** 816
31:30	**Vol. 2:** 815

Ecclesiastes

1:1	**Vol. 3:** 606
1:2	**Vol. 1:** 551
1:3	**Vol. 1:** 262, 728 **Vol. 3:** 137
1:6–20	**Vol. 3:** 1056
1:11	**Vol. 1:** 665 **Vol. 3:** 236, 238
1:13	**Vol. 3:** 1027
1:15	**Vol. 3:** 953
1:16	**Vol. 2:** 830 **Vol. 3:** 1027
1:18	**Vol. 3:** 1027
2:1	**Vol. 1:** 551 **Vol. 3:** 799
2:2	**Vol. 2:** 431, 433
2:3	**Vol. 3:** 1027
2:5	**Vol. 2:** 761
2:8	**Vol. 2:** 838 **Vol. 3:** 673
2:9	**Vol. 3:** 1027
2:11	**Vol. 3:** 137
2:12 f	**Vol. 3:** 1024
2:12	**Vol. 2:** 744 **Vol. 3:** 1027
2:13 f	**Vol. 1:** 728
2:13	**Vol. 3:** 137, 1027
2:14 ff	**Vol. 3:** 1024
2:14	**Vol. 3:** 1028
2:14b	**Vol. 1:** 728
2:15	**Vol. 3:** 1024, 1028
2:16	**Vol. 3:** 236, 238, 1028
2:18 ff	**Vol. 1:** 262
2:18–22	**Vol. 1:** 262
2:19	**Vol. 3:** 1024, 1028
2:21	**Vol. 2:** 830 **Vol. 3:** 1027
2:25	**Vol. 1:** 551
2:26	**Vol. 3:** 1027
3:1 ff	**Vol. 3:** 835
3:1	**Vol. 3:** 835, 842
3:2	**Vol. 3:** 835
3:9	**Vol. 3:** 137
3:10	**Vol. 3:** 799
3:12	**Vol. 2:** 100
3:13	**Vol. 1:** 551
3:16	**Vol. 2:** 93
3:19 f	**Vol. 1:** 434
3:19	**Vol. 1:** 728 **Vol. 3:** 137, 690
3:20	**Vol. 1:** 520
3:21	**Vol. 3:** 690
4:2	**Vol. 3:** 816
4:5	**Vol. 3:** 1024
4:6	**Vol. 3:** 255
4:8	**Vol. 1:** 230 **Vol. 2:** 841 **Vol. 3:** 799
4:9	**Vol. 2:** 139
4:10	**Vol. 1:** 608
4:13	**Vol. 2:** 822 **Vol. 3:** 1024, 1028
4:14	**Vol. 2:** 820
4:17*†	**Vol. 2:** 53 **Vol. 3:** 1024
5:1	**Vol. 1:** 614
5:2 f	**Vol. 3:** 1024
5:2	**Vol. 3:** 799
5:7	**Vol. 1:** 512 **Vol. 2:** 625, 820
5:8	**Vol. 3:** 137
5:11	**Vol. 2:** 841
5:12	**Vol. 2:** 841
5:13	**Vol. 3:** 799
5:15	**Vol. 3:** 137, 690
5:17	**Vol. 2:** 100
5:18	**Vol. 2:** 841
5:19	**Vol. 2:** 845
6:2	**Vol. 1:** 728 **Vol. 2:** 841, 845 **Vol. 3:** 953
6:3	**Vol. 1:** 182
6:8	**Vol. 1:** 728 **Vol. 2:** 257 **Vol. 3:** 137, 1024, 1028
6:9 f	**Vol. 1:** 728
7:2–6	**Vol. 2:** 433
7:4 ff*	**Vol. 3:** 1024
7:4 f*	**Vol. 3:** 1028
7:4*	**Vol. 2:** 431
7:5*	**Vol. 3:** 673
7:6	**Vol. 2:** 431
7:7*	**Vol. 2:** 431 **Vol. 3:** 1028
7:8	**Vol. 3:** 691

Ecclesiastes *(cont'd)*

7:9*	**Vol. 3:** 254, 1024
7:10 ff*	**Vol. 3:** 1027
7:10	**Vol. 1:** 240
7:11 f*	**Vol. 3:** 137
7:12	**Vol. 1:** 728
7:14	**Vol. 1:** 551
7:15	**Vol. 2:** 890
7:16*	**Vol. 3:** 1028, 1033
7:17	**Vol. 1:** 530 **Vol. 3:** 835
7:19*	**Vol. 1:** 728 **Vol. 3:** 1027–1028
7:20	**Vol. 2:** 100
7:23*	**Vol. 3:** 799, 1027–1028
7:25*†	**Vol. 3:** 1024, 1027
7:26	**Vol. 1:** 266
7:27*	**Vol. 1:** 343 **Vol. 3:** 823
7:29*	**Vol. 3:** 823
8:1*	**Vol. 1:** 577, 581 **Vol. 3:** 1027–1028
8:5	**Vol. 2:** 395 **Vol. 3:** 1028
8:8	**Vol. 2:** 222, 887 **Vol. 3:** 209, 842
8:10	**Vol. 3:** 816
8:11 f	**Vol. 3:** 1153
8:14	**Vol. 3:** 140
8:15	**Vol. 3:** 816
8:16	**Vol. 3:** 799, 1027
8:17	**Vol. 2:** 395 **Vol. 3:** 1028
9:1	**Vol. 3:** 1028
9:4	**Vol. 1:** 444, 641
9:5	**Vol. 1:** 444 **Vol. 2:** 139 **Vol. 3:** 237–238, 255
9:6	**Vol. 2:** 139
9:7 ff	**Vol. 1:** 551
9:7	**Vol. 2:** 272
9:9	**Vol. 2:** 478, 890
9:10	**Vol. 3:** 823, 946, 1027
9:11	**Vol. 2:** 116, 841 **Vol. 3:** 1028
9:13	**Vol. 3:** 1024, 1027
9:14	**Vol. 3:** 952
9:15 f	**Vol. 2:** 822 **Vol. 3:** 1027
9:15	**Vol. 3:** 209, 1028
9:17	**Vol. 3:** 255, 1024, 1028
9:18	**Vol. 3:** 1027
10:1	**Vol. 3:** 1024, 1027
10:2	**Vol. 2:** 148 **Vol. 3:** 1024, 1028
10:3	**Vol. 3:** 823, 953, 1024
10:4	**Vol. 3:** 255
10:6	**Vol. 2:** 261, 841 **Vol. 3:** 1024
10:10 f	**Vol. 3:** 137
10:10	**Vol. 3:** 919, 1027
10:11	**Vol. 2:** 554
10:12	**Vol. 3:** 1024, 1028
10:13	**Vol. 3:** 1024
10:14	**Vol. 1:** 493 **Vol. 3:** 1024
10:15	**Vol. 3:** 1024
10:19	**Vol. 2:** 431
10:20	**Vol. 1:** 349 **Vol. 2:** 841
11:5	**Vol. 1:** 240
11:6	**Vol. 2:** 452
11:9†	**Vol. 2:** 355, 890 **Vol. 3:** 924, 943

11:10	**Vol. 3:** 125
12:1	**Vol. 1:** 379 **Vol. 2:** 890 **Vol. 3:** 957
12:2	**Vol. 3:** 733, 735
12:4	**Vol. 1:** 267 **Vol. 3:** 673
12:7	**Vol. 1:** 520 **Vol. 3:** 690
12:9	**Vol. 3:** 760, 1028
12:11	**Vol. 3:** 1028
12:13	**Vol. 1:** 728
12:14	**Vol. 2:** 216

Song of Solomon, or Canticles

1:1	**Vol. 3:** 606, 673
1:3	**Vol. 2:** 87 **Vol. 3:** 1071–1072
1:5	**Vol. 1:** 203
1:7	**Vol. 1:** 259 **Vol. 3:** 680
1:9	**Vol. 1:** 531
1:11	**Vol. 2:** 96, 572
1:13	**Vol. 1:** 240
2:2	**Vol. 1:** 725
2:15	**Vol. 3:** 950
2:17	**Vol. 1:** 559 **Vol. 2:** 501
3:2	**Vol. 1:** 267
3:4	**Vol. 3:** 716
3:6	**Vol. 2:** 293–294
3:8	**Vol. 3:** 760
3:11	**Vol. 2:** 578
4:2	**Vol. 1:** 152
4:6	**Vol. 1:** 559 **Vol. 2:** 293–294
4:10	**Vol. 3:** 600
4:12	**Vol. 3:** 498
4:13	**Vol. 2:** 761
4:14	**Vol. 2:** 293–294
4:16	**Vol. 1:** 683 **Vol. 3:** 600
5:1	**Vol. 2:** 294
5:2	**Vol. 1:** 510 **Vol. 2:** 881
5:3	**Vol. 1:** 449
5:5	**Vol. 2:** 294
5:10	**Vol. 1:** 205
5:13	**Vol. 2:** 294
6:6	**Vol. 1:** 152
6:8*	**Vol. 2:** 87 **Vol. 3:** 816, 1071–1072
6:9*	**Vol. 1:** 510 **Vol. 3:** 385
6:10	**Vol. 3:** 730, 733
7:2*	**Vol. 3:** 950
7:4*	**Vol. 3:** 992
7:5*	**Vol. 1:** 171 **Vol. 3:** 992
7:8	**Vol. 2:** 501
7:10	**Vol. 3:** 273
7:13*	**Vol. 2:** 675
8:5	**Vol. 3:** 858
8:6	**Vol. 2:** 540
8:7	**Vol. 2:** 475 **Vol. 3:** 109
8:9 f	**Vol. 3:** 948
8:10	**Vol. 2:** 735
8:13	**Vol. 1:** 259
8:14	**Vol. 1:** 559

Isaiah

1:1 ff	**Vol. 3:** 155

Isaiah *(cont'd)*

1:1	**Vol. 3:** 208, 311, 1093
1:2–3	**Vol. 2:** 432
1:2	**Vol. 1:** 288 **Vol. 2:** 174, 363
1:3	**Vol. 1:** 173 **Vol. 2:** 395, 797
1:4 ff	**Vol. 3:** 578
1:4	**Vol. 3:** 342, 1051
1:5 f	**Vol. 3:** 997–998
1:5	**Vol. 2:** 181, 420
1:6	**Vol. 1:** 120 **Vol. 2:** 712 **Vol. 3:** 857
1:7	**Vol. 3:** 1005
1:8	**Vol. 2:** 326
1:9 f	**Vol. 3:** 93
1:9	**Vol. 2:** 69, 767 **Vol. 3:** 251–252
1:10 ff	**Vol. 3:** 783
1:10–17	**Vol. 2:** 42 **Vol. 3:** 78
1:10	**Vol. 2:** 174, 440
1:11–31	**Vol. 3:** 427
1:11	**Vol. 1:** 732 **Vol. 3:** 159, 1016
1:13 f	**Vol. 1:** 626
1:13	**Vol. 2:** 765 **Vol. 3:** 407, 421
1:15 ff	**Vol. 2:** 285
1:15–17	**Vol. 2:** 864
1:15 f	**Vol. 2:** 864
1:15	**Vol. 2:** 174 **Vol. 3:** 159, 427
1:16	**Vol. 1:** 699
1:17–23	**Vol. 3:** 1074
1:17	**Vol. 1:** 484–485 **Vol. 2:** 103, 737 **Vol. 3:** 355
1:18	**Vol. 1:** 204–205, 699
1:22	**Vol. 3:** 808
1:23	**Vol. 1:** 717 **Vol. 2:** 363 **Vol. 3:** 1074
1:24	**Vol. 1:** 554 **Vol. 2:** 509
1:25	**Vol. 2:** 96 **Vol. 3:** 29
1:26	**Vol. 2:** 803
1:27	**Vol. 2:** 595
1:28	**Vol. 3:** 908
1:29	**Vol. 3:** 562
1:31	**Vol. 3:** 109
2	**Vol. 3:** 382
2:1	**Vol. 3:** 311, 1094
2:2 ff	**Vol. 1:** 96 **Vol. 2:** 56, 326
2:2–5	**Vol. 2:** 495 **Vol. 3:** 1094
2:2–4	**Vol. 2:** 791 **Vol. 3:** 1010
2:2 f	**Vol. 1:** 661 **Vol. 2:** 325 **Vol. 3:** 791
2:2	**Vol. 2:** 56, 489, 899 **Vol. 3:** 786, 1012
2:3	**Vol. 1:** 321 **Vol. 3:** 1095
2:4	**Vol. 1:** 484 **Vol. 2:** 141
2:5	**Vol. 2:** 302, 492 **Vol. 3:** 1012
2:6	**Vol. 2:** 554, 742
2:7	**Vol. 2:** 257, 683
2:8	**Vol. 2:** 876
2:9	**Vol. 2:** 260
2:10 f	**Vol. 2:** 218
2:10	**Vol. 2:** 215 **Vol. 3:** 714
2:11 f	**Vol. 2:** 887
2:11	**Vol. 2:** 202, 260
2:12–18	**Vol. 2:** 363
2:12	**Vol. 2:** 890 **Vol. 3:** 29
2:17	**Vol. 2:** 199, 202, 260, 887 **Vol. 3:** 29
2:18 ff	**Vol. 2:** 285
2:19	**Vol. 3:** 381, 714
2:20	**Vol. 1:** 551 **Vol. 2:** 876
2:22	**Vol. 1:** 108
2:23	**Vol. 3:** 866
2:24	**Vol. 3:** 70
3:1	**Vol. 2:** 509
3:2	**Vol. 2:** 554
3:3	**Vol. 1:** 279 **Vol. 2:** 175, 554–555 **Vol. 3:** 1028
3:6	**Vol. 3:** 747
3:7	**Vol. 2:** 167
3:8	**Vol. 1:** 589 **Vol. 3:** 1079
3:9	**Vol. 1:** 565 **Vol. 2:** 489 **Vol. 3:** 93
3:10 f	**Vol. 3:** 1149
3:10	**Vol. 2:** 272
3:14 f	**Vol. 2:** 257, 821–822
3:16 f	**Vol. 2:** 326
3:18	**Vol. 1:** 522
3:20	**Vol. 3:** 498
3:24	**Vol. 3:** 120
3:26	**Vol. 2:** 422
4:1	**Vol. 2:** 649 **Vol. 3:** 340
4:2–5	**Vol. 1:** 146
4:2	**Vol. 2:** 201 **Vol. 3:** 867
4:3 f	**Vol. 1:** 699
4:3	**Vol. 1:** 243
4:4	**Vol. 1:** 479 **Vol. 3:** 695, 1178
4:5 f	**Vol. 1:** 653
4:5	**Vol. 1:** 655
5:1 ff	**Vol. 2:** 364
5:1–7	**Vol. 2:** 154, 301, 746 **Vol. 3:** 918, 920
5:1 f	**Vol. 3:** 866
5:1	**Vol. 3:** 673, 866
5:2	**Vol. 1:** 725 **Vol. 3:** 951
5:3	**Vol. 2:** 324
5:4	**Vol. 1:** 725 **Vol. 3:** 867
5:5	**Vol. 3:** 950
5:6	**Vol. 1:** 726 **Vol. 3:** 867
5:7	**Vol. 2:** 248, 305, 432 **Vol. 3:** 357
5:8 ff	**Vol. 2:** 841
5:8 f	**Vol. 2:** 822
5:8	**Vol. 1:** 641
5:9	**Vol. 2:** 178 **Vol. 3:** 1005
5:10	**Vol. 3:** 402, 911, 1161
5:11	**Vol. 3:** 919
5:12	**Vol. 3:** 126, 513, 673
5:13	**Vol. 2:** 275 **Vol. 3:** 590
5:14	**Vol. 2:** 206
5:15	**Vol. 2:** 260
5:18	**Vol. 3:** 1161
5:19	**Vol. 2:** 53 **Vol. 3:** 1016
5:20	**Vol. 1:** 423
5:22	**Vol. 3:** 911, 919
5:23	**Vol. 3:** 355
5:24	**Vol. 2:** 440 **Vol. 3:** 342, 866, 1118
5:25–30	**Vol. 3:** 1094
5:25	**Vol. 1:** 233 **Vol. 2:** 797
5:27	**Vol. 3:** 177

Isaiah *(cont'd)*

5:28   **Vol. 3:** 823
5:29   **Vol. 2:** 421
5:30   **Vol. 2:** 421
6   **Vol. 3:** 330, 389
6:1 ff   **Vol. 2:** 173, 191 **Vol. 3:** 514
6:1–13   **Vol. 2:** 613
6:1–8   **Vol. 1:** 273
6:1–4   **Vol. 1:** 655
6:1   **Vol. 1:** 54, 509 **Vol. 2:** 613, 632 **Vol. 3:** 786
6:2–6   **Vol. 1:** 280
6:2 f   **Vol. 2:** 689
6:2   **Vol. 1:** 101 **Vol. 2:** 212
6:3 ff   **Vol. 2:** 190
6:3–7   **Vol. 2:** 225
6:3 f   **Vol. 1:** 409
6:3   **Vol. 1:** 735 **Vol. 2:** 45, 70
6:4   **Vol. 3:** 559
6:5 ff   **Vol. 3:** 860
6:5   **Vol. 1:** 108, 585 **Vol. 2:** 375 **Vol. 3:** 104, 514
6:6   **Vol. 1:** 655
6:7   **Vol. 1:** 368, 699 **Vol. 3:** 154
6:8   **Vol. 1:** 127–128
6:8b   **Vol. 3:** 1095
6:9 ff   **Vol. 2:** 174, 178
6:9–11   **Vol. 3:** 1094
6:9 f   **Vol. 2:** 155–156, 630, 753, 799 **Vol. 3:** 128, 131–132, 313, 1094
6:9   **Vol. 2:** 175
6:10   **Vol. 1:** 219, 230, 261 **Vol. 2:** 154, 168, 632, 753, 799 **Vol. 3:** 125
6:11   **Vol. 2:** 154 **Vol. 3:** 1006
6:13   **Vol. 3:** 249, 867
7   **Vol. 1:** 178 **Vol. 3:** 267
7:1–25   **Vol. 1:** 504
7:1–9   **Vol. 2:** 306
7:3   **Vol. 2:** 649 **Vol. 3:** 79
7:7   **Vol. 3:** 226
7:9   **Vol. 1:** 596 **Vol. 3:** 389, 1211
7:10 ff   **Vol. 2:** 626
7:10   **Vol. 2:** 351
7:11 f   **Vol. 2:** 856
7:11   **Vol. 2:** 198–199
7:12   **Vol. 3:** 799–800
7:14 ff   **Vol. 2:** 627
7:14   **Vol. 1:** 186, 737 **Vol. 2:** 86, 649, 715 **Vol. 3:** 662, 697, 1072
7:18   **Vol. 3:** 985
7:19   **Vol. 3:** 254
7:20   **Vol. 2:** 139, 418 **Vol. 3:** 985
7:21   **Vol. 2:** 412
8   **Vol. 3:** 267
8:1 ff   **Vol. 2:** 626
8:1   **Vol. 1:** 368 **Vol. 3:** 483
8:2   **Vol. 1:** 595 **Vol. 3:** 1041
8:3 f   **Vol. 3:** 79
8:3   **Vol. 2:** 649 **Vol. 3:** 1057

8:5–8   **Vol. 3:** 1090
8:6   **Vol. 1:** 543, 581
8:7   **Vol. 3:** 713, 985
8:8   **Vol. 2:** 86
8:9 f   **Vol. 3:** 185
8:9   **Vol. 2:** 791
8:10   **Vol. 3:** 226
8:11–15   **Vol. 3:** 391
8:11   **Vol. 3:** 1054
8:12   **Vol. 3:** 709
8:13 ff   **Vol. 3:** 382
8:13   **Vol. 1:** 622
8:14 f   **Vol. 2:** 706
8:14   **Vol. 1:** 609 **Vol. 2:** 705–706, 708–709 **Vol. 3:** 382–384, 389, 391–393
8:15   **Vol. 1:** 610, 663
8:16 ff   **Vol. 3:** 1094
8:16   **Vol. 2:** 763
8:17   **Vol. 1:** 592, 596 **Vol. 2:** 240
8:18   **Vol. 2:** 190, 325, 627, 633
8:19   **Vol. 1:** 450 **Vol. 2:** 554, 559
8:20   **Vol. 2:** 559
8:22   **Vol. 1:** 422 **Vol. 2:** 807
9   **Vol. 1:** 178
9:1 f   **Vol. 2:** 596
9:1†   **Vol. 1:** 422, 435 **Vol. 2:** 793 **Vol. 3:** 555
9:2–7*   **Vol. 2:** 335, 374 **Vol. 3:** 637
9:2   **Vol. 1:** 422–423 **Vol. 3:** 198, 212, 555, 569, 940
9:3*   **Vol. 2:** 889 **Vol. 3:** 1161
9:4*   **Vol. 3:** 166
9:5 f   **Vol. 2:** 778
9:5   **Vol. 2:** 779 **Vol. 3:** 722
9:6 f*   **Vol. 1:** 210 **Vol. 3:** 648
9:6*   **Vol. 1:** 326, 427 **Vol. 2:** 86, 779 **Vol. 3:** 637, 649, 1016, 1068
9:7–20   **Vol. 3:** 1094
9:7*   **Vol. 1:** 426–427 **Vol. 2:** 376, 448 **Vol. 3:** 841–842, 1094, 1166–1167
9:9*   **Vol. 3:** 29
9:12*   **Vol. 2:** 124
9:13   **Vol. 2:** 889 **Vol. 3:** 531
9:14*   **Vol. 2:** 158 **Vol. 3:** 760
9:17*   **Vol. 1:** 565
9:18 f   **Vol. 1:** 109
10:1–4   **Vol. 1:** 717
10:2   **Vol. 2:** 822 **Vol. 3:** 601, 1074
10:4   **Vol. 1:** 368
10:5 ff   **Vol. 3:** 97
10:5   **Vol. 1:** 111 **Vol. 2:** 791 **Vol. 3:** 549
10:6   **Vol. 1:** 332 **Vol. 3:** 209
10:7 ff   **Vol. 3:** 234
10:7–11   **Vol. 3:** 32
10:7   **Vol. 3:** 125, 823
10:7b   **Vol. 3:** 125
10:8 ff   **Vol. 3:** 342
10:10   **Vol. 2:** 887

Isaiah *(cont'd)*

10:11   **Vol. 2:** 285
10:13   **Vol. 3:** 1027
10:14   **Vol. 1:** 519   **Vol. 3:** 747
10:16   **Vol. 2:** 49
10:19   **Vol. 3:** 248
10:20 ff   **Vol. 3:** 249
10:20   **Vol. 1:** 589
10:21   **Vol. 2:** 86
10:22 f   **Vol. 2:** 513   **Vol. 3:** 251
10:22   **Vol. 2:** 684   **Vol. 3:** 251
10:23   **Vol. 1:** 519
10:25   **Vol. 1:** 109
10:27   **Vol. 2:** 891   **Vol. 3:** 1161
10:33 f   **Vol. 2:** 260
10:33   **Vol. 2:** 509   **Vol. 3:** 29
10:34   **Vol. 3:** 867
11   **Vol. 1:** 210   **Vol. 2:** 333   **Vol. 3:** 637, 692
11:1 ff   **Vol. 1:** 185, 210   **Vol. 2:** 335, 614, 830   **Vol. 3:** 79, 649
11:1–10   **Vol. 3:** 639, 649
11:1–9   **Vol. 1:** 426   **Vol. 2:** 374   **Vol. 3:** 637
11:1–8   **Vol. 3:** 692
11:1–5   **Vol. 3:** 650
11:1–4   **Vol. 3:** 650
11:1 f   **Vol. 2:** 376
11:1   **Vol. 1:** 321, 407, 427   **Vol. 2:** 333, 715   **Vol. 3:** 649–650, 652, 869
11:2 ff   **Vol. 3:** 650
11:2   **Vol. 1:** 122   **Vol. 2:** 93, 654   **Vol. 3:** 130, 254–257, 639, 691, 1016, 1027, 1029
11:3 f   **Vol. 2:** 141
11:4   **Vol. 2:** 257, 686   **Vol. 3:** 192, 639, 690
11:5   **Vol. 1:** 239   **Vol. 3:** 121, 207, 879, 966
11:6–9   **Vol. 2:** 779
11:6 f   **Vol. 3:** 515
11:6   **Vol. 2:** 428, 888   **Vol. 3:** 951
11:8   **Vol. 1:** 281, 510   **Vol. 2:** 586
11:9   **Vol. 2:** 229
11:10   **Vol. 1:** 427   **Vol. 2:** 554   **Vol. 3:** 255, 649, 652, 867, 869
11:11 ff   **Vol. 3:** 249
11:11   **Vol. 1:** 531
11:12   **Vol. 1:** 297   **Vol. 2:** 689
11:13   **Vol. 3:** 1161
11:15   **Vol. 3:** 985
11:16   **Vol. 2:** 889
12:1*   **Vol. 1:** 368
12:2   **Vol. 3:** 218
12:3   **Vol. 3:** 208, 986, 988
12:4   **Vol. 2:** 650   **Vol. 3:** 668
12:5   **Vol. 3:** 46, 668
12:6   **Vol. 2:** 425
13–23   **Vol. 3:** 960
13   **Vol. 1:** 141–142, 519
13:1   **Vol. 3:** 325
13:2   **Vol. 3:** 1009

13:3   **Vol. 1:** 109
13:4   **Vol. 1:** 332
13:6   **Vol. 2:** 53, 888, 890   **Vol. 3:** 729
13:7   **Vol. 3:** 178
13:8   **Vol. 1:** 186   **Vol. 3:** 858
13:9   **Vol. 2:** 363, 890
13:10   **Vol. 1:** 203, 425   **Vol. 2:** 38, 484, 916   **Vol. 3:** 559, 731, 733, 735
13:11   **Vol. 1:** 332   **Vol. 3:** 29
13:13   **Vol. 1:** 108   **Vol. 2:** 189   **Vol. 3:** 29
13:14   **Vol. 2:** 458
13:17   **Vol. 3:** 823, 957
13:19   **Vol. 3:** 93, 560
13:20 f   **Vol. 3:** 255
13:20   **Vol. 3:** 828, 842
13:21 f   **Vol. 3:** 1005
13:21   **Vol. 1:** 451   **Vol. 3:** 255
13:22   **Vol. 3:** 782
14   **Vol. 1:** 142, 519
14:1–23   **Vol. 1:** 141
14:1   **Vol. 1:** 688   **Vol. 3:** 254
14:2   **Vol. 3:** 590
14:3–21   **Vol. 2:** 432
14:3   **Vol. 2:** 890   **Vol. 3:** 254, 256
14:4–21   **Vol. 1:** 141
14:4   **Vol. 2:** 745   **Vol. 3:** 255
14:5   **Vol. 3:** 1161
14:6   **Vol. 3:** 254
14:8   **Vol. 1:** 389
14:9 ff   **Vol. 2:** 206
14:12   **Vol. 1:** 610   **Vol. 2:** 495   **Vol. 3:** 468, 734
14:13 f   **Vol. 3:** 622
14:13   **Vol. 2:** 613
14:16   **Vol. 3:** 557
14:17   **Vol. 3:** 177
14:20   **Vol. 3:** 842
14:21   **Vol. 3:** 117
14:22   **Vol. 3:** 633
14:24   **Vol. 3:** 224
14:25   **Vol. 3:** 1161
14:26   **Vol. 2:** 201   **Vol. 3:** 1016
14:29   **Vol. 3:** 1161
14:30   **Vol. 2:** 777   **Vol. 3:** 255
14:32   **Vol. 1:** 661   **Vol. 2:** 260
15:2–3   **Vol. 2:** 418
15:2 f   **Vol. 2:** 416
15:2   **Vol. 2:** 418   **Vol. 3:** 418
15:5   **Vol. 3:** 557
15:6   **Vol. 1:** 743
16:2   **Vol. 2:** 746
16:4   **Vol. 1:** 690
16:5   **Vol. 3:** 880
16:6   **Vol. 3:** 29
16:8   **Vol. 2:** 422
16:9   **Vol. 3:** 525
16:10   **Vol. 3:** 673
16:12   **Vol. 2:** 862   **Vol. 3:** 418, 786
17:2   **Vol. 2:** 586   **Vol. 3:** 255
17:4   **Vol. 2:** 44

Isaiah *(cont'd)*

17:5	**Vol. 2:** 32 **Vol. 3:** 526
17:6	**Vol. 3:** 867
17:7 f	**Vol. 1:** 589
17:8	**Vol. 3:** 418
17:10	**Vol. 2:** 705 **Vol. 3:** 207, 218, 275
17:11	**Vol. 3:** 525
17:12	**Vol. 3:** 112
17:13	**Vol. 1:** 520 **Vol. 3:** 711
18:1	**Vol. 3:** 836
18:2	**Vol. 1:** 419
18:4	**Vol. 1:** 663 **Vol. 3:** 526
18:5	**Vol. 3:** 526
18:7	**Vol. 2:** 41 **Vol. 3:** 155, 786
19	**Vol. 1:** 531
19:1	**Vol. 2:** 38, 190, 917 **Vol. 3:** 1001
19:3	**Vol. 2:** 554–555, 879 **Vol. 3:** 691
19:4	**Vol. 3:** 1025
19:5–8	**Vol. 3:** 985
19:5	**Vol. 1:** 515
19:6	**Vol. 1:** 515
19:8	**Vol. 2:** 422–423
19:10	**Vol. 3:** 820, 1161
19:11 f	**Vol. 3:** 1028
19:11	**Vol. 1:** 531 **Vol. 3:** 1016, 1025
19:12	**Vol. 3:** 482
19:13 f	**Vol. 2:** 458
19:13	**Vol. 3:** 870
19:14	**Vol. 1:** 513 **Vol. 3:** 911, 913
19:17	**Vol. 1:** 622
19:20	**Vol. 3:** 462
19:25	**Vol. 2:** 297
20	**Vol. 1:** 531
20:1 ff	**Vol. 2:** 626
20:2 f	**Vol. 2:** 754
20:2	**Vol. 3:** 79, 121
20:3	**Vol. 2:** 633, 741
20:4	**Vol. 1:** 193
20:5	**Vol. 3:** 562
20:6	**Vol. 3:** 209
21:1–10	**Vol. 1:** 141 **Vol. 3:** 1091
21:3	**Vol. 1:** 239 **Vol. 3:** 1169
21:4	**Vol. 1:** 144
21:9	**Vol. 1:** 610
21:16	**Vol. 2:** 139
22:4	**Vol. 1:** 201
22:10	**Vol. 3:** 948
22:11	**Vol. 1:** 380
22:13	**Vol. 2:** 272
22:14	**Vol. 1:** 698
22:16	**Vol. 3:** 239
22:19	**Vol. 2:** 254
22:21	**Vol. 2:** 254 **Vol. 3:** 120
22:22	**Vol. 2:** 726–727, 730, 732–733 **Vol. 3:** 387, 652
22:23	**Vol. 3:** 878
22:25	**Vol. 3:** 878
23	**Vol. 1:** 519 **Vol. 2:** 767 **Vol. 3:** 1052
23:4	**Vol. 2:** 201 **Vol. 3:** 858
23:7	**Vol. 3:** 29
23:9	**Vol. 3:** 29
23:12	**Vol. 3:** 29, 255
23:13	**Vol. 3:** 255
23:15	**Vol. 2:** 690 **Vol. 3:** 673, 842
23:16	**Vol. 3:** 673
23:18	**Vol. 2:** 139
24–28	**Vol. 2:** 306
24–27	**Vol. 1:** 50 **Vol. 3:** 80, 829, 961
24:2	**Vol. 2:** 666
24:4	**Vol. 2:** 422 **Vol. 3:** 203, 1071
24:5	**Vol. 1:** 322, 368
24:7	**Vol. 2:** 422–423
24:8 f	**Vol. 3:** 673
24:8	**Vol. 2:** 842
24:16	**Vol. 2:** 93
24:18	**Vol. 1:** 609, 661
24:21	**Vol. 2:** 888
24:23	**Vol. 1:** 195 **Vol. 2:** 326, 376, 495 **Vol. 3:** 733
25:1–5	**Vol. 2:** 261
25:1	**Vol. 3:** 668, 673, 1016, 1157
25:4	**Vol. 3:** 201
25:5	**Vol. 3:** 554
25:6 ff	**Vol. 2:** 727
25:6–8	**Vol. 2:** 522, 791
25:6	**Vol. 1:** 210 **Vol. 2:** 532, 580, 632 **Vol. 3:** 951
25:8	**Vol. 2:** 631 **Vol. 3:** 267–268, 1112
25:9	**Vol. 2:** 240, 353, 773 **Vol. 3:** 218
25:10	**Vol. 3:** 255–256
25:11	**Vol. 3:** 29
26	**Vol. 1:** 124
26:1	**Vol. 3:** 673
26:2	**Vol. 2:** 726
26:6	**Vol. 2:** 257, 260, 778
26:7	**Vol. 2:** 93
26:8	**Vol. 2:** 650 **Vol. 3:** 237
26:9	**Vol. 1:** 484 **Vol. 3:** 673
26:11	**Vol. 2:** 395 **Vol. 3:** 28, 1167
26:12	**Vol. 1:** 210 **Vol. 2:** 778
26:13	**Vol. 3:** 238
26:14	**Vol. 1:** 444 **Vol. 2:** 569 **Vol. 3:** 237
26:16 ff	**Vol. 3:** 1068
26:16–21	**Vol. 3:** 722
26:17 f	**Vol. 1:** 186
26:17	**Vol. 1:** 409
26:19	**Vol. 1:** 434, 444 **Vol. 2:** 479 **Vol. 3:** 268, 273
26:20	**Vol. 1:** 109 **Vol. 2:** 429 **Vol. 3:** 367, 843
26:21	**Vol. 1:** 410 **Vol. 3:** 786
27:1	**Vol. 1:** 205, 210, 508, 523 **Vol. 2:** 891 **Vol. 3:** 983
27:5	**Vol. 2:** 782 **Vol. 3:** 1153
27:9	**Vol. 3:** 153–154, 203, 418, 865
27:10	**Vol. 3:** 255
27:12	**Vol. 2:** 720 **Vol. 3:** 526, 985
27:13	**Vol. 2:** 38, 876, 917 **Vol. 3:** 874
28:1	**Vol. 1:** 513 **Vol. 2:** 139 **Vol. 3:** 29

Isaiah (*cont'd*)

28:2   **Vol. 3:** 255, 711
28:3   **Vol. 2:** 139   **Vol. 3:** 29
28:5 f   **Vol. 3:** 249
28:6   **Vol. 3:** 238
28:7   **Vol. 1:** 513, 527   **Vol. 2:** 458   **Vol. 3:** 919
28:9 ff   **Vol. 3:** 483
28:9–10   **Vol. 2:** 432
28:9   **Vol. 3:** 771
28:11 f   **Vol. 2:** 444, 446, 513, 740   **Vol. 3:** 1079–1080
28:11   **Vol. 2:** 175
28:12   **Vol. 2:** 154   **Vol. 3:** 255–256, 389, 530
28:13   **Vol. 1:** 419   **Vol. 3:** 1118
28:14–18   **Vol. 1:** 366
28:15   **Vol. 1:** 368   **Vol. 2:** 471, 479   **Vol. 3:** 388–389
28:16   **Vol. 1:** 477, 541, 596, 661   **Vol. 2:** 327, 706, 709   **Vol. 3:** 382, 384, 388–393, 490–491, 500, 563, 1211–1212
28:17   **Vol. 2:** 471
28:17a   **Vol. 3:** 389
28:18   **Vol. 1:** 368   **Vol. 3:** 226
28:21   **Vol. 1:** 202, 688   **Vol. 3:** 1148
28:22*   **Vol. 3:** 713, 1157
28:23–25   **Vol. 2:** 747
28:25   **Vol. 2:** 211
28:27   **Vol. 2:** 211
28:28   **Vol. 1:** 202
29:2   **Vol. 2:** 842
29:3   **Vol. 3:** 951–952
29:4   **Vol. 2:** 554
29:5   **Vol. 2:** 842
29:6   **Vol. 3:** 557
29:7 f   **Vol. 2:** 842
29:8   **Vol. 1:** 546
29:9 f   **Vol. 1:** 219
29:9   **Vol. 3:** 178
29:10   **Vol. 3:** 692
29:11   **Vol. 3:** 498, 500
29:13   **Vol. 1:** 552   **Vol. 2:** 43, 53, 93, 150, 181, 469, 799, 813, 864   **Vol. 3:** 184, 427, 760, 769–770, 807
29:14   **Vol. 1:** 74, 463   **Vol. 3:** 130–132, 504, 1027–1028
29:15   **Vol. 1:** 422   **Vol. 3:** 1149
29:16 f   **Vol. 3:** 823
29:16   **Vol. 2:** 434, 609   **Vol. 3:** 911–912, 915–917
29:17–24   **Vol. 2:** 779
29:18–20   **Vol. 3:** 697
29:18 f   **Vol. 2:** 379
29:18   **Vol. 1:** 218–219
29:19   **Vol. 2:** 257, 823, 891
29:20   **Vol. 3:** 29
29:21   **Vol. 2:** 141
29:23   **Vol. 2:** 653   **Vol. 3:** 1148
29:24   **Vol. 2:** 777   **Vol. 3:** 691–692

30–31   **Vol. 1:** 531
30:1   **Vol. 1:** 607
30:4   **Vol. 2:** 926
30:6   **Vol. 2:** 807, 842   **Vol. 3:** 1005
30:7   **Vol. 1:** 546
30:8   **Vol. 1:** 245   **Vol. 3:** 484, 1094
30:10   **Vol. 2:** 432   **Vol. 3:** 77
30:12   **Vol. 3:** 1094
30:13   **Vol. 2:** 898
30:14   **Vol. 3:** 914
30:15 ff   **Vol. 3:** 249
30:15   **Vol. 2:** 320   **Vol. 3:** 206, 249, 389
30:17   **Vol. 3:** 1009
30:18   **Vol. 1:** 216   **Vol. 2:** 364   **Vol. 3:** 224
30:19   **Vol. 2:** 416
30:20   **Vol. 3:** 766
30:23–25   **Vol. 3:** 986
30:24   **Vol. 2:** 34   **Vol. 3:** 444
30:25   **Vol. 1:** 609
30:26   **Vol. 2:** 690, 890   **Vol. 3:** 731, 733
30:27 f   **Vol. 1:** 108
30:27   **Vol. 1:** 109
30:28   **Vol. 1:** 241   **Vol. 3:** 695, 1178
30:30   **Vol. 2:** 836   **Vol. 3:** 711
30:33   **Vol. 3:** 117
31:1   **Vol. 2:** 257   **Vol. 3:** 531
31:2   **Vol. 3:** 1028, 1094
31:3 f   **Vol. 2:** 602
31:3   **Vol. 1:** 673, 677, 679   **Vol. 3:** 691
31:7   **Vol. 1:** 455
31:9   **Vol. 2:** 208
32:1   **Vol. 2:** 591
32:3   **Vol. 1:** 589
32:4   **Vol. 2:** 777
32:5 f   **Vol. 3:** 1025
32:6   **Vol. 3:** 1025
32:7   **Vol. 2:** 257
32:8   **Vol. 2:** 93
32:9 ff   **Vol. 2:** 326
32:9   **Vol. 2:** 841
32:10   **Vol. 3:** 238
32:11   **Vol. 1:** 239, 314
32:13   **Vol. 1:** 240, 743   **Vol. 2:** 841
32:14   **Vol. 2:** 842
32:15 ff   **Vol. 3:** 355
32:15–20   **Vol. 3:** 692
32:15 f   **Vol. 3:** 1006
32:15   **Vol. 1:** 322   **Vol. 2:** 199, 854   **Vol. 3:** 823
32:16   **Vol. 3:** 255
32:17   **Vol. 3:** 255
32:18†   **Vol. 2:** 803, 842   **Vol. 3:** 254
33:1–24   **Vol. 3:** 78
33:1   **Vol. 3:** 859
33:2   **Vol. 3:** 836
33:3   **Vol. 2:** 34   **Vol. 3:** 207
33:5   **Vol. 2:** 199
33:6   **Vol. 2:** 93, 830   **Vol. 3:** 1027
33:7–10   **Vol. 1:** 91
33:7   **Vol. 1:** 201

Isaiah *(cont'd)*

33:8	**Vol. 1:** 368 **Vol. 3:** 823
33:9	**Vol. 2:** 422
33:13	**Vol. 2:** 53
33:14	**Vol. 1:** 655
33:15 f	**Vol. 3:** 367
33:15	**Vol. 3:** 924, 946
33:16	**Vol. 2:** 199
33:18	**Vol. 3:** 482
33:19	**Vol. 2:** 740
33:20	**Vol. 2:** 841 **Vol. 3:** 842
33:23	**Vol. 2:** 415
33:24	**Vol. 1:** 698
34:1	**Vol. 1:** 519
34:2	**Vol. 1:** 414 **Vol. 2:** 684
34:4	**Vol. 1:** 610, 724 **Vol. 2:** 38, 189, 916 **Vol. 3:** 180, 557, 559, 735–736
34:5	**Vol. 1:** 414, 513 **Vol. 2:** 189
34:6	**Vol. 3:** 159
34:7	**Vol. 1:** 513
34:10	**Vol. 3:** 109, 842
34:11	**Vol. 1:** 173
34:13–15	**Vol. 3:** 1005
34:13	**Vol. 1:** 726
34:14	**Vol. 1:** 451 **Vol. 3:** 255
34:15*	**Vol. 1:** 663 **Vol. 2:** 32
34:17	**Vol. 3:** 255, 842
35	**Vol. 1:** 124 **Vol. 2:** 110
35:1	**Vol. 2:** 266
35:2–7	**Vol. 1:** 91
35:2	**Vol. 2:** 44
35:3–6	**Vol. 2:** 168
35:3–5	**Vol. 3:** 697
35:3	**Vol. 2:** 859
35:4 ff	**Vol. 2:** 170
35:4	**Vol. 1:** 320 **Vol. 3:** 125
35:5–6	**Vol. 1:** 429
35:5 f†	**Vol. 1:** 445 **Vol. 2:** 379 **Vol. 3:** 1006
35:5	**Vol. 1:** 218–219 **Vol. 2:** 726 **Vol. 3:** 56
35:6 f	**Vol. 2:** 266
35:6	**Vol. 2:** 415
35:7	**Vol. 3:** 986
35:8	**Vol. 1:** 272 **Vol. 2:** 458
35:9	**Vol. 1:** 113 **Vol. 3:** 192
35:10	**Vol. 2:** 355, 420 **Vol. 3:** 193
36 ff	**Vol. 2:** 325
36:3	**Vol. 2:** 254
36:6	**Vol. 1:** 589
36:13	**Vol. 1:** 410
36:14–20	**Vol. 3:** 202
36:15	**Vol. 3:** 201
36:18 ff	**Vol. 3:** 342
36:19 f	**Vol. 2:** 285
36:19	**Vol. 3:** 202
36:22	**Vol. 2:** 254
37:2	**Vol. 2:** 254
37:3	**Vol. 2:** 140, 890 **Vol. 3:** 858
37:10 ff	**Vol. 3:** 342
37:15	**Vol. 2:** 862
37:16	**Vol. 1:** 280 **Vol. 2:** 70, 724
37:17	**Vol. 2:** 726
37:20*	**Vol. 3:** 1040
37:21	**Vol. 2:** 862
37:23	**Vol. 2:** 201
37:24	**Vol. 3:** 1009
37:25	**Vol. 3:** 1005
37:26	**Vol. 1:** 165
37:27	**Vol. 1:** 743
37:28	**Vol. 3:** 255
37:32	**Vol. 3:** 1167
37:33	**Vol. 3:** 951
37:36 ff	**Vol. 3:** 342
37:37	**Vol. 2:** 679
37:38	**Vol. 2:** 876
38	**Vol. 2:** 628
38:2	**Vol. 2:** 862
38:3	**Vol. 3:** 235
38:5	**Vol. 2:** 863 **Vol. 3:** 842
38:7 ff	**Vol. 2:** 627
38:8	**Vol. 3:** 554, 846
38:9	**Vol. 2:** 863 **Vol. 3:** 673, 999
38:10	**Vol. 2:** 29–30
38:11	**Vol. 1:** 433
38:12	**Vol. 3:** 811
38:13	**Vol. 1:** 240 **Vol. 3:** 342
38:17	**Vol. 1:** 233 **Vol. 3:** 262, 997
38:18	**Vol. 3:** 226, 816, 880
38:19	**Vol. 1:** 617 **Vol. 3:** 354
38:21	**Vol. 2:** 169
39:2	**Vol. 2:** 357, 607
39:6	**Vol. 2:** 890
39:7	**Vol. 3:** 786
39:8	**Vol. 2:** 100 **Vol. 3:** 354
40–66	**Vol. 1:** 52, 686
40–55	**Vol. 1:** 54, 699 **Vol. 2:** 226 **Vol. 3:** 1101, 1105
40	**Vol. 1:** 383 **Vol. 2:** 326 **Vol. 3:** 828
40:1–31	**Vol. 3:** 69
40:1–8	**Vol. 3:** 1101
40:1–7	**Vol. 3:** 257
40:1–5	**Vol. 3:** 1101
40:1	**Vol. 1:** 569
40:2	**Vol. 1:** 109 **Vol. 3:** 177, 668, 960
40:3 ff	**Vol. 1:** 409 **Vol. 2:** 262
40:3–5	**Vol. 3:** 1011
40:3	**Vol. 1:** 410–412 **Vol. 2:** 715 **Vol. 3:** 53, 55, 118–119, 937, 939–940, 1005–1007
40:4	**Vol. 3:** 392, 1010, 1012
40:5 f	**Vol. 1:** 672 **Vol. 2:** 799
40:5	**Vol. 2:** 45 **Vol. 3:** 221
40:6 ff	**Vol. 1:** 273 **Vol. 2:** 844
40:6 f	**Vol. 3:** 1101
40:6–8	**Vol. 1:** 678
40:6	**Vol. 1:** 411, 673, 743 **Vol. 2:** 211 **Vol. 3:** 1101
40:7	**Vol. 1:** 516, 609, 743–744 **Vol. 2:** 211, 746 **Vol. 3:** 690

Isaiah *(cont'd)*

40:8   **Vol. 1:** 411, 673, 744   **Vol. 3:** 224, 1101, 1122
40:9   **Vol. 2:** 109, 111, 327, 803
40:10 f   **Vol. 1:** 320   **Vol. 3:** 565
40:10   **Vol. 2:** 139, 279
40:11   **Vol. 2:** 32, 34, 412   **Vol. 3:** 565
40:12   **Vol. 3:** 1010, 1160
40:13 f   **Vol. 3:** 129, 1032
40:13   **Vol. 1:** 363   **Vol. 2:** 279, 513, 772   **Vol. 3:** 125, 129
40:15   **Vol. 3:** 823, 1160
40:18 ff   **Vol. 2:** 285
40:18   **Vol. 2:** 502
40:19 f   **Vol. 2:** 287
40:19   **Vol. 3:** 119
40:20   **Vol. 1:** 390, 537
40:22   **Vol. 2:** 189
40:25   **Vol. 2:** 70, 71, 226
40:26   **Vol. 1:** 273, 380   **Vol. 2:** 199   **Vol. 3:** 1102
40:27–31   **Vol. 2:** 266
40:27   **Vol. 2:** 215
40:28   **Vol. 1:** 262   **Vol. 2:** 616   **Vol. 3:** 119, 841
40:29   **Vol. 2:** 215
40:30 f   **Vol. 1:** 262
40:30   **Vol. 1:** 262
40:31   **Vol. 1:** 173   **Vol. 2:** 240, 773
41 f   **Vol. 2:** 309
41–45   **Vol. 3:** 1153
41:1 ff   **Vol. 2:** 364
41:2   **Vol. 1:** 273   **Vol. 3:** 357, 746
41:4   **Vol. 1:** 273, 665   **Vol. 2:** 59, 64, 69–70, 157
41:8 ff   **Vol. 3:** 1102
41:8   **Vol. 1:** 77, 273, 538   **Vol. 2:** 596   **Vol. 3:** 369, 867
41:10 f   **Vol. 3:** 355
41:10   **Vol. 1:** 623
41:11   **Vol. 3:** 562
41:13   **Vol. 1:** 622–623   **Vol. 2:** 149   **Vol. 3:** 716
41:14   **Vol. 3:** 192
41:15   **Vol. 3:** 392, 1010
41:16   **Vol. 2:** 34
41:17 ff   **Vol. 3:** 79
41:17 f   **Vol. 2:** 266
41:17   **Vol. 2:** 257, 823
41:18   **Vol. 3:** 986, 1006
41:19   **Vol. 2:** 266, 711
41:20   **Vol. 1:** 380   **Vol. 2:** 395
41:21   **Vol. 2:** 375–376
41:22   **Vol. 3:** 125
41:23   **Vol. 2:** 56
41:25   **Vol. 3:** 911, 915–916
41:26 f   **Vol. 3:** 1101
41:27   **Vol. 1:** 665   **Vol. 2:** 109
41:28   **Vol. 2:** 879

41:29   **Vol. 2:** 720
42   **Vol. 3:** 110
42:1–9   **Vol. 3:** 609
42:1–4   **Vol. 1:** 374, 651   **Vol. 3:** 48, 69, 110, 609, 612, 692, 1041, 1163
42:1   **Vol. 1:** 534, 538   **Vol. 2:** 543, 819, 888   **Vol. 3:** 258, 609–611, 638–641, 685, 698, 807, 864, 987
42:2 f   **Vol. 2:** 258
42:2   **Vol. 1:** 409
42:3 f   **Vol. 3:** 609
42:3   **Vol. 2:** 888   **Vol. 3:** 109–110
42:4   **Vol. 2:** 240–241, 654   **Vol. 3:** 109
42:5   **Vol. 2:** 77, 164, 190   **Vol. 3:** 690
42:6 ff   **Vol. 1:** 688   **Vol. 2:** 333
42:6   **Vol. 1:** 273   **Vol. 2:** 492, 494, 728, 799, 888   **Vol. 3:** 313, 716
42:7   **Vol. 1:** 422   **Vol. 2:** 596, 726   **Vol. 3:** 592, 609
42:8   **Vol. 2:** 44, 70   **Vol. 3:** 926
42:9   **Vol. 2:** 670, 672   **Vol. 3:** 45, 704
42:10   **Vol. 3:** 669, 675
42:12   **Vol. 2:** 44   **Vol. 3:** 926
42:13   **Vol. 3:** 1167
42:14   **Vol. 2:** 765, 767   **Vol. 3:** 908
42:15   **Vol. 1:** 515   **Vol. 3:** 986
42:16   **Vol. 1:** 422
42:17   **Vol. 2:** 728
42:18   **Vol. 3:** 519
42:21   **Vol. 3:** 140, 355
42:24   **Vol. 2:** 440
42:25   **Vol. 1:** 109
43:1 ff   **Vol. 2:** 337   **Vol. 3:** 79
43:1   **Vol. 1:** 273   **Vol. 2:** 649   **Vol. 3:** 192
43:2   **Vol. 3:** 695, 983, 986
43:3 ff   **Vol. 3:** 623
43:3 f   **Vol. 1:** 479   **Vol. 3:** 192
43:3   **Vol. 2:** 367   **Vol. 3:** 153, 192, 1196
43:4   **Vol. 2:** 541
43:5 ff   **Vol. 3:** 208
43:5   **Vol. 1:** 297   **Vol. 2:** 32
43:6   **Vol. 3:** 718
43:7   **Vol. 1:** 380   **Vol. 2:** 777   **Vol. 3:** 119
43:8 ff   **Vol. 2:** 307
43:8   **Vol. 1:** 428–429
43:9 f   **Vol. 3:** 1101
`43:9   **Vol. 3:** 355, 881
43:10 ff   **Vol. 2:** 70
43:10   **Vol. 1:** 273, 538   **Vol. 2:** 720, 888   **Vol. 3:** 130, 1041
43:11   **Vol. 2:** 279
43:12   **Vol. 3:** 1041
43:14   **Vol. 2:** 226   **Vol. 3:** 192
43:15   **Vol. 1:** 382   **Vol. 2:** 226
43:16–21   **Vol. 2:** 670
43:16   **Vol. 3:** 937
43:17   **Vol. 1:** 442   **Vol. 3:** 109
43:18 ff   **Vol. 2:** 671
43:18 f   **Vol. 2:** 670, 672
43:18   **Vol. 3:** 236

Isaiah *(cont'd)*

43:19–21   **Vol. 3:** 986
43:19 f   **Vol. 3:** 1006
43:19   **Vol. 3:** 180, 937, 1006
43:20   **Vol. 2:** 266   **Vol. 3:** 986
43:21   **Vol. 3:** 926–927
43:22–25   **Vol. 3:** 150
43:22–24   **Vol. 3:** 625
43:22   **Vol. 1:** 262
43:23   **Vol. 2:** 221
43:24   **Vol. 1:** 194
43:25   **Vol. 1:** 471   **Vol. 3:** 167, 235, 631
43:26   **Vol. 3:** 355
43:28   **Vol. 1:** 414
44   **Vol. 3:** 828
44:1   **Vol. 3:** 1102
44:2   **Vol. 1:** 622   **Vol. 3:** 807
44:3   **Vol. 2:** 266   **Vol. 3:** 490, 692, 986–989
44:4   **Vol. 1:** 743
44:5   **Vol. 2:** 572   **Vol. 3:** 498
44:6   **Vol. 1:** 665, 667   **Vol. 2:** 59, 64, 70, 279, 282, 375–376   **Vol. 3:** 201–202
44:7 ff   **Vol. 3:** 45
44:7   **Vol. 2:** 498   **Vol. 3:** 704, 1101
44:8   **Vol. 2:** 720   **Vol. 3:** 1041
44:9–20   **Vol. 2:** 285, 432
44:9   **Vol. 3:** 1153
44:12 ff   **Vol. 1:** 654
44:13 ff   **Vol. 1:** 390
44:13   **Vol. 1:** 706
44:15   **Vol. 1:** 654   **Vol. 2:** 876
44:17   **Vol. 2:** 862, 876   **Vol. 3:** 248
44:19   **Vol. 2:** 876   **Vol. 3:** 248, 823
44:21   **Vol. 3:** 236
44:22 ff   **Vol. 3:** 192
44:23   **Vol. 2:** 356
44:24   **Vol. 1:** 95, 522   **Vol. 2:** 189, 279
44:25   **Vol. 2:** 554–555   **Vol. 3:** 1025, 1101
44:26   **Vol. 3:** 1101
44:27   **Vol. 3:** 986, 1005, 1101
44:28   **Vol. 1:** 111   **Vol. 3:** 97, 566, 786, 1019, 1154
45–48   **Vol. 2:** 285
45   **Vol. 3:** 218, 960
45:1 ff   **Vol. 2:** 791
45:1   **Vol. 1:** 111   **Vol. 2:** 335–336   **Vol. 3:** 97, 218, 716
45:2   **Vol. 3:** 1010
45:3   **Vol. 1:** 273   **Vol. 2:** 70, 215, 396, 830, 835
45:5   **Vol. 2:** 279
45:6 f   **Vol. 2:** 396
45:6   **Vol. 2:** 70
45:7   **Vol. 1:** 379, 422   **Vol. 2:** 491, 778   **Vol. 3:** 119
45:9 ff   **Vol. 3:** 1102
45:9   **Vol. 2:** 434, 609   **Vol. 3:** 119, 911–912, 916–917
45:10   **Vol. 3:** 858

45:11   **Vol. 2:** 226
45:13   **Vol. 3:** 190, 192, 590
45:13a   **Vol. 3:** 279
45:14 ff   **Vol. 1:** 688
45:14   **Vol. 2:** 862, 876
45:15   **Vol. 2:** 215   **Vol. 3:** 218
45:17   **Vol. 3:** 218, 828
45:19   **Vol. 3:** 502
45:20   **Vol. 2:** 32, 862   **Vol. 3:** 206, 250
45:21 f   **Vol. 3:** 218
45:21   **Vol. 3:** 218, 355, 1101
45:22   **Vol. 2:** 279, 888   **Vol. 3:** 208
45:23 f   **Vol. 2:** 514
45:23   **Vol. 1:** 321   **Vol. 2:** 369, 513, 650, 859, 925   **Vol. 3:** 1079, 1101
45:24   **Vol. 3:** 355
45:25*   **Vol. 3:** 355
46:1 f   **Vol. 2:** 285
46:2   **Vol. 3:** 209
46:3 f   **Vol. 3:** 250, 805
46:3   **Vol. 2:** 305
46:4   **Vol. 2:** 765   **Vol. 3:** 250
46:5   **Vol. 2:** 501
46:6   **Vol. 2:** 139, 876   **Vol. 3:** 1153, 1161
46:7   **Vol. 3:** 206
46:9   **Vol. 3:** 236
46:10   **Vol. 3:** 45
46:12 f   **Vol. 3:** 357
46:13   **Vol. 2:** 53, 326
47   **Vol. 1:** 141
47:1   **Vol. 3:** 588
47:2   **Vol. 3:** 394
47:3   **Vol. 2:** 212
47:4   **Vol. 3:** 192, 202
47:6   **Vol. 1:** 448   **Vol. 2:** 297   **Vol. 3:** 1161
47:7   **Vol. 3:** 125, 232
47:8 f   **Vol. 3:** 1074
47:8   **Vol. 2:** 395
47:9   **Vol. 2:** 554
47:10   **Vol. 2:** 830   **Vol. 3:** 1028
47:11   **Vol. 1:** 320   **Vol. 2:** 395   **Vol. 3:** 152, 154
47:12   **Vol. 2:** 554
47:13   **Vol. 2:** 189, 555   **Vol. 3:** 735
47:14   **Vol. 3:** 206
48:1 ff   **Vol. 2:** 364
48:1   **Vol. 3:** 232
48:2   **Vol. 2:** 325, 803
48:4   **Vol. 1:** 241
48:6   **Vol. 2:** 670
48:10   **Vol. 1:** 268
48:11   **Vol. 2:** 70
48:12–16a   **Vol. 1:** 141
48:12   **Vol. 1:** 665, 667   **Vol. 2:** 59, 64, 69–70, 279
48:13   **Vol. 2:** 149
48:14 f   **Vol. 1:** 273
48:14   **Vol. 2:** 32   **Vol. 3:** 1101
48:16   **Vol. 3:** 202, 258, 502
48:17   **Vol. 3:** 201–202

105

Isaiah *(cont'd)*

48:18 f	**Vol. 3:** 355
48:18	**Vol. 2:** 777–778 **Vol. 3:** 987
48:20–22	**Vol. 1:** 141
48:20	**Vol. 2:** 55–56, 318 **Vol. 3:** 202, 594
48:21	**Vol. 1:** 683 **Vol. 2:** 266 **Vol. 3:** 543
48:22	**Vol. 2:** 357, 777–778
49	**Vol. 2:** 309
49:1 ff	**Vol. 2:** 279, 337
49:1 f	**Vol. 3:** 609
49:1–11	**Vol. 3:** 609
49:1–6	**Vol. 1:** 374 **Vol. 3:** 69, 609, 692, 1041
49:1	**Vol. 3:** 612
49:2	**Vol. 2:** 686 **Vol. 3:** 554, 609, 967, 1102
49:3	**Vol. 3:** 609
49:4	**Vol. 1:** 262, 551
49:5 f	**Vol. 3:** 609
49:6 ff	**Vol. 2:** 333
49:6	**Vol. 1:** 477, 544, 641, 685 **Vol. 2:** 34, 55–56, 69, 492, 494–495, 888 **Vol. 3:** 69, 208, 218, 613
49:7	**Vol. 2:** 876 **Vol. 3:** 201–202
49:8	**Vol. 2:** 175, 178, 297, 890 **Vol. 3:** 214, 746, 838
49:9 f	**Vol. 2:** 266
49:9	**Vol. 1:** 422 **Vol. 3:** 565, 592, 609
49:10	**Vol. 2:** 267, 825 **Vol. 3:** 986
49:11	**Vol. 3:** 1012
49:13	**Vol. 2:** 71, 193, 257, 260, 356, 823
49:14 ff	**Vol. 3:** 1102
49:15	**Vol. 3:** 1069
49:16	**Vol. 2:** 149
49:18	**Vol. 2:** 32, 585
49:21	**Vol. 2:** 724 **Vol. 3:** 1068
49:22	**Vol. 1:** 240
49:23	**Vol. 2:** 396, 773, 876
49:24 f	**Vol. 2:** 631 **Vol. 3:** 209, 713
49:25 f	**Vol. 3:** 202
49:25	**Vol. 3:** 201
49:26	**Vol. 1:** 513 **Vol. 2:** 69, 396
50:1 ff	**Vol. 2:** 364
50:1	**Vol. 1:** 268, 505 **Vol. 2:** 307, 576–577 **Vol. 3:** 594, 1068–1069
50:2	**Vol. 1:** 272, 670 **Vol. 2:** 140, 179 **Vol. 3:** 202, 983, 986
50:3	**Vol. 1:** 203 **Vol. 2:** 189 **Vol. 3:** 1102
50:4 ff	**Vol. 2:** 279, 337
50:4–9	**Vol. 3:** 69, 609, 1041
50:4 f	**Vol. 3:** 609
50:4	**Vol. 3:** 1027, 1102
50:5	**Vol. 2:** 178, 726
50:7	**Vol. 3:** 382
50:8	**Vol. 2:** 53 **Vol. 3:** 355
50:9	**Vol. 1:** 316 **Vol. 2:** 714 **Vol. 3:** 357
50:11	**Vol. 1:** 442
51:1 f	**Vol. 3:** 393
51:1	**Vol. 3:** 382, 520
51:2	**Vol. 1:** 80 **Vol. 2:** 720 **Vol. 3:** 369, 382, 520, 858, 867
51:3	**Vol. 2:** 761
51:4	**Vol. 2:** 492
51:5 f	**Vol. 3:** 355
51:5–8	**Vol. 3:** 357
51:5	**Vol. 2:** 53, 239–240, 773
51:6	**Vol. 1:** 316 **Vol. 2:** 189, 714 **Vol. 3:** 520
51:7	**Vol. 2:** 181
51:8	**Vol. 1:** 316, 508 **Vol. 3:** 842
51:9 ff	**Vol. 2:** 672
51:9 f	**Vol. 3:** 983
51:10	**Vol. 2:** 197 **Vol. 3:** 202, 937, 1005
51:11	**Vol. 2:** 420 **Vol. 3:** 192–193
51:12	**Vol. 1:** 743 **Vol. 3:** 613
51:15	**Vol. 2:** 650
51:16	**Vol. 3:** 554, 1102
51:17 f	**Vol. 2:** 276
51:17	**Vol. 1:** 109 **Vol. 2:** 275 **Vol. 3:** 208, 357, 922
51:21 ff	**Vol. 2:** 823
51:22	**Vol. 1:** 109 **Vol. 3:** 922
52	**Vol. 3:** 610
52:1	**Vol. 1:** 154, 314 **Vol. 2:** 325, 803
52:2	**Vol. 3:** 560
52:3	**Vol. 3:** 192, 196, 200, 435
52:4	**Vol. 3:** 711
52:5	**Vol. 3:** 341–343
52:6	**Vol. 2:** 891 **Vol. 3:** 341
52:7	**Vol. 1:** 239 **Vol. 2:** 70, 100, 109, 111, 375–376, 778, 782 **Vol. 3:** 48, 612, 966
52:8	**Vol. 2:** 201
52:9	**Vol. 3:** 202
52:10	**Vol. 3:** 55, 118, 311
52:11	**Vol. 1:** 607 **Vol. 2:** 513 **Vol. 3:** 860
52:12	**Vol. 2:** 355
52:13 ff	**Vol. 2:** 337
52:13–53:12	**Vol. 1:** 374, 426 **Vol. 2:** 307 **Vol. 3:** 69, 269, 357, 609–610, 1041
52:13	**Vol. 3:** 196, 593, 607, 611, 624, 630, 632
52:14 f	**Vol. 1:** 96
52:15	**Vol. 3:** 48, 131–132, 613
53	**Vol. 1:** 96–97, 437, 549, 581, 699, 707 **Vol. 2:** 313, 411, 540 **Vol. 3:** 195–196, 435, 567, 578, 582, 597, 610–612, 621, 638, 697, 723, 748, 825
53:1 ff	**Vol. 2:** 258
53:1–3	**Vol. 1:** 427
53:1	**Vol. 2:** 173, 175, 513, 632 **Vol. 3:** 311–312, 314, 321, 613
53:2 f	**Vol. 1:** 704
53:2	**Vol. 3:** 867
53:3–8	**Vol. 2:** 51
53:3 f	**Vol. 1:** 163 **Vol. 3:** 823
53:3	**Vol. 1:** 162 **Vol. 2:** 49 **Vol. 3:** 999
53:4–6	**Vol. 3:** 721, 1200
53:4	**Vol. 1:** 162, 390 **Vol. 2:** 165 **Vol. 3:** 748, 998–999, 1195
53:5–12	**Vol. 3:** 491

Isaiah *(cont'd)*

53:5	**Vol. 2:** 368, 778 **Vol. 3:** 723, 777–778
53:6	**Vol. 2:** 412, 458–459 **Vol. 3:** 170, 938
53:7 f	**Vol. 2:** 263, 381 **Vol. 3:** 66, 609
53:7–12	**Vol. 1:** 581 **Vol. 2:** 263
53:7	**Vol. 1:** 548 **Vol. 2:** 410, 728 **Vol. 3:** 200, 347, 435
53:8	**Vol. 1:** 548, 576 **Vol. 2:** 38, 260 **Vol. 3:** 624
53:9	**Vol. 2:** 841 **Vol. 3:** 529, 723
53:10 ff	**Vol. 3:** 269
53:10–12	**Vol. 3:** 195, 1200
53:10 f	**Vol. 3:** 293, 420
53:10	**Vol. 3:** 171, 196, 522, 611, 624, 1016
53:10b	**Vol. 3:** 1200
53:11 f	**Vol. 1:** 96 **Vol. 2:** 532 **Vol. 3:** 195
53:11	**Vol. 2:** 854 **Vol. 3:** 196, 355, 1180
53:11a	**Vol. 3:** 1200
53:12	**Vol. 1:** 390, 548 **Vol. 2:** 62, 445, 525, 854 **Vol. 3:** 379, 491, 611–612, 625, 638, 823–826, 967, 1184, 1195
54:1 ff	**Vol. 3:** 1057
54:1	**Vol. 1:** 288, 321, 411 **Vol. 3:** 858, 1065, 1068, 1070
54:2	**Vol. 3:** 713
54:3	**Vol. 3:** 1005–1006
54:4 ff	**Vol. 3:** 1102
54:4–8	**Vol. 2:** 541
54:5 f	**Vol. 3:** 1068
54:5	**Vol. 3:** 201–202, 1068
54:6 f	**Vol. 2:** 541
54:7 ff	**Vol. 3:** 167
54:7 f	**Vol. 1:** 109 **Vol. 3:** 827
54:7	**Vol. 3:** 842, 1200
54:8–10	**Vol. 1:** 109
54:8	**Vol. 2:** 71, 215 **Vol. 3:** 201–202
54:9 f	**Vol. 2:** 672, 681
54:9	**Vol. 3:** 841
54:10	**Vol. 1:** 367 **Vol. 2:** 778–779 **Vol. 3:** 152, 1012
54:11 ff	**Vol. 2:** 823
54:11 f	**Vol. 3:** 397–398
54:11	**Vol. 1:** 661 **Vol. 2:** 260
54:12	**Vol. 3:** 395–396
54:13	**Vol. 2:** 778 **Vol. 3:** 764
54:14†	**Vol. 3:** 161
54:16	**Vol. 1:** 379, 468
54:17	**Vol. 2:** 142, 164 **Vol. 3:** 355, 609
55:1 ff	**Vol. 1:** 210
55:1	**Vol. 2:** 266–267, 275, 277 **Vol. 3:** 490, 813, 986, 988, 1051
55:2	**Vol. 2:** 735
55:3	**Vol. 1:** 367, 426 **Vol. 2:** 237–238 **Vol. 3:** 649, 828
55:5	**Vol. 2:** 226
55:6–13	**Vol. 1:** 699
55:6	**Vol. 3:** 528, 531
55:7	**Vol. 1:** 698 **Vol. 3:** 528, 938
55:8 f	**Vol. 3:** 937
55:8	**Vol. 3:** 528
55:9	**Vol. 3:** 125
55:10 f	**Vol. 2:** 626
55:10	**Vol. 1:** 186, 513, 733 **Vol. 2:** 189, 274 **Vol. 3:** 522
55:11	**Vol. 3:** 1094, 1101
55:12	**Vol. 2:** 778 **Vol. 3:** 761
55:13	**Vol. 2:** 650
56–66	**Vol. 1:** 54 **Vol. 3:** 451
56–59	**Vol. 3:** 357
56:1–8	**Vol. 1:** 688
56:1	**Vol. 2:** 53 **Vol. 3:** 311, 355, 357, 367
56:2	**Vol. 3:** 407
56:3 ff	**Vol. 1:** 560 **Vol. 2:** 117
56:3	**Vol. 1:** 515 **Vol. 3:** 866
56:5	**Vol. 2:** 149
56:6–11	**Vol. 3:** 1101
56:6	**Vol. 3:** 609
56:7	**Vol. 1:** 272 **Vol. 2:** 236, 248, 325, 379, 610, 863 **Vol. 3:** 378, 380, 421, 430, 791
56:8	**Vol. 2:** 32
56:10	**Vol. 2:** 547, 586
56:11 f	**Vol. 3:** 919
56:11	**Vol. 3:** 137, 566
57:2	**Vol. 2:** 778
57:3	**Vol. 2:** 554–555
57:4	**Vol. 2:** 735
57:5	**Vol. 3:** 865
57:6	**Vol. 2:** 298, 854 **Vol. 3:** 423, 919
57:7	**Vol. 2:** 587
57:8	**Vol. 3:** 237
57:9	**Vol. 1:** 194
57:15	**Vol. 2:** 199, 825 **Vol. 3:** 255
57:17 f	**Vol. 1:** 329
57:17	**Vol. 3:** 137
57:18	**Vol. 2:** 777
57:19	**Vol. 2:** 53, 778 **Vol. 3:** 515
57:20	**Vol. 3:** 255
57:21	**Vol. 2:** 357, 777
58:2	**Vol. 1:** 456 **Vol. 2:** 856
58:3 ff	**Vol. 3:** 161
58:3–10	**Vol. 2:** 864
58:3–7	**Vol. 1:** 612
58:3	**Vol. 1:** 495, 612 **Vol. 2:** 260
58:5	**Vol. 1:** 495
58:6–7	**Vol. 2:** 104
58:6	**Vol. 3:** 177
58:7	**Vol. 1:** 250, 312 **Vol. 2:** 265–266, 272
58:8 ff	**Vol. 3:** 357
58:10	**Vol. 1:** 250 **Vol. 2:** 265–266, 492
58:11	**Vol. 3:** 490, 813, 986–988
58:12	**Vol. 3:** 1006
58:13	**Vol. 2:** 890 **Vol. 3:** 1102
58:14	**Vol. 2:** 735
58:23	**Vol. 3:** 407
59:1 f	**Vol. 2:** 175, 864
59:3	**Vol. 1:** 449
59:4	**Vol. 1:** 186
59:6	**Vol. 3:** 1149

Isaiah *(cont'd)*

59:7   **Vol. 3:** 159, 820, 859, 966
59:8   **Vol. 2:** 778
59:9   **Vol. 1:** 606
59:10   **Vol. 1:** 218
59:11   **Vol. 1:** 607   **Vol. 2:** 423
59:13   **Vol. 2:** 471   **Vol. 3:** 881
59:14   **Vol. 1:** 607   **Vol. 3:** 881
59:15   **Vol. 3:** 881
59:17   **Vol. 3:** 966
59:19   **Vol. 3:** 987
59:20 f   **Vol. 2:** 329   **Vol. 3:** 203
59:20   **Vol. 1:** 320, 355   **Vol. 2:** 319,
            327   **Vol. 3:** 202–203
59:21   **Vol. 3:** 692
60   **Vol. 1:** 686
60:1 ff   **Vol. 2:** 45, 302, 585
60:1 f   **Vol. 2:** 596
60:1   **Vol. 1:** 320   **Vol. 2:** 45, 495   **Vol. 3:**
            634, 1068
60:2   **Vol. 1:** 422   **Vol. 2:** 212
60:3   **Vol. 2:** 492, 793
60:4   **Vol. 2:** 32
60:5 f   **Vol. 1:** 320
60:5   **Vol. 2:** 793, 842
60:6   **Vol. 2:** 294
60:7   **Vol. 2:** 863
60:9   **Vol. 2:** 773
60:10 ff   **Vol. 2:** 888
60:10   **Vol. 1:** 474
60:12   **Vol. 3:** 1005
60:13   **Vol. 3:** 786
60:15   **Vol. 1:** 555
60:16   **Vol. 2:** 842
60:17   **Vol. 1:** 190   **Vol. 2:** 777–778   **Vol. 3:**
            357
60:19 f   **Vol. 2:** 491   **Vol. 3:** 731
60:19†   **Vol. 2:** 495   **Vol. 3:** 733
60:20 ff   **Vol. 3:** 836
60:20   **Vol. 2:** 422   **Vol. 3:** 720, 733
60:21†   **Vol. 1:** 184   **Vol. 3:** 357, 722, 866–867
60:22   **Vol. 1:** 297   **Vol. 2:** 428, 698, 887
61   **Vol. 2:** 109, 353   **Vol. 3:** 520
61:1 ff   **Vol. 1:** 445
61:1–4   **Vol. 2:** 823
61:1–3   **Vol. 3:** 612
61:1–2   **Vol. 1:** 429   **Vol. 3:** 639
61:1 f   **Vol. 1:** 91, 738   **Vol. 2:** 168,
            379   **Vol. 3:** 56, 71, 612, 639,
            696–697, 762, 1108
61:1   **Vol. 1:** 122, 698, 717   **Vol. 2:** 109–110,
            257, 279, 337, 779, 824–825   **Vol. 3:**
            51, 258, 591, 698, 1061
61:2   **Vol. 1:** 272   **Vol. 2:** 779, 890   **Vol. 3:**
            746
61:3   **Vol. 1:** 120   **Vol. 2:** 711, 891
61:4   **Vol. 3:** 1006
61:5   **Vol. 2:** 742, 888   **Vol. 3:** 918

61:6   **Vol. 1:** 272   **Vol. 2:** 380, 625,
            842   **Vol. 3:** 37, 1175
61:7   **Vol. 3:** 354
61:8   **Vol. 3:** 354
61:10   **Vol. 1:** 316–317, 522   **Vol. 2:**
            584   **Vol. 3:** 207–208, 357
62:1–9   **Vol. 2:** 779
62:1   **Vol. 2:** 485, 779   **Vol. 3:** 355
62:2   **Vol. 2:** 649, 779
62:4   **Vol. 1:** 519   **Vol. 3:** 1006
62:5   **Vol. 2:** 578, 584–585   **Vol. 3:** 1065
62:8   **Vol. 1:** 554
62:9   **Vol. 2:** 32   **Vol. 3:** 816
62:11   **Vol. 2:** 139, 327, 379   **Vol. 3:** 218
62:12   **Vol. 3:** 192
63:1 ff   **Vol. 1:** 109
63:1 f   **Vol. 1:** 111
63:1   **Vol. 3:** 711, 820
63:2 f   **Vol. 1:** 224
63:2–6   **Vol. 3:** 919
63:3   **Vol. 3:** 919
63:4   **Vol. 2:** 890   **Vol. 3:** 193
63:5   **Vol. 3:** 202
63:7   **Vol. 3:** 926
63:7b   **Vol. 2:** 595
63:9   **Vol. 3:** 192
63:10 f   **Vol. 2:** 227
63:11–14   **Vol. 3:** 692
63:11 f   **Vol. 2:** 639
63:11   **Vol. 2:** 412
63:15–64:11 **Vol. 1:** 77
63:15   **Vol. 2:** 598, 765   **Vol. 3:** 1166–1167
63:16   **Vol. 1:** 77, 164, 617   **Vol. 2:**
            71   **Vol. 3:** 202
63:17   **Vol. 2:** 458
63:19 f   **Vol. 3:** 1010
63:19   **Vol. 1:** 164   **Vol. 2:** 649
64:1*   **Vol. 2:** 189–190   **Vol. 3:** 543
64:2   **Vol. 3:** 318
64:3*   **Vol. 2:** 773   **Vol. 3:** 504
64:4*   **Vol. 2:** 219, 773   **Vol. 3:** 533
64:6 f   **Vol. 3:** 578
64:7   **Vol. 1:** 272
64:8*   **Vol. 1:** 617   **Vol. 3:** 234, 638
64:12   **Vol. 2:** 765
65:1 f   **Vol. 2:** 176
65:1   **Vol. 1:** 112   **Vol. 2:** 489, 636,
            879–880   **Vol. 3:** 528
65:2   **Vol. 1:** 492   **Vol. 2:** 490, 880
65:3   **Vol. 1:** 451
65:4   **Vol. 1:** 117, 449   **Vol. 3:** 238
65:6   **Vol. 1:** 243
65:8   **Vol. 3:** 919
65:10   **Vol. 3:** 255
65:11   **Vol. 1:** 451   **Vol. 2:** 175, 518   **Vol. 3:**
            919
65:12   **Vol. 1:** 272   **Vol. 2:** 367   **Vol. 3:** 1016
65:13   **Vol. 2:** 265, 522, 532   **Vol. 3:** 1053
65:15   **Vol. 1:** 272
65:16   **Vol. 1:** 98–99

Isaiah *(cont'd)*

65:17 f	**Vol. 1:** 380 **Vol. 2:** 670
65:17–25	**Vol. 1:** 210
65:17–19	**Vol. 2:** 779
65:17	**Vol. 1:** 185 **Vol. 2:** 189, 219, 888 **Vol. 3:** 180, 533
65:19	**Vol. 2:** 353, 355
65:20	**Vol. 3:** 842
65:21	**Vol. 2:** 888
65:22	**Vol. 1:** 538 **Vol. 3:** 866
65:23	**Vol. 1:** 262, 546
65:23b	**Vol. 1:** 215
65:24	**Vol. 2:** 179
65:25	**Vol. 1:** 250
66	**Vol. 3:** 786
66:1 f	**Vol. 3:** 465, 785, 793
66:1	**Vol. 1:** 518 **Vol. 2:** 193, 247, 252, 613 **Vol. 3:** 256, 258, 741
66:2	**Vol. 1:** 185 **Vol. 2:** 257, 414
66:2b	**Vol. 2:** 260
66:3	**Vol. 1:** 117 **Vol. 3:** 341
66:4	**Vol. 2:** 179 **Vol. 3:** 1016
66:7 ff	**Vol. 3:** 732
66:7–11	**Vol. 3:** 1068
66:7	**Vol. 1:** 186 **Vol. 2:** 569–570
66:8	**Vol. 1:** 186 **Vol. 2:** 717
66:9	**Vol. 3:** 637
66:10–19	**Vol. 1:** 91
66:10	**Vol. 2:** 356–357
66:11	**Vol. 1:** 240 **Vol. 2:** 735
66:12	**Vol. 2:** 778 **Vol. 3:** 987
66:13	**Vol. 3:** 1069
66:14	**Vol. 1:** 91, 240 **Vol. 2:** 357 **Vol. 3:** 269
66:15 f	**Vol. 1:** 655 **Vol. 2:** 836
66:15	**Vol. 1:** 657 **Vol. 2:** 96
66:18 ff	**Vol. 3:** 250
66:18	**Vol. 1:** 320 **Vol. 2:** 32 **Vol. 3:** 823
66:19	**Vol. 1:** 688 **Vol. 2:** 48, 124, 888
66:20	**Vol. 3:** 38, 431
66:22	**Vol. 2:** 48 **Vol. 3:** 180, 224
66:23	**Vol. 2:** 876
66:24	**Vol. 1:** 655, 657 **Vol. 2:** 208 **Vol. 3:** 109–110, 447–448

Jeremiah

1–25	**Vol. 3:** 1095
1:1	**Vol. 3:** 311, 1092–1093, 1120
1:3	**Vol. 3:** 590
1:4–10	**Vol. 3:** 1088, 1095
1:5	**Vol. 2:** 226, 395 **Vol. 3:** 1095
1:6	**Vol. 1:** 272 **Vol. 3:** 1095
1:8	**Vol. 3:** 1095
1:9 f	**Vol. 2:** 252
1:9	**Vol. 3:** 1088, 1095
1:10	**Vol. 2:** 252 **Vol. 3:** 1095
1:11 ff	**Vol. 2:** 173
1:11–12	**Vol. 2:** 432
1:12	**Vol. 3:** 1096, 1153
1:16	**Vol. 2:** 876
1:18	**Vol. 2:** 98
2–4:5†	**Vol. 3:** 1095
2	**Vol. 3:** 263
2:1 ff	**Vol. 2:** 541
2:2	**Vol. 2:** 576, 583, 585 **Vol. 3:** 235
2:3	**Vol. 1:** 565 **Vol. 3:** 420, 987
2:4–9	**Vol. 2:** 364
2:4	**Vol. 2:** 174
2:5	**Vol. 1:** 481, 492, 551–552
2:6	**Vol. 1:** 531 **Vol. 2:** 206, 275 **Vol. 3:** 1005
2:7	**Vol. 2:** 296 **Vol. 3:** 104
2:8	**Vol. 2:** 440 **Vol. 3:** 78, 565
2:10	**Vol. 2:** 576 **Vol. 3:** 125
2:11	**Vol. 2:** 70, 720
2:12	**Vol. 2:** 363
2:13	**Vol. 2:** 479 **Vol. 3:** 1153
2:15	**Vol. 3:** 1005
2:18	**Vol. 1:** 531
2:19	**Vol. 1:** 607 **Vol. 2:** 141
2:20	**Vol. 3:** 592, 1161–1162
2:21	**Vol. 2:** 248, 313 **Vol. 3:** 918
2:23	**Vol. 1:** 492 **Vol. 3:** 104
2:24	**Vol. 3:** 680
2:25	**Vol. 2:** 540, 576
2:26	**Vol. 3:** 562
2:27 f	**Vol. 3:** 206
2:27	**Vol. 3:** 865
2:29	**Vol. 3:** 578
2:30	**Vol. 1:** 551 **Vol. 3:** 745
2:31	**Vol. 2:** 206
2:32	**Vol. 1:** 522
2:36	**Vol. 1:** 531
2:37	**Vol. 2:** 149
3:1–25	**Vol. 2:** 576
3:1–10	**Vol. 2:** 583
3:1–9	**Vol. 1:** 499
3:2	**Vol. 3:** 1098
3:3	**Vol. 3:** 1098
3:4 f	**Vol. 1:** 618
3:4	**Vol. 1:** 618
3:6–10	**Vol. 2:** 541 **Vol. 3:** 1068
3:8	**Vol. 2:** 576
3:9	**Vol. 1:** 390
3:10	**Vol. 3:** 578
3:11 ff	**Vol. 2:** 306
3:11	**Vol. 3:** 355
3:12	**Vol. 1:** 245 **Vol. 2:** 595
3:13	**Vol. 2:** 179
3:14	**Vol. 1:** 607 **Vol. 2:** 519
3:15	**Vol. 3:** 565–566
3:16	**Vol. 2:** 128 **Vol. 3:** 788
3:17	**Vol. 1:** 492, 709 **Vol. 2:** 325–326, 612, 888 **Vol. 3:** 836
3:19	**Vol. 1:** 537, 618 **Vol. 2:** 69 **Vol. 3:** 717
3:20	**Vol. 3:** 1068
3:23	**Vol. 3:** 206
3:25	**Vol. 2:** 179

Jeremiah *(cont'd)*

4:2   Vol. 3: 816
4:3 f   Vol. 2: 326
4:3   Vol. 3: 522
4:4   Vol. 1: 109, 154, 308 – 309   Vol. 2: 184   Vol. 3: 109
4:5 – 6:30   Vol. 3: 1095
4:7   Vol. 3: 1006
4:9   Vol. 2: 622
4:10   Vol. 2: 509
4:11 f   Vol. 3: 695
4:11   Vol. 2: 34   Vol. 3: 836
4:13   Vol. 3: 859
4:14   Vol. 3: 820, 823
4:16   Vol. 3: 240
4:19 – 21   Vol. 3: 1091, 1096, 1099
4:19   Vol. 2: 181, 391   Vol. 3: 1097
4:20   Vol. 3: 859
4:22   Vol. 3: 1024, 1028
4:23 – 26   Vol. 2: 189
4:24   Vol. 3: 1010
4:26 f   Vol. 3: 1005
4:28   Vol. 1: 356   Vol. 2: 422
4:29   Vol. 2: 218   Vol. 3: 381, 383
4:30   Vol. 1: 522
4:31   Vol. 3: 178, 1068
5:1 ff   Vol. 1: 124
5:1   Vol. 3: 157
5:3   Vol. 3: 382, 514, 745, 777
5:4   Vol. 3: 937
5:5   Vol. 3: 592, 908, 1161 – 1162
5:6   Vol. 1: 465   Vol. 2: 136
5:7 ff   Vol. 1: 499
5:7   Vol. 1: 743   Vol. 2: 583   Vol. 3: 157
5:12   Vol. 2: 471
5:13   Vol. 3: 1095
5:14   Vol. 3: 1096
5:17   Vol. 1: 724   Vol. 3: 865
5:19   Vol. 1: 688
5:21   Vol. 3: 131, 1025
5:22   Vol. 2: 91
5:24   Vol. 3: 1001
5:26 ff Vol. 2: 841
5:26   Vol. 1: 343
5:27   Vol. 1: 172   Vol. 2: 841
5:28   Vol. 2: 363, 737
5:30   Vol. 1: 527
5:31   Vol. 2: 470   Vol. 3: 574
6:4   Vol. 3: 119
6:10   Vol. 3: 1016
6:11   Vol. 1: 108, 288
6:13   Vol. 2: 778   Vol. 3: 137
6:14   Vol. 2: 778
6:15   Vol. 2: 49   Vol. 3: 836
6:16   Vol. 3: 530, 938
6:18   Vol. 1: 293
6:19   Vol. 1: 721   Vol. 2: 440
6:20   Vol. 3: 421, 427, 745
6:21   Vol. 3: 994

6:22 ff Vol. 2: 326
6:22*   Vol. 2: 55, 841
6:24   Vol. 3: 858
6:27   Vol. 3: 808
6:29   Vol. 1: 654
7:1 ff   Vol. 3: 1103
7:1 – 15   Vol. 3: 78
7:1 – 7   Vol. 2: 297
7:1   Vol. 3: 1096
7:2   Vol. 2: 174
7:3 ff   Vol. 3: 82
7:3   Vol. 3: 786
7:4   Vol. 1: 589   Vol. 2: 325   Vol. 3: 783, 786, 788, 1096
7:5 ff   Vol. 3: 1096
7:5 f   Vol. 1: 717
7:6   Vol. 1: 492   Vol. 2: 525, 737, 862   Vol. 3: 1074
7:8   Vol. 3: 1096
7:9   Vol. 1: 492   Vol. 3: 377, 1103
7:10   Vol. 2: 650
7:11   Vol. 2: 236, 379, 610   Vol. 3: 377 – 378, 380 – 381, 427, 430, 788, 791
7:12 ff Vol. 3: 426
7:12   Vol. 3: 786
7:13   Vol. 1: 272   Vol. 2: 174
7:14   Vol. 1: 227, 272   Vol. 3: 1096
7:17 f   Vol. 3: 427
7:18   Vol. 1: 586, 654   Vol. 2: 854   Vol. 3: 423, 465, 919
7:20   Vol. 1: 109   Vol. 3: 109
7:21 f   Vol. 3: 427
7:22   Vol. 2: 889   Vol. 3: 427
7:23 f   Vol. 3: 938
7:23   Vol. 1: 368   Vol. 2: 797   Vol. 3: 946
7:24   Vol. 1: 562
7:28   Vol. 3: 745
7:30   Vol. 3: 104
7:31   Vol. 1: 655   Vol. 3: 110, 418, 426
7:32   Vol. 2: 208, 890
7:33   Vol. 1: 444   Vol. 2: 268
7:34   Vol. 2: 578, 584   Vol. 3: 394, 1006
8:1   Vol. 3: 836
8:2   Vol. 2: 876   Vol. 3: 731, 735
8:3   Vol. 1: 534
8:4   Vol. 1: 609 – 610
8:6   Vol. 1: 357
8:7   Vol. 1: 173   Vol. 2: 395   Vol. 3: 835
8:8 f   Vol. 3: 1028, 1096
8:8   Vol. 2: 440   Vol. 3: 478
8:9   Vol. 3: 563, 1027
8:10   Vol. 3: 137
8:11   Vol. 2: 778
8:13   Vol. 1: 724   Vol. 3: 866 – 867
8:15   Vol. 2: 778
8:16   Vol. 3: 557
8:17   Vol. 2: 554
8:18 – 23   Vol. 3: 1096
8:19   Vol. 1: 551   Vol. 3: 200
8:20   Vol. 3: 526

Jeremiah *(cont'd)*

8:22   **Vol. 2:** 167
9:2   **Vol. 3:** 1079
9:4   **Vol. 2:** 431   **Vol. 3:** 881
9:5   **Vol. 3:** 881
9:6*   **Vol. 3:** 808
9:7   **Vol. 3:** 1079
9:10 f   **Vol. 3:** 1008
9:10   **Vol. 2:** 249, 418
9:13–16   **Vol. 2:** 285
9:13*   **Vol. 3:** 760
9:14*   **Vol. 2:** 663
9:15*   **Vol. 1:** 202   **Vol. 2:** 27, 29
9:16–21   **Vol. 2:** 418
9:16*   **Vol. 3:** 1028
9:18   **Vol. 1:** 683   **Vol. 2:** 418
9:19*   **Vol. 3:** 760
9:20*   **Vol. 2:** 174   **Vol. 3:** 745
9:22*   **Vol. 2:** 32, 841   **Vol. 3:** 1027–1028
9:23 f   **Vol. 1:** 227
9:23   **Vol. 3:** 130, 1019
9:24   **Vol. 1:** 228   **Vol. 2:** 890   **Vol. 3:** 130, 357
9:25   **Vol. 1:** 308
10:1   **Vol. 2:** 305
10:2   **Vol. 2:** 189, 555   **Vol. 3:** 735
10:6   **Vol. 2:** 498
10:7   **Vol. 2:** 375, 791
10:10–15   **Vol. 2:** 285
10:10   **Vol. 3:** 892
10:11   **Vol. 1:** 51
10:12   **Vol. 2:** 616   **Vol. 3:** 1027
10:13   **Vol. 3:** 1001
10:14   **Vol. 3:** 690, 1025
10:15   **Vol. 1:** 551   **Vol. 3:** 836
10:16   **Vol. 1:** 522   **Vol. 2:** 297, 650
10:17   **Vol. 1:** 711
10:19   **Vol. 3:** 857, 1051
10:20   **Vol. 3:** 859
10:21   **Vol. 2:** 104   **Vol. 3:** 125, 531, 565–566
10:22   **Vol. 2:** 173, 586   **Vol. 3:** 557
10:24   **Vol. 3:** 777
10:25   **Vol. 1:** 272
11:1 ff   **Vol. 3:** 1095
11:3 ff   **Vol. 2:** 797
11:4   **Vol. 1:** 368   **Vol. 2:** 797, 889
11:5   **Vol. 1:** 98, 683
11:6   **Vol. 1:** 245
11:7   **Vol. 2:** 889
11:12   **Vol. 3:** 206
11:13   **Vol. 3:** 418
11:14   **Vol. 2:** 860, 862–863
11:16   **Vol. 2:** 711
11:19   **Vol. 3:** 237, 823
11:20   **Vol. 2:** 181, 183   **Vol. 3:** 357, 808
11:21   **Vol. 3:** 531
11:23   **Vol. 1:** 190
12:1–5   **Vol. 3:** 342
12:2   **Vol. 2:** 468

12:3   **Vol. 3:** 808
12:5   **Vol. 2:** 746
12:6   **Vol. 3:** 1212
12:8   **Vol. 1:** 555
12:9   **Vol. 1:** 113
12:12   **Vol. 1:** 518   **Vol. 2:** 778
12:14 ff   **Vol. 2:** 252
12:15 ff   **Vol. 2:** 252
12:16   **Vol. 3:** 760
13:1 ff   **Vol. 3:** 121
13:1–11   **Vol. 2:** 754   **Vol. 3:** 1099
13:9   **Vol. 3:** 29–30
13:10   **Vol. 1:** 272   **Vol. 2:** 876
13:11   **Vol. 2:** 349
13:14   **Vol. 1:** 685   **Vol. 2:** 34
13:17   **Vol. 3:** 29, 565
13:19   **Vol. 1:** 357   **Vol. 2:** 60, 778   **Vol. 3:** 1099
13:21   **Vol. 1:** 485   **Vol. 3:** 760, 1068
13:22   **Vol. 2:** 212, 583
13:23   **Vol. 1:** 184
13:26   **Vol. 2:** 583
14 ff   **Vol. 2:** 307
14   **Vol. 1:** 210
14:1–15:4 **Vol. 3:** 1096
14:2–12   **Vol. 3:** 235
14:3   **Vol. 1:** 546
14:5†   **Vol. 1:** 520   **Vol. 2:** 211
14:7   **Vol. 3:** 1096
14:8   **Vol. 2:** 239, 772–773   **Vol. 3:** 207, 836
14:9   **Vol. 1:** 272   **Vol. 3:** 206, 1096
14:10   **Vol. 3:** 1096
14:11–12   **Vol. 1:** 612
14:11   **Vol. 2:** 862   **Vol. 3:** 1097
14:12   **Vol. 1:** 612   **Vol. 2:** 817, 864
14:13   **Vol. 2:** 777–778
14:14 f   **Vol. 2:** 651
14:14   **Vol. 2:** 181, 554
14:19–22   **Vol. 3:** 1096
14:19   **Vol. 1:** 538   **Vol. 2:** 326, 773, 778   **Vol. 3:** 836
14:21   **Vol. 2:** 612   **Vol. 3:** 234–235
14:22   **Vol. 2:** 285, 773
15:1–4   **Vol. 3:** 1096
15:1   **Vol. 2:** 636, 639   **Vol. 3:** 1097
15:2   **Vol. 3:** 590–591
15:3   **Vol. 1:** 113   **Vol. 2:** 268
15:4   **Vol. 2:** 663
15:5–9   **Vol. 3:** 1068
15:7   **Vol. 1:** 685   **Vol. 2:** 34
15:9   **Vol. 3:** 680, 731, 1068
15:10   **Vol. 3:** 721
15:11   **Vol. 2:** 509   **Vol. 3:** 836
15:13   **Vol. 3:** 166
15:15–18   **Vol. 3:** 235
15:15   **Vol. 2:** 769, 806   **Vol. 3:** 134
15:16–21   **Vol. 3:** 342
15:16   **Vol. 2:** 355, 357, 830   **Vol. 3:** 1097–1098
15:17   **Vol. 2:** 724   **Vol. 3:** 1097

Jeremiah *(cont'd)*

15:19	**Vol. 3**: 81
15:20	**Vol. 3**: 207
15:21	**Vol. 3**: 192
16:1–9	**Vol. 3**: 1097
16:2	**Vol. 3**: 79
16:5–7	**Vol. 2**: 417
16:5 f	**Vol. 2**: 417
16:5	**Vol. 2**: 777–778 **Vol. 3**: 79
16:6	**Vol. 2**: 573
16:8	**Vol. 3**: 79
16:9	**Vol. 2**: 578, 584 **Vol. 3**: 394
16:11	**Vol. 2**: 876, 890
16:12	**Vol. 1**: 492
16:15	**Vol. 3**: 147
16:17	**Vol. 3**: 574, 938
16:19 ff	**Vol. 2**: 888
16:19	**Vol. 1**: 320
16:21	**Vol. 3**: 316
17:1–4	**Vol. 1**: 686
17:3	**Vol. 3**: 426
17:5	**Vol. 1**: 607, 673, 679
17:6	**Vol. 3**: 444
17:7	**Vol. 3**: 866
17:8	**Vol. 1**: 652 **Vol. 3**: 866
17:9 f	**Vol. 2**: 183
17:9	**Vol. 2**: 183
17:10	**Vol. 1**: 721 **Vol. 2**: 181 **Vol. 3**: 648, 808
17:11	**Vol. 2**: 841 **Vol. 3**: 1024–1025
17:12	**Vol. 1**: 668
17:13	**Vol. 1**: 607 **Vol. 2**: 239, 478–479, 754, 772–773
17:14	**Vol. 3**: 207
17:15	**Vol. 3**: 1097
17:16 ff	**Vol. 2**: 890
17:22	**Vol. 2**: 890
17:24	**Vol. 2**: 890
17:26	**Vol. 3**: 423, 1009
17:27	**Vol. 2**: 890 **Vol. 3**: 94, 109
18	**Vol. 1**: 93
18:1–12	**Vol. 3**: 916
18:1–6	**Vol. 2**: 747
18:2	**Vol. 3**: 911–912
18:3	**Vol. 3**: 911
18:6	**Vol. 2**: 609 **Vol. 3**: 911–912, 915–916
18:8	**Vol. 1**: 354, 357 **Vol. 3**: 823
18:11	**Vol. 3**: 823
18:13	**Vol. 3**: 1071
18:15	**Vol. 1**: 546 **Vol. 3**: 994
18:18	**Vol. 3**: 721, 823
18:20	**Vol. 3**: 98, 235
18:22	**Vol. 3**: 377
18:23	**Vol. 3**: 152, 154, 836, 994
19	**Vol. 1**: 93 **Vol. 2**: 754
19:1 ff	**Vol. 2**: 626
19:1–20:6	**Vol. 3**: 1097
19:1	**Vol. 3**: 914
19:2	**Vol. 3**: 912
19:3	**Vol. 3**: 786
19:5	**Vol. 2**: 199 **Vol. 3**: 421
19:6 f	**Vol. 2**: 208
19:6	**Vol. 2**: 890
19:7	**Vol. 1**: 444 **Vol. 2**: 268
19:11	**Vol. 3**: 249, 914
19:13	**Vol. 2**: 854 **Vol. 3**: 423, 465, 919
20:7–10	**Vol. 3**: 342
20:7–9	**Vol. 3**: 1097
20:7	**Vol. 2**: 431 **Vol. 3**: 341, 716
20:8 ff	**Vol. 3**: 235
20:8	**Vol. 2**: 431 **Vol. 3**: 1097
20:9	**Vol. 3**: 1054
20:9a	**Vol. 3**: 1097
20:10	**Vol. 2**: 132, 777
20:11	**Vol. 1**: 485 **Vol. 2**: 806
20:12	**Vol. 2**: 181 **Vol. 3**: 808
20:13	**Vol. 3**: 673, 816
20:14 ff	**Vol. 2**: 478 **Vol. 3**: 721
20:15	**Vol. 2**: 109, 569
21:8	**Vol. 1**: 434 **Vol. 2**: 479, 481 **Vol. 3**: 929, 940
21:8b	**Vol. 3**: 926
21:12	**Vol. 3**: 109
22:3	**Vol. 2**: 737 **Vol. 3**: 1073–1074
22:6	**Vol. 1**: 165
22:7	**Vol. 1**: 465
22:9	**Vol. 2**: 876
22:10	**Vol. 2**: 416
22:13	**Vol. 2**: 41, 139
22:14	**Vol. 2**: 334
22:15 f	**Vol. 2**: 396
22:17	**Vol. 1**: 137 **Vol. 3**: 137
22:18	**Vol. 2**: 418
22:22	**Vol. 3**: 566
22:24–30	**Vol. 3**: 655
22:28 f	**Vol. 1**: 505
22:28	**Vol. 3**: 957
23:1 ff	**Vol. 2**: 412
23:1 f	**Vol. 2**: 104
23:1–5	**Vol. 3**: 566
23:2	**Vol. 3**: 565
23:3	**Vol. 2**: 128 **Vol. 3**: 745
23:4	**Vol. 3**: 566
23:5 ff	**Vol. 2**: 337
23:5 f	**Vol. 2**: 374
23:5	**Vol. 2**: 591, 890 **Vol. 3**: 649–650, 867
23:6	**Vol. 2**: 591
23:7	**Vol. 2**: 890
23:8	**Vol. 3**: 147
23:9–40	**Vol. 3**: 1097
23:9	**Vol. 1**: 527
23:10	**Vol. 2**: 422
23:11	**Vol. 1**: 449
23:12	**Vol. 1**: 190
23:14	**Vol. 3**: 93
23:15	**Vol. 1**: 201–202, 449 **Vol. 2**: 27, 29, 468
23:16 ff	**Vol. 1**: 550–551 **Vol. 3**: 1097
23:16 f	**Vol. 1**: 527

Jeremiah *(cont'd)*

23:17	**Vol. 2:** 778
23:18	**Vol. 3:** 1097
23:19	**Vol. 3:** 557
23:20	**Vol. 2:** 56
23:22	**Vol. 1:** 712 **Vol. 3:** 1097
23:23	**Vol. 2:** 53
23:24	**Vol. 1:** 735 **Vol. 2:** 214–215 **Vol. 3:** 465
23:25	**Vol. 2:** 651
23:26	**Vol. 3:** 1019
23:27	**Vol. 3:** 823
23:28	**Vol. 3:** 1097
23:29	**Vol. 1:** 655 **Vol. 3:** 382, 1097
23:30	**Vol. 3:** 377
23:32	**Vol. 1:** 512 **Vol. 2:** 458
23:34	**Vol. 2:** 796
23:40	**Vol. 2:** 49
24	**Vol. 1:** 724
24:1 f	**Vol. 3:** 866
24:1	**Vol. 2:** 841 **Vol. 3:** 786
24:2 f	**Vol. 2:** 105
24:5	**Vol. 2:** 105
24:6	**Vol. 2:** 252 **Vol. 3:** 147
24:7	**Vol. 1:** 184, 354 **Vol. 2:** 797
24:8	**Vol. 3:** 249
24:9	**Vol. 1:** 416
25:3 ff	**Vol. 3:** 1104
25:5	**Vol. 3:** 938
25:6	**Vol. 2:** 876
25:9	**Vol. 1:** 141 **Vol. 3:** 608
25:10	**Vol. 2:** 485, 578 **Vol. 3:** 394
25:11	**Vol. 2:** 696
25:12	**Vol. 1:** 734
25:14	**Vol. 3:** 134
25:15 ff	**Vol. 1:** 109 **Vol. 2:** 275–276
25:15–28	**Vol. 1:** 106
25:15 f	**Vol. 3:** 922
25:15	**Vol. 1:** 111 **Vol. 3:** 208
25:16	**Vol. 1:** 529
25:27 f	**Vol. 3:** 922
25:28	**Vol. 3:** 745
25:29*	**Vol. 1:** 273 **Vol. 2:** 650
25:30*	**Vol. 3:** 324
25:34 ff	**Vol. 3:** 566
25:34	**Vol. 3:** 566
25:36	**Vol. 1:** 465
25:37 f	**Vol. 1:** 109
25:37	**Vol. 2:** 778
25:38*	**Vol. 3:** 794
26	**Vol. 2:** 363 **Vol. 3:** 1096
26:1 ff	**Vol. 3:** 82
26:1	**Vol. 3:** 1096
26:2 ff	**Vol. 3:** 1104
26:2*	**Vol. 2:** 876 **Vol. 3:** 324
26:3*	**Vol. 3:** 823–824
26:6	**Vol. 1:** 416 **Vol. 3:** 426
26:8 f	**Vol. 3:** 94
26:9	**Vol. 1:** 485 **Vol. 3:** 426
26:16*	**Vol. 2:** 124
26:17	**Vol. 1:** 196
26:19	**Vol. 1:** 699 **Vol. 2:** 860
26:21*	**Vol. 3:** 836
26:23*	**Vol. 3:** 238–239
27:1 ff	**Vol. 2:** 626
27:2–11	**Vol. 3:** 1161
27:4*	**Vol. 3:** 836
27:5*	**Vol. 3:** 821
27:6 f	**Vol. 1:** 141 **Vol. 2:** 148
27:8*	**Vol. 3:** 1161
27:9 f	**Vol. 2:** 555
27:9	**Vol. 1:** 512 **Vol. 2:** 554
27:11*	**Vol. 3:** 1161
27:16*	**Vol. 2:** 124
27:20*	**Vol. 3:** 836
27:22	**Vol. 2:** 890
27:27*	**Vol. 3:** 836
27:29*	**Vol. 1:** 340
28 f	**Vol. 3:** 1099
28:2 ff	**Vol. 3:** 79, 1097
28:2–11	**Vol. 3:** 1161
28:2*	**Vol. 3:** 1161
28:4*	**Vol. 3:** 1161
28:6*	**Vol. 1:** 98 **Vol. 3:** 836
28:9	**Vol. 2:** 778, 891 **Vol. 3:** 1098
28:11*	**Vol. 3:** 1098, 1161
28:12 ff	**Vol. 3:** 1098
28:12	**Vol. 3:** 1098
28:13–17	**Vol. 3:** 1161
28:14*	**Vol. 3:** 1161
28:15	**Vol. 3:** 117
28:27*	**Vol. 1:** 340
28:36*	**Vol. 1:** 515
29:1 ff	**Vol. 2:** 240
29:1	**Vol. 1:** 196
29:3*	**Vol. 3:** 557
29:4–23	**Vol. 1:** 246
29:8*	**Vol. 3:** 842
29:9	**Vol. 2:** 651
29:11*	**Vol. 1:** 562 **Vol. 2:** 240, 777–778 **Vol. 3:** 528–529, 823–824
29:11c	**Vol. 1:** 562
29:12 ff	**Vol. 2:** 864
29:12*	**Vol. 2:** 862–863 **Vol. 3:** 528
29:13 f	**Vol. 3:** 531
29:13*	**Vol. 2:** 881 **Vol. 3:** 528
29:14*	**Vol. 3:** 318
29:17	**Vol. 1:** 724
29:23*	**Vol. 2:** 803 **Vol. 3:** 324
29:26*	**Vol. 1:** 529
29:27*	**Vol. 3:** 346
30 f	**Vol. 2:** 307
30–32	**Vol. 3:** 1095
30:2*	**Vol. 3:** 324
30:3	**Vol. 2:** 890
30:8*	**Vol. 3:** 1161
30:9	**Vol. 3:** 649
30:12 f	**Vol. 3:** 997
30:19*	**Vol. 2:** 131 **Vol. 3:** 673

Jeremiah *(cont'd)*

30:22	**Vol. 1:** 368 **Vol. 2:** 797
30:23 f	**Vol. 1:** 108
30:24	**Vol. 2:** 56
31	**Vol. 3:** 576, 578
31:2*	**Vol. 3:** 1005
31:3	**Vol. 2:** 541
31:4 f	**Vol. 3:** 673
31:4	**Vol. 2:** 252, 541 **Vol. 3:** 1071
31:5*	**Vol. 3:** 816
31:6*	**Vol. 1:** 272 **Vol. 2:** 326
31:7	**Vol. 3:** 208, 673
31:8*	**Vol. 1:** 218, 292, 297 **Vol. 2:** 800
31:9	**Vol. 1:** 617 **Vol. 2:** 71 **Vol. 3:** 636
31:10*	**Vol. 2:** 32 **Vol. 3:** 565
31:11*	**Vol. 3:** 192
31:12	**Vol. 2:** 266, 711 **Vol. 3:** 919
31:15–20	**Vol. 3:** 235
31:15	**Vol. 1:** 170, 737 **Vol. 2:** 417, 715
31:16	**Vol. 2:** 139
31:17	**Vol. 2:** 240
31:18*	**Vol. 1:** 184, 354 **Vol. 3:** 760
31:19	**Vol. 1:** 356 **Vol. 2:** 418
31:20*	**Vol. 1:** 617 **Vol. 3:** 238
31:21	**Vol. 3:** 1071
31:22	**Vol. 1:** 380
31:26*	**Vol. 2:** 431
31:27	**Vol. 2:** 890 **Vol. 3:** 522
31:29 ff	**Vol. 1:** 434
31:31 ff*	**Vol. 1:** 354 **Vol. 2:** 78, 248, 364, 525–526, 533, 536, 661, 670–671 **Vol. 3:** 167, 327, 765
31:31–35	**Vol. 2:** 716
31:31–34	**Vol. 1:** 224, 248, 366, 368–369, 371 **Vol. 2:** 145, 240, 306, 320, 533, 671, 786, 854 **Vol. 3:** 69, 74, 160, 702
31:31–33	**Vol. 2:** 797 **Vol. 3:** 493
31:31	**Vol. 1:** 367 **Vol. 2:** 890
31:32	**Vol. 2:** 889 **Vol. 3:** 227, 747
31:33 f	**Vol. 2:** 127, 155 **Vol. 3:** 74, 701
31:33	**Vol. 1:** 184, 368 **Vol. 2:** 42, 177, 872, 923 **Vol. 3:** 127, 484, 490
31:34*	**Vol. 1:** 701 **Vol. 2:** 448, 596, 803–804 **Vol. 3:** 157, 203, 235, 241, 575, 760
31:34b	**Vol. 2:** 526, 533, 536
31:35*	**Vol. 2:** 491 **Vol. 3:** 733
31:36*	**Vol. 2:** 441
31:38 ff	**Vol. 2:** 325
31:38	**Vol. 2:** 803, 890
31:39	**Vol. 2:** 431
32:4*	**Vol. 2:** 367 **Vol. 3:** 209, 772
32:6 ff	**Vol. 2:** 240, 626
32:7 ff	**Vol. 2:** 754
32:7–9	**Vol. 1:** 93
32:7	**Vol. 3:** 190
32:8	**Vol. 3:** 190
32:10 ff	**Vol. 3:** 484
32:10–12	**Vol. 3:** 478
32:10*	**Vol. 3:** 1041, 1160
32:12 f	**Vol. 1:** 485
32:14	**Vol. 3:** 914
32:15*	**Vol. 1:** 380
32:16*	**Vol. 2:** 862
32:19	**Vol. 3:** 938
32:20 f	**Vol. 2:** 627
32:25*	**Vol. 3:** 1041
32:29*	**Vol. 1:** 203 **Vol. 3:** 423
32:31*	**Vol. 3:** 166
32:33*	**Vol. 3:** 760
32:35*	**Vol. 2:** 208 **Vol. 3:** 110, 418, 421
32:38–40	**Vol. 2:** 797
32:38	**Vol. 1:** 368 **Vol. 2:** 797 **Vol. 3:** 813
32:40	**Vol. 2:** 181
32:41	**Vol. 2:** 100
33:6	**Vol. 2:** 778
33:7	**Vol. 2:** 252
33:8	**Vol. 1:** 606, 701 **Vol. 3:** 105
33:9*	**Vol. 2:** 425, 778
33:10–12*	**Vol. 3:** 1006
33:11	**Vol. 3:** 423
33:12*	**Vol. 3:** 794
33:14	**Vol. 2:** 890
33:15 f	**Vol. 2:** 591
33:15	**Vol. 3:** 649–650, 867
33:21	**Vol. 1:** 366
33:24	**Vol. 1:** 262 **Vol. 3:** 513
33:25	**Vol. 1:** 366
34:1*	**Vol. 1:** 165
34:2*	**Vol. 3:** 772
34:3*	**Vol. 1:** 127
34:5*	**Vol. 2:** 418, 602
34:8 ff	**Vol. 1:** 366, 716 **Vol. 3:** 608
34:8–11	**Vol. 2:** 841
34:8	**Vol. 1:** 698
34:9	**Vol. 2:** 306
34:11	**Vol. 1:** 716
34:13	**Vol. 2:** 889
34:14–22	**Vol. 3:** 191
34:14	**Vol. 2:** 306
34:15	**Vol. 1:** 698
34:17*	**Vol. 1:** 272, 685, 698, 716
34:18 ff	**Vol. 3:** 425
34:18	**Vol. 1:** 368
34:22	**Vol. 2:** 215
35	**Vol. 3:** 565
35:6 f	**Vol. 3:** 919
35:6–10	**Vol. 3:** 811
35:7	**Vol. 3:** 1005
35:9 f	**Vol. 3:** 1005
36	**Vol. 3:** 1097
36:2 f	**Vol. 3:** 1104
36:2*	**Vol. 1:** 716
36:3*	**Vol. 3:** 157, 823–824
36:4	**Vol. 3:** 478, 484
36:5 ff	**Vol. 1:** 245
36:7	**Vol. 1:** 109
36:11	**Vol. 3:** 478
36:12	**Vol. 3:** 478

Jeremiah *(cont'd)*

36:18	**Vol. 3:** 478
36:19	**Vol. 3:** 962
36:23*	**Vol. 3:** 1041, 1097
36:26	**Vol. 3:** 962
36:32	**Vol. 3:** 478, 1097
37:3*	**Vol. 2:** 862
37:5	**Vol. 1:** 531
37:6*	**Vol. 2:** 569
37:7 ff	**Vol. 2:** 306
37:7	**Vol. 1:** 531
37:10	**Vol. 3:** 811–812
37:15 f	**Vol. 2:** 96
37:15	**Vol. 3:** 478
38:1*	**Vol. 2:** 800
38:7	**Vol. 3:** 816
38:9	**Vol. 3:** 351
38:28*	**Vol. 2:** 136
39:10 f*	**Vol. 3:** 498
39:13	**Vol. 3:** 115
39:17*	**Vol. 2:** 602
39:18*	**Vol. 1:** 596 **Vol. 2:** 698 **Vol. 3:** 115
39:24*	**Vol. 1:** 343
39:44*	**Vol. 3:** 498
40:4*	**Vol. 3:** 177, 951
40:8	**Vol. 3:** 232
40:10	**Vol. 2:** 711
40:11–15	**Vol. 3:** 249
40:11*	**Vol. 2:** 105
41:1 f	**Vol. 2:** 521
41:1	**Vol. 3:** 115
41:5	**Vol. 2:** 325, 573 **Vol. 3:** 426, 788
41:8	**Vol. 2:** 711
41:17	**Vol. 1:** 531
42–44	**Vol. 1:** 531
42:2*	**Vol. 2:** 862
42:4*	**Vol. 2:** 862
42:5*	**Vol. 3:** 1041
42:10*	**Vol. 3:** 255
42:18	**Vol. 1:** 109
42:20*	**Vol. 2:** 862
43:7	**Vol. 2:** 613
43:30*	**Vol. 1:** 652
44:3 f	**Vol. 1:** 555
44:3*	**Vol. 1:** 203
44:7	**Vol. 1:** 288
44:8*	**Vol. 1:** 203
44:15–19	**Vol. 2:** 285
44:15	**Vol. 1:** 293
44:17–25	**Vol. 3:** 423
44:23*	**Vol. 2:** 441
44:25*	**Vol. 1:** 344 **Vol. 3:** 226
44:28*	**Vol. 1:** 531 **Vol. 3:** 226
45:3*	**Vol. 3:** 255
45:28*	**Vol. 3:** 841
46–51	**Vol. 3:** 960
46	**Vol. 1:** 531
46:1	**Vol. 3:** 1095
46:6	**Vol. 3:** 209
46:9*	**Vol. 3:** 119
46:10	**Vol. 2:** 363
46:10b	**Vol. 3:** 160
46:18	**Vol. 2:** 375
46:21*	**Vol. 1:** 688 **Vol. 2:** 139, 890 **Vol. 3:** 908
46:27*	**Vol. 3:** 111, 208
46:28	**Vol. 3:** 777
47:1	**Vol. 3:** 1095
47:4	**Vol. 2:** 890
47:5	**Vol. 2:** 573
47:6*	**Vol. 3:** 255
48:2*	**Vol. 3:** 823
48:6	**Vol. 3:** 209
48:8	**Vol. 3:** 209
48:11*	**Vol. 3:** 255, 600
48:12	**Vol. 2:** 890 **Vol. 3:** 911
48:15	**Vol. 2:** 375
48:19	**Vol. 3:** 209
48:29*	**Vol. 3:** 29
48:32	**Vol. 3:** 866
48:33	**Vol. 3:** 673
48:35*	**Vol. 3:** 418
48:37	**Vol. 2:** 573
48:38	**Vol. 3:** 957
48:39*	**Vol. 3:** 166
48:42*	**Vol. 2:** 800
48:44	**Vol. 1:** 609
49:2	**Vol. 2:** 890
49:7*	**Vol. 3:** 1027
49:9	**Vol. 1:** 420
49:11	**Vol. 3:** 1073
49:16	**Vol. 1:** 173
49:18	**Vol. 3:** 93, 560
49:19	**Vol. 2:** 498
49:20*	**Vol. 3:** 823–824
49:22	**Vol. 1:** 173
49:23*	**Vol. 3:** 255
49:30*	**Vol. 3:** 823
49:34	**Vol. 2:** 376 **Vol. 3:** 1095
49:36	**Vol. 2:** 189, 689 **Vol. 3:** 389
49:39	**Vol. 2:** 56
50	**Vol. 1:** 141
50:5	**Vol. 1:** 366
50:6*	**Vol. 2:** 586 **Vol. 3:** 454, 566
50:12	**Vol. 3:** 1069
50:13	**Vol. 1:** 109
50:19	**Vol. 3:** 565
50:20*	**Vol. 3:** 157
50:21	**Vol. 1:** 414
50:25*	**Vol. 2:** 830
50:26	**Vol. 1:** 414
50:27	**Vol. 3:** 835
50:28	**Vol. 3:** 786
50:29	**Vol. 3:** 134
50:30	**Vol. 3:** 835
50:32*	**Vol. 3:** 29
50:34*	**Vol. 3:** 192
50:35	**Vol. 3:** 1028
50:40	**Vol. 3:** 93, 560

Jeremiah *(cont'd)*

50:42*	**Vol. 3:** 119
50:45*	**Vol. 3:** 820, 823–824
50:46*	**Vol. 3:** 557
51	**Vol. 1:** 141
51:2*	**Vol. 3:** 29
51:6	**Vol. 3:** 209
51:7	**Vol. 1:** 111
51:8	**Vol. 1:** 120, 610
51:9*	**Vol. 2:** 349
51:10	**Vol. 2:** 363
51:11*	**Vol. 3:** 119, 786
51:13	**Vol. 3:** 137
51:15*	**Vol. 3:** 1027
51:17*	**Vol. 3:** 1025
51:18	**Vol. 1:** 551
51:19	**Vol. 2:** 297
51:20*	**Vol. 3:** 823
51:23*	**Vol. 2:** 34
51:25	**Vol. 3:** 1010, 1013
51:26	**Vol. 1:** 661
51:33	**Vol. 3:** 526
51:34 f	**Vol. 1:** 673
51:35 f	**Vol. 1:** 221
51:36*	**Vol. 3:** 1005
51:39	**Vol. 1:** 442
51:42	**Vol. 3:** 983
51:45	**Vol. 2:** 800 **Vol. 3:** 209
51:47	**Vol. 2:** 890
51:48	**Vol. 2:** 356
51:52	**Vol. 2:** 423, 890
51:57*	**Vol. 2:** 375 **Vol. 3:** 1028
51:60–63	**Vol. 3:** 394
52	**Vol. 1:** 61 **Vol. 3:** 1087
52:16	**Vol. 3:** 918
52:25	**Vol. 3:** 478

Lamentations

1:3	**Vol. 3:** 255
1:5	**Vol. 1:** 281
1:5b	**Vol. 2:** 261
1:6	**Vol. 3:** 255
1:7	**Vol. 2:** 430, 890
1:8	**Vol. 2:** 423
1:8b	**Vol. 2:** 261
1:10	**Vol. 3:** 786
1:12	**Vol. 2:** 888–889
1:12c	**Vol. 2:** 261
1:13	**Vol. 2:** 199
1:14	**Vol. 2:** 136
1:15	**Vol. 3:** 1071
1:16	**Vol. 2:** 416
1:18	**Vol. 3:** 357, 1071
1:20	**Vol. 2:** 261, 888
1:21	**Vol. 2:** 423
2:1	**Vol. 2:** 888–889
2:5c	**Vol. 2:** 261
2:7	**Vol. 3:** 560, 948
2:8	**Vol. 2:** 422 **Vol. 3:** 402, 908

2:10	**Vol. 1:** 520
2:11	**Vol. 1:** 230
2:12	**Vol. 3:** 178, 680
2:13	**Vol. 3:** 1071
2:14	**Vol. 1:** 550 **Vol. 3:** 1024
2:16	**Vol. 2:** 421
2:18	**Vol. 2:** 261
2:19	**Vol. 3:** 178
2:20	**Vol. 2:** 261 **Vol. 3:** 786
2:21 f	**Vol. 2:** 888–889
3:4	**Vol. 2:** 190
3:8	**Vol. 2:** 863
3:9	**Vol. 3:** 951
3:10 f	**Vol. 3:** 342
3:10	**Vol. 2:** 214–215
3:11	**Vol. 3:** 255
3:13	**Vol. 2:** 27
3:14	**Vol. 2:** 431
3:15	**Vol. 1:** 202, 743 **Vol. 2:** 27, 29
3:17	**Vol. 2:** 777
3:19	**Vol. 1:** 202 **Vol. 2:** 29
3:20	**Vol. 3:** 680
3:21	**Vol. 2:** 773
3:24	**Vol. 2:** 297, 773
3:25	**Vol. 2:** 773
3:26	**Vol. 2:** 773
3:27	**Vol. 3:** 1161
3:29	**Vol. 1:** 743
3:31	**Vol. 2:** 261
3:32–34	**Vol. 2:** 261
3:34 ff	**Vol. 3:** 514
3:36	**Vol. 2:** 370
3:37 f	**Vol. 2:** 261
3:40	**Vol. 3:** 533
3:42 f	**Vol. 1:** 109
3:42	**Vol. 3:** 155
3:44	**Vol. 2:** 863
3:56	**Vol. 2:** 215
3:57	**Vol. 2:** 889
3:58	**Vol. 3:** 192
3:60 f	**Vol. 3:** 820
4:2	**Vol. 3:** 823, 914
4:3	**Vol. 1:** 240
4:4	**Vol. 2:** 349
4:6	**Vol. 3:** 93
4:11	**Vol. 1:** 661
4:12	**Vol. 1:** 519
4:14	**Vol. 1:** 218
4:16	**Vol. 1:** 109
4:18	**Vol. 2:** 898
4:19	**Vol. 1:** 173
4:20	**Vol. 2:** 336
4:21	**Vol. 2:** 357
5:1	**Vol. 3:** 234
5:2	**Vol. 1:** 688
5:5	**Vol. 3:** 254
5:8	**Vol. 3:** 192
5:13	**Vol. 1:** 393–394
5:14	**Vol. 3:** 255
5:21	**Vol. 1:** 354

Ezekiel

1 f	**Vol. 2:** 191
1	**Vol. 2:** 615 **Vol. 3:** 398, 618, 1089
1:1 f	**Vol. 3:** 502, 590
1:1 – 3:15	**Vol. 3:** 1100
1:1	**Vol. 3:** 311, 514, 986
1:3	**Vol. 3:** 986
1:4 ff	**Vol. 2:** 688
1:4 – 28	**Vol. 2:** 613
1:4	**Vol. 2:** 97, 501
1:5 ff	**Vol. 1:** 280
1:5 – 22	**Vol. 2:** 689
1:5 – 12	**Vol. 1:** 101
1:5	**Vol. 2:** 501
1:7	**Vol. 2:** 45
1:10	**Vol. 1:** 116, 173, 585
1:11	**Vol. 1:** 233 **Vol. 3:** 1162
1:13	**Vol. 2:** 45, 485
1:15 ff	**Vol. 2:** 688
1:16	**Vol. 2:** 501
1:20 f	**Vol. 2:** 479
1:22 f	**Vol. 1:** 523
1:22	**Vol. 2:** 501, 613
1:23	**Vol. 1:** 233 **Vol. 3:** 1162
1:24	**Vol. 3:** 255, 729, 990
1:26 – 28	**Vol. 3:** 398
1:26	**Vol. 2:** 501
1:27	**Vol. 1:** 655 – 656 **Vol. 2:** 97
1:28	**Vol. 1:** 610 **Vol. 3:** 514
2:1 ff	**Vol. 1:** 273
2:1*	**Vol. 2:** 501
2:2	**Vol. 3:** 691
2:4	**Vol. 3:** 1098
2:5	**Vol. 3:** 1100
2:6	**Vol. 1:** 510
2:8 ff	**Vol. 1:** 243
2:8	**Vol. 2:** 726
2:9 – 3:3	**Vol. 3:** 1098
2:9 f	**Vol. 1:** 244 **Vol. 3:** 500
2:10	**Vol. 3:** 1098
3:1 ff	**Vol. 2:** 273
3:1	**Vol. 3:** 1098
3:3	**Vol. 1:** 169
3:4	**Vol. 3:** 1099
3:7	**Vol. 2:** 174
3:9	**Vol. 1:** 203 **Vol. 3:** 382
3:12 f	**Vol. 3:** 557
3:12	**Vol. 3:** 691
3:14	**Vol. 1:** 108
3:15 ff	**Vol. 3:** 986
3:15	**Vol. 3:** 986
3:17 ff	**Vol. 1:** 222
3:18 ff	**Vol. 2:** 479
3:20	**Vol. 3:** 585 – 586, 856
3:23	**Vol. 3:** 986
3:25 – 5:4	**Vol. 3:** 1099
3:26	**Vol. 2:** 141
4 – 5	**Vol. 2:** 626
4:1 – 5:4	**Vol. 3:** 1099
4:1	**Vol. 2:** 573
4:2	**Vol. 3:** 951
4:4 – 8	**Vol. 3:** 1099
4:5 f	**Vol. 3:** 804
4:8	**Vol. 2:** 124
4:11	**Vol. 3:** 402
4:16	**Vol. 3:** 402
5	**Vol. 3:** 960
5:2	**Vol. 2:** 34, 687
5:5	**Vol. 2:** 529
5:6 f	**Vol. 3:** 354
5:10	**Vol. 2:** 34
5:11	**Vol. 1:** 74 **Vol. 3:** 786
5:12	**Vol. 2:** 687
5:14	**Vol. 3:** 1005
5:15 f	**Vol. 2:** 265
5:17	**Vol. 1:** 113
6:3	**Vol. 2:** 199 **Vol. 3:** 426
6:4 ff	**Vol. 2:** 284 – 285
6:5	**Vol. 1:** 610 **Vol. 2:** 34
6:6	**Vol. 3:** 426
6:7	**Vol. 2:** 395
6:9	**Vol. 3:** 236
6:10	**Vol. 2:** 41 **Vol. 3:** 236
6:11 ff	**Vol. 1:** 109
6:11	**Vol. 2:** 149
6:12	**Vol. 2:** 53
6:13	**Vol. 2:** 284 – 285, 395 **Vol. 3:** 865
6:14	**Vol. 1:** 465 **Vol. 2:** 395
7:3	**Vol. 1:** 110
7:4	**Vol. 2:** 395
7:7	**Vol. 2:** 53, 888 **Vol. 3:** 836
7:8	**Vol. 2:** 854
7:10	**Vol. 1:** 320 **Vol. 3:** 29 – 30
7:12	**Vol. 1:** 320 **Vol. 3:** 836
7:13	**Vol. 3:** 601
7:17	**Vol. 3:** 178
7:18	**Vol. 2:** 157, 212, 621
7:19	**Vol. 1:** 110 **Vol. 3:** 856
7:20	**Vol. 2:** 287 **Vol. 3:** 29 – 30
7:23	**Vol. 2:** 803
7:26	**Vol. 2:** 440
7:27†	**Vol. 1:** 165, 314
8	**Vol. 1:** 74 **Vol. 2:** 285 **Vol. 3:** 427
8:1 ff	**Vol. 1:** 196
8:1	**Vol. 3:** 588
8:2	**Vol. 2:** 45, 97, 501
8:3	**Vol. 3:** 691, 794
8:5	**Vol. 2:** 287
8:6	**Vol. 3:** 786
8:10	**Vol. 2:** 285, 502
8:11	**Vol. 2:** 293
8:13 f	**Vol. 3:** 275
8:16	**Vol. 2:** 876 **Vol. 3:** 731, 783
8:17 f	**Vol. 2:** 285
8:17	**Vol. 2:** 558
8:18	**Vol. 2:** 174
9:2	**Vol. 3:** 478
9:3	**Vol. 1:** 280
9:4 ff	**Vol. 3:** 498

117

Ezekiel *(cont'd)*

9:4	**Vol. 2:** 423, 572–573 **Vol. 3:** 483, 500
9:6	**Vol. 1:** 281 **Vol. 3:** 786
9:7	**Vol. 1:** 444
9:8–10	**Vol. 1:** 109
9:8	**Vol. 3:** 249
9:10	**Vol. 2:** 158
10	**Vol. 1:** 280 **Vol. 2:** 502
10:1	**Vol. 2:** 501–502 **Vol. 3:** 398
10:10	**Vol. 2:** 501–502
10:15	**Vol. 3:** 986
10:17	**Vol. 2:** 479
10:19–22	**Vol. 1:** 101
10:20	**Vol. 3:** 986
10:21 f	**Vol. 2:** 501–502
10:22	**Vol. 1:** 674
11:1	**Vol. 3:** 691
11:2	**Vol. 3:** 823
11:5	**Vol. 1:** 609 **Vol. 3:** 691
11:6	**Vol. 1:** 444
11:7	**Vol. 1:** 444
11:10	**Vol. 2:** 395
11:11 f	**Vol. 2:** 395
11:13	**Vol. 1:** 609 **Vol. 3:** 249
11:15	**Vol. 3:** 190
11:19 f	**Vol. 3:** 692
11:19	**Vol. 1:** 184, 248, 354 **Vol. 2:** 565, 670
11:20	**Vol. 2:** 134, 797 **Vol. 3:** 354
11:22	**Vol. 1:** 101
11:24	**Vol. 3:** 691
12:1 ff	**Vol. 3:** 1099
12:1–16	**Vol. 3:** 1099
12:3 ff	**Vol. 2:** 627
12:6	**Vol. 2:** 633
12:9	**Vol. 1:** 203
12:11	**Vol. 2:** 529, 633
12:14 f	**Vol. 2:** 395
12:15	**Vol. 1:** 686
12:16	**Vol. 2:** 395 **Vol. 3:** 249
12:17 ff	**Vol. 2:** 627
12:17–20	**Vol. 3:** 1099
12:21 ff	**Vol. 3:** 1099
12:22	**Vol. 2:** 53
12:24	**Vol. 2:** 116
12:25	**Vol. 3:** 1099
12:27	**Vol. 2:** 53 **Vol. 3:** 1099
13:5	**Vol. 2:** 890
13:6 ff	**Vol. 1:** 550
13:6	**Vol. 2:** 554
13:8	**Vol. 2:** 471
13:9	**Vol. 2:** 554
13:10 ff	**Vol. 1:** 205
13:10–16	**Vol. 1:** 120 **Vol. 3:** 948
13:10	**Vol. 2:** 779
13:13	**Vol. 3:** 1001
13:14	**Vol. 3:** 310
13:16	**Vol. 2:** 779
13:18 f	**Vol. 2:** 565
13:18	**Vol. 1:** 92
13:19	**Vol. 2:** 470
13:21	**Vol. 3:** 201
13:23	**Vol. 2:** 554 **Vol. 3:** 201
14:3 ff	**Vol. 3:** 687
14:3 f	**Vol. 3:** 125
14:3	**Vol. 3:** 98
14:4	**Vol. 2:** 285 **Vol. 3:** 98
14:7	**Vol. 3:** 98
14:9	**Vol. 2:** 458
14:11	**Vol. 1:** 448 **Vol. 2:** 797 **Vol. 3:** 585–586
14:13	**Vol. 1:** 609 **Vol. 3:** 585
14:14	**Vol. 2:** 681
14:16	**Vol. 1:** 465 **Vol. 2:** 724
14:20	**Vol. 2:** 479, 681 **Vol. 3:** 202
14:21	**Vol. 1:** 113
14:22	**Vol. 3:** 249
15:1–8	**Vol. 3:** 918
15:4	**Vol. 2:** 60
15:8	**Vol. 1:** 609 **Vol. 3:** 585
16	**Vol. 1:** 499 **Vol. 2:** 349, 576, 747 **Vol. 3:** 263
16:1–63	**Vol. 2:** 583
16:2 ff	**Vol. 2:** 324
16:4 f	**Vol. 2:** 889
16:4	**Vol. 3:** 444, 447
16:5	**Vol. 3:** 720
16:8–14	**Vol. 3:** 1068
16:8	**Vol. 1:** 344, 366 **Vol. 2:** 212, 578 **Vol. 3:** 1068
16:9	**Vol. 1:** 121–122 **Vol. 2:** 711
16:10–13	**Vol. 2:** 349
16:12	**Vol. 1:** 229
16:13	**Vol. 2:** 711
16:15	**Vol. 3:** 1069
16:17	**Vol. 2:** 287
16:18 f	**Vol. 2:** 711
16:22	**Vol. 1:** 312 **Vol. 3:** 236
16:23	**Vol. 3:** 1051
16:26	**Vol. 1:** 672
16:31	**Vol. 2:** 139
16:32	**Vol. 2:** 139
16:33	**Vol. 2:** 139
16:34	**Vol. 2:** 139
16:36 f†	**Vol. 3:** 310, 563
16:37	**Vol. 1:** 555 **Vol. 2:** 540
16:38 ff	**Vol. 3:** 538
16:38	**Vol. 3:** 154, 1167
16:40	**Vol. 1:** 292 **Vol. 2:** 582, 800
16:41	**Vol. 2:** 139
16:42	**Vol. 3:** 154, 255
16:46–56	**Vol. 3:** 93
16:49	**Vol. 3:** 29
16:51 f	**Vol. 3:** 355
16:52	**Vol. 3:** 356, 856
16:54	**Vol. 3:** 856
16:55	**Vol. 3:** 147
16:56	**Vol. 3:** 29–30
16:57†	**Vol. 3:** 310
16:59–63	**Vol. 2:** 307

Ezekiel *(cont'd)*

16:59	**Vol. 3:** 583
16:60	**Vol. 3:** 235
16:61	**Vol. 3:** 236
16:62	**Vol. 3:** 236
16:63	**Vol. 2:** 49, 727 **Vol. 3:** 153–154
17	**Vol. 2:** 747
17:1–10	**Vol. 3:** 918
17:2	**Vol. 2:** 745
17:5 ff	**Vol. 3:** 866
17:6	**Vol. 3:** 866
17:8	**Vol. 3:** 866
17:12–21	**Vol. 2:** 747
17:15 ff	**Vol. 3:** 583
17:15	**Vol. 1:** 531, 606 **Vol. 3:** 209
17:17	**Vol. 1:** 292–293 **Vol. 2:** 800
17:18	**Vol. 3:** 209
17:21	**Vol. 3:** 249
17:22 ff	**Vol. 2:** 374
17:22 f	**Vol. 2:** 337
17:23	**Vol. 1:** 531 **Vol. 3:** 255, 554, 867–868
17:24	**Vol. 1:** 515 **Vol. 2:** 260 **Vol. 3:** 866
18	**Vol. 3:** 135, 720
18:1 ff	**Vol. 3:** 1104
18:1–32	**Vol. 3:** 69
18:2	**Vol. 1:** 434 **Vol. 2:** 745
18:4	**Vol. 1:** 221 **Vol. 2:** 479
18:7	**Vol. 2:** 266, 666
18:9	**Vol. 2:** 479 **Vol. 3:** 354
18:12	**Vol. 2:** 820
18:13	**Vol. 2:** 479
18:16	**Vol. 2:** 266
18:17	**Vol. 2:** 479 **Vol. 3:** 354
18:19	**Vol. 3:** 354
18:20 ff	**Vol. 2:** 479
18:20	**Vol. 2:** 139
18:21 ff	**Vol. 1:** 434
18:21 f	**Vol. 1:** 333
18:21	**Vol. 3:** 354
18:22	**Vol. 3:** 585–586
18:23	**Vol. 3:** 1019
18:24	**Vol. 1:** 609 **Vol. 3:** 585
18:26	**Vol. 3:** 585–586
18:27	**Vol. 3:** 368
18:30	**Vol. 3:** 98
18:31 f	**Vol. 1:** 434
18:31	**Vol. 1:** 354 **Vol. 2:** 670 **Vol. 3:** 692
19	**Vol. 2:** 418, 747
19:3	**Vol. 1:** 484
19:4	**Vol. 1:** 531
19:5	**Vol. 1:** 712
19:6	**Vol. 1:** 484
19:10–14	**Vol. 3:** 918
19:10	**Vol. 3:** 866
19:11	**Vol. 3:** 867
19:12 f	**Vol. 3:** 867
19:13	**Vol. 3:** 1005
19:14	**Vol. 3:** 867
20	**Vol. 1:** 531 **Vol. 3:** 1005
20:6	**Vol. 3:** 117
20:9	**Vol. 2:** 307
20:10–26	**Vol. 3:** 1005
20:11	**Vol. 3:** 354
20:12–20	**Vol. 2:** 396
20:13	**Vol. 3:** 354
20:14	**Vol. 2:** 307
20:16	**Vol. 1:** 492 **Vol. 3:** 354
20:18	**Vol. 3:** 354
20:19	**Vol. 3:** 354
20:21	**Vol. 3:** 354
20:22	**Vol. 2:** 307
20:24 f	**Vol. 3:** 354
20:25 f	**Vol. 3:** 421
20:27	**Vol. 1:** 609 **Vol. 3:** 585
20:28	**Vol. 2:** 43 **Vol. 3:** 423
20:29	**Vol. 3:** 426
20:31	**Vol. 3:** 416
20:32	**Vol. 1:** 390 **Vol. 3:** 549
20:33–38	**Vol. 2:** 364
20:33	**Vol. 1:** 503
20:34	**Vol. 3:** 745
20:35	**Vol. 3:** 1006
20:36	**Vol. 3:** 1005
20:37 f	**Vol. 3:** 772
20:38	**Vol. 1:** 537, 606
20:40	**Vol. 3:** 415–416
20:43	**Vol. 3:** 236
20:44	**Vol. 3:** 236
21:3 f*	**Vol. 3:** 109
21:6 f*	**Vol. 2:** 423
21:11 f	**Vol. 2:** 627
21:18*	**Vol. 3:** 355
21:21*	**Vol. 2:** 296
21:22*	**Vol. 3:** 951
21:23	**Vol. 3:** 1099
21:26 ff	**Vol. 2:** 554
21:26*	**Vol. 2:** 260, 262
21:28 f*	**Vol. 3:** 240
21:29*	**Vol. 1:** 241 **Vol. 3:** 310
21:31	**Vol. 2:** 596
21:37*	**Vol. 3:** 238
22	**Vol. 3:** 1103
22:2–4	**Vol. 2:** 803
22:2	**Vol. 3:** 159
22:4	**Vol. 3:** 585
22:7	**Vol. 1:** 415 **Vol. 2:** 737 **Vol. 3:** 1074
22:10 f	**Vol. 2:** 260
22:10	**Vol. 3:** 310, 861, 1074
22:13	**Vol. 3:** 137
22:26	**Vol. 1:** 74 **Vol. 2:** 440
22:27	**Vol. 1:** 118, 137
22:28	**Vol. 2:** 470, 555
22:29	**Vol. 2:** 823
22:30	**Vol. 3:** 933
22:31	**Vol. 1:** 109
23	**Vol. 1:** 499 **Vol. 2:** 576, 747 **Vol. 3:** 263
23:10	**Vol. 1:** 429 **Vol. 3:** 310, 563
23:11–32	**Vol. 1:** 141

Ezekiel *(cont'd)*

23:14	**Vol. 2:** 287
23:15	**Vol. 2:** 501–502 **Vol. 3:** 120
23:18	**Vol. 1:** 607 **Vol. 3:** 310, 563
23:19	**Vol. 3:** 236, 240
23:20	**Vol. 1:** 672 **Vol. 3:** 561
23:21	**Vol. 3:** 794
23:24	**Vol. 2:** 796, 800–801
23:27	**Vol. 3:** 236, 1167
23:28	**Vol. 1:** 555
23:29	**Vol. 2:** 926 **Vol. 3:** 310
23:31–35	**Vol. 3:** 922
23:32†	**Vol. 2:** 431
23:33†	**Vol. 1:** 513
23:37–45	**Vol. 2:** 583
23:41	**Vol. 2:** 711
23:46 f	**Vol. 2:** 800
24:6	**Vol. 2:** 27, 296 **Vol. 3:** 159
24:7 f	**Vol. 2:** 212
24:9	**Vol. 3:** 159
24:11 f	**Vol. 2:** 27
24:15 ff	**Vol. 2:** 626
24:15–24	**Vol. 3:** 1099
24:17	**Vol. 2:** 423
24:18	**Vol. 2:** 689
24:24	**Vol. 2:** 627, 633
24:27	**Vol. 2:** 627, 633
25–32	**Vol. 1:** 688 **Vol. 3:** 960
25:3	**Vol. 3:** 786
25:5	**Vol. 2:** 395
25:10	**Vol. 3:** 238
25:12	**Vol. 3:** 93
25:17	**Vol. 2:** 650
26:2 ff†	**Vol. 2:** 767 **Vol. 3:** 1099
26:8	**Vol. 3:** 951
26:10	**Vol. 3:** 557
26:11	**Vol. 1:** 712
26:12	**Vol. 2:** 842
26:15	**Vol. 2:** 423
26:16	**Vol. 1:** 527
26:18	**Vol. 2:** 890
26:19 f	**Vol. 3:** 989, 1006
26:19	**Vol. 3:** 1006
26:20	**Vol. 2:** 197 **Vol. 3:** 1006
27	**Vol. 1:** 142
27:6	**Vol. 3:** 785
27:7	**Vol. 1:** 531
27:8 ff	**Vol. 3:** 1028
27:8	**Vol. 1:** 194
27:11	**Vol. 2:** 60
27:12–22	**Vol. 1:** 267
27:13	**Vol. 2:** 124
27:15	**Vol. 2:** 139
27:17	**Vol. 2:** 711
27:26	**Vol. 3:** 786
27:27 f	**Vol. 1:** 194
27:27	**Vol. 1:** 293 **Vol. 2:** 139, 890
27:28	**Vol. 3:** 786
27:29 ff	**Vol. 3:** 1054

27:30–34	**Vol. 2:** 418
27:33	**Vol. 2:** 139, 841
27:35	**Vol. 1:** 527
28	**Vol. 1:** 142 **Vol. 3:** 396
28:2	**Vol. 2:** 201, 279
28:3	**Vol. 3:** 1028
28:5	**Vol. 2:** 201
28:9	**Vol. 2:** 279
28:13 ff	**Vol. 2:** 761
28:13	**Vol. 1:** 380 **Vol. 3:** 395–396
28:14–16	**Vol. 1:** 280
28:15	**Vol. 3:** 924
28:17	**Vol. 2:** 291
28:18	**Vol. 3:** 785
28:22	**Vol. 2:** 226
28:24	**Vol. 1:** 725–726
28:25	**Vol. 3:** 608
28:26	**Vol. 2:** 395
29–32	**Vol. 1:** 531
29:3	**Vol. 1:** 205, 508
29:4	**Vol. 1:** 670
29:5	**Vol. 2:** 32
29:7	**Vol. 1:** 239 **Vol. 3:** 255
29:10	**Vol. 3:** 1005
29:16	**Vol. 1:** 492 **Vol. 3:** 240
29:18 f	**Vol. 2:** 139
29:21	**Vol. 2:** 727
30:3 ff	**Vol. 2:** 363
30:3	**Vol. 2:** 53, 888, 890
30:6	**Vol. 3:** 29
30:12	**Vol. 3:** 1005
30:13	**Vol. 3:** 255
30:15	**Vol. 1:** 109
30:18	**Vol. 3:** 29
30:21	**Vol. 3:** 713
30:24 f	**Vol. 1:** 141
30:24	**Vol. 3:** 713
30:26	**Vol. 2:** 34
31	**Vol. 2:** 747
31:3 f	**Vol. 3:** 866
31:4	**Vol. 2:** 201
31:5	**Vol. 3:** 867
31:6	**Vol. 3:** 554, 867–868
31:8 f	**Vol. 2:** 761
31:10	**Vol. 2:** 201
31:12	**Vol. 2:** 796 **Vol. 3:** 867
31:13	**Vol. 3:** 255
31:14	**Vol. 2:** 197, 199
31:15 ff	**Vol. 1:** 91
31:15	**Vol. 2:** 222, 422, 889
31:18	**Vol. 2:** 197
32:1 ff	**Vol. 3:** 1104
32:1–16	**Vol. 2:** 418
32:2	**Vol. 1:** 508 **Vol. 3:** 709
32:7	**Vol. 1:** 203, 425 **Vol. 2:** 38, 916 **Vol. 3:** 109, 559, 731, 733, 735
32:10	**Vol. 2:** 890
32:12	**Vol. 3:** 29
32:13	**Vol. 3:** 709
32:14	**Vol. 2:** 711

Ezekiel *(cont'd)*

32:18 f	**Vol. 2:** 197
32:19 ff	**Vol. 1:** 442
32:20 ff	**Vol. 2:** 206
32:22	**Vol. 1:** 293
32:23 f	**Vol. 3:** 238
32:23	**Vol. 1:** 292
32:24	**Vol. 2:** 197 **Vol. 3:** 856
32:26	**Vol. 3:** 238
32:30	**Vol. 3:** 856
33:1–9	**Vol. 3:** 1100
33:4	**Vol. 2:** 158
33:5	**Vol. 3:** 209
33:7	**Vol. 3:** 1100
33:8	**Vol. 1:** 607 **Vol. 3:** 1100
33:9	**Vol. 1:** 354
33:10	**Vol. 3:** 269, 823
33:11	**Vol. 1:** 354 **Vol. 2:** 479
33:13	**Vol. 3:** 232, 240
33:14 ff	**Vol. 1:** 354
33:16	**Vol. 3:** 240
33:28	**Vol. 3:** 29
33:29	**Vol. 2:** 278
33:30	**Vol. 2:** 720
33:31	**Vol. 1:** 492 **Vol. 3:** 137
33:33	**Vol. 2:** 891
34	**Vol. 2:** 459, 747 **Vol. 3:** 567
34:1 ff	**Vol. 3:** 564–565
34:2–10	**Vol. 3:** 566
34:5 f	**Vol. 2:** 104, 412
34:5	**Vol. 2:** 34, 412–413 **Vol. 3:** 567
34:6	**Vol. 2:** 412
34:11 f	**Vol. 3:** 565
34:12–16	**Vol. 3:** 531
34:12	**Vol. 2:** 887, 889
34:13	**Vol. 2:** 34
34:14 f	**Vol. 3:** 255
34:15	**Vol. 3:** 567
34:16	**Vol. 2:** 34
34:17	**Vol. 1:** 503–504
34:23 f	**Vol. 2:** 337 **Vol. 3:** 609
34:23	**Vol. 2:** 412 **Vol. 3:** 566, 649
34:25	**Vol. 1:** 113, 185 **Vol. 2:** 778 **Vol. 3:** 1005–1006
34:27	**Vol. 2:** 777 **Vol. 3:** 1161
34:29	**Vol. 2:** 266, 825
34:30†	**Vol. 2:** 650
34:31	**Vol. 3:** 565
35:4	**Vol. 3:** 1005
35:9	**Vol. 3:** 1005
35:12 f	**Vol. 3:** 341–342
36 f	**Vol. 2:** 297
36–48	**Vol. 2:** 701
36	**Vol. 2:** 240
36:6	**Vol. 3:** 1166
36:9	**Vol. 3:** 522
36:10	**Vol. 3:** 1006
36:17 f	**Vol. 2:** 284
36:23	**Vol. 2:** 226, 229, 653 **Vol. 3:** 236
36:24 f	**Vol. 1:** 185
36:24	**Vol. 1:** 225
36:25 ff†	**Vol. 3:** 989
36:25–27	**Vol. 3:** 987–988
36:25	**Vol. 1:** 144, 151–152, 225 **Vol. 2:** 284
36:26 ff	**Vol. 2:** 797
36:26–37	**Vol. 3:** 69
36:26 f	**Vol. 1:** 184, 354 **Vol. 2:** 155, 184, 786 **Vol. 3:** 692
36:26	**Vol. 1:** 225 **Vol. 2:** 670
36:27	**Vol. 1:** 225 **Vol. 3:** 354
36:29	**Vol. 1:** 699
36:31	**Vol. 3:** 236
36:33 ff	**Vol. 3:** 1006
36:33	**Vol. 1:** 699 **Vol. 2:** 890
36:36	**Vol. 2:** 278
37–48	**Vol. 1:** 124
37	**Vol. 2:** 240 **Vol. 3:** 269, 578
37:1–14	**Vol. 3:** 692, 1100
37:3	**Vol. 3:** 269
37:4 ff	**Vol. 3:** 269
37:4–6	**Vol. 3:** 1100
37:4	**Vol. 3:** 1100
37:5	**Vol. 2:** 479
37:6	**Vol. 1:** 672 **Vol. 2:** 278, 395
37:7–11	**Vol. 3:** 269
37:7	**Vol. 3:** 557
37:8	**Vol. 1:** 672 **Vol. 3:** 690
37:9–10	**Vol. 3:** 1100
37:9	**Vol. 1:** 444 **Vol. 2:** 787 **Vol. 3:** 690, 703, 1100
37:10	**Vol. 1:** 296 **Vol. 2:** 479 **Vol. 3:** 690, 1185
37:11–14	**Vol. 3:** 269, 1100
37:11	**Vol. 3:** 1100
37:12	**Vol. 3:** 238
37:13	**Vol. 2:** 278
37:14	**Vol. 1:** 354 **Vol. 2:** 786
37:16	**Vol. 3:** 483
37:21	**Vol. 1:** 297
37:22	**Vol. 1:** 534 **Vol. 3:** 566
37:23	**Vol. 2:** 284–285 **Vol. 3:** 200
37:24 f	**Vol. 2:** 337 **Vol. 3:** 609
37:24	**Vol. 2:** 376 **Vol. 3:** 566, 649
37:25 f	**Vol. 1:** 185
37:25	**Vol. 2:** 448 **Vol. 3:** 608
37:26	**Vol. 2:** 778
37:27	**Vol. 2:** 800 **Vol. 3:** 784, 813
38 f	**Vol. 3:** 80, 389
38–39	**Vol. 3:** 962
38:4	**Vol. 1:** 296
38:7	**Vol. 1:** 296
38:8	**Vol. 2:** 777 **Vol. 3:** 1006
38:10	**Vol. 3:** 823
38:11	**Vol. 2:** 777 **Vol. 3:** 111
38:12	**Vol. 1:** 523 **Vol. 3:** 1006
38:14	**Vol. 2:** 777
38:16	**Vol. 2:** 56, 296
38:17	**Vol. 2:** 307
38:18	**Vol. 2:** 890

Ezekiel *(cont'd)*

38:19 f   **Vol. 3:** 557
38:19   **Vol. 3:** 557, 1166
38:20   **Vol. 1:** 610, 670   **Vol. 3:** 1010
38:22   **Vol. 1:** 655
38:23   **Vol. 2:** 56
39:6   **Vol. 1:** 655   **Vol. 2:** 777
39:8   **Vol. 2:** 890
39:11   **Vol. 3:** 239
39:13   **Vol. 2:** 890
39:17   **Vol. 2:** 32
39:21 f   **Vol. 2:** 45
39:24   **Vol. 3:** 105
39:26   **Vol. 2:** 777
39:27   **Vol. 1:** 96
39:28   **Vol. 2:** 278   **Vol. 3:** 318
39:29   **Vol. 2:** 854   **Vol. 3:** 692
40 ff   **Vol. 3:** 784
40–48   **Vol. 2:** 226   **Vol. 3:** 402, 404, 509
40–46   **Vol. 3:** 551
40–43   **Vol. 3:** 783, 787–788
40:3   **Vol. 1:** 101
40:5–9   **Vol. 2:** 498
40:5   **Vol. 3:** 436
40:17   **Vol. 3:** 796
40:38   **Vol. 3:** 421
40:39   **Vol. 3:** 421
40:42   **Vol. 3:** 421
40:43   **Vol. 2:** 43
40:46   **Vol. 2:** 53
41:1   **Vol. 3:** 783, 786
41:4   **Vol. 3:** 783
41:6   **Vol. 3:** 860
41:7 ff   **Vol. 3:** 786
41:15   **Vol. 3:** 783
41:21   **Vol. 3:** 783, 786
41:23   **Vol. 3:** 783, 786
41:25   **Vol. 3:** 783
42:13 f   **Vol. 3:** 786
42:15   **Vol. 2:** 290
42:16–20   **Vol. 3:** 690
42:19   **Vol. 3:** 783
42:20   **Vol. 3:** 436
43:2   **Vol. 2:** 45   **Vol. 3:** 990
43:11   **Vol. 1:** 712   **Vol. 3:** 98, 354
43:13–17   **Vol. 3:** 419
43:14   **Vol. 3:** 156
43:17   **Vol. 3:** 156
43:20   **Vol. 3:** 149, 156, 419
43:22 ff   **Vol. 3:** 200
43:22 f   **Vol. 3:** 435, 924
43:22   **Vol. 3:** 149
43:23–26   **Vol. 3:** 419
43:23   **Vol. 3:** 149, 152
43:24   **Vol. 2:** 746   **Vol. 3:** 445
43:25   **Vol. 3:** 924
43:26   **Vol. 3:** 152, 419
44:7 ff   **Vol. 3:** 593, 786
44:7   **Vol. 1:** 154, 309, 672

44:9   **Vol. 1:** 308, 672
44:11   **Vol. 3:** 421, 786
44:12   **Vol. 3:** 98, 552
44:13   **Vol. 2:** 53
44:15 f   **Vol. 3:** 786
44:15   **Vol. 2:** 34
44:16   **Vol. 1:** 322   **Vol. 3:** 424
44:17 ff   **Vol. 1:** 204
44:18   **Vol. 3:** 711
44:19   **Vol. 3:** 786
44:21   **Vol. 3:** 919
44:22   **Vol. 2:** 592
44:23†   **Vol. 3:** 760
44:24   **Vol. 3:** 354–355
44:27   **Vol. 3:** 156, 786
44:28   **Vol. 1:** 636   **Vol. 2:** 297
44:29   **Vol. 1:** 414
44:30 ff   **Vol. 3:** 853
44:30   **Vol. 3:** 415–416
45:1–6   **Vol. 2:** 698
45:1   **Vol. 2:** 297   **Vol. 3:** 416, 1160
45:2   **Vol. 3:** 786
45:3 f   **Vol. 3:** 786
45:6 f   **Vol. 3:** 416
45:10   **Vol. 3:** 356, 1160
45:11   **Vol. 3:** 1160
45:13   **Vol. 3:** 416
45:14   **Vol. 2:** 711
45:15   **Vol. 3:** 152, 423
45:16   **Vol. 3:** 416
45:17   **Vol. 3:** 152–153, 159, 423
45:18   **Vol. 3:** 786, 924
45:19   **Vol. 3:** 152, 786
45:20   **Vol. 3:** 152–153
45:21   **Vol. 1:** 632   **Vol. 2:** 463
45:23   **Vol. 3:** 421, 924
45:24 f   **Vol. 2:** 711
46:1   **Vol. 2:** 890
46:2 f   **Vol. 2:** 876
46:2   **Vol. 3:** 423
46:4   **Vol. 2:** 410, 890   **Vol. 3:** 421, 924
46:5   **Vol. 2:** 711
46:6   **Vol. 3:** 924
46:7   **Vol. 2:** 711
46:9   **Vol. 2:** 876
46:11   **Vol. 2:** 410, 711
46:12   **Vol. 1:** 344   **Vol. 2:** 890   **Vol. 3:** 423
46:13   **Vol. 3:** 421, 924
46:14 f   **Vol. 2:** 711
46:15   **Vol. 3:** 421
46:17   **Vol. 1:** 698
46:18   **Vol. 2:** 34
46:19   **Vol. 3:** 786
46:24   **Vol. 3:** 422
47:1 ff   **Vol. 2:** 326   **Vol. 3:** 813
47:1–12   **Vol. 3:** 962, 986, 987
47:1   **Vol. 3:** 988
47:6 ff   **Vol. 2:** 685
47:9   **Vol. 1:** 670
47:11   **Vol. 3:** 444

Ezekiel *(cont'd)*

47:12 f	**Vol. 3:** 865
47:12	**Vol. 3:** 786
47:13 f	**Vol. 2:** 297
47:22 f	**Vol. 1:** 688, 691 **Vol. 2:** 297
48:8 ff	**Vol. 3:** 416
48:8–35	**Vol. 2:** 698
48:10	**Vol. 3:** 786
48:12	**Vol. 3:** 416
48:18	**Vol. 3:** 416
48:20 f	**Vol. 3:** 416
48:28	**Vol. 3:** 983
48:29	**Vol. 2:** 297
48:30–34	**Vol. 3:** 871
48:30	**Vol. 3:** 397

Daniel

1:2	**Vol. 3:** 786
1:3	**Vol. 3:** 115
1:4	**Vol. 1:** 140 **Vol. 2:** 557, 616 **Vol. 3:** 760, 924, 1027
1:8	**Vol. 2:** 521
1:9	**Vol. 2:** 116
1:10	**Vol. 2:** 370
1:12 ff	**Vol. 2:** 692
1:12	**Vol. 3:** 799
1:13	**Vol. 2:** 521
1:14	**Vol. 3:** 799
1:15	**Vol. 1:** 672 **Vol. 2:** 521
1:16	**Vol. 2:** 521
1:17	**Vol. 1:** 140 **Vol. 3:** 1027
1:19	**Vol. 3:** 528
1:20	**Vol. 2:** 555 **Vol. 3:** 1035
2	**Vol. 1:** 141, 512 **Vol. 2:** 745 **Vol. 3:** 316
2:1	**Vol. 2:** 808
2:2 f	**Vol. 2:** 557
2:2	**Vol. 2:** 479, 554–555
2:3 ff	**Vol. 2:** 56
2:4–7:28	**Vol. 1:** 51
2:5 ff	**Vol. 3:** 316
2:5	**Vol. 2:** 291
2:8	**Vol. 1:** 267
2:10	**Vol. 3:** 1028
2:11	**Vol. 1:** 679
2:12	**Vol. 3:** 1028
2:13	**Vol. 1:** 330
2:18 f	**Vol. 2:** 190
2:18	**Vol. 1:** 340
2:20–23	**Vol. 3:** 640
2:20 f	**Vol. 3:** 1027
2:20	**Vol. 2:** 555
2:21	**Vol. 2:** 607 **Vol. 3:** 131, 835, 1028
2:22	**Vol. 2:** 215, 491
2:23	**Vol. 3:** 816, 1027
2:27–30	**Vol. 3:** 311
2:27–28	**Vol. 1:** 512
2:27	**Vol. 2:** 555 **Vol. 3:** 1028
2:28 f	**Vol. 2:** 808 **Vol. 3:** 502
2:28	**Vol. 2:** 56, 190, 665, 808, 912 **Vol. 3:** 316, 502
2:29 f	**Vol. 3:** 820
2:29	**Vol. 2:** 665 **Vol. 3:** 316
2:30	**Vol. 3:** 316, 1027
2:31 f	**Vol. 2:** 158
2:31	**Vol. 2:** 287
2:33	**Vol. 3:** 914
2:34 f	**Vol. 2:** 287 **Vol. 3:** 392, 394
2:34	**Vol. 1:** 610 **Vol. 3:** 384, 393, 914
2:37	**Vol. 2:** 49, 190
2:38	**Vol. 2:** 96
2:41	**Vol. 3:** 914
2:42	**Vol. 3:** 914
2:44 f	**Vol. 3:** 392
2:44	**Vol. 1:** 610 **Vol. 2:** 190, 888
2:45	**Vol. 2:** 56, 665, 808
2:46	**Vol. 2:** 876
2:47	**Vol. 2:** 514 **Vol. 3:** 311
2:48	**Vol. 3:** 1029
3	**Vol. 2:** 628 **Vol. 3:** 669
3:1–18	**Vol. 2:** 287
3:4	**Vol. 1:** 340 **Vol. 2:** 799–800 **Vol. 3:** 48, 50–51
3:5 ff	**Vol. 2:** 876
3:5	**Vol. 3:** 594
3:6	**Vol. 1:** 235 **Vol. 3:** 846
3:10 ff	**Vol. 2:** 876
3:14	**Vol. 2:** 876
3:15	**Vol. 3:** 846
3:18	**Vol. 2:** 876 **Vol. 3:** 962
3:19	**Vol. 1:** 706
3:22	**Vol. 1:** 476 **Vol. 2:** 628, 815
3:24 f	**Vol. 2:** 863
3:27	**Vol. 3:** 860
3:28*	**Vol. 2:** 876
3:29*	**Vol. 3:** 341
3:54*	**Vol. 3:** 669
3:56*	**Vol. 3:** 669
3:88*	**Vol. 3:** 201
3:92*	**Vol. 3:** 177
4	**Vol. 2:** 431, 745
4:1–7*	**Vol. 1:** 246
4:3	**Vol. 2:** 376
4:6	**Vol. 3:** 502
4:7*	**Vol. 2:** 555
4:10 f	**Vol. 3:** 866
4:13–33	**Vol. 1:** 113
4:13*	**Vol. 1:** 101
4:15	**Vol. 3:** 866
4:16	**Vol. 1:** 527 **Vol. 3:** 820, 845
4:17*	**Vol. 1:** 101
4:18	**Vol. 3:** 502
4:19	**Vol. 3:** 29
4:21 f	**Vol. 3:** 867–868
4:23	**Vol. 2:** 191
4:24	**Vol. 3:** 192, 585
4:26	**Vol. 3:** 866
4:27	**Vol. 2:** 594
4:30*	**Vol. 1:** 142 **Vol. 3:** 846

Daniel *(cont'd)*

4:31	**Vol. 2:** 607
4:32	**Vol. 3:** 200, 823
4:33 f	**Vol. 3:** 147
4:34*	**Vol. 2:** 791 **Vol. 3:** 29, 193, 601
5:1	**Vol. 2:** 521 **Vol. 3:** 745, 816
5:2 ff	**Vol. 3:** 788
5:4	**Vol. 2:** 77
5:5	**Vol. 2:** 485 **Vol. 3:** 846
5:6	**Vol. 1:** 239 **Vol. 3:** 820
5:7	**Vol. 2:** 555
5:10	**Vol. 3:** 232, 820
5:11 f	**Vol. 3:** 1029
5:11	**Vol. 2:** 555
5:12	**Vol. 1:** 729 **Vol. 2:** 616 **Vol. 3:** 177
5:14	**Vol. 1:** 729 **Vol. 3:** 1027
5:20	**Vol. 3:** 29
5:21	**Vol. 1:** 113
5:23	**Vol. 3:** 788, 816, 938
5:27	**Vol. 3:** 953, 1160
6	**Vol. 2:** 628
6:3	**Vol. 3:** 691
6:5*	**Vol. 3:** 585–586
6:6*	**Vol. 2:** 441
6:11*	**Vol. 2:** 863 **Vol. 3:** 550
6:13*	**Vol. 2:** 882 **Vol. 3:** 98, 226
6:16	**Vol. 1:** 327 **Vol. 3:** 550
6:18	**Vol. 3:** 498–499
6:19	**Vol. 1:** 694
6:20	**Vol. 3:** 203
6:22	**Vol. 2:** 628 **Vol. 3:** 951
6:23*	**Vol. 3:** 585
6:24	**Vol. 3:** 1212
6:25*	**Vol. 3:** 1041
6:26	**Vol. 1:** 732 **Vol. 3:** 224
6:27*	**Vol. 2:** 876
6:28*	**Vol. 2:** 876 **Vol. 3:** 192
7–12	**Vol. 1:** 124
7	**Vol. 1:** 113–114, 118, 141 **Vol. 2:** 80, 604, 607, 745, 891 **Vol. 3:** 196, 510, 616–618, 620, 622, 627, 632, 697, 983, 1114
7:1–8	**Vol. 1:** 119
7:1	**Vol. 3:** 513
7:2	**Vol. 1:** 420 **Vol. 2:** 189
7:3	**Vol. 3:** 984
7:4	**Vol. 1:** 665
7:6	**Vol. 2:** 124
7:7 ff	**Vol. 1:** 126
7:7 f	**Vol. 1:** 508
7:7	**Vol. 2:** 98, 621, 808 **Vol. 3:** 715
7:9 ff	**Vol. 2:** 190
7:9–28	**Vol. 2:** 731
7:9–10	**Vol. 3:** 588
7:9 f	**Vol. 2:** 191 **Vol. 3:** 615
7:9	**Vol. 1:** 204 **Vol. 2:** 613
7:10	**Vol. 1:** 101, 243 **Vol. 2:** 698, 700 **Vol. 3:** 630, 695
7:12	**Vol. 2:** 376, 607 **Vol. 3:** 835

7:13 ff	**Vol. 2:** 190, 337
7:13 f	**Vol. 2:** 376, 912 **Vol. 3:** 614, 863
7:13	**Vol. 1:** 321, 323 **Vol. 2:** 38, 147, 194, 313, 503, 808, 917–918 **Vol. 3:** 195, 384, 513, 613, 615, 621, 627–629, 633, 638
7:14	**Vol. 2:** 376, 448, 607, 610 **Vol. 3:** 615, 630
7:15	**Vol. 2:** 279 **Vol. 3:** 820
7:16	**Vol. 3:** 316
7:17 ff	**Vol. 2:** 56
7:18	**Vol. 2:** 227, 731 **Vol. 3:** 614, 638
7:19–22	**Vol. 3:** 695
7:19	**Vol. 2:** 98
7:21 ff	**Vol. 2:** 227
7:21	**Vol. 3:** 126, 962
7:22	**Vol. 1:** 321 **Vol. 2:** 202
7:22a	**Vol. 3:** 614
7:24	**Vol. 2:** 693 **Vol. 3:** 715
7:25	**Vol. 2:** 441, 688, 700 **Vol. 3:** 614
7:26	**Vol. 3:** 588
7:27	**Vol. 1:** 165, 321, 589 **Vol. 2:** 376, 425, 607, 888 **Vol. 3:** 614
7:28	**Vol. 2:** 279 **Vol. 3:** 820
8	**Vol. 2:** 745
8:3	**Vol. 3:** 715
8:10	**Vol. 2:** 687 **Vol. 3:** 28, 735
8:12	**Vol. 3:** 881, 885
8:13	**Vol. 3:** 786, 1006
8:14	**Vol. 2:** 688
8:16	**Vol. 1:** 101, 103
8:17*	**Vol. 1:** 103, 610 **Vol. 3:** 613, 847
8:18	**Vol. 3:** 279, 860
8:19 ff	**Vol. 2:** 56
8:19*	**Vol. 1:** 110 **Vol. 2:** 61 **Vol. 3:** 847
8:21	**Vol. 2:** 124
8:23 ff	**Vol. 1:** 125
8:23	**Vol. 1:** 734
8:24	**Vol. 2:** 789
8:25	**Vol. 3:** 1161
8:26 f†	**Vol. 3:** 614
8:26	**Vol. 3:** 950
8:27	**Vol. 2:** 622, 625 **Vol. 3:** 993
9	**Vol. 2:** 892
9:1	**Vol. 2:** 376
9:2	**Vol. 1:** 243 **Vol. 3:** 87
9:3–19	**Vol. 1:** 345
9:3	**Vol. 1:** 612 **Vol. 2:** 863
9:4	**Vol. 2:** 132, 134, 622, 862
9:5	**Vol. 1:** 606
9:6	**Vol. 2:** 791
9:8	**Vol. 2:** 509
9:9–11	**Vol. 1:** 607
9:9	**Vol. 1:** 606 **Vol. 3:** 152, 156
9:11	**Vol. 2:** 440, 639
9:13	**Vol. 2:** 639, 860 **Vol. 3:** 881
9:14	**Vol. 2:** 136 **Vol. 3:** 87
9:15 ff	**Vol. 2:** 509
9:15 f	**Vol. 1:** 109
9:15	**Vol. 1:** 531 **Vol. 2:** 406

Daniel *(cont'd)*

9:16	**Vol. 2:** 789 **Vol. 3:** 156, 355
9:17	**Vol. 2:** 863 **Vol. 3:** 318
9:18	**Vol. 2:** 863 **Vol. 3:** 356
9:19	**Vol. 2:** 509 **Vol. 3:** 155–156
9:20	**Vol. 2:** 862–863
9:21*	**Vol. 1:** 101, 103, 164 **Vol. 2:** 863 **Vol. 3:** 847
9:22	**Vol. 1:** 103 **Vol. 3:** 125
9:24	**Vol. 2:** 696 **Vol. 3:** 152–154, 498, 786
9:26	**Vol. 3:** 786
9:27	**Vol. 1:** 74, 125 **Vol. 2:** 912 **Vol. 3:** 255, 1006
10:3	**Vol. 1:** 120, 672
10:5 f	**Vol. 1:** 101 **Vol. 2:** 45 **Vol. 3:** 629, 861
10:5	**Vol. 3:** 120, 633
10:6	**Vol. 1:** 233 **Vol. 2:** 485, 800
10:9	**Vol. 1:** 610
10:13	**Vol. 1:** 102, 104, 165
10:14	**Vol. 2:** 56
10:16	**Vol. 2:** 502, 727
10:20	**Vol. 1:** 104 **Vol. 2:** 124
10:21	**Vol. 1:** 102
11:2	**Vol. 2:** 124, 841–842
11:3	**Vol. 3:** 1019
11:4	**Vol. 3:** 761
11:10–13	**Vol. 2:** 800
11:11	**Vol. 2:** 800
11:13	**Vol. 2:** 845
11:14	**Vol. 3:** 994
11:17	**Vol. 3:** 228, 711
11:18	**Vol. 3:** 255
11:19	**Vol. 3:** 994
11:24 f	**Vol. 3:** 823
11:24	**Vol. 2:** 845 **Vol. 3:** 820
11:25	**Vol. 3:** 125
11:26	**Vol. 1:** 277
11:27	**Vol. 2:** 61, 521 **Vol. 3:** 836
11:28	**Vol. 2:** 845
11:31	**Vol. 1:** 74 **Vol. 3:** 786, 1006
11:33 ff	**Vol. 3:** 994
11:35	**Vol. 1:** 204
11:37	**Vol. 1:** 694
11:39	**Vol. 3:** 140
11:40–12:3	**Vol. 3:** 961
11:40*	**Vol. 3:** 847
11:41	**Vol. 2:** 707–708
11:43	**Vol. 2:** 215
11:45*	**Vol. 3:** 847
12	**Vol. 3:** 270
12:1 f	**Vol. 3:** 836
12:1	**Vol. 1:** 101, 104, 243 **Vol. 2:** 807–808, 912, 916 **Vol. 3:** 209, 270, 803, 836
12:2	**Vol. 1:** 254, 434, 685 **Vol. 2:** 49, 928 **Vol. 3:** 270, 275, 303, 558, 832
12:3	**Vol. 1:** 586 **Vol. 2:** 486 **Vol. 3:** 196, 270, 734, 861

12:4	**Vol. 1:** 244 **Vol. 2:** 763 **Vol. 3:** 498, 500, 760
12:5 ff	**Vol. 2:** 56
12:5–7	**Vol. 3:** 742
12:7	**Vol. 2:** 700 **Vol. 3:** 841
12:9 f	**Vol. 3:** 362
12:9	**Vol. 1:** 244 **Vol. 3:** 498, 500, 836
12:10	**Vol. 1:** 204 **Vol. 3:** 799
12:11	**Vol. 1:** 74, 125 **Vol. 2:** 688, 912 **Vol. 3:** 1006
12:12	**Vol. 1:** 216 **Vol. 2:** 688, 772–774 **Vol. 3:** 226
12:13	**Vol. 1:** 734 **Vol. 2:** 298 **Vol. 3:** 254, 845

Hosea

1 ff	**Vol. 2:** 576
1–3	**Vol. 2:** 626 **Vol. 3:** 721
1:1	**Vol. 3:** 311, 1090, 1092–1093
1:2 ff	**Vol. 2:** 754 **Vol. 3:** 1093
1:2–9	**Vol. 3:** 1093
1:2	**Vol. 1:** 492 **Vol. 2:** 577 **Vol. 3:** 208, 1093
1:4	**Vol. 3:** 79, 134, 159, 255, 1093
1:6 ff	**Vol. 2:** 581
1:6	**Vol. 3:** 79
1:7	**Vol. 3:** 206
1:9	**Vol. 2:** 541, 797 **Vol. 3:** 79, 1103
1:10 ff*	**Vol. 1:** 288
1:10–2:1*	**Vol. 1:** 255
1:10*	**Vol. 1:** 272, 275 **Vol. 2:** 782, 800 **Vol. 3:** 251, 718
2	**Vol. 2:** 240 **Vol. 3:** 263, 578
2:1–5	**Vol. 2:** 746
2:1	**Vol. 1:** 290
2:2 ff*	**Vol. 2:** 583
2:2	**Vol. 1:** 240
2:4	**Vol. 3:** 1069
2:5*	**Vol. 1:** 186 **Vol. 2:** 711 **Vol. 3:** 147
2:6*	**Vol. 3:** 950–951
2:7*	**Vol. 1:** 481, 492 **Vol. 3:** 1069
2:8	**Vol. 1:** 726 **Vol. 2:** 711
2:9	**Vol. 3:** 835, 846
2:10*	**Vol. 1:** 498
2:11	**Vol. 3:** 407
2:12*	**Vol. 1:** 724 **Vol. 3:** 865, 1040
2:13 ff	**Vol. 3:** 427
2:13	**Vol. 3:** 267
2:14*	**Vol. 2:** 139
2:15	**Vol. 1:** 492 **Vol. 2:** 887 **Vol. 3:** 918
2:16–25	**Vol. 3:** 1005
2:16*	**Vol. 2:** 511 **Vol. 3:** 1006
2:17	**Vol. 1:** 281 **Vol. 2:** 889
2:18	**Vol. 2:** 511 **Vol. 3:** 1093
2:19 f	**Vol. 2:** 541 **Vol. 3:** 1068
2:20	**Vol. 1:** 113
2:21*	**Vol. 2:** 595
2:22	**Vol. 2:** 711
2:23 f	**Vol. 3:** 1093

Hosea (*cont'd*)

2:23* **Vol. 1:** 275, 369 **Vol. 2:** 541, 581, 597, 797 **Vol. 3:** 251, 422, 522
3 **Vol. 3:** 1093
3:1–5 **Vol. 3:** 1093
3:1 **Vol. 1:** 258 **Vol. 2:** 540
3:2 **Vol. 2:** 139
3:4 **Vol. 2:** 374 **Vol. 3:** 36
3:5 **Vol. 1:** 354 **Vol. 2:** 56, 583
4–14 **Vol. 3:** 1093
4:1 ff **Vol. 2:** 285
4:1 f **Vol. 2:** 396 **Vol. 3:** 70
4:1 **Vol. 2:** 364 **Vol. 3:** 880, 1093
4:2 **Vol. 3:** 159, 1103
4:3 **Vol. 1:** 113, 670 **Vol. 2:** 422
4:4–19 **Vol. 1:** 499
4:4 **Vol. 2:** 141 **Vol. 3:** 78
4:5 **Vol. 3:** 994, 1068
4:6 ff **Vol. 2:** 797
4:6 **Vol. 2:** 396, 440 **Vol. 3:** 1052
4:9 **Vol. 3:** 134
4:10 **Vol. 2:** 272
4:11 ff **Vol. 3:** 427
4:11 **Vol. 3:** 745, 919
4:12 ff **Vol. 2:** 583
4:12 **Vol. 3:** 691–692
4:13 ff **Vol. 3:** 1069
4:14 **Vol. 2:** 60 **Vol. 3:** 134
4:16 **Vol. 2:** 312
4:18 **Vol. 2:** 540
5:1 **Vol. 2:** 305
5:3 **Vol. 2:** 395
5:4 **Vol. 1:** 354 **Vol. 2:** 396
5:5 **Vol. 3:** 29–30, 994
5:6 **Vol. 3:** 78
5:7 ff **Vol. 2:** 583
5:8 **Vol. 3:** 50–51
5:9 **Vol. 2:** 141
5:10 **Vol. 2:** 312
5:13 **Vol. 3:** 997
5:14–6:2 **Vol. 2:** 807
5:14 **Vol. 3:** 601
5:15 **Vol. 3:** 786
6:1–7:2 **Vol. 3:** 235
6:1–3 **Vol. 3:** 267
6:1 f **Vol. 3:** 784
6:1 **Vol. 3:** 601
6:2 ff **Vol. 3:** 168
6:2 **Vol. 2:** 687, 893 **Vol. 3:** 283, 287, 297, 1200
6:3 **Vol. 3:** 514
6:4 **Vol. 2:** 541 **Vol. 3:** 267, 269
6:5 **Vol. 3:** 1093
6:6 **Vol. 1:** 259, 622 **Vol. 2:** 227, 396, 596, 813 **Vol. 3:** 37, 267, 427, 429, 792, 1022
6:7 **Vol. 1:** 461 **Vol. 3:** 267, 583
6:9 **Vol. 2:** 746
6:10 **Vol. 3:** 267

6:11* **Vol. 1:** 448 **Vol. 3:** 526
7:2 **Vol. 1:** 230 **Vol. 3:** 673
7:3 **Vol. 2:** 374
7:4 **Vol. 1:** 249
7:5 **Vol. 3:** 919
7:6 f **Vol. 1:** 249
7:7 **Vol. 1:** 318
7:10 **Vol. 3:** 29–30
7:11 **Vol. 1:** 175, 531
7:12 **Vol. 1:** 172, 293 **Vol. 3:** 776
7:13 **Vol. 3:** 192, 345
7:15 **Vol. 3:** 823
7:16 **Vol. 1:** 531
8:1 **Vol. 1:** 173 **Vol. 2:** 440 **Vol. 3:** 583
8:2 **Vol. 2:** 396
8:4 f **Vol. 2:** 285
8:7 **Vol. 2:** 432 **Vol. 3:** 526
8:8 **Vol. 3:** 235
8:10 **Vol. 2:** 791 **Vol. 3:** 745
8:11 ff **Vol. 3:** 235
8:12 **Vol. 1:** 70 **Vol. 3:** 823
8:13 **Vol. 1:** 531 **Vol. 3:** 134
8:14† **Vol. 3:** 78, 786
9:1 ff **Vol. 2:** 583
9:2 **Vol. 3:** 267
9:3 **Vol. 1:** 531
9:6 **Vol. 3:** 859
9:7 **Vol. 1:** 320, 527 **Vol. 2:** 890 **Vol. 3:** 77, 93, 134
9:9 **Vol. 1:** 468 **Vol. 3:** 235
9:10 **Vol. 1:** 724 **Vol. 3:** 919, 1005
9:14 **Vol. 1:** 515
9:15 **Vol. 1:** 555
9:17 **Vol. 2:** 174
10:1 **Vol. 2:** 248 **Vol. 3:** 918
10:2 **Vol. 3:** 355
10:6 **Vol. 3:** 421
10:8 **Vol. 1:** 610, 726 **Vol. 2:** 218 **Vol. 3:** 382, 418
10:10 **Vol. 3:** 268, 776
10:11 **Vol. 3:** 760
10:12 **Vol. 1:** 733 **Vol. 2:** 480 **Vol. 3:** 522, 526
10:13 **Vol. 1:** 596, 721, 732 **Vol. 2:** 471 **Vol. 3:** 574
10:14 **Vol. 2:** 889
11:1 ff **Vol. 1:** 617 **Vol. 2:** 541
11:1 **Vol. 1:** 281, 290, 531–532, 737 **Vol. 2:** 71, 540, 640, 715 **Vol. 3:** 69, 642, 1005, 1007
11:3 **Vol. 3:** 805
11:4 **Vol. 3:** 592
11:5 **Vol. 1:** 354, 531
11:6 **Vol. 3:** 255
11:8 f **Vol. 2:** 541
11:8 **Vol. 1:** 617
11:9 **Vol. 2:** 70–71, 225
11:11 **Vol. 1:** 531 **Vol. 3:** 147
12 **Vol. 3:** 578
12:1 **Vol. 1:** 531, 596 **Vol. 2:** 711

Hosea *(cont'd)*

12:3 f	**Vol. 1:** 61
12:4	**Vol. 2:** 305, 860
12:6*	**Vol. 2:** 69, 797 **Vol. 3:** 237, 717
12:7*	**Vol. 2:** 53, 240
12:8 f	**Vol. 3:** 727
12:8*	**Vol. 3:** 1160
12:9*	**Vol. 1:** 531 **Vol. 2:** 841
12:10*	**Vol. 3:** 1005–1006
12:11	**Vol. 2:** 432
12:13	**Vol. 1:** 531
12:14	**Vol. 2:** 636
13:1	**Vol. 3:** 354
13:2	**Vol. 2:** 285, 287 **Vol. 3:** 427
13:4 f	**Vol. 3:** 1005
13:4	**Vol. 2:** 396
13:5–9	**Vol. 2:** 364
13:6	**Vol. 3:** 727
13:7	**Vol. 1:** 119
13:8	**Vol. 1:** 520
13:10 f	**Vol. 2:** 374
13:10	**Vol. 3:** 206
13:11	**Vol. 1:** 109
13:12	**Vol. 3:** 498
13:14	**Vol. 1:** 511 **Vol. 2:** 215 **Vol. 3:** 192, 201, 267
13:15	**Vol. 3:** 1005
14:3	**Vol. 2:** 738 **Vol. 3:** 206–207
14:4	**Vol. 1:** 109 **Vol. 3:** 206
14:5 ff*	**Vol. 1:** 354
14:5–10	**Vol. 3:** 1006
14:5 f	**Vol. 3:** 866
14:5	**Vol. 3:** 269
14:6	**Vol. 2:** 711
14:8 f	**Vol. 3:** 357
14:8*	**Vol. 2:** 285 **Vol. 3:** 866
14:9	**Vol. 3:** 940, 942
14:10	**Vol. 3:** 1028

Joel

1:1	**Vol. 3:** 1093
1:2–12	**Vol. 1:** 724
1:5	**Vol. 1:** 513
1:6	**Vol. 2:** 296
1:8	**Vol. 3:** 1071
1:10	**Vol. 2:** 711
1:11	**Vol. 3:** 525
1:12	**Vol. 1:** 515
1:14	**Vol. 2:** 864 **Vol. 3:** 51
1:15	**Vol. 2:** 53, 887–888, 890 **Vol. 3:** 729
1:19	**Vol. 3:** 865
2	**Vol. 1:** 425 **Vol. 3:** 829
2:1 ff	**Vol. 3:** 828
2:1–2	**Vol. 3:** 874
2:1	**Vol. 2:** 53, 888, 890, 898 **Vol. 3:** 50–51
2:2	**Vol. 1:** 423 **Vol. 2:** 887 **Vol. 3:** 1001
2:10 f	**Vol. 1:** 425

2:10	**Vol. 1:** 203, 423 **Vol. 2:** 916 **Vol. 3:** 731, 733, 735
2:11	**Vol. 2:** 890 **Vol. 3:** 318
2:12 ff	**Vol. 1:** 423
2:12	**Vol. 2:** 181, 864
2:13 f	**Vol. 1:** 357
2:13	**Vol. 2:** 769
2:15–17	**Vol. 2:** 864
2:15	**Vol. 3:** 51
2:16	**Vol. 1:** 295
2:17 f	**Vol. 2:** 297
2:19–24	**Vol. 2:** 711
2:19	**Vol. 2:** 711
2:21	**Vol. 2:** 357
2:22	**Vol. 1:** 724 **Vol. 3:** 865
2:23	**Vol. 1:** 286 **Vol. 2:** 357 **Vol. 3:** 355, 766
2:24	**Vol. 2:** 711 **Vol. 3:** 919
2:25–28	**Vol. 2:** 740
2:25	**Vol. 1:** 119 **Vol. 2:** 124
2:26	**Vol. 3:** 816
2:28 ff	**Vol. 2:** 42 **Vol. 3:** 87
2:28–32	**Vol. 2:** 38, 58, 916 **Vol. 3:** 699, 707, 732, 1079
2:28–29*	**Vol. 2:** 854–855 **Vol. 3:** 693
2:28 f	**Vol. 3:** 692
2:28*	**Vol. 1:** 198 **Vol. 2:** 117, 785–786
2:29*	**Vol. 3:** 594
2:30–31	**Vol. 3:** 732
2:30*	**Vol. 1:** 224, 655 **Vol. 2:** 629
2:31*	**Vol. 1:** 203, 224, 320 **Vol. 3:** 318–319, 731, 733–734
2:32*	**Vol. 2:** 329, 654 **Vol. 3:** 209, 213, 250
3–4	**Vol. 2:** 916
3:1*	**Vol. 1:** 512 **Vol. 3:** 836, 986
3:2†	**Vol. 1:** 503 **Vol. 2:** 363
3:2*	**Vol. 2:** 297
3:3*	**Vol. 2:** 296, 633
3:4	**Vol. 2:** 767, 890
3:6*	**Vol. 2:** 124, 324
3:9	**Vol. 3:** 51
3:13	**Vol. 1:** 111 **Vol. 3:** 526, 919
3:14†	**Vol. 2:** 890
3:14*	**Vol. 2:** 887–888
3:15	**Vol. 3:** 731, 735
3:17*	**Vol. 1:** 684 **Vol. 2:** 326, 803 **Vol. 3:** 160
3:18	**Vol. 1:** 683 **Vol. 3:** 813, 919, 986–987, 1010
3:19†	**Vol. 1:** 531 **Vol. 3:** 355
4:2	**Vol. 1:** 503 **Vol. 2:** 363
4:14	**Vol. 2:** 890

Amos

1–2	**Vol. 3:** 960
1	**Vol. 3:** 93
1:1	**Vol. 3:** 311, 557, 1092
1:2	**Vol. 2:** 190, 363
1:3–16	**Vol. 2:** 139

Amos *(cont'd)*

1:3	**Vol. 2:** 98 **Vol. 3:** 1092
1:4 ff	**Vol. 1:** 661
1:4	**Vol. 1:** 654–655
1:5	**Vol. 3:** 1092
1:6	**Vol. 3:** 1092
1:7	**Vol. 1:** 655
1:8	**Vol. 3:** 1092
1:9 f	**Vol. 2:** 767
1:9	**Vol. 3:** 1092
1:11	**Vol. 3:** 1040, 1092
1:13	**Vol. 3:** 1092
1:14	**Vol. 3:** 1092
1:15	**Vol. 1:** 165 **Vol. 3:** 908
2	**Vol. 3:** 93
2:1	**Vol. 1:** 264 **Vol. 3:** 1092
2:3	**Vol. 3:** 1092
2:4	**Vol. 2:** 440, 458, 471 **Vol. 3:** 1092
2:5	**Vol. 1:** 661
2:6 ff	**Vol. 2:** 841
2:6–16	**Vol. 1:** 716
2:6–14	**Vol. 3:** 960
2:6 f	**Vol. 1:** 717 **Vol. 3:** 357
2:6	**Vol. 2:** 96, 260, 820 **Vol. 3:** 594, 1092
2:7 f	**Vol. 3:** 1103
2:7	**Vol. 2:** 225, 257, 260, 649, 822
2:9	**Vol. 3:** 866
2:10	**Vol. 1:** 531
2:11	**Vol. 3:** 1092
2:13 ff	**Vol. 2:** 260
2:13	**Vol. 1:** 743
2:14 f	**Vol. 3:** 209
2:16	**Vol. 3:** 1092
3–5	**Vol. 3:** 1092
3:1 ff	**Vol. 2:** 364
3:2	**Vol. 1:** 538 **Vol. 2:** 395 **Vol. 3:** 135
3:4	**Vol. 3:** 601
3:5	**Vol. 1:** 172, 609 **Vol. 2:** 707
3:6	**Vol. 3:** 113, 720, 874
3:7 f	**Vol. 3:** 502
3:7	**Vol. 3:** 311
3:8	**Vol. 2:** 746 **Vol. 3:** 1092
3:9 f	**Vol. 3:** 1103
3:12	**Vol. 3:** 1092
3:13†	**Vol. 2:** 69, 318 **Vol. 3:** 717, 1041
3:14	**Vol. 3:** 78, 93, 134
3:15	**Vol. 3:** 1092
4:1 ff	**Vol. 1:** 717 **Vol. 3:** 93
4:1–3	**Vol. 3:** 1090
4:1	**Vol. 2:** 820, 822
4:2	**Vol. 2:** 225
4:3	**Vol. 3:** 1092
4:4 f	**Vol. 3:** 427
4:4	**Vol. 1:** 732 **Vol. 2:** 693 **Vol. 3:** 185
4:5 f	**Vol. 3:** 1092
4:5	**Vol. 1:** 344 **Vol. 3:** 423
4:6–8	**Vol. 1:** 354
4:6	**Vol. 1:** 357
4:7	**Vol. 2:** 765 **Vol. 3:** 1001
4:8–11	**Vol. 3:** 1092
4:9	**Vol. 1:** 119
4:10	**Vol. 1:** 429
4:11	**Vol. 3:** 93, 560
4:12	**Vol. 3:** 117
4:13	**Vol. 1:** 379, 523 **Vol. 2:** 69, 650 **Vol. 3:** 690
5:1–2	**Vol. 2:** 418
5:1	**Vol. 2:** 305
5:2	**Vol. 1:** 610 **Vol. 3:** 1071
5:3 f	**Vol. 3:** 1092
5:3	**Vol. 2:** 698
5:4	**Vol. 1:** 357 **Vol. 2:** 442, 479 **Vol. 3:** 355, 367
5:5	**Vol. 3:** 426
5:6 f	**Vol. 1:** 622
5:6	**Vol. 3:** 109, 355
5:7	**Vol. 1:** 717 **Vol. 3:** 355
5:8	**Vol. 1:** 422, 523 **Vol. 3:** 902
5:10 ff	**Vol. 2:** 841
5:10	**Vol. 1:** 555 **Vol. 2:** 141
5:11 ff	**Vol. 1:** 717
5:11	**Vol. 2:** 822
5:12–15	**Vol. 3:** 357
5:12	**Vol. 2:** 820 **Vol. 3:** 166, 192
5:13	**Vol. 3:** 836
5:14 ff	**Vol. 3:** 717
5:14 f	**Vol. 1:** 565 **Vol. 2:** 285 **Vol. 3:** 249
5:14	**Vol. 2:** 69, 479 **Vol. 3:** 355
5:15	**Vol. 1:** 555 **Vol. 3:** 147
5:16–17	**Vol. 2:** 418
5:16	**Vol. 2:** 418, 422 **Vol. 3:** 720
5:17	**Vol. 3:** 1092
5:18	**Vol. 2:** 364, 887, 890, 926
5:19	**Vol. 3:** 948
5:20	**Vol. 1:** 423 **Vol. 2:** 887, 890
5:21 ff	**Vol. 3:** 783
5:21–27	**Vol. 3:** 427
5:21	**Vol. 1:** 626 **Vol. 3:** 600
5:22	**Vol. 3:** 422
5:23 f	**Vol. 2:** 864
5:23	**Vol. 3:** 673
5:25 ff†	**Vol. 3:** 964
5:25–27	**Vol. 2:** 248
5:25	**Vol. 3:** 427, 431
5:26	**Vol. 2:** 85 **Vol. 3:** 735, 904–905
5:27	**Vol. 3:** 465
6:1	**Vol. 1:** 165, 357
6:2	**Vol. 3:** 717
6:3	**Vol. 2:** 53, 888, 890
6:5	**Vol. 3:** 823
6:6	**Vol. 1:** 121, 665 **Vol. 2:** 711 **Vol. 3:** 720
6:7	**Vol. 3:** 590
6:8	**Vol. 3:** 29–30, 740
6:10	**Vol. 1:** 194
6:11	**Vol. 2:** 428
6:12	**Vol. 1:** 202 **Vol. 2:** 746 **Vol. 3:** 355, 525
7–9	**Vol. 2:** 173

Amos *(cont'd)*

7	**Vol. 1:** 699
7:1 ff	**Vol. 1:** 210
7:1–8	**Vol. 3:** 1092
7:1	**Vol. 3:** 569
7:2	**Vol. 3:** 152
7:3	**Vol. 1:** 357 **Vol. 3:** 1092
7:4	**Vol. 3:** 93, 569, 695
7:6	**Vol. 1:** 357
7:7	**Vol. 3:** 569
7:8	**Vol. 2:** 797
7:9	**Vol. 1:** 81 **Vol. 2:** 431 **Vol. 3:** 418, 786
7:10	**Vol. 3:** 1092
7:13	**Vol. 3:** 786, 1092
7:15	**Vol. 2:** 412, 797 **Vol. 3:** 1092
7:17	**Vol. 3:** 104
8	**Vol. 2:** 364
8:1 ff	**Vol. 1:** 716
8:1 f	**Vol. 2:** 432
8:1–2	**Vol. 3:** 1092
8:2	**Vol. 2:** 797 **Vol. 3:** 1090, 1092
8:3	**Vol. 2:** 891
8:4	**Vol. 2:** 257, 820, 822
8:5	**Vol. 2:** 370, 830 **Vol. 3:** 402, 407, 1160
8:6	**Vol. 1:** 268 **Vol. 2:** 260, 820, 822
8:7 f	**Vol. 2:** 260
8:7	**Vol. 3:** 29–30
8:8	**Vol. 1:** 531
8:9	**Vol. 1:** 203, 423 **Vol. 2:** 38, 887, 916 **Vol. 3:** 559, 731
8:10	**Vol. 1:** 626 **Vol. 2:** 422, 890 **Vol. 3:** 673
8:11–13	**Vol. 2:** 266
8:11 f	**Vol. 3:** 1092
8:11	**Vol. 2:** 275
8:13	**Vol. 3:** 1071
8:14	**Vol. 1:** 610 **Vol. 3:** 152, 156
9	**Vol. 2:** 364
9:1 ff	**Vol. 2:** 307
9:1–4	**Vol. 3:** 1092
9:1	**Vol. 1:** 429 **Vol. 3:** 157, 209
9:2	**Vol. 2:** 206
9:3	**Vol. 1:** 508, 523
9:5 f	**Vol. 1:** 523
9:5	**Vol. 1:** 531
9:6	**Vol. 2:** 189
9:7 ff	**Vol. 3:** 82
9:7	**Vol. 1:** 531, 688
9:8	**Vol. 3:** 514
9:9	**Vol. 2:** 791
9:10	**Vol. 1:** 430 **Vol. 2:** 888
9:11 ff	**Vol. 3:** 514
9:11 f	**Vol. 3:** 651
9:11–15	**Vol. 2:** 374
9:11–12	**Vol. 3:** 812
9:11	**Vol. 2:** 248, 252 **Vol. 3:** 650, 828
9:12	**Vol. 1:** 276 **Vol. 3:** 251, 532, 1010
9:13	**Vol. 2:** 890 **Vol. 3:** 144, 522, 919
9:15	**Vol. 3:** 1092

Obadiah

1	**Vol. 3:** 311
3	**Vol. 3:** 29
8	**Vol. 3:** 1028
4	**Vol. 1:** 173 **Vol. 3:** 734
5	**Vol. 3:** 377, 728
11	**Vol. 2:** 296, 889
14	**Vol. 2:** 889
15	**Vol. 2:** 888, 890
17	**Vol. 3:** 250
21	**Vol. 2:** 376

Jonah

1:2	**Vol. 2:** 351, 679
1:3 ff	**Vol. 2:** 350
1:3	**Vol. 2:** 215
1:4	**Vol. 2:** 680
1:6	**Vol. 3:** 115
1:7	**Vol. 1:** 609 **Vol. 2:** 296
1:9	**Vol. 1:** 515
1:10	**Vol. 2:** 680
1:12	**Vol. 2:** 680
1:13	**Vol. 3:** 711
1:14	**Vol. 3:** 355
1:15	**Vol. 2:** 680 **Vol. 3:** 559
1:17*	**Vol. 1:** 169, 420 **Vol. 2:** 687
2	**Vol. 3:** 297
2:1*	**Vol. 1:** 670
2:2	**Vol. 2:** 351, 862
2:3	**Vol. 3:** 673
2:4*	**Vol. 2:** 197 **Vol. 3:** 786
2:5*	**Vol. 1:** 314
2:6	**Vol. 2:** 351
2:7*	**Vol. 2:** 185 **Vol. 3:** 786
2:8	**Vol. 2:** 863 **Vol. 3:** 236
2:9	**Vol. 1:** 551
2:11*	**Vol. 1:** 670
2:23*	**Vol. 2:** 268
3:1–10	**Vol. 2:** 680
3:2	**Vol. 2:** 679 **Vol. 3:** 51
3:3	**Vol. 2:** 679
3:4–10	**Vol. 1:** 612
3:4	**Vol. 2:** 351, 679 **Vol. 3:** 51
3:5	**Vol. 2:** 679 **Vol. 3:** 51, 209
3:6	**Vol. 2:** 679 **Vol. 3:** 588
3:7–10	**Vol. 1:** 109
3:7	**Vol. 2:** 269, 679 **Vol. 3:** 50–51
3:8 ff	**Vol. 3:** 1104
3:9 f	**Vol. 1:** 354, 356
3:10 ff	**Vol. 2:** 351
3:10	**Vol. 1:** 354 **Vol. 2:** 679
4:2	**Vol. 2:** 351, 769, 862
4:3	**Vol. 2:** 509
4:5	**Vol. 3:** 554
4:6	**Vol. 2:** 356 **Vol. 3:** 554
4:11	**Vol. 2:** 395, 679

Micah

1	**Vol. 2:** 364
1:1	**Vol. 3:** 1093
1:2	**Vol. 2:** 174, 888 **Vol. 3:** 786
1:3	**Vol. 2:** 925 **Vol. 3:** 786
1:4	**Vol. 3:** 1010
1:5	**Vol. 2:** 305
1:7	**Vol. 2:** 139, 285
1:8	**Vol. 2:** 418, 926
1:10	**Vol. 2:** 431
2:1 f	**Vol. 2:** 841
2:1	**Vol. 1:** 562 **Vol. 2:** 586 **Vol. 3:** 823
2:2	**Vol. 2:** 822
2:3	**Vol. 3:** 351, 823
2:4	**Vol. 3:** 859
2:5	**Vol. 1:** 295
2:10	**Vol. 3:** 255
2:11	**Vol. 2:** 470 **Vol. 3:** 919
2:12 f	**Vol. 3:** 250
2:12*	**Vol. 2:** 32, 586
3:1–4	**Vol. 2:** 864
3:1–3	**Vol. 1:** 717
3:2 ff	**Vol. 2:** 822
3:2 f	**Vol. 1:** 673
3:2	**Vol. 3:** 357, 601
3:4	**Vol. 1:** 409 **Vol. 3:** 836
3:5	**Vol. 3:** 51
3:6 f	**Vol. 2:** 554
3:6	**Vol. 3:** 731
3:7	**Vol. 3:** 345
3:8	**Vol. 3:** 713
3:9–12	**Vol. 3:** 78
3:11	**Vol. 2:** 139, 554 **Vol. 3:** 78, 255
3:12	**Vol. 3:** 82, 786
4:1 ff	**Vol. 2:** 56
4:1 f	**Vol. 1:** 661 **Vol. 2:** 325
4:1–3	**Vol. 2:** 791 **Vol. 3:** 70, 1010, 1012, 1094
4:1	**Vol. 2:** 56, 489
4:2	**Vol. 2:** 440
4:3 f	**Vol. 1:** 210
4:3	**Vol. 1:** 484 **Vol. 2:** 141
4:4	**Vol. 1:** 724 **Vol. 2:** 888 **Vol. 3:** 254–255, 866
4:6 f	**Vol. 1:** 185 **Vol. 3:** 565
4:6	**Vol. 2:** 32 **Vol. 3:** 745
4:7	**Vol. 3:** 828
4:8	**Vol. 1:** 165
4:9 f	**Vol. 3:** 1068
4:10	**Vol. 3:** 192, 201
4:12	**Vol. 2:** 32 **Vol. 3:** 823, 1016
4:13	**Vol. 2:** 98 **Vol. 3:** 650, 715
5	**Vol. 3:** 649
5:2 ff	**Vol. 2:** 374
5:2–6*	**Vol. 2:** 335
5:2*	**Vol. 1:** 164, 170, 321 **Vol. 2:** 320, 715, 888 **Vol. 3:** 490, 828
5:3*	**Vol. 3:** 567, 827, 835
5:4*	**Vol. 2:** 649, 888
5:5*	**Vol. 2:** 778 **Vol. 3:** 201
5:6	**Vol. 3:** 269
5:7 f	**Vol. 3:** 250
5:9	**Vol. 1:** 554
5:11	**Vol. 2:** 554
5:12	**Vol. 2:** 555
5:13	**Vol. 2:** 876
5:14	**Vol. 1:** 109
5:15	**Vol. 1:** 109
6:1	**Vol. 2:** 363
6:2	**Vol. 1:** 661
6:4	**Vol. 2:** 636, 639 **Vol. 3:** 192
6:5	**Vol. 2:** 396 **Vol. 3:** 236, 355–356
6:6 ff	**Vol. 3:** 155, 427
6:6–8	**Vol. 2:** 42
6:7	**Vol. 1:** 721 **Vol. 2:** 711 **Vol. 3:** 421
6:8	**Vol. 1:** 116, 261 **Vol. 2:** 100, 103, 174, 307 **Vol. 3:** 46, 70, 117, 367
6:10	**Vol. 3:** 29
6:11	**Vol. 3:** 355, 1160
6:12	**Vol. 2:** 842
6:15	**Vol. 2:** 711 **Vol. 3:** 144
6:16	**Vol. 3:** 354
7:1–6	**Vol. 1:** 724–725
7:1	**Vol. 1:** 724 **Vol. 3:** 866
7:2	**Vol. 2:** 91
7:3	**Vol. 1:** 717
7:4	**Vol. 2:** 416, 890 **Vol. 3:** 399, 950
7:6	**Vol. 1:** 725 **Vol. 2:** 250
7:7	**Vol. 2:** 240, 773 **Vol. 3:** 218
7:8	**Vol. 1:** 422, 609 **Vol. 3:** 1040
7:9	**Vol. 3:** 355
7:10	**Vol. 3:** 650
7:14	**Vol. 1:** 162 **Vol. 3:** 565
7:15	**Vol. 1:** 531
7:18	**Vol. 1:** 699 **Vol. 2:** 297 **Vol. 3:** 250
7:19	**Vol. 1:** 699 **Vol. 2:** 197
7:20	**Vol. 2:** 596 **Vol. 3:** 523

Nahum

1:1	**Vol. 2:** 679
1:3	**Vol. 2:** 769 **Vol. 3:** 514
1:5	**Vol. 3:** 1010
1:6	**Vol. 2:** 836 **Vol. 3:** 382
1:7	**Vol. 2:** 91
1:9 ff	**Vol. 3:** 823
1:9	**Vol. 3:** 823
1:11	**Vol. 3:** 823
1:13	**Vol. 3:** 592
1:15	**Vol. 2:** 111
2:1*	**Vol. 2:** 778
2:2*	**Vol. 3:** 29
2:4*	**Vol. 2:** 485–486
2:5	**Vol. 3:** 994
2:6	**Vol. 2:** 679
2:7	**Vol. 1:** 710 **Vol. 2:** 418
2:12	**Vol. 1:** 226
3:1	**Vol. 3:** 159
3:2	**Vol. 3:** 557

Nahum *(cont'd)*

3:3	**Vol. 3:** 994
3:4	**Vol. 2:** 554–555
3:7	**Vol. 2:** 423, 679
3:10	**Vol. 2:** 296
3:11	**Vol. 1:** 553
3:12	**Vol. 1:** 724
3:13	**Vol. 1:** 553
3:14	**Vol. 3:** 916
3:17	**Vol. 3:** 478
3:18	**Vol. 3:** 566

Habakkuk

1:2	**Vol. 2:** 69
1:4	**Vol. 2:** 60
1:5	**Vol. 1:** 461–462 **Vol. 2:** 625
1:6	**Vol. 1:** 201
1:7	**Vol. 3:** 318
1:8	**Vol. 1:** 173, 175
1:11	**Vol. 3:** 152
1:12	**Vol. 1:** 164
1:14	**Vol. 1:** 670
2:2	**Vol. 3:** 484
2:3 f	**Vol. 1:** 597, 604 **Vol. 3:** 366–367
2:3	**Vol. 2:** 240, 772–773 **Vol. 3:** 953
2:4	**Vol. 1:** 598 **Vol. 2:** 442, 817–818 **Vol. 3:** 359, 365, 367, 685, 1177, 1189
2:5	**Vol. 1:** 461 **Vol. 2:** 435 **Vol. 3:** 30, 919
2:6	**Vol. 1:** 575 **Vol. 2:** 745
2:9	**Vol. 1:** 137
2:11	**Vol. 3:** 393
2:14	**Vol. 1:** 735 **Vol. 2:** 229
2:16	**Vol. 3:** 922
2:18 f	**Vol. 2:** 285
2:18	**Vol. 1:** 428, 596 **Vol. 3:** 766
2:20	**Vol. 3:** 786
3:1	**Vol. 2:** 863 **Vol. 3:** 673
3:2	**Vol. 1:** 108–109
3:3–6	**Vol. 3:** 960
3:3	**Vol. 2:** 71, 190 **Vol. 3:** 926
3:4	**Vol. 2:** 491 **Vol. 3:** 514
3:5	**Vol. 2:** 167 **Vol. 3:** 1116
3:6	**Vol. 3:** 711, 1010
3:8	**Vol. 3:** 983
3:11	**Vol. 3:** 731, 733
3:12	**Vol. 1:** 109
3:13	**Vol. 1:** 241 **Vol. 2:** 336 **Vol. 3:** 207
3:16	**Vol. 2:** 807, 863, 890 **Vol. 3:** 254
3:17	**Vol. 1:** 724 **Vol. 2:** 711 **Vol. 3:** 153
3:18	**Vol. 2:** 353 **Vol. 3:** 218–220
3:19	**Vol. 2:** 60 **Vol. 3:** 673

Zephaniah

1:1	**Vol. 3:** 311, 1090, 1093
1:3	**Vol. 2:** 708 **Vol. 3:** 994
1:5	**Vol. 2:** 876
1:7–18	**Vol. 2:** 363
1:7 f	**Vol. 3:** 117, 160
1:7	**Vol. 2:** 53, 890
1:14–16	**Vol. 3:** 874
1:14	**Vol. 2:** 53, 888
1:15	**Vol. 1:** 110, 425 **Vol. 2:** 663, 887
1:18	**Vol. 2:** 836
2:2 f	**Vol. 1:** 110
2:2	**Vol. 1:** 110
2:3	**Vol. 1:** 110 **Vol. 2:** 257, 260 **Vol. 3:** 355, 1148
2:7	**Vol. 1:** 189 **Vol. 3:** 250
2:9†	**Vol. 3:** 93, 250, 444, 560
2:10	**Vol. 2:** 69 **Vol. 3:** 29–30
2:11	**Vol. 2:** 876
2:13	**Vol. 2:** 679
2:14	**Vol. 1:** 173 **Vol. 2:** 680 **Vol. 3:** 113
3	**Vol. 2:** 472
3:2	**Vol. 3:** 745
3:3	**Vol. 1:** 118
3:4	**Vol. 1:** 461 **Vol. 2:** 440
3:5	**Vol. 3:** 357
3:6	**Vol. 3:** 29
3:7	**Vol. 3:** 745
3:8	**Vol. 2:** 773, 836 **Vol. 3:** 1040
3:10	**Vol. 2:** 888 **Vol. 3:** 155, 421
3:11	**Vol. 3:** 29
3:12	**Vol. 2:** 91, 257, 260
3:13	**Vol. 1:** 551 **Vol. 2:** 471
3:14	**Vol. 3:** 50–51
3:16	**Vol. 1:** 328 **Vol. 3:** 836
3:17	**Vol. 3:** 207
3:18	**Vol. 2:** 772
3:19 f	**Vol. 3:** 745, 836

Haggai

1:6	**Vol. 2:** 139
1:8	**Vol. 3:** 786
1:10	**Vol. 2:** 765
1:11	**Vol. 2:** 711
1:12	**Vol. 3:** 208
1:13	**Vol. 3:** 46
1:14	**Vol. 3:** 208
2:3	**Vol. 2:** 44
2:5	**Vol. 1:** 328, 531 **Vol. 3:** 692
2:6 ff	**Vol. 1:** 686
2:6	**Vol. 2:** 717 **Vol. 3:** 317, 560
2:7	**Vol. 1:** 320, 537 **Vol. 3:** 257
2:9	**Vol. 1:** 380, 735 **Vol. 2:** 778
2:10–14	**Vol. 3:** 451
2:10	**Vol. 3:** 1090
2:11 ff	**Vol. 2:** 226
2:11*	**Vol. 2:** 441
2:12	**Vol. 2:** 711
2:15	**Vol. 2:** 889 **Vol. 3:** 786
2:16	**Vol. 3:** 557
2:18 f	**Vol. 2:** 889
2:18	**Vol. 3:** 786
2:20–23	**Vol. 2:** 307

131

Haggai *(cont'd)*

2:20	**Vol. 3:** 1090
2:21	**Vol. 1:** 515
2:22	**Vol. 1:** 465
2:23	**Vol. 1:** 534 **Vol. 2:** 336, 891 **Vol. 3:** 609

Zechariah

1:1	**Vol. 3:** 82, 311, 430
1:3–17	**Vol. 3:** 717
1:4	**Vol. 1:** 354
1:7–6:8	**Vol. 3:** 80
1:8	**Vol. 1:** 118, 204–205, 420, 657
1:9	**Vol. 1:** 101
1:11 ff	**Vol. 1:** 101
1:12	**Vol. 2:** 509
1:14	**Vol. 1:** 558
1:15	**Vol. 2:** 807
1:16	**Vol. 3:** 402
1:18 ff	**Vol. 2:** 689
2 f	**Vol. 2:** 190
2:1	**Vol. 3:** 436
2:2–5*	**Vol. 1:** 101
2:5–11*	**Vol. 2:** 45
2:6*	**Vol. 2:** 38, 189, 194, 917
2:8*	**Vol. 3:** 860
2:11 f	**Vol. 2:** 797
2:11	**Vol. 2:** 888 **Vol. 3:** 209
3:1 f	**Vol. 3:** 468
3:1	**Vol. 2:** 146 **Vol. 3:** 192, 569
3:2	**Vol. 1:** 572 **Vol. 3:** 345
3:3 f	**Vol. 1:** 556
3:4 f	**Vol. 1:** 479
3:6*	**Vol. 3:** 1041
3:7	**Vol. 1:** 503
3:8–10	**Vol. 1:** 426
3:8 f	**Vol. 3:** 392
3:8	**Vol. 2:** 336 **Vol. 3:** 609, 649, 867
3:9	**Vol. 3:** 1161
3:10	**Vol. 1:** 724 **Vol. 3:** 866
4:1 ff	**Vol. 2:** 335
4:1	**Vol. 2:** 485
4:2–14	**Vol. 2:** 712
4:2–3	**Vol. 2:** 686
4:3	**Vol. 2:** 487
4:6	**Vol. 2:** 712 **Vol. 3:** 392, 692
4:7–10	**Vol. 3:** 391
4:7	**Vol. 2:** 116 **Vol. 3:** 392
4:9	**Vol. 3:** 392
4:10	**Vol. 2:** 690, 889 **Vol. 3:** 392
4:11 ff	**Vol. 2:** 335
4:11–14	**Vol. 2:** 487, 686
5:6 ff	**Vol. 3:** 402
6:1–8	**Vol. 1:** 118
6:2 ff	**Vol. 1:** 657
6:2	**Vol. 1:** 203, 205
6:5	**Vol. 2:** 189, 689
6:8	**Vol. 3:** 254
6:9 ff	**Vol. 3:** 782
6:9–15	**Vol. 2:** 307
6:10	**Vol. 2:** 891
6:12–15	**Vol. 3:** 786
6:12	**Vol. 1:** 426 **Vol. 2:** 649 **Vol. 3:** 649, 867
6:13	**Vol. 1:** 426 **Vol. 2:** 778 **Vol. 3:** 926
6:14	**Vol. 2:** 773 **Vol. 3:** 237
7:2	**Vol. 3:** 149, 152, 155
7:3–5	**Vol. 1:** 612
7:8–14	**Vol. 2:** 174
7:9	**Vol. 2:** 595
7:10†	**Vol. 2:** 257, 737 **Vol. 3:** 1074
8:1–23	**Vol. 3:** 717
8:3	**Vol. 3:** 250
8:4 f	**Vol. 3:** 79
8:7	**Vol. 3:** 208
8:8	**Vol. 2:** 797 **Vol. 3:** 813, 880
8:9	**Vol. 2:** 889 **Vol. 3:** 786
8:10 ff	**Vol. 2:** 778
8:10	**Vol. 2:** 139
8:11 f	**Vol. 3:** 250
8:13	**Vol. 1:** 328
8:15	**Vol. 1:** 328 **Vol. 2:** 326
8:16	**Vol. 2:** 777 **Vol. 3:** 881, 886
8:17	**Vol. 1:** 555 **Vol. 3:** 823, 825, 881
8:19	**Vol. 1:** 612
8:20 ff	**Vol. 1:** 686
8:20–23	**Vol. 2:** 791
8:21 f	**Vol. 1:** 586
8:21	**Vol. 2:** 860
8:22 f	**Vol. 2:** 888
8:22	**Vol. 3:** 149, 152, 155
9:2 ff	**Vol. 2:** 767
9:5	**Vol. 3:** 585
9:6	**Vol. 3:** 29
9:7	**Vol. 2:** 698 **Vol. 3:** 250
9:9 f	**Vol. 1:** 210, 623 **Vol. 2:** 888, 899
9:9	**Vol. 1:** 100, 117, 321 **Vol. 2:** 257–258, 324–327, 379, 754 **Vol. 3:** 50–51, 218, 462, 509–510, 557
9:10	**Vol. 2:** 257, 591, 778
9:11	**Vol. 2:** 533
9:13	**Vol. 1:** 286 **Vol. 2:** 124
9:14	**Vol. 3:** 559
9:17	**Vol. 1:** 210
10:1	**Vol. 3:** 846
10:2	**Vol. 1:** 512, 550 **Vol. 2:** 554–555
10:3	**Vol. 3:** 565–566
10:7	**Vol. 2:** 357 **Vol. 3:** 919
10:8	**Vol. 3:** 192
10:9	**Vol. 3:** 522
10:10	**Vol. 1:** 531
10:11	**Vol. 2:** 197 **Vol. 3:** 29
11–14	**Vol. 3:** 961
11:5 f	**Vol. 3:** 566
11:5	**Vol. 2:** 841 **Vol. 3:** 720
11:12	**Vol. 1:** 93 **Vol. 2:** 139
11:13	**Vol. 1:** 93, 520 **Vol. 3:** 808
11:14	**Vol. 3:** 451
11:16 f	**Vol. 3:** 566

Zechariah *(cont'd)*

12:3	**Vol. 3:** 28, 803
12:4	**Vol. 1:** 527
12:5 f	**Vol. 2:** 698
12:6	**Vol. 2:** 485
12:8	**Vol. 3:** 649, 966
12:10 ff	**Vol. 2:** 917
12:10–14	**Vol. 1:** 518 **Vol. 2:** 38
12:10	**Vol. 2:** 117, 324, 854 , **Vol. 3:** 566, 629, 649
12:11	**Vol. 3:** 275, 962
13:1 f	**Vol. 3:** 986–987, 989
13:1	**Vol. 1:** 151 **Vol. 3:** 649, 813
13:2	**Vol. 3:** 238
13:4	**Vol. 1:** 116 **Vol. 3:** 121
13:7	**Vol. 1:** 163 **Vol. 2:** 34, 413, 459, 803 **Vol. 3:** 329, 564, 566–567
13:8 f	**Vol. 3:** 250
13:9	**Vol. 2:** 96 **Vol. 3:** 808
13:14	**Vol. 1:** 119
14:1	**Vol. 1:** 320 **Vol. 2:** 926
14:2	**Vol. 3:** 250, 962
14:3	**Vol. 2:** 889–890
14:4	**Vol. 2:** 713 **Vol. 3:** 543, 558, 1010, 1012
14:5 ff	**Vol. 1:** 320
14:5	**Vol. 1:** 101 **Vol. 2:** 376 **Vol. 3:** 557
14:7	**Vol. 1:** 420 **Vol. 2:** 887
14:8	**Vol. 3:** 813, 962, 986–987
14:9	**Vol. 2:** 376, 650
14:10 f	**Vol. 1:** 185
14:11	**Vol. 1:** 413–414
14:12	**Vol. 1:** 683
14:13	**Vol. 3:** 747
14:16	**Vol. 1:** 185, 688 **Vol. 2:** 797, 876 **Vol. 3:** 813
14:18–19	**Vol. 1:** 531
14:18	**Vol. 3:** 813
14:19	**Vol. 3:** 813
14:21	**Vol. 2:** 891

Malachi

1:1	**Vol. 3:** 311
1:2 f	**Vol. 1:** 556
1:2	**Vol. 2:** 318–319
1:3	**Vol. 2:** 318–319
1:4–14	**Vol. 3:** 717
1:6	**Vol. 1:** 617–618 **Vol. 3:** 636
1:7 ff	**Vol. 2:** 415

1:9	**Vol. 1:** 586 **Vol. 3:** 149, 152, 155
1:10	**Vol. 2:** 41 **Vol. 3:** 1019
1:11	**Vol. 2:** 650
1:14	**Vol. 2:** 569 **Vol. 3:** 318
2:2	**Vol. 1:** 416
2:3	**Vol. 2:** 34
2:4	**Vol. 1:** 544
2:5 f	**Vol. 2:** 778
2:5	**Vol. 2:** 478
2:7	**Vol. 2:** 141
2:8	**Vol. 3:** 937
2:10	**Vol. 1:** 379, 617–618 **Vol. 2:** 720
2:14 ff	**Vol. 2:** 583
2:14–16	**Vol. 1:** 505
2:14	**Vol. 2:** 578 **Vol. 3:** 1041
2:16	**Vol. 1:** 555
2:17	**Vol. 2:** 103, 817 **Vol. 3:** 354
3:1 ff	**Vol. 1:** 151 **Vol. 3:** 430
3:1 f	**Vol. 3:** 695
3:1–6	**Vol. 1:** 146
3:1	**Vol. 1:** 102, 544 **Vol. 2:** 38, 596, 891 **Vol. 3:** 46, 80, 119, 121, 212, 786, 937, 940
3:2 ff	**Vol. 2:** 363
3:2	**Vol. 2:** 773
3:3	**Vol. 2:** 96, 891
3:4	**Vol. 2:** 815
3:5†	**Vol. 1:** 410 **Vol. 2:** 139, 554–555 **Vol. 3:** 379, 1073–1074
3:7	**Vol. 1:** 354
3:8	**Vol. 2:** 693 **Vol. 3:** 416, 853
3:10	**Vol. 2:** 693 **Vol. 3:** 853
3:11	**Vol. 1:** 721 **Vol. 2:** 831
3:13	**Vol. 3:** 345
3:14	**Vol. 1:** 551
3:15	**Vol. 3:** 209, 800
3:16–4:3	**Vol. 2:** 833, 838
3:16	**Vol. 2:** 91 **Vol. 3:** 236, 345
3:17	**Vol. 1:** 534 **Vol. 2:** 838
3:19–21*	**Vol. 2:** 891
3:22*	**Vol. 3:** 354
3:23*	**Vol. 3:** 318
3:24*	**Vol. 1:** 414
4:1–6*	**Vol. 3:** 80
4:1	**Vol. 1:** 655 **Vol. 2:** 890 **Vol. 3:** 695
4:2*	**Vol. 2:** 591 **Vol. 3:** 198, 212, 731
4:4	**Vol. 2:** 639
4:5 f*	**Vol. 1:** 354, 543–544 **Vol. 3:** 147
4:5	**Vol. 1:** 320, 323, 593 **Vol. 2:** 443, 596, 890 **Vol. 3:** 86, 121, 198, 212, 863
4:6	**Vol. 1:** 544 **Vol. 3:** 147

New Testament

Matthew

1	**Vol. 2:** 36, 685 **Vol. 3:** 656
1:1 ff	**Vol. 1:** 427
1:1–17	**Vol. 1:** 77 **Vol. 2:** 79, 314 **Vol. 3:** 654–655
1:1	**Vol. 1:** 177, 182, 244 **Vol. 3:** 63
1:2–27	**Vol. 1:** 182
1:2–16	**Vol. 3:** 656
1:2	**Vol. 1:** 81, 182 **Vol. 2:** 318, 320 **Vol. 3:** 658
1:3	**Vol. 1:** 178 **Vol. 2:** 320 **Vol. 3:** 1062
1:5 f	**Vol. 1:** 178
1:5	**Vol. 3:** 1062
1:6 f	**Vol. 3:** 606–607
1:6	**Vol. 1:** 177 **Vol. 2:** 378 **Vol. 3:** 656, 1062
1:7	**Vol. 3:** 659
1:10	**Vol. 3:** 659
1:11	**Vol. 1:** 141
1:12	**Vol. 3:** 655
1:15 f	**Vol. 2:** 318
1:15	**Vol. 2:** 318, 640
1:16	**Vol. 1:** 177, 187 **Vol. 2:** 318 **Vol. 3:** 652, 658, 662, 1073
1:17 f	**Vol. 2:** 691
1:17	**Vol. 1:** 141 **Vol. 2:** 35 **Vol. 3:** 63, 657
1:18 ff	**Vol. 3:** 642, 656, 1062
1:18–25	**Vol. 1:** 506 **Vol. 3:** 697
1:18	**Vol. 1:** 181–182, 322 **Vol. 3:** 1188
1:19	**Vol. 1:** 506 **Vol. 2:** 291, 563 **Vol. 3:** 189, 360, 570, 660
1:20	**Vol. 1:** 102, 106, 177, 288, 512 **Vol. 2:** 488, 513, 585 **Vol. 3:** 517, 652, 658, 660, 1058, 1073
1:21	**Vol. 1:** 273 **Vol. 2:** 332, 654, 799 **Vol. 3:** 212, 221, 580
1:22 f	**Vol. 2:** 715 **Vol. 3:** 82, 1072, 1163
1:22	**Vol. 1:** 736 **Vol. 3:** 489, 657, 1198
1:23	**Vol. 1:** 186, 581, 737 **Vol. 2:** 86–87, 654 **Vol. 3:** 1058, 1072, 1163
1:24	**Vol. 1:** 442, 476 **Vol. 2:** 585 **Vol. 3:** 280, 1058, 1073
1:25	**Vol. 2:** 398 **Vol. 3:** 660
2	**Vol. 3:** 317
2:1 ff	**Vol. 2:** 378, 630
2:1–23	**Vol. 2:** 640 **Vol. 3:** 83, 1068, 1071
2:1–16	**Vol. 2:** 557
2:1–12	**Vol. 3:** 735
2:1	**Vol. 1:** 170, 178
2:2	**Vol. 1:** 321 **Vol. 2:** 315, 877
2:3	**Vol. 3:** 710
2:4	**Vol. 1:** 178 **Vol. 2:** 32, 799 **Vol. 3:** 480
2:5 f	**Vol. 2:** 715 **Vol. 3:** 82
2:5	**Vol. 1:** 170, 736 **Vol. 2:** 320
2:6	**Vol. 1:** 270, 321, 518 **Vol. 2:** 320 **Vol. 3:** 567, 1163
2:7	**Vol. 1:** 110, 274 **Vol. 2:** 488 **Vol. 3:** 844
2:8	**Vol. 1:** 170 **Vol. 3:** 46
2:9	**Vol. 2:** 175
2:10	**Vol. 2:** 356
2:11	**Vol. 1:** 266, 609 **Vol. 2:** 41, 96, 248, 294, 728, 831
2:12 ff	**Vol. 2:** 630
2:12	**Vol. 1:** 421, 512 **Vol. 3:** 324
2:13 ff	**Vol. 3:** 603
2:13 f	**Vol. 3:** 604
2:13–15	**Vol. 3:** 1007
2:13	**Vol. 1:** 102, 326, 421, 463, 512, 532, 559 **Vol. 2:** 513 **Vol. 3:** 517
2:14	**Vol. 3:** 280
2:15	**Vol. 1:** 290, 532, 736–737 **Vol. 2:** 715 **Vol. 3:** 82, 489, 642, 657, 1005, 1007, 1163
2:16	**Vol. 1:** 106, 109 **Vol. 3:** 341, 844
2:17–18	**Vol. 1:** 170
2:17 f	**Vol. 2:** 715 **Vol. 3:** 82, 1163
2:17	**Vol. 1:** 736 **Vol. 3:** 81, 489, 503
2:18	**Vol. 1:** 737 **Vol. 2:** 417 **Vol. 3:** 113
2:19–21	**Vol. 3:** 1007
2:19	**Vol. 1:** 102, 430, 512, 532 **Vol. 3:** 517
2:20 f	**Vol. 3:** 604
2:20	**Vol. 1:** 288, 518 **Vol. 2:** 640
2:22	**Vol. 1:** 421, 512 **Vol. 2:** 303, 381 **Vol. 3:** 324, 1179, 1193
2:23	**Vol. 2:** 333, 715 **Vol. 3:** 81–82, 489, 503, 1163
3:1 ff	**Vol. 3:** 82
3:1	**Vol. 1:** 150, 156 **Vol. 3:** 55, 1007
3:2	**Vol. 1:** 358, 599 **Vol. 2:** 54, 193, 382, 384 **Vol. 3:** 55, 580
3:3	**Vol. 1:** 411, 736 **Vol. 2:** 715 **Vol. 3:** 53, 118, 503, 940
3:4	**Vol. 1:** 116, 119, 240
3:5	**Vol. 1:** 94
3:6	**Vol. 2:** 533 **Vol. 3:** 987, 991, 1208, 1210
3:7 ff	**Vol. 1:** 358
3:7–12	**Vol. 3:** 695
3:7–9	**Vol. 3:** 439
3:7	**Vol. 1:** 111, 327, 509, 559 **Vol. 2:** 311 **Vol. 3:** 439, 644
3:8	**Vol. 1:** 358, 722 **Vol. 3:** 869
3:9	**Vol. 1:** 77, 286, 599 **Vol. 3:** 281, 360, 393, 822

Matthew *(cont'd)*

3:10   Vol. 1: 156, 358, 656, 722   Vol. 2: 104, 749   Vol. 3: 868–869

3:11   Vol. 1: 144, 146, 323, 358, 493, 653   Vol. 2: 785–786   Vol. 3: 55, 110, 447, 714, 1178, 1187, 1208–1210

3:12   Vol. 1: 156   Vol. 2: 32, 411   Vol. 3: 111, 527, 695, 804, 1210

3:13–17   Vol. 3: 113, 170, 990

3:13   Vol. 3: 987, 991, 1208

3:14 f   Vol. 3: 170

3:14   Vol. 3: 1208

3:15   Vol. 1: 549, 738   Vol. 2: 669, 715   Vol. 3: 360

3:16 f   Vol. 2: 194

3:16   Vol. 1: 175, 704   Vol. 2: 75, 185, 193, 314, 726, 728   Vol. 3: 258, 543, 987, 1180

3:17   Vol. 1: 290   Vol. 2: 193, 543, 725, 819   Vol. 3: 114, 611, 697, 807, 1070

4:1 ff   Vol. 2: 630

4:1–11   Vol. 1: 125, 384   Vol. 3: 83, 470, 657, 797, 800,

4:1 f   Vol. 2: 640   Vol. 3: 1007 804, 979, 1007, 1011

4:1   Vol. 3: 469, 602, 697, 1197

4:2   Vol. 1: 421, 613   Vol. 2: 267, 689, 696, 887, 893   Vol. 3: 954

4:3   Vol. 1: 290   Vol. 3: 643

4:4   Vol. 1: 250, 252   Vol. 2: 267, 480, 872, 893   Vol. 3: 329, 805, 807, 1181, 1193

4:5 ff   Vol. 2: 631   Vol. 3: 790, 796

4:5   Vol. 2: 235, 327, 803   Vol. 3: 469

4:6 f   Vol. 1: 290

4:6   Vol. 1: 239, 335   Vol. 2: 706   Vol. 3: 643, 805

4:7   Vol. 2: 893   Vol. 3: 802, 805, 809

4:8 f   Vol. 3: 806

4:8   Vol. 1: 524   Vol. 2: 46, 199, 381   Vol. 3: 469, 569, 1010

4:9   Vol. 1: 609   Vol. 2: 877

4:10   Vol. 2: 877, 893   Vol. 3: 469, 550, 806

4:11   Vol. 3: 469, 517, 546

4:12   Vol. 2: 333, 368

4:13–26   Vol. 3: 1163

4:13   Vol. 3: 251, 1052

4:14   Vol. 1: 736   Vol. 3: 489, 657

4:15   Vol. 2: 793   Vol. 3: 757

4:16   Vol. 1: 423, 435   Vol. 3: 555, 658

4:17   Vol. 1: 167, 358, 482, 599, 720   Vol. 2: 54, 193, 381, 384   Vol. 3: 55, 1163

4:18–22   Vol. 2: 825   Vol. 3: 985

4:18   Vol. 3: 983–984

4:19   Vol. 2: 433, 565

4:20   Vol. 3: 838

4:21   Vol. 1: 274   Vol. 3: 350

4:22   Vol. 3: 838

4:23 f   Vol. 2: 164

4:23   Vol. 2: 110, 112, 164, 630–631, 750, 799   Vol. 3: 52, 56–57, 197, 761, 785, 999, 1110

4:24   Vol. 2: 165, 175, 415   Vol. 3: 475, 734, 856, 999

4:25   Vol. 1: 482   Vol. 2: 327, 801

5–9   Vol. 3: 1110

5–7   Vol. 2: 164, 449   Vol. 3: 1011, 1109–1110

5   Vol. 2: 583   Vol. 3: 184, 1009

5:1 ff   Vol. 3: 83

5:1–12   Vol. 2: 203

5:1 f   Vol. 2: 110

5:1   Vol. 1: 322   Vol. 2: 185, 640, 801   Vol. 3: 589

5:2 ff   Vol. 3: 580

5:2 f   Vol. 3: 763

5:2   Vol. 2: 726–727   Vol. 3: 761, 763

5:3 ff   Vol. 1: 495   Vol. 2: 640

5:3–11   Vol. 2: 543

5:3–10   Vol. 1: 217   Vol. 2: 386, 388

5:3–6   Vol. 3: 696

5:3   Vol. 1: 216, 285, 358   Vol. 2: 258, 300, 381, 386, 824   Vol. 3: 693, 978

5:4   Vol. 1: 571   Vol. 2: 381, 420, 422

5:5 ff   Vol. 1: 453

5:5   Vol. 2: 258, 300, 311, 380   Vol. 3: 807

5:6   Vol. 1: 744   Vol. 2: 267, 433   Vol. 3: 360

5:7   Vol. 2: 595

5:8   Vol. 1: 587   Vol. 2: 183, 756   Vol. 3: 106, 335, 515, 518

5:9   Vol. 1: 274, 288, 290   Vol. 2: 780, 782   Vol. 3: 1155

5:10 ff   Vol. 2: 806

5:10   Vol. 2: 193, 300   Vol. 3: 360

5:11 ff   Vol. 3: 142

5:11 f   Vol. 1: 217   Vol. 2: 359, 806

5:11   Vol. 1: 556, 567   Vol. 3: 257, 340, 627

5:12   Vol. 2: 193, 353–354, 358, 806   Vol. 3: 83, 311

5:13   Vol. 2: 46, 749–750, 757   Vol. 3: 445, 447–448, 713, 944, 1012, 1025

5:14 ff   Vol. 2: 217, 749

5:14   Vol. 2: 313, 493, 746   Vol. 3: 445

5:14b   Vol. 3: 1012

5:15 ff   Vol. 2: 487

5:15 f   Vol. 2: 486

5:15   Vol. 2: 750, 757

5:16   Vol. 2: 47, 101, 104, 193, 493   Vol. 3: 343, 1012, 1150

5:17 ff   Vol. 3: 184

5:17–20   Vol. 2: 640   Vol. 3: 181

5:17–19   Vol. 2: 443

5:17 f   Vol. 2: 450, 715, 721, 872   Vol. 3: 185, 327, 329, 428–429, 541, 584, 807, 1163

5:17   Vol. 1: 322, 335, 719, 737–738   Vol. 2: 281, 313–314, 382, 443–444, 714   Vol. 3: 81, 181–183, 189, 311, 313, 492

Matthew *(cont'd)*

5:18 ff   **Vol. 1:** 488, 738
5:18 f   **Vol. 1:** 719
5:18   **Vol. 1:** 322, 518   **Vol. 2:** 192, 437, 443–444, 720   **Vol. 3:** 181–183, 484, 742
5:19–20   **Vol. 2:** 426, 443   **Vol. 3:** 184
5:19   **Vol. 1:** 334   **Vol. 3:** 183, 187, 482, 763
5:20   **Vol. 1:** 729   **Vol. 2:** 101, 133, 385, 443   **Vol. 3:** 183, 360, 763, 941, 1162
5:21 ff   **Vol. 1:** 738   **Vol. 3:** 183, 360, 762–763, 1107
5:21–48   **Vol. 1:** 335   **Vol. 2:** 281, 443   **Vol. 3:** 1163
5:21 f   **Vol. 1:** 364   **Vol. 2:** 143
5:21   **Vol. 1:** 167   **Vol. 2:** 177, 365, 437, 443
5:22   **Vol. 1:** 110, 417–418   **Vol. 2:** 443   **Vol. 3:** 696, 742, 1025
5:23 ff   **Vol. 2:** 366
5:23–24   **Vol. 1:** 702   **Vol. 2:** 41, 443, 868   **Vol. 3:** 173, 428–429, 435–436
5:24   **Vol. 1:** 666   **Vol. 3:** 167, 173
5:25 f   **Vol. 3:** 173, 1157
5:25   **Vol. 1:** 554   **Vol. 2:** 136, 365, 368   **Vol. 3:** 547, 939
5:26   **Vol. 2:** 850
5:27 ff   **Vol. 3:** 183, 539
5:27–32   **Vol. 3:** 172
5:27–31   **Vol. 2:** 580
5:27 f   **Vol. 2:** 580, 583
5:27   **Vol. 1:** 167   **Vol. 2:** 443
5:28   **Vol. 1:** 457   **Vol. 2:** 443   **Vol. 3:** 515, 742, 1058, 1175
5:29 f   **Vol. 1:** 138, 231, 561   **Vol. 2:** 708, 710   **Vol. 3:** 448
5:29   **Vol. 1:** 234   **Vol. 2:** 710   **Vol. 3:** 516
5:30   **Vol. 2:** 149, 385, 710
5:31 ff   **Vol. 3:** 183
5:31 f   **Vol. 1:** 506   **Vol. 2:** 580, 583   **Vol. 3:** 188–189, 980, 1058
5:31   **Vol. 1:** 606   **Vol. 2:** 443
5:32   **Vol. 1:** 500, 506   **Vol. 2:** 443, 580, 583   **Vol. 3:** 535, 538, 540, 742, 1155, 1195
5:33–37   **Vol. 3:** 183, 429, 740, 792
5:33   **Vol. 2:** 443   **Vol. 3:** 135, 738, 740
5:34–36   **Vol. 3:** 741
5:34 f   **Vol. 1:** 518   **Vol. 2:** 192
5:34   **Vol. 2:** 74, 193, 443, 614   **Vol. 3:** 740–742
5:35   **Vol. 1:** 50, 239   **Vol. 2:** 74, 327, 803   **Vol. 3:** 741
5:36   **Vol. 1:** 203   **Vol. 2:** 159, 175   **Vol. 3:** 1155
5:37   **Vol. 1:** 730   **Vol. 3:** 741, 1106
5:38 ff   **Vol. 3:** 979
5:38–48   **Vol. 1:** 702
5:38–42   **Vol. 2:** 386   **Vol. 3:** 97, 183
5:38   **Vol. 2:** 443   **Vol. 3:** 94, 1179

5:39 ff   **Vol. 3:** 380
5:39   **Vol. 2:** 443, 739   **Vol. 3:** 742
5:39a   **Vol. 1:** 566
5:40   **Vol. 2:** 365, 433
5:41   **Vol. 2:** 720   **Vol. 3:** 183
5:42   **Vol. 2:** 43, 856–857
5:43 ff   **Vol. 1:** 258, 556   **Vol. 2:** 366, 542   **Vol. 3:** 183
5:43–48   **Vol. 1:** 258, 701   **Vol. 2:** 544   **Vol. 3:** 576
5:43 f   **Vol. 1:** 554, 556
5:43   **Vol. 2:** 443
5:44 ff   **Vol. 1:** 620
5:44 f   **Vol. 3:** 360
5:44   **Vol. 1:** 417 · **Vol. 2:** 443, 543, 806, 868   **Vol. 3:** 97, 742, 755
5:45 ff   **Vol. 1:** 556
5:45†   **Vol. 1:** 620   **Vol. 2:** 100, 193   **Vol. 3:** 331, 360, 575, 731, 1002
5:46 f   **Vol. 3:** 580, 757
5:46   **Vol. 2:** 118, 443
5:47   **Vol. 1:** 729   **Vol. 2:** 724, 795
5:48   **Vol. 1:** 335, 492, 730   **Vol. 2:** 63, 65, 77, 101, 192, 229, 443, 566, 778, 782   **Vol. 3:** 185, 927
6:1 ff   **Vol. 3:** 141, 184, 402
6:1–18   **Vol. 3:** 657
6:1–4   **Vol. 2:** 596   **Vol. 3:** 874
6:1   **Vol. 2:** 193   **Vol. 3:** 141, 360, 1198
6:2 ff   **Vol. 2:** 462, 469
6:2 f   **Vol. 3:** 1155
6:2–18   **Vol. 3:** 1162
6:2   **Vol. 1:** 99   **Vol. 2:** 47, 433   **Vol. 3:** 141, 674, 785, 874
6:3   **Vol. 3:** 142
6:4   **Vol. 2:** 76, 214, 216   **Vol. 3:** 517
6:5 ff   **Vol. 2:** 469
6:5–15   **Vol. 2:** 868
6:5   **Vol. 1:** 99   **Vol. 2:** 433, 488, 548, 813   **Vol. 3:** 141, 389, 785
6:6–9   **Vol. 2:** 867
6:6   **Vol. 2:** 30, 76, 214, 216, 730, 869
6:7 ff   **Vol. 3:** 402
6:7   **Vol. 2:** 178, 795   **Vol. 3:** 822, 1175, 1190, 1192
6:8   **Vol. 1:** 620   **Vol. 2:** 726, 857
6:9 ff   **Vol. 2:** 868
6:9–15   **Vol. 2:** 561
6:9–13   **Vol. 2:** 832, 869
6:9   **Vol. 1:** 618, 621   **Vol. 2:** 74, 76, 193, 229, 653, 871
6:10   **Vol. 1:** 323   **Vol. 2:** 74, 194, 267, 382, 921   **Vol. 3:** 1022
6:11   **Vol. 1:** 250–251   **Vol. 2:** 871, 895
6:12   **Vol. 1:** 701–702   **Vol. 2:** 566, 668
6:13   **Vol. 1:** 567   **Vol. 2:** 868   **Vol. 3:** 204, 470, 803
6:13a   **Vol. 1:** 567   **Vol. 3:** 1198
6:13b   **Vol. 1:** 566–567   **Vol. 2:** 878   **Vol. 3:** 1176

Matthew *(cont'd)*

6:14 ff	**Vol. 2:** 668 **Vol. 3:** 402
6:14 f	**Vol. 1:** 701 **Vol. 2:** 770 **Vol. 3:** 586
6:14	**Vol. 1:** 702 **Vol. 2:** 192
6:15	**Vol. 2:** 301 **Vol. 3:** 142
6:16 ff	**Vol. 3:** 331
6:16 f	**Vol. 1:** 586
6:16–18	**Vol. 1:** 613
6:16	**Vol. 1:** 99 **Vol. 2:** 433, 488, 813 **Vol. 3:** 141
6:17	**Vol. 1:** 120 **Vol. 2:** 159, 712
6:18	**Vol. 2:** 76, 214, 216, 488 **Vol. 3:** 142
6:19 ff	**Vol. 2:** 749, 831
6:19 f	**Vol. 1:** 119 **Vol. 3:** 378
6:19–34	**Vol. 3:** 402
6:19	**Vol. 2:** 268
6:20	**Vol. 2:** 193 **Vol. 3:** 1149
6:21	**Vol. 2:** 757, 832
6:22 f	**Vol. 1:** 423 **Vol. 2:** 706, 749–750, 757 **Vol. 3:** 516
6:22	**Vol. 1:** 234 **Vol. 2:** 487 **Vol. 3:** 572
6:23	**Vol. 1:** 565
6:24 ff	**Vol. 1:** 384
6:24	**Vol. 1:** 138, 461 **Vol. 2:** 73, 286, 686, 749–750, 832, 838 **Vol. 3:** 595
6:25 ff	**Vol. 2:** 275, 480
6:25–34	**Vol. 1:** 277, 642
6:25–33	**Vol. 1:** 251 **Vol. 2:** 386
6:25–32	**Vol. 2:** 843
6:25	**Vol. 1:** 234, 277 **Vol. 2:** 272 **Vol. 3:** 683
6:26 ff	**Vol. 2:** 749 **Vol. 3:** 331
6:26–32	**Vol. 2:** 76
6:26	**Vol. 1:** 173, 278 **Vol. 2:** 32, 192 **Vol. 3:** 520, 526
6:26a	**Vol. 1:** 384
6:26b	**Vol. 2:** 566
6:27	**Vol. 1:** 92, 277
6:28	**Vol. 1:** 263 **Vol. 2:** 129
6:29	**Vol. 2:** 46–47 **Vol. 3:** 606–607
6:30	**Vol. 1:** 278, 744 **Vol. 2:** 211
6:31	**Vol. 2:** 275
6:32	**Vol. 1:** 142, 278, 620 **Vol. 2:** 192, 793 **Vol. 3:** 532, 958
6:33	**Vol. 1:** 278, 384, 666 **Vol. 2:** 267, 275, 387, 832 **Vol. 3:** 360, 372, 517, 530–532
6:34	**Vol. 1:** 251, 277, 563 **Vol. 2:** 757, 832 **Vol. 3:** 727–728
7:1 ff	**Vol. 2:** 365
7:1–5	**Vol. 2:** 366, 449
7:1 f	**Vol. 2:** 364
7:1	**Vol. 2:** 366 **Vol. 3:** 402
7:2	**Vol. 1:** 572 **Vol. 3:** 402, 1173
7:3 ff	**Vol. 2:** 469
7:3	**Vol. 1:** 116 **Vol. 2:** 433, 749 **Vol. 3:** 129
7:4	**Vol. 1:** 453 **Vol. 2:** 757
7:5	**Vol. 1:** 667 **Vol. 2:** 749 **Vol. 3:** 944

7:6	**Vol. 1:** 117 **Vol. 2:** 746, 749 **Vol. 3:** 395, 944
7:7–12	**Vol. 2:** 178
7:7–11	**Vol. 2:** 857
7:7 f	**Vol. 2:** 857, 881 **Vol. 3:** 529, 532
7:7	**Vol. 2:** 42, 728, 856, 881 **Vol. 3:** 530
7:8	**Vol. 2:** 856–857
7:9–11	**Vol. 2:** 857
7:9	**Vol. 3:** 805
7:10	**Vol. 1:** 509
7:11	**Vol. 1:** 286, 565, 620 **Vol. 2:** 41–42, 193, 565, 857 **Vol. 3:** 698
7:12 f	**Vol. 2:** 513
7:12	**Vol. 2:** 442 **Vol. 3:** 183, 762
7:13 ff	**Vol. 3:** 603
7:13 f	**Vol. 2:** 29, 31, 481, 746, 749, 881 **Vol. 3:** 940
7:13	**Vol. 1:** 254, 464 **Vol. 2:** 387, 728, 807–808
7:14	**Vol. 3:** 530
7:15–20	**Vol. 2:** 749
7:15	**Vol. 1:** 114, 118 **Vol. 2:** 472 **Vol. 3:** 81, 84, 604
7:16 ff	**Vol. 1:** 722
7:16 f	**Vol. 3:** 869
7:16	**Vol. 1:** 722, 726 **Vol. 2:** 33, 398 **Vol. 3:** 896, 1174
7:17–19	**Vol. 1:** 722
7:17 f	**Vol. 1:** 565 **Vol. 2:** 104
7:17	**Vol. 3:** 868
7:18	**Vol. 2:** 757
7:19	**Vol. 1:** 656, 722 **Vol. 3:** 869
7:20	**Vol. 1:** 722
7:21 ff	**Vol. 1:** 97 **Vol. 2:** 272, 276
7:21	**Vol. 2:** 193, 385, 514, 750 **Vol. 3:** 1022, 1155
7:22 f	**Vol. 2:** 358 **Vol. 3:** 84
7:22	**Vol. 1:** 453 **Vol. 3:** 81, 475–476
7:23	**Vol. 1:** 347 **Vol. 2:** 383, 398 **Vol. 3:** 476, 1150
7:24 ff	**Vol. 2:** 177 **Vol. 3:** 1155
7:24–27†	**Vol. 2:** 248, 383, 386, 749 **Vol. 3:** 1025
7:24 f	**Vol. 1:** 662 **Vol. 3:** 382
7:24	**Vol. 2:** 175, 619–620 **Vol. 3:** 1108
7:25	**Vol. 1:** 610 **Vol. 3:** 707, 982, 984, 987, 1001
7:26	**Vol. 2:** 620
7:27	**Vol. 1:** 610 **Vol. 3:** 707, 982, 984, 987, 1001
7:28 ff	**Vol. 2:** 177
7:28 f	**Vol. 3:** 1163
7:28	**Vol. 2:** 63 **Vol. 3:** 769
7:29	**Vol. 2:** 610, 623 **Vol. 3:** 83, 480–481, 1108
8 f	**Vol. 3:** 1110
8–9	**Vol. 2:** 164 **Vol. 3:** 851
8:1–15	**Vol. 3:** 657
8:1	**Vol. 1:** 482
8:2–4	**Vol. 2:** 631 **Vol. 3:** 106
8:2	**Vol. 2:** 860, 877 **Vol. 3:** 758

Matthew *(cont'd)*

8:3   **Vol. 2:** 150, 466   **Vol. 3:** 1022
8:4   **Vol. 2:** 41   **Vol. 3:** 37, 569, 1043
8:5–15   **Vol. 3:** 106
8:5–13   **Vol. 3:** 456, 980
8:5   **Vol. 1:** 570   **Vol. 3:** 964
8:6   **Vol. 1:** 283   **Vol. 2:** 415   **Vol. 3:** 856, 999
8:7   **Vol. 2:** 165
8:8 f   **Vol. 3:** 758
8:8–10   **Vol. 2:** 165
8:8   **Vol. 2:** 168–169   **Vol. 3:** 729, 964, 1108, 1110
8:9   **Vol. 1:** 290   **Vol. 2:** 608   **Vol. 3:** 595, 964
8:10 f   **Vol. 2:** 793
8:10   **Vol. 1:** 99, 599   **Vol. 2:** 624, 631   **Vol. 3:** 530, 964
8:11 f   **Vol. 1:** 78   **Vol. 2:** 57
8:11   **Vol. 1:** 81, 321, 667   **Vol. 2:** 319, 385, 727   **Vol. 3:** 922
8:12   **Vol. 1:** 289, 424–425   **Vol. 2:** 382, 385, 421, 877
8:13   **Vol. 2:** 165, 168–169   **Vol. 3:** 847–848, 964
8:14 f   **Vol. 3:** 1059
8:14   **Vol. 1:** 656
8:15   **Vol. 3:** 546
8:16   **Vol. 1:** 453–454   **Vol. 2:** 165   **Vol. 3:** 475, 694, 1108, 1110
8:17   **Vol. 1:** 736   **Vol. 2:** 165   **Vol. 3:** 489, 748, 998–999
8:18   **Vol. 1:** 341   **Vol. 2:** 630
8:19–26   **Vol. 1:** 489
8:19–22   **Vol. 1:** 464
8:19   **Vol. 3:** 481, 767
8:20 f   **Vol. 1:** 488
8:20   **Vol. 1:** 118, 173   **Vol. 2:** 192, 825   **Vol. 3:** 620, 623, 813
8:21–22   **Vol. 1:** 265, 482
8:22   **Vol. 1:** 439, 444, 446, 482
8:23–37   **Vol. 2:** 630
8:23–27   **Vol. 1:** 419   **Vol. 3:** 984–985
8:23   **Vol. 3:** 984
8:24   **Vol. 2:** 212   **Vol. 3:** 557
8:25   **Vol. 3:** 115, 211, 767
8:26 f   **Vol. 3:** 1002
8:26   **Vol. 1:** 181   **Vol. 3:** 280
8:27   **Vol. 2:** 179, 623
8:28 ff   **Vol. 3:** 475
8:28–34   **Vol. 2:** 631
8:28   **Vol. 1:** 66, 325, 420   **Vol. 3:** 247
8:29   **Vol. 1:** 290, 409, 452–453   **Vol. 2:** 208, 559   **Vol. 3:** 474, 856
8:30–34   **Vol. 1:** 117
8:30   **Vol. 2:** 631   **Vol. 3:** 1011
8:31   **Vol. 1:** 570   **Vol. 3:** 293
8:32   **Vol. 3:** 475, 984–985, 990, 1199
8:34   **Vol. 1:** 325   **Vol. 2:** 803

9   **Vol. 3:** 558
9:2–8   **Vol. 2:** 610, 631
9:2   **Vol. 1:** 286, 328   **Vol. 2:** 415   **Vol. 3:** 999
9:3   **Vol. 2:** 182, 728   **Vol. 3:** 342, 481
9:4   **Vol. 1:** 106, 567
9:5   **Vol. 2:** 434
9:6   **Vol. 2:** 415   **Vol. 3:** 999
9:7   **Vol. 2:** 248
9:8   **Vol. 3:** 622
9:9–13   **Vol. 2:** 523, 630   **Vol. 3:** 758
9:9   **Vol. 1:** 482   **Vol. 2:** 754   **Vol. 3:** 275, 757, 759
9:10 f   **Vol. 3:** 580
9:10   **Vol. 3:** 580, 757
9:11   **Vol. 2:** 813   **Vol. 3:** 481, 767
9:12 ff   **Vol. 2:** 813
9:12 f   **Vol. 3:** 428, 998
9:12   **Vol. 2:** 386   **Vol. 3:** 758
9:13   **Vol. 1:** 274, 322, 486   **Vol. 2:** 566, 596, 757   **Vol. 3:** 360, 427, 492, 580, 1022
9:14 ff   **Vol. 1:** 495
9:14–17   **Vol. 2:** 754   **Vol. 3:** 921
9:14 f   **Vol. 2:** 359
9:14   **Vol. 1:** 487   **Vol. 3:** 481
9:15   **Vol. 1:** 321   **Vol. 2:** 358, 383, 422, 585
9:16 f   **Vol. 2:** 714
9:16   **Vol. 3:** 543
9:17   **Vol. 2:** 670, 675–676, 854
9:18–26   **Vol. 2:** 168, 630   **Vol. 3:** 1059
9:18   **Vol. 1:** 168, 430   **Vol. 2:** 151, 877
9:20 ff   **Vol. 2:** 560
9:20 f   **Vol. 1:** 316   **Vol. 3:** 860
9:20   **Vol. 2:** 696   **Vol. 3:** 1058
9:21   **Vol. 2:** 714, 724
9:22   **Vol. 1:** 328   **Vol. 2:** 714   **Vol. 3:** 212, 846–848
9:23 ff   **Vol. 1:** 445
9:23   **Vol. 1:** 168   **Vol. 2:** 418, 623   **Vol. 3:** 674
9:24   **Vol. 1:** 283, 443   **Vol. 2:** 433, 510
9:25   **Vol. 3:** 280, 717, 1110
9:26   **Vol. 1:** 322
9:27 ff   **Vol. 2:** 165
9:27–31   **Vol. 1:** 219
9:27   **Vol. 1:** 409   **Vol. 2:** 595   **Vol. 3:** 652
9:28 f   **Vol. 2:** 631
9:29   **Vol. 2:** 630
9:30   **Vol. 2:** 726
9:32 ff   **Vol. 3:** 475
9:32   **Vol. 1:** 429   **Vol. 2:** 631
9:33   **Vol. 1:** 429   **Vol. 2:** 488, 623, 801
9:34   **Vol. 1:** 168, 429, 453   **Vol. 2:** 510   **Vol. 3:** 472, 481, 802, 1190, 1198, 1210
9:35–10:42 **Vol. 2:** 733
9:35–38   **Vol. 2:** 750
9:35   **Vol. 2:** 110, 112, 164, 630–631   **Vol. 3:** 52, 56–57, 761, 785, 999, 1110
9:36   **Vol. 2:** 413, 599   **Vol. 3:** 567

Matthew *(cont'd)*

9:37 f   **Vol. 2:** 746 **Vol. 3:** 144, 1150
9:37   **Vol. 1:** 204 **Vol. 3:** 526
9:38   **Vol. 1:** 453 **Vol. 2:** 514, 861 **Vol. 3:** 526
10   **Vol. 2:** 57 **Vol. 3:** 1109
10:1–16   **Vol. 1:** 213 **Vol. 2:** 825 **Vol. 3:** 453
10:1–5   **Vol. 1:** 131
10:1   **Vol. 1:** 274, 454, 500 **Vol. 2:** 165, 610, 695 **Vol. 3:** 475, 999
10:2 ff   **Vol. 2:** 652
10:2–4   **Vol. 1:** 136
10:2   **Vol. 1:** 129, 134, 136 **Vol. 2:** 695 **Vol. 3:** 384
10:3   **Vol. 2:** 550
10:4   **Vol. 1:** 299 **Vol. 2:** 321 **Vol. 3:** 1167
10:5 f   **Vol. 1:** 482 **Vol. 2:** 314 **Vol. 3:** 453–454, 626
10:5   **Vol. 1:** 340 **Vol. 2:** 695, 793 **Vol. 3:** 454, 940
10:6 f   **Vol. 3:** 946
10:6   **Vol. 2:** 248, 315, 385, 413, 459, 695 **Vol. 3:** 567
10:7 ff   **Vol. 3:** 57
10:7 f   **Vol. 2:** 632
10:7–8a   **Vol. 1:** 213
10:7   **Vol. 1:** 482 **Vol. 2:** 54 **Vol. 3:** 55–56
10:8   **Vol. 1:** 446, 454 **Vol. 2:** 41, 165, 184 **Vol. 3:** 281, 475, 994
10:8b   **Vol. 2:** 43
10:9   **Vol. 1:** 142 **Vol. 2:** 96–97 **Vol. 3:** 121
10:10   **Vol. 1:** 143, 407 **Vol. 2:** 272 **Vol. 3:** 349, 794, 855
10:11 ff   **Vol. 1:** 689
10:11   **Vol. 3:** 349
10:12–15   **Vol. 1:** 171
10:12 f   **Vol. 3:** 258
10:12   **Vol. 1:** 213
10:13 ff   **Vol. 2:** 223
10:13   **Vol. 1:** 213, 355 **Vol. 2:** 780–781 **Vol. 3:** 349
10:14   **Vol. 1:** 239 **Vol. 2:** 413 **Vol. 3:** 560
10:15   **Vol. 2:** 203, 366, 767, 894 **Vol. 3:** 93
10:16   **Vol. 1:** 118, 175, 510 **Vol. 2:** 413, 619, 746 **Vol. 3:** 447
10:17 ff   **Vol. 1:** 489 **Vol. 2:** 386
10:17   **Vol. 1:** 163, 364 **Vol. 2:** 368 **Vol. 3:** 785
10:18   **Vol. 1:** 270 **Vol. 2:** 169 **Vol. 3:** 1043
10:19 f   **Vol. 3:** 257
10:19   **Vol. 1:** 278 **Vol. 3:** 849
10:20   **Vol. 1:** 90 **Vol. 2:** 75
10:21   **Vol. 1:** 286–287, 725
10:22   **Vol. 1:** 556 **Vol. 2:** 62, 654, 773, 806 **Vol. 3:** 257
10:23 ff   **Vol. 2:** 450
10:23   **Vol. 1:** 99, 559 **Vol. 2:** 63, 382, 806, 930 **Vol. 3:** 454, 620, 626
10:24 ff   **Vol. 1:** 486

10:24 f   **Vol. 1:** 482, 488–489 **Vol. 2:** 513 **Vol. 3:** 767
10:24   **Vol. 1:** 404, 549 **Vol. 2:** 510 **Vol. 3:** 629
10:25 f   **Vol. 1:** 305
10:25   **Vol. 1:** 168 **Vol. 2:** 509 **Vol. 3:** 472, 727
10:26 f   **Vol. 3:** 314
10:26   **Vol. 1:** 623 **Vol. 2:** 212, 216–217 **Vol. 3:** 312, 657
10:27   **Vol. 1:** 423 **Vol. 2:** 212, 217, 493 **Vol. 3:** 54
10:28   **Vol. 1:** 436, 464, 623 **Vol. 2:** 208–209, 366, 480 **Vol. 3:** 304, 657, 686
10:29–31   **Vol. 2:** 76
10:29 f   **Vol. 2:** 566
10:29   **Vol. 1:** 173, 609
10:30 f   **Vol. 1:** 623
10:30   **Vol. 1:** 203 **Vol. 2:** 159
10:31   **Vol. 3:** 657
10:32 f   **Vol. 1:** 323, 347 **Vol. 2:** 193, 565 **Vol. 3:** 625–626
10:32   **Vol. 1:** 205 **Vol. 2:** 383 **Vol. 3:** 62, 86, 142, 621
10:33   **Vol. 2:** 76
10:34–37   **Vol. 1:** 159
10:34–36   **Vol. 3:** 697
10:34   **Vol. 2:** 780 **Vol. 3:** 181, 967, 978, 1070
10:35 f   **Vol. 1:** 725 **Vol. 2:** 250
10:35   **Vol. 2:** 585
10:37 ff   **Vol. 2:** 544, 825
10:37   **Vol. 1:** 289, 488, 619 **Vol. 2:** 386, 548 **Vol. 3:** 349
10:38   **Vol. 1:** 324, 402, 404, 482, 489, 493 **Vol. 3:** 60, 349, 748
10:39   **Vol. 1:** 464 **Vol. 3:** 529, 682, 1163
10:40 ff   **Vol. 1:** 130
10:40   **Vol. 1:** 91, 285 **Vol. 2:** 176, 920 **Vol. 3:** 56, 314, 326, 629, 746
10:41   **Vol. 2:** 652 **Vol. 3:** 360
10:42   **Vol. 1:** 318 **Vol. 2:** 429 **Vol. 3:** 141–142, 980, 989
11:1   **Vol. 2:** 63, 695 **Vol. 3:** 56, 761
11:2 ff   **Vol. 2:** 631
11:2–6   **Vol. 2:** 314, 379
11:2   **Vol. 1:** 487 **Vol. 2:** 686 **Vol. 3:** 1150
11:3   **Vol. 1:** 323 **Vol. 2:** 245, 379, 739 **Vol. 3:** 367, 378
11:4   **Vol. 2:** 176, 351
11:5 f   **Vol. 2:** 110
11:5   **Vol. 1:** 217–219, 428, 445 **Vol. 2:** 110, 118, 358, 379, 415, 464, 824–825 **Vol. 3:** 281, 519, 696–697, 1110
11:6   **Vol. 1:** 358 **Vol. 2:** 110, 708 **Vol. 3:** 697
11:7–19   **Vol. 2:** 443
11:7   **Vol. 1:** 167 **Vol. 3:** 559, 1007
11:8 ff   **Vol. 3:** 82
11:8   **Vol. 2:** 565

Matthew *(cont'd)*

11:9	**Vol. 1:** 729 **Vol. 3:** 83
11:10–14	**Vol. 1:** 545
11:10	**Vol. 1:** 102 **Vol. 3:** 80, 119, 329, 940
11:11–15	**Vol. 2:** 443
11:11 f	**Vol. 3:** 82
11:11	**Vol. 2:** 427 **Vol. 3:** 184
11:12 f	**Vol. 2:** 383
11:12	**Vol. 3:** 603, 711–712, 1180
11:13	**Vol. 2:** 443 **Vol. 3:** 183
11:14	**Vol. 1:** 323, 545 **Vol. 2:** 443
11:15	**Vol. 2:** 178, 750
11:16	**Vol. 1:** 259, 267, 283
11:17	**Vol. 2:** 418 **Vol. 3:** 674
11:18 f	**Vol. 2:** 276 **Vol. 3:** 623, 921
11:18	**Vol. 1:** 323, 637 **Vol. 2:** 272 **Vol. 3:** 921
11:19	**Vol. 1:** 286, 384, 495, 561 **Vol. 2:** 272, 549 **Vol. 3:** 360, 580, 623, 758, 1030, 1174
11:20 ff	**Vol. 2:** 366
11:20–24	**Vol. 1:** 358
11:20	**Vol. 1:** 167 **Vol. 2:** 803 **Vol. 3:** 340
11:21 ff	**Vol. 2:** 383
11:21	**Vol. 1:** 181 **Vol. 2:** 714 **Vol. 3:** 1052
11:22	**Vol. 2:** 767
11:23 f	**Vol. 3:** 93
11:23	**Vol. 2:** 207 **Vol. 3:** 224
11:24	**Vol. 2:** 767
11:25 ff	**Vol. 1:** 290, 615 **Vol. 3:** 313, 640
11:25–30	**Vol. 1:** 375
11:25–27	**Vol. 1:** 619 **Vol. 3:** 640
11:25 f	**Vol. 1:** 620 **Vol. 2:** 76
11:25	**Vol. 1:** 282, 284, 345–346 **Vol. 2:** 192–193, 216, 354, 514 **Vol. 3:** 533, 821, 837
11:26	**Vol. 2:** 818–819 **Vol. 3:** 1017, 1175
11:27 ff	**Vol. 3:** 326
11:27	**Vol. 1:** 90, 95, 375 **Vol. 2:** 193, 313, 368, 404, 610, 653 **Vol. 3:** 313, 639–640, 642, 645, 1017, 1107, 1163
11:28 ff	**Vol. 1:** 262, 335, 339 **Vol. 2:** 118–119, 262 **Vol. 3:** 256
11:28–30	**Vol. 2:** 281, 443 **Vol. 3:** 1162
11:28 f	**Vol. 3:** 640
11:28	**Vol. 1:** 263, 729 **Vol. 3:** 411, 580, 1162
11:29 f	**Vol. 3:** 1162, 1164
11:29	**Vol. 1:** 486, 570 **Vol. 2:** 106, 258, 262, 281 **Vol. 3:** 529–530, 683
11:30	**Vol. 2:** 106
12	**Vol. 3:** 1109
12:1–12	**Vol. 1:** 631
12:1–8	**Vol. 2:** 267, 754 **Vol. 3:** 37, 408, 423, 1163
12:1	**Vol. 3:** 837, 1163
12:2 ff	**Vol. 2:** 813
12:2	**Vol. 3:** 516
12:3–7	**Vol. 3:** 792
12:3	**Vol. 1:** 427 **Vol. 3:** 329
12:4	**Vol. 1:** 586 **Vol. 2:** 248, 724 **Vol. 3:** 792
12:5	**Vol. 2:** 139, 444
12:6	**Vol. 2:** 426 **Vol. 3:** 380, 429, 658, 792
12:7 f	**Vol. 3:** 429
12:7	**Vol. 2:** 139, 370, 596, 813 **Vol. 3:** 427, 429, 1022
12:8	**Vol. 3:** 792
12:9–16	**Vol. 3:** 1163
12:9–14	**Vol. 3:** 409
12:9	**Vol. 3:** 785
12:10	**Vol. 2:** 165, 610
12:11 f	**Vol. 2:** 459
12:11	**Vol. 1:** 115, 516, 609 **Vol. 2:** 413 **Vol. 3:** 717
12:12	**Vol. 2:** 434, 565, 610
12:13	**Vol. 2:** 150, 170, 739 **Vol. 3:** 147, 442
12:14	**Vol. 1:** 363 **Vol. 2:** 812–813
12:15	**Vol. 2:** 165
12:16	**Vol. 3:** 320
12:17–21	**Vol. 3:** 1163
12:17	**Vol. 1:** 736 **Vol. 3:** 489
12:18 ff	**Vol. 3:** 48
12:18†	**Vol. 1:** 534 **Vol. 2:** 75, 365, 543, 819 **Vol. 3:** 110, 442, 610, 685, 698
12:19	**Vol. 1:** 409
12:20	**Vol. 1:** 421, 651 **Vol. 3:** 109
12:21†	**Vol. 2:** 241, 654 **Vol. 3:** 110
12:22–32	**Vol. 3:** 1163
12:22–30	**Vol. 2:** 603
12:22–28	**Vol. 1:** 454
12:22	**Vol. 1:** 219, 429, 718 **Vol. 3:** 515
12:23 ff	**Vol. 3:** 474
12:23	**Vol. 1:** 427 **Vol. 3:** 652
12:24–37	**Vol. 2:** 177
12:24–32	**Vol. 2:** 813 **Vol. 3:** 481
12:24–29	**Vol. 3:** 696
12:24	**Vol. 1:** 168 **Vol. 2:** 510, 631 **Vol. 3:** 472, 481, 802, 869, 1210
12:25–37	**Vol. 2:** 560 **Vol. 3:** 83, 472
12:25–29	**Vol. 3:** 695
12:25	**Vol. 1:** 106 **Vol. 3:** 128, 1008
12:26 f	**Vol. 1:** 453
12:26	**Vol. 2:** 381 **Vol. 3:** 474
12:27–29	**Vol. 3:** 470
12:27 f	**Vol. 3:** 695
12:27	**Vol. 1:** 487 **Vol. 2:** 365 **Vol. 3:** 472, 474, 476, 696
12:28	**Vol. 1:** 453 **Vol. 2:** 75, 150, 381–382, 921 **Vol. 3:** 475, 696, 985, 1163, 1193–1194, 1210
12:29	**Vol. 1:** 53, 508, 651, 666 **Vol. 2:** 382, 603, 631, 702, 733 **Vol. 3:** 602, 913
12:30 ff	**Vol. 1:** 703
12:30	**Vol. 1:** 297 **Vol. 2:** 32, 34 **Vol. 3:** 568
12:31 f	**Vol. 3:** 696
12:31	**Vol. 3:** 343, 628
12:32 f	**Vol. 1:** 347
12:32	**Vol. 1:** 327, 701 **Vol. 3:** 343–344, 658, 831, 1106

Matthew *(cont'd)*

12:33 ff   **Vol. 2:** 749
12:33–37   **Vol. 3:** 1163
12:33 f   **Vol. 3:** 869
12:33   **Vol. 1:** 722   **Vol. 3:** 868
12:34   **Vol. 1:** 565, 729
12:35–37   **Vol. 1:** 427
12:35   **Vol. 1:** 453, 566–567   **Vol. 2:** 100, 831
12:36   **Vol. 2:** 894   **Vol. 3:** 1121, 1142–1143
12:37   **Vol. 2:** 370   **Vol. 3:** 360
12:38 ff   **Vol. 2:** 629
12:38–42   **Vol. 2:** 750   **Vol. 3:** 481, 1163
12:38–41   **Vol. 2:** 350
12:38   **Vol. 3:** 481
12:39 f   **Vol. 2:** 680   **Vol. 3:** 628
12:39   **Vol. 1:** 565   **Vol. 2:** 36, 351, 582, 584   **Vol. 3:** 532, 579
12:40   **Vol. 1:** 169, 421, 518, 671   **Vol. 2:** 207, 351, 687
12:41 f   **Vol. 2:** 366   **Vol. 3:** 658, 1163
12:41   **Vol. 1:** 358   **Vol. 2:** 352, 365, 680   **Vol. 3:** 52–53, 83, 275, 516, 1187
12:42   **Vol. 1:** 517   **Vol. 2:** 381, 385, 680   **Vol. 3:** 606–607, 1003, 1030
12:43 ff   **Vol. 2:** 691   **Vol. 3:** 475
12:43–45   **Vol. 3:** 1163
12:43   **Vol. 3:** 256, 529–530, 1006
12:44   **Vol. 1:** 477, 524   **Vol. 3:** 474
12:45   **Vol. 2:** 251   **Vol. 3:** 474, 579, 657
12:45c   **Vol. 3:** 256
12:46 ff   **Vol. 3:** 1070
12:46–50   **Vol. 1:** 488   **Vol. 2:** 750   **Vol. 3:** 1062
12:46–49   **Vol. 3:** 1163
12:49   **Vol. 2:** 150
12:50   **Vol. 2:** 193   **Vol. 3:** 1022, 1163
13   **Vol. 2:** 691, 749   **Vol. 3:** 1109
13:1–58   **Vol. 3:** 1163
13:1–9   **Vol. 2:** 748, 750   **Vol. 3:** 522
13:1–2   **Vol. 3:** 589
13:1   **Vol. 3:** 984
13:2   **Vol. 1:** 297   **Vol. 2:** 32
13:3   **Vol. 1:** 464
13:4–8   **Vol. 1:** 609
13:4   **Vol. 1:** 174
13:5   **Vol. 1:** 464, 517   **Vol. 2:** 197, 739   **Vol. 3:** 382
13:6   **Vol. 1:** 516, 653   **Vol. 3:** 731
13:7 f   **Vol. 2:** 739
13:7   **Vol. 1:** 226, 726   **Vol. 2:** 185
13:8–23   **Vol. 3:** 522
13:8   **Vol. 1:** 722
13:9   **Vol. 2:** 178, 750
13:10–17   **Vol. 2:** 750
13:10–15   **Vol. 2:** 752
13:11   **Vol. 1:** 742   **Vol. 2:** 178, 401   **Vol. 3:** 314, 503, 533
13:12   **Vol. 1:** 730
13:13 ff   **Vol. 2:** 178   **Vol. 3:** 313
13:13 f   **Vol. 3:** 517

13:13   **Vol. 3:** 131
13:14   **Vol. 1:** 736   **Vol. 2:** 175   **Vol. 3:** 81, 515
13:15   **Vol. 1:** 261   **Vol. 2:** 156, 799   **Vol. 3:** 131
13:16 f   **Vol. 1:** 217, 742   **Vol. 2:** 176, 630
13:16   **Vol. 2:** 110   **Vol. 3:** 313
13:17   **Vol. 1:** 457   **Vol. 3:** 360, 1163
13:18–23   **Vol. 2:** 748, 750   **Vol. 3:** 868
13:19   **Vol. 1:** 174, 566, 742   **Vol. 3:** 470, 712
13:20 f   **Vol. 3:** 382
13:20   **Vol. 2:** 358   **Vol. 3:** 382, 837
13:21   **Vol. 1:** 608   **Vol. 2:** 708, 808
13:22   **Vol. 1:** 460, 726   **Vol. 2:** 459–460, 842–843, 845
13:23   **Vol. 1:** 742   **Vol. 2:** 104, 177, 773   **Vol. 3:** 868
13:24 ff   **Vol. 1:** 554   **Vol. 3:** 527
13:24–43   **Vol. 1:** 299
13:24–30   **Vol. 2:** 708, 750   **Vol. 3:** 470, 523
13:24 f   **Vol. 3:** 868
13:24   **Vol. 1:** 520   **Vol. 2:** 104, 502
13:26   **Vol. 1:** 744   **Vol. 2:** 211, 488
13:27   **Vol. 2:** 104, 510   **Vol. 3:** 115
13:28   **Vol. 2:** 33
13:29   **Vol. 2:** 33
13:30 f   **Vol. 2:** 364
13:30   **Vol. 1:** 171   **Vol. 2:** 32–33   **Vol. 3:** 526
13:31 f   **Vol. 2:** 385, 429, 747, 750   **Vol. 3:** 523
13:31   **Vol. 2:** 502
13:32   **Vol. 1:** 174   **Vol. 2:** 129   **Vol. 3:** 813, 868–869
13:33   **Vol. 2:** 216, 385, 433, 461–462, 502, 747, 750   **Vol. 3:** 1058, 1178
13:34 f   **Vol. 2:** 750, 753
13:34   **Vol. 2:** 801
13:35   **Vol. 1:** 377–378, 736   **Vol. 2:** 217, 727   **Vol. 3:** 489
13:36–51   **Vol. 2:** 833, 838
13:36–43   **Vol. 2:** 750   **Vol. 3:** 831
13:36   **Vol. 1:** 489, 701
13:37–43   **Vol. 3:** 627
13:37   **Vol. 2:** 104   **Vol. 3:** 868
13:38   **Vol. 1:** 289, 566   **Vol. 2:** 104, 709   **Vol. 3:** 868
13:39 f   **Vol. 2:** 62   **Vol. 3:** 658
13:39   **Vol. 1:** 566   **Vol. 3:** 526, 829
13:40 ff   **Vol. 1:** 289
13:40 f   **Vol. 2:** 364, 917
13:40   **Vol. 2:** 33
13:41   **Vol. 2:** 33, 387, 708–709
13:42   **Vol. 1:** 657   **Vol. 2:** 208, 421
13:43   **Vol. 2:** 486, 750   **Vol. 3:** 360, 732
13:44 ff   **Vol. 1:** 647   **Vol. 2:** 750   **Vol. 3:** 530
13:44–46   **Vol. 2:** 386, 749
13:44   **Vol. 1:** 268   **Vol. 2:** 216, 502, 832–833, 846   **Vol. 3:** 528–529
13:45 f   **Vol. 2:** 833   **Vol. 3:** 395
13:45   **Vol. 2:** 502   **Vol. 3:** 529, 532
13:46   **Vol. 2:** 846   **Vol. 3:** 395

Matthew *(cont'd)*

13:47–50	**Vol. 2:** 750
13:47	**Vol. 2:** 32, 502
13:48	**Vol. 2:** 33
13:49 f	**Vol. 1:** 566
13:49	**Vol. 1:** 102, 473 **Vol. 2:** 62, 364 **Vol. 3:** 360, 658, 831
13:50	**Vol. 2:** 208, 421
13:51 f	**Vol. 2:** 750
13:51	**Vol. 3:** 132, 503
13:52	**Vol. 1:** 453 **Vol. 2:** 509, 670, 714, 834 **Vol. 3:** 184, 482
13:53–58	**Vol. 2:** 631 **Vol. 3:** 88
13:53	**Vol. 2:** 63
13:54	**Vol. 1:** 616 **Vol. 3:** 761, 785, 1030
13:55	**Vol. 1:** 279 **Vol. 2:** 320 **Vol. 3:** 660
13:56	**Vol. 3:** 1204
13:57	**Vol. 2:** 248, 708, 757 **Vol. 3:** 696
13:58	**Vol. 3:** 1163
14:1 f	**Vol. 2:** 342
14:1	**Vol. 1:** 418 **Vol. 2:** 175 **Vol. 3:** 39
14:2 ff	**Vol. 3:** 82
14:2	**Vol. 1:** 283 **Vol. 3:** 1152
14:3	**Vol. 1:** 171 **Vol. 2:** 136 **Vol. 3:** 540, 717
14:4	**Vol. 1:** 637
14:5	**Vol. 1:** 430, 623 **Vol. 2:** 801
14:7	**Vol. 1:** 346 **Vol. 2:** 856 **Vol. 3:** 742
14:8	**Vol. 2:** 159, 378 **Vol. 3:** 1071
14:9	**Vol. 1:** 341
14:10	**Vol. 2:** 136
14:11	**Vol. 2:** 159 **Vol. 3:** 1071
14:12	**Vol. 1:** 265, 610
14:13–21	**Vol. 1:** 250, 729 **Vol. 2:** 272, 523, 630
14:13	**Vol. 2:** 839 **Vol. 3:** 1007
14:14	**Vol. 1:** 321 **Vol. 2:** 165, 459, 599, 750
14:15	**Vol. 2:** 268 **Vol. 3:** 189, 847
14:17	**Vol. 1:** 670
14:18	**Vol. 2:** 192
14:19	**Vol. 1:** 341, 744 **Vol. 2:** 211, 801 **Vol. 3:** 519
14:20	**Vol. 1:** 743
14:21	**Vol. 1:** 283 **Vol. 2:** 563, 699
14:22–33	**Vol. 2:** 630 **Vol. 3:** 985, 990
14:22–23	**Vol. 2:** 281 **Vol. 3:** 984
14:22	**Vol. 2:** 663 **Vol. 3:** 189
14:23	**Vol. 2:** 185, 839, 869 **Vol. 3:** 1010
14:24 ff	**Vol. 3:** 1002
14:24	**Vol. 1:** 517 **Vol. 3:** 856
14:25	**Vol. 1:** 420 **Vol. 2:** 136
14:26	**Vol. 1:** 409 **Vol. 2:** 559 **Vol. 3:** 324, 474, 710
14:27	**Vol. 1:** 328, 623
14:28–31	**Vol. 3:** 990
14:30	**Vol. 1:** 409 **Vol. 3:** 211, 990
14:31	**Vol. 1:** 504 **Vol. 3:** 750, 1187
14:33	**Vol. 1:** 290 **Vol. 2:** 550, 877 **Vol. 3:** 132
14:34	**Vol. 3:** 1059
14:36	**Vol. 3:** 211, 860
15	**Vol. 3:** 572, 584
15:1 ff	**Vol. 2:** 813 **Vol. 3:** 584
15:1–20	**Vol. 2:** 715, 813 **Vol. 3:** 481, 763, 990
15:1–11	**Vol. 3:** 183
15:2 ff	**Vol. 2:** 469
15:2 f	**Vol. 3:** 584
15:2	**Vol. 1:** 199 **Vol. 3:** 481, 774
15:3–9	**Vol. 3:** 184
15:3	**Vol. 1:** 335 **Vol. 3:** 868
15:4 f	**Vol. 1:** 730
15:4	**Vol. 1:** 415, 430 **Vol. 3:** 95, 1070
15:5 f	**Vol. 3:** 1070
15:5	**Vol. 1:** 415 **Vol. 2:** 42–43
15:6	**Vol. 1:** 415 **Vol. 2:** 715 **Vol. 3:** 184
15:7 ff	**Vol. 2:** 469 **Vol. 3:** 807
15:7	**Vol. 1:** 736 **Vol. 2:** 43 **Vol. 3:** 81
15:8 ff	**Vol. 2:** 150
15:8	**Vol. 2:** 183, 799
15:9	**Vol. 1:** 552 **Vol. 2:** 93 **Vol. 3:** 57, 184, 770
15:10–20	**Vol. 1:** 169 **Vol. 2:** 150
15:10	**Vol. 1:** 274 **Vol. 2:** 177–178
15:11	**Vol. 1:** 384, 448, 642 **Vol. 3:** 106, 860
15:12	**Vol. 2:** 708 **Vol. 3:** 1106, 1108
15:13	**Vol. 2:** 192, 708, 746 **Vol. 3:** 523, 869
15:14	**Vol. 1:** 220, 424, 609–610 **Vol. 2:** 709, 757 **Vol. 3:** 184, 942
15:15	**Vol. 2:** 746 **Vol. 3:** 384
15:16 f	**Vol. 3:** 106
15:17	**Vol. 1:** 742
15:18 f	**Vol. 1:** 322
15:18	**Vol. 1:** 448, 642 **Vol. 2:** 568
15:19	**Vol. 1:** 169, 564, 566 **Vol. 2:** 182, 472, 568 **Vol. 3:** 820
15:20	**Vol. 1:** 448
15:21 ff	**Vol. 2:** 165 **Vol. 3:** 475
15:21–28	**Vol. 3:** 106, 1059
15:21	**Vol. 1:** 169 **Vol. 2:** 170, 303
15:22 f	**Vol. 1:** 409
15:22	**Vol. 1:** 427 **Vol. 2:** 595 **Vol. 3:** 652
15:23	**Vol. 2:** 880 **Vol. 3:** 189
15:24 f	**Vol. 2:** 315
15:24	**Vol. 1:** 482 **Vol. 2:** 248, 314, 413, 695, 793 **Vol. 3:** 454, 567
15:25	**Vol. 2:** 877
15:26	**Vol. 1:** 117 **Vol. 2:** 434
15:27	**Vol. 1:** 117, 609 **Vol. 2:** 513
15:28	**Vol. 2:** 168–169 **Vol. 3:** 758, 846–848, 1058
15:29	**Vol. 2:** 185
15:30–31	**Vol. 1:** 429 **Vol. 2:** 414–415
15:30	**Vol. 1:** 219 **Vol. 2:** 165
15:31	**Vol. 2:** 73, 170, 623
15:32–39	**Vol. 1:** 250, 729 **Vol. 2:** 272, 523, 630
15:32	**Vol. 2:** 599 **Vol. 3:** 189, 228, 939, 1022
15:33	**Vol. 1:** 743 **Vol. 3:** 1007
15:34	**Vol. 2:** 692 **Vol. 3:** 657
15:35	**Vol. 1:** 340–341
15:36	**Vol. 1:** 670 **Vol. 2:** 692 **Vol. 3:** 819

Matthew *(cont'd)*

15:37	**Vol. 1:** 729 **Vol. 2:** 692 **Vol. 3:** 657
15:38	**Vol. 1:** 283 **Vol. 2:** 699
15:39	**Vol. 3:** 189
16:1 ff	**Vol. 2:** 629
16:1–16	**Vol. 3:** 439
16:1–4	**Vol. 2:** 631, 750 **Vol. 3:** 867
16:1	**Vol. 2:** 192, 351, 629, 680, 880 **Vol. 3:** 439, 442, 804
16:2 f	**Vol. 1:** 656
16:2	**Vol. 2:** 192 **Vol. 3:** 1002
16:3 f	**Vol. 3:** 393
16:3	**Vol. 1:** 503, 586 **Vol. 2:** 398 **Vol. 3:** 848
16:4	**Vol. 1:** 220 **Vol. 2:** 350–351, 582, 584, 687 **Vol. 3:** 532
16:5–12	**Vol. 3:** 132
16:6	**Vol. 3:** 184, 439, 442
16:7 f	**Vol. 3:** 820
16:7	**Vol. 2:** 182
16:8	**Vol. 2:** 398
16:9	**Vol. 3:** 240
16:10	**Vol. 2:** 692
16:11 f	**Vol. 2:** 462
16:11	**Vol. 3:** 184, 439
16:12	**Vol. 3:** 439, 769
16:13 ff	**Vol. 2:** 680
16:13–23	**Vol. 2:** 341 **Vol. 3:** 1061
16:13	**Vol. 2:** 550, 879 **Vol. 3:** 623
16:14	**Vol. 1:** 736 **Vol. 3:** 82–83
16:15 ff	**Vol. 1:** 200, 489
16:16 ff	**Vol. 3:** 132
16:16–19	**Vol. 3:** 386
16:16 f	**Vol. 3:** 387
16:16	**Vol. 1:** 290 **Vol. 2:** 231, 480 **Vol. 3:** 385
16:17 ff	**Vol. 2:** 733
16:17	**Vol. 1:** 217, 222, 677–678 **Vol. 2:** 75–76 **Vol. 3:** 314, 330, 336, 384, 533
16:18 f	**Vol. 2:** 207, 786
16:18	**Vol. 1:** 297–298, 302–304, 662 **Vol. 2:** 30, 38, 207, 252, 433 **Vol. 3:** 382–385, 390, 713, 763
16:19	**Vol. 1:** 171, 702–703 **Vol. 2:** 194, 727, 732 **Vol. 3:** 188, 387, 482, 717
16:21	**Vol. 1:** 167 **Vol. 2:** 327, 665, 893 **Vol. 3:** 39, 276, 294, 480, 569, 723
16:22 ff	**Vol. 1:** 489
16:22 f	**Vol. 3:** 455, 804
16:22	**Vol. 2:** 708 **Vol. 3:** 160, 751
16:23	**Vol. 1:** 111, 493 **Vol. 2:** 618, 708 **Vol. 3:** 384, 470, 807
16:24 f	**Vol. 1:** 489 **Vol. 3:** 1022
16:24	**Vol. 1:** 324, 394, 402, 455, 464, 493, 718
16:25 f	**Vol. 3:** 174
16:25	**Vol. 1:** 489, 718 **Vol. 2:** 433 **Vol. 3:** 212, 530, 682
16:26	**Vol. 3:** 136–137, 167, 174
16:27	**Vol. 1:** 102, 323, 327 **Vol. 2:** 46, 369 **Vol. 3:** 136, 1158, 1200
16:28	**Vol. 1:** 323 **Vol. 2:** 271, 382, 386–387 **Vol. 3:** 627, 863
17:1–8	**Vol. 2:** 48 **Vol. 3:** 114, 330
17:1 f	**Vol. 3:** 604
17:1	**Vol. 2:** 199, 686 **Vol. 3:** 384, 751, 862–863, 1010, 1012
17:2–5	**Vol. 2:** 47
17:2	**Vol. 1:** 204, 587, 704, 706, 708 **Vol. 2:** 486, 493 **Vol. 3:** 731, 861–862
17:3	**Vol. 2:** 559
17:4	**Vol. 2:** 514 **Vol. 3:** 384
17:5 ff	**Vol. 3:** 132
17:5	**Vol. 2:** 176, 493, 543, 725, 819 **Vol. 3:** 114, 555, 611, 864, 1003
17:6	**Vol. 1:** 290, 586, 610
17:7	**Vol. 1:** 623
17:8	**Vol. 2:** 724
17:9	**Vol. 1:** 335 **Vol. 3:** 276, 294, 515, 862, 1012
17:10–13	**Vol. 2:** 443
17:10	**Vol. 1:** 323, 544 **Vol. 3:** 480
17:11	**Vol. 3:** 80, 147, 480
17:12 f	**Vol. 3:** 658
17:12	**Vol. 1:** 326 **Vol. 2:** 399 **Vol. 3:** 723
17:13	**Vol. 3:** 82
17:14 ff	**Vol. 3:** 475
17:14	**Vol. 2:** 860
17:15	**Vol. 1:** 609 **Vol. 2:** 595, 600 **Vol. 3:** 475, 734, 990
17:16 ff	**Vol. 2:** 165
17:16	**Vol. 2:** 165
17:17	**Vol. 2:** 36, 766 **Vol. 3:** 1204
17:18	**Vol. 1:** 718 **Vol. 2:** 165 **Vol. 3:** 846–848
17:19	**Vol. 1:** 453
17:20	**Vol. 1:** 504, 600 **Vol. 3:** 1012
17:21	**Vol. 1:** 613
17:22	**Vol. 1:** 326 **Vol. 2:** 150, 368 **Vol. 3:** 984
17:23	**Vol. 1:** 162 **Vol. 3:** 276, 294, 1122
17:24 ff	**Vol. 1:** 525
17:24–27	**Vol. 2:** 630, 851 **Vol. 3:** 753, 792, 985
17:24	**Vol. 2:** 62 **Vol. 3:** 384, 767, 853, 1179
17:25	**Vol. 1:** 684 **Vol. 2:** 62, 378, 742 **Vol. 3:** 822
17:26	**Vol. 1:** 717
17:27	**Vol. 1:** 666, 671 **Vol. 2:** 708, 728, 851 **Vol. 3:** 1179–1180
18	**Vol. 2:** 770–771 **Vol. 3:** 1109
18:1 ff	**Vol. 1:** 489
18:1–25	**Vol. 3:** 1071
18:1–6	**Vol. 2:** 429 **Vol. 3:** 1052
18:1–5	**Vol. 2:** 262, 427
18:1	**Vol. 3:** 847
18:2	**Vol. 1:** 274
18:3 f	**Vol. 1:** 285

143

Matthew *(cont'd)*

18:3	**Vol. 1:** 284, 321, 355, 358 **Vol. 2:** 385 **Vol. 3:** 746
18:4	**Vol. 2:** 262, 427
18:5	**Vol. 2:** 176, 772 **Vol. 3:** 746
18:6	**Vol. 1:** 241, 489 **Vol. 2:** 708–709 **Vol. 3:** 1212
18:7	**Vol. 2:** 664, 708 **Vol. 3:** 1052, 1180
18:7b	**Vol. 2:** 709
18:8 f	**Vol. 1:** 657 **Vol. 2:** 385, 710 **Vol. 3:** 941
18:8	**Vol. 1:** 239 **Vol. 2:** 149, 414–415 **Vol. 3:** 99, 394, 830, 832
18:10	**Vol. 1:** 102, 358, 462, 586 **Vol. 2:** 192, 194, 429 **Vol. 3:** 518, 1052
18:11	**Vol. 3:** 628
18:12 ff	**Vol. 3:** 566
18:12–14	**Vol. 3:** 567–568
18:12 f	**Vol. 2:** 459
18:12	**Vol. 2:** 459–460 **Vol. 3:** 822
18:13	**Vol. 3:** 530
18:14	**Vol. 1:** 358 **Vol. 2:** 429, 818 **Vol. 3:** 1175
18:15 ff	**Vol. 1:** 535 **Vol. 2:** 142, 897
18:15–20	**Vol. 1:** 466 **Vol. 2:** 769, 898
18:15	**Vol. 2:** 724 **Vol. 3:** 138, 579
18:16	**Vol. 1:** 302 **Vol. 2:** 686 **Vol. 3:** 1043, 1122
18:17	**Vol. 1:** 297–298, 302–303 **Vol. 2:** 175, 731, 795 **Vol. 3:** 757–758
18:18	**Vol. 1:** 171, 702–703 **Vol. 2:** 481, 733, 897 **Vol. 3:** 188, 387, 482, 717
18:19	**Vol. 2:** 192, 194, 857–858, 869, 897 **Vol. 3:** 1158
18:20	**Vol. 1:** 90, 285 **Vol. 2:** 32, 895, 897–898, 901
18:21 f	**Vol. 2:** 513 **Vol. 3:** 657
18:21–35	**Vol. 2:** 769, 898
18:21–34	**Vol. 2:** 118
18:21	**Vol. 1:** 701 **Vol. 2:** 691 **Vol. 3:** 384
18:23 ff	**Vol. 3:** 135
18:23–35	**Vol. 2:** 301, 596, 600, 667, 749–750 **Vol. 3:** 173, 758
18:23	**Vol. 2:** 502, 667
18:24	**Vol. 2:** 770
18:25	**Vol. 1:** 268, 286, 341 **Vol. 2:** 513, 846
18:26	**Vol. 1:** 609 **Vol. 2:** 769–770, 772, 877
18:27	**Vol. 1:** 505, 700 **Vol. 2:** 513, 596, 600 **Vol. 3:** 189, 595
18:28	**Vol. 1:** 226 **Vol. 2:** 667 **Vol. 3:** 717
18:29	**Vol. 1:** 570, 609 **Vol. 2:** 769–770
18:30	**Vol. 2:** 136
18:32–35	**Vol. 1:** 702
18:32	**Vol. 1:** 565, 700
18:33 f	**Vol. 2:** 597
18:33	**Vol. 2:** 595–596, 667
18:34	**Vol. 1:** 111 **Vol. 2:** 600, 770 **Vol. 3:** 595, 856
18:35	**Vol. 2:** 192, 596, 770
19:1–12	**Vol. 3:** 538
19:1–9	**Vol. 3:** 980
19:1	**Vol. 2:** 63 **Vol. 3:** 456, 540, 991
19:2	**Vol. 2:** 165
19:3–12	**Vol. 3:** 172
19:3–9	**Vol. 2:** 580 **Vol. 3:** 188, 534
19:3	**Vol. 1:** 506 **Vol. 2:** 138, 563, 580 **Vol. 3:** 189, 534, 539
19:4 f	**Vol. 2:** 579 **Vol. 3:** 329
19:4	**Vol. 1:** 166, 384 **Vol. 2:** 563, 570 **Vol. 3:** 329
19:5 ff	**Vol. 3:** 539
19:5 f	**Vol. 2:** 580 **Vol. 3:** 1175
19:5	**Vol. 2:** 349, 565, 570, 722 **Vol. 3:** 251, 1070
19:5b	**Vol. 1:** 678
19:6–9	**Vol. 2:** 581
19:6	**Vol. 1:** 678 **Vol. 2:** 570 **Vol. 3:** 534–535, 542, 1164
19:7 ff	**Vol. 3:** 189
19:7–9	**Vol. 1:** 506
19:7	**Vol. 1:** 244, 335, 506, 606
19:8	**Vol. 1:** 166 **Vol. 2:** 156 **Vol. 3:** 538, 763, 1204
19:9–12	**Vol. 2:** 580
19:9	**Vol. 1:** 500, 506, 742 **Vol. 2:** 563, 580, 583 **Vol. 3:** 183, 535, 538, 540, 542, 1171, 1195
19:10 ff	**Vol. 3:** 541
19:10	**Vol. 1:** 742 **Vol. 2:** 139 **Vol. 3:** 541–542
19:11 f	**Vol. 1:** 742
19:11	**Vol. 3:** 541–542
19:12	**Vol. 1:** 178, 560, 742 **Vol. 2:** 385, 580–581, 710 **Vol. 3:** 541–542, 1071
19:13 ff	**Vol. 1:** 283–284 **Vol. 3:** 861
19:13	**Vol. 2:** 151
19:14	**Vol. 1:** 284 **Vol. 2:** 222
19:15	**Vol. 1:** 284 **Vol. 2:** 151, 578
19:16–30	**Vol. 1:** 335 **Vol. 2:** 301
19:16–22	**Vol. 2:** 825, 844
19:16–20	**Vol. 3:** 1163
19:16	**Vol. 2:** 480–481 **Vol. 3:** 832
19:17	**Vol. 1:** 336 **Vol. 2:** 100, 133, 879 **Vol. 3:** 1022
19:18 f	**Vol. 2:** 583
19:18	**Vol. 3:** 377, 379, 755
19:20	**Vol. 2:** 135 **Vol. 3:** 954
19:21	**Vol. 1:** 482, 495 **Vol. 2:** 63, 65, 720, 824, 833, 845–846 **Vol. 3:** 141, 1022
19:22	**Vol. 2:** 845–846
19:23 ff	**Vol. 1:** 489
19:23–30	**Vol. 2:** 750
19:23 f	**Vol. 2:** 385, 842–843
19:23	**Vol. 2:** 845
19:24†	**Vol. 1:** 116, 730 **Vol. 2:** 381, 843
19:25	**Vol. 1:** 730 **Vol. 2:** 623, 843
19:26	**Vol. 1:** 730 **Vol. 2:** 603, 606, 843 **Vol. 3:** 213, 519, 1121
19:27	**Vol. 2:** 840 **Vol. 3:** 384, 920

Matthew (cont'd)

19:28†	**Vol. 1:** 99, 153, 179, 185–186, 482 **Vol. 2:** 48, 313, 365, 385, 387, 613–614, 695, 786 **Vol. 3:** 180, 454, 588, 629, 871, 920, 1177
19:29	**Vol. 2:** 250, 300–301 **Vol. 3:** 142, 832, 920
19:30	**Vol. 1:** 666 **Vol. 2:** 57
20	**Vol. 3:** 572
20:1–16	**Vol. 2:** 118, 749, 751 **Vol. 3:** 141, 920
20:1–15	**Vol. 2:** 386
20:1–6	**Vol. 3:** 1150
20:1	**Vol. 2:** 315, 502, 510 **Vol. 3:** 1150
20:2 ff	**Vol. 2:** 770
20:2–13	**Vol. 2:** 711
20:2	**Vol. 2:** 851 **Vol. 3:** 1150
20:3	**Vol. 1:** 267 **Vol. 2:** 739 **Vol. 3:** 847
20:4	**Vol. 3:** 360
20:5 f	**Vol. 3:** 847
20:5	**Vol. 3:** 847
20:6	**Vol. 2:** 739 **Vol. 3:** 847
20:8 ff	**Vol. 1:** 666
20:8	**Vol. 1:** 274 **Vol. 3:** 135, 1150
20:9	**Vol. 3:** 847
20:11 ff	**Vol. 3:** 1155
20:11	**Vol. 2:** 510
20:12	**Vol. 1:** 261 **Vol. 2:** 499 **Vol. 3:** 141, 847
20:13–16	**Vol. 3:** 920
20:13–15	**Vol. 3:** 360
20:13	**Vol. 1:** 260 **Vol. 3:** 575
20:14	**Vol. 2:** 846
20:15	**Vol. 3:** 141, 516
20:16	**Vol. 1:** 540, 667 **Vol. 2:** 57, 566
20:17	**Vol. 2:** 695 **Vol. 3:** 751
20:18	**Vol. 2:** 365, 368 **Vol. 3:** 39
20:19	**Vol. 1:** 162, 394 **Vol. 2:** 368 **Vol. 3:** 276, 340
20:20	**Vol. 2:** 276 **Vol. 3:** 1071
20:21	**Vol. 2:** 148, 386, 388 **Vol. 3:** 1019
20:22	**Vol. 1:** 326 **Vol. 2:** 276
20:23	**Vol. 2:** 148 **Vol. 3:** 118, 1178
20:25–28	**Vol. 3:** 979
20:25	**Vol. 1:** 168 **Vol. 2:** 519, 793
20:26	**Vol. 1:** 285 **Vol. 2:** 427 **Vol. 3:** 546–547
20:27 f	**Vol. 1:** 667
20:27	**Vol. 3:** 596, 598
20:28–32	**Vol. 3:** 920
20:28	**Vol. 1:** 96–97, 322, 369 **Vol. 2:** 262 **Vol. 3:** 195, 197, 420, 429, 546–547, 611, 682–683, 1180
20:29–34	**Vol. 1:** 49 **Vol. 2:** 754
20:30	**Vol. 3:** 652, 658, 939
20:31 f	**Vol. 3:** 920
20:32	**Vol. 3:** 1022
20:33	**Vol. 2:** 726, 728
20:34	**Vol. 2:** 599, 631
21:1–9	**Vol. 2:** 379, 754 **Vol. 3:** 791

21:1	**Vol. 2:** 54, 315, 686, 713
21:2	**Vol. 1:** 116–117 **Vol. 3:** 179
21:3	**Vol. 2:** 488
21:4	**Vol. 1:** 736 **Vol. 3:** 489
21:5	**Vol. 2:** 258, 327
21:6	**Vol. 1:** 477
21:7	**Vol. 1:** 117
21:9	**Vol. 1:** 100, 281, 323, 482 **Vol. 3:** 652
21:10–17	**Vol. 1:** 281 **Vol. 3:** 429, 791
21:10	**Vol. 2:** 803 **Vol. 3:** 557
21:11	**Vol. 2:** 333 **Vol. 3:** 83
21:12–17	**Vol. 3:** 1168
21:12 f	**Vol. 2:** 379, 610, 754 **Vol. 3:** 39
21:12	**Vol. 1:** 111, 175
21:13 f	**Vol. 2:** 584
21:13	**Vol. 2:** 248 **Vol. 3:** 329, 378, 380, 430, 788
21:14	**Vol. 1:** 219 **Vol. 2:** 415 **Vol. 3:** 792
21:15 f	**Vol. 1:** 284, 724 **Vol. 3:** 792
21:15	**Vol. 1:** 281, 427 **Vol. 2:** 623 **Vol. 3:** 480–481, 652
21:16	**Vol. 1:** 281 **Vol. 3:** 329, 350, 817
21:17	**Vol. 2:** 528
21:18 f	**Vol. 2:** 267, 630, 750, 754 **Vol. 3:** 793, 868–869
21:18–22	**Vol. 1:** 724
21:19	**Vol. 1:** 181, 515, 722 **Vol. 2:** 488 **Vol. 3:** 528, 829–830
21:20	**Vol. 1:** 515
21:21	**Vol. 1:** 504 **Vol. 2:** 724, 871 **Vol. 3:** 984
21:22	**Vol. 2:** 856–857
21:23–24:1	**Vol. 2:** 236
21:23–27	**Vol. 3:** 792, 1154
21:23	**Vol. 1:** 174, 199 **Vol. 2:** 799 **Vol. 3:** 481, 761, 791, 869
21:24	**Vol. 2:** 879 **Vol. 3:** 1106
21:25	**Vol. 1:** 599 **Vol. 2:** 182, 434
21:26	**Vol. 2:** 801
21:28–32	**Vol. 1:** 356 **Vol. 2:** 751 **Vol. 3:** 869
21:28	**Vol. 1:** 286 **Vol. 2:** 686 **Vol. 3:** 822, 1150
21:29 ff	**Vol. 2:** 514
21:29	**Vol. 1:** 356 **Vol. 3:** 954
21:31 f	**Vol. 1:** 499 **Vol. 3:** 1062
21:31	**Vol. 2:** 381 **Vol. 3:** 757, 953, 1022, 1155
21:32	**Vol. 1:** 339, 356, 599 **Vol. 3:** 360, 517, 758, 940, 954
21:33–46	**Vol. 2:** 746, 751 **Vol. 3:** 641, 869, 920
21:33–41	**Vol. 2:** 301
21:33 f	**Vol. 3:** 868
21:33	**Vol. 2:** 510, 790 **Vol. 3:** 951
21:34	**Vol. 1:** 722 **Vol. 3:** 837
21:35 ff	**Vol. 3:** 748
21:35 f	**Vol. 1:** 547
21:35	**Vol. 1:** 163
21:37 f	**Vol. 1:** 290
21:37	**Vol. 2:** 720 **Vol. 3:** 954
21:38	**Vol. 2:** 182, 543

Matthew *(cont'd)*

21:41 ff	**Vol. 1:** 723
21:41	**Vol. 1:** 564 **Vol. 3:** 920
21:42	**Vol. 2:** 129, 159, 253, 313, 622–623, 706 **Vol. 3:** 329, 389–390, 490, 492, 809, 1175
21:43	**Vol. 2:** 381, 385
21:45 f	**Vol. 3:** 39
21:46	**Vol. 2:** 801 **Vol. 3:** 83
22:1 ff	**Vol. 2:** 339
22:1–14	**Vol. 1:** 324 **Vol. 2:** 580, 727, 750–751 **Vol. 3:** 869, 922
22:1–13	**Vol. 3:** 253
22:1–10	**Vol. 2:** 386, 388, 578
22:1	**Vol. 2:** 748
22:2–10	**Vol. 1:** 274 **Vol. 2:** 747
22:2 f	**Vol. 2:** 358
22:2	**Vol. 2:** 502
22:4	**Vol. 1:** 116 **Vol. 3:** 118
22:6	**Vol. 3:** 28, 252, 717
22:7	**Vol. 1:** 111, 464 **Vol. 3:** 964
22:8	**Vol. 3:** 118, 349
22:9	**Vol. 3:** 528–529, 940
22:10	**Vol. 1:** 566 **Vol. 2:** 32, 100
22:11 ff	**Vol. 1:** 317
22:11 f	**Vol. 1:** 316 **Vol. 2:** 579
22:11	**Vol. 3:** 516
22:12 ff	**Vol. 2:** 236
22:12	**Vol. 1:** 260
22:13 f	**Vol. 1:** 171, 566
22:13	**Vol. 1:** 425 **Vol. 2:** 149, 421 **Vol. 3:** 546
22:14	**Vol. 1:** 96–97, 274, 540
22:15 ff	**Vol. 3:** 378
22:15–40	**Vol. 3:** 657
22:15–22	**Vol. 3:** 549, 754, 1168
22:15	**Vol. 1:** 363 **Vol. 3:** 884, 1108
22:16	**Vol. 1:** 304, 487 **Vol. 2:** 343 **Vol. 3:** 441–442, 940
22:17	**Vol. 3:** 754, 822
22:18	**Vol. 2:** 469
22:19	**Vol. 3:** 754
22:20	**Vol. 2:** 288 **Vol. 3:** 489
22:21	**Vol. 2:** 79
22:22–33	**Vol. 2:** 578
22:22	**Vol. 2:** 624
22:23–40	**Vol. 2:** 516
22:23–33	**Vol. 2:** 580 **Vol. 3:** 263, 792
22:23–32	**Vol. 3:** 439
22:23	**Vol. 1:** 174 **Vol. 3:** 277, 439
22:24–40	**Vol. 3:** 455
22:24	**Vol. 3:** 275, 1074
22:25	**Vol. 1:** 430, 666
22:27	**Vol. 3:** 252, 954
22:28	**Vol. 3:** 277
22:29	**Vol. 2:** 459–460 **Vol. 3:** 305, 490, 492
22:30 f	**Vol. 1:** 290
22:30	**Vol. 1:** 103 **Vol. 2:** 578, 581 **Vol. 3:** 278
22:31 f	**Vol. 2:** 481 **Vol. 3:** 263, 277
22:31	**Vol. 3:** 329, 489
22:32	**Vol. 1:** 78, 81, 445 **Vol. 2:** 73, 319, 480, 578
22:33	**Vol. 2:** 623 **Vol. 3:** 769
22:34–40	**Vol. 1:** 334 **Vol. 2:** 543, 813, 870 **Vol. 3:** 173, 791
22:34–39	**Vol. 2:** 443
22:34	**Vol. 2:** 32 **Vol. 3:** 439, 1194
22:35	**Vol. 3:** 480, 657, 804
22:36 ff	**Vol. 2:** 544 **Vol. 3:** 1155
22:36	**Vol. 1:** 334 **Vol. 2:** 426 **Vol. 3:** 127
22:37 ff	**Vol. 1:** 259
22:37–40	**Vol. 2:** 42
22:37 f	**Vol. 3:** 542
22:37	**Vol. 2:** 73, 147 **Vol. 3:** 685, 763
22:38	**Vol. 1:** 334 **Vol. 2:** 426
22:39 f	**Vol. 1:** 335
22:39	**Vol. 1:** 738 **Vol. 2:** 177, 503 **Vol. 3:** 378, 1064
22:40	**Vol. 2:** 174, 177 **Vol. 3:** 183, 185
22:41–46	**Vol. 2:** 147, 515 **Vol. 3:** 651
22:41–45	**Vol. 1:** 427
22:41	**Vol. 2:** 32 **Vol. 3:** 481
22:42–44	**Vol. 3:** 653
22:42	**Vol. 3:** 652, 658, 822
22:43 f	**Vol. 1:** 177
22:43	**Vol. 3:** 671
22:44	**Vol. 1:** 239, 554 **Vol. 2:** 515 **Vol. 3:** 1178
22:45	**Vol. 3:** 652, 658
22:46	**Vol. 1:** 365 **Vol. 2:** 880
23	**Vol. 1:** 111 **Vol. 2:** 327, 434 **Vol. 3:** 253, 480–481, 657, 1109, 1162
23:1 ff	**Vol. 2:** 261
23:1–25:46	**Vol. 2:** 469
23:1–39	**Vol. 2:** 715 **Vol. 3:** 183
23:1–36	**Vol. 2:** 813 **Vol. 3:** 580
23:1	**Vol. 1:** 174 **Vol. 2:** 799
23:2 f	**Vol. 2:** 640
23:2	**Vol. 1:** 297 **Vol. 2:** 640 **Vol. 3:** 87, 184, 482, 589, 883
23:3	**Vol. 2:** 133 **Vol. 3:** 184, 883, 1149
23:4 ff	**Vol. 3:** 184
23:4	**Vol. 1:** 261, 335 **Vol. 2:** 150 **Vol. 3:** 883, 1162
23:5	**Vol. 1:** 254 **Vol. 2:** 136, 864 **Vol. 3:** 559, 1149–1150
23:6 f	**Vol. 3:** 481
23:6	**Vol. 1:** 666 **Vol. 2:** 548 **Vol. 3:** 785
23:7 ff	**Vol. 1:** 489
23:7–12	**Vol. 3:** 1152
23:7 f	**Vol. 1:** 273
23:7	**Vol. 3:** 115
23:8 ff	**Vol. 2:** 721–722
23:8–12	**Vol. 3:** 482
23:8–10	**Vol. 2:** 84
23:8	**Vol. 3:** 115, 767–768
23:9	**Vol. 1:** 274, 619 **Vol. 2:** 73, 192

Matthew (*cont'd*)

23:11	**Vol. 1:** 285 **Vol. 2:** 427 **Vol. 3:** 546–547, 1152
23:12	**Vol. 1:** 285 **Vol. 2:** 202, 262
23:13 ff	**Vol. 2:** 470, 640, 691 **Vol. 3:** 1052
23:13–36	**Vol. 3:** 482
23:13–16	**Vol. 2:** 443
23:13	**Vol. 2:** 222, 311, 385, 462, 730, 732, 813 **Vol. 3:** 253, 387, 1052
23:15	**Vol. 1:** 289, 361, 516, 688 **Vol. 2:** 208, 720, 732, 792, 813 **Vol. 3:** 360, 480, 984, 1052
23:16 ff	**Vol. 2:** 470 **Vol. 3:** 785
23:16–22	**Vol. 3:** 183, 741, 792, 1052
23:16 f	**Vol. 1:** 220 **Vol. 3:** 429
23:16	**Vol. 3:** 942
23:17	**Vol. 2:** 228–229 **Vol. 3:** 1025
23:18 ff	**Vol. 3:** 435–436
23:18 f	**Vol. 2:** 41
23:18–22	**Vol. 3:** 429
23:19	**Vol. 1:** 220 **Vol. 2:** 228–229
23:22	**Vol. 2:** 74 **Vol. 3:** 588
23:23 f	**Vol. 1:** 116 **Vol. 3:** 1053
23:23	**Vol. 1:** 261 **Vol. 2:** 211, 365, 443, 596, 694, 813 **Vol. 3:** 883
23:24	**Vol. 1:** 116 **Vol. 3:** 883, 942
23:25 f	**Vol. 3:** 106, 990, 1053
23:25	**Vol. 1:** 495, 743 **Vol. 2:** 443, 532, 813 **Vol. 3:** 604
23:26	**Vol. 1:** 220 **Vol. 2:** 813
23:27 ff	**Vol. 2:** 813
23:27 f	**Vol. 2:** 488 **Vol. 3:** 360, 1053
23:27	**Vol. 1:** 205, 241, 265 **Vol. 2:** 443, 501–502 **Vol. 3:** 197
23:28 f	**Vol. 3:** 360
23:29–36	**Vol. 1:** 174
23:29–33	**Vol. 3:** 1053
23:29–31	**Vol. 1:** 265
23:29	**Vol. 2:** 443 **Vol. 3:** 247, 360
23:30	**Vol. 1:** 222, 643
23:31 f	**Vol. 3:** 83
23:31	**Vol. 1:** 288 **Vol. 3:** 82, 1043
23:32	**Vol. 1:** 740 **Vol. 3:** 403, 1053
23:33	**Vol. 1:** 509, 559 **Vol. 2:** 208 **Vol. 3:** 854
23:34 ff	**Vol. 3:** 1030
23:34–36	**Vol. 3:** 83
23:34	**Vol. 1:** 163, 174, 395 **Vol. 2:** 352, 714 **Vol. 3:** 184, 482, 785
23:35 ff	**Vol. 1:** 75
23:35	**Vol. 1:** 163, 221–222 **Vol. 2:** 525, 854 **Vol. 3:** 82, 360, 430, 435–436, 789
23:37 ff	**Vol. 1:** 174 **Vol. 2:** 328 **Vol. 3:** 229
23:37–39	**Vol. 2:** 37 **Vol. 3:** 83, 1052
23:37 f	**Vol. 3:** 1008
23:37	**Vol. 1:** 174, 286, 430 **Vol. 2:** 33, 328, 754, 803 **Vol. 3:** 82
23:38	**Vol. 2:** 328 **Vol. 3:** 1008
23:39	**Vol. 1:** 174, 213 **Vol. 2:** 328, 653
24 f	**Vol. 3:** 831, 844
24	**Vol. 1:** 125 **Vol. 2:** 904, 911 **Vol. 3:** 560, 984, 1109
24:1–3	**Vol. 2:** 713 **Vol. 3:** 1011
24:1	**Vol. 1:** 174 **Vol. 2:** 236 **Vol. 3:** 791–792
24:2 ff	**Vol. 2:** 803
24:2	**Vol. 2:** 450 **Vol. 3:** 185, 189, 1177, 1184
24:3	**Vol. 2:** 37, 62, 629, 900 **Vol. 3:** 658, 831
24:4 ff	**Vol. 2:** 460
24:4 f	**Vol. 2:** 459, 461, 808
24:4–36	**Vol. 2:** 702
24:4–35	**Vol. 2:** 915
24:5	**Vol. 2:** 281
24:6	**Vol. 1:** 326 **Vol. 2:** 62–63, 665, 808, 918 **Vol. 3:** 962
24:7	**Vol. 2:** 266, 793 **Vol. 3:** 280, 558
24:8	**Vol. 2:** 244, 808 **Vol. 3:** 858
24:9–12	**Vol. 1:** 608
24:9	**Vol. 1:** 430 **Vol. 2:** 368, 654, 773, 793, 808
24:10 ff	**Vol. 2:** 773
24:10	**Vol. 1:** 556 **Vol. 2:** 708–709
24:11	**Vol. 2:** 459, 461, 472, 808 **Vol. 3:** 280
24:12	**Vol. 1:** 96, 318, 733 **Vol. 2:** 447, 911 **Vol. 3:** 56
24:13	**Vol. 2:** 62, 773
24:14	**Vol. 1:** 519 **Vol. 2:** 62, 110, 112, 665 **Vol. 3:** 52, 56
24:15–22	**Vol. 3:** 793
24:15	**Vol. 1:** 74 **Vol. 2:** 228 **Vol. 3:** 128, 489, 792, 1008
24:16	**Vol. 1:** 559 **Vol. 3:** 1011
24:17	**Vol. 2:** 845
24:19	**Vol. 3:** 1053
24:20	**Vol. 1:** 559 **Vol. 3:** 410, 698
24:21 f	**Vol. 3:** 803
24:21	**Vol. 2:** 426, 808, 916
24:22	**Vol. 1:** 678 **Vol. 2:** 916
24:23–27	**Vol. 1:** 175
24:24	**Vol. 1:** 323 **Vol. 2:** 426, 459, 461, 472, 629, 633, 808 **Vol. 3:** 84, 280
24:26	**Vol. 3:** 1007
24:27	**Vol. 1:** 610 **Vol. 2:** 488, 900–901 **Vol. 3:** 620, 1001
24:28	**Vol. 1:** 175, 610 **Vol. 2:** 32, 695, 746, 757
24:29 ff	**Vol. 2:** 916
24:29	**Vol. 1:** 203, 425, 610 **Vol. 2:** 37, 192, 484 **Vol. 3:** 559, 732, 734, 736
24:30 f	**Vol. 2:** 900
24:30	**Vol. 1:** 323, 518 **Vol. 2:** 46, 48, 194, 488, 604, 630, 808, 917 **Vol. 3:** 633–634, 1003
24:31	**Vol. 1:** 517, 686, 725 **Vol. 2:** 33, 194, 364, 426, 689, 911, 917 **Vol. 3:** 674, 874

Matthew *(cont'd)*

24:32–36   **Vol. 2:** 751
24:32 f   **Vol. 1:** 725   **Vol. 2:** 382
24:32   **Vol. 2:** 54, 604   **Vol. 3:** 867
24:33   **Vol. 2:** 30
24:34   **Vol. 1:** 99   **Vol. 2:** 36, 38, 271,
    911–912, 916
24:35   **Vol. 1:** 322, 518   **Vol. 2:** 192–193
24:36 ff   **Vol. 1:** 725
24:36–25:46 **Vol. 2:** 915
24:36   **Vol. 1:** 323   **Vol. 2:** 192, 901,
    916   **Vol. 3:** 847–848
24:37 ff   **Vol. 2:** 382   **Vol. 3:** 833
24:37–44   **Vol. 2:** 751   **Vol. 3:** 628
24:37–39   **Vol. 2:** 682   **Vol. 3:** 618
24:37 f   **Vol. 2:** 901
24:37   **Vol. 2:** 900   **Vol. 3:** 620
24:38 ff   **Vol. 2:** 275
24:38 f   **Vol. 3:** 991
24:38   **Vol. 2:** 272, 580–581   **Vol. 3:** 278
24:39   **Vol. 2:** 900–901   **Vol. 3:** 604
24:40 ff   **Vol. 2:** 364
24:40–41   **Vol. 2:** 686, 720   **Vol. 3:** 604
24:40   **Vol. 3:** 751, 1058
24:41   **Vol. 3:** 394
24:42–25:13 **Vol. 2:** 749
24:42 f   **Vol. 1:** 323
24:42   **Vol. 2:** 137, 894
24:43 f   **Vol. 2:** 382   **Vol. 3:** 618
24:43   **Vol. 2:** 136, 400, 433, 509–510, 831,
    926   **Vol. 3:** 202, 378
24:44   **Vol. 1:** 323   **Vol. 3:** 118, 604, 822, 848
24:45 ff   **Vol. 2:** 254, 382
24:45–51   **Vol. 2:** 751
24:45   **Vol. 1:** 472   **Vol. 2:** 619   **Vol. 3:** 595,
    837
24:46   **Vol. 1:** 217   **Vol. 3:** 529–530
24:48 ff   **Vol. 2:** 275
24:48   **Vol. 1:** 564   **Vol. 3:** 843
24:49   **Vol. 1:** 513–514   **Vol. 3:** 903
24:50   **Vol. 2:** 245   **Vol. 3:** 847–848
24:51   **Vol. 2:** 304, 421
25   **Vol. 2:** 912
25:1 ff   **Vol. 2:** 619
25:1–46   **Vol. 2:** 917
25:1–13   **Vol. 2:** 382, 581, 585, 751   **Vol. 3:** 529,
    1025
25:1–12   **Vol. 3:** 253, 1072
25:1–3   **Vol. 3:** 1059
25:1   **Vol. 1:** 325   **Vol. 2:** 486, 502,
    585   **Vol. 3:** 1072
25:2 f   **Vol. 2:** 620
25:3 ff   **Vol. 2:** 711
25:3 f   **Vol. 2:** 486
25:3–7   **Vol. 3:** 481
25:5   **Vol. 3:** 843, 1072
25:6   **Vol. 2:** 578, 585
25:7 f   **Vol. 2:** 486
25:7   **Vol. 1:** 524   **Vol. 2:** 578   **Vol. 3:** 280

25:8   **Vol. 2:** 620   **Vol. 3:** 109
25:9   **Vol. 2:** 711   **Vol. 3:** 727
25:10   **Vol. 2:** 30–31, 730   **Vol. 3:** 118
25:11   **Vol. 2:** 513, 728   **Vol. 3:** 252–253, 954,
    1072
25:13 ff   **Vol. 2:** 751
25:13   **Vol. 1:** 323   **Vol. 2:** 137, 894   **Vol. 3:**
    847–848
25:14 ff   **Vol. 2:** 255
25:14–40   **Vol. 2:** 751
25:14–30   **Vol. 2:** 749, 751, 838   **Vol. 3:** 529
25:14 f   **Vol. 2:** 499, 916
25:14   **Vol. 2:** 746, 790, 845
25:15   **Vol. 2:** 790, 839   **Vol. 3:** 1019
25:16 ff   **Vol. 3:** 137–138
25:18   **Vol. 2:** 216
25:19   **Vol. 2:** 513   **Vol. 3:** 843
25:20 ff   **Vol. 2:** 513
25:20   **Vol. 2:** 689
25:21 ff   **Vol. 2:** 255
25:21   **Vol. 2:** 100, 358, 428, 751   **Vol. 3:** 941,
    1193
25:23   **Vol. 2:** 358, 428   **Vol. 3:** 941
25:24   **Vol. 2:** 32, 34, 155   **Vol. 3:** 141, 526
25:25   **Vol. 2:** 216, 846
25:26   **Vol. 2:** 32, 34   **Vol. 3:** 526
25:27   **Vol. 2:** 846
25:30   **Vol. 1:** 425   **Vol. 2:** 421   **Vol. 3:** 595
25:31 ff   **Vol. 2:** 146, 339, 364, 481, 544, 614,
    894, 928
25:31–46   **Vol. 1:** 91, 299, 689   **Vol. 2:** 301, 369,
    751, 826   **Vol. 3:** 135, 277
25:31–45   **Vol. 2:** 101
25:31   **Vol. 1:** 102   **Vol. 2:** 339, 383,
    614   **Vol. 3:** 197, 589, 620, 629
25:32 f   **Vol. 2:** 413
25:32   **Vol. 1:** 115, 297, 473   **Vol. 2:**
    32   **Vol. 3:** 565, 567
25:33   **Vol. 2:** 148
25:34 ff   **Vol. 1:** 495
25:34–40   **Vol. 2:** 144
25:34   **Vol. 1:** 215, 378   **Vol. 2:** 300, 339, 382,
    385, 388, 894   **Vol. 3:** 118, 832
25:35–45   **Vol. 1:** 285
25:35 f   **Vol. 3:** 359, 547
25:35   **Vol. 2:** 32, 268, 766   **Vol. 3:** 989
25:36   **Vol. 1:** 190–191, 313
25:37   **Vol. 2:** 268, 275   **Vol. 3:** 360
25:38   **Vol. 1:** 313   **Vol. 2:** 32
25:40   **Vol. 1:** 99   **Vol. 2:** 104, 339, 429,
    597   **Vol. 3:** 142, 547, 1155
25:41   **Vol. 1:** 103, 417, 452, 657   **Vol. 2:** 148,
    208, 272, 276, 894   **Vol. 3:** 99, 118,
    469–471, 830, 832, 947
25:42   **Vol. 2:** 268, 275   **Vol. 3:** 989
25:43 f   **Vol. 1:** 313
25:43   **Vol. 1:** 190–191   **Vol. 2:** 32
25:44   **Vol. 3:** 546
25:45   **Vol. 2:** 429, 597   **Vol. 3:** 142, 1155

Matthew *(cont'd)*

25:46 **Vol. 2:** 208, 480–481 **Vol. 3:** 98–99, 303, 360, 830, 832
26 **Vol. 1:** 633
26:1 **Vol. 2:** 63
26:2 **Vol. 1:** 394, 633 **Vol. 2:** 368 **Vol. 3:** 627
26:3 **Vol. 1:** 199, 297 **Vol. 2:** 32 **Vol. 3:** 39, 480
26:4 **Vol. 1:** 363
26:5 **Vol. 2:** 623, 799
26:6 ff **Vol. 2:** 549
26:6–13 **Vol. 3:** 980, 1060
26:6 **Vol. 2:** 464, 528 **Vol. 3:** 1061
26:7 **Vol. 2:** 159, 295.
26:10 **Vol. 3:** 1149–1150
26:11 **Vol. 2:** 824
26:12 **Vol. 1:** 265 **Vol. 2:** 295
26:13 **Vol. 2:** 110, 112 **Vol. 3:** 52, 242, 244
26:14 **Vol. 1:** 299 **Vol. 2:** 695, 720
26:15 **Vol. 2:** 96, 851
26:16 **Vol. 3:** 532
26:17 ff **Vol. 2:** 527
26:17 **Vol. 1:** 633 **Vol. 2:** 277 **Vol. 3:** 118, 1019
26:18 **Vol. 1:** 633 **Vol. 3:** 837, 1204
26:19 **Vol. 1:** 633 **Vol. 3:** 118
26:20–25 **Vol. 2:** 531 **Vol. 3:** 804
26:20 **Vol. 2:** 528, 623, 695 **Vol. 3:** 954
26:22 **Vol. 1:** 167 **Vol. 2:** 720
26:24 **Vol. 3:** 329, 1053
26:25 **Vol. 1:** 299 **Vol. 3:** 115
26:26–29 **Vol. 1:** 237 **Vol. 2:** 523
26:26 f **Vol. 1:** 213 **Vol. 2:** 530
26:26 **Vol. 2:** 533
26:27 **Vol. 3:** 819, 857
26:27b **Vol. 2:** 533
26:28 **Vol. 1:** 96–97, 154, 223, 369, 438, 701–702 **Vol. 2:** 535, 543, 671, 854 **Vol. 3:** 166, 429, 580, 611, 1174
26:28b **Vol. 2:** 533
26:29 **Vol. 1:** 251 **Vol. 2:** 526, 581, 894, 896 **Vol. 3:** 922
26:30–35 **Vol. 3:** 386, 803
26:30† **Vol. 2:** 528 **Vol. 3:** 669
26:31 f **Vol. 3:** 567
26:31 **Vol. 1:** 163 **Vol. 2:** 34, 413, 459, 708 **Vol. 3:** 188, 329
26:33–75 **Vol. 3:** 384
26:33 **Vol. 2:** 708
26:34 **Vol. 1:** 173, 421 **Vol. 3:** 114
26:36 ff **Vol. 1:** 420
26:36–46 **Vol. 2:** 178, 561, 868
26:37 **Vol. 1:** 167 **Vol. 2:** 420, 686 **Vol. 3:** 751
26:38 **Vol. 2:** 420 **Vol. 3:** 224, 683
26:39–44 **Vol. 3:** 657
26:39 **Vol. 1:** 335, 609, 620 **Vol. 2:** 83, 276, 869, 871 **Vol. 3:** 1022

26:40 **Vol. 1:** 442 **Vol. 3:** 713, 847
26:41 **Vol. 2:** 137, 871 **Vol. 3:** 694, 994
26:42 **Vol. 1:** 620 **Vol. 2:** 222 **Vol. 3:** 1022
26:43 **Vol. 1:** 261
26:45 **Vol. 2:** 54, 150, 543 **Vol. 3:** 252, 256, 580
26:46 **Vol. 2:** 54
26:47 ff **Vol. 1:** 299
26:47 **Vol. 1:** 199, 390 **Vol. 3:** 967
26:48 f **Vol. 2:** 549
26:48 **Vol. 2:** 629 **Vol. 3:** 717
26:49 **Vol. 2:** 358 **Vol. 3:** 115
26:50 **Vol. 1:** 260
26:51 ff. **Vol. 2:** 630
26:51 f **Vol. 3:** 967
26:52 **Vol. 1:** 464 **Vol. 3:** 591
26:53–56 **Vol. 3:** 329
26:53 **Vol. 1:** 260, 570 **Vol. 3:** 822
26:54 **Vol. 2:** 666 **Vol. 3:** 188, 490, 492
26:55 **Vol. 2:** 895 **Vol. 3:** 379, 589, 761, 791, 846, 967, 1204
26:56 **Vol. 1:** 736 **Vol. 3:** 490, 492
26:57–75 **Vol. 2:** 379 **Vol. 3:** 386, 803
26:57–68 **Vol. 3:** 409
26:57 **Vol. 1:** 297 **Vol. 2:** 32 **Vol. 3:** 39, 481, 1204
26:58 **Vol. 2:** 62–63 **Vol. 3:** 547
26:59 **Vol. 1:** 364 **Vol. 2:** 472
26:60 **Vol. 2:** 472, 686
26:61 **Vol. 2:** 252, 450, 687, 732 **Vol. 3:** 185, 189, 343, 509, 784, 792
26:62 **Vol. 3:** 39, 275, 1042
26:63 f **Vol. 3:** 712, 742
26:63 **Vol. 1:** 290 **Vol. 2:** 480 **Vol. 3:** 473, 738
26:64 **Vol. 1:** 323 **Vol. 2:** 147, 194, 380, 515, 930 **Vol. 3:** 457, 1003
26:65 **Vol. 1:** 317 **Vol. 3:** 342, 1043
26:66 **Vol. 2:** 143 **Vol. 3:** 822
26:67 **Vol. 1:** 162–163
26:68 **Vol. 3:** 81, 83
26:69 **Vol. 2:** 333
26:70 **Vol. 1:** 455
26:71 **Vol. 2:** 30, 333
26:72 **Vol. 1:** 455
26:73 **Vol. 3:** 316
26:74 **Vol. 1:** 415, 455 **Vol. 2:** 565 **Vol. 3:** 114, 742
26:75 **Vol. 1:** 201 **Vol. 2:** 417 **Vol. 3:** 240, 1122
27 **Vol. 1:** 633 **Vol. 2:** 378
27:1 f **Vol. 1:** 394
27:1 **Vol. 1:** 199, 363
27:2 **Vol. 1:** 270 **Vol. 2:** 368, 379
27:3–10 **Vol. 1:** 93 **Vol. 3:** 804, 912, 1008
27:3 **Vol. 1:** 93, 299, 356 **Vol. 2:** 365
27:4 **Vol. 1:** 222 **Vol. 3:** 360
27:5 **Vol. 1:** 94 **Vol. 2:** 321 **Vol. 3:** 793
27:6 **Vol. 1:** 222 **Vol. 2:** 43
27:7 f **Vol. 1:** 520

149

Matthew *(cont'd)*

27:7   **Vol. 1:** 93, 363, 689   **Vol. 3:** 912
27:8   **Vol. 1:** 93, 222, 265
27:9   **Vol. 1:** 93, 736   **Vol. 2:** 49   **Vol. 3:** 489
27:10   **Vol. 1:** 520   **Vol. 3:** 912
27:11–61   **Vol. 1:** 394
27:11   **Vol. 1:** 270   **Vol. 2:** 315, 378
27:12   **Vol. 1:** 199
27:13   **Vol. 3:** 1042
27:14 f   **Vol. 1:** 270
27:14   **Vol. 2:** 624   **Vol. 3:** 1121
27:15–26   **Vol. 1:** 396   **Vol. 3:** 189
27:15 f   **Vol. 3:** 592
27:16 f   **Vol. 2:** 331
27:17   **Vol. 2:** 32, 339, 378
27:18   **Vol. 1:** 396
27:19   **Vol. 1:** 395   **Vol. 2:** 369   **Vol. 3:** 360–361, 723
27:20   **Vol. 1:** 199, 395, 463, 589   **Vol. 2:** 801, 856
27:21   **Vol. 1:** 270
27:23   **Vol. 1:** 409, 564
27:24 f   **Vol. 1:** 395
27:24   **Vol. 1:** 222   **Vol. 2:** 149–150, 623   **Vol. 3:** 360, 990
27:25 f   **Vol. 2:** 799
27:25   **Vol. 1:** 222, 286   **Vol. 2:** 158–159
27:26   **Vol. 1:** 162
27:27   **Vol. 1:** 270   **Vol. 2:** 32   **Vol. 3:** 964
27:28   **Vol. 1:** 314
27:29 f   **Vol. 2:** 159
27:29   **Vol. 1:** 406, 726   **Vol. 2:** 315, 358, 378, 859   **Vol. 3:** 340, 1188
27:30   **Vol. 3:** 903
27:31   **Vol. 1:** 314–316   **Vol. 3:** 340
27:32   **Vol. 2:** 740
27:34   **Vol. 2:** 27–28, 269   **Vol. 3:** 922
27:35   **Vol. 1:** 396   **Vol. 2:** 82, 299
27:36   **Vol. 2:** 133
27:37   **Vol. 2:** 139, 159, 315, 339, 379   **Vol. 3:** 509
27:38   **Vol. 2:** 148   **Vol. 3:** 379
27:39 ff.   **Vol. 2:** 630
27:39–44   **Vol. 3:** 347
27:39–43   **Vol. 1:** 397
27:39 f   **Vol. 3:** 211, 343
27:39   **Vol. 1:** 396   **Vol. 2:** 82, 159
27:40   **Vol. 1:** 290   **Vol. 2:** 687   **Vol. 3:** 185, 189, 509, 784, 792
27:41   **Vol. 1:** 199   **Vol. 3:** 340
27:42   **Vol. 1:** 323   **Vol. 2:** 315, 379   **Vol. 3:** 1212
27:43   **Vol. 1:** 290, 396, 592   **Vol. 2:** 82
27:44   **Vol. 3:** 340, 379
27:45   **Vol. 1:** 423   **Vol. 3:** 732, 847
27:46 ff   **Vol. 1:** 544
27:46   **Vol. 1:** 396, 411, 620   **Vol. 2:** 82   **Vol. 3:** 113, 253, 670
27:47   **Vol. 3:** 114

27:48   **Vol. 2:** 28   **Vol. 3:** 947
27:49   **Vol. 3:** 211, 253
27:50   **Vol. 1:** 409   **Vol. 2:** 426   **Vol. 3:** 113, 694
27:51–54   **Vol. 3:** 558
27:51   **Vol. 2:** 328   **Vol. 3:** 382, 543, 793, 795
27:52–54   **Vol. 3:** 558
27:52–53   **Vol. 1:** 266
27:52 f   **Vol. 2:** 328   **Vol. 3:** 247
27:52   **Vol. 1:** 234, 443   **Vol. 2:** 728
27:53   **Vol. 2:** 228, 327, 489, 803   **Vol. 3:** 280
27:54   **Vol. 1:** 290   **Vol. 3:** 557, 964
27:55 f   **Vol. 3:** 1059, 1070
27:55   **Vol. 3:** 516, 546
27:56   **Vol. 3:** 662, 1071
27:57   **Vol. 2:** 842–843   **Vol. 3:** 1053
27:58   **Vol. 1:** 234, 341   **Vol. 3:** 135
27:60   **Vol. 2:** 30, 670   **Vol. 3:** 247, 382, 393
27:62–66   **Vol. 3:** 283
27:62   **Vol. 2:** 32   **Vol. 3:** 120, 408, 410
27:63 f   **Vol. 3:** 499
27:63   **Vol. 2:** 459–460, 513, 687   **Vol. 3:** 281
27:64 ff   **Vol. 1:** 663
27:64   **Vol. 1:** 341, 445   **Vol. 2:** 459, 799   **Vol. 3:** 285, 378
27:65   **Vol. 2:** 136
27:66   **Vol. 3:** 499
28   **Vol. 3:** 518
28:1 ff   **Vol. 3:** 1059
28:1–20   **Vol. 3:** 294
28:1   **Vol. 2:** 518, 720   **Vol. 3:** 412, 1060
28:2 f   **Vol. 2:** 486, 493
28:2   **Vol. 1:** 102   **Vol. 2:** 193, 513   **Vol. 3:** 393, 517, 557
28:3   **Vol. 1:** 204   **Vol. 2:** 624   **Vol. 3:** 1001, 1004
28:4   **Vol. 1:** 446, 622   **Vol. 3:** 277, 283, 557
28:5   **Vol. 1:** 102, 623   **Vol. 2:** 624   **Vol. 3:** 517
28:7†   **Vol. 1:** 445, 504   **Vol. 3:** 515, 1174
28:8   **Vol. 2:** 358, 624, 721   **Vol. 3:** 48, 247, 276, 947
28:9   **Vol. 2:** 358, 877   **Vol. 3:** 717
28:10 f   **Vol. 3:** 48
28:10   **Vol. 1:** 623   **Vol. 2:** 721   **Vol. 3:** 48, 276
28:11–17   **Vol. 3:** 288
28:11–15   **Vol. 3:** 283
28:11   **Vol. 3:** 46
28:12   **Vol. 1:** 363   **Vol. 2:** 32   **Vol. 3:** 964
28:13   **Vol. 1:** 442   **Vol. 3:** 285, 291, 378
28:14   **Vol. 1:** 270, 590
28:15   **Vol. 2:** 315   **Vol. 3:** 748, 1106
28:16 ff   **Vol. 3:** 286
28:16–20   **Vol. 1:** 136   **Vol. 2:** 83, 282
28:16   **Vol. 3:** 1011
28:17   **Vol. 2:** 877   **Vol. 3:** 518
28:18 ff   **Vol. 1:** 95, 146   **Vol. 2:** 176, 461   **Vol. 3:** 807
28:18–20   **Vol. 2:** 611

Matthew *(cont'd)*

28:18   **Vol. 1:** 95, 258, 720   **Vol. 2:** 81, 194, 282, 368, 610, 653   **Vol. 3:** 1163

28:19 f   **Vol. 1:** 90

28:19   **Vol. 1:** 145, 290   **Vol. 2:** 84, 653, 655, 687, 793   **Vol. 3:** 327, 648, 698, 946, 1186, 1209

28:20   **Vol. 1:** 214, 335   **Vol. 2:** 62, 133, 895, 901   **Vol. 3:** 57, 763, 829

Mark

1:1   **Vol. 1:** 165   **Vol. 2:** 110, 112–113   **Vol. 3:** 63, 213, 652

1:2   **Vol. 1:** 102, 545, 586, 736   **Vol. 3:** 80, 119, 940

1:3–8   **Vol. 1:** 111

1:3   **Vol. 1:** 411   **Vol. 3:** 53, 118, 940

1:4 f   **Vol. 1:** 701

1:4   **Vol. 1:** 146, 358, 599, 701   **Vol. 2:** 533   **Vol. 3:** 52, 55–56, 212, 580, 1007, 1178, 1208, 1210

1:5 f   **Vol. 2:** 275

1:5   **Vol. 1:** 346   **Vol. 2:** 325, 327   **Vol. 3:** 987, 991, 1208, 1210

1:6   **Vol. 1:** 116, 482, 520   **Vol. 2:** 272   **Vol. 3:** 121

1:7   **Vol. 1:** 323, 493   **Vol. 3:** 55–56, 179, 714, 729

1:8 ff   **Vol. 3:** 990

1:8   **Vol. 1:** 158   **Vol. 2:** 603, 785   **Vol. 3:** 697, 714, 1210

1:9 ff   **Vol. 3:** 170

1:9–11   **Vol. 3:** 113

1:9   **Vol. 1:** 146   **Vol. 3:** 987, 991, 1174, 1208–1210

1:10 f   **Vol. 3:** 987

1:10   **Vol. 1:** 175, 704   **Vol. 2:** 185, 193, 314   **Vol. 3:** 543, 697, 1070, 1180

1:11   **Vol. 2:** 193, 543, 819   **Vol. 3:** 114, 611–612, 621, 639–641, 643, 651, 697, 807

1:12 f   **Vol. 2:** 267   **Vol. 3:** 470, 804, 1007–1008

1:12   **Vol. 1:** 453, 739   **Vol. 3:** 602, 697

1:13   **Vol. 1:** 114   **Vol. 2:** 689, 696, 893

1:14 ff   **Vol. 3:** 762, 1108

1:14 f   **Vol. 3:** 762

1:14   **Vol. 2:** 110, 112   **Vol. 3:** 37, 52

1:15   **Vol. 1:** 358, 482, 599, 702, 738   **Vol. 2:** 54, 110, 112, 381–382, 384, 387, 566   **Vol. 3:** 762, 837, 1212–1213

1:16 ff   **Vol. 1:** 482, 488

1:16–20   **Vol. 2:** 825   **Vol. 3:** 985

1:16   **Vol. 3:** 983–984

1:17   **Vol. 1:** 181, 488–489, 493

1:18   **Vol. 1:** 701   **Vol. 3:** 838

1:19   **Vol. 3:** 350

1:20   **Vol. 1:** 274, 321, 324, 493, 701

1:21 ff   **Vol. 2:** 228

1:21–38   **Vol. 3:** 1108

1:21 f   **Vol. 3:** 761

1:21   **Vol. 1:** 628   **Vol. 3:** 88, 761, 785

1:22   **Vol. 1:** 530   **Vol. 2:** 36, 177, 610, 623, 671   **Vol. 3:** 83, 313, 480, 769

1:23 ff   **Vol. 3:** 506

1:23 f   **Vol. 3:** 998

1:23   **Vol. 1:** 409   **Vol. 3:** 694, 785

1:24   **Vol. 1:** 454, 464   **Vol. 2:** 228, 231, 333, 559   **Vol. 3:** 474, 503

1:25–28   **Vol. 3:** 508

1:25 f   **Vol. 1:** 322   **Vol. 3:** 1108

1:25   **Vol. 1:** 572   **Vol. 3:** 475

1:26 f   **Vol. 3:** 694

1:26   **Vol. 3:** 113–114, 475

1:27   **Vol. 2:** 36, 179, 610, 623–624, 670–671   **Vol. 3:** 313, 769

1:28   **Vol. 3:** 508

1:29 ff   **Vol. 3:** 1059

1:29   **Vol. 1:** 689   **Vol. 3:** 785

1:30   **Vol. 1:** 656

1:31   **Vol. 2:** 630   **Vol. 3:** 546, 717

1:32   **Vol. 1:** 314   **Vol. 3:** 731

1:33   **Vol. 2:** 30, 33, 803

1:34   **Vol. 1:** 701   **Vol. 2:** 165   **Vol. 3:** 474, 506, 860

1:35 ff   **Vol. 3:** 1108

1:35–39   **Vol. 2:** 868

1:35   **Vol. 1:** 321   **Vol. 2:** 869   **Vol. 3:** 275, 509, 1007

1:36   **Vol. 2:** 806, 911

1:38 f   **Vol. 1:** 322   **Vol. 2:** 630   **Vol. 3:** 56

1:38   **Vol. 1:** 322   **Vol. 3:** 54, 509, 1108

1:39   **Vol. 1:** 454   **Vol. 2:** 631   **Vol. 3:** 56, 475, 785

1:40 ff   **Vol. 3:** 860

1:40   **Vol. 2:** 860

1:41 f   **Vol. 2:** 464

1:41   **Vol. 2:** 599, 630   **Vol. 3:** 1022

1:42   **Vol. 2:** 466

1:43 ff   **Vol. 3:** 506, 508

1:44   **Vol. 1:** 476   **Vol. 2:** 631, 640   **Vol. 3:** 507, 569, 1043, 1109

1:45   **Vol. 3:** 56, 320, 508, 1007, 1106, 1108–1109

2   **Vol. 1:** 317   **Vol. 3:** 507

2:1–3:6   **Vol. 3:** 510, 1109

2:1–12   **Vol. 1:** 701

2:2   **Vol. 1:** 297, 742   **Vol. 2:** 30   **Vol. 3:** 1109

2:3 ff   **Vol. 3:** 999–1000

2:3–12   **Vol. 2:** 610, 631

2:3–5   **Vol. 2:** 415

2:3   **Vol. 2:** 689

2:4   **Vol. 3:** 912

2:5 ff   **Vol. 3:** 998

2:5   **Vol. 1:** 286, 599, 701   **Vol. 2:** 631   **Vol. 3:** 1108

2:6   **Vol. 3:** 820

Mark *(cont'd)*

2:7   **Vol. 1:** 701   **Vol. 2:** 720   **Vol. 3:** 342, 481
2:8   **Vol. 3:** 694
2:9 f   **Vol. 2:** 415
2:9   **Vol. 2:** 415, 434
2:10   **Vol. 1:** 518, 701   **Vol. 3:** 508, 622
2:11   **Vol. 3:** 1108
2:12   **Vol. 1:** 528   **Vol. 3:** 508
2:13–17   **Vol. 2:** 523, 630   **Vol. 3:** 106, 428
2:13   **Vol. 3:** 761–762
2:14   **Vol. 1:** 488, 493   **Vol. 2:** 467, 754   **Vol. 3:** 275, 759, 1061, 1108
2:15 ff   **Vol. 1:** 689
2:15 f   **Vol. 3:** 580
2:16 f   **Vol. 2:** 272, 276
2:16   **Vol. 2:** 272, 276, 813   **Vol. 3:** 480–481
2:17   **Vol. 1:** 274, 322   **Vol. 2:** 170, 386, 434, 746, 757, 813   **Vol. 3:** 360, 492, 508, 580, 713, 758, 958, 998
2:18 ff   **Vol. 1:** 384   **Vol. 2:** 630, 732
2:18–22   **Vol. 2:** 585, 754   **Vol. 3:** 921
2:18 f   **Vol. 1:** 495   **Vol. 2:** 359
2:18   **Vol. 1:** 487, 612   **Vol. 2:** 272   **Vol. 3:** 481
2:19 f   **Vol. 2:** 585
2:19   **Vol. 1:** 612   **Vol. 2:** 272, 358, 383, 746   **Vol. 3:** 844
2:20   **Vol. 1:** 321
2:21 f   **Vol. 1:** 317, 613   **Vol. 2:** 671, 714
2:21   **Vol. 1:** 316   **Vol. 2:** 670   **Vol. 3:** 543
2:22   **Vol. 1:** 114   **Vol. 2:** 675–676
2:23 ff   **Vol. 2:** 437
2:23–28   **Vol. 2:** 267, 442, 754   **Vol. 3:** 37, 423, 429
2:23–27   **Vol. 1:** 335   **Vol. 3:** 1168
2:23–26   **Vol. 3:** 408
2:24   **Vol. 3:** 516
2:25 f   **Vol. 3:** 812, 814
2:25   **Vol. 1:** 245, 427   **Vol. 3:** 329, 957
2:26   **Vol. 1:** 586   **Vol. 2:** 248
2:27 f   **Vol. 3:** 623
2:27   **Vol. 1:** 384   **Vol. 3:** 410–411, 1184
2:28 f   **Vol. 2:** 514
2:28   **Vol. 3:** 508
3   **Vol. 3:** 507
3:1 ff   **Vol. 3:** 1168
3:1–6   **Vol. 3:** 409
3:1   **Vol. 1:** 516   **Vol. 3:** 785
3:2 ff   **Vol. 2:** 437
3:2   **Vol. 1:** 83   **Vol. 2:** 133, 165
3:3 ff   **Vol. 1:** 256   **Vol. 3:** 508
3:4   **Vol. 1:** 500, 563   **Vol. 2:** 434, 610
3:5   **Vol. 1:** 111   **Vol. 2:** 150, 156, 568   **Vol. 3:** 147
3:6   **Vol. 1:** 463   **Vol. 2:** 343, 812–813   **Vol. 3:** 441–443
3:7–6:6   **Vol. 3:** 1109
3:7   **Vol. 1:** 733

3:8   **Vol. 3:** 1174
3:9   **Vol. 2:** 768, 807–808
3:10 f   **Vol. 2:** 165   **Vol. 3:** 860
3:10   **Vol. 1:** 163   **Vol. 2:** 165   **Vol. 3:** 860
3:11 f   **Vol. 3:** 506
3:11   **Vol. 3:** 474, 643
3:12 f   **Vol. 1:** 256
3:12   **Vol. 1:** 572   **Vol. 3:** 320, 474
3:13 ff   **Vol. 2:** 630
3:13–19   **Vol. 3:** 453
3:13   **Vol. 1:** 274   **Vol. 2:** 185   **Vol. 3:** 1010
3:14 f   **Vol. 1:** 482   **Vol. 2:** 632, 695   **Vol. 3:** 57
3:14   **Vol. 1:** 136   **Vol. 2:** 695   **Vol. 3:** 54, 56
3:15   **Vol. 2:** 610   **Vol. 3:** 473, 475
3:16 ff   **Vol. 2:** 652
3:16–19   **Vol. 1:** 136
3:16   **Vol. 3:** 383
3:17   **Vol. 1:** 289   **Vol. 2:** 652   **Vol. 3:** 1002
3:18   **Vol. 2:** 550   **Vol. 3:** 1061, 1167
3:19   **Vol. 2:** 321
3:20 ff   **Vol. 1:** 452
3:20 f   **Vol. 2:** 750
3:20   **Vol. 1:** 322   **Vol. 3:** 508
3:21   **Vol. 1:** 528   **Vol. 3:** 1109
3:22–30   **Vol. 1:** 563   **Vol. 2:** 603   **Vol. 3:** 481
3:22–29   **Vol. 3:** 696
3:22   **Vol. 1:** 168, 637   **Vol. 2:** 327, 631   **Vol. 3:** 472, 481, 507, 1109
3:23–30   **Vol. 2:** 560   **Vol. 3:** 83, 472
3:23–27   **Vol. 3:** 695
3:23   **Vol. 3:** 1109
3:26   **Vol. 2:** 62   **Vol. 3:** 275
3:27   **Vol. 1:** 53, 508, 651   **Vol. 2:** 382, 603, 631, 702, 733, 900   **Vol. 3:** 473, 508, 696, 713, 913, 998
3:28 ff   **Vol. 3:** 580
3:28–30   **Vol. 3:** 1206
3:28 f   **Vol. 3:** 628, 696
3:28   **Vol. 1:** 289   **Vol. 3:** 343, 579, 1107
3:29   **Vol. 1:** 327   **Vol. 2:** 143   **Vol. 3:** 99, 343, 473, 579, 658, 830, 832
3:30   **Vol. 1:** 637   **Vol. 3:** 696
3:31 ff   **Vol. 3:** 1070
3:31–35   **Vol. 1:** 256, 488   **Vol. 2:** 750
3:31   **Vol. 1:** 274
3:32   **Vol. 3:** 516
3:33 ff   **Vol. 1:** 256
3:34 f   **Vol. 3:** 1062
3:35   **Vol. 3:** 503, 1022
4   **Vol. 2:** 36, 749
4:1 f   **Vol. 3:** 761
4:1–34   **Vol. 2:** 748
4:1–9   **Vol. 2:** 748, 750   **Vol. 3:** 522
4:1   **Vol. 1:** 297   **Vol. 2:** 36   **Vol. 3:** 984, 1201
4:2   **Vol. 2:** 36   **Vol. 3:** 762
4:4   **Vol. 1:** 174   **Vol. 3:** 1201
4:5   **Vol. 2:** 197   **Vol. 3:** 382
4:6   **Vol. 1:** 516, 653   **Vol. 3:** 731

Mark *(cont'd)*

4:7   **Vol. 1:** 226
4:8   **Vol. 2:** 129
4:9   **Vol. 2:** 178, 750   **Vol. 3:** 510
4:10 ff   **Vol. 2:** 750, 752
4:10–12   **Vol. 3:** 131
4:10 f   **Vol. 1:** 489
4:10   **Vol. 2:** 695, 724, 879
4:11 ff   **Vol. 3:** 507
4:11–12   **Vol. 2:** 434
4:11   **Vol. 1:** 578   **Vol. 2:** 178, 401   **Vol. 3:** 314, 503, 507
4:11b   **Vol. 2:** 753
4:12   **Vol. 1:** 261, 355   **Vol. 2:** 178, 753   **Vol. 3:** 131, 517
4:13–20   **Vol. 1:** 737   **Vol. 2:** 748, 750   **Vol. 3:** 522, 868, 1106
4:14 ff   **Vol. 3:** 1114
4:14–20   **Vol. 1:** 577–578
4:15   **Vol. 1:** 174, 566   **Vol. 3:** 470, 868
4:16–20   **Vol. 3:** 868
4:16 f   **Vol. 3:** 869
4:16   **Vol. 2:** 177, 358   **Vol. 3:** 382, 748
4:17   **Vol. 1:** 608   **Vol. 2:** 808
4:19   **Vol. 1:** 278, 457, 460, 723   **Vol. 2:** 459–460, 842–843, 845   **Vol. 3:** 252, 829
4:20   **Vol. 2:** 104, 773   **Vol. 3:** 868
4:21   **Vol. 2:** 749–750
4:22   **Vol. 1:** 181   **Vol. 2:** 212, 216   **Vol. 3:** 312, 320
4:23   **Vol. 2:** 750
4:24   **Vol. 2:** 178, 499   **Vol. 3:** 402, 822
4:25   **Vol. 2:** 750
4:26–29   **Vol. 2:** 385, 750   **Vol. 3:** 523
4:28   **Vol. 1:** 723, 744
4:29   **Vol. 3:** 526–527
4:30 ff   **Vol. 2:** 385, 429, 750   **Vol. 3:** 523
4:30 f   **Vol. 2:** 502
4:30   **Vol. 3:** 868
4:31   **Vol. 2:** 502
4:32   **Vol. 1:** 174   **Vol. 2:** 192   **Vol. 3:** 555, 813, 869
4:33 f   **Vol. 2:** 750, 753   **Vol. 3:** 1109
4:33   **Vol. 3:** 1109
4:34   **Vol. 1:** 577   **Vol. 3:** 507–508
4:35 ff   **Vol. 3:** 984
4:35–51   **Vol. 3:** 984
4:35–41   **Vol. 2:** 630   **Vol. 3:** 985
4:36–41   **Vol. 1:** 419
4:37   **Vol. 3:** 1002–1003
4:38   **Vol. 1:** 464   **Vol. 3:** 115, 767
4:39   **Vol. 1:** 572   **Vol. 3:** 989, 1002
4:40 f   **Vol. 3:** 131
4:41   **Vol. 1:** 384   **Vol. 2:** 179, 623   **Vol. 3:** 989
5:1 ff   **Vol. 2:** 168   **Vol. 3:** 475, 998
5:1–17   **Vol. 2:** 631
5:2   **Vol. 3:** 247, 1175

5:3–7   **Vol. 1:** 481
5:3   **Vol. 3:** 246
5:4   **Vol. 3:** 714
5:5   **Vol. 1:** 409
5:6 f   **Vol. 3:** 506
5:6   **Vol. 2:** 877   **Vol. 3:** 947
5:7   **Vol. 2:** 74   **Vol. 3:** 113, 474, 643, 737, 856
5:9   **Vol. 2:** 653
5:11   **Vol. 3:** 1011
5:12   **Vol. 1:** 570
5:13   **Vol. 2:** 398, 699   **Vol. 3:** 984–985, 990
5:14   **Vol. 1:** 559   **Vol. 3:** 46
5:15   **Vol. 1:** 502
5:16   **Vol. 1:** 576
5:18 ff   **Vol. 2:** 631
5:19 f   **Vol. 3:** 508
5:19   **Vol. 1:** 701   **Vol. 2:** 595
5:20   **Vol. 2:** 623   **Vol. 3:** 56
5:21–43   **Vol. 2:** 168, 630   **Vol. 3:** 1059
5:21   **Vol. 1:** 297
5:22   **Vol. 1:** 239, 609
5:23   **Vol. 2:** 151, 480
5:25 ff   **Vol. 2:** 170
5:25–34   **Vol. 2:** 560
5:25   **Vol. 1:** 221, 683   **Vol. 2:** 696   **Vol. 3:** 1175
5:26 ff   **Vol. 2:** 168
5:26   **Vol. 2:** 846   **Vol. 3:** 723
5:27–30   **Vol. 3:** 860
5:27   **Vol. 3:** 860
5:29 f   **Vol. 2:** 398
5:29   **Vol. 1:** 163, 234, 516   **Vol. 3:** 987
5:30 ff   **Vol. 2:** 169
5:30   **Vol. 3:** 860
5:31   **Vol. 3:** 861
5:33   **Vol. 1:** 610, 622   **Vol. 3:** 884
5:34   **Vol. 1:** 599   **Vol. 2:** 165, 631, 780   **Vol. 3:** 212, 861
5:35 ff   **Vol. 2:** 480
5:36   **Vol. 1:** 439, 599, 623   **Vol. 3:** 1211
5:37 ff   **Vol. 3:** 508
5:37   **Vol. 1:** 701   **Vol. 3:** 508
5:38 f   **Vol. 2:** 623   **Vol. 3:** 1174, 1185
5:38   **Vol. 1:** 329   **Vol. 2:** 416, 418, 623
5:39   **Vol. 1:** 283   **Vol. 2:** 623   **Vol. 3:** 280
5:40   **Vol. 2:** 433   **Vol. 3:** 280, 507, 751, 1071
5:41   **Vol. 1:** 581   **Vol. 2:** 630   **Vol. 3:** 280, 717
5:42   **Vol. 1:** 528   **Vol. 2:** 696
5:43   **Vol. 2:** 398, 631   **Vol. 3:** 506, 1109
6:1–6   **Vol. 2:** 631   **Vol. 3:** 88, 507
6:2 f   **Vol. 3:** 508
6:2   **Vol. 1:** 96, 488, 530   **Vol. 2:** 149, 603, 624   **Vol. 3:** 761–762, 785, 1030
6:3   **Vol. 1:** 256, 279, 668   **Vol. 2:** 320, 333, 708   **Vol. 3:** 660, 1204
6:4   **Vol. 2:** 248, 757   **Vol. 3:** 83, 696
6:5 f   **Vol. 1:** 600   **Vol. 2:** 165
6:5   **Vol. 2:** 151, 165, 603–604

Mark *(cont'd)*

6:6   **Vol. 2:** 165, 624, 631, 750   **Vol. 3:** 761
6:7 ff   **Vol. 2:** 632
6:7–13   **Vol. 1:** 130, 489   **Vol. 2:** 733
6:7–11   **Vol. 1:** 131
6:7   **Vol. 1:** 129, 167, 274   **Vol. 2:** 610, 686, 695   **Vol. 3:** 475
6:8–11   **Vol. 3:** 453
6:8   **Vol. 1:** 142–143, 340, 407   **Vol. 2:** 97   **Vol. 3:** 120–121
6:11   **Vol. 1:** 239, 520   **Vol. 2:** 767   **Vol. 3:** 93, 560, 1043
6:12 f   **Vol. 3:** 57
6:12   **Vol. 1:** 359   **Vol. 3:** 54, 56
6:13   **Vol. 1:** 120–121   **Vol. 2:** 165, 169, 712   **Vol. 3:** 475
6:14 ff   **Vol. 2:** 342   **Vol. 3:** 508
6:14 f   **Vol. 3:** 507
6:14   **Vol. 1:** 446   **Vol. 2:** 603, 652   **Vol. 3:** 320
6:15   **Vol. 1:** 545   **Vol. 3:** 83
6:17–20   **Vol. 1:** 156
6:17   **Vol. 2:** 136, 550, 579   **Vol. 3:** 717
6:18   **Vol. 3:** 540
6:19   **Vol. 1:** 430
6:20   **Vol. 2:** 229   **Vol. 3:** 361
6:21   **Vol. 1:** 666   **Vol. 2:** 699, 887
6:23   **Vol. 2:** 381   **Vol. 3:** 742
6:24–28   **Vol. 2:** 159
6:24   **Vol. 3:** 1071
6:25   **Vol. 3:** 82
6:26   **Vol. 1:** 74
6:27   **Vol. 2:** 136
6:28   **Vol. 3:** 1071
6:29   **Vol. 1:** 265, 487   **Vol. 3:** 247
6:30–44   **Vol. 1:** 729   **Vol. 2:** 523   **Vol. 3:** 508
6:30   **Vol. 1:** 129, 134, 136, 297   **Vol. 3:** 763
6:31   **Vol. 3:** 256, 508
6:32–14   **Vol. 2:** 630
6:32   **Vol. 3:** 1007
6:33   **Vol. 2:** 398   **Vol. 3:** 947
6:34 ff   **Vol. 2:** 272
6:34   **Vol. 2:** 413, 459, 599, 750   **Vol. 3:** 567, 761–762
6:35   **Vol. 3:** 847
6:36   **Vol. 1:** 505   **Vol. 3:** 189
6:37   **Vol. 2:** 711
6:39   **Vol. 1:** 744
6:41   **Vol. 1:** 213, 250   **Vol. 2:** 192   **Vol. 3:** 519
6:42–52   **Vol. 3:** 985
6:42   **Vol. 1:** 743
6:44   **Vol. 2:** 699
6:45–52   **Vol. 2:** 630   **Vol. 3:** 984–985, 990
6:45   **Vol. 1:** 505   **Vol. 3:** 189, 951
6:46   **Vol. 1:** 321   **Vol. 3:** 509, 1010
6:47 ff   **Vol. 3:** 1002
6:48   **Vol. 1:** 322   **Vol. 2:** 136   **Vol. 3:** 856
6:48c   **Vol. 2:** 281

6:49   **Vol. 1:** 409   **Vol. 2:** 281, 559   **Vol. 3:** 293, 324, 822
6:50   **Vol. 1:** 623   **Vol. 2:** 281   **Vol. 3:** 710
6:51   **Vol. 1:** 729
6:52   **Vol. 2:** 155   **Vol. 3:** 131–132
6:53   **Vol. 3:** 1059
6:55   **Vol. 3:** 860
6:56   **Vol. 1:** 267   **Vol. 3:** 860, 994
7   **Vol. 3:** 774
7:1 ff   **Vol. 2:** 272
7:1–23   **Vol. 2:** 715, 813   **Vol. 3:** 481, 763
7:1–4   **Vol. 2:** 150
7:1   **Vol. 1:** 297   **Vol. 2:** 327
7:2–23   **Vol. 3:** 990
7:2   **Vol. 1:** 153, 448   **Vol. 2:** 139, 144
7:3 f   **Vol. 1:** 225   **Vol. 3:** 105, 717, 990
7:3   **Vol. 1:** 153, 199   **Vol. 2:** 150, 315, 813   **Vol. 3:** 774
7:4   **Vol. 1:** 144, 149   **Vol. 3:** 748, 990
7:5 ff   **Vol. 1:** 153   **Vol. 2:** 469
7:5   **Vol. 1:** 199, 448   **Vol. 2:** 813   **Vol. 3:** 481, 774
7:6 ff   **Vol. 2:** 150
7:6–13   **Vol. 3:** 181, 184
7:6 f   **Vol. 2:** 43, 469
7:6   **Vol. 1:** 736   **Vol. 2:** 183
7:7   **Vol. 1:** 552   **Vol. 2:** 93   **Vol. 3:** 770
7:8 f   **Vol. 1:** 336
7:8   **Vol. 1:** 335, 701   **Vol. 3:** 717, 774–775
7:9–13   **Vol. 1:** 289, 619
7:9   **Vol. 1:** 74, 335   **Vol. 2:** 133
7:10 f   **Vol. 2:** 640
7:10   **Vol. 1:** 415, 430   **Vol. 3:** 95, 1070
7:11 f   **Vol. 3:** 1070
7:11   **Vol. 2:** 41–43
7:13   **Vol. 2:** 43, 503   **Vol. 3:** 773–774
7:14 ff   **Vol. 1:** 153
7:14–23   **Vol. 1:** 169   **Vol. 2:** 150
7:14 f   **Vol. 2:** 437, 640
7:14   **Vol. 1:** 274, 448
7:15   **Vol. 1:** 448, 642   **Vol. 3:** 106, 762, 1168
7:17–23   **Vol. 3:** 507–508
7:17   **Vol. 2:** 746   **Vol. 3:** 507
7:18 f   **Vol. 2:** 268
7:18   **Vol. 1:** 448, 642   **Vol. 3:** 106, 131
7:19   **Vol. 2:** 268
7:19c   **Vol. 3:** 106
7:20   **Vol. 1:** 448   **Vol. 3:** 106
7:21 ff   **Vol. 3:** 31
7:21–23   **Vol. 3:** 106
7:21 f   **Vol. 1:** 563
7:21   **Vol. 1:** 499, 564   **Vol. 2:** 182   **Vol. 3:** 820
7:22   **Vol. 1:** 138   **Vol. 3:** 30, 516
7:23   **Vol. 1:** 448
7:24 ff   **Vol. 3:** 475
7:24–30   **Vol. 3:** 980, 1059
7:24   **Vol. 3:** 275, 506–508
7:25   **Vol. 1:** 609, 637
7:26   **Vol. 2:** 126

Mark *(cont'd)*

7:27 f **Vol. 1:** 117
7:27 **Vol. 1:** 666–667, 744 **Vol. 2:** 434
7:28 **Vol. 1:** 117, 283, 744
7:29 **Vol. 2:** 631
7:30 **Vol. 2:** 248
7:31–37 **Vol. 3:** 508
7:31 f **Vol. 3:** 475
7:32 ff **Vol. 2:** 560
7:32 **Vol. 1:** 428 **Vol. 2:** 151
7:33 f **Vol. 3:** 860
7:33 **Vol. 3:** 507, 751, 1079
7:34 **Vol. 1:** 429 **Vol. 2:** 192, 423, 729 **Vol. 3:** 519
7:35 **Vol. 1:** 428 **Vol. 2:** 175, 726, 728–729 **Vol. 3:** 180, 592, 1079
7:36 f **Vol. 3:** 508
7:36 **Vol. 1:** 729 **Vol. 2:** 631 **Vol. 3:** 56, 506, 1109
7:37 **Vol. 1:** 428, 729 **Vol. 2:** 170, 623, 632 **Vol. 3:** 56
8:1 ff **Vol. 2:** 272
8:1–21 **Vol. 3:** 508
8:1–10 **Vol. 1:** 729 **Vol. 2:** 523, 630
8:2 **Vol. 2:** 599 **Vol. 3:** 228
8:3 **Vol. 1:** 505 **Vol. 3:** 189, 939
8:4 **Vol. 1:** 743 **Vol. 3:** 1007
8:5 **Vol. 2:** 692, 879
8:6 f **Vol. 1:** 213
8:6 **Vol. 1:** 250, 340, 517 **Vol. 3:** 819
8:8 **Vol. 1:** 729, 743 **Vol. 2:** 692
8:9 **Vol. 1:** 505 **Vol. 2:** 699 **Vol. 3:** 189
8:11 f **Vol. 2:** 192, 631, 750
8:11 **Vol. 2:** 629 **Vol. 3:** 83, 480, 804
8:12 ff **Vol. 2:** 630
8:12 **Vol. 3:** 531, 694, 1107
8:14–21 **Vol. 3:** 132
8:15–21 **Vol. 3:** 508
8:15 **Vol. 2:** 462 **Vol. 3:** 442
8:16 f **Vol. 3:** 820
8:17–21 **Vol. 3:** 510
8:17–18 **Vol. 2:** 434
8:17 f **Vol. 2:** 178 **Vol. 3:** 131
8:17 **Vol. 2:** 155 **Vol. 3:** 131, 503
8:18 **Vol. 3:** 131, 240, 517
8:19 **Vol. 2:** 696, 699
8:20 **Vol. 2:** 692, 699
8:21 **Vol. 3:** 131
8:22–26 **Vol. 3:** 508
8:22–25 **Vol. 1:** 219
8:22 **Vol. 3:** 507
8:23 **Vol. 2:** 151, 170, 560, 803 **Vol. 3:** 749
8:24 **Vol. 3:** 519
8:25 **Vol. 3:** 147, 519
8:26 **Vol. 3:** 506–507, 1174
8:27 ff **Vol. 1:** 708 **Vol. 2:** 680
8:27–9:1 **Vol. 3:** 864
8:27–33 **Vol. 2:** 341 **Vol. 3:** 508, 1061
8:27–30 **Vol. 3:** 509
8:27 **Vol. 2:** 550
8:28 **Vol. 1:** 545 **Vol. 3:** 82–83, 507–508
8:29–31 **Vol. 3:** 629
8:29 **Vol. 2:** 76, 231 **Vol. 3:** 384
8:30 **Vol. 1:** 572 **Vol. 3:** 506
8:31 ff **Vol. 3:** 508
8:31 f **Vol. 1:** 545
8:31 **Vol. 1:** 74, 198, 430 **Vol. 2:** 327, 526, 665, 687, 893 **Vol. 3:** 39, 276, 294, 507, 509, 623–624, 723, 761, 809, 1109, 1198
8:32 f **Vol. 3:** 455
8:32 **Vol. 1:** 572 **Vol. 3:** 751, 1109
8:33† **Vol. 1:** 111, 572 **Vol. 2:** 618 **Vol. 3:** 197, 394, 470, 509, 807
8:34 **Vol. 1:** 324, 394, 402, 455, 482, 493 **Vol. 3:** 60
8:35 f **Vol. 3:** 174
8:35 **Vol. 1:** 464 **Vol. 2:** 110, 112, 433 **Vol. 3:** 212–213, 530, 682
8:36 **Vol. 1:** 524 **Vol. 3:** 137, 142
8:37 **Vol. 2:** 480 **Vol. 3:** 167, 174, 196
8:38 f **Vol. 2:** 654
8:38 **Vol. 1:** 205, 323, 347 **Vol. 2:** 36, 46, 228, 582, 584 **Vol. 3:** 135, 508, 563, 579–580, 618, 620–621, 625, 1108
9:1 **Vol. 2:** 38, 271, 382, 386–387, 604, 910, 930 **Vol. 3:** 627, 863, 1107
9:2 ff **Vol. 1:** 708
9:2–8 **Vol. 2:** 48 **Vol. 3:** 114
9:2–7 **Vol. 2:** 47 Sr 9:2 f **Vol. 2:** 486
9:2 **Vol. 1:** 704, 706 **Vol. 2:** 199, 686 **Vol. 3:** 508, 861–863, 1010, 1012
9:3 **Vol. 1:** 204
9:4 f **Vol. 1:** 545 **Vol. 2:** 640
9:4 **Vol. 2:** 559 **Vol. 3:** 474
9:5 **Vol. 1:** 488 **Vol. 2:** 514 **Vol. 3:** 115, 555, 767
9:7 **Vol. 2:** 176, 543, 725 **Vol. 3:** 114, 611, 621, 639, 643, 651, 864, 1003
9:8 **Vol. 2:** 724
9:9 **Vol. 1:** 335, 576 **Vol. 3:** 276, 294, 506, 862, 1012
9:10 **Vol. 3:** 131, 717, 1106
9:11 ff **Vol. 1:** 545
9:11 **Vol. 1:** 323, 544–545, 667 **Vol. 3:** 624
9:12 f **Vol. 1:** 545 **Vol. 3:** 188, 329
9:12 **Vol. 1:** 74, 581 **Vol. 3:** 80, 147, 623–624, 723
9:13 **Vol. 1:** 545 **Vol. 3:** 489
9:14 ff **Vol. 3:** 475
9:14 **Vol. 3:** 1010
9:15 **Vol. 2:** 623–624
9:17 **Vol. 1:** 428 **Vol. 2:** 595 **Vol. 3:** 475, 767
9:18 **Vol. 1:** 516 **Vol. 3:** 750
9:19 **Vol. 2:** 36, 766 **Vol. 3:** 1204
9:20 **Vol. 1:** 609 **Vol. 3:** 506
9:22 **Vol. 1:** 463, 656 **Vol. 2:** 600 **Vol. 3:** 990

Mark (cont'd)

9:23 f	**Vol. 2:** 631 **Vol. 3:** 1211
9:23	**Vol. 1:** 600 **Vol. 2:** 604
9:24	**Vol. 1:** 283
9:25	**Vol. 1:** 428–429, 572 **Vol. 3:** 475, 507, 694, 1108
9:26	**Vol. 1:** 96, 446 **Vol. 3:** 475
9:28–32	**Vol. 1:** 130
9:28 f	**Vol. 3:** 507
9:29	**Vol. 1:** 613 **Vol. 3:** 474
9:30 ff	**Vol. 3:** 508
9:30 f	**Vol. 3:** 507
9:30	**Vol. 3:** 946, 1010
9:31 f	**Vol. 3:** 508
9:31	**Vol. 1:** 162, 430 **Vol. 2:** 150, 368, 526–527, 893 **Vol. 3:** 276, 294, 507, 623–624
9:32	**Vol. 2:** 216, 406, 880 **Vol. 3:** 131, 507, 1122
9:33–37	**Vol. 1:** 285 **Vol. 2:** 427
9:33–34	**Vol. 2:** 429 **Vol. 3:** 821
9:34	**Vol. 3:** 447
9:35	**Vol. 2:** 57, 695 **Vol. 3:** 114, 447, 761, 979
9:36	**Vol. 1:** 239
9:37	**Vol. 1:** 285 **Vol. 2:** 176, 429 **Vol. 3:** 746
9:38	**Vol. 2:** 653 **Vol. 3:** 475, 767
9:39	**Vol. 1:** 415
9:40	**Vol. 2:** 34, 813
9:41	**Vol. 1:** 285 **Vol. 3:** 141, 980, 989, 1107
9:42–50	**Vol. 3:** 446, 448
9:42–48	**Vol. 2:** 387 **Vol. 3:** 1052
9:42 f	**Vol. 3:** 447
9:42	**Vol. 2:** 429, 652 **Vol. 3:** 394, 984, 1212
9:43 ff	**Vol. 2:** 385
9:43–48	**Vol. 2:** 385, 710 **Vol. 3:** 99
9:43	**Vol. 1:** 657 **Vol. 2:** 208, 387, 414–415, 481 **Vol. 3:** 111, 447
9:45	**Vol. 1:** 239, 657 **Vol. 2:** 208, 415, 481
9:46	**Vol. 2:** 387
9:47 f	**Vol. 2:** 208
9:47	**Vol. 1:** 453, 657 **Vol. 2:** 387
9:48	**Vol. 1:** 430, 657 **Vol. 2:** 709 **Vol. 3:** 109–110, 447–448
9:49 f	**Vol. 2:** 749–750
9:49	**Vol. 1:** 657 **Vol. 2:** 746 **Vol. 3:** 446–447, 697
9:50	**Vol. 2:** 757, 781 **Vol. 3:** 445, 447
9:50a	**Vol. 3:** 447
10:1 ff	**Vol. 3:** 762
10:1–12†	**Vol. 1:** 506 **Vol. 2:** 442 **Vol. 3:** 181–182, 538
10:1	**Vol. 3:** 275, 540, 761, 991
10:2 ff	**Vol. 1:** 737
10:2–12†	**Vol. 1:** 500 **Vol. 2:** 580 **Vol. 3:** 172, 188
10:2–9	**Vol. 3:** 534, 980
10:2	**Vol. 1:** 506 **Vol. 2:** 563 **Vol. 3:** 189, 539, 804
10:3	**Vol. 1:** 335
10:4	**Vol. 1:** 243–244, 506, 606 **Vol. 3:** 189
10:5	**Vol. 1:** 335 **Vol. 2:** 156, 184 **Vol. 3:** 182, 538
10:6 ff	**Vol. 1:** 500
10:6–9	**Vol. 3:** 539
10:6 f	**Vol. 2:** 579
10:6	**Vol. 1:** 166, 384 **Vol. 2:** 563, 570 **Vol. 3:** 1058, 1154
10:7 f	**Vol. 2:** 570 **Vol. 3:** 1070
10:7	**Vol. 3:** 251
10:8 f	**Vol. 2:** 570
10:8	**Vol. 2:** 583, 722
10:9 ff	**Vol. 2:** 581
10:9	**Vol. 2:** 565 **Vol. 3:** 1164
10:10	**Vol. 3:** 507
10:11 f	**Vol. 1:** 506 **Vol. 2:** 580, 583
10:11	**Vol. 1:** 500, 506 **Vol. 2:** 564 **Vol. 3:** 189, 540
10:12	**Vol. 1:** 506 **Vol. 2:** 563 **Vol. 3:** 189, 540
10:13 ff	**Vol. 1:** 283, 489
10:13–16	**Vol. 1:** 160, 213, 284 **Vol. 3:** 861
10:13	**Vol. 1:** 572
10:14 f	**Vol. 1:** 284
10:14	**Vol. 1:** 149 **Vol. 2:** 222–223
10:15	**Vol. 1:** 213, 284 **Vol. 2:** 262, 385 **Vol. 3:** 746, 1107
10:16	**Vol. 1:** 74, 212, 239, 284 **Vol. 2:** 151
10:17 ff	**Vol. 1:** 482 **Vol. 3:** 978
10:17–31	**Vol. 1:** 335 **Vol. 2:** 301
10:17–22	**Vol. 2:** 844
10:17 f	**Vol. 2:** 100
10:17	**Vol. 2:** 388, 480–481, 860 **Vol. 3:** 832
10:18	**Vol. 1:** 565
10:19	**Vol. 1:** 619 **Vol. 2:** 583 **Vol. 3:** 377, 379, 755
10:20	**Vol. 2:** 135, 675
10:21	**Vol. 1:** 268 **Vol. 2:** 720, 824, 833, 846 **Vol. 3:** 141, 519, 954
10:22	**Vol. 2:** 845–846 **Vol. 3:** 1108
10:23 ff	**Vol. 2:** 843
10:23–31	**Vol. 2:** 750
10:23	**Vol. 2:** 845, 910
10:24	**Vol. 1:** 286, 591 **Vol. 2:** 623
10:25	**Vol. 1:** 116 **Vol. 2:** 842
10:26 ff	**Vol. 2:** 118
10:26	**Vol. 1:** 730 **Vol. 2:** 623 **Vol. 3:** 213
10:27	**Vol. 2:** 74, 603, 606 **Vol. 3:** 213, 519
10:28 ff	**Vol. 1:** 256
10:28–31	**Vol. 2:** 57
10:28	**Vol. 1:** 701 **Vol. 2:** 840 **Vol. 3:** 516
10:29 f	**Vol. 1:** 287, 619 **Vol. 2:** 250
10:29	**Vol. 2:** 110, 112, 301, 387 **Vol. 3:** 213, 1107
10:30	**Vol. 2:** 480, 840 **Vol. 3:** 142, 748, 832, 837–839
10:31	**Vol. 2:** 57

Mark *(cont'd)*

10:32 ff	**Vol. 3:** 507–508
10:32	**Vol. 1:** 482, 489 **Vol. 2:** 623–624, 695
10:33 f	**Vol. 2:** 327, 526
10:33	**Vol. 2:** 368 **Vol. 3:** 39, 516, 623
10:34	**Vol. 1:** 162, 430 **Vol. 2:** 893 **Vol. 3:** 276, 340, 967
10:35–45	**Vol. 2:** 385
10:35–37	**Vol. 2:** 276
10:35	**Vol. 2:** 858
10:37–40	**Vol. 3:** 588
10:37	**Vol. 2:** 41, 148, 386, 388
10:38 f	**Vol. 1:** 144 **Vol. 3:** 697
10:38	**Vol. 1:** 394 **Vol. 2:** 63, 276
10:39	**Vol. 3:** 118
10:40	**Vol. 1:** 730 **Vol. 2:** 148 **Vol. 3:** 1198
10:42–45	**Vol. 3:** 979
10:42	**Vol. 1:** 167–168 **Vol. 2:** 519 **Vol. 3:** 822
10:43 f	**Vol. 2:** 427 **Vol. 3:** 1022
10:43	**Vol. 3:** 546–547
10:44	**Vol. 3:** 611
10:45	**Vol. 1:** 96–97, 322, 369, 398, 437–438, 492, 549, 701–702 **Vol. 2:** 42, 262, 532, 543 **Vol. 3:** 195–197, 508, 546–547, 611–612, 625, 682–683, 1064, 1180
10:45b	**Vol. 2:** 525
10:46 ff	**Vol. 3:** 507–508
10:46–52	**Vol. 1:** 219
10:46†	**Vol. 1:** 288 **Vol. 3:** 589, 939–940, 1201
10:47 f	**Vol. 2:** 341 **Vol. 3:** 507
10:47	**Vol. 2:** 333, 595
10:48	**Vol. 1:** 489, 572 **Vol. 2:** 595 **Vol. 3:** 651
10:49	**Vol. 1:** 328
10:51	**Vol. 3:** 115, 519
10:52	**Vol. 1:** 599 **Vol. 2:** 631 **Vol. 3:** 212, 508, 519, 939
11:1–11	**Vol. 3:** 509
11:1–10	**Vol. 2:** 379, 754 **Vol. 3:** 791
11:1	**Vol. 1:** 725 **Vol. 2:** 54, 713 **Vol. 3:** 1174
11:2	**Vol. 1:** 117, 171 **Vol. 3:** 179
11:3	**Vol. 3:** 1154
11:4 f	**Vol. 1:** 117
11:4	**Vol. 2:** 30 **Vol. 3:** 179
11:5	**Vol. 2:** 869 **Vol. 3:** 179, 1154
11:7 f	**Vol. 1:** 317
11:7	**Vol. 1:** 117 **Vol. 3:** 378
11:9 f	**Vol. 1:** 323
11:9	**Vol. 1:** 100, 213 **Vol. 3:** 378
11:10	**Vol. 1:** 213
11:11–17	**Vol. 2:** 610
11:11	**Vol. 2:** 528, 695 **Vol. 3:** 429, 792, 847
11:12 ff	**Vol. 1:** 724 **Vol. 2:** 267, 750, 754 **Vol. 3:** 793
11:12–25	**Vol. 3:** 784
11:12 f	**Vol. 3:** 868–869
11:13	**Vol. 1:** 724 **Vol. 3:** 837, 958
11:15 ff	**Vol. 1:** 111 **Vol. 2:** 236, 754 **Vol. 3:** 429, 784
11:15–19	**Vol. 2:** 379 **Vol. 3:** 181, 791, 1168
11:15–17	**Vol. 2:** 327
11:15	**Vol. 1:** 175 **Vol. 2:** 236
11:16	**Vol. 3:** 913
11:17	**Vol. 1:** 274 **Vol. 2:** 248, 793 **Vol. 3:** 329, 380, 430, 761–762, 788, 791
11:18	**Vol. 1:** 463 **Vol. 2:** 36, 327, 623, 799 **Vol. 3:** 39, 531, 769
11:19 f	**Vol. 2:** 653
11:19	**Vol. 2:** 528
11:20–26	**Vol. 3:** 1012
11:20	**Vol. 1:** 515
11:21	**Vol. 1:** 417, 488, 515 **Vol. 3:** 115, 767
11:22 ff	**Vol. 1:** 600
11:22	**Vol. 1:** 600
11:23	**Vol. 1:** 504, 600 **Vol. 3:** 984, 1107
11:24 f	**Vol. 1:** 600
11:24	**Vol. 2:** 858, 868
11:25 f	**Vol. 1:** 701 **Vol. 2:** 871
11:25	**Vol. 1:** 620, 702 **Vol. 2:** 868
11:27 ff	**Vol. 3:** 1154
11:27–13:1	**Vol. 2:** 236
11:27–33	**Vol. 3:** 792
11:27	**Vol. 1:** 199 **Vol. 3:** 789, 791
11:29	**Vol. 2:** 880
11:30	**Vol. 2:** 193, 434
11:31	**Vol. 3:** 821, 1211
12:1 f	**Vol. 3:** 868
12:1–12	**Vol. 2:** 301, 746, 751 **Vol. 3:** 641, 869, 920
12:1	**Vol. 2:** 790 **Vol. 3:** 951
12:2	**Vol. 1:** 724 **Vol. 3:** 837
12:3	**Vol. 1:** 163, 547
12:4 ff	**Vol. 2:** 236
12:4	**Vol. 2:** 50, 157
12:5 ff	**Vol. 1:** 430
12:5	**Vol. 1:** 163
12:6	**Vol. 2:** 58, 543, 720
12:9	**Vol. 1:** 464 **Vol. 2:** 513
12:10 f	**Vol. 2:** 129, 313, 622
12:10	**Vol. 1:** 245 **Vol. 2:** 159, 253, 706 **Vol. 3:** 329, 390, 393, 490, 492, 809
12:11	**Vol. 2:** 623
12:12	**Vol. 1:** 724 **Vol. 3:** 508, 717
12:13–17	**Vol. 1:** 269 **Vol. 3:** 549, 754, 979, 1168
12:13	**Vol. 2:** 343, 812 **Vol. 3:** 441, 1108
12:14 ff	**Vol. 3:** 762
12:14–17	**Vol. 3:** 979
12:14	**Vol. 1:** 586–587 **Vol. 3:** 754, 757, 884, 940
12:15	**Vol. 2:** 469 **Vol. 3:** 804
12:16	**Vol. 2:** 288 **Vol. 3:** 489
12:17	**Vol. 2:** 623–624 **Vol. 3:** 978
12:18 ff	**Vol. 1:** 488 **Vol. 2:** 691 **Vol. 3:** 767
12:18–27	**Vol. 2:** 578, 580 **Vol. 3:** 263, 439, 792

Mark *(cont'd)*

12:19	**Vol. 2:** 640
12:24	**Vol. 2:** 459–460, 603 **Vol. 3:** 304, 490, 492, 1174
12:25 f	**Vol. 1:** 290, 446
12:25	**Vol. 1:** 103 **Vol. 2:** 192, 578, 581
12:26 f	**Vol. 1:** 78 **Vol. 2:** 481 **Vol. 3:** 263
12:26	**Vol. 1:** 81, 244 **Vol. 2:** 73, 319, 640 **Vol. 3:** 329
12:27	**Vol. 1:** 445 **Vol. 2:** 460, 480, 578
12:28 ff	**Vol. 1:** 259, 339
12:28–34	**Vol. 2:** 516, 543, 813, 870 **Vol. 3:** 173, 455, 791
12:28	**Vol. 1:** 334 **Vol. 2:** 177, 426, 544 **Vol. 3:** 439
12:29 f	**Vol. 1:** 334 **Vol. 2:** 73, 177
12:29	**Vol. 2:** 720–721
12:30 f	**Vol. 3:** 542
12:30	**Vol. 3:** 127, 685, 713
12:31	**Vol. 1:** 334–335 **Vol. 2:** 177 **Vol. 3:** 1064
12:32	**Vol. 2:** 721, 739 **Vol. 3:** 884
12:33	**Vol. 1:** 730 **Vol. 3:** 131, 431
12:34	**Vol. 2:** 54
12:35 ff	**Vol. 2:** 147 **Vol. 3:** 508, 791
12:35–37	**Vol. 2:** 515 **Vol. 3:** 651
12:35 f	**Vol. 2:** 79 **Vol. 3:** 762
12:35	**Vol. 3:** 481, 761, 791
12:36	**Vol. 1:** 239, 477, 554 **Vol. 2:** 515 **Vol. 3:** 697
12:37–40	**Vol. 2:** 469 **Vol. 3:** 580
12:37	**Vol. 2:** 516
12:38–40	**Vol. 3:** 481
12:38	**Vol. 1:** 267, 312 **Vol. 2:** 36 **Vol. 3:** 769, 1019
12:39	**Vol. 1:** 666 **Vol. 3:** 589, 785
12:40	**Vol. 2:** 738 **Vol. 3:** 482, 748, 1074
12:41–44	**Vol. 2:** 43, 751, 824 **Vol. 3:** 789, 791, 1062, 1074
12:41	**Vol. 2:** 97, 842 **Vol. 3:** 796
12:42	**Vol. 2:** 821, 850
12:43	**Vol. 1:** 274 **Vol. 3:** 796, 1107
12:44	**Vol. 1:** 729 **Vol. 2:** 475, 846 **Vol. 3:** 791, 955
13	**Vol. 1:** 125, 541 **Vol. 2:** 65, 894, 909–915 **Vol. 3:** 65, 490, 560, 844, 984
13:1 ff	**Vol. 2:** 39, 236
13:1–36	**Vol. 2:** 36
13:1–4	**Vol. 2:** 36–37, 713 **Vol. 3:** 1011
13:1	**Vol. 3:** 791
13:2 ff	**Vol. 2:** 803
13:2 f	**Vol. 3:** 792
13:2	**Vol. 1:** 75 **Vol. 2:** 426, 450 **Vol. 3:** 185, 211, 275, 343, 393, 1177
13:3 ff	**Vol. 3:** 507
13:3 f	**Vol. 3:** 508
13:4–23	**Vol. 2:** 915
13:4	**Vol. 2:** 37, 629, 892, 904, 912
13:5–37	**Vol. 2:** 702
13:5–31	**Vol. 2:** 904
13:5–27	**Vol. 3:** 956
13:5–13	**Vol. 2:** 904, 915
13:5 f	**Vol. 2:** 459, 461
13:5	**Vol. 2:** 911, 914
13:5b–23	**Vol. 2:** 913
13:5b	**Vol. 2:** 914
13:6	**Vol. 2:** 281, 913–914
13:7	**Vol. 2:** 62, 665, 892, 912, 918 **Vol. 3:** 962
13:7a	**Vol. 2:** 914
13:7b	**Vol. 2:** 913–914
13:8	**Vol. 1:** 165 **Vol. 2:** 266, 793, 913–914 **Vol. 3:** 558, 858, 956
13:9–13	**Vol. 2:** 904, 911
13:9	**Vol. 1:** 163, 270, 364 **Vol. 2:** 913–914 **Vol. 3:** 785, 1043
13:10	**Vol. 2:** 110, 665 **Vol. 3:** 52, 56, 213
13:11	**Vol. 1:** 90, 277 **Vol. 2:** 913 **Vol. 3:** 83, 697–698, 704, 849
13:12	**Vol. 1:** 286–287, 289, 725 **Vol. 2:** 368
13:13	**Vol. 1:** 556 **Vol. 2:** 38, 62, 773, 806, 916 **Vol. 3:** 257
13:13a	**Vol. 2:** 773, 913
13:13b–17	**Vol. 2:** 913
13:13b	**Vol. 2:** 914
13:14 f	**Vol. 2:** 916
13:14–23	**Vol. 2:** 904
13:14–20	**Vol. 2:** 37, 914 **Vol. 3:** 793
13:14–19	**Vol. 2:** 914
13:14	**Vol. 1:** 74–75 **Vol. 2:** 373, 911–912 **Vol. 3:** 792, 1011
13:15 f	**Vol. 2:** 910
13:16 f	**Vol. 2:** 911
13:17	**Vol. 3:** 1053
13:18	**Vol. 2:** 913
13:19 f	**Vol. 3:** 803
13:19	**Vol. 1:** 166 **Vol. 2:** 664, 808, 912–913, 916
13:20	**Vol. 1:** 539, 542 **Vol. 2:** 916
13:20a	**Vol. 2:** 913
13:21 ff	**Vol. 2:** 904
13:21	**Vol. 2:** 914 **Vol. 3:** 1211
13:22 f	**Vol. 1:** 323
13:22	**Vol. 2:** 472, 629, 633, 911, 913–914 **Vol. 3:** 84, 803
13:23	**Vol. 2:** 911, 914
13:24 f	**Vol. 2:** 916
13:24–31	**Vol. 2:** 904
13:24–30	**Vol. 2:** 38
13:24–27	**Vol. 2:** 913–914, 916
13:24	**Vol. 1:** 203, 425 **Vol. 2:** 37–38, 484, 892 **Vol. 3:** 732, 734
13:25	**Vol. 1:** 610 **Vol. 2:** 192, 603 **Vol. 3:** 559, 736
13:26 f	**Vol. 2:** 252, 911
13:26	**Vol. 1:** 323 **Vol. 2:** 46, 385, 604, 912, 917 **Vol. 3:** 527, 620, 622, 629, 1003

Mark *(cont'd)*

13:27 **Vol. 1:** 102, 518, 725 **Vol. 2:** 33, 194, 313, 689, 911, 917 **Vol. 3:** 527

13:28 ff **Vol. 2:** 904

13:28–37 **Vol. 2:** 913

13:28–32 **Vol. 2:** 751

13:28 f **Vol. 2:** 382, 398, 912, 914

13:28 **Vol. 1:** 486, 725 **Vol. 2:** 604 **Vol. 3:** 867

13:28b **Vol. 2:** 913

13:29 **Vol. 2:** 30, 387, 727, 911

13:30 **Vol. 2:** 36–38, 382, 910–912, 917, 930 **Vol. 3:** 1107

13:31 **Vol. 2:** 193, 911, 913 **Vol. 3:** 1108

13:32 ff **Vol. 2:** 912

13:32 f **Vol. 2:** 911, 930

13:32 **Vol. 1:** 323, 548 **Vol. 2:** 75, 192, 894, 904, 910, 913, 916–917 **Vol. 3:** 642, 844, 847–848

13:33–37 **Vol. 2:** 751, 914, 916

13:33 f **Vol. 2:** 913

13:33 **Vol. 2:** 137, 911, 914 **Vol. 3:** 515, 517, 838

13:34–37 **Vol. 1:** 725

13:34 **Vol. 2:** 502, 732, 751, 913–914

13:35 f **Vol. 2:** 911

13:35 **Vol. 2:** 136–137, 751, 914

13:36 **Vol. 1:** 489

13:37 **Vol. 2:** 137, 911, 914

14 **Vol. 1:** 633

14:1 **Vol. 1:** 199, 633 **Vol. 3:** 531, 717

14:2 **Vol. 2:** 623, 799

14:3 ff **Vol. 2:** 295, 549

14:3–9 **Vol. 3:** 1060

14:3 **Vol. 2:** 159, 464, 528 **Vol. 3:** 408, 1061

14:4 **Vol. 1:** 464 **Vol. 3:** 1060

14:5 **Vol. 2:** 112

14:6–9 **Vol. 3:** 1060

14:6 **Vol. 2:** 104 **Vol. 3:** 1149–1150

14:7 **Vol. 2:** 824

14:8 **Vol. 1:** 265 **Vol. 3:** 243, 750

14:9 **Vol. 2:** 110 **Vol. 3:** 52, 213, 242–244, 547

14:10 f **Vol. 2:** 526

14:10 **Vol. 1:** 299 **Vol. 2:** 695

14:11 **Vol. 3:** 70–71, 531–532

14:12–26 **Vol. 1:** 633

14:12 **Vol. 1:** 633–634 **Vol. 2:** 277, 463, 527 **Vol. 3:** 118, 1019

14:13 **Vol. 1:** 325 **Vol. 3:** 911, 990

14:14 **Vol. 2:** 510, 527, 549 **Vol. 3:** 767–768

14:15 **Vol. 3:** 569

14:16 **Vol. 2:** 527 **Vol. 3:** 118

14:17–21 **Vol. 2:** 531 **Vol. 3:** 804

14:17 **Vol. 2:** 528, 695

14:18–25 **Vol. 2:** 526 **Vol. 3:** 1107

14:18 **Vol. 2:** 272, 521, 526

14:19 **Vol. 2:** 720

14:20 **Vol. 2:** 695

14:21 **Vol. 2:** 526–527 **Vol. 3:** 329, 1053

14:22–25 **Vol. 1:** 237 **Vol. 2:** 523–524 **Vol. 3:** 508

14:22–24 **Vol. 1:** 634

14:22 f **Vol. 1:** 213

14:22 **Vol. 1:** 251 **Vol. 2:** 523–525, 535

14:22c **Vol. 2:** 524, 532

14:23 **Vol. 2:** 533 **Vol. 3:** 819

14:24 **Vol. 1:** 96–97, 223, 369, 437–438 **Vol. 2:** 523–526, 530, 532–533, 535–536, 543, 671, 854 **Vol. 3:** 166, 611–612

14:25 **Vol. 2:** 382, 385, 524, 531–532, 535, 727, 882, 894, 896 **Vol. 3:** 180, 922

14:26–31 **Vol. 3:** 386, 803

14:26 **Vol. 2:** 528, 713 **Vol. 3:** 245, 669

14:27 f **Vol. 3:** 567

14:27 **Vol. 2:** 34, 413, 459 **Vol. 3:** 188, 329, 697, 1122

14:28 **Vol. 2:** 732 **Vol. 3:** 281

14:30 **Vol. 1:** 173, 455 **Vol. 3:** 114, 1107, 1122

14:31 **Vol. 1:** 435

14:32 ff **Vol. 2:** 526

14:32–42 **Vol. 2:** 178, 561, 868

14:32 **Vol. 2:** 713

14:33 **Vol. 2:** 623–624, 686

14:34 **Vol. 3:** 683

14:35 ff **Vol. 3:** 804

14:35 f **Vol. 3:** 509

14:35 **Vol. 1:** 322 **Vol. 2:** 603

14:36 **Vol. 1:** 335, 614–615, 620 **Vol. 2:** 76, 83, 276, 871, 896 **Vol. 3:** 639, 697, 1022

14:37 **Vol. 1:** 442 **Vol. 3:** 713

14:38 **Vol. 1:** 677 **Vol. 2:** 137, 871 **Vol. 3:** 694, 802–803, 994

14:39 **Vol. 1:** 321 **Vol. 2:** 222 **Vol. 3:** 980

14:41 f **Vol. 3:** 516

14:41 **Vol. 2:** 150, 527, 543 **Vol. 3:** 252, 256, 580

14:42 **Vol. 2:** 54

14:43 ff **Vol. 1:** 395

14:43 **Vol. 1:** 299, 390 **Vol. 2:** 695, 801 **Vol. 3:** 967

14:44 f **Vol. 2:** 549

14:44 **Vol. 1:** 663 **Vol. 2:** 526 **Vol. 3:** 717

14:45 **Vol. 3:** 115

14:46 **Vol. 3:** 717

14:47 f **Vol. 3:** 967

14:47 **Vol. 1:** 489 **Vol. 3:** 978

14:48 **Vol. 1:** 343 **Vol. 3:** 379

14:49 **Vol. 1:** 736 **Vol. 2:** 895 **Vol. 3:** 329, 490, 761, 791, 1204

14:50 **Vol. 1:** 559

14:51 **Vol. 1:** 481 **Vol. 3:** 717

14:52 **Vol. 1:** 313, 559

14:53 ff **Vol. 1:** 395

14:53–72 **Vol. 2:** 379 **Vol. 3:** 386, 803–804

14:53–65 **Vol. 3:** 409

Mark *(cont'd)*

14:54	**Vol. 1:** 318 **Vol. 2:** 493
14:55	**Vol. 1:** 364 **Vol. 3:** 1043
14:56	**Vol. 2:** 499 **Vol. 3:** 1043
14:57 f	**Vol. 3:** 792
14:57	**Vol. 3:** 275
14:58	**Vol. 2:** 150, 236, 252, 450, 687, 732 **Vol. 3:** 185, 211, 343, 509, 784
14:59	**Vol. 2:** 499 **Vol. 3:** 1043
14:60	**Vol. 3:** 39, 275, 1042
14:61 f	**Vol. 2:** 282 **Vol. 3:** 712
14:61†	**Vol. 1:** 212 **Vol. 3:** 509
14:62	**Vol. 1:** 323 **Vol. 2:** 147, 194, 380, 385, 515, 603, 731–732, 917 **Vol. 3:** 457, 509, 588, 620, 627, 629, 1003
14:63	**Vol. 3:** 958, 1043
14:64	**Vol. 2:** 143, 175, 282, 365, 488 **Vol. 3:** 342
14:65	**Vol. 1:** 162–163 **Vol. 3:** 83, 347, 857
14:67	**Vol. 1:** 318 **Vol. 2:** 333 **Vol. 3:** 520
14:68	**Vol. 1:** 455
14:70 ff	**Vol. 1:** 455
14:70	**Vol. 1:** 455
14:71	**Vol. 1:** 415 **Vol. 2:** 398, 565 **Vol. 3:** 742
14:72	**Vol. 1:** 173 **Vol. 3:** 114, 240
15	**Vol. 2:** 378
15:1 ff	**Vol. 2:** 630
15:1–47	**Vol. 1:** 394
15:1–15	**Vol. 1:** 395
15:1	**Vol. 1:** 199, 363–364 **Vol. 2:** 526
15:2	**Vol. 2:** 315, 378–379 **Vol. 3:** 509
15:3 f	**Vol. 1:** 83
15:3	**Vol. 1:** 199
15:5	**Vol. 2:** 624
15:6–15	**Vol. 1:** 396, 505 **Vol. 3:** 189
15:6	**Vol. 2:** 858
15:7	**Vol. 1:** 633 **Vol. 2:** 331
15:8	**Vol. 1:** 411
15:9	**Vol. 2:** 315, 378 **Vol. 3:** 509
15:10	**Vol. 1:** 396, 558 **Vol. 2:** 526
15:11	**Vol. 1:** 199 **Vol. 3:** 558
15:12	**Vol. 2:** 315 **Vol. 3:** 509
15:13 f	**Vol. 1:** 409
15:14	**Vol. 3:** 189
15:15	**Vol. 1:** 162 **Vol. 2:** 526, 801 **Vol. 3:** 1017
15:16–19	**Vol. 3:** 347
15:16	**Vol. 3:** 964
15:17	**Vol. 1:** 205, 406, 726
15:18	**Vol. 2:** 315, 358, 378
15:19	**Vol. 2:** 159, 859, 877 **Vol. 3:** 903
15:20	**Vol. 1:** 205, 314 **Vol. 3:** 341
15:20b	**Vol. 1:** 396
15:21	**Vol. 1:** 396, 520 **Vol. 2:** 740
15:22	**Vol. 1:** 581
15:23	**Vol. 2:** 28, 295 **Vol. 3:** 922
15:24	**Vol. 1:** 396 **Vol. 2:** 82, 299 **Vol. 3:** 287, 670

15:25	**Vol. 3:** 847
15:26	**Vol. 2:** 139, 315, 339, 379 **Vol. 3:** 489, 509
15:27	**Vol. 2:** 148 **Vol. 3:** 379
15:28	**Vol. 1:** 736 **Vol. 2:** 445 **Vol. 3:** 379, 490, 824
15:29 ff	**Vol. 2:** 630 **Vol. 3:** 211
15:29–32	**Vol. 1:** 395, 397 **Vol. 3:** 347
15:29 f	**Vol. 3:** 792
15:29	**Vol. 1:** 396 **Vol. 2:** 82, 159, 339, 687 **Vol. 3:** 185, 287, 343, 509, 785
15:31 f	**Vol. 3:** 965
15:31	**Vol. 1:** 199, 323 **Vol. 3:** 341
15:32	**Vol. 2:** 379 **Vol. 3:** 340, 509
15:33 f	**Vol. 3:** 847
15:33	**Vol. 1:** 423 **Vol. 3:** 732
15:34 f	**Vol. 1:** 544
15:34	**Vol. 1:** 396, 411, 581, 615, 620 **Vol. 2:** 82 **Vol. 3:** 113, 1187
15:35	**Vol. 3:** 114
15:36	**Vol. 2:** 28 **Vol. 3:** 947
15:37	**Vol. 2:** 426 **Vol. 3:** 113, 708
15:38	**Vol. 2:** 328 **Vol. 3:** 543, 793, 795
15:39	**Vol. 3:** 503, 508, 708, 964–965
15:40 f	**Vol. 3:** 1059–1060, 1070
15:40	**Vol. 3:** 1071
15:41	**Vol. 3:** 546
15:42	**Vol. 3:** 120, 408, 410
15:43	**Vol. 1:** 234, 365 **Vol. 2:** 387
15:44 f	**Vol. 3:** 964
15:44	**Vol. 1:** 274 **Vol. 2:** 624, 714
15:45	**Vol. 1:** 610 **Vol. 2:** 41
15:46 ff	**Vol. 3:** 296
15:46	**Vol. 3:** 246–247, 382, 393
16	**Vol. 1:** 633
16:1 ff	**Vol. 3:** 1059
16:1 f	**Vol. 3:** 288
16:1–8a	**Vol. 3:** 286
16:1–8	**Vol. 3:** 294
16:1	**Vol. 1:** 120 **Vol. 2:** 295 **Vol. 3:** 1060
16:2 f	**Vol. 3:** 247
16:2	**Vol. 3:** 246, 412, 731
16:3	**Vol. 2:** 30
16:4	**Vol. 3:** 519
16:5 f	**Vol. 2:** 623
16:5	**Vol. 1:** 204 **Vol. 2:** 146, 624 **Vol. 3:** 247
16:6 ff	**Vol. 3:** 294
16:6	**Vol. 2:** 333 **Vol. 3:** 281, 285
16:7	**Vol. 1:** 136 **Vol. 3:** 289, 515
16:8	**Vol. 2:** 358–359 **Vol. 3:** 247, 296
16:9–20	**Vol. 1:** 510 **Vol. 2:** 632
16:9–19	**Vol. 3:** 294
16:9	**Vol. 2:** 488 **Vol. 3:** 412, 1059
16:10	**Vol. 2:** 422 **Vol. 3:** 48
16:12	**Vol. 1:** 706, 708 **Vol. 2:** 739 **Vol. 3:** 320
16:13	**Vol. 3:** 48, 251–252
16:14	**Vol. 2:** 183–184 **Vol. 3:** 320, 340
16:15 ff	**Vol. 2:** 632

Mark *(cont'd)*

16:15	**Vol. 1:** 95, 384 **Vol. 2:** 110, 176
16:16	**Vol. 1:** 489 **Vol. 2:** 366
16:17 ff	**Vol. 1:** 446
16:17 f	**Vol. 2:** 560
16:17	**Vol. 3:** 475
16:18	**Vol. 1:** 510
16:19	**Vol. 2:** 515 **Vol. 3:** 749
16:20	**Vol. 1:** 658–659 **Vol. 2:** 632 **Vol. 3:** 1152

Luke

1–2	**Vol. 3:** 700
1	**Vol. 2:** 624 **Vol. 3:** 931, 1072
1:1–4	**Vol. 2:** 113, 787 **Vol. 3:** 773
1:1	**Vol. 1:** 576, 737 **Vol. 3:** 772, 1158
1:2	**Vol. 1:** 166 **Vol. 2:** 718 **Vol. 3:** 546, 773–774
1:3 f	**Vol. 1:** 247 **Vol. 3:** 489
1:3	**Vol. 2:** 86 **Vol. 3:** 718, 822
1:4	**Vol. 1:** 663 **Vol. 2:** 920 **Vol. 3:** 771
1:5–80	**Vol. 3:** 790
1:5–25	**Vol. 2:** 327 **Vol. 3:** 1071
1:5	**Vol. 2:** 34, 378 **Vol. 3:** 37
1:6	**Vol. 1:** 335 **Vol. 2:** 144 **Vol. 3:** 361, 947
1:7	**Vol. 2:** 139, 400
1:8–23	**Vol. 3:** 790
1:8	**Vol. 2:** 34 **Vol. 3:** 37
1:9–11	**Vol. 2:** 294
1:9	**Vol. 1:** 321, 478 **Vol. 2:** 437 **Vol. 3:** 785
1:10	**Vol. 1:** 733 **Vol. 2:** 294, 799 **Vol. 3:** 847
1:11–20	**Vol. 1:** 104
1:11	**Vol. 2:** 294, 513 **Vol. 3:** 436
1:12	**Vol. 1:** 609, 622 **Vol. 3:** 710
1:13	**Vol. 1:** 178, 187, 274, 288, 623 **Vol. 2:** 178, 860
1:14	**Vol. 1:** 181 **Vol. 2:** 353–354, 358
1:15	**Vol. 1:** 739 **Vol. 3:** 457, 698, 921, 1071
1:16–28	**Vol. 1:** 129
1:16 f	**Vol. 1:** 355, 545
1:17	**Vol. 1:** 128, 322–323, 593 **Vol. 2:** 443, 620 **Vol. 3:** 80, 118–119, 361, 694, 698, 940
1:18	**Vol. 1:** 197
1:19	**Vol. 1:** 102–103, 474 **Vol. 3:** 57
1:20	**Vol. 1:** 736 **Vol. 3:** 1211
1:21 f	**Vol. 2:** 624 **Vol. 3:** 785
1:21	**Vol. 3:** 843
1:22	**Vol. 1:** 429 **Vol. 3:** 515
1:23	**Vol. 1:** 737 **Vol. 3:** 552
1:24	**Vol. 1:** 343 **Vol. 2:** 214
1:25	**Vol. 3:** 340
1:26 ff	**Vol. 3:** 1071
1:26–38	**Vol. 1:** 104
1:26	**Vol. 3:** 324
1:27	**Vol. 1:** 427, 668 **Vol. 2:** 248 **Vol. 3:** 652, 1072
1:28	**Vol. 2:** 119, 358
1:30	**Vol. 1:** 104, 623 **Vol. 2:** 118 **Vol. 3:** 530
1:31	**Vol. 1:** 274, 343 **Vol. 2:** 332
1:32 ff	**Vol. 3:** 642
1:32–35	**Vol. 3:** 637
1:32	**Vol. 1:** 274, 427 **Vol. 2:** 74, 200, 513, 614 **Vol. 3:** 457, 652
1:33	**Vol. 2:** 62, 248, 319, 381 **Vol. 3:** 662
1:33b	**Vol. 1:** 177
1:34 f	**Vol. 1:** 85 **Vol. 3:** 662
1:34	**Vol. 1:** 668 **Vol. 2:** 398 **Vol. 3:** 660, 662
1:35	**Vol. 1:** 187, 274, 322 **Vol. 2:** 87, 200, 228, 603 **Vol. 3:** 555, 660, 697–698, 1073
1:35b	**Vol. 1:** 177
1:36	**Vol. 1:** 343 **Vol. 3:** 1073
1:37	**Vol. 3:** 1121
1:38	**Vol. 1:** 607 **Vol. 2:** 119, 262 **Vol. 3:** 30, 1121
1:39	**Vol. 2:** 320 **Vol. 3:** 275, 456, 1008, 1169
1:41 f	**Vol. 3:** 84
1:41	**Vol. 1:** 283, 739 **Vol. 3:** 698, 700
1:42	**Vol. 1:** 213, 411, 722
1:44	**Vol. 1:** 283 **Vol. 2:** 353, 358
1:45	**Vol. 1:** 216–217 **Vol. 2:** 63 **Vol. 3:** 1198, 1211
1:46–55	**Vol. 2:** 596 **Vol. 3:** 30, 674, 1071
1:46–48	**Vol. 3:** 30
1:46	**Vol. 2:** 596 **Vol. 3:** 683
1:47	**Vol. 2:** 353, 358 **Vol. 3:** 219, 693
1:48	**Vol. 1:** 216 **Vol. 2:** 35, 262, 596, 603
1:49–50	**Vol. 3:** 30
1:49	**Vol. 2:** 228, 426
1:50 ff	**Vol. 2:** 543
1:50	**Vol. 2:** 35, 596
1:51–53	**Vol. 3:** 30
1:51	**Vol. 2:** 34 **Vol. 3:** 30, 127, 718
1:52	**Vol. 2:** 203, 262, 596
1:53	**Vol. 1:** 128, 735 **Vol. 2:** 266–267, 596, 842–843
1:54 f	**Vol. 3:** 30
1:54	**Vol. 2:** 596 **Vol. 3:** 241, 612
1:55	**Vol. 2:** 358, 596 **Vol. 3:** 523, 829–830
1:57	**Vol. 1:** 737 **Vol. 3:** 834, 843
1:58	**Vol. 2:** 595
1:59	**Vol. 1:** 284, 309 **Vol. 2:** 692
1:63	**Vol. 2:** 624, 858 **Vol. 3:** 489
1:64	**Vol. 1:** 213 **Vol. 2:** 726, 728 **Vol. 3:** 1079
1:65	**Vol. 3:** 1008
1:66	**Vol. 2:** 149, 513
1:67	**Vol. 1:** 739 **Vol. 3:** 84, 698, 700
1:68 ff	**Vol. 2:** 358
1:68–79	**Vol. 2:** 596 **Vol. 3:** 674, 715

Luke *(cont'd)*

1:68   **Vol. 1:** 191, 212   **Vol. 2:** 73, 358, 596, 799   **Vol. 3:** 198
1:69   **Vol. 1:** 427   **Vol. 2:** 248, 596   **Vol. 3:** 198, 212, 612, 652, 715
1:70   **Vol. 2:** 228, 358   **Vol. 3:** 830
1:71   **Vol. 1:** 554, 557   **Vol. 2:** 596   **Vol. 3:** 198, 212
1:72   **Vol. 2:** 228, 596   **Vol. 3:** 241
1:73   **Vol. 3:** 198, 742
1:74   **Vol. 1:** 554, 566   **Vol. 2:** 596   **Vol. 3:** 550
1:75   **Vol. 2:** 237, 480   **Vol. 3:** 361
1:76   **Vol. 1:** 545   **Vol. 2:** 200, 332, 596   **Vol. 3:** 80, 86, 118, 198, 940
1:77   **Vol. 1:** 701   **Vol. 2:** 596, 799   **Vol. 3:** 198, 212, 580
1:78 f   **Vol. 3:** 212
1:78   **Vol. 2:** 78, 199, 495, 596, 599   **Vol. 3:** 198
1:79   **Vol. 1:** 423   **Vol. 2:** 596, 780–781   **Vol. 3:** 198, 319, 555, 940
1:80   **Vol. 1:** 92   **Vol. 2:** 129   **Vol. 3:** 570, 694, 718, 1007
2   **Vol. 2:** 624   **Vol. 3:** 317, 931, 1073
2:1 ff   **Vol. 3:** 642
2:1–52   **Vol. 3:** 1071
2:1–3   **Vol. 1:** 171
2:1–2   **Vol. 1:** 669
2:1   **Vol. 1:** 269, 322, 330, 519
2:2   **Vol. 1:** 666
2:4   **Vol. 1:** 427, 616   **Vol. 2:** 185, 248, 803   **Vol. 3:** 63, 652, 1174, 1180
2:5   **Vol. 3:** 1073
2:6 f   **Vol. 1:** 187
2:6   **Vol. 1:** 737
2:7   **Vol. 1:** 668   **Vol. 3:** 189
2:8–14   **Vol. 3:** 1007
2:8 f   **Vol. 1:** 421   **Vol. 3:** 566
2:8   **Vol. 2:** 135–136
2:9   **Vol. 1:** 102, 622   **Vol. 2:** 46, 486, 513
2:10   **Vol. 1:** 623   **Vol. 2:** 799   **Vol. 3:** 57
2:11   **Vol. 1:** 427   **Vol. 2:** 332, 358   **Vol. 3:** 219, 652, 838
2:12   **Vol. 1:** 283   **Vol. 2:** 629
2:13   **Vol. 1:** 102, 733   **Vol. 2:** 191   **Vol. 3:** 517, 817, 964
2:14   **Vol. 1:** 288   **Vol. 2:** 46, 358, 566, 780–781, 819   **Vol. 3:** 219
2:15   **Vol. 1:** 169, 171   **Vol. 2:** 193, 358   **Vol. 3:** 314, 1121–1122
2:16   **Vol. 1:** 283   **Vol. 3:** 1169
2:17   **Vol. 3:** 314, 1121
2:18   **Vol. 2:** 624
2:19   **Vol. 3:** 1121–1122
2:20   **Vol. 2:** 176   **Vol. 3:** 817
2:21 f   **Vol. 1:** 737
2:21   **Vol. 1:** 98, 169, 309, 343   **Vol. 2:** 692
2:22 ff   **Vol. 2:** 327

2:22–52   **Vol. 3:** 790
2:22   **Vol. 1:** 474   **Vol. 2:** 444   **Vol. 3:** 409, 1058
2:23   **Vol. 1:** 736   **Vol. 2:** 228, 444, 570, 729   **Vol. 3:** 660
2:24   **Vol. 1:** 172, 175   **Vol. 2:** 41, 444   **Vol. 3:** 430, 790, 1164
2:25–38   **Vol. 3:** 1059
2:25–27   **Vol. 3:** 698
2:25 f   **Vol. 3:** 790
2:25   **Vol. 1:** 329, 570   **Vol. 2:** 91, 245   **Vol. 3:** 84, 361
2:26   **Vol. 3:** 517
2:27   **Vol. 2:** 444
2:28 f   **Vol. 1:** 213
2:28   **Vol. 1:** 239
2:29–32   **Vol. 3:** 674, 790
2:29   **Vol. 1:** 505   **Vol. 2:** 509   **Vol. 3:** 189, 1121–1122
2:30–32   **Vol. 2:** 314
2:30 f   **Vol. 3:** 118
2:30   **Vol. 3:** 221, 515
2:31 f   **Vol. 2:** 799
2:31   **Vol. 1:** 586
2:32   **Vol. 2:** 494, 799   **Vol. 3:** 313
2:33   **Vol. 2:** 624
2:34   **Vol. 1:** 207, 213, 471, 610   **Vol. 2:** 367, 629, 706, 708–709   **Vol. 3:** 276, 516, 821
2:35   **Vol. 3:** 312, 684, 821, 967
2:36   **Vol. 3:** 81, 84, 872–873, 1072
2:37   **Vol. 1:** 607   **Vol. 3:** 550
2:38   **Vol. 2:** 245, 314   **Vol. 3:** 198, 790, 846
2:39   **Vol. 2:** 63, 444
2:40   **Vol. 1:** 92   **Vol. 2:** 118, 129   **Vol. 3:** 718, 1030, 1194
2:41–51   **Vol. 1:** 256
2:41   **Vol. 1:** 169, 632–633   **Vol. 3:** 409
2:42   **Vol. 1:** 169   **Vol. 2:** 437, 696
2:43   **Vol. 1:** 283, 737   **Vol. 2:** 63, 773
2:44   **Vol. 3:** 489, 940
2:46   **Vol. 2:** 236, 327, 880   **Vol. 3:** 767, 789
2:47   **Vol. 3:** 132
2:48   **Vol. 1:** 530
2:49   **Vol. 2:** 327, 665   **Vol. 3:** 698, 1070
2:50   **Vol. 3:** 132, 1122
2:51   **Vol. 3:** 931, 1070
2:52   **Vol. 1:** 92   **Vol. 2:** 118, 130   **Vol. 3:** 1030
3   **Vol. 2:** 36
3:1 ff   **Vol. 2:** 262
3:1   **Vol. 1:** 269   **Vol. 2:** 550
3:2–17   **Vol. 1:** 111
3:2   **Vol. 3:** 39–40, 1007, 1107, 1121, 1193
3:3   **Vol. 3:** 52, 55, 580, 1208
3:4–6   **Vol. 3:** 1011
3:4   **Vol. 1:** 244, 411, 736   **Vol. 3:** 53, 118, 940
3:5   **Vol. 2:** 262
3:6   **Vol. 3:** 118, 221, 1011

Luke *(cont'd)*

3:7–9   **Vol. 3:** 695
3:7   **Vol. 1:** 559   **Vol. 2:** 801   **Vol. 3:** 1208
3:8   **Vol. 1:** 77, 167, 286   **Vol. 3:** 393, 822, 869
3:9   **Vol. 1:** 156, 656, 722   **Vol. 2:** 104, 749   **Vol. 3:** 869
3:10   **Vol. 2:** 801   **Vol. 3:** 869
3:11   **Vol. 2:** 41   **Vol. 3:** 1155
3:12 f   **Vol. 3:** 758
3:12   **Vol. 3:** 767
3:13   **Vol. 3:** 1022, 1157
3:14   **Vol. 3:** 144, 558, 727, 965
3:15–18   **Vol. 3:** 695
3:15   **Vol. 3:** 820
3:16 f   **Vol. 2:** 921
3:16   **Vol. 1:** 323   **Vol. 2:** 785–786, 921   **Vol. 3:** 55, 110, 179, 447, 714, 1210
3:17   **Vol. 1:** 156   **Vol. 2:** 32, 411   **Vol. 3:** 111, 804
3:18   **Vol. 1:** 571   **Vol. 2:** 113   **Vol. 3:** 57, 87
3:19   **Vol. 2:** 141   **Vol. 3:** 540
3:20   **Vol. 2:** 136   **Vol. 3:** 1193
3:21 f   **Vol. 2:** 873   **Vol. 3:** 113
3:21   **Vol. 2:** 193, 728, 799   **Vol. 3:** 170, 543, 990
3:22   **Vol. 1:** 175, 179, 704   **Vol. 2:** 193, 314, 543, 566, 819   **Vol. 3:** 114, 499, 611, 639, 641, 659, 697–698, 807, 987, 1070
3:23 ff   **Vol. 2:** 691
3:23–38   **Vol. 1:** 77, 177–178   **Vol. 2:** 79, 314   **Vol. 3:** 654
3:23   **Vol. 1:** 167   **Vol. 2:** 333   **Vol. 3:** 655, 658–659, 662, 1073
3:24   **Vol. 2:** 467
3:26   **Vol. 2:** 320   **Vol. 3:** 397
3:27   **Vol. 3:** 655
3:29   **Vol. 2:** 331, 467
3:31   **Vol. 1:** 427   **Vol. 3:** 63, 652
3:33   **Vol. 2:** 320
3:34   **Vol. 1:** 77, 81   **Vol. 2:** 318, 320
3:36   **Vol. 3:** 543
3:37   **Vol. 2:** 236
3:38   **Vol. 1:** 85   **Vol. 2:** 920   **Vol. 3:** 659
4:1 f   **Vol. 3:** 1007
4:1–14   **Vol. 3:** 698
4:1–13   **Vol. 3:** 470, 804, 979, 1007
4:1–4   **Vol. 2:** 630
4:1   **Vol. 1:** 739   **Vol. 3:** 602, 697–698, 700, 991
4:2   **Vol. 2:** 267, 689, 696, 893
4:3   **Vol. 3:** 659
4:4   **Vol. 2:** 267, 872   **Vol. 3:** 805
4:5 f   **Vol. 3:** 806
4:5   **Vol. 1:** 519, 524   **Vol. 2:** 381   **Vol. 3:** 569, 843
4:6   **Vol. 2:** 42, 46, 368, 610
4:7   **Vol. 2:** 877, 893   **Vol. 3:** 806–807

4:8   **Vol. 2:** 877, 893   **Vol. 3:** 550
4:9–12   **Vol. 2:** 631   **Vol. 3:** 790, 796, 1011
4:9   **Vol. 2:** 235   **Vol. 3:** 659
4:10 f   **Vol. 3:** 805
4:10   **Vol. 1:** 335
4:11   **Vol. 2:** 706
4:12   **Vol. 2:** 893   **Vol. 3:** 802, 805
4:13   **Vol. 1:** 607   **Vol. 2:** 728   **Vol. 3:** 804
4:14 ff   **Vol. 2:** 631   **Vol. 3:** 762
4:14   **Vol. 2:** 603   **Vol. 3:** 698
4:15 f   **Vol. 3:** 785
4:15   **Vol. 3:** 761
4:16 ff   **Vol. 3:** 88, 761–762, 764
4:16–30   **Vol. 2:** 631
4:16–27   **Vol. 2:** 379
4:16–21   **Vol. 3:** 589, 821
4:16 f   **Vol. 1:** 245
4:16   **Vol. 1:** 245, 321, 628   **Vol. 2:** 333, 437, 887   **Vol. 3:** 56, 275, 409
4:17   **Vol. 1:** 244, 736   **Vol. 2:** 728   **Vol. 3:** 485
4:18 ff   **Vol. 1:** 701
4:18–21   **Vol. 1:** 701
4:18 f   **Vol. 1:** 738   **Vol. 2:** 118   **Vol. 3:** 612, 639, 696
4:18   **Vol. 1:** 122–123, 701   **Vol. 2:** 110, 113, 712, 825   **Vol. 3:** 499, 591, 698, 733, 1061, 1108
4:19   **Vol. 3:** 744, 746
4:20   **Vol. 3:** 135, 520, 785
4:21   **Vol. 1:** 167, 736, 738   **Vol. 2:** 118   **Vol. 3:** 71, 329, 490, 492, 762–763, 1178
4:22   **Vol. 1:** 96   **Vol. 2:** 118, 333, 757   **Vol. 3:** 660
4:22a   **Vol. 2:** 624
4:23   **Vol. 1:** 616   **Vol. 2:** 164, 746, 757
4:24   **Vol. 2:** 231, 641   **Vol. 3:** 83, 86, 746
4:25 f   **Vol. 1:** 544   **Vol. 3:** 1062
4:25   **Vol. 1:** 98   **Vol. 2:** 31, 193, 266, 688, 730   **Vol. 3:** 883
4:27   **Vol. 2:** 464
4:28   **Vol. 1:** 106, 110, 739   **Vol. 3:** 785
4:29   **Vol. 2:** 624   **Vol. 3:** 275
4:30   **Vol. 3:** 1178
4:31   **Vol. 3:** 88
4:32   **Vol. 2:** 610, 623   **Vol. 3:** 83, 532, 1106
4:33   **Vol. 1:** 637   **Vol. 2:** 426   **Vol. 3:** 113, 785
4:34   **Vol. 2:** 228, 333, 559
4:35 f   **Vol. 3:** 1059
4:36   **Vol. 2:** 610, 623–624   **Vol. 3:** 475, 694, 1106
4:37   **Vol. 3:** 112
4:38   **Vol. 1:** 656   **Vol. 2:** 880   **Vol. 3:** 785
4:39   **Vol. 1:** 572   **Vol. 3:** 275, 546
4:40 f   **Vol. 2:** 165
4:40   **Vol. 1:** 314   **Vol. 3:** 731
4:42   **Vol. 3:** 1007
4:43   **Vol. 2:** 113, 665   **Vol. 3:** 54

Luke *(cont'd)*

4:44	**Vol. 1:** 297 **Vol. 2:** 631 **Vol. 3:** 56, 785, 1174
5:1–11	**Vol. 2:** 630, 825 **Vol. 3:** 985
5:1	**Vol. 1:** 181 **Vol. 3:** 315, 984, 992, 1114
5:2	**Vol. 3:** 992
5:3	**Vol. 3:** 761
5:4	**Vol. 2:** 197 **Vol. 3:** 803
5:5–8	**Vol. 3:** 1122
5:5	**Vol. 1:** 263 **Vol. 2:** 595 **Vol. 3:** 115, 1193
5:6	**Vol. 1:** 671, 733 **Vol. 3:** 543
5:7	**Vol. 1:** 344, 736 **Vol. 2:** 739
5:8	**Vol. 1:** 610 **Vol. 2:** 563, 859 **Vol. 3:** 580
5:9	**Vol. 1:** 344 **Vol. 2:** 623–624
5:10	**Vol. 1:** 489, 623, 642
5:11	**Vol. 1:** 482
5:12–16	**Vol. 2:** 631
5:12 f	**Vol. 2:** 466
5:12	**Vol. 1:** 586, 609 **Vol. 2:** 860 **Vol. 3:** 1022
5:13	**Vol. 2:** 150 **Vol. 3:** 1022
5:14	**Vol. 1:** 340 **Vol. 3:** 37, 569, 1043
5:15	**Vol. 3:** 1106
5:16	**Vol. 2:** 869 **Vol. 3:** 1007
5:17	**Vol. 2:** 170 **Vol. 3:** 480, 761, 768
5:18 ff	**Vol. 3:** 1000
5:18–26	**Vol. 2:** 610, 631
5:18	**Vol. 3:** 999
5:19	**Vol. 3:** 912
5:21 ff	**Vol. 2:** 170
5:21	**Vol. 2:** 170, 720, 724 **Vol. 3:** 342, 481
5:22	**Vol. 3:** 820
5:23 f	**Vol. 2:** 920 **Vol. 3:** 280
5:23	**Vol. 2:** 193, 434
5:24	**Vol. 2:** 415 **Vol. 3:** 999
5:26	**Vol. 1:** 528 **Vol. 3:** 748
5:27–32	**Vol. 2:** 523 **Vol. 3:** 428, 980
5:27	**Vol. 2:** 467, 754 **Vol. 3:** 759
5:28	**Vol. 3:** 251, 275, 757
5:29 f	**Vol. 2:** 630
5:29	**Vol. 2:** 467 **Vol. 3:** 757
5:30	**Vol. 2:** 170, 276, 813
5:31	**Vol. 2:** 170, 386, 757 **Vol. 3:** 758, 998
5:32	**Vol. 1:** 274, 322, 358 **Vol. 2:** 276 **Vol. 3:** 361, 492, 580
5:33 ff	**Vol. 1:** 495
5:33–39	**Vol. 2:** 754
5:33–38	**Vol. 3:** 921
5:33 f	**Vol. 2:** 359
5:33	**Vol. 1:** 487, 637 **Vol. 2:** 170, 276
5:34	**Vol. 2:** 358, 383, 585, 799
5:35	**Vol. 2:** 585
5:36 f†	**Vol. 2:** 714
5:36	**Vol. 2:** 670 **Vol. 3:** 543
5:37	**Vol. 2:** 854
5:38	**Vol. 2:** 675–676
5:39	**Vol. 2:** 105, 714 **Vol. 3:** 921
6	**Vol. 1:** 217 **Vol. 3:** 1009
6:1–5	**Vol. 2:** 267, 754 **Vol. 3:** 37, 408, 423, 429
6:2	**Vol. 2:** 170
6:3	**Vol. 1:** 427 **Vol. 3:** 329
6:4	**Vol. 1:** 586 **Vol. 2:** 248 **Vol. 3:** 792
6:5	**Vol. 1:** 216
6:6–11	**Vol. 3:** 409, 442
6:6	**Vol. 1:** 129, 516 **Vol. 3:** 761–762, 785
6:7	**Vol. 1:** 83 **Vol. 2:** 133, 165, 170, 813
6:8	**Vol. 3:** 275, 820
6:9	**Vol. 1:** 463 **Vol. 2:** 102, 434, 880
6:10	**Vol. 2:** 150 **Vol. 3:** 147
6:11	**Vol. 1:** 739 **Vol. 2:** 813 **Vol. 3:** 128
6:12–16	**Vol. 1:** 135 **Vol. 3:** 453, 980
6:12 f	**Vol. 2:** 873
6:12	**Vol. 1:** 420 **Vol. 2:** 869 **Vol. 3:** 1009–1010
6:13	**Vol. 1:** 128, 136, 540, 542 **Vol. 2:** 655, 695 **Vol. 3:** 54
6:14 ff	**Vol. 1:** 136 **Vol. 2:** 652
6:14	**Vol. 2:** 550, 655
6:15	**Vol. 1:** 274, 488 **Vol. 3:** 1167
6:16	**Vol. 1:** 299 **Vol. 2:** 320–321 **Vol. 3:** 1011
6:17–49	**Vol. 2:** 150
6:17	**Vol. 1:** 733 **Vol. 2:** 327, 801 **Vol. 3:** 1009
6:18	**Vol. 2:** 164 **Vol. 3:** 475
6:19	**Vol. 2:** 169, 757 **Vol. 3:** 860, 1201
6:20 ff	**Vol. 1:** 216–217, 495 **Vol. 2:** 386, 388, 449, 543
6:20–49	**Vol. 2:** 598
6:20 f	**Vol. 3:** 696
6:20	**Vol. 2:** 300, 381, 824 **Vol. 3:** 978
6:21	**Vol. 1:** 217, 744 **Vol. 2:** 266–267, 416
6:21b	**Vol. 2:** 433
6:22 ff	**Vol. 2:** 544
6:22	**Vol. 1:** 453, 473, 566 **Vol. 3:** 257, 340, 627
6:23	**Vol. 2:** 353, 426, 894 **Vol. 3:** 83
6:24 ff	**Vol. 2:** 824–825, 843
6:24–26	**Vol. 3:** 1053
6:24	**Vol. 1:** 571 **Vol. 2:** 842
6:25 f	**Vol. 2:** 416
6:25	**Vol. 1:** 735 **Vol. 2:** 267, 417, 422
6:25b	**Vol. 2:** 433
6:26	**Vol. 2:** 472 **Vol. 3:** 83, 1155
6:27 ff	**Vol. 3:** 979
6:27 f	**Vol. 1:** 215 **Vol. 2:** 386, 544 **Vol. 3:** 183
6:27	**Vol. 1:** 556 **Vol. 2:** 543 **Vol. 3:** 97
6:28	**Vol. 1:** 417 **Vol. 3:** 755
6:29 f	**Vol. 3:** 183
6:29	**Vol. 2:** 222 **Vol. 3:** 903
6:30	**Vol. 2:** 846
6:30b	**Vol. 2:** 858
6:32 ff	**Vol. 3:** 580
6:32–36	**Vol. 2:** 386, 544 **Vol. 3:** 183
6:32–34	**Vol. 2:** 118

Luke *(cont'd)*

6:32	**Vol. 2:** 366
6:33	**Vol. 2:** 102 **Vol. 3:** 757
6:34	**Vol. 2:** 241, 498–499 **Vol. 3:** 751
6:35	**Vol. 1:** 556, 566 **Vol. 2:** 102, 106, 426, 929
6:36†	**Vol. 1:** 620 **Vol. 2:** 63, 543, 598
6:37	**Vol. 1:** 505, 702 **Vol. 2:** 370 **Vol. 3:** 189
6:38	**Vol. 1:** 240 **Vol. 2:** 43 **Vol. 3:** 402, 559, 1173
6:39	**Vol. 1:** 220, 610 **Vol. 2:** 757 **Vol. 3:** 942
6:40	**Vol. 1:** 404, 486
6:41 f	**Vol. 2:** 469, 749
6:41	**Vol. 1:** 116 **Vol. 3:** 129
6:42	**Vol. 2:** 757
6:43 ff	**Vol. 2:** 104, 749 **Vol. 3:** 868
6:43 f	**Vol. 3:** 869
6:43	**Vol. 1:** 722 **Vol. 2:** 757
6:44	**Vol. 2:** 33 **Vol. 3:** 1174
6:45	**Vol. 2:** 100, 831
6:45b	**Vol. 1:** 567
6:46	**Vol. 1:** 274 **Vol. 2:** 272, 276, 513–514 **Vol. 3:** 1155
6:47 ff	**Vol. 2:** 383, 749 **Vol. 3:** 1155
6:48 f	**Vol. 1:** 661 **Vol. 3:** 987
6:48	**Vol. 3:** 559
7	**Vol. 3:** 558, 1061
7:1 ff	**Vol. 3:** 999
7:1–10	**Vol. 3:** 456
7:1	**Vol. 2:** 799
7:2 f	**Vol. 3:** 611
7:2	**Vol. 1:** 326 **Vol. 3:** 964
7:3	**Vol. 1:** 197, 199 **Vol. 2:** 315 **Vol. 3:** 211
7:4	**Vol. 1:** 570 **Vol. 3:** 1169
7:5	**Vol. 1:** 297 **Vol. 2:** 793 **Vol. 3:** 785
7:6	**Vol. 2:** 549 **Vol. 3:** 964
7:7 f	**Vol. 3:** 611
7:7	**Vol. 1:** 283 **Vol. 2:** 169 **Vol. 3:** 348
7:8	**Vol. 2:** 608 **Vol. 3:** 964
7:9 f	**Vol. 2:** 245
7:9	**Vol. 2:** 624 **Vol. 3:** 964
7:10	**Vol. 2:** 170
7:11 ff	**Vol. 1:** 445 **Vol. 2:** 168
7:11–17	**Vol. 2:** 630 **Vol. 3:** 303, 1059
7:11 f	**Vol. 2:** 480
7:12	**Vol. 1:** 329 **Vol. 2:** 29 **Vol. 3:** 1071, 1202
7:13	**Vol. 2:** 416, 419, 600 **Vol. 3:** 280
7:14 f	**Vol. 3:** 1108
7:14	**Vol. 3:** 280
7:15	**Vol. 1:** 167, 445 **Vol. 3:** 1071
7:16	**Vol. 1:** 191 **Vol. 2:** 632, 641, 799 **Vol. 3:** 83, 86, 457, 748
7:18 ff	**Vol. 2:** 631
7:19 f	**Vol. 2:** 379
7:19	**Vol. 3:** 367, 378
7:20	**Vol. 3:** 82
7:21 ff	**Vol. 3:** 848
7:21	**Vol. 1:** 163, 219 **Vol. 3:** 475, 515, 847
7:22 f	**Vol. 3:** 1122
7:22	**Vol. 1:** 428, 445 **Vol. 2:** 110, 176, 358, 379, 415, 464, 825 **Vol. 3:** 519, 696–697, 733
7:23	**Vol. 2:** 170, 708
7:24	**Vol. 1:** 102 **Vol. 2:** 799 **Vol. 3:** 559, 1007, 1022, 1198
7:25	**Vol. 2:** 47
7:26 f	**Vol. 3:** 1122
7:26	**Vol. 3:** 83, 86–87
7:27	**Vol. 1:** 102 **Vol. 3:** 80, 119, 329, 940
7:28	**Vol. 2:** 427, 429
7:29	**Vol. 2:** 799 **Vol. 3:** 361, 758
7:30	**Vol. 1:** 74 **Vol. 2:** 170 **Vol. 3:** 480, 1017, 1208
7:31	**Vol. 2:** 433
7:32	**Vol. 2:** 416, 418 **Vol. 3:** 674
7:33 f	**Vol. 3:** 921
7:33	**Vol. 1:** 250 **Vol. 3:** 82, 623, 921
7:34	**Vol. 2:** 276, 549 **Vol. 3:** 628, 758
7:35	**Vol. 1:** 286 **Vol. 3:** 1030, 1180, 1198
7:36 ff	**Vol. 1:** 689 **Vol. 2:** 549 **Vol. 3:** 475, 580
7:36–50	**Vol. 1:** 701 **Vol. 2:** 118 **Vol. 3:** 1059, 1061
7:36 f	**Vol. 2:** 812
7:36	**Vol. 2:** 170, 272, 880 **Vol. 3:** 1061
7:37 f	**Vol. 2:** 295
7:38 ff	**Vol. 1:** 120
7:38–46	**Vol. 1:** 239
7:38	**Vol. 1:** 120, 167 **Vol. 2:** 417 **Vol. 3:** 1002
7:39 f	**Vol. 3:** 88
7:39	**Vol. 3:** 83, 86–87, 860
7:40	**Vol. 3:** 767, 1061
7:41 ff	**Vol. 2:** 750
7:41–43	**Vol. 2:** 386, 668
7:41	**Vol. 2:** 502
7:43 f	**Vol. 3:** 1061
7:43	**Vol. 2:** 364 **Vol. 3:** 749
7:44 ff	**Vol. 3:** 545, 547
7:44 f	**Vol. 2:** 812
7:44	**Vol. 3:** 989, 1002
7:45	**Vol. 3:** 251
7:46	**Vol. 1:** 120 **Vol. 2:** 159, 295, 712
7:47 ff	**Vol. 1:** 701
7:47	**Vol. 1:** 97 **Vol. 2:** 544
7:49	**Vol. 1:** 167, 701
7:50	**Vol. 3:** 212
8	**Vol. 2:** 749
8:1–3	**Vol. 1:** 642 **Vol. 3:** 1059
8:1	**Vol. 2:** 113, 695, 750 **Vol. 3:** 52, 54
8:2	**Vol. 1:** 274 **Vol. 2:** 691 **Vol. 3:** 475, 1059
8:3	**Vol. 2:** 845–846 **Vol. 3:** 546–547, 1053
8:4–8	**Vol. 2:** 748, 750 **Vol. 3:** 522

Luke *(cont'd)*

8:5	**Vol. 1:** 174 **Vol. 2:** 192 **Vol. 3:** 944
8:6 ff	**Vol. 2:** 739
8:6	**Vol. 1:** 516 **Vol. 3:** 382
8:7	**Vol. 1:** 226
8:8	**Vol. 2:** 178, 750 **Vol. 3:** 114
8:9 f	**Vol. 2:** 750, 753 **Vol. 3:** 132
8:9	**Vol. 1:** 340
8:10	**Vol. 2:** 178 **Vol. 3:** 251–253, 313–314, 503
8:11–15	**Vol. 2:** 748, 750 **Vol. 3:** 522, 868
8:11	**Vol. 3:** 746
8:12	**Vol. 1:** 174, 566 **Vol. 3:** 470
8:13	**Vol. 1:** 607–608 **Vol. 2:** 177, 358, 708, 808 **Vol. 3:** 382, 746, 803, 837–838
8:14	**Vol. 1:** 459, 726 **Vol. 2:** 475, 842–843, 846
8:15	**Vol. 2:** 104, 178, 183, 773 **Vol. 3:** 868
8:16	**Vol. 2:** 212, 487, 493, 749 **Vol. 3:** 860, 913
8:17	**Vol. 2:** 212, 216 **Vol. 3:** 312, 320
8:18	**Vol. 2:** 750 **Vol. 3:** 822
8:19 ff	**Vol. 2:** 750 **Vol. 3:** 1062, 1070
8:20	**Vol. 3:** 46
8:21	**Vol. 2:** 733 **Vol. 3:** 315
8:22 ff	**Vol. 3:** 992
8:22–25	**Vol. 2:** 630 **Vol. 3:** 984–985
8:22	**Vol. 3:** 984
8:23 ff	**Vol. 3:** 1002
8:23	**Vol. 1:** 419, 736 **Vol. 3:** 1003
8:24 f	**Vol. 3:** 989
8:24	**Vol. 2:** 595 **Vol. 3:** 115, 767
8:25	**Vol. 2:** 179, 623
8:26 ff	**Vol. 3:** 475
8:26–37	**Vol. 2:** 631
8:27	**Vol. 1:** 325 **Vol. 3:** 246, 729, 843
8:28	**Vol. 2:** 860 **Vol. 3:** 856
8:29	**Vol. 3:** 592, 843, 1008
8:31	**Vol. 2:** 205 **Vol. 3:** 474
8:32	**Vol. 1:** 570 **Vol. 3:** 1011
8:33	**Vol. 1:** 226 **Vol. 3:** 984–985, 990
8:35	**Vol. 1:** 239, 502 **Vol. 2:** 433
8:37	**Vol. 1:** 733
8:39	**Vol. 1:** 576 **Vol. 3:** 56
8:40–56	**Vol. 2:** 168, 630 **Vol. 3:** 1059
8:40	**Vol. 3:** 746
8:41	**Vol. 1:** 168 **Vol. 3:** 785
8:42	**Vol. 1:** 226 **Vol. 2:** 696, 799 **Vol. 3:** 1202
8:43 ff	**Vol. 2:** 165
8:43–48	**Vol. 1:** 77
8:43 f	**Vol. 1:** 683
8:43	**Vol. 2:** 164, 696, 846 **Vol. 3:** 714
8:44 f	**Vol. 3:** 860
8:45 f	**Vol. 3:** 860
8:45	**Vol. 2:** 595 **Vol. 3:** 115, 767
8:47	**Vol. 2:** 138, 168, 799
8:48	**Vol. 1:** 328 **Vol. 3:** 212
8:50	**Vol. 1:** 623
8:51	**Vol. 1:** 284 **Vol. 3:** 1071
8:52	**Vol. 2:** 418
8:54 f	**Vol. 3:** 280
8:54	**Vol. 3:** 114, 717
8:55	**Vol. 2:** 919 **Vol. 3:** 694
8:56	**Vol. 1:** 340 **Vol. 2:** 631
9	**Vol. 3:** 862
9:1 f	**Vol. 2:** 632
9:1–6	**Vol. 2:** 733, 825
9:1	**Vol. 2:** 165, 169, 609–610, 695 **Vol. 3:** 475
9:2–5	**Vol. 3:** 453
9:2	**Vol. 2:** 168–169 **Vol. 3:** 52
9:3	**Vol. 1:** 143, 407
9:5	**Vol. 1:** 239 **Vol. 3:** 560, 946
9:6	**Vol. 2:** 113, 165, 632 **Vol. 3:** 54, 57
9:7 f	**Vol. 2:** 342
9:8	**Vol. 1:** 167 **Vol. 2:** 488 **Vol. 3:** 83, 86
9:10–17	**Vol. 1:** 729 **Vol. 2:** 150, 272, 523
9:10	**Vol. 1:** 131, 136, 576 **Vol. 2:** 401 **Vol. 3:** 131
9:11–17	**Vol. 2:** 630
9:11	**Vol. 2:** 168, 459, 630
9:12	**Vol. 1:** 520 **Vol. 2:** 695 **Vol. 3:** 189, 1007
9:14	**Vol. 2:** 381, 699
9:15	**Vol. 3:** 1043
9:16	**Vol. 2:** 192, 801 **Vol. 3:** 519
9:17	**Vol. 1:** 743
9:18 ff	**Vol. 2:** 680
9:18–22	**Vol. 2:** 341 **Vol. 3:** 1061
9:18	**Vol. 2:** 724, 869, 873
9:19	**Vol. 1:** 167 **Vol. 3:** 82–83, 86
9:20	**Vol. 2:** 76, 231 **Vol. 3:** 384, 809
9:21	**Vol. 1:** 340
9:22	**Vol. 2:** 63, 665, 893 **Vol. 3:** 39, 276, 294, 723
9:23	**Vol. 1:** 324, 394, 402–403, 455 **Vol. 2:** 895 **Vol. 3:** 683
9:24 f	**Vol. 3:** 174
9:24	**Vol. 2:** 433, 919 **Vol. 3:** 212, 530, 682
9:25	**Vol. 3:** 137, 174
9:26	**Vol. 1:** 323 **Vol. 2:** 228 **Vol. 3:** 135, 563
9:27	**Vol. 1:** 98 **Vol. 2:** 271, 382 **Vol. 3:** 863, 883
9:28 ff	**Vol. 2:** 873
9:28–36	**Vol. 2:** 48 **Vol. 3:** 114
9:28	**Vol. 1:** 181 **Vol. 2:** 185, 686, 692 **Vol. 3:** 604, 862, 1010–1012
9:29–35	**Vol. 2:** 47
9:29	**Vol. 1:** 204, 704, 708 **Vol. 2:** 486, 739 **Vol. 3:** 862
9:30 f	**Vol. 2:** 559
9:31	**Vol. 1:** 326, 545 **Vol. 2:** 46, 327 **Vol. 3:** 863, 940, 1011
9:32	**Vol. 1:** 261, 442 **Vol. 2:** 46, 48
9:33	**Vol. 2:** 514, 595 **Vol. 3:** 115, 812
9:34–38	**Vol. 2:** 560
9:34 f	**Vol. 3:** 1003

Luke (cont'd)

9:34   **Vol. 3:** 555
9:35   **Vol. 1:** 541   **Vol. 2:** 176, 543   **Vol. 3:** 611
9:36   **Vol. 3:** 48
9:37 ff   **Vol. 3:** 475
9:37   **Vol. 1:** 325   **Vol. 3:** 862, 1010, 1012
9:38   **Vol. 1:** 411   **Vol. 2:** 595, 860   **Vol. 3:** 1202
9:39   **Vol. 1:** 409   **Vol. 3:** 748
9:40   **Vol. 3:** 174
9:41   **Vol. 2:** 766   **Vol. 3:** 1204
9:42   **Vol. 2:** 168
9:43   **Vol. 1:** 530   **Vol. 2:** 426, 623
9:44   **Vol. 1:** 326   **Vol. 2:** 150, 368   **Vol. 3:** 624
9:45   **Vol. 1:** 657   **Vol. 2:** 216, 406, 879–880   **Vol. 3:** 1122
9:46 ff   **Vol. 1:** 285   **Vol. 2:** 427, 429
9:46 f   **Vol. 3:** 821
9:47   **Vol. 3:** 749, 1201
9:48   **Vol. 2:** 176   **Vol. 3:** 746, 821, 979
9:49   **Vol. 3:** 115, 475, 767
9:50   **Vol. 2:** 34
9:51 ff   **Vol. 2:** 337, 630
9:51–56   **Vol. 3:** 454–455, 980
9:51†   **Vol. 1:** 586, 737   **Vol. 3:** 455, 749, 762
9:52 f   **Vol. 3:** 454
9:52   **Vol. 1:** 102
9:53†   **Vol. 3:** 455
9:54 f   **Vol. 3:** 454–455
9:54   **Vol. 1:** 544   **Vol. 2:** 653   **Vol. 3:** 454, 697
9:55   **Vol. 1:** 572   **Vol. 3:** 455, 694
9:56   **Vol. 1:** 464   **Vol. 3:** 455, 628
9:58   **Vol. 1:** 118, 173   **Vol. 2:** 825   **Vol. 3:** 628, 813
9:59–62   **Vol. 1:** 488
9:59–60   **Vol. 1:** 265
9:59 f   **Vol. 1:** 482
9:59   **Vol. 1:** 666–667
9:60   **Vol. 1:** 446   **Vol. 3:** 46
9:61   **Vol. 1:** 666–667   **Vol. 3:** 1174
9:62   **Vol. 1:** 493   **Vol. 2:** 385
10   **Vol. 2:** 920
10:1 ff   **Vol. 2:** 690–691
10:1–24   **Vol. 2:** 733
10:1–20   **Vol. 2:** 150
10:1–16   **Vol. 1:** 129
10:1–13   **Vol. 1:** 489
10:1–12   **Vol. 2:** 754, 825   **Vol. 3:** 453
10:1 f   **Vol. 3:** 144
10:1   **Vol. 1:** 129, 326   **Vol. 2:** 641, 697, 739   **Vol. 3:** 569
10:2   **Vol. 2:** 513, 750   **Vol. 3:** 526
10:3   **Vol. 1:** 118   **Vol. 2:** 411, 413   **Vol. 3:** 455
10:4   **Vol. 1:** 142–143
10:5 ff   **Vol. 1:** 689

10:5 f   **Vol. 2:** 781   **Vol. 3:** 258, 455
10:6   **Vol. 1:** 355   **Vol. 3:** 258
10:7 f   **Vol. 3:** 794
10:7   **Vol. 2:** 272, 275   **Vol. 3:** 349, 492, 855
10:8 ff   **Vol. 3:** 454
10:9   **Vol. 2:** 54, 632, 920   **Vol. 3:** 56, 1194
10:10 f   **Vol. 3:** 455
10:11   **Vol. 2:** 54, 349, 400, 920
10:12   **Vol. 2:** 203, 767, 894   **Vol. 3:** 93, 455
10:13 ff   **Vol. 2:** 383
10:13   **Vol. 2:** 714   **Vol. 3:** 589, 1052
10:14   **Vol. 2:** 767
10:15   **Vol. 2:** 203, 207
10:16   **Vol. 1:** 91, 130, 285   **Vol. 2:** 176, 920   **Vol. 3:** 314, 326, 746
10:17 ff   **Vol. 2:** 641
10:17–20   **Vol. 3:** 455
10:17 f   **Vol. 2:** 702   **Vol. 3:** 695
10:17   **Vol. 2:** 358, 654   **Vol. 3:** 470, 475
10:18   **Vol. 1:** 83, 610   **Vol. 2:** 38, 193, 382, 631, 920   **Vol. 3:** 470, 733, 1001
10:19   **Vol. 1:** 510–511, 554   **Vol. 2:** 603, 610   **Vol. 3:** 575, 806, 944
10:20   **Vol. 1:** 244   **Vol. 2:** 193, 358, 560   **Vol. 3:** 475, 490
10:21 f   **Vol. 1:** 620   **Vol. 3:** 313
10:21   **Vol. 1:** 282, 346, 620   **Vol. 2:** 216, 354, 514, 653, 818   **Vol. 3:** 640, 698, 847
10:22   **Vol. 1:** 90   **Vol. 2:** 368, 404, 610   **Vol. 3:** 313, 326, 639–640, 645, 1017
10:23 f   **Vol. 2:** 176, 630   **Vol. 3:** 313
10:24   **Vol. 3:** 83, 733
10:25 ff   **Vol. 1:** 334, 338   **Vol. 2:** 427
10:25–40   **Vol. 2:** 177
10:25–38   **Vol. 1:** 334
10:25–37   **Vol. 1:** 259, 335   **Vol. 2:** 301, 444   **Vol. 3:** 173, 539, 980
10:25–29   **Vol. 2:** 170
10:25–28   **Vol. 2:** 443, 543, 813, 870   **Vol. 3:** 455, 542, 791
10:25   **Vol. 2:** 481   **Vol. 3:** 275, 480, 767, 802, 804, 832
10:26   **Vol. 2:** 444
10:27   **Vol. 1:** 335   **Vol. 2:** 73   **Vol. 3:** 127, 713, 1064
10:28   **Vol. 2:** 442   **Vol. 3:** 351
10:29–37   **Vol. 1:** 67, 257–258   **Vol. 2:** 750
10:29   **Vol. 1:** 335   **Vol. 3:** 361, 455
10:30 ff   **Vol. 2:** 104
10:30–37   **Vol. 2:** 600, 747, 749   **Vol. 3:** 455–456
10:30–35   **Vol. 3:** 545
10:30   **Vol. 1:** 314   **Vol. 2:** 327, 502   **Vol. 3:** 378, 749, 857
10:31 f   **Vol. 2:** 467
10:31   **Vol. 2:** 600   **Vol. 3:** 37
10:32   **Vol. 2:** 600
10:33 f   **Vol. 1:** 335
10:33b   **Vol. 1:** 259
10:34 f   **Vol. 1:** 689

Luke *(cont'd)*

10:34	**Vol. 1:** 114, 688 **Vol. 2:** 712 **Vol. 3:** 922
10:35	**Vol. 1:** 453
10:36 f	**Vol. 3:** 455
10:36	**Vol. 3:** 378, 822
10:37 f	**Vol. 2:** 600
10:37	**Vol. 1:** 258–259, 335 **Vol. 2:** 444, 544, 595–596, 747 **Vol. 3:** 455
10:37a	**Vol. 2:** 600
10:38 ff	**Vol. 1:** 689
10:38–42	**Vol. 1:** 278 **Vol. 3:** 1059–1060
10:38	**Vol. 3:** 1061
10:39	**Vol. 1:** 239 **Vol. 3:** 589, 1106
10:40	**Vol. 2:** 724 **Vol. 3:** 546
10:42	**Vol. 1:** 540 **Vol. 2:** 304
11	**Vol. 2:** 868
11:1–13	**Vol. 2:** 768, 868
11:1	**Vol. 1:** 487 **Vol. 2:** 873 **Vol. 3:** 762
11:2 ff	**Vol. 1:** 615 **Vol. 2:** 868–869 **Vol. 3:** 204
11:2–4	**Vol. 2:** 561
11:2	**Vol. 1:** 323, 621 **Vol. 2:** 76, 229, 795, 867, 871 **Vol. 3:** 696
11:3	**Vol. 1:** 251 **Vol. 2:** 871, 895
11:4	**Vol. 2:** 668
11:5 ff	**Vol. 1:** 689
11:5–13	**Vol. 2:** 178
11:5–8	**Vol. 2:** 747, 750, 881
11:5 f	**Vol. 2:** 549
11:7	**Vol. 1:** 284 **Vol. 2:** 30, 587, 730 **Vol. 3:** 1174
11:8	**Vol. 2:** 881 **Vol. 3:** 958
11:9 f	**Vol. 2:** 728, 881 **Vol. 3:** 532
11:9	**Vol. 2:** 881 **Vol. 3:** 530
11:11	**Vol. 1:** 509 **Vol. 3:** 1179
11:12	**Vol. 1:** 511
11:13	**Vol. 1:** 286 **Vol. 2:** 41–42, 728, 857, 881 **Vol. 3:** 698
11:14–26	**Vol. 2:** 728
11:14	**Vol. 1:** 429 **Vol. 2:** 623 **Vol. 3:** 475
11:15–23	**Vol. 3:** 696
11:15–22	**Vol. 3:** 481
11:15	**Vol. 1:** 168 **Vol. 2:** 631 **Vol. 3:** 472
11:16	**Vol. 2:** 629, 750 **Vol. 3:** 481, 804
11:17–23	**Vol. 2:** 560 **Vol. 3:** 83, 472
11:17	**Vol. 3:** 128, 1008
11:18 f	**Vol. 3:** 472
11:19–32	**Vol. 2:** 750
11:19 f	**Vol. 3:** 695
11:19	**Vol. 3:** 476, 696
11:20	**Vol. 1:** 358, 651 **Vol. 2:** 74, 150, 382, 631, 920 **Vol. 3:** 475, 696, 985, 998
11:21 f	**Vol. 1:** 508
11:21	**Vol. 2:** 135, 382, 780, 845
11:22	**Vol. 1:** 322, 591, 651 **Vol. 2:** 603
11:23 ff	**Vol. 1:** 739
11:23	**Vol. 2:** 32, 34 **Vol. 3:** 568
11:24 ff	**Vol. 3:** 475
11:24	**Vol. 3:** 128, 256, 530, 694, 1006, 1008
11:25 f	**Vol. 3:** 586
11:25	**Vol. 3:** 474
11:26	**Vol. 1:** 666 **Vol. 2:** 251, 691 **Vol. 3:** 474, 604, 694, 1059
11:27 f	**Vol. 3:** 1062, 1070
11:27	**Vol. 1:** 169, 240
11:28	**Vol. 2:** 177
11:29 ff	**Vol. 2:** 629
11:29–32	**Vol. 2:** 350, 687 **Vol. 3:** 481
11:29 f	**Vol. 3:** 628
11:29	**Vol. 1:** 565 **Vol. 2:** 33, 36, 351, 631, 680
11:29b–30	**Vol. 3:** 628
11:30	**Vol. 2:** 351, 680
11:31 f	**Vol. 2:** 921
11:31	**Vol. 2:** 381, 385, 563 **Vol. 3:** 86, 606, 1003, 1030
11:32	**Vol. 2:** 352, 680 **Vol. 3:** 52–53, 83, 275, 303, 1187
11:33 f	**Vol. 2:** 486
11:33	**Vol. 2:** 214, 484, 487, 493, 749–750, 757 **Vol. 3:** 860
11:34 ff	**Vol. 2:** 706, 749–750
11:34–46	**Vol. 1:** 423
11:34 f	**Vol. 2:** 757
11:34	**Vol. 1:** 565 **Vol. 3:** 572
11:36	**Vol. 2:** 303 **Vol. 3:** 1001
11:37–54	**Vol. 2:** 170
11:37–41	**Vol. 3:** 990
11:37	**Vol. 2:** 812, 880
11:38–42	**Vol. 2:** 813
11:38	**Vol. 1:** 666 **Vol. 2:** 623, 812
11:39	**Vol. 1:** 743 **Vol. 3:** 184, 604, 990, 1053
11:40	**Vol. 3:** 1025
11:41	**Vol. 2:** 596
11:42 ff	**Vol. 2:** 443
11:42–52	**Vol. 2:** 470 **Vol. 3:** 1052
11:42	**Vol. 2:** 211, 665, 693–694 **Vol. 3:** 197, 854
11:43–54	**Vol. 2:** 813
11:43	**Vol. 2:** 543, 548 **Vol. 3:** 785
11:44	**Vol. 1:** 205, 265 **Vol. 2:** 746 **Vol. 3:** 247, 1053
11:45–52	**Vol. 1:** 174 **Vol. 3:** 181
11:45 f	**Vol. 3:** 480
11:45†	**Vol. 3:** 28, 767
11:46 f	**Vol. 2:** 443
11:46	**Vol. 1:** 261, 335 **Vol. 2:** 150 **Vol. 3:** 883
11:47 f	**Vol. 3:** 1053
11:47	**Vol. 3:** 247
11:48	**Vol. 3:** 1043
11:49	**Vol. 1:** 128, 136, 174 **Vol. 3:** 84, 86, 492, 1030
11:50 f	**Vol. 1:** 222 **Vol. 3:** 532
11:50	**Vol. 1:** 378 **Vol. 2:** 854
11:51	**Vol. 1:** 464 **Vol. 2:** 248 **Vol. 3:** 82, 430, 436
11:52	**Vol. 2:** 222, 443, 730 **Vol. 3:** 480, 1052

Luke *(cont'd)*

11:53   **Vol. 3:** 480
12   **Vol. 2:** 832
12:1   **Vol. 2:** 33, 170, 462   **Vol. 3:** 944
12:2   **Vol. 2:** 212, 216   **Vol. 3:** 312
12:3   **Vol. 1:** 423   **Vol. 2:** 493   **Vol. 3:** 54
12:4 f   **Vol. 1:** 623
12:4   **Vol. 1:** 623, 731   **Vol. 2:** 549
12:5   **Vol. 1:** 623   **Vol. 2:** 209, 609   **Vol. 3:** 686
12:6   **Vol. 1:** 173
12:7   **Vol. 1:** 203   **Vol. 2:** 159
12:8 f   **Vol. 1:** 347, 490   **Vol. 3:** 618, 622, 625–626, 628
12:8   **Vol. 1:** 205   **Vol. 2:** 383   **Vol. 3:** 621, 633
12:9   **Vol. 1:** 455
12:10   **Vol. 3:** 343, 472, 580, 628, 658, 696
12:11   **Vol. 1:** 166   **Vol. 2:** 608   **Vol. 3:** 785
12:12   **Vol. 3:** 762–763, 849
12:13 ff   **Vol. 1:** 142
12:13–21   **Vol. 2:** 825
12:13 f   **Vol. 1:** 488   **Vol. 3:** 767
12:13   **Vol. 2:** 300   **Vol. 3:** 767
12:14 f   **Vol. 2:** 833
12:14   **Vol. 2:** 365
12:15   **Vol. 1:** 138, 729   **Vol. 2:** 135, 480, 845–846
12:16–21   **Vol. 2:** 747, 750, 833, 846   **Vol. 3:** 978
12:16–20   **Vol. 2:** 749, 843
12:16   **Vol. 2:** 502, 842
12:17 f   **Vol. 3:** 1155
12:17   **Vol. 1:** 722   **Vol. 2:** 32   **Vol. 3:** 820
12:18   **Vol. 2:** 32
12:19   **Vol. 2:** 272, 275, 355, 846, 919   **Vol. 3:** 683
12:20 f   **Vol. 2:** 833
12:20   **Vol. 2:** 382, 430, 480, 858, 918–919   **Vol. 3:** 1025
12:21   **Vol. 2:** 842
12:22–31   **Vol. 1:** 277   **Vol. 2:** 386
12:22 f   **Vol. 2:** 919
12:22   **Vol. 2:** 831
12:24–28   **Vol. 2:** 749
12:24   **Vol. 1:** 98, 173
12:25   **Vol. 1:** 92
12:26   **Vol. 3:** 252
12:27   **Vol. 2:** 47   **Vol. 3:** 606
12:28   **Vol. 1:** 744
12:29   **Vol. 2:** 275
12:30   **Vol. 1:** 620   **Vol. 2:** 793   **Vol. 3:** 532, 958
12:31   **Vol. 2:** 275   **Vol. 3:** 532
12:32   **Vol. 1:** 620, 623   **Vol. 2:** 382–383, 385, 429, 818–819, 832
12:33 f   **Vol. 2:** 749–750, 831   **Vol. 3:** 378
12:33   **Vol. 1:** 119, 142, 268, 468, 495   **Vol. 2:** 596, 757, 832, 845–846   **Vol. 3:** 1149
12:34 ff   **Vol. 2:** 727

12:34   **Vol. 2:** 832
12:35–38   **Vol. 2:** 751
12:35   **Vol. 1:** 240   **Vol. 2:** 487, 493   **Vol. 3:** 121
12:36–40   **Vol. 2:** 581
12:36 f   **Vol. 2:** 513
12:36   **Vol. 2:** 728, 881   **Vol. 3:** 85, 626
12:37 f   **Vol. 1:** 217
12:37   **Vol. 1:** 322   **Vol. 3:** 546
12:38   **Vol. 2:** 136
12:39 f   **Vol. 2:** 382, 751   **Vol. 3:** 848
12:39   **Vol. 1:** 323   **Vol. 2:** 831   **Vol. 3:** 85, 378, 1157
12:40   **Vol. 3:** 118, 822
12:41–48   **Vol. 2:** 469
12:41–46   **Vol. 2:** 751
12:42 ff   **Vol. 2:** 254
12:42–46   **Vol. 2:** 382
12:42   **Vol. 2:** 164, 254–255, 619, 732
12:43 ff   **Vol. 3:** 472
12:44   **Vol. 2:** 845   **Vol. 3:** 883, 1193
12:45   **Vol. 1:** 284, 513–514   **Vol. 3:** 843, 903
12:46 ff   **Vol. 2:** 398
12:46   **Vol. 2:** 255, 304, 513   **Vol. 3:** 847–848
12:47   **Vol. 3:** 118, 1204
12:48   **Vol. 1:** 730   **Vol. 2:** 858
12:49 f   **Vol. 3:** 697
12:49–50   **Vol. 3:** 697
12:49   **Vol. 1:** 322, 656–657
12:50   **Vol. 1:** 144   **Vol. 2:** 63
12:51 ff   **Vol. 2:** 781
12:51–53   **Vol. 3:** 697
12:51   **Vol. 3:** 822, 967, 978
12:52   **Vol. 2:** 689
12:53   **Vol. 1:** 725   **Vol. 2:** 250, 585   **Vol. 3:** 1070
12:54 ff   **Vol. 3:** 173
12:54   **Vol. 3:** 1003
12:55   **Vol. 3:** 707, 1003
12:56   **Vol. 2:** 192, 469   **Vol. 3:** 808, 838, 848, 1187
12:57   **Vol. 2:** 365   **Vol. 3:** 361
12:58 f   **Vol. 3:** 173–174
12:58   **Vol. 1:** 168, 554   **Vol. 2:** 136, 365, 368   **Vol. 3:** 167, 1150
12:59   **Vol. 2:** 850
13:1 ff   **Vol. 1:** 75   **Vol. 3:** 998
13:1–9   **Vol. 2:** 750
13:1–8   **Vol. 1:** 725
13:1–5   **Vol. 1:** 564   **Vol. 2:** 366
13:1–3   **Vol. 1:** 633
13:1   **Vol. 1:** 221   **Vol. 3:** 430, 788, 837
13:2   **Vol. 3:** 723, 822
13:3–6   **Vol. 2:** 813
13:3   **Vol. 1:** 286, 464   **Vol. 3:** 173, 430
13:4   **Vol. 1:** 609   **Vol. 2:** 327   **Vol. 3:** 822
13:5   **Vol. 1:** 464, 725   **Vol. 3:** 173, 869
13:5b   **Vol. 3:** 920
13:6 ff   **Vol. 1:** 722   **Vol. 2:** 366

Luke *(cont'd)*

13:6–9 **Vol. 1:** 417 **Vol. 2:** 630, 749 **Vol. 3:** 174, 868–869, 919
13:6–8 **Vol. 2:** 118
13:6 f **Vol. 3:** 868
13:6 **Vol. 1:** 722, 725 **Vol. 3:** 532, 918
13:7 **Vol. 1:** 73
13:8 **Vol. 1:** 480 **Vol. 2:** 513
13:9 **Vol. 1:** 326
13:10–17 **Vol. 3:** 409
13:10 **Vol. 3:** 761, 785
13:11 **Vol. 1:** 452, 637 **Vol. 2:** 168 **Vol. 3:** 994, 998, 1058, 1142
13:12 **Vol. 1:** 505 **Vol. 3:** 189
13:13 **Vol. 2:** 151 **Vol. 3:** 86
13:14 **Vol. 2:** 165, 665, 692 **Vol. 3:** 1150
13:15 **Vol. 1:** 115, 117 **Vol. 3:** 180
13:16 **Vol. 1:** 452, 718 **Vol. 2:** 665, 920 **Vol. 3:** 179, 470, 592, 857, 998
13:17 **Vol. 2:** 47, 358
13:18–21 **Vol. 2:** 749
13:18 f **Vol. 2:** 429, 750 **Vol. 3:** 523, 868
13:19 **Vol. 1:** 174 **Vol. 2:** 129 **Vol. 3:** 813, 869
13:20 f **Vol. 2:** 502, 750 **Vol. 3:** 1058
13:20 **Vol. 2:** 747
13:21 **Vol. 2:** 216, 461–462
13:22–30 **Vol. 3:** 174
13:22 **Vol. 3:** 761
13:23 f **Vol. 2:** 481, 749
13:23 **Vol. 1:** 607
13:24 **Vol. 1:** 646–647 **Vol. 2:** 29, 31
13:25 ff **Vol. 2:** 510
13:25–28 **Vol. 2:** 751
13:25 **Vol. 2:** 31, 728, 881 **Vol. 3:** 280
13:26 ff **Vol. 2:** 272
13:26 **Vol. 1:** 607 **Vol. 2:** 272, 276 **Vol. 3:** 761–762
13:27 **Vol. 1:** 607 **Vol. 2:** 276, 383 **Vol. 3:** 575
13:28 ff **Vol. 2:** 57
13:28–30 **Vol. 1:** 667
13:28 f **Vol. 1:** 78
13:28 **Vol. 1:** 81 **Vol. 2:** 385, 421
13:29 **Vol. 1:** 689 **Vol. 3:** 1003
13:30 **Vol. 2:** 57
13:31 **Vol. 2:** 812 **Vol. 3:** 847
13:32 f **Vol. 3:** 979
13:32 **Vol. 1:** 118, 453 **Vol. 2:** 63, 630, 688 **Vol. 3:** 475, 838
13:33 **Vol. 1:** 163, 464 **Vol. 2:** 170, 328, 641, 665, 803, 825 **Vol. 3:** 83, 696, 723
13:34 ff **Vol. 2:** 328
13:34 f **Vol. 1:** 174 **Vol. 2:** 754 **Vol. 3:** 230
13:34 **Vol. 1:** 286 **Vol. 2:** 33, 37, 757 **Vol. 3:** 82, 1008
13:35 **Vol. 1:** 174 **Vol. 2:** 37 **Vol. 3:** 392, 1008
14:1 ff **Vol. 2:** 170

14:1–6 **Vol. 3:** 409
14:1 **Vol. 1:** 168 **Vol. 2:** 133, 812
14:3 **Vol. 2:** 610 **Vol. 3:** 480
14:4 **Vol. 3:** 111, 749–750
14:5 **Vol. 1:** 115, 117
14:6 **Vol. 3:** 714
14:7–10 **Vol. 3:** 589
14:7 **Vol. 1:** 540, 666
14:8 **Vol. 1:** 666 **Vol. 2:** 578
14:9 **Vol. 2:** 57
14:10 **Vol. 2:** 549
14:11 **Vol. 2:** 202, 262
14:12 ff **Vol. 2:** 825, 844
14:12 **Vol. 2:** 549, 842 **Vol. 3:** 114, 135
14:13 f **Vol. 2:** 203
14:13 **Vol. 1:** 219 **Vol. 2:** 415
14:14 **Vol. 1:** 129, 217, 495 **Vol. 3:** 277, 361
14:15–24 **Vol. 2:** 750
14:15 **Vol. 1:** 250 **Vol. 2:** 272
14:16 ff **Vol. 1:** 689
14:16–25 **Vol. 1:** 274
14:16–24 **Vol. 1:** 324 **Vol. 2:** 747
14:17–20 **Vol. 3:** 695
14:17 **Vol. 3:** 118
14:18 f **Vol. 2:** 858, 880
14:18 **Vol. 1:** 520, 666 **Vol. 2:** 663
14:19 **Vol. 2:** 689 **Vol. 3:** 1164
14:20 **Vol. 2:** 579
14:21 **Vol. 1:** 110–111, 219 **Vol. 2:** 415, 510, 825
14:23 **Vol. 2:** 663 **Vol. 3:** 951
14:24 **Vol. 2:** 270
14:25–34 **Vol. 3:** 448
14:25–33 **Vol. 2:** 825
14:26 f **Vol. 1:** 289, 305, 488
14:26 **Vol. 1:** 256, 287, 556, 619 **Vol. 3:** 682–683
14:27 **Vol. 1:** 324, 394, 402, 404 **Vol. 2:** 203 **Vol. 3:** 60
14:28–33 **Vol. 2:** 747, 750
14:28–32 **Vol. 2:** 386, 752
14:28 **Vol. 1:** 667
14:29 **Vol. 1:** 661 **Vol. 3:** 341, 516, 714
14:31 **Vol. 1:** 667 **Vol. 2:** 699 **Vol. 3:** 1190
14:32 **Vol. 1:** 197 **Vol. 2:** 780
14:33 **Vol. 1:** 305, 358, 495 **Vol. 2:** 845
14:34 f **Vol. 2:** 749–750
14:34 **Vol. 2:** 757 **Vol. 3:** 445, 447, 1025
14:35 **Vol. 1:** 480 **Vol. 2:** 750
15 **Vol. 2:** 118, 332, 443, 566 **Vol. 3:** 920
15:1 ff **Vol. 3:** 580, 762
15:1–32 **Vol. 3:** 213, 314
15:1–7 **Vol. 2:** 750
15:1–6 **Vol. 3:** 529
15:1 f **Vol. 2:** 524, 754
15:1 **Vol. 2:** 790
15:2 ff **Vol. 1:** 129
15:2 **Vol. 2:** 170
15:4 ff **Vol. 2:** 460
15:4–10 **Vol. 2:** 747

Luke *(cont'd)*

15:4–7   **Vol. 2:** 386, 388   **Vol. 3:** 567
15:4–6   **Vol. 3:** 566
15:4 f   **Vol. 3:** 530, 566
15:4   **Vol. 1:** 463   **Vol. 2:** 413, 459   **Vol. 3:** 565, 1008
15:5   **Vol. 3:** 530
15:6   **Vol. 1:** 463   **Vol. 2:** 358, 549   **Vol. 3:** 529
15:7   **Vol. 2:** 358, 416, 720   **Vol. 3:** 361, 529
15:8 ff   **Vol. 2:** 750   **Vol. 3:** 1058
15:8–10   **Vol. 2:** 386, 388   **Vol. 3:** 529
15:8 f   **Vol. 2:** 851
15:8   **Vol. 1:** 463   **Vol. 2:** 487, 493   **Vol. 3:** 531–532, 860
15:9   **Vol. 2:** 358, 549
15:10   **Vol. 1:** 103   **Vol. 2:** 358   **Vol. 3:** 529
15:11 ff   **Vol. 1:** 556, 701   **Vol. 2:** 76
15:11–32   **Vol. 2:** 386, 388, 600, 749–750   **Vol. 3:** 580, 920, 1061
15:12 f   **Vol. 2:** 846
15:12   **Vol. 1:** 535   **Vol. 2:** 303, 475, 675, 846, 871
15:13   **Vol. 2:** 32, 34, 480, 790
15:14   **Vol. 1:** 167   **Vol. 2:** 266   **Vol. 3:** 713, 954
15:15 f   **Vol. 1:** 117
15:15   **Vol. 2:** 349, 804   **Vol. 3:** 920
15:16   **Vol. 1:** 169, 457   **Vol. 3:** 1174
15:17   **Vol. 1:** 250, 464, 729   **Vol. 2:** 266, 566
15:18   **Vol. 2:** 193
15:19   **Vol. 3:** 348
15:20 ff   **Vol. 1:** 701
15:20   **Vol. 1:** 241, 609   **Vol. 2:** 549, 600   **Vol. 3:** 529, 947
15:21   **Vol. 2:** 193   **Vol. 3:** 348, 529
15:22–24   **Vol. 3:** 529
15:22   **Vol. 1:** 666
15:23   **Vol. 1:** 116   **Vol. 2:** 272, 356, 358   **Vol. 3:** 529
15:24   **Vol. 1:** 359, 436, 446, 463   **Vol. 2:** 170, 480   **Vol. 3:** 278, 529
15:25   **Vol. 1:** 198   **Vol. 3:** 674
15:26   **Vol. 1:** 284
15:27   **Vol. 1:** 116   **Vol. 2:** 170   **Vol. 3:** 751
15:28–32   **Vol. 2:** 170
15:28   **Vol. 1:** 110, 570   **Vol. 2:** 600
15:29   **Vol. 1:** 114, 322   **Vol. 2:** 356, 549
15:30   **Vol. 1:** 116   **Vol. 2:** 475, 846
15:31   **Vol. 1:** 286   **Vol. 2:** 846
15:32   **Vol. 1:** 359, 446, 463   **Vol. 2:** 356, 358, 480   **Vol. 3:** 529
16:1 ff   **Vol. 2:** 254, 732   **Vol. 3:** 576
16:1–17   **Vol. 2:** 254
16:1–14   **Vol. 2:** 832
16:1–9   **Vol. 2:** 750
16:1–8   **Vol. 2:** 749, 837
16:1   **Vol. 2:** 34, 842, 845   **Vol. 3:** 468
16:2   **Vol. 2:** 254   **Vol. 3:** 114

16:3   **Vol. 2:** 513   **Vol. 3:** 1155
16:5–7   **Vol. 2:** 668
16:5   **Vol. 2:** 513
16:6 f   **Vol. 3:** 489
16:6   **Vol. 2:** 711   **Vol. 3:** 492–493
16:8 f   **Vol. 3:** 575
16:8   **Vol. 1:** 289   **Vol. 2:** 495, 619, 837
16:9   **Vol. 2:** 255, 381–382, 549, 749, 832, 837, 844   **Vol. 3:** 811–812, 832, 1180
16:10 f   **Vol. 2:** 255
16:11   **Vol. 1:** 684   **Vol. 2:** 837, 844   **Vol. 3:** 884, 1211
16:12   **Vol. 1:** 684   **Vol. 2:** 742, 846
16:13   **Vol. 1:** 138, 461   **Vol. 2:** 749–750, 838
16:14 f   **Vol. 3:** 603
16:14   **Vol. 2:** 170, 550, 843   **Vol. 3:** 341, 712
16:15   **Vol. 2:** 183, 200   **Vol. 3:** 361, 1010
16:16   **Vol. 2:** 113, 383, 443   **Vol. 3:** 603, 711–712, 1107
16:17   **Vol. 1:** 609   **Vol. 2:** 443–444   **Vol. 3:** 182
16:18   **Vol. 1:** 500, 506   **Vol. 2:** 580–581, 583   **Vol. 3:** 172, 188–189, 534, 538
16:18a   **Vol. 1:** 506   **Vol. 3:** 540
16:18b   **Vol. 1:** 506   **Vol. 2:** 564   **Vol. 3:** 540
16:19–31   **Vol. 2:** 267, 747, 750, 843, 846   **Vol. 3:** 99, 978, 1061
16:19 f   **Vol. 2:** 272
16:19   **Vol. 2:** 355, 486, 842, 895
16:20   **Vol. 2:** 30, 466, 825   **Vol. 3:** 1061
16:21 f   **Vol. 2:** 842
16:21   **Vol. 1:** 117, 744
16:22 ff   **Vol. 1:** 78
16:22   **Vol. 1:** 78, 103, 240   **Vol. 2:** 825
16:23–31†   **Vol. 2:** 433
16:23   **Vol. 1:** 240   **Vol. 2:** 85, 207   **Vol. 3:** 682, 856
16:24 f   **Vol. 2:** 597
16:24   **Vol. 1:** 145   **Vol. 2:** 150, 595–596   **Vol. 3:** 114, 989, 1079
16:25   **Vol. 1:** 286, 564, 571   **Vol. 2:** 843   **Vol. 3:** 240, 751
16:26   **Vol. 2:** 207
16:27 ff   **Vol. 2:** 630
16:28   **Vol. 2:** 689   **Vol. 3:** 856
16:29–31   **Vol. 2:** 641
16:29   **Vol. 2:** 174
16:31   **Vol. 1:** 591   **Vol. 2:** 352   **Vol. 3:** 1061
17   **Vol. 2:** 904, 918   **Vol. 3:** 430
17:1 f   **Vol. 2:** 429   **Vol. 3:** 394
17:1   **Vol. 1:** 136   **Vol. 2:** 709   **Vol. 3:** 1052
17:2   **Vol. 2:** 429   **Vol. 3:** 393
17:3 f   **Vol. 3:** 579
17:3   **Vol. 1:** 572
17:4   **Vol. 2:** 691
17:5 f   **Vol. 1:** 600
17:5   **Vol. 1:** 136, 489, 600
17:6   **Vol. 1:** 600   **Vol. 3:** 984, 1012
17:7–10   **Vol. 2:** 747, 750, 838   **Vol. 3:** 595
17:7 f   **Vol. 2:** 271

171

Luke *(cont'd)*

17:8   **Vol. 3:** 121, 546
17:9 f   **Vol. 3:** 1155
17:9   **Vol. 2:** 118
17:10   **Vol. 3:** 141, 1149–1150
17:11 ff   **Vol. 2:** 631
17:11–19   **Vol. 3:** 106, 455–456, 980
17:11   **Vol. 3:** 449
17:12 ff   **Vol. 2:** 466
17:12   **Vol. 1:** 325   **Vol. 2:** 464   **Vol. 3:** 997
17:13   **Vol. 2:** 595, 838   **Vol. 3:** 115
17:14–17   **Vol. 3:** 106
17:14   **Vol. 3:** 37
17:15 f   **Vol. 3:** 456
17:15–16   **Vol. 3:** 113
17:16–18   **Vol. 1:** 67
17:16   **Vol. 1:** 609   **Vol. 3:** 818
17:17 ff   **Vol. 2:** 566
17:18   **Vol. 1:** 685   **Vol. 2:** 46, 742   **Vol. 3:** 455, 529
17:19   **Vol. 3:** 212
17:19c   **Vol. 3:** 106
17:20 f   **Vol. 2:** 37, 170, 340, 382, 384, 921   **Vol. 3:** 762
17:20   **Vol. 2:** 133, 382, 385
17:21 ff   **Vol. 2:** 921
17:21   **Vol. 1:** 358   **Vol. 3:** 844
17:22 ff   **Vol. 3:** 605
17:22–37   **Vol. 3:** 628
17:22 f   **Vol. 2:** 918
17:22   **Vol. 2:** 930   **Vol. 3:** 620, 628, 633
17:23 ff   **Vol. 1:** 175
17:23 f   **Vol. 2:** 900   **Vol. 3:** 618
17:23   **Vol. 2:** 806
17:24   **Vol. 2:** 486, 894   **Vol. 3:** 633, 1001
17:25   **Vol. 1:** 74, 667   **Vol. 2:** 665   **Vol. 3:** 623–624, 723
17:26 ff   **Vol. 2:** 382   **Vol. 3:** 633
17:26–36   **Vol. 2:** 751
17:26 f   **Vol. 2:** 682
17:26   **Vol. 2:** 385, 580
17:27 ff   **Vol. 2:** 275
17:27   **Vol. 2:** 581   **Vol. 3:** 991
17:29   **Vol. 1:** 657   **Vol. 2:** 193, 767   **Vol. 3:** 93, 1002
17:30   **Vol. 3:** 620
17:31 f   **Vol. 1:** 493
17:31   **Vol. 3:** 913
17:32   **Vol. 3:** 93, 240, 1058
17:33   **Vol. 1:** 464   **Vol. 2:** 203, 838–839, 920   **Vol. 3:** 682
17:34 f   **Vol. 2:** 920   **Vol. 3:** 604
17:34   **Vol. 1:** 421   **Vol. 2:** 918
17:35   **Vol. 3:** 1058, 1194
17:37   **Vol. 1:** 175, 234   **Vol. 2:** 33, 746, 757   **Vol. 3:** 1054
18:1 ff   **Vol. 3:** 576, 1074
18:1–8   **Vol. 2:** 750, 768   **Vol. 3:** 1059
18:1–6   **Vol. 2:** 771

18:1   **Vol. 1:** 563   **Vol. 2:** 666, 771   **Vol. 3:** 1204
18:2 ff   **Vol. 2:** 747
18:2   **Vol. 1:** 623   **Vol. 2:** 365
18:3 ff   **Vol. 2:** 96   **Vol. 3:** 97
18:3   **Vol. 1:** 554
18:4   **Vol. 1:** 623
18:5   **Vol. 2:** 62
18:6   **Vol. 3:** 575
18:7 f   **Vol. 3:** 93, 199
18:7   **Vol. 1:** 411, 541   **Vol. 2:** 771
18:8   **Vol. 2:** 37   **Vol. 3:** 529–530, 620, 626–627
18:9 ff   **Vol. 2:** 366   **Vol. 3:** 580
18:9–27   **Vol. 2:** 443
18:9–14   **Vol. 2:** 261, 442, 584, 694, 750   **Vol. 3:** 253, 361
18:9   **Vol. 1:** 591   **Vol. 3:** 161, 252–253, 361
18:10–14   **Vol. 2:** 747   **Vol. 3:** 790
18:10   **Vol. 2:** 185, 236, 868   **Vol. 3:** 837
18:11 f   **Vol. 3:** 819
18:11   **Vol. 2:** 869   **Vol. 3:** 252–253, 575, 604, 757
18:12   **Vol. 2:** 693   **Vol. 3:** 854
18:13   **Vol. 2:** 192, 869   **Vol. 3:** 160, 903
18:14   **Vol. 2:** 202, 262, 868   **Vol. 3:** 161, 361, 1202
18:15 ff   **Vol. 1:** 284   **Vol. 2:** 223   **Vol. 3:** 861
18:15–17   **Vol. 1:** 160
18:15   **Vol. 1:** 283
18:16 f   **Vol. 1:** 283
18:16   **Vol. 2:** 222
18:17   **Vol. 1:** 284–285   **Vol. 2:** 385, 757   **Vol. 3:** 746
18:18–30   **Vol. 1:** 335   **Vol. 2:** 301
18:18–24   **Vol. 2:** 825
18:18–23   **Vol. 2:** 844
18:18 f   **Vol. 2:** 100
18:18   **Vol. 1:** 168   **Vol. 2:** 300, 480–481   **Vol. 3:** 832
18:20   **Vol. 2:** 583   **Vol. 3:** 377, 379, 755
18:21   **Vol. 2:** 135, 675, 871
18:22   **Vol. 2:** 368, 720, 824, 833, 846   **Vol. 3:** 141, 251, 253
18:23   **Vol. 2:** 842, 845–846
18:24–30   **Vol. 2:** 750
18:24   **Vol. 2:** 845
18:25   **Vol. 1:** 116   **Vol. 2:** 842
18:26 f   **Vol. 3:** 546
18:26   **Vol. 1:** 730   **Vol. 3:** 213, 546
18:27   **Vol. 2:** 603, 606
18:28   **Vol. 2:** 840, 846
18:29 f   **Vol. 2:** 250, 840
18:29   **Vol. 2:** 112–113, 301, 387
18:30   **Vol. 3:** 142, 751, 832
18:31 ff   **Vol. 3:** 329
18:31   **Vol. 2:** 63–64, 695   **Vol. 3:** 39, 488
18:32   **Vol. 3:** 28, 340
18:33   **Vol. 1:** 162   **Vol. 2:** 63   **Vol. 3:** 276

Luke *(cont'd)*

18:34	**Vol. 1:** 489 **Vol. 2:** 216, 398 **Vol. 3:** 132, 1122
18:35	**Vol. 3:** 455
18:37	**Vol. 1:** 322 **Vol. 2:** 333
18:38	**Vol. 1:** 411
18:40	**Vol. 1:** 341
18:41	**Vol. 3:** 519
18:42	**Vol. 3:** 212
18:43	**Vol. 2:** 631 **Vol. 3:** 817
19:1 ff	**Vol. 3:** 580
19:1–10	**Vol. 1:** 701 **Vol. 3:** 980
19:1–6	**Vol. 2:** 434
19:1	**Vol. 3:** 455
19:2	**Vol. 2:** 842 **Vol. 3:** 758
19:3	**Vol. 1:** 92 **Vol. 2:** 428 **Vol. 3:** 1180
19:4	**Vol. 1:** 326
19:5 f	**Vol. 2:** 524, 754 **Vol. 3:** 1169
19:5	**Vol. 3:** 224, 519, 838
19:6	**Vol. 2:** 358
19:7†	**Vol. 2:** 563, 630 **Vol. 3:** 189
19:8	**Vol. 2:** 825, 844–846 **Vol. 3:** 758
19:9 f	**Vol. 2:** 118 **Vol. 3:** 213
19:9	**Vol. 1:** 77 **Vol. 3:** 212, 838
19:10 ff	**Vol. 2:** 813
19:10	**Vol. 1:** 322, 464 **Vol. 2:** 513 **Vol. 3:** 532, 567, 628
19:11 ff	**Vol. 2:** 255
19:11–27	**Vol. 2:** 751, 838
19:11	**Vol. 1:** 326 **Vol. 2:** 920 **Vol. 3:** 455, 822
19:12–27	**Vol. 3:** 809
19:12 f	**Vol. 2:** 916
19:12	**Vol. 1:** 188 **Vol. 2:** 381
19:13	**Vol. 1:** 274 **Vol. 3:** 1158
19:14	**Vol. 1:** 197 **Vol. 2:** 804
19:15	**Vol. 2:** 381 **Vol. 3:** 1158
19:16	**Vol. 2:** 739
19:17 ff	**Vol. 2:** 255
19:17	**Vol. 2:** 100, 428, 608, 751 **Vol. 3:** 141
19:18	**Vol. 2:** 739
19:19 f	**Vol. 2:** 751
19:19	**Vol. 3:** 141
19:20	**Vol. 2:** 739
19:21	**Vol. 3:** 526
19:22	**Vol. 2:** 365 **Vol. 3:** 526
19:23	**Vol. 3:** 1157
19:24	**Vol. 1:** 190
19:28–40	**Vol. 2:** 754
19:28–38	**Vol. 2:** 379 **Vol. 3:** 791
19:28	**Vol. 2:** 713 **Vol. 3:** 455
19:29–44	**Vol. 2:** 713
19:29	**Vol. 1:** 274 **Vol. 2:** 54
19:30 f	**Vol. 3:** 179
19:30	**Vol. 1:** 117
19:33	**Vol. 1:** 117 **Vol. 2:** 513 **Vol. 3:** 179
19:35	**Vol. 1:** 117
19:37–38	**Vol. 3:** 113, 817
19:37	**Vol. 1:** 733 **Vol. 2:** 603 **Vol. 3:** 817
19:38	**Vol. 1:** 323 **Vol. 2:** 46, 781 **Vol. 3:** 652
19:39	**Vol. 1:** 572 **Vol. 2:** 170
19:40	**Vol. 1:** 409–410, 724 **Vol. 3:** 393
19:41 ff	**Vol. 1:** 75, 725
19:41–44	**Vol. 2:** 37
19:42	**Vol. 1:** 600 **Vol. 2:** 216, 328, 780–781
19:43 f	**Vol. 2:** 328
19:43	**Vol. 1:** 554 **Vol. 3:** 952, 965
19:44	**Vol. 1:** 286 **Vol. 3:** 838
19:45 ff	**Vol. 2:** 236, 327
19:45–48	**Vol. 3:** 791
19:45 f	**Vol. 1:** 111 **Vol. 2:** 610, 754 **Vol. 3:** 429, 784, 789, 1168
19:46	**Vol. 2:** 248 **Vol. 3:** 329, 378, 380, 430, 788
19:47 f	**Vol. 2:** 379 **Vol. 3:** 784
19:47	**Vol. 2:** 799 **Vol. 3:** 39, 761, 789, 791
19:48	**Vol. 2:** 799
20 f	**Vol. 3:** 762
20–21	**Vol. 3:** 785
20:1–21:38	**Vol. 2:** 236
20:1–8	**Vol. 3:** 792, 1154
20:1	**Vol. 1:** 199 **Vol. 2:** 113, 799 **Vol. 3:** 791
20:3	**Vol. 2:** 879
20:4	**Vol. 2:** 434
20:6	**Vol. 1:** 591 **Vol. 3:** 86
20:7	**Vol. 2:** 129
20:9–19	**Vol. 2:** 301, 746, 751 **Vol. 3:** 641, 869, 920
20:9 f	**Vol. 3:** 843, 868
20:9	**Vol. 2:** 790, 799
20:10 f	**Vol. 1:** 128, 163, 547
20:10	**Vol. 1:** 722–723 **Vol. 3:** 837
20:11	**Vol. 2:** 50
20:13	**Vol. 2:** 543, 720
20:14	**Vol. 1:** 181 **Vol. 3:** 820
20:17 f	**Vol. 2:** 920 **Vol. 3:** 393
20:17	**Vol. 2:** 159, 253, 313, 622, 706 **Vol. 3:** 188, 329, 390, 492, 519, 809
20:18	**Vol. 1:** 610 **Vol. 2:** 706 **Vol. 3:** 393
20:19	**Vol. 3:** 39, 846–847
20:20–26	**Vol. 3:** 442, 549, 754, 1168
20:20	**Vol. 1:** 166, 270 **Vol. 2:** 133, 469, 608 **Vol. 3:** 361, 749, 1106, 1108
20:21	**Vol. 3:** 351, 940
20:22	**Vol. 3:** 754
20:23	**Vol. 1:** 239, 413 **Vol. 3:** 129, 361
20:24	**Vol. 2:** 288 **Vol. 3:** 489
20:26	**Vol. 2:** 624 **Vol. 3:** 714, 1122
20:27–40	**Vol. 3:** 263, 792
20:27–39	**Vol. 3:** 439
20:27–38	**Vol. 2:** 578, 580
20:27	**Vol. 3:** 439, 685
20:34 f†	**Vol. 2:** 581
20:34	**Vol. 1:** 289
20:35	**Vol. 3:** 349
20:36 f	**Vol. 2:** 481

Luke *(cont'd)*

20:36   **Vol. 1:** 103, 289–290   **Vol. 2:** 578, 920, 929   **Vol. 3:** 278
20:37 f   **Vol. 1:** 78   **Vol. 3:** 263
20:37   **Vol. 1:** 81   **Vol. 2:** 73, 319
20:38   **Vol. 1:** 445   **Vol. 2:** 480, 578, 920
20:39 f   **Vol. 1:** 334
20:41–44   **Vol. 1:** 427   **Vol. 2:** 147   **Vol. 3:** 651–652, 791–792
20:41   **Vol. 2:** 79, 515
20:42 f   **Vol. 1:** 177   **Vol. 2:** 515
20:42   **Vol. 1:** 244   **Vol. 3:** 671, 675
20:43   **Vol. 1:** 477, 554
20:44   **Vol. 2:** 515–516
20:45 ff   **Vol. 2:** 469–470   **Vol. 3:** 580
20:45   **Vol. 2:** 799
20:46 f   **Vol. 3:** 481
20:46   **Vol. 1:** 297   **Vol. 2:** 548   **Vol. 3:** 785, 1019
20:47–48   **Vol. 1:** 265
20:47   **Vol. 1:** 730   **Vol. 3:** 482, 1074
21   **Vol. 1:** 125   **Vol. 2:** 904, 911   **Vol. 3:** 65, 430
21:1–4   **Vol. 2:** 41, 43, 751, 824   **Vol. 3:** 791, 1062, 1074
21:1   **Vol. 2:** 41, 842   **Vol. 3:** 519, 796
21:2   **Vol. 1:** 564–565   **Vol. 2:** 821, 850
21:3   **Vol. 1:** 98   **Vol. 3:** 883
21:4   **Vol. 2:** 41, 475, 846   **Vol. 3:** 955
21:5–7   **Vol. 2:** 713   **Vol. 3:** 1011
21:5 f   **Vol. 3:** 792
21:5   **Vol. 1:** 414   **Vol. 2:** 236   **Vol. 3:** 791
21:6 ff   **Vol. 2:** 803
21:6   **Vol. 3:** 185, 189
21:7   **Vol. 1:** 320, 326
21:8–36   **Vol. 2:** 702
21:8 f   **Vol. 2:** 920
21:8   **Vol. 1:** 493   **Vol. 2:** 281, 459, 461, 911   **Vol. 3:** 838
21:9   **Vol. 1:** 667   **Vol. 2:** 62, 665, 918   **Vol. 3:** 962
21:10   **Vol. 2:** 266, 793
21:11   **Vol. 1:** 622   **Vol. 2:** 426, 629   **Vol. 3:** 558
21:12   **Vol. 1:** 270, 297   **Vol. 2:** 136, 368   **Vol. 3:** 785
21:13   **Vol. 3:** 1043
21:15 f   **Vol. 2:** 629
21:15   **Vol. 1:** 91   **Vol. 3:** 1030
21:16   **Vol. 1:** 287   **Vol. 2:** 549
21:17   **Vol. 1:** 556   **Vol. 2:** 773, 806   **Vol. 3:** 257
21:18   **Vol. 1:** 203   **Vol. 2:** 159
21:19   **Vol. 2:** 773
21:20 ff   **Vol. 2:** 54
21:20–24   **Vol. 2:** 37   **Vol. 3:** 793
21:20   **Vol. 1:** 75   **Vol. 2:** 328, 664   **Vol. 3:** 792, 964, 1008
21:21   **Vol. 1:** 559   **Vol. 3:** 1011

21:22   **Vol. 1:** 736   **Vol. 3:** 97, 329, 488–489
21:23 f   **Vol. 3:** 1062
21:23   **Vol. 1:** 111   **Vol. 2:** 664   **Vol. 3:** 1053
21:24–35   **Vol. 2:** 911
21:24   **Vol. 1:** 610, 737   **Vol. 2:** 328–329, 664, 793   **Vol. 3:** 591, 803, 837, 944, 967
21:25–28   **Vol. 2:** 916
21:25   **Vol. 2:** 192   **Vol. 3:** 112, 560, 732, 734, 736, 984
21:26   **Vol. 1:** 322, 519, 622   **Vol. 2:** 244   **Vol. 3:** 559, 736
21:27–30   **Vol. 2:** 912
21:27   **Vol. 1:** 323   **Vol. 2:** 46, 604, 920   **Vol. 3:** 629, 1003
21:28   **Vol. 1:** 725   **Vol. 2:** 54, 388, 894   **Vol. 3:** 199, 633
21:29 ff   **Vol. 2:** 382
21:29–33   **Vol. 2:** 751
21:29   **Vol. 1:** 725   **Vol. 2:** 604   **Vol. 3:** 867
21:31   **Vol. 2:** 54, 382, 387–388
21:32   **Vol. 2:** 36, 38, 193, 911–912, 916
21:33   **Vol. 2:** 193
21:34 ff   **Vol. 2:** 751
21:34–36   **Vol. 2:** 37
21:34 f   **Vol. 1:** 725   **Vol. 2:** 894
21:34   **Vol. 1:** 261, 278, 513–514   **Vol. 2:** 182   **Vol. 3:** 922
21:35   **Vol. 1:** 322, 586
21:36   **Vol. 2:** 137, 861, 911   **Vol. 3:** 620, 627, 839
21:37 f   **Vol. 3:** 791
21:37   **Vol. 2:** 713   **Vol. 3:** 761
22   **Vol. 1:** 633
22:1   **Vol. 1:** 633   **Vol. 2:** 463
22:2   **Vol. 2:** 799   **Vol. 3:** 39
22:3   **Vol. 1:** 299   **Vol. 2:** 684, 695   **Vol. 3:** 470, 473
22:4   **Vol. 3:** 964
22:6   **Vol. 1:** 346   **Vol. 3:** 532
22:7   **Vol. 1:** 633   **Vol. 2:** 277, 527
22:8   **Vol. 1:** 633
22:9   **Vol. 3:** 118
22:10   **Vol. 3:** 911, 990
22:11   **Vol. 1:** 633   **Vol. 2:** 510, 527   **Vol. 3:** 189
22:12   **Vol. 2:** 527   **Vol. 3:** 569
22:13   **Vol. 1:** 633   **Vol. 3:** 118
22:14   **Vol. 1:** 136, 634   **Vol. 2:** 528   **Vol. 3:** 804
22:15–20   **Vol. 2:** 523, 531, 534
22:15   **Vol. 1:** 457, 633   **Vol. 2:** 277, 527–528   **Vol. 3:** 670
22:16   **Vol. 2:** 534, 894
22:17   **Vol. 2:** 523   **Vol. 3:** 819
22:18   **Vol. 2:** 382, 531, 534
22:19 f†   **Vol. 1:** 237, 439, 634
22:19   **Vol. 1:** 641   **Vol. 2:** 42, 523, 530, 534, 536   **Vol. 3:** 243
22:20   **Vol. 1:** 223, 369   **Vol. 2:** 312, 523, 529–530, 534, 536, 671, 854   **Vol. 3:** 166, 1174

Luke *(cont'd)*

22:21 ff   **Vol. 3:** 804
22:21–23   **Vol. 2:** 531   **Vol. 3:** 624
22:21   **Vol. 3:** 470
22:22   **Vol. 1:** 473   **Vol. 3:** 946, 1053
22:23   **Vol. 1:** 326   **Vol. 3:** 1157
22:24 ff   **Vol. 2:** 276
22:24   **Vol. 2:** 550   **Vol. 3:** 822
22:25–27   **Vol. 3:** 979
22:25 f   **Vol. 2:** 339
22:25   **Vol. 1:** 143, 274   **Vol. 2:** 378, 518   **Vol. 3:** 1152
22:26 f   **Vol. 2:** 427, 518   **Vol. 3:** 546
22:26   **Vol. 1:** 197   **Vol. 2:** 675   **Vol. 3:** 547, 1152
22:27   **Vol. 1:** 549   **Vol. 2:** 262   **Vol. 3:** 195, 546–547, 625
22:28 ff   **Vol. 2:** 385, 727, 882, 920–921
22:28–34   **Vol. 3:** 803
22:28   **Vol. 1:** 185   **Vol. 3:** 804
22:29 f   **Vol. 1:** 323   **Vol. 3:** 85
22:29   **Vol. 1:** 369   **Vol. 2:** 382, 385   **Vol. 3:** 697, 871
22:30   **Vol. 1:** 251   **Vol. 2:** 48, 272, 276, 313, 365, 387, 581, 695   **Vol. 3:** 180, 629, 871
22:31 ff   **Vol. 2:** 731
22:31–34   **Vol. 3:** 386
22:31   **Vol. 2:** 858
22:32   **Vol. 1:** 355, 359, 489   **Vol. 2:** 857, 861
22:33   **Vol. 2:** 136   **Vol. 3:** 118
22:34   **Vol. 1:** 173   **Vol. 3:** 114
22:35–38   **Vol. 3:** 978
22:35 f   **Vol. 1:** 142
22:35   **Vol. 1:** 142, 384   **Vol. 3:** 729, 954
22:36 ff   **Vol. 3:** 977
22:36   **Vol. 1:** 143, 268   **Vol. 3:** 967
22:37 f   **Vol. 1:** 489
22:37   **Vol. 1:** 581   **Vol. 2:** 62–64, 445   **Vol. 3:** 612, 824–826, 967
22:38   **Vol. 3:** 729, 967
22:39   **Vol. 2:** 437
22:40–46   **Vol. 2:** 178, 561, 868
22:41   **Vol. 2:** 859
22:42   **Vol. 1:** 335, 620   **Vol. 2:** 83, 276, 871   **Vol. 3:** 1017–1018, 1022
22:43   **Vol. 1:** 102   **Vol. 2:** 193   **Vol. 3:** 517
22:44   **Vol. 1:** 646   **Vol. 2:** 861, 873
22:45   **Vol. 1:** 305, 442   **Vol. 2:** 420   **Vol. 3:** 275
22:46   **Vol. 2:** 871
22:47   **Vol. 1:** 299   **Vol. 2:** 549, 695
22:48   **Vol. 3:** 624
22:49 ff   **Vol. 3:** 729
22:49   **Vol. 3:** 967, 1175, 1190
22:51   **Vol. 2:** 168
22:52   **Vol. 3:** 379, 964, 967
22:53   **Vol. 1:** 423   **Vol. 2:** 150, 610, 895   **Vol. 3:** 470, 791

22:54–71   **Vol. 2:** 379   **Vol. 3:** 386, 409, 804
22:54   **Vol. 1:** 343
22:55   **Vol. 1:** 656
22:56   **Vol. 2:** 493   **Vol. 3:** 519–520
22:57 ff   **Vol. 1:** 455
22:60   **Vol. 3:** 114, 742
22:61   **Vol. 1:** 201–202   **Vol. 3:** 240, 519
22:62   **Vol. 3:** 1122
22:63   **Vol. 1:** 162   **Vol. 3:** 341
22:64   **Vol. 3:** 83
22:65   **Vol. 3:** 343
22:66   **Vol. 1:** 199, 297, 364   **Vol. 2:** 32
22:67   **Vol. 3:** 1211
22:69   **Vol. 1:** 323   **Vol. 2:** 147, 194, 380, 515   **Vol. 3:** 457, 621, 627, 629, 838
22:71   **Vol. 3:** 1043
23   **Vol. 1:** 633   **Vol. 2:** 378   **Vol. 3:** 1174
23:1–56   **Vol. 1:** 394
23:1   **Vol. 1:** 733
23:2   **Vol. 1:** 269, 395   **Vol. 2:** 222, 378, 793   **Vol. 3:** 652, 754
23:3   **Vol. 2:** 315, 378–379
23:4   **Vol. 2:** 139   **Vol. 3:** 529
23:5   **Vol. 1:** 395   **Vol. 2:** 799   **Vol. 3:** 558, 762
23:7   **Vol. 2:** 608
23:8   **Vol. 2:** 241   **Vol. 3:** 517, 843
23:10   **Vol. 1:** 83, 395
23:11   **Vol. 2:** 486   **Vol. 3:** 341, 964
23:12   **Vol. 1:** 554   **Vol. 2:** 549
23:13 ff   **Vol. 1:** 395
23:13   **Vol. 1:** 168
23:14   **Vol. 1:** 83   **Vol. 2:** 139, 365   **Vol. 3:** 529
23:15   **Vol. 3:** 1157
23:16–25   **Vol. 3:** 189
23:16   **Vol. 1:** 162   **Vol. 3:** 778
23:17–25   **Vol. 1:** 396
23:17   **Vol. 2:** 378
23:18   **Vol. 1:** 409
23:19   **Vol. 2:** 136   **Vol. 3:** 1191
23:21   **Vol. 1:** 409
23:22   **Vol. 2:** 139   **Vol. 3:** 529, 778
23:22b   **Vol. 1:** 395
23:23   **Vol. 2:** 856   **Vol. 3:** 113, 713
23:24   **Vol. 2:** 76, 858
23:25   **Vol. 2:** 136
23:25b   **Vol. 1:** 395
23:26–31   **Vol. 3:** 980
23:26   **Vol. 1:** 493   **Vol. 2:** 740   **Vol. 3:** 749
23:27   **Vol. 1:** 733   **Vol. 2:** 418
23:28 ff   **Vol. 1:** 75   **Vol. 2:** 328
23:28–32   **Vol. 2:** 37
23:28–31   **Vol. 1:** 395
23:28   **Vol. 1:** 286, 395   **Vol. 3:** 1062
23:29   **Vol. 1:** 240
23:30   **Vol. 1:** 610   **Vol. 2:** 212, 216, 218
23:31   **Vol. 1:** 390, 515   **Vol. 2:** 382
23:32 ff   **Vol. 3:** 725
23:32   **Vol. 1:** 564

Luke *(cont'd)*

23:33	**Vol. 1:** 564 **Vol. 2:** 148 **Vol. 3:** 379
23:34	**Vol. 1:** 620 **Vol. 2:** 82, 299, 543, 871, 873
23:34b	**Vol. 1:** 396
23:35 ff	**Vol. 1:** 397
23:35–39	**Vol. 3:** 347
23:35	**Vol. 1:** 168, 323, 396, 539, 541 **Vol. 2:** 82, 379, 630–631 **Vol. 3:** 341
23:36	**Vol. 2:** 28, 339 **Vol. 3:** 341
23:37 f	**Vol. 2:** 315
23:37	**Vol. 2:** 379, 418
23:38	**Vol. 2:** 379 **Vol. 3:** 489, 492, 509
23:39	**Vol. 1:** 564 **Vol. 3:** 211
23:40	**Vol. 1:** 572 **Vol. 2:** 739
23:41	**Vol. 3:** 361, 725, 751, 1157
23:42	**Vol. 1:** 320 **Vol. 2:** 763 **Vol. 3:** 241
23:43	**Vol. 1:** 701 **Vol. 2:** 543, 761, 918, 921 **Vol. 3:** 211, 302, 504, 682, 838
23:44	**Vol. 1:** 423 **Vol. 3:** 847
23:45	**Vol. 1:** 203 **Vol. 3:** 543, 732, 793, 795
23:46	**Vol. 1:** 409, 620 **Vol. 2:** 149, 426, 871, 919 **Vol. 3:** 113, 694, 708
23:47	**Vol. 3:** 361, 964–965
23:48	**Vol. 3:** 903
23:49	**Vol. 1:** 481 **Vol. 3:** 1059, 1070
23:50–56	**Vol. 3:** 980
23:50	**Vol. 2:** 563 **Vol. 3:** 361
23:51	**Vol. 2:** 315, 385 **Vol. 3:** 1017, 1158
23:52	**Vol. 1:** 234
23:53	**Vol. 3:** 246, 1190
23:54	**Vol. 3:** 408, 410
23:55–24:11	**Vol. 3:** 1060
23:55	**Vol. 1:** 234, 322 **Vol. 3:** 247, 516
23:56†	**Vol. 1:** 335 **Vol. 2:** 295 **Vol. 3:** 111
24	**Vol. 3:** 287–288, 297, 518
24:1–53	**Vol. 3:** 294
24:1	**Vol. 2:** 198, 295 **Vol. 3:** 246, 412, 1059
24:2	**Vol. 3:** 247, 393
24:4	**Vol. 1:** 204
24:5	**Vol. 1:** 445 **Vol. 3:** 277
24:6 ff	**Vol. 3:** 48
24:7	**Vol. 2:** 63, 663, 665
24:8	**Vol. 3:** 1122
24:9	**Vol. 2:** 358 **Vol. 3:** 48, 247, 252
24:10	**Vol. 1:** 136 **Vol. 3:** 252, 1060
24:11	**Vol. 2:** 359, 488, 911 **Vol. 3:** 296, 1060
24:12	**Vol. 2:** 624, 724 **Vol. 3:** 247, 947
24:13	**Vol. 2:** 686
24:16	**Vol. 2:** 398, 739 **Vol. 3:** 276, 717
24:18	**Vol. 1:** 691 **Vol. 3:** 1061
24:19 ff	**Vol. 2:** 340
24:19	**Vol. 2:** 333, 341, 603, 641, 799 **Vol. 3:** 83, 86, 1149–1150
24:20	**Vol. 1:** 168, 394–395 **Vol. 2:** 365, 368
24:21	**Vol. 1:** 326 **Vol. 2:** 241, 313–314 **Vol. 3:** 198–200, 296
24:22	**Vol. 1:** 528 **Vol. 3:** 247
24:23	**Vol. 3:** 515
24:24	**Vol. 2:** 314 **Vol. 3:** 247
24:25 ff	**Vol. 3:** 329
24:25	**Vol. 2:** 183 **Vol. 3:** 129, 188, 492, 1212
24:26	**Vol. 2:** 46, 339–340, 663, 665 **Vol. 3:** 503–504, 723–724
24:27	**Vol. 1:** 167, 581 **Vol. 2:** 444, 641 **Vol. 3:** 490, 492, 830
24:29 f	**Vol. 3:** 276
24:29	**Vol. 3:** 224
24:30 f	**Vol. 2:** 524
24:30	**Vol. 1:** 213 **Vol. 2:** 48, 524
24:31 f	**Vol. 2:** 729
24:31	**Vol. 2:** 726, 729 **Vol. 3:** 276, 518
24:32	**Vol. 1:** 581 **Vol. 2:** 183, 342, 729 **Vol. 3:** 490, 492
24:33	**Vol. 2:** 33 **Vol. 3:** 846
24:34–40	**Vol. 3:** 297
24:34	**Vol. 3:** 285, 297
24:35	**Vol. 1:** 576 **Vol. 2:** 524, 897
24:36 ff	**Vol. 1:** 128
24:36–49	**Vol. 3:** 295, 297
24:36 f	**Vol. 3:** 518
24:37 ff	**Vol. 3:** 474
24:37–41	**Vol. 2:** 559
24:37	**Vol. 2:** 624 **Vol. 3:** 324, 694, 822
24:38	**Vol. 2:** 185, 282 **Vol. 3:** 710
24:39 f	**Vol. 1:** 239
24:39	**Vol. 1:** 241, 393, 677, 679 **Vol. 2:** 149, 282 **Vol. 3:** 276, 323, 694
24:41–43	**Vol. 3:** 449
24:41	**Vol. 2:** 282, 359, 624
24:43	**Vol. 2:** 524, 920
24:44–47	**Vol. 3:** 329
24:44	**Vol. 1:** 736 **Vol. 2:** 314, 444, 641, 665 **Vol. 3:** 485, 671, 675
24:45	**Vol. 3:** 132, 490
24:46 ff	**Vol. 1:** 136 **Vol. 2:** 176
24:46 f	**Vol. 1:** 702
24:46	**Vol. 2:** 63, 359 **Vol. 3:** 723
24:47	**Vol. 1:** 359, 701, 720 **Vol. 2:** 328, 359 **Vol. 3:** 56
24:48 f	**Vol. 1:** 90
24:48	**Vol. 3:** 1044
24:49	**Vol. 2:** 200, 328, 786 **Vol. 3:** 70–71, 229, 698
24:50–51	**Vol. 1:** 214 **Vol. 2:** 713
24:51	**Vol. 1:** 607
24:52 f	**Vol. 3:** 793
24:52	**Vol. 2:** 328, 359, 877
24:53	**Vol. 1:** 213 **Vol. 2:** 236, 327–328

John

1:1 ff	**Vol. 1:** 63, 175, 549 **Vol. 2:** 405, 546, 840, 927 **Vol. 3:** 462, 1116–1117
1:1–18	**Vol. 1:** 628 **Vol. 3:** 791, 1114–1115
1:1–14	**Vol. 3:** 582
1:1–12	**Vol. 1:** 66
1:1–4	**Vol. 3:** 1114–1115
1:1–3	**Vol. 3:** 1115

John *(cont'd)*

1:1 f   **Vol. 3:** 1116
1:1   **Vol. 1:** 166, 383–384   **Vol. 2:** 81, 654   **Vol. 3:** 61, 326, 1106, 1114–1115, 1176, 1186
1:1a   **Vol. 3:** 1204
1:1b   **Vol. 3:** 1172, 1185, 1204–1205
1:2   **Vol. 3:** 1115
1:3 f   **Vol. 3:** 1115
1:3   **Vol. 1:** 95, 181, 384, 524   **Vol. 3:** 1182
1:4–9   **Vol. 3:** 916
1:4 f   **Vol. 3:** 314, 1115
1:4   **Vol. 1:** 168   **Vol. 2:** 80, 482, 494   **Vol. 3:** 314
1:5 ff   **Vol. 3:** 1115
1:5–13   **Vol. 3:** 1115
1:5   **Vol. 1:** 424   **Vol. 2:** 488   **Vol. 3:** 723, 750, 1114–1115
1:6 ff   **Vol. 1:** 111   **Vol. 2:** 494   **Vol. 3:** 82
1:6–8   **Vol. 3:** 1115
1:6   **Vol. 3:** 1201, 1203
1:7   **Vol. 1:** 323, 603   **Vol. 3:** 1045, 1211
1:8 f   **Vol. 2:** 80
1:8   **Vol. 3:** 697, 1045
1:9–11   **Vol. 3:** 1114–1115
1:9   **Vol. 1:** 323, 524   **Vol. 2:** 280, 494   **Vol. 3:** 893, 1115
1:10 f   **Vol. 3:** 1116
1:10   **Vol. 1:** 303, 524–525   **Vol. 2:** 400   **Vol. 3:** 1182
1:11   **Vol. 2:** 839, 846   **Vol. 3:** 321, 460, 723, 750–751
1:12 f   **Vol. 1:** 158, 179, 256, 287, 290, 303, 526   **Vol. 2:** 928   **Vol. 3:** 1115
1:12   **Vol. 1:** 599   **Vol. 2:** 610, 929   **Vol. 3:** 646–647, 748, 1213
1:13   **Vol. 1:** 148, 159, 221, 678   **Vol. 2:** 76   **Vol. 3:** 647, 661, 1188
1:14 f   **Vol. 3:** 1117
1:14–18   **Vol. 3:** 890, 1115
1:14   **Vol. 1:** 347, 678–679, 739–740   **Vol. 2:** 47–48, 75–76, 80, 119, 122, 176, 185, 404, 567, 632, 725, 928   **Vol. 3:** 313, 323, 326, 516, 630, 697, 813, 889–890, 1106, 1114–1115, 1117, 1202
1:15   **Vol. 1:** 323, 409, 493   **Vol. 3:** 1045, 1115, 1176
1:16 f   **Vol. 2:** 120
1:16   **Vol. 1:** 739   **Vol. 3:** 749, 1115, 1179
1:17 f   **Vol. 3:** 1115
1:17   **Vol. 1:** 374   **Vol. 2:** 80, 119, 232, 339, 443, 448, 641–642, 673   **Vol. 3:** 631, 889–890, 1022, 1116
1:18   **Vol. 1:** 240, 573, 575–576, 620   **Vol. 2:** 75, 79, 81, 404, 505, 725   **Vol. 3:** 314, 462, 517, 646, 1174, 1176, 1185–1186
1:19 ff   **Vol. 3:** 1045
1:19–34   **Vol. 3:** 697, 791

1:19–28   **Vol. 1:** 111
1:19 f   **Vol. 2:** 339
1:19   **Vol. 2:** 315, 467, 879   **Vol. 3:** 455
1:20   **Vol. 1:** 346–347, 455   **Vol. 2:** 282
1:21   **Vol. 1:** 544–545   **Vol. 2:** 443, 640, 879
1:23   **Vol. 1:** 411, 736   **Vol. 3:** 940
1:25 ff   **Vol. 1:** 487
1:25   **Vol. 1:** 544–545   **Vol. 2:** 640, 879
1:26 f   **Vol. 3:** 55
1:26   **Vol. 3:** 990, 1210
1:27   **Vol. 1:** 323, 493   **Vol. 3:** 179, 348
1:28   **Vol. 3:** 991
1:29 ff   **Vol. 1:** 629
1:29–36   **Vol. 1:** 629
1:29–34   **Vol. 3:** 170
1:29   **Vol. 1:** 525, 701–702   **Vol. 2:** 411, 527, 927   **Vol. 3:** 516, 582, 611, 1117, 1196
1:30   **Vol. 1:** 493   **Vol. 3:** 1174, 1176
1:31   **Vol. 2:** 315   **Vol. 3:** 312, 314, 321, 323, 990, 1210
1:32 ff   **Vol. 3:** 516
1:32–34   **Vol. 2:** 411
1:32 f   **Vol. 2:** 878   **Vol. 3:** 460, 704, 987
1:32   **Vol. 1:** 175   **Vol. 3:** 225, 258, 516, 1045
1:33   **Vol. 1:** 158   **Vol. 2:** 231   **Vol. 3:** 697, 704, 990, 1070, 1210
1:34   **Vol. 1:** 539, 541   **Vol. 3:** 611, 1045
1:35 ff   **Vol. 2:** 686
1:35–51   **Vol. 2:** 825   **Vol. 3:** 791, 985
1:35–43   **Vol. 1:** 136
1:35   **Vol. 1:** 487
1:36   **Vol. 2:** 80, 411, 434   **Vol. 3:** 520, 611
1:37   **Vol. 1:** 487
1:38–40   **Vol. 2:** 311
1:38   **Vol. 1:** 488, 581   **Vol. 3:** 115, 224, 516, 767
1:39 ff   **Vol. 2:** 231
1:39   **Vol. 1:** 321   **Vol. 3:** 847, 1205
1:41   **Vol. 2:** 334, 338–339   **Vol. 3:** 462, 528, 530
1:42   **Vol. 1:** 273, 581   **Vol. 3:** 382–383, 386, 520
1:43 ff   **Vol. 1:** 483
1:43   **Vol. 1:** 482, 488, 581
1:44–47   **Vol. 2:** 550
1:44   **Vol. 3:** 1180
1:45   **Vol. 2:** 333, 339   **Vol. 3:** 489, 528–529
1:46   **Vol. 2:** 101, 334
1:47 ff   **Vol. 2:** 339
1:47   **Vol. 1:** 321   **Vol. 2:** 310, 314   **Vol. 3:** 516, 894
1:48   **Vol. 2:** 398   **Vol. 3:** 114, 460, 517
1:49 ff   **Vol. 2:** 231
1:49   **Vol. 2:** 315, 550   **Vol. 3:** 115, 460, 652
1:51   **Vol. 1:** 102   **Vol. 2:** 185–186, 194, 319, 726–728   **Vol. 3:** 543, 620, 630, 632
2:1 ff   **Vol. 2:** 630, 632
2:1–11   **Vol. 2:** 580, 676   **Vol. 3:** 791, 922, 990
2:1 f   **Vol. 2:** 579
2:2   **Vol. 1:** 274   **Vol. 2:** 578

John (*cont'd*)

2:4	**Vol. 1:** 321, 738 **Vol. 2:** 927 **Vol. 3:** 848, 890, 1058, 1070
2:5	**Vol. 3:** 546
2:6	**Vol. 1:** 742 **Vol. 3:** 105, 990
2:9	**Vol. 2:** 269, 585 **Vol. 3:** 546, 922
2:10	**Vol. 1:** 513 **Vol. 2:** 133, 428
2:11	**Vol. 1:** 489 **Vol. 2:** 47–48, 629, 632 **Vol. 3:** 312, 314, 516–517
2:12–22	**Vol. 1:** 629
2:13 ff	**Vol. 2:** 328
2:13–22	**Vol. 3:** 430
2:13–17	**Vol. 2:** 610, 754 **Vol. 3:** 39, 429, 791, 1168
2:13	**Vol. 1:** 629, 633–634 **Vol. 2:** 54, 315, 927
2:14 ff	**Vol. 1:** 111 **Vol. 3:** 789
2:14	**Vol. 1:** 175 **Vol. 2:** 413
2:15	**Vol. 2:** 854
2:16 f	**Vol. 2:** 248
2:16	**Vol. 2:** 236 **Vol. 3:** 430, 516
2:17	**Vol. 3:** 430, 1167
2:18 ff	**Vol. 3:** 784
2:18–22	**Vol. 3:** 791–792
2:18†	**Vol. 2:** 434, 629 **Vol. 3:** 569
2:19 ff	**Vol. 2:** 252
2:19–22	**Vol. 2:** 434 **Vol. 3:** 813
2:19–21	**Vol. 2:** 450 **Vol. 3:** 784
2:19–20	**Vol. 2:** 687
2:19	**Vol. 2:** 236, 252, 732 **Vol. 3:** 180, 185, 211, 343, 509
2:20	**Vol. 2:** 434, 685 **Vol. 3:** 185, 788
2:21	**Vol. 1:** 234 **Vol. 3:** 185, 890
2:22	**Vol. 3:** 185, 491–492
2:23 ff	**Vol. 2:** 632 **Vol. 3:** 791
2:23†	**Vol. 1:** 633 **Vol. 2:** 629, 927 **Vol. 3:** 1213
2:24	**Vol. 3:** 1211, 1213
2:25	**Vol. 2:** 879 **Vol. 3:** 517, 1044
3	**Vol. 1:** 284, 510
3:1–36	**Vol. 2:** 751
3:1–15	**Vol. 3:** 791
3:1	**Vol. 1:** 168 **Vol. 2:** 812
3:2	**Vol. 1:** 420, 488 **Vol. 2:** 79, 604, 629 **Vol. 3:** 115, 768
3:3 ff	**Vol. 1:** 303 **Vol. 2:** 567
3:3–8	**Vol. 3:** 460
3:3–7	**Vol. 3:** 1132
3:3 f	**Vol. 1:** 180 **Vol. 3:** 185
3:3	**Vol. 1:** 179 **Vol. 2:** 385, 604, 661, 787, 928 **Vol. 3:** 518, 647, 1178
3:4	**Vol. 1:** 179 **Vol. 2:** 434, 812 **Vol. 3:** 1071
3:5–8	**Vol. 1:** 179 **Vol. 2:** 878 **Vol. 3:** 703, 705
3:5	**Vol. 1:** 147–148, 154, 158, 160, 179–180, 185, 290, 526 **Vol. 2:** 385, 604, 661, 929 **Vol. 3:** 459, 647, 704, 1178

3:6	**Vol. 1:** 179, 678–679 **Vol. 2:** 567, 928
3:7	**Vol. 1:** 179 **Vol. 2:** 625, 666 **Vol. 3:** 1178
3:8	**Vol. 1:** 147, 179, 656 **Vol. 3:** 113, 703, 708, 1022
3:9	**Vol. 2:** 625, 812
3:10	**Vol. 3:** 767
3:11	**Vol. 3:** 516, 1045
3:12 f	**Vol. 2:** 196
3:13	**Vol. 2:** 185, 787, 928 **Vol. 3:** 622, 629–631, 646
3:14 ff	**Vol. 2:** 642
3:14 f	**Vol. 1:** 147, 510
3:14	**Vol. 1:** 390, 509 **Vol. 2:** 202, 204, 339, 665 **Vol. 3:** 630–631, 1007
3:15 ff	**Vol. 2:** 42
3:15 f†	**Vol. 1:** 638 **Vol. 2:** 80 **Vol. 3:** 832
3:15	**Vol. 2:** 388 **Vol. 3:** 832, 1178, 1212
3:16 ff	**Vol. 1:** 525, 603 **Vol. 2:** 367
3:16–21	**Vol. 1:** 290 **Vol. 2:** 928 **Vol. 3:** 791
3:16	**Vol. 1:** 287, 338, 464, 638, 702 **Vol. 2:** 42, 75, 78–79, 122, 404, 542, 546, 548, 610, 725 **Vol. 3:** 321, 643, 646, 825, 1202
3:17 f	**Vol. 2:** 365
3:17	**Vol. 1:** 525 **Vol. 3:** 216, 445, 643, 646, 1022
3:18 f	**Vol. 1:** 424 **Vol. 2:** 894, 928
3:18	**Vol. 1:** 599 **Vol. 2:** 75, 654, 702, 725 **Vol. 3:** 646, 1202, 1213
3:18b	**Vol. 3:** 1211
3:19–21	**Vol. 3:** 1150
3:19	**Vol. 1:** 323, 424, 524–525, 566 **Vol. 2:** 366, 494, 543, 928 **Vol. 3:** 1150
3:20	**Vol. 1:** 556, 564, 603 **Vol. 2:** 141 **Vol. 3:** 1158
3:21	**Vol. 1:** 490 **Vol. 2:** 232 **Vol. 3:** 312, 314, 321, 891, 1149–1150
3:22–26	**Vol. 1:** 487
3:22	**Vol. 3:** 1205
3:23	**Vol. 2:** 592 **Vol. 3:** 1210
3:25 f	**Vol. 3:** 1205
3:25	**Vol. 1:** 487 **Vol. 3:** 532
3:26	**Vol. 3:** 115, 991, 1045
3:27	**Vol. 3:** 193, 359
3:28	**Vol. 3:** 1044
3:29 f	**Vol. 2:** 585
3:29	**Vol. 1:** 741 **Vol. 2:** 356, 549, 585, 751 **Vol. 3:** 113
3:31 f	**Vol. 2:** 196 **Vol. 3:** 1045
3:31	**Vol. 2:** 928 **Vol. 3:** 629
3:32	**Vol. 3:** 314, 516, 1045
3:33	**Vol. 2:** 77 **Vol. 3:** 499, 749, 1046
3:34	**Vol. 2:** 878 **Vol. 3:** 403, 697, 704, 1114, 1122
3:35	**Vol. 1:** 620 **Vol. 2:** 81, 149, 542, 546, 610, 653 **Vol. 3:** 313, 645–646, 1122, 1174, 1185
3:36	**Vol. 1:** 111–113, 593, 638 **Vol. 2:** 388, 404, 546 **Vol. 3:** 226, 832, 837

John *(cont'd)*

4   **Vol. 3:** 143, 459, 461
4:1 ff   **Vol. 1:** 146
4:1–45   **Vol. 3:** 455
4:1–42   **Vol. 1:** 67   **Vol. 2:** 751   **Vol. 3:** 456, 458, 980
4:1 f   **Vol. 1:** 160
4:1   **Vol. 2:** 398
4:2   **Vol. 1:** 179
4:3   **Vol. 3:** 115
4:4   **Vol. 3:** 449
4:5 ff   **Vol. 3:** 987
4:5   **Vol. 1:** 258   **Vol. 2:** 318   **Vol. 3:** 454, 457–458
4:6   **Vol. 1:** 263   **Vol. 2:** 318   **Vol. 3:** 459, 847, 1180
4:6b   **Vol. 3:** 458
4:7 ff   **Vol. 3:** 459
4:7–27   **Vol. 3:** 1059
4:7   **Vol. 3:** 989
4:8   **Vol. 3:** 454, 458
4:9   **Vol. 2:** 315   **Vol. 3:** 460, 1058
4:10 ff   **Vol. 2:** 277   **Vol. 3:** 185
4:10–15   **Vol. 3:** 459, 991
4:10–14   **Vol. 2:** 928
4:10   **Vol. 1:** 683   **Vol. 2:** 41–42   **Vol. 3:** 459, 1132
4:11 f   **Vol. 3:** 459
4:11   **Vol. 2:** 198, 277, 434
4:12   **Vol. 1:** 116   **Vol. 2:** 318, 426   **Vol. 3:** 461
4:13 ff   **Vol. 2:** 80
4:13 f   **Vol. 3:** 459, 987, 989
4:13   **Vol. 2:** 267, 277
4:14 f   **Vol. 2:** 267, 514
4:14   **Vol. 2:** 277, 482, 787   **Vol. 3:** 459, 462, 703, 830, 832
4:16–19   **Vol. 3:** 460
4:17 f   **Vol. 3:** 460
4:18   **Vol. 3:** 460, 890
4:19   **Vol. 1:** 66   **Vol. 3:** 83, 460, 462, 516–517
4:20 ff   **Vol. 2:** 927
4:20   **Vol. 2:** 878   **Vol. 3:** 459–460, 789
4:21–24   **Vol. 3:** 460
4:21   **Vol. 2:** 878, 927   **Vol. 3:** 460–461, 1211–1212
4:22 ff   **Vol. 2:** 878
4:22 f   **Vol. 3:** 458
4:22   **Vol. 2:** 314   **Vol. 3:** 212, 216, 219, 460–463
4:23 f   **Vol. 2:** 80, 873, 927   **Vol. 3:** 460–461, 551, 705
4:23   **Vol. 1:** 324   **Vol. 2:** 280, 878   **Vol. 3:** 532, 890–891, 893
4:24   **Vol. 2:** 66, 75, 666   **Vol. 3:** 891
4:25 f   **Vol. 2:** 339, 927   **Vol. 3:** 462
4:25   **Vol. 2:** 231, 334, 338   **Vol. 3:** 47–48, 461–462

4:26   **Vol. 3:** 462
4:27   **Vol. 3:** 1058–1059
4:29   **Vol. 3:** 462
4:31–34   **Vol. 3:** 1132
4:31   **Vol. 1:** 488   **Vol. 2:** 879
4:32 f   **Vol. 3:** 185
4:32   **Vol. 2:** 268–269, 434
4:34   **Vol. 1:** 128   **Vol. 2:** 64, 268–269, 359, 561   **Vol. 3:** 1022, 1150
4:35–38   **Vol. 2:** 927
4:35 f   **Vol. 2:** 359
4:35   **Vol. 1:** 204   **Vol. 2:** 750   **Vol. 3:** 516, 526
4:36 ff   **Vol. 3:** 144
4:36–38   **Vol. 3:** 526
4:36   **Vol. 1:** 723   **Vol. 2:** 32   **Vol. 3:** 832
4:37   **Vol. 2:** 280   **Vol. 3:** 893
4:38   **Vol. 1:** 263   **Vol. 3:** 458
4:39–42   **Vol. 3:** 462
4:39   **Vol. 3:** 1046
4:40   **Vol. 2:** 879   **Vol. 3:** 454, 1205
4:41   **Vol. 3:** 1106
4:42   **Vol. 1:** 525, 603   **Vol. 3:** 219, 460, 462
4:43 f   **Vol. 3:** 460
4:44   **Vol. 1:** 616   **Vol. 3:** 83, 696
4:45   **Vol. 2:** 927
4:46   **Vol. 3:** 994
4:47 ff   **Vol. 2:** 480, 632
4:47   **Vol. 1:** 326   **Vol. 2:** 879
4:48   **Vol. 2:** 629
4:49   **Vol. 1:** 284
4:50   **Vol. 1:** 284   **Vol. 2:** 631   **Vol. 3:** 280, 1211
4:51   **Vol. 1:** 284   **Vol. 3:** 46
4:52 f   **Vol. 3:** 848
4:53   **Vol. 2:** 248, 250
5   **Vol. 3:** 630
5:1 ff   **Vol. 2:** 328, 632
5:1–9   **Vol. 3:** 409
5:1   **Vol. 1:** 629   **Vol. 2:** 927
5:2   **Vol. 2:** 309
5:3   **Vol. 1:** 516   **Vol. 2:** 415
5:4   **Vol. 3:** 709, 990, 998
5:5   **Vol. 2:** 685
5:6   **Vol. 3:** 843, 1022
5:7   **Vol. 1:** 637   **Vol. 2:** 514   **Vol. 3:** 709, 990, 994
5:8 ff   **Vol. 2:** 168
5:9 ff   **Vol. 2:** 170
5:10   **Vol. 2:** 610
5:12   **Vol. 2:** 879
5:13 f   **Vol. 2:** 169
5:14   **Vol. 2:** 236   **Vol. 3:** 792, 998
5:16   **Vol. 2:** 806   **Vol. 3:** 409, 533
5:17–47   **Vol. 1:** 704
5:17–30   **Vol. 3:** 646
5:17   **Vol. 2:** 74, 499   **Vol. 3:** 186, 409, 604, 1150
5:18   **Vol. 2:** 449, 500   **Vol. 3:** 186–187, 532, 604

John (*cont'd*)

5:19 ff	**Vol. 2:** 500
5:19–47	**Vol. 2:** 751
5:19	**Vol. 1:** 549 **Vol. 2:** 313, 604 **Vol. 3:** 645–646
5:20	**Vol. 2:** 426, 542, 548, 625, 653 **Vol. 3:** 569, 646
5:21	**Vol. 3:** 304, 647, 1022
5:21a	**Vol. 3:** 303
5:22	**Vol. 2:** 365 **Vol. 3:** 645
5:23	**Vol. 2:** 50 **Vol. 3:** 645–646
5:24 ff	**Vol. 3:** 848
5:24–25	**Vol. 3:** 114
5:24	**Vol. 1:** 436, 439, 637 **Vol. 2:** 186, 366, 482, 567, 702, 929 **Vol. 3:** 277, 517, 832, 1114, 1212
5:25–28	**Vol. 2:** 929
5:25	**Vol. 1:** 324 **Vol. 2:** 178 **Vol. 3:** 113, 837
5:26	**Vol. 3:** 304, 645, 1183
5:27	**Vol. 2:** 610 **Vol. 3:** 618, 630–631
5:28 f	**Vol. 1:** 440 **Vol. 2:** 625 **Vol. 3:** 303, 839
5:28–29	**Vol. 3:** 113
5:28	**Vol. 2:** 178 **Vol. 3:** 247
5:29 f	**Vol. 2:** 365
5:29	**Vol. 1:** 324, 564 **Vol. 2:** 101, 366 **Vol. 3:** 303, 1157–1158
5:30	**Vol. 2:** 366, 561, 604 **Vol. 3:** 362, 532
5:30a	**Vol. 3:** 1022
5:30b	**Vol. 3:** 1022
5:31 f	**Vol. 3:** 890
5:31	**Vol. 3:** 890, 1045
5:32	**Vol. 2:** 739 **Vol. 3:** 1045
5:33	**Vol. 3:** 1045
5:34	**Vol. 3:** 216
5:35 f	**Vol. 2:** 494
5:35	**Vol. 2:** 353, 487–488 **Vol. 3:** 848
5:36	**Vol. 1:** 128 **Vol. 2:** 64, 313, 426 **Vol. 3:** 1045, 1149–1150
5:37	**Vol. 1:** 704 **Vol. 3:** 461, 1045
5:38 ff	**Vol. 1:** 638
5:38	**Vol. 1:** 704 **Vol. 3:** 1212
5:39–47	**Vol. 3:** 329
5:39 f	**Vol. 2:** 399
5:39	**Vol. 1:** 246, 737 **Vol. 2:** 314, 448, 641, 927 **Vol. 3:** 188, 215, 429, 490, 492, 499, 517, 533, 822, 832, 1045, 1212
5:40	**Vol. 1:** 324 **Vol. 3:** 1212
5:41	**Vol. 2:** 46–47
5:42	**Vol. 3:** 461
5:43	**Vol. 1:** 323 **Vol. 3:** 748
5:44	**Vol. 2:** 46–47, 724 **Vol. 3:** 532
5:45 ff	**Vol. 2:** 641
5:45	**Vol. 1:** 83 **Vol. 2:** 241 **Vol. 3:** 533, 631, 822
5:46	**Vol. 3:** 489, 1212
5:47	**Vol. 3:** 493, 1212
6	**Vol. 1:** 629–630 **Vol. 2:** 534–535 **Vol. 3:** 631
6:1 ff	**Vol. 2:** 267, 339, 632 **Vol. 3:** 499
6:1–13	**Vol. 1:** 729 **Vol. 2:** 272, 523
6:1	**Vol. 3:** 984
6:2	**Vol. 3:** 994
6:4	**Vol. 1:** 633–634 **Vol. 2:** 927
6:5–13	**Vol. 2:** 630
6:5	**Vol. 2:** 274, 550, 801
6:6	**Vol. 1:** 326
6:7	**Vol. 2:** 550, 711 **Vol. 3:** 727
6:9	**Vol. 1:** 284
6:10	**Vol. 1:** 744 **Vol. 2:** 684
6:11	**Vol. 1:** 670
6:12	**Vol. 1:** 464 **Vol. 2:** 32
6:13	**Vol. 1:** 729 **Vol. 2:** 32
6:14 f	**Vol. 3:** 509
6:14	**Vol. 2:** 641 **Vol. 3:** 80, 83
6:15–21	**Vol. 2:** 281, 630
6:15	**Vol. 1:** 326, 629, 633 **Vol. 2:** 379 **Vol. 3:** 602
6:16 ff	**Vol. 3:** 984
6:16–21	**Vol. 3:** 985, 990
6:17	**Vol. 1:** 423
6:18	**Vol. 3:** 707
6:20	**Vol. 2:** 434
6:22–66	**Vol. 2:** 751
6:22	**Vol. 1:** 321
6:25	**Vol. 2:** 736 **Vol. 3:** 115
6:26	**Vol. 1:** 743
6:27–59	**Vol. 2:** 58
6:27 f	**Vol. 3:** 1202
6:27†	**Vol. 1:** 464 **Vol. 2:** 268–269, 273, 482, 928–929 **Vol. 3:** 499, 631, 832, 1022
6:28	**Vol. 3:** 1149
6:29	**Vol. 2:** 736 **Vol. 3:** 136, 144, 1150, 1212
6:30	**Vol. 2:** 629, 750, 894 **Vol. 3:** 1211–1212
6:31–35	**Vol. 3:** 1132
6:31–34	**Vol. 1:** 253
6:31 f	**Vol. 2:** 194
6:31	**Vol. 3:** 1007
6:32 ff	**Vol. 3:** 185
6:32–35	**Vol. 2:** 642
6:32	**Vol. 2:** 273, 280 **Vol. 3:** 893
6:33 ff	**Vol. 2:** 218
6:33	**Vol. 2:** 185, 482 **Vol. 3:** 1176
6:34	**Vol. 1:** 250 **Vol. 2:** 514
6:35 ff	**Vol. 2:** 727, 882
6:35–58	**Vol. 3:** 383
6:35	**Vol. 1:** 251 **Vol. 2:** 80, 267, 269, 273, 279–280, 482, 535 **Vol. 3:** 1212
6:36	**Vol. 1:** 678
6:37	**Vol. 1:** 324, 453 **Vol. 3:** 1204, 1212
6:38	**Vol. 2:** 185, 194 **Vol. 3:** 1022, 1176
6:39 ff	**Vol. 2:** 900
6:39 f	**Vol. 2:** 58, 929 **Vol. 3:** 277
6:39	**Vol. 1:** 324, 464 **Vol. 2:** 894 **Vol. 3:** 304, 529, 1022

John *(cont'd)*

6:40	**Vol. 2:** 482 **Vol. 3:** 304, 517, 645, 832, 1022
6:41 f	**Vol. 2:** 185, 194
6:41	**Vol. 2:** 269, 279–280 **Vol. 3:** 1176
6:42	**Vol. 2:** 333 **Vol. 3:** 1176
6:44 f	**Vol. 3:** 1212
6:44	**Vol. 1:** 303, 324 **Vol. 2:** 58, 567, 604, 929 **Vol. 3:** 304
6:45	**Vol. 1:** 486 **Vol. 3:** 81, 764
6:46	**Vol. 2:** 505 **Vol. 3:** 516, 518, 1185, 1202
6:47	**Vol. 2:** 280, 482, 535 **Vol. 3:** 832
6:48–51	**Vol. 2:** 642
6:48	**Vol. 2:** 80, 273, 279–280, 482
6:49 f	**Vol. 2:** 273
6:49–51a	**Vol. 1:** 253
6:49	**Vol. 3:** 1007
6:50 f	**Vol. 2:** 194
6:50	**Vol. 2:** 186
6:51 ff	**Vol. 2:** 80, 273, 277, 535 **Vol. 3:** 323
6:51–58	**Vol. 1:** 678 **Vol. 2:** 523, 534 **Vol. 3:** 704
6:51–56	**Vol. 1:** 679
6:51	**Vol. 1:** 253 **Vol. 2:** 279–280 **Vol. 3:** 445, 611, 830
6:51c–58	**Vol. 2:** 534
6:51c	**Vol. 2:** 523, 535
6:52	**Vol. 3:** 963
6:53 ff	**Vol. 1:** 701 **Vol. 2:** 727, 882
6:53–58	**Vol. 3:** 704
6:53–56	**Vol. 1:** 224
6:53	**Vol. 3:** 631
6:54	**Vol. 1:** 324 **Vol. 2:** 58, 535, 929 **Vol. 3:** 277, 304, 832
6:55†	**Vol. 2:** 268–269 **Vol. 3:** 891
6:56	**Vol. 2:** 535 **Vol. 3:** 226, 1192
6:57	**Vol. 1:** 620 **Vol. 2:** 929 **Vol. 3:** 226, 1022, 1185
6:57a	**Vol. 3:** 1183
6:58	**Vol. 2:** 186 **Vol. 3:** 830
6:59	**Vol. 3:** 764, 785
6:60 f	**Vol. 2:** 709
6:60	**Vol. 1:** 490 **Vol. 2:** 155
6:61	**Vol. 2:** 708 **Vol. 3:** 1117
6:62 f	**Vol. 2:** 787 **Vol. 3:** 704
6:62	**Vol. 1:** 678 **Vol. 2:** 185 **Vol. 3:** 629, 631
6:63	**Vol. 1:** 679 **Vol. 2:** 80, 535, 709, 878, 928–929 **Vol. 3:** 244, 459–460, 703–704, 1114, 1117, 1122
6:64	**Vol. 1:** 166
6:65	**Vol. 2:** 567 **Vol. 3:** 1045, 1180, 1212
6:66†	**Vol. 1:** 321, 490, 493, 608 **Vol. 2:** 268, 709
6:67	**Vol. 2:** 695
6:68 f	**Vol. 2:** 76
6:68	**Vol. 2:** 482 **Vol. 3:** 114, 384, 462, 832, 1114, 1122
6:69†	**Vol. 1:** 489, 603 **Vol. 2:** 231, 404 **Vol. 3:** 384
6:70 f	**Vol. 3:** 582
6:70	**Vol. 1:** 540, 542 **Vol. 2:** 695 **Vol. 3:** 470, 472
6:71	**Vol. 2:** 695
7	**Vol. 2:** 57
7:1–52	**Vol. 2:** 751
7:1	**Vol. 1:** 430 **Vol. 3:** 532
7:2 ff	**Vol. 2:** 217
7:2	**Vol. 2:** 927 **Vol. 3:** 813
7:3–9	**Vol. 3:** 813
7:4	**Vol. 2:** 736 **Vol. 3:** 312, 314, 321
7:5	**Vol. 1:** 256 **Vol. 3:** 321
7:6 f	**Vol. 3:** 837
7:6	**Vol. 2:** 899 **Vol. 3:** 118, 321
7:7	**Vol. 1:** 525, 556, 603 **Vol. 3:** 1150
7:8 ff	**Vol. 2:** 185
7:8–10	**Vol. 2:** 217
7:8	**Vol. 1:** 738 **Vol. 2:** 217, 927
7:10 ff	**Vol. 2:** 328
7:10 f	**Vol. 2:** 927
7:10	**Vol. 2:** 217 **Vol. 3:** 320
7:11	**Vol. 2:** 315
7:12	**Vol. 2:** 101, 460, 739, 801
7:13	**Vol. 1:** 622 **Vol. 2:** 736
7:14	**Vol. 2:** 236, 927 **Vol. 3:** 764, 792, 813
7:15–36	**Vol. 3:** 813
7:15 f	**Vol. 2:** 641
7:15	**Vol. 1:** 488 **Vol. 2:** 624 **Vol. 3:** 481, 493
7:16 f	**Vol. 3:** 769
7:16	**Vol. 1:** 128, 549 **Vol. 2:** 624
7:17	**Vol. 2:** 641 **Vol. 3:** 1022, 1155, 1188
7:18	**Vol. 2:** 46 **Vol. 3:** 532, 575–576, 645
7:19 ff	**Vol. 1:** 430
7:19	**Vol. 2:** 448, 450, 641 **Vol. 3:** 532
7:20	**Vol. 1:** 453, 529, 637
7:21	**Vol. 2:** 624 **Vol. 3:** 1149
7:22 f	**Vol. 1:** 309
7:22	**Vol. 3:** 405, 409
7:23	**Vol. 2:** 170, 448, 625 **Vol. 3:** 186–187
7:24	**Vol. 1:** 678, 680 **Vol. 2:** 365 **Vol. 3:** 362
7:25	**Vol. 2:** 325
7:26	**Vol. 1:** 168 **Vol. 2:** 736
7:27	**Vol. 3:** 652
7:28	**Vol. 1:** 409 **Vol. 2:** 280 **Vol. 3:** 461, 764, 792
7:29	**Vol. 1:** 128 **Vol. 2:** 236, 279, 653 **Vol. 3:** 1202
7:30	**Vol. 1:** 738 **Vol. 3:** 848
7:31	**Vol. 2:** 801
7:33	**Vol. 2:** 429 **Vol. 3:** 843
7:34 ff	**Vol. 3:** 185
7:34	**Vol. 3:** 529
7:35	**Vol. 1:** 326, 686 **Vol. 2:** 35, 126 **Vol. 3:** 764
7:36	**Vol. 2:** 277
7:37 ff	**Vol. 2:** 787 **Vol. 3:** 83

John *(cont'd)*

7:37 f   **Vol. 1:** 409   **Vol. 3:** 459, 813, 988, 991
7:37   **Vol. 1:** 324, 629, 683   **Vol. 2:** 277, 894, 927   **Vol. 3:** 383, 748, 1212
7:38 f   **Vol. 2:** 785, 787, 929   **Vol. 3:** 703–704
7:38   **Vol. 1:** 169, 683   **Vol. 2:** 80   **Vol. 3:** 490, 492, 704
7:39   **Vol. 1:** 147, 326   **Vol. 2:** 46, 878   **Vol. 3:** 459, 749, 813, 988, 991
7:40   **Vol. 3:** 80, 83
7:41 f   **Vol. 3:** 1176
7:42   **Vol. 1:** 170, 427   **Vol. 2:** 399, 803   **Vol. 3:** 490, 492, 652
7:43   **Vol. 2:** 801   **Vol. 3:** 543
7:44   **Vol. 3:** 1019
7:47   **Vol. 2:** 459–460
7:48 f   **Vol. 2:** 801
7:48   **Vol. 1:** 168
7:49   **Vol. 1:** 417   **Vol. 2:** 399, 448, 801
7:50   **Vol. 2:** 812
7:51   **Vol. 1:** 666   **Vol. 2:** 399, 448   **Vol. 3:** 1062
7:52   **Vol. 2:** 448   **Vol. 3:** 83, 533
7:53 ff   **Vol. 2:** 754
7:53–8:11   **Vol. 1:** 506   **Vol. 2:** 448, 580   **Vol. 3:** 480
8   **Vol. 3:** 463
8:1–11   **Vol. 3:** 536, 538, 541
8:2   **Vol. 3:** 764, 792, 796
8:3–11   **Vol. 2:** 584
8:3   **Vol. 3:** 480
8:5 ff   **Vol. 2:** 448
8:5   **Vol. 2:** 448, 582
8:6   **Vol. 2:** 150   **Vol. 3:** 489, 804
8:7 ff   **Vol. 3:** 539
8:7   **Vol. 2:** 96, 879   **Vol. 3:** 227, 579, 1062
8:8   **Vol. 2:** 150   **Vol. 3:** 489
8:9   **Vol. 1:** 167, 198, 350
8:10   **Vol. 2:** 365
8:11   **Vol. 1:** 701   **Vol. 2:** 365   **Vol. 3:** 536, 1062
8:12–59   **Vol. 2:** 751
8:12   **Vol. 1:** 323, 424, 483, 638   **Vol. 2:** 80, 217, 279–280, 482, 494, 749   **Vol. 3:** 314, 814, 916, 945
8:13–58   **Vol. 3:** 890
8:13   **Vol. 2:** 187   **Vol. 3:** 1045
8:14   **Vol. 1:** 689   **Vol. 3:** 1045
8:15   **Vol. 1:** 678, 680   **Vol. 3:** 890
8:16   **Vol. 2:** 280, 724–725   **Vol. 3:** 893
8:17   **Vol. 2:** 448, 686   **Vol. 3:** 890, 1043–1045, 1123
8:18   **Vol. 3:** 890, 1044
8:19   **Vol. 1:** 689
8:20   **Vol. 1:** 738   **Vol. 2:** 236, 927   **Vol. 3:** 764, 792, 796, 848
8:23   **Vol. 1:** 179   **Vol. 2:** 187, 928
8:24   **Vol. 3:** 582
8:25 ff   **Vol. 1:** 689

8:25   **Vol. 1:** 166
8:26–29   **Vol. 1:** 620
8:26   **Vol. 2:** 178   **Vol. 3:** 314
8:28   **Vol. 2:** 202, 204   **Vol. 3:** 631, 764
8:29   **Vol. 2:** 725, 816   **Vol. 3:** 646
8:30–40   **Vol. 1:** 79
8:30   **Vol. 1:** 742   **Vol. 3:** 1212
8:31 ff   **Vol. 2:** 567
8:31–36   **Vol. 1:** 718
8:31 f   **Vol. 1:** 719   **Vol. 2:** 63
8:31   **Vol. 1:** 490, 720, 742   **Vol. 3:** 226, 1149, 1211–1212
8:32–36   **Vol. 1:** 717
8:32   **Vol. 1:** 717, 742   **Vol. 2:** 80
8:33   **Vol. 1:** 717   **Vol. 3:** 1163
8:34 ff   **Vol. 1:** 720
8:34–44   **Vol. 3:** 1155
8:34   **Vol. 1:** 742   **Vol. 3:** 596
8:35   **Vol. 2:** 751   **Vol. 3:** 225, 830
8:36   **Vol. 1:** 719   **Vol. 3:** 596
8:37   **Vol. 1:** 742   **Vol. 3:** 532
8:38   **Vol. 1:** 720   **Vol. 3:** 516, 1201, 1205
8:39 f   **Vol. 1:** 79
8:39   **Vol. 1:** 286, 718
8:40   **Vol. 2:** 175, 178
8:41–47   **Vol. 2:** 473, 567
8:41–44   **Vol. 2:** 312
8:41   **Vol. 1:** 637   **Vol. 3:** 661, 1150
8:42–47   **Vol. 2:** 403
8:42 f   **Vol. 2:** 405
8:42   **Vol. 1:** 179, 322–323   **Vol. 2:** 505, 546   **Vol. 3:** 1203
8:43   **Vol. 1:** 529   **Vol. 2:** 604
8:44 f   **Vol. 3:** 582
8:44   **Vol. 1:** 166, 458, 567   **Vol. 2:** 472   **Vol. 3:** 470, 472, 890, 892, 1150
8:45 f   **Vol. 3:** 1212
8:45   **Vol. 3:** 517, 892
8:46   **Vol. 2:** 141   **Vol. 3:** 170
8:47   **Vol. 2:** 567   **Vol. 3:** 1114, 1122, 1188
8:48–59   **Vol. 1:** 79   **Vol. 3:** 472
8:48 f   **Vol. 1:** 453   **Vol. 3:** 462
8:48   **Vol. 1:** 637   **Vol. 3:** 456, 462–463, 465
8:49   **Vol. 1:** 453   **Vol. 2:** 50, 314   **Vol. 3:** 463
8:50   **Vol. 2:** 46–47   **Vol. 3:** 532
8:50b   **Vol. 3:** 531
8:51 f   **Vol. 1:** 337   **Vol. 3:** 830
8:51   **Vol. 1:** 79, 436, 439   **Vol. 2:** 133   **Vol. 3:** 517, 832, 1114
8:52   **Vol. 1:** 79, 453, 529   **Vol. 2:** 271
8:53   **Vol. 2:** 426
8:54 f   **Vol. 3:** 461
8:55   **Vol. 1:** 337   **Vol. 2:** 503
8:56   **Vol. 1:** 80   **Vol. 2:** 354, 359, 630
8:58   **Vol. 1:** 80
8:59   **Vol. 2:** 217   **Vol. 3:** 792
9–12   **Vol. 1:** 384
9   **Vol. 3:** 409
9:1 ff   **Vol. 1:** 219   **Vol. 2:** 632

John *(cont'd)*

9:1	**Vol. 3:** 1180
9:2 ff	**Vol. 2:** 169 **Vol. 3:** 998
9:2 f	**Vol. 2:** 366
9:2	**Vol. 1:** 219 **Vol. 2:** 879 **Vol. 3:** 115, 409, 997
9:3	**Vol. 1:** 163, 219 **Vol. 3:** 312, 314, 321
9:4	**Vol. 1:** 421 **Vol. 2:** 79 **Vol. 3:** 1149–1150
9:5	**Vol. 1:** 629 **Vol. 2:** 80, 494 **Vol. 3:** 916
9:6–15	**Vol. 3:** 916
9:7	**Vol. 1:** 581, 629
9:8	**Vol. 3:** 516, 589·
9:10	**Vol. 2:** 726, 728 **Vol. 3:** 519
9:11	**Vol. 3:** 519
9:14	**Vol. 2:** 726, 728 **Vol. 3:** 519
9:15	**Vol. 2:** 879 **Vol. 3:** 519
9:16–41	**Vol. 3:** 582
9:16	**Vol. 2:** 133, 604 **Vol. 3:** 543
9:17	**Vol. 2:** 726, 728 **Vol. 3:** 83, 519
9:18	**Vol. 3:** 519, 1211
9:19	**Vol. 2:** 879
9:21	**Vol. 1:** 92 **Vol. 2:** 726, 728, 879 **Vol. 3:** 519
9:22	**Vol. 1:** 347 **Vol. 2:** 312
9:23	**Vol. 1:** 92 **Vol. 2:** 879
9:25	**Vol. 2:** 720
9:26	**Vol. 2:** 726, 728 **Vol. 3:** 519
9:28	**Vol. 1:** 487 **Vol. 2:** 642 **Vol. 3:** 347
9:29 f	**Vol. 1:** 689
9:30	**Vol. 1:** 487 **Vol. 2:** 623, 726, 728 **Vol. 3:** 519
9:31	**Vol. 2:** 85, 94 **Vol. 3:** 1022
9:32	**Vol. 2:** 726, 728 **Vol. 3:** 519, 830
9:33	**Vol. 3:** 1202–1203
9:34 f	**Vol. 1:** 453
9:34	**Vol. 1:** 178 **Vol. 3:** 764
9:35–39	**Vol. 3:** 631
9:38	**Vol. 2:** 859, 877
9:39	**Vol. 1:** 525 **Vol. 2:** 217, 279, 365, 750
9:41	**Vol. 3:** 582, 890
10 f	**Vol. 3:** 1115
10	**Vol. 1:** 303 **Vol. 2:** 459 **Vol. 3:** 187, 567
10:1–42	**Vol. 2:** 751
10:1–30	**Vol. 3:** 567
10:1–11	**Vol. 2:** 413
10:1–5	**Vol. 2:** 751
10:1–3	**Vol. 2:** 31
10:1 f	**Vol. 2:** 30
10:1	**Vol. 3:** 378
10:2 f	**Vol. 3:** 314
10:3 f	**Vol. 2:** 839 **Vol. 3:** 566
10:3	**Vol. 2:** 652, 728 **Vol. 3:** 114, 314
10:4	**Vol. 1:** 453, 483 **Vol. 3:** 568
10:5	**Vol. 1:** 559, 684 **Vol. 2:** 742
10:6	**Vol. 2:** 757
10:7–9	**Vol. 1:** 303
10:7	**Vol. 2:** 31, 279–280
10:8	**Vol. 2:** 280 **Vol. 3:** 378
10:9	**Vol. 2:** 31, 80, 279–280 **Vol. 3:** 216
10:10 ff	**Vol. 2:** 80
10:10	**Vol. 1:** 323, 464, 729 **Vol. 2:** 482 **Vol. 3:** 378, 445, 728
10:11 ff	**Vol. 1:** 464
10:11	**Vol. 1:** 398 **Vol. 2:** 101, 104, 279–280 **Vol. 3:** 611, 683
10:12	**Vol. 1:** 118, 559 **Vol. 2:** 34 **Vol. 3:** 602
10:14 ff	**Vol. 2:** 721, 723
10:14 f	**Vol. 2:** 403–404
10:14	**Vol. 2:** 101, 104, 279–280
10:15	**Vol. 1:** 438 **Vol. 2:** 610, 653, 747 **Vol. 3:** 313, 611, 640
10:15a	**Vol. 1:** 620
10:15b	**Vol. 2:** 42
10:16	**Vol. 1:** 338 **Vol. 2:** 177, 413, 928 **Vol. 3:** 114, 463, 567
10:17 f	**Vol. 1:** 260 **Vol. 3:** 611
10:17	**Vol. 1:** 337 **Vol. 2:** 217, 546 **Vol. 3:** 683
10:18	**Vol. 1:** 337 **Vol. 2:** 217, 610 **Vol. 3:** 567, 748
10:19	**Vol. 3:** 543
10:20 f	**Vol. 1:** 453, 637
10:20	**Vol. 1:** 529
10:21	**Vol. 2:** 604, 726, 728 **Vol. 3:** 1122
10:22–29	**Vol. 1:** 629
10:22	**Vol. 3:** 366
10:23	**Vol. 2:** 236 **Vol. 3:** 789, 792
10:24 f	**Vol. 2:** 653, 736
10:24	**Vol. 2:** 736 **Vol. 3:** 683
10:25	**Vol. 3:** 1045, 1150
10:26 ff	**Vol. 1:** 304
10:27–29	**Vol. 2:** 101
10:27–28	**Vol. 3:** 114
10:27 f	**Vol. 3:** 568, 837
10:27	**Vol. 1:** 483 **Vol. 2:** 177 **Vol. 3:** 114
10:28 f	**Vol. 2:** 42
10:28	**Vol. 1:** 440, 464 **Vol. 2:** 80, 149, 482 **Vol. 3:** 602, 830, 832
10:29	**Vol. 2:** 149, 426 **Vol. 3:** 602
10:30	**Vol. 1:** 620 **Vol. 2:** 79, 217, 505, 721–722, 725
10:32	**Vol. 3:** 187, 1045
10:33–36	**Vol. 3:** 629
10:33	**Vol. 2:** 231, 565 **Vol. 3:** 187
10:34–38	**Vol. 3:** 622
10:34–36	**Vol. 3:** 187
10:34†	**Vol. 2:** 448 **Vol. 3:** 187
10:35 f	**Vol. 3:** 186, 329
10:35	**Vol. 3:** 188, 491–492
10:36	**Vol. 2:** 231· **Vol. 3:** 187, 342, 611
10:37	**Vol. 3:** 187, 1149, 1212
10:38	**Vol. 3:** 187, 1192
10:38a	**Vol. 3:** 1212
10:39	**Vol. 3:** 187
10:40	**Vol. 3:** 991

183

John *(cont'd)*

10:41 f	**Vol. 3:** 1197
10:41	**Vol. 3:** 890
10:42	**Vol. 1:** 702
11	**Vol. 1:** 265, 445 **Vol. 2:** 630 **Vol. 3:** 558, 980
11:1 ff	**Vol. 2:** 168, 480, 632
11:1 – 12:8	**Vol. 3:** 1060
11:1 – 44	**Vol. 3:** 303, 1059
11:1	**Vol. 3:** 1174, 1176, 1180
11:2	**Vol. 1:** 120, 239 **Vol. 2:** 295
11:3	**Vol. 2:** 548
11:4	**Vol. 2:** 46, 48, 632 **Vol. 3:** 998, 1206
11:6	**Vol. 1:** 265
11:7 – 10	**Vol. 2:** 706
11:8	**Vol. 3:** 115
11:9 f	**Vol. 2:** 706, 751 **Vol. 3:** 945
11:9	**Vol. 3:** 847
11:10	**Vol. 1:** 421 **Vol. 2:** 493
11:11 – 14	**Vol. 1:** 443
11:11	**Vol. 2:** 549 **Vol. 3:** 280
11:12	**Vol. 3:** 216
11:13	**Vol. 1:** 442 **Vol. 3:** 822
11:14	**Vol. 2:** 736, 873
11:15	**Vol. 3:** 911
11:16	**Vol. 1:** 488
11:17	**Vol. 1:** 265 **Vol. 2:** 418, 689 **Vol. 3:** 247
11:19	**Vol. 1:** 329 **Vol. 2:** 418
11:20 ff	**Vol. 3:** 1060
11:24	**Vol. 2:** 57 – 58, 894, 900 **Vol. 3:** 277, 280
11:25 ff	**Vol. 2:** 546
11:25 f	**Vol. 1:** 324 **Vol. 2:** 42, 367, 567 **Vol. 3:** 832
11:25	**Vol. 1:** 436, 603 **Vol. 2:** 81, 279 – 280, 388, 482, 928 – 929 **Vol. 3:** 277, 280, 647
11:26	**Vol. 2:** 900 **Vol. 3:** 830
11:26b	**Vol. 3:** 1211
11:27 f	**Vol. 3:** 768
11:27	**Vol. 3:** 646
11:28	**Vol. 2:** 899
11:30	**Vol. 2:** 418
11:31 ff	**Vol. 3:** 1060
11:31	**Vol. 1:** 329 **Vol. 2:** 416, 418 **Vol. 3:** 247, 822
11:32	**Vol. 1:** 609
11:33	**Vol. 2:** 416, 418, 878 **Vol. 3:** 694, 710
11:35	**Vol. 2:** 418
11:36	**Vol. 2:** 542, 548
11:37	**Vol. 3:** 280
11:38	**Vol. 2:** 418 **Vol. 3:** 247, 381
11:39	**Vol. 1:** 430 **Vol. 3:** 1060
11:40	**Vol. 2:** 631 – 632 **Vol. 3:** 280, 313 – 314
11:41 f	**Vol. 3:** 819
11:41	**Vol. 1:** 620 **Vol. 2:** 76, 178, 187 **Vol. 3:** 646
11:42	**Vol. 3:** 1184
11:43	**Vol. 2:** 178 **Vol. 3:** 113, 280
11:44	**Vol. 1:** 265, 489 **Vol. 2:** 149 **Vol. 3:** 179
11:46 f	**Vol. 2:** 812
11:47 ff	**Vol. 3:** 440
11:47	**Vol. 1:** 364 **Vol. 2:** 32
11:48	**Vol. 2:** 793 **Vol. 3:** 39
11:49 ff	**Vol. 2:** 399
11:49	**Vol. 1:** 397 **Vol. 3:** 39
11:49b – 53	**Vol. 3:** 39
11:50 ff	**Vol. 2:** 793
11:50 f	**Vol. 3:** 611
11:50	**Vol. 1:** 398 **Vol. 2:** 434, 721, 723, 799 **Vol. 3:** 824, 826, 1174, 1197
11:51 f	**Vol. 3:** 1197
11:51	**Vol. 1:** 326 **Vol. 3:** 39
11:52	**Vol. 1:** 297 **Vol. 2:** 32, 34, 722 – 723, 928
11:53	**Vol. 1:** 430
11:54	**Vol. 2:** 217
11:55 f	**Vol. 2:** 927
11:55	**Vol. 1:** 265, 629, 632 – 634 **Vol. 3:** 101
11:56	**Vol. 3:** 792, 822
11:57	**Vol. 1:** 337 **Vol. 2:** 812
12 ff	**Vol. 1:** 629
12	**Vol. 1:** 630
12:1 ff	**Vol. 1:** 630
12:1 – 11	**Vol. 3:** 980
12:1	**Vol. 1:** 445, 630, 633 **Vol. 3:** 1061
12:2 – 11	**Vol. 1:** 265
12:2	**Vol. 3:** 546, 1060
12:3	**Vol. 1:** 120, 239, 736 **Vol. 2:** 295 **Vol. 3:** 600, 1060
12:4 ff	**Vol. 1:** 642 **Vol. 3:** 1060
12:5	**Vol. 2:** 295
12:6	**Vol. 1:** 143 **Vol. 3:** 378
12:7 f	**Vol. 3:** 1060
12:7	**Vol. 1:** 265 **Vol. 2:** 133, 434
12:8	**Vol. 2:** 824
12:9	**Vol. 1:** 445 **Vol. 2:** 801
12:10	**Vol. 3:** 39
12:12 ff	**Vol. 1:** 630 **Vol. 2:** 328, 339
12:12 – 19	**Vol. 2:** 379 **Vol. 3:** 791
12:12 – 15	**Vol. 1:** 629
12:12	**Vol. 2:** 927
12:13	**Vol. 1:** 100, 212, 409 **Vol. 2:** 231 **Vol. 3:** 652
12:14	**Vol. 1:** 117 **Vol. 3:** 188
12:15	**Vol. 1:** 117, 623, 718 **Vol. 2:** 327
12:16	**Vol. 2:** 46, 546 **Vol. 3:** 1122
12:17	**Vol. 3:** 114, 247, 1044
12:19	**Vol. 1:** 493
12:20 ff	**Vol. 2:** 126
12:20	**Vol. 2:** 877, 927
12:21 f	**Vol. 2:** 550
12:21	**Vol. 2:** 513, 879
12:23 ff	**Vol. 2:** 546
12:23 – 28	**Vol. 2:** 48
12:23	**Vol. 2:** 927 **Vol. 3:** 631
12:24 – 26	**Vol. 1:** 441

John *(cont'd)*

12:24   **Vol. 1:** 609, 722 **Vol. 2:** 724, 751 **Vol. 3:** 524

12:25 f   **Vol. 2:** 433 **Vol. 3:** 530

12:25   **Vol. 1:** 464, 556 **Vol. 2:** 135, 482 **Vol. 3:** 174, 212, 682, 832, 843

12:26 ff   **Vol. 1:** 482

12:26   **Vol. 1:** 483 **Vol. 2:** 50 **Vol. 3:** 546

12:27 f   **Vol. 1:** 620 **Vol. 2:** 873 **Vol. 3:** 646

12:27   **Vol. 2:** 83, 927 **Vol. 3:** 211, 216, 710, 848

12:28   **Vol. 2:** 193, 653 **Vol. 3:** 114, 848

12:29   **Vol. 3:** 1002

12:30   **Vol. 3:** 1184

12:31   **Vol. 1:** 83, 168, 525–526 **Vol. 2:** 38, 193, 609, 631, 702 **Vol. 3:** 470, 582, 802

12:32   **Vol. 1:** 483, 510 **Vol. 2:** 202, 204, 567, 928

12:33   **Vol. 1:** 326, 438, 738

12:34   **Vol. 2:** 202, 204, 339, 448 **Vol. 3:** 631, 830

12:35 f   **Vol. 1:** 638 **Vol. 3:** 945

12:35   **Vol. 1:** 424 **Vol. 2:** 80, 429 **Vol. 3:** 750, 945

12:36   **Vol. 1:** 289 **Vol. 2:** 494 **Vol. 3:** 1213

12:37 ff   **Vol. 2:** 632 **Vol. 3:** 460

12:37–43   **Vol. 2:** 632

12:37–41   **Vol. 3:** 131

12:38 f   **Vol. 1:** 736

12:38   **Vol. 1:** 736 **Vol. 3:** 312, 314, 321

12:39 ff   **Vol. 1:** 261 **Vol. 3:** 313

12:40   **Vol. 1:** 355 **Vol. 2:** 155, 178, 753 **Vol. 3:** 128, 132

12:41   **Vol. 1:** 736 **Vol. 2:** 46, 48

12:42   **Vol. 1:** 168, 181, 347 **Vol. 2:** 312

12:43   **Vol. 2:** 543

12:44 ff   **Vol. 1:** 409

12:44   **Vol. 1:** 483 **Vol. 3:** 314

12:44c   **Vol. 3:** 1214

12:45   **Vol. 1:** 587 **Vol. 2:** 79, 404 **Vol. 3:** 517

12:46 f   **Vol. 1:** 323

12:46   **Vol. 1:** 424 **Vol. 2:** 494

12:47 f   **Vol. 1:** 171 **Vol. 3:** 1114

12:47   **Vol. 1:** 525 **Vol. 2:** 135 **Vol. 3:** 216

12:48   **Vol. 1:** 74, 637 **Vol. 2:** 58, 929 **Vol. 3:** 136, 748–749, 1114

12:49 f   **Vol. 1:** 337, 620 **Vol. 2:** 930

12:49   **Vol. 1:** 337 **Vol. 3:** 645

12:50   **Vol. 1:** 337 **Vol. 2:** 482 **Vol. 3:** 832

13–17   **Vol. 1:** 490 **Vol. 2:** 911

13   **Vol. 2:** 434

13:1 ff   **Vol. 2:** 754

13:1–17:26 **Vol. 2:** 751

13:1–30   **Vol. 2:** 526, 534

13:1–20   **Vol. 3:** 226, 990

13:1–15   **Vol. 3:** 547

13:1   **Vol. 1:** 630, 633, 738 **Vol. 2:** 64, 186, 217, 528, 927 **Vol. 3:** 848

13:2 ff   **Vol. 3:** 804

13:2   **Vol. 1:** 299 **Vol. 2:** 526 **Vol. 3:** 470

13:3   **Vol. 1:** 322 **Vol. 2:** 79, 149, 610, 653, 738 **Vol. 3:** 1174

13:4 ff   **Vol. 3:** 611

13:4–16   **Vol. 1:** 549

13:4 f   **Vol. 3:** 121

13:4   **Vol. 2:** 264

13:5–14   **Vol. 1:** 239

13:5   **Vol. 1:** 167, 239 **Vol. 3:** 989

13:6   **Vol. 2:** 514

13:7   **Vol. 1:** 154 **Vol. 2:** 398

13:8   **Vol. 1:** 241 **Vol. 2:** 304 **Vol. 3:** 829–830

13:9   **Vol. 2:** 159

13:10   **Vol. 1:** 152–153 **Vol. 3:** 107, 704

13:13 ff   **Vol. 1:** 154

13:13 f   **Vol. 3:** 768

13:13   **Vol. 3:** 116

13:14   **Vol. 2:** 535 **Vol. 3:** 116, 945

13:15   **Vol. 1:** 492 **Vol. 2:** 291 **Vol. 3:** 547, 597, 905, 1155

13:16   **Vol. 1:** 129, 134, 404 **Vol. 3:** 629

13:17   **Vol. 1:** 217

13:18   **Vol. 1:** 540, 542, 736 **Vol. 3:** 188, 329, 490, 492

13:20   **Vol. 1:** 91, 285 **Vol. 2:** 176, 535, 920 **Vol. 3:** 314, 326, 629, 746, 748

13:21   **Vol. 2:** 878 **Vol. 3:** 694

13:23   **Vol. 1:** 78, 240 **Vol. 3:** 589, 1174, 1186

13:25   **Vol. 3:** 589

13:26–30 **Vol. 2:** 321

13:26   **Vol. 1:** 145 **Vol. 2:** 528

13:27   **Vol. 3:** 470, 473

13:29   **Vol. 1:** 143, 642 **Vol. 2:** 927 **Vol. 3:** 822

13:30   **Vol. 1:** 421 **Vol. 2:** 528

13:31 ff   **Vol. 1:** 630

13:31 f   **Vol. 2:** 46 **Vol. 3:** 631

13:31   **Vol. 3:** 631

13:33   **Vol. 1:** 286 **Vol. 2:** 429

13:34 f   **Vol. 1:** 303, 490, 526, 719

13:34   **Vol. 1:** 335, 337–338, 738 **Vol. 2:** 43, 546, 671, 673

13:35 f   **Vol. 1:** 483

13:35   **Vol. 1:** 338, 490 **Vol. 2:** 398, 404

13:36   **Vol. 3:** 954

13:37 f   **Vol. 3:** 683

13:38   **Vol. 1:** 702

14–16   **Vol. 2:** 339, 780 **Vol. 3:** 697

14:1–6   **Vol. 3:** 941

14:1   **Vol. 1:** 355 **Vol. 3:** 710

14:1a   **Vol. 3:** 1214

14:2 ff   **Vol. 2:** 751

14:2 f   **Vol. 1:** 440 **Vol. 2:** 727, 929 **Vol. 3:** 118, 946

14:2   **Vol. 2:** 250 **Vol. 3:** 229

14:3   **Vol. 3:** 751

John *(cont'd)*

14:4 f   **Vol. 3:** 185
14:6–10   **Vol. 3:** 326
14:6   **Vol. 1:** 355, 375, 489, 620   **Vol. 2:** 31, 48, 80–81, 279, 281, 460, 482, 610, 751   **Vol. 3:** 163, 395, 647, 742, 832, 890–891, 893, 941, 1114
14:7 ff   **Vol. 3:** 185
14:7   **Vol. 1:** 620   **Vol. 2:** 404   **Vol. 3:** 314
14:8 f   **Vol. 2:** 550   **Vol. 3:** 569
14:8   **Vol. 3:** 728
14:9   **Vol. 1:** 338, 587, 620   **Vol. 2:** 79, 288, 404, 722, 766   **Vol. 3:** 314, 517, 891
14:10 f   **Vol. 1:** 620   **Vol. 3:** 1192
14:10   **Vol. 2:** 79, 505   **Vol. 3:** 224–225, 1114, 1122, 1149
14:10b   **Vol. 3:** 1193
14:11   **Vol. 3:** 1150, 1212
14:12 ff   **Vol. 3:** 1155
14:12   **Vol. 3:** 946, 1149–1150, 1155
14:13 f   **Vol. 2:** 654, 857–858
14:14   **Vol. 3:** 1114
14:15 ff   **Vol. 1:** 630
14:15–17   **Vol. 1:** 490
14:15   **Vol. 1:** 337–338, 526   **Vol. 2:** 133
14:16 ff   **Vol. 1:** 324
14:16–28   **Vol. 3:** 704
14:16 f   **Vol. 1:** 89   **Vol. 2:** 787
14:16   **Vol. 1:** 90, 324   **Vol. 2:** 359, 857, 878–879   **Vol. 3:** 704, 830
14:17   **Vol. 1:** 89–90, 303   **Vol. 2:** 403, 604, 878   **Vol. 3:** 225, 892, 1114, 1205
14:18–24   **Vol. 2:** 787
14:18   **Vol. 2:** 359, 738
14:19   **Vol. 2:** 359, 429
14:19b   **Vol. 1:** 701
14:20   **Vol. 2:** 359   **Vol. 3:** 1192
14:21 ff   **Vol. 2:** 546
14:21 f   **Vol. 2:** 489   **Vol. 3:** 314
14:21   **Vol. 1:** 337–338   **Vol. 2:** 133
14:22 ff   **Vol. 3:** 185
14:22   **Vol. 1:** 326
14:23 f   **Vol. 2:** 133, 546
14:23   **Vol. 1:** 337, 526   **Vol. 2:** 727   **Vol. 3:** 229, 1205
14:24   **Vol. 1:** 128, 337   **Vol. 3:** 229, 1114
14:25   **Vol. 3:** 764, 1205
14:26   **Vol. 1:** 89–90, 123, 324   **Vol. 2:** 231, 359, 654, 687, 878   **Vol. 3:** 242, 314, 403, 704, 763–764, 942–943, 1203
14:27   **Vol. 1:** 622   **Vol. 2:** 359, 780–781   **Vol. 3:** 710
14:28   **Vol. 2:** 426, 500   **Vol. 3:** 946
14:30   **Vol. 1:** 168   **Vol. 2:** 609   **Vol. 3:** 470, 802
14:31   **Vol. 1:** 337   **Vol. 2:** 404, 546   **Vol. 3:** 280
15   **Vol. 3:** 567
15:1 ff   **Vol. 1:** 303

15:1 f   **Vol. 3:** 868–869
15:1–16   **Vol. 2:** 751
15:1–11   **Vol. 3:** 921
15:1–8   **Vol. 2:** 313   **Vol. 3:** 226
15:1   **Vol. 2:** 279–281   **Vol. 3:** 893
15:2 ff   **Vol. 1:** 722   **Vol. 2:** 449
15:2   **Vol. 1:** 723   **Vol. 3:** 102
15:3   **Vol. 3:** 107, 1114
15:4 ff   **Vol. 1:** 285   **Vol. 2:** 546
15:4 f   **Vol. 3:** 225, 1192
15:4   **Vol. 2:** 359   **Vol. 3:** 226
15:5 ff   **Vol. 2:** 101
15:5   **Vol. 1:** 723   **Vol. 2:** 279, 281   **Vol. 3:** 226, 1155
15:6   **Vol. 1:** 515, 608, 656   **Vol. 2:** 32   **Vol. 3:** 226
15:7 ff   **Vol. 1:** 290
15:7   **Vol. 2:** 359, 857–858   **Vol. 3:** 226, 921, 1114, 1122
15:8   **Vol. 1:** 490, 723
15:9 ff   **Vol. 1:** 526, 630
15:9–17   **Vol. 2:** 482   **Vol. 3:** 226
15:9 f   **Vol. 2:** 546
15:9   **Vol. 2:** 359, 404, 546   **Vol. 3:** 226, 921
15:10   **Vol. 1:** 337–338, 549   **Vol. 2:** 133   **Vol. 3:** 226, 921
15:11   **Vol. 1:** 741   **Vol. 2:** 359   **Vol. 3:** 921
15:12 ff   **Vol. 1:** 338
15:12   **Vol. 1:** 337–338   **Vol. 2:** 546
15:13   **Vol. 1:** 257   **Vol. 2:** 359, 549, 673
15:14   **Vol. 2:** 750   **Vol. 3:** 1062
15:15   **Vol. 2:** 178   **Vol. 3:** 314, 613
15:16   **Vol. 1:** 540, 542, 723   **Vol. 2:** 359, 654, 857–858   **Vol. 3:** 226
15:17   **Vol. 1:** 338   **Vol. 2:** 546
15:18 ff   **Vol. 1:** 525, 556   **Vol. 2:** 806
15:18–27   **Vol. 2:** 709
15:18   **Vol. 1:** 603   **Vol. 2:** 398, 403
15:19   **Vol. 1:** 525–526, 540, 542   **Vol. 2:** 359, 542, 548   **Vol. 3:** 1171, 1188
15:20   **Vol. 1:** 337, 404, 549   **Vol. 2:** 806
15:21   **Vol. 3:** 257
15:22 ff   **Vol. 3:** 1150
15:22–24   **Vol. 3:** 582
15:23   **Vol. 1:** 603
15:24   **Vol. 3:** 1149–1150
15:25   **Vol. 1:** 556, 736   **Vol. 2:** 41, 448   **Vol. 3:** 329, 489
15:26 f   **Vol. 1:** 490, 683
15:26   **Vol. 1:** 89–90, 123, 324   **Vol. 2:** 687, 878   **Vol. 3:** 314, 403, 704, 892, 1046, 1202–1203
15:27   **Vol. 1:** 166   **Vol. 3:** 1046
16:1 ff   **Vol. 3:** 849
16:1   **Vol. 2:** 708–709
16:2 ff   **Vol. 2:** 751
16:2 f   **Vol. 2:** 403
16:2   **Vol. 2:** 359   **Vol. 3:** 551, 822, 848
16:4   **Vol. 1:** 166
16:5–15   **Vol. 2:** 895

John *(cont'd)*

16:5	**Vol. 1:** 630 **Vol. 2:** 879
16:6	**Vol. 1:** 297
16:7 ff	**Vol. 1:** 91
16:7	**Vol. 1:** 89–90, 324 **Vol. 2:** 878, 929 **Vol. 3:** 890, 946
16:8 ff	**Vol. 2:** 141
16:8–11	**Vol. 1:** 270 **Vol. 2:** 48 **Vol. 3:** 705
16:8 f	**Vol. 3:** 582
16:8	**Vol. 1:** 89 **Vol. 2:** 141, 927 **Vol. 3:** 362
16:9 ff	**Vol. 1:** 89
16:9	**Vol. 3:** 136
16:10	**Vol. 2:** 359, 699 **Vol. 3:** 362
16:11	**Vol. 1:** 168, 525–526 **Vol. 2:** 365, 609 **Vol. 3:** 470, 582, 802
16:12 ff	**Vol. 1:** 90, 324
16:12 f	**Vol. 3:** 704
16:13 f	**Vol. 1:** 89, 123
16:13	**Vol. 1:** 90 **Vol. 2:** 878 **Vol. 3:** 47, 258, 314–315, 892, 942
16:14	**Vol. 2:** 84 **Vol. 3:** 47, 704
16:15a	**Vol. 1:** 620
16:16 ff	**Vol. 2:** 895
16:16–19	**Vol. 2:** 429
16:16 f	**Vol. 3:** 515
16:16	**Vol. 1:** 741
16:17 f	**Vol. 3:** 185
16:19	**Vol. 2:** 879
16:20–24	**Vol. 2:** 482
16:20–22	**Vol. 2:** 420
16:20	**Vol. 1:** 741 **Vol. 2:** 417–419
16:21	**Vol. 1:** 178, 187, 284 **Vol. 2:** 751, 809 **Vol. 3:** 848
16:22	**Vol. 1:** 91, 741 **Vol. 2:** 359, 421, 809
16:23–26	**Vol. 2:** 857
16:23 f	**Vol. 2:** 178, 857
16:23	**Vol. 2:** 857, 879
16:24	**Vol. 1:** 741 **Vol. 2:** 357, 858
16:25	**Vol. 2:** 757–758 **Vol. 3:** 47
16:26 f	**Vol. 2:** 857
16:26	**Vol. 2:** 857–858
16:27 f	**Vol. 2:** 79 **Vol. 3:** 1202
16:27	**Vol. 2:** 542, 548 **Vol. 3:** 1174
16:28	**Vol. 1:** 323 **Vol. 3:** 946, 1174
16:29	**Vol. 2:** 757–758
16:30	**Vol. 2:** 879 **Vol. 3:** 1174, 1192
16:32	**Vol. 2:** 34, 725, 839 **Vol. 3:** 516, 646, 848
16:33	**Vol. 1:** 328, 526, 638, 651 **Vol. 2:** 359, 780–781, 809, 911 **Vol. 3:** 1212
17	**Vol. 2:** 653, 723 **Vol. 3:** 38
17:1 ff	**Vol. 1:** 290
17:1	**Vol. 1:** 620, 738 **Vol. 2:** 46, 74, 76, 192, 217, 873, 927 **Vol. 3:** 646
17:2 f	**Vol. 2:** 80 **Vol. 3:** 832
17:2	**Vol. 1:** 303, 678 **Vol. 2:** 482, 610
17:3	**Vol. 2:** 42, 73, 280, 339, 403–404, 482, 724 **Vol. 3:** 630, 643, 645, 893
17:4 f	**Vol. 2:** 46
17:4	**Vol. 1:** 549 **Vol. 2:** 64, 79 **Vol. 3:** 1150
17:5	**Vol. 1:** 620 **Vol. 2:** 46, 76, 204 **Vol. 3:** 1205
17:6	**Vol. 1:** 304, 337 **Vol. 2:** 42, 217, 653 **Vol. 3:** 312, 314, 321
17:8	**Vol. 1:** 603 **Vol. 2:** 404 **Vol. 3:** 748–749, 1114, 1122, 1202
17:9	**Vol. 2:** 879
17:11 f	**Vol. 2:** 135, 653 **Vol. 3:** 645
17:11	**Vol. 1:** 620 **Vol. 2:** 76, 79, 133, 228, 231, 721–722 **Vol. 3:** 1188
17:12	**Vol. 1:** 299, 464, 736 **Vol. 2:** 135, 653 **Vol. 3:** 188, 329, 491, 529
17:13	**Vol. 1:** 741 **Vol. 2:** 359
17:14	**Vol. 1:** 526, 556 **Vol. 3:** 1114, 1171, 1188
17:14b	**Vol. 3:** 1188
17:15	**Vol. 1:** 526, 566 **Vol. 2:** 133, 879 **Vol. 3:** 472, 1188
17:16	**Vol. 1:** 526 **Vol. 3:** 1171, 1188
17:17	**Vol. 2:** 232 **Vol. 3:** 890, 892, 1114
17:18	**Vol. 1:** 526 **Vol. 3:** 892
17:19	**Vol. 2:** 232 **Vol. 3:** 38, 40
17:20 ff	**Vol. 1:** 338
17:20 f	**Vol. 2:** 413
17:20	**Vol. 1:** 158 **Vol. 2:** 879, 928 **Vol. 3:** 1106
17:21 ff	**Vol. 2:** 404, 721
17:21	**Vol. 1:** 128, 304, 620 **Vol. 2:** 64, 79, 722–723 **Vol. 3:** 1192
17:22	**Vol. 2:** 46–47 **Vol. 3:** 529
17:23 ff	**Vol. 2:** 546
17:23	**Vol. 2:** 64, 404, 722 **Vol. 3:** 1192
17:24 f	**Vol. 1:** 620
17:24	**Vol. 1:** 377–378 **Vol. 2:** 46, 482, 929 **Vol. 3:** 518
17:25 f	**Vol. 1:** 620
17:25	**Vol. 1:** 128 **Vol. 2:** 610, 653 **Vol. 3:** 362
17:26	**Vol. 2:** 404, 546, 653 **Vol. 3:** 314
18 f	**Vol. 2:** 378
18–21	**Vol. 1:** 305
18	**Vol. 1:** 633
18:1 ff	**Vol. 1:** 630
18:1–2	**Vol. 2:** 713
18:2–11	**Vol. 2:** 526
18:2	**Vol. 2:** 32
18:3 f	**Vol. 3:** 39
18:3	**Vol. 2:** 486 **Vol. 3:** 40, 547, 964
18:5	**Vol. 2:** 333
18:6	**Vol. 1:** 610
18:7	**Vol. 2:** 333
18:9	**Vol. 1:** 464, 736 **Vol. 3:** 529
18:10 f	**Vol. 3:** 967
18:11	**Vol. 2:** 276
18:12	**Vol. 1:** 343 **Vol. 2:** 315, 699 **Vol. 3:** 547
18:13–24	**Vol. 3:** 409

John (cont'd)

18:13	**Vol. 1:** 630 **Vol. 3:** 39
18:14	**Vol. 1:** 363 **Vol. 3:** 611, 1197
18:15	**Vol. 1:** 321
18:16 ff	**Vol. 3:** 1122
18:16	**Vol. 2:** 30
18:17	**Vol. 3:** 804
18:18 ff	**Vol. 1:** 318
18:18	**Vol. 1:** 318 **Vol. 3:** 547
18:19	**Vol. 2:** 879 **Vol. 3:** 769
18:20	**Vol. 2:** 217 **Vol. 3:** 761, 764, 785, 791
18:21	**Vol. 2:** 879
18:22 ff	**Vol. 1:** 299
18:22 f	**Vol. 2:** 451
18:22	**Vol. 3:** 547
18:23	**Vol. 3:** 1044
18:24	**Vol. 1:** 630 **Vol. 3:** 39–40
18:25 ff	**Vol. 1:** 455 **Vol. 3:** 804, 1122
18:27	**Vol. 1:** 173
18:28–19:24	**Vol. 1:** 394
18:28	**Vol. 1:** 265, 448, 630, 633–634 **Vol. 2:** 527–528, 927 **Vol. 3:** 39
18:29	**Vol. 1:** 83
18:31	**Vol. 1:** 364, 395 **Vol. 2:** 365, 449, 451
18:32	**Vol. 1:** 326, 438, 736
18:33 ff	**Vol. 2:** 339
18:33	**Vol. 2:** 315
18:35	**Vol. 2:** 315, 793
18:36 f	**Vol. 2:** 339
18:36–37	**Vol. 3:** 977
18:36	**Vol. 1:** 646 **Vol. 2:** 387, 641 **Vol. 3:** 1188
18:37	**Vol. 1:** 304, 323, 427, 603 **Vol. 3:** 114, 462, 652, 892, 1045
18:37d	**Vol. 3:** 890
18:38	**Vol. 1:** 270 **Vol. 2:** 139 **Vol. 3:** 529, 893
18:38b	**Vol. 1:** 395
18:39	**Vol. 1:** 633 **Vol. 2:** 315, 927 **Vol. 3:** 189
18:40	**Vol. 1:** 409 **Vol. 3:** 378
19	**Vol. 1:** 630, 633
19:1	**Vol. 1:** 162
19:2	**Vol. 1:** 205, 316, 406 **Vol. 2:** 159 **Vol. 3:** 964
19:3	**Vol. 1:** 162 **Vol. 2:** 315, 358
19:4	**Vol. 1:** 395 **Vol. 2:** 139, 398 **Vol. 3:** 529
19:5	**Vol. 1:** 205, 406, 726 **Vol. 2:** 565
19:6 f	**Vol. 1:** 395
19:6	**Vol. 2:** 139 **Vol. 3:** 39, 529, 916
19:7	**Vol. 2:** 443, 448–449
19:10	**Vol. 3:** 189
19:11	**Vol. 1:** 179 **Vol. 3:** 97, 582, 916
19:12–16	**Vol. 1:** 270
19:12 f	**Vol. 1:** 395
19:12	**Vol. 1:** 409 **Vol. 2:** 549 **Vol. 3:** 189, 1154
19:13	**Vol. 2:** 309, 369 **Vol. 3:** 588–589, 1185
19:14	**Vol. 1:** 629–630, 633–634 **Vol. 2:** 463, 527–528, 927 **Vol. 3:** 120, 410, 847, 916
19:15	**Vol. 3:** 39, 916
19:15b	**Vol. 1:** 395
19:17	**Vol. 2:** 309
19:19 ff	**Vol. 1:** 323 **Vol. 2:** 315, 339
19:19	**Vol. 2:** 315, 333–334, 379 **Vol. 3:** 509, 652
19:20	**Vol. 2:** 54, 126, 309
19:21 f	**Vol. 2:** 339
19:21	**Vol. 2:** 315
19:23	**Vol. 2:** 303, 689
19:24	**Vol. 1:** 396, 478, 736 **Vol. 2:** 299 **Vol. 3:** 490, 492, 543, 670
19:25	**Vol. 2:** 82 **Vol. 3:** 662, 1060–1061, 1201, 1205
19:26 f	**Vol. 3:** 1070
19:26	**Vol. 3:** 1058
19:27	**Vol. 2:** 839 **Vol. 3:** 846
19:28	**Vol. 1:** 736 **Vol. 2:** 64, 267 **Vol. 3:** 491–492
19:29 f	**Vol. 2:** 28
19:29	**Vol. 3:** 913
19:30	**Vol. 1:** 335 **Vol. 2:** 64, 159, 368, 787, 929 **Vol. 3:** 704
19:31	**Vol. 1:** 234 **Vol. 2:** 463, 879–880 **Vol. 3:** 120, 408, 410
19:32–36	**Vol. 1:** 629
19:32	**Vol. 1:** 393, 666
19:34	**Vol. 1:** 221 **Vol. 2:** 787 **Vol. 3:** 704, 990
19:35	**Vol. 2:** 280 **Vol. 3:** 517–518
19:36 f	**Vol. 3:** 490
19:36	**Vol. 1:** 241, 634, 720, 736 **Vol. 2:** 527 **Vol. 3:** 492
19:37†	**Vol. 2:** 739
19:38	**Vol. 2:** 217, 879
19:39	**Vol. 1:** 265 **Vol. 2:** 295, 812 **Vol. 3:** 294
19:40	**Vol. 2:** 295, 437 **Vol. 3:** 296
19:41 f	**Vol. 3:** 247
19:41	**Vol. 2:** 670
19:42	**Vol. 3:** 120, 408, 410
20	**Vol. 2:** 780 **Vol. 3:** 276, 283
20:1 ff	**Vol. 1:** 630
20:1–21:25	**Vol. 3:** 294
20:1–18	**Vol. 3:** 1060
20:1–4	**Vol. 3:** 247
20:1	**Vol. 1:** 423 **Vol. 3:** 393, 412
20:2	**Vol. 3:** 288, 296, 947
20:3–6	**Vol. 3:** 1185
20:3	**Vol. 3:** 1174
20:4	**Vol. 1:** 666 **Vol. 3:** 947
20:6	**Vol. 3:** 247
20:7 f	**Vol. 3:** 297
20:7	**Vol. 2:** 159
20:8	**Vol. 3:** 247, 517, 1185

John *(cont'd)*

20:9   **Vol. 1:** 445   **Vol. 2:** 666   **Vol. 3:** 490, 492
20:11   **Vol. 3:** 247
20:12   **Vol. 1:** 204   **Vol. 2:** 159   **Vol. 3:** 294
20:13   **Vol. 3:** 285
20:14 ff   **Vol. 3:** 287
20:14–29   **Vol. 3:** 518
20:15   **Vol. 2:** 513, 739   **Vol. 3:** 822
20:16   **Vol. 2:** 309   **Vol. 3:** 115, 767
20:17   **Vol. 2:** 185   **Vol. 3:** 276, 860, 941
20:18   **Vol. 3:** 46, 48, 1060
20:19–23   **Vol. 3:** 286, 295
20:19   **Vol. 1:** 622   **Vol. 2:** 30, 730, 780   **Vol. 3:** 297
20:20   **Vol. 1:** 393   **Vol. 2:** 359, 624   **Vol. 3:** 569
20:21 ff   **Vol. 1:** 136
20:21–29   **Vol. 3:** 295
20:21   **Vol. 1:** 526   **Vol. 2:** 176, 654, 733, 780, 787, 927   **Vol. 3:** 286
20:22 f   **Vol. 3:** 705
20:22   **Vol. 2:** 231, 787, 878, 929   **Vol. 3:** 460, 694, 698, 703–704, 749
20:23   **Vol. 1:** 303, 702–703   **Vol. 2:** 733, 787   **Vol. 3:** 387, 580, 717
20:24–29   **Vol. 3:** 289
20:24   **Vol. 2:** 695
20:25 ff   **Vol. 1:** 393
20:25   **Vol. 2:** 150   **Vol. 3:** 518
20:25a   **Vol. 3:** 904
20:26   **Vol. 2:** 692, 730, 780   **Vol. 3:** 297
20:27   **Vol. 1:** 602   **Vol. 2:** 150   **Vol. 3:** 276
20:28   **Vol. 2:** 81, 513–515, 725
20:29   **Vol. 1:** 217, 603   **Vol. 3:** 517
20:30 f   **Vol. 1:** 136, 244   **Vol. 3:** 489
20:30   **Vol. 1:** 244   **Vol. 2:** 632
20:31   **Vol. 1:** 148, 287, 290, 599   **Vol. 2:** 80, 231, 339   **Vol. 3:** 646, 1213
20:31a   **Vol. 3:** 1211
21   **Vol. 3:** 276, 283
21:1–23   **Vol. 3:** 295
21:1–19   **Vol. 2:** 630
21:1–11   **Vol. 3:** 985
21:1   **Vol. 3:** 312, 314, 321, 984
21:3–10   **Vol. 3:** 295
21:3   **Vol. 3:** 757
21:6   **Vol. 1:** 671, 733   **Vol. 2:** 146, 303
21:7   **Vol. 1:** 313   **Vol. 3:** 121
21:9   **Vol. 1:** 670
21:11–17   **Vol. 3:** 295
21:11   **Vol. 2:** 684–685   **Vol. 3:** 543
21:12 f   **Vol. 3:** 276
21:12   **Vol. 1:** 365   **Vol. 2:** 624
21:13   **Vol. 2:** 524
21:14   **Vol. 1:** 445   **Vol. 3:** 312, 314, 321
21:15 ff   **Vol. 1:** 136   **Vol. 2:** 542, 548, 928
21:15–17   **Vol. 3:** 568
21:15   **Vol. 2:** 411, 548   **Vol. 3:** 386

21:16 ff   **Vol. 3:** 387
21:16   **Vol. 2:** 548   **Vol. 3:** 568
21:17   **Vol. 2:** 398, 548   **Vol. 3:** 386
21:18   **Vol. 2:** 150, 675   **Vol. 3:** 121
21:19 ff   **Vol. 1:** 482
21:20   **Vol. 3:** 589
21:22 f   **Vol. 2:** 930
21:24   **Vol. 1:** 136   **Vol. 3:** 489
21:25   **Vol. 1:** 244, 742

Acts

1–12   **Vol. 3:** 1114
1–7   **Vol. 3:** 1114
1–5   **Vol. 2:** 314
1   **Vol. 1:** 90   **Vol. 3:** 387
1:1 ff   **Vol. 2:** 787
1:1   **Vol. 1:** 167, 247   **Vol. 2:** 86   **Vol. 3:** 88, 764, 1106
1:2–16   **Vol. 2:** 921
1:2   **Vol. 1:** 335   **Vol. 3:** 276, 698, 749
1:3   **Vol. 1:** 128, 474   **Vol. 2:** 689, 696   **Vol. 3:** 516, 723, 1181
1:4   **Vol. 1:** 128, 340   **Vol. 2:** 245, 328, 786   **Vol. 3:** 70–71, 228, 296, 449, 534
1:5   **Vol. 1:** 158, 303   **Vol. 2:** 786   **Vol. 3:** 697–698, 990, 1210
1:6 ff   **Vol. 2:** 921   **Vol. 3:** 147
1:6–8   **Vol. 2:** 610
1:6 f   **Vol. 3:** 844
1:6   **Vol. 2:** 313, 315, 786, 879–880, 920
1:7   **Vol. 1:** 477   **Vol. 2:** 75, 609   **Vol. 3:** 838
1:8   **Vol. 1:** 129, 136, 303, 322, 335, 517   **Vol. 2:** 57, 176, 603, 632, 740, 786   **Vol. 3:** 87, 449, 456, 698, 700, 909, 1044, 1114
1:9 ff   **Vol. 2:** 918
1:9   **Vol. 3:** 276, 749, 1003, 1114
1:10 f   **Vol. 2:** 194   **Vol. 3:** 947
1:10   **Vol. 1:** 102, 204   **Vol. 3:** 520
1:11   **Vol. 2:** 192, 333, 713, 920   **Vol. 3:** 520, 749
1:12   **Vol. 2:** 54, 713   **Vol. 3:** 940–941
1:13–26   **Vol. 1:** 135
1:13   **Vol. 1:** 136, 488   **Vol. 2:** 320, 550   **Vol. 3:** 1167
1:14   **Vol. 1:** 256   **Vol. 2:** 768, 873   **Vol. 3:** 908, 1065
1:15   **Vol. 2:** 652, 740, 801   **Vol. 3:** 1194
1:16   **Vol. 1:** 343, 427, 736   **Vol. 2:** 663   **Vol. 3:** 490, 699, 942
1:17 ff   **Vol. 1:** 299
1:17   **Vol. 1:** 478   **Vol. 2:** 299   **Vol. 3:** 546
1:18–20   **Vol. 3:** 1008
1:18   **Vol. 1:** 93–94   **Vol. 2:** 600, 854   **Vol. 3:** 912
1:19   **Vol. 1:** 93
1:20   **Vol. 1:** 190, 244   **Vol. 3:** 671, 675, 1008

Acts *(cont'd)*

1:21 f   **Vol. 1:** 183   **Vol. 2:** 299, 786   **Vol. 3:** 764

1:21   **Vol. 1:** 322   **Vol. 2:** 663   **Vol. 3:** 769, 843–844

1:22   **Vol. 1:** 136   **Vol. 3:** 276–277, 660, 749, 1044

1:24 f   **Vol. 2:** 299, 873

1:24   **Vol. 1:** 540, 542   **Vol. 2:** 183   **Vol. 3:** 569

1:25   **Vol. 1:** 299   **Vol. 3:** 584

1:26   **Vol. 1:** 609   **Vol. 2:** 299, 787

2–5   **Vol. 3:** 699, 785

2   **Vol. 1:** 90, 129, 528   **Vol. 2:** 732, 784–785   **Vol. 3:** 387, 704, 1080

2:1 ff   **Vol. 2:** 328   **Vol. 3:** 86

2:1–13   **Vol. 2:** 784–785

2:1   **Vol. 1:** 737   **Vol. 2:** 784, 786   **Vol. 3:** 1194

2:2 f   **Vol. 2:** 632

2:2   **Vol. 1:** 736   **Vol. 2:** 193, 310   **Vol. 3:** 112, 559, 589, 707, 711

2:3 f   **Vol. 3:** 110

2:3   **Vol. 1:** 656   **Vol. 3:** 109, 571

2:4 ff   **Vol. 1:** 303

2:4–38   **Vol. 2:** 921

2:4   **Vol. 1:** 739   **Vol. 2:** 739, 786   **Vol. 3:** 699–700, 1080

2:5–11   **Vol. 3:** 700

2:5   **Vol. 2:** 91, 563, 786   **Vol. 3:** 197

2:6   **Vol. 2:** 786

2:7 f   **Vol. 2:** 740

2:7   **Vol. 2:** 625, 740

2:8   **Vol. 2:** 786

2:9–11   **Vol. 2:** 309, 786

2:9   **Vol. 1:** 427

2:10   **Vol. 1:** 532   **Vol. 2:** 740

2:11   **Vol. 1:** 361   **Vol. 2:** 426, 740, 786   **Vol. 3:** 1079–1080

2:13   **Vol. 2:** 739–740   **Vol. 3:** 700, 922

2:14–39   **Vol. 3:** 62

2:14–36   **Vol. 3:** 87

2:14   **Vol. 2:** 175   **Vol. 3:** 1070, 1080, 1122

2:15–21   **Vol. 2:** 38

2:15   **Vol. 1:** 514   **Vol. 3:** 749, 847

2:16 f   **Vol. 3:** 1191

2:16–21   **Vol. 3:** 1079

2:17 ff   **Vol. 3:** 699

2:17–36   **Vol. 2:** 315

2:17–21   **Vol. 2:** 654, 740, 916   **Vol. 3:** 71, 707, 732

2:17–18   **Vol. 2:** 855

2:17 f   **Vol. 2:** 42, 194, 785–786   **Vol. 3:** 86–87, 699–700, 1194

2:17   **Vol. 1:** 198, 512   **Vol. 2:** 58, 785, 787   **Vol. 3:** 87, 515, 700

2:18   **Vol. 2:** 786

2:19–20   **Vol. 3:** 732

2:19   **Vol. 1:** 224   **Vol. 2:** 187, 629   **Vol. 3:** 700

2:20   **Vol. 1:** 203–204, 224, 425   **Vol. 3:** 213, 318–319, 732, 734

2:21   **Vol. 3:** 732

2:22   **Vol. 2:** 333, 603, 629   **Vol. 3:** 570–571, 1154, 1198

2:23–32   **Vol. 3:** 1200

2:23 f   **Vol. 3:** 299

2:23   **Vol. 1:** 473, 693   **Vol. 3:** 1017

2:24   **Vol. 2:** 78   **Vol. 3:** 180, 717, 793, 858

2:25–35   **Vol. 2:** 186

2:25–28   **Vol. 3:** 262

2:25   **Vol. 1:** 427, 695   **Vol. 3:** 559

2:26 f   **Vol. 3:** 297

2:26   **Vol. 2:** 354, 356   **Vol. 3:** 813, 1079

2:27 ff   **Vol. 1:** 266

2:27   **Vol. 1:** 468, 470   **Vol. 2:** 207, 238, 919   **Vol. 3:** 651, 683

2:28   **Vol. 2:** 356   **Vol. 3:** 314, 940–941

2:29 f   **Vol. 1:** 66

2:29   **Vol. 1:** 65, 430   **Vol. 2:** 736   **Vol. 3:** 246

2:30   **Vol. 1:** 240, 722   **Vol. 2:** 79   **Vol. 3:** 742

2:31   **Vol. 1:** 468, 470, 677, 695   **Vol. 2:** 207, 340, 919   **Vol. 3:** 262, 276, 491, 515

2:32–36   **Vol. 2:** 194   **Vol. 3:** 71

2:32 f   **Vol. 3:** 298

2:32   **Vol. 2:** 78   **Vol. 3:** 56, 1044

2:33   **Vol. 1:** 153   **Vol. 2:** 148, 176, 202–203, 785–786, 855, 921   **Vol. 3:** 87–88, 698, 700, 705, 748

2:34   **Vol. 1:** 427   **Vol. 2:** 148, 185, 515   **Vol. 3:** 276

2:35   **Vol. 1:** 239, 477, 554

2:36   **Vol. 1:** 168, 394–395, 663   **Vol. 2:** 81, 203, 248, 315, 340, 386, 400, 515   **Vol. 3:** 65, 299, 658, 698

2:37   **Vol. 2:** 183   **Vol. 3:** 252

2:38–40   **Vol. 3:** 71

2:38 f   **Vol. 1:** 159   **Vol. 2:** 786   **Vol. 3:** 71, 699

2:38   **Vol. 1:** 146, 148, 152, 154, 157–158, 185, 359, 701–702   **Vol. 2:** 41–42, 533, 611, 655, 785–786   **Vol. 3:** 56, 499, 580, 732, 990, 1187, 1208–1210

2:39   **Vol. 1:** 159, 286   **Vol. 2:** 73, 786

2:40   **Vol. 1:** 571   **Vol. 2:** 36, 860   **Vol. 3:** 87, 213, 732

2:41   **Vol. 1:** 149   **Vol. 2:** 699, 786   **Vol. 3:** 686, 746

2:42   **Vol. 1:** 251, 642   **Vol. 2:** 523, 530, 768, 786   **Vol. 3:** 769, 964

2:43–47   **Vol. 2:** 786

2:43   **Vol. 2:** 169, 629   **Vol. 3:** 683, 700

2:44 f   **Vol. 1:** 496   **Vol. 3:** 499

2:44   **Vol. 3:** 545, 1194, 1211, 1213

2:45   **Vol. 2:** 845–846   **Vol. 3:** 957

2:46 f   **Vol. 2:** 869, 895   **Vol. 3:** 908

Acts *(cont'd)*

2:46	**Vol. 1:** 369 **Vol. 2:** 236, 250, 272, 328, 354, 523, 768, 895 **Vol. 3:** 750, 793, 1201
2:47	**Vol. 2:** 119, 354, 895 **Vol. 3:** 817, 1194
3 f	**Vol. 3:** 611
3	**Vol. 1:** 214
3:1 ff	**Vol. 2:** 328, 632 **Vol. 3:** 785
3:1–10	**Vol. 3:** 793
3:1–8	**Vol. 2:** 597
3:1	**Vol. 2:** 185 **Vol. 3:** 101, 847
3:2 ff	**Vol. 2:** 415
3:2	**Vol. 1:** 169 **Vol. 2:** 29–30, 415, 895 **Vol. 3:** 1071
3:3	**Vol. 1:** 326
3:4	**Vol. 3:** 520
3:6–8	**Vol. 3:** 520
3:6	**Vol. 2:** 333, 597, 654 **Vol. 3:** 61, 213
3:7	**Vol. 2:** 415
3:8	**Vol. 3:** 817
3:9	**Vol. 2:** 799 **Vol. 3:** 817
3:10	**Vol. 1:** 528 **Vol. 2:** 29, 623, 625
3:11	**Vol. 2:** 236, 623 **Vol. 3:** 717, 789, 947
3:12–26	**Vol. 3:** 87
3:12 f	**Vol. 1:** 78
3:12	**Vol. 2:** 310, 625 **Vol. 3:** 520
3:13 ff	**Vol. 3:** 299
3:13–26	**Vol. 3:** 62
3:13 f	**Vol. 1:** 455 **Vol. 3:** 793
3:13	**Vol. 1:** 81 **Vol. 2:** 73, 319, 364 **Vol. 3:** 189, 610–611, 624
3:14 f	**Vol. 2:** 808
3:14	**Vol. 1:** 261 **Vol. 2:** 116, 119, 229, 563 **Vol. 3:** 361
3:15	**Vol. 1:** 168, 445, 669 **Vol. 3:** 199, 723, 1044
3:16	**Vol. 3:** 1193, 1211
3:17	**Vol. 1:** 168, 455 **Vol. 2:** 407 **Vol. 3:** 1157
3:18	**Vol. 1:** 736 **Vol. 3:** 46, 48, 81, 699, 723
3:19 ff	**Vol. 3:** 148
3:19–21	**Vol. 3:** 66
3:19 f	**Vol. 2:** 785
3:19†	**Vol. 1:** 355, 359, 471 **Vol. 3:** 732
3:20 f	**Vol. 2:** 614
3:20	**Vol. 3:** 658, 686
3:21	**Vol. 1:** 186 **Vol. 2:** 194, 665, 920 **Vol. 3:** 81, 147–148, 830
3:22–26	**Vol. 2:** 315
3:22 f	**Vol. 2:** 638 **Vol. 3:** 80, 83, 86, 1007
3:22	**Vol. 2:** 641 **Vol. 3:** 88
3:23†	**Vol. 1:** 465 **Vol. 3:** 683, 732
3:24	**Vol. 3:** 48
3:25 f	**Vol. 1:** 214
3:25	**Vol. 1:** 78, 212, 288, 616 **Vol. 2:** 786 **Vol. 3:** 1012
3:26	**Vol. 1:** 355 **Vol. 3:** 213, 610–611, 624
4	**Vol. 1:** 364
4:1 ff	**Vol. 2:** 827
4:1	**Vol. 3:** 439, 964
4:2	**Vol. 3:** 47, 56, 440, 763–764, 1191
4:4	**Vol. 2:** 684, 699 **Vol. 3:** 686, 941, 1114
4:5	**Vol. 1:** 168, 297 **Vol. 2:** 32 **Vol. 3:** 481
4:6	**Vol. 3:** 39–40
4:7	**Vol. 2:** 253, 603, 654
4:8 ff	**Vol. 3:** 387
4:8–12	**Vol. 3:** 87
4:8	**Vol. 1:** 168, 739 **Vol. 2:** 786, 921 **Vol. 3:** 699–700
4:9 f	**Vol. 3:** 213
4:9	**Vol. 2:** 365, 799 **Vol. 3:** 1152
4:10 ff	**Vol. 3:** 62, 793
4:10 f	**Vol. 3:** 393
4:10	**Vol. 1:** 394, 445 **Vol. 2:** 170, 333, 799 **Vol. 3:** 56, 61, 212
4:11	**Vol. 1:** 74 **Vol. 2:** 129, 159, 249, 313, 622, 706 **Vol. 3:** 389
4:12	**Vol. 2:** 654, 666, 722 **Vol. 3:** 213, 732, 1210
4:13	**Vol. 2:** 456, 625, 736 **Vol. 3:** 516, 699, 750
4:15	**Vol. 1:** 341
4:16	**Vol. 2:** 629, 632 **Vol. 3:** 320
4:18	**Vol. 1:** 340 **Vol. 3:** 763–764
4:19	**Vol. 2:** 364 **Vol. 3:** 361
4:20	**Vol. 2:** 176 **Vol. 3:** 313, 1044
4:21	**Vol. 3:** 98, 529
4:22	**Vol. 2:** 629, 632
4:23	**Vol. 3:** 189
4:24	**Vol. 2:** 192–193, 509 **Vol. 3:** 908, 984, 1154
4:25 ff	**Vol. 2:** 799
4:25 f	**Vol. 1:** 168
4:25	**Vol. 1:** 177, 427 **Vol. 2:** 793, 921 **Vol. 3:** 611–612, 699
4:26	**Vol. 2:** 33, 378 **Vol. 3:** 1194
4:27 f	**Vol. 1:** 696
4:27	**Vol. 1:** 122–123 **Vol. 2:** 33, 229, 712 **Vol. 3:** 611, 1061
4:28	**Vol. 1:** 1017
4:29–31	**Vol. 3:** 699
4:29 f	**Vol. 2:** 632
4:29	**Vol. 2:** 736 **Vol. 3:** 1113–1114
4:30 f	**Vol. 3:** 700
4:30	**Vol. 2:** 149–150, 629 **Vol. 3:** 611
4:31 ff	**Vol. 1:** 303
4:31	**Vol. 1:** 297, 739 **Vol. 2:** 32, 736, 786, 921 **Vol. 3:** 559, 699–700, 1114
4:32 ff	**Vol. 1:** 642
4:32	**Vol. 1:** 496, 504, 733 **Vol. 2:** 722, 845–846 **Vol. 3:** 685, 1213
4:33	**Vol. 2:** 119, 603 **Vol. 3:** 276, 1044
4:34	**Vol. 1:** 268
4:35	**Vol. 3:** 957, 1201
4:36 f	**Vol. 2:** 499, 846
4:36	**Vol. 1:** 276, 289, 571, 581, 642 **Vol. 2:** 467 **Vol. 3:** 87
4:37	**Vol. 1:** 520 **Vol. 2:** 845

Acts *(cont'd)*

5:1–11   **Vol. 1:** 466, 642, 703   **Vol. 3:** 387
5:1–10   **Vol. 3:** 700, 1206
5:1 f   **Vol. 2:** 846
5:1   **Vol. 2:** 845
5:2   **Vol. 1:** 350
5:3   **Vol. 1:** 739   **Vol. 2:** 473, 845, 847, 921   **Vol. 3:** 87, 471
5:4   **Vol. 1:** 567   **Vol. 2:** 473   **Vol. 3:** 547, 1158
5:5 ff   **Vol. 1:** 265   **Vol. 3:** 471
5:5   **Vol. 1:** 610
5:6   **Vol. 2:** 675
5:7   **Vol. 3:** 847
5:8   **Vol. 2:** 845   **Vol. 3:** 135
5:9   **Vol. 2:** 30, 513, 921   **Vol. 3:** 802
5:10   **Vol. 1:** 446, 610
5:11   **Vol. 1:** 303
5:12   **Vol. 2:** 149, 236, 629, 632   **Vol. 3:** 789, 793, 908
5:13   **Vol. 1:** 365   **Vol. 2:** 349   **Vol. 3:** 252
5:14   **Vol. 1:** 603, 733   **Vol. 2:** 517   **Vol. 3:** 686, 1058
5:15 f   **Vol. 2:** 168
5:15   **Vol. 1:** 340   **Vol. 3:** 387, 555
5:16   **Vol. 1:** 733   **Vol. 2:** 165, 921   **Vol. 3:** 475
5:17 ff   **Vol. 2:** 827
5:17–32   **Vol. 2:** 434
5:17 f   **Vol. 1:** 364   **Vol. 2:** 654
5:17   **Vol. 1:** 535, 739   **Vol. 3:** 439, 1167
5:18   **Vol. 2:** 790, 839
5:19   **Vol. 1:** 103, 421   **Vol. 2:** 30, 136, 513, 630, 726, 729
5:20 f   **Vol. 2:** 328   **Vol. 3:** 793
5:20   **Vol. 3:** 61, 1122
5:21   **Vol. 1:** 363   **Vol. 2:** 236   **Vol. 3:** 39, 764
5:22   **Vol. 2:** 136   **Vol. 3:** 934
5:23   **Vol. 1:** 663   **Vol. 2:** 30, 136, 729–730
5:24   **Vol. 3:** 39, 964
5:25   **Vol. 2:** 136, 236, 328   **Vol. 3:** 764
5:26   **Vol. 3:** 711
5:27   **Vol. 3:** 39
5:28   **Vol. 1:** 222, 340   **Vol. 2:** 654   **Vol. 3:** 763–764
5:29   **Vol. 1:** 593   **Vol. 2:** 565   **Vol. 3:** 387
5:30 ff   **Vol. 3:** 62
5:30 f   **Vol. 3:** 298
5:30   **Vol. 1:** 266, 390   **Vol. 2:** 73   **Vol. 3:** 793, 868
5:31   **Vol. 1:** 168, 359, 669, 701–702   **Vol. 2:** 148, 202–203   **Vol. 3:** 199, 219, 580
5:32   **Vol. 1:** 593   **Vol. 2:** 921   **Vol. 3:** 700, 704, 1122
5:33   **Vol. 2:** 183
5:34   **Vol. 1:** 341   **Vol. 2:** 799, 812   **Vol. 3:** 480, 768
5:35   **Vol. 1:** 326   **Vol. 2:** 310   **Vol. 3:** 1157

5:36 f   **Vol. 1:** 591   **Vol. 2:** 339   **Vol. 3:** 378
5:36   **Vol. 2:** 34, 689   **Vol. 3:** 275
5:37 f   **Vol. 3:** 768
5:37   **Vol. 1:** 493, 607, 717   **Vol. 2:** 34, 320
5:38 f   **Vol. 3:** 189
5:38   **Vol. 1:** 607   **Vol. 3:** 1017, 1149
5:39   **Vol. 1:** 179, 590, 646   **Vol. 2:** 74   **Vol. 3:** 529, 763, 963
5:40   **Vol. 1:** 163, 340, 590   **Vol. 2:** 654   **Vol. 3:** 189
5:41   **Vol. 2:** 50, 359, 361, 654   **Vol. 3:** 349
5:42   **Vol. 2:** 113, 236, 250, 328   **Vol. 3:** 57, 763–764, 1201
6   **Vol. 1:** 305   **Vol. 3:** 548, 1066–1067
6:1 ff   **Vol. 2:** 547, 740, 827   **Vol. 3:** 909, 1075
6:1–7   **Vol. 2:** 847
6:1–6   **Vol. 3:** 548
6:1 f   **Vol. 1:** 490
6:1   **Vol. 1:** 181, 490   **Vol. 2:** 126, 310–311   **Vol. 3:** 465–466, 546–547, 1201
6:2 ff   **Vol. 1:** 135
6:2   **Vol. 1:** 274, 733   **Vol. 2:** 695, 816   **Vol. 3:** 251, 546, 1113
6:3 ff   **Vol. 2:** 785
6:3   **Vol. 1:** 174, 191, 472, 735, 739   **Vol. 2:** 563, 921   **Vol. 3:** 88, 700, 958, 1030, 1043
6:4   **Vol. 2:** 768   **Vol. 3:** 546
6:5   **Vol. 1:** 361, 540, 733, 735, 739   **Vol. 2:** 114, 550, 563, 677, 921   **Vol. 3:** 65, 700
6:6   **Vol. 2:** 152, 873   **Vol. 3:** 66
6:7   **Vol. 1:** 490   **Vol. 2:** 130, 179   **Vol. 3:** 37, 1113–1114
6:8 ff   **Vol. 3:** 88, 548
6:8–15   **Vol. 3:** 65
6:8–10   **Vol. 2:** 603
6:8 f   **Vol. 1:** 364
6:8   **Vol. 1:** 739   **Vol. 2:** 119, 603, 629, 632   **Vol. 3:** 700, 1067
6:9 ff   **Vol. 3:** 87
6:9   **Vol. 1:** 297   **Vol. 2:** 740   **Vol. 3:** 275, 598, 785, 1180
6:10   **Vol. 1:** 739   **Vol. 2:** 365, 632, 786, 921   **Vol. 3:** 700, 714, 1030
6:11 ff   **Vol. 2:** 641
6:11   **Vol. 1:** 739   **Vol. 2:** 450   **Vol. 3:** 342, 345, 1122
6:12 ff   **Vol. 2:** 827
6:12   **Vol. 2:** 799   **Vol. 3:** 481
6:13 f   **Vol. 1:** 174
6:13   **Vol. 2:** 450   **Vol. 3:** 1043, 1122, 1199
6:14   **Vol. 2:** 236, 333, 437, 920   **Vol. 3:** 167, 185, 189, 343, 464, 509, 773–774, 792
6:15   **Vol. 3:** 257, 520, 588
7   **Vol. 1:** 532   **Vol. 3:** 65, 431, 464–465, 607
7:1–60   **Vol. 3:** 1067
7:2–53   **Vol. 2:** 315   **Vol. 3:** 87, 464, 466

Acts *(cont'd)*

7:2	**Vol. 2:** 46, 76 **Vol. 3:** 71
7:4	**Vol. 3:** 464–465
7:5 ff	**Vol. 3:** 464
7:5 f	**Vol. 3:** 523
7:5	**Vol. 1:** 286 **Vol. 2:** 300, 369 **Vol. 3:** 71, 464, 1043
7:6	**Vol. 1:** 684 **Vol. 2:** 689, 742
7:7	**Vol. 2:** 793 **Vol. 3:** 464, 550
7:8 f	**Vol. 1:** 65
7:8	**Vol. 1:** 81, 154, 309 **Vol. 2:** 318, 695
7:9	**Vol. 3:** 1167
7:10	**Vol. 2:** 378 **Vol. 3:** 1030
7:11	**Vol. 1:** 744 **Vol. 2:** 266
7:12	**Vol. 2:** 318
7:13	**Vol. 3:** 314, 320
7:14	**Vol. 2:** 318 **Vol. 3:** 683
7:15 f	**Vol. 3:** 458, 464
7:15	**Vol. 1:** 430
7:17†	**Vol. 1:** 346, 732, 733 **Vol. 2:** 130 **Vol. 3:** 71
7:18	**Vol. 3:** 275
7:20	**Vol. 3:** 837
7:22	**Vol. 2:** 641 **Vol. 3:** 197, 778, 1149
7:23	**Vol. 1:** 191, 737 **Vol. 2:** 636, 696 **Vol. 3:** 843
7:24	**Vol. 3:** 97, 575
7:25 ff	**Vol. 2:** 641
7:25	**Vol. 2:** 149
7:26	**Vol. 1:** 251 **Vol. 2:** 780 **Vol. 3:** 575, 963
7:27	**Vol. 1:** 168, 258 **Vol. 3:** 575
7:29	**Vol. 1:** 518, 559, 691 **Vol. 3:** 1175, 1192
7:30 ff	**Vol. 3:** 1007
7:30	**Vol. 1:** 656, 737 **Vol. 2:** 636, 696 **Vol. 3:** 465, 1014
7:31	**Vol. 2:** 625 **Vol. 3:** 862
7:32	**Vol. 1:** 81, 365 **Vol. 2:** 73 **Vol. 3:** 464–465
7:33	**Vol. 3:** 179
7:34	**Vol. 2:** 178, 424
7:35	**Vol. 2:** 149, 641 **Vol. 3:** 199, 465
7:36	**Vol. 1:** 518 **Vol. 2:** 629, 636, 696 **Vol. 3:** 80, 984
7:37	**Vol. 2:** 638, 641 **Vol. 3:** 83, 86, 464, 1007
7:38	**Vol. 1:** 303 **Vol. 3:** 465, 1014, 1106, 1118
7:39	**Vol. 1:** 532 **Vol. 2:** 179–180
7:41–43	**Vol. 3:** 1008
7:41	**Vol. 2:** 356 **Vol. 3:** 431
7:42 f	**Vol. 2:** 164 **Vol. 3:** 465
7:42–43	**Vol. 2:** 248
7:42	**Vol. 2:** 193, 368, 696 **Vol. 3:** 465, 550
7:43	**Vol. 1:** 141 **Vol. 2:** 85 **Vol. 3:** 736, 749, 905
7:44–50	**Vol. 3:** 793
7:44	**Vol. 3:** 811, 905
7:45 f	**Vol. 3:** 465
7:45	**Vol. 1:** 427 **Vol. 2:** 331
7:46–50	**Vol. 2:** 248
7:46	**Vol. 2:** 248, 319 **Vol. 3:** 530, 815
7:47–58	**Vol. 1:** 174
7:47–50	**Vol. 3:** 465
7:47	**Vol. 2:** 248, 315 **Vol. 3:** 606
7:48 ff	**Vol. 3:** 785
7:48 f	**Vol. 2:** 450
7:48	**Vol. 2:** 74, 150, 200, 248, 920 **Vol. 3:** 461, 793
7:49	**Vol. 1:** 239, 518 **Vol. 2:** 74, 193 **Vol. 3:** 258, 465
7:50	**Vol. 2:** 149 **Vol. 3:** 607
7:51 f	**Vol. 2:** 229
7:51	**Vol. 1:** 309, 311 **Vol. 2:** 155, 178, 921 **Vol. 3:** 700
7:52	**Vol. 1:** 320 **Vol. 2:** 806 **Vol. 3:** 46, 82, 199, 361, 793
7:53	**Vol. 1:** 103 **Vol. 2:** 135, 450 **Vol. 3:** 345, 465, 1174, 1187
7:54 ff	**Vol. 1:** 440 **Vol. 2:** 827
7:54	**Vol. 2:** 183, 421
7:55 ff	**Vol. 1:** 303
7:55 f	**Vol. 2:** 148 **Vol. 3:** 287
7:55	**Vol. 1:** 739 **Vol. 2:** 46, 192, 359, 921 **Vol. 3:** 257, 504, 520, 699–700
7:56	**Vol. 2:** 729, 919, 921 **Vol. 3:** 543, 621, 633
7:57 ff	**Vol. 2:** 450
7:57 f	**Vol. 3:** 909
7:57	**Vol. 2:** 96, 178 **Vol. 3:** 113, 908
7:58	**Vol. 2:** 762 **Vol. 3:** 1043
7:59	**Vol. 1:** 276 **Vol. 2:** 921 **Vol. 3:** 694
7:60	**Vol. 1:** 410, 443 **Vol. 2:** 859 **Vol. 3:** 113, 292
8–12	**Vol. 3:** 1114
8	**Vol. 3:** 456
8:1	**Vol. 1:** 303, 686 **Vol. 2:** 34, 381 **Vol. 3:** 449, 456, 909
8:2	**Vol. 2:** 91, 418
8:3	**Vol. 1:** 303 **Vol. 2:** 136, 368
8:4 ff	**Vol. 3:** 57, 1067
8:4–25	**Vol. 3:** 453, 456–457
8:4–13	**Vol. 3:** 456
8:4	**Vol. 1:** 686 **Vol. 3:** 1113
8:5 ff	**Vol. 2:** 114
8:5–40	**Vol. 2:** 550
8:5	**Vol. 3:** 52, 56, 456
8:6 ff	**Vol. 2:** 632
8:6 f	**Vol. 3:** 457
8:6	**Vol. 2:** 629 **Vol. 3:** 908
8:7–29	**Vol. 2:** 921
8:7	**Vol. 1:** 411 **Vol. 2:** 165, 415 **Vol. 3:** 113, 475, 999
8:8	**Vol. 2:** 359 **Vol. 3:** 456
8:9 ff	**Vol. 3:** 457
8:9–24	**Vol. 3:** 88
8:9–13	**Vol. 3:** 700

Acts *(cont'd)*

8:9	**Vol. 1:** 528 **Vol. 2:** 74, 558 **Vol. 3:** 457, 463
8:10	**Vol. 2:** 426, 428 **Vol. 3:** 457, 462
8:11	**Vol. 1:** 528 **Vol. 2:** 558 **Vol. 3:** 457
8:12 ff	**Vol. 3:** 699
8:12	**Vol. 1:** 160 **Vol. 2:** 387, 654 **Vol. 3:** 1211
8:13	**Vol. 2:** 603, 768 **Vol. 3:** 457
8:14 ff	**Vol. 1:** 135, 146, 148
8:14–17	**Vol. 2:** 785
8:14 f	**Vol. 2:** 114
8:14	**Vol. 1:** 136 **Vol. 2:** 328 **Vol. 3:** 746, 1114
8:15–19	**Vol. 3:** 699
8:15–17	**Vol. 1:** 158
8:16	**Vol. 1:** 609 **Vol. 2:** 655, 724 **Vol. 3:** 61, 1209
8:17 ff	**Vol. 2:** 152
8:17	**Vol. 2:** 42
8:18 ff	**Vol. 2:** 152
8:18–24	**Vol. 3:** 458
8:18–20	**Vol. 2:** 605
8:18	**Vol. 2:** 845, 847
8:19–24	**Vol. 2:** 557
8:19	**Vol. 2:** 611
8:20	**Vol. 1:** 464 **Vol. 2:** 845
8:21 ff	**Vol. 3:** 87
8:21	**Vol. 2:** 302, 304 **Vol. 3:** 1106
8:22	**Vol. 1:** 563 **Vol. 2:** 861
8:23	**Vol. 1:** 202 **Vol. 2:** 28 **Vol. 3:** 575
8:24	**Vol. 2:** 860–861 **Vol. 3:** 1174
8:25	**Vol. 2:** 113, 513 **Vol. 3:** 1044, 1113
8:26–40	**Vol. 3:** 65
8:26	**Vol. 1:** 103 **Vol. 2:** 513 **Vol. 3:** 275, 941, 1008
8:27	**Vol. 1:** 560 **Vol. 2:** 381, 511, 877
8:28	**Vol. 1:** 245, 736
8:29	**Vol. 2:** 349, 847 **Vol. 3:** 700
8:30–35	**Vol. 3:** 87
8:30	**Vol. 1:** 736
8:31	**Vol. 1:** 570 **Vol. 3:** 943
8:32 f	**Vol. 2:** 381
8:32	**Vol. 1:** 581 **Vol. 2:** 410–411, 413, 728 **Vol. 3:** 490
8:33	**Vol. 1:** 576, 581 **Vol. 2:** 38, 365
8:34	**Vol. 3:** 609
8:35	**Vol. 2:** 263, 410, 726–728 **Vol. 3:** 490
8:36	**Vol. 2:** 223 **Vol. 3:** 941, 990
8:37	**Vol. 3:** 639, 646, 1211
8:38 f	**Vol. 3:** 990, 1180
8:38	**Vol. 1:** 341
8:39	**Vol. 2:** 359, 513 **Vol. 3:** 602, 700, 941
8:40	**Vol. 3:** 529
9	**Vol. 1:** 305
9:1–19	**Vol. 1:** 136
9:1 f	**Vol. 2:** 827 **Vol. 3:** 380, 1199
9:1	**Vol. 1:** 490 **Vol. 3:** 708
9:2	**Vol. 1:** 171 **Vol. 2:** 856 **Vol. 3:** 785, 941
9:3–9	**Vol. 3:** 330
9:3–6	**Vol. 1:** 183
9:3	**Vol. 2:** 193, 493
9:4 ff	**Vol. 3:** 85
9:4 f	**Vol. 2:** 806
9:4	**Vol. 1:** 174, 358, 610 **Vol. 2:** 155 **Vol. 3:** 114
9:5	**Vol. 1:** 511 **Vol. 2:** 513 **Vol. 3:** 88
9:6	**Vol. 2:** 623, 666 **Vol. 3:** 275
9:7	**Vol. 3:** 114
9:8	**Vol. 2:** 726, 728 **Vol. 3:** 520
9:9	**Vol. 2:** 272
9:10 f	**Vol. 3:** 85
9:10–16	**Vol. 2:** 867
9:10	**Vol. 1:** 490 **Vol. 3:** 87, 515, 517, 700, 862
9:11	**Vol. 2:** 320, 861, 867, 873 **Vol. 3:** 275
9:12	**Vol. 3:** 515, 517, 519, 862
9:13	**Vol. 1:** 305
9:14	**Vol. 1:** 276 **Vol. 2:** 654
9:15	**Vol. 1:** 136, 540 **Vol. 3:** 38, 912, 1065
9:16	**Vol. 2:** 654, 666 **Vol. 3:** 257, 725
9:17	**Vol. 1:** 739 **Vol. 2:** 152, 921 **Vol. 3:** 285, 458, 519, 699–700, 941, 1191
9:18	**Vol. 3:** 519
9:19	**Vol. 1:** 490 **Vol. 2:** 523
9:20 ff	**Vol. 3:** 87
9:20	**Vol. 3:** 52, 56, 62, 639, 644, 785
9:22	**Vol. 3:** 1199
9:23	**Vol. 1:** 363, 737
9:24	**Vol. 2:** 29, 133
9:25 f	**Vol. 1:** 490
9:25	**Vol. 1:** 420 **Vol. 3:** 948
9:26–30	**Vol. 3:** 65
9:26	**Vol. 2:** 349 **Vol. 3:** 802
9:27 f	**Vol. 2:** 736
9:27	**Vol. 1:** 136, 576 **Vol. 2:** 736 **Vol. 3:** 749, 941, 1191
9:29	**Vol. 2:** 126, 311 **Vol. 3:** 908
9:30	**Vol. 2:** 328
9:31	**Vol. 1:** 303, 623, 733 **Vol. 2:** 252, 921 **Vol. 3:** 87, 449, 456, 699, 947
9:32 ff	**Vol. 2:** 632
9:32	**Vol. 3:** 387
9:33	**Vol. 3:** 999
9:34 f	**Vol. 2:** 867
9:34	**Vol. 2:** 654 **Vol. 3:** 275
9:35	**Vol. 1:** 355
9:36–42	**Vol. 2:** 433
9:36	**Vol. 1:** 581, 735 **Vol. 2:** 596 **Vol. 3:** 1065
9:37	**Vol. 2:** 596 **Vol. 3:** 994
9:38	**Vol. 1:** 490
9:39	**Vol. 1:** 316 **Vol. 2:** 416 **Vol. 3:** 1065, 1154
9:40	**Vol. 2:** 726, 728, 859
9:42	**Vol. 3:** 1212
10 f	**Vol. 3:** 456

Acts *(cont'd)*

10   **Vol. 1:** 90   **Vol. 2:** 732   **Vol. 3:** 387, 793
10:1 ff   **Vol. 3:** 66
10:1–11:18 **Vol. 1:** 361   **Vol. 3:** 106
10:1   **Vol. 1:** 274   **Vol. 3:** 85, 964
10:2   **Vol. 1:** 361, 623   **Vol. 2:** 94, 596, 800, 861
10:3–8   **Vol. 1:** 103
10:3   **Vol. 3:** 320, 515, 517, 700, 847, 862
10:4   **Vol. 2:** 185, 513, 596   **Vol. 3:** 242, 520
10:6   **Vol. 1:** 689   **Vol. 3:** 984
10:7   **Vol. 2:** 768   **Vol. 3:** 700, 964
10:8   **Vol. 1:** 576
10:9 ff   **Vol. 2:** 873
10:9–16   **Vol. 2:** 434   **Vol. 3:** 113
10:9   **Vol. 2:** 873   **Vol. 3:** 847, 941
10:10–16   **Vol. 3:** 700
10:10   **Vol. 1:** 528   **Vol. 2:** 269   **Vol. 3:** 87, 119, 410, 1193
10:11   **Vol. 1:** 166   **Vol. 2:** 689, 729   **Vol. 3:** 543, 913
10:12   **Vol. 1:** 175   **Vol. 2:** 192
10:13–14   **Vol. 3:** 113
10:13   **Vol. 3:** 88
10:14 f   **Vol. 2:** 268
10:14   **Vol. 1:** 448, 642   **Vol. 2:** 275
10:15   **Vol. 1:** 448, 642   **Vol. 3:** 106
10:16   **Vol. 3:** 749, 913
10:17   **Vol. 2:** 30   **Vol. 3:** 862
10:18   **Vol. 3:** 114
10:19–47   **Vol. 2:** 921
10:19   **Vol. 3:** 700, 862
10:20   **Vol. 1:** 504
10:21   **Vol. 2:** 138
10:22   **Vol. 1:** 361, 623   **Vol. 2:** 228, 793   **Vol. 3:** 325, 361, 964, 1043, 1122
10:23   **Vol. 1:** 690
10:24   **Vol. 2:** 549, 663
10:25 f   **Vol. 2:** 877
10:25   **Vol. 1:** 325, 609
10:28   **Vol. 1:** 448, 685   **Vol. 2:** 349, 563, 742   **Vol. 3:** 569
10:29   **Vol. 3:** 1106
10:30 ff   **Vol. 2:** 873
10:30   **Vol. 2:** 486   **Vol. 3:** 847
10:31   **Vol. 2:** 178, 596   **Vol. 3:** 242
10:32   **Vol. 3:** 984
10:33   **Vol. 1:** 477   **Vol. 2:** 899   **Vol. 3:** 1198
10:34   **Vol. 1:** 587   **Vol. 2:** 726–728   **Vol. 3:** 750
10:35   **Vol. 2:** 794   **Vol. 3:** 361, 746
10:36 ff   **Vol. 3:** 660
10:36–43   **Vol. 3:** 62, 66
10:36 f   **Vol. 3:** 1113
10:36   **Vol. 1:** 239   **Vol. 2:** 780, 782   **Vol. 3:** 1113
10:37–41   **Vol. 3:** 62
10:37 f   **Vol. 3:** 499

10:37   **Vol. 1:** 167   **Vol. 3:** 52, 1113
10:38   **Vol. 1:** 122, 453   **Vol. 2:** 168–169, 333, 603, 632, 712   **Vol. 3:** 470, 698, 713, 1061, 1152
10:39   **Vol. 1:** 266, 390   **Vol. 2:** 328   **Vol. 3:** 793, 868
10:40 f   **Vol. 1:** 445
10:40   **Vol. 2:** 489, 687
10:41   **Vol. 1:** 478   **Vol. 2:** 272, 524, 799, 897   **Vol. 3:** 283, 449
10:42 f   **Vol. 1:** 701
10:42   **Vol. 1:** 340–341, 445, 473   **Vol. 2:** 365, 480
10:43   **Vol. 2:** 654   **Vol. 3:** 213, 580, 748, 1212
10:44 ff   **Vol. 1:** 148   **Vol. 3:** 286, 699
10:44–48   **Vol. 1:** 158   **Vol. 2:** 611, 785
10:44–47   **Vol. 3:** 699
10:44 f   **Vol. 1:** 146   **Vol. 2:** 596
10:44   **Vol. 1:** 528, 609   **Vol. 3:** 1122
10:45   **Vol. 1:** 310   **Vol. 2:** 785, 794, 855   **Vol. 3:** 1194
10:46   **Vol. 1:** 528   **Vol. 2:** 740, 786   **Vol. 3:** 1080
10:47 f   **Vol. 2:** 596
10:47   **Vol. 2:** 42, 223   **Vol. 3:** 499, 990
10:48   **Vol. 1:** 160, 476   **Vol. 2:** 655, 880, 895   **Vol. 3:** 227, 1210
11:1 ff   **Vol. 1:** 135, 302
11:1   **Vol. 2:** 794   **Vol. 3:** 746
11:2   **Vol. 1:** 310, 504
11:3   **Vol. 1:** 309–310
11:4   **Vol. 1:** 167
11:5   **Vol. 1:** 528   **Vol. 2:** 689   **Vol. 3:** 862, 913
11:6   **Vol. 1:** 114, 175   **Vol. 2:** 192   **Vol. 3:** 520
11:7–9   **Vol. 3:** 113
11:8   **Vol. 1:** 448
11:9   **Vol. 1:** 448
11:12–28   **Vol. 2:** 921
11:12   **Vol. 1:** 503   **Vol. 3:** 85, 700
11:14   **Vol. 1:** 148   **Vol. 2:** 250
11:15–18   **Vol. 3:** 699
11:15 f   **Vol. 3:** 699
11:15   **Vol. 1:** 166–167, 528, 609
11:16   **Vol. 1:** 158   **Vol. 2:** 514, 786   **Vol. 3:** 241, 990, 1122, 1210
11:17   **Vol. 1:** 528   **Vol. 2:** 223, 499   **Vol. 3:** 61, 1212, 1214
11:18   **Vol. 1:** 359   **Vol. 2:** 794   **Vol. 3:** 111
11:19 f   **Vol. 3:** 458
11:19   **Vol. 1:** 686   **Vol. 2:** 34, 809   **Vol. 3:** 941, 1113–1114
11:20   **Vol. 2:** 113, 126, 740   **Vol. 3:** 61
11:21   **Vol. 1:** 355   **Vol. 2:** 149, 513
11:22   **Vol. 1:** 303   **Vol. 2:** 328   **Vol. 3:** 1106
11:23   **Vol. 1:** 571, 697   **Vol. 2:** 119, 359   **Vol. 3:** 87, 228
11:24   **Vol. 1:** 739   **Vol. 3:** 700, 729
11:25   **Vol. 2:** 328

Acts *(cont'd)*

11:26   **Vol. 1:** 123, 199, 490   **Vol. 2:** 32, 333, 343, 523, 654   **Vol. 3:** 764
11:26c   **Vol. 3:** 325
11:27 ff   **Vol. 2:** 827
11:27 f   **Vol. 3:** 86–87, 700
11:27   **Vol. 2:** 328   **Vol. 3:** 458
11:28 ff   **Vol. 2:** 268
11:28–30   **Vol. 2:** 694
11:28   **Vol. 1:** 326, 519   **Vol. 2:** 266   **Vol. 3:** 86–87, 1183
11:29 f   **Vol. 2:** 827
11:29   **Vol. 1:** 473, 490   **Vol. 2:** 694   **Vol. 3:** 546–547
11:30   **Vol. 1:** 199   **Vol. 2:** 149   **Vol. 3:** 1155
12   **Vol. 3:** 387
12:1 ff   **Vol. 2:** 827
12:1–3   **Vol. 1:** 343
12:1   **Vol. 1:** 303   **Vol. 2:** 378   **Vol. 3:** 837, 1180
12:2   **Vol. 3:** 292, 967
12:3 ff   **Vol. 2:** 630
12:3   **Vol. 2:** 816
12:4 f   **Vol. 2:** 136
12:4   **Vol. 1:** 633   **Vol. 2:** 135, 368, 689, 799
12:5   **Vol. 1:** 303   **Vol. 2:** 868
12:6–11   **Vol. 2:** 919
12:6   **Vol. 1:** 326, 442   **Vol. 2:** 30, 136
12:7–10   **Vol. 1:** 103
12:7   **Vol. 1:** 421   **Vol. 2:** 486, 493, 513
12:8   **Vol. 3:** 121
12:9   **Vol. 3:** 822, 862
12:10   **Vol. 1:** 607, 666   **Vol. 2:** 29, 136, 726, 729
12:11 f   **Vol. 2:** 244
12:11   **Vol. 2:** 150
12:12–16   **Vol. 2:** 434
12:12   **Vol. 1:** 276, 642   **Vol. 2:** 33, 847, 869   **Vol. 3:** 1065, 1071
12:13   **Vol. 2:** 30, 179, 881
12:14   **Vol. 2:** 30, 726, 729   **Vol. 3:** 113, 1180
12:15   **Vol. 1:** 102, 529
12:16   **Vol. 2:** 729, 881   **Vol. 3:** 227
12:17   **Vol. 1:** 576   **Vol. 3:** 558
12:18   **Vol. 1:** 181   **Vol. 3:** 709–710
12:19   **Vol. 1:** 341   **Vol. 2:** 136, 365   **Vol. 3:** 532
12:20   **Vol. 1:** 589   **Vol. 2:** 378, 780   **Vol. 3:** 908
12:21–22   **Vol. 3:** 113
12:21   **Vol. 2:** 369   **Vol. 3:** 588
12:22   **Vol. 1:** 410   **Vol. 2:** 789
12:23   **Vol. 1:** 103, 181   **Vol. 2:** 46, 168   **Vol. 3:** 998
12:24   **Vol. 1:** 733   **Vol. 2:** 130, 513   **Vol. 3:** 1113–1114
12:25   **Vol. 2:** 827   **Vol. 3:** 546–547
13–28   **Vol. 3:** 1114
13   **Vol. 3:** 64–65

13:1–4   **Vol. 1:** 135
13:1   **Vol. 1:** 303   **Vol. 2:** 740   **Vol. 3:** 86–87, 700, 767–768
13:2   **Vol. 1:** 274, 474   **Vol. 2:** 873, 921   **Vol. 3:** 85, 552, 700
13:3   **Vol. 1:** 613   **Vol. 2:** 152, 873   **Vol. 3:** 55
13:4–12   **Vol. 2:** 467, 557
13:4   **Vol. 2:** 921   **Vol. 3:** 700
13:5   **Vol. 1:** 297   **Vol. 2:** 113   **Vol. 3:** 47, 87, 410, 785, 1113–1114
13:6 ff   **Vol. 3:** 88
13:6   **Vol. 1:** 623   **Vol. 2:** 74, 331, 472, 557
13:7 f   **Vol. 1:** 270
13:7   **Vol. 2:** 176   **Vol. 3:** 532, 1113–1114
13:8   **Vol. 1:** 581   **Vol. 2:** 557
13:9–11   **Vol. 3:** 700
13:9   **Vol. 1:** 739   **Vol. 2:** 786, 921   **Vol. 3:** 520, 699–700
13:10   **Vol. 1:** 289, 554   **Vol. 3:** 197, 361, 471, 941–942
13:11   **Vol. 1:** 219, 424, 466, 609   **Vol. 2:** 149   **Vol. 3:** 87, 731
13:12   **Vol. 1:** 270, 530   **Vol. 3:** 769, 942, 1214
13:13   **Vol. 3:** 1203
13:14–52   **Vol. 3:** 203
13:14   **Vol. 2:** 314   **Vol. 3:** 410, 589, 785
13:15   **Vol. 1:** 245   **Vol. 2:** 799   **Vol. 3:** 87, 485
13:16 ff   **Vol. 1:** 691
13:16–41   **Vol. 3:** 62, 65, 87
13:16   **Vol. 1:** 361   **Vol. 2:** 310   **Vol. 3:** 558
13:17   **Vol. 1:** 532, 541   **Vol. 2:** 73, 200, 202, 799   **Vol. 3:** 1010
13:18   **Vol. 2:** 696   **Vol. 3:** 843, 1007
13:19   **Vol. 2:** 300, 793
13:20   **Vol. 2:** 41, 689
13:21   **Vol. 2:** 696   **Vol. 3:** 872
13:22   **Vol. 1:** 427   **Vol. 2:** 378   **Vol. 3:** 1018
13:23–31   **Vol. 3:** 62
13:23   **Vol. 2:** 786   **Vol. 3:** 71, 219, 523
13:24   **Vol. 1:** 358   **Vol. 3:** 660, 940, 1208
13:25   **Vol. 2:** 62   **Vol. 3:** 179, 348, 947
13:26   **Vol. 1:** 78, 257, 361, 623   **Vol. 3:** 213, 1113
13:27 ff   **Vol. 3:** 793
13:27   **Vol. 1:** 168, 245, 736   **Vol. 2:** 328, 407   **Vol. 3:** 114
13:28   **Vol. 2:** 139   **Vol. 3:** 529
13:29   **Vol. 1:** 266   **Vol. 2:** 63   **Vol. 3:** 247, 488–489
13:30   **Vol. 1:** 445
13:31   **Vol. 2:** 328, 799   **Vol. 3:** 285, 1044, 1181
13:32 f   **Vol. 3:** 71
13:32   **Vol. 2:** 786   **Vol. 3:** 71
13:33 ff   **Vol. 3:** 523
13:33   **Vol. 1:** 177–179, 286, 736   **Vol. 3:** 639, 641, 644, 671, 675, 698
13:34 ff   **Vol. 3:** 1017

Acts *(cont'd)*

13:34–37 **Vol. 3:** 1200
13:34 f **Vol. 1:** 468
13:34 **Vol. 1:** 427, 445 **Vol. 2:** 238 **Vol. 3:** 303
13:35 ff **Vol. 1:** 470
13:35–37 **Vol. 1:** 266
13:35 **Vol. 2:** 238 **Vol. 3:** 491
13:36 f **Vol. 3:** 1017
13:36 **Vol. 1:** 427, 443 **Vol. 2:** 35 **Vol. 3:** 547, 1017
13:37 **Vol. 2:** 919 **Vol. 3:** 651
13:38 f **Vol. 1:** 158 **Vol. 3:** 361, 1113
13:38 **Vol. 1:** 701 **Vol. 2:** 113, 451, 641 **Vol. 3:** 47, 213
13:41 **Vol. 1:** 462 **Vol. 2:** 625 **Vol. 3:** 1148–1149
13:42 **Vol. 1:** 570 **Vol. 3:** 1122
13:43 **Vol. 1:** 361, 589 **Vol. 2:** 85, 94, 119 **Vol. 3:** 179–180, 228, 785
13:44 **Vol. 2:** 33, 176 **Vol. 3:** 410, 1113–1114
13:45 **Vol. 1:** 739 **Vol. 3:** 343, 1167
13:46 **Vol. 2:** 315, 364, 663, 736, 794 **Vol. 3:** 832, 1113–1114
13:47† **Vol. 1:** 341, 477 **Vol. 2:** 57, 495 **Vol. 3:** 613
13:48 f **Vol. 2:** 513
13:48 **Vol. 1:** 476 **Vol. 2:** 359 **Vol. 3:** 832, 1114, 1186
13:49 **Vol. 3:** 1113
13:50 **Vol. 1:** 361 **Vol. 2:** 94
13:51 **Vol. 1:** 239 **Vol. 3:** 561
13:52 **Vol. 1:** 490, 739 **Vol. 2:** 359, 921 **Vol. 3:** 699
14 **Vol. 3:** 327
14:1–20 **Vol. 3:** 203
14:1† **Vol. 1:** 297, 361, 733 **Vol. 2:** 126, 314 **Vol. 3:** 410, 785
14:2 **Vol. 1:** 563, 593 **Vol. 3:** 685
14:3 f **Vol. 2:** 736
14:3 **Vol. 2:** 119, 629, 632, 736 **Vol. 3:** 843
14:4 **Vol. 1:** 136, 733 **Vol. 3:** 544
14:5 **Vol. 3:** 27
14:6 **Vol. 2:** 606
14:8–18 **Vol. 2:** 85
14:8 **Vol. 2:** 415
14:9 **Vol. 3:** 212, 520
14:10 **Vol. 2:** 654 **Vol. 3:** 113, 351
14:11 f **Vol. 3:** 457
14:11 **Vol. 2:** 503
14:13 **Vol. 1:** 116, 405 **Vol. 2:** 30
14:14 **Vol. 1:** 128, 130, 136, 317, 410
14:15 **Vol. 1:** 355, 551 **Vol. 2:** 73, 193, 503 **Vol. 3:** 200, 984
14:16 **Vol. 2:** 35, 407, 793 **Vol. 3:** 940–941, 947
14:17 **Vol. 1:** 701 **Vol. 2:** 77, 102, 182, 193, 356 **Vol. 3:** 310, 331, 837, 1004

14:18 **Vol. 2:** 839 **Vol. 3:** 258, 1071
14:19 **Vol. 1:** 322, 589 **Vol. 3:** 558
14:20 **Vol. 1:** 490
14:22 **Vol. 1:** 490, 571 **Vol. 2:** 809, 920 **Vol. 3:** 87, 226
14:23 **Vol. 1:** 199–200, 303, 478, 613 **Vol. 2:** 150 **Vol. 3:** 1201, 1212
14:25 **Vol. 3:** 1113
14:26 **Vol. 2:** 119, 368
14:27 **Vol. 1:** 303 **Vol. 2:** 31–32, 726–727, 729 **Vol. 3:** 47
14:28–29 **Vol. 3:** 101
14:28 **Vol. 1:** 490
15 **Vol. 1:** 62, 129 **Vol. 2:** 795 **Vol. 3:** 387, 1164
15:1 ff **Vol. 2:** 328
15:1–21 **Vol. 2:** 641
15:1 **Vol. 1:** 310 **Vol. 2:** 437 **Vol. 3:** 458, 764
15:2 **Vol. 1:** 136, 199, 310 **Vol. 3:** 458, 532
15:3 **Vol. 1:** 355 **Vol. 2:** 359 **Vol. 3:** 449, 458, 1174
15:4 **Vol. 1:** 199 **Vol. 3:** 47, 1174, 1198
15:5 **Vol. 1:** 310, 341, 535 **Vol. 2:** 450, 812 **Vol. 3:** 804
15:6 **Vol. 1:** 199, 297 **Vol. 2:** 32
15:7–11 **Vol. 1:** 157
15:7 **Vol. 1:** 158, 168, 541 **Vol. 2:** 110, 112, 563 **Vol. 3:** 1114
15:8 **Vol. 2:** 183, 921 **Vol. 3:** 699
15:9 **Vol. 1:** 158, 503 **Vol. 3:** 106
15:10 f **Vol. 2:** 119 **Vol. 3:** 213
15:10 **Vol. 1:** 241, 490 **Vol. 3:** 802, 1164
15:11 **Vol. 3:** 909, 1211
15:12 **Vol. 1:** 131, 576, 733 **Vol. 2:** 629, 632 **Vol. 3:** 812
15:13–21 **Vol. 2:** 563
15:13 **Vol. 2:** 563
15:14 **Vol. 1:** 191, 576 **Vol. 2:** 73, 800
15:16 f **Vol. 3:** 651
15:16 **Vol. 1:** 355, 427 **Vol. 2:** 248, 252, 920 **Vol. 3:** 650, 934
15:17 ff **Vol. 3:** 387
15:17–18 **Vol. 3:** 812
15:17 **Vol. 1:** 276 **Vol. 3:** 251, 532
15:18 **Vol. 2:** 451 **Vol. 3:** 830
15:19 ff **Vol. 3:** 387
15:19 f **Vol. 1:** 310
15:19 **Vol. 1:** 355 **Vol. 2:** 364 **Vol. 3:** 812
15:20 **Vol. 1:** 221, 226 **Vol. 2:** 286, 678, 682, 826 **Vol. 3:** 538, 931, 1195
15:21 **Vol. 1:** 245 **Vol. 2:** 35, 286 **Vol. 3:** 56, 785
15:22 f **Vol. 1:** 199
15:22 **Vol. 1:** 540 **Vol. 2:** 321 **Vol. 3:** 87, 822
15:23–29 **Vol. 1:** 247
15:23 **Vol. 1:** 247, 256 **Vol. 2:** 358 **Vol. 3:** 458
15:24 **Vol. 3:** 710
15:25 **Vol. 1:** 540 **Vol. 3:** 822, 908

Acts (cont'd)

15:26   **Vol. 2:** 368   **Vol. 3:** 257, 683
15:27   **Vol. 3:** 1106
15:28 ff   **Vol. 2:** 309
15:28 f   **Vol. 1:** 261   **Vol. 2:** 450–451, 921
15:28   **Vol. 3:** 700, 822
15:29   **Vol. 1:** 226   **Vol. 2:** 284–286, 678, 682   **Vol. 3:** 106, 432, 538, 931, 1157, 1195
15:30   **Vol. 1:** 297, 733   **Vol. 2:** 32   **Vol. 3:** 189
15:31   **Vol. 1:** 245   **Vol. 2:** 359
15:32   **Vol. 1:** 570–571   **Vol. 3:** 86–87, 700
15:33   **Vol. 3:** 189, 843, 1198
15:34   **Vol. 3:** 822
15:35 f   **Vol. 3:** 1113
15:35   **Vol. 2:** 513   **Vol. 3:** 763–764
15:36–40   **Vol. 1:** 129
15:36   **Vol. 1:** 191   **Vol. 2:** 113   **Vol. 3:** 1113–1114
15:37 ff   **Vol. 3:** 909
15:37   **Vol. 1:** 274
15:38   **Vol. 1:** 607
15:39   **Vol. 1:** 110   **Vol. 2:** 467
15:40   **Vol. 2:** 119
15:41   **Vol. 1:** 303
16:1 ff   **Vol. 3:** 491
16:1–5   **Vol. 3:** 203
16:1–3   **Vol. 1:** 159
16:1   **Vol. 1:** 324, 490   **Vol. 2:** 126
16:2   **Vol. 3:** 1043
16:3   **Vol. 1:** 310   **Vol. 2:** 451, 641   **Vol. 3:** 431
16:4   **Vol. 1:** 136, 199, 330–331   **Vol. 2:** 135, 451, 718   **Vol. 3:** 773–774
16:5   **Vol. 1:** 303   **Vol. 2:** 895
16:6–18   **Vol. 2:** 921
16:6 f   **Vol. 2:** 786   **Vol. 3:** 700
16:6   **Vol. 2:** 222–223
16:7   **Vol. 3:** 88, 700, 802
16:8   **Vol. 1:** 341
16:9 f   **Vol. 1:** 476, 570   **Vol. 3:** 700
16:9   **Vol. 1:** 421, 512   **Vol. 3:** 87, 515, 862
16:10–17   **Vol. 1:** 490
16:10   **Vol. 1:** 274   **Vol. 3:** 862
16:12   **Vol. 2:** 304, 550, 895
16:13   **Vol. 1:** 628   **Vol. 2:** 29, 875   **Vol. 3:** 410, 987, 990, 1063
16:14 f   **Vol. 3:** 1065
16:14   **Vol. 1:** 205, 361   **Vol. 2:** 94, 183
16:15   **Vol. 1:** 159, 689   **Vol. 2:** 250, 364   **Vol. 3:** 1063, 1065
16:16 ff   **Vol. 3:** 475
16:16–18   **Vol. 3:** 474
16:16   **Vol. 2:** 558, 875   **Vol. 3:** 81, 88
16:17   **Vol. 1:** 410   **Vol. 2:** 74, 113   **Vol. 3:** 47, 213, 941–942
16:18   **Vol. 1:** 340   **Vol. 2:** 609, 654   **Vol. 3:** 475, 846

16:19   **Vol. 1:** 168, 267   **Vol. 3:** 749
16:20   **Vol. 3:** 964
16:21   **Vol. 2:** 438
16:22 ff   **Vol. 3:** 87
16:22   **Vol. 1:** 163, 341, 407   **Vol. 3:** 964
16:23 f   **Vol. 1:** 340
16:23   **Vol. 1:** 163, 663   **Vol. 2:** 133, 136   **Vol. 3:** 857
16:24   **Vol. 1:** 663   **Vol. 2:** 136   **Vol. 3:** 794
16:25 ff   **Vol. 2:** 630   **Vol. 3:** 592
16:25   **Vol. 1:** 420   **Vol. 2:** 175   **Vol. 3:** 669–670, 675
16:26 f   **Vol. 2:** 30, 729
16:26   **Vol. 1:** 661   **Vol. 3:** 558–559
16:27   **Vol. 1:** 326   **Vol. 2:** 136   **Vol. 3:** 967
16:28   **Vol. 1:** 564   **Vol. 3:** 1157
16:29   **Vol. 1:** 610   **Vol. 2:** 493, 858
16:30   **Vol. 1:** 663   **Vol. 2:** 513   **Vol. 3:** 252
16:31–34   **Vol. 1:** 159
16:31   **Vol. 1:** 604   **Vol. 2:** 250   **Vol. 3:** 61, 213, 1212
16:32 f   **Vol. 2:** 176
16:32   **Vol. 3:** 1113
16:33   **Vol. 1:** 148–149, 152, 163   **Vol. 2:** 250
16:34   **Vol. 1:** 603   **Vol. 2:** 250, 354   **Vol. 3:** 1211, 1214
16:35 f   **Vol. 3:** 189, 964
16:35   **Vol. 1:** 407
16:37   **Vol. 1:** 163, 453   **Vol. 2:** 136, 139, 790
16:38   **Vol. 1:** 407   **Vol. 3:** 46, 964
16:39   **Vol. 1:** 571
16:40   **Vol. 1:** 570   **Vol. 2:** 136   **Vol. 3:** 87, 1063
17–24   **Vol. 3:** 821
17   **Vol. 3:** 65, 327
17:1–9   **Vol. 1:** 269
17:1   **Vol. 1:** 297   **Vol. 3:** 785
17:2   **Vol. 1:** 590   **Vol. 2:** 437   **Vol. 3:** 87, 410, 490, 492, 821
17:3   **Vol. 2:** 729   **Vol. 3:** 48, 723–724, 1199
17:4   **Vol. 1:** 361, 590   **Vol. 2:** 126, 300, 302   **Vol. 3:** 1063, 1065
17:5   **Vol. 1:** 267, 566   **Vol. 2:** 623, 789   **Vol. 3:** 750–751, 1167
17:6   **Vol. 1:** 411, 519, 691   **Vol. 2:** 285, 804
17:7   **Vol. 1:** 269, 330–331   **Vol. 2:** 380, 804   **Vol. 3:** 1157
17:8   **Vol. 2:** 804   **Vol. 3:** 710
17:9   **Vol. 3:** 252
17:10 f   **Vol. 3:** 87
17:10   **Vol. 1:** 297   **Vol. 3:** 785
17:11   **Vol. 1:** 188   **Vol. 2:** 364   **Vol. 3:** 490, 492, 746, 1114
17:12   **Vol. 2:** 126   **Vol. 3:** 1063, 1065
17:13   **Vol. 3:** 559, 710, 1113–1114
17:14   **Vol. 3:** 984
17:15   **Vol. 1:** 337, 472
17:16   **Vol. 1:** 110   **Vol. 2:** 74, 245   **Vol. 3:** 694

Acts *(cont'd)*

17:17	**Vol. 1:** 267, 361 **Vol. 3:** 87, 410, 785, 821
17:18	**Vol. 1:** 689 **Vol. 2:** 550 **Vol. 3:** 46, 261, 277, 822, 1036
17:19	**Vol. 2:** 85, 574, 670 **Vol. 3:** 749, 769
17:20	**Vol. 1:** 689 **Vol. 2:** 175
17:21	**Vol. 1:** 689 **Vol. 2:** 670
17:22–31	**Vol. 3:** 87
17:22	**Vol. 1:** 257, 453 **Vol. 2:** 85 **Vol. 3:** 431
17:23	**Vol. 1:** 689 **Vol. 2:** 74, 77, 93–94, 113, 406–407, 503 **Vol. 3:** 460–461, 489
17:24 f	**Vol. 2:** 73, 164
17:24	**Vol. 1:** 524 **Vol. 2:** 74, 77, 150, 193, 514, 721, 920 **Vol. 3:** 784–785, 793
17:25	**Vol. 2:** 149, 164, 480, 861 **Vol. 3:** 461, 707
17:26–29	**Vol. 3:** 331
17:26	**Vol. 1:** 221, 473, 477, 586 **Vol. 2:** 721, 921
17:27 f	**Vol. 2:** 85
17:27	**Vol. 3:** 529, 532
17:28 f	**Vol. 2:** 565
17:28	**Vol. 1:** 85 **Vol. 2:** 77, 480, 919–920 **Vol. 3:** 927, 1155
17:29	**Vol. 1:** 106, 175, 279 **Vol. 2:** 86, 96, 503 **Vol. 3:** 331
17:30	**Vol. 1:** 340–341 **Vol. 2:** 407 **Vol. 3:** 47, 844, 1113
17:31 f	**Vol. 3:** 261
17:31	**Vol. 1:** 326, 473 **Vol. 2:** 238, 365, 894, 920 **Vol. 3:** 361, 1210
17:32	**Vol. 3:** 277
17:32a	**Vol. 3:** 303
17:34	**Vol. 2:** 349
18–25	**Vol. 2:** 785
18:1	**Vol. 3:** 534, 1174
18:2	**Vol. 1:** 476 **Vol. 2:** 847 **Vol. 3:** 240, 534, 1065
18:3	**Vol. 1:** 279 **Vol. 3:** 812
18:4	**Vol. 1:** 361, 589 **Vol. 3:** 87, 410, 785, 821
18:5 ff	**Vol. 3:** 203
18:5	**Vol. 3:** 1044
18:6	**Vol. 1:** 222, 317 **Vol. 2:** 158, 794 **Vol. 3:** 343, 561
18:7	**Vol. 1:** 297, 361 **Vol. 2:** 85, 94 **Vol. 3:** 785
18:8	**Vol. 1:** 148, 159–160, 603 **Vol. 2:** 176, 250, 517
18:9	**Vol. 1:** 421, 512, 623 **Vol. 3:** 85, 515, 862
18:10	**Vol. 2:** 800
18:11	**Vol. 2:** 895 **Vol. 3:** 764, 1113
18:12 f	**Vol. 3:** 908
18:12–17	**Vol. 1:** 270
18:12	**Vol. 1:** 270 **Vol. 2:** 369
18:13	**Vol. 1:** 361 **Vol. 2:** 450 **Vol. 3:** 909
18:14	**Vol. 1:** 326 **Vol. 2:** 726, 728, 766 **Vol. 3:** 575
18:15	**Vol. 2:** 451
18:16 f	**Vol. 2:** 369
18:17	**Vol. 3:** 749, 903
18:18	**Vol. 1:** 203 **Vol. 2:** 157, 159, 162, 641, 867, 895 **Vol. 3:** 228, 431
18:19	**Vol. 1:** 297, 324 **Vol. 3:** 251, 785, 821
18:20	**Vol. 2:** 880 **Vol. 3:** 843
18:21	**Vol. 3:** 1021
18:23	**Vol. 1:** 490 **Vol. 3:** 843
18:24–28	**Vol. 3:** 87
18:24	**Vol. 1:** 324 **Vol. 3:** 490, 492, 1106, 1117
18:25 f	**Vol. 3:** 941
18:25	**Vol. 1:** 318 **Vol. 2:** 921 **Vol. 3:** 110, 694, 699–700, 763–764, 771, 942, 1117
18:26	**Vol. 2:** 736 **Vol. 3:** 751, 785, 942, 1065
18:27	**Vol. 1:** 261, 490 **Vol. 2:** 119 **Vol. 3:** 489, 746
18:28	**Vol. 2:** 790 **Vol. 3:** 490, 492, 764
19:1 ff	**Vol. 1:** 146, 148 **Vol. 3:** 699
19:1–21	**Vol. 2:** 921
19:1–7	**Vol. 2:** 785 **Vol. 3:** 458
19:1 f	**Vol. 3:** 699
19:1	**Vol. 1:** 490 **Vol. 3:** 1017
19:2	**Vol. 3:** 941
19:4 f	**Vol. 1:** 157–158
19:4	**Vol. 1:** 359 **Vol. 3:** 1208, 1212
19:5	**Vol. 2:** 176 **Vol. 3:** 61, 1209
19:6	**Vol. 1:** 528 **Vol. 2:** 42, 152, 611, 740, 786 **Vol. 3:** 86–87, 699–700, 1080
19:7	**Vol. 2:** 696 **Vol. 3:** 458
19:8 f	**Vol. 3:** 821
19:8	**Vol. 1:** 590 **Vol. 2:** 736 **Vol. 3:** 87, 410, 785
19:9	**Vol. 1:** 415, 473, 490, 593, 607, 733 **Vol. 2:** 155, 794, 895 **Vol. 3:** 941
19:10	**Vol. 2:** 126 **Vol. 3:** 1113–1114
19:11	**Vol. 2:** 603
19:12 f	**Vol. 3:** 694
19:12	**Vol. 3:** 167, 174, 475
19:13 ff	**Vol. 2:** 74 **Vol. 3:** 476
19:13 f	**Vol. 3:** 473
19:13–20	**Vol. 3:** 88
19:13–16	**Vol. 2:** 654 **Vol. 3:** 476
19:13	**Vol. 1:** 322 **Vol. 3:** 52, 473, 475, 737–738
19:15 f	**Vol. 3:** 694
19:15	**Vol. 2:** 655 **Vol. 3:** 475
19:16	**Vol. 1:** 313 **Vol. 2:** 519
19:17	**Vol. 1:** 609
19:18	**Vol. 1:** 346, 702 **Vol. 2:** 556–557
19:19	**Vol. 1:** 243, 267 **Vol. 2:** 74, 556–557 **Vol. 3:** 1157
19:20	**Vol. 2:** 130, 557 **Vol. 3:** 714, 718, 1113–1114
19:21–21:16	**Vol. 2:** 827
19:21–41	**Vol. 2:** 85

Acts *(cont'd)*

19:21   **Vol. 1:** 737   **Vol. 2:** 328, 666   **Vol. 3:** 700, 1183
19:22   **Vol. 3:** 843
19:23 ff   **Vol. 2:** 623
19:23–41   **Vol. 2:** 74
19:23–40   **Vol. 3:** 203
19:23   **Vol. 3:** 709–710, 837, 941
19:24   **Vol. 1:** 279   **Vol. 2:** 96   **Vol. 3:** 784–785
19:25–27   **Vol. 2:** 568
19:26 f   **Vol. 2:** 235
19:26   **Vol. 1:** 589   **Vol. 2:** 73, 801   **Vol. 3:** 784
19:27   **Vol. 1:** 419, 519   **Vol. 2:** 94, 235, 303, 426   **Vol. 3:** 824, 826, 1175
19:28   **Vol. 1:** 106, 110, 410, 739   **Vol. 3:** 947
19:29   **Vol. 3:** 521
19:30   **Vol. 1:** 490   **Vol. 2:** 789
19:31   **Vol. 2:** 549
19:32   **Vol. 1:** 303   **Vol. 3:** 521
19:33   **Vol. 2:** 789   **Vol. 3:** 558
19:34   **Vol. 3:** 114, 847
19:35–41   **Vol. 1:** 270
19:35   **Vol. 3:** 480, 796
19:36   **Vol. 3:** 1157
19:37   **Vol. 2:** 235
19:38   **Vol. 1:** 84, 267, 270, 279
19:39 f   **Vol. 1:** 303
19:39   **Vol. 1:** 577–578   **Vol. 2:** 789   **Vol. 3:** 521, 532
19:40   **Vol. 1:** 84, 419   **Vol. 2:** 139   **Vol. 3:** 189
19:41   **Vol. 3:** 521
20   **Vol. 1:** 364
20:1   **Vol. 1:** 490   **Vol. 2:** 623
20:2   **Vol. 2:** 126   **Vol. 3:** 87, 164
20:3   **Vol. 1:** 326   **Vol. 2:** 398, 827
20:4   **Vol. 1:** 656
20:5–15   **Vol. 1:** 490
20:5   **Vol. 1:** 322   **Vol. 3:** 224
20:6   **Vol. 1:** 634   **Vol. 2:** 550, 692
20:7 ff   **Vol. 2:** 632
20:7 f   **Vol. 1:** 297
20:7   **Vol. 1:** 326, 631   **Vol. 2:** 32, 518, 523   **Vol. 3:** 410, 412, 821
20:8   **Vol. 2:** 32, 486
20:9–12   **Vol. 1:** 446
20:9   **Vol. 1:** 609   **Vol. 2:** 198   **Vol. 3:** 589, 821, 1198
20:10   **Vol. 2:** 623, 919
20:11   **Vol. 2:** 289, 523
20:13 f   **Vol. 3:** 749
20:13   **Vol. 1:** 326
20:15   **Vol. 2:** 739
20:16   **Vol. 2:** 785   **Vol. 3:** 843
20:17–37   **Vol. 3:** 65
20:17   **Vol. 1:** 199   **Vol. 3:** 568
20:18 ff   **Vol. 3:** 844

20:18   **Vol. 3:** 843
20:19   **Vol. 2:** 263   **Vol. 3:** 802
20:20   **Vol. 2:** 250, 790   **Vol. 3:** 764
20:21   **Vol. 1:** 359   **Vol. 3:** 1213
20:22 f   **Vol. 2:** 921   **Vol. 3:** 1183
20:22   **Vol. 1:** 171, 325   **Vol. 3:** 700
20:23   **Vol. 2:** 809, 827   **Vol. 3:** 87, 224, 592, 700
20:24   **Vol. 2:** 62, 110, 112, 119, 359, 827   **Vol. 3:** 546, 947, 1044
20:25   **Vol. 3:** 52, 56, 87, 517
20:26 ff   **Vol. 3:** 1018
20:26   **Vol. 1:** 222
20:27   **Vol. 2:** 77   **Vol. 3:** 1017–1018
20:28   **Vol. 1:** 191–192, 199, 223, 303, 477   **Vol. 2:** 73, 83, 838, 921   **Vol. 3:** 166, 395, 568, 700, 1018
20:29   **Vol. 1:** 118, 261
20:30   **Vol. 1:** 490, 493
20:31   **Vol. 1:** 568   **Vol. 2:** 137
20:32   **Vol. 2:** 119, 230, 249, 252, 302   **Vol. 3:** 1114
20:33   **Vol. 2:** 96
20:34   **Vol. 3:** 547, 958
20:35   **Vol. 2:** 41, 514, 694   **Vol. 3:** 967, 994
20:36   **Vol. 2:** 859
20:37   **Vol. 1:** 241, 609   **Vol. 2:** 549
21:1–18   **Vol. 1:** 490
21:3   **Vol. 2:** 148
21:4   **Vol. 1:** 490   **Vol. 2:** 692, 827, 921   **Vol. 3:** 227, 700, 1022, 1183
21:5   **Vol. 1:** 286   **Vol. 2:** 859, 869   **Vol. 3:** 351
21:6   **Vol. 2:** 839
21:8   **Vol. 2:** 114, 550   **Vol. 3:** 548, 1067
21:9 ff   **Vol. 3:** 86
21:9–11   **Vol. 3:** 700
21:9   **Vol. 2:** 212, 689   **Vol. 3:** 81, 87, 1072
21:10 ff   **Vol. 2:** 827, 900
21:10 f   **Vol. 3:** 86
21:10   **Vol. 3:** 87, 227
21:11   **Vol. 2:** 149–150, 921   **Vol. 3:** 85–87, 121, 1183
21:12–14   **Vol. 3:** 1183
21:12   **Vol. 3:** 1183
21:13   **Vol. 2:** 416, 623   **Vol. 3:** 118, 257, 546
21:14   **Vol. 1:** 591   **Vol. 3:** 111
21:15–20   **Vol. 2:** 451
21:15   **Vol. 2:** 328
21:16   **Vol. 1:** 167, 490
21:17–26   **Vol. 1:** 310
21:17   **Vol. 3:** 746
21:18 ff   **Vol. 3:** 592
21:18–26   **Vol. 3:** 101
21:18   **Vol. 1:** 199   **Vol. 2:** 328
21:19   **Vol. 1:** 576
21:20 ff   **Vol. 2:** 641
21:20   **Vol. 2:** 450   **Vol. 3:** 686
21:21   **Vol. 1:** 310, 607   **Vol. 2:** 450, 795   **Vol. 3:** 764, 771, 944

Acts *(cont'd)*

21:22	**Vol. 1:** 733
21:23	**Vol. 2:** 689, 867
21:24 ff	**Vol. 2:** 641
21:24–26	**Vol. 3:** 101
21:24	**Vol. 1:** 203 **Vol. 2:** 135, 450, 452 **Vol. 3:** 771
21:25	**Vol. 1:** 226 **Vol. 2:** 135, 284–286, 682 **Vol. 3:** 432, 931
21:26 ff	**Vol. 2:** 236
21:26	**Vol. 2:** 451 **Vol. 3:** 46–47, 101, 431, 793
21:27 f	**Vol. 2:** 451
21:28 f	**Vol. 3:** 949
21:28	**Vol. 1:** 641–642 **Vol. 2:** 126, 310, 438, 450, 799 **Vol. 3:** 764
21:29	**Vol. 1:** 695 **Vol. 3:** 515
21:30 ff	**Vol. 2:** 623
21:30	**Vol. 2:** 30, 730 **Vol. 3:** 749
21:31 ff	**Vol. 2:** 699
21:31–35	**Vol. 3:** 788
21:31	**Vol. 1:** 430
21:32	**Vol. 3:** 903, 964
21:33	**Vol. 1:** 341 **Vol. 3:** 749
21:34	**Vol. 1:** 410 **Vol. 2:** 623 **Vol. 3:** 965
21:35	**Vol. 3:** 711
21:36	**Vol. 2:** 799
21:37–40	**Vol. 2:** 434
21:37	**Vol. 2:** 126, 699 **Vol. 3:** 965
21:38 ff	**Vol. 3:** 729
21:38	**Vol. 1:** 532, 717 **Vol. 2:** 699 **Vol. 3:** 1007
21:39	**Vol. 2:** 328, 804, 860
21:40	**Vol. 2:** 309 **Vol. 3:** 558
22:1–21	**Vol. 1:** 136
22:2	**Vol. 2:** 309 **Vol. 3:** 111
22:3	**Vol. 2:** 315, 328, 451 **Vol. 3:** 778, 873, 1167, 1178
22:4–16	**Vol. 1:** 183
22:4	**Vol. 2:** 136, 368, 806 **Vol. 3:** 941–942
22:5	**Vol. 1:** 197 **Vol. 3:** 1043
22:6–11	**Vol. 3:** 330
22:6	**Vol. 2:** 193, 493 **Vol. 3:** 1203
22:7 f	**Vol. 2:** 806
22:7	**Vol. 3:** 114
22:8	**Vol. 2:** 333, 513
22:9	**Vol. 2:** 493 **Vol. 3:** 114
22:10	**Vol. 1:** 476 **Vol. 2:** 513
22:11	**Vol. 2:** 46, 493 **Vol. 3:** 520, 1180
22:12	**Vol. 2:** 91, 451 **Vol. 3:** 1043
22:13	**Vol. 3:** 519, 846
22:14	**Vol. 1:** 476 **Vol. 2:** 73, 176 **Vol. 3:** 114, 361, 1022, 1191
22:15	**Vol. 2:** 176 **Vol. 3:** 1044
22:16	**Vol. 1:** 146, 148, 152, 154, 157–158, 276 **Vol. 3:** 990, 1210
22:17 ff	**Vol. 3:** 87
22:17–21	**Vol. 1:** 476
22:17 f	**Vol. 3:** 700
22:17	**Vol. 1:** 528 **Vol. 2:** 236 **Vol. 3:** 793, 913
22:18	**Vol. 3:** 88
22:19	**Vol. 1:** 163 **Vol. 2:** 136 **Vol. 3:** 785, 1212
22:20	**Vol. 2:** 854 **Vol. 3:** 1044
22:21	**Vol. 1:** 136 **Vol. 3:** 38
22:23	**Vol. 1:** 449
22:24	**Vol. 1:** 163, 341, 410 **Vol. 2:** 139, 699 **Vol. 3:** 965
22:25 f	**Vol. 3:** 964
22:26–29	**Vol. 2:** 699
22:28	**Vol. 2:** 157, 804
22:29	**Vol. 1:** 607
22:30–23:10	**Vol. 1:** 364 **Vol. 3:** 40
22:30	**Vol. 1:** 83, 341 **Vol. 3:** 179, 1198
23:1 ff	**Vol. 3:** 39
23:1	**Vol. 1:** 353 **Vol. 2:** 101, 804 **Vol. 3:** 520
23:2 f	**Vol. 3:** 903
23:3 ff	**Vol. 3:** 40
23:3	**Vol. 1:** 205, 265, 341 **Vol. 2:** 365, 451 **Vol. 3:** 588, 948
23:4 f	**Vol. 3:** 35, 347
23:5	**Vol. 1:** 168
23:6–9	**Vol. 3:** 440
23:6	**Vol. 1:** 288, 446 **Vol. 2:** 242, 303, 365 **Vol. 3:** 439
23:7	**Vol. 1:** 733 **Vol. 3:** 439, 544
23:8 ff	**Vol. 1:** 346
23:8 f	**Vol. 3:** 695
23:8	**Vol. 1:** 101 **Vol. 2:** 812 **Vol. 3:** 439
23:9	**Vol. 1:** 564 **Vol. 2:** 303, 812 **Vol. 3:** 482, 529
23:10	**Vol. 1:** 341, 623 **Vol. 2:** 91, 699 **Vol. 3:** 602, 964–965
23:11	**Vol. 1:** 328, 421, 476, 512 **Vol. 2:** 666 **Vol. 3:** 85, 88, 1043
23:12–14	**Vol. 1:** 430
23:12	**Vol. 2:** 689
23:14	**Vol. 1:** 415
23:15	**Vol. 1:** 326 **Vol. 2:** 489, 699
23:16	**Vol. 3:** 965
23:17 ff	**Vol. 2:** 699
23:17	**Vol. 3:** 964
23:18	**Vol. 3:** 592
23:19	**Vol. 3:** 749
23:21	**Vol. 1:** 591
23:22	**Vol. 1:** 340 **Vol. 2:** 489, 699
23:23	**Vol. 3:** 964
23:24	**Vol. 1:** 270 **Vol. 3:** 211
23:25	**Vol. 3:** 489, 904
23:26–30	**Vol. 1:** 247
23:26	**Vol. 1:** 247, 270 **Vol. 2:** 358 **Vol. 3:** 718
23:27	**Vol. 1:** 344, 486 **Vol. 3:** 964
23:28	**Vol. 1:** 84 **Vol. 2:** 139
23:29	**Vol. 1:** 84 **Vol. 2:** 450–451 **Vol. 3:** 592
23:30	**Vol. 1:** 83, 340

Acts *(cont'd)*

23:31	**Vol. 3:** 749, 1181
23:32	**Vol. 3:** 965
23:33	**Vol. 1:** 270
23:34	**Vol. 1:** 114 **Vol. 3:** 1188
23:35	**Vol. 1:** 83, 341 **Vol. 2:** 135
24	**Vol. 3:** 65
24:1	**Vol. 1:** 270 **Vol. 2:** 489 **Vol. 3:** 40
24:2	**Vol. 1:** 83 **Vol. 2:** 780
24:3	**Vol. 1:** 695 **Vol. 3:** 718, 818
24:4	**Vol. 2:** 221, 258
24:5	**Vol. 1:** 519, 535 **Vol. 2:** 333, 438
24:6	**Vol. 2:** 365 **Vol. 3:** 717, 793, 802
24:7	**Vol. 2:** 699
24:8	**Vol. 1:** 341 **Vol. 2:** 365
24:10	**Vol. 1:** 270
24:11	**Vol. 2:** 696, 877
24:12	**Vol. 1:** 297 **Vol. 2:** 236 **Vol. 3:** 785, 793, 821
24:13	**Vol. 1:** 83
24:14	**Vol. 1:** 535, 604 **Vol. 2:** 451 **Vol. 3:** 550, 941, 1211
24:15	**Vol. 1:** 326 **Vol. 2:** 73, 242, 245 **Vol. 3:** 303, 361, 575
24:16	**Vol. 1:** 350, 353, 495 **Vol. 2:** 707 **Vol. 3:** 1175, 1192
24:17 f	**Vol. 3:** 431
24:17	**Vol. 2:** 597
24:18	**Vol. 2:** 236, 623 **Vol. 3:** 101, 793
24:19	**Vol. 1:** 83 **Vol. 2:** 899
24:20	**Vol. 1:** 364 **Vol. 3:** 529, 575
24:21	**Vol. 3:** 114
24:22	**Vol. 2:** 699 **Vol. 3:** 941
24:23	**Vol. 2:** 222 **Vol. 3:** 547, 717, 964
24:24	**Vol. 3:** 1213
24:25	**Vol. 1:** 495 **Vol. 2:** 365 **Vol. 3:** 361, 750, 821
24:26	**Vol. 2:** 845
24:27	**Vol. 1:** 737 **Vol. 2:** 119
25 – 28	**Vol. 1:** 276
25:2	**Vol. 2:** 489 **Vol. 3:** 39
25:3	**Vol. 2:** 119 **Vol. 3:** 941
25:5	**Vol. 1:** 83
25:6	**Vol. 1:** 341 **Vol. 2:** 369
25:7	**Vol. 1:** 261 **Vol. 3:** 570 – 571
25:8	**Vol. 1:** 269 **Vol. 2:** 236, 450 **Vol. 3:** 793
25:9	**Vol. 2:** 119
25:10 f	**Vol. 3:** 575
25:10	**Vol. 2:** 369
25:11	**Vol. 1:** 83, 269 **Vol. 2:** 116, 119, 858 **Vol. 3:** 349, 1157
25:12	**Vol. 1:** 363
25:13 f	**Vol. 2:** 378
25:14	**Vol. 3:** 592
25:15	**Vol. 2:** 370, 489
25:16	**Vol. 1:** 83 – 84 **Vol. 2:** 116, 119, 438
25:17	**Vol. 1:** 341 **Vol. 2:** 369
25:18	**Vol. 1:** 83 **Vol. 2:** 139

25:19	**Vol. 1:** 453
25:20	**Vol. 3:** 532
25:21	**Vol. 1:** 269, 341 **Vol. 2:** 93
25:22	**Vol. 3:** 1017
25:23	**Vol. 1:** 341 **Vol. 2:** 699
25:24	**Vol. 1:** 411, 733 **Vol. 2:** 882
25:25	**Vol. 2:** 93 **Vol. 3:** 750, 1157
25:26	**Vol. 3:** 349, 489
25:27	**Vol. 2:** 139 **Vol. 3:** 592, 822, 1118
26	**Vol. 3:** 65
26:1	**Vol. 2:** 150
26:2 – 18	**Vol. 1:** 136
26:2	**Vol. 1:** 84
26:3	**Vol. 2:** 437, 860
26:4	**Vol. 1:** 166 **Vol. 2:** 675
26:5	**Vol. 1:** 535, 693 **Vol. 2:** 451 **Vol. 3:** 551, 1043
26:6	**Vol. 2:** 786 **Vol. 3:** 71, 550
26:7	**Vol. 1:** 84 **Vol. 2:** 139, 695 **Vol. 3:** 550, 871
26:8	**Vol. 2:** 364 **Vol. 3:** 304
26:9 – 18	**Vol. 1:** 183
26:9 – 11	**Vol. 3:** 1199
26:9	**Vol. 2:** 333 **Vol. 3:** 822, 1157
26:10	**Vol. 1:** 305 **Vol. 2:** 136 **Vol. 3:** 482
26:11	**Vol. 1:** 730 **Vol. 3:** 785
26:12 – 18	**Vol. 3:** 330
26:13	**Vol. 2:** 193, 486, 493 **Vol. 3:** 732, 941
26:14 f	**Vol. 2:** 806
26:14	**Vol. 1:** 511 **Vol. 2:** 155, 309 **Vol. 3:** 114
26:15 – 18	**Vol. 2:** 302
26:15	**Vol. 2:** 513
26:16 f	**Vol. 1:** 136
26:16	**Vol. 1:** 476 **Vol. 3:** 285, 515, 546, 1044, 1191
26:17 f	**Vol. 3:** 38
26:18	**Vol. 1:** 355, 359, 424 **Vol. 2:** 230, 654, 726, 728, 920 **Vol. 3:** 213, 471, 1213
26:19	**Vol. 1:** 593 **Vol. 3:** 1191
26:20	**Vol. 1:** 355, 359 **Vol. 3:** 47, 1150
26:21	**Vol. 3:** 793, 802
26:22	**Vol. 1:** 326 **Vol. 2:** 426, 641
26:23	**Vol. 1:** 326, 667 – 668 **Vol. 2:** 113, 793 **Vol. 3:** 304, 722, 724, 1113
26:24	**Vol. 1:** 529 **Vol. 3:** 113, 493
26:25	**Vol. 1:** 502, 529 **Vol. 3:** 718, 884, 1122
26:26	**Vol. 1:** 591 **Vol. 2:** 736 **Vol. 3:** 389
26:27	**Vol. 1:** 604
26:27a	**Vol. 3:** 1211
26:28	**Vol. 1:** 123, 590 **Vol. 2:** 343
26:29	**Vol. 2:** 867
26:30	**Vol. 1:** 270 **Vol. 3:** 588
26:31	**Vol. 3:** 592, 1157
26:32	**Vol. 1:** 269 **Vol. 3:** 189
27:1 – 28:16	**Vol. 1:** 490
27:1	**Vol. 2:** 93 **Vol. 3:** 964
27:3	**Vol. 2:** 549 – 550, 739
27:4	**Vol. 3:** 1002
27:6	**Vol. 3:** 964

Acts *(cont'd)*

27:7	**Vol. 3:** 1002
27:9	**Vol. 3:** 843
27:10	**Vol. 3:** 27
27:11	**Vol. 1:** 198, 591, 593 **Vol. 3:** 964
27:12	**Vol. 3:** 1017
27:13	**Vol. 1:** 697 **Vol. 3:** 822, 1003
27:14	**Vol. 3:** 1002, 1199
27:15	**Vol. 3:** 1002
27:20	**Vol. 3:** 211, 252, 317, 319, 731, 735
27:21	**Vol. 1:** 593 **Vol. 3:** 27, 136
27:22	**Vol. 3:** 87, 683
27:23–24	**Vol. 1:** 512
27:23	**Vol. 1:** 421, 474 **Vol. 3:** 87
27:24	**Vol. 1:** 269, 474, 623 **Vol. 2:** 116, 119, 666
27:25	**Vol. 3:** 1211
27:27 f	**Vol. 1:** 103
27:29	**Vol. 2:** 689, 867
27:30	**Vol. 1:** 326, 559 **Vol. 3:** 984
27:31	**Vol. 3:** 211, 964
27:33	**Vol. 3:** 717, 750–751
27:34	**Vol. 1:** 203, 609 **Vol. 3:** 211, 1204
27:35	**Vol. 3:** 819
27:36	**Vol. 3:** 751
27:37	**Vol. 3:** 683
27:38	**Vol. 3:** 984
27:39	**Vol. 1:** 240
27:40	**Vol. 3:** 984
27:41	**Vol. 3:** 180, 560, 711
27:42	**Vol. 3:** 1017
27:43	**Vol. 1:** 341 **Vol. 2:** 222 **Vol. 3:** 211, 964, 1017
27:44	**Vol. 3:** 211, 252
28	**Vol. 1:** 364
28:1–6	**Vol. 1:** 510
28:1	**Vol. 3:** 211
28:2 f	**Vol. 1:** 656
28:2	**Vol. 1:** 318 **Vol. 2:** 550 **Vol. 3:** 860, 1004
28:3	**Vol. 2:** 33
28:4	**Vol. 2:** 96 **Vol. 3:** 211, 984
28:5	**Vol. 1:** 564, 656 **Vol. 2:** 921 **Vol. 3:** 561, 723
28:6	**Vol. 1:** 610
28:7	**Vol. 1:** 690 **Vol. 2:** 550
28:8	**Vol. 1:** 656 **Vol. 2:** 151
28:9	**Vol. 3:** 252
28:10	**Vol. 2:** 50 **Vol. 3:** 958
28:12	**Vol. 3:** 227
28:13	**Vol. 1:** 322 **Vol. 3:** 1003
28:14	**Vol. 1:** 570 **Vol. 2:** 692 **Vol. 3:** 227
28:15	**Vol. 1:** 325
28:16	**Vol. 3:** 964
28:17	**Vol. 2:** 437, 799 **Vol. 3:** 592
28:18	**Vol. 2:** 139, 365 **Vol. 3:** 189
28:19	**Vol. 1:** 83, 269 **Vol. 2:** 663
28:20	**Vol. 1:** 570 **Vol. 2:** 314–315
28:21	**Vol. 1:** 567 **Vol. 3:** 492
28:22	**Vol. 1:** 535 **Vol. 2:** 617
28:23	**Vol. 2:** 314, 444, 641 **Vol. 3:** 65, 87, 1044
28:24–28	**Vol. 2:** 37
28:24	**Vol. 1:** 591
28:25–28	**Vol. 3:** 87
28:25	**Vol. 1:** 736 **Vol. 3:** 699
28:26 f	**Vol. 2:** 753, 799 **Vol. 3:** 131–132, 313
28:27	**Vol. 1:** 261 **Vol. 2:** 156, 178
28:28	**Vol. 3:** 221
28:30 f	**Vol. 3:** 226, 1114
28:30	**Vol. 3:** 746
28:31	**Vol. 1:** 590 **Vol. 2:** 340, 387, 736 **Vol. 3:** 52, 56, 764

Romans

1–11	**Vol. 1:** 65
1–8	**Vol. 1:** 370 **Vol. 3:** 251, 368, 580
1–7	**Vol. 3:** 38
1–4	**Vol. 1:** 436 **Vol. 2:** 800
1–3	**Vol. 1:** 112 **Vol. 2:** 366–367, 400 **Vol. 3:** 164
1	**Vol. 2:** 570 **Vol. 3:** 372
1:1 ff	**Vol. 2:** 111
1:1–7	**Vol. 1:** 247
1:1–4	**Vol. 3:** 62
1:1	**Vol. 1:** 276, 474, 638, 718, 720 **Vol. 2:** 111 **Vol. 3:** 596, 601
1:2–4	**Vol. 3:** 1122
1:2	**Vol. 2:** 176, 228, 605 **Vol. 3:** 70, 313, 487–492
1:3 f	**Vol. 3:** 61, 243, 299, 323, 639, 1110, 1171, 1188
1:3–4	**Vol. 3:** 643, 651
1:3	**Vol. 1:** 427, 473, 675 **Vol. 2:** 79, 314, 378 **Vol. 3:** 643–644, 661, 1073, 1199
1:4	**Vol. 1:** 323, 675 **Vol. 2:** 79, 81, 203, 230, 340, 604–605 **Vol. 3:** 129, 277, 299–300, 304, 643, 703, 705, 1073
1:5	**Vol. 1:** 129 **Vol. 2:** 121, 179, 654, 793–794 **Vol. 3:** 38, 314, 748–749, 1150
1:6 f	**Vol. 1:** 275, 298
1:7	**Vol. 1:** 275, 300, 305, 620 **Vol. 2:** 229, 516, 544, 780–781
1:7b	**Vol. 2:** 874
1:8 ff	**Vol. 2:** 874
1:8–12	**Vol. 1:** 247
1:8	**Vol. 1:** 599, 601 **Vol. 2:** 73, 873 **Vol. 3:** 611, 818
1:9 f	**Vol. 2:** 874–875
1:9	**Vol. 3:** 230, 246, 550–551, 643–644, 693, 742, 1043
1:10 ff	**Vol. 2:** 826
1:10	**Vol. 2:** 861, 874 **Vol. 3:** 943, 1021
1:11 f	**Vol. 1:** 129
1:11	**Vol. 1:** 458 **Vol. 2:** 41, 43 **Vol. 3:** 703, 706–707
1:12 f	**Vol. 1:** 399

Romans *(cont'd)*

1:13	**Vol. 1:** 697, 723 **Vol. 2:** 223, 406 **Vol. 3:** 252, 1022
1:14	**Vol. 2:** 126–127, 668
1:15	**Vol. 2:** 112 **Vol. 3:** 214
1:16 f	**Vol. 2:** 111 **Vol. 3:** 365, 371, 1031
1:16	**Vol. 1:** 397, 601, 666–667 **Vol. 2:** 78, 127, 314, 604–605 **Vol. 3:** 214, 367, 563
1:17	**Vol. 1:** 289 **Vol. 2:** 78, 111, 447 **Vol. 3:** 312, 315, 321, 362, 365, 1171, 1177, 1189–1190
1:18 ff	**Vol. 2:** 460, 566, 682 **Vol. 3:** 315, 332, 576, 1031
1:18–5:21	**Vol. 1:** 401
1:18–4:25	**Vol. 3:** 368
1:18–3:20	**Vol. 1:** 112 **Vol. 2:** 472 **Vol. 3:** 580, 584
1:18–32	**Vol. 2:** 127, 286, 793 **Vol. 3:** 163, 1202
1:18–23	**Vol. 3:** 310
1:18	**Vol. 1:** 112, 417 **Vol. 2:** 76, 94, 193, 399 **Vol. 3:** 197, 575–576, 580, 885, 1199
1:19 ff	**Vol. 2:** 77 **Vol. 3:** 327, 331
1:19–23	**Vol. 3:** 331
1:19 f	**Vol. 2:** 400, 503
1:19	**Vol. 3:** 320–321
1:20 ff	**Vol. 1:** 382
1:20	**Vol. 1:** 385 **Vol. 2:** 77–78, 86, 139, 604 **Vol. 3:** 128, 321, 515, 829, 885, 1154, 1185, 1187
1:20b	**Vol. 1:** 386
1:21 ff	**Vol. 1:** 112 **Vol. 2:** 566
1:21 f	**Vol. 2:** 78 **Vol. 3:** 132
1:21	**Vol. 1:** 424, 551–552 **Vol. 2:** 47, 161, 183, 399, 874 **Vol. 3:** 132, 200, 333, 576, 819, 821, 1192
1:22 f	**Vol. 2:** 400
1:23	**Vol. 1:** 175, 469 **Vol. 2:** 46, 76–77, 503, 874 **Vol. 3:** 167, 304, 331
1:24	**Vol. 1:** 235, 457 **Vol. 2:** 51, 155–156, 182, 368, 567 **Vol. 3:** 1175, 1192
1:25	**Vol. 1:** 99, 385, 461 **Vol. 2:** 93–94, 399, 472, 874 **Vol. 3:** 167, 550, 576, 830, 885
1:25b	**Vol. 1:** 213
1:26 ff	**Vol. 2:** 563
1:26–32	**Vol. 3:** 929
1:26	**Vol. 2:** 50–51, 155, 660 **Vol. 3:** 167, 722
1:27	**Vol. 1:** 460–461, 701 **Vol. 2:** 459–460, 569–570 **Vol. 3:** 197, 751
1:28 ff	**Vol. 3:** 1157
1:28	**Vol. 2:** 155, 399 **Vol. 3:** 28, 808–809
1:29 ff	**Vol. 3:** 31
1:29–32	**Vol. 2:** 597
1:29–31	**Vol. 3:** 31
1:29 f	**Vol. 3:** 28
1:29	**Vol. 1:** 138, 557, 563 **Vol. 3:** 197, 346, 576
1:30	**Vol. 1:** 589, 593 **Vol. 2:** 86, 435 **Vol. 3:** 28, 30, 32, 345–346
1:31	**Vol. 2:** 539, 542 **Vol. 3:** 132
1:32	**Vol. 2:** 77, 399, 446 **Vol. 3:** 332, 349, 363, 581, 1155, 1157
2 f	**Vol. 3:** 168
2	**Vol. 3:** 372
2:1–3:20	**Vol. 3:** 163
2:1	**Vol. 2:** 139, 365, 566, 739
2:2 f	**Vol. 2:** 365
2:2	**Vol. 2:** 449
2:3	**Vol. 2:** 766 **Vol. 3:** 824–825
2:4	**Vol. 1:** 461 **Vol. 2:** 79, 106, 766, 770
2:5 f	**Vol. 3:** 1151
2:5	**Vol. 1:** 106, 112, 358, 417 **Vol. 2:** 76, 155–156, 183–184, 834, 836, 894, 926 **Vol. 3:** 315
2:6 f	**Vol. 2:** 446
2:6	**Vol. 1:** 323 **Vol. 3:** 136, 142, 1200
2:7	**Vol. 1:** 113, 470 **Vol. 2:** 47, 50, 101, 446, 774–775 **Vol. 3:** 142, 302, 368, 832
2:8	**Vol. 1:** 106, 591 **Vol. 3:** 575–576, 885
2:9 f†	**Vol. 1:** 667 **Vol. 2:** 127
2:9	**Vol. 1:** 106, 666 **Vol. 2:** 127, 446, 808 **Vol. 3:** 683
2:10	**Vol. 1:** 666 **Vol. 2:** 47, 50 **Vol. 3:** 1151
2:11 f	**Vol. 2:** 446
2:11	**Vol. 1:** 587
2:12–16	**Vol. 2:** 77 **Vol. 3:** 327
2:12	**Vol. 2:** 365, 445–446 **Vol. 3:** 163
2:13	**Vol. 2:** 176–177, 445–446 **Vol. 3:** 362–363, 1155, 1202
2:14 ff	**Vol. 1:** 350
2:14–16	**Vol. 2:** 127, 660
2:14 f	**Vol. 2:** 794, 905 **Vol. 3:** 584
2:14	**Vol. 2:** 177, 444, 922–923 **Vol. 3:** 927
2:15	**Vol. 1:** 83, 350, 353 **Vol. 2:** 183, 444, 446, 567 **Vol. 3:** 490, 824, 1042
2:16	**Vol. 2:** 111, 113, 218, 365, 446 **Vol. 3:** 61–62, 611
2:17 ff	**Vol. 2:** 566 **Vol. 3:** 1020
2:17–29	**Vol. 3:** 584
2:17–24	**Vol. 2:** 448
2:17–20	**Vol. 2:** 216, 655
2:17	**Vol. 2:** 444, 652, 655 **Vol. 3:** 258
2:18	**Vol. 2:** 399 **Vol. 3:** 771, 808
2:19	**Vol. 1:** 220, 424, 592 **Vol. 3:** 942
2:20	**Vol. 1:** 282, 637, 708 **Vol. 2:** 216, 399 **Vol. 3:** 778, 885
2:21	**Vol. 3:** 54, 764
2:22–24	**Vol. 1:** 282
2:22	**Vol. 2:** 235
2:23 ff	**Vol. 3:** 584
2:23	**Vol. 1:** 228, 637
2:24	**Vol. 2:** 653 **Vol. 3:** 342–343
2:25–29	**Vol. 2:** 573

Romans (*cont'd*)

2:25	**Vol. 1:** 311 **Vol. 3:** 1158
2:26	**Vol. 2:** 135 **Vol. 3:** 363, 824, 1175
2:27	**Vol. 2:** 62, 660 **Vol. 3:** 493, 1183
2:28 f	**Vol. 2:** 786 **Vol. 3:** 702, 1199
2:28	**Vol. 2:** 218 **Vol. 3:** 164, 320
2:29	**Vol. 2:** 218 **Vol. 3:** 142, 320, 493, 701, 817
3 f	**Vol. 3:** 168
3	**Vol. 3:** 165, 432
3:1 f	**Vol. 1:** 311
3:1–4	**Vol. 3:** 320
3:1	**Vol. 1:** 730
3:2	**Vol. 3:** 1106, 1118, 1211
3:3	**Vol. 1:** 73 **Vol. 2:** 77 **Vol. 3:** 378
3:4	**Vol. 1:** 181, 743 **Vol. 2:** 472 **Vol. 3:** 363, 886
3:5 ff	**Vol. 3:** 364
3:5	**Vol. 2:** 565 **Vol. 3:** 362, 372, 575–576
3:6	**Vol. 1:** 524 **Vol. 2:** 365
3:7	**Vol. 1:** 730
3:8	**Vol. 2:** 365
3:9	**Vol. 1:** 202 **Vol. 2:** 127
3:10	**Vol. 3:** 362
3:11	**Vol. 3:** 131–132, 532
3:12	**Vol. 2:** 781
3:13	**Vol. 1:** 265 **Vol. 2:** 28, 726 **Vol. 3:** 1079
3:13a	**Vol. 2:** 727
3:14	**Vol. 1:** 202, 416
3:15	**Vol. 1:** 222, 239 **Vol. 2:** 28, 443, 854
3:16	**Vol. 3:** 859, 940
3:17	**Vol. 2:** 781 **Vol. 3:** 940
3:18	**Vol. 2:** 28
3:19 ff	**Vol. 1:** 719
3:19 f	**Vol. 2:** 450
3:19	**Vol. 1:** 417, 524 **Vol. 2:** 444 **Vol. 3:** 951
3:20–27	**Vol. 3:** 161
3:20	**Vol. 1:** 675, 730 **Vol. 2:** 101, 398, 446 **Vol. 3:** 363–364, 580, 1151, 1178, 1190
3:21 ff	**Vol. 1:** 385, 702 **Vol. 2:** 119 **Vol. 3:** 364, 372, 581
3:21–31	**Vol. 2:** 120
3:21–30	**Vol. 1:** 157
3:21–28	**Vol. 1:** 702
3:21–26	**Vol. 3:** 163, 954
3:21 f	**Vol. 3:** 362
3:21	**Vol. 2:** 282, 446 **Vol. 3:** 81, 312, 315, 321, 365, 831, 837, 1043
3:21b	**Vol. 2:** 444
3:22 ff	**Vol. 1:** 158
3:22 f	**Vol. 3:** 1190
3:22	**Vol. 1:** 601 **Vol. 2:** 566 **Vol. 3:** 1190
3:23 ff	**Vol. 2:** 366
3:23	**Vol. 1:** 719 **Vol. 2:** 46, 161, 446 **Vol. 3:** 954
3:24 ff	**Vol. 2:** 119
3:24	**Vol. 2:** 41–42, 120 **Vol. 3:** 199, 363–364, 576, 701, 1190, 1192
3:25 f	**Vol. 1:** 398, 437 **Vol. 2:** 446 **Vol. 3:** 169, 362, 364, 581, 1176, 1185, 1190
3:25†	**Vol. 1:** 223, 417, 697, 701–702 **Vol. 2:** 339, 407, 766–767 **Vol. 3:** 163, 165, 170, 198–199, 431, 435, 579, 1175, 1184, 1190, 1212
3:25b	**Vol. 3:** 165
3:26	**Vol. 3:** 165, 362–363, 365, 576, 837, 1190
3:27–31	**Vol. 1:** 601
3:27 f	**Vol. 3:** 1151
3:27	**Vol. 1:** 228 **Vol. 2:** 446
3:28	**Vol. 2:** 444, 446 **Vol. 3:** 363, 824–825
3:29 f	**Vol. 2:** 127, 446, 721
3:29	**Vol. 2:** 434, 566, 793
3:30	**Vol. 1:** 309–311, 375 **Vol. 2:** 73 **Vol. 3:** 363, 372, 1171, 1176, 1189
3:31	**Vol. 1:** 73, 719 **Vol. 2:** 445, 450 **Vol. 3:** 185, 320, 580
3:35	**Vol. 3:** 165
4	**Vol. 3:** 366, 825–826, 906
4:1–5:1	**Vol. 1:** 289
4:1–25	**Vol. 3:** 1151
4:1–13	**Vol. 1:** 78
4:1–3	**Vol. 1:** 79
4:1	**Vol. 3:** 529, 1199
4:2	**Vol. 1:** 228 **Vol. 2:** 120 **Vol. 3:** 363
4:3 ff	**Vol. 3:** 168
4:3–8	**Vol. 3:** 169
4:3–6	**Vol. 3:** 825
4:3	**Vol. 1:** 78, 157, 596, 604 **Vol. 2:** 73, 301 **Vol. 3:** 169, 362, 369, 490, 824, 1175, 1187, 1214
4:4–8	**Vol. 1:** 79
4:4	**Vol. 1:** 675 **Vol. 2:** 118, 120 **Vol. 3:** 142, 824
4:5	**Vol. 1:** 157 **Vol. 2:** 94, 388 **Vol. 3:** 362–363, 824, 1212, 1214
4:6	**Vol. 1:** 216, 427 **Vol. 3:** 362, 824, 1151
4:7–12	**Vol. 1:** 311
4:7	**Vol. 1:** 702 **Vol. 3:** 169
4:8	**Vol. 2:** 513 **Vol. 3:** 824–825
4:9 ff	**Vol. 1:** 601 **Vol. 3:** 824
4:9–25	**Vol. 3:** 393
4:9–12	**Vol. 1:** 79
4:9	**Vol. 1:** 216, 596 **Vol. 3:** 362–363, 1187–1188
4:10	**Vol. 1:** 309–310 **Vol. 3:** 825
4:11 f	**Vol. 1:** 311
4:11	**Vol. 1:** 154, 157, 601 **Vol. 3:** 362–364, 368, 499, 1182, 1187, 1190
4:12	**Vol. 2:** 452 **Vol. 3:** 1189
4:13 ff	**Vol. 2:** 300, 312
4:13–16	**Vol. 3:** 584
4:13 f	**Vol. 2:** 302
4:13	**Vol. 1:** 79 **Vol. 2:** 301 **Vol. 3:** 72, 362, 364, 368
4:14–20	**Vol. 3:** 585

Romans *(cont'd)*

4:14	**Vol. 1:** 547 **Vol. 2:** 301 **Vol. 3:** 72, 1188
4:15	**Vol. 1:** 112 **Vol. 2:** 444 **Vol. 3:** 584
4:16 ff	**Vol. 3:** 523
4:16 f	**Vol. 2:** 794
4:16	**Vol. 1:** 79, 157, 659 **Vol. 2:** 120 **Vol. 3:** 1184, 1187
4:17 ff	**Vol. 1:** 601
4:17	**Vol. 1:** 275, 384, 436, 440, 445–446, 477 **Vol. 2:** 480, 605 **Vol. 3:** 71, 304, 368, 1214
4:18–22	**Vol. 1:** 79
4:18	**Vol. 2:** 73, 243 **Vol. 3:** 1178, 1187
4:19–25	**Vol. 1:** 157
4:19	**Vol. 1:** 80, 235, 445, 504 **Vol. 3:** 1067
4:20 f	**Vol. 1:** 504
4:20	**Vol. 1:** 504 **Vol. 2:** 46, 874 **Vol. 3:** 1187
4:21	**Vol. 3:** 71, 1154
4:22 ff	**Vol. 3:** 489, 824–825
4:22 f	**Vol. 1:** 596
4:22	**Vol. 1:** 702 **Vol. 3:** 362, 1187
4:23 ff	**Vol. 3:** 825
4:23 f	**Vol. 3:** 906
4:24 f	**Vol. 2:** 343
4:24	**Vol. 1:** 326, 446 **Vol. 3:** 281, 1212, 1214
4:25	**Vol. 1:** 86, 437, 702 **Vol. 2:** 120, 339, 380, 527 **Vol. 3:** 363, 371, 586, 611, 643, 1184
5	**Vol. 1:** 97 **Vol. 2:** 774 **Vol. 3:** 581
5:1 ff	**Vol. 3:** 171, 581
5:1 f	**Vol. 3:** 941
5:1–8:39	**Vol. 3:** 368
5:1	**Vol. 1:** 638 **Vol. 2:** 83, 370, 605, 781 **Vol. 3:** 171, 363, 368, 372, 1190
5:2 f	**Vol. 2:** 874
5:2	**Vol. 1:** 229, 611, 638 **Vol. 2:** 47, 83, 121, 242–243, 774 **Vol. 3:** 40
5:3 ff	**Vol. 2:** 774–775, 809
5:3	**Vol. 1:** 229 **Vol. 2:** 774, 809 **Vol. 3:** 1192
5:4	**Vol. 3:** 809
5:5	**Vol. 1:** 564 **Vol. 2:** 79, 183, 545, 785, 855 **Vol. 3:** 563, 701–702
5:5b	**Vol. 3:** 171
5:6 ff	**Vol. 1:** 437
5:6	**Vol. 2:** 94, 338 **Vol. 3:** 198, 837, 995, 1197
5:7	**Vol. 1:** 365 **Vol. 3:** 362
5:8 ff	**Vol. 3:** 169
5:8–10	**Vol. 3:** 1111
5:8 f	**Vol. 1:** 112 **Vol. 2:** 179
5:8	**Vol. 1:** 435, 438 **Vol. 2:** 94, 338, 544, 604 **Vol. 3:** 581, 995, 1197
5:9 ff	**Vol. 2:** 566
5:9 f	**Vol. 3:** 1184
5:9	**Vol. 1:** 437 **Vol. 3:** 166, 168, 214, 363, 644, 1175, 1182
5:10 f	**Vol. 1:** 398, 702 **Vol. 3:** 168, 1193
5:10	**Vol. 1:** 554 **Vol. 2:** 481 **Vol. 3:** 167–168, 171, 643–644, 1193
5:11	**Vol. 1:** 228 **Vol. 2:** 517, 874 **Vol. 3:** 167–168, 581, 838, 1182, 1193
5:12 ff	**Vol. 1:** 524 **Vol. 2:** 481, 682, 721 **Vol. 3:** 168
5:12–21	**Vol. 1:** 86, 436, 472 **Vol. 2:** 57 **Vol. 3:** 580
5:12–20	**Vol. 2:** 723
5:12	**Vol. 1:** 86, 96, 321, 436 **Vol. 2:** 723 **Vol. 3:** 204, 304, 581, 1194
5:13–18	**Vol. 3:** 165
5:13	**Vol. 2:** 783 **Vol. 3:** 702
5:14 ff	**Vol. 1:** 86
5:14	**Vol. 1:** 71, 86, 327 **Vol. 2:** 380, 504, 641 **Vol. 3:** 378, 585, 906
5:15 ff	**Vol. 2:** 723 **Vol. 3:** 586
5:15–21	**Vol. 1:** 96 **Vol. 2:** 120
5:15–17	**Vol. 2:** 42
5:15 f	**Vol. 2:** 121
5:15	**Vol. 1:** 96, 730 **Vol. 2:** 41, 120, 504, 718, 723 **Vol. 3:** 581, 586
5:16–19	**Vol. 3:** 363
5:16	**Vol. 1:** 97 **Vol. 2:** 41, 365 **Vol. 3:** 363, 371
5:17 f	**Vol. 3:** 586
5:17	**Vol. 1:** 649 **Vol. 2:** 41, 380, 723 **Vol. 3:** 138, 362, 364, 368, 746, 749
5:18 f	**Vol. 3:** 1194
5:18	**Vol. 1:** 96, 398, 738 **Vol. 2:** 365 **Vol. 3:** 363, 365, 368, 371, 586
5:19	**Vol. 1:** 96, 223, 472 **Vol. 2:** 175, 179 **Vol. 3:** 362, 365
5:20 f	**Vol. 2:** 445
5:20	**Vol. 1:** 322, 370, 719, 730 **Vol. 2:** 131, 445 **Vol. 3:** 580, 586
5:20a	**Vol. 3:** 1183
5:20b	**Vol. 2:** 120, 122, 445
5:21	**Vol. 2:** 120, 380, 617 **Vol. 3:** 204, 362, 368, 581, 832
6–8	**Vol. 1:** 717
6	**Vol. 2:** 388, 463 **Vol. 3:** 1210
6:1 ff	**Vol. 1:** 148, 152, 225, 604, 701 **Vol. 2:** 131 **Vol. 3:** 368
6:1 f	**Vol. 2:** 120
6:1–11	**Vol. 2:** 655 **Vol. 3:** 278, 581
6:1	**Vol. 2:** 120, 123, 131, 434, 678, 718 **Vol. 3:** 227
6:2	**Vol. 1:** 400, 718
6:3 ff	**Vol. 1:** 147, 289, 300 **Vol. 2:** 218, 715 **Vol. 3:** 581
6:3–13†	**Vol. 2:** 403
6:3–11	**Vol. 1:** 158
6:3 f	**Vol. 1:** 150, 438 **Vol. 2:** 519
6:3	**Vol. 1:** 146, 181, 186, 401 **Vol. 2:** 406, 718 **Vol. 3:** 1209–1210

Romans *(cont'd)*

6:4 f   **Vol. 1:** 315, 455
6:4   **Vol. 1:** 146–147, 266, 602 **Vol. 2:** 46–47, 76, 338, 481, 605, 671, 718, 920 **Vol. 3:** 281, 368, 944
6:5–9   **Vol. 2:** 718
6:5   **Vol. 2:** 504 **Vol. 3:** 277
6:6 ff   **Vol. 2:** 566
6:6   **Vol. 1:** 73, 236, 399, 401–402, 438, 466, 643, 718 **Vol. 2:** 401, 420, 566, 715 **Vol. 3:** 581
6:7 ff   **Vol. 2:** 340
6:7   **Vol. 3:** 363–364
6:8   **Vol. 1:** 181, 643 **Vol. 2:** 243 **Vol. 3:** 1211
6:9   **Vol. 1:** 146 **Vol. 2:** 338, 519 **Vol. 3:** 281, 303
6:9b   **Vol. 3:** 581
6:10 f   **Vol. 1:** 439 **Vol. 2:** 481
6:10–13   **Vol. 2:** 920
6:10   **Vol. 1:** 400–401, 438 **Vol. 2:** 717–718 **Vol. 3:** 363, 368, 723, 1209
6:11   **Vol. 1:** 181, 446, 718 **Vol. 2:** 120, 718 **Vol. 3:** 277, 364, 368, 824
6:12 ff   **Vol. 1:** 457 **Vol. 3:** 581
6:12–23   **Vol. 2:** 120
6:12   **Vol. 1:** 234, 236, 457, 718 **Vol. 2:** 179, 380
6:13 ff   **Vol. 3:** 372
6:13–19   **Vol. 1:** 475
6:13   **Vol. 1:** 231, 446, 475 **Vol. 3:** 362, 364, 368, 964, 1070
6:14 f   **Vol. 2:** 120
6:14   **Vol. 1:** 718 **Vol. 2:** 519
6:15   **Vol. 1:** 719 **Vol. 2:** 120
6:16   **Vol. 3:** 362, 581, 596, 854
6:17 f   **Vol. 2:** 874
6:17   **Vol. 2:** 121, 183, 718 **Vol. 3:** 61, 581, 596, 770, 773, 904
6:18 ff   **Vol. 1:** 720
6:18–22   **Vol. 1:** 718
6:18   **Vol. 1:** 717–718 **Vol. 3:** 362, 364–365, 596–597
6:19–22   **Vol. 2:** 230
6:19   **Vol. 1:** 231, 718 **Vol. 2:** 565 **Vol. 3:** 364, 994
6:20–23   **Vol. 1:** 718
6:20   **Vol. 1:** 718
6:21 ff   **Vol. 2:** 120
6:21 f   **Vol. 2:** 61
6:21   **Vol. 1:** 719
6:22 f   **Vol. 3:** 832
6:22   **Vol. 1:** 717–718 **Vol. 2:** 61, 230, 482 **Vol. 3:** 364, 368, 597
6:23   **Vol. 1:** 86, 436, 470, 719 **Vol. 2:** 101, 121, 419, 517, 617 **Vol. 3:** 142, 144–145, 204, 368
7 f   **Vol. 3:** 168

7   **Vol. 1:** 78 **Vol. 2:** 282–283 **Vol. 3:** 363, 538
7:1 ff   **Vol. 2:** 480
7:1–25   **Vol. 3:** 161
7:1–24   **Vol. 1:** 335
7:1–3   **Vol. 1:** 507 **Vol. 3:** 535
7:1   **Vol. 2:** 399, 406, 444, 519
7:2 ff   **Vol. 3:** 538
7:2–9   **Vol. 3:** 538
7:2 f   **Vol. 2:** 563 **Vol. 3:** 537
7:2   **Vol. 1:** 73, 171
7:2b   **Vol. 2:** 444
7:3–6   **Vol. 1:** 718
7:3   **Vol. 1:** 718 **Vol. 2:** 583
7:3a   **Vol. 3:** 325
7:4 f   **Vol. 1:** 723
7:4   **Vol. 1:** 437 **Vol. 2:** 715
7:5 ff   **Vol. 3:** 581
7:5 f   **Vol. 3:** 839
7:5   **Vol. 1:** 231, 458, 676, 679 **Vol. 3:** 538, 722, 1152, 1187, 1200
7:6   **Vol. 1:** 438 **Vol. 2:** 446, 519, 671–672, 675, 714–716, 786 **Vol. 3:** 493, 596–597, 701–702, 944
7:7 ff   **Vol. 1:** 86, 336 **Vol. 2:** 282 **Vol. 3:** 580, 964
7:7–13   **Vol. 1:** 719 **Vol. 3:** 1021
7:7–12   **Vol. 3:** 585
7:7–10   **Vol. 1:** 337
7:7 f   **Vol. 1:** 458
7:7   **Vol. 2:** 398, 434, 444, 446 **Vol. 3:** 278
7:8 ff   **Vol. 3:** 278
7:8–13   **Vol. 2:** 445
7:8   **Vol. 1:** 336 **Vol. 3:** 197
7:9 ff   **Vol. 3:** 581
7:9 f   **Vol. 1:** 336, 437 **Vol. 2:** 445
7:9   **Vol. 3:** 278, 538
7:10 ff   **Vol. 2:** 715
7:10 f   **Vol. 1:** 719
7:10   **Vol. 1:** 336, 719 **Vol. 2:** 446 **Vol. 3:** 368
7:11   **Vol. 1:** 336, 430 **Vol. 2:** 459–460 **Vol. 3:** 278
7:11c   **Vol. 2:** 446
7:12 ff   **Vol. 2:** 447
7:12   **Vol. 1:** 336, 370, 719 **Vol. 2:** 228, 443–445, 447 **Vol. 3:** 362, 779
7:13–25   **Vol. 3:** 581
7:13   **Vol. 2:** 446, 488
7:14 ff   **Vol. 1:** 236 **Vol. 2:** 566 **Vol. 3:** 1158
7:14–25   **Vol. 3:** 702
7:14   **Vol. 1:** 236, 268, 336, 719 **Vol. 3:** 706
7:15 ff   **Vol. 3:** 1021
7:15   **Vol. 1:** 556, 564 **Vol. 2:** 398
7:17 ff   **Vol. 1:** 564
7:17   **Vol. 2:** 251, 443
7:18 ff   **Vol. 2:** 101
7:18 f   **Vol. 2:** 446, 566 **Vol. 3:** 1021
7:18   **Vol. 1:** 676 **Vol. 2:** 104, 251
7:19   **Vol. 1:** 564 **Vol. 3:** 1021

Romans *(cont'd)*

7:20   **Vol. 2:** 251
7:21–25   **Vol. 2:** 282
7:21   **Vol. 1:** 564   **Vol. 2:** 104, 446   **Vol. 3:**
            529, 1021
7:22 f   **Vol. 3:** 591
7:22   **Vol. 1:** 231
7:23 f   **Vol. 1:** 719
7:23   **Vol. 1:** 231, 564   **Vol. 2:** 444,
            741   **Vol. 3:** 127, 515, 597
7:24   **Vol. 1:** 236, 336, 436, 566   **Vol. 2:** 446,
            874   **Vol. 3:** 204, 859
7:25   **Vol. 1:** 231, 335–336, 564   **Vol. 2:** 121,
            446, 517, 741, 873–874   **Vol. 3:** 127,
            204, 596
7:25b   **Vol. 2:** 444
8   **Vol. 1:** 651   **Vol. 2:** 242, 282, 617,
            885   **Vol. 3:** 1119
8:1 ff   **Vol. 1:** 336, 398, 719   **Vol. 2:**
            566   **Vol. 3:** 581
8:1–17   **Vol. 2:** 566
8:1–11   **Vol. 2:** 883
8:1   **Vol. 1:** 702   **Vol. 2:** 282, 365, 370,
            884   **Vol. 3:** 1192
8:2 ff   **Vol. 1:** 718
8:2–27   **Vol. 3:** 38
8:2   **Vol. 1:** 335   **Vol. 2:** 444, 481   **Vol. 3:**
            304, 368, 701, 1021, 1178, 1183
8:3   **Vol. 1:** 236, 473, 676, 679, 718,
            738   **Vol. 2:** 366, 446, 504,
            725   **Vol. 3:** 170–171, 323, 597,
            643–644, 1117, 1175, 1203
8:3b   **Vol. 3:** 204
8:4 ff   **Vol. 1:** 602
8:4–14   **Vol. 2:** 75
8:4–6   **Vol. 3:** 702
8:4 f   **Vol. 2:** 816
8:4   **Vol. 1:** 168, 675, 681, 738   **Vol. 2:**
            445–446   **Vol. 3:** 161, 204, 363, 944,
            995
8:5 ff   **Vol. 1:** 236
8:5–11   **Vol. 2:** 715
8:5–9   **Vol. 1:** 681
8:5–8   **Vol. 1:** 680
8:5   **Vol. 1:** 681   **Vol. 2:** 617–618   **Vol. 3:**
            204, 1200
8:6–17   **Vol. 3:** 204
8:6   **Vol. 1:** 719   **Vol. 2:** 481, 617, 781,
            816   **Vol. 3:** 368
8:7 f   **Vol. 2:** 605
8:7   **Vol. 1:** 555, 681   **Vol. 2:** 617, 816
8:8 f   **Vol. 1:** 676   **Vol. 3:** 1200
8:8   **Vol. 2:** 816
8:9 ff   **Vol. 1:** 458   **Vol. 3:** 225
8:9–17   **Vol. 3:** 581
8:9 f   **Vol. 1:** 147, 168
8:9   **Vol. 1:** 638, 679, 681   **Vol. 2:** 251, 424,
            785, 816   **Vol. 3:** 701, 703
8:10 f   **Vol. 2:** 481

8:10   **Vol. 1:** 446   **Vol. 2:** 338   **Vol. 3:** 362,
            368, 702, 1192
8:11   **Vol. 1:** 638   **Vol. 2:** 78, 83, 243, 251,
            605, 816   **Vol. 3:** 281, 304, 699,
            702–703, 1183
8:12–17   **Vol. 1:** 256
8:12 f   **Vol. 1:** 299, 719   **Vol. 3:** 702
8:12   **Vol. 1:** 236, 681   **Vol. 2:** 668
8:13–17   **Vol. 1:** 286
8:13   **Vol. 1:** 235, 286, 326–327, 681   **Vol. 2:**
            816   **Vol. 3:** 368, 581, 702, 1158
8:14 ff   **Vol. 1:** 615   **Vol. 2:** 605   **Vol. 3:** 613
8:14–17   **Vol. 1:** 620   **Vol. 3:** 698
8:14–16   **Vol. 3:** 701
8:14 f   **Vol. 2:** 785
8:14   **Vol. 1:** 256, 289, 638   **Vol. 2:** 230,
            873   **Vol. 3:** 645, 702–703
8:15 ff   **Vol. 2:** 218
8:15–17   **Vol. 3:** 701
8:15 f   **Vol. 1:** 289   **Vol. 2:** 786, 874   **Vol. 3:**
            702–703
8:15   **Vol. 1:** 410, 614–615, 621, 623,
            681   **Vol. 2:** 76, 867, 871, 873, 883,
            896   **Vol. 3:** 597, 639, 694, 705, 749
8:16 f   **Vol. 1:** 256
8:16   **Vol. 2:** 76, 424, 567, 816, 873   **Vol. 3:**
            693–694, 1042
8:17   **Vol. 1:** 643, 669   **Vol. 2:** 46–47, 300,
            360–361, 419, 482, 809, 926   **Vol. 3:**
            724–725
8:18 ff   **Vol. 2:** 671   **Vol. 3:** 725
8:18–25   **Vol. 3:** 702
8:18–23   **Vol. 1:** 720
8:18 f   **Vol. 3:** 316
8:18   **Vol. 1:** 327   **Vol. 2:** 46, 48,
            419   **Vol. 3:** 349, 722, 725, 824–825,
            837–839
8:19 ff   **Vol. 1:** 384
8:19–23   **Vol. 1:** 286
8:19–22   **Vol. 1:** 437   **Vol. 3:** 180
8:19   **Vol. 1:** 552   **Vol. 2:** 244–245   **Vol. 3:**
            645
8:20–23   **Vol. 2:** 243
8:20–22   **Vol. 1:** 524
8:20   **Vol. 1:** 385, 552   **Vol. 3:** 1193
8:21   **Vol. 1:** 385, 470, 518, 552,
            717–718   **Vol. 2:** 46, 48   **Vol. 3:** 595,
            597, 884
8:22 f   **Vol. 2:** 883   **Vol. 3:** 204
8:22   **Vol. 1:** 385, 552   **Vol. 2:** 424
8:23   **Vol. 1:** 289, 315, 385, 440, 638,
            669   **Vol. 2:** 40, 243, 245, 423–424,
            774, 785–786, 874, 884, 926   **Vol. 3:**
            199, 320, 417, 701–702
8:24 ff   **Vol. 2:** 243
8:24 f   **Vol. 3:** 563
8:24   **Vol. 1:** 601   **Vol. 2:** 241, 245,
            774   **Vol. 3:** 61, 214
8:25   **Vol. 2:** 243, 245, 774–775
8:26 f   **Vol. 2:** 874, 882, 884   **Vol. 3:** 702

Romans (*cont'd*)

8:26	**Vol. 1:** 90 **Vol. 2:** 424, 666, 873–874, 884 **Vol. 3:** 995
8:27	**Vol. 2:** 183, 424, 885 **Vol. 3:** 533, 1200
8:28 ff	**Vol. 1:** 697
8:28–39	**Vol. 1:** 173
8:28–30	**Vol. 3:** 529
8:28	**Vol. 1:** 275, 696–697 **Vol. 2:** 101, 121–122 **Vol. 3:** 701–702, 1018, 1152, 1201
8:29 f	**Vol. 1:** 275, 298, 542
8:29	**Vol. 1:** 256, 668–669, 693, 695, 707 **Vol. 2:** 288, 725 **Vol. 3:** 214, 303, 305, 643, 645
8:30	**Vol. 1:** 696 **Vol. 2:** 46, 48 **Vol. 3:** 363
8:31 ff	**Vol. 2:** 121
8:31–39	**Vol. 2:** 102
8:31–32	**Vol. 2:** 411
8:31 f	**Vol. 2:** 360
8:31	**Vol. 2:** 83 **Vol. 3:** 1199
8:32	**Vol. 1:** 702 **Vol. 2:** 78, 119, 122, 242, 368, 527, 725 **Vol. 3:** 643–644, 1197
8:33 f	**Vol. 1:** 83 **Vol. 3:** 925, 1199
8:33	**Vol. 1:** 84, 542 **Vol. 2:** 229, 882 **Vol. 3:** 363
8:34	**Vol. 1:** 90 **Vol. 2:** 80, 147, 338, 365, 874, 883 **Vol. 3:** 40, 61–62, 281, 287, 303, 612
8:35 ff	**Vol. 2:** 544
8:35–39	**Vol. 2:** 806 **Vol. 3:** 534
8:35–36	**Vol. 3:** 534
8:35	**Vol. 1:** 313, 419, 564 **Vol. 2:** 267, 808–809 **Vol. 3:** 967
8:35a	**Vol. 3:** 534
8:36 ff	**Vol. 1:** 440
8:36	**Vol. 2:** 413 **Vol. 3:** 824
8:37 ff	**Vol. 1:** 564 **Vol. 2:** 545
8:37	**Vol. 1:** 651 **Vol. 2:** 545, 809
8:38 f	**Vol. 1:** 103, 719 **Vol. 2:** 605
8:38–39	**Vol. 3:** 534
8:38	**Vol. 1:** 103, 167, 326, 441, 591, 718 **Vol. 2:** 243, 518, 603, 895
8:39	**Vol. 1:** 385 **Vol. 2:** 198, 200 **Vol. 3:** 534, 1192
9–11	**Vol. 1:** 159, 256, 370, 467, 540, 593, 619 **Vol. 2:** 156, 314–316, 340, 794, 800 **Vol. 3:** 38, 168, 251, 1112
9	**Vol. 2:** 545
9:1–11:36	**Vol. 3:** 320
9:1–3	**Vol. 2:** 874
9:1	**Vol. 1:** 350, 353 **Vol. 3:** 702, 742, 885, 1042
9:2	**Vol. 1:** 370 **Vol. 2:** 425 **Vol. 3:** 229
9:3	**Vol. 1:** 414, 675 **Vol. 2:** 867, 874–875 **Vol. 3:** 229, 1199
9:4 f	**Vol. 1:** 286, 370, 637 **Vol. 2:** 122, 794, 800
9:4	**Vol. 2:** 285, 310, 445 **Vol. 3:** 551
9:5	**Vol. 1:** 99, 213, 675 **Vol. 2:** 80–81, 195, 314, 725, 874 **Vol. 3:** 1188, 1193, 1199
9:6 ff	**Vol. 2:** 77
9:6–29	**Vol. 1:** 159
9:6–13	**Vol. 2:** 319
9:6 f	**Vol. 1:** 286, 299 **Vol. 3:** 524
9:6	**Vol. 1:** 609 **Vol. 3:** 1112
9:7 f	**Vol. 1:** 286, 557
9:7	**Vol. 1:** 79, 81, 275 **Vol. 3:** 523
9:8	**Vol. 1:** 286, 675 **Vol. 3:** 824–825, 1175
9:9	**Vol. 1:** 80 **Vol. 3:** 846, 1067, 1112
9:10	**Vol. 1:** 81, 619 **Vol. 2:** 587
9:11 f	**Vol. 1:** 541, 557
9:11	**Vol. 1:** 275, 540, 564, 697 **Vol. 2:** 319 **Vol. 3:** 225, 251, 1018
9:12	**Vol. 2:** 428, 587 **Vol. 3:** 1151
9:13 ff	**Vol. 2:** 544
9:13	**Vol. 1:** 556
9:14 ff	**Vol. 3:** 1020
9:14	**Vol. 3:** 576
9:15–18	**Vol. 3:** 912
9:15 f	**Vol. 2:** 641
9:15	**Vol. 2:** 118, 597–598
9:16	**Vol. 1:** 469 **Vol. 2:** 597, 807 **Vol. 3:** 947
9:17	**Vol. 3:** 46, 48, 329, 490, 492
9:18	**Vol. 2:** 155, 597 **Vol. 3:** 1018
9:19 ff	**Vol. 3:** 912
9:19–33	**Vol. 3:** 912
9:19	**Vol. 1:** 416 **Vol. 2:** 139, 144–145 **Vol. 3:** 912, 1017–1018
9:20–23	**Vol. 2:** 434
9:20–21	**Vol. 3:** 917
9:20	**Vol. 3:** 912
9:21 ff	**Vol. 3:** 913, 1065
9:21	**Vol. 2:** 609 **Vol. 3:** 912, 917
9:22 ff	**Vol. 3:** 912
9:22–33	**Vol. 3:** 917
9:22	**Vol. 1:** 112, 464 **Vol. 2:** 76, 770 **Vol. 3:** 350, 1020, 1187
9:23 f	**Vol. 2:** 597 **Vol. 3:** 314
9:23	**Vol. 1:** 112 **Vol. 2:** 842, 844 **Vol. 3:** 118, 1187
9:24 ff	**Vol. 3:** 1020
9:24	**Vol. 2:** 800 **Vol. 3:** 251
9:25 f	**Vol. 2:** 581, 597 **Vol. 3:** 251
9:25	**Vol. 1:** 275, 369
9:26	**Vol. 1:** 274–275, 290 **Vol. 3:** 645
9:27	**Vol. 1:** 410, 736 **Vol. 2:** 684 **Vol. 3:** 251
9:28 f	**Vol. 2:** 513
9:29	**Vol. 1:** 736 **Vol. 2:** 69, 767 **Vol. 3:** 93, 251
9:30 f	**Vol. 2:** 807 **Vol. 3:** 362
9:30	**Vol. 2:** 78, 794 **Vol. 3:** 364, 368, 383, 750, 1188, 1190
9:31 f	**Vol. 3:** 383
9:31	**Vol. 3:** 363

Romans *(cont'd)*

9:32 f	**Vol. 3:** 393
9:32	**Vol. 2:** 706 **Vol. 3:** 363, 1151, 1190
9:33	**Vol. 1:** 477 **Vol. 2:** 327, 706, 708–709 **Vol. 3:** 382–383, 390, 563, 1020, 1212
10:1–4	**Vol. 3:** 1200
10:1	**Vol. 2:** 818, 861, 874 **Vol. 3:** 1174
10:2	**Vol. 1:** 637 **Vol. 2:** 400, 570 **Vol. 3:** 1043, 1167
10:3	**Vol. 2:** 78, 407 **Vol. 3:** 362–363, 372, 532, 581
10:4 ff	**Vol. 3:** 362
10:4	**Vol. 1:** 311, 370, 719, 730 **Vol. 2:** 61, 445, 451 **Vol. 3:** 363–364, 779, 1150, 1177, 1187
10:5	**Vol. 1:** 719 **Vol. 2:** 641 **Vol. 3:** 323, 363, 368, 1177
10:6–10	**Vol. 2:** 183
10:6 f	**Vol. 2:** 185
10:6	**Vol. 3:** 364, 368, 613, 1188
10:7	**Vol. 1:** 719 **Vol. 2:** 205
10:8 ff	**Vol. 1:** 347 **Vol. 3:** 55
10:8 f	**Vol. 3:** 62
10:8	**Vol. 2:** 719 **Vol. 3:** 1122
10:9 ff	**Vol. 1:** 205
10:9–11	**Vol. 3:** 1213
10:9	**Vol. 1:** 147, 153, 599 **Vol. 2:** 75, 78 **Vol. 3:** 61, 1142, 1199, 1211
10:9a	**Vol. 2:** 514
10:10	**Vol. 3:** 362, 364, 1187
10:11	**Vol. 2:** 186, 706 **Vol. 3:** 490, 1212
10:12 ff	**Vol. 1:** 276 **Vol. 2:** 874
10:12 f	**Vol. 3:** 1199
10:12	**Vol. 1:** 730 **Vol. 2:** 126–127, 566, 842
10:13	**Vol. 2:** 654
10:14 ff	**Vol. 1:** 719 **Vol. 2:** 176
10:14	**Vol. 3:** 1142, 1212
10:15	**Vol. 1:** 129, 239 **Vol. 2:** 111 **Vol. 3:** 55
10:16 ff	**Vol. 3:** 1020
10:16	**Vol. 1:** 736 **Vol. 2:** 175, 513
10:17	**Vol. 1:** 158 **Vol. 2:** 175 **Vol. 3:** 1020, 1122, 1190
10:18	**Vol. 1:** 519 **Vol. 3:** 1020, 1122
10:19	**Vol. 1:** 110, 112 **Vol. 2:** 641, 794 **Vol. 3:** 131–132
10:20	**Vol. 1:** 736 **Vol. 2:** 489, 880 **Vol. 3:** 528
10:21	**Vol. 1:** 593 **Vol. 2:** 490, 880
11	**Vol. 1:** 541 **Vol. 2:** 598
11:1–32	**Vol. 1:** 159
11:1 f	**Vol. 2:** 799–800
11:1	**Vol. 1:** 79, 370 **Vol. 2:** 310 **Vol. 3:** 505, 872
11:2 ff	**Vol. 1:** 545
11:2–5	**Vol. 2:** 874
11:2	**Vol. 1:** 667, 693 **Vol. 2:** 882 **Vol. 3:** 490
11:3	**Vol. 2:** 513, 724 **Vol. 3:** 252, 436
11:4 ff	**Vol. 3:** 436
11:4	**Vol. 2:** 85, 690–691, 699, 859 **Vol. 3:** 252, 325
11:5 f	**Vol. 2:** 120
11:5	**Vol. 1:** 159, 181, 540–541 **Vol. 2:** 699 **Vol. 3:** 251–252, 325, 837
11:6	**Vol. 2:** 699 **Vol. 3:** 1151
11:7	**Vol. 1:** 159, 540–541 **Vol. 2:** 156 **Vol. 3:** 251–253, 532
11:8	**Vol. 2:** 178 **Vol. 3:** 313, 694
11:9 f	**Vol. 3:** 505
11:9	**Vol. 1:** 427 **Vol. 2:** 708 **Vol. 3:** 135
11:10	**Vol. 1:** 424
11:11–16	**Vol. 1:** 370
11:11 f	**Vol. 2:** 794 **Vol. 3:** 586
11:11	**Vol. 1:** 611, 730 **Vol. 2:** 794
11:12	**Vol. 1:** 739 **Vol. 2:** 794, 844 **Vol. 3:** 252
11:13 f	**Vol. 2:** 451, 794
11:13	**Vol. 1:** 129 **Vol. 2:** 794 **Vol. 3:** 546, 548
11:14	**Vol. 1:** 675 **Vol. 3:** 214
11:15	**Vol. 1:** 702 **Vol. 3:** 167–168, 581, 751, 1189
11:16 ff	**Vol. 1:** 79
11:16 f	**Vol. 3:** 869
11:16	**Vol. 2:** 691 **Vol. 3:** 869–870, 917
11:17–24	**Vol. 1:** 311 **Vol. 2:** 712, 747 **Vol. 3:** 921
11:17 f	**Vol. 1:** 228 **Vol. 3:** 868–869
11:17	**Vol. 1:** 644 **Vol. 2:** 794 **Vol. 3:** 870
11:18	**Vol. 3:** 869–870
11:19	**Vol. 3:** 869
11:20	**Vol. 2:** 200, 617–618 **Vol. 3:** 505, 1010
11:21	**Vol. 2:** 660
11:22 f	**Vol. 3:** 227
11:22	**Vol. 1:** 611 **Vol. 2:** 106
11:24	**Vol. 2:** 660 **Vol. 3:** 869
11:25 ff	**Vol. 1:** 667
11:25 f	**Vol. 2:** 800 **Vol. 3:** 84, 214
11:25	**Vol. 1:** 321, 370, 739 **Vol. 2:** 37, 156, 304, 406, 620, 794 **Vol. 3:** 505
11:26 f	**Vol. 1:** 370
11:26	**Vol. 2:** 37, 313, 315, 319, 327, 329 **Vol. 3:** 202, 205, 871
11:28 ff	**Vol. 1:** 541
11:28	**Vol. 1:** 540–541, 554 **Vol. 2:** 544 **Vol. 3:** 1184
11:29	**Vol. 1:** 275, 356–357, 370 **Vol. 2:** 77, 122
11:30	**Vol. 1:** 593 **Vol. 2:** 597
11:31	**Vol. 2:** 597
11:32–36	**Vol. 2:** 101
11:32	**Vol. 1:** 96, 593, 730 **Vol. 2:** 499, 597, 800 **Vol. 3:** 1187
11:33 ff	**Vol. 3:** 505
11:33–36	**Vol. 1:** 370–371 **Vol. 2:** 926 **Vol. 3:** 168

Romans *(cont'd)*

11:33 f	**Vol. 3:** 1032
11:33	**Vol. 2:** 75, 198, 365–366, 400 **Vol. 3:** 533, 940, 1032
11:34	**Vol. 1:** 363 **Vol. 3:** 129
11:36	**Vol. 1:** 94–95, 99, 238 **Vol. 2:** 46, 73, 874 **Vol. 3:** 830, 1182–1183
12–16	**Vol. 2:** 883
12–15	**Vol. 1:** 65
12	**Vol. 1:** 232, 301 **Vol. 2:** 885 **Vol. 3:** 1119
12:1 ff	**Vol. 1:** 300, 604
12:1 f	**Vol. 2:** 816
12:1	**Vol. 1:** 234–235, 475, 570 **Vol. 2:** 42, 78, 230, 263, 568, 597–598, 885 **Vol. 3:** 38, 368, 432, 447, 550–551, 746, 838, 1106, 1118
12:2	**Vol. 1:** 185, 708–709 **Vol. 2:** 62, 567–568, 673 **Vol. 3:** 130, 702, 808, 810, 831, 861, 864, 931, 970, 1020–1021, 1187
12:3 ff	**Vol. 2:** 42 **Vol. 3:** 1119
12:3–5	**Vol. 2:** 121
12:3	**Vol. 1:** 502, 570 **Vol. 2:** 121, 499, 617–618 **Vol. 3:** 403, 703, 928, 1183
12:4 ff	**Vol. 1:** 300
12:4–8	**Vol. 3:** 702–703, 1067
12:4 f	**Vol. 1:** 231, 235 **Vol. 2:** 884
12:4	**Vol. 3:** 572, 1158
12:5	**Vol. 1:** 96, 237
12:6 ff	**Vol. 2:** 499 **Vol. 3:** 1119
12:6–8	**Vol. 2:** 121 **Vol. 3:** 703
12:6	**Vol. 1:** 50 **Vol. 2:** 121 **Vol. 3:** 81, 707
12:7	**Vol. 3:** 546–547, 764, 770
12:8	**Vol. 1:** 197, 570–571 **Vol. 2:** 41, 43, 597 **Vol. 3:** 572, 1169
12:9	**Vol. 1:** 567 **Vol. 2:** 350, 470 **Vol. 3:** 927
12:10	**Vol. 1:** 257 **Vol. 2:** 51, 539, 542, 549–550 **Vol. 3:** 928
12:11	**Vol. 1:** 318 **Vol. 3:** 110, 596–597, 694, 1169
12:12 f	**Vol. 2:** 774
12:12	**Vol. 2:** 241, 244, 359–360, 768
12:12c	**Vol. 2:** 874
12:13	**Vol. 1:** 690 **Vol. 2:** 230, 550, 617, 807 **Vol. 3:** 752, 958
12:14	**Vol. 1:** 215, 417 **Vol. 3:** 806, 874 **Vol. 3:** 755
12:15	**Vol. 2:** 361, 416
12:16	**Vol. 2:** 200, 263, 617–618, 620 **Vol. 3:** 1010
12:17 f	**Vol. 2:** 816
12:17	**Vol. 1:** 564, 695 **Vol. 3:** 136, 183, 755, 1179
12:18	**Vol. 2:** 781
12:19 ff	**Vol. 1:** 702
12:19–21	**Vol. 3:** 929
12:19 f	**Vol. 3:** 97

12:19	**Vol. 1:** 111, 417 **Vol. 2:** 157, 513 **Vol. 3:** 345
12:20	**Vol. 1:** 554, 657 **Vol. 2:** 157, 268, 757
12:21	**Vol. 1:** 564, 651 **Vol. 3:** 755
13	**Vol. 2:** 885, 903, 905, 924–925 **Vol. 3:** 549
13:1 ff	**Vol. 3:** 97
13:1–11	**Vol. 2:** 922
13:1–7	**Vol. 2:** 609 **Vol. 3:** 930
13:1–4	**Vol. 2:** 101
13:1	**Vol. 1:** 476, 564 **Vol. 2:** 158, 608 **Vol. 3:** 97, 683, 755
13:2 ff	**Vol. 3:** 755
13:3 f	**Vol. 1:** 564 **Vol. 3:** 817
13:3	**Vol. 1:** 168, 564, 622 **Vol. 2:** 609
13:4 f	**Vol. 3:** 755
13:4	**Vol. 1:** 111, 564 **Vol. 3:** 97, 546, 549, 967, 1157
13:5	**Vol. 1:** 350, 353 **Vol. 2:** 664 **Vol. 3:** 1184
13:6 f	**Vol. 3:** 754
13:6	**Vol. 2:** 62, 768 **Vol. 3:** 553
13:7	**Vol. 2:** 50, 62, 668
13:8 ff	**Vol. 2:** 546 **Vol. 3:** 755
13:8–10	**Vol. 2:** 481
13:8	**Vol. 1:** 738 **Vol. 2:** 668, 739 **Vol. 3:** 377, 752
13:9 f	**Vol. 3:** 378
13:9	**Vol. 1:** 259, 336, 338 **Vol. 2:** 163, 544, 583 **Vol. 3:** 755
13:10	**Vol. 1:** 564, 738–739 **Vol. 3:** 755
13:10b	**Vol. 2:** 445 **Vol. 3:** 779
13:11 ff	**Vol. 3:** 849
13:11–14	**Vol. 1:** 563 **Vol. 2:** 922
13:11	**Vol. 2:** 925 **Vol. 3:** 214, 838–839, 848
13:12	**Vol. 1:** 315–316, 421, 424 **Vol. 2:** 54, 130, 495, 894, 922, 925
13:13	**Vol. 1:** 513 **Vol. 2:** 587, 894, 925–926 **Vol. 3:** 31, 945, 1167
13:14	**Vol. 1:** 316, 676, 695 **Vol. 2:** 587, 926
14 f	**Vol. 2:** 273
14:1–15:13	**Vol. 3:** 995
14:1	**Vol. 1:** 350, 504, 602 **Vol. 2:** 130 **Vol. 3:** 821, 995
14:2	**Vol. 2:** 211 **Vol. 3:** 996, 1211
14:3 ff	**Vol. 2:** 364
14:3	**Vol. 3:** 751
14:4	**Vol. 1:** 610, 684 **Vol. 2:** 450, 742
14:5 ff	**Vol. 1:** 631
14:5	**Vol. 2:** 364 **Vol. 3:** 107, 130, 996, 1202
14:6	**Vol. 2:** 874 **Vol. 3:** 819
14:7 ff	**Vol. 3:** 944
14:7	**Vol. 2:** 481
14:8	**Vol. 1:** 441 **Vol. 2:** 481, 517
14:9	**Vol. 1:** 445, 702 **Vol. 2:** 81, 204, 207, 481, 514, 519
14:10 ff	**Vol. 2:** 369
14:10	**Vol. 1:** 323, 474 **Vol. 2:** 369, 925–926 **Vol. 3:** 1151
14:11 ff	**Vol. 2:** 481

Romans *(cont'd)*

14:11	**Vol. 2:** 513, 859, 874, 925 **Vol. 3:** 1079
14:12	**Vol. 3:** 854, 1106
14:13	**Vol. 2:** 364, 706–708, 710 **Vol. 3:** 996
14:14	**Vol. 1:** 448, 591 **Vol. 2:** 517 **Vol. 3:** 824–825, 996
14:15	**Vol. 1:** 464 **Vol. 2:** 268 **Vol. 3:** 944, 1197
14:17	**Vol. 1:** 300 **Vol. 2:** 268, 277, 360, 482, 781 **Vol. 3:** 362, 701–702
14:18	**Vol. 2:** 817 **Vol. 3:** 596–597, 808, 931
14:19	**Vol. 2:** 781, 807 **Vol. 3:** 189
14:20	**Vol. 2:** 268, 710 **Vol. 3:** 107, 189, 996
14:21	**Vol. 2:** 272, 275, 706, 710 **Vol. 3:** 107, 922, 996, 1192
14:22	**Vol. 1:** 217 **Vol. 3:** 809
14:23	**Vol. 1:** 504, 602 **Vol. 2:** 366, 446, 618 **Vol. 3:** 581, 996
15	**Vol. 3:** 553
15:1 ff	**Vol. 2:** 668
15:1–3	**Vol. 2:** 815
15:1	**Vol. 2:** 606, 815 **Vol. 3:** 995–996
15:2	**Vol. 2:** 101, 815
15:3–6	**Vol. 2:** 774
15:3	**Vol. 1:** 492 **Vol. 2:** 619, 815, 828, 835 **Vol. 3:** 340, 770
15:4 f	**Vol. 3:** 87
15:4	**Vol. 1:** 571 **Vol. 3:** 489–490, 492, 770
15:5 ff	**Vol. 1:** 311 **Vol. 3:** 909
15:5 f	**Vol. 2:** 874
15:5	**Vol. 2:** 121, 618–619
15:6	**Vol. 1:** 620 **Vol. 2:** 76, 722, 874 **Vol. 3:** 908
15:7	**Vol. 1:** 492 **Vol. 2:** 46 **Vol. 3:** 751
15:8 f	**Vol. 3:** 38
15:8	**Vol. 1:** 311, 659 **Vol. 2:** 179 **Vol. 3:** 72, 546, 1118
15:9 ff	**Vol. 2:** 874
15:9	**Vol. 1:** 346 **Vol. 2:** 111, 597, 874 **Vol. 3:** 671–672, 675
15:10	**Vol. 2:** 186, 356, 799
15:11	**Vol. 2:** 513, 793, 799 **Vol. 3:** 817
15:12	**Vol. 1:** 167, 736 **Vol. 3:** 869
15:13	**Vol. 1:** 730 **Vol. 2:** 241, 243, 360, 781, 874 **Vol. 3:** 38, 702
15:14	**Vol. 1:** 569, 591 **Vol. 2:** 101
15:15	**Vol. 1:** 365 **Vol. 2:** 304 **Vol. 3:** 38, 489, 1183
15:16–19	**Vol. 3:** 703
15:16	**Vol. 2:** 78, 111, 235 **Vol. 3:** 38, 431, 552, 746
15:17 ff	**Vol. 2:** 874
15:17	**Vol. 1:** 228 **Vol. 2:** 388
15:18 f	**Vol. 2:** 632
15:18	**Vol. 1:** 130, 365 **Vol. 3:** 314
15:19	**Vol. 1:** 129 **Vol. 2:** 328, 605, 629, 903 **Vol. 3:** 752
15:20 f	**Vol. 3:** 400
15:20	**Vol. 1:** 662, 684 **Vol. 2:** 550, 742
15:21	**Vol. 3:** 48, 131–132, 613
15:22	**Vol. 2:** 220–221
15:23 f	**Vol. 3:** 400
15:23	**Vol. 1:** 458 **Vol. 2:** 903 **Vol. 3:** 730
15:24	**Vol. 2:** 826 **Vol. 3:** 516
15:25–28	**Vol. 3:** 854
15:25	**Vol. 2:** 826 **Vol. 3:** 546
15:26 ff	**Vol. 2:** 818
15:26	**Vol. 1:** 642 **Vol. 2:** 826 **Vol. 3:** 854
15:27	**Vol. 2:** 328, 668, 826 **Vol. 3:** 552, 707, 752
15:28	**Vol. 2:** 826 **Vol. 3:** 499
15:29	**Vol. 1:** 214, 739
15:30 ff	**Vol. 2:** 874
15:30–33	**Vol. 2:** 874
15:30	**Vol. 1:** 570, 646–647 **Vol. 2:** 517, 545, 868 **Vol. 3:** 702
15:31	**Vol. 1:** 593 **Vol. 2:** 329, 826 **Vol. 3:** 546, 746, 752, 1176
15:32	**Vol. 3:** 1021
15:33	**Vol. 1:** 99 **Vol. 2:** 78, 780, 874
16	**Vol. 3:** 1063
16:1 f	**Vol. 3:** 1063
16:1	**Vol. 1:** 301 **Vol. 3:** 546, 549, 1065
16:2	**Vol. 1:** 474 **Vol. 2:** 517 **Vol. 3:** 958, 1158
16:3 f	**Vol. 3:** 1065
16:3	**Vol. 3:** 548, 1063
16:4	**Vol. 1:** 241, 398 **Vol. 3:** 683, 818
16:5	**Vol. 1:** 301 **Vol. 2:** 550 **Vol. 3:** 416
16:6	**Vol. 1:** 263 **Vol. 3:** 1063
16:7	**Vol. 1:** 130 **Vol. 3:** 591, 601, 1192
16:8	**Vol. 2:** 517
16:9	**Vol. 3:** 548
16:10 f	**Vol. 2:** 550
16:10	**Vol. 3:** 808, 810
16:12	**Vol. 1:** 263 **Vol. 3:** 1063
16:13	**Vol. 1:** 539 **Vol. 2:** 517
16:15	**Vol. 2:** 550 **Vol. 3:** 378, 1063
16:16	**Vol. 1:** 299 **Vol. 2:** 530, 547, 549 **Vol. 3:** 701
16:17	**Vol. 1:** 486, 535 **Vol. 2:** 708, 710, 719 **Vol. 3:** 770
16:18	**Vol. 1:** 169, 212, 563 **Vol. 2:** 460 **Vol. 3:** 596
16:19	**Vol. 1:** 564 **Vol. 2:** 101, 179 **Vol. 3:** 1022
16:20	**Vol. 1:** 239 **Vol. 2:** 78, 780–781, 874 **Vol. 3:** 471
16:21	**Vol. 2:** 517 **Vol. 3:** 548
16:22	**Vol. 1:** 247 **Vol. 2:** 517
16:23	**Vol. 1:** 689 **Vol. 2:** 254
16:25 ff	**Vol. 2:** 724, 874 **Vol. 3:** 322
16:25 f	**Vol. 3:** 832, 837
16:25	**Vol. 2:** 112, 217 **Vol. 3:** 52–53, 61, 314, 504, 844
16:26	**Vol. 2:** 77, 179 **Vol. 3:** 81, 314, 491–492, 1150
16:27	**Vol. 1:** 99 **Vol. 2:** 46, 77, 724 **Vol. 3:** 1032

1 Corinthians

1–3	**Vol. 3:** 1030
1:1 ff	**Vol. 1:** 247
1:1–9	**Vol. 3:** 1165
1:1	**Vol. 1:** 129, 276 **Vol. 3:** 1020
1:2	**Vol. 1:** 275–276, 298–300, 305 **Vol. 2:** 229, 654, 874
1:3	**Vol. 1:** 620 **Vol. 2:** 516, 780–781, 874 **Vol. 3:** 1178
1:4 ff	**Vol. 2:** 121, 874
1:4–7	**Vol. 3:** 701
1:4	**Vol. 2:** 73, 119 **Vol. 3:** 818
1:5	**Vol. 2:** 400, 828, 842, 844 **Vol. 3:** 197, 954
1:6	**Vol. 1:** 659–660 **Vol. 3:** 905, 1043
1:7	**Vol. 2:** 518 **Vol. 3:** 315, 707, 954
1:8	**Vol. 1:** 467, 660 **Vol. 2:** 61, 140, 517, 874, 894 **Vol. 3:** 169, 924
1:9	**Vol. 1:** 275, 643 **Vol. 2:** 77 **Vol. 3:** 643, 924, 1182
1:10 ff	**Vol. 1:** 535
1:10–4:21	**Vol. 1:** 400
1:10	**Vol. 1:** 570 **Vol. 2:** 398, 654 **Vol. 3:** 130, 350, 482, 544
1:11	**Vol. 3:** 316, 544, 905
1:12	**Vol. 2:** 311 **Vol. 3:** 297, 383, 387, 544, 1117, 1209
1:13–17	**Vol. 1:** 146
1:13	**Vol. 1:** 398 **Vol. 2:** 655 **Vol. 3:** 387, 544, 1209
1:14 ff	**Vol. 1:** 147
1:14–17	**Vol. 1:** 179
1:14	**Vol. 1:** 160 **Vol. 2:** 874 **Vol. 3:** 819
1:15	**Vol. 2:** 655 **Vol. 3:** 1209
1:16	**Vol. 1:** 159, 675 **Vol. 2:** 248, 250 **Vol. 3:** 252
1:17 f	**Vol. 1:** 397
1:17	**Vol. 1:** 129, 147, 399–400, 547, 602, 638 **Vol. 2:** 111 **Vol. 3:** 1031
1:18 ff	**Vol. 2:** 171 **Vol. 3:** 1031
1:18–3:20	**Vol. 3:** 1111
1:18–2:16	**Vol. 2:** 401
1:18–31	**Vol. 2:** 430 **Vol. 3:** 581
1:18–25	**Vol. 1:** 397
1:18–24	**Vol. 1:** 400
1:18	**Vol. 1:** 397, 399, 464 **Vol. 2:** 78, 338, 604 **Vol. 3:** 61, 169, 214, 714, 1026
1:19 ff	**Vol. 1:** 397, 399
1:19	**Vol. 1:** 74, 463 **Vol. 3:** 131–132, 504, 1031
1:20	**Vol. 3:** 831, 1026, 1030
1:21–25	**Vol. 3:** 820
1:21	**Vol. 1:** 397, 601 **Vol. 2:** 400, 819 **Vol. 3:** 52–53, 214, 1031
1:22 ff	**Vol. 3:** 1111
1:22 f	**Vol. 2:** 127
1:22–24	**Vol. 2:** 127
1:22	**Vol. 1:** 398 **Vol. 2:** 629, 680, 858 **Vol. 3:** 532, 1031
1:23 f	**Vol. 1:** 439
1:23	**Vol. 1:** 399–400, 638 **Vol. 2:** 706, 708, 794 **Vol. 3:** 52, 55, 504, 1025, 1031
1:24 ff	**Vol. 3:** 1111
1:24	**Vol. 1:** 174, 275, 551 **Vol. 2:** 78, 126, 604 **Vol. 3:** 1030–1032
1:25 f	**Vol. 3:** 714
1:25	**Vol. 3:** 995, 1026
1:26 ff	**Vol. 3:** 1031
1:26–29	**Vol. 1:** 248, 399 **Vol. 2:** 605
1:26 f	**Vol. 3:** 504
1:26	**Vol. 1:** 188, 275, 680 **Vol. 3:** 515
1:27 f	**Vol. 1:** 542
1:27	**Vol. 2:** 605 **Vol. 3:** 563, 995
1:28	**Vol. 1:** 73
1:29 ff	**Vol. 2:** 874
1:29	**Vol. 1:** 228, 675 **Vol. 3:** 1031
1:30 f	**Vol. 2:** 119–120
1:30	**Vol. 1:** 417 **Vol. 2:** 78, 217, 229, 591, 605 **Vol. 3:** 163, 199, 258, 326, 362, 364, 372, 1031–1032
1:31	**Vol. 1:** 228 **Vol. 3:** 504, 1031
2	**Vol. 1:** 183
2:1–16	**Vol. 3:** 967
2:1–5	**Vol. 1:** 400
2:1 f	**Vol. 1:** 248, 397
2:1	**Vol. 3:** 47, 504, 1031, 1043, 1112
2:2 f	**Vol. 3:** 995
2:2	**Vol. 1:** 248, 399 **Vol. 2:** 364 **Vol. 3:** 55, 504, 1031, 1111
2:3	**Vol. 1:** 183, 622 **Vol. 2:** 434 **Vol. 3:** 504
2:4–16	**Vol. 3:** 336
2:4 f	**Vol. 3:** 701, 703, 1031
2:4	**Vol. 1:** 588, 592, 602 **Vol. 2:** 605, 632 **Vol. 3:** 52–53, 570–571, 963, 1112, 1125
2:5	**Vol. 1:** 601 **Vol. 2:** 78
2:6–16	**Vol. 3:** 327, 1031
2:6–13	**Vol. 2:** 569
2:6–8	**Vol. 2:** 435
2:6 f	**Vol. 3:** 1031
2:6	**Vol. 1:** 73, 168, 675 **Vol. 2:** 62 **Vol. 3:** 185, 504, 802, 829
2:7–16	**Vol. 3:** 345
2:7	**Vol. 1:** 696 **Vol. 2:** 46, 217 **Vol. 3:** 504, 830
2:8	**Vol. 1:** 167, 169 **Vol. 2:** 46, 513 **Vol. 3:** 802, 1111
2:9–16	**Vol. 2:** 874
2:9	**Vol. 2:** 176, 183, 185, 219 **Vol. 3:** 118, 492, 504, 515, 533
2:10–16	**Vol. 1:** 680 **Vol. 2:** 567 **Vol. 3:** 1031
2:10–12	**Vol. 3:** 701
2:10 f	**Vol. 2:** 217
2:10	**Vol. 1:** 465 **Vol. 2:** 75, 198, 217 **Vol. 3:** 314, 533
2:11 ff	**Vol. 2:** 883
2:11	**Vol. 2:** 75, 400 **Vol. 3:** 694
2:12–3:4	**Vol. 3:** 705

1 Corinthians *(cont'd)*

2:12–14	**Vol. 3:** 703
2:12 f	**Vol. 2:** 605
2:12	**Vol. 2:** 75, 122 **Vol. 3:** 129, 504, 694, 701, 749, 1203
2:12a	**Vol. 3:** 1174, 1188
2:12b	**Vol. 3:** 1174
2:13–3:1	**Vol. 3:** 706
2:13–15	**Vol. 3:** 707
2:13 f	**Vol. 3:** 703
2:13	**Vol. 2:** 364, 605 **Vol. 3:** 707, 764, 1031, 1112
2:14 f	**Vol. 2:** 75
2:14	**Vol. 1:** 246 **Vol. 2:** 365, 400 **Vol. 3:** 504, 684
2:15 ff	**Vol. 1:** 248
2:15	**Vol. 2:** 605 **Vol. 3:** 504, 707, 1200
2:16	**Vol. 1:** 638, 739 **Vol. 2:** 900 **Vol. 3:** 129
3:1–3	**Vol. 1:** 679
3:1	**Vol. 1:** 282 **Vol. 2:** 605 **Vol. 3:** 707, 963, 1200
3:2	**Vol. 2:** 268–269
3:3	**Vol. 1:** 535, 681 **Vol. 2:** 565 **Vol. 3:** 944–945, 1167, 1200
3:4–10	**Vol. 1:** 301
3:4	**Vol. 1:** 681 **Vol. 2:** 311 **Vol. 3:** 544
3:5 ff	**Vol. 1:** 400
3:5–17	**Vol. 2:** 252
3:5–11	**Vol. 2:** 129
3:5	**Vol. 2:** 517 **Vol. 3:** 548, 809, 1117, 1211
3:6 ff	**Vol. 2:** 248
3:6 f	**Vol. 2:** 129
3:6	**Vol. 3:** 164, 868
3:8	**Vol. 1:** 263 **Vol. 2:** 839 **Vol. 3:** 1200
3:9 ff	**Vol. 3:** 390
3:9	**Vol. 1:** 248, 300 **Vol. 2:** 252 **Vol. 3:** 1152
3:10 ff	**Vol. 1:** 279 **Vol. 3:** 500
3:10–14†	**Vol. 2:** 253
3:10–13	**Vol. 2:** 747
3:10–12	**Vol. 2:** 249
3:10	**Vol. 1:** 662 **Vol. 2:** 121, 249 **Vol. 3:** 143, 1032
3:11 f	**Vol. 3:** 1151
3:11	**Vol. 1:** 662 **Vol. 2:** 129, 739 **Vol. 3:** 387, 390
3:12 ff	**Vol. 1:** 662
3:12–15	**Vol. 3:** 387
3:12	**Vol. 1:** 390, 744 **Vol. 2:** 96, 211, 249, 756
3:13 ff	**Vol. 2:** 370 **Vol. 3:** 136
3:13	**Vol. 1:** 467, 657 **Vol. 2:** 756, 894 **Vol. 3:** 315, 317, 320, 446, 808–809, 1178
3:14	**Vol. 2:** 249 **Vol. 3:** 142, 224
3:15	**Vol. 1:** 467, 662 **Vol. 3:** 99, 143, 214, 1181
3:16 f	**Vol. 2:** 249 **Vol. 3:** 387, 784
3:16	**Vol. 1:** 638 **Vol. 2:** 83, 249, 251–252 **Vol. 3:** 701, 809
3:17	**Vol. 1:** 467–468 **Vol. 3:** 84, 86
3:18 ff	**Vol. 3:** 1031
3:18–23	**Vol. 3:** 1032
3:18 f	**Vol. 3:** 1031
3:18	**Vol. 2:** 460 **Vol. 3:** 822, 831, 1026, 1032
3:19 f	**Vol. 3:** 1031
3:19	**Vol. 1:** 413, 524 **Vol. 3:** 1026, 1030, 1036, 1202
3:20	**Vol. 1:** 551 **Vol. 2:** 513 **Vol. 3:** 821
3:21 ff	**Vol. 1:** 525
3:21	**Vol. 1:** 228, 718 **Vol. 3:** 504
3:22 f	**Vol. 1:** 441
3:22	**Vol. 1:** 95, 326 **Vol. 3:** 383
3:23	**Vol. 1:** 718 **Vol. 2:** 160
4:1	**Vol. 1:** 129 **Vol. 2:** 75, 255, 732 **Vol. 3:** 504, 546, 824–825
4:2	**Vol. 2:** 255 **Vol. 3:** 252, 529, 532
4:3 ff	**Vol. 3:** 810
4:3	**Vol. 2:** 365
4:4	**Vol. 1:** 350, 352 **Vol. 3:** 363, 365, 432, 1192
4:5	**Vol. 1:** 425 **Vol. 2:** 183, 218, 364, 495, 518 **Vol. 3:** 321, 817, 838–839, 1017
4:6 ff	**Vol. 1:** 399
4:6	**Vol. 1:** 400, 486, 709 **Vol. 3:** 864, 1196, 1199
4:7	**Vol. 1:** 228, 504, 639 **Vol. 3:** 749
4:8	**Vol. 1:** 638 **Vol. 2:** 267, 380, 668, 828, 842, 844 **Vol. 3:** 143, 305, 1111
4:9 ff	**Vol. 3:** 143
4:9–13	**Vol. 1:** 129 **Vol. 2:** 57
4:9	**Vol. 1:** 103 **Vol. 2:** 434, 565 **Vol. 3:** 521, 570–571, 600, 822
4:10	**Vol. 1:** 183, 281, 638 **Vol. 2:** 47, 51, 620 **Vol. 3:** 432, 714, 995, 1026
4:11	**Vol. 1:** 163 **Vol. 3:** 847, 857
4:12	**Vol. 1:** 215, 263 **Vol. 2:** 766, 806, 839 **Vol. 3:** 347
4:13	**Vol. 1:** 479 **Vol. 3:** 102
4:14 ff	**Vol. 1:** 619
4:14 f	**Vol. 1:** 180
4:14	**Vol. 1:** 286, 568 **Vol. 3:** 489
4:15	**Vol. 1:** 180 **Vol. 2:** 692, 697, 834
4:16 f	**Vol. 1:** 571
4:16	**Vol. 1:** 129, 400, 491
4:17	**Vol. 1:** 180, 286, 491 **Vol. 2:** 517 **Vol. 3:** 241–242, 764, 940, 942
4:19 f	**Vol. 2:** 605–606
4:19	**Vol. 2:** 399, 517 **Vol. 3:** 1021, 1106, 1125
4:20	**Vol. 1:** 300 **Vol. 3:** 1125
4:21	**Vol. 1:** 407 **Vol. 2:** 258 **Vol. 3:** 694, 1175
5 ff	**Vol. 2:** 581
5–7	**Vol. 3:** 802
5	**Vol. 3:** 535

1 Corinthians *(cont'd)*

5:1 ff	**Vol. 1:** 500
5:1 – 13	**Vol. 3:** 214
5:1 – 8	**Vol. 1:** 628
5:1 – 6	**Vol. 2:** 676
5:1 – 5	**Vol. 1:** 703
5:1	**Vol. 2:** 794 **Vol. 3:** 1195
5:2	**Vol. 1:** 466 **Vol. 2:** 422 **Vol. 3:** 1157
5:3 ff	**Vol. 2:** 874
5:3 – 5	**Vol. 1:** 466
5:3	**Vol. 1:** 235 **Vol. 2:** 364, 875, 899 **Vol. 3:** 694
5:4	**Vol. 1:** 466 **Vol. 2:** 33, 605, 654
5:5	**Vol. 1:** 466 – 467 **Vol. 2:** 368, 517 **Vol. 3:** 214, 470 – 471, 535, 694
5:6 ff	**Vol. 2:** 755
5:6 – 8	**Vol. 2:** 716
5:6	**Vol. 1:** 228 **Vol. 2:** 428, 462 **Vol. 3:** 489, 917
5:7 – 8	**Vol. 1:** 634 **Vol. 2:** 463, 716 **Vol. 3:** 417, 431
5:7	**Vol. 1:** 437, 629, 633 – 634 **Vol. 2:** 338, 463, 527, 534, 675 – 676, 714 **Vol. 3:** 102, 917
5:8	**Vol. 1:** 563, 630 **Vol. 2:** 676 **Vol. 3:** 886
5:9 ff	**Vol. 1:** 500 **Vol. 3:** 536
5:9 – 12	**Vol. 2:** 576
5:9 f	**Vol. 3:** 1165
5:9	**Vol. 2:** 922 **Vol. 3:** 489
5:10 f	**Vol. 1:** 138 **Vol. 2:** 286 **Vol. 3:** 31, 604
5:10	**Vol. 1:** 524 – 525 **Vol. 2:** 926
5:11	**Vol. 1:** 138, 257, 513 **Vol. 2:** 273, 655 **Vol. 3:** 347, 489
5:12 f	**Vol. 3:** 1199
5:12	**Vol. 2:** 365 – 366
5:13	**Vol. 1:** 566 **Vol. 2:** 463 **Vol. 3:** 535
5:14	**Vol. 1:** 720 **Vol. 2:** 604
6	**Vol. 3:** 380
6:1 f	**Vol. 2:** 230
6:1 – 11	**Vol. 1:** 400 **Vol. 3:** 576
6:1 – 6	**Vol. 3:** 1165
6:1	**Vol. 1:** 365 **Vol. 3:** 576, 1158, 1204
6:2 f	**Vol. 1:** 649 **Vol. 2:** 365 **Vol. 3:** 1165
6:2	**Vol. 1:** 440 **Vol. 2:** 366, 613
6:4	**Vol. 3:** 588
6:5	**Vol. 1:** 373, 504 **Vol. 3:** 1032
6:6	**Vol. 2:** 365
6:7 f	**Vol. 3:** 575
6:7	**Vol. 2:** 365 **Vol. 3:** 380
6:8	**Vol. 3:** 380
6:9 ff	**Vol. 2:** 584 **Vol. 3:** 536 – 537, 1165
6:9 – 10	**Vol. 2:** 583 **Vol. 3:** 31, 832, 929
6:9 – 20	**Vol. 1:** 500
6:9 – 11	**Vol. 3:** 701
6:9	**Vol. 2:** 300, 459 – 460, 570 **Vol. 3:** 576, 929
6:10 f	**Vol. 1:** 138
6:10	**Vol. 1:** 138, 513 **Vol. 3:** 347, 377, 604, 929
6:11	**Vol. 1:** 152 **Vol. 2:** 75, 230, 463, 654 **Vol. 3:** 61, 363, 499, 536, 701, 990
6:12 – 20	**Vol. 2:** 402, 576
6:12	**Vol. 2:** 611
6:13 – 20	**Vol. 1:** 235
6:13	**Vol. 1:** 73, 169, 500 **Vol. 2:** 268, 517 **Vol. 3:** 718
6:14	**Vol. 2:** 606, 923 **Vol. 3:** 304
6:15 ff	**Vol. 1:** 500
6:15 – 19	**Vol. 1:** 501
6:15 f	**Vol. 1:** 507
6:15	**Vol. 1:** 231, 235 **Vol. 2:** 273
6:16	**Vol. 1:** 232 **Vol. 2:** 350, 579, 722
6:17	**Vol. 2:** 350, 722 **Vol. 3:** 694, 701, 703
6:18 f	**Vol. 1:** 718
6:18	**Vol. 1:** 500, 559 **Vol. 2:** 273 **Vol. 3:** 197, 535, 579, 1165
6:19 f	**Vol. 1:** 235 **Vol. 2:** 463 **Vol. 3:** 701
6:19	**Vol. 1:** 638 **Vol. 2:** 249, 566 **Vol. 3:** 784
6:20	**Vol. 1:** 268 **Vol. 2:** 47, 49, 874 **Vol. 3:** 198, 200, 854
6:25 ff	**Vol. 3:** 535
7 – 16	**Vol. 3:** 1203
7 – 10	**Vol. 1:** 717
7	**Vol. 2:** 903, 923 **Vol. 3:** 188, 534 – 537, 1072
7:1 – 24	**Vol. 3:** 535
7:1 – 16	**Vol. 2:** 563
7:1 – 9	**Vol. 2:** 580 **Vol. 3:** 541 – 542
7:1 – 7	**Vol. 3:** 1072
7:1 – 2	**Vol. 3:** 534
7:1	**Vol. 1:** 496 **Vol. 2:** 104, 565, 581 **Vol. 3:** 536, 1203
7:2 ff	**Vol. 3:** 1058, 1065
7:2 – 7	**Vol. 3:** 189, 539
7:2	**Vol. 1:** 501 **Vol. 2:** 923 **Vol. 3:** 536
7:3 – 7	**Vol. 3:** 534
7:3 – 5	**Vol. 3:** 1201
7:3 f	**Vol. 1:** 338 **Vol. 3:** 536
7:3	**Vol. 2:** 579, 668
7:4	**Vol. 1:** 235 **Vol. 2:** 273 **Vol. 3:** 1064, 1067
7:5	**Vol. 1:** 322, 495 – 496 **Vol. 3:** 380, 471, 536, 802, 837, 1067, 1194
7:7	**Vol. 1:** 496 **Vol. 2:** 121, 273, 581 **Vol. 3:** 536, 1022, 1188
7:7b	**Vol. 3:** 536
7:8 f	**Vol. 2:** 564 **Vol. 3:** 225
7:8 – 9	**Vol. 3:** 534
7:8	**Vol. 2:** 104 **Vol. 3:** 536, 1075
7:9	**Vol. 1:** 495 – 496, 656 **Vol. 3:** 536 188, 535 – 536
7:10 – 16	**Vol. 2:** 580
7:10 – 11	**Vol. 3:** 534 – 535
7:10 f	**Vol. 1:** 507 **Vol. 2:** 580 **Vol. 3:** 172, 183,

1 Corinthians *(cont'd)*

7:10   **Vol. 1:** 130   **Vol. 2:** 514, 581, 900   **Vol. 3:** 85, 534, 931, 967
7:10b   **Vol. 3:** 535
7:11–13   **Vol. 1:** 701
7:11   **Vol. 3:** 167, 535–537
7:12–16   **Vol. 2:** 581   **Vol. 3:** 173, 534, 536, 1165
7:12 f   **Vol. 2:** 250
7:12   **Vol. 1:** 130   **Vol. 2:** 900   **Vol. 3:** 85, 252, 535
7:13–16   **Vol. 3:** 173
7:14   **Vol. 1:** 149, 159   **Vol. 2:** 230   **Vol. 3:** 1175, 1192
7:15–24   **Vol. 1:** 275
7:15   **Vol. 1:** 275   **Vol. 2:** 781   **Vol. 3:** 535, 537, 540, 1191
7:16   **Vol. 3:** 214, 535
7:17 ff   **Vol. 1:** 299
7:17–24   **Vol. 3:** 932
7:17   **Vol. 1:** 301   **Vol. 2:** 517
7:18   **Vol. 1:** 310
7:19   **Vol. 1:** 311, 336, 338, 602   **Vol. 2:** 133
7:20 ff   **Vol. 1:** 525
7:20–24   **Vol. 3:** 596
7:20   **Vol. 1:** 275
7:21 ff   **Vol. 3:** 582, 1162
7:21   **Vol. 3:** 225, 596, 860
7:22 ff   **Vol. 3:** 596
7:22 f   **Vol. 2:** 51
7:22   **Vol. 1:** 638, 717–718, 720   **Vol. 3:** 598, 613, 854
7:23   **Vol. 1:** 268   **Vol. 3:** 198, 200
7:24   **Vol. 3:** 1202
7:25 ff   **Vol. 3:** 1072
7:25–38   **Vol. 3:** 1072
7:25–28   **Vol. 3:** 537
7:25   **Vol. 1:** 341   **Vol. 2:** 398, 597   **Vol. 3:** 85, 535–536, 1066, 1072, 1203
7:26–35   **Vol. 3:** 537
7:26–29   **Vol. 2:** 580
7:26   **Vol. 1:** 496   **Vol. 2:** 104, 664   **Vol. 3:** 536
7:27 f   **Vol. 3:** 173, 537, 540
7:27   **Vol. 1:** 171   **Vol. 3:** 188, 537
7:28   **Vol. 1:** 496, 675   **Vol. 3:** 189, 536, 1072
7:29 ff   **Vol. 1:** 525, 639, 675   **Vol. 2:** 581   **Vol. 3:** 188, 536, 1165
7:29–31   **Vol. 3:** 121
7:29   **Vol. 1:** 278   **Vol. 2:** 62, 922   **Vol. 3:** 252, 838
7:30   **Vol. 2:** 361, 416
7:31   **Vol. 1:** 278, 325, 525, 709   **Vol. 2:** 62
7:32 ff   **Vol. 1:** 278   **Vol. 3:** 536
7:32   **Vol. 2:** 816   **Vol. 3:** 536, 1022
7:34   **Vol. 1:** 235   **Vol. 3:** 536, 694
7:36 ff   **Vol. 2:** 581, 588   **Vol. 3:** 536, 538, 541
7:36   **Vol. 2:** 588   **Vol. 3:** 1021, 1072
7:37   **Vol. 1:** 661   **Vol. 2:** 133, 364, 663   **Vol. 3:** 1019

7:38   **Vol. 2:** 581, 588
7:39 f   **Vol. 2:** 564
7:39   **Vol. 1:** 171, 443   **Vol. 2:** 517   **Vol. 3:** 173, 535, 537, 843, 1165, 1191
7:40   **Vol. 1:** 217   **Vol. 2:** 398   **Vol. 3:** 85, 224, 703, 822, 967
8   **Vol. 3:** 802
8:1 ff   **Vol. 1:** 352   **Vol. 3:** 996
8:1–11:1   **Vol. 1:** 400
8:1–13   **Vol. 3:** 433
8:1–7   **Vol. 2:** 74
8:1–6   **Vol. 2:** 286
8:1 f   **Vol. 3:** 432
8:1   **Vol. 1:** 638   **Vol. 2:** 253, 284–285, 401–402, 546   **Vol. 3:** 432, 996, 1203
8:2   **Vol. 2:** 402   **Vol. 3:** 822
8:3   **Vol. 2:** 400, 402–403, 545
8:4 ff   **Vol. 2:** 721–722   **Vol. 3:** 433
8:4–6   **Vol. 1:** 628
8:4   **Vol. 2:** 73, 268–269, 284–286, 721–722, 831   **Vol. 3:** 432, 996
8:5 f   **Vol. 2:** 73, 515
8:5   **Vol. 2:** 895
8:6   **Vol. 1:** 95, 384, 620   **Vol. 2:** 73, 84, 160, 195, 515–516, 671, 721–722   **Vol. 3:** 61, 996, 1063, 1182, 1198
8:7 ff   **Vol. 1:** 350
8:7   **Vol. 1:** 352, 449   **Vol. 2:** 284–285, 402   **Vol. 3:** 432, 995–996
8:8†   **Vol. 1:** 475, 731   **Vol. 2:** 268
8:9 ff   **Vol. 2:** 273
8:9–13   **Vol. 2:** 286
8:9   **Vol. 2:** 402, 706   **Vol. 3:** 996
8:10 ff   **Vol. 3:** 433
8:10 f   **Vol. 3:** 1165
8:10   **Vol. 1:** 352   **Vol. 2:** 284–285   **Vol. 3:** 432, 995–996, 1208
8:11   **Vol. 1:** 257   **Vol. 3:** 996, 1197
8:12   **Vol. 1:** 352   **Vol. 3:** 903
8:13   **Vol. 1:** 352   **Vol. 2:** 268, 708, 710   **Vol. 3:** 829–830, 996
9   **Vol. 3:** 854, 1053
9:1 ff   **Vol. 1:** 136
9:1   **Vol. 1:** 183, 229, 528   **Vol. 3:** 284, 314, 1151
9:2   **Vol. 3:** 499
9:3–18   **Vol. 3:** 771
9:3 f   **Vol. 3:** 855
9:3   **Vol. 2:** 365
9:4–6   **Vol. 2:** 611
9:4   **Vol. 2:** 223, 275
9:5   **Vol. 1:** 131–132, 256   **Vol. 2:** 121   **Vol. 3:** 252, 383, 387
9:7 ff   **Vol. 2:** 223
9:7   **Vol. 1:** 723   **Vol. 2:** 816   **Vol. 3:** 144, 525, 568, 868, 964
9:8 ff   **Vol. 1:** 49   **Vol. 2:** 446
9:8–18   **Vol. 3:** 854
9:8   **Vol. 2:** 444

1 Corinthians *(cont'd)*

9:9   **Vol. 1:** 115, 737   **Vol. 2:** 641, 746, 755
9:10   **Vol. 3:** 489, 492, 1193
9:11   **Vol. 3:** 525, 707, 752
9:12 f   **Vol. 2:** 706
9:12   **Vol. 2:** 111, 221   **Vol. 3:** 142
9:13 f   **Vol. 3:** 794
9:13   **Vol. 2:** 235, 694   **Vol. 3:** 433, 436, 793
9:14   **Vol. 2:** 111, 272   **Vol. 3:** 47, 349, 773, 1053
9:15–18   **Vol. 2:** 435
9:15   **Vol. 1:** 229   **Vol. 3:** 142, 1053
9:16   **Vol. 1:** 229   **Vol. 2:** 112, 664   **Vol. 3:** 142, 504
9:17 f   **Vol. 3:** 142
9:17   **Vol. 2:** 255   **Vol. 3:** 1158
9:18   **Vol. 2:** 111   **Vol. 3:** 964
9:19 ff   **Vol. 1:** 720   **Vol. 2:** 451   **Vol. 3:** 137
9:19–23   **Vol. 3:** 793
9:19 f   **Vol. 2:** 706
9:19   **Vol. 1:** 718, 720   **Vol. 3:** 137, 596
9:20 f   **Vol. 3:** 431
9:20   **Vol. 1:** 310   **Vol. 2:** 314, 445
9:21 f   **Vol. 3:** 1165
9:21   **Vol. 2:** 445–446   **Vol. 3:** 1151
9:22   **Vol. 1:** 310   **Vol. 2:** 816   **Vol. 3:** 137, 214, 431
9:23   **Vol. 1:** 644   **Vol. 2:** 112
9:24 ff   **Vol. 1:** 648   **Vol. 3:** 838, 947
9:24–27   **Vol. 1:** 469, 647   **Vol. 3:** 214
9:24   **Vol. 1:** 649   **Vol. 3:** 142, 750
9:25   **Vol. 1:** 406, 495–496, 645   **Vol. 2:** 244
9:26   **Vol. 1:** 449
9:27   **Vol. 1:** 163, 235, 647   **Vol. 3:** 54, 808, 810
10   **Vol. 3:** 806, 984
10:1 ff   **Vol. 1:** 149
10:1–13   **Vol. 1:** 467   **Vol. 3:** 1007
10:1–5   **Vol. 2:** 719
10:1–4   **Vol. 3:** 706
10:1 f   **Vol. 3:** 990, 1003
10:1   **Vol. 1:** 619   **Vol. 2:** 406   **Vol. 3:** 984, 1022
10:2–5   **Vol. 2:** 641
10:2   **Vol. 1:** 144   **Vol. 3:** 1209–1210
10:3 f   **Vol. 2:** 276   **Vol. 3:** 382–383, 706–707
10:3   **Vol. 2:** 268–269
10:4   **Vol. 1:** 677   **Vol. 2:** 276, 755   **Vol. 3:** 459
10:5   **Vol. 2:** 819   **Vol. 3:** 1007–1008
10:6   **Vol. 1:** 71, 564   **Vol. 2:** 277   **Vol. 3:** 724
10:7–10   **Vol. 2:** 286
10:7 f   **Vol. 3:** 802
10:7   **Vol. 2:** 286
10:8   **Vol. 1:** 501, 610   **Vol. 2:** 699
10:9 f   **Vol. 1:** 464
10:9   **Vol. 3:** 802, 809
10:10   **Vol. 1:** 467

10:11   **Vol. 1:** 325, 568–569, 581   **Vol. 3:** 489, 759, 829, 831, 906, 1204
10:12   **Vol. 1:** 610   **Vol. 3:** 822
10:13   **Vol. 2:** 77, 565, 611   **Vol. 3:** 802–803, 809
10:14 ff   **Vol. 2:** 273
10:14–22   **Vol. 2:** 286
10:14   **Vol. 1:** 500, 559   **Vol. 2:** 286
10:15   **Vol. 2:** 364, 620
10:16 f   **Vol. 1:** 237   **Vol. 2:** 277
10:16   **Vol. 1:** 213, 223, 251, 643   **Vol. 2:** 273, 521, 523, 529, 536   **Vol. 3:** 166, 819
10:16b   **Vol. 1:** 369
10:17   **Vol. 1:** 96, 639   **Vol. 2:** 277, 534
10:18   **Vol. 1:** 257, 643, 675   **Vol. 2:** 218, 312, 339   **Vol. 3:** 433, 436
10:19 ff.   **Vol. 3:** 433
10:19†   **Vol. 2:** 284–285   **Vol. 3:** 432–433
10:20 ff   **Vol. 2:** 273
10:20 f   **Vol. 1:** 452   **Vol. 3:** 1208
10:20   **Vol. 2:** 74, 85, 520   **Vol. 3:** 310, 1008
10:21   **Vol. 1:** 639   **Vol. 2:** 516, 518, 520, 522   **Vol. 3:** 1165
10:22   **Vol. 2:** 516, 522   **Vol. 3:** 714
10:23–30   **Vol. 3:** 433
10:23 f   **Vol. 1:** 352, 638   **Vol. 2:** 611
10:23   **Vol. 1:** 300   **Vol. 2:** 253, 611
10:24   **Vol. 2:** 739
10:25 ff   **Vol. 1:** 352
10:25–30   **Vol. 2:** 286
10:25   **Vol. 2:** 273, 364
10:27 ff   **Vol. 3:** 1165
10:27   **Vol. 1:** 275, 299, 352   **Vol. 2:** 269, 364
10:28   **Vol. 1:** 352   **Vol. 2:** 235, 284–285, 611
10:29   **Vol. 1:** 352   **Vol. 2:** 364
10:30   **Vol. 2:** 121, 874   **Vol. 3:** 819
10:31 ff   **Vol. 1:** 352   **Vol. 2:** 235, 611   **Vol. 3:** 433
10:31   **Vol. 2:** 46–47, 272, 874   **Vol. 3:** 1155, 1187
10:32   **Vol. 2:** 126–127, 159, 273, 286, 707   **Vol. 3:** 1165
10:33–11:1   **Vol. 2:** 160
10:33   **Vol. 2:** 816   **Vol. 3:** 214, 531–532
11   **Vol. 2:** 530, 547   **Vol. 3:** 1066
11:1–6   **Vol. 2:** 212
11:1   **Vol. 1:** 400, 491   **Vol. 3:** 60, 724, 729
11:2 ff   **Vol. 2:** 51
11:2–16   **Vol. 3:** 1063
11:2–15   **Vol. 2:** 159
11:2   **Vol. 2:** 718–719   **Vol. 3:** 241, 773–774, 817
11:3 ff   **Vol. 2:** 563
11:3   **Vol. 2:** 160, 579   **Vol. 3:** 1022, 1063
11:4–6   **Vol. 2:** 160
11:4–5   **Vol. 2:** 212
11:4 f   **Vol. 2:** 869, 874
11:4   **Vol. 2:** 160   **Vol. 3:** 1199
11:5   **Vol. 2:** 160–161, 212, 883   **Vol. 3:** 1066

217

1 Corinthians *(cont'd)*

11:6–7	**Vol. 2:** 212
11:6	**Vol. 3:** 564
11:7–9	**Vol. 2:** 160
11:7	**Vol. 2:** 46, 51, 160–161, 288, 563, 668
11:8	**Vol. 2:** 213
11:9	**Vol. 1:** 385 **Vol. 2:** 161, 213 **Vol. 3:** 1177, 1183
11:10	**Vol. 1:** 102 **Vol. 2:** 160–161, 213, 668, 874
11:11 f	**Vol. 1:** 385
11:11	**Vol. 3:** 1183
11:12	**Vol. 2:** 160 **Vol. 3:** 1063, 1177
11:12b	**Vol. 3:** 1188
11:13 ff	**Vol. 2:** 563
11:13 f	**Vol. 2:** 365
11:13–15	**Vol. 2:** 162
11:13	**Vol. 2:** 212–213, 669, 874, 883 **Vol. 3:** 1066
11:14	**Vol. 2:** 50–51, 162, 661 **Vol. 3:** 764
11:15	**Vol. 2:** 162 **Vol. 3:** 1066, 1179
11:16	**Vol. 1:** 299, 301 **Vol. 2:** 162, 213, 550 **Vol. 3:** 822
11:17 ff	**Vol. 1:** 322
11:17–34	**Vol. 3:** 349, 547
11:17–22	**Vol. 3:** 544
11:17	**Vol. 1:** 341 **Vol. 3:** 817, 1187
11:18 f	**Vol. 1:** 535
11:18	**Vol. 1:** 299 **Vol. 3:** 544, 1194, 1211
11:19	**Vol. 3:** 320, 808, 1052
11:20 ff	**Vol. 2:** 272
11:20–29	**Vol. 2:** 221
11:20	**Vol. 1:** 514 **Vol. 2:** 516, 518, 522, 534 **Vol. 3:** 411, 1194
11:21	**Vol. 1:** 514 **Vol. 2:** 267, 273, 534 **Vol. 3:** 750
11:22	**Vol. 1:** 299, 461 **Vol. 2:** 846 **Vol. 3:** 817
11:23 ff	**Vol. 3:** 62
11:23–26	**Vol. 1:** 131, 237 **Vol. 2:** 277
11:23–25	**Vol. 2:** 523–524
11:23	**Vol. 1:** 129, 251, 630 **Vol. 2:** 368, 523, 527–528, 719 **Vol. 3:** 61, 322, 611, 751, 773–774, 1171, 1181
11:24 f	**Vol. 1:** 398, 437 **Vol. 2:** 523 **Vol. 3:** 243
11:24	**Vol. 1:** 237, 437–439 **Vol. 2:** 368, 524, 530, 536, 874 **Vol. 3:** 819
11:25	**Vol. 1:** 223, 369–370 **Vol. 2:** 312, 316, 524–525, 529–530, 533, 536, 671, 786 **Vol. 3:** 166, 819
11:26 ff	**Vol. 2:** 530
11:26	**Vol. 1:** 237, 437 **Vol. 2:** 273, 516, 523, 530–531, 894, 896 **Vol. 3:** 47, 245–246
11:27–32	**Vol. 1:** 369
11:27 f	**Vol. 2:** 523
11:27	**Vol. 1:** 223, 237 **Vol. 2:** 143, 516, 522, 531 **Vol. 3:** 349
11:28	**Vol. 1:** 414 **Vol. 3:** 808
11:29	**Vol. 1:** 301, 504 **Vol. 2:** 273
11:30–32	**Vol. 3:** 1206
11:30 f	**Vol. 1:** 163
11:30	**Vol. 1:** 467 **Vol. 3:** 730, 998
11:31 f	**Vol. 2:** 522
11:31	**Vol. 1:** 503
11:32	**Vol. 2:** 366, 516 **Vol. 3:** 778, 998
11:32b	**Vol. 3:** 779
11:33–34	**Vol. 3:** 544
11:33	**Vol. 2:** 245
11:34	**Vol. 2:** 267 **Vol. 3:** 252
12–14	**Vol. 2:** 176 **Vol. 3:** 707
12	**Vol. 1:** 232, 238, 301 **Vol. 2:** 168–169, 566, 723 **Vol. 3:** 1079
12:1 ff	**Vol. 2:** 42
12:1	**Vol. 2:** 406 **Vol. 3:** 84, 706–707, 1203
12:2	**Vol. 2:** 793 **Vol. 3:** 1079
12:3	**Vol. 1:** 205, 369, 414 **Vol. 2:** 75, 402, 514, 516 **Vol. 3:** 61, 314, 475, 703, 780, 967
12:4 ff	**Vol. 1:** 535 **Vol. 2:** 84
12:4–31	**Vol. 3:** 1067
12:4	**Vol. 3:** 297
12:5	**Vol. 2:** 517 **Vol. 3:** 546–548
12:6	**Vol. 3:** 1021, 1151–1152
12:7	**Vol. 1:** 232 **Vol. 3:** 323, 1210
12:8 ff	**Vol. 2:** 632
12:8–11	**Vol. 3:** 703
12:8	**Vol. 1:** 602 **Vol. 3:** 1031, 1210
12:9 ff	**Vol. 2:** 121
12:9	**Vol. 1:** 601 **Vol. 2:** 721 **Vol. 3:** 1210
12:10	**Vol. 1:** 452, 504, 581–582 **Vol. 2:** 605, 740 **Vol. 3:** 475, 695, 1080, 1152
12:11–27	**Vol. 2:** 121
12:11	**Vol. 1:** 535 **Vol. 2:** 721, 839 **Vol. 3:** 1017–1018, 1021, 1152, 1210
12:12 ff	**Vol. 1:** 231, 467 **Vol. 2:** 499
12:12–30	**Vol. 1:** 237
12:12–27	**Vol. 1:** 300
12:12–26	**Vol. 1:** 235 **Vol. 3:** 544
12:12 f	**Vol. 1:** 237 **Vol. 2:** 722 **Vol. 3:** 1062
12:13	**Vol. 1:** 96, 147–148, 152, 237, 720 **Vol. 2:** 51, 126–127, 309, 721, 785, 800 **Vol. 3:** 499, 701–702, 1187, 1209–1210
12:14 ff	**Vol. 1:** 300
12:14–26	**Vol. 1:** 237 **Vol. 2:** 434 **Vol. 3:** 703
12:17	**Vol. 2:** 175
12:18 f	**Vol. 2:** 720
12:18	**Vol. 1:** 477 **Vol. 3:** 1021
12:22 f	**Vol. 3:** 822
12:23 f	**Vol. 2:** 51
12:23	**Vol. 2:** 50
12:24	**Vol. 3:** 955, **1021**
12:25–38	**Vol. 1:** 129
12:25	**Vol. 1:** 278 **Vol. 2:** 514 **Vol. 3:** 544
12:26	**Vol. 2:** 722 **Vol. 3:** 724
12:27	**Vol. 1:** 237, 300, 535 **Vol. 2:** 273, 304
12:28 ff	**Vol. 2:** 121, 499

1 Corinthians *(cont'd)*

12:28 f	**Vol. 3:** 84
12:28†	**Vol. 1:** 198, 667 **Vol. 2:** 605, 632 **Vol. 3:** 88, 703, 767–768
12:29 ff	**Vol. 1:** 66
12:30	**Vol. 1:** 581 **Vol. 2:** 740
12:31	**Vol. 2:** 121, 123, 425 **Vol. 3:** 88, 569, 1167
12:31b	**Vol. 3:** 942
13	**Vol. 1:** 300, 720 **Vol. 2:** 79, 499, 544–545, 723
13:1–14:1	**Vol. 1:** 352
13:1	**Vol. 1:** 103 **Vol. 2:** 97, 221, 565, 786, 884 **Vol. 3:** 112, 674
13:2	**Vol. 1:** 602, 638 **Vol. 2:** 545 **Vol. 3:** 84, 505
13:3	**Vol. 1:** 235–236 **Vol. 2:** 845, 847
13:4	**Vol. 2:** 106, 771 **Vol. 3:** 1167
13:5	**Vol. 1:** 110, 564 **Vol. 3:** 532, 824–825
13:6	**Vol. 3:** 576, 887
13:7	**Vol. 2:** 243, 545, 774 **Vol. 3:** 887, 1211
13:8	**Vol. 1:** 73, 609 **Vol. 2:** 400, 545 **Vol. 3:** 225
13:9 f	**Vol. 2:** 304
13:9	**Vol. 2:** 62, 546
13:10	**Vol. 1:** 73 **Vol. 2:** 62, 304
13:11	**Vol. 1:** 73, 282 **Vol. 2:** 563, 617 **Vol. 3:** 824
13:12 f	**Vol. 2:** 401
13:12	**Vol. 1:** 282, 587 **Vol. 2:** 218, 304, 400, 402–403, 482, 503, 546, 746 **Vol. 3:** 335
13:13†	**Vol. 1:** 236, 282, 601, 609 **Vol. 2:** 242, 425, 545–546, 687 **Vol. 3:** 225
14	**Vol. 2:** 884 **Vol. 3:** 77, 89, 505, 967, 1032, 1066, 1079
14:1–6	**Vol. 1:** 582
14:1–5	**Vol. 3:** 703
14:1–4	**Vol. 2:** 740
14:1	**Vol. 2:** 546, 807, 868 **Vol. 3:** 88, 706–707, 942, 967, 1167
14:2–19	**Vol. 2:** 741
14:2–6	**Vol. 1:** 582
14:2 f	**Vol. 3:** 87
14:2	**Vol. 1:** 582 **Vol. 2:** 786 **Vol. 3:** 505, 1080
14:3–5	**Vol. 2:** 253
14:3 f	**Vol. 1:** 329
14:3	**Vol. 3:** 81, 84
14:4 f	**Vol. 1:** 300
14:4	**Vol. 2:** 253
14:5–1?	**Vol. 3:** 112
14:5	**Vol. 1:** 581–582 **Vol. 3:** 748, 1022, 1080
14:6 f	**Vol. 2:** 874 **Vol. 3:** 819
14:6	**Vol. 2:** 400 **Vol. 3:** 81, 315, 770, 962
14:7–12	**Vol. 2:** 883
14:7 f	**Vol. 2:** 434, 883 **Vol. 3:** 674
14:7	**Vol. 2:** 398
14:8–9	**Vol. 3:** 874
14:8	**Vol. 3:** 119, 410, 874, 962
14:9	**Vol. 1:** 449 **Vol. 3:** 1113
14:11 f	**Vol. 3:** 962
14:11	**Vol. 3:** 1191
14:12	**Vol. 1:** 300, 731 **Vol. 2:** 253 **Vol. 3:** 390, 695, 703, 707, 1167
14:13 ff	**Vol. 2:** 883
14:13–16:26	**Vol. 2:** 869
14:13–19	**Vol. 3:** 703
14:13	**Vol. 1:** 581–582 **Vol. 2:** 874, 884 **Vol. 3:** 505
14:14 ff	**Vol. 3:** 1080
14:14–17	**Vol. 3:** 702
14:14–16	**Vol. 2:** 873
14:14 f	**Vol. 2:** 874 **Vol. 3:** 672
14:14	**Vol. 1:** 582, 723 **Vol. 3:** 129, 694
14:15 f	**Vol. 3:** 84
14:15	**Vol. 3:** 671–672, 675, 705
14:16–19	**Vol. 3:** 672
14:16	**Vol. 1:** 99, 213, 582 **Vol. 2:** 456, 874 **Vol. 3:** 505
14:17	**Vol. 2:** 253
14:18	**Vol. 1:** 528 **Vol. 2:** 121, 874 **Vol. 3:** 819, 1080
14:19	**Vol. 1:** 300, 528, 582 **Vol. 2:** 253, 567, 692, 873 **Vol. 3:** 112, 129, 771, 1080, 1113
14:20	**Vol. 1:** 282, 284 **Vol. 2:** 62
14:21	**Vol. 2:** 175, 444, 446, 513, 740 **Vol. 3:** 1079
14:22	**Vol. 2:** 741, 883 **Vol. 3:** 1080
14:23 f	**Vol. 2:** 741 **Vol. 3:** 84, 962
14:23	**Vol. 1:** 300, 322, 528–529, 582 **Vol. 2:** 402, 456–457 **Vol. 3:** 1080
14:24 f	**Vol. 3:** 84, 703, 705, 1080
14:24	**Vol. 2:** 141, 364, 456–457 **Vol. 3:** 129, 1165
14:25 f	**Vol. 3:** 671
14:25	**Vol. 1:** 610 **Vol. 2:** 218, 874 **Vol. 3:** 47, 320
14:26 ff	**Vol. 2:** 884 **Vol. 3:** 1080
14:26	**Vol. 1:** 322, 581 **Vol. 2:** 253 **Vol. 3:** 110, 315, 671, 703, 770
14:27 ff	**Vol. 3:** 962
14:27	**Vol. 1:** 581–582 **Vol. 2:** 304, 400
14:28	**Vol. 1:** 300, 581–582 **Vol. 2:** 874
14:28b	**Vol. 3:** 1080
14:29	**Vol. 1:** 503
14:30 f	**Vol. 1:** 570
14:30	**Vol. 1:** 667 **Vol. 3:** 84, 315, 589
14:31	**Vol. 1:** 571 **Vol. 3:** 81, 84
14:32	**Vol. 3:** 84, 694
14:33 f	**Vol. 1:** 301
14:33–38	**Vol. 3:** 932
14:33	**Vol. 1:** 300, 667 **Vol. 2:** 78, 780
14:33a	**Vol. 3:** 84
14:33b–36	**Vol. 3:** 1066
14:34 f	**Vol. 3:** 1063
14:34	**Vol. 2:** 446

1 Corinthians *(cont'd)*

14:35   **Vol. 2:** 880   **Vol. 3:** 564, 1066
14:36   **Vol. 1:** 322, 325   **Vol. 2:** 517   **Vol. 3:** 61, 1110
14:37   **Vol. 1:** 337   **Vol. 2:** 403, 407, 605   **Vol. 3:** 706–707, 822
14:38   **Vol. 2:** 403, 407   **Vol. 3:** 84
14:39   **Vol. 2:** 222   **Vol. 3:** 1167
14:39b   **Vol. 3:** 1080
14:40   **Vol. 1:** 667
15   **Vol. 1:** 236, 266, 445, 651   **Vol. 2:** 208, 903, 905, 923–925   **Vol. 3:** 276–277, 280–281, 287, 304
15:1 ff   **Vol. 1:** 394–395   **Vol. 2:** 111, 338
15:1–8   **Vol. 3:** 1047
15:1–7   **Vol. 1:** 131   **Vol. 3:** 62
15:1–5   **Vol. 3:** 61
15:1–3   **Vol. 2:** 719   **Vol. 3:** 1110
15:1 f   **Vol. 3:** 55, 1111
15:1   **Vol. 3:** 61, 314.
15:2   **Vol. 1:** 601   **Vol. 2:** 111   **Vol. 3:** 214, 1106
15:3 ff   **Vol. 1:** 298, 437, 445   **Vol. 3:** 61, 773–774
15:3–4:11   **Vol. 1:** 601
15:3–10   **Vol. 3:** 283
15:3–8   **Vol. 3:** 55, 288, 297
15:3–7   **Vol. 3:** 62
15:3–5   **Vol. 2:** 338   **Vol. 3:** 286, 612, 1110
15:3 f   **Vol. 1:** 150   **Vol. 2:** 380   **Vol. 3:** 491, 1200
15:3   **Vol. 1:** 398, 435, 438, 680   **Vol. 2:** 532, 926   **Vol. 3:** 166, 196, 322, 581, 751, 773, 1184, 1197
15:4–7   **Vol. 3:** 285
15:4   **Vol. 1:** 266   **Vol. 2:** 340, 481, 687, 893   **Vol. 3:** 283, 292
15:5 ff   **Vol. 2:** 524   **Vol. 3:** 518
15:5–9   **Vol. 1:** 136
15:5–8   **Vol. 2:** 786   **Vol. 3:** 281
15:5–7   **Vol. 3:** 285
15:5   **Vol. 2:** 695   **Vol. 3:** 285, 383–384
15:6 f   **Vol. 3:** 286
15:6   **Vol. 1:** 443   **Vol. 2:** 717, 925   **Vol. 3:** 224, 285
15:7   **Vol. 1:** 129–130, 133, 256   **Vol. 3:** 285
15:8 ff   **Vol. 2:** 171
15:8   **Vol. 1:** 86, 130, 182–183, 528   **Vol. 2:** 57   **Vol. 3:** 284–285, 314
15:9 ff   **Vol. 3:** 288
15:9   **Vol. 1:** 183, 274–275, 301   **Vol. 2:** 176, 429, 806   **Vol. 3:** 184, 581, 729
15:10 f   **Vol. 3:** 581
15:10   **Vol. 1:** 263   **Vol. 2:** 121   **Vol. 3:** 701
15:11   **Vol. 1:** 131, 601   **Vol. 3:** 55, 314
15:12 ff   **Vol. 1:** 440, 446   **Vol. 2:** 338, 924   **Vol. 3:** 831
15:12–24   **Vol. 2:** 926

15:12   **Vol. 1:** 638   **Vol. 2:** 402, 924   **Vol. 3:** 52, 55, 277–278, 304–305
15:13–17   **Vol. 3:** 281
15:14–17   **Vol. 3:** 281
15:14   **Vol. 1:** 547, 551, 601   **Vol. 2:** 242   **Vol. 3:** 52–53, 284, 417
15:15   **Vol. 2:** 472   **Vol. 3:** 529, 1043
15:16 f   **Vol. 2:** 338
15:17–19   **Vol. 2:** 559
15:17   **Vol. 1:** 86, 551, 601, 702   **Vol. 2:** 242   **Vol. 3:** 281
15:18   **Vol. 1:** 443   **Vol. 2:** 925   **Vol. 3:** 1207
15:19   **Vol. 2:** 597, 724   **Vol. 3:** 417
15:20 ff   **Vol. 2:** 242, 481–482, 895   **Vol. 3:** 831
15:20–28   **Vol. 2:** 702
15:20–22   **Vol. 1:** 86
15:20   **Vol. 1:** 86, 443, 731   **Vol. 2:** 48, 338, 786, 925   **Vol. 3:** 303, 417, 558, 1189
15:21 f   **Vol. 1:** 436   **Vol. 2:** 57, 566
15:21   **Vol. 3:** 1198
15:22 ff   **Vol. 1:** 467
15:22 f   **Vol. 3:** 1191
15:22   **Vol. 1:** 86, 96, 440   **Vol. 2:** 481, 721   **Vol. 3:** 304, 1192, 1194
15:23 ff   **Vol. 2:** 58, 924
15:23–28   **Vol. 2:** 665   **Vol. 3:** 644
15:23 f   **Vol. 3:** 277
15:23   **Vol. 1:** 446, 649   **Vol. 2:** 338, 786, 839, 900, 924, 926   **Vol. 3:** 297, 303–304, 417, 1189
15:24 ff   **Vol. 2:** 926
15:24–28   **Vol. 1:** 238   **Vol. 2:** 388
15:24–27   **Vol. 1:** 467
15:24   **Vol. 1:** 73, 103, 167, 718   **Vol. 2:** 62, 74, 195, 368, 518, 603, 609
15:25 f   **Vol. 3:** 276
15:25   **Vol. 1:** 177, 239, 477, 554   **Vol. 2:** 147, 339, 381, 514–515, 665
15:26 ff   **Vol. 2:** 58
15:26†   **Vol. 1:** 73, 440, 719   **Vol. 2:** 482–483, 631, 874, 926
15:27   **Vol. 1:** 239   **Vol. 3:** 148, 316, 632
15:28   **Vol. 2:** 74, 80, 242, 482, 514, 926   **Vol. 3:** 643–644, 839, 1191
15:29   **Vol. 1:** 147, 398, 400   **Vol. 2:** 874   **Vol. 3:** 990, 1197, 1207–1208
15:30 ff   **Vol. 1:** 129, 400
15:30–32   **Vol. 3:** 1208
15:30   **Vol. 1:** 419   **Vol. 3:** 848
15:31 f   **Vol. 2:** 895
15:31   **Vol. 1:** 228   **Vol. 2:** 895
15:32   **Vol. 1:** 431   **Vol. 2:** 272, 275, 565   **Vol. 3:** 674
15:33   **Vol. 1:** 468–469, 564   **Vol. 2:** 437–438, 459–460, 757
15:34   **Vol. 1:** 515   **Vol. 2:** 402, 924   **Vol. 3:** 304, 363
15:35 ff   **Vol. 1:** 722   **Vol. 2:** 482, 566   **Vol. 3:** 286
15:35–42a   **Vol. 1:** 470

1 Corinthians *(cont'd)*

15:35   **Vol. 3:** 684
15:36 ff   **Vol. 2:** 923   **Vol. 3:** 524
15:37   **Vol. 1:** 313   **Vol. 3:** 252
15:38   **Vol. 1:** 236   **Vol. 3:** 278, 1020
15:39 ff   **Vol. 2:** 739
15:39   **Vol. 1:** 114, 670, 674, 679   **Vol. 2:** 565
15:40 f   **Vol. 2:** 46
15:40   **Vol. 1:** 518
15:41   **Vol. 3:** 731, 735
15:42 ff   **Vol. 1:** 470
15:42–50   **Vol. 3:** 694, 701
15:42–44   **Vol. 3:** 281
15:42   **Vol. 1:** 236   **Vol. 3:** 302–305
15:42b   **Vol. 1:** 470
15:43 f   **Vol. 2:** 789
15:43   **Vol. 2:** 48, 50–51
15:44 ff   **Vol. 3:** 684
15:44–49   **Vol. 3:** 702
15:44–46   **Vol. 3:** 706
15:44   **Vol. 1:** 236, 470   **Vol. 2:** 566–567   **Vol. 3:** 297, 303, 305, 706, 1195
15:44b   **Vol. 1:** 87
15:45 ff†   **Vol. 1:** 86   **Vol. 2:** 566
15:45–49   **Vol. 1:** 86
15:45–48   **Vol. 3:** 661
15:45   **Vol. 1:** 179, 665   **Vol. 2:** 57, 242, 481, 504   **Vol. 3:** 632, 683–684, 703, 705, 1175, 1178, 1183
15:46–49   **Vol. 2:** 160
15:46   **Vol. 3:** 303, 706
15:47 f   **Vol. 3:** 632
15:47–49   **Vol. 1:** 520
15:47   **Vol. 1:** 518   **Vol. 2:** 57
15:48–53   **Vol. 2:** 789
15:48 f   **Vol. 2:** 196
15:49   **Vol. 2:** 288   **Vol. 3:** 283, 303, 305
15:50–54   **Vol. 3:** 304
15:50   **Vol. 1:** 222, 236, 290, 470, 675, 679   **Vol. 2:** 566   **Vol. 3:** 301–303, 305
15:50a   **Vol. 2:** 300–301
15:50b   **Vol. 2:** 300
15:51 ff   **Vol. 2:** 482
15:51 f   **Vol. 2:** 925   **Vol. 3:** 84, 167
15:51   **Vol. 1:** 443   **Vol. 2:** 922, 924–925   **Vol. 3:** 305, 505
15:52 ff   **Vol. 2:** 242   **Vol. 3:** 304
15:52 f   **Vol. 2:** 665
15:52   **Vol. 1:** 470   **Vol. 2:** 894, 924   **Vol. 3:** 281, 305, 874
15:53 f   **Vol. 1:** 435   **Vol. 2:** 923   **Vol. 3:** 302
15:53   **Vol. 1:** 316, 440   **Vol. 3:** 283, 305
15:54 f   **Vol. 1:** 440, 651   **Vol. 3:** 267, 304
15:54   **Vol. 1:** 470   **Vol. 3:** 267, 1106, 1112
15:55 ff   **Vol. 2:** 545
15:55   **Vol. 1:** 511, 719   **Vol. 3:** 267

15:56   **Vol. 1:** 437, 511, 719   **Vol. 2:** 605   **Vol. 3:** 581
15:56b   **Vol. 2:** 445
15:57   **Vol. 1:** 440, 470, 651   **Vol. 2:** 121, 517, 874
15:58   **Vol. 1:** 257, 602, 661–662, 730   **Vol. 2:** 517, 924   **Vol. 3:** 1151
16:1–4   **Vol. 2:** 826
16:1–3   **Vol. 3:** 854
16:1–2   **Vol. 3:** 752
16:1 f   **Vol. 3:** 854
16:1   **Vol. 1:** 301, 305   **Vol. 2:** 826   **Vol. 3:** 1155, 1203
16:2   **Vol. 1:** 631   **Vol. 2:** 329, 518, 694, 826, 834   **Vol. 3:** 410, 412, 854, 943
16:3   **Vol. 2:** 121, 826   **Vol. 3:** 752, 809, 854
16:4   **Vol. 2:** 826
16:5–9   **Vol. 1:** 247
16:6 f   **Vol. 3:** 1204
16:6   **Vol. 3:** 228
16:7 f   **Vol. 3:** 227
16:7   **Vol. 2:** 517   **Vol. 3:** 843
16:8   **Vol. 3:** 417
16:9   **Vol. 2:** 30, 726–727
16:10   **Vol. 1:** 181   **Vol. 3:** 1149, 1151
16:11   **Vol. 2:** 245, 780
16:12   **Vol. 3:** 1019
16:13   **Vol. 1:** 421   **Vol. 2:** 137, 563
16:14   **Vol. 2:** 546
16:15   **Vol. 2:** 248   **Vol. 3:** 416, 546–547
16:16   **Vol. 1:** 263
16:17   **Vol. 1:** 741   **Vol. 2:** 899–900   **Vol. 3:** 955
16:18   **Vol. 2:** 399, 785   **Vol. 3:** 256, 694
16:19   **Vol. 1:** 301, 718   **Vol. 2:** 517   **Vol. 3:** 1065
16:20–22   **Vol. 2:** 530
16:20   **Vol. 2:** 523, 530, 549
16:20a   **Vol. 2:** 531
16:21   **Vol. 1:** 247   **Vol. 2:** 62, 148   **Vol. 3:** 489
16:22 f   **Vol. 2:** 874
16:22   **Vol. 1:** 323, 414   **Vol. 2:** 229, 515–516, 523, 531, 543, 548, 895–896   **Vol. 3:** 84, 319
16:22a   **Vol. 2:** 530, 874
16:22b   **Vol. 2:** 530
16:23   **Vol. 2:** 516, 874

2 Corinthians

1–9   **Vol. 2:** 922
1:1   **Vol. 1:** 129, 299   **Vol. 2:** 83, 229
1:2   **Vol. 1:** 299, 620   **Vol. 2:** 83, 780, 874   **Vol. 3:** 934
1:3 ff   **Vol. 1:** 571   **Vol. 2:** 874
1:3   **Vol. 1:** 212, 620   **Vol. 2:** 73, 76, 78, 516, 598
1:4   **Vol. 2:** 808–809
1:5 ff   **Vol. 3:** 722, 998

2 Corinthians *(cont'd)*

1:5	**Vol. 1:** 639 **Vol. 2:** 808 **Vol. 3:** 724
1:6 f	**Vol. 3:** 724
1:6	**Vol. 2:** 774, 808–809
1:7 f	**Vol. 3:** 1174
1:7	**Vol. 1:** 643 **Vol. 2:** 243, 874–875 **Vol. 3:** 725
1:8–11	**Vol. 2:** 924
1:8	**Vol. 1:** 261 **Vol. 2:** 406, 809, 924
1:9	**Vol. 1:** 591–592 **Vol. 3:** 304
1:10	**Vol. 3:** 203
1:11	**Vol. 1:** 586 **Vol. 2:** 121, 861, 874 **Vol. 3:** 818, 1174
1:12 ff	**Vol. 2:** 874
1:12	**Vol. 1:** 229, 350, 353, 524, 731 **Vol. 2:** 120, 739 **Vol. 3:** 504, 934, 1031, 1043
1:13 f	**Vol. 1:** 592
1:13	**Vol. 1:** 245 **Vol. 2:** 61
1:14	**Vol. 1:** 228, 742 **Vol. 2:** 304, 517, 874, 894 **Vol. 3:** 1180
1:15 f	**Vol. 3:** 1184
1:15	**Vol. 1:** 592
1:17	**Vol. 1:** 675 **Vol. 3:** 963
1:18	**Vol. 2:** 77 **Vol. 3:** 1112
1:19 f	**Vol. 3:** 1112, 1116
1:19	**Vol. 1:** 130 **Vol. 3:** 52, 55, 643, 1198
1:20	**Vol. 1:** 99 **Vol. 2:** 874 **Vol. 3:** 55, 72, 742
1:21 f	**Vol. 3:** 499
1:21	**Vol. 1:** 123, 660
1:22	**Vol. 1:** 123, 147, 372, 638, 669 **Vol. 2:** 40, 42, 183 **Vol. 3:** 304, 499, 701
1:23	**Vol. 1:** 276 **Vol. 2:** 874 **Vol. 3:** 683, 742, 1043
1:24	**Vol. 2:** 360, 519 **Vol. 3:** 1152
2:1 ff	**Vol. 2:** 420
2:1	**Vol. 2:** 182 **Vol. 3:** 471, 1020
2:2	**Vol. 2:** 356
2:3	**Vol. 1:** 591 **Vol. 2:** 360
2:4	**Vol. 2:** 360, 546, 809 **Vol. 3:** 489
2:5–11	**Vol. 1:** 467
2:5	**Vol. 1:** 261 **Vol. 2:** 304, 420 **Vol. 3:** 1180
2:6	**Vol. 1:** 572
2:7	**Vol. 1:** 467 **Vol. 2:** 122
2:8	**Vol. 1:** 664
2:9	**Vol. 2:** 179 **Vol. 3:** 809–810, 1113
2:10	**Vol. 2:** 122 **Vol. 3:** 214
2:11	**Vol. 1:** 138, 467, 718 **Vol. 3:** 128, 471, 591
2:12 f	**Vol. 2:** 924
2:12	**Vol. 2:** 30, 111, 517, 726–727 **Vol. 3:** 1177
2:13	**Vol. 3:** 694
2:14 ff	**Vol. 3:** 170, 600
2:14–17	**Vol. 1:** 650
2:14	**Vol. 1:** 649–650 **Vol. 2:** 121, 403, 874 **Vol. 3:** 322, 600–601
2:15 f	**Vol. 1:** 248 **Vol. 3:** 601
2:15	**Vol. 1:** 464 **Vol. 3:** 214, 600
2:16	**Vol. 1:** 439 **Vol. 3:** 729
2:17	**Vol. 1:** 96, 138, 248 **Vol. 3:** 1110, 1112
3	**Vol. 2:** 786 **Vol. 3:** 495
3:1–3	**Vol. 3:** 499
3:1	**Vol. 1:** 248 **Vol. 3:** 958
3:2 f	**Vol. 1:** 247–248
3:2	**Vol. 1:** 245 **Vol. 3:** 490, 935
3:3	**Vol. 1:** 203, 248, 592 **Vol. 3:** 493, 546, 701–702
3:4–18	**Vol. 2:** 312 **Vol. 3:** 327
3:4–6	**Vol. 2:** 703
3:4	**Vol. 1:** 592 **Vol. 2:** 73
3:5 f	**Vol. 1:** 592 **Vol. 3:** 729
3:5	**Vol. 1:** 130, 248 **Vol. 3:** 729, 824, 914, 1176
3:5b	**Vol. 3:** 1188
3:6 ff	**Vol. 2:** 316
3:6–4:15	**Vol. 3:** 336
3:6–8	**Vol. 3:** 701
3:6	**Vol. 1:** 154, 248, 430 **Vol. 2:** 312, 446, 605, 671, 715 **Vol. 3:** 493, 546, 548, 702, 729, 1178, 1183
3:7 ff	**Vol. 1:** 737
3:7–18	**Vol. 3:** 706, 795
3:7–11	**Vol. 2:** 47 **Vol. 3:** 225
3:7 f	**Vol. 3:** 546
3:7	**Vol. 1:** 73 **Vol. 2:** 46, 641 **Vol. 3:** 493, 520, 547
3:8 f	**Vol. 2:** 482 **Vol. 3:** 546–547
3:9 f	**Vol. 1:** 730
3:9†	**Vol. 2:** 365, 641 **Vol. 3:** 362, 364–365, 372, 547
3:10	**Vol. 2:** 303
3:11 f	**Vol. 2:** 736
3:11	**Vol. 1:** 73 **Vol. 2:** 213 **Vol. 3:** 1176
3:12–18	**Vol. 3:** 861
3:12	**Vol. 2:** 242
3:13–18	**Vol. 3:** 701
3:13–16	**Vol. 2:** 213
3:13	**Vol. 1:** 73, 587 **Vol. 2:** 46, 61, 214 **Vol. 3:** 520
3:14 ff	**Vol. 1:** 245 **Vol. 3:** 313
3:14–17	**Vol. 3:** 701
3:14 f	**Vol. 1:** 245, 587 **Vol. 2:** 182–183, 213
3:14	**Vol. 1:** 73, 666 **Vol. 2:** 156, 213, 716 **Vol. 3:** 128, 215, 591, 1192
3:15	**Vol. 1:** 587 **Vol. 2:** 641
3:16 f	**Vol. 3:** 1178
3:16	**Vol. 1:** 245, 355, 587 **Vol. 2:** 213, 641 **Vol. 3:** 1204
3:17 f	**Vol. 2:** 641
3:17	**Vol. 1:** 147, 246, 248, 717, 719 **Vol. 2:** 81, 84, 213, 516, 873 **Vol. 3:** 493, 701
3:18	**Vol. 1:** 707 **Vol. 2:** 46–48, 213–214, 288, 756 **Vol. 3:** 303–304, 701–703, 861, 864, 1178, 1183, 1189, 1198
4	**Vol. 2:** 834
4:1	**Vol. 1:** 563 **Vol. 2:** 597 **Vol. 3:** 546, 548

2 Corinthians *(cont'd)*

4:2	**Vol. 1:** 130, 350, 413 **Vol. 2:** 217 **Vol. 3:** 323, 564, 885–886, 945, 1110, 1112
4:3	**Vol. 1:** 464 **Vol. 2:** 112, 214
4:4 ff	**Vol. 2:** 161
4:4	**Vol. 1:** 466, 587 **Vol. 2:** 46–47, 213–214, 288–289, 493–495, 609 **Vol. 3:** 128, 591, 694, 831, 1191
4:5	**Vol. 2:** 112 **Vol. 3:** 55, 596
4:6	**Vol. 1:** 175, 384, 424, 587 **Vol. 2:** 46–47, 183, 213, 402, 486, 493–495, 567, 672, 834 **Vol. 3:** 701, 914
4:7 ff	**Vol. 2:** 806
4:7–15	**Vol. 3:** 278
4:7–12	**Vol. 1:** 129, 400 **Vol. 3:** 601
4:7	**Vol. 1:** 638 **Vol. 2:** 78, 605, 830, 834 **Vol. 3:** 912, 914
4:8 ff	**Vol. 2:** 420
4:8	**Vol. 2:** 51, 808–809
4:9 f	**Vol. 2:** 481
4:9	**Vol. 1:** 464
4:10 ff	**Vol. 1:** 479, 638 **Vol. 3:** 322
4:10 f	**Vol. 2:** 566, 808
4:10	**Vol. 1:** 438, 445, 639, 679 **Vol. 2:** 47, 481, 655, 808
4:11 f	**Vol. 1:** 440
4:11	**Vol. 1:** 679 **Vol. 2:** 420, 668
4:12	**Vol. 2:** 922 **Vol. 3:** 1152
4:13	**Vol. 3:** 694, 1211
4:14	**Vol. 1:** 474 **Vol. 2:** 606, 925–926 **Vol. 3:** 281
4:14b	**Vol. 3:** 304
4:15	**Vol. 1:** 94 **Vol. 2:** 121, 131, 874 **Vol. 3:** 819, 1187
4:16	**Vol. 1:** 185, 467, 470 **Vol. 2:** 566, 671, 673, 895
4:17 f	**Vol. 3:** 832
4:17	**Vol. 1:** 261 **Vol. 2:** 46, 48, 51, 809 **Vol. 3:** 257
4:18	**Vol. 1:** 602 **Vol. 2:** 789 **Vol. 3:** 839
5	**Vol. 2:** 923–925 **Vol. 3:** 825, 1032
5:1 ff	**Vol. 2:** 482
5:1–10	**Vol. 1:** 236, 440 **Vol. 2:** 903 **Vol. 3:** 283, 304
5:1–7	**Vol. 3:** 814
5:1–5	**Vol. 1:** 470 **Vol. 3:** 702
5:1 f	**Vol. 2:** 193
5:1	**Vol. 1:** 518, 638 **Vol. 2:** 252–253, 925 **Vol. 3:** 189, 305, 814, 832, 1188
5:2 f	**Vol. 2:** 207, 925
5:2	**Vol. 1:** 313, 316, 458 **Vol. 2:** 423, 925 **Vol. 3:** 814, 1195
5:3	**Vol. 1:** 313, 316
5:4 f	**Vol. 3:** 304
5:4	**Vol. 1:** 261, 315–316, 467 **Vol. 2:** 423, 922, 925 **Vol. 3:** 302, 814, 1194–1195
5:5	**Vol. 1:** 638 **Vol. 2:** 40, 42, 605, 789 **Vol. 3:** 499, 701, 1195
5:6–9	**Vol. 2:** 789
5:6–8	**Vol. 3:** 814
5:6	**Vol. 1:** 315, 328 **Vol. 2:** 517 **Vol. 3:** 814, 1205
5:7 ff	**Vol. 3:** 945
5:7	**Vol. 1:** 601–602, 704 **Vol. 2:** 243, 482, 789 **Vol. 3:** 1031, 1182
5:8 f	**Vol. 2:** 244
5:8	**Vol. 1:** 328 **Vol. 2:** 207, 244, 482, 517, 762, 789, 818, 925–926 **Vol. 3:** 302, 1172, 1204–1205, 1207
5:9	**Vol. 2:** 550, 789, 816 **Vol. 3:** 931
5:10 f	**Vol. 3:** 322, 324
5:10	**Vol. 1:** 112, 248, 323, 564 **Vol. 2:** 102, 365, 369, 665, 789, 894 **Vol. 3:** 136, 142, 214, 277, 322, 584, 1151, 1182, 1204
5:11–21	**Vol. 2:** 398
5:11	**Vol. 1:** 350, 590, 623 **Vol. 2:** 398 **Vol. 3:** 322
5:12	**Vol. 2:** 182, 398–399 **Vol. 3:** 1199
5:13	**Vol. 1:** 502, 528 **Vol. 2:** 398
5:14 ff	**Vol. 1:** 437
5:14–20	**Vol. 3:** 572
5:14 f	**Vol. 1:** 437–438 **Vol. 2:** 398, 672 **Vol. 3:** 1197
5:14	**Vol. 1:** 375, 492 **Vol. 2:** 364, 399, 545, 721, 723 **Vol. 3:** 169, 225, 1111, 1197
5:15	**Vol. 1:** 248, 718 **Vol. 2:** 481
5:15b	**Vol. 1:** 702
5:16	**Vol. 1:** 675, 680 **Vol. 2:** 398–399, 672 **Vol. 3:** 276, 1178, 1200
5:16b	**Vol. 2:** 399 **Vol. 3:** 1199
5:17 ff	**Vol. 3:** 171
5:17	**Vol. 1:** 168, 186, 248, 299, 384–385, 440, 602, 666, 680, 702 **Vol. 2:** 83, 399, 545, 566, 671–672, 714, 781 **Vol. 3:** 831, 1192, 1207
5:18 ff	**Vol. 2:** 544 **Vol. 3:** 54, 547
5:18–21	**Vol. 3:** 168, 198
5:18–20	**Vol. 3:** 167
5:18 f	**Vol. 1:** 702 **Vol. 3:** 167, 581
5:18	**Vol. 1:** 702 **Vol. 2:** 83 **Vol. 3:** 167–169, 171, 546, 1182, 1188, 1193
5:19 ff	**Vol. 1:** 398, 525 **Vol. 2:** 545, 605
5:19 f	**Vol. 1:** 299
5:19	**Vol. 1:** 477, 524, 702 **Vol. 2:** 80, 83 **Vol. 3:** 167–169, 171–172, 586, 824, 1111–1112, 1193
5:19a	**Vol. 3:** 1192
5:20 f	**Vol. 1:** 719 **Vol. 2:** 370
5:20	**Vol. 1:** 129, 197, 398, 570 **Vol. 2:** 860 **Vol. 3:** 87, 169, 171
5:21	**Vol. 1:** 390, 417, 437, 702 **Vol. 2:** 78, 83, 366, 398, 445 **Vol. 3:** 168–171, 362–363, 576, 581, 825, 1192, 1197
6:1 ff	**Vol. 2:** 771
6:1–9	**Vol. 2:** 121
6:1	**Vol. 1:** 547, 571 **Vol. 2:** 121 **Vol. 3:** 701, 746, 1152

2 Corinthians *(cont'd)*

6:2 ff	**Vol. 2:** 894
6:2	**Vol. 1:** 638 **Vol. 2:** 178, 186, 894 **Vol. 3:** 214, 744, 746, 838
6:3 – 10	**Vol. 2:** 420
6:3 – 7a	**Vol. 3:** 1190
6:3	**Vol. 2:** 705 **Vol. 3:** 546
6:4 – 10	**Vol. 2:** 605, 809
6:4 – 7	**Vol. 3:** 886
6:4	**Vol. 2:** 664, 774, 808 **Vol. 3:** 546, 548
6:5	**Vol. 1:** 263, 613 **Vol. 2:** 136 – 137 **Vol. 3:** 857
6:6	**Vol. 2:** 470 **Vol. 3:** 702, 1177
6:7 f	**Vol. 2:** 51
6:7	**Vol. 2:** 148, 605 **Vol. 3:** 362, 886, 963
6:8 f	**Vol. 2:** 481
6:8	**Vol. 2:** 47, 50, 459 – 460
6:9	**Vol. 2:** 407 **Vol. 3:** 779, 808
6:10	**Vol. 1:** 479, 639 **Vol. 2:** 360 – 361, 420, 828, 842, 844
6:11	**Vol. 1:** 254 **Vol. 2:** 726 – 727
6:12	**Vol. 1:** 742 **Vol. 2:** 567, 600, 807 – 808
6:13	**Vol. 1:** 286, 742 **Vol. 3:** 197
6:14 ff	**Vol. 2:** 800 **Vol. 3:** 471, 934, 1165
6:14 – 7:1	**Vol. 2:** 922
6:14 – 18	**Vol. 1:** 563
6:14	**Vol. 1:** 424, 639 **Vol. 2:** 494, 741 – 742 **Vol. 3:** 362, 1160, 1164
6:15	**Vol. 1:** 125 **Vol. 2:** 304 **Vol. 3:** 471
6:16 ff	**Vol. 1:** 256
6:16	**Vol. 1:** 254, 368 **Vol. 2:** 73, 83, 249, 251 **Vol. 3:** 471, 784, 813, 944 – 945
6:16a	**Vol. 3:** 1165
6:17	**Vol. 1:** 473 **Vol. 2:** 513 **Vol. 3:** 745, 860
6:18	**Vol. 1:** 256, 615 **Vol. 2:** 69 **Vol. 3:** 645, 718, 1175
7:1	**Vol. 1:** 449, 623 **Vol. 3:** 72, 197, 694
7:2	**Vol. 1:** 138, 468, 742 **Vol. 3:** 575
7:3	**Vol. 1:** 435, 643 **Vol. 2:** 365
7:4 ff	**Vol. 1:** 571
7:4 f	**Vol. 2:** 809
7:4	**Vol. 1:** 228 **Vol. 2:** 727, 874
7:5 f	**Vol. 2:** 263
7:5	**Vol. 1:** 647, 674 **Vol. 2:** 179, 360, 924
7:6 f	**Vol. 2:** 899 – 900
7:7	**Vol. 1:** 458 **Vol. 3:** 47, 1167
7:8 – 11	**Vol. 2:** 420
7:8 – 10	**Vol. 1:** 356
7:8	**Vol. 1:** 356
7:9 f	**Vol. 1:** 359 **Vol. 3:** 1187
7:9	**Vol. 3:** 1174, 1200
7:10	**Vol. 1:** 356, 467 **Vol. 2:** 360, 420 **Vol. 3:** 1200
7:11 f	**Vol. 3:** 1169
7:11	**Vol. 1:** 458 **Vol. 2:** 360 **Vol. 3:** 97, 101, 1158, 1167, 1200
7:12	**Vol. 3:** 322, 575
7:13	**Vol. 2:** 360 **Vol. 3:** 256, 694, 1174, 1193, 1198
7:14	**Vol. 1:** 228 **Vol. 3:** 563, 885, 1174
7:15	**Vol. 1:** 622 **Vol. 2:** 567, 600 **Vol. 3:** 746
7:16	**Vol. 1:** 328 **Vol. 2:** 360
8 f	**Vol. 2:** 311
8 – 9	**Vol. 3:** 854
8	**Vol. 1:** 138 **Vol. 2:** 826 **Vol. 3:** 553
8:1 – 5	**Vol. 3:** 854
8:1 – 3	**Vol. 2:** 694
8:1	**Vol. 1:** 301 **Vol. 2:** 121 **Vol. 3:** 314
8:2	**Vol. 1:** 731 **Vol. 2:** 197, 809, 842, 844 **Vol. 3:** 572, 809 – 810, 1199
8:3 f	**Vol. 3:** 547
8:3	**Vol. 3:** 1043
8:4	**Vol. 2:** 860 **Vol. 3:** 546, 548, 854
8:5	**Vol. 2:** 42 **Vol. 3:** 547, 1021
8:6	**Vol. 2:** 121, 826 **Vol. 3:** 1169, 1187
8:7 f	**Vol. 2:** 329
8:7	**Vol. 2:** 121, 400, 546, 694 **Vol. 3:** 752, 1169, 1188
8:8 – 9	**Vol. 1:** 731 **Vol. 2:** 694
8:8	**Vol. 2:** 694, 826 **Vol. 3:** 1169
8:9 ff	**Vol. 2:** 400
8:9	**Vol. 1:** 492, 547 **Vol. 2:** 824, 826, 828, 842, 844 **Vol. 3:** 547, 810, 854
8:10 f	**Vol. 3:** 1021
8:10	**Vol. 2:** 826 **Vol. 3:** 1021, 1174
8:11	**Vol. 2:** 846 **Vol. 3:** 1021
8:12	**Vol. 3:** 746, 1180
8:13	**Vol. 2:** 499
8:14 f	**Vol. 2:** 329
8:14	**Vol. 2:** 499 **Vol. 3:** 837, 955
8:15 f	**Vol. 2:** 826
8:15	**Vol. 2:** 131
8:16 f	**Vol. 2:** 874
8:16	**Vol. 2:** 121 **Vol. 3:** 1169, 1190
8:18 f	**Vol. 2:** 826
8:18	**Vol. 2:** 111 **Vol. 3:** 817
8:19 ff	**Vol. 2:** 47
8:19	**Vol. 1:** 301, 478 **Vol. 2:** 121, 150, 694 **Vol. 3:** 546, 752
8:21	**Vol. 1:** 695
8:22 f	**Vol. 2:** 826
8:22	**Vol. 1:** 592 **Vol. 3:** 809, 1213
8:23	**Vol. 1:** 130, 642 **Vol. 2:** 826 **Vol. 3:** 548, 1174
8:24	**Vol. 1:** 228 **Vol. 3:** 752
9	**Vol. 2:** 826 **Vol. 3:** 553
9:1 – 5	**Vol. 3:** 547
9:1 – 4	**Vol. 2:** 826
9:1	**Vol. 3:** 546, 548, 752, 854
9:2 f	**Vol. 3:** 119, 410
9:2	**Vol. 3:** 1167, 1174
9:3	**Vol. 1:** 547 **Vol. 2:** 303
9:4	**Vol. 1:** 712 **Vol. 3:** 563
9:5 – 14	**Vol. 3:** 752
9:5 – 10	**Vol. 2:** 694
9:5 f	**Vol. 1:** 214

2 Corinthians *(cont'd)*

9:5	**Vol. 1:** 138, 322 **Vol. 2:** 694, 826 **Vol. 3:** 70, 350, 752, 854
9:6–13	**Vol. 1:** 347
9:6–11	**Vol. 2:** 129
9:6–9	**Vol. 3:** 854
9:6 f	**Vol. 2:** 827
9:6	**Vol. 3:** 525, 854
9:7	**Vol. 2:** 43, 329, 567, 663, 694 **Vol. 3:** 547, 854, 1180
9:8	**Vol. 1:** 731 **Vol. 2:** 121 **Vol. 3:** 197, 727–728
9:9 f	**Vol. 3:** 362
9:9	**Vol. 2:** 34, 821, 827
9:10 ff	**Vol. 2:** 844
9:10	**Vol. 1:** 733 **Vol. 2:** 129, 268, 831
9:11 f	**Vol. 2:** 874 **Vol. 3:** 819
9:11	**Vol. 2:** 842 **Vol. 3:** 572
9:12–15	**Vol. 3:** 547
9:12–13	**Vol. 2:** 694 **Vol. 3:** 752
9:12 f	**Vol. 3:** 546, 548
9:12	**Vol. 1:** 731, 741 **Vol. 2:** 329 **Vol. 3:** 552, 854, 955
9:13 ff	**Vol. 2:** 827
9:13	**Vol. 1:** 346–347, 642 **Vol. 2:** 874 **Vol. 3:** 547, 572, 809
9:14	**Vol. 1:** 458 **Vol. 2:** 121, 861, 874–875
9:15	**Vol. 2:** 41–42, 121, 694
10–13	**Vol. 2:** 111, 923–924, 927 **Vol. 3:** 1190
10–12	**Vol. 2:** 874
10:1–13:10	**Vol. 2:** 922
10:1–13:4	**Vol. 2:** 435
10:1 f	**Vol. 3:** 1190
10:1	**Vol. 1:** 328, 492, 570 **Vol. 2:** 258, 263 **Vol. 3:** 914, 929
10:2 f	**Vol. 1:** 675
10:2	**Vol. 1:** 328, 365, 592 **Vol. 2:** 860, 899 **Vol. 3:** 824–825
10:3 f	**Vol. 2:** 927
10:3	**Vol. 1:** 646, 676, 679 **Vol. 3:** 944, 963, 1188, 1200
10:4 f	**Vol. 3:** 824, 963
10:4	**Vol. 3:** 963
10:5 f	**Vol. 2:** 179
10:5	**Vol. 2:** 179, 200, 399 **Vol. 3:** 128, 197, 591, 824
10:6	**Vol. 2:** 175 **Vol. 3:** 97, 118
10:7	**Vol. 3:** 515, 824–825
10:8	**Vol. 1:** 228, 731 **Vol. 2:** 252, 517, 611
10:9	**Vol. 3:** 822
10:10 f	**Vol. 3:** 1190
10:10	**Vol. 1:** 261 **Vol. 2:** 899–900 **Vol. 3:** 714, 914, 994, 1106, 1113
10:11	**Vol. 2:** 899 **Vol. 3:** 824, 1149
10:12	**Vol. 1:** 365 **Vol. 2:** 364 **Vol. 3:** 131, 403
10:13–16	**Vol. 2:** 112 **Vol. 3:** 400
10:13	**Vol. 3:** 400, 403–404
10:15 f	**Vol. 1:** 684 **Vol. 2:** 130, 742
10:15	**Vol. 1:** 602 **Vol. 2:** 129, 425 **Vol. 3:** 404
10:16	**Vol. 1:** 662
10:17 f	**Vol. 1:** 228
10:18	**Vol. 2:** 112 **Vol. 3:** 808
10:27	**Vol. 1:** 592
10:32	**Vol. 2:** 83
11	**Vol. 2:** 311 **Vol. 3:** 1026, 1072
11:1–12:10	**Vol. 3:** 170
11:1	**Vol. 2:** 429, 668, 765 **Vol. 3:** 1026
11:2 f	**Vol. 3:** 572
11:2	**Vol. 1:** 87, 475 **Vol. 2:** 563, 581, 585 **Vol. 3:** 101, 1072, 1167
11:3	**Vol. 1:** 87, 413, 468–469, 510 **Vol. 2:** 459–460, 585 **Vol. 3:** 128
11:4	**Vol. 2:** 112, 741, 766 **Vol. 3:** 52, 55, 694–695, 701, 746, 885
11:5	**Vol. 2:** 765 **Vol. 3:** 824–825, 955
11:6	**Vol. 2:** 456 **Vol. 3:** 322, 914
11:7	**Vol. 2:** 41, 111, 263
11:8	**Vol. 3:** 144, 379, 546
11:9	**Vol. 1:** 741 **Vol. 2:** 899 **Vol. 3:** 953, 955, 1204
11:10	**Vol. 3:** 951
11:12 ff	**Vol. 1:** 228
11:12–15	**Vol. 2:** 927
11:13 ff	**Vol. 1:** 710
11:13–15	**Vol. 1:** 710
11:13	**Vol. 2:** 472 **Vol. 3:** 864
11:14	**Vol. 2:** 495, 622, 625 **Vol. 3:** 471, 864
11:15	**Vol. 1:** 710 **Vol. 2:** 61 **Vol. 3:** 362, 364, 546, 864
11:16 ff	**Vol. 1:** 229, 727
11:16–12:10	**Vol. 2:** 809
11:16 f	**Vol. 3:** 1026
11:16	**Vol. 2:** 83, 429 **Vol. 3:** 822
11:17	**Vol. 1:** 712
11:18	**Vol. 1:** 228, 675
11:19 f	**Vol. 2:** 766
11:19	**Vol. 2:** 620 **Vol. 3:** 1026
11:20 f	**Vol. 3:** 1190
11:20	**Vol. 1:** 586
11:21–12:10	**Vol. 3:** 601
11:21	**Vol. 1:** 365 **Vol. 3:** 1026
11:22	**Vol. 1:** 79, 370 **Vol. 2:** 83, 310, 315
11:23 ff	**Vol. 2:** 420 **Vol. 3:** 724, 998
11:23–30	**Vol. 1:** 727
11:23–29	**Vol. 1:** 129 **Vol. 2:** 263
11:23	**Vol. 1:** 163, 263, 731 **Vol. 2:** 136 **Vol. 3:** 546, 548, 857, 1172
11:24	**Vol. 1:** 163 **Vol. 2:** 96, 696
11:25	**Vol. 1:** 163, 407 **Vol. 2:** 717
11:26	**Vol. 1:** 257, 419 **Vol. 2:** 472 **Vol. 3:** 379, 984, 987, 1007–1008
11:27	**Vol. 1:** 263, 313, 318, 613 **Vol. 2:** 137, 267
11:28	**Vol. 1:** 278 **Vol. 2:** 895
11:29	**Vol. 1:** 656 **Vol. 2:** 708

225

2 Corinthians *(cont'd)*

11:30	**Vol. 1:** 183, 229 **Vol. 2:** 762 **Vol. 3:** 995, 1026, 1190
11:31	**Vol. 1:** 213, 620 **Vol. 2:** 472, 516, 874
11:32	**Vol. 2:** 135, 378
11:33	**Vol. 2:** 150 **Vol. 3:** 948
12	**Vol. 1:** 528 **Vol. 3:** 1026
12:1 ff	**Vol. 2:** 176, 900 **Vol. 3:** 315
12:1	**Vol. 1:** 133, 727 **Vol. 2:** 517 **Vol. 3:** 297, 515, 517
12:2 ff	**Vol. 1:** 528 **Vol. 3:** 602
12:2–4	**Vol. 2:** 192 **Vol. 3:** 694
12:2 f	**Vol. 3:** 602
12:2	**Vol. 2:** 688, 762 **Vol. 3:** 602, 1192
12:4	**Vol. 1:** 528 **Vol. 2:** 176, 688, 762–763 **Vol. 3:** 602, 1121
12:5–10	**Vol. 2:** 884
12:5	**Vol. 1:** 229 **Vol. 2:** 762 **Vol. 3:** 995, 1192
12:6 ff	**Vol. 3:** 571
12:6	**Vol. 1:** 228, 727 **Vol. 2:** 175 **Vol. 3:** 824–825
12:7 ff	**Vol. 1:** 183 **Vol. 3:** 728, 998
12:7–10	**Vol. 2:** 263
12:7	**Vol. 1:** 102–103, 163, 467, 674, 726–727 **Vol. 2:** 221 **Vol. 3:** 203, 469–471, 474, 714, 802, 857, 998
12:8 f	**Vol. 2:** 867
12:8	**Vol. 1:** 607 **Vol. 2:** 874 **Vol. 3:** 1174
12:9–10	**Vol. 3:** 914
12:9 f	**Vol. 1:** 399, 727 **Vol. 2:** 605, 762 **Vol. 3:** 995, 1190
12:9	**Vol. 1:** 163, 229, 467, 731 **Vol. 2:** 62, 121 **Vol. 3:** 315, 714, 814, 857, 971, 995, 1026, 1190, 1192, 1194
12:10	**Vol. 2:** 435, 664, 806, 808, 818 **Vol. 3:** 27, 998
12:11	**Vol. 3:** 955, 1026
12:12	**Vol. 1:** 129 **Vol. 2:** 605, 629, 632, 774 **Vol. 3:** 571
12:13	**Vol. 2:** 122 **Vol. 3:** 252
12:14	**Vol. 2:** 668, 834 **Vol. 3:** 118
12:15	**Vol. 1:** 731 **Vol. 2:** 567
12:16	**Vol. 1:** 261, 413
12:17 f	**Vol. 1:** 138
12:17	**Vol. 1:** 138
12:18	**Vol. 3:** 694
12:19	**Vol. 2:** 252, 714 **Vol. 3:** 822
12:20	**Vol. 1:** 106 **Vol. 2:** 263 **Vol. 3:** 31, 346, 928, 1167
12:21	**Vol. 1:** 359, 500 **Vol. 2:** 73, 263, 422 **Vol. 3:** 1157
12:24 ff	**Vol. 1:** 235
13:1	**Vol. 2:** 686 **Vol. 3:** 1043, 1123
13:2	**Vol. 2:** 899 **Vol. 3:** 252
13:3 f	**Vol. 2:** 605
13:3–4	**Vol. 3:** 914
13:3	**Vol. 2:** 179 **Vol. 3:** 314, 809–810
13:4	**Vol. 1:** 400 **Vol. 2:** 481, 604, 606 **Vol. 3:** 995, 1171, 1190
13:5	**Vol. 2:** 402 **Vol. 3:** 802, 808, 810, 1192
13:7	**Vol. 1:** 564 **Vol. 2:** 104, 488, 867, 874–875
13:8	**Vol. 3:** 885–886, 1199
13:9 f	**Vol. 3:** 1190
13:9	**Vol. 2:** 867, 874–875 **Vol. 3:** 350, 995
13:10	**Vol. 2:** 252, 517, 611, 899
13:11	**Vol. 1:** 571 **Vol. 2:** 79, 360, 544, 618, 780–781, 874 **Vol. 3:** 252, 350
13:12	**Vol. 2:** 549
13:13	**Vol. 1:** 643 **Vol. 2:** 84, 119, 516, 544, 687
13:14	**Vol. 2:** 874 **Vol. 3:** 327, 702
15:9	**Vol. 2:** 83
15:12	**Vol. 1:** 228
20:19	**Vol. 2:** 263

Galatians

1 f	**Vol. 2:** 311
1:1–5	**Vol. 1:** 247
1:1	**Vol. 1:** 129, 133 **Vol. 2:** 328 **Vol. 3:** 1110
1:2	**Vol. 1:** 301
1:3 f	**Vol. 3:** 62
1:3	**Vol. 2:** 516, 780, 874
1:4	**Vol. 1:** 566 **Vol. 2:** 42 **Vol. 3:** 61, 198, 611, 831, 1019, 1174, 1197
1:5	**Vol. 1:** 99 **Vol. 2:** 46, 874
1:6 ff	**Vol. 1:** 399 **Vol. 2:** 741 **Vol. 3:** 774
1:6–10	**Vol. 2:** 112
1:6–9	**Vol. 1:** 247 **Vol. 2:** 112
1:6	**Vol. 1:** 275 **Vol. 2:** 625
1:7	**Vol. 2:** 221 **Vol. 3:** 710
1:8 f	**Vol. 1:** 719 **Vol. 2:** 874 **Vol. 3:** 1201
1:8	**Vol. 1:** 103, 415 **Vol. 2:** 193, 741
1:9	**Vol. 1:** 415
1:10	**Vol. 1:** 590 **Vol. 2:** 112 **Vol. 3:** 596
1:11–17	**Vol. 3:** 55
1:11	**Vol. 2:** 111 **Vol. 3:** 314
1:12–17	**Vol. 1:** 136
1:12	**Vol. 1:** 129 **Vol. 2:** 217, 565, 900 **Vol. 3:** 322, 384, 701, 764
1:13 ff	**Vol. 2:** 282
1:13 f	**Vol. 2:** 310
1:13	**Vol. 1:** 299, 301 **Vol. 2:** 83, 806 **Vol. 3:** 934, 963
1:14	**Vol. 1:** 730 **Vol. 2:** 130 **Vol. 3:** 312, 764, 774, 1167
1:15 f	**Vol. 3:** 701, 1110
1:15	**Vol. 1:** 275, 474 **Vol. 2:** 819 **Vol. 3:** 284, 612, 701, 1071
1:16	**Vol. 1:** 129, 183, 222, 528, 675 **Vol. 2:** 111–112, 126, 794 **Vol. 3:** 643, 773, 1191
1:17 f	**Vol. 2:** 328
1:17	**Vol. 1:** 130, 133 **Vol. 2:** 523 **Vol. 3:** 1008

Galatians *(cont'd)*

1:18–20	**Vol. 2:** 328
1:18 f	**Vol. 1:** 130, 132 **Vol. 3:** 288
1:18	**Vol. 2:** 895 **Vol. 3:** 227, 383, 1204
1:19	**Vol. 1:** 130, 256
1:20	**Vol. 2:** 472 **Vol. 3:** 742
1:22 f	**Vol. 3:** 1193
1:22	**Vol. 1:** 299, 301 **Vol. 2:** 407
1:23	**Vol. 2:** 719, 806 **Vol. 3:** 61, 963
1:24	**Vol. 2:** 874
1:33	**Vol. 3:** 934
2–5	**Vol. 1:** 717
2:1 ff	**Vol. 2:** 328
2:1–14	**Vol. 3:** 549
2:1	**Vol. 1:** 129–130 **Vol. 2:** 185
2:2	**Vol. 1:** 469, 547 **Vol. 2:** 111, 328 **Vol. 3:** 52, 54, 61, 315, 563, 822, 947
2:3	**Vol. 1:** 257, 310 **Vol. 2:** 663
2:4	**Vol. 1:** 322, 717–718 **Vol. 2:** 472
2:5	**Vol. 3:** 884
2:6 ff	**Vol. 1:** 310
2:6	**Vol. 1:** 587 **Vol. 3:** 822
2:7 ff	**Vol. 3:** 454
2:7–9	**Vol. 2:** 794
2:7 f	**Vol. 2:** 111
2:7	**Vol. 1:** 132, 310 **Vol. 2:** 112 **Vol. 3:** 1211
2:8 f	**Vol. 3:** 38
2:8	**Vol. 1:** 129 **Vol. 2:** 112 **Vol. 3:** 384, 387
2:9	**Vol. 1:** 129–131, 302, 643 **Vol. 2:** 121, 126, 146 **Vol. 3:** 383, 387, 795, 822, 1184
2:10	**Vol. 2:** 826–828 **Vol. 3:** 241, 246, 1169
2:11 ff	**Vol. 3:** 386, 1066
2:11–21	**Vol. 3:** 387
2:11–14	**Vol. 1:** 310
2:11	**Vol. 2:** 365 **Vol. 3:** 383
2:12	**Vol. 1:** 310, 473 **Vol. 2:** 272, 794
2:13	**Vol. 1:** 130 **Vol. 2:** 469 **Vol. 3:** 252
2:14	**Vol. 2:** 310, 795 **Vol. 3:** 352, 383–384, 1204
2:15 f	**Vol. 3:** 549
2:15	**Vol. 2:** 660, 793 **Vol. 3:** 549
2:16 ff	**Vol. 1:** 158
2:16 f	**Vol. 3:** 363
2:16	**Vol. 1:** 157, 599, 675 **Vol. 3:** 363, 372, 549, 1151, 1178, 1190, 1212–1213
2:17	**Vol. 2:** 434 **Vol. 3:** 365, 529, 532, 546, 549
2:18–21	**Vol. 3:** 549
2:18 f	**Vol. 1:** 719
2:18	**Vol. 3:** 189
2:19 ff	**Vol. 1:** 399
2:19 f	**Vol. 1:** 439
2:19	**Vol. 1:** 397, 400–401
2:20 f	**Vol. 2:** 119, 338, 605
2:20	**Vol. 1:** 148, 235, 289, 676, 679, 727 **Vol. 2:** 368, 481, 544–545, 900 **Vol. 3:** 198, 323, 372, 643–644, 1192, 1197, 1200
2:21	**Vol. 1:** 74, 437, 602 **Vol. 2:** 41, 120 **Vol. 3:** 362–363
3	**Vol. 1:** 311 **Vol. 3:** 372, 906
3:1–4:7	**Vol. 2:** 786
3:1–5	**Vol. 1:** 719 **Vol. 3:** 967
3:1	**Vol. 1:** 301, 397, 399 **Vol. 2:** 559 **Vol. 3:** 55, 62, 129, 463, 490, 1111
3:2 f	**Vol. 3:** 701
3:2	**Vol. 1:** 158, 486 **Vol. 2:** 175 **Vol. 3:** 1151, 1178
3:3	**Vol. 1:** 680 **Vol. 3:** 129
3:4	**Vol. 3:** 723
3:5 ff	**Vol. 1:** 289
3:5	**Vol. 2:** 175, 605, 632 **Vol. 3:** 701, 1178
3:6 ff	**Vol. 1:** 78
3:6–18	**Vol. 3:** 1151
3:6–14	**Vol. 3:** 1112
3:6–9	**Vol. 1:** 78, 702
3:6 f	**Vol. 3:** 869
3:6	**Vol. 1:** 78, 157, 596, 604 **Vol. 2:** 73, 301 **Vol. 3:** 169, 362–363, 824–825, 1187, 1214
3:7	**Vol. 1:** 286, 289, 299 **Vol. 2:** 794 **Vol. 3:** 1188
3:8–14	**Vol. 1:** 214
3:8	**Vol. 1:** 157, 212, 214, 695 **Vol. 2:** 793 **Vol. 3:** 329, 363, 491–492, 515, 1012
3:9	**Vol. 3:** 1188
3:10 ff	**Vol. 1:** 601 **Vol. 2:** 101 **Vol. 3:** 161, 491
3:10–14	**Vol. 3:** 581, 1164
3:10–13	**Vol. 1:** 417 **Vol. 2:** 312
3:10	**Vol. 1:** 78, 244, 417, 719 **Vol. 2:** 102, 445, 449 **Vol. 3:** 226, 1151, 1178
3:11	**Vol. 2:** 447 **Vol. 3:** 316, 362–363, 365, 367, 369, 1177
3:12–19	**Vol. 1:** 375
3:12	**Vol. 3:** 1022
3:12b	**Vol. 2:** 445
3:13 f	**Vol. 2:** 794 **Vol. 3:** 171
3:13	**Vol. 1:** 214–215, 266, 268, 389–390, 398, 438, 509, 719 **Vol. 2:** 83, 366, 445, 504, 709 **Vol. 3:** 597, 868, 1197
3:14	**Vol. 1:** 158, 181, 214, 417 **Vol. 3:** 72, 701, 749
3:15 ff	**Vol. 2:** 445
3:15–18	**Vol. 3:** 72, 366
3:15	**Vol. 1:** 74, 369–370, 664
3:16 f	**Vol. 1:** 79
3:16–19	**Vol. 3:** 523
3:16	**Vol. 1:** 370 **Vol. 2:** 186, 338, 755 **Vol. 3:** 73, 400
3:17 ff	**Vol. 1:** 601 **Vol. 2:** 641

227

Galatians *(cont'd)*

3:17   **Vol. 1:** 73, 370, 664   **Vol. 2:** 445, 689   **Vol. 3:** 1187
3:18   **Vol. 2:** 122, 302   **Vol. 3:** 72
3:19–29   **Vol. 2:** 445
3:19 f   **Vol. 1:** 374–375
3:19   **Vol. 1:** 103, 719   **Vol. 2:** 445   **Vol. 3:** 345, 465, 585, 1182
3:20   **Vol. 2:** 73
3:21 f   **Vol. 3:** 72
3:21   **Vol. 2:** 445, 605   **Vol. 3:** 362–363
3:22 ff   **Vol. 3:** 585
3:22 f   **Vol. 2:** 445
3:22   **Vol. 3:** 492, 580
3:23 ff   **Vol. 1:** 289, 601   **Vol. 3:** 580
3:23–39   **Vol. 2:** 302
3:23   **Vol. 1:** 321, 326   **Vol. 2:** 135   **Vol. 3:** 315
3:24 ff   **Vol. 3:** 779
3:24   **Vol. 1:** 78, 370   **Vol. 2:** 445   **Vol. 3:** 363
3:25   **Vol. 1:** 321   **Vol. 2:** 445   **Vol. 3:** 779
3:26 ff   **Vol. 1:** 371   **Vol. 2:** 800
3:26–29   **Vol. 1:** 601   **Vol. 2:** 127, 794   **Vol. 3:** 1200
3:26 f   **Vol. 1:** 157–158, 289   **Vol. 2:** 445
3:26   **Vol. 1:** 146, 256   **Vol. 3:** 645, 1190, 1212
3:27 ff   **Vol. 1:** 147, 300
3:27–29   **Vol. 3:** 932
3:27   **Vol. 1:** 146, 148, 158, 186, 315–316   **Vol. 3:** 1209
3:28†   **Vol. 1:** 385, 718, 720   **Vol. 2:** 126, 309, 563, 566, 570, 722   **Vol. 3:** 1062, 1067, 1190, 1192, 1209
3:29   **Vol. 1:** 289   **Vol. 2:** 301, 570   **Vol. 3:** 523–524, 869
4   **Vol. 2:** 452
4:1 ff   **Vol. 1:** 289, 620
4:1–11   **Vol. 2:** 453
4:1–7   **Vol. 2:** 828   **Vol. 3:** 613
4:1   **Vol. 2:** 301   **Vol. 3:** 779, 843
4:2   **Vol. 1:** 477   **Vol. 2:** 254
4:3 ff   **Vol. 3:** 839
4:3   **Vol. 1:** 103, 282, 718–719   **Vol. 2:** 452–453, 828   **Vol. 3:** 596
4:4 ff   **Vol. 2:** 84
4:4–7   **Vol. 1:** 615
4:4 f   **Vol. 1:** 738   **Vol. 2:** 828   **Vol. 3:** 643, 843
4:4   **Vol. 1:** 181, 187, 268, 282, 321, 374, 549   **Vol. 2:** 78–79   **Vol. 3:** 198, 597, 661, 831, 834, 1058, 1073, 1198
4:5 ff   **Vol. 1:** 417
4:5 f   **Vol. 1:** 286
4:5   **Vol. 1:** 283, 289   **Vol. 2:** 453, 672   **Vol. 3:** 751
4:6 ff   **Vol. 2:** 605

4:6 f   **Vol. 1:** 289   **Vol. 2:** 183   **Vol. 3:** 645, 698, 701
4:6   **Vol. 1:** 410, 614–615, 621, 623, 681   **Vol. 2:** 76, 218, 605, 786, 867, 871, 873–874, 883, 896   **Vol. 3:** 62, 639, 643, 701, 703
4:7   **Vol. 2:** 301
4:8 ff   **Vol. 2:** 73
4:8–11   **Vol. 1:** 631
4:8 f   **Vol. 2:** 73, 400   **Vol. 3:** 596, 838, 1164
4:8   **Vol. 2:** 453   **Vol. 3:** 597
4:9 ff   **Vol. 3:** 837
4:9   **Vol. 1:** 718   **Vol. 2:** 400, 402, 452–453, 545, 645, 828   **Vol. 3:** 994
4:10   **Vol. 2:** 133, 828, 887   **Vol. 3:** 410
4:11   **Vol. 1:** 263, 623
4:12   **Vol. 2:** 860   **Vol. 3:** 575
4:13 f   **Vol. 3:** 998
4:13–15   **Vol. 1:** 727
4:13   **Vol. 1:** 674, 679   **Vol. 3:** 994
4:14   **Vol. 1:** 674   **Vol. 2:** 176, 559   **Vol. 3:** 746, 802
4:15   **Vol. 1:** 163, 216   **Vol. 3:** 802, 857, 1043
4:16   **Vol. 1:** 554   **Vol. 3:** 887
4:17   **Vol. 2:** 221
4:18   **Vol. 2:** 899   **Vol. 3:** 1167, 1204
4:19   **Vol. 1:** 178, 180, 286, 708   **Vol. 3:** 858, 1070
4:20   **Vol. 2:** 899   **Vol. 3:** 113, 167, 1204
4:21–31   **Vol. 1:** 80–81, 532, 601, 718, 720   **Vol. 2:** 312, 755   **Vol. 3:** 1014, 1200
4:21–26   **Vol. 1:** 49
4:21 f   **Vol. 1:** 286
4:21   **Vol. 1:** 245, 412   **Vol. 2:** 444
4:22 ff   **Vol. 2:** 452
4:22–31   **Vol. 3:** 706
4:22 f   **Vol. 1:** 284, 718
4:22   **Vol. 3:** 491
4:23 f   **Vol. 3:** 661
4:23   **Vol. 1:** 178, 286, 370
4:23a   **Vol. 3:** 1200
4:24 ff   **Vol. 2:** 316
4:24 f   **Vol. 3:** 1014
4:24   **Vol. 1:** 176, 370   **Vol. 2:** 746, 755
4:25 f   **Vol. 2:** 188, 803
4:25   **Vol. 1:** 81, 286, 371   **Vol. 2:** 329, 452
4:26 ff   **Vol. 1:** 371
4:26 f   **Vol. 3:** 1070
4:26   **Vol. 1:** 686, 689, 718   **Vol. 2:** 194, 329, 755   **Vol. 3:** 203, 1014, 1069
4:27   **Vol. 1:** 187, 411   **Vol. 2:** 356   **Vol. 3:** 858
4:28   **Vol. 1:** 81, 286, 412   **Vol. 3:** 1200
4:29   **Vol. 1:** 286   **Vol. 2:** 806   **Vol. 3:** 701, 1189, 1200
4:30 f   **Vol. 1:** 284
4:30   **Vol. 1:** 453   **Vol. 2:** 302   **Vol. 3:** 490, 492
4:31   **Vol. 1:** 286, 718

Galatians *(cont'd)*

5:1–26   **Vol. 3:** 1164
5:1–13   **Vol. 1:** 718
5:1–12   **Vol. 2:** 926
5:1–6   **Vol. 2:** 120
5:1   **Vol. 1:** 717–719   **Vol. 2:** 338   **Vol. 3:** 702, 1164
5:3 f   **Vol. 3:** 1164
5:3   **Vol. 2:** 444, 668
5:4   **Vol. 1:** 73, 611   **Vol. 2:** 120, 123   **Vol. 3:** 363
5:5   **Vol. 2:** 241–242, 245, 924   **Vol. 3:** 362, 365, 702
5:6   **Vol. 1:** 311, 336, 338, 602, 624   **Vol. 2:** 545   **Vol. 3:** 713–714, 1152, 1182
5:7   **Vol. 1:** 469, 591   **Vol. 2:** 221   **Vol. 3:** 884, 947
5:8   **Vol. 1:** 588, 592–593
5:9   **Vol. 1:** 628   **Vol. 2:** 428, 462   **Vol. 3:** 917
5:10   **Vol. 1:** 591–592   **Vol. 2:** 618   **Vol. 3:** 710, 1213
5:11 ff   **Vol. 1:** 719
5:11   **Vol. 1:** 73, 399   **Vol. 2:** 708, 806   **Vol. 3:** 54
5:12   **Vol. 2:** 668
5:13 ff   **Vol. 3:** 581
5:13–22   **Vol. 2:** 546
5:13 f   **Vol. 1:** 719–720
5:13   **Vol. 1:** 718   **Vol. 3:** 596–597, 944, 1193
5:14   **Vol. 1:** 94, 259, 738   **Vol. 2:** 445, 544, 546, 720   **Vol. 3:** 185
5:15–26   **Vol. 1:** 604
5:16 ff   **Vol. 1:** 236, 602
5:16–26   **Vol. 3:** 581
5:16–24   **Vol. 3:** 701, 1200
5:16–21   **Vol. 1:** 457
5:16 f   **Vol. 3:** 702
5:16   **Vol. 1:** 106, 457–458, 676   **Vol. 2:** 62   **Vol. 3:** 702, 944, 1167
5:17   **Vol. 1:** 676   **Vol. 3:** 1021, 1199–1200
5:18–23   **Vol. 3:** 702
5:18   **Vol. 1:** 106, 719   **Vol. 2:** 445   **Vol. 3:** 698, 702, 1164
5:19 ff†   **Vol. 1:** 535, 554   **Vol. 2:** 286   **Vol. 3:** 31, 1157
5:19–24   **Vol. 1:** 557
5:19–23   **Vol. 3:** 31, 928
5:19–21   **Vol. 1:** 681
5:19 f   **Vol. 1:** 106, 496
5:19   **Vol. 1:** 501, 676, 739   **Vol. 3:** 320, 581, 1151, 1158
5:20   **Vol. 1:** 106, 452, 535, 555   **Vol. 2:** 558   **Vol. 3:** 1167
5:21   **Vol. 1:** 513   **Vol. 2:** 300–301, 503, 924   **Vol. 3:** 84, 1158
5:22   **Vol. 1:** 106, 720, 723, 739   **Vol. 2:** 106, 360, 445, 545, 771, 780, 782   **Vol. 3:** 927
5:23   **Vol. 1:** 495–496   **Vol. 2:** 258–259
5:24   **Vol. 1:** 148, 236, 401, 676   **Vol. 3:** 581, 722
5:25   **Vol. 1:** 106, 739   **Vol. 2:** 481, 673   **Vol. 3:** 702
5:25b   **Vol. 2:** 452
5:26   **Vol. 1:** 557   **Vol. 2:** 47, 481
6:1   **Vol. 2:** 258, 605   **Vol. 3:** 350, 586, 694, 702, 707, 750, 802
6:2   **Vol. 1:** 261, 738   **Vol. 2:** 444, 446, 722   **Vol. 3:** 1151
6:3   **Vol. 3:** 822
6:4   **Vol. 1:** 229   **Vol. 2:** 724, 739   **Vol. 3:** 808
6:5   **Vol. 1:** 261
6:6   **Vol. 2:** 101   **Vol. 3:** 61, 771, 1110
6:7 ff   **Vol. 3:** 134
6:7–10   **Vol. 2:** 926–927
6:7 f   **Vol. 1:** 469   **Vol. 3:** 204, 525
6:7   **Vol. 2:** 459–460   **Vol. 3:** 341, 525
6:8   **Vol. 1:** 681, 719   **Vol. 2:** 482, 924   **Vol. 3:** 701–702, 832
6:9   **Vol. 2:** 102, 104   **Vol. 3:** 189, 839, 1155
6:10   **Vol. 1:** 256   **Vol. 2:** 101, 249, 251, 719   **Vol. 3:** 752, 838, 1151, 1199, 1204
6:11   **Vol. 1:** 163, 247, 727   **Vol. 2:** 148   **Vol. 3:** 489, 492, 802
6:12 ff   **Vol. 1:** 310
6:12 f   **Vol. 1:** 310
6:12   **Vol. 1:** 399, 675   **Vol. 2:** 806
6:13 f   **Vol. 1:** 311
6:13   **Vol. 1:** 228, 675, 680   **Vol. 2:** 135   **Vol. 3:** 1158
6:14 f   **Vol. 1:** 385
6:14   **Vol. 1:** 228, 397, 399, 401, 438, 680   **Vol. 2:** 420, 671
6:15   **Vol. 1:** 311, 336, 384, 602   **Vol. 2:** 452, 671–672, 781   **Vol. 3:** 400
6:16   **Vol. 1:** 51, 61, 257   **Vol. 2:** 218, 313, 339, 452, 573, 597, 780, 874   **Vol. 3:** 400, 871
6:17   **Vol. 1:** 163, 235, 399, 727   **Vol. 2:** 573   **Vol. 3:** 252, 1113
6:18   **Vol. 1:** 99   **Vol. 2:** 874   **Vol. 3:** 693

Ephesians

1:1   **Vol. 1:** 130   **Vol. 3:** 1020
1:2   **Vol. 2:** 780, 874
1:3–14   **Vol. 2:** 302
1:3–11   **Vol. 2:** 77
1:3–6   **Vol. 3:** 817
1:3   **Vol. 1:** 212, 214, 620   **Vol. 2:** 73, 76, 196, 516, 874   **Vol. 3:** 72, 197, 706, 967
1:4   **Vol. 1:** 377–378, 542   **Vol. 2:** 302   **Vol. 3:** 925
1:5 ff   **Vol. 2:** 129
1:5   **Vol. 1:** 696   **Vol. 2:** 819   **Vol. 3:** 1019
1:6 f   **Vol. 2:** 122

Ephesians *(cont'd)*

1:6   **Vol. 2:** 122, 874   **Vol. 3:** 504
1:7 ff   **Vol. 1:** 730
1:7 f   **Vol. 3:** 701
1:7   **Vol. 1:** 221, 223–224, 398, 701   **Vol. 2:** 79, 122, 302, 844   **Vol. 3:** 166, 198–200, 586
1:8   **Vol. 3:** 197, 966, 1032
1:9 f   **Vol. 3:** 504
1:9   **Vol. 1:** 697, 738   **Vol. 2:** 620, 819   **Vol. 3:** 314, 1019
1:10–23 **Vol. 2:** 195
1:10   **Vol. 1:** 738   **Vol. 2:** 129, 163, 195, 255, 302   **Vol. 3:** 504, 1019, 1032, 1176
1:11–14 **Vol. 2:** 300
1:11 f   **Vol. 2:** 302   **Vol. 3:** 1018
1:11   **Vol. 1:** 696–697   **Vol. 2:** 299–300, 819   **Vol. 3:** 1017–1019, 1152
1:12   **Vol. 2:** 241, 874
1:13 f   **Vol. 3:** 701
1:13   **Vol. 1:** 147, 158   **Vol. 2:** 113, 176, 302   **Vol. 3:** 214, 499, 701, 1212
1:14   **Vol. 1:** 372   **Vol. 2:** 839, 874   **Vol. 3:** 199, 499, 702
1:15 ff **Vol. 2:** 874
1:15 f   **Vol. 3:** 818
1:15   **Vol. 2:** 230, 546   **Vol. 3:** 1212
1:16–23 **Vol. 2:** 874–875
1:16   **Vol. 3:** 246
1:17 f   **Vol. 3:** 258, 702
1:17   **Vol. 1:** 437   **Vol. 2:** 46, 400, 516   **Vol. 3:** 315, 694, 701, 1032
1:18   **Vol. 2:** 47, 243, 300, 302, 844   **Vol. 3:** 516
1:19 ff **Vol. 3:** 287
1:19   **Vol. 2:** 78, 605   **Vol. 3:** 714, 718
1:20–23 **Vol. 2:** 209
1:20 f   **Vol. 1:** 103, 302   **Vol. 2:** 514, 518, 604
1:20   **Vol. 1:** 402, 445   **Vol. 2:** 80–81, 147, 196, 515   **Vol. 3:** 588, 1152
1:21 f   **Vol. 2:** 162
1:21   **Vol. 1:** 103, 326   **Vol. 2:** 603, 609   **Vol. 3:** 197, 795, 831
1:22 f   **Vol. 1:** 237
1:22   **Vol. 1:** 95   **Vol. 2:** 243   **Vol. 3:** 390
1:23   **Vol. 1:** 740   **Vol. 2:** 81, 83, 195   **Vol. 3:** 1191
2 f   **Vol. 2:** 794
2   **Vol. 3:** 185
2:1 ff   **Vol. 3:** 934, 944
2:1–3:6 **Vol. 2:** 302
2:1   **Vol. 1:** 310, 355, 402, 446   **Vol. 3:** 586, 1176
2:2 f   **Vol. 1:** 676
2:2   **Vol. 1:** 169, 289, 449, 452, 524, 593   **Vol. 2:** 193   **Vol. 3:** 471, 694, 802, 944, 1152
2:3   **Vol. 1:** 112, 286, 457   **Vol. 2:** 660, 794   **Vol. 3:** 252, 934

2:4–9   **Vol. 2:** 597
2:4   **Vol. 2:** 597, 842
2:5–10   **Vol. 2:** 660
2:5–8   **Vol. 1:** 157   **Vol. 3:** 204
2:5   **Vol. 1:** 446, 643   **Vol. 2:** 122   **Vol. 3:** 586
2:6   **Vol. 1:** 402, 643, 689   **Vol. 2:** 196, 380   **Vol. 3:** 277, 588, 966
2:7   **Vol. 1:** 322   **Vol. 2:** 106, 122, 844
2:8 f   **Vol. 1:** 228   **Vol. 2:** 122
2:8   **Vol. 1:** 158   **Vol. 2:** 41–42   **Vol. 3:** 214, 701, 1190
2:10   **Vol. 1:** 386   **Vol. 2:** 83, 101, 129   **Vol. 3:** 118, 143, 1154, 1193
2:11 ff **Vol. 1:** 689
2:11–22 **Vol. 3:** 390, 1018
2:11–21 **Vol. 3:** 1200
2:11 f   **Vol. 1:** 676   **Vol. 2:** 794
2:11   **Vol. 2:** 150
2:12 ff **Vol. 1:** 301
2:12   **Vol. 1:** 685   **Vol. 2:** 241–242, 742, 804   **Vol. 3:** 73, 172, 837
2:13–16 **Vol. 2:** 722
2:13   **Vol. 1:** 223, 398   **Vol. 3:** 166, 172
2:14 ff **Vol. 1:** 311   **Vol. 3:** 674
2:14–22 **Vol. 2:** 163
2:14–18 **Vol. 2:** 443, 781   **Vol. 3:** 172
2:14 f   **Vol. 2:** 591   **Vol. 3:** 1154
2:14   **Vol. 1:** 331, 555   **Vol. 2:** 328, 646   **Vol. 3:** 180, 185–186, 323, 795, 949
2:15 f   **Vol. 3:** 186
2:15   **Vol. 1:** 73, 330–331, 336–337, 385, 402, 679   **Vol. 2:** 122, 163, 447, 566, 671   **Vol. 3:** 500, 949
2:16   **Vol. 1:** 402, 430, 555   **Vol. 3:** 167, 171–172, 432, 949
2:17–22 **Vol. 2:** 794
2:17   **Vol. 2:** 113, 780, 782
2:18 f   **Vol. 3:** 941
2:18   **Vol. 1:** 223   **Vol. 2:** 83, 605, 721   **Vol. 3:** 40, 315, 327, 336, 500, 504, 701, 1210
2:19 ff **Vol. 2:** 253
2:19–22 **Vol. 2:** 249, 251
2:19 f   **Vol. 3:** 387
2:19   **Vol. 1:** 256, 689, 691   **Vol. 2:** 83, 129, 228, 249, 251, 794, 804
2:20 ff **Vol. 1:** 331   **Vol. 2:** 129
2:20–22 **Vol. 1:** 662   **Vol. 3:** 393
2:20 f   **Vol. 2:** 129   **Vol. 3:** 504
2:20   **Vol. 1:** 661–662   **Vol. 2:** 249, 253, 313   **Vol. 3:** 84, 387, 390, 393, 397, 500
2:21   **Vol. 1:** 623   **Vol. 2:** 83   **Vol. 3:** 186, 784
2:22   **Vol. 2:** 163, 249, 253
2:28   **Vol. 3:** 542
3:1–13   **Vol. 2:** 794
3:1–9   **Vol. 2:** 113

Ephesians *(cont'd)*

3:1–6   **Vol. 1:** 129
3:1   **Vol. 2:** 573, 794   **Vol. 3:** 592
3:2   **Vol. 2:** 255
3:3   **Vol. 2:** 900   **Vol. 3:** 314, 490, 533
3:4   **Vol. 3:** 129, 132
3:5 ff   **Vol. 2:** 217
3:5   **Vol. 1:** 289   **Vol. 2:** 35   **Vol. 3:** 84, 314, 321–322, 533, 701, 967
3:6 f   **Vol. 2:** 126
3:6   **Vol. 2:** 302   **Vol. 3:** 73, 504
3:7   **Vol. 3:** 546, 548, 1152
3:8 ff   **Vol. 1:** 697   **Vol. 3:** 837
3:8–10   **Vol. 2:** 75
3:8   **Vol. 2:** 217, 429, 842   **Vol. 3:** 504, 966
3:9 f   **Vol. 3:** 1032
3:9   **Vol. 2:** 255, 655   **Vol. 3:** 504, 830
3:10   **Vol. 1:** 302   **Vol. 2:** 193, 196, 609   **Vol. 3:** 314
3:11 f   **Vol. 3:** 941
3:12   **Vol. 1:** 592, 638   **Vol. 3:** 966
3:13 f   **Vol. 2:** 856
3:13   **Vol. 1:** 563   **Vol. 2:** 573, 809   **Vol. 3:** 505
3:14 ff   **Vol. 3:** 505
3:14–19   **Vol. 2:** 874
3:14 f   **Vol. 1:** 621   **Vol. 2:** 655, 867
3:14   **Vol. 2:** 859, 869   **Vol. 3:** 1204
3:15   **Vol. 1:** 616   **Vol. 2:** 192, 195, 655   **Vol. 3:** 504, 1133
3:16 f   **Vol. 2:** 605   **Vol. 3:** 701
3:16   **Vol. 2:** 46–47, 76, 78, 844
3:17 ff   **Vol. 2:** 546
3:17   **Vol. 1:** 148, 662   **Vol. 2:** 183, 251   **Vol. 3:** 868
3:18   **Vol. 1:** 254   **Vol. 2:** 198   **Vol. 3:** 750
3:19   **Vol. 1:** 740   **Vol. 2:** 78, 545
3:20 f   **Vol. 2:** 874
3:20   **Vol. 1:** 730   **Vol. 2:** 78
3:21   **Vol. 1:** 99, 662   **Vol. 2:** 35, 46
4   **Vol. 2:** 723
4:1–16   **Vol. 2:** 722   **Vol. 3:** 548
4:1   **Vol. 1:** 275, 571   **Vol. 2:** 263, 517   **Vol. 3:** 349, 592, 945, 965–966
4:2 ff   **Vol. 3:** 927
4:2   **Vol. 2:** 259, 263, 765, 771
4:3 ff   **Vol. 1:** 302
4:3 f   **Vol. 2:** 163   **Vol. 3:** 702
4:3   **Vol. 1:** 602   **Vol. 2:** 133, 669, 721–722, 780, 782   **Vol. 3:** 592, 1169
4:4 ff   **Vol. 2:** 84, 721
4:4–6   **Vol. 1:** 147
4:4   **Vol. 2:** 243, 721–722
4:5 f   **Vol. 2:** 515
4:5   **Vol. 1:** 146–147, 602   **Vol. 2:** 515, 721   **Vol. 3:** 61
4:6   **Vol. 1:** 375, 620   **Vol. 2:** 73
4:7   **Vol. 1:** 93, 638   **Vol. 2:** 41, 122, 517   **Vol. 3:** 403

4:8 ff   **Vol. 1:** 302   **Vol. 2:** 186   **Vol. 3:** 494
4:8   **Vol. 2:** 42, 185–186, 199, 209, 785   **Vol. 3:** 87, 203, 591, 965
4:9   **Vol. 2:** 122, 195, 303
4:10   **Vol. 2:** 195
4:11 ff   **Vol. 3:** 1067
4:11–16   **Vol. 3:** 703
4:11   **Vol. 1:** 66, 129, 302, 486   **Vol. 2:** 114   **Vol. 3:** 84, 568, 703, 767–768
4:12   **Vol. 1:** 92, 237, 302   **Vol. 2:** 249, 253   **Vol. 3:** 350, 546–547
4:13   **Vol. 1:** 92–93, 282, 302, 325, 602, 740   **Vol. 2:** 62, 162–163, 563, 722   **Vol. 3:** 350, 403
4:14 ff   **Vol. 1:** 325
4:14   **Vol. 1:** 92, 238, 282, 413, 740   **Vol. 2:** 459–460   **Vol. 3:** 770, 943, 1002, 1204
4:15 f   **Vol. 1:** 238   **Vol. 2:** 129
4:15   **Vol. 1:** 282   **Vol. 2:** 162, 568   **Vol. 3:** 886–887
4:16   **Vol. 1:** 92, 241   **Vol. 2:** 128, 162, 249, 253, 304, 499, 546, 568   **Vol. 3:** 403, 1152, 1190
4:17   **Vol. 1:** 552   **Vol. 2:** 517, 793   **Vol. 3:** 130
4:18   **Vol. 1:** 424, 685   **Vol. 2:** 183, 567, 742   **Vol. 3:** 127
4:19   **Vol. 1:** 138   **Vol. 2:** 368   **Vol. 3:** 197
4:20 f   **Vol. 2:** 176
4:20   **Vol. 1:** 486–487   **Vol. 3:** 931
4:21   **Vol. 3:** 765, 886
4:22 ff   **Vol. 1:** 457   **Vol. 2:** 566
4:22   **Vol. 1:** 315, 457, 468–469, 718   **Vol. 2:** 460, 473, 675, 715   **Vol. 3:** 886, 934
4:23 f   **Vol. 2:** 673
4:23   **Vol. 1:** 106, 458   **Vol. 2:** 675–676   **Vol. 3:** 130, 694
4:24   **Vol. 1:** 106, 315–316, 386   **Vol. 2:** 237, 473, 671   **Vol. 3:** 362, 365, 886, 1200
4:25 ff   **Vol. 1:** 259
4:25   **Vol. 1:** 231–232, 315   **Vol. 2:** 473   **Vol. 3:** 886, 967
4:26   **Vol. 1:** 110–111   **Vol. 3:** 731
4:27   **Vol. 3:** 470
4:28   **Vol. 1:** 639   **Vol. 2:** 41, 694   **Vol. 3:** 378, 854
4:29   **Vol. 2:** 118, 249, 253   **Vol. 3:** 449, 967
4:30   **Vol. 1:** 147   **Vol. 2:** 894   **Vol. 3:** 499, 701, 703
4:31   **Vol. 1:** 106, 110, 202   **Vol. 3:** 31, 343
4:32–5:2   **Vol. 3:** 927
4:32   **Vol. 1:** 110, 702   **Vol. 2:** 122, 600
5:1   **Vol. 1:** 287, 491–492
5:2   **Vol. 1:** 492   **Vol. 2:** 42, 209, 544   **Vol. 3:** 198, 432, 600–601, 944, 1197
5:3 ff   **Vol. 3:** 31
5:3   **Vol. 1:** 138, 501   **Vol. 2:** 655   **Vol. 3:** 197
5:4   **Vol. 2:** 874   **Vol. 3:** 819, 1026

Ephesians *(cont'd)*

5:5   **Vol. 1:** 138   **Vol. 2:** 286, 300, 388, 400
5:6   **Vol. 1:** 110, 112, 289, 321, 547, 593   **Vol. 2:** 76, 459   **Vol. 3:** 572
5:8 ff   **Vol. 3:** 945
5:8 f   **Vol. 3:** 838
5:8   **Vol. 1:** 286, 355, 424   **Vol. 2:** 493, 495, 517   **Vol. 3:** 446, 839, 944
5:9   **Vol. 1:** 723   **Vol. 2:** 495   **Vol. 3:** 362, 365
5:10   **Vol. 2:** 816   **Vol. 3:** 808, 810, 931
5:11   **Vol. 1:** 424, 644
5:12   **Vol. 2:** 214, 217   **Vol. 3:** 564
5:13   **Vol. 2:** 141   **Vol. 3:** 322, 967
5:14   **Vol. 2:** 186   **Vol. 3:** 276, 492
5:15 f   **Vol. 2:** 256   **Vol. 3:** 446–447
5:15   **Vol. 3:** 133, 945, 1026, 1032
5:16   **Vol. 1:** 268   **Vol. 3:** 838–839
5:17 f   **Vol. 3:** 1020
5:17   **Vol. 3:** 131, 133, 1026
5:18 ff   **Vol. 3:** 671, 674–675
5:18–20   **Vol. 1:** 514
5:18 f   **Vol. 3:** 703, 967
5:18   **Vol. 1:** 514   **Vol. 3:** 922, 1210
5:19   **Vol. 2:** 874   **Vol. 3:** 669–671, 673, 706, 967
5:20   **Vol. 1:** 620   **Vol. 2:** 654, 874   **Vol. 3:** 675, 819
5:21–6:9   **Vol. 1:** 59, 514
5:21–33   **Vol. 1:** 496   **Vol. 2:** 579, 905, 923   **Vol. 3:** 219, 535, 539, 1067
5:21   **Vol. 1:** 623   **Vol. 3:** 929, 1064
5:22 ff   **Vol. 2:** 160, 545, 563, 581
5:22–6:9   **Vol. 3:** 929, 932
5:22–32   **Vol. 2:** 585
5:22   **Vol. 3:** 1064
5:23   **Vol. 2:** 349, 579   **Vol. 3:** 220
5:25 ff   **Vol. 3:** 220
5:25–27   **Vol. 1:** 302
5:25   **Vol. 1:** 492   **Vol. 2:** 209, 368, 563   **Vol. 3:** 1063–1064, 1197
5:26 f   **Vol. 2:** 349
5:26   **Vol. 1:** 147, 153–154, 157–158, 185   **Vol. 3:** 107, 967, 990
5:27   **Vol. 1:** 475   **Vol. 2:** 47   **Vol. 3:** 924–925
5:28–33   **Vol. 2:** 722
5:28   **Vol. 2:** 563   **Vol. 3:** 1064
5:30   **Vol. 1:** 231–232, 241
5:31   **Vol. 2:** 349, 579, 722   **Vol. 3:** 535, 1064, 1070
5:32   **Vol. 2:** 349, 581   **Vol. 3:** 505, 1064, 1068
6:1 ff   **Vol. 1:** 289
6:1–9   **Vol. 2:** 180
6:1–4   **Vol. 1:** 619
6:1–3   **Vol. 1:** 160
6:1   **Vol. 1:** 286   **Vol. 3:** 362
6:2   **Vol. 1:** 336   **Vol. 3:** 95

6:4   **Vol. 1:** 110, 286, 568–569   **Vol. 3:** 777, 779
6:5–8   **Vol. 3:** 582
6:5   **Vol. 1:** 623   **Vol. 2:** 509, 513   **Vol. 3:** 596
6:6   **Vol. 2:** 815–817   **Vol. 3:** 685, 854
6:7   **Vol. 2:** 565
6:8   **Vol. 1:** 718
6:9   **Vol. 1:** 587   **Vol. 2:** 51, 513   **Vol. 3:** 583, 598
6:10 ff   **Vol. 1:** 647, 718
6:10–17   **Vol. 3:** 364, 802, 965
6:10   **Vol. 2:** 517, 604   **Vol. 3:** 252, 714, 718
6:11–17   **Vol. 2:** 925
6:11   **Vol. 1:** 316   **Vol. 3:** 470–471, 943, 965
6:12   **Vol. 1:** 167, 222, 424, 449, 452, 566, 647, 676, 679, 718   **Vol. 2:** 193, 514, 518, 559   **Vol. 3:** 707, 718, 838
6:13   **Vol. 1:** 566   **Vol. 2:** 887   **Vol. 3:** 749, 965
6:14   **Vol. 1:** 240   **Vol. 3:** 121, 362, 365, 886, 966
6:15   **Vol. 1:** 239   **Vol. 2:** 113, 780   **Vol. 3:** 117–118, 966
6:16   **Vol. 1:** 566, 656   **Vol. 3:** 109, 471, 749, 966
6:17–20   **Vol. 2:** 868
6:17   **Vol. 3:** 703, 966–967
6:18 ff   **Vol. 2:** 874   **Vol. 3:** 802
6:18 f   **Vol. 2:** 768   **Vol. 3:** 1174, 1176
6:18   **Vol. 2:** 137, 768, 861, 873, 883   **Vol. 3:** 702, 705, 839
6:19   **Vol. 2:** 726–727, 736   **Vol. 3:** 314, 322
6:20   **Vol. 1:** 197   **Vol. 2:** 736   **Vol. 3:** 169
6:21–33   **Vol. 2:** 51
6:21   **Vol. 3:** 314, 546, 548, 1157
6:23 f   **Vol. 2:** 874
6:23   **Vol. 2:** 545, 780
6:24   **Vol. 1:** 469   **Vol. 3:** 302

Philippians

1   **Vol. 2:** 924–925
1:1   **Vol. 1:** 191, 300, 718, 720   **Vol. 2:** 550   **Vol. 3:** 546, 548, 596, 613
1:2   **Vol. 2:** 516, 780, 874
1:3 ff   **Vol. 2:** 874
1:3–11   **Vol. 1:** 247
1:3   **Vol. 2:** 73   **Vol. 3:** 246
1:4   **Vol. 2:** 861, 874–875
1:5 f   **Vol. 2:** 360
1:5   **Vol. 1:** 643   **Vol. 2:** 360   **Vol. 3:** 818
1:6   **Vol. 2:** 102, 130, 243, 894, 922, 926   **Vol. 3:** 1151
1:7   **Vol. 1:** 637, 644, 658–659   **Vol. 2:** 121, 617   **Vol. 3:** 362, 592
1:8   **Vol. 2:** 567, 600   **Vol. 3:** 1043
1:9 ff   **Vol. 2:** 874–875
1:9   **Vol. 1:** 730   **Vol. 2:** 391, 400, 707   **Vol. 3:** 197

Philippians *(cont'd)*

1:10 f   **Vol. 1:** 467
1:10   **Vol. 2:** 391, 707, 894, 922, 926   **Vol. 3:** 279, 808, 810, 1187
1:11   **Vol. 1:** 723, 739   **Vol. 2:** 874   **Vol. 3:** 362, 365, 817, 1187
1:12 ff   **Vol. 3:** 38, 592
1:12   **Vol. 2:** 398
1:13 f   **Vol. 3:** 592
1:13   **Vol. 3:** 252, 320, 1192
1:14   **Vol. 1:** 592, 731   **Vol. 3:** 61, 1110
1:15 ff   **Vol. 2:** 360
1:15–18   **Vol. 2:** 360
1:15   **Vol. 1:** 558   **Vol. 2:** 818   **Vol. 3:** 52, 55
1:16   **Vol. 1:** 471
1:17–26   **Vol. 3:** 38
1:17   **Vol. 2:** 809   **Vol. 3:** 101, 280, 592
1:18   **Vol. 2:** 360   **Vol. 3:** 54
1:19–26   **Vol. 3:** 432
1:19 f   **Vol. 2:** 874
1:19   **Vol. 2:** 605, 861   **Vol. 3:** 703
1:20 ff   **Vol. 3:** 203
1:20–26   **Vol. 3:** 279
1:20   **Vol. 1:** 440–441   **Vol. 2:** 244–245, 360, 566, 736
1:21   **Vol. 1:** 440   **Vol. 2:** 481   **Vol. 3:** 137, 227, 279
1:22–24   **Vol. 1:** 676
1:22   **Vol. 1:** 534, 723   **Vol. 2:** 925   **Vol. 3:** 314, 323
1:23   **Vol. 1:** 315, 457, 679   **Vol. 2:** 187, 207, 482, 762, 925–926   **Vol. 3:** 302, 1205, 1207
1:24   **Vol. 1:** 679   **Vol. 3:** 227, 323
1:25 f   **Vol. 2:** 130
1:25   **Vol. 1:** 592   **Vol. 2:** 130, 360, 924   **Vol. 3:** 228
1:26   **Vol. 1:** 229, 730   **Vol. 2:** 605, 874, 899–900   **Vol. 3:** 1204
1:27   **Vol. 1:** 646–647   **Vol. 2:** 111, 804   **Vol. 3:** 349, 685, 702
1:28   **Vol. 1:** 464, 623
1:29   **Vol. 2:** 122   **Vol. 3:** 725, 1212–1213
1:30   **Vol. 1:** 648
2   **Vol. 1:** 400, 549, 714   **Vol. 2:** 500, 620
2:1 ff   **Vol. 1:** 400   **Vol. 2:** 187, 546   **Vol. 3:** 942
2:1–18   **Vol. 3:** 687
2:1–4   **Vol. 3:** 597
2:1 f   **Vol. 2:** 360
2:1   **Vol. 1:** 328–329, 570   **Vol. 2:** 598, 600   **Vol. 3:** 702
2:2   **Vol. 2:** 618, 722   **Vol. 3:** 687
2:3   **Vol. 2:** 47, 262, 617   **Vol. 3:** 928
2:4 ff   **Vol. 1:** 301   **Vol. 3:** 929
2:5 ff   **Vol. 1:** 492   **Vol. 2:** 343, 618   **Vol. 3:** 137, 529–530, 597
2:5–11   **Vol. 1:** 472, 483, 706   **Vol. 2:** 203, 504, 514, 844   **Vol. 3:** 603–604, 644

2:5   **Vol. 2:** 179, 262, 504, 619   **Vol. 3:** 1192
2:6 ff   **Vol. 1:** 707   **Vol. 2:** 262, 289, 828
2:6–11   **Vol. 1:** 147, 398, 547, 706–707   **Vol. 2:** 262, 500, 618   **Vol. 3:** 61, 612, 674
2:6–8   **Vol. 2:** 203
2:6 f   **Vol. 2:** 500
2:6   **Vol. 1:** 400, 547, 705   **Vol. 2:** 80–82, 498   **Vol. 3:** 603, 712
2:6b   **Vol. 3:** 604
2:7 f   **Vol. 1:** 437
2:7   **Vol. 1:** 455, 546, 548–549, 709   **Vol. 2:** 187, 262, 504, 565, 855   **Vol. 3:** 583, 596, 604, 661, 748, 1064
2:8 ff   **Vol. 1:** 399   **Vol. 2:** 91, 119
2:8–11   **Vol. 2:** 926   **Vol. 3:** 55
2:8 f   **Vol. 3:** 298
2:8   **Vol. 1:** 223, 335, 398, 549   **Vol. 2:** 80, 179, 187, 445, 500   **Vol. 3:** 165, 364, 529–530, 1190
2:8b   **Vol. 2:** 445   **Vol. 3:** 597
2:8c   **Vol. 2:** 262
2:9 ff   **Vol. 1:** 95, 102–103   **Vol. 2:** 514
2:9–11   **Vol. 2:** 81, 203, 386
2:9 f   **Vol. 2:** 195, 654
2:9   **Vol. 1:** 123, 406   **Vol. 2:** 203, 332
2:10 f   **Vol. 2:** 196, 262, 369, 619, 926   **Vol. 3:** 279
2:10   **Vol. 1:** 518   **Vol. 2:** 187, 194, 859, 925
2:11   **Vol. 1:** 168, 205, 347   **Vol. 2:** 187, 514–515, 874   **Vol. 3:** 1079, 1187
2:12–16   **Vol. 2:** 187, 230
2:12–15   **Vol. 1:** 491
2:12   **Vol. 1:** 299, 622–623   **Vol. 2:** 91, 179, 724, 899–900   **Vol. 3:** 214
2:12b   **Vol. 2:** 566
2:13 f   **Vol. 2:** 819
2:13   **Vol. 1:** 623   **Vol. 2:** 83, 566   **Vol. 3:** 143, 1021, 1152, 1178
2:14   **Vol. 3:** 821, 1155
2:15   **Vol. 1:** 525   **Vol. 2:** 36, 139, 144, 488, 493, 495   **Vol. 3:** 924–925
2:16–17   **Vol. 1:** 649
2:16   **Vol. 1:** 229, 263, 547   **Vol. 2:** 47, 481, 874, 894, 922   **Vol. 3:** 61, 563, 947, 1111
2:17 f   **Vol. 2:** 360
2:17   **Vol. 1:** 479, 648   **Vol. 2:** 42, 360   **Vol. 3:** 38, 431, 552
2:19   **Vol. 1:** 299
2:20 f   **Vol. 2:** 360
2:20   **Vol. 1:** 278, 637   **Vol. 2:** 498–499
2:21   **Vol. 1:** 278   **Vol. 2:** 360, 605   **Vol. 3:** 532
2:22   **Vol. 1:** 286   **Vol. 3:** 596, 809–810
2:24   **Vol. 1:** 591–592
2:25 ff   **Vol. 3:** 1164
2:25–30   **Vol. 2:** 221
2:25   **Vol. 1:** 130   **Vol. 2:** 816   **Vol. 3:** 548, 553, 957
2:26   **Vol. 3:** 1193

Philippians *(cont'd)*

2:27	**Vol. 2:** 597
2:28	**Vol. 3:** 1169
2:29	**Vol. 2:** 51, 517
2:30	**Vol. 1:** 741 **Vol. 3:** 553, 683, 955, 1151
3	**Vol. 3:** 278
3:1	**Vol. 2:** 359–360, 517 **Vol. 3:** 252, 1194
3:2 ff	**Vol. 2:** 401, 924
3:2 f	**Vol. 1:** 117
3:2	**Vol. 1:** 309, 311, 564 **Vol. 3:** 517
3:3–7	**Vol. 1:** 681
3:3 f	**Vol. 1:** 592, 675, 679
3:3	**Vol. 1:** 228, 311 **Vol. 2:** 218, 573, 786, 874 **Vol. 3:** 550, 701–702, 1192
3:4	**Vol. 1:** 592 **Vol. 3:** 822
3:5–11	**Vol. 2:** 444
3:5	**Vol. 1:** 309, 311, 370 **Vol. 2:** 310, 315, 692, 695, 812 **Vol. 3:** 465, 872
3:6	**Vol. 1:** 301, 556, 681 **Vol. 2:** 139, 282, 806 **Vol. 3:** 161, 363, 1167
3:7 ff	**Vol. 1:** 400
3:7 f	**Vol. 3:** 873
3:7	**Vol. 2:** 835 **Vol. 3:** 136
3:8 ff	**Vol. 1:** 638 **Vol. 2:** 605
3:8–11	**Vol. 1:** 675
3:8	**Vol. 1:** 480 **Vol. 2:** 403 **Vol. 3:** 137, 278
3:9	**Vol. 1:** 649, 681 **Vol. 2:** 78 **Vol. 3:** 137, 278, 362–364, 367, 529–530, 1177, 1188
3:10–16	**Vol. 2:** 402
3:10–14	**Vol. 1:** 649
3:10 f	**Vol. 2:** 420 **Vol. 3:** 278
3:10†	**Vol. 1:** 401, 643, 648–649, 707 **Vol. 2:** 402–403, 604, 606, 808 **Vol. 3:** 276–278, 722, 724–725
3:11	**Vol. 1:** 325 **Vol. 3:** 278, 489
3:12 ff	**Vol. 2:** 807 **Vol. 3:** 749
3:12–16	**Vol. 2:** 569 **Vol. 3:** 278
3:12–15	**Vol. 2:** 129
3:12 f	**Vol. 2:** 741 **Vol. 3:** 750
3:12	**Vol. 1:** 491, 649 **Vol. 2:** 62, 806
3:13	**Vol. 1:** 493 **Vol. 3:** 824–825
3:14	**Vol. 1:** 275, 649 **Vol. 2:** 52, 62, 188, 194, 741, 806 **Vol. 3:** 142
3:15	**Vol. 1:** 649 **Vol. 2:** 62, 618, 741 **Vol. 3:** 315
3:16	**Vol. 2:** 144, 452 **Vol. 3:** 400
3:17	**Vol. 1:** 129, 400–401, 491 **Vol. 3:** 905
3:18 f	**Vol. 1:** 400, 464
3:18	**Vol. 1:** 400, 554 **Vol. 2:** 402, 804, 926
3:19 ff	**Vol. 2:** 924
3:19	**Vol. 1:** 518 **Vol. 2:** 61, 65, 73, 402, 619 **Vol. 3:** 564
3:20 f	**Vol. 2:** 48, 926
3:20	**Vol. 1:** 299, 686, 689–690 **Vol. 2:** 194, 245, 387, 518, 804, 903, 922, 925 **Vol. 3:** 219, 221, 279
3:21	**Vol. 1:** 707, 709 **Vol. 2:** 46, 48, 83, 263, 288, 566, 606, 741, 926 **Vol. 3:** 199, 278–279, 297, 864, 1152
4:1	**Vol. 1:** 257, 406 **Vol. 2:** 517, 924
4:2	**Vol. 1:** 570–571 **Vol. 2:** 618–619 **Vol. 3:** 1063
4:3	**Vol. 1:** 244, 344, 646–647 **Vol. 3:** 252, 548, 1164
4:4	**Vol. 2:** 359–360
4:5	**Vol. 1:** 278 **Vol. 2:** 54, 258, 360, 518, 896, 903, 922
4:6 f	**Vol. 2:** 874
4:6	**Vol. 1:** 278 **Vol. 2:** 858, 861, 868, 874 **Vol. 3:** 314, 819
4:7	**Vol. 2:** 135, 182, 780–781 **Vol. 3:** 128
4:8	**Vol. 2:** 95 **Vol. 3:** 101, 252, 362, 824–825, 927–928
4:9	**Vol. 1:** 486 **Vol. 2:** 78, 780, 874 **Vol. 3:** 751, 1158
4:9b	**Vol. 2:** 874
4:10	**Vol. 2:** 359–360, 617 **Vol. 3:** 837, 1194
4:11	**Vol. 3:** 727–728, 955
4:12 f	**Vol. 2:** 263
4:12	**Vol. 1:** 731, 744 **Vol. 2:** 267 **Vol. 3:** 954–955
4:13	**Vol. 2:** 604, 606 **Vol. 3:** 714, 1210
4:14	**Vol. 1:** 644 **Vol. 2:** 360, 809
4:15	**Vol. 1:** 138, 166 **Vol. 2:** 131, 550 **Vol. 3:** 1106
4:16	**Vol. 2:** 360, 717 **Vol. 3:** 957–958
4:17	**Vol. 2:** 42, 131 **Vol. 3:** 532
4:18	**Vol. 1:** 731 **Vol. 2:** 131, 816 **Vol. 3:** 242, 431, 600–601, 746
4:19	**Vol. 2:** 73, 874 **Vol. 3:** 957–958
4:20	**Vol. 1:** 99 **Vol. 2:** 46, 874
4:22	**Vol. 1:** 269
4:23	**Vol. 2:** 874 **Vol. 3:** 693

Colossians

1:1	**Vol. 1:** 130
1:2 f	**Vol. 2:** 874
1:2	**Vol. 2:** 229, 780
1:2b	**Vol. 2:** 874
1:3 ff	**Vol. 2:** 874
1:3 f	**Vol. 3:** 818
1:3†	**Vol. 2:** 76, 516, 875
1:3b	**Vol. 2:** 874
1:4 f	**Vol. 1:** 601
1:4	**Vol. 2:** 243 **Vol. 3:** 1212
1:5	**Vol. 2:** 111, 241, 243
1:5b	**Vol. 2:** 122
1:6	**Vol. 2:** 129, 899
1:7	**Vol. 1:** 257, 486 **Vol. 3:** 546, 548, 1196
1:8	**Vol. 3:** 316, 702
1:9–14†	**Vol. 2:** 874–875
1:9–12	**Vol. 2:** 857
1:9 f	**Vol. 2:** 400
1:9	**Vol. 2:** 856 **Vol. 3:** 133, 706, 1032

Colossians *(cont'd)*

1:10 f	**Vol. 2:** 129
1:10	**Vol. 1:** 723 **Vol. 2:** 101, 817 **Vol. 3:** 349, 945, 1032
1:11	**Vol. 2:** 46–47, 360, 605, 771, 774 **Vol. 3:** 718
1:12	**Vol. 1:** 620 **Vol. 2:** 228, 230, 302, 304, 495 **Vol. 3:** 729, 819
1:13–20	**Vol. 1:** 147
1:13 f	**Vol. 3:** 644
1:13	**Vol. 1:** 301, 424, 566 **Vol. 2:** 609 **Vol. 3:** 204, 831
1:14	**Vol. 1:** 221, 638, 701 **Vol. 3:** 198–199, 204
1:15 ff	**Vol. 1:** 95, 103, 302
1:15–23	**Vol. 2:** 195
1:15–20	**Vol. 1:** 237 **Vol. 2:** 614 **Vol. 3:** 674
1:15–18	**Vol. 1:** 628, 740
1:15–17	**Vol. 3:** 647
1:15 f	**Vol. 1:** 95 **Vol. 2:** 77 **Vol. 3:** 515, 647
1:15	**Vol. 1:** 256, 668–669 **Vol. 2:** 79, 288–289, 834 **Vol. 3:** 518
1:16 ff	**Vol. 1:** 95, 258 **Vol. 3:** 172
1:16 f	**Vol. 1:** 94 **Vol. 2:** 195
1:16	**Vol. 1:** 103, 167, 384, 668 **Vol. 2:** 160, 195, 518, 609, 612 **Vol. 3:** 1182, 1186
1:17	**Vol. 1:** 166, 549, 668 **Vol. 3:** 1177
1:17b	**Vol. 3:** 1186
1:18 ff	**Vol. 3:** 287
1:18 f	**Vol. 2:** 81
1:18	**Vol. 1:** 86, 166, 256, 301, 445, 662, 666, 668–669, 740 **Vol. 2:** 162 **Vol. 3:** 303, 504, 1189
1:18a	**Vol. 1:** 237
1:19–22	**Vol. 3:** 171, 1111, 1193
1:19 f	**Vol. 1:** 95, 237, 402, 669 **Vol. 3:** 169
1:19	**Vol. 1:** 740 **Vol. 2:** 203, 251, 819, 834 **Vol. 3:** 172, 1193
1:20	**Vol. 1:** 167, 224, 301, 740 **Vol. 2:** 80, 195, 203, 781–782, 808 **Vol. 3:** 166–167, 171, 504, 1182, 1193
1:21 ff	**Vol. 3:** 228, 934
1:21 f	**Vol. 3:** 172
1:21	**Vol. 1:** 554, 566, 685 **Vol. 2:** 742 **Vol. 3:** 127, 1175, 1192
1:22	**Vol. 1:** 437, 474–475, 676, 740 **Vol. 2:** 140, 808 **Vol. 3:** 167, 171, 323, 924–925, 1193
1:23	**Vol. 1:** 95, 661–662, 741 **Vol. 2:** 243 **Vol. 3:** 52, 172, 227–228, 546, 548, 925
1:24	**Vol. 1:** 301, 438, 479, 643, 648, 676, 679, 741 **Vol. 2:** 360, 573, 808 **Vol. 3:** 504, 722, 724, 953, 955
1:25 ff	**Vol. 2:** 217
1:25 f	**Vol. 3:** 322
1:25	**Vol. 1:** 741 **Vol. 2:** 255 **Vol. 3:** 315, 546, 548, 1111
1:26	**Vol. 2:** 35, 401 **Vol. 3:** 321–322, 504, 830–831, 837
1:27	**Vol. 2:** 47, 217, 242 **Vol. 3:** 314, 504, 1020, 1192
1:28 f	**Vol. 3:** 956
1:28	**Vol. 1:** 474, 568, 647 **Vol. 2:** 62 **Vol. 3:** 504, 765
1:29–2:3	**Vol. 2:** 874–875
1:29	**Vol. 1:** 263, 647 **Vol. 2:** 874 **Vol. 3:** 1152
2:1–15	**Vol. 1:** 740
2:1–3	**Vol. 2:** 874
2:1 f	**Vol. 1:** 647
2:2 f	**Vol. 2:** 402 **Vol. 3:** 132
2:2	**Vol. 2:** 401, 546, 834 **Vol. 3:** 133
2:3	**Vol. 1:** 174 **Vol. 2:** 216–217, 830, 834 **Vol. 3:** 1032
2:4–23	**Vol. 2:** 401
2:4	**Vol. 1:** 592 **Vol. 2:** 459
2:5	**Vol. 2:** 360, 874–875 **Vol. 3:** 694, 1213
2:6	**Vol. 2:** 514, 517 **Vol. 3:** 61, 751, 775, 944
2:7	**Vol. 1:** 660, 730 **Vol. 2:** 249, 253, 874 **Vol. 3:** 61, 765, 819, 868
2:7c	**Vol. 3:** 1190
2:8–17	**Vol. 1:** 631
2:8	**Vol. 1:** 525 **Vol. 2:** 200, 269, 401, 452–453, 459–460, 550, 559, 828 **Vol. 3:** 379, 774, 1035
2:9	**Vol. 1:** 95, 676, 740 **Vol. 2:** 79, 81, 86, 187, 251, 343 **Vol. 3:** 172, 1193
2:10–15	**Vol. 2:** 453
2:10 f	**Vol. 1:** 167
2:10	**Vol. 1:** 167, 740 **Vol. 2:** 83, 162, 514, 609 **Vol. 3:** 1192
2:11 f	**Vol. 1:** 148, 154, 158, 311 **Vol. 2:** 218 **Vol. 3:** 499
2:11–14	**Vol. 3:** 956
2:11–13	**Vol. 2:** 573
2:11	**Vol. 1:** 315, 676 **Vol. 2:** 786 **Vol. 3:** 204
2:12 ff	**Vol. 1:** 740
2:12–15	**Vol. 3:** 204
2:12 f	**Vol. 1:** 154, 157–158
2:12	**Vol. 1:** 146, 148, 158, 266, 315, 401, 643 **Vol. 2:** 217, 655 **Vol. 3:** 278, 1152
2:13 ff	**Vol. 1:** 224 **Vol. 2:** 366, 783 **Vol. 3:** 172
2:13	**Vol. 1:** 445–446, 643, 676 **Vol. 2:** 122 **Vol. 3:** 204, 277, 586, 825, 1176
2:14 f	**Vol. 1:** 167, 302, 402 **Vol. 3:** 1196
2:14	**Vol. 1:** 330, 471 **Vol. 3:** 410, 994, 1199
2:15	**Vol. 1:** 315, 467, 525, 649 **Vol. 2:** 291, 559, 645, 702, 736 **Vol. 3:** 172, 570
2:16 f	**Vol. 2:** 268
2:16	**Vol. 1:** 648 **Vol. 2:** 268, 277, 304, 364 **Vol. 3:** 410
2:17	**Vol. 1:** 327 **Vol. 3:** 556

Colossians *(cont'd)*

2:18	**Vol. 1:** 103, 648, 676 **Vol. 2:** 263, 559 **Vol. 3:** 551, 1035, 1198
2:19	**Vol. 1:** 241, 302 **Vol. 2:** 128
2:20–4:1	**Vol. 2:** 463
2:20–23	**Vol. 2:** 270
2:20	**Vol. 1:** 302, 330, 401, 438–439, 525 **Vol. 2:** 195, 200, 452–453, 559, 828 **Vol. 3:** 278
2:21 ff	**Vol. 2:** 453
2:21–23	**Vol. 2:** 559
2:21	**Vol. 1:** 330 **Vol. 2:** 269 **Vol. 3:** 860
2:22	**Vol. 1:** 402 **Vol. 3:** 572, 770
2:23	**Vol. 2:** 51, 263 **Vol. 3:** 1204
3:1–4:6	**Vol. 2:** 566
3:1–17	**Vol. 3:** 934
3:1–5	**Vol. 2:** 920
3:1–4	**Vol. 1:** 290 **Vol. 3:** 204
3:1 f	**Vol. 2:** 188
3:1	**Vol. 1:** 402, 643 **Vol. 2:** 147, 263, 453, 515, 619, 702 **Vol. 3:** 278, 298
3:2	**Vol. 1:** 518 **Vol. 2:** 619
3:3 f	**Vol. 1:** 138 **Vol. 2:** 218
3:3	**Vol. 1:** 401 **Vol. 2:** 217, 481, 672, 834
3:4	**Vol. 2:** 48, 481 **Vol. 3:** 163, 257, 322, 956, 1207
3:5–10	**Vol. 2:** 127
3:5–9	**Vol. 1:** 401
3:5	**Vol. 1:** 138, 231, 401, 445, 518, 564 **Vol. 2:** 286 **Vol. 3:** 31, 722, 928–929
3:6	**Vol. 1:** 110, 112
3:8 f	**Vol. 1:** 106
3:8	**Vol. 1:** 106, 110 **Vol. 3:** 31, 343, 564
3:9 ff	**Vol. 1:** 311 **Vol. 2:** 566 **Vol. 3:** 1062
3:9 f	**Vol. 2:** 675
3:9	**Vol. 1:** 315, 718 **Vol. 2:** 473, 673, 715
3:10–12	**Vol. 1:** 386
3:10 f	**Vol. 2:** 51
3:10	**Vol. 1:** 185, 315–316 **Vol. 2:** 161, 288, 400, 473, 671, 673, 675 **Vol. 3:** 303, 1063, 1187, 1200
3:11	**Vol. 1:** 95, 258, 311, 718, 720 **Vol. 2:** 126–127, 800 **Vol. 3:** 1191
3:12 f	**Vol. 2:** 62, 127
3:12	**Vol. 1:** 316, 542 **Vol. 2:** 79, 106, 229, 259, 263, 544, 598, 600, 673, 771, 920 **Vol. 3:** 927–928
3:13	**Vol. 1:** 147, 702 **Vol. 2:** 122, 765
3:14	**Vol. 1:** 110 **Vol. 2:** 62 **Vol. 3:** 592, 1193
3:15 ff	**Vol. 2:** 874
3:15	**Vol. 1:** 275, 648 **Vol. 2:** 183, 722, 781 **Vol. 3:** 818–819
3:16	**Vol. 1:** 568–569 **Vol. 2:** 121, 251, 842, 874 **Vol. 3:** 669–671, 673, 675, 706, 765, 1178
3:17	**Vol. 2:** 654 **Vol. 3:** 819, 1155
3:18 ff	**Vol. 2:** 51 539, 1067
3:18–4:11	**Vol. 1:** 59
3:18–4:1	**Vol. 3:** 929–930
3:18–20	**Vol. 2:** 180
3:18 f	**Vol. 1:** 496 **Vol. 2:** 160, 579, 905, 923 **Vol. 3:**
3:18	**Vol. 3:** 930, 1064
3:19	**Vol. 1:** 202 **Vol. 2:** 563 **Vol. 3:** 1064
3:20 f	**Vol. 1:** 619
3:20	**Vol. 1:** 160, 286 **Vol. 2:** 816 **Vol. 3:** 930, 1191
3:21	**Vol. 1:** 286
3:22 ff	**Vol. 2:** 517
3:22–25	**Vol. 3:** 582
3:22	**Vol. 1:** 587, 623, 680 **Vol. 2:** 509, 513, 817 **Vol. 3:** 596
3:23	**Vol. 3:** 685, 1155
3:24	**Vol. 2:** 302 **Vol. 3:** 135–136, 596–597, 751
3:25	**Vol. 1:** 587 **Vol. 3:** 575, 930
4:1	**Vol. 1:** 637 **Vol. 2:** 499 **Vol. 3:** 362, 583
4:2 ff	**Vol. 2:** 874
4:2 f	**Vol. 2:** 768
4:2	**Vol. 2:** 137, 768, 869, 874 **Vol. 3:** 819
4:2c	**Vol. 3:** 1190
4:3	**Vol. 1:** 171, 647 **Vol. 2:** 30, 726–727 **Vol. 3:** 504
4:4	**Vol. 3:** 322
4:5	**Vol. 1:** 268 **Vol. 2:** 256 **Vol. 3:** 838, 945, 1032
4:6	**Vol. 2:** 118 **Vol. 3:** 449
4:7	**Vol. 1:** 257 **Vol. 3:** 314, 546, 548, 596
4:9	**Vol. 3:** 314
4:10	**Vol. 1:** 337 **Vol. 2:** 467 **Vol. 3:** 591, 601, 746
4:11	**Vol. 1:** 310 **Vol. 2:** 331 **Vol. 3:** 548, 1152
4:12	**Vol. 1:** 647 **Vol. 2:** 62, 868, 874–875 **Vol. 3:** 596, 613
4:13	**Vol. 1:** 319 **Vol. 3:** 1043
4:14	**Vol. 2:** 168
4:15 f	**Vol. 1:** 302
4:15	**Vol. 1:** 301
4:16	**Vol. 1:** 245–246 **Vol. 3:** 489
4:17	**Vol. 2:** 517 **Vol. 3:** 546
4:18	**Vol. 2:** 874

1 Thessalonians

1:1 ff	**Vol. 2:** 874
1:1 f	**Vol. 1:** 298
1:1	**Vol. 1:** 130, 299 **Vol. 2:** 780
1:1b	**Vol. 2:** 874
1:2 ff	**Vol. 2:** 874
1:2–10	**Vol. 1:** 247
1:2 f	**Vol. 2:** 874–875 **Vol. 3:** 242, 818
1:2	**Vol. 3:** 230, 246
1:3	**Vol. 1:** 263 **Vol. 2:** 242–243, 545, 774 **Vol. 3:** 818
1:4	**Vol. 1:** 540–542

1 Thessalonians *(cont'd)*

1:5   **Vol. 2:** 632   **Vol. 3:** 701, 703, 1106
1:6   **Vol. 1:** 491   **Vol. 2:** 360, 809   **Vol. 3:** 60–61, 529, 701, 746, 905, 1110
1:7   **Vol. 3:** 905
1:8   **Vol. 1:** 599   **Vol. 3:** 1110, 1211, 1214
1:9 f   **Vol. 3:** 644, 1112
1:9   **Vol. 1:** 355, 720   **Vol. 2:** 73–74, 285–286   **Vol. 3:** 304, 597, 888, 940
1:10   **Vol. 1:** 112, 445, 566   **Vol. 2:** 76, 194, 245, 544, 925   **Vol. 3:** 62, 205, 214, 643
2:1   **Vol. 1:** 329   **Vol. 3:** 940
2:2   **Vol. 2:** 78, 111, 550, 736   **Vol. 3:** 27, 54
2:3 ff   **Vol. 3:** 50
2:3   **Vol. 1:** 329   **Vol. 2:** 460
2:4   **Vol. 2:** 183, 816   **Vol. 3:** 809, 1211
2:5   **Vol. 1:** 138   **Vol. 3:** 1043, 1112
2:6   **Vol. 2:** 46–47   **Vol. 3:** 1174, 1176
2:7   **Vol. 1:** 261, 282, 286   **Vol. 3:** 1070
2:8   **Vol. 2:** 41, 43, 818   **Vol. 3:** 54, 683
2:9   **Vol. 1:** 138, 261, 263   **Vol. 2:** 111   **Vol. 3:** 52, 54
2:10   **Vol. 2:** 139, 144   **Vol. 3:** 363, 1043
2:11   **Vol. 1:** 286, 329
2:12   **Vol. 1:** 275, 300, 329, 571   **Vol. 2:** 46, 76   **Vol. 3:** 54, 87, 945
2:13 ff   **Vol. 2:** 874
2:13   **Vol. 1:** 325   **Vol. 2:** 175   **Vol. 3:** 230, 314, 329, 746, 751, 819, 888, 1110, 1112
2:14–16   **Vol. 2:** 312
2:14 f   **Vol. 2:** 312
2:14   **Vol. 1:** 299, 491   **Vol. 2:** 83   **Vol. 3:** 724
2:15 f   **Vol. 1:** 394–395   **Vol. 2:** 221   **Vol. 3:** 203
2:15   **Vol. 1:** 430, 740   **Vol. 2:** 806, 816
2:16   **Vol. 1:** 112, 740   **Vol. 2:** 61, 222, 794   **Vol. 3:** 214
2:17–3:13   **Vol. 3:** 955
2:17   **Vol. 1:** 457, 731   **Vol. 2:** 182   **Vol. 3:** 837, 848, 1169
2:18   **Vol. 2:** 221, 901   **Vol. 3:** 471
2:19 f   **Vol. 2:** 47
2:19   **Vol. 1:** 229, 406   **Vol. 2:** 243, 874, 900–901
2:20   **Vol. 2:** 360
3:1   **Vol. 2:** 818
3:2   **Vol. 1:** 570   **Vol. 3:** 87, 548, 1152
3:3   **Vol. 1:** 471   **Vol. 2:** 360, 809
3:4   **Vol. 1:** 326   **Vol. 2:** 809   **Vol. 3:** 84, 1204
3:5   **Vol. 1:** 547, 601, 718   **Vol. 3:** 471, 563, 802, 809
3:6   **Vol. 2:** 545   **Vol. 3:** 246, 1204
3:7   **Vol. 1:** 571   **Vol. 2:** 664, 809
3:8   **Vol. 1:** 601
3:9 f   **Vol. 3:** 819

3:9   **Vol. 2:** 360, 874
3:10–13   **Vol. 2:** 874
3:10   **Vol. 1:** 730   **Vol. 2:** 130, 860, 874–875   **Vol. 3:** 350, 955
3:11 ff   **Vol. 2:** 874
3:12 f   **Vol. 2:** 517
3:12   **Vol. 1:** 730   **Vol. 2:** 131, 144
3:13   **Vol. 2:** 139, 144, 228, 900   **Vol. 3:** 1207
4–5   **Vol. 2:** 924
4   **Vol. 2:** 925
4:1–8   **Vol. 3:** 955
4:1   **Vol. 1:** 570–571, 730   **Vol. 2:** 517, 666, 816   **Vol. 3:** 252, 751, 944, 1192
4:2   **Vol. 1:** 341   **Vol. 2:** 517
4:3–8   **Vol. 3:** 1064
4:3–7   **Vol. 2:** 230
4:3   **Vol. 1:** 501   **Vol. 3:** 1064
4:4   **Vol. 2:** 50, 580   **Vol. 3:** 913, 1064, 1067
4:5   **Vol. 2:** 73, 793   **Vol. 3:** 722, 1064
4:6   **Vol. 1:** 138   **Vol. 3:** 97, 584, 1042, 1064, 1158
4:7   **Vol. 3:** 1191, 1193
4:8   **Vol. 1:** 74   **Vol. 2:** 42, 786   **Vol. 3:** 701
4:9–12   **Vol. 3:** 955
4:9   **Vol. 2:** 549
4:10   **Vol. 1:** 571, 730
4:11   **Vol. 1:** 341   **Vol. 2:** 550   **Vol. 3:** 112, 1157
4:12   **Vol. 3:** 945
4:13 ff   **Vol. 2:** 925   **Vol. 3:** 55
4:13–5:11   **Vol. 3:** 955
4:13–18   **Vol. 2:** 559, 903, 924   **Vol. 3:** 1200
4:13–17   **Vol. 2:** 482
4:13 f   **Vol. 1:** 441
4:13   **Vol. 1:** 443   **Vol. 2:** 242, 406, 794, 901   **Vol. 3:** 251–252
4:14–17   **Vol. 1:** 649
4:14   **Vol. 1:** 443, 599   **Vol. 2:** 925–926   **Vol. 3:** 61, 1178, 1211
4:15 ff   **Vol. 2:** 911, 922, 926
4:15   **Vol. 1:** 443   **Vol. 2:** 514, 900–901, 923–924, 926   **Vol. 3:** 305, 967
4:16 ff   **Vol. 2:** 924–925
4:16   **Vol. 1:** 103, 342, 410, 446, 667   **Vol. 2:** 38, 186, 194, 924–925   **Vol. 3:** 113, 277, 558, 674, 874, 1207
4:17   **Vol. 1:** 325, 449, 643, 649   **Vol. 2:** 482, 517, 923–926   **Vol. 3:** 278, 602, 1003, 1207
4:18   **Vol. 1:** 571   **Vol. 2:** 244, 924
5   **Vol. 2:** 925
5:1 ff   **Vol. 2:** 702, 900   **Vol. 3:** 833, 838, 844
5:1–5   **Vol. 2:** 911
5:1   **Vol. 2:** 922, 924, 926
5:2 f   **Vol. 2:** 360
5:2   **Vol. 1:** 323, 421   **Vol. 2:** 75, 517, 894, 925–926   **Vol. 3:** 378
5:3   **Vol. 1:** 466   **Vol. 3:** 858
5:4–10   **Vol. 2:** 911
5:4–6   **Vol. 1:** 425

1 Thessalonians (cont'd)

5:4   **Vol. 2:** 894, 925   **Vol. 3:** 378, 750
5:5–7   **Vol. 1:** 421
5:5   **Vol. 1:** 289, 421   **Vol. 2:** 495, 925
5:6 ff   **Vol. 2:** 911
5:6–8   **Vol. 1:** 514
5:6   **Vol. 1:** 421, 442, 513   **Vol. 2:** 137, 794, 894, 925   **Vol. 3:** 252
5:7   **Vol. 1:** 421, 513   **Vol. 2:** 925
5:8 f   **Vol. 3:** 214
5:8   **Vol. 1:** 316   **Vol. 2:** 242, 244, 545, 925   **Vol. 3:** 965–966
5:9 f   **Vol. 3:** 61
5:9   **Vol. 1:** 112, 477   **Vol. 2:** 839   **Vol. 3:** 214
5:10   **Vol. 1:** 437, 443   **Vol. 2:** 137, 923, 925–926   **Vol. 3:** 1197, 1207
5:11   **Vol. 1:** 571   **Vol. 2:** 253
5:12   **Vol. 1:** 197, 263, 569   **Vol. 3:** 930
5:13   **Vol. 3:** 930
5:14   **Vol. 1:** 329, 569   **Vol. 2:** 771   **Vol. 3:** 687, 955
5:15   **Vol. 2:** 101, 807   **Vol. 3:** 136, 1179
5:16   **Vol. 2:** 360
5:17 f   **Vol. 2:** 874
5:17   **Vol. 3:** 230
5:18   **Vol. 2:** 874   **Vol. 3:** 819
5:19–22   **Vol. 3:** 695, 703
5:19 f   **Vol. 3:** 703
5:19   **Vol. 3:** 109
5:20   **Vol. 3:** 110
5:21   **Vol. 3:** 808, 810
5:22   **Vol. 1:** 567, 704
5:23 f   **Vol. 2:** 874
5:23   **Vol. 1:** 235   **Vol. 2:** 78, 133, 139, 144, 230, 568, 780–781, 874, 900–901   **Vol. 3:** 684, 694
5:24 f   **Vol. 2:** 874
5:24   **Vol. 3:** 1154
5:25   **Vol. 1:** 647   **Vol. 2:** 868, 874
5:26   **Vol. 2:** 549
5:27   **Vol. 1:** 245–247   **Vol. 3:** 489, 738
5:28   **Vol. 2:** 874
6:16 f   **Vol. 2:** 518

2 Thessalonians

1:1 ff   **Vol. 2:** 875
1:1 f   **Vol. 1:** 298
1:1   **Vol. 1:** 130
1:2   **Vol. 2:** 516, 780, 874
1:3 ff   **Vol. 2:** 874, 911
1:3 f   **Vol. 2:** 806
1:3   **Vol. 2:** 129–131, 546, 668   **Vol. 3:** 819
1:4 f   **Vol. 3:** 725
1:4   **Vol. 1:** 228, 299, 301   **Vol. 2:** 83, 766, 774
1:5–12   **Vol. 2:** 903
1:5 f   **Vol. 3:** 362

1:5   **Vol. 1:** 300   **Vol. 2:** 366   **Vol. 3:** 349, 725
1:6 f   **Vol. 2:** 809
1:6–10   **Vol. 2:** 911
1:7   **Vol. 1:** 102   **Vol. 2:** 194   **Vol. 3:** 315
1:8   **Vol. 1:** 657   **Vol. 2:** 96, 179
1:9†   **Vol. 1:** 466–467   **Vol. 2:** 46, 96, 518   **Vol. 3:** 99, 714, 830, 832
1:10   **Vol. 2:** 47, 625   **Vol. 3:** 1043, 1211, 1213
1:11 f   **Vol. 2:** 605, 874, 911
1:11   **Vol. 2:** 101, 819
1:12   **Vol. 2:** 47, 81, 654
2   **Vol. 2:** 461
2:1 ff   **Vol. 3:** 838
2:1–15   **Vol. 2:** 903
2:1–12   **Vol. 2:** 447, 702   **Vol. 3:** 319
2:1–2   **Vol. 3:** 112
2:1 f   **Vol. 2:** 911
2:1   **Vol. 2:** 33, 518, 900   **Vol. 3:** 1174
2:2 f   **Vol. 1:** 247
2:2   **Vol. 2:** 517, 901, 921   **Vol. 3:** 315, 412, 559, 695
2:3 ff   **Vol. 1:** 125   **Vol. 2:** 633
2:3–12   **Vol. 3:** 471
2:3 f   **Vol. 1:** 667   **Vol. 3:** 505
2:3   **Vol. 1:** 464, 607   **Vol. 2:** 447, 459–460, 911, 924   **Vol. 3:** 315
2:4 ff   **Vol. 2:** 911
2:4   **Vol. 1:** 75   **Vol. 2:** 93   **Vol. 3:** 570–571, 784
2:5   **Vol. 1:** 269   **Vol. 3:** 1204
2:6 f   **Vol. 3:** 319
2:6   **Vol. 3:** 315
2:7 ff   **Vol. 2:** 901
2:7   **Vol. 2:** 447, 911   **Vol. 3:** 319, 505
2:8–12   **Vol. 2:** 911
2:8 f   **Vol. 2:** 900
2:8   **Vol. 1:** 73   **Vol. 2:** 74, 447, 518   **Vol. 3:** 315, 319, 694, 703
2:9–12   **Vol. 3:** 576
2:9   **Vol. 2:** 603, 629   **Vol. 3:** 319, 471, 1152
2:10   **Vol. 1:** 464   **Vol. 2:** 459–460   **Vol. 3:** 746, 886
2:11   **Vol. 2:** 459   **Vol. 3:** 1152
2:12   **Vol. 2:** 365, 818   **Vol. 3:** 127, 575
2:13 f   **Vol. 3:** 214
2:13   **Vol. 1:** 166, 534   **Vol. 2:** 230, 544, 668, 874, 911   **Vol. 3:** 214, 416, 701, 818, 885
2:14   **Vol. 1:** 275   **Vol. 2:** 46–47, 839
2:15   **Vol. 1:** 247   **Vol. 2:** 718, 911   **Vol. 3:** 61, 717, 765, 774
2:16 f   **Vol. 2:** 874
2:16   **Vol. 1:** 571   **Vol. 2:** 243–244   **Vol. 3:** 832
2:17   **Vol. 1:** 660   **Vol. 3:** 87, 197, 1149, 1151
3:1–3   **Vol. 2:** 874
3:1   **Vol. 1:** 647   **Vol. 2:** 868   **Vol. 3:** 61, 252, 947

2 Thessalonians *(cont'd)*

3:2	**Vol. 1:** 565 **Vol. 3:** 203, 1176
3:3	**Vol. 1:** 566 **Vol. 2:** 135
3:4	**Vol. 1:** 341, 591 **Vol. 2:** 615
3:5	**Vol. 2:** 183, 775, 874
3:6	**Vol. 1:** 341 **Vol. 2:** 654, 718 **Vol. 3:** 751, 774, 905, 945
3:7	**Vol. 1:** 491 **Vol. 2:** 666
3:8	**Vol. 1:** 250, 261 **Vol. 2:** 41
3:9	**Vol. 1:** 491 **Vol. 2:** 611 **Vol. 3:** 905
3:10 ff	**Vol. 1:** 341
3:10	**Vol. 2:** 272, 901 **Vol. 3:** 1204
3:11	**Vol. 1:** 267 **Vol. 2:** 434
3:12	**Vol. 1:** 341, 571 **Vol. 3:** 112
3:13	**Vol. 1:** 563 **Vol. 2:** 102
3:14	**Vol. 2:** 179
3:15	**Vol. 1:** 554, 569
3:16	**Vol. 2:** 513, 517, 780–781, 874
3:17	**Vol. 2:** 629 **Vol. 3:** 489
3:18	**Vol. 2:** 874

1 Timothy

1:1 ff	**Vol. 2:** 171
1:1	**Vol. 1:** 130 **Vol. 2:** 78 **Vol. 3:** 220
1:2	**Vol. 1:** 180, 286, 619 **Vol. 2:** 516, 597, 780
1:3–7	**Vol. 3:** 380
1:3	**Vol. 1:** 341 **Vol. 2:** 718 **Vol. 3:** 228
1:4	**Vol. 2:** 36, 131, 644 **Vol. 3:** 532, 768, 1119
1:5	**Vol. 1:** 341, 351, 353, 552, 604 **Vol. 2:** 62, 101, 183, 470 **Vol. 3:** 107
1:6 ff	**Vol. 2:** 171
1:6	**Vol. 1:** 552, 608 **Vol. 3:** 903
1:7	**Vol. 2:** 447 **Vol. 3:** 480, 768
1:8	**Vol. 2:** 104, 447, 549
1:9–10	**Vol. 3:** 31
1:9 f	**Vol. 2:** 447 **Vol. 3:** 31, 380
1:9	**Vol. 2:** 94, 237, 447 **Vol. 3:** 362, 365
1:10	**Vol. 2:** 170–171, 570, 584 **Vol. 3:** 738, 770
1:11	**Vol. 1:** 217 **Vol. 2:** 46, 77–78 **Vol. 3:** 1211
1:12 ff	**Vol. 2:** 122
1:12	**Vol. 1:** 477 **Vol. 2:** 121, 604
1:13	**Vol. 2:** 407, 597, 806 **Vol. 3:** 27–28, 343, 345
1:14	**Vol. 2:** 545 **Vol. 3:** 1020
1:15	**Vol. 3:** 214, 581, 744, 765
1:15a	**Vol. 3:** 746
1:16	**Vol. 1:** 326, 666 **Vol. 2:** 597 **Vol. 3:** 832, 1184, 1212
1:17	**Vol. 1:** 469 **Vol. 2:** 46, 50, 73, 77, 724 **Vol. 3:** 515, 518
1:18	**Vol. 1:** 341, 619 **Vol. 2:** 104 **Vol. 3:** 963
1:19	**Vol. 1:** 351, 353, 608 **Vol. 2:** 101 **Vol. 3:** 61
1:20	**Vol. 1:** 415 **Vol. 2:** 368 **Vol. 3:** 470–471, 779
2:1 ff	**Vol. 3:** 930
2:1–15	**Vol. 1:** 59
2:1	**Vol. 2:** 861 **Vol. 3:** 819
2:2	**Vol. 2:** 95, 378, 475, 846 **Vol. 3:** 112
2:3	**Vol. 2:** 78 **Vol. 3:** 745–746, 768
2:4 ff	**Vol. 1:** 375 **Vol. 3:** 197
2:4	**Vol. 2:** 78, 405, 721 **Vol. 3:** 214, 887, 1020
2:5 f	**Vol. 2:** 722 **Vol. 3:** 61
2:5	**Vol. 1:** 374–375 **Vol. 2:** 73, 84, 565, 721
2:6	**Vol. 1:** 398 **Vol. 2:** 42 **Vol. 3:** 195, 197–198, 214, 611, 1180, 1197
2:7	**Vol. 1:** 130, 477 **Vol. 2:** 126 **Vol. 3:** 52, 170, 767–768
2:8	**Vol. 1:** 110 **Vol. 2:** 237, 869 **Vol. 3:** 821, 1017
2:9–15	**Vol. 3:** 929, 932
2:9	**Vol. 1:** 502, 524 **Vol. 2:** 96 **Vol. 3:** 395, 561
2:10	**Vol. 2:** 85, 95, 669 **Vol. 3:** 70, 561
2:11 ff	**Vol. 2:** 160
2:11–15	**Vol. 3:** 1063
2:11	**Vol. 3:** 112
2:12	**Vol. 1:** 87 **Vol. 3:** 112, 349, 765, 1066
2:13 ff	**Vol. 1:** 85
2:13	**Vol. 1:** 87 **Vol. 3:** 401
2:14	**Vol. 2:** 459–460 **Vol. 3:** 585
2:15	**Vol. 1:** 187, 285, 502, 603 **Vol. 3:** 215, 225, 1177
3	**Vol. 3:** 930
3:1–13	**Vol. 3:** 929
3:1–7	**Vol. 3:** 548
3:1	**Vol. 1:** 190, 192, 457, 460–461 **Vol. 2:** 104 **Vol. 3:** 765
3:2	**Vol. 1:** 191, 496, 502, 515, 524, 690 **Vol. 2:** 550, 563, 580–581 **Vol. 3:** 750, 765
3:3	**Vol. 1:** 514, 646 **Vol. 2:** 258 **Vol. 3:** 922
3:4	**Vol. 1:** 197, 286 **Vol. 2:** 95
3:5	**Vol. 1:** 197 **Vol. 2:** 83
3:6 f	**Vol. 3:** 470
3:6	**Vol. 1:** 609
3:7	**Vol. 1:** 198, 609 **Vol. 2:** 104 **Vol. 3:** 340, 471
3:8–13	**Vol. 3:** 546, 548, 1067
3:8	**Vol. 2:** 95 **Vol. 3:** 137, 564, 922
3:9	**Vol. 1:** 351, 353 **Vol. 3:** 107, 505
3:10	**Vol. 2:** 140 **Vol. 3:** 546, 808, 924
3:11	**Vol. 1:** 515 **Vol. 3:** 470, 546, 549, 1065
3:12	**Vol. 1:** 197 **Vol. 2:** 563, 580–581
3:13	**Vol. 2:** 104, 736, 838 **Vol. 3:** 546, 1212
3:15	**Vol. 1:** 300, 661–662 **Vol. 2:** 83, 249 **Vol. 3:** 500, 794–795, 934
3:16	**Vol. 1:** 662, 677, 679 **Vol. 2:** 46, 48, 94, 203, 289, 340 **Vol. 3:** 61, 322, 363, 505, 674, 694, 705, 749

1 Timothy *(cont'd)*

4:1–3   **Vol. 2:** 447
4:1   **Vol. 1:** 452, 607–608   **Vol. 2:** 459–460   **Vol. 3:** 380, 694, 705, 770, 838, 953
4:2   **Vol. 1:** 351–352   **Vol. 2:** 469, 472, 574
4:3 ff   **Vol. 2:** 268
4:3 f   **Vol. 1:** 385
4:3   **Vol. 2:** 579   **Vol. 3:** 750, 819, 1119
4:4   **Vol. 2:** 104, 268
4:6   **Vol. 2:** 104, 718   **Vol. 3:** 61, 546, 770
4:7 f   **Vol. 2:** 95
4:7   **Vol. 1:** 313, 647   **Vol. 2:** 401, 405, 645, 858
4:8   **Vol. 1:** 313, 327, 406   **Vol. 2:** 95, 429, 480
4:9   **Vol. 3:** 744, 746, 765
4:10   **Vol. 1:** 263, 647   **Vol. 2:** 78   **Vol. 3:** 220
4:11 ff   **Vol. 3:** 934
4:11   **Vol. 3:** 765
4:12   **Vol. 1:** 462, 603   **Vol. 2:** 675   **Vol. 3:** 101, 905, 934
4:13   **Vol. 3:** 771
4:14   **Vol. 1:** 199   **Vol. 2:** 122, 152   **Vol. 3:** 705, 1182
4:15   **Vol. 2:** 130   **Vol. 3:** 320
4:16   **Vol. 3:** 215, 228, 770
5:1–21   **Vol. 1:** 59
5:1 f   **Vol. 2:** 675
5:1   **Vol. 3:** 1042
5:2   **Vol. 1:** 198   **Vol. 3:** 101, 1070
5:3–16   **Vol. 3:** 930
5:3   **Vol. 2:** 50, 405   **Vol. 3:** 1075
5:4–16   **Vol. 3:** 1075
5:4   **Vol. 1:** 286   **Vol. 2:** 95   **Vol. 3:** 745–746, 1075
5:5   **Vol. 2:** 861   **Vol. 3:** 228, 1075
5:7   **Vol. 1:** 341   **Vol. 3:** 750
5:8   **Vol. 1:** 455   **Vol. 2:** 251
5:9†   **Vol. 2:** 428, 564   **Vol. 3:** 1065, 1075
5:10   **Vol. 1:** 187, 239, 496, 690   **Vol. 2:** 104   **Vol. 3:** 1075, 1151
5:11   **Vol. 2:** 858
5:12   **Vol. 1:** 74, 712
5:13   **Vol. 1:** 267, 322, 487   **Vol. 2:** 557   **Vol. 3:** 903, 1075
5:14 f   **Vol. 1:** 285, 496
5:14   **Vol. 1:** 187   **Vol. 2:** 510   **Vol. 3:** 347, 1017, 1075
5:15   **Vol. 1:** 493   **Vol. 3:** 470–471, 903
5:16   **Vol. 1:** 261   **Vol. 3:** 1075
5:17   **Vol. 1:** 198–199, 263   **Vol. 2:** 50   **Vol. 3:** 572, 771
5:18†   **Vol. 1:** 115   **Vol. 2:** 755   **Vol. 3:** 349, 490, 492
5:19   **Vol. 1:** 83, 199   **Vol. 2:** 686   **Vol. 3:** 1043, 1193
5:20   **Vol. 2:** 141   **Vol. 3:** 252
5:21   **Vol. 2:** 135, 364   **Vol. 3:** 1044
5:22   **Vol. 1:** 685   **Vol. 2:** 133, 152, 742   **Vol. 3:** 101
5:23   **Vol. 3:** 922
5:24   **Vol. 2:** 366
5:25   **Vol. 2:** 104, 217   **Vol. 3:** 1151
6:1 f   **Vol. 1:** 59   **Vol. 3:** 582
6:1   **Vol. 2:** 50, 509, 653   **Vol. 3:** 342–343, 596, 771, 1162
6:2   **Vol. 1:** 462   **Vol. 3:** 765, 1152
6:3 ff   **Vol. 3:** 1119
6:3–5   **Vol. 3:** 380
6:3   **Vol. 1:** 322   **Vol. 2:** 94, 170–171   **Vol. 3:** 768, 770
6:4   **Vol. 1:** 558   **Vol. 3:** 343, 532, 998
6:5 f   **Vol. 2:** 95
6:5   **Vol. 1:** 607   **Vol. 2:** 859   **Vol. 3:** 127, 887
6:6   **Vol. 3:** 727
6:7   **Vol. 3:** 317
6:8   **Vol. 1:** 318   **Vol. 3:** 727
6:9 f   **Vol. 2:** 845
6:9   **Vol. 1:** 457, 466–467, 609   **Vol. 2:** 842   **Vol. 3:** 802
6:10   **Vol. 1:** 138, 460–461, 564   **Vol. 2:** 459–460, 550, 843   **Vol. 3:** 868
6:11 ff   **Vol. 3:** 838
6:11   **Vol. 1:** 559, 603   **Vol. 2:** 94, 258, 775, 807   **Vol. 3:** 363, 365
6:12–16   **Vol. 2:** 724
6:12 f   **Vol. 1:** 346   **Vol. 3:** 1047
6:12   **Vol. 1:** 346, 647   **Vol. 2:** 104   **Vol. 3:** 319, 750, 832
6:13 f   **Vol. 1:** 341   **Vol. 3:** 61
6:13   **Vol. 3:** 198
6:14   **Vol. 1:** 337, 341   **Vol. 2:** 133, 518   **Vol. 3:** 319, 838
6:15 f   **Vol. 2:** 724   **Vol. 3:** 304
6:15   **Vol. 1:** 217   **Vol. 2:** 77, 381, 514, 519   **Vol. 3:** 198, 569
6:16   **Vol. 1:** 435   **Vol. 2:** 50, 250, 494   **Vol. 3:** 302, 518, 718, 832
6:17 ff   **Vol. 2:** 844
6:17   **Vol. 1:** 341   **Vol. 2:** 198, 842
6:18   **Vol. 1:** 642   **Vol. 2:** 100, 102, 104, 694   **Vol. 3:** 1151
6:19   **Vol. 1:** 326   **Vol. 2:** 104   **Vol. 3:** 1017, 1149
6:20   **Vol. 1:** 337   **Vol. 2:** 135, 401, 405, 652, 655, 677   **Vol. 3:** 61, 770, 903, 1119
6:21   **Vol. 1:** 608   **Vol. 3:** 70, 903

2 Timothy

1:1   **Vol. 1:** 130   **Vol. 3:** 1020
1:2   **Vol. 1:** 286, 619   **Vol. 2:** 516, 597, 780
1:3   **Vol. 1:** 351, 353   **Vol. 2:** 121, 861   **Vol. 3:** 230, 246
1:4   **Vol. 3:** 705

2 Timothy *(cont'd)*

1:5   **Vol. 1:** 159, 591, 604   **Vol. 2:** 251, 470   **Vol. 3:** 241, 247, 1070

1:6   **Vol. 2:** 138, 152   **Vol. 3:** 110, 240, 243, 705, 1182

1:7   **Vol. 1:** 622–623   **Vol. 3:** 258, 705

1:8 f   **Vol. 2:** 604

1:8   **Vol. 3:** 563, 724–725

1:9   **Vol. 1:** 697   **Vol. 2:** 122   **Vol. 3:** 215, 832, 844

1:10   **Vol. 1:** 73, 437, 469   **Vol. 2:** 113, 480–481, 495   **Vol. 3:** 220–221, 302, 304, 312, 319, 323

1:11   **Vol. 1:** 477   **Vol. 2:** 113   **Vol. 3:** 52, 88, 170, 767

1:12   **Vol. 1:** 591   **Vol. 2:** 135, 138, 894, 922   **Vol. 3:** 203, 770, 1211

1:13   **Vol. 2:** 170   **Vol. 3:** 61

1:14   **Vol. 2:** 104, 135, 251   **Vol. 3:** 61, 770

1:16†   **Vol. 2:** 248, 250, 517, 597, 874   **Vol. 3:** 563, 686

1:17   **Vol. 3:** 529, 694, 1169

1:18†   **Vol. 2:** 597, 874, 922   **Vol. 3:** 546, 831

2:1 f   **Vol. 2:** 718

2:1   **Vol. 1:** 180, 286, 619   **Vol. 2:** 122, 604

2:2   **Vol. 2:** 718   **Vol. 3:** 729, 765

2:3 f   **Vol. 3:** 964

2:3   **Vol. 2:** 104   **Vol. 3:** 724

2:4   **Vol. 1:** 646   **Vol. 2:** 475, 816, 846   **Vol. 3:** 1158

2:5   **Vol. 1:** 406, 645–646   **Vol. 2:** 258, 447

2:6   **Vol. 1:** 263, 723   **Vol. 3:** 197, 750

2:7   **Vol. 2:** 405, 517   **Vol. 3:** 132

2:8   **Vol. 1:** 427, 445   **Vol. 2:** 79, 113   **Vol. 3:** 61, 243, 299, 651

2:9   **Vol. 1:** 171, 564   **Vol. 2:** 74, 113   **Vol. 3:** 725

2:10   **Vol. 2:** 47, 775   **Vol. 3:** 215, 832

2:11 ff   **Vol. 2:** 775   **Vol. 3:** 203

2:11 f   **Vol. 1:** 455

2:11   **Vol. 1:** 130, 435, 441   **Vol. 3:** 278, 765, 1063, 1066

2:12   **Vol. 1:** 323, 455, 643   **Vol. 2:** 380, 775

2:13   **Vol. 1:** 455

2:14–19   **Vol. 3:** 915

2:14–18   **Vol. 3:** 1119

2:14   **Vol. 3:** 241, 1042, 1044, 1119

2:15   **Vol. 1:** 309, 475   **Vol. 3:** 352, 809, 1169

2:16   **Vol. 2:** 94, 130

2:17 f   **Vol. 3:** 305

2:17   **Vol. 2:** 550   **Vol. 3:** 999

2:18   **Vol. 1:** 608   **Vol. 2:** 550   **Vol. 3:** 277–278

2:18b   **Vol. 2:** 402

2:19   **Vol. 1:** 299, 662   **Vol. 2:** 249, 400, 655   **Vol. 3:** 500, 576

2:20 f   **Vol. 1:** 662   **Vol. 3:** 913

2:20   **Vol. 2:** 50–51   **Vol. 3:** 915

2:21   **Vol. 2:** 509   **Vol. 3:** 102, 118, 912, 915, 1065

2:22–26   **Vol. 3:** 915

2:22   **Vol. 1:** 559, 603   **Vol. 2:** 782, 807   **Vol. 3:** 107, 363, 365

2:23–26   **Vol. 3:** 903

2:23†   **Vol. 1:** 176   **Vol. 2:** 858   **Vol. 3:** 532, 963, 1026

2:24   **Vol. 3:** 765

2:25   **Vol. 2:** 405, 874   **Vol. 3:** 1187

2:26   **Vol. 1:** 515   **Vol. 3:** 470–471, 1178, 1187

3:1 ff   **Vol. 1:** 496   **Vol. 2:** 58

3:1–5   **Vol. 1:** 460

3:1   **Vol. 1:** 420   **Vol. 2:** 894   **Vol. 3:** 839, 954, 1191

3:2–5   **Vol. 3:** 31

3:2–4   **Vol. 1:** 420   **Vol. 3:** 903

3:2   **Vol. 1:** 593   **Vol. 2:** 237, 435, 550, 843   **Vol. 3:** 30–32, 343, 345

3:3   **Vol. 1:** 495–496   **Vol. 2:** 539, 542   **Vol. 3:** 470

3:4   **Vol. 2:** 550, 605

3:5   **Vol. 1:** 455, 708   **Vol. 2:** 95   **Vol. 3:** 31, 903

3:6   **Vol. 1:** 457   **Vol. 3:** 591, 1058

3:7   **Vol. 1:** 487   **Vol. 2:** 405   **Vol. 3:** 887

3:8   **Vol. 2:** 219, 557–558, 642   **Vol. 3:** 127, 808

3:9   **Vol. 2:** 130   **Vol. 3:** 128

3:10 f   **Vol. 3:** 724

3:10   **Vol. 1:** 697   **Vol. 2:** 770–771, 775   **Vol. 3:** 771, 935

3:11   **Vol. 2:** 806   **Vol. 3:** 203, 722

3:12   **Vol. 2:** 94, 480, 806   **Vol. 3:** 935

3:13   **Vol. 1:** 565   **Vol. 2:** 130, 459–460, 558

3:14 ff   **Vol. 3:** 491

3:14 f   **Vol. 3:** 215, 1033

3:14   **Vol. 1:** 486   **Vol. 3:** 224–225, 935

3:15   **Vol. 1:** 159, 284   **Vol. 2:** 235   **Vol. 3:** 487, 493, 1212

3:16 f   **Vol. 3:** 492

3:16   **Vol. 2:** 141–142   **Vol. 3:** 327, 329, 352, 363, 365, 401, 490–491, 708, 771, 779

3:17   **Vol. 3:** 350

4:1   **Vol. 1:** 327   **Vol. 2:** 365, 387   **Vol. 3:** 61, 1042, 1044

4:2   **Vol. 1:** 572   **Vol. 2:** 141, 770   **Vol. 3:** 770, 838

4:3 f   **Vol. 2:** 171, 718

4:3   **Vol. 2:** 170, 766   **Vol. 3:** 61, 768, 770, 839, 887

4:4   **Vol. 2:** 645   **Vol. 3:** 887, 903

4:5   **Vol. 1:** 514–515, 647, 735   **Vol. 2:** 114   **Vol. 3:** 546, 548, 1149

4:6 ff   **Vol. 3:** 203

4:6-†   **Vol. 1:** 648   **Vol. 2:** 855

4:7 f   **Vol. 1:** 441   **Vol. 3:** 365

4:7   **Vol. 1:** 647   **Vol. 2:** 62, 104, 133   **Vol. 3:** 947

2 Timothy *(cont'd)*

4:8	**Vol. 1:** 406 **Vol. 2:** 365, 894 **Vol. 3:** 252, 319, 362–363
4:9	**Vol. 3:** 1169
4:10	**Vol. 2:** 543
4:11	**Vol. 3:** 546, 749
4:14	**Vol. 3:** 136, 1200
4:15	**Vol. 2:** 135
4:16	**Vol. 2:** 874–875 **Vol. 3:** 824–825
4:17 f	**Vol. 3:** 203
4:17	**Vol. 1:** 118, 474, 735 **Vol. 2:** 604 **Vol. 3:** 52–53
4:18	**Vol. 1:** 566 **Vol. 2:** 46, 196, 387 **Vol. 3:** 203, 215, 1176
4:19	**Vol. 2:** 248, 250 **Vol. 3:** 1065
4:21	**Vol. 3:** 1169
4:22	**Vol. 3:** 693

Titus

1:1–3	**Vol. 2:** 171
1:1	**Vol. 1:** 130, 542 **Vol. 2:** 94, 405 **Vol. 3:** 613
1:2 f	**Vol. 2:** 481
1:2	**Vol. 2:** 77, 242, 472 **Vol. 3:** 71, 73, 832, 844, 1193
1:3	**Vol. 2:** 78 **Vol. 3:** 52–53, 198, 220, 323, 839, 1211
1:4	**Vol. 1:** 286, 619 **Vol. 2:** 138, 597, 780
1:5–9	**Vol. 3:** 929
1:5	**Vol. 1:** 199–200, 472 **Vol. 3:** 251, 253
1:6 ff	**Vol. 3:** 930
1:6 f	**Vol. 2:** 140 **Vol. 3:** 924
1:6	**Vol. 1:** 83, 286, 496 **Vol. 2:** 563, 581
1:7†	**Vol. 1:** 110, 191–192, 199, 514 **Vol. 2:** 255 **Vol. 3:** 137, 564
1:8	**Vol. 1:** 496, 502 **Vol. 2:** 550 **Vol. 3:** 362, 365
1:9	**Vol. 2:** 141, 170, 718 **Vol. 3:** 61, 604, 770
1:10	**Vol. 1:** 309, 552
1:11	**Vol. 3:** 137, 765
1:12	**Vol. 1:** 114, 564 **Vol. 3:** 81, 887
1:13	**Vol. 1:** 604 **Vol. 2:** 141, 170 **Vol. 3:** 61, 887
1:14 ff	**Vol. 3:** 1119
1:14	**Vol. 1:** 336 **Vol. 2:** 310
1:15	**Vol. 1:** 351–352, 448 **Vol. 3:** 107, 127
1:16	**Vol. 1:** 347, 496, 593 **Vol. 3:** 197, 808, 1151
2:1	**Vol. 2:** 170, 669 **Vol. 3:** 770
2:2 ff	**Vol. 3:** 930
2:2–10	**Vol. 3:** 929
2:2 f	**Vol. 1:** 197
2:2	**Vol. 1:** 502, 515, 604 **Vol. 2:** 95, 170–171, 775
2:3 ff	**Vol. 3:** 1065
2:3–5	**Vol. 3:** 112
2:3	**Vol. 2:** 235 **Vol. 3:** 470, 768, 922
2:4 f	**Vol. 3:** 1063

2:4	**Vol. 2:** 549–550, 675
2:5	**Vol. 1:** 502 **Vol. 3:** 101, 342–343
2:6	**Vol. 1:** 502 **Vol. 2:** 675
2:7	**Vol. 2:** 95, 104 **Vol. 3:** 771, 905, 1151
2:8	**Vol. 1:** 564 **Vol. 2:** 170
2:9 f	**Vol. 3:** 582
2:9	**Vol. 2:** 509, 816 **Vol. 3:** 596
2:10	**Vol. 1:** 524 **Vol. 3:** 220, 771
2:11–13	**Vol. 3:** 779
2:11	**Vol. 2:** 78, 122 **Vol. 3:** 220–221, 312, 319
2:12 ff	**Vol. 1:** 457
2:12	**Vol. 1:** 186, 524 **Vol. 2:** 94 **Vol. 3:** 363, 365
2:13 f	**Vol. 3:** 779
2:13	**Vol. 1:** 217 **Vol. 2:** 46, 76, 78, 81–82, 241, 245, 725 **Vol. 3:** 220, 319
2:14	**Vol. 2:** 104, 447, 800, 839 **Vol. 3:** 200, 1151, 1167, 1197
2:15	**Vol. 1:** 462 **Vol. 2:** 141
3:1	**Vol. 1:** 166, 593 **Vol. 2:** 608 **Vol. 3:** 97, 118, 197, 243
3:2	**Vol. 1:** 646 **Vol. 2:** 258
3:3 ff	**Vol. 1:** 459
3:3	**Vol. 1:** 185, 457, 460, 556–557, 593 **Vol. 2:** 459–460 **Vol. 3:** 31, 596, 929, 1193
3:4	**Vol. 1:** 185 **Vol. 2:** 78–79, 106, 550 **Vol. 3:** 220–221, 312, 319
3:5 f	**Vol. 2:** 122 **Vol. 3:** 220
3:5–7	**Vol. 1:** 154, 158 **Vol. 2:** 786
3:5	**Vol. 1:** 147–148, 153, 158, 184–186, 290 **Vol. 2:** 597, 672–673 **Vol. 3:** 215, 363, 365, 705
3:6	**Vol. 2:** 785, 843, 855 **Vol. 3:** 1194
3:7 f	**Vol. 1:** 441
3:7	**Vol. 2:** 122, 242, 300–301 **Vol. 3:** 220, 365, 832
3:8	**Vol. 1:** 197, 277 **Vol. 2:** 73, 104 **Vol. 3:** 765, 1017, 1151, 1211, 1214
3:9	**Vol. 2:** 36, 447, 645 **Vol. 3:** 532, 963, 1119
3:10	**Vol. 1:** 535, 568–569 **Vol. 2:** 858–859
3:11	**Vol. 2:** 365
3:12	**Vol. 2:** 364 **Vol. 3:** 1169
3:13	**Vol. 2:** 447 **Vol. 3:** 251, 253, 480, 1169
3:14	**Vol. 1:** 197, 723 **Vol. 2:** 104, 645 **Vol. 3:** 958, 1151, 1187
3:15	**Vol. 2:** 549

Philemon

1	**Vol. 1:** 192
2	**Vol. 1:** 301 **Vol. 2:** 250, 816
3	**Vol. 2:** 516, 780, 874
3	**Vol. 2:** 416
4 ff	**Vol. 2:** 874–875
4 f	**Vol. 3:** 818
4	**Vol. 2:** 73, 874 **Vol. 3:** 246

Philemon *(cont'd)*

5	**Vol. 3:** 1174, 1176, 1185, 1211
6	**Vol. 1:** 643 **Vol. 2:** 403, 874
7	**Vol. 2:** 567, 600 **Vol. 3:** 256
8	**Vol. 2:** 736
9	**Vol. 1:** 197 **Vol. 3:** 170, 592
10	**Vol. 1:** 180, 619 **Vol. 3:** 1070
11	**Vol. 2:** 434
12	**Vol. 2:** 567, 600
13	**Vol. 1:** 398 **Vol. 3:** 1017, 1174, 1196, 1204
14	**Vol. 2:** 663
15	**Vol. 2:** 179 **Vol. 3:** 534, 832, 848, 1184
16	**Vol. 3:** 583
17	**Vol. 1:** 642 **Vol. 3:** 930
18	**Vol. 3:** 575, 930
19	**Vol. 1:** 247 **Vol. 3:** 489
20	**Vol. 2:** 434, 600 **Vol. 3:** 256
21	**Vol. 1:** 592 **Vol. 3:** 1155
22	**Vol. 1:** 690 **Vol. 2:** 116, 122, 874
23 f	**Vol. 2:** 331
23	**Vol. 3:** 591, 601
25	**Vol. 2:** 516 **Vol. 3:** 693

Hebrews

1:1 ff	**Vol. 2:** 75
1:1–4	**Vol. 3:** 1113
1:1 f	**Vol. 3:** 216, 312
1:1	**Vol. 1:** 576, 619 **Vol. 2:** 675, 714 **Vol. 3:** 82
1:2 ff	**Vol. 2:** 81
1:2 f	**Vol. 3:** 647
1:2	**Vol. 1:** 63, 384, 477, 576 **Vol. 2:** 57–58, 289, 301, 514 **Vol. 3:** 326, 647, 829–831, 1118, 1174, 1191
1:3–4	**Vol. 3:** 588
1:3	**Vol. 1:** 123, 549, 712–713 **Vol. 2:** 64, 147, 195, 199, 288–290, 426, 515 **Vol. 3:** 107, 287, 298, 588, 674, 1010, 1154, 1186
1:4–14	**Vol. 1:** 102
1:4 f	**Vol. 2:** 654
1:4	**Vol. 1:** 123, 659 **Vol. 2:** 301
1:5 ff	**Vol. 1:** 123 **Vol. 3:** 1113
1:5–2:18	**Vol. 3:** 433
1:5–14	**Vol. 3:** 40
1:5	**Vol. 1:** 177–179, 668 **Vol. 2:** 622 **Vol. 3:** 641, 647
1:6	**Vol. 1:** 519, 668
1:7	**Vol. 3:** 553, 695, 1204
1:8 f	**Vol. 3:** 553
1:8	**Vol. 1:** 123, 164, 408 **Vol. 3:** 365, 647, 830
1:9	**Vol. 1:** 122–123, 556 **Vol. 2:** 204, 354, 448, 712 **Vol. 3:** 365, 575, 1061
1:10	**Vol. 1:** 384 **Vol. 2:** 149 **Vol. 3:** 1148
1:11 f	**Vol. 1:** 384
1:11	**Vol. 1:** 316–317, 464
1:12	**Vol. 3:** 167
1:13	**Vol. 1:** 177, 239, 477, 554 **Vol. 2:** 147, 204, 515 **Vol. 3:** 298
1:14	**Vol. 1:** 326 **Vol. 2:** 300 **Vol. 3:** 216, 546, 553, 695
2:1	**Vol. 1:** 683, 731
2:2 f	**Vol. 1:** 658
2:2	**Vol. 1:** 103, 659 **Vol. 2:** 175 **Vol. 3:** 585, 1113, 1180
2:3 ff	**Vol. 2:** 632
2:3 f	**Vol. 3:** 216
2:3	**Vol. 1:** 299, 659 **Vol. 2:** 176 **Vol. 3:** 1113
2:4	**Vol. 1:** 659 **Vol. 2:** 629, 785 **Vol. 3:** 705, 1023
2:5 ff	**Vol. 3:** 632
2:5	**Vol. 1:** 326, 519
2:6 ff	**Vol. 3:** 632
2:6	**Vol. 1:** 190–191, 289
2:7–19	**Vol. 3:** 143
2:7	**Vol. 1:** 406 **Vol. 2:** 204
2:8	**Vol. 1:** 239 **Vol. 3:** 632, 839
2:9 f	**Vol. 1:** 437 **Vol. 3:** 722–723
2:9	**Vol. 1:** 123, 406 **Vol. 2:** 123, 270–271 **Vol. 3:** 515, 723, 1178
2:10	**Vol. 1:** 168, 669 **Vol. 2:** 46–47, 63, 669 **Vol. 3:** 63, 215, 725, 941, 1177, 1183
2:11 f	**Vol. 1:** 256
2:11	**Vol. 1:** 669 **Vol. 2:** 138, 230, 722 **Vol. 3:** 563
2:12	**Vol. 1:** 304, 396 **Vol. 2:** 82, 722 **Vol. 3:** 48, 669–670, 675
2:13	**Vol. 1:** 284, 592
2:14–18	**Vol. 1:** 396
2:14 f	**Vol. 1:** 222, 437–438 **Vol. 2:** 271 **Vol. 3:** 174
2:14	**Vol. 1:** 73, 284, 436–437, 677 **Vol. 2:** 207, 525 **Vol. 3:** 471, 718
2:15	**Vol. 1:** 435, 437, 622–623 **Vol. 2:** 143 **Vol. 3:** 167, 174, 596–597
2:16	**Vol. 1:** 80 **Vol. 3:** 750
2:17	**Vol. 1:** 256 **Vol. 2:** 505, 598, 668, 800 **Vol. 3:** 41, 161
2:18	**Vol. 3:** 63, 724, 801, 804, 1175
3 f	**Vol. 3:** 1007
3	**Vol. 2:** 719 **Vol. 3:** 434
3:1 ff	**Vol. 3:** 433
3:1–4:16	**Vol. 2:** 718
3:1–6	**Vol. 2:** 249, 447 **Vol. 3:** 1007
3:1	**Vol. 1:** 130, 276, 346 **Vol. 2:** 194, 230 **Vol. 3:** 40, 61, 129, 397
3:2 ff	**Vol. 2:** 642
3:2	**Vol. 2:** 248
3:3 f	**Vol. 3:** 120
3:4–6	**Vol. 3:** 198
3:4	**Vol. 1:** 383 **Vol. 2:** 74 **Vol. 3:** 1148
3:5	**Vol. 2:** 164, 248 **Vol. 3:** 198
3:6	**Vol. 1:** 660, 712 **Vol. 2:** 243, 736 **Vol. 3:** 647, 794
3:6b	**Vol. 2:** 249

Hebrews *(cont'd)*

3:7 ff — **Vol. 3:** 954
3:7–4:14 — **Vol. 1:** 299
3:7–4:13 — **Vol. 3:** 433
3:7–19 — **Vol. 1:** 372
3:7–11 — **Vol. 2:** 178, 775
3:7 — **Vol. 1:** 372　**Vol. 3:** 705, 838
3:8 f — **Vol. 3:** 802
3:8 — **Vol. 1:** 203, 473　**Vol. 2:** 155　**Vol. 3:** 1007–1008
3:9 — **Vol. 2:** 696　**Vol. 3:** 1148
3:10 — **Vol. 2:** 459–460　**Vol. 3:** 940
3:11 — **Vol. 1:** 321, 327　**Vol. 3:** 257, 742
3:12 f — **Vol. 3:** 838
3:12 — **Vol. 1:** 607–608　**Vol. 2:** 183　**Vol. 3:** 325, 434, 586
3:13 — **Vol. 2:** 155, 459–460, 568
3:14 — **Vol. 1:** 165, 326, 396, 608, 639, 660, 712　**Vol. 2:** 64
3:15 ff — **Vol. 3:** 227
3:15 — **Vol. 1:** 203, 372　**Vol. 2:** 155, 775　**Vol. 3:** 838
3:16 — **Vol. 1:** 203, 532　**Vol. 2:** 642
3:17 — **Vol. 1:** 610–611　**Vol. 2:** 696　**Vol. 3:** 1007–1008
3:18 — **Vol. 1:** 321, 327, 593　**Vol. 3:** 257, 742
4 — **Vol. 2:** 719　**Vol. 3:** 434
4:1 ff — **Vol. 3:** 257
4:1–13 — **Vol. 1:** 372　**Vol. 3:** 143, 227
4:1–9 — **Vol. 3:** 73
4:1 — **Vol. 3:** 257, 954, 1113
4:2 — **Vol. 2:** 175　**Vol. 3:** 73, 215, 954
4:3 ff — **Vol. 1:** 327
4:3–11 — **Vol. 2:** 178, 775
4:3 — **Vol. 1:** 375, 378　**Vol. 3:** 257, 742
4:4 — **Vol. 2:** 690　**Vol. 3:** 257, 457
4:5 — **Vol. 3:** 257
4:6 — **Vol. 1:** 593
4:7 — **Vol. 1:** 372, 427, 473　**Vol. 2:** 155　**Vol. 3:** 838
4:8 — **Vol. 2:** 331　**Vol. 3:** 257
4:9–11 — **Vol. 3:** 742
4:9 — **Vol. 1:** 372　**Vol. 2:** 800　**Vol. 3:** 74, 410
4:10 f — **Vol. 3:** 257
4:11 — **Vol. 1:** 593, 611　**Vol. 2:** 291　**Vol. 3:** 905, 1113, 1169
4:12 — **Vol. 1:** 63, 106, 241　**Vol. 2:** 365, 686　**Vol. 3:** 128, 684, 693, 724, 967, 1113, 1152
4:13 — **Vol. 1:** 313, 386　**Vol. 3:** 516, 1204
4:14–7:21 — **Vol. 3:** 433
4:14–5:10 — **Vol. 2:** 447
4:14 f — **Vol. 1:** 396
4:14 — **Vol. 1:** 321, 346, 637　**Vol. 2:** 195　**Vol. 3:** 61, 647, 717
4:15 f — **Vol. 2:** 614
4:15 — **Vol. 2:** 504–505, 598　**Vol. 3:** 41, 63, 582, 663, 722, 724, 801, 804, 995

4:16 — **Vol. 1:** 322　**Vol. 2:** 598, 614, 736　**Vol. 3:** 41, 530, 748
5:1 ff — **Vol. 2:** 42
5:1 — **Vol. 1:** 472　**Vol. 2:** 41　**Vol. 3:** 41, 433, 1174, 1197, 1203
5:2 — **Vol. 2:** 407, 459–460　**Vol. 3:** 41
5:3 — **Vol. 2:** 668, 799　**Vol. 3:** 41, 1174, 1203
5:4 f — **Vol. 2:** 47
5:4 — **Vol. 2:** 50　**Vol. 3:** 41
5:5 — **Vol. 1:** 178–179　**Vol. 2:** 204
5:6 — **Vol. 2:** 591　**Vol. 3:** 41, 830
5:7 ff — **Vol. 3:** 41
5:7–10 — **Vol. 1:** 396
5:7–9 — **Vol. 3:** 432
5:7 f — **Vol. 2:** 64, 178　**Vol. 3:** 582
5:7 — **Vol. 1:** 646, 677, 679　**Vol. 2:** 91, 178, 861　**Vol. 3:** 63, 211, 323, 713, 1171, 1180–1181
5:8 — **Vol. 1:** 223, 487　**Vol. 2:** 91, 289　**Vol. 3:** 647, 724
5:9 f — **Vol. 1:** 123　**Vol. 2:** 178
5:9 — **Vol. 2:** 63, 138　**Vol. 3:** 215–216
5:10 — **Vol. 1:** 168　**Vol. 2:** 591　**Vol. 3:** 42
5:11–6:19 — **Vol. 2:** 591
5:11 — **Vol. 3:** 1106, 1180
5:12 f — **Vol. 3:** 844
5:12 — **Vol. 1:** 166　**Vol. 2:** 64, 452　**Vol. 3:** 765, 768, 1106, 1118
5:13 f — **Vol. 1:** 282
5:13 — **Vol. 3:** 365
5:14 — **Vol. 1:** 313, 504　**Vol. 2:** 64, 391
6:1 ff — **Vol. 2:** 452　**Vol. 3:** 765
6:1–20 — **Vol. 2:** 718
6:1–12 — **Vol. 1:** 299
6:1–8 — **Vol. 3:** 227
6:1 f — **Vol. 3:** 216
6:1 — **Vol. 1:** 166, 446, 599, 662, 702　**Vol. 2:** 64, 73　**Vol. 3:** 1212, 1214
6:2 — **Vol. 1:** 146, 149　**Vol. 2:** 152, 365　**Vol. 3:** 61, 99, 277, 830
6:4 ff — **Vol. 2:** 156, 270, 487, 717–718　**Vol. 3:** 582, 705, 750, 809
6:4–10 — **Vol. 1:** 417
6:4–8 — **Vol. 1:** 359, 372　**Vol. 3:** 143, 434, 1206
6:4 — **Vol. 1:** 639, 703　**Vol. 2:** 41, 194, 606　**Vol. 3:** 990
6:5 — **Vol. 1:** 187, 327　**Vol. 2:** 632, 785　**Vol. 3:** 830, 832
6:6 — **Vol. 1:** 394, 397, 608, 702　**Vol. 2:** 291　**Vol. 3:** 586, 647, 1187
6:7 f — **Vol. 1:** 214
6:7 — **Vol. 2:** 211　**Vol. 3:** 750, 1004
6:8 — **Vol. 1:** 359, 416, 726　**Vol. 2:** 64　**Vol. 3:** 808–809
6:9–15 — **Vol. 2:** 769
6:9 — **Vol. 1:** 591　**Vol. 3:** 216
6:10 — **Vol. 3:** 546
6:11 f — **Vol. 2:** 771　**Vol. 3:** 74
6:11 — **Vol. 1:** 457, 492　**Vol. 2:** 64　**Vol. 3:** 1169

Hebrews (*cont'd*)

6:12 ff   **Vol. 3:** 73
6:12   **Vol. 1:** 215, 491–492, 712   **Vol. 2:** 300–301
6:13 ff   **Vol. 3:** 366
6:13   **Vol. 1:** 80   **Vol. 3:** 74, 742
6:14   **Vol. 1:** 214, 732   **Vol. 3:** 73
6:15   **Vol. 1:** 215   **Vol. 2:** 771   **Vol. 3:** 73
6:16 ff   **Vol. 1:** 659
6:16 f   **Vol. 3:** 742
6:16   **Vol. 1:** 658, 660
6:17   **Vol. 1:** 374–375, 731   **Vol. 2:** 300–301, 686   **Vol. 3:** 1017–1018
6:18 f   **Vol. 2:** 244
6:18   **Vol. 1:** 571   **Vol. 2:** 77, 301, 472, 606   **Vol. 3:** 713, 717, 1158, 1180
6:19–20   **Vol. 3:** 543
6:19   **Vol. 1:** 372, 658, 660   **Vol. 3:** 684, 794–795
6:20   **Vol. 1:** 168   **Vol. 2:** 301   **Vol. 3:** 795, 830, 941, 947
7–10   **Vol. 3:** 366
7   **Vol. 2:** 693   **Vol. 3:** 228
7:1 ff   **Vol. 2:** 378   **Vol. 3:** 41, 1113
7:1–10   **Vol. 2:** 447, 591, 694
7:1–7   **Vol. 1:** 214
7:1–3   **Vol. 2:** 591
7:1   **Vol. 1:** 325   **Vol. 2:** 74, 591   **Vol. 3:** 163, 435
7:2   **Vol. 1:** 49, 80, 581   **Vol. 2:** 59, 694, 781   **Vol. 3:** 365, 448, 854, 1174
7:2b   **Vol. 2:** 591, 694
7:3   **Vol. 1:** 166, 616, 619   **Vol. 2:** 36, 64, 480, 505, 591, 694   **Vol. 3:** 41, 647
7:3b   **Vol. 2:** 592
7:3c   **Vol. 2:** 592
7:4 ff   **Vol. 1:** 80
7:4–10   **Vol. 2:** 592, 694
7:4–7   **Vol. 2:** 694
7:4   **Vol. 1:** 65   **Vol. 2:** 694   **Vol. 3:** 1174
7:5 ff   **Vol. 3:** 41
7:5   **Vol. 1:** 240, 337   **Vol. 2:** 447, 467, 592, 693   **Vol. 3:** 854
7:6–8   **Vol. 2:** 447
7:6   **Vol. 2:** 36, 592, 694   **Vol. 3:** 73
7:7   **Vol. 2:** 592
7:8   **Vol. 2:** 592, 694
7:9–10   **Vol. 2:** 694
7:9   **Vol. 2:** 467
7:10   **Vol. 1:** 240, 325
7:11–28   **Vol. 2:** 591–592
7:11   **Vol. 2:** 64, 448, 467   **Vol. 3:** 41, 275, 585
7:12   **Vol. 2:** 320, 447, 663
7:13 ff   **Vol. 2:** 447
7:13 f   **Vol. 1:** 619   **Vol. 3:** 872
7:13   **Vol. 3:** 435–436
7:14   **Vol. 2:** 320, 642   **Vol. 3:** 397, 435

7:15   **Vol. 1:** 731   **Vol. 2:** 447, 505   **Vol. 3:** 275
7:16   **Vol. 1:** 337, 677   **Vol. 2:** 207, 447, 505, 592   **Vol. 3:** 41, 189
7:17   **Vol. 3:** 830
7:18 f   **Vol. 3:** 41–42
7:18   **Vol. 1:** 337   **Vol. 2:** 447   **Vol. 3:** 995
7:19   **Vol. 2:** 55, 64, 447, 448   **Vol. 3:** 1113
7:20 ff   **Vol. 1:** 375
7:20–22   **Vol. 3:** 742
7:20 f   **Vol. 3:** 41, 738
7:21   **Vol. 1:** 356   **Vol. 3:** 830
7:22   **Vol. 1:** 371–372, 375
7:23 f   **Vol. 3:** 228
7:23   **Vol. 2:** 222   **Vol. 3:** 41
7:24   **Vol. 2:** 592   **Vol. 3:** 41, 225, 584–585, 830
7:25–27   **Vol. 3:** 582
7:25   **Vol. 1:** 90   **Vol. 2:** 294, 592, 882   **Vol. 3:** 41, 62, 215, 612
7:26–28   **Vol. 2:** 42
7:26   **Vol. 1:** 563   **Vol. 2:** 195, 199, 238, 669   **Vol. 3:** 41, 534, 663, 925, 1010
7:27 f   **Vol. 2:** 717
7:27   **Vol. 1:** 372, 448   **Vol. 2:** 717, 799, 895   **Vol. 3:** 41, 162, 433, 723, 1154, 1196–1197
7:28   **Vol. 2:** 63, 65, 592   **Vol. 3:** 41, 647, 738, 830, 995, 1113
7:28b   **Vol. 2:** 447
8–9   **Vol. 3:** 814
8:1–2   **Vol. 2:** 195   **Vol. 3:** 814
8:1   **Vol. 1:** 637   **Vol. 2:** 81, 147, 157, 193, 195, 426   **Vol. 3:** 298, 435
8:2   **Vol. 2:** 230   **Vol. 3:** 42, 552, 811, 888–889
8:3 f   **Vol. 2:** 41–42
8:3   **Vol. 1:** 472   **Vol. 3:** 41, 433
8:4 f   **Vol. 1:** 518   **Vol. 2:** 447
8:5   **Vol. 1:** 326, 371   **Vol. 2:** 194, 291, 642, 804   **Vol. 3:** 42, 550, 555–556, 569, 814, 905
8:5b   **Vol. 2:** 447
8:6 ff   **Vol. 3:** 42
8:6–13   **Vol. 1:** 154   **Vol. 3:** 227
8:6   **Vol. 1:** 371–372, 374–375, 666   **Vol. 2:** 447–448, 671   **Vol. 3:** 73, 552
8:7–13   **Vol. 3:** 433
8:7   **Vol. 1:** 666   **Vol. 2:** 139, 145, 671   **Vol. 3:** 531
8:8 ff   **Vol. 2:** 316
8:8–12   **Vol. 1:** 256, 371   **Vol. 2:** 145   **Vol. 3:** 74
8:8   **Vol. 1:** 666   **Vol. 2:** 139, 144–145, 248, 315, 320, 671
8:9 f   **Vol. 2:** 156
8:9   **Vol. 1:** 532   **Vol. 2:** 145   **Vol. 3:** 227, 750

Hebrews *(cont'd)*

8:10   **Vol. 1:** 368   **Vol. 2:** 42, 248   **Vol. 3:** 127, 227, 490
8:11   **Vol. 2:** 428, 804   **Vol. 3:** 765
8:12   **Vol. 3:** 160, 241, 575–576
8:13   **Vol. 1:** 371, 666   **Vol. 2:** 447, 671, 675, 716
9–10   **Vol. 2:** 199
9   **Vol. 3:** 366
9:1–10:39   **Vol. 3:** 433
9:1–10   **Vol. 3:** 120
9:1–5   **Vol. 3:** 163
9:1   **Vol. 1:** 524   **Vol. 3:** 42, 365, 551
9:2–5   **Vol. 3:** 814
9:2–3   **Vol. 2:** 230   **Vol. 3:** 814
9:2   **Vol. 1:** 586, 666   **Vol. 2:** 487   **Vol. 3:** 120
9:4 f   **Vol. 3:** 787
9:4   **Vol. 1:** 252–253, 408   **Vol. 2:** 294
9:5   **Vol. 1:** 280, 371   **Vol. 2:** 304, 614   **Vol. 3:** 163–164
9:5a   **Vol. 3:** 163
9:6–8   **Vol. 3:** 814
9:6   **Vol. 1:** 666   **Vol. 3:** 120, 551
9:7   **Vol. 1:** 222   **Vol. 2:** 406, 717, 724   **Vol. 3:** 41
9:8 ff   **Vol. 3:** 832
9:8   **Vol. 1:** 666   **Vol. 3:** 317, 323, 543, 705, 941
9:9   **Vol. 1:** 351–352   **Vol. 2:** 41, 63, 746, 804   **Vol. 3:** 433, 550, 555, 831
9:10   **Vol. 1:** 146, 149, 677   **Vol. 2:** 268   **Vol. 3:** 351, 365, 831
9:11 ff   **Vol. 3:** 166, 336
9:11 f   **Vol. 3:** 199, 1177
9:11   **Vol. 1:** 327, 386   **Vol. 2:** 64, 102, 150, 195   **Vol. 3:** 42, 317, 814–815, 1178
9:12 ff   **Vol. 1:** 223
9:12 f   **Vol. 1:** 114, 222
9:12   **Vol. 1:** 116, 372   **Vol. 2:** 230, 717–718   **Vol. 3:** 63, 162, 198, 200, 529, 723, 812
9:13 ff   **Vol. 1:** 225, 371
9:13–14   **Vol. 1:** 224, 677   **Vol. 3:** 41, 107
9:13   **Vol. 1:** 115–116, 448
9:14   **Vol. 1:** 116, 223, 351–352, 355, 446   **Vol. 2:** 718   **Vol. 3:** 41, 199–200, 432, 435, 550, 705, 925
9:15 f   **Vol. 3:** 323
9:15   **Vol. 1:** 276, 371, 374–375, 659   **Vol. 2:** 80, 300, 671   **Vol. 3:** 73, 199, 584–585
9:16 f   **Vol. 1:** 371
9:16   **Vol. 1:** 369   **Vol. 2:** 663
9:17   **Vol. 1:** 659   **Vol. 3:** 713
9:18 ff   **Vol. 1:** 224–225
9:18–22   **Vol. 1:** 222
9:18   **Vol. 2:** 673   **Vol. 3:** 366
9:19 ff   **Vol. 1:** 222   **Vol. 2:** 447
9:19 f   **Vol. 1:** 337

9:19   **Vol. 1:** 114, 116, 223, 244
9:20   **Vol. 2:** 533
9:21   **Vol. 3:** 552, 913
9:22   **Vol. 1:** 222, 701–702   **Vol. 2:** 854   **Vol. 3:** 41, 107, 199–200
9:23–28   **Vol. 1:** 115
9:23 f   **Vol. 2:** 194–195
9:23   **Vol. 2:** 291, 663   **Vol. 3:** 433
9:24 ff   **Vol. 2:** 447
9:24 f   **Vol. 3:** 794
9:24   **Vol. 1:** 587   **Vol. 2:** 80, 150, 199, 230, 489   **Vol. 3:** 42, 63, 814, 888–889, 905
9:25 ff   **Vol. 2:** 42
9:25 f   **Vol. 2:** 664   **Vol. 3:** 199, 433
9:25   **Vol. 1:** 222, 685   **Vol. 2:** 742   **Vol. 3:** 1175
9:26 ff   **Vol. 2:** 717
9:26   **Vol. 1:** 325, 378   **Vol. 3:** 41, 162, 323, 829–832
9:27   **Vol. 2:** 366
9:28   **Vol. 1:** 96–97, 438   **Vol. 2:** 194   **Vol. 3:** 199, 215, 612
10   **Vol. 3:** 366, 905
10:1 ff   **Vol. 3:** 41, 588
10:1–4   **Vol. 3:** 107
10:1   **Vol. 1:** 115, 327, 371   **Vol. 2:** 63, 102, 288, 447, 804   **Vol. 3:** 41, 63, 433, 555–556, 905, 1158
10:1c   **Vol. 2:** 448
10:2 f   **Vol. 2:** 717
10:2   **Vol. 1:** 351–352   **Vol. 2:** 315, 717   **Vol. 3:** 550
10:2b   **Vol. 2:** 447
10:3   **Vol. 2:** 717   **Vol. 3:** 243, 245
10:4–10   **Vol. 3:** 582
10:4   **Vol. 1:** 114–116, 222, 225   **Vol. 2:** 606
10:5 ff   **Vol. 3:** 41–42, 434, 1023
10:5–10   **Vol. 3:** 432–433, 1023
10:5–9   **Vol. 3:** 63
10:5   **Vol. 1:** 234   **Vol. 3:** 350, 1023
10:6   **Vol. 2:** 818   **Vol. 3:** 431, 1203
10:7   **Vol. 2:** 157   **Vol. 3:** 1023
10:8   **Vol. 2:** 448, 818   **Vol. 3:** 431, 434, 1023, 1203
10:9 f   **Vol. 3:** 1023
10:9a   **Vol. 2:** 448
10:9b   **Vol. 2:** 447
10:10 ff   **Vol. 2:** 42
10:10   **Vol. 1:** 234, 372   **Vol. 2:** 230, 448, 717   **Vol. 3:** 434, 552, 1023
10:11–13   **Vol. 3:** 588
10:11 f   **Vol. 3:** 433
10:11   **Vol. 2:** 895   **Vol. 3:** 552
10:12 ff   **Vol. 1:** 371
10:12 f   **Vol. 2:** 80, 515
10:12   **Vol. 2:** 147, 204, 717–718, 720   **Vol. 3:** 162, 298
10:13   **Vol. 1:** 239, 477, 554   **Vol. 2:** 245   **Vol. 3:** 252
10:14–18   **Vol. 3:** 227

Hebrews *(cont'd)*

10:14	**Vol. 2:** 64, 230, 717, 720 **Vol. 3:** 433
10:15 ff	**Vol. 3:** 433
10:15–18	**Vol. 1:** 154
10:15 f	**Vol. 2:** 786
10:15	**Vol. 3:** 705
10:16 ff	**Vol. 1:** 371 **Vol. 2:** 316
10:16 f	**Vol. 1:** 371 **Vol. 3:** 42, 74
10:16	**Vol. 3:** 127, 490
10:17	**Vol. 2:** 448 **Vol. 3:** 241
10:18	**Vol. 2:** 448, 736 **Vol. 3:** 42, 433, 582, 1203
10:19 ff	**Vol. 2:** 505 **Vol. 3:** 41
10:19–25	**Vol. 2:** 718, 881
10:19–22	**Vol. 3:** 366
10:19–20	**Vol. 3:** 543, 941
10:19	**Vol. 1:** 223 **Vol. 2:** 230 **Vol. 3:** 41, 166, 366, 812, 832, 940
10:20	**Vol. 1:** 677 **Vol. 2:** 673, 675 **Vol. 3:** 63, 795, 1180
10:21	**Vol. 1:** 637 **Vol. 3:** 794
10:22	**Vol. 1:** 152, 154, 157–158, 223–225, 322, 351–352 **Vol. 2:** 183 **Vol. 3:** 38, 41, 107, 888–889, 941, 990
10:23	**Vol. 1:** 346 **Vol. 2:** 244 **Vol. 3:** 61, 74
10:24	**Vol. 1:** 110 **Vol. 3:** 129
10:25 ff	**Vol. 3:** 434
10:25	**Vol. 1:** 713 **Vol. 2:** 55, 438 **Vol. 3:** 74, 143
10:26 ff	**Vol. 1:** 372
10:26–39	**Vol. 1:** 299 **Vol. 2:** 718
10:26–31	**Vol. 3:** 1206
10:26–30	**Vol. 3:** 136
10:26 f	**Vol. 1:** 359, 703 **Vol. 3:** 582
10:26	**Vol. 2:** 405 **Vol. 3:** 28, 434, 586, 888, 1203
10:27 f	**Vol. 2:** 244
10:27	**Vol. 1:** 326, 623 **Vol. 2:** 366
10:28 f	**Vol. 2:** 598
10:28	**Vol. 1:** 74 **Vol. 2:** 686 **Vol. 3:** 1043
10:29 f	**Vol. 2:** 230
10:29	**Vol. 1:** 223, 371, 448 **Vol. 2:** 123, 533, 786 **Vol. 3:** 28, 166, 434, 647, 705, 944
10:30	**Vol. 1:** 111 **Vol. 2:** 158, 365, 800 **Vol. 3:** 97
10:31	**Vol. 1:** 609, 611, 623 **Vol. 2:** 149
10:32	**Vol. 1:** 646 **Vol. 2:** 495, 775 **Vol. 3:** 240, 722–723, 725
10:33	**Vol. 1:** 644 **Vol. 3:** 340, 521, 934
10:34	**Vol. 2:** 361, 775, 845, 847 **Vol. 3:** 225, 604, 722, 724
10:35 ff	**Vol. 3:** 143
10:35	**Vol. 2:** 736 **Vol. 3:** 74, 143
10:36	**Vol. 2:** 300, 361, 775 **Vol. 3:** 1023
10:37 f	**Vol. 1:** 604 **Vol. 3:** 366
10:37	**Vol. 2:** 429 **Vol. 3:** 74, 843
10:38 f	**Vol. 1:** 372
10:38†	**Vol. 2:** 818 **Vol. 3:** 362, 365, 685
10:39	**Vol. 2:** 775, 839 **Vol. 3:** 685
11	**Vol. 1:** 714 **Vol. 2:** 835 **Vol. 3:** 367, 433, 582, 1047
11:1	**Vol. 1:** 604, 712–713 **Vol. 2:** 142, 243, 768 **Vol. 3:** 1158
11:2	**Vol. 1:** 198 **Vol. 3:** 1047
11:3	**Vol. 1:** 713 **Vol. 2:** 488, 768 **Vol. 3:** 128, 350, 829–831, 1187
11:4	**Vol. 2:** 41 **Vol. 3:** 365, 434, 436, 1047
11:5 f	**Vol. 2:** 817
11:5	**Vol. 2:** 627 **Vol. 3:** 264, 265, 325, 602, 1047
11:6	**Vol. 1:** 322 **Vol. 2:** 606 **Vol. 3:** 73, 143, 532
11:7	**Vol. 2:** 91, 300–301, 365, 682 **Vol. 3:** 120, 211, 365, 1181, 1188
11:8–12	**Vol. 1:** 80
11:8–10	**Vol. 3:** 1007
11:8	**Vol. 1:** 326, 461 **Vol. 2:** 180, 301
11:9–10	**Vol. 1:** 691 **Vol. 3:** 811
11:9	**Vol. 1:** 81, 460, 684 **Vol. 2:** 318 **Vol. 3:** 565, 815
11:10–16	**Vol. 3:** 73
11:10	**Vol. 1:** 279, 327, 387, 661, 690 **Vol. 2:** 245, 803
11:11	**Vol. 1:** 80, 92, 378 **Vol. 3:** 73, 1067
11:12	**Vol. 1:** 241, 445, 732 **Vol. 2:** 435 **Vol. 3:** 735
11:13	**Vol. 1:** 346, 460, 689–691 **Vol. 2:** 630, 790, 804 **Vol. 3:** 565, 815
11:14	**Vol. 1:** 460, 616 **Vol. 2:** 489 **Vol. 3:** 532
11:15 f	**Vol. 1:** 689
11:15	**Vol. 1:** 460 **Vol. 3:** 241
11:16	**Vol. 1:** 327, 460 **Vol. 2:** 73, 194, 725, 803, 847 **Vol. 3:** 563
11:17–19	**Vol. 1:** 80
11:17–18	**Vol. 1:** 81
11:17	**Vol. 1:** 461 **Vol. 2:** 76
11:18	**Vol. 3:** 523
11:19	**Vol. 2:** 604, 746 **Vol. 3:** 304, 824, 826
11:20	**Vol. 1:** 81, 214, 326
11:21	**Vol. 1:** 214, 408 **Vol. 2:** 318
11:22	**Vol. 1:** 337, 430 **Vol. 3:** 940
11:23 ff	**Vol. 2:** 642
11:23	**Vol. 1:** 284, 330, 623 **Vol. 2:** 216, 378 **Vol. 3:** 365
11:24–28	**Vol. 2:** 768
11:24–27	**Vol. 1:** 532
11:24	**Vol. 1:** 455 **Vol. 3:** 457
11:25 f	**Vol. 3:** 839, 1180
11:25	**Vol. 1:** 534 **Vol. 2:** 73
11:26	**Vol. 2:** 830, 835, 844 **Vol. 3:** 143, 340
11:27	**Vol. 1:** 623 **Vol. 2:** 77, 378, 768, 835
11:28	**Vol. 1:** 222–223, 465, 633 **Vol. 2:** 854
11:29	**Vol. 1:** 356, 516 **Vol. 3:** 802, 984
11:30	**Vol. 1:** 609 **Vol. 2:** 690 **Vol. 3:** 948
11:31	**Vol. 1:** 499, 593 **Vol. 3:** 1067
11:32	**Vol. 1:** 427, 576 **Vol. 3:** 843
11:33 f	**Vol. 3:** 365

Hebrews *(cont'd)*

11:33	**Vol. 1:** 118, 646 **Vol. 3:** 70, 951
11:34	**Vol. 1:** 559, 656, 685 **Vol. 2:** 742 **Vol. 3:** 109–110, 713, 961–962, 967
11:35 f	**Vol. 2:** 739
11:35	**Vol. 3:** 200, 277, 1067
11:36	**Vol. 1:** 163 **Vol. 2:** 136 **Vol. 3:** 802
11:37	**Vol. 1:** 114, 322 **Vol. 3:** 967
11:38	**Vol. 2:** 459 **Vol. 3:** 381, 1007
11:39	**Vol. 2:** 64 **Vol. 3:** 70, 73, 1047
11:40	**Vol. 2:** 64
12	**Vol. 1:** 400 **Vol. 2:** 775 **Vol. 3:** 1014
12:1 f	**Vol. 3:** 367
12:1–29	**Vol. 1:** 372 **Vol. 2:** 718
12:1–11	**Vol. 1:** 604
12:1–4	**Vol. 1:** 648 **Vol. 3:** 582
12:1	**Vol. 1:** 406, 712 **Vol. 2:** 775 **Vol. 3:** 73, 947, 1047, 1180
12:2 f	**Vol. 2:** 775
12:2	**Vol. 1:** 168, 394, 400, 461, 604 **Vol. 2:** 51, 60–61, 64, 147, 204, 331, 361, 505, 515, 775 **Vol. 3:** 298, 563, 941, 1180
12:3 ff	**Vol. 3:** 143
12:3 f	**Vol. 1:** 647
12:3	**Vol. 2:** 64, 775 **Vol. 3:** 189, 685
12:4 ff	**Vol. 3:** 998
12:4	**Vol. 1:** 222, 646 **Vol. 3:** 240
12:5–11	**Vol. 3:** 365
12:5 f	**Vol. 2:** 757 **Vol. 3:** 778
12:5	**Vol. 1:** 462, 571 **Vol. 2:** 142 **Vol. 3:** 189, 821
12:6	**Vol. 1:** 163, 639 **Vol. 2:** 549 **Vol. 3:** 778
12:7–11	**Vol. 3:** 778
12:7	**Vol. 2:** 775 **Vol. 3:** 647, 1187
12:8	**Vol. 1:** 188, 639
12:9	**Vol. 1:** 621 **Vol. 3:** 647, 695, 778
12:10	**Vol. 2:** 230 **Vol. 3:** 750, 778
12:11	**Vol. 1:** 313, 723 **Vol. 2:** 361, 780, 782, 899 **Vol. 3:** 363, 365, 778, 822, 954
12:12 ff	**Vol. 3:** 143
12:12–28	**Vol. 1:** 299
12:12	**Vol. 2:** 859
12:13	**Vol. 2:** 415 **Vol. 3:** 351, 903
12:14	**Vol. 2:** 230, 244, 782, 807
12:15 ff	**Vol. 2:** 123, 847 **Vol. 3:** 143
12:15	**Vol. 1:** 96–97, 191, 202, 448 **Vol. 2:** 782 **Vol. 3:** 868, 954
12:16 f	**Vol. 3:** 582
12:16	**Vol. 1:** 501 **Vol. 2:** 268, 318, 782 **Vol. 3:** 869, 1179
12:17	**Vol. 1:** 215, 359 **Vol. 2:** 300, 318, 361 **Vol. 3:** 532, 809
12:18 ff	**Vol. 1:** 656
12:18–29	**Vol. 3:** 433, 1014
12:18–24	**Vol. 3:** 1007
12:18–19	**Vol. 2:** 642 **Vol. 3:** 874
12:19	**Vol. 2:** 785, 858 **Vol. 3:** 112, 674
12:20	**Vol. 3:** 568
12:21	**Vol. 1:** 623 **Vol. 3:** 324
12:22 ff	**Vol. 2:** 803 **Vol. 3:** 550
12:22 f	**Vol. 1:** 689
12:22	**Vol. 1:** 327 **Vol. 2:** 194, 207, 327, 329 **Vol. 3:** 1014
12:23	**Vol. 1:** 304, 669 **Vol. 2:** 64, 193, 354, 365 **Vol. 3:** 38, 365, 694
12:24	**Vol. 1:** 224–225, 371, 374–375 **Vol. 2:** 675 **Vol. 3:** 1014
12:25 ff	**Vol. 3:** 143
12:25	**Vol. 2:** 193, 642, 858 **Vol. 3:** 325, 1014
12:26	**Vol. 2:** 717 **Vol. 3:** 557, 560
12:27	**Vol. 1:** 214 **Vol. 3:** 265, 317, 1154
12:28 f	**Vol. 3:** 1014
12:28	**Vol. 2:** 91, 121 **Vol. 3:** 74, 550, 560–561, 931, 1181
12:29	**Vol. 1:** 656 **Vol. 2:** 91
13:1 ff	**Vol. 2:** 718
13:1	**Vol. 2:** 549
13:2	**Vol. 1:** 690 **Vol. 2:** 550
13:3	**Vol. 3:** 241
13:4	**Vol. 1:** 448 **Vol. 2:** 365, 580, 583–584, 587 **Vol. 3:** 925
13:5	**Vol. 2:** 899 **Vol. 3:** 727–728
13:6	**Vol. 1:** 328, 623
13:7	**Vol. 1:** 491–492 **Vol. 3:** 934
13:8	**Vol. 3:** 830, 839
13:9	**Vol. 1:** 689 **Vol. 2:** 123, 183, 268 **Vol. 3:** 770, 944
13:10 ff	**Vol. 3:** 817
13:10–13	**Vol. 3:** 434
13:10	**Vol. 2:** 273 **Vol. 3:** 38, 433, 435–436, 550, 815
13:11–13	**Vol. 3:** 723
13:11	**Vol. 1:** 222 **Vol. 2:** 476 **Vol. 3:** 794, 965, 1182, 1203
13:12 f	**Vol. 3:** 724
13:12	**Vol. 1:** 223 **Vol. 2:** 230, 800 **Vol. 3:** 166, 723
13:13	**Vol. 3:** 340, 435, 965
13:14	**Vol. 1:** 689, 720 **Vol. 2:** 329, 804 **Vol. 3:** 74, 225, 434, 532, 832, 965, 970
13:15 f	**Vol. 2:** 42 **Vol. 3:** 42, 242, 434
13:15	**Vol. 1:** 346 **Vol. 3:** 817, 965
13:16	**Vol. 2:** 694, 817 **Vol. 3:** 435
13:17	**Vol. 1:** 591 **Vol. 2:** 137, 423 **Vol. 3:** 685, 930
13:18	**Vol. 1:** 223, 351, 591, 647
13:19	**Vol. 3:** 147
13:20 ff	**Vol. 2:** 718 **Vol. 3:** 287
13:20 f	**Vol. 2:** 875
13:20	**Vol. 1:** 223, 371, 437 **Vol. 2:** 78, 413, 533, 671, 780–781 **Vol. 3:** 166, 298
13:21	**Vol. 1:** 99 **Vol. 2:** 46, 817 **Vol. 3:** 197, 350, 830, 1023
13:22	**Vol. 1:** 571 **Vol. 2:** 766 **Vol. 3:** 1113

James

1:1	**Vol. 1:** 55, 247, 686 **Vol. 2:** 34, 358, 695, 804 **Vol. 3:** 370, 613
1:2 f	**Vol. 2:** 809 **Vol. 3:** 810
1:2	**Vol. 1:** 406, 460, 609 **Vol. 2:** 361 **Vol. 3:** 802
1:3 f	**Vol. 2:** 775
1:3	**Vol. 1:** 604 **Vol. 2:** 400 **Vol. 3:** 809
1:4 f	**Vol. 3:** 251
1:4	**Vol. 2:** 63, 65 **Vol. 3:** 253
1:5–7	**Vol. 2:** 868
1:5 f	**Vol. 2:** 857
1:5	**Vol. 2:** 43, 857 **Vol. 3:** 253, 340, 572, 1032
1:6 ff	**Vol. 1:** 604 **Vol. 2:** 435
1:6–8	**Vol. 1:** 504
1:6	**Vol. 3:** 984, 1003
1:7	**Vol. 2:** 565, 857
1:8	**Vol. 1:** 505 **Vol. 3:** 572, 686–687, 940
1:9 f	**Vol. 2:** 263
1:9	**Vol. 2:** 200
1:10 f	**Vol. 2:** 842, 844
1:10	**Vol. 1:** 744 **Vol. 2:** 211 **Vol. 3:** 523
1:10c	**Vol. 2:** 263
1:11	**Vol. 1:** 515, 586, 609, 744 **Vol. 2:** 211 **Vol. 3:** 523, 731
1:12	**Vol. 1:** 217, 406 **Vol. 2:** 775 **Vol. 3:** 802, 809
1:13–16	**Vol. 3:** 888
1:13	**Vol. 1:** 563 **Vol. 3:** 802–803
1:13a	**Vol. 3:** 1198
1:13c	**Vol. 3:** 1198
1:14	**Vol. 1:** 458 **Vol. 3:** 802, 809
1:15	**Vol. 1:** 178, 187, 343, 458 **Vol. 3:** 582
1:16	**Vol. 2:** 459–460
1:17 f	**Vol. 2:** 186
1:17	**Vol. 1:** 621 **Vol. 2:** 41–42, 63, 495 **Vol. 3:** 554, 556, 888, 1018
1:18	**Vol. 1:** 158, 178, 187, 289, 386 **Vol. 3:** 416, 888, 1017
1:19 f	**Vol. 1:** 110
1:19	**Vol. 3:** 1143
1:20	**Vol. 2:** 563 **Vol. 3:** 369–370, 372
1:21	**Vol. 1:** 479, 731 **Vol. 3:** 685, 868, 1118
1:22–25	**Vol. 3:** 1154
1:22 f	**Vol. 2:** 177
1:22	**Vol. 2:** 176, 449, 459 **Vol. 3:** 1155
1:23 f	**Vol. 3:** 228
1:23	**Vol. 1:** 181 **Vol. 2:** 176 **Vol. 3:** 1155
1:25	**Vol. 1:** 717–718, 720 **Vol. 2:** 63, 176, 449 **Vol. 3:** 1150–1151, 1154–1155
1:26 f	**Vol. 3:** 551
1:26	**Vol. 1:** 551–552 **Vol. 2:** 460 **Vol. 3:** 551, 822, 1079
1:27	**Vol. 1:** 190–191, 448 **Vol. 2:** 738 **Vol. 3:** 107, 925, 1074, 1202
2:1 ff	**Vol. 2:** 566
2:1	**Vol. 1:** 587
2:2–4	**Vol. 3:** 589
2:2 f	**Vol. 2:** 486, 825
2:2	**Vol. 1:** 296, 479
2:3	**Vol. 1:** 239 **Vol. 3:** 589
2:4	**Vol. 1:** 505, 566 **Vol. 2:** 365
2:5	**Vol. 1:** 542 **Vol. 2:** 300–301, 380, 826, 842, 844
2:6 f	**Vol. 2:** 825
2:6	**Vol. 2:** 50, 842, 844
2:7	**Vol. 1:** 146, 276 **Vol. 2:** 105, 654
2:8	**Vol. 1:** 259 **Vol. 2:** 63, 449, 544 **Vol. 3:** 490–491
2:9 ff	**Vol. 3:** 584
2:9–11	**Vol. 3:** 584
2:9	**Vol. 1:** 587
2:10 f	**Vol. 2:** 449
2:10	**Vol. 2:** 133, 143, 720 **Vol. 3:** 184
2:11	**Vol. 1:** 607 **Vol. 2:** 583
2:12	**Vol. 1:** 717–718, 720 **Vol. 2:** 449
2:13	**Vol. 1:** 228 **Vol. 2:** 449, 597, 826 **Vol. 3:** 1155
2:14–26	**Vol. 1:** 79 **Vol. 3:** 369, 1182
2:14–18	**Vol. 3:** 369
2:15–16	**Vol. 2:** 694
2:15	**Vol. 3:** 251, 253
2:16	**Vol. 1:** 234, 318, 744 **Vol. 2:** 435
2:17	**Vol. 1:** 446, 605 **Vol. 2:** 63 **Vol. 3:** 1151
2:18	**Vol. 3:** 569
2:19	**Vol. 1:** 453 **Vol. 2:** 73
2:19a	**Vol. 3:** 1211
2:20	**Vol. 2:** 63, 398
2:21	**Vol. 1:** 81 **Vol. 3:** 369–370, 436, 1196
2:22	**Vol. 1:** 604 **Vol. 2:** 63 **Vol. 3:** 228, 362, 370, 1151–1152
2:23	**Vol. 1:** 596, 604, 736 **Vol. 2:** 73, 549 **Vol. 3:** 169, 369, 490, 492, 824–826, 1187
2:24	**Vol. 3:** 369, 1151
2:25	**Vol. 1:** 102, 453, 499 **Vol. 3:** 369
2:26	**Vol. 1:** 446 **Vol. 3:** 370, 694
3:1 ff	**Vol. 3:** 369
3:1–6	**Vol. 2:** 435
3:1	**Vol. 3:** 767–768
3:2	**Vol. 2:** 63, 563
3:3	**Vol. 1:** 118, 591 **Vol. 3:** 1187
3:4	**Vol. 2:** 155
3:5 ff	**Vol. 1:** 231
3:5 f	**Vol. 1:** 656 **Vol. 3:** 1079
3:5	**Vol. 1:** 231 **Vol. 2:** 757 **Vol. 3:** 370, 1143
3:6–10	**Vol. 1:** 564
3:6	**Vol. 1:** 182, 231 **Vol. 3:** 576, 1143
3:7	**Vol. 1:** 114, 175 **Vol. 2:** 661
3:8	**Vol. 2:** 28, 661 **Vol. 3:** 1079, 1143
3:9 f	**Vol. 1:** 213, 417
3:9	**Vol. 2:** 505
3:10	**Vol. 3:** 958
3:11 ff	**Vol. 3:** 369
3:11 f	**Vol. 3:** 988
3:11	**Vol. 1:** 201 **Vol. 3:** 987

James *(cont'd)*

3:12	**Vol. 1:** 725 **Vol. 2:** 711, 757 **Vol. 3:** 449
3:13 ff	**Vol. 3:** 369
3:13	**Vol. 2:** 105, 258 **Vol. 3:** 569, 1032
3:14	**Vol. 1:** 201, 228–229 **Vol. 2:** 567 **Vol. 3:** 888, 1167
3:15 f	**Vol. 3:** 1032
3:15	**Vol. 1:** 452 **Vol. 3:** 684
3:16	**Vol. 1:** 564 **Vol. 3:** 1158, 1167
3:17	**Vol. 1:** 505 **Vol. 2:** 258, 470, 597, 780, 782 **Vol. 3:** 101, 1032
3:18	**Vol. 1:** 723 **Vol. 2:** 780, 782 **Vol. 3:** 363, 365, 369–370, 525
4:1	**Vol. 1:** 231, 459, 646 **Vol. 3:** 962, 964
4:2	**Vol. 1:** 639 **Vol. 3:** 963
4:3	**Vol. 1:** 459 **Vol. 2:** 858
4:4	**Vol. 1:** 257, 472 **Vol. 2:** 548–549, 584
4:5	**Vol. 1:** 558 **Vol. 2:** 251 **Vol. 3:** 491–492, 693, 705, 822
4:6	**Vol. 2:** 123, 757 **Vol. 3:** 30–31
4:6b	**Vol. 2:** 263
4:7	**Vol. 1:** 559 **Vol. 3:** 471
4:8–10	**Vol. 2:** 422
4:8	**Vol. 2:** 55, 422 **Vol. 3:** 101, 572
4:9 f	**Vol. 2:** 361, 417
4:9	**Vol. 2:** 417, 422, 433 **Vol. 3:** 859
4:10	**Vol. 2:** 203, 263
4:11 f	**Vol. 2:** 449 **Vol. 3:** 346
4:11	**Vol. 2:** 365
4:12	**Vol. 1:** 464 **Vol. 2:** 365, 450, 721–722
4:13	**Vol. 1:** 268 **Vol. 3:** 137, 1154
4:14	**Vol. 2:** 480, 488
4:15	**Vol. 2:** 480 **Vol. 3:** 31, 1023, 1179
4:16	**Vol. 1:** 228 **Vol. 3:** 31
4:17	**Vol. 2:** 105 **Vol. 3:** 31, 582
5:1 ff	**Vol. 3:** 369
5:1–6	**Vol. 2:** 844
5:1	**Vol. 1:** 322 **Vol. 3:** 859
5:2	**Vol. 2:** 842
5:3	**Vol. 1:** 119 **Vol. 2:** 28, 96, 836 **Vol. 3:** 1190
5:4	**Vol. 1:** 410–411 **Vol. 2:** 69, 178 **Vol. 3:** 526
5:5	**Vol. 2:** 182
5:6	**Vol. 2:** 370 **Vol. 3:** 369–370
5:7 f	**Vol. 2:** 518, 771, 900–901
5:7–11	**Vol. 2:** 769, 771
5:7	**Vol. 1:** 722 **Vol. 2:** 245, 771 **Vol. 3:** 1003
5:8	**Vol. 2:** 55, 387, 771
5:9	**Vol. 2:** 30, 365, 423, 727, 771
5:10	**Vol. 2:** 291, 513, 771 **Vol. 3:** 724, 905
5:11	**Vol. 1:** 216 **Vol. 2:** 63, 598, 600, 775
5:12	**Vol. 1:** 609 **Vol. 3:** 183, 741
5:13 ff	**Vol. 1:** 121 **Vol. 2:** 875
5:13	**Vol. 3:** 671–672, 722
5:14–18	**Vol. 2:** 868
5:14 f	**Vol. 2:** 632
5:14	**Vol. 1:** 120–121, 198–199, 274, 304 **Vol. 2:** 513, 712
5:15 ff	**Vol. 3:** 582
5:15 f	**Vol. 1:** 703
5:15	**Vol. 2:** 861, 867 **Vol. 3:** 212, 216
5:16	**Vol. 1:** 346, 702 **Vol. 2:** 169, 861, 867 **Vol. 3:** 369–370, 713
5:17 f	**Vol. 2:** 193, 730
5:17	**Vol. 1:** 544 **Vol. 2:** 503, 688, 861 **Vol. 3:** 1002
5:18	**Vol. 3:** 1004
5:19 f	**Vol. 1:** 355 **Vol. 2:** 460
5:19	**Vol. 2:** 459 **Vol. 3:** 888, 942
5:20	**Vol. 1:** 733 **Vol. 2:** 214, 400, 460 **Vol. 3:** 685, 940

1 Peter

1:1–2:10	**Vol. 1:** 180
1:1 f	**Vol. 1:** 305 **Vol. 2:** 230 **Vol. 3:** 1201
1:1	**Vol. 1:** 55, 130, 141, 305, 686, 690 **Vol. 2:** 34, 695, 790, 804 **Vol. 3:** 336, 435, 871
1:2	**Vol. 1:** 223–224, 693, 733 **Vol. 2:** 179, 230, 687, 780–781 **Vol. 3:** 166, 257, 705
1:2a	**Vol. 3:** 435
1:3	**Vol. 1:** 180, 212, 290 **Vol. 2:** 73, 76, 242, 516, 597 **Vol. 3:** 215, 276–277, 1189
1:3a	**Vol. 3:** 1201
1:3b	**Vol. 3:** 1201
1:4 ff	**Vol. 3:** 257
1:4	**Vol. 1:** 290, 469 **Vol. 2:** 193, 300 **Vol. 3:** 925, 1173
1:5 ff	**Vol. 3:** 316
1:5 f	**Vol. 3:** 839
1:5	**Vol. 1:** 180 **Vol. 2:** 135, 605 **Vol. 3:** 118, 215, 838
1:6 f	**Vol. 3:** 810
1:6	**Vol. 2:** 354 **Vol. 3:** 802
1:7	**Vol. 1:** 464, 604, 656 **Vol. 2:** 50–51 **Vol. 3:** 257, 446, 529, 809, 817, 1151
1:8 f	**Vol. 2:** 361
1:8	**Vol. 1:** 603 **Vol. 2:** 354 **Vol. 3:** 1212
1:9	**Vol. 2:** 61, 63 **Vol. 3:** 215, 685
1:10 ff	**Vol. 2:** 630 **Vol. 3:** 257, 837
1:10 f	**Vol. 3:** 83
1:10	**Vol. 2:** 123 **Vol. 3:** 215, 532–533
1:11 f	**Vol. 3:** 313
1:11	**Vol. 3:** 63, 81, 257, 317, 533, 705, 722–723
1:12	**Vol. 2:** 113, 193 **Vol. 3:** 312–313, 316, 546, 705
1:13 ff	**Vol. 1:** 223
1:13–19	**Vol. 1:** 634
1:13	**Vol. 1:** 180, 240, 515, 634 **Vol. 2:** 63, 123, 270 **Vol. 3:** 128, 257, 316
1:14–18	**Vol. 1:** 552

1 Peter *(cont'd)*

1:14 f	**Vol. 2:** 230
1:14	**Vol. 1:** 458, 709 **Vol. 2:** 179 **Vol. 3:** 934
1:15 ff	**Vol. 2:** 270
1:15 f	**Vol. 2:** 228
1:15–18	**Vol. 3:** 935
1:15	**Vol. 1:** 275–276, 305 **Vol. 2:** 76 **Vol. 3:** 934
1:17	**Vol. 1:** 587, 621, 623, 634, 691 **Vol. 2:** 50, 270, 365 **Vol. 3:** 844, 934, 1200
1:18 f	**Vol. 1:** 223, 437 **Vol. 3:** 200, 435, 1175
1:18	**Vol. 1:** 551–552 **Vol. 2:** 96, 270 **Vol. 3:** 215, 435
1:19	**Vol. 1:** 629, 634 **Vol. 2:** 411, 463 **Vol. 3:** 166, 257, 924–925
1:20	**Vol. 1:** 378, 693 **Vol. 2:** 58 **Vol. 3:** 63, 323, 843–844, 1191
1:21	**Vol. 1:** 305 **Vol. 2:** 73 **Vol. 3:** 1214
1:21a	**Vol. 3:** 1211
1:21b	**Vol. 3:** 1213
1:22	**Vol. 1:** 180 **Vol. 2:** 179, 470, 549, 868 **Vol. 3:** 101, 107, 685, 888
1:23 ff	**Vol. 3:** 329
1:23–35	**Vol. 1:** 158
1:23–25†	**Vol. 2:** 113
1:23 f	**Vol. 3:** 1118
1:23	**Vol. 1:** 180, 289–290, 469 **Vol. 2:** 270 **Vol. 3:** 224–225, 1176, 1201
1:24 f	**Vol. 3:** 1122
1:24	**Vol. 1:** 516, 609, 678, 744 **Vol. 2:** 46, 211
1:25	**Vol. 3:** 61, 224
2	**Vol. 2:** 775
2:1–3	**Vol. 3:** 346
2:1	**Vol. 2:** 270, 469
2:2	**Vol. 1:** 284, 558 **Vol. 2:** 270 **Vol. 3:** 215, 1106, 1118
2:3	**Vol. 2:** 270
2:4 ff	**Vol. 1:** 661 **Vol. 2:** 706
2:4–10	**Vol. 2:** 381
2:4–8	**Vol. 3:** 393
2:4 f	**Vol. 2:** 249 **Vol. 3:** 435
2:4	**Vol. 1:** 539, 541 **Vol. 2:** 49, 83, 249, 270 **Vol. 3:** 390, 393, 809
2:5 ff	**Vol. 1:** 305 **Vol. 2:** 732
2:5	**Vol. 1:** 662 **Vol. 2:** 42, 230, 249, 253 **Vol. 3:** 37, 383, 387, 390, 393, 706–707, 746
2:6–8	**Vol. 2:** 313, 706
2:6 f	**Vol. 3:** 393
2:6†	**Vol. 1:** 477, 539, 541 **Vol. 2:** 49, 327, 709 **Vol. 3:** 390, 397, 491, 563, 1212
2:7	**Vol. 1:** 593 **Vol. 2:** 50, 129, 159, 253, 622, 706 **Vol. 3:** 383, 389–390
2:8	**Vol. 1:** 593 **Vol. 2:** 706, 708–709 **Vol. 3:** 382–383, 389–390, 397, 1186
2:9 f	**Vol. 1:** 256
2:9	**Vol. 1:** 276, 305, 424, 539, 541 **Vol. 2:** 73, 83, 380, 623, 800, 839 **Vol. 3:** 37, 46–47, 336, 435, 927
2:10	**Vol. 1:** 369 **Vol. 2:** 597
2:11 f	**Vol. 3:** 934
2:11	**Vol. 1:** 458, 646, 677, 690–691 **Vol. 2:** 790, 804 **Vol. 3:** 336, 685, 964
2:12	**Vol. 1:** 190 **Vol. 2:** 105, 794 **Vol. 3:** 346, 515, 725, 935, 1150–1151
2:13 ff	**Vol. 3:** 97, 755
2:13–3:7	**Vol. 1:** 59
2:13–18	**Vol. 2:** 775
2:13–17	**Vol. 3:** 549, 930
2:13 f	**Vol. 1:** 270
2:13	**Vol. 1:** 386 **Vol. 2:** 378, 517
2:14	**Vol. 1:** 270 **Vol. 2:** 101 **Vol. 3:** 817, 1155
2:15	**Vol. 2:** 102 **Vol. 3:** 1023, 1026
2:16	**Vol. 1:** 718–719 **Vol. 3:** 854
2:17	**Vol. 1:** 257, 305, 623 **Vol. 2:** 50–51
2:18–3:7	**Vol. 3:** 929
2:18	**Vol. 1:** 623 **Vol. 2:** 58, 258, 509 **Vol. 3:** 596
2:19 f	**Vol. 2:** 123 **Vol. 3:** 725
2:19	**Vol. 1:** 350, 353 **Vol. 3:** 183, 575–576, 725
2:20	**Vol. 1:** 163 **Vol. 2:** 102, 775 **Vol. 3:** 857, 1202
2:21 ff	**Vol. 1:** 305
2:21–25	**Vol. 2:** 775 **Vol. 3:** 257, 582
2:21–24	**Vol. 1:** 702
2:21	**Vol. 1:** 276 **Vol. 2:** 291, 338, 809 **Vol. 3:** 490, 723–724, 905
2:22–25	**Vol. 3:** 435
2:22 f	**Vol. 3:** 63
2:22	**Vol. 3:** 435, 529, 723
2:23 f	**Vol. 2:** 51
2:23	**Vol. 3:** 347, 370–371
2:24 ff	**Vol. 3:** 371
2:24	**Vol. 1:** 163, 181, 234, 266, 390 **Vol. 3:** 370–371, 723, 868
2:24a	**Vol. 3:** 1171, 1195
2:25	**Vol. 1:** 191, 355 **Vol. 2:** 413, 459–460 **Vol. 3:** 568, 685
3:1–7	**Vol. 2:** 923 **Vol. 3:** 932, 1067
3:1	**Vol. 1:** 593 **Vol. 2:** 50 **Vol. 3:** 138, 935
3:2	**Vol. 1:** 623 **Vol. 2:** 218 **Vol. 3:** 101, 515
3:3 ff	**Vol. 3:** 346
3:3 f	**Vol. 1:** 469
3:3	**Vol. 1:** 524
3:4	**Vol. 1:** 386 **Vol. 2:** 182, 218, 258 **Vol. 3:** 112, 693
3:5	**Vol. 2:** 73, 218
3:6	**Vol. 1:** 80 **Vol. 2:** 102, 218, 513 **Vol. 3:** 1067
3:7	**Vol. 2:** 50, 221, 223, 301, 400, 563 **Vol. 3:** 913, 994, 1058, 1065, 1067, 1200–1201

1 Peter *(cont'd)*

3:8	**Vol. 1:** 257 **Vol. 2:** 63, 549–550, 600 **Vol. 3:** 257
3:9	**Vol. 1:** 215, 276 **Vol. 2:** 300–301 **Vol. 3:** 136, 183, 347, 1179
3:10 ff	**Vol. 2:** 270
3:10	**Vol. 1:** 564 **Vol. 2:** 887 **Vol. 3:** 1023, 1079
3:11	**Vol. 1:** 564 **Vol. 2:** 782, 807 **Vol. 3:** 531
3:12	**Vol. 2:** 178, 861 **Vol. 3:** 370–371, 516
3:13–17	**Vol. 3:** 964
3:13	**Vol. 2:** 51 **Vol. 3:** 1167
3:14	**Vol. 1:** 623 **Vol. 3:** 370–371, 710, 725
3:15	**Vol. 1:** 51 **Vol. 2:** 244, 858 **Vol. 3:** 118
3:16	**Vol. 1:** 350–351, 353 **Vol. 2:** 258 **Vol. 3:** 257, 346, 934–935
3:17	**Vol. 1:** 563 **Vol. 2:** 51, 102 **Vol. 3:** 1023
3:18 ff	**Vol. 3:** 61
3:18–22	**Vol. 3:** 63, 674, 964
3:18 f	**Vol. 3:** 694
3:18	**Vol. 1:** 437, 479, 677 **Vol. 2:** 338, 717 **Vol. 3:** 40, 257, 323, 370–371, 575–576, 582, 705, 723, 1174, 1203
3:19 ff	**Vol. 2:** 207–208, 682
3:19 f	**Vol. 1:** 103
3:19	**Vol. 1:** 438 **Vol. 2:** 136, 207 **Vol. 3:** 54, 947
3:20 f	**Vol. 3:** 990
3:20	**Vol. 1:** 593, 677 **Vol. 2:** 692, 770, 881 **Vol. 3:** 119, 211, 215, 683, 1177
3:21 f	**Vol. 1:** 290
3:21	**Vol. 1:** 146–148, 158, 350–352, 479, 677 **Vol. 2:** 102, 682, 880–881 **Vol. 3:** 211, 215, 276–277, 906, 990, 1208
3:22	**Vol. 2:** 80–81, 147, 514, 603 **Vol. 3:** 947
4:1–3	**Vol. 1:** 677
4:1	**Vol. 1:** 679 **Vol. 3:** 128, 323, 582, 722, 724, 964
4:2 ff	**Vol. 3:** 964
4:2	**Vol. 1:** 458 **Vol. 2:** 475 **Vol. 3:** 844, 1023
4:3	**Vol. 1:** 322, 458, 514 **Vol. 2:** 274, 475 **Vol. 3:** 31, 727, 922, 929, 947, 1017
4:4 f	**Vol. 1:** 677
4:4	**Vol. 1:** 689 **Vol. 3:** 343, 947
4:5 f	**Vol. 2:** 365
4:5	**Vol. 1:** 445 **Vol. 3:** 118
4:6	**Vol. 1:** 677 **Vol. 2:** 207–208, 565 **Vol. 3:** 694, 705, 1200
4:7	**Vol. 1:** 515, 656 **Vol. 2:** 54–55, 63, 563, 923 **Vol. 3:** 794
4:8	**Vol. 1:** 502, 733 **Vol. 2:** 214
4:9	**Vol. 1:** 690 **Vol. 2:** 550
4:10 f	**Vol. 3:** 546
4:10	**Vol. 1:** 305 **Vol. 2:** 105, 121, 123, 255, 732 **Vol. 3:** 547, 854, 1118
4:11	**Vol. 2:** 46 **Vol. 3:** 718, 1106, 1118
4:12 ff	**Vol. 1:** 141, 305
4:12	**Vol. 1:** 656, 689 **Vol. 3:** 110, 446, 802
4:13	**Vol. 2:** 46, 354, 361, 808 **Vol. 3:** 257, 316, 722, 724
4:14	**Vol. 1:** 286 **Vol. 2:** 75, 654 **Vol. 3:** 257, 340, 705, 1194
4:15	**Vol. 2:** 742 **Vol. 3:** 377, 725
4:16	**Vol. 1:** 123 **Vol. 2:** 343, 654 **Vol. 3:** 563, 724–725
4:17 f	**Vol. 3:** 839
4:17	**Vol. 1:** 167, 593, 667 **Vol. 2:** 63, 78, 249, 365
4:18	**Vol. 2:** 94, 488 **Vol. 3:** 215, 370–371
4:19	**Vol. 1:** 383, 386 **Vol. 2:** 102 **Vol. 3:** 686, 725, 1023, 1155
5:1 ff	**Vol. 1:** 305
5:1	**Vol. 1:** 198, 643 **Vol. 2:** 47–48 **Vol. 3:** 257, 316, 568, 722, 724–725
5:2 f	**Vol. 2:** 519
5:2–4	**Vol. 3:** 568
5:2	**Vol. 1:** 190 **Vol. 3:** 137, 1200
5:3 f	**Vol. 3:** 568
5:3	**Vol. 2:** 302 **Vol. 3:** 905
5:4	**Vol. 1:** 406 **Vol. 2:** 47 **Vol. 3:** 257, 323
5:5 f	**Vol. 3:** 161
5:5	**Vol. 1:** 198 **Vol. 2:** 117, 123, 262–264, 618, 675 **Vol. 3:** 30–31
5:6	**Vol. 2:** 149, 203, 263 **Vol. 3:** 718, 839
5:7	**Vol. 1:** 278
5:8 f	**Vol. 1:** 141, 305
5:8	**Vol. 1:** 118, 421, 515, 554, 718 **Vol. 2:** 137 **Vol. 3:** 203, 469, 471, 531, 802, 944
5:9	**Vol. 1:** 257, 305, 660 **Vol. 3:** 722, 724–725
5:10	**Vol. 1:** 276, 290, 660, 662 **Vol. 2:** 47, 78, 123 **Vol. 3:** 350, 725
5:11	**Vol. 2:** 47 **Vol. 3:** 718
5:12	**Vol. 2:** 78, 123 **Vol. 3:** 489, 824, 826, 888, 1042, 1174
5:13	**Vol. 1:** 141, 180, 619 **Vol. 3:** 388
5:14	**Vol. 2:** 547, 549, 780–781

2 Peter

1:1 f	**Vol. 3:** 221
1:1	**Vol. 1:** 130, 478 **Vol. 2:** 73, 498–499 **Vol. 3:** 370
1:2	**Vol. 1:** 733 **Vol. 2:** 400, 405, 780
1:3 f	**Vol. 1:** 276 **Vol. 2:** 86 **Vol. 3:** 927
1:3–8	**Vol. 2:** 95
1:3	**Vol. 1:** 644 **Vol. 2:** 41–42, 405, 661 **Vol. 3:** 927, 1182

2 Peter *(cont'd)*

1:4	**Vol. 1:** 448, 458, 469, 559, 644 **Vol. 2:** 661 **Vol. 3:** 71, 302, 304, 832, 927, 1177
1:5 ff	**Vol. 3:** 927
1:5 f	**Vol. 2:** 405
1:5	**Vol. 1:** 497 **Vol. 2:** 400 **Vol. 3:** 927, 1169
1:6	**Vol. 1:** 496–497 **Vol. 2:** 775
1:7	**Vol. 2:** 542, 549
1:8	**Vol. 1:** 472, 723 **Vol. 2:** 131, 405, 661
1:9	**Vol. 2:** 714, 899
1:10	**Vol. 1:** 540, 542, 660 **Vol. 2:** 661 **Vol. 3:** 1155, 1169
1:11	**Vol. 2:** 387, 661, 843 **Vol. 3:** 221, 815, 832, 940–941
1:12 f	**Vol. 3:** 241–242
1:12	**Vol. 1:** 326 **Vol. 2:** 899
1:13 f	**Vol. 3:** 815
1:13	**Vol. 3:** 247, 370
1:14	**Vol. 1:** 315 **Vol. 3:** 317, 815
1:15	**Vol. 3:** 240, 815, 940, 1169
1:16–18	**Vol. 3:** 862
1:16	**Vol. 2:** 426, 645, 900–901 **Vol. 3:** 314, 832, 863, 1033
1:17	**Vol. 2:** 46–47, 819 **Vol. 3:** 114, 863
1:19	**Vol. 1:** 659–660 **Vol. 2:** 289, 487–488, 493, 495–496, 558 **Vol. 3:** 81
1:20 f	**Vol. 3:** 329
1:20	**Vol. 1:** 181, 577–578 **Vol. 2:** 839 **Vol. 3:** 490, 492
1:21	**Vol. 1:** 578–579 **Vol. 3:** 705, 1022–1023
2	**Vol. 3:** 862
2:1 f	**Vol. 2:** 449
2:1	**Vol. 1:** 268, 438, 455, 464, 535 **Vol. 2:** 472, 509 **Vol. 3:** 768
2:2	**Vol. 3:** 343, 888, 942
2:3	**Vol. 1:** 138, 268 **Vol. 2:** 365
2:4–10	**Vol. 3:** 832
2:4 f	**Vol. 2:** 682
2:4	**Vol. 1:** 103, 452
2:5 f	**Vol. 2:** 95
2:5	**Vol. 1:** 168, 666 **Vol. 2:** 135, 692 **Vol. 3:** 52, 170, 203, 370, 991
2:6	**Vol. 1:** 326 **Vol. 2:** 291, 366, 767 **Vol. 3:** 93, 203, 905
2:7 f	**Vol. 3:** 240, 370
2:7	**Vol. 3:** 204, 934
2:8	**Vol. 2:** 175, 449 **Vol. 3:** 856, 934
2:9	**Vol. 2:** 95, 366, 700, 894 **Vol. 3:** 98, 203, 576, 802–803, 1176
2:10 ff†	**Vol. 3:** 342
2:10	**Vol. 1:** 365, 448, 458, 462, 493, 677 **Vol. 2:** 46, 518 **Vol. 3:** 947
2:11	**Vol. 2:** 365 **Vol. 3:** 345, 371, 714, 1202
2:12	**Vol. 1:** 468–469 **Vol. 2:** 406, 476, 661 **Vol. 3:** 1118
2:13 ff	**Vol. 1:** 459
2:13	**Vol. 1:** 460 **Vol. 2:** 459–460, 547 **Vol. 3:** 575–576
2:14	**Vol. 1:** 138, 286, 313, 416 **Vol. 2:** 584 **Vol. 3:** 516
2:15	**Vol. 2:** 459–460, 677 **Vol. 3:** 576, 942
2:16	**Vol. 2:** 142
2:17	**Vol. 1:** 425 **Vol. 3:** 987–988, 1003
2:18	**Vol. 1:** 458, 552, 559 **Vol. 2:** 459–460
2:19	**Vol. 1:** 718 **Vol. 3:** 70
2:20 f	**Vol. 3:** 942
2:20	**Vol. 1:** 448, 559 **Vol. 2:** 405 **Vol. 3:** 221
2:21	**Vol. 1:** 339, 355 **Vol. 2:** 405 **Vol. 3:** 221, 370, 774, 942, 1174
2:22	**Vol. 1:** 117, 355 **Vol. 2:** 757 **Vol. 3:** 888, 990
3	**Vol. 2:** 461, 771 **Vol. 3:** 127, 241, 247, 489
3:1	**Vol. 1:** 339 **Vol. 3:** 221, 241, 1122
3:2	**Vol. 2:** 584
3:3–7	**Vol. 2:** 58, 894 **Vol. 3:** 341, 947
3:3	**Vol. 2:** 769, 901
3:4 ff	**Vol. 1:** 166, 443 **Vol. 2:** 900, 930
3:4	**Vol. 3:** 832
3:5–10	**Vol. 2:** 682
3:5–7	**Vol. 2:** 836 **Vol. 3:** 1019, 1023, 1176
3:5	**Vol. 1:** 464
3:6	**Vol. 1:** 657 **Vol. 2:** 95, 193, 366
3:7	**Vol. 2:** 698–699, 894 **Vol. 3:** 684
3:8	**Vol. 2:** 772
3:9 f	**Vol. 1:** 359, 464, 742 **Vol. 2:** 771 **Vol. 3:** 1017–1018
3:9	
3:10 ff	**Vol. 2:** 38
3:10–12	**Vol. 3:** 180
3:10	**Vol. 1:** 657 **Vol. 2:** 193, 452, 894 **Vol. 3:** 378
3:11 ff	**Vol. 1:** 441
3:11 f	**Vol. 2:** 95 **Vol. 3:** 832
3:11	**Vol. 3:** 180
3:12	**Vol. 1:** 657 **Vol. 2:** 193, 245, 452, 887, 894, 900 **Vol. 3:** 1169
3:13	**Vol. 1:** 186, 518 **Vol. 2:** 193, 245, 671, 714 **Vol. 3:** 71, 371, 832
3:14	**Vol. 2:** 780 **Vol. 3:** 529, 925, 1169
3:15 f	**Vol. 1:** 693 **Vol. 3:** 401, 492
3:15	**Vol. 2:** 770–771 **Vol. 3:** 215
3:16	**Vol. 1:** 247, 578 **Vol. 3:** 129, 252, 490, 492
3:17	**Vol. 1:** 611, 693 **Vol. 2:** 135, 459–460
3:18	**Vol. 2:** 46, 123, 129–130, 405 **Vol. 3:** 221, 832

1 John

1:1 ff	**Vol. 3:** 276
1:1–10	**Vol. 1:** 338
1:1–4	**Vol. 2:** 404
1:1–3	**Vol. 1:** 638
1:1 f	**Vol. 2:** 482

1 John *(cont'd)*

1:1†   **Vol. 1:** 63, 166   **Vol. 2:** 176   **Vol. 3:** 47, 61, 313, 517, 825, 1114, 1185
1:2 f   **Vol. 3:** 47
1:2   **Vol. 3:** 312, 314, 321, 323, 1046, 1204
1:3   **Vol. 1:** 644   **Vol. 3:** 646
1:4   **Vol. 1:** 741   **Vol. 2:** 359   **Vol. 3:** 582
1:5–10   **Vol. 3:** 162
1:5 f   **Vol. 1:** 126
1:5   **Vol. 1:** 424   **Vol. 2:** 175, 494   **Vol. 3:** 46–47
1:6 f   **Vol. 1:** 638   **Vol. 2:** 494   **Vol. 3:** 945
1:6   **Vol. 1:** 424, 644   **Vol. 2:** 473   **Vol. 3:** 891, 945
1:7 ff   **Vol. 3:** 163
1:7–10   **Vol. 1:** 223
1:7   **Vol. 1:** 223, 644   **Vol. 2:** 183   **Vol. 3:** 47, 107, 163, 166, 582, 646
1:8   **Vol. 2:** 449, 459–460   **Vol. 3:** 362, 582, 890
1:9–2:2   **Vol. 3:** 362
1:9   **Vol. 1:** 148, 346, 602, 702   **Vol. 2:** 449   **Vol. 3:** 107, 163, 362, 576, 582
1:10   **Vol. 2:** 449, 473, 567
2:1 f   **Vol. 1:** 89
2:1–6   **Vol. 2:** 716
2:1   **Vol. 1:** 90–91, 286, 324, 637   **Vol. 2:** 84   **Vol. 3:** 40, 162–163, 362, 704
2:1b   **Vol. 2:** 449
2:2   **Vol. 1:** 525   **Vol. 3:** 162, 582, 1203
2:3 ff   **Vol. 1:** 638
2:3 f   **Vol. 1:** 166, 338
2:3   **Vol. 1:** 638   **Vol. 2:** 133, 398
2:4 f   **Vol. 1:** 126, 338
2:4   **Vol. 2:** 473
2:5   **Vol. 2:** 64, 398
2:6   **Vol. 1:** 638   **Vol. 2:** 668   **Vol. 3:** 226, 945
2:7 ff   **Vol. 2:** 673
2:7–11   **Vol. 2:** 404
2:7 f   **Vol. 1:** 338
2:7   **Vol. 1:** 166, 338–339   **Vol. 2:** 671, 673, 716   **Vol. 3:** 582
2:8 ff   **Vol. 2:** 494
2:8–11   **Vol. 2:** 673
2:8   **Vol. 1:** 338–339, 424   **Vol. 2:** 280, 488, 494, 671
2:9 ff   **Vol. 3:** 98
2:9   **Vol. 1:** 257, 424, 556
2:10   **Vol. 2:** 494, 708–709   **Vol. 3:** 47, 226
2:11   **Vol. 1:** 424   **Vol. 2:** 709   **Vol. 3:** 945
2:12   **Vol. 1:** 286   **Vol. 2:** 654   **Vol. 3:** 582
2:13 f   **Vol. 1:** 651   **Vol. 3:** 472
2:13   **Vol. 1:** 566
2:14   **Vol. 1:** 566   **Vol. 2:** 405
2:15 ff   **Vol. 1:** 603
2:15   **Vol. 1:** 526   **Vol. 2:** 548   **Vol. 3:** 32
2:16   **Vol. 1:** 458, 678   **Vol. 2:** 475, 846   **Vol. 3:** 31

2:17   **Vol. 1:** 458, 526   **Vol. 3:** 226, 830, 1022–1023, 1155
2:18–27   **Vol. 3:** 1206
2:18   **Vol. 1:** 123, 126   **Vol. 2:** 58, 435, 645   **Vol. 3:** 849
2:19   **Vol. 3:** 312, 314, 321
2:20   **Vol. 1:** 123, 638   **Vol. 2:** 228, 231   **Vol. 3:** 703–704
2:21   **Vol. 3:** 489, 764
2:22 ff   **Vol. 2:** 231
2:22 f   **Vol. 1:** 126, 455   **Vol. 3:** 646
2:22   **Vol. 1:** 347, 455   **Vol. 2:** 339, 473, 567   **Vol. 3:** 1206
2:23   **Vol. 1:** 347, 455   **Vol. 2:** 78, 302
2:24   **Vol. 1:** 166   **Vol. 3:** 226
2:26†   **Vol. 2:** 459–460   **Vol. 3:** 1141
2:27   **Vol. 1:** 123, 638   **Vol. 3:** 225, 703–704, 764, 890
2:28   **Vol. 1:** 123, 286   **Vol. 2:** 64, 736–737, 900–901   **Vol. 3:** 312, 314, 321
2:29   **Vol. 1:** 179   **Vol. 2:** 76   **Vol. 3:** 362, 647, 1155
3   **Vol. 2:** 449
3:1–10   **Vol. 3:** 582
3:1 f   **Vol. 1:** 620
3:1   **Vol. 1:** 274   **Vol. 2:** 546   **Vol. 3:** 517, 646–647
3:2 f   **Vol. 2:** 242
3:2   **Vol. 2:** 242, 503   **Vol. 3:** 278, 312, 314, 321, 515
3:3   **Vol. 2:** 244   **Vol. 3:** 101–102
3:5   **Vol. 3:** 312, 314, 321, 323, 582, 1117
3:6 ff   **Vol. 1:** 126
3:6   **Vol. 2:** 404, 449   **Vol. 3:** 226
3:7 ff   **Vol. 3:** 1155
3:7 f   **Vol. 3:** 362
3:7   **Vol. 1:** 286   **Vol. 2:** 459–460   **Vol. 3:** 362
3:8 f   **Vol. 3:** 582
3:8   **Vol. 1:** 166   **Vol. 3:** 312, 314, 321, 323, 362, 471–472, 646, 1150
3:9 f   **Vol. 3:** 647
3:9   **Vol. 1:** 179   **Vol. 2:** 76   **Vol. 3:** 524, 703–704, 1188
3:10   **Vol. 1:** 179, 287   **Vol. 2:** 546   **Vol. 3:** 320, 362, 472, 582, 646
3:11–18   **Vol. 3:** 98
3:11   **Vol. 1:** 166   **Vol. 3:** 46–47
3:12   **Vol. 1:** 566   **Vol. 3:** 362, 472, 1150
3:13   **Vol. 1:** 556   **Vol. 2:** 625
3:14 ff   **Vol. 2:** 546
3:14 f   **Vol. 3:** 226
3:14   **Vol. 1:** 439   **Vol. 2:** 186, 482
3:15   **Vol. 1:** 556
3:16 f   **Vol. 2:** 76   **Vol. 3:** 945
3:16   **Vol. 1:** 257   **Vol. 2:** 404, 546, 668   **Vol. 3:** 163, 547, 1206
3:17   **Vol. 2:** 475, 600, 694, 733, 846   **Vol. 3:** 957
3:18   **Vol. 1:** 286   **Vol. 3:** 1079, 1176

1 John *(cont'd)*

3:19   **Vol. 1:** 590
3:20 f   **Vol. 2:** 365
3:21 ff   **Vol. 1:** 338
3:21 f   **Vol. 3:** 1206
3:21   **Vol. 1:** 590   **Vol. 2:** 736
3:22 ff   **Vol. 2:** 449
3:22   **Vol. 1:** 338–339   **Vol. 2:** 133, 816, 857–858
3:23   **Vol. 1:** 338–339   **Vol. 2:** 654   **Vol. 3:** 1213
3:24   **Vol. 1:** 338   **Vol. 3:** 703–704, 764, 1192
4   **Vol. 2:** 449
4:1 ff   **Vol. 1:** 123
4:1–3   **Vol. 3:** 630, 704
4:1 f   **Vol. 1:** 347
4:1   **Vol. 1:** 452   **Vol. 2:** 472   **Vol. 3:** 81, 475, 695, 808, 810, 988
4:2 f   **Vol. 1:** 126, 347   **Vol. 3:** 1206
4:2   **Vol. 1:** 323, 347, 638, 678–679   **Vol. 2:** 339   **Vol. 3:** 323, 475
4:3   **Vol. 1:** 126   **Vol. 3:** 695
4:4 f   **Vol. 1:** 651
4:4   **Vol. 1:** 286   **Vol. 2:** 76   **Vol. 3:** 1188
4:5   **Vol. 2:** 567
4:6   **Vol. 1:** 603   **Vol. 2:** 404, 459–460   **Vol. 3:** 694–695, 704, 892, 1188
4:7 ff   **Vol. 2:** 546   **Vol. 3:** 162
4:7–12   **Vol. 3:** 98
4:7 f   **Vol. 2:** 404, 546
4:7   **Vol. 1:** 179   **Vol. 2:** 76, 79   **Vol. 3:** 582, 647, 1188
4:8   **Vol. 2:** 79, 404, 542, 546
4:9–14   **Vol. 3:** 646
4:9 f   **Vol. 2:** 404
4:9   **Vol. 2:** 75, 482, 546   **Vol. 3:** 162, 312, 314, 321, 643, 1202
4:10   **Vol. 2:** 78–79   **Vol. 3:** 162–163, 582, 643
4:11   **Vol. 3:** 945
4:12 ff   **Vol. 2:** 546
4:12   **Vol. 2:** 64
4:13 ff   **Vol. 1:** 638
4:13–21   **Vol. 3:** 162
4:13   **Vol. 2:** 41   **Vol. 3:** 703–704, 1192
4:14 f   **Vol. 3:** 225
4:14   **Vol. 3:** 643, 1046
4:15 f   **Vol. 3:** 1192
4:15   **Vol. 1:** 347, 638   **Vol. 3:** 646
4:16   **Vol. 2:** 76, 404, 542, 546   **Vol. 3:** 1211
4:17   **Vol. 2:** 64, 366, 736, 894   **Vol. 3:** 98, 163
4:18   **Vol. 1:** 624   **Vol. 2:** 64   **Vol. 3:** 98
4:19   **Vol. 3:** 98, 945
4:20   **Vol. 1:** 556   **Vol. 2:** 473, 546   **Vol. 3:** 337
4:21   **Vol. 1:** 287, 339   **Vol. 2:** 546

5:1–12   **Vol. 2:** 449
5:1 f   **Vol. 1:** 126
5:1   **Vol. 2:** 339   **Vol. 3:** 647, 1188
5:2 f   **Vol. 1:** 338
5:2   **Vol. 1:** 339   **Vol. 3:** 1155
5:3 f   **Vol. 1:** 339
5:3   **Vol. 1:** 262, 624
5:4 f   **Vol. 1:** 651   **Vol. 3:** 780
5:4   **Vol. 1:** 602, 651   **Vol. 3:** 647, 1188
5:5   **Vol. 3:** 646
5:6–8   **Vol. 3:** 704
5:6   **Vol. 3:** 163, 166, 892, 990, 1046
5:8   **Vol. 2:** 84, 687   **Vol. 3:** 990
5:10   **Vol. 1:** 638   **Vol. 2:** 473, 567   **Vol. 3:** 1046, 1187
5:10b   **Vol. 3:** 1211
5:10c   **Vol. 3:** 1213
5:11   **Vol. 2:** 78   **Vol. 3:** 1046
5:12   **Vol. 1:** 637   **Vol. 2:** 78, 302, 482
5:13   **Vol. 2:** 654   **Vol. 3:** 489, 1213
5:14 ff   **Vol. 3:** 1022, 1205
5:14 f   **Vol. 2:** 857
5:14   **Vol. 2:** 178, 736–737, 857   **Vol. 3:** 1023
5:15   **Vol. 2:** 858
5:16–21   **Vol. 3:** 582
5:16 f   **Vol. 3:** 1172, 1185, 1205–1206
5:16   **Vol. 1:** 703   **Vol. 2:** 856, 879
5:16a   **Vol. 2:** 449   **Vol. 3:** 1206
5:16b   **Vol. 2:** 449
5:17   **Vol. 2:** 449   **Vol. 3:** 575–576
5:18 f   **Vol. 1:** 566
5:18   **Vol. 1:** 525   **Vol. 2:** 133   **Vol. 3:** 647
5:18a   **Vol. 3:** 1188
5:19   **Vol. 1:** 566   **Vol. 3:** 1188
5:20   **Vol. 2:** 82, 280, 403, 482   **Vol. 3:** 127, 646
5:21   **Vol. 1:** 286   **Vol. 2:** 135

2 John

1   **Vol. 1:** 286, 539   **Vol. 2:** 518
2   **Vol. 3:** 830
3   **Vol. 2:** 597, 780
4 ff   **Vol. 1:** 338
4   **Vol. 1:** 286, 338–339   **Vol. 2:** 518   **Vol. 3:** 528, 945
5 f   **Vol. 1:** 339
5   **Vol. 1:** 166   **Vol. 2:** 518, 546, 670, 673, 880
6   **Vol. 1:** 166, 338–339   **Vol. 2:** 518, 880   **Vol. 3:** 945
7–11   **Vol. 3:** 646
7   **Vol. 1:** 126, 638, 678–679   **Vol. 2:** 339, 459–460   **Vol. 3:** 323, 630, 1176, 1206
8   **Vol. 3:** 144, 749, 751
9 f   **Vol. 3:** 770
9   **Vol. 1:** 247, 637–638   **Vol. 2:** 78, 302   **Vol. 3:** 224
10   **Vol. 1:** 535   **Vol. 2:** 358

2 John *(cont'd)*

11	**Vol. 1:** 566
12	**Vol. 1:** 203, 741 **Vol. 2:** 359
13	**Vol. 1:** 286, 539 **Vol. 2:** 518

3 John

2	**Vol. 2:** 170, 867 **Vol. 3:** 684, 943
3 f	**Vol. 3:** 945
3	**Vol. 3:** 1044–1045
4	**Vol. 1:** 286
5	**Vol. 1:** 689
6	**Vol. 1:** 304 **Vol. 3:** 1044–1045
7	**Vol. 2:** 654
8	**Vol. 3:** 751, 1152
9	**Vol. 1:** 304 **Vol. 2:** 550
10	**Vol. 1:** 304, 453, 566 **Vol. 3:** 241, 1149–1150
11	**Vol. 1:** 491, 563–564 **Vol. 2:** 102 **Vol. 3:** 1188
12	**Vol. 3:** 1044–1045
13	**Vol. 1:** 203

Jude

3b	**Vol. 2:** 719
23a	**Vol. 2:** 597
2	**Vol. 1:** 733 **Vol. 2:** 597, 780–781
3	**Vol. 1:** 646 **Vol. 2:** 717–718 **Vol. 3:** 61, 216, 774, 1199
4	**Vol. 1:** 455 **Vol. 2:** 95, 123, 714, 725 **Vol. 3:** 490
5	**Vol. 1:** 532 **Vol. 2:** 717, 719 **Vol. 3:** 216, 241
6	**Vol. 1:** 103, 452 **Vol. 2:** 161, 366, 894
7	**Vol. 1:** 321, 493, 657, 677 **Vol. 2:** 96, 767 **Vol. 3:** 93, 99, 344, 570, 830
8	**Vol. 1:** 74, 448 **Vol. 2:** 46, 518 **Vol. 3:** 344
9	**Vol. 1:** 103–104, 365, 504, 572 **Vol. 2:** 365 **Vol. 3:** 344, 471, 492, 821
10	**Vol. 1:** 468–469 **Vol. 2:** 661 **Vol. 3:** 345, 1118
11	**Vol. 2:** 459, 677 **Vol. 3:** 942, 947, 1054
12	**Vol. 1:** 723 **Vol. 2:** 547 **Vol. 3:** 868–869, 1003
13	**Vol. 1:** 425, 520 **Vol. 2:** 459 **Vol. 3:** 564, 684, 736
14 f	**Vol. 2:** 817, 897 **Vol. 3:** 265, 492
14	**Vol. 1:** 85 **Vol. 2:** 219, 228, 692 **Vol. 3:** 602
15	**Vol. 2:** 95, 141, 155
16	**Vol. 1:** 587 **Vol. 2:** 145, 625 **Vol. 3:** 947
17	**Vol. 2:** 718 **Vol. 3:** 241, 1122
18	**Vol. 2:** 58, 95 **Vol. 3:** 844, 947
19–20	**Vol. 3:** 705
20	**Vol. 2:** 249, 718, 883 **Vol. 3:** 61
21–23	**Vol. 2:** 597
21	**Vol. 2:** 245 **Vol. 3:** 832
22	**Vol. 1:** 504
23	**Vol. 1:** 556 **Vol. 3:** 216, 602
24	**Vol. 2:** 46, 135, 354 **Vol. 3:** 925
25	**Vol. 2:** 46, 73, 426 **Vol. 3:** 221, 830

Revelation

1–3	**Vol. 2:** 691 **Vol. 3:** 85
1	**Vol. 2:** 674
1:1	**Vol. 1:** 103, 247 **Vol. 2:** 665 **Vol. 3:** 85, 88, 312, 316, 569, 613
1:2	**Vol. 3:** 89, 1046
1:3	**Vol. 3:** 85, 489–490, 838
1:4	**Vol. 1:** 114, 304 **Vol. 2:** 687, 691, 780–781 **Vol. 3:** 706, 1171, 1181
1:5	**Vol. 1:** 152, 223, 256, 445, 602, 668 **Vol. 2:** 340, 378, 514 **Vol. 3:** 166, 180, 200, 303, 582, 990, 1046, 1174
1:6	**Vol. 2:** 231, 380 **Vol. 3:** 37, 718, 1154
1:7	**Vol. 1:** 99, 518 **Vol. 3:** 629, 871, 1003
1:8	**Vol. 2:** 59, 64, 69, 80, 282, 513–514, 674 **Vol. 3:** 718
1:9 ff	**Vol. 2:** 826 **Vol. 3:** 287
1:9	**Vol. 1:** 642 **Vol. 2:** 775 **Vol. 3:** 89, 517, 1046
1:10 ff	**Vol. 3:** 490
1:10–12	**Vol. 3:** 113
1:10	**Vol. 1:** 528, 631 **Vol. 2:** 176, 426, 518, 674 **Vol. 3:** 113, 411–412, 706, 874
1:11	**Vol. 1:** 244, 257, 304 **Vol. 2:** 550, 691
1:12–20	**Vol. 2:** 674
1:12 f	**Vol. 2:** 487
1:12	**Vol. 2:** 486
1:13 ff	**Vol. 2:** 80, 482
1:13	**Vol. 1:** 240 **Vol. 2:** 503 **Vol. 3:** 121, 527, 629, 633
1:14	**Vol. 1:** 204 **Vol. 3:** 1004
1:15	**Vol. 1:** 239, 656 **Vol. 2:** 97 **Vol. 3:** 113
1:16	**Vol. 2:** 488, 686 **Vol. 3:** 732, 735, 967
1:17 f	**Vol. 1:** 437–438 **Vol. 2:** 282, 482
1:17	**Vol. 1:** 239, 610, 623, 667 **Vol. 2:** 58, 64, 80 **Vol. 3:** 839
1:18	**Vol. 2:** 207, 340, 727, 733 **Vol. 3:** 387
1:19	**Vol. 1:** 326 **Vol. 3:** 505
1:20	**Vol. 1:** 103, 304 **Vol. 2:** 486–487 **Vol. 3:** 505, 735–736
2 f	**Vol. 2:** 691
2	**Vol. 1:** 651 **Vol. 2:** 42 **Vol. 3:** 88, 490
2:1	**Vol. 1:** 103, 304 **Vol. 2:** 486–487 **Vol. 3:** 718, 735, 944
2:2 f	**Vol. 2:** 775
2:2	**Vol. 1:** 263, 564, 603 **Vol. 2:** 473, 567, 677 **Vol. 3:** 88, 529, 802
2:3	**Vol. 1:** 263 **Vol. 3:** 257
2:4	**Vol. 2:** 388
2:5	**Vol. 1:** 611 **Vol. 2:** 487 **Vol. 3:** 1150
2:6	**Vol. 1:** 556 **Vol. 2:** 388, 676

Revelation *(cont'd)*

2:7   **Vol. 1:** 390, 651   **Vol. 2:** 41, 178, 763   **Vol. 3:** 706, 868

2:8   **Vol. 1:** 304, 406, 445, 667   **Vol. 2:** 58, 64

2:9 f   **Vol. 3:** 471

2:9   **Vol. 1:** 296–297   **Vol. 2:** 315, 826, 842, 844   **Vol. 3:** 343

2:10   **Vol. 1:** 406, 455, 602, 623   **Vol. 2:** 136, 692, 894   **Vol. 3:** 722, 803

2:11   **Vol. 1:** 441, 651   **Vol. 2:** 178   **Vol. 3:** 575–576, 706

2:12   **Vol. 1:** 304   **Vol. 2:** 686   **Vol. 3:** 967

2:13   **Vol. 1:** 455, 602   **Vol. 2:** 654   **Vol. 3:** 717, 1008, 1047

2:14–15 **Vol. 2:** 677

2:14 f **Vol. 3:** 717

2:14   **Vol. 1:** 253, 471   **Vol. 2:** 284–286, 315, 708   **Vol. 3:** 432, 765, 770

2:15   **Vol. 2:** 676–677   **Vol. 3:** 770

2:16   **Vol. 2:** 686   **Vol. 3:** 963

2:17   **Vol. 1:** 205, 251, 253   **Vol. 2:** 41, 178, 218, 653, 671, 674   **Vol. 3:** 490, 706, 967

2:18   **Vol. 1:** 239, 304, 656   **Vol. 2:** 503   **Vol. 3:** 648

2:19   **Vol. 1:** 602–603   **Vol. 2:** 775   **Vol. 3:** 546

2:20 ff **Vol. 2:** 582

2:20 f **Vol. 3:** 844

2:20   **Vol. 2:** 284–286, 459, 677   **Vol. 3:** 81, 432, 765, 1067

2:21 f **Vol. 1:** 359

2:21   **Vol. 3:** 1023

2:22   **Vol. 2:** 808

2:23   **Vol. 1:** 436   **Vol. 2:** 181, 183, 399   **Vol. 3:** 533, 648, 1151, 1200

2:24   **Vol. 1:** 261   **Vol. 2:** 198, 401, 677   **Vol. 3:** 86, 770

2:25   **Vol. 3:** 717

2:26–28 **Vol. 2:** 677

2:26 f **Vol. 2:** 795   **Vol. 3:** 648

2:26   **Vol. 2:** 64, 133

2:27–28 **Vol. 1:** 407

2:27   **Vol. 1:** 164, 177, 408   **Vol. 2:** 98   **Vol. 3:** 913

2:28   **Vol. 3:** 736, 748

2:29   **Vol. 2:** 178   **Vol. 3:** 706

3   **Vol. 1:** 651   **Vol. 2:** 42   **Vol. 3:** 88, 490

3:1   **Vol. 1:** 304   **Vol. 2:** 652   **Vol. 3:** 706, 736

3:2 f   **Vol. 2:** 137

3:2   **Vol. 1:** 326, 436   **Vol. 3:** 252

3:3   **Vol. 2:** 133, 926   **Vol. 3:** 848

3:4 f   **Vol. 1:** 204

3:4   **Vol. 1:** 317, 449, 556   **Vol. 2:** 652   **Vol. 3:** 349, 944

3:5   **Vol. 1:** 244, 317, 323, 347, 471   **Vol. 2:** 653

3:6   **Vol. 2:** 178   **Vol. 3:** 706

3:7 f   **Vol. 2:** 727, 733

3:7   **Vol. 1:** 257, 304   **Vol. 2:** 31, 76, 228, 550, 730   **Vol. 3:** 387, 652, 893

3:8   **Vol. 1:** 427, 455   **Vol. 2:** 30–31, 133, 654, 727   **Vol. 3:** 257

3:9   **Vol. 1:** 239, 296–297   **Vol. 2:** 312, 314–315, 399, 474

3:10   **Vol. 1:** 326, 519   **Vol. 2:** 133, 245, 776, 808   **Vol. 3:** 803, 848

3:11   **Vol. 1:** 406   **Vol. 3:** 717, 748

3:12   **Vol. 2:** 186, 194, 329, 654, 671, 804   **Vol. 3:** 490, 784, 795, 1154

3:13   **Vol. 2:** 178   **Vol. 3:** 706

3:14   **Vol. 1:** 99, 166, 304, 384   **Vol. 3:** 893, 1046

3:15–16 **Vol. 1:** 318

3:15   **Vol. 2:** 668

3:17 f **Vol. 2:** 842, 844

3:17   **Vol. 1:** 313–314   **Vol. 2:** 597, 826, 842   **Vol. 3:** 519, 859, 958

3:18   **Vol. 1:** 204, 313–314, 317, 363, 656   **Vol. 3:** 321, 518, 564

3:18b **Vol. 1:** 319

3:19   **Vol. 1:** 318   **Vol. 2:** 142, 549   **Vol. 3:** 779

3:20   **Vol. 1:** 319   **Vol. 2:** 31, 726–727, 881   **Vol. 3:** 85

3:21   **Vol. 2:** 41   **Vol. 3:** 588

3:22   **Vol. 2:** 178   **Vol. 3:** 706

4   **Vol. 3:** 398

4:1–8:2 **Vol. 2:** 691

4:1 f   **Vol. 1:** 528

4:1   **Vol. 2:** 31, 665   **Vol. 3:** 113, 569, 874

4:2–10 **Vol. 2:** 702   **Vol. 3:** 588

4:2   **Vol. 3:** 706, 1193

4:3   **Vol. 2:** 503   **Vol. 3:** 397–398, 515, 1003

4:4 ff **Vol. 1:** 200

4:4   **Vol. 1:** 200, 204, 406   **Vol. 2:** 159, 614–615

4:5   **Vol. 1:** 656   **Vol. 2:** 486, 691   **Vol. 3:** 706, 1001–1002

4:6–8 **Vol. 1:** 280

4:6   **Vol. 2:** 503, 615, 689   **Vol. 3:** 398, 984

4:7   **Vol. 1:** 116, 118, 173, 175   **Vol. 2:** 503, 689

4:8–11 **Vol. 2:** 868, 877

4:8   **Vol. 2:** 69, 76, 228–229, 514, 687, 689   **Vol. 3:** 256, 718

4:9 f   **Vol. 2:** 482   **Vol. 3:** 1193

4:9   **Vol. 2:** 46, 689   **Vol. 3:** 718, 819

4:10 f **Vol. 1:** 200

4:10   **Vol. 1:** 406, 610   **Vol. 2:** 615

4:11   **Vol. 1:** 386   **Vol. 2:** 50, 73, 513–514, 604, 615, 878   **Vol. 3:** 349, 1023

5:1 ff **Vol. 1:** 244   **Vol. 2:** 340

5:1–13 **Vol. 3:** 588

5:1   **Vol. 2:** 691   **Vol. 3:** 490, 500

5:2 ff **Vol. 2:** 726

Revelation *(cont'd)*

5:2–10   **Vol. 3:** 500
5:2–9   **Vol. 2:** 727
5:2   **Vol. 2:** 426, 653   **Vol. 3:** 54, 180, 349, 714
5:3 f   **Vol. 3:** 515
5:3   **Vol. 2:** 194
5:4   **Vol. 3:** 349, 529
5:5 ff   **Vol. 2:** 674
5:5 f   **Vol. 2:** 194
5:5   **Vol. 1:** 114, 118, 200, 427   **Vol. 2:** 320, 340   **Vol. 3:** 180, 397, 652, 869, 872
5:6 ff   **Vol. 1:** 200   **Vol. 2:** 80, 615
5:6–13   **Vol. 2:** 702
5:6   **Vol. 1:** 114, 118, 629, 634   **Vol. 2:** 147, 411, 689, 691   **Vol. 3:** 706, 715
5:8 ff   **Vol. 1:** 114
5:8–14   **Vol. 2:** 868
5:8–10   **Vol. 2:** 877
5:8   **Vol. 1:** 164   **Vol. 2:** 294, 411, 689, 867
5:9 ff   **Vol. 3:** 672
5:9 f   **Vol. 2:** 795
5:9   **Vol. 1:** 223, 268, 629, 634   **Vol. 2:** 411, 671, 674, 878   **Vol. 3:** 166, 181, 200, 349, 672–675, 1079, 1175
5:10   **Vol. 2:** 231, 380, 388, 411   **Vol. 3:** 37
5:11 ff   **Vol. 2:** 194
5:11–12   **Vol. 3:** 113
5:11   **Vol. 1:** 103   **Vol. 2:** 176, 684, 689, 692, 697, 700
5:12 ff   **Vol. 2:** 700
5:12 f   **Vol. 2:** 411   **Vol. 3:** 674
5:12–14   **Vol. 2:** 877
5:12   **Vol. 1:** 213, 629, 634   **Vol. 2:** 426, 844, 878   **Vol. 3:** 113, 349, 714, 748, 1032
5:13   **Vol. 1:** 386   **Vol. 2:** 176, 604, 615   **Vol. 3:** 718
5:13b   **Vol. 1:** 213
5:14   **Vol. 2:** 689
6 f   **Vol. 3:** 180
6–19   **Vol. 1:** 114
6   **Vol. 2:** 911
6:1–8   **Vol. 1:** 657
6:1   **Vol. 2:** 689   **Vol. 3:** 500, 1002
6:2–8   **Vol. 1:** 118
6:2   **Vol. 1:** 118, 205, 651
6:3   **Vol. 2:** 689   **Vol. 3:** 500
6:4   **Vol. 1:** 118, 205, 656   **Vol. 3:** 748, 967, 1174
6:5   **Vol. 1:** 203   **Vol. 2:** 689   **Vol. 3:** 500, 1162
6:6   **Vol. 1:** 118   **Vol. 2:** 689, 711   **Vol. 3:** 575–576, 922, 1162
6:7   **Vol. 2:** 689   **Vol. 3:** 500
6:8   **Vol. 1:** 114, 118, 205, 430   **Vol. 2:** 266, 609, 711, 926   **Vol. 3:** 967, 998, 1175, 1198
6:9–10   **Vol. 3:** 113
6:9 f   **Vol. 3:** 245, 436

6:9   **Vol. 2:** 207   **Vol. 3:** 89, 500, 686, 1046–1047
6:10 f   **Vol. 1:** 222
6:10   **Vol. 1:** 410   **Vol. 2:** 228, 426, 509   **Vol. 3:** 97, 893
6:11   **Vol. 1:** 204, 430   **Vol. 2:** 772   **Vol. 3:** 97, 256
6:12–17   **Vol. 2:** 38
6:12   **Vol. 1:** 204, 224   **Vol. 3:** 500, 558, 732, 734
6:13   **Vol. 1:** 610, 725   **Vol. 2:** 192   **Vol. 3:** 557, 736
6:14   **Vol. 3:** 736, 1013
6:15–17   **Vol. 3:** 382
6:15 f   **Vol. 2:** 844
6:15   **Vol. 1:** 217, 314, 718   **Vol. 2:** 218, 378, 699   **Vol. 3:** 381, 713
6:16   **Vol. 1:** 111, 610   **Vol. 2:** 216, 412   **Vol. 3:** 588
6:17   **Vol. 2:** 76, 426, 894
7:1–8   **Vol. 2:** 314
7:1   **Vol. 1:** 103, 517   **Vol. 2:** 689   **Vol. 3:** 179, 389, 707, 718, 868, 984, 1002
7:2 f   **Vol. 2:** 573   **Vol. 3:** 575–576, 984
7:2   **Vol. 1:** 410   **Vol. 2:** 426   **Vol. 3:** 731
7:3 ff   **Vol. 2:** 574
7:3   **Vol. 3:** 613, 868
7:4 ff   **Vol. 2:** 695
7:4–8   **Vol. 2:** 700   **Vol. 3:** 871
7:4   **Vol. 2:** 315, 684, 696, 700   **Vol. 3:** 871
7:5–8   **Vol. 2:** 700   **Vol. 3:** 397, 872
7:5   **Vol. 2:** 320   **Vol. 3:** 397
7:7   **Vol. 2:** 467
7:9–17   **Vol. 2:** 702, 868
7:9–10   **Vol. 3:** 113
7:9   **Vol. 1:** 204   **Vol. 2:** 207, 695–696, 700, 795, 799, 801   **Vol. 3:** 1079
7:10 ff   **Vol. 3:** 500
7:10–17   **Vol. 3:** 588
7:10–12   **Vol. 2:** 877
7:10   **Vol. 1:** 410   **Vol. 2:** 412, 426, 878   **Vol. 3:** 216
7:11   **Vol. 1:** 103, 200   **Vol. 2:** 689
7:12   **Vol. 1:** 99, 213   **Vol. 2:** 73, 604, 878   **Vol. 3:** 672, 714, 718, 819, 1032
7:13   **Vol. 1:** 200, 204
7:14   **Vol. 1:** 152, 223, 317   **Vol. 2:** 193, 513, 808   **Vol. 3:** 166, 181
7:15   **Vol. 3:** 784, 813
7:16 f   **Vol. 2:** 631
7:16   **Vol. 1:** 653   **Vol. 2:** 267   **Vol. 3:** 731
7:17   **Vol. 1:** 471   **Vol. 2:** 420   **Vol. 3:** 568, 943, 988–990, 1178
8–9   **Vol. 2:** 711
8   **Vol. 2:** 687
8:1   **Vol. 3:** 500
8:2 ff†   **Vol. 2:** 691
8:2–9:21   **Vol. 3:** 874
8:2 f   **Vol. 1:** 103
8:2   **Vol. 1:** 103

Revelation *(cont'd)*

8:3–11:18   **Vol. 2:** 691
8:3   **Vol. 2:** 161, 294, 702   **Vol. 3:** 436
8:4   **Vol. 2:** 294
8:5   **Vol. 2:** 294   **Vol. 3:** 436, 558,
          1001–1002
8:7 f   **Vol. 1:** 103
8:7   **Vol. 1:** 224, 657, 744   **Vol. 3:** 868, 1004
8:8 f   **Vol. 1:** 387
8:8   **Vol. 3:** 984, 1013
8:9   **Vol. 1:** 224   **Vol. 3:** 683
8:10 ff   **Vol. 3:** 737, 989
8:10   **Vol. 1:** 103, 610   **Vol. 2:** 192,
          486   **Vol. 3:** 984, 987
8:11   **Vol. 1:** 202   **Vol. 2:** 27, 29   **Vol. 3:** 874
8:12   **Vol. 1:** 103, 421, 425   **Vol. 2:**
          488   **Vol. 3:** 732, 734, 736
8:13†   **Vol. 1:** 165   **Vol. 2:** 687   **Vol. 3:** 1054
9:1 f   **Vol. 2:** 205
9:1   **Vol. 1:** 103, 610   **Vol. 2:** 192   **Vol. 3:**
          737
9:2   **Vol. 1:** 425   **Vol. 2:** 727   **Vol. 3:** 93,
          732
9:3 ff   **Vol. 2:** 205
9:3   **Vol. 1:** 118, 511   **Vol. 2:** 609
9:4   **Vol. 1:** 744   **Vol. 2:** 565, 573   **Vol. 3:**
          500–501, 575–576, 868
9:5   **Vol. 1:** 511   **Vol. 2:** 690   **Vol. 3:** 856
9:6   **Vol. 1:** 559   **Vol. 2:** 894   **Vol. 3:**
          528–529, 531
9:7 ff   **Vol. 1:** 119
9:7   **Vol. 1:** 118   **Vol. 2:** 503   **Vol. 3:** 962
9:8   **Vol. 1:** 118   **Vol. 3:** 1067
9:9   **Vol. 1:** 118   **Vol. 2:** 98   **Vol. 3:** 947,
          962
9:10   **Vol. 1:** 511   **Vol. 2:** 609, 690   **Vol. 3:**
          575–576
9:11   **Vol. 1:** 464   **Vol. 2:** 205, 309
9:12   **Vol. 1:** 204, 321, 449   **Vol. 2:** 159
9:13   **Vol. 1:** 103   **Vol. 2:** 689   **Vol. 3:** 436,
          715
9:14 f   **Vol. 2:** 689   **Vol. 3:** 179
9:14   **Vol. 3:** 987
9:15–18   **Vol. 1:** 430
9:17   **Vol. 1:** 118   **Vol. 3:** 515
9:18   **Vol. 3:** 857, 1198
9:19   **Vol. 1:** 118, 510   **Vol. 2:** 609   **Vol. 3:**
          575–576
9:20 f   **Vol. 1:** 163, 452   **Vol. 2:** 286   **Vol. 3:**
          179
9:20   **Vol. 1:** 452   **Vol. 2:** 96–97, 178, 286,
          794, 877   **Vol. 3:** 251, 857, 1008
9:21   **Vol. 1:** 501   **Vol. 2:** 558
10:1 ff   **Vol. 1:** 103
10:1   **Vol. 1:** 239, 656   **Vol. 2:** 193   **Vol. 3:**
          714, 732, 1003
10:2   **Vol. 2:** 148
10:3 f   **Vol. 3:** 1002
10:3   **Vol. 1:** 118, 410   **Vol. 2:** 426

10:4 ff   **Vol. 2:** 691
10:4   **Vol. 1:** 326   **Vol. 2:** 193   **Vol. 3:** 500
10:5   **Vol. 2:** 192
10:6   **Vol. 1:** 387   **Vol. 2:** 74, 193   **Vol. 3:**
          742, 844, 984
10:7   **Vol. 1:** 326   **Vol. 2:** 64, 894   **Vol. 3:**
          88, 505, 613
10:8 ff   **Vol. 1:** 103
10:8   **Vol. 2:** 193   **Vol. 3:** 113
10:9 f   **Vol. 1:** 169, 202
10:9   **Vol. 2:** 273
10:11   **Vol. 2:** 793, 799   **Vol. 3:** 1079
11:1 ff   **Vol. 2:** 329
11:1 f   **Vol. 3:** 404, 784, 948
11:1   **Vol. 3:** 436
11:2   **Vol. 1:** 453   **Vol. 2:** 688, 700, 795,
          803   **Vol. 3:** 436, 944
11:3 ff   **Vol. 1:** 545
11:3–6   **Vol. 1:** 545
11:3   **Vol. 1:** 545   **Vol. 2:** 688, 700   **Vol. 3:**
          1047
11:4–11   **Vol. 2:** 686
11:4   **Vol. 1:** 321   **Vol. 2:** 487, 712
11:5   **Vol. 1:** 554, 657   **Vol. 2:** 665   **Vol. 3:**
          575–576
11:6   **Vol. 1:** 163, 224, 544   **Vol. 2:** 31, 193,
          686   **Vol. 3:** 81, 987–988, 1002, 1004
11:7 ff   **Vol. 2:** 700
11:7   **Vol. 1:** 114, 430, 651   **Vol. 2:** 64,
          205   **Vol. 3:** 962, 1047
11:8 f   **Vol. 1:** 610
11:8   **Vol. 1:** 394, 532   **Vol. 2:** 329, 365,
          803   **Vol. 3:** 93, 706
11:9   **Vol. 1:** 265   **Vol. 2:** 688, 795,
          799   **Vol. 3:** 246, 1079
11:10   **Vol. 2:** 41, 356   **Vol. 3:** 88, 856
11:11   **Vol. 1:** 239, 609   **Vol. 3:** 694, 706, 1185
11:12   **Vol. 1:** 554   **Vol. 2:** 193   **Vol. 3:** 113
11:13   **Vol. 1:** 610   **Vol. 2:** 46, 193, 652,
          700   **Vol. 3:** 253, 558
11:15–19   **Vol. 3:** 874
11:15–18   **Vol. 2:** 868, 877
11:15   **Vol. 1:** 103   **Vol. 2:** 381, 388, 426,
          514   **Vol. 3:** 113, 672, 913
11:16 ff   **Vol. 1:** 200
11:16   **Vol. 3:** 857
11:17 f   **Vol. 3:** 672
11:17   **Vol. 2:** 69, 229, 381, 514, 604   **Vol. 3:**
          718, 819
11:18   **Vol. 1:** 111, 446, 468, 623   **Vol. 2:** 76,
          426   **Vol. 3:** 88, 613, 839
11:19–16:1   **Vol. 2:** 691
11:19   **Vol. 2:** 194, 727   **Vol. 3:** 558, 784,
          1001–1002, 1004
12 ff   **Vol. 2:** 273
12   **Vol. 1:** 508   **Vol. 2:** 653, 918   **Vol. 3:**
          732, 737, 1067–1068
12:1   **Vol. 1:** 239   **Vol. 2:** 192, 695   **Vol. 3:**
          732, 734, 736, 1067
12:2–6   **Vol. 2:** 700

Revelation *(cont'd)*

12:2   **Vol. 1:** 178, 187, 410 **Vol. 2:** 615 **Vol. 3:** 856, 858

12:3   **Vol. 1:** 187, 205, 405, 657 **Vol. 2:** 192, 691, 693 **Vol. 3:** 715

12:4 f   **Vol. 1:** 326 **Vol. 2:** 653

12:4   **Vol. 2:** 192, 687, 700 **Vol. 3:** 737, 1046, 1067

12:5   **Vol. 1:** 164, 187, 407 **Vol. 2:** 98, 570, 702, 795 **Vol. 3:** 470, 602–603

12:6   **Vol. 1:** 559 **Vol. 2:** 688, 700 **Vol. 3:** 1007–1008, 1067, 1198

12:7 ff   **Vol. 1:** 83, 103, 508

12:7–12   **Vol. 3:** 470

12:7   **Vol. 1:** 103–104 **Vol. 2:** 688 **Vol. 3:** 962–963

12:8   **Vol. 3:** 714

12:9 ff   **Vol. 2:** 702

12:9   **Vol. 1:** 168, 508, 510, 519 **Vol. 2:** 459–461 **Vol. 3:** 470, 472

12:10 ff   **Vol. 3:** 672, 674

12:10 f   **Vol. 2:** 877

12:10   **Vol. 1:** 83 **Vol. 2:** 388, 604 **Vol. 3:** 216, 470

12:11   **Vol. 1:** 164, 223, 629, 634 **Vol. 3:** 166, 471, 683, 1046, 1183

12:12   **Vol. 2:** 193, 356 **Vol. 3:** 471, 813, 839, 1054

12:13 ff   **Vol. 1:** 508 **Vol. 3:** 984

12:13   **Vol. 2:** 570, 806

12:14–17   **Vol. 3:** 1067

12:14   **Vol. 1:** 339 **Vol. 3:** 1007

12:15 f   **Vol. 3:** 987

12:15   **Vol. 3:** 989

12:16 f   **Vol. 3:** 471

12:16   **Vol. 2:** 701

12:17   **Vol. 1:** 111, 339 **Vol. 2:** 133, 653, 695 **Vol. 3:** 89, 253, 523, 962, 1046, 1068

13   **Vol. 1:** 75, 125, 608 **Vol. 2:** 687 **Vol. 3:** 253

13:1 ff   **Vol. 2:** 625

13:1–14   **Vol. 2:** 604

13:1   **Vol. 1:** 114, 405 **Vol. 2:** 159, 381, 653, 693 **Vol. 3:** 715, 983–984

13:2   **Vol. 1:** 114, 118–119, 239, 508 **Vol. 2:** 603–604, 610

13:3   **Vol. 1:** 114, 493 **Vol. 2:** 625 **Vol. 3:** 857

13:4 ff   **Vol. 2:** 615

13:4   **Vol. 1:** 114, 508 **Vol. 2:** 610, 877 **Vol. 3:** 963

13:5   **Vol. 2:** 688, 700

13:6   **Vol. 3:** 342, 813

13:7 ff   **Vol. 1:** 111

13:7 f   **Vol. 1:** 114 **Vol. 2:** 795

13:7   **Vol. 1:** 651 **Vol. 3:** 962, 1079

13:8   **Vol. 1:** 244, 378 **Vol. 2:** 877 **Vol. 3:** 490

13:10   **Vol. 1:** 602 **Vol. 2:** 776 **Vol. 3:** 591, 967

13:11 ff   **Vol. 2:** 633

13:11–18   **Vol. 2:** 574

13:11   **Vol. 1:** 114

13:12   **Vol. 1:** 119 **Vol. 2:** 610, 674, 877

13:13   **Vol. 1:** 114, 657 **Vol. 2:** 192

13:14   **Vol. 1:** 114 **Vol. 2:** 459, 461 **Vol. 3:** 857, 967

13:15   **Vol. 1:** 114 **Vol. 2:** 288, 574 **Vol. 3:** 694, 706

13:16 f   **Vol. 1:** 114 **Vol. 3:** 500

13:16   **Vol. 2:** 428, 826, 842 **Vol. 3:** 490

13:17 ff   **Vol. 2:** 653

13:17 f   **Vol. 2:** 684

13:17   **Vol. 2:** 574, 653 **Vol. 3:** 471

13:18   **Vol. 1:** 119, 126 **Vol. 2:** 574 **Vol. 3:** 129, 1032

14:1   **Vol. 2:** 327, 329, 573, 654, 700 **Vol. 3:** 490, 500

14:2   **Vol. 3:** 990

14:3   **Vol. 1:** 200, 268, 486 **Vol. 2:** 207, 671, 674, 689, 695, 700, 702, 763 **Vol. 3:** 673, 675

14:4   **Vol. 1:** 449, 482 **Vol. 3:** 416, 568, 1067, 1072

14:5   **Vol. 2:** 473, 702 **Vol. 3:** 925

14:6 ff   **Vol. 1:** 103

14:6   **Vol. 2:** 795 **Vol. 3:** 1079

14:7   **Vol. 2:** 193, 366, 877 **Vol. 3:** 113, 848, 984, 987, 989–990, 1154

14:8   **Vol. 1:** 106, 142, 610 **Vol. 2:** 793, 795 **Vol. 3:** 922

14:9 ff   **Vol. 3:** 501

14:9   **Vol. 2:** 574 **Vol. 3:** 113, 500

14:10   **Vol. 1:** 106, 111, 657 **Vol. 2:** 76, 228 **Vol. 3:** 856, 913, 922

14:11   **Vol. 2:** 574 **Vol. 3:** 256, 500, 856

14:12   **Vol. 1:** 602 **Vol. 2:** 133, 776

14:13   **Vol. 1:** 216, 263, 441, 446 **Vol. 2:** 193 **Vol. 3:** 256, 706

14:14 ff   **Vol. 3:** 1003

14:14   **Vol. 1:** 204 **Vol. 2:** 503 **Vol. 3:** 633

14:15 ff   **Vol. 3:** 784

14:15   **Vol. 1:** 103, 410, 516 **Vol. 3:** 527, 633, 848

14:16   **Vol. 3:** 527

14:17 ff   **Vol. 1:** 103

14:18   **Vol. 1:** 657 **Vol. 2:** 33 **Vol. 3:** 114, 436

14:19 f   **Vol. 1:** 224

14:19   **Vol. 1:** 106, 111 **Vol. 2:** 33

14:20   **Vol. 2:** 697, 700 **Vol. 3:** 919

15:1 ff   **Vol. 2:** 58

15:1   **Vol. 1:** 103, 106, 111, 163 **Vol. 2:** 64, 192, 623, 625 **Vol. 3:** 857

15:2 ff   **Vol. 1:** 651 **Vol. 2:** 868

15:2–18:24   **Vol. 2:** 691

15:2   **Vol. 1:** 114, 656 **Vol. 2:** 625, 684 **Vol. 3:** 984

Revelation *(cont'd)*

15:3 f   **Vol. 2:** 793, 877   **Vol. 3:** 672
15:3   **Vol. 2:** 58, 69, 74, 237, 378, 623, 642,
             793   **Vol. 3:** 362, 672–675, 718, 893,
             940
15:4   **Vol. 2:** 76, 237, 724   **Vol. 3:** 321, 362
15:5–8   **Vol. 3:** 784
15:5   **Vol. 2:** 727   **Vol. 3:** 811
15:6 f   **Vol. 1:** 103
15:6   **Vol. 2:** 486   **Vol. 3:** 105, 107, 120, 857
15:7   **Vol. 1:** 106, 743   **Vol. 2:** 689
15:8   **Vol. 2:** 46, 64, 76   **Vol. 3:** 857
16   **Vol. 2:** 855
16:1   **Vol. 1:** 106   **Vol. 2:** 426   **Vol. 3:** 784
16:2   **Vol. 1:** 564   **Vol. 2:** 574   **Vol. 3:** 998
16:3 f   **Vol. 1:** 224
16:3   **Vol. 3:** 683, 984
16:4   **Vol. 3:** 984, 987, 989
16:5 ff   **Vol. 2:** 868
16:5–7   **Vol. 2:** 877
16:5   **Vol. 2:** 237   **Vol. 3:** 362, 988, 990
16:6 f   **Vol. 1:** 222
16:6   **Vol. 2:** 854   **Vol. 3:** 88
16:7   **Vol. 2:** 69, 514   **Vol. 3:** 362, 436, 718,
             893
16:8   **Vol. 1:** 653   **Vol. 3:** 731
16:9   **Vol. 1:** 359, 653   **Vol. 2:** 654   **Vol. 3:**
             342, 857
16:10–12   **Vol. 3:** 1180
16:10 f   **Vol. 3:** 97
16:10   **Vol. 1:** 425   **Vol. 2:** 381, 615   **Vol. 3:**
             1079
16:11   **Vol. 2:** 193   **Vol. 3:** 342
16:12   **Vol. 1:** 516   **Vol. 2:** 378   **Vol. 3:** 731,
             987
16:13 f   **Vol. 1:** 452   **Vol. 3:** 694
16:13   **Vol. 1:** 114   **Vol. 2:** 472, 474   **Vol. 3:**
             988
16:14   **Vol. 1:** 519   **Vol. 2:** 33, 69, 378, 633,
             894   **Vol. 3:** 718, 962
16:15   **Vol. 1:** 216, 313   **Vol. 2:** 133,
             137   **Vol. 3:** 85
16:16   **Vol. 1:** 274   **Vol. 2:** 33, 309   **Vol. 3:**
             962
16:17   **Vol. 1:** 449   **Vol. 3:** 113, 784
16:18   **Vol. 3:** 558, 1001–1002
16:19   **Vol. 1:** 106, 111, 142, 610   **Vol. 2:**
             795   **Vol. 3:** 241, 246, 922
16:20   **Vol. 1:** 559   **Vol. 3:** 1013
16:21   **Vol. 3:** 342, 857, 1004
17–19   **Vol. 1:** 501
17 f   **Vol. 3:** 179
17   **Vol. 1:** 75   **Vol. 3:** 1047
17:1–19:10   **Vol. 1:** 142
17:1–18   **Vol. 3:** 1068
17:1   **Vol. 1:** 103, 142   **Vol. 2:** 365, 582, 653
17:2 ff   **Vol. 2:** 378
17:2   **Vol. 1:** 514   **Vol. 3:** 922
17:3 f   **Vol. 1:** 142

17:3   **Vol. 1:** 205, 743   **Vol. 2:** 159, 653,
             693   **Vol. 3:** 706, 715, 1008, 1067
17:4   **Vol. 1:** 111, 142, 205, 743   **Vol. 3:**
             395–396, 1067
17:5   **Vol. 1:** 142, 518   **Vol. 2:** 582, 625,
             653   **Vol. 3:** 490, 1069
17:6 ff   **Vol. 2:** 625
17:6 f   **Vol. 3:** 1067
17:6   **Vol. 1:** 222, 514   **Vol. 2:** 623,
             625   **Vol. 3:** 1047
17:7   **Vol. 2:** 625, 693   **Vol. 3:** 505, 715
17:8   **Vol. 1:** 114, 244, 378, 464   **Vol. 2:** 205,
             625, 899
17:9 ff   **Vol. 2:** 378
17:9 f   **Vol. 3:** 1067
17:9   **Vol. 1:** 142   **Vol. 3:** 129, 1013, 1032,
             1070
17:10   **Vol. 1:** 610   **Vol. 2:** 665, 692
17:11   **Vol. 1:** 114
17:12 ff   **Vol. 3:** 715
17:12   **Vol. 2:** 381, 693   **Vol. 3:** 715
17:13 f   **Vol. 2:** 603
17:13   **Vol. 2:** 398, 722
17:14   **Vol. 1:** 652   **Vol. 2:** 378, 514   **Vol. 3:**
             963
17:15   **Vol. 2:** 799, 801   **Vol. 3:** 1079
17:16–18   **Vol. 3:** 1008
17:16   **Vol. 1:** 656   **Vol. 2:** 693   **Vol. 3:** 715,
             1008
17:17   **Vol. 2:** 64
17:18   **Vol. 3:** 1067
18   **Vol. 3:** 1054
18:1–2   **Vol. 1:** 103   **Vol. 3:** 113
18:1   **Vol. 2:** 38, 46, 193, 486
18:2–24   **Vol. 3:** 1008
18:2   **Vol. 1:** 410, 557, 610   **Vol. 2:** 136, 249,
             426   **Vol. 3:** 505, 694, 714, 1008
18:3 ff   **Vol. 2:** 378
18:3   **Vol. 1:** 106, 111   **Vol. 2:** 795,
             844   **Vol. 3:** 922
18:4   **Vol. 1:** 642, 644   **Vol. 2:** 193,
             800   **Vol. 3:** 857
18:5   **Vol. 2:** 349   **Vol. 3:** 241–242, 575
18:6   **Vol. 3:** 572, 913
18:7 ff   **Vol. 3:** 856
18:7 f   **Vol. 2:** 423
18:7   **Vol. 2:** 381   **Vol. 3:** 588, 1074, 1149
18:8   **Vol. 1:** 656   **Vol. 2:** 266, 720   **Vol. 3:**
             714, 857
18:9   **Vol. 1:** 656   **Vol. 2:** 417   **Vol. 3:** 1054
18:10   **Vol. 1:** 321   **Vol. 2:** 426   **Vol. 3:** 714,
             848, 856
18:11   **Vol. 2:** 422   **Vol. 3:** 1054
18:12   **Vol. 1:** 390   **Vol. 2:** 97–98   **Vol. 3:**
             393, 395, 913
18:13   **Vol. 1:** 114, 234   **Vol. 2:** 294–295,
             711   **Vol. 3:** 922
18:14   **Vol. 1:** 457   **Vol. 2:** 486
18:15   **Vol. 2:** 422, 842, 844   **Vol. 3:** 856

Revelation *(cont'd)*

18:16   **Vol. 1:** 205 **Vol. 2:** 426 **Vol. 3:** 393, 395

18:17   **Vol. 1:** 198 **Vol. 2:** 842, 844 **Vol. 3:** 848, 1008, 1054

18:18 f   **Vol. 2:** 426

18:18   **Vol. 1:** 656

18:19   **Vol. 1:** 520 **Vol. 2:** 159, 422, 844 **Vol. 3:** 848, 1008

18:20   **Vol. 2:** 193, 228, 356 **Vol. 3:** 84, 88

18:21   **Vol. 2:** 426 **Vol. 3:** 394, 714, 1013

18:22   **Vol. 1:** 279 **Vol. 3:** 394, 874

18:23   **Vol. 1:** 452 **Vol. 2:** 459–461, 487–488, 493, 558, 578, 585, 795

18:24   **Vol. 1:** 222 **Vol. 3:** 88

19:1 f   **Vol. 3:** 672, 674

19:1–21:8   **Vol. 2:** 692

19:1–8   **Vol. 2:** 868

19:1–7   **Vol. 2:** 877

19:1   **Vol. 1:** 99 **Vol. 2:** 46, 192, 426, 604, 878 **Vol. 3:** 113, 216

19:2   **Vol. 1:** 222, 405, 468–469 **Vol. 3:** 97, 362, 613, 893

19:3   **Vol. 1:** 99 **Vol. 2:** 878

19:4 f   **Vol. 2:** 702

19:4   **Vol. 1:** 99 **Vol. 2:** 689, 878

19:5   **Vol. 2:** 73, 428 **Vol. 3:** 817

19:6 ff   **Vol. 3:** 672

19:6   **Vol. 1:** 99 **Vol. 2:** 381, 514 **Vol. 3:** 505, 674, 718, 990, 1002

19:7 ff   **Vol. 2:** 58, 581 **Vol. 3:** 1068

19:7–9   **Vol. 2:** 354

19:7 f   **Vol. 1:** 657

19:7   **Vol. 1:** 164 **Vol. 2:** 354, 358, 412, 585 **Vol. 3:** 118, 1067

19:8   **Vol. 2:** 486 **Vol. 3:** 107, 362, 714

19:9   **Vol. 1:** 164, 216, 274 **Vol. 2:** 358, 412, 585 **Vol. 3:** 489, 893

19:10   **Vol. 1:** 103, 239, 609 **Vol. 2:** 877 **Vol. 3:** 81, 89, 706

19:11–21   **Vol. 2:** 700

19:11   **Vol. 1:** 118, 205 **Vol. 2:** 727 **Vol. 3:** 362, 963

19:12   **Vol. 1:** 656 **Vol. 2:** 654 **Vol. 3:** 365, 490

19:13   **Vol. 1:** 63, 145, 164, 224 **Vol. 2:** 654, 686 **Vol. 3:** 326, 1114

19:14   **Vol. 1:** 118, 204–205 **Vol. 3:** 107, 964

19:15 f   **Vol. 2:** 514

19:15   **Vol. 1:** 106, 111, 164, 407 **Vol. 2:** 69, 98, 686, 795 **Vol. 3:** 718, 922, 967

19:16   **Vol. 1:** 168 **Vol. 2:** 378, 654 **Vol. 3:** 490, 964

19:17 ff   **Vol. 3:** 716

19:17–21   **Vol. 1:** 118

19:17   **Vol. 1:** 103, 410 **Vol. 2:** 33 **Vol. 3:** 732

19:18 ff   **Vol. 2:** 378

19:18   **Vol. 2:** 428, 699

19:19 f   **Vol. 1:** 114

19:19   **Vol. 2:** 33 **Vol. 3:** 964

19:20   **Vol. 1:** 114, 657 **Vol. 2:** 209, 459, 472, 474, 574, 633 **Vol. 3:** 992

19:21   **Vol. 1:** 430, 744 **Vol. 3:** 252, 967

20   **Vol. 1:** 53 **Vol. 2:** 701–703

20:1 ff   **Vol. 1:** 103 **Vol. 2:** 65, 631

20:1–7   **Vol. 2:** 389, 697

20:1–5   **Vol. 1:** 52

20:1–3   **Vol. 2:** 702

20:1   **Vol. 2:** 205, 734

20:2 f   **Vol. 1:** 508

20:2–7   **Vol. 2:** 700–701

20:2   **Vol. 1:** 168, 508, 510 **Vol. 3:** 718

20:3   **Vol. 1:** 508 **Vol. 2:** 64, 205, 459, 461, 665, 702, 734, 795 **Vol. 3:** 179, 499

20:4 ff   **Vol. 3:** 277, 303

20:4   **Vol. 1:** 205 **Vol. 2:** 207, 365, 380, 574, 613 **Vol. 3:** 89, 278, 490, 686, 1046

20:5 f   **Vol. 3:** 278

20:5   **Vol. 1:** 446 **Vol. 2:** 64, 380 **Vol. 3:** 252

20:6   **Vol. 1:** 649 **Vol. 2:** 231, 304, 380 **Vol. 3:** 37, 304

20:7 ff   **Vol. 1:** 111 **Vol. 3:** 389

20:7–10   **Vol. 3:** 962

20:7   **Vol. 2:** 64, 136, 207 **Vol. 3:** 179, 471, 962

20:8–15   **Vol. 2:** 701

20:8–10   **Vol. 2:** 460

20:8   **Vol. 1:** 508 **Vol. 2:** 33, 459, 461, 684, 689, 795 **Vol. 3:** 962

20:9   **Vol. 1:** 254, 657 **Vol. 2:** 193 **Vol. 3:** 965, 1174

20:10 ff   **Vol. 3:** 992

20:10   **Vol. 1:** 114, 508, 657 **Vol. 2:** 209, 459–460, 472, 474, 631 **Vol. 3:** 99, 471, 856

20:11 ff   **Vol. 3:** 277

20:11–15   **Vol. 3:** 136, 277, 303

20:11   **Vol. 1:** 204, 559 **Vol. 2:** 193 **Vol. 3:** 589, 1013

20:12 f   **Vol. 1:** 446 **Vol. 2:** 365

20:12   **Vol. 1:** 244 **Vol. 2:** 426 **Vol. 3:** 136

20:13 f   **Vol. 1:** 441 **Vol. 2:** 207, 926

20:13   **Vol. 2:** 207 **Vol. 3:** 984

20:14 f   **Vol. 2:** 209 **Vol. 3:** 99

20:14   **Vol. 1:** 437, 657 **Vol. 2:** 207 **Vol. 3:** 304, 471

20:15   **Vol. 3:** 136, 490, 528

21 f   **Vol. 2:** 764

21   **Vol. 2:** 303 **Vol. 3:** 396–398, 948

21:1 ff   **Vol. 1:** 387 **Vol. 2:** 632

21:1–25:5   **Vol. 1:** 142

21:1–5   **Vol. 1:** 185

21:1–4   **Vol. 2:** 779

21:1   **Vol. 1:** 321, 518 **Vol. 2:** 193, 631, 671, 674 **Vol. 3:** 558, 984, 1013

21:2 f   **Vol. 3:** 1068

Revelation *(cont'd)*

21:2   **Vol. 2:** 186, 194, 231, 329, 563, 585, 671, 674, 722, 804   **Vol. 3:** 118
21:3 f   **Vol. 2:** 483
21:3   **Vol. 1:** 368   **Vol. 2:** 193, 426, 800   **Vol. 3:** 518, 784, 813
21:4   **Vol. 1:** 321   **Vol. 2:** 419–420, 423, 631, 674   **Vol. 3:** 872
21:5   **Vol. 1:** 186, 387   **Vol. 2:** 674   **Vol. 3:** 588, 893, 1154, 1193
21:6   **Vol. 1:** 166   **Vol. 2:** 41, 59, 64, 80, 267, 282, 482   **Vol. 3:** 988, 991
21:7   **Vol. 1:** 651   **Vol. 2:** 300
21:8   **Vol. 1:** 452, 657   **Vol. 2:** 74, 286, 304, 473, 495, 558, 584   **Vol. 3:** 304, 992, 1067
21:9 ff   **Vol. 2:** 585
21:9 f   **Vol. 3:** 569
21:9–22:21   **Vol. 2:** 692
21:9   **Vol. 1:** 743   **Vol. 2:** 58, 585   **Vol. 3:** 857, 1068
21:10 ff   **Vol. 2:** 804
21:10 f   **Vol. 2:** 48, 329
21:10   **Vol. 2:** 186, 194, 199, 231   **Vol. 3:** 706, 1010
21:11   **Vol. 2:** 76, 493   **Vol. 3:** 393, 396–398
21:12 ff   **Vol. 1:** 200   **Vol. 2:** 696
21:12 f   **Vol. 2:** 30, 329
21:12   **Vol. 2:** 199, 315, 652   **Vol. 3:** 397, 490, 871, 948, 1010
21:13   **Vol. 2:** 687   **Vol. 3:** 397, 1003
21:14   **Vol. 1:** 130, 134, 661   **Vol. 2:** 412, 652   **Vol. 3:** 88, 387, 395, 397
21:15   **Vol. 3:** 404
21:16   **Vol. 1:** 254   **Vol. 2:** 199, 498, 700
21:17–21   **Vol. 3:** 948
21:17   **Vol. 3:** 404, 948
21:18   **Vol. 2:** 96   **Vol. 3:** 107
21:19–21   **Vol. 3:** 396
21:19 f   **Vol. 3:** 872
21:19   **Vol. 1:** 661   **Vol. 3:** 393, 395, 398
21:21   **Vol. 2:** 30, 96   **Vol. 3:** 107, 395
21:22   **Vol. 2:** 58, 69, 194, 231, 329, 514   **Vol. 3:** 37, 718, 784, 1068
21:23 f   **Vol. 2:** 495
21:23   **Vol. 2:** 76, 412, 487–488   **Vol. 3:** 398, 732, 734

21:24   **Vol. 2:** 378, 793, 795   **Vol. 3:** 944
21:25   **Vol. 1:** 421   **Vol. 2:** 30   **Vol. 3:** 387, 395, 948
21:26   **Vol. 2:** 795
21:27   **Vol. 1:** 448, 641   **Vol. 2:** 74, 473, 495   **Vol. 3:** 490
22:1 f   **Vol. 2:** 763   **Vol. 3:** 962, 988
22:1   **Vol. 2:** 482, 486, 615, 702   **Vol. 3:** 569, 988–989, 991, 1203
22:2–14   **Vol. 2:** 482
22:2   **Vol. 1:** 390, 723   **Vol. 3:** 868
22:3   **Vol. 1:** 415   **Vol. 2:** 495, 665, 702   **Vol. 3:** 613
22:4   **Vol. 1:** 587   **Vol. 2:** 573, 654, 804   **Vol. 3:** 490, 500
22:5   **Vol. 1:** 421   **Vol. 2:** 388, 487, 493, 495   **Vol. 3:** 397, 732
22:6   **Vol. 2:** 514, 665   **Vol. 3:** 88, 569, 694, 893
22:7   **Vol. 3:** 85
22:8 f   **Vol. 1:** 103   **Vol. 2:** 877
22:8   **Vol. 1:** 239, 609   **Vol. 3:** 569
22:9   **Vol. 3:** 88
22:10   **Vol. 3:** 500, 838
22:11   **Vol. 1:** 479   **Vol. 2:** 495   **Vol. 3:** 362, 575–576
22:12   **Vol. 3:** 136
22:13   **Vol. 1:** 166, 667   **Vol. 2:** 58–59, 64, 80, 282, 674
22:14   **Vol. 1:** 339, 390–391   **Vol. 2:** 30, 763   **Vol. 3:** 868
22:15   **Vol. 1:** 452   **Vol. 2:** 286, 473, 558, 584   **Vol. 3:** 99, 948
22:16   **Vol. 1:** 117, 304, 407, 427   **Vol. 2:** 340, 486, 495, 558   **Vol. 3:** 652, 735–737, 869
22:17–21   **Vol. 2:** 516, 523, 530
22:17   **Vol. 2:** 41, 267, 482, 585, 883   **Vol. 3:** 706, 988, 991, 1023
22:18 f   **Vol. 2:** 495   **Vol. 3:** 88, 489–490
22:18   **Vol. 3:** 857
22:19   **Vol. 1:** 390–391   **Vol. 2:** 231, 304, 482   **Vol. 3:** 868
22:20   **Vol. 1:** 99, 323   **Vol. 2:** 229, 530–531, 585, 674, 896   **Vol. 3:** 316, 319

Index to
Extrabiblical Literature

Old Testament Apocrypha and Pseudepigrapha

Addition to Daniel: Susanna
(Ad. Dan. Sus.)

5	**Vol. 3:** 570, 821
13	**Vol. 3:** 943
37	**Vol. 3:** 255

Addition to Daniel: Bel and the Dragon
(Ad. Dan. Bel)

1	**Vol. 3:** 873	
3	**Vol. 2:** 876	
5	**Vol. 1:** 380	
7	**Vol. 2:** 431	
9	**Vol. 2:** 284	**Vol. 3:** 342, 570
11	**Vol. 3:** 911	
12	**Vol. 2:** 730	
14	**Vol. 2:** 285	**Vol. 3:** 557
15	**Vol. 2:** 437	
18	**Vol. 2:** 431	
19	**Vol. 2:** 431	
23	**Vol. 2:** 876	
30	**Vol. 2:** 801	

Additions to Esther (Ad. Est.)

13.1–6	**Vol. 1:** 246
13.12 ff	**Vol. 2:** 310
16.4	**Vol. 3:** 818

Apocalypse of Ezra. *See* 2 Esdras

Aristeas, Letter of (Aristeas)

47–50	**Vol. 2:** 697
84	**Vol. 3:** 229
102	**Vol. 3:** 570
139	**Vol. 3:** 186
178	**Vol. 3:** 908
225	**Vol. 2:** 116

Assumption of Moses (Ass. Mos.)

3.9	**Vol. 3:** 263	
6 ff	**Vol. 1:** 125	
7	**Vol. 2:** 311	
10.1	**Vol. 2:** 602	
10.5	**Vol. 1:** 203	**Vol. 3:** 731, 733
10.7–10	**Vol. 3:** 961	

10.12	**Vol. 2:** 892
11.17	**Vol. 3:** 46
12.10	**Vol. 1:** 334

1 Baruch (Bar.). *See also* Epistle of Jeremy

1–3	**Vol. 1:** 345	
1.10 ff	**Vol. 1:** 700	
1.11	**Vol. 2:** 863	
1.12	**Vol. 3:** 555	
1.13	**Vol. 2:** 863	
1.20	**Vol. 1:** 683	**Vol. 3:** 610
2.6	**Vol. 3:** 1163	
2.8	**Vol. 3:** 125	
2.9	**Vol. 2:** 136	
2.11	**Vol. 2:** 627	
2.12	**Vol. 3:** 354	
2.17	**Vol. 3:** 233, 354	
2.19	**Vol. 3:** 354	
2.20	**Vol. 3:** 610	
2.28	**Vol. 3:** 610	
2.32	**Vol. 3:** 816	
3.6 f	**Vol. 3:** 816	
3.12 f	**Vol. 2:** 840	
3.12	**Vol. 3:** 842	
3.13	**Vol. 3:** 842	
3.14	**Vol. 1:** 485	
3.23	**Vol. 2:** 644	
3.27–28	**Vol. 3:** 641	
3.34	**Vol. 3:** 735	
4.7	**Vol. 1:** 451	
4.8–23	**Vol. 3:** 1068	
4.10	**Vol. 3:** 1194	
4.13	**Vol. 3:** 354	
4.22	**Vol. 3:** 218	
4.24	**Vol. 3:** 209	
4.27	**Vol. 3:** 238	
4.29	**Vol. 3:** 209	
5.5	**Vol. 3:** 238	
5.7	**Vol. 1:** 663	
5.8	**Vol. 3:** 555	
6	**Vol. 2:** 285	
6.18	**Vol. 3:** 379	
6.28	**Vol. 3:** 444–445	

2 Baruch. *See* Syriac Apocalypse of Baruch

3 Baruch. *See* Greek Book of Baruch

Ecclesiasticus. *See* Sirach, Book of

1 Enoch. *See* Ethiopic Book of Enoch

2 Enoch. *See* Slavonic Book of Enoch

3 Enoch. *See* Hebrew Book of Enoch

Epistle of Jeremy (Ep. Jer.)
[appears at end of 1 Baruch
(= Bar. 6)]

5 f	**Vol. 2:** 876
9	**Vol. 3:** 119
12	**Vol. 2:** 27
24	**Vol. 2:** 27
37	**Vol. 2:** 663
45 f	**Vol. 3:** 119
60	**Vol. 3:** 735
65	**Vol. 1:** 416

1 Esdras (1 Esd.) [LXX and English versions, 3 Esd. in Vulgate]

1.5	**Vol. 2:** 425
1.8	**Vol. 3:** 786
1.20	**Vol. 3:** 841
1.48	**Vol. 3:** 583
1.55	**Vol. 3:** 177
1.57	**Vol. 1:** 735
2.2	**Vol. 3:** 51
2.20	**Vol. 3:** 1147
2.28	**Vol. 1:** 694
3.5	**Vol. 3:** 1028
3.7	**Vol. 3:** 1027
3.8	**Vol. 3:** 498
3.9	**Vol. 3:** 1028
4.20	**Vol. 2:** 349
4.22	**Vol. 3:** 241
4.31	**Vol. 2:** 431
4.37	**Vol. 3:** 1149
4.39	**Vol. 2:** 817
4.40	**Vol. 2:** 425
4.42	**Vol. 3:** 1028
4.44	**Vol. 3:** 534
4.56	**Vol. 3:** 144
4.57	**Vol. 3:** 534
4.59 f	**Vol. 3:** 1027
5.6	**Vol. 3:** 1028
5.39	**Vol. 3:** 534
5.43	**Vol. 3:** 786
5.50	**Vol. 3:** 813
5.53	**Vol. 1:** 380
5.60	**Vol. 3:** 669

5.62	**Vol. 3:** 669
5.63	**Vol. 1:** 695
6.13	**Vol. 1:** 380
6.15	**Vol. 2:** 191
6.31	**Vol. 2:** 839
7.13	**Vol. 3:** 534
8 f	**Vol. 3:** 456
8.7	**Vol. 3:** 760
8.11	**Vol. 3:** 821
8.17	**Vol. 3:** 957
8.18	**Vol. 3:** 786
8.23	**Vol. 3:** 760, 1027
8.24	**Vol. 3:** 98
8.46	**Vol. 3:** 820
8.47	**Vol. 3:** 873
8.62	**Vol. 3:** 846
8.64	**Vol. 3:** 786
8.76	**Vol. 3:** 841
8.94	**Vol. 1:** 589
9.3	**Vol. 3:** 51
9.9	**Vol. 3:** 534
9.13	**Vol. 3:** 177
9.36	**Vol. 1:** 505
9.40	**Vol. 3:** 808
9.41	**Vol. 3:** 125
9.42	**Vol. 2:** 369
9.46	**Vol. 3:** 177
9.47	**Vol. 1:** 409
9.48 f	**Vol. 3:** 760
9.53	**Vol. 1:** 341
9.55	**Vol. 3:** 760

2 Esdras (2 Esd.)

3.7	**Vol. 1:** 434	**Vol. 2:** 791
3.10 f	**Vol. 3:** 816	
3.12	**Vol. 2:** 791, 800	
4.5	**Vol. 2:** 139	
4.21	**Vol. 1:** 73	
4.23	**Vol. 1:** 73	
4.28 ff	**Vol. 3:** 522	
4.33	**Vol. 2:** 892	
4.35	**Vol. 2:** 892	
4.36	**Vol. 2:** 925	
4.38	**Vol. 3:** 1148	
4.43	**Vol. 3:** 1148	
4.51 ff	**Vol. 3:** 575	
4.51 f	**Vol. 2:** 629	
5.2 ff	**Vol. 2:** 892	
5.4	**Vol. 2:** 688	**Vol. 3:** 731, 733
5.5	**Vol. 1:** 73	**Vol. 3:** 393
5.8	**Vol. 1:** 124	
5.23 ff	**Vol. 1:** 539	
5.23	**Vol. 2:** 313	
5.26	**Vol. 2:** 314	
5.45	**Vol. 2:** 207	**Vol. 3:** 210
5.50 ff	**Vol. 1:** 124	
6.5 ff	**Vol. 2:** 830	
6.7	**Vol. 2:** 56	
6.8	**Vol. 1:** 73	

2 Esdras (2 Esd.) *(cont'd)*

6.10	**Vol. 2:** 863
6.11 f	**Vol. 2:** 629
6.11	**Vol. 2:** 839
6.15	**Vol. 3:** 559
6.21	**Vol. 1:** 124
6.23–24	**Vol. 3:** 874
6.23	**Vol. 2:** 925
6.26	**Vol. 1:** 545
6.27 f	**Vol. 3:** 462
6.29	**Vol. 3:** 559
6.34	**Vol. 2:** 56
6.55 ff	**Vol. 2:** 798
6.58	**Vol. 2:** 798
7	**Vol. 2:** 364, 842 **Vol. 3:** 271, 293
7.7 ff	**Vol. 2:** 481 **Vol. 3:** 940
7.7 f	**Vol. 3:** 940
7.7	**Vol. 3:** 672
7.11	**Vol. 2:** 310
7.12 f	**Vol. 2:** 928
7.13	**Vol. 2:** 420
7.20	**Vol. 3:** 957
7.24	**Vol. 3:** 673
7.25	**Vol. 3:** 1027
7.26	**Vol. 2:** 803 **Vol. 3:** 772
7.28 f	**Vol. 2:** 701 **Vol. 3:** 610, 637, 642
7.28–31	**Vol. 3:** 271
7.28	**Vol. 3:** 652
7.29	**Vol. 2:** 893
7.31 ff	**Vol. 1:** 434
7.32–38	**Vol. 3:** 303
7.32–36	**Vol. 3:** 271
7.36	**Vol. 2:** 208
7.37 ff	**Vol. 3:** 271
7.38	**Vol. 1:** 656
7.77	**Vol. 2:** 830
7.78 ff	**Vol. 3:** 682
7.78–100	**Vol. 2:** 207
7.88 ff	**Vol. 1:** 435
7.88	**Vol. 2:** 565
7.89	**Vol. 3:** 271
7.97	**Vol. 2:** 486 **Vol. 3:** 271
7.98 ff	**Vol. 2:** 736
7.98	**Vol. 3:** 106
7.100	**Vol. 2:** 565
7.113	**Vol. 2:** 56
7.119	**Vol. 3:** 70, 1149
7.132–139	**Vol. 2:** 651
8.3	**Vol. 3:** 210
8.17	**Vol. 3:** 673
8.25	**Vol. 3:** 416
8.31–33	**Vol. 2:** 118
8.31	**Vol. 3:** 201
8.36	**Vol. 1:** 710 **Vol. 2:** 118
8.41	**Vol. 3:** 210
8.47–54	**Vol. 2:** 261
8.52 ff	**Vol. 2:** 928
8.52	**Vol. 2:** 803
8.59	**Vol. 2:** 265
8.63	**Vol. 2:** 629
9.7 f	**Vol. 3:** 250
9.7	**Vol. 1:** 598 **Vol. 3:** 210
9.13	**Vol. 3:** 210
9.17	**Vol. 3:** 522
9.26–13.56	**Vol. 2:** 745
9.31	**Vol. 3:** 522
9.38–10.59	**Vol. 3:** 1068
9.38–10.27	**Vol. 3:** 509
10.1	**Vol. 2:** 863
10.2	**Vol. 2:** 578, 773
10.6	**Vol. 3:** 796
10.7	**Vol. 3:** 1069
10.19	**Vol. 1:** 569
10.23	**Vol. 3:** 498
10.24	**Vol. 3:** 672
10.27	**Vol. 2:** 326
10.54	**Vol. 2:** 326
12.22	**Vol. 3:** 650
12.31	**Vol. 3:** 650
12.33	**Vol. 3:** 961
12.34	**Vol. 3:** 250
12.36 ff	**Vol. 3:** 502
13.1–13	**Vol. 3:** 616
13.5 ff	**Vol. 3:** 962
13.10 f	**Vol. 1:** 656 **Vol. 2:** 836
13.23	**Vol. 3:** 210
13.25 ff	**Vol. 2:** 326
13.25	**Vol. 3:** 652
13.26	**Vol. 3:** 250, 616
13.32	**Vol. 3:** 610, 616, 637, 642
13.36	**Vol. 2:** 326
13.37	**Vol. 3:** 610, 616, 637, 642
13.48	**Vol. 3:** 250
13.52	**Vol. 3:** 610, 616, 637, 642
13.54	**Vol. 3:** 616
14.5	**Vol. 2:** 56
14.9	**Vol. 2:** 202 **Vol. 3:** 610, 637, 642
14.22	**Vol. 3:** 939
14.23	**Vol. 2:** 696
14.29	**Vol. 3:** 210
14.34	**Vol. 3:** 210
14.35	**Vol. 3:** 210
14.42–47	**Vol. 1:** 243–244
14.49	**Vol. 2:** 202

3 Esdras. *See* 1 Esdras

**Ethiopic Book of Enoch
(Eth. Enoch)**

1–36	**Vol. 3:** 265, 272
1.3–9	**Vol. 2:** 897
1.6–9	**Vol. 2:** 836
1.9	**Vol. 1:** 85 **Vol. 2:** 155, 219, 817, 897 **Vol. 3:** 265, 492
5.4	**Vol. 1:** 607
5.6	**Vol. 3:** 210
5.8 f	**Vol. 2:** 892
6 ff	**Vol. 3:** 636

269

Ethiopic Book of Enoch
(Eth. Enoch) *(cont'd)*

6–16	**Vol. 1:** 102
6–11	**Vol. 2:** 681
6	**Vol. 2:** 213 **Vol. 3:** 801
6.6	**Vol. 1:** 451
6.7	**Vol. 2:** 651
7.2 ff	**Vol. 1:** 452
7.5–9.3	**Vol. 1:** 410
8.1	**Vol. 1:** 452
9.1	**Vol. 1:** 103
9.3	**Vol. 2:** 882
9.9–10	**Vol. 1:** 103
10.4 ff	**Vol. 2:** 205
10.4	**Vol. 3:** 1006
10.6	**Vol. 2:** 364
10.10	**Vol. 2:** 928
10.17 ff	**Vol. 1:** 729
10.17	**Vol. 2:** 698
10.19˙	**Vol. 2:** 698
14.9–22	**Vol. 1:** 655
14.11	**Vol. 1:** 280
14.16–20	**Vol. 3:** 789
14.18 ff	**Vol. 2:** 613
14.18 f	**Vol. 2:** 613
14.18	**Vol. 1:** 280
14.22	**Vol. 2:** 698
15.4	**Vol. 3:** 693
15.6–10	**Vol. 3:** 693
15.6	**Vol. 3:** 693
15.7	**Vol. 3:** 229
15.10	**Vol. 3:** 229
17.3	**Vol. 2:** 830
17.6	**Vol. 1:** 423, 674
18.2	**Vol. 2:** 689
18.11 ff	**Vol. 2:** 205
18.13–16	**Vol. 2:** 459
19–21	**Vol. 1:** 102
19	**Vol. 3:** 801
19.1	**Vol. 3:** 459
20.2	**Vol. 1:** 464
20.5	**Vol. 1:** 104
20.7	**Vol. 1:** 103, 280
21.1–10	**Vol. 2:** 459
22	**Vol. 2:** 207
22.7	**Vol. 1:** 410
22.9 ff	**Vol. 3:** 229
22.9	**Vol. 2:** 274
22.12	**Vol. 1:** 410
22.13	**Vol. 3:** 272
24.4	**Vol. 2:** 763
25.3	**Vol. 3:** 789
25.4 f	**Vol. 1:** 389–390 **Vol. 2:** 763
26.1 f	**Vol. 3:** 789
26.1	**Vol. 1:** 523
27.1 f	**Vol. 2:** 208
37–71	**Vol. 3:** 196, 265, 610, 614, 789
37.4	**Vol. 2:** 928 **Vol. 3:** 640
38.1	**Vol. 2:** 731
38.2	**Vol. 2:** 899
38.3	**Vol. 3:** 502
39.3 f	**Vol. 2:** 762
39.3	**Vol. 2:** 202
39.4 ff	**Vol. 3:** 229, 692
39.4 f	**Vol. 3:** 682
40.1	**Vol. 2:** 698
40.3	**Vol. 1:** 103
40.6	**Vol. 1:** 103
40.9	**Vol. 1:** 103 **Vol. 2:** 602–603, 928
42	**Vol. 3:** 1029
42.1 ff	**Vol. 3:** 1116
42.1 f	**Vol. 2:** 840 **Vol. 3:** 1115
45.3	**Vol. 2:** 250, 614
46	**Vol. 3:** 615, 961
46.3 ff	**Vol. 3:** 615
46.3 f	**Vol. 1:** 321
46.3	**Vol. 2:** 216, 835 **Vol. 3:** 615
46.6	**Vol. 3:** 272
46.7 f	**Vol. 2:** 652
46.8	**Vol. 3:** 615
47.1 f	**Vol. 3:** 242
47.1–4	**Vol. 3:** 956
48.1	**Vol. 1:** 729 **Vol. 3:** 459, 986
48.2 ff	**Vol. 3:** 615
48.2	**Vol. 1:** 321
48.7	**Vol. 2:** 228, 928 **Vol. 3:** 210, 575
48.8 f	**Vol. 2:** 228
49.3	**Vol. 1:** 175
49.4	**Vol. 2:** 899
50.3	**Vol. 3:** 210
51	**Vol. 3:** 961
51.1 f	**Vol. 3:** 272
51.1	**Vol. 2:** 207
51.2	**Vol. 3:** 633
51.3	**Vol. 2:** 216, 613
51.5 f	**Vol. 1:** 729
51.5	**Vol. 2:** 486
52.1	**Vol. 2:** 202, 762
52.6	**Vol. 2:** 836
53	**Vol. 3:** 961
53.6	**Vol. 2:** 731 **Vol. 3:** 615
54.1 ff	**Vol. 2:** 208
54.6	**Vol. 1:** 103 **Vol. 3:** 469
54.7–55.2	**Vol. 2:** 681
55 f	**Vol. 3:** 961
55.4	**Vol. 2:** 613
56.3 f	**Vol. 2:** 208
56.5	**Vol. 3:** 615
58.2	**Vol. 1:** 216
60	**Vol. 2:** 681
60.7	**Vol. 3:** 983
60.8	**Vol. 3:** 1006
60.16	**Vol. 3:** 983
61.8	**Vol. 3:** 1161
61.10	**Vol. 2:** 518, 602–603, 608 **Vol. 3:** 983
62	**Vol. 3:** 961
62.2	**Vol. 2:** 613–614
62.3	**Vol. 2:** 369, 613–614, 926
62.5 ff	**Vol. 2:** 613–614

Ethiopic Book of Enoch (Eth. Enoch) (cont'd)

62.5	Vol. 2: 369, 926
62.7 ff	Vol. 3: 615
62.8	Vol. 731 Vol. 3: 615
62.11–15	Vol. 1: 539
62.12	Vol. 1: 110
62.13–16	Vol. 3: 272
62.13	Vol. 3: 210
62.14 ff	Vol. 1: 204
62.14	Vol. 2: 532
63.6	Vol. 1: 423
63.10	Vol. 2: 207
65.1–69.25	Vol. 2: 681
66.2	Vol. 3: 983
68.1	Vol. 3: 502
69.2 f	Vol. 2: 655–656
69.4	Vol. 2: 195
69.13–21	Vol. 2: 652
69.22	Vol. 3: 983
70 f	Vol. 3: 615, 618
71	Vol. 3: 615
71.1	Vol. 2: 195
71.11	Vol. 1: 409, 527
71.14	Vol. 2: 817
71.15 f	Vol. 3: 229
71.15	Vol. 2: 928
71.16	Vol. 3: 682
72–82	Vol. 2: 191 Vol. 3: 265
72–74	Vol. 3: 731
72.7–32	Vol. 1: 627
76.1 ff	Vol. 2: 695
77.1 ff	Vol. 2: 689
77.1	Vol. 1: 212
78	Vol. 3: 731
80.4 ff	Vol. 1: 124
80.4	Vol. 3: 733
81.4	Vol. 1: 243
82.8	Vol. 2: 602–603
82.11 ff	Vol. 2: 689
82.11	Vol. 2: 695
83–90	Vol. 3: 265
83.7	Vol. 3: 502
83.8	Vol. 2: 731 Vol. 3: 250
84.5	Vol. 2: 731
85–90	Vol. 2: 745 Vol. 3: 789
86.1–88.3	Vol. 3: 468
89.52	Vol. 2: 202
89.59 ff	Vol. 2: 696
89.59 f	Vol. 2: 690
89.61–64	Vol. 1: 243
89.76	Vol. 3: 35
90.9	Vol. 3: 715
90.19	Vol. 3: 961
90.26 f	Vol. 2: 208
90.29	Vol. 3: 509
90.30	Vol. 3: 250
90.31	Vol. 1: 545 Vol. 2: 202
90.33	Vol. 2: 311 Vol. 3: 272
90.37 f	Vol. 3: 715
91–104	Vol. 3: 265
91–94	Vol. 2: 892
91.1	Vol. 3: 693
91.5 ff	Vol. 3: 575
91.9	Vol. 1: 655–656
91.10	Vol. 1: 442
91.12 f	Vol. 2: 701
91.16	Vol. 2: 602–603
92.3	Vol. 1: 442
93.1–14	Vol. 2: 701
93.9	Vol. 1: 607
94	Vol. 3: 961
94.7	Vol. 3: 961
94.9	Vol. 3: 961
94.10	Vol. 3: 961
95.3 ff	Vol. 3: 272
95.3	Vol. 3: 961
96.4	Vol. 2: 842
98.10	Vol. 3: 193–194, 196, 210
98.14	Vol. 3: 210
99	Vol. 1: 124
99.1	Vol. 3: 210
99.7	Vol. 1: 452 Vol. 3: 806
100.1–5	Vol. 3: 961
100.6	Vol. 2: 842
100.9	Vol. 1: 655–656
102 ff	Vol. 1: 435
102.1	Vol. 1: 656 Vol. 3: 210
102.5	Vol. 2: 207
103.2 ff	Vol. 3: 502
103.4 f	Vol. 2: 842
103.4	Vol. 3: 272, 682
103.5	Vol. 1: 216
103.7	Vol. 2: 207 Vol. 3: 682
104.2–6	Vol. 3: 272
105.1–2	Vol. 3: 637
105.2	Vol. 2: 405 Vol. 3: 642
106	Vol. 2: 681 Vol. 3: 642
106.1–19	Vol. 2: 681
106.5	Vol. 2: 195
106.16	Vol. 3: 209
107	Vol. 2: 681
108.11 ff	Vol. 1: 423
108.12	Vol. 2: 279

4 Ezra. See 2 Esdras

Greek Book of Baruch (Gr. Bar.)

2 ff	Vol. 2: 202
2.2	Vol. 2: 762
4	Vol. 2: 207
4.17	Vol. 3: 31
6–9	Vol. 3: 731
8.5	Vol. 3: 31
13.2	Vol. 1: 554
13.4	Vol. 3: 31

Hebrew Book of Enoch (Heb. Enoch)

5.6	Vol. 2: 158
11.1	Vol. 3: 502
48C.7	Vol. 3: 35, 640
48D.1	Vol. 3: 35

Jubilees, Book of (Jub.)

1.11	Vol. 1: 452	
1.16	Vol. 2: 158	
1.17	Vol. 3: 509	
1.20	Vol. 3: 939	
1.22–25	Vol. 3: 637	
1.24 f	Vol. 1: 615, 618	
1.27 f	Vol. 3: 509	
1.27	Vol. 1: 104	
1.28	Vol. 1: 618	
1.29	Vol. 1: 104	
2.1	Vol. 1: 104	
2.2 f	Vol. 2: 603	
2.4	Vol. 3: 984	
2.17–33	Vol. 3: 407	
2.18	Vol. 3: 623	
2.20	Vol. 3: 637	
3.10	Vol. 1: 656	
4.17	Vol. 2: 817	Vol. 3: 265
4.20	Vol. 2: 698	
4.25	Vol. 3: 35	
5.1–12	Vol. 3: 468	
5.1	Vol. 1: 452	
5.6 ff	Vol. 2: 205	
5.14	Vol. 1: 423	
6.7	Vol. 1: 221	
6.12 ff	Vol. 1: 221	
6.17–21	Vol. 2: 784	
6.23–32	Vol. 1: 627	
6.32–38	Vol. 1: 627	
7.19	Vol. 3: 962	
7.27	Vol. 1: 452	
8.19	Vol. 1: 523	
8.25	Vol. 3: 962	
9.8	Vol. 3: 962	
9.15	Vol. 1: 656	
10.1 ff	Vol. 1: 452	
10.8	Vol. 3: 468	
10.17	Vol. 2: 817	
10.22	Vol. 2: 791	
11.19	Vol. 1: 572	
15	Vol. 1: 309	
15.13	Vol. 3: 669	
16.13	Vol. 3: 669	
16.18	Vol. 3: 37	
16.26	Vol. 3: 867	
17–19	Vol. 3: 801	
17	Vol. 3: 801	
19.9	Vol. 1: 243	
19.28	Vol. 3: 468	
19.29	Vol. 1: 618	Vol. 3: 637
22.1	Vol. 1: 104	
22.17	Vol. 1: 452	
23	Vol. 3: 692	
23.26	Vol. 3: 939	
23.30	Vol. 3: 610, 961	
24.22	Vol. 2: 279	
24.28	Vol. 1: 110	
24.30	Vol. 1: 110	
26–31	Vol. 3: 692	
30.5	Vol. 3: 456	
30.19 ff	Vol. 3: 486	
33.13	Vol. 1: 499	
33.18	Vol. 1: 499	
34.19	Vol. 3: 243	
36.10	Vol. 2: 767	
45.3	Vol. 3: 263	
47.5 f	Vol. 2: 309	
49.6	Vol. 3: 919	
50.5	Vol. 3: 160	
50.11	Vol. 3: 428	

Judith (Jud.)

2.2	Vol. 3: 502, 1016
2.15	Vol. 1: 341
2.20	Vol. 2: 396
3.8	Vol. 3: 821
4.9	Vol. 1: 612
4.12	Vol. 3: 908
4.13	Vol. 1: 612
5.8	Vol. 2: 876
5.19	Vol. 1: 685
6.1	Vol. 3: 255
6.14	Vol. 3: 177
6.16	Vol. 1: 197
6.18	Vol. 2: 876
6.19	Vol. 3: 30
6.21	Vol. 1: 197
7.18	Vol. 2: 801
8.1	Vol. 3: 873
8.6	Vol. 1: 626
8.12	Vol. 3: 799
8.14	Vol. 3: 125, 533, 823
8.16	Vol. 3: 613
8.18	Vol. 2: 876
8.25 f	Vol. 3: 799
8.25–27	Vol. 3: 778
8.25	Vol. 3: 818
8.26	Vol. 3: 800
8.31	Vol. 2: 93
9.2	Vol. 3: 177, 456, 873
9.6	Vol. 1: 693
9.8	Vol. 3: 256
9.11	Vol. 3: 263
9.12	Vol. 1: 381
10.2	Vol. 1: 626
10.5	Vol. 1: 143
10.8	Vol. 2: 876
10.15	Vol. 3: 209
10.18	Vol. 2: 898
10.23	Vol. 2: 876
11.3	Vol. 3: 209

Judith (Jud.) *(cont'd)*

11.13	**Vol. 3:** 416
11.17	**Vol. 2:** 863
11.19	**Vol. 1:** 693
12.1	**Vol. 1:** 341
12.6	**Vol. 2:** 863
12.7	**Vol. 1:** 144 **Vol. 3:** 228
12.9	**Vol. 3:** 228
12.10	**Vol. 1:** 272 **Vol. 3:** 957
13.3	**Vol. 2:** 863
13.5	**Vol. 3:** 836
13.6	**Vol. 3:** 399
13.7	**Vol. 3:** 716
13.10	**Vol. 1:** 143 **Vol. 2:** 863
13.13	**Vol. 3:** 860
13.14	**Vol. 3:** 816
13.15	**Vol. 1:** 143
13.17	**Vol. 2:** 876
13.18	**Vol. 1:** 380
13.19	**Vol. 3:** 233
14.7	**Vol. 2:** 876
15.2	**Vol. 3:** 908
15.5	**Vol. 3:** 908
15.9	**Vol. 3:** 908
15.11	**Vol. 3:** 1161
16.2	**Vol. 3:** 672
16.14	**Vol. 1:** 381
16.14b	**Vol. 1:** 381
16.17	**Vol. 3:** 110
16.18 f	**Vol. 1:** 414
16.18	**Vol. 2:** 876

1 Maccabees (1 Macc.)

1.1	**Vol. 2:** 124
1.10	**Vol. 2:** 124 **Vol. 3:** 318
1.11–15	**Vol. 1:** 688
1.13	**Vol. 3:** 354
1.15	**Vol. 1:** 268 **Vol. 2:** 228 **Vol. 3:** 799, 1161
1.17	**Vol. 2:** 801
1.20	**Vol. 2:** 801
1.21	**Vol. 3:** 29, 419, 788
1.22	**Vol. 3:** 794
1.23	**Vol. 2:** 215
1.24	**Vol. 3:** 29
1.29	**Vol. 2:** 801
1.36	**Vol. 3:** 468
1.38	**Vol. 1:** 286
1.39	**Vol. 1:** 626
1.43	**Vol. 3:** 550
1.45	**Vol. 1:** 626 **Vol. 3:** 428
1.46	**Vol. 2:** 227 **Vol. 3:** 418
1.47	**Vol. 1:** 641
1.48 ff	**Vol. 1:** 309
1.49	**Vol. 3:** 354
1.54 ff	**Vol. 1:** 74–75
1.54	**Vol. 3:** 418–419, 788, 1006
1.59	**Vol. 3:** 418
1.60 f	**Vol. 1:** 309

1.62	**Vol. 1:** 448
1.63	**Vol. 2:** 228
2.6	**Vol. 3:** 342
2.19	**Vol. 1:** 607 **Vol. 3:** 550
2.21	**Vol. 3:** 157, 354
2.22	**Vol. 3:** 550
2.23 ff	**Vol. 3:** 418
2.28	**Vol. 3:** 381
2.40	**Vol. 3:** 354
2.42	**Vol. 2:** 237, 810
2.44	**Vol. 3:** 209
2.45	**Vol. 3:** 418
2.47	**Vol. 3:** 29
2.49	**Vol. 3:** 29
2.52	**Vol. 3:** 369, 799, 823, 1188
2.53	**Vol. 2:** 134
2.54	**Vol. 3:** 36
2.57	**Vol. 3:** 649
2.58	**Vol. 3:** 747
2.60	**Vol. 3:** 202, 951
2.63	**Vol. 3:** 820
2.68	**Vol. 3:** 428
3.2	**Vol. 2:** 349
3.6	**Vol. 3:** 209
3.18 f	**Vol. 2:** 191
3.18	**Vol. 3:** 209
3.19	**Vol. 1:** 650
3.20	**Vol. 3:** 29
3.26	**Vol. 1:** 574
3.28	**Vol. 3:** 144, 796
3.30	**Vol. 1:** 729
3.34	**Vol. 2:** 310
3.44	**Vol. 2:** 863
3.45	**Vol. 3:** 794
3.46	**Vol. 2:** 863
3.52	**Vol. 3:** 823
4.9	**Vol. 3:** 209
4.10 f	**Vol. 2:** 191
4.11	**Vol. 3:** 192, 194, 209
4.18	**Vol. 2:** 735
4.23	**Vol. 2:** 842
4.24	**Vol. 3:** 669
4.25	**Vol. 3:** 209
4.30	**Vol. 2:** 863 **Vol. 3:** 218
4.33	**Vol. 3:** 669, 816
4.35	**Vol. 3:** 823
4.36–59	**Vol. 1:** 629 **Vol. 3:** 788
4.36–41	**Vol. 1:** 626
4.42	**Vol. 3:** 924
4.44–49	**Vol. 3:** 419
4.46 ff	**Vol. 3:** 80, 311
4.49 ff	**Vol. 3:** 788
4.51	**Vol. 3:** 794
4.54–59	**Vol. 3:** 366
4.54	**Vol. 3:** 673
4.55	**Vol. 2:** 876
5.19	**Vol. 1:** 194
5.33	**Vol. 2:** 863
5.39	**Vol. 2:** 139
5.49	**Vol. 3:** 51

273

1 Maccabees (1 Macc.) *(cont'd)*

5.58	Vol. 1: 340
5.62	Vol. 3: 209
5.68	Vol. 3: 418
6.1	Vol. 2: 842
6.2	Vol. 2: 124, 841
6.9	Vol. 3: 823
6.10	Vol. 1: 277
6.15	Vol. 3: 498
6.17	Vol. 2: 675
6.19	Vol. 3: 823
6.21	Vol. 2: 349
6.29	Vol. 2: 139
6.38	Vol. 3: 557
6.40	Vol. 1: 663
6.44	Vol. 3: 209
6.49	Vol. 3: 191
6.53	Vol. 3: 191
6.60	Vol. 2: 776, 815
6.63	Vol. 3: 711
7.7	Vol. 3: 98
7.12 ff	Vol. 3: 479
7.12	Vol. 3: 358
7.13	Vol. 2: 237, 810
7.16	Vol. 3: 479
7.18	Vol. 3: 882
7.31	Vol. 3: 311
7.37	Vol. 2: 863
7.38	Vol. 3: 229
7.40	Vol. 2: 863
8.9	Vol. 2: 124
8.12	Vol. 3: 255
8.18	Vol. 2: 124 Vol. 3: 1161
8.23 ff	Vol. 2: 310
8.23	Vol. 1: 515
8.26	Vol. 2: 134 Vol. 3: 821
8.28	Vol. 2: 134 Vol. 3: 821
8.29	Vol. 2: 789
8.31	Vol. 3: 1161
8.32	Vol. 1: 515
9.9	Vol. 3: 209
9.10	Vol. 2: 138
9.12–13·	Vol. 3: 874
9.21	Vol. 3: 209
9.27	Vol. 3: 80, 311
9.35	Vol. 2: 801
9.39	Vol. 2: 578
9.46	Vol. 3: 209
9.58	Vol. 3: 111
9.73	Vol. 3: 255
10.3	Vol. 1: 246
10.7	Vol. 1: 246
10.17–20	Vol. 1: 246
10.20 f	Vol. 3: 35
10.24	Vol. 2: 199
10.26 f	Vol. 3: 226
10.29	Vol. 1: 406 Vol. 3: 444
10.31	Vol. 3: 756
10.34	Vol. 3: 570
10.37	Vol. 3: 957
10.38	Vol. 2: 173 Vol. 3: 452, 823
10.42	Vol. 3: 957
10.43	Vol. 2: 667
10.47	Vol. 2: 817
10.52	Vol. 3: 716
10.63 f	Vol. 3: 51
10.83	Vol. 2: 284 Vol. 3: 209
10.84	Vol. 3: 785
10.89	Vol. 2: 437
11.4	Vol. 3: 785
11.8	Vol. 3: 820, 823
11.24	Vol. 3: 452
11.28	Vol. 3: 70
11.29–37	Vol. 1: 246
11.33	Vol. 3: 358
11.35	Vol. 3: 444, 756, 992
11.48	Vol. 3: 209
11.54	Vol. 2: 675
11.57	Vol. 2: 675 Vol. 3: 452
11.58	Vol. 3: 545
11.71	Vol. 2: 863
12.5–23	Vol. 1: 246
12.6	Vol. 2: 789
12.9	Vol. 1: 243
12.10	Vol. 3: 799
12.11	Vol. 2: 669, 863 Vol. 3: 229
12.15	Vol. 2: 191
12.25	Vol. 2: 765
12.27	Vol. 2: 136
12.29	Vol. 2: 227
12.45	Vol. 3: 957
13.15	Vol. 3: 957
13.31	Vol. 2: 675
13.37	Vol. 1: 406 Vol. 3: 957
13.39	Vol. 2: 667 Vol. 3: 756
13.45	Vol. 1: 410
13.47	Vol. 2: 285 Vol. 3: 669
13.51	Vol. 3: 669, 673, 675
14.9	Vol. 1: 314
14.11	Vol. 2: 357
14.20–25	Vol. 2: 789
14.22	Vol. 3: 1016
14.23	Vol. 3: 570
14.32	Vol. 3: 144
14.36	Vol. 3: 101
14.41	Vol. 2: 817 Vol. 3: 80, 311
14.49	Vol. 3: 796
15.3	Vol. 3: 147
15.8	Vol. 2: 666
15.9	Vol. 3: 786
15.17	Vol. 2: 789
15.20	Vol. 3: 821
15.22 f	Vol. 2: 309
16.2	Vol. 3: 201

2 Maccabees (2 Macc.)

1.1–9	Vol. 1: 246
1.2	Vol. 2: 318

2 Maccabees (2 Macc.) *(cont'd)*

1.4	**Vol. 1:** 341
1.5	**Vol. 3:** 166–167
1.6	**Vol. 2:** 863
1.9	**Vol. 3:** 813
1.10–2.18	**Vol. 1:** 246
1.10	**Vol. 3:** 766
1.11	**Vol. 3:** 818
1.13	**Vol. 3:** 821
1.16	**Vol. 2:** 215 **Vol. 3:** 381
1.19 ff	**Vol. 3:** 428
1.20	**Vol. 1:** 341 **Vol. 3:** 821
1.23 f	**Vol. 2:** 863
1.23	**Vol. 1:** 409
1.24 ff	**Vol. 1:** 382
1.24	**Vol. 2:** 105
1.25	**Vol. 3:** 209
1.27	**Vol. 1:** 685
1.28	**Vol. 3:** 29
1.30	**Vol. 3:** 669
1.34	**Vol. 3:** 808
1.36	**Vol. 1:** 580
2.4 ff	**Vol. 1:** 252
2.4	**Vol. 3:** 325
2.7	**Vol. 3:** 157
2.8	**Vol. 3:** 316
2.9	**Vol. 3:** 786
2.10†	**Vol. 2:** 863
2.13	**Vol. 1:** 377, 414, 574
2.17	**Vol. 3:** 37
2.19	**Vol. 3:** 418
2.21	**Vol. 2:** 310
2.22	**Vol. 3:** 157, 178
2.23	**Vol. 3:** 799
2.24	**Vol. 3:** 318
2.25	**Vol. 3:** 238
2.27	**Vol. 3:** 119, 818
2.29	**Vol. 1:** 377 **Vol. 3:** 821
3.1 ff	**Vol. 3:** 428
3.6	**Vol. 3:** 796
3.7	**Vol. 1:** 476
3.8	**Vol. 1:** 696
3.10	**Vol. 3:** 1074
3.12	**Vol. 2:** 93
3.22	**Vol. 1:** 663
3.24	**Vol. 3:** 796
3.26	**Vol. 3:** 229
3.28	**Vol. 3:** 796
3.29	**Vol. 3:** 209, 1147
3.32 ff	**Vol. 3:** 428
3.32	**Vol. 3:** 209
3.33	**Vol. 3:** 156
3.40	**Vol. 3:** 796
4.1	**Vol. 1:** 387
4.2	**Vol. 1:** 415
4.3	**Vol. 3:** 808
4.5	**Vol. 2:** 803
4.6	**Vol. 1:** 694 **Vol. 3:** 125
4.10	**Vol. 2:** 124
4.11	**Vol. 1:** 645 **Vol. 2:** 803
4.12–15	**Vol. 3:** 35
4.13	**Vol. 2:** 311
4.14	**Vol. 3:** 550
4.15	**Vol. 2:** 124
4.18	**Vol. 1:** 645
4.21	**Vol. 1:** 324, 663
4.24	**Vol. 1:** 324
4.27	**Vol. 3:** 716
4.34	**Vol. 3:** 561
4.36	**Vol. 2:** 124
4.38	**Vol. 3:** 98
4.40	**Vol. 3:** 125
4.41	**Vol. 3:** 381
4.42	**Vol. 2:** 138 **Vol. 3:** 796
4.44	**Vol. 1:** 324
4.47	**Vol. 3:** 859
4.50	**Vol. 1:** 137 **Vol. 2:** 803
5.5	**Vol. 3:** 604
5.6	**Vol. 2:** 803 **Vol. 3:** 821
5.8	**Vol. 1:** 607 **Vol. 2:** 803 **Vol. 3:** 933
5.12	**Vol. 1:** 341
5.15	**Vol. 3:** 727
5.18	**Vol. 3:** 796
5.20	**Vol. 3:** 166
5.21	**Vol. 3:** 29
5.23	**Vol. 2:** 803
5.25	**Vol. 2:** 468
6.1 ff	**Vol. 2:** 125
6.1	**Vol. 2:** 803
6.6 f	**Vol. 1:** 626
6.7	**Vol. 2:** 663
6.8	**Vol. 2:** 124
6.9	**Vol. 2:** 124
6.11	**Vol. 2:** 93 **Vol. 3:** 381
6.12–17	**Vol. 3:** 778
6.12–16	**Vol. 1:** 734
6.12	**Vol. 1:** 734 **Vol. 3:** 823
6.13	**Vol. 1:** 734
6.14	**Vol. 1:** 324, 735 **Vol. 3:** 98
6.20	**Vol. 2:** 773
6.21	**Vol. 2:** 468 **Vol. 3:** 119
6.23	**Vol. 2:** 803 **Vol. 3:** 823, 933
6.24	**Vol. 2:** 207, 468
6.28	**Vol. 2:** 93, 290
6.30	**Vol. 3:** 721
6.31	**Vol. 1:** 435 **Vol. 2:** 290 **Vol. 3:** 926
7.5	**Vol. 1:** 341
7.6	**Vol. 3:** 673
7.7	**Vol. 1:** 665
7.8	**Vol. 3:** 1153
7.9	**Vol. 1:** 506 **Vol. 2:** 928 **Vol. 3:** 200, 270–271
7.11 f	**Vol. 3:** 270
7.11	**Vol. 3:** 200, 270–271
7.13 f	**Vol. 3:** 270
7.13	**Vol. 3:** 856
7.14	**Vol. 2:** 928 **Vol. 3:** 200, 271
7.16	**Vol. 3:** 821
7.18	**Vol. 3:** 721

275

2 Maccabees (2 Macc.) *(cont'd)*

7.20	**Vol. 3:** 238, 348
7.21	**Vol. 2:** 569 **Vol. 3:** 823
7.22 f	**Vol. 3:** 271
7.23	**Vol. 1:** 382 **Vol. 3:** 270
7.24	**Vol. 2:** 841 **Vol. 3:** 957
7.25	**Vol. 3:** 209
7.29	**Vol. 3:** 270–271
7.32	**Vol. 3:** 721
7.33	**Vol. 3:** 166–167, 610
7.34	**Vol. 2:** 191
7.36 f	**Vol. 3:** 270
7.36	**Vol. 3:** 29
7.37	**Vol. 1:** 235, 345 **Vol. 3:** 157, 195–196
8.1	**Vol. 2:** 310
8.3	**Vol. 1:** 410
8.4	**Vol. 3:** 341–342
8.9	**Vol. 1:** 476
8.10	**Vol. 1:** 734
8.11	**Vol. 3:** 93
8.12	**Vol. 2:** 898
8.15	**Vol. 2:** 93
8.16	**Vol. 2:** 684
8.17	**Vol. 2:** 803 **Vol. 3:** 29
8.18	**Vol. 2:** 69
8.21	**Vol. 2:** 480
8.23	**Vol. 1:** 245
8.27	**Vol. 3:** 209
8.28	**Vol. 3:** 1074
8.29	**Vol. 3:** 166–167
8.30	**Vol. 2:** 498 **Vol. 3:** 1074
8.33	**Vol. 2:** 139
9.4	**Vol. 3:** 30, 229, 342
9.5	**Vol. 2:** 599
9.6	**Vol. 2:** 599
9.7 f	**Vol. 3:** 29
9.7	**Vol. 1:** 341
9.8	**Vol. 3:** 30, 821
9.10	**Vol. 3:** 734, 821
9.11	**Vol. 3:** 29
9.12	**Vol. 2:** 498, 765 **Vol. 3:** 29–30, 342
9.18	**Vol. 3:** 358
9.19	**Vol. 2:** 170, 803
9.21	**Vol. 1:** 663
9.27	**Vol. 2:** 257
9.28†	**Vol. 3:** 341–342
10.1–8	**Vol. 1:** 626
10.2	**Vol. 1:** 387 **Vol. 3:** 418
10.4	**Vol. 3:** 341–342, 585
10.6	**Vol. 3:** 381
10.7	**Vol. 3:** 669, 818
10.8	**Vol. 1:** 330
10.12	**Vol. 3:** 799
10.19	**Vol. 3:** 534
10.26	**Vol. 3:** 157, 484
10.28	**Vol. 1:** 372
10.34	**Vol. 3:** 341–342
10.35	**Vol. 3:** 342
10.38	**Vol. 3:** 669
11.2	**Vol. 2:** 124 **Vol. 3:** 823
11.6	**Vol. 3:** 209
11.14	**Vol. 3:** 358
11.17	**Vol. 3:** 325
11.19	**Vol. 3:** 799
11.20	**Vol. 3:** 820
11.24	**Vol. 2:** 124
11.25	**Vol. 2:** 437, 803
11.34	**Vol. 2:** 789
12.7	**Vol. 2:** 803
12.12	**Vol. 3:** 534
12.14	**Vol. 3:** 342, 346
12.15	**Vol. 3:** 841
12.16	**Vol. 3:** 992
12.25	**Vol. 3:** 209
12.31	**Vol. 3:** 818
12.32	**Vol. 2:** 783
12.37	**Vol. 3:** 669
12.41	**Vol. 2:** 216
12.43 f	**Vol. 3:** 270
12.43	**Vol. 3:** 271, 820
12.44	**Vol. 2:** 863
13.2	**Vol. 2:** 124
13.3	**Vol. 3:** 209
13.4	**Vol. 2:** 437
13.8	**Vol. 3:** 418
13.9	**Vol. 1:** 261
13.10	**Vol. 1:** 340
13.12	**Vol. 1:** 341 **Vol. 3:** 229
13.14	**Vol. 1:** 382 **Vol. 2:** 803
13.15	**Vol. 1:** 650
13.21	**Vol. 3:** 502
13.22	**Vol. 3:** 358
14.3	**Vol. 3:** 209
14.4	**Vol. 1:** 406
14.5	**Vol. 3:** 125
14.6	**Vol. 2:** 237, 810
14.8	**Vol. 2:** 803
14.9	**Vol. 1:** 694
14.12	**Vol. 1:** 476
14.14	**Vol. 3:** 821
14.15	**Vol. 3:** 318
14.23	**Vol. 2:** 801
14.26	**Vol. 3:** 570
14.27	**Vol. 1:** 341
14.31	**Vol. 1:** 341
14.33	**Vol. 3:** 318
14.36	**Vol. 3:** 923–924
14.38	**Vol. 2:** 310
14.40	**Vol. 3:** 821
14.41	**Vol. 3:** 711
14.42	**Vol. 3:** 29
14.43	**Vol. 2:** 801
14.45 f	**Vol. 2:** 801
14.46	**Vol. 3:** 270–271
15.1	**Vol. 1:** 663 **Vol. 3:** 256
15.2	**Vol. 2:** 224, 663
15.4	**Vol. 1:** 341, 495
15.5	**Vol. 3:** 957
15.6	**Vol. 3:** 30

2 Maccabees (2 Macc.) *(cont'd)*

15.7	**Vol. 3:** 229
15.8 f	**Vol. 1:** 329
15.8	**Vol. 3:** 125
15.10	**Vol. 3:** 584
15.11 ff	**Vol. 1:** 512
15.11	**Vol. 1:** 663
15.14	**Vol. 2:** 863
15.17	**Vol. 3:** 926
15.20	**Vol. 2:** 303
15.21	**Vol. 2:** 898
15.23	**Vol. 2:** 191
15.24	**Vol. 3:** 342
15.27	**Vol. 3:** 318
15.30	**Vol. 2:** 803
15.33	**Vol. 3:** 125
15.34	**Vol. 3:** 318, 923–924
15.36	**Vol. 1:** 330 **Vol. 3:** 411
15.37	**Vol. 3:** 255

3 Maccabees (3 Macc.)

1.3	**Vol. 1:** 330 **Vol. 3:** 98
1.4	**Vol. 3:** 177
1.16	**Vol. 2:** 663
1.19	**Vol. 3:** 561
1.22	**Vol. 1:** 696 **Vol. 2:** 765, 803
1.23	**Vol. 3:** 902
1.25	**Vol. 3:** 799
1.26	**Vol. 3:** 821
1.27	**Vol. 3:** 29
1.29	**Vol. 3:** 821
2.2	**Vol. 2:** 191
2.3	**Vol. 1:** 380 **Vol. 3:** 29
2.5	**Vol. 3:** 29
2.6	**Vol. 3:** 808
2.7	**Vol. 2:** 801
2.8	**Vol. 3:** 816
2.9	**Vol. 1:** 380
2.10	**Vol. 3:** 70
2.17	**Vol. 3:** 29
2.19	**Vol. 3:** 318
2.21	**Vol. 3:** 29
2.22	**Vol. 3:** 113
2.26	**Vol. 1:** 696
2.27	**Vol. 1:** 696
2.28	**Vol. 3:** 711
2.29	**Vol. 2:** 574
2.30	**Vol. 2:** 498 **Vol. 3:** 502
2.32	**Vol. 3:** 201, 799
3.4 ff	**Vol. 2:** 310
3.4	**Vol. 2:** 803
3.7	**Vol. 2:** 876
3.8	**Vol. 2:** 124
3.15	**Vol. 3:** 711
3.16	**Vol. 3:** 125, 786
3.17	**Vol. 2:** 898
3.20	**Vol. 2:** 669 **Vol. 3:** 125
3.21	**Vol. 2:** 233
3.24	**Vol. 1:** 694 **Vol. 3:** 571

3.25	**Vol. 2:** 669 **Vol. 3:** 29
3.26	**Vol. 3:** 98
3.28	**Vol. 2:** 846
3.29	**Vol. 2:** 658
3.30	**Vol. 3:** 904
4.1	**Vol. 2:** 735
4.4	**Vol. 3:** 823, 908
4.5	**Vol. 3:** 561
4.6	**Vol. 3:** 908
4.7	**Vol. 3:** 711
4.9	**Vol. 2:** 663 **Vol. 3:** 1161
4.16	**Vol. 3:** 816
4.20	**Vol. 3:** 570
4.21	**Vol. 3:** 1147
5.2	**Vol. 2:** 684
5.5 f	**Vol. 3:** 821
5.6	**Vol. 2:** 663
5.7	**Vol. 1:** 618
5.11	**Vol. 1:** 382
5.12	**Vol. 1:** 696 **Vol. 3:** 823, 1147
5.13	**Vol. 3:** 29, 816
5.14	**Vol. 1:** 272
5.16	**Vol. 3:** 823
5.22	**Vol. 3:** 821
5.28	**Vol. 3:** 1147
5.29	**Vol. 1:** 696
5.30	**Vol. 1:** 694 **Vol. 3:** 125
5.31	**Vol. 3:** 570, 923
5.35	**Vol. 3:** 318, 816
5.40	**Vol. 3:** 821
5.49	**Vol. 3:** 821
5.51	**Vol. 2:** 30
6.1	**Vol. 2:** 863
6.2	**Vol. 2:** 69
6.3	**Vol. 1:** 618
6.4	**Vol. 3:** 29, 318
6.8	**Vol. 1:** 618
6.9	**Vol. 3:** 29, 318
6.10	**Vol. 3:** 201
6.11	**Vol. 3:** 202
6.12	**Vol. 3:** 29
6.13	**Vol. 3:** 209
6.16	**Vol. 2:** 863
6.19	**Vol. 1:** 622
6.27	**Vol. 2:** 839 **Vol. 3:** 177
6.29	**Vol. 3:** 177, 218
6.30	**Vol. 3:** 166, 821
6.32	**Vol. 3:** 218, 673, 816
6.33	**Vol. 3:** 209, 229
6.34	**Vol. 3:** 109
6.36	**Vol. 3:** 209
6.37	**Vol. 2:** 839
7.3	**Vol. 3:** 98
7.6	**Vol. 1:** 663
7.8	**Vol. 2:** 839
7.12	**Vol. 2:** 735
7.13	**Vol. 1:** 409 **Vol. 2:** 669
7.14	**Vol. 2:** 291 **Vol. 3:** 98
7.16	**Vol. 3:** 209, 218, 263, 669, 818
7.17	**Vol. 3:** 228, 1016

277

3 Maccabees (3 Macc.) *(cont'd)*

7.19	**Vol. 1:** 691	**Vol. 2:** 669
7.20	**Vol. 2:** 863	**Vol. 3:** 209
7.21	**Vol. 3:** 557	
7.22	**Vol. 3:** 209	

4 Maccabees (4 Macc.)

1.1–35	**Vol. 3:** 823	
1.1	**Vol. 2:** 93	**Vol. 3:** 1035
1.2	**Vol. 3:** 926	
1.5	**Vol. 3:** 716	
1.7	**Vol. 2:** 93	
1.8	**Vol. 3:** 570, 926	
1.10	**Vol. 2:** 49	**Vol. 3:** 816, 926
1.11	**Vol. 2:** 773	**Vol. 3:** 611
1.14	**Vol. 1:** 503	
1.15	**Vol. 2:** 475, 846	
1.16	**Vol. 2:** 138	
1.17	**Vol. 2:** 93	
1.20	**Vol. 2:** 658	
1.26	**Vol. 3:** 30	
1.29	**Vol. 2:** 437	
1.30	**Vol. 3:** 926	
1.33	**Vol. 3:** 902	
1.35	**Vol. 2:** 765	**Vol. 3:** 125
2.2–24†	**Vol. 3:** 823	
2.2	**Vol. 3:** 816	
2.3	**Vol. 2:** 675	
2.7	**Vol. 2:** 437	
2.8	**Vol. 2:** 803	**Vol. 3:** 711
2.11	**Vol. 3:** 98	
2.15	**Vol. 3:** 30	
2.16	**Vol. 3:** 125	
2.21 f	**Vol. 2:** 565	
2.21	**Vol. 2:** 437	
2.23	**Vol. 2:** 377, 803	
3.1–19	**Vol. 3:** 823	
3.9	**Vol. 2:** 521	
3.11	**Vol. 3:** 177	
3.15	**Vol. 3:** 823	
3.17	**Vol. 1:** 650	**Vol. 2:** 663 **Vol. 3:** 109
3.19	**Vol. 3:** 570	
3.20	**Vol. 2:** 803	**Vol. 3:** 1156
4.3	**Vol. 3:** 786, 796	
4.4	**Vol. 3:** 816	
4.6	**Vol. 3:** 796	
4.11	**Vol. 2:** 191, 863	
4.12	**Vol. 3:** 669	
4.14	**Vol. 3:** 209	
4.15	**Vol. 3:** 29	
4.22	**Vol. 2:** 325	
4.23	**Vol. 1:** 330	**Vol. 2:** 803
4.26	**Vol. 2:** 310	**Vol. 3:** 856
5.2	**Vol. 2:** 284	
5.6	**Vol. 3:** 561, 821, 856, 1035	
5.8 f	**Vol. 3:** 126	
5.8	**Vol. 2:** 658	
5.9	**Vol. 3:** 821	
5.10	**Vol. 3:** 823, 1035	

5.11	**Vol. 3:** 1035	
5.12	**Vol. 2:** 876	
5.13	**Vol. 2:** 663	
5.16	**Vol. 2:** 663, 803	
5.18	**Vol. 2:** 93	
5.20	**Vol. 1:** 334	
5.22	**Vol. 3:** 1035	
5.23	**Vol. 2:** 773	
5.24	**Vol. 2:** 93, 437, 498 **Vol. 3:** 761	
5.25	**Vol. 1:** 382 **Vol. 2:** 658	
5.28	**Vol. 2:** 431	
5.29	**Vol. 2:** 134	
5.30	**Vol. 2:** 599	
5.31	**Vol. 2:** 93 **Vol. 3:** 823	
5.34	**Vol. 1:** 495	
5.35	**Vol. 3:** 1035	
5.36	**Vol. 2:** 93, 475	
5.37	**Vol. 2:** 663 **Vol. 3:** 682	
5.38	**Vol. 2:** 93 **Vol. 3:** 823	
6.2	**Vol. 2:** 93	
6.4	**Vol. 3:** 50	
6.5	**Vol. 3:** 856	
6.7	**Vol. 3:** 823	
6.9	**Vol. 1:** 461 **Vol. 2:** 663, 773	
6.10 f	**Vol. 3:** 856	
6.11	**Vol. 3:** 904	
6.15	**Vol. 2:** 468	
6.16	**Vol. 1:** 410	
6.17	**Vol. 2:** 468	
6.18	**Vol. 2:** 134	
6.19	**Vol. 2:** 675	
6.22	**Vol. 2:** 93	
6.24	**Vol. 2:** 663	
6.27	**Vol. 3:** 856	
6.28 f	**Vol. 3:** 193, 611	
6.28	**Vol. 3:** 157, 195–196, 727	
6.30–35	**Vol. 3:** 823	
6.30	**Vol. 3:** 856	
6.31	**Vol. 2:** 93	
6.33	**Vol. 1:** 650	
7.1–24	**Vol. 3:** 823	
7.2	**Vol. 3:** 856	
7.7	**Vol. 2:** 475, 846 **Vol. 3:** 1035	
7.9	**Vol. 2:** 773 **Vol. 3:** 1035	
7.11	**Vol. 2:** 293	
7.13	**Vol. 3:** 177	
7.15	**Vol. 2:** 93, 475	
7.16	**Vol. 1:** 461 **Vol. 2:** 93 **Vol. 3:** 856	
7.18	**Vol. 1:** 694	
7.19	**Vol. 2:** 480	
7.21	**Vol. 2:** 93 **Vol. 3:** 399, 1035	
7.22	**Vol. 2:** 773 **Vol. 3:** 926	
7.23	**Vol. 3:** 1028	
7.24	**Vol. 3:** 1035	
8 ff	**Vol. 2:** 690	
8.2	**Vol. 3:** 856	
8.5	**Vol. 1:** 529 **Vol. 3:** 856	
8.6	**Vol. 3:** 98	
8.7	**Vol. 1:** 455 **Vol. 2:** 803	
8.8	**Vol. 2:** 124, 846	

4 Maccabees (4 Macc.) *(cont'd)*

8.9	**Vol. 3:** 98, 856
8.11	**Vol. 3:** 820
8.14	**Vol. 2:** 663 **Vol. 3:** 157
8.16	**Vol. 3:** 823
8.17	**Vol. 3:** 126
8.19	**Vol. 3:** 30, 823, 856
8.22	**Vol. 2:** 663
8.23	**Vol. 2:** 475
8.24†	**Vol. 2:** 663 **Vol. 3:** 711
8.26	**Vol. 3:** 957
8.27	**Vol. 3:** 856
9.4	**Vol. 3:** 209
9.5 f	**Vol. 3:** 856
9.6	**Vol. 2:** 93, 663, 773 **Vol. 3:** 856
9.7	**Vol. 3:** 799, 856
9.8	**Vol. 2:** 773 **Vol. 3:** 926
9.9	**Vol. 2:** 767 **Vol. 3:** 856
9.15	**Vol. 3:** 856
9.16	**Vol. 3:** 166, 856
9.17	**Vol. 3:** 545, 823
9.18	**Vol. 3:** 856, 926
9.20	**Vol. 3:** 109
9.22	**Vol. 1:** 709 **Vol. 2:** 773
9.24	**Vol. 1:** 694 **Vol. 2:** 157
9.27	**Vol. 3:** 856
9.28	**Vol. 2:** 767
9.30	**Vol. 2:** 773 **Vol. 3:** 29, 821, 823, 856
9.32	**Vol. 1:** 491 **Vol. 3:** 856
10.1 f	**Vol. 2:** 767
10.1	**Vol. 1:** 435
10.2	**Vol. 1:** 410
10.5	**Vol. 2:** 735
10.8	**Vol. 2:** 599
10.10	**Vol. 3:** 926
10.11	**Vol. 3:** 856
10.13	**Vol. 1:** 529
10.15	**Vol. 1:** 455 **Vol. 2:** 93 **Vol. 3:** 827
10.16	**Vol. 3:** 856
10.19	**Vol. 3:** 823
10.21	**Vol. 3:** 119, 669
11.1	**Vol. 3:** 856
11.2	**Vol. 3:** 856, 926
11.5	**Vol. 1:** 382 **Vol. 2:** 93 **Vol. 3:** 821
11.6	**Vol. 3:** 856
11.8	**Vol. 2:** 93
11.12	**Vol. 2:** 117
11.16	**Vol. 3:** 821, 856
11.20	**Vol. 1:** 645 **Vol. 3:** 856
11.23	**Vol. 2:** 93 **Vol. 3:** 856
11.25	**Vol. 3:** 711, 823
11.26	**Vol. 3:** 711
11.27	**Vol. 3:** 823
12.3	**Vol. 3:** 799
12.4	**Vol. 3:** 856
12.6	**Vol. 3:** 209
12.8 f	**Vol. 3:** 177
12.12	**Vol. 3:** 856
12.13	**Vol. 2:** 452 **Vol. 3:** 856
12.18	**Vol. 3:** 157
13.1	**Vol. 3:** 823
13.3	**Vol. 3:** 816, 823
13.7	**Vol. 3:** 98
13.9	**Vol. 1:** 491
13.10	**Vol. 3:** 570
13.11	**Vol. 2:** 767
13.12	**Vol. 2:** 773
13.14	**Vol. 3:** 821
13.15	**Vol. 3:** 856
13.16	**Vol. 3:** 823
13.17	**Vol. 3:** 682, 816
13.19	**Vol. 1:** 694
13.24	**Vol. 2:** 542
13.27	**Vol. 2:** 437, 658, 765 **Vol. 3:** 856
14.1	**Vol. 1:** 461
14.2	**Vol. 3:** 823
14.5	**Vol. 3:** 682, 856, 946
14.8	**Vol. 3:** 856
14.9	**Vol. 2:** 767
14.11	**Vol. 3:** 823, 856
15.1	**Vol. 3:** 823
15.2	**Vol. 3:** 209
15.3	**Vol. 2:** 480, 542 **Vol. 3:** 119, 209
15.4	**Vol. 2:** 502
15.8	**Vol. 3:** 209
15.10	**Vol. 2:** 134
15.11	**Vol. 3:** 823, 856
15.12	**Vol. 2:** 480
15.16	**Vol. 3:** 799
15.18–22	**Vol. 3:** 856
15.22	**Vol. 2:** 574, 599 **Vol. 3:** 856
15.23	**Vol. 3:** 823
15.24	**Vol. 1:** 598 **Vol. 3:** 1211
15.25	**Vol. 2:** 658
15.27	**Vol. 3:** 209
15.29	**Vol. 2:** 599, 690
15.30	**Vol. 2:** 569, 773
15.31 f	**Vol. 2:** 773
15.32	**Vol. 3:** 856
16.1 f	**Vol. 3:** 856
16.1	**Vol. 2:** 773 **Vol. 3:** 823
16.2	**Vol. 3:** 570
16.3	**Vol. 2:** 658 **Vol. 3:** 856, 951
16.4	**Vol. 3:** 823
16.8	**Vol. 2:** 773
16.13	**Vol. 1:** 435
16.15	**Vol. 3:** 856
16.16–23	**Vol. 1:** 714
16.17	**Vol. 2:** 773 **Vol. 3:** 856
16.18	**Vol. 3:** 240
16.19	**Vol. 2:** 773
16.21	**Vol. 2:** 773 **Vol. 3:** 951
16.22	**Vol. 1:** 598 **Vol. 3:** 1211
16.25	**Vol. 2:** 480
17.2	**Vol. 1:** 598 **Vol. 3:** 711
17.3	**Vol. 3:** 856
17.4	**Vol. 2:** 773
17.5	**Vol. 2:** 93
17.7	**Vol. 2:** 773 **Vol. 3:** 856

4 Maccabees (4 Macc.) (cont'd)

17.9	Vol. 3: 711
17.10	Vol. 2: 773 Vol. 3: 856
17.11	Vol. 1: 645
17.12	Vol. 1: 435 Vol. 2: 480, 773 Vol. 3: 682, 808, 926
17.14 ff	Vol. 1: 646
17.17	Vol. 2: 773 Vol. 3: 926
17.18 ff	Vol. 3: 348
17.18	Vol. 1: 474
17.19	Vol. 2: 803
17.20 f	Vol. 3: 611
17.20	Vol. 2: 49
17.21 f	Vol. 3: 195–196
17.22	Vol. 1: 694 Vol. 3: 157, 164–165, 193, 209
17.23	Vol. 2: 290, 773 Vol. 3: 856, 926
18.2	Vol. 2: 93 Vol. 3: 823
18.3	Vol. 1: 235
18.5	Vol. 2: 437 Vol. 3: 98
18.6	Vol. 3: 354
18.7	Vol. 2: 134
18.10	Vol. 3: 761
18.11 ff	Vol. 3: 1042
18.12	Vol. 3: 761
18.13	Vol. 3: 951
18.15	Vol. 3: 669
18.18	Vol. 3: 673, 761
18.19	Vol. 2: 480
18.20	Vol. 2: 124 Vol. 3: 109, 856
18.22	Vol. 2: 325

Manasses, Prayer of (Man.)

5	Vol. 1: 109
9 f	Vol. 1: 108

Martyrdom of Isaiah (Mart. Isa.)

2.1	Vol. 1: 125
2.3 ff	Vol. 3: 806
2.8–11	Vol. 3: 1006–1007
3.11	Vol. 1: 125

Psalms of Solomon (Pss. Sol.)

2.1 f	Vol. 3: 815
2.6	Vol. 2: 573
2.10	Vol. 3: 358
2.15	Vol. 3: 358
2.18	Vol. 3: 358
2.30 f	Vol. 3: 815
2.32	Vol. 3: 358
2.34	Vol. 3: 358
3.1 ff	Vol. 2: 364
3.3	Vol. 3: 358
3.4–8	Vol. 3: 358
3.4	Vol. 3: 778
3.5	Vol. 3: 210, 358
3.16	Vol. 2: 480, 928
4	Vol. 3: 749
4.7	Vol. 2: 815
4.8	Vol. 2: 815
4.9	Vol. 3: 358
4.19	Vol. 2: 815
4.21	Vol. 3: 233
5.1–12	Vol. 2: 266
5.1	Vol. 3: 358
5.2	Vol. 2: 824
5.6	Vol. 2: 811
5.11	Vol. 2: 824
6.1	Vol. 3: 210
8.7	Vol. 3: 358
8.8	Vol. 3: 358
8.14	Vol. 3: 913
8.16 ff	Vol. 1: 125
8.22	Vol. 2: 818
8.23	Vol. 3: 358
8.26	Vol. 3: 358
8.28	Vol. 1: 685
9.1	Vol. 3: 193
9.2	Vol. 3: 358
9.6 f	Vol. 2: 867
9.9	Vol. 2: 831
9.12	Vol. 1: 345
10.1–6	Vol. 2: 266
10.2	Vol. 3: 165
10.4	Vol. 3: 241
10.5	Vol. 3: 358
10.6	Vol. 2: 824
10.7	Vol. 2: 824
10.8	Vol. 3: 210
12.6	Vol. 2: 867 Vol. 3: 193, 210
13.2	Vol. 3: 210
13.7–10	Vol. 2: 266
13.7	Vol. 3: 210
13.9	Vol. 3: 778
14.2	Vol. 3: 946
14.6 f	Vol. 2: 207
14.6	Vol. 2: 928
15.1	Vol. 2: 824
15.6 ff	Vol. 3: 498, 500
15.6–9	Vol. 2: 573
15.6	Vol. 3: 210, 358
15.8–10	Vol. 2: 574
15.11	Vol. 2: 207
15.15	Vol. 2: 480
16.2	Vol. 2: 30
16.4 f	Vol. 3: 210
16.5–13	Vol. 2: 867
17	Vol. 3: 210, 649
17.13	Vol. 1: 125
17.21 ff	Vol. 2: 337 Vol. 3: 961
17.21–42	Vol. 2: 867
17.21	Vol. 3: 656
17.23–18.9	Vol. 2: 812
17.23	Vol. 1: 178
17.24	Vol. 1: 710 Vol. 2: 602
17.29	Vol. 3: 575
17.30	Vol. 2: 782 Vol. 3: 430
17.32	Vol. 3: 358

Psalms of Solomon (Pss. Sol.) *(cont'd)*

17.35 f	**Vol. 3:** 649
17.36	**Vol. 3:** 575
17.37	**Vol. 1:** 175
17.40 f	**Vol. 3:** 170
17.41–46	**Vol. 2:** 498
17.42 f	**Vol. 2:** 602
17.45	**Vol. 3:** 508, 566
17.51	**Vol. 2:** 602
18	**Vol. 3:** 210, 749
18.2	**Vol. 2:** 824
18.4	**Vol. 2:** 310
18.5 ff	**Vol. 2:** 337

Sibylline Oracles (Sib.)

1.20	**Vol. 2:** 405
1.29	**Vol. 1:** 87
1.103	**Vol. 2:** 208
1.125 ff	**Vol. 2:** 682
2.54	**Vol. 2:** 115
2.186 ff	**Vol. 1:** 656
2.187–213	**Vol. 2:** 836
2.230	**Vol. 1:** 705
2.238 ff	**Vol. 1:** 656
3	**Vol. 2:** 364
3.63 ff	**Vol. 1:** 125
3.83–92	**Vol. 2:** 836
3.88 ff	**Vol. 1:** 125
3.256	**Vol. 3:** 1013
3.271	**Vol. 2:** 309
3.319 ff	**Vol. 3:** 962
3.429 f	**Vol. 2:** 396
3.570–579	**Vol. 3:** 428
3.582 ff	**Vol. 3:** 693
3.652–660	**Vol. 2:** 701
3.662 ff	**Vol. 3:** 962
3.663 ff	**Vol. 2:** 326
3.787	**Vol. 2:** 326
3.796 ff	**Vol. 2:** 629
3.801 f	**Vol. 3:** 731
3.811 f	**Vol. 2:** 744
3.812	**Vol. 2:** 756
4.28	**Vol. 1:** 428
4.45–87	**Vol. 2:** 692
4.46	**Vol. 1:** 729
4.165–167	**Vol. 1:** 155
4.171–182	**Vol. 2:** 836
4.173–174	**Vol. 3:** 874
4.178–190	**Vol. 2:** 207
4.189	**Vol. 1:** 729
5.12 ff	**Vol. 2:** 684
5.138 ff	**Vol. 2:** 684
5.155–161	**Vol. 2:** 836
5.249	**Vol. 2:** 310
5.251 f	**Vol. 2:** 326
5.264	**Vol. 3:** 160
5.495	**Vol. 3:** 913
8.14	**Vol. 3:** 394
8.239	**Vol. 3:** 874

Sirach, Book of (Sir.)

Prol. 3	**Vol. 3:** 816
Prol. 4	**Vol. 3:** 1027
Prol. 10	**Vol. 3:** 1027
Prol. 14	**Vol. 3:** 821
Prol. 27	**Vol. 2:** 437
1.1–10	**Vol. 3:** 641
1.1	**Vol. 3:** 1027
1.2	**Vol. 3:** 828
1.3 f	**Vol. 3:** 1027
1.4	**Vol. 1:** 380 **Vol. 3:** 1027
1.6–20	**Vol. 3:** 1069
1.6	**Vol. 1:** 412 **Vol. 3:** 311, 1027
1.8	**Vol. 3:** 1028
1.9 f	**Vol. 1:** 380
1.11 ff	**Vol. 1:** 622
1.12	**Vol. 2:** 357
1.14	**Vol. 1:** 580 **Vol. 3:** 1027
1.16	**Vol. 3:** 1027
1.18	**Vol. 3:** 1027
1.19 f	**Vol. 3:** 130
1.20	**Vol. 3:** 1027
1.21	**Vol. 3:** 355
1.24 ff	**Vol. 3:** 1027
1.25	**Vol. 2:** 835
1.27	**Vol. 2:** 258, 818
1.28	**Vol. 3:** 687
1.29	**Vol. 2:** 468
1.30	**Vol. 1:** 609
2.1	**Vol. 3:** 117, 799
2.2	**Vol. 2:** 767
2.3	**Vol. 2:** 349
2.5	**Vol. 3:** 745, 808
2.7	**Vol. 1:** 609
2.8	**Vol. 2:** 139
2.10	**Vol. 3:** 226
2.14	**Vol. 2:** 773
2.17	**Vol. 2:** 264 **Vol. 3:** 117
2.18	**Vol. 1:** 609
3.3–16	**Vol. 2:** 49
3.3	**Vol. 3:** 150
3.5	**Vol. 2:** 863
3.6	**Vol. 3:** 255
3.15	**Vol. 3:** 240
3.16	**Vol. 3:** 341
3.17	**Vol. 3:** 745
3.18	**Vol. 2:** 203
3.21	**Vol. 1:** 420
3.28	**Vol. 3:** 29
3.29	**Vol. 2:** 175 **Vol. 3:** 1028
3.30	**Vol. 3:** 150, 153, 157
4.1–10	**Vol. 3:** 638
4.8	**Vol. 2:** 258
4.10	**Vol. 3:** 638
4.11	**Vol. 3:** 1027
4.15	**Vol. 2:** 179
4.17	**Vol. 1:** 622 **Vol. 3:** 354
4.23	**Vol. 3:** 209
4.24	**Vol. 3:** 1027

Sirach, Book of (Sir.) *(cont'd)*

4.26	**Vol. 3:** 711
4.27	**Vol. 3:** 1025
4.28	**Vol. 1:** 645
5.5 f	**Vol. 3:** 152
5.6	**Vol. 1:** 732 **Vol. 3:** 150, 255
5.7 ff	**Vol. 1:** 110
5.7	**Vol. 1:** 109 **Vol. 3:** 836
5.13	**Vol. 1:** 609 **Vol. 2:** 49
5.15	**Vol. 1:** 381
6.8	**Vol. 3:** 228
6.10	**Vol. 3:** 228
6.11	**Vol. 2:** 735
6.15	**Vol. 3:** 167
6.16	**Vol. 1:** 329
6.18 f	**Vol. 1:** 322
6.18	**Vol. 3:** 1027
6.20	**Vol. 3:** 226
6.22	**Vol. 3:** 1027
6.24	**Vol. 3:** 1161
6.26	**Vol. 3:** 685, 938, 1161
6.27	**Vol. 1:** 495
6.28	**Vol. 3:** 255–256
6.30	**Vol. 3:** 1161
6.32	**Vol. 1:** 412
6.33 f	**Vol. 3:** 1028
6.34 f	**Vol. 1:** 92
6.35	**Vol. 1:** 575 **Vol. 2:** 757
6.37	**Vol. 3:** 1027
7.2	**Vol. 1:** 607
7.5	**Vol. 3:** 358, 1028, 1033
7.11	**Vol. 2:** 261–262
7.17	**Vol. 3:** 110
7.19	**Vol. 3:** 1028
7.20	**Vol. 2:** 139 **Vol. 3:** 882
7.22	**Vol. 3:** 226
7.29	**Vol. 3:** 479
7.31	**Vol. 3:** 416
7.33	**Vol. 2:** 115
8.1	**Vol. 1:** 609
8.2	**Vol. 2:** 841
8.8	**Vol. 2:** 757 **Vol. 3:** 1027–1028
8.14	**Vol. 2:** 818
8.15	**Vol. 3:** 1024
9.2	**Vol. 3:** 921
9.3	**Vol. 1:** 609
9.5	**Vol. 2:** 707
9.8	**Vol. 1:** 655
9.10	**Vol. 2:** 675
9.12	**Vol. 2:** 818 **Vol. 3:** 355
9.14	**Vol. 3:** 1028
9.15	**Vol. 1:** 575 **Vol. 3:** 820
9.17	**Vol. 3:** 816, 1028
10.1	**Vol. 3:** 1028
10.6	**Vol. 3:** 29
10.7	**Vol. 3:** 29
10.8	**Vol. 3:** 29
10.9	**Vol. 3:** 29
10.11	**Vol. 3:** 271
10.12 f	**Vol. 3:** 29
10.12	**Vol. 1:** 607 **Vol. 3:** 30
10.15 ff	**Vol. 2:** 261
10.17	**Vol. 3:** 255
10.18	**Vol. 1:** 381 **Vol. 3:** 29
10.19	**Vol. 2:** 49
10.22	**Vol. 2:** 841
10.23	**Vol. 2:** 49 **Vol. 3:** 358
10.25	**Vol. 3:** 1028
10.26	**Vol. 3:** 1028
10.28	**Vol. 2:** 258
10.29	**Vol. 3:** 355, 358
10.30	**Vol. 2:** 823, 841
11.1	**Vol. 3:** 1027
11.7	**Vol. 1:** 572
11.11–13	**Vol. 3:** 953
11.12 f	**Vol. 2:** 261
11.12	**Vol. 1:** 729
11.13	**Vol. 2:** 621
11.17	**Vol. 2:** 91, 93, 818 **Vol. 3:** 228
11.18 f	**Vol. 2:** 845
11.18	**Vol. 2:** 139, 841
11.19	**Vol. 3:** 255, 528
11.21	**Vol. 2:** 841 **Vol. 3:** 226
11.22	**Vol. 2:** 93, 139 **Vol. 3:** 847
11.27	**Vol. 3:** 310–311, 847
11.28	**Vol. 3:** 271
11.30	**Vol. 3:** 29
11.32	**Vol. 1:** 655
12.1	**Vol. 2:** 117
12.2	**Vol. 2:** 93
12.4	**Vol. 2:** 93
12.15	**Vol. 2:** 767
13.1	**Vol. 2:** 501
13.2 f	**Vol. 2:** 841
13.11	**Vol. 2:** 498
13.13	**Vol. 1:** 381
13.18–23	**Vol. 2:** 841
13.20	**Vol. 2:** 259–260 **Vol. 3:** 29
13.22	**Vol. 3:** 355, 358
13.26	**Vol. 3:** 820
14.16	**Vol. 3:** 270
14.18 f	**Vol. 1:** 433
14.18	**Vol. 1:** 221, 673
14.20–27	**Vol. 3:** 1029
14.20	**Vol. 1:** 216 **Vol. 3:** 1027
14.25	**Vol. 3:** 794
14.27	**Vol. 1:** 653
15.1	**Vol. 3:** 748
15.3	**Vol. 3:** 459, 1027
15.7	**Vol. 3:** 131
15.8	**Vol. 3:** 29
15.10	**Vol. 3:** 1027
15.12	**Vol. 3:** 957
15.15	**Vol. 2:** 818
15.18	**Vol. 3:** 1027
16.7	**Vol. 1:** 109 **Vol. 3:** 152
16.8	**Vol. 3:** 29
16.10	**Vol. 2:** 184
16.12	**Vol. 1:** 110 **Vol. 3:** 167

Sirach, Book of (Sir.) *(cont'd)*

16.13	**Vol. 2:** 773
16.17	**Vol. 1:** 381
16.22	**Vol. 2:** 773
16.23	**Vol. 3:** 1024–1025
17.1	**Vol. 1:** 381
17.2	**Vol. 3:** 835
17.3 f	**Vol. 2:** 287
17.3	**Vol. 2:** 287
17.10	**Vol. 3:** 816
17.15	**Vol. 2:** 215
17.20	**Vol. 2:** 215
17.22	**Vol. 2:** 117
17.24	**Vol. 2:** 773
17.27 f	**Vol. 3:** 233, 270, 816
17.31	**Vol. 1:** 221
18.2	**Vol. 3:** 355
18.6	**Vol. 2:** 622
18.10	**Vol. 2:** 698
18.13	**Vol. 2:** 141 **Vol. 3:** 565, 761
18.14	**Vol. 3:** 776
18.15	**Vol. 1:** 495
18.16	**Vol. 3:** 255
18.17	**Vol. 2:** 116
18.18	**Vol. 3:** 1025
18.20	**Vol. 3:** 847
18.21	**Vol. 3:** 836
18.22	**Vol. 3:** 355, 358
18.23	**Vol. 3:** 117, 799, 801
18.24	**Vol. 3:** 836
18.25	**Vol. 2:** 842
18.27	**Vol. 2:** 90 **Vol. 3:** 1028
18.28	**Vol. 3:** 271, 1027
18.29	**Vol. 2:** 757 **Vol. 3:** 1028
18.30	**Vol. 1:** 460, 495
18.31	**Vol. 2:** 817
18.33	**Vol. 1:** 142
19.1	**Vol. 2:** 841
19.2	**Vol. 2:** 349
19.11 ff	**Vol. 3:** 1025
19.20	**Vol. 3:** 1027
19.22 f	**Vol. 3:** 1027
19.23	**Vol. 3:** 1024
19.24	**Vol. 1:** 729
19.25	**Vol. 1:** 412
19.30	**Vol. 2:** 369, 431
20.4	**Vol. 3:** 711
20.5	**Vol. 3:** 1028
20.7	**Vol. 3:** 1024, 1028
20.13	**Vol. 3:** 1025, 1028
20.14	**Vol. 3:** 1024
20.15	**Vol. 3:** 50
20.16	**Vol. 3:** 1025
20.19	**Vol. 2:** 644
20.20	**Vol. 3:** 1025
20.21	**Vol. 3:** 255
20.22	**Vol. 3:** 1024
20.26	**Vol. 2:** 437
20.27	**Vol. 3:** 1028
20.28	**Vol. 3:** 150
20.29	**Vol. 3:** 902, 1028
20.30 f	**Vol. 3:** 1027
20.31	**Vol. 3:** 1025
21.2	**Vol. 1:** 559
21.4	**Vol. 2:** 842 **Vol. 3:** 29
21.10	**Vol. 1:** 254
21.11	**Vol. 3:** 125, 1027
21.12	**Vol. 1:** 412
21.13	**Vol. 3:** 991, 1028
21.14	**Vol. 3:** 1025
21.15	**Vol. 3:** 816, 1028
21.16	**Vol. 1:** 574 **Vol. 3:** 1025
21.18	**Vol. 3:** 1025, 1027
21.19	**Vol. 3:** 126
21.20	**Vol. 1:** 412 **Vol. 2:** 431, 433 **Vol. 3:** 1025
21.22	**Vol. 3:** 1025
21.23	**Vol. 3:** 1024
21.25	**Vol. 3:** 1161
21.26	**Vol. 3:** 1025, 1028
22.6	**Vol. 1:** 575 **Vol. 3:** 1027
22.7 f	**Vol. 3:** 1025
22.7	**Vol. 3:** 761, 914
22.11 f	**Vol. 3:** 1025
22.11	**Vol. 3:** 255, 270
22.13	**Vol. 3:** 255, 1024
22.14	**Vol. 3:** 1025
22.18	**Vol. 2:** 773 **Vol. 3:** 1025
22.22	**Vol. 1:** 559 **Vol. 3:** 29, 310–311, 502
22.24	**Vol. 1:** 655 **Vol. 3:** 346
22.27	**Vol. 3:** 498
23.1	**Vol. 1:** 618 **Vol. 2:** 509
23.2	**Vol. 3:** 1027
23.3	**Vol. 1:** 732 **Vol. 2:** 131
23.4	**Vol. 1:** 618
23.6	**Vol. 1:** 460
23.8	**Vol. 2:** 707 **Vol. 3:** 29, 346
23.9 ff	**Vol. 3:** 740
23.11	**Vol. 3:** 355
23.12	**Vol. 1:** 607
23.14	**Vol. 3:** 1025
23.16 ff	**Vol. 1:** 233
23.16	**Vol. 1:** 655, 732 **Vol. 3:** 109
23.18	**Vol. 2:** 586
23.19	**Vol. 3:** 730
23.20	**Vol. 1:** 381
23.21	**Vol. 3:** 98
23.23	**Vol. 3:** 1195
24	**Vol. 3:** 1032
24.1	**Vol. 3:** 816, 1027
24.3–12	**Vol. 3:** 1116
24.6	**Vol. 2:** 840
24.7	**Vol. 3:** 255–256
24.8 ff	**Vol. 3:** 1029
24.8 f	**Vol. 1:** 380
24.8	**Vol. 1:** 382 **Vol. 3:** 255
24.9	**Vol. 3:** 416
24.11	**Vol. 3:** 255
24.12	**Vol. 3:** 808

Sirach, Book of (Sir.) *(cont'd)*

24.15	**Vol. 2:** 294 **Vol. 3:** 600–601
24.17	**Vol. 2:** 842 **Vol. 3:** 919
24.18 ff	**Vol. 3:** 640
24.22	**Vol. 2:** 179
24.23 ff	**Vol. 3:** 1029
24.23	**Vol. 3:** 459
24.25–34	**Vol. 3:** 459
24.25	**Vol. 3:** 1027
24.30–33	**Vol. 3:** 986
24.33	**Vol. 3:** 769
25.2	**Vol. 2:** 583, 841 **Vol. 3:** 29, 1025
25.4 ff	**Vol. 1:** 92
25.5	**Vol. 3:** 125, 1027
25.7–10	**Vol. 1:** 216
25.8	**Vol. 1:** 216
25.10	**Vol. 3:** 1027
25.18	**Vol. 1:** 504
25.21	**Vol. 1:** 109
25.24	**Vol. 1:** 434
25.25	**Vol. 1:** 565 **Vol. 2:** 735
26.4	**Vol. 2:** 841
26.5	**Vol. 2:** 90
26.14	**Vol. 3:** 167
26.16	**Vol. 3:** 730, 1068
26.28	**Vol. 3:** 953
26.29	**Vol. 3:** 355
27.1 ff	**Vol. 2:** 845
27.3	**Vol. 3:** 1169
27.4 f	**Vol. 3:** 823
27.4	**Vol. 1:** 480
27.5	**Vol. 3:** 799, 808, 820, 911
27.7	**Vol. 3:** 799, 816, 823
27.8	**Vol. 3:** 748
27.11	**Vol. 1:** 575 **Vol. 3:** 733, 1024, 1027–1028
27.13	**Vol. 2:** 431, 433 **Vol. 3:** 1025
27.15	**Vol. 2:** 854 **Vol. 3:** 29
27.16 f	**Vol. 3:** 502
27.21	**Vol. 3:** 346, 502
27.23	**Vol. 2:** 621
27.28	**Vol. 3:** 29
27.30	**Vol. 1:** 109
28.1	**Vol. 3:** 717
28.2	**Vol. 3:** 177
28.6	**Vol. 3:** 226
28.10 f	**Vol. 1:** 654
28.10	**Vol. 1:** 109 **Vol. 2:** 842
28.12	**Vol. 3:** 109
28.16	**Vol. 3:** 255
28.19 f	**Vol. 3:** 1161
28.23	**Vol. 3:** 109
28.25	**Vol. 3:** 1161
29.1 ff	**Vol. 2:** 769
29.6	**Vol. 3:** 346, 823
29.15	**Vol. 1:** 372
30.2	**Vol. 3:** 816
30.3	**Vol. 3:** 761
30.9	**Vol. 2:** 621
30.14	**Vol. 2:** 822, 841
30.16	**Vol. 2:** 357
30.17	**Vol. 3:** 255–256, 271
30.20	**Vol. 3:** 711
30.21 ff	**Vol. 2:** 420
30.24	**Vol. 1:** 277
30.27	**Vol. 3:** 761
31.3 f	**Vol. 3:** 255
31.3	**Vol. 2:** 841, 845
31.5 f	**Vol. 2:** 845
31.5	**Vol. 3:** 355
31.7	**Vol. 3:** 1024
31.8	**Vol. 1:** 492 **Vol. 2:** 841 **Vol. 3:** 924
31.10	**Vol. 3:** 808
31.11	**Vol. 3:** 1027
31.18	**Vol. 2:** 41
31.21	**Vol. 3:** 255, 711
31.24	**Vol. 2:** 509
31.26	**Vol. 3:** 808
31.27	**Vol. 1:** 381
31.30	**Vol. 3:** 1024, 1079
32.2	**Vol. 3:** 957
32.3	**Vol. 2:** 669
32.4	**Vol. 3:** 1028, 1033
32.12	**Vol. 3:** 29
32.17	**Vol. 3:** 1019
32.18	**Vol. 3:** 125
32.23	**Vol. 2:** 132
33.1	**Vol. 2:** 509 **Vol. 3:** 799–800, 1025
33.2	**Vol. 3:** 1028
33.3	**Vol. 2:** 879
33.5 f	**Vol. 3:** 1025
33.5	**Vol. 3:** 820
33.8	**Vol. 1:** 626
33.10–13	**Vol. 3:** 916
33.10	**Vol. 1:** 381
33.13	**Vol. 2:** 818 **Vol. 3:** 911
33.25	**Vol. 3:** 255
33.26	**Vol. 2:** 569 **Vol. 3:** 1161
33.28	**Vol. 1:** 589 **Vol. 2:** 669
34.1 f	**Vol. 2:** 137
34.1	**Vol. 3:** 1024
34.2	**Vol. 3:** 555
34.5 ff	**Vol. 1:** 512
34.8	**Vol. 3:** 1027
34.10	**Vol. 3:** 799
34.19	**Vol. 3:** 150
34.20	**Vol. 2:** 137
34.22	**Vol. 2:** 139
34.23 f	**Vol. 3:** 1041
34.25	**Vol. 1:** 144, 152
34.26	**Vol. 2:** 863
35.1	**Vol. 2:** 131
35.2	**Vol. 2:** 117
35.3	**Vol. 1:** 607
35.5 f	**Vol. 3:** 498
35.6	**Vol. 3:** 479
35.8	**Vol. 3:** 416
35.15	**Vol. 2:** 468, 707
35.17	**Vol. 2:** 863

Sirach, Book of (Sir.) *(cont'd)*

36.2	**Vol. 2:** 468
36.4 f	**Vol. 2:** 396
36.12 f	**Vol. 2:** 609, 803
36.13	**Vol. 2:** 818
36.15	**Vol. 1:** 381 **Vol. 3:** 255
36.18	**Vol. 2:** 139, 773
36.24	**Vol. 3:** 255
37.11	**Vol. 2:** 139 **Vol. 3:** 818
37.20 f	**Vol. 3:** 1027
37.20	**Vol. 3:** 1028
37.22 ff	**Vol. 3:** 1028
37.26	**Vol. 3:** 1028
37.27	**Vol. 3:** 799
38.1 f	**Vol. 2:** 167
38.1	**Vol. 1:** 381 **Vol. 2:** 50
38.4	**Vol. 1:** 381
38.6	**Vol. 2:** 622
38.9–14	**Vol. 2:** 167
38.12	**Vol. 1:** 381
38.14	**Vol. 3:** 255
38.19	**Vol. 3:** 228
38.21	**Vol. 3:** 271
38.23	**Vol. 3:** 255
38.24 f	**Vol. 3:** 1028
38.24–39.11	**Vol. 3:** 479
38.24–34	**Vol. 3:** 911
38.24	**Vol. 3:** 1027
38.25 ff	**Vol. 3:** 479
38.25	**Vol. 1:** 575
38.27	**Vol. 2:** 773 **Vol. 3:** 497
38.28	**Vol. 1:** 654
38.29–30	**Vol. 3:** 911
38.30	**Vol. 2:** 115
38.31	**Vol. 3:** 1028, 1212
38.34	**Vol. 1:** 382
39.1	**Vol. 3:** 479, 1027
39.2	**Vol. 1:** 575
39.3	**Vol. 2:** 757
39.4	**Vol. 3:** 479, 799
39.5	**Vol. 2:** 863
39.6	**Vol. 3:** 479, 1120
39.7 f	**Vol. 3:** 479
39.7	**Vol. 2:** 863 **Vol. 3:** 1027
39.8	**Vol. 1:** 227, 735 **Vol. 3:** 769
39.9 f	**Vol. 1:** 735
39.9	**Vol. 3:** 271, 816
39.10	**Vol. 3:** 1027
39.11	**Vol. 3:** 226, 255
39.14	**Vol. 3:** 600–601, 673, 816
39.18	**Vol. 2:** 818
39.19	**Vol. 2:** 215
39.21–30	**Vol. 1:** 381
39.22	**Vol. 3:** 991
39.26	**Vol. 3:** 444, 919
39.33 f	**Vol. 3:** 846
39.34	**Vol. 3:** 808
40.1	**Vol. 3:** 937, 1161
40.2	**Vol. 3:** 820
40.5 f	**Vol. 3:** 255
40.7	**Vol. 3:** 209
40.9	**Vol. 2:** 265
40.10	**Vol. 1:** 381 **Vol. 3:** 991
40.14	**Vol. 3:** 381
40.17	**Vol. 2:** 117
40.19	**Vol. 3:** 823, 924
40.20	**Vol. 3:** 1027
40.24	**Vol. 3:** 201–202
40.28	**Vol. 2:** 823
40.29	**Vol. 3:** 820, 823
41.1 f	**Vol. 3:** 232
41.1–4	**Vol. 1:** 433
41.1	**Vol. 2:** 271
41.2	**Vol. 2:** 773
41.11 ff	**Vol. 3:** 271
41.14 f	**Vol. 3:** 1027
41.15	**Vol. 3:** 1025
42.1	**Vol. 3:** 310–311
42.2	**Vol. 3:** 358
42.4	**Vol. 3:** 1161
42.8	**Vol. 2:** 675 **Vol. 3:** 126, 808, 1025
42.9	**Vol. 1:** 277
42.15	**Vol. 3:** 262
42.16	**Vol. 2:** 491
42.17	**Vol. 2:** 622
42.18	**Vol. 1:** 349
42.19	**Vol. 1:** 322 **Vol. 2:** 215
42.21	**Vol. 3:** 1027
43.1 ff	**Vol. 2:** 491
43.2 ff	**Vol. 2:** 491
43.2	**Vol. 2:** 622
43.3	**Vol. 1:** 652
43.5	**Vol. 3:** 255
43.6 ff	**Vol. 2:** 491
43.6–8	**Vol. 3:** 733
43.6	**Vol. 3:** 842
43.8	**Vol. 2:** 128, 622
43.13	**Vol. 3:** 255
43.19	**Vol. 1:** 726
43.23	**Vol. 3:** 823, 983
43.24 f	**Vol. 1:** 381
43.24	**Vol. 1:** 419
43.31	**Vol. 1:** 575–576
43.33	**Vol. 3:** 1027
44–50	**Vol. 1:** 714
44.1 ff	**Vol. 1:** 617
44.2	**Vol. 1:** 381
44.4	**Vol. 3:** 1028
44.6	**Vol. 2:** 841
44.8	**Vol. 3:** 271
44.15	**Vol. 3:** 1027
44.16	**Vol. 2:** 290, 815, 817 **Vol. 3:** 265–266, 602
44.17 ff	**Vol. 3:** 991
44.17 f	**Vol. 2:** 681
44.17	**Vol. 3:** 167, 836
44.19 ff	**Vol. 3:** 369
44.21	**Vol. 2:** 499
44.23	**Vol. 3:** 255

Sirach, Book of (Sir.) *(cont'd)*

45.3	**Vol. 3:** 255
45.4	**Vol. 2:** 257
45.6–26	**Vol. 3:** 479
45.8	**Vol. 3:** 36
45.17	**Vol. 3:** 761
45.20	**Vol. 3:** 416
45.24	**Vol. 3:** 36
45.26	**Vol. 3:** 1027
46.1	**Vol. 3:** 209, 479
46.5	**Vol. 2:** 70
46.6	**Vol. 2:** 70
46.10	**Vol. 1:** 492
46.12	**Vol. 3:** 271
46.19	**Vol. 3:** 270
47.6	**Vol. 1:** 405 **Vol. 3:** 816
47.11	**Vol. 3:** 649
47.12 f	**Vol. 3:** 255
47.13	**Vol. 2:** 655
47.14	**Vol. 3:** 1028
47.17	**Vol. 1:** 580 **Vol. 2:** 757
47.19	**Vol. 1:** 233
47.20 ff	**Vol. 1:** 108–109
47.20	**Vol. 3:** 1024
47.23	**Vol. 3:** 255, 1024
48.3	**Vol. 1:** 544 **Vol. 2:** 765
48.5	**Vol. 1:** 444
48.7	**Vol. 3:** 1013
48.8	**Vol. 3:** 209
48.9	**Vol. 3:** 262, 265, 747
48.10	**Vol. 1:** 544 **Vol. 2:** 337
48.12	**Vol. 1:** 735 **Vol. 3:** 693
48.14	**Vol. 2:** 622 **Vol. 3:** 1148
48.15	**Vol. 1:** 607
48.18	**Vol. 3:** 29
48.19	**Vol. 3:** 1068
48.20	**Vol. 3:** 192, 194
48.25	**Vol. 2:** 215
49.3	**Vol. 2:** 93
49.10	**Vol. 3:** 192, 194
49.12	**Vol. 3:** 117
49.14 f	**Vol. 3:** 265
49.14	**Vol. 3:** 602, 747
49.16	**Vol. 1:** 84
50	**Vol. 1:** 700
50.5	**Vol. 3:** 794
50.6	**Vol. 3:** 733–734
50.15	**Vol. 3:** 919
50.20	**Vol. 1:** 216
50.21	**Vol. 2:** 876
50.24	**Vol. 3:** 192–194
50.25 f	**Vol. 3:** 456, 461
50.26	**Vol. 3:** 1025
50.27	**Vol. 2:** 325, 331, 573 **Vol. 3:** 479, 1027
50.28	**Vol. 3:** 1028, 1033
51.1–12	**Vol. 1:** 345
51.1	**Vol. 1:** 618 **Vol. 2:** 514, 863 **Vol. 3:** 218, 220
51.2 f	**Vol. 3:** 192, 194

51.2	**Vol. 3:** 193
51.3	**Vol. 2:** 421
51.6	**Vol. 3:** 816
51.8	**Vol. 2:** 773
51.10	**Vol. 1:** 618 **Vol. 3:** 29
51.13	**Vol. 2:** 863 **Vol. 3:** 1027
51.17	**Vol. 3:** 1027
51.22	**Vol. 2:** 139
51.23–30	**Vol. 2:** 262
51.23	**Vol. 3:** 479
51.24	**Vol. 2:** 266
51.25 f	**Vol. 3:** 1161–1162
51.26	**Vol. 3:** 1161
51.27	**Vol. 3:** 255–256
51.30	**Vol. 2:** 139 **Vol. 3:** 836

Slavonic Book of Enoch (Sl. Enoch)

2–20	**Vol. 2:** 613
3–21	**Vol. 2:** 688
3.1	**Vol. 2:** 925
3.3	**Vol. 3:** 984
7	**Vol. 2:** 762
8	**Vol. 2:** 762–763
8.1–8	**Vol. 2:** 191
8.1	**Vol. 2:** 761
10.4 f	**Vol. 3:** 31
11–16	**Vol. 3:** 731
11	**Vol. 2:** 762
17	**Vol. 2:** 763
18	**Vol. 2:** 762
19.4	**Vol. 3:** 983
20	**Vol. 2:** 614
21.3	**Vol. 1:** 103
22.4 ff	**Vol. 3:** 35
22.8	**Vol. 1:** 204
24.1	**Vol. 1:** 103
30.15	**Vol. 1:** 254 **Vol. 2:** 493 **Vol. 3:** 939
31	**Vol. 1:** 449
33.1	**Vol. 2:** 698
33.4	**Vol. 2:** 698
39.2	**Vol. 2:** 279
49.2	**Vol. 3:** 1161
52.1 ff	**Vol. 1:** 216
55.2	**Vol. 2:** 326
58.6	**Vol. 1:** 410
61.2	**Vol. 3:** 229
64.5a	**Vol. 3:** 35–36
65.7 f	**Vol. 3:** 836

Syriac Apocalypse of Baruch (Syr. Bar.)

4.2 ff	**Vol. 2:** 326
4.2–6	**Vol. 3:** 789
6	**Vol. 2:** 56
8	**Vol. 2:** 56
13.3	**Vol. 2:** 202
14.12	**Vol. 3:** 1149

Syriac Apocalypse of Baruch (Syr. Bar.) *(cont'd)*

22.1	**Vol. 3:** 543	
25–30	**Vol. 3:** 695	
25.4	**Vol. 2:** 892	
27	**Vol. 2:** 892	
27.6	**Vol. 2:** 266	
29.3	**Vol. 2:** 701	**Vol. 3:** 652
29.5–8	**Vol. 1:** 729	
29.5	**Vol. 2:** 698	**Vol. 3:** 919
29.6 ff	**Vol. 2:** 272	
29.6	**Vol. 2:** 842	
29.7 f	**Vol. 2:** 892	
29.8	**Vol. 1:** 252	**Vol. 2:** 218
30.1–5	**Vol. 2:** 701	
30.2	**Vol. 3:** 956	
37.1	**Vol. 1:** 656	
39.7	**Vol. 3:** 919	
40.2 f	**Vol. 3:** 961	
40.2	**Vol. 3:** 250	
40.3	**Vol. 2:** 701	
44.3	**Vol. 3:** 939	
44.7	**Vol. 1:** 570	
44.15	**Vol. 1:** 656	
48.38	**Vol. 3:** 1149	
48.39	**Vol. 1:** 656	
50–51	**Vol. 3:** 297	
50.2	**Vol. 3:** 271	
50.3 f	**Vol. 3:** 271	
51.1–12	**Vol. 3:** 861	
51.1	**Vol. 1:** 706	
51.3	**Vol. 3:** 271	
51.5	**Vol. 3:** 271	
51.12–52	**Vol. 2:** 842	
51.15	**Vol. 3:** 174	
54.2	**Vol. 3:** 1149	
54.5	**Vol. 1:** 598	
54.16	**Vol. 1:** 598	
54.17 f	**Vol. 2:** 396	
54.19	**Vol. 1:** 434	
54.21	**Vol. 1:** 598	
56	**Vol. 2:** 213	
57.2	**Vol. 1:** 77, 598	
59.10	**Vol. 2:** 208	
66.2	**Vol. 3:** 160	
67.6	**Vol. 3:** 601	
70.2	**Vol. 3:** 526	
70.9	**Vol. 3:** 610	
76.4	**Vol. 2:** 696	
85.3	**Vol. 3:** 311	
85.13	**Vol. 2:** 208	

Testament of Asher (Test. Ash.)

1.3	**Vol. 2:** 481	**Vol. 3:** 939–940
1.5	**Vol. 2:** 481	**Vol. 3:** 939–940
1.9	**Vol. 3:** 939	
4.3	**Vol. 1:** 491	

5.2	**Vol. 2:** 928	**Vol. 3:** 210
6	**Vol. 3:** 693	
6.6	**Vol. 3:** 210	
7.2†	**Vol. 1:** 685	
7.3	**Vol. 3:** 210, 961	

Testament of Benjamin (Test. Ben.)

3.1	**Vol. 1:** 491	
3.8	**Vol. 3:** 165, 195	
4.1	**Vol. 1:** 405, 491	**Vol. 3:** 210
4.5	**Vol. 3:** 1152	
5	**Vol. 3:** 807	
6	**Vol. 3:** 807	
6.4	**Vol. 3:** 963	
8.2	**Vol. 3:** 125	
8.3	**Vol. 3:** 125–126	
9.1	**Vol. 1:** 499	
10	**Vol. 2:** 207	
10.1	**Vol. 2:** 136	
10.3 f	**Vol. 1:** 334	
10.5	**Vol. 3:** 210	
10.6–9	**Vol. 3:** 272	
10.11	**Vol. 2:** 313	
11.2	**Vol. 2:** 397	
11.5	**Vol. 3:** 953	

Testament of Dan (Test. Dan)

5.1	**Vol. 1:** 334	
5.10 f	**Vol. 3:** 961	
5.10	**Vol. 3:** 210	
5.13–6.4	**Vol. 2:** 602	
6.2	**Vol. 1:** 104	**Vol. 3:** 35
6.3 f	**Vol. 1:** 554	
6.9	**Vol. 3:** 210	
6.10	**Vol. 3:** 372	

Testament of Gad (Test. Gad)

2.5	**Vol. 3:** 263	
4.7	**Vol. 3:** 210, 1152	
5.1	**Vol. 3:** 963	
5.3	**Vol. 2:** 261	
5.4	**Vol. 3:** 346	
5.7	**Vol. 3:** 210	
7.5	**Vol. 3:** 210	

Testament of Issachar (Test. Iss.)

1.11	**Vol. 1:** 742	
3.8	**Vol. 3:** 572, 1152	
5.2	**Vol. 1:** 334	**Vol. 2:** 427
7	**Vol. 3:** 807	

Testament of Joseph (Test. Jos.)

1.6	**Vol. 2:** 116	
2.2	**Vol. 3:** 263	
2.7	**Vol. 3:** 570	

Testament of Joseph (Test. Jos.) *(cont'd)*

4.6 ff	**Vol. 2:** 583
5.1	**Vol. 2:** 583
6.7	**Vol. 3:** 263
8.3	**Vol. 1:** 528
8.5	**Vol. 3:** 670
10.3	**Vol. 3:** 210
12.2 f	**Vol. 2:** 309
13.3	**Vol. 2:** 309
14.5	**Vol. 3:** 570
17.4	**Vol. 1:** 569
19 f	**Vol. 2:** 311
19.11	**Vol. 3:** 210

Testament of Judah (Test. Jud.)

6	**Vol. 1:** 499
11.1	**Vol. 3:** 125
13	**Vol. 1:** 499
14.2 f	**Vol. 3:** 126
14.3	**Vol. 1:** 233
14.4	**Vol. 1:** 514
14.6	**Vol. 1:** 334
14.7	**Vol. 3:** 957
15.4	**Vol. 2:** 272
16.1	**Vol. 3:** 31
16.3 f	**Vol. 1:** 334
16.3	**Vol. 3:** 963
20	**Vol. 3:** 693
20.1	**Vol. 3:** 929
21.2	**Vol. 3:** 35–36
21.4	**Vol. 3:** 36
22.2	**Vol. 2:** 899 **Vol. 3:** 210
24.1–5	**Vol. 2:** 495
24.1	**Vol. 1:** 407 **Vol. 2:** 558 **Vol. 3:** 35, 170
24.4–6	**Vol. 3:** 650
25	**Vol. 2:** 433
25.1–4	**Vol. 3:** 272
25.1	**Vol. 2:** 480
25.4	**Vol. 1:** 442

Testament of Levi (Test. Lev.)

2–5	**Vol. 1:** 512
2	**Vol. 2:** 688
2.4	**Vol. 3:** 210
2.7	**Vol. 3:** 984
2.10	**Vol. 3:** 210
3	**Vol. 2:** 614, 688
3.4 ff	**Vol. 3:** 789
3.8	**Vol. 2:** 608
4.1	**Vol. 1:** 515 **Vol. 3:** 180, 210
4.3	**Vol. 2:** 397
5.1 f	**Vol. 3:** 789
5.6	**Vol. 1:** 104
6	**Vol. 3:** 455
7	**Vol. 3:** 461, 693
8.14 f	**Vol. 2:** 899
8.15	**Vol. 3:** 656

11	**Vol. 3:** 693
13.2	**Vol. 3:** 229
13.5	**Vol. 2:** 831
14.1	**Vol. 3:** 487
14.2	**Vol. 1:** 334
14.3	**Vol. 2:** 313
14.4	**Vol. 2:** 312
14.6	**Vol. 1:** 155, 334
18	**Vol. 3:** 693
18.1–14	**Vol. 1:** 81
18.2	**Vol. 3:** 35
18.3 f	**Vol. 2:** 558
18.3	**Vol. 1:** 407 **Vol. 2:** 397, 495
18.6 ff	**Vol. 1:** 175
18.9 ff	**Vol. 3:** 80
18.9	**Vol. 3:** 170
18.11	**Vol. 2:** 763
19.1	**Vol. 3:** 929, 939

Testament of Naphtali (Test. Naph.)

2.5	**Vol. 3:** 125
4.1	**Vol. 3:** 487
5–7	**Vol. 1:** 512
8.2 f	**Vol. 3:** 210
8.4	**Vol. 3:** 807

Testament of Reuben (Test. Reub.)

1	**Vol. 1:** 499
2	**Vol. 3:** 939
3	**Vol. 3:** 693, 939
3.3–6	**Vol. 3:** 31
3.9	**Vol. 3:** 210
4.1	**Vol. 3:** 1164
4.4	**Vol. 1:** 569
4.10	**Vol. 3:** 263
5	**Vol. 2:** 213
5.5	**Vol. 3:** 98, 210
6	**Vol. 1:** 499
6.8	**Vol. 3:** 35
6.12	**Vol. 3:** 961
7.2	**Vol. 3:** 380

Testament of Simeon (Test. Sim.)

2.8	**Vol. 3:** 263
2.12	**Vol. 1:** 515 **Vol. 2:** 222
4.8	**Vol. 3:** 963
5.5	**Vol. 3:** 961
6.2	**Vol. 2:** 313
6.5	**Vol. 2:** 313
7.1 f	**Vol. 3:** 210
7.2	**Vol. 2:** 313

Testament of Zebulun
(Test. Zeb.)

2.7	**Vol. 1:** 515
3.4	**Vol. 3:** 487
7.3	**Vol. 2:** 599 **Vol. 3:** 957
8.2	**Vol. 2:** 599
8.6	**Vol. 2:** 599
9	**Vol. 2:** 158
10.3	**Vol. 3:** 210
10.4	**Vol. 3:** 272

Tobit (Tob.)

1.1	**Vol. 1:** 243 **Vol. 3:** 873
1.4	**Vol. 2:** 675
1.6	**Vol. 1:** 626 **Vol. 3:** 416
1.11 f	**Vol. 3:** 233
1.14	**Vol. 1:** 142
1.18	**Vol. 2:** 310 **Vol. 3:** 342, 377
1.22	**Vol. 3:** 498
2.1	**Vol. 2:** 783
2.2	**Vol. 3:** 228, 233
2.6	**Vol. 2:** 433
2.8	**Vol. 1:** 444
2.12	**Vol. 2:** 139
2.13	**Vol. 2:** 607
2.14	**Vol. 2:** 139
3.1–6	**Vol. 1:** 345
3.1	**Vol. 2:** 863
3.2	**Vol. 3:** 358
3.6	**Vol. 1:** 506 **Vol. 2:** 663
3.8	**Vol. 3:** 570
3.10	**Vol. 2:** 478 **Vol. 3:** 823
3.13	**Vol. 1:** 506
3.15	**Vol. 3:** 821, 1202
3.16	**Vol. 2:** 863
3.17	**Vol. 3:** 177
4.8 ff	**Vol. 2:** 830
4.9	**Vol. 2:** 663
4.14	**Vol. 2:** 139 **Vol. 3:** 933
4.21	**Vol. 1:** 607
5.3	**Vol. 2:** 139
5.5	**Vol. 3:** 1185
5.6	**Vol. 1:** 688
5.7	**Vol. 2:** 139, 773
5.8	**Vol. 2:** 767
5.9	**Vol. 2:** 139
5.10	**Vol. 1:** 665
5.13	**Vol. 2:** 876
5.14 f	**Vol. 2:** 139
5.15	**Vol. 1:** 663
5.16	**Vol. 1:** 212
5.18	**Vol. 1:** 479
6.1 ff	**Vol. 1:** 670
6.2 f	**Vol. 1:** 283
6.5	**Vol. 1:** 218
6.7	**Vol. 1:** 451
6.9	**Vol. 1:** 218
6.11 f	**Vol. 3:** 355
6.13 f	**Vol. 1:** 451

6.17	**Vol. 2:** 863
7.3	**Vol. 3:** 873
7.6	**Vol. 1:** 212
7.7	**Vol. 1:** 212
7.8	**Vol. 2:** 521
7.10	**Vol. 2:** 577 **Vol. 3:** 882
7.14	**Vol. 3:** 498
7.18	**Vol. 2:** 514
8.1	**Vol. 2:** 521
8.2	**Vol. 1:** 142
8.3	**Vol. 3:** 1005–1007
8.4 f	**Vol. 2:** 863
8.5	**Vol. 1:** 381 **Vol. 2:** 191
8.6	**Vol. 1:** 87
8.13	**Vol. 3:** 860
8.15	**Vol. 1:** 381
8.18	**Vol. 1:** 341
8.19	**Vol. 2:** 578 **Vol. 3:** 119
9.5	**Vol. 3:** 498–499
9.6	**Vol. 1:** 212
10.1	**Vol. 3:** 823
10.8	**Vol. 3:** 316
10.12	**Vol. 1:** 212
11.12 ff	**Vol. 1:** 218
12.1 ff	**Vol. 2:** 139
12.1	**Vol. 1:** 322
12.4	**Vol. 3:** 355
12.5	**Vol. 2:** 139
12.6	**Vol. 3:** 669
12.7	**Vol. 3:** 502
12.8	**Vol. 2:** 863
12.9	**Vol. 3:** 358
12.12	**Vol. 1:** 444 **Vol. 2:** 863 **Vol. 3:** 242
12.14	**Vol. 3:** 799
12.15	**Vol. 2:** 227, 863
12.18	**Vol. 3:** 669
12.22	**Vol. 3:** 669
13.1	**Vol. 2:** 863
13.2	**Vol. 2:** 209
13.4	**Vol. 1:** 618
13.10 f	**Vol. 2:** 326
13.11	**Vol. 3:** 816
13.14 f	**Vol. 1:** 216
13.14	**Vol. 2:** 357
13.16 ff	**Vol. 2:** 326
13.16–18	**Vol. 3:** 397
13.18	**Vol. 3:** 816
14	**Vol. 1:** 737
14.4	**Vol. 1:** 734 **Vol. 3:** 209, 823
14.5	**Vol. 1:** 734, 740
14.7 ff	**Vol. 3:** 233
14.7	**Vol. 3:** 209
14.9	**Vol. 3:** 358
14.10	**Vol. 1:** 609
14.11	**Vol. 3:** 358
14.13	**Vol. 2:** 846

Wisdom of Solomon (Wis.)

1.1 f	**Vol. 3:** 648

289

Wisdom of Solomon (Wis.) *(cont'd)*

1.1	**Vol. 2:** 512
1.2	**Vol. 1:** 598 **Vol. 3:** 799, 801
1.3 f	**Vol. 3:** 648
1.3	**Vol. 3:** 648, 808, 823, 1024
1.4–6	**Vol. 3:** 1027
1.5	**Vol. 3:** 823
1.6	**Vol. 3:** 341, 1041
1.7	**Vol. 1:** 735 **Vol. 2:** 512 **Vol. 3:** 693
1.8	**Vol. 3:** 93
1.9	**Vol. 2:** 512
1.11	**Vol. 3:** 345
1.14	**Vol. 1:** 380
1.15	**Vol. 3:** 358
2–5	**Vol. 3:** 618
2.1 ff	**Vol. 1:** 598
2.1	**Vol. 2:** 475 **Vol. 3:** 823
2.3	**Vol. 3:** 109
2.4	**Vol. 2:** 475
2.5	**Vol. 2:** 475 **Vol. 3:** 498, 555
2.6	**Vol. 1:** 381
2.9	**Vol. 3:** 29
2.10–20	**Vol. 2:** 202
2.10	**Vol. 3:** 358, 1074
2.13–18	**Vol. 3:** 638
2.13	**Vol. 2:** 512, 782 **Vol. 3:** 610
2.14	**Vol. 3:** 125
2.16 ff	**Vol. 1:** 618
2.16	**Vol. 3:** 30, 823
2.17	**Vol. 3:** 624, 799
2.18 ff	**Vol. 3:** 202
2.18	**Vol. 1:** 288 **Vol. 2:** 782
2.19	**Vol. 2:** 257 **Vol. 3:** 808
2.20	**Vol. 2:** 370 **Vol. 3:** 624
2.21	**Vol. 3:** 823
2.22	**Vol. 2:** 139 **Vol. 3:** 502, 924
2.23	**Vol. 1:** 380 **Vol. 2:** 287
2.24	**Vol. 1:** 557 **Vol. 3:** 468, 799
3.1 ff	**Vol. 1:** 598
3.1	**Vol. 3:** 358, 680, 856
3.2	**Vol. 3:** 821, 823, 1024
3.4	**Vol. 1:** 435 **Vol. 3:** 98
3.5	**Vol. 3:** 799–800
3.6	**Vol. 3:** 808
3.7–10	**Vol. 2:** 202
3.7	**Vol. 3:** 836
3.9	**Vol. 1:** 598 **Vol. 3:** 228, 882
3.10	**Vol. 1:** 572 **Vol. 3:** 823
3.11	**Vol. 3:** 1027
3.12	**Vol. 3:** 1024
3.13	**Vol. 2:** 586 **Vol. 3:** 585, 923
3.14–5.5	**Vol. 2:** 49
3.14	**Vol. 2:** 117
3.16	**Vol. 2:** 586
3.17	**Vol. 3:** 823
3.18	**Vol. 1:** 329
3.19	**Vol. 1:** 420
4.1	**Vol. 1:** 435 **Vol. 3:** 238, 926
4.2	**Vol. 1:** 491, 645 **Vol. 3:** 923
4.3	**Vol. 1:** 663
4.4	**Vol. 3:** 711
4.7	**Vol. 3:** 255
4.8 f	**Vol. 2:** 480
4.9	**Vol. 2:** 846
4.10 ff	**Vol. 2:** 627, 817 **Vol. 3:** 266
4.10	**Vol. 2:** 202, 815 **Vol. 3:** 265, 602
4.11	**Vol. 3:** 601
4.12	**Vol. 3:** 125
4.13	**Vol. 3:** 842
4.17	**Vol. 1:** 663 **Vol. 3:** 1028
4.18	**Vol. 3:** 29
4.19	**Vol. 2:** 502 **Vol. 3:** 238
5.1–5	**Vol. 2:** 202
5.1	**Vol. 2:** 735
5.2	**Vol. 3:** 209
5.3	**Vol. 2:** 431
5.4	**Vol. 2:** 846 **Vol. 3:** 823, 1024
5.5	**Vol. 3:** 638
5.6	**Vol. 3:** 730
5.8	**Vol. 2:** 842 **Vol. 3:** 29–30
5.9	**Vol. 1:** 322 **Vol. 3:** 555
5.11	**Vol. 3:** 571, 711
5.13	**Vol. 3:** 926
5.14	**Vol. 3:** 238
5.15	**Vol. 2:** 139
5.16	**Vol. 1:** 405
5.17	**Vol. 1:** 381
5.18	**Vol. 3:** 358
5.19	**Vol. 2:** 237 **Vol. 3:** 966
5.22	**Vol. 3:** 983
6.2	**Vol. 2:** 801
6.7	**Vol. 1:** 694 **Vol. 2:** 509
6.9	**Vol. 1:** 485, 609 **Vol. 3:** 585, 1027
6.10	**Vol. 3:** 760–761
6.12	**Vol. 3:** 1027
6.13	**Vol. 1:** 692
6.14	**Vol. 2:** 842
6.15	**Vol. 2:** 61
6.18	**Vol. 2:** 132
6.20–23	**Vol. 3:** 1027
6.20	**Vol. 2:** 377
6.22	**Vol. 2:** 215 **Vol. 3:** 502, 882
6.24	**Vol. 3:** 209, 1028
6.25	**Vol. 3:** 1120
7.2	**Vol. 1:** 322, 459
7.3	**Vol. 2:** 498
7.6†	**Vol. 2:** 498 **Vol. 3:** 937
7.7	**Vol. 3:** 1027
7.8	**Vol. 2:** 842
7.9	**Vol. 3:** 823
7.11	**Vol. 2:** 842
7.12–22	**Vol. 3:** 1056, 1069
7.12	**Vol. 3:** 1027, 1029
7.13	**Vol. 1:** 485 **Vol. 2:** 842
7.15	**Vol. 3:** 937, 1027–1028
7.17	**Vol. 2:** 452 **Vol. 3:** 1147
7.18	**Vol. 3:** 835
7.20	**Vol. 2:** 658 **Vol. 3:** 711, 820
7.22	**Vol. 3:** 760–761, 1027

Wisdom of Solomon (Wis.) *(cont'd)*

7.23	**Vol. 1:** 663
7.24	**Vol. 3:** 1027
7.25 f	**Vol. 2:** 290, 603 **Vol. 3:** 647
7.25	**Vol. 2:** 506
7.26	**Vol. 2:** 287, 290 **Vol. 3:** 827, 1147
7.27	**Vol. 3:** 1029
7.28	**Vol. 3:** 1027
7.29	**Vol. 3:** 730, 734
7.30	**Vol. 3:** 1027
8.3 f	**Vol. 3:** 641
8.3	**Vol. 2:** 509
8.4	**Vol. 3:** 502
8.5	**Vol. 2:** 841–842 **Vol. 3:** 1027
8.7	**Vol. 1:** 502 **Vol. 3:** 926
8.8	**Vol. 1:** 692 **Vol. 3:** 835
8.12	**Vol. 3:** 228
8.13	**Vol. 3:** 238
8.17	**Vol. 3:** 823, 1027
8.18	**Vol. 2:** 842
8.19 f	**Vol. 2:** 480
8.20	**Vol. 1:** 233 **Vol. 3:** 923
8.21	**Vol. 2:** 882
9.1	**Vol. 3:** 263, 1116
9.2	**Vol. 1:** 381 **Vol. 3:** 1027
9.4 f	**Vol. 3:** 610
9.4	**Vol. 3:** 1027, 1029
9.6	**Vol. 3:** 823, 1027
9.8	**Vol. 1:** 491
9.9	**Vol. 3:** 1027
9.10	**Vol. 2:** 191, 815
9.14	**Vol. 3:** 823
9.15	**Vol. 1:** 233 **Vol. 3:** 680, 811, 814
9.17 f	**Vol. 3:** 1027
9.17	**Vol. 3:** 86
9.18	**Vol. 2:** 452 **Vol. 3:** 209, 760–761
10	**Vol. 1:** 714
10.1	**Vol. 1:** 380 **Vol. 3:** 586
10.2	**Vol. 3:** 585
10.3	**Vol. 1:** 109
10.4	**Vol. 2:** 681 **Vol. 3:** 1027
10.5	**Vol. 2:** 143 **Vol. 3:** 924
10.6 ff	**Vol. 3:** 240
10.7	**Vol. 3:** 1040
10.8 f	**Vol. 3:** 1027
10.8	**Vol. 3:** 238
10.11	**Vol 2:** 841
10.12	**Vol. 1:** 648, 663 **Vol. 2:** 93
10.15	**Vol. 2:** 143 **Vol. 3:** 924
10.16	**Vol. 2:** 627
10.17	**Vol. 2:** 139
10.18	**Vol. 3:** 1024
10.19	**Vol. 3:** 255
10.20	**Vol. 3:** 669, 816, 908
10.21	**Vol. 1:** 428 **Vol. 3:** 1027
11.2–19.22	**Vol. 3:** 916
11.5	**Vol. 3:** 98
11.8	**Vol. 3:** 98
11.9†	**Vol. 1:** 109 **Vol. 3:** 799–800
11.10	**Vol. 1:** 568 **Vol. 2:** 370 **Vol. 3:** 808
11.12	**Vol. 3:** 238
11.13	**Vol. 3:** 98
11.15	**Vol. 3:** 823
11.16	**Vol. 3:** 98
11.17	**Vol. 1:** 380
11.20	**Vol. 3:** 402
12 f	**Vol. 3:** 331
12.1	**Vol. 1:** 468 **Vol. 3:** 692–693
12.2	**Vol. 1:** 568, 609 **Vol. 3:** 232, 585, 1212–1213
12.5	**Vol. 3:** 502
12.7	**Vol. 3:** 610
12.10	**Vol. 3:** 823
12.14 f	**Vol. 3:** 98
12.15	**Vol. 2:** 370 **Vol. 3:** 358
12.16	**Vol. 3:** 358
12.18	**Vol. 2:** 257
12.19–21	**Vol. 3:** 638
12.19	**Vol. 3:** 721, 760–761
12.20	**Vol. 3:** 610, 721, 842
12.21	**Vol. 3:** 721
12.22	**Vol. 3:** 721, 727
12.23	**Vol. 3:** 1024
12.24	**Vol. 3:** 1024
12.25–27	**Vol. 3:** 721
12.26	**Vol. 1:** 568 **Vol. 3:** 799
12.27	**Vol. 1:** 455 **Vol. 2:** 370 **Vol. 3:** 98, 821
13–15	**Vol. 2:** 287
13	**Vol. 3:** 885
13.1 f	**Vol. 2:** 491
13.1–10	**Vol. 3:** 885
13.1–9	**Vol. 2:** 396
13.1	**Vol. 1:** 387 **Vol. 2:** 400, 658, 660
13.2	**Vol. 3:** 735
13.3	**Vol. 1:** 380
13.4	**Vol. 3:** 128, 1147
13.5	**Vol. 1:** 382, 385
13.6	**Vol. 2:** 144 **Vol. 3:** 528
13.7	**Vol. 2:** 863
13.10	**Vol. 1:** 444 **Vol. 2:** 77
13.13	**Vol. 2:** 287
13.14	**Vol. 3:** 885
13.15	**Vol. 1:** 663
13.16	**Vol. 1:** 694 **Vol. 2:** 287
14	**Vol. 3:** 885
14.1	**Vol. 1:** 520
14.2	**Vol. 3:** 1027
14.3	**Vol. 1:** 618, 663, 694
14.5	**Vol. 3:** 1027
14.6	**Vol. 3:** 29
14.10	**Vol. 3:** 98
14.11	**Vol. 1:** 382 **Vol. 3:** 1024
14.15	**Vol. 2:** 285, 287
14.17	**Vol. 2:** 287 **Vol. 3:** 1169
14.20	**Vol. 3:** 823
14.23–26	**Vol. 3:** 929
14.23	**Vol. 3:** 502
14.25 f	**Vol. 3:** 31

Wisdom of Solomon (Wis.) *(cont'd)*

14.26	**Vol. 3:** 680
14.27 f	**Vol. 1:** 499
14.27	**Vol. 2:** 138
14.31	**Vol. 3:** 584
15.1 ff	**Vol. 2:** 769
15.1	**Vol. 3:** 882
15.2	**Vol. 3:** 823
15.3	**Vol. 1:** 435 **Vol. 3:** 358
15.5	**Vol. 1:** 444 **Vol. 2:** 287 **Vol. 3:** 1024
15.7–17	**Vol. 3:** 916
15.7	**Vol. 2:** 609 **Vol. 3:** 912, 916
15.8	**Vol. 3:** 916
15.9	**Vol. 1:** 491 **Vol. 3:** 916
15.10	**Vol. 3:** 916
15.11	**Vol. 2:** 787 **Vol. 3:** 692, 703, 1147
15.12	**Vol. 3:** 823
15.13	**Vol. 1:** 387 **Vol. 3:** 916
15.14	**Vol. 3:** 1024
15.15	**Vol. 2:** 175 **Vol. 3:** 823
15.18	**Vol. 3:** 125
16.1	**Vol. 3:** 98
16.2 f	**Vol. 1:** 460
16.2	**Vol. 3:** 98
16.6	**Vol. 1:** 568–569 **Vol. 3:** 209, 239
16.7	**Vol. 3:** 209, 462
16.9	**Vol. 3:** 98, 680
16.11	**Vol. 3:** 867
16.12	**Vol. 2:** 167
16.13	**Vol. 2:** 30
16.16	**Vol. 1:** 455
16.17	**Vol. 1:** 509 **Vol. 3:** 109, 218, 1147
16.20	**Vol. 1:** 459
16.21	**Vol. 1:** 711
16.22	**Vol. 2:** 773
16.24	**Vol. 1:** 381 **Vol. 3:** 98
16.27	**Vol. 3:** 572
16.28	**Vol. 2:** 882 **Vol. 3:** 818
16.29	**Vol. 1:** 683
17.2	**Vol. 1:** 694
17.4	**Vol. 2:** 644
17.5	**Vol. 2:** 773 **Vol. 3:** 711, 735
17.7	**Vol. 3:** 30
17.8	**Vol. 2:** 91
17.9	**Vol. 1:** 622
17.10	**Vol. 1:** 455 **Vol. 3:** 748
17.11	**Vol. 1:** 349, 420 **Vol. 2:** 370
17.12	**Vol. 3:** 823
17.13	**Vol. 2:** 138, 621 **Vol. 3:** 823
17.14 f	**Vol. 1:** 420
17.14	**Vol. 3:** 324
17.18	**Vol. 3:** 711
17.21	**Vol. 2:** 287
18.2	**Vol. 3:** 818
18.5	**Vol. 3:** 209, 908, 1114
18.6	**Vol. 1:** 663, 692
18.7	**Vol. 3:** 209
18.11	**Vol. 3:** 93, 98
18.14 ff	**Vol. 3:** 1116
18.18	**Vol. 2:** 138
18.19	**Vol. 2:** 621
18.20 ff	**Vol. 3:** 36
18.20	**Vol. 1:** 109
18.21	**Vol. 2:** 143, 863 **Vol. 3:** 552, 924
18.22	**Vol. 3:** 98, 1147
18.25	**Vol. 1:** 465
19.1	**Vol. 1:** 109
19.3	**Vol. 3:** 125, 823
19.4	**Vol. 1:** 734 **Vol. 3:** 98
19.5	**Vol. 3:** 799
19.6	**Vol. 1:** 381 **Vol. 3:** 610
19.7	**Vol. 3:** 555
19.9	**Vol. 3:** 816
19.13	**Vol. 1:** 420 **Vol. 3:** 571, 711
19.20b	**Vol. 2:** 658

Qumran Writings (Dead Sea Scrolls)

The Blessings (1QSb)

3.22	**Vol. 2:** 34
3.28	**Vol. 2:** 799
4.23	**Vol. 2:** 298 **Vol. 3:** 35
4.25 f	**Vol. 2:** 298
5.20 ff	**Vol. 3:** 650
5.25	**Vol. 3:** 961
5.27	**Vol. 2:** 558, 799

Commentary on Habakkuk
(1QpHab)

1.9	**Vol. 3:** 823
1.13	**Vol. 3:** 359, 766
2.2	**Vol. 3:** 359, 766
2.3	**Vol. 2:** 312
2.5 f	**Vol. 2:** 56
2.5–9	**Vol. 3:** 1120
2.6	**Vol. 2:** 893
2.7 ff	**Vol. 3:** 492

Commentary on Habakkuk (1QpHab) *(cont'd)*

2.8 f	**Vol. 2:** 34
2.9	**Vol. 3:** 610
4.29	**Vol. 1:** 679
5.3	**Vol. 2:** 793, 798
5.4 ff	**Vol. 1:** 539
5.4	**Vol. 2:** 793
5.5	**Vol. 2:** 798
5.10	**Vol. 3:** 359, 766
6.14	**Vol. 3:** 484
7.1 ff	**Vol. 3:** 492
7.1–5	**Vol. 3:** 80
7.2	**Vol. 2:** 61 **Vol. 3:** 842
7.4–8	**Vol. 3:** 1120
7.4	**Vol. 3:** 359, 766
7.7 f	**Vol. 3:** 503
7.7	**Vol. 2:** 61
7.12	**Vol. 2:** 61
7.13 f	**Vol. 1:** 627
7.13	**Vol. 3:** 842
7.14	**Vol. 1:** 412
8.1–3	**Vol. 1:** 598 **Vol. 2:** 314 **Vol. 3:** 359, 367
8.3	**Vol. 3:** 766
8.8	**Vol. 2:** 34
9.2	**Vol. 1:** 676
9.6	**Vol. 2:** 893
9.9 ff	**Vol. 2:** 34
9.9	**Vol. 2:** 56 **Vol. 3:** 766
10.7	**Vol. 3:** 484
10.9 f	**Vol. 2:** 312
10.9	**Vol. 3:** 39, 801
10.10	**Vol. 1:** 296
10.14	**Vol. 3:** 484
11.1	**Vol. 2:** 397
11.5	**Vol. 3:** 766
11.8	**Vol. 3:** 801
11.10	**Vol. 3:** 484
11.15	**Vol. 3:** 359
12.3	**Vol. 2:** 824
12.6	**Vol. 2:** 824
12.10	**Vol. 2:** 824
12.13 f	**Vol. 2:** 893
12.13	**Vol. 2:** 792
12.14	**Vol. 3:** 842
13.1 ff	**Vol. 2:** 893
13.2 ff	**Vol. 3:** 842
13.3 f	**Vol. 2:** 792

Community Rule (1QS)

1	**Vol. 1:** 556
1.1	**Vol. 3:** 531
1.2 f	**Vol. 1:** 556
1.3 f	**Vol. 2:** 542
1.3	**Vol. 1:** 333, 554 **Vol. 2:** 640 **Vol. 3:** 610
1.4	**Vol. 1:** 539
1.5	**Vol. 3:** 883

1.6	**Vol. 1:** 499 **Vol. 3:** 934
1.8 f	**Vol. 2:** 782
1.8	**Vol. 2:** 61, 595 **Vol. 3:** 934
1.9 ff	**Vol. 1:** 345
1.9 f	**Vol. 1:** 554
1.9–11	**Vol. 1:** 556
1.9	**Vol. 1:** 627 **Vol. 2:** 492 **Vol. 3:** 637
1.10	**Vol. 2:** 298, 312 **Vol. 3:** 469
1.11 f	**Vol. 1:** 641
1.12	**Vol. 2:** 842
1.14 f	**Vol. 3:** 842
1.15	**Vol. 3:** 882, 934
1.16–2.18	**Vol. 2:** 493, 784
1.17	**Vol. 1:** 333
1.18 f	**Vol. 3:** 210
1.18	**Vol. 1:** 452 **Vol. 2:** 492, 608 **Vol. 3:** 469
1.20	**Vol. 1:** 98
1.21	**Vol. 2:** 599
1.22	**Vol. 2:** 595
1.23 f	**Vol. 2:** 608
1.23	**Vol. 1:** 452
1.24	**Vol. 1:** 345 **Vol. 2:** 492
1.25	**Vol. 3:** 934
2.1	**Vol. 2:** 595, 599 **Vol. 3:** 828
2.2–4	**Vol. 1:** 212
2.2	**Vol. 2:** 61, 298 **Vol. 3:** 934
2.3 f	**Vol. 3:** 828
2.3	**Vol. 2:** 782 **Vol. 3:** 126
2.4 ff	**Vol. 1:** 416, 452
2.4 f	**Vol. 2:** 312
2.4–9	**Vol. 1:** 554 **Vol. 3:** 469
2.4	**Vol. 2:** 595, 779
2.5	**Vol. 2:** 298, 492 **Vol. 3:** 469
2.7 f	**Vol. 2:** 493
2.8	**Vol. 1:** 656, 700 **Vol. 3:** 160, 828
2.11	**Vol. 2:** 285
2.12	**Vol. 2:** 706–707
2.13 f	**Vol. 3:** 28
2.13	**Vol. 3:** 1120
2.14	**Vol. 3:** 934
2.15	**Vol. 1:** 109 **Vol. 3:** 828
2.16	**Vol. 2:** 492 **Vol. 3:** 637
2.17	**Vol. 2:** 285, 298, 706–707 **Vol. 3:** 828
2.18	**Vol. 1:** 98
2.19 f	**Vol. 2:** 34
2.19	**Vol. 2:** 492, 608 **Vol. 3:** 469
2.20	**Vol. 1:** 98, 102
2.21 f	**Vol. 2:** 699
2.21	**Vol. 2:** 799
2.22	**Vol. 2:** 397, 472
2.23	**Vol. 2:** 298
2.24	**Vol. 2:** 105, 261, 595 **Vol. 3:** 926, 928
2.25–3.12	**Vol. 1:** 144
2.25	**Vol. 3:** 828
2.26	**Vol. 1:** 700 **Vol. 3:** 934
3	**Vol. 2:** 364
3.1	**Vol. 3:** 680, 823, 842
3.2	**Vol. 1:** 641
3.3	**Vol. 2:** 493

Community Rule (1QS) *(cont'd)*

3.4 f	**Vol. 1:** 152
3.4–12	**Vol. 3:** 105, 989
3.4	**Vol. 3:** 28, 823
3.6 ff	**Vol. 2:** 878
3.6–12	**Vol. 1:** 700
3.6	**Vol. 2:** 141 **Vol. 3:** 882
3.7 ff	**Vol. 1:** 700
3.7 f	**Vol. 3:** 693
3.7–9	**Vol. 3:** 695
3.7	**Vol. 2:** 480
3.8 f	**Vol. 1:** 152
3.8	**Vol. 2:** 261 **Vol. 3:** 680
3.9	**Vol. 3:** 934
3.10	**Vol. 1:** 627
3.13 ff	**Vol. 1:** 563
3.13–4.26	**Vol. 2:** 565 **Vol. 3:** 126, 693
3.13	**Vol. 2:** 492 **Vol. 3:** 761, 766
3.15	**Vol. 2:** 71–72, 397 **Vol. 3:** 503
3.16	**Vol. 1:** 735
3.17 ff	**Vol. 3:** 939, 964
3.17 f	**Vol. 1:** 382
3.17–25	**Vol. 1:** 452
3.18 ff	**Vol. 1:** 102 **Vol. 3:** 943–944
3.18	**Vol. 2:** 56 **Vol. 3:** 837, 934
3.19 ff	**Vol. 2:** 492
3.19–26	**Vol. 2:** 71
3.20 ff	**Vol. 3:** 940
3.20 f	**Vol. 2:** 493 **Vol. 3:** 934, 944
3.20–23	**Vol. 3:** 469
3.20	**Vol. 2:** 481, 492 **Vol. 3:** 503, 704
3.21 f	**Vol. 3:** 503
3.21–24	**Vol. 1:** 423
3.21	**Vol. 2:** 459, 492 **Vol. 3:** 503, 801
3.23	**Vol. 2:** 56, 608 **Vol. 3:** 842
3.24 ff	**Vol. 3:** 994
3.24 f	**Vol. 1:** 102
3.24	**Vol. 2:** 707–708 **Vol. 3:** 801, 882
3.25	**Vol. 1:** 102, 382 **Vol. 2:** 71
3.26	**Vol. 2:** 492
4	**Vol. 2:** 364 **Vol. 3:** 273
4.1–5.13	**Vol. 3:** 250
4.1	**Vol. 1:** 452
4.3 f	**Vol. 3:** 928
4.3–14	**Vol. 3:** 926
4.3	**Vol. 2:** 105, 261, 824
4.4 f	**Vol. 2:** 595
4.5	**Vol. 2:** 285 **Vol. 3:** 926
4.6 ff	**Vol. 2:** 493
4.6	**Vol. 1:** 333 **Vol. 2:** 216 **Vol. 3:** 926
4.7 f	**Vol. 1:** 423 **Vol. 3:** 273
4.7	**Vol. 2:** 480, 779
4.8	**Vol. 3:** 1025
4.9–11	**Vol. 1:** 452 **Vol. 3:** 31, 1025
4.9	**Vol. 1:** 333 **Vol. 2:** 471 **Vol. 3:** 926
4.10	**Vol. 1:** 109, 499 **Vol. 3:** 926
4.11	**Vol. 2:** 34
4.12 f	**Vol. 2:** 493 **Vol. 3:** 842
4.12	**Vol. 1:** 110, 452
4.13	**Vol. 1:** 656
4.15 ff	**Vol. 2:** 298
4.15	**Vol. 2:** 707
4.16	**Vol. 3:** 939
4.17	**Vol. 2:** 105 **Vol. 3:** 882
4.18 ff	**Vol. 2:** 56 **Vol. 3:** 837
4.18	**Vol. 3:** 126, 1029
4.20 f	**Vol. 1:** 673 **Vol. 2:** 878 **Vol. 3:** 105
4.20–21	**Vol. 3:** 883
4.20	**Vol. 3:** 1029
4.21 f	**Vol. 1:** 225 **Vol. 3:** 639, 989, 1029
4.21	**Vol. 3:** 695
4.22	**Vol. 1:** 102, 288, 539 **Vol. 2:** 71, 782 **Vol. 3:** 1029
4.24	**Vol. 3:** 882, 1025
4.25	**Vol. 2:** 397 **Vol. 3:** 842
4.26	**Vol. 2:** 298
5.1	**Vol. 1:** 333, 357
5.2	**Vol. 1:** 732 **Vol. 2:** 34, 134, 842
5.3 f	**Vol. 3:** 928
5.3	**Vol. 2:** 261, 299 **Vol. 3:** 626
5.4	**Vol. 2:** 105, 595 **Vol. 3:** 801, 883, 926
5.5 f	**Vol. 2:** 312
5.5	**Vol. 1:** 309
5.6	**Vol. 2:** 248 **Vol. 3:** 160
5.7–11	**Vol. 3:** 740
5.7	**Vol. 3:** 1194
5.8	**Vol. 1:** 333, 357 **Vol. 2:** 640
5.9	**Vol. 1:** 732 **Vol. 2:** 34, 134
5.10 f	**Vol. 3:** 939
5.10	**Vol. 3:** 944
5.11	**Vol. 2:** 397 **Vol. 3:** 801, 823
5.12	**Vol. 1:** 110
5.13 f	**Vol. 3:** 989
5.14	**Vol. 3:** 1120
5.15	**Vol. 3:** 487
5.17 f	**Vol. 3:** 823
5.17	**Vol. 3:** 487
5.19	**Vol. 3:** 1120
5.21 ff	**Vol. 2:** 397
5.21	**Vol. 3:** 692
5.22	**Vol. 1:** 333 **Vol. 2:** 842
5.23 f	**Vol. 3:** 486
5.24	**Vol. 2:** 782 **Vol. 3:** 692
5.25	**Vol. 2:** 105, 261, 595 **Vol. 3:** 928
6.1	**Vol. 3:** 1120, 1122
6.3	**Vol. 2:** 34
6.4 f	**Vol. 1:** 630
6.4–6	**Vol. 2:** 522
6.4	**Vol. 3:** 1120
6.7 f	**Vol. 3:** 486
6.8	**Vol. 1:** 197
6.9	**Vol. 2:** 799
6.10 f	**Vol. 3:** 486
6.12	**Vol. 1:** 190
6.14	**Vol. 1:** 190
6.15	**Vol. 3:** 882
6.16 f	**Vol. 3:** 105
6.16	**Vol. 2:** 54, 299 **Vol. 3:** 1120
6.17	**Vol. 2:** 842

294

Community Rule (1QS) (cont'd)

6.18	**Vol. 2:** 299
6.19 f	**Vol. 1:** 641
6.19	**Vol. 1:** 732 **Vol. 2:** 54, 842
6.20	**Vol. 1:** 190
6.21	**Vol. 2:** 299
6.22	**Vol. 2:** 54
6.25	**Vol. 3:** 105
6.26	**Vol. 3:** 486
6.27	**Vol. 3:** 233
7	**Vol. 3:** 842
7.1	**Vol. 3:** 486
7.3	**Vol. 3:** 105
7.6	**Vol. 2:** 842 **Vol. 3:** 1016
7.16	**Vol. 3:** 105
7.18 ff	**Vol. 1:** 607
7.18	**Vol. 3:** 692
7.20	**Vol. 1:** 735
7.22 ff	**Vol. 1:** 607
7.22	**Vol. 1:** 735
7.23	**Vol. 3:** 692
8	**Vol. 3:** 1006
8.1–15	**Vol. 1:** 539
8.1	**Vol. 2:** 782
8.2	**Vol. 2:** 105, 595 **Vol. 3:** 883, 926
8.3	**Vol. 2:** 134 **Vol. 3:** 160, 692
8.4 ff	**Vol. 2:** 61
8.4–9	**Vol. 2:** 779
8.5 ff	**Vol. 1:** 661 **Vol. 2:** 228
8.5 f	**Vol. 2:** 878
8.5–10	**Vol. 3:** 169
8.5–9	**Vol. 2:** 312
8.5	**Vol. 2:** 248, 312 **Vol. 3:** 783
8.6	**Vol. 2:** 818 **Vol. 3:** 160, 883
8.7 f	**Vol. 3:** 382, 392
8.9	**Vol. 2:** 248, 782
8.10	**Vol. 3:** 160
8.11 f	**Vol. 3:** 1120
8.12	**Vol. 3:** 692
8.13	**Vol. 2:** 228 **Vol. 3:** 939
8.14	**Vol. 3:** 487
8.15	**Vol. 2:** 640
8.18	**Vol. 2:** 782
8.20	**Vol. 2:** 61, 782
8.21	**Vol. 2:** 228
8.22	**Vol. 2:** 640
8.35	**Vol. 2:** 707
9.2	**Vol. 2:** 782
9.3 ff	**Vol. 2:** 228
9.3–6	**Vol. 2:** 878
9.3	**Vol. 1:** 661
9.4 f	**Vol. 2:** 118
9.5 f	**Vol. 2:** 782
9.5	**Vol. 2:** 312
9.6	**Vol. 2:** 248 **Vol. 3:** 783
9.8 f	**Vol. 2:** 782
9.10 f	**Vol. 2:** 899 **Vol. 3:** 35
9.11	**Vol. 1:** 321 **Vol. 3:** 80
9.12 ff	**Vol. 1:** 333 **Vol. 3:** 836
9.12	**Vol. 3:** 766
9.13 f	**Vol. 1:** 627
9.13	**Vol. 3:** 761, 1016
9.14	**Vol. 3:** 359
9.15	**Vol. 3:** 1016
9.17	**Vol. 2:** 216 **Vol. 3:** 883
9.18 ff	**Vol. 3:** 836
9.18	**Vol. 3:** 640
9.19 f	**Vol. 3:** 1006
9.19	**Vol. 2:** 782
9.21–23	**Vol. 1:** 556
9.21	**Vol. 2:** 707 **Vol. 3:** 766
9.22	**Vol. 2:** 261
9.23	**Vol. 3:** 1016
9.26	**Vol. 3:** 842
9.27	**Vol. 2:** 707
10.1 ff	**Vol. 3:** 842
10.1–8	**Vol. 1:** 627
10.4	**Vol. 2:** 595
10.6	**Vol. 2:** 118
10.9	**Vol. 2:** 397
10.11	**Vol. 2:** 353
10.12	**Vol. 2:** 72, 397
10.16	**Vol. 2:** 72, 595
10.17	**Vol. 3:** 210
10.18 ff	**Vol. 2:** 56
10.18	**Vol. 2:** 72, 707
10.19	**Vol. 1:** 109 **Vol. 2:** 893
10.20	**Vol. 1:** 357 **Vol. 3:** 926
10.22	**Vol. 3:** 926
10.25 f	**Vol. 3:** 926
10.25	**Vol. 3:** 372
10.26	**Vol. 2:** 595
11.1–14	**Vol. 3:** 160
11.1	**Vol. 2:** 261 **Vol. 3:** 801
11.2 f	**Vol. 3:** 161
11.2	**Vol. 3:** 359
11.3	**Vol. 1:** 700 **Vol. 3:** 359
11.4	**Vol. 3:** 882
11.5	**Vol. 2:** 71, 493 **Vol. 3:** 161, 359
11.6	**Vol. 2:** 216, 397
11.7 f	**Vol. 2:** 298 **Vol. 3:** 614
11.7	**Vol. 2:** 302
11.8	**Vol. 2:** 228, 302
11.9	**Vol. 1:** 673
11.10	**Vol. 3:** 944
11.11	**Vol. 2:** 72, 782
11.12 f	**Vol. 2:** 118, 595
11.12	**Vol. 1:** 673 **Vol. 2:** 707 **Vol. 3:** 359, 372, 801
11.13 f	**Vol. 2:** 72
11.14	**Vol. 2:** 72
11.15–20	**Vol. 3:** 640
11.15	**Vol. 2:** 397
11.17	**Vol. 2:** 72, 782 **Vol. 3:** 1016
11.18	**Vol. 2:** 118 **Vol. 3:** 359
11.19	**Vol. 2:** 72, 197
11.21	**Vol. 3:** 823
12 ff	**Vol. 3:** 1006
14.13	**Vol. 2:** 118

Community Rule (1QS) *(cont'd)*

16.9	**Vol. 3:** 359
16.15	**Vol. 2:** 707
17.4	**Vol. 2:** 707

Damascus Document (CD)

1.3	**Vol. 2:** 312
1.4	**Vol. 2:** 779 **Vol. 3:** 234, 250
1.5 f	**Vol. 1:** 110
1.5–11	**Vol. 3:** 783
1.7	**Vol. 2:** 312
1.11	**Vol. 3:** 359, 766
1.13	**Vol. 3:** 487, 939
1.14	**Vol. 2:** 312
1.15	**Vol. 3:** 801
1.21	**Vol. 1:** 110
2.3 f	**Vol. 1:** 700
2.3	**Vol. 3:** 640
2.4	**Vol. 1:** 412 **Vol. 2:** 397
2.6	**Vol. 3:** 250, 939
2.12 f	**Vol. 2:** 337
2.13	**Vol. 3:** 801
2.14	**Vol. 2:** 279
2.16	**Vol. 1:** 499
2.17	**Vol. 2:** 459 **Vol. 3:** 801
2.18–21	**Vol. 3:** 468
2.18	**Vol. 1:** 102 **Vol. 2:** 134
2.21	**Vol. 1:** 333 **Vol. 2:** 134
3.1	**Vol. 3:** 801
3.2 f	**Vol. 2:** 134
3.3 f	**Vol. 3:** 486
3.4	**Vol. 2:** 459 **Vol. 3:** 801
3.8	**Vol. 1:** 110
3.13 f	**Vol. 3:** 639
3.14 ff	**Vol. 3:** 503
3.14	**Vol. 2:** 459 **Vol. 3:** 801
3.15	**Vol. 3:** 1016
3.16	**Vol. 3:** 459
3.18	**Vol. 1:** 700
3.19	**Vol. 2:** 248, 312
3.20	**Vol. 2:** 45, 480
3.21	**Vol. 2:** 34
4.1	**Vol. 3:** 801
4.2	**Vol. 1:** 357
4.3	**Vol. 2:** 312
4.4	**Vol. 1:** 273 **Vol. 2:** 56
4.6 ff	**Vol. 3:** 160
4.11	**Vol. 2:** 312
4.12b–5.14a	**Vol. 3:** 538
4.13	**Vol. 2:** 314, 779 **Vol. 3:** 469
4.15	**Vol. 3:** 469
4.16	**Vol. 2:** 314
4.17	**Vol. 1:** 499
4.20	**Vol. 1:** 499
4.21	**Vol. 1:** 383
5.1 f	**Vol. 3:** 487
5.2 f	**Vol. 3:** 486
5.2	**Vol. 3:** 499
5.8	**Vol. 2:** 640
5.18	**Vol. 1:** 102 **Vol. 2:** 492, 640 **Vol. 3:** 704
5.19	**Vol. 3:** 210
5.20	**Vol. 3:** 801
5.21	**Vol. 2:** 640
6.1	**Vol. 2:** 312
6.2 f	**Vol. 2:** 312, 314
6.2	**Vol. 3:** 234
6.4	**Vol. 3:** 459
6.11	**Vol. 2:** 56
6.14–7.4	**Vol. 3:** 173, 428
6.14	**Vol. 2:** 134
6.17	**Vol. 2:** 738
6.18 f	**Vol. 1:** 627
6.18	**Vol. 2:** 134
6.19	**Vol. 1:** 368 **Vol. 2:** 312
7.2	**Vol. 2:** 141
7.6	**Vol. 2:** 699
7.10	**Vol. 3:** 1120
7.15 ff	**Vol. 3:** 486
7.15	**Vol. 3:** 650
7.16	**Vol. 3:** 651
7.18 ff	**Vol. 3:** 487
7.18 f	**Vol. 2:** 313
7.18–20	**Vol. 3:** 650
7.18	**Vol. 3:** 531
7.19 f	**Vol. 2:** 558
7.19–20	**Vol. 3:** 735
7.20 f	**Vol. 3:** 961
8.1	**Vol. 2:** 893
8.2 f	**Vol. 2:** 56
8.2	**Vol. 2:** 314
8.3	**Vol. 1:** 109, 333 **Vol. 2:** 312
8.5	**Vol. 3:** 926
8.6	**Vol. 3:** 926
8.8–18	**Vol. 2:** 579
8.14	**Vol. 2:** 640
8.16	**Vol. 2:** 312
8.20	**Vol. 3:** 1120
8.21	**Vol. 2:** 312
8.40	**Vol. 2:** 312
9.1–10.3	**Vol. 3:** 740
9.4	**Vol. 1:** 197
9.10–12	**Vol. 2:** 573
9.11	**Vol. 2:** 640
10.2	**Vol. 1:** 333
10.6	**Vol. 3:** 487
10.14–11.18	**Vol. 3:** 408
10.14	**Vol. 2:** 134
10.16	**Vol. 2:** 134
11.22	**Vol. 1:** 296
12.2	**Vol. 3:** 469
12.3	**Vol. 3:** 801
12.6	**Vol. 1:** 296
12.20	**Vol. 1:** 333
12.21	**Vol. 3:** 766
12.23 f	**Vol. 3:** 35
12.23	**Vol. 1:** 321
13.1 f	**Vol. 2:** 699
13.4	**Vol. 2:** 299

Damascus Document (CD) *(cont'd)*

13.6 f	**Vol. 1:** 190	
13.9	**Vol. 1:** 190	**Vol. 3:** 566
13.11	**Vol. 3:** 126	
13.12	**Vol. 2:** 298	
13.18	**Vol. 2:** 595	
13.22	**Vol. 3:** 766	
14.3 ff	**Vol. 1:** 360	
14.3–6	**Vol. 2:** 311	
14.4 ff	**Vol. 3:** 486	
14.9–12	**Vol. 1:** 190	
14.12 ff	**Vol. 3:** 545	
14.14	**Vol. 2:** 738	
14.16	**Vol. 3:** 193	
15.2	**Vol. 2:** 640	**Vol. 3:** 234
15.5	**Vol. 3:** 740	
15.9	**Vol. 2:** 640	
15.12	**Vol. 2:** 640	
15.15 ff	**Vol. 2:** 161	
15.15	**Vol. 3:** 1025	
16.1–9	**Vol. 3:** 680	
16.2	**Vol. 2:** 640	
16.3 f	**Vol. 3:** 487	
16.4 f	**Vol. 2:** 605	
16.5	**Vol. 1:** 102	**Vol. 2:** 640
16.7	**Vol. 2:** 134	
16.8	**Vol. 3:** 194	
19.1 f	**Vol. 2:** 134, 699	
19.1	**Vol. 2:** 595	
19.5–16	**Vol. 2:** 56	
19.9	**Vol. 2:** 56, 134	
19.15 f	**Vol. 1:** 109	
19.16	**Vol. 1:** 357	
19.17	**Vol. 3:** 926	
19.18	**Vol. 3:** 926	
19.26 f	**Vol. 2:** 312	
19.26	**Vol. 2:** 640	
19.28	**Vol. 2:** 134	
19.34	**Vol. 2:** 459	
19.35	**Vol. 2:** 798	**Vol. 3:** 823
20.1	**Vol. 1:** 321	**Vol. 3:** 766
20.2	**Vol. 1:** 333	
20.3 f	**Vol. 2:** 299	
20.9	**Vol. 2:** 285	
20.11	**Vol. 2:** 459	
20.14 f	**Vol. 3:** 272	
20.14	**Vol. 3:** 766	
20.17	**Vol. 2:** 134	
20.19	**Vol. 3:** 486, 823	
20.21	**Vol. 2:** 595	
20.22	**Vol. 2:** 134, 699	
20.27 f	**Vol. 2:** 56	
20.32	**Vol. 3:** 359, 766	
20.33 f	**Vol. 2:** 56	
20.33	**Vol. 2:** 355	
20.34	**Vol. 1:** 288	**Vol. 3:** 160

Florilegium (4Qflor)

1.7 ff	**Vol. 3:** 650

1.8	**Vol. 3:** 801	
1.9	**Vol. 3:** 823	
1.10 ff	**Vol. 1:** 178	
1.11	**Vol. 3:** 531, 650	
1.12 f	**Vol. 3:** 651	
1.12	**Vol. 3:** 650	
1.17	**Vol. 2:** 285	
1.19	**Vol. 2:** 56	
2.3	**Vol. 2:** 640	

Genesis Apocryphon (1QGenAp)

2	**Vol. 2:** 682	**Vol. 3:** 642
2.1	**Vol. 1:** 102	
2.4	**Vol. 2:** 71	
2.16	**Vol. 1:** 102	
20.12	**Vol. 2:** 71	
20.13	**Vol. 2:** 71	
20.16 ff	**Vol. 1:** 452	
20.28 f	**Vol. 1:** 452	

Hymns, Hodayot (1QH)

1.3	**Vol. 3:** 828	
1.5–39	**Vol. 1:** 700	
1.7 f	**Vol. 1:** 382	**Vol. 3:** 828
1.7	**Vol. 2:** 397	
1.8	**Vol. 3:** 1016	
1.9 ff	**Vol. 3:** 503	
1.10	**Vol. 1:** 333	
1.12	**Vol. 3:** 52	
1.13 f	**Vol. 1:** 382	
1.17	**Vol. 2:** 779	
1.20	**Vol. 2:** 72	
1.21	**Vol. 3:** 312	
1.26	**Vol. 2:** 71	
1.27 f	**Vol. 1:** 382	
1.28 f	**Vol. 3:** 1120	
1.30	**Vol. 2:** 622, 651	
1.31	**Vol. 2:** 397	
1.32	**Vol. 2:** 595	
1.33	**Vol. 2:** 622	
2.2	**Vol. 1:** 296	
2.3	**Vol. 1:** 102	
2.7–35	**Vol. 3:** 680	
2.9	**Vol. 1:** 357	
2.10	**Vol. 1:** 102	
2.13 f	**Vol. 3:** 503, 1029	
2.13	**Vol. 2:** 818	**Vol. 3:** 359
2.14	**Vol. 2:** 459	**Vol. 3:** 801
2.16 f	**Vol. 3:** 469	
2.17	**Vol. 3:** 761	
2.18	**Vol. 2:** 397	
2.19	**Vol. 2:** 459	
2.20	**Vol. 1:** 345	**Vol. 2:** 480
2.23	**Vol. 2:** 118, 595	
2.25 f	**Vol. 1:** 656	
2.25	**Vol. 2:** 118, 595	
2.30	**Vol. 2:** 651	
2.31	**Vol. 1:** 345	**Vol. 2:** 480
2.32	**Vol. 3:** 193, 210, 823	

Hymns, Hodayot (1QH) *(cont'd)*

2.35	Vol. 3: 193
3.5–18	Vol. 3: 722
3.6	Vol. 3: 680, 823
3.7–10	Vol. 3: 1068
3.12–18	Vol. 2: 311
3.19–23	Vol. 2: 161
3.19	Vol. 3: 193, 680
3.20	Vol. 3: 52
3.21 f	Vol. 2: 298
3.22	Vol. 2: 298
3.23	Vol. 2: 622, 651
3.24 f	Vol. 2: 298
3.24	Vol. 3: 823
3.25 ff	Vol. 1: 110, 656
3.28	Vol. 1: 110
3.29–39	Vol. 3: 559
3.29–36	Vol. 2: 836
3.29	Vol. 3: 469
3.32	Vol. 3: 469
3.34 ff	Vol. 3: 272
3.36	Vol. 1: 102 Vol. 3: 842
4.7	Vol. 2: 459
4.8 f	Vol. 3: 823
4.10–16	Vol. 2: 314
4.10	Vol. 2: 471
4.12	Vol. 2: 459 Vol. 3: 801
4.14	Vol. 3: 687, 823, 883
4.16	Vol. 3: 801
4.20	Vol. 2: 72 Vol. 3: 801
4.23	Vol. 2: 602 Vol. 3: 823
4.25	Vol. 3: 801
4.26	Vol. 2: 799
4.27	Vol. 1: 96
4.28 f	Vol. 2: 602
4.28	Vol. 2: 622
4.29	Vol. 2: 622 Vol. 3: 503
4.30	Vol. 1: 673 Vol. 3: 359
4.31	Vol. 3: 693
4.32 f	Vol. 2: 566 Vol. 3: 637
4.32	Vol. 1: 288 Vol. 2: 72
4.33	Vol. 2: 818
4.34 f	Vol. 3: 234
4.35	Vol. 3: 1120
4.37	Vol. 1: 700 Vol. 2: 72, 118, 595 Vol. 3: 160
4.38	Vol. 1: 382
5.9	Vol. 3: 312
5.11 f	Vol. 3: 210
5.12–39	Vol. 3: 680
5.12	Vol. 2: 808
5.20 ff	Vol. 2: 194
5.20	Vol. 2: 738
5.21	Vol. 1: 102
5.22	Vol. 2: 595
5.23 f	Vol. 2: 521
5.25	Vol. 1: 288 Vol. 2: 216
5.26 f	Vol. 2: 312
5.26	Vol. 3: 823
5.28	Vol. 2: 707 Vol. 3: 801
5.36	Vol. 2: 707 Vol. 3: 801
5.38	Vol. 3: 823
5.39	Vol. 3: 469
6.4	Vol. 3: 312
6.8	Vol. 2: 798
6.9	Vol. 2: 595
6.11	Vol. 2: 622
6.12 f	Vol. 2: 793
6.13	Vol. 1: 102
6.21	Vol. 3: 469
6.26	Vol. 3: 382
6.28 ff	Vol. 3: 961
6.29 f	Vol. 3: 272
6.30 f	Vol. 2: 56
6.30	Vol. 1: 288 Vol. 2: 602
6.34	Vol. 3: 273
7.4	Vol. 3: 469
7.6 f	Vol. 2: 602, 878
7.8 f	Vol. 2: 249
7.8	Vol. 3: 382
7.10	Vol. 3: 610
7.12	Vol. 2: 312
7.15	Vol. 2: 779
7.18	Vol. 1: 700 Vol. 2: 595
7.20	Vol. 1: 288 Vol. 2: 595 Vol. 3: 637
7.27	Vol. 2: 118, 595
7.30 f	Vol. 2: 72
7.30	Vol. 1: 700
7.34	Vol. 1: 296 Vol. 2: 72
7.35	Vol. 1: 700 Vol. 2: 118, 595
8.1–8	Vol. 3: 722
8.4–14	Vol. 3: 986
8.10 f	Vol. 2: 216
8.11	Vol. 3: 499, 823
8.14	Vol. 3: 823
8.36	Vol. 2: 707 Vol. 3: 610, 801
9	Vol. 3: 722
9.7 f	Vol. 3: 680
9.7	Vol. 2: 595
9.9	Vol. 2: 397
9.10	Vol. 2: 118, 595
9.11	Vol. 2: 779
9.14	Vol. 2: 118, 595
9.17	Vol. 2: 72
9.24	Vol. 2: 357
9.28 f	Vol. 3: 212
9.28	Vol. 2: 808 Vol. 3: 680
9.29 f	Vol. 1: 539
9.30	Vol. 2: 72
9.32 f	Vol. 2: 72
9.33	Vol. 2: 780 Vol. 3: 680
9.34	Vol. 2: 72
9.35 f	Vol. 1: 618
9.35	Vol. 2: 71
9.38	Vol. 2: 651
9.66	Vol. 2: 480
10.2	Vol. 2: 818 Vol. 3: 1016
10.3	Vol. 2: 71
10.5 f	Vol. 2: 72

Hymns, Hodayot (1QH) *(cont'd)*

10.5	**Vol. 3:** 823
10.6	**Vol. 2:** 818
10.8	**Vol. 2:** 71
10.9	**Vol. 2:** 72, 818 **Vol. 3:** 1016
10.14	**Vol. 2:** 72, 595
10.16	**Vol. 2:** 72, 595
10.20	**Vol. 3:** 52
10.21	**Vol. 1:** 700
10.34 f	**Vol. 1:** 102
11.5	**Vol. 2:** 595
11.6	**Vol. 2:** 651 **Vol. 3:** 52
11.7	**Vol. 2:** 72
11.9 f	**Vol. 2:** 72
11.9	**Vol. 1:** 700 **Vol. 2:** 566, 818
11.11 f	**Vol. 2:** 298
11.12	**Vol. 2:** 228
11.13	**Vol. 1:** 102
11.14	**Vol. 2:** 397
11.17 f	**Vol. 2:** 595
11.17	**Vol. 2:** 72
11.18	**Vol. 2:** 72
11.23 f	**Vol. 3:** 210
11.23	**Vol. 2:** 355
11.24	**Vol. 2:** 397
11.25	**Vol. 2:** 651
11.28	**Vol. 2:** 595 **Vol. 3:** 126
11.29	**Vol. 2:** 72
11.30 f	**Vol. 2:** 595
11.30	**Vol. 2:** 355, 357
11.31	**Vol. 2:** 118
11.33	**Vol. 2:** 72
12.3	**Vol. 2:** 651
12.4–11	**Vol. 1:** 627
12.5	**Vol. 1:** 333
12.10	**Vol. 2:** 72
12.11 ff	**Vol. 3:** 1029
12.11 f	**Vol. 2:** 878
12.11	**Vol. 3:** 693
12.13	**Vol. 2:** 71, 397 **Vol. 3:** 126
12.14	**Vol. 2:** 595
12.21	**Vol. 2:** 595
12.30	**Vol. 3:** 52
13.5	**Vol. 2:** 595
13.6	**Vol. 2:** 357
13.11 f	**Vol. 1:** 383
13.11	**Vol. 3:** 52
13.13 f	**Vol. 1:** 673
13.13	**Vol. 2:** 72 **Vol. 3:** 126
13.16	**Vol. 2:** 633
13.18 f	**Vol. 2:** 878 **Vol. 3:** 610
13.19	**Vol. 2:** 72 **Vol. 3:** 693
14.12 f	**Vol. 3:** 487
14.13	**Vol. 2:** 818 **Vol. 3:** 1016
14.15 ff	**Vol. 2:** 72
14.15	**Vol. 2:** 72, 397
14.17	**Vol. 2:** 397
14.19	**Vol. 2:** 298
14.24	**Vol. 1:** 700
14.25	**Vol. 2:** 878 **Vol. 3:** 610
15.11	**Vol. 1:** 333
15.12	**Vol. 2:** 397
15.14 f	**Vol. 1:** 382
15.15	**Vol. 3:** 211
15.16 f	**Vol. 1:** 673
15.16	**Vol. 2:** 779, 808 **Vol. 3:** 210
15.17	**Vol. 1:** 110, 382 **Vol. 2:** 72, 893
15.18 f	**Vol. 1:** 333
15.20	**Vol. 2:** 397, 633
15.22	**Vol. 3:** 693
15.25	**Vol. 2:** 72 **Vol. 3:** 882
16.1 ff	**Vol. 3:** 487
16.5	**Vol. 2:** 707 **Vol. 3:** 801
16.6 f	**Vol. 2:** 878
16.9	**Vol. 2:** 595
16.10	**Vol. 3:** 610
16.11 f	**Vol. 2:** 878
16.12	**Vol. 2:** 118, 595
16.14	**Vol. 3:** 610
16.16	**Vol. 2:** 595
16.17	**Vol. 3:** 883
16.18	**Vol. 3:** 610
16.20	**Vol. 2:** 459
17.12	**Vol. 2:** 640
17.13	**Vol. 1:** 656
17.15	**Vol. 2:** 45, 298
17.17	**Vol. 3:** 52
17.20	**Vol. 2:** 651 **Vol. 3:** 194
17.22	**Vol. 2:** 261
17.23	**Vol. 2:** 707 **Vol. 3:** 801
17.26	**Vol. 2:** 878
18.5	**Vol. 3:** 211
18.8	**Vol. 2:** 651
18.14 f	**Vol. 3:** 610
18.14	**Vol. 3:** 52
18.15	**Vol. 2:** 355
18.20	**Vol. 1:** 309
18.22	**Vol. 2:** 72
18.26	**Vol. 3:** 823
18.30	**Vol. 2:** 779

Manual of Discipline.
See Community Rule

Messianic Rule (1QSa)

1.1	**Vol. 2:** 56
1.3 f	**Vol. 1:** 296
1.3	**Vol. 3:** 160
1.5	**Vol. 1:** 333
1.6–11	**Vol. 2:** 579
1.7	**Vol. 3:** 761
1.9	**Vol. 1:** 296
1.13	**Vol. 1:** 296
1.14	**Vol. 2:** 699
1.15	**Vol. 3:** 871
1.21	**Vol. 3:** 961
1.26	**Vol. 3:** 961
1.29	**Vol. 2:** 699 **Vol. 3:** 871

Messianic Rule (1QSa) *(cont'd)*

2.4	**Vol. 1:** 296
2.5 ff	**Vol. 1:** 219
2.5–9	**Vol. 2:** 161
2.5	**Vol. 1:** 296
2.7 f	**Vol. 1:** 296
2.8 f	**Vol. 2:** 161, 298 **Vol. 3:** 961
2.9 f	**Vol. 2:** 194
2.11 f	**Vol. 3:** 637
2.11–22	**Vol. 3:** 509
2.11–21	**Vol. 2:** 34, 314
2.11	**Vol. 1:** 178, 273
2.12 ff	**Vol. 3:** 35
2.12	**Vol. 2:** 312
2.17 ff	**Vol. 3:** 545
2.17–22	**Vol. 1:** 630
2.17–21	**Vol. 2:** 522
2.21	**Vol. 1:** 296

Testimonies (4Qtest)

1	**Vol. 2:** 640
5 ff	**Vol. 2:** 640
12 f	**Vol. 2:** 558 **Vol. 3:** 735
12	**Vol. 3:** 650
23	**Vol. 3:** 469

War Scroll (1QM)

1	**Vol. 3:** 961
1.1–7	**Vol. 2:** 793
1.1	**Vol. 2:** 298, 3i2 **Vol. 3:** 469, 961
1.5	**Vol. 2:** 72, 298
1.6	**Vol. 3:** 250
1.9 f	**Vol. 2:** 71, 779
1.9	**Vol. 2:** 480, 893
1.10 f	**Vol. 1:** 102, 452
1.10	**Vol. 1:** 296
1.11	**Vol. 2:** 298, 779, 893
1.12 f	**Vol. 3:** 193
1.12	**Vol. 2:** 798, 808 **Vol. 3:** 193, 210–211
1.13–15	**Vol. 1:** 452
1.13	**Vol. 3:** 469
2	**Vol. 3:** 961
2.1	**Vol. 2:** 34
2.2 f	**Vol. 3:** 871
2.4	**Vol. 1:** 333
2.5	**Vol. 2:** 118
2.6	**Vol. 2:** 651, 696
2.7	**Vol. 1:** 273
2.10–15	**Vol. 2:** 793
3–9	**Vol. 3:** 961
3	**Vol. 2:** 117
3.2 ff	**Vol. 3:** 486
3.2	**Vol. 1:** 273
3.4	**Vol. 2:** 651
3.5	**Vol. 2:** 780
3.9–19	**Vol. 2:** 364
3.9	**Vol. 1:** 110
3.11	**Vol. 2:** 780

3.12–4.17	**Vol. 3:** 871
3.13 ff	**Vol. 2:** 651 **Vol. 3:** 486
3.14 f	**Vol. 3:** 871
4.1 f	**Vol. 3:** 469
4.1–13	**Vol. 2:** 651
4.1	**Vol. 1:** 110 **Vol. 3:** 828
4.2	**Vol. 2:** 298, 699 **Vol. 3:** 250
4.3	**Vol. 3:** 828
4.6	**Vol. 3:** 372, 882
4.7 f	**Vol. 3:** 828
4.10	**Vol. 1:** 273, 296
4.13	**Vol. 3:** 210
4.14	**Vol. 2:** 780
4.15	**Vol. 2:** 285
4.19	**Vol. 2:** 285
4.32	**Vol. 2:** 842
5.1 ff	**Vol. 2:** 651
5.5	**Vol. 3:** 823
5.14	**Vol. 3:** 823
6.1–6	**Vol. 1:** 646
6.2 f	**Vol. 3:** 486
6.6	**Vol. 2:** 228, 793, 798
6.9	**Vol. 2:** 842
6.12 f	**Vol. 3:** 761
7.4 f	**Vol. 1:** 219
7.5	**Vol. 2:** 893
7.6	**Vol. 1:** 102 **Vol. 2:** 161, 298
7.10–9.9	**Vol. 2:** 34
7.11	**Vol. 3:** 823
7.12	**Vol. 2:** 34
7.27	**Vol. 2:** 842
8.4 ff	**Vol. 3:** 389
8.9	**Vol. 2:** 799
9.1	**Vol. 2:** 798
9.7 f	**Vol. 1:** 321
9.14 f	**Vol. 3:** 486
9.14–16	**Vol. 1:** 103–104
9.34	**Vol. 2:** 842
10–14	**Vol. 3:** 961
10.2	**Vol. 2:** 798 **Vol. 3:** 761
10.4 f	**Vol. 3:** 210
10.6	**Vol. 2:** 640
10.7	**Vol. 3:** 233–234
10.8	**Vol. 3:** 263
10.9 f	**Vol. 1:** 539
10.9	**Vol. 2:** 798
10.10 f	**Vol. 2:** 299
10.10	**Vol. 2:** 798 **Vol. 3:** 761
10.11 f	**Vol. 1:** 102
10.11	**Vol. 2:** 197
10.12	**Vol. 1:** 333, 382
10.14	**Vol. 2:** 799
10.15	**Vol. 2:** 298
10.24	**Vol. 2:** 842
11.1–12.5	**Vol. 2:** 602
11.2 f	**Vol. 2:** 651
11.3	**Vol. 3:** 210
11.5–7	**Vol. 3:** 735
11.6 f	**Vol. 2:** 495
11.6	**Vol. 2:** 558 **Vol. 3:** 650

War Scroll (1QM) *(cont'd)*

11.7	**Vol. 2:** 337
11.8 f	**Vol. 2:** 793 **Vol. 3:** 469
11.9	**Vol. 3:** 194
11.12 ff	**Vol. 3:** 273
11.13	**Vol. 2:** 799
12	**Vol. 2:** 117
12.1 f	**Vol. 2:** 298
12.1	**Vol. 2:** 798 **Vol. 3:** 961
12.2	**Vol. 2:** 651
12.3	**Vol. 2:** 480, 595, 779
12.4	**Vol. 2:** 699
12.5	**Vol. 2:** 818
12.7 f	**Vol. 1:** 102
12.7	**Vol. 1:** 296
12.8	**Vol. 1:** 333 **Vol. 2:** 161, 512
12.9	**Vol. 1:** 102 **Vol. 2:** 602
12.11	**Vol. 2:** 792
12.12 ff	**Vol. 1:** 735
12.13	**Vol. 2:** 355
12.14	**Vol. 2:** 793
12.18	**Vol. 2:** 512
13.1–5	**Vol. 1:** 452
13.1	**Vol. 1:** 197
13.2–5	**Vol. 2:** 298
13.4 f	**Vol. 3:** 469
13.5 f	**Vol. 2:** 608
13.7	**Vol. 2:** 651, 798
13.8	**Vol. 3:** 250
13.9	**Vol. 2:** 298, 798
13.10	**Vol. 1:** 102 **Vol. 2:** 492 **Vol. 3:** 704
13.11 f	**Vol. 1:** 423, 452
13.12 ff	**Vol. 2:** 355
13.12 f	**Vol. 2:** 357
13.12	**Vol. 3:** 469
13.14	**Vol. 2:** 893 **Vol. 3:** 194
14.4 f	**Vol. 3:** 210
14.4	**Vol. 1:** 735 **Vol. 2:** 71, 357, 595, 651
14.5 f	**Vol. 3:** 193
14.5	**Vol. 1:** 273, 296 **Vol. 2:** 707, 798 **Vol. 3:** 193, 211, 250, 801
14.6	**Vol. 3:** 761
14.7	**Vol. 2:** 793, 824
14.8 f	**Vol. 2:** 595 **Vol. 3:** 250
14.8	**Vol. 2:** 651
14.9	**Vol. 2:** 608 **Vol. 3:** 469
14.10	**Vol. 3:** 194
14.12	**Vol. 2:** 228, 651
14.14 ff	**Vol. 3:** 503
14.15	**Vol. 1:** 102
14.16	**Vol. 2:** 71
15.1 f	**Vol. 3:** 211
15.1	**Vol. 2:** 808 **Vol. 3:** 194
15.2 f	**Vol. 2:** 893
15.3	**Vol. 3:** 469
15.4	**Vol. 2:** 34
15.5	**Vol. 3:** 487
15.9	**Vol. 1:** 296
15.14	**Vol. 1:** 102
16.1	**Vol. 2:** 799
16.3 ff	**Vol. 1:** 646
16.7	**Vol. 2:** 799
16.10 ff	**Vol. 1:** 646
17	**Vol. 2:** 34
17.1	**Vol. 2:** 779
17.2	**Vol. 3:** 233–234
17.5 f	**Vol. 2:** 608
17.6	**Vol. 3:** 194
17.7 f	**Vol. 1:** 102 **Vol. 2:** 355
17.9	**Vol. 1:** 735
18	**Vol. 2:** 34
18.1	**Vol. 3:** 469
18.3	**Vol. 3:** 469
18.5	**Vol. 2:** 893
18.6	**Vol. 2:** 71, 651
18.7 f	**Vol. 2:** 608
18.7	**Vol. 3:** 210
18.8	**Vol. 2:** 357, 651
18.11	**Vol. 2:** 595 **Vol. 3:** 194, 211
18.14	**Vol. 2:** 109
19.1	**Vol. 2:** 72
19.4	**Vol. 2:** 298
19.6	**Vol. 2:** 793

Words of Moses (1Q22)

1.1	**Vol. 2:** 640
1.7	**Vol. 2:** 285
1.11	**Vol. 2:** 640
2.5	**Vol. 2:** 640
2.8	**Vol. 1:** 333
2.11	**Vol. 2:** 640
4.3	**Vol. 2:** 640

Jewish Hellenistic Writers

The following references to the works of Josephus reflect the Loeb Classical Library numbering system. For the few articles that cite the Whiston numbering system, the Loeb equivilant of the Whiston citation is used to list the reference while the citation actually found in the article is given in parentheses following the page number.

Josephus, *Against Apion (Ap.)*

1.1	**Vol. 1:** 711
1.8	**Vol. 3:** 485
1.21	**Vol. 3:** 419
1.31 ff	**Vol. 3:** 491
1.31	**Vol. 3:** 36
1.42	**Vol. 1:** 330
1.114 f	**Vol. 2:** 756
1.119	**Vol. 3:** 279
1.155	**Vol. 3:** 570
1.167	**Vol. 2:** 43
1.199	**Vol. 2:** 570
1.219–2.150	**Vol. 2:** 310
1.224	**Vol. 2:** 659
1.282	**Vol. 3:** 996
1.289	**Vol. 3:** 480
1.290	**Vol. 3:** 479
1.292	**Vol. 3:** 380
2.29	**Vol. 1:** 264
2.121–124	**Vol. 2:** 310, 792 (2.10)
2.145–150	**Vol. 2:** 310
2.169	**Vol. 1:** 599
2.190–219	**Vol. 3:** 931
2.190	**Vol. 3:** 572
2.193	**Vol. 3:** 789
2.211	**Vol. 1:** 264
2.218	**Vol. 1:** 185
2.255–261	**Vol. 2:** 792 (2.36)
2.256	**Vol. 1:** 599
2.273	**Vol. 2:** 660
2.275	**Vol. 2:** 660
2.282	**Vol. 1:** 627

Josephus, *Jewish Antiquities (Ant.)*

1.33	**Vol. 3:** 407
1.40–51	**Vol. 3:** 638 (1.1.4)
1.43	**Vol. 1:** 334
1.49	**Vol. 1:** 87
1.60	**Vol. 3:** 98
1.74	**Vol. 2:** 682
1.75–79	**Vol. 2:** 660 (1.3.2)
1.85	**Vol. 3:** 265
1.98	**Vol. 3:** 952
1.104–108	**Vol. 3:** 638 (1.3.9)
1.116	**Vol. 1:** 529

1.155	**Vol. 1:** 387
1.179	**Vol. 2:** 779
1.180 f	**Vol. 3:** 36
1.215–219	**Vol. 1:** 698 (1.12.3)
1.222	**Vol. 3:** 1202
1.255	**Vol. 3:** 318
1.331	**Vol. 3:** 324
1.333	**Vol. 3:** 324
2.9	**Vol. 3:** 681
2.63	**Vol. 1:** 511
2.72	**Vol. 1:** 580
2.136–159	**Vol. 3:** 638 (2.6.8)
2.138	**Vol. 1:** 363
2.205	**Vol. 3:** 480
2.209	**Vol. 3:** 876
2.243–253	**Vol. 2:** 381 (2.10.2)
2.275 f	**Vol. 2:** 651 (2.12.4 f)
2.275	**Vol. 3:** 785
2.277–280	**Vol. 2:** 309 (2.13.1)
2.301	**Vol. 2:** 798
2.315–317	**Vol. 2:** 463 (2.15.1)
2.339	**Vol. 3:** 318
3.8	**Vol. 2:** 899
3.26–32	**Vol. 1:** 252 (3.1.6)
3.96	**Vol. 3:** 265
3.100	**Vol. 3:** 789
3.122–133	**Vol. 2:** 659 (3.6.4)
3.123	**Vol. 3:** 789
3.133	**Vol. 3:** 27
3.139–143	**Vol. 1:** 586 (3.6.6)
3.144–146	**Vol. 2:** 258 (3.6.7)
3.151 ff	**Vol. 1:** 204 (3.7.1 ff)
3.166–171	**Vol. 3:** 396
3.172–178	**Vol. 2:** 651 (3.7.6)
3.179–187	**Vol. 2:** 659 (3.7.7)
3.180 ff	**Vol. 3:** 789
3.189	**Vol. 3:** 37
3.202	**Vol. 2:** 899 **Vol. 3:** 789
3.212	**Vol. 3:** 324
3.234	**Vol. 3:** 919
3.237–254	**Vol. 1:** 627
3.252 ff	**Vol. 2:** 783
3.252 f	**Vol. 2:** 461
3.252	**Vol. 2:** 783
3.255–257	**Vol. 1:** 586 (3.10.7)
3.259–260	**Vol. 1:** 221 (3.11.2)
3.290	**Vol. 3:** 789

Josephus, Jewish Antiquities (Ant.) *(cont'd)*

3.310	**Vol. 3:** 318
3.312	**Vol. 3:** 721
3.317–322	**Vol. 2:** 827 (3.15.3)
4.6	**Vol. 2:** 677
4.24	**Vol. 2:** 608
4.73	**Vol. 2:** 43
4.114	**Vol. 2:** 796
4.188	**Vol. 1:** 419
4.207	**Vol. 2:** 235 (4.8.10), 651 (4.8.10)
4.209	**Vol. 3:** 813
4.228	**Vol. 2:** 742 **Vol. 3:** 1160, 1164
4.231–239	**Vol. 1:** 163 (4.8.21) **Vol. 2:** 696 (4.8.21)
4.238	**Vol. 2:** 96
4.244–259	**Vol. 2:** 696 (4.8.23)
4.267–270	**Vol. 2:** 659 (4.8.26)
4.270	**Vol. 3:** 721
4.320–326	**Vol. 2:** 659 (4.8.48)
4.326	**Vol. 3:** 265
5.5	**Vol. 3:** 126
5.39	**Vol. 3:** 571, 594
5.93–99	**Vol. 3:** 638 (5.1.25)
5.109	**Vol. 2:** 608
5.166–174	**Vol. 2:** 258 (5.2.12)
5.205–209	**Vol. 2:** 659 (5.5.4)
5.214	**Vol. 3:** 952
5.215–217	**Vol. 2:** 659 (5.6.3)
5.249	**Vol. 1:** 515
5.264	**Vol. 3:** 1202
6.7–12	**Vol. 2:** 258 (6.1.2)
6.92	**Vol. 1:** 700
6.123	**Vol. 2:** 879
6.126 ff	**Vol. 2:** 677
6.156–165	**Vol. 2:** 815 (6.8.1)
6.170–174	**Vol. 2:** 659 (6.9.1)
6.185	**Vol. 1:** 143
6.225	**Vol. 3:** 875–876
6.237 f	**Vol. 3:** 92
6.240	**Vol. 3:** 218
6.262–268	**Vol. 2:** 806 (6.12.7)
6.309	**Vol. 3:** 1164
6.328	**Vol. 2:** 879
6.347	**Vol. 3:** 744
6.374	**Vol. 3:** 785
7.110	**Vol. 3:** 480
7.117–121	**Vol. 2:** 258 (7.6.1)
7.130–140	**Vol. 2:** 660 (7.7.1)
7.169	**Vol. 1:** 511
7.209	**Vol. 3:** 721
7.244	**Vol. 2:** 33
7.319	**Vol. 3:** 480
7.332	**Vol. 3:** 572
7.338	**Vol. 1:** 334
7.342	**Vol. 1:** 334
7.365	**Vol. 2:** 34
7.380	**Vol. 1:** 387, 618
8.23	**Vol. 3:** 125
8.44–49	**Vol. 3:** 651
8.45 ff	**Vol. 3:** 476
8.45	**Vol. 3:** 996
8.71	**Vol. 3:** 795, 948
8.88	**Vol. 3:** 418
8.94	**Vol. 1:** 334
8.100	**Vol. 3:** 813
8.102	**Vol. 3:** 789
8.106	**Vol. 3:** 789
8.107	**Vol. 3:** 789
8.111–117	**Vol. 2:** 651 (8.4.3)
8.114	**Vol. 3:** 789
8.115	**Vol. 3:** 210
8.117	**Vol. 3:** 789
8.120	**Vol. 1:** 334
8.123	**Vol. 3:** 813
8.124–129	**Vol. 1:** 345 (8.4.6)
8.131	**Vol. 3:** 789
8.141–149	**Vol. 3:** 279 (8.5.3)
8.165 f	**Vol. 2:** 381 (8.6.5 f)
8.167	**Vol. 1:** 577
8.230	**Vol. 3:** 418
8.251–255	**Vol. 3:** 575 (8.10.2)
8.256–262	**Vol. 1:** 345 (8.10.3)
8.280	**Vol. 2:** 61
8.318	**Vol. 3:** 125
8.335–342	**Vol. 2:** 659 (8.13.5)
8.337	**Vol. 1:** 334
8.355–362	**Vol. 1:** 345 (8.13.8)
8.360	**Vol. 3:** 876
8.376	**Vol. 1:** 513
8.404	**Vol. 2:** 33
8.405	**Vol. 2:** 779
9.34	**Vol. 2:** 879
9.43	**Vol. 3:** 721
9.55	**Vol. 2:** 899
9.60	**Vol. 3:** 318
9.176	**Vol. 3:** 744
9.208–214	**Vol. 2:** 679 (9.10.2)
9.214	**Vol. 1:** 700
9.239–242	**Vol. 2:** 679 (9.11.3)
9.240	**Vol. 3:** 681
9.258–262	**Vol. 2:** 659 (9.13.1)
9.280	**Vol. 3:** 456
9.287	**Vol. 3:** 460
10.2	**Vol. 3:** 756
10.24–29	**Vol. 2:** 628 (10.2.1)
10.51	**Vol. 3:** 772
10.70	**Vol. 3:** 102
10.75	**Vol. 3:** 51
10.81–83	**Vol. 2:** 659 (10.5.2)
10.142	**Vol. 2:** 659 (10.8.3)
10.155	**Vol. 3:** 756
10.184	**Vol. 3:** 450
10.195	**Vol. 1:** 511
10.209 f	**Vol. 2:** 899
10.216	**Vol. 2:** 557
10.267	**Vol. 2:** 899
10.276	**Vol. 2:** 899
10.281	**Vol. 3:** 923

Josephus, Jewish
Antiquities (Ant.) *(cont'd)*

11.3	**Vol. 3:** 570
11.28	**Vol. 1:** 341
11.47	**Vol. 2:** 136
11.63	**Vol. 3:** 147
11.66	**Vol. 1:** 185
11.88–94	**Vol. 3:** 610 (11.4.4)
11.88	**Vol. 3:** 450
11.97–103	**Vol. 3:** 610 (11.4.6)
11.114	**Vol. 1:** 700
11.128	**Vol. 3:** 478
11.133	**Vol. 3:** 871
11.154	**Vol. 3:** 813
11.159–167	**Vol. 1:** 151 (11.5.6)
11.169	**Vol. 1:** 694
11.192	**Vol. 1:** 574
11.213	**Vol. 3:** 248
11.216	**Vol. 2:** 779
11.240	**Vol. 3:** 681
11.261	**Vol. 1:** 394
11.266 f	**Vol. 1:** 394
11.291	**Vol. 3:** 451
11.302–347	**Vol. 3:** 451
11.303	**Vol. 3:** 450
11.306 ff	**Vol. 3:** 451
11.312	**Vol. 3:** 451
11.321–324	**Vol. 3:** 451
11.327	**Vol. 3:** 39
11.329–339	**Vol. 1:** 207 (11.8.5) **Vol. 2:** 651 (11.8.5)
11.340	**Vol. 3:** 450–451
11.341	**Vol. 3:** 451
11.344	**Vol. 3:** 450
11.345	**Vol. 3:** 453
11.346	**Vol. 3:** 451, 465
12.7–10	**Vol. 3:** 453
12.7	**Vol. 1:** 580
12.10	**Vol. 3:** 450, 460
12.18	**Vol. 2:** 882
12.23	**Vol. 1:** 387
12.40 ff	**Vol. 1:** 196 (12.2.5 ff)
12.40–50	**Vol. 2:** 697 (12.2.5)
12.57–59	**Vol. 2:** 697 (12.2.7)
12.99	**Vol. 2:** 879
12.129–144	**Vol. 1:** 406 (12.3.3)
12.136	**Vol. 3:** 318
12.138–153	**Vol. 3:** 756
12.141	**Vol. 3:** 756
12.142	**Vol. 3:** 478
12.176	**Vol. 3:** 758
12.186 ff	**Vol. 2:** 578
12.258–262	**Vol. 3:** 450
12.258–261	**Vol. 3:** 452
12.258	**Vol. 3:** 450
12.259	**Vol. 3:** 461
12.261	**Vol. 3:** 455, 461
12.262	**Vol. 3:** 450
12.278	**Vol. 2:** 33
12.322	**Vol. 2:** 899
12.323–325	**Vol. 1:** 627
12.378	**Vol. 3:** 191
12.387 f	**Vol. 3:** 451
12.413–419	**Vol. 2:** 332 (12.10.6)
13.49–57	**Vol. 3:** 756
13.62–73	**Vol. 3:** 451
13.74–79	**Vol. 3:** 453, 460
13.76	**Vol. 3:** 461
13.78 f	**Vol. 3:** 461
13.117 ff	**Vol. 3:** 439
13.173	**Vol. 3:** 439
13.242	**Vol. 3:** 813
13.252	**Vol. 2:** 783
13.254–258	**Vol. 1:** 309 (13.9.1)
13.255 f	**Vol. 3:** 452
13.255	**Vol. 3:** 456
13.256	**Vol. 3:** 451
13.257	**Vol. 3:** 872
13.288–292	**Vol. 2:** 815 (13.10.5)
13.293–298	**Vol. 2:** 811 (13.10.6)
13.293 ff	**Vol. 3:** 439
13.293	**Vol. 3:** 439
13.297 f	**Vol. 3:** 488
13.297	**Vol. 3:** 439, 772
13.299	**Vol. 3:** 39
13.311 ff	**Vol. 3:** 80
13.318	**Vol. 3:** 872
13.372	**Vol. 3:** 813
13.380	**Vol. 2:** 578
13.409	**Vol. 3:** 772
14.19–24	**Vol. 2:** 463 (14.2.1)
14.71 f	**Vol. 3:** 815
14.91	**Vol. 1:** 363
14.107	**Vol. 3:** 196
14.110–118	**Vol. 2:** 309 (14.7.2)
14.158–162	**Vol. 2:** 308 (14.9.2)
14.192	**Vol. 1:** 363
14.202	**Vol. 3:** 191
14.255	**Vol. 1:** 615
14.267	**Vol. 3:** 1211
14.285	**Vol. 3:** 745
14.302	**Vol. 2:** 607
14.337	**Vol. 2:** 783
14.411	**Vol. 3:** 452
14.415	**Vol. 3:** 380
14.450	**Vol. 3:** 441
14.468	**Vol. 3:** 452
14.480	**Vol. 3:** 716
15.22	**Vol. 3:** 443
15.39–41	**Vol. 3:** 443
15.50	**Vol. 3:** 813
15.98	**Vol. 1:** 419
15.118 ff	**Vol. 3:** 789
15.127–146	**Vol. 1:** 102 (15.5.3)
15.200	**Vol. 3:** 952
15.253	**Vol. 3:** 37
15.259	**Vol. 1:** 505 **Vol. 3:** 189, 534
15.320–322	**Vol. 3:** 443
15.403 ff	**Vol. 3:** 789

Josephus, Jewish Antiquities (Ant.) *(cont'd)*

15.410–416 Vol. 3: 789
15.416   Vol. 3: 783
15.417   Vol. 3: 486, 789
15.421   Vol. 1: 627
16.10   Vol. 2: 33
16.11   Vol. 3: 1164
16.27–30   Vol. 2: 651 (16.2.3)
16.93   Vol. 3: 681
16.151   Vol. 1: 89
16.162–165 Vol. 3: 752 (16.6.2)
16.163   Vol. 1: 363   Vol. 3: 408
16.167 f   Vol. 3: 752 (16.6.4 f)
16.170   Vol. 2: 882
16.172   Vol. 3: 415
16.187   Vol. 3: 36
16.244   Vol. 3: 996
16.301   Vol. 3: 681
17.19 f   Vol. 2: 578
17.99   Vol. 3: 570
17.130   Vol. 3: 925
17.140   Vol. 1: 342
17.149   Vol. 1: 574
17.199   Vol. 1: 342
17.213–223 Vol. 2: 699 (17.9.3)
17.226   Vol. 3: 486
17.254   Vol. 2: 783
17.289   Vol. 3: 923
17.295–298 Vol. 3: 530 (17.10.10)
17.295   Vol. 1: 394
17.299–303 Vol. 1: 127 (17.11.1)
17.319   Vol. 3: 449
17.320   Vol. 3: 756
18   Vol. 2: 320
18.1   Vol. 2: 565
18.4   Vol. 3: 756
18.6   Vol. 3: 1167
18.11   Vol. 3: 439, 1035
18.12–25   Vol. 2: 810 (18.1.3–6)
18.12–15   Vol. 2: 811 (18.1.3)
18.14   Vol. 2: 207
18.16 f   Vol. 3: 439
18.16   Vol. 3: 439
18.17   Vol. 3: 439
18.18   Vol. 3: 681
18.21   Vol. 3: 545
18.23–25   Vol. 1: 270 (18.1.6)
18.24   Vol. 1: 710
18.25   Vol. 3: 996
18.29 f   Vol. 3: 452
18.35   Vol. 3: 39
18.59   Vol. 3: 1029
18.65–80   Vol. 2: 521 (18.3.4)
18.65   Vol. 3: 785
18.81   Vol. 1: 574
18.82   Vol. 3: 1029
18.85 ff   Vol. 1: 396
18.85–89   Vol. 3: 452

18.85   Vol. 3: 147
18.90   Vol. 3: 756
18.95   Vol. 3: 39
18.116–119 Vol. 3: 1006
18.135   Vol. 1: 428
18.167   Vol. 3: 452, 456
18.266   Vol. 3: 925
18.284   Vol. 2: 899
18.293   Vol. 3: 439
18.310–317 Vol. 3: 752 (18.9.1), 853 (18.9.1)
18.356   Vol. 2: 136
19.96   Vol. 1: 546
19.110   Vol. 1: 342
19.294   Vol. 3: 796
19.317–325 Vol. 2: 521 (19.7.1)
19.328–331 Vol. 2: 258 (19.7.3)
20.38–48   Vol. 2: 792 (20.2.4)
20.40   Vol. 3: 1052
20.49–53   Vol. 2: 827 (20.2.5)
20.83   Vol. 3: 681
20.97 ff   Vol. 1: 396, 629
20.100–104 Vol. 2: 827 (20.5.2)
20.102   Vol. 1: 394
20.103   Vol. 3: 40
20.106 f   Vol. 1: 629
20.118–136 Vol. 3: 454
20.118–124 Vol. 3: 452
20.118   Vol. 3: 452
20.124   Vol. 2: 33
20.129   Vol. 1: 394
20.131 ff   Vol. 3: 40
20.132   Vol. 1: 341
20.142   Vol. 2: 557
20.161   Vol. 1: 394
20.169 ff   Vol. 1: 396, 532, 629
20.179–181 Vol. 2: 467 (20.8.8)
20.181   Vol. 3: 853
20.193   Vol. 2: 608
20.197–203 Vol. 2: 331 (20.9.1)
20.199   Vol. 3: 439
20.205 ff   Vol. 3: 40
20.206 f   Vol. 3: 853

Josephus, *The Jewish War (War)*

1.19   Vol. 2: 688
1.27   Vol. 1: 503
1.33   Vol. 3: 451
1.63   Vol. 3: 452
1.76   Vol. 3: 993
1.97   Vol. 2: 578
1.139   Vol. 3: 441
1.152 f   Vol. 3: 815
1.170   Vol. 1: 363
1.204–207   Vol. 2: 660 (1.10.5)
1.213   Vol. 3: 452
1.253   Vol. 2: 783
1.302 f   Vol. 3: 452
1.352   Vol. 3: 716
1.355   Vol. 3: 452

Josephus, The Jewish War (War) *(cont'd)*

1.430	**Vol. 3:** 681
1.488	**Vol. 1:** 560
1.493	**Vol. 3:** 681
1.511	**Vol. 2:** 578
1.540	**Vol. 2:** 879
1.562	**Vol. 2:** 578
1.625	**Vol. 3:** 486
1.649	**Vol. 1:** 574
1.666	**Vol. 2:** 839
2.8	**Vol. 2:** 565
2.10	**Vol. 2:** 463
2.20	**Vol. 1:** 513
2.42	**Vol. 1:** 330 **Vol. 2:** 783
2.55–65	**Vol. 2:** 313 (2.4.1–3)
2.97	**Vol. 3:** 756
2.112	**Vol. 1:** 511
2.117–166	**Vol. 2:** 811 (2.8)
2.117–118	**Vol. 2:** 659 (2.8.1)
2.118	**Vol. 3:** 1029, 1168
2.119–166	**Vol. 2:** 810 (2.8.2–14)
2.119–161	**Vol. 1:** 641
2.119–121	**Vol. 2:** 579 (2.8.2)
2.119	**Vol. 3:** 439, 1035
2.120	**Vol. 1:** 495
2.122–123	**Vol. 2:** 842 (2.8.3)
2.125	**Vol. 3:** 978
2.129–131	**Vol. 1:** 630
2.129	**Vol. 3:** 989
2.134–136	**Vol. 3:** 740 (2.8.6)
2.135	**Vol. 2:** 779
2.137–142	**Vol. 1:** 102 (2.8.7), 554 (2.8.7) **Vol. 2:** 651 (2.8.7) **Vol. 3:** 740 (2.8.7)
2.138	**Vol. 1:** 495
2.140	**Vol. 2:** 608
2.149	**Vol. 3:** 989
2.150	**Vol. 1:** 495
2.151 ff	**Vol. 3:** 1042
2.151	**Vol. 2:** 49 **Vol. 3:** 572
2.154	**Vol. 3:** 681
2.155	**Vol. 3:** 229
2.159 f	**Vol. 1:** 145 (2.8.12 f)
2.160–161	**Vol. 1:** 152 (2.8.13) **Vol. 2:** 579 (2.8.13)
2.162 ff	**Vol. 3:** 439
2.163	**Vol. 2:** 207 **Vol. 3:** 681
2.164	**Vol. 3:** 439
2.165	**Vol. 3:** 439
2.166	**Vol. 3:** 439
2.170 f	**Vol. 3:** 1168
2.175	**Vol. 2:** 43 **Vol. 3:** 430
2.196	**Vol. 3:** 721
2.232–246	**Vol. 3:** 452, 454
2.232	**Vol. 3:** 452
2.258–263	**Vol. 3:** 1006
2.260	**Vol. 1:** 377
2.261 ff†	**Vol. 1:** 396
2.261	**Vol. 1:** 532
2.313 f	**Vol. 2:** 160
2.350	**Vol. 2:** 608
2.367	**Vol. 2:** 776
2.385	**Vol. 1:** 511
2.420	**Vol. 2:** 109
2.425	**Vol. 1:** 627
2.427	**Vol. 3:** 1168
2.441	**Vol. 3:** 40
2.454	**Vol. 3:** 1168
2.515	**Vol. 3:** 813
2.517–522	**Vol. 2:** 309 (2.19.2)
2.549	**Vol. 1:** 342
2.624	**Vol. 3:** 51
3.9	**Vol. 3:** 1168
3.92	**Vol. 3:** 51
3.110–114	**Vol. 3:** 528 (3.6.1)
3.164	**Vol. 3:** 229
3.228	**Vol. 1:** 515
3.241	**Vol. 3:** 229
3.307–315	**Vol. 3:** 452
3.352	**Vol. 3:** 39
3.361–382	**Vol. 2:** 659 (3.8.5)
3.375	**Vol. 2:** 207
3.398	**Vol. 1:** 663
3.419–427	**Vol. 2:** 660 (3.9.3)
3.436	**Vol. 1:** 688
3.516–521	**Vol. 3:** 754 (3.10.8)
4.188	**Vol. 3:** 839
4.224	**Vol. 3:** 1168
4.236–269	**Vol. 2:** 660 (4.4.3)
4.326 f	**Vol. 3:** 1168
4.334–344	**Vol. 3:** 82 (4.5.4)
4.406	**Vol. 1:** 230
4.414	**Vol. 3:** 248
4.449	**Vol. 3:** 457
4.503–508	**Vol. 3:** 608 (4.9.3)
4.508	**Vol. 3:** 1168
4.514	**Vol. 3:** 1168
4.528	**Vol. 2:** 839
4.544	**Vol. 3:** 1168
4.567	**Vol. 3:** 1168
4.656	**Vol. 2:** 109
5.1–10	**Vol. 2:** 313 (5.1.1–2)
5.5	**Vol. 3:** 185, 788–789
5.31	**Vol. 3:** 229
5.193	**Vol. 3:** 949
5.199	**Vol. 3:** 1058
5.200	**Vol. 3:** 796
5.210	**Vol. 3:** 921
5.212–217	**Vol. 3:** 789
5.233–235	**Vol. 3:** 396
5.250	**Vol. 3:** 1168
5.262	**Vol. 3:** 952
5.264	**Vol. 3:** 952
5.375–419	**Vol. 1:** 345 (5.9.4)
5.405	**Vol. 3:** 756
5.415	**Vol. 1:** 700
5.429–438	**Vol. 2:** 651 (5.10.3)
5.449 ff	**Vol. 1:** 394
5.469 ff	**Vol. 3:** 952

Josephus, The Jewish War (War) *(cont'd)*

5.480	**Vol. 3:** 210
5.510	**Vol. 2:** 136
5.532	**Vol. 3:** 480
5.565	**Vol. 3:** 1162
6.4 ff	**Vol. 3:** 789
6.50	**Vol. 2:** 563
6.68–80	**Vol. 3:** 847 (6.1.7)
6.105	**Vol. 1:** 683
6.130	**Vol. 1:** 742
6.142	**Vol. 1:** 262
6.170	**Vol. 3:** 131
6.190	**Vol. 1:** 89
6.196	**Vol. 1:** 513
6.282	**Vol. 3:** 796
6.285	**Vol. 3:** 210
6.288–309	**Vol. 3:** 634 (6.5.3)
6.291	**Vol. 3:** 480
6.299	**Vol. 2:** 783
6.310–315	**Vol. 2:** 921 (6.5.4)
6.313	**Vol. 2:** 899
6.351	**Vol. 3:** 1006
6.435–442	**Vol. 2:** 591 (6.10.1)
6.438	**Vol. 3:** 36
7.8	**Vol. 2:** 565
7.67	**Vol. 3:** 210
7.123	**Vol. 3:** 785
7.132–152	**Vol. 2:** 660 (7.5.5)
7.171–177	**Vol. 2:** 659 (7.6.2)
7.203	**Vol. 1:** 392
7.216–218	**Vol. 3:** 753 (7.6.6)
7.325 f	**Vol. 1:** 435
7.330	**Vol. 2:** 140
7.337–388	**Vol. 2:** 480 (7.8.7)
7.340	**Vol. 1:** 435
7.341 ff	**Vol. 1:** 435 **Vol. 3:** 681
7.341	**Vol. 1:** 435
7.349	**Vol. 2:** 762
7.372	**Vol. 1:** 435
7.388	**Vol. 1:** 435
7.405	**Vol. 3:** 109
7.418	**Vol. 1:** 345
7.420–736	**Vol. 3:** 451
7.447	**Vol. 2:** 140
7.450	**Vol. 3:** 92
7.453	**Vol. 1:** 694

Josephus, *Life of Flavius Josephus (Life)*

1†	**Vol. 3:** 871
7	**Vol. 1:** 152 (2)
10 ff	**Vol. 2:** 311
10	**Vol. 3:** 439
72	**Vol. 2:** 607–608
80–83	**Vol. 2:** 467 (15)
112	**Vol. 2:** 607
198	**Vol. 3:** 36
258	**Vol. 3:** 737

Philo, *De Abrahamo (Abr.)*

5	**Vol. 2:** 660
17 f	**Vol. 3:** 266
26	**Vol. 2:** 61
27	**Vol. 2:** 681
32	**Vol. 3:** 1118
35	**Vol. 2:** 681
42–44	**Vol. 1:** 80
44	**Vol. 3:** 126
51	**Vol. 2:** 651
56	**Vol. 3:** 37
87	**Vol. 2:** 659 **Vol. 3:** 531
90	**Vol. 3:** 744
103	**Vol. 3:** 575
116	**Vol. 1:** 342
153	**Vol. 2:** 756
157	**Vol. 2:** 659
163	**Vol. 3:** 1157
167	**Vol. 3:** 369
198	**Vol. 3:** 35
201–207	**Vol. 2:** 357
208	**Vol. 2:** 659
223	**Vol. 2:** 169
235	**Vol. 2:** 757
248	**Vol. 2:** 659
261	**Vol. 2:** 377
268 ff	**Vol. 1:** 598
272 ff	**Vol. 1:** 598
275	**Vol. 2:** 169

Philo, *De Aeternitate Mundi (Aet. Mund.)*

2	**Vol. 1:** 512
8	**Vol. 1:** 178
9	**Vol. 1:** 178
28	**Vol. 2:** 659
34	**Vol. 2:** 659
84	**Vol. 3:** 681
88	**Vol. 1:** 711
89 ff	**Vol. 1:** 184
92	**Vol. 1:** 711
112	**Vol. 3:** 570
116	**Vol. 3:** 570
143	**Vol. 1:** 468

Philo, *De Agricultura (Agric.)*

16	**Vol. 1:** 577
40	**Vol. 3:** 98
63	**Vol. 3:** 681
95–99	**Vol. 1:** 509
136	**Vol. 3:** 1120
160	**Vol. 3:** 716

Philo, *De Cherubin (Cher.)*

14	**Vol. 3:** 533
40–47	**Vol. 3:** 642
52	**Vol. 3:** 522

Philo, De Cherubin (Cher.) *(cont'd)*

87	Vol. 3: 407
88	Vol. 3: 842
94 f	Vol. 3: 789
115	Vol. 3: 716
125 ff	Vol. 3: 1117

Philo, De Confusione Linguarum (Conf. Ling.)

8	Vol. 2: 740
63	Vol. 3: 639
101	Vol. 3: 716
103	Vol. 3: 716
109	Vol. 3: 486
134 ff	Vol. 1: 734
152	Vol. 3: 522, 526
161	Vol. 3: 681

Philo, De Congressu Eruditionis Gratia (Congr.)

34	Vol. 3: 486
90	Vol. 2: 681 Vol. 3: 486
99	Vol. 2: 590–591 Vol. 3: 36
109	Vol. 3: 194
159	Vol. 3: 877
161 ff	Vol. 1: 627

Philo, De Decalogo (Decal.)

25	Vol. 2: 658
30 f	Vol. 3: 842
33	Vol. 2: 784
41	Vol. 2: 658
46	Vol. 2: 784
47	Vol. 3: 1120
49	Vol. 2: 496
87	Vol. 1: 349 Vol. 2: 659
93 f	Vol. 2: 651
100	Vol. 3: 407
101	Vol. 2: 659 Vol. 3: 842
102	Vol. 2: 192
121 f	Vol. 2: 583
124	Vol. 2: 583
126	Vol. 2: 583
129	Vol. 2: 583
131	Vol. 2: 583
149	Vol. 3: 716
160	Vol. 2: 783
165 ff	Vol. 3: 931

Philo, Quod Deterius Potiori Insidiari Soleat (Det. Pot. Ins.)

13	Vol. 3: 533
20	Vol. 3: 789
29	Vol. 3: 125
56	Vol. 3: 595
57	Vol. 3: 533
59	Vol. 3: 681

83	Vol. 2: 288
84	Vol. 3: 681
86	Vol. 3: 125
175	Vol. 2: 763

Philo, Quod Deus Sit Immutabilis (Deus Imm.)

20	Vol. 2: 833
29	Vol. 1: 695
31	Vol. 1: 523
35	Vol. 2: 658
37	Vol. 2: 658
52–56	Vol. 1: 674
54	Vol. 3: 769
60 f	Vol. 3: 1166
76	Vol. 3: 98
91	Vol. 2: 833
131 ff	Vol. 3: 35
135	Vol. 2: 493 Vol. 3: 789
143	Vol. 3: 126

Philo, De Ebrietate (Ebr.)

30	Vol. 1: 523
44	Vol. 2: 496
65	Vol. 3: 36
72	Vol. 3: 210
75	Vol. 3: 716
76	Vol. 3: 35
97	Vol. 2: 779
98	Vol. 1: 409
105	Vol. 3: 716
111	Vol. 3: 210
126	Vol. 3: 36
133	Vol. 2: 288
137	Vol. 2: 288 Vol. 3: 126
142	Vol. 1: 468

Philo, De Exsecrationibus (Exsec.)

6	Vol. 3: 867, 869

Philo, In Flaccum (Flacc.)

1	Vol. 3: 479
4	Vol. 3: 479
41–96	Vol. 2: 310
45 f	Vol. 2: 309
111	Vol. 2: 689
164	Vol. 1: 511

Philo, De Fuga et Inventione (Fug.)

72	Vol. 2: 659
79	Vol. 2: 830
108	Vol. 3: 36
109	Vol. 3: 35
165	Vol. 3: 533

Philo, *De Gigantibus (Gig.)*

22	**Vol. 2:** 187
31 ff	**Vol. 3:** 692
51	**Vol. 3:** 963
52	**Vol. 1:** 330
54	**Vol. 3:** 760

Philo, *De Josepho (Jos.)*

1	**Vol. 3:** 769
2	**Vol. 1:** 89
39	**Vol. 1:** 89
57	**Vol. 2:** 779
67	**Vol. 2:** 608
68	**Vol. 2:** 493
145	**Vol. 2:** 493

Philo, *Legum Allegoriae (Leg. All.)*

1.10	**Vol. 2:** 588
1.20	**Vol. 3:** 842
1.31 f	**Vol. 1:** 520
1.39	**Vol. 3:** 681
1.44	**Vol. 1:** 734
1.52	**Vol. 1:** 228
1.54 f	**Vol. 1:** 330
1.73	**Vol. 3:** 716
1.80	**Vol. 3:** 522
1.86	**Vol. 3:** 926
1.95	**Vol. 2:** 608
1.100	**Vol. 3:** 716
1.105 ff	**Vol. 1:** 435
1.107	**Vol. 1:** 435
2.23	**Vol. 2:** 658
2.28†	**Vol. 1:** 341
2.31	**Vol. 3:** 126
2.34	**Vol. 1:** 465
2.57	**Vol. 2:** 480, 763
2.70	**Vol. 3:** 126
2.79–81	**Vol. 1:** 509
2.81	**Vol. 1:** 87
2.89	**Vol. 1:** 599 **Vol. 2:** 659
2.98	**Vol. 3:** 939
2.106 f	**Vol. 1:** 412
3.4	**Vol. 1:** 734
3.21	**Vol. 2:** 480 **Vol. 3:** 194
3.25 f	**Vol. 3:** 451
3.26	**Vol. 3:** 458
3.27	**Vol. 3:** 639
3.32 f	**Vol. 3:** 377
3.36	**Vol. 1:** 468
3.78	**Vol. 2:** 115
3.79 ff	**Vol. 3:** 36
3.79	**Vol. 2:** 590, 592
3.81	**Vol. 2:** 590
3.82	**Vol. 3:** 922
3.84	**Vol. 3:** 533
3.92	**Vol. 3:** 716
3.95–104	**Vol. 2:** 288
3.96	**Vol. 3:** 1117
3.98 f	**Vol. 3:** 842
3.99 f	**Vol. 3:** 554
3.100–103	**Vol. 3:** 515
3.102	**Vol. 2:** 290 **Vol. 3:** 904
3.103 f	**Vol. 3:** 554
3.105	**Vol. 2:** 830
3.108	**Vol. 2:** 290
3.151	**Vol. 2:** 480
3.152	**Vol. 1:** 674
3.159	**Vol. 2:** 61
3.162	**Vol. 2:** 659
3.171 f	**Vol. 2:** 493
3.185	**Vol. 3:** 522
3.203 ff	**Vol. 3:** 41
3.211	**Vol. 3:** 996
3.228	**Vol. 3:** 369
3.229	**Vol. 3:** 877
3.234	**Vol. 3:** 125
4.108	**Vol. 3:** 939

Philo, *Legatio ad Gaium (Leg. Gai.)*

26	**Vol. 2:** 608
53	**Vol. 3:** 779
54	**Vol. 2:** 608
120–139	**Vol. 2:** 310
137 f	**Vol. 3:** 598
155	**Vol. 3:** 598
156 f	**Vol. 3:** 598
190	**Vol. 2:** 608
281–283	**Vol. 2:** 309
293	**Vol. 3:** 526
353	**Vol. 1:** 580

Philo, *De Migratione Abrahami (Migr. Abr.)*

2	**Vol. 3:** 210
18	**Vol. 3:** 681
34 f	**Vol. 2:** 397, 762
34	**Vol. 3:** 681
39 f	**Vol. 2:** 493
71	**Vol. 2:** 289
97	**Vol. 2:** 377
122–125	**Vol. 3:** 210
124	**Vol. 3:** 210
133	**Vol. 3:** 946
170	**Vol. 3:** 939
171	**Vol. 3:** 939
176 f	**Vol. 3:** 465
192	**Vol. 2:** 659 **Vol. 3:** 126
195	**Vol. 3:** 939
204	**Vol. 3:** 946
218	**Vol. 3:** 1029

Philo, *De Mutatione Nominum (Mut. Nom.)*

4	**Vol. 1:** 428
11 f	**Vol. 2:** 651
29–32	**Vol. 1:** 387

Philo, De Mutatione Nominum (Mut. Nom.) *(cont'd)*

121	**Vol. 2:** 332
181	**Vol. 2:** 289
197	**Vol. 1:** 428 **Vol. 3:** 1157
269	**Vol. 3:** 526

Philo, Quod Omnis Probus Liber Sit (Omn. Prob. Lib.)

12 f	**Vol. 1:** 641
12	**Vol. 3:** 545
62	**Vol. 2:** 659
81 f	**Vol. 3:** 487
87	**Vol. 3:** 545
114	**Vol. 3:** 194
160	**Vol. 2:** 659

Philo, De Opificio Mundi (Op. Mund.)

3	**Vol. 2:** 660 **Vol. 3:** 332
10	**Vol. 1:** 387
16	**Vol. 1:** 523 **Vol. 3:** 904
17	**Vol. 2:** 608
19	**Vol. 3:** 904
23	**Vol. 1:** 89
25	**Vol. 1:** 523
26	**Vol. 3:** 842
29	**Vol. 2:** 192 **Vol. 3:** 904
31	**Vol. 1:** 580
36	**Vol. 2:** 659 **Vol. 3:** 904
60	**Vol. 3:** 843
79	**Vol. 3:** 769
80	**Vol. 3:** 92
82	**Vol. 2:** 192
89	**Vol. 1:** 618, 627
117	**Vol. 2:** 192
129	**Vol. 3:** 904
132	**Vol. 1:** 377
134 ff	**Vol. 1:** 520
135	**Vol. 3:** 125
137	**Vol. 3:** 789
143	**Vol. 3:** 486
146	**Vol. 2:** 289
155 f	**Vol. 2:** 480
155	**Vol. 3:** 681
165	**Vol. 1:** 89
171	**Vol. 1:** 694

Philo, De Plantatione (Plant.)

14	**Vol. 3:** 681
18	**Vol. 2:** 288
48	**Vol. 3:** 522
50	**Vol. 2:** 289
91	**Vol. 2:** 659
93	**Vol. 2:** 61

Philo, De Posteritate Caini (Post. C.)

38	**Vol. 3:** 942
42	**Vol. 3:** 716
57 f	**Vol. 2:** 493
124	**Vol. 1:** 185
143	**Vol. 1:** 742
150	**Vol. 2:** 659
154	**Vol. 3:** 939
233	**Vol. 3:** 942

Philo, De Praemiis et Poenis (Praem.)

13	**Vol. 2:** 659
16	**Vol. 2:** 899
17	**Vol. 3:** 266
65	**Vol. 2:** 659
72	**Vol. 1:** 695
79	**Vol. 1:** 334
91–97	**Vol. 2:** 899
101	**Vol. 1:** 334
117	**Vol. 1:** 342 **Vol. 3:** 939
123	**Vol. 2:** 798
125	**Vol. 2:** 798
153	**Vol. 1:** 627

Philo, Quis Rerum Divinarum Heres Sit (Rer. Div. Her.)

5–29	**Vol. 2:** 736
8	**Vol. 1:** 334
38	**Vol. 2:** 288
44	**Vol. 3:** 194
55	**Vol. 3:** 681
70	**Vol. 2:** 187
75	**Vol. 1:** 523
76	**Vol. 2:** 830
94	**Vol. 3:** 369
98	**Vol. 2:** 99
124	**Vol. 3:** 194
133	**Vol. 1:** 387
166	**Vol. 3:** 98
182	**Vol. 3:** 36
186	**Vol. 3:** 194
205 f	**Vol. 3:** 36
263 ff	**Vol. 3:** 491
265	**Vol. 3:** 126
269	**Vol. 3:** 716
293	**Vol. 3:** 147
302	**Vol. 2:** 659
315	**Vol. 2:** 355, 357

Philo, De Sacrificiis Abelis et Caini (Sacr.)

5	**Vol. 3:** 681
6 f	**Vol. 2:** 798
22	**Vol. 3:** 926
27	**Vol. 3:** 926

Philo, De Sacrificiis Abelis et Caini (Sacr.) *(cont'd)*

49	**Vol. 2:** 377
60	**Vol. 2:** 608
63	**Vol. 1:** 674
67	**Vol. 1:** 734
69	**Vol. 3:** 838
95	**Vol. 1:** 468
100	**Vol. 2:** 658
114	**Vol. 3:** 194
117 ff	**Vol. 3:** 194

Philo, *De Sobrietate (Sobr.)*

42	**Vol. 3:** 575
55	**Vol. 3:** 210
56	**Vol. 3:** 639
66	**Vol. 3:** 37

Philo, *De Somniis (Som.)*

1.6	**Vol. 3:** 459	
1.33	**Vol. 2:** 659	
1.36	**Vol. 2:** 762	
1.71	**Vol. 2:** 289	
1.75	**Vol. 2:** 493	
1.76	**Vol. 1:** 387	
1.86	**Vol. 3:** 210	
1.115	**Vol. 2:** 289	
1.135	**Vol. 3:** 681	
1.139	**Vol. 2:** 187	
1.149	**Vol. 3:** 789	
1.163	**Vol. 2:** 512	
1.181	**Vol. 3:** 681	
1.206	**Vol. 2:** 290	**Vol. 3:** 904
1.214 f	**Vol. 3:** 36	
1.215	**Vol. 3:** 35	
1.239	**Vol. 2:** 290	
1.256	**Vol. 3:** 925	
2.23	**Vol. 3:** 526	
2.31	**Vol. 2:** 744	
2.175	**Vol. 1:** 334	
2.226	**Vol. 2:** 397	
2.244	**Vol. 2:** 377	
2.248	**Vol. 3:** 789	
2.253	**Vol. 2:** 779	
2.354	**Vol. 2:** 651	

Philo, *De Specialibus Legibus (Spec. Leg.)*

1	**Vol. 1:** 89
1.1–11	**Vol. 1:** 309
1.18	**Vol. 3:** 126
1.20†	**Vol. 3:** 515
1.32–35	**Vol. 3:** 515
1.44	**Vol. 1:** 742
1.58	**Vol. 2:** 573
1.59	**Vol. 3:** 760
1.65	**Vol. 3:** 491

1.66	**Vol. 3:** 681	
1.77 ff	**Vol. 3:** 752	
1.77	**Vol. 3:** 194	
1.81	**Vol. 3:** 1117	
1.82–97	**Vol. 3:** 36	
1.96	**Vol. 1:** 618	
1.135	**Vol. 3:** 194	
1.149	**Vol. 1:** 495	**Vol. 2:** 99
1.169–189	**Vol. 1:** 627	
1.173	**Vol. 1:** 495	
1.190	**Vol. 1:** 700	
1.199	**Vol. 1:** 230	
1.209	**Vol. 3:** 925	
1.212	**Vol. 3:** 422	
1.221	**Vol. 2:** 518	
1.224	**Vol. 3:** 422	
1.243	**Vol. 3:** 35	
1.269	**Vol. 1:** 330	
1.271	**Vol. 3:** 422	
1.285 ff	**Vol. 3:** 418	
1.288	**Vol. 2:** 493	
1.290	**Vol. 3:** 418	
1.300	**Vol. 1:** 334	
1.302	**Vol. 2:** 192	
1.333	**Vol. 1:** 228	
1.345	**Vol. 3:** 531	
2.2–38	**Vol. 3:** 740	
2.6	**Vol. 1:** 618	**Vol. 2:** 659
2.8	**Vol. 2:** 651	
2.27	**Vol. 2:** 659	
2.41	**Vol. 1:** 627	
2.42–55	**Vol. 1:** 627	
2.42	**Vol. 2:** 659	
2.54 f	**Vol. 2:** 357	
2.95	**Vol. 3:** 194	
2.116	**Vol. 3:** 194	
2.121 f	**Vol. 3:** 194	
2.159	**Vol. 1:** 574	
2.164	**Vol. 3:** 36	
2.176 ff	**Vol. 2:** 785	
2.176–188	**Vol. 2:** 783	
2.176	**Vol. 2:** 783	
2.185	**Vol. 2:** 462	
2.192	**Vol. 2:** 782	
2.195	**Vol. 1:** 495	
2.196	**Vol. 3:** 98	
2.201	**Vol. 2:** 266	
2.225	**Vol. 2:** 659	
3.1 f	**Vol. 2:** 762	
3.40	**Vol. 3:** 785	
3.54	**Vol. 2:** 140	
3.63	**Vol. 3:** 926	
3.145	**Vol. 3:** 194	
3.189	**Vol. 1:** 694	
3.209	**Vol. 3:** 575	
4.40	**Vol. 2:** 651	
4.49	**Vol. 3:** 491	
4.112	**Vol. 1:** 495	
4.123	**Vol. 2:** 289, 659	
4.147	**Vol. 2:** 99	

311

**Philo, De Specialibus Legibus
(Spec. Leg.)** *(cont'd)*

4.150	**Vol. 3:** 772
4.170	**Vol. 1:** 228
4.176–179	**Vol. 2:** 738
4.180	**Vol. 3:** 416
4.203	**Vol. 2:** 742 **Vol. 3:** 1160, 1164
4.231	**Vol. 2:** 497
5.741d	**Vol. 1:** 589

Philo, *De Virtutibus (Virt.)*

5	**Vol. 2:** 659
18	**Vol. 2:** 659
57	**Vol. 3:** 125
90	**Vol. 2:** 821
188	**Vol. 3:** 789
215 f	**Vol. 2:** 396
217	**Vol. 3:** 681

Philo, *De Vita Contemplativa
(Vit. Cont.)*

25	**Vol. 1:** 641 **Vol. 3:** 669
28	**Vol. 1:** 580 **Vol. 2:** 744
31	**Vol. 1:** 580
65 f	**Vol. 2:** 785
75	**Vol. 1:** 577
78	**Vol. 1:** 574

Philo, *De Vita Mosis (Vit. Mos.)*

1.23	**Vol. 3:** 772
1.48	**Vol. 3:** 877
1.54	**Vol. 2:** 677
1.75	**Vol. 2:** 651

1.95	**Vol. 3:** 570
1.156	**Vol. 2:** 757
1.158	**Vol. 1:** 639–640 **Vol. 3:** 126, 486
1.187	**Vol. 1:** 513
1.235	**Vol. 3:** 875
1.279	**Vol. 3:** 522
1.287	**Vol. 3:** 486
1.295 ff	**Vol. 2:** 677
2.4	**Vol. 2:** 792
2.7	**Vol. 2:** 792
2.14	**Vol. 2:** 659
2.20–24	**Vol. 1:** 627
2.29	**Vol. 2:** 757
2.65	**Vol. 1:** 185
2.74 ff	**Vol. 3:** 904
2.76	**Vol. 2:** 290
2.101–104	**Vol. 3:** 789
2.109–135	**Vol. 3:** 36
2.122–135	**Vol. 3:** 396
2.125	**Vol. 1:** 578
2.134	**Vol. 1:** 89, 523
2.138	**Vol. 3:** 989
2.141	**Vol. 3:** 904
2.147	**Vol. 1:** 700
2.160–173	**Vol. 3:** 871
2.167	**Vol. 3:** 875
2.185	**Vol. 1:** 514
2.196	**Vol. 3:** 418
2.203	**Vol. 3:** 486
2.238	**Vol. 1:** 734
2.284	**Vol. 3:** 877
2.290	**Vol. 3:** 486
2.291	**Vol. 3:** 345
2.292	**Vol. 3:** 486
3.171	**Vol. 1:** 469

Early Christian Literature

Barnabas, Letter of (Barn.)

4.6	**Vol. 2:** 316
4.9	**Vol. 1:** 204
4.11	**Vol. 1:** 339
4.14	**Vol. 2:** 316
6.6	**Vol. 2:** 299
6.7	**Vol. 2:** 316
8.1–3	**Vol. 2:** 316
8.7	**Vol. 2:** 316
9.3	**Vol. 1:** 411
9.9	**Vol. 3:** 770
10.12	**Vol. 2:** 316
11.1	**Vol. 2:** 316

12.2	**Vol. 2:** 316
12.5 ff	**Vol. 1:** 510
12.5	**Vol. 2:** 316
12.8 ff	**Vol. 2:** 332
12.10	**Vol. 3:** 653
15.3–9	**Vol. 2:** 701
15.4–5	**Vol. 2:** 697
15.8–9	**Vol. 2:** 692
15.9	**Vol. 1:** 631
16.5	**Vol. 2:** 316
18–20	**Vol. 3:** 929
18.1	**Vol. 2:** 481 **Vol. 3:** 940
19 ff	**Vol. 1:** 339

Barnabas, Letter of (Barn.) *(cont'd)*

19.12	**Vol. 2:** 776
20.1	**Vol. 1:** 204

1 Clement

1.2	**Vol. 2:** 94
1.3	**Vol. 2:** 539
3.2	**Vol. 3:** 963
4.8	**Vol. 1:** 619
4.13	**Vol. 2:** 316
6.1	**Vol. 3:** 856
7.6	**Vol. 2:** 682
8.3	**Vol. 1:** 618 **Vol. 2:** 316
9.3	**Vol. 3:** 265
9.4	**Vol. 2:** 682
13.3	**Vol. 1:** 339
16.17	**Vol. 3:** 1163
18.10	**Vol. 2:** 673
20.11	**Vol. 1:** 387
21.6−8	**Vol. 3:** 929
22.6	**Vol. 3:** 516
23.2 ff	**Vol. 3:** 687
25.2	**Vol. 2:** 725
29.2 f	**Vol. 2:** 316
30.1	**Vol. 3:** 346
30.3	**Vol. 3:** 346
31.2−4	**Vol. 2:** 316
31.2	**Vol. 1:** 619
32.4	**Vol. 2:** 81
33.5	**Vol. 2:** 570
33.6	**Vol. 2:** 130
34.7	**Vol. 3:** 1194
35.5	**Vol. 3:** 346, 931
40.5	**Vol. 2:** 457
41.1	**Vol. 3:** 931
42.1 f	**Vol. 3:** 548
43	**Vol. 2:** 316
43.4	**Vol. 3:** 37
46.5	**Vol. 1:** 535 **Vol. 3:** 963
47.3	**Vol. 3:** 383
49.5	**Vol. 2:** 214
50.5	**Vol. 1:** 339
55.3 ff	**Vol. 3:** 962
55.6	**Vol. 2:** 316
59.2 ff	**Vol. 3:** 611
59.2−4	**Vol. 3:** 611
59.4	**Vol. 3:** 319
60.3	**Vol. 3:** 319
60.4	**Vol. 1:** 619
62.2	**Vol. 3:** 931

2 Clement

2.1 f	**Vol. 1:** 411
2.4	**Vol. 3:** 492
4	**Vol. 3:** 929
4.5	**Vol. 1:** 339
6.1	**Vol. 2:** 838
6.7	**Vol. 1:** 339

7.6	**Vol. 3:** 499
8.2	**Vol. 3:** 912
8.4	**Vol. 1:** 339
8.6	**Vol. 3:** 499
11.2 ff	**Vol. 3:** 687
13.1	**Vol. 2:** 817
14.2	**Vol. 2:** 570
16.3	**Vol. 3:** 180
16.4	**Vol. 2:** 214
17.1	**Vol. 3:** 772
17.7	**Vol. 3:** 856
19.2	**Vol. 3:** 687

Didache (Did.)

1−5	**Vol. 3:** 929
1.1	**Vol. 2:** 481 **Vol. 3:** 940
1.3	**Vol. 1:** 613
2.1	**Vol. 3:** 770
4.3	**Vol. 2:** 776
6.1	**Vol. 3:** 770
6.3	**Vol. 2:** 284
7.1−3	**Vol. 3:** 648
7.3	**Vol. 3:** 648
8.1	**Vol. 1:** 630 **Vol. 3:** 408
8.2	**Vol. 2:** 870
9 f	**Vol. 3:** 611
9	**Vol. 1:** 117 **Vol. 2:** 896
9.2	**Vol. 1:** 641
9.5	**Vol. 3:** 395
10	**Vol. 2:** 896
10.5 f	**Vol. 3:** 245
10.5	**Vol. 2:** 531
10.6†	**Vol. 2:** 531, 895−896
10.7	**Vol. 3:** 89
11.2	**Vol. 3:** 770
11.3	**Vol. 3:** 84
11.7−12	**Vol. 3:** 89
13	**Vol. 1:** 198
13.1−7	**Vol. 3:** 89
13.1	**Vol. 3:** 349
13.2	**Vol. 3:** 768
14.1	**Vol. 1:** 631
15.1 f	**Vol. 3:** 84
16.3	**Vol. 2:** 130
16.5	**Vol. 1:** 656
16.6	**Vol. 3:** 634

Epistle to Diognetus (Ep. Diog.)

2.2	**Vol. 3:** 913
2.7	**Vol. 3:** 913
3.1	**Vol. 2:** 85
5	**Vol. 2:** 804
6.3	**Vol. 3:** 1188
7.2	**Vol. 1:** 387
9.2	**Vol. 3:** 1196
9.5	**Vol. 3:** 1196

313

Gospel of Thomas (Gos. Thom.)

6	**Vol. 1:** 92
7	**Vol. 2:** 752
8	**Vol. 2:** 751
10	**Vol. 3:** 697
16	**Vol. 3:** 697
17	**Vol. 2:** 219
20	**Vol. 2:** 751, 926
22	**Vol. 1:** 284
24	**Vol. 2:** 706
25	**Vol. 2:** 752
27	**Vol. 2:** 751
37	**Vol. 2:** 926
38	**Vol. 3:** 634
47	**Vol. 2:** 838
64	**Vol. 2:** 751
65	**Vol. 2:** 751
66	**Vol. 2:** 751
82	**Vol. 2:** 752 **Vol. 3:** 697
90	**Vol. 3:** 640
94	**Vol. 2:** 752
95	**Vol. 2:** 752
104	**Vol. 2:** 752

Hermas, *Commandments* or *Mandates* *(Com.* or *Man.)*

2.2 f	**Vol. 3:** 346
3 f	**Vol. 3:** 983
4.1	**Vol. 3:** 316
4.3	**Vol. 3:** 316
6.1	**Vol. 3:** 929
8.3	**Vol. 3:** 346
8.8	**Vol. 3:** 316
8.12	**Vol. 1:** 339
11.1 ff	**Vol. 3:** 687

Hermas, *Similitudes (Sim.)*

5.3.1	**Vol. 1:** 577
5.3.2	**Vol. 1:** 577
5.4.2	**Vol. 1:** 577
5.5.1	**Vol. 1:** 577
5.6.8	**Vol. 1:** 577
6.5.5	**Vol. 3:** 345
8.6.3	**Vol. 3:** 499
8.11.1	**Vol. 1:** 577
9.11.9	**Vol. 1:** 577
9.12.3 f	**Vol. 2:** 31
10.4.1†	**Vol. 1:** 339

Hermas, *Visions (Vis.)*

3.5.3	**Vol. 1:** 339
3.9.7	**Vol. 1:** 666
3.10.6	**Vol. 3:** 515
4.3.3	**Vol. 2:** 836
5.5 ff	**Vol. 1:** 339

Ignatius, *Letter to the* *Ephesians (Eph.)*

4.1 f	**Vol. 3:** 675
5.3	**Vol. 3:** 1194
7.2	**Vol. 3:** 724
9.2	**Vol. 1:** 339
10.3	**Vol. 3:** 529
13.1	**Vol. 3:** 1194
18.2	**Vol. 3:** 653
20	**Vol. 2:** 271
20.2	**Vol. 3:** 653

Ignatius, *Letter to the* *Magnesians (Mag.)*

2.1	**Vol. 3:** 548
5	**Vol. 3:** 929
6.1	**Vol. 3:** 548
7.1	**Vol. 3:** 1194
8	**Vol. 2:** 316
9.1	**Vol. 1:** 631 **Vol. 3:** 411
10.3	**Vol. 2:** 316

Ignatius, *Letter to the* *Philadelphians (Phil.)*

6	**Vol. 2:** 677
6.2	**Vol. 3:** 1194
9.1	**Vol. 2:** 31
10.1	**Vol. 3:** 1194

Ignatius, *Letter to* *Polycarp (Pol.)*

3.2	**Vol. 3:** 724
4.1–6.2	**Vol. 3:** 929
4.2	**Vol. 3:** 724

Ignatius, *Letter to the* *Romans (Rom.)*

7.3	**Vol. 3:** 653
9.2	**Vol. 1:** 183

Ignatius, *Letter to the* *Smyrnaeans (Smy.)*

1.1	**Vol. 3:** 653, 661
4.2	**Vol. 3:** 724
8.2	**Vol. 2:** 547

Ignatius, *Letter to the* *Trallians (Trall.)*

2.1	**Vol. 3:** 548
6.1	**Vol. 1:** 535
9.1	**Vol. 3:** 653
11	**Vol. 2:** 677
13.2	**Vol. 1:** 339

Martyrdom of Polycarp

2.2	**Vol. 3:** 257
2.3	**Vol. 3:** 856
14.1 ff	**Vol. 3:** 611
14.1	**Vol. 3:** 611
14.3	**Vol. 3:** 611

Polycarp, *To the Philippians* (Polycarp)

4.2 – 6.1	**Vol. 3:** 929
4.2	**Vol. 2:** 539
8.1	**Vol. 2:** 40

Rabbinic Writings

Mishnah

Aboth (= Pirke Aboth)

1.1	**Vol. 3:** 772
1.3	**Vol. 2:** 191 **Vol. 3:** 1149
1.5	**Vol. 3:** 536, 1058
1.9	**Vol. 3:** 1154
1.10	**Vol. 2:** 608
1.11	**Vol. 2:** 191
1.12	**Vol. 2:** 779
1.17	**Vol. 3:** 1121
2.1	**Vol. 3:** 614
2.3	**Vol. 2:** 608 **Vol. 3:** 614
2.12 f	**Vol. 2:** 481 **Vol. 3:** 940
2.12	**Vol. 2:** 837
2.16	**Vol. 3:** 140
3.5	**Vol. 3:** 1161 – 1162
3.14 ff	**Vol. 2:** 812
3.14	**Vol. 2:** 798 **Vol. 3:** 773
3.15 f	**Vol. 2:** 608
3.16	**Vol. 3:** 140
4.11	**Vol. 1:** 83
4.17	**Vol. 1:** 405
4.22	**Vol. 3:** 1154
5.19	**Vol. 3:** 942
5.21	**Vol. 2:** 261
6.2	**Vol. 3:** 488, 769, 1162
6.5	**Vol. 1:** 405
6.6	**Vol. 2:** 34, 652
6.10	**Vol. 2:** 310
6.11	**Vol. 3:** 140

Arakhin

7.3 ff	**Vol. 3:** 194
9.1 – 4	**Vol. 3:** 194

Baba Bathra

6.8	**Vol. 3:** 381

Baba Kamma

3.5	**Vol. 2:** 608
5.3	**Vol. 2:** 608
10.1	**Vol. 3:** 756
10.2	**Vol. 3:** 754

Berakoth

1.4	**Vol. 2:** 864
3.3	**Vol. 3:** 1058
5.5	**Vol. 1:** 128
6.1	**Vol. 2:** 521
7.2	**Vol. 3:** 1058
7.3	**Vol. 1:** 212 **Vol. 2:** 521
9.2	**Vol. 3:** 1154

Erubin

6.2	**Vol. 3:** 439

Gittin

1.1	**Vol. 3:** 498
1.3	**Vol. 3:** 498
4.9	**Vol. 3:** 194

Hagigah

2.1	**Vol. 2:** 397 **Vol. 3:** 502, 748
2.7	**Vol. 3:** 105

Hallah

3.3	**Vol. 3:** 194

Hullin

3.6	**Vol. 1:** 172

Kelim

13.6	Vol. 3: 498
13.7	Vol. 3: 479

Ketuboth

4.3	Vol. 1: 159
4.6	Vol. 3: 921
9.5	Vol. 2: 608
9.9	Vol. 1: 159

Kiddushin

1.10	Vol. 3: 761
4.9	Vol. 2: 608

Kilaim

8.2	Vol. 3: 1160

Makkoth

1.6	Vol. 3: 439
3.16	Vol. 3: 140

Megillah

4.4	Vol. 3: 485

Menahoth

10.3	Vol. 2: 785

Middoth

1.2	Vol. 1: 314
2.6	Vol. 3: 1162
3	Vol. 3: 419
3.8	Vol. 3: 921

Moed Katan

3.7 ff	Vol. 1: 329

Nazir

1.3	Vol. 2: 61

Nedarim

1	Vol. 2: 43
3	Vol. 2: 43
3.2	Vol. 2: 43
3.4	Vol. 3: 757
8	Vol. 2: 43
9	Vol. 2: 43
9.1	Vol. 2: 43
10.2–4	Vol. 2: 608
11	Vol. 2: 43

Niddah

4.2	Vol. 3: 439

Oholoth

17.5	Vol. 3: 498

Parah

3.3	Vol. 3: 439
3.7	Vol. 3: 439

Peah

2.6	Vol. 3: 772
4.7	Vol. 3: 194
8.9	Vol. 1: 219

Pesahim

2.5	Vol. 3: 194
8.8	Vol. 1: 155
10.2–7	Vol. 2: 522
10.5 f	Vol. 3: 194
10.5	Vol. 2: 313

Rosh ha-Shanah

1.1	Vol. 1: 628
3.8	Vol. 1: 509

Sanhedrin

3.2	Vol. 1: 203 Vol. 2: 159 Vol. 3: 741
4.1	Vol. 1: 630
4.5	Vol. 3: 498
6.1	Vol. 3: 51
7.4	Vol. 3: 227
7.5	Vol. 3: 341–343
9.1	Vol. 1: 235
10.1	Vol. 2: 798, 811
11.1–4	Vol. 1: 196
11.1	Vol. 2: 311, 313 Vol. 3: 227
11.3	Vol. 3: 479

Shabbath

3.1	Vol. 2: 811
6.5	Vol. 3: 444
7.2	Vol. 3: 408
8.5	Vol. 3: 498
14.4	Vol. 2: 798
16.2	Vol. 3: 408

Shebuoth

6.13	Vol. 3: 741

Shekalim

1.7	Vol. 2: 823
2.5	Vol. 2: 823
5.3	Vol. 3: 498
5.4	Vol. 3: 498

Sotah

1.7	**Vol. 3:** 402
3.4	**Vol. 3:** 1058
7.7 f	**Vol. 2:** 158
9.9	**Vol. 1:** 724
9.14	**Vol. 2:** 126
9.15	**Vol. 1:** 544, 724 **Vol. 2:** 811

Sukkah

4.9	**Vol. 3:** 814
5.2 ff	**Vol. 1:** 629
5.2–5	**Vol. 3:** 814

Taanith

2.1 f	**Vol. 3:** 389

Terumoth

6.5	**Vol. 3:** 194

Tohoroth

3.6	**Vol. 1:** 155
7.6	**Vol. 3:** 756
7.7	**Vol. 3:** 498

Yadaim

4.6	**Vol. 3:** 439
4.7	**Vol. 3:** 439

Yebamoth

1.1	**Vol. 2:** 61
2.29	**Vol. 1:** 145
4.11	**Vol. 2:** 608
8.5	**Vol. 2:** 311
9.3	**Vol. 3:** 1121
11.2	**Vol. 1:** 159

Yoma

2.4	**Vol. 2:** 294
3.8	**Vol. 3:** 159
3.9b	**Vol. 3:** 233
4.2	**Vol. 3:** 159
6.2	**Vol. 3:** 159
8.8 f	**Vol. 3:** 428
8.9	**Vol. 3:** 173, 428

Yom Tob (= Betzah)

3.1	**Vol. 2:** 811

Zabim

2.1	**Vol. 1:** 155

Babylonian Talmud

Abodah Zarah

17a	**Vol. 2:** 833

Baba Bathra

14b	**Vol. 3:** 485
16a	**Vol. 1:** 83 **Vol. 3:** 469
73a	**Vol. 3:** 983
75a	**Vol. 3:** 396

Baba Kamma

38a	**Vol. 2:** 309
113a	**Vol. 3:** 756

Baba Metzia

59b	**Vol. 2:** 687

Bekhoroth

30b	**Vol. 3:** 756

Berakoth

3a	**Vol. 3:** 448
5a	**Vol. 3:** 447
8b	**Vol. 1:** 230 **Vol. 3:** 1121
17a	**Vol. 3:** 105
27b	**Vol. 2:** 608
28b–29a	**Vol. 2:** 312
31a	**Vol. 2:** 433
32b	**Vol. 3:** 396
34b	**Vol. 3:** 638
35a	**Vol. 1:** 212
40a	**Vol. 1:** 614
46a	**Vol. 2:** 521
47b	**Vol. 1:** 485
50a	**Vol. 2:** 521
51a	**Vol. 3:** 921
55a	**Vol. 2:** 480
55b	**Vol. 1:** 116
60b	**Vol. 2:** 313 **Vol. 3:** 1152
61b	**Vol. 2:** 720, 837
2.2	**Vol. 3:** 1161
60 ff	**Vol. 1:** 231

Erubin

13b	**Vol. 3:** 1121
53b	**Vol. 3:** 1058

Gittin

60b	**Vol. 3:** 488
88a	**Vol. 2:** 730

Hagigah

12b	**Vol. 3:** 35
13 ff	**Vol. 1:** 527
14b	**Vol. 1:** 216
15a	**Vol. 1:** 175 **Vol. 2:** 608

Hullin

92a	**Vol. 2:** 309
106a	**Vol. 2:** 608
131	**Vol. 2:** 467

Kiddushin

29b	**Vol. 3:** 445
76a	**Vol. 3:** 455
81a	**Vol. 3:** 536

Makkoth

22a–22b	**Vol. 2:** 696
23b–24a	**Vol. 2:** 442
23b	**Vol. 3:** 367
24a–24b	**Vol. 2:** 310

Megillah

10b	**Vol. 3:** 656
12b–13a	**Vol. 2:** 310
13b	**Vol. 2:** 310
14b	**Vol. 3:** 656
23a	**Vol. 3:** 1058
27b	**Vol. 2:** 479
29a	**Vol. 2:** 310
31a	**Vol. 2:** 350

Menahoth

20b	**Vol. 3:** 445
65a–66a	**Vol. 1:** 627
85a	**Vol. 2:** 557
93b	**Vol. 1:** 223
104b	**Vol. 3:** 422
110a	**Vol. 3:** 422

Nedarim

32b	**Vol. 2:** 591
41a	**Vol. 2:** 824

Niddah

23a	**Vol. 3:** 1121

31a	**Vol. 3:** 1121

Ketuboth

50a	**Vol. 2:** 738
66b	**Vol. 3:** 445
67a–67b	**Vol. 2:** 738

Pesahim

3a	**Vol. 1:** 641
13a	**Vol. 1:** 641
54a	**Vol. 3:** 487
68b	**Vol. 2:** 784
87b	**Vol. 2:** 309
91b	**Vol. 1:** 145
112b	**Vol. 2:** 608
174b	**Vol. 3:** 195
7	**Vol. 1:** 641
27	**Vol. 3:** 195
68	**Vol. 3:** 408

Rosh ha-Shanah

10b–11a	**Vol. 1:** 628
21a	**Vol. 3:** 51
12	**Vol. 1:** 628

Sanhedrin

5a	**Vol. 2:** 608
19b	**Vol. 1:** 180 **Vol. 2:** 738
21b	**Vol. 2:** 141
25b	**Vol. 3:** 756
38a	**Vol. 2:** 608, 730 **Vol. 3:** 392
39a	**Vol. 3:** 447
40b	**Vol. 3:** 183
41a	**Vol. 3:** 538
43a	**Vol. 1:** 630 **Vol. 2:** 28, 295 **Vol. 3:** 51, 472
46b	**Vol. 1:** 265
56a–56b	**Vol. 2:** 309
59a	**Vol. 2:** 34
70b	**Vol. 1:** 614
88b	**Vol. 2:** 880
90b	**Vol. 3:** 274
91a	**Vol. 1:** 674 **Vol. 3:** 682
93b	**Vol. 2:** 314
94b	**Vol. 3:** 1161
97a–97b	**Vol. 2:** 698
97a	**Vol. 2:** 712 **Vol. 3:** 575
98a–98b	**Vol. 3:** 610
98b	**Vol. 2:** 314
99a	**Vol. 2:** 696
99b	**Vol. 1:** 180
102b	**Vol. 1:** 455
107b	**Vol. 3:** 472
108b	**Vol. 2:** 591
111b	**Vol. 3:** 1161

Shabbath

4a	**Vol. 3:** 183
12b	**Vol. 2:** 313
17b	**Vol. 3:** 1121
31a–31b	**Vol. 2:** 730
31a	**Vol. 1:** 485 **Vol. 2:** 311, 442, 811 **Vol. 3:** 488
33b	**Vol. 3:** 756
63a	**Vol. 2:** 314
88b	**Vol. 3:** 1121
104a	**Vol. 3:** 488
116a	**Vol. 1:** 455
119a	**Vol. 3:** 408, 753
129a	**Vol. 3:** 1121
132a	**Vol. 1:** 310
137b	**Vol. 1:** 309

Sotah

12b	**Vol. 1:** 598
22a	**Vol. 3:** 463
28b	**Vol. 3:** 1121
33a	**Vol. 3:** 39
47a	**Vol. 3:** 472
47b	**Vol. 3:** 1161
48b	**Vol. 1:** 597
49a	**Vol. 2:** 712
49b	**Vol. 2:** 126
47	**Vol. 3:** 227

Sukkah

45b	**Vol. 3:** 161

52a	**Vol. 1:** 178
52b	**Vol. 3:** 36

Taanith

8a	**Vol. 1:** 597
19a	**Vol. 3:** 638
19b–20a	**Vol. 3:** 638
20b	**Vol. 2:** 479–480
21a	**Vol. 3:** 1152
23b	**Vol. 1:** 614 **Vol. 3:** 639
24a	**Vol. 2:** 823

Yebamoth

15b	**Vol. 2:** 579
22a	**Vol. 1:** 180
62b	**Vol. 2:** 562
63a	**Vol. 3:** 867
63b	**Vol. 2:** 579
86	**Vol. 2:** 467

Yoma

5a	**Vol. 1:** 223
9a	**Vol. 1:** 555
22b	**Vol. 3:** 170
53b	**Vol. 3:** 39
72b	**Vol. 1:** 405

Zebahim

6a	**Vol. 1:** 223

Index of
Hebrew and Aramaic Words

Index of Hebrew
and Aramaic Words

'āḇ **Vol. 1:** 617 f., 621
Vol. 3: 870
'āḇaḏ **Vol. 1:** 463
'ᵃḇaddôn **Vol. 1:** 463 f.
'āḇâh **Vol. 3:** 1016, 1019
'āḇal **Vol. 2:** 422 f.
'āḇaq **Vol. 1:** 645
'abbā' **Vol. 1:** 614 f., 620
Vol. 2: 867, 869, 896
Vol. 3: 639
'āḇî **Vol. 1:** 614
'āḇîḇ **Vol. 2:** 675
Vol. 3: 422
'aḇnēṭ **Vol. 3:** 120
'aḇrāhām **Vol. 1:** 76
'āḏām **Vol. 1:** 84
Vol. 2: 160, 502, 564, 571
Vol. 3: 613
'ᵃḏāmâh **Vol. 1:** 84
Vol. 2: 564
'ᵃḏarkōnîm
Vol. 2: 848
'āḏōm **Vol. 1:** 205
'āḏôn **Vol. 2:** 509, 511 f., 562,
590
'ᵃḏōnay **Vol. 1:** 71
Vol. 2: 69, 71, 512
Vol. 3: 786
'āḡam **Vol. 3:** 992
'āḡam **Vol. 2:** 423
'āḥ **Vol. 1:** 255, 258, 260
Vol. 2: 739
'ahaḇ **Vol. 2:** 551
'ahᵃḇâh **Vol. 2:** 105, 539, 547
'ahᵃḇaṭ ḥeseḏ **Vol. 2:** 105
'ᵃḥāḏîm **Vol. 2:** 716
'aḥar **Vol. 1:** 492
Vol. 2: 55 f.
Vol. 3: 178, 262
'aḥᵃrê **Vol. 1:** 321, 481
'aḥᵃrîṭ hayyāmîm **Vol. 2:** 56
'aḥᵃrôn **Vol. 1:** 326
Vol. 2: 61
'aḥaṭ **Vol. 2:** 716 f., 720
'āḥaz **Vol. 2:** 860
'āhēḇ **Vol. 2:** 539, 547
'ᵃḥiyâh **Vol. 2:** 521
'ᵃḥiyâhû **Vol. 2:** 521
'ᵃḥuzzâh **Vol. 3:** 256
'āḵal **Vol. 2:** 268
'al **Vol. 3:** 153
'ālâh **Vol. 3:** 474, 739

'ālēp **Vol. 3:** 760
'alᵉpê yiśrā'ēl **Vol. 2:** 698
'allâp **Vol. 3:** 769
'allûp **Vol. 2:** 698
'almānâh **Vol. 3:** 1073, 1077
'āmal **Vol. 2:** 422
'āman **Vol. 1:** 97, 100, 595–
597, 599, 601
Vol. 2: 837
Vol. 3: 368, 878, 902
'ᵃmānâh **Vol. 1:** 598
'āmar **Vol. 2:** 488
Vol. 3: 821, 1087, 1144 f.
'āmēn **Vol. 1:** 97 f.
'ᵃmorā'îm **Vol. 1:** 69
'ānâh **Vol. 2:** 423
'ānaḥ **Vol. 2:** 423
'ānaq **Vol. 2:** 423
'ᵃnāqâh **Vol. 2:** 423
'ᵃnî **Vol. 2:** 278
'ᵃnî hû' **Vol. 2:** 279
'ᵃnî YHWH **Vol. 2:** 278
'ānōḵî **Vol. 2:** 278
'anšê 'ᵃmānâh **Vol. 1:** 598
'anšê gᵉ'ullāṭeḵā **Vol. 3:** 190
'ap **Vol. 1:** 106, 108
'apîq **Vol. 3:** 985
'āreṣ **Vol. 1:** 539
Vol. 2: 456
'armôn **Vol. 1:** 661
'ārôn **Vol. 3:** 812
'ārûr **Vol. 1:** 416
'āšām **Vol. 2:** 406
Vol. 3: 171, 420, 437 f., 856
'āsap **Vol. 2:** 32
Vol. 3: 255
'ᵃsar **Vol. 2:** 732
Vol. 3: 188
'āsar **Vol. 1:** 171, 472
Vol. 2: 732
Vol. 3: 591, 1161
'āšar **Vol. 1:** 215
'ᵃšer **Vol. 2:** 68, 888
'ašᵉrê **Vol. 1:** 215 f.
'ašērîm **Vol. 3:** 865
'ašmâh **Vol. 3:** 156
'āsôn **Vol. 3:** 999
'aššāp **Vol. 3:** 1035
'aššapîm **Vol. 2:** 555
'aṭā' **Vol. 2:** 895
'āṭam **Vol. 3:** 950
'āwâh **Vol. 1:** 456

'āwen **Vol. 1:** 550
Vol. 3: 1024
'ᵃwîl **Vol. 3:** 1037
'ayyēh **Vol. 3:** 267
'āzal **Vol. 1:** 698
'āzar **Vol. 2:** 222
'ᵃzārâh **Vol. 3:** 156
'azkārâh **Vol. 3:** 233, 238 f.,
423
'dm **Vol. 1:** 84
'ēḇel **Vol. 2:** 422
Vol. 3: 720
'eḇen **Vol. 3:** 388, 391, 398
'eḇen yiśra'ēl **Vol. 3:** 398
'eḇyôn **Vol. 2:** 820–822, 829
Vol. 3: 93
'eḥāḏ **Vol. 1:** 665, 678
Vol. 2: 498, 716, 720, 725
'eḥᵉzeh **Vol. 3:** 178
'eḥî **Vol. 3:** 267
'ehyeh 'ᵃšer 'ehyeh **Vol. 2:** 68
'el **Vol. 3:** 1090
'ēl **Vol. 1:** 103, 190, 296
Vol. 2: 67, 70, 86 f., 304 f.
'ēl-'elyôn **Vol. 3:** 36, 457
'elep **Vol. 2:** 698
'ēlî **Vol. 2:** 82, 637
'ēliyyâh, 'ēliyyâhû **Vol. 1:** 543
'ēlleh **Vol. 3:** 739
'ᵉlôah **Vol. 2:** 67, 70
Vol. 3: 178
'ᵉlôhêkem **Vol. 3:** 239
'ᵉlōhēnû **Vol. 2:** 720
'ᵉlōhîm **Vol. 1:** 56
Vol. 2: 67, 70, 502, 591
Vol. 3: 264, 631
'elōi **Vol. 2:** 82
'ēm **Vol. 1:** 87
Vol. 3: 1069, 1077
'ēmer **Vol. 3:** 1087
'ᵉmeṭ **Vol. 2:** 119
Vol. 3: 354, 358, 877–892,
902
'ᵉmûnâh **Vol. 1:** 597, 601, 714
Vol. 3: 368, 878 f., 882
'ēn mispār **Vol. 2:** 683
'ēn qēṣeh **Vol. 2:** 683
'ᵉnôš **Vol. 2:** 562, 564
Vol. 3: 613
'ēpôḏ **Vol. 3:** 36
'eppattaḥ **Vol. 2:** 560, 729
'ereḵ 'appayim **Vol. 2:** 769

'ereṣ **Vol. 1:** 517
  Vol. 2: 209
  Vol. 3: 105, 160, 249
'ēš **Vol. 1:** 654, 658
'eṣba' **Vol. 2:** 150
'ēṣer **Vol. 1:** 215
'ēšeṭ ba'ªlaṭ-'ôḇ **Vol. 2:** 554
'eškār **Vol. 3:** 139
'eṭ **Vol. 3:** 777
'eṭnâh **Vol. 3:** 139
'eṭnan **Vol. 3:** 139
'eṭnān **Vol. 3:** 139
'eṭpattaḥ **Vol. 2:** 560, 729
'ᵉwîl **Vol. 3:** 126, 1024 f.
'î **Vol. 3:** 1051
'iggereṭ **Vol. 1:** 246
'iḵabôḏ **Vol. 2:** 45
'im **Vol. 1:** 210
  Vol. 3: 420
'immā' **Vol. 1:** 614
'imrâh **Vol. 3:** 1087
'îš **Vol. 2:** 562, 564, 571, 739
  Vol. 3: 680, 1075
'îš hā'ᵉlōhîm **Vol. 3:** 77
'iššâh **Vol. 2:** 587
  Vol. 3: 1055, 1065, 1075, 1077
'istallaq **Vol. 3:** 631
'iṭṭer **Vol. 2:** 414
'iṭṭîm **Vol. 2:** 555
'iwweleṭ **Vol. 3:** 125 f., 1024 f.
'mn **Vol. 1:** 100, 606
  Vol. 2: 837
  Vol. 3: 877 f.
'ōhel **Vol. 1:** 294
  Vol. 3: 811
'ōhel 'ēḏûṭ **Vol. 3:** 811
'ōhel mô'ēḏ **Vol. 3:** 811, 815
'ōmnâh **Vol. 3:** 878
'ôr **Vol. 2:** 488, 496
  Vol. 3: 318
'ôṣār **Vol. 2:** 830
'ôṭ **Vol. 2:** 350, 501, 626 f., 629, 634
'ōṭô **Vol. 3:** 264
'ōṭōṭ ûmôp̄ᵉṭîm **Vol. 2:** 627
'ôy **Vol. 3:** 1051
'ôyēḇ **Vol. 1:** 553
'ōzen **Vol. 3:** 125
'ûlām **Vol. 3:** 782
'wn' **Vol. 3:** 229
'zn **Vol. 2:** 175

'āḇaḏ **Vol. 2:** 164, 876
  Vol. 3: 550, 1148
'ªḇāḏîm **Vol. 3:** 593, 608 f.
'āḇar **Vol. 1:** 699
  Vol. 3: 255, 583
'aḇdê hammeleḵ **Vol. 3:** 608
'aḇdekā **Vol. 3:** 244
'aḇdî **Vol. 3:** 639
'ªḇôḏâh **Vol. 3:** 552, 595
'āḏap̄ **Vol. 2:** 130
'ªḏî **Vol. 1:** 522

'al **Vol. 1:** 632, 636
  Vol. 2: 184
  Vol. 3: 178
'al habbayiṭ **Vol. 2:** 254
'ālâh **Vol. 2:** 185
  Vol. 3: 421, 860
'ālaz **Vol. 3:** 29
'ālᵉmā' **Vol. 1:** 523
  Vol. 2: 514
'ªlî **Vol. 3:** 459
'allîz **Vol. 3:** 29
'almâh **Vol. 2:** 87
  Vol. 3: 1071 f.
'ām **Vol. 1:** 292–294, 539
  Vol. 2: 456, 789 f., 792 f., 796–801
  Vol. 3: 105
'am hā'āreṣ **Vol. 1:** 539
  Vol. 2: 456, 801, 805
  Vol. 3: 105, 756
'am sᵉḡullâh **Vol. 2:** 839 f.
'am YHWH **Vol. 2:** 796
'āmaḏ **Vol. 1:** 380, 474
  Vol. 2: 136
  Vol. 3: 224, 228, 279
'āmāl **Vol. 1:** 262
'ammî **Vol. 2:** 796
'ammîm **Vol. 1:** 96
  Vol. 2: 790, 792, 799
'ammûḏ **Vol. 3:** 795
'āmōq **Vol. 2:** 197
'anā **Vol. 3:** 822
'ānaḡ **Vol. 2:** 735
'ānâh **Vol. 2:** 175, 179, 260, 468, 821
  Vol. 3: 1041
'ānāw **Vol. 2:** 257, 829
'ªnāwâh **Vol. 2:** 260, 264
'ānî **Vol. 2:** 257 f., 820–822, 829
'ānî wᵉ'eḇyôn **Vol. 2:** 822
'ªniyyîm **Vol. 2:** 829
'āp̄ār **Vol. 1:** 520
  Vol. 3: 178
'āqaḇ **Vol. 2:** 431
'aqrāḇ **Vol. 1:** 510
'ªrāḇâh **Vol. 1:** 411
'ārâh **Vol. 1:** 549
  Vol. 2: 854
'ārap̄ **Vol. 3:** 192
'ārîṣ **Vol. 3:** 29
'ārōm **Vol. 1:** 412
'āśâh **Vol. 3:** 1148, 1153, 1156, 1159
'āśâh ṣᵉḏāqâh **Vol. 2:** 597
'āšaq **Vol. 3:** 379, 574
'āšar **Vol. 3:** 693
'ªśārâh **Vol. 2:** 234
'āṣēl **Vol. 3:** 1024
'āśᵉmû missappēr **Vol. 2:** 683
'āšîr **Vol. 3:** 841
'āšûq **Vol. 2:** 138
'aṭar **Vol. 2:** 862 f.
'ªṭārâh **Vol. 1:** 405

'āṭēq **Vol. 2:** 714
'aṭîḏ **Vol. 1:** 326
'āwâh **Vol. 3:** 859
'āwaṭ **Vol. 2:** 370
'āwel **Vol. 3:** 586 f.
'awlâh **Vol. 3:** 574
'āwōn **Vol. 2:** 138
  Vol. 3: 574, 577, 587
'ªwōnōṭām **Vol. 3:** 420
'āyēp̄ **Vol. 2:** 265
'ayin **Vol. 2:** 501
  Vol. 3: 985
'ªzā'zēl **Vol. 1:** 451, 698
'āzaḇ **Vol. 3:** 248
'ªzaḇṭānî **Vol. 2:** 82
'bd **Vol. 3:** 593
'eḇeḏ **Vol. 1:** 283
  Vol. 2: 164
  Vol. 3: 593, 597, 607–611, 618, 637, 639–641, 664
'eḇeḏ kᵉna'ªnî **Vol. 3:** 593
'ēḇer **Vol. 2:** 305
'eḇrâh **Vol. 1:** 108
'ēḏ **Vol. 3:** 1041
'ēḏâh **Vol. 1:** 190, 292–296, 302
'ēḏen **Vol. 2:** 761
'ēḏer **Vol. 3:** 564
'ēḏûṭ **Vol. 3:** 1040
'ērāḇôn **Vol. 2:** 39
'erwâh **Vol. 3:** 310, 562
'erwaṭ dāḇār **Vol. 3:** 1195
'ēṣ **Vol. 3:** 865, 870
'ēṣâh **Vol. 3:** 1016
'ēśeḇ **Vol. 1:** 743
  Vol. 2: 211
'eśer **Vol. 3:** 851
'eštōnôṭ **Vol. 3:** 820
'ēṭ **Vol. 3:** 827, 835, 841, 850
'ēzer **Vol. 2:** 576, 637
'iḇrî **Vol. 2:** 305
  Vol. 3: 593
'immānû 'ēl **Vol. 2:** 86
'innâh **Vol. 1:** 495, 612
'inyân **Vol. 3:** 799
'îr **Vol. 2:** 802
'iwwēr **Vol. 1:** 218
'izzaḇôn **Vol. 3:** 139
'ōl **Vol. 3:** 1161
'ōlâh **Vol. 3:** 421–423, 432, 434, 438
'ōlāl, 'ôlēl **Vol. 1:** 281
'ôlām **Vol. 1:** 164, 476, 523, 526
  Vol. 2: 67, 105, 514, 931
  Vol. 3: 237, 827–829, 850
'ôlām habbā' **Vol. 3:** 70, 829
'ôlām lᵉḏōrōṭām **Vol. 3:** 828
'ōmer **Vol. 3:** 421
'ôp̄ **Vol. 1:** 172
'ôrî **Vol. 3:** 178
'orlaṭ lēḇāḇ **Vol. 2:** 184
'ormâh **Vol. 1:** 412
'ōšer **Vol. 2:** 841

'ōz **Vol. 2:** 602
'ôz **Vol. 2:** 602
Vol. 3: 817
'šr **Vol. 2:** 841
'ûr **Vol. 3:** 279

ba'al **Vol. 1:** 75
Vol. 2: 511, 562, 677
Vol. 3: 469, 1006, 1065
ba'al habayiṯ **Vol. 2:** 510
ba'al 'iššâh **Vol. 3:** 1065
ba'al šāmēm **Vol. 3:** 1006
ba'al zᵉḇûḇ, zᵉḇûḇ **Vol. 3:** 469
ba'al zᵉḇûl **Vol. 3:** 469
ba'al zibbûl **Vol. 3:** 469
ba'ar **Vol. 3:** 1024 f.
bā'ar **Vol. 3:** 1024
bāḇel **Vol. 1:** 140
baḏ **Vol. 2:** 723
baḏ bᵉḇaḏ yihyeh **Vol. 2:** 723
bāḏāḏ **Vol. 2:** 723
bāḏal **Vol. 3:** 392
bāḡaḏ **Vol. 1:** 461
bāhal **Vol. 3:** 1169
bāhan **Vol. 1:** 503
Vol. 3: 355, 808
bāhar **Vol. 1:** 503, 534, 537 f.
bahereṯ **Vol. 2:** 465
bāḥîr **Vol. 1:** 537 f.
Vol. 3: 641
bāḥûr **Vol. 1:** 537 f.
bākâh **Vol. 2:** 416, 422
bāḵar **Vol. 1:** 667 f.
bala' **Vol. 2:** 677
bālaḡ **Vol. 3:** 254
bālâh **Vol. 2:** 714
bālal **Vol. 2:** 649
bāmâh **Vol. 2:** 199, 205
Vol. 3: 418, 426
bammeh **Vol. 2:** 116
bāmôṯ **Vol. 2:** 199
Vol. 3: 1010
bānâh **Vol. 2:** 251
bāqar **Vol. 1:** 189
bāqaš **Vol. 2:** 164
Vol. 3: 530
bar **Vol. 2:** 144, 331
Vol. 3: 924
bar 'ᵉnāš **Vol. 3:** 614
bar 'ᵉnāšā' **Vol. 3:** 614
bar nāšā' **Vol. 3:** 614 f., 617,
619, 623 f., 627, 630, 665
bārā' **Vol. 1:** 378–380, 388,
672
Vol. 3: 119, 1153
bārah **Vol. 1:** 558
bāraḵ **Vol. 1:** 207–209, 218
Vol. 2: 778
Vol. 3: 816
bārar **Vol. 1:** 537
bārûḵ **Vol. 1:** 210
bārûḵ 'attâh **Vol. 1:** 207
barzel **Vol. 2:** 97

bāṣa' **Vol. 3:** 137
bāṣār **Vol. 3:** 1145
bāśār **Vol. 1:** 233, 434, 672 f.,
675 f., 678
Vol. 2: 477, 565, 571
Vol. 3: 178
baššîr **Vol. 3:** 669
baṭ **Vol. 3:** 403, 911
baṭ qôl **Vol. 2:** 174
Vol. 3: 51, 80, 113
bāṭah **Vol. 1:** 327, 589, 596,
599, 601
Vol. 2: 240
Vol. 3: 70
baṭṭēl **Vol. 3:** 187
bayiṯ **Vol. 2:** 247, 254, 256,
510
Vol. 3: 782, 786
bayyôm hahû' **Vol. 2:** 890
bāzâh **Vol. 1:** 461
bᵉ **Vol. 3:** 1175, 1190, 1192,
1210–1212
be'ᵉmûnāṯô **Vol. 3:** 366
bᵉ'ēr **Vol. 3:** 986
be'aḏ **Vol. 3:** 153, 160
be'el dᵉḇāḇā **Vol. 3:** 469
be'ēl diḇaḇā **Vol. 3:** 469
bᵉ'ēnê **Vol. 3:** 821
bᵉaḥᵃrîṯ hayyāmîm **Vol. 2:** 56
beḡeḏ **Vol. 1:** 316
bᵉḵî **Vol. 2:** 416
bᵉḵôr **Vol. 1:** 667
Vol. 3: 416
bᵉliyya'al **Vol. 3:** 1024
bᵉlēḇ šālēm **Vol. 3:** 572
bēn **Vol. 1:** 283, 285, 287
Vol. 3: 244
ben 'āḏām **Vol. 1:** 84
Vol. 2: 502
Vol. 3: 613 f., 617, 619,
622 f.
ben Dāwîḏ **Vol. 3:** 619, 652
bᵉnê **Vol. 2:** 652
bᵉnê 'āḏām **Vol. 3:** 613 f.
bᵉnê hā'āḏām **Vol. 3:** 613
bᵉnê yiśrā'ēl **Vol. 2:** 791
bᵉrāḵâh **Vol. 1:** 217 f.
Vol. 2: 779
bᵉrāḵôṯ **Vol. 1:** 212
bᵉrēḵâh **Vol. 3:** 992
bᵉrî'ē bāśār **Vol. 1:** 672
bᵉrî'ôṯ **Vol. 3:** 614
bᵉrîṯ **Vol. 1:** 224, 365–368, 376
Vol. 2: 600
bᵉriyyâh ḥᵃḏāšâh **Vol. 2:** 672
beṣa' **Vol. 3:** 29, 137
bᵉselem'elôhîm **Vol. 2:** 292
bᵉšēm **Vol. 2:** 650, 652, 656
bᵉśôrâh **Vol. 2:** 108 f.
bêṯ **Vol. 1:** 170
bêṯ 'āḇ **Vol. 3:** 870
bêṯ 'ᵃḇāḏîm **Vol. 3:** 593
bêṯ hakkapporeṯ **Vol. 3:** 156
bêṯ'ēl **Vol. 2:** 67

beṭah **Vol. 1:** 663
Vol. 2: 777
bᵉṭāḥâh **Vol. 3:** 70
beṭen **Vol. 2:** 599
bᵉṯûlâh **Vol. 3:** 1071 f., 1076
bᵉyāḏ **Vol. 2:** 149
bᵉyarkᵉṯê **Vol. 3:** 794
bᵉyōšer lᵉḇabô **Vol. 3:** 572
bî **Vol. 2:** 860
biḡlal **Vol. 2:** 116
bikkûrîm **Vol. 2:** 675
bimᵉṯē mᵉ'āṭ **Vol. 2:** 683
bîn **Vol. 1:** 694
Vol. 2: 397, 616
Vol. 3: 124 f., 130, 351, 760,
1028 f.
bînâh **Vol. 3:** 125, 130, 1027
biśrā' **Vol. 2:** 532
biśśar **Vol. 2:** 108 f.
biṭṭāḥôn **Vol. 1:** 589, 600 f.
biyḏê **Vol. 1:** 636
bô' **Vol. 2:** 898
bō' **Vol. 1:** 327
bôḡereṯ **Vol. 2:** 588
bôhan **Vol. 3:** 388 f.
bôḵ **Vol. 2:** 416
bôš **Vol. 3:** 562, 1024
bôšeṯ **Vol. 3:** 562
brk **Vol. 1:** 218, 263
Vol. 3: 799
bsr **Vol. 1:** 682
bûšâh **Vol. 3:** 562
bûz **Vol. 1:** 461

dā'aḵ **Vol. 3:** 109
da'aṯ **Vol. 1:** 600
Vol. 2: 391, 397, 616
Vol. 3: 640, 1027, 1029
dāḇaq **Vol. 2:** 349
dāḇār **Vol. 1:** 63, 597
Vol. 2: 173, 512
Vol. 3: 345, 483, 502, 820,
878, 1087, 1094, 1096,
1103, 1116, 1119–1121,
1125, 1195
dāḡ **Vol. 1:** 670 f.
dāḡâh **Vol. 1:** 670
dakā' **Vol. 2:** 260
dāḵâh **Vol. 2:** 260
dakkā' **Vol. 2:** 261
dal **Vol. 2:** 260, 820, 822
dālal **Vol. 2:** 260
dām **Vol. 1:** 224, 226
Vol. 3: 158
dāmâh **Vol. 2:** 501
dāraḵ **Vol. 2:** 369
dāraš **Vol. 1:** 64, 580
Vol. 2: 489, 554
Vol. 3: 93, 531
darkᵉmônîm **Vol. 2:** 848
dāṯ **Vol. 2:** 439, 441
dāwîḏ **Vol. 1:** 425
Vol. 3: 244, 652
day **Vol. 3:** 728–730

dbr **Vol. 1:** 332
    Vol. 3: 268
dᵉbar YHWH **Vol. 3:** 1087, 1090
dᵉḇāreykā **Vol. 3:** 267
deber **Vol. 3:** 1116
dᵉḡaṭ-hayyām **Vol. 1:** 670
deleṭ **Vol. 2:** 30
dᵉmā' **Vol. 2:** 532
dᵉmûṯ **Vol. 2:** 287, 501 f.
dᵉp̄ûs **Vol. 3:** 904
dᵉraš **Vol. 2:** 488
derek **Vol. 3:** 937
deše' **Vol. 1:** 743
    Vol. 2: 211
diḇaḇā **Vol. 3:** 469
dibbâh **Vol. 3:** 346
dibber **Vol. 3:** 324
dibbēr **Vol. 1:** 333
    Vol. 3: 1121
dibbᵉrâh **Vol. 3:** 1120
dibbᵉrôṯ **Vol. 3:** 1120
dibbûr **Vol. 3:** 1121
diḇrê hamᵉ'ōrôṯ **Vol. 2:** 512
diḵṯîḇ **Vol. 3:** 487
dîlêh **Vol. 2:** 840
dîn **Vol. 1:** 503
    Vol. 2: 363
dōḇer **Vol. 2:** 586
dôr **Vol. 2:** 35 f.
dōrēš el hammēṭîm **Vol. 2:** 554
dûmiyyâh **Vol. 2:** 669

g'l **Vol. 3:** 222
gā'âh **Vol. 3:** 29
gā'al **Vol. 1:** 267
    Vol. 3: 178, 190–194, 201 f.,
    222
ga'ᵃyôn **Vol. 3:** 29
gā'ar **Vol. 3:** 346
gāḇah **Vol. 2:** 199, 201
gāḇar **Vol. 1:** 103
gāḇiš **Vol. 3:** 394
gāḇōah **Vol. 3:** 29
gaḇrā' **Vol. 3:** 614
gaḇrî'ēl **Vol. 1:** 103
gāḏaḏ **Vol. 3:** 377
gāḏal **Vol. 2:** 201, 369
gāḏap̄ **Vol. 3:** 341, 345
gāḏēr **Vol. 3:** 950
gāḏôl **Vol. 1:** 188, 670 f.
    Vol. 2: 425
    Vol. 3: 1087
gālâh **Vol. 2:** 212
    Vol. 3: 310, 318, 590
gālûṯ **Vol. 1:** 685
    Vol. 3: 590
gan **Vol. 2:** 761
gānaḇ **Vol. 2:** 377
gannāḇ **Vol. 2:** 377
gannâh **Vol. 2:** 761
gāra' **Vol. 3:** 379
gāraš **Vol. 1:** 453
gaṭ šᵉmānê **Vol. 2:** 710

gāzal **Vol. 2:** 377, 601
gdl **Vol. 2:** 425
gē hinnōm **Vol. 2:** 208
gē' **Vol. 3:** 29
gᵉ'ālēnû **Vol. 3:** 194
gē'eh **Vol. 3:** 29
gᵉ'ûlîm **Vol. 3:** 193
gᵉ'ullâh **Vol. 3:** 190, 193
gᵉḇal **Vol. 1:** 243
gᵉḇîr **Vol. 2:** 511
gᵉḇûrâh **Vol. 2:** 602
gᵉḇûrōṯ **Vol. 2:** 602 f.
gᵉḏērâh **Vol. 3:** 950
gᵉḏûḏ **Vol. 3:** 377
gᵉḏûlâh **Vol. 2:** 116
gēhinnām **Vol. 2:** 208
gᵉmar haqqēṣ **Vol. 2:** 61
gᵉmārā' **Vol. 1:** 58
gᵉnāzim **Vol. 3:** 796
gepen **Vol. 3:** 918
gēr **Vol. 1:** 258, 360, 684,
    689 f.
    Vol. 2: 636
gᵉûrâh **Vol. 2:** 602
gēwâh **Vol. 3:** 29
gᵉwiyyaṯ bᵉśārô **Vol. 1:** 676
geza' **Vol. 3:** 867
gᵉzerâh **Vol. 1:** 580
gibbôr **Vol. 2:** 562, 602
gibbôrîm **Vol. 2:** 602
gîl **Vol. 2:** 353, 356
gillûlîm **Vol. 2:** 284 f.
gō'ᵃlî **Vol. 3:** 178
gō'ēl **Vol. 3:** 178, 190–192,
    194, 218
gōlâh **Vol. 1:** 685
    Vol. 3: 590
gôrāl **Vol. 2:** 296, 298
gôy **Vol. 2:** 790–792, 796, 805
gôyim **Vol. 1:** 58, 96
    Vol. 2: 790–793
gupā' **Vol. 2:** 532
gûr **Vol. 1:** 684, 690
    Vol. 2: 730
    Vol. 3: 91

h'myn **Vol. 3:** 368, 800
hā'eben habbᵉḏîl **Vol. 3:** 391 f.
hā'eben hārō'šâh **Vol. 3:** 391
ha'ᵃṭîdîm **Vol. 1:** 326
hā'ēḏ **Vol. 3:** 1041
hā'ôlām habbā' **Vol. 3:** 829
hā'ôlām hazzeh **Vol. 3:** 829
hāḏar **Vol. 3:** 30
haddāḡâh **Vol. 1:** 670
hāḡār **Vol. 1:** 80
haggāḏâh **Vol. 1:** 58, 581,
    633 f.
    Vol. 2: 522
hahî' gaḇrā' **Vol. 3:** 614
hahû' gaḇrā' **Vol. 3:** 614
hahozîm bakkôḵāḇîm **Vol. 2:**
    555

hakkōhēn haggāḏôl **Vol. 3:** 35
hakkōl **Vol. 1:** 522
hālak **Vol. 1:** 481, 683
    Vol. 2: 777, 815
    Vol. 3: 264, 933, 943, 946,
    1156
hᵃlāḵâh **Vol. 1:** 59
hālal **Vol. 1:** 99
    Vol. 2: 422, 862
    Vol. 3: 668 f., 816
hālam **Vol. 3:** 396
halᵉlû-'eth-yahweh **Vol. 1:** 99
halᵉlûyâh **Vol. 1:** 99
    Vol. 2: 862
    Vol. 3: 669
hallēl **Vol. 1:** 633
    Vol. 3: 817
hāmâh **Vol. 2:** 423
    Vol. 3: 112
hamᵉ'ōrōṯ **Vol. 2:** 512
hāmôn **Vol. 2:** 800, 842
hanniš'ārîm bā'āreṣ **Vol. 3:** 249
hap̄ṭārâh **Vol. 3:** 485
haqqēṣ hā'aḥᵃrôn **Vol. 2:** 61
har **Vol. 3:** 1009
hāraḡ **Vol. 1:** 429
hārâh **Vol. 1:** 176, 186, 343
hašḥîṯ **Vol. 1:** 685
hattaḥtîṯ **Vol. 2:** 209
hāwâh **Vol. 3:** 760
hāyâh **Vol. 3:** 823, 1091, 1175
hāyâh kᵉ **Vol. 3:** 821
hayyôm **Vol. 2:** 890
he'ᵉmîn **Vol. 1:** 597
    Vol. 3: 1211–1213
he'ᵉzîn **Vol. 2:** 175
he'ᵉrâh nap̄šô **Vol. 1:** 548
hē'îḏ **Vol. 3:** 1042
hebel **Vol. 1:** 550 f.
heḏyôṭ **Vol. 2:** 456
hêḵāl **Vol. 3:** 782 f., 786 f.
hêlēl **Vol. 2:** 495
    Vol. 3: 468
hēmānûṯa' **Vol. 1:** 98
hēqîm bᵉrîṯ **Vol. 1:** 368
hērôn **Vol. 2:** 423
hēšîḇ **Vol. 3:** 134, 420
hēsîr **Vol. 1:** 606
hēzîḏ **Vol. 3:** 28
hî **Vol. 3:** 1051
higgāyôn **Vol. 3:** 673
hillēl **Vol. 3:** 817
himnon **Vol. 3:** 669
hiqtîr **Vol. 2:** 293
hištaḥᵃwâh **Vol. 2:** 862, 876
hiṯhallēl **Vol. 1:** 227
hiṯnabbē' **Vol. 1:** 527
hittîr **Vol. 2:** 732
hô **Vol. 3:** 1051
hôḇēl **Vol. 1:** 194
hôḏ **Vol. 3:** 926
hôlîḏ **Vol. 1:** 177
hôn **Vol. 1:** 381
    Vol. 3: 727

hôp̄ia' **Vol. 2:** 735
hôšēa' **Vol. 3:** 208
hôšî'âh **Vol. 3:** 207
hôsî'âh nā' **Vol. 1:** 100
hôwâh **Vol. 3:** 1051
hôy **Vol. 3:** 1051
hû' **Vol. 2:** 279
hûm **Vol. 3:** 112
hwh **Vol. 2:** 68
hwy **Vol. 2:** 68

ḥāḇā' **Vol. 2:** 214
ḥāḇal **Vol. 1:** 468
Vol. 3: 858
ḥāḇar **Vol. 1:** 636, 641
Vol. 3: 1162
ḥāḇēr **Vol. 1:** 259
ḥᵃḇērîm **Vol. 2:** 810
ḥᵃḇûrâh **Vol. 1:** 641, 643
Vol. 2: 810
ḥad **Vol. 1:** 665
ḥāḏāš **Vol. 2:** 670, 675
ḥag **Vol. 1:** 626
ḥag ḥᵃmiššîm yôm **Vol. 2:** 783
ḥag šāḇu'ôṯ **Vol. 2:** 783
ḥāg̱ar **Vol. 3:** 120
ḥᵃg̱ôr **Vol. 3:** 120
ḥᵃg̱ôrâh **Vol. 3:** 120
ḥai **Vol. 1:** 87
ḥākâh **Vol. 2:** 239, 772 f.
Vol. 3: 226
ḥākām **Vol. 1:** 486
Vol. 2: 616
Vol. 3: 479, 1024, 1027 f.
ḥᵃkam ḥᵃrāšîm **Vol. 2:** 555
ḥᵃkāmîm **Vol. 3:** 479
ḥāḵîm **Vol. 3:** 1028
ḥālâh **Vol. 2:** 164, 860
Vol. 3: 720, 997
ḥālal **Vol. 1:** 164
ḥālāl **Vol. 1:** 444
ḥālāq **Vol. 2:** 116
ḥālaq **Vol. 1:** 534
ḥālaṣ **Vol. 3:** 201
ḥalḥālâh **Vol. 3:** 858
ḥᵃlîp̄âh **Vol. 3:** 166
ḥāmaḏ **Vol. 1:** 456
ḥāmâh **Vol. 3:** 948
ḥāmal **Vol. 3:** 720
ḥāmam **Vol. 1:** 318
ḥāmās **Vol. 3:** 574
ḥᵃmîšî **Vol. 2:** 303
ḥānan **Vol. 2:** 594, 778, 860
ḥānaṭ **Vol. 1:** 264
ḥānēp̄ **Vol. 2:** 468
ḥᵃnôḵ **Vol. 3:** 264
ḥap̄ **Vol. 2:** 144
Vol. 3: 924
ḥāp̄aś **Vol. 3:** 533
ḥāp̄ēṣ **Vol. 1:** 534
Vol. 3: 1016, 1019
ḥāqaq **Vol. 1:** 333
ḥāqar **Vol. 3:** 808
ḥᵃqēl d'mā' **Vol. 1:** 93

ḥāraq **Vol. 2:** 421
ḥārāš **Vol. 1:** 279
ḥᵃrāšîm **Vol. 2:** 555
ḥārēḇ **Vol. 3:** 1004 f.
ḥārōḇ **Vol. 3:** 1005
ḥārôn **Vol. 1:** 108
ḥārûṭ **Vol. 3:** 488
ḥarṭōm **Vol. 2:** 555
ḥarṭummîm **Vol. 1:** 574
Vol. 2: 555
ḥārûṣ **Vol. 2:** 95
ḥāšaḇ **Vol. 3:** 820 f., 823–825, 1187
ḥāsâh **Vol. 1:** 589
Vol. 2: 91
ḥāṣâh **Vol. 1:** 534
Vol. 2: 240
ḥᵃsar-lēḇ **Vol. 3:** 1024
ḥāsîḏ **Vol. 2:** 237 f., 600 f.
ḥᵃsîḏîm **Vol. 2:** 237, 810
Vol. 3: 270
ḥāṣîr **Vol. 1:** 743
Vol. 2: 211
ḥašmal **Vol. 2:** 97
ḥᵃṣōṣᵉrâh **Vol. 3:** 873
ḥāṭā' **Vol. 3:** 101, 104, 419
ḥᵃṭā'âh **Vol. 3:** 171
ḥāṭāh **Vol. 3:** 166
ḥāṭam **Vol. 3:** 497
ḥaṭṭā'ṭ **Vol. 3:** 156, 171, 419, 434, 437, 577, 1203
ḥawwâh **Vol. 1:** 87
ḥay **Vol. 2:** 477
Vol. 3: 743
ḥāyâh **Vol. 2:** 477, 483
Vol. 3: 206, 255
ḥayil **Vol. 2:** 602, 800, 842
ḥaylâh **Vol. 3:** 457
ḥayyâh **Vol. 1:** 113
Vol. 2: 478 f.
Vol. 3: 679
ḥayyîm **Vol. 2:** 477
ḥāzâh **Vol. 2:** 395
Vol. 3: 513
ḥāzaq **Vol. 1:** 663
Vol. 2: 154, 767
Vol. 3: 713, 716
ḥāzāq **Vol. 3:** 112
ḥāzôn **Vol. 1:** 574
Vol. 3: 1093
ḥbwrh **Vol. 2:** 814
ḥē **Vol. 3:** 743
ḥebel **Vol. 2:** 298
Vol. 3: 858
ḥeka **Vol. 2:** 848
ḥêl **Vol. 3:** 949
ḥel'âh **Vol. 2:** 27
ḥēleḇ **Vol. 3:** 416
ḥeleḏ **Vol. 1:** 711
ḥēleq **Vol. 2:** 298, 303
ḥelqâh **Vol. 2:** 303
ḥēmâh **Vol. 1:** 106, 108
Vol. 2: 27
ḥēn **Vol. 2:** 116 f., 123, 356,

600, 815
Vol. 3: 528, 818
ḥēq **Vol. 1:** 78
ḥērem **Vol. 1:** 413
ḥereš **Vol. 2:** 555
ḥerûṭ **Vol. 3:** 488
ḥesed **Vol. 1:** 367
Vol. 2: 105, 116 f., 119, 123 f., 237, 540, 550, 594 f., 600 f.
Vol. 3: 354, 358, 429, 879 f., 882, 889
ḥēṭ' **Vol. 3:** 419
ḥezyôn **Vol. 2:** 622
ḥgg **Vol. 1:** 626
ḥîḏâh **Vol. 1:** 575
Vol. 2: 745
ḥîl **Vol. 3:** 858
ḥillâh **Vol. 3:** 149, 152
ḥillēl **Vol. 2:** 224
ḥinnâm **Vol. 1:** 550
Vol. 2: 41
ḥiṭṭē' **Vol. 3:** 149, 152, 419
ḥiwyā' **Vol. 1:** 87
ḥkm **Vol. 3:** 1027
ḥnn **Vol. 2:** 117, 123, 598
ḥōḇ **Vol. 2:** 666–668
ḥôḇâh **Vol. 2:** 667
ḥōḇēr ḥāḇēr **Vol. 2:** 554
ḥōḇrê šāmayim **Vol. 2:** 555
ḥōḏeš **Vol. 3:** 733
ḥoḵmâh **Vol. 3:** 130, 1027, 1029
ḥōl **Vol. 2:** 224
Vol. 3: 104
ḥᵒlî **Vol. 3:** 997, 999
ḥōm **Vol. 1:** 652
ḥômâh **Vol. 3:** 948
ḥômōṭayim **Vol. 3:** 948
ḥōnāḵ **Vol. 2:** 815
ḥōq **Vol. 1:** 332 f.
Vol. 2: 439 f.
Vol. 3: 354
ḥorbâh **Vol. 3:** 1005
ḥōreḇ **Vol. 1:** 652
ḥôrēḇ **Vol. 3:** 1013
ḥōrîm **Vol. 1:** 716
ḥōṭām, ḥōṭām **Vol. 3:** 497
ḥōṯer **Vol. 1:** 407
Vol. 3: 867
ḥôzeh **Vol. 3:** 77, 513
ḥqq **Vol. 2:** 573
ḥṭ' **Vol. 3:** 587
ḥûḇ **Vol. 2:** 370
ḥûl **Vol. 1:** 324
Vol. 3: 350, 858
ḥuqqâh **Vol. 1:** 332 f.
Vol. 2: 439, 441
Vol. 3: 354
ḥuqqaṭ 'ôlām **Vol. 3:** 237
ḥuqqōṭ **Vol. 2:** 441
ḥwh **Vol. 3:** 316

kāḇaḥ **Vol. 3:** 109

kābēḏ **Vol. 1:** 230, 261
kāḇôḏ **Vol. 1:** 122, 211, 261, 735
  Vol. 2: 45–47, 49, 336, 485, 502
  Vol. 3: 262, 514
kāḏaḏ **Vol. 3:** 396
kaḏkōḏ **Vol. 3:** 396
kāhan **Vol. 2:** 234
  Vol. 3: 36
kāhaš **Vol. 1:** 455
  Vol. 2: 470, 474
kālā' **Vol. 2:** 222
kālâh **Vol. 2:** 60
  Vol. 3: 255
kālam **Vol. 3:** 98, 345
kālîl **Vol. 3:** 421
kallâh **Vol. 2:** 584
kammōn **Vol. 2:** 211
kāna' **Vol. 2:** 260
kānan **Vol. 3:** 350
kānāp̄ **Vol. 1:** 172
  Vol. 3: 797
kāpar **Vol. 1:** 455
  Vol. 3: 176
kappōreṯ **Vol. 3:** 153, 156, 163, 812
kar **Vol. 3:** 951
kāra' **Vol. 2:** 876
kārâh **Vol. 3:** 139
kārar **Vol. 3:** 951
kāraṯ **Vol. 1:** 307, 368
kāraz **Vol. 3:** 51
kārōz **Vol. 2:** 682
  Vol. 3: 51
karpas **Vol. 2:** 522
kāsal **Vol. 3:** 1024 f.
kāšal **Vol. 2:** 705, 707
  Vol. 3: 801, 994
kāšēr **Vol. 2:** 452
kāṯaḇ **Vol. 3:** 483, 487
kāṯûḇ **Vol. 3:** 485, 487
kāzāḇ **Vol. 1:** 550
  Vol. 2: 471
kbd **Vol. 1:** 261
  Vol. 2: 52
kᵉ **Vol. 2:** 498, 501
  Vol. 3: 614, 821
kᵉʿerkî **Vol. 2:** 498
kᵉḇar 'ᵉnāš **Vol. 3:** 614
kᵉḇēḏuṯ **Vol. 3:** 711
keḇeś **Vol. 2:** 410, 412
kᵉḥunnâh **Vol. 3:** 36
kᵉlal **Vol. 3:** 350
kᵉlāyôṯ **Vol. 2:** 181
kᵉlî **Vol. 1: 522**
  Vol. 3: 1065
kᵉlimmâh **Vol. 3:** 856
kᵉmišpāṭ **Vol. 2:** 437
kᵉmô **Vol. 2:** 501
kᵉnā'âh **Vol. 1:** 711
kᵉna'ᵃnî **Vol. 3:** 593
kᵉništā' **Vol. 1:** 295
kēp̄ **Vol. 3:** 381

kēp̄ā' **Vol. 3:** 381, 383, 386
kerem **Vol. 3:** 918
kerem bᵉyaḇneh **Vol. 3:** 921
kᵉrîṯûṯ **Vol. 1:** 505
kᵉrûḇ **Vol. 1:** 279
kesel **Vol. 3:** 1024
kesep̄ **Vol. 2:** 96
kᵉsîl **Vol. 3:** 1024, 1037
kᵉsîlûṯ **Vol. 3:** 1024
kᵉṯāḇ **Vol. 3:** 487
keṯer **Vol. 1:** 405
  Vol. 3: 182
kᵉṯîḇ **Vol. 3:** 487
kᵉṯûḇîm **Vol. 3:** 485, 487
khd **Vol. 2:** 215
kî **Vol. 3:** 264, 1211
kipper **Vol. 1:** 698
  Vol. 3: 149–155, 160, 190, 192, 196, 419, 423
kippurîm **Vol. 3:** 153, 156
kislâh **Vol. 3:** 1024
kissâh **Vol. 2:** 212
kissē' **Vol. 2:** 612
kiššēp̄ **Vol. 2:** 555
kiṯᵉḇê-haqqōḏeš **Vol. 3:** 487
kôᵃh **Vol. 2:** 602
kôah **Vol. 2:** 602
  Vol. 3: 713
kōhēn **Vol. 2:** 234
  Vol. 3: 33
kōhēn hārō'š **Vol. 3:** 35
kōhēn-ṣeḏeq **Vol. 2:** 591
  Vol. 3: 36
kôḵîm **Vol. 1:** 264
kōl **Vol. 1:** 87, 97, 522
kōnām **Vol. 2:** 43
kōp̄er **Vol. 3:** 153, 155, 166, 190, 192, 1179
kōrēm **Vol. 3:** 918
kōṯeret **Vol. 3:** 389
kpr **Vol. 2:** 294
ktb **Vol. 3:** 483
kûl **Vol. 2:** 773
kûn **Vol. 1:** 380
  Vol. 2: 69, 489
  Vol. 3: 117, 350, 966

la'ᵃnâh **Vol. 2:** 27, 663
lāḇān **Vol. 1:** 204
lāḇaš **Vol. 1:** 314
lāham **Vol. 3:** 959
lahaṣ **Vol. 2:** 807
lāhaṣ **Vol. 2:** 807
lāhaš **Vol. 2:** 554
lahḏā' **Vol. 3:** 1194
lāmaḏ **Vol. 1:** 69, 484–486
  Vol. 3: 760, 766
lāmâh **Vol. 2:** 82
lamᵉnaṣṣēaḥ **Vol. 2:** 60
lāneṣaḥ **Vol. 2:** 60
lappîḏ **Vol. 2:** 485
lāqaḥ **Vol. 1:** 364, 475
  Vol. 3: 262, 264–266, 745, 747

lāšan **Vol. 3:** 345
lāšôn **Vol. 3:** 29, 1078
ld't **Vol. 3:** 800
lᵉ **Vol. 2:** 502, 876
  Vol. 3: 1175, 1187, 1208, 1210 f.
lᵉ'azkārâh **Vol. 3:** 239
lᵉummîm **Vol. 2:** 793
lēḇ **Vol. 1:** 230, 349
  Vol. 2: 181 f., 184, 565
  Vol. 3: 124 f., 679, 1024
lēḇāḇ **Vol. 1:** 230
  Vol. 2: 177, 181, 184, 565
  Vol. 3: 124 f.
lᵉḇaḏ **Vol. 2:** 723
lᵉḇāḏāḏ **Vol. 2:** 723
lᵉḇārek **Vol. 1:** 217
lᵉḇônâh **Vol. 2:** 293
lᵉḥaṭṭā'ṯ **Vol. 3:** 171
lehem **Vol. 1:** 170, 249
  Vol. 2: 521
  Vol. 3: 423, 814
lehem hamma'ᵃreḵeṯ **Vol. 3:** 814
lehem happānîm **Vol. 3:** 814
lehem-pānîm **Vol. 3:** 423
lᵉḵapper bᵉ'aḏ hā-'āreṣ **Vol. 3:** 160
lᵉlammēḏ **Vol. 3:** 769
lᵉp̄ānāyw **Vol. 3:** 267
leqaḥ **Vol. 2:** 777
lᵉrō'š pinnâh **Vol. 3:** 388
lešem **Vol. 3:** 396
lᵉšēm **Vol. 2:** 652, 655
  Vol. 3: 1209
lᵉšēm haššēm **Vol. 2:** 652
lᵉšēm šāmayim **Vol. 2:** 652
lēṣṭāyûṭ **Vol. 3:** 377
lēṣṭēs **Vol. 3:** 377
lēṣṭyā' **Vol. 3:** 377
lᵉšûm **Vol. 3:** 1209
lᵉṭabbālā' **Vol. 3:** 448
lᵉwāṭ **Vol. 3:** 1205
lēwî **Vol. 2:** 466
lᵉyômā' **Vol. 1:** 251
lᵉzabbālā' **Vol. 3:** 448
lᵉzikkārôn **Vol. 3:** 239
lîḏē **Vol. 2:** 149
lîlîṭ **Vol. 1:** 451
limmaḏ **Vol. 3:** 760 f., 763 f., 766
lîn **Vol. 3:** 178, 255
lip̄nê **Vol. 3:** 1173, 1175
lip̄nê yhwh **Vol. 3:** 239, 422
lîṣ **Vol. 1:** 194, 580
lišān **Vol. 3:** 1078
liškâh **Vol. 3:** 796
liwyāṯān **Vol. 1:** 670
lmḏ **Vol. 3:** 760 f.
lō' 'ammî **Vol. 2:** 581, 797
lō' hākām **Vol. 3:** 1024
lō' kiḥēḏû **Vol. 2:** 489
lō' nuppāh **Vol. 3:** 111
lō' ruhāmâh **Vol. 2:** 581

lōṭ Vol. 2: 294
lû Vol. 2: 666
lû' Vol. 2: 666
lûn Vol. 3: 178
lûṣ Vol. 1: 580
 Vol. 3: 29, 1024

m'ûm Vol. 3: 924
m'l Vol. 3: 587
mā'as Vol. 1: 455
mā'ēn Vol. 3: 1016, 1019
ma'al Vol. 3: 586
mā'al Vol. 1: 606, 609
 Vol. 3: 585 f.
mā'ᵃmāḏ Vol. 1: 711
ma'ᵃmaqqîm Vol. 2: 197
ma'ᵃśēr Vol. 2: 693
 Vol. 3: 416, 851
mā'ôn Vol. 2: 586
ma'yān Vol. 3: 985
mabbua' Vol. 3: 985
mabbûl Vol. 3: 991
māḏaḏ Vol. 3: 402
māḏôn Vol. 3: 346
māhah Vol. 2: 773
 Vol. 3: 227
māhâh Vol. 1: 471
mahᵃlâh Vol. 3: 999
mahᵃlōqeṭ Vol. 1: 534
mahᵃluyîm Vol. 3: 999
māhār Vol. 1: 251
mahᵃšāḇâh Vol. 3: 125, 820
mahᵃšeḇeṭ Vol. 3: 1027
mahšāk Vol. 3: 859
mak'ôḇ Vol. 3: 999
mākar Vol. 1: 268
mal'āk Vol. 1: 104 f., 194
mālah Vol. 3: 444
mālak Vol. 2: 373
mālaṭ Vol. 1: 186
 Vol. 3: 206, 209
mālē' Vol. 1: 734 f., 743
malᵉkût Vol. 2: 376, 389
malᵉkût šāmayim Vol. 2: 376
malᵉkût YHWH Vol. 2: 376
malkî-ṣeḏeq Vol. 2: 590
 Vol. 3: 36
mamleket kōhᵃnîm Vol. 3: 36
māmôn Vol. 2: 836
māmônā' Vol. 2: 836
mān Vol. 1: 252
mān hû' Vol. 1: 252
māna' Vol. 2: 222
mānâh Vol. 2: 303
 Vol. 3: 823
mānôah Vol. 3: 255
mānôṭ Vol. 3: 255
mapṭēah Vol. 2: 730
māqaq Vol. 1: 689
 Vol. 3: 559
māqôm Vol. 1: 538
 Vol. 2: 191, 369
 Vol. 3: 786 f.
māqôr Vol. 3: 985

mār Vol. 2: 513
mar'eh Vol. 1: 704
mārā' Vol. 2: 511, 514
mara' 'aṭa' ('aṭe') Vol. 2: 897
māraḏ Vol. 1: 606
mārâh Vol. 1: 589
māran Vol. 2: 513, 895
māran 'ᵃṭā' Vol. 2: 895
māranā' Vol. 2: 895
māranā' ṭā Vol. 2: 895
mārē' Vol. 2: 513 f.
mārē' 'ālᵉmā' Vol. 2: 514
mārî Vol. 2: 513 f.
 Vol. 3: 115
mārôm Vol. 2: 199
māṣā' Vol. 3: 318, 528, 727
māšah Vol. 1: 120 f.
 Vol. 2: 335
mašâh Vol. 2: 636
māsāk Vol. 3: 794
māšāl Vol. 2: 202, 744–746,
 757 f.
māšal Vol. 1: 165
 Vol. 2: 518
māsar Vol. 3: 772, 1181
mašber Vol. 3: 858
māšîah Vol. 1: 53, 63
 Vol. 2: 334 f.
 Vol. 3: 244
maśkîl Vol. 3: 766
maśkōreṭ Vol. 3: 139
māṣôr Vol. 3: 951
māsōreṭ Vol. 1: 63
 Vol. 3: 772
mašrîṭā' Vol. 1: 295
maśśā' Vol. 1: 712
 Vol. 3: 673
maṣṣāḇ Vol. 1: 711
massâh Vol. 3: 799
maṣṣēḇâh Vol. 1: 711
maṣṣeḇeṭ Vol. 3: 867
maṣṣōṭ Vol. 1: 249, 625 f., 628,
 632 f.
 Vol. 3: 422
maṭlā' Vol. 2: 745
maṭṭeh Vol. 1: 407 f.
 Vol. 3: 870
māweṭ Vol. 1: 432
 Vol. 3: 267, 388
mayim Vol. 3: 988
mazkîr Vol. 3: 233, 247
mazzîqîm Vol. 1: 451
mᵉ'ûrâh Vol. 2: 586
mᵉ'ārâh Vol. 3: 380
mē'aṭ Vol. 2: 428
mᵉ'aṭ mᵉ'ᵉlōhîm Vol. 2: 502
mᵉ'ōnâh Vol. 2: 586
mᵉ'ônēn Vol. 2: 554
mᵉḇaqqēr Vol. 1: 190
 Vol. 3: 196
mᵉḇaśśēr Vol. 2: 109
mᵉḇukâh Vol. 2: 416
mᵉḏînā' Vol. 3: 456
mᵉhabbᵉlîm Vol. 1: 451

mᵉhîr Vol. 3: 139, 166, 190
mᵉkaššēp̄ Vol. 2: 554
mekes Vol. 3: 756
melah Vol. 3: 444
mᵉlahᵃšîm Vol. 2: 554
melek Vol. 1: 581
 Vol. 2: 375 f., 390
mēlîṣ Vol. 1: 373
mᵉlummāḏâh Vol. 3: 769
mêm Vol. 3: 488
mêmrā' Vol. 1: 63
 Vol. 3: 1116, 1120
memšālâh Vol. 1: 165
 Vol. 2: 607 f.
mᵉnahᵃmîm Vol. 1: 89
mᵉnahēš Vol. 2: 554
mᵉnaṭ Vol. 2: 303
mᵉnûhâh Vol. 3: 255 f., 258
mᵉqalᵉlîm Vol. 1: 416
mᵉqôm haqqōḏeš Vol. 3: 787
mᵉqôm miqdāšî Vol. 3: 786
mᵉqôm qoḏšô Vol. 3: 786
mᵉrōrâh Vol. 2: 27
mᵉšārēṭ Vol. 1: 485
mᵉšîhā' Vol. 2: 334 f.
mᵉšo'âh Vol. 3: 859
mᵉṣôḏîm Vol. 3: 952
mᵉšōmēm Vol. 3: 1006
mᵉṣōrā' Vol. 2: 464
mᵉśûkkâh Vol. 3: 950
mᵉṣûlâh Vol. 2: 197
mᵉṣûqâh Vol. 2: 663
mēṭ Vol. 1: 444
mᵉṭabbal Vol. 3: 447
mēṭeka Vol. 3: 268
mᵉṭurgām Vol. 1: 580
mᵉṭurḡᵉman Vol. 3: 485
mᵉzimmâh Vol. 3: 820
mibbᵉśārî Vol. 1: 434, 672
 Vol. 3: 178
mibbēṭ lᵉ Vol. 3: 794
miḏbār Vol. 1: 411
 Vol. 3: 1004
middâh Vol. 2: 683
 Vol. 3: 402
middôṭ Vol. 1: 580
miḏrāk Vol. 3: 369
miḏrāš Vol. 1: 64, 580 f.
 Vol. 3: 483
miḏyān Vol. 3: 346
miḡdāl Vol. 2: 369
mihyâh Vol. 1: 711
 Vol. 2: 169
mîkā'ēl Vol. 1: 104
mikᵉsâh Vol. 3: 756
miksâh Vol. 2: 683
mikšōl Vol. 2: 705, 707
 Vol. 3: 98, 856, 994
miktāḇ Vol. 1: 246
milhāmâh Vol. 1: 645
 Vol. 3: 959
millâh Vol. 3: 1087, 1120
millē' Vol. 2: 60
millᵉṭā' Vol. 3: 1120

329

millû'îm **Vol. 2:** 61
mîn **Vol. 1:** 534
   Vol. 2: 35, 501
   Vol. 3: 463
min **Vol. 2:** 312
   Vol. 3: 178, 1181
min hā'ôlām wᵉ'aḏ hā'ôlām
   Vol. 3: 828
minḥâh **Vol. 1:** 250
   Vol. 2: 41
   Vol. 3: 38, 421 f., 431 f., 434
minyān **Vol. 2:** 683
miplāś **Vol. 1:** 503
miqdāš **Vol. 2:** 224
   Vol. 3: 786
miqdaš 'ᵉlōhâw **Vol. 3:** 786
miqdāšî **Vol. 3:** 786
miqneh **Vol. 2:** 837
miqrā' **Vol. 1:** 272
   Vol. 3: 485
miqweh **Vol. 2:** 773
miškāḇ **Vol. 2:** 586 f.
miškān **Vol. 3:** 811
miskēn **Vol. 2:** 822
miskēnuṯ **Vol. 2:** 822
mišnâh **Vol. 1:** 54, 64
mišpāḥâh **Vol. 2:** 698, 789
   Vol. 3: 870 f.
mišpāḥôṯ **Vol. 1:** 194
mispār **Vol. 1:** 574 f.
   Vol. 2: 683
mišpāṭ **Vol. 2:** 777
   Vol. 3: 354, 359
mispô' **Vol. 1:** 743
miṣrayim **Vol. 1:** 530
mišteh **Vol. 2:** 576
   Vol. 3: 745
miṣwâh **Vol. 1:** 331–333
mittaḇal **Vol. 3:** 447
miṭṭâh **Vol. 1:** 408
miṭṭᵉḇel **Vol. 3:** 447
mizbēaḥ **Vol. 3:** 418
mizmôr **Vol. 3:** 671, 673
mizreh **Vol. 1:** 685
mlk **Vol. 2:** 389
mlṭ **Vol. 3:** 253
mō'znayim **Vol. 3:** 1160
mō'znayyā' **Vol. 3:** 1160
mō'ēḏ **Vol. 1:** 294, 626
   Vol. 3: 835, 1040–1042
mōhar **Vol. 2:** 578
mōkîaḥ **Vol. 1:** 373
mōleḏeṯ **Vol. 1:** 181
mōlek **Vol. 2:** 375
mōpēṯ **Vol. 2:** 350, 627, 633
mōqēš **Vol. 2:** 705, 707
mōr, môr **Vol. 2:** 294
mōreh **Vol. 3:** 766
mōšeh **Vol. 2:** 635
mōšᵉkôṯ **Vol. 3:** 950
mōsēr **Vol. 3:** 591
mōšîa' **Vol. 3:** 217
mōṣôq **Vol. 2:** 663
mšh **Vol. 1:** 124

mûl **Vol. 1:** 307
mûsāḏ **Vol. 3:** 388
mûsar **Vol. 3:** 1027
mûsār **Vol. 3:** 776 f.
muṣṣāḇ **Vol. 3:** 951
mûssāḏ **Vol. 3:** 388
mûṭ **Vol. 1:** 429 f., 432
mûṭ **Vol. 3:** 559

nā' **Vol. 2:** 860
nā'âh **Vol. 2:** 669
nā'ap **Vol. 1:** 498
   Vol. 2: 582
nā'aq **Vol. 2:** 423
nā'ar **Vol. 3:** 560
nā'aṣ **Vol. 3:** 341
nā'weh **Vol. 2:** 668
nā'al **Vol. 2:** 730
na'ar **Vol. 1:** 281, 283
   Vol. 2: 675
na'ᵃrâh **Vol. 3:** 1071 f.
nāḇā' **Vol. 3:** 77
nāḇal **Vol. 3:** 1024 f.
nāḇāl **Vol. 3:** 1024 f., 1037
nāḇaṭ **Vol. 3:** 126
nāḇî' **Vol. 3:** 77
nāḇôn **Vol. 3:** 351
nāḏaḇ **Vol. 3:** 821
nāḏâh **Vol. 1:** 414
nāḏān **Vol. 3:** 139
nāḏar **Vol. 1:** 344
nāḏîḇ **Vol. 3:** 821
nāḡa' **Vol. 2:** 349
   Vol. 3: 860
nāḡaḏ **Vol. 3:** 45
nāḡah **Vol. 2:** 485
nāḡan **Vol. 3:** 671
nāḡap **Vol. 2:** 705
nāḡaś **Vol. 2:** 53, 349
nāhal **Vol. 3:** 255
nahal **Vol. 3:** 985
naḥᵃlâh **Vol. 2:** 298, 300
   Vol. 3: 140
naḥᵃlaṯ YHWH **Vol. 3:** 140
naham **Vol. 2:** 421
nāham **Vol. 2:** 423
nāham **Vol. 1:** 356, 569
   Vol. 3: 155, 255
nāhār **Vol. 3:** 985
nāhāš **Vol. 1:** 509
nahaṭ **Vol. 3:** 255
nākā' **Vol. 3:** 109
nākeh **Vol. 2:** 414
nākôaḥ **Vol. 3:** 1028
nāmaqqû **Vol. 3:** 559
nāpal **Vol. 1:** 608
   Vol. 2: 863
nāpaṣ **Vol. 2:** 33 f.
nāpaš **Vol. 3:** 255
napšām **Vol. 3:** 158
napšô **Vol. 3:** 420
nāqaḇ **Vol. 3:** 341
nāqam **Vol. 3:** 93, 134
nāqām **Vol. 3:** 93

nāqap **Vol. 3:** 178
nāqî **Vol. 2:** 144
   Vol. 3: 103, 355
nāqî' **Vol. 3:** 355
nāśā' **Vol. 1:** 587, 698, 743
   Vol. 2: 201
   Vol. 3: 152, 177, 266, 559, 747, 821, 1195
nāśā' pānîm **Vol. 2:** 622
nāšā' **Vol. 2:** 666
nāṣaḇ **Vol. 3:** 951
nāṣaḥ **Vol. 1:** 650
nāsâh **Vol. 3:** 799 f.
nāsak **Vol. 1:** 476
   Vol. 2: 854
nāṣal **Vol. 3:** 201, 211
nāšal **Vol. 3:** 177
nāšaq **Vol. 2:** 876
nāṣar **Vol. 2:** 132, 134, 349
   Vol. 3: 201
nāsî **Vol. 1:** 165
nāśî' **Vol. 2:** 562
nāṭâh **Vol. 1:** 407
   Vol. 2: 199
   Vol. 3: 870
nāṯan **Vol. 2:** 41, 69, 367, 587
nāṭar **Vol. 3:** 177, 183
nāṭaṣ **Vol. 3:** 178
nāṭaš **Vol. 3:** 560
nāzâh **Vol. 1:** 144, 152, 225
nāzal **Vol. 1:** 683
   Vol. 3: 988
nāzar **Vol. 1:** 405
nāzîr **Vol. 2:** 224
nᵉ'āqâh **Vol. 2:** 423 f.
ne'aṣâh **Vol. 3:** 341
nᵉ'um YHWH **Vol. 2:** 173
   Vol. 3: 1098
nᵉḇālâh **Vol. 3:** 1024 f.
nᵉḇēlāṯî **Vol. 3:** 268
nᵉḇî'îm **Vol. 3:** 485
nebraštā' **Vol. 2:** 485
nᵉḏāḇâh **Vol. 1:** 344, 534
   Vol. 3: 423
nēḏer **Vol. 1:** 344
   Vol. 2: 41
   Vol. 3: 423
neḡeḇ **Vol. 3:** 1004
nᵉḡînâh **Vol. 3:** 669
nᵉḡînôṯ **Vol. 3:** 673
nᵉhar **Vol. 3:** 985
nᵉḥōšeṯ **Vol. 2:** 97
nepeš **Vol. 1:** 444, 495, 548, 555, 612
   Vol. 2: 158, 181, 477 f., 565
   Vol. 3: 158, 234, 420, 679 f., 687–689
nᵉqāmâh **Vol. 3:** 93
nᵉqēḇâh **Vol. 2:** 569
nᵉqûddâh **Vol. 3:** 182
nēs **Vol. 2:** 350
nēsaḥ **Vol. 1:** 650
nᵉšāmâh **Vol. 3:** 680, 690, 707
nesek **Vol. 3:** 423

nēṣer **Vol. 2:** 333
 Vol. 3: 867
nešer **Vol. 1:** 172
nᵉṣûrê **Vol. 1:** 685
nĕṭaḥ **Vol. 1:** 230
nēzer **Vol. 1:** 405
niddah **Vol. 1:** 685
niddûy **Vol. 1:** 414
niham **Vol. 1:** 357
 Vol. 3: 149, 152
ninᵉwēh **Vol. 2:** 679
niplā'ôṭ **Vol. 2:** 622
niqqᵉpû **Vol. 3:** 178
nirpaś **Vol. 3:** 950
niškâh **Vol. 3:** 796
niṣṣāḥôn **Vol. 1:** 648
nō'am **Vol. 2:** 485
ⁿôaḥ **Vol. 3:** 255
nōaḥ **Vol. 2:** 681
nokrî **Vol. 2:** 360, 684, 687
 Vol. 2: 742
nōpeh **Vol. 3:** 396
nôrā' **Vol. 2:** 622
 Vol. 3: 318
nôrā'ôt **Vol. 3:** 318
noṣrî **Vol. 2:** 333
nṣrṭ **Vol. 2:** 333 f.
nûaḥ **Vol. 2:** 681
 Vol. 3: 254–256, 258
nûb **Vol. 1:** 683
nûḏ **Vol. 2:** 422 f.
nûs **Vol. 1:** 558 f.
nûš **Vol. 3:** 859

pā'âh **Vol. 2:** 767
pā'al **Vol. 3:** 350, 1148, 1156
pa'am **Vol. 2:** 716
pāḏâh **Vol. 3:** 190, 192–194, 201 f., 223
pāhaḏ **Vol. 1:** 622
 Vol. 3: 557
pālā' **Vol. 2:** 622
pālal **Vol. 2:** 862 f.
pālaṭ **Vol. 3:** 201, 248
pallēṭ **Vol. 3:** 192
pānîm **Vol. 1:** 211, 585 f.
 Vol. 2: 622
pāqaḏ **Vol. 1:** 189, 332 f.
 Vol. 3: 93, 134
pāqaḥ **Vol. 2:** 726
pāqîḏ **Vol. 1:** 190
pāraḏ **Vol. 1:** 472
pārâh **Vol. 1:** 128
pāraq **Vol. 3:** 192
pārar **Vol. 3:** 166, 583
pāraṣ **Vol. 3:** 377, 950
pāraš **Vol. 1:** 581
 Vol. 2: 810
 Vol. 3: 760
pārāšâh **Vol. 3:** 69
pardēs **Vol. 2:** 761
pāriṣ **Vol. 3:** 377
parnāsîm **Vol. 3:** 545
parnēs **Vol. 3:** 545

pārōkeṭ **Vol. 3:** 794
pārûš **Vol. 2:** 810
parzel **Vol. 2:** 97
pāša' **Vol. 1:** 606
pāsah **Vol. 1:** 632
pāṣâh **Vol. 2:** 726
 Vol. 2: 192, 201
pāṣaḥ **Vol. 3:** 673
pāšar **Vol. 1:** 581
pāšaṭ **Vol. 1:** 581
pashā' **Vol. 1:** 632
pāṭâh **Vol. 2:** 458
pāṭaḥ **Vol. 1:** 581
 Vol. 2: 726
 Vol. 3: 177
pāṭar **Vol. 1:** 581
paṭbaḡ **Vol. 2:** 521
pᵉ'ullâh **Vol. 3:** 139
pᵉḏûyîm **Vol. 3:** 190
pᵉḡa'îm **Vol. 1:** 451
peh **Vol. 2:** 726
pele' **Vol. 3:** 503
pᵉlištîm **Vol. 2:** 124
pᵉnîmî **Vol. 3:** 794
pᵉnînîm **Vol. 3:** 395
pᵉqûḏâh **Vol. 1:** 189
pᵉquddâh **Vol. 1:** 189, 333
 Vol. 2: 684, 777
pᵉraq **Vol. 3:** 192
pᵉraqlēṭ **Vol. 1:** 89
pērēk **Vol. 3:** 711
pereṣ **Vol. 3:** 950
pᵉrî **Vol. 1:** 721
pᵉrîšayyā' **Vol. 2:** 810
peša' **Vol. 3:** 574, 577, 586
pᵉšā'îm **Vol. 1:** 555
pesah **Vol. 1:** 626, 628, 632
pᵉšar **Vol. 1:** 65
pᵉšaṭ **Vol. 3:** 488
pēšer **Vol. 1:** 581, 629
peṭah **Vol. 2:** 29 f.
pᵉṭah **Vol. 2:** 560, 729
peṭî **Vol. 1:** 281
 Vol. 3: 1024
piḏyôm **Vol. 3:** 190
piḏyôn **Vol. 3:** 190
pillēl **Vol. 3:** 152
pinnaṭ **Vol. 3:** 388
piqqûḏîm **Vol. 1:** 332 f.
pišrô **Vol. 3:** 487
pisseah **Vol. 2:** 415
plṭ **Vol. 3:** 253
pō'al **Vol. 3:** 139
pqd **Vol. 1:** 332 f.
pṭb **Vol. 3:** 268
pûṣ **Vol. 2:** 33

qābar **Vol. 1:** 264
qābas **Vol. 2:** 32; 3: 745
qabbālâh **Vol. 3:** 1121
qāḏar **Vol. 2:** 422
qāḏôš **Vol. 3:** 224
 Vol. 3: 101, 104, 787
qāhāl **Vol. 1:** 292–298, 302,

 304 f., 641
 Vol. 2: 796, 800
 Vol. 3: 670
qālal **Vol. 3:** 29
qallēl **Vol. 1:** 415 f.
qan'ān **Vol. 3:** 1167
qānâh **Vol. 1:** 380
 Vol. 2: 649
 Vol. 3: 192
qānēh **Vol. 3:** 399
qārā' **Vol. 1:** 271, 409–411
 Vol. 3: 823
qārab **Vol. 1:** 322
 Vol. 2: 53
 Vol. 3: 860
qārâh **Vol. 3:** 48, 50 f.
qārōb **Vol. 2:** 53
qāšâh **Vol. 2:** 154
qāšar **Vol. 3:** 525
qāṣeh **Vol. 2:** 60, 303
qāṣîn **Vol. 1:** 165
qāṣîr **Vol. 3:** 525 f.
qāṭābkā **Vol. 3:** 267
qāṭān **Vol. 2:** 428, 675
qāṭēḡôr **Vol. 1:** 83
qāṭēḡôr **Vol. 1:** 83
qāṭōn **Vol. 2:** 428, 675
qāw **Vol. 2:** 239
qāwâh **Vol. 2:** 239 f., 772 f.
qayiṣ **Vol. 2:** 432
qeber **Vol. 1:** 264
 Vol. 3: 238
qᵉbûrâh **Vol. 1:** 264
 Vol. 3: 238 f.
qedem **Vol. 1:** 164, 665
qᵉḏēšôṭ **Vol. 1:** 625
qᵉhillā' **Vol. 1:** 295 f.
qᵉlālâh **Vol. 1:** 416
qᵉrē' **Vol. 3:** 487
qeren **Vol. 1:** 721
 Vol. 3: 714
qereš **Vol. 3:** 795
qēṣ **Vol. 2:** 56, 60 f., 432
 Vol. 3: 835
qᵉṣāṭ **Vol. 2:** 60
qeseṗ **Vol. 1:** 108
qešeṭ **Vol. 3:** 1002
qᵉṭōreṭ **Vol. 2:** 293
qhl **Vol. 1:** 307
 Vol. 2: 805
qibbēl **Vol. 3:** 748, 1181
qiddûš **Vol. 2:** 522
qin'âh **Vol. 1:** 558
qinyān **Vol. 1:** 381
qîr **Vol. 3:** 948
qiryâh **Vol. 2:** 802
qiṭrēḡ **Vol. 1:** 83
qiṭṭēr **Vol. 2:** 293
qōḏeš **Vol. 1:** 272
 Vol. 3: 786
qoḏšô **Vol. 3:** 786
qôl **Vol. 1:** 292
 Vol. 2: 174, 863
 Vol. 3: 51, 113

qōmâh **Vol. 2:** 199
qômâh **Vol. 1:** 92
qômᵉmiyyûṭ **Vol. 2:** 735
qôr **Vol. 1:** 318
qôrâh **Vol. 3:** 948
qorbān **Vol. 2:** 41, 43
    Vol. 3: 423
qōṣ **Vol. 3:** 182
qôṣâh **Vol. 3:** 182
qôsēm qᵉsāmîm **Vol. 2:** 554
qr' **Vol. 3:** 543
qsr nrwn **Vol. 2:** 684
qûm **Vol. 2:** 773
    Vol. 3: 224, 226, 279
quppâh **Vol. 3:** 545
qwh **Vol. 2:** 246

r'š **Vol. 3:** 743
rā'âh **Vol. 2:** 395, 488 f.
    Vol. 3: 126, 318, 513, 569 f.
ra' **Vol. 1:** 459, 562, 565
    Vol. 2: 103
    Vol. 3: 1087
rā'aḇ **Vol. 2:** 265
rā'âh **Vol. 1:** 258, 451, 562
    Vol. 3: 564, 569
rā'ap **Vol. 1:** 683
rā'aš **Vol. 3:** 556 f.
rā'ēḇ **Vol. 2:** 265
ra'yôn **Vol. 3:** 820
raḇ **Vol. 3:** 115, 766, 889
rāḇâh **Vol. 1:** 732
    Vol. 2: 130
rāḇaṣ **Vol. 2:** 349, 586
    Vol. 3: 255
rabbaṭ **Vol. 2:** 511
rabbî **Vol. 1:** 67
    Vol. 3: 115, 766 f.
rabbî ûmārî **Vol. 3:** 116
rabbîm **Vol. 1:** 95 f.
    Vol. 2: 800
    Vol. 3: 195 f.
rabbûnî **Vol. 3:** 115
rabym **Vol. 3:** 196
rāḏap **Vol. 2:** 805
rāḡa' **Vol. 3:** 255
rāḡaz **Vol. 3:** 557
rahaḇ **Vol. 1:** 670
    Vol. 3: 29
raham **Vol. 2:** 116
rāham **Vol. 2:** 594
rāhām **Vol. 1:** 172
raḥᵃmîm **Vol. 2:** 105, 594, 598 f.
rāhaq **Vol. 2:** 53
rāhaṣ **Vol. 1:** 144, 151 f., 225
rānan **Vol. 2:** 353, 355
    Vol. 3: 668
rāpā' **Vol. 2:** 167
rāpâh **Vol. 3:** 255
rāpaś **Vol. 3:** 950
rāqia' **Vol. 1:** 523
rāš **Vol. 2:** 820, 822
rāšā' **Vol. 2:** 370

Vol. 3: 577
rāšâh **Vol. 2:** 817
    Vol. 3: 177, 745
rāṣôn **Vol. 2:** 116–118, 818
    Vol. 3: 745
rāšûṭ **Vol. 2:** 608
rāwaḥ **Vol. 3:** 255
rāz **Vol. 3:** 502 f.
rāzîm **Vol. 1:** 578
rb **Vol. 3:** 196
rē'šîṭ **Vol. 1:** 165
    Vol. 3: 415
rēa' **Vol. 1:** 255, 258 f.
    Vol. 2: 548, 739, 803
    Vol. 3: 820
rēḇeṣ **Vol. 2:** 586
    Vol. 3: 255
reḡa' **Vol. 3:** 255, 827
rᵉḡaz **Vol. 2:** 653
reḡeš **Vol. 2:** 653
rēqā' **Vol. 1:** 417 f.
rêqā' **Vol. 1:** 417
rᵉšā'îm **Vol. 2:** 829
rᵉshûṭā' **Vol. 2:** 608
rᵉšûṭ **Vol. 2:** 608
rᵉšûyôṭ **Vol. 2:** 608
rḥm **Vol. 2:** 544, 598 f.
ri'šôn **Vol. 1:** 165, 665, 667
rîḇ **Vol. 2:** 363
    Vol. 3: 93, 346, 355, 820, 1050 f.
ribbônô šel 'ôlām **Vol. 2:** 514
riḡšā' **Vol. 2:** 653
riham **Vol. 3:** 152
rinnâh **Vol. 2:** 860
rîq **Vol. 1:** 417, 546
rô'eh **Vol. 3:** 77
rō'š **Vol. 1:** 165, 665
    Vol. 2: 27, 157 f., 683
    Vol. 3: 388
rōḇ **Vol. 1:** 732
    Vol. 2: 842
rōḡez **Vol. 1:** 108
    Vol. 2: 652
rûa' **Vol. 3:** 50, 816
rûah **Vol. 1:** 102, 451, 672, 674
    Vol. 2: 479, 565
    Vol. 3: 125, 680, 690 f., 694, 708
rûḥôṭ **Vol. 1:** 102, 674
rûm **Vol. 2:** 199, 201
    Vol. 3: 29
ruqqamtî **Vol. 1:** 712
rûṣ **Vol. 3:** 946
rwb **Vol. 3:** 196

sāḡar **Vol. 2:** 730
sāḵal **Vol. 3:** 1024 f.
sāḵan **Vol. 3:** 760
sālaḥ **Vol. 1:** 698
    Vol. 3: 149, 152, 155, 157
sālal **Vol. 3:** 951
sāmaḵ yāḏayim **Vol. 2:** 151
sanheḏrîn **Vol. 1:** 363

sāpaḏ **Vol. 2:** 417
sāpar **Vol. 1:** 574
    Vol. 3: 52, 478
sappahaṭ **Vol. 2:** 465
sārîs **Vol. 1:** 560
sarsōr **Vol. 1:** 374
sāṭam **Vol. 3:** 950
sāṭān **Vol. 3:** 468
sāṭāna' **Vol. 3:** 468
ṣdq **Vol. 3:** 358
sᵉ'ārâh **Vol. 3:** 266, 559
sᵉḡiḏ **Vol. 2:** 876
sᵉḡullâh **Vol. 2:** 297 f., 838–840
sekel **Vol. 3:** 1024
sela' **Vol. 3:** 381
sᵉlîhâh **Vol. 3:** 156
sēmān **Vol. 3:** 904
semel **Vol. 2:** 287
sēmel **Vol. 2:** 287
sᵉmîkâh **Vol. 3:** 115
sᵉnêḡôr **Vol. 1:** 83
sēper **Vol. 1:** 243, 246, 505
    Vol. 3: 483
sᵉṭar **Vol. 3:** 177
sēṭîm **Vol. 3:** 583
sîḡ **Vol. 3:** 808
siḵlûṭ **Vol. 3:** 1024
sînay **Vol. 3:** 1013
sôḏ **Vol. 1:** 611, 712
    Vol. 3: 311, 502 f.
sôlᵉlâh **Vol. 3:** 951
sôleṭ **Vol. 3:** 422
sômēm **Vol. 1:** 75
sôpēr, sōpēr **Vol. 1:** 64
    Vol. 3: 247, 478 f., 485
sōpᵉrîm **Vol. 3:** 478
sr' **Vol. 3:** 447
sry **Vol. 3:** 447
sûḡ **Vol. 3:** 950
sûḵ **Vol. 1:** 120 f.
sukkâh **Vol. 3:** 811
sûr **Vol. 1:** 606
    Vol. 3: 166, 583
sûṭ **Vol. 3:** 557

ṣā'îr **Vol. 2:** 675
ṣā'aq **Vol. 1:** 409 f.
ṣāḇā' **Vol. 1:** 522
    Vol. 2: 602, 684
ṣāḇâh **Vol. 3:** 959
ṣāḏaq **Vol. 2:** 144
    Vol. 3: 355, 376, 924
ṣaddîq **Vol. 3:** 354, 357, 366, 766
ṣāḏaq **Vol. 3:** 439
ṣāhal **Vol. 1:** 411
ṣah **Vol. 2:** 777
ṣāhah **Vol. 2:** 485
ṣāhaq **Vol. 2:** 430–432
ṣalmāweṭ **Vol. 3:** 554
ṣāmē' **Vol. 2:** 265
ṣāmek **Vol. 3:** 488
ṣāpâh **Vol. 3:** 126
ṣar **Vol. 1:** 553

Vol. 2: 663, 807
ṣāra' Vol. 2: 464
ṣāra'aṭ Vol. 2: 464 f.
ṣārâh Vol. 2: 423, 663
ṣārar Vol. 2: 807
ṣārebeṭ Vol. 2: 288
ṣārûa' Vol. 2: 464
ṣdq Vol. 3: 354, 356-358, 376 f.
ṣᵉbā' Vol. 3: 821
ṣᵉbā'ôṭ Vol. 2: 69, 602
   Vol. 3: 717, 959
ṣᵉdāqâh Vol. 2: 363, 594 f., 777
   Vol. 3: 354, 357 f., 375 f., 766
ṣedeq Vol. 1: 581
   Vol. 2: 591
   Vol. 3: 354, 376
ṣēl Vol. 3: 554
ṣᵉla' Vol. 2: 863
ṣᵉlēm Vol. 1: 706
   Vol. 2: 287
ṣelem Vol. 2: 287, 502
   Vol. 3: 904
ṣemaḥ Vol. 3: 867, 870
ṣemeḏ Vol. 3: 1161
ṣidqōṭ YHWH Vol. 3: 356
ṣippôr Vol. 1: 172
ṣîr Vol. 1: 194
   Vol. 3: 858
ṣiwwâh Vol. 1: 331, 333
ṣiyyâh Vol. 2: 265
ṣiyyôn Vol. 2: 324
ṣō'n Vol. 2: 412 f.
   Vol. 3: 564
ṣōrēr Vol. 3: 468
ṣûḏ Vol. 3: 952
ṣûm Vol. 1: 612
ṣûr Vol. 3: 381, 399
ṣûrî Vol. 3: 178
ṣwh Vol. 1: 331
ṣwwḥ Vol. 1: 409

śāba' Vol. 1: 734, 743
śābar Vol. 2: 239
śāḡaḇ Vol. 3: 192
śāhaq Vol. 2: 430 f.
śākak Vol. 3: 950
śākal Vol. 2: 397
   Vol. 3: 125, 1025
śākār Vol. 3: 138-140
śakîr Vol. 3: 139
śāmaḥ Vol. 2: 355-357, 430
śānē' Vol. 1: 555
śār Vol. 3: 468
śar Vol. 1: 102, 165
   Vol. 2: 376
śārâ Vol. 1: 80
śāraḏ Vol. 3: 248
śārâh Vol. 1: 80
   Vol. 2: 305
śārap Vol. 3: 255
śārar Vol. 2: 305
śārîḏ Vol. 3: 248, 251

śāśôn Vol. 2: 356
śāṭâh Vol. 3: 583
śāṭān Vol. 3: 468 f.
śe'ēṭ Vol. 2: 465
śē'îr Vol. 1: 451
śᵉḥôq Vol. 2: 431, 433
śᵉkar ha-niṣṣāḥôn Vol. 1: 648
śekel Vol. 3: 1027, 1029
śeker Vol. 3: 139
śᵉmō'l Vol. 2: 148
śᵉrāpîm Vol. 1: 509
śîaḥ Vol. 1: 574
   Vol. 2: 140
śîḇ Vol. 1: 196
śiddîm Vol. 3: 444
śîm Vol. 1: 696
śimḥâh Vol. 2: 356 f.
śîś Vol. 2: 355 f.
śûk Vol. 3: 950

š'r Vol. 3: 254
šā'aḡ Vol. 3: 324
šā'âh Vol. 3: 112, 859
šā'al Vol. 2: 856, 879
šā'al bᵉšālôm Vol. 2: 779
šā'an Vol. 3: 255
šā'ar Vol. 3: 248
šā'ōn Vol. 3: 859
šā'an Vol. 3: 255
ša'ar Vol. 2: 29
šāba' Vol. 1: 344
   Vol. 3: 474, 739
šāḇâh Vol. 3: 590
šāḇaḥ Vol. 3: 816
šāḇar Vol. 3: 109
šāḇaṭ Vol. 3: 255 f., 405 f.
šabbāṭ Vol. 1: 625
   Vol. 3: 255 f., 405
šabbāṭôn Vol. 3: 255
šāḏaḏ Vol. 3: 377, 859
šadday Vol. 2: 67, 87, 513
   Vol. 3: 717, 729
šāhâh Vol. 2: 876
šāhaḥ Vol. 2: 260
šahaṣ Vol. 3: 30
šahaṭ Vol. 1: 470
   Vol. 3: 262
šāḥaṭ Vol. 1: 468, 470
šāḥōr Vol. 1: 203
šākaḇ Vol. 1: 442
   Vol. 2: 586
šākan Vol. 1: 272, 380
   Vol. 3: 255
šāḵēn Vol. 3: 255
šālâh Vol. 3: 341
šālaḥ Vol. 1: 127, 246, 475, 581
   Vol. 3: 860
šālēm Vol. 1: 734
   Vol. 2: 60, 65, 592 f.
   Vol. 3: 134, 422
šālîaḥ Vol. 1: 127-134, 194
   Vol. 3: 746
šallîṭ Vol. 2: 512

šālôm Vol. 1: 208, 211, 213
   Vol. 2: 169, 237, 357, 593, 777-780, 782 f.
   Vol. 3: 422, 448, 528
šālû Vol. 3: 341
šālûaḥ Vol. 1: 127 f.
šalwâh Vol. 2: 777
šāma' Vol. 1: 340
   Vol. 2: 172 f., 175, 179, 395
šāmam Vol. 2: 622
šāmar Vol. 2: 132, 134, 778
šāmaṭ Vol. 1: 698
šāmayim Vol. 1: 75
   Vol. 2: 71, 191, 376 f., 652
šāmēm Vol. 1: 75, 530
   Vol. 3: 1004-1006
šāmᵉrîm Vol. 3: 451
šāmîr Vol. 1: 743
šānâh Vol. 1: 64
   Vol. 3: 1126
šāpâh Vol. 3: 870
šāpak Vol. 2: 854
šāpal Vol. 2: 260
šāpaṭ Vol. 1: 503
   Vol. 2: 363
   Vol. 3: 355
šāqaḏ Vol. 2: 136 f.
šāqâh Vol. 2: 274
šāqaṭ Vol. 2: 777
   Vol. 3: 255
šāqēḏ Vol. 3: 1096
šāraṭ Vol. 3: 673
šāṭ Vol. 3: 350
šāṭâh Vol. 2: 274
šāṭar Vol. 3: 477
šāw' Vol. 1: 550
šaw'âh Vol. 2: 860
šāwa' Vol. 2: 423
šāwâh Vol. 1: 580
šb' Vol. 3: 743
šbṭ Vol. 3: 414
še Vol. 3: 729
šᵉ'ār Vol. 3: 248 f., 254
šᵉ'ār yāšûḇ Vol. 3: 249
šᵉ'ēlâh Vol. 3: 879
šᵉ'ēr Vol. 1: 672 f., 675
šᵉ'ēr bᵉśārô Vol. 1: 675
šᵉ'ērîṭ Vol. 3: 248
šᵉ'ôl Vol. 1: 264, 523
   Vol. 2: 206
   Vol. 3: 262, 267
šᵉ'ārîm Vol. 2: 802
šᵉba' Vol. 2: 690
   Vol. 3: 739
šebbᵉ'alpē Vol. 3: 488
šebbikṭaḇ Vol. 3: 488
šebeṭ Vol. 3: 255
šēbeṭ Vol. 3: 870
šēbeṭ Vol. 1: 407
   Vol. 3: 870
šᵉbî Vol. 3: 590
šᵉbô Vol. 3: 396
šᵉbû'âh Vol. 3: 739
šeḏ Vol. 1: 451

šᵉḏûḏâh **Vol. 3:** 859
šᵉḵâḇâh **Vol. 2:** 586
   Vol. 3: 255
šᵉḵem **Vol. 3:** 458
šeker **Vol. 3:** 859
šᵉḵînâh **Vol. 1:** 586
   Vol. 2: 377
šᵉḵōḇeṭ **Vol. 2:** 587
šᵉlāmîm **Vol. 3:** 422 f., 425
šᵉlēṭ **Vol. 3:** 570, 860
šᵉlîm **Vol. 2:** 487
šᵉlōmōh **Vol. 3:** 605
šēm **Vol. 1:** 68, 272
   Vol. 2: 71, 88, 190, 649 f., 652, 654
   Vol. 3: 233, 237, 1209
šēmaʿ **Vol. 2:** 173, 177
šᵉmaʿ **Vol. 2:** 720, 864
šᵉmaʿ yiśrāʾēl **Vol. 2:** 173
šᵉmayîn **Vol. 3:** 1006
šemen **Vol. 2:** 710
šemeš **Vol. 3:** 731
šᵉmiṭṭâh **Vol. 2:** 667
šᵉmōneh ʿeśrēh **Vol. 2:** 864
šᵉmûʾâh **Vol. 2:** 173
šēnâʾ **Vol. 1:** 442
šenneʾᵉmar **Vol. 3:** 487
šᵉpaʿ **Vol. 2:** 842
šᵉpar **Vol. 2:** 815
šeqel **Vol. 3:** 752
šeqer **Vol. 2:** 470
   Vol. 3: 574–576
šᵉrāʾ **Vol. 1:** 167
   Vol. 2: 732
   Vol. 3: 177, 188
šērēṭ **Vol. 3:** 551
šeṭep **Vol. 3:** 991
šêziḇ **Vol. 3:** 192, 201
šibbōleṭ **Vol. 3:** 867
šiḡyōnôṭ **Vol. 3:** 673
šikḇaṭ-zeraʿ **Vol. 2:** 586
šikmâh **Vol. 2:** 730
šillēm **Vol. 3:** 420, 422
šilōaḥ **Vol. 1:** 581
šimᵃmâh **Vol. 3:** 1005
šiqqûṣ **Vol. 1:** 74 f.
   Vol. 3: 1006
šîr **Vol. 2:** 357
   Vol. 3: 668, 669, 671–673, 816
šîrâh **Vol. 3:** 673
šlm **Vol. 2:** 778
   Vol. 3: 607
šôʾēl ʾôḇ **Vol. 2:** 554
šôḏ **Vol. 3:** 729, 859
šôḏēḏ **Vol. 3:** 377
šoltānāʾ **Vol. 2:** 607
šômēm **Vol. 1:** 74
šômᵉrîm **Vol. 3:** 451
šômᵉrôn **Vol. 3:** 449
šôpār **Vol. 3:** 873
šôqēḏ **Vol. 3:** 1096
šôreš **Vol. 3:** 867
šôṭēr **Vol. 3:** 477

šōṭᵉrîm **Vol. 1:** 196
šqr **Vol. 3:** 587
šûaʿ **Vol. 2:** 69, 332
šûḇ **Vol. 1:** 354, 357 f., 362
   Vol. 2: 222
   Vol. 3: 134, 146, 255, 823, 933
šûr **Vol. 1:** 694

tāʿâh **Vol. 2:** 458
   Vol. 3: 801
tabbel **Vol. 3:** 447
taḇnîṭ **Vol. 1:** 706
   Vol. 2: 501 f.
   Vol. 3: 904
tāḡāʾ **Vol. 3:** 182
tahᵃlûʾîm **Vol. 3:** 999
tahᵃnûn **Vol. 2:** 860, 863
tahᵃnûnîm **Vol. 2:** 117
tahaṭ **Vol. 2:** 586
tahbûlôṭ **Vol. 1:** 194
tahtî **Vol. 2:** 197
tālâh **Vol. 1:** 393
talmîḏ **Vol. 1:** 69, 481, 485–488
talmidîm **Vol. 3:** 767
talmûḏ **Vol. 1:** 69
   Vol. 3: 769
tām **Vol. 2:** 60 f., 144, 487
   Vol. 3: 924
tāmâh **Vol. 2:** 622
tāmak **Vol. 1:** 663
   Vol. 3: 350
tāmam **Vol. 1:** 734
   Vol. 2: 60
tamhûy **Vol. 3:** 545
tāmîm **Vol. 2:** 60 f., 65, 144, 782
   Vol. 3: 923 f.
tannaʾîm **Vol. 1:** 69
tannîn **Vol. 1:** 670
tannînîm gᵉḏōlîm **Vol. 1:** 670
tāpēl **Vol. 3:** 1024
targēm **Vol. 1:** 69, 580 f.
targûm **Vol. 1:** 69
tāśîm **Vol. 3:** 420
tbl **Vol. 3:** 447
tᵉʾēnâh **Vol. 1:** 723
ṭēḇēl **Vol. 3:** 448
tᵉḇûnâh **Vol. 2:** 287
   Vol. 3: 130, 1027
tᵉhillâh **Vol. 3:** 926
tᵉhillâh **Vol. 1:** 164
   Vol. 3: 669
tᵉhinnâh **Vol. 2:** 860, 863
tᵉhôm **Vol. 2:** 197, 205
   Vol. 3: 983
tᵉkûnâh **Vol. 1:** 712
tᵉmûnâh **Vol. 1:** 706
   Vol. 2: 501
tᵉmûrâh **Vol. 3:** 166
tᵉnak **Vol. 3:** 485
tᵉnûʾâh **Vol. 2:** 144
tᵉnûpâh **Vol. 3:** 416, 424

tᵉpillâh **Vol. 2:** 862 f.
   Vol. 3: 669
tēqaʿ **Vol. 3:** 112
tᵉqal **Vol. 3:** 994
tᵉrāpîm **Vol. 2:** 284, 317
   Vol. 3: 528
tᵉrûmâh **Vol. 3:** 415
tᵉšûʾâh **Vol. 2:** 144
tipʾereṭ **Vol. 1:** 227, 522
tiplâh **Vol. 3:** 1024
tiqqāhēnî **Vol. 3:** 262
tiqwâh **Vol. 1:** 712
   Vol. 2: 239, 773
tîrôš **Vol. 3:** 918
tîrōš **Vol. 3:** 918
tmm **Vol. 2:** 778
tōʾar **Vol. 1:** 704
tōʿēḇâh **Vol. 1:** 75
tôḏâh **Vol. 1:** 344
   Vol. 3: 233, 423, 673
tôheleṭ **Vol. 1:** 712
tōhû **Vol. 1:** 550
tôkahaṭ **Vol. 2:** 140
tolēḏōṭ **Vol. 1:** 181
tôrâh **Vol. 1:** 54, 70, 333, 714
   Vol. 2: 296, 439–441
   Vol. 3: 485, 488
tôrâh šebbᵉʿalpē **Vol. 3:** 488
tôrâh šebbiḵtaḇ **Vol. 3:** 488
tôšāḇ **Vol. 1:** 684, 690
   Vol. 2: 789
tpl **Vol. 3:** 447
tûḇ **Vol. 3:** 147
twḏh **Vol. 2:** 550

ṭaʿam **Vol. 1:** 459
ṭāʿam **Vol. 2:** 269
ṭāʿan **Vol. 1:** 743
ṭāḇal **Vol. 1:** 144 f., 152
ṭabbaʿaṭ **Vol. 3:** 497
ṭāhar **Vol. 3:** 116
ṭāhēr **Vol. 2:** 144
   Vol. 3: 924
ṭāhôr **Vol. 3:** 101, 103
ṭalyāʾ **Vol. 2:** 411
   Vol. 3: 611
ṭāman **Vol. 2:** 773
ṭāmēʾ **Vol. 1:** 447
   Vol. 3: 103
ṭap **Vol. 1:** 281, 283
ṭārap **Vol. 3:** 601
ṭbl **Vol. 3:** 447
ṭᵉḇîlâh **Vol. 1:** 150
ṭᵉlîṭāʾ qûm **Vol. 1:** 581
ṭihar **Vol. 3:** 419
ṭôḇ **Vol. 2:** 99, 103, 105, 116
   Vol. 3: 351, 821
ṭôḇ ʿôlāmîm **Vol. 2:** 105
ṭôḇ wārāʾ **Vol. 2:** 103
ṭôṭāpōṭ **Vol. 3:** 559
ṭûaḥ **Vol. 1:** 120
ṭumʾâh **Vol. 3:** 103
ṭûpôs **Vol. 3:** 904

wāw **Vol. 3:** 182
wayᵉhî . . . wa **Vol. 1:** 181
wayᵉhî dᵉbar YHWH **Vol. 2:** 173
   Vol. 3: 1090
wayišbōṭ **Vol. 3:** 405
wayyinnāhem **Vol. 3:** 155
wayyiššā'er **Vol. 3:** 248
wayyiṯhallēk **Vol. 3:** 264
wᵉ'aḥar **Vol. 3:** 262
wᵉ'ēnennû **Vol. 3:** 264
wᵉ'attâh **Vol. 1:** 246
wᵉhāyû **Vol. 3:** 239
wᵉhiš'arti **Vol. 3:** 248
wᵉnihyeh **Vol. 3:** 267
wᵉnislaḥ lô **Vol. 3:** 155
wᵉnizkartem **Vol. 3:** 239

y'd **Vol. 1:** 626
Ya-huwa **Vol. 2:** 67
yā'al **Vol. 1:** 164
yā'aḏ **Vol. 1:** 293
yā'al **Vol. 3:** 137
yā'aṣ **Vol. 1:** 363
yā'ēp **Vol. 2:** 265
yābēš **Vol. 3:** 999
yāḏ **Vol. 1:** 636
   Vol. 2: 60, 148 f., 153, 414
   Vol. 3: 860
yaḏ yᵉmînô **Vol. 2:** 414
yāḏa' **Vol. 2:** 395, 397, 408,
   488 f., 587
   Vol. 3: 316, 668, 760
yāḏāh **Vol. 1:** 344 f., 574
   Vol. 2: 305
   Vol. 3: 233, 668, 816
yāga' **Vol. 1:** 262
yāh **Vol. 1:** 99
   Vol. 2: 862
yahaḏ **Vol. 3:** 766, 908
yāhal **Vol. 2:** 239 f., 772 f.
yahᵃlōm **Vol. 3:** 395
yāhaś **Vol. 2:** 683
yahdāw **Vol. 3:** 908
yāḥiḏ **Vol. 2:** 76, 725
   Vol. 3: 766
yāḥîr **Vol. 3:** 30
Yahweh **Vol. 2:** 67, 590
yākaḥ **Vol. 2:** 140
   Vol. 3: 341
yālaḏ **Vol. 1:** 176 f., 186
   Vol. 3: 858
yām **Vol. 1:** 670
   Vol. 2: 56
   Vol. 3: 983
yāmîm **Vol. 2:** 475, 889
yāmîn **Vol. 1:** 146, 414
yāpa' **Vol. 2:** 735
yāpeh **Vol. 2:** 103
yārâh **Vol. 1:** 574
   Vol. 2: 296
   Vol. 3: 760, 771
yāraš **Vol. 1:** 453
   Vol. 2: 298, 304
yardēn **Vol. 3:** 991

yārē' **Vol. 1:** 327
   Vol. 2: 91, 93
   Vol. 3: 318
yāṣā' **Vol. 3:** 760
yāša' **Vol. 2:** 331
   Vol. 3: 201 f., 206–208, 211,
   217, 223, 588
yāṣab **Vol. 1:** 474
yāšab **Vol. 2:** 164, 773
   Vol. 3: 224, 228, 254 f.
yāsaḏ **Vol. 1:** 379 f., 661
   Vol. 3: 350
yāšān **Vol. 2:** 713
yāsar **Vol. 3:** 776
yāṣar **Vol. 1:** 380
   Vol. 3: 119
yāšār **Vol. 2:** 144, 237
   Vol. 3: 351, 355, 821, 924
yāšᵉpēh **Vol. 3:** 395 f.
yāṣûa' **Vol. 2:** 587
yāšûb **Vol. 3:** 251
yāšûbû **Vol. 3:** 233
yāṯar **Vol. 1:** 728
   Vol. 3: 248
yāṯôm **Vol. 2:** 737 f.
yāwān **Vol. 2:** 124
yayin **Vol. 3:** 918
yᵉ'ôr **Vol. 3:** 985
yᵉ'ôr **Vol. 3:** 985
yᵉhāb **Vol. 1:** 277
yᵉhayyēnû **Vol. 3:** 267
Yᵉhôsēp **Vol. 2:** 331
yᵉhôšûa' **Vol. 3:** 330–332
   Vol. 3: 208
yᵉhôšua' **Vol. 3:** 208
yᵉhôwâh **Vol. 2:** 69
Yehuḏ **Vol. 2:** 848
yᵉhûḏâh **Vol. 1:** 61
   Vol. 2: 305, 319
yᵉhûḏî **Vol. 2:** 305
yᵉhûḏîṯ **Vol. 2:** 305
yᵉkappēr **Vol. 3:** 155
yeleḏ **Vol. 1:** 283
   Vol. 2: 675
yᵉnahᵃmēnû **Vol. 2:** 681
yᵉqimēnû **Vol. 3:** 267
yᵉqûm **Vol. 1:** 711
yᵉqûmûn **Vol. 3:** 268
yᵉrûšālayim **Vol. 2:** 324, 592
yēša' **Vol. 3:** 217
yᵉša'yāhû **Vol. 3:** 208
yēṣer hā-ra' **Vol. 1:** 459
yᵉsôḏ **Vol. 1:** 661
Yēšû **Vol. 2:** 332
yᵉšû'âh **Vol. 3:** 207, 217
yᵉšû'āṯekā **Vol. 3:** 207
Yēšua' **Vol. 3:** 330–332
yēšûa' **Vol. 2:** 69
   Vol. 3: 208
yeṭer **Vol. 1:** 728
   Vol. 3: 248
yᵉwānîm **Vol. 2:** 124
yhw **Vol. 2:** 305
YHWH **Vol. 1:** 71 f., 208, 210 f.

   Vol. 2: 68–70, 88, 173, 278,
   376, 389, 512, 656, 720,
   796, 887
   Vol. 3: 140, 155, 239, 356,
   597, 607, 777, 786, 1087,
   1098, 1181
YHWH 'ᵉlōhēnû YHWH 'eḥāḏ
   Vol. 2: 720
YHWH ṣᵉbā'ôṯ **Vol. 3:** 959
yidd'ōnî **Vol. 2:** 554
yiggâh **Vol. 2:** 260
yihyeh **Vol. 3:** 366
yihyû **Vol. 3:** 268
yiqqahēnî **Vol. 3:** 262
yiqraṯ **Vol. 3:** 388
yir'ê šāmayîm **Vol. 1:** 360
yiṣḥāq **Vol. 1:** 80
   Vol. 2: 431
yišhār **Vol. 2:** 710
yiśrā'ēl **Vol. 1:** 61, 294
   Vol. 2: 67, 173, 304, 322,
   698, 791
yissᵉḏû **Vol. 3:** 391
yiṭkappēr **Vol. 3:** 155
yiṭrōn **Vol. 3:** 137
yizkᵉrû **Vol. 3:** 233
yizzākēr **Vol. 3:** 232
yôbēl **Vol. 1:** 698
   Vol. 3: 191
yôḏ **Vol. 3:** 182, 484
yôm **Vol. 2:** 475, 887–890, 931
   Vol. 3: 835, 841
yônâh **Vol. 2:** 350
yônēq **Vol. 1:** 281
yôṣēr **Vol. 3:** 911
yrd **Vol. 3:** 991
yš' **Vol. 2:** 332

za'am **Vol. 1:** 108
zā'ap **Vol. 3:** 559
zā'aq **Vol. 1:** 409
   Vol. 2: 423
   Vol. 3: 50
za'ᵃwâh **Vol. 1:** 685
   Vol. 2: 663
zābaḏ **Vol. 2:** 41
zābaḥ **Vol. 3:** 418
zāḏôn **Vol. 3:** 29
zāhāb **Vol. 2:** 95
zāhar **Vol. 2:** 485
zak **Vol. 3:** 101
zākâh **Vol. 2:** 144
   Vol. 3: 348, 355, 924
zākak **Vol. 2:** 144
   Vol. 3: 103, 924
zākar **Vol. 3:** 232–234, 236,
   238 f., 245
zākār **Vol. 2:** 569, 587
zākār ûnᵉqēbâh **Vol. 2:** 569
zāmām **Vol. 3:** 820
zāmar **Vol. 3:** 668, 671
zammar **Vol. 3:** 673
zānâh **Vol. 1:** 498

335

zāqēn **Vol. 1:** 193, 196
  Vol. 2: 562
zār **Vol. 1:** 684
  Vol. 2: 742
zāra' **Vol. 3:** 521 f.
zārâh **Vol. 2:** 33 f.
zārah **Vol. 3:** 318
zar^aḳā **Vol. 3:** 524
zayiṭ **Vol. 2:** 711
zbh **Vol. 3:** 422
zebaḥ **Vol. 3:** 418, 422, 434, 438
zebaḥ hayyamîm **Vol. 3:** 437

zebel **Vol. 3:** 469
z^ebūḇ **Vol. 3:** 469
z^ebūl **Vol. 3:** 469
zēḏ **Vol. 3:** 29
zēker **Vol. 3:** 236–238
z^eḵūṭ '^emûnāh **Vol. 1:** 714
z^eḵūṭ tôrâh **Vol. 1:** 714
z^enūṭ **Vol. 1:** 499
  Vol. 3: 1195
zera' **Vol. 1:** 177
  Vol. 3: 521–523
z^ewā'âh **Vol. 2:** 663
zibbūl, zibbûl **Vol. 3:** 469

zikkārōn **Vol. 3:** 233, 236, 239
zikrōn **Vol. 3:** 238, 244
zikrōnôṭ **Vol. 3:** 233
zimmâh **Vol. 3:** 1024
zimrâh **Vol. 3:** 669
zirmâh **Vol. 3:** 561
zkr **Vol. 3:** 235 f.
zō'ṭ **Vol. 3:** 178
zûā' **Vol. 2:** 876
zûḇ **Vol. 1:** 682
zûḏ **Vol. 3:** 29

Index of Greek Words

Index of Greek Words

(*chief references in* **bold figures**)

a- **Vol. 2:** 206
abba **Vol. 1: 614,** 619–621
  Vol. 2: 868, **870 f.**
Abraam **Vol. 1: 76,** 181
  Vol. 3: 72 f.
abyssos **Vol. 1:** 449
  Vol. 2: 197, **205, 207, 210**
  Vol. 3: 474, 983, 989
achatēs **Vol. 3: 396**
acheiropoiētos **Vol. 3:** 185
Acheldamach **Vol. 1:** 93
achrēston **Vol. 2:** 434
achri **Vol. 2:** 64, 530 f.
  Vol. 3: 148
achri telous **Vol. 2:** 64
Adam **Vol. 1: 84,** 179
  Vol. 2: 57
adēlōs **Vol. 1:** 648
adelphē **Vol. 1: 254 f.,** 539
  Vol. 3: 1065
adelphia **Vol. 1:** 257
adelphos **Vol. 1:** 138, **254–257,**
  259 f., 305, 373
  Vol. 2: 505, 538, 547 f.
  Vol. 3: 1065
adelphotēs **Vol. 1: 254,** 257,
  305
adiakritos **Vol. 1: 503,** 505
adialeiptos **Vol. 3: 229**
adialeiptōs **Vol. 3: 229 f.**
adikēma **Vol. 3: 573–575,** 577
adikeo **Vol. 1:** 467
  Vol. 3: 573–576, 586
adikia **Vol. 2:** 92–94, 458, 844
  Vol. 3: 102, 137, 150, **352,**
  573–576, 577, 580, 584, 887,
  1148, 1150
adikos **Vol. 2:** 92 f.
  Vol. 3: 573–576, 587
adikōs **Vol. 3: 573–575**
adō **Vol. 2:** 436
  Vol. 3: 672–675, 676
adokimos **Vol. 1:** 163, 557
  Vol. 3: 808–810
adolos **Vol. 3:** 1118
adynatos **Vol. 2: 601, 606**
  Vol. 3: 995
aei **Vol. 2:** 420
  Vol. 3: 827, 839
aeidō **Vol. 3:** 672
aēr **Vol. 1:** 449
  Vol. 2: 189, 476

  Vol. 3: 471
aetos **Vol.1:** 175
  Vol. 3: 1054
agalliaō **Vol. 2:** 355, 436
  Vol. 3: 673
agalliaomai **Vol. 2: 352–354,**
  357 f., **361,** 780
agalliasis **Vol. 2: 352–354,** 358
agallō **Vol. 2:** 352
agallomai **Vol. 2:** 352
agamos **Vol. 3: 536 f.**
agan **Vol. 3:** 103
agapaō **Vol. 2: 538–540, 542–**
  544, 547–549, 551
  Vol. 3: 173, 455, 942
agapē **Vol. 1:** 180, 256 f., 667,
  695, 738
  Vol. 2: 106, 123, 242 f., 427,
  469 f., **538–551,** 765, 780
  Vol. 3: 562, 582, 746, 929,
  931, 942, 1151, 1182, 1211
agapētos **Vol. 1:** 257, 287, 541
  Vol. 2: 538 f., 543 f., 551,
  725
  Vol. 3: 641
agathoergeō **Vol. 2: 98, 100,**
  102
agathon **Vol. 2:** 98 f., 101
  Vol. 3: 138, 775, 1021
agathopoieō **Vol. 2: 98, 100,**
  102
agathopoiia **Vol. 2: 98, 102**
  Vol. 3: 1153, 1155
agathopoios **Vol. 2: 98, 101**
  Vol. 3: 1153, 1155
agathos **Vol. 1:** 348, 351, 561,
  564
  Vol. 2: 60, **98–106,** 239, 241,
  243, 403, 476, 683, 781, 846
  Vol. 3: 45, 138, 775, 1148,
  1158
agathōsynē **Vol. 2: 98, 100f.,**
  819
agathotēs **Vol. 2:** 290
agauos **Vol. 2:** 643
agenealogētos **Vol. 2: 35 f.**
agērochia **Vol. 3:** 29
agnoēma **Vol. 2: 406**
agnoeō **Vol. 2:** 391, 400, **406–**
  408
  Vol. 3: 431, 573, 1036
agnoia **Vol. 1:** 422

  Vol. 2: 406 f., 458
  Vol. 3: 573, 577, 997
agnōsia **Vol. 1:** 513
  Vol. 2: 402, **406**
agnōstos **Vol. 1:** 670
  Vol. 2: 77, 394, **406 f.**
agnōstos patēr **Vol. 2:** 394
agnōstos propatōr **Vol. 2:** 394
agnōstos theos **Vol. 2:** 394
agō **Vol. 1:** 645
  Vol. 2: 643, 735
agōgē **Vol. 3: 935**
agōn **Vol. 1: 644–649,** 652
  Vol. 3: 946
agōnia **Vol. 1: 645 f.**
agōnizomai **Vol. 1: 644–647**
agora **Vol. 1:** 267, 291
agoraias **Vol. 1:** 267
agorazō **Vol. 1: 267 f.**
  Vol. 3: 200
agoreuō **Vol. 2:** 744
agrammatos **Vol. 2:** 456
  Vol. 3: 1197
agraphos **Vol. 3:** 574, 930
agrielaios **Vol. 2:** 710, 712
  Vol. 3: 869
agrios **Vol. 1:** 520
agros **Vol. 1:** 93, 222, 520
agrypneō **Vol. 2:** 137
agrypnia **Vol. 2:** 137
ahoratos **Vol. 3:** 511 f., 515
aianēs **Vol. 2:** 206
aichmalōsia **Vol. 1:** 685
  Vol. 3: 590 f.
aichmalōteuō **Vol. 3: 590**
aichmalōtizō **Vol. 3: 590 f.**
aichmalōtos **Vol. 3:** 589, **590,**
  597, 599
aichmē **Vol. 3:** 590
Aïdas **Vol. 2:** 206
aideomai **Vol. 3: 561**
Aïdēs **Vol. 2:** 206
adiaphron **Vol. 3:** 835
aidios **Vol. 2:** 290
  Vol. 3: 826 f., 829
aidoion **Vol. 3: 561**
aidōs **Vol. 3: 561 f.,** 564
Aigyptios **Vol. 1: 530**
Aigyptos **Vol. 1: 530**
  Vol. 2: 835
aineō **Vol. 1:** 344
  Vol. 2: 744, **855,** 868

339

Vol. 3: 233, **816 f.**, 819
ainesis **Vol. 3: 816 f.**
ainigma **Vol. 2: 743–746, 756, 760**
ainos **Vol. 3: 816 f.**, 819
aiōn **Vol. 1**: 105, 125, 164, 179, 325 f., 476, 523 f., 601, 708, 718, 737
  Vol. 2: 37, 62, 158, 543, 609, 887, 928
  Vol. 3: 276, 312, **826–833, 841**, 850, 864
aiōnes **Vol. 3**: 832
aiōnios **Vol. 1**: 442, 464
  Vol. 2: 388, 480, 483, 928
  Vol. 3: 98 f., 199, 517, 812, **826 f., 829 f., 832**, 844, 850, 1212
aipys **Vol. 1**: 465
airō **Vol. 1**: 701
  Vol. 2: 411
aisch- **Vol. 3**: 562
aischrokerdēs **Vol. 3: 564**
aischrologia **Vol. 3: 564**
aischron **Vol. 3**: 562
aischron estin **Vol. 3: 564**
aischros **Vol. 2**: 50, 476, 658
  Vol. 3: 562–564
aischrotēs **Vol. 3: 562**
aischynē **Vol. 2**: 212
  Vol. 3: 561, **562–564**
aischynesthai **Vol. 3**: 562
aischynō **Vol. 3: 562–564**
aischynomai **Vol. 3**: 564
aisthanomai **Vol. 2: 390–392, 408**
aisthēsis **Vol. 2: 390 f.**, 591
aisthētērion **Vol. 2**: 391
aisthētos **Vol. 1**: 523
  Vol. 2: 192
aitēma **Vol. 2: 855, 858**, 861
aiteō **Vol. 2: 855–858**, 859, 861, 868
  Vol. 3: 683
aiteomai **Vol. 2: 856**
aitia **Vol. 2: 137–139**
  Vol. 3: 573
aitiama **Vol. 2**: 138
aitiōma **Vol. 2: 137–139**
aition **Vol. 2**: 139
aitios **Vol. 2: 137 f.**
  Vol. 3: 215
akaireomai **Vol. 3**: 833, 837
akairos **Vol. 2**: 644
  Vol. 3: 833
akairōs **Vol. 3: 837 f.**
akakos **Vol. 1: 561, 563**
akantha **Vol. 1: 725 f.**
akanthinos **Vol. 1**: 725
akarpos **Vol. 1: 721, 723**
akatakalyptos **Vol. 2**: 212
akatalytos **Vol. 1**: 337
  Vol. 3: 177, 189

akatastasia **Vol. 2**: 780
akatharsia **Vol. 3: 102 f.**
akathartos **Vol. 1**: 500, 637
  Vol. 3: 102 f., 473, 475
akautēriastos **Vol. 2: 574**
Akeldaimach **Vol. 1: 93**
Akeldama **Vol. 1: 93**
Akeldamach **Vol. 1: 93**
Akeldamak **Vol. 1: 93**
akmaios **Vol. 2: 588**
akmazō **Vol. 2: 588**
akmē **Vol. 2**: 587 f.
akoē **Vol. 2: 172 f., 175**
akoloutheō **Vol. 1**: 324, **480–483**, 488, 493
  Vol. 2: 614, 658
  Vol. 3: 946
akolouthos **Vol. 1**: 484
akouō **Vol. 1**: 261
  Vol. 2: 172–180, 427, 443, 643, 812, 864
  Vol. 3: 113 f., 127, 173, 544, 573, 1161
akrasia **Vol. 1: 494–496**
akratēs **Vol. 1: 494–496**
akris **Vol. 1**: 119
akroatēs **Vol. 2: 172, 175, 177**, 554 f.
akrobystia **Vol. 1: 307, 309 f.**
  Vol. 2: 660
  Vol. 3: 1182, 1189
akrogōniaios **Vol. 1**: 541
  Vol. 3: 388–390, 393, 398 f.
alalētos **Vol. 2**: 424, 882, 884
alalos **Vol. 1**: 428
alaomai **Vol. 3**: 29
alazōn **Vol. 2**: 430, **435**
  Vol. 3: 28, 30–32
alazoneia **Vol. 1**: 228
  Vol. 3: 28–32
alazoneuomai **Vol. 3**: 29 f.
aleiphō **Vol. 1: 119–121**, 124, 471
  Vol. 2: 335, 712 f.
  Vol. 3: 1060
alektorophōnia **Vol. 2**: 136
alētheia **Vol. 1**: 90, 98, 708
  Vol. 2: 460, 468, 470, 472, 878
  Vol. 3: 72, 242, 316, 323, 575 f., 746, **874–878, 882–893**, 902, 1045, 1191, 1199, 1202
alēthēs **Vol. 3: 874–877, 882–884, 888–891, 893**
alētheuō **Vol. 3: 874, 877, 886–888**
alēthinos **Vol. 1**: 98
  Vol. 2: 280, 477, 724, 837, 878
  Vol. 3: 874, 877, 883 f., 888 f., 891, 893
alēthōs **Vol. 1**: 98
  Vol. 3: 462, **874, 877, 883,**

888, 893
alisgēmata **Vol. 2**: 286
Alkinoos **Vol. 2**: 233
allagma **Vol. 3**: 1196
allassō **Vol. 3**: 146, **166 f.**, 175
allēgoreō **Vol. 2: 743, 746, 755 f., 760**
allēgoria **Vol. 1**: 49
  Vol. 2: 743 f., 746, 748
allēlōn **Vol. 2**: 765
allēlous **Vol. 2**: 542
  Vol. 3: 353, 447
allogenēs **Vol. 1: 684 f.**, 687
  Vol. 2: 739, 742
  Vol. 3: 455 f.
allophylos **Vol. 1: 684 f.**
  Vol. 2: 349, **739, 742**
allos **Vol. 1**: 666, 684, 691
  Vol. 2: 423, 618, **739, 741 f.**, 744, 785 f.
  Vol. 3: 166, 185, 1080, 1176
allōs **Vol. 2: 739**
allotriepiskopos **Vol. 2: 742**
allotrioō **Vol. 1: 684**
allotrios **Vol. 1: 683–685**, 687
  Vol. 2: 739, 742
  Vol. 3: 400
alogos **Vol. 1**: 674
  Vol. 2: 476, 661
  Vol. 3: 1081, 1118
alōpēx **Vol. 1**: 118
Alypis **Vol. 3**: 160
amachos **Vol. 2**: 646
amēchanos **Vol. 1**: 107
amemptos **Vol. 2: 137, 139, 143–145**
  Vol. 3: 348, **923–925**
amemptōs **Vol. 2**: 139, **143 f.**
  Vol. 3: 924
amēn **Vol. 1: 97–100**
  Vol. 3: 742, 883, 1107
amerimnos **Vol. 1**: 278
ametamelētos **Vol. 1: 356 f.**
ametanoētos **Vol. 1: 357 f.**
  Vol. 2: 183
ametatheton **Vol. 3**: 1018
amethystos **Vol. 3: 396 f.**
amētōr **Vol. 1**: 616
ametros **Vol. 2**: 400, **402, 404**
amiantos **Vol. 1: 447 f.**
  Vol. 3: 923, 925
amnos **Vol. 2**: 194, **410–414**
  Vol. 3: 611, 925
amnos tou theou **Vol. 3: 611**
amōmētos **Vol. 3**: 923
amōmos **Vol. 2**: 144
  Vol. 3: 923–925
amōmotēs **Vol. 3: 924**
ampelōn **Vol. 3: 918 f.**
ampelos **Vol. 3**: 226, **918, 922 f.**
ampelourgos **Vol. 3: 919**
amphiballō **Vol. 1**: 504
amphisbēteō **Vol. 1**: 504
amphoteros **Vol. 3**: 172

amyētos **Vol. 3:** 679
ana **Vol. 1:** 373, 391, 413
  Vol. 2: 765
  Vol. 3: 1172, 1174, 1195, 1199
ana- **Vol. 3:** 231, 519, 1195
ana meros **Vol. 2: 303 f.**
ana meson **Vol. 1:** 373
anabainō **Vol. 2:** 42, 184 f., 199, 204, 209
  Vol. 3: 203, 242, 494, 591, 941, 946, 1180
anabasis **Vol. 3: 936**
anabioō **Vol. 3: 259**
anabiōsis **Vol. 1:** 184
  Vol. 3: 259
anabioskomai **Vol. 3: 259**
anablepō **Vol. 2:** 735
  Vol. 3: 519
anaboaō **Vol. 1: 410 f.**
anachōreō **Vol. 3:** 265
anadeiknymi **Vol. 3: 569**
anadeixis **Vol. 3: 569**
anagennaō **Vol. 1: 176, 178, 180 f.,** 184 f., 188
  Vol. 3: 215
anagennēsis **Vol. 1:** 178
anaginōskō **Vol. 1:** 243, **245,** 248
  Vol. 3: 485
anagnōsis **Vol. 1:** 245
anaitios **Vol. 2: 137, 139**
anakainizō **Vol. 2:** 670
anakainoō **Vol. 2: 670–673**
anakainoomai **Vol. 2:** 675
anakainōsis **Vol. 1:** 178, 185, 708
  Vol. 2: 670, 673
anakainousthai **Vol. 1:** 185
anakalyptō **Vol. 2: 212 f.**
  Vol. 3: 311
anakeimai **Vol. 3:** 589
anakekalymmenos **Vol. 2:** 213
anakephalaioomai **Vol. 2: 156 f.,** 163
anakephalaōsis **Vol. 2:** 163
anaklinomai **Vol. 3:** 589
anakremannymi **Vol. 1:** 391
anakrinō **Vol. 2:** 362, 364
analambanō **Vol. 2:** 203
  Vol. 3: 747, 749
analēmpsis **Vol. 1:** 738
  Vol. 3: 747, 749
analmos **Vol. 3:** 443
analogia **Vol. 1:** 49 f.
analos **Vol. 3: 443**
analyō **Vol. 2:** 925
anamenō **Vol. 2:** 245
anamimnēskesthai **Vol. 3:** 231
anamimnēskō **Vol. 3: 230, 232, 239–241, 243**
anamnēsis **Vol. 1:** 370, 483
  Vol. 2: 533, 717
  Vol. 3: 230 f., 238 f., 241,

243–245, 247, 260
ananeoō **Vol. 2: 674, 676**
ananeoomai **Vol. 2:** 675
ananēphō **Vol. 1:** 514 f.
anangellō **Vol. 3: 44–48,** 68
anank- **Vol. 2:** 663
anankaios **Vol. 2:** 663
anankastōs **Vol. 2:** 663
anankazō **Vol. 2: 663, 669**
  Vol. 3: 951
anankē **Vol. 2: 662–664**
  Vol. 3: 1054
anapauma **Vol. 3: 255**
anapauō **Vol. 3: 254, 256–258**
anapausis **Vol. 2:** 281
  Vol. 3: 254–256, 407
anapherō **Vol. 3:** 435, 1195 f.
anapiptō **Vol. 3:** 589
anaplēroō **Vol. 1: 733 f.,** 736, **738, 340 f.**
anaplērōsis **Vol. 1:** 735
anapologētos **Vol. 2: 137–139**
anapsychō **Vol. 3: 686**
anapsyxis **Vol. 3:** 148, **686**
anaseiō **Vol. 3: 556, 558**
anaskolopizō **Vol. 1:** 391
anastasis **Vol. 1:** 434,445
  Vol. 2: 504, 924
  Vol. 3: 167, 231, **259, 261, 276, 278** f., 280, 299, 304, 439, 558, 579, 602, 677 f., 683, 936, 1189
anastatēria **Vol. 3:** 261
anastauroō **Vol. 1: 391, 394, 397**
  Vol. 2: 291
anastrephō **Vol. 1:** 354
  Vol. 3: 933
anastrephomai **Vol. 3: 933**
anastrophē **Vol. 3: 933, 935**
anatassomai **Vol. 1:** 576
anatellō **Vol. 2:** 557
anathema **Vol. 1: 413–415,** 418
  Vol. 2: 516, 520, 741, 896
  Vol. 3: 171
anathēma **Vol. 1: 413 f.**
anathematizō **Vol. 1: 413, 415**
anatlōn **Vol. 3:** 178
anatolē **Vol. 3:** 178, 867
anatrechō **Vol. 2:** 655
anax **Vol. 2:** 372
anaxios **Vol. 3: 348**
anaxiōs **Vol. 3: 349**
anazaō **Vol. 3: 259, 278**
anchisteuō **Vol. 3:** 191
anchisteus **Vol. 3:** 191
andrapodistēs **Vol. 3:** 380
andreia **Vol. 1:** 501
  Vol. 3: 354, 925
andrizesche **Vol. 2: 563**
andrizomai **Vol. 2: 562 f., 571**
anechō **Vol. 2:** 776
anechomai **Vol. 2: 764–766**
  Vol. 3: 165, 364

anēkō **Vol. 3:** 930
anektos **Vol. 2: 765, 767**
anektoteros **Vol. 2:** 767
aneleēmōn **Vol. 2: 594, 597**
anēleēs **Vol. 2:** 594
anelēmpthē **Vol. 2:** 203
aneleos **Vol. 2: 594, 597**
anemos **Vol. 2:** 155
  Vol. 3: 690, 770, **1000 f.,** 1198
anenenkai **Vol. 3:** 435
anenklētos **Vol. 2: 137, 139**
  Vol. 3: 923–925, 932
aneōgmenos **Vol. 2:** 727
anepilēmptos **Vol. 2: 750**
anēr **Vol. 1:** 92, 546, 550
  Vol. 2: 91, 161 f., 234, 466, 561, **562–564,** 565, **571,** 581, 606, 615, 634, 699
  Vol. 3: 172, 223, 361, 636, 680, 687, 1055, 1075, 1117
anēthon **Vol. 2: 210 f.**
anexeraunētos **Vol. 3: 532 f.**
angel- **Vol. 3:** 68
angelia **Vol. 3: 44–47,** 67
angellō **Vol. 2:** 107
  Vol. 3: 44–46, 48, 50 f., 54, 68, 232
angeloi Dios **Vol. 3:** 49
angelos **Vol. 1:** 101 f., **104,** 127
  Vol. 2: 107, 502, 578, 791
  Vol. 3: 45 f., 49, 990
anhamartētos **Vol. 3:** 579
anhistēmi **Vol. 2:** 680, 925
  Vol. 3: 178, **259, 261,** 267 f., **275 f.,** 279, 281, 307, 624
anhypokritos **Vol. 1:** 351
  Vol. 2: 468–470
anhypostatos **Vol. 1:** 710
aniptos **Vol. 1:** 153
ankalē **Vol. 1:** 239
ankos **Vol. 1:** 239
anō **Vol. 1:** 179
  Vol. 2: 184, **187,** 191 f., 329, 619
  Vol. 3: 1199
anochē **Vol. 2: 765–767,** 771
anoētos **Vol. 3: 122, 124, 126, 129**
anoia **Vol. 3:** 122 f., 125, 128
anoignymi **Vol. 2:** 726
anoigō **Vol. 2: 726–728,** 730
  Vol. 3: 543, 950
anoixis **Vol. 2:** 726
anomia **Vol. 1:** 125, 556, 639
  Vol. 2: 438, 440, 447–449, 709
  Vol. 3: 137, 505, 573, 584, 717
anomos **Vol. 2: 438, 440, 445, 447, 449,** 468
  Vol. 3: 137, 574
anomōs **Vol. 2: 446**
anosios **Vol. 2: 236 f.**

341

anōthen Vol. 1: 179
 Vol. 2: 187 f.
 Vol. 3: 1178
ant- Vol. 1: 645
antagōnizomai Vol. 1: **644**
antallagē Vol. 3: 1196
antallagma Vol. 2: 835
 Vol. 3: 153, **166, 174**
antanaplēroō Vol. 1: 741
antapodidōmi Vol. 3: 134 f.
antapodoma Vol. 3: 134 f.
antapodosis Vol. 3: 134 f.
anthos Vol. 3: 523, 867
anthrax Vol. 3: **396**
anthrōpareskos Vol. 2: **815, 817**
anthrōpinos Vol. 2: **564 f.**, 661
 Vol. 3: 719, 995
anthrōpologia Vol. 1: 682
anthrōpos Vol. 1: 50, 162, 192,
 335, 374, 377, 401, 407,
 535, 701
 Vol. 2: 155, 160, 165, 194,
 216, 233, 337, 376, 380,
 385, 387, 447, 456, 473,
 502–504, 510, 514, 543,
 562–566, 571, 607, 630, 672,
 675 f., 723, 781, 819 f., 840,
 900, 912
 Vol. 3: 127, 147, 174, 181,
 195, 505, 530, 539, 607,
 613, 617, 620, 630, 632,
 665, 680, 684, 718, 734,
 770, 775, 831, 1144, 1176,
 1190, 1194, 1200
anthypatos Vol. 1: 270
anti Vol. 1: 124, 400
 Vol. 2: 119
 Vol. 3: 195–197, 611,
 1171 f., 1174, 1179 f., 1196 f.
anti hēmōn Vol. 3: 1197
anti pollōn Vol. 3: 195, 611,
 1180
Antichristos Vol. 1: **124**
 Vol. 2: 435
antidikos Vol. 1: **553 f.**
 Vol. 3: 173, 469
antiloidoreō Vol. 3: **346**
antilytron Vol. 3: **189,** 195, **197,**
 1180, 1197
antimisthia Vol. 3: 197
Antiocheus Vol. 1: 361
antipsychon Vol. 3: 195
antipsychos Vol. 3: 157
antis Vol. 3: 1179
antitheos Vol. 1: 124
antitypon Vol. 3: **903–906**
antitypos Vol. 3: **888, 903**
aoidē Vol. 3: 672
aoidos Vol. 3: 672
aoratos Vol. 2: 768
 Vol. 3: 128
ap- Vol. 2: 241, 856
ap' allōn Vol. 3: 1176
apaideutos Vol. 3: 1026

apaiteō Vol. 2: **855, 858**
apallassō Vol. 3: 166 f., **173 f.**
apallotrioō Vol. 1: 684 f.
 Vol. 2: **742**
apangellō Vol. 3: **44–48,** 68,
 1046
apantaō Vol. 1: **324 f.**
apantēsis Vol. 1: **324 f.**
 Vol. 3: 603
aparabatos Vol. 3: **583–585**
aparaklētos Vol. 1: 89
aparaskeuastos Vol. 3: **119**
aparchē Vol. 1: 166, 669
 Vol. 2: 40, 288, 883 f.
 Vol. 3: 72, 277, 303, **415–
 417,** 437, 701, 1078
aparneomai Vol. 1: **454 f.**
apataō Vol. 2: **457–461**
apatē Vol. 2: **457–459,** 843 f.
 Vol. 3: 875
apatheia Vol. 3: 719
apathēs Vol. 3: 724
apatōr Vol. 1: **615 f.,** 619, **621**
apaugasma Vol. 2: 284, **289 f.,**
 293
apechō Vol. 2: 433
apechomai Vol. 2: 765
apedokimasan Vol. 1: 74
apeirastos Vol. 3: **798 f.,** 802,
 809
apeiron Vol. 2: 244
apeiros Vol. 3: 840
apeitheia Vol. 1: **588 f.,** 593
apeitheō Vol. 1: **588 f.,** 591, 593
apeithēs Vol. 1: **588 f.,** 593
apekdechomai Vol. 1: **289**
 Vol. 2: **244 f.,** 774, 883
 Vol. 3: **745**
apekdyō Vol. 1: 314 f.
apekdyomai Vol. 1: **314**
apekdysis Vol. 1: 314 f.
apeleutheros Vol. 1: **715, 717 f.**
 Vol. 3: 598
apelpizō Vol. 2: **238, 241,** 244
apēlthen Vol. 2: 217
aperchomai Vol. 1: **320 f.,** 608
 Vol. 2: 217
aperitmētos Vol. 1: **307, 309**
apestalmenos Vol. 1: 127, 581
apestrepsen Vol. 2: 215
aph' hymōn Vol. 3: 1176
aphaireō Vol. 3: 153
aphanizō Vol. 2: 433, 831
aphesis Vol. 1: 160, **697 f.,
 700–703**
 Vol. 2: 533, 667
 Vol. 3: 52, 55, 191, 1178,
 1184
aphiēmi Vol. 1: **697 f., 700–703**
 Vol. 2: 668
 Vol. 3: 167, 172, 188
aphistēmi Vol. 1: **606–608,** 611
 Vol. 3: 585 f.
aphobōs Vol. 1: 181

aphōmoiōmenos Vol. 2: 505
aphomoioō Vol. 2: **500–502,**
 505 f.
aphorizō Vol. 1: **472 f.**
aphormē Vol. 1: 336
Aphroditē Vol. 3: 318
aphrōn Vol. 2: 766
 Vol. 3: **1023–1026**
aphrosynē Vol. 3: **1023–1026**
aphtharsia Vol. 1: **467–470**
 Vol. 2: 480, 924
 Vol. 3: 281, 302, 995
aphthartos Vol. 1: **467 f.**
 Vol. 3: 1201
aphthoros Vol. 3: 1071
apisteō Vol. 1: 591, **594**
apistia Vol. 1: **594**
 Vol. 3: 227
apistos Vol. 1: **594,** 602
 Vol. 2: 457
apo Vol. 1: 51, 126, 181, 284,
 320, 377, 414, 476, 487,
 607, 622 f., 684, 697
 Vol. 2: 35, 55, 91, 172, 175,
 222, 241, 244 f., 586, 780,
 789, 912
 Vol. 2: 173, 181, 188, 204,
 309 f., 318, 375, 416, 773,
 828 f., 834, **1171–1175, 1178,**
 1180 f., **1188 f., 1198,** 1214
apo merous Vol. 2: 303 f.
apoblepō Vol. 2: 835
apodechomai Vol. 3: **744, 746**
apodeiknymi Vol. 3: **570 f.**
apodeixis Vol. 1: 588
 Vol. 3: **570**
apodekateuō Vol. 2: **693 f.**
 Vol. 3: **851**
apodekatoō Vol. 2: **693 f.**
 Vol. 3: **851**
apodektos Vol. 3: **744–746**
apodēmeō Vol. 2: **790**
apodidōmi Vol. 2: 115
 Vol. 3: **134–136,** 145, 754
apodochē Vol. 3: **744, 746**
apodokimasthēnai Vol. 3: 723
apodokimazō Vol. 3: **808 f.**
apogegrammenos Vol. 1: 304
apoginomai Vol. 3: **181**
apoginōskō Vol. 2: 244
apographō Vol. 1: 304
apoikesia Vol. 1: 685
apoikia Vol. 1: 685
apoikismos Vol. 1: 685
apoinos Vol. 3: 152
apokalypuis Vol. 1: 50, 737
 Vol. 2: 517
 Vol. 3: 310 f., **313–316,** 502
apokalyptō Vol. 2: 212
 Vol. 3: **309–312, 314,** 316,
 321
apokaradokeō Vol. 2: 244
apokaradokia Vol. 2: **238,
 244–246**

Vol. 3: 745
apokatallassō **Vol. 3: 166 f.,
171 f.**
apokatastasis **Vol. 1:** 521
Vol. 2: 920
Vol. 3: 146–148, 192
apokathistanō **Vol. 3: 146**
apokathistēmi **Vol. 3: 146 f.**
apokekrymmenēn **Vol. 2:** 217
apokoptō **Vol. 2:** 418
apokrypha **Vol. 2:** 214
apokryphos **Vol. 1:** 50
Vol. 2: 214–216
apokryptō **Vol. 1:** 50
Vol. 2: 214–217
apokteinō **Vol. 1: 429 f.,** 463
Vol. 3: 172
apokyeō **Vol. 1:** 178, 187
apolambanō **Vol. 3: 747, 751**
apolauō **Vol. 3:** 377
apolaustikos **Vol. 2:** 475
apolegō **Vol. 2:** 244
apōleia **Vol. 1: 462–466,** 471
Vol. 2: 126
Vol. 3: 1187
Apollōn **Vol. 1:** 463
apollymi **Vol. 1: 462–464,** 471
Vol. 3: 530
apollyō **Vol. 1:** 463
Vol. 2: 460
Apollyōn **Vol. 1: 462–464,** 471
apolō **Vol. 1:** 74
apologeomai **Vol. 1:** 51
apologia **Vol. 1:** 51
Vol. 3: 38, 97, 1018
apolouō **Vol. 1: 150–152**
apolouomai **Vol. 1:** 701
apolyō **Vol. 1: 505**
Vol. 3: 177, 188 f., 534
apolytrōsis **Vol. 1:** 268, 301,
701
Vol. 2: 388, 839, 883
Vol. 3: 189 f., 193, 199 f.
apōn **Vol. 2:** 899
apopheugō **Vol. 1: 558 f.**
apophthengesthai **Vol. 3: 1080**
apoplanaō **Vol. 2: 457, 459**
apoplanaomai **Vol. 2: 457, 459**
apopnigō **Vol. 1:** 226
aposkiasma **Vol. 3: 553–556**
apostasia **Vol. 1:** 51, **606 f.**
apostasion **Vol. 1: 505 f. 606 f.**
Vol. 3: 1064
apostasis **Vol. 1:** 606
apostatēs **Vol. 1:** 606
apostellō **Vol. 1: 126–128,
133 f., 136,** 332
apostereō **Vol. 3: 379 f.**
apostolē **Vol. 2:** 111, 299
apostolos **Vol. 1: 126–130,
133 f., 136,** 199, 275
Vol. 2: 695
Vol. 3: 48, 52, 767
apostrephō **Vol. 1: 354 f.,** 608

Vol. 2: 215
aposynagōgos **Vol. 1:** 181
apothanōn **Vol. 2:** 375
apothaumazō **Vol. 2:** 621
apothesis **Vol. 1: 314 f.**
Vol. 3: 815
apothnēskō **Vol. 1:** 327, **430 f.,
435,** 443
Vol. 3: 375, 1197
apotinassō **Vol. 3: 560 f.**
apotithēmi **Vol. 1: 314 f.**
Vol. 3: 886
apotrepō **Vol. 3: 902 f.**
apotrepomai **Vol. 3: 903**
aproskopos **Vol. 2: 705–707**
aprosōpolēmptōs **Vol. 1: 585,
587**
apseudēs **Vol. 2: 470, 472**
Vol. 3: 71, 876
apsinthia **Vol. 2:** 27
apsinthion **Vol. 2:** 27
apsinthos **Vol. 2: 27–29**
Vol. 3: 737
ar- **Vol. 2:** 815
Vol. 3: 349, 834, 1004
ara **Vol. 1: 416,** 418
Vol. 2: 683
araomai **Vol. 1:** 416
arariskō **Vol. 3: 925**
archai **Vol. 2: 608 f.,** 614
archaia **Vol. 1:** 165
archaios **Vol. 1: 164 f., 167,**
508, 666
Vol. 2: 671, 713
archangelos **Vol. 1: 101, 103**
Vol. 3: 622
archē **Vol. 1:** 64 f., **164–167,
169,** 377, 383, 536, 588,
628, 665, 712
Vol. 2: 49, 59, 61, 64, 157 f.,
162, 452, 608, 614, 669, 912
Vol. 3: 215, 416, 723, 1118,
1204
archēgos **Vol. 1: 164 f., 168,**
668 f.
Vol. 2: 64, 505
Vol. 3: 199, 215, 723
archētypos **Vol. 3: 554, 904**
archieraomai **Vol. 2:** 234
archierateuō **Vol. 2:** 234
archieratikos **Vol. 3: 32, 40**
archiereus **Vol. 1:** 198 f.
Vol. 2: 232–236, 238
Vol. 3: 32, 35, 39 f., 44, 162
archierōsynē **Vol. 2:** 234
archipoimēn **Vol. 3: 564, 568**
architektōn **Vol. 1: 279,** 377
Vol. 2: 555
architelōnēs **Vol. 3: 755, 758**
archō **164 f., 167, 169**
Vol. 3: 509, 822
archōn **Vol. 1:** 105, **164 f.,
168 f.,** 407, 536 f., 665
Vol. 2: 609, 777

Vol. 3: 199, 469 f.
arēn **Vol. 2: 410 f.**
Arēs **Vol. 3:** 318
areskeia **Vol. 2: 814 f.,** 817
areskō **Vol. 1:** 537
Vol. 2: 814–816, 820
Vol. 3: 264, 925
areskos **Vol. 2: 815**
arestos **Vol. 2: 814–816**
Vol. 3: 925
aretē **Vol. 1:** 459, 645
Vol. 2: 61, 290, 477, 815
Vol. 3: 138, 354, 562, 776,
923, **925–927,** 932, 936,
1148
argia **Vol. 3:** 407, 409
argos **Vol. 1:** 73
Vol. 2: 96
argyrion **Vol. 2: 96,** 845, **851**
argyros **Vol. 2: 96,** 845
argyrous **Vol. 2: 96**
ari- **Vol. 3: 925**
aristeros **Vol. 2: 148**
aristos **Vol. 3: 925**
arithmeō **Vol. 2: 703**
arithmos **Vol. 1:** 665
Vol. 2: 683 f., 703
arkeisthai **Vol. 3: 727**
arkeō **Vol. 3: 726–728,** 730
arketos **Vol. 3: 727**
arkos **Vol. 1:** 118
arneomai **Vol. 1:** 347, **454–456,**
608
Vol. 3: 1050
arnion **Vol. 2: 410–413**
Vol. 3: 568
arnos **Vol. 2:** 413
arōma **Vol. 2:** 295
arrabōn **Vol. 1:** 372, 375,
638 f.
Vol. 2: 39 f., 44
Vol. 3: 72, 499, 701
arrēn **Vol. 2:** 569 f.
arrhētos **Vol. 2:** 763
arrostēma **Vol. 3: 997**
arrōsteō **Vol. 3: 997**
arrostia **Vol. 3: 997**
arsēn **Vol. 2:** 562 f., **569 f.**
arsenokoitēs **Vol. 2: 569 f.**
Artemisia **Vol. 2:** 27
arthmos **Vol. 2:** 683
arti **Vol. 1:** 282
Vol. 2: 756
Vol. 3: 409, **833 f., 837,** 850
artios **Vol. 3:** 348, **349 f.,** 352
artiōs **Vol. 3:** 350
artos **Vol. 1: 249,** 251, 253, 586
Vol. 2: 194, 520, 524, 530
Vol. 3: 814
artynō **Vol. 3:** 349
artyō **Vol. 3:** 349, 445, 449
asaleutos **Vol. 3: 558–560**
asbestinos **Vol. 3:** 111
asbestos **Vol. 3: 110 f.,** 447

aschēmōn **Vol. 3:** 1195
asebeia **Vol. 1:** 622
　Vol. 2: 91–94
　Vol. 3: 49, 573, 576, 580,
　584
asebeō **Vol. 2:** 93
asebēs **Vol. 2: 91–95,** 468
　Vol. 3: 574 f., 577, 580, 995,
　1197
aselgeia **Vol. 2:** 587
askeō **Vol. 1: 494 f.,** 503
askēsis **Vol. 2:** 659
askētēs **Vol. 1:** 495
asma **Vol. 3:** 673
asophos **Vol. 3: 1026**
asōtōs **Vol. 2:** 480
aspasmos **Vol. 1: 206 f.**
aspazomai **Vol. 1: 206, 213,**
　218
asphaleia **Vol. 1: 663 f.**
　Vol. 3: 771
asphalēs **Vol. 1:** 660, **663**
asphalizō **Vol. 1: 663**
asphalōs **Vol. 1: 663**
aspilos **Vol. 3: 923–925,** 932
aspis **Vol. 3:** 966
astēr **Vol. 2:** 27, 555, 557
　Vol. 3: 734–737
astheneia **Vol. 3:** 281, **993–996,**
　998, 1190
astheneō **Vol. 3: 993–995,** 997
asthenēs **Vol. 2:** 828
　Vol. 3: 993–995, 1000
asthenōn **Vol. 3: 993–995**
asthenountes **Vol. 3:** 994 f.
astocheō **Vol. 1:** 608
astorgos **Vol. 2: 538 f.,** 542
astrapē **Vol. 3: 1000 f.**
astrologoi tou ouranou **Vol. 2:**
　555
astrologos **Vol. 2:** 555
astron **Vol. 3: 734–737**
asynetos **Vol. 3: 131 f.**
ata **Vol. 2:** 349
ataraxia **Vol. 1:** 68
atē **Vol. 2:** 349
atelestos **Vol. 3:** 679
atenizō **Vol. 3:** 519, **520**
athanasia **Vol. 1:** 58, **430–432,**
　435
　Vol. 2: 477
　Vol. 3: 302
athanatos **Vol. 2:** 232, 476, 480
Athēna **Vol. 3:** 1036, 1144
Athēnaiōn **Vol. 2:** 847
atheos **Vol. 2:** 639
atheotēs **Vol. 2:** 92
atheteō **Vol. 1: 74,** 462
athetēsis **Vol. 1:** 337
athetēsō **Vol. 1:** 74
athleō **Vol. 1:** 645 f.
athlēsis **Vol. 1:** 645 f.
athlētēs **Vol. 1:** 646
athlon **Vol. 1:** 648

athōoō **Vol. 3:** 152
athroizō **Vol. 2:** 31, **33**
atimazō **Vol. 2: 48, 50**
atimazomai **Vol. 2:** 50
atimia **Vol. 2: 48–50**
　Vol. 3: 281
atimos **Vol. 2: 48–50**
atomos **Vol. 2:** 925
atychēma **Vol. 3:** 577
aucheō **Vol. 1:** 227
augazō **Vol. 2: 289,293**
augē **Vol. 1:** 711
　Vol. 2: 289 f.
aulē **Vol. 3:** 565, 568
auleō **Vol. 2:** 436
autarkeia **Vol. 2:** 820
　Vol. 3: 727 f.
autarkēs **Vol. 3: 727**
authentein **Vol. 3:** 1066
auto **Vol. 2:** 363
autokatakritos **Vol. 2:** 363, **365**
autolexei **Vol. 1:** 580
automaton **Vol. 2:** 657
automatos **Vol. 1:** 723
autos **Vol. 1:** 181, 400 f., 569,
　591, 669, 704, 707 f., 712,
　731, 741
　Vol. 2: 288, 290, 387, 433,
　437, 452, 477, 489, 495,
　502–504, 586, 618 f., 661,
　692, 733, 735, 766, 772,
　781, 839, 882, 900 f.
　Vol. 3: 53, 71 f., 128, 166,
　168, 170–174, 180, 185,
　195, 207, 210, 218, 228,
　242, 258, 264, 267, 276,
　278, 392, 420, 509, 519,
　603, 660, 711 f., 716, 765,
　828, 846, 850, 892, 908,
　925, 1018, 1022, 1073,
　1177–1180, 1182 f., 1186,
　1188, 1194, 1199, 1201,
　1210–1214
auxanō **Vol. 1:** 732
　Vol. 2: 128–130
auxēsis **Vol. 2: 128**
auxō **Vol. 2:** 128 f.
axioō **Vol. 3:** 348
axios **Vol. 3:** 348 f., 352, 673,
　1157
axiōs **Vol. 3:** 55, **348 f.,** 933,
　944
azyma **Vol. 2: 463**
azymos **Vol. 2: 461, 463**

Babylōn **Vol. 1: 140**
bainō **Vol. 1:** 658
　Vol. 2: 184, 196
balantion **Vol. 1: 142**
ballantion **Vol. 1: 142 f.**
ballō **Vol. 1:** 376, 454
　Vol. 2: 299, 743
　Vol. 3: 468
baptisma **Vol. 1: 144, 146,**

　149 f., 160, 703
　Vol. 3: 52, 55
baptismos **Vol. 1: 144, 146,**
　149 f.
　Vol. 3: 770
baptistēs **Vol. 1:** 145, 149 f.
　Vol. 3: 1208
baptizō **Vol. 1: 143–146, 149,**
　152 f., 224 f.
　Vol. 2: 672
　Vol. 3: 205, 447, 501, **1172,**
　1187 f., 1196, **1207–1210,**
　1213 f.
baptizomenos **Vol. 3: 1208**
baptizōn **Vol. 3: 1208**
baptō **Vol. 1: 143–145,** 152,
　160, 224
barbaros **Vol. 2:** 790
bareisthai **Vol. 1:** 261
bareō **Vol. 1: 260 f.**
bareōs **Vol. 1:** 261
baros **Vol. 1: 260 f.,** 263
barynō **Vol. 1: 260 f.**
barys **Vol. 1: 260–262**
　Vol. 3: 1162
baryteros **Vol. 1:** 261
barytimos **Vol. 1:** 260
basanismos **Vol. 3: 855 f.**
basanistēs **Vol. 3:** 758, **855 f.**
basanizō **Vol. 3: 855 f.**
basanos **Vol. 3:** 353, **855 f.,** 859
basileia **Vol. 1:** 298, 300–302,
　329, 369, 508, 657
　Vol. 2: 54, 74, 112, 192,
　234, **372–382, 386–388,** 502,
　580, 613, 714
　Vol. 3: 52, 55 f., 181, 511,
　584, 746, 832
basileia tōn ouranōn **Vol. 2:**
　192, 376, **381,** 502, 714
　Vol. 3: 55, 181
basileia tou theou **Vol. 2:** 381 f.,
　386–388
　Vol. 3: 511, 746, 832
basilēiē **Vol. 2:** 373
basileion hierateuma **Vol. 3:** 37
basileios **Vol. 1:** 305
　Vol. 2: 372 f., 380
basileuō **Vol. 2:** 120, **372 f.,**
　377 f., 380 f.,
basileus **Vol. 1:** 665
　Vol. 2: 69, **372 f., 377 f., 389,**
　449, 511, 615, 781
　Vol. 3: 608
basilikos **Vol. 3:** 372 f., 449
basilis **Vol. 2:** 373
basilissa **Vol. 2: 372 f., 381,** 511
basis **Vol. 2:** 415
baskainō **Vol. 2: 552, 559**
bassa **Vol. 2:** 197
bastazō **Vol. 1:** 403
bathos **Vol. 2: 197–199,** 204
bathy **Vol. 2:** 197
bathys **Vol. 2: 197 f.**

Vol. 3: 1199
battalogeō Vol. 2: 795
bdelygma Vol. 2: 284
bdelygma tēs erēmōseōs Vol. 1:
74 f.
Vol. 2: 912
Vol. 3: 1006, 1008
bebaioō Vol. 1: 658 f.
Vol. 3: 924
bebaios Vol. 1: 658–660, 663
bebaiōsis Vol. 1: 658 f.
Beelzeboub Vol. 3: 468 f.
Beelzeboul Vol. 3: 344, 469,
472
Beelzebul Vol. 3: 468
Beezeboul Vol. 3: 468 f., 472,
476
Belial Vol. 3: 468
Beliar Vol. 3: 468, 476
belos Vol. 3: 959, 966
bēma Vol. 2: 362, 369
Vol. 3: 322
bēma podos Vol. 2: 369
bēryllos Vol. 3: 396 f.
bēssa Vol. 2: 197
Bēthleem Vol. 1: 169
bia Vol. 2: 601
Vol. 3: 574, 711, 925
biaios Vol. 3: 711, 987
biastēs Vol. 3: 603, 711 f., 718
biazō Vol. 2: 383
Vol. 3: 603, 711
biazomai Vol. 3: 712, 718
biblion Vol. 1: 243 f., 248
Vol. 3: 1120
biblos Vol. 1: 65, 181, 242–244,
248
Vol. 2: 189
Vol. 3: 490, 656
biē Vol. 3: 353
bioō Vol. 2: 474 f.
bios Vol. 1: 460, 640
Vol. 2: 474 f., 476–478,
845 f.
Vol. 3: 32, 839, 935
biōtikos Vol. 1: 278
Vol. 2: 474 f.
blaisos Vol. 2: 414
blapsis Vol. 3: 340
blaptō Vol. 3: 340
blasphēmeō Vol. 1: 413
Vol. 2: 143
Vol. 3: 340–342, 344, 346,
347, 364, 471, 473, 696
blasphēmia Vol. 3: 341 f., 344 f.
blasphēmos Vol. 3: 27, 341 f.,
345
blastanō Vol. 3: 865
blepō Vol. 1: 602, 713
Vol. 2: 142, 243, 488, 756,
914
Vol. 3: 126, 511 f., 515, 517,
520
Boanērges Vol. 2: 652

boaō Vol. 1: 410–412
Vol. 2: 855
Vol. 3: 53, 55, 118
boē Vol. 1: 410 f.
Vol. 2: 855
boēthos Vol. 2: 576
Vol. 3: 178, 210
bōmos Vol. 3: 418, 431
borboros Vol. 3: 679
boskō Vol. 2: 210, 411
botanē Vol. 2: 210 f.
boulē Vol. 1: 292, 693
Vol. 2: 149, 819
Vol. 3: 1015–1018, 1149
boulēma Vol. 3: 1015, 1017 f.
bouleuomai Vol. 1: 430, 537
Vol. 3: 1157
boulomai Vol. 1: 533 f., 569
Vol. 3: 1015–1018, 1019–
1021, 1023
bous Vol. 1: 115
brabeion Vol. 1: 470, 644 f.,
647–649
brabeuō Vol. 1: 648, 652
brabeus Vol. 1: 648
brachys Vol. 2: 502, 643
brechō Vol. 3: 1000 f.
brephos Vol. 1: 160, 280 f.,
283 f.
briaros Vol. 3: 27
brithō Vol. 3: 27
brochē Vol. 3: 1000 f.
brōma Vol. 2: 264, 268 f., 277
brōmata Vol. 3: 766
brontē Vol. 3: 1000, 1002
brōsimos Vol. 3: 268
brōsis Vol. 2: 268 f., 831
Vol. 3: 1179
brychō Vol. 2: 416 f., 421, 424
brygmos Vol. 2: 421
byblos Vol. 1: 243

chair- Vol. 3: 817
chaire Vol. 2: 356, 358
chairein Vol. 2: 356, 358, 777,
781
chairete Vol. 2: 356, 358
chairō Vol. 1: 206, 246 f., 739
Vol. 2: 352–355, 356–359,
420, 436
chalaza Vol. 3: 1000, 1004
chalepos Vol. 1: 419 f.
chalkēdōn Vol. 3: 396 f.
chalkeus Vol. 2: 96
chalkion Vol. 2: 96
chalkolibanon Vol. 2: 97
chalkos Vol. 2: 96
char- Vol. 3: 817
chara Vol. 1: 400, 459 f., 731,
741
Vol. 2: 115, 355, 356–359,
388, 420, 423, 431, 433
Vol. 3: 1180
charagma Vol. 1: 114

Vol. 2: 573–575
charaktēr Vol. 1: 712
Vol. 2: 284, 288–290, 292
charassō Vol. 2: 288, 573–575
Vol. 3: 951
charax Vol. 3: 951 f.
charis Vol. 1: 52, 112, 247,
300, 571, 601, 739
Vol. 2: 115–124, 131, 356,
360, 543, 546, 614, 780
Vol. 3: 252, 717, 746, 817,
854, 889, 1151, 1179
charisamenos Vol. 2: 116
charisma Vol. 1: 52, 300
Vol. 2: 39, 42, 79, 115, 118–
124, 172, 499
Vol. 3: 81, 702 f., 706 f., 927,
1091, 1167
charitēs Vol. 2: 115
charitoō Vol. 2: 115 f., 118 f.,
122
charizomai Vol. 1: 703
Vol. 2: 115 f., 118 f., 122
Vol. 3: 72, 210
charma Vol. 2: 115
cheilos Vol. 2: 740
cheir Vol. 1: 475, 478
Vol. 2: 144, 146, 148–151,
153, 367, 710
Vol. 3: 102, 475, 696, 716 f.,
763, 1148, 1174, 1182
cheires Vol. 2: 148 f.
cheirographon Vol. 3: 1199
cheiropoiētos Vol. 3: 185, 793,
888
cheirothesia Vol. 2: 153
cheirotoneō Vol. 1: 471, 478
cheirotonia Vol. 2: 153
cheō Vol. 1: 520
Vol. 2: 853
chēra Vol. 3: 228, 549, 1055,
1058, 1065, 1073–1076
chēreia Vol. 3: 1074
chernētis Vol. 3: 875
chēros Vol. 3: 1073
cheroub Vol. 1: 279
cheroubeim, cheroubein Vol. 1:
279
cheroubim, cheroubin Vol. 1:
279
chiliades Vol. 2: 698 f.
chiliarchos Vol. 1: 666
Vol. 2: 489, 699
chilias Vol. 2: 389, 690, 697–
700, 703, 734, 795, 809, 887,
901, 931
Vol. 3: 179, 277, 305, 417,
470 f., 500
chilioi Vol. 1: 52
Vol. 2: 697. 699 f., 703 f.
chiōn Vol. 3: 1000, 1004
chliaros Vol. 1: 317–319
chliarotēs Vol. 1: 318
chliō Vol. 1: 318

chloē **Vol. 2:** 27
chlōros **Vol. 1:** 205
Chobar **Vol. 3:** 986
choikos **Vol. 1:** 520
choiros **Vol. 1:** 117
cholē **Vol. 2:** 27 f.
cholos **Vol. 1:** 107
chōlos **Vol. 2:** 415
chōra **Vol. 1:** 741
   Vol. 3: 1008
Chōrēb **Vol. 3:** 1013
chōreō **Vol. 1:** 728, **741 f.**
chōria **Vol. 2:** 807
chōrion **Vol. 1:** 93
   Vol. 2: 845
chōris **Vol. 2:** 446
chōrizō **Vol. 3:** 172 f., 188 f.,
   534 f., 537, 539, 1064, 1070,
   1072, 1164, 1195
chōros **Vol. 1:** 728, 741
chortasma **Vol. 1: 743 f.**
chortazō **Vol. 1:** 728, **743 f.**
   Vol. 2: 211
chortos **Vol. 1: 743 f.**
   Vol. 2: 210 f.
   Vol. 3: 523
chous **Vol. 1: 520**
Chouthaios **Vol. 3:** 450, 456
chraomai **Vol. 3:** 599, 835
chrē **Vol. 2:** 845
   Vol. 3: 324, **956–958**
chreia **Vol. 3: 956–958**
chrēma **Vol. 1:** 138, 465
   Vol. 2: 829, 844, **845,** 852
   Vol. 3: 324, 403, 604
chrēmata **Vol. 3: 324**
chrēmatismos **Vol. 3: 324 f.**
chrēmatizō **Vol. 3: 324 f.**
chrēsmos **Vol. 3:** 324
chrēsteuomai **Vol. 2: 105**
chrēstologia **Vol. 1:** 212
chrēston **Vol. 2:** 105
chrēstos **Vol. 2:** 98, 103, **105 f.,**
   281, 335, 343, 659, 714
   Vol. 3: 882
chrēstotēs **Vol. 2: 105–107,** 766,
   770 f.
   Vol. 3: 227
chrēzō **Vol. 3: 956–958**
chrima **Vol. 1:** 121
chriō **Vol. 1:** 53, **119–123**
   Vol. 2: 334 f., 347, 711
   Vol. 3: 499, 1060
chrisis **Vol. 1:** 121
chrisma **Vol. 1: 119, 121–123**
   Vol. 2: 435
   Vol. 3: 764
Christianos **Vol. 1:** 123, 199,
   590
   Vol. 2: 333, **343**
   Vol. 3: 325
Christos **Vol. 1:** 53, 63, 122–
   125, 181, 214, 237, 242,
   278, 299, 302, 321, 399,

414, 476, 592, 639, 647,
   708, 718, 720, 739
   Vol. 2: 94, **334 f., 338–340,**
   343, 348, 374, 379, 401,
   403, 454, 495, 515, 517,
   519, 545 f., 558, 619, 671,
   775, 808, 812, 835, 885
   Vol. 3: 52–56, 73, 89, 129,
   147, 170, 243, 257, 276,
   299, 462, 504, 509, 572,
   592, 596, 614, 638, 650,
   652, 658, 666, 675, 724,
   764 f., 770, 1033, 1060,
   1172, 1182, 1190, 1192 f.,
   1199, 1205, 1207, 1209,
   1212–1215
chronizō **Vol. 3: 839, 843**
chronos **Vol. 1:** 326, 734, 738
   Vol. 3: 148, 826 f., 833–835,
   839–844
chronotribeō **Vol. 3: 839 f., 843**
chrysion **Vol. 2: 95,** 683
   Vol. 3: 396
chrysolithos **Vol. 3: 396 f.**
chrysoō **Vol. 2: 95**
chrysoprasos **Vol. 3: 396 f.**
chrysos **Vol. 2: 95**
chrysous **Vol. 2: 95,** 574
   Vol. 3: 814
chthōn **Vol. 1:** 263

dai- **Vol. 2:** 788
daimōn **Vol. 1:** 102, 168, **449–454**
   Vol. 2: 85, 498
   Vol. 3: 473, 727
daimonion **Vol. 1: 450–452,**
   636 f.
   Vol. 2: 284, 520, 691
   Vol. 3: 468, 473, 475
daimonizomai **Vol. 1: 450, 453**
daiomai **Vol. 1:** 450
daktylios **Vol. 3:** 497
daktylos **Vol. 2: 148, 150,** 153
dalancha **Vol. 3:** 982
damalis **Vol. 1:** 115
daneistēs **Vol. 2:** 667
Dauid **Vol. 1:** 181, **425**
   Vol. 2: 374
   Vol. 3: 245, 607, 648, 658,
   671, 1073, 1188
dea Roma **Vol. 3:** 217
dechomai **Vol. 1:** 534
   Vol. 2: 146, 244, 817
   Vol. 3: 744–746, 751, 808
deēsis **Vol. 2:** 855, **860 f.**
   Vol. 3: 1174
dei **Vol. 2:** 139, **662–669,** 808,
   878, 912
   Vol. 3: 39, 504, 624, 723,
   957
deidō **Vol. 1:** 453
   Vol. 2: 85
deigma **Vol. 3: 570**

deigmatizō **Vol. 2:** 291
   Vol. 3: 570
deiknymi **Vol. 3: 569,** 571
deilia **Vol. 1:** 622
deiliaō **Vol. 1:** 622
deinon **Vol. 3:** 561
deinos **Vol. 1:** 348
deipneō **Vol. 2: 520 f., 536**
deipnon **Vol. 2:** 273, 518, **520,**
   522, 536
   Vol. 3: 411, 669 f., 750
deisidaimōn **Vol. 1: 450, 453**
   Vol. 2: 85
deisidaimonesterous **Vol. 2:** 85
deisidaimonia **Vol. 1: 450, 453**
   Vol. 2: 85
dek- **Vol. 2: 238,** 245
   Vol. 3: 759, 808
deka **Vol. 1:** 54
   Vol. 2: 692, 699
   Vol. 3: 851
dekatē **Vol. 2: 692–694**
   Vol. 3: 851, 1174
dekatoō **Vol. 2: 692–694**
   Vol. 3: 851
dekatos **Vol. 2: 692**
   Vol. 3: 851
dekteos **Vol. 3:** 744
dekton **Vol. 3:** 745
dektos **Vol. 3: 744–746**
dēloō **Vol. 3:** 309, 311 f.,
   316 f., 323
dēlos **Vol. 3:** 309, **316**
delphys **Vol. 1:** 254
dēmiourgeō **Vol. 1:** 378, 387
   Vol. 3: 1156
dēmiourgos **Vol. 1:** 279, 383,
   387, 389, 513, 521
dēmos **Vol. 1:** 292, 690
   Vol. 2: 788 f., 798
   Vol. 3: 871, 1205
dēmosia **Vol. 2:** 790
dēmosiōnēs **Vol. 3:** 757
dēmosios **Vol. 2: 788, 790**
dendron **Vol. 3:** 865 f., 868
deō **Vol. 1:** 171 f.
   Vol. 2: 732–734
   Vol. 3: 188, 537
deomai **Vol. 2:** 855, 857, 859,
   860 f., 874, 885
deon estin **Vol. 2: 664 f.**
derkomai **Vol. 1:** 507
derma **Vol. 3:** 178
derō **Vol. 1: 161–163**
desm- **Vol. 3:** 591
desmē **Vol. 3:** 591
desmeuō **Vol. 3: 591**
desmios **Vol. 3:** 589, **591 f.,** 599
desmophylax **Vol. 3: 591**
desmos **Vol. 3:** 180, 589, **591 f.,**
   599
desmōtērion **Vol. 3: 591,** 679
desmōtēs **Vol. 3: 591**
despotēs **Vol. 1:** 345

Vol. 2: 508–510
Vol. 3: 876, 1162
deuro **Vol. 3:** 280
deute **Vol. 1:** 493
deuteronomion **Vol. 1:** 54
deuteros **Vol. 1:** 54 f., 666
Vol. 3: 814
dexia **Vol. 2: 146**
Vol. 3: 588, 749
dexiai **Vol. 2:** 146
dexios **Vol. 2: 146 f.**, 152, 188, 194, 614
Vol. 3: 1178
dhala **Vol. 3:** 983
di' ainigmatōn **Vol. 2: 756**
di' hēmōn **Vol. 1:** 570
dia **Vol. 1:** 123, 187, 197, 503, 558, 570, 601, 704, 736
Vol. 2: 27, 120 f., 243, 245, 356, 436, 517, 573, 580, 621, 654, 756, 767, 769, 774, 781
Vol. 3: 53, 72, 152, 163, 166, 171 f., 185, 204, 391, 468, 489, 491, 611, 675, 839, 1033, 1083, **1171–1174, 1176–1178, 1181–1184, 1186, 1189–1191, 1193, 1197 f.**, 1201, 1210 f., 1214
dia charagmatōn **Vol. 2: 573**
dia cheiros tinos **Vol. 2:** 149
dia eidous **Vol. 1:** 704
dia phthonon **Vol. 1:** 558
dia pisteōs **Vol. 1:** 601
Vol. 3: 163, 166, 204, 373
diaballō **Vol. 3: 468**, 476
diabolos **Vol. 1:** 168, 449 f.
Vol. 2: 381, 458
Vol. 3: 468–473, 474, 476, 628, 804, 1178
diachōrizesthai **Vol. 3:** 534
diadēma **Vol. 1: 405**
diadeō **Vol. 1:** 405
diairesis **Vol. 3:** 932
diakoneō **Vol. 2:** 427, 823, 847
Vol. 3: 171, 195, **544–548**, 553, 593, 596, 598, 625, 724, 1065 f.
diakonia **Vol. 2:** 299
Vol. 3: 168, **544–548**, 854, 1112
diakonos **Vol. 1:** 192, 198, 667
Vol. 2: 826
Vol. 3: 195, **544–546, 548 f.**, 553, 596, 1065
diakrinō **Vol. 1: 503–505**
diakrisis **Vol. 1: 503 f.**
dialegomai **Vol. 3: 820 f.**, 826, 1083
dialeipō **Vol. 3: 247 f.**, 251
dialektos **Vol. 3:** 1079
diallassō **Vol. 1:** 569
Vol. 3: 166
diallassomai **Vol. 3: 166 f.**, 173

dialogismos **Vol. 1:** 350, 566
Vol. 3: 820 f., 826
dialogizomai **Vol. 1:** 589
Vol. 3: 820, 826
dialyō **Vol. 2:** 33 f.
diamartyreō **Vol. 3: 1042, 1044**
diamartyromai **Vol. 3: 1038 f.**, 1041, 1044
diamerismos **Vol. 3:** 978
diangellō **Vol. 3: 44–47**
dianoēma **Vol. 3: 122 f., 125, 128**
dianoia **Vol. 1:** 671, 673
Vol. 2: 177, 181, 403, 493
Vol. 3: 122–125, 127 f.
dianoichthēti **Vol. 2: 729**
dianoigō **Vol. 1:** 581, 667
Vol. 2: 726, 729
dianyktereuō **Vol. 1:** 420
diaphtheirō **Vol. 1:** 463, **467 f.**, 470
diaphthora **Vol. 1: 467 f.**, 470
Vol. 3: 262
diapragmateuomai **Vol. 3:** 1158
diarrhēgnymi **Vol. 3:** 592
diaseiō **Vol. 3: 556–558**
diaskorpizō **Vol. 2:** 33 f.
diasōzō **Vol. 3:** 157, **205, 211 f.**, 860, 1177
diaspeirō **Vol. 1:** 55, 685
Vol. 2: 33 f.
diaspora **Vol. 1:** 55, 683, **685 f.**, 691 f.
Vol. 2: 33–35
diastellō **Vol. 1:** 335
diatagma **Vol. 1:** 330
diatassō **Vol. 3:** 854
diatēreō **Vol. 3:** 717
diathēkē **Vol. 1:** 226, **365 f.**, 368 f., **371 f.**, **374, 376**, 659, 666, 682
Vol. 2: 132, 183, 329, 524, 670 f.
Vol. 3: 72, 224, 484, 784, 815
diatithemai **Vol. 1:** 365, 368 f.
diatithēmi **Vol. 1:** 365, 376
Vol. 2: 385
Vol. 3: 871
diaugazō **Vol. 2: 289**
diazonnymi **Vol. 3:** 120
dichostasia **Vol. 1:** 535
didachē **Vol. 1:** 55, 62
Vol. 2: 36 f., 671
Vol. 3: 60 f., 63, 768–771, 907
didaktikos **Vol. 3: 759, 765**
didaktos **Vol. 3: 759, 764**
didask– **Vol. 3:** 766
didaskalia **Vol. 2:** 121, 170, 766
Vol. 3: 228, 765, **768–771**
didaskalos **Vol. 1:** 484

Vol. 2: 36, 510, 595
Vol. 3: 115, 480, 568, 764, **765–768**, 779, 781
didaskō **Vol. 1:** 191, 568, 573
Vol. 2: 36, 113, 165
Vol. 3: 44, 54, 56 f., 181, 228, 509, **759–765**, 769, 774, 821
didaskōn **Vol. 1:** 197
Vol. 3: 766
didōmi **Vol. 1:** 331, 363, 454
Vol. 2: 39–41, 44, 274, 299, 489
Vol. 3: 168, 173 f., 195, 197, 420, 611, 683, 737, 748, 1180
didrachmon **Vol. 3: 752 f.**
didymos **Vol. 1:** 394
diēgeomai **Vol. 1: 573, 575 f.**
diēgēsis **Vol. 1: 573–576**
Vol. 2: 113
Vol. 3: 773
diemai **Vol. 2:** 805
dierchomai **Vol. 1: 320 f.**
diermēneia **Vol. 1:** 579
diermēneuō **Vol. 1: 579–581**
diermēneuomai **Vol. 1:** 581
diermēneutēs **Vol. 1: 579, 581**
diexhodos **Vol. 3: 940**
dihaireō **Vol. 1: 533–535**
dihairesis **Vol. 1: 533–535**
dikaia lambanein **Vol. 3:** 353
dikaiokrisia **Vol. 3:** 315
dikaiōma **Vol. 1:** 332 f., 677, 738
Vol. 3: 352, 354, 361–363, 365, 371 f., 760
dikaion **Vol. 3:** 353
dikaioō **Vol. 1:** 701
Vol. 2: 122, 370
Vol. 3: 161, 168, **352, 354 f., 358, 360–363, 365, 369 f.**, **372, 375**
dikaios **Vol. 2:** 91, 93, 144, 236 f., 497, 620, 658 f.
Vol. 3: 352–355, 358, 360–363, 365–370, 374 f., 573, 575, 732, 924, 1177
dikaiōs **Vol. 2:** 94
Vol. 3: 352 f., 361, 363, 370
dikaiōsis **Vol. 1:** 701
Vol. 3: 352, 354, 363, 371 f., 1184
dikaiosynē **Vol. 1:** 112, 501, 639, 701, 723
Vol. 2: 78, 245, 387 f., 497, 543, 546, 595, 884
Vol. 3: 72, 92 f., 161, 166, 168, 170, 184, **352–354, 358, 360–365, 369–372, 374–377**, 436, 573, 575, 825 f., 925, 966, 1149, 1155, 1177, 1187 f.
dikastikos **Vol. 3:** 354

dikē **Vol. 1:** 558, 645, 700
   Vol. 3: 32, **92 f.**, **96**, 100, 267, 353, 375 f., 573, 583
dio **Vol. 2:** 186, 664
dio legei **Vol. 2:** 186
diōgmos **Vol. 2: 805 f.**, 808
   Vol. 3: 27
diōkō **Vol. 1:** 553, 558, 649
   Vol. 2: 805 f.
   Vol. 3: 942
diōkōn **Vol. 1:** 558
diōktēs **Vol. 3:** 27
diorthōsis **Vol. 3: 351**, 831
dioryssō **Vol. 2:** 831
Dios **Vol. 3:** 1002
diotrephēs **Vol. 2:** 372
diplous **Vol. 3:** 572
dipsaō **Vol. 2: 264–268, 277**
dipsos **Vol. 2:** 265
dipsychos **Vol. 1:** 505
   Vol. 3: 572, **686 f.**
dischilioi **Vol. 2: 699**
dissos **Vol. 3:** 1083
distazō **Vol. 1:** 504
distomos **Vol. 2:** 686
dizēmai **Vol. 3:** 530
dochē **Vol. 3: 744 f.**
dōdeka **Vol. 1:** 131, 489
   Vol. 2: 694, 700, **703**
   Vol. 3: 404
dōdekaphylon **Vol. 2:** 695
dogma **Vol. 1: 330 f.**, 336, 342, 533
   Vol. 2: 135, 442, 447, 453
   Vol. 3: 773, 822, 877
dogmatizō **Vol. 1: 330**
   Vol. 2: 453
dok– **Vol. 2: 238**, 245
dokaō **Vol. 3:** 808
dokei **Vol. 3: 821 f.**
dokeō **Vol. 1:** 55, 330
   Vol. 2: 44, 52, 393
   Vol. 3: 387, 808, **821 f.**, 826, 877
dokimasia **Vol. 3: 808**
dokimasis **Vol. 3: 808**
dokimazō **Vol. 3: 808–810**
dokimē **Vol. 3: 808 f.**
dokimion **Vol. 3: 808 f.**
dokimos **Vol. 3: 808**, 810
dokountes **Vol. 3: 822**
doloō **Vol. 3:** 886
dōma **Vol. 2:** 40–42
domos **Vol. 2:** 509
dōrea **Vol. 2: 40–42**, 122
   Vol. 3: 364
dōrean **Vol. 2: 40 f.**, 120
dōrēma **Vol. 2: 40–42**
dōreomai **Vol. 2: 40 f.**
dōron **Vol. 2: 39–43**, 120
   Vol. 3: 38, 1203
dosis **Vol. 2:** 40 f., 131
dotēs **Vol. 2:** 43
doulagōgō **Vol. 1:** 647

douleia **Vol. 1:** 707
   Vol. 3: 590, **592 f.**, **595–598**
douleuō **Vol. 2:** 817
   Vol. 3: 545, 550, **592–595**, **598**
doulos **Vol. 1:** 256, 283, 647, 650, 706, 709, 718, 720
   Vol. 2: 254 f., 508–511, 573
   Vol. 3: 548, 589–591, **592–597**, 599, 608–611, 613, 758, 854, 1162
dounai **Vol. 1:** 331
   Vol. 3: 683
doxa **Vol. 1:** 261, 327, 483, 546, 587, 594, 599, 696, 732, 735, 740
   Vol. 2: 44–52, 119, 146, 162, 190, 204, 213, 242, 289 f., 336, 377, 393, 482, 485, 543, 546, 563, 605, 612, 724, 781, 839
   Vol. 3: 214, 257, 262, 281, 283 f., 316, 344, 514, 516 f., 554, 717, 723, 817, 821, 848, 925, 927, 1176, 1187, 1189
doxasthēnai **Vol. 2:** 546
   Vol. 3: 848
doxazō **Vol. 1:** 483
   Vol. 2: 44 f., 203, **874**
doxazomai **Vol. 2:** 47, 546
drakōn **Vol. 1: 507 f.**, 510 f.
   Vol. 3: 470
drama **Vol. 2:** 644
draō **Vol. 2:** 644
drepanon **Vol. 3:** 527
dromos **Vol. 3: 945, 947**
dyna– **Vol. 2:** 601
dynamai **Vol. 2: 601**, **603 f.**, **615**
   Vol. 3: 152, 186 f., 491, 1033
dynameis **Vol. 2:** 148, 608 f.
   Vol. 3: 927
dynamenos **Vol. 2:** 450
dynamis **Vol. 1:** 104, 167, 337, 398, 400
   Vol. 2: 69 f., 177, 388, 561, **601–606**, 607–609, 615 f., 654
   Vol. 3: 276, 278, 281, 299, 371, 457, 711, 714, 717, 736, 927, 993, 995, 1026
dynamoō **Vol. 2: 601, 603**
dynastēs **Vol. 2:** 70, **601**
dynateō **Vol. 2: 601, 603**
dynaton **Vol. 2:** 498
dynatos **Vol. 2: 601**, 606
   Vol. 3: 995
dynō **Vol. 1: 314**
dyo **Vol. 3:** 1040
dyō **Vol. 1:** 312 f., **314**, 317, 470
   Vol. 2: 686, 688, 697
dyomai **Vol. 1:** 314

dysexēgētos **Vol. 3:** 124
dysnoētos **Vol. 3: 122, 124, 129**
dysparaklētos **Vol. 1:** 89
dyssebēs **Vol. 3:** 353

ē agnoeite **Vol. 2:** 406
ean **Vol. 1:** 210, 591
   Vol. 2: 588
   Vol. 3: 181, 227, 243, 420, 446, 535
echē **Vol. 3:** 112
ēcheō **Vol. 3: 112**, 114
echō **Vol. 1:** 137, 337, 560, 600, **635–638**, 640, 739
   Vol. 2: 62, 78, 115, 121, 145, 242, 435, 587, 594, 622, 643, 735, 846
   Vol. 3: 129, 216, 822, 998, 1212
ēchōn **Vol. 3:** 112
ēchos **Vol. 3: 112**
echthos **Vol. 1:** 553
echthra **Vol. 1: 553–555**
   Vol. 3: 172
echthros **Vol. 1:** 553 f., 557.
   Vol. 2: 742
   Vol. 3: 469
ēdē **Vol. 2:** 62
   Vol. 3: 869
edō **Vol. 1:** 611
egeirō **Vol. 1:** 445
   Vol. 2: 136, 252, 925
   Vol. 3: 185, 259, 268, 276, 279 f., 307, 715
egeneto **Vol. 1:** 384
   Vol. 2: 351, 398
   Vol. 3: 313, 351
egersis **Vol. 3: 279 f.**
egō **Vol. 1:** 418, 542, 588, 590, 607
   Vol. 2: 278–283, 289, 498, 663
   Vol. 3: 127, 136, 185, 195, 204, 505, 591, 742, 773, 1022, 1172, 1213
egō de legō hymin **Vol. 2: 281**
egō eimi **Vol. 2:** 79, **278–283**, 715, 741
   Vol. 3: 204, 343, 510, 591, 1022
egrēgora **Vol. 2:** 136
ei **Vol. 1:** 592
   Vol. 2: 270, 671
   Vol. 3: 187, 228, 257, 278 f., 1018
ei kai **Vol. 3:** 596
ei mē **Vol. 1:** 130, 399, 575
   Vol. 2: 100
   Vol. 3: 1195
ei pōs **Vol. 3:** 278 f.,
eidenai **Vol. 2:** 391
   Vol. 3: 1064, 1078

eidō Vol. 1: 703
eidōleion Vol. 2: **284**
eidōlion Vol. 2: **284**
eidōlolatrēs Vol. 2: **284 f.**
eidōlolatria Vol. 1: 138, 500
   Vol. 2: **284–286**
eidōlon Vol. 1: 138
   Vol. 2: **284**, 287, **292**, 471
   Vol. 3: 207, 678 f., **891**
eidōlothyton Vol. 2: **284 f.**
   Vol. 3: **417, 432**
eidon Vol. 3: **511, 513, 515**
eidos Vol. 1: **703 f.**, 705, 708, 714
   Vol. 2: 393
   Vol. 3: 513, 554, 1183
eiē Vol. 3: 160
eike Vol. 2: 286
eikō Vol. 2: 256
eikōn Vol. 1: 95, 114, 371, 707
   Vol. 2: 158, 284, **286–288**, 289 f., **292 f.**, 501–503, 743
   Vol. 3: 554 f., 904 f., 1158
eikos Vol. 2: 256
eikosi Vol. 2: 699
eimi Vol. 1: 414
   Vol. 2: 57, 79, **278–283**, 290, 724
   Vol. 3: 195, 204, 343, 510, 591, 1022
einai Vol. 1: 179, 181, 271, 592
   Vol. 2: 234, 351, 390, 500, 503 f., 658, 665 f., 683
   Vol. 3: 72, 112, 149, 152, 157, 173, 218, 239, 354, 387, 391, 445, 489, 555, 564, 660, 727, 822, 834, 967, 1026, 1162, 1172, 1175, 1177, 1181, 1185, 1193 f., 1204–1207
einai syn Christō Vol. 3: **1172, 1205, 1207**
eiōthos Vol. 2: 437
eipein Vol. 2: 236
eipon Vol. 1: 341
   Vol. 3: 490, 510
eirēnē Vol. 1: 213
   Vol. 2: 357, 388, 593, **776–783**
   Vol. 3: 171, 966, 1181, 1191
eirēneuō Vol. 2: **776, 780**
   Vol. 3: 447
eirēnikē Vol. 3: **422**
eirēnikos Vol. 3: **776, 780, 782**
eirēnopoieō Vol. 2: **776, 782**
eirēnopoios Vol. 2: **776, 780, 782**
eirgasmenos Vol. 1: 348
eirōn Vol. 2: **430**
eirōtaō Vol. 2: 879
eis Vol. 1: 107, 227, 245, 305, 320, 325, 358, 502, 547, 591 f., 599, 601, 647, 659, 730, 740–742

   Vol. 2: 35, 60–62, 64, 115, 131, 162, 209, 241, 268, 320, 367, 387, 403, 420, 533, 542, 655, 657, 661, 735, 769, 771, 773–775, 809, 835, 839, 882, 900
   Vol. 3: 52, 55, 99, 161, 171, 199, 218, 239, 242–245, 278, 313, 371, 388, 400, 432, 448, 505, 511, 519, 563, 572, 603, 711 f., 718, 737, 769, 803, 828–830, 839, 841, 845 f., 935, 1033, 1043, 1045, **1171–1178, 1182–1191, 1201, 1204, 1208–1215**
eis andra teleion Vol. 2: 162
eis bebaiōsin Vol. 1: 659
eis cheiras Vol. 2: 149
eis Christon (Iēsoun) Vol. 3: 1209, 1213
eis doxan Vol. 3: **1189**
eis geneas kai geneas Vol. 2: 35
eis pistin Vol. 1: 601
   Vol. 3: **1189**
eis telos Vol. 2: 60–62, 64, 773
eis to onoma Vol. 3: **1209–1211**
eisakouō Vol. 2: 91, **172 f.**, 175, 177
   Vol. 3: 1181
eisdechomai Vol. 3: **744 f.**
eiselthein Vol. 2: 387
eiserchomai Vol. 1: **320 f.**, 647
   Vol. 2: 385, 387
eishodos Vol. 3: **935–937, 940 f.**
eiskaleō Vol. 1: 273
eispherō Vol. 3: 803
eita Vol. 2: 735
eite Vol. 2: 789
ek Vol. 1: 179, 289, 291, 301, 310, 320, 377, 445, 534, 601, 669
   Vol. 2: 55, 120, 172, 175, 179, 193, 244, 464, 599, 657, 789, 846
   Vol. 3: 40, 180, 200, 278, 299, 364, 367 f., 373, 685, 713, 793, 829 f., 839, 922, 1073, 1148, **1171–1174, 1176–1178, 1180–1183, 1185, 1188–1190, 1198, 1201–1203**, 1214
ek merous Vol. 2: **303 f.**
ek pisteōs Vol. 1: 601
   Vol. 3: **364, 367 f.**, 373, 1177, **1188–1190**
ek tou patros Vol. 3: **1203**
ekballō Vol. 1: 449, **453**, 739
   Vol. 3: 473
ekcheō Vol. 2: **523–525, 853–855**
ekchynnō Vol. 2: **853 f.**
ekchynō Vol. 2: 854
ekchysis Vol. 2: 854

ekdechomai Vol. 2: **244 f.**
   Vol. 3: **745**
ekdēmeō Vol. 2: **788–790**
ekdēmos Vol. 2: **788**
ekdiēgeomai Vol. 1: 575
ekdikazō Vol. 3: 92
ekdikeō Vol. 3: **92 f., 96 f.**, 100
ekdikēsis Vol. 3: **92 f.**, **97**, 136, 836
ekdikos Vol. 3: **92, 97**
ekdiōkō Vol. 2: **805 f.**
ekdochē Vol. 2: **244**
ekdotos Vol. 1: 693
ekdyō Vol. 1: **313 f.**
ekdyomai Vol. 1: 315
ekei Vol. 2: **421**
ekeinos Vol. 1: 522, 575
   Vol. 2: 122, 826
   Vol. 3: 836, 846, 850
ekkaleō Vol. 1: 291
   Vol. 3: 51
ekkathairō Vol. 3: **102**, 154, 167
ekklaō Vol. 3: 869
ekklēsia Vol. 1: 10, 56, 271 f., **291–293, 295–304, 306 f.**, 490, 519, 535, 643
   Vol. 2: 30, 83, 328, 349, **731**, 734, 796, 805
   Vol. 3: 49, 335, 384, 387, 521, 567 f., 670, 675, 1141, 1194, 1201
ekklēsiazō Vol. 1: 292
ekkoptō Vol. 3: 869
eklampō Vol. 2: **484–486**
eklegō Vol. 1: 537
eklegomai Vol. 1: 273, 533 f., **536–542**, 598
   Vol. 2: 237
   Vol. 3: 253, 636, 641
ekleipō Vol. 3: **248**
eklektos Vol. 1: 97, 305, **536–541**, 598
   Vol. 2: 237
   Vol. 3: 388, 641, 1117
eklelegmenos Vol. 1: 541
ekloge Vol. 1: **536 f.**, 539 f.
   Vol. 2: 120
   Vol. 3: 251 f.
eklyō Vol. 3: **177 f., 189**
ekmyktērizō Vol. 3: 341
eknēphō Vol. 1: **514 f.**
ekniptō Vol. 1: 153
ekpeirazō Vol. 3: **798 f., 802**, 809
ekphainō Vol. 3: 311
ekpheugō Vol. 1: 558
ekpiptō Vol. 1: **608**
ekplēroō Vol. 2: 734
   Vol. 3: 71
ekplēssō Vol. 1: 527, **529 f.**
ekplēssomai Vol. 1: 530
   Vol. 2: 623
ekpneō Vol. 3: **689, 708**

ekporeuomai **Vol. 3:** 1181, 1202 f.
ekptyō **Vol. 2:** 559
ekpyrōsis **Vol. 1:** 178, 184, 654
Vol. 2: 836
ekrhizoō **Vol. 3: 865 f., 869**
ekrybēn **Vol. 2:** 214
ekstasis **Vol. 1: 527 f.,** 530
Vol. 2: 625
Vol. 3: 315
ekteinō **Vol. 2:** 150
ektenōs **Vol. 2:** 868
ekthambeō **Vol. 2: 621, 623 f.**
ekthambos **Vol. 2: 621, 623**
ekthaumazō **Vol. 2: 621, 623**
ektinaktron **Vol. 3:** 560
ektinassō **Vol. 3: 560**
ektitrōskō **Vol. 1:** 182
ektrapē **Vol. 3: 903**
ektrechō **Vol. 2:** 588
ektrephō **Vol. 3:** 779
ektrepō **Vol. 3: 902 f.**
ektrepomai **Vol. 3: 903**
ektrōma **Vol. 1:** 176, **182 f.,** 188
Vol. 2: 57
Vol. 3: 284, 314
ekzēteō **Vol. 3: 530–532**
ekzētēsis **Vol. 3: 532**
elachistos **Vol. 2: 427–429**
Vol. 3: 181
elachistoteros **Vol. 2: 428 f.**
elaia **Vol. 2:** 710 f.
Vol. 3: 868, 870
elaion **Vol. 1:** 119
Vol. 2: 710–713
Vol. 3: 869. 921 f., 1162
elaiōn **Vol. 2:** 710 f.
elassōn **Vol. 2: 427 f.**
eleaō **Vol. 2: 594**
eleeinos **Vol. 2: 594, 597**
eleeinoteros **Vol. 2: 597**
eleēmōn **Vol. 2: 594–596**
Vol. 3: 162
eleēmosynas poieō **Vol. 2: 597**
eleēmosynē **Vol. 2: 594–597**
eleeō **Vol. 2:** 543 f., **594 f.,** 597 f.
eleēson **Vol. 2: 594**
elegmos **Vol. 2: 140 f.**
ēleimmenos **Vol. 2:** 335
ēlektron **Vol. 2:** 97
elenchō **Vol. 1:** 89, 349
Vol. 2: 137, **140–142,** 145, 768
Vol. 3: 573, 892
elenchōn **Vol. 1:** 373
elenchos **Vol. 1:** 713
Vol. 2: 140–142
elenxis **Vol. 2: 140, 142**
eleōn **Vol. 1:** 197
eleos **Vol. 1:** 112
Vol. 2: 117 f., 123, 449, 543 f., 546, **593–597,** 598 f.,

600
Vol. 3: 241, 889, 1201
elephantiasis **Vol. 2: 464**
elephas **Vol. 2: 464**
eleusis **Vol. 1: 320**
eleutheria **Vol. 1: 715–719,** 721
Vol. 2: 449, 735 f.
Vol. 3: 561, 597, 1151, 1193
eleutheroō **Vol. 1: 715, 717**
eleutheros **Vol. 1: 715–718**
ēli ēli lema sabachtani **Vol. 2:** 82
elleipsis **Vol. 1:** 56
ellogeō **Vol. 3:** 587
elōi elōi lama sabachthani **Vol. 2:** 82
elpis **Vol. 1:** 180, 589, 730
Vol. 2: 238–246, 545, 736, 774
Vol. 3: 214, 1151
elpizō **Vol. 1:** 589, 596, 714
Vol. 2: 142, **238–246**
elpizomena **Vol. 2:** 238
elthe **Vol. 1:** 320, 738
ēlthon **Vol. 1:** 569
emballō **Vol. 1:** 477
emblepō **Vol. 3: 519 f.**
embrimaomai **Vol. 3:** 710
emeō **Vol. 1:** 318
Emmanouēl **Vol. 1:** 186
Vol. 2: 86, 627. 654, 799
Vol. 3: 664, 1072 f.
emmenō **Vol. 3: 223, 226**
emon **Vol. 2: 846**
emos **Vol. 1:** 738
empaigmonē **Vol. 3:** 341
empaizō **Vol. 2:** 436
Vol. 3: 340 f.
empeiria **Vol. 1:** 56
empeirikos **Vol. 1:** 56
emperipateō **Vol. 3: 943–945**
emphanēs **Vol. 2: 488 f.**
emphanizō **Vol. 2: 488 f.**
Vol. 3: 314, 316, 320
emphasis **Vol. 1:** 711
emphysaō **Vol. 2:** 787
emphytos **Vol. 3: 865, 868**
empimplēmi **Vol. 1: 733, 735**
empneō **Vol. 3: 689**
emporeuomai **Vol. 1:** 268
emprosthen **Vol. 2:** 818
Vol. 3: 242, 1173, 1175, **1205**
empsychos **Vol. 2:** 476
en **Vol. 1:** 92, 94, 138, 162, 227 f., 275, 299, 304, 334, 336, 351, 390, 394, 469, 569, 571, 590, 592, 679, 685, 704, 706, 708, 712, 730, 732, 737 f., 742
Vol. 2: 115, 146, 170, 220, 241 f., 289, 354, 356, 358–360, 368, 388, 399, 403, 420, 436, 445, 503 f., 517,

519, 524, 545–547, 563, 574, 586, 604, 615, 619, 621, 643, 655, 657, 671, 675, 680, 683, 708, 715, 726, 735 f., 740, 746, 756, 765, 767 f., 773 f., 781, 789, 816, 819, 878, 883, 900, 912, 925
Vol. 3: 31, 53, 82, 102, 112, 121, 166, 168, 170–172, 180 f., 185, 195, 224 f., 227, 242, 257, 268, 299, 315, 320, 322, 354, 391, 400, 403, 445, 447, 456, 464, 491, 504, 521, 554, 671, 675, 685, 695, 713, 737, 765, 793, 836, 839, 845–847, 850, 876, 884 f., 891 f., 909, 914, 933, 939, 944, 946, 966, 1033, 1045, 1079, 1150, **1171–1178, 1182 f., 1185 f., 1188, 1190–1194, 1198, 1200 f., 1204, 1207–1210, 1212–1214**
en ainigmati **Vol. 2:** 756
en alētheia **Vol. 3: 1191**
en aphtharsia **Vol. 1:** 469
en apokryphō **Vol. 2:** 215
en archē **Vol. 3: 1204**
en Christō **Vol. 1:** 299
Vol. 2: 545, 671
Vol. 3: 1171, 1190–1193, 1207
en Christō Iēsou **Vol. 2:** 619
en dexia **Vol. 2:** 146
en eidei **Vol. 2:** 704
en hēlikia **Vol. 1:** 92
en heni sōmati **Vol. 3: 1191**
en hō **Vol. 3: 1175, 1212**
en hymin **Vol. 3:** 504, **1192**
en kryptō **Vol. 3:** 320
en kyriō **Vol. 1:** 571
Vol. 2: 359 f., 619
Vol. 3: 1191
en merei **Vol. 2: 304**
en panti **Vol. 1:** 94
en pneumati **Vol. 2:** 242
Vol. 3: 695, 1177, **1190–1192**
en prosōpō **Vol. 2:** 399
en sarki **Vol. 1:** 592
Vol. 2: 242, 816
Vol. 3: 322, **1200**
en tō Iēsou **Vol. 3: 1191**
en tō kryptō **Vol. 2:** 214, 216, 218
en tō onomati **Vol. 3: 1210**
en tō phanerō **Vol. 2:** 218
enankalizomai **Vol. 1:** 239
enanthrōpeō **Vol. 2:** 661
enanti **Vol. 2:** 735
Vol. 3: 239
enantion **Vol. 2:** 876
endeixis **Vol. 1:** 573
endēmeō **Vol. 2: 788–790**

Vol. 3: 1205
endoxazō **Vol. 2: 44**
endoxazomai **Vol. 2:** 47
endoxos **Vol. 2: 44, 47**
Vol. 3: 318
endyma gamou **Vol. 2: 579**
endynameō **Vol. 2:** 604
endynamoō **Vol. 2: 601**
endyō **Vol. 1:** 314 f.
Vol. 2: 925
enechō **Vol. 2:** 142, 145
enedra **Vol. 1:** 710
enekrypsen **Vol. 2:** 216
enepō **Vol. 2:** 643
energeia **Vol. 3:** 403, **1147, 1151**
energēma **Vol. 3: 1147, 1151**
energeō **Vol. 3:** 719, 1021, **1147, 1151 f.**, 1182
energēs **Vol. 3: 1147, 1151**
energos **Vol. 3:** 1147
energoumenē **Vol. 2:** 861
enestēkos **Vol. 3:** 831
eneulogeō **Vol. 1: 206, 212**
eneulogeomai **Vol. 1:** 206
engastrimythos **Vol. 2: 554**
engizō **Vol. 2: 53–55,** 382, 387, 901, 932
Vol. 3: 55
engraphē **Vol. 3: 482**
engraphō **Vol. 3: 482 f.,** 486, **490**
engyaō **Vol. 1:** 372
engyos **Vol. 1:** 372 f., 375 f.
Vol. 2: 40
engys **Vol. 2: 52–54,** 65, 382
Vol. 3: 1172 f.
enhorkizō **Vol. 3: 737 f.**
enhybrizō **Vol. 3: 27 f.**
eniautos **Vol. 3:** 826, **841**
eniautous treis kai mēnas hex **Vol. 2: 688,** 700
enischyō **Vol. 3:** 713
enkainizō **Vol. 2: 670, 673,** 675
Vol. 3: 366
enkakeō **Vol. 1: 561, 563**
enkaleō **Vol. 1: 84**
enkauchaomai **Vol. 1:** 227 f.
enkentris **Vol. 3: 865**
enkentrisis **Vol. 3: 865**
enkentrizō **Vol. 3: 865, 867, 869**
enklēma **Vol. 1: 84**
Vol. 3: 923
enkopē **Vol. 2: 220 f.,** 418
enkopēn didonai tini **Vol. 2:** 220
enkoptō **Vol. 2: 220 f.,** 222, 418
enkrateia **Vol. 1: 494–496,** 502 f.
Vol. 2: 99
Vol. 3: 102, 214
enkratēs **Vol. 1: 494–496**
enkrateuomai **Vol. 1: 494–496,**

647
enkryptō **Vol. 2:** 216
ennoia **Vol. 3: 122 f., 125. 128,** 457
ennomos **Vol. 1:** 578
Vol. 2: 437 f., **446,** 454
Vol. 3: 521
Enōch **Vol. 3:** 264
enochleō **Vol. 3:** 997
enochō **Vol. 2:** 142
enochos **Vol. 2:** 137, 139, **142 f.**
Vol. 3: 573
enoikeō **Vol. 2: 247, 251,** 324
enōpion **Vol. 2:** 876
Vol. 3: 242, 267, 712, 1044
enōtizō **Vol. 2:** 172
enōtizomai **Vol. 2:** 175
entaphiasmos **Vol. 1: 263–265**
entaphiastēs **Vol. 1:** 264
entaphiazō **Vol. 1: 263–265**
entellomai **Vol. 1: 331 f.,** 335, **337 f.,** 341 f.
entetalmenon **Vol. 1:** 331
enteuxis **Vol. 2: 860 f.**
enthousiasmos **Vol. 2:** 233
enthymeomai **Vol. 1: 105 f.**
enthymēsis **Vol. 1: 105 f.**
Vol. 3: 128
entimos **Vol. 2: 48 f.**
Vol. 3: 388
entolē **Vol. 1: 330–337,** 341 f., 430
Vol. 2: 133, 177, 426 f., 441, 443, 445, 451, 664, 673, 778
Vol. 3: 127, 173, 181, 239, 455, 584, 774
entos **Vol. 2:** 383, 390
entynchanō **Vol. 2:** 424, **882**
Vol. 3: 130, 199, 325, 417, 432, 550, 702, 1080, 1119
enypion **Vol. 1:** 511 f.
enypniazomai **Vol. 2:** 586
eoika **Vol. 2:** 286
ep- **Vol. 1:** 645
Vol. 3: 563
ep' alētheias **Vol. 3: 883 f.**
epaeidōn epaidēn **Vol. 2: 554**
epagōnizomai **Vol. 1: 644**
epaineō **Vol. 3: 816 f.**
epainos **Vol. 3: 874**
Vol. 3: 668, 816 f.
epaischynomai **Vol. 3: 562–564**
epakoloutheō **Vol. 1: 480 f.**
epakouō **Vol. 2: 172 f.,** 175, 178
epakroaomai **Vol. 2:** 172, 175
epanapauō **Vol. 3:** 258
epanapauomai **Vol. 3: 254 f.**
epangeilamenos **Vol. 3:** 69
epangelia **Vol. 1:** 271, 372, 557
Vol. 2: 111, 122
Vol. 3: 68–72, 143
epangellō **Vol. 3:** 74
epangellomai **Vol. 3: 68, 70**
epangelma **Vol. 3: 68, 71**

epanorthoō **Vol. 3: 351**
epanorthōsis **Vol. 3: 351 f.**
eparatos **Vol. 1: 416 f.**
epeimi **Vol. 1:** 251
epeisan **Vol. 1:** 589
epēkoos **Vol. 2:** 173
epekteinomai **Vol. 1:** 649
epelpizō **Vol. 1:** 589
ependyomai **Vol. 1:** 313 f., 316
Vol. 3: 1195
eperchomai **Vol. 1: 320, 322**
eperōtaō **Vol. 2:** 856, **879 f.**
eperōtēma **Vol. 2: 879–881**
eperōtōn tous nekrous **Vol. 2:** 554
eph' hō **Vol. 3: 1171, 1194,** 1215
eph' hymas **Vol. 3:** 257
ephapax **Vol. 2: 716–718, 725**
Vol. 3: 434, 723
ephphatha **Vol. 2: 560, 729,** 932
ephybrizō **Vol. 3:** 27
epi **Vol. 1:** 98, 107, 188, 227, 251, 276, 393, 506, 591 f.
Vol. 2: 56, 58, 241, 243 f., 356 f., 504, 654 f., 769, 772, 835, 876
Vol. 3: 27, 40, 153, 178 257 f., 392, 432, 540, 712, 737, 750, 763, 839, 883 f., 908, 990, 1085, **1171–1177,** 1181, **1193–1196, 1201, 1210,** 1212–1215
epi- **Vol. 3:** 231
epi ti **Vol. 3:** 935
epi to auto **Vol. 3: 1171, 1194,** 1214
epi tō onomati **Vol. 3:** 1210
epibareō **Vol. 1:** 261
epiboulos **Vol. 3:** 468
epieikeia **Vol. 2: 256–259,** 264
epieikēs **Vol. 2: 256–259**
epigeios **Vol. 1: 517 f.**
Vol. 2: 619
epiginōskō **Vol. 2:** 392, **397–399,** 405
Vol. 3: 771, 808, 810
epignōsis **Vol. 2:** 392, 397, **400 f., 403, 405,** 408
epigraphē **Vol. 1:** 66
Vol. 3: 489
epigraphō **Vol. 3: 489 f.**
epigrapsō **Vol. 3:** 490
epihorkeō **Vol. 3: 737 f.**
epihorkos **Vol. 3: 737 f.**
epikaleō **Vol. 1:** 271 f., 345
Vol. 2: 27, **874**
epikaleomai **Vol. 1: 270–273, 276**
Vol. 3: 232
epikataraomai **Vol. 1:** 416
epikataratos **Vol. 1: 416 f.**
epiklēsis **Vol. 2:** 556

epilambanō **Vol. 3: 747, 749 f.**
epilambanomai **Vol. 3: 747**
epilampō **Vol. 3:** 867
epilegō **Vol. 1:** 537
epilyō **Vol. 1: 576–578**
epilyomai **Vol. 1:** 577
epilysis **Vol. 1: 576–578**
epimartyreō **Vol. 3: 1042**
epimartyromai **Vol. 3: 1041**
epimeleisthai **Vol. 3:** 678
epimenō **Vol. 3: 223, 227 f.**
epinoia **Vol. 1:** 711
ēpios **Vol. 1:** 282
epiousa **Vol. 1:** 251
epiousios **Vol. 1:** 143, 249, **251,**
253
Vol. 2: 268, 868, 871, 895
epiphainō **Vol. 2:** 122
Vol. 3: 317–319
epiphaneia **Vol. 1:** 504, 658
Vol. 2: 518, 900 f.
Vol. 3: 220, 310, 316, **317–**
319, 505
epiphanēs **Vol. 3: 317–319**
epipherō **Vol. 3:** 344
epiphōneō **Vol. 1: 408–410**
epipnoia **Vol. 3:** 690
epipotheō **Vol. 1:** 456–458
Vol. 3: 1195
epipothēsis **Vol. 1:** 458
epipothia **Vol. 1:** 458
episeiō **Vol. 3: 556–558**
episkēnoō **Vol. 3: 814**
episkepsis **Vol. 1:** 189
episkeptomai **Vol. 1: 188–191,**
200
episkiazō **Vol. 3: 553, 555**
episkopē **Vol. 1: 188–190, 192**
Vol. 3: 836, 847
episkopeō **Vol. 1: 188–190**
episkopos **Vol. 1:** 110, **188–**
191, 198 f., 333
Vol. 2: 777
Vol. 3: 134, 568, 1065
epispasmos **Vol. 1:** 309
epistamai **Vol. 3:** 122
epistatēs **Vol. 2:** 514, 595
Vol. 3: 115, 767, 781
epistellō **Vol. 1: 246 f., 249**
epistēmē **Vol. 1:** 671
Vol. 2: 493
epistērizō **Vol. 3:** 87
epistolē **Vol. 1:** 242, **246–248**
Vol. 2: 781
Vol. 3: 490, 499
epistrephō **Vol. 1: 353–355,**
357, 359
Vol. 3: 233, 823, 1212
epistrophē **Vol. 1: 354 f.**
episynagō **Vol. 2: 31, 33**
episynagōgē **Vol. 2:** 31, **33**
episystasis **Vol. 1:** 292
epitassō **Vol. 1:** 341
epiteleisthai **Vol. 3:** 725

epithema **Vol. 3:** 164, 424
epithesis **Vol. 2:** 149 f., 153
epithesis tōn cheirōn **Vol. 2:**
149–151, 153
epithymeō **Vol. 1:** 106, **456 f.**
Vol. 3: 1199
epithymia **Vol. 1:** 106, **456–458,**
460 f., 645
Vol. 2: 458, 588
Vol. 3: 32, 678, 802
epitimaō **Vol. 1: 572 f.**
Vol. 3: 344
epitimia **Vol. 1: 572**
epitithēmi **Vol. 2:** 146, 151
Vol. 3: 243, 857
epitithēmi tas cheiras **Vol. 2:**
146, **150 f.**
epithesis **Vol. 3:** 1182
epitropos **Vol. 1:** 349
Vol. 2: 254
epizēteō **Vol. 1:** 460
Vol. 3: 530 f.
epoikodomeō **Vol. 2:** 249, **251,**
253
eponomazō **Vol. 2: 648, 652,**
655
epōnymos **Vol. 2:** 651
epoptēs **Vol. 1:** 189
epopteuō **Vol. 1:** 189
Vol. 3: 512, 515
erō **Vol. 3:** 1119
epos **Vol. 3:** 1081, 1086
epourania **Vol. 2:** 195 f.
epouranioi **Vol. 2: 188**
epouranion **Vol. 3:** 215
epouranios **Vol. 2: 188, 191 f.,**
194, 196, 329, 387
eprepen **Vol. 2: 668 f.**
era **Vol. 3:** 1004
eranos **Vol. 1:** 291
eraō **Vol. 2: 538–540, 542**
Vol. 3: 845
eraunaō **Vol. 3:** 527, **532 f.**
erchomai **Vol. 1:** 179, **319–322,**
327, 358, 438, 569, 738
Vol. 2: 184, 379, 530 f., 664,
758, 839, 912
Vol. 3: 181, 195, 843, 941,
998, 1173, 1181, 1212
erchomenos **Vol. 2:** 379
erēm- **Vol. 3:** 1007
erēmia **Vol. 3: 1004, 1007**
erēmoō **Vol. 3: 1004–1008**
erēmos **Vol. 3: 1004,** 1007,
1014
erēmos topos **Vol. 3:** 1004, 1007
erēmōsis **Vol. 1:** 74 f.
Vol. 2: 912
Vol. 3: 1004–1008
erēmousthai **Vol. 3:** 1007 f.
ereō **Vol. 3:** 532
ereunaō **Vol. 2:** 856
ergasia **Vol. 3:** 173, **1147,**
1149 f.

ergatēs **Vol. 3: 1147, 1149 f.**
ergazomai **Vol. 1:** 266 f.
Vol. 2: 434
Vol. 3: 793, **1147, 1149 f.**
1156–1158
ergon **Vol. 1:** 197, 228 f., 271,
446, 535, 566, 603, 723
Vol. 2: 104, 120, 449
Vol. 3: 123, 548, 551, 719,
876, **1147–1152,** 1154, 1158
f., 1176, 1178
eriphion **Vol. 1:** 114
eriphos **Vol. 1:** 114
eris **Vol. 1:** 106, 535, 558
Vol. 2: 587
Vol. 3: 544
eritheia **Vol. 1:** 106, 535
erō **Vol. 2:** 734
erōs **Vol. 2:** 103, 123, 493,
538–540, 542, 551
Vol. 3: 877
erōtaō **Vol. 2: 855–857, 879 f.,**
885
erxai **Vol. 3:** 719
eschata **Vol. 1:** 165
Vol. 2: 245
eschaton **Vol. 1:** 56, 211
Vol. 2: 55, 402 904, 909
Vol. 3: 286
eschatos **Vol. 1:** 179, 517,
665–667
Vol. 2: 52 f., **55–59,** 65, 241,
402, 772
Vol. 3: 218, 836, 838, 848 f.,
1190
eschatōs **Vol. 2: 55**
ēse **Vol. 3:** 673
esō **Vol. 2:** 566
Vol. 3: 127, 718
esomena **Vol. 2:** 665
esoptron **Vol. 2:** 756
esōteron **Vol. 3: 794**
esōteros **Vol. 3: 794**
estērigmenai **Vol. 3:** 878
esthēs **Vol. 1:** 312
esthiō **Vol. 1:** 253, 743 f.
Vol. 2: 264, **271,** 275, **277,**
521, 523
Vol. 3: 793
ethē **Vol. 3:** 583
ethelō **Vol. 3:** 1015 f., 1018
ethnē **Vol. 2: 788,** 790 f., **793–**
796, 799 f.
Vol. 3: 38, 73, 454, 567
ethnikoi **Vol. 2: 788**
ethnikos **Vol. 2: 790, 795**
Vol. 3: 580, 757
ethnikōs **Vol. 2: 790, 795**
ethnos **Vol. 1:** 541
Vol. 2: 37, 124, 127, 378,
788, **790** f., **793–796,** 798–
801, **805,** 839
Vol. 3: 38, 73, 313, 454,
567, 940, 1191, 1197

ethos **Vol. 2: 436–438**, 450, 455, 657, 662, 790
ēthos **Vol. 1:** 56
    Vol. 2: 436–438
eti **Vol. 3:** 253
etymos **Vol. 1:** 56
eu **Vol. 1:** 206
    Vol. 2: 92, 817
    Vol. 3: 48, 719, 817, 1002, 1156 f.
euangelia **Vol. 2:** 108, 113
euangelia thyein **Vol. 2:** 108
euangelion **Vol. 1:** 310, 397
    Vol. 2: 107–114
    Vol. 3: 38, 45, 52, 54, 61, 68 f., 71, 217, 746, 959, 966
euangelistēs **Vol. 2: 107, 114**
    Vol. 3: 768
euangelizō **Vol. 2: 107, 110**
    Vol. 3: 54, 57
euangelizomai **Vol. 2: 107–114**, 443, 782
    Vol. 3: 46–48, 54, 57, 61, 67 f., 71, 764, 774, 1191
euangelizomenos **Vol. 2:** 109
euangelos **Vol. 2:** 107
euaresteō **Vol. 2: 814–817**
    Vol. 3: 264
euarestos **Vol. 2: 814–816**
    Vol. 3: 930 f., 1021
eucharisteō **Vol. 1:** 206, 213
    Vol. 2: 855, 868, 874
    Vol. 3: 675, **817–820**
eucharistia **Vol. 1:** 206, 213, 730
    Vol. 2: 874
    Vol. 3: 817–819, 820
eucharistos **Vol. 2: 874**
    Vol. 3: 817
euchē **Vol. 2: 861, 867**
euchomai **Vol. 1:** 227
    Vol. 2: 861 f., 867, 873
    Vol. 3: 572
euchos **Vol. 2:** 52
euchrēston **Vol. 2:** 434
eudaimonia **Vol. 2:** 60, 419
    Vol. 3: 138, 926
eudia **Vol. 3: 1000, 1002**
eudokeō **Vol. 1:** 534
    Vol. 2: 383, 780 f., 817 f., 820
    Vol. 3: 219
eudokēsis **Vol. 2:** 817
eudokia **Vol. 1:** 558
    Vol. 2: 358, 566, **817–820**
eudokos **Vol. 2:** 817
eudokoumenē zōē **Vol. 2:** 817
euergesia **Vol. 3: 1152**
euergeteō **Vol. 2:** 99
    Vol. 3: 1147, 1152
euergetēs **Vol. 1:** 519
    Vol. 2: 372
    Vol. 3: 1147, 1152
euēthēs **Vol. 2:** 643
euēthia **Vol. 1:** 206

eugenēs **Vol. 1: 187 f.**
euharmostia **Vol. 1:** 206
euhilateuō **Vol. 3:** 152
euhodoō **Vol. 3: 943**
eukaireō **Vol. 3: 833, 837**
eukairia **Vol. 3: 833, 837**
eukairos **Vol. 3: 833, 837**
eukairōs **Vol. 3: 833, 837 f.**
eulabeia **Vol. 2: 90 f.**
    Vol. 3: 561, 1181
eulabeomai **Vol. 1:** 622
    Vol. 2: 90 f.
    Vol. 3: 823, 1181
eulabēs **Vol. 2: 90 f.**, 95
eulabētheis **Vol. 2:** 91
eulogēmenos **Vol. 1:** 206, 213
eulogeō **Vol. 1: 206 f., 212 f.,** 217
eulogeomai **Vol. 2: 874**
eulogētos **Vol. 1: 206 f., 210, 212 f.**
eulogia **Vol. 1: 206, 212–214,** 216, 416
    Vol. 3: 70, 233, 752, 819, 854
eunē **Vol. 1:** 560
euneō **Vol. 3:** 173
eunomia **Vol. 3:** 27
eunouchizō **Vol. 1: 559 f.**
eunouchos **Vol. 1: 559–561**
-euō **Vol. 3:** 775
euōdia **Vol. 3:** 432, **599–601**
euōnymos **Vol. 2: 148**
euphrainō **Vol. 2:** 352, **354– 357, 361,** 436
euphrosynē **Vol. 2: 354 f.,** 419
euprosdektos **Vol. 3: 744, 746,** 838
eupsycheō **Vol. 3: 687**
eurhythmia **Vol. 1:** 206
euschēmosynē **Vol. 1:** 206
eusebeia **Vol. 1:** 228, 595, 622, 708
    Vol. 2: 91–95, 99
    Vol. 3: 505, 561, 574, 770
eusebeō **Vol. 2: 91–93**
eusebēs **Vol. 2:** 91–94, 596, 659
eusebōs **Vol. 2:** 93 f., 480
eusplanchnos **Vol. 2: 599 f.**
eutheōs **Vol. 2:** 37
    Vol. 3: 833 f., 837
euthymia **Vol. 2:** 60
euthys **Vol. 3: 833 f., 837,** 1169
ex **Vol. 2:** 436, 722, 756
ex ainigmatōn **Vol. 2:** 756
ex anastasis **Vol. 3:** 299
ex haireseōs **Vol. 1:** 534
ex henos **Vol. 2:** 722
exagorazō **Vol. 1: 267 f.**
exaiteomai **Vol. 2: 855 f., 858**
exakoloutheō **Vol. 1: 480 f.**
    Vol. 3: 1033
exaleiphō **Vol. 1: 471**

exanastasis **Vol. 3: 259, 278**
exangellō **Vol. 3: 44–46**
exanhistēmi **Vol. 3: 259,** 307
exapataō **Vol. 2: 457–459**
exapostellō **Vol. 1: 126–128,** 136
exartizō **Vol. 3: 349–351**
exēgēma **Vol. 1:** 573
exēgēmatikos **Vol. 1:** 573
exēgeomai **Vol. 1:** 57, **573–576**
    Vol. 2: 555
exēgēsis **Vol. 1:** 57, **573 f.,** 576, 580
exēgētēs **Vol. 1: 573–575,** 584
    Vol. 2: 555
exeimi **Vol. 2:** 606
exekklēsiazomai **Vol. 1:** 292
exeleutheros **Vol. 3:** 598
exeraunō **Vol. 3: 532 f.**
exerchomai **Vol. 1:** 179, 320 f.
    Vol. 2: 663
    Vol. 3: 1180, 1202
exērtismenos **Vol. 3:** 350
exesti **Vol. 2:** 253, **606, 611**
exhilasis **Vol. 3: 150 f.,** 153
exhilaskomai **Vol. 3:** 104, 146, **148–155, 160,** 167
exhilasma **Vol. 3:** 174, 192
exhilasmos **Vol. 3: 150–153**
exhistēmi **Vol. 1: 527 f.,** 729
    Vol. 3: 1109
exhodos **Vol. 3: 935–937, 940**
exhomologeō **Vol. 1: 344–346**
exhomologeomai **Vol. 1:** 344
    Vol. 2: 874
    Vol. 3: 675, 1208
exhomologēsis **Vol. 1:** 344
exhorkistēs **Vol. 3: 473, 476, 737 f.**
exhorkizō **Vol. 3: 473, 476, 737 f.**
exhorkoō **Vol. 3:** 473
exhypnizō **Vol. 1:** 442
existamai **Vol. 1: 526 f.**
existanō **Vol. 1:** 527
exō **Vol. 2:** 566, 672
    Vol. 3: 280, 1172
exodos **Vol. 1:** 57
    Vol. 3: 863
exolethreuō **Vol. 1: 465**
exolethreuomai **Vol. 1:** 465
exoudeneō **Vol. 1: 74**
exousia **Vol. 1:** 104 f., 166 f., 228, 301, 564, 638
    Vol. 2: 161, 191, 213, 221, 561, 601, **606–611,** 614, **615 f.,** 671
    Vol. 3: 97, 482, 549, 617, 645, 711, 755
exousiai **Vol. 2: 608 f.,** 616
exousiazō **Vol. 2:** 606, 611
exoutheneō **Vol. 1: 74,** 455

Gabriēl **Vol. 1:** 103

353

Gaios **Vol. 2:** 683
gala **Vol. 1:** 282
  Vol. 2: 268 f., 277
  Vol. 3: 1118
galēnē **Vol. 2:** 776
Galilaia **Vol. 3:** 456
gam- **Vol. 2:** 575
gameō **Vol. 2:** 564, **575 f., 581,**
  583–585, **588 f.**
  Vol. 3: 191, 263, 356, 539,
  845, 1055, 1057, 1072
gamiskō **Vol. 2: 575, 581**
gamizō **Vol. 2: 575, 581, 588**
gamizōn **Vol. 2:** 588
gamos **Vol. 1:** 498, 560, 625
  Vol. 2: 575 f., 579 f., 584, 589
gar **Vol. 1:** 351, 569
  Vol. 2: 106, 661, 766, 768,
  835
  Vol. 3: 55, 174, 178, 195,
  214, 375, 487, 549, 767,
  773, 963, 1026, 1033, 1152
gazophylakion **Vol. 3:** 791,
  795 f.
gē **Vol. 1: 517 f.,** 684
  Vol. 2: 55, 57, 104, 188,
  205, 207, 209
  Vol. 3: 178, 182, 218; 445,
  448
gegrammenon **Vol. 3: 483,**
  488 f.
gegraptai **Vol. 3:** 329, **483,**
  487 f.
gehenna **Vol. 1:** 231, 623
  Vol. 2: 143, 205, 207, **208–**
  210
  Vol. 3: 110, 446
gelaō **Vol. 2: 429, 432 f., 436**
gelōs **Vol. 2: 429–431, 433**
gem- **Vol. 2:** 575
gemistos **Vol. 1: 742**
gemizō **Vol. 1: 742 f.**
gemō **Vol. 1:** 728, **742 f.**
genea **Vol. 1:** 176, 187
  Vol. 2: 35–39, 382, 584, 910,
  912
  Vol. 3: 828
genealogeō **Vol. 2: 35**
genealogeomai **Vol. 2:** 35 f.
genealogia **Vol. 2: 35**
genēma **Vol. 3:** 922
genesis **Vol. 1:** 176, 181 f., 184
  Vol. 2: 658
  Vol. 3: 647, 656, 679
genna **Vol. 1:** 176
gennaō **Vol. 1: 176–179,** 181,
  185–188
  Vol. 2: 75 f., 188, 505, 575,
  661, 725
  Vol. 3: 642, 654 f., 661,
  1200
gennaomai **Vol. 3:** 1202
gennēma **Vol. 2:** 505
gennēthēnai **Vol. 1:** 179 f.

genoito **Vol. 1:** 98
  Vol. 2: 119
genomenon **Vol. 3:** 1113
genos **Vol. 1:** 305, 539, 541,
  684
  Vol. 2: 35, 75, 232, 349
  Vol. 3: 40, 454–456, 1202
gēraskō **Vol. 2:** 716
gerōn **Vol. 2:** 674
gerousia **Vol. 1:** 194–196,
  199 f., 363
gēs **Vol. 1:** 186
Gethsēmani **Vol. 2: 710**
geuma **Vol. 1:** 459
geuomai **Vol. 2:** 264, **269, 277**
geus **Vol. 2:** 269
gignomai **Vol. 1:** 181
  Vol. 3: 152 f., 1202
gignōskō **Vol. 1:** 245
  Vol. 3: 1148
ginomai **Vol. 1:** 176, **181,** 184,
  188, 370, 384, 536, 578,
  590, 708
  Vol. 2: 35, 351, 392, 398,
  489, 504, 665, 671, 707,
  818, 912
  Vol. 3: 143, 149, 168, 170,
  181 f., 312 f., 351, 661,
  1022, 1073, 1107, 1113,
  1175
ginōskō **Vol. 1:** 233, 245, 432,
  484, 692, 716, 724
  Vol. 2: 158, 202, 221, **390–**
  408, 448, 460, 490, 586, 757
  Vol. 3: 125, 168, 170, 205 f.,
  310, 316, 630, 639, 679,
  720, 835, 1031, 1199
gleukos **Vol. 3:** 922
glōchin **Vol. 3:** 1078
glōssa **Vol. 1:** 143, 530
  Vol. 2: 126, 505, 785 f.
  Vol. 3: 75, 180, 346, 505,
  576, 770, **1078 f.,** 1143,
  1176
glōssokomeion **Vol. 1:** 143
glōssokomon **Vol. 1: 142 f.**
glōtta **Vol. 3:** 1078
glykeia **Vol. 2:** 239
glykys **Vol. 2:** 239
  Vol. 3: 449
gnēsios **Vol. 3:** 1164
gno- **Vol. 2:** 392
gnōmē **Vol. 1:** 107
  Vol. 2: 392, **397 f.,** 757
gnōrimos **Vol. 1:** 484
gnōrizō **Vol. 3:** 44, 310, **314**
gnōsis **Vol. 1:** 58, 73, 422, 513,
  708
  Vol. 2: 219, 391, **392–406,**
  408, 477, 480, 539, 545,
  646, 655, 677, 685
  Vol. 3: 206, 310, 640, 647,
  885, 932, 936, 996, 1201
gnōstos **Vol. 2: 392, 397**

  Vol. 3: 88
gnōthi seauton **Vol. 2:** 392
  Vol. 3: 103
goaō **Vol. 2:** 558
goēs **Vol. 2: 552, 558, 561**
Gōg **Vol. 3: 959**
gonata **Vol. 2: 859**
gōnia **Vol. 2:** 129, 159
  Vol. 3: 382, 387, **388 f.,** 391,
  393, 398
gony **Vol. 2: 859**
gonypeteō **Vol. 1:** 610
  Vol. 2: 855 f., 859
gramma **Vol. 1:** 431
  Vol. 2: 233, 641, 675, 715
  Vol. 3: 477, **482 f.,** 486,
  492 f., 495, 1183
grammata **Vol. 3: 483, 487,** 491
grammateus **Vol. 1:** 199
  Vol. 2: 714, 834
  Vol. 3: 184, **477–480,** 482
graph- **Vol. 3:** 483
graphai **Vol. 3: 490 f.**
graphē **Vol. 1:** 246, 558, 580,
  736
  Vol. 2: 774
  Vol. 3: 71, 186 f., 311, 327,
  482 f., 486 f., 489–492, 690,
  708, 763, 1200
graphō **Vol. 1:** 736
  Vol. 3: 329, **482 f., 488–492,**
  496, 1141, 1196 f.
grapsō **Vol. 3:** 490
graptos **Vol. 3:** 490
graus **Vol. 2:** 645
grēgoreō **Vol. 2: 136,** 563, 914
gymnasia **Vol. 1:** 312 f.
gymnazō **Vol. 1:** 312 f.
gymnikos **Vol. 1:** 645
gymnos **Vol. 1: 312–314,** 315–
  317
gymnotēs **Vol. 1: 312–314,** 316
gynaikarion **Vol. 3: 1055, 1058**
gynaikeion **Vol. 3: 1058**
gynaikeios **Vol. 3: 1055**
gynaikōnitis **Vol. 3:** 1058
gynē **Vol. 2:** 562–564, 585
  Vol. 3: 188, 875, 913, **1055,**
  1058, 1069, 1073, 1076,
  1183
gynē engastrimythos **Vol. 2: 554**
gypsos **Vol. 2:** 574
gys **Vol. 2:** 269

ha- **Vol. 2:** 716
  Vol. 3: 572
hadēs **Vol. 1:** 264, 433, 463
  Vol. 2: 85, 188, 191, **205–210**
  Vol. 3: 262, 267, 388, 858,
  947, 984
Hagar **Vol. 1:** 80
  Vol. 2: 329, 755
hagia **Vol. 2:** 230
  Vol. 3: 794

hagiasma Vol. 2: **224**
hagiasmos Vol. 2: **224**
hagiastērion Vol. 2: **224**
hagiazō Vol. 1: 669
 Vol. 2: **224**, 229, 231 f.
 Vol. 3: 38, 152
hagiographa Vol. 1: 58
hagioi Vol. 2: 229, 302
hagiomai Vol. 2: 224
 Vol. 3: 100
hagios Vol. 1: 105, 272, 275,
 300, 305
 Vol. 2: 93, **223 f.**, 227, 229,
 231 f., 237, 388, 547, 549,
 653, 669, 673, 683, 826,
 839, 868
 Vol. 3: 38, 101, 104 f., 107,
 487, 491, 695, 774, 794,
 814, 925, 1047, 1176–1178,
 1210 f.
hagiōsynē Vol. 2: **224**
 Vol. 3: 299, 1188 f.
hagiotēs Vol. 2: **224**, 230
hagizō Vol. 2: 224
hagneia Vol. 3: 100 f.
hagnismos Vol. 3: 100 f.
hagnizō Vol. 3: 100 f.
hagnos Vol. 1: 495
 Vol. 3: **100–102**
hagnōs Vol. 3: 101
hagnotēs Vol. 3: 100 f.
haima Vol. 1: 93, **220–223**,
 226, 376, 647, 685, 699
 Vol. 2: 477, **524 f.**, **532**,
 535 f., 854
 Vol. 3: 158, 166, 180, 1175
haimatekchysia Vol. 1: 222
 Vol. 2: **536**, **853 f.**
 Vol. 3: 158
haireō Vol. 1: 533
haireomai Vol. 1: **533**, 537, 542
 Vol. 3: 252
hairesis Vol. 1: **533–535**
 Vol. 3: 941
hairetikos Vol. 1: **533–535**
hairetizō Vol. 1: 533 f., 537
hairetos Vol. 1: 533
hala Vol. 3: 444
halas Vol. 3: **443–446**, 448 f.
halia Vol. 1: 291
haliskomai Vol. 3: 590
halizō Vol. 3: **443–445**, 447
hallēlouia Vol. 1: 99 f.
 Vol. 2: 862
 Vol. 3: 669
hallomai Vol. 3: 459
halōn Vol. 3: 527
halōsis Vol. 1: 469
hals Vol. 3: 443 f., **446**, 1155
halykos Vol. 3: 443 f., **449**
hama Vol. 2: 500
 Vol. 3: **908**, **1173**
hamart- Vol. 3: 577
hamartanō Vol. 2: 406

Vol. 3: 103, **577**, **579**, 587,
 1194
hamartēma Vol. 2: 767
 Vol. 3: **577**, **579**
hamartētikos Vol. 3: **576**
hamartia Vol. 1: 86, 125, 160,
 430, 446, 461, 562 f., 682,
 699, 701, 703, 733, 741
 Vol. 2: 93 f., 120, 411, 457,
 460, 504, 533, 566, 668, 717
 Vol. 3: 52, 55, 152, 161 f.,
 168, 170 f., 180, 243, 375,
 419 f., 434, 549, **573**, **575–**
 577, **579–582**, **584**, 587,
 596 f., 717, 811, 1178,
 1197, 1203
hamartinoos Vol. 3: **576**
hamartōlos Vol. 2: 94
 Vol. 3: 161, **577**, **579 f.**, 757,
 995, 998
hapas Vol. 1: 94
 Vol. 2: 770
hapax Vol. 1: 667
 Vol. 2: **716–719**, 720, 723,
 725
 Vol. 3: 723
haphē Vol. 1: 241
haplōs Vol. 1: 572
haplotēs Vol. 3: **571 f.**
haplous Vol. 2: 487, 744
 Vol. 3: **571 f.**
haptō Vol. 1: 241
 Vol. 3: **859 f.**
haptomai Vol. 3: **859 f.**
Har Magedōn Vol. 3: **962**
harma Vol. 3: 353
Harmaged(d)ōn Vol. 3: **959**
harmonia Vol. 2: 683
harmos Vol. 1: 241
harmozō Vol. 1: 241
harpagē Vol. 2: 847
 Vol. 3: **601**, **604**
harpagmos Vol. 1: 552
 Vol. 2: 500
 Vol. 3: **601**, **603–605**
harpax Vol. 3: **601**, **604**
harpazō Vol. 3: **601–603**, 605,
 712
Hasidioi Vol. 2: 810
hatheudō Vol. 2: 927
hautē (fem. of → *houtos*)
hazomai Vol. 2: 224
 Vol. 3: 100
heautos Vol. 1: 547, 592, 706,
 729
 Vol. 2: 259, 262, 618, 725,
 815 f., 833, 883
 Vol. 3: 168, 197, 353, 611,
 925, 1064, 1078, 1156,
 1176, 1193
hebdomēkonta Vol. 2: **696**
Hebraios Vol. 2: **304 f.**
 Vol. 3: 465
Hebraïs Vol. 2: **304**, 309

Hebraïsti Vol. 2: 309
heddomēkonta Vol. 2: 691
hēdeōs Vol. 2: 766
hēdonē Vol. 1: 231, 233, 456,
 458–461, 671
 Vol. 2: 419
hēdos Vol. 1: 458
hedra Vol. 1: 363, 661
hedraiōma Vol. 1: 658, **660–**
 662
hedraios Vol. 1: 658, **660–663**
hēdyosmon Vol. 2: **210 f.**
hēdys Vol. 1: 458
 Vol. 2: 211, 475
hēgemōn Vol. 1: 270
 Vol. 2: 377
 Vol. 3: 939
hēgemonia Vol. 2: 377
hēgemonikon Vol. 1: 450
 Vol. 2: 157, 182
 Vol. 3: 679, 681, 684
hēgeomai Vol. 1: 584
 Vol. 2: 500, 835
 Vol. 3: 28
heilkōmenos Vol. 2: 466
heima Vol. 1: 316
heis Vol. 1: 94, 232, 576, 602,
 664, 669, 678, 682
 Vol. 2: 100, 309, 349, 477,
 517, 563 f., 566, 589, 618,
 716, 717, **719 f.**, **722**, 724 f.,
 932
 Vol. 3: 172, 181, 231, 253,
 403, 622, 675, 685, 767,
 866, 909, 1175, 1187, 1191,
 1194, 1197, 1210
hekastos Vol. 1: 94, 576
 Vol. 3: 403
hekatontarchēs Vol. 3: **958**, **964**
hekatonarchos Vol. 3: **958**, **964**
hēkō Vol. 1: 320 f., 327
Hēlias Vol. 1: 543
 Vol. 3: 863 f.
hēlikia Vol. 1: 92 f., 277
 Vol. 2: 588
 Vol. 3: 350, 403
hēlios Vol. 2: 289, 486
 Vol. 3: **730–733**, 734
Hellas Vol. 2: 124, 126
Hellēn Vol. 1: 59, 686
 Vol. 2: 124, 126 f.
Hellēnes Vol. 2: 126 f.
Hellēnikos Vol. 2: **124**, **126**
Hellēnis Vol. 2: 124, 126
Hellēnistēs Vol. 2: 124, 126
Hellēnisti Vol. 2: 124, 126
Hellēnizein Vol. 2: 126
hēmera Vol. 1: 204, 251, 267,
 320, 402, 421, 477, 738
 Vol. 2: 56, 58, 363, 518,
 693, 783, **887**, **889**, **895**, 899
 f., 926, **931**
 Vol. 3: 185, 208, 315, 318,
 320, 351, 826, 835, 841 f.,

hēmera (cont'd)
845, 924, 940, 1001, 1181, 1190, 1201
hēmera kai hēmera **Vol. 2: 895**
hēmeteron **Vol. 2: 846**
hēmeteros **Vol. 2:** 502
Vol. 3: 1196
hen (neuter of → *heis*)
heneka **Vol. 3:** 161, 1083
heneken **Vol. 2:** 387
hennymi **Vol. 1:** 316
henotēs **Vol. 2: 719, 721**
Vol. 3: 675
heōrakōs **Vol. 3:** 517
heortazō **Vol. 1: 624, 631, 634**
heortē **Vol. 1:** 291, **624, 626, 628, 632,** 635
Vol. 3: 232, 813
heōs **Vol. 1:** 184, 517
Vol. 2: 55, 57, 61, 901, 912
Vol. 3: 181 f., 218, 409, 683, 828, 834
heōsphoros **Vol. 2: 495**
Vol. 3: 468, 734
hepta **Vol. 2: 690,** 702 f., 893, 931
Vol. 3: 88, 179 f., 500, 706, 715
heptakis **Vol. 2: 690**
hermēneia **Vol. 1:** 59, **579–582, 584**
hermēneuō **Vol. 1:** 59, **579–581, 584**
Vol. 2: 729
Vol. 3: 898
hermēneuomai **Vol. 1:** 581
hermēneus **Vol. 1:** 579 f.
hermēneutēs **Vol. 1: 579 f.,** 582
hermēneutikos **Vol. 1:** 579
Hērōdeios **Vol. 3:** 441
Hērōdianos **Vol. 2:** 343
Vol. 3: 441
Hērōdos **Vol. 3:** 441
hēsychazō **Vol. 3: 111 f.**
hēsychia **Vol. 3: 111 f.**
hēsychios **Vol. 3: 111 f.**
hetaerae **Vol. 1:** 497 f.
hetairos **Vol. 1:** 254, **259 f.,** 484
Vol. 2: 548
Vol. 3: 49
hetera **Vol. 2: 739**
heterodidaskaleō **Vol. 3: 766, 768**
heteroglōssos **Vol. 2: 739–741**
Vol. 3: 1078 f.
heteroi **Vol. 2: 739**
heteros **Vol. 1:** 666, 708
Vol. 2: 380, **739 f., 742,** 785 f.
Vol. 3: 1080
heterōs **Vol. 1: 739, 741**
heterozygeō **Vol. 2: 739, 741**
Vol. 3: 1160, 1164
heterozygos **Vol. 3: 1160**

hetoim- **Vol. 3:** 966
hetoima **Vol. 1:** 475
hetoimasia **Vol. 3: 116–118,** 966
hetoimassō **Vol. 3:** 117
hetoimazō **Vol. 1:** 363
Vol. 2: 382
Vol. 3: 116 f., 119
hetoimos **Vol. 3: 116,** 122
hēttēma **Vol. 3:** 573
hēttō **Vol. 3:** 1083
Heua **Vol. 1: 87**
Vol. 2: 649
Vol. 3: 585, 1063
heurēka **Vol. 3:** 528
heuriskō **Vol. 1:** 709
Vol. 2: 724
Vol. 3: 199, 264, **527–530,** 533
hex **Vol. 2:** 688, 700
hexis **Vol. 2:** 657
Vol. 3: 562, 926
hiēmi **Vol. 1:** 697
hiera **Vol. 2: 233–235**
Vol. 3: 487, 491, 785
hiera grammata **Vol. 3: 487, 491**
hierachēs **Vol. 2: 234**
hieraomai **Vol. 2:** 233
hierapolos **Vol. 2: 234**
hierateia **Vol. 2: 232–235**
Vol. 3: 32, 36
hierateuma **Vol. 1:** 305
Vol. 2: 232–235, 380
Vol. 3: 32, 43
hierateuō **Vol. 2: 232–234**
Vol. 3: 32, 37
hieratikos **Vol. 2: 233 f.**
hiereia **Vol. 2:** 234
hiereuō **Vol. 2:** 234
hiereus **Vol. 2: 232–236**
Vol. 3: 32 f., 35, 37, **40,** 347, 582
hierodoulos **Vol. 2:** 234
Vol. 3: 415
hierogrammateus **Vol. 3:** 480
hierōma **Vol. 2:** 234
hieron **Vol. 2: 232–235**
Vol. 3: 690, 781, 784, **785, 793,** 795 f., 798, 807, 812, 941, 1058
hieroprepēs **Vol. 1:** 645
Vol. 2: 232 f., 235
hieroprepestatos **Vol. 2: 235**
hieros **Vol. 1:** 243, 498, 560, 625
Vol. 2: 223 f., **232–238,** 324, 572, 576, 584, 644
Vol. 3: 32, 43, 478, 772, 781, 785, 1085
hieros gamos **Vol. 2: 576, 584**
Hierosolyma **Vol. 2: 324–326**
Hierosolymitēs **Vol. 2: 324 f.**
hierosyleō **Vol. 2: 232–235**

hierosylos **Vol. 2: 235**
hierōsynē **Vol. 2: 232–234**
Vol. 3: 32, 36, 41
hierothyta **Vol. 2: 233**
hierothyton **Vol. 2: 285**
hierothytos **Vol. 2: 232–235**
hierourgeō **Vol. 2: 232–235**
Vol. 3: 32, 38, 44, 552
hierourgia **Vol. 2: 234**
hierourgōn **Vol. 2: 235**
hikanō **Vol. 3:** 728
hikanoō **Vol. 3: 728 f.**
hikanos **Vol. 3:** 726, **728 f.,** 839
hikanotēs **Vol. 1:** 248
Vol. 3: 728 f.
hikesios **Vol. 1:** 687
hiketeia **Vol. 2:** 859
hiketēria **Vol. 2: 860 f.,** 885
hilaos **Vol. 3:** 148
hilaros **Vol. 2:** 239
Vol. 3: 148
hilarōs **Vol. 2:** 735
hilaskomai **Vol. 1:** 89, 437, 694, 697, 699
Vol. 2: 614
Vol. 3: 146, **148 f., 151–155, 160–162,** 167, 169, 190, 192 f., 195 f., 199, 364, 419, 423, 425, 431, 435, 579, 611, 720, 788, 812, 815
hilasmos **Vol. 1:** 89
Vol. 3: 148–151, 156, 162 f.
hilastērion **Vol. 1:** 398
Vol. 2: 614, 766
Vol. 3: 148–150, 153, 156 f., 163–165, 170, 175, 431, 435, 812, 815
hilastērios **Vol. 3:** 149
hilasthēnai **Vol. 3:** 149
hilasthēti **Vol. 3:** 149, 161
hilēmi **Vol. 3:** 148
hileō poiein **Vol. 3:** 148 f.
hileos **Vol. 3:** 148
hileōs **Vol. 2:** 123
Vol. 3: 148 f., 152 f., 157, 160, 192
himation **Vol. 1:** 312, **316 f.**
Vol. 2: 714
hina **Vol. 1:** 181, 647, 736
Vol. 2: 661, 753, 760, 826
Vol. 3: 53, 71, 168, 170, 186, 241, 312, 489, 643, 771, 1184, 1186, 1191, 1212
hina mē **Vol. 2:** 709
hina plērōthē **Vol. 2:** 753
Vol. 3: 71, 489
hippikos **Vol. 1:** 645
hippos **Vol. 1:** 118
hiron **Vol. 2:** 224
Vol. 3: 117, 785
histēmi **Vol. 1:** 51, 471, 474, 606
Vol. 2: 563
Vol. 3: 259, 892

historeō **Vol. 3:** 398
hodēgeō **Vol. 3: 935–937, 942**
hodēgos **Vol. 1:** 220
　Vol. 3: 935–937, 939, 942
hodoio **Vol. 3:** 1155
hodoiporeō **Vol. 3: 941**
hodos **Vol. 2:** 458–460, 481
　Vol. 3: 352, 584, **935–937, 939–941,** 943, 946 f., 1006
hoios **Vol. 2:** 912
　Vol. 3: 391
holokarpōma **Vol. 3:** 421
holokarpōsis **Vol. 3:** 421
holokautōma **Vol. 3: 417, 421, 430, 434**
holokautōsis **Vol. 3:** 421
holos **Vol. 1:** 94, 231, 377
　Vol. 2: 659
　Vol. 3: 456
holōs **Vol. 3:** 740
homichlē **Vol. 3: 1000, 1003**
homo- **Vol. 3:** 908
homoia **Vol. 2: 503**
homoiōma **Vol. 2:** 284, **500–504**
　Vol. 3: 904
homoioō **Vol. 2: 500–505**
homoiopathēs **Vol. 2: 500–503**
homoios **Vol. 2: 497,** 498, **500–503,** 516
　Vol. 3: 123, 404, 904
homoiōs **Vol. 2: 500, 502, 508**
homoiōsis **Vol. 2: 500–502, 505,** 743
homoiotēs **Vol. 2: 500–502, 505**
homoiousthai **Vol. 2:** 498
homologeō **Vol. 1: 344–348,** 454
　Vol. 3: 54, 232 f., 774
homologia **Vol. 1: 344,** 346 f.
homonoia **Vol. 2:** 776
　Vol. 3: 217
homoousios **Vol. 2: 497, 505–508,** 516
homos **Vol. 1:** 344
　Vol. 2: 500, 719
homothymadon **Vol. 3: 908 f.**
hoplizō **Vol. 3: 959, 964**
hoplon **Vol. 3: 959, 963 f.**
hopōs **Vol. 1:** 736
hōra **Vol. 2:** 758, 927
　Vol. 3: 826, 833, 835, 841, **845–849,** 850
hōraios **Vol. 3: 845, 847**
horama **Vol. 3:** 310, **511–513,** 515, 517, 862
horaō **Vol. 1:** 695
　Vol. 2: 134, 173, 176, 180, 555, 768
　Vol. 3: 281, 284 f., 509, **511–513,** 515 f., 521, 1046, 1206
horasis **Vol. 3: 512, 515**
horatos **Vol. 3:** 511 f., **515**

hōrē **Vol. 3:** 845
horion **Vol. 1:** 472
hōrismenos **Vol. 1:** 473
horisthentos **Vol. 2:** 203
horizō **Vol. 1:** 471, **472 f.,** 478, 533, 693, 695
　Vol. 2: 203
　Vol. 3: 299 f., 504
horkia **Vol. 1:** 594
horkios **Vol. 3:** 738
horkizō **Vol. 3:** 473, **737, 739 f.,** 1073
horkōmosia **Vol. 3: 737 f.,** 742
horkos **Vol. 3:** 583, **737–740,** 743
hormē **Vol. 1:** 710
horōn **Vol. 3:** 513
horōntes tou asteras **Vol. 2: 555**
horos **Vol. 1:** 472
hōs **Vol. 1:** 197, 285, 287, 446, 710
　Vol. 2: 116, 290, 411, 420, 437, 502, 578, 699, 768, 778
　Vol. 3: 152, 170, 195, 210, 354, 622, 1202
hōs kecharismenoi **Vol. 2:** 116
hōs mē **Vol. 1:** 278
　Vol. 2: 581
hosa echeis **Vol. 2: 846**
hosakis **Vol. 3:** 243
hōsanna **Vol. 1:** 100
　Vol. 3: 509
hosia **Vol. 2:** 237
hosiē **Vol. 2: 236**
hosios **Vol. 2:** 93, 223, 232, **236–238**
hosiotēs **Vol. 2: 236 f.**
hosos **Vol. 2:** 429
　Vol. 3: 1162
hōsper **Vol. 1:** 176
　Vol. 2: 234, 498, 502
　Vol. 3: 195, 564, 876
hōsperei **Vol. 1:** 182
hostē **Vol. 2:** 671
hote **Vol. 1:** 738
　Vol. 2: 758, 766
　Vol. 3: 843
hoti **Vol. 1:** 348, 591, 599
　Vol. 2: 213, 356, 826, 901
　Vol. 3: 181, 186, 241, 257, 264, 316, 510, 892, 1039, 1194, 1211, 1213
houtos **Vol. 1:** 522, 524–526, 569, 708, 712
　Vol. 2: 58, 155, 524, 545, 609, 654, 773, 799, 910, 912
　Vol. 3: 71, 178, 181, 185, 240 f., 243, 245, 400, 464, 469 f., 673, 763, 829 f., 838, 1120, 1141, 1184, 1194
hyakinthos **Vol. 3: 396 f.**
hyalinos **Vol. 3:** 984
hybris **Vol. 2:** 259
　Vol. 3: 27, 29 f., **32,** 561

hybristēs **Vol. 3: 27–29, 31**
hybristikos **Vol. 3:** 27
hybrizō **Vol. 3:** 27–29
hydata **Vol. 3: 987–990**
hydōr **Vol. 1:** 179 f.
　Vol. 2: 140, 274
　Vol. 3: 449, 982 f., 987, **998–990,** 992, 1177 f., 1180, 1210
hydōr tou elegmou **Vol. 2:** 140
hyetos **Vol. 3: 1000, 1003**
hygiaine **Vol. 2:** 169
hygiaino **Vol. 2:** 164, **169–171,** 766
　Vol. 3: 267, 770, 887
hygiēs **Vol. 2:** 164, **169–171**
　Vol. 3: 428, 1022
hygros **Vol. 1:** 390
hyios **Vol. 1:** 181, 256, 280 f., 284, **286–290,** 487, 523, 595, 615, 619, 667 f.
　Vol. 2: 81, 194, 216, 324, 337, 374, 376, 380, 385, 387, 502 f., 514, 565, 585, 607, 630, 656, 725, 900, 912
　Vol. 3: 147, 195, 299, 530, 597, 607, 609, 611–613, 617, 620, 630, 634 f., 639, 641, 648, 651, 658, 665 f., 751, 831, 1085, 1144, 1202
hyios Dauid **Vol. 3:** 607, **648,** 658, 666
hyios tou anthrōpou **Vol. 2:** 194, 216, 337, 376, 380, 385, 387, 502 f., 514, 565, 607, 630, 900, 912
　Vol. 3: 147, 195, 530, 607, **613, 617, 620, 630,** 665, 831, 1144
hyios tou theou **Vol. 1:** 281, 615
　Vol. 3: 299, 607, 611, **634,** 651, 1085
hyiothesia **Vol. 1:** 282, **286 f., 289**
　Vol. 2: 883
　Vol. 3: 72, 597, 666, 751
hylē **Vol. 1:** 164, 704 f.
hymnagorēs **Vol. 3: 668**
hymneō **Vol. 3: 668–670,** 673, 675, 817
hymnēsis **Vol. 3: 668 f.**
hymnētos **Vol. 3:** 669
hymnōdeō **Vol. 3:** 669
hymnographos **Vol. 3: 669**
hymnologia **Vol. 3:** 668
hymnos **Vol. 1:** 213
　Vol. 2: 874
　Vol. 3: 668–670, 672, 674 f., 816
hypakoē **Vol. 1:** 604
　Vol. 2: 172, 177, **179**
　Vol. 3: 1150 f.
hypakouō **Vol. 2:** 172 f., 177,

hypakouō (*cont'd*)
179
Vol. 3: 107
hypantaō Vol. 1: 324 f.
hypantēsis Vol. 1: 324 f.
hyparchōn Vol. 1: 706
Vol. 2: 833
hyparchonta Vol. 2: 845–847
hyparxis Vol. 1: 711
Vol. 2: 829, 844, 845–847
hypatos Vol. 1: 270
hypēkoos Vol. 2: 179
hypenantion Vol. 3: 1199
hyper Vol. 1: 197, 227, 398, 647, 728 f.
Vol. 2: 486, 523 f., 543, 587, 617, 819
Vol. 3: 153, 168, 170, 195, 197, 611, **1171–1174, 1176, 1180, 1193, 1196 f., 1199, 1203, 1207 f.**, 1214
hyper hēmōn Vol. 2: 882
Vol. 3: 168, 170, **1196 f.**
hyper hymōn Vol. 2: 368, **523 f.**
hyper pantōn Vol. 3: 195, 197, 1180, **1197 f.**
hyper pollōn Vol. 2: **524, 543**
Vol. 3: 611, 1174
hyperakmos Vol. 2: 581, **587 f.**
Vol. 3: 538, 1072
hyperaspizō Vol. 3: 1196
hyperauxanō Vol. 2: 128
hyperbainō Vol. 1: 138
Vol. 3: **583 f.**
hyperechō Vol. 2: 609
hyperekperissōs Vol. 1: 728
hyperekperissou Vol. 1: 730 f.
hyperēnoreōn Vol. 3: 28
hyperentynchanō Vol. 2: **874, 882**
hyperēphaneia Vol. 3: 29 f.
hyperēphaneuomai Vol. 3: 29
hyperēphania Vol. 3: **28–30**
hyperēphanos Vol. 3: **27–32,** 127
hyperēphanōs Vol. 3: 30
hypēreteō Vol. 3: **544, 547**
hypēretēs Vol. 3: **544, 546,** 609
hyperhypsoō Vol. 2: **200 f.,** 203
hypernikaō Vol. 1: 650 f.
hyperperisseuō Vol. 1: 730
Vol. 2: 131
hyperperissōs Vol. 1: **728 f.**
hyperphroneō Vol. 2: 617
hyperpleonazō Vol. 2: **130 f.**
hyphistamai Vol. 1: 710 f.
hyphistēmi Vol. 1: 710
hypnoō Vol. 1: 442
hypnos Vol. 1: 429, **441–443,** 446
hypo Vol. 1: 263, 736
Vol. 2: 772
Vol. 3: 489, 1162, **1171– 1174, 1181 f., 1193, 1198,**

1202, 1208, 1210
hypo- **Vol.** 3: 231
hypodeigma Vol. 2: **284, 290, 293**
Vol. 3: 555, 570, 905
hypogrammos Vol. 2: **291**
Vol. 3: 724, 905
hypographō Vol. 2: 291
Vol. 3: **483**
hypokeimenon Vol. 1: 711
hypokrinō Vol. 2: **467 f.,** 813
hypokrinomai Vol. 2: **468, 474**
hypokrisis Vol. 2: **468 f.**
hypokritēs Vol. 2: **468–470**
hypolambanō Vol. 3: **747, 749**
hypoleimma Vol. 3: **247 f.,** 251
hypoleipō Vol. 3: **247 f.**
hypoleipomai Vol. 3: 251
hypomenō Vol. 2: 240, 243– 245, **764, 772–774, 776**
Vol. 3: 229
hypomimnēskō Vol. 3: **230, 240–243**
hypomnēsis Vol. 3: **230, 241– 243,** 247
hypomonē Vol. 1: 646
Vol. 2: 243, 245, **772–776,** 782, 809
Vol. 3: 73, 555
hypōpiazō Vol. 1: **162 f.,** 647
hyposchismos Vol. 3: 543
hypostasis Vol. 1: 703, **710–714**
Vol. 2: 142, 243, 288–290, 488, 507, 768
hypostolē Vol. 1: 713
Vol. 2: 775
hypotagē Vol. 1: 347
hypotassomai Vol. 2: 180, 664
Vol. 3: 931
hypothesis Vol. 1: 61
hypotypōsis Vol. 3: **903–905**
hyps- Vol. 3: 29
hypsēlo- Vol. 3: 29
hypsēlophroneō Vol. 2: 198
hypsēlos Vol. 2: **198–200,** 617 f.
Vol. 3: **1009 f.**
hypsistos Vol. 2: **198–200,** 591
hypsōma Vol. 2: **198, 200**
Vol. 3: 824
hypsoō Vol. 1: 288
Vol. 2: 185, 199, **200–204,** 423
Vol. 3: 161, 624, 630 f., 715
hypsos Vol. 1: 123
Vol. 2: 197, **198–200,** 204
hys Vol. 1: 117
hysterēma Vol. 1: 741
Vol. 3: 573, **952 f., 955**
hystereō Vol. 3: **952–954**
hysterēsis Vol. 3: **952 f., 955**
hysteron Vol. 3: **952 f.**
hysteros Vol. 3: **952 f.,** 958

Ia Vol. 2: **556**

Iakōb Vol. 2: 284, 305, **316– 319,** 431, 649
Vol. 3: 203, 987
Iakōbos Vol. 2: **316–319**
iama Vol. 2: **166–169**
Iaō Vol. 2: 512, **556**
iaomai Vol. 2: 151, 164, **166– 170,** 634
Vol. 3: 997 f.
iasis Vol. 2: **166,** 168
Vol. 3: 261
Iasōn Vol. 2: 332
iaspis Vol. 3: **395–398**
iatros Vol. 2: **166, 168,** 172
ichthydion Vol. 1: **670**
ichthyophagos Vol. 1: 670
ichthys Vol. 1: **670**
id- Vol. 3: 511 f.
ide Vol. 3: 521
idea Vol. 2: 284, 590
Vol. 3: 224, 513
idein Vol. 2: 206, 663
Vol. 3: 513, 519, 1206
idia Vol. 2; **838–840,** 846
idioi Vol. 2: 839
idion einai Vol. 2: **846**
idios Vol. 1: 197, 578 f.
Vol. 2: 273, 456, 725, **839 f.**
Vol. 3: 750, 964
idiōtēs Vol. 2: **456 f.**
idou Vol. 2: 103, 671
Vol. 3: **516,** 521
ienai Vol. 3: 935
Ierousalēm Vol. 2: **324–330**
Iēsō Vol. 3: 261
Iēsous Vol. 1: 181, 235, 278, 399, 445, 476
Vol. 2: 94, **330–332,** 338– 340, **344,** 373, 379, 508, 514, 517, 527, 619, 654, 885
Vol. 3: 52, 55 f., 89, 209, 212, 243, 261, 276, 299, 592, 596, 611, 675, 763 f., 770, 1033, 1172, 1191, 1209, 1211, 1213
-ikos Vol. 3: 690
Ioda Vol. 2: 320
Iōnas Vol. 2: **350–352**
Iordanēs Vol. 3: **991,** 992, 1209 f.
ios Vol. 2: **27–29,** 831
iōta Vol. 3: 181 f.
Iouda Vol. 2: **319 f.**
Vol. 3: 456
Ioudaia Vol. 1: 94
Vol. 2: **305, 316,** 320
Vol. 3: 456
Ioudaikos Vol. 2: 310
Ioudaikōs Vol. 2: **304,** 310
Ioudaios Vol. 1: 297, 361
Vol. 2: **304 f.,** 378, 660, 789
Vol. 3: 450
Ioudaïsmos Vol. 2: 310
ioudaïzō Vol. 2: 310

Ioudas Vol. 2: **316, 319 f.**
iris Vol. 3: **1000, 1002**
isa Vol. 2: **498,** 500
Isaak Vol. 1: **81**
  Vol. 2: 329, 431, 649
isangelos Vol. 1: **101, 103**
  Vol. 2: 578
  Vol. 3: 278
ischyō Vol. 2: 170
  Vol. 3: **712–714,** 718
ischyros Vol. 2: 70
  Vol. 3: **712–714,** 993
ischyroteros Vol. 3: 55
ischys Vol. 1: 262, 732
  Vol. 2: 177, 601 f.
  Vol. 3: 711, **712–714,** 717
isēgoreomai Vol. 2: **498**
isodaimōn Vol. 2: **498**
isomoiros Vol. 2: **498**
isonomeō Vol. 2: **498**
isoō Vol. 2: **498**
isopolitēs Vol. 2: **498**
isopsychos Vol. 2: **497–499**
isos Vol. 2: **497–500, 502, 505, 508**
  Vol. 3: 353
isotēs Vol. 2: **497–499**
isotheos Vol. 2: **498**
isotimos Vol. 2: **497–499**
Israēl Vol. 1: 329, 370
  Vol. 2: **304,** 317, 319, **322,** 378, 799
  Vol. 3: 198
Israēlitēs Vol. 2: **304, 310**
ithys Vol. 3: 834

kai Vol. 1: 592
  Vol. 2: 722
  Vol. 3: 492, 979, 1175, 1178
kai egeneto . . .kai Vol. 1: 181
kainē ktisis Vol. 2: 545
kainizō Vol. 2: **670**
kainoō Vol. 2: **670**
kainos Vol. 1: 335, 384, 388 f., 666
  Vol. 2: 473, 524, 545, 566 **669–676,** 714
  Vol. 3: 168
kainotēs Vol. 2: **670–672,** 675, 715
kaiō Vol. 2: 487
kairos Vol. 1: 268, 337, 477, 629, 722, 724, 738
  Vol. 2: 37, 588, 899, 925
  Vol. 3: 148, 686, 750, 826 f., 831, **833–838, 841,** 843 f., 846–849, 754, 1041
Kaisar Vol. 1: **269,** 345
  Vol. 2: 549
  Vol. 3: 745
kakia Vol. 1: **561, 563–565,** 731
  Vol. 2: 458
  Vol. 3: 577, 886, 936
kako- Vol. 2: 419

kakologeō Vol. 1: 206 f., 413, 415, 418
kakoō Vol. 1: **561–563**
kakopatheia Vol. 3: **724**
kakopatheō Vol. 3: **719, 722, 725**
kakopoieō Vol. 1: **561, 563**
kakopoios Vol. 1: **561, 563**
kakos Vol. 1: 107, 125, 138, 228, 513, **561–565,** 567
  Vol. 3: 124, 200, 724, 1021, 1148, 1150, 1157, 1179
kakōs Vol. 3: **719,** 998
kakōsis Vol. 3: 847
kakourgos Vol. 1: **561,** 564
  Vol. 3: 379
kala Vol. 2: 103
kalamos Vol. 3: 404
kaleō Vol. 1: 84, **270–273, 275 f.,** 291, 306, 533, 569
  Vol. 2: 243, 544, 809
  Vol. 3: 51, 54, 398. 767
kaleomai Vol. 1: 271, 274
  Vol. 3: 181
kallielaios Vol. 2: **710, 712**
  Vol. 3: 869
kalodidaskalos Vol. 3: **765, 768**
kalon Vol. 2: 98,103
kalopoieō Vol. 2: **102**
kalos Vol. 1: 197, 722
  Vol. 2: **98–106**
  Vol. 3: 391, 770, 775, 963, 1021, 1148
kalōs Vol. 2: 766
  Vol. 3: 1156
kalos kagathos Vol. 2: 102 f.
  Vol. 3: 775
kaloumenos Vol. 1: 271, 273
kalymma Vol. 2: **212 f.**
  Vol. 3: **794 f.**
kalyptō Vol. 1: 701
  Vol. 2: **211 f.,** 214, 216, 220
  Vol. 3: 309 f., 313, 323 f., 795
kamēlos Vol. 1: 116
kamptō Vol. 2: 859
kananaios Vol. 3: **1167**
kanōn Vol. 1: 51
  Vol. 3: **399 f.,** 403 f., 485, 493
kapēleuō Vol. 1: 138
kara Vol. 2: 244
karadokeō Vol. 2: **244**
kardia Vol. 1: 169. 230, 350 f., 742
  Vol. 2: 40, 177, **180–184,** 207, 262, 566 f.
  Vol. 3: 124, 127 f., 229, 572, 679, 710
kardiognōstēs Vol. 2: **180, 183**
karpōma Vol. 3: 421
karpophoreō Vol. 1: **721 f.**
karpos Vol. 1: **721–723,** 727
  Vol. 2: 104

  Vol. 3: 522, 526, 1149
karpōsis Vol. 2: 421
kartereō Vol. 2: **764, 767 f., 776,** 868
kassiterinos Vol. 3: 391
kat- Vol. 1: 645
  Vol. 3: 563
kat' agnoian Vol. 2: **406**
kat' allēlōn Vol. 2: 423
kat' aretēn Vol. 2: 477
kat' eklogēn Vol. 3: **251 f.**
kat' eleon Vol. 2: 594
kat' oikon Vol. 3: **1201**
kat' opsin Vol. 1: 680
kata Vol. 1: 50, 188, 227 f., 257, 376, 504, 534, 576, 675, 680, 719
  Vol. 2: 120, 242, 303 f., 400, 406, 420, 423, 436 f., 476 f., 489, 502, 505, 519, 565, 594, 656 f., 659 f., 671, 723, 766, 774, 882
  Vol. 3: 251 f., 299, 365, 400, 403, 456, 491, 516, 585, 595, 737, 770, 926, 944, 1018 f., 1035, 1073, **1172 f., 1188–1190, 1198–1201,** 1214
kata anthrōpon Vol. 2: 565
kata anthrōpous Vol. 2: 565
  Vol. 3: **1200**
kata charin Vol. 2: 120
kata Christon Iēsoun Vol. 2: 619
kata epignōsin Vol. 2: 400
kata gnōsin Vol. 2: 400
  Vol. 3: **1201**
kata hairesin Vol. 1: 534
kata logon Vol. 2: 476 f., 766
kata meros Vol. 2: **303 f.**
kata monas Vol. 2: **723 f.**
kata opheilēma Vol. 2: 120
kata physin Vol. 2: 476 f., 657, 659
  Vol. 3: 595, 926
kata pistin Vol. 3: 365
kata pneuma Vol. 1: **675,** 719
  Vol. 2: 242, 617
  Vol. 3: 299, **1172, 1188 f., 1199 f.**
kata prothesin Vol. 3: **1201**
kata sarka Vol. 1: 188, 228, 257, **675,** 680, 719
  Vol. 2: 242, 617
  Vol. 3: 1073, **1172, 1188, 1199 f.**
kata tas graphas Vol. 3: **491, 1200**
kata tēn graphēn Vol. 3: **491**
kata theon Vol. 2: 420, 882
  Vol. 3: **1200**
kata tychēn Vol. 3: 585
katabainō Vol. 2: **184–186**
  Vol. 3: 1176
kataballō Vol. 1: **376 f.**

katabareō **Vol. 1:** 261
katabolē **Vol. 1:** 376–378, 383, 388, 542
katabrabeuō **Vol. 1: 648**
katachthonios **Vol. 1:** 518
katadendros **Vol. 2:** 285
katadikazō **Vol. 2:** 362, **370**
katadikē **Vol. 2:** 370
katadiōkō **Vol. 2: 805 f.**
katagelaō **Vol. 2: 429, 433**
　Vol. 3: 563
kataginōskō **Vol. 2:** 362 f., **365**
katagōnizomai **Vol. 1:** 644
kataischynō **Vol. 3:** 562–564
katakalymma **Vol. 2:** 212
katakalyptō **Vol. 2:** 212
katakalyptomai **Vol. 2:** 212
katakauchaomai **Vol. 1: 227 f.**
kataklysmos **Vol. 3:** 982, **991**
katakrima **Vol. 2:** 362, **365**
katakrinō **Vol. 2:** 362, **365**
katakrisis **Vol. 2:** 362, **365**
katakyrieuō **Vol. 2: 510, 519**
katalaleō **Vol. 1:** 413
　Vol. 3: 340, **345–347**
katalalia **Vol. 3:** 345 f.
katalalos **Vol. 3:** 345 f.
katalambanō **Vol. 1:** 649
　Vol. 3: 747, 749 f.
katalambanomai **Vol. 3:** 750
kataleimma **Vol. 3:** 247 f., **251**
kataleipō **Vol. 2:** 724
　Vol. 3: 247 f., **251**
katallagē **Vol. 1:** 701
　Vol. 2: 545
　Vol. 3: 166–168, 581, 1112
katallassō **Vol. 1:** 701
　Vol. 3: 146, **166–169, 171 f.,** 186, 188, 196, 363, 581, 824, 1192
kataloipoi **Vol. 3:** 251
kataloipos **Vol. 3:** 247 f., **251**
katalyma **Vol. 3: 177, 189**
katalyō **Vol. 2:** 252
　Vol. 3: 177, 181, 183, 185, 189
katamartyreō **Vol. 3: 1038 f., 1041–1043**
katangeleus **Vol. 3: 44–46**
katangellō **Vol. 2:** 111, 113
　Vol. 3: 44–48, 54, 57, 764, 1043
kalanoeō **Vol. 3: 122, 124, 126, 129**
katantaō **Vol. 1:** 324 f., 327, 649
　Vol. 3: 278
katapateō **Vol. 3:** 28, **943 f.**
katapauma **Vol. 3:** 255
katapauō **Vol. 3: 254, 256–258**
katapauomai **Vol. 3:** 255
katapausis **Vol. 3:** 73, **254 f., 257 f.**
katapetasma **Vol. 3: 794,** 798,
814
katapheugō **Vol. 1:** 558
kataphileō **Vol. 2: 547, 549**
kataphroneō **Vol. 1: 461 f.**
kataphronētēs **Vol. 1: 461 f.**
kataphyteuō **Vol. 3: 866**
katapinō **Vol. 2:** 274
katapiptō **Vol. 1:** 608
katara **Vol. 1: 416**
　Vol. 3: 1197
kataraomai **Vol. 1:** 207, 413, **416–418**
katargeō **Vol. 1:** 73 f., 466
katartisis **Vol. 3:** 349 f.
katartismos **Vol. 1:** 302
　Vol. 3: 349 f.
katartizō **Vol. 3:** 349 f., 1187
kataseiō **Vol. 3: 556–558**
kataskēnoō **Vol. 3:** 813
kataskēnōsis **Vol. 3: 813**
kataskeuazō **Vol. 1:** 383
　Vol. 3: 116, **118–120**
kataskopos **Vol. 3:** 50
katasphragizō **Vol. 3: 497**
katathema **Vol. 1: 413, 415**
katathematizō **413, 415**
katatomē **Vol. 1: 307, 309**
kataxioō **Vol. 3:** 348 f., 627
katēcheō **Vol. 3:** 44, **771 f.,** 780
katēchēsis **Vol. 3:** 771
katechō **Vol. 3:** 505, 885
katechōn **Vol. 3:** 771
katēchoumenos **Vol. 3:** 771
katēgor **Vol. 1: 82 f.,**
　Vol. 3: 470
katēgoreō **Vol. 1:** 82 f.
katēgoria **Vol. 1:** 82 f.
katēgorōn **Vol. 1:** 83
katēgoros **Vol. 1: 82–84**
kateidōlos **Vol. 2: 284 f.**
katenōpion **Vol. 3:** 925
katēphēs **Vol. 3:** 28
katēramenos **Vol. 1:** 416
kateulogeō **Vol. 1:** 212
katexousiazō **Vol. 2: 606 f.**
　Vol. 2: 895
　Vol. 3: 1201
kath' hēmōn **Vol. 3:** 1199
kath' homoiosin **Vol. 2:** 505
kath' homoiotēta **Vol. 2:** 505
kath' hypomonēn **Vol. 2:** 774
kathairō **Vol. 3:** 102
katharismos **Vol. 3:** 102
katharizō **Vol. 3:** 102, 104, 152
katharma **Vol. 1:** 479
katharmos **Vol. 3:** 102
katharoi **Vol. 3:** 108
katharos **Vol. 1:** 351
　Vol. 2: 144
　Vol. 3: 100 f., 102 f., **105,** 108, 167, 924, 997
katharotēs **Vol. 3:** 102
katharsis **Vol. 2:** 477, 594
kathedra **Vol. 3:** 184, **587**
kathēkō **Vol. 3:** 930
kathēmai **Vol. 2:** 612, **615**
　Vol. 3: 587–589
kathēmenos **Vol. 3:** 1193
katheudō **Vol. 1:** 429 f., **441–443,** 447
　Vol. 2: 927
kathezomai **Vol. 3:** 587
kathistēmi **Vol. 1: 471 f.,** 478, 533
　Vol. 3: 363
kathizō **Vol. 3: 587–589**
kathodēgos **Vol. 3: 935 f.,**
katholikos **Vol. 1:** 52
kathoraō **Vol. 3:** 128, **511 f., 515**
kathōs **Vol. 1:** 338
　Vol. 2: 669
　Vol. 3: 488, 492, 1018
kathōs gegraptai **Vol. 1:** 736
　Vol. 3: 488, 492
katischyō **Vol. 3:** 627, **712 f.**
katō **Vol. 1:** 179
　Vol. 2: 184, **187,** 209 f., 304
　Vol. 3: 1199
katoikeō **Vol. 2:** 247, 251
　Vol. 3: 793
katoikētērion **Vol. 2:** 247, 249, 251
katoikizō **247, 251**
katoptrizontes **Vol. 2:** 756
katōteros **Vol. 2:** 205, **209**
kauchaomai **Vol. 1: 227 f.**
　Vol. 2: 243, 354, **874**
kauchēma **Vol. 1: 227–229**
　Vol. 2: 243
　Vol. 3: 1151
kauchēsis **Vol. 1:** 227 f., 712
kauma **Vol. 1: 652 f.**
kaumatizō **Vol. 1: 652 f.**
kaustēriazō **Vol. 2: 574 f.**
kaustēriazomai **Vol. 2:** 575
kaustērion **Vol. 2:** 574
kautērion **Vol. 2:** 574
kecharitōmenē **Vol. 2:** 119
keimai **Vol. 1:** 441, 471
　Vol. 2: 809, 846
keiō **Vol. 1:** 670
keisthai **Vol. 1:** 635
kekalymmenon **Vol. 2:** 214
kekasthai **Vol. 2:** 643
kekatharmenos **Vol. 3:** 103
kekaustēriasmenōn **Vol. 2:** 574
keklēmenos **Vol. 1:** 272
kekrymmenos **Vol. 2:** 217
kel **Vol. 1:** 408
keleuma **Vol. 1:** 408
keleuō **Vol. 1:** 271, **341**
keleusma **Vol. 1:** 341 f., **408–410,** 412
keleustēs **Vol. 1:** 408
keleuthos **Vol. 3:** 1155
keleuthros **Vol. 1:** 481

kenodoxia **Vol. 1:** 228, **546**
  Vol. 2: 44, 47
kenodoxos **Vol. 1: 546**
  Vol. 2: 44, 47
kenoō **Vol. 1: 546 f.,** 706
  Vol. 2: 301, 500, 514
  Vol. 3: 597
kenos **Vol. 1: 546 f.,** 550 f.,
  553, 671, 706 f., 709
  Vol. 2: 262, 343, 445, 828,
  844, 854
  Vol. 3: 281, 563, 604, 645
kenōsis 548 f.
kēnsos **Vol. 3: 752–754**
kentron **Vol. 1: 511**
  Vol. 3: 267
kentyriōn **Vol. 3: 958, 964**
kephalaion **Vol. 2:** 157, 163
kephalaioō **Vol. 2:** 157
kephalē **Vol. 1:** 238, 301, 665
  Vol. 2: 156–163, 579
  Vol. 3: 1063, 1066
kephalē gōnias **Vol. 3: 388–390,**
  398 f.
kephalis **Vol. 2:** 157
kēphas **Vol. 3: 381, 383 f.,** 398
keraia **Vol. 3:** 181 f.
kerameia **Vol. 3: 910**
kerameikos **Vol. 3: 910**
kerameus **Vol. 3: 910–912**
keramikos **Vol. 3: 910–913**
keramion **Vol. 3: 910 f.**
keramos 910, 912
kerannymi **Vol. 3: 910 f.,** 913
keras **Vol. 2:** 601
  Vol. 3: 198, 711, **714 f.**
kerdainō **Vol. 3: 136 f.**
kerdos **Vol. 3:** 134, **136 f.**
kērygma **Vol. 1:** 62, 247, 369,
  397
  Vol. 2: 36, 248, 398, 401,
  647
  Vol. 3: 48, 51–53, 60–63,
  67 f., 166, 285 f., 328, 401,
  629 f., 643–645
kēryssō **Vol. 1:** 397
  Vol. 2: 111, 113
  Vol. 3: 44, 46 f., **48, 50–52,
  54–57,** 170, 285, 767, 774,
  1112
kēryx **Vol. 1:** 127
  Vol. 2: 682
  Vol. 3: 48–53, 67, 170, 767
kēteios **Vol. 1:** 670
kētos 670 f.
kibōtos **Vol. 3:** 812, 815, 1040,
  1042
kindyneuō **Vol. 1: 419**
kindynos **Vol. 1: 419**
kinyra **Vol. 3:** 671
klados **Vol. 3: 865, 867, 869 f.**
klaiō **Vol. 2: 416 f., 424**
klaō **Vol. 2:** 296, **524**
klasis **Vol. 2: 520, 524, 530**

klasis tou artou **Vol. 2: 520,
  524,** 530
klasma **Vol. 1:** 729
klauthmos **Vol. 2: 416 f.,** 421
klēdonizomenos **Vol. 2: 554**
kleiō **Vol. 2: 729 f.,** 733
kleis **Vol. 2:** 727, **729 f.,** 897
  Vol. 3: 188, 384, 387 f., 652,
  717, 763
kleisē ta splanchna **Vol. 2:** 733
klēma **Vol. 3:** 226, **865, 869**
kleos **Vol. 2:** 52
  Vol. 3: 1156
kleptēs **Vol. 3: 377 f.,** 381
kleptō **Vol. 3:** 54, **377 f.,** 381
kleptōn **Vol. 3:** 377
klēronomeō **Vol. 1:** 301
  Vol. 2: 258, **295–300**
klēronomia **Vol. 2: 295–302**
  Vol. 3: 72, 391
klēronomos **Vol. 2: 295–300**
  Vol. 3: 72
klēroō **Vol. 1:** 534
  Vol. 2: 295 f., 299, 380
klēros **Vol. 1:** 534
  Vol. 2: 295–304
  Vol. 3: 647
klēsis **Vol. 1: 270 f., 273–275**
  Vol. 2: 243, 556
klētos **Vol. 1:** 92, **270–275,** 298,
  540
  Vol. 2: 544
  Vol. 3: 1201
koilia **Vol. 1:** 169, 742
koimaō **Vol. 1:** 441
  Vol. 2: 925
koimaomai **Vol. 1:** 429 f.,
  441–443
  Vol. 2: 925
  Vol. 3: 1207
koinē **Vol. 1:** 62
  Vol. 2: 657
koinon **Vol. 1:** 639
koinōneō **Vol. 1: 636, 639, 641**
koinōnia **Vol. 1:** 448, 635,
  639–644, 649
  Vol. 2: 530, 826
  Vol. 3: 104, 278, 547, 572,
  702, 724, 854
koinōnikos **Vol. 1: 639 f.,** 642
koinōnos **Vol. 1: 639, 642 f.,**
  Vol. 2: 520, 661
koinoō **Vol. 1:** 448, **639, 642**
koinos **Vol. 1:** 291 f., 448,
  639–642, 644
  Vol. 2: 499
  Vol. 3: 28, 104, 1083
koitē **Vol. 2:** 570, **586 f.**
kokkinos **Vol. 1:** 205 f.
kolaphizō **Vol. 1: 161–164**
  Vol. 3: 857, 859
kolaphos **Vol. 3:** 857
kolasis **Vol. 1: 568**
  Vol. 3: 98 f.

kolazō **Vol. 1:** 568
  Vol. 3: 98, 100
kolla **Vol. 2:** 248
kollaō **Vol. 2: 350**
kollaomai **Vol. 2: 348 f.**
kollourion **Vol. 3:** 518
koloboō **Vol. 1:** 542
  Vol. 2: 916, 932
kolos **Vol. 2:** 222
kolpoō **Vol. 1:** 240
kolpos **Vol. 1:** 240
  Vol. 3: 1174, 1185 f.
kōlyō **Vol. 1:** 149
  Vol. 2: 220–223
kōmē **Vol. 2:** 803
komizomai **Vol. 1:** 713
kōmos **Vol. 2:** 587
kondrantēn **Vol. 2:** 850
koniaō **Vol. 1:** 205, 265
konis **Vol. 1:** 520
  Vol. 3: 545
kōnōps **Vol. 1:** 116
kopetos **Vol. 2:** 223, **417 f., 424**
kōphos **Vol. 1: 428 f.**
kopiaō **Vol. 1: 262 f.**
  Vol. 3: 1162
kopos **Vol. 1:** 260, **262 f.,** 647
kopria **Vol. 1: 480**
  Vol. 3: 448
koprion **Vol. 1: 480**
kopron **Vol. 1: 480**
kopros **Vol. 1: 480**
koptō **Vol. 2:** 220, **416–418,**
  705
koptomai **Vol. 2: 417**
korakinos **Vol. 3:** 754
korasion **Vol. 1:** 283
  Vol. 3: 1071
korban **Vol. 2: 43 f.,** 469, 813
  Vol. 3: 423, 763, 1070
korbanas **Vol. 2: 43**
koreō **Vol. 2:** 796
Korinthos **Vol. 1:** 299
kosmeō **Vol. 1: 521, 524, 526**
  Vol. 2: 236
kosmikon **Vol. 3:** 814
kosmikos **Vol. 1: 521, 524**
kosmios **Vol. 1: 521, 524**
kosmiōs **Vol. 2:** 476
kosmokratōr **Vol. 2:** 514
  Vol. 3: 716–718
kosmos **Vol. 1:** 53, 105, 377,
  401, 517, 519, **521–526,** 542,
  613, 651
  Vol. 2: 200, 280, 411, 420,
  452, 476, 494, 511, 548,
  559, 567, 609, 840
  Vol. 3: 72, 168 f., 217, 445,
  469 f., 574, 582, 789, 829,
  1035, 1045, 1164, 1188,
  1193
kotos **Vol. 1:** 107
kpei **Vol. 1:** 378
kraipalē **Vol. 1:** 514

krat- **Vol. 1:** 494
krataioō **Vol. 3: 716, 718**
krataios **Vol. 3: 716, 718**
krateō **Vol. 1:** 703
 Vol. 3: 716 f.
kratistos **Vol. 3: 716–718**
kratos **Vol. 2:** 601, 767
 Vol. 3: 711, **716–718**
kraugazō **Vol. 1:** 409
krazō **Vol. 1:** 271 f., **408–410,**
 412
 Vol. 2: 855, 873
 Vol. 3: 114
kreas **Vol. 1: 671 f., 674**
kreissōn **Vol. 3:** 216
kreittō **Vol. 3:** 1083
kreittōn **Vol. 1:** 371, 666
 Vol. 2: 847
 Vol. 3: 73
kremannymi **Vol. 1: 391, 394**
krima **Vol. 1:** 210
 Vol. 2: 362–366
 Vol. 3: 96, 648, 760
krinō **Vol. 1:** 60, 503, 648
 Vol. 2: 361–365, 370, **371,**
 468
krisis **Vol. 1:** 386
 Vol. 2: 143, **362, 365 f.,** 371,
 680
 Vol. 3: 344 f., 582
kritēs **Vol. 2: 362 f., 365**
kritikos **Vol. 2: 362, 365**
krouō **Vol. 2: 855,** 857, **881,**
 885
 Vol. 3: 529, 532
krybō **Vol. 2:** 214
kryphaiọs **Vol. 2: 214, 216**
kryphē **Vol. 2:** 214
kryphios **Vol. 2: 214**
krypta **Vol. 2:** 214
kryptō **Vol. 2:** 210 f., **214,**
 216 f., 220, 835
 Vol. 3: 247, 312, 493
krypton **Vol. 2:** 212
 Vol. 3: 320
kryptos **Vol. 2: 214–216**
krystallizō **Vol. 2:** 398
krystallos **Vol. 3: 398**
ktaomai **Vol. 1:** 380
 Vol. 2: 773, 845
 Vol. 3: 1064 f., 1078
kteinō **Vol. 1:** 429
ktēma **Vol. 2:** 829, 844, **845 f.**
ktēmata **Vol. 2: 845**
ktēnos **Vol. 1:** 114
 Vol. 3: 1160
ktēsis **Vol. 1:** 381
kti **Vol. 1:** 378
ktisis **Vol. 1: 376–378, 381,**
 383–386, 388 f.
 Vol. 2: 243 f., 545, 671 f.,
 912
 Vol. 3: 642
ktisma **Vol. 1: 378, 381–383,**

385–387
ktistēs **Vol. 1: 378, 382 f., 387**
ktizō **Vol. 1:** 178, 376, **378–**
 380, 383 f., 387 f.
 Vol. 2: 912
 Vol. 3: 1182
kybernaō **Vol. 1:** 193 f., 198
kybernēsis **Vol. 1: 192–194, 198**
kybernētēs **Vol. 1:** 193 f., 198
kydos **Vol. 2:** 52
kyklos **Vol. 3:** 679
kyllos **Vol. 2: 414 f.**
kyminon **Vol. 2: 210 f.**
kynarion **Vol. 1:** 117
kyōn **Vol. 1:** 117
kyria **Vol. 1:** 539
 Vol. 2: 510 f., 518
kyriakē **Vol. 3:** 410, **411 f.,** 413
kyriakē hēmera **Vol. 2: 518,**
 934
kyriakon deipnon **Vol. 2: 518,**
 520, 522
 Vol. 3: 411
kyriakos **Vol. 2: 510, 518**
kyrie **Vol. 2: 509 f.,** 514
kyrieuō **Vol. 1:** 445
 Vol. 2: 510, 518
kyrioi **Vol. 2: 510, 512,** 516 f.,
 595
kyrios **Vol. 1:** 71, 168, 197,
 210, 212, 228, 295, 325,
 469, 475, 484, 486, 571, 718
 Vol. 2: 63 f., 72, 80 f., 155,
 186, 191, 194, 203, 213,
 247, 332, 338, 359, 373,
 386 f., **508–520,** 522, 527,
 530, 533, 536, 548, 562,
 595, 651 f., 664, 720, 735,
 789, 800, 837, 867, 900 f.,
 932
 Vol. 3: 56, 115, 160, 171,
 178, 221, 239, 245, 299,
 341, 344, 372, 411, 484,
 531, 567 f., 595 f., 643, 651,
 709, 763, 780, 940, 1151,
 1178, 1181, 1191, 1198,
 1202, 1205, 1207, 1211
kyriotēs **Vol. 1:** 462
 Vol. 2: 510, 518, 614
 Vol. 3: 284, 344
kyroō **Vol. 1: 664**
kyros **Vol. 1:** 664
 Vol. 2: 510

labete **Vol. 2:** 524
lachainō **Vol. 2:** 210
lachanon **Vol. 2: 210 f.**
laikos **Vol. 2:** 457
lailaps **Vol. 3: 1000, 1003**
lakaō **Vol. 1:** 94
laleō **Vol. 2:** 111, 113
 Vol. 3: 54, 574, **1081, 1106,**
 1109
laleō tō theō **Vol. 2: 874**

lalia **Vol. 3:** 316
lambanō **Vol. 1:** 336, 343, 363,
 475, 536, 587, 709
 Vol. 2: 524, 594
 Vol. 3: 241, 253, 262, 353,
 596, 737, 744–746, **747–751,**
 753, 835
lampades **Vol. 2:** 486
lampas **Vol. 2: 484–486,** 487
lampō **Vol. 2: 484–486, 496**
lampros **Vol. 2:** 484, 486
lamprōs **Vol. 2: 484, 486**
lamprotēs **Vol. 2: 484–486**
lanchanō **Vol. 1:** 471, **478**
lanthanō **Vol. 3:** 875, 878
laoi **Vol. 2:** 799
laos **Vol. 1:** 199, 299, 305, 307,
 569, 732
 Vol. 2: 127, 457, 788, 790 f.,
 793, **795–801, 805,** 839
 Vol. 3: 161, 551, 1197
laos ex ethnōn **Vol. 2:** 805
laskō **Vol. 1:** 94
latreia **Vol. 2:** 285, 885
 Vol. 3: 549–551, 1119
latreuō **Vol. 2:** 94, 885
 Vol. 3: 432, 544 f., **549 f.,**
 553
latron **Vol. 3:** 549
leg- **Vol. 3:** 1081
legō **Vol. 1:** 344, 418, 536
 Vol. 2: 173, 180, 186, 281,
 356, 379, 645
 Vol. 3: 54. 457, 489 f., 505,
 822, 995, **1081 f., 1087,**
 1106 f., 1144, 1156 f.
legomenos **Vol. 1:** 310
leia 377
leimma **Vol. 3: 247 f., 251 f.**
leipō **Vol. 3: 247 f., 251,** 253
leipsanon **Vol. 3: 248**
leitourgeō **Vol. 1:** 474
 544 f., 549 f., **551–553,** 755
leitourgia **Vol. 3: 551–553,** 913
leitourgikos **Vol. 3: 551 f.**
leitourgos **Vol. 2:** 885
 Vol. 3: 38, **551–553,** 755
lēkeō **Vol. 1:** 94
lēmpsis **Vol. 2:** 131
leōn **Vol. 1:** 118
 Vol. 2: 411
lēos, leōs **Vol. 2:** 795, 798
 Vol. 3: 551
lepra **Vol. 2: 464,** 466
 Vol. 3: 997
lepros **Vol. 2: 463 f.,** 466
lepton **Vol. 2:** 850
 Vol. 3: 791
lēstēs **Vol. 3: 377–379,** 380 f.
lēthē **Vol. 3:** 231
lēthō **Vol. 3:** 875, 878, 884
Leuei **Vol. 2:** 467
Leueitikos **Vol. 2:** 466
Leui **Vol. 2: 466 f.**

Leuis **Vol. 2: 466**
Leuitēs **Vol. 2: 466**
leuk **Vol. 2:** 487
leukē **Vol. 2:** 464, 675
leukos **Vol. 1:** 203, **204,** 206, 317
　Vol. 2: 484
　Vol. 3: 40, 143, 347, 349, 360, 362
lexis **Vol. 3:** 1086
lian **Vol. 1:** 729
　Vol. 2: 103
liaros **Vol. 1:** 318
libanos **Vol. 2: 293–295**
libanōtos **Vol. 2: 293–295**
libertinos **Vol. 3:** 590, **598**
ligyrion **Vol. 3:** 396
limnē **Vol. 3:** 984 f., **992**
limos **Vol. 2: 264–266**
lithinos **Vol. 3: 390,** 398
lithos **Vol. 1:** 541, 660
　Vol. 3: 363, 381 f., 388 f., **390 f., 393 f.,** 396, 398, 855
log- **Vol. 3:** 822
logeia **Vol. 3: 751 f.,** 759, 854
logikos **Vol. 2:** 476, 885
　Vol. 3: 1081, 1105, 1118 f.
logion **Vol. 1:** 62, 504
　Vol. 2: 57, 630
　Vol. 3: 1081, 1106, 1118
logios **Vol. 3: 1081, 1106,** 1117
logismos **Vol. 1:** 350
　Vol. 3: 75, 678, **822–824,** 826
logistikos **Vol. 3:** 122
logizesthai eis **Vol. 3: 1171**
logizomai **Vol. 1:** 472
　Vol. 2: 458
　Vol. 3: 168 f., **822–826,** 1175, 1187 f.
logographos **Vol. 2:** 643
logomacheō **Vol. 3: 1119**
logomachia **Vol. 3: 1119**
logos **Vol. 1:** 54, 56, 63, 107, 138, 337, 344, 397, 459, 468, 513, 546, 571, 579, 592. 636, 654, 659, 671, 736
　Vol. 2: 79, 81, 113, 131, 133, 155, 158, 169 f., 175, 456, 476 f., 493, 518, 546, 591, 594, 643 f., 657, 659, 683, 744, 766
　Vol. 3: 53, 69, 122, 168 f., 313, 353, 489, 540, 542, 744, 746, 765, 771 f., 868, 876, 886, 941, 1026, 1031, 1036 f., 1044, 1046, 1078, **1081–1087, 1106, 1108–1110, 1112, 1119–1123,** 1143–1145, 1149, 1176, 1195, 1204 f.
loidoreō **Vol. 1:** 413
　Vol. 3: 340 f., **346 f.**
loidoria **Vol. 3: 346,** 1179

loidoros **Vol. 3: 346 f.**
loipoi **Vol. 2: 794**
　Vol. 3: 253
loipon **Vol. 3: 252**
loipos **Vol. 3: 247 f., 251–253**
louō **Vol. 1:** 143 f., **150–154,** 160, 224, 701
　Vol. 3: 180, 989, 1007
loutron **Vol. 1: 150–153**
lychnia **Vol. 2:** 484, **486 f.**
　Vol. 3: 814
lychnos **Vol. 2:** 484, **486 f.,** 488, **495 f.**
lydia **Vol. 3:** 855
lykos **Vol. 1:** 118
lyō **Vol. 1:** 152
　Vol. 2: 732
　Vol. 3: 174, **177, 179–181, 183–189,** 201, 222, 261, 329, 435, 484, 491 f., **537,** 544, 763, 795
lypē **Vol. 2:** 360, 419–421, 424
　Vol. 3: 725
lypeō **Vol. 1:** 178
　Vol. 2: 416, **419 f.**
lypeomai **Vol. 2: 419 f.**
lysis **Vol. 1:** 577, 581
　Vol. 3: 177, 188, 537
lythēnai 491
lytra **Vol. 3: 190,** 192
lytron **Vol. 1:** 438
　Vol. 2: 425
　Vol. 3: 174, 177 f., **189–192, 194–197,** 214, 219, 420, 429, 435, 546, 611, 682, 1179 f., 1196
lytroō **Vol. 3:** 174, **189 f.,** 192, 215
lytrōsis **Vol. 1:** 191
　Vol. 2: 174, **189 f., 193, 198 f.**
lytrōtēs **Vol. 3:** 178, **189 f., 193, 199**
lytrōtos **Vol. 3:** 193
lytroumenos **Vol. 3:** 192
lytrousthai **Vol. 3: 192 f., 198, 200**

-ma **Vol. 3:** 689
machaira **Vol. 3: 958, 967**
machē **Vol. 1:** 262, 644–646
　Vol. 2: 447
　Vol. 3: 958 f., 963
machomai **Vol. 1:** 645 f.
　Vol. 3: 959, 963, 981
mageia **Vol. 2: 552, 557 f.,** 729, 831, 847
　Vol. 3: 180, 270, 324, 457, 474, 735, 844, 860
mageuō **Vol. 2: 552, 557 f.**
Magōg **Vol. 3:** 959
magos **Vol. 2: 552, 557, 561**
mainomai **Vol. 1: 527–530**
　Vol. 3: 76, 230

makar **Vol. 1:** 215
makarios **Vol. 1: 215 f.**
　Vol. 2: 543, 659, 825
　Vol. 3: 257, 719
makarismos **Vol. 1: 215 f.**
makarizō **Vol. 1: 215 f.**
Makkabaios **Vol. 1:** 63
makran **Vol. 2: 52–54**
makrothen **Vol. 3:** 53
makrothymeō **Vol. 2: 768–772,** 901
makrothymia **Vol. 1:** 646
　Vol. 2: 764–771, 774, **776,** 901
makrothymos **Vol. 2: 768 f.**
malakia **Vol. 3: 996 f.,** 999
mallon **Vol. 1:** 534, 591, 729
　Vol. 2: 504
　Vol. 3: 596, 599
mamōnas, mammōnas **Vol. 1:** 138, 277, 684
　Vol. 2: 255, 549, 829, 831, **836 f., 843–846, 852**
　Vol. 3: 576, 595, 812
mania **Vol. 1: 528 f.**
　Vol. 2: 471
manna **Vol. 1:** 205, 249, **252 f.**
　Vol. 2: 218, 268 f., 628
manteuomai **Vol. 3:** 74, 81
manteuomenos manteian **Vol. 2:** 554
manthanō **Vol. 1: 483–487,** 493
　Vol. 3: 765
mantikos **Vol. 3:** 75
mantis **Vol. 2:** 234
　Vol. 3: 75 f.
marana tha **Vol. 2:** 895
maranatha **Vol. 1:** 323, 415
　Vol. 2: 515, 518, 520, 527, 530 f., **537,** 543, 887, **895–898, 931 f.**
　Vol. 3: 245, 316
margaritēs **Vol. 3: 394,** 396, 399
martyr **Vol. 3:** 1038
martyreō **Vol. 1:** 348
　Vol. 2: 110
　Vol. 3: 46, 53 f., **1038, 1041–1047,** 1203
martyria **Vol. 2:** 110
　Vol. 3: 53, 89, 749, **1038–1046,** 1050, 1213
martyrion **Vol. 3:** 198, 811, **1038–1040, 1042–1044**
martyromai **Vol. 3:** 1038
martyros **Vol. 3:** 1038
martys **Vol. 1:** 189
　Vol. 3: 53, **1038, 1041–1044, 1046 f.,** 1050 f.
mastigoō **Vol. 1: 161–164**
　Vol. 3: 998
mastix **Vol. 1: 161–163**
　Vol. 3: 996
mastizō **Vol. 1:** 161 f.

mastos **Vol. 1:** 240
mataiologia **Vol. 1: 550, 552**
mataiologos **Vol. 1: 550, 552**
mataioō **Vol. 1: 549, 551 f.**
mataios **Vol. 1:** 546, **549–552**
Vol. 2: 285, 400
Vol. 2: 200, 281, 554
mataiotēs **Vol. 1: 549–552**
matē **Vol. 1:** 550
matēn **Vol. 1:** 549 f., **552**
math- **Vol. 1:** 483
mathēsis **Vol. 2:** 659
mathētēs **Vol. 1:** 167, 303 f.,
480 f., **483–487, 489 f.,** 492
Vol. 2: 695
Vol. 3: 509
mathēteuō **Vol. 2:** 714 f.
mathos **Vol. 2:** 419
matia **Vol. 1:** 550
Mattaios **Vol. 2: 715**
mazos **Vol. 1:** 240
mē **Vol. 2:** 220, 222, 459 f.,
709
Vol. 3: 152, 168, 170, 181,
188, 377, 534, 539 f., 543,
563, 710, 740, 767, 803,
822, 825, 886, 1119, 1195 f.
mē anakalyptomenon **Vol. 2:**
213
mē eis kenon **Vol. 1:** 547
mē genoito **Vol. 1:** 181
Vol. 3: 505
mē mataion **Vol. 1:** 550
mē ou **Vol. 2:** 220
mē thaumasēs **Vol. 2:** 625
mechri **Vol. 1:** 734
Vol. 3: 64
mēdeis **Vol. 3:** 103, 558
mēden agan **Vol. 2:** 103
mega (neut. of → *megas*)
megal- **Vol. 3:** 29
megalē (fem. of → *megas*)
megaleia **Vol. 2: 424–426**
megaleios **Vol. 2:** 425
megaleiotēs **Vol. 2: 424–426**
megalōsynē **Vol. 1:** 732
Vol. 2: 424–426
megalynō **Vol. 2: 424 f.**
Vol. 3: 400
megas **Vol. 1:** 228, 334
Vol. 2: 177, 356, **424–426,**
428, **429,** 443, 623
Vol. 3: 113 f., 143, 318, 394,
455, 457, 568, 1013
megistanes **Vol. 1:** 666
megistos **Vol. 2:** 425
meizōn **Vol. 1:** 334
Vol. 2: 425–427, 545, 835
melan **Vol. 1:** 203
melas **Vol. 1:** 203, 205 f.
Melchisedek **Vol. 2: 590, 593**
mellō **Vol. 1: 325–327**
Vol. 2: 480
mellōn **Vol. 1: 325–327**

Vol. 3: 198, 829 f., 833
melō **Vol. 1: 276, 278,** 356
melos **Vol. 1: 229, 231,** 235,
241, 445
memnēmai **Vol. 3:** 230
memona **Vol. 3:** 230
memphomai **Vol. 2:** 139, **143–
145**
Vol. 3: 932
mempsimoiros **Vol. 2: 143, 145**
mempsis **Vol. 2: 143 f.**
men- **Vol. 1:** 528
Vol. 2: 245
mēn **Vol. 2:** 675, 688, 700
Vol. 3: 152, 826
menein en **Vol. 2: 546**
Vol. 3: 225
mēnis **Vol. 1:** 107
menō **Vol. 1:** 608
Vol. 2: 213, 772, 847
Vol. 3: 223–225, 228–230
menontes **Vol. 3:** 224
menos **Vol. 2:** 233
Vol. 3: 230
mēpote **Vol. 2:** 753
merimna **Vol. 1: 276–278**
merimnaō **Vol. 1: 276–278**
Vol. 3: 1038
meris **Vol. 2:** 298, 306, **303 f.,**
783
merizō **Vol. 3:** 400
mermēros **Vol. 3:** 1038
meros **Vol. 2:** 209, 295, **303 f.**
Vol. 3: 403
mesidios **Vol. 1:** 373
mesitēs **Vol. 1: 372–376**
Vol. 2: 343
Vol. 3: 215
mesiteuō **Vol. 1: 373–375**
mesonyktion **Vol. 1:** 420
Vol. 2: 136
mesos **Vol. 1:** 94, 372 f.
Vol. 2: 615
Vol. 3: 195, 795, 948, 1178
mesotēs **Vol. 3:** 926
mesotoichon **Vol. 3:** 185, **795,**
798, **948 f.**
Mesrain **Vol. 1:** 530
messa **Vol. 1:** 665
Messias **Vol. 2:** 334
Vol. 3: 462
mestos **Vol. 2:** 597
Vol. 3: 102
meta **Vol. 1:** 357, 442, 445
Vol. 2: 233, 359, 423, 445,
604, 680, 699
Vol. 3: 262, 561, 1120,
**1172–1174, 1182, 1190, 1201,
1204–1207,** 1214 f.
metabainō **Vol. 2: 184, 186**
metadidōmi **Vol. 2:** 40 f.
metakaleomai **Vol. 1:** 273
metalambanō **Vol. 3: 747, 750**
metalēmpsis **Vol. 3: 747, 750**

metallassō **Vol. 3: 166 f.**
metamelomai **Vol. 1:** 353–355,
356
metamorphoō **Vol. 3: 861, 864**
metamorphoomai **Vol. 1: 705,
708**
Vol. 2: 673
metanoeō **Vol. 1:** 353–356,
357–359, 362, 600
Vol. 3: 103
metanoia **Vol. 1:** 111, 160,
355 f., **357 f.,** 362, 422,
702 f., 742
Vol. 2: 183, 770
Vol. 3: 48, 52, 55, 1158
metaphora **Vol. 2:** 743
metaschēmatizō **Vol. 1:** 707,
708–710
Vol. 3: 864
metathesis **Vol. 3:** 265 f.
metatithēmi **Vol. 1:** 608
Vol. 2: 123
Vol. 3: 264–266, **601 f.**
metechō **Vol. 1: 635 f.,** 639
meteōros **Vol. 3:** 29
mētēr **Vol. 1:** 187, 569, 615
Vol. 2: 497
Vol. 3: 1055, 1061, **1068–
1070,** 1076
meth' hymōn **Vol. 3: 1204**
methē **Vol. 1: 513–515**
Vol. 2: 587
methermēneuō **Vol. 1:** 579 f.
methermēneuomai **Vol. 1:** 581
methodeia **Vol. 3: 935, 943**
methodeuō **Vol. 3:** 936
methodos **Vol. 3:** 935 f., 943
methyō **Vol. 1: 513 f.,**
methyskō **Vol. 1: 513**
methyskomai **Vol. 1:** 513
methysma **Vol. 1: 513**
methysos **Vol. 1: 513**
metochē **Vol. 1: 635 f.**
metochos **Vol. 1: 635 f.,** 639
metoikesia **Vol. 1:** 685
mētra **Vol. 1:** 667
metreō **Vol. 3:** 402
metrētēs **Vol. 3: 403**
metron **Vol. 1:** 605, 711, 740
Vol. 2: 618
Vol. 3: 400, **402–404,** 430,
436, 561
mētropolis **Vol. 3:** 1069
mi **Vol. 1:** 490
mia (fem. of → *heis*)
miainō **Vol. 1: 447–449**
Vol. 3: 925
miasma **Vol. 1: 447 f.**
miasmos **Vol. 1: 447 f.**
Michaēl **Vol. 1:** 104
Vol. 3: 345, 471
mikron **Vol. 2:** 429
mikros **Vol. 2:** 194, 424, **427–
429,** 709

Vol. 3: 839
mimēma **Vol. 1:** 491
Vol. 2: 289
Vol. 3: 876
mimeomai **Vol. 1:** 480, 483, **490 f.**, 493
Vol. 3: 60
mimēsis **Vol. 1:** 491
mimētēs **Vol. 1:** 287, **490 f.**
Vol. 3: 60
mimnēskō **Vol. 3:** 230, 233, 240–242, 245
mimnēskomai **Vol. 2:** 533
Vol. 3: 230, 240 f., 247
mimos **Vol. 1:** 490
miseō **Vol. 1:** 553, **555–557**
Vol. 2: 547
miseomai **Vol. 1:** 555
misthapodosia **Vol. 2:** 835
Vol. 3: 138, 141, 143
misthapodotēs **Vol. 3:** 138, 141, 143
misthios **Vol. 3:** 138 f.
misthōma **Vol. 3:** 138 f.
misthoō **Vol. 3:** 138 f.
misthos **Vol. 2:** 193, 499, 813
Vol. 3: 134, 136, 138 f., 141–145
misthōtēs **Vol. 3:** 139
misthōtos **Vol. 3:** 138f., 567
mnaomai **Vol. 1:** 264
Vol. 3: 353
mnē– **Vol. 3:** 231–233, 246
mneia **Vol. 3:** 230, 238, 242, 246
mnēma **Vol. 1:** 263–265
Vol. 3: 230, 238, 246
mnēmē **Vol. 3:** 230 f., 238, 240
mnēmeion **Vol. 1:** 263–265
Vol. 3: 238, 246, 268
mnēmōn **Vol. 3:** 230
mnēmoneuō **Vol. 3:** 230, 240–243
Mnēmosynē **Vol. 3:** 231
mnēmosynon **Vol. 3:** 230, 233, 236, 238, 242
mochthos **Vol. 1:** 262
mogilalos **Vol. 1:** 428
moichalidēs **Vol. 2:** 584
moichalis **Vol. 2:** 351, **582**, 584
moichaō **Vol. 2:** 582
moicheia **Vol. 1:** 500
Vol. 2: 582
Vol. 3: 538
moicheuō **Vol. 1:** 494, 498
Vol. 2: 582, 589
Vol. 3: 325, 538, 1167
moichos **Vol. 2:** 582
moira **Vol. 2:** 145, 303, 501, 664
Vol. 3: 729
mōlōps **Vol. 1:** 163 f.
molynō **Vol. 1:** 448 f.
molysmos **Vol. 1:** 448 f.

monastr̄ion **Vol. 1:** 641
monē **Vol. 3:** 224, 229
monogenēs **Vol. 1:** 668
Vol. 2: 75 f., 81, **723–725**
Vol. 3: 1202
monon **Vol. 2:** 723 f.
monos **Vol. 1:** 216, 664 f., 667
Vol. 2: 75, 394, **716**, 720, **723 f.**
Vol. 3: 314, 1202
mōnos **Vol. 2:** 723
Vol. 3: 186
monōs **Vol. 2:** 723
monōtatos **Vol. 2:** 724
mōrainō **Vol. 3:** 1023, 1025
mōrainomai **Vol. 3:** 447, **1024**
mōreuō **Vol. 3:** 1025
mōria **Vol. 2:** 143, 619, 709
Vol. 3: 53, **1023**, 1025 f.
mōrologia **Vol. 3:** 1026
mōron **Vol. 3:** 1026
mōros **Vol. 1:** 281, 418
Vol. 2: 619 f.
Vol. 3: 126, **1023–1026**, 1036
morphē **Vol. 1:** 50, 204, 355, 703 f., **705–708**, 709, 714
Vol. 2: 203, 290, 500, 673
Vol. 3: 596 f., 604, 645
morphoō **Vol. 1:** 705, 708
morphōsis **Vol. 1:** 705, 708
Vol. 3: 885
moschos **Vol. 1:** 116
mousikos **Vol. 1:** 645
Mōÿsēs **Vol. 2:** 635, **638**, 642
Vol. 3: 186, 484
mychos **Vol. 2:** 644
myeō **Vol. 3:** 501, 510
myktērizō **Vol. 3:** 341, 347
mylikos **Vol. 3:** 390, 394
mylinos **Vol. 3:** 390, 394, 1013
mylos **Vol. 3:** 390, 394
myō **Vol. 3:** 501
myron **Vol. 1:** 119, 124
Vol. 2: 294 f., 712
mystērion **Vol. 1:** 64, 370, 539, 578
Vol. 2: 255, 401, 581, 835
Vol. 3: 314, **501–505**, 510 f.
mystēs **Vol. 1:** 184, 327
Vol. 3: 205
mythōdes **Vol. 2:** 643
mythologos **Vol. 2:** 644
mythos **Vol. 2:** 613, **643–645**, 647
Vol. 3: 274, 1033, 1081

naiō **Vol. 3:** 781
naos **Vol. 1:** 234
Vol. 2: 233, 235 f., 250
Vol. 3: 185, **781–785**, 789, 792 f., 796 f.
nauageō **Vol. 1:** 608
Nazaraios **Vol. 1:** 535

Nazarēnos **Vol. 2:** 332–334, 343, 346
Nazaret **Vol. 2:** 333
Nazōraios **Vol. 2:** 332–334, 343, 346
nē Dia **Vol. 3:** 738
nea **Vol. 2:** 675
neanis **Vol. 3:** 1071 f.
neaniskos **Vol. 1:** 192
nekroō **Vol. 1:** 443, 445
nekros **Vol. 1:** 429, 436, **443–446**
Vol. 2: 554
Vol. 3: 268, 278, 299, 303, 1176, 1189, 1207 f.
nekrōsis **Vol. 1:** 443, 445
nektar **Vol. 1:** 513
nekys **Vol. 1:** 443
nēlees **Vol. 2:** 594
nemō **Vol. 2:** 296, 438
neōkoros **Vol. 3:** 796
neomēnia **Vol. 3:** 733
neophytos **Vol. 2:** 674
neos **Vol. 2:** 669–671, 674–676, 714
Vol. 3: 457, 785
neōs **Vol. 3:** 796
neōteros **Vol. 2:** 674 f.
neotēs **Vol. 2:** 674 f.
nēphalios **Vol. 1:** 513–515
nephelē **Vol. 2:** 912
Vol. 3: 1000, 1003
nēphō **Vol. 1:** 514 f.
Vol. 2: 137
nephos **Vol. 3:** 1003
nephros **Vol. 2:** 181
nēpios **Vol. 1:** 92, 238, 280–282, 290
Vol. 3: 607
nēsteia **Vol. 1:** 611 f.
nēsteuō **Vol. 1:** 611–613
nēstis **Vol. 1:** 611–613
nikaō **Vol. 1:** 648, **650**, 652
nikē **Vol. 1:** 644, **650 f.**
Nikolaitēs **Vol. 2:** 676
Nikolaos **Vol. 2:** 676
nikōn **Vol. 1:** 651
nikos **Vol. 1:** 650
Vol. 3: 267
Nineuē **Vol. 2:** 678
Nineui **Vol. 2:** 678
Nineuitēs **Vol. 2:** 678
Ninos **Vol. 2:** 678
Ninus **Vol. 2:** 678
niptō **Vol. 1:** 143 f., 150–152, 153 f., 160, 224 f.
Vol. 2: 144, 150
Nōe **Vol. 2:** 681
noēma **Vol. 1:** 711
Vol. 2: 182
Vol. 3: 122–125, 128, 824, 1082
noeō **Vol. 1:** 693
Vol. 3: 122–129, 132 f.

noētos **Vol. 1:** 523
  Vol. 2: 192
  Vol. 3: 124
nomē **Vol. 2:** 438
nomeus **Vol. 3:** 564
nomikos **Vol. 2: 438, 443, 447**
  Vol. 3: 353, 409, **477, 480**
nomimos **Vol. 2:** 475
  Vol. 3: 930
nomimōs **Vol. 1:** 645
  Vol. 2: 438, 447
nomizō **Vol. 1:** 595
  Vol. 2: 234, 439
  Vol. 3: 181
nomodidaskalos **Vol. 2: 438, 447**
  Vol. 3: 477, 480, 765, 768
nomophylakōn **Vol. 1:** 193
nomos **Vol. 1:** 54, 94, 228, 245, 282, 334, 336 f., 715, 738
  Vol. 2: 120, 131, 436 f., **437–450,** 452, **455,** 519, 540 f., 544, 546, 658 f., 662, 715
  Vol. 3: 72, 181, 185 f., 239, 353 f., 480, 493, 573 f., 580, 583 f., 593, 596 f., 885, 1151, 1178, 1188
nomothesia **Vol. 2: 438, 445**
nomotheteō **Vol. 2: 438, 448**
nomothetēs **Vol. 2: 438, 450**
noos **Vol. 3:** 133
noos theoudēs **Vol. 3:** 27
nosēma **Vol. 3: 996, 998**
noseō **Vol. 3: 996–998**
nosos **Vol. 3:** 993 f., **996–999,** 1000, 1119
nossia **Vol. 1:** 174
nothos **Vol. 1: 187 f.**
  Vol. 2: 657
notos **Vol. 3: 1000, 1003**
nous **Vol. 1:** 232, 355–357, 443 f., 481, 521, 546, 557, 568, 595, 636, 638, 671, 676, 693, 706, 708, 739
  Vol. 2: 182, 212, 439, 476, 493, 564 f., 567, 590 f.
  Vol. 3: 122–130, 133, 224, 351, 572, 672, 678, 681, 689, 809, 936, 939, 1198
nous praktikos **Vol. 3:** 123
nous theōrētikos **Vol. 3:** 123
nouthesia **Vol. 1: 568 f.**
noutheteō **Vol. 1:** 329, **567 f.,** 573
nymphē **Vol. 1:** 153
  Vol. 2: 549, 579, 581, **584 f.**
  Vol. 3: 1071, 1167
nymphios **Vol. 1:** 325
  Vol. 2: 549, **584 f.**
nymphōn **Vol. 2: 584 f.**
nyn **Vol. 2:** 282, 329, 416, 480, 543, 912
  Vol. 3: 826, 831, **833 f., 837,**

841, 843, 850, 1169
nyn aiōn **Vol. 2:** 543
nyn chronos **Vol. 3: 834**
nyni **Vol. 1:** 282
  Vol. 2: 282
  Vol. 3: 831, **833 f., 837,** 924
nyx **Vol. 1: 420 f.,** 425
  Vol. 2: 134, 368, 490
  Vol. 3: 1181

obryzos **Vol. 2:** 574
ochlos **Vol. 1:** 292 f.
  Vol. 2: 448, 788 f., 796, 799, **800 f., 805**
ochyrōma **Vol. 3:** 963
ochyros **Vol. 3:** 963
ōdē **Vol. 2: 874**
  Vol. 3: 668, 670 f., **672–675,** 676
ōdin **Vol. 3:** 180, **857–859**
ōdinō **Vol. 3:** 178, 180
  Vol. 3: 857–859
ōdis **Vol. 3:** 858
odmē **Vol. 3:** 599
ōdos **Vol. 3:** 672
odous **Vol. 2:** 421
odynē **Vol. 1:** 726
  Vol. 2: 419
  Vol. 3: 229
odyrmos **Vol. 2:** 417
ogdoos autos **Vol. 2:** 692
oida **Vol. 2:** 391 f., 398, 719
  Vol. 3: 1064, 1205
oikeia **Vol. 1:** 673
oikeios **Vol. 1:** 673
  Vol. 2: 247, 249, **251,** 794
oikeiotaton **Vol. 3:** 1157
oikeō **Vol. 1:** 518
  Vol. 2: 247, **250 f.**
oikētērion **Vol. 3:** 814
oiketēs **Vol. 2:** 509
  Vol. 3: 609
oikia **Vol. 2:** 257 f., 250
oikodespoteō **Vol. 2: 508, 510**
oikodespotēs **Vol. 2: 508–510,** 714, 790
oikodespotēsis **Vol. 2: 509**
oikodomē **Vol. 1:** 329, 662
  Vol. 2: 193, 249, **251–253,** 256
oikodomeō **Vol. 1:** 300, 302
  Vol. 2: 129, 249, **251–253**
  Vol. 3: 185
oikonomeō **Vol. 2: 253–255**
oikonomia **Vol. 1:** 697, 738
  Vol. 2: 253–256, 302, 714, 832, 837
  Vol. 3: 468, 504, 1032
oikonomos **Vol. 2: 253–255**
oikos **Vol. 1:** 149, 197, 300, 662, 690
  Vol. 2: 129, **247–256,** 873
  Vol. 3: 229, 465, 504, 593, 782, 794, 1201

oikoumenē **Vol. 1:** 59, 326, **517–519,** 521, 523, 526
  Vol. 3: 217
oikourēma **Vol. 1:** 498
oiktirmōn **Vol. 2: 598**
oiktirmos **Vol. 2:** 116, 543, **593,** 594, 597, **598,** 599 f., 733
oiktirō **Vol. 2: 598, 600**
oiktizō **Vol. 2:** 598
oiktos **Vol. 2:** 593, 598
oiktros **Vol. 2:** 598
oimē **Vol. 2:** 756
oinophlygia **Vol. 1:** 514
  Vol. 3: 918, 922
oinopotēs **Vol. 3: 918, 921**
oinos **Vol. 1:** 106
  Vol. 3: 918, 922 f.
oitōnizomenos **Vol. 2: 554**
oktō **Vol. 2:** 692
olethreuō **Vol. 1:** 471
olethros **Vol. 1:** 462, 464, **465–467,** 500
  Vol. 2: 33, 368
  Vol. 3: 97, 214, 471, 477, 535, 537
oligon **Vol. 2:** 429
oligopsychos **Vol. 3: 687**
oligōreō **Vol. 1: 462**
oligos **Vol. 1:** 462, 590
  Vol. 2: 427 f.
  Vol. 3: 839
ollymi **Vol. 1:** 462 f., 465
olothreuō **Vol. 1: 465**
olothreuōn **Vol. 1:** 465
olothreutēs **Vol. 1:** 465
ombros **Vol. 3: 1000, 1003**
omma **Vol. 2:** 393
  Vol. 3: 512
omnymi **Vol. 3:** 737
omnyō **Vol. 3: 737–740,** 743, 792, 840
omosai **Vol. 3:** 740
omosu **Vol. 1:** 64
  Vol. 2: 278, 617, 826
  Vol. 3: 122, 876, 891, 1075, 1181, 1185 f., 1200, 1202
onaimēn **Vol. 2:** 434
onar **Vol. 1: 511–513**
onarion **Vol. 1:** 117
oneidismos **Vol. 2:** 835
  Vol. 3: 340
oneidizō **Vol. 2:** 835
  Vol. 3: 257, 340 f.
oneidos **Vol. 3:** 340, 347
ōneomai **Vol. 3:** 144
onēsimos **Vol. 2:** 434
onikos **Vol. 3:** 394
oninēmi **Vol. 2:** 434
onkos **Vol. 1:** 671, 674
onoma **Vol. 1:** 272
  Vol. 2: 229, **648, 651 f., 654–656**
  Vol. 3: 161, 257, 341, 763, 1119, 1172, 1187, 1196,

366

1209–1211, 1213
onomazō **Vol. 2: 648, 655**
  Vol. 3: 233, 341
onos **Vol. 1:** 117
onta **Vol. 3:** 876, 891
onychion **Vol. 3: 396**
op– **Vol. 3:** 511 f.
opheil– **Vol. 2:** 666
opheilē **Vol. 2: 666, 668**
  Vol. 3: 754
opheilēma **Vol. 1:** 701
  Vol. 2: 120, **666–668**
opheiletēs **Vol. 2: 666–668**
opheilō **Vol. 2: 662 f., 666–669**
  Vol. 3: 152, 573
ōpheleia **Vol. 3:** 137
ōpheleō **Vol. 1:** 463
  Vol. 2: 115, 505
ophelon **Vol. 2: 666, 668**
ophis **Vol. 1:** 390, 507, **508 f.,** 511
  Vol. 2: 638, 642
  Vol. 3: 470
ophthalmos **Vol. 2:** 710, 925
  Vol. 3: 32, **511 f., 516,** 1179
ōphthē **Vol. 3:** 281, 284 f.
ōphthēn **Vol. 3: 511 f., 518**
opi **Vol. 1:** 492
opisō **Vol. 1:** 321, 324, 481 f., **492 f.**
  Vol. 3: 471, 946
opisthen **Vol. 1:** 492 f.
ops **Vol. 1:** 585
  Vol. 2: 564
opsarion **Vol. 1: 670**
opse **Vol. 2:** 136
opsimos **Vol. 3: 1000, 1003**
opsis **Vol. 1:** 680
  Vol. 3: 512
opsomai **Vol. 3: 511, 515**
opson **Vol. 3:** 144
opsōnia **Vol. 3: 144 f.**
opsōnion **Vol. 3:** 134, **144 f.,** 379, 964
optanomai **Vol. 3: 516,** 1181
optanomenos **Vol. 3:** 1181
optasia **Vol. 3:** 310, **511 f., 515, 517**
orcheomai **Vol. 2:** 436
oregō **Vol. 1:** 460
oregomai **Vol. 1:** 457, **460 f.**
  Vol. 3: 587
oreinos **Vol. 3: 1008**
orexis **Vol. 1: 460 f.**
  Vol. 3: 587
orgaō **Vol. 1:** 107
orgē **Vol. 1: 106–108, 110–113,** 464
  Vol. 2: 412, 544, 834, 924
  Vol. 3: 205, 315, 580, 836, 1166, 1187
orgilos **Vol. 1: 107, 110**
orgizō **Vol. 1: 107**
  Vol. 2: 419

orgizomai **Vol. 1:** 110
Oriōn **Vol. 3:** 950
ornis **Vol. 1:** 174
oros **Vol. 2:** 591
  Vol. 3: 1009, 1013 f., 1094
orphanos **Vol. 2: 737 f.**
orthon **Vol. 3:** 577
orthopodeō **Vol. 3: 351 f.**
orthos **Vol. 1:** 307, 348, 599
  Vol. 2: 475, 659
  Vol. 3: 348, **351 f.,** 1084
orthōs **Vol. 3: 351,** 933
orthotomeō **Vol. 1:** 307, 309
  Vol. 3: 351 f.
Osiris **Vol. 2:** 274
osmaomai **Vol. 2:** 211
osmē **Vol. 3:** 432, **599–601**
osphys **Vol. 1:** 239
osteon **Vol. 1:** 240
ostraka **Vol. 3: 913**
ostrakeus **Vol. 3: 913**
ostrakinos **Vol. 3:** 912, **913–915**
ostrakizō **Vol. 3: 913**
ostrakon **Vol. 3: 913**
ouai **Vol. 3: 1051–1054**
oudeis **Vol. 1:** 351
  Vol. 2: 100, 683
  Vol. 3: 353, 521
ouden kōlyei **Vol. 2:** 222
oulē **Vol. 2:** 465
oupō **Vol. 1:** 738
ouranioi **Vol. 2:** 188
ouranios **Vol. 2: 188, 191 f.,** 778
ouranos **Vol. 1:** 304, 517
  Vol. 2: 54, 184, **188–196,** 376 f., 381, 502, 555, 714, 735
  Vol. 3: 55, 181 f., 391, 543, 941, 1176
ouranos aisthētos **Vol. 2:** 192
ouranos noētos **Vol. 2:** 192
ouranothen **Vol. 2: 188, 193,** 486
ous **Vol. 2:** 175, 180
  Vol. 3: 125
ousia **Vol. 1:** 711
  Vol. 2: 507, **845 f.**
ousiōdēs **Vol. 3:** 647
oxos **Vol. 2:** 28
oxythymia **Vol. 2:** 769

pachynō **Vol. 2:** 153 f., 156
pachys **Vol. 2:** 153 f.
pagis **Vol. 3:** 802, 1178
pagos **Vol. 2:** 716
paidagōgos **Vol. 1: 370**
  Vol. 2: 445
  Vol. 3: 580, **775, 778 f.,** 935
paidarion **Vol. 1: 283 f.**
  Vol. 2: 428
paideia **Vol. 1:** 462, 568 f., 639
  Vol. 2: 140 f., 745
  Vol. 3: 311, 688, 745, **775–**

777, 779, 998
paideuō **Vol. 1:** 162, 164, 494, 502, 568, 573
  Vol. 2: 122, 140–142, 446
  Vol. 3: 775–778, 780
paideutēs **Vol. 3: 775, 778**
paidia **Vol. 3:** 1027
paidion **Vol. 1:** 280, **283–285**
  Vol. 3: 352
paidiskē **Vol. 1:** 283 f.
pais **Vol. 1:** 96, 273, 280 f., **283 f.,** 286, 290, 538, 552, 597, 707
  Vol. 2: 151, 229, 337, 364, 643
  Vol. 3: 590, 593, 607–612, 634 f., 637, 640, 664, 721, 775
pais theou **Vol. 1:** 281, 283, 538
  Vol. 3: 597, **607,** 610–612, 634 f., 640, 664, 721
paizō **Vol. 2:** 436
  Vol. 3: 347
palai **Vol. 1:** 165
  Vol. 2: 669 f., 675, **713 f.,** 716, 834
palaioō **Vol. 1:** 645
  Vol. 2: 671, 675, **713 f.,** 716
palaios **Vol. 1:** 192, 339, 401, 666, 671, 682
  Vol. 2: 473, 566, 669, 675 f., **713 f.,** 716
palaiotēs **Vol. 2:** 671, 675, **713–715**
palin **Vol. 1:** 184
palingenesia **Vol. 1:** 176, 178, 180, **184 f.,** 188, 290, 521
  Vol. 2: 566, 625, 673, 836
  Vol. 3: 215, 220, 629
pan **Vol. 2:** 734
panēgyris **Vol. 1:** 304
panoplia **Vol. 3: 959, 965**
panourgia **Vol. 1: 412 f.**
panourgos **Vol. 1: 412 f.**
panta **Vol. 1:** 165, 383, 577 f.
panta en pasin **Vol. 3: 1191**
pantelēs **Vol. 3:** 210
pantes **Vol. 1:** 96
pantodapos **Vol. 3:** 197
pantoios **Vol. 3:** 197
pantokratōr **Vol. 2:** 69, 513
  Vol. 3: 716–718, 729
pantote **Vol. 1:** 741
  Vol. 2: 882
par– **Vol. 2:** 856
para **Vol. 1:** 239, 690, 714
  Vol. 2: 172, 175, 243, 291, 450, 502, 618, 659 f., 743, 756, 846
  Vol. 3: 178, 228, 835, 869, 939, 1036, **1171–1174, 1181, 1185, 1198, 1201–1205,** 1214
para kairon **Vol. 3:** 835

para kyriō **Vol. 3: 1202**
para patros **Vol. 3: 1202**
para physin **Vol. 2:** 659 f.
 Vol. 3: 869
para theō **Vol. 3: 1202**
para theou **Vol. 3: 1203**
parabainō **Vol. 2:** 586
 Vol. 3: 583 f., 587
paraballō **Vol. 2:** 743
parabasis **Vol. 1:** 85
 Vol. 3: 573 f., **583–585**
parabatēs **Vol. 3: 583 f.**
parabolē **Vol. 1:** 577
 Vol. 2: 502, **743 f., 746, 748,**
 753, 757 f., 803
 Vol. 3: 131, 503, 555, 906,
 1014, 1070, 1106
paradeigma **Vol. 2:** 290, 743
 Vol. 3: 904, 907
paradeigmatizō **Vol. 2:** 284,
 291, 293
 Vol. 3: 570
paradeisos **Vol. 2: 760 f., 764**
 Vol. 3: 315, 602
paradidomai **Vol. 2:** 527
paradidōmi **Vol. 2:** 146, 339,
 361, 367 f., 543, 719, 854
 Vol. 3: 55, 61, 171, 611,
 643, **772–774,** 1181
paradosis **Vol. 1:** 199, 335, 485
 Vol. 2: 367 f.
 Vol. 3: 61, 584, 764, **772,**
 774
paraineō **Vol. 1:** 65
 Vol. 2: 744
paraiteomai **Vol. 2: 855 f., 858**
parakaleō **Vol. 1:** 88 f., 91,
 197, 249, 271, 329, 568,
 569–571, 573
 Vol. 2: 381
 Vol. 3: 54, 87 f., 170, 1042
parakalōn **Vol. 1:** 197
paraklēsis **Vol. 1:** 329, **569–571**
 Vol. 2: 121, 766, 774
 Vol. 3: 87 f., 751
paraklētōr **Vol. 1:** 89
paraklētos **Vol. 1: 88–92,** 271,
 324, 329, 571
 Vol. 2: 359, 878, 895
 Vol. 3: 162 f., 225, 242, **704**
parakoē **Vol. 2: 172, 175**
 Vol. 3: 573, 585
parakoloutheō **Vol. 1: 480 f.**
parakouō **Vol. 2: 172, 175**
paralambanō **Vol. 2:** 839 f.
 Vol. 3: 61, 604, **747 f., 751,**
 773 f., 1181
paralelymenos **Vol. 3: 999**
paralogizomai **Vol. 2: 457–459**
paralyō **Vol. 3: 999**
paralytikos **Vol. 2: 415**
 Vol. 3: 999
paralytos **Vol. 2:** 415
paramenō **Vol. 3: 223, 228**

paramytheomai **Vol. 1: 328 f.**
 Vol. 3: 54
paramythia **Vol. 1: 328 f.**
paramythion **Vol. 1: 328 f.**
parangelia **Vol. 1: 340 f.**
parangellō **Vol. 1:** 330, **340–342**
parangelma **Vol. 1:** 339 f.
paranomeō **Vol. 2: 438, 451**
paranomos **Vol. 2:** 586
paranymphios **Vol. 3:** 1072
paraphora **Vol. 2:** 744
parapikrainō **Vol. 1: 202 f.**
parapikrasmos **Vol. 1: 203**
parapiptō **Vol. 1: 608 f.**
 Vol. 2: 717
 Vol. 3: 573, **585**
paraplēsion **Vol. 3:** 1173
paraptōma **Vol. 1:** 446, 606,
 608, 701
 Vol. 2: 120, 586
 Vol. 3: 168, 573, **585** f.,
 1176, 1184
pararrheō **Vol. 1: 682 f.**
paraskeuazō **Vol. 3:** 116, **118–**
 120, 410
paraskeuē **Vol. 3:** 119 f., **405,**
 408, 410, 413
parastēsai **Vol. 3:** 925
paratēreō **Vol. 2: 132 f.**
 Vol. 3: 410, 717
paratērēsis **Vol. 2: 132 f.**
parathēkē **Vol. 3:** 61, 770 f.
pardalis **Vol. 1:** 119
paredothē **Vol. 2:** 339
pareimi **Vol. 2: 898 f.**
 Vol. 3: 242
pareiserchomai **Vol. 1: 320, 322**
parektos **Vol. 3:** 540, 1195
paremballō **Vol. 3: 959, 965**
parembolē **Vol. 3: 959, 965**
parepidēmeō **Vol. 2:** 790
parepidēmos **Vol. 1:** 305, 683,
 689, **690,** 691
 Vol. 2: 788–790, 794, 803
parerchomai **Vol. 1: 320, 322**
 Vol. 2: 671
 Vol. 3: 181
paresis **Vol. 1:** 573, **697** f.,
 701 f.
 Vol. 2: 767
 Vol. 3: 1184
pariēmi **Vol. 1:** 698
paristanō **Vol. 1:** 474, 478
paristēmi **Vol. 1:** 471, **474** f.,
 478, 533
 Vol. 3: 925, 1181
paroikeō **Vol. 1: 690 f.**
paroikia **Vol. 1:** 685, **690 f.**
 Vol. 3: 844
paroikos **Vol. 1:** 683 f., 686–
 689, **690 f.**
 Vol. 2: 249, 251
paroimia **Vol. 2:** 736, **743,** 745,
 756 f., 760

paroinos **Vol. 1:** 514
paromoiazō **Vol. 2: 500–502**
paromoios **Vol. 2: 500** f., 503
parōn **Vol. 2:** 899
parorgismos **Vol. 2: 107, 110**
parorgizō **Vol. 1: 107, 110**
parousia **Vol. 1:** 65, 73, 406
 Vol. 2: 54, 144, 192, 387,
 503, 518, 630, **887,** 894 f.,
 897, **898–903, 907,** 909,
 924–926, **932–934**
 Vol. 3: 30, 55, 252, 310,
 315, 319, 658, 863
paroxynō **Vol. 1:** 107
paroxynomai **Vol. 1:** 110
paroxysmos **Vol. 1: 107, 110**
parrhēsia **Vol. 1:** 660, 715
 Vol. 2: 734 –737, 758
 Vol. 3: 74, 143, 1145
parrhēsiazomai **Vol. 2: 734–737**
parthenia **Vol. 3:** 1072
parthenikos **Vol. 3:** 1071
parthenos **Vol. 1:** 186
 Vol. 2: 87, 585, 588
 Vol. 3: 536, ·667, 1055,
 1058, **1071** f., 1076, 1078
pas **Vol. 1: 94,** 138, 186, 504,
 518, 524, 647, 669, 674,
 740, 742
 Vol. 2: 234, 253, 403, 477,
 502, 505, 511, 655, 657,
 661, 694, 709, 714, 719,
 723, 768, 774, 781, 793,
 799, 819, 840, 846, 910
 Vol. 3: 148, 171, 181 f., 195,
 197, 327, 354, 391, 403,
 456, 488, 567, 711, 754,
 765, 770, 841, 875, 887,
 913, 1153, 1158, 1162,
 1176 f., 1180, 1182, 1186,
 1190 f., 1194, 1197 f., 1201,
 1211 f.
pascha **Vol. 1:** 624 f., **632–635**
 Vol. 2: 277, 441, 521, **537,**
 716, 783
 Vol. 3: 431, 669
paschō **Vol. 1:** 487, 632
 Vol. 3: 92, **719–725,** 997
patassō **Vol. 1: 161–164**
pateō **Vol. 3: 943** f., 947
patēr **Vol. 1:** 65, 298, 326, 442,
 614–619, 621, 740
 Vol. 2: 250, 394, 401, 476,
 506 f., 655, 778, 780, 868 f.,
 871, 878
 Vol. 3: 162, 472, 636, 638,
 675, 772, 774, 1185 f.,
 1202 f.
path- **Vol. 3:** 719
pathē **Vol. 3:** 678
pathēma **Vol. 3: 719, 722** f.
pathētos **Vol. 3: 719, 722,** 724
pathos **Vol. 1:** 108, 674
 Vol. 2: 419, 658

Vol. 3: 719 f., 722, 997
patria Vol. 1: 615 f., 621
  Vol. 2: 655 f.
patrikos Vol. 3: 764
patrios Vol. 3: 1035
patris Vol. 1: 615 f.
  Vol. 2: 476
pau Vol. 1: 283
Paulos Vol. 2: 489
  Vol. 3: 592, 1203
pax Vol. 2: 716
pedinos Vol. 3: 1009
pēganon Vol. 2: 210 f.
pēgē Vol. 3: 982, 985–987, 988–990
pēgnymi Vol. 2: 716
peinaō Vol. 2: 264–268, 274, 277
peira Vol. 3: 798 f., 802, 810
peiraō Vol. 3: 798 f.
peiraomai Vol. 3: 802
peirasmos Vol. 1: 461, 682
  Vol. 2: 808
  Vol. 3: 587, 798–800, 802 f., 809, 811, 1176
peirazō Vol. 3: 790, 798 f., 801 f., 808–810, 1198
peismonē Vol. 1: 588, 591 f.
peith- Vol. 1: 588
peitharcheō Vol. 3: 588 f., 593
peitharchos Vol. 1: 588
peithō Vol. 1: 228, 588–593, 605
  Vol. 3: 1213
peithomai Vol. 1: 328, 587–593, 598
  Vol. 2: 122, 470
peithos Vol. 1: 588, 592
  Vol. 3: 53
pel- Vol. 3: 572
pelas Vol. 1: 258
pelazō Vol. 1: 258
pēlos Vol. 3: 911, 915 f.
pelta Vol. 3: 966
pempō Vol. 1: 126–128
  Vol. 3: 1203
penēs Vol. 2: 257, 264, 820–822, 828
penia Vol. 1: 564
  Vol. 2: 820
penichros Vol. 1: 564
  Vol. 2: 820 f.
penomai Vol. 1: 564
pentakischilioi Vol. 2: 699
pentateuchos Vol. 1: 65
pentē Vol. 2: 689, 693, 699
pentēkostē Vol. 1: 738
  Vol. 2: 783, 788
pentēkostos Vol. 2: 783
penth- Vol. 3: 719
pentheō Vol. 2: 416–418, 420, 421–423
penthos Vol. 2: 421–424
  Vol. 3: 720

pepausthai Vol. 3: 845
pepeismai Vol. 1: 588
  Vol. 2: 243
pepoitha Vol. 1: 587–589, 591 f.
pepoithenai Vol. 1: 228, 596
pepoithēsis Vol. 1: 588 f., 592
pepoithōs Vol. 1: 598
  Vol. 2: 243
pepyrōmena Vol. 3: 966
pēra Vol. 1: 143
  Vol. 2: 825
peras Vol. 3: 836
peri Vol. 1: 84, 227, 266, 335, 599
  Vol. 2: 140, 356, 489, 504, 621
  Vol. 3: 153, 162, 171, 419 f., 434, 611, 763, 771, 1045, 1119, 1172–1174, 1176, 1211, 1214
peri hamartias Vol. 3: 171, 419 f., 434, 1203
peri pollōn Vol. 3: 611, 1174
peribolaion Vol. 3: 1179
peribolon Vol. 3: 679
periechō Vol. 3: 491
periekryben Vol. 2: 214
perierchomai Vol. 1: 320, 322
perierga Vol. 2: 557
periergazomai Vol. 1: 266 f.
  Vol. 2: 434
  Vol. 3: 152
periergon Vol. 2: 557
periergos Vol. 1: 266 f.
  Vol. 2: 552
perikathairaō Vol. 1: 479
  Vol. 2: 102
perikatharma Vol. 1: 479 f.
  Vol. 2: 57
  Vol. 3: 102
perikephalaia Vol. 3: 959, 966
perikopē Vol. 1: 65
perikoptō Vol. 1: 65
perilampō Vol. 2: 484, 486
perileipō Vol. 3: 248
perileipomai Vol. 3: 247
periloipos Vol. 3: 248
perimenō 245
  Vol. 3: 224, 228
periousiasmos Vol. 2: 838
periousios Vol. 2: 298, 800, 838–840
peripateō Vol. 3: 935, 942, 943–945, 947, 1183
peripherō Vol. 3: 770
periphora Vol. 2: 744
periphroneō Vol. 1: 461 f.
peripiptō Vol. 1: 608
peripoieō Vol. 2: 838
peripoieomai Vol. 2: 833, 838 f.
  Vol. 3: 751
peripoiēsis Vol. 1: 305
  Vol. 2: 829, 838 f.
peripsaō Vol. 1: 479

peripsēma Vol. 1: 479 f.
  Vol. 2: 57
perisseia Vol. 1: 728–731
  Vol. 3: 137 f., 400
perisseuma Vol. 1: 728 f.
perisseuō Vol. 1: 728–731, 735, 744
  Vol. 2: 131, 504
  Vol. 3: 137, 728
perisseuon Vol. 1: 729
perisson Vol. 1: 729–731
  Vol. 3: 728
perissos Vol. 1: 728
  Vol. 3: 349
perissōs Vol. 1: 728, 730
perissoteron Vol. 1: 729–731
perissoteros Vol. 1: 728
perissoterōs Vol. 1: 728, 731
peristera Vol. 1: 175
peritemnō Vol. 1: 307, 309, 312
peritomē Vol. 1: 307, 309 f.
  Vol. 3: 1183, 1189
perizōnnymi Vol. 3: 120 f., 711
pernēmi Vol. 1: 497
pēroō Vol. 2: 153
pēros Vol. 2: 153
pērōsis Vol. 2: 153
perysi Vol. 3: 1174
petannymi Vol. 1: 172
peteinon Vol. 1: 172
  Vol. 2: 729
peteinos Vol. 1: 172
petomai Vol. 1: 172
petra Vol. 2: 433, 732
  Vol. 3: 381–384, 386, 390, 393, 398, 623
petrōdēs Vol. 3: 382
petros Vol. 2: 433, 652, 732
  Vol. 3: 381–383 f., 386, 398
phainō Vol. 2: 433, 484, 487 f., 496
  Vol. 3: 310, 312, 317, 320
phainomai Vol. 2: 484, 487 f.
  Vol. 3: 310
-phan- Vol. 3: 310
phaneroō Vol. 2: 122
  Vol. 3: 310, 312, 314, 316, 317, 320–323
phaneros Vol. 3: 312, 317, 320
phanerōs Vol. 3: 317, 320
phanerōsis Vol. 3: 317, 323
phantasia Vol. 3: 891
phantasma Vol. 2: 552, 559
  Vol. 3: 317, 324, 513, 876
phantazō Vol. 3: 317, 324
phantazomenon Vol. 3: 324
phaos Vol. 2: 490
Pharisaios Vol. 1: 487, 535
  Vol. 3: 810, 814
pharmakeia Vol. 2: 286, 552, 558
pharmakeus Vol. 2: 552, 558
pharmakon Vol. 1: 58
  Vol. 2: 552, 558

pharmakos **Vol. 2: 552, 554, 555, 558**
phasma **Vol. 2:** 622
phatis **Vol. 2:** 52
phatos **Vol. 2:** 674
phaulos **Vol. 1: 561, 564**
 Vol. 3: 1158
-phē- **Vol. 3: 74 f.**
pheidomenōs **Vol. 1:** 214
phēmi **Vol. 3:** 341
phengos **Vol. 2:** 484
pherō **Vol. 1:** 722
 Vol. 3: 1195
pheugō **Vol. 1: 558 f.**
pheugōn **Vol. 1:** 558
phil– **Vol. 2:** 547
Philadelpheia **Vol. 2:** 550
philadelphia **Vol. 1: 254, 257**
 Vol. 2: 470, 538, 542, **547, 549 f.**
philadelphos **Vol. 1: 254, 257**
 Vol. 2: 549
philagathos **Vol. 2: 549**
philandros **Vol. 2:** 549
philanthrōpia **Vol. 2: 547, 549, 551**
philanthrōpōs **Vol. 2: 550**
philargyria **Vol. 1: 138**
 Vol. 2: 550, 845
philargyros **Vol. 2: 550,** 843
philautia **Vol. 1:** 228
philautos **Vol. 2: 550**
philē **Vol. 2: 547 f.**
philēdonas **Vol. 1: 458, 460**
 Vol. 2: 550
philēma **Vol. 1:** 206
 Vol. 2: 538, 547–549
Philēmon **Vol. 2: 550**
phileō **Vol. 1:** 206
 Vol. 2: 86, **538 f., 542 f., 547–551,** 585
Philētos **Vol. 2: 550**
philia **Vol. 1:** 257
 Vol. 2: 538, 547 f., 551, 735, 776
Philippēsios **Vol. 2: 550**
Philippoi **Vol. 2: 550**
Philippos **Vol. 2:** 538, **550**
philodēmos **Vol. 2:** 657
Philologos **Vol. 2: 550**
philoneikia **Vol. 2: 550**
philoneikos **Vol. 2: 550**
philonikia **Vol. 2: 550**
philonikos **Vol. 2: 550**
philophrōn **Vol. 2: 550**
philophronōs **Vol. 2: 550**
philoprōteuō **Vol. 2: 550**
philos **Vol. 1:** 259, 665
 Vol. 2: 538, **547–551,** 585, 663
 Vol. 3: 1034
philosopheō **Vol. 3: 1034 f.**
philosophia **Vol. 1:** 664
 Vol. 2: 538, **550**

 Vol. 3: 877, 1027, **1034–1036**
philosophos **Vol. 2: 550**
 Vol. 3: 1034–1036
philostorgos **Vol. 2: 538 f., 542, 550**
philoteknia **Vol. 2:** 658
philoteknos **Vol. 2: 550**
philotheos **Vol. 1:** 460
 Vol. 2: 550
philotimeomai **Vol. 2: 550**
philotimia **Vol. 1:** 137
philoxenia **Vol. 1: 686, 690**
 Vol. 2: 538, **547, 550**
philoxenos **Vol. 1: 686, 690**
 Vol. 2: 550
phobeō **Vol. 1:** 328, 621, 623 f.
 Vol. 2: 596
phobeomai **Vol. 1:** 361, 484, **621–623**
 Vol. 2: 91, 94
phoberos **Vol. 1: 621–623**
 Vol. 3: 318
phobētheis **Vol. 2:** 91
phobēthron **Vol. 1:** 622
phobētron **Vol. 1:** 622
phobos **Vol. 1: 621 f.**
 Vol. 2: 93 f., 396
 Vol. 3: 561, 721
phobos theou **Vol. 2:** 93 f.
phoboumenos **Vol. 1:** 359, 361
 Vol. 2: 94
phoboumenos ton theon **Vol. 1:** 359, **361,** 623
phoinix **Vol. 1:** 648
phoitazō **Vol. 3:** 391
phōnē **Vol. 2:** 426
 Vol. 3: 51, 80, **113 f.,** 394, 675, 1078, 1143
phōneō **Vol. 3: 113 f.**
phonos **Vol. 1:** 558
 Vol. 2: 674
phoros **Vol. 3: 752, 754**
phortion **Vol. 1:** 260 f., 335
 Vol. 3: 1162
phortizō **Vol. 1:** 260, 262
 Vol. 3: 1162
phortos **Vol. 1:** 260
phōs **Vol. 1:** 421–424, 723
 Vol. 2: 290, 397, 477, 480, 484–487, **490, 493, 496**
 Vol. 3: 312 f., 317, 554, 734
phōsphoros **Vol. 2: 490, 493, 495**
phōstēr **Vol. 2: 490, 493**
phōteinos **Vol. 2: 490, 493**
phōtismos **Vol. 2: 490, 493**
phōtizō **Vol. 2:** 485, **490, 493–495**
 Vol. 3: 893
phragellion **Vol. 1: 162**
phragelloō **Vol. 1: 162**
phragmos **Vol. 3:** 185, 949, **950 f.**
phrassō **Vol. 3: 950 f.**

phrattō **Vol. 3:** 950
phrear **Vol. 3:** 986
phren– **Vol. 2:** 616
phrēn **Vol. 1:** 501, 671
 Vol. 2: 620, 643
 Vol. 3: 1036, 1172
phronēma **Vol. 1:** 680
 Vol. 2: 616 f.
phroneō **Vol. 1:** 502
 Vol. 2: 259, **616–619,** 781
 Vol. 3: 124, 441
phronēsis **Vol. 1:** 485
 Vol. 2: 616 f., 620
 Vol. 3: 354, 898, 1032
phronimos **Vol. 2: 616–620**
 Vol. 3: 1025 f.
phronimōs **Vol. 2: 617, 619**
phrontis **Vol. 1:** 276 f.
phrontisteon **Vol. 1:** 377
phrontizō **Vol. 1:** 276 f.
 Vol. 3: 823
phroureō **Vol. 2: 134 f.**
phthanō **Vol. 2:** 932
phthartos **Vol. 1:** 468, 470
phtheirō **Vol. 1:** 462, **467–469,** 471
phthoneō **Vol. 1: 557**
phthonos **Vol. 1: 557 f.**
phthora **Vol. 1: 467–470,** 681
 Vol. 2: 661
 Vol. 3: 281, 995
phy– **Vol. 2:** 656
phyē **Vol. 3:** 866
phygē **Vol. 1: 558 f.**
phylakē **Vol. 2: 134, 136,** 207
phylakizō **Vol. 2:** 136
phylaktērion **Vol. 2:** 136
phylassō **Vol. 2:** 132 f., **134 f.,** 137, 177, 450, 452, 864
phylassomai **Vol. 1:** 332
phylax **Vol. 2:** 136
phylē **Vol. 1:** 518, 684
 Vol. 2: 306
 Vol. 3: 870 f., 873
phyllon **Vol. 3: 865**
phylon **Vol. 3:** 454
phyō **Vol. 2:** 656
 Vol. 3: 870
phyraō **Vol. 3:** 917
phyrama **Vol. 2:** 676
 Vol. 3: 917
physeion **Vol. 2:** 657
physika **Vol. 1:** 63
physikos **Vol. 2: 656,** 660 f.
physikōs **Vol. 2:** 661
physioō **Vol. 2:** 422
physis **Vol. 1:** 460, 481, 714
 Vol. 2: 394, 439, 476, 648, **656–662**
 Vol. 3: 71, 595, 647, 869, 926 f.
phyteia **Vol. 3:** 523, **865, 868**
phyteuma **Vol. 3:** 866
phyteuō **Vol. 3: 865, 868**

pikrainō Vol. 1: 202
pikria Vol. 1: 106, **202**, 726
pikros Vol. 1: **201**, 203
  Vol. 2: 27
pikrōs Vol. 1: **201**
pimplēmi Vol. 1: 728, **733–739**
pimprēni Vol. 1: 94
pinō Vol. 2: 264, 269, 272,
  274, 277, 524, 535, 755
  Vol. 3: 243, 383, 707, 723
piotēs Vol. 3: 870
pipraskō Vol. 1: **268**
piptō Vol. 1: 608, **610 f.**
  Vol. 2: 835
  Vol. 3: 586
pisteuō Vol. 1: 324, 354 f., 397,
  588, **593 f., 597, 599, 601**
  Vol. 2: 243, 837
  Vol. 3: 53, 491, 746, 800,
  1031, 1172, 1188, 1196,
  1211–1213
pisteuōn Vol. 1: 601
  Vol. 3: 392, 1212
pistis Vol. 1: 50, 289, 351, 446,
  504, 587, **593–595, 597–606,**
  660, 704, 712 f.
  Vol. 2: 94, 117, 133, 142,
  170, 175, 239, 242 f., 342,
  450, 469, 488, 543, 545 f.,
  560, 563, 618, 768
  Vol. 3: 72, 163, 204, 226,
  228, 315, 364–368, 373,
  403 f., 505, 581, 584, 774,
  878, 882, 885, 966, 1033,
  1150 f., 1172, 1176 f., 1182,
  1188–1191, **1211–1213**
pistoō Vol. 1: 594
pistos Vol. 1: 305, 310, **593 f.,**
  598, 602
  Vol. 2: 837
  Vol. 3: 162, 765, 1046 f.,
  1211
pith- Vol. 1: 588
pithanologia Vol. 1: 588 f., 592
pithanos Vol. 1: 588
plan- Vol. 2: 457 f.
planaō Vol. 1: 608
  Vol. 2: 457–461, 469
planaomai Vol. 2: **457, 459**
  Vol. 3: 573
planē Vol. 2: **457–461**
planēs Vol. 2: 459
planētēs Vol. 2: **457, 459**
planōntes Vol. 3: 766
planos Vol. 2: **457, 459**
plasas Vol. 3: 766
plassō Vol. 1: 383
plateia Vol. 2: 735
platos Vol. 1: 253
platynō Vol. 1: 253 f.
platys Vol. 1: 253 f.
plax Vol. 3: 1040
plē- Vol. 1: 733
plēgē Vol. 1: **161–163**

  Vol. 3: 857
pleion Vol. 1: 729
plēmmeleia Vol. 3: 420
plēn Vol. 1: 98
pleon Vol. 1: 137
  Vol. 2: 130, 236
pleonazō Vol. 2: 128, **130 f.**
pleonekteō Vol. 1: **137–139**
  Vol. 2: 845
pleonektēs Vol. 1: **137–139**
  Vol. 2: 845
pleonexia Vol. 1: **137–139**, 214
  Vol. 2: 286, **845 f.**
plērēs Vol. 1: 546, **733–735,**
  738 f., 744
  Vol. 3: 102, 572, 700
plērōma Vol. 1: 522, 728,
  733–735, 738–740, 744
  Vol. 2: 83, 163
  Vol. 3: 252, 350, 827, 843
plēroō Vol. 1: 93, 171, 532,
  552, 728, **733–738, 740, 741,**
  744
  Vol. 2: 77, 83, 87, 251, 359,
  417, 629, 640, 669, 715,
  753, 819
  Vol. 3: 53, 71, 82, 172, 181
  f., 187, 329, 489, 491, 494,
  505, 642, 804, 827, 1073,
  1121
plērophoreō Vol. 1: **733, 735,**
  737
plērophoria Vol. 1: **733, 735**
plēsion Vol. 1: 255, 257, **258–**
  260
  Vol. 2: 503, 540, 544, 548,
  551
  Vol. 3: 173, 455, 1155
plēsios Vol. 1: 254, 257 f.
plēthos Vol. 1: 292, 728, **731–**
  733
  Vol. 2: 799
plēthynō Vol. 1: 728, **732**
  Vol. 2: 128
plousios Vol. 2: 820 f., 826,
  840–842, 844–846
plousiōs Vol. 2: **840, 842**
plouteō Vol. 2: 826, **840–842,**
  845
ploutizō Vol. 2: **840–842**
ploutos Vol. 1: 138
  Vol. 2: 824, 829, 834 f.,
  840–844, 845 f., **852**
  Vol. 3: 545
plynō Vol. 1: 150, 152 f.
pneō Vol. 3: **689, 707**
pneu- Vol. 3: 689
pneuma Vol. 1: 66, 90, 232,
  234–236, 449, 452, 470,
  500 f., 637, 674 f., 719, 739
  Vol. 2: 213, 233, 242, 388,
  476, 479, 520, 546, 559,
  617, 641, 672 f., 675, 691,
  715, 784, 824, 878, 899, 919

  Vol. 3: 75, 129, 257 f., 299,
  471, 473, 475, 493, 495,
  597, 672, 678, 680 f., 685,
  689 f., 693–695, 700, 706,
  708 f., 711, 831, 967, 1046,
  1172, 1177 f., 1183, 1188–
  1192, 1199 f., 1202 f., 1210
pneuma mantikon Vol. 3: 75
pneumatikos Vol. 1: 236, 242,
  336, 566
  Vol. 2: 276, 567, 605
  Vol. 3: 281, 283, 303, 308,
  435, 504, 647, 674 f., 684,
  687, **689 f., 706 f.**, 1037,
  1200
pneumatikōs Vol. 3: 689
pnigō Vol. 1: 220, **226**
pniktos Vol. 1: 220, **226**
pnoē Vol. 3: 680, **689, 707**
podes kai cheires Vol. 2: 149
poiēma Vol. 3: 719, **1152–1154**
poieō Vol. 1: 363, 377 f., 380,
  383, 387, 590, 722
  Vol. 2: 100, 221, 597, 664,
  709
  Vol. 3: 148 f., 168, 170,
  242 f., 245, 316, 353, 372,
  719, 859, 1021 f., 1083,
  1148 f., **1152–1158**
poieomai Vol. 1: 536
  Vol. 2: 128
poiēsis Vol. 3: **1152–1155**
poiētēs Vol. 2: 655
  Vol. 3: 1150, **1153–1155**
poiētikos Vol. 3: 123
poimainō Vol. 1: 408
  Vol. 3: 564, 566, 568
poimēn Vol. 1: 191 f.
  Vol. 2: 104, 412
  Vol. 3: 564, 566, 568 f.
poimnē Vol. 3: 564, **566–568**
poimnion Vol. 2: 586
  Vol. 3: 564–566
poith- Vol. 1: 588
polemeō Vol. 3: **958 f., 963,**
  981
polemikos Vol. 2: 776
polemos Vol. 1: 644 f., 652
  Vol. 3: 958 f., 961–963, 981
pōleō Vol. 1: **268**
  Vol. 2: 846
polis Vol. 1: 230, 291, 372,
  431, 536, 687, 715
  Vol. 2: 92, 236, 320, 324,
  439, 477, 788, **801–803, 805,**
  840
  Vol. 3: 49f., 219, 353, 454,
  456 f., 545, 564, 574, 755,
  925, 1156, 1173
politarchēs Vol. 2: **801, 804**
politeia Vol. 2: **801–804**
politēs Vol. 1: 372 f.
  Vol. 2: 801–804
politeuma Vol. 1: 299

politeuma (cont'd)
  Vol. 2: 801–805
politeuō Vol. 1: 373
politeuomai Vol. 2: 801–804
politikos Vol. 2: 475, 657
pollō mallon Vol. 2: 504
polloi Vol. 1: 94–97, 576
  Vol. 2: 530, 537
  Vol. 3: 195, 197, 229, 275, 363
pōlos Vol. 1: 117
polyeleos Vol. 3: 889
polypragmoneō Vol. 3: 152
polys Vol. 1: 94 f.
  Vol. 2: 104, 130, 417, 503 f., 524, 543, 840, 846
  Vol. 3: 247, 611, 723, 839, 989 f., 1174, 1180, 1201
polysplanchnos Vol. 2: 598–600, 1201
polytelēs Vol. 3: 388
poma Vol. 2: 274
poneō Vol. 1: 262, 564
ponēreuomai Vol. 1: 562
ponēria Vol. 1: 564–566
  Vol. 3: 886
ponēro- Vol. 2: 419
ponēros Vol. 1: 228, 348, 561–563, 564–567, 656, 722
  Vol. 2: 103, 351, 584, 868
  Vol. 3: 124, 204, 469 f., 473, 475, 572, 579, 1148, 1150, 1176
ponos Vol. 1: 260, 262, 271, 459, 564, 647
  Vol. 2: 820
ponth- Vol. 3: 719
pōpote Vol. 3: 521
poreuō Vol. 1: 481
poreuomai Vol. 3: 937, 943, 945–947
pornē Vol. 1: 497 f., 500–502
  Vol. 2: 365
  Vol. 3: 1195
porneia Vol. 1: 106, 494, 496 f., 499–501, 503
  Vol. 2: 580, 582 f.
  Vol. 3: 538, 540 f., 886, 1064, 1195
porneuō Vol. 1: 233, 494, 497, 506
  Vol. 2: 575, 579 f., 583, 722
  Vol. 3: 538
pornos Vol. 1: 497
  Vol. 2: 586
pōroō Vol. 2: 153–155
pōros Vol. 2: 153
pōrōsis Vol. 2: 153, 156
porphyra Vol. 1: 205
porphyros Vol. 1: 205
porrō Vol. 2: 53
posis Vol. 2: 274, 509
potamophorētos Vol. 3: 987, 992

potamos Vol. 3: 982, 985, 987, 989 f., 992
pote Vol. 3: 683, 964
potērion Vol. 2: 274, 276 f., 524, 536
potis Vol. 2: 509
potizō Vol. 2: 274 f.
poton Vol. 2: 274
potos Vol. 2: 274
pou Vol. 1: 283
  Vol. 3: 267, 482
pous Vol. 1: 239
  Vol. 2: 149, 369
pragma Vol. 1: 138, 271
  Vol. 2: 142
  Vol. 3: 772, 876, 1155–1158, 1195
pragmateia Vol. 3: 1155, 1158
pragmateuomai Vol. 3: 1155, 1158
praktikos Vol. 2: 475
  Vol. 3: 123
praktōr Vol. 3: 1157
prassō Vol. 3: 719, 1148, 1150, 1155–1159
prattō Vol. 3: 353, 1155–1157
praxis Vol. 2: 556
  Vol. 3: 719, 1155–1158
praÿpatheia Vol. 2: 256, 264
praÿpathia Vol. 2: 256
praÿs Vol. 2: 201, 256–264, 771, 822
  Vol. 3: 218, 807, 1032
praÿtēs Vol. 2: 256–259, 263, 771
praÿthymos Vol. 2: 261
prēgma Vol. 2: 674
prēnēs Vol. 1: 94
prepei Vol. 1: 669
  Vol. 2: 668 f.
prepō Vol. 2: 668 f.
prepon estin Vol. 2: 669
presbeia Vol. 1: 192 f., 197
presbeion Vol. 1: 193
presbeuō Vol. 1: 192–194, 197
  Vol. 3: 169 f.
presbeuteros Vol. 3: 774, 1065, 1201
presbeutēs Vol. 1: 193 f.
  Vol. 3: 170
presbys Vol. 1: 192, 194, 200
  Vol. 3: 50
presbytatos Vol. 1: 192
presbyterion Vol. 1: 192, 194, 197 f., 201
presbyteron Vol. 1: 192
presbyteros Vol. 1: 188, 190 f., 192–200, 485
  Vol. 2: 674
  Vol. 3: 39, 170, 568
presbytēs Vol. 1: 192 f., 197, 536
presbytis Vol. 1: 192, 197
prēssō Vol. 3: 1155

pro Vol. 1: 475, 478, 542, 664, 692 f., 695 f.
  Vol. 2: 134, 674
  Vol. 3: 747, 750, 829, 844, 1172 f., 1175, 1177, 1214
pro- Vol. 3: 74, 82
proagoreuō Vol. 3: 75
proangellō Vol. 3: 45
probainō Vol. 2: 412
probaton Vol. 2: 410, 412–414, 458
  Vol. 3: 567 f.
problēma Vol. 2: 745
procheirizō Vol. 1: 471, 475 f., 478
procheiros Vol. 1: 475
procheirotoneō Vol. 1: 478
prodokia Vol. 2: 238 f., 241, 244
prodromos Vol. 3: 945, 947
proelpizō Vol. 2: 238, 241
proepangellomai Vol. 3: 68, 70
proerchomai Vol. 1: 320, 322
proginomai Vol. 2: 767
proginōskō Vol. 1: 471, 692 f., 695
prognōsis Vol. 1: 542, 692 f.
prographō Vol. 3: 482
prohēgoumenos Vol. 1: 666
prohetoimazō Vol. 3: 116 f., 1187
prohistamenos Vol. 1: 193, 197
prohistēmi Vol. 1: 192–194, 197, 201
prohoraō Vol. 1: 471, 695
  Vol. 3: 491, 511 f. 515
prohorizō Vol. 1: 471, 478, 533, 692, 695 f., 697
  Vol. 2: 79
  Vol. 3: 299, 1018
prōi Vol. 2: 136
proidein Vol. 1: 695
proïdousa Vol. 3: 491
proïmos Vol. 3: 1000, 1003
prōinos Vol. 3: 736
prokatangellō Vol. 3: 44, 46, 48
prokatartizō Vol. 3: 349 f.
prokeimai Vol. 1: 400
  Vol. 3: 1180
prokopē Vol. 2: 128, 130 f.
prokoptō Vol. 1: 92
  Vol. 2: 128, 130
prokrima Vol. 2: 363 f.
prokyroō Vol. 1: 664
prolambanō Vol. 3: 747, 750
prolegō Vol. 3: 75
promantis Vol. 3: 75 f.
promerimnaō Vol. 1: 276
pronoeō Vol. 1: 471, 692–695, 697
pronoia Vol. 1: 692–695
  Vol. 2: 108
propatōr Vol. 2: 394
prophēmi Vol. 3: 74

prophēteia Vol. 1: 736
  Vol. 2: 545
  Vol. 3: 74 f., 81, 1046, 1182
prophētēs Vol. 1: 66
  Vol. 2: 915
  Vol. 3: 74 f., 81, 90 f., 181, 195, 490 f., 1187, 1198
prophēteuō Vol. 1: 527, 529
  Vol. 2: 443
  Vol. 3: 74–76, 87, 533
prophētikos Vol. 3: 74 f., 81, 491
prophētis Vol. 3: 74 f.
propheugō Vol. 1: 558
prophōneō Vol. 3: 75
pros Vol. 1: 107, 181, 187, 302, 558, 585, 592, 598
  Vol. 2: 115 f., 244, 290, 349, 518, 727, 769, 789, 876, 899
  Vol. 3: 162, 265, 353, 712, 737, 747, 1171–1176, 1184–1186, 1204–1206, 1211 f., 1214
pros phthonon Vol. 1: 558
pros thanaton Vol. 3: 1206
pros to paron Vol. 2: 899
pros ton theon Vol. 1: 592
  Vol. 3: 1204, 1211
prosagōgē Vol. 1: 592
prosanaplēroō Vol. 1: 734, 741
proschysis Vol. 1: 223
  Vol. 2: 853 f.
prosdechomai Vol. 2: 238, 244 f.
  Vol. 3: 744 f.
prosdeomai Vol. 2: 860 f.
prosdokaō Vol. 2: 238, 244–246
prosechō Vol. 3: 908
prosēgoria Vol. 2: 651
prosēlytos Vol. 1: 180, 359–362, 560, 589, 623, 684, 688 f.
  Vol. 2: 86, 90, 93 f., 126, 792
proserchomai Vol. 1: 320, 322, 360
proseuchē Vol. 2: 530, 860, 861, 863, 867, 875
proseuchomai Vol. 2: 194, 396, 803, 855 f., 859 f., 861 f., 867, 873 f., 882
  Vol. 3: 194, 232, 470, 638 f., 670, 1012, 1022, 1176
proskairos Vol. 3: 833, 837
proskaleō Vol. 1: 272
proskaleomai Vol. 1: 270 f., 273–275
proskartereō Vol. 2: 767 f.
proskarterēsis Vol. 2: 767 f.
prosklēroō Vol. 2: 300, 302
prosklēsis Vol. 1: 271
proskollaō Vol. 2: 350
proskollaomai Vol. 2: 348 f.
proskomma Vol. 2: 220, 705–707, 708

  Vol. 3: 363, 382, 996
proskopē Vol. 2: 705 f.
proskoptō Vol. 2: 705 f., 710
  Vol. 3: 996
proskyneō Vol. 1: 207, 610
  Vol. 2: 855, 859 f., 862, 867, 873, 874–878, 885, 927
  Vol. 3: 219, 460, 551
proskynēsis Vol. 2: 859, 876
proskynētēs Vol. 2: 875, 878
proslambanō Vol. 3: 262, 747 f., 750 f.
proslēmpsis Vol. 3: 747, 751
prosmenō Vol. 3: 223, 228
prosōpolēmpsia Vol. 1: 585, 587
prosōpolēmpteō Vol. 1: 585, 587
prosōpolēmptēs Vol. 1: 585, 587
prosōpon Vol. 1: 181, 211, 585–587, 704, 708
  Vol. 2: 399, 622, 625
  Vol. 3: 514, 531, 1175
prosphatos Vol. 2: 674 f.
prospherō Vol. 2: 41
  Vol. 3: 925
prosphora Vol. 2: 40–42
  Vol. 3: 38, 417, 431–434
prostassō Vol. 1: 477
prostithēmi Vol. 1: 600
prōta Vol. 1: 664, 666
protassō Vol. 1: 477
proteron Vol. 1: 664, 666
prōteuō Vol. 1: 664–666
prothesis Vol. 1: 542, 692, 695, 696 f.
  Vol. 2: 120, 819
  Vol. 3: 814, 1018, 1201
prothesmia Vol. 1: 471, 477
prothymia Vol. 1: 188
protithēmi Vol. 1: 471, 477, 692, 696 f.
  Vol. 3: 163
prōtokathedria Vol. 1: 664, 666
  Vol. 3: 587
prōtokathedritēs Vol. 1: 664, 666
prōtoklisia Vol. 1: 664, 666
  Vol. 3: 587
prōton Vol. 1: 664, 666
prōtos Vol. 1: 165, 334, 377, 664–667, 668 f.
  Vol. 2: 55, 57 f., 657, 671, 720
  Vol. 3: 457
prōtostatēs Vol. 1: 535
prōtotokos Vol. 1: 288, 304, 445, 664–666, 667–669
  Vol. 2: 157, 725, 729
  Vol. 3: 38, 416
psallō Vol. 1: 344
  Vol. 2: 436, 874
  Vol. 3: 670–675

psalmos Vol. 2: 874
  Vol. 3: 668, 670 f., 674 f.
psekas Vol. 3: 1004
psēphos Vol. 2: 674
pseud- Vol. 2: 468, 470, 472, 648
pseudadelphos Vol. 1: 254, 257
  Vol. 2: 472
pseudapostolos Vol. 2: 472
pseudēs Vol. 1: 66
  Vol. 2: 470–473
pseudochristos Vol. 1: 124 f.
  Vol. 2: 472
pseudodidaskalos Vol. 1: 535
  Vol. 2: 472
  Vol. 3: 766, 768
pseudologos Vol. 2: 472
pseudomai Vol. 1: 454
  Vol. 2: 468 f., 470, 472, 567
  Vol. 3: 877
pseudomartyr Vol. 3: 1043
pseudomartyreō Vol. 2: 470
  Vol. 3: 1038 f., 1041
pseudomartyria Vol. 2: 472
  Vol. 3: 1038 f.
pseudomartys Vol. 2: 472
  Vol. 3: 1038 f.
pseudōnymos Vol. 2: 648, 652, 655
pseudoprophētēs Vol. 1: 125
  Vol. 2: 472, 474
  Vol. 3: 74, 81
pseudos Vol. 2: 468, 470, 472–474, 724
  Vol. 3: 875, 885 f.
pseudōs Vol. 1: 66
pseustēs Vol. 2: 470, 472, 503
psithyrismos Vol. 3: 346
psithyristes Vol. 3: 346
psychē Vol. 1: 229, 235, 443 f., 450, 465, 671
  Vol. 2: 157, 181, 393, 476–478, 564 f., 773, 838 f., 919
  Vol. 3: 158, 174, 195, 215, 223, 278, 281, 531, 611, 676 f., 679–688, 689, 706, 827, 1196
psychikos Vol. 1: 236
  Vol. 2: 567
  Vol. 3: 281, 301, 504, 676, 684, 686 f.
psychō Vol. 1: 317 f.
psychos Vol. 1: 317–319
psychron Vol. 1: 317
  Vol. 2: 274
psychros Vol. 1: 317 f.
  Vol. 2: 826
ptaiō Vol. 3: 573
ptē Vol. 2: 821
pterna Vol. 1: 241
pternismos Vol. 1: 241
pterygas Vol. 1: 174
pterygion Vol. 3: 790, 796, 805
pteryx Vol. 3: 796 f., 805

373

ptēssō **Vol. 2:** 821
ptōcheia **Vol. 2: 821 f., 824, 826**
ptōcheuō **Vol. 2: 821, 824, 826, 828**
ptōchos **Vol. 2:** 110, 257, 264, 453, 820, **821–824, 828,** 834, 843 f., 846, **852**
  Vol. 3: 70, 119, 241, 351, 499, 525, 545 f., 548, 553, 572, 727, 752, 810
ptoliethron **Vol. 2:** 802
ptolis **Vol. 2:** 801
ptōma **Vol. 1: 608–610**
ptōsis **Vol. 1: 608 f.**
ptōssō **Vol. 2:** 821
ptōx **Vol. 2:** 821
ptyon **Vol. 3:** 527
pygmē **Vol. 2: 148, 150,** 153
pylē **Vol. 2: 29–31**
pylōn **Vol. 2: 29 f.**
pyr **Vol. 1:** 205, 263, **652–654, 656 f.**
  Vol. 2: 485, 746, 836
  Vol. 3: 96, 446 f., 695, 1178
pyra **Vol. 1: 653, 656**
pyressō **Vol. 1: 653, 656**
pyretos **Vol. 1:** 377, **653, 656**
pyrinos **Vol. 1: 653, 657**
pyroō **Vol. 1:** 205, **653, 656**
  Vol. 3: 966
pyrōsis **Vol. 1: 653 f., 656**
  Vol. 3: 110
pyrrazō **Vol. 1: 653, 656**
pyrros **Vol. 1: 205 f., 653, 656 f.**
pythōn **Vol. 2: 552, 558 f.**
  Vol. 3: 474

rhabbi **Vol. 2:** 514
  Vol. 3: 115 f., 766 f., 780
rhabbouni **Vol. 3: 115 f.,** 780
rhabdizō **Vol. 1: 161, 163,** 407
rhabdos **Vol. 1: 161–164, 407 f.**
  Vol. 2: 795
  Vol. 3: 404, 867
rhabdouchos **Vol. 1:** 407
rhacha **Vol. 1:** 417
rhainō **Vol. 1:** 144, 151, 153, 224
rhaka **Vol. 1:** 413, **417 f.**
  Vol. 2: 143
  Vol. 3: 1025
rhantismos **Vol. 1: 224 f.**
rhantizō **Vol. 1:** 144, 151 f., 220, **224–226**
rhapisma **Vol. 1: 162**
rhapizō **Vol. 1: 162**
rhē **Vol. 3:** 1119
rhēka **Vol. 1:** 417
rhēma **Vol. 3:** 749, 967, 1078, 1081, 1087, 1106 f., 1113 f., **1119–1122,** 1143–1145
rhēmata **Vol. 3:** 1122
rheō **Vol. 1: 682 f.**

rhēsis **Vol. 2:** 734
  Vol. 3: 1119
rhēthen **Vol. 1:** 736
  Vol. 3: 489
rhētōr **Vol. 3:** 1119
rhipē **Vol. 2:** 925
rhipizō **Vol. 3: 1000, 1003**
rhiza **Vol. 1:** 138
  Vol. 3: 865–868, 870
rhizoō **Vol. 3: 865, 868**
rhizoomai **Vol. 1:** 660
rhomphaia **Vol. 2:** 686
  Vol. 3: 959, 967
rhyomai **Vol. 3:** 177, 192, 198, **200–202, 204,** 212, 222, 1176
rhypainō **Vol. 1: 479**
rhypaō **Vol. 1: 479**
rhypareuō **Vol. 1: 479**
rhyparia **Vol. 3: 479**
rhyparos **Vol. 1: 479**
  Vol. 3: 102
rhypoō **Vol. 1: 479**
rhypos **Vol. 1: 479**
rhysamenos **Vol. 3:** 192
rhysis **Vol. 1: 682 f.**

sabaōth **Vol. 2:** 69
sabbata **Vol. 3: 405**
sabbatismos **Vol. 3: 411,** 413
sabbaton **Vol. 3:** 186, 258, **405,** 413, 940
Saddouk **Vol. 3:** 439
Saddoukaios **Vol. 1:** 535
  Vol. 3: 439, 443
Saleim **Vol. 2:** 592
Salēm **Vol. 2:** 590 f., **592 f.**
saleuō **Vol. 3:** 557, **558,** 561
Salōmōn **Vol. 3: 605,** 1120
salos **Vol. 3: 558–561**
salpinx **Vol. 2:** 925
  Vol. 3: 873 f.
salpistēs **Vol. 3: 874**
salpizō **Vol. 3: 873 f.**
Samareia **Vol. 3: 449, 456 f.,** 466
Samareitēs **Vol. 3:** 450
Samareitikon **Vol. 3:** 449
Samareitis **Vol. 3:** 449 f.
Samareus **Vol. 3:** 450
Samaria **Vol. 3:** 449
Samaritēs **Vol. 3: 449 f.,** 454, 463, 466
Samaritis **Vol. 3:** 450
saphēs **Vol. 3:** 477
sappheiros **Vol. 3: 396 f.**
sapros **Vol. 1:** 565, 722
Sarapis **Vol. 2:** 520
sardion **Vol. 3: 396–398**
sardonyx **Vol. 3: 396 f.**
sarkikos **Vol. 1: 671, 674, 677, 682**
  Vol. 2: 120
  Vol. 3: 963, 1200

sarkinos **Vol. 1:** 236, 337, **671, 674, 682**
Sarra **Vol. 1: 80**
  Vol. 2: 329, 431
  Vol. 3: 1072
sarx **Vol. 1:** 188, 221 f., 228, 233, 236, 257, 446, 457, 461, 535, 592, 647, **671 f., 674–682,** 719
  Vol. 2: 242, 273, 349, 477, 504, 525, 535, 566, 579, 589, 617, 816, 919
  Vol. 3: 32, 54, 171, 227, 313, 322 f., 581, 587, 724, 811, 994, 1073, 1115, 1117, 1151, 1158, 1172, 1175 f., 1188, 1195 f., 1199 f.
Satan **Vol. 3: 468**
Satanas **Vol. 1:** 102, 297, 454
  Vol. 3: 468–470, 477, 579, 804
sbennymi **Vol. 3: 109–111,** 447
schēma **Vol. 1:** 703, 707, **708 f.,** 714
  Vol. 2: 203, 500, 673
  Vol. 3: 564, 604, 864
schēsis **Vol. 1:** 271
schisma **Vol. 1:** 535
  Vol. 3: 543 f.
schizō **Vol. 3: 543 f.**
schoinisma **Vol. 2:** 298
seb- **Vol. 2:** 91 f.
sebas **Vol. 2:** 92
sebasma **Vol. 2: 91–93**
Sebastē **Vol. 3:** 449
sebastos **Vol. 2:** 93, 234
sebazomai **Vol. 2: 91–93**
sebō **Vol. 2:** 85, 92
sebomai **Vol. 1:** 112, 361, 622, 624, 687
  Vol. 2: 85, **90–95,** 232, 439
  Vol. 3: 100, 573, 577
sebomenoi ton theon **Vol. 2:** 85
sebomenos **Vol. 1:** 361
  Vol. 2: 85, 90, 94
sebomenos ton theon **Vol. 1: 359, 361**
  Vol. 2: 85
seiō **Vol. 3: 556 f.,** 561
seismos **Vol. 3: 556 f.,** 561
selēnē **Vol. 3:** 475, **733 f.**
selēniazomai **Vol. 3:** 475, **733 f.**
sēma **Vol. 2:** 626, 629
  Vol. 3: 310
sēmainō **Vol. 3:** 310
sēmainomenon **Vol. 3:** 1129
sēmainon **Vol. 3:** 1129
sēmantikos **Vol. 1:** 68
sēmasia **Vol. 2:** 465
sēmeia kai terata **Vol. 2:** 626 f., 629
sēmeion **Vol. 2:** 192, 350, 352, 621, 625, **626 f., 629,** 633 f., 858

Vol. 3: 110, 233, 516, 554, 904, 1108, 1150
sēmeron **Vol. 1:** 251
Vol. 3: 71, 826, **833 f., 837, 841,** 849, 1169
semnos **Vol. 2: 91–93,** 232
Vol. 3: 727
semnōs **Vol. 2:** 93
semnotēs **Vol. 2: 91–93,** 95
sēs **Vol. 1:** 119
Vol. 2: 831
sidēros **Vol. 2: 97,** 795
sidērous **Vol. 2: 97**
Sidōnios **Vol. 3:** 450
Sikimitēs **Vol. 3:** 450
Sikimois **Vol. 3:** 450
Sina **Vol. 3:** 1009, 1011, **1013 f.**
sinapi **Vol. 3:** 523
sindōn **Vol. 3:** 296
siniazō **Vol. 3:** 804
siō **Vol. 3:** 556
Siōn **Vol. 2: 324, 326, 330**
siteutos **Vol. 1:** 116
sitista **Vol. 1:** 116
sitos **Vol. 3:** 523 f., 527
skallō **Vol. 1:** 726
skandalēthron **Vol. 2:** 707
skandalizō **Vol. 2: 705, 707–710**
Vol. 3: 446, 996
skandalon **Vol. 1:** 535, 608
Vol. 2: 429, 664, 705 f., **707–710**
Vol. 3: 382, 394, 399, 996, 1052
skēnē **Vol. 3:** 465, **811–814,** 1040, 1042
skēnōma **Vol. 2:** 248
Vol. 3: 465, **811,** 815
skēnoō **Vol. 3: 811,** 813
skēnopēgia **Vol. 3: 813**
skēnopoios **Vol. 3: 811 f.**
skēnos **Vol. 3: 811,** 814
skepē **Vol. 3:** 554
skēptō **Vol. 1:** 407
skēptron **Vol. 1:** 405, **407**
skeuazō **Vol. 3:** 119
skeuos **Vol. 1:** 540
Vol. 3: 116, 910, 912–914, 917, 1064 f., 1067, 1076, 1078, 1187
skia **Vol. 2:** 291, 717
Vol. 3: 553–556, 660, 905
skiaō **Vol. 3:** 554
skiazō **Vol. 3:** 554
skiē **Vol. 3:** 553
sklērokardia **Vol. 2: 153, 156, 180, 184**
sklēros **Vol. 2: 153–156**
sklērotēs **Vol. 2: 153,** 155
sklērotrachēlos **Vol. 2: 153,** 155
sklērynō **Vol. 2: 153,** 155
skolops **Vol. 1: 726 f.**
Vol. 2: 762, 809

Vol. 3: 40, 203, 257, 470 f., 714, 728, 802, 814, 857, 995, 998, 1000, 1026
skopeō **Vol. 1:** 188
Vol. 2: 393
skopos **Vol. 1:** 188
Vol. 2: 52, 65
skorpios **Vol. 1: 510**
skorpizō **Vol. 2: 32–34**
skoteinos **Vol. 1: 421–423**
skotia **Vol. 1: 420 f., 423 f.**
skotizō **Vol. 1: 421, 423**
skotoō **Vol. 1: 421, 423**
skotos **Vol. 1:** 301, **420 f., 423, 425**
Vol. 2: 484, 490, 543
Vol. 3: 554, 831, 1151
skybalon **Vol. 1:** 480
Vol. 3: 278
skytotomos **Vol. 3:** 812
smaragdinos **Vol. 3:** 398
smaragdos **Vol. 3: 396 f.**
smyrna **Vol. 2: 294 f.**
smyrnizō **Vol. 2:** 295
societas **Vol. 1:** 643
Solomōn **Vol. 3: 605,** 607
sōma **Vol. 1:** 87, 229, **232–237,** 241 f., 275, 300–302, 399, 443 f., 446, 501, 647, 671 f., 675 f., 679, 707
Vol. 2: 158, 162, 263, 273, 476, **523–525,** 531 f., 534, **537,** 546, 564, 566 f., 789, 818, 883, 899, 919
Vol. 3: 171 f., 283, 303, 308, 554, 556, 680, 683 f., 1158, 1182, 1187, 1191, 1195
sōmatikos **Vol. 1:** 704
sōmatikōs **Vol. 1:** 740
son **Vol. 2: 846**
sophia **Vol. 1:** 165, 228, 400, 485, 501, 592, 692, 696
Vol. 2: 61, 99, 120, 127, 355, 406, 493, 616, 620
Vol. 3: 53, 68, 76, 129 f., 678, 765, 898, 925, **1026–1028, 1030–1032,** 1033, 1036 f., 1144
sophistēs **Vol. 3: 1034**
sophizō **Vol. 3: 1026, 1028, 1033**
sophos **Vol. 1:** 192
Vol. 2: 555
Vol. 3: 129, **1026–1028, 1032,** 1034, 1037
sōphrōn **Vol. 1:** 494, **501 f.**
sōphroneō **Vol. 1: 501 f.,** 528
Vol. 2: 617
sōphronōs **Vol. 1: 501 f.**
Vol. 2: 94
sōphrosynē **Vol. 1:** 494, 501 f., 529, 550
Vol. 3: 27, 354, 561 f., 925
sōs **Vol. 1:** 501

Vol. 2: 617
sōson **Vol. 1:** 100
sōtēr **Vol. 1:** 519
Vol. 2: 78, 158, 332, 349, 584
Vol. 3: 71, 177, 205, 210, **216–223,** 318, 462, 1022, 1046
sōtēria **Vol. 1:** 68, 168, 397, 454, 464 f.
Vol. 2: 332, 388, 777, 839
Vol. 3: 198, **205–207, 209–216, 218 f.,** 223, 371, 501, 528, 715, 723, 1033
sōtērion **Vol. 3:** 207, 422, 966
sōtērios **Vol. 2:** 122
Vol. 3: 216 f., 221
sōzō **Vol. 1:** 210, 397, 463, 519, 697
Vol. 2: 122, 158, 343, 394, 560, 773, 780, 819
Vol. 3: 177, 201 f., **204–206, 209–219,** 223, 253, 501, 642, 1177
sōzōn **Vol. 3:** 218
speios **Vol. 3:** 380
speirō **Vol. 3: 521 f., 525,** 527, 868
speirōn **Vol. 3:** 868
spēlaion **Vol. 3:** 378, **380 f.,** 793
spendō **Vol. 2: 853–855**
Vol. 3: 432
speos **Vol. 3:** 380
sperma **Vol. 1:** 377 f.
Vol. 2: 104, 586
Vol. 3: 72 f., 251, **521–524,** 527, 684, 1073, 1188
spermatikos **Vol. 3:** 1084 f.
spermologos **Vol. 3: 525**
speudō **Vol. 2:** 245
Vol. 3: 1168
speudontes **Vol. 2:** 245
sphazō **Vol. 2:** 411
sphodra **Vol. 2:** 846
sphragis **Vol. 3:** 73, **497, 499,** 501
sphragizō **Vol. 3: 497, 499,** 1212
sphryon **Vol. 2:** 415
splanchna **Vol. 1:** 258
Vol. 2: 116, 567, **593,** 596, 598, **599 f.,** 733
splanchneuō **Vol. 2:** 599
splanchnizomai **Vol. 2: 599 f.**
splanchnon **Vol. 2: 599 f.**
spondē **Vol. 3:** 423
spora **Vol. 3:** 527, 1201
sporos **Vol. 3: 521, 523**
spoudaios **Vol. 3: 1168 f.**
spoudazō **Vol. 3: 1168 f.**
spoudē **Vol. 1:** 197
Vol. 3: 1166, **1168 f.**
stachys **Vol. 3:** 523

staktē **Vol. 2**: 294
stasis **Vol. 1**: 377
statēr **Vol. 2**: 851
   Vol. 3: 752 f., 792
stauroō **Vol. 1**: **391, 393 f., 397, 399**
   Vol. 3: 1190
stauros **Vol. 1**: 197, 228, 389, **391–399, 403 f.**, 437, 726
   Vol. 2: 139, 379
   Vol. 3: 172, 641, 1026, 1199
stegō **Vol. 3**: 887
steinos **Vol. 2**: 807
stēkete **Vol. 2**: 563
stellō **Vol. 1**: 126
stemma **Vol. 1**: **405**
stenagmos **Vol. 2**: **423 f.**, 882–884
stenazō **Vol. 2**: 416, **423 f.**, 883 f.
   Vol. 3: 1195
stenochōreō **Vol. 1**: 742
   Vol. 2: **807 f.**
stenochōria **Vol. 2**: **807 f.**
stenos **Vol. 1**: 807
stephanēphoros **Vol. 1**: 648
stephanoō **Vol. 1**: **405 f.**
stephanos **Vol. 1**: **405 f.**
stephō **Vol. 1**: 405
stereos **Vol. 1**: 660
stergō **Vol. 2**: 538 f., **542**
stērizō **Vol. 1**: 660
   Vol. 3: 87
sthenos **Vol. 3**: 715, 993
stichaomai **Vol. 2**: 451
stichos **Vol. 2**: 451
stigma **Vol. 1**: 235
   Vol. 2: 572, 574, **575**
stigmata **Vol. 2**: **572 f.**
stigmatias **Vol. 2**: 572
stizō **Vol. 2**: 572
stoa **Vol. 1**: 68
stoicheia **Vol. 2**: 73, 200, 446, **451, 828**
   Vol. 3: 180, 775, 1035, 1118, 1164
stoicheion **Vol. 1**: 104 f., 282, 331 f., 401
   Vol. 2: 73, 436, 451 f., 559
stoicheō **Vol. 2**: **451 f., 454**
stoichos **Vol. 2**: 451
stolē **Vol. 1**: 312, 317
stoma **Vol. 2**: 726 f.
   Vol. 3: 909
stratēgos **Vol. 1**: 407, 475, 569
   Vol. 3: **958, 964**
strateia **Vol. 3**: **958, 963**
strateuma **Vol. 3**: 877, **958, 964**
strateuō **Vol. 3**: **958, 963 f.**
strateuomai **Vol. 1**: 646
   Vol. 3: 981
stratia **Vol. 3**: **958, 964**
stratiōtēs **Vol. 3**: **958, 964**
stratologeō **Vol. 3**: **958, 964**

stratopedarchēs **Vol. 3**: **958, 964**
stratopedon **Vol. 3**: **958, 964**
strephō **Vol. 1**: 285, **354 f.**, 358, 362
   Vol. 3: 933, 947
strouthion **Vol. 1**: 173
stygeō **Vol. 2**: 86
stylos **Vol. 3**: 387, **795**, 822
Sychar **Vol. 3**: 457
sykē **Vol. 1**: 417, **723**
   Vol. 2: 267, 382, 623, 630, 754, 871, 912, 916
   Vol. 3: 174, 249, 532, 793, 865, 868 f., 1012
sykea **Vol. 1**: 723
sylagōgeō **Vol. 2**: 453
   Vol. 3: **379**
sylaō **Vol. 3**: **379**
syleuō **Vol. 3**: **379**
syllambanō **Vol. 1**: 187, **343 f.**
syllēbdēn **Vol. 3**: 354
syllegō **Vol. 2**: 31, **33**
syllogismos **Vol. 1**: 664
symbasileuō **Vol. 1**: 643
   Vol. 2: **372 f.**
symbolon **Vol. 3**: 76
symbouleuō **Vol. 1**: **362 f.**
   Vol. 3: 129
symboulia **Vol. 1**: **362**
symboulion **Vol. 1**: **362 f.**
symboulos **Vol. 1**: **362 f.**
symmartyreō **Vol. 1**: 350
   Vol. 3: **1038 f., 1042**
symmetria **Vol. 2**: 102
symmimētēs **Vol. 1**: **490 f.**
symmorphizomai **Vol. 1**: **705, 707**
symmorphoomai **Vol. 1**: **705**
symmorphos **Vol. 1**: **705, 707**
sympaschō **Vol. 1**: 643
   Vol. 3: **719, 722, 724**
sympatheō **Vol. 3**: **719, 722, 724**
symphōnia **Vol. 3**: 674
symphytos **Vol. 2**: 504
symplēroō **Vol. 1**: **736–738**
sympnigō **Vol. 1**: 226
sympolitēs **Vol. 2**: 794, 804
sympsychos **Vol. 3**: **687**
syn **Vol. 1**: 343, 363, 645, 647
   Vol. 2: 115, 481
   Vol. 3: **1172 f., 1190, 1201, 1205–1207**, 1214 f.
syn Christō **Vol. 3**: **1172, 1205, 1207**, 1214 f.
synagō **Vol. 1**: **291 f., 297, 299, 303**
   Vol. 2: 31, **33**
synagōgē **Vol. 1**: 69, 245, 272, **291–293, 295–297, 307**, 589
   Vol. 3: 479, 868
synagōnizomai **Vol. 1**: **645, 647**
synaichmalōtos **Vol. 3**: 591
synakoloutheō **Vol. 1**: **480 f.**
synalizō **Vol. 3**: **443, 449**

synantaō **Vol. 1**: 325
synapothnēskō **Vol. 1**: **430 f.**, **435**
synarchias **Vol. 1**: 193
synathleō **Vol. 1**: **645–647**
synathroizō 31, **33**
synaulizomai **Vol. 3**: 449
synchairō **Vol. 2**: 431
syndesmos **Vol. 2**: 62
   Vol. 3: **590, 591 f.**
syndikos **Vol. 1**: 89
syndoulos **Vol. 1**: 256
   Vol. 3: 596
syndoxazō **Vol. 1**: 643
   Vol. 2: **44**
syndoxazomai **Vol. 2**: 47
-synē **Vol. 3**: 353
synechō **Vol. 2**: 733
synedreuō **Vol. 1**: 363
synedrion **Vol. 1**: 363
   Vol. 2: 143
synedros **Vol. 1**: 363
synegeiresthai **Vol. 1**: 643
synēgoros **Vol. 1**: 83, 89
syneidēsis **Vol. 1**: **348–351, 353**
   Vol. 2: 567, 707
   Vol. 3: 365, 995
syneiserchomai **Vol. 1**: 321
synerchomai **Vol. 1**: **320, 322**
synergeō **Vol. 3**: **1147 f., 1152**
synergos **Vol. 2**: 360
   Vol. 3: 548, **1147, 1152**
synesis **Vol. 1**: 348, 485
   Vol. 3: 122, 129, **130**, 1026, 1032
synetos **Vol. 2**: 555
syngeneia **Vol. 1**: 194, 669
syngenēs **Vol. 2**: 549
syngraphē **Vol. 1**: 505
synhypokrinomai **Vol. 2**: **469**
syniēmi **Vol. 2**: 398
   Vol. 3: 124 f., **130, 132 f.**, 1036
synistēmi **Vol. 1**: 166
   Vol. 3: 1186
synkakopatheō **Vol. 3**: **719, 722**
synkalyptō **Vol. 3**: 210
synkekalymmenon **Vol. 2**: 212
synkerannymi **Vol. 1**: 69
synkleiō **Vol. 3**: 491
synklēronomein **Vol. 1**: 643
synklēronomos **Vol. 2**: **295 f., 300**
   Vol. 3: 73
synkoinōneō **Vol. 1**: **639, 642, 644**
synkoinōnos **Vol. 1**: **639, 642, 644**
synkrinō **Vol. 2**: 362, 364
synodos **Vol. 1**: 292
synoida **Vol. 1**: 348, 350 f., 353
synoikodomeō **Vol. 2**: 249, 251, **253**
synopsis **Vol. 1**: 69

synopsizō **Vol. 1:** 69
synstenazō **Vol. 2:** 884
synteleia **Vol. 2: 59–62**
   Vol. 3: 836, 847
synteleō **Vol. 2:** 37, **59**
   Vol. 3: 178
synthaptō **Vol. 1:** 266, 401
synthēkē **Vol. 1:** 365 f.
syntrechō **Vol. 3:** 947
Śyriakē **Vol. 3:** 411
syschēmatizō **Vol. 1: 708 f.**
   Vol. 2: 673
sysseismos **Vol. 3:** 266
systauroō **Vol. 1: 391, 394, 397–399, 401**
systauroumai **Vol. 1:** 643
systoicheō **Vol. 2: 451 f.**
systrephō **Vol. 2:** 31, **33**
syzaō **Vol. 1:** 643
syzeugnymi **Vol. 3:** 539, **1160, 1162, 1164**
syzoōpoieō **Vol. 1:** 643
syzygos **Vol. 3: 1160, 1164**

tachinos **Vol. 3:** 847
tachy **Vol. 3:** 173
tachys **Vol. 3:** 1169
tainia **Vol. 1:** 648
talaipōreō **Vol. 2:** 423
   Vol. 3: 858 f.
talaipōria **Vol. 3: 858 f.**
talaipōros **Vol. 3: 858 f.**
talitha, koum **Vol. 1:** 581
tapeinōma **Vol. 2:** 198
tapeinoō **Vol. 1:** 569, 731
   Vol. 2: 259–264
tapeinophrōn **Vol. 2: 259–264**
tapeinophroneō **Vol. 2:** 259
tapeinophrosynē **Vol. 2: 259–264**, 617
   Vol. 3: 928
tapeinos **Vol. 2:** 200, 257, **259–264**, 617 f., 620
tapeinōsis **Vol. 2:** 200, **259–264**
tapeinotēs **Vol. 2:** 259
taphē **Vol. 1: 263 f.**
taphos **Vol. 1: 263–265**
   Vol. 2: 727
tarach- **Vol. 3:** 709
tarachē **Vol. 3: 709**
tarachos **Vol. 3: 709 f.**
tarachthēnai **Vol. 3:** 563
tarassō **Vol. 3: 709 f.**
tarassomai **Vol. 3:** 710
tassō **Vol. 1:** 471, **476,** 478, 533
   Vol. 3: 1186
tauotēs **Vol. 2:** 506
tauros **Vol. 1:** 116
tauta (neut. pl. of → houtos)
taxis **Vol. 1:** 271, 504
   Vol. 2: 102
tē emē cheiri **Vol. 2:** 148
technē 271, **279**
   Vol. 2: 657

technitēs **Vol. 1: 279,** 387
teichos **Vol. 3: 948**
teinō **Vol. 1:** 478
tekein **Vol. 1:** 667
tekmērion **Vol. 3:** 571
tekna theou **Vol. 3:** 647
teknion **Vol. 1: 285 f.**
teknogoneō **Vol. 1:** 187, 285
teknogonia **Vol. 1:** 187, 285
   Vol. 3: 1177
teknon **Vol. 1:** 256, 280, **284–287,** 290 f., 416
   Vol. 3: 607, 647
teknoō **Vol. 1:** 176
teknopoieō **Vol. 1:** 285
teknotropheō **Vol. 1:** 187
tēkō **Vol. 3:** 559
tektōn **Vol. 1:** 279
tēlaugēma **Vol. 2:** 465
tēle **Vol. 2:** 713
teleioō **Vol. 2: 59–66**
   Vol. 3: 491, 756
teleios **Vol. 1:** 92, 649
   Vol. 2: 59–65, 77, 162, 449, 477, 563, 741, 778, 782
   Vol. 3: 350, 502, 504, 1021, 1031
teleiōs **Vol. 2:** 63
teleiōsis **Vol. 1:** 668
   Vol. 2: 59, 61, 63 f.
teleiotēs **Vol. 2: 59–64**
teleiōtēs **Vol. 2:** 59, 61
Tēlemachos **Vol. 2:** 233
teleō **Vol. 1:** 737
   Vol. 2: 59–65
   Vol. 3: 752–756
teleutaō **Vol. 1: 429 f.**
   Vol. 2: 59
teleutē **Vol. 2:** 59
telōneō **Vol. 3:** 756
telōnēs **Vol. 3:** 755, **757,** 759
telōnion **Vol. 3: 755–757, 759**
telos **Vol. 1:** 69, 164, 429, 741
   Vol. 2: 52, 58, **59–66,** 157, 445, 713, 715, 741, 904
   Vol. 3: 277, 363, 725, **752, 754–756,** 759, 779, 838, 924
temenos **Vol. 2:** 233
   Vol. 3: 781 f., 785
temnō **Vol. 1:** 307
   Vol. 3: 352
teras **Vol. 2:** 621, 626 f., 629, 633 f.
teratoskopos **Vol. 2:** 554
tēreō **Vol. 1:** 336 f.
   Vol. 2: 132 f., 135, 137
tērēsis **Vol. 2: 132 f.**
tessarakonta, tesserakonta **Vol. 2: 689, 696,** 893
   Vol. 3: 1181
tessares **Vol. 2: 688, 703**
tetelestai **Vol. 2:** 64
tethnēkōs **Vol. 1:** 444

tetokōs **Vol. 1:** 177
tetradion **Vol. 2: 689**
tetrakischilioi **Vol. 2: 699**
tetrakosioi **Vol. 2: 689**
thalamos **Vol. 3:** 983
thalassa **Vol. 3: 982–985,** 989, 992
thalatta **Vol. 3:** 982
thalattan **Vol. 2:** 726
thambeō **Vol. 2: 621,** 623 f.
thambos **Vol. 2: 621, 623–625,** 633
thanatoō **Vol. 1: 430 f.,** 435
thanatos **Vol. 1:** 398, **429–431, 435, 441–443,** 446, 463, 707
   Vol. 2: 136, 143, 365, 479, 504, 781, 925, 927
   Vol. 3: 145, 157, 171, 180, 267, 554, 581, 723, 858, 984, 1157, 1178, 1194, 1206
thaptō **Vol. 1: 263 f.**
   Vol. 3: 292
tharreō **Vol. 1: 327–329**
tharseō **Vol. 1:** 327 f.
thauma **Vol. 1:** 528
   Vol. 2: 621–623, 633
thaumasios **Vol. 2: 621–623**
thaumasthēnai **Vol. 2:** 625
thaumastos **Vol. 2: 621–623,** 625 f.
thaumazō **Vol. 1:** 528, 587
   Vol. 2: 621–625
thea **Vol. 2:** 477
   Vol. 3: 512, 1085
theaomai **Vol. 2:** 621
   Vol. 3: 511 f., 516
theatēs **Vol. 3:** 512
theatrizomai **Vol. 3:** 521
theatrizomenos **Vol. 1:** 646
theatron **Vol. 3:** 512, **520 f.**
theia physis **Vol. 3:** 71
theioi anthrōpoi **Vol. 2:** 165
theion **Vol. 2:** 72, 86
   Vol. 3: 265, 876
theios **Vol. 1:** 645
   Vol. 2: 66, 81, 86, 165, 475, 561, 606, 615, 634, 661
   Vol. 3: 49, 71, 564, 635 f., 927
theios anēr **Vol. 3:** 636
theiotata **Vol. 3:** 1083
theiotēs **Vol. 2: 66,** 86
thēkē **Vol. 3:** 867
thēlazōn **Vol. 1:** 281
thelēma **Vol. 2:** 819
   Vol. 3: 1016, **1018 f., 1021–1023**
thelēsis **Vol. 3: 1018, 1023**
thelō **Vol. 1:** 534, 569
   Vol. 2: 406
   Vol. 3: 1015 f., **1018–1023,** 1152, 1195
thēlys **Vol. 2:** 569
   Vol. 3: 1058

377

thematikos **Vol. 1:** 648
themeilia **Vol. 1:** 660
themelioō **Vol. 1:** 383, **660**
　Vol. 3: 391
themelios **Vol. 1:** 658, **660–663**
　Vol. 2: 129, 249, 706
　Vol. 3: 382, 387–390
themethla **Vol. 1:** 660
theo- **Vol. 3:** 491
theoi **Vol. 2:** 498, 674
theologeō **Vol. 1:** 70
theomachos **Vol. 1:** 646
　Vol. 3: 963
Theophilos **Vol. 2:** 86
theophorētos **Vol. 3:** 491
theopneustos **Vol. 3:** 327, 401,
　491, **689 f.**, 708
theopoieō **Vol. 2:** 661
thēpreō **Vol. 2:** 393, 482
　Vol. 3: 511 f., **516**
theōrētikos **Vol. 2:** 475, 478
　Vol. 3: 123
theōria **Vol. 2:** 60
theos **Vol. 1:** 70, 96, 98, 111 f.,
　138, 164, 179, 192, 197,
　212, 257, 273, 281, 283,
　287, 289, 295, 298–300,
　303, 305, 336, 359, 361,
　374, 484, 523, 538, 552,
　569, 579, 592, 597–600,
　615, 623, 670, 674, 678,
　693, 706 f., 734
　Vol. 2: 53, **66–86**, 88, 93 f.,
　99 f., 121, 127, 183, ·229,
　231, 247 f., 250, 289, 299,
　337, 364, 381 f., 386–388,
　393 f., 401 f., 408, 411 f.,
　420, 424, 472, 498, 500,
　503, 511–516, 520, 543,
　549, 565, 596, 602, 609,
　636, 649, 651, 653, 655,
　661, 687, 720, 725, 767,
　780, 791, 794, 800, 878,
　882, 884, 912, 923, 932
　Vol. 3: 38, 54, 71 f., 128 f.,
　152, 160, 162 f., 168, 170,
　172, 202, 205, 211, 217 f.,
　223, 239, 242, 257 f., 264,
　299, 315 f., 318 f., 331, 341,
　371 f., 374, 376 f., 391, 400,
　431 f., 457, 461, 484, 511,
　515, 521, 531, 549, 576,
　580, 593, 597, 607, 610–
　612, 634 f., 640, 647, 651,
　664, 670, 738, 746, 749,
　794, 824, 832, 848, 867,
　886, 925, 959, 965, 967,
　1017–1019, 1021, 1026,
　1036, 1043 f., 1046, 1085,
　1107, 1118, 1150, 1152,
　1186–1188, 1193, 1198,
　1200, 1202–1205, 1211
theosebeia **Vol. 2:** 85, **91 f.**
　Vol. 3: 70

theosebeō **Vol. 2:** 85
theosebēs **Vol. 1:** 361
　Vol. 2: 85, **91, 94**
theostygēs **Vol. 2:** 86
　Vol. 3: 28
theotēs **Vol. 1:** 740
　Vol. 2: 66, 86
theou hyios **Vol. 3: 635**
thēr **Vol. 1:** 113
therapeia **Vol. 2: 164, 171**
therapeuō **Vol. 2: 164–170**
　Vol. 3: 57
therapōn **Vol. 2:** 164
　Vol. 3: 609 f.
thērion **Vol. 1: 113 f., 119,** 507
　Vol. 2: 381, 574, 625, 653,
　661, 684, 693, 776, 809, 826
　Vol. 3: 256, 342, 471, 500,
　715, 856, 1198
therismos **Vol. 2:** 522, **525–527**
theristēs **Vol. 3: 525 f.**
therizō **Vol. 3: 525–527**
thermainō **Vol. 1:** 318
thermē **Vol. 1: 317 f.**
thermos **Vol. 1:** 318 f.
theros **Vol. 3:** 525
thēsaurizō **Vol. 2: 829–831,**
　834, 836
thēsaurizōn **Vol. 2: 833**
thēsauros **Vol. 2:** 191, **829–831,**
　834–836, 838, 843 f., 846 f.,
　852
　Vol. 3: 143, 184, 340
thesmos **Vol. 1:** 477
Thessalonikeus **Vol. 1:** 299
thiasos **Vol. 1:** 291
thlaō **Vol. 2:** 807
thlibō **Vol. 2: 807–809**
thlibonta **Vol. 2:** 807
thlipsis **Vol. 1:** 741
　Vol. 2: 360, 664, 766, 774,
　781, **807–809,** 912
　Vol. 3: 956
thnēskō **Vol. 1: 430 f., 435**
thnētos **Vol. 1: 430 f., 435**
　Vol. 2: 476
thōrax **Vol. 3: 959, 966**
thorybazō **Vol. 2:** 621
thorybeō **Vol. 2: 621,** 623
thorybos **Vol. 2: 621, 623**
thremma **Vol. 1:** 116
thrēneō **Vol. 2: 416–418,** 424
thrēnos **Vol. 2:** 417, 611
thrēskeia **Vol. 3: 549, 551,** 1074
thrēskō **Vol. 3:** 164
thrēskos **Vol. 3: 549, 551**
thriambeuō **Vol. 1:** 644, **649,**
　652
thriambos **Vol. 1:** 649
thrix **Vol. 2:** 197
thronoi **Vol. 2: 612, 614**
thronos **Vol. 2:** 147, 601,
　611 f., 614 f.
　Vol. 3: 274, 588, 1193

thygatēr **Vol. 1:** 280
　Vol. 2: 325
thym **Vol. 1:** 105
thymiama **Vol. 2: 293 f.**
thymiaō **Vol. 2: 293 f.**
thymiatērion **Vol. 2: 293 f.**
　Vol. 3: 814
thymoō **Vol. 2:** 419
thymoomai **Vol. 1: 105 f.**
thymos **Vol. 1: 105 f.,** 107 f.,
　110 f., 113, 456, 471
　Vol. 2: 768 f.
　Vol. 3: 586, 676–678, 908,
　1166
thyō **Vol. 2:** 108, 293, 689
　Vol. 3: 417, 428, 437, 552,
　582, 676, 686, 715, 785,
　812, 81·4, 908
thyra **Vol. 2: 29–31,** 280, 734
　Vol. 3: 966
thyreos **Vol. 3:** 109, **959, 966**
thysia **Vol. 2:** 41 f.
　**Vol. 3: 415, 417, 421, 428,
　432 f., 434 f.,** 437, 1023
thysiasma **Vol. 3: 421**
thysiastērion **Vol. 3: 417 f., 428,
　434 f.,** 437, 1196
ti **Vol. 1:** 326
ti kōlyei **Vol. 2:** 222
tiara **Vol. 1:** 405
tiktō **Vol. 1:** 176, 178, **186 f.,**
　280, 285, 668
　Vol. 3: 858
timaō **Vol. 2: 48–50**
timē **Vol. 1:** 222
　Vol. 2: 44, **47–50, 52**
　Vol. 3: 138, 174, 198, 200,
　717, 817
timios **Vol. 3:** 391, 396
timiōtatos **Vol. 3:** 398
tis **Vol. 1:** 94, 182, 592, 594,
　689
　Vol. 2: 115 f., 149, 220, 222,
　241, 303, 367, 498, 502,
　625, 671, 708, 735, 826, 882
　Vol. 3: 174, 353, 445, 719,
　822, 946, 1172, 1205, 1209
tithēmi **Vol. 1:** 413, 471, **477 f.,**
　568, 660, 696
　Vol. 2: 859
　Vol. 3: 168, 611, 683, 1046,
　1186
titlos **Vol. 1:** 392, 396
toichon **Vol. 3:** 795
toichos **Vol. 3: 948**
toioutos **Vol. 1:** 284
　Vol. 2: 503, 912
tokos **Vol. 3:** 1156
tolma **Vol. 1:** 710
tolmaō **Vol. 1:** 364 f.
　Vol. 3: 344
tolmēros **Vol. 1: 364 f.**
tolmērotoron **Vol. 1:** 365
tolmētēs **Vol. 1: 364 f.**

topazion Vol. 3: **396 f.**
topos Vol. 1: 538
  Vol. 3: 461, 464, 584, 856, 1004, 1007
topos pedinos Vol. 3: **1009**
tote Vol. 1: 282, 666
touto (neut. sing. of → *houtos*)
toxon Vol. 3: 1002
trachēlos Vol. 1: 241
trachys Vol. 3: 709
tragos Vol. 1: 114
trapeza Vol. 2: 518, **520, 522**
  Vol. 3: 814
trapeza daimoniōn Vol. 2: 520
trapeza kyriou Vol. 2: 518, **522**
trapeza tou theou Vol. 2: 520
trechō Vol. 1: 648
  Vol. 3: **945–947**
treis Vol. 2: 545, **686–688,** 700, 703, 763, 893
  Vol. 3: 185
tria Vol. 2: **686**
tria tauta Vol. 2: 545
tribō Vol. 3: 840
tribolos Vol. 1: **726**
tris Vol. 2: 659, **686, 703**
trischilioi Vol. 2: **699**
tritos Vol. 1: 666
  Vol. 2: 63, **687, 703,** 893
trochos Vol. 1: 182
trōgō Vol. 2: **535 f.**
tromos Vol. 1: 622
-tron Vol. 3: 189
trōō Vol. 1: 182
trophos Vol. 1: 282
tropos Vol. 2: 662, 781
trygaō Vol. 2: 31, **33**
tychē Vol. 2: 657
tymbos Vol. 1: 264
tynchanon Vol. 3: 1129
typhlos Vol. 1: **218, 220**
typikōs Vol. 2: 277
  Vol. 3: **903**
typōma Vol. 3: 904

typoō Vol. 3: 904
typos Vol. 1: 71, 86, 371, 491, 744
  Vol. 2: 277, 284, 290, 760
  Vol. 3: 61, 555, **903–907,** 1015
typōsis Vol. 3: 904
typtō Vol. 3: 903
tyrannikos Vol. 2: 855
tyrannos Vol. 2: 372
  Vol. 3: 152
Tyrou hieras kai asylou Vol. 2: **851**

xenia Vol. 1: 690
xenizō Vol. 1: 689 f.
xenodocheō Vol. 1: **686**
Xenophōn Vol. 1: 569
xenos Vol. 1: 683, **686–689,** 691
  Vol. 2: 99, 538, 742, 794, 803
xērainō Vol. 1: **515**
  Vol. 3: 999
xēros Vol. 1: 390, **515 f.**
xylon Vol. 1: 214, **389 f.,** 394, 404
  Vol. 3: 391, **865 f., 868,** 870, 1195 f.

zaō Vol. 1: 181, 739
  Vol. 2: 94, **476–483,** 658, 882
  Vol. 3: 267, 366–368, 926, 1118, 1177
zēleō Vol. 3: **1167**
zēleuō Vol. 1: 318
zēloō Vol. 2: 121, 806
  Vol. 3: **1166 f.**
zēlos Vol. 1: 106, 535, 557 f.
  Vol. 2: 587
  Vol. 3: **1166 f.,** 1170
zēlōtēs Vol. 1: 72
  Vol. 3: **1166 f.**

zēmia Vol. 3: 134, **136 f.**
zēmioomai Vol. 3: 136
Zēn Vol. 1: 588
zeō Vol. 1: 318 f.
zestos Vol. 1: **317–319**
zēteō Vol. 1: 278, 430, 580
  Vol. 2: 806, 879
  Vol. 3: 188, 527–529, **530–533,** 1026, 1119, 1166
zētēsis Vol. 3: **530, 532,** 887
zeugnymi Vol. 3: **1160 f., 1164**
zeugos Vol. 3: **1160 f., 1164**
Zeus Vol. 1: 687
  Vol. 3: 1002
zizanion Vol. 3: 523
zō Vol. 2: 476
zōa Vol. 1: 443
  Vol. 2: 661
zōē Vol. 1: 337, 431, 464, 657
  Vol. 2: 387 f., 474, **475–483,** 546, 780, 817, 928
  Vol. 3: 99, 216, 309, 313, 353, 517, 832, 987, 1084, 1206, 1212
zōē aiōnios Vol. 2: 388, 480, 483, 928
  Vol. 3: 99, 517, **832,** 1212
zōnē Vol. 1: 142
  Vol. 3: **120**
zōnnymi Vol. 3: 116, **120,** 122
zōogoneō Vol. 2: **476**
zōon Vol. 1: 640
  Vol. 2: 476, 658, 689
  Vol. 3: 391, 679, 684
zōopoieō Vol. 1: 445
  Vol. 2: **476, 481**
  Vol. 3: 72
zōsa Vol. 1: 180
zygon Vol. 3: **1160 f.**
zygos Vol. 1: 261
  Vol. 2: 106, 119
  Vol. 3: 590, 592, **1160–1162**
zymē Vol. 2: **461–463,** 675
zymoō Vol. 2: 461 f.

General Index

General Index

(*chief references in* **bold figures**)

Aaron **Vol. 1:** 151, 224, 294, 544, 580
  Vol. 2: 228, 312, 314, 466, 592, 636, 777
  Vol. 3: 33–36, 77, 80, 155, 159, 164, 239,
  418, 424, 445, 508, 588, 650, 654, 827, 853,
  878, 1013, 1057
Aaronic blessing **Vol. 1:** 98, 211 f.
  Vol. 3: 126, 318
Aaron's rod **Vol. 1:** 408
  Vol. 2: 638
  Vol. 3: 787
Abaddon **Vol. 3:** 262
Abandon **Vol. 1:** 455, 488, 513, 526, 541, 549,
  606, 613, 681, 701, 720
  Vol. 2: 123, 155, 307, 396
  Vol. 3: 584
Abandoned **Vol. 3: 1004–1008**
Abandonment **Vol. 1:** 51, 411, 559, 595
  Vol. 2: 82 f., 307, 314, 419
  Vol. 3: 586, 1073
Abase **Vol. 1:** 731
  Vol. 2: 263
Abasement **Vol. 2: 259–264**
Abba **Vol. 1:** 286, 289, 410, **614 f.**, 623
  Vol. 2: 76, 883
  Vol. 3: 703
Abdicate **Vol. 2:** 160
Abdomen **Vol. 1:** 169
Abednego **Vol. 2:** 628
  Vol. 3: 110
Abel **Vol. 1:** 72, 87, 174, 375, 410, 713
  Vol. 3: 82, 143, 421, 425, 430, 434, 436,
  616 f., 621, 627, 630, 1014
Abhor **Vol. 1:** 555
  Vol. 3: 560
Abib **Vol. 2:** 675
Abide **Vol. 1:** 166, 282, 338, 458, 608, 611,
  637 f., 669, 723
  Vol. 2: 76, 359, 449, 535, 736
  Vol. 3: 225, 255, 921
Abide by **Vol. 3: 223–229**
Abiding **Vol. 1:** 73, 469, 719
Abihu **Vol. 2:** 638
Ability **Vol. 1:** 248, 278, 481, 676, 681, 731
  Vol. 2: 156, 354, 391, 395, 403, **601–616**
  Vol. 3: 116, 677, 691, **728–730**, 760, 763, 925,
  1026
Abimelech **Vol. 2:** 140, 431
  Vol. 3: 394, 739
Abinu malkenu litany **Vol. 1:** 618
Abiram **Vol. 1:** 195
  Vol. 2: 638
Able **Vol. 3:** 728–730

Ablutions **Vol. 1:** 144, 149 f., 152 f.
  Vol. 3: 30, 982, 989, 1007
Abner **Vol. 1:** 366
Abnormal **Vol. 2:** 568
Abode **Vol. 1:** 523, 661
  Vol. 2: 71, 184, 205, 295
  Vol. 3: 224–229
Abolish **Vol. 1: 73,** 368, 414, 462, 469, 591, 622,
  676, 685, 738
  Vol. 2: 160, 275, 443
  Vol. 3: 177–189, 323, 434
Abolition **Vol. 1:** 719
Abomination **Vol. 1:** 109, 142, 225, 382, 448,
  743
  Vol. 2: 200, 284, 296, 555
  Vol. 3: 104
Abomination of desolation **Vol. 1: 74 f.,,** 125,
  566
  Vol. 2: 65, 373, 809, 912, 916, 931
  Vol. 3: 419, 788, 793, 797, 803, 1006, 1008
Abomination of the Gentiles **Vol. 2:** 791
Aborted **Vol. 1:** 182
Abound **Vol. 1:** 683, **728–744**
  Vol. 2: 130 f., 144
Above **Vol. 1:** 518, 665
  Vol. 2: 184–196, 200–204, 259, 386
  Vol. 3: 767
Abracadabra **Vol. 2:** 560, 729
Abraham **Vol. 1:** 53, 65, 72, **76–80,** 141, 159,
  194, 208 f., 214, 227 f., 235, 286, 308 f., 311,
  346, 366, 370, 402, 417, 444 f., 452, 477,
  504, 531, 538 f., 574, 596 f., 601, 604, 617,
  640, 669, 684, 690 f., 693, 706, 713 f.
  Vol. 2: 68, 73, 76, 117, 120, 127 f., 140, 168,
  180, 216, 243, 245, 297, 301 f., 314, 316–
  319, 321, 329, 354, 359, 426, 431, 437, 452,
  549, 570, 576, 590–593, 596, 627 f., 649,
  651, 682, 691, 693 f., 755, 771, 793, 847,
  865, 899, 917
  Vol. 3: 36, 41, 69, 71–73, 77, 140, 146, 171,
  202, 213, 240 f., 263, 281, 359, 363, 366,
  369 f., 382, 393, 416, 418, 421, 425, 436,
  460, 495, 499, 514, 522–524, 529, 569, 579,
  581, 584, 617, 626 f., 639, 642 f., 652 f., 656
  f., 659, 701, 735, 739, 786, 800–802, 806,
  825 f., 841, 854, 867, 869, 871, 879, 965, 969
  f., 1012, 1055, 1072, 1091, 1112, 1135, 1151,
  1163, 1179, 1188
Abraham's bosom **Vol. 1: 78,** 240
  Vol. 3: 682
Abraoth **Vol. 3:** 476
Abrasax **Vol. 2:** 683

Abroad **Vol. 1:** 689
  Vol. 2: 788
Abrogate **Vol. 1:** 500
  Vol. 2: 675
Absalom **Vol. 2:** 649
Absence **Vol. 1:** 598, 724
  Vol. 2: 420, 422
Absent **Vol. 1:** 466
  Vol. 3: 1205
Absolute **Vol. 1:** 500, 522, 616, 636, 718
  Vol. 2: 279, 441, 444
Absolution **Vol. 1:** 639
  Vol. 3: 35, 685
Absolutism **Vol. 1:** 543
Absolve **Vol. 1:** 529
Absorb **Vol. 1:** 709
Abstain **Vol. 1:** 261, 494, 541, 611, 690 f., 704,
  Vol. 2: 135
  Vol. 3: 919
Abstemious **Vol. 1:** 515
  Vol. 2: 272
Abstention **Vol. 3:** 380, 934
Abstinence **Vol. 1:** 494–496, 514, 611 f., 625
  Vol. 2: 271
  Vol. 3: 101 f., 107, 536, 837, 996
Abstract **Vol. 1:** 450, 537, 562, 609
  Vol. 2: 240, 242, 746
Abstract thought **Vol. 3:** 234
Abstraction **Vol. 1:** 601, 641
  Vol. 3: 353
Abstruse **Vol. 1:** 421
Absurd **Vol. 1:** 637
Abundance **Vol. 1:** 727–732
  Vol. 2: 92, 105, 128, 130 f., 842
  Vol. 3: 137, 559, 791, 919, 922, 955
Abuse **Vol. 1:** 183, 264, 413, 418, 646
  Vol. 2: 123, 155, 310, 412, 772, 835
  Vol. 3: 27, 143, 340, **346 f.**, 755, 818
Abusive **Vol. 3: 346 f.**
Abyss **Vol. 1:** 449, 508
  Vol. 2: 126, **205–210,** 459, 727, 734, 826
  Vol. 3: 474, 983
Accad **Vol. 1:** 140
Accadian **Vol. 2:** 305
Accede **Vol. 1:** 320, 322
Accent **Vol. 3:** 316
Accept **Vol. 1:** 110, 112, 368, 375, 414, 425,
  483 f., 486–488, 556, 568, 578, 590, 629,
  666, 695
  Vol. 2: 178, 237 f., 245, 309, 311, 377, 794,
  817
  Vol. 3: 177, 220, 358, 434, 728, **744–746,** 759,
  777
Accept as proved **Vol. 3: 808–810**
Accept into one's society **Vol. 3: 747–751**
Accept opinion **Vol. 3:** 821
Acceptable **Vol. 1:** 235, 675, 708
  Vol. 2: 92, 116, 146, 171, 230, **814–817,** 884 f.
  Vol. 3: 358, **744–746,** 1014
Acceptance **Vol. 1:** 534, 588, 593, 603, 655, 701
  f.
  Vol. 2: 116, 173, 177, 230, 272, 309, 400,
  407, 812, 832,
  Vol. 3: 142, 505, **744–751,** 1062

Access **Vol. 1:** 223, 324, 390, 485, 592, 603,
  611, 638, 742
  Vol. 2: 31, 83, 230, 280, 443, 500, 591, 721,
  727, 733, 736, 855
  Vol. 3: 37, 40–42, 106, 235, 244, 336, 366,
  395, 470, 504, 543, 814, **935–943**
Accessible **Vol. 1:** 602
  Vol. 2: 342
Accession **Vol. 1:** 177, 626
  Vol. 2: 109, 146
  Vol. 3: 45, 317
Accident **Vol. 2:** 167, 414 f., 419, 665
  Vol. 3: 244, 474, 999
Accidental **Vol. 3:** 585, 997
Acclamation **Vol. 1:** 122, 629, 630
  Vol. 2: 424
  Vol. 3: 643, 673
Accommodate **Vol. 1:** 548
  Vol. 2: 814–817
Accompaniment **Vol. 3:** 668, 673
Accompany **Vol. 1:** 322, 480 f., 585
Accomplish **Vol. 1:** 696, 733, 737
  Vol. 2: 59, 64, 83, 120
  Vol. 3: 489, 911, **1147–1158**
Accomplishment **Vol. 1:** 653, 680, 697
  Vol. 2: 120
  Vol. 3: 68
Accord **Vol. 2:** 304
  Vol. 3: 349
Accost **Vol. 2:** 856
Account **Vol. 1:** 56, 378, 386, 573, 577, 588,
  725
  Vol. 2: 131, 244, 255, 858
  Vol. 3: 820, 823, 1081
Accountability **Vol. 1:** 349, 522
  Vol. 3: 844, 912
Accountant **Vol. 2:** 254
Accredit **Vol. 3:** 571
Accuracy **Vol. 3:** 65, 875
Accursed **Vol. 1:** 265, 390, 413 f., 416 f.
  Vol. 2: 399
  Vol. 3: 229
Accusation **Vol. 1:** 82–84, 281, 373, 402, 577,
  594, 609, 612, 631
  Vol. 2: 138 f., 178, 252, 434, 450
  Vol. 3: 483, 573, 1043
Accuse **Vol. 1:** 82–84, 349 f., 410, 473
  Vol. 2: 137, 140, 193, 236, 378, 380, 451
  Vol. 3: 51, 346, **468–473,** 804, 824, **923–928**
Accuser **Vol. 1:** 82–84, 454, 554, 610
  Vol. 2: 191, 313
  Vol. 3: 174, 232, 275
Accustom **Vol. 1:** 483 f.
  Vol. 2: 235
  Vol. 3: 775
Accustomed **Vol. 2:** 436
Achaemenidae **Vol. 3:** 372, 848
Achaia **Vol. 2:** 766, 826
  Vol. 3: 119, 416, 499, 976
Achaicus **Vol. 1:** 741
Achan **Vol. 1:** 345
Achieve **Vol. 2:** 62, 327, 394
  Vol. 3: 702
Achievement **Vol. 1:** 398, 431 f., 485, 492 f., 502,

Achievement (cont'd)
  612, 645, 647, 650 f., 676, 697, 722 f.
  Vol. 2: 120, 122, 798
  Vol. 3: 141 f., 817, 924, 946, **1147–1152**
Achilles **Vol. 2:** 232
  Vol. 3: 49, 959
Achsah **Vol. 3:** 557
Acknowledge **Vol. 1:** 265, 489, 549, 587
  Vol. 2: 180, 362, 383, 403, 417, 427, 877
  Vol. 3: 749, 853
Acknowledgment **Vol. 1:** 415
  Vol. 3: 637
Acquaint **Vol. 1:** 692
Acquaintance **Vol. 2:** 392
Acquiesce **Vol. 2:** 769
Acquire **Vol. 1:** 482–484, 635, 639
  Vol. 2: 298, 301, **838–840**
  Vol. 3: 192, 529
Acquisition **Vol. 1:** 533
  Vol. 2: 838–840
Acquit **Vol. 1:** 205, 352, 439, 505, 558, 698
Acquittal **Vol. 2:** 121, 674
  Vol. 3: 352–377
Act **Vol. 2:** 74, 108
  Vol. 3: 151, 1155–1158
Act of offering **Vol. 3: 417–436**
Act rightly **Vol. 3: 351 f.**
Act unjustly **Vol. 3:** 574
Act violently **Vol. 3:** 377
Action **Vol. 1:** 207, 484, 504 f., 552, 556, 564,
  585, 589–591, 600, 603, 639, 679 f., 693,
  697, 702, 713 f., 721 f., 741 f.
  Vol. 2: 47, 62, 79, 118, 200, 223, 395 f.
  Vol. 3: 54, 1021, 1123, **1147–1152, 1155–1158**
Active **Vol. 1:** 400, 605, 624
  Vol. 2: 149, 169, 475, 660, 861
  Vol. 3: 1147–1152, 1168
Activity **Vol. 1:** 489, 491, 595, 627, 655, 686,
  693, 695–697
  Vol. 2: 425
  Vol. 3: 1147, 1155
Actor **Vol. 1:** 706, 708
  Vol. 2: 468, 748
  Vol. 3: 138
Acts, Book of **Vol. 1:** 136, 148, 158, 181, 198,
  257, 266, 303, 324, 361, 364, 490, 589, 591,
  603
  Vol. 2: 130, 147, 252, 315, 333, 359
  Vol. 3: 62–65, 86
Acts, apocryphal books of **Vol. 1:** 50 f.,
  Vol. 2: 168
Acts of Andrew **Vol. 1:** 51
Acts of John **Vol. 1:** 50
  Vol. 2: 219
Acts of Paul **Vol. 1:** 51
  Vol. 2: 219, 557
Acts of Peter **Vol. 1:** 51
  Vol. 2: 219, 557
Acts of Thomas **Vol. 1:** 51, 646
  Vol. 2: 219
  Vol. 3: 231
Actual **Vol. 1:** 710 f.
Actuality **Vol. 3:** 1142
Actualization **Vol. 1:** 711, 713

  Vol. 3: 238
Adam **Vol. 1:** 53, 71, 77, **84–88**, 96, 179, 182,
  327, 390, 433 f., 436, 440, 446, 451, 472,
  548, 567, 621, 669, 730
  Vol. 2: 45, 57 f., 103, 158, 175, 179, 242, 481,
  483, 504, 564, 566, 570 f., 611, 649, 662,
  680 f., 691, 721, 723, 761, 763 f., 893, 897,
  920
  Vol. 3: 35, 186, 264 f., 273, 277, 302, 363,
  460, 469, 495, 522, 578 f., 581, 585 f., 613,
  617, 623, 632, 656, 659, 661, 663, 684, 687,
  906, 1063, 1075, 1158, 1194
Adapa **Vol. 2:** 201
  Vol. 3: 617
Adapt **Vol. 1:** 481, 483
  Vol. 2: 314
Adaptation **Vol. 2:** 307
Adar **Vol. 3:** 1053
Add **Vol. 1:** 540
  Vol. 3: 489
Addict **Vol. 1:** 514
Addiction **Vol. 3:** 996
Address **Vol. 1:** 66, 285 f., 488, 582, 614–617,
  620, 622
  Vol. 2: 315, 354, 358, 513 f., 651, 856, 860,
  867
  Vol. 3: 718
Address enthusiastically **Vol. 3:** 1080
Adequacy **Vol. 1:** 576
Adequate **Vol. 1:** 690
  Vol. 3: 727 f.
Adherence **Vol. 2:** 270
Adherent **Vol. 1:** 487, 489, 535
  Vol. 2: 298
Adiabene **Vol. 2:** 792
Adjuration **Vol. 1:** 97 f.
Adjure **Vol. 3:** 473, **737–743, 1038–1050**
Adjustment **Vol. 1:** 602, 679, 715
  Vol. 2: 569
Adjutant **Vol. 3:** 49
Administer **Vol. 1:** 536
  Vol. 2: 253–256, 451, 802
Administer **Vol. 3:** 188
Administer oath **Vol. 3:** 473
Administration **Vol. 1:** 192, 738
  Vol. 2: 121, 254, 377
  Vol. 3: 482, 548, 605, 880, 912
Administrative **Vol. 1:** 198
Administrator **Vol. 1:** 190, 198, 373
  Vol. 3: 478
Admiration **Vol. 1:** 99, 435
  Vol. 2: 92
  Vol. 3: 1166
Admission **Vol. 2:** 449
  Vol. 3: 747–751, 754
Admit **Vol. 1:** 680
  Vol. 3: 744–746, 747
Admonish **Vol. 3:** 675, 687
Admonition **Vol. 1:** 110, 319, 462, 502, 568 f.
  Vol. 2: 262, 360
Adonai **Vol. 2:** 556
  Vol. 3: 1116
Adonis **Vol. 1:** 64
  Vol. 3: 104, 274 f.

Adonizedek **Vol. 2:** 590
Adopt **Vol. 1:** 483, 632
  Vol. 2: 309, 318
Adoption **Vol. 1:** 123, 177–179, **280–291**, 410,
  534, 615, 668, 708, 738
  Vol. 2: 76, 374, 672, 884
  Vol. 3: 637, 751
Adoptionism **Vol. 3:** 300
Adoptionist **Vol. 1:** 473
  Vol. 2: 506
  Vol. 3: 639
Adoration **Vol. 2:** 855, 859, 868, 876
  Vol. 3: 531
Adore **Vol. 2:** 615
  Vol. 3: 233
Adorn **Vol. 1:** 469, 520, 524, 684
  Vol. 2: 95, 217, 236, 352
  Vol. 3: 771
Adornment **Vol. 3:** 562, 1067
Adulation **Vol. 1:** 99
Adult **Vol. 1:** 213, 281 f., 284, 568, 614
  Vol. 2: 62, 64, 562, 656
Adulterer **Vol. 2: 582–584**
  Vol. 3: 757
Adulteress **Vol. 1:** 650
  Vol. 2: 541, **582–584**, 800
  Vol. 3: 325, 537, 570, 580, 656
Adulterous **Vol. 2:** 36, 351
Adulterous generation **Vol. 2:** 582, 584, 680
Adultery **Vol. 1:** 51, 97, 235, 240, 349, 390,
  495, 498–500, 505–507, 655
  Vol. 2: 440, 448, **575–590**, 871
  Vol. 3: 104, 182 f., 227, 448, **535–541**, 792,
  796, 1062, 1064
Adulthood **Vol. 2:** 59
Advance **Vol. 1:** 320, 322, 473, 692–695
  Vol. 2: 128, 130, 238
  Vol. 3: 74
Advance payment **Vol. 2:** 40
Advanced **Vol. 2:** 61
Advantage **Vol. 1:** 137–139, 434, 437, 467 f.,
  539, 728–731
  Vol. 2: 115, 519
  Vol. 3: 31 f., 134, 136 f., 532, 833
Advent **Vol. 1:** 320, 737
  Vol. 2: 382, 887, **898–901**, 904, 931
  Vol. 3: 120, 733
Adversary **Vol. 1:** 91, 271, 516, 553, 647
  Vol. 2: 202, 368, 618, 877
  Vol. 3: 468–473, 784, 1068
Adverse **Vol. 1:** 572
  Vol. 2: 364
Adversity **Vol. 1:** 262, 411, 622
  Vol. 2: 478, 764
  Vol. 3: 672
Advertising **Vol. 3:** 900
Advice **Vol. 1:** 211, 340, 362 f., 568, 591
  Vol. 2: 141
  Vol. 3: 136
Advise **Vol. 1:** 65, 91, 362 f., 450, 568
  Vol. 2: 744
  Vol. 3: 677
Adviser **Vol. 1:** 89, 362 f.
  Vol. 3: 1029

Advisory **Vol. 1:** 193
Advocate **Vol. 1:** 78, **88–92**, 266, 271, 324, 329,
  571 f., 637
  Vol. 2: 84, 231, 266, 359, 709, 787, 878, 883,
  885, 895
  Vol. 3: 47, 93, 162 f., 225, 242, 315, 362, 460,
  633, 704, 1046, 1050
Aegina **Vol. 2:** 847
Aegisthus **Vol. 2:** 887
Aelia Capitolina **Vol. 2:** 308
Aelius Aristides **Vol. 1:** 406
  Vol. 2: 116, 621
Aeolian **Vol. 2:** 124
Aeon **Vol. 2:** 488
  Vol. 3: 826–833
Aeschylus **Vol. 1:** 550
  Vol. 3: 852
Aesculapius **Vol. 3:** 261, 915
Aesthetic **Vol. 1:** 459, 536
  Vol. 2: 93, 95, 98, 100, 102 f.
Afar **Vol. 2:** 53
Affair **Vol. 3:** 324
Affairs **Vol. 2:** 146
Affect **Vol. 1:** 654, 658
  Vol. 2: 366
Affection **Vol. 1:** 177, 254, 742
  Vol. 2: 538, 599, 861
  Vol. 3: 678
Affection, without natural **Vol. 2: 538–547**
Affectionate **Vol. 2: 538–547**
Affiliation **Vol. 2:** 310
Affinity **Vol. 1:** 482
Affirm **Vol. 1:** 83, 98, 487, 545
  Vol. 2: 318
  Vol. 3: 742, 1038–1050
Affirmation **Vol. 2:** 149, 297, 313, 317, 340, 343
  Vol. 3: 741
Afflatus **Vol. 2:** 233
Afflict **Vol. 1:** 188 f., 467, 612
  Vol. 2: 260, 267, **807–809**
Affliction **Vol. 1:** 68, 163, 171, 188, 202, 260–
  262, 329, 410, 422, 539, 648, 652 f., 687,
  725, 727, 731, 741
  Vol. 2: 257, 263, 357, 359–361, 414, 416,
  423, 663, 700, 766, **805–809**, 865
  Vol. 3: 200, 212, 256, 322, 701, **719–725**, 801,
  836, 856
Afflictions of Christ **Vol. 2:** 808
  Vol. 3: 956
Affluence **Vol. 2:** 320
Affrontery **Vol. 1:** 364
Aflame **Vol. 3:** 225
Afraid **Vol. 1:** 453, 621–623, 646, 688
  Vol. 2: 90
After **Vol. 1:** 321, **480–494**
  Vol. 2: 55
  Vol. 3: 952–956
After-life **Vol. 1:** 204
  Vol. 2: 432 f.
  Vol. 3: 99, 178, 270, 274 f.
Afternoon **Vol. 1:** 634
Agabus **Vol. 2:** 827
  Vol. 3: 86 f., 121, 1183
Agamemnon **Vol. 3:** 851

Agape **Vol. 3:** 547 f.
Agate **Vol. 3:** 396
Age **Vol. 1:** 92 f., 124, 165, 192–194, 277, 280, 282–289, 298, 368, 431, 477, 522, 524, 566, 620, 638, 675, 683, 709, 718
  Vol. 2: 35, 58, 62, 75, 129, 170, 254, 353, 359, 398, 428 f., 433, 588, 674, 689 f., 698, 700, **713–716**, 737, 892, 907, 917, 919 f., 928
  Vol. 3: 312, 350, 403, 492, 558, 561, 698, 759, **826–833**, 841
Age to come **Vol. 1:** 86, 145, 282, 326 f., 518, 688
  Vol. 2: 74, 270, 298, 420, 672, 718, 836, 840, 919 f., 928
  Vol. 3: 142, 364, 809
Age of marriage **Vol. 2:** 578, 584, 588
Aged **Vol. 3:** 545
Agent **Vol. 1:** 205, 208, 476 f., 538, 540, 542, 566
  Vol. 2: 195, 502, 516, 552, 658, 718
Aggrandizement **Vol. 3:** 703
Aggravate **Vol. 1:** 496
Agitate **Vol. 3:** 556, **709f.**
Agitation **Vol. 1:** 108
  Vol. 2: 652
Agitator **Vol. 1:** 396
Agni cult **Vol. 1:** 653
Agony **Vol. 1:** 393, 645 f.
Agree **Vol. 1:** 344, 454
  Vol. 2: 897
Agreeable **Vol. 1:** 675
  Vol. 2: 116
  Vol. 3: 744
Agreement **Vol. 1:** 356, 365, 368, 415, 588, 590, 594, 687
  Vol. 2: 146, 236, 317, 328, 436, **500–508**, 584, 660, 879
  Vol. 3: 224, 816, 1039, 1083, 1165
Agricultural festivals **Vol. 1:** 625
Agriculture **Vol. 3:** 102, 835
Agrippa (→Herod)
Ahab **Vol. 1:** 195, 640
  Vol. 2: 458, 582
  Vol. 3: 426, 876, 1057, 1091
Ahabah prayer **Vol. 1:** 618
  Vol. 2: 313
Ahasuerus **Vol. 3:** 279, 756, 1057
Ahaz **Vol. 1:** 596, 655
  Vol. 2: 86, 628
  Vol. 3: 249
Ahaziah **Vol. 3:** 1091
Ahijah **Vol. 1:** 127
  Vol. 2: 521
Ahikam **Vol. 3:** 478
Ahithophel **Vol. 1:** 433
Ahriman **Vol. 1:** 563
  Vol. 3: 693
Ahura Mazda **Vol. 1:** 563
Ai **Vol. 1:** 394
Aid **Vol. 1:** 261
  Vol. 2: 363
  Vol. 3: 544–549, 553, **1147–1152**
Ailing **Vol. 3: 996–999**
Ailment **Vol. 1:** 119, 515, 727

Aim **Vol. 1:** 270, 470, 488, 541, 604, 644, 676, 695, 697, 720
  Vol. 2: 78, 335, 339, 353
  Vol. 3: 365
Aimless **Vol. 1:** 546, 550
Aion **Vol. 2:** 158
  Vol. 3: 827
Air **Vol. 1:** 164, **449–454**, 708
  Vol. 2: 189, 192 f., 232, 452
  Vol. 3: 678, 689
Akedah **Vol. 3:** 195
Akeldama **Vol. 1:** 93 f., 224
  Vol. 2: 321, 854
  Vol. 3: 912
Akiba, Rabbi **Vol. 1:** 67
  Vol. 2: 337, 544, 608, 640, 720
Akitu **Vol. 2:** 644
Akkadian **Vol. 1:** 68
Aland, Kurt **Vol. 1:** 149
Alarm **Vol. 1:** 621, 646
  Vol. 2: 621–626
  Vol. 3: 50, 239, 709, 1169
Alas **Vol. 3: 1051–1055**
Alazon **Vol. 3:** 28
Albrektson, B. **Vol. 3: 333**
Alchemical **Vol. 3:** 310
Alcimus **Vol. 3:** 479
Alcinous **Vol. 2:** 233
Alcohol **Vol. 1:** 625
  Vol. 3: 101, 107
Aleppo **Vol. 3:** 446
Alert **Vol. 1:** 513, 515
  Vol. 2: 136 f.
Alexander **Vol. 1:** 466
  Vol. 3: 471, 558
Alexander Balas **Vol. 2:** 817
Alexander the Great **Vol. 1:** 59, 255, 405
  Vol. 2: 33, 95, 124 f., 307, 372 f., 512, 612, 651, 849
  Vol. 3: 80, 269, 450, 634, 715
Alexander (high priest) **Vol. 3:** 40
Alexander Janneus (→ Jonathan)
Alexander, Rabbi **Vol. 2:** 462
Alexandra **Vol. 2:** 810
Alexandria **Vol. 1:** 49, 68
  Vol. 2: 126, 331 f., 754
  Vol. 3: 385, 453, 485, 598, 778, 827, 976
Alexandrian **Vol. 3:** 41
Alexandrians, synagogue of **Vol. 1:** 297
Alexandrines **Vol. 3:** 843
Alien **Vol. 1:** 221, 411, **683–692**
  Vol. 2: 297, 540, **739–742**
  Vol. 3: 256, 381
Alien speech **Vol. 3: 1078–1081**
Alienate **Vol. 1:** 684 f.
  Vol. 2: 156, 265
  Vol. 3: 172
Alienation **Vol. 2:** 94, 170, 663
Alive **Vol. 1:** 359, 401, 445, 474, 509, 653, 722
  Vol. 2: 122, 269, 922, 924
  Vol. 3: 689
All **Vol. 1:** 94–97, 383, 524, 577, 639, 654, 665, 668 f., 678, 694, 718, 720, 730, 735, 740
  Vol. 2: 67, 188, 195, 209, 242, 398, 401, 425,

387

428, 530, 690, 799
Vol. 3: 195, 197, 275, 906
All in all **Vol. 2:** 74
All-Sovereign **Vol. 2:** 513
All-sufficiency **Vol. 3:** 723
Allay **Vol. 3:** 109
Allegation **Vol. 2:** 139
Allegiance **Vol. 1:** 302, 304, 406, 424, 492
  Vol. 2: 311, 377, 380, 382
  Vol. 3: 136, 544, 780
Allegorical **Vol. 2:** 56, 125, 277, 280, 329, 446, 685
  Vol. 3: 486
Allegorize **Vol. 1:** 577
  Vol. 2: 442, 590
  Vol. 3: 789
Allegory **Vol. 1: 49**, 71, 81, 116, 259, 289, 368, 574, 577, 737
  Vol. 2: 252, 279, 584 f., **743–760**
  Vol. 3: 920
Alleviation **Vol. 1:** 328, 727
  Vol. 2: 28
Alliance **Vol. 1:** 141, 594, 718
  Vol. 3: 33, 391, 444, 605
Alliteration **Vol. 2:** 831
Allocate **Vol. 1:** 365, 533, 640
Allot **Vol. 2:** 296, 298, 300
Allotment **Vol. 1:** 475, 533
Allow **Vol. 1:** 506 f., 529, 587, 676, 686, 691, 698
  Vol. 2: 223, 236, 369, 435
  Vol. 3: 188, 475
Allowance **Vol. 3:** 144
Alloy **Vol. 2:** 97
Allurement **Vol. 1:** 457 f., 726
Allusion **Vol. 3:** 489, 494, 612
Ally **Vol. 1:** 531
Almighty **Vol. 1:** 111, 356, 409
  Vol. 2: 69 f., 74, 231, 240, 290, 329, 509, 513, 601, 857, 859, 862
  Vol. 3: 544, **716–718**, 721, 729
Almond **Vol. 3:** 1096
Almost **Vol. 2:** 428
Alms **Vol. 2: 594–598**, 820, 823
  Vol. 3: 242, 545, 748, 874
Almsgiving **Vol. 2:** 104, 216, 469, 824, 830–832
  Vol. 3: 157
Aloes **Vol. 1:** 122, 265
  Vol. 2: 295
Alone **Vol. 1:** 492
  Vol. 2: 307, **723–725**
  Vol. 3: 436, 542
Alongside **Vol. 2:** 743
Aloof **Vol. 1:** 528, 606 f.
  Vol. 2: 315
Aloud **Vol. 3:** 75
Alpha and Omega **Vol. 2:** 59, 282
Alphabet **Vol. 2:** 282
  Vol. 3: 483 f., 492
Alphaeus **Vol. 2:** 467
Altar **Vol. 1:** 75, 122, 221, 223, 387, 559, 653, 655, 687
  Vol. 2: 77, 85, 191, 207, 212, 226, 273, 373, 556, 689

Vol. 3: 34, 94, 104, 151, 154, 157 f., 173, 245, 259, 404, **415–436**, 489, 497, 686, 715, 789, 794, 918, 1006
Altar of burnt offering **Vol. 1:** 633
  Vol. 3: 812, 919
Altar of incense **Vol. 1:** 114
  Vol. 2: 294
  Vol. 3: 418, 424, 436, 787 f., 812, 814 f.
Altar of sacrifice **Vol. 2:** 97
Alter **Vol. 1:** 608, 704
  Vol. 2: 437
  Vol. 3: 166
Alteration **Vol. 1:** 658
Alves, Rubem **Vol. 3:** 973
Amalekites **Vol. 2:** 637, 639
  Vol. 3: 139, 236, 427, 1009
Amanuensis **Vol. 3:** 478
Amarna letters **Vol. 1:** 170, 207
  Vol. 2: 324
Amaze **Vol. 1:** 527, 529 f.
  Vol. 2: 621–626
Amazement **Vol. 2:** 359, **621–626**
Amaziah **Vol. 3:** 1092
Ambassador **Vol. 1:** 101, 126, 129, 192–194
  Vol. 2: 608
  Vol. 3: 49, 168–170, 547
Ambiguity **Vol. 2:** 313
Ambiguity in translation **Vol. 3:** 1177
Ambiguous **Vol. 3:** 352
Ambition **Vol. 1:** 106, 137, 427, 676
  Vol. 2: 121, 518
  Vol. 3: 112, 821, 888, 1052
Ambrose **Vol. 1:** 315
Ambrosiaster **Vol. 2:** 219
Amen **Vol. 1: 97–99, 250**
  Vol. 2: 456, 837, 862, 878
  Vol. 3: 509, 626, 669, 675, 742, 883, 1046, 1106, 1112
Amen-formula **Vol. 3:** 1107
Amethyst **Vol. 3:** 396 f.
Ami, Rabbi **Vol. 1:** 597
Amiable **Vol. 2:** 115
Amillenarianism **Vol. 2:** 389
Amillennialist **Vol. 1:** 53, 508
  Vol. 2: 702
Ammon **Vol. 2:** 395
  Vol. 3: 634
Ammonites **Vol. 1:** 426
  Vol. 2: 373
Amnesty **Vol. 2:** 168
Amoraim **Vol. 1:** 49, 69
Amorite **Vol. 1:** 734
  Vol. 2: 555, 636, 888
  Vol. 3: 94, 458
Amorite dynasty **Vol. 3:** 94 f.
Amos **Vol. 1:** 66, 109, 244, 661
  Vol. 3: 79, 93, 139, 249, 366, 659, 1089–1092, 1103
Amount **Vol. 1:** 734
  Vol. 2: 683
Amphictyony **Vol. 2:** 325, 695
Amphitheatre **Vol. 3:** 571
Amputation **Vol. 2:** 415
  Vol. 3: 448

Amulet **Vol. 1:** 451
  Vol. 2: 136, 556
Amun **Vol. 1:** 177
'Amwas **Vol. 3:** 453
Anabaptists **Vol. 3:** 108
Anakim **Vol. 3:** 248
Analogical **Vol. 3:** 996
Analogical correspondence **Vol. 3:** 326
Analogy **Vol. 1: 49,** 50, 60, 71, 580
  Vol. 2: 110, 501
  Vol. 3: 278, 301 f., 570, 912, 1007, 1064, 1132 f., 1138
Analyse **Vol. 1:** 353
Analytical study **Vol. 1:** 580
Ananias **Vol. 1:** 136
  Vol. 2: 91, 320
  Vol. 3: 912
Ananias (high priest) **Vol. 1:** 205, 476
  Vol. 2: 451
  Vol. 3: 40, 347, 948 f.
Ananias and Sapphira **Vol. 1:** 466 f., 642
  Vol. 2: 473, 846
  Vol. 3: 387
Ananus **Vol. 3:** 39
Anarchy **Vol. 1:** 654, 667
Anastasis **Vol. 3:** 261
Anastasius Sinaita **Vol. 1:** 649
Anath **Vol. 2:** 553
Anathema **Vol. 2:** 402, 530, 897
Anatolia **Vol. 3:** 421
Anatolian **Vol. 2:** 97
Anatomy **Vol. 1:** 241
Anaximander **Vol. 2:** 137
  Vol. 3: 840
Ancestor **Vol. 1:** 167, 240, 255, 288, 615
  Vol. 2: 92, 206, 318, 320, 331, 437
Ancestral **Vol. 1:** 573 f., 616
Ancestry **Vol. 1:** 187, 427
  Vol. 2: 36
  Vol. 3: 654 f.
Ancestry of Messiah **Vol. 3:** 656
Anchor **Vol. 1:** 372, 658, 660
  Vol. 2: 244
  Vol. 3: 684, 913
Ancient **Vol. 1:** 164, 641, 657, 720
Ancient of Days **Vol. 1:** 204
  Vol. 2: 80, 613, 917
  Vol. 3: 614, 621
Ancient paths **Vol. 3:** 938
Andrew **Vol. 3:** 383
Androgynous **Vol. 2:** 570
  Vol. 3: 1056
Andronicus **Vol. 1:** 130
Andronicus Rhodius **Vol. 1:** 64
Andros **Vol. 2:** 214
  Vol. 3: 760
Angel **Vol. 1:** 54, **101–105,** 127, 166 f., 202, 204, 219, 233, 252, 280, 331, 335, 339, 345, 374, 408–410, 449–452, 464 f., 474, 476, 478, 489 f., 508, 512, 517, 544, 570, 585 f., 622 f., 648, 656 f., 659, 677, 690, 733, 736
  Vol. 2: 37, 46, 69, 86, 107, 126, 146 f., 149, 161, 175, 185, 191 f., 194–196, 199, 213, 228 f., 263, 298 f., 302, 332, 365, 381, 426, 434,

452, 459, 486, 488, 492 f., 502, 513 f., 518, 556, 559, 561, 565, 577, 591, 602 f., 608 f., 612–615, 624 f., 651, 655, 681 f., 689, 691, 696, 707, 709, 727, 791, 793, 811, 819, 832, 837, 860, 877, 884, 904, 916, 930
  Vol. 3: 35, 40, 45 f., 48, 54, 57, 80, 99, 113, 120, 135, 172, 179, 186 f., 199, 216, 218, 242, 265, 270 f., 278, 313, 316, 322, 342, 344 f., 389, 394, 433, 436, 440, 457, 465, 469 f., 500, 506, 514 f., 517, 527, 546, 551, 557, 579, 621, 630, 632 f., 636 f., 642, 660, 681, 693, 695, 707, 709, 714, 732, 736, 795, 802, 805, 807, 812, 829, 844, 847, 856, 860, 939, 948, 1001, 1003–1005, 1011, 1013 f., 1054, 1060, 1071, 1113, 1121
Angel of Darkness **Vol. 2:** 492, 708
  Vol. 3: 469, 801, 842, 939, 944
Angel of death **Vol. 1:** 83, 509
  Vol. 3: 468, 471
Angel of destruction **Vol. 3:** 469
Angel of light **Vol. 1:** 710
  Vol. 2: 495
  Vol. 3: 471, 864
Angel of the waters **Vol. 3:** 990
Angelic **Vol. 1:** 462, 676
  Vol. 2: 45 f., 196, 270
Angelology **Vol. 1:** 102
  Vol. 3: 457, 704
Angelophany **Vol. 3:** 288
Angels of the Churches **Vol. 1:** 103, 304
Anger **Vol. 1: 105–113,** 202 f., 316, 329, 364, 381, 465, 467, 535, 555, 654, 657, 679, 681, 715, 734
  Vol. 2: 28, 58, 70, 76, 139, 180, 224, 256, 261, 272, 275, 366, 419, 421, 484, 544, 550, 599 f., 768 f., 834, 854
  Vol. 3: 99, 174, 205, 214, 221, 255, 347, 369, 580, 586, 689, 691, 1051, 1166
Angites **Vol. 3:** 987
Angler **Vol. 1:** 670
Angry **Vol. 1:** 105, 107, 202, 364, 418, 479
  Vol. 3: 559
Anguish **Vol. 1:** 411, 422, 526
  Vol. 2: 83, 364, 416, 423
  Vol. 3: 229, 858
Animal **Vol. 1:** 84 f., 101, **113–119,** 151 f., 173, 175, 178, 186, 218–226, 232, 234, 239–241, 260, 272, 342 f., 371, 393, 419, 443, 468 f., 490, 507, 509, 511, 520, 560, 565, 585, 609 f., 625, 627, 632, 671 f., 674, 699, 721, 725, 743
  Vol. 2: 30, 37, 50, 59, 151, 159, 167, 180, 192, 205, 208, 230, 233, 236, 256 f., 268, 274 f., 286, 288, 320, 381, 410–414, 461, 474, 476, 483, 501, 533, 562, 564 f., 569, 572, 577, 586, 599, 625, 631, 649, 653, 659, 661 f., 684, 689, 693, 728, 741, 746, 754, 776, 809, 826, 843
  Vol. 3: 27, 41, 95, 103 f., 108, 113, 117, 151, 158 f., 189 f., 192, 200, 212 f., 256, 260, 342, 345, 377, 381, 407, 409, 417, 419–425, 427, 434 f., 444, 471, 476, 497, 500, 532, 560, 565, 568, 604, 713, 715, 739, 791, 797, 856, 858, 860, 923, 925, 965, 986, 990, 1055 f.,

1078, 1160 f., 1164.
Animal worship **Vol. 3:** 104
Animate 522 f.
   Vol. 3: 678
Animation **Vol. 1:** 444, 521
Animism **Vol. 1:** 450
   Vol. 2: 520
   Vol. 3: 424
Ankle **Vol. 1:** 393
   Vol. 2: 415
Anna **Vol. 2:** 245
   Vol. 3: 81, 198, 790, 872 f., 1059, 1072
Annas **Vol. 3:** 39 f., 381
Annexation **Vol. 2:** 325
Annihilation **Vol. 1:** 109, 413 f., 462 f., 465,
   610, 688, 719
   Vol. 2: 58, 363, 367
   Vol. 3: 248, 590
Annius of Viterbo **Vol. 3:** 655
Anniversary **Vol. 1:** 628
Announce **Vol. 1:** 246, 301, 655
   Vol. 2: 107 f., 326, 343, 375
   Vol. 3: 44–48, 52, **68–74**, 316
Announcement **Vol. 1:** 62, 293, 696
   Vol. 2: 340, 368, 384
   Vol. 3: 44, **48–57, 68–74**, 1090
Annoy **Vol. 1:** 557
Annual **Vol. 1:** 632
   Vol. 2: 211
Annul **Vol. 1:** 370, 416, 578
   Vol. 2: 437
   Vol. 3: 177–189
Anodyne **Vol. 2:** 295
Anoint **Vol. 1:** 53, 63, 119–124, 178, 427, 471,
   512, 544
   Vol. 2: 159, 203 f., 227, 294, **334–343**, 354,
   374, 435, 710–713, 791, 812, 835, 875, 899
   Vol. 3: 153, 221, 242, 499, 650, 696–698,
   703, 750, 764, 1059–1061, 1150
Anointing oil **Vol. 2:** 226, 294
Anonymous 733
Another **Vol. 1:** 684 f.
   Vol. 2: 625, 838
Answer **Vol. 1:** 51, 98 f., 272, 332, 339, 345,
   409, 411, 480, 583, 727
   Vol. 2: 173, 175, 178 f., 244, 296, 446, **468–
470**, 856, 864
   Vol. 3: 324 f., 347, 449, 528, 777, 849
Answerable **Vol. 1:** 222, 365
   Vol. 2: 475, 510
Ant **Vol. 1:** 252
Antagonism **Vol. 2:** 826
   Vol. 3: 1049
Antagonist **Vol. 2:** 383
Anthology **Vol. 2:** 315
Anthropocentric **Vol. 1:** 383
   Vol. 2: 260
Anthropological **Vol. 1:** 233, 382, 401, 523,
   672 f., 687, 706
   Vol. 2: 64, 94, 253, 919
Anthropology **Vol. 1:** 236, 675
   Vol. 2: 397, 919
Anthropomorphism **Vol. 1: 50**, 63, 66, 239, 472,
   585

Vol. 2: 66
   Vol. 3: 341, 345, 513, 943, 1167
Anti-Christian **Vol. 1:** 607, 733
   Vol. 2: 625
   Vol. 3: 36, 856
Anti-docetic **Vol. 2:** 535 f.
Anti-gnostic **Vol. 1:** 603
   Vol. 2: 402, 405
Anti-God **Vol. 1:** 124 f.
   Vol. 2: 394
Anti-Jewish **Vol. 2:** 309 f., 316
Anti-Judaistic **Vol. 2:** 135
Anti-legal **Vol. 2:** 135
Anti-monarchical **Vol. 2:** 374, 376
Anti-mystical **Vol. 2:** 133
Anti-Semitism **Vol. 1:** 360
   Vol. 2: 316
Anti-social **Vol. 2:** 92
   Vol. 3: 584
Anti-speculative **Vol. 1:** 603
Antichrist **Vol. 1:** 75, 114, **124–126**, 323, 464,
   544, 566
   Vol. 2: 58, 192, 205, 435, 447, 460 f., 610,
   615, 633, 645, 653, 684, 809, 901, 905, 931
   Vol. 3: 319, 471, 476, 505, 706, 716, 803, 872
Anticipate **Vol. 1:** 651, 733, 737
   Vol. 2: 367, 380, 394
   Vol. 3: 624, **747–751**
Anticipation **Vol. 2:** 87, 238 f., 244 f., 309, 315,
   354, 402, 918 f.
   Vol. 3: 633, 922
Antidote **Vol. 2:** 271
Antinomian **Vol. 1:** 302, 338, 720
   Vol. 2: 394
Antinomianism **Vol. 2:** 447, 677 f., 718
Antioch **Vol. 1:** 133, 303, 361, 462, 473
   Vol. 2: 316, 321, 343, 368, 523, 729, 795,
   827, 849, 895
   Vol. 3: 87, 106, 203, 226, 228, 252, 284, 325,
   352, 385
Antioch of Pisidia **Vol. 3:** 65, 180, 228
Antiochus III **Vol. 1:** 196
   Vol. 3: 478
Antiochus IV Epiphanes **Vol. 1:** 75, 125, 235,
   309, 529
   Vol. 2: 125, 372, 628, 688, 849
   Vol. 3: 35, 50, 270 f., 318, 419, 452, 460, 498,
   788, 1006, 1035
Antiochus VII **Vol. 3:** 147
Antiochus Philopappus **Vol. 1:** 640
Antipas **Vol. 3:** 1047
Antipathy **Vol. 1:** 555
   Vol. 2: 332
Antiphon the Sophist
   Vol. 3: 1019
Antiquity **Vol. 1:** 164, 531
   Vol. 3: 828 f.
Antiseptic **Vol. 3:** 444
Antithesis **Vol. 1:** 335, 600, 705
   Vol. 2: 314, 419, 422 f.
   Vol. 3: 1107
Antithetical **Vol. 2:** 122
Antithetical argumentation **Vol. 3:** 1082
Antitype **Vol. 1:** 71, 86, 142, 222, 327

Antitype (cont'd)
  Vol. 2: 835
  Vol. 3: 41, 632, **903–906**, 1007
Antonia Vol. 3: 788, 977
Antony Vol. 2: 849
Anxiety Vol. 1: **276–278**, 421, 455, 597, 622, 646, 651, 715, 723, 726
  Vol. 2: 90, 240, 244, 360, 664, 832 f., 841, 868
  Vol. 3: 103, 128, 683, 691, 710, 728
Apartheid Vol. 3: 975
Apathy Vol. 1: 359
  Vol. 3: 821
A-personal Vol. 2: 197
Aphorism Vol. 1: 555
  Vol. 2: 757, 890
Aphrodite Vol. 2: 85, 224
  Vol. 3: 318
Apiece Vol. 2: 158
Apion Vol. 2: 310
Apiru Vol. 1: 170
Apocalypse Vol. 1: **50**, 430, 528, 541, 656
  Vol. 2: 914
  Vol. 3: 85
Apocalypse, Little Vol. 2: 903
Apocalypse of Baruch Vol. 3: 271
Apocalypse of Elijah Vol. 2: 219
Acocalypse of Enoch Vol. 2: 219
Apocalypse of Peter Vol. 2: 219
  Vol. 3: 312
Apocalypses, Apocryphal Vol. 1: 50
Apocalyptic Vol. 1: **50**, 54, 56, 65, 110, 116, 118, 124, 175, 203, 210 f., 216 f., 224, 243 f., 304, 313, 326, 409, 425, 433, 442, 463, 519, 524, 527, 539, 545, 559, 598, 607, 610, 638, 651, 655, 706, 742
Apocalyptic Vol. 2: 37, 45, 54, 56, 58, 65, 71 f., 133, 173, 191, 193, 202, 208, 215 f., 219, 237, 252, 276, 279, 329, 364, 366 f., 376 f., 382 – 386, 389, 397, 447, 458 f., 482, 629, 633, 664 f., 674, 684, 688 f., 692, 695 f., 698, 700 f., 703, 762, 835 f., 888, 891 f., 894, 899, 901, 903, 905 f., 911, 913 f., 918, 920 f., 923, 925–927, 930
  Vol. 3: 70, 80, 88, 250, 253, 277, 280, 302, 312, 319, 332, 373, 403, 489, 502–504, 522, 526, 559, 576, 610, 613–621, 624, 628–631, 633, 639 f., 644, 658 f., 695, 718, **730–737**, 829–831, 836, 842 f., 847, 851, 862, 888 f., 928, 956, 961 f., 989, 1007, 1011, 1033, 1054, 1109, 1161
Apocalypticism Vol. 3: 58
Apocalyptist Vol. 1: **50**
  Vol. 2: 191, 311, 892
  Vol. 3: 979
Apocrypha Vol. 1: **50,** 63, 66–68, 341, 618, 626, 646
  Vol. 2: 41, 93, 138, **219**, 324 f., 331
Apocryphal Vol. 1: 243
  Vol. 2: 204, 218 f.
  Vol. 3: 58, 85, 401, 493
Apodictic law Vol. 3: 931
Apokatastasis Vol. 3: 148
Apollinarianism Vol. 3: 1176

Apollo Vol. 1: 189, 508, 574 f.
  Vol. 2: 85, 166, 224, 558, 756
  Vol. 3: 75, 103, 738
Apollonius of Tyana Vol. 2: 107, 393
  Vol. 3: 259, 261, 635
Apollos Vol. 1: 709
  Vol. 3: 387, 699, 1117
Apollyon Vol. 1: 462
  Vol. 2: 126
Apolodorous of Athens Vol. 3: 92
Apologetic Vol. 1: 338, 383, 736, 737
  Vol. 2: 310, 312, 332
  Vol. 3: 64, 66, 494
Apologetics Vol. 1: 51, 688
Apologia Vol. 3: 621
Apologist Vol. 1: 51, 63
  Vol. 3: 1048
Apology Vol. 1: **51**
  Vol. 2: 357, 856, 858
Apophthegm Vol. 1: 269
  Vol. 2: 757
Apostasy Vol. 1: **51**, 108, 124, 141, 281, 309, 347, 357, 390, 397, 469, 499, 512, 606–608, 611, 693, 703
  Vol. 2: 37, 270, 288, 291, 449, 487, 573, 576, 581 f., 606, 629, 633, 678, 708, 718 f., 798
  Vol. 3: 28, 96, 135 f., 469, 578, 582, 606, 637, 692, 750, 764, 803, 1069, 1104
Apostate Vol. 1: 51, 109, 448, 607, 611
  Vol. 2: 291, 555, 688, 705, 779, 866 f.
  Vol. 3: 343, 601, 883, 961
Apostatize Vol. 2: 125
Apostle Vol. 1: 71, **126–137**, 172, 174, 183, 191 f., 194, 198–200, 214, 246 f., 256, 274 f., 298, 301, 307, 332, 337, 340, 474–479, 489, 493, 519, 540, 542, 547, 568, 571, 576, 592, 619, 623, 643, 662, 686, 707, 710, 723
  Vol. 2: 50, 57, 62, 77, 109, 111–114, 119, 121, 129, 135, 152, 176, 179, 187, 196, 217, 244, 253, 299, 359, 365, 385, 398, 412, 434, 443, 446, 451, 460 f., 472, 517, 550, 573, 597, 603, 611, 620, 655, 695, 718, 729, 732, 734, 736, 740, 765, 768, 787, 789, 799, 873, 877
  Vol. 3: 52, 54, 59 f., 63, 65, 67, 84, 88, 128, 212, 241, 252, 296, 313–315, 384, 387, 390, 393 f., 504, 547 f., 553, 568, 571, 724, 729, 746, 767–769, 793, 817, 822, 857, 862, 872, 955, 1044, 1047 f., 1059, 1113, 1122, 1151 f.
Apostles' Creed Vol. 2: 210
Apostleship Vol. 1: 130–134, 183
  Vol. 2: 112, 120 f., 299, 399, 827
  Vol. 3: 170, 322, 749
Apostolate Vol. 1: 130–135
  Vol. 2: 121
  Vol. 3: 1020
Apostolic Vol. 1: 469, 478, 491, 496, 592, 644, 733, 742
  Vol. 2: 75, 121, 252, 255, 263, 329, 403
  Vol. 3: 458
Apostolic Council Vol. 1: 310
  Vol. 2: 328
  Vol. 3: 315
Apostolic decree Vol. 2: 450 f., 678

Vol. 3: 106, 931
Apostolic Fathers Vol. 1: 51, 52, 339, 535
    Vol. 2: 123, 219
Apostolic generation Vol. 1: 132
Apostolic ministry Vol. 1: 419
Apostolic office Vol. 1: 247
Apostolic succession Vol. 1: 129
Apostolic tradition Vol. 1: 70, 200, 247, 302
Apotropaic Vol. 3: 982
Apotropaic function Vol. 3: 103
Appal Vol. 1: 530
Apparent Vol. 1: 686
    Vol. 2: 420
Apparition Vol. 2: 552–562
    Vol. 3: 310, 317–324
Appeal Vol. 1: 206, 269–271, 349–351, 487,
    492, 569 f., 615, 736
    Vol. 2: 155, 162, 281, 312, 364, 860, 879–881,
    882
    Vol. 3: 238, 359
Appeal to Caesar Vol. 1: 276
    Vol. 2: 882
Appear Vol. 1: 55, 185, 320, 383, 471, 544, 587,
    597, 710, 712, 723
    Vol. 2: 82, 318, 328, 386, 447, 484, 518
    Vol. 3: 221, 259, 275, 281, 310, 317–324,
    821 f.
Appearance Vol. 1: 87, 183 f., 204, 248, 298,
    328, 341, 393, 474, 491, 503, 515, 522, 545,
    550, 585–588, 597, 607, 622 f., 654, 656,
    678, 680, 703–711, 734
    Vol. 2: 45, 49, 102 f., 176, 182, 270, 281, 284,
    286–289, 343, 399, 500–508, 566, 657, 724,
    786 f., 909, 918
    Vol. 3: 121, 282, 286, 290, 292, 297–299,
    301, 310, 317–324, 513, 516, 558, 571, 649,
    686, 734, 813, 861–864, 875, 877, 889, 914,
    994, 1005, 1011, 1034, 1112
Appearing Vol. 2: 898–901
    Vol. 3: 220
Appease Vol. 1: 450
    Vol. 2: 164, 166, 860
    Vol. 3: 149, 152, 154, 254, 996
Appetite Vol. 1: 106, 672
    Vol. 2: 460
    Vol. 3: 692
Applicable Vol. 3: 712
Application Vol. 1: 577, 601, 647, 703, 709
    Vol. 2: 150, 161
    Vol. 3: 184, 480
Appoint Vol. 1: 189 f., 275, 293, 331, 369, 427,
    471–478, 533 f., 538, 540, 626 f., 696
    Vol. 2: 152, 244, 299, 301, 374, 376, 385,
    412, 447
    Vol. 3: 569, 570 f.
Appointed day Vol. 1: 706
Appointed time Vol. 1: 722, 738
Appointment Vol. 1: 664
    Vol. 2: 122, 151, 297, 336
    Vol. 3: 259, 1040
Apportion Vol. 1: 534 f.
    Vol. 2: 296 f.
    Vol. 3: 402–404
Appreciate Vol. 2: 386

Apprehend Vol. 1: 343 f., 425, 523, 692
    Vol. 3: 122–130
Apprehension Vol. 1: 73, 277
    Vol. 2: 172, 390
    Vol. 3: 899
Apprentice Vol. 1: 484, 486
    Vol. 3: 759, 910
Approach Vol. 1: 151, 251, 258, 320, 322, 360,
    514, 627
    Vol. 2: 53 f., 151, 215, 856, 882–885
Approbation Vol. 2: 815 f.
    Vol. 3: 744
Appropriate Vol. 1: 223 f., 486, 616
    Vol. 2: 302, 342, 380, 400, 438, 446, 668 f.
    Vol. 3: 348 f., 353, 833
Appropriation Vol. 1: 603
    Vol. 2: 273
Approval Vol. 1: 681, 742
    Vol. 2: 308, 815
    Vol. 3: 559, 744–746
Approve Vol. 1: 475, 672
    Vol. 2: 123, 362, 364, 744, 817
    Vol. 3: 798–810, 816
Approved Vol. 3: 808
Approximation Vol. 2: 686
Apsu Vol. 2: 553
Aptitude Vol. 3: 349
Apuleius Vol. 2: 556
    Vol. 3: 861
Aquarius Vol. 2: 688
Aqueduct Vol. 1: 318
Aquila Vol. 1: 89, 279, 379, 539
    Vol. 2: 141, 335, 707, 847
    Vol. 3: 485, 494, 812, 1065
Aquinas, Thomas Vol. 1: 49, 65, 374
    Vol. 2: 103
    Vol. 3: 244, 1133
Aquit Vol. 3: 352–377
Arabia Vol. 1: 81
    Vol. 2: 95, 293 f., 381, 636
Arabian desert Vol. 3: 1008
Arabic Vol. 1: 68
Arable Vol. 1: 517
    Vol. 3: 1006
Arabs Vol. 1: 68
Arabs in Palestine Vol. 2: 308
Arad Vol. 3: 483
Aramaeans Vol. 1: 68
Aramaic Vol. 1: 51, 63, 68 f., 614 f., 618, 620,
    632
    Vol. 2: 125, 192, 229, 309, 311, 502, 515,
    795, 870, 911
    Vol. 3: 112, 483, 485, 613, 622, 628, 914
Aramaism Vol. 2: 525 f., 529, 780
    Vol. 3: 456
Arâq el-'Emir Vol. 3: 451
Aratus Vol. 1: 85
    Vol. 2: 77, 85
    Vol. 3: 331
Araunah Vol. 3: 787
Aravacae Vol. 2: 291
Arbitrariness Vol. 1: 367, 579, 713
Arbitrary Vol. 3: 160, 281, 824, 1017, 1019
Arbitrator Vol. 1: 373

Arch of Titus **Vol. 3:** 789
Archaeology **Vol. 3:** 327
Archangel **Vol. 1:** 101, 342, 410
  Vol. 2: 191, 608, 922, 924 f.
  Vol. 3: 113, 622
Archelaus (→Herod)
Archetypal **Vol. 2:** 284, 655
Archetype **Vol. 1:** 491 f., 522
  Vol. 2: 103, 160, 191, 460, 546
  Vol. 3: 630, 776, 1047
Archimedes **Vol. 3:** 528
Architecture **Vol. 3:** 397
Archon **Vol. 3:** 49
Ardour **Vol. 1:** 652
Arduous **Vol. 2:** 266
Arena **Vol. 3:** 203
Areopagus **Vol. 1:** 473
  Vol. 2: 77, 85, 503, 919
  Vol. 3: 65, 431, 793, 1036
Ares **Vol. 2:** 85
  Vol. 3: 318, 959
Aretas **Vol. 2:** 378, 579
Argue **Vol. 3:** 821
Argument **Vol. 1:** 545, 547, 590, 592, 663, 680
  Vol. 2: 140, 223, 312, 427, 434
  Vol. 3: 82, 119, **530–532, 820–826**
Argumentum ad hominem **Vol. 3:** 188
Argus **Vol. 3:** 512
Arian **Vol. 1:** 549
  Vol. 2: 81, 497, 506, 725
  Vol. 3: 1133
Arian controversy **Vol. 2: 505–508**
Arianism **Vol. 2:** 76
Arise **Vol. 1:** 181, 679, 681
  Vol. 2: 281, 366, 381
  Vol. 3: 224
Aristarchus **Vol. 3:** 521
Aristeas **Vol. 1:** 68, 221, 377, 575
  Vol. 2: 690, 697, 707
Aristides **Vol. 1:** 51
  Vol. 2: 648
Aristobulus **Vol. 3:** 766, 872
Aristocracy **Vol. 1:** 640
  Vol. 2: 102, 372
Aristocratic **Vol. 1:** 196, 363 f., 536
Aristogeiton **Vol. 2:** 372
Aristomachus **Vol. 2:** 291
Aristonicus **Vol. 1:** 640
Aristotle **Vol. 1:** 63, 65, 232, 521, 579, 635, 646, 705
  Vol. 2: 99, 180, 257, 439, 475, 657, 757, 772
  Vol. 3: 123, 354, 570, 678, 776, 841, 875 f., 926 f., 1027, 1034, 1083, 1086, 1169
Arius **Vol. 2:** 505
Ark of the covenant **Vol. 1:** 122, 143, 195, 252, 280, 293 f., 492, 537
  Vol. 2: 69, 186, 212, 225 f., 325, 613, 650
  Vol. 3: 33, 117, 207, 497, 673, 787, 812, 815, 1004, 1010
Ark of Noah **Vol. 1:** 713
  Vol. 3: 120, 211, 248, 310, 683, 851
Ark of testimony **Vol. 3:** 156, 1040
Arm **Vol. 1:** 239, 284, 427, 648, 673, 679
  Vol. 2: 239, 864, 877

Vol. 3: 311, 713, **959–967**
Armageddon **Vol. 1:** 114
  Vol. 3: 959–967
Armed **Vol. 1:** 651
Armenia **Vol. 2:** 95
Armies of heaven **Vol. 1:** 118, 205
Armour **Vol. 2:** 137, 431, 868
  Vol. 3: 120, 200, 471, 886, **959–967**
Armour of God **Vol. 3:** 749, 965
Armour of light **Vol. 2:** 495, 925
Armourer **Vol. 2:** 97
Arms **Vol. 3:** 119
Arms-bearer **Vol. 1:** 283
Army **Vol. 1:** 254, 293, 295, 505, 521, 536, 685
  Vol. 2: 32, 69, 146, 325, 374, 795–801, 845
  Vol. 3: 45, 179, 256, 469, 478, 811, 958
Army in battle array **Vol. 3: 959–967**
Aroma **Vol. 3: 599–601**
Aromatic **Vol. 2:** 211, 293
Arouse **Vol. 1:** 609
  Vol. 2: 418
Arraign **Vol. 3:** 242
Arrange **Vol. 1:** 241, 476 f., 503 f., 521, 692
  Vol. 3: 349
Arrange in advance **Vol. 3: 349–351**
Arrangement **Vol. 1:** 712
  Vol. 3: 1147
Array **Vol. 2:** 225
Arrears **Vol. 2:** 667
  Vol. 3: 757
Arrest **Vol. 1:** 343, 364, 395, 423, 630, 633, 663
  Vol. 2: 368, 429, 448, 451, 486, 526 f., 713, 801
  Vol. 3: 38, 592, 716 f., 848
Arrival **Vol. 1:** 320, 324
  Vol. 2: 109, 382, 432, 909
Arrive **Vol. 1:** 540, 649
Arrogance **Vol. 1:** 108, 227 f., 364 f., 385, 597
  Vol. 2: 201, 259–261, 366, 399, 422, 435, 462
  Vol. 3: 27 f., 132, 341, 565, 888, 1079
Arrow **Vol. 1:** 656, 698
  Vol. 2: 27, 334
  Vol. 3: 268, **959–967**, 1079
Art **Vol. 1:** 279, 459, 579, 588, 592
  Vol. 2: 683
  Vol. 3: 331, 347, 399, 926, 1028
Artemis **Vol. 1:** 189, 560
  Vol. 2: 74, 85, 235, 426, 484, 678
  Vol. 3: 784, 796, 1068, 1071
Articulation **Vol. 1:** 579 f.
  Vol. 2: 390
  Vol. 3: 1084
Artificer **Vol. 1:** 387
Artificial **Vol. 3:** 655, 657, 886
Artisan **Vol. 1:** 279, 382, 412
  Vol. 3: 551
Artist **Vol. 2:** 574
Arts **Vol. 1:** 490
  Vol. 2: 102, 679
Asa **Vol. 3:** 659
Asahel **Vol. 1:** 170
Asaph **Vol. 3:** 659
Asbestos **Vol. 3:** 111
Ascend **Vol. 2: 184–196**, 377

Vol. 3: 631, 941
Ascended **Vol. 1:** 384, 403
  Vol. 3: 244
Ascension **Vol. 1:** 123, 128, 183, 204, 372, 631, 668
  Vol. 2: 184, 203 f., 692, 713, 718, 787, 918, 920
  Vol. 3: 198, 298, 323, 433, 602, 704, 1003, 1060, 1186
Ascent **Vol. 2: 184,** 209, 646
  Vol. 3: 629 f.
Ascetic **Vol. 1:** 250, 284, 313, 489, 496, 613, 641, 645
  Vol. 2: 268, 272, 394, 581, 843
  Vol. 3: 108, 536, 996, 1007
Asceticism **Vol. 1:** 445, 495 f., 612, 647, 674, 715
  Vol. 2: 51, 100, 263, 265, 267, 271 f., 447, 481
  Vol. 3: 121, 758
Asclepas of Gaza **Vol. 2:** 506
Asclepieion of Cos **Vol. 2:** 166
Asclepius **Vol. 1:** 594
  Vol. 2: 151, 166, 602, 621, 666, 674
  Vol. 3: 103, 216, 519, 738, 859
Ascribe **Vol. 2:** 363
Ascription **Vol. 1:** 427
  Vol. 2: 80
Ash **Vol. 3:** 989
Ashamed **Vol. 2:** 51
  Vol. 3: 135, 352, 367, **562–564**
Ashdod **Vol. 3:** 248
Asher **Vol. 2:** 317
  Vol. 3: 872 f.
Asherah **Vol. 1:** 625
  Vol. 3: 865
Asherim **Vol. 2:** 226, 284
Ashes **Vol. 1:** 115
  Vol. 2: 32, 157, 366, 583
  Vol. 3: 557, 589
Ashmedai **Vol. 1:** 451
Ashtaroth **Vol. 3:** 787
Ashur **Vol. 1:** 140
Ashurbanipal **Vol. 2:** 679
Asia Minor **Vol. 1:** 55, 64, 199, 264, 301, 560, 634, 651
  Vol. 2: 34, 108, 135, 222, 270, 451, 685, 918, 924
  Vol. 3: 118, 185, 203, 217, 416, 598, 757, 795 f., 844, 1035
Asians, Synagogue of the **Vol. 1:** 297
Ask **Vol. 1:** 227, 504, 509, 569–571, 600, 639, 730
  Vol. 2: 359, **855–886**
  Vol. 3: 348, 531
Askar **Vol. 3:** 458
Asleep **Vol. 1:** 314
  Vol. 2: 419, 900, 917, 922
  Vol. 3: 303
Asp **Vol. 2:** 28
Aspect **Vol. 1:** 585, 601
  Vol. 2: 287
Aspersion **Vol. 1:** 151
Aspiration **Vol. 1:** 426, 456, 533

Vol. 3: 893
Aspire **Vol. 2:** 550
  Vol. 3: 531
Ass **Vol. 1:** ¹15, 117, 409, 725
  Vol. 2: 25 ƒ., 510
  Vol. 3: 557, 560, 1160
Assassin **Vol. 3:** 1167
Assassination **Vol. 1:** 340
Assault **Vol. 1:** 241, 710
  Vol. 2: 383
  Vol. 3: 94 f.
Assemble **Vol. 1:** 320, 322, 340
  Vol. 2: 32 f., 267, 328
  Vol. 3: 443–449
Assembly **Vol. 1:** 56, 69, 199, 291–298, 301–304, 466, 475, 535, 578, 626, 669, 728, 731–733
  Vol. 2: 234, 798, 800
  Vol. 3: 49, **520 f.,** 1016
Assent **Vol. 1:** 271, 331, 454, 594
  Vol. 2: 648
  Vol. 3: 369
Assert **Vol. 1:** 83, 541, 596
  Vol. 2: 283, 862
Assert claims **Vol. 3:** 531
Asserting on oath **Vol. 3: 737–743**
Assertive oaths **Vol. 3:** 738
Assessment **Vol. 1:** 680
  Vol. 2: 239, 361–363, 374, 417
Asseveration **Vol. 3:** 742
Asset **Vol. 3:** 758
Assign **Vol. 2:** 300, 438 f.
Assist **Vol. 1:** 343 f., 570, 650
Assistance **Vol. 1:** 694
  Vol. 2: 266
Assistant **Vol. 3:** 544, 1147–1152
Assmann, Hugo **Vol. 3:** 973
Associate **Vol. 1:** 259, 678, 702
  Vol. 2: 263, 349
Association **Vol. 1:** 414, 488, 493, 606, 639
  Vol. 2: 342
  Vol. 3: 433, 1165
Assume **Vol. 1:** 709 f.
  Vol. 2: 165, 430
  Vol. 3: 747–751, 821
Assumption **Vol. 1:** 402, 697
Assumption of Moses **Vol. 1:** 66, 104
  Vol. 2: 642
  Vol. 3: 345, 471
Assurance **Vol. 1:** 223, 225, 328, 351, 409, 492, 542, 604, 659 f., 663, 703, 713, 733, 735, 740
  Vol. 2: 83, 213, 239, 243, 358, 394, 531, 536, 783, 873, 924
  Vol. 3: 490, 889
Assure **Vol. 1:** 733
  Vol. 2: 374
Assured **Vol. 1:** 719
Assyras **Vol. 2:** 679
Assyria **Vol. 1:** 61, 111, 140 f., 293, 531 f.
  Vol. 2: 306, 320, 679 f.
  Vol. 3: 179, 202, 341, 590, 867, 1088
Assyrian **Vol. 2:** 166, 189, 285, 306, 320
  Vol. 3: 115, 460, 715
Assyrian Law **Vol. 3:** 95

Assyrians **Vol. 1:** 52, 55, 67 f., 531, 670, 673
  Vol. 2: 740
  Vol. 3: 951
Asleep **Vol. 3:** 252, 280
Astarte **Vol. 3:** 785, 1068 f.
Astarte–Anath **Vol. 1:** 625
Astonishment **Vol. 1: 526–530**, 729
  Vol. 2: 620–626, 736
Astound **Vol. 1:** 527–529, 729
  Vol. 2: 621–626
Astral **Vol. 1:** 631
Astrologer **Vol. 2:** 558
  Vol. 3: 206
Astrological **Vol. 3:** 310
Astrological calculations **Vol. 3:** 844
Astrology **Vol. 1:** 521
  Vol. 2: 189, 198, 200, 214, 509, 555
  Vol. 3: 397, 735
Astronomical **Vol. 1:** 200
  Vol. 2: 37, 191, 690, 694, 916
Astronomy **Vol. 1:** 140
  Vol. 2: 743
  Vol. 3: 146, 399
Asunder **Vol. 3:** 539
Asylum **Vol. 1:** 687, 691
  Vol. 3: 594
At once **Vol. 3: 833–839**
Athanasius **Vol. 1:** 52, 318
  Vol. 2: 505–507, 661
  Vol. 3: 53, 401 f.
Atheism **Vol. 1:** 595
  Vol. 3: 1096
Atheist **Vol. 2:** 92
Athena **Vol. 3:** 457
Athene **Vol. 1:** 588
  Vol. 2: 85, 233, 847–849
  Vol. 3: 959, 1071
Athenians **Vol. 1:** 453, 475, 478, 497 f., 689
  Vol. 2: 85, 92, 820, 847
  Vol. 3: 525, 784, 870, 1055
Athens **Vol. 1:** 68, 189, 267, 291, 475, 478, 497, 529, 573, 611, 640, 687, 732
  Vol. 2: 74, 77, 233, 285, 372, 407, 788, 802, 818
  Vol. 3: 431, 453, 477, 755, 775, 785, 910, 913, 1015, 1071
Athlete **Vol. 1:** 470, 495 f., 645 f.
Athletics **Vol. 1:** 312 f., 406, 469
Atlas **Vol. 2:** 188
Atom **Vol. 1:** 671
Atomism **Vol. 1:** 640
Atomist **Vol. 3:** 1085
Atone **Vol. 2:** 321, 410 f., 800, 855
  Vol. 3: 104, **145–176**, 693
Atonement **Vol. 1:** 57, 152, 172, 220 f., 223 f., 301, 339, 371, 415, 418, 466 f., 698–700
  Vol. 2: 72, 294, 407, 525
  Vol. 3: 104, **145–176**, 194–197, 236, 364, 372, 419, 423, 428, 579, 724, 812, 941, 989, 999
Atoning **Vol. 2:** 49, 78, 368, 532, 535
  Vol. 3: 35, 41 f., 215, 432, 722
Atoning sacrifice **Vol. 3:** 723
Atoning value **Vol. 3:** 194 f.
Atrocity **Vol. 3:** 872

Attachment **Vol. 1:** 486, 493
  Vol. 2: 103
Attack **Vol. 1:** 117, 303, 396, 430, 509, 551, 562, 602, 660
  Vol. 2: 150, 166, 320, 398
  Vol. 3: 121, 748, 799, 859 f.
Attacker **Vol. 1:** 451
Attain **Vol. 1:** 635, 644, 723
  Vol. 3: 489, 727, **747–751**
Attainment **Vol. 1:** 734
  Vol. 2: 262
Attalus II Philadelphus **Vol. 2:** 550
Attempt **Vol. 1:** 541
  Vol. 2: 321
  Vol. 3: 798–808
Attend **Vol. 1:** 691, 693
  Vol. 2: 134, 172
  Vol. 3: 511
Attendance **Vol. 2:** 164
Attendant **Vol. 1:** 102, 407, 485
  Vol. 2: 228
  Vol. 3: 32, 49, 609
Attendant circumstances **Vol. 3:** 1182
Attention **Vol. 1:** 457, 591, 731
  Vol. 2: 132, 134, 350, 435
  Vol. 3: 558
Attentive **Vol. 1:** 458
  Vol. 2: 172
Attestation **Vol. 1:** 668
  Vol. 3: 1038–1050
Attic Greek **Vol. 1:** 62
Attis **Vol. 1:** 64, 560
  Vol. 3: 501
Attitude **Vol. 1:** 70, 217, 275, 331, 333, 349, 355, 484 f., 492, 496, 510, 553, 571, 583, 589, 591 f., 596, 598, 600, 602 f., 609, 611, 616, 621 f., 627, 629, 635, 639, 641, 680, 686 f., 691, 701, 709 f., 714 f., 725, 737
  Vol. 2: 90, 92–94, 99, 147, 170, 177, 179, 239–241, 243, 256, 258–261, 265, 275, 286, 310, 312, 316, 327, 341 f., 353 f., 383, 393 f., 422, 426, 430–432, 435, 437 f., 451, 471, 568, 598, 624, 815 f., 825, 857 f., 864, 878
  Vol. 3: 27, 127, 142, 183 f., 251, 314, 346, 351, 407, 424, 427, 493, 691, 727, 945, 1055
Attorney **Vol. 3:** 325
Attract attention **Vol. 3:** 1051
Attraction **Vol. 2:** 115, 308, 350, 538
  Vol. 3: 225, 320
Attractive **Vol. 1:** 206, 498
  Vol. 2: 116
Attribute **Vol. 1:** 529, 548 f., 616, 740
  Vol. 2: 70, 76, 332, 372, 424
  Vol. 3: 100, 220, 344, 357, 717
Atom **Vol. 3:** 1125
Auction **Vol. 3:** 755
Auctioneer **Vol. 3:** 50
Audacious **Vol. 1:** 364
Augment **Vol. 2:** 130
Augur **Vol. 2:** 554
August **Vol. 2:** 128, 232
Augustine **Vol. 1:** 59, 116, 299, 315
  Vol. 2: 103, 685, 701, 755
  Vol. 3: 402

Augustus **Vol. 1:** 59, 269, 330, 519
   Vol. 2: 93, 108, 233, 373, 511, 850
   Vol. 3: 217, 219, 457, 755 f., 959
Austin, J. L. **Vol. 3:** 895–897, 1125, 1139
Authentication **Vol. 1:** 596, 603, 736
   Vol. 2: 351, 398, 626
   Vol. 3: 489, 499, 648
Authenticity **Vol. 1: 51**, 68, 247, 266, 419, 513, 598, 620
   Vol. 3: 628
Author **Vol. 1:** 168, 380, 427, 736
   Vol. 2: 110–112, 114
Authoritarian **Vol. 1:** 191
   Vol. 3: 1064
Authoritative **Vol. 1:** 71, 123, 131 f., 216, 220, 334, 410, 450, 533, 572, 576, 594
   Vol. 2: 157, 219, 398, 401, 436, 630, 632, 718, 915
   Vol. 3: 48, 59, 440, 481, 492, 696, 1152
Authorities **Vol. 1:** 102, 163, 166, 168 f., 288, 330, 340 f., 363, 392, 590, 593, 649, 717
   Vol. 2: 50, 101, 158, 230, 238, 255, 282, 365, 451, 607 f., 885
   Vol. 3: 49, 51, 97, 243
Authority **Vol. 1:** 50, 74, 76, 79, 85, 87, 89, 95, 99, 103, 119, 122 f., 127–134, 146, 164–166, 171, 190, 192, 194, 196, 200, 219, 222, 228, 247, 261, 269–271, 281, 301, 303, 335, 337, 341, 349, 363, 365, 385, 392, 402, 407 f., 427, 451, 454, 458, 476, 482, 485–487, 489, 491, 510 f., 528, 534, 548, 564, 572, 574, 578, 588, 590, 596, 614–617, 638, 664, 667, 700, 703 f., 718, 720, 729
   Vol. 2: 31, 72 f., 79, 118, 121, 146, 151, 160–162, 174, 177, 179 f., 194, 196, 203 f., 213, 218, 236, 238, 267, 282, 287, 327, 335 f., 362, 365, 375 f., 426, 446, 468, 508, 510–515, 517, 595, **600–616**, 624, 632, 640, 652, 654, 671, 674, 686, 721, 727–730, 787, 795, 797, 880, 917, 921, 930
   Vol. 3: 37, 46, 55, 57, 75, 82, 88, 93, 97, 112 f., 115, 120, 128, 139, 188, 311, 313, 322, 329, 340, 342, 344, 384 f., 387, 401, 474, 476, 479, 481, 484, 488, 495, 497–499, 510, 514, 547, 554, 563, 588 f., 617 f., 622 f., 627, 631, 645, 647 f., 700, 711, 741, 754 f., 763, 769, 792, 807, 817, 822, 848, 869, 871, 930, 953, 964, 967, 1022, 1055, 1063, 1066 f., 1103, 1107–1109, 1113, 1122, 1163
Authorization **Vol. 1:** 127, 131–134, 146, 303
   Vol. 2: 152, 351, 607
Authorized **Vol. 2:** 176, 362, 365, 654
   Vol. 3: 49, 162, 1044
Authorized Version **Vol. 1:** 70
Autobiographical **Vol. 2:** 282
Automatic **Vol. 1:** 541, 678, 694, 740
   Vol. 2: 128
Autonomous **Vol. 1:** 424, 439, 494, 565, 595, 605
   Vol. 2: 295, 432, 446
   Vol. 3: 927 f.
Autonomy **Vol. 1:** 693
   Vol. 2: 120, 306, 790
   Vol. 3: 1045

Autumn **Vol. 1:** 626
   Vol. 3: 269
Avail **Vol. 1:** 602
   Vol. 3: 713
Avarice **Vol. 1: 137–139**, 169, 644
   Vol. 2: 550, 845 f., 852
Avenge **Vol. 1:** 222
   Vol. 2: 157, 167
   Vol. 3: 92–97, 134
Avenger **Vol. 3: 92–97**, 159
Avenger of blood **Vol. 3:** 94, 178, 190, 194
Avert **Vol. 3:** 159
Avestas **Vol. 3:** 617
Avoid **Vol. 1:** 272, 423, 432, 485, 514, 558 f., 625, 684, 687, 699
   Vol. 2: 260, 268, 290, 358, 447
   Vol. 3: 136, 902 f.
Avow **Vol. 1:** 346
Await **Vol. 1:** 504, 544, 738
   Vol. 2: 82, 338, 385, 387, 764, 772
   Vol. 3: 220
Awake **Vol. 1:** 323, 342, 421, 445, 458
   Vol. 2: 137
   Vol. 3: 512
Awaken **Vol. 2:** 240
   Vol. 3: 259–281, 861
Awakening **Vol. 3: 279–281**
Award **Vol. 1:** 648
Aware **Vol. 1:** 483, 513, 549, 569
   Vol. 2: 327
   Vol. 3: 513
Awareness **Vol. 2:** 80, 432
   Vol. 3: 694
Awe **Vol. 1: 621–624**, 653
   Vol. 2: 90, 181, 224, 359
   Vol. 3: 100, 561
Awe-inspiring **Vol. 2:** 622
Awkward **Vol. 3:** 1024 f.
Axe-head **Vol. 2:** 97, 628
Axios-acclamation **Vol. 3:** 673
Ayer, A. J. **Vol. 3:** 897, 1135 f.
Azazel **Vol. 1:** 451, 698
   Vol. 3: 150, 469, 1005

Baal **Vol. 1:** 209, 497 f., 527, 543, 625
   Vol. 2: 85, 190, 224, 234, 265, 297, 432, 582, 699, 724, 797, 848, 863
   Vol. 3: 77, 248, 266 f., 325, 426, 436, 617, 1009, 1013, 1057, 1091, 1095
Baal-berith **Vol. 1:** 367
Baal-Melqart **Vol. 2:** 851
Baal-peor **Vol. 2:** 60, 291
Baal-Tars **Vol. 2:** 848
Baal-worship **Vol. 3:** 267
Baalam **Vol. 3:** 311, 468, 1054, 1120
Baalization **Vol. 1:** 499
Bab-ilani **Vol. 1:** 140
Baba Rabba **Vol. 3:** 452
Babbler **Vol. 3:** 525
Babbling **Vol. 3:** 77
   Vol. 2: 269 f., 354
   Vol. 3: 313

Babel **Vol. 1:** 72, 140, 451, 529
  Vol. 2: 117, 649
  Vol. 3: 578, 782, 787
Babila **Vol. 1:** 140
Baby **Vol. 1:** 239, 281–283
  Vol. 2: 269 f., 354
  Vol. 3: 313
Babylon **Vol. 1:** 67, 106, 111, 120, **140–142**, 340, 409 f., 469, 497, 501, 531
  Vol. 2: 38, 96, 136, 185, 189, 212, 307, 321, 367, 381, 422 f., 432, 486 f., 495, 541, 582, 625, 644, 649, 653, 691, 696, 795, 844, 916
  Vol. 3: 179, 193, 216, 218, 241, 394, 396, 468, 476, 526, 557, 590, 594, 622, 713, 731, 848, 856, 866, 913, 916, 922, 959, 1005, 1008, 1013, 1028, 1054, 1068, 1070, 1074, 1101 f., 1104, 1161
Babylonia **Vol. 1:** 76
  Vol. 2: 375, 466
  Vol. 3: 1088
Babylonian **Vol. 1:** 124, 126, 141, 219, 308, 379, 497, 508, 531, 616, 625, 717
  Vol. 2: 96 f., 166, 174, 201, 239, 266, 285, 287, 305 f., 330, 555, 688, 690
  Vol. 3: 51, 94 f., 115, 135, 192, 209, 274, 405, 564, 617, 715, 782, 851, 937, 986, 997
Babylonian creation myth **Vol. 1:** 523
  Vol. 2: 200 f., 553
Babylonian law **Vol. 3:** 95, 259
Babylonian Talmud (→Talmud, Babylonian)
Babylonians **Vol. 1:** 52, 55
  Vol. 2: 679, 681
  Vol. 3: 788
Bacchantes **Vol. 1:** 528
Bacchic ceremonies **Vol. 3:** 679
Bacchides **Vol. 3:** 479
Bacchus **Vol. 1:** 64, 528
  Vol. 3: 919
Back **Vol. 1:** 233
Backsliding **Vol. 1:** 481
  Vol. 3: 692, 1095
Bad **Vol. 1:** 56, 106, 236, 349 f., 357, 419, 422, 456, 459, 469, 504, 557, **561–567**, 610, 657, 680, 721 f., 739
  Vol. 2: 363, 395, 419, 476
  Vol. 3: 124, 127, 1148
Badness **Vol. 3:** 936
Badge **Vol. 1:** 407
  Vol. 3: 120
Bag **Vol. 1: 142 f.**
  Vol. 2: 726, 825
  Vol. 3: 120
Baggage train **Vol. 2:** 845
Bailiff **Vol. 3:** 1157
Bait **Vol. 2:** 707 f.
Bake **Vol. 3:** 422
Baker **Vol. 1:** 560
  Vol. 3: 446
Balaam **Vol. 1:** 208, 407, 416, 527, 578
  Vol. 2: 431, 558, 638, 677 f., 745
Balak **Vol. 1:** 208, 416
  Vol. 2: 558, 638
  Vol. 3: 311
Balance **Vol. 1:** 118, 203
    Vol. 2: 130, 256

    Vol. 3: 1160–1165
Balance arm **Vol. 3:** 399
Baldness **Vol. 2:** 465
Balsam **Vol. 1:** 120
  Vol. 3: 758
Balustrade **Vol. 3:** 795
Ban **Vol. 1:** 171, 413–417
  Vol. 2: 166, 296, 830
  Vol. 3: 139, 471
Band **Vol. 1:** 527
Bandit **Vol. 3: 377–379**
Banish **Vol. 1:** 476, 558
  Vol. 2: 359, 420, 463
Banishment **Vol. 1:** 687
  Vol. 2: 318
  Vol. 3: 590, 913
Banking **Vol. 1:** 319
Banner **Vol. 1:** 652
  Vol. 2: 350, 357
Banquet **Vol. 1:** 210, 274, 460, 689
  Vol. 2: 270, 276, 354 f., 358, **520–538**, 711 f., 825
  Vol. 3: 744, 951
Banus the Eremite **Vol. 1:** 152
Baptism **Vol. 1:** 77, 122 f., **143–154**, 179 f., 184–186, 224–226, 237, 266, 275, 285, 289–291, 300, 311, 315 f., 346, 351, 358, 360, 400 f., 438, 446, 466, 487, 570, 601–603, 653, 676 f., 701–704, 739
  Vol. 2: 40, 63, 75, 130, 144, 150, 152, 176, 185, 193 f., 217 f., 223, 228, 250, 276, 309, 314, 354, 401, 411, 504, 566, 641, 655, 669, 672, 682, 715, 718, 721, 728, 819, 880 f., 885
  Vol. 3: 31, 38, 52, 55, 61, 71, 82, 105, 107 f., 113, 120, 170, 204 f., 211, 215, 227, 277, 281, 317, 361, 373, 387, 499, 501, 510, 543, 580 f., 602, 611 f., 639, 641, 647 f., 658–660, 695, 697, 699, 701, 704, 807, 831, 861, 906, 934, 940, 984, 989–992, 1007, 1061, 1070, 1168, 1178, **1208–1210**
Baptism for the dead **Vol. 3: 1208**
Baptism by fire **Vol. 3:** 447
Baptism, Infant **Vol. 1: 148 f., 154–161,** 284
  Vol. 2: 223, 250
Baptismal **Vol. 3:** 278, 772
Baptismal confession **Vol. 3:** 646 f.
Baptismal formula **Vol. 2:** 84
  Vol. 3: 1062
Baptismal hymn **Vol. 2:** 270
Baptismal liturgy **Vol. 2:** 533, 785
Baptists (→John the Baptist) **Vol. 2:** 311
Baptize **Vol. 1:** 129, 144, 237, 359, 602, 634, 657
  Vol. 2: 127, 231, 359, 519
  Vol. 3: 320, 713
Baptizer in Spirit **Vol. 3:** 697
bar Hunnah, Rabbah **Vol. 2:** 730
Bar-Jesus **Vol. 1:** 424
  Vol. 2: 557
Bar Kokhba **Vol. 1:** 62, 407
  Vol. 2: 308, 313, 316, 337, 495, 558
  Vol. 3: 452, 510, 735
Bar Mitzwah **Vol. 1:** 284
Barabbas **Vol. 1:** 409
  Vol. 2: 136, 331

Vol. 3: 378
Baraitha **Vol. 1: 51**
Barak **Vol. 3:** 1001, 1057
Barbarian **Vol. 1:** 518
  Vol. 2: 124, 127, 657
Barbarianism **Vol. 3:** 353
Barbarity **Vol. 1:** 686
Bare **Vol. 1:** 312 f.
  Vol. 2: 854
Baris **Vol. 3:** 82
Barley **Vol. 1:** 118, 249, 648
  Vol. 2: 349, 711, 783
  Vol. 3: 422
Barn **Vol. 2:** 32, 831
Barnabas **Vol. 1:** 130, 136, 191, 274, 337, 405, 478, 552, 571, 642 f., 739
  Vol. 2: 85, 152, 321, 368, 467, 469, 503, 557, 809, 827
  Vol. 3: 87, 226, 228, 241, 683, 770, 1113
Barnabas, Epistle of **Vol. 1:** 51 f.
  Vol. 2: 316
Barr, James **Vol. 3:** 333, 1123, 1126 f., 1140 f.
Barracks **Vol. 3: 959–967**
Barren **Vol. 1:** 187, 411, 723, 725
  Vol. 2: 324
  Vol. 3: 444, 475, 1062, 1072
Barricade **Vol. 3:** 951
Barrier **Vol. 1:** 385, 488, 541, 560, 583, 638, 685
  Vol. 2: 315, 376, 611
  Vol. 3: 106, 795, 949
Barter **Vol. 2:** 822
Barth, Karl **Vol. 3:** 148, 298, 325–328, 371, 663, 1056
Bartimaeus **Vol. 1:** 328
  Vol. 3: 115, 507 f.
Baruch **Vol. 1:** 50, 124, 485
  Vol. 3: 82, 478, 484
Base **Vol. 1:** 557, 596, 660, 662, 736
  Vol. 3: 562–564, 809
Baseless **Vol. 1:** 555
Baseness **Vol. 3:** 125
Bashan **Vol. 3:** 248
Basic **Vol. 1:** 653 f., 662, 711, 717, 738
  Vol. 2: 264, 288, 313, 407
Basil of Ancyra **Vol. 2:** 507
Basil the Great **Vol. 2:** 505, 507
Basilides **Vol. 2:** 401
Basilisk **Vol. 1:** 705
Basis **Vol. 1:** 539–541, 546, 601, 605, 620, 637, 640, 659–662, 676, 681, 697, 710, 712, 730
  Vol. 2: 243, 313, 352, 360, 365, 448, 583
  Vol. 3: 887
Basket **Vol. 2:** 586
  Vol. 3: 545, 657
Bat **Vol. 3:** 678
Bath **Vol. 1:** 144, 149–153
  Vol. 3: 447, 642
Bath Qol **Vol. 3:** 113 f.
Bathe **Vol. 2:** 334
Bathsheba **Vol. 1:** 349
  Vol. 3: 605, 656, 1062, 1069
Battering-rams **Vol. 3:** 951
Battle **Vol. 1:** 103 f., 245, 264, 273, 294, 332,

432 f., 452, 476, 508, 516, 521, 563, 574, 594, 608, 624, 644–646, 654, 656, 741
  Vol. 2: 31–33, 56, 69, 154, 244, 274, 334, 357, 362, 367, 385, 435, 602, 674, 698, 796 f., 893, 907
  Vol. 3: 119, 200, 207, 874, **958–967**
Battle–cry **Vol. 3:** 51, 353
Battle-line **Vol. 2:** 451
  Vol. 3: 959–967
Battle-mace **Vol. 2:** 98
Battle-trained **Vol. 3:** 761
Battlefield **Vol. 1:** 315
Battlement **Vol. 3:** 796
Bay **Vol. 1:** 240
Bay-leaves **Vol. 3:** 75
Bazaars of Annas **Vol. 3:** 381
Be **Vol. 2:** 68
Beacon **Vol. 3:** 1009
Beam **Vol. 1:** 116, 391, 666
  Vol. 2: 290, **484–486**
Beans **Vol. 1:** 249
Bear (*animal*) **Vol. 1:** 118 f., 520
  Vol. 2: 215, 423
Bear **Vol. 1: 176–188**, 280, 285, 391, 498, 541, 560, 616, 638 f., 645, 667 f., 683, 722, 727, 742 f.
  Vol. 2: 343, 668, **765–767**
  Vol. 3: 250, 1195
Bear burden **Vol. 3:** 448
Bear children **Vol. 3:** 1055
Bear cross **Vol. 1:** 394, 396, 402 f.
  Vol. 2: 314
Bear false witness **Vol. 3: 1038–1050**
Bear fruit **Vol. 1:** 721
  Vol. 2: 101, 154, 177, 230, 773, 827
  Vol. 3: 173, 921
Bear name **Vol. 3: 324 f.**
Bear sin **Vol. 1:** 96, 234, 266, 390, 398, 525
  Vol. 2: 80, 411 f., 854
  Vol. 3: 195, 581 f., 1195
Bear testimony **Vol. 3:** 1068
Bear witness **Vol. 1:** 83, 89, 275, 323, 339, 350, 364, 535, 541, 556, 659, 704, 731
  Vol. 2: 111, 130, 152, 183, 240, 245, 308, 332, 840, 867, 927
  Vol. 3: 54–56, 163, 241, 317, 434, 651, 935, **1038–1050**, 1123
Bearable **Vol. 2: 765–767**
Beard **Vol. 2:** 418
  Vol. 3: 950
Bearer **Vol. 1:** 617
  Vol. 2: 308
  Vol. 3: 314
Bearer of authority **Vol. 2: 606–611**
Bearing **Vol. 1:** 708 f.
Bearing light **Vol. 2: 490–496**
Beast **Vol. 1:** 111, 113, 119, 125 f., 142, 244, 405, 430, 434, 444, 469, 507 f., 520, 523, 545, 667, 728
  Vol. 2: 157, 192, 205, 208, 288, 376, 381, 457, 502, 574, 625, 653, 684, 688, 693, 701, 724, 776, 795, 826, 890, 899
  Vol. 3: 99, 249, 253, 256, 490, 500, 715, 856, 867, 967, 1047

Beast of prey **Vol. 3:** 601
Beat **Vol. 1: 161–164**, 235, 647
  Vol. 2: 95, **705–707**
  Vol. 3: 96 f., 99, 725, 903
Beat the breast **Vol. 2:** 416, **417–419**
Beating **Vol. 3: 857**
Beatitudes **Vol. 1:** 215, 217, 290, 744
  Vol. 2: 267, 300, 353, 380, 386, 388, 422,
  543, 782, 824 f., 843
  Vol. 3: 696, 807, 978, 1009
Beautification **Vol. 1:** 119
Beautiful **Vol. 1:** 459
  Vol. 2: 60, **98–107**, 201, 271, 329, **484–486**,
  806, 815
  Vol. 3: 845–849
Beauty **Vol. 1:** 119 f., 227, 229, 277, 380, 382,
  411, 521 f., 650, 673, 704
  Vol. 2: 60, 100, 103, 115 f., 250, 326, 539
  Vol. 3: 128, 398, 730, 734, 1067
Beckon **Vol. 3:** 556
Become **Vol. 1: 176–188**, 285, 481, 548, 667
Become loose **Vol. 3: 177–189**
Become reconciled **Vol. 3: 166–174**
Become weak **Vol. 3: 177–189**
Become weary **Vol. 3: 177–189**
Becoming **Vol. 2:** 256
Bed **Vol. 1:** 408, 560
  Vol. 2: 232, **586 f**.
  Vol. 3: 399, 1058
Bedouin **Vol. 1:** 81
Beelzeboul **Vol. 3: 468–476**
Beelzebub, Beelzebul **Vol. 1:** 168, 637
  Vol. 2: 510, 560, 728
  Vol. 3: 83, 344, **468–473**, 507, 1109
Beer-sheba **Vol. 1:** 76
  Vol. 3: 426
Befall **Vol. 1:** 325, 608 f., 689
Before **Vol. 1:** 668, 696
  Vol. 3: 74
Beforehand **Vol. 1:** 664, 666, 693, 736
Beg **Vol. 1:** 43
  Vol. 2: 737, 821 f., **855–886**
Beget **Vol. 1: 176–188**, 285–287, 378, 445, 617,
  674
  Vol. 2: 75 f., 392, 575, 738
  Vol. 3: 521, 647, 681, 865, 1070
Beggar **Vol. 1:** 259, 686
  Vol. 2: 386, 820–822
  Vol. 3: 589
Beggar-king **Vol. 2:** 258
Beggarly **Vol. 2:** 453
Begin **Vol. 1:** 581, 591, 666, 680
  Vol. 3: 723, 818, 832
Begin to fade **Vol. 2: 587–589**
Beginner **Vol. 2:** 61, 64
Beginning **Vol. 1:** 65, 95, **164–169**, 174, 315,
  376 f., 383, 482, 521 f., 526, 536, 538, 545,
  589, 594, 619, 625, 628, 665 f., 669, 678
  Vol. 2: 52, 56, 59, 61, 64 f., 78, 81, 112 f.,
  128, 138, 156 f., 162, 217, 228, 358, 391,
  452, 608 f., 615, 669, 716, 777, 786
  Vol. 3: 215, 415, 469, 827, 1028
Beginning and end **Vol. 2:** 64, 289
Begotten **Vol. 1:** 616

Beguiling speech **Vol. 1:** 592
  Vol. 2: 459
Behave **Vol. 3: 933–935**
Behave childishly **Vol. 3:** 340
Behaviour **Vol. 1:** 229, 334, 340, 354, 412, 421,
  450, 480, 491, 496 f., 505, 526–530, 535,
  541, 553, 562 f., 567–569, 591, 593, 596 f.,
  607, 644, 701, 714, 720
  Vol. 2: 65, 101 f., 118, 143, 178, 235, 259,
  272, 285, 299, 312, 342, 361, 379, 400, 457,
  469, 493, 597, 619, 624, 707, 709
  Vol. 3: 54, 76, 79, 101, 104, 110, 136, 138,
  149, 343, 347, 349, 353, 355, 373, 527, 562,
  586, 691, 762, 771, 926 f., 929, **933–935**,
  1020 f., 1023, 1028, 1041, 1084, 1156
Behaviourist schools **Vol. 2:** 568
Behead **Vol. 1:** 393
Behemoth **Vol. 3:** 1006
Behind **Vol. 1:** 481, 492 f.
  Vol. 2: 55
  Vol. 3: 952–956
Behold **Vol. 2:** 213
  Vol. 3: 511–518
Being **Vol. 1:** 64, 87, 491, 547, 550, 571, 576,
  587, 643, 703–712, 740
  Vol. 2: 67 f., 70, 77–80, 83, 85, 289, 396, 400,
  402, 439, 566, 651, 656, 659, 719
  Vol. 3: 42, 167, 646 f., 827, 840, 885, 1139
Beit Lahm **Vol. 1:** 170
Bel and the Dragon **Vol. 1:** 50
  Vol. 2: 285
  Vol. 3: 557
Belial, Beliar **Vol. 1:** 98, 124 f., 288, 296, 423,
  452, 554, 563, 587
  Vol. 2: 71 f., 298, 304, 314, 472, 542, 779
  Vol. 3: 468–473, 801, 939
Belief **Vol. 1:** 69, 76 f., 81, 101 f., 179, 216, 253,
  286, 308, 311, 322, 324, 330, 347, 354, 372,
  395, 415, 417, 432 f., 437, 439, 446, 451,
  476, 483, 505, 524–526, 539, 545, 567, 583,
  586–606, 607, 633, 637, 660, 672, 678, 680,
  721, 730
  Vol. 2: 75, 80, 82, 124 f., 195, 287, 309,
  313 f., 431, 491, 535, 654, 718 f., 929
  Vol. 3: 104, 462, 582, 1052
Believe **Vol. 2:** 78 f., 119, 127, 135, 177, 243,
  267, 269, 301, 310, 315, 340, 366, 379,
  404 f., 429, 453, 494, 642, 709, 715, 824,
  868, 874, 929
  Vol. 3: 121, 130, 168, 185, 233, 251, 322,
  391 f., 394, 685, 821 f., 1046, 1060, **1211–
  1214**
Believer **Vol. 1:** 92, 96, 112, 123, 146–148, 159,
  167, 179, 181, 183, 185, 203, 214, 224 f.,
  227, 232, 252, 256, 275, 305, 310, 315, 325,
  327, 338, 346, 351, 375, 377, 385, 397, 400
  f., 412, 424, 440, 464, 469, 473 f., 478, 491 f.,
  497, 504 f., 507, 526, 534, 551, 559, 571,
  578, 595 f., 598, 600–603, 605, 607, 611,
  625, 637 f., 644, 651, 659 f., 666, 676, 679,
  683, 690 f., 693, 709, 718 f., 723, 730, 733,
  740
  Vol. 2: 32, 40, 47 f., 71, 74–79, 83, 94, 101 f.,
  119, 129 f., 136, 157 f., 177 f., 186, 203 f.,

211, 230 f., 242., f., 251, 253, 266, 271, 283, 295, 300–302, 304, 313, 329, 343, 350, 353 f., 359, 361, 370, 380, 387, 391, 394, 420, 424, 445, 460, 463, 542, 545 f., 587, 604 f., 609–611, 619 f., 653, 664, 671 f., 675, 709, 712, 715, 722, 734, 736, 775, 781, 787, 809, 819, 828, 834, 855, 861, 882, 895, 901, 922–927
Vol. 3: 32, 42, 47, 73, 89, 109, 173, 186, 189, 198, 200, 204, 214, 216, 220, 225, 229, 250, 257 f., 278 f., 292 f., 303, 305, 364–366, 371 f., 383, 398, 402 f., 417, 476, 499 f., 521, 523 f., 535, 549, 581, 588, 604, 648, 701 f., 705, 710, 718, 750, 795, 801 f., 813, 814, 815, 838, 864, 869, 893, 954, 963, 1020 f., 1025, 1052, 1114, 1122, 1149 f., 1152, 1155, 1165
Believing **Vol. 3:** 471
Bellicose **Vol. 1:** 657
  Vol. 2: 776
Belly **Vol. 1:** 73, **169**, 212, 671
  Vol. 2: 73, 266, 351, 599, 619
Belong **Vol. 1:** 308, 463, 525, 684, 686–688, 715, 718
  Vol. 2: 42, 122, **247–251**, 270, 312, 317, 328, 359, 374, 438, 456, 845–847
  Vol. 3: 592
Belong to Christ **Vol. 3:** 417
Belongings **Vol. 1:** 381, 414
Beloved **Vol. 1:** 256 f., 287, 568
  Vol. 2: 79, 307, 326, 517, **538–547**, 819
  Vol. 3: 204, 600, 641, 872
Below **Vol. 2:** 184, **187 f.**, 259
Belshazzar **Vol. 3:** 788, 846, 953, 1160
Belt **Vol. 3: 120 f.**, 966
ben Dosa, R. Hanina **Vol. 2:** 168
ben Hyrcanus, Eliezer **Vol. 1:** 597
  Vol. 2: 696
ben Jose, Rabbi Eliezer **Vol. 1:** 581
ben Kosebah, Simeon **Vol. 2:** 337, 339
ben Yochai, Rabbi Simeon **Vol. 2:** 791
ben Zakkai, R. Johanan **Vol. 1:** 216, 588
  Vol. 2: 313, 689
  Vol. 3: 682
Bend **Vol. 2:** 260, 370, 414, 856, 876
Benedictine School **Vol. 3:** 232
Benediction **Vol. 1:** 212, 219, 416
  Vol. 2: 521 f., 529, 864
  Vol. 3: 819
Benedictus **Vol. 3:** 84, 198, 202, 212, 219, 241, 612, 674
Benefaction **Vol. 2:** 666
Benefactor **Vol. 1:** 258, 519
  Vol. 2: 108, 372
  Vol. 3: 217, 818, **1147–1152**
Beneficence **Vol. 2:** 121
Beneficial **Vol. 2:** 103, 434
  Vol. 3: 982, 988
Benefit **Vol. 1:** 115, 384, 467, 475, 479, 536, 581, 624, 694, 709, 722
  Vol. 2: 30, 115, 141, 352, 382
  Vol. 3: 707, 750 f., 818, **1147–1152**
Benevolence **Vol. 2:** 34, 116 f.
  Vol. 3: 689

Benevolent **Vol. 1:** 328, 389
  Vol. 2: 100, 256, 550, 552
  Vol. 3: 148, 747
Bengel, J. A. **Vol. 3:** 148
Benjamin **Vol. 1:** 52, 61, 544
  Vol. 2: 146, 317–319
  Vol. 3: 194, 396, 872 f., 953, 1179
Benjaminite **Vol. 2:** 374
Bereave **Vol. 3:** 379
Bereaved **Vol. 1:** 520
  Vol. 2: 737
Bereavement **Vol. 1:** 569
  Vol. 2: 737 f.
Berechiah **Vol. 3:** 82, 430
Berkeley, Bishop George **Vol. 3:** 56, 899
Bernice **Vol. 1:** 453,
  Vol. 2: 160
Beroea **Vol. 1:** 188
  Vol. 3: 1063, 1065
Beryl **Vol. 3:** 396
Beseech **Vol. 2:** 860 f.
Besiege **Vol. 1:** 554
Best **Vol. 1:** 666
  Vol. 2: 121
Best man **Vol. 2:** 585
Best seat **Vol. 3: 587–589**
Bestow **Vol. 1:** 208 f., 211, 237, 271, 406, 542, 625, 668, 714, 722, 728, 732, 739
  Vol. 2: 122, 266, 277, 342
  Vol. 3: 1080
Bestowal **Vol. 2:** 40
Beth-Dagan **Vol. 3:** 453
Bet Se'an **Vol. 3:** 453
Beth-peor **Vol. 3:** 345
Bethany **Vol. 1:** 630
  Vol. 2: 104, 418, 528, 549, 801
  Vol. 3: 600, 1060 f.
Bethel **Vol. 1:** 52, 140, 511, 531
  Vol. 2: 67, 194, 225, 306, 317–319, 711
  Vol. 3: 33, 78, 426, 782, 786
Bethesda **Vol. 1:** 637
  Vol. 3: 709
Bethlehem **Vol. 1: 169–171**, 330, 737
  Vol. 2: 320, 416, 579
  Vol. 3: 158, 191, 567, 652 f., 664, 735, 1008, 1071
Bethsaida **Vol. 1:** 282
Bethshemesh **Vol. 3:** 426
Bethuel **Vol. 3:** 879
Bethzatha **Vol. 3:** 186
Betray **Vol. 1:** 83, 260, 268, 327, 346, 356, 421, 473, 520, 555
  Vol. 2: 367 f., 543
  Vol. 3: 316, 378, 470, 532, 1156
Betrayal **Vol. 1:** 630
  Vol. 2: 321, 339, 368, 526 f., 531, 808
  Vol. 3: 804, 912, 1157
Betrothal **Vol. 1:** 128, 506
  Vol. 2: 588
Betrothed **Vol. 2:** 563, 798
  Vol. 3: 95, 1058
Better **Vol. 1:** 371, 374, 482, 489, 666, 731
  Vol. 2: 364, 447 f., 676, 714
  Vol. 3: 73, 216

Bewail **Vol. 2:** 416
Beware **Vol. 2:** 135, 462
Bewitch **Vol. 1:** 507
    Vol. 2: 552–562
Beyond **Vol. 1:** 604, 687, 721
    Vol. 2: 125, 195, 206, 208, 240, 587
    Vol. 3: 252
Bezalel **Vol. 2:** 290
    Vol. 3: 788
Bias **Vol. 1:** 585, 587
Bible **Vol. 1:** 243
    Vol. 2: 309
    Vol. 3: 485
Biblical criticism (→Criticism, Biblical)
Biblical exegesis **Vol. 3:** 1140
iblical scholar **Vol. 3: 477–482**
Bigamy **Vol. 1:** 383
Bile **Vol. 2:** 27
Bilhah **Vol. 2:** 317
    Vol. 3: 1057
Bilingual **Vol. 2:** 308
Bill **Vol. 3:** 489, 492
Bill of divorce **Vol. 1:** 606
    Vol. 2: 307
    Vol. 3: 484
Binary **Vol. 3:** 1142
Bind **Vol. 1: 171 f.**, 259, 394, 405, 415, 452, 472, 484, 488, 491, 508, 594, 600, 638, 650 f., 669, 703
    Vol. 2: 86, 167, 194, 244, 335, 382, 732, 795, 890, 897
    Vol. 3: 97, 120, 388, 394, 472, 537, **591 f.**, 1160–1165
Binding **Vol. 1:** 98 f., 241, 331, 338, 341, 346, 397, 472, 595, 619
    Vol. 2: 43, 437–439, 701 f., 811, 813
    Vol. 3: 50, 57, 72, 105, 184, 384, 410, 429, 471, 479, 717, 740, 792, 883, 932, 1044, 1052, 1122
Binding and loosing **Vol. 1:** 171, 466
    Vol. 2: 731–733
    Vol. 3: 179, 188
Biographical **Vol. 3:** 58
Biography **Vol. 2:** 113
    Vol. 3: 720
Biological **Vol. 1:** 617
Bird **Vol. 1:** 119, **172–176**, 262, 277, 286, 557, 610, 671 f., 674
    Vol. 2: 32 f., 136, 275, 314, 386, 570, 586, 637, 661 f., 729, 746
    Vol. 3: 113, 260, 422, 555, 672, 790 f., 797, 867, 1164
Birth **Vol. 1:** 147, 151, 159 f., 172, **176–188**, 191, 207, 256, 280, 286, 295, 303, 309, 330, 343, 361, 458, 508, 521, 560, 617, 619, 643, 653, 668, 697, 708, 710, 721, 737
    Vol. 2: 35, 57, 75 f., 86, 126, 188, 270, 305, 309, 318 f., 332, 343, 358, 392, 394, 430, 483, 498, 505, 566 f., 570, 599, 627 f., 660 f., 666, 673, 694, 715, 836
    Vol. 3: 103, 215, 219 f., 284, 314, 317, 405, 444, 652, **660–664**, 697, 703 f., 735, 790, 835, 846, 848, **857 f.**, 937, 989, 1058, 1068, 1071 f., 1178

Birth of Jesus **Vol. 1:** 171, 187, 256
    Vol. 2: 36, 86 f., 819
Birth narratives **Vol. 1:** 104, 182, 187, 256, 283, 512, 737
    Vol. 2: 358, 624
    Vol. 3: 324, 657, 674, 735, 790, 931
Birth–pangs **Vol. 1:** 124, 178, 180
    Vol. 2: 808, 904
    Vol. 3: 1068
Birthday **Vol. 1:** 627
    Vol. 2: 786, 887
    Vol. 3: 742
Birthright **Vol. 2:** 316, 318, 782
    Vol. 3: 869
Bishop **Vol. 1:** 110, 136, **188–201**, 247, 300, 307, 333, 339, 493, 514 f., 646, 666, 690
    Vol. 2: 152, 255, 258, 406, 563, 777
    Vol. 3: 39, 42, 50, 88, 134, 170, 365, 548, 553, 568, 685, 750, 765, 922, 924, 1065
Bit **Vol. 1:** 118
Bit-lahmi **Vol. 1:** 170
Bite **Vol. 2:** 167, 421
    Vol. 3: 748
Bithynia **Vol. 2:** 34
Bitter **Vol. 1: 201–203**
    Vol. 2: 27–29, 270, 273, 293, 890
    Vol. 3: 444, 737
Bitter herbs **Vol. 1:** 633
    Vol. 2: 522, 529
Bitterness **Vol. 1:** 96, 106, 724, 743
    Vol. 2: 27, 271
Black **Vol. 1:** 115, **203–206**, 319, 656 f.
    Vol. 2: 470, 496
    Vol. 3: 40, 143, 347, 349, 360, 362, 396
Black, Max **Vol. 3:** 1127
Blacksmith **Vol. 2:** 98
Blade **Vol. 2:** 97 f.
Blame **Vol. 1:** 247
    Vol. 2: 137–145
Blameless **Vol. 2:** 60, 133, 137, 139 f., 143 f., 255, 282, 593, **705–707**
    Vol. 3: 101, 171, 228, 361, 435, 529, 534, **923–928**, 933
Blandishments **Vol. 3:** 1143
Blaspheme **Vol. 3: 340–347**
Blasphemer **Vol. 2:** 235
    Vol. 3: 27, 1025
Blasphemous **Vol. 3: 341–345**
Blasphemy **Vol. 1:** 79, 126, 270, 294, 317, 327, 394, 396, 466, 637, 700
    Vol. 2: 143, 175, 231, 248, 282, 307, 651, 653
    Vol. 3: 94, 187, 364, 471 f., 481, 628, 1054
Blazing **Vol. 1:** 653
Blemish **Vol. 1:** 116, 219, 371, 468, 634
    Vol. 2: 144, 354, 410 f., 415, 569
    Vol. 3: 200, 421 f., 656, **923–928**
Bless **Vol. 1: 206–218**, 416 f.
    Vol. 2: 71, 92, 122, 561, 649 f., 874
    Vol. 3: 69, 207, 816, 861, 1107
Blessed **Vol. 1:** 100, **206–218**, 288, 321, 412, 556, 649, 690, 729
    Vol. 2: 77 f., 80–82, 110, 245, 258, 266, 289, 380, 433, 449, 654, 763, 774, 840, 865 f.
    Vol. 3: 41, 98, 257, 313, 360, 580, 645, 1062

Blessedness **Vol. 3:** 839, 969
Blessing **Vol. 1:** 78, 81, 97 f., 122, 149, 184, 191, **206–218**, 237, 240, 247, 250, 276, 280, 284, 286, 288, 300, 308, 332, 367, 369, 380, 408, 413, 416, 431, 463, 498, 531, 585, 603, 617, 633, 683, 713, 731–733, 735
   Vol. 2: 116 f., 128, 147 f., 151, 176 f., 196, 237, 242, 275, 300, 317–319, 326, 328, 357, 400, 478 f., 485, 505, 521, 529, 543, 640, 650, 652, 681, 711 f., 776–779, 792, 806, 818, 825 f., 844, 874, 885, 900, 920
   Vol. 3: 33, 45, 70, 72, 84, 98, 105, 139 f., 233, 242, 246, 256, 347, 406, 422, 424 f., 449, 523, 697, 731, 733 f., 737, 740, 743, 750, 799, 819, 829, 832, 847, 853 f., 865, 868, 871, 919, 928, 938, 1009, 1012, 1078, 1087, 1125
Blessing of Moses **Vol. 2:** 639
   Vol. 3: 872
Blighted **Vol. 1:** 725
Blind **Vol. 1: 218–220**, 319, 341, 355, 420 f., 424, 429, 473, 513, 525, 572, 610
   Vol. 2: 153, 167, 170 f., 214, 216 f., 351, 358, 366, 414, 434, 458, 469 f., 560, 599, 630, 633, 707, 709, 728, 754
   Vol. 3: 128, 132, 147, 184, 319, 321, 328, 409, 474, 481, 505, 517, 519, 521, 533, 543, 731 f., 749, 792, 916, 998, 1000, 1020
Blind guide **Vol. 3:** 942
Bliss **Vol. 1:** 216, 240, 563
   Vol. 2: 60
Blood **Vol. 1:** 93 f., 96 f., 114–116, 144, 151 f., 174, 186, **220–226**, 230, 237, 254 f., 258, 261, 268, 289, 304, 317, 324, 328, 351, 369, 371, 375, 395, 398, 402, 410, 448, 470, 513 f., 516, 541, 548, 555, 633 f., 638, 643 f., 647, 651, 655, 662, 671, 673, 675–677, 679, 683, 685, 694, 699 f., 702 f., 713, 730
   Vol. 2: 122, 142 f., 150, 159, 164, 183, 200, 230, 269, 277, 302, 329, 339, 410–414, 457, 477, 494, 521–536, 542, 552, 560, 568, 571, 606, 625 f., 637, 671, 675, 682, 690, 718, 782, 787, 800, 846, 853–855, 929
   Vol. 3: 28, 41, 93, 103, 107, 150 f., 154, 157–160, 163 f., 166, 171 f., 174, 179–181, 198–201, 227, 243–245, 301, 314, 323, 337, 364, 366, 372, 403, 418, 422–425, 428, 432–436, 448, 471, 532, 673, 676, 678, 680 f., 686, 723, 733 f., 758, 788, 794, 812, 815, 861, 919, 941, 965, 984, 989, 1014, 1047, 1059, 1100, 1103
Blood of the covenant **Vol. 2:** 525, 532 f.
Blood-group **Vol. 3:** 871
Blood-guilt **Vol. 2:** 138
   Vol. 3: 100, 159
Blood-money **Vol. 1:** 222, 689
   Vol. 2: 44
Bloodshed **Vol. 1:** 380, 452, 657, 724
   Vol. 3: 579
Bloodthirstiness **Vol. 1:** 205
Blot out **Vol. 1:** 244, 370, 374, 471
   Vol. 3: 484
Blow **Vol. 1:** 161 f., 241, 263, 317
   Vol. 3: 689–708, 857, **1000–1004**

Blunt **Vol. 1:** 428
   Vol. 2: 295
Boanerges **Vol. 2:** 652
   Vol. 3: 1002
Boar **Vol. 3:** 950
Boast **Vol. 1:** 78, 112, **227–229**, 320, 399, 499, 547, 566, 601, 637, 675, 680, 684, 727
   Vol. 2: 122, 263, 352, 354, 434 f., 676, 762, 826, 844, 862, 874
   Vol. 3: 32, 142, 581, 814, 995, 1031
Boastful **Vol. 1:** 546, 712
   Vol. 2: 44, 430
   Vol. 3: 28–32
Boat **Vol. 1:** 559
   Vol. 2: 303
   Vol. 3: 1003
Boaz **Vol. 2:** 116, 577
   Vol. 3: 191, 656, 1041, 1057
Bochim **Vol. 3:** 425
Bodilessness **Vol. 1:** 314 f., 435
   Vol. 2: 926
   Vol. 3: 179, 231, 681
Bodily **Vol. 1:** 422, 704, 709, 740
   Vol. 2: 79, 181 f., 196, 288, 343, 447
Bodily training **Vol. 2:** 429
Body **Vol. 1:** 66, 87, 93, 96, 119 f., 152 f., 169, 182, 209, 225, **229–242**, 250, 266, 275, 277 f., 300, 302, 307, 310, 312–315, 351, 354, 365, 385, 390 f., 393, 399, 401 f., 423, 432, 435 f., 438, 440, 442–445, 459, 463, 466, 470, 473, 477, 480, 487, 495, 497 f., 500 f., 504, 517, 521, 525, 527, 532, 535, 539, 562, 610, 617, 623, 629, 636, 638 f., 643 f., 647 f., 652 f., 671–676, 679, 682, 687, 695, 705, 707, 709, 711, 715, 721 f., 727 f., 732 f., 739, 741
   Vol. 2: 40, 50 f., 83, 102, 127, 129, 143 f., 148, 158 f., 162, 171, 179 f., 184, 188, 195, 207 f., 230, 241–243, 245, 249, 253, 256, 263, 265 f., 270, 273, 277, 295, 303 f., 334, 349 f., 360, 369, 384, 391, 394, 402, 414 f., 434, 457, 465, 476–478, 482, 487, 499, 506, 516 f., 521–536, 565–568, 571 f., 606, 619, 642, 659, 709 f., 715, 718, 722 f., 762, 787, 789, 816, 818, 837, 883–885, 919, 924
   Vol. 3: 48, 120, 124, 172, 185 f., 189, 219 f., 225, 242–245, 256, 272 f., 275–278, 281, 283, 290, 292 f., 296, 298, 303, 322, 337, 344 f., 366, 378, 403, 417, 425, 430, 432 f., 443, 504, 522, 524, 534–536, 542, 544, 546–548, 554, 556, 563, 572, 577, 602, 677–680, 684 f., 687, 689, 692, 694, 701 f., 706, 712, 717, 720, 724, 750, 785, 791 f., 811, 814 f., 864, 914 f., 1037, 1060, 1064 f., 1067, 1119, 1152, 1158, 1205, 1209
Body of Christ **Vol. 1:** 10, 55, 92, 147 f., 153, 237 f., 301, 327, 398, 400, 467, 501, 541, 662, 723, 740 f.
   Vol. 2: 42, 83, 162 f., 169, 273, 277, 350, 534, 536, 566, 646, 715, 722, 885
   Vol. 3: 685, 1141
Body of death **Vol. 1:** 236, 436
   Vol. 3: 204, 228
Body of Moses **Vol. 1:** 104
Body of sin **Vol. 1:** 73, 236

Body of troops **Vol. 3: 958–967**
Boethus **Vol. 3:** 35
Boethusian **Vol. 3:** 441
Boiling **Vol. 1:** 317
Boils **Vol. 2:** 637
Boldness **Vol. 1:** 328 f., **364 f.**, 435, 490, 592, 710, 715, 739, 743
   Vol. 2: 118, 263, 625, **734–737**
   Vol. 3: 699
Boman, T. **Vol. 3:** 59, 1126, 1141
Bond **Vol. 1:** 202, 259, 402, 471, 507, 594, 640, 663, 698, 715, 719, 723
   Vol. 2: 62, 121
   Vol. 3: 591 f.
Bond of the tongue **Vol. 3:** 180
Bondage **Vol. 1:** 275, 282, 284, 335, 385, 412, 470, 531, 552, 623, 707, 715 f., 718, 742
   Vol. 2: 28, 74, 101, 121, 158, 182, 884
   Vol. 3: 174, 177, 192, 196, 202, 609, 793, 944, 1014, 1070, 1162 f.
Bonds **Vol. 2:** 30
   Vol. 3: 179
Bondwoman **Vol. 1:** 531
Bone **Vol. 1:** 205, 240, 337, 629, 652, 671 f., 677
   Vol. 2: 153
   Vol. 3: 269, 557
Bonino, José Miquez **Vol. 3:** 971 f.
Book **Vol. 1:** 53, **242–249,** 292
   Vol. 2: 113 f., 189, 192, 358, 781
   Vol. 3: 236, 404, 484, 490, 495, 499, 1094, 1099
Book of the covenant **Vol. 1:** 308, 360
   Vol. 2: 441, 639, **822,** 841
   Vol. 3: 418, 484, 1103
Book of the law **Vol. 1:** 243
   Vol. 2: 369, 440
   Vol. 3: 485
Book of life **Vol. 1:** 448, 471
   Vol. 2: 312, 795, 866
   Vol. 3: 99, 136, 209, 490, 528
Book of Noah **Vol. 3:** 265
Booth **Vol. 3:** 554, **811–815**
Booth of David **Vol. 3:** 650 f.
Booty **Vol. 2:** 32, 41, 296, 497, 844
   Vol. 3: 137, 236, 377, 590, **601–605,** 756, 960
Border **Vol. 2:** 60, 303
Born **Vol. 1:** 181, 295, 308, 412, 473, 526, 549, 608, 616, 667, 678, 709, 738
   Vol. 2: 228, 288, 353
   Vol. 3: 323, 362, 843
Born again **Vol. 1:** 154, 176, 185, 290, 386, 469, 706
   Vol. 2: 270, 661, 715
   Vol. 3: 215, 225
Born of God **Vol. 3:** 582
Bornhäuser, K. **Vol. 3: 292**
Bornkamm, G. **Vol. 3: 331 f.**
Borrow **Vol. 2:** 254
Bosom **Vol. 1:** 240, 575
   Vol. 3: 1185 f.
Bottle **Vol. 1:** 114, 613
Bottomless **Vol. 2:** 197, 205
Bought **Vol. 1:** 308

Boulder **Vol. 3:** 393
Bound **Vol. 1:** 715—718
   Vol. 2: 367
   Vol. 3: 280
Boundary **Vol. 1:** 472 f., 517, 539
   Vol. 2: 60, 131, 312
   Vol. 3: 444
Boundary-marks **Vol. 3:** 949
Boundary-stone **Vol. 3:** 391
Boundless **Vol. 1:** 600
Bounds **Vol. 1:** 729
Bounty **Vol. 2:** 735
Bow **Vol. 1:** 118, 587
   Vol. 2: 196, 232, 260, 354, 859, 876, 925
   Vol. 3: 379, 1079
Bowels **Vol. 1:** 169
   Vol. 2: 567, 600, 854
Bowl **Vol. 1:** 106, 449, 653
   Vol. 2: 96, 691, 855
   Vol. 3: 545, 1004
Box **Vol. 1: 142 f.**
   Vol. 2: 586, 726
Boxer **Vol. 1:** 645
Boy **Vol. 1: 280–291,** 428
   Vol. 2: 411, 428
   Vol. 3: 553, 611, 775
Brackish **Vol. 1:** 201
   Vol. 3: 988
Bradley, F. H. **Vol. 3:** 896, 901, 1136
Brag **Vol. 3:** 29
Braggart **Vol. 2:** 435
   Vol. 3: 32
Bragging **Vol. 1:** 228
   Vol. 2: 862
Brain **Vol. 1:** 230, 679
   Vol. 2: 182, 568
Branch **Vol. 1:** 515, 644, 648, 722
   Vol. 2: 32, 712 f.
   Vol. 3: 226, 416, 567, 649, 811, 813, **865–870,** 921
Branch of David **Vol. 2:** 337, 374
Brand **Vol. 1:** 114,
   Vol. 2: 291, **572–575**
   Vol. 3: 594
Branding iron **Vol. 2:** 574
Brandish **Vol. 3:** 556
Brandon, S. G. F. **Vol. 3:** 58, 976–979
Brass **Vol. 2:** 96 f.
Brass-founder **Vol. 2:** 97
Brave **Vol. 1:** 364
Bray **Vol. 1:** 409
Brazen **Vol. 2:** 188
Breach **Vol. 1:** 308, 630, 641, 687, 717
   Vol. 2: 288
Bread **Vol. 1:** 143, 170, 205, 237, **249–253,** 341, 384, 586, 597, 612 f., 629–631, 633, 642, 670, 729
   Vol. 2: 80, 143, 157, 186, 194, 218, 225, 267–269, 271, 273, 277, 279 f., 354, 417, 463, 479, 521–536, 590 f., 628, 632 f., 637, 642, 676, 868, 871 f., 928 f.
   Vol. 3: 47, 144, 239, 243–245, 383, 435, 444, 446, 519, 631, 703, 727, 748, 800, 804 f., 819, 893

Bread of affliction **Vol. 2:** 522
Bread of the face **Vol. 3:** 814
Bread of the first fruits **Vol. 3:** 424
Bread of the Presence **Vol. 1:** 586
  Vol. 3: 423 f., 436
Bread of setting in order **Vol. 3:** 814
Bread-offering **Vol. 3:** 423
Breadth **Vol. 1:** 253, 254
Break **Vol. 1:** 408, 686
  Vol. 2: 231, 296
  Vol. 3: 166, 377, 583
Break bread **Vol. 2:** 271, 354, **520–538**, 768
  Vol. 3: 908
Break down **Vol. 1:** 541, 676
  Vol. 2: 252
Break faith **Vol. 1:** 74
Break in **Vol. 1:** 729
Break the law **Vol. 2: 438–451**
Break loose **Vol. 1:** 639
Break off relations **Vol. 3:** 379
Break one's oath **Vol. 3: 737–743**
Break through **Vol. 1:** 488
  Vol. 3: 711
Break up **Vol. 2:** 33
Breakdown **Vol. 2:** 569
Breaking of bread **Vol. 2:** 32
Breast **Vol. 1:** 240, 515
  Vol. 2: 416–419
  Vol. 3: 1062
Breastplate, breastpiece **Vol. 1:** 205, 657
  Vol. 2: 226, **296**, 674, 925
  Vol. 3: 236, 396 f., 959
Breastplate of faith **Vol. 3:** 966
Breastplate of judgment **Vol. 3:** 966
Breath **Vol. 1:** 66, 84, 105, 382, 434, 550 f., 729
  Vol. 2: 77, 290, 457, 476, 478
  Vol. 3: 269, 555, 676, 678 f., **689–708**, 916, 1100
Breathe **Vol. 1:** 317
  Vol. 2: 231, 289, 787
Breathe out **Vol. 3: 689–708**
Breathing **Vol. 3:** 689
Breed **Vol. 2:** 742
Brethren **Vol. 1:** 287, 329, 424, 439, 473, 570, 666, 669, 675, 689, 707
  Vol. 2: 76, 230, 844
  Vol. 3: 98
Brevity **Vol. 1:** 743
Bribe **Vol. 2:** 41
  Vol. 3: 139, 149, 192, 290, 425, 747, 880
Bribery **Vol. 1:** 137, 219, 268, 468
  Vol. 2: 837
  Vol. 3: 35
Brick **Vol. 3:** 1099
Brick-kiln **Vol. 2:** 628
Bride **Vol. 1:** 120, 145, 153, 475, 507
  Vol. 2: 307, 329, 349, 412, 541, **575–590**, 798
  Vol. 3: 572, 594, 782, 813, 1057, 1068, 1071 f., 1141
Bride chamber **Vol. 2: 584 f.**
Bride of Christ **Vol. 1:** 10, 153, 474
Bridegroom **Vol. 1:** 325, 475, 507, 612
  Vol. 2: 358 f., 382 f., 562, **575–590**
  Vol. 3: 118, 844, 921

Bridge **Vol. 1:** 640
  Vol. 2: 185
  Vol. 3: 756
Bridle **Vol. 1:** 627, 735
Brier **Vol. 1:** 726
  Vol. 3: 950
Bright **Vol. 1:** 204
  Vol. 2: 239, **484–486, 490–496**
  Vol. 3: 103
Brightness **Vol. 2:** 61, 290, 484, **490–496**
Brilliance **Vol. 2: 484–486, 490–496**
Brimstone **Vol. 1:** 657
  Vol. 3: 992
Bring **Vol. 1:** 471, 666, 731, 741
  Vol. 2: 41, 314, 326, 337
Bring about **Vol. 1:** 552
  Vol. 2: 129
  Vol. 3: 1147–1152
Bring to account **Vol. 2:** 140
Bring back **Vol. 3:** 146
Bring to birth **Vol. 3:** 722
Bring charges **Vol. 3: 468–473**
Bring forth **Vol. 1:** 186 f., 386, 566, 721 f., 739
  Vol. 2: 575
Bring in **Vol. 1:** 471
  Vol. 2: 443
Bring into light **Vol. 3:** 312
Bring to light **Vol. 1:** 106, 469
  Vol. 2: 140, 216, 218, 365, 484, **490–496**
  Vol. 3: 323, 840, 892
Bring low **Vol. 2:** 201, 865
Bring to mind **Vol. 1:** 123
Bring to pass **Vol. 1:** 471
  Vol. 2: 240
Bring to perfection **Vol. 3:** 1148
Bring to rest **Vol. 3: 254–258**
Bring safely through **Vol. 3: 205–216**
Bring to safety **Vol. 3:** 201
Bring salvation **Vol. 3: 216–221**
Bring together **Vol. 1:** 69, 292, 735
  Vol. 2: 31, 716
  Vol. 3: 443
Bring to trial **Vol. 2:** 365
Bring up **Vol. 1:** 569
  Vol. 2: 95, 201, 738
  Vol. 3: 241, **775–780**, 1075
Bringing **Vol. 3:** 417
British in Palestine **Vol. 2:** 308
Brittle **Vol. 2:** 293
Broad **Vol. 1: 253 f.**
Broken **Vol. 1:** 629, 641
  Vol. 3: 692
Broken-hearted **Vol. 3:** 359
Bronze **Vol. 1:** 509 f.
  Vol. 2: 27, **95–98**
  Vol. 3: 392
Bronze altar **Vol. 3:** 787
Bronze laver **Vol. 3:** 787
Brood **Vol. 1:** 174
Brothel **Vol. 2:** 350
Brother **Vol. 1:** 191, 237, **254–260**, 305, 318, 339, 341, 352, 364, 418, 504, 556 f., 572, 637, 664, 666, 669, 672, 675, 691
  Vol. 2: 53, 141, 217, 250, 268 f., 311, 318 f.,

Brother (cont'd)
368, 404, 450, 472, 499, 503, 521, 538, 540,
542, 544–550, 571, 600, 606, 655, 709, 722,
739, 749, 769 f., 795, 803, 805, 823, 879
Vol. 3: 49, 173 f., 201, 346, 428, 455, 547,
563, 580, 657, 728, 922, 930, 945, 1055,
1062, 1065, 1069, 1074, 1155, 1163
Brother-in-law Vol. 1: 254, 499
Brotherhood Vol. 1: 254–257, 305, 640
Vol. 2: 185
Brotherly Vol. 1: 640 f.
Vol. 2: 116, 328
Brotherly love Vol. 2: 547–550
Brown, R. E. Vol. 3: 300 f.
Brutality Vol. 2: 256
Vol. 3: 27
Brutish Vol. 3: 1024 f.
Buddhism Vol. 3: 1155
Bugle Vol. 3: 962
Bugle-blast Vol. 3: 873 f.
Bühler, Karl Vol. 3: 1125
Build Vol. 1: 300, 302, 329, 378, 390, 395, 458,
600, 660, 662, 684
Vol. 2: 119, 177, 230, 247–256
Vol. 3: 118–120, 350, 382, 387, 532
Build up Vol. 1: 214, 329, 582, 638, 723, 730 f.,
740 f.
Vol. 2: 78, 263, 307, 402, 611, 741, 815
Vol. 3: 110, 703, 819
Builder Vol. 1: 279, 657
Vol. 2: 622
Vol. 3: 382, 388, 391, 624
Building Vol. 1: 300, 305, 377, 389 f., 426, 490,
521, 529, 609, 658, 660–662, 744
Vol. 2: 29, 129, 193, 236, 247–256, 646, 732
Vol. 3: 189, 388–391, 605 f., 752
Building material Vol. 2: 211
Bull Vol. 1: 114, 116, 224 f., 677
Vol. 2: 606
Vol. 3: 199, 420, 715
Bultmann, Rudolf Vol. 1: 54, 90, 583
Vol. 2: 906 f.
Vol. 3: 53, 57, 60, 84 f., 281 f., 328 f., 372,
618, 899, 1138–1140
Bundle Vol. 2: 33
Vol. 3: 591
Burden Vol. 1: 241, 250, 260–263, 271, 277,
335 f., 438, 441, 564, 570, 647, 674, 712,
Vol. 2: 83, 151, 160, 301, 307, 386, 453, 636,
820, 824
Vol. 3: 105, 407, 448, 692, 758, 1095, 1148,
1166–1169
Burglar Vol. 2: 382
Burglary Vol. 3: 379
Buri and Eschatology Vol. 2: 903
Burial Vol. 1: 93, 144, 150, 263 f., 626, 630, 643
Vol. 2: 32, 218, 236, 295, 417 f., 437
Vol. 3: 286, 750, 1047
Burial ground Vol. 1: 520, 689
Vol. 2: 206
Burlesque Vol. 2: 430
Burn Vol. 1: 94, 109, 205, 235, 279, 390, 466,
509, 515, 652–657
Vol. 2: 32, 74, 293, 304

Vol. 3: 159, 255, 421, 434, 536, 1058
Burn incense Vol. 2: 293 f.
Burning Vol. 3: 96
Burning bush Vol. 2: 68, 173, 215, 636
Vol. 3: 179, 199, 1014
Burning coals Vol. 2: 157
Burnt-offering Vol. 1: 172
Vol. 2: 410
Vol. 3: 239, 417, 447, 787, 873, 1162
Burst Vol. 1: 94
Bury Vol. 1: 104, 147, 204, 263–266, 315, 390,
393, 401, 435, 437, 438, 446, 455, 487, 671
Vol. 2: 187, 217, 318, 326 f., 340, 417, 424
Vol. 3: 239, 247
Bush Vol. 1: 725
Business   Vol. 1: 138, 267, 268, 292, 319, 373,
402, 594
Vol. 2: 39, 235, 254, 303
Vol. 3: 75, 324, 482, 823, 1147–1152
Busy Vol. 3: 407, 1168
Busybody Vol. 1: 266 f.
Vol. 2: 434, 557
Vol. 3: 112
Butler Vol. 1: 560
Button Vol. 3: 497
Buy Vol. 1: 267 f., 380
Vol. 2: 240, 273, 286, 847
Vol. 3: 139, 191, 200, 566
Buy back Vol. 3: 178, 201
Buzzing Vol. 3: 678
By-product Vol. 1: 681
Byblos Vol. 1: 243
Bystander Vol. 3: 583
Byzantine Vol. 1: 70
Vol. 3: 674

Caesar Vol. 1: 83, 169, 269 f., 276, 330 f., 345,
474, 652
Vol. 2: 108, 288, 377, 389, 549, 604, 615,
625, 684, 804, 849–851
Vol. 3: 217, 318, 441, 549, 635, 731, 754,
792, 953, 978 f.
Caesarea Vol. 1: 629
Vol. 2: 333, 369, 596, 732
Vol. 3: 40, 453, 1080, 1183
Caesarea Philippi Vol. 2: 341
Vol. 3: 294, 509
Caiaphas Vol. 1: 397
Vol. 3: 39 f., 381, 826, 1197
Cain Vol. 1: 72, 87, 429
Vol. 2: 138, 572, 626, 649, 690, 770
Vol. 3: 421, 425, 434, 1054
Cainites Vol. 3: 1054
Cairo Vol. 1: 530
Cakes Vol. 3: 422
Calah Vol. 1: 140
Calamity Vol. 1: 239, 423, 451, 565, 727
Vol. 2: 136, 240, 364, 470, 688, 844, 890
Vol. 3: 207, 249, 996
Calamus Vol. 1: 121
Calculate Vol. 2: 458
Vol. 3: 822, 824
Calculating Vol. 3: 142

Calculation **Vol. 2:** 244, 914
Calendar **Vol. 1:** 61, 272, 624–628, 632
  Vol. 2: 189, 228, 528
  Vol. 3: 412
Calf **Vol. 1:** 116
  Vol. 2: 356, 817
  Vol. 3: 33, 431
Caliga **Vol. 3:** 966
Caligula **Vol. 1:** 119, 125
  Vol. 2: 511, 850
Call **Vol. 1:** 76, 84, 97, 129, 136, 163, 167, 215, 244, 262, **270–276**, 285, 289, 291, 295, 298, 300 f., 303, 311, 319, 322, 329, 340, 342, 344 f., 357–359, 367, 408–410, 422, 446, 480, 482 f., 488 f., 493, 508 f., 532 f., 540, 542, 544, 569, 592, 598 f., 601, 603, 621, 634, 651, 657, 662, 689–691, 695–697, 703, 719, 729 f.
  Vol. 2: 62, 68, 83, 101, 114, 119, 154, 160, 173, 185, 188, 194, 215, 225, 230, 243, 259, 262, 267, 272, 285, 291, 302, 317, 351, 356, 358, 374, 394, 400, 403, 405, 413, 418, 422, 527, 530, 544, 566, 636, 641, **648–656**, 712, 721, 778, 794, 796 f., 804, 839, 846, 862, 877
  Vol. 3: 51, 53, 55, 76 f., **113 f.**, 171, 215, 221, 225, 231 f., 311, **324 f.**, 360, 371, 400, 424, 428, 431, 435, 528, 532, 542, 563, 628, 638, 641, 644, 647 f., 672, 725, 729, 757–759, 823, 924, 945, 985 f., 1012, 1019, 1059, 1088, 1095, 1098, 1108, 1117
Call to account **Vol. 1:** 332 f.
  Vol. 2: 275, 856
Call away **Vol. 1:** 607
Call for **Vol. 1:** 84
Call in **Vol. 1:** 84, 88, 91, 569
Call on **Vol. 1:** 410
  Vol. 2: 874
Call out **Vol. 3:** 52
Call together **Vol. 3:** 51
Called **Vol. 1:** 97, 133, 534
  Vol. 2: 229 f., 243, 297, 350, 353, 363, 380, 544, 839
Calling **Vol. 3:** 41, 121, 215
Callous **Vol. 3:** 542
Callus **Vol. 2:** 153
Calm **Vol. 3:** 254, 256
Calmness **Vol. 1:** 68, 432
  Vol. 2: 776
  Vol. 3: 558
Calumny **Vol. 3:** 340
Calvary **Vol. 2:** 232, 911
  Vol. 3: 158, 246, 558
Calvin, John **Vol. 1:** 248, 299, 374
Calvinistic tradition **Vol. 2:** 219
Cambyses **Vol. 3:** 428
Camel **Vol. 1:** 116
  Vol. 2: 317
  Vol. 3: 213, 256
Camp **Vol. 1:** 295
  Vol. 2: 298
  Vol. 3: 951, **958–967**
Camp commander **Vol. 3:** **958–967**
Camp-followers **Vol. 2:** 801
Campaign **Vol. 3:** **958–967**

Cana **Vol. 2:** 676
  Vol. 3: 317, 321, 403, 922, 1070
Canaan **Vol. 1:** 53, 77, 141, 209, 281, 625, 688
  Vol. 2: 69, 99, 258, 265, 318 f., 324, 573, 627, 802
  Vol. 3: 135, 150, 201, 421, 425, 564, 740, 811 f., 919, 960, 993
Canaanite **Vol. 1:** 101, 121, 195, 543, 640
  Vol. 2: 49, 67, 85, 98, 154, 190, 199, 265, 297 f., 300, 305, 307, 319, 324 f., 353, 434, 441, 541, 553, 576, 583, 590 f., 602, 636
  Vol. 3: 94 f., 104, 356, 405, 418, 424, 427, 454, 593, 787, 1010, 1068 f., 1093
Canaanite mythology **Vol. 3:** 617
Canaanite religion **Vol. 3:** 274
Canaanite script **Vol. 3:** 483 f.
Canal **Vol. 3:** 146
Cancel **Vol. 1:** 73 f., 402, 471, 697–699, 701
  Vol. 3: 152, 154, 277
Cancelled **Vol. 3:** 510
Candace **Vol. 1:** 560
  Vol. 2: 381, 511
Candelabra **Vol. 3:** 424, 736, 788 f.
Candid **Vol. 2:** 470
Cane **Vol. 3:** 399
Cane-grass **Vol. 3:** 559
Cannibalism **Vol. 2:** 520
Canon **Vol. 1:** 50, **51 f.**, 53, 65 f., 70, 134 f., 243 f.
  Vol. 2: 219, 406, 442, 452
  Vol. 3: 315, **399–402**, 486, 493, 774
Canopy **Vol. 1:** 653
Capability **Vol. 1:** 502, 526, 675, 723
  Vol. 2: **601–616**, 839
Capable **Vol. 2:** 103, 394
  Vol. 3: **349–351**
Capable of suffering **Vol. 3:** 719
Capacity **Vol. 1:** 239, 445, 579, 583, 681, 697, 719, 723, 742
  Vol. 2: 121, 287, 390, 842
Capernaum **Vol. 1:** 282
  Vol. 2: 231, 624, 851
  Vol. 3: 348, 753, 757, 759, 856, 964, 1052
Capital **Vol. 1:** 271, 392 f., 395, 403, 721
  Vol. 2: 139, 157, 325, 327, 335, 845
Capital offence **Vol. 3:** 593
Capital punishment **Vol. 2:** 365
  Vol. 3: 95, 537, 541
Cappadocia **Vol. 2:** 34
Capricious **Vol. 1:** 692
  Vol. 3: 1018
Capstone **Vol. 3:** **388–390**
Captain **Vol. 2:** 698
Captive **Vol. 1:** 698, 717
  Vol. 2: 186, 296, 367, 453
  Vol. 3: 51, 379, **589–599**
Captivity **Vol. 1:** **52**, 53–55, 57, 61, 67, 354, 685, 701, 717
  Vol. 2: 696
  Vol. 3: 135, 192, 657, 937
Capture **Vol. 1:** 343, 364, 724
  Vol. 2: 308, 325
  Vol. 3: 590 f.
Caravan **Vol. 3:** 757

Carcass **Vol. 1:** 230, 232, 610
  Vol. 2: 33
Cardinal virtues **Vol. 1:** 501 f.
  Vol. 2: 377
  Vol. 3: 354, 925
Care **Vol. 1:** 102, 115, 173, 188 f., 191, 199, 203, 239, 250, **276–278**, 335, 464, 498, 523, 587, 612, 616, 620, 642, 676, 689, 692–695, 726
  Vol. 2: 43, 76, 117, 123, 137, 149, 164, 211, 227, 234, 275, 303, 358–360, 386, 395, 413, 538, 737 f., 777, 821, 823, 832, 832, 843, 924
  Vol. 3: 54, 138, 330, 402, 545, 548 f., 564 f., 677 f., 683, 728, 776, 810, 823, 854, 922, 937, 980, 1043, 1059, 1075, 1162
Care of souls **Vol. 3:** 678
Career **Vol. 1:** 476
  Vol. 3: 947
Careful **Vol. 2:** 275
  Vol. 3: 875
Careless **Vol. 1:** 563
Cargo **Vol. 1:** 260
Caricature **Vol. 1:** 114
Carmel **Vol. 1:** 209, 527, 543
  Vol. 2: 628
  Vol. 3: 418, 426, 453, 962, 1009, 1013, 1091
Carnal **Vol. 1:** 236, 315
  Vol. 2: 392
Carnality **Vol. 1:** 673
Carnap, Rudolf **Vol. 3:** 897, 1136
Carnelian **Vol. 3:** 396
Carousing **Vol. 1:** 458
Carpenter **Vol. 1:** 279
Carpet **Vol. 1:** 317
Carry **Vol. 2:** 151, 236
  Vol. 3: 250
Carry away **Vol. 1:** 529
Carry off as booty **Vol. 3:** 379
Carry out **Vol. 1:** 733–735, 742
  Vol. 2: 59, 441, 601
  Vol. 3: 756
Carrying ring **Vol. 2:** 97
Cartesian view **Vol. 3:** 1135
Carthage **Vol. 1:** 52, 392
  Vol. 2: 126, 664
  Vol. 3: 385, 402
Cart-wheel **Vol. 3:** 820
Carve **Vol. 1:** 332, 390
  Vol. 3: 483
Case **Vol. 1:** 52, 484, 645
  Vol. 2: 369, 489
  Vol. 3: 92 f., **1119–1123**
Cash **Vol. 2:** 130
Cassiver, E. **Vol. 3:** 1125
Cast **Vol. 2:** 95, 97
Cast ashore **Vol. 1:** 608
Cast die **Vol. 2:** 573
Cast down **Vol. 2:** 225
  Vol. 3: 28, 473
Cast lots **Vol. 1:** 70, 478
  Vol. 2: **295–303**
Cast off **Vol. 1:** 574
Cast the ostracon **Vol. 3:** 913
Cast out **Vol. 1:** 168, 415, 446, **449–454**, 541,

572, 623, 651
  Vol. 2: 34, 75, 165, 379, 382, 559, 63!, 921
  Vol. 3: 344, 472 f., **474–476**, 696, 713, 734, 998
Castaway **Vol. 1:** 299
Castle **Vol. 3:** 948
Castrate **Vol. 1:** 559–561
Casual **Vol. 1:** 529
Casuistic **Vol. 3:** 741, 1149
Casuistry **Vol. 1:** **52**, 67, 334 f., 485, 700, 730
  Vol. 2: 281, 427, 442, 596, 671, 811, 813
  Vol. 3: 105, 482, 762, 777, 785, 1052
Cat-fish **Vol. 3:** 754
Catastrophe **Vol. 1:** 108, 224, 450, 596, 610 f., 622, 657
  Vol. 2: 54, 56, 189, 225, 238, 313, 382, 384 f., 418, 422 f., 893 f.
Catch **Vol. 1:** 469, 609, 671
  Vol. 2: 624, 922
  Vol. 3: **747–751**
Catch in the act **Vol. 2:** 363
Catch the eye **Vol. 2:** 350
Catch out **Vol. 3:** 749
Catch sight **Vol. 1:** 694
Catchword **Vol. 1:** 351
Catechesis **Vol. 3:** 30 f., 648
Catechetical **Vol. 2:** 158, 270, 338
  Vol. 3: 61, 286, 940
Catechism **Vol. 1:** 599
Catechumen **Vol. 2:** 457
  Vol. 3: 772
Catechumenate **Vol. 1:** 158
Category **Vol. 1:** 635, 681, 694
Cathari **Vol. 3:** 108
Cathartic **Vol. 3:** 989
Catholic **Vol. 3:** 62
Catholic Epistles **Vol. 1:** **52**
Cattle **Vol. 1:** 114–116, 209, 743
  Vol. 2: 572, 637, 742, 837
  Vol. 3: 256, 564
Causal relations **Vol. 3:** 1130
Causality **Vol. 1:** 69
Cause **Vol. 1:** 60, 69, 164, 166, 219, 436, 550, 556, 607, 673, 731
  Vol. 2: 41, **137–145**, 154, 166, 265, 357, 364, 370, 707, 768
  Vol. 3: 545, 573, 577, 1034, 1183
Cause to ascend **Vol. 3:** 421
Cause to quake **Vol. 3:** **556–558**
Cause of stumbling **Vol. 3:** 1052
Cause to swear **Vol. 3:** **737–743**
Cauterize **Vol. 3:** 448
Caution **Vol. 1:** 663
  Vol. 2: 90
  Vol. 3: 564
Cavalry **Vol. 1:** 510
Cave **Vol. 1:** 264, 393
  Vol. 2: 218, 318
  Vol. 3: **380 f.**, 794, 1007, 1011
Cavity **Vol. 1:** 673
Cease **Vol. 1:** 181, 606, 640, 726
  Vol. 2: 241, 764
  Vol. 3: 247 f., 251, 255, 405
Cedar **Vol. 3:** 866 f.

Celebrate **Vol. 1:** 360, 525, 624–634, 649, 700, 727
  Vol. 2: 108, 374
  Vol. 3: 232, 388, **417–436**, 668, 672
Celebration **Vol. 2:** 273, 355
Celestial **Vol. 1:** 104
Celibacy **Vol. 1:** 192, 495 f., 560
  Vol. 2: 121, 580 f., 588
  Vol. 3: 534–536, 538, 541, 934
Cellar **Vol. 2:** 214
Celsus **Vol. 3:** 291, 635
Cemetery **Vol. 1:** 451
Cenchreae **Vol. 3:** 1063, 1065
Censer **Vol. 1:** 649, 655
  Vol. 2: 293 f.
  Vol. 3: 436
Censorious **Vol. 2:** 130
Censure **Vol. 1:** 461, 572
  Vol. 2: 140 f., 144, 335
Census **Vol. 1:** 171, 519
  Vol. 2: 569
  Vol. 3: 192, 468, 480, 752
Centauros **Vol. 3:** 1000
Centre **Vol. 1:** 681
  Vol. 2: 180, 242, 325, 327 f., 615
Centurion **Vol. 1:** 283, 341, 591
  Vol. 2: 222, 624
  Vol. 3: 106, 211, 242, 348, 361, 508, 856, 958
Cephas **Vol. 3:** 297, 352, **381–388**, 795
Cereal-offering **Vol. 2:** 293, 461, 583, 711
  Vol. 3: 236, **422**, 425
Cereals **Vol. 1:** 250
  Vol. 2: 211, 693
  Vol. 3: 415, 417, 445, 447
Ceremonial **Vol. 1:** 122 f., 295, 373, 629, 641, 649
  Vol. 2: 585
  Vol. 3: 45, 106, 358
Ceremonial cleanness **Vol. 1:** 155, 448, 685
Ceremonial defilement **Vol. 2:** 463
Ceremonial impurity **Vol. 2:** 415
Ceremonial law (→Law, ceremonial)
Ceremony **Vol. 1:** 152, 155–158, 186, 224 f., 282, 288, 308, 366, 426, 452, 616, 625
  Vol. 2: 236, 375
  Vol. 3: 159
Cerinthus **Vol. 2:** 677, 701
Certain **Vol. 1:** 97–99, 326, 678, 680, 723
Certainty **Vol. 1:** 339, 591, 638, **658–664**, 697, 713 f.
  Vol. 2; 175, 178, 239, 242 f., 245, 307, 340, 391, 857 f., 887
  Vol. 3: 319, 646, 771, **874–901**
Certificate **Vol. 1:** 244
Certify **Vol. 3:** 1039
Cessation **Vol. 1:** 551
  Vol. 2: 61, 65
  Vol. 3: 255
Cessation of prophecy **Vol. 3:** 80
Chaff **Vol. 3:** 526, 804
Chain **Vol. 3:** 170, 589, 829
Chain up **Vol. 3:** 591
Chained **Vol. 1:** 452
Chair **Vol. 1:** 661

  Vol. 2: 611
Chairemon **Vol. 2:** 310
Chalcedony **Vol. 2:** 396
Chalcis **Vol. 3:** 40
Chaldean astrology **Vol. 3:** 1035
Chaldeans **Vol. 1:** 140, 267
  Vol. 2: 557
Chalice **Vol. 3:** 641
Chalk **Vol. 1:** 265
Challenge **Vol. 1:** 258
  Vol. 2: 286, 379, 432
  Vol. 3: 252
Champion **Vol. 1:** 104
Chance **Vol. 1:** 687, 694, 725
  Vol. 2: 497, 665
  Vol. 3: 776, 869
Change **Vol. 1:** 354 f., 416, 470, 475, 477, 527, 596, 599, 608 f., 624, 630, 632, 654, 700, 705, 708
  Vol. 2: 183, 214, 288, 317, 320, 328, 922
  Vol. 3: 119, 166, 271, 305, 505, 561, 596, **601–605**, 841, 848
Change into another form **Vol. 3: 861–864**
Change guard **Vol. 3:** 873
Change of heart **Vol. 3:** 155, 860
Change of masters **Vol. 3:** 597
Change mind **Vol. 1:** 356–358, 468
  Vol. 2: 183
Change position **Vol. 3: 601–605**
Changeable **Vol. 2:** 393
  Vol. 3: 224
Changed life **Vol. 1:** 223, 358, 604
Chanin Hanechba, Rabbi **Vol. 1:** 614 f.
Channel **Vol. 1:** 581, 683
  Vol. 3: 985
Chaos **Vol. 1:** 113 f., 422, 507 f., 522
  Vol. 2: 200, 367, 607, 631
  Vol. 3: 207, 807, 983
Character **Vol. 1:** 56, 187 f., 206, 236, 239, 271, 274, 479, 491, 532, 535, 542 f., 561, 565, 601, 603, 642, 644, 651, 678, 693, 704–710, 731, 733
  Vol. 2: 75, 141, 256, 288, 304, 309 f., 335, 352, 363 f., 366, 369, 377, 382, 429, 453, 657–659, 767, 774 f., 798, 857
  Vol. 3: 50, 56, 106, 153, 156, 162 f., 197, 358, 368, 606, 677, 721, **808–810**, 899, 911, 996, 1012, 1053, 1067
Character-formation **Vol. 2:** 289
Characteristic **Vol 1:** 114, 284, 304, 310, 488 f., 614, 629, 636, 686, 723, 739
  Vol. 2: 106, 115, 127, 155, 158, 226, 243, 261, 288 f., 353–355, 376, 430, 435, 458, 470, 602, 657 f., 774, 843, 864
  Vol. 3: 31, 49
Characterize **Vol. 1:** 697, 706, 714, 736, 741
  Vol. 2: 383, 427, 430 f., 449, 816
Charge **Vol. 1:** 84, 261, 335, 340, 349, 474, 477, 505, 528, 558, 604, 643, 688, 690
  Vol. 2: 111, 113, 137–139, 144, 263, 378 f., 451, 773
  Vol. 3: 68, 342, 454, 879, **1038–1050**
Charge under oath **Vol. 3:** 737
Charger **Vol. 1:** 117

Chariot **Vol. 1:** 280, 531, 537
   Vol. 2: 98, 226, 349, 485, 688 f.
   Vol. 3: 266, 557, 560, 605, 1001
Charioteer **Vol. 1:** 558
   Vol. 3: 583
Charis **Vol. 2:** 115
Charisma **Vol. 1: 52**
   Vol. 2: 633
   Vol. 3: 635
Charismatic **Vol. 1: 52**, 192, 198, 208, 570, 601, 739
   Vol. 2: 231, 374, 400, 627, 771, 785, 787, 883 f.
   Vol. 3: 83 f., 86, 199, 257, 456, 458, 460, 547, 638 f., 698, 701 f., 705, 768, 774, 1018, 1021, 1066, 1118 f.
Charitable acts **Vol. 3:** 545
Charity **Vol. 1:** 259
   Vol. 2: 34, 415, 450, **594–598**, 823, 827
   Vol. 3: 358, 754, 756, 854, 973 f.
Charlatan **Vol. 3:** 32
Charlemagne **Vol. 3:** 855
Charm **Vol. 2:** 115 f., 136, **552–562**
Charmer **Vol. 2:** 554
Charming **Vol. 3:** 818
Chase **Vol. 1:** 481
Chassidim **Vol. 1:** 67
Chaste **Vol. 1:** 496, 502
   Vol. 3: 101
Chasten **Vol. 1:** 373
   Vol. 2: 366
Chastening **Vol. 1:** 426
   Vol. 3: 779, 998, 1027
Chastise **Vol. 1: 161–164**, 568
   Vol. 3: 776–778
Chastisement **Vol. 1:** 407, 639, 734
   Vol. 2: 261, 357
   Vol. 3: 98, 636
Chastity **Vol. 2:** 132
   Vol. 3: 33, **100–102**, 1055, 1071
Chat **Vol. 3: 1081–1119**
Chattels **Vol. 1:** 498
   Vol. 2: 844 f.
   Vol. 3: 380, 593 f.
Chatter **Vol. 2:** 401
Cheap grace **Vol. 1:** 112
   Vol. 2: 106, 123
Cheat **Vol. 1:** 137–139
   Vol. 2: 257, **457–461**
   Vol. 3: 379
Cheating **Vol. 3:** 377
Chebar **Vol. 3:** 986
Check **Vol. 1:** 352, 495, 722
   Vol. 2: 270
   Vol. 3: 109
Chedorlaomer **Vol. 2:** 590, 694
Cheek **Vol. 2:** 417
   Vol. 3: 979
Cheer **Vol. 1:** 328
   Vol. 2: 809
Cheerful **Vol. 2:** 43, 827
   Vol. 3: 148, 672
Cheerfulness **Vol. 1:** 513
   Vol. 2: 354–356, 419

Chenara **Vol. 3:** 983
Chepre **Vol. 2:** 279
Cherub **Vol. 1:** 101, 279 f., 674
   Vol. 2: 476, 612 f., 689, 761
   Vol. 3: 156, 163, 256, 794, 812
Chest **Vol. 1:** 142 f.
   Vol. 2: 829–836
   Vol. 3: 789
Chiasmus **Vol. 3:** 170
Chief **Vol. 1:** 270
   Vol. 2: 160, 234
   Vol. 3: 415
Chief magistrate **Vol. 3: 958–967**
Chief men **Vol. 1:** 168
Chief priest (→Priest, Chief)
Chief seat **Vol. 1:** 666
Chief Shepherd **Vol. 1:** 305
   Vol. 3: 564–568
Chief tax-collector **Vol. 3: 755–759**
Child **Vol. 1:** 92, 177, 240, 256, **280–291**, 360, 378, 407, 423, 508, 523, 568, 595, 614, 617–619, 621, 639, 708
   Vol. 2: 76, 86 f., 127, 129, 151, 228, 242, 262, 312, 353, 358, 385, 416, 427, 429, 539, 542, 570 f., 588, 675, 708, 710
   Vol. 3: 103, 553, 590, 593, 607, 611, 634, 647 f., 775, 777, 821
Child-bearing **Vol. 1:** 187–378
Child-sacrifice **Vol. 1:** 463
   Vol. 2: 208
Childbirth **Vol. 1:** 85, 187, 288, 409 f., 654
   Vol. 2: 478
   Vol. 3: 103, **857 f.**
Childish **Vol. 1:** 615
Childless **Vol. 1:** 288, 499, 531
   Vol. 2: 435, 577, 628, 638
   Vol. 3: 340, 1055, 1074
Childlike **Vol. 1:** 616
   Vol. 2: 867
Children **Vol. 1:** 149, 155, 160, 212 f., 219, 238, 254, 256, 267, 277, 293, 308, 329, 332, 358, 395, 411, 431, 445, 498, 507, 510, 551, 556, 569, 572, 614–619, 637, 655, 660, 668, 693, 708, 744
   Vol. 2: 50, 95, 129, 151, 188, 222, 230, 250, 539, 550, 562, 581, 599, 656, 709, 737, 816, 834
   Vol. 3: 594, 746, 779, 861, 928–930, 1056, 1058
Children of Abraham **Vol. 1:** 77, 111
   Vol. 2: 794, 798
Children of the curse **Vol. 1:** 416
Children of darkness **Vol. 2:** 602
   Vol. 3: 926, 970
Children of the Devil **Vol. 1:** 567
   Vol. 3: 372
Children of falsehood **Vol. 2:** 492
Children of God **Vol. 1:** 83, 179, 274, 284, 286, 287 f., 339, 437, 462, 470, 617 f., 620, 649, 651, 717
   Vol. 2: 76, 191, 218, 244 f., 610, 798, 929
   Vol. 3: 646
Children of hell **Vol. 1:** 361
Children of the Kingdom **Vol. 2:** 417

Children of light **Vol. 1:** 333, 656
  Vol. 2: 36, 459, 495, 542, 602
  Vol. 3: 126, 926, 944, 979
Children of obedience **Vol. 2:** 179
Children of promise **Vol. 1:** 81, 299, 371
Children of righteousness **Vol. 2:** 492
Children of wisdom **Vol. 1:** 286
Children of wrath **Vol. 2:** 660
Chiliasm **Vol. 1:** 50, **52** f., 64
  Vol. 2: 64, 136, 207, 389, 701
Chiliast **Vol. 1: 52**
Chirping **Vol. 3:** 678
Chiyya bar Abba, Rabbi **Vol. 2:** 462
Choice **Vol. 1:** 123, 275, 435, 474, 476, 478, 531, **533–543**, 609
  Vol. 2: 120, 139, 260, 309, 327, 478, 581, 584, 818 f.
  Vol. 3: 260, 598, 918
Choir **Vol. 1:** 665
  Vol. 2: 353
Choke **Vol. 1:** 226, 457, 460
  Vol. 2: 843
  Vol. 3: 474
Chomsky, Noam **Vol. 3:** 1124, 1131, 1134, 1142
Choose **Vol. 1:** 273, 435, 472, 481, 503, **533–543**, 556, 563, 680, 693, 714
  Vol. 2: 86, 106, 260, 395
  Vol. 3: 313, 344, 786, 1060
Chorazin **Vol. 1:** 282
  Vol. 3: 1052
Chorus **Vol. 2:** 233
Chorus-master **Vol. 3:** 760, 766
Chosen **Vol. 1:** 97, 271, 274, 356, 379, 426, 474, 512, 534, 546, 625, 668, 685, 688
  Vol. 2: 73, 83, 117, 216, 294, 296, 298 f., 301, 335 f., 378, 380, 517, 542, 673, 790, 792, 795, 798, 819, **838–840**, 844
  Vol. 3: 367, 392, 565, 640, 648, 783, 864, 913
Chosen people **Vol. 1:** 99, 485, 618, 636
  Vol. 2: 71, 99, 191, 297, 307, 364
  Vol. 3: 137
Chosen race **Vol. 2:** 380, 839
Christ **Vol. 1: 53**, 63, 73 f., 80 f., 83, 86, 89 f., 92, 95 f., 99, 103, 110–112, 114–116, 118, 122–126, 129, 131–133, 135 f., 138, 142, 144, 146–150, 152 f., 155, 158 f., 166–169, 171, 175, 178–186, 191, 197, 204 f., 212–215, 221–225, 228 f., 231–235, 237 f., 241, 244–248, 251, 253 f., 256 f., 259, 266, 268, 275 f., 278 f., 282, 285, 287, 289 f., 297–303, 305, 311, 313, 315 f., 319–327, 329, 331, 335–342, 346 f., 351 f., 355, 361, 363, 370–372, 374 f., 378, 382, 384–386, 389 f., 394 f., 397–409, 411, 414, 417, 419, 421, 424 f., 427, 434–441, 445 f., 448 f., 452 f., 455 f., 458, 461 f., 464, 466 f., 469 f., 472–474, 476–479, 483, 486–488, 491–493, 496, 501, 508, 510, 513, 517–519, 525, 528, 535, 539–542, 547–549, 551 f., 554 f., 559, 563 f., 566–568, 570–572, 575 f., 581 f., 586–590, 592 f., 602, 604, 607, 610 f., 615, 619 f., 622 f., 631 f., 637–639, 643 f., 647–651, 656, 659–662, 664, 668 f., 675–677, 679–681, 683–686, 689, 691, 693, 696 f., 701–703,

706–709, 712, 717–720, 723, 727, 730 f., 738–741
  Vol. 2: 30–33, 35, 38–40, 42, 46–48, 51, 55, 57–59, 61–65, 73, 75–84, 87, 94, 98, 101 f., 104, 106, 109, 111–114, 119–123, 127, 129 f., 133, 135–140, 147, 149, 152, 156, 159–165, 168–171, 174, 176 f., 179 f., 183, 185–188, 193–196, 198–200, 203 f., 207–210, 213, 217 f., 228–231, 238, 241 f., 244 f., 249, 251–255, 258 f., 262 f., 267–271, 273, 275–277, 281–283, 286–291, 300–304, 313–315, 320 f., 329, **330–348**, 349 f., 353 f., 356–361, 365–369, 374, 378–380, 386–389, 398–403, 407, 411–413, 416 f., 419–422, 434, 437, 443–451, 453, 459–461, 463, 473, 495, 519, 545, 565, 570, 581, 585, 615, 619, 632, 640, 645, 653, 664–666, 671–674, 691, 706, 712, 716, 718, 720–723, 732 f., 762 f., 774, 780 f., 800, 806, 812, 815–819, 826–828, 834 f., 842, 844, 855, 859, 867 f., 873, 875, 877, 882 f., 885, 894 f., 900–903, 905–909, 918 f., 922, 924–928, 930 f.
  Vol. 3: 37, 40–42, 48, 50, 52–58, 60–62, 65–67, 71–73, 81–84, 86, 89, 98, 101 f., 107 f., 110, 113 f., 118, 120 f., 127–129, 132, 135–138, 142 f., 147 f., 161–164, 167–172, 177, 195–200, 204, 209, 211–213, 215 f., 219–221, 225–229, 232, 240–246, 251–253, 257 f., 267, 270, 276–279, 281–290, 292, 297–300, 302–305, 312–316, 319–331, 334, 336 f., 346 f., 349, 351 f., 360–365, 367 f., 370–373, 379 f., 383–388, 390, 393, 398, 400, 403, 410, 412, 417, 431–435, 445 f., 449, 462, 471, 475, 481, 490 f., 493, 495, 499 f., 503–506, 509 f., 516–518, 522–524, 529 f., 534–537, 541, 543, 546–549, 552 f., 556, 558, 563, 567–569, 571 f., 576, 580–582, 584–586, 588 f., 591 f., 596–598, 600–604, 606 f., 613 f., 621, 631 f., 636, 643, 647 f., 652 f., 656, 658–664, 670, 672, 674 f., 683, 685 f., 697, 700–706, 714, 716, 718, 722–725, 728 f., 731, 733, 736, 746, 748–752, 763–766, 768–771, 774 f., 779, 790, 793 f., 802, 807, 810, 812–815, 818 f., 824–826, 830–833, 837–839, 843 f., 848, 854, 856, 858, 861–863, 868–870, 873 f., 886, 888, 890, 892 f., 898, 901, 904–906, 908 f., 912 f., 917, 924 f., 928 f., 931 f., 934 f., 944 f., 947, 949 f., 954–956, 963–965, 968, 971, 974–977, 980, 985, 990 f., 995, 998 f., 1003, 1010, 1018–1021, 1023, 1025 f., 1030–1033, 1035, 1043–1050, 1053 f., 1060, 1063–1065, 1067, 1073, 1075, 1079, 1106, 1111–1115, 1118 f., 1122 f., 1131, 1138, 1141, 1143, 1150–1152, 1155, 1162–1165, 1167, 1176–1180, 1182, 1184–1187, 1189–1194, 1196–1203, 1205–1214
Christ, Person of **Vol. 1:** 53, 237, 375, 409, 424, 454 f., 488, 548 f., 578, 581, 610, 680, 729
  Vol. 2: 119, 314, 342 f., 354, 383–388, 402, 535, 676, 691, 732, 903, 906, 920
  Vol. 3: 48, 56–67, 83, 115 f., 162, 168–170, 185–188, 195–200, 204 f., 212 f., 219–221, 243–247, 276 f., 281–305, 313 f., 321–323,

Christ, Person of (*cont'd*)
393, 503–510, 567 f., 581 f., 607–664, 695–699, 703 f., 723–725, 790 f., 804–807, 889 f., 920 f., 941, 967–981, 1030–1033, 1046, 1106–1117, 1122
Christ, work of **Vol. 1:** 53, 91, 215, 237, 369, 372, 375, 409, 540, 581, 611, 651, 701, 730
Vol. 2: 39, 42, 54, 80, 84, 113, 119, 193, 196, 262, 343, 361, 402, 426, 443 f., 595, 609, 624 f., 630, 732 f., 789, 839, 903, 906
Vol. 3: 40, 42, 57, 120, 131, 138, 162, 168, 171, 177, 191, 204, 220, 395
Christ-event **Vol. 1:** 445
Vol. 2: 314, 316, 907, 930
Christ-hymn **Vol. 1:** 58, 707
Vol. 3: 347
Christendom **Vol. 2:** 328
Christening **Vol. 1:** 707
Christian **Vol. 1:** 81, 88, 123, 129, 132, 138, 141, 144–150, 152, 155–159, 167, 170, 175, 179, 190, 195, 198, 200–202, 204, 215, 219, 222, 228 f., 231, 236 f, 241, 246–248, 256 f., 261, 265 f., 268 f., 275, 281 f., 289, 295, 297–300, 303–305, 314, 316, 319, 325, 331, 336, 339, 346 f., 351–353, 355, 359–361, 364 f., 369–371, 379, 384–387, 397, 403, 406, 410, 415–417, 419, 425, 429, 438–441, 445 f., 453, 458–460, 462, 465 f., 469, 473, 477, 480, 490, 496, 502, 505, 507 f., 510, 513 f., 518 f., 525 f., 534 f., 547, 551 f., 556, 563, 566, 569 f., 572, 578 f., 581, 590, 593, 597, 599, 601 f., 604, 607, 610 f., 613, 619 f., 623 f., 627–632, 634, 637, 641, 644–649, 651 f., 655 f., 659 f., 662, 669, 675, 675, 679 f., 684 f., 689–691, 693 f., 696 f., 701 f., 709, 713, 719 f., 727, 739 f.
Vol. 2: 32–34, 36–38, 42 f., 47, 51 f., 54, 58 f., 64 f., 72–77, 83, 85 f., 92, 94 f., 102 f., 106, 110, 114–116, 120–123, 125 f., 129 f., 133, 137, 139 f., 144, 147, 158, 160 f., 163, 175 f., 179, 188, 193 f., 196, 198, 200, 203, 208f., 211–213, 217 f., 221, 223, 230 f., 235–237, 241–244, 248–253, 258, 264, 275, 268–272, 275, 278 f., 282 f., 285 f., 288, 294, 304, 308, 316, **330–348,** 349, 352, 354, 359, 361, 365, 368, 373, 380, 383 f., 391, 394, 399, 402 f., 405, 407, 410, 413, 415, 418–420, 422, 424, 429 f., 435, 437 f., 445, 450 f., 453, 457, 460, 473, 487, 494, 499, 517, 519, 600, 606, 609, 611, 618, 623, 625, 654, 665 f., 678, 707, 712, 775, 786, 793, 803 f., 806–809, 812, 815 f., 819, 842, 858, 861, 866, 868, 882 f., 893, 895, 897 f., 900, 904, 906, 909 f., 913–915, 917 f., 921, 924, 926 f.
Vol. 3: 27, 30 f., 42, 48, 53, 58–61, 63, 81 f., 84–89, 97, 101 f., 106–108, 112 f., 115, 118 f., 127–130, 136, 142 f., 163–166, 181, 184, 186, 189, 194, 197, 200, 204–206, 213–215, 219 f., 225, 230, 240, 243, 246, 251–253, 256 f., 265, 270, 272, 277, 283, 287, 289, 291, 300 f., 303 f., 309, 312 f., 315 f., 319, 322, 324 f., 327 f., 330, 335 f., 345–347, 349, 352, 362, 364, 368, 370 f., 373, 379 f., 389 f., 393, 400, 403, 408, 410–412, 416,

418, 431–433, 435, 440, 446–449, 453 f., 458, 465, 470 f., 482, 485 f., 489, 491–495, 501, 507, 515, 524, 526, 534–536, 546, 548, 550, 552, 559, 562 f., 568, 572, 576, 579, 581, 583 f., 586, 588 f., 591, 598, 602–604, 610, 612 f., 615, 617, 621, 623, 627, 629 f., 632, 635 f., 639, 645, 647, 652, 656 f., 662, 668, 670, 672, 674 f., 685 f., 697–699, 701, 706 f., 710, 717, 724 f., 728–730, 741, 746, 752 f., 755, 757 f., 765, 768, 770–774, 778, 780, 785, 793, 802, 804, 809 f., 815, 817–819, 830, 832 f., 837, 839, 844, 846, 853–857, 862–864, 869, 871 f., 886–888, 891 f., 894, 896, 903, 905, 913, 921, 923–925, 927–931, 934–936, 940–943, 945, 947, 949, 953, 957, 963 f., 966, 968–976, 999, 1030, 1033, 1036, 1040, 1047–1049, 1063, 1070, 1075, 1080, 1109, 1112, 1115 f., 1118 f., 1121, 1123, 1132 f., 1135, 1137, 1143, 1151, 1155, 1157, 1163–1165, 1167, 1169, 1179, 1187 f., 1190–1192, 1194 f., 1199–1201, 1206–1208, 1213
Christian Platonists **Vol. 2:** 754
Christian prophets **Vol. 3: 84–89**
Christianity **Vol. 3:** 240, 633
Christianity, break with Judaism **Vol. 1:** 634
Christmas **Vol. 1:** 631
Vol. 2: 176, 358, 624
Vol. 3: 1122
Christocentric **Vol. 1: 53**
Christocratic reign **Vol. 3:** 843
Christological **Vol. 1: 53,** 214 f., 239, 281, 337, 411, 435, 438, 440, 599, 621, 737
Vol. 2: 113, 338 f., 343, 354, 380, 386, 403, 749, 809, 827, 834 f., 925
Vol. 3: 39, 83, 167, 172, 200, 224, 568, 576, 607, 627, 640, 767 f., 830, 832, 848, 863, 920
Christology **Vol. 1: 53,** 63, 220, 347, 371, 548 f., 620, 712
Vol. 2: 81 f., 204, 231, 314, 340, 342 f., 387 f., 402, 434, 500
Vol. 3: 40, 42, 65 f., 107, 462, 464, 558, 635, 637, 639, 644, 646, 648, 650 f., 704, 762 f., 1030 f., 1107
Christophany **Vol. 3:** 288
Chromosome **Vol. 3:** 663
Chronicle **Vol. 1:** 243
Chronicler **Vol. 1: 53,** 55, 295
Chronicles **Vol. 1:** 53, 165, 170, 537 f.
Chronological **Vol. 3:** 64
Chronological speculation **Vol. 3:** 653
Chronology **Vol. 1:** 301, 630, 634
Chrysippus **Vol. 1:** 694
Vol. 2: 658
Vol. 3: 679
Chrysolite **Vol. 3:** 396
Chrysoprase **Vol. 3:** 396
Chrysostom **Vol. 2:** 506
Chthonic **Vol. 1:** 498
Church **Vol. 1:** 10, 50–52, 56, 58 f., 61–63, 65 f., 71, 87, 89–92, 95 f., 99, 106, 114, 117, 121, 123, 125 f., 129–135, 138, 146–150, 154, 157, 159 f., 166–168, 172, 175, 178, 183, 185, 187 f., 191 f., 197–200, 214 f., 223 f.,

228, 231 f., 235, 237 f., 242–244, 246–248,
251, 254, 257 f., 261, 263, 267, 271 f., 275 f.,
278 f., 285–287, 289, **291–307**, 310 f., 322–
325, 328–331, 339–341, 343 f., 346 f., 351,
359, 361, 363–365, 369 f., 372, 384, 390,
393–400, 403, 406, 411, 414 f., 424, 436,
441, 449, 453, 461 f., 466–469, 473–475,
477 f., 490, 496, 500, 506, 508, 510, 519,
525 f., 528 f., 534 f., 539–542, 545, 548, 551,
554, 556, 561, 566, 568–572, 578 f., 582,
589, 591 f., 599–605, 611, 613, 615, 619,
621, 623, 628, 630–632, 634, 638, 640–644,
646, 648, 651, 653, 660, 662, 664, 666 f.,
669, 675, 686, 689–691, 697, 702–704, 720,
723, 728, 730–733, 736, 739–741
Vol. 2: 30, 32 f., 37, 42 f., 50 f., 58, 62, 83 f.,
95, 106, 110–112, 114, 122, 127, 129, 133,
135, 137, 141 f., 147, 152, 159, 162 f., 165,
169, 171, 174, 178, 186 f., 203, 207, 210,
212 f., 218 f., 221–223, 228, 231, 235, 243,
249 f., 252, 256, 258, 263 f., 270, 272 f., 275,
277, 282, 287, 289, 301–304, 308, 315 f.,
328 f., 333, 337–340, 349, 354, 356, 359–
361, 365 f., 381, 386 f., 398 f., 402, 404–407,
410–413, 418–421, 438, 443, 446, 448,
450 f., 456 f., 460–462, 473 f., 505, 515–518,
523 f., 526 f., 529–531, 533–536, 542, 545,
547, 550, 563 f., 566, 571, 573, 581 f., 585,
590, 596–598, 604 f., 610 f., 618–620, 632 f.,
641 f., 646, 654, 676–678, 684, 691, 695,
699–702, 706 f., 709 f., 712, 718 f., 721–723,
727, 729, 731–734, 741, 748, 763, 766, 768,
774 f., 780 f., 785 f., 792, 794–796, 799 f.,
805 f., 808 f., 812, 816, 818, 825–828, 838 f.,
842, 844, 846 f., 858 f., 867, 869–871, 873,
875, 882–885, 894–898, 900–903, 905,
914 f., 917 f., 921 f., 927, 930
Vol. 3: 31, 38, 52 f., 57 f., 60, 62 f., 66, 81,
84 f., 87–89, 97, 107, 109 f., 112, 118, 120 f.,
127, 129, 131 f., 142, 147 f., 169 f., 173, 182,
188 f., 195, 205, 213 f., 219–221, 227, 241–
246, 251–253, 257, 278, 284, 286, 290, 298–
300 J15, 319–322, 326, 335, 337, 343, 346,
350, 352, 365, 369, 379, **383–388**, 390, 394 f.,
397, 401–404, 408, 432, 440, 446–449, 458,
464, 470, 482, 489 f., 494, 499 f., 503–506,
525, 529, 535 f., 540, 544–549, 553, 568–
570, 572, 581, 602, 607, 611–613, 618, 622,
628, 643, 646, 651, 653 f., 659 f., 670, 683,
685, 687, 698, 703, 710, 714, 724, 742, 750,
752–754, 763–765, 767 f., 770, 772–774,
779, 783–785, 793, 802 f., 809 f., 817–819,
825, 831, 838, 854 f., 860, 868, 871, 903,
905, 908 f., 915, 920, 924, 927 f., 930–932,
944, 950, 954, 956, 958, 963, 965, 968, 974,
987, 995, 1020 f., 1032, 1043, 1047, 1053 f.,
1061, 1063–1065, 1066–1068, 1074 f.,
1079 f., 1106, 1113, 1119, 1141, 1162, 1165,
1167, 1169
Church of England **Vol. 1:** 149
Vol. 2: 219
Church of Scotland **Vol. 1:** 148
Chuza **Vol. 3:** 1059
Cicero **Vol. 1:** 406

Vol. 2: 711
Vol. 3: 757
Cilicia **Vol. 3:** 598
Cilician haircloth **Vol. 3:** 813
Cilicians, synagogue of the **Vol. 1:** 297
Cinnamon **Vol. 1:** 121
Cipher **Vol. 2:** 683 f.
Circle **Vol. 1:** 439
Circular **Vol. 2:** 52
Circularity **Vol. 3:** 1143
Circumcision **Vol. 1:** 50, 61 f., 73, 78 f., 145,
149, 154–160, 235, 283, **307–312**, 336, 340,
360 f., 368, 371, 385, 424, 504, 552, 602,
626, 641, 675 f., 680, 691, 699
Vol. 2: 86, 94, 119, 218, 309, 437, 443, 450 f.,
569 f., 573, 625 f., 636, 641, 652, 660, 668,
671, 692, 708, 721, 741, 827f.
Vol. 3: 54, 137, 186 f., 204, 320, 352, 405,
407, 408 f., 431, 452, 493, 498–500, 549,
551, 608, 637, 714, 764, 949, 1010, 1057,
1066, 1071, 1158, 1164
Circumcision party **Vol. 3:** 387
Circumlocution **Vol. 1:** 586
Vol. 2: 381, 602 f., 846
Vol. 3: 342, 489, 510, 562, 622, 684, 741,
748, 816
Circumspection **Vol. 2:** 90 f.
Circumstances **Vol. 1:** 520, 540, 542, 591, 678
Vol. 2: 116, 129, 197, 222, 400
Circus **Vol. 1:** 645
Cisterns **Vol. 3:** 982
Cite **Vol. 1:** 736
Vol. 2: 318
Cities of refuge **Vol. 3:** 35, 94
Citium **Vol. 1:** 68
Citizen **Vol. 1:** 291, 299, 360, 392, 479, 497,
640, 685, 687, 689–691, 715, 732
Vol. 2: 49, 325, 329, 349, 363, 456, 497, 500,
788, 794, **801–804**
Vol. 3: 49, 738, 913
Citizenship **Vol. 2:** 149, 193, **801–804**
City **Vol. 1:** 230, 272, 279, 286, 291, 319, 325–
327, 394, 396, 431, 463, 554, 559, 562, 610,
615, 616, 642, 648, 654, 660 f., 663, 682,
688, 690 f., 714, 741
Vol. 2: 29, 125, 132, 134, 217, 233 f., 236,
245, 297, 324–330, 375, 412, 426, **788–805**
Vol. 3: 49, 74, 93, 146, 206, 210, 217, 225,
434 f., 497, 557, 951, 1012
City of David **Vol. 1:** 272
Vol. 2: 324 f.
Vol. 3: 652
City of God **Vol. 2:** 243, 696, 803
Vol. 3: 1008
City wall **Vol. 3:** **948–950**
City-state **Vol. 1:** 287
Vol. 2: 92, 439, 788, **801–804**
Vol. 3: 49, 593, 755
Civic **Vol. 2:** 290
Civic magistrate **Vol. 2:** **801–804**
Civil authorities **Vol. 2:** 101, 369
Civil code **Vol. 1:** 373
Civilization **Vol. 3:** 1068
Civilized **Vol. 3:** 353

Claim **Vol. 1:** 84, 258, 271, 273, 311, 399, 455, 473, 527, 537 f., 543 f., 550, 587, 590, 595 f., 605, 610, 618, 637 f., 719 f., 723
Vol. 2: 111, 118, 139, 159, 165, 202, 241, 256, 276, 282, 287, 298, 307, 309, 334, 337 f., 352, 375, 378–381, 383, 385, 394, 396, 398 f., 401, 426, 434, 443 f., 600, 606, 794
Vol. 3: 144, 202, 348, 361, 508, 629, 635 f., 641, 645, 648, 651, 696, 824, 881, 888, 908, 917, 1045, 1070, 1088, 1155
Clan **Vol. 1:** 194, 196, 294, 534, 615 f., 625, 632
Vol. 2: 35, 247, 317, 582, 789 f.
Vol. 3: 870–87
Clarify **Vol. 2:** 390
Vol. 3: 316
Clarity of mind **Vol. 1:** 514 f.
Class **Vol. 1:** 501
Vol. 2: 102, 284, 298, 303, 311, 437, 826
Vol. 3: 561, 757 f., 929, 1147
Class distinction **Vol. 3:** 589
Class-ethic **Vol. 2:** 103
Classical Greek **Vol. 1:** 62
Classification **Vol. 1:** 533
Classify **Vol. 1:** 534
Claudius Caesar **Vol. 1:** 476
Vol. 2: 827, 847
Vol. 3: 40
Claudius Lysias **Vol. 1:** 340
Vol. 2: 451
Clay **Vol. 1:** 243
Vol. 2: 98
Vol. 3: 392, **910–917**
Clean **Vol. 1:** 62, 172, 265, 349, 351 f., 379, 479, 488
Vol. 2: 144, 225, 237, 261, 275
Vol. 3: 100–108, 355, 1053
Cleanliness **Vol. 1:** 330
Cleanse **Vol. 1:** 115, 119, 122, 144, 146, 148, 150–154, 158, 223–225, 239, 281, 433, 629, 634, 644, 677, 698, 725
Vol. 2: 72, 159, 183, 285, 326, 358, 379, 410, 412, 423, 448, 464, 477, 586, 610, 890
Vol. 3: 30, **102–108**, 152 f., 163, 199 f., 212, 220, 604, 882, 989
Cleansing **Vol. 3:** 695, 1149, 1168
Cleansing of temple **Vol. 3:** 429, 791, 869, 977
Cleansing the hands **Vol. 3:** 106
Cleanthes **Vol. 1:** 232, 616
Vol. 2: 85, 430
Vol. 3: 331
Clear **Vol. 1:** 204, 313, 680
Vol. 3: 309, **316 f.**, 572
Clearchus **Vol. 2:** 757
Cleave to **Vol. 2: 348–350**, 579
Vol. 3: 1069
Cleft **Vol. 2:** 197
Vol. 3: 543
Clement of Alexandria **Vol. 1:** 49
Vol. 2: 506, 754
Clement of Rome **Vol. 1:** 51
Vol. 2: 214, 316, 457
Clement, First Epistle of **Vol. 2:** 264
Vol. 3: 388

Clement, Second Epistle of **Vol. 1:** 51
Cleopas **Vol. 1:** 576
Cleopatra **Vol. 2:** 550
Clergy **Vol. 2:** 457
Clerk **Vol. 3: 477–482**
Clever **Vol. 1:** 412, 509, 551, 692
Vol. 3: 31, 130, 136, 926, 1017
Cliff **Vol. 3:** 381
Climax **Vol. 1:** 647, 669, 725
Climb **Vol. 2:** 184 f.
Climb over **Vol. 1:** 71
Cling **Vol. 1:** 700
Vol. 2: 349
Clique **Vol. 3:** 543 f.
Clopas **Vol. 3:** 1061
Close **Vol. 1:** 620, 678
Vol. 2: 59, 349, 407, **726–734**
Vol. 3: 950 f., 1007
Closed **Vol. 2:** 31
Cloth **Vol. 2:** 205, **312–317**
Vol. 2: 212
Clothe **Vol. 1: 312–317**, 467, 470, 744
Vol. 2: 40, 714 f., 925
Vol. 3: 121, 358, 691, 732
Clothing **Vol. 1:** 114, 116, 204, 207, 234, **312–317**, 318, 395, 449, 468, 470, 479, 563, 625, 630, 636, 672, 706–709
Vol. 2: 264, 295, 465, 823, 831, 833
Vol. 3: 105, 497, 519, 543, 547, 560, 683, 727, 862 f., 1074
Cloud **Vol. 1:** 144, 151, 204, 323, 503, 649, 655
Vol. 2: 154, 190, 194, 212, 376, 380, 493, 905, 912, 916 f., 922, 925
Vol. 3: 114, 267, 509, 554 f., 613 f., 617, 633, 749, 863, **1000–1004**, 1013
Cloud of witnesses **Vol. 3:** 1047
Club **Vol. 1:** 162, 407
Clumsy **Vol. 2:** 146
Cluster **Vol. 1:** 724
Vol. 3: 919
Coals of fire **Vol. 2:** 157
Vol. 3: 97
Coat **Vol. 1:** 478
Cock **Vol. 1:** 173
Vol. 2: 666
Vol. 3: 114, 240, 803, 845
Cock-crow **Vol. 2:** 136
Code **Vol. 2:** 683 f.
Code of Hammurabi **Vol. 2:** 555, 582
Vol. 3: 94
Codex **Vol. 1: 53**, 69
Vol. 3: 478
Coercion **Vol. 3:** 1163
Coercive **Vol. 3:** 711
Coffin **Vol. 1:** 674
Cognition **Vol. 2:** 390, 395
Co-heirs **Vol. 3:** 73
Coherence **Vol. 3:** 689 f., 894
Coherence theory of truth **Vol. 3:** 896
Cohort **Vol. 2:** 32, 93, 699
Coin **Vol. 1:** 463, 592, 643
Vol. 2: 95–97, 287–289, 308–310, 358, 386, 573 f., 630, 651, 728, **847–852**, 898
Vol. 3: 217, 489, 498, **752–755**, 791, 808, 904,

920, 1058
Coin in fish's mouth **Vol. 3: 753**
Coincide **Vol. 1:** 555
Coincidence **Vol. 2:** 342
Coitus **Vol. 2:** 586
Colani and Eschatology **Vol. 2: 903 f.**
Cold **Vol. 1:** 96, **317–319**, 733
    Vol. 2: 274, 597, 727, 826, 844, 881
    Vol. 3: 260, 321
Collapse **Vol. 1:** 608–610
    Vol. 2: 337, 679
Colleague **Vol. 3:** 1147
Collect **Vol. 1:** 508, 536
    Vol. 2: 31–33
    Vol. 3: 443, 745, **1081–1119**
Collect taxes **Vol. 3:** 747
Collect tithe **Vol. 2: 693 f.**
    Vol. 3: 851–855
Collecting box **Vol. 3:** 752, 796
Collection **Vol. 1:** 128, 138, 214, 301, 332, 478,
    642, 731
    Vol. 2: 121, 400, 818, 826–828, 834, 844
    Vol. 3: 70, 119, 351, 369, 499, 546, 548, 553,
    572, **751 f.**, 810, 819, 854, 943, 955
College **Vol. 1:** 573
Collegiate **Vol. 1:** 199
Collyrium **Vol. 3:** 518
Colonnade **Vol. 2:** 236
Colony **Vol. 1:** 685
    Vol. 2: 801–804
    Vol. 3: 964
Colossae **Vol. 1:** 319
    Vol. 2: 270, 302, 453, 550
    Vol. 3: 379, 930
Colosseum **Vol. 3:** 203
Colossian heresy **Vol. 2:** 559
Colossians **Vol. 1:** 55, 160, 237, 301, 525, 740
    Vol. 2: 217, 269, 646, 774, 817
    Vol. 3: 775, 1035
Colour **Vol. 1: 203–206**, 224, 447, 656 f.
    Vol. 2: 27, 37, 310
    Vol. 3: 396 f., 919
Colpe, C. **Vol. 3: 620**
Colt **Vol. 1:** 117
    Vol. 3: 179
Column **Vol. 2:** 157
    Vol. 3: 795
Combat **Vol. 1:** 644 f., 650
Combustible **Vol. 1:** 653, 656
Combustion **Vol. 1:** 654
Come **Vol. 1:** 174, **319–327**, 438, 545, 609
    Vol. 2: 184, 281, 338, 379, 382, 384, 388,
    585, 886, **895–898**
    Vol. 3: 118, 316, 617, 941
Come of age **Vol. 2:** 65
Come between **Vol. 1:** 373
Come down **Vol. 2:** 379, 928
Come to an end **Vol. 3:** 248
Come forth **Vol. 3:** 592
Come to grief **Vol. 3:** 573
Come to know **Vol. 2: 392–406**
Come to life again **Vol. 3: 259–281**, 529
Come near **Vol. 1:** 586
    Vol. 2: 54

Come to pass **Vol. 1:** 737
    Vol. 3: 1104
Come short **Vol. 3: 952–956**
Come to terms **Vol. 3:** 192
Come together **Vol. 1:** 97
    Vol. 2: 659
Come too late **Vol. 3: 952–956**
Come into view **Vol. 2: 487 f.**
Comedy **Vol. 2: 430 f.**
Comet **Vol. 2:** 558
Comfort **Vol. 1:** 88, 95, 244, **327–329**, 431, 547,
    568–571, 639, 681
    Vol. 2: 78, 206, 215, 242, 244, 257, 259, 261,
    263, 297, 352, 357, 381, 386, 418, 429, 774,
    793
    Vol. 3: 54, 79, 84, 118, 255 f., 359, 783, 845
Comforter **Vol. 1:** 89, 91
    Vol. 2: 307
Coming **Vol. 1:** 65, 111, 124, 175, 269, 358,
    411, 438, 474 f., 489, 516, 519, 525, 544 f.,
    571, 581, 596, 610, 613, 620, 633, 639, 651,
    678, 688, 695, 699, 704, 708, 741
    Vol. 2: 87, 95, 110 f., 129, 155 f., 170, 194,
    196, 218, 229, 240–242, 262, 266 f., 271,
    273, 298, 335, 340, 351, 353, 358, 366, 377,
    380, 382 f., 385, 387, 433, 496, 503, 517 f.,
    530, 535, 675, 701, 736, 738, 771, 785, 811,
    887, 894, **898–901**, 905, 912–914, 916 f.,
    921 f., 925
    Vol. 3: 55, 141, 215, 229, 257, 312, 321, 351,
    433, 509, 604 f., 618, 628 f., 634, 672, 703,
    707, 863, 1001, 1011, 1033
Coming One **Vol. 1:** 100, 437
    Vol. 2: 379, 384
    Vol. 3: 367, 378, 462, 695, 1045
Commagene **Vol. 1:** 640
Command **Vol. 1:** 74, 121, 165, 193, 208, 226,
    230 f., 255, 260, 271 f., 274, 292–292, 303,
    308, 310, 322, **330–343**, 381, 389, 408–410,
    415, 453 f., 461, 469, 476, 491, 506, 526,
    532, 554–556, 559 f., 572, 604, 617, 622 f.,
    683, 714, 731, 741
    Vol. 2: 43, 75, 77, 109, 123, 133, 135, 137,
    154 f., 173, 180, 193, 229, 268, 272, 298,
    328, 336, 398, 403 f., 407, 427, 429, 436,
    440–442, 444 f., 447, 453, 473, 503, 516,
    540–544, 546, 548, 550, 631, 637, 642, 650,
    653, 664, 668, 720, 779, 826, 867
    Vol. 3: 45, 47 f., 51, 93, 105, 114, 127, 173,
    310, 455, 485, 595, 648, 685, 822, 832, 964,
    1001
Commander **Vol. 1:** 164, 270
    Vol. 2: 189, 363, 511, 699
    Vol. 3: 51, 478
Commander-in-chief **Vol. 2:** 374
Commandment (→Decalogue) **Vol. 1:** 61, 67,
    86, 95, 166, 196, 215 f., 245, 257–262, 293 f.,
    316, 331–333, 337–341, 355, 357, 402, 415,
    417 f., 422, 430, 433, 437, 451, 455 f., 458,
    494, 506, 526, 533, 538, 551, 554, 571, 597,
    604, 618 f., 623, 626 f., 632, 638, 676, 689,
    691, 730
    Vol. 2: 42, 62 f., 68, 93, 106, 132, 135, 141,
    144 f., 147, 149, 163, 167, 177, 215, 223,

Commandment (*cont'd*)
288, 297, 306 f., 309, 313, 325, 355, 426 f.,
441–443, 446, 449, 451, 458, 489, 492, 499,
542 f., 579 f., 640 f., 652, 660, 698 f., 716,
792, 816, 823, 848, 858, 864, 870–873, 889,
893, 930
Vol. 3: 54, 74, 181, 183 f., 186, 221, 239, 278,
352–377, 378–380, 420, 455, 484, 487, 490,
542, 545, 550, 572 f., 578, 584 f., 740, 745,
777, 790 f., 800 f., 806, 863, 892, 916, 933,
937 f., 946 f., 949, 1040, 1068–1070, 1087,
1096, 1102, 1107, 1118, 1120 f., 1151, 1153,
1161, 1168
Commemorate **Vol. 1:** 626
Commemoration **Vol. 3:** 407
Commencement **Vol. 2:** 656
Commend **Vol. 1:** 278, 731
Vol. 2: 112, 135, 368, 398, 744
Vol. 3: 403, 431
Commendation **Vol. 1:** 592
Vol. 3: 489
Commentaries of Philo **Vol. 3:** 486
Commentaries of Qumran **Vol. 3:** 487
Commentary **Vol. 2:** 315
Vol. 3: 483
Commerce **Vol. 1:** 670
Vol. 2: 711, 841
Vol. 2: 605 f., 1054
Commercial **Vol. 1:** 268, 344, 484, 721
Vol. 3: 134, 138
Commercialism **Vol. 3:** 791
Commiseration **Vol. 2:** 117
Commission **Vol. 1:** 98, 103, 122 f., 127–136,
195, 213, 246, 263, 271, 274, 294, 298,
300 f., 332, 381, 382, 455, 464, 489, 533,
538, 542, 550, 592, 596, 600, 703
Vol. 2: 83, 146, 152, 154, 169, 173, 176, 212,
217, 255, 269, 302, 307, 328, 358, 426, 435,
469, 608–610, 640, 651, 654, 695, 728
Vol. 3: 49, 53, 55, 57, 83, 128, 142, 284,
314, 427, 453, 456, 569, 629–631, 645 f.,
698, 748, 779, 892, 998, 1044, 1053, 1057,
1093–1095, 1098 f., 1103
Commit **Vol. 1:** 730, 733
Vol. 2: 151, 159, 368, 376, 442
Commit injustice **Vol. 3:** **573–576**
Commit perjury **Vol. 3:** 737
Commitment **Vol. 1:** 239, 284, 344, 368, 496,
502, 514, 680
Vol. 2: 841
Vol. 3: 336, 425, 436, 793, 1058
Commodity **Vol. 2:** 97, 254
Common **Vol. 1:** 62, 433, 448, 473, 539, 547 f.,
583, 624, 639, 642 f., 677, 728
Vol. 2: 272 f., 307, 311, 313, 316, 350, 355 f.,
394, 448, 452, 456, 501, 625, 657, 659, 722,
785, 840
Vol. 3: 702 f., 724, 756, 908, 914
Common meal **Vol. 2:** 520
Common sense **Vol. 3:** 898
Commoner **Vol. 2:** 102
Commonwealth **Vol. 2:** **801–804**
Vol. 3: 219
Commotion **Vol. 2:** **621–626,** 653, 842

Vol. 3: 536, **709 f.**
Communal **Vol. 1:** 448, 484, 533, 633, 639,
641 f., 717, 720
Vol. 2: 247, 316, 355, 438, 846, 869
Vol. 3: 234
Commune **Vol. 3:** 160
Comunicate **Vol. 3:** 760, 898
Communication **Vol. 1:** 511, 574, 578 f., 639,
678, 692
Vol. 2: 559
Vol. 3: 44, 54, 705, 874, 1078
Communion **Vol. 1:** 152, 160, 314, 460, 635,
639, 642
Vol. 2: 40, 161, 245, 273, 286, 288, 359, 518,
781, 905
Vol. 3: 262, 362, 403, 646, 705
Communism **Vol. 1:** 642
Communistic **Vol. 1:** 640
Community **Vol. 1:** 58, 77, 96 f., 128, 133, 144,
159 f., 171, 175, 189–191, 194–197, 211,
214, 219, 224 f., 237, 244, 256–259, 267,
269, 273, 279, 295 f., 298, 300, 302 f., 305,
308, 310, 317, 330, 333, 338, 355, 357, 361,
368, 414, 433, 435, 466, 474, 479, 488, 490,
497, 500, 520, 526, 534–536, 538, 542, 544,
554, 560, 577–579, 582, 598, 607, 613,
624 f., 628 f., 631 f., 634, 640–643, 656, 658,
661 f., 668, 673, 681, 684–687, 690, 693,
700, 715, 720, 732 f.
Vol. 2: 49, 53 f., 56, 73, 83, 92, 121, 123,
129 f., 132, 134, 141, 147, 152, 155, 157 f.,
161, 174, 176, 194, 203, 216, 225, 228, 231,
234, 237, 242, 247–253, 255, 257, 261, 298
f., 302, 306–315, 328 f., 339, 354, 363, 384,
427, 429, 438, 441, 459, 463, 511, 516 f.,
523, 534, 542, 546, 566, 785, 788, 799, 803,
810, 820, 840, 842, 864, 882 f., 897, 906,
915, 918
Vol. 3: 27, 34 f., 56, 66, 85 f., 88, 95–97,
105 f., 110, 142, 162, 164, 188, 196 f., 256,
268, 285–287, 289, 296, 299, 344, 346, 359,
384, 390, 392, 398, 420 f., 428, 448, 471,
486, 488, 495, 523, 532, 536, 545, 550 f.,
553, 566, 568, 571, 574, 576, 593, 595 f.,
598, 614 f., 619, 634, 637, 639, 671, 674 f.,
695, 700, 702, 707, 720, 745, 758, 775, 783
f., 790, 792, 810, 830, 842, 852, 871, 882 f.,
892, 899, 906, 925 f., 928, 934 f., 942, 961,
964, 970, 974, 1018, 1032, 1054, 1059, 1062
f., 1068, 1075, 1080, 1083, 1107, 1109, 1113,
1122 f., 1143, 1155, 1169
Community of hope **Vol. 3:** 970
Community Rule **Vol. 1:** 67
Community theology **Vol. 1: 58**
Companion **Vol. 1:** 254 f., 259, 283, 480, 635,
639, 642 f., 690
Vol. 3: 49, 201, 583
Companionship **Vol. 1:** 643
Company **Vol. 1:** 259, 469, 484, 542, 555, 641,
673, 733
Vol. 2: 355, 386, 790, 800
Comparable **Vol. 1:** 729
Comparative ethics (→Ethics, Comparative)
Comparative theology (→Theology, Compara-

tive)
Compare **Vol. 2: 362–367, 500–508, 743–756**
  Vol. 3: 348
Comparison **Vol. 1**: 580, 724
  Vol. 2: 128, 287, 351–354, 411, 424, 459, 501, 743–756
Compass **Vol. 2**: 688
Compassion **Vol. 1**: 110, 112 f., 214, 258, 334 f., 486, 569, 679, 699
  Vol. 2: 116 f., 121, 123, 364, 418, 543, **593–601**, 667, 733, 738, 779, 801, 825, 857, 866
  Vol. 3: 152, 156, 267, 311, **719–725**, 957, 989, 1073
Compassionate **Vol. 2**: 63, 632, 652, 812
Compel **Vol. 1**: 505, 718
  Vol. 2: 245, **662–669**
  Vol. 3: 951
Compensation **Vol. 2**: 48, 583, 666 f.
  Vol. 3: 96, 153, 256, 605, 677
Compete **Vol. 1**: 645–647
  Vol. 2: 308, 316
Competence **Vol. 3: 728–730**
Competent **Vol. 2**: 362, 372, 562
  Vol. 3: 726, **728–730**
Competition **Vol. 1**: 625
  Vol. 3: 775, 799, 1166
Compile **Vol. 1**: 576
Complacency **Vol. 2**: 448
  Vol. 3: 369, 603, 692
Complain **Vol. 1**: 574
  Vol. 2: 190, 416, 423, 854
  Vol. 3: 237
Complaint **Vol. 1**: 598, 652
  Vol. 2: 140, 143 f.
Complaint psalm **Vol. 3**: 234 f.
Complete **Vol. 1**: 58, 263, 282, 429, 591, 605, 678, 733 f., 741
  Vol. 2: 52–66, 118, 144, 162, 195, 244, 313, 359, 451, 778
  Vol. 3: 349–351, 776
Completeness **Vol. 2**: 191, 653, 701, 716
  Vol. 3: 723, 872
Completion **Vol. 1**: 627
  Vol. 2: 59, 65
Complimen **Vol. 1**: 461
Complutensian Polyglot **Vol. 1**: 70
Comply **Vol. 2**: 132
  Vol. 3: 231
Component **Vol. 2**: 452
Compose **Vol. 1**: 676
Composition **Vol. 3**: 65
Compound **Vol. 2**: 293
Comprehend **Vol. 1**: 431, 481, 678
  Vol. 2: 392–406
  Vol. 3: 124, **130–133**, 512, 747
Comprehension **Vol. 1**: 676
  Vol. 2: 392–406
Comprehensive **Vol. 2**: 690
  Vol. 3: 894
Compromise **Vol. 2**: 285, 308
  Vol. 3: 209, 884
Compulsion **Vol. 1**: 272, 401, 496, 718 f.
  Vol. 2: 160, 393, 447, **662–669**, 827
  Vol. 3: 108, 589, 854, 1049

Compulsory **Vol. 3**: 551, 593, 775, 934
Comrade **Vol. 1**: 254, 259
  Vol. 2: 810
  Vol. 3: 583, **1160–1165**
Conceal **Vol. 1**: 50, 577
  Vol. 2: 61, 195, **211–220**, 379, 416, 746, 752
  Vol. 3: 309 f., 884, 914
Conceit **Vol. 1**: 546
  Vol. 3: 380
Conceive **Vol. 1**: 176, 186, **343 f.**, 425
  Vol. 2: 86, 176
  Vol. 3: 511
Concentration **Vol. 2**: 868
  Vol. 3: 911
Concept **Vol. 1**: 612, 711
Conception **Vol. 1**: 152, 186 f., 343, 625, 708
  Vol. 2: 87, 229, 587, 599
  Vol. 3: 660, 1073
Concepts, Moral (→Moral concepts)
Conceptual **Vol. 1**: 582
  Vol. 3: 123
Concern **Vol. 1**: 102, 191 f., 276 f., 646, 595, 731
  Vol. 2: 140, 235, 303, 395, 429, 538, 825
  Vol. 3: 138, 357, 402, 507, 519, 560, 835, 853, 859, 1053
Concession **Vol. 1**: 310, 496, 506, 709
Conciliate **Vol. 3: 148–166**
Conciliator **Vol. 1**: 373
Conciseness **Vol. 2**: 748
Conclude **Vol. 1**: 330
Conclusion **Vol. 1**: 664
  Vol. 2: 32, 59 f., 139, 157
  Vol. 3: 1086
Concord **Vol. 2**: 776, 782
  Vol. 3: 33
Concordism **Vol. 2**: 889
Concrete **Vol. 2**: 746
Concubinage **Vol. 2**: 578
Concubine **Vol. 1**: 230, 498 f.
  Vol. 2: 575
  Vol. 3: 1055
Condemn **Vol. 2**: 78, 142, 150, 205, 237 f., 282, **362–367, 370**, 379, 381, 383, 435, 445–447, 736
  Vol. 3: 211, 402, 1062, 1151
Condemn to death **Vol. 2**: 57
Condemnation **Vol. 1**: 171, 191, 217, 220, 349, 356, 372, 392, 394–396, 403, 417, 424, 433, 437, 452, 513, 515, 542, 547, 550, 566, 579, 590, 597, 607, 609 f., 613, 633, 648, 655, 675, 688, 722, 730, 738
  Vol. 2: 139, 185, 222, 267, 271, 285 f., 361, **362–367, 370**, 443, 445, 449, 584, 709, 723
  Vol. 3: 164, 270, 354, 403, 748, 1052
Condemnatory **Vol. 1**: 397
Condescension **Vol. 1**: 426
  Vol. 2: 116, 118
Condiment **Vol. 3**: 443 f.
Condition **Vol. 1**: 165, 271, 275, 367, 536, 541, 543, 548, 564, 582, 600, 606, 618, 672, 679, 703, 739
  Vol. 2: 147, 163, 230, 235, 308, 325, 343, 359, 366, 415, 421, 445, 500, 548, 568, **656–**

Condition (cont'd)
661, 859
Vol. 3: 144, 858, 1156
Conditional **Vol. 3:** 172
Conditioned **Vol. 1:** 71, 526
Conduct **Vol. 1:** 59, 201, 349 f., 352, 418, 472, 482, 487, 491, 550, 571, 594, 597 f., 601, 604, 616, 620, 623 f., 723
Vol. 2: 61, 95, 103, 123, 218, 230, 246, 365, 391, 396, 407, 431, 436, 445, 452, 666, 669, 776, 786, **801–804**, 815 f., 819, 828, 846
Vol. 3: 60, 124, 137, 204, 347, 356–358, 400, 447, 525, 561, 604, 692, 761, 774, **933–947**, 1027 f., 1043, 1052, 1058, 1169
Confederacy **Vol. 2:** 375
Confederate **Vol. 2:** 810
Confederation **Vol. 2:** 373
Confer **Vol. 1:** 208, 650, 675
Vol. 2: 152, 335
Confess **Vol. 1:** 115, 205, 223, 276, **344–348**, 424, 455, 469, 493, 545, 574, 677 f.
Vol. 2: 42, 114, 215, 217, 263, 309, 343, 373, 377, 380, 382 f., 430, 449, 473, 516, 519, 559, 874, 885
Vol. 3: 44, 47, 54, 136, 163, 225, 233, 243, 249, 362, 625, 668, 816, 1050
Confession **Vol. 1:** 51, 142, 149, 153, 158, 227, 244, 272, 290, 309, 332, 336, 340, 344, 347, 349, 380, 382, 384, 396, 404, 435, 437, 491, 519, 597–599, 604, 636, 638, 662, 668 f., 679, 700, 702, 708, 735
Vol. 2: 73, 75, 78, 118, 133, 174, 176, 231, 239, 243 f., 251, 315, 340–342, 404, 514 f., 614, 654, 722, 724 f., 897
Vol. 3: 42, 60 f., 74, 114, 142, 164, 167, 233, 342, 384–386, 401, 474, 490, 505, 509, 563, 578, 611, 630, 639, 643, 646, 651–653, 675, 703, 729, 742, 774, 777, 836 f., 899, 965
Confessional **Vol. 1:** 600, 628
Vol. 2: 338 f.
Confessional formula **Vol. 3:** 299
Confidence **Vol. 1:** 223, 227, 229, 261, 311, 327 f., 364 f., 384, 399, 425, 433, 444, 492, 505, 531, 587 f., 591 f., 658–660, 675, 679–681, 703, 710, 712 f.
Vol. 2: 42, 165, 218, 230, 240, 243 f., 249, 360, 367, 385, 387, **734–737**, 843 f., 863, 866, 868, 873, 900
Vol. 3: 47, 74, 143, 249, 366, 728, 1096
Confidential **Vol. 2:** 395
Vol. 3: 502, 589
Confine **Vol. 1:** 735
Vol. 2: 135, 445, **807–809**
Confirm **Vol. 1:** 97–99, 415, 538, 545, 594, 596 f., 600, 658–664, 667, 708, 734
Vol. 2: 119, 123, 341, 350, 797
Vol. 3: 344, 499, 1104, **1038–1050**
Confiscation **Vol. 3:** 604
Conflagration **Vol. 1:** 463, 521, 656 f.
Conflict **Vol. 1:** 270, 273, 373, 429 f., 452, 487, 561, 563, 592, 600–604, 631, 644–653
Vol. 2: 111, 119, 282 f., 308, 310 f., 313, 401, 781
Vol. 3: 111, 753, **958–967**

Conflicting **Vol. 1:** 505
Conform **Vol. 1:** 708 f.
Vol. 2: 234, 242, 255, 262, 289, 361, 436, 439, 446, **451–453**, 673, 885
Vol. 3: 577, 701
Conforming to the law **Vol. 2:** **438–451**
Conformity **Vol. 1:** 371, 400, 481, 603, 693, 705, 707
Vol. 2: 259, 403, 443
Vol. 3: 1200
Confront **Vol. 2:** 327, 378
Confrontation **Vol. 1:** 499, 502, 505, 524 f., 550, 624, 651
Vol. 2: 396, 437
Vol. 3: 145, 472
Confounded **Vol. 3:** 562, 733
Confuse **Vol. 2:** 416
Confusion **Vol. 1:** 468, 527
Vol. 2: 461
Vol. 3: 556, **709 f.**, 731
Confute **Vol. 1:** 577
Vol. 3: 492
Congenital **Vol. 2:** 414 f.
Congratulate **Vol. 2:** 92
Congregation **Vol. 1:** 96 f., 99, 190, 219, 245, 247, 255, 272, 291, 293 f., 296 f., 300–305, 496, 500 f., 572, 582, 618, 643, 732
Vol. 2: 51, 73 f., 121, 126, 152, 161, 201, 235, 237, 247 f., 250 f., 412, 523, 533, 547, 668, 676, 800, 816, 818
Vol. 3: 88, 159, 670, 675, 746, 868, 905, 930, 1058
Congregation of wickedness **Vol. 2:** 364
Conjecture **Vol. 1:** 326
Vol. 2: 44 f.
Conjugal rights **Vol. 3:** 536, 539
Conjuror **Vol. 2:** 555
Connection **Vol. 2:** 386, 683
Connive **Vol. 2:** 767
Conquer **Vol. 1:** 118, 252, 400, 434, 445, 458, 460, 563 f., 644, 650, 688, 718
Vol. 2: 218, 308, 373, **510–520**, 795
Conqueror **Vol. 1:** 126, 244, 407 f., 413, 651
Vol. 2: 329, 419
Conquest **Vol. 1:** 402, 445 f., 533, 686, 713, 716
Vol. 2: 257
Vol. 3: 256, 1104
Conquest of Canaan **Vol. 1:** **53**, 55, 61, 66, 72
Vol. 2: **297 f.**, 373, 802, 841
Conscience **Vol. 1:** 116, 147, 152, 223, 225, 341, **348–353**, 448 f., 495, 552, 566, 572, 604, 677
Vol. 2: 63, 101 f., 121, 140, 149, 182, 235, 268, 286, 493, 567, 574 f., 611, 659, 706 f., 735, 881
Vol. 3: 35, 41, 107, 127, 133, 322 f., 365 f., 426, 432 f., 550, 725, 755, 759, 824, 874, 889, 903, 927, 941, 989, 995 f., 1042 f.
Conscious **Vol. 1:** 549, 647, 696, 736
Vol. 2: 417
Vol. 3: 513, 1017
Consciousness **Vol. 1:** 348, 351, 353, 485, 491, 497, 527 f., 538 f., 699 f.
Vol. 2: 295, 310, 340, 379, 435
Vol. 3: 125, 127, 514, 677, 681, 899

Conscription **Vol. 1:** 536
Consecrate **Vol. 1:** 210, 224, 239, 294 f., 405, 413–415, 474, 497, 507, 688
   Vol. 2: 40, 43, 60, 63, **223–238**, 354, 650, **670–674**, 675, 862
   Vol. 3: 160, 415, 892
Consecration **Vol. 2:** 61, 215, **223–238**, 294, 579, 581, 638, 711, 782
   Vol. 3: 38, 422 f., 989
Consent **Vol. 1:** 344
   Vol. 2: 501, 817
   Vol. 3: 1057
Consequence **Vol. 1:** 268, 396, 419, 437, 478, 541, 611, 679, 687, 702, 716–718, 721, 725
   Vol. 2: 119, 138 f., 159, 314, 360, 384, 399, 583
   Vol. 3: 134, 185, 201, 525, 578 f., 586, 720, 919, 1094
Conservation **Vol. 3:** 820
Conservative **Vol. 3:** 440
Consider **Vol. 2:** **362–367**, 458
   Vol. 3: **122–130**, 230, 232, 511, 519 f., **820–826**
Consider worthy **Vol. 3:** **348 f.**
Considerate **Vol. 2:** **256–259**, 400
Consideration **Vol. 1:** 105 f., 537, 675, 680, 723
   Vol. 2: 286, 386
   Vol. 3: 128, **820–826**, 1015
Consign **Vol. 1:** 730
Consistency **Vol. 1:** 725 f.
Consistent **Vol. 2:** 335
Consolation **Vol. 1:** 216 f., 328 f.
   Vol. 2: 359, 418, 420
   Vol. 3: 88
Consolation of Israel **Vol. 1:** 329, 570
   Vol. 2: 245
   Vol. 3: 790
Console **Vol. 1:** 88, 328 f., 341, **567–573**
   Vol. 2: 418
   Vol. 3: 255
Consolidate **Vol. 1:** 604
Consolidation **Vol. 2:** 129
Consort **Vol. 2:** 349
Conspicuous **Vol. 1:** 267
Conspiracy **Vol. 1:** 246
   Vol. 2: 521
Constancy **Vol. 1:** 367, 710
   Vol. 2: 452, 868
Constant **Vol. 3:** **229 f.**
Constantine **Vol. 2:** 506
Constellation **Vol. 1:** 670
   Vol. 2: 187, 688
   Vol. 3: 146, 312, 396 f., 554, **734–737**, 842 f.
Constitute **Vol. 1:** 710
   Vol. 2: 441
Constitution **Vol. 1:** 189, 521, 640, 711
   Vol. 2: 657
   Vol. 3: 755
Constraint **Vol. 1:** 496, 525, 693
   Vol. 2: 360
   Vol. 3: 711, 739
Construct **Vol. 3:** **118–120**
Construction **Vol. 1:** 521 f., 713
   Vol. 2: 683

Consubstantial **Vol. 2:** **505**
   Vol. 3: 1186
Consul **Vol. 1:** 169, **269 f.**, 407
Consult **Vol. 2:** 367, 856, 879
Consultation **Vol. 1:** 293
   Vol. 2: 32
Consume **Vol. 1:** 390
   Vol. 2: **268 f.**, 831
Consuming **Vol. 3:** 982
Consummation **Vol. 1:** 52, 251 f., 506, 508, 655, 668, 692
   Vol. 2: 52, 59, 61 f., 65, 147, 178, 271, 329, 383, 532, 575, 585, 692, 789, 877, 918, 920 f., 926
   Vol. 3: 71, 73, 256, 702, 733, 842, 844, 847
Consumption **Vol. 1:** 642
   Vol. 2: 271
Contact **Vol. 1:** 444, 512, 583
   Vol. 2: 225 f., 267, 285
   Vol. 3: 103
Contagious magic **Vol. 2:** 553
Contain **Vol. 1:** 636, 741
   Vol. 2: 773
Contaminate **Vol. 3:** 759
Contaminated **Vol. 1:** 653
Contamination **Vol. 2:** 223
   Vol. 3: 231
Contemn **Vol. 3:** 341
Contemplate **Vol. 3:** **122–130**
Contemplation **Vol. 1:** 529
   Vol. 2: 60
   Vol. 3: 845
Contemplative **Vol. 2:** 475, 478
   Vol. 3: 210
Contemporary **Vol. 1:** 334
   Vol. 2: 35, 314, 331, 338
   Vol. 3: 335
Contempt **Vol. 1:** 74 f., 254, 397, 461, 479, 481, 539, 647, 726
   Vol. 2: 124, 270, 284, 310, 334, 428, 449, 718

   Vol. 3: 28 f., 426, 556, 593, 809
Contemptuously **Vol. 3:** 943
Contend **Vol. 1:** 645–647, 719
   Vol. 2: 305, 718
   Vol. 3: 355
Content **Vol. 1:** 546, 600, 681, 704, 727, 741
   Vol. 2: 111 f., 143, 243, 777, 817
   Vol. 3: 54, 70, 74, 76, 143, **727 f.**, 1083
Contentiousness **Vol. 1:** 106, 641, 646
   Vol. 3: 1119
Contentment **Vol. 1:** 433
   Vol. 2: 60
   Vol. 3: 257, **727 f.**, 955
Contest **Vol. 1:** 454, 469, 645
   Vol. 2: 316
   Vol. 3: 873, 946
Contestant **Vol. 1:** 646 f.
Context **Vol. 1:** 57, 582, 698, 737
   Vol. 3: 153 f., 206, 877, 892, 899, 1140
Continence **Vol. 3:** 536
Contingent proposition **Vol. 3:** 894
Continue **Vol. 1:** 674
   Vol. 3: 238

Continue in **Vol. 3:** 223–229
Continuity **Vol. 1:** 299, 736
  Vol. 2: 231, 314, 695, 700, 721, 787, 891, 918–920
  Vol. 3: 236, 292, 654
Contract **Vol. 1:** 121, 243, 291, 344
  Vol. 2: 40, 146, 305, 879
  Vol. 3: 353
Contract price **Vol. 3: 138–144**, 539
Contractor **Vol. 1:** 279
Contradict **Vol. 1:** 601, 630, 659, 693
  Vol. 2: 342
Contradiction **Vol. 2:** 281, 401
  Vol. 3: 779
Contradictory **Vol. 2:** 214, 229
Contrary **Vol. 1:** 597, 606
  Vol. 2: 420, 438, 445
Contrast **Vol. 1:** 609, 629, 631, 643, 666
  Vol. 2: 281, 288, 304, 329, 334, 349, 357
  Vol. 3: 889
Contravention **Vol. 1:** 447
Contribution **Vol. 1:** 642, 740
  Vol. 2: 131, 320, 594, 823, 826 f.
  Vol. 3: 153, 415
Contrite **Vol. 2:** 422
Contrition **Vol. 2:** 157
Contrive **Vol. 1:** 599
  Vol. 2: 236, 888
Control **Vol. 1:** 208, 260, 273, 365, 429, 436, 450, 452, 458, 494 f., 501 f., 517, 527, 595, 650 f., 654, 671, 692, 697, 715, 720, 733, 738
  Vol. 2: 99, 120, 149 f., 159, 182, 191, 262, 287, 296 f., 299, 430, 446, 510, 512, 561, 609, 617, 736
  Vol. 3: 122, 177, 234, 474, 689, 693, 917, 1087
Controversy **Vol. 1:** 133, 487, 544, 558, 631
  Vol. 2: 362, 402, 405, 426, 446, 448, 451, 580
  Vol. 3: 762, 887, 909, 999, 1026, 1086, 1119
Convene **Vol. 2:** 31
Convenient **Vol. 3: 833–839**
Convention **Vol. 3:** 895, 1123, 1141
Conversation **Vol. 1:** 575, 612
  Vol. 2: 861, 867, 869, 873
  Vol. 3: 1058, 1083
Conversion **Vol. 1:** 77, 111, 136, 144–146, 149, 158–160, 163, 180, 182 f., 245, 291, 346, 349, **353–362**, 422, 511, 557, 560, 589 f., 623, 685, 688, 691, 702 f.
  Vol. 2: 74, 86, 90, 93 f., 126, 181, 183, 240, 250, 266, 270, 314, 405, 407, 413, 453, 568, 584, 596, 716, 749, 785, 792, 825, 828, 877
  Vol. 3: 48, 54, 82, 106, 148, 322, 361, 373, 542, 549, 582, 586, 628, 675, 698 f., 705, 751, 765, 775, 955, 1158
Convert **Vol. 1:** 191, 247, 350, 413, 689
  Vol. 2: 158, 227, 443 f., 563, 881
  Vol. 3: 233, 352, 410, 416, 686, 1052, 1164
Convey **Vol. 3:** 706, 1140
Convey property **Vol. 3:** 806
Conveyance **Vol. 1:** 606
Convict **Vol. 1:** 91, 130, 349
  Vol. 2: 137–145, 158, 447, 768
  Vol. 3: 573

Conviction **Vol. 1:** 365, 392, 482, 492, 545, 587, 595, 604, 710, 713, 731, 735
  Vol. 2: 140, 152
  Vol. 3: 705, 709
Convictor **Vol. 1:** 373
Convince **Vol. 1:** 504, 572, 588–590, 594, 663, 681
  Vol. 2: 140
  Vol. 3: 362, 1087
Convincer **Vol. 1:** 91
Convivial **Vol. 2:** 356
Conzelmann, H. **Vol. 3:** 86
Cook **Vol. 2:** 254
Co-operate **Vol. 3:** 1147–1152
Co-operation **Vol. 2:** 446
Co-ordinate **Vol. 1:** 523
  Vol. 2: 80
Coping **Vol. 2:** 157
Coponius **Vol. 2:** 849
  Vol. 3: 452
Copper **Vol. 2:** 96 f.
  Vol. 3: 606
Copper-smith **Vol. 2:** 96
Copy **Vol. 1:** 491, 521, 643
  Vol. 2: 192, 194, **284**, 287, **290 f.**, 310, 447, 497, **503–508**, 655, 804
  Vol. 3: 433, 478, 645, 647, 876, 888, **903–906**
Copyist **Vol. 2:** 309, 715
Coral **Vol. 3:** 498
Corban **Vol. 2: 39–44**
  Vol. 3: 481
Cord **Vol. 3:** 592
Cords of death **Vol. 3:** 858
Cords of Sheol **Vol. 3:** 858
Co-regent **Vol. 2:** 146 f.
Corinth **Vol. 1:** 138, 183, 261, 299, 313, 315, 317, 328 f., 352, 361, 399, 468, 497, 500, 514, 568, 571, 638, 727
  Vol. 2: 74, 127, 159, 212 f., 231, 235, 254, 267, 273, 286, 311, 365, 369, 451, 576, 597, 605, 611, 756, 762 f., 809, 849, 851, 895, 898 f., 923
  Vol. 3: 84, 127, 170, 203, 225, 297, 305, 346, 369, 379, 432, 534, 541, 548, 561, 714, 742, 802, 831, 905, 955, 994 f., 1021, 1025, 1065 f., 1073, 1080, 1110
Corinthian **Vol. 3:** 412, 499, 544, 570, 707, 932, 1026, 1030 f., 1053
Corinthians **Vol. 1:** 214, 236, 275, 279, 328, 351 f., 356, 365, 397 f., 400, 419, 466, 469, 491, 496, 500, 514, 559, 571, 592, 639, 664, 680 f., 709, 731, 741 f.
  Vol. 2: 57, 74, 159 f., 175, 179, 253, 263, 273, 338, 360, 399, 402 f., 420, 422, 519, 530, 676, 727, 756, 765, 826, 834, 880, 884, 922
  Vol. 3: 61, 85, 118, 130, 142, 241 f., 380, 431, 576, 727, 752, 773, 954 f., 1151
Corn **Vol. 1:** 115, 204, 498, 625
  Vol. 2: 267, 675, 711
  Vol. 3: 194, 792
Cornelian **Vol. 3:** 396
Cornelius **Vol. 1:** 148, 361, 504, 576, 690
  Vol. 2: 178, 596, 800, 895
  Vol. 3: 66, 105 f., 242, 324, 361, 699, 1043

Corner **Vol. 2:** 159, 688 f.
  Vol. 3: 388–390
Cornerstone **Vol. 1:** 377, 541, 596, 661 f.
  Vol. 2: 129, 249, 253, 313, 622 f., 706
  Vol. 3: 84, **381–399**, 504, 809
Coronation **Vol. 1:** 121, 426
  Vol. 2: 200
  Vol. 3: 873
Corporate **Vol. 1:** 229, 237, 294, 301, 305, 733
  Vol. 2: 353, 920
  Vol. 3: 373, 523 f.
Corporeality **Vol. 1:** 87, 233, 500
  Vol. 3: 680
Corpse **Vol. 1:** 113, 229, 232–234, 393, 429,
  443 f., 446, 450, 480, 608, 610, 653–655
  Vol. 3: 100, 303, 694, 860, 953, 989
Corpus Hermeticum (→Hermetic Literature)
Correct **Vol. 1:** 163, 707
  Vol. 2: 123, 140, 327
  Vol. 3: 351 f., 776, **874–901**
Correcting **Vol. 3: 351 f.**
Correction **Vol. 1:** 349, 462, 551, 555, 568 f.
  Vol. 2: 140–142
  Vol. 3: 745
Correctly **Vol. 3: 351 f.**
Corrector **Vol. 1:** 708
Correlation **Vol. 1:** 60
Correspond **Vol. 1:** 246, 491, 731
  Vol. 2: 289, 380, **451–453, 497–500**
  Vol. 3: 348, 397, 884 f., 904, 1104, 1200
Correspondence theory of truth **Vol. 3: 894–896**
Corresponding **Vol. 2: 497–500**
  Vol. 3: 903–906
Corroboration **Vol. 3:** 326
Corroborative oath **Vol. 3:** 740
Corrupt **Vol. 1:** 96, 350, 402, 464, 467–469,
  565, 588, 589, 724
  Vol. 2: 183, 326, 461
  Vol. 3: 310, 578
Corruptibility **Vol. 1:** 552
  Vol. 2: 96
Corrupting **Vol. 3:** 886
Corruption **Vol. 1:** 76, 266, 299, 381, 458,
  467 f., 470, 559, 562, 590, 611, 677, 681
  Vol. 2: 96, 183, 661, 692, 714
  Vol. 3: 140, 271, 281, 444, 449, 525, 651,
  685, 939
Cosmetics **Vol. 1:** 119
  Vol. 2: 334, 711 f.
Cosmic **Vol. 1: 53**, 102, 167, 186, 224, 237 f.,
  257, 290, 298, 301–303, 374, 383, 396,
  401 f., 423, 432, 498, 521, 523, 549, 562,
  610, 637, 707
  Vol. 2: 38, 54, 56, 65, 73, 75, 167, 188 f., 196,
  200 f., 290, 375, 385, 389, 393 f., 436, 439,
  482, 609, 629, 665, 828, 916
  Vol. 3: 148, 172, 353, 397, 502, 559, 595 f.,
  630, 678 f., 718, 722, 847, 1147
Cosmic cycle **Vol. 3:** 146
Cosmic egg **Vol. 2:** 188
Cosmic dualism **Vol. 3:** 802
Cosmic harmony **Vol. 2:** 498
Cosmic sabbath **Vol. 2:** 697
Cosmic signs **Vol. 3:** 372 f.

Cosmic week **Vol. 2:** 697 f., 701
Cosmogony **Vol. 1: 53**
  Vol. 2: 189, 394
Cosmological **Vol. 1:** 166, 386, 452, 523, 616,
  674
  Vol. 2: 71, 190–193, 195, 645, 887
  Vol. 3: 630, 645, 719, 789, 865, 984
Cosmological argument **Vol. 3:** 331
Cosmology **Vol. 1: 53**, 69, 491, 521 f., 594, 655
  Vol. 2: 187, 394, 397, 677, 763
  Vol. 3: 146, 148, 693
Cosmopolitanism **Vol. 1:** 640
Cosmos **Vol. 1:** 94, 164, 167, 184, 232 f., 237,
  387, 432, 450, 470, 507, 521–526, 595, 616,
  715 f.
  Vol. 2: 66, 158, 165, 188, 192, 199, 270, 394,
  405, 603
  Vol. 3: 831, 994, 1085
Cost **Vol. 1:** 404, 414, 679
  Vol. 2: 104, 699
Costas, Orlando E. **Vol. 3:** 973
Costly **Vol. 3:** 398
Council **Vol. 1:** 52, 102, 192, 194, 196, 199,
  273, 297, 350, **362–364**, 418, 580, 591, 712
  Vol. 2: 32, 368
  Vol. 3: 35, 39, 42, 49, 97, 99, 241, 1016
Council of Alexandria **Vol. 2:** 507
Council of Antioch **Vol. 2: 506–508**
Council of Constantinople **Vol. 2: 505–508**
Council of the Five Hundred **Vol. 3:** 1015
Council of Jerusalem (→Jerusalem Council)
Council of Nicaea **Vol. 2:** 316, **505–507**
Council of Trent **Vol. 3:** 244, 371, 401
Counsel **Vol. 1:** 89, 362 f., 425, 451, 552, 569,
  625, 684, 696, 738
  Vol. 2: 77, 300, 440, 856
  Vol. 3: 79, 224, 258, 311, 916, 1016 f.
Counsellor **Vol. 1:** 91, 665
  Vol. 3: 230, 242, 704, 1068
Count **Vol. 1:** 480, 536, 540, 546, 556, 675, 723,
  732 f.
  Vol. 2: 144, 429, 683
  Vol. 3: 1081–1119
Countenance **Vol. 1:** 212, 708
  Vol. 2: 491
Counter **Vol. 2:** 266
Counteract **Vol. 1:** 693
Counterfeit **Vol. 1:** 187
  Vol. 3: 916
Counterpart **Vol. 2:** 291
Countless **Vol. 2:** 700
Country **Vol. 1:** 517, 606, 615, 685, 741
  Vol. 2: 92, 349, 788
Countryside **Vol. 1:** 520
Courage **Vol. 1:** 314, 327, **364 f.**, 431, 501, 536,
  720, 731
  Vol. 2: 180, 244, 736
  Vol. 3: 676, 689, 715, 747, 925 f., 1059
Course **Vol. 1:** 492, 524, 608, 610, 667, 694,
  730, 741
  Vol. 2: 62, 457
  Vol. 3: 945–947, 1086
Court **Vol. 1:** 101 f., 267, 271, 315, 321, 344,
  347, 349 f., 363 f., 373, 393, 414 f., 478, 554,

Court (cont'd)
560, 580, 665
Vol. 2: 116, 137, 142 f., 225, 367 f., 392, 613 f., 841, 922
Vol. 3: 49, 78, 212, 324, 380, 404, 441, 537, 545, 547, 588, 608, 633, 636, 741, 756, 849, 954, 1032, 1048, 1165
Court of the Gentiles **Vol. 2:** 236
Vol. 3: 789, 795, 949
Court of Israel **Vol. 3:** 789
Court of men **Vol. 2:** 236
Court of the women **Vol. 2:** 236
Vol. 3: 789, 796, 1058
Court prophet **Vol. 2:** 306
Courtesan **Vol. 1:** 497
Courtesy **Vol. 2:** 549, 712, 812, 860
Courtly style **Vol. 2:** 79, 428, 818
Vol. 3: 564
Courtyard **Vol. 1:** 632
Cousin **Vol. 1:** 256
Covenant **Vol. 1:** 58 f., 61, 71, 77, 79, 81, 96, 98, 108 f., 123, 149, 154, 159 f., 185, 189, 195, 199, 210, 221–225, 243, 248, 258, 280, 293–296, 308 f., 311, 332 f., 349 f., 354, 357, **365–376**, 382 f., 386, 412, 414, 416, 423, 433, 437, 448, 452, 463, 481, 531, 538, 541 f., 589, 593, 596, 601, 617, 626, 636, 638, 641, 655, 659, 666, 685, 690 f., 702, 717
Vol. 2: 40, 47, 63 f., 73, 75, 77, 105, 117, 122, 132, 134, 139, 145, 155, 176, 183, 213, 228, 230, 237, 275 f., 287, 295, 298, 304, 307, 314, 316, 318, 320, 328 f., 343, 356, 367, 374, 385, 396, 441 f., 444, 447 f., 453, 471, 478 f., 486, 492, 512, 521, 524 f., 532 f., 535 f., 540 f., 569, 576, 581, 591–595, 597, 626, 637, 671, 681, 716 f., 741, 772, 779, 784–786, 794, 797 f., 854, 891, 923
Vol. 3: 28, 42, 70, 72–74, 79, 89, 113, 135 f., 140, 150, 166 f., 172, 190 f., 200, 215, 224, 227, 233, 235, 237, 239, 241, 243, 246, 263 f., 273, 311, 313, 316, 320, 323, 332, 342, 354, 356 f., 363, 365 f., 372 f., 390 f., 397, 407, 411, 415, 422, 425, 433, 435 f., 445, 484, 486, 499, 522–524, 531, 574, 578, 583 f., 590, 592, 626 f., 649 f., 692, 740, 743, 761, 782, 784, 790, 793, 799 f., 803, 805, 811, 815, 824, 828, 836, 870–872, 879, 882, 890, 938, 941, 944 f., 1002 f., 1013 f., 1018, 1030, 1040 f., 1057, 1074, 1087, 1091, 1096, 1102, 1105 f., 1148, 1158
Covenant loyalty **Vol. 3:** 889
Cover **Vol. 1:** 555, 587, 653, 698, 701, 707, 733, 735
Vol. 2: 157, 160–162, **211–214**, 225, 259, 294
Vol. 3: 149, 154, 156, 192, **553–556**
Cover over **Vol. 3:** 150
Cover up **Vol. 3:** 310
Covering **Vol. 3:** **794 f.**
Covet **Vol. 1:** 432, 457, 727
Vol. 2: 871
Vol. 3: 142, 1057
Covetous **Vol. 1:** 137 f., 231, 336
Vol. 2: 286
Covetousness **Vol. 2:** 96, 669, 833

Cow **Vol. 1:** 537, 672, 686
Cowardice **Vol. 1:** 365, 559
Vol. 2: 180, 430
Cozbi **Vol. 3:** 159
Crack **Vol. 1:** 94
Craft **Vol. 1:** 279, 654, 743
Vol. 3: 377
Craftsman **Vol. 1:** **279**, 383, 387, 419, 735
Vol. 2: 574
Vol. 3: 691, 728, 787
Craftsmanship **Vol. 1:** 723, 735
Crafty **Vol. 1:** 412
Vol. 2: 469, 616
Vol. 3: 935
Crag **Vol. 3:** 381
Cramp **Vol. 2:** **807–809**
Cranfield, C. E. B. **Vol. 3:** **299 f.**
Crave **Vol. 1:** 456, 671
Vol. 2: 539
Craving **Vol. 3:** 676, 805
Crazed **Vol. 1:** 529
Create **Vol. 1:** 257, 272, 349, 378, 380, 383, 402, 422, 493, 563, 590, 672 f., 678
Vol. 2: 77, 106, 111, 128, 149, 158, 183, 190, 193
Vol. 3: 119, 1058, 1147, 1153
Created **Vol. 1:** 181, 301, 390, 474, 509, 518, 524, 572, 600, 625, 668, 670
Vol. 2: 83, 101, 161, 163, 310, 660, 798
Creation **Vol. 1:** 54, 56, 58, 60, 63, 65 f., 70, 72, 84 f., 87, 95, 99, 101, 116, 165–169, 175, 180, 185, 211, 213, 216, 230, 236, 256, 279, 313, 333, 355, **376–389**, 424, 431, 433, 437, 470, 496, 506, 517 f., 521 f., 524–526, 552, 565, 617, 628, 630, 636, 665, 668–671, 694, 713, 732 f.
Vol. 2: 45, 47–49, 51 f., 58, 64, 72, 78, 83, 99, 128, 149, 160, 189, 194 f., 243–245, 275, 285, 356, 396 f., 405, 420, 441 f., 447, 483, 488, 491, 496, 516, 548, 553, 564, 569, 574, 590, 602, 608, 613, 615, 622, 629, 643, 657–662, 671 f., 690 f., 714, 720 f., 761, 834, 877, 883 f., 889, 912, 927, 931
Vol. 3: 36, 52, 117–120, 128, 148, 180, 182, 199, 204, 207, 210, 250, 256, 293, 319, 330, 349, 372 f., 402, 406, 416 f., 502–504, 515, 460, 616, 642, 647, 656, 674, 681, 683, 689, 707, 725, 730, 734, 831, 833, 837, 843, 845 f., 885, 912, 917, 922, 980, 983, 986, 990, 995, 1029, 1031, 1033, 1055 f., 1063 f., 1087 f., 1100, 1102, 1116 f., 1133, 1143, **1152–1155**, 1157, 1182
Creation of man **Vol. 3:** 915
Creation myth **Vol. 2:** **200 f.**, 553
Creation, New **Vol. 1:** 86 f., 153, 185 f., 222, 225, 248, 257, 275, 299, 311, 336, 359, 385, 390, 434, 470, 538, 628, 680
Vol. 2: 48, 78, 83, 307, 399, 482, 545, 661, 670–673, 675, 691 f., 764, 780, 836
Vol. 3: 71, 168, 171, 656, 703, 785, 817, 831, 886, 927
Creation ordinances **Vol. 1:** 333
Vol. 2: 570
Vol. 3: 392

421

Creative **Vol. 1:** 384, 400, 643, 692
  Vol. 2: 128, 425, 488, 920
Creative intuition **Vol. 3:** 898
Creative word **Vol. 3:** 1088, 1100, 1105 f., 1108, 1120
Creator **Vol. 1:** 92, 112, 138, 175, 178, 216, 227, 375, 378–387, 422, 502, 518, 522 f., 552, 616 f., 621, 639, 665, 669–671, 688, 723, 728
  Vol. 2: 58 f., 64, 70–72, 74, 92, 94, 158, 160, 164, 175, 187, 226, 375, 472, 478, 480, 485, 491, 512, 514, 633, 649, 655, 658, 672, 724, 799, 839, 877
  Vol. 3: 36, 128, 172, 233, 644, 692, 826, 835, 842, 846, 885, 912, 916, 984, 986, 1020, 1032, 1105, 1148 f., 1182, 1202
Creature **Vol. 1:** 138, 222, **376–389**, 439, 471, 521, 674, 679, 723
  Vol. 2: 94, 105, 117, 472, 485, 613, 657, 661
Creatureliness **Vol. 1:** 85, 221, 233, 552, 678 f., 700
  Vol. 2: 564 f.
Credal form **Vol. 1:** 58, 473, 677
Credentials **Vol. 3:** 354
Credibility **Vol. 1:** 505, 588, 594, 724
  Vol. 2: 444, 858
  Vol. 3: 290
Credit **Vol. 1:** 594
  Vol. 2: 131, 400, 434
  Vol. 3: 822–826
Creditor **Vol. 2:** 667, 858
Creed **Vol. 1:** 147, 379, 473, 620
  Vol. 2: 406
Creep **Vol. 2:** 412
Cremation **Vol. 1:** 264
Crenides **Vol. 2:** 550
Creon **Vol. 1:** 550
Cretans **Vol. 3:** 81, 887
Crete **Vol. 2:** 612, 645
  Vol. 3: 137, 253, 782
Crime **Vol. 1:** 151, 392, 410, 519
  Vol. 2: 139, 142, 521
  Vol. 3: 93 f., 574
Criminal **Vol. 1:** 264, 390 f., 402, 417, 466, 479, 564, 649, 655, 669, 698
  Vol. 2: 137, 238, 392, 572
  Vol. 3: 149, 203, 211, 242, 575
Cripple **Vol. 1:** 507
  Vol. 2: 414 f.
  Vol. 3: 520, 710
Crisis **Vol. 1:** 436, 724 f.
  Vol. 2: 117, 309, **362–367**, 382 f., 706
  Vol. 3: 826
Crispus **Vol. 1:** 160
Criterion **Vol. 2:** 460, 847
Criterion of judgment **Vol. 3:** 399
Critic **Vol. 2:** 362
Critical **Vol. 1:** 583 f., 602
  Vol. 2: 159, 401
Critical faculty **Vol. 3:** 124
Criticism **Vol. 1:** 512, 568, 603
  Vol. 2: 214
Criticism, Biblical **Vol. 1:** 70, 582
Criticism, Historical **Vol. 1:** 57, **60**, 61, 548

  Vol. 2: 340, 389
  Vol. 3: 282
Criticism, Literary **Vol. 1:** 51, 57, 60, **62**, 68
Criticism, Redaction (→Redaction Criticism)
Criticism, Scientific **Vol. 1:** 71
Criticism, Textual **Vol. 1:** 57, **69 f**, 71
Crocodile **Vol. 2:** 485
  Vol. 3: 557
Cronus **Vol. 2:** 188
Crooked **Vol. 2:** 36, 370, **414 f.**
Crops **Vol. 1:** 520, 724, 729
  Vol. 2: 32, 211, 693, 711
  Vol. 3: 525, 756
Cross **Vol. 1:** 54 f., 57, 73 f., 113, 147, 167 f., 191, 198, 214, 223 f., 228, 237, 248, 254, 279, 323, 330, 375, 385, **389–405**, 409, 411, 417, 430, 437, 439, 455, 461, 464, 473, 479, 483, 510, 540, 544, 547–549, 551, 555, 564, 572, 601 f., 615, 638, 647, 649, 651, 669, 680, 685, 702 f., 707, 719, 722, 726 f., 740
  Vol. 2: 42, 61, 64, 78, 80, 83, 112, 126 f., 139, 145, 156, 179, 185 f., 199, 204 f., 262 f., 267, 273, 314, 334, 338–340, 343, 354, 361, 367, 378–380, 387 f., 402, 419 f., 426, 433, 435, 443–445, 481, 543, 559, 572 f., 575, 604–606, 610, 620, 671, 708, 710, 722, 766 f., 775, 782 f., 794, 804, 819, 909, 918
  Vol. 3: 96 f., 99, 169, 171 f., 174, 183, 186, 204, 211 f., 214, 221, 245, 253, 278, 299, 315, 328, 343, 347, 366, 372, 374, 400, 415, 432, 448, 471, 489, 503 f., 510, 552, 563, 571, 580, 601, 631, 641, 670, 725, 743, 779, 785, 824 f., **865–870**, 871, 883, 922, 949 f., 956, 965, 995, 1017, 1025 f., 1030–1032, 1062, 1108–1110 f., 113, 1154, 1195
Cross over **Vol. 3:** 583
Cross-examine **Vol. 2:** 362
Crossan, J.D. **Vol. 3:** 899
Crouch **Vol. 2:** 260
Crowd **Vol. 1:** 292–295, 322, 409, 411, 482, 646, 679, 728 f., 731 f., 744
  Vol. 2: 32 f., 599, 625, **788–805, 807–809**, 842
  Vol. 3: 112 f., 711
Crown **Vol. 1:** 118, 163, 204, **405–408**, 470, 648, 652
  Vol. 2: 96, 200, 204, 244, 691, 695, 795
  Vol. 3: 182, 483, 748, 750, 809, 1067
Crown of boasting **Vol. 1:** 229
  Vol. 2: 901
Crown of glory **Vol. 3:** 323
Crown of life **Vol. 2:** 136, 775
Crown of thorns **Vol. 1:** 726
Crucified **Vol. 1:** 135, 178, 244, 248, 300, 387, 393–396, 439, 455, 466, 473, 564, 629, 633, 643, 727
  Vol. 2: 203 f., 242, 267, 273, 282, 291, 340, 367, 388, 400, 412, 420, 715, 718
  Vol. 3: 55, 60, 71, 276
Crucifixion **Vol. 1:** 154, 162 f., 168, 290, 298, 304, 390–396, 516, 630
  Vol. 2: 32, 150, 204, 295, 299, 327, 368, 379, 526 f.
  Vol. 3: 185, 202, 211, 243, 583, 732, 1047, 1059

Crucify **Vol. 2:** 270, 544, 718
Cruel **Vol. 1:** 108, 392 f., 520, 652
Cruelty **Vol. 2:** 98, 680
  Vol. 3: 542
Crumb **Vol. 1:** 252
Crusaders in Palestine **Vol. 2:** 308
Crush **Vol. 1:** 261, 610
  Vol. 2: 260 f., 807
Cry **Vol. 1:** 342, 360, **408–412**, 464, 610, 615,
  623, 724
  Vol. 2: 82 f., 175, 178 f., 215, 229, 328, 355,
  361, 416–424, 426, 631, 855, 862, 873, 922
  Vol. 3: 50, 53, 54, 118, 202, 782
Cry aloud **Vol. 3:** 48
Cry out **Vol. 3:** 114
Cryptic **Vol. 1:** 619
Crystal, D. **Vol. 3:** 394, 396, 398, 1127
Crystal sea **Vol. 2:** 615
Cuff **Vol. 1:** 163
Culinary **Vol. 2:** 211
Cullmann, Oscar **Vol. 1:** 148
  Vol. 2: 907 f.
  Vol. 3: 333, 618
Culmination **Vol. 1:** 541
  Vol. 2: 59, 917
Culpable **Vol. 1:** 364
  Vol. 2: 139
  Vol. 3: 132, 342, 1025, 1052
Culprit **Vol. 1:** 415
Cult **Vol. 1:** 53, 64, 66, 69, 101 f., 109, 123, 142,
  207, 224, 226, 255, 294, 340, 367, 444,
  498 f., 514, 529, 560, 587, 595, 599, 625,
  649, 653, 655, 687, 698, 708
  Vol. 2: 42, 60, 74, 92, 97, 108 f., 164, 185,
  190 f., 206, 226, 228, 233, 235, 265, 285 f.,
  307, 310, 327, 335, 375, 440, 650, 726, 891,
  923
  Vol. 3: 33, 37, 42, 50, 78 f., 101, 104, 150,
  161, 205, 217, 221, 234 f., 237, 239, 317 f.,
  427, 531, 544, 608, 672 f., **781–797**, 847, 852,
  1010, 1105
Cultic **Vol. 1:** 58, 66, 99 f., 122, 150, 210 f.,
  219 f., 223, 250, 291 f., 296, 304, 307, 310,
  322, 351, 367, 390, 401, 403, 438, 447, 468,
  479, 495, 497, 499, 538, 586, 607, 650, 687,
  699, 716, 742
  Vol. 2: 41, 53, 61, 63, 92–95, 134, 164, 185,
  223, 225, 227 f., 234, 288, 296 f., 306, 336,
  349, 353–355, 410, 461, 511, 520, 525, 778,
  887
  Vol. 3: 45, 77, 94, 98, 101 f., 105, 118, 149,
  154 f., 157, 162, 167, 190, 194, 207 f., 236,
  239, 267, 417, 503, 549, 551 f., 556, 653,
  668, 738, 782, 925, 982, 1055, 1068, 1148,
  1154
Cultic centre **Vol. 2:** 325 f.
Cultic prostitution **Vol. 3:** 1068 f.
Cultic regulations **Vol. 2: 441**
Cultivate **Vol. 1:** 681
  Vol. 2: 211, 275, 710
Cultivated **Vol. 2:** 660
Cultivation **Vol. 1:** 416, 520, 726
Cultural **Vol. 1:** 518, 583
  Vol. 2: 373

  Vol. 3: 1066
Cultural equality **Vol. 2:** 309
Cultural pluralism **Vol. 3:** 1048
Culture **Vol. 1:** 59, 68, 70, 452, 522, 543, 598,
  625, 640, 732
  Vol. 2: 124–126, 161 f., 287, 308, 311, 462,
  582, 640, 645, 680, 820, 841
  Vol. 3: 776 f., 851, 1063, 1124, 1147
Cultured **Vol. 3: 1081–1119**
Cumanus **Vol. 3:** 452
Cumber **Vol. 1:** 73
Cummin **Vol. 2: 210 f.**
Cuneiform **Vol. 1:** 68
Cunning **Vol. 1:** 282, **412 f.,** 509
  Vol. 2: 616
  Vol. 3: 136, 943
Cup **Vol. 1:** 109, 111, 213, 369, 529, 633
  Vol. 2: 96, **274–277,** 297, 516, **521–536,** 854
  Vol. 3: 242, 245, 604, 670, 1018
Cup of blessing **Vol. 1: 521 f.,** 529, 532
Cup of consolation **Vol. 2:** 417
Cup of fury **Vol. 3:** 242
Cup of salvation **Vol. 3:** 208
Cup of suffering **Vol. 2:** 276
  Vol. 3: 723
Cup of wrath **Vol. 3:** 745
Cup-shaped **Vol. 1:** 240
Cupbearer **Vol. 3:** 49
Cure **Vol. 1:** 119, 218, 428
  Vol. 2: 164, **166–171**
  Vol. 3: 938
Curetes **Vol. 2:** 552
Curiosity **Vol. 3:** 76, 79
Curious **Vol. 1:** 266
  Vol. 2: 552–562
Currency **Vol. 2:** 96, 574
  Vol. 3: 791, 808
Curse **Vol. 1:** 78, 85, 97 f., 108, 113, 173, 202,
  207–210, 214 f., 219, 266, 286, 332, 367,
  369, 389 f., **413–418,** 421, 452, 463 f., 509,
  547, 554, 673, 719, 724–726, 743
  Vol. 2: 143, 157, 166, 245, 257, 267, 402,
  445, 478, 504 f., 516, 519, 561, 623, 630,
  638, 650, 709, 723, 741, 874, 885, 896
  Vol. 3: 72, 76, 84, 95, 98, 226 f., 256, 311,
  340, 345, 347, 363, 424, 444, 449, 469, 471,
  474, 520, 581, 597, 620, 683, 738–740, 743,
  853, 928, 1009, 1025, 1036, 1055, 1069,
  1074, 1078, 1087, 1103 f., 1107, 1112, 1125,
  1148
Curtain **Vol. 1:** 280, 677
  Vol. 2: 212, 673
  Vol. 3: 543, **794 f.,** 814
Cushite **Vol. 2:** 638, 684
Custodian **Vol. 1:** 370, 573, 579
  Vol. 2: 445
  Vol. 3: 580, **775–780,** 935
Custody **Vol. 2:** 132, 134
  Vol. 3: 591
Custom **Vol. 1:** 70, 164, 196, 257, 288, 308–
  310, 314 f., 364, 394, 402, 406, 511, 570,
  586, 611, 626 f., 629, 631, 655, 687
  Vol. 2: 132 f., 159, 162, 221, 254, 310 f., 317,
  331, 335 f., **417, 436–456,** 581, 584, 641, 657,

714, 790, 799
  Vol. 3: 409 f., 488, 573, 764, 773, 819, 944, 1059
Customary Vol. 1: 709
Customs duties Vol. 3: 752–759
Customs house Vol. 3: 755–759
Customs officer Vol. 3: 756
Cut Vol. 1: 309, 368, 527
  Vol. 2: 220
  Vol. 3: 377, 392
Cut down Vol. 1: 725
  Vol. 3: 867, 919
Cut off Vol. 1: 65, 239, 308, 463, 465, 467, 472, 561, 654
  Vol. 2: 314, 385
  Vol. 3: 98, 227, 229, 262, 447, 538, 590, 1059
Cut oneself Vol. 2: 417
Cut short Vol. 2: 222
Cut straight Vol. 3: 351 f.
Cutheans Vol. 3: 450, 456
Cutting-edge Vol. 2: 97
Cybele Vol. 1: 142, 560
Cycle Vol. 1: 182, 635–630, 654
  Vol. 2: 375
  Vol. 3: 842 f.
Cycle of births Vol. 3: 679
Cyclical history Vol. 2: 891
Cyclical pattern Vol. 3: 260
Cymbals Vol. 3: 76, 112
Cyme Vol. 2: 289
Cynics Vol. 1: 127, 137, 143, 459, 645
  Vol. 2: 735, 841
  Vol. 3: 50, 593, 1039
Cypress Vol. 1: 389
  Vol. 3: 866
Cyprian Vol. 2: 869
  Vol. 3: 385
Cyprus Vol. 1: 68, 167, 497
  Vol. 2: 74, 467, 557, 740
Cyrene Vol. 2: 740
  Vol. 3: 598 f.
Cyrenean synagogue Vol. 1: 297
Cyrus Vol. 1: 52, 54, 111, 273, 340, 393, 686
  Vol. 2: 335 f., 791, 830
  Vol. 3: 51, 218, 566, 788, 851, 960

Dagger Vol. 3: 966, 978
Dagon Vol. 1: 625
  Vol. 3: 785–787, 817
Daily Vol. 1: 249–253, 261, 278, 624, 630, 702
  Vol. 2: 268, 326, 328, 871, 883, 885, 895
Daily offering Vol. 2: 294
Dais Vol. 2: 369
Damage Vol. 1: 182, 563, 678
  Vol. 2: 307, 705
  Vol. 3: 27, 136–138, 561
Damage to crops Vol. 3: 95
Damages Vol. 3: 94, 95 f.
Damaging Vol. 2: 309
Damascus Vol. 1: 368, 528
  Vol. 2: 320, 486, 513, 523, 895
  Vol. 3: 114, 284, 288, 453, 520, 731 f., 751, 757, 948, 1110

Damascus Rule Vol. 1: 67
Damasus of Rome Vol. 1: 71
  Vol. 2: 508
Damnation Vol. 1: 423, 657
  Vol. 2: 362, 365
  Vol. 3: 579
Damning Vol. 1: 413
Dan Vol. 1: 52, 70
  Vol. 2: 306, 317, 319, 789
  Vol. 3: 33, 426, 782, 872
Dance Vol. 2: 436
  Vol. 3: 673
Dancing Vol. 1: 108, 625 f., 709
  Vol. 2: 418
Danger Vol. 1: 116, 187, 241, 278, 299, 372, 381, 419 f., 430, 440, 455, 482, 484, 489 f., 496, 510, 553, 559, 594, 611 f., 622, 651, 663, 693, 695, 703, 715
  Vol. 2: 86, 96, 123, 137, 307, 328, 385, 412, 460, 843 f.
  Vol. 3: 177, 184, 200, 205, 216, 475, 681, 685, 748, 802, 805, 833, 908, 983, 1003, 1008, 1058
Dangerous Vol. 1: 108, 509, 565, 585
  Vol. 3: 103
Daniel Vol. 1: 50, 52, 75, 103 f., 340, 345, 512, 672
  Vol. 2: 96, 174, 215 f., 373 f., 555, 586, 610, 622, 627 f., 905, 912 f.
  Vol. 3: 80, 270, 275, 279, 557, 616, 860, 881, 914, 950 f., 960, 983, 1029
Dare Vol. 1: 364
  Vol. 2: 432
Daric Vol. 2: 848
Darius Vol. 1: 393
  Vol. 2: 847
  Vol. 3: 427
Dark Vol. 1: 203, 218, 257, 647
  Vol. 2: 193, 199, 351
Dark saying Vol. 2: 756–758
Darken Vol. 1: 421, 449
  Vol. 2: 156, 183, 422
  Vol. 3: 731, 733–736
Darkness Vol. 1: 102, 110, 204, 276, 301, 333, 338, 355, 359, 379, 382, 420–425, 450, 452, 462, 483, 490, 519, 522, 525, 556, 563, 609 f., 656, 723
  Vol. 2: 53, 71, 185, 190, 206, 212, 215–218, 302, 380, 382, 471, 473, 484 f., 487, 490–496, 514, 543, 548, 586, 604, 608 f., 632, 637, 645, 672, 709, 742, 834, 839, 868, 928
  Vol. 3: 47, 204, 260, 262, 270, 344, 435, 469–471, 495, 503, 553–556, 592, 693, 732, 736, 750, 807, 831, 839, 849, 872, 891, 902, 929, 939, 944, 963, 979, 1149, 1151
Darnel Vol. 3: 523
Dart Vol. 1: 656, 682
  Vol. 3: 959–967
Datames Vol. 2: 848
Date Vol. 1: 477, 627 f., 630 f., 634, 739
  Vol. 2: 894, 901
  Vol. 3: 191, 653, 838, 844
Dathan Vol. 1: 195
  Vol. 2: 638

Daughter **Vol. 1:** 256, 283, 395, 499, 614 f., 655
  Vol. 2: 213, 317, 325–327, 548, 575, 581, 588, 677
  Vol. 3: 180, 1057 f., 1062, 1074
Daughter of Abraham **Vol. 3:** 180
Daughter of Jerusalem **Vol. 2:** 325
  Vol. 3: 1062
Daughter of Judah **Vol. 3:** 1071
Daughter of Zion **Vol. 2:** 327
Daughter-in-law **Vol. 2:** 584
Daughter's inheritance **Vol. 3:** 1057
David **Vol. 1:** 53, 61, 65 f., 100, 108, 117 f., 122, 141, 170, 177, 195, 209, 266, 332, 349, 366, **425–428,** 430, 473, 538, 544
  Vol. 2: 35, 79, 98, 113, 116 f., 138, 147, 186, 237 f., 248, 260, 306, 324 f., 329, 335–337, 340, 354, 376, 378, 431, 515, 540, 591, 691, 727, 733, 802, 815, 838, 848
  Vol. 3: 73, 77, 117, 121, 158 f., 187, 191, 203, 206, 212, 219, 245, 300, 311, 366 f., 408, 418, 423, 426, 439, 468, 478–480, 494, 522 f., 557, 565 f., 572, 588, 594, 605, 607–609, 611 f., 616, 621, 636 f., 643, **648–662,** 673, 692, 699, 715, 736, 742, 783, 787 f., 794, 797, 812, 815, 836, 872 f., 875 f., 879, 957, 960, 1010, 1017, 1055, 1057, 1104 f., 1188
David *redivivus* **Vol. 1:** 426
Davidic descent **Vol. 3:** 651 f., 662
Davidic dynasty **Vol. 1:** 596
  Vol. 2: 306, 325, 374, 612
  Vol. 3: 461
Davidic king **Vol. 1:** 100, 210, 405
  Vol. 2: 227, 335, 701
  Vol. 3: 462, 650
Davidic messiah **Vol. 3:** 566, 650, 657 f.
Davidic sonship **Vol. 3:** 652, 791, 1073
Davidic tradition **Vol. 3:** 639
Dawn **Vol. 1:** 630
  Vol. 2: 109, 151, 289, 495
  Vol. 3: 267
Day **Vol. 1:** 272, 321, 366, 422 f., 425, 451, 473, 477, 513 f., 612, 619, 627–631, 731, 737
  Vol. 2: 232, 245 f., 351, 359, 364, 426, 491, 496, 658, 691, **886–935**
  Vol. 3: 74, 410, 628, 633, 730 f., 826, 841, 846 f., 849, 996
Day of atonement **Vol. 1:** 114, 116, 151, 221, 223 f., 351, 612, 626, 628, 700
  Vol. 2: 29, 151, 199, 294, 296, 350, 598, 652, 718
  Vol. 3: 35, 38 f., 41, 150 f., 156, 161–165, 173, 192, 194, 198 f., 243, 323, 366, 418 f., 428, 433 f., 753, 788, 794, 812, 815, 941, 947, 989
Day of Christ **Vol. 1:** 147, 229, 742
  Vol. 2: 47, 130, 360, 707, 894, 922
  Vol. 3: 315
Day of conflict **Vol. 1:** 382
Day of favour **Vol. 1:** 382
Day of God **Vol. 2:** 245, 266, 894
Day of judgment **Vol. 1:** 289, 329, 358, 467
  Vol. 2: 64, 218, 366 f., 383, 385, 413, 438, 605, 894, 909

  Vol. 3: 51, 96, 98, 117, 197, 203, 272, 316, 318 f., 359, 370, 567, 633, 809, 817, 836, 842, 961
Day of the Lord **Vol. 1:** 75, 466 f.
  Vol. 2: 37, 140, 517, 700, 887 f., 890 f., 893 f., 901, 916, 924, 926
  Vol. 3: 315, 318, 731, 750, 836, 842, 844, 847, 924 f., 1001
Day of massacre **Vol. 2:** 72
Day of opportunity **Vol. 1:** 115, 174
Day of preparation **Vol. 3: 119 f., 405–411,** 472
Day of rest **Vol. 3:** 256, **405–415**
Day of salvation **Vol. 1:** 440, 638
  Vol. 2: 242, 353 f., 894
  Vol. 3: 214, 838
Day of the Son of man **Vol. 2:** 894
Day of testing **Vol. 1:** 473
Day of tribulation **Vol. 3:** 197
Day of vengeance **Vol. 3:** 93
Day of visitation **Vol. 1:** 190
Day of wrath **Vol. 1:** 110
  Vol. 2: 894
Day of Yahweh **Vol. 1:** 190, 423, 655
  Vol. 2: 53, 58, 363, 887 f., 890 f., 893
  Vol. 3: 381
Day-star **Vol. 2:** 495
  Vol. 3: 468, 734
Daybreak **Vol. 2:** 289
  Vol. 3: 736
Daylight **Vol. 2:** 490
Days of the Messiah **Vol. 3:** 829
Dayspring **Vol. 1:** 191
Dazzling **Vol. 1:** 708
Deacon **Vol. 1:** 198, 472
  Vol. 2: 238, 563, 838
  Vol. 3: 544–553, 808, 922, 924, 930, 1066 f.
Dead **Vol. 1:** 79, 103, 120, 125, 147, 166, 186, 204 f., 221, 225, 232–234, 240, 254, 256, 261, 263–265, 290, 312 f., 329, 342, 346, 352, 359, 384 f., 390, 400–402, 410, 421, 429–447, 450–452, 463, 469 f., 475, 484, 499, 523, 544, 569, 591 f., 605, 609 f., 612, 625, 649, 653, 668 f., 676 f., 696
  Vol. 2: 29 f., 32, 50, 58, 63, 78 f., 91 f., 113, 122, 178, 190, 204–210, 303, 340, 358, 365 f., 387 f., 403, 417–424, 433, 435, 477–483, 554, 559, 577, 603–606, 612, 625, 630 f., 643, 680, 701 f., 714, 763 f., 796, 830, 865, 893 f., 922, 924, 929
  Vol. 3: 56, 104, 113, 149, 204 f., 246, 254, 259 f., 262, 272, 276, 312, 387, 553, 651, 832, 984, 989, 1100
Dead orthodoxy **Vol. 3:** 1151
Dead Sea **Vol. 2:** 319
  Vol. 3: 444, 983, 1008
Dead Sea Scrolls (→ Qumran)
Dead works **Vol. 1:** 116, 351, 599
Deadly **Vol. 1:** 645
Deaf **Vol. 1:** 220, **428 f.,** 509
  Vol. 2: 170 f., 175, 358, 414, 633, 729
  Vol. 3: 180, 475, 519, 860, 1000
Deaf-mute **Vol. 2:** 560, 630
Deal justly **Vol. 3:** 192
Deal out **Vol. 2:** 438

Vol. 3: 402–404
Deal unjustly **Vol. 3: 573–576**
Dealer **Vol. 2:** 236
Dealings **Vol. 1:** 548, 680
  Vol. 2: 235, 287, 309 f., 342, 353, 366
  Vol. 3: 139
Dear **Vol. 2:** 547
  Vol. 3: 677
Death **Vol. 1:** 73, 78, 84–86, 93, 96, 113, 118,
  120, 131, 142, 144, 147 f., 150 f., 154, 158,
  168, 173, 180 f., 187, 205, 207 f., 221–224,
  231–237, 240, 248, 257, 264–266, 288, 301–
  303, 309 f., 314 f., 321, 323, 326–328, 331,
  336, 343, 346, 354, 359, 364–367, 371,
  374 f., 380, 387, 389–395, 398–406, 409,
  416–424, **429–447,** 455, 458, 463–474, 482 f.,
  500 f., 505, 507, 511 f., 518, 524, 525, 529,
  543, 548 f., 552, 556–559, 563 f., 571, 586,
  611, 619, 622 f., 628–630, 634, 638, 643 f.,
  646, 649–651, 654, 659, 672–677, 681 f.,
  686, 702, 707–709, 718 f., 722 f., 738, 740
  Vol. 2: 28–30, 42, 48 f., 57–59, 61, 78–80, 83,
  101 f., 106, 111, 119 f., 123, 126, 131, 133,
  136, 138, 142 f., 150, 179, 185 f., 191, 204–
  210, 212, 217, 222, 224, 229, 232, 234, 239,
  242, 245, 262 f., 270 f., 273, 276, 282, 291,
  300, 303 f., 318, 327, 333, 338–343, 351,
  360, 364 f., 367 f., 370, 380, 382, 398, 403,
  411, 416–424, 431, 433 f., 441–443, 445 f.,
  449 f., 471–474, 478–484, 498, 504 f., 512,
  514, 516 f., 519, 522, 525, 527, 532–536,
  543, 545 f., 552 f., 555, 564, 568, 570, 577,
  581–584, 592, 598, 604, 617, 624, 631 f.,
  636, 638, 641, 644, 655, 663, 665, 671,
  674 f., 680, 687, 691 f., 694, 696, 706, 708,
  715–718, 723, 727, 732 f., 736, 738, 761–
  764, 777, 781 f., 787, 808, 811, 816, 824,
  840, 854, 858, 882, 887, 889, 893, 897, 900,
  903, 908, 911, 914, 917–920, 924–930
  Vol. 3: 35, 38, 42, 55, 59, 62, 66, 74, 82,
  94–96, 99, 102 f., 107, 113, 129, 137, 140,
  142, 145, 151, 155, 157–160, 162–165, 167–
  169, 171–174, 178–180, 183, 186, 188 f.,
  193–196, 198 f., 200–202, 205 f., 210–212,
  220, 224, 226, 231, 237, 242, 244 f., 257,
  260–262, 266–268, 270, 277, 279–281, 302,
  322 f., 341–343, 349, 364, 366, 388, 400,
  405, 408, 410, 415, 424 f., 429, 432 f., 436,
  444, 465, 471, 473, 487, 489, 493 f., 498,
  501, 504, 514, 528–530, 534, 552, 554,
  557 f., 563, 566 f., 571, 576, 578–582, 584–
  586, 590, 594, 596 f., 600–603, 612, 624,
  631, 641, 680, 682, 685 f., 692, 694, 697 f.,
  702, 704 f., 718, 720 f., 723, 748, 750 f., 772,
  774, 778 f., 785, 790, 793, 795, 806, 812,
  815, 825, 832, 835, 837 f., 840, 844, 846–
  848, 858, 910, 915, 921, 935–941, 956, 984,
  995, 997 f., 1005, 1011, 1017, 1019, 1021,
  1030, 1040, 1043 f., 1047, 1049, 1061, 1073,
  1079, 1092, 1099, 1101, 1109, 1112, 1117,
  1152, 1154
Death-duty **Vol. 3:** 415
Death-penalty **Vol. 3:** 448, 1069
Death-warrant **Vol. 1:** 471

Deathbed **Vol. 1:** 586
Debar **Vol. 2:** 286
Debased **Vol. 1:** 671
Debate **Vol. 1:** 601, 631, 715
  Vol. 2: 311, 362, 448
  Vol. 3: 530–532, 820, 1082 f.
Debauchery **Vol. 1:** 458, 496, 654
  Vol. 3: 918, 947
Debit **Vol. 1:** 471
Deborah **Vol. 2:** 796
  Vol. 3: 556, 836, 1001, 1057
Debt **Vol. 1:** 226, 402, 698, 701
  Vol. 2: 39, 115, 118, 120, **666–668,** 822, 837
  Vol. 3: 96, 172, 191, 594, 758, 943
Debtor **Vol. 1:** 505, 702
  Vol. 2: 40, 168, 254, **666–668,** 858, 898
  Vol. 3: 189, 758
Decadence **Vol. 3:** 396
Decalogue **Vol. 1:** 54, 336 f., 717
  Vol. 2: 68, 173, 278, 284, 441, 444, 637, 639
  Vol. 3: 377, 405 f., 418, 484, 488, 787, 1013,
  1041, 1102, 1118, 1120 f., 1148
Decapitate **Vol. 1:** 391
Decay **Vol. 1:** 266, 385, 470, 480, 500, 552, 683
  Vol. 2: 206, 244, 714, 884
  Vol. 3: 292, 302
Deceased **Vol. 1:** 265, 431
Deceit **Vol. 1:** 296, 299, 421, 509, 551
  Vol. 2: 437, **457–461**
  Vol. 3: 136, 574, 880
Deceitful **Vol. 2: 457–461, 470–474**
Deceitfulness **Vol. 2:** 155, 183, **457–461,** 844
Deceive **Vol. 1:** 85, 124–126, 212, 336, 413,
  430, 468, 481, 508, 552, 592, 657
  Vol. 2: 457–461, 470–474, 701 f., 795, 914
  Vol. 3: 361 f., 468, 573,. 706, 755, 873
Deceiver **Vol. 2: 457–461**
  Vol. 3: 475
Decency **Vol. 1:** 501
  Vol. 2: 95
  Vol. 3: 573
Decent **Vol. 2:** 256
Deception **Vol. 1:** 87, 126, 550, 693
  Vol. 2: 317, **457–461,** 555
  Vol. 3: 278, 876, 892 f., 936
Deceptive **Vol. 1:** 546, 550, 709, 726
Decide **Vol. 1:** 60, 472, 533, 565, 610, 648, 651,
  695
  Vol. 2: 314, **362–367**
Decide upon **Vol. 2:** 817
Decimal **Vol. 1:** 692
Decimate **Vol. 2:** 698
Decision **Vol. 1:** 107, 112, 123, 129, 190, 195,
  217, 244, 273, 291, 293, 304, 308, 330, 356,
  365, 373, 395, 423 f., 457, 476 f., 482, 485,
  488, 491, 503, 533 f., 536 f., 540–542, 547,
  562, 567, 586, 600 f., 607, 609, 625, 681,
  695, 697, 703, 720, 732
  Vol. 2: 55, 116, 130, 135, 181, 223, 311, 313,
  342, **362–367,** 377 f., 384–386, 391, 567, 727,
  736, 873
  Vol. 3: 125, 128, 177, 235, 480 f., 582, 691,
  745, 821, 834, 838, 849, 938, 944, 1017,
  1111, 1117, 1121, 1157

Decisive **Vol. 1**: 482, 488, 597, 739
 Vol. 2: 87, 119, 122, 157, 338, 357, 407, 907
 Vol. 3: 258, 833
Declaration **Vol. 1**: 402, 702, 738
 Vol. 2: 379, 396, 547
Declaratory **Vol. 1**: 596
Declaratory formula **Vol. 3**: 104, 745
Declare **Vol. 1**: 344, 574–576, 604 f., 719, 736
 Vol. 2: 380
 Vol. 3: 47, 316, 760
Declare openly **Vol. 3**: 1080
Declare useless **Vol. 3**: **808–810**
Decline **Vol. 1**: 454
 Vol. 2: **855–859**
Decompose **Vol. 3**: 293
Decomposition **Vol. 1**: 265
Decoration **Vol. 1**: 495, 522, 524
 Vol. 3: 119
Decrease **Vol. 2**: 130
Decree **Vol. 1**: 244, 322, 326, 330, 363, 393, 402, 414, 563, 690, 693, 695 f., 734
 Vol. 2: 79, 108, 233, 237, 296, 366, 399, 441, 450, 574, 622
 Vol. 3: 51, 311, 325, 354, 484, 503 f., 882
Decry **Vol. 1**: 727
Dedicate **Vol. 1**: 413 f.
 Vol. 2: 43, 673
 Vol. 3: 194, 406 f.
Dedication **Vol. 1**: 273, 414, 470, 492, 537, 633, 705
 Vol. 2: 855, 889
 Vol. 3: 157, 207, 366, 415, 552, 873
Dedication of Temple **Vol. 1**: 629
Deduction **Vol. 2**: 391, 396, 402
 Vol. 3: 824
Deed **Vol. 1**: 79, 212, 214, 236, 243 f., 254, 271, 457, 482, 546, 556, 568, 572, 679, 713, 719, 722 f.
 Vol. 2: 42, 118, 366, 380, 386, 443, 819
 Vol. 3: 45, 52, 215, 318, 484, 882 f., 1038, **1147–1158**
Dead of cession **Vol. 1**: 505
Deed of sale **Vol. 3**: 478, 498
Deem **Vol. 1**: 595
Deem worthy **Vol. 3**: 348 f.
Deep **Vol. 1**: 522, 670
 Vol. 2: 197 f., 205, 424
Deep things **Vol. 2**: 198, 401
Deep-seated **Vol. 2**: 197
Deepen **Vol. 2**: 405
Defamation **Vol. 3**: **341–345**
Defame **Vol. 3**: **341–345**
Defamer **Vol. 3**: **345 f.**
Default **Vol. 3**: 379
Defeat **Vol. 1**: 433, 438–440, 470, 508, 525, 644, 646, 649 f.
 Vol. 2: 147, 211, 320, 367
 Vol. 3: 45, 573, 601
Defect **Vol. 1**: 56, 107, 219
 Vol. 2: 98, 160, 415
 Vol. 3: 925
Defection **Vol. 1**: 606–608
Defective **Vol. 1**: 352, 593
Defence **Vol. 1**: 51, 373, 528, 590, 612, 726

 Vol. 2: 75, 138, 148, 307, 319, 398, 450
 Vol. 3: 97, 118, 950
Defence force **Vol. 2**: 306
Defenceless **Vol. 1**: 416
 Vol. 2: 257, 411–413, 615, 710
 Vol. 3: 557
Defend **Vol. 2**: 865
 Vol. 3: 93, 824
Defendant **Vol. 1**: 558
Defender **Vol. 1**: 89
Defending Counsel **Vol. 1**: 83, 89
Defer **Vol. 2**: 779
Deference **Vol. 2**: 94
 Vol. 3: 112
Deferential **Vol. 1**: 609
Defiance **Vol. 2**: 360
 Vol. 3: 475
Deficiency **Vol. 3**: **952–956**
Defile **Vol. 1**: 96, 205, 265, 384, 390, 393, **447–449**, 468, 499, 639, 642, 671
 Vol. 2: 126, 224, 230, 285
 Vol. 3: 106, 108, 173, 344, 925, 932, 953
Defilement **Vol. 1**: 152, 204, 225, 479 f., 507, 559, 641, 677, 688
 Vol. 2: 586 f.
 Vol. 3: 153, 428, 440, 469, 793, 869, 914, 1165
Define **Vol. 1**: 710
Definite **Vol. 1**: 693, 734
Definition **Vol. 1**: 331, 501, 506, 681
 Vol. 3: 1086
Deformed **Vol. 1**: 287, 479
 Vol. 2: 415
Defraud **Vol. 1**: 137 f.
 Vol. 3: **379 f.**
Degenerate **Vol. 2**: 361
 Vol. 3: 95
Degradation **Vol. 2**: 50 f., 299, 772
 Vol. 3: 1062
Degrading **Vol. 2**: 162, 661
Degree **Vol. 2**: 304
Dehistorizing **Vol. 1**: 380
Deification **Vol. 1**: 616, 705
 Vol. 2: 99, 239, 394, 404, 498, 876, 898
 Vol. 3: 634
Deism **Vol. 1**: **70,** 71
 Vol. 2: 902
Deists **Vol. 3**: 290
Deity **Vol. 1**: 75, 676, 740
 Vol. 2: 49, **66,** 81, 86, 92, 99, 166, 271, 284, 287, 303, 318, 342, 352, 378, 396, 430, 584
 Vol. 3: 100, 124
Dejection **Vol. 2**: 417, 433
Delay **Vol. 1**: 693, 742
 Vol. 2: 220 f., 698, 765, 771 f., 900 f., 912, 921
 Vol. 3: 97, 215, 578, **839–845**
Delegate **Vol. 1**: 130, 132, 408
 Vol. 2: 376, 607
Delegation **Vol. 1**: 197
Deliberate **Vol. 1**: 372, 473, 502, 722
 Vol. 2: 273, 407, 445
 Vol. 3: 28, 125, 585
Delight **Vol. 1**: 534

Vol. 2: 60, 115, 282 f., 355, 478, **817–820**
Vol. 3: 407, 648, 1019
Delinquent **Vol. 1:** 561
Deliver **Vol. 1:** 195, 236, 238, 326, 409, 414 f., 436, 459, 466, 547, 558, 566, 599 f., 623, 650, 734
 Vol. 2: 78, 82, 146, 150, 353, **361–371,** 387, 394, 418, 442, 447, 479, 681, 817
 Vol. 3: 30, 174, **177–221**
Deliver up **Vol. 1:** 693
 Vol. 2: 340, 411, 526, 534
Deliverance **Vol. 1:** 68, 70, 99, 141, 315, 345, 438 f., 531 f., 544, 554, 566, 596, 655, 699, 701 f.
 Vol. 2: 55, 83, 363, 413, 421, 485, 642, 807, 824, 863, 868, 920
 Vol. 3: 135, **177–221,** 357, 425, 470, 724, 911, 960, 1097, 1102, 1111
Deliverer **Vol. 1:** 54, 320
 Vol. 2: 329, 363
Delivering **Vol. 3: 216–221**
Delivery **Vol. 3:** 53
Delphi **Vol. 1:** 653
 Vol. 2: 392, 558 f.
 Vol. 3: 75, 103, 379, 474, 782, 851
Delphic Apollo **Vol. 1:** 574 f.
 Vol. 3: 739
Delphic oracle **Vol. 3:** 310
Delta **Vol. 1:** 531
Delude **Vol. 1:** 552
 Vol. 2: 457–461
Deluge **Vol. 3: 991**
Delusion **Vol. 1:** 546
 Vol. 2: 349, **457–461,** 473
Demand **Vol. 1:** 84, 271, 334, 368, 396, 398, 402,.406, 426, 482, 489, 491 f., 510, 538, 571, 588, 595, 598–600, 602, 616, 626 f., 640, 643, 647, 714, 719, 730, 738
 Vol. 2: 75, 77, 102, 123, 132, 135, 147, 184, 224, 244, 262, 281, 285, 301, 394, 396, 399, 427, 445, 469, 812, 833, **855–859**
 Vol. 3: 46, 72, 531, 766
Demean **Vol. 1:** 449
 Vol. 2: 259
Demented **Vol. 1:** 529
Demeter **Vol. 1:** 215
 Vol. 2: 233
 Vol. 3: 739
Demetrius **Vol. 1:** 419
 Vol. 2: 139
 Vol. 3: 784, 1045
Demiurge **Vol. 1:** 387, 521
Democracy **Vol. 1:** 732
Democritus **Vol. 1:** 521
 Vol. 2: 233
 Vol. 3: 840
Demolish **Vol. 3: 177–189**
Demon **Vol. 1:** 54, 95, 102, 119, 121, 168, 219, 322, 382, 409, 415, 431, 446, **449–454,** 508 f., 529 f., 567, 572, 611, 625, 632, 636 f., 643, 651
 Vol. 2: 34, 74, 85, 159, 165–167, 189, 196, 205, 208, 210, 225, 228, 251, 273, 284, 286, 379, 382, 426, 452, 518, 556, 561, 600, 610,

615, 630 f., 648 f., 691, 702, 877, 921
 Vol. 3: 108, 149, 344, 444, 462, 468, 470–473, 476, 586, 643, 657, 693 f., 696, 713, 725, 738, 770, 806, 810, 856, 910, 939, 982, 984, 1004–1006, 1059, 1061, 1109
Demon-possessed **Vol. 1:** 79, 453
 Vol. 2: 595
Demon-possessed land **Vol. 3:** 463
Demon-possession **Vol. 2:** 165, 631
Demoniac **Vol. 1:** 117, 340, 420, 427, 572, 576
 Vol. 2: 231, 623
 Vol. 3: 592, 714
Demonic **Vol. 1:** 114, 139, 151, 408, 414, 449, 452, 500, 510 f., 522, 527, 611, 613, 644, 650 f.
 Vol. 2: 73 f., 136, 179, 195, 270, 284–286, 485
 Vol. 3: 97, 102 f., 180, 310, 343, 433, 592, 690, 831, 983–987, 989 f., 998, 1008
Demonstrate **Vol. 2:** 404
 Vol. 3: 569–571, 759
Demonstration **Vol. 1:** 411, 613, 628
 Vol. 2: 165, 315, 352, 398, 416, 422, 427, 461
 Vol. 3: 570 f.
Demosthenes **Vol. 1:** 498
 Vol. 3: 679
Demythologization **Vol. 1: 54,** 57, 59, 380, 523, 583
 Vol. 2: 189, 202, **645 f., 906 f.**
 Vol. 3: 328, 1048
Den **Vol. 2:** 586, 628
 Vol. 3: 378, **380 f.,** 430
Denarius **Vol. 1:** 118
 Vol. 2: 288, 850 f.
 Vol. 3: 920, 979
Denck, Hans **Vol. 3:** 148
Denial **Vol. 2:** 265, 291, 394, 924
 Vol. 3: 208, 212, 240, 903
Denizen **Vol. 1:** 510
Denounce **Vol. 1:** 641
 Vol. 2: 311, 380
Denunciation **Vol. 1:** 410
 Vol. 2: 312
Deny **Vol. 1:** 74, 126, 202, 268, 346 f., 421, 427, 433, **454–456,** 469, 482, 489 f., 493, 525, 535, 552, 562, 608, 611, 644, 657, 678, 691, 708, 718, 730
 Vol. 2: 135, 161, 222, 229, 296, 361, 398, 444, 459, 471, 473, 707, 775
 Vol. 3: 200, 281, 343, 625, 646, 683, 1025, 1050
Depart **Vol. 1:** 181, 209, 320, 442, 558 f., 606 f., 611, 634
 Vol. 2: 312, 421, 924
 Vol. 3: 121, **534–543,** 580
Departed **Vol. 2:** 559
Departure **Vol. 1:** 607, 676
 Vol. 2: 317, 420, 777
 Vol. 3: 863, **935–943,** 946
Depend on **Vol. 1:** 591, 649, 659
 Vol. 2: 120, 446
Dependable **Vol. 1:** 97, 594, 596
Dependence **Vol. 1:** 84, 311, 355, 375, 385 f., 484, 616, 664, 673, 681, 700

Dependence (*cont'd*)
  Vol. 2: 116, 162, 416 f., 432, 667, 821 f.
  Vol. 3: 342, 498, 552, 589, 595, 677, 869 f.
Dependent **Vol. 1:** 385, 427, 440, 480, 541 f., 612, 730
  Vol. 2: 121, 132, 262, 306, 336
  Vol. 3: 728, 813
Depersonalize **Vol. 1:** 566, 612
Depict **Vol. 1:** 689 f.
Deplore **Vol. 2:** 594
Depopulate **Vol. 3: 1004–1008**
Depopulation **Vol. 1:** 109
  Vol. 2: 60
Deport **Vol. 1:** 686
Deportation **Vol. 2:** 306, 691
  Vol. 3: 249, 590
Depose **Vol. 1:** 315
  Vol. 3: 254
Deposit **Vol. 2:** 27, 39, 586
  Vol. 3: 61, 73, 255
Depravation **Vol. 3:** 396
Depraved **Vol. 1:** 398, 565
  Vol. 3: 361, 579
Depravity **Vol. 1:** 559, 677
  Vol. 3: 996
Depreciation **Vol. 1:** 524
  Vol. 2: 315
  Vol. 3: 1058
Depreciatory **Vol. 2:** 259
Depression **Vol. 1:** 163, 262
Deprivation **Vol. 2:** 267
Deprive **Vol. 1:** 679
  Vol. 2: 49, 201, 257, 361
  Vol. 3: 379 f.
Depth **Vol. 1:** 253
  Vol. 2: 183, **197–205**, 209, 212, 677
  Vol. 3: 504
Dereliction **Vol. 1:** 615
  Vol. 3: 211
Derision **Vol. 2:** 358, 432
  Vol. 3: 29
Derivation **Vol. 1:** 56 f., 662, 674, 696
Derogatory **Vol. 1:** 732
  Vol. 2: 259, 263, 305, 372, 428, 452
Descartes, R. **Vol. 1:** 504
  Vol. 3: 899
Descend **Vol. 1:** 675, 704
  Vol. 2: 184 f., 205, 209, 326, 329, 922
  Vol. 3: 630 f., 691
Descendant **Vol. 1:** 81, 285 f., 288, 427, 434, 473
  Vol. 2: 247, 297, 369
  Vol. 3: 251, 524, 634, 652, 734
Descendants of Abraham **Vol. 1: 79**, 80, 366
  Vol. 2: 120, 301, 314, 452, 570
Descendants of Adam **Vol. 1:** 96
Descendants of David **Vol. 1:** 366
  Vol. 2: 337, 378
Descendants of Joseph **Vol. 2:** 636
Descendants of Levi **Vol. 2:** 447, 592, 693
Descendants of Noah **Vol. 1:** 366
Descendants of patriarchs **Vol. 2:** 317
Descent **Vol. 1:** 187, 283, 289, 427, 433, 438, 525, 541, 557, 616, 619, 667, 677, 681, 683

  Vol. 2: 35, **185**, 312, 381, 447, 452, 656, 660, 796, 924 f.
  Vol. 3: 393, 471, 629, 632, 870
Descent into hell **Vol. 1:** 677
  Vol. 2: 303
Descent of Jesus **Vol. 1:** 77, 619
  Vol. 2: 79, 113, 320
Describe **Vol. 1:** 57, 573–576, 580
  Vol. 2: 385
Description **Vol. 1:** 57, 614
  Vol. 2: 343
Descriptive Ethics (→ Ethics, Descriptive)
Desecration **Vol. 1:** 75, 125, 448, 626
  Vol. 2: 38, 223
  Vol. 3: 452, 173
Desecularization **Vol. 1:** 122
Desert **Vol. 1:** 411, 451, 509, 550, 729, 739
  Vol. 2: 265 f., 305, 635
  Vol. 3: 189, 508, 534, **1004–1014**
Deserted **Vol. 3: 1004–1008**
Deserter **Vol. 1:** 606
  Vol. 2: 572
Desertion **Vol. 1:** 716
Deserts **Vol. 1:** 722
Deserve **Vol. 1:** 434, 489
  Vol. 2: 142, 718
  Vol. 3: 144, 349
Deserving **Vol. 3:** 348
Design **Vol. 1:** 556, 670
  Vol. 2: 675, 819
  Vol. 3: 902
Designation **Vol. 1:** 332, 473, 501, 623, 626, 735
  Vol. 2: 79, 333, 648
Designer **Vol. 1:** 279
  Vol. 3: 331
Desirable **Vol. 1:** 729
Desire **Vol. 1:** 98, 106, 137, 169, 187, 211, 231, 233, 236, 336, 343, 359, 401, 412, 424, **456–461**, 494 f., 501 f., 509, 528, 530, 533 f., 537, 555, 557, 611, 630, 645 f., 671 f., 676, 678, 680 f., 692, 723 f., 726, 734
  Vol. 2: 47, 62, 116, 121, 182 f., 200, 262, 265, 274, 356, 377, 391, 419, 458, 460, 478, **538–547**, 583, 588, 599, 814–816, **817–820**, 843, 856, 874, 925
  Vol. 3: 231, 676 f., 680, 702, 799, 866, 934, **1015–1023**
Desist **Vol. 3:** 255
Desolate **Vol. 1:** 174, 411
  Vol. 3: 1004–1008
Desolation **Vol. 1:** 75, 114, 173 f., 411, 610
  Vol. 2: 54, 82 f., 299, 738
  Vol. 3: 444, **1004–1008**
Desolation, abomination of (→ Abomination of desolation)
Despair **Vol. 1:** 106, 314, 411
  Vol. 2: 478
  Vol. 3: 560, 565, 691, 1051
Despise **Vol. 1:** 74, 400, 453, 455, **461 f.**, 542, 555
  Vol. 2: 221, 258, 310, 363, 435, 440, 838
  Vol. 3: 27 f., 215, 777
Despised **Vol. 2:** 48, 50 f.

429

Vol. 3: 593
Despoil **Vol. 1:** 651
  Vol. 3: 379, 859
Despondency **Vol. 1:** 622
  Vol. 2: 259
Despot **Vol. 1:** 272
Despotic rule **Vol. 2:** 607
Destination **Vol. 2:** 184 f., 327
  Vol. 3: 121, 352
Destined **Vol. 3:** 382, 686, 1018
Destiny **Vol. 1:** 50, 107, 260, 377, 379 f., 431,
  434, 436, 450, 464, 477, 489, 534, 595, 677,
  692 f., 716
  Vol. 2: 52, 70, 138, 209, 288, 308, 383, 412,
  430, 481, 510, 709, 782
  Vol. 3: 117, 206, 260, 265, 269, 272, 507,
  610, 616, 623, 629, 650, 677 f., 686, 835,
  940, 1045
Destitute **Vol. 1:** 318
  Vol. 2: 254
  Vol. 3: 853
Destitution **Vol. 3:** 191, 748
Destroy **Vol. 1:** 104, 110 f., 151, 163, 168, 219,
  254, 322, 390, 395, 399, 401, 414, 425, 434,
  436, 446, 451, 459, **462–471**, 500, 521, 530,
  546, 552, 554 f., 563, 608, 623, 638, 655–
  657, 661, 672, 698, 701
  Vol. 2: 33, 58, 99, 126, 151, 154, 195, 226,
  252, 285, 306 f., 328, 363, 368, 373, 378,
  435, 460, 715, 798, 831, 893
  Vol. 3: 97, 99, 166, **177–189**, 214, 250, 471,
  535, 537, 574, 686, 934, 949
Destroyer **Vol. 1:** 101, 379, 462, 465, 467
  Vol. 2: 677
  Vol. 3: 859, 1091
Destroying angel **Vol. 1:** 101
Destruction **Vol. 1:** 103, 113, 141, 205, 222,
  236, 248, 254, 354, 413–415, 425, 431, 452,
  462–469, 525, 554, 593, 608, 610–612, 629,
  654, 657, 685, 692, 724
  Vol. 2: 33, 61, 72, 110, 149, 154, 225, 236,
  238, 271, 275, 306, 366, 413, 418, 422, 446,
  552, 661, 679, 681 f., 705, 709, 844, 846,
  914–916
  Vol. 3: 159, 193, 201, 210, 214, 262, 266,
  268, 474, 748, 779, 784, 790–792, 795, 804,
  820, 853, 866, 869, 938, 940, 992, **1004–1008**,
  1058
Destruction of Jerusalem **Vol. 2:** 37 f., 312
Destructive **Vol. 1:** 207, 210, 413, 416, 418,
  452, 457, 459, 461, 463, 555, 561, 563
  Vol. 2: 27
  Vol. 3: 986, 1096
Detach **Vol. 1:** 674, 715
Detachment **Vol. 3: 958–967**
Detail **Vol. 2:** 385
Detain **Vol. 2:** 221
Detention **Vol. 2:** 132
Determination **Vol. 1:** 240, 648
  Vol. 2: 818 f.
Determine **Vol. 1:** 54, 326, 457 f., **471–478**, 533,
  540, 542, 571, 648, 695–697, 722, 734 f., 737
  Vol. 2: 64, 66, 75, 123, 132, 156, 160, 162,
  203, 332, 339, 383 f., 430, 432, 609, 662 f.

Vol. 3: 121, 504, 1073
Determine by lot **Vol. 2: 295–303**
Determinism **Vol. 1: 54**
  Vol. 3: 577
Deterministic **Vol. 2:** 56, 72
Deterrent **Vol. 1:** 392, 568
  Vol. 3: 448
Detest **Vol. 2:** 350
Deucalion **Vol. 2:** 124
Deutero-Isaiah **Vol. 1: 54**
  Vol. 3: 609
Deutero-Pauline **Vol. 1:** 55, 247
Deuteronomic **Vol. 1: 55**, 332, 426
Deuteronomic reform **Vol. 3:** 1096
Deuteronomic school **Vol. 1:** 53, **55**
Deuteronomist **Vol. 1: 55**
  Vol. 2: 258, 367
Deuteronomistic **Vol. 1: 55**
  Vol. 2: 325, 355, 374
Deuteronomistic circles **Vol. 3:** 1093
Deuteronomy **Vol. 1:** 53, **54f**., 61, 65, 209, 331,
  463, 484, 538
  Vol. 2: 317, 355, 823
  Vol. 3: 139, 249, 406, 805
Devalue **Vol. 1:** 674
  Vol. 2: 310, 313, 427
Devastate **Vol. 3: 1004–1008**
Devastation **Vol. 1:** 109, 380, 734
  Vol. 3: 729, 859, **1004–1008**, 1068
Develop **Vol. 1:** 164, 485, 686, 692, 694, 740
  Vol. 2: 223, 310, 391, 841
Development **Vol. 2:** 65, 131, 288, 367, 387 f.,
  923
  Vol. 3: 58, 280, 760
Deviant **Vol. 1:** 514
Deviate **Vol. 2:** 363, 457
  Vol. 3: 583
Deviation **Vol. 3:** 577, 583, 903
Device **Vol. 2:** 289
  Vol. 3: 1027
Devil **Vol. 1:** 73, 104, 110, 118, 166–168, 173,
  204, 223, 287, 335, 436, 438, 458, 504, 509,
  515, 542, 557, 559, 561, 563, 565–567,
  609 f., 651
  Vol. 2: 143, 207, 267, 312, 365, 381 f., 403,
  472, 602, 608 f., 701, 728, 811, 893
  Vol. 3: 99, 174, 321, 362, **468–476**, 499, 523,
  718, 796, 807, 831, 892, 944, 962, 1054,
  1150, 1155
Devilish **Vol. 1:** 432
Devious **Vol. 2:** 235
Devise **Vol. 1:** 532
  Vol. 3: 820
Devise craftily **Vol. 3: 1026–1034**
Devoid **Vol. 1:** 546
Devote **Vol. 1:** 151, 641 f., 645
  Vol. 2: 768
Devoted **Vol. 2: 232–236**, 262, 399, 838
  Vol. 3: 377
Devotion **Vol. 1:** 58, 239, 265, 329, 413, 469,
  492, 510
  Vol. 2: 136, 236, 270, 538, 547, 572
  Vol. 3: 322, 572, 687, 954
Devotion to duty **Vol. 3:** 565 f.

Devour **Vol. 1:** 508, 655 f., 730
  Vol. 2: 421
Devout **Vol. 1:** 537, 539, 597, 641, 666, 691, 708
  Vol. 2: 53, 85, 90–92, 94, 167, **223–238**, 265, 272, 302, 353, 418, 451, 471, 550, 803
  Vol. 3: 361
Dew **Vol. 1:** 177
  Vol. 2: 307, 586, 865 f.
  Vol. 3: 255, 267–269
Dewey, John **Vol. 3:** 896
Diachronic linguistics **Vol. 3:** 1140
Diachrony **Vol. 3:** 1140, 1142
Diadem **Vol. 1:** 405
  Vol. 2: 693
Diadochoi **Vol. 2:** 372
Diagnosis **Vol. 2:** 464
Dialect **Vol. 3:** 1078
Dialectic **Vol. 1:** 533
  Vol. 2: 171
  Vol. 3: 1086
Dialectical Theology **Vol. 3:** 326, 328
Dialogue **Vol. 2:** 867
  Vol. 3: 492, 1083 f., 1086
Diamond **Vol. 3:** 391, 396
Diana **Vol. 2:** 85
  Vol. 3: 1071
Dianoetic virtues **Vol. 3:** 926
Diary **Vol. 1:** 243
Diaspora **Vol. 1:** 55, 66, 68, 128, 197, 246, 360, 364, 475, 499, 544, 607, 617 f., 626, 693
  Vol. 2: 33 f., 91, 398, 449, 695, 792, 795
  Vol. 3: 38, 287, 485, 644, 752, 853, 1040
Dibelius, M. **Vol. 3:** 63, 85
Dichotomy **Vol. 1:** 233
Dictate **Vol. 1:** 247 f., 573
  Vol. 3: 329
Dictation **Vol. 3:** 491
Dictator **Vol. 1:** 475
Didache **Vol. 1:** 51, **55**, 370
  Vol. 2: 219, 870, 895 f.
  Vol. 3: 89, 402, 412, 770, 929
Didactic **Vol. 2:** 628, 743
Die **Vol. 1:** 181, 219, 234, 256, 314, 327, 352, 397, 400 f., 429–447, 460, 466, 505, 520, 525, 585, 610, 625, 629 f., 659, 676 f., 681, 689, 717 f.
  Vol. 2: 59, 120, 207, 226, 232, 269, 271, 289, 326, 339, 350, 368, 398 f., 411, 927
  Vol. 3: 254, 293, 364, 631, 689, 719, 826
Dietary laws **Vol. 1:** 473
  Vol. 2: 211
  Vol. 3: 931
Difference **Vol. 1:** 601 f., 631
  Vol. 2: 101, 127, 307, 397, 499, 657, 739
  Vol. 3: 534
Different **Vol. 1:** 485, 500, 539, 670, 673, 707–709
  Vol. 2: 739–742, 794
  Vol. 3: 638, 1056
Differentiate **Vol. 1:** 504
  Vol. 2: 310
  Vol. 3: 353
Difficult **Vol. 1:** 364, 419, 536

  Vol. 2: 155, 308, 316
  Vol. 3: 177
Difficulty **Vol. 1:** 164, 229, 260, 262, 419 f., 516, 581, 725
  Vol. 2: 257, 320, 414, **807–809**
Dig **Vol. 2:** 210
  Vol. 3: 434
Digest **Vol. 2:** 269
Dignify **Vol. 3:** 30
Dignity **Vol. 1:** 193, 537, 668
  Vol. 2: 49 f., 91, 101, 146, 159 f., 262, 340, 563
  Vol. 3: 545, 583, 596, 1059
Digression **Vol. 2:** 458
Dike **Vol. 2:** 729
  Vol. 3: 353
Dilepton **Vol. 2:** 850
Diligence **Vol. 2:** 271
Diligent **Vol. 2:** 255
  Vol. 3: 953
Dill **Vol. 2:** 210 f.
Dilthey, W. **Vol. 3:** 1138
Dilute **Vol. 3:** 911, 913
Dimension **Vol. 1:** 680
  Vol. 2: 103, 197
Diminish **Vol. 2:** 288
Diminutive **Vol. 2:** 410 f.
Dinner **Vol. 2:** 358, **520–538**
Dio Cassius **Vol. 2:** 324, 679, 792
Diodore of Tarsus **Vol. 2:** 505
Diodorus **Vol. 2:** 679
Diodorus Siculus **Vol. 1:** 580
  Vol. 2: 116
Diogenes of Apollonia **Vol. 2:** 476
Diogenes Laertius **Vol. 2:** 430
  Vol. 3: 727
Diogenian **Vol. 2:** 757
Diognetus, Epistle to **Vol. 1:** 51
Dionsysiac **Vol. 2:** 539
Dionysius of Alexandria **Vol. 2:** 507
Dionysius of Halicarnassus **Vol. 1:** 314, 320, 580
  Vol. 2: 116, 476
Dionysius of Syracuse **Vol. 1:** 640
Dionysus **Vol. 1:** 64, 184, 513 f., 528 f., 625, 647, 649
  Vol. 2: 430, 674
  Vol. 3: 318, 919, 1085
Dioscuri **Vol. 1:** 687
Diotrephes **Vol. 1:** 453
  Vol. 3: 241
Dip **Vol. 1:** 144 f.
  Vol. 2: 150
Diplomatic **Vol. 3:** 51
Direct **Vol. 1:** 330 f., 340, 483, 486, 509, 597, 693, 696, 718, 737
  Vol. 2: 50
  Vol. 3: 45, 834
Direction **Vol. 1:** 357, 423, 481, 484, 492, 512
  Vol. 2: 236, 271, 377, 406
  Vol. 3: 121, 351, 572, 820, 945 f., 1153
Directive **Vol. 1:** 341, 476
Director **Vol. 1:** 279
Dirge **Vol. 2:** **416–424**
  Vol. 3: 673 f.

Dirt **Vol. 1:** 315, **479 f.**, 520
　Vol. 2: 57
　Vol. 3: 108, 278, 916
Dirty **Vol. 3:** 102
Disability **Vol. 1:** 727
　Vol. 2: 414 f.
　Vol. 3: 475, 932
Disadvantage **Vol. 1:** 288
　Vol. 3: 134, **136–138**
Disagreement **Vol. 1:** 107, 110, 628, 693
Disappear **Vol. 1:** 675, 699, 718
　Vol. 2: 312
Disappearance **Vol. 1:** 607, 654, 671, 683
Disappoint **Vol. 2:** 240
　Vol. 3: 209
Disappointed **Vol. 3: 562–564**
Disappointment **Vol. 1:** 202, 585, 594, 724 f.
　Vol. 2: 241, 316, 420, 618
Disapproval **Vol. 1:** 572, 681
Disarm **Vol. 1:** 314, 649, 651
　Vol. 2: 382
Disaster **Vol. 1:** 450, 462, 565, 608, 725
　Vol. 2: 56, 225, 417, 435
　Vol. 3: 27, 393, 919, 1089
Disastrous **Vol. 1:** 699
Disbelief **Vol. 1:** 504, 591, 594
　Vol. 2: 473, 544
　Vol. 3: 313, 911
Disc **Vol. 1:** 523
　Vol. 2: 188, 556
Discard **Vol. 1:** 674
Discern **Vol. 1:** 123, 353, 504, 673
　Vol. 2: 328
　Vol. 3: 173, 358, 517
Discernment **Vol. 3:** 522, 533, 695, 703, 770, 776, 1023, 1027
Discernment of spirits **Vol. 1:** 300, 452
Discerner **Vol. 2:** 365
Discerning **Vol. 2:** 616
Discernment **Vol. 2:** 391, 616
Discharge **Vol. 1:** 74, 577, 683, 697 f.
　Vol. 2: 586
　Vol. 3: 103, **177–189**
Disciple **Vol. 1:** 136, 148, 153, 166 f., 183, 200, 203 f., 213 f., 239, 251 f., 256, 262, 266, 274, 276, 284–290, 298, 303–307, 321, 323 f., 328, 335, 337 f., 340, 358, 402 f., 415, 417, 419, 430, 439, 443, 453–455, 464, **480–494**, 504, 510, 528, 540, 542, 545, 556, 559, 561, 572, 577 f., 600, 603, 612 f., 615, 617, 619 f., 623, 628, 630, 642, 644, 659, 684, 686, 689, 722, 729, 733, 741 f.
　Vol. 2: 31, 34, 38, 57, 63, 76, 84, 87, 104, 106, 112, 136 f., 144, 150, 155, 159, 164 f., 168 f., 176, 178, 180, 183, 193 f., 216 f., 222 f., 229, 232, 250, 255, 262, 267, 272, 276, 281 f., 291, 311, 328, 330 f., 339, 341–343, 350, 358 f., 365, 382 f., 387 f., 401, 403, 405, 411, 413, 417, 420, 427–430, 432, 434, 450, 462, 473, 482, 486 f., 493, 510, 518, 523 f., 528, 532, 535, 544, 550, 597, 610, 614, 619, 632, 642, 652–654, 666, 695, 697, 702, 706, 709, 713–715, 732 f., 736–739, 752, 754, 766, 773, 781, 787, 795, 801, 806, 809,
825, 827, 831 f., 834, 838, 843, 846, 856, 867, 879 f., 902, 904, 909, 911, 916 f., 921, 929 f.
　Vol. 3: 56 f., 59, 115, 118, 121, 129, 131 f., 136, 147, 184, 188, 204, 213, 226, 228, 240, 242, 253, 256–258, 276 f., 289, 291, 293, 313 f., 321, 325, 340, 343, 347, 378, 393 f., 409, 429, 445–447, 449, 453, 456, 470 f., 474, 476, 480 f., 503, 506 f., 509, 540, 546, 628, 648, 670, 697, 705, 708, 710, 713, 717, 723, 734, 741, 746, 763, 767, 792, 803 f., 806 f., 821, 848 f., 854, 920, 922, 941, 947, 954, 967, 985, 995, 1003, 1012, 1043 f., 1061, 1079, 1108, 1113, 1164
Discipleship **Vol. 1: 480–494,** 541, 607, 722
　Vol. 2: 104, 139, 203, 262, 543 f., 631, 699, 782, 824 f.
　Vol. 3: 107, 253, 623, 625, 757, 1053, 1108
Disciplina arcana **Vol. 3:** 461
Disciplinary **Vol. 1:** 392, 414
Discipline **Vol. 1:** 152, 171, 192, 233, 288, 299, 415, 460, 462, **494–503,** 506, 515, 535, 539, 561, 569, 572, 639, 647, 652
　Vol. 2: 140 f., 230, 243 f., 266, 350, 367, 391, 459, 575, 579, 582 f., 588, 668, 722, 733, 775, 782, 867 f., 897
　Vol. 3: 95, 97, 99, 102, 214 f., 384, 471, 535, 538, 544, 561, 745, 750, **759–780,** 821, 954, 998, 1024, 1064, 1075
Disclaim **Vol. 1:** 592
　Vol. 2: 150, 470
Disclose **Vol. 1:** 50, 313
　Vol. 2: 212
　Vol. 3: 310–316
Disclosure **Vol. 3: 310–324**
Disclosure situation **Vol. 3:** 336
Disconcerted **Vol. 3:** 562
Discontent **Vol. 3:** 556, 805
Discontinuity **Vol. 2:** 919 f.
　Vol. 3: 236
Discord **Vol. 1:** 646
Discount **Vol. 1:** 399
Discourage **Vol. 2:** 259, 266
Discouragement **Vol. 3:** 494
Discourse **Vol. 1:** 62, 575, 578
　Vol. 3: 1086 f., 1106
Discover **Vol. 2:** 296
　Vol. 3: 527–530
Discredit **Vol. 1:** 529
　Vol. 2: 340
Discreet **Vol. 2:** 103
Discrepancy **Vol. 2:** 261
　Vol. 3: 184, 883
Discretion **Vol. 1:** 555
　Vol. 2: 90
　Vol. 3: 354, 957
Discrimination **Vol. 1:** 219, 737
　Vol. 2: 362, 391
　Vol. 3: 395
Discuss **Vol. 3:** 668, **820 f.**
Discussion **Vol. 1:** 338, 488, 506, 552, 595
　Vol. 3: 530–532, 1083
Disdain **Vol. 1:** 112, 587
　Vol. 3: 27

Disdainful **Vol. 2:** 284
Disease **Vol. 1:** 119, 124, 234, 451, 505, 515, 527, 636
   Vol. 2: 138, 164, 170, 349, 414, 421, 463 f., 553
   Vol. 3: 104, 178, 189, 473, 748, 858, 860, 910, **993–996** (*also* → Sickness)
Disfavour **Vol. 2:** 261, 267
Disfigure **Vol. 2:** 433, 831
   Vol. 3: 562
Disgrace **Vol. 1:** 288, 391–393
   Vol. 2: 48 f., 51, 140, 284, 572, 583, 658
   Vol. 3: 240, **562–564**, 856
Disgraceful **Vol. 3: 562–564**
Disguise **Vol. 1:** 709 f.
   Vol. 3: 864, 948
Dish **Vol. 1:** 633
   Vol. 2: 556
Disharmony **Vol. 2:** 781
Dishonesty **Vol. 1:** 137
   Vol. 2: 282, 837
   Vol. 3: 377, 566
Dishonour **Vol. 1:** 282, 393
   Vol. 2: 47–51, 160
   Vol. 3: 377, **562–564**
Disillusionment **Vol. 1:** 679, 743
Disinherit **Vol. 2:** 257
Disintegrate **Vol. 1:** 470
   Vol. 3: 446
Dislike **Vol. 2:** 705
Dislocation **Vol. 3:** 903
Disloyal **Vol. 2:** 312, 396
Dismay **Vol. 3:** 166
Dismembered **Vol. 1:** 230
Dismiss **Vol. 1:** 505, 701
   Vol. 3: 177–189
Disobedience **Vol. 1:** 86, 110, 203, 211, 356 f., 367, 385, 390, 399, 422 f., 433, 463, 465, 472, 509, 555, 588 f., 591, 598, 607, 611, 659, 730
   Vol. 2: 144, 172, 175, 179, 272, 400, 407, 459 f., 473, 564 f., 627, 667, 682, 716, 820, 864
   Vol. 3: 97, 118, 130, 134 f., 139, 185, 382, 481, 563, 565, 573, 585, 740, 779, 799, 809, 938, 1155
Disobedient **Vol. 1:** 102, 109, 202, 219, 449, 569, 588 f., 593 f.
   Vol. 2: 181, 183, 202, 301, 367, 478, 481, 490, 653, 721, 880
   Vol. 3: 691, 1008, 1014
Disorder **Vol. 1:** 468
   Vol. 2: 458, 621–626, 780
   Vol. 3: 148
Disown **Vol. 1:** 454 f., 684
   Vol. 2: 383, 641
   Vol. 3: 560
Disparage **Vol. 1:** 413, 461
   Vol. 3: 346
Disparate **Vol. 1:** 525
Dispatch **Vol. 1:** 698
Dispensation **Vol. 1:** 53, 81, 372, 730
   Vol. 2: 40, 115, 365, 443, 641
Dispense **Vol. 1:** 211, 503 f.

Vol. 2: 363, 370
Dispenser of the Spirit **Vol. 3:** 697 f.
Disperse **Vol. 2:** 33 f., 413
Dispersion **Vol. 1:** 55, 141, 361, 394, 671, **683–692**
   Vol. 2: 33, 35, 126, 306, 308, 310 f., 316, 324, 326, 331 f., 426, 740
   Vol. 3: 65 (*also* → Diaspora)
Display **Vol. 1:** 649, 696 f.
Display in public **Vol. 3:** 571
Displeasure **Vol. 1:** 318, 740
   Vol. 2: 149, 419
Disposal **Vol. 1:** 414, 536, 723
   Vol. 2: 275, 368
   Vol. 3: 268
Dispose **Vol. 1:** 369, 539, 640, 657, 715
   Vol. 3: 263
Disposed **Vol. 2:** 259
Disposition **Vol. 1:** 107, 485, 511
   Vol. 2: 102, 392, 501, 622, 659
   Vol. 3: 111 f., 123, 125, 127, 684, 912
Dispossess **Vol. 2:** 265
Disproof **Vol. 3:** 202
Disproportion **Vol. 1:** 743
Disprove **Vol. 1:** 74
   Vol. 2: 340
Disputation **Vol. 3:** 1086
Dispute **Vol. 1:** 104, 285, 294, 373, 453–455, 504, 535, 558, 578, 687
   Vol. 2: 140–142, **362–367**, 550, 680
   Vol. 3: 281, 346, 532, 820 f., 887, **958–967**, 999, 1119, **1155–1158**
Disqualified **Vol. 3: 808–810**
Disqualify **Vol. 1:** 163, 235, 514
   Vol. 2: 415, 424
Disregard **Vol. 1:** 333, 454, 461 f., 607
   Vol. 2: 325, 402, 448, 683
Disrepair **Vol. 3:** 788
Disrepute **Vol. 2:** 363
Disrespectful **Vol. 2:** 334, 432
   Vol. 3: 1055
Disruption **Vol. 2:** 250
   Vol. 3: 468
Dissatisfaction **Vol. 1:** 459
   Vol. 3: 1051
Dissection **Vol. 1:** 533
Dissension **Vol. 1:** 535
   Vol. 2: 362, 708
   Vol. 3: 1119
Dissimulate **Vol. 2: 468–470**
Dissipation **Vol. 1:** 261, 514, 686
   Vol. 3: 922
Dissociation **Vol. 2:** 334
Dissolute **Vol. 1:** 496
   Vol. 2: 480
   Vol. 3: 856
Dissolution **Vol. 1:** 496, 578
   Vol. 2: 325, 629
   Vol. 3: 832
Dissolve **Vol. 1:** 688, 698, 707
   Vol. 2: 33, 452
   Vol. 3: 178, 559
Dissuade **Vol. 1:** 450
   Vol. 3: 902

Distance **Vol. 1:** 583, 618, 679, 693
  Vol. 2: 90, 94, 197, 215, 876
  Vol. 3: 595
Distant **Vol. 2:** 53, 713
Distinct **Vol. 3:** 874
Distinction **Vol. 1:** 227, 385, 503, 533, 662, 720
  Vol. 2: 80, 302, 308, 355; 399, 403, 425, 457, 660, 683
  Vol. 3: 85, 106, 317, 534
Distinctiveness **Vol. 1:** 240
Distinguish **Vol. 1:** 60, **503–505**, 527, 533, 599, 614, 705, 723, 735, 737
  Vol. 2: 84, 121, 226, 319, 333, 358, 362, 364, 391, 395, 397 f., 442
  Vol. 3: 108, 127, 475, 526, 535, 701, 707
Distort **Vol. 3:** 332
Distraction **Vol. 1:** **526–530**
Distress **Vol. 1:** 106, 111, 260, 262, 345, 409 f., 422, 461, 645
  Vol. 2: 63, 82, 215, 229, 265, 353, 357, 360 f., 419, 423 f., 594, **621–626**, 663–665, 715, **807–809**, 855, 863, 890, 904
  Vol. 3: 210, 239, 388, 505, 514, 558, 560, 836, **858 f.**, 860, 1011
Distribute **Vol. 1:** 365, 453, 533–535, 641
  Vol. 2: 33, 436, 438 f.
Distribution of alms **Vol. 3:** **544–549**, 957
District **Vol. 2:** 303 f., 788
Distrust **Vol. 2:** 167
Disturb **Vol. 1:** 698
  Vol. 3: 556, **709 f.**
Disturbance **Vol. 2:** 623, 777
  Vol. 3: 112, 558
Disunite **Vol. 1:** 108
Disunity **Vol. 1:** 535
Diversity **Vol. 1:** 602, 654
  Vol. 2: 719
Divert **Vol. 1:** 741
  Vol. 2: 458
Dives **Vol. 2:** 267, 846
  Vol. 3: 240, 856
Divest **Vol. 1:** 549
Divi filius **Vol. 3:** 635
Divide **Vol. 1:** 398, 503 f., 523, 533–535
  Vol. 2: 189, 296 f., 362, 788, 810
  Vol. 3: 468, 472, **534–544**
Divide asunder **Vol. 3:** 684
Divided monarchy **Vol. 2:** 320
Divided heart **Vol. 3:** 687
Dividing wall **Vol. 3:** 185 f., **795, 948–950**
Divination **Vol. 2:** 296, **552–562**
  Vol. 3: 33
Divine **Vol. 2:** **66**, 72, 86, 94, 112, 120, 147, 149, 188, 224, 233, 236, 247, 255, 267, 269, 280, 287 f., 290, 293, 335 f., 351, 355, 357, 362, 365, 372 f., 378, 393, 402–404, 439, 475, 520, 659, 663, 719, 818
  Vol. 3: 33, 36, 41, 49, 117, 123, 635, 690
Divine attributes **Vol. 3:** 373
Divine honours **Vol. 3:** 217
Divine man **Vol. 2:** 107, 165, 498, 606
Divine nature **Vol. 1:** 216, 548, 706, 740
  Vol. 2: 80, 374
  Vol. 3: 71, 372, 832, 927

Divine origin **Vol. 1:** 85
  Vol. 2: 394
Divine passive **Vol. 3:** 1047
Divine philosophy **Vol. 3:** 1035
Divine secret **Vol. 1:** 578
Divine statement **Vol. 3:** **324 f.**
Divine warrior **Vol. 3:** 960
Diviner **Vol. 1:** 573, 575, 579
  Vol. 2: 234
  Vol. 3: 33
Divinity **Vol. 1:** 548 f., 551, 576, 616
  Vol. 2: **66**, 81 f., 86, **232–236**, 294, 373, 378
  Vol. 3: 663, 678, 965
Divinity of Jesus **Vol. 2:** 36, **80–83**, 504
Divinization **Vol. 1:** 498, 595, 643, 707
Division **Vol. 1:** 503, 533 f., 628, 631
  Vol. 2: 62, 306, 311, 315, 319, 708, 736, 794, 799, 887
  Vol. 3: 130, **543 f.**, 978
Division of day **Vol. 3:** 847
Division of time **Vol. 3:** 845–847
Divisive **Vol. 1:** 300, 400
Divorce **Vol. 1:** 243 f., 335, 340, 384, 453, 500, 502, **505–507**, 555, 607, 678, 698, 701
  Vol. 2: 138, 349 f., 563 f., 570, 588, 715
  Vol. 3: 95, 99, 172 f., **177–189**, 487, 498, **534–543**, 544, 660, 980, 1057, 1064, 1069, 1075, 1164, 1195
Dix, Gregory **Vol. 3:** 244, 675
Dizziness **Vol. 1:** 514
Do **Vol. 3:** **1147–1158**
Do business **Vol. 3:** **1155–1158**
Do good **Vol. 2:** 98, 101 f., 326, 429
  Vol. 3: 745
Do well **Vol. 1:** 610
Do wrong **Vol. 2:** 137
  Vol. 3: **573–576**, 859
Docetic **Vol. 1:** 339
  Vol. 2: 314, 402
Docetism **Vol. 1:** **55**, 58, 338
  Vol. 2: 504
  Vol. 3: 724
Doctor **Vol. 1:** 381
  Vol. 2: 59, 164, 167
  Vol. 3: 138, 217, 840
Doctrinal opinion **Vol. 2:** 311
Doctrine **Vol. 1:** 62, 70, 238, 247, 279, 282, 330, 341, 346, 544, 636–638, 662, 738–740
  Vol. 2: 64, 78, 95, 118 f., 152, 165, 170 f., 191, 219, 270, 273, 311, 358, 361, 367 f., 452, 460, 598, 652, 859
  Vol. 3: 51, 53, 61, 765, 769 f., 773 f., 1002
Document **Vol. 1:** 243, 246
  Vol. 3: 231, **482–495**, 497, 500, 1038, 1040 f., 1043
Dodd, C. H. **Vol. 1:** 56
  Vol. 2: **904–906**
  Vol. 3: 59, 62 f., 151
Doer **Vol. 3:** **1153–1155**
Dog **Vol. 1:** 117 f., 444, 744
  Vol. 2: 27, 539
Dogma **Vol. 1:** 50, 330, 533, 694
Dogmatics **Vol. 1:** 65, 707
Dogmatism **Vol. 1:** 486

Doing good **Vol. 3: 1153–1155**
Doing the truth **Vol. 3: 891**
Domain **Vol. 1:** 671
  Vol. 2: 381
Dome of the Rock **Vol. 3:** 787
Domestic **Vol. 1:** 574
  Vol. 2: 254, 410, 412
  Vol. 3: 443
Dominant **Vol. 2:** 442
  Vol. 3: 712–714
Dominate **Vol. 1:** 407, 424, 436, 457 f., 466
  Vol. 2: 182
Domination **Vol. 1:** 670
  Vol. 2: 688
Domineer **Vol. 3:** 1066
Dominion **Vol. 1:** 74, 102, 114, 165, 300, 381–383, 454, 462, 522, 524, 526, 610, 651, 701, 734
  Vol. 2: 51, 83, 120, 203, 208, 210, 287, 319, 388, **510–520**, 607, 649
  Vol. 3: 204, 648 f., 716
Domitian **Vol. 1:** 126
  Vol. 2: 378, 511, 514, 678, 684
  Vol. 3: 621, 653, 789
Donated **Vol. 3:** 140
Donation **Vol. 2:** 115
  Vol. 3: 874
Donatists **Vol. 3:** 108
Donkey **Vol. 1:** 117, 317
Donkey stone **Vol. 3:** 394
Doom **Vol. 1:** 85, 464, 610, 693, 699
  Vol. 2: 38, 367, 438
Door **Vol. 1:** 303, 646, 690
  Vol. 2: 29–31, 179, 194, 280, 434, 510, 726 f., 729, 881
  Vol. 3: 227, 556, 567, 936
Doorkeeper **Vol. 2:** 382, 912
Doorpost **Vol. 1:** 221
  Vol. 2: 410
  Vol. 3: 484
Doors of knowledge **Vol. 3:** 936
Dooyeweerd, H. **Vol. 3:** 899
Dorak **Vol. 2:** 98
Dorcas **Vol. 2:** 596
  Vol. 3: 1065
Dorian **Vol. 1:** 498
  Vol. 3: 1055
Doric **Vol. 2:** 124
  Vol. 3: 870
Dositheus **Vol. 3:** 463, 635
Double birth **Vol. 1:** 653
Double entendre **Vol. 3: 1177 f.**
Double heart **Vol. 2:** 468
  Vol. 3: 883
Double portion **Vol. 2:** 317
Double-minded **Vol. 1:** 505
  Vol. 2: 435
  Vol. 3: 572, 686 f.
Doubt **Vol. 1:** 76, 323, **503–505**, 596, 609
  Vol. 2: 142, 182, 241, 244, 282, 393, 419, 857, 863, 868
  Vol. 3: 341, 494, 528, 572, 778, 805, 809, 820, 1096
Dough **Vol. 1:** 249

  Vol. 2: 461–463, 675 f.
  Vol. 3: 194, 416, 917
Dove **Vol. 1:** 172, 175, 704
  Vol. 2: 313
  Vol. 3: 516
Dovetail **Vol. 1:** 241
Down payment **Vol. 2:** 39
  Vol. 3: 416
Downcast **Vol. 2:** 259 f.
Downfall **Vol. 1:** 462 f., 610
  Vol. 2: 320, 432, 890
  Vol. 3: 866
Downing, F. G. **Vol. 3: 329 f.**
Downwards **Vol. 2: 187**, 617
Dowry **Vol. 2:** 588
  Vol. 3: 1057
Doxology **Vol. 1:** 97–99, 210, 212 f., 620
  Vol. 2: 80 f., 122, 290, 724
  Vol. 3: 830, 1058
Drachma **Vol. 2:** 851 f.
  Vol. 3: 532, **752–755**
Dragon **Vol. 1:** 87, 104, 111, 114, 119, 125, 175, 187, 205, 390, 405, **507–511**, 562, 657
  Vol. 2: 29, 570 f., 613, 615, 625, 638, 642, 691, 693, 701
  Vol. 3: 216, 253, 470, 474, 476, 603, 714 f., 718, 737, 983 f., 987, 1046, 1068
Drain **Vol. 2:** 854
Drain cup **Vol. 3:** 919
Drama **Vol. 2:** 748
Dramatic **Vol. 2:** 430, 432
Draw **Vol. 1:** 458, 538
  Vol. 3: 483
Draw attention **Vol. 1:** 618
  Vol. 3: 516
Draw conclusion **Vol. 3:** 822 f.
Draw lots **Vol. 1: 478**
  Vol. 3: 49, 260
Draw near **Vol. 2:** 53, 388, 422
  Vol. 3: 860
Draw off blood **Vol. 3:** 448
Draw together **Vol. 2:** 113
Draw up **Vol. 1:** 576
Drawn out **Vol. 2:** 265, 636
Dread **Vol. 2:** 90, 224, 420
Dream **Vol. 1:** 393, 395, 420 f., 429, **511–513**, 574, 577, 580, 692
  Vol. 2: 92, 96, 185, 240, 307, 317, 319, 362, 433, 457, 468, 488, 555, 561, 586, 616, 898
  Vol. 3: 87, 316, 324, 392, 502, 517, 521, 555, 660, 723, 806, 1097
Dregs **Vol. 1:** 710
Dress **Vol. 1: 312–317**
  Vol. 2: 275, 303
  Vol. 3: 562
Dressing **Vol. 1:** 477
Drift **Vol. 1:** 481, 608, 682 f.
Drink **Vol. 1:** 106, 109, 451, 494, 504, 513, 528, 611 f., 625, 633, 683
  Vol. 2: 157, **264–277**, 295, 355, 357, 382, 387, 417, 520, 530, 929
  Vol. 3: 243, 245, 276, 359, 556, 706, 859, 988 f.
Drink-offering **Vol. 2: 853–855**

Vol. 3: 208, **423**
Drink toast **Vol. 2:** 356
Drip **Vol. 1:** 683
Drive **Vol. 1:** 494, 496, 590, 645, 675 f., 739
Drive across **Vol. 3:** 799
Drive away **Vol. 1:** 686
  Vol. 2: 417, 485, **805–807**
  Vol. 3: 558–560
Drive out **Vol. 1:** 453, 529 f., 608, 726, 740
  Vol. 2: 64, 151, 363
Driven by the wind **Vol. 3:** 1002
Drizzle **Vol. 3:** 1004
Drop **Vol. 1:** 608, 698
  Vol. 3: 255
Drop off **Vol. 1:** 682
Dropsy **Vol. 3:** 749
Drought **Vol. 1:** 209, 354, 543 f.
  Vol. 2: 193, 264, 688
  Vol. 3: 79
Drover **Vol. 3:** 268
Drown **Vol. 1:** 226, 508
  Vol. 2: 426
  Vol. 3: 109, 985, 990
Druids **Vol. 3:** 259
Drunkard **Vol. 1:** 513
  Vol. 3: 921
Drunken **Vol. 1:** 261, 420 f., 458, **513–515,**
  528 f., 561
  Vol. 2: 137, 458, 587, 625, 925
  Vol. 3: 918–922, 1047
Drunkenness **Vol. 3:** 556, 674, 913, **918–922**
Dry **Vol. 1:** 390, 513, 516
  Vol. 2: 153, 265
Dry up **Vol. 1:** 515 f., 652
  Vol. 3: 109, 867, 999
Dualism **Vol. 1: 55,** 58, 102, 124, 233, 333, 382,
  422, 432, 435, 446, 452, 461, 494, 496, 500,
  518, 522, 524 f., 562 f., 656, 674, 734
  Vol. 2: 71, 376, 402 f., 405 f., 434, 472, 492 f.,
  565, 567, 608, 610, 736, 840, 905, 919
  Vol. 3: 42, 631, 695, 831, 833, 891, 895, 899,
  1029, 1082, 1084
Dualistic **Vol. 3:** 41, 470, 595, 926, 939, 945,
  1101
Dualistic redemption **Vol. 2:** 201
Duality **Vol. 3:** 1056
Dubious **Vol. 1:** 352, 539
Due **Vol. 2:** 358
  Vol. 3: 134–136, 353 f., 753, **755–759**
Dull **Vol. 1:** 281, 428
  Vol. 2: 28, 183
Dumb **Vol. 1:** 220, **428 f.**
  Vol. 2: 171, 410, 729, 863
  Vol. 3: 474 f., 750, 1118
Dung **Vol. 1:** 480
  Vol. 3: 469, 915
Dupe **Vol. 2:** 458
Duplicity **Vol. 3:** 886, 889
Durable **Vol. 1:** 97, 658
Duration **Vol. 1:** 589 f., 711, 732
  Vol. 2: 374, 475, 478, 698
  Vol. 3: 827, 830
Durkheim, E. **Vol. 3:** 1125
Dust **Vol. 1:** 239, 254, 433 f., 520, 672, 705

Vol. 2: 261, 349, 478
  Vol. 3: 268, 545, 560, 683, 915
Duty **Vol. 1:** 190, 287, 295 f., 302, 358, 386,
  490, 505, 569 f., 606, 628, 633, 684, 687 f.,
  696
  Vol. 2: 43, 47, 223, 227, 327, 437, 439, 663,
  825
  Vol. 3: 49, 104, 608, **755–759,** 765, 810, 908
Dwell **Vol. 1:** 272, 519, 558, 676, 684, 691, 726,
  740
  Vol. 2: 75, 79, 164, 190, 193, 195, 215, 245,
  247–251, 326, 343, 866
  Vol. 3: 228, 254 f., 588, 781, **811–815**
Dwelling **Vol. 1:** 688
  Vol. 2: 190, 199, **247–251,** 586, 925
  Vol. 3: 224–229, 225, 784, **811–815**
Dwelling-place **Vol. 3: 224–229,** 465
Dye **Vol. 1:** 205
Dying **Vol. 1:** 145, 147, 225, 359, 401, 455, 470,
  638 f., 648
  Vol. 2: 83, 201, 525 f., 532, 644
  Vol. 3: 205, 227
Dynamic **Vol. 1:** 602, 681
  Vol. 2: 65, 171, 480
  Vol. 3: 1091, 1155
Dynamic monotheism **Vol. 2:** 71
Dynamic view of language **Vol. 3:** 1125
Dynasty **Vol. 1:** 596
  Vol. 2: 306, 325, 374

E source **Vol. 1: 56,** 57, 61, 511
E-temen-an-ki **Vol. 1:** 140 f.
Ea **Vol. 3:** 259
Ea-Enki **Vol. 2:** 553
Each **Vol. 1:** 94
  Vol. 2: 720
Eager **Vol. 2:** 244, 868
Eagle **Vol. 1:** 116, 173, 175, 262
  Vol. 2: 201
  Vol. 3: 805, 918, 1054
Ear **Vol. 1:** 230, 234, 261, 689
  Vol. 2: 110, 154, 172–176, 178, 267, 414, 726
  Vol. 3: 312, 434, 516 f., 594
Earlier **Vol. 1:** 666
  Vol. 2: 187, **713–716**
Earliest **Vol. 1:** 668
Early **Vol. 2:** 136
Early Catholicism **Vol. 2:** 918 f.
Early rain **Vol. 3: 1000–1004**
Earn **Vol. 1:** 78, 329, 437
  Vol. 2: 102, 200, 302, 499
  Vol. 3: 140, 142, 595
Earnest **Vol. 2:** 39 f., 883
Earnestness **Vol. 1:** 492, 612 f., 730
  Vol. 2: 859
Ears of corn **Vol. 3:** 408
Earth **Vol. 1:** 54, 95, 254, 272, 302, 313, 322,
  380 f., 383, 387, 402, 443, 449, 466, 469,
  498, 508 f., **517–526,** 585, 587, 621, 627, 661,
  663, 672, 674, 689–691, 722, 734 f., 743
  Vol. 2: 55, 70, 74, 77, 80, 84, 131, 149, 164,
  174, 184–190, 192, 194–196, 205, 207,
  209 f., 212, 215, 232, 271, 274, 279 f., 282,
  299 f., 303 f., 327, 329, 353, 355, 363, 375–

Earth (cont'd)
   377, 380 f., 396, 399, 402, 411, 452, 494,
   564, 571, 619, 626, 650, 655 f., 664, 688,
   700, 819, 836, 840, 866, 876, 918–920
   Vol. 3: 69, 117, 171, 258, 269, 574, 578, 674,
   692, 741, 865, 941, 1054, 1068, 1148, 1176
Earth-bound **Vol. 1:** 422
Earthen vessel **Vol. 1:** 638
Earthenware **Vol. 3: 910–915**
Earthly **Vol. 1:** 401, 520, 547, 587, 638 f., 642 f.,
   706 f., 709, 720, 728, 738
   Vol. 2: 244, 326, 342, 359, 373, 385, 403, 659
Earthly man **Vol. 1:** 85
Earthly nature **Vol. 1:** 168
Earthquake **Vol. 1:** 124, 319, 610
   Vol. 2: 426, 700, 911
   Vol. 3: 79, 292, 382, 543, **556–558**, 592, 1001,
   1091
Ease **Vol. 1:** 724
   Vol. 2: 777
   Vol. 3: 255
East **Vol. 1:** 164, 205, 665
   Vol. 2: 378
   Vol. 3: 730
Easter **Vol. 1:** 323, 423, 474, 599, 603, 631,
   634, 659
   Vol. 2: 176, 203, 341 f., 387, 524, 610 f., 624,
   654, 695, 738, 897
   Vol. 3: 131, 276, 282, 411, 844
Easter legends **Vol. 3: 282 f.**
Eat **Vol. 1:** 175, 225 f., 250, 308, 341, 350–352,
   390, 444, 448, 504, 597, 611 f., 620, 633,
   643, 670, 673, 678, 691, 724, 731, 743 f.
   Vol. 2: 157, 226, **264–277**, 286, 355, 357, 387,
   402, 417, 421, 520, 530, 533, 711, 889, 929
   Vol. 3: 158 f., 239, 245, 276, 423, 859
Eat (salt) with **Vol. 3: 443–449**
Eatable **Vol. 2: 268 f.**
Eating **Vol. 2: 268 f.**
Eating meat **Vol. 3:** 106
Ebal **Vol. 1:** 67, 210
   Vol. 2: 639
   Vol. 3: 451, 788, 1009
Ebeling, G. **Vol. 3:** 898, 1139 f.
Ebionites **Vol. 2:** 36
   Vol. 3: 621, 632, 661
Ecclesiastes **Vol. 1:** 59, 211
   Vol. 3: 606
Ecclesiastical **Vol. 2:** 536
   Vol. 3: 112
Ecclesiasticus (Sirach) **Vol. 1:** 50, 575 f., 580
   Vol. 2: 331, 355, 622
Ecclesiology **Vol. 1: 56**
Echo **Vol. 3:** 80, 112 f.
Economic **Vol. 1:** 501, 642, 710
   Vol. 2: 259
Economics **Vol. 1:** 643
Economy **Vol. 1:** 738
   Vol. 2: 306, 822
   Vol. 3: 593
Ecstasy **Vol. 1:** 399, 414, 502, 514, **526–530**
   Vol. 2: 103, 477, 539, 621, 764
   Vol. 3: 76–79, 84, 89, 126, 129, 283, 315,
   476, 690 f., 720, 1000

Ecstatic **Vol. 1:** 582, 598
   Vol. 2: 202, 355, 394, 398, 739 f., 785, 883
   Vol. 3: 225, 515, 571, 691, 698, 700, 707,
   1079
Ecumenical **Vol. 1:** 304, 519
Eden **Vol. 1:** 168, 389, 453
   Vol. 2: 482
   Vol. 3: 986, 988
Edge **Vol. 2:** 303
   Vol. 3: 796 f.
Edict **Vol. 1:** 330 f., 393, 476, 623, 686
   Vol. 3: 48, 1015
Edification **Vol. 1:** 50
   Vol. 2: 763, 924
   Vol. 3: 390, 547, 675, 703, 748, 962, 1080
Edificatory **Vol. 1:** 741
Edifice **Vol. 1:** 658
Edify **Vol. 2:** 253
   Vol. 3: 84, 675, 770
Editorial adaptation **Vol. 1:** 57
Edom **Vol. 2:** 38
   Vol. 3: 1005
Edomites **Vol. 2:** 373
   Vol. 3: 341, 871
Educate **Vol. 1:** 352, 617
   Vol. 2: 265
   Vol. 3: 759–780
Educated **Vol. 1:** 498
Education **Vol. 1:** 567–569
   Vol. 2: 102 f., 140–142, 288, 309, 406, 430,
   437, 513, 737
   Vol. 3: 75, **759–780**, 880, 996, 1028, 1055
Educational **Vol. 2:** 103, 419, 432, 445
   Vol. 3: 721, 1066
Educator **Vol. 1:** 640
Efface **Vol. 2:** 288
Effect **Vol. 1:** 469, 513–515, 546, 550, 601, 610,
   652, 733, 738, 742
   Vol. 2: 245, 360, 362, 422, 428
   Vol. 3: 905, 1147–1152
Effective **Vol. 1:** 311, 515, 540, 547
   Vol. 2: 109, 122, 130, 148, 327, 426, 861
   Vol. 3: 1147–1152
Efficacious **Vol. 2:** 592, 873
   Vol. 3: 1091, 1108
Efficacy **Vol. 1:** 216, 609, 659
   Vol. 3: 242
Effort **Vol. 1:** 241, 386, 429, 437, 439, 456, 464,
   478, 502, 550 f., 645 f., 649, 660, 675, 681,
   716, 718, 723
   Vol. 2: 261, 271
   Vol. 3: 111, 141, 252, 359, 526, 555, 603,
   799, 946, 1150
Effulgence **Vol. 1:** 712
   Vol. 2: 284, **289 f.**
Ego **Vol. 2:** 182
Egocentric **Vol. 2:** 242
Egypt **Vol. 1:** 53, 55, 64, 117, 119 f., 162, 173,
   177, 193 f., 209 f., 249 f., 264, 270, 281, 290,
   293, 380, 393 f., 422, 512, **530–532**, 559, 574,
   616, 626, 632 f., 684, 688, 691 f., 716, 737
   Vol. 2: 38, 68 f., 95 f., 99, 125, 130, 134, 157,
   166, 202, 219, 255, 305, 318 f., 321, 329,
   367, 424, 461, 464, 492, 512, 521, 541, 554–

558, 586, 627, 643, 699, 717, 719, 796, 822, 830, 835 f., 849, 863, 889 f., 916
Vol. 3: 35, 135, 143, 159, 190, 192 f., 211, 216, 227, 259, 311, 359, 388, 405 f., 421, 428, 451, 453, 460, 476, 551, 592–594, 605, 642, 731, 788, 811, 846, 857, 870, 918, 937, 940, 960, 970, 984, 1001, 1005, 1007, 1028 f., 1068, 1088, 1103, 1162, 1167, 1179
Egyptian **Vol. 1:** 172, 205, 264, 266, 288, 307, 393, 523, **530–532**, 546, 574, 616, 625, 633, 692 f.
Vol. 2: 97, 157, 166, 201, 234, 279, 305, 318, 374, 489, 848, 876, 891
Vol. 3: 208, 274, 560, 617, 634, 636, 713, 827, 1068, 1085
Egyptian king myth **Vol. 2:** 200 f.
Eichhorn, J.G. **Vol. 3:** 1138
Eight **Vol. 2: 692**
Eighteen Benedictions **Vol. 1:** 444
Vol. 2: 311–313, 803, **864–867**
Vol. 3: 194, 638, 650, 871
Eighth **Vol. 2:** 692, 698
Eighth day **Vol. 1:** 309 f.
Vol. 2: 692
Eisler, Robert **Vol. 3:** 977
Ekron **Vol. 3:** 469
El **Vol. 1:** 616, 625
Vol. 2: 67, 190, 553
Vol. 3: 617
El-berith **Vol. 1:** 367
Elath **Vol. 2:** 97
Elation **Vol. 1:** 163, 727
Elder **Vol. 1:** 83, 92, 121, 136, **188–201**, 285, 288, 293 f., 300, 303, 305, 310, 356, 364, 472, 478, 496, 499, 515, 527, 529, 536, 568
Vol. 2: 50, 152, 319, 356, 363, 519, 521, 563, 615, 638 f., 696, 715, 799, 880
Vol. 3: 33, 39, 77, 88, 95, 185, 191, 241, 478, 480 f., 568, 588, 924, 930, 1065
Eleatic school **Vol. 2:** 719
Eleazar **Vol. 1:** 435, 529
Vol. 2: 792
Vol. 3: 681, 926, 1168
Elect **Vol. 1:** 84, 159, 189, 216, 273, 275, 296, 305, 345, 381, 403, 475 f., 478, 485, **533–543**, 545, 617, 646 f., 655, 673, 697
Vol. 2: 32–34, 45, 56, 73, 118, 156, 194, 228 f., 241, 298, 307, 313 f., 354, 357, 364, 367, 395, 413, 428, 540, 566, 689, 771, 775, 798, 817, 893, 916
Vol. 3: 118, 168, 196, 215, 253, 272, 398, 505, 524, 610, 614–616, 636 f., 641, 748, 783, 874, 1016, 1029, 1117, 1165
Elect of righteousness **Vol. 3:** 359
Election **Vol. 1:** 77, 80 f., 123, 129, 159, 166, 177, 273 f., 288, 298, 300, 305, 378 f., 474, 484 f., **533–543**, 589, 617, 644, 669, 690, 693, 697, 700, 720, 730
Vol. 2: 73, 77, 117 f., 237, 259, 301 f., 307, 311 f., 321, 357 f., 385, 400, 402, 544 f., 604, 609, 661, 709, 797, 818 f., 863, 889
Vol. 3: 135 f., 221, 224, 251 f., 332, 482, 639, 648, 721, 818, 1018, 1031, 1087, 1095, 1102, 1112, 1121

Electrum **Vol. 2:** 97
Elemental powers, spirits **Vol. 1:** 282, 331, 401, 439
Vol. 2: 200, 270, 559, 645
Elemental principle **Vol. 3:** 689
Elemental spirits **Vol. 3:** 775, 994
Elementary **Vol. 1:** 166
Vol. 2: 452
Vol. 3: 216
Elementary propositions **Vol. 3:** 894
Elements **Vol. 1:** 102, 419, 525, 653 f., 664, 707
Vol. 2: 270, **436–456**, 657, 659
Vol. 3: 27, 180, 690, 1035
Elephant **Vol. 1:** 116
Elephantine **Vol. 1:** 207
Vol. 2: 576
Vol. 3: 427, 451, 457, 752
Eleusinian deities **Vol. 2:** 484
Eleusinian mysteries **Vol. 1:** 408
Vol. 2: 643
Vol. 3: 50, 138, 491 f., 593
Eleusis **Vol. 1:** 573
Vol. 3: 501
Elevation **Vol. 1:** 432
Elevated **Vol. 1:** 123
Eleven **Vol. 3:** 340
Elhanan **Vol. 1:** 170
Eli **Vol. 1:** 193
Vol. 2: 116, 856
Vol. 3: 33 f., 155, 426, 451, 655, 740
Eliakim **Vol. 2:** 727, 730, 732 f.
Elias **Vol. 1:** 543, 545
Eliashib **Vol. 3:** 35
Eliezer **Vol. 2:** 637
Vol. 3: 879
Eliezer ben Hyrkanos, Rabbi **Vol. 3:** 1058
Eligible **Vol. 1:** 533
Elihu **Vol. 1:** 511
Elijah **Vol. 1:** 128, 173, 209 f., 273, 323, 328, 481, 485, 527, **543–545**, 593, 640
Vol. 2: 82, 281, 337, 399, 432 f., 443, 488, 503, 559, 582, 627 f., 640, 686, 688, 724, 730, 861, 863, 882, 893, 902
Vol. 3: 78, 80, 83, 89, 119, 121, 211, 248, 252 f., 261 f., 266 f., 293, 325, 361, 418, 426, 436, 454, 480, 495, 507, 558, 579, 602, 621, 650, 658, 707, 721, 747, 812, 863 f., 880, 962, 1002, 1005, 1009, 1013 f., 1062, 1067, 1090 f., 1120
Elijah *redivivus* **Vol. 3:** 121, 147
Elimination **Vol. 1:** 508, 643 f.
Vol. 2: 372
Eliphaz **Vol. 3:** 209, 1041
Elis **Vol. 1:** 189
Elisha **Vol. 1:** 210, 481, 485
Vol. 2: 225, 337, 433, 464, 627 f.
Vol. 3: 77 f., 121, 211, 261, 266 f., 293, 444, 558, 962, 987, 1007, 1089, 1091
Elite **Vol. 1:** 489, 536 f., 539
Elizabeth **Vol. 1:** 187, 739
Vol. 2: 353, 358
Vol. 3: 84, 340, 361, 843, 1009, 1071, 1073
Elkanah **Vol. 3:** 1057
Ellipse **Vol. 1:** 56

Ellipsis **Vol. 1: 56**
Elliptical **Vol. 1: 56**
Eloah **Vol. 2:** 67
Elohim **Vol. 2: 56**
   Vol. 2: 67
Elohist **Vol. 1: 56**, 65, 72
Elohistic narrative **Vol. 3:** 484
Elohistic source (→ E source) **Vol. 1: 56**
Eloquence **Vol. 1:** 212
   Vol. 2: 873
   Vol. 3: 322, **1081–1119**
Elucidate **Vol. 1:** 581
Elymas **Vol. 2:** 557
Elysian fields **Vol. 2:** 761
Elzevir edition **Vol. 1:** 70
Emanate **Vol. 1:** 616, 705
Emanation **Vol. 2:** 67, 290
   Vol. 3: 831
Emancipation **Vol. 3:** 1168
Embalm **Vol. 1:** 264, 266
   Vol. 2: 293
Embassy **Vol. 1:** 192, 197
   Vol. 2: 311
Embellish **Vol. 1:** 265
Embezzlement **Vol. 2:** 471
   Vol. 3: 377
Embitter **Vol. 1:** 201 f., 561, 563
Emblem **Vol. 1:** 406–408
Embodiment **Vol. 1:** 501, 545, 705, 708, 712
   Vol. 2: 289, 325, 625
   Vol. 3: 686, 694, 815, 1205
Emboss **Vol. 2:** 288
Embrace **Vol. 1:** 206 f., 239, 742
Embryo **Vol. 1:** 183, 283, 712
   Vol. 3: 997
Emerald **Vol. 3:** 391, 396, 1003
Emergency **Vol. 3:** 408, 410
Emigrate **Vol. 2: 788–790**
Emissary **Vol. 2:** 328
Emission **Vol. 2:** 586
   Vol. 3: 104
Emmanuel **Vol. 1:** 581, 737
   Vol. 2: 86 f., 654
   Vol. 3: 697
Emmaus **Vol. 1:** 576
   Vol. 2: 342, 729
   Vol. 3: 132, 198, 283, 287, 453, 717
Emotion **Vol. 1:** 106, 230, 239 f., 461, 555, 567, 656
   Vol. 2: 70, 180–183, 244, 352, 355, 416–424, 478, 552, 567, 593, 599 f., 765
   Vol. 3: 125, 676 f., 680 f., 684, 691, 710, 719, 748, 823
Emotional strain **Vol. 3:** 858
Empathy **Vol. 1:** 583
Empedocles of Agrigentum **Vol. 1:** 594
   Vol. 3: 635
Emperor **Vol. 1:** 119, 125, 269 f., 474, 519
   Vol. 2: 167, 233 f., 288, 378, 380, 511, 572, 574, 624, 665, 693, 782, 898
   Vol. 3: 45, 217, 411, 635, 715, 718, 736, 959, 1168
Emperor-cult **Vol. 2:** 309, 373, 674, 876
Emperor-worship **Vol. 2: 511**

   Vol. 3: 959
Emphasis **Vol. 1:** 99, 359, 538, 609, 732
   Vol. 2: 112
Emphasize **Vol. 2:** 327
Emphatic **Vol. 1:** 600
Empire **Vol. 1:** 126, 519
   Vol. 2: 376, 381, 689, 788, 802, 918
   Vol. 3: 555
Empirical **Vol. 1: 56**, 522, 711
   Vol. 2: 395
Empiricism **Vol. 1: 56**, 64
Empiricist **Vol. 1: 56**
   Vol. 3: 1136
Employ **Vol. 1:** 653
Employer **Vol. 2:** 513
Employment **Vol. 1:** 267
   Vol. 3: 758
Empower **Vol. 2:** 146, 165
Emptiness **Vol. 1:** 482, 512
   Vol. 2: 432
   Vol. 3: 407
Empty **Vol. 1:** 137, 266, 455, **545–553**, 611 f., 623, 706 f., 709, 714
   Vol. 2: 150, 203, 242, 262, 264, 285, 343, 400, 445, 471, 500, 620, 683, 828, 844, 854
   Vol. 3: 200, 281, 417, 554, 597, 604, 645, 815, 1101
Empty-handed **Vol. 1:** 546 f.
Empty-headed **Vol. 1:** 417 f.
Enable **Vol. 1:** 681
   Vol. 2: 357, 359
   Vol. 3: 728–730
Enact **Vol. 1:** 369
   Vol. 2: 438–451
Enallage **Vol. 3:** 1174
Encaenia **Vol. 3:** 366
Encamp **Vol. 3: 811–815**
Enchanter **Vol. 2:** 555
Enchantment **Vol. 2:** 166
Enclose **Vol. 1:** 54, 240
Enclosure **Vol. 3:** 565, 948
Encompass **Vol. 1:** 405
Encounter **Vol. 1:** 335, 611, 623
   Vol. 2: 223, 317, 342, 396, 631
   Vol. 3: 56, 310, 336, 493, 694
Encouragement **Vol. 1:** 88, 258, 263, 303, **327–329**, 342, 512 f., 567–570, 600, 679, 722
   Vol. 2: 199, 266, 317, 431, 857
   Vol. 3: 44, 54, 204, 492, 844, 930, 1043
End **Vol. 1:** 56, 69, 95, 164, 289, 298, 311, 342, 403, 410, 429, 432–434, 463, 470, 492, 513, 515, 521, 544, 550, 581, 589, 597, 610, 619, 642, 651, 654, 666 f., 669, 671, 680–682, 696, 698, 712, 719, 734 f., 737, 739
   Vol. 2: 37, **52–66**, 128, 157, 229, 275, 303, 313, 351, 385, 443, 445, 451, 461, 629, 633, 657, 665, 701, 748, 786, 892, 904, 908, 910–912, 914 f., 918, 926
   Vol. 3: 42, 254, 659, 725, 756, 759, **796 f**, 936, 969
End of the age **Vol. 1:** 124, 325
   Vol. 2: 37, 218, 282, 326, 329, 844, 900 f., 921
End of time **Vol. 1:** 389, 657

Vol. 2: 48, 300, 354, 376 f., 388, 417, 610
Vol. 3: 504, 621, 701
End of the world **Vol. 1:** 56, 216 f., 496, 519, 630
Vol. 2: 37 f., 52, 54, 61 f., 383 f., 458, 893, 903, 918
Vol. 3: 559, 812, 829, 844
End-time **Vol. 1:** 65, 185, 244, 545, 610, 622, 629, 656, 729, 733, 735
Vol. 2: 34, 54, 56, 250, 266, 306, 308 f., 315, 382, 717, 736, 785, 808, 833, 889, 914 f., 929
Vol. 3: 31, 80, 88, 105, 213, 301, 531, 650, 695 f., 832, 918
Endanger **Vol. 1:** 241, 500, 687
Vol. 2: 370
Endeavour **Vol. 1:** 319, 695, 723
Vol. 2: 617
Vol. 3: 42, **798–808**
Endless **Vol. 2:** 891
Endor **Vol. 2:** 554
Vol. 3: 270
Endorse **Vol. 1:** 99, 679
Endow **Vol. 1:** 207, 654, 739
Endowment **Vol. 1:** 122, 735, 739
Vol. 2: 121, 658
Vol. 3: 69
Ends of the earth **Vol. 2:** 55
Endurable **Vol. 2: 765–767**
Endurance **Vol. 1:** 123, 215, 257, 304, 400, 541, 570, 639, 644, 646, 650, 673, 710, 727
Vol. 2: 98, 123, 245, 291, 301, 696, **764–776**
Vol. 3: 680, 1040
Endure **Vol. 2:** 269, 357, 420, **764–767**, 773
Vol. 3: 224, 347, 490, **719–725**
Endure hard labour **Vol. 3: 858 f.**
Endure hardship **Vol. 3: 719–725**
Enduring **Vol. 1:** 711, 739
Vol. 2: 96, 318
Vol. 3: 558–560
Enemy **Vol. 1:** 125, 187, 208, 210, 215, 239, 248, 252, 257, 259, 264 f., 295, 345, 400, 416 f., 440, 453, 463 f., 477, 487, 508, 541, **553–557**, 567, 572, 610, 622, 649 f., 652, 655, 657, 662, 679, 686, 702, 726
Vol. 2: 58, 61, 71, 105 f., 110, 144, 146 f., 149, 157 f., 187, 206, 211, 215, 220, 245, 256, 263, 266, 268, 363 f., 366, 385 f., 402, 413, 416, 432 f., 438, 486, 499, 543 f., 547, 549, 613, 632, 665, 674, 679, 868
Vol. 3: 49, 93, 96 f., 145, 167, 183, 193, 202, 207, 210, 212, 216, 218, 234, 237, 249, 256, 269, 275, 341, 355 f., 360, 379, 425, 444, 469 f., 559, 562 f., 576, 581, 590, 609, 633, 678, 721, 757, 802, 806, 818, 842, 868, 873, 908 f., 916, 951, 960, 983, 987, 994, 1006, 1017, 1099
Energetic **Vol. 2:** 861
Energy **Vol. 1:** 671
Vol. 2: 148, 658
Vol. 3: 599, 683, 691
Engage **Vol. 1:** 372, 494, 656
Engaged **Vol. 2:** 582, 585
Engagement **Vol. 2:** 584
Engelmann, P. **Vol. 3:** 1136

Engrave **Vol. 1:** 332
Vol. 2: 573
Vol. 3: 483, 488
Enigmatic **Vol. 1:** 203
Enjoy **Vol. 2: 269–271**, 352, 428, 477, 817, 843
Vol. 3: 372, 922
Enjoyment **Vol. 1:** 212, 239 f., 431, 434, 457 f., 494, 529, 687, 689 f., 722, 728
Vol. 2: 264, 273, **352–361**, 458
Vol. 3: 677, 845, 852
Enlarge **Vol. 1:** 253, 732 f.
Enlightener **Vol. 2:** 290
Enlightenment **Vol. 1:** 421–423, 562
Vol. 2: 243, 265, 270, **490–496**, 718
Vol. 3: 932, 1083
Enlist soldiers **Vol. 3: 958–967**
Enmeduranna **Vol. 3:** 264 f.
Enmity **Vol. 1:** 85, 223, 289, 370, 417, 458, 501, 525, **553–557**, 603, 644, 681
Vol. 2: 258, 309, 426, 548, 663
Vol. 3: 168 f., 171, 315, 949
Enoch **Vol. 1:** 50, 66, 85, 124, 316, 545
Vol. 2: 202, 216, 219, 227, 290, 627, 681, 815, 817, 842, 897, 905
Vol. 3: 35, 262, 264–266, 272, 487, 558, 579, 602, 615–617, 621, 627, 682, 747
Enosh **Vol. 1:** 451
Enough **Vol. 1:** 597, 699, 728, 731
Vol. 2: 131, 272
Vol. 3: 726–730
Enquire **Vol. 2:** 140, 286, 362, 364
Vol. 3: 531
Enquiry **Vol. 1:** 607
Vol. 3: 570
Enrage **Vol. 1:** 107
Enraptured **Vol. 3:** 230
Enrich **Vol. 2:** 405, 842
Enrobe **Vol. 1:** 122
Enrol **Vol. 3:** 486, 1014
Enrolment **Vol. 1:** 330, 669
Enslave **Vol. 1:** 138, 364, 399, 401, 437 f., 457 f., 460, 466, 469, 613, 717
Vol. 2: 94, 154, 182 f., 195, 229, 265, 401, 449, 718, 828, 843
Vol. 3: 96
Ensure **Vol. 2:** 364
Entanglement **Vol. 2:** 457
Enter **Vol. 1:** 320, 646, 682, 688
Vol. 2: 223, 244, 295, 385, 387 f., 813
Vol. 3: 691, 910
Enterprise **Vol. 1:** 710, 712
Vol. 2: 254
Entertain **Vol. 1:** 625, 690
Vol. 2: 674
Enthronement **Vol. 1:** 121–123, 177, 668
Vol. 2: 58, 108 f., 201–203, 374–376, 918
Vol. 3: 637, 643, 673, 863
Enthronement festival **Vol. 2:** 375, 613
Enthronement Psalms **Vol. 2:** 336, 375, 613
Enthusiasm **Vol. 1:** 528 f., 594, 598, 600 f., 604, 642, 679
Vol. 2: 160, 171, 241, 386, 429, 785 f., 883
Vol. 3: 58, 199, 932, 1166
Enthusiast **Vol. 1:** 638

Enthusiast (cont'd)
  Vol. 2: 253, 267, 611, 741
  Vol. 3: 690
Entice Vol. 1: 458
  Vol. 3: 809
Enticement Vol. 2: 458, 708, 845
Entirely Vol. 2: 63
Entirety Vol. 1: 740
Entity Vol. 1: 522
Entrails Vol. 2: 599 f.
  Vol. 3: 423
Entrance Vol. 2: 29–31, 54, 179, 245
  Vol. 3: 213, 221, 310, 395, 794, 935–943, 948
Entranced Vol. 1: 528
Entreat Vol. 2: 861–864, 867–875
Entreat favour Vol. 3: 149
Entreaty Vol. 2: 860 f., 862–864, 867–875
Entrenchment Vol. 3: 952
Entrust Vol. 1: 273, 332, 594, 596, 684, 730
  Vol. 2: 113, 255 f., 366, 438, 837
  Vol. 3: 686
Entry Vol. 1: 317, 325, 629, 724
  Vol. 2: 379, 415, 902
  Vol. 3: 652, 669, 791
Enûma Eliš Vol. 2: 200, 552
Envious Vol. 1: 557
  Vol. 2: 356
Environment Vol. 1: 679, 693, 720
  Vol. 2: 307–309, 487
  Vol. 3: 935
Envoy Vol. 1: 126 f., 130, 193 f., 596
  Vol. 3: 50
Envy Vol. 1: 397, 509, 557 f.
  Vol. 2: 594
  Vol. 3: 149, 532, 707, 1119, 1166
Epaenetus Vol. 3: 416
Epaphras Vol. 2: 597
  Vol. 3: 596
Epaphroditus Vol. 1: 130, 741
  Vol. 3: 553, 955, 957, 1164
Epexegetical kai Vol. 3: 241
Ephemeral Vol. 2: 358
Ephesians Vol. 1: 55, 148, 160, 237, 301, 487
  Vol. 2: 85, 217, 302
  Vol. 3: 66, 315, 592, 699
Ephesus Vol. 1: 199, 263, 303, 419, 560, 568,
  578, 654
  Vol. 2: 74, 85, 155, 235, 360, 557, 623, 644,
  676, 678, 763, 775
  Vol. 3: 65, 203, 480, 521, 529, 757, 768, 784,
  796, 903, 915, 949, 967, 1080
Ephod Vol. 2: 296
Ephphatha Vol. 3: 860
Ephraim Vol. 2: 306, 318, 541, 649
  Vol. 3: 450
Ephrath Vol. 1: 170
Ephrathah Vol. 1: 170
Ephron Vol. 3: 51, 146
Epic literature Vol. 3: 1081
Epictetus Vol. 2: 140, 259, 776
  Vol. 3: 50, 123, 491, 634, 739, 766
Epicureans Vol. 1: 246, 555, 672, 676
  Vol. 2: 817
  Vol. 3: 525, 1034, 1036, 115

Epicurus Vol. 1: 469, 671, 673
  Vol. 3: 217, 678
Epidaurus Vol. 1: 594
  Vol. 2: 166
  Vol. 3: 103, 520, 915
Epilepsy Vol. 1: 163, 727
  Vol. 3: 475, 734, 750
Epimenides Vol. 2: 77, 85
  Vol. 3: 81, 331, 887
Epiphanius Vol. 2: 506 f.
  Vol. 3: 36
Epiphany Vol. 2: 245, 862
  Vol. 3: 317, 514, 862
Episcopacy Vol. 1: 188–201
Epistle Vol. 1: 246
Epistles, Apocryphal Vol. 1: 50 f.
Epistolary style Vol. 1: 247
Epitaph Vol. 1: 431
Epoch Vol. 1: 477
  Vol. 3: 826–833
Eponym Vol. 2: 318 f.
Equal Vol. 2: 291, 438, 496–508, 825
  Vol. 3: 409
Equal rights Vol. 1: 720
Equal status Vol. 2: 160 f.
Equality Vol. 1: 366, 368, 640–642, 691
  Vol. 2: 80, 146, 160, 309, 311, 403, 426,
  496–508, 823
  Vol. 3: 604
Equality of the sexes Vol. 2: 563
Equate Vol. 2: 338, 387
Equestrian order Vol. 3: 718, 755
Equilibrium Vol. 3: 560
Equip Vol. 2: 152, 606
  Vol. 3: 118, 349–351, 959–967
Equipment Vol. 3: 349–351
Equivalent Vol. 3: 153, 1179
Era Vol. 3: 829
Erase Vol. 1: 471
  Vol. 2: 312
  Vol. 3: 109, 840
Erasmus Vol. 1: 70
Erastus Vol. 2: 254
Erech Vol. 1: 140
Erect Vol. 2: 251, 373
  Vol. 3: 118–120, 279
Erigena, John Scotus Vol. 3: 148
Erinyes Vol. 1: 687
Eros Vol. 2: 539, 643
Erotic Vol. 1: 631
  Vol. 2: 584
  Vol. 3: 676
Err Vol. 1: 400, 467, 608
  Vol. 2: 142
  Vol. 3: 585 f.
Errant Vol. 1: 664
Erroneous Vol. 1: 708
  Vol. 2: 239
Error Vol. 1: 355, 438, 546, 680, 700, 733
  Vol. 2: 95, 141, 214, 406–408, 457–461
  Vol. 3: 328, 379, 585 f., 770
Eryx Vol. 1: 497
Esau Vol. 1: 81, 214, 556 f., 667
  Vol. 2: 116, 316–319, 369, 431, 782, 796, 847

Vol. 3: 869, 1179
Escape **Vol. 1:** 268, 358, 420 f., **558 f.**, 657, 677, 717
  Vol. 2: 136, 366 f., 393, 434, 445, 573
  Vol. 3: 120, 209, 227, 528, 1053
Eschatological **Vol. 1: 56**, 87, 99, 111, 123 f., 126, 131, 133 f., 147, 170 175 f., 179, 184–186, 204, 215–217, 224 f., 231, 237, 244, 260, 262 f., 269, 278, 289, 296–305, 317, 321, 336, 338, 347, 358, 368, 373, 383, 400, 414, 423, 425, 449, 452, 463, 465 f., 482, 496, 505, 513, 515, 518, 535, 539, 544 f., 551, 554, 566, 578, 601 f., 604, 607, 610, 615, 620, 630, 634, 638, 640 f., 656 f., 661, 668, 701, 709, 728, 735 f.
  Vol. 2: 31, 33, 45, 47 f., 50, 56–65, 72, 100, 102, 109, 111, 117, 122, 130 f., 135, 147, 150, 162, 168, 186, 189 f., 192, 194, 200, 203, 205, 208, 228 f., 240–242, 244 f., 252, 261 f., 264, 275 f., 288, 298, 300, 303, 312–315, 325 f., 329, 337, 353–359, 367, 374–377, 382, 384, 386, 399, 402, 411 f., 420, 426, 429, 435, 479, 487, 491 f., 495, 499, 504, 518, 522, 524, 530 f., 534–536, 573, 580, 585, 591, 595, 602, 604, 609–611, 614, 625, 631 f., 640, 665 f., 670, 672, 676, 691, 693, 695 f., 698, 709, 727 f., 733, 754, 767, 773, 779 f., 786, 793, 797, 807–809, 819, 823, 825, 842, 844, 875, 887 f., 890–894, 900–935
  Vol. 3: 35–37, 46 f., 74, 79, 82–84, 88, 111 f., 121, 141–143, 147 f., 182, 196 f., 204 f., 207 f., 210, 214 f., 218, 233, 245, 256, 272, 274, 276, 279, 281, 287 f., 292, 297, 301, 318–320, 328, 334, 352, 361, 368, 372 f., 417, 430, 460, 462, 502, 514, 545 f., 556, 558, 560, 615, 618–620, 623–627, 630 f., 637 f., 641, 643, 645, 647, 649, 669, 675, 682, 685 f., 693, 696 f., 699, 701, 703, 705, 710, 725, 731–737, 745, 749, 784, 792, 803, 842–844, 848, 856, 863, 871, 890, 905 f., 922, 924, 934, 953, 961 f., 965, 969, 973, 986–989, 1005 f., 1008, 1010 f., 1041, 1117, 1149, 1158, 1168
Eschatology **Vol. 1:** 50, 53, **56**, 65, 111, 382, 563, 601, 639
  Vol. 2: 47 f., 110, 139, 376, **383–385**, 388 f., 447, 517, 749, 764, 785, 824, 886, 890, 892, 894, 899, **901–935**
  Vol. 3: 46, 66 f., 80, 86, 146, 277, 305, 332, 453, 603, 648, 658, 830–833, 991
Eschatology, consistent **Vol. 2: 383, 902 f**.
Eschatology, futurist **Vol. 2: 384**, 388, 924, 927–929
Eschatology, realized **Vol. 1: 56**, 111
  Vol. 2: 242, **384**, 883, **904–906**, 927 f., 930
Eschatology, thorough-going **Vol. 2: 383**
  Vol. 3: 506
Eschaton **Vol. 3:** 642, 733
1 Esdras **Vol. 1:** 50
2 Esdras **Vol. 1:** 124
  Vol. 3: 271
3 Esdras **Vol. 3:** 312
Eshnuna **Vol. 3:** 594

Esoteric **Vol. 1:** 577
  Vol. 2: 401
  Vol. 3: 481, 502
Especial **Vol. 2: 838–840**
Espouse **Vol. 2:** 364
Essence **Vol. 1:** 703, 705, 710–712
  Vol. 2: 84, 287 f.
  Vol. 3: 513, 1186
Essenes **Vol. 1:** 67, 102, 145, 151, 153, 204, 309, 495, 534, 554, 627, 630, 641 f., 688
  Vol. 2: 71, 207, 377, 579, 651, 785, 810 f., 823
  Vol. 3: 80, 105, 108, 160, 273, 486 f., 495, 531, 545, 595, 608, 623, 681, 740, 753, 802, 978 f., 989, 1006, 1035
Essential **Vol. 1:** 549, 701, 703–709, 715
  Vol. 2: 106, 335, 406, 438
Establish **Vol. 1:** 123, 329, 368, 380, 426, 472, 522, 596, 626, 639, 660, 664, 681, 688, 696
  Vol. 2: 69, 183, 489
  Vol. 3: 117, 242, 350, 434
Establishment **Vol. 3:** 970
Estate **Vol. 1:** 641
  Vol. 2: 254, 303, 317, 823, 844
Esteem **Vol. 1:** 106, 197, 553
  Vol. 2: 48, 130, 364, 438
  Vol. 3: 317
Esteemed **Vol. 3: 808–810**
Estha **Vol. 3:** 655
Esther **Vol. 1:** 50, 59, 364, 560, 626, 637
  Vol. 2: 116, 291, 860
  Vol. 3: 960, 962, 1057
Estimate **Vol. 1:** 480
  Vol. 2: 365
Estrangement **Vol. 1:** 421, 459, 474, 684 f.
  Vol. 2: 468, 742
  Vol. 3: 171 f., 227
Etana **Vol. 2:** 201
Etch **Vol. 2:** 573
Eternal **Vol. 1:** 79, 240, 243, 382 f., 386, 406, 408, 442, 452, 464, 544, 563, 596, 611, 619, 657, 665, 694, 697
  Vol. 2: 52, 70, 72, 77, 86, 103, 105, 138, 179, 213, 230, 253, 271, 274, 290, 303, 355, 365, 412, 585, 792
  Vol. 3: 41, 99, 189, 209, 229, 260, 583, 686, **826–833**, 1034
Eternal death **Vol. 1:** 434
  Vol. 3: 685, 833
Eternal destruction **Vol. 1:** 423, 466, 610
  Vol. 2: 61
  Vol. 3: 96
Eternal fire **Vol. 3:** 96, 99, 470
Eternal habitations **Vol. 2:** 382
  Vol. 3: 812
Eternal judgment **Vol. 3:** 99
Eternal life **Vol. 1:** 78 f., 112, 244, 250, 253 f., 337, 406, 423, 434, 439–441, 464, 476, 482, 603, 625, 637 f., 701, 723
  Vol. 2: 32, 42, 47, 51, 79, 82 f., 120, 194, 207, 230, 265, 269, 273, 277, 280, 295, 300–304, 388, 403 f., 415, 419, 480–483, 517, 535, 606, 632, 642, 654, 727, 770, 774, 824, 830, 833, 840, 905, 927 f., 930

Eternal life (*cont'd*)
Vol. 3: 47, 71, 73, 99, 114, 142, 145, 216, 302, 321, 368, 517, 525, 533, 631, 647, 681 f., 685 f., 750, 809, 831, **832 f.**, 837, 920, 1046, 1122
Eternal punishment **Vol. 1:** 339
   Vol. 3: 98 f., 210
Eternal rejection **Vol. 3:** 99
Eternal sin **Vol. 3:** 99
Eternity **Vol. 1:** 222, 311, 347, 380, 440, 464, 470, 473, 616, 669, 719
   Vol. 2: 255, 276, 592, 719, 878, 906, 919
   Vol. 3: 686, **826–833**, 841
Eternity-formula **Vol. 3:** 828
Ether **Vol. 1:** 449
   Vol. 2: 188
Ethic **Vol. 1:** 489, 494 f., 498
Ethical **Vol. 1:** 333 f., 339, 412, 420, 448, 460, 483, 490, 501, 514, 543, 546, 561 f., 565, 607, 612, 626, 640, 649
   Vol. 2: 65, 95, 98, 103, 116, 128, 132, 223, 232, 258 f., 262, 367, 377, 383, 391, 437, 439, 443, 475, 781 f.
   Vol. 3: 102 f., 107, 138, 149, 357, 373, 572, 766, 844, 928, 933, 945, 1148, 1166
Ethical values **Vol. 2:** 224
Ethics **Vol. 1:** 52, 54, **56**, 59, 62, 65, 68, 147, 338, 494, 571, 687
   Vol. 2: 60, 65, 102, 123, 133, 140, 166, 394, 397, 544, 719, 858
   Vol. 3: 54, 75, 103, 107, 215, 351, 561, 582, 849, 1022, 1034
Ethics, comparative **Vol. 1: 56**
Ethics, descriptive **Vol. 1: 56**
Ethics, negative **Vol. 2:** 394
Ethics, normative **Vol. 1: 56**
Ethics, philosophical **Vol. 1: 56**, 68, 494
Ethiopia **Vol. 2:** 294, 367, 381
   Vol. 3: 526
Ethiopian **Vol. 1:** 341
   Vol. 2: 349, 381
Ethiopian eunuch **Vol. 3:** 65 f., 602, 609
Ethiopic **Vol. 1:** 68
Ethiopic Enoch **Vol. 3:** 265, 272
Ethnic origin **Vol. 2:** 124, 305
Etruscans **Vol. 1:** 68
   Vol. 3: 851
Etymology **Vol. 1: 56 f.**, 61
   Vol. 3: 206, 878
Euboea **Vol. 2:** 233
Eucharist **Vol. 1:** 154, 702
   Vol. 2: 535, 591, 897
   Vol. 3: 158, 412, **816–819**
Eucharistic **Vol. 1:** 437
Eucharistic sacrifice **Vol. 3:** 244 f.
Eudaemonism **Vol. 1:** 501
   Vol. 3: 1034
Eudaimonia **Vol. 2:** 271
Eulogy **Vol. 3:** 816
Eumenides **Vol. 1:** 421, 588
Eumolpidae **Vol. 1:** 573
Eunice **Vol. 3:** 1070
Eunuch **Vol. 1:** 341, **559–561**
   Vol. 2: 381, 385, 580, 710, 728

Vol. 3: 541, 866
Euodia **Vol. 1:** 344
   Vol. 3: 1164
Euphemism **Vol. 1:** 429
   Vol. 2: 59, 148, 925, 927
   Vol. 3: 910, 1053
Euphrates **Vol. 1:** 516, 531
   Vol. 2: 555, 754
   Vol. 3: 179, 871, 985–987
Europe **Vol. 2:** 222
Eusebius **Vol. 1:** 582
   Vol. 2: 505
Eustathius of Antioch **Vol. 2:** 506
Evade **Vol. 1:** 602
   Vol. 2: 254
   Vol. 3: 835
Evaluation **Vol. 1:** 348, 480, 504, 528, 666, 679 f., 736
   Vol. 2: 103, 473, 847, 905
   Vol. 3: 402, 824
Evangelism **Vol. 1:** 95, 129, 662
Evangelist **Vol. 1:** 116, 213
   Vol. 2: 107–115, 187
   Vol. 3: 768, 1067
Evangelize **Vol. 2:** 83, **107–115**
Evans, C. F. **Vol. 3:** 299
Evaporate **Vol. 3:** 109
Evaporation **Vol. 3:** 689
Eve **Vol. 1: 84–88**, 187, 390, 413, 451, 468
   Vol. 3: 585, 691
   Vol. 3: 215, 579, 585
Evening **Vol. 1:** 629, 632, 634
   Vol. 2: 136, 887
   Vol. 3: 846
Event **Vol. 1:** 71, 667, 693, 707, 713, 733, 735, 737 f.
   Vol. 2: 137
   Vol. 3: 53, 65, 1090, **1119–1123**
Ever **Vol. 2:** 60 f.
Everlasting **Vol. 1:** 367, 423
   Vol. 2: 357, 374
Everlasting God **Vol. 2:** 67
Everyday **Vol. 1:** 614 f., 703
   Vol. 2: 334
   Vol. 3: 313
Everyone **Vol. 1:** 94
Evidence **Vol. 1:** 365, 428, 436, 726
   Vol. 2: 140, 142, 368, 498
   Vol. 3: 1038–1050
Evident **Vol. 2:** 377
   Vol. 3: 316, **317–324**
Evil **Vol. 1:** 55, 84 f., 104, 106 f., 118, 124, 138, 152, 163, 167, 169, 201, 205, 212, 223, 228, 231, 240, 265, 268, 322, 348, 351, 354 f., 357, 359, 370, 381, 385, 387, 389, 402, 411, 413, 416, 419 f., 422, 424, 429, 431, 433– 435, 449–453, 456 f., 463, 466 f., 473, 509, 522, 529, 556, 558 f., **561–567**, 568, 609, 631, 644, 649, 651, 653, 656, 671, 673 f., 676, 700, 704, 719, 731, 743
   Vol. 2: 28, 36, 86, 94, 97–101, 103, 127, 150 f., 157 f., 166, 181 f., 191, 193, 229, 236, 239, 266, 272, 274, 328, 350 f., 358, 366, 369, 387, 391, 396, 406, 419, 446, 458,

462 f., 490, 497, 568, 659, 676, 680, 716, 733, 794, 798, 811, 817, 868, 889 f., 928
Vol. 3: 103, 125, 130, 140, 172, 174, 179, 201, 203 f., 212, 231, 265, 321, 358, 439, 476, 522, 534, 572, 579, 586, 647, 651, 691–693, 695, 718, 720, 725, 734, 807, 810, 865, 868 f., 938, 1021, 1054, 1079, 1148, 1158, 1176
Evil eye Vol. 1: 423
　Vol. 2: 553
　Vol. 3: 520
Evil generation Vol. 3: 256
Evil impulse, inclination Vol. 1: 83, 231, 336, 459
　Vol. 2: 459
　Vol. 3: 363, 468 f., 579, 801, 805, 939
Evil one Vol. 1: 420, 510, 526, 651
　Vol. 2: 135, 376, 709, 868
　Vol. 3: 121, 469, 1176
Evil powers Vol. 2: 30, 193, 582
Evil speech Vol. 3: 345 f.
Evil spirits Vol. 2: 75, 358, 383, 459, 630, 653
Evil spirits and good spirits Vol. 3: 694 f.
Evil thoughts Vol. 3: 106
Evil-doers Vol. 1: 293, 433, 452, 537, 555, 561, 563, 641
　Vol. 2: 101, 237, 893
　Vol. 3: 359, 527, 583
Evil-speaking Vol. 3: 345
Evolve Vol. 1: 694
Exact Vol. 1: 712
Exaction Vol. 1: 572
　Vol. 2: 318, 364
　Vol. 3: 756
Exaggerate Vol. 1: 528
　Vol. 2: 433
Exalt Vol. 2: 197–205, 265, 417, 422 f.
　Vol. 3: 393
Exaltation Vol. 1: 83, 95, 168, 179, 224, 375, 399, 402, 437 f., 483, 500, 510, 549, 648, 668
　Vol. 2: 122, 148, 178, 184, 195, 198–204, 262 f., 343, 603 f., 609 f., 718, 900, 903, 918, 920
　Vol. 3: 42, 55, 162, 297, 366, 510, 552, 588, 615 f., 620, 630, 632, 652, 698, 812, 1111
Exalted Vol. 1: 133, 135, 168, 214, 244, 248, 269, 300, 305, 338, 375, 387, 403, 482, 491, 532, 540, 565, 603, 643, 656
　Vol. 2: 46, 58 f., 64, 84, 93 f., 119, 128, 147, 165, 194, 196, 198–200, 210, 225, 242, 262, 277, 329, 340, 386, 493, 503, 514, 516–518, 530, 604, 611, 786, 795, 921
　Vol. 3: 29, 62, 85, 88, 195, 276, 349, 534, 630, 670, 838
Examination Vol. 1: 163, 602
　Vol. 2: 341
　Vol. 3: 533, 758, 855, 1080
Examine Vol. 1: 189, 485, 503, 591
　Vol. 2: 140, 183, 362–367, 393, 856
　Vol. 3: 533
Example Vol. 1: 71, 156, 214, 239, 276, 299, 311, 400 f., 440, 448, 491 f., 532, 544, 572, 578, 593, 600, 643, 667, 694, 714
　Vol. 2: 47, 95, 180, 219, 258, 262, 277, 284–

293, 318, 350, 381, 400, 429, 471, 519, 619, 770, 773, 806, 811, 826
　Vol. 3: 60, 73, 183, 346, 490, 547, 570, 582, 724, 775, 821, 854, 980, 1157
Excavate Vol. 1: 520
Exceed Vol. 1: 729
　Vol. 2: 128, 131
　Vol. 3: 360
Exceeding Vol. 1: 728
Excel Vol. 1: 728
Excellence Vol. 1: 537
　Vol. 2: 98, 105
　Vol. 3: 730, 1034
Excellent Vol. 2: 102
　Vol. 3: 716–718
Exception Vol. 1: 674
Exceptive clause Vol. 1: 500
　Vol. 3: 538, 540 f., 1195
Excess Vol. 1: 108, 169, 495, 501, 625, 728 f.
　Vol. 2: 314
Excessive Vol. 3: 922
Exchange Vol. 1: 469
　Vol. 2: 96, 503
　Vol. 3: 166–174, 197, 885, 1179
Excite Vol. 1: 733
　Vol. 2: 350
　Vol. 3: 556–558
Excited Vol. 1: 107, 528
　Vol. 2: 244
Excitement Vol. 1: 646
　Vol. 2: 149, 181, 652
　Vol. 3: 676, 710
Exclude Vol. 1: 607 f., 612, 632, 644, 659, 684, 687, 689, 694, 700, 740
　Vol. 2: 286
　Vol. 3: 105, 402, 470, 954
Exclusion Vol. 1: 414, 433, 463, 466 f., 473, 500, 560, 566, 666
　Vol. 2: 312, 316, 530, 709, 813
　Vol. 3: 534
Exclusive Vol. 1: 539
　Vol. 2: 273, 724, 888
Exclusiveness Vol. 2: 73, 275, 494
　Vol. 3: 479, 1167
Exclusivism Vol. 3: 191
Excommunication Vol. 1: 413, 415
　Vol. 2: 33, 302
　Vol. 3: 188, 535, 756, 779
Excuse Vol. 1: 270, 385
　Vol. 2: 138 f., 183, 366, 400, 408, 855–859
　Vol. 3: 128, 885, 951, 1150
Execrate Vol. 1: 413, 415 f.
Execute Vol. 1: 657, 669, 735
Execution Vol. 1: 264, 345, 389–396, 429, 466, 693, 737
　Vol. 2: 59, 291, 368, 370, 437, 527
　Vol. 3: 96, 159, 538, 796, 865
Executor Vol. 2: 368
Exegesis Vol. 1: 57, 59 f., 62, 64 f., 68 f., 71, 575, 579
　Vol. 2: 406
　Vol. 3: 42, 264, 1120
Exemplar Vol. 3: 360
Exemplary Vol. 1: 568, 598

Exemplary (*cont'd*)
  Vol. 2: 102
Exempt **Vol. 1:** 482, 604, 698, 716
  Vol. 2: 370, 578, 775
  Vol. 3: 1032
Exercise **Vol. 1:** 312 f., 495 f., 522, 645, 647, 671
  Vol. 2: 267, 336, 361, 372
Exercise authority **Vol. 2: 606–611**
Exert oneself **Vol. 3:** 799
Exertion **Vol. 1:** 262 f., 495, 540, 568, 729
  Vol. 3: 936
Exhalation **Vol. 3:** 679
Exhaustion **Vol. 1:** 262 f., 393, 395, 730
  Vol. 2: 265, 295
Exhibit **Vol. 1:** 371, 696 f.
  Vol. 2: 291, 434, 488
  Vol. 3: 570 f.
Exhilaration **Vol. 1:** 173
Exhort **Vol. 1:** 65, 88 f., 197, 199, 271, 328 f., 339, 341, 346, 446, **567–573**, 623, 634, 644, 687, 713, 739, 742
  Vol. 2: 359, 417, 744
  Vol. 3: 69, 84, 87 f., 170, 214
Exhortation **Vol. 1:** 65, 336 f., 341, 400–402, 491 f., 510, 542, 570, 602–604, 607, 623, 630
  Vol. 2: 101, 106, 121, 123, 203, 214, 239, 263 f., 272, 423, 435, 438, 517, 598, 766, 912, 924
  Vol. 3: 54, 87, 118, 197, 219, 351, 685, 928, 1027, 1088, 1113, 1118
Exile **Vol. 1:** 52–56, 61 f., 141, 196, 262, 294, 379, 410, 414, 531, 539, 612, 632, 683, 685 f., 689 f., 700, 716, 734
  Vol. 2: 32, 100, 105, 226, 266, 330, 376, 541, 691, 801, 866, 889
  Vol. 3: 69, 79, 94, 147, 149, 190, 193, 249 f., 336, 355, 566, 590, 654, 777, 815, 845, 866 f., 873, 960, 986, 1074, 1099, 1100 f., 1104
Existence **Vol. 1:** 57, 65 f., 70 f., 95, 166, 222, 229, 234, 236, 238, 423, 431, 433, 436, 444, 470, 472 f., 475, 483, 485 f., 492, 500, 516, 539–541, 544, 551 f., 562, 564 f., 595, 597 f., 601 f., 607, 619, 644, 654, 661, 675 f., 678 f., 697, 706 f., 711, 713, 719, 727, 735
  Vol. 2: 52, 68, 100, 158, 286, 295, 307, 311, 314, 350, 361, 364, 394, 402, 453, 471, 476, 479, 493, 657, 662, 671, 719, 721
  Vol. 3: 122, 224
Existential **Vol. 2:** 384, 399, 906
Existential ontology **Vol. 1:** 65
Existential truth **Vol. 3:** 894
Existentialism **Vol. 1:** 54, **57**, 64 f.
  Vol. 3: 328
Existentialist **Vol. 1:** 681
  Vol. 3: 58
Existentialist philosophy **Vol. 1:** 54
Exodus **Vol. 1:** 53, **57**, 65, 99, 173, 249, 281, 290, 531 f., 539, 632 f., 737
  Vol. 2: 99, 150, 227, 410, 492, 521, 534, 540, 602, 636 f., 640, 871, 889
  Vol. 3: 47, 181, 194, 201, 238, 332, 336, 359, 406, 423, 559, 653, 836, 863, 940, 960,

969 f., 975, 1011
Exorcism **Vol. 1:** 121, 384, 451, 453, 572
  Vol. 2: 519, 556, 560, 610
  Vol. 3: 61, 81, 103, **468–476**, 507 f., 651, 695 f.
Exorcist **Vol. 1:** 322, 670
  Vol. 2: 165
  Vol. 3: 394, **473–476**, 643, **737–743**
Expand **Vol. 1:** 253
Expansion **Vol. 2:** 359, 462
Expect **Vol. 2: 238–246**, 295, 309, 313, 354, 359, 860, 921
  Vol. 3: 744–746
Expectation **Vol. 1:** 296, 329, 423, 440, 482, 544 f., 553, 598, 633 f., 642, 660, 689 f., 702, 706, 712 f., 720, 722, 725, 729, 735
  Vol. 2: 44, 95, 110, **238–246**, 264, 294, 307, 325, 329, 337, 340, 377, 383, 385–387, 402, 420, 427, 606, 664 f., 674, 698, 709, 731, 737, 772 f., 857, 875, 894, 900, 902, 905, 912, 915, 923
  Vol. 3: 30, 40, 63, 80, 121, 203, 225, 272, 274, 301, 318, 460, 462, 545, 615, 618, 632, 650, 695, 726, 731, 831, 836, 838, 840, 848, 886, 1155
Expediency **Vol. 1:** 397
  Vol. 2: 721
  Vol. 3: 541, 826
Expedition **Vol. 3: 958–967**
Expel **Vol. 1:** 453, 529
  Vol. 2: 463
Expel spirit **Vol. 3:** 473
Expend **Vol. 1:** 479
  Vol. 3: 840
Expense **Vol. 2:** 518
  Vol. 3: 551
Expensive **Vol. 1:** 260
  Vol. 2: 293, 547
Experience **Vol. 1:** 56, 192, 253, 258, 278, 352, 359, 411, 483 f., 514, 527 f., 536, 540, 564, 571, 583, 585, 594, 618, 620, 629, 640, 649, 654, 669, 691, 699, 716, 727
  Vol. 2: 78, 103, 115 f., 211, 261, **269–271**, 315, 351, 353 f., 359 f., **390–409**, 420, 422 f., 445, 568, 593, 909, 923
  Vol. 3: 55 f., 123, 232, 237, 260, 493, 511, 513, 516, 602, 676, 719, 761, 799, 812, 888, 894, **1147–1152**
Experience distress **Vol. 3: 858 f.**
Experienced **Vol. 1:** 56, 332
  Vol. 2: 362
Experiential profession **Vol. 2:** 405
Experiment **Vol. 3: 798–810**
Expert **Vol. 1:** 484, 512
  Vol. 2: 222, 392, 456
Expert in Jewish law **Vol. 3: 477–482**
Expiate **Vol. 3:** 146, **148–166**, 167
Expiation **Vol. 1:** 700
  Vol. 2: 261, 766
  Vol. 3: 353, 364, 422, 574
Expiatory **Vol. 1:** 107, 344, 479, 612, 699
  Vol. 2: 582
  Vol. 3: 102, 198, 779
Expire **Vol. 1:** 430 f., 734, 737

445

Vol. 2: 368
Vol. 3: 708
Explain Vol. 1: 57, 59, 506, **573–584**
  Vol. 2: 362, 401, 555, **726–729**, 907
  Vol. 3: 310, **316 f.**, 335, 337, 495, 569 f., 768, 898, 906, 1078, 1137, 1143
Explanation Vol. 1: 57, 59, 573
  Vol. 2: 139, 169, 823
Exploit Vol. 3: 379, 834
Exploitation Vol. 1: 268, 547
  Vol. 2: 257, 308, 448, 737, 822
Exponent Vol. 1: 574
Expose Vol. 1: 349, 390, 416, 422, 425, 459, 489, 577, 602, 718
  Vol. 2: 140, 284, 339, 350, 368, 448, 542
  Vol. 3: 203, 310, 570, 886, 892
Expose to public disgrace Vol. 2: **291**
Exposition Vol. 1: 69, 573 f., 580, 628 f., 709
  Vol. 2: 174, 209
  Vol. 3: 88, 112, 775, 821, 1052
Expositor Vol. 2: 281
Exposure Vol. 3: 96
Expound Vol. 1: 67, 573, 576 f., 579, 581, 737
  Vol. 2: 327, 362, 441, 448
  Vol. 3: 352, 478, 761, 767
Express Vol. 1: 669, 722
  Vol. 2: 353, 431, 648, 884
Expression Vol. 1: 579, 580, 602, 642, 655, 705, 727
  Vol. 2: 115, 334, 391, 417–424, 430, 547
  Vol. 3: 128
Expulsion Vol. 1: 466, 687
  Vol. 2: 847
Extend Vol. 1: 742
  Vol. 2: 131
Extend hand Vol. 3: 759
Extension Vol. 1: 565
  Vol. 2: 197 f., 314, 316
Extent Vol. 2: 197, 329, 683
Extermination Vol. 1: 465, 468
  Vol. 2: 308
  Vol. 3: 342
External Vol. 1: 261, 680, 704 f., 708 f., 714, 717, 720
  Vol. 2: 102 f., 136, 336, 605
  Vol. 3: 30 f., 106, 234
Extinct Vol. 3: 109
Extinction Vol. 1: 429, 463 f., 499, 526
Extinguish Vol. 2: 658
  Vol. 3: **109–111**
Extinguisher Vol. 1: 63
Extort Vol. 1: 212
  Vol. 2: 44, 201, 862
  Vol. 3: 557 f., 574, 758
Extortion Vol. 3: 756
Extortioner Vol. 3: 757
Extra-marital Vol. 1: 497–500
  Vol. 2: 582
Extraction Vol. 2: 660
Extradition Vol. 3: 594
Extraordinary Vol. 2: 621 f.
Extravagance Vol. 3: 395
Extravagant Vol. 2: 128
Extreme Vol. 2: 55

Extremity Vol. 1: 687
  Vol. 2: 197
Exult Vol. 1: 227
  Vol. 2: **352–354**, 436, 862
  Vol. 3: 29
Exultation Vol. 2: **352–354**, 432
Eye Vol. 1: 118, 162 f., 189, 218, 230 f., 234, 261, 319, 381, 423 f., 453, 458, 561, 565, 585, 613, 656, 667, 683, 695, 726 f., 731
  Vol. 2: 28, 110, 116, 153 f., 174, 176, 187, 192, 215 f., 279, 302, 350 f., 484, 487, 552, 579, 690, 726, 728, 873, 925
  Vol. 3: 192, 312, **511–521**, 717, 916 f., 993, 1002
Eye of a needle Vol. 1: 116
  Vol. 2: 843
  Vol. 3: 213
Eye-salve Vol. 3: **518 f.**
Eye-service Vol. 1: 587
  Vol. 3: 572
Eyesight Vol. 2: 490
Eyewitness Vol. 1: 266, 395
  Vol. 2: 645
  Vol. 3: 60, 290, 773, 894, 1033, 1122
Ezekiel Vol. 1: 52, 66, 128, 280, 499, 531
  Vol. 2: 189, 226, 240, 583, 670, 711, 823
  Vol. 3: 79, 104, 139, 249, 269 f., 418, 439, 609, 692, 784, 788, 986, 1098–1101, 1103
Ezekiel's vision Vol. 2: 97, 612 f.
  Vol. 3: 419, 787 f., 871, 1098
Ezra Vol. 1: 50, 52 f., 64, 66, 245
  Vol. 2: 307, 369, 439, 466, 636, 848
  Vol. 3: 34, 51, 250, 451, 478 f., 485

Fable Vol. 2: 643, 645, 757
  Vol. 3: 816
Face Vol. 1: 181, 211, 431, **585–587**, 609
  Vol. 2: 46, 61, 161, 212 f., 263, 326, 384, 395, 482, 484, 572, 793
  Vol. 3: 512, 514, 521, 531, 862–864
Face of God Vol. 1: 211, **585**
  Vol. 2: 68, 215, 218, 312, 317
Fact Vol. 2: 407
Factions Vol. 1: 533
  Vol. 3: 1031
Factor Vol. 1: 692, 738
Facts Vol. 3: 759, 876, 888
Factual narrative Vol. 2: 643
Factual truth Vol. 3: 894
Faculty Vol. 2: **391**
  Vol. 3: 128, 131
Faculty of comprehension Vol. 3: **130–133**
Fade Vol. 1: 411, 673, 678, 724
Fail Vol. 1: 609 f., 673
  Vol. 2: 400, 406, 445
  Vol. 3: 839, **952–956**, 1104
Fail to reach Vol. 3: **952–956**
Failing Vol. 3: **346 f.**
Failure Vol. 1: 219, 378, 426, 544, 597, 607, 723, 725 f., 736, 742
  Vol. 2: 92, 165, 178, 263, 265, 282, 308, 315, 395, 399, 407, 435, 443, 478, 665, 820
  Vol. 3: 542, 573, 577, 585, 802, 807

Faint **Vol. 1:** 262
  Vol. 2: 265
Faint-hearted **Vol. 1:** 329, 504
  Vol. 2: 259
  Vol. 3: 687, 955
Fair **Vol. 1:** 204, 625, 637
  Vol. 2: 102 f., 438
  Vol. 3: 845–849
Fair weather **Vol. 3: 1000–1004**
Fairness **Vol. 2: 497–500**
Faith **Vol. 1:** 50 f., 57, 59 f., 74, 76, 78–81, 93, 95, 97, 110, 112, 116, 120, 123, 138, 148–150, 154, 157–160, 163, 166, 180, 185, 191, 215, 222 f., 225, 228, 236, 238, 244, 248, 255–257, 261, 275, 277, 281 f., 286, 289, 297 f., 300 f., 303 f., 308 f., 311, 316, 318, 321–325, 328, 330, 333, 336, 341, 346, 350 f., 354 f., 358 f., 361, 372, 379 f., 382, 384, 386, 397 f., 401, 408, 414, 417, 422, 424, 426, 433 f., 439–441, 452, 455, 459–461, 467, 472, 475, 478, 480, 483, 486, 489, 491–493, 496 f., 499, 502, 504 f., 509 f., 525, 528 f., 532, 534, 540, 542 f., 547, 551 f., 559, 562, 571, **587–606**, 607–609, 619, 624, 633, 637, 639, 641, 643 f., 647, 649–651, 656, 659–662, 675, 689, 691, 695, 698 f., 704, 712–714, 719, 722 f., 730 f., 735–740
  Vol. 2: 31, 45, 47, 63 f., 68, 73, 78, 94 f., 99, 111 f., 117, 120–123, 125 f., 129–133, 135 f., 142, 156, 162, 168, 170, 175–177, 179 f., 182 f., 186, 190, 194, 196, 198, 200, 207 f., 213, 215, 217 f., 221, 223, 229, 239–243, 250 f., 266, 273, 277, 280, 286, 297, 300–303, 310, 314 f., 318 f., 327, 330 f., 335, 338, 340, 342, 349, 354, 360 f., 364, 374 f., 396, 404 f., 407, 418, 443, 445–447, 449–452, 460, 462, 469–471, 473, 482, 488, 504, 509, 515 f., 535, 542 f., 545–549, 560, 563, 581, 595, 597, 603, 605 f., 615, 617 f., 620 f., 624 f., 636, 641 f., 645, 654 f., 658, 672, 676, 678, 682, 708, 716–721, 724, 729, 736, 766, 768, 771, 776, 786, 789, 793–795, 800, 804, 809, 812, 817 f., 827, 835, 839, 843 f., 857–859, 861, 868, 871, 873, 875, 877, 881, 884, 891, 894, 900, 906, 925 f.
  Vol. 3: 48, 55, 57, 61, 71–73, 106–110, 118, 120, 127, 129, 132, 136, 142–144, 161, 163, 165 f., 168, 171 f., 191, 202–204, 211 f., 214 f., 220 f., 225–228, 232 f., 236, 240, 246, 252, 257, 264, 270, 277 f., 280–282, 286 f., 289, 291 f., 296, 299 f., 310, 313, 315, 317, 319, 325, 328, 333, 337, 342 f., 347, 363–368, 372 f., 383, 385 f., 389, 391, 393 f., 403, 416–418, 420, 433 f., 447, 463, 470 f., 489, 492, 499, 505, 507, 516 f., 520, 523, 529 f., 532, 535, 548–550. 576, 580–582, 584–586, 591, 602, 613, 646, 675, 685, 710, 728, 746, 751, 764, 768, 771, 774, 779 f., 783, 793, 800 f., 803, 809, 814, 818, 821, 824–826, 832, 837–839, 842, 844, 846, 849, 861, 869, 878, 889, 891, 899, 903, 908, 915, 917, 925, 927, 934, 945, 951, 954 f., 965–968, 973, 990, 995, 1011 f., 1021 f., 1031, 1033, 1042, 1045–1047, 1053, 1067, 1070, 1111–1150 f., 1158, 1188 f., **1211–1214**
Faithful **Vol. 1:** 99, 118, 217, 293, 406, 424, 455, 513, 532, 568, 571, 594, 627, 656, 684
  Vol. 2: 73, 136, 159, 229, 237, 239, 249, 308 f., 312, 315, 353, 358, 360, 367, 837
  Vol. 3: 228, 357, 362, 367, 526, 800, 809, **874–901**, 1046 f., 1065
Faithfulness **Vol. 1:** 74, 227, 251, 311, 346, 357, 367, 386, 490, 499, 591, 594, 597 f., 603, 659
  Vol. 2: 77, 105, 119, 181, 240, 255, 261, 263, 315, 364, 396, 428, 498, 540, 797 f.
  Vol. 3: 45, 70, 79, 121, 135, 157, 166 f., 192, 215, 234, 320, 354, 366–368, 373, 391, 514, 565, 578, 626, 649, 685, 729, 776, 810, **874–901**, 966
Faithless **Vol. 1:** 423, 448, 455, 511
  Vol. 2: 36, 418, 479
Faithlessness **Vol. 2:** 49, 307, 351, 541
  Vol. 3: 1054
Fake **Vol. 2:** 556
Fall **Vol. 1:** 52, 57, 72, 79, 86 f., 113, 336, 352, 433 f., 524, 542, 567, **606–611**, 682, 692 f., 724
  Vol. 2: 45, 51, 123, 245, 287, 354, 366 f., 394, 405, 420, 423, 460, 478, 504, 651, 681, 692, 705 f., 708, 710, 714 f., 764, 778, 791, 794, 888 f., 910, 914, 916 f., 930
  Vol. 3: 277, 468, 470, 578, 585 f., 725, 733, 735, 806, 810, 954, 996, 1063, 1100, 1148
Fall away **Vol. 1:** 416, 554, **606–611**
  Vol. 2: 123, 285, 325, 708 f., 717, 775, 791
  Vol. 3: 803, 838
Fall behind **Vol. 3:** 251
Fall beside **Vol. 3: 585 f.**
Fall down **Vol. 3:** 806
Fall of angels **Vol. 1:** 102 f.
Fall from grace **Vol. 1:** 611
  Vol. 2: 120
  Vol. 3: 363
Fall of Satan **Vol. 1:** 83
Fall short **Vol. 1:** 56, 546, 675
  Vol. 2: 161, 380
Fallacy **Vol. 1:** 550, 577
Fallen **Vol. 1:** 102, 222, 384, 451 f., 468, 525
  Vol. 2: 237, 568, 723
Fallen angels **Vol. 2:** 213
  Vol. 3: 829
Fallen humanity **Vol. 3:** 32
Fallen spirits **Vol. 2:** 205
Falling stars **Vol. 3:** 736
Fallible **Vol. 1:** 678 f.
  Vol. 2: 439
Fallow **Vol. 2:** 822
  Vol. 3: 190, 918
False **Vol. 1:** 66, 124, 228, 347, 357, 456, 496, 504, 512, 591 f., 607, 679, 681
  Vol. 2: 51, 169, 225, 314, 407, 473, 491, 606, 724, 921
  Vol. 3: 201, 988, 1054
False accusation **Vol. 3:** 95
False alternatives **Vol. 3:** 942
False apostle **Vol. 1:** 228, 710
  Vol. 2: 472, 677
  Vol. 3: 88, 886

False brother **Vol. 1:** 254, 322
  Vol. 2: 472
False Christ **Vol. 1:** 124
  Vol. 2: 472, 915 f., 930
False claim **Vol. 3:** 81, 932
False confidence **Vol. 1:** 308
False congregation **Vol. 1:** 296
False divination **Vol. 3:** 201
False doctrine **Vol. 1:** 352, 487
  Vol. 2: 78, 133, 135, 171, 286, 625, 710
  Vol. 3: 887
False estimate **Vol. 3:** 888
False evidence **Vol. 3:** 1041
False expectations **Vol. 2:** 902
  Vol. 3: 804
False freedom **Vol. 3:** 70
False gods **Vol. 2:** 73 f., 285 f., 453, 503
  Vol. 3: 919
False gospel **Vol. 1:** 415
False hope **Vol. 2:** 240
False idea **Vol. 3:** 930
False independence **Vol. 3:** 604
False lips **Vol. 2:** 468
False messiah **Vol. 3:** 378
False name **Vol. 2: 648–656**
False oath **Vol. 3:** 76, 881
False outlook **Vol. 2:** 49
False peace **Vol. 2:** 781
False piety **Vol. 3:** 141
False practice **Vol. 1:** 352
False prayer **Vol. 2: 864**
False prophecy **Vol. 3:** 94, 1097
False prophet **Vol. 1:** 114, 125, 323, 383, 512, 527, 550, 567
  Vol. 2: 154, 208, 240, 458, 470, 472, 474, 629, 633, 651, 701, 754, 773, 778, 904
  Vol. 3: 51, **74–89**, 99, 210, 377, 475, 628, 768, 800, 803, 856, 868, 888, 962, 1098
False prophetess **Vol. 3:** 844
False reasoning **Vol. 2:** 458
False reliance **Vol. 3:** 788
False representation **Vol. 3:** 341
False saviour **Vol. 3:** 803
False security **Vol. 1:** 79, 424, 542, 596, 610
  Vol. 2: 841
False shepherd **Vol. 1:** 559
  Vol. 2: 413
False standard **Vol. 1:** 566
  Vol. 3: 825
False step **Vol. 2: 705–707**
  Vol. 3: 585 f.
False teacher **Vol. 1:** 138, 261, 311, 402, 425, 443, 460, 535, 578, 637
  Vol. 2: 94 f., 152, 221, 447, 453, 459 f., 463, 472 f., 509, 518, 574, 579, 645, 766
  Vol. 3: 128, 137, 344, 500, 710, 765 f., 864, 888, 915, 942, 954, 1003, 1054
False teaching **Vol. 1:** 238, 257, 460, 469, 604, 611
  Vol. 2: 268, 509
  Vol. 3: 70, 380, 999
False way **Vol. 3:** 938
False witness **Vol. 2:** 470, 472, 686, 871
  Vol. 3: 529, 880, **1038–1050**

False words **Vol. 3:** 876
Falsehood **Vol. 1:** 66, 225, 232, 359, 448, 653
  Vol. 2: 71 f., 492
  Vol. 3: 576, 876, 880, 882, 889–893, 1079
Falsify **Vol. 2:** 370
Fame **Vol. 1:** 400
  Vol. 2: 46, 265
  Vol. 3: 840, 1156
Familiar **Vol. 1:** 484, 614 f.
  Vol. 2: 392, 395
Familiar spirit **Vol. 2:** 554
Family **Vol. 1:** 159, 165, 182, 192, 194–198, 207 f., 240, 254, 256 f., 264 f., 286 f., 289, 294, 308, 512, 530 f., 614 f., 617, 619, 621, 624–626, 629, 634, 640
  Vol. 2: 35, 92, 95, 206, 225, 234, 247 f., 250 f., 317, 363, 386 f., 428, 508, 538 f., 548 f., 582, 608, 655, 692, 711, 737, 789, 905
  Vol. 3: 36, 355, 448, 673, 756, 777, 852, 865, 870 f., 928, 930, 1053, 1093
Family gods **Vol. 2:** 317
Family of manuscripts **Vol. 1:** 70
Family ties **Vol. 2:** 825
Family tree **Vol. 2:** 35 f.
  Vol. 3: 652, 658, 872
Famine **Vol. 1:** 118, 203, 380, 531, 642, 716
  Vol. 2: 264–268, 274, 318, 688, 711, 730, 827, 836, 911
  Vol. 3: 201, 249, 498, 590, 713
Famous **Vol. 1:** 381
Fan **Vol. 2:** 411
Fanatical **Vol. 2:** 101
Fanaticism **Vol. 2:** 386
  Vol. 3: 1052
Fantasy **Vol. 1:** 679
  Vol. 2: 181, 430
Far **Vol. 2:** 52 f.
Far off **Vol. 1:** 523, 691
  Vol. 2: 113
Far-reaching **Vol. 2:** 428
Farce **Vol. 2:** 168
Farewell **Vol. 2:** 169, 356, 549, 914
  Vol. 3: 757
Farm **Vol. 2:** 29
Farmer **Vol. 1:** 625, 656
  Vol. 2: 245, 822
Farmer of taxes **Vol. 3: 755–759**
Farrer, Austin **Vol. 3: 334**
Fascination **Vol. 1:** 625
Fashion **Vol. 1:** 380, 492, 521, 708
Fast **Vol. 1:** 120, 143, 245, 384, 487, 495, 515, **611–613**, 625, 630, 672
  Vol. 2: 159, 216, 260, 264, 267, 272, 277, 358, 383, 534, 585, 714, 754, 864, 885, 893
  Vol. 3: 51, 408, 543, 804, 921, 954, 996, 1007
Fasten **Vol. 1:** 171, 241, 663
  Vol. 3: 859
Fat **Vol. 1:** 119, 261, 672
  Vol. 2: 154, 335
  Vol. 3: 159, 416, 423
Fatal **Vol. 1:** 336, 422, 510, 647, 699
  Vol. 2: 138, 226, 435
Fatalism **Vol. 3:** 834
Fate **Vol. 1:** 103, 163, 243, 257, 267, 277, 313,

Fate (*cont'd*)
315, 390, 403 f., 419, 431, 434, 436, 439,
450, 453, 464, 472, 516, 545, 594, 597, 692 f.
Vol. 2: 61, 63, 66, 80, 120, 136, 138, 192,
205, 259, 298, 303, 393, 406, 416, 449,
457 f., 501, 510, 657, 662, **664–666,** 920
Vol. 3: 27, 205, 260, 270, 421, 439 f., 561,
577, 583, 602, 626, 628, 717, 719–721, 744,
776, 833 f., 1054
Fate of spirits **Vol. 3: 475**
Father **Vol. 1:** 49, 65 f., 76 f., 79, 90, 173, 176 f.,
190, 198, 203, 213, 222, 238, 240, 251,
255 f., 277 f., 282, 286–289, 298, 301, 311,
323 f., 326, 329, 336–338, 346, 356, 359,
375, 409 f., 440, 442, 453, 461 f., 464, 469 f.,
486 f., 492, 509, 511, 522, 526, 549, 556,
570, 575, **614–621,** 637–639, 651, 655, 667,
674, 681, 693, 704, 712, 716, 720, 729 f., 740
Vol. 2: 46, 62–64, 71, 73, 75 f., 78 f., 81, 83 f.,
101, 120, 125, 137, 165, 170, 178 f., 185 f.,
192, 194 f., 203 f., 216 f., 229, 231 f., 243,
245, 247, 250, 254, 262, 269, 276, 278,
289 f., 303, 307, 317–319, 332, 342, 349,
358 f., 366, 381, 383, 386, 388, 401, 403 f.,
426, 435, 437, 450, 486, 495, 497, 499 f.,
505–507, 516 f., 541 f., 546, 548 f., 561, 566,
571, 578, 588, 604, 607, 610, 624 f., 645,
653, 655, 686, 718, 721–723, 725, 737 f.,
770, 780 f., 799, 825, 830, 832, 834, 857,
867–873, 878 f., 881, 883, 885, 896 f., 899,
904, 917, 921, 927–930
Vol. 3: 32, 47, 61, 71, 78, 114, 135, 172, 174,
186 f., 202, 225, 228, 242, 244, 257, 281,
286, 313 f., 320, 326 f., 343, 362, 395, 403,
409, 416, 435, 463, 472, 504, 509, 517, 523,
527, 529, 569, 588, 624, 635–642, 644–648,
650, 652, 656, 659 f., 675, 683, 710, 728,
731, 748, 770, 776–779, 790, 803, 807, 848,
863, 865, 871, 891, 935, 941, 946, 965,
1017 f., 1045 f., 1055, 1057 f., 1060, 1069,
1074 f., 1107, 1114, 1122, 1133, 1135, 1150,
1152, 1154, 1163, 1178, 1186, 1204
Father in heaven **Vol. 2: 193**
Father of glory **Vol. 2:** 46
Father of lies **Vol. 1:** 458
Father of lights **Vol. 2:** 495
  Vol. 3: 556
Father of mercies **Vol. 2:** 598
Father of nations **Vol. 1:** 79
Fatherhood **Vol. 1:** 619–621
Fatherland **Vol. 1:** 615 f.
  Vol. 2: 476
Fatherless **Vol. 1:** 615 f
  Vol. 2: 737 f.
  Vol. 3: 1074
Fatherly **Vol. 2:** 106
Fatigue **Vol. 1:** 262
Fatten **Vol. 1:** 743
Fault **Vol. 1:** 261, 345 f., 525, 550, 574, 608
  Vol. 2: 63, 142, 144 f., 215
  Vol. 3: 92, 529, 573
Fault-finding **Vol. 2:** 143
Faultless **Vol. 3:** 101, 923
Favour **Vol. 1:** 52, 216, 395, 501, 540–542, 590,

622
  Vol. 2: 72, 115 f., 119, 122, 167, 190, 257,
263, 308, 317, 356, 385, 428, 438, 485, 538,
547, 622, 815 f., **817–820,** 837, 863
  Vol. 3: 149, 151, 167, 918, 1053
Favourable **Vol. 3: 744–746**
Favourable opportunity **Vol. 3: 833–839**
Fear **Vol. 1:** 111, 168, 173, 239, 265, 276, 310,
327, 329, 360 f., 409, 412, 420–422, 431–
435, 439, 448, 452–456, 484, 507, 510, 530,
537, 559, 570, 577, 586, 590, 609, 611, **621–
624,** 646, 652, 675, 679, 686–688, 691, 715,
719
  Vol. 2: 49, 64, 85, 90 f., 93–95, 99, 178, 180,
213, 217 f., 227, 239 f., 242, 245, 261, 263,
266, 271, 281, 349, 357–360, 391, 396,
419 f., 434, 449, 478, 484, 491, 594, 604,
621–626, 705, 736, 772, 807, 817, 819, 830,
855, 866, 894, 926
  Vol. 3: 27, 30, 39, 98, 117, 130, 136, 157,
202, 249, 258, 318, 324, 341, 382, 557,
561 f., 597, 657, 710 f., 721, 747, 800, 953,
1028, 1036, 1095
Fearful **Vol. 1:** 364, 403
  Vol. 2: 238, 241, 244
  Vol. 3: 982
Fearlessness **Vol. 2:** 103, 734
  Vol. 3: 592, 1095
Feast **Vol. 1:** 53, 59, 116, 122, 224, 274, 291,
308, 332, 384, 416, 515, **624–635,** 641, 654,
666, 691, 743
  Vol. 2: 226, 273, 277, 314, 354–356, 385,
410, 437, 441, 461, 463, 478, 521 f., 536,
674, 690, 716, 727, 737, 755, 783–788, 880,
885, 887, 927
  Vol. 3: 51, 69, 407, 410, 421, 424, 431, 436,
440, 478, 568, 608, 669, 673, 745, 781, 873,
919, 1074 (*also* → Festival)
Feast of Booths **Vol. 3:** 813
Feast of the Covenant **Vol. 2:** 441
Feast of Dedication **Vol. 1:** 626, 629
  Vol. 3: 165
Feast of Lots **Vol. 1:** 626
Feast of New Wine **Vol. 3:** 1162
Feast of Oil **Vol. 3:** 1162
Feast of Renewal of Covenant **Vol. 1:** 627
  Vol. 2: 441, 784
Feast of Tabernacles **Vol. 1:** 100, 626, 628 f.,
632
  Vol. 2: 217, 355, 644
  Vol. 3: 789, **811–814,** 1005
Feast of Unleavened Bread **Vol. 1:** 249, 633
  Vol. 2: 461, 463
Feast of Weeks **Vol. 1:** 625–628, 631
  Vol. 2: 783
Feast-offering **Vol. 2:** 410
Feature **Vol. 2:** 335 f.
Fee **Vol. 1:** 484
Feeble **Vol. 1:** 192
  Vol. 2: 211, 263
  Vol. 3: 178
Feed **Vol. 1:** 250, 277, 320, 341, 617, 629, 670,
687, 743
  Vol. 2: 411, 543, 823

449

Vol. 3: 358, 545
Feeding the five thousand **Vol. 1:** 250, 283, 341, 384, 729, 743
 Vol. 2: 379, 523, 534, 630, 699
 Vol. 3: 240, 508 f.
Feeding the four thousand **Vol. 1:** 250, 283, 341, 729, 743
 Vol. 2: 523, 630, 699
Feel **Vol. 2:** 398
Feel compassion **Vol. 2: 594–598**
Feel pain **Vol. 2: 419–421**
Feeling **Vol. 1:** 106, 230, 555, 568, 622
 Vol. 2: 116, **180–184,** 245, 257, 312, 352, 357, 419, 547, 568, 599, 875
 Vol. 3: 122 f., 557, 677, 680, 719, 908, 1134
Feet-washing **Vol. 1:** 153, 630
 Vol. 2: 303, 535, 754, 812
 Vol. 3: 547, 597, 611, 848
Felix **Vol. 1:** 270, 341, 346, 495, 695
 Vol. 2: 258, 451, 596, 707
 Vol. 3: 40, 65, 718
Fell **Vol. 1:** 867
Fellow **Vol. 1:** 255 f., 258 f., 680, 689, 691
Fellow-citizen **Vol. 2:** 794
Fellow-heir **Vol. 2: 295–303**
Fellow-worker **Vol. 3:** 548, **1147–1152**
Fellowship **Vol. 1:** 95, 97, 126, 148, 175, 213, 219, 222, 225, 232, 237, 257, 259, 291 f., 294, 298–301, 304, 315, 319, 347, 367, 369 f., 386, 424, 434, 440 f., 448, 452, 455, 467, 482 f., 489–493, 519, 554, 586, 596, **635–644,** 657, 685, 688, 691, 696, 702, 719, 722 f.
 Vol. 2: 31, 39, 48, 75 f., 78, 104, 121, 129 f., 152, 162, 237, 242, 249–251, 253, 271 f., 275, 277, 286, 302, 304, 319, 360, 386, 402–404, 427, 444, 473, 478 f., 499, 520, 533, 536, 546 f., 549, 596, 653, 655, 705, 742, 762 f., 768, 789, 795, 810, 812, 826 f., 859, 861, 879
 Vol. 3: 47, 57, 104, 106, 129, 135, 163, 225, 227, 245, 256, 262 f., 346, 349, 378, 459, 518, 535 f., 547, 553, 572, 580, 602, 614, 681, 693, 702, 724 f., 745, 749, 751, 793, 832, 848, 854, 891, 924, 934, 937, 941, 945, 1025
Female **Vol. 2:** 161, 287, **569–571**
 Vol. 3: 1055–1075
Fence **Vol. 3:** 140, 773, 949, **950 f.**
Ferment **Vol. 2: 461–463**
Ferocity **Vol. 1:** 420, 515
 Vol. 3: 230
Fertile **Vol. 2:** 211, 265
Fertility **Vol. 1:** 208 f., 354, 497 f., 560, 611 f., 624 f.
 Vol. 2: 791
 Vol. 3: 274, 425, 692, 782, 866, 918 f., 986, 1069, 1071, 1093
Fertility cult **Vol. 2:** 539, 541, 573
Fertility gods **Vol. 2:** 265
Fertility rites **Vol. 2:** 69, 567, 583
Fertilize **Vol. 1:** 377, 498
Fertilizer **Vol. 3:** 445, 448
Fervent **Vol. 2:** 868

Fervour **Vol. 1:** 318
Festal **Vol. 3:** 208
Fester **Vol. 1:** 683
Festival **Vol. 1:** 245, 249 f., 272, 274, 304, 360, 612, **624–635,** 700
 Vol. 2: 311, 326, 355, 521, 676, 783–788
 Vol. 3: 50, 107, 232 f., 237, 255, 408, 424, 501, 556, 692, 669, 733, 835 (also→Feast)
Festival of enthronement **Vol. 2:** 374 f., 644
Festival of Lights **Vol. 1:** 627, 631
Festival of Wood-carrying **Vol. 1:** 627
Festive **Vol. 2:** 353–355, 358
Festus **Vol. 1:** 270, 341, 453, 529
 Vol. 2: 369, 450
 Vol. 3: 718, 884
Fetter **Vol. 1:** 171, 190
 Vol. 3: 591 f.
Fever **Vol. 1:** 94, 377, 572, 636, 652 f., 656
Few **Vol. 1:** 97, 283, 735, 739
 Vol. 2: 427–429, 683, 692, 720
Fiancée **Vol. 3:** 1055
Fickleness **Vol. 3:** 833, 887
Fiction **Vol. 1:** 550
 Vol. 2: 152, 643
Fiction **Vol. 3:** 554, 1081
Fidelity **Vol. 1:** 589, 594 f., 603
 Vol. 2: 694
 Vol. 3: 354, 879
Field **Vol. 1:** 93, 209, 222, 263, 267, 277, 411, 517, 519 f., 525, 647, 673, 689, 744
 Vol. 2: 30, 216, 245, 296, 833
 Vol. 3: 119, 191, 229, 526, 1058
Field of blood **Vol. 1:** 93
Field semantics **Vol. 3:** 1141
Fierce **Vol. 1:** 260 f., 520, 653
Fiery **Vol. 1:** 653–656
Fifth Commandment **Vol. 3:** 95
Fiftieth **Vol. 2:** 783
Fig **Vol. 1:** 73, 417, 515, 600, **721–728**
 Vol. 2: 267, 382, 623, 630, 871, 912, 916 f.
 Vol. 3: 256, 517, 532, 557, 736, 865, 867–869
Fight **Vol. 1:** 164, 431, 435, 470, 544, **644–652,** 653, 662, 675
 Vol. 2: 135, 138, 305, 360, 362
 Vol. 3: 250, 601, 677, 946 f., **958–967,** 981
Figurative **Vol. 1:** 122, 229, 268
 Vol. 2: 53, 149, 266, 269, 738, 743–760
 Vol. 3: 99, 102, 180, 311, 499, 710, 737, 754, 858, 936, 949, 986, 994
Figure **Vol. 1:** 71, 234, 266, 375, 585, 708 f.
 Vol. 2: 284, 287, 291, 337, 380, **743–756**
 Vol. 3: 483
Figure of speech **Vol. 2:** 278
Figurines **Vol. 3:** 915 f.
Fill **Vol. 1:** 318, 514, 728, 732, 736
 Vol. 2: 128, 195, 209, 215, 229, 358 f., 386, 855
Fill the hand **Vol. 2:** 60, 149
Fill up **Vol. 3:** 955
Filth **Vol. 1: 479 f.**
Filthiness **Vol. 1:** 448
Final **Vol. 1:** 423, 433, 443, 446, 499, 554, 563, 566, 583, 587, 628, 651, 653, 656 f., 667, 674, 693, 699, 725, 737

Final (cont'd)
  Vol. 2: 53, 56, 58, 100, 136, 154, 197, 300, 353, 357, 363, 383, 403, 461, 625, 785
Final hour **Vol. 3:** 849
Final judgment **Vol. 2:** 47, 202 f., 208, 301, 366, 383, 417, 597, 630, 665, 767, 826
  Vol. 3: 140, 193, 360, 500, 658, 695, 731, 778 f., 838, 947
Final state **Vol. 1:** 445
Final time **Vol. 2:** 58
Finality **Vol. 1:** 359
  Vol. 2: 718
Finality of judgment **Vol. 3:** 99
Finally **Vol. 2:** 55, 62 f.
  Vol. 3: 252, **952–956**
Financial **Vol. 1:** 477, 642
Financial help **Vol. 2:** 328
Financial support **Vol. 3:** 525
Find **Vol. 1:** 630, 709, 724
  Vol. 2: 833
  Vol. 3: 513, **527–533,** 754
Find fault **Vol. 2:** 139, 143
Find favour **Vol. 2:** 116
Find out **Vol. 1:** 676
  Vol. 2: 398
Fine **Vol. 2:** 98, 104, 577, 582
  Vol. 3: 96, 420
Fine linen **Vol. 3:** 794
Finery **Vol. 2:** 217
Finger **Vol. 1:** 683
  Vol. 2: 148
Finger of God **Vol. 1:** 651
  Vol. 2: 74, 150
  Vol. 3: 475
Finish **Vol. 1:** 429, 581, 734
  Vol. 2: 59 f., 64, 382
  Vol. 3: 349–351, 499
Finishing-post **Vol. 1:** 493
Finite **Vol. 2:** 77
Fir **Vol. 1:** 723
Fire **Vol. 1:** 144, 146, 151, 182, 205, 209, 224, 231, 314, 318, 322, 380, 387, 390, 414, 418, 420, 467, **652–658,** 700, 711
  Vol. 2: 45, 157, 193, 205, 208, 210, 304, 435, 452, 461, 485, 490, 493, 682, 746, 779, 785, 836
  Vol. 3: 93, 95 f., 99, 109–111, 143 f., 210, 239, 266, 315 f., 421 f., 426, 436, 443, 445–448, 470, 526 f., 639, 695, 713 f., 808 f., 859 f., 912, 914 f., 947, 952, 962, 982 f., 989 f., 992, 1014, 1079, 1091, 1096 f., 1178
Fire and brimstone **Vol. 3:** 1002
Firebrand **Vol. 3:** 557
Fireplace **Vol. 1:** 652
Firm **Vol. 1:** 97, **658–664,** 735
  Vol. 2: 129, 153, 267, 489, 611, 659, 706, 716
  Vol. 3: 387, 390, 394, **558–560,** 797, 878
Firmament **Vol. 1:** 522 f.
  Vol. 2: 184, 188–190, 192 f.
Firmicus Maternus **Vol. 1:** 327
Firmness **Vol. 2:** 123
First **Vol. 1:** 164 f., 177, 193, 195, 288, 334, **664–670,** 712
  Vol. 2: 44, 55, 157, 550, 693, 703, 720, 725, 729
  Vol. 3: 190, 415 f., 598, 855, 920
First cause **Vol. 3:** 331
First day **Vol. 1:** 630 f.
  Vol. 3: 410
First and last **Vol. 2:** 55, 57 f., 70, 80, 279, 282, 482
First man (→ Man, first)
First-born **Vol. 1:** 166, 177, 193 f., 208, 221, 256, 288, 304, 445, 519, **664–670,** 692, 707, 713
  Vol. 2: 310, 317, 491, 637, 703, 798, 835
  Vol. 3: 38, 190, 266, 636, 638, 644, 872, 1014
First-fruits **Vol. 1:** 166, 187, 210, 386, 638
  Vol. 2: 40, 48, 186, 226, 242 f., 288, 672, 675, 783, 884
  Vol. 3: 72, 199, 204, 297, 303, **415–436,** 701, 852
First-ripe **Vol. 1:** 724
Fiscal term **Vol. 3:** 854
Fish **Vol. 1:** 119, 175, 249 f., 344, 509, 518, 623, 666, **670–671,** 674, 725, 733
  Vol. 2: 32 f., 233, 351 f., 624, 630, 662, 685, 728
  Vol. 3: 444, 543, 753, 757, 985
Fish-costume **Vol. 1:** 670
Fisherman **Vol. 1:** 488 f., 493, 642
  Vol. 3: 313, 757
Fishlike **Vol. 1:** 670
Fist **Vol. 1:** 163
  Vol. 2: 148, 150
  Vol. 3: 857
Fit **Vol. 1:** 241, 505, 515
  Vol. 2: 102, 385
  Vol. 3: 348 f.
Fitness **Vol. 3:** 348
Fitting **Vol. 2:** 101, 212, **668 f.,** 683
  Vol. 3: 349, 353
Five **Vol. 2:** 685, **689 f.,** 692 f.
Fix **Vol. 1:** 332, 477, 658, 734 f.
Fixed order **Vol. 3:** 730, 734
Flame **Vol. 1:** 653, 656
  Vol. 3: 110
Flame-coloured **Vol. 1:** 653
Flamen Dialis **Vol. 2:** 461
Flash **Vol. 1:** 610
Flattery **Vol. 2:** 116, 259, 470
  Vol. 3: 1053
Flavia Neapolis **Vol. 3:** 457
Flavour **Vol. 1:** 657
  Vol. 2: 211
Flay **Vol. 1:** 162
  Vol. 3: 377, 421
Flee **Vol. 1:** 431, 493, 500, 512, **558 f.**
  Vol. 2: 215
Fleeting **Vol. 1:** 433, 512, 516, 651
  Vol. 2: 475
  Vol. 3: 691
Flesh **Vol. 1:** 54, 87, 106, 114, 138, 163, 169, 184, 221 f., 225, 229 f., 232 f., 236, 240, 257, 282, 286, 290, 299, 308, 311, 315, 323, 327, 336 f., 401 f., 411, 424, 446, 448, 455, 457 f., 461, 466 f., 469 f., 473, 506, 522, 535, 555–557, 592, 602, 625, 629, 637 f., 647, 670,

671–682, 683, 690 f., 695, 719, 726 f., 738 f., 741
Vol. 2: 62, 71, 75, 79 f., 91, 94, 163, 169, 171, 185, 209, 218, 225, 233, 235, 242, 269 f., 282, 339, 349, 366, 378, 398 f., 404, 445 f., 459, 477, 504 f., 521, 523, 532, 558, 565 f., 571 f., 579, 587, 602, 611, 617, 668, 673, 682, 709, 722, 806, 816, 818, 836, 919, 925, 928 f.
Vol. 3: 32, 54, 158, 174, 178, 186, 204, 227 f., 269, 273, 301, 313 f., 322, 364, 423 f., 447, 534 f., 538, 581, 597, 630, 645, 680, 685, 687, 691 f., 702, 724, 802, 813, 826, 939, 944 f., 949, 964, 994 f., 1021, 1064, 1101, 1117, 1158, 1176, 1199 f.
Flesh and blood **Vol. 2:** 599
Flew, Anthony **Vol. 3:** 1137
Flexibility **Vol. 3:** 1067
Flies **Vol. 2:** 637
Flight **Vol. 1:** 280, 558 f., 674, 685
    Vol. 2: 317, 350, 461
    Vol. 3: 1007, 1011
Flock **Vol. 1:** 115, 252, 286, 303, 305, 320, 503, 623, 632, 684
    Vol. 2: 31 f., 34, 56, 136, 383, 412 f., 429, 519, 586, 721, 723, 819, 832, 838, 841, 928
    Vol. 3: 421, **564–568**
Flog **Vol. 1:** 161 f., 407
Flood **Vol. 1:** 72, 168, 185, 382, 508, 522, 531, 593, 610, 657
    Vol. 2: 205, 382, 569, 613, 681 f.
    Vol. 3: 203, 248, 259, 469, 605, 628, 634, 653, 695, 851, 906, 982 f., 989 f., **991**
Florilegium **Vol. 3:** 487
Flour **Vol. 1:** 249 f.
    Vol. 3: 422, 917
Flourish **Vol. 1:** 678
    Vol. 2: 211, 360
Flow **Vol. 1: 682 f.**
    Vol. 2: 119
Flower **Vol. 1:** 277, 411, 609, 648, 673, 678
    Vol. 3: 521–527
Flowing water **Vol. 3:** 985
Fluid **Vol. 1:** 741
Flute **Vol. 2:** 436
Flutter **Vol. 2:** 422 f.
Fly **Vol. 1:** 172, 608
    Vol. 3: 469
Foal **Vol. 1:** 117
Focus **Vol. 2:** 325–329
Fodder **Vol. 1:** 743
    Vol. 2: 211
    Vol. 3: 444
Fodor, J. A. **Vol. 3:** 1134
Foe **Vol. 1:** 241, 531
    Vol. 2: 63, 83
Fog **Vol. 3: 1000–1004**
Fold **Vol. 2:** 31, 586
    Vol. 3: 572
Folk lore **Vol. 3:** 59
Follow **Vol. 1:** 118, 324, 335, 359, 402, 423 f., 446, 464, 480–494, 588, 591, 593, 600, 605, 615, 619, 644, 649, 651, 659, 667, 684, 702, 733

Vol. 2: 30, 133 f., 160, 173, 177, 262 f., 291, 301 f., 350, 413, 431, 444, 825, 833, 846
    Vol. 3: 233, 349, 448, 946, 1108, 1163
Follower **Vol. 1:** 173, 213, 274, 361, 396, 480, 533, 616, 669
    Vol. 2: 57, 94, 96, 112, 279 f., 311, 339, 341–343, 368, 413, 426, 624, 806, 920
    Vol. 3: 529 f., 724, 998, 1059
Folly **Vol. 1:** 227, 277, 281, 397, 418, 550, 555, 673
    Vol. 2: 127, 143, 148, 171, 181, 189, 391, 400, 479, 620
    Vol. 3: 122–130, 240, 995
Fond **Vol. 2: 547–550**
Food **Vol. 1:** 61, 73, 119, 169, 172 f., 203, 207, 226, 249 f., 252, 277, 282, 318, 330, 352, 360, 384 f., 393, 451, 464, 480, 494 f., 497, 500, 509, 565, 586, 611, 670, 672, 674, 691, 696, 711, 728 f., 731, 743 f.
    Vol. 2: 201, 218, **264–277,** 318, 370, 402, 434, 452, 475, 590, 631, 682, 709 f., 801, 811, 831, 833
    Vol. 3: 106, 117, 144, 417, 424, 445, 449, 499, 545, 547, 556, 680, 683, 706, 750 f., 793, 804, 860, 865
Food of immortality **Vol. 2:** 534
Food-laws **Vol. 3:** 113
Food-offering **Vol. 3:** 421
Fool **Vol. 1:** 108, 281, **413–418,** 550, 574, 728
    Vol. 2: 239, 430, 583, 833
    Vol. 3: 820, 914, 953
Foolhardy **Vol. 1:** 364
Foolish **Vol. 1:** 85, 106, 258, 277, 280 f., 513, 542, 546, 551, 670, 675, 708, 727
    Vol. 2: 430, 619, 658
    Vol. 3: 122–133, 447, 563
Foolishness **Vol. 3:** 53, 714, 938, **1023–1036,** 1058
Foot **Vol. 1:** 239, 393, 449, 674
    Vol. 2: 28, 149, 212, 282, 349, 369, 414 f.
    Vol. 3: 107, 560, 805, 914, 943, 966, 989, 1059
Foothold **Vol. 1:** 710
Footstep **Vol. 2:** 358, 452
Footstool **Vol. 1:** 477
    Vol. 2: 74, 245, 611
Forbearance **Vol. 1:** 398, 699, 734
    Vol. 2: 63, 79, **256–259,** 700, **764–767,** 834, 863
    Vol. 3: 128, 163, 215, 364, 818, 825, 1020
Forbearing **Vol. 2:** 652
Forbid **Vol. 1:** 332, 413, 415, 456, 572, 619, 625, 687
    Vol. 2: 154, 206, **220–223,** 244, 296, 446
    Vol. 3: 56, 188
Forbidden **Vol. 1:** 87, 139, 171, 221, 389 f., 426, 499, 505, 611, 630 f., 655, 670, 685
    Vol. 2: 458, 573, 811
Forbidden degrees **Vol. 2: 577**
    Vol. 3: 96
    Vol. 3: 95, 538
Force **Vol. 1:** 453, 508, 543, 651, 653, 678 f., 692, 694, 717, 720, 733
    Vol. 2: 67, 258, 540, **601–606, 663 f.,** 812

Force (*cont'd*)
  Vol. 3: 711–718, 951, **967–981,** 1083
Ford **Vol. 3:** 758
Forearm **Vol. 1:** 393
Forebear **Vol. 1:** 287
Forecast **Vol. 1:** 699
Forecourt **Vol. 1:** 633
Forefather **Vol. 1:** 280, 285, 324, 615, 665
  Vol. 2: 378
  Vol. 3: 234 f.
Forehead **Vol. 2:** 572, 864, 869
  Vol. 3: 498, 500
Foreign **Vol. 1:** 305, 505, 522, 550 f., 553, 622,
  655, **683–692**
  Vol. 2: 35, 99, 159, 251, 288, 308, 328, 349,
  538, 540, 735, **739–742,** 790, 794, 801, 803.
  805
Foreign landlords **Vol. 3:** 641, 951
Foreign policy **Vol. 2:** 320
Foreigner **Vol. 1:** 308, 392, 474, 715
  Vol. 2: 305, 309–311, 335, 519, 735, **788–790,**
  823
  Vol. 3: 193, 455, 757, 789, 980
Foreknowledge **Vol. 1:** 273, 278, 378, 382 f.,
  471, 477 f., 540, 542, 668, **692–697**
  Vol. 2: 118, 397, 608, 819
  Vol. 3: 517, 1018
Foreman **Vol. 2:** 595
  Vol. 3: 268
Forensic **Vol. 1:** 438
  Vol. 2: 122
  Vol. 3: 166, 372 f.
Foreordained **Vol. 2:** 299
  Vol. 3: 132
Forerunner **Vol. 1:** 125, 150, 544 f.
  Vol. 2: 109, 305, 353
  Vol. 3: 121, 795, 940, **945–947,** 1045
Foresee **Vol. 1:** 471, 693, 695
  Vol. 2: 352, 430, 602, 917
  Vol. 3: 492, **511–518**
Foreshadow **Vol. 1:** 115, 158, 266, 290, 545
  Vol. 2: 313
  Vol. 3: 73, 863
Foresight **Vol. 1:** 692–694
  Vol. 2: 318
  Vol. 3: 39
Foreskin **Vol. 1:** 307–309, 672
Forest **Vol. 3:** 352
Forestall **Vol. 2:** 415
  Vol. 3: 747
Foretaste **Vol. 2:** 271
Foretell **Vol. 1:** 528
  Vol. 3: 44–48, 74–89
Forethought **Vol. 1:** 692 f.
Forfeit **Vol. 1:** 240, 484
  Vol. 2: 155
  Vol. 3: 136–138, 174, 178, 190
Forgery **Vol. 3:** 448
Forget **Vol. 1:** 441, 484, 546, 570, 728
  Vol. 2: 272, 275, 366, 440, 606, 781
  Vol. 3: 316, 806
Forgetfulness **Vol. 3:** 840, 847
Forgiveness **Vol. 1:** 86 f., 97, 110, 146, 148,
  155–158, 191, 216, 222–225, 301, 303, 317,

327 f., 333, 346, 351, 354 f., 358 f., 371, 375,
  467, 492, 499 f., 545, 643, 673, **697–703,** 722,
  730
  Vol. 2: 74, 116, 122 f., 137, 156, 168, 212,
  214, 237, 239 f., 270, 302, 332, 366, 386,
  400, 407, 448 f., 494, 521, 523 f., 533, 536,
  543, 545 f., 595, 631, 654 f., 667 f., 691, 696,
  732 f., 767, 769, 771, 787, 813, 861, 868,
  870 f., 898
  Vol. 3: 48, 52, 55 f., 62, 71, 73, 98, 107, 135,
  149 f., 152–155, 157, 161, 167, 174, 199,
  212 f., 221, 343, 374, 402, 481, 508, 528 f.,
  565, 576, 579 f., 582, 586, 618, 622, 657,
  696, 705, 728, 748, 803, 838, 997 f., 1012,
  1059, 1061, 1108, 1143
Foregiving **Vol. 1:** 617, 620, 640
  Vol. 2: 652
Form **Vol. 1:** 50, 66, 71, 204, 234, 299, 355,
  371, 380, 525, 547, 636, 678, **703–714,** 722,
  737
  Vol. 2: 67, 74, 80, 82, 99, 125, 142, 203, 243,
  284, **286–289,** 290 f., 488, 500, 502, 590, 657,
  673, 739, 768
  Vol. 3: 70, 119, 260, 513 f., 516, 554 f., 597,
  604, 644 f., 864, **903–906,** 1027
Form criticism **Vol. 1: 57,** 58, 67 f., 576
  Vol. 3: 58, 234, 333
Form-history **Vol. 1:** 57
Formal **Vol. 1:** 664, 714, 738
  Vol. 2: 276, 287, 312
Formalism **Vol. 2:** 812
Formality **Vol. 1:** 394
Formalized **Vol. 3:** 705
Former **Vol. 1:** 665
  Vol. 2: 419
Former Prophets **Vol. 1: 66**
Formerly **Vol. 2: 713–716**
Formless **Vol. 1:** 380
Formula **Vol. 2:** 279, 281 f., 319, 330, 339 f.,
  356, 424, 552, 619, 653, 655, 659, 729, 797,
  897
  Vol. 3: 61, 234, 373, 476
Formula quotations in Matthew **Vol. 3:** 657
Formulation **Vol. 1:** 579, 705
Fornication **Vol. 1:** 106, 233, 469, 496–501,
  559, 672
  Vol. 2: 586 f., 677 f., 682
  Vol. 3: 95, 1165
Forsake **Vol. 1:** 493, 552
  Vol. 2: 387, 450
  Vol. 3: 560
Forsaken **Vol. 1:** 113, 174
  Vol. 2: 82, 738
Fort **Vol. 3:** 948
Forthteller **Vol. 3:** 77
Forthwith **Vol. 3:** 834
Fortified camp **Vol. 3: 959–967**
Fortify **Vol. 3:** 605, 950
Fortitude **Vol. 3:** 354
Fortress **Vol. 1:** 636
  Vol. 2: 324, 801
  Vol. 3: 1010
Fortuitous **Vol. 3:** 720
Fortunate **Vol. 1:** 215

Vol. 2: 840
Fortunatus Vol. 1: 741
Fortune Vol. 1: 208, 435, 482, 489, 543, 585, 596, 671, 673
  Vol. 2: 49, 108, 116, 146, 148, 320, 594, 898
  Vol. 3: 45, 138 f., 925, 936
Fortune-teller Vol. 1: 463
Fortune-telling Vol. 3: 1104
Forty Vol. 2: 689, **696**, 697, 893
Forty stripes Vol. 3: 96
Forty-two months Vol. 2: **688**
Forum Vol. 2: 142
Forum Romanum Vol. 3: 789
Forward Vol. 1: 665
Foul Vol. 1: 110, 114
Found Vol. 1: 376 f., 383
Foundation Vol. 1: 244, 279, 302, 327, 329, 375, **376–389**, 390 f., 540, 542 f., 596, 598, 602, **658–664**, 684, 693, 697
  Vol. 2: 64, 129, 189, 217, 245, 249, 302, 314, 452, 582, 659, 706
  Vol. 3: 84, 350, 384 f., 387–395, 397, 500, 795, 797, 865, 872, 948
Foundation of Salem Vol. 2: 324
Foundation-stone Vol. 2: 652
  Vol. 3: 391
Founder Vol. 1: 168, 641, 669
  Vol. 3: 69
Foundling Vol. 1: 616
Fountain Vol. 1: 151, 552
  Vol. 3: 498
Four Vol. 2: 658, 687, **688 f.**, 690, 697, 769
  Vol. 3: 179
Four hundred Vol. 2: 689, 697
Foursquare Vol. 2: 700
Fourteen Vol. 2: 685, 691
Fourth Vol. 2: 693, 711
Fourth school of Jewish philosophers
  Vol. 3: 1168
Fourth philosophy Vol. 2: 810
Fox Vol. 1: 118, 173
  Vol. 3: 950
Fracture Vol. 1: 302
  Vol. 2: 414
Fragile Vol. 1: 678
  Vol. 3: 910, 915
Fragment Vol. 1: 464
  Vol. 2: 32, 296
Fragmentary Vol. 2: 304
Fragmentation of truth Vol. 3: 899
Fragrance Vol. 1: 122, 439, 650
  Vol. 2: **293 f.**
  Vol. 3: **599–601**, 689
Frailty Vol. 1: 678 f.
  Vol. 2: 498
  Vol. 3: 212
Frame of mind Vol. 2: **616–620**
Frankincense Vol. 1: 586
  Vol. 2: **293 f.**
  Vol. 3: 238 f., 423
Frankness Vol. 1: 329, 715
  Vol. 2: **734–737**
Fraternal Vol. 1: 572
Fratricide Vol. 3: 578

Fraud Vol. 2: 470
  Vol. 3: 574
Fraudulent Vol. 3: 574
Free Vol. 1: 120, 223, 275, 310, 346, 371, 401, 432, 439, 452, 470, 482, 506, 525 f., 529, 534, 536 f., 540, 542, 562, 572, 632, 651, 666, 677, 684, 697, 699, 702, **715–721**, 723, 728, 742
  Vol. 2: 40, 42, 63, 74, 122, 126, 143, 158, 164, 166, 188, 245, 259, 265, 306, 329, 367, 406, 415, 420, 453, 595, 652, 715, 718, 788, 820, 890
  Vol. 3: 102 f., 142, **177–221**, 407, 537, 545, 590, 753, 991, 1062
Free from guilt Vol. 3: 152
Free will (→ Will, free)
Freeborn Vol. 1: 411, 715
Freedman Vol. 1: 297, 715, 718
  Vol. 3: **589–599**
Freedom Vol. 1: 54, 62, 79, 81, 148, 219, 238, 248, 286, 289, 298, 310, 360, 383, 386, 400, 412, 435, 439, 447, 458, 475, 483, 494, 500, 525, 534, 569, 629, 633, 642, 667, 674, **715–721**, 728, 731, 737
  Vol. 2: 63, 103, 132, 160 f., 245, 265, 273, 275, 307, 329, 335, 393, 402 f., 451, 516, 605, 607, 609, 611, 631, 706, 727, 734–736, 873
  Vol. 3: 37, 79, 120, 129, 141, **177–221**, 352, 488, 561, 590, 592–594, 597–599, 674, 776, 824, 838, 917, 944, 1017, 1055, 1162, 1164
Freedom movements Vol. 1: 717
Freedom of choice Vol. 2: **606–611**
Freedom of Israel Vol. 2: **308**
Freedom of Jerusalem Vol. 2: **308**
Freedom-loving Vol. 2: 660
Freeman Vol. 1: 299, 392
  Vol. 2: 412
Freethinkers Vol. 1: 62, 555
Freewill-offering Vol. 1: 344, 534
  Vol. 2: 329
  Vol. 3: **422 f.** 432, 753, 854 f.
Freeze Vol. 1: 671
Frege, G. Vol. 3: 1128
Frenzy Vol. 1: 528
Fresh Vol. 2: 670, **674–676**
Fresh water Vol. 3: 986
Fretful Vol. 2: 599
Friend Vol. 1: 77, 206, 215, **254–260**, 270, 284, 365, 484, 555, 557, 559, 571, 640, 663, 665
  Vol. 2: 63, 83, 256, 356, 359, 392, 538, 541 f., **547–550**, 585, 663, 735, 881
  Vol. 3: 49, 217, 369, 443, 448, 502, 577, 580, 625, 639, 1017
Friend of the bridegroom Vol. 2: 383, 549, 585
Friendliness Vol. 2: 105, 311, 622
Friendship Vol. 1: 338, 553 f., 687
  Vol. 2: 134, 538, **547–550**, 683, 776, 798
Fright Vol. 1: 621, 673
Frighten Vol. 1: 226, 328, 527
  Vol. 2: 621
Fringes Vol. 1: 254
Frivolity Vol. 1: 501
Frivolous Vol. 3: 903

Frogs **Vol. 1:** 114, 408
  Vol. 2: 637
  Vol. 3: 672
Front **Vol. 1:** 665
Frontier **Vol. 2:** 337
Frost **Vol. 1:** 652
Frostbite **Vol. 1:** 652
Frozen **Vol. 1:** 443
Fructify **Vol. 1:** 498
  Vol. 2: 188
Frugal **Vol. 1:** 597
  Vol. 2: 419
Fruit **Vol. 1:** 77, 85, 87, 112, 139, 178, 181, 187,
  228, 240, 297, 358, 382, 389 f., 417, 496,
  515, 540, 557, 565, 633, 669, 671, 681–683,
  686, **721–728,** 739 f., 743
  Vol. 2: 32, 44, 104, 130 f., 154, 230, 245, 261,
  267, 271, 343, 360, 397, 432, 458, 545, 623,
  662, 693, 711, 736, 754, 761 f., 771, 781 f.,
  809, 871, 912, 916
  Vol. 3: 40, 174, 203, 226, 249, 257, 320, 421,
  470 f., 522, 525 f., 532, 678, 702, 714, 728,
  793, 802, 809, 814, 855, 857, 865–870, 918,
  920, 922, 927, 995, 998, 1000, 1012, 1026,
  1149, 1158
Fruit of the light **Vol. 2: 495**
Fruit-bearing **Vol. 1:** 542
Fruit-trees **Vol. 3:** 952
Fruitful **Vol. 1:** 180, 211, 214, 496
  Vol. 2: 128, 193, 232
  Vol. 3: 508
Fruitfulness **Vol. 1:** 723
  Vol. 2: 711
  Vol. 3: 415
Fruitless **Vol. 1:** 263, 547, 549, 721, 723
  Vol. 2: 32, 142
  Vol. 3: 869
Frustrate **Vol. 2:** 435
  Vol. 3: 166
Frustration **Vol. 1:** 468, 681
  Vol. 2: 828
  Vol. 3: 236, 801, 814, 858
Fuchs, E. **Vol. 3:** 898, 1139 f.
Fuel **Vol. 1:** 389
  Vol. 2: 710 f.
Fugitive **Vol. 3:** 594
Fulfil **Vol. 1:** 99, 178, 216, 289, 322, 335, 337,
  349, 352, 367, 369, 409, 417, 492, 509, 545,
  556, 596, 604, 640, 658, 674, 711, 713, 719,
  728–744
  Vol. 2: 59 f., 62–64, 77, 127, 132, 149, 154,
  156, 165, 168, 235, 238, 297, 313, 328 f.,
  332, 342, 374, 410, 417 f., 442 f., 445 f., 470,
  474, 543, 546, 642, 665, 716, 812 f., 819, 926
  Vol. 3: 187, 360, 489, 491
Fulfiller **Vol. 1:** 303
Fulfilment **Vol. 1:** 72, 95, 117, 138, 170, 175,
  214, 223, 228, 243, 251, 290, 305, 311, 329,
  339, 368, 370, 372, 374 f., 411, 416, 428 f.,
  439, 445, 460, 485, 492, 532, 536, 538, 545,
  560, 570, 581, 587, 592, 601–603, 615, 624,
  626, 634, 637, 647, 657, 697, 701, 719, 736 f.
  Vol. 2: 39, 59, 62 f., 73, 82, 86 f., 100, 108–
  111, 170, 174, 195, 203, 240–242, 245, 258,

262, 281, 294, 299 f., 303, 314, 327, 338,
  351, 356 f., 379, 403, 441, 443, 490, 585,
  691, 714, 732, 786, 819, 909, 920 f., 923 f.,
  927
  Vol. 3: 47 f., 69, 71–74, 82, 188, 202, 204,
  220, 257, 329, 378, 390, 494 f., 500, 516,
  632, 702, 732 f., 749, 756, 762, 806 f., 813,
  836 f., 845, 890, 1013, 1023, 1073, 1096,
  1105, 1112, 1121, 1149
Full **Vol. 1:** 546, 732
  Vol. 2: 416
  Vol. 3: 102
Full of idols **Vol. 2: 284–286**
Full moon **Vol. 3:** 734
Fuller **Vol. 1:** 151
Fuller, R. H. **Vol. 3: 287–289**
Fullness **Vol. 1:** 93, 95, 171, 237 f., 323, 402,
  417, 522, 532, 552, 601, 638, 676, 697, 723,
  728–744
  Vol. 2: 39, 67, 77–79, 83, 87, 106, 119, 131,
  163, 187, 197, 211, 246, 251, 257, 342 f.,
  359, 453, 477, 504, 629, 640, 653, 669, 690,
  715, 722, 782 f., 798 f., 819, 834, 844, 855
  Vol. 3: 53, 71, 74, 82, 137, 171 f., 182, 252,
  329, 403, 489, 494 f., 505, 510, 642, 728,
  730, 804, 827, 838, 849, 1073, 1121
Fullness of time **Vol. 3:** 843
Fully-grown **Vol. 2:** 59
Fumes **Vol. 2:** 294
Fumigation **Vol. 2:** 293
Function **Vol. 1:** 128 f., 133, 188–190, 193 f.,
  196–198, 219, 230 f., 237, 280, 300, 302,
  336, 349, 352, 373, 375, 378, 486, 533, 536,
  544, 549, 572, 648, 667, 681, 711, 737
  Vol. 2: 59, 121, 147, 181, 230, 243, 255, 290,
  296, 328, 391, 414, 445, 447
  Vol. 3: 49–51, 76, 86, 88, 681, 704, 1067,
  1139, **1155–1158**
Function of genealogies **Vol. 3: 653–660**
Functionary **Vol. 2:** 327
Fundamental **Vol. 2:** 43
Funeral **Vol. 1:** 263, 431, 654
  Vol. 2: 416, 418
  Vol. 3: 260
Funeral song **Vol. 2: 418**
Fungi **Vol. 2:** 465
Funk, R. W. **Vol. 3:** 899
Furies **Vol. 1:** 420
Furnace **Vol. 2:** 628
Furnish **Vol. 3: 118–120, 349–351**
Furnishings **Vol. 2:** 291
Furrow **Vol. 1:** 493
Further **Vol. 3: 1147–1152**
Furtherance **Vol. 2:** 128
Furthest **Vol. 1:** 665
Furtiveness **Vol. 1:** 421
Fury **Vol. 1:** 108 f., 739
  Vol. 2: 854 f.
Fusion **Vol. 1:** 584, 643 f.
Futile **Vol. 2:** 239, 242, 399, 683
  Vol. 3: 200, 810, 821, 903, 935
Futility **Vol. 1:** 385, 431, 524 f., 546, 549, 551 f.
  Vol. 2: 119, 400, 473, 793
  Vol. 3: 219, 431, 914

Future **Vol. 1:** 56 f., 184, 237, 243 f., 289, 311, 323–327, 372, 383, 438, 482, 489, 496, 508, 512, 519, 525, 531, 551, 554, 562, 587, 592 f., 596–598, 601 f., 604, 611, 638 f., 654, 659–661, 670 f., 673, 676, 681, 690, 692, 695, 704, 706, 713 f., 719
   Vol. 2: 35–37, 40, 56–58, 62, 65, 102, 108, 119, 122 f., 142, 203, 215, 218, 225, 231, 239 f., 242 f., 244, 254, 266 f., 271, 288, 295, 298, 300 f., 306, 313, 319, 325, 333, 337 f., 350, 353 f., 365, 367, 376, 382, 384–386, 388, 393, 396, 415, 417 f., 423, 461, 515, 517, 521, 532, 606, 665 f., 670, 717, 732, 737, 789 f., 797, 823, 844, 886–888, 891, 900, 905, 908 f., 911, 917, 921, 924–926, 928 f.
   Vol. 3: 47, 77, 79, 87 f., 194, 203, 213 f., 252, 316, 349, 529, 728, 826, 829, 831 f., 834, 836, 840, 1099

Gaal **Vol. 2:** 521
Gabinius **Vol. 1:** 363
Gabriel **Vol. 1:** 101 f., **103 f.,** 474
   Vol. 3: 279, 660, 1071
Gad **Vol. 1:** 543
   Vol. 2: 317
   Vol. 3: 1092
Gadamer, H.-G. **Vol. 3:** 898, 1123, 1127, 1140
Gadarene **Vol. 1:** 117, 420
   Vol. 2: 631
   Vol. 3: 985
Gadites **Vol. 2:** 638
Gaia **Vol. 1:** 420
Gain **Vol. 1:** 138, 533, 651, 700, 728, 733
   Vol. 2: 288, 835, 837–840, 845, 918
   Vol. 3: 134–145, 196, 227, 564, 752, 765, 935, 1054, 1119
Gain attention **Vol. 3:** 874
Gain influence **Vol. 3:** 1078
Gain insight **Vol. 3: 122–130**
Gain mastery **Vol. 3:** 716, 1078
Gaius **Vol. 1:** 689
   Vol. 3: 521, 1045
Galatia **Vol. 1:** 301
   Vol. 2: 34
   Vol. 3: 524, 710, 742
Galatians **Vol. 1:** 158, 235, 397, 478, 593, 708, 727
   Vol. 2: 120, 559, 573, 625, 826, 828, 899
   Vol. 3: 129, 314, 752, 1111
Galaxy **Vol. 3:** 397
Gale **Vol. 3:** 557, 736
Galilean **Vol. 1:** 171, 581
   Vol. 2: 740
   Vol. 3: 430
Galilee **Vol. 1:** 67, 167, 170, 303, 629, 642, 670
   Vol. 2: 328, 332 f., 381, 767, 804, 849, 918
   Vol. 3: 283, 288, 296, 313, 340, 442 f., 454, 456, 458, 481, 508 f., 641, 757, 983 f., 992, 1010, 1060 f.
Gall **Vol. 1:** 107, 202
   Vol. 2: 27–29, 267, 295, 831, 836
   Vol. 3: 922

Gallio **Vol. 1:** 361
   Vol. 2: 369, 451, 766
Gallows **Vol. 1:** 389, 394
Gamaliel **Vol. 1:** 341, 591
   Vol. 2: 34
   Vol. 3: 189, 480, 768, 778, 873, 1157
Gamaliel II **Vol. 3:** 273
Game **Vol. 1:** 625
   Vol. 3: 149, 261, 422, 929
Game-tree principle **Vol. 3:** 1142
Ganymedes **Vol. 3:** 259
Gap **Vol. 1:** 614, 734
Garden **Vol. 1:** 559
   Vol. 2: 210, 266, 274, 760
   Vol. 3: 986
Garden of Eden **Vol. 1:** 139, 389, 433
   Vol. 2: 298, 761, 889
Gardener **Vol. 3: 918–922,** 1060
Garland **Vol. 1:** 405
Garment **Vol. 1:** 204 f., 240, **312–317,** 556, 613, 666, 671
   Vol. 2: 40, 188, 226, 263, 299, 486, 491, 493, 556, 671, 673, 714
   Vol. 3: 107, 860, 921
Garrison **Vol. 1:** 710
   Vol. 2: 134
   Vol. 3: 605
Gate **Vol. 1:** 254, 303
   Vol. 2: 29–31, 207, 210, 280, 363, 441, 652, 733 f., 807
   Vol. 3: 388, 395, 397, 603, 871, 940, 948
Gate of God **Vol. 1:** 140
Gates of Hell **Vol. 3:** 383, 385, 713
Gath **Vol. 3:** 248
Gather **Vol. 1:** 273, 291, 297 f., 304 f., 466, 490, 544, 610, 724 f.
   Vol. 2: 31–35, 131, 161, 194, 226, 237, 310, 328, 359, 413, 531, **829–836,** 866, 928
   Vol. 3: 255, 526, 531, 567, 745, 804
Gather an army **Vol. 3: 958–967**
Gayomart **Vol. 2:** 645
   Vol. 3: 617
Gaza **Vol. 2:** 848
   Vol. 3: 248, 453
Gaze on **Vol. 3: 520**
Gazelle **Vol. 3:** 1065
Ge **Vol. 2:** 188
Gear **Vol. 3:** 913
Geba **Vol. 3:** 426
Gebul **Vol. 3:** 446
Gedaliah **Vol. 3:** 249, 478
Gehazi **Vol. 1:** 485
Gehenna **Vol. 1:** 231, 418, 656, 700
   Vol. 2: 205–210, 298
   Vol. 3: 265, 271, 682
Gehinnom **Vol. 2:** 208 f.
Gem **Vol. 2:** 556
   Vol. 3: 394–396, 753
Gemara **Vol. 1: 58,** 69
   Vol. 3: 485
Gematria **Vol. 2: 683–685**
   Vol. 3: 657
Gemeinde **Vol. 1: 58,** 59
Genealogies of Jesus Christ **Vol. 3: 653–660**

Genealogy **Vol. 1:** 65 f., 72, 77, 81, 85, 141, 176, 181 f., 208, 244, 255, 619
 Vol. 2: 35 f., 124, 318, 331, 467, 644 f., 684 f., 691, 694
 Vol. 3: 63, 191, 653–660, 664, 768, 872, 1026, 1062, 1073, 1119
Genealogy of Moses **Vol. 3:** 660
Genera **Vol. 2:** 158
General **Vol. 1:** 475
 Vol. 3: 601, **958–967**
General resurrection **Vol. 3:** 277, 287
General revelation **Vol. 3:** 336
General semantics **Vol. 3:** 1125
Generate **Vol. 1:** 452, 497 f.
 Vol. 3: 1153
Generation **Vol. 1:** 176, 179, 181, 187, 208, 294, 305, 308, 565, 596, 603
 Vol. 2: 35–39, 54, 248, 271, 365, 381, 387, 582, 584, 629 f., 635, 680, 682, 689, 691 f., 696, 766, 798, 892, 910–912, 916 f., 923
 Vol. 3: 213, 242, 283, 732, 827 f., 1030
Generation of vipers **Vol. 2:** 311
Generative **Vol. 2:** 657
Generative poetics **Vol. 3:** 1142
Generosity **Vol. 2:** 49, 98, 400, 694, 857
 Vol. 3: 141, 853 f., 926, 955
Generous **Vol. 1:** 254, 642, 715
 Vol. 2: 539, 652
 Vol. 3: 752
Genesis **Vol. 1:** 65, 181, 510 f.
 Vol. 3: 980
Genesis Apocryphon **Vol. 3:** 487
Genius **Vol. 1:** 653
Gennesaret **Vol. 3:** 983–985, 992, 1059
Genre, Literary **Vol. 1:** 57, **58**, 68, 582
Gentile **Vol. 1: 58,** 62, 115, 129, 155–157, 159, 167 f., 175, 202, 277, 307, 309 f., 320, 346, 350, 360, 375, 402, 417, 419, 434, 448, 473, 476–478, 508, 514, 531, 541, 544, 554 f ., 593, 601, 619, 627, 632, 642, 644, 659, 667, 684–686, 689, 691, 695, 730 f., 733, 737, 740
 Vol. 2: 31, 35, 37, 77, 83, 85 f., 94, 111–113, 126 f., 129, 139, 156, 158, 163, 178, 183, 223, 235–237, 251, 261, 275, 294, 302, 310, 312, 315–317, 325, 328, 340, 356, 359, 368, 378, 385, 399 f., 413, 437, 443 f., 446, 453, 495, 499, 519, 558, 567, 573, 581, 587, 592, 596 f., 641, 655, 664, 682, 688 f., 695, 702, 712, 721 f., 728–731, 736, 741, 773, **788–805,** 827, 844, 867, 880, 888, 898, 922 f.
 Vol. 3: 38, 53 f., 56, 68, 63, 66, 71–73, 101, 106, 125, 163, 168, 172, 182, 186, 193 f., 194, 197, 198, 203, 214, 227, 241, 251 f., 296, 324, 327, 352, 361, 363, 378, 387, 389, 410, 431, 453 f., 457 f., 491, 504 f., 515, 523, 549, 552, 555, 560, 569, 576, 579 f., 584, 591, 629, 656, 662, 672, 675, 686, 714, 750, 752, 755, 757, 793, 795, 812, 869 f., 909, 913, 916, 922, 929, 931, 944, 949, 951, 954, 956, 961, 976, 1010, 1018 f., 1043, 1052, 1164, 1184, 1189 f., 1199
Gentile Christians **Vol. 1:** 145, 226, 228, 256, 261, 310 f., 340, 473, 552, 593
 Vol. 2: 241, 286, 315 f., 328 f., 398, 437,

660 f., 732, 795
 Vol. 3: 101
Gentile churches **Vol. 1:** 61, 632, 739
 Vol. 2: 315 f., 329
Gentle **Vol. 1:** 282, 431, 469, 570
 Vol. 2: 218, **256–259**
Gentleman **Vol. 2:** 562
Gentleness **Vol. 2:** 105, **256–259,** 360
 Vol. 3: 525
Genuflexion **Vol. 1:** 207
Genuine **Vol. 1:** 356, 607, 637, 681
 Vol. 2: 102, 105, 280, **468–470,** 574, 858
 Vol. 3: 808–810, 874–901
Genuineness **Vol. 3:** 631
Geographical **Vol. 1:** 517 f.
Geological eras **Vol. 2:** 889
Gerar **Vol. 2:** 140
Gerasene **Vol. 2:** 623, 699
 Vol. 3: 592
Gerassa **Vol. 1:** 226
Gerhardsson, B. **Vol. 3:** 59
Gerizim **Vol. 1:** 67, 210
 Vol. 2: 591, 878, 927
 Vol. 3: 450–452, 458, 460–462, 465, 789, 1010
German idealism **Vol. 3:** 686
Gersham **Vol. 2:** 636 f.
Geschichte **Vol. 1:** 58, **60**
Gesture **Vol. 1:** 413
 Vol. 2: 150–152, 157, 630, 859
Get **Vol. 3:** 192, **747–751**
Get back **Vol. 3: 747–751**
Get ready **Vol. 3: 116–120, 349–351**
Get through **Vol. 3:** 255
Get up **Vol. 3:** 279
Get well **Vol. 3:** 259
Gethsemane **Vol. 1:** 305, 343, 442, 490, 559, 615, 646
 Vol. 2: 32, 82, 178, 420, 429, 624, **710–713,** 851, 868, 871 f., 911
 Vol. 3: 211, 378, 591, 657, 803, 978, 1022
Ghetto **Vol. 2:** 309
Ghost **Vol. 1:** 452
 Vol. 2: 281, **552–562**
 Vol. 3: 324
Giant **Vol. 1:** 452
Gibeah **Vol. 3:** 426
Gibeon **Vol. 1:** 195, 511
 Vol. 3: 426, 812
Gibeonites **Vol. 3:** 154, 159
Gideon **Vol. 2:** 260, 374, 428, 627, 777
 Vol. 3: 201, 206, 514, 874, 962, 994
Gift **Vol. 1: 52,** 90, 92, 97, 122, 138, 146, 148 f., 158, 168, 192, 195, 198, 212, 214, 216, 218, 225, 228, 232 f., 236, 244, 250 f., 279, 287, 289 f., 300 f., 305, 329, 357–359, 371 f., 375, 385, 389, 413–415, 428, 478, 485, 496, 498, 502, 511, 531 f., 535 f., 558, 571, 573, 586, 601 f., 607, 609, 617, 620, 637 f., 642, 648, 655, 661, 691, 699, 716, 718, 722 f., 731, 733, 739, 742
 Vol. 2: 39–44, 62 f., 74, 76 f., 79, 83, 96, 102, 106–108, 115–123, 152, 162, 167, 169, 178, 186 f., 194, 210, 218, 228, 230, 240, 242 f.,

253, 255 f., 266, 270 f., 275, 277, 288, 294 f., 297, 302, 310, 326, 329, 336, 355 f., 360, 374, 385 f., 400, 410, 419, 445, 447, 469, 475, 480 f., 492, 498 f., 533, 540, 548, 550, 566, 580 f., 590, 594–598, 602, 611, 617 f., 632, 638, 641, 650, 675, 687, 693, 718, 721, 723, 728, 771, 777 f., 780 f., 785, 787, 789, 794, 798, 812 f., 816, 824, 826, 828, 830, 832, 834 f., 841, 844, 852, 859, 861, 868, 873, 877, 881, 883, 885, 918, 928, 930
Vol. 3: 69, 72, **74–89,** 110, 124, 131 f., 135, 138–140, 143 f., 149, 163, 168, 189 f., 199, 216, 228, 240, 243, 257, 315, 323, 349, 357, 360, 363 f., 372 f., 402 f., **415–418,** 421–423, 428, 433 f., 436, 458, 472, 499, 530, 536, 541 f., 547, 589, 600, 638–640, 647, 649, 691, 693, 699–702, 704, 706–708, 713 f., 728 f., 745 f., 748 f., 763, 789, 791, 810, 819, 853, 855, 874, 919, 922, 927, 944, 955, 967, 986, 988, 1002, 1004, 1016, 1018, 1029 f., 1032, 1059, 1067, 1070, 1169
Gift of first fruits **Vol. 3: 415–417**
Gihon **Vol. 1:** 122
Vol. 3: 986
Gilgal **Vol. 2:** 225
Vol. 3: 78, 426
Gilgamesh epic **Vol. 3:** 265, 602, 613
Gird **Vol. 3: 116–122,** 966
Gird up **Vol. 3:** 128
Girdle **Vol. 3:** 120 f., 966
Girl **Vol. 1:** 283, 287, 505
Vol. 3: 1071
Gischala **Vol. 2:** 804
Give **Vol. 1:** 235, 300, 319, 454, 509, 548, 642, 651, 659, 703, 717, 730, 738, 740, 742
Vol. 2: 39–44, 63, 116, 121, 131, 186, 269, 277, 280, 282, 357, 359, 411, 499, 594–598
Vol. 3: 153, 727, 748, 854 f.
Give account **Vol. 2:** 137, 244, 369 f.
Give an address **Vol. 3:** 821
Give attention **Vol. 3:** 125
Give away **Vol. 2:** 367, 596
Vol. 3: 134–136
Give back **Vol. 3: 134–136,** 146
Give birth **Vol. 2:** 318, 329
Give drink **Vol. 2: 274–277**
Give God glory **Vol. 1:** 345
Vol. 2: 46, 816
Give ground **Vol. 1:** 741
Give impression **Vol. 3:** 821
Give information **Vol. 3: 316 f.**
Give life **Vol. 2:** 280, **476–484**
Give lot **Vol. 2: 299**
Give in marriage **Vol. 2: 575–582**
Give mind to **Vol. 2: 616–620**
Give notice **Vol. 3:** 47
Give offence **Vol. 3:** 433
Give out **Vol. 3: 402–404, 952–956**
Give rest **Vol. 3: 254–258**
Give up **Vol. 1:** 413, 698
Vol. 2: 156, 217, 241, 244, 361, **367 f.**
Vol. 3: 134–136
Give up ghost **Vol. 3:** 680
Give way **Vol. 1:** 741

Vol. 2: 256
Giver **Vol. 1:** 375, 498, 543, 716, 718, 738
Vol. 2: 827
Vol. 3: 417
Giving **Vol. 1:** 732
Vol. 2: 594–598, 694, 827 f.
Giving birth **Vol. 3: 857 f.**
Glad **Vol. 2: 356–361,** 436
Glad tidings **Vol. 2: 107–115**
Gladden **Vol. 2: 354–356**
Gladness **Vol. 2:** 107, 353, **354–356,** 590
Vol. 3: 121, 680, 919
Glaucus **Vol. 3:** 75
Glaze **Vol. 3:** 914
Gleam **Vol. 3:** 395
Gleaming **Vol. 2: 484–486**
Gleaning **Vol. 1:** 541, 724
Vol. 3: 867, 918, 1074
Glib **Vol. 1:** 682
Glitter **Vol. 3:** 395
Gloom **Vol. 1:** 110, 421–423, 425
Vol. 2: 215
Gloomy **Vol. 2:** 206
Glorification **Vol. 2:** 203, 372, 400, 787, 809
Vol. 3: 725, 863
Glorified Christ **Vol. 1:** 131, 399, 587, 709
Vol. 2: 48, 289, 332, 625, 787, 819
Glorify **Vol. 1:** 89, 211, 235, 312, 643, 649, 706 f.
Vol. 2: 44, 79, 128, 229, 272, 306, 352 f., 360, 394, 425, 606, 819, 862, 874
Vol. 3: 672, 848 f.
Glorious **Vol. 1:** 435, 707, 717
Vol. 2: 44, 263
Vol. 3: 317
Glory **Vol. 1:** 73, 100, 204, 222, 227 f., 235, 261, 280, 311, 313 f., 323, 327, 329, 345 f., 352, 381, 386, 401, 405 f., 411, 464, 469 f., 504, 508, 546, 560, 574, 576, 587, 592, 637–639, 643–645, 653, 655 f., 669, 673, 675, 677 f., 688, 696, 704, 706, 712, 730, 732, 735, 740
Vol. 2: 44–52, 71, 75, 78 f., 82 f., 112, 119, 131, 146, 160–162, 176, 190, 196, 203 f., 213, 217 f., 229, 235, 240, 242–245, 272, 278, 289 f., 303, 328 f., 336, 354, 357, 360, 366, 377, 380, 388, 397, 420, 425, 473, 482, 485–488, 493, 503, 543, 546, 563, 605, 607, 614 f., 627 f., 632, 637, 641, 650, 653 f., 669, 672, 694, 696, 718, 724, 736, 774, 779, 781, 834, 839, 844, 863, 877, 894, 909, 916, 928 f.
Vol. 3: 55, 117 f., 128, 138, 163, 165, 199 f., 214, 220, 262, 277, 281, 313 f., 316 f., 320–323, 343, 349, 373, 397 f., 416, 433, 504, 514, 516, 518, 532, 554, 563, 588 f., 606, 621, 631, 633 f., 645, 705, 717, 722 f., 725, 733–735, 749, 790, 806, 821, 825 f., 838, 848, 860, 863 f., 890, 914, 925, 954, 1006, 1008, 1020, 1155, 1166
Glossalalia (→ Tongues, speaking in)
Glue **Vol. 2:** 348 f.
Gluttony **Vol. 1:** 169, 561
Vol. 2: 271, 274
Vol. 3: 921

Gnash the teeth **Vol. 2:** 416 f., **421**
Gnat **Vol. 1:** 116
Gnaw **Vol. 2:** 421
Gnomic discourse **Vol. 2:** 890
Gnosis **Vol. 1:** 55
  Vol. 2: 393
  Vol. 3: 1073
Gnostic **Vol. 1:** 55, **58**, 60, 103, 123, 127, 133–135, 212, 237 f., 313–316, 338 f., 347, 455, 479, 500, 524, 534, 547, 570, 604, 638, 680, 706, 709, 740
  Vol. 2: 36, 72, 159, 171, 185, 187 f., 195, 219, 221, 248, 250, 253, 265, 280, 286, 310, 314, 393 f., 397, 403 f., 439, 447, 449, 457, 481 f., 506, 557, 584, 601, 608, 655, 674, 677 f., 683, 701, 830, 840, 919, 928
  Vol. 3: 40, 85, 123, 128, 205, 220, 344, 602, 622, 640, 643, 645–647, 661, 825, 832, 891, 930, 932, 939–941, 945, 1020, 1029–1031, 1054, 1115 f., 1118
Gnosticism **Vol. 1:** 50, 54 f., **58**, 86, 133, 179, 230, 233 f., 247, 301, 387, 422, 432, 438 f., 487, 500, 510, 513, 522 f., 525, 601, 616, 669, 678 f., 705, 708, 740
  Vol. 2: 60, 129, 158, 219, 251, 391, **393 f.**, 401, 404, 419, 448, 453, 477, 480, 485, 490 f., 493, 495, 567, 645 f., 717, 719, 906
  Vol. 3: 206, 231, 273, 324, 457, 502 f., 595, 617, 630–632, 706, 772, 827, 832, 936, 1034 f., 1046, 1119
Go **Vol. 3: 945–947**
Go about **Vol. 3: 943–945**
Go after **Vol. 3:** 860
Go aside **Vol. 3: 583–585**
Go astray **Vol. 1:** 541, 608
  Vol. 2: 457–461, 708
  Vol. 3: 585 f.
Go away **Vol. 1:** 320, 606, 608
  Vol. 2: 359
  Vol. 3: 362
Go before **Vol. 2:** 412
Go forth **Vol. 1:** 713
Go forward **Vol. 2:** 128
Go to law **Vol. 2:** 365
Go up **Vol. 2: 184–187**, 326
  Vol. 3: 421
Goad **Vol. 1:** 511
  Vol. 2: 155
Goal **Vol. 1:** 69, 92 f., 95, 168, 186, 188, 250, 263, 289, 314, 319, 325, 358, 384 f., 432, 451, 460 f., 481, 484 f., 489, 491, 538, 540 f., 583, 597, 600–605, 640, 647, 713, 719, 731
  Vol. 2: 48, **52–66**, 75, 77, 95 f., 99, 106, 120, 130, 157, 162, 194 f., 204, 231, 241, 243–245, 252, 287, 313, 402, 404, 443, 445, 453, 569, 665, 703, 715, 741, 772, 806 f., 817, 819 f., 886, 891, 908
  Vol. 3: 216, 225, 350 f., 363, 617, 725, 728, 752, 755 f., 759, 762, 779, 831, 839, 843, 849, 935, 938 f., 946, 991, 1020, 1158, 1177
Goat **Vol. 1:** 114–116, 224 f., 299
  Vol. 2: 148, 151, 296, 413, 606
  Vol. 3: 98, 164, 199, 420, 423, 564, 567
Goblet **Vol. 2:** 274

Goel **Vol. 3:** 191
Gog and Magog **Vol. 1:** 508, 657
  Vol. 2: 701, 792
  Vol. 3: 389, **959–967**
God **Vol. 1:** 70, 73–79, 81, 84–87, 89, 94 f., 97–99, 101–104, 106, 108–114, 116, 119, 122–126, 129, 133, 136, 138–140, 142 f., 147–149, 151 f., 154, 157, 159 f., 162–169, 171–175, 177–180, 183–191, 195, 197, 200, 202–205, 208–210, 212–219, 221–225, 227–229, 231, 234–240, 243–245, 248, 250–253, 255–257, 259, 261, 263, 268–270, 272–281, 284–290, 294 f., 297–300, 302–305, 308 f., 311–327, 329–336, 338–347, 349–361, 363, 365–387, 389 f., 397–402, 408–418, 420–427, 430, 433 f., 436 f., 439–441, 444–462, 464–479, 481–492, 494–496, 499–514, 516–518, 520–535, 537 f., 540–560, 562–568, 570–572, 574–576, 580–582, 585–605, 607–612, 614–629, 632 f., 636–641, 644–647, 649–654, 656–662, 665, 667–669, 672–681, 684–686, 688–691, 693–702, 704, 706–708, 712–714, 716–720, 722 f., 726, 728–738, 740–744
  Vol. 2: 29 f., 32–35, 37–39, 41–51, 53–55, 57–61, 63–65, **66–90**, 91–96, 98–102, 105 f., 109–113, 115–125, 127–129, 131–135, 137, 139–142, 144–149, 151 f., 154–156, 158–165, 167–170, 173–179, 181–204, 206, 208, 211–218, 220, 222 f., 225–232, 235–245, 247–253, 255–263, 265–268, 270–275, 277–279, 281 f., 284 f., 287–290, 294–307, 309–313, 315, 317, 325–329, 332, 335–340, 342 f., 349–351, 353–358, 360, 363–369, 373, 376–389, 391, 393–405, 407 f., 411–413, 415–420, 422, 424–436, 440–451, 453, 456, 458, 460, 462, 501–503, 508–514, 516, 519, 521, 539, 565, 567, 576, 602, 609, 619, 627, 631, 635–638, 646, 648–661, 674, 687, 718, 720 f., 725, 727, 736, 765, 772, 777, 794, 813, 815–819, 832, 842, 855–882, 884 f., 888 f., 891–894, 898 f., 902, 904–906, 908 f., 911, 916–923, 927, 929
  Vol. 3: 28–31, 36–38, 41, 45–48, 53–58, 65 f., 69–74, 77–79, 81–83, 93, 95–98, 101, 105 f., 111, 113, 117–121, 125–132, 134–136, 138–145, 148 f., 151–153, 155, 160–173, 177–181, 186–191, 195, 197–200, 202, 204 f., 207, 210–216, 218–221, 224–230, 232–257, 262–266, 268–281, 284–287, 289 f., 293, 297–304, 309–337, 340–353, 355–373, 377, 380–383, 386–393, 395, 397 f., 400–411, 416 f., 425, 428–436, 445, 457, 460–462, 465–476, 479, 482, 484–488, 490–492, 495, 498–509, 512–518, 522–526, 528–537, 539 f., 542–544, 546–552, 554–559, 561–563, 565–567, 571 f., 574, 576, 578–586, 588–591, 593–598, 600–605, 607–616, 618–651, 653, 658 f., 662–664, 670–675, 678, 681–687, 689–696, 698, 701 f., 704 f., 707 f., 710–718, 720–726, 728–734, 737, 740–743, 745–751, 754 f., 760–766, 768 f., 771–773, 776–779, 782–787, 789–795, 797, 799–815, 817–821, 824–833, 835–839, 841–844, 846–

849, 851–857, 860, 863–866, 868–872, 874, 876–886, 888–894, 899–901, 904–906, 909, 911–917, 919 f., 922–924 f., 927 f., 934, 937–947, 950 f., 953–956, 959–961, 963–973, 975, 978–981, 983 f., 986–991, 995, 997 f., 1000–1014, 1016–1023, 1025 f., 1028–1033, 1036, 1040–1050, 1053 f., 1056, 1058, 1060, 1066, 1068–1070, 1073 f., 1078–1081, 1084, 1087–1123, 1132 f., 1137, 1148–1155, 1157 f., 1161, 1163–1169, 1176–1178, 1180, 1182, 1184 f., 1187–1196, 1198, 1200–1206, 1209, 1211, 1213 f.
God Almighty **Vol. 2:** 67
God, concepts of **Vol. 1:** 54 f.
God, to have **Vol. 2:** 78
God Most High **Vol. 2:** 67, 375, 591
God, names of **Vol. 1: 56,** 71, 98
    Vol. 2: 67 f., 318, **375, 649–656**
God of Abraham **Vol. 2:** 73
God of this age **Vol. 3:** 831
God of the Amen **Vol. 1:** 98
God of Bethel **Vol. 2:** 67
God of eternity **Vol. 3:** 827
God of the future **Vol. 3: 969**
God of glory **Vol. 2:** 46
God of heaven **Vol. 2: 193**
    Vol. 3: 485
God of hope **Vol. 3: 969**
God of Isaac **Vol. 2:** 73
God of Israel **Vol. 1:** 208, 272, 280, 383, 476, 626
    Vol. 2: 29, 53, 67, 69–73, 215, 285, 309, 335, 492, 512, 796 f., 830, 863, 867, 876, 909
    Vol. 3: 318, 794, 828, 881
God of Jacob **Vol. 2:** 73
God of Seeing **Vol. 2:** 67
God of Truth **Vol. 1:** 98
    Vol. 3: 877, 882, 901
God of this world **Vol. 2:** 381, 494, 609
    Vol. 3: 694
God-breathed **Vol. 3:** 327, 491, **689–708**
God-fearer **Vol. 1:** 359–361, 688
    Vol. 2: 85
    Vol. 3: 931
God-fearing **Vol. 1:** 227, 542, 623
    Vol. 2: 85, 91, 492
Goddess **Vol. 2:** 85
    Vol. 3: 231, 845, 861, 1055, 1068 f., 1071
Goddess of fate **Vol. 2:** 303
Godforsaken **Vol. 2:** 86
Godhead **Vol. 1:** 204, 740
    Vol. 2: 70, 506, 819
    Vol. 3: 310
Godless **Vol. 1:** 109, 125, 259, 277, 416, 449, 552, 586, 598, 687, 734
    Vol. 2: 49, 53, 56, 71, 91, 155, 239, 265, 304, 310, 312, 405 f., 417, 442, **468–470,** 475, 479, 486, 549, 705, 707, 777, 810
    Vol. 3: 31, 96, 140, 224, 394, 574, 578, 580, 836, 839, 847, 983, 1024 f., 1068, 1149
Godlessness **Vol. 1:** 716 f., 719
    Vol. 2: 91, 94, 265, 474
    Vol. 3: 573, 580, 1079
Godliness **Vol. 1:** 112, 228, 240, 327, 361, 496,

559, 622, 687
    Vol. 2: 85, **90–95,** 131, 232, 439, 468, 621, 659
    Vol. 3: 33, 100, 353, 561, 574, 577, 584, 692, 727, 768, 1119
Godly **Vol. 1:** 125, 186, 467, 474, 551, 555, 575, 597
    Vol. 2: 91, 94, 181, 475, 485
    Vol. 3: 203
Godly sorrow **Vol. 2:** 420
Gods **Vol. 1:** 128, 189, 481, 492, 497, 528, 537, 569, 585, 616
    Vol. 2: 66–90, 92, 164, 166 f., 184, 188, 190, 224 f., 232–237, 239, 259 f., 265, 271, 284–287, 309, 396, 407, 425, 430, 432, 439, 452, 498, 510, 564, 572, 612, 633, 644, 649, 657, 662–664, 705, 722, 859, 871, 876
    Vol. 3: 27, 45, 49 f., 69, 76, 103 f., 123, 138, 146, 148 f., 186 f., 200–202, 205 f., 209, 216 f., 224, 260 f., 317 f., 340, 353, 388, 397, 415, 432, 460, 515, 549 f., 561 f., 583, 593, 634 f., 679, 715–717, 719, 727, 739, 760, 781 f., 806, 840, 851, 916, 919, 925, 930, 936 f., 959, 1000 f., 1006, 1009, 1024, 1029, 1039, 1068, 1081, 1101, 1148
Gold **Vol. 1:** 204, 380, 319, 390, 464, 498, 537, 648, 656, 682, 743
    Vol. 2: 28, **95–98,** 102, 235, 349, 572, 574, 683, 728, 795, 831, 836, 844, 852
    Vol. 3: 107, 200, 391 f., 518, 809, 812, 814, 855, 914 f., 957
Golden **Vol. 2:** 95
Golden age **Vol. 1:** 508, 640
    Vol. 2: 95 f., 337, 888
    Vol. 3: 217
Golden altar **Vol. 3:** 812
Golden calf **Vol. 2:** 356, 637
    Vol. 3: 1013
Golden girdle **Vol. 3:** 120 f.
Golden rule **Vol. 2:** 442
Goldsmith **Vol. 2:** 95
Golgotha **Vol. 1:** 581
    Vol. 2: 718
Gomer **Vol. 2:** 754
Gomorrah **Vol. 1:** 657, 677
    Vol. 2: 366, 767
    Vol. 3: 93, 96, 203, 240, 344, 444, 560, 628
Gong **Vol. 2:** 97
Good **Vol. 1:** 55 f., 85, 118, 163, 168, 212, 232 f., 236, 336, 348–351, 356, 370, 389, 413, 434, 458, 463, 468 f., 473, 490, 495, 501, 504, 509 f., 523, 536 f., 540, 543, 552, 556, 561–565, 568, 570, 585, 604, 612, 623, 649, 653 f., 671, 673, 676 f., 680 f., 708, 715, 720–723, 731
    Vol. 2: 62, 86, **98–107,** 115 f., 118, 130, 157 f., 178, 182 f., 206, 239, 241, 243, 269, 271 f., 274, 279–281, 286, 288, 334, 350, 357, 367, 369, 391, 394 f., 403, 445–447, 476, 490, 497, 506, 659, 683, 714, 719, 770, 781, 806 f., 811, 815, 817, 844, 857, 866, 889
    Vol. 3: 73, 127, 130, 138, 140, 227, 351, 358, 410, 522, 693, 720, 751, 775, 779, 807, 865, 869, 933, 938, 1021, 1054, 1148, 1156

Good behaviour **Vol. 3:** 140
Good day **Vol. 3: 1000–1004**
Good deed **Vol. 2:** 425
 Vol. 3: 1147–1152
Good Friday **Vol. 1:** 634
Good health **Vol. 2:** 356
Good news **Vol. 2: 107–115,** 387, 410, 611
 Vol. 3: 45 f., 69, 71, 696
Good order **Vol. 3:** 27
Good pleasure **Vol. 2: 817–820**
Good sense **Vol. 2: 616–620**
Good turn **Vol. 2:** 115
Good works **Vol. 1:** 316, 604, 735
 Vol. 2: 83, 95, 101, 117, 129, 191, 242, 266,
 384, 446, 597, 645, 830, 834 f., 842, 844, 846
 Vol. 3: 129, 135
Goodness **Vol. 1:** 84, 86, 185, 345, 380, 484,
 562, 566, 616, 620, 695, 700
 Vol. 2: 72, 76, 79, 98, 105, 139, 270, 290,
 386, 397, 718, 812, 905
 Vol. 3: 356, 572, 687, 762
Goods **Vol. 1:** 381, 457, 537, 588, 639, 642,
 728 f.
 Vol. 2: 255, 361, 844 f.
 Vol. 3: 201, 913
Goodwill **Vol. 1:** 558
 Vol. 2: 115, 358, **817–820**
 Vol. 3: 151, 169, 745, 1169
Gore, Charles **Vol. 1:** 548 f.
Gorgias **Vol. 3:** 138, 1083, 1086
Gospel **Vol. 1:** 50, 54, 62, 74, 95, 123, 129 f.,
 132 f., 146–148, 150, 153, 157 f., 165 f., 168,
 171, 180, 182, 222, 238 f., 248, 258 f., 269,
 275, 297, 310 f., 322, 331, 336, 338, 350,
 367, 370, 384, 396–399, 437, 464, 469, 474,
 476 f., 489, 496, 505, 508, 517, 524, 540,
 547, 551, 554, 558, 560, 566, 576, 590, 593,
 599, 601–603, 605, 607, 613, 638, 643 f.,
 647, 658 f., 675, 677, 683, 702, 719, 722,
 727, 733
 Vol. 2: 30, 43, 75, 77 f., **107–115,** 119, 122,
 126, 129, 149, 156, 161, 169, 176, 179, 214,
 221 f., 235, 242, 250, 254 f., 263, 302, 328 f.,
 338, 356–360, 367, 379, 387, 404, 435, 443,
 451, 453, 494, 559, 569, 597, 604 f., 610 f.,
 625, 627, 645 f., 665, 673, 678, 702, 706,
 709, 726, 741, 780, 782, 786, 794 f., 812,
 818, 825, 839, 844, 875, 899, 901, 903, 906,
 910 f., 913, 915
 Vol. 3: 38, 44–46, 50, 52, 54 f., 58 f., 61, 63 f.,
 67–73, 85, 108, 118, 128, 142, 169, 174, 198,
 212–214, 217, 228, 241–243, 280, 313–315,
 323 f., 347, 349, 352, 367, 384, 393, 400,
 495, 510, 526, 546, 548, 551 f., 560, 563,
 570, 586, 592, 596, 600, 705, 710, 718, 725,
 742, 746, 751, 771, 773 f., 794, 818, 830,
 862, 864, 868, 884–888, 914, 922, 935, 959,
 964, 966, 975, 980, 1021, 1025, 1043 f.,
 1053 f., 1060, 1080, 1110, 1114, 1122, 1152
Gospel according to the Egyptians **Vol. 1:** 50
 Vol. 2: 219
Gospel according to the Hebrews **Vol. 1:** 50
 Vol. 2: 219
Gospel, another **Vol. 2:** 112, 766

Gospel of Marcion **Vol. 1:** 50
Gospel of the Nazarenes **Vol. 1:** 576
 Vol. 3: 795
Gospel of Peter **Vol. 1:** 50
 Vol. 3: 285, 297
Gospel of Philip **Vol. 1:** 50
 Vol. 2: 310
 Vol. 3: 661
Gospel of Thomas **Vol. 1:** 50
 Vol. 2: 168, 219, 462, 751 f., 757
Gospel of Truth **Vol. 1:** 616
Gospel of the Twelve Apostles **Vol. 1:** 50
Gossip **Vol. 3:** 45, 346 f., 525
Gourd **Vol. 1:** 241
Govern **Vol. 1:** 194, 573, 662
 Vol. 2: 374, 381, 663
 Vol. 3: 217, 678, 944 f.
Governing **Vol. 2:** 158
Government **Vol. 1:** 193, 199, 291, 588, 654
 Vol. 2: 373, 607 f., 801–804, 859
 Vol. 3: 97, 324, 353, 755, 758, 1028
Government of God **Vol. 1:** 152, 379, 551
Governor **Vol. 1:** 169, 190, **269 f.,** 363, 519, 649
 Vol. 2: 254, 377, 511, 608
Grace **Vol. 1:** 52, 74, 93, 97, 112, 129, 147, 154,
 157, 163, 180, 190, 211, 227 f., 290, 300,
 305, 311, 324, 326, 356, 358, 370 f., 397,
 436, 439–441, 455, 466 f., 478, 488, 509,
 532, 535, 538, 541 f., 547, 571, 585, 587,
 589, 596, 601, 605, 607, 609, 611, 622, 655,
 659, 660, 668, 680, 698, 700, 703, 727, 730,
 732, 739 f.
 Vol. 2: 39, 42, 44, 72–79, 83, 94, 106, **115–
 124,** 129, 131, 139, 152, 183, 198, 208, 215,
 243 f., 253, 255, 261, 264, 302, 356, 360,
 364, 366, 368, 393 f., 396, 400, 445, 498 f.,
 504, 516, 519, 522, 536, 540, 543, 546, 550,
 565, 581, 594, 597 f., 649, 660, 699, 708,
 713, 718, 741, 769, 771, 791, 797, 815, 818,
 826 f., 842–844, 859, 862 f., 866, 878, 928
 Vol. 3: 28, 31, 69, 71 f., 81, 84, 97, 118, 135,
 138, 140, 142–145, 161, 163, 167 f., 199,
 214 f., 221, 228, 235, 251 f., 315 f., 325, 344,
 348, 350, 354, 356, 359, 363–365, 373, 402,
 436, 449, 505, 528 f., 536, 552, 578, 581,
 586, 649, 705, 717, 725, 728, 746, 748 f.,
 762, 779, 801, 809, 817–819, 825, 842, 844,
 854, 857, 869, 879, 883, 888 f., 912, 920,
 954, 969, 1020, 1067, 1151, 1163, 1167,
 1178–1180
Grace and truth **Vol. 3: 889 f.**
Graceful **Vol. 2:** 115
 Vol. 3: 818
Gracious **Vol. 1:** 212, 345, 357, 386, 540, 585 f.,
 597, 611, 622, 638, 699, 716, 731
 Vol. 2: 68, 77, 86, 105, 115 f., 216, 240, 242,
 275, 357, 360, 395, 598, 624, 652, 812, 819
 Vol. 3: 148–166, 167, 448
Graciousness **Vol. 2: 256–259**
Grade **Vol. 2:** 50
Gradually **Vol. 3:** 839
Graft **Vol. 1:** 644
 Vol. 2: 660, 712 f., 794
 Vol. 3: 227, 320, **865–870**

Grain **Vol. 1:** 249, 252, 289, 313
  Vol. 2: 32
  Vol. 3: 421 f., 526, 852, 1053, 1163
Grammar **Vol. 3:** 206, 1081, 1085–1087, 1119 f., 1141
Grammatical structure **Vol. 3:** 1124
Granary **Vol. 2:** 830
Grandchildren **Vol. 3:** 1056
Grandeur **Vol. 1:** 474, 638
  Vol. 2: 92, 261, **424–427**
Grandson **Vol. 1:** 287
Grant **Vol. 1:** 454, 506, 649
  Vol. 2: 40 f., 116, 175, 353, 368, 438
Grant life **Vol. 2:** 119
Grapes **Vol. 1:** 224, 725
  Vol. 2: 32 f., 737
  Vol. 3: 866 f., **918–922**
Grapevine **Vol. 3: 918–922**
Grasp **Vol. 1:** 241, 533, 607, 649, 713, 742
  Vol. 2: 391, 406
  Vol. 3: 130, **716–718, 747–751,** 822
Grass **Vol. 1:** 411, 515, 627, 673, 678, 743 f.
  Vol. 2: 27, 210 f.
  Vol. 3: 521–527, 1009, 1101
Grass, Hans **Vol. 3:** 282 f.
Grasshopper **Vol. 2:** 831
  Vol. 3: 112
Grassland **Vol. 3:** 1004
Grateful **Vol. 2:** 115, 121, 395
Gratification **Vol. 1:** 457
Gratitude **Vol. 1:** 183, 335, 702, 728
  Vol. 2: 108, 115, 202, 353, 400, 444, 668, 825, 874
  Vol. 3: 207, **816–819**
Grave **Vol. 1: 263–266,** 470, 655
  Vol. 2: 138, 206, 328, 331, 341, 418, 726 f., 780, 924, 928
  Vol. 3: 239, 246, 256, 262, 269, 499, 1053, 1100
Graven **Vol. 3:** 488, 916
Graven image **Vol. 2:** 226
Graven object **Vol. 2: 573 f.**
Graze **Vol. 3:** 565
Grease **Vol. 2:** 335
Great **Vol. 1:** 600
  Vol. 2: 130, 363, 369, **424–427,** 428
  Vol. 3: 115, 457
Great commandment **Vol. 2:** 147, 426
Great God **Vol. 2:** 82
Great year **Vol. 3:** 653
Greater **Vol. 1:** 728, 730
  Vol. 2: 426
  Vol. 3: 792, 1030
Greatest **Vol. 1:** 285
  Vol. 2: 427
Greatness **Vol. 1:** 732
  Vol. 2: 105, 197, 272, 316, 426, 429
Greece **Vol. 1:** 55, 140 f., 193, 243, 264, 279, 392, 493, 497 f., 616, 624 f., 641
  Vol. 2: 92, 96, 102, 124, 166, 802 f., 830, 898, 918
  Vol. 3: 49, 103, 259, 421, 679, 739, 851
Greed **Vol. 1: 137–139,** 456, 611
  Vol. 2: 115, 421

  Vol. 3: 381, 756 f., 820, 1053 f.
Greediness **Vol. 3: 601–605**
Greedy **Vol. 3:** 564
Greek **Vol. 1:** 59, **62,** 140, 220, 228, 307, 309, 311, 349, 351, 361, 369, 382, 397, 408, 422, 431, 444, 502, 510–512, 524, 560, 575, 589, 622, 686 f., 691, 709, 715
  Vol. 2: 85, 92, 99, 102 f., **124–127,** 159, 166 f., 170, 173, 180, 188, 208, 212, 223, 234, 257, 260, 266, 274, 302, 315, 321, 372, 430, 657, 707, 790, 802, 805, 847–851, 876, 879
  Vol. 3: 65, 106, 277, 513, 730, 791, 834, 840, 852, 980
Greek prepositions **Vol. 3: 1171–1215**
Greek view of truth **Vol. 3:** 889
Green **Vol. 1:** 390, 653, 744
  Vol. 3: 396
Greet **Vol. 1:** 206, 585, 724
  Vol. 2: 328, 517, 549, 779
Greet by name **Vol. 3:** 1063
Greeting **Vol. 1:** 206 f., 212 f., 241, 246 f., 427, 587, 609, 732
  Vol. 2: 170, 352, **356–358,** 516, 549, 597, 777, 780 f.
  Vol. 3: 258
Gregarious **Vol. 2:** 412
Gregory Nazianzen **Vol. 2:** 505
Gregory of Nyssa **Vol. 3:** 148
Grey **Vol. 1:** 205, 227
Griddle **Vol. 1:** 249
Grief **Vol. 1:** 202, 311, 467, 520, 529, 593, 673
  Vol. 2: 157, 227, 360, 416–420, **421–423**
  Vol. 3: 691, 1051, 1167
Grieve **Vol. 2:** 260, **421–423,** 807
Griffin-vulture **Vol. 1:** 173
Grind the teeth **Vol. 2:** 421
Grinding **Vol. 3:** 1058
Grip **Vol. 1:** 675
  Vol. 3: 747
Groan **Vol. 1:** 385
  Vol. 2: 416–424, 862, 884, 925
  Vol. 3: 180, 702
Grope **Vol. 1:** 421
Grotto **Vol. 3:** 782
Ground **Vol. 1:** 70, 376, 416, 433, 470, 500, 513, 517, 604, 609, 623, 633, 637, 653, 658, 662, 669, 679, 693, 695 f., 699 f., 702, 710 f., 721, 743
  Vol. 2: 67, 104, 137–139, 143, 232, 253, 298, 302, 318, 359 f., 439
  Vol. 3: 1183
Groundless **Vol. 1:** 550
Groundwork **Vol. 1:** 662
Group **Vol. 1:** 208, 229, 237, 274, 280, 286–288, 297, 301–304, 311, 341, 463, 487, 489, 498, 505, 533–536, 539, 602, 627 f., 632 f., 643 f., 693, 712, 732 f., 742
  Vol. 2: 306, 310–313, 315 f.
Grove **Vol. 2:** 233
  Vol. 3: 782, 785
Grovelling **Vol. 2:** 259
Grow **Vol. 1:** 181, 284, 289, 504, 557, 681, 722, 728, 732
  Vol. 2: 123, **128–131,** 162, 201, 223, 252 f.,

Grow (cont'd)
271, 656 f., 668
Vol. 3: 57, 870, 1033, 1118
Grow luxuriantly **Vol. 3:** 27
Grow old **Vol. 2: 713–716**
Grow up **Vol. 2:** 270, 369
Vol. 3: 215, 352
Grow weary **Vol. 3:** 628
Growl **Vol. 2:** 421, 423
Grown **Vol. 2:** 65, 425
Growth **Vol. 1:** 92, 174, 214, 238, 282, 302, 305, 343, 602, 625, 722 f., 725 f., 731, 744
Vol. 2: 128–131, 169, 185, 230, 360, 400
Vol. 3: 835
Grudge **Vol. 1:** 107, 557
Grudging **Vol. 1:** 214
Vol. 3: 818
Gruesome **Vol. 2:** 206
Grumble **Vol. 1:** 465
Vol. 2: 144 f., 175, 261, 423, 771
Vol. 3: 805
Guarantee **Vol. 1:** 99, 247, 308, **365–376,** 594, 637, 658 f., 713
Vol. 2: 40, 120, 243, 265, 272, 300, 382, 406, 789, 839
Vol. 3: 489, 497, 500, 701, 738
Guarantor **Vol. 1:** 371–375, 641
Vol. 2: 239
Guard **Vol. 1:** 247, 280, 335, 366, 395, 610, 614, 663
Vol. 2: 132–137, 177, 379, 413, 438, 864
Vol. 3: 201, 215, 277, 497, 512, 557, 565, 948
Guardian **Vol. 1:** 188, 191, 196, 477, 498, 560
Vol. 2: 161, 213, 215, 254, 307, 581, 737, 838
Vol. 3: 566
Guardian angel **Vol. 1:** 102, 304
Vol. 2: 194
Gudea **Vol. 2:** 679
Guest **Vol. 1:** 249, 271, 612, 686 f.
Vol. 2: 32, 521, 712, 825
Vol. 3: 49, 160, 424, 589, 744 f., 759
Guest room **Vol. 1:** 690
Vol. 3: 177–189
Guidance **Vol. 1:** 308, 485, 512, 579, 655
Vol. 2: 215, 296, 460, 875
Vol. 3: 334, 702, 720, 753, 777, 938
Guide **Vol. 1:** 118, 225, 351 f., 423, 484, 543, 565, 567–570, 585, 654
Vol. 2: 70, 216, 364, 412, 509
Vol. 3: 105, 163, **775–780, 935–943,** 1020
Guideline **Vol. 3:** 399
Guild **Vol. 1:** 291 f.
Guile **Vol. 2:** 270
Vol. 3: 469
Guileless **Vol. 1:** 561
Vol. 2: 470–474
Vol. 3: 691
Guilt **Vol. 1:** 85, 89, 221–224, 237, 294, 324, 331, 344, 349, 374, 397, 433, 436–438, 448, 452, 463, 479, 554, 556, 562 f., 590, 608, 611, 652, 674, 698 f., 702, 732
Vol. 2: 72, 78, **137–145,** 151, 155, 166, 175, 197, 215, 225–227, 239, 263, 366, 386, 400, 405 f., 416 f., 420, 457, 460, 544, 567 f.,

583 f., 768 f.
Vol. 3: 41, 98, 105, 150 f., 153 f., 156, 162, 196, 202, 359, 430, 514, 529, 535, 573 f., 577–579, 586, 720, 725, 756, 779, 818, 823 f., 856, 923, 925, 932, 1040
Guilt-offering **Vol. 3:** 155, 196, 428, 856
Guiltless **Vol. 1:** 563
Vol. 3: 257
Guilty **Vol. 1:** 373, 390, 413, 436, 449, 458, 500, 506, 516, 524, 578, 607, 609
Vol. 2: 137, 237, 363, 365, 368, 370, 407, 463, 667, 727
Vol. 3: 310, 342 f., 355, 420, 448, 574, 740
Gulf **Vol. 1:** 240, 303, 640,. 670
Vol. 2: 185
Gullet **Vol. 3:** 679
Gum **Vol. 2:** 293 f., 349
Gunkel, Hermann **Vol. 1:** 68
Vol. 3: 85
Gush **Vol. 1:** 682
Gutiérrez, Gustavo **Vol. 3:** 973–975
Güttgemanns, E. **Vol. 3:** 1123, 1142

H source **Vol. 1: 61**
Haaraloth **Vol. 3:** 1010
Habakkuk **Vol. 1:** 66
Vol. 3: 78, 366
Habiru **Vol. 2:** 305
Habit **Vol. 2:** 437 f., 547, 790
Habitation **Vol. 2: 247–251,** 925 f.
Habitual **Vol. 2:** 391
Hack **Vol. 1:** 726
Hadad-rimmon **Vol. 3:** 275
Hades **Vol. 1:** 101, 118, 205, 303, 419–421, 438, 464, 674, 677
Vol. 2: 29 f., 85, 186, **205–210,** 284, 433, 482, 490, 701, 727, 731
Vol. 3: 54, 260, 383, 387, 678, 683, 856, 946, 984
Hadrian **Vol. 1:** 309, 328
Vol. 2: 308, 333, 792, 898
Vol. 3: 217, 735
Haemorrhage **Vol. 1:** 682 f.
Vol. 3: 987
Haenchen, E. **Vol. 3:** 63
Hagar **Vol. 1:** 76, **80 f.,** 411, 531 f., 650
Vol. 2: 452, 755
Vol. 3: 594, 1014, 1057, 1070
Haggadah **Vol. 1: 58,** 59, 64, 67, 69 f., 485, 599
Vol. 2: 333, 534, 661
Vol. 3: 244, 669
Haggai **Vol. 1:** 52, 66
Vol. 2: 337
Vol. 3: 78, 783
Hagiographa **Vol. 1: 58 f.,** 63, 66
Vol. 3: 485, 638
Hail **Vol. 1:** 206, 380
Vol. 2: 189, 356, 637, 830
Vol. 3: 846, **1000–1004**
Hair **Vol. 1:** 116, 203 f., 227, 609, 671 f., 682
Vol. 2: 50, 159 f., 162, 197, 465, 657, 661
Vol. 3: 741, 1004, 1099
Hair shirt **Vol. 3:** 120
Hair-splitting **Vol. 3:** 428

463

Halachah **Vol. 1:** 58, **59,** 64, 67, 69, 334, 485
  Vol. 2: 610, 811
  Vol. 3: 654, 773 f.
Half-hearted **Vol. 1:** 318
Half-shekel **Vol. 1:** 684
  Vol. 3: 752–755, 853, 1179
Halicarnassus **Vol. 3:** 217, 219
Hall **Vol. 1:** 68
Hallel **Vol. 2:** 522, 528
  Vol. 3: 669 f.
Hallel cup **Vol. 2: 522**
Hallelujah **Vol. 1:** 97, **99 f.**
  Vol. 2: 878
Hallow **Vol. 1:** 310
  Vol. 2: 74, 229, 650, 653
Halo **Vol. 3:** 1002 f.
Halt **Vol. 2:** 359, 415
  Vol. 3: 254
Ham **Vol. 2:** 622
Hammer **Vol. 2:** 97
  Vol. 3: 1097
Hammerer **Vol. 1:** 63
Hammurabi **Vol. 1:** 140
  Vol. 2: 200, 555, 582, 612, 677
  Vol. 3: 593 f.
Hamper **Vol. 1:** 674
  Vol. 2: 221–223, 414
Hananiah **Vol. 3:** 1097 f., 1161
Hand **Vol. 1:** 197, 206, 225, 231, 315, 393, 395,
  478 f., 515 f., 540, 546, 561, 609, 636, 645,
  650
  Vol. 2: 28, 60, 77, 144, **146–153,** 163, 188,
  190, 192, 194, 201, 203 f., 225, 230, 235,
  237, 252 f., 282, 285, 287, 367 f., 378, 380,
  385, 411, 414 f., 423, 513, 571 f., 614, 710,
  726, 813, 820, 839, 866, 869, 877
  Vol. 3: 105, 108, 212, 243, 256, 475, 588,
  696, 716, 749 f., 763, 793, 805, 860, 989, 992
Hand down **Vol. 2:** 311
  Vol. 3: 765, **772–775**
Hand of God **Vol. 1:** 623, 655, 738
  Vol. 2: 49, 72, 86, 188, 194, 196, 199, 204,
  614
  Vol. 3: 554, 633, 680, 713, 717, 747, 825, 916
Hand on **Vol. 2:** 171
Hand over **Vol. 2:** 119, 361, **367 f.,** 543
  Vol. 3: 135, 471, 1058
Handicraft **Vol. 3:** 1028
Handiwork **Vol. 2:** 574
Handle **Vol. 2:** 270, 275
Handle shamefully **Vol. 2:** 50
Handmaid **Vol. 2:** 119, 262
Handshake **Vol. 2:** 146
Handwriting **Vol. 2:** 146, 148
Handy **Vol. 1:** 475
Hang **Vol. 1:** 265, 389–394, 417
  Vol. 2: 291, 321
  Vol. 3: 96
Hanker **Vol. 1:** 677
Hannah **Vol. 2:** 116, 260, 856
  Vol. 3: 30, 235, 263, 1057 f., 1069, 1072
Hannas **Vol. 3:** 35
Hannibal **Vol. 2:** 290
Hansen's disease **Vol. 2: 464**

Hanukkah **Vol. 1:** 626, 631
  Vol. 3: 165
Happen **Vol. 1:** 181
Happiness **Vol. 1:** 216, 501, 640
  Vol. 2: 60, 108, 352, 419, 484, 490, 780 f.
  Vol. 3: 138, 260, 559, 926, 1034
Happy **Vol. 1:** 79, **206–218**
Harass **Vol. 1:** 226, 727
  Vol. 2: 413, 599
Harassment **Vol. 2:** 374
Harbour **Vol. 1:** 645, 743
  Vol. 2: 102, 660
Hard **Vol. 1:** 419 f.
  Vol. 2: 97, **153–156,** 178, 183 f., 304, 388,
  407, 710, 843
  Vol. 3: 132, 396, 586
Hard to interpret **Vol. 3:** 124
Hard to understand **Vol. 3: 122–130**
Hard work **Vol. 3:** 858, 936
Hardened, hardening **Vol. 1:** 106, 220, 317, 357,
  370–372, 424, 467, 565
  Vol. 2: 153–156, 174, 178, 304, 315, 741
  Vol. 3: 251, 253, 1020, 1094
Harder **Vol. 2:** 281
Hardhearted **Vol. 2:** 153, 155
Hardness **Vol. 2:** 98, **153–156,** 182
Hardness of heart **Vol. 1:** 384, 429
  Vol. 2: 37, **180–184,** 627, 834
  Vol. 3: 132, 538
Hardship **Vol. 1:** 262, 420, 563, 645, 647, 727
  Vol. 2: 419, 544
  Vol. 3: 27, 256, 719–725, **858 f.,** 1162
Harem **Vol. 1:** 560
  Vol. 2: 578
  Vol. 3: 606, 673, 1058
Harlot **Vol. 1:** 100, 141, 142, 356, 470, 497–
  499, 501, 593
  Vol. 2: 349 f., 365, 475, 486, 575 582 f., 587,
  653, 692, 795
  Vol. 3: 95, 139, 490, 656, 757, 856, 920,
  1068, 1070
Harlotry **Vol. 3:** 267
Harm **Vol. 1:** 443, 451 f., 510, 553, 561, 563,
  565, 572
  Vol. 2: 28, 862
  Vol. 3: 27, 341, 693
Harmful **Vol. 1:** 422, 561, 565, 625
  Vol. 2: 27
Harmless **Vol. 1:** 563
  Vol. 2: 286
Harmonic **Vol. 1:** 522
Harmonious **Vol. 3:** 687
Harmonization **Vol. 1:** 130, 241
  Vol. 3: 283, 296, 654 f., 704
Harmony **Vol. 1:** 113, 206, 209, 498, 595, 627,
  692, 716
  Vol. 2: 62, 78, 163, 363, 439, 619, 658, 660,
  780–782
  Vol. 3: 33, 678, 818, 909, 927
Harp **Vol. 3:** 671
Harris, M. J. **Vol. 3: 302–305**
Harrow **Vol. 1:** 726
Harsh **Vol. 1:** 202, 420, 520
  Vol. 3: 709

Harshness **Vol. 2:** 256
Harvest **Vol. 1:** 171, 204, 249, 263, 289, 292, 296, 516, 624–627, 719, 722, 724, 733
  Vol. 2: 35, 265, 271, 359, 364, 514, 662, 737, 783, 785, 861
  Vol. 3: 134, 143, 189, 278, 304, 407, 503, **521–527,** 701, 846, 918
Harvest festival **Vol. 2:** 463, 783
Hasidim **Vol. 2:** 810
  Vol. 3: 270, 461
Hasmon **Vol. 1:** 63
Hasmoneans **Vol. 1:** 59, 63, 309, 363
  Vol. 2: 308, 310, 337, 810, 812, 849 f.
  Vol. 3: 34, 440, 442, 452, 649, 960
Haste **Vol. 1:** 596, 684
Hasten **Vol. 1:** 558
  Vol. 2: 246, 315, 385
  Vol. 3: 320, 1168
Hasty **Vol. 3:** 953
Hat **Vol. 2:** 160, 162
Hate **Vol. 1:** 202, 255, 359, 409, 424, 525, **553–557,** 727
  Vol. 2: 86, 100, 288, 310, 318, 386, 540, 549, 659, 824, 838
  Vol. 3: 28, 212, 683, 777, 832, 945, 1045
Hatra-Khorsabad-Nimrud **Vol. 2:** 679
Hatred **Vol. 1:** 458, 539, 553, 555
  Vol. 2: 105, 180, 261, 309, 316, 359, 403, 405, 420, 449, 473, 478, 548, 625, 806, 808
  Vol. 3: 681, 908, 926
Haughtiness **Vol. 2:** 263, 618
  Vol. 3: 29 f.
Haunt **Vol. 2:** 136
Haustafeln **Vol. 3: 928–932,** 1075
Have **Vol. 1:** 137, **635–644**
Have need of **Vol. 3: 956–958**
Have no opportunity **Vol. 3: 833–839**
Have no time **Vol. 3: 833–839**
Have in view **Vol. 2:** 132
Havoc **Vol. 3:** 729
Hay **Vol. 1:** 743 f.
  Vol. 2: 210 f.
Hazael **Vol. 3:** 248
Hazardous **Vol. 1:** 725 f.
He who is **Vol. 2:** 69
Head **Vol. 1:** 120, 166 f., 192, 196 f., 203, 230, 232, 238, 241, 294, 301 f., 305, 520, 609, 614, 617, 633 f., 648, 676, 726
  Vol. 2: 129, 151, **156–163,** 184, 195, 212 f., 232, 234, 243 f., 249 f., 259, 268, 363, 370, 388, 562 f., 568, 571, 579, 661, 668 f., 691, 722 f.
  Vol. 3: 108, 159, 219 f., 298, 310, 390, 403, 504, 556, 670, 741, 865, 1060, 1066
Head of the corner **Vol. 2:** 159
Head of gold **Vol. 2:** 96
Head-covering **Vol. 2: 213**
Head-dress **Vol. 1:** 405
  Vol. 3: 715
Headache **Vol. 1:** 163
Headquarters **Vol. 3: 959–967**
Headship **Vol. 3:** 1063 f.
Heal **Vol. 2:** 150, 153 f., **163–172,** 414, 466, 561, 630, 633, 754, 875

  Vol. 3: 56, 106, 211, 216, 348, 428, 476, 725, 861, 1000
Healer **Vol. 1:** 600
  Vol. 2: 490
  Vol. 3: 782, 859
Healing **Vol. 1:** 83, 117, 119–121, 163, 198, 213 f., 219 f., 234, 261, 267, 300, 328 f., 340, 384, 390, 427–429, 443, 454, 487, 489, 509, 516, 529–531, 572, 656, 685, 701, 729
  Vol. 2: 85, 121, 141, 151, **163–172,** 185, 379, 396, 448, 464, 466, 553, 560, 595, 597, 601 f., 606, 610, 623, 625, 628, 630 f., 665 f., 712, 715, 801, 865, 920
  Vol. 3: 37, 57, 61, 147, 180, 212 f., 261, 357, 408 f., 441 f., 444, 475, 481, 508, 519 f., 651 f., 657, 680, 731, 792, 840, 848, 859–861, 916, 922, 982, 987, 990 f., 997 f., 1043, 1059, 1061, 1108–1110, 1152
Health **Vol. 1:** 119, 240, 727
  Vol. 2: 102, **163,** 352, 356 f., 478, 552, 777, 781
  Vol. 3: 693, 805
Healthy **Vol. 2:** 102, **169–171**
  Vol. 3: 125, 712 f.
Heap **Vol. 1:** 520, 610
  Vol. 2: 157
Hear **Vol. 1:** 97, 230, 261, 272, 340, 347, 372, 409, 419, 427, 439, 480, 485 f., 529, 548, 591, 594, 604, 637, 688, 704, 727, 734 f., 742
  Vol. 2: 91, 110, 154–156, **172–180,** 203, 257, 285, 313, 358 f., 366, 369, 383, 395, 398, 405, 413, 427, 440, 443, 473, 720, 812, 857 f., 860, 862, 864, 866, 868, 877, 929
  Vol. 3: 105, 113 f., 127, 139, 173, 216, 218, 310, 313 f., 513, 528, 544, 744, 822, 868, 1161
Hearer **Vol. 1:** 577, 583, 599, 603, 725
  Vol. 2: 269, 379, 459
  Vol. 3: 363
Hearing **Vol. 1:** 630, 738
  Vol. 3: 1062
Heart **Vol. 1:** 106 f., 151, 169, 184, 212, 225, 230, 232, 240, 248, 261, 308, 311, 318 f., 322, 341, 347, 349–351, 357, 368, 371 f., 379, 418, 424 f., 448, 456 f., 460, 492, 501, 506, 509, 518, 552, 566, 587, 592, 604, 648, 660, 673, 682, 726, 729, 741 f.
  Vol. 2: 40, 60, 63, 96, 105, 123, 139, 150, 154–156, 176–178, **180–184,** 197, 217 f., 225, 262, 285, 306, 351, 355, 365, 420 f., 423 f., 444, 446, 468, 470, 492, 565–567, 571, 580, 588, **599 f.,** 641, 670, 727, 736, 831 f., 855, 857, 864
  Vol. 3: 69, 102, 106–108, 124 f., 128, 313, 351, 474, 484, 490, 493, 531, 550, 572, 578 f., 685–687, 691, 710, 809, 820, 823 f., 868, 888, 903
Heart of the earth **Vol. 2:** 351 f.
Hearth **Vol. 1:** 653 f.
Heartless **Vol. 2:** 542
Heat **Vol. 1:** 108, 317, 515 f., 652–654, 656, 743
  Vol. 2: 601, 628
  Vol. 3: 260, 446, 730 f.
Heathen **Vol. 1:** 115, 117, 145, 219–221, 226,

309, 320 f., 398, 416, 424, 451 f., 469, 519, 586, 655, 684 f., 688 f.
Vol. 2: 73 f., 77, 127, 284–286, 296, 307 f., 349 f., 385, 396, 400, 418, 426, 503, 581, 650, 660, 684, 705, **790–795,** 876 f.
Vol. 3: 32, 130, 193, 209, 310, 341–343, 552, 757, 934 f., 940, 944, 1032, 1058, 1064 f.
Heathenism **Vol. 1:** 626
   Vol. 2: 407
Heaven **Vol. 1:** 54, 58, 95, 123, 252, 272, 302, 304, 322 f., 379 f., 383, 387, 402, 410, 446, 449, 451, 464, 466, 474, 497, 508 f., 517 f., 522 f., 525 f., 544, 610, 618, 621, 627, 629, 637, 655, 657, 661–665, 669, 674, 689 f., 735
   Vol. 2: 29, 31, 37, 40, 42, 45 f., 48, 70 f., 74, 77, 84, 96, 149, 164, 174, **184–196,** 199–202, 204 f., 209 f., 215, 225, 245, 262, 269, 279 f., 282, 299 f., 317, 319, 329, 349, 351, 353, 355, 358 f., 363, 376 f., 380, 383, 391, 452, 459, 486, 494, 499, 555, 614 f., 619, 642, 646, 650, 652 f., 655, 688 f., 691, 727–730, 734, 761, 764, 804, 818 f., 836, 873, 918–920, 928, 931
   Vol. 3: 114, 117, 171, 189, 203, 205, 218, 229, 258, 266, 305, 362, 389, 469, 494, 514, 519, 588, 591, 602, 620, 630 f., 634, 674, 687, 692, 694, 736, 741, 781, 807, 813, 941, 946, 984, 1006, 1054, 1148
Heaven of heavens **Vol. 2: 189**
Heaven, new (→ New heaven)
Heavenly **Vol. 1:** 547, 609, 619, 627
   Vol. 2: 144, 147, 281, 294, 326, 332, 387, 925
   Vol. 3: 42, 231
Heavenly army **Vol. 1:** 104
   Vol. 2: 191
Heavenly banquet **Vol. 3:** 652 f.
Heavenly beings **Vol. 1:** 101, 619
   Vol. 2: 376
   Vol. 3: 287
Heavenly bodies **Vol. 3: 733–737,** 835, 842
Heavenly body (→ Resurrection body)
Heavenly calling **Vol. 2:** 62
Heavenly city **Vol. 1:** 279, 327, 387, 691
   Vol. 3: 397
Heavenly council **Vol. 1:** 363
Heavenly dress **Vol. 1:** 314
Heavenly gift **Vol. 1:** 372
   Vol. 2: 270
   Vol. 3: 809
Heavenly home **Vol. 1:** 460, 684, 691
Heavenly host **Vol. 1:** 100
   Vol. 2: 602
   Vol. 3: 964
Heavenly Jerusalem (→ Jerusalem, Heavenly)
Heavenly man **Vol. 1:** 85
   Vol. 2: 192, 646
   Vol. 3: 632
Heavenly powers **Vol. 1:** 90
   Vol. 2: 608 f.
Heavenly sanctuary **Vol. 1:** 587, 677
   Vol. 2: 64, 80
   Vol. 3: 795, 888
Heavenly sea **Vol. 3:** 984
Heavenly temple **Vol. 3:** 789

Heavenly wall **Vol. 2:** 646
Heavenly world **Vol. 1:** 103, 586, 740
   Vol. 2: 48
   Vol. 3: 829, 936, 941
Heavy **Vol. 1: 260–263**
   Vol. 2: 154
   Vol. 3: 184
Heavy shower **Vol. 3: 1000–1004**
Heavy-laden **Vol. 1:** 262
   Vol. 2: 262
Hebraism **Vol. 1:** 286, 290, 615
   Vol. 2: 175, 832, 837, 876, 895
Hebrew **Vol. 1:** 51, 68 f., 71
   Vol. 2: 125 f., 258, **304–323,** 556, 849, 928
   Vol. 3: 481, 484 f.
Hebrew view of truth **Vol. 3:** 889
Hebrews **Vol. 1:** 52, 68, 304, 359, 371, 531, 619
   Vol. 2: 42, 199, 204, 318, 635
   Vol. 3: 107
Hebron **Vol. 3:** 464
Hecataeus **Vol. 2:** 639
Hecate **Vol. 2:** 485
Hedge **Vol. 3:** 407, **948–952**
Hedonism **Vol. 2:** 677
Heed **Vol. 1:** 410, 704
   Vol. 2: 172, 351, 370
   Vol. 3: 114, 758, 1154
Heedlessness **Vol. 3:** 394
Heel **Vol. 1:** 241
   Vol. 2: 431
Hegel, G. W. F. **Vol. 3:** 896, 900 f.
Hegesippus **Vol. 3:** 621, 653, 796
Heidegger, Martin **Vol. 1:** 57, 65
   Vol. 3: 898, 1123, 1127, 1130, 1139 f., 1143
Heifer **Vol. 1:** 115
   Vol. 3: 154, 159
Height **Vol. 1:** 92, 123, 253, 288, 608
   Vol. 2: 184 f., 195 f., **197–205,** 209, 225, 423, 610
   Vol. 3: 32, 630, 1014
Heilsgeschichte **Vol. 1: 59**
Heir **Vol. 1:** 80, 185, 208, 214, 286, 289, 532, 556, 669, 719, 731
   Vol. 2: 122, 183, 238, 247, **295–304,** 570, 828
   Vol. 3: 72, 211, 634, 642, 647, 920, 1057, 1067
Heiress **Vol. 2:** 577
   Vol. 3: 1074
Helena **Vol. 3:** 457
Heli **Vol. 3:** 662
Heliodorus **Vol. 3:** 156
Heliopolis **Vol. 2:** 639
Helios **Vol. 3:** 730
Hell **Vol. 1:** 54, 101, 173, 231, 264, 433, 436, 449, 462 f., 509, 559, 623, 653, 655–657
   Vol. 2: 30, 37, 85, 136, 143, 184, 186, 188, 191, 196 f., 204, **205–210,** 265, 298, 351, 370, 385, 490 f., 733 f., 764, 791 f., 931
   Vol. 3: 99, 110 f., 201, 262, 265, 305 f., 359, 388, 446, 448, 470, 476, 586, 602, 686 f., 946, 984, 1054
Hellanicus of Tripolis **Vol. 2:** 506
Hellas **Vol. 2:** 898
Hellen **Vol. 2:** 124

Hellene **Vol. 2:** 790
Hellenism **Vol. 1: 59,** 63, 68 f., 124, 377, 432, 444, 493, 539, 570, 640, 646
  Vol. 2: 92, 224, 277, 307, 311, 324, 372 f., 638, 664
  Vol. 3: 31, 97, 127, 287, 325, 428, 440, 479, 577, 634, 685, 729, 740, 748, 776, 924, 931, 959, 1035, 1079, 1147
Hellenist **Vol. 1:** 642
  Vol. 2: 124, 152, 311, 740
  Vol. 3: 59, 65 f., 465, 548, 908
Hellenist source **Vol. 3:** 700
Hellenistic **Vol. 1:** 399, 409, 435, 442, 468, 474, 496, 514, 539, 547, 560, 562, 570, 601, 613, 645 f., 674, 677 f., 692, 705, 707, 711
  Vol. 2: 73, 93, 99, 104, 108 f., 111, 113, 125, 140, 142, 159, 173, 187, 207, 214, 234, 250, 257 f., 281, 284 f., 311, 324, 372 f., 400, 403, 660, 811, 849, 862, 898, 900, 926, 928
  Vol. 3: 35, 58 f., 69 f., 101, 138, 199, 217, 220 f., 324, 331, 333, 453, 458, 610 f., 613, 618, 626, 631–633, 635 f., 644–647, 651, 680–682, 685, 689 f., 692, 761, 779, 832, 855, 861–863, 889, 891, 928, 930 f., 933, 940, 958, 989, 998 f., 1029, 1033–1035, 1074 f.
Hellenistic Christianity **Vol. 1:** 601
  Vol. 2: 103, 785
  Vol. 3: 195
Hellenistic Judaism **Vol. 1:** 77, 216, 357, 487, 499, 502, 512, 522–524, 598, 604, 645, 648, 674, 685, 688, 742
  Vol. 2: 77, 93, 99, 241, 324, 396, 638, 651, 661, 745, 804, 810, 821, 823
  Vol. 3: 41, 59, 853, 931, 1029, 1033, 1052, 1072, 1117, 1149, 1167
Hellenistic period **Vol. 1:** 62, 64
  Vol. 2: 311
  Vol. 3: 638, 739, 741, 781, 913, 952
Hellenistic philosophy **Vol. 2:** 399
  Vol. 3: 827, 1034 f., 1169
Hellenistic religion **Vol. 1:** 61
  Vol. 3: 861
Hellenizing **Vol. 2:** 70, 125, 321, 372
  Vol. 3: 452, 635
Hellespont **Vol. 2:** 233
Helmet **Vol. 2:** 97, 244, 925
  Vol. 3: 200
Helmsman **Vol. 1:** 198
Help **Vol. 1:** 98, 101, 198, 248, 252, 287 f., 294, 328, 332, 344, 409 f., 464, 468, 474, 509, 522, 531, 544, 546, 563, 567, 607, 614, 625, 645, 678, 686
  Vol. 2: 71, 83, 105, 116, 121, 128, 141, 175, 230, 255, 257, 261, 265–267, 299, 326, 331 f., 353, 355, 363, 423, 428 f., 446, 468, 593, 600, 622, 628, 631, 654, 710, 806, 820 f., 825, 844, 855, 860, 877
  Vol. 3: 30, 95, 210, 232 f., 341, 356, 727, 782, 802, 836
Helper **Vol. 1: 88–92,** 259, 600, 637
  Vol. 2: 262, 281, 332, 363, 576, 709, 724
  Vol. 3: 544–549
Helpful **Vol. 3: 544–549**

Helpless **Vol. 1:** 218, 280 f., 284, 288, 312, 358, 407, 548, 716
  Vol. 2: 168, 260, 413, 435, 737, 813
  Vol. 3: 380, 1073
Hen **Vol. 1:** 174
Henceforth **Vol. 3:** 252
Henderson, I. **Vol. 3:** 1139
Hendiadys **Vol. 2:** 878
  Vol. 3: 319, 814
Hengel, Martin **Vol. 3:** 979
Hephaestus **Vol. 1:** 654
  Vol. 2: 115
Hera **Vol. 2:** 85
Heracleitus' antitheses **Vol. 3:** 929
Heracles **Vol. 2:** 643, 849
  Vol. 3: 634
Heraclitus **Vol. 1:** 63, 654
  Vol. 3: 1081 f., 1084
Herald **Vol. 1:** 298, 407, 410, 477, 648, 699
  Vol. 2: 108, 111, 682
  Vol. 3: 45, **48–57,** 170, 634
Herb **Vol. 1:** 116, 633
  Vol. 2: 210 f., 522, 558, 693 f., 813
  Vol. 3: 1053
Herculanum **Vol. 3:** 394
Hercules **Vol. 2:** 232, 430
Herd **Vol. 1:** 252, 625
  Vol. 2: 410, 412, 841
  Vol. 3: 564–568
Herder, J. G. **Vol. 3:** 1123
Herdsman **Vol. 3:** 811
Hereditary **Vol. 1:** 407
  Vol. 2: 372, 374
Heresy **Vol. 1:** 50, 247, 556, 740
  Vol. 2: 171, 405, 432, 449, 559
  Vol. 3: 181, 314, 768, 770 f., 930, 1018
Heretic **Vol. 1:** 117, 413, 416, 462, 466, 533, 535, 632, 708
  Vol. 2: 152, 312, 557, 574, 866, 903
  Vol. 3: 70, 401, 439, 765, 768, 844, 942, 988, 1119
Heretical **Vol. 1:** 347, 533 f., 607
  Vol. 2: 358, 406, 608, 718, 920
Heritage **Vol. 1:** 78, 190
  Vol. 2: 295–304, 311, 845
  Vol. 3: 140
Hermas **Vol. 1:** 51, 339, 577
  Vol. 2: 219, 264
  Vol. 3: 929
Hermeneutic, New **Vol. 1:** 584
Hermeneutical circle **Vol. 1:** 584
Hermeneutics **Vol. 1:** 57, **59,** 581–584
  Vol. 2: 907
  Vol. 3: 335, 1137, 1142
Hermes **Vol. 1:** 60, 101, 552, 579, 654
  Vol. 2: 85, 214, 503
  Vol. 3: 50, 679, 717, 1085
Hermetic **Vol. 3:** 645
Hermetic literature **Vol. 1: 60,** 522, 595
  Vol. 2: 99
  Vol. 3: 123, 146, 206, 483, 719, 936, 952, 1034
Hermodios **Vol. 2:** 372
Hermon **Vol. 3:** 1010, 1012

467

Hero **Vol. 1:** 101, 431, 490, 645
   Vol. 2: 92, 498, 562, 602
   Vol. 3: 346, 644, 673
Herod Agrippa I **Vol. 1:** 341, 343, 410
   Vol. 2: 378, 511, 789, 850
   Vol. 3: 908
Herod Agrippa II **Vol. 1:** 324, 453, 590, 593
   Vol. 2: 378, 451, 511, 695
   Vol. 3: 40, 65, 389
Herod Antipas (tetrarch) **Vol. 1:** 118, 156, 168,
   283, 346, 430, 554, 696
   Vol. 2: 63, 378, 383, 464, 550, 799, 801, 812,
   849
   Vol. 3: 361, 441–443, 507, 540 f., 603, 742,
   757,1059
Herod Archelaus **Vol. 2:** 849
   Vol. 3: 324, 1179
Herod the Great **Vol. 1:** 125, 170, 430, 512,
   560, 737
   Vol. 2: 235, 308, 378, 511, 550, 578, 849
   Vol. 3: 35, 324, 341, 419, 441–443, 452, 710,
   756, 783, 788, 872, 921, 1058, 1068, 1179
Herod, king of Chalcis **Vol. 3:** 40
Herod Philip (→ Philip, Herod)
Herodians **Vol. 2:** 462, 850
   Vol. 3: 441–443, 884, 979
Herodias **Vol. 3:** 361, 540 f., 742, 1071
Herodotos **Vol. 1:** 319
   Vol. 2: 247, 557, 643, 678
Herod's temple **Vol. 3:** 788 f.
Heroism **Vol. 1:** 433, 435, 437
Hertz, H. **Vol. 3:** 899
Hesiod **Vol. 1:** 640
   Vol. 2: 95–97
Hesitate **Vol. 1:** 326
   Vol. 2: 374
   Vol. 3: 839
Hestia **Vol. 1:** 653 f.
Heyne, C.G. **Vol. 3:** 1138
Hezekiah **Vol. 1:** 295, 509
   Vol. 2: 320, 627
   Vol. 3: 202, 235, 426, 609, 788, 853, 879, 951
Hiddekel **Vol. 3:** 986
Hidden **Vol. 1:** 50, 244, 252, 282, 313, 385, 425,
   504, 587, 604, 609 f., 629, 651, 676, 692, 720
   Vol. 2: 83, 112, 147, 149, 176, 183, 190, 197,
   211–220, 255, 263, 288, 354, 377, 397, 401,
   461 f., 490, 762, 833 f.
   Vol. 3: 54, 77, 132, 138, 310, 317, 321 f., 344,
   445, 517, 652, 833, 1031
Hide **Vol. 1:** 50, 313, 346, 401, 585, 701
   Vol. 2: 211–220, 240, 312, 401, 412, 773, 835
   Vol. 3: 309, 312 f., 324, 401, 493, 500, 514
Hideout **Vol. 3:** 380
Hierapolis **Vol. 1:** 319
Hierarchical **Vol. 1:** 302
   Vol. 3: 1063
Hierarchy **Vol. 1:** 382, 636, 667, 725, 740
   Vol. 3: 548
Hieroglyphics **Vol. 1:** 574
High **Vol. 2: 198–208,** 617 f.
   Vol. 3: 29, **1009–1013**
High D. M. **Vol. 3:** 1130
High calling **Vol. 3:** 142

High God **Vol. 3:** 982
High place **Vol. 2:** 199
   Vol. 3: 1010
High position **Vol. 2:** 200
High priest (→ Priest, High)
High priestly prayer **Vol. 2:** 231, 654, 723, 929
   Vol. 3: 38, 321, 362
High-born **Vol. 1:** 188
High-handed **Vol. 1:** 400
   Vol. 2: 510
High-sounding **Vol. 2:** 198
Higher **Vol. 1:** 674
   Vol. 2: 259
Higher families **Vol. 2:** 195
Highest   **Vol. 2:** 71, **198–200**
Highway **Vol. 1:** 411
   Vol. 3: 935–943
Highwayman **Vol. 3: 377–379**
Hilary **Vol. 2:** 507
Hilkiah **Vol. 2:** 555
   Vol. 3: 485, 878
Hill **Vol. 1:** 239 f., 683
   Vol. 2: 217, 225, 262, 326, 329
Hill, D. **Vol. 3:** 85 f., 154
Hill of Salt **Vol. 3:** 444
Hillel **Vol. 1:** 67, 69, 153, 155, 499, 506, 580
   Vol. 2: 311, 442, 579
   Vol. 3: 494, 534, 538
Hilly **Vol. 3: 1008 f.**
Hind **Vol. 1:** 520
Hinder **Vol. 1:** 149, 284, 592 f., 636, 730, 740
   Vol. 2: 220–223, 285, 418, 435, 708, 781, 843
   Vol. 3: 254, 320, 719
Hindrance **Vol. 2: 220,** 864, 868, 875
   Vol. 3: 857, 994
Hinge **Vol. 2:** 59
Hinnom **Vol. 1:** 93
   Vol. 2: 208
   Vol. 3: 110, 426, 912
Hippo, synod of **Vol. 1:** 52
Hippocrates **Vol. 2:** 414, 464
Hippocratic oath **Vol. 2:** 166
   Vol. 3: 738 f., 840
Hippodrome **Vol. 1:** 645
Hippolytus **Vol. 2:** 506
   Vol. 3: 36, 245
Hiram **Vol. 2:** 97
Hire **Vol. 2:** 317, 386
   Vol. 3: 138–144, 349
Hired servant **Vol. 3: 138–144,** 847
Hired shepherd **Vol. 3:** 565
Hireling **Vol. 1:** 559
   Vol. 3: 567
Hisda, Rabbi **Vol. 3:** 488
Historian **Vol. 2:** 335
   Vol. 3: 289, 297, 336
Historical **Vol. 1:** 437, 472, 518, 524, 597, 601,
   603, 605, 617, 638, 686, 707
   Vol. 2: 56, 100, 112, 289, 316, 628, 636, 646,
   695, 718
   Vol. 3: 58, 64 f., 287, 299, 301, 922
Historical background **Vol. 1:** 57–59, 68, 70,
   130, 582, 628 f.
Historical criticism (→ Criticism, Historical)

Historical perspective **Vol. 1:** 60
Historical process **Vol. 3:** 826, 831
Historical relativity **Vol. 1:** 583
Historical reliability **Vol. 3:** 654
Historical truth **Vol. 3:** 894
Historical value **Vol. 3:** 862
Historicality **Vol. 1:** 583
Historicism **Vol. 1: 60**
Historicity **Vol. 1:** 678
  Vol. 2: 621, 812
  Vol. 3: 284, 293, 302, 334, 509, 627, 662
Historie **Vol. 1:** 58, **60**
Historiography **Vol. 2:** 890
  Vol. 3: 65
History **Vol. 1:** 50, 53, 56, 59 f., 66, 71 f., 101,
  109–111, 124, 126, 137, 142, 167 f., 182,
  190, 200, 208 f., 224, 243 f., 258, 272, 290,
  308, 333, 336, 338, 345, 347, 366 f., 373,
  377–381, 383, 398, 411, 426, 434, 477, 504,
  523, 531, 538, 541, 551, 563, 583, 596, 599,
  604, 626, 632, 634, 640 f., 655, 679, 694,
  700, 713, 716, 737
  Vol. 2: 37, 48, 52, 69 f., 72, 100, 109, 116 f.,
  119, 129, 158, 190, 194 f., 204, 206, 229,
  240, 260, 262, 268, 278 f., 285, 289, 295,
  297 f., 300, 305 f., 310, 312, 314, 316, 320,
  328, 331, 340, 342 f., 353, 361, 393 f., 396 f.,
  404, 407, 425, 442, 472, 509, 514, 540, 566,
  590, 609, 622, 626, 644, 663–666, 691 f.,
  697, 714, 716–718, 727, 784, 863, 888, 891,
  906–908, 914, 917–919, 922, 927 f., 931
  Vol. 3: 56, 58, 64 f., 69, 79 f., 86, 88 f., 117,
  135, 180, 190 f., 193, 202, 210, 218, 225,
  235–238, 246, 257, 268, 275, 280, 289,
  301 f., 312, 319, 325, 332–336, 399, 440,
  452, 495, 502–505, 543, 550, 578, 631 f.,
  636 f., 643, 649, 652–654, 657 f., 660, 680,
  720, 731, 734, 771, 785, 828 f., 836, 841–
  844, 846, 871, 899, 905, 926, 969, 986, 1014,
  1018, 1020, 1032 f., 1069, 1087 f., 1094 f.,
  1099–1105, 1112, 1114, 1147 f., 1153, 1166
History of ideas **Vol. 1:** 694
  Vol. 2: 490
History of Judah **Vol. 2: 306–308**
History of Israel **Vol. 2:** 35, 70, **306–308**, 315,
  319, 797, 807, 862, 871
History of redaction **Vol. 1: 67**
History of religions **Vol. 1:** 60 f., 130
  Vol. 2: 223, 453, 493
  Vol. 3: 464
History of religions school **Vol. 3:** 635 f.
Hittite code **Vol. 3:** 419
Hittite law **Vol. 3:** 94 f.
Hittites **Vol. 2:** 98
  Vol. 3: 656
Hivites **Vol. 2:** 636
Hjelmsley, L. **Vol. 3:** 1126
Hoar frost **Vol. 1:** 683
Hodayot **Vol. 2:** 622
  Vol. 3: 487, 669
Hold **Vol. 1:** 560, 595, 597, 635 f., 712, 741 f.
  Vol. 2: 64, 133, 135, 142, 244, 611
  Vol. 3: 716–718
Hold back **Vol. 1:** 607, 722

  Vol. 2: 222
Hold fast **Vol. 1:** 455
  Vol. 2: 301, 315, 350, 654
  Vol. 3: 737, 860, 1047
Hold out **Vol. 2:** 240
Hold to **Vol. 2: 451–453**
Hold together **Vol. 2:** 263, 546
Holiness **Vol. 1:** 101, 151, 175, 204, 219, 221,
  225, 258, 304, 386, 473, 538, 627, 655, 673,
  675
  Vol. 2: 76, 79, 91, 129, 144, 217, **224–232,**
  236–238, 244, 253, 307, 415, 447, 492, 676,
  689, 782, 807 878
  Vol. 3: 79, 215, 342, 361, 514, 578, 651, 750,
  776, 778, 786, 805, 934, 1064
Holiness code **Vol. 1: 61,** 65, 626
Hollow **Vol. 1:** 546
Holocaust **Vol. 3:** 421
Holy **Vol. 1:** 74, 108, 117, 189, 235, 243, 300,
  305, 336, 339, 368, 370, 424, 451, 474, 542,
  545, 585, 621, 634, 645, 647, 653 f., 657, 719
  Vol. 2: 56, 70–72, 78, 91–93, 129, 187 f.,
  223–238, 248, 253, 293, 302, 307, 324, 326,
  445, 473, 549, 650, 653, 669, 862 f., 865,
  868, 885
  Vol. 3: 32, 36, 38, 93, **100–102,** 105, 107 f.,
  171, 174, 207, 221, 228, 321, 395, 407, 534,
  645, 690, 779, 785, 794, 852, 870, 892
Holy assembly **Vol. 1:** 272
Holy city **Vol. 1:** 200
  Vol. 2: 231, 327, 700, 803
  Vol. 3: 436, 490, 734
Holy communion **Vol. 2:** 644
Holy congregation **Vol. 1:** 296
Holy family **Vol. 1:** 290
Holy garments **Vol. 1:** 151
Holy of holies **Vol. 1:** 223, 280
  Vol. 2: 190, 230, 293 f.
  Vol. 3: 156, 543, 794 f., 812, 814 f., 941
Holy nation **Vol. 2:** 380, 839
Holy one **Vol. 1:** 101, 266, 293
  Vol. 2: 71, 221, 227, 231, 238, 541
  Vol. 3: 474, 636, 800, 893, 1028
Holy One of Israel **Vol. 2:** 225 f.
Holy ones **Vol. 2:** 298, 302
Holy people **Vol. 2: 226 f.,** 307, 380, 797 f.
Holy place **Vol. 1:** 114, 121 f., 478, 685, 687
  Vol. 2: 230, 325, 328, 718, 866
  Vol. 3: 41, 104, 199, 239, 323, 418, 433, 436,
  543, 785–787, 794 f., 812, 814, 1005
Holy race **Vol. 2: 232**
Holy Roman emperors **Vol. 3:** 386
Holy root **Vol. 3:** 869
Holy seed **Vol. 3:** 654
Holy servant **Vol. 2:** 229
Holy Spirit (→ Spirit, Holy)
Holy tent **Vol. 1:** 211
Holy war **Vol. 1:** 382, 429, 646, 650
  Vol. 2: 225, 374, 650, 830, 888
  Vol. 3: 248, 590, 960, 963
Holy writings **Vol. 1:** 58
  Vol. 3: 483
Homage **Vol. 1:** 246, 347
  Vol. 2: 92 f., 186, 194, 201, 615, 859, 876 f.

Home **Vol. 1:** 327 f., 449, 460, 615 f., 652, 654, 672, 687, 690
Vol. 2: 193 f., 244, 251, 305, 394, 461, 575, 788, 818, 839 f.
Vol. 3: 205, 231, 286, 476, 562
Home, be at **Vol. 2: 788–790**
Homeland **Vol. 1:** 615, 684, 686, 690
Vol. 2: 194, 266, 311, 788
Homeless **Vol. 2:** 386, 822
Vol. 3: 547, 560, 623
Homer **Vol. 3:** 49
Homesickness **Vol. 1:** 460
Homicide **Vol. 1:** 429
Homiletic **Vol. 1:** 628
Homily **Vol. 1:** 737
Homoeopathic **Vol. 3:** 982
Homonymy **Vol. 3:** 1124
Homosexual **Vol. 1:** 448, 461, 497
Vol. 2: 569–571
Homosexuality **Vol. 2:** 142
Vol. 3: 95, 104
Honest **Vol. 3:** 351, 379, 758, 875, 882
Honesty **Vol. 1:** 413, 695
Vol. 3: 564, 572, 785, 879
Honey **Vol. 1:** 682 f.
Vol. 3: 382
Honi the circle-drawer **Vol. 3:** 638
Honorarium **Vol. 1:** 198
Vol. 2: 50
Honour **Vol. 1:** 111, 120, 122, 192, 195, 198–200, 220, 255, 287, 290, 304, 315, 336, 344, 386, 405, 415, 431, 435, 453, 470, 474, 478, 552 f., 572, 594, 616 f., 619, 645, 647–649, 665, 668 f., 687 f., 715, 717, 722
Vol. 2: 44–52, 73, 80, 91 f., 94, 101, 105, 116, 119, 127, 134, 146, 159, 191, 203 f., 229, 257, 265, 278, 295, 305, 319, 334, 336, 340, 343, 349, 352, 363, 367, 417, 424, 435, 538, 550, 674, 712, 772, 806, 840, 844, 863, 871, 878, 890
Vol. 3: 52, 138, 142, 262, 281, 342, 388, 588, 594 f., 652, 672, 717, 752, 755, 800, 809, 863, 871, 948, 953, 1007, 1053, 1055, 1064
Honourable **Vol. 1:** 442, 521, 524
Vol. 2: 91, 95, 105, 587, 654
Honourable purpose **Vol. 3:** 912
Hook **Vol. 3:** 182
Hope **Vol. 1:** 56, 78 f., 98, 109, 147, 180, 216 f., 229, 236, 261 f., 274, 279, 282, 289 f., 305, 320, 323 f., 328 f., 337, 372, 385 f., 400 f., 406, 426 f., 434, 440, 444, 466 f., 492, 504 f., 547, 554, 562, 564, 571, 586, 589, 592, 596, 598, 601, 604, 608 f., 629, 638 f., 641, 644, 658, 672, 679, 683, 694, 697, 710, 712–714, 724 f., 730
Vol. 2: 47, 51, 54, 73, 82, 111, 118 f., 122 f., 142, 178, 208, 218, **238–246,** 249, 263, 266, 301, 307, 313, 315, 337, 339, 342, 357, 360, 366, 377, 385, 399, 418 f., 447, 479, 495, 515, 531, 545, 550, 654, 674, 736, 764, 771–774, 776, 783, 789, 791, 807, 809, 822, 842, 858, 874, 887, 896, 901, 909, 914, 919, 925 f.
Vol. 3: 74, 141, 143, 200, 202, 214, 220, 225, 228, 249 f., 252, 257, 286, 317, 320, 341,

361 f., 389, 528 f., 556, 563, 578, 649, 682, 687, 702, 725, 744, 810, 813, 818, 836, 839, 845, 866 f., **968–970,** 1005, 1025, 1047, 1094, 1151
Hope of glory **Vol. 2:** 47
Hope of Israel **Vol. 2:** 772
Hope of salvation **Vol. 3:** 965
Hopeless **Vol. 1:** 336, 464, 596, 716
Vol. 2: 118, 215, 283, 413, 418 f.
Hopelessness **Vol. 2:** 131, 138
Hophra **Vol. 3:** 918
Horace **Vol. 2:** 239
Horae **Vol. 3:** 845
Horeb **Vol. 2:** 281, 636 f., 892
Vol. 3: 252, 1005, 1013, 1091
Horizon **Vol. 1:** 583 f., 681
Vol. 2: 198
Horn **Vol. 1:** 114, 118, 121
Vol. 2: 689, 693, 754
Vol. 3: 191, 198, 212, 419, 436, **714–716,** 815, 873
Horn of salvation **Vol. 3:** 715
Horned One **Vol. 3:** 715
Horror **Vol. 1:** 75, 114, 431, 437, **526–530,** 610, 622
Vol. 2: 622
Horse **Vol. 1:** 117, 203, 205, 510, 657, 743
Vol. 2: 189, 226, 232, 257, 538, 550, 572, 574
Vol. 3: 209, 266, 362, 490, 557, 1162
Hort, F. J. A. **Vol. 1:** 70
Hosanna **Vol. 1:** 97, **100,** 281
Vol. 3: 792
Hosea **Vol. 1:** 66, 109, 255, 290, 320, 368, 498, 532
Vol. 2: 240, 374, 396, 541, 576, 580, 583, 597, 754
Vol. 3: 79, 208, 267, 355, 592, 721, 1093, 1103
Hosea's children **Vol. 2:** 581, 797
Hosius of Cordova **Vol. 2:** 506
Hospice **Vol. 1:** 687 f.
Vol. 2: 823
Hospitable **Vol. 1:** 686
Hospitality **Vol. 1:** 686–690
Vol. 2: 358, 538, **547–550,** 590, 807
Vol. 3: 443 f., 561, 568, 744, 746, 1065, 1075
Host **Vol. 1:** 102, 280, 332, 380, 522, 647, 666, 690, 733
Vol. 2: 69, 189
Vol. 3: 589
Host of heaven **Vol. 2: 189,** 368
Hostages **Vol. 3:** 146
Hostile **Vol. 1:** 113, 269, 328, 407, 422, 451, 501, 507, 510, 512, 553, 555, 597, 610, 650, 680 f., 683 f., 687, 693
Vol. 2: 124, 150, 239, 309, 394, 491, 712, **739–742,** 816
Vol. 3: 127 f., 171, 198, 227, 346, 747, 983, 1006
Hostilities **Vol. 1:** 625
Hostility **Vol. 1:** 398, 402, 419, 430, 515, 555, 688, 724
Vol. 2: 311, 806 f., 827
Vol. 3: 39, 172, 185, 345, 452, 721, 1049

Hot **Vol. 1: 317–319**
  Vol. 2: 727, 844, 881
  Vol. 3: 321
Hour **Vol. 1:** 321, 324, 420, 423, 627, 629, 710
  Vol. 2: 55, 217, 359, 384, 892, 917, 927
  Vol. 3: 605, 826, 833, **845–849**
House **Vol. 1:** 149, 170, 174, 225, 272, 274, 292, 300–303, 308, 426, 440, 498, 596, 598, 617, 632, 638, 641 f., 655, 658, 660–662, 687 f., 695, 697, 716, 730, 734, 738
  Vol. 2: 40, 129, 177, 189, 193, 236, **247–256,** 285, 290, 428, 489, 509, 714, 732, 738, 832, 837, 873, 925, 929
  Vol. 3: 120, 189, 225, 229, 382, 390 f., 435, 465, 468, 472, 504, 647–650, 707, 782 f., 786, 789, 910, 915, 1001, 1005, 1032, 1108
House of David **Vol. 1: 426,** 544
  Vol. 2: 248, 319, 336 f., 342, 374, 730, 732 f., 866
  Vol. 3: 649 f., 652, 715, 873, 1073
House of God **Vol. 1:** 140
  Vol. 2: 67, 194, 247–249, 317, 327
  Vol. 3: 647, 783, 786, 789, 792, 853
House of holiness **Vol. 2:** 312
House of Israel **Vol. 1:** 174, 368, 726
  Vol. 2: 226, **305,** 314 f., 320, 400, 695, 732
  Vol. 3: 65, 453 f., 567
House of Jacob **Vol. 3:** 1012
House of the Lord **Vol. 2:** 247
House of prayer **Vol. 2:** 325
  Vol. 3: 430, 791
House of steadfastness **Vol. 2:** 312
House of truth **Vol. 2:** 312
House-church **Vol. 1:** 301 f.
  Vol. 2: 250, 550
  Vol. 3: 547
House-owner **Vol. 2:** 608
House-steward **Vol. 2:** 254
House-tables **Vol. 3: 928–932**
House-wall **Vol. 3: 948–950**
Household **Vol. 1:** 156, 159 f., 167, 194, 198, 256, 303, 472, 614, 633, 689, 691
  Vol. 2: 83, 122, **247–256,** 318, 487, 510, 562, 794
  Vol. 3: 928 f.
Household of God **Vol. 3:** 934
Household gods **Vol. 3:** 377, 533
Household servant **Vol. 2:** 164
  Vol. 3: 609
Householder **Vol. 2:** 714
  Vol. 3: 378
Howl **Vol. 3:** 1051
Huldah **Vol. 3:** 1057
Huleh **Vol. 3:** 991
Human **Vol. 2:** 355, 359, 362, 439, **564–569,** 659
Human life **Vol. 1:** 58
Human nature **Vol. 3:** 926
Human race **Vol. 1:** 665
Human sacrifice **Vol. 1:** 352
  Vol. 3: 421, **425 f.**
Humane **Vol. 3:** 429, 448, 981
Humanistic attitude **Vol. 2:** 99
Humanitarian **Vol. 2:** 43, 667
  Vol. 3: 406, 410–412, 746

Humanity **Vol. 1:** 86, 233, 255, 427, 474, 521, 524, 547, 556, 625, 631, 672, 675, 678, 680, 694, 709, 718 f.
  Vol. 2: 57 f., 126, 267, 287, 349, 441, 564 f., 607, 671, 799, 912
  Vol. 3: 653, 724
Humanity of Jesus **Vol. 2:** 36
Humble **Vol. 1:** 109, 308, 345, 479, 495, 547, 584, 587, 609, 612
  Vol. 2: 149, 203, 225, 244, **256–264,** 417, 422, 427, 435, 617 f., 821, 825, 856, 864
  Vol. 3: 445, 685, 691, 718, 800, 914
Humble-minded **Vol. 2: 259–264,** 617 f.
Humbling **Vol. 2:** 202, 265
Humboldt, W. von **Vol. 3:** 1123, 1127
Hume, David **Vol. 1:** 56
Humiliate **Vol. 2:** 260, 430
  Vol. 3: 345
Humiliated **Vol. 3:** 588
Humiliation **Vol. 1:** 154, 256, 398, 400, 520, 548, 569, 712
  Vol. 2: 203 f., 212, **259–264,** 903
  Vol. 3: 618, 620, 625, 630, 1017
Humility **Vol. 1:** 117, 135, 154, 227, 239, 285, 400, 489, 548 f., 700
  Vol. 2: 117, 200 f., 203, 240, **256–264,** 423, 428 f., 617 f., 771, 822, 828, 859, 862, 919
  Vol. 3: 27, 30, 32, 161, 218, 525, 544, 546, 589, 693, 727, 807, 859, 926, 928, 1032, 1143
Humour **Vol. 2: 430–436**
Hundred and forty-four thousand **Vol. 2:** 320, 700
  Vol. 3: 416 f.
Hunger **Vol. 1:** 109, 217, 250, 252 f., 272, 277, 381, 497, 613, 651, 653, 671
  Vol. 2: 264–277, 463, 478, 521, 523 f., 536, 596, 633, 665
  Vol. 3: 360, 383, 677, 707, 723, 728, 1092
Hungry **Vol. 2:** 157, 237, 263, **264–277,** 386, 824 f.
  Vol. 3: 189, 358, 424, 547
Hunt **Vol. 1:** 609
  Vol. 2: 805–807
Hur **Vol. 2:** 637
  Vol. 3: 878
Hurt **Vol. 1:** 413, 656, 726
Husband **Vol. 1:** 84, 87, 232, 235, 302, 395, 453, 506 f., 623
  Vol. 2: 50 f., 349, 400, 512, 539, 541, 549, 562 f., 582 f., 880
  Vol. 3: 138, 172, 189, 219, 325, **534–543,** 660, 928 f., 1055, 1057, 1064, 1066–1068, 1070, 1073
Husbandry **Vol. 1:** 498
Hush-money **Vol. 3:** 556
Husk **Vol. 1:** 704 f.
Hybris **Vol. 3:** 353
Hygiene **Vol. 1:** 119 f., 309
Hygienic purpose **Vol. 2:** 461
Hymenaeus **Vol. 1:** 466
  Vol. 2: 550
  Vol. 3: 471, 915
Hymn **Vol. 1:** 67, 147, 212 f., 237, 381 f., 386,

398, 400, 402, 547, 598, 628, 649, 651, 669, 706
  Vol. 2: 45, 49, 105, 261 f., 270, 289 f., 343, 358, 445, 500, 504, 528, 614, 618, 775, 782, 874, 877 f., 926
  Vol. 3: 77, 172, 235, 322, 505, 603, 610, 612, **668–676,** 714, 721, 816 f., 890, 967, 1032, 1115 f.
Hymn to Zeus **Vol. 3:** 331
Hyperbole **Vol. 1:** 116, 168, 713
  Vol. 2: 385
  Vol. 3: 758
Hypocrisy **Vol. 1:** 282, 299
  Vol. 2: 43, 448, 462, **467–474,** 813, 831
  Vol. 3: 180, 183 f., 482, 883, 1032, 1052 f.
Hypocrite **Vol. 1:** 205, 261, 416
  Vol. 2: 222, 304, 311, **467–474,** 730, 813
  Vol. 3: 251, 389
Hypostasis **Vol. 2:** 67, 442, 444, 507, 650
  Vol. 3: 1116
Hypostatic appearance **Vol. 1:** 101
Hypostatize **Vol. 3:** 356
Hypostatized **Vol. 1:** 382, 586
  Vol. 2: 290
Hypothesis **Vol. 1: 61**
Hypothetical **Vol. 1:** 591, 601
Hyssop **Vol. 1:** 225
Hysteria **Vol. 1:** 163

I am **Vol. 1:** 79, 250, 323, 628
  Vol. 2: 31, 68, 79 f., 119, **278–283,** 482, 494, 715, 741
  Vol. 3: 204, 567 f., 591, 631, 969, 1022
I-saying **Vol. 3:** 614, 622, 624 f.
I-style **Vol. 2:** 278 f.
I-Thou **Vol. 2:** 71, 75, 287
  Vol. 3: 330
Iaba **Vol. 3:** 476
Iae **Vol. 3:** 476
Iamblichus **Vol. 2:** 214, 556
Ibzan **Vol. 1:** 170
Ice **Vol. 3:** 1105
Ichabod **Vol. 2:** 45
Iconium **Vol. 3:** 203, 226, 544
Idaean Dactyls **Vol. 2:** 553
Idea **Vol. 1:** 66, 87, 105, 130, 242, 358, 460, 483, 491, 598, 616, 636, 641, 643, 679, 704
  Vol. 2: 72, 99, 103, 169, 185, 192, 207, 284, 314, 392 f., 434, 719
  Vol. 3: 123, 126, 224, 231, 513, 531, 682, 778, 1027
Ideal **Vol. 1:** 426, 460, 491 f., 502, 640–642, 670
  Vol. 2: 92, 99, 102 f., 130, 141, 234, 325, 337, 618, 820
  Vol. 3: 217, 777, 779
Idealism **Vol. 1:** 694
  Vol. 3: 931
Idealization **Vol. 2:** 250, 824
  Vol. 3: 57
Idealized **Vol. 1:** 627
Ideational theory **Vol. 3:** 1129
Identification **Vol. 1:** 709
  Vol. 2: 282, 302, 314, 343, 796, 825, 920
Identification formula **Vol. 2: 279**

Identify **Vol. 1:** 439, 481, 489, 634, 707, 709 f.
  Vol. 2: 77, 123, 312, 318, 411, 618
Identity **Vol. 1:** 316, 444, 598, 707
  Vol. 2: 80, 82, 282, 308, 632, 669, 835, 923
  Vol. 3: 277 f., 292, 305, 454, 543
Ideology **Vol. 2:** 111, 373
Idiom **Vol. 3:** 481
Idle **Vol. 1:** 73
  Vol. 2: 265
  Vol. 3: 687, 945, 955
Idle words **Vol. 3:** 1143
Idol **Vol. 1:** 75, 120, 138, 239, 252, 261, 350–352, 382, 390, 428, 444, 537, 546, 550–552, 589, 643, 731
  Vol. 2: 92, 96 f., 135, 158, 175, 178, 235, 268 f., 273, **284–293,** 309, 325, 402, 432, 458, 470, 555, 650, 677, 722, 793, 859, 877, 893
  Vol. 3: 45, 94, 119, 206, 209, 248, 310, 331, 432 f., 471, 690, 782, 802, 828, 888, 904, 913, 1101 f., 1165
Idol-worship **Vol. 3:** 310
Idolater **Vol. 1:** 467
  Vol. 2: 284–286, 660
  Vol. 3: 1072
Idolatrous **Vol. 1:** 75, 151, 410, 532
  Vol. 3: 469, 806, 964, 1008
Idolatry **Vol. 1:** 75, 138, 141, 231, 451 f., 496, 499 f., 514, 531, 550 f., 555, 559, 681, 688
  Vol. 2: 96, 138, **284–286,** 436, 587, 678, 682, 699, 720, 791, 794
  Vol. 3: 28, 31, 33, 79, 81, 93 f., 96, 104, 200, 250, 579, 582, 606, 692, 786, 802, 872, 914, 931, 989, 1055, 1121, 1165
Idumea **Vol. 1:** 269, 309
Idumean **Vol. 3:** 788, 1168
Ignatius **Vol. 1:** 51, 339, 535
  Vol. 2: 271, 316, 550
  Vol. 3: 724, 950
Ignoble **Vol. 2:** 50
  Vol. 3: 912
Ignominy **Vol. 3: 562–564**
Ignorance **Vol. 1:** 85, 417, 422, 455, 501, 561, 737
  Vol. 2: 166, 230, 261, **390–409,** 430, 458, 882, 912 f., 916
  Vol. 3: 844, 936, 997, 1022, 1026
Ignorant **Vol. 2: 406–408,** 661, 801
Ignore **Vol. 2:** 29, 683, 767
  Vol. 3: 57
Ilium **Vol. 2:** 233
Ill (→ Sick)
Ill-disposed **Vol. 1:** 202
  Vol. 2: 259
Ill-fortune **Vol. 2:** 148
Ill-repute **Vol. 3:** 341
Ill-temper **Vol. 1:** 681
Ill-timed **Vol. 3: 833–839**
Ill-treat **Vol. 2:** 202
  Vol. 3: 27 f.
Ill-treated **Vol. 1:** 644
  Vol. 2: 420
Ill-will **Vol. 1:** 557
  Vol. 3: 1019, 1166
Illegal **Vol. 2:** 451

Illegitimate **Vol. 1:** 500
   Vol. 2: 141, 311, 372
Illicit union **Vol. 2:** 586 f.
Illiterate **Vol. 3:** 1058
Illness (→ Sickness)
Illuminate **Vol. 1:** 212, 246
   Vol. 2: 289, 394
   Vol. 3: 318
Illumination **Vol. 2: 490–496**
   Vol. 3: 705, 893
Illuminations **Vol. 1:** 629
Illumine **Vol. 1:** 422
   Vol. 2: 183, 412, 484 f., **490–496**
Illusion **Vol. 1:** 546, 551, 713
   Vol. 2: 44, 458
   Vol. 3: 123, 597
Illusory **Vol. 1:** 546
Illustrate **Vol. 1:** 547, 627, 670
Illustration **Vol. 2:** 434, 501
Illustrative stories **Vol. 2:** 743–760
Illustrious **Vol. 2:** 291
   Vol. 3: 716–718
Image **Vol. 1:** 71, 75, 86, 87, 95, 107, 114, 138,
   168, 175, 203, 205, 236 f., 339 f., 360, 380,
   382, 386, 407, 469, 491, 522, 552, 580, 586,
   609, 654, 657, 661 f., 693, 707, 714
   Vol. 2: 57, 65, 85, 98, 158, 161, 196, 226,
   233, 242, 247, 253, 259, 277 f., **284–293,**
   318 f., 393, 470, **500–508,** 571, 650, 672, 693,
   743, 746, 834, 871, 876, 926
   Vol. 3: 50, 76, 207, 214, 219, 334, 392, 485,
   489, 498, 513, 554, 570 f., 644 f., 649, 701,
   705, 724, **903–906,** 913, 915 f., 1056, 1063,
   1068, 1075, 1158
Image of the beast **Vol. 2: 288**
Image of God **Vol. 2:** 51, 79, 161, **284, 287–289,**
   502, 505, 565, 569
Imagery **Vol. 1:** 118, 204, 406, 523, 549, 645,
   647–649
   Vol. 2: 38, 104, 231, 385
   Vol. 3: 522, 526, 686, 736, 863, 1008, 1048
Imagination **Vol. 1:** 330, 550
   Vol. 2: 44
   Vol. 3: 127, 513
Imbecile **Vol. 1:** 509
Imhotep **Vol. 2:** 166
Imitate **Vol. 1:** 214, 287, 400 f., **480–494,** 498,
   522, 638, 702
   Vol. 2: 160, 291, 350, 510, 552, 782
   Vol. 3: 724
Imitation **Vol. 3:** 775
Imitator **Vol. 3:** 942
Immaculate conception **Vol. 3:** 663
Immanence **Vol. 1:** 71, 522
   Vol. 3: 353, 1117
Immanent **Vol. 1:** 70, 460, 661, 688, 711
   Vol. 2: 376
Immaterial **Vol. 1:** 229, 602
   Vol. 2: 192
   Vol. 3: 875
Immature **Vol. 1:** 282
   Vol. 2: 428, 675
Immeasurable **Vol. 3:** 827
Immediacy **Vol. 3:** 703 f.

Immediate **Vol. 1:** 512
Immerse **Vol. 1:** 144, 147, 155, 224
Immersion **Vol. 1:** 143 f., 149 f., 152, 225
   Vol. 3: 105, 695
Immigrant **Vol. 1:** 625
Imminence **Vol. 1:** 322 f., 496, 513–515, 612,
   725
   Vol. 2: 53, 438, 732, 894, 921
   Vol. 3: 440, 838
Imminent **Vol. 2:** 55, 315, 382 f., 891, 900, 910,
   915, 922, 925, 930
Immobilization **Vol. 1:** 239
Immoderate **Vol. 1:** 625
Immodesty **Vol. 1:** 496
Immolate **Vol. 1:** 235
Immoral **Vol. 1:** 467, 497
   Vol. 2: 224, 438, 782
Immorality **Vol. 1:** 138, 231, 466, **494–503,** 555,
   681
   Vol. 2: 263, 402, 422, 669, 676–678, 792
   Vol. 3: 535 f., 802, 903, 926, 931, 945, 1064,
   1067, 1165
Immortal **Vol. 1:** 66, 229, 233, 432 f., 435,
   467–469, 705
   Vol. 2: 40, 77, 188, 232, 271, 274, 476, 565,
   658 f.
   Vol. 3: 99, 122, 125, 220, 263, 679, 690, 1034
Immortality **Vol. 1:** 58, 430–432, 435, 444, 463,
   467–470, 709
   Vol. 2: 47, 113, 125, 201, 207, 239, 241, 268,
   477, 480, 539, 661, 761, 763, 925
   Vol. 3: 231, 260, 267, 271–274, 323, 679,
   681 f., 686, 692, 926, 936, 939, 946
Immovable **Vol. 1:** 586, 663
Immune **Vol. 2:** 309, 573
Immutability **Vol. 3:** 553
Impact **Vol. 1:** 733
Impaired **Vol. 2:** 415
Impale **Vol. 1:** 391, 393
Impart **Vol. 1:** 207 f., 479, 620
   Vol. 2: 645
Impart knowledge **Vol. 3:** 766
Impart revelation **Vol. 3: 324 f.**
Impartial **Vol. 1:** 503, 505, 587, 639
   Vol. 2: 438, 497
   Vol. 3: 353, 356
Impassibility **Vol. 1:** 108
   Vol. 3: 724
Impatient **Vol. 2:** 238
   Vol. 3: 691
Impede **Vol. 2:** 414
Impediment **Vol. 1:** 163, 428
   Vol. 2: 155, 220
   Vol. 3: 180, 860
Impel **Vol. 1:** 408, 497
   Vol. 3: 691
Impending **Vol. 1:** 725
   Vol. 2: 382, 384
Impenetrable **Vol. 1:** 422
Impenitence **Vol. 2:** 155, 713
Impenitent **Vol. 1:** 106, 357 f.
   Vol. 2: 183, 352, 584, 834
   Vol. 3: 315, 1096
Imperative **Vol. 1:** 571, 602

Imperfect **Vol. 1:** 491, 518, 587
  Vol. 2: 62, 304, 473, 717
  Vol. 3: 199
Imperial **Vol. 1:** 395
  Vol. 2: 93, 518, 574
  Vol. 3: 221
Imperial cult **Vol. 2:** 108 f., 111, 234
Imperishable **Vol. 1:** 236, 467–470, 647
  Vol. 2: 56, 218, 300, 349, 597, 657
  Vol. 3: 267, 303, 995
Imperium **Vol. 2:** 373
Impermanence **Vol. 1:** 437
  Vol. 3: 814, 995
Impersonal **Vol. 1:** 484, 566, 693
  Vol. 3: 676 f.
Impervious **Vol. 2:** 154
Impiety **Vol. 1:** 461, 622
  Vol. 2: 91 f.
Implanted **Vol. 1:** 731
  Vol. 3: 865–870
Implement **Vol. 2:** 96
Implication **Vol. 1:** 482, 668
  Vol. 2: 333
  Vol. 3: 370, 373
Implicit **Vol. 2:** 387
Implore **Vol. 1:** 569 f.
  Vol. 2: 860
  Vol. 3: 473, **737–743**
Imply **Vol. 1:** 608, 680
  Vol. 2: 121
Importance **Vol. 1:** 260, 375, 528, 538, 627, 662, 679, 690
  Vol. 2: 130, 165, 325, 327, 333, 378, 428
  Vol. 3: 589
Important **Vol. 1:** 625 f., 666, 676, 739
  Vol. 2: 146, 275, 425
Imports **Vol. 3:** 851
Importunate widow **Vol. 3:** 1059
Importuner **Vol. 3:** 29
Importunity **Vol. 2:** 730, 881
Impose **Vol. 1:** 537, 552, 613
  Vol. 3: 108
Impossible **Vol. 1:** 669, 699, 719
  Vol. 2: 243, 606, 718
  Vol. 3: 914
Imposter **Vol. 2: 457–461,** 558
  Vol. 3: 32, 757
Imposture **Vol. 1:** 550
Impotence **Vol. 1:** 497
  Vol. 2: 285, 449, **601–616**
  Vol. 3: 691, 714, 1102
Impoverishment **Vol. 1:** 642
Impregnable **Vol. 1:** 659
Impress **Vol. 1:** 712
  Vol. 2: 288 f.
  Vol. 3: 32, 497, 500, 1112
Impression **Vol. 2:** 44 f., 284, 390
  Vol. 3: 904
Impressive **Vol. 3:** 570, 792
Imprint **Vol. 2: 284–293**
Imprison **Vol. 2:** 136, 207
  Vol. 3: 590 f.
Imprisoned **Vol. 3:** 547
Imprisonment **Vol. 1:** 219, 323, 432, 564, 731

  Vol. 2: 30, 206, 368
  Vol. 3: 96, **591 f.**
Improve **Vol. 2:** 326, 823
  Vol. 3: 721
Improvement **Vol. 3:** 146, **351 f.**
Impulse **Vol. 1:** 107, 354, 456 f., 459 f., 555, 636, 710
  Vol. 3: 719
Impure **Vol. 1:** 451, 639
  Vol. 2: 225
Impurity **Vol. 1:** 138, 152, 155, 231, 448, 475, 479, 496
  Vol. 2: 415, 579, 669
  Vol. 3: 104, 425, 926, 989, 1005
Imputation **Vol. 1:** 671
Imputed relation **Vol. 3:** 1130
Imputed righteousness **Vol. 3:** 371
Imputed sin **Vol. 3:** 825
In Christ **Vol. 3: 1192 f.**
In line with **Vol. 2: 451–453**
Inability **Vol. 1:** 556, 561
  Vol. 2: 100, 156
  Vol. 3: 132, 341, 995
Inaccessible **Vol. 1:** 445
Inactivity **Vol. 1:** 73, 240, 441
  Vol. 2: 240
  Vol. 3: 111, 1155
Inadequacy **Vol. 1:** 319
  Vol. 2: 821
  Vol. 3: 177, 814
Inalienable **Vol. 1:** 669
  Vol. 2: 298
  Vol. 3: 649
Inanimate **Vol. 1:** 429
Inappropriate **Vol. 2:** 431, 433
Inarticulate **Vol. 1:** 409
Inattentive **Vol. 2:** 172
Inauguration **Vol. 1:** 724
  Vol. 2: 262, 384, 673
Incalculable **Vol. 3:** 824
Incantation **Vol. 1:** 409, 450
  Vol. 2: 168, 552
  Vol. 3: 673, 1087
Incapable **Vol. 1:** 681
  Vol. 2: 405, 446
Incapacity **Vol. 1:** 742
  Vol. 3: 993
Incarcerate **Vol. 1:** 452
Incarnate **Vol. 1:** 575, 671, 678, 739
  Vol. 3: 645
Incarnation **Vol. 1:** 58, 66, 179, 347, 438, 547–549, 644, 668, 678 f., 706
  Vol. 2: 86, 111, 343, 373, 378, 500, 504, 535 f., 590, 661, 828, 835, 907, 927 f.
  Vol. 3: 174, 323, 630, 646, 661, 663, 679, 843, 931, 1070, 1115, 1117
Incense **Vol. 1:** 151, 478, 509, 655
  Vol. 2: 28, 96, 226, **293–295,** 713, 723, 728, 831
  Vol. 3: 156, 159, 419, 422, 436, 445, 447, 600, 790, 847
Incense-altar (→ Altar of incense)
Incest **Vol. 1:** 499 f.
  Vol. 2: 33, 142

Incest (cont'd)
  Vol. 3: 95, 574
Incite Vol. 1: 107, 110, 674
  Vol. 3: 516, **556–558,** 559
Inclination Vol. 1: 334, 533, 682
  Vol. 2: 116, 710
  Vol. 3: 939
  (also → Evil inclination)
Include Vol. 2: 313, 400
Inclusion Vol. 1: 739
  Vol. 2: 316
Incognito Vol. 2: 268
Income Vol. 2: 898
  Vol. 3: 417, 852
Incomparability of God Vol. 2: 501 f.
Incomparable Vol. 1: 615, 619, 729
  Vol. 2: 245
Incompatible Vol. 1: 501, 506, 513 f., 681
  Vol. 2: 82, 309, 439
  Vol. 3: 542
Incomplete Vol. 2: 100, 304
Incomprehensible Vol. 1: 363, 529·
  Vol. 2: 100, 105 f.
  Vol. 3: 75
Incomprehension Vol. 3: 507
Incongruous Vol. 1: 724
Inconsistency Vol. 1: 506
  Vol. 2: 349, 451
  Vol. 3: 369
Inconstant Vol. 2: 457
Incorporation Vol. 1: 237, 285, 303, 481, 643
  Vol. 3: 869, 1209
Incorporeal Vol. 3: 178, 677
Incorruptible Vol. 1: 467 f., 674
  Vol. 2: 242
  Vol. 3: 281
Incorruption Vol. 1: 380, 470
  Vol. 2: 924
Increase Vol. 1: 411, 600, 728, 730, 732 f., 742
  Vol. 2: 128–131, 317, 445
Incredibility Vol. 1: 594
Incredible Vol. 2: 263
Inculcate Vol. 1: 598
Inculpate Vol. 2: 370
Incur Vol. 1: 611
  Vol. 2: 405
Indebted Vol. 1: 648
  Vol. 2: **666–668**
  Vol. 3: 752
Indecency Vol. 1: 505
Indecision Vol. 3: 119
Indeed Vol. 3: **874–901**
Indefinite Vol. 2: 697
Indelible Vol. 1: 310, 680
Indemnity Vol. 3: 152
Indent Vol. 2: 288
Independence Vol. 1: 102, 190, 263, 377, 422, 484, 522, 537, 542, 680 f., 742
  Vol. 2: 84, 202
  Vol. 3: 78, 811, 960
Independent Vol. 1: 604, 627, 642 f., 697, 718
  Vol. 2: 195, 265, 325, 336, 441, 650
  Vol. 3: 455, 592, 677, 692, **727 f.,** 834
Indestructible Vol. 1: 337, 468

Vol. 2: 96, 325
  Vol. 3: **177–189**
Indeterminism Vol. 1: **54**
India Vol. 1: 653
  Vol. 2: 278, 293
Indicate Vol. 2: 648
  Vol. 3: 310
Indicative Vol. 1: 602
Indict Vol. 1: 349
Indictment Vol. 1: 84
  Vol. 3: 1041
Indifference Vol. 1: 318, 459, 553, 647, 737
  Vol. 2: 435, 438, 481, 699
  Vol. 3: 57, 370
Indifferent Vol. 3: 369
Indigence Vol. 3: 1055
Indignation Vol. 1: 106–108, 656
Indignity Vol. 1: 264 f.
  Vol. 3: 739
Indirect Vol. 1: 578
  Vol. 2: 150
Indispensability Vol. 3: 445
Indispensable Vol. 1: 618
Indissolubility Vol. 1: 384
  Vol. 2: 349, 583, 592
Indistinct image Vol. 2: **743–756**
Individual Vol. 1: 94, 156, 195, 215, 224, 233, 235, 237, 275, 294, 303, 305, 308, 354 f., 357, 367, 379, 382, 387, 409, 432–435, 463, 482, 485, 505, 520, 525, 536 f., 539, 568 f., 595, 597, 600, 612, 617 f., 620, 624, 626, 632 f., 636, 640–643, 647, 658, 662, 680, 682, 699, 702, 707, 711, 716, 721, 723, 732, 739
  Vol. 2: 71 f., 79, 99, 115, 117 f., 121 f., 133 f., 145, 158 f., 220, 222, 241 f., 249, 259, 273, 288, 298, 301, 303 f., 310–313, 320, 329, 353–355, 376, 385, 388, 410, 412, 422, 445, 476, 565, 611, 800, 864, 889
  Vol. 3: 54, 139, 146, 193, 200–202, 234, 236, 261, 268 f., 277, 232, 355, 358, 393, 421, 470, 546, 550, 578 f., 613, 653, 663, 692, 694, 699–701, 707, 720, 746, 776, 783, 799, 810, 834, 842, 847, 866, 868, 912, 937, 1052, 1088 f., 1100, 1102
Individualistic Vol. 2: 253·
Individualization Vol. 1: 433, 625
Indivisible Vol. 1: 501
Indolence Vol. 2: 772
Induce Vol. 1: 589
  Vol. 2: 266
Indulge Vol. 2: 116, 419
Indulgence Vol. 1: 77, 625, 698
  Vol. 2: 270 f., 462
Indulgent Vol. 2: 256, 817
Industrial Vol. 3: 138
Industry Vol. 3: 605
Indwelling Vol. 2: 243
  Vol. 3: 226
Ineffable Vol. 1: 705
Ineffective Vol. 1: 207, 319, 546 f.
Ineffectual Vol. 1: 546, 550
Inefficacy Vol. 1: 547
Inertia Vol. 3: 709
Inescapable Vol. 1: 609

Vol. 2: 138
Inevitable **Vol. 1:** 326 f., 418, 431 f., 437, 681, 719
  Vol. 2: 128, 138, 155, 399
  Vol. 3: 324
Inexcusable **Vol. 2:** 137
Inexhaustible **Vol. 2:** 165
Inexperience **Vol. 1:** 280 f.
  Vol. 2: 391, 468, 674
Inexplicable **Vol. 3:** 528
Inexpressible **Vol. 1:** 669
Inextinguishable **Vol. 3: 110 f.**
Infallible **Vol. 1:** 351, 527
Infamous **Vol. 2:** 291
Infancy stories (→ Birth narratives)
Infant **Vol. 1:** 280 f., 283, 290, 308, 512, 737
  Vol. 2: 294
  Vol. 3: 447
Infant baptism (→ Baptism, infant)
Infant communion **Vol. 1:** 160
Infant mortality **Vol. 1:** 498
Infant sacrifice **Vol. 3:** 84
Infatuation **Vol. 3:** 577, 1024
Infection **Vol. 1:** 611
  Vol. 2: 461 f.
Inference **Vol. 1:** 580
Inferior **Vol. 1:** 208, 259, 387
  Vol. 2: 412, 513
  Vol. 3: 344, 695, **952–956**
Inferiority **Vol. 1:** 734
  Vol. 2: 447
Infertility **Vol. 3:** 444
Infiltration **Vol. 1:** 539
Infinite **Vol. 1:** 164
Infirmity **Vol. 1:** 183, 452, 674, 679
  Vol. 2: 164 f.
  Vol. 3: 180, 409
Inflame **Vol. 1:** 418, 656
Inflammation **Vol. 3:** 109
Inflation **Vol. 3:** 1162
Inflict blow **Vol. 3:** 857
Inflict pain **Vol. 2: 419–421**
Influence **Vol. 1:** 165, 196, 302, 414, 423, 543, 564, 567 f., 587, 590 f., 611, 618, 624, 655, 676
  Vol. 2: 49, 66 f., 126, 130, 136, 159, 206, 221, 259, 307, 309, 319, 333, 338, 349, 366, 372, 393, 403, 406, 462, 582, 866
  Vol. 3: 50, 103, 415, 479, 481, 834, 864, 1054, 1123
Influential **Vol. 1:** 188
  Vol. 2: 915
  Vol. 3: 480
Inform **Vol. 1:** 246, 350
  Vol. 3: 49, 468, 759, **771 f.**
Information **Vol. 2:** 32, 234, 341, 858
  Vol. 3: 44, 47, 50, 55, 57, 69, 76, 766, 875, 1106
Informed **Vol. 2:** 406
Ingathering **Vol. 1:** 686, 724
  Vol. 2: 359
Ingrafting **Vol. 1:** 159
Ingratiate **Vol. 2:** 254, 837
Ingratitude **Vol. 1:** 399, 552

Vol. 2: 400
Ingredient **Vol. 2:** 294
Inhabit **Vol. 1:** 690
  Vol. 2: 247–251
Inhabitant **Vol. 1:** 286, 508, 519, 521, 726
  Vol. 2: 324, 326–328, 367, 802
Inhabited **Vol. 1:** 518
Inharmonious **Vol. 2:** 393
Inherent **Vol. 1:** 673
Inherit **Vol. 1:** 215, 222, 276, 287, 301, 433, 436, 470, 518, 552, 563, 625, 643, 667, 675
  Vol. 2: 258, **295–304,** 388, 608
Inheritance **Vol. 1:** 289, 390, 448, 469, 636, 640, 651, 696
  Vol. 2: 40, 135, 193, 230, 247, 258, **295–304,** 311, 339, 380, 438, 495, 671, 839
  Vol. 3: 72 f., 136, 191, 200, 391, 633, 701, 777, 807, 819, 853, 1057, 1073 f.
Inheritor **Vol. 1:** 79
  Vol. 2: 295–303
Inhibit **Vol. 2:** 628
Inhospitable **Vol. 1:** 657
Inhuman **Vol. 1:** 670
  Vol. 2: 542
Inhumane **Vol. 3:** 594
Inhumation **Vol. 1:** 264
Iniquity **Vol. 1:** 115, 202, 231, 296, 308, 607, 673, 734
  Vol. 2: 138, 261, 742
  Vol. 3: 154, 164, 171, 241, 693
Initiate **Vol. 1:** 176, 178, 189, 255, 316, 430, 596, 625, 705, 716
  Vol. 2: 60, 118
  Vol. 3: 61, 103, 205, **501–506,** 1085
Initiated **Vol. 1:** 577, 616, 654
  Vol. 2: 233
Initiation **Vol. 1:** 144, 149, 151, 154 f., 159 f., 237, 286, 288, 432, 470, 611, 616
  Vol. 3: 740
Initiative **Vol. 1:** 157, 275, 488
  Vol. 2: 119, 317, 334, 374, 582, 792
  Vol. 3: 75 f., 266
Initiator **Vol. 2:** 78
Injunct **Vol. 3: 324 f.**
Injure **Vol. 1:** 182, 687
  Vol. 3: 573–576, 583
Injury **Vol. 1:** 241, 463
  Vol. 2: 166 f.
  Vol. 3: 94, 152
Injury to livestock **Vol. 3:** 95
Injustice **Vol. 1:** 219, 410, 687, 716
  Vol. 2: 93, 258, 363, 365, 458, 822, 841, 864
  Vol. 3: 92, 514, **573–576,** 586
Ink **Vol. 1:** 203, 247
  Vol. 3: 490, 493
Inlay **Vol. 2:** 349
Inn **Vol. 1:** 688
  Vol. 3: 229
Innate **Vol. 1:** 481, 525
Inner **Vol. 1:** 679 f.
  Vol. 2: 283
  Vol. 3: 208, **794**
Inner life **Vol. 2:** 181 f.
  Vol. 3: 125, 684 f.

Inner man **Vol. 1:** 169
  Vol. 2: 78, 244
  Vol. 3: 127, 679, 681, 683
Inner powers **Vol. 3:** 680
Inner shrine **Vol. 3: 794**
Innermost being **Vol. 1:** 683
  Vol. 2: 180
Innocence **Vol. 1:** 221 f., 269, 287 f., 390, 395, 507, 510, 561
  Vol. 2: 149, 318, 429, 583
  Vol. 3: 266, 563, 740, 1055
Innocent **Vol. 1:** 737
  Vol. 2: 137, 139, 367, 417
  Vol. 3: 101, 103, 125, 154, 165, 201, 342, 355, 358, 537, 542, 721, 809, **923–928,** 1071
Innocent blood **Vol. 3:** 159
Innocuous association **Vol. 3:** 802
Innovation **Vol. 3:** 61
Innumerable **Vol. 2:** 683
Inopportune **Vol. 3: 833–839**
Insatiable **Vol. 1:** 137–139, 459 f.
Inscribe **Vol. 2:** 573
Inscription **Vol. 2:** 139, 173, 308 f., 331, 333 f., 339, 378 f., 433
  Vol. 3: 482–495, 500
Inscrutability **Vol. 2:** 197, 363
Insect **Vol. 1:** 172, 252
  Vol. 2: 268
Insecurity **Vol. 2:** 138
Insensible **Vol. 2:** 575
Insensitive **Vol. 2:** 153 f.
Inseparable **Vol. 2:** 386
Insight **Vol. 1:** 129, 421, 437, 483–485, 567 f., 597, 662, 671, 680, 742
  Vol. 2: 220, 316, 353, 391–393, 400, 444, 457, 517, 616
  Vol. 3: 122–133, 513, 684, 693, 720, 745, 778, 926, 1025, 1028 f., 1032
Insignificance **Vol. 1:** 174, 290, 381
  Vol. 2: 101, 260, 354, 605, 899
  Vol. 3: 868, 993
Insincerity **Vol. 2:** 270
Insinuation **Vol. 1:** 565
  Vol. 2: 263
Insipid **Vol. 3: 443–449,** 1024 f.
Insistene **Vol. 1:** 700
Insolence **Vol. 2:** 260
  Vol. 3: 27–29, 1024
Insolvency **Vol. 3:** 594
Inspect **Vol. 1:** 128, 188 f.
  Vol. 2: 393
  Vol. 3: 129
Inspiration **Vol. 2:** 147, 233, 342
  Vol. 3: 75 f., 86, 327, 491, 689 f., 696 f., 1117
Inspire **Vol. 1:** 427, 529, 578, 629, 734
  Vol. 2: 372, 445, 819
Inspired by God **Vol. 3: 689–708,** 771
Inspirer of prophecy **Vol. 3:** 705
Install **Vol. 2:** 149, 200
Installation **Vol. 2:** 151
Instalment **Vol. 2:** 39 f.
Instantaneous **Vol. 2:** 168
Instigate **Vol. 1:** 643
Instinct **Vol. 1:** 457 f., 460, 497, 502, 650

Vol. 2: 180, 182, 660 f.
Institution (*also* → Words of institution) **Vol. 1:** 71, 120, 130, 192, 194, 238, 297–300, 302, 304, 425 f., 473, 486, 667
  Vol. 2: 101, 125, 231, 335, 373 f., 579 f., 657, 922
  Vol. 3: 42, 50, 52, 79, 97, 181, 188, 191, 407, 440, 561
Institutionalize **Vol. 2:** 123
  Vol. 3: 84, 705
Instruct **Vol. 1:** 330, 340, 349, 421, 526, 574, 597, 680, 735
  Vol. 2: 112, 298
  Vol. 3: 45, 352, **501–506, 759–780, 1026–1034**
Instruction **Vol. 1:** 52, 64, 69 f., 246, 281, 332, 341, 462, 487, 491, 567 f., 570, 578, 593, 595, 600, 603, 617, 627
  Vol. 2: 32, 72, 141, 219, 235, 307 f., 310 f., 315, 328, 332, 440, 696, 719, 873
  Vol. 3: 33, 44, 57, 75, 119, 135, 353, 408, 483, 485, 531, 756, **759–780,** 809, 1095, 1106
Instructor **Vol. 1:** 333
  Vol. 3: 759
Instructress **Vol. 3:** 353
Instrument **Vol. 1:** 125, 136, 141, 231, 273, 353, 381, 389–392, 395, 414, 509 f., 523, 540, 655, 726
  Vol. 2: 97, 195, 302, 335, 364, 434, 436, 486, 836, 863
  Vol. 3: 113, 189, 268, 324, 364, 873 f., 913, 1182
Insubordination **Vol. 3:** 1054
Insubstantial **Vol. 1:** 512, 744
Insult **Vol. 1:** 259, 395, **413–418,** 566, 727
  Vol. 2: 49, 140, 257
  Vol. 3: 27 f., 340, **346 f.,** 430, 447, 872
Insupportable **Vol. 2:** 266
Insurrection **Vol. 2:** 320
Intact **Vol. 2:** 60
Integration **Vol. 1:** 190
  Vol. 2: 336
Integrity **Vol. 1:** 396, 467, 643
  Vol. 2: 61, 237
  Vol. 3: 50, 102, 291, 572, 692, 879, 882
Intellect **Vol. 1:** 399, 420, 568
  Vol. 2: 171, 567, 617
  Vol. 3: 122–130, 531, 823
Intellectual **Vol. 1:** 437, 444, 486, 494 f., 536, 567, 595, 616, 742
  Vol. 2: 59, 93, 166, 181 f., 265, 391, 397 f., 400, 405, 407, 478
  Vol. 3: 122–133, 230, 337, 349, 713, 825, 935, 1078, **1081–1119**
Intellectual death **Vol. 1:** 431
Intelligence **Vol. 2: 616–620**
  Vol. 3: 122–130
Intelligent **Vol. 2:** 256, 392, **616–620**
  Vol. 3: 130–133
Intelligible **Vol. 1:** 522, 582
  Vol. 2: 884
  Vol. 3: 124, 130
Intemperance **Vol. 1:** 672
Intend **Vol. 1:** 471, 696, 704, 718
  Vol. 2: 342

Vol. 3: 230, 823
Intense Vol. 1: 726
    Vol. 2: 244, 312, 356
Intensification Vol. 1: 631
    Vol. 2: 876
Intensity Vol. 1: 654
    Vol. 2: 197
Intention Vol. 1: 59, 119, 325, 426, 433, 496, 534, 573, 577 f., 600, 608, 677, 693, 695–697, 711, 719
    Vol. 2: 39, 150, 181, 281, 306, 315, 326, 443, 867
    Vol. 3: 49, 68, 88, 122 f., 506, 691, 914, 916, 947, **1015–1023**, 1143, 1149
Intentional Vol. 1: 609
Interact Vol. 1: 680
Intercalary days Vol. 1: 627
Intercede Vol. 1: 210, 647, 688
    Vol. 2: 307, 861, 874, **882–885**
    Vol. 3: 152, 682, 1079
Intercession Vol. 1: 78, 103 f., 213, 504, 699 f., 727
    Vol. 2: 117, 152, 199, 294, 424, 637 f., 857, 861, 863, 868, 874 f., 882–884
    Vol. 3: 40, 42, 130, 155, 230, 232, 244, 505, 746, 819, 1097, 1205 f.
Intercessor Vol. 1: 83, 88 f., 544
    Vol. 2: 147, 313, 874, 884
    Vol. 3: 33
Interchangeable Vol. 2: 84
Intercommunion Vol. 3: 1186
Intercourse Vol. 1: 235, 496–498, 506, 639, 678
    Vol. 2: 577, **586 f.**
    Vol. 3: 95 f., 100, 103 f.
Interdependence Vol. 2: 329
Interest Vol. 1: 278, 324, 366, 641, 721
    Vol. 2: 254, 395, 497, 830, 837, 861
    Vol. 3: 519, 532
Interesting Vol. 2: 670
Interfere Vol. 2: 317
Interim judgment Vol. 2: 363
Intermediary Vol. 1: 104, 372, 449
    Vol. 2: 442
    Vol. 3: 215, 284, 465, 640, 645
Intermediate beings Vol. 1: 101, 451
Intermediate state Vol. 1: 313, 315, 442
    Vol. 2: 761
    Vol. 3: 272, 279
Internal Vol. 1: 704, 708
    Vol. 2: 102
Interpose Vol. 1: 731
    Vol. 2: 650
Interpret Vol. 1: 57, 59, 69, 103, **573–584,** 679
    Vol. 2: 125, 305, 339 f., **362–367,** 468, 555, 621
    Vol. 3: 75, 316, 492, 962
Interpretation Vol. 1: 57–59, 65 f., 69, 71, 333, 398, 411, 415, 485, 512, 539, 566, **573–584,** 598, 616, 628, 737
    Vol. 2: 83, 121, 294, 312, 314, 329, 332, 342, 351, 383, 386, 388, 391, 442 f., 549, 616, 811, 839, 903
    Vol. 3: 76, 87, 89, 112, 184, 203, 316, 392, 484, 487 f., 494, 761–763, 777, 789, 1080,

1099, 1120, 1142, 1163
Interpretation of tongues Vol. 3: **1080**
Interpreter Vol. 1: 69, 220, 373 f., 512, 573
    Vol. 2: 401
    Vol. 3: 210, 480, 485, 704
Interrogate Vol. 2: 362, 365, 451
Interrupt Vol. 1: 625
Intertestamental period Vol. 1: 527
    Vol. 2: 227, 308
    Vol. 3: 135, 193, 440
Interval Vol. 1: 503, 540
    Vol. 2: 429
Intervene Vol. 2: 111, 200, 510
    Vol. 3: 263
Intervention Vol. 1: 379, 381, 385, 512, 521, 543 f., 551, 609, 643, 670, 716, 738
    Vol. 2: 48, 117, 166, 184, 201 f.
    Vol. 3: 48, 93, 177, 318 f., 355 f., 846
Intestines Vol. 2: 599
Intimacy Vol. 3: 860
Intimate Vol. 1: 482, 672, 712
Intimidation Vol. 3: 557
Intoxication Vol. 1: 513, 515, 528
    Vol. 3: 859
Intrigue Vol. 3: 820
Introduce Vol. 1: 544
    Vol. 2: 408, 437
Introduction Vol. 1: 167
Introductory formula Vol. 3: **487–492,** 1107
Introductory greeting Vol. 3: 818
Introspection Vol. 2: 407
Introspective Vol. 2: 355
Intuition Vol. 2: 393
Invader Vol. 3: 916
Invalid Vol. 1: 514, 720
    Vol. 3: 224, 890
Invariable Vol. 1: 351
Invasion Vol. 3: 93, 391, 1009
Invective Vol. 1: 413
Invention Vol. 1: 675
    Vol. 2: 111
    Vol. 3: 65, 506
Invest Vol. 1: 207
    Vol. 2: 80, 151
Investigate Vol. 1: 64, 189, 266, 580
    Vol. 2: **362–367,** 392
    Vol. 3: 492, 531
Investigation Vol. 3: **530–532,** 935
Investiture Vol. 3: 36
Invincible Vol. 1: 443
Inviolability Vol. 2: 325, 443, 592
    Vol. 3: 583, 805
Invisible Vol. 1: 95, 299, 360, 374, 385, 469, 491, 576, 580, 595, 602, 704
    Vol. 2: 77–79, 86, 163, 190 243, 288, 399, 613 f.
    Vol. 3: 128, 365, **511–518,** 647
Invitation Vol. 1: 270, 272–274, 324, 339, 483
    Vol. 2: 262, 307, 520
    Vol. 3: 53, 55, 114, 118, 529, 869
Invite Vol. 1: 409, 529, 542, 569 f.
    Vol. 2: 32, 270, 386, 812, 825
    Vol. 3: 49, 1029
Invocation Vol. 1: 271, 276, 367, 569 f., 615–

Invocation (*cont'd*)
618, 620 f.
Vol. 2: 76, 168, 512, 530 f., 556, 862
Vol. 3: 565, 741, 1039
Invocation of saints **Vol. 1:** 78
Involuntary **Vol. 1:** 561
Vol. 3: 434
Involved **Vol. 1:** 601
Involvement **Vol. 2:** 351, 358, 477 f., 816
Inward **Vol. 1:** 612
Vol. 3: 320
Inward parts **Vol. 2: 599 f.**
Ionians **Vol. 1:** 497
Ionic **Vol. 3:** 870
Ionic philosophy **Vol. 2:** 657
Iota **Vol. 3:** 181 f.
Iranian **Vol. 1:** 434
Vol. 2: 645 f., 836
Vol. 3: 275, 928, 1035
Iranian cosmology **Vol. 3:** 693
Irenaeus **Vol. 1:** 59, 116, 154, 180
Vol. 2: 506, 645, 677
Vol. 3: 855
Iris **Vol. 3:** 1000, 1002
Iron **Vol. 1:** 164, 407, 463, 726
Vol. 2: 27, **95–98**, 188
Vol. 3: 392, 914
Iron age **Vol. 2:** 97
Iron furnace **Vol. 2:** 98
Irony **Vol. 1:** 277, 382, 411, 413, 479, 590, 710
Vol. 2: 170, 263, 358, 380, 398 f., 402 f.,
430–436, 620, 714, 828, 834, 836
Vol. 3: 386, 394, 452, 768, 887, 967
Irrational **Vol. 2:** 659
Vol. 3: 681, **1081–1119**
Irreconcilable **Vol. 1:** 473, 501, 553
Vol. 3: 104
Irregular **Vol. 2:** 138, 459
Irregularity **Vol. 2:** 273
Vol. 3: 731
Irrelevant **Vol. 1:** 680
Vol. 2: 402
Irreligion **Vol. 1:** 74, 186
Vol. 3: 200
Irreligious **Vol. 2:** 94, 782
Irreproachable **Vol. 2:** 137, 139
Vol. 3: 171, 228, **923–928**
Irresistible **Vol. 1:** 459, 609
Irresponsibility **Vol. 1:** 559
Vol. 2: 272
Irreverence **Vol. 1:** 112
Vol. 2: 430, 436
Irrevocable **Vol. 1:** 207, 356 f., 365, 416, 443,
572, 611, 718 f.
Vol. 2: 77, 307, 681
Vol. 3: 72, 174
Irrigation **Vol. 3:** 986–988
Irritable **Vol. 1:** 107
Irruption **Vol. 1:** 612
Vol. 2: 382
Isaac **Vol. 1:** 65, 76, **81,** 82, 214, 411, 532, 556,
574, 617
Vol. 2: 68, 73, 76, 316–319, 431, 587, 627,
649, 651, 691, 725, 746, 865

Vol. 3: 69, 73, 195, 263, 359, 369 f., 418, 421,
425, 514, 523 f., 600, 608, 642, 661, 800,
806, 965, 969, 1009, 1057, 1091, 1112, 1135,
1179
Isaac, sacrifice of **Vol. 1:** 76, 79, 81 f., 403, 604,
713
Vol. 3: 369 f. (*also* → Akedah)
Isaiah **Vol. 1:** 54, 66, 109, 127, 273, 378, 407,
485, 531, 538 f., 596, 673, 737, 743
Vol. 2: 86 f., 109, 111, 154, 174, 183, 189,
225, 306, 355, 374, 420, 432, 613, 649, 740,
754
Vol. 3: 69, 79, 248, 367, 388 f., 391, 427, 430,
494, 609, 842, 912, 916, 920, 1001, 1006,
1093 f., 1101
Isaiah Apocalypse **Vol. 1:** 50
Iscariot **Vol. 2: 321** (*also* → Judas Iscariot)
Ishmael **Vol. 1:** 80 f., 411, 532
Vol. 2: 128
Vol. 3: 249, 661
Ishmael, Rabbi **Vol. 2:** 591
Ishtar **Vol. 2:** 201, 553
Isis **Vol. 1:** 64, 176, 206, 271, 595
Vol. 2: 67, 214, 224, 289 f., 521, 539, 554
Vol. 3: 138, 216, 501, 717, 785, 861, 1068,
1085
Isis-hymn **Vol. 3:** 760
Island **Vol. 2:** 233, 353
Isles of the blessed **Vol. 2:** 761
Isolated **Vol. 2:** 195, 295
Isolation **Vol. 3:** 710, 1097
Israel **Vol. 1:** 49, **61,** 65, 67, 71, 74, 76, 80 f.,
101 f., 104, 111 f., 117, 121, 134, 151 f., 155,
170, 172–174, 177, 190, 194 f., 199, 205,
219 f., 225, 245, 249, 252, 255, 257 f., 281,
286, 288 f., 293 f., 296 f., 299, 302 f., 305 f.,
308, 320, 324, 333, 355–357, 366 f., 369 f.,
372 f., 377, 380–383, 390, 393, 405, 407,
411, 414, 416, 423, 425 f., 429, 433, 444,
450, 460, 467, 481, 484 f., 487, 489, 497–
499, 509 f., 518, 527, 531 f., 538–541, 543 f.,
546, 551, 553–555, 557, 560, 585 f., 593,
610–612, 617, 619, 622, 625 f., 628 f., 632,
637, 640 f., 650, 655, 661, 667, 673, 675,
684–691, 698–700, 713, 716, 724 f., 734, 737
f.
Vol. 2: 37 f., 45, 53, 56, 63, 68–73, 77, 80 f.,
86, 100, 104, 111, 122, 125, 127, 130, 134,
142, 146, 149, 154–156, 158, 173 f., 177,
190, 202 f., 206, 218, 222 f., 225, 229–231,
237, 239–242, 245, 247, 249, 252, 257 f.,
265, 269, 275, 284 f., 287, 296–298, 300–
302, 304, **304–323,** 325 f., 328 f., 331, 335 f., 339,
342 f., 350, 353, 358, 363 f., 367–369, 373–
375, 377–379, 382, 385, 396, 410, 412 f.,
415, 425 f., 431 f., 441 f., 445, 453, 458, 485,
490, 495, 521, 534, 541, 545, 558, 573,
576 f., 580, 583–585, 597, 602, 607 f., 610,
612, 615, 627, 629, 636, 641 f., 644, 649 f.,
652, 660, 664, 670, 677, 679 f., 688, 690 f.,
695 f., 698, 700, 712, 730, 754, 772, 777,
779, 782, 786, 790–794, 796–800, 802, 805,
810, 812, 822, 825, 835, 838, 840, 844, 848,
850, 859, 862 f., 865 f., 872, 880, 882, 888,

890, 893, 916–918, 921
Vol. 3: 30, 33 f., 36–38, 50, 65 f., 69, 71–73, 77, 79 f., 95, 97, 104 f., 117, 135, 147, 150, 172, 190, 192–194, 198 f., 201–203, 206–212, 216, 218 f., 229, 232, 234–239, 241, 249, 251–253, 268–270, 299 f., 311, 318, 333, 341, 355–357, 359 f., 363, 382, 387, 392, 397, 400, 405–407, 416, 418, 420, 426 f., 431, 450, 454–456, 468 f., 478, 484 f., 505, 522, 531, 545, 557, 564 f., 567, 586, 590, 594, 605 f., 608, 611 f., 614, 621, 626, 630, 636–638, 642, 644 f., 650, 652–654, 658, 692, 720 f., 729, 734, 745, 762, 769, 776 f., 787, 790, 793 f., 800, 806 f., 828, 851 f., 866, 871–873, 881, 893, 905, 911 f., 914, 916, 918, 920, 937 f., 940, 950, 952 f., 960, 962, 964, 970, 984, 986, 1006 f., 1009, 1013 f., 1016 f., 1019, 1028 f., 1032, 1041, 1057, 1063, 1068 f., 1071, 1092, 1095, 1100 f., 1103–1105, 1112, 1121, 1148, 1162
Israel, modern **Vol. 2:** 308
Israel of God **Vol. 1:** 61, 257
   Vol. 3: 400, 871
Israel and sonship **Vol. 3: 636**
Israelite **Vol. 1:** 123, 170, 177, 180, 195, 208, 216, 218, 221, 245, 250, 252, 288, 299, 309, 321, 349, 360, 379 f., 434, 451, 485, 509, 527, 543, 559, 622, 640, 688, 690–692, 716
   Vol. 2: 53, 70, 134, 174 f., 180, 213, 239, **304–316,** 324–326, 336, 353, 373, 424, 428, 441, 462, 592, 626, 819, 822, 835
   Vol. 3: 36, 65, 77, 93, 96, 140, 150, 190, 207, 238, 262, 272, 274 f., 341, 379, 421, 424, 427, 429, 455, 460, 531, 590, 593–595, 609f., 653, 656, 740, 752, 806, 811, 836, 841, 851–853, 870, 953, 960, 962, 964 f., 1010, 1028, 1057, 1104, 1162
Issachar **Vol. 2:** 317
   Vol. 3: 139
Issue **Vol. 1:** 604, 703
   Vol. 2: 62, 138, 846
Issue of blood **Vol. 3:** 1059
Isthmian games **Vol. 1:** 406
Italian Cohort **Vol. 2:** 596
Italy **Vol. 1:** 55
Ithaca **Vol. 2:** 372
Itinerant **Vol. 1:** 132, 322
Ivory **Vol. 2:** 349
Ivy **Vol. 1:** 648

J source **Vol. 1:** 57, 61, 66, 72, 512
Jabbok **Vol. 2:** 317
Jabesh **Vol. 1:** 574
Jabez **Vol. 3:** 478
Jabneh **Vol. 3:** 453, 921
Jacinth **Vol. 3:** 396
Jackal **Vol. 3:** 950, 1051
Jacob **Vol. 1:** 61, 65, 76 f., 116, 140, 182, 208, 214, 255, 264, 272, 320, 408, 430, 511, 531, 538, 556, 574, 596, 617, 645, 648, 697
   Vol. 2: 68 f., 73, 116, 128, 140, 185, 247, **304–323,** 329, 337, 375, 416, 426, 431, 466 f., 558, 578, 649, 651, 791, 796, 860, 865, 899

Vol. 3: 73, 139, 194, 203, 263, 359, 418, 425, 458 f., 461, 514, 608, 642, 649, 655, 658, 683, 734, 736, 739, 806, 815, 852, 860, 872, 879, 965, 969, 1012, 1040 f., 1059, 1091, 1094, 1135
Jacob's ladder **Vol. 3:** 630
Jacob's well **Vol. 3:** 459, 461, 987
Jael **Vol. 1:** 687
Jairus **Vol. 1:** 340
   Vol. 2: 418, 433, 623, 630
   Vol. 3: 280, 293, 558, 1059
Jambres **Vol. 2:** 219, 557 f., 642
James **Vol. 2: 316**
James, apostle **Vol. 1:** 643
   Vol. 2: 148, 652, 816
   Vol. 3: 241, 283, 297, 346, 454, 588, 795, 822
James, epistle **Vol. 1:** 304, 318, 346, 604 f., 731
   Vol. 2: 28, 63, 370, 422 f., 435, 449 f., 738, 771, 775, 825, 868
   Vol. 3: 52, 107, 346, 369, 525, 582, 687, 1151
James, the Lord's brother **Vol. 1:** 256, 310
   Vol. 3: 130, 256, 288, 387, 621, 796
James, William **Vol. 3:** 896
James the younger **Vol. 2:** 320
   Vol. 3: 1060
James and Zoker **Vol. 3:** 621
Jamnia **Vol. 1:** 51
   Vol. 2: 313
   Vol. 3: 401, 485, 921
Janik, A. **Vol. 3:** 1136
Jannes **Vol. 2:** 219, 557 f., 642
Jar **Vol. 3: 910–913**
Jason **Vol. 2:** 804
Jasper **Vol. 3:** 395 f., 395–397, 948
Javan **Vol. 2:** 124
Jaw **Vol. 1:** 694
   Vol. 2: 30
Jealous **Vol. 1:** 108, 543, 667
   Vol. 3: 156, 572
Jealousy **Vol. 1:** 106, 201, 557 f., 681, 739
   Vol. 2: 587, 618, 818
   Vol. 3: 243, 691, 1054, 1166 f.
Jebel Musa **Vol. 3:** 1013
Jebel Usdum **Vol. 3:** 444
Jebus **Vol. 2:** 324
Jebusite **Vol. 2:** 186, 324, 375, 636
   Vol. 3: 783, 787, 1010
Jeconiah **Vol. 1:** 683
   Vol. 3: 655, 912, 957
Jedidiah **Vol. 3:** 605
Jehoiachin **Vol. 2:** 69
   Vol. 3: 609, 1104
Jehoiada **Vol. 3:** 82, 430
Jehoiakim **Vol. 1:** 652
   Vol. 3: 478, 1096
Jehoshaphat **Vol. 2:** 754
   Vol. 3: 478
Jehovah **Vol. 1:** 71 f.
   Vol. 2: 69
Jehovah-shalom **Vol. 2:** 777
Jehovah's Witnesses **Vol. 2:** 81
Jehu **Vol. 1:** 543
   Vol. 3: 1092
Jeopardize **Vol. 2:** 415

Jeopardy **Vol. 2:** 360
  Vol. 3: 577
Jephthah **Vol. 1:** 352
  Vol. 3: 421, 425 f.
Jeremiah **Vol. 1:** 52, 66, 93, 245 f., 368, 409,
  485, 499, 531, 717
  Vol. 2: 70, 105, 154, 183, 226, 239 f., 252,
  285, 306 f., 374, 479, 541, 583, 612, 754
  Vol. 3: 79, 83, 94, 96, 159 f., 234 f., 249, 381,
  427, 430, 484, 609, 701, 721, 788, 811, 866,
  881, 912, 914, 916, 961, 1068, 1091, 1095–
  1098, 1103, 1120, 1161
Jeremias, Joachim **Vol. 1:** 148
  Vol. 3: 83, 620
Jeremy, Epistle of **Vol. 1:** 50
Jericho **Vol. 1:** 49, 593, 713
  Vol. 2: 225, 754
  Vol. 3: 78, 444, 469, 758, 788, 874, 948
Jeroboam I **Vol. 1:** 127, 332, 515
  Vol. 2: 374
  Vol. 3: 426, 872, 999
Jeroboam II **Vol. 3:** 1092
Jerome **Vol. 1:** 50, 53, 71, 251
  Vol. 2: 75, 219, 804
  Vol. 3: 402
Jerubbaal **Vol. 1:** 195
Jerusalem **Vol. 1:** 52 f., 61 f., 72, 75, 108, 116 f.,
  125, 129, 131, 133, 136, 138, 166, 170,
  174 f., 196, 199, 210, 214, 240, 286, 296 f.,
  301, 303–305, 310, 317, 320, 323 f., 333,
  340, 344, 361, 363 f., 366, 390, 393, 395 f.,
  411, 416, 473, 478, 528, 532, 538, 554, 559,
  586, 610, 612, 629, 632, 640, 642, 683, 686,
  691, 724 f., 731, 735–737
  Vol. 2: 33, 37 f., 45, 54, 56, 63, 112, 125, 174,
  185 f., 188, 190, 194, 208, 216 f., 225, 227,
  229, 231, 234, 245, 271, 296, 305, 308, 311,
  321, **324–330,** 331, 335, 349, 363, 373, 375 f.,
  379, 381, 400, 418, 450–452, 467 f., 489,
  528, 592 f., 597, 612, 623 f., 649 f., 664, 679,
  681, 688, 693, 700 f., 706, 713, 740, 754 f.,
  761, 763, 778, 785, 793, 802–804, 809, 815,
  818, 826 f., 834, 844, 846 f., 849, 852, 864–
  866, 878, 888, 895, 902, 904, 909 f., 914–
  918, 921, 927, 930
  Vol. 3: 28, 34–38, 40, 62–66, 71, 82, 87 f., 94,
  101, 106, 112, 118 f., 160, 177, 198, 203,
  229, 236, 250 f., 269, 271, 286 f., 289 f.,
  295 f., 315, 320 f., 380, 391, 410, 426, 428,
  430, 435, 441, 443, 451 f., 456, 458, 460, 464
  f., 499, 509, 546, 553, 557, 559 f., 591 f., 598
  f., 605, 615, 624, 642, 653, 669, 692, 698,
  700, 709f., 721, 723, 735 f., 741, 752 f., 758,
  762, 782–786, 791 f., 795, 807, 838, 854,
  856, 871 f., 908, 912, 914, 920, 944, 948 f.,
  952, 957, 960, 962, 965, 976 f., 1006, 1008,
  1010 f., **1014,** 1047, 1052, 1062, 1067–1070,
  1074, 1094, 1097, 1100, 1103, 1114, 1168,
  1183, 1201
Jerusalem above **Vol. 2:** 329, 356, 803
  Vol. 3: 1070
Jerusalem Council **Vol. 1:** 62, 135, 157, 221,
  261, 310, 330 f., 363
  Vol. 2: 321, 795, 827

  Vol. 3: 106, 410, 812, 1164
Jerusalem decree **Vol. 3:** 87
Jerusalem, heavenly **Vol. 1:** 142, 304, 411, 421
  Vol. 2: 186, 188, 191, 194, 207, **326,** 329,
  487 f., 585
  Vol. 3: 143, 203, 871, 944
Jerusalem, new **Vol. 1:** 185, 380, 390, 448, 587
  Vol. 2: 30, 199, 231, 329, 423, 473f., 482,
  495, 615, 652, 671, 674, 692, 696, 700 f.,
  763, 795, 803 f., 931
  Vol. 3: 99, 107, 387, 395, 397 f., 404, 558,
  732, 734, 784, 813, 948, 1010, 1012, 1068
Jerusalem Talmud (→ Talmud, Jerusalem)
Jesse **Vol. 1:** 407
  Vol. 3: 649, 867
Jesus **Vol. 1:** 66, 75, 77, 79, 83, 85 f., 89–93,
  95–100, 102, 104, 106, 111 f., 117 f., 120,
  122–125, 127–136, 141–149, 153, 160,
  162 f., 167 f., 170–174, 176–180, 182 f., 185,
  187, 191, 198 f., 204 f., 212, 215, 217, 219–
  224, 226, 228, 231, 234 f., 239, 245, 250 f.,
  253, 255–263, 265–267, 296 f., 273 f., 278 f.,
  281–287, 289 f., 296–298, 302, 304 f., 309–
  311, 313, 317, 321–324, 328, 334–341, 343,
  346 f., 351, 356, 358 f., 361, 363–365, 369,
  372, 374 f., 377 f., 382, 384 f., 389–404, 407,
  409, 411, 413–415, 417 f., 420 f., 423–425,
  427–430, 435–441, 443, 445 f., 448, 452–
  455, 457, 461, 466 f., 469 f., 473–478, 480,
  482 f., 486–491, 493, 495, 499 f., 504, 506,
  509–512, 515 f., 520, 525, 528–530, 532,
  539–542, 544 f., 548 f., 551 f., 554, 556,
  558–561, 564–566, 570, 572, 575, 577 f.,
  581–583, 590, 592 f., 599–604, 612 f., 615,
  619 f., 623, 628–634, 637–639, 642–644,
  646, 649–651, 657, 659, 662 f., 666–670,
  675–680, 684 f., 689, 691, 693, 701 f., 704,
  707 f., 717, 720, 722–725, 729, 736–742, 744
  Vol. 2: 36, 69, 73, 79, 109 f., 113, 174, 194,
  223, 230, 241, 253, 299–301, 314, 321, **330–
  348,** 373 f., 379, 383, 398, 400, 404 f., 459,
  495, 519, **653–656,** 691, 695, 702, 708–710,
  713, 716, 721–725, 728 f., 775, 785, 794,
  799–801, 812, 818 f., 824 f., 831–846, 851,
  855–861, 867–882, 893, 895 f., 898–922,
  928–930
  Vol. 3: 30 f., 37–39, 41 f., 48, 50, 55–64, 66 f.,
  71–74, 81–89, 99, 106 f., 110, 114 f., 118,
  120, 129, 131 f., 135 f., 143, 147 f., 160–163,
  170 f., 173 f., 179–189, 195–199, 202, 204 f.,
  209, 211–213, 215, 219–221, 225 f., 228 f.,
  240–246, 253, 257, 261, 263 f., 276–278,
  280–287, 289–294, 296–302, 313–316, 319–
  323, 325 f., 329 f., 333, 340, 342–344, 347 f.,
  360–362, 364, 366, 370, 372, 378–380, 382–
  387, 390, 392–395, 402–404, 408–410, 415,
  423, 428–435, 440, 442, 445–448, 454–456,
  460, 462 f., 470–476, 481 f., 489–492, 494 f.,
  499, 506–510, 516 f., 519, 522 f., 526 f.,
  529 f., 532, 536, 538–543, 545–547, 556–
  560, 567–569, 571, 579–582, 584, 589, 592,
  595–598, 603, 605, 607, 610–612, 614, 617–
  634, 636, 639–646, 648, 651–654, 656–664,
  669 f., 674 f., 682 f., 685, 695–698, 700–706,

481

710, 712, 717, 725, 729, 731 f., 737, 740–
742, 746, 748–751, 753–755, 757 f., 761–
764, 767–770, 773–775, 784 f., 789–796,
801–807, 809, 813–815, 818 f., 822, 824–
826, 832, 837–839, 843 f., 847–849, 860–
864, 867–869, 873 f., 883 f., 886, 890–893,
901, 909, 911 f., 916, 919–922, 924 f., 931,
934, 939, 941 f., 945 f., 951 f., 954, 956, 962,
964 f., 967–970, 975–980, 984 f., 987 f., 990,
998, 1002 f., 1007, 1009–1012, 1014, 1017 f.,
1021 f., 1025, 1033, 1043–1047, 1049, 1052,
1059–1062, 1067 f., 1070 f., 1073, 1079,
1106–1110, 1113–1116, 1118–1122, 1132 f.,
1137, 1140, 1143, 1149 f., 1152, 1154 f.,
1157, 1161–1164, 1168, 1176, 1178, 1180,
1182, 1191 f., 1199, 1201, 1206, 1209–1212
Jesus and Moses **Vol. 2: 640–642,** 893
Jesus and revolution **Vol. 3: 967–981**
Jesus as truth **Vol. 3: 891 f.**
Jesus as the Word **Vol. 3: 1114–1117**
Jesus' equality with God **Vol. 2: 499 f.**
Jesus ben Sirach **Vol. 1:** 626
   Vol. 2: 331, 622
   Vol. 3: 270, 479, 911, 916 (*also* → Ecclesias-
ticus)
Jesus-groups **Vol. 2:** 308, 311
Jethro **Vol. 1:** 195
   Vol. 2: 636 f.
   Vol. 3: 33
Jew **Vol. 1:** 67, 117, 141, 155 f., 194, 199, 202,
228, 253, 257 f., 261, 266, 279, 282, 296 f.,
308–311, 317, 340, 350, 361, 363, 366, 385,
394–397, 402 f., 417, 419, 424, 434 f., 453,
462, 473, 476, 487, 503, 506, 510, 529, 545,
554, 565, 575, 589–591, 593, 601, 615, 618,
622, 627 f., 630, 637, 642, 659, 684–686,
688, 694, 708, 720, 730, 737, 739 f., 742
   Vol. 2: 35, 69, 83, 94, 104, 113, 124–127,
129 f., 135, 139, 148, 155 f., 159, 163, 177 f.,
213 f., 216–218, 221, 241, 254, 261, 282, 285
f., 288, 303, **304–323,** 328, 331 f., 338, 349,
353, 356, 358, 369, 372, 378 f., 381, 399 f.,
405, 407, 413, 444–446, 448–451, 460, 467,
474, 499, 652, 655, 660 f., 682, 695, 707,
712, 721 f., 727, 729, 736, 740, 786, 789, 793
f., 799–801, 804, 816, 818, 828, 834, 849 f.,
877 f., 917, 930
   Vol. 3: 34, 38, 51, 65 f., 82, 97, 101, 106, 132,
147, 163, 168, 172, 186–188, 190, 199, 203,
213 f., 216, 229, 237, 240, 251 f., 269, 275,
277, 280, 287, 313, 320, 342, 352, 361–363,
378, 408, 431, 435, 441 f., 452 f., 455, 459–
463, 465, 470, 490, 493 f., 504, 509, 523,
529, 532 f., 549, 558, 561, 571, 579, 582, 584
f., 641, 658, 671, 686, 701, 714, 751 f., 754,
756 f., 778, 785, 790, 795, 813, 818, 853,
870, 872 f., 883, 885, 892, 908 f., 940, 949,
951, 954, 964, 976 f., 997 f., 1020, 1025,
1035, 1040, 1043, 1048, 1062, 1101, 1111,
1113, 1122, 1132, 1149, 1163, 1165, 1184,
1189 f., 1195, 1199
Jewel **Vol. 1:** 469
   Vol. 2: 218
   Vol. 3: 391, 395, 397, 872, 948

Jewellery **Vol. 1:** 522
   Vol. 2: 96
Jewish **Vol. 1:** 144, 154–159, 182, 199 f., 228,
230, 236, 243 f., 252, 257, 264 f., 267, 272,
277, 296 f., 304 f., 308–311, 313–316, 322,
331, 334, 336 f., 347 f., 350, 360, 363 f., 370,
374, 377, 390, 394–396, 399, 403, 409,
414 f., 423, 427 f., 434 f., 442, 444, 446, 449,
455, 463, 465, 474 f., 487, 499, 505 f., 508 f.,
514 f., 527, 534, 539, 545, 559, 580 f., 590,
597, 607, 616, 618, 624, 627 f., 631 f., 641,
655, 661, 686, 691, 694, 706, 714, 725, 742
   Vol. 2: 30, 32, 35, 41, 46, 51, 70 f., 73, 80, 91,
112, 120, 125, 128, 133–135, 140, 144, 150,
152, 158, 160, 169, 178, 191, 204, 208 f.,
211, 215, 218, 221 f., 228, 234, 236 f., 241,
250, 254, 261, 266 f., 269, 271, 275, 279,
284, 291, 294, 302, **304–316,** 324, 327, 329,
331–335, 339, 350, 352 f., 368, 407, 410,
426 f., 429, 437 f., 442, 446, 448, 461 f., 826
f., 849 f., 888, 927
   Vol. 3: 31, 35, 38–41, 50, 58 f., 63, 70–72, 80,
85, 89, 98, 101, 106, 148, 163–165, 168,
181 f., 184–189, 191, 195–197, 227, 240,
253, 265, 270, 272, 282, 287, 291, 293, 300,
311 f., 320, 324, 361 f., 369 f., 373, 383, 390,
393, 397, 401, 403, 408–410, 418, 431, 439–
441, 452–454, 458, 460 f., 464, 466, 471 f.,
476, 479, 482, 491 f., 494 f., 502, 510, 526,
558–560, 580, 584, 599, 603 f., 606, 611,
615–619, 622, 629–632, 636 f., 644, 647,
652, 656 f., 659, 662, 669, 693, 715, 717,
728, 735, 741, 754–756, 762, 764–766, 768,
774 f., 783–785, 789 f., 793, 803, 805, 813,
817–819, 829 f., 832, 847, 861, 867–869,
872, 877, 882, 885, 888, 892, 908, 913, 919–
921, 924, 929, 931–934, 939 f., 944, 962,
964, 976–979, 984, 986 f., 990 f., 1014,
1029–1032, 1035, 1043, 1059, 1061, 1063 f.,
1066 f., 1073, 1111, 1116, 1119, 1163 f.,
1184, 1197, 1199
Jewish Christians **Vol. 1:** 55, **61,** 62, 157, 226,
310 f., 340, 368, 473, 632, 689
   Vol. 2: 126, 135, 221, 236, 241, **314–316,** 331,
333, 437, 499
Jewish missionary activity **Vol. 2:** 792
Jewry **Vol. 1:** 473
Jezebel **Vol. 1:** 416
   Vol. 2: 555, 582, 677 f., 724
   Vol. 3: 81, 426, 844, 846, 1005, 1013, 1057,
1067
Jinn **Vol. 1:** 509
Joab **Vol. 1:** 324
   Vol. 2: 116
Joanan **Vol. 2:** 320
Joanna **Vol. 3:** 1060
Job **Vol. 1:** 211, 434, 467, 547, 562, 568, 645,
652, 672
   Vol. 2: 67, 93, 144, 274, 432, 771, 773, 775,
841, 860
   Vol. 3: 140, 177–179, 209, 234 f., 261, 342,
346, 425, 468, 528, 564, 609, 721, 800, 802,
842, 866, 915, 950, 997, 1041, 1160
Job's comforters **Vol. 1: 89**

Job's comforters (cont'd)
Vol. 3: 209
Joda Vol. 2: 320
Joel Vol. 1: 66, 224, 512, 531, 683
Vol. 2: 329, 690, 785
Vol. 3: 87, 213, 250, 594, 693, 699 f., 732, 1001
Johanan, Rabbi Vol. 2: 784
Johanan ben Zakkai Vol. 3: 921
John Vol. 1: 52, 63, 116, 134, 199, 202, 204 f., 244, 303, 347, 359, 424, 438–441, 458, 483, 490, 524 f., 528, 538 f., 542, 603, 612, 623, 628–631, 633, 637 f., 643, 678 f.
Vol. 2: 34, 76, 114, 148, 193, 204, 217, 302, 315, 339, 359, 367, 403 f., 480, 494, 546, 557, 567, 625, 652, 736, 775, 786, 907, 927
Vol. 3: 40, 46 f., 98, 107, 136, 241, 320, 454, 481, 495, 529, 559, 588, 717, 795, 822, 908, 1010, 1113
John the Baptist Vol. 1: 77, 111, 116, 128, 145 f., 149 f., 155-158, 187, 219, 273, 309, 323, 335, 343, 346, 356, 358, 409, 411, 428, 430, 446, 541, 545, 559, 571, 599, 612, 638, 657, 722, 729, 739
Vol. 2: 104, 110, 113, 130, 136, 159, 176, 229, 245, 262, 272, 275 f., 311, 338, 353, 358 f., 366, 368, 379, 383, 399, 410, 427, 429, 443, 467, 487, 494, 550, 580, 585, 592, 624, 669, 676, 708, 786, 799, 801, 902
Vol. 3: 39, 52, 55 f., 63, 81–83, 86 f., 110, 115, 118 f., 121, 144, 179, 182, 198, 202, 212, 321, 360 f., 393, 436, 439, 489, 507, 516, 519, 527, 540, 555, 558 f., 570, 580, 603, 620, 623, 644, 658, 660 f., 674, 695, 697, 711, 713, 717, 742, 758, 767, 790 f., 804, 822, 848, 869, 890, 893, 920 f., 940, 947, 965, 969, 987, 990 f., 1006–1009, 1017, 1030, 1044 f., 1048, 1062, 1071 f., 1107, 1115, 1121, 1154, 1157, 1208, 1210
John of Gischala Vol. 3: 1168
John, high priest Vol. 3: 40
John Hyranus I Vol. 1: 309
Vol. 2: 810, 815, 849
Vol. 3: 439, 450, 452, 872
John Hyranus II Vol. 2: 850
Vol. 3: 39
Join Vol. 2: 300, 348–350, 353, 356, 395, 579
Vol. 3: 535, 539, 1160–1165
Joiner Vol. 1: 241
Joint Vol. 1: 238, 241
Joke Vol. 2: 430
Jonah Vol. 1: 66, 358, 517, 671
Vol. 2: 215, 350–352, 381, 629 f., 679 f., 687, 831, 888
Vol. 3: 52–54, 83, 89, 236, 628
Jonathan Vol. 2: 69, 116, 540, 849
Vol. 3: 190, 195, 218, 875 f., 962
Jonathan (Alexander Janneus) Vol. 1: 394
Vol. 2: 659, 849 f.
Jonathan (son of Ananus) Vol. 3: 39
Jonathan (high priest) Vol. 3: 34 f., 51
Joppa Vol. 1: 528
Vol. 2: 596
Vol. 3: 1065

Jordan Vol. 1: 55, 67, 144, 629
Vol. 2: 185, 639
Vol. 3: 237, 559, 695–698, 704, 758, 788, 951, 985 f., 991
Joseph Vol. 1: 104, 264, 337, 408, 430, 512, 531, 555, 580, 650
Vol. 2: 116, 306, 317–320, 331, 416, 431 f., 558, 636 f.
Vol. 3: 458–460, 479, 531, 591, 658, 670, 720, 739, 872, 880, 1167, 1179
Joseph of Arimathea Vol. 1: 265
Vol. 2: 216, 387
Vol. 3: 292, 361, 1017
Joseph Barsabbas Vol. 2: 299
Joseph of Nazareth Vol. 1: 256, 279, 506, 530, 559
Vol. 2: 86, 333
Vol. 3: 243, 249, 320, 324, 430, 652–655, 658–663, 931, 1062, 1070 f., 1073
Joseph, son of Tobias Vol. 3: 758
Josephus, Flavius Vol. 1: 87, 102, 149, 151, 156, 178, 201–204, 221, 230, 243, 252 f., 258 f., 269 f., 277, 313, 329, 334, 341–343, 345, 355, 363, 365, 377, 387, 394, 396, 409 f., 412, 428, 435, 442, 450 f., 472, 495, 510 f., 513, 515, 529 f., 532–534, 554, 559 f., 574, 578, 580, 586, 599, 615, 618, 627, 629, 641, 646, 683, 694 f., 698, 700, 709
Vol. 2: 33, 43, 61, 109, 125, 136, 150, 160, 182, 207, 222, 234 f., 258, 259, 308–311, 320, 324, 331, 373, 377, 381, 461, 463, 512, 557, 565, 570, 578 f., 591 f., 607 f., 651, 659 f., 679, 688, 707, 779, 792, 810 f., 879, 899
Vol. 3: 34, 36, 39 f., 51, 80, 96, 98, 119, 125 f., 210, 218, 273, 279, 439, 449–451, 459, 479 f., 485 f., 545, 575, 606, 680 f., 756, 758, 769, 772, 783, 789, 795, 813, 871, 939, 948, 989, 1042, 1058, 1162, 1164
Joses Vol. 3: 1060
Joshua Vol. 1: 53, 66, 208, 332, 340, 393, 485
Vol. 2: 69, 151, 297, 330–332, 466, 628, 638, 712, 878
Vol. 3: 78, 208 f., 212, 418, 469, 609, 772, 841, 867, 926, 948, 962
Joshua ben Levi, Rabbi Vol. 3: 488, 1162
Joshua's long day Vol. 2: 628
Josiah Vol. 1: 55, 632
Vol. 2: 306, 325, 466, 521, 555, 778, 797
Vol. 3: 34, 426, 478, 485, 783, 878, 1057, 1095 f.
Journey Vol. 1: 173, 263, 626, 649
Vol. 2: 191, 266, 317 f., 327, 679
Vol. 3: 121, 229, 454, 602, 630, 679, 935, 945–947
Joy Vol. 1: 119 f., 122, 217, 227, 263, 335, 358 f., 381, 400, 411 f., 423, 459 f., 490, 530, 561, 603, 607, 612, 633, 648, 729–731, 734, 741
Vol. 2: 103, 107, 115, 122, 130, 149, 180 f., 218, 247, 268, 276, 352–361, 386, 388, 408, 416, 419–421, 423 f., 429–431, 433, 435 f., 450, 462, 482, 519, 521, 524, 585, 590, 711 f., 780 f., 783, 809, 817, 833, 862, 873 f., 887,

894, 901
Vol. 3: 168, 268, 361, 529, 567, 668, 672, 674, 682, 687, 701, 721, 783, 817, 835, 848, 921, 941, 956, 1152
Joyful **Vol. 2:** 239, 244, 272, 735
Joyous **Vol. 2:** 240
Jubilation **Vol. 1:** 410
Vol. 2: 353, 540
Jubilee **Vol. 1:** 698
Vol. 3: 191, 594, 756
Jubilees, Book of **Vol. 2:** 528
Vol. 3: 487
Judah **Vol. 1:** 49, **61 f.,** 72, 118, 140 f., 518, 544, 597
Vol. 2: 38, 226, 247, 272, **304–323,** 325 f., 335 f., 374, 577, 592, 636, 696, 815, 823, 848, 899, 916
Vol. 3: 94, 249 f., 256, 356, 359, 367, 397, 435, 526, 557, 649, 654, 821, 853, 872 f., 1071, 1100, 1104, 1179
Judah ben Elai, Rabbi **Vol. 3:** 1058
Judah the Prince, Rabbi **Vol. 3:** 488
Judaism **Vol. 1:** 61, 63 f., 67, **69,** 72, 76–78, 85, 92, 99, 101, 109, 120, 127 f., 145, 153–156, 160, 166, 169, 174, 178, 180, 195, 200, 212 f., 216, 219, 221, 227, 235, 245, 259, 261, 264, 280, 284, 288, 295, 302, 308 f., 311 f., 326, 329 f., 334, 345, 351, 354, 356, 360, 371, 381 f., 387, 394–396, 399, 402, 405, 407, 414, 416, 435, 437, 449, 451, 472, 485–488, 503, 509, 511, 515, 524, 534 f., 543 f., 555, 565, 580, 595, 597–599, 601, 614, 617 f., 629, 632–634, 643, 645, 656, 669, 672 f., 686, 688 f., 691, 700, 714, 717, 721, 729 f., 736 f.
Vol. 2: 37, 43, 48 f., 53 f., 56, 67, 71, 73, 82, 100, 104 f., 109, 125, 131, 141, 147, 149, 151, 159, 168, 174 f., 182, 186, 191, 207, 211, 216, 227, 237, 240 f., 248, 266, 280 f., 283, 285, 287, 298, **307–316,** 324, 336 f., 340, 353, 355, 357, 377, 383, 385, 396–398, 418, 420, 427, 437, 440–442, 450, 468, 479, 486, 499, 516, 556, 565, 578, 591, 599, 603, 612–614, 640 f., 660, 663, 667, 672, 676, 678, 689 f., 715, 720, 761, 773, 784, 786, 792, 794, 798, 803, 808, 810–814, 818, 823, 830, 833, 867 f., 880 f., 892, 903, 919 f., 928, 930
Vol. 3: 28, 31, 41, 45, 54, 59, 66, 86, 96, 105 f., 108, 142, 157, 167, 181, 183, 192–194, 220, 233, 250–253, 256, 266, 274, 293, 296, 300, 311, 331, 342, 348, 358, 361, 377, 383, 392, 397, 407, 428, 434, 439, 441, 450, 453, 460 f., 466, 485–491, 494, 498, 522, 528, 543, 545, 550, 552, 566, 568, 575, 579 f., 595, 610 f., 613 f., 623, 637, 648 f., 652, 654, 659, 668, 671 f., 682, 685, 692 f., 696, 729, 740, 746, 748, 761 f., 766, 769, 772, 777 f., 784, 789, 808, 825, 828 f., 832, 836, 843, 853 f., 867, 892, 920, 931 f., 938, 983 f., 989 f., 1006 f., 1029, 1033, 1035, 1042, 1052, 1054, 1056, 1072, 1074, 1117, 1120, 1149–1151, 1154, 1161, 1167
Judaism, liberal **Vol. 1:** 69
Judaism, Talmudic **Vol. 1:** 69

Vol. 2: 332
Judaizers **Vol. 1:** 61, **62,** 78 f., 157 f., 331
Vol. 2: 570, 741, 828
Vol. 3: 524, 884, 1164
Judaizing **Vol. 1:** 309, 487
Vol. 2: 133
Judas **Vol. 2:** **316–321**
Judas Barsabbas **Vol. 2:** **321**
Vol. 3: 87, 908
Judas, brother of Jesus **Vol. 2:** 320
Judas of Damascus   **Vol. 2:** 320
Judas the Galilean **Vol. 1:** 591
Vol. 2: 34, **320**
Vol. 3: 378, 1167 f.
Judas Iscariot **Vol. 1:** 93, 129, 143, 222, 299, 356, 364, 464, 478, 520, 689, 725
Vol. 2: 44, 299, **321,** 339, 368. 437, 526–528, 549, 851, 854
Vol. 3: 70, 115, 378, 387, 397, 448, 470, 472, 532, 569, 582, 584, 793, 804, 912, 1053, 1060
Judas Maccabaeus **Vol. 1:** 63, 340, 627
Vol. 2: 810, 849
Vol. 3: 51, 318, 961 f.
Judas, son of James **Vol. 2:** 320
Judas the prophet **Vol. 1:** 570 f.
Jude **Vol. 1:** 52
Vol. 2: 320, 459, 897
Vol. 3: 344, 653
Judea **Vol. 1:** 67, 94, 166, 269 f., 297, 301, 303, 395, 512
Vol. 2: 54, **305, 316,** 320, 826, 921
Vol. 3: 63, 324, 456, 458, 460, 478, 508, 756–758, 1008, 1093, 1114, 1168, 1179
Judge **Vol. 1:** 60, 97, 107, 112, 115, 118, 168, 185, 189 f., 196, 219 f., 248, 273, 320, 323, 327, 344 f., 349, 356, 373, 399, 410, 425, 445, 464, 469, 473, 482, 503–505, 519, 525, 529, 531, 539, 566, 587, 637, 648, 655 f., 674, 678, 680, 684
Vol. 2: 71, 119 f., 140, 143, 148, 194, 204, 209, 216, 230, 238, 253, 257, 259 f., 298, 314, 327, 358, **361–371,** 372, 381, 383, 385, 390–392, 411, 440, 450, 456, 468, 490, 503, 510, 518, 574, 604 f., 607, 609 f., 612, 614, **616–620,** 622, 721, 727, 771, 818, 833, 859, 865 f., 877, 894, 899, 929
Vol. 3: 95, 115, 118, 124, 134, 136, 144, 173, 201, 216, 218, 279, 343, 346, 355, 361 f., 373, 402 f., 492, 576, 584, 588, 617 f., 621, 627, 630, 633, 639, 646, 674, 686, 691, 738, 740, 749, 812, 830, 840, 865, 871, 885, 935, 1054, 1057, 1062, 1104, 1108, 1150, 1152, 1158, 1161
Judges **Vol. 1:** 53, 55, 66, 426, 716, 739
Vol. 2: 98
Vol. 3: 49, 73, 279
Judge's oath **Vol. 3:** 740
Judgment **Vol. 1:** 77, 79, 83 f., 86, 89, 91, 102 f., 106 f., 109–113, 115, 146, 156, 163, 167, 171–173, 175, 185, 190 f., 203, 205, 209 f., 219, 224, 228, 231, 233, 240, 243 f., 320 f., 326 f., 343, 345, 347–350, 353, 356, 358 f., 364, 372, 386, 390, 396, 414–418, 423, 425,

Judgment (cont'd)
429 f., 433 f., 439–441, 443, 446, 449, 452, 462, 465–468, 471 f., 474, 486, 495, 499 f., 503 f., 514, 516–518, 524 f., 531, 533, 536, 542, 546, 550 f., 554, 559, 564, 566, 583, 585, 597 f., 602, 610 f., 623 f., 652 f., 655–657, 667, 670, 674, 676, 703, 705, 722, 724 f., 737
Vol. 2: 28, 31–33, 37–39, 47, 53, 56, 58, 70, 72, 75, 98, 101–103, 111, 117 f., 136, 141, 143, 146–148, 154–156, 169; 174, 178, 189, 191, 193, 198, 202 f., 205, 208, 210, 214–218, 228, 230, 237, 239 f., 243, 245, 249, 252, 257, 260, 262, 265, 267, 271, 275 f., 283, 285 f., 294, 296, 301, 306 f., 313, 326, 328, 335, 339, 351 f., 354, **361–371**, 381, 391 f., 395 f., 398 f., 401, 407, 413, 417 f., 422, 440, 446, 449 f., 457, 468, 471, 482 f., 485, 526, 540, 544, 570, 583–585, 591, 595–597, 602, 609 f., 614 f., 618, 620, 625, 630, 633, 638, 642 f., 654, 665, 679–681, 692, 698–702, 706, 709 f., 714, 717, 720, 724, 735 f., 740 f., 762–764, 766, 777, 779, 791–793, 795, 797, 809, 811, 813, 815, 822, 834, 836, 841, 843 f., 854, 866, 875, 887–894, 898, 909, 915–918, 920, 928–931
Vol. 3: 28 f., 31, 51, 53, 69, 79, 82 f., 87, 96 f., 99, 113, 117, 127 f., 130, 136, 140–143, 145, 161, 163, 173 f., 187 f., 193, 196, 203–205, 221, 224, 232, 240, 247, 249, 253, 265, 267, 271, 277, 279, 303, 305, 311 f., 319, 321, 342, 344 f., 354, 356, 360, 362, 366, 371, 374, 380, 391, 394, 402, 430, 436, 470, 476, 478, 498, 500, 502, 508, 526 f., 557, 560, 562 f., 566, 576, 582, 586, 589, 591, 604 f., 626, 629 f., 633, 636, 643, 645, 648 f., 677, 679, 682, 692, 695, 697, 714, 728 f., 731–733, 735–737, 740, 745, 760, 768, 772 f., 778, 790 f., 793, 801, 822, 824 f., 832, 836, 846, 848, 856, 867, 869, 874, 893, 895, 911–913, 918 f., 938, 962, 964, 967, 983 f., 994, 997, 1001, 1003, 1008 f., 1012, 1040 f., 1043, 1050, 1054, 1058, 1073, 1080, 1086, 1089–1098, 1100 f., 1103, 1105, 1111, 1114, 1148 f., 1151 (also → Last judgment)
Judgment seat Vol. 1: 347
Vol. 2: 361, **369–371**, 875, 925 f.
Vol. 3: 322, 589, 710
Judicial Vol. 1: 196, 267, 395, 415, 471, 572, 640
Vol. 2: 137, 362, 365, 439
Vol. 3: 93, 168
Judicious Vol. 2: 169, 616
Judith Vol. 1: 50, 626
Vol. 3: 873, 962
Jug Vol. 1: 742
Juggler Vol. 2: **552–562**
Julius Africanus Vol. 3: 655, 872
Julius Caesar Vol. 1: 269
Junction Vol. 1: 241
Jung, G.C. Vol. 3: 1137
Junias Vol. 1: 130
Juno Vol. 1: 108
Vol. 2: 85

Jupiter Vol. 1: 705
Vol. 2: 85, 308, 558
Vol. 3: 735
Jupiter Capitolinus Vol. 3: 753
Jupiter Lapis Vol. 3: 739
Juridical Vol. 1: 132, 195, 199
Vol. 2: 407
Jurisdiction Vol. 1: 360, 364, 395, 610, 627
Vol. 2: 608
Jurist Vol. 2: **438–451**
Juror Vol. 1: 205
Vol. 2: 674
Just Vol. 1: 137, 304, 336, 370, 554, 593, 637, 659, 673, 719, 738
Vol. 2: 72, 78, 237, 354, 363, 365, 372, 417, 447, 497, 499, 566
Vol. 3: **352–377**, 758, **833–839**, 924, 1002
Just One Vol. 1: 476
Justice Vol. 1: 116, 261, 332, 356, 396, 410, 438, 447, 501, 503 f., 543, 640, 651, 666
Vol. 2: 93, 119, 139, 141, 201, 226, 233, 260, 363, 368, 396, 443, 484, 486, 510, 612, 614, 658, 665, 694, 737 f.
Vol. 3: 27, **97–99**, 103, 117, 130, 138, 183, 261, 353, 356, 389, 479, 561, 575, 606, 640, 645, 648 f., 777, 1053, 1074, 1079, 1087, 1102–1104
Justification Vol. 1: 73, 78, 86, 97, 152, 154, 157 f., 223, 228, 275, 347, 379, 398–401, 437, 439, 472, 475, 547, 564, 571, 602, 604 f., 639, 662, 673, 681, 687, 695 f., 701 f., 720
Vol. 2: 42, 72, 78, 95, 118–120, 122 f., 129, 203, 214, 242, 359, 387, 444, 450 f., 504, 645, 723, 844, 882, 884
Vol. 3: 142–144, 161, 168 f., 171, 227, 436, 549, 951, 1122, 1184
Justify Vol. 2: 73, 75, 118, 120, 122, 282, 370, 388, 408, 445, 447
Vol. 3: 168, 220, **352–377**
Justifying Vol. 1: 601, 730
Justin Martyr Vol. 1: 51, 154, 180, 535
Vol. 2: 316, 556, 832
Vol. 3: 58, 453, 855
Justly Vol. 3: **352–377**
Justus Vol. 2: 299, 331

Kaddish Vol. 2: 229
Kadesh Vol. 2: 635
Vol. 3: 33, 1013 f.
Kähler, Martin Vol. 1: 60
Kairos Vol. 3: 834
Kakia Vol. 2: 271
Kalach Vol. 1: 140
Kalendarium of Antiochus Vol. 2: 128
Kali Vol. 3: 1068
Kalneh Vol. 1: 140
Kamithos Vol. 1: 35
Kant, Immanuel Vol. 1: 64
Vol. 3: 899
Karaites Vol. 1: 67
Vol. 2: 126
Karma Vol. 3: 679
Käsemann, E. Vol. 3: 58, 84, 372, **619**

Katz J.J. **Vol. 3:** 1134
Keep **Vol. 1:** 332, 337–341, 526, 611, 623, 635, 638, 691
  Vol. 2: 132–137, 177 f., 191, 266, 271, 282, 297, 300, 327, 333, 354 f., 440, 444, 653, 838
Keep alive **Vol. 2: 476–484**
Keep clear of **Vol. 3:** 903
Keep faith **Vol. 2:** 798
Keep from harm **Vol. 3: 205–216,** 686
Keep holy **Vol. 3:** 406
Keep peace **Vol. 2: 776–783**
Keep safe **Vol. 2:** 838
Keep silence **Vol. 3:** 873, 1066, 1109
Keep in touch **Vol. 3:** 774
Keep watch **Vol. 3:** 134
Kegel, G. **Vol. 3:** 300
Kenites **Vol. 3:** 405, 478
Kenotic **Vol. 3:** 1117
Kenoticism **Vol. 1:** 548 f.
  Vol. 2: 500
Kepler, Johannes **Vol. 3:** 735
Keret, Legend of King **Vol. 1:** 511
  Vol. 2: 553
Kernel **Vol. 1:** 704 f.
Kernel-texts **Vol. 3:** 1142
Kerygma **Vol. 1:** 54 f., 57, 59, **62,** 65, 397, 400, 547, 551, 601, 605
  Vol. 2: 339, 341, 343, 380, 387 f., 430, 633, 906
  Vol. 3: 44–68, 213 f., 281 f., 322, 333
Kethubim **Vol. 3:** 671
Key **Vol. 2:** 207, 223, **726–734**
  Vol. 3: 498, 1052
Keys of the kingdom of heaven **Vol. 2: 731–733**
  Vol. 3: 384, 387, 763
Keystone **Vol. 3: 388–390**
Kfar Bilu **Vol. 3:** 453
Kibroth-hatta'avah **Vol. 1:** 456
Kick **Vol. 1:** 511
  Vol. 2: 155
  Vol. 3: 560
Kid **Vol. 1:** 114
  Vol. 2: 521
Kidnapper **Vol. 3: 380**
Kidnapping **Vol. 1:** 717
  Vol. 3: 95, 593
Kidney **Vol. 1:** 230
  Vol. 2: 181
Kidron **Vol. 2:** 236, 713
  Vol. 3: 796
Kieffer, R. **Vol. 3:** 1123
Kierkegaard, Søren **Vol. 1:** 57
  Vol. 3: 897–899, 1143, 901
Kill **Vol. 1:** 174 f., 220, 222 f., 336, 390, 394 f., 401, **429–447,** 451, 463, 468 f., 508, 608, 610, 623, 629, 632–634, 740
  Vol. 2: 202, 229, 234, 312, 327 f., 370, 446, 624, 871
  Vol. 3: 253 f., **417–436,** 769, 860
Kiln **Vol. 2:** 574
Kin **Vol. 1:** 673
Kind **Vol. 1:** 704
  Vol. 2: 35, 75, **98–107,** 116, **256–259,** 284, **500–508,** 550, **656–661**

Kindle **Vol. 1:** 241, 653 f.
  Vol. 3: 859
Kindly **Vol. 3:** 148
Kindness **Vol. 1:** 461, 665
  Vol. 2: 79, 105 f., 115, 158, 237 f., 270, 594, 770, 834
  Vol. 3: 227, 572, **1147–1152**
Kindred **Vol. 1:** 181, 626
  Vol. 3: 190
King **Vol. 1:** 100, 115, 117, 121, 123, 177 f., 195, 210, 269 f., 293, 317, 321, 323, 331 f., 366, 373, 375, 405, 408, 425–427, 464, 511, 537 f., 543, 581, 606, 609, 617 f., 622 f., 649, 651 f., 684, 732
  Vol. 2: 49, 55, 57, 70 f., 74, 77, 96, 109, 167, 175, 190, 218, 234, 257 f., 294, 296, 306–308, 319 f., 325–327, 335–338, 341 f., 358, 363 f., **372–390,** 411–413, 432, 434, 441, 449, 458, 502, 510, 518, 521, 585, 590, 607, 612 f., 615, 641, 644, 649, 693 f., 701, 703, 711, 721, 781, 788, 797, 877, 898, 905, 931
  Vol. 3: 37, 78 f., 94, 97, 121, 140, 143, 154, 197, 201, 206, 208, 217 f., 269, 275, 335, 342, 355, 357, 481, 490, 497, 509, 561, 588, 593–595, 605–609, 614, 636 f., 648, 650, 652, 715, 718, 735, 754, 758, 851, 937, 1060, 1089, 1154
King of ages **Vol. 1:** 469
King of Israel **Vol. 1:** 100, 395, 617
  Vol. 2: 146, 375, 378, 380
King of Jacob **Vol. 2:** 375
King James' Version **Vol. 1:** 70
King of the Jews **Vol. 1:** 63, 205
  Vol. 2: 315, 378–380, 449
King of kings **Vol. 2:** 378, 514
King Solomon's mines **Vol. 2:** 97
Kingdom **Vol. 1:** 406, 424, 451 f., 508, 516, 519, 523 f., 526, 578, 649, 689, 720, 729, 734
  Vol. 2: 37 f., 56, 62, 70, 74, 76, 85, 95, 98, 104, 112, 129, 150, 158, 193, 196, 227, 229, 241, 258, 271, 306, **372–390,** 469, 486, 510, 531 f., 585, 604, 607–609, 613, 641, 653, 661, 701, 703, 709, 717, 749, 758, 779, 795, 832, 842, 868, 881, 894, 904, 924, 929, 931
  Vol. 3: 52, 74, 147, 204, 213, 215, 245 f., 312, 317, 319, 360, 392, 472, 621, 648, 650, 695, 803, 806, 940, 1044
Kingdom of Christ **Vol. 1:** 701
  Vol. 2: 388
Kingdom of David **Vol. 1:** 100
Kingdom of the dead **Vol. 3:** 989
Kingdom of the Father **Vol. 2:** 381
Kingdom of glory **Vol. 2:** 202
Kingdom of God **Vol. 1:** 10, 62, 77, 86 f., 116, 124 f., 138, 146–149, 160, 167, 174, 179, 213 f., 216 f., 219, 222, 238, 250, 263, 275, 277 f., 284 f., 290, 298, 300, 321–323, 326, 329, 358, 369, 381, 384, 434, 453 f., 470, 482, 489, 518, 525, 560 f., 563, 590, 599, 612, 620, 646, 651, 657, 666, 675 f., 679, 691
  Vol. 2: 31, 37, 54, 57, 74, 98, 110, 113, 118, 147, 151, 168, 178, 216, 222 f., 241, 250, 267 f., 270, 272, 275, 277, 295, 300–303, **376 f., 381,** 382, 386–389, 401, 426 f., 429, 443, 462,

Kingdom of God (cont'd)
502, 535, 543, 548 f., 580, 583, 604, 619,
640, 653, 695, 714 f., 727 f., 730–734, 749,
752 f., 781, 791, 809, 813, 819, 824, 832–
834, 840, 843, 846, 857, 871, 888, 899, 902,
904, 906, 911, 920 f.
    Vol. 3: 55, 65, 81, 106, 131, 141 f., 181, 184,
221, 225 f., 314, 360, 365, 392, 503, 507,
514, 518, 522, 530, 532, 576, 603, 618–620,
685, 696, 701, 711 f., 725, 746, 762, 792,
803, 807, 830, 832, 844, 866, 920, 922, 941,
965, 969 f., 998, 1052, 1059, 1062, 1070,
1106, 1152, 1158, 1178
Kingdom of heaven (→ Kingdom of God)
Kingdom of Israel **Vol. 1: 52,** 61
Kingdom of Judah **Vol. 1: 52,** 61
    Vol. 2: 319 f.
Kingdom of priests **Vol. 2:** 380
    Vol. 3: 36
Kingly **Vol. 2:** 242, 335–337, **372–389**
Kings, Books of **Vol. 1:** 66, 68, 537 f., 625
Kings of the east **Vol. 2:** 378
King's scribe **Vol. 3:** 478
Kingship **Vol. 1:** 210, 241, 374, 405 f., 425–427
    Vol. 2: 139, 234, 339, **372–389,** 432, 644
    Vol. 3: 349, 649
Kingu **Vol. 2:** 200
Kinsfolk **Vol. 1:** 194
Kinship **Vol. 1:** 207, 414, 675
    Vol. 3: 635, 653, 871, 1163
Kinsman **Vol. 2:** 226
    Vol. 3: 178, 190 f., 193
Kiss **Vol. 1:** 206 f.
    Vol. 2: 530, 538, **547–550,** 812, 859, 876
Kittim **Vol. 3:** 961
Klausner, J. **Vol. 3:** 292
Knapsack **Vol. 1:** 143
Knead **Vol. 3:** 916 f.
Knee **Vol. 2:** 196, 414, 856, **859–861,** 925
Kneel **Vol. 2: 855–886**
Knife **Vol. 1:** 308
Knock **Vol. 2:** 220, 705, **855–881 f.**
    Vol. 3: 227
Know **Vol. 2:** 240, 262, 276, 280, 289, **390–409,**
413, 445, 488 f., 543
    Vol. 3: 130, 267, 460, 861
Know the name **Vol. 2:** 648
Knowability **Vol. 2:** 397
Knower of hearts **Vol. 2: 180–184**
Knowing ones **Vol. 2:** 397
Knowledge **Vol. 1:** 58, 60, 85, 93, 107, 123, 138,
197, 212, 222, 225, 233, 238, 244 f., 247,
277, 281 f., 303, 325, 334, 347 f., 352, 386,
389, 421 f., 432, 442, 444, 453, 481, 483 f.,
486, 488, 496 f., 500, 504, 512, 525, 530, 538
f., 555, 562, 565, 567 f., 587, 595, 597 f.,
600–603, 605, 620, 637 f., 644, 650, 675,
684 f., 692–697, 707 f., 716, 735, 740, 742 f.
    Vol. 2: 60, 71 f., 75, 78, 103, 118, 122, 129,
158, 181–183, 188, 198, 202, 216–218, 220
f., 223, 227, 229, 243 f., 252 f., 267, 269, 271,
274, 287, 298, 304, 357, **390–409,** 446, 448,
453, 456, 460 f., 469, 480, 490 f., 493 f., 503,
538 f., 545, 567, 597, 620, 626, 645 f., 648,

655, 661, 720–722, 730, 757, 830, 834 f.,
865, 879, 922
    Vol. 3: 36 f., 39, 44, 46, 58, 73, 84, 133, 206,
212, 214 f., 221, 258, 265, 310, 313 f., 316 f.,
327, 332, 335 f., 358, 403, 427, 431, 433, 461
f., 476, 481, 483, 493, 501 f., 515, 517, 521 f.,
528, 530, 533, 542, 554, 573, 580, 600, 630,
638–642, 679 f., 719 f., 749, 759, 761, 765 f.,
775 f., 777, 799, 809, 819, 826 f., 885, 887,
903, 912, 914, 926, 934 f., 939, 963, 995 f.,
1017, 1022, 1025–1032, 1034 f., 1052, 1073,
1083 f., 1086 f., 1111, 1156
Known **Vol. 2:** 338, 746 f.
Koine **Vol. 1:** 59, **62**
Korah **Vol. 1:** 294
    Vol. 2: 638
    Vol. 3: 1054
Korzybski, A. **Vol. 3:** 1125
Krishna **Vol. 3:** 330
Kronos **Vol. 2:** 232
Künneth, W. **Vol. 3:** 292
Kuthites **Vol. 3:** 450

Laban **Vol. 1:** 574
    Vol. 2: 140, 317, 521, 578
    Vol. 3: 139, 533, 739, 879, 1040 f.
Labour **Vol. 1:** 85, 115, 180, 186 f., **260–263,**
271, 466, 519, 551, 564, 722 f.
    Vol. 2: 262, 269, 317, 475, 839, 890
    Vol. 3: 54, 144, **857 f., 1147–1152**
Labour-pains **Vol. 3:** 856
Labourer **Vol. 1:** 430
    Vol. 2: 386, 711, 861
    Vol. 3: 349, 847, 920
Lachesis **Vol. 3:** 260
Lachish **Vol. 3:** 428, 483
Lack **Vol. 1:** 384, 489, 494, 504, 516, 541, 562,
593, 648, 723, 731 f., 740 f.
    Vol. 2: 183, 217, 221, 264 f., 269, 274, 286,
391, 395 f., 401, 406–408, 422, 434, 456,
459, 499
    Vol. 3: 247–253, 573, **952–958**
Lack of sense **Vol. 3:** 1023–1026
Lad **Vol. 1:** 283 f.
Ladanum **Vol. 2:** 294
Ladd, G.E. **Vol. 3:** 293
Ladder **Vol. 1:** 140
    Vol. 2: 185, 317, 319
Laden **Vol. 1:** 565, 699, 742
Lady **Vol. 2: 510–520**
Lahama **Vol. 1:** 170
Lair **Vol. 2:** 586
Laity **Vol. 1:** 629
Lake **Vol. 3:** 557, **982–992**
Lake, K. **Vol. 3:** 292
Lake of fire **Vol. 2:** 304, 701
    Vol. 3: 99, 962
Lamb **Vol. 1:** 111, 114 f., 118 f., 142, 164, 223,
240 f., 274, 317, 386, 448, 482, 525, 629 f.,
633 f., 651 f., 691, 702
    Vol. 2: 58, 80, 147, 194, 218, 231, 280, 329,
410–414, 458, 461, 463, 473, 482, 495, 521 f.,
527–529, 532, 534, 543, 569, 581, 585, 615,

625, 654, 665, 674, 676, 691, 700, 727 f.,
763, 799, 801, 844
  Vol. 3: 181, 200, 216, 335, 349, 398, 416 f.,
  421, 423, 431, 435, 454, 471, 500, 516,
  568, 582, 611, 633, 674, 714 f., 925, 943,
  988, 990, 1032, 1068, 1072
Lamb of God **Vol. 1:** 525, 629, 702
  Vol. 2: 411
Lame **Vol. 1:** 637
  Vol. 2: 153, 167, 170 f., 358, **414 f.,** 597, 606,
  625, 630, 633
  Vol. 3: 213, 320, 351, 792, 902, 1000
Lamech **Vol. 2:** 681, 770
  Vol. 3: 578
Lament **Vol. 1:** 178, 286, 547
  Vol. 2: 361, **416–424,** 433, 436, 598, 862, 890
  Vol. 3: 78, 670, 720, 725, 908, 911
Lamentation **Vol. 1:** 262, 378, 410, 551
  Vol. 2: 33, 167, **416–424,** 806, 823, 860
  Vol. 3: 668, 672 f., 1051
Lamentations, Book of **Vol. 1:** 59, 717
Lamp **Vol. 1:** 234
  Vol. 2: 212, **484–496,** 556, 710 f.
  Vol. 3: 445, 732, 748, 882
Lamp-bearer **Vol. 2:** 578
Lampe, G.W.H. **Vol. 3:** 292
Lampstand **Vol. 1:** 304
  Vol. 2: 217, 484 f., **486 f.,** 691, 712
  Vol. 3: 736, 787 f., 812, 814
Lance **Vol. 3:** 590
Land **Vol. 1:** 76, 243, 360, 390, 498 f., 515 f.,
  517–526, 537, 565, 607, 625, 640 f., 684, 688,
  710, 726, 735, 741
  Vol. 2: 187, 248, 257, 265, 275, **295–304,** 305,
  307, 309, 311, 315–317, 357, 362 f., 367,
  374, 448, 511, 540, 691, 698, 788, 822
  Vol. 3: 33, 70, 94, 102, 104, 117, 135, 190,
  195, 210, 235, 269, 274, 355, 357, 522, 853
Land of promise (→ Promised land)
Landed property **Vol. 2: 845–847**
Landowner **Vol. 2:** 297, 788, 843
  Vol. 3: 852
Landscape **Vol. 2:** 92, 303
Langer, S.K. **Vol. 3:** 1130
Language **Vol. 1:** 59, 62
  Vol. 2: 124, 157, 308 f., 648, 740, 784, 786,
  791, 907, 925, 927
  Vol. 3: 78, **113 f.,** 335, 483, 757, **1078–1081,**
  1121
Language, function of **Vol. 3:** 335, 895, **1078–
1123**
Language and meaning in religion **Vol. 3: 1123–
1143**
Language and thought **Vol. 3: 1126 f.**
Language-event **Vol. 1:** 583
  Vol. 3: 1140
Language-game **Vol. 3:** 1131, 1135, 1138
Languish **Vol. 2:** 422
Laodicea **Vol. 1:** 318 f. 363
  Vol. 2: 597, 727, 826, 844, 881
  Vol. 3: 321, 402, 518 f., 958
Laodiceans, Epistle to the **Vol. 1:** 51
  Vol. 2: 219
Lapis lazuli **Vol. 3:** 396, 398

Lapse **Vol. 1:** 359, 608
  Vol. 3: 573, 577, 586
Large **Vol. 2:** 177, 194, **424–429,** 443, 709
  Vol. 3: 455
Large-heartedness **Vol. 2: 484–486**
Lasciviousness **Vol. 3:** 996
Lash **Vol. 1:** 161 f.
  Vol. 3: 1079
Last **Vol. 1:** 56, 97, 326, 653, 665–667, 669
  Vol. 2: 52–66
  Vol. 3: 920
Last Adam **Vol. 2:** 57, 481, 504, 566
  Vol. 3: 684
Last day **Vol. 1:** 421
  Vol. 2: 53, 118, 298, 364, 378, 861, 887, 894,
  929
  Vol. 3: 411, 749
Last days **Vol. 1:** 151, 218, 224, 244, 420, 460,
  496, 612, 556, 566, 607, 610
  Vol. 2: 75, 219, 302, 354, 377, 379, 397, 413,
  443, 604, 607, 609, 642, 649, 654, 709, 727,
  740, 772, 785, 787, 875
  Vol. 3: 34, 40, 71, 209 f., 299, 341, 469, 700,
  836, 842, 847, 1118
Last enemy **Vol. 1:** 440
Last hour **Vol. 2:** 384
  Vol. 3: 845, 848 f.
Last judgment **Vol. 1:** 56, 65, 83, 324, 333, 417,
  473, 742
  Vol. 2: 191, 205, 208, 245, 262, 365, 481,
  488, 499, 682, 700 f., 867, 928 f.
  Vol. 3: 97, 135 f., 143, 242, 634 (*also* →
  Judgment)
Last Supper (→ Lord's Supper)
Last things **Vol. 1: 56**
  Vol. 2: 245, 691
  Vol. 3: 312
Last times **Vol. 1:** 452, 675
  Vol. 2: 61
  Vol. 3: 215, 838
Last will and testament **Vol. 2:** 317
Lasting **Vol. 2:** 96, 393
Late **Vol. 1:** 607
  Vol. 3: 839
Late rain **Vol. 3: 1000–1004**
Latent **Vol. 1:** 711
Later **Vol. 1:** 665
  Vol. 3: 952–956
Lateran Council **Vol. 3:** 244
Latin **Vol. 2:** 126
Latinism **Vol. 1:** 363
  Vol. 3: 448
Latter **Vol. 3: 952–956**
Latter days **Vol. 2:** 337
Latter Prophets **Vol. 1:** 66
Laud **Vol. 3:** 816
Laugh **Vol. 2:** 357, 361, 416 f., 422, 424, **429–
436**
  Vol. 3: 347
Laughter **Vol. 2: 429–436**
  Vol. 3: 280
Laurel **Vol. 1:** 470, 648
Laver **Vol. 3:** 812
Lavish **Vol. 1:** 730

Law **Vol. 1:** 52–54, 58 f., 62, 64 f., 67, 70, 73 f., 77–79, 86, 98, 102 f., 107, 109, 112 f., 116 f., 129, 157, 164, 183 f., 190, 196–198, 214, 218–221, 228, 230 f., 234, 243, 245, 252, 258, 261, 263–265, 268 f., 271, 282, 284, 293–297, 302, 309–311, 321 f., 327 f., 331–336, 340 f., 347, 349 f., 353, 355, 357 f., 360 f., 365, 367 f., 370 f., 373 f., 390, 397 f., 402, 412, 416–418, 424, 430, 434, 436–439, 446, 448, 452, 457 f., 461, 463, 468, 471–473, 477 f., 481, 484–487, 499 f., 503, 506, 512, 532, 543 f., 547, 554, 556, 564, 570, 573–575, 579, 589, 591 f., 595, 597 f., 601, 606 f., 609 f., 612, 622, 625, 627, 630 f., 637, 645, 654, 659, 663, 667, 674–676, 678, 680 f., 685–688, 690 f., 694, 699, 708, 714 f., 717–720, 729 f., 733–735, 738
Vol. 2: 59, 61–64, 73, 77, 86, 91 f., 94, 99–101, 103, 111 f., 114, 116–120, 122 f., 125–127, 131–138, 141 f., 144, 148, 174, 176 f., 180 f., 186, 188, 211, 216, 222, 228, 235, 237, 241 f., 247, 254–256, 259, 261 f., 266, 281–283, 288, 296, 298, 301, 307, 312, 320, 327, 329, 349, 355, 357, 365, 368, 385, 398 f., 406, **436–456**, 460, 468 f., 475, 488, 492, 498 f., 503 f., 510 f., 513, 516, 519, 540–544, 546, 550, 552, 555, 559, 566, 576–579, 583, 590, 595 f., 605, 607, 610, 617, 621, 631, 637, 639–642, 645, 656–660, 662–668, 673, 678, 686, 693 f., 708 f., 714–716, 719, 727, 737, 741 f., 748, 754, 767, 776 f., 784, 786, 793–795, 797, 799, 801, 810–813, 816, 822, 827 f., 830, 833, 837, 842, 889, 922
Vol. 3: 33 f., 36 f., 41 f., 49, 51, 56, 65, 69 f., 72 f., 84, 86, 89, 92, 94, 97–99, 101, 105 f., 108, 115 f., 127, 135, 137, 140, 150, 161, 163, 167 f., 172, 181–187, 189, 192, 200, 204, 224, 226 f., 239, 251, 253, 257 f., 271, 277 f., 311, 320, 329 f., 332, 346, 348, 352–356, 358–361, 363–365, 374, 380, 383, 390, 393, 405 f., 408, 427 f., 431, 439 f., 442, 459, 465, 478–485, 488, 493, 533, 537, 541, 544, 549, 556, 559, 561, 572–574, 578–581, 583–586, 591, 593 f., 596 f., 606, 620, 625, 650, 670, 680, 691, 701 f., 706, 711, 722, 738, 742, 760–769, 772–775, 777–779, 787, 792, 800, 824, 843, 852 f., 855, 882, 884 f., 892, 937, 939, 944, 946, 948 f., 954, 995, 1014, 1020, 1026, 1029, 1035, 1040, 1043 f., 1050, 1052 f., 1057 f., 1094–1096, 1103 f., 1106 f., 1109, 1121 f., 1148–1151, 1153–1155, 1157 f., 1162–1164, 1167, 1177
Law, apodeictic **Vol. 2: 41**
Law, casuistic **Vol. 2: 441**
Law, ceremonial **Vol. 1:** 75
Law, summary of **Vol. 2:** 177
Law and prophets **Vol. 2: 174,** 177, 444
   Vol. 3: 311
Law of Christ **Vol. 2: 446**
Law of evidence **Vol. 2:** 686
Law of God **Vol. 2:** 440
Law of holiness **Vol. 2: 226**
Law of the land **Vol. 2:** 439
Law of liberty **Vol. 2: 449 f.**

   Vol. 3: 228
Law of sin **Vol. 2:** 282
Law of Yahweh **Vol. 2:** 440
Law-book **Vol. 1:** 243
Law-breaker **Vol. 2:** 29, 143, 572
Lawbreaking **Vol. 3:** 577
Lawcourt **Vol. 2:** 142, 362
   Vol. 3: 234, 236, 740, 1048
Lawful **Vol. 1:** 500, 535
   Vol. 2: 104, 138, 253, 281, **606–611**
   Vol. 3: 409, 534, 707, 758
Lawgiver **Vol. 2: 438–451,** 485, 580, 635–642, 677, 721, 871
   Vol. 3: 346, 564
Lawgiving **Vol. 2: 438–451,** 784–786
Lawless **Vol. 2: 438–451,** 468, 677, 810, 901
   Vol. 3: 365, 1149
Lawlessness **Vol. 1:** 125, 556, 639, 681
   Vol. 2: 438–451, 494, 901
   Vol. 3: 137, 471, 505, 571
Lawsuit **Vol. 1:** 267, 345
   Vol. 2: 363
   Vol. 3: 93, 1041, **1155–1158**
Lawyer **Vol. 2:** 147, 177, 223, **438–451,** 730
   Vol. 3: 477–482, 883, 1052
Lax **Vol. 1:** 333, 560
   Vol. 2: 801
Laxity **Vol. 3:** 369
Lay **Vol. 1:** 413, 477, 662, 684, 696
Lay aside **Vol. 1:** 314, 470
   Vol. 3: 120, 815
Lay down **Vol. 1:** 660
   Vol. 2: 439
   Vol. 3: 254
Lay down life **Vol. 2:** 42, 101, 359, 413
   Vol. 3: 547, 567, 683
Lay foundation **Vol. 2:** 64
Lay hold **Vol. 1:** 596
   Vol. 3: 747–751
Lay to heart **Vol. 1:** 106
Lay waste **Vol. 1:** 468
   Vol. 3: 1004–1014
Layard, Austen **Vol. 2:** 679
Layer **Vol. 2:** 586
Laying on of hands **Vol. 1:** 197, 207, 284, 684, 735
   Vol. 2: 28, 122, **146–153,** 875
   Vol. 3: 115, 240, 422, 916
Layman **Vol. 1:** 98
   Vol. 2: 456 f.
Lazarus **Vol. 1:** 117, 265, 409, 430, 443
   Vol. 2: 178, 267, 418, 433, 466, 548, 630, 706, 801, 825, 846, 929
   Vol. 3: 39, 99, 179, 240, 280, 293, 303, 381, 558, 682, 819, 856, 1044, 1059, 1061, 1079
Lazy **Vol. 3:** 1024
Lead **Vol. 1:** 471, 486, 489, 509, 532, 570, 573, 575, 579, 585, 604, 623, 638, 645, 648–650, 669, 680, 719 f.
   Vol. 2: 70, 72, 149, 152, 222, 230, 358, 377, 408, 410, 846, 871
   Vol. 3: 314, 392, **935–943**
Lead astray **Vol. 1:** 413, 423, 452, 460, 468 f., 487, 493, 510, 566, 570, 588, 602 f., 689

Vol. 2: 156, 281, 407, **457–461,** 469, 471, 474, **707–710,** 793, 808, 841
Vol. 3: 81, 499, 801, 810, 939, 996
Lead away **Vol. 1:** 685, 688
Lead back **Vol. 2:** 462
Lead out **Vol. 2:** 313
Lead in a straight way**Vol. 3: 351 f.**
Lead in triumph **Vol. 3:** 600
Leader **Vol. 1:** 132, 164 f., 168, 191, 193, 198, 200, 220, 270, 293 f., 424, 462, 475, 568, 591, 596, 610, 629, 664–666, 725, 739 f.
Vol. 2: 50, 95, 372, 379, 514, 724, 799
Vol. 3: 199, 219, 384, 568, 593, 642, 795, 809, 930, **935–943,** 1007, 1054
Leaderless **Vol. 2:** 800
Leadership **Vol. 1:** 196 f., 199, 300, 425
Vol. 2: 114, 121, 317, 374
Vol. 3: 700, 915, 1169
Leaf **Vol. 1:** 515, 652
Vol. 3: 865–870
League **Vol. 2:** 306
Leah **Vol. 1:** 61
Vol. 2: 305 f., 317, 319, 578, 796
Vol. 3: 139, 993
Lean **Vol. 1:** 255
Leaney, A.R.C. **Vol. 3:** 288 f.
Leap over **Vol. 1:** 632
Learn **Vol. 1:** 69, 333, 481, 483–485, 599
Vol. 2: 179, 289, 291, 313, 392, 395, 398, 422
Vol. 3: 78, 513, 724, 820
Learn Christ **Vol. 3:** 765
Learn by heart **Vol. 3:** 59
Learned in law **Vol. 2: 438–451**
Learner **Vol. 1:** 136, 483–485
Vol. 2: 291
Learning **Vol. 2:** 61, 140, 659
Vol. 3: 483, 493
Least **Vol. 3:** 55, **427–429**
Leather **Vol. 1:** 243, 254
Vol. 2: 465
Vol. 3: 109, 120 f., 483
Leather-worker **Vol. 1:** 279
Vol. 3: 811–815
Leave **Vol. 1:** 488, 607, 697 f., 701
Vol. 2: 394
Vol. 3: 247–253, 254, 560
Leave behind **Vol. 3: 247–253**
Leave country **Vol. 2: 788–790**
Leave off **Vol. 3:** 251
Leave over **Vol. 3: 243–253**
Leaven **Vol. 1:** 249, 630, 634
Vol. 2: 216, 385, 428, **461–463,** 675 f., 714, 716, 755, 834
Vol. 3: 132, 184, 422 f., 431, 442, 1058
Leaves **Vol. 1:** 390, 723 f.
Vol. 2: 382
Lebanon **Vol. 1:** 165
Lectionary **Vol. 1:** 245
Vol. 3: 485
Lecture **Vol. 3:** 1087
Leda **Vol. 3:** 216
Left hand **Vol. 1:** 103
Vol. 2: 146–153
Left-handed **Vol. 2:** 414

Leg **Vol. 1:** 393, 656
Vol. 2: 414 f., 817
Legal **Vol. 1:** 258, 286, 337, 344, 365, 368, 373, 375, 392, 395 f., 402, 468, 475, 477, 488, 503–506, 543, 558, 606, 645, 650, 658–660, 664, 668, 687, 697 f.
Vol. 2: 121, 132, 137, 139, 141–143, 254, 256, 296,. 305, 307, 312, 335, 349, 362–364, 366 f., 369, 372, 427, 437–451, 510, 512, 662 f., 716
Vol. 3: 68, 92, 97, 134, 144, 194, 355, 359, 497, 530, 1039, 1043
Legal concept **Vol. 2:** 39
Legal demands **Vol. 3:** 583
Legal due **Vol. 3:** 753
Legal expert **Vol. 2: 438–451**
Legalism **Vol. 1:** 259, 331, 335, 338 f., 361, 371, 397, 399–402, 487, 532, 597, 602, 681
Vol. 2: 134, 267, 327, 730
Vol. 3: 71, 370, 934
Legalistic **Vol. 2:** 106, 133, 221, 361, 671
Vol. 3: 72, 105, 107, 996
Legend **Vol. 1:** 58
Vol. 2: 784 f.
Vol. 3: 662, 706, 876
Legendary **Vol. 1:** 594
Legion **Vol. 1:** 175, 475
Vol. 3: 475
Legislate **Vol. 2:** 438–451, 738
Legislation **Vol. 1:** 506
Vol. 2: 438–451
Legitimacy **Vol. 1:** 599
Vol. 3: 653 f., 656
Legitimate **Vol. 1:** 498
Vol. 2: 372
Vol. 3: 571, 1044
Legitimation **Vol. 2:** 329
Vol. 3: 643
Leibniz, G.W. **Vol. 3:** 896, 899
Leiden magical papyrus **Vol. 2:** 683
Leisure **Vol. 2:** 360
Leivestad, R. **Vol. 3: 619**
Lend **Vol. 2:** 241
Vol. 3: 953
Length **Vol. 1:** 253
Leniency **Vol. 1:** 467, 698, 700
Vol. 2: 257, 769, 817
Lent **Vol. 3:** 146
Lentils **Vol. 1:** 249
Leo **Vol. 2:** 688
Léon–Dufour, X. **Vol. 3: 300**
Leontopolis **Vol. 2:** 331
Vol. 3: 35, 451
Leopard **Vol. 1:** 119
Leper **Vol. 2:** 358, 410, 414, **463–466,** 599, 630 f.
Vol. 3: 37, 106, 159, 419 f., 508, 569, 860, 1000, 1061
Leprosy **Vol. 1:** 151, 163, 204, 225, 241, 685
Vol. 2: 171, 349, 396, **463–466,** 633
Vol. 3: 104, 108, 986, 989, 997, 1061
Leprous **Vol. 2: 463–466**
Lepton **Vol. 2:** 849 f., 852
Lesbian **Vol. 1:** 498

Less than **Vol. 3: 952–956**
Lesson **Vol. 3:** 330, 719
Let alone **Vol. 1:** 698
Let go **Vol. 1:** 698, 701
  Vol. 3: 177
Let know **Vol. 3:** 316
Let loose **Vol. 3:** 469
Let pass **Vol. 1:** 697 f.
Let slip **Vol. 1:** 682 f.
Lethargy **Vol. 3:** 279
Leto **Vol. 1:** 508
  Vol. 3: 1071
Letter **Vol. 1:** 62, **242–249,** 255, 261, 292, 356,
  430, 656, 727, 737
  Vol. 2: 113 f., 291, 356, 358, 446, 448, 452,
  530, 641, 671, 675
  Vol. 3: 112, 477, **482–495,** 498, 742, 744, 765,
  904, 1169
Letter to Aristides **Vol. 3:** 872
Letter of commendation **Vol. 1:** 592
  Vol. 3: 935
Letters of Paul **Vol. 3:** 492
Level **Vol. 1:** 709
  Vol. 2: 259, 563
Level place **Vol. 3: 1009**
Levelling **Vol. 3:** 1011, 1013
Levi **Vol. 1:** 487, 544
  Vol. 2: 237, 317, 320, 447, **466 f.,** 592, 639,
  693 f.
  Vol. 3: 34, 435, 455 f., 658, 757, 853 f., 871,
  873
Leviathan **Vol. 1:** 205, 326, 523
  Vol. 2: 485
  Vol. 3: 983
Levirate marriage **Vol. 1:** 499
  Vol. 2: 564, 576, **577 f.,** 588, 691
  Vol. 3: 95, 191, 263, 275, 356, 655, 1055,
  1074
Levite **Vol. 1:** 65, 98, 170, 230, 294, 360, 538,
  554, 636
  Vol. 2: 227, 237, 297, 300, 304, 311, 321, **466
  f.,** 592, 636, 638, 649, 693 f., 730, 799, 813,
  823
  Vol. 3: 33–35, 38, 41 f., 415, 424, 433, 478,
  551, 565, 852 f., 989
Levitical **Vol. 1:** 80, 211, 245, 314, 337, 341,
  408, 619, 677
  Vol. 2: 64, 290, 320, 448, **466 f.,** 694
  Vol. 3: 38, 41 f., 164, 228, 410, 439, 742, 947
Levitical messiah **Vol. 3:** 657
Levitical scribe **Vol. 3:** 478
Leviticus **Vol. 1:** 65
Levy **Vol. 1:** 296, 537
  Vol. 3: 752
Lex talionis **Vol. 3:** 94, 96, 928, 1179
Lexicography **Vol. 3:** 1140 f.
Liability **Vol. 1:** 373
  Vol. 2: 362
  Vol. 3: 420, 753 f.
Liable **Vol. 1:** 418, 550, 657
  Vol. 2: 142, 156, 667, 775
Liar **Vol. 1:** 166, 350, 423 f.
  Vol. 2: 470–474, 503
  Vol. 3: 281, 529, 887

Libation **Vol. 1:** 648
  Vol. 2: 854 f.
  Vol. 3: 919
Liberal **Vol. 1:** 639, 642
  Vol. 2: 827
Liberal Judaism (→ Judaism, liberal)
Liberality **Vol. 1:** 731
Liberally **Vol. 3:** 403
Liberate **Vol. 1:** 399, 401
  Vol. 2: 64, 131
Liberating union **Vol. 3:** 590
Liberating word **Vol. 1:** 384, 397
Liberation **Vol. 1:** 58, 138, 209, 277, 385, 432,
  435, 522, 524, **715–721**
  Vol. 2: 110
  Vol. 3: 41, 277, 592, 598, 679, 720, 860,
  972–974
Liberator **Vol. 2:** 560
Libertine **Vol. 3: 598 f.,** 942
Libertini, Synagogue of the **Vol. 1:** 297
Libertinism **Vol. 1: 62,** 336, 339, 448, 556, 638,
  720
  Vol. 2: 394, 447, 584, 611, 677
Liberty **Vol. 1:** 62, 331, 435, 458, 470, **715–721**
  Vol. 2: 161 f., 211, 444, 884
  Vol. 3: 51, 227, 380, 488, 536, 678, 705,
  1053, 1151
Libophoenicia **Vol. 2:** 126
Library **Vol. 1:** 377
Lice **Vol. 2:** 637
Licence **Vol. 2:** 678
  Vol. 3: 922, 932, 1064
Licentiousness **Vol. 1:** 494, 500, 681
  Vol. 2: 256, 436, 587, 868, 892
  Vol. 3: 1059
Lick up **Vol. 1:** 520
Lictor **Vol. 1:** 407
Lie **Vol. 1:** 424, 454 f., 458, 461, 466, 471,
  550 f., 563, 660, 670
  Vol. 2: 72, 77, 312, 393, **467–474,** 555, 567,
  736, 813, 831, 847
  Vol. 3: 291, 574, 576, 586, 741, 875, 885 f.,
  892 f., 926, 946, 1041
Lie down **Vol. 1:** 442
  Vol. 2: 586
  Vol. 3: 255
Lie fallow **Vol. 2:** 822
Lie in wait **Vol. 2:** 132 f., 215, 460
Life **Vol. 1:** 60, 78, 84, 96, 105, 107, 139, 148,
  168, 180, 182, 212, 221 f., 226, 229, 231,
  234, 236, 241, 243 f., 248, 250 f., 253, 260,
  262, 265, 274, 277 f., 281 f., 296 f., 300, 303,
  311, 321, 323, 327, 329, 332 f., 335, 337,
  347, 350, 354 f., 359, 367, 381, 384, 391,
  399–401, 403, 406, 416 f., 421–424, 427,
  429–438, 441 f., 444–446, 456–460, 462–
  465, 467–471, 479f., 483, 488–494, 496, 500,
  502, 505 f., 509, 512–515, 517, 521, 524 f.,
  528, 533 f., 537, 541, 543, 546–552, 556 f.,
  561, 565, 568, 570 f., 574 f., 597, 601, 603 f.,
  608–610, 615, 617, 619, 621, 624 f., 627 f.,
  630, 634, 637 f., 640–645, 649–651, 653 f.,
  656–659, 662, 666, 669, 671–673, 676–682,
  689, 697, 703, 709–711, 713 f., 716–720, 722

f., 726 f., 729, 733, 736, 738, 740 f., 743 f.
Vol. 2: 31, 42, 54, 58, 60 f., 77, 80, 83, 87, 95, 99 f., 102–104, 106, 108, 111, 113, 116–124, 129, 132, 136, 156–159, 162, 166, 178, 180–182, 185f., 201, 203, 205 f., 209, 211, 217f., 221, 225, 228, 239, 242, 244, 258 f., 260, 264 f., 267, 269–271, 274 f., 278–280, 282, 295, 310, 316, 332, 339, 343, 350 f., 353, 357, 361, 366, 368, 370, 387 f., 394 f., 400 f., 404, 406 f., 416, 419–421, 426, 428, 430, 433, 436–439, 441 f., 446 f., 449, 452 f., 458, 460, 472, **474–484,** 485 f., 488, 490–492, 494, 510, 512, 517, 523, 535, 538, 567–569, 571 f., 583, 598, 605 f., 617, 625, 631, 636, 642, 657, 665 f., 671 f., 675 f., 691, 705, 714–716, 718 f., 736, 764, 778, 780, 787, 789, 794, 807, 811, 815–819, 825, 828, 830, 833 f., 837 f., 840, 843, **845–847,** 861, 864, 892, 903, 911, 918 f., 926, 928 f.
Vol. 3: 50, 55 f., 62, 99, 105, 121, 136 f., 140, 145, 151, 153, 155, 157 f., 160, 163, 167, 178, 189–192, 195–197, 199 f., 204 f., 208 f., 212–216, 219f., 225, 227–229, 240, 244, 258, 260–264, 276, 280, 303, 313, 315, 321–323, 347, 353, 359, 378, 400, 416, 424, 432, 435, 440, 444 f., 480, 487, 493, 515, 523 f., 528–530, 533, 546, 555, 581 f., 597, 600 f., 623–625, 631, 638, 645–647, 675, **676–687,** 701–707, 730 f., 746, 748, 772, 774, 809, 811, 819, 827 f., 834, 839, 842, 860, 866, 883, 886, 891, 894, 905, 916, 921, 928 f., **933–947,** 953, 973, 986, 988 f., 993, 1030, 1032, 1045 f., 1053, 1058, 1067, 1079, 1084, 1093, 1095, 1103, 1106, 1114, 1122, 1131, 1163, 1169
Life-bringing **Vol. 3:** 982
Life-destroying **Vol. 1:** 653
Life-force **Vol. 3:** 600, 681, 690 f.
Life-giving **Vol. 1:** 329, 430, 436, 649, 653, 665, 722 f.
  Vol. 2: 186, 274, 520, 929
  Vol. 3: 280, 599, 703
Life-span **Vol. 1:** 92, 431
  Vol. 2: 478, 690
  Vol. 3: 826–833, 841–843
Life-style **Vol. 1:** 110, 185, 598
Lifeless **Vol. 1:** 429, 441
  Vol. 3: 913
Lifelong **Vol. 1:** 623
  Vol. 3: 537
Lifetime **Vol. 2:** 382, 887, 921
Lift up **Vol. 1:** 211, 510, 585
  Vol. 2: 187, 204, 225, 259, 642, 764, 873
  Vol. 3: 153
Lift up the countenance **Vol. 2:** 621
Light **Vol. 1:** 60, 102, 174, 203, 219 f., 261, 286, 320, 323, 333, 338, 355, 359, 379, 382, 420–425, 432, 477, 483, 490, 513, 522, 525, 556, 562 f., 566, 580, 586, 592, 616, 638, 644, 652, 705, 711, 723
  Vol. 2: 46, 70 f., 77, 80, 105, 119, 130, 183, 185, 189, 193, 200, 213 f., 216 f., 232, 250, 278–281, 290, 302, 307, 313, 353, 380, 408, 428, **484–496,** 517, 565, 609, 645, 672, 691, 706, 713, 719, 742, 761, 795, 830, 834, 839,
889, 928
  Vol. 3: 47, 110, 118, 163, 184, 204, 212, 268, 276, 310, 312, 314, 316 f., 320–322, 335, 344, 398, 435, 445 f., 468, 471, 495, 503, 554 f., 634, 646, 679, 693, 730–737, 807, 860, 862, 882, 893, 916, 929, 939, 944, 963, 1001, 1012, 1045, 1115, 1150, 1158
Light of knowledge **Vol. 3:** 936
Light and truth **Vol. 3:** 881
Light up **Vol. 2: 490–496**
Light-bearers **Vol. 2:** 493
Lighten **Vol. 1:** 699
Lighthearted **Vol. 2:** 431, 435
Lightness **Vol. 2:** 461
Lightning **Vol. 1:** 610, 654
  Vol. 2: 484
  Vol. 3: 984, **1000–1004**
Like **Vol. 1:** 206, 491
  Vol. 2: 80, 284, 286, 291, 307, **496–508,** 516, 744, 817
  Vol. 3: 123, 904
Like-minded **Vol. 2: 500–508**
Like-value **Vol. 3: 348 f.**
Likeness **Vol. 1:** 587, 676, 707, 709
  Vol. 2: 242, **284, 286–288, 496–508**
  Vol. 3: 555, **903–906**
Liking **Vol. 2:** 116
Lilies of the field **Vol. 2:** 386
Lilith **Vol. 1:** 451
Limb **Vol. 1:** 152, **229–242,** 300
  Vol. 2: 414 f.
Lime **Vol. 3:** 111
Limestone **Vol. 3:** 381
Limit **Vol. 1:** 54, 352, 384, 386, 389, 422, 488 f., 494, 500, 548 f., 565, 625, 669, 671, 680 f., 734
  Vol. 2: 106, 244, 309, 360, 689, 692, 873
  Vol. 3: 27, 400
Limitation **Vol. 3:** 678, 814
Limited period **Vol. 2: 765–767**
Limitless **Vol. 2:** 694
Limp **Vol. 2:** 414 f.
Lindos **Vol. 3:** 317
Line **Vol. 1:** 426 f.
  Vol. 2: 337, 436, 451
Line of argumentation **Vol. 3:** 1086
Lineage **Vol. 1:** 220, 616
  Vol. 2: 656
Linear history **Vol. 2:** 891
Linen **Vol. 1:** 204 f., 531
  Vol. 3: 120, 794
Linger **Vol. 2:** 773
  Vol. 3: 227, **839–845**
Linguistic categories **Vol. 3:** 1138
Linguistics **Vol. 1:** 56, 582
  Vol. 3: 1123–1143
Link **Vol. 1:** 259, 731
Lintel **Vol. 2:** 410
Lion **Vol. 1:** 116, 118 f., 444, 520, 694
  Vol. 2: 215, 320, 411, 421, 628
  Vol. 3: 180, 203, 471, 601, 650, 713, 944, 951, 1092
Lion of Judah **Vol. 2:** 340
  Vol. 3: 649

Lip **Vol. 3:** 498
Lip-service **Vol. 2:** 93
Liparians **Vol. 3:** 851
Lipit-Ishtar Code **Vol. 2:** 582
Lips **Vol. 1:** 382, 424, 455
 Vol. 2: 28, 30, 864
Liquefy **Vol. 1:** 682
Liquid **Vol. 1:** 513, 520, 626
 Vol. 2: 854
 Vol. 3: 403
List **Vol. 3:** 399, 483
Listen **Vol. 1:** 210, 485, 510, 529, 584, 591
 Vol. 2: 155, **172–180,** 316, 413, 435, 444, 867
 Vol. 3: 112, 800, 1092
Listener **Vol. 2:** 175, 748
Literal **Vol. 1:** 323, 713
 Vol. 2: 266, 415, 685, 917, 927
 Vol. 3: 486, 730, 733
Literalism **Vol. 2:** 905
Literary analysis **Vol. 3:** 333
Literary criticism (→ Criticism, literary)
Literary forms (→ Form-criticism)
Literary genre (→ Genre, literary)
Literature **Vol. 3:** 483
Litigant **Vol. 2:** 369
Litigate **Vol. 2:** 363
Litigation **Vol. 2:** 317
Little **Vol. 1:** 283, 358, 461 f., 586, 623
 Vol. 2: 157, **427–429**
Little Apocalypse **Vol. 1:** 541
 Vol. 2: 65
 Vol. 3: 56
Little ones **Vol. 2:** 428, 709
 Vol. 3: 394
Little while **Vol. 2:** 429
Little woman **Vol. 3:** **1055–1068**
Liturgical **Vol. 1:** 98 f., 280, 346, 514, 618, 620, 628, 642
 Vol. 2: 253, 512, 870, 874
 Vol. 3: 47, 50, 208, 233, 244, 668, 673, 702, 720
Liturgy **Vol. 1:** 100, 297, 414, 416, 627 f., 633
 Vol. 2: 45, 200 f., 353, 530–536
 Vol. 3: 78, 462, 638, 674 f., 846
Live **Vol. 1:** 181, 234, 435, 444, 513, 517, 597, 600, 613, 621, 643, 661, 676 f., 679, 682, 685 f., 690 f., 713, 723, 739
 Vol. 2: 95, 120, 123, 267, 269, 271, 297, 335, 393, 438, 445, **474–484, 801–804,** 815–819
 Vol. 3: 255, 269, 366–368, 760, 805, **811–815**
Live as a Jew **Vol. 2:** 310
Live in **Vol. 2:** **247–251**
Live in peace **Vol. 2:** **776–783**
Livelihood **Vol. 1:** 277, 357
 Vol. 2: 297, 475, 678
Liver **Vol. 1:** 230
Livestock **Vol. 2:** 410, 412, 693
Living **Vol. 1:** 87, 147, 240, 469, 535, 641 f., 659, 665, 683, 690, 711, 723, 736
 Vol. 2: 74, 204, 233, 267, 275, 282, 285, 319, 365, 924
 Vol. 3: 791
Living creature **Vol. 1:** 280
 Vol. 2: **476–484**

Living One **Vol. 2:** 197
Living soul **Vol. 3:** 683
Living stone **Vol. 1:** 305
 Vol. 2: 83, 230, 249, 253
 Vol. 3: 390, 393, 435
Living water **Vol. 2:** 267
 Vol. 3: 459, 813 f., 943, 982, **986–988**
Load **Vol. 1:** 260, 711, 728, 742 f.
 Vol. 2: 281
Loaf, loaves **Vol. 1:** 249 f., 586
 Vol. 2: 534
 Vol. 3: 657, 904
Loafer **Vol. 1:** 267
Loan **Vol. 2:** 254, 666, 856, 858
Loan-word **Vol. 2:** 125, 333
Loathe **Vol. 1:** 555, 557
Local **Vol. 1:** 624, 626, 643
Locality **Vol. 2:** 303, 376
Location **Vol. 1:** 527
 Vol. 3: 602
Lock **Vol. 2:** 207
 Vol. 3: 498
Locke, John **Vol. 1:** 56
 Vol. 3: 1130
Locusts **Vol. 1:** 118 f., 342, 409, 511, 612
 Vol. 2: 628, 637, 690, 831
 Vol. 3: 248, 256, 560, 846, 856, 1001
Lodge **Vol. 3:** 255
Lodging **Vol. 1:** 687
 Vol. 3: **177–189**
Loft **Vol. 2:** 189
Logia **Vol. 1:** 57 f., **62 f.,** 67 f.
 Vol. 2: 757
 Vol. 3: 84 f., 1030
Logic **Vol. 1:** 49, 481, 664
 Vol. 2: 284
 Vol. 3: 119, 379, 571, 876, 1034, 1081, 1085–1087
Logical **Vol. 1:** 333
 Vol. 2: 392 f.
Logical antimony **Vol. 3:** 887
Logical necessity **Vol. 3:** 894
Logical positivism **Vol. 3:** 1136
Logos **Vol. 1:** 60, **63,** 102, 166, 178, 374, 438, 575 f., 595, 711, 739
 Vol. 2: 125, 140, 185, 288, 355, 404, 535 f., 590
 Vol. 3: 35 f., 41, 554, 643, 689, 704, 723, 890, 922, 1033, 1069, 1084 f., **1114–1117,** 1204
Loins **Vol. 1:** 239 f.
 Vol. 3: 966
Lois **Vol. 3:** 1070
Loneliness **Vol. 1:** 679
 Vol. 2: 307, 360, 420, 478
 Vol. 3: 1004, 1073
Long **Vol. 1:** 523
 Vol. 2: 239
Long time **Vol. 3:** **826–833**
Longing **Vol. 1:** 385, 456, 522, 524, 610, 672
 Vol. 2: 103, 108, 238, 244, 247, 265, 267, 270, 325, 394, 420, 423, 539, 789, 900
 Vol. 3: 421, 680, 820, 858, 996, 1092
Longsuffering **Vol. 2:** 764, 766, **768–772**
Look **Vol. 1:** 231, 456, 510, 585, 694

493

Vol. 3: 126, **519 f.**
Look at **Vol. 2:** 393
  Vol. 3: 511–520
Look back **Vol. 1:** 493
Look cheerful **Vol. 3:** 254
Look in the face **Vol. 3: 519 f.**
Look for **Vol. 1:** 189
  Vol. 2: 244–246
Look forward **Vol. 1:** 633
Look into **Vol. 2:** 393
Look up **Vol. 2:** 194
  Vol. 3: 519
Loose (→ Binding and loosing) **Vol. 1:** 171, 190, 577, 698
  Vol. 2: 402, 732 f.
  Vol. 3: 177–221, 537, 544
Loosen **Vol. 3:** 558
Lord **Vol. 1:** 71, 102, 128, 165–168, 187, 205, 209, 221 f., 256, 270, 325, 346, 355, 381 f., 396, 427, 441, 475 f., 489, 519, 522 f., 526, 540, 546, 549, 559, 569, 571 f., 574, 592, 596, 601, 603 f., 607, 610, 626, 643 f., 652, 659, 662, 665, 668 f., 674 f., 688, 695, 704, 720, 722, 726–728, 733–736
  Vol. 2: 47, 58, 68–72, 74, 76 f., 79–81, 84, 112, 119, 129–131, 139, 143 f., 147, 149, 155, 157, 162, 164 f., 173, 180, 186 f., 191, 193 f., 202–204, 213–215, 218, 226, 230 f., 238, 240, 242–244, 250, 263 f., 274, 278 f., 287, 297, 299, 312, 317 f., 325, 329 f., 332, 336, 343, 350, 353, 357, 359, 361, 363, 366, 369, 373, 383, 386, 388, 399, 403, 405, 407, 411–413, 460, 491, **508–520,** 522, 528, 535, 548, 562, 580, 582, 590, 595, 619, 649, 652, 654, 674, 677, 722, 725, 800, 818, 859, 863, 867, 869, 877, 891, 895 f., 915, 922
  Vol. 3: 37, 45, 47, 53, 55 f., 60, 62, 66, 69f., 83–85, 88, 95, 98, 115, 118, 120, 130, 135, 140, 155 f., 158–160, 166, 177 f., 191, 195, 202–209, 212, 218 f., 221, 226 f., 233, 239, 241 f., 250, 255, 257 f., 265, 267–269, 272, 277–279, 281–283, 285, 289, 296, 298 f., 313, 317–320, 324, 341–343, 347, 349, 357, 363, 378–380, 386, 388–390, 405–407, 411 f., 420, 422, 426 f., 430, 433, 474–476, 484, 492, 500, 502, 505, 510, 518, 520, 529, 531, 536 f., 541, 544, 548, 560, 567–569, 583, 588, 590–592, 595–597, 600, 602–604, 623, 638 f., 649, 651, 653, 660, 669, 674 f., 683, 685, 687, 698, 701, 710, 718, 728, 731 f., 764, 768, 773, 777 f., 780, 784, 786, 790, 792, 794, 800 f., 805 f., 812, 815, 819, 824 f., 829, 833, 835, 837, 841, 844, 846, 852 f., 857, 860 f., 867, 873, 889, 908, 913, 918, 921, 924 f., 929 f., 938, 942, 945–947, 962, 967, 973–978, 986, 990, 996, 1004, 1011 f., 1016 f., 1022, 1026, 1032 f., 1044, 1058, 1060, 1064, 1079, 1093–1099, 1103, 1106 f., 1114, 1119–1122, 1155, 1166, 1178, 1181, 1192, 1194, 1199, 1205, 1209
Lord it over **Vol. 2: 510–520**
Lord of the flies **Vol. 3:** 469
Lord of heaven **Vol. 1:** 75
Lord of hosts **Vol. 1:** 280

Vol. 2: 69, 326, 375
  Vol. 3: 959
Lord of lords **Vol. 2:** 514
Lord of the sabbath **Vol. 3:** 410
Lord of spirits **Vol. 1:** 452
  Vol. 3: 272, 615
Lord of time **Vol. 3:** 841
Lord's Day **Vol. 1:** 631
  Vol. 2: 518
  Vol. 3: 405–415
Lord's Prayer **Vol. 1:** 249–251, 384, 566 f., 615, 619, 621
  Vol. 2: 229, 267, 561, 653, 668, 832, **868–873**
  Vol. 3: 204, 696, 803, 1022, 1176
Lord's Supper **Vol. 1:** 117, 157, 213, 237, 250 f., 253, 298, 301, 369 f., 414, 467, 473, 513, 629 f., 633 f., 639, 643, 689, 701 f.
  Vol. 2: 42, 221, 250, 269, 273–277, 286, 314, 554, 368, 391, **516,** 518, **520–538,** 543, 547, 581, 671, 732, 754, 854, 882, 885, 894–897, 920
  Vol. 3: 47, 61, 166, 195, 227, 239, 243–247, 277, 322, 337, 349, 383, 395, 411, 415, 420, 429, 436, 448, 510, 553, 568, 580, 589, 669 f., 704, 706, 724, 750, 773, 778, 819, 905, 922, 990, 1165
Lord's table **Vol. 3:** 435
Lordship **Vol. 1:** 203, 237 f., 248, 298, 302, 355, 462, 475, 492, 522, 637, 639
  Vol. 2: 81, 163, 203 f., 374 f., 399, 425, **510–520,** 619, 649, 722, 754
  Vol. 3: 45, 55 f., 604, 703, 780, 929, 1006, 1064, 1105 f., 1155
Lose **Vol. 1:** 462, 608–611, 639, 651
  Vol. 2: 314, 385, 838
Lose heart **Vol. 1:** 561, 563
Lose life **Vol. 1:** 439, 464, 698
  Vol. 2: 203, 918, 920
  Vol. 3: 137, 212, 677, 682
Lose way **Vol. 1:** 608
Loss **Vol. 1:** 463, 465, 497, 608, 611, 640, 679, 716
  Vol. 2: 31, 318, 420, 422 f., 775
  Vol. 3: 134, 278
Lost **Vol. 1:** 322, 332, 359, 463 f., 472, 525, 541, 729
  Vol. 2: 287 f., 314, 356, 358, 366, 386, 394, 412 f., 439, 446, 459–461, 857
  Vol. 3: 143, 319, 529 f., 532, 567, 580, 628, 750, 754, 920, 1058 f.
Lost tribes **Vol. 3:** 873
Lot **Vol. 1:** 216, 255, 433, 452, 478, 482, 488 f., 491, 554, 689, 741
  Vol. 2: 72, 247, 294, **295–304,** 361, 787, 835
  Vol. 3: 204, 370, 633, 856, 1058
Lot's wife **Vol. 3:** 240
Loud **Vol. 2:** 201, 426
Love **Vol. 1:** 55, 96, 102 f., 108–110, 112, 126, 166 f., 171, 173, 180, 190 f., 197, 206 f., 215, 232, 235 f., 238–240, 254–260, 262 f., 270, 275, 277 f., 282, 287, 300, 303, 311, 318, 324 f., 329, 334–339, 341, 347, 351 f., 464, 469, 484, 490–492, 496, 498, 502, 525 f., 528, 530, 538, 541 f., 548 f., 552–557, 559,

Love (*cont'd*)
564, 566, 568–570, 574, 590, 596, 601–604, 607, 609, 611, 616 f., 620, 622–626, 630, 638 f., 642, 644, 651 f., 655, 662, 664, 666–668, 679, 687 f., 693, 695 f., 719 f., 722, 730 f., 733 f., 738, 740
Vol. 2: 43, 51, 62 f., 64, 70 f., 76, 78 f., 83, 86, 97, 101, 103–106, 117, 119, 121, 129, 131 f., 134, 141, 144, 147, 149, 162 f., 176 f., 180, 183, 185, 198, 214, 217, 221, 227, 230, 242 f., 253, 258, 264, 267, 269, 286, 301, 304, 310, 318, 328, 358 f., 364, 366, 386, 391 f., 395, 400, 402–405, 413, 418, 422, 426 f., 444–446, 449, 469 f., 473, 475, 478, 482, 493 f., 499, 503, **538–551**, 563, 585, 597, **599 f**, 604 f., 625, 632, 653, 658 f., 665, 668, 673, 681, 698, 706, 709, 720 f., 733, 736, 745, 771, 774–776, 779 f., 791, 798, 807, 812 f., 815, 817, 824, 826 f., 838, 847, 855, 857, 868, 880, 905, 925, 929
Vol. 3: 32, 45, 47, 54, 79, 97 f., 106 f., 113, 118, 129, 162, 167 f., 171, 173, 183, 192, 198, 202, 215, 219, 225 f., 229, 256, 261, 296, 315, 319, 321 f., 349 f., 360, 378, 380, 427 f., 431 f., 455, 489 f., 505, 519, 532, 534, 536, 543, 545, 547, 553, 562, 565 f., 569, 576, 582, 592, 596 f., 644, 646, 677, 680, 685, 687, 701, 707, 713, 722, 746, 750, 752, 755, 776–779, 800, 806, 810, 818, 832, 838, 848, 868 f., 879, 886 f., 903, 921, 926 f., 929, 932, 942, 944 f., 965, 996, 998, 1001 f., 1034, 1059, 1061, 1063 f., 1093, 1148, 1151, 1155
Love feast **Vol. 2:** 547
Love for mankind **Vol. 2: 547–550**
Love of money **Vol. 2:** 550, 845
   Vol. 3: 868
Love of wisdom **Vol. 3: 1034–1036**
Loveless **Vol. 2:** 143, 864, 868
   Vol. 3: 377
Lovely **Vol. 3:** 1148
Lover **Vol. 1:** 481, 492, 506, 558
Lovingkindness **Vol. 2:** 237, 261
   Vol. 3: 354
Low **Vol. 1:** 566
   Vol. 2: 259, 263, 822
Lower **Vol. 1:** 674, 707
   Vol. 2: 209 f., 719
Lower regions **Vol. 2: 205–210**
Lowest **Vol. 2:** 55, 57
Lowliness **Vol. 2: 259–264**, 334, 379
Lowly **Vol. 2:** 200, 203, **259–264**, 821
Loyal **Vol. 2:** 125, 149, 237, 319
Loyalty **Vol. 1:** 189, 270, 281, 308, 367, 529, 618, 688
   Vol. 2: 71, 117, 132, 134, 146, 218, 239, 397, 451, 487, 595, 785
   Vol. 3: 157, 213, 358, 444, 537, 871, 879, 927
Lucian **Vol. 1:** 281
   Vol. 2: 556
   Vol. 3: 494
Lucifer **Vol. 3:** 468
Lucius of Cyrene **Vol. 2:** 740
Lucky **Vol. 2:** 146
   Vol. 3: 31

Ludicrous **Vol. 2:** 285
Luke **Vol. 1:** 69, 116, 135 f., 162, 181, 199, 303, 440, 490, 539–541, 571, 586, 590, 642, 735
   Vol. 2: 118, 168, 222 f., 236, 254, 272, 327, 333, 356
   Vol. 3: 47, 52, 57, 64 f., 86 f., 654–659, 732, 909
Luke's view of history **Vol. 3:** 86
Lukewarm **Vol. 1: 317–319**
   Vol. 2: 727, 844, 881
   Vol. 3: 321
Lull **Vol. 1:** 441
Luminary **Vol. 1:** 422, 451, 523
   Vol. 2: 490–496
   Vol. 3: 730–737
Lump **Vol. 1:** 634
   Vol. 2: 462
   Vol. 3: 917
Lunacy **Vol. 3:** 734
Lunar calendar **Vol. 3:** 733
Lunar cycle **Vol. 1:** 626
Lunatic **Vol. 2:** 165
   Vol. 3: 475
Lure **Vol. 1:** 458, 681
   Vol. 2: 707
Lurk **Vol. 1:** 241
Lust **Vol. 1:** 106, 137, 231, 448, **456–461**, 469, 559, 627, 645, 671, 677, 690 f.
   Vol. 2: 368, 478, 580, 779
   Vol. 3: 32, 97, 183, 582, 596, 680, 685, 1054, 1064
Lustration **Vol. 1:** 144 f., 151, 155 f., 186, 225
   Vol. 3: 990
Luther, Martin **Vol. 1:** 50, 77, 299
   Vol. 2: 219, 244, 258, 361
   Vol. 3: 655, 928
Luxuriant **Vol. 3:** 918
Luxury **Vol. 1:** 118, 205, 531, 671
   Vol. 2: 486
Luz **Vol. 2:** 317
LXX (→ Septuagint)
Lycaonia **Vol. 3:** 773
Lycia **Vol. 1:** 573
Lydia **Vol. 1:** 344, 361
   Vol. 2: 550, 847
   Vol. 3: 1063, 1065 f.
Lying **Vol. 1:** 350, 512, 550, 555
   Vol. 2: 469, 586
Lying in state **Vol. 1:** 696
Lying spirit **Vol. 2:** 458
Lynch **Vol. 1:** 344
   Vol. 2: 450
Lyre **Vol. 3:** 671
Lysander **Vol. 3:** 635
Lysimachus **Vol. 2:** 310, 849
Lystra **Vol. 1:** 405
   Vol. 2: 606
   Vol. 3: 203, 226, 457, 558

Macarius of 'Aelia' **Vol. 2:** 506
Maccabean **Vol. 1:** 650, 717
   Vol. 3: 270, 818
Maccabean rebellion **Vol. 1:** 75, 688
   Vol. 2: 290, **307**

Vol. 3: 35, 479
Maccabees **Vol. 1:** 50, 59, 62, **63**, 233, 645
  Vol. 2: 125, 237, 241, 337, 810
  Vol. 3: 164, 419, 452, 461, 783, 788, 961
Mace-head **Vol. 2:** 97
Macedonia **Vol. 1:** 301
  Vol. 2: 550, 809, 818, 826
  Vol. 3: 499, 955, 1021
Macedonian **Vol. 1:** 712
  Vol. 2: 33, 372, 802, 804
  Vol. 3: 450
Machpelah **Vol. 2:** 318, 847
Macquarrie, John **Vol. 3:** **329 f.**
Macrocosm **Vol. 3:** 513
Macrocosmic time **Vol. 3:** 834
Madman **Vol. 3:** 577, 1008
Madness **Vol. 1:** 450, **526–530**
  Vol. 2: 27, 431
  Vol. 3: 123, 996
Madonna-cult **Vol. 3:** 1070
Magi **Vol. 1:** 170
  Vol. 2: 294, **552–562**, 728, 831
  Vol. 3: 341, 1071
Magic **Vol. 1:** 95, 119–121, 186, 207 f., 219,
  243, 254, 266 f., 320, 346, 409, 420, 450–
  454, 550, 577, 611, 625, 686, 718
  Vol. 2: 74, 151, 168, 170, 214, 286 f., 296,
  393, 479, 520, **552–562**, 601 f., 605, 621,
  629 f., 648, 650, 652, 654, 656, 662, 728 f.,
  831, 847
  Vol. 3: 180, 206, 231 f., 270, 324, 340, 342,
  457, 471 f., 476, 483, 520, 606, 735, 800,
  844, 860 f., 982, 1087, 1100, 1157
Magic arts **Vol. 2:** 557
Magic potion **Vol. 2:** **552–562**
Magical **Vol. 3:** 202, 1087
Magical ceremony **Vol. 2:** **556**
Magician **Vol. 1:** 424
  Vol. 2: **552–562**, 639, 642
  Vol. 3: 463
Magistrate **Vol. 1:** 163, 168, 193, 341, 407
  Vol. 2: 234
  Vol. 3: 173, 478
Magna Mater **Vol. 1:** 560
Magnanimous **Vol. 1:** 715
Magnesia **Vol. 3:** 757
Magnificat **Vol. 2:** 34, 261
  Vol. 3: 30, 219, 241, 612, 674, 718, 1071
Magnificent **Vol. 2:** 425
  Vol. 3: 28
Magnify **Vol. 2:** 44, 202, 360, **424–427**
Magus **Vol. 2:** **552–562**
Maiden **Vol. 1:** 283 f., 498
  Vol. 2: 317
  Vol. 3: 1055, **1071–1073**
Maieutic dialogue **Vol. 3:** 1086
Maim **Vol. 2:** 153, **414 f.**
  Vol. 3: 98, 594
Main meal **Vol. 2:** **520–538**
Main point **Vol. 2:** 157
Maintain **Vol. 1:** 717
  Vol. 2: 326 f.
  Vol. 3: 212
Maintenance **Vol. 1:** 414, 525, 602

Vol. 2: 135, 271, 737
  Vol. 3: 525
Majestic **Vol. 2:** 46, 92
Majesty **Vol. 1:** 95, 99, 163, 185, 344, 559, 618,
  732
  Vol. 2: 44, 46, 71, 80, 146, 217, 338, **424–427**,
  432
  Vol. 3: 52, 317, 342, 381, 514, 632, 718, 848,
  1033
Majority **Vol. 1:** 95, 97, 541, 686, 732
Make **Vol. 1:** 378, 383, 387, 471, 474, 477, 520,
  523, 732
  Vol. 2: 77, 252
  Vol. 3: 350, **1152–1155**
Make alive **Vol. 1:** 643, 677
  Vol. 2: **476–484**, 865
  Vol. 3: 257
Make amends **Vol. 1:** 308
Make clear **Vol. 3:** **316 f.**
Make crooked **Vol. 2:** 370
Make desolate **Vol. 3:** **1004–1008**
Make example of **Vol. 2:** 291
Make foolish **Vol. 3:** **1023–1026**
Make friends **Vol. 2:** 832, 837
Make fun of **Vol. 2:** 436
  Vol. 3: 340
Make great **Vol. 2:** 202, **424–427**
Make holy **Vol. 2:** **224–232**
Make judgments **Vol. 3:** 880
Make known **Vol. 1:** 71, 83, 420, 575 f., 701
  Vol. 2: 217, 358, **488–490**
  Vol. 3: **44–48**, 54, 231, 310 f., 314, 316, **317–
  324**, 569, 760
Make large **Vol. 2:** **424–427**
Make laws **Vol. 2:** **438–451**
Make like **Vol. 2:** **500–508**
  Vol. 3: 350
Make low **Vol. 2:** **259–264**
Make merry **Vol. 2:** 356
Make new **Vol. 2:** 604, **670–674**
Make one **Vol. 3:** 172
Make one's own **Vol. 3:** **747–751**
Make peace **Vol. 2:** **776–783**
Make plain **Vol. 2:** 488
Make ready **Vol. 3:** **118–120**
Make righteous **Vol. 2:** 94
Make room **Vol. 1:** **728–744**
Make ruler **Vol. 3:** 570
Make a show **Vol. 2:** 352
Make a speech **Vol. 3:** 820
Make sport **Vol. 2:** 436
Make straight **Vol. 1:** 411
Make strong **Vol. 3:** **716–718**
Make sufficient **Vol. 3:** **728–730**
Make visible **Vol. 3:** 312, **317–324**
Make void **Vol. 2:** 43
  Vol. 3: 773
Make war **Vol. 3:** 362, **958–967**
Make waste **Vol. 3:** 867
Make wise **Vol. 3:** **1026–1034**
Make worthy **Vol. 3:** **348 f.**
Maker **Vol. 1:** **376–389**
  Vol. 2: 655
  Vol. 3: **1153–1155**

Makeshift **Vol. 1:** 610
Malachi **Vol. 1:** 66
  Vol. 2: 318
  Vol. 3: 79, 853, 1089
Malachite **Vol. 3:** 396
Malady **Vol. 2:** 167
Malaria **Vol. 1:** 163
Malaysian tribes **Vol. 1:** 308
Malcontent **Vol. 2:** 145
Male **Vol. 1:** 308
  Vol. 2: 161, 287, 410, 562, **569–571**
  Vol. 3: 1055, 1062 f., 1065, 1067, 1072
Malediction **Vol. 1:** 416
Malefactor **Vol. 2:** 148
  Vol. 3: 27, 965
Malevolent **Vol. 2:** 552
Malformation **Vol. 1:** 560
Malice **Vol. 1:** 110, 231, 259, 631
  Vol. 2: 270, 379, 463, 676
Malicious **Vol. 2:** 149
Malignant **Vol. 1:** 203, 520
Malinowski, B. **Vol. 3:** 1125
Malta **Vol. 3:** 561, 683
Maltese **Vol. 3:** 96
Maltreat **Vol. 1:** 162, 285
  Vol. 2: 50
Mambres **Vol. 2:** 557
Mammon **Vol. 1:** 138, 684
  Vol. 2: 73, 255, 286, 382, **829–853**
  Vol. 3: 576, 1054
Mamre **Vol. 2:** 557
  Vol. 3: 782
Man **Vol. 1:** 50, 57, 59, 84, 87, 103, 114–116, 126, 242, 382, 472, 521 f., 547 f., 621, 640, 665, 667, 672, 674, 677–679, 701, 705, 708, 720, 722, 732
  Vol. 2: 46, 65, 94, 160–162, 180–185, 196, 266, 287, 349, 390, 483, 508, 545, **562–572**, 581, 600, 646, 661–663, 715, 739, 781, 813, 819, 889
  Vol. 3: 41, 117, 133, 167, 359, 614 f., 620, 630, 632, 678, 680, 687, 691, 776, 915, 1055 f., 1058, 1148
Man, first **Vol. 2:** 46, 159, 504
Man, second **Vol. 1:** 86, 520, 665
Man of God **Vol. 3:** 77 f.
Man of lawlessness **Vol. 2:** 447
  Vol. 3: 319
Man of sin **Vol. 1:** 73, 125
Man-centred **Vol. 1:** 501
Manage **Vol. 2:** 247–256
Management **Vol. 2:** 253–256
Manager **Vol. 2:** 254
Manasseh **Vol. 1:** 655
  Vol. 2: 306, 318, 374, 555, 649
  Vol. 3: 426, 450, 872, 962
Mandaean **Vol. 1:** 89, 422, 653
  Vol. 3: 921, 936
Mandaeism **Vol. 2:** 278, 491, 646, 830
Mandate **Vol. 2:** 607
Manetho **Vol. 2:** 310
Manhood **Vol. 1:** 93, 302
Mania **Vol. 3:** 1024
Manichaean **Vol. 3:** 108, 231

Manichaeism **Vol. 1:** 422
  Vol. 2: 491, 674
Manifest **Vol. 1:** 711
  Vol. 2: 216 f., 359, **487 f.**
  Vol. 3: 309 f., 316
Manifestation **Vol. 1:** 232, 542, 586, 609, 648, 677, 679, 711
  Vol. 2: 447
  Vol. 3: 570
Manilius **Vol. 3:** 124
Manipulate **Vol. 2:** 556
  Vol. 3: 1098
Mankind **Vol. 1:** 96, 211, 470, 548, 616 f., 672 f., 675, 677 f., 694, 720 f., 737
  Vol. 2: 332, 342
  Vol. 3: 628
Manliness **Vol. 2:** 562
  Vol. 3: 926
Manna **Vol. 1:** 195, 205, **248–253**
  Vol. 2: 218, 268 f., 272, 628, 637, 674, 871 f., 928
  Vol. 3: 383, 427, 508, 706, 787, 804, 815, 893
Manner **Vol. 1:** 708
  Vol. 2: 369, 437, 550
Manner of life **Vol. 1:** 469, 623
  Vol. 2: 95, 243, 264, 308, 475
  Vol. 3: 349
Manning **Vol. 1:** 733
Mansion **Vol. 3:** 229
Manslaughter **Vol. 1:** 151
Mantle **Vol. 3:** 739
Mantology **Vol. 2:** 621
Manual work **Vol. 2:** 820
  Vol. 3: 813
Manufacture **Vol. 1:** 378, 723
Manumission **Vol. 1:** 267
  Vol. 3: 95, 379, 593 f., 597 f.
Manure **Vol. 3:** 469
Manuscripts **Vol. 1:** 53, 70
Many **Vol. 1:** **95–97**, 514, 575
  Vol. 2: 130, 179, 525 f., 530, 532, 543, 719, 800, 854
  Vol. 3: 115, 195–197, 275, 611 f., 682
Many waters **Vol. 3:** 1006
Map **Vol. 3:** 483
Mar **Vol. 1:** 468
  Vol. 2: 287 f.
Marah **Vol. 1:** 202
  Vol. 2: 637
Maranatha **Vol. 2:** 530 f., **886–935**
  Vol. 3: 245, 826
Marathon **Vol. 1:** 624
Marble **Vol. 3:** 391
Marcellus of Ancyra **Vol. 2:** 506 f.
March **Vol. 1:** 342, 409
  Vol. 2: 451
  Vol. 3: 945
Marcion **Vol. 1:** 55, 379
  Vol. 3: 108, 401
Marcosians **Vol. 3:** 640
Marcus Aurelius **Vol. 1:** 68, 232, 720
  Vol. 2: 657, 776
  Vol. 3: 739
Marduk **Vol. 1:** 140

Vol. 2: 200, 553
  Vol. 3: 1102, 1105, 1125
Marduk-Ellil hymns **Vol. 3:** 1088
Mari **Vol. 3:** 46, 1089
Mariamne **Vol. 2:** 550
Marinus **Vol. 3:** 453
Marital **Vol. 1:** 506
Mark **Vol. 1:** 69, 114–116, 134, 199, 235, 399,
  556, 655, 727, 735, 739
  Vol. 2: 33, 149, 182, 284, 291, 329, 390, 411,
  431, **572–575,** 626, 701, 847
  Vol. 3: 60, 63 f., 108, 310, 490, 497, 500,
  1065
Mark, ending of **Vol. 3:** 294
Mark Antony **Vol. 3:** 731
Mark of the beast **Vol. 2:** 574
Mark of Cain **Vol. 2:** 572, 626
Mark of esteem **Vol. 3:** 816
Markah **Vol. 3:** 453
Market **Vol. 1:** 189, 225, **267 f.,** 283, 352, 625
  Vol. 2: 273, 286
  Vol. 3: 50, 378, 381, 432, 943
Marriage **Vol. 1:** 103, 138, 153, 155, 207, 278,
  308, 335, 368, 384, 408, 414, 426, 448, 457,
  494–496, 498–500, 502, 505, 507, 544, 560
  f., 625 f., 675, 678, 682, 688, 698, 717
  Vol. 2: 32, 59, 126, 139, 141, 188, 221, 230,
  311, 317, 349, 400, 412, 444, 517, 541, 545,
  549, 564, 570 f., **575–590,** 691, 722, 923
  Vol. 3: 35, 95 f., 181 f., 188, 191, 219, 225,
  325, 356, 380, 497, 534–544, 562, 583, 606,
  913, 1055, 1057, 1059, 1064 f., 1072, 1075,
  1093, 1164 f., 1167
Marriage bed **Vol. 2:** **586 f**
Marriage ceremony **Vol. 2:** 576, 578
Marriage feast **Vol. 1:** 274
  Vol. 3: 869
Marriage laws **Vol. 1:** 61
  Vol. 2: 511, **576–581,** 585
Marriage supper **Vol. 3:** 1068
Married **Vol. 1:** 145, 152, 411, 496 f.
  Vol. 2: 87
  Vol. 3: 173, 1055
Marry **Vol. 2:** **575–582,** 608, 715, 738
  Vol. 3: 545
Mars **Vol. 2:** 85
Marsh **Vol. 3:** 992
Marshall **Vol. 1:** 521
Martha **Vol. 1:** 278
  Vol. 2: 418, 929
  Vol. 3: 980, 1059–1061
Martyr **Vol. 1:** 222, 257, 312, 406, 435, 438,
  440, 455, 474, 529, 645, 649, 694, 709
  Vol. 2: 49, 117, 133, 193, 207, 290, 365, 412,
  712, 724, 767, 854
  Vol. 3: 97, 113, 157, 193–196, 245, 271, 436,
  592, 686, 865, 893, 926, 1035
Martyr-theology **Vol. 3:** 165
Martyrdom **Vol. 1:** 163, 235, 403, 440, 647,
  651, 653, 707
  Vol. 2: 117, 361, 542, 824, 854 f.
  Vol. 3: 82, 121, 137, 165, 212, 240, 279, 291,
  387, 432, 579, 1042, 1168
Martyrology **Vol. 2:** 368

Marvel **Vol. 1:** 381
  Vol. 2: **621–626**
Marvellous **Vol. 2:** **621–626,** 669
Marx, Karl **Vol. 3:** 968
Marxist analysis **Vol. 3:** 971
Marxsen, Willi **Vol. 3:** **284–286**
Mary **Vol. 1:** 104, 120, 187, 213, 256, 278, 506,
  512, 530, 559, 623, 668
  Vol. 2: 34, 86, 118 f., 261, 332 f., 353, 358
  Vol. 3: 30, 430, 555, 652, 655 f., **660–664,**
  674, 908, 1009, 1060–1062, 1068, 1070–
  1073
Mary of Bethany **Vol. 1:** 540
  Vol. 2: 418
  Vol. 3: 980, 1059–1061
Mary Magdalene **Vol. 1:** 266
  Vol. 3: 115, 276, 287 f., 296, 475, 860, 980,
  1059–1061
Mary, mother of James and Joses **Vol. 3:** 1060,
  1071
Mary, mother of John Mark **Vol. 1:** 642
  Vol. 2: 847
  Vol. 3: 1065, 1071
Mary, wife of Clopas **Vol. 3:** 1061
Masada **Vol. 1:** 435, 627
  Vol. 3: 681, 1117 f.
Mascall, E.L. **Vol. 3:** **334**
Mask **Vol. 1:** 316, 586
Mason **Vol. 1:** 279
  Vol. 3: 915
Masonry **Vol. 1:** 241
Masoretes **Vol. 1:** **63**
Masoretic text **Vol. 1:** 50, **63,** 68, 71
Masquerade **Vol. 3:** 864
Mass **Vol. 1:** 528, 732
  Vol. 2: 788
Mass media **Vol. 3:** 900
Massah **Vol. 2:** 635
  Vol. 3: 800 f., 806
Massilia **Vol. 3:** 149
Mast **Vol. 1:** 241
Mastema **Vol. 1:** 125, 452
  Vol. 3: 468
Master **Vol. 1:** 67, 239, 266, 275, 285, 305, 404,
  416, 440, 462, 474, 480, 482, 484–486, 488,
  494, 609 f., 617, 623, 637 f., 680, 715–717,
  720
  Vol. 2: 84, 155, 180, 258, 281, 330, 435, 450,
  499, **508–520,** 539, 581, 595, 611, 653, 721,
  737, 775, 816 f., 833, 837 f., 859, 890
  Vol. 3: 29, 49, 78, **115 f.,** 121, 572, 582 f.,
  589–599, 716, 759, **765–768,** 776, 916, 928 f.,
  1065, 1152, 1157
Master-builder **Vol. 1:** 377
  Vol. 3: 142 f., 1032
Mastery **Vol. 1:** 265, 460, 571
  Vol. 2: 165
  Vol. 3: 678
Match-maker **Vol. 1:** 475
Material **Vol. 1:** 209, 458 f., 513, 522, 537, 562,
  589, 639, 642, 676, 680, 687, 710, 716, 744
  Vol. 2: 99, 187, 200, 265 f., 284, 287, 659,
  837, 840 f., 844, 846
  Vol. 3: 208, 276, 435, 678, 1058

Material things **Vol. 2:** 32, 328, 356
Material world **Vol. 1:** 58, 139, 233, 250, 387
Materialism **Vol. 1:** 532
  Vol. 2: 488
Materialistic **Vol. 1:** 186, 583
  Vol. 2: 275
Materialization **Vol. 2:** 337
Mathematics **Vol. 1:** 140, 665
  Vol. 2: 743
  Vol. 3: 349, 399, 823, 1081
Mattathias **Vol. 1:** 63
  Vol. 3: 658, 961
Matter **Vol. 1:** 55, 66, 236, 380, 443, 450, 562, 704 f., 711
  Vol. 2: 394, 402, 452, 505
  Vol. 3: 146, 273, 595, 941, **1119–1123, 1147–1152, 1155–1158**
Matthan **Vol. 3:** 655
Matthat **Vol. 3:** 655
Matthew **Vol. 1:** 69, 116, 134, 181 f., 199, 571
  Vol. 2: 217, 315, 351 f., 467, 691, 715
  Vol. 3: 52, 482, 494 f., 654–659, 757–759
Matthias **Vol. 1:** 129, 132
  Vol. 2: 299, 787
  Vol. 3: 387
Mature **Vol. 2:** 62, 269, 391
  Vol. 3: 350, 779, 1031
Maturity **Vol. 1:** 92 f., 284, 302, 325, 474, 565, 568, 647
  Vol. 2: 59, 64 f., 103, 129, 187, 563, 721
  Vol. 3: 403, 702, 775, 1118
Maxim **Vol. 2:** 757
Maximilla **Vol. 3:** 89
Mazaeus **Vol. 2:** 848
Mazdaism **Vol. 1:** 107, 653
  Vol. 2: 492
Mazzoth **Vol. 2:** 522
Meagre **Vol. 2:** 821, 826
Meal **Vol. 1:** 212 f., 219, 250, 272, 282, 292, 308, 367, 369, 414, 480, 629 f., 632–634, 641
  Vol. 2: 74, 150, 228, 271–274, 276, 286, 354–356, 520, 522, 581, 599
  Vol. 3: 105, 119, 144, 208, 422, 431, 443, 508, 545, 547 f., 588, 706, 744 f., 750, 819, 845 f., 922, 1074
Meal-offering **Vol. 3:** 238, 243, 423
Mean **Vol. 3:** 820–826
Meaning **Vol. 1:** 57, 68, 250, 338, 381, 551, 574, 614, 629, 632 f., 676, 678, 737
  Vol. 2: 67, 103, 106, 213, 281, 326, 332, 377, 384, 434, 891
  Vol. 3: 102 f., 112, 520, 533, 878, **1081–1119,** 1124, 1137, 1140, 1143
Meaningless **Vol. 1:** 522
  Vol. 2: 683, 729
  Vol. 3: 1136
Means **Vol. 1:** 580 f., 681
  Vol. 2: 164, 167, **845–847**
  Vol. 3: 324 f., 1182
Means of deliverance **Vol. 3: 216–221**
Means of ordering **Vol. 3:** 1078
Means of testing **Vol. 3: 808–810**
Measure **Vol. 1:** 602, 711, 728, 733–735, 738, 740 f.

Vol. 2: 122, 131, 266, 362, 366, 369, 424, 448, 683, 698, 891
  Vol. 3: 399–404, 436, 559, 799, 841, 935, 948, 1085
Measurement **Vol. 3:** 399
Measuring-line **Vol. 2:** 298
Meat **Vol. 1:** 226, 230, 249, 261, 350–352, 630, 643, 671, 731
  Vol. 2: 235, 268 f., 272 f., **284–286**
  Vol. 3: 432, 444 f., 566, 802
Meat offered to idols **Vol. 2: 284–286,** 721
Mebaqqer **Vol. 3:** 566
Mechanistic **Vol. 3:** 162
Meddle **266 f.**
Meddlesome **Vol. 2: 552–562**
Medea **Vol. 2:** 553
Medes **Vol. 2:** 678 f.
  Vol. 3: 957
Media **Vol. 1:** 141
Medians **Vol. 2:** 557
Mediate **Vol. 1:** 102, 210, 375, 380 f., 466
  Vol. 2: 388, 402–404
  Vol. 3: 646
Mediation **Vol. 1:** 282, 346, 374, 570 f.
Mediator **Vol. 1:** 101, 103, 127, 238, 294, 304, **365–376,** 380, 382, 450 f., 485, 617, 668 f.
  Vol. 2: 72, 80, 84, 117, 167, 178, 343, 442 f., 448, 492, 603 f., 721, 781, 874
  Vol. 3: 85, 197, 206, 216, 287, 314, 641, 644, 647, 751, 1029
Mediatorial **Vol. 3:** 554
Medical **Vol. 1:** 302, 443, 692
  Vol. 2: 153, **164,** 166–168, 170, 414
  Vol. 3: 112, 148
Medical prescriptions **Vol. 3:** 915
Medical test **Vol. 3:** 799
Medicament **Vol. 3:** 448
Medicinal **Vol. 1:** 120, 319
  Vol. 2: 211, 710, 712
  Vol. 3: 443
Medicine **Vol. 1:** 119, 140, 381, 484, 577, 742
  Vol. 2: 166–168, 256, 271, **552–562**
  Vol. 3: 709, 738
Meditation **Vol. 1:** 245, 338, 521, 653
  Vol. 3: 178
Mediterranean **Vol. 2:** 319
  Vol. 3: 757, 983 f.
Medium **Vol. 1:** 512
  Vol. 2: 96, 554
  Vol. 3: 76, 270, 474
Mediumship **Vol. 2: 559**
Meek **Vol. 1:** 217, 518, 570
  Vol. 2: 194, **256–264,** 380
  Vol. 3: 807
Meekness **Vol. 1:** 731
  Vol. 2: 256–264
Meet **Vol. 1:** 734
  Vol. 2: 882–885
  Vol. 3: 119, 603, 860
Meet together **Vol. 3:** 143
Meeting **Vol. 1:** 267, 291, 296, 302, 324 f., 363, 466, 587, 698, 713
  Vol. 2: 161, 231, 416
  Vol. 3: 179, 185

Meeting place **Vol. 2:** 250
  Vol. 3: 255
Megara **Vol. 1:** 414
Megiddo **Vol. 3:** 962
Megilloth **Vol. 1:** 58, **63**
Meir, Rabbi **Vol. 1:** 67
Melchi **Vol. 3:** 655, 658
Melchizedek **Vol. 1:** 80, 99 f., 208, 214, 581,
  619, 677, 731
  Vol. 2: 36, 67, 178, 378, 447, 467, 505, 508,
  590–593, 614, 693 f., 781
  Vol. 3: 36, 41 f., 187, 189, 228, 365, 433,
  435 f., 457, 616, 627, 852, 854, 922, 947
Melchizedekians **Vol. 3:** 36
Melito **Vol. 3:** 401
Melody **Vol. 3:** 674
Melt **Vol. 1:** 682 f.
  Vol. 2: 95, 452
  Vol. 3: 1105
Memar Markah **Vol. 3:** 452, 462
Member **Vol. 1:** 153, 189, **229–242**, 275, 278,
  301, 303, 305, 310, 341, 344, 368, 433, 475,
  484, 496, 500 f., 518, 534, 539, 542, 554–
  556, 568, 596, 598, 601, 607, 614, 618, 625,
  628, 633, 641 f., 653, 689, 691, 700, 732,
  739, 741
  Vol. 2: 51, 83, 141, 148, 157–160, **247–251**,
  273, 312, 314, 350, 363, 366, 385, 414 f.,
  450, 499, 518, 619, 794
  Vol. 3: 364, 701, 1180
Membership **Vol. 1:** 144, 148, 159, 181, 280,
  287 f., 299, 308, 364, 414, 539, 641, 693
  Vol. 2: 310 f., 377, 441
  Vol. 3: 1180
Memorial **Vol. 1:** 263, 624, 632
  Vol. 3: 230, 237, 244, 246, 423, 840
Memorial sign **Vol. 3:** 236
Memory **Vol. 1:** 431, 471, 627, 629, 631, 683
  Vol. 2: 335, 410, 568
  Vol. 3: 64, **230–247**, 477, 488, 493, 593, 657,
  680, 776, 1054, 1060, 1122
Memphis **Vol. 1:** 530
  Vol. 3: 1088
Memra **Vol. 1:** **63**
  Vol. 3: 1116
Men of faithfulness **Vol. 1:** 598
Men Tyrannus **Vol. 3:** 153
Menander **Vol. 1:** 469
  Vol. 2: 438, 457, 648, 757
  Vol. 3: 279, 463
Mendacious **Vol. 2:** **470–474**
Menelaus **Vol. 3:** 259
Menial **Vol. 1:** 239
  Vol. 3: 609, 917
Menorah **Vol. 3:** 789
Menstruation **Vol. 1:** 151
  Vol. 2: 577
  Vol. 3: 102–104
Mental **Vol. 1:** 240, 527, 676, 680 f., 711, 715
  Vol. 2: 163, 284
Mental strain **Vol. 3:** 858
Mentality **Vol. 2:** **616–620**
Mention **Vol. 1:** 619
  Vol. 3: **230–247**

Mention honourably **Vol. 3:** 816
Mercenaries **Vol. 2:** 325, 801
  Vol. 3: 139, 1054
Merchandise **Vol. 2:** 97 f., 236
Merchant **Vol. 1:** 117
  Vol. 2: 502
  Vol. 3: 395, 1054
Merciful **Vol. 1:** 349, 356, 616 f.
  Vol. 2: **594–598**, 652
  Vol. 3: **148–166**, 167
Merciless **Vol. 2:** 97, 154, **594–598**
  Vol. 3: 1074
Mercury **Vol. 2:** 85
Mercy **Vol. 1:** 112 f., 116, 180, 185, 189, 191,
  197, 228, 258, 261, 335, 345, 356, 359, 464,
  570, 593, 611, 615, 620, 666, 671, 679, 687,
  730, 732 f.
  Vol. 2: 68, 71 f., 78, 104 f., 117 f., 121, 123,
  146, 154, 168, 245, 257, 267, 353, 357 f.,
  364, 388, 407, 413, 435, 443, 449, 492, 517,
  543 f., 546, 550, 567, **593–601**, 607, 694, 770,
  807, 824, 826, 840, 842, 865, 867, 875
  Vol. 3: 52, 56, 98, 118, 152, 161, 202, 211,
  215, 224, 241, 358 f., 365, 409, 428 f., 528,
  553, 578, 672, 912, 917, 947, 1053 f., 1074,
  1166
Mercy-seat **Vol. 1:** 114, 151, 280
  Vol. 2: 294, 614
  Vol. 3: **148–166**, 812, 815
Meribah **Vol. 2:** 635, 638
  Vol. 3: 800 f.
Merit **Vol. 1:** 329, 399, 478, 489, 538 f.
  Vol. 2: 44, 141, 301, 813
  Vol. 3: 136, 140–144, 342, 348, 358 f., 370,
  825, 853, 1053
Meritorious **Vol. 1:** 702
  Vol. 2: 873
  Vol. 3: 722
Merkabah **Vol. 1:** 527
Merneptah **Vol. 2:** 305
Meron **Vol. 3:** 1010, 1012
Merriment **Vol. 2:** 354, 430
Mesha Stone (→ Moabite Stone)
Meshach **Vol. 2:** 628
  Vol. 3: 110
Mesopotamia **Vol. 1:** 177
  Vol. 3: 407, 421, 730, 782, 787, 1009, 1029,
  1088
Mespila **Vol. 2:** 678
Mess of pottage **Vol. 2:** 316
Message **Vol. 1:** 133, 171, 197, 202, 217, 239,
  244, 246–248, 275, 282, 325, 334, 358, 397,
  399–401, 409, 411, 468, 482, 486, 489,
  511 f., 527, 529, 541, 551, 600 f., 638, 647,
  659, 717, 719
  Vol. 2: 37, 74 f., 77 f., 107, 109, 112–114,
  126 f., 135, 171–173, 175 f., 179, 217, 233,
  243, 281, 315, 332, 338, 356–359, 383 f.,
  387, 403 f., 435, 627, 718 f., 749, 765, 843 f.,
  918
  Vol. 3: **44–48**, 52 f., 55–57, 168, 170 f., 174,
  522, 570, 601, 630, 758, 764, 779, 838, 905,
  914, 942, 950, 1089, 1094, 1103 f., 1110,
  1113, 1120, 1154

Messenger **Vol. 1: 101–104**, 127–130, 133–135, 163, 279, 280, 283, 301, 304, 416, 430, 450, 467, 475, 509, 595, 623, 686, 690, 727
Vol. 2: 107, 109–111, 179, 185, 192, 314, 328, 403, 426, 503, 806
Vol. 3: 45, 49 f., 52, 212, 231, 471, 642 f., 746, 848, 857, 1001, 1043, 1089, 1095, 1097 f., 1107
Messenger of Satan **Vol. 3:** 857
Messiah **Vol. 1: 53**, 63, 72, 77, 79, 123–125, 141, 144–146, 170 f., 177 f., 213, 252 f., 276, 296, 302, 305, 321, 323, 330, 347, 373, 381, 407, 409, 414, 426–428, 451, 455, 470, 473, 544 f., 560, 581, 586, 607, 610, 612 f., 627, 629, 633, 661, 665, 675, 700, 717, 720, 724
Vol. 2: 30, 32, 56, 61, 75, 101, 109, 147 f., 159, 170, 176, 241, 245, 252, 257 f., 282, 294, 308, **313 f**, 328, **334–343**, 353, 375, 377–379, 385, 400, 411, 458, 498, 503, 515, 521, 558, 580 f., 585, 591 f., 602–604, 607, 609 f., 612–614, 640, 701, 708, 712, 739, 762, 791 f., 794, 808, 811 f., 819, 888, 892, 898 f., 902–904, 927, 930
Vol. 3: 30, 34–36, 46–48, 59, 62, 66, 79 f., 82, 121, 147, 170, 192, 194, 212, 218, 221, 225, 244 f., 250, 271, 293 f., 296, 299 f., 311 f., 358, 378, 397, 432, 462, 490, 506, 517, 522, 524, 529 f., 557, 566, 575, 607, 610, 616, 618–621, 633 f., 637, 639, 642 f., 646, 651 f., 654, 657 f., 662, 690, 693, 699, 710, 715, 722, 735, 804, 829, 858, 863, 867, 883, 906, 919, 926, 956, 967, 1007, 1016, 1044, 1072, 1109 f., 1112, 1122
Messiah, Davidic **Vol. 1:** 426
Vol. 2: 337
Messiah, dying (→ Suffering messiah)
Messiah of hope **Vol. 3: 969 f**.
Messiahship **Vol. 1:** 428, 473
Vol. 2: 282, 339–341, 343, 379
Vol. 3: 110, 131, 717, 864, 1061
Messianic **Vol. 1:** 72, 114, 123, 174, 210, 219, 250, 320–323, 329, 406–408, 473, 599, 633, 666
Vol. 2: 31, 100, 104, 110 f., 165, 241, 252, 309, 313 f., **334–343**, 353, 368, 375 f., 379, 389, 495, 515, 566, 581, 591 f., 599, 604, 610, 629 f., 638, 654, 672, 677, 706, 712, 717, 730 f., 761, 780
Vol. 3: 114, 221, 342, 382 f., 390, 392 f., 395, 430, 519, 610, 615 f., 618 f., 621, 633, 639, 642, 646, 649–652, 655, 657, 663, 697–699, 735, 791, 831, 851, 863, 921, 961, 1006 f., 1060, 1070, 1161
Messianic age **Vol. 1:** 175, 185, 253, 354, 510, 543 f., 700, 724
Vol. 2: 151, 294, 585, 591, 629, 640, 698 f., 792, 798, 859, 892
Vol. 3: 378, 649, 658, 951, 1121
Messianic banquet **Vol. 2:** 270, 276, 761, 871
Messianic claims **Vol. 3:** 343, 442, 462, 649
Messianic community **Vol. 1:** 302
Vol. 2: 30, 34, 207, 731–733
Vol. 3: 182, 699
Messianic consciousness **Vol. 2:** 340 f., 731

Messianic expectation **Vol. 2:** 110, 245, 335, 337 f., 341, 590
Vol. 3: 462, 616, 637, 654, 843, 872
Messianic hope **Vol. 1:** 426, 570, 629
Vol. 2: 174, 337
Vol. 3: 147 f., 636, 648, 651, 867
Messianic interpretation **Vol. 2:** 31, 557
Messianic king **Vol. 1:** 100, 210
Vol. 2: 374, 412, 701
Messianic kingdom **Vol. 3:** 579
Messianic presence **Vol. 2:** 279
Messianic pretender **Vol. 2:** 313
Messianic rule **Vol. 1:** 67
Messianic secret **Vol. 1:** 335
Vol. 2: 341, 379, 752 f., 916
Vol. 3: 131, 320, 503, **506–510**, 619
Messianic shepherd **Vol. 3:** 567 f.
Messianic speculation **Vol. 3:** 655 f.
Messianic titles **Vol. 1: 63**
Vol. 2: 378, 380
Vol. 3: 219, 367, 615, 656
Messianic typology **Vol. 3:** 191
Messianic week **Vol. 3:** 658
Messianic woes **Vol. 3:** 695, 697, 722, 956
Messianic work **Vol. 2:** 165
Messianism **Vol. 1:** 427
Vol. 2: 258, 337–339, 379, 903, 921
Vol. 3: 30, 656
Metal **Vol. 1:** 653 f.
Vol. 2: 96 f., 288
Vol. 3: 396, 483, 498, 808
Metallurgy **Vol. 2:** 98
Metaphor **Vol. 1:** 50, 93, 122, 144, 169, 186 f., 202, 204, 219 f., 224, 239–241, 247, 255, 259 f., 281 f., 284 f., 290, 300, 305 f., 313, 315–317, 320–322, 324 f., 364, 372, 386 f., 390, 405 f., 409, 421, 423 f., 431, 438, 444, 447–449, 471, 477, 479, 481 f., 527, 538, 546, 556, 558 f., 565, 577, 586, 609 f., 617, 635, 643, 645, 648, 650 f., 654, 656–658, 670, 721, 723, 726
Vol. 2: 27–30, 40–42, 91, 155–158, 166, 169 f., 180–182, 185, 211, 224, 234 f., 247–252, 254 f., 259, 264, 266, 268 f., 278 f., 285, 291, 303, 307, 313, 349, 351, 364, 370, 385, 412–415, 421, 423, 444, 451, 462, 479, 484, 486 f., 490, 493, 506, 509, 573, 583–585, 587, 598 f., 612, 705, 707 f., 711, 714, 727 f., 732 f., 738, 743–760. 764. 806. 810, 821, 855, 881, 927
Vol. 3: 50, 99, 109 f., 112, 119, 121, 155, 158, 177, 189, 203, 208, 224, 272, 379, 432, 446 f., 449, 477, 497 f., 505, 525, 529, 534, 557–559, 564–567, 597, 600 f., 674, 690, 695, 701, 703, 722, 730 f., 733–735, 794, 858, 865, 867 f., 871, 874, 902, 911, 914, 948, 951 f., 963, 991 f., 996, 1002, 1010 f., 1049, 1055, 1069, 1072, 1074, 1134, 1137 f.
Metaphysical **Vol. 1:** 422, 492, 561 f.
Vol. 2: 184, 242, 396
Vol. 3: 646–648, 906, 1133, 1136
Metaphysical proof **Vol. 2:** 77
Metaphysics **Vol. 1:** 53, 57, **63 f.**, 665
Vol. 3: 1034, 1081, 1085

Metatron **Vol. 3:** 35
Mete out **Vol. 1:** 572
Metempsychosis **Vol. 1:** 594
Meteorite **Vol. 1:** 610
Meteorological **Vol. 2:** 191
Method **Vol. 1:** 486, 533, 569, 582, 684
   Vol. 2: 311, 903
   Vol. 3: 59, **935–943**
Methuselah **Vol. 2:** 681, 698
Metonymy **Vol. 1:** 267
   Vol. 2: 273
   Vol. 3: 198, 434, 815
Micah **Vol. 1:** 66, 109, 170
   Vol. 2: 250
   Vol. 3: 33, 79, 367, 1006
Micaiah **Vol. 2:** 458
   Vol. 3: 478
Mice **Vol. 2:** 831
Michael **Vol. 1:** 83, 101–103, **104**, 452, 504, 508, 572
   Vol. 2: 191, 591, 608, 642, 763, 779
   Vol. 3: 35, 270, 345, 457, 471, 616, 1054
Michal **Vol. 3:** 1057
Microcosm **Vol. 1:** 232, 521
   Vol. 3: 513
Midday **Vol. 3:** 846
Middle **Vol. 1:** 372
Middle Assyrian laws **Vol. 3:** 94
Middle way **Vol. 3:** 939
Middleman **Vol. 1:** 374
   Vol. 3: 50
Midian **Vol. 1:** 691
   Vol. 2: 636
   Vol. 3: 33, 201, 459, 1013
Midianites **Vol. 2:** 367, 635, 638
   Vol. 3: 206, 874
Midnight **Vol. 1:** 284, 420, 633
   Vol. 2: 136, 881
Midrash **Vol. 1:** **64**, 67, 485, 628, 630
   Vol. 2: 125, 187, 755, 913
   Vol. 3: 487, 494, 654, 656, 706, 804
Mien **Vol. 1:** 708
Might **Vol. 1:** 95, 142, 167, 175, 228, 336, 347, 466, 531, 638, 649
   Vol. 2: 70, 78, 191, 200, 510, **601–616**, 650, 654, 843, 859
   Vol. 3: 45, 97, 99, 121, 230, 258, 274, 549, 588, 617, 645, 711, **712–714, 716–718**, 736, 755, 783, 993, 995
Mighty **Vol. 2:** 49, 369, 601–616
   Vol. 3: **712–714, 716–718**
Mighty deeds **Vol. 2:** **424–427**
Mighty God **Vol. 2:** 86
Mighty One **Vol. 2:** 70, 602
Mighty works **Vol. 1:** 600
   Vol. 2: 383
Migrate **Vol. 2:** 308
Mikwaoth **Vol. 3:** 989
Mild **Vol. 2:** 105, **256–259**
Military **Vol. 1:** 340, 377, 475 f., 505, 536, 553, 645–647, 650, 680, 710, 732
   Vol. 2: 104, 220, 788, 898
   Vol. 3: 51, 145, 248 f., 502
Military commander **Vol. 3:** **958–967**

Military force **Vol. 2:** 601 f.
Military scribe **Vol. 3:** 478
Military service **Vol. 1:** 687
   Vol. 2: 306, 578
Military terms **Vol. 3:** **958–967**
Milk **Vol. 1:** 282, 682 f.
   Vol. 2: **268 f.**, 452
   Vol. 3: 566
Milkless **Vol. 1:** 515
Mill **Vol. 3:** **390–394**, 1058
Millenarianism **Vol. 2:** 905
Millennium **Vol. 1:** **52**, 53, 64, 254, 508
   Vol. 2: 389, 690, **697–703**, 795, 809, 901, 931
   Vol. 3: 179, 277, 305, 470 f.
Millstone **Vol. 3:** **390–394**, 1013
Mind **Vol. 1:** 106, 231–233, 245, 266, 350, 355–357, 398, 413, 443, 448, 459 f., 501 f., 514 f., 518, 523, 546 f., 549, 555, 557, 568, 587, 594 f., 636, 638, 676, 678, 680, 700, 706, 708, 723, 739, 742
   Vol. 2: 156, 172, 174, 177, 181 f., 212 f., 260, 282, 360, 390–393, 398, 406 f., 422, 437, 476, 564 f., 567, 590, **616–620**, 676, 781, 832, 884 f.
   Vol. 3: 101, **122–133**, 204, 221, **230–247**, 558, 672, 712, 724, 760, 789, 824, 826, 1036
Mind of Christ **Vol. 3:** 129
Mindful **Vol. 3:** 230, 1038
Minerva **Vol. 2:** 85
   Vol. 3: 1071
Mingle **Vol. 3:** 430
Mining **Vol. 2:** 96 f.
Minister **Vol. 1:** 74, 462, 476
   Vol. 2: 381
   Vol. 3: 115, 228, 545, 729, 754 f., 758, 807, 813, 853, 855
Minister of death **Vol. 1:** 101
Ministry **Vol. 1:** 175, 192, 219, 329, 403, 419, 429, 477 f., 488, 515 f., 559, 568, 570, 613, 684, 689, 724 f., 735, 742
   Vol. 2: 75, 118, 148, 163, 168, 187, 193, 299, 341, 447, 517, 543, 799, 898, 902, 927, 929
   Vol. 3: 58, 59, 88 f., 168 f., 171, 182, 323, 552, 603, 659, 696–698, 790, 804, 866, 980, 1011, 1060 f., 1067
Ministry of reconciliation **Vol. 3:** 1111 f.
Ministry of women **Vol. 3:** **1065–1067**
Minor **Vol. 1:** 92, 280 f., 477, 509, 568
Minor judges **Vol. 2:** 363
Minor Prophets **Vol. 1:** **66**
Minority **Vol. 1:** 95, 97, 686
   Vol. 2: 254
Mint **Vol. 1:** 704
   Vol. 2: **210 f.**, 573, 847
Miracle **Vol. 1:** 57 f., 114, 195, 218, 220, 248, 252 f., 313, 341, 384, 427 f., 470, 487, 574, 583, 596, 599 f., 617, 620, 623, 659, 670, 724
   Vol. 2: 85, 91, 151, 164–171, 192, 228, 267, 272, 287, 328, 358, 379, 466, 560 f., 603 f., **620–635**, 654, 749, 858, 863, 901, 920
   Vol. 3: 46, 78 f., 110, 212, 216, 233, 261, 503, 516, 520, 554, 571, 638, 664, 700, 714, 717, 763, 769, 800, 804, 806, 848, 851, 922, 984, 1073, 1108, 1110, 1148, 1150

Miracle-worker **Vol. 3:** 643
Miraculous **Vol. 1:** 398, 595, 616, 619, 629, 671, 739
  Vol. 2: 166–168, 385
Mire **Vol. 3: 915–917**
Miriam **Vol. 2:** 635, 638
  Vol. 3: 77, 1057
Mirror **Vol. 1:** 181
  Vol. 2: 284, 290, 603, 756
Miscarriage **Vol. 1:** 124, **176–188**
Mischief **Vol. 1:** 186
Misconceive **Vol. 1:** 715
Misconduct **Vol. 1:** 506
Miserable **Vol. 1:** 561, 565
  Vol. 2: 825
  Vol. 3: 859
Miserliness **Vol. 1:** 138
Misery **Vol. 1:** 450, 734
  Vol. 2: 393, 595
Misfit **Vol. 2:** 92
Misfortune **Vol. 1:** 84, 162, 203, 561, 563 f., 608, 611, 688, 705
  Vol. 2: 108, 215, 266, 285, 422, 598, 707
  Vol. 3: 264, 528, **719–725**, 856
Mishap **Vol. 1:** 52, 608
Mishmarot **Vol. 1:** 628
Mishnah **Vol. 1:** 51 f., 58 f., **64**, 67, 69 f., 128, 155, 172, 212, 280, 364, 485, 509
  Vol. 2: 43, 174, 583, 881
  Vol. 3: 488, 493, 741, 752, 761, 989
Misinterpretation **Vol. 1:** 429
Mislead **Vol. 1:** 174, 555, 589, 606, 680
  Vol. 2: 457–461, 708
Mismated **Vol. 2: 739–742**
  Vol. 3: 1160–1165
Misogyny **Vol. 3:** 1064
Misplaced **Vol. 1:** 531, 729
Misrepresent **Vol. 1:** 644
  Vol. 2: 281, 655
  Vol. 3: 468, 636
Miss **Vol. 1:** 718
  Vol. 2: 172, 460
  Vol. 3: 835, **952–956**
Miss goal **Vol. 3:** 419
Miss mark **Vol. 1:** 608
  Vol. 2: 457
  Vol. 3: 577
Miss way **Vol. 3:** 419, 585
Missiles **Vol. 3:** 109
Missing **Vol. 1:** 332
  Vol. 3: 910
Mission **Vol. 1:** 95, 127–129, 133, 135, 142, 146, 155, 214, 256, 282, 331, 339, 361, 403, 411, 488, 510, 536, 538, 547, 581, 596, 599, 601, 603, 620, 657, 667, 678, 700, 736
  Vol. 2: 32, 111, 119–121, 126, 150, 169, 173, 222, 257, 272, 275, 309, 314–316, 327, 338, 517, 645, 668, 706, 728, 732, 773, 786 f., 794, 828, 875, 888, 902, 920 f., 924
  Vol. 3: 51, 88, 137, 197, 242, 258, 293, 454, 456, 463, 465 f., 472 f., 506, 526, 532, 546, 567, 580, 613, 626, 644, 682, 695, 698–700, 705, 729, 746, 812, 864, 954, 977, 1108, 1114, 1150

Mission-field **Vol. 3:** 985
Missionary **Vol. 1:** 77, 128, 131–134, 166, 192, 214, 247, 263, 303, 329, 335, 350, 355, 359 f., 547, 551, 570, 599, 650, 662, 686, 688 f., 723, 733, 739
  Vol. 2: 34, 73, 77, 111, 114, 125, 130, 250, 272, 311, 315 f., 360, 493, 573, 727, 740, 781, 927
  Vol. 3: 59 f., 63, 144, 214, 410, 724, 857, 931, 934, 941, 1041, 1152, 1167
Mist **Vol. 2:** 488
  Vol. 3: 1000–1004
Mistake **Vol. 2:** 406, 457, 459, 910, 915
  Vol. 3: 99, 351, 577, 585, 778
Mistress **Vol. 1:** 239, 498
  Vol. 2: 510–520
  Vol. 3: 1055
Mistrust **Vol. 1:** 86, 594
Misunderstanding **Vol. 1:** 121, 443, 498, 502, 544, 601, 643, 680, 693, 719 f.
  Vol. 2: 28, 312, 316, 434
  Vol. 3: 185, 215, 508
Misuse **Vol. 1:** 459, 579, 719
  Vol. 2: 123, 606
Misuse authority **Vol. 2: 606–611**
Mite **Vol. 2:** 850
Mithras **Vol. 1:** 64, 176, 255, 374
  Vol. 3: 138, 501
Mithras liturgy **Vol. 3:** 690
Mitigate **Vol. 2:** 256
Mitigating **Vol. 1:** 500
Mix **Vol. 1:** 69, 289
  Vol. 2: 95 f.
  Vol. 3: 543, **910–917**, 1160
Mixed **Vol. 3:** 470
Mixed marriages **Vol. 1:** 155, 688
  Vol. 2: 126, 250, 581
  Vol. 3: 451, 535 f., 1165
Mixed population **Vol. 2:** 801
Mixer of potions **Vol. 2: 552–562**
Mixture **Vol. 3: 917**
Mnason **Vol. 1:** 167
Mnemonic **Vol. 2:** 685
Moab **Vol. 1:** 208
  Vol. 3: 345, 600, 786, 806, 866, 911, 957
Moabite stone **Vol. 3:** 483
Moabites **Vol. 2:** 373, 677
Mob **Vol. 2: 800 f.**
  Vol. 3: 559, 711, 713
Mock **Vol. 2: 429–436**
  Vol. 3: 253, 340, 343, 563, 570
Mockery **Vol. 1:** 205, 246, 395, 406, 410, 541
  Vol. 2: 287, 378 f., 421, **429–436**
  Vol. 3: 29, 589, 785, 1096
Mode **Vol. 1:** 547, 706 f.
Model **Vol. 1:** 491
  Vol. 2: 151, 284, **290 f.**, 427
  Vol. 3: 99, 336, 854, 899, **903–906**, 1061, 1133, 1135
Moderation **Vol. 1:** 494, 501 f., 647
  Vol. 2: 99, 103, 130, 266
  Vol. 3: 103, 833, 922
Modest **Vol. 2:** 260
Modesty **Vol. 1:** 501

503

Vol. 2: 257
Vol. 3: 27, 445, **561–564**, 1034
Modia **Vol. 3:** 961
Modification **Vol. 1:** 541
Moira **Vol. 2:** 303
Moisten **Vol. 2:** 188
Mold **Vol. 2:** 465
Molech **Vol. 1:** 655
   Vol. 2: 375
Molest **Vol. 3:** 997
Moloch **Vol. 1:** 463
   Vol. 2; 83, 375
   Vol. 3: 94
Moltmann, Jürgen **Vol. 2:** 908 f.
   Vol. 3: 968–972, 975
Moment **Vol. 2:** 925
   Vol. 3: 255, 827, **833–839**
Monarchical **Vol. 1:** 190, 192, 198, 200
Monarchy **Vol. 1:** 52, 55, 109, 121 f., 195 f.,
   425 f., 478, 716
   Vol. 2: 319 f., 335, **373–389**, 822, 841
   Vol. 3: 33, 79, 828
Monastery **Vol. 1:** 641
Monastic **Vol. 1:** 641
Monastic comunities **Vol. 3:** 78
Monday lections **Vol. 1:** 245
Monepiscopacy **Vol. 1:** 192
Money **Vol. 1:** 93, 142 f., 265, 377, 406, 461,
   465, 497, 520, 564, 641, 648, 671, 684, 715,
   731
   Vol. 2: 32, 42, 49, 96, 131, 216, 221, 226,
   321, 326, 497, 583, 666 f., 822, **829–853**, 854,
   Vol. 3: 69 f., 120, 155, 189, 200 f., 236, **324 f.**,
   379, 420, 545, 547, 557 f., 677, 748, **751–759**,
   808, 852, 868
Money, love of **Vol. 1:** **137–139**
Money-box **Vol. 1:** 142 f.
Money-changers **Vol. 1:** 704
   Vol. 2: 236
   Vol. 3: 756, 791
Monism **Vol. 1:** 255
Monistic anthropology **Vol. 2:** 919
Monogamy **Vol. 1:** 166, 335, 383 f.
   Vol. 2: 575 f.
   Vol. 3: 1064
Monologue **Vol. 2:** 867
Monotheism **Vol. 1:** 77, 452, 543
   Vol. 2: 70, 515, 606, 720
Monotheistic **Vol. 2:** 67, 71
Monster **Vol. 1:** 113 f., 431, 508
Monstrous **Vol. 1:** 670
Montanist **Vol. 3:** 108
Montanism **Vol. 3:** 89
Montanus **Vol. 2:** 507
   Vol. 3: 89
Month **Vol. 1:** 390, 723
   Vol. 2: 157, 689, 694, 887
   Vol. 3: 396, 826, 841, 847
Monument **Vol. 1:** 431
   Vol. 2: 149, 649
   Vol. 3: 246, 777, 1040, 1053
Mood **Vol. 1:** 107
Moon **Vol. 1:** 124, 224, 420, 425, 449, 451
   Vol. 2: 128, 192, 484, 487 f., 491, 495 f., 622,

628, 690 f., 889, 916
   Vol. 3: 475, **730–737**, 1067
Moon-cult **Vol. 1:** 616
   Vol. 2: 67
Moon-goddess **Vol. 3:** 733
Moon-struck **Vol. 3:** **733 f.**
Moore, G.E. **Vol. 3:** 897, 1135 f.
Moral **Vol. 1:** 114, 206, 334, 348, 352 f., 365, 419
   f., 432, 441, 447–449, 460, 462, 468, 479 f.,
   498, 502, 524, 559, 562 f., 565, 570 f., 595,
   607 f., 628, 645, 699, 708 f., 722, 725 f., 732
   Vol. 2: 93, 100, 105, 143 f., 150, 241, 280, 363,
   372, 377, 383, 394, 471, 582, 657, 666, 781
   Vol. 3: 49, 68, 125 f., 130, 136, 149, 160, 349,
   426, 512, 677, 945, 993, 1039, 1053, 1148,
   1154
Moral awareness **Vol. 3:** 678
Moral concepts **Vol. 1:** 56
Moral conviction **Vol. 3:** 682
Moral corruption **Vol. 2:** 58
Moral evil **Vol. 1:** 422
Moral freedom **Vol. 1:** 62
Moral goodness **Vol. 2:** 98
Moral impurity **Vol. 1:** 155
Moral instruction **Vol. 3:** 929
Moral language **Vol. 1:** 56
Moral lapse **Vol. 2:** 51
Moral perfection **Vol. 2:** 77
Moral philosophy **Vol. 1:** 56, 502
   Vol. 3: 930
Moral powers **Vol. 3:** 684
Moral struggle **Vol. 3:** 679
Morality **Vol. 1:** 483 f.
   Vol. 2: 223 f., 420, 660
   Vol. 3: 50, 101, 103, 1052 f.
Moralize **Vol. 2:** 67
Morally good **Vol. 2:** 102
Morals **Vol. 1:** 56, 107, 206, 469, 687
   Vol. 2: 92, 457, 575
   Vol. 3: 573, 583
Mordecai **Vol. 2:** 291
   Vol. 3: 51, 873
More **Vol. 1:** 137, 728
   Vol. 2: 130
Morning **Vol. 2:** 136
   Vol. 3: 846, 902
Morning offering **Vol. 3:** 423
Morning star **Vol. 2:** 486, **490–496**
   Vol. 3: 736 f.
Morris, Leon **Vol. 3:** 152, 154
Morrow **Vol. 1:** 251
Morsel **Vol. 2:** 528
Mortal **Vol. 1:** 169, 233 f., 430–432, 435–438,
   440, 468–470, 499, 679, 705
   Vol. 2: 83, 263, 476, 503, 659, 879
   Vol. 3: 267, 575, 681
Mortality **Vol. 2:** 564, 923
Mortification **Vol. 1:** 443
Mosaic dispensation **Vol. 1:** 73
Mosaic legislation **Vol. 1:** 70, 330, 368, 444, 500
   Vol. 2: 123, 133
   Vol. 3: 95, 182
Mosaic tradition **Vol. 2:** 327
Mosaics in synagogues **Vol. 3:** 396

Moses **Vol. 1:** 53, 55 f., 65 f., 72, 104, 108, 128, 167 f., 173, 194 f., 252 f., 255, 272 f., 297, 309, 311, 326, 330, 332 f., 357, 365, 373–375, 399, 476, 485, 487, 505, 508 f., 532, 539, 543–545, 556, 559, 580, 587, 591, 595 f., 633, 639, 691, 704, 713, 729, 736
Vol. 2: 46, 48, 68 f., 117, 151, 154, 173 f., 180, 186, 202, 209, 212 f., 215 f., 219, 225, 249, 281, 287, 290, 306, 331, 337, 369, 437, 440, 442, 447–451, 453, 460, 488 f., 521, 557, 559, 580, 592, 598, 625, 627, 631, **635–643**, 677, 684, 686, 696, 724, 745, 762, 768, 777, 795–797, 835, 844, 847, 893
Vol. 3: 33, 42, 51, 56, 65, 77 f., 80, 86, 89, 117, 143, 154 f., 159, 179, 181, 186 f., 194, 199, 201 f., 207 f., 225, 234 f., 311, 324, 330, 344 f., 359, 367, 382, 418, 433, 459, 465, 479–482, 484 f., 487, 493–495, 508, 514, 520, 531, 550, 554, 559, 566, 568, 579, 594, 608–610, 630 f., 642 f., 650, 660, 673 f., 692, 699, 701, 721, 729, 740, 752, 764, 772 f., 778, 788, 800, 806, 812, 814 f., 828, 836, 861–864, 875, 877–880, 890, 893, 905, 969, 1001, 1003, 1007, 1009, 1011, 1013 f., 1043, 1057, 1103–1105, 1107, 1118, 1162 f.
Moses' seat **Vol. 1:** 297
Vol. 3: 87, 482, 589, 1162
Most High **Vol. 1:** 225, 321, 380 f.
Vol. 2: 376, 865, 899
Vol. 3: 36, 250, 271, 311, 424, 474, 555, 614, 616, 629, 637, 650, 660, 785, 793
Most honourable **Vol. 3: 716–718**
Mosul **Vol. 2:** 678
Mot **Vol. 2:** 554
Moth **Vol. 1:** 119, 468
Vol. 2: 831
Mother **Vol. 1:** 87, 239 f., 288, 336, 461, 501, 517, 556, 615, 619, 739
Vol. 2: 188, 226, 229, 250, 261, 312, 317, 329, 332, 358, 548, 571, 575, 737, 803
Vol. 3: 215, 987, **1055–1075**, 1163
Mother of God **Vol. 3:** 1070
Mother goddess **Vol. 2:** 85
Mother of harlots **Vol. 1:** 142
Vol. 3: 1070
Mother of Israel **Vol. 3:** 1069
Mother-in-law **Vol. 3:** 1059
Mother-love **Vol. 2:** 599
Motherhood **Vol. 3: 1068–1071**
Motherless **Vol. 1:** 616
Motion **Vol. 3: 556–558**, 681
Motivate **Vol. 1:** 537
Vol. 2: 364
Motivation **Vol. 1:** 358, 397, 558, 686, 691
Vol. 3: 854
Motive **Vol. 1:** 265, 270, 352, 395, 418, 549, 558, 603, 611 f., 622–625, 641, 738
Vol. 2: 43, 103, 137, 181, 244, 331, 350, 360, 437, 858
Vol. 3: 123, 1106
Motiveless **Vol. 1:** 546
Mould **Vol. 1:** 543, 676, 681, 708
Vol. 2: 95, 285
Vol. 3: 904, 917

Moule, C.F.D. **Vol. 3:** 60, 292 f.
Mound **Vol. 3: 951 f**.
Mount **Vol. 2:** 131, **184**
Mount of Olives **Vol. 1:** 629
Vol. 2: 713
Vol. 3: 381, 558, 1010–1012
Mount of transfiguration **Vol. 3:** 863, 1010, 1012
Mountain **Vol. 1:** 379, 387, 504, 559, 600, 602, 610, 661
Vol. 2: 157, 184, 187, 199, 218, 262, 297, 324 f., 353, 489, 870 f., 878
Vol. 3: 117, 391 f., 460, 543, 806, 862 f., 865, **1004–1014**, 1094
Mountain chain **Vol. 3: 1009–1013**
Mountain of God **Vol. 2:** 185, 202, 635
Mountain region **Vol. 3: 1009–1013**
Mountainous **Vol. 2:** 305
Vol. 3: 1008 f.
Mourn **Vol. 2: 417–423**, 433
Vol. 3: 120, 359
Mourner **Vol. 3:** 588
Mournful **Vol. 1:** 705
Mourning **Vol. 1:** 120, 203, 217, 239, 265, 329, 520, 569, 571, 612, 625, 630
Vol. 2: 267, 357 f., **417–423**, 714, 777, 887, 917
Vol. 3: 672 f.
Mourning women **Vol. 2:** 418
Mouth **Vol. 1:** 347, 414, 476, 508, 657, 729
Vol. 2: 28, 72, 80, 83, 132, 157, 216, 237, 252, 267, 451, 726 f.
Vol. 3: 81, 497, 639, 967, 1095
Move **Vol. 1:** 741
Vol. 2: 116, 266
Move quickly **Vol. 3: 945–947**
Movement **Vol. 1:** 487, 521, 602, 720
Vol. 2: 457
Vol. 3: 259, 677 f., 689 f., 707, 841 f., 933
Much **Vol. 2:** 130, 840
Mud **Vol. 3: 915–917**
Muddy **Vol. 3:** 950
Multiform **Vol. 1:** 705
Multiple meaning **Vol. 3:** 878
Multiply **Vol. 1:** 728, 732 f.
Vol. 2: 128, 130 f.
Multitude **Vol. 1:** 95, 292 f., 529, 670, **728–744**
Vol. 2: 214, 696 f., 795, 811, 842
Mummy **Vol. 1:** 263
Mundane **Vol. 1:** 644
Murder **Vol. 1:** 51, 309, 364, 410, 418, 420, 429, 443, 468, 499, 546, 558, 640
Vol. 2: 63, 138, 489, 854
Vol. 3: 82, 94, 96, 103, 201, 422, 680, 708, 1053
Murderer **Vol. 1:** 166, 168, 458, 556
Vol. 2: 472
Vol. 3: 35, 159, 190, 472, 756, 1054
Murderous **Vol. 1:** 657
Murex **Vol. 1:** 205
Murmur **Vol. 1:** 195, 509
Vol. 2: 423
Vol. 3: 799
Muses **Vol. 2:** 372
Music **Vol. 1:** 625
Vol. 2: 92

505

Vol. 3: 668–676, 873
Musical instruments **Vol. 3:** 77, 669, 671, 689, 873 f.
Musician **Vol. 2:** 578
  Vol. 3: 34
Musonius Rufus **Vol. 1:** 498
Must **Vol. 2: 662–669,** 808 f.
Mustard **Vol. 1:** 173
  Vol. 2: 129, 385, 429, 462, 714, 834
  Vol. 3: 523, 555, 868, 1012
Muster **Vol. 1:** 189, 292 f., 296, 332 f.
  Vol. 2: 683 f.
  Vol. 3: 478
Mute **Vol. 1:** 428, 509
Mutilation **Vol. 1:** 307, 309, 311
  Vol. 3: 96
Mutual **Vol. 1:** 240, 300, 303, 385, 639, 643, 662, 686, 724, 733
  Vol. 2: 51, 313, 317, 404
Muzzle **Vol. 1:** 115
Mycenae **Vol. 3:** 851
Mylitta **Vol. 1:** 497
Myrrh **Vol. 1:** 120–122, 265 f.
  Vol. 2: 28, **293–295,** 712
  Vol. 3: 154
Myrtle **Vol. 1:** 648
Mysteries of Aion **Vol. 3:** 827
Mysterious **Vol. 2:** 364
Mystery **Vol. 1:** 64, 129, 167, 169, 171, 179, 351, 370 f., 427, 498, 509, 541, 565 f., 661, 677, 737, 740
  Vol. 2: 64, 69, 72, 75, 176, 178, 197 f., 255, 274, 341 f., 349, 401, 726, 736, 794, 835, 922
  Vol. 3: 49 f., 84, 138, 169, 311, 314, 316, 321 f., **501–506,** 664, 721, 833, 844, 1019 f., 1031–1033, 1109
Mystery of lawlessness **Vol. 2:** 447, 901
Mystery religions **Vol. 1:** 59, **64,** 123, 150, 176, 186, 230, 271, 282, 284., 286, 288, 316, 327, 373, 432, 438 f., 470, 484, 595, 611, 616, 625, 643, 650, 654, 705–708, 716
  Vol. 2: 60, 202, 214, 233, 239, 265, 274, 276, 457, 539, 763, 862, 898
  Vol. 3: 103, 205, 231, 497, 501–503, 577, 593, 647, 706, 748, 772 f., 831, 928, 1031, 1033 f., 1085
Mystic **Vol. 2:** 185, 357
  Vol. 3: 128, 640, 720, 724, 1079
Mystical **Vol. 1:** 66, 123, 302, 337, 500, 513 f., 636, 638, 643 f.
  Vol. 2: 201, 539, 584
  Vol. 3: 225
Mystical identity **Vol. 3:** 425
Mysticism **Vol. 1:** 432, 527, 643
  Vol. 2: 76 f., 173, 393, 403, 479, 762
  Vol. 3: 232
Myth **Vol. 1:** 53 f., 57, 87, 230, 336, 507 f., 523, 640, 669
  Vol. 2: 60, 125, 196, 200, 204, 310, 314, 394, 404 f., 408, 613, 633, **643–647,** 761, 858, 906 f.
  Vol. 3: 35, 40, 237, 274, 281 f., 317, 328, 618, 765, 768, 887, 921, 1029, 1031, 1033, 1047, 1081, 1119, 1138 f.
Myth of Er **Vol. 2:** 762

Vol. 3: 260
Myth and ritual school **Vol. 2:** 644
Mythical **Vol. 1:** 498, 508, 523, 594, 616
  Vol. 2: 280, 297, 405
  Vol. 3: 996, 1106
Mythological **Vol. 1:** 617
  Vol. 2: 201 f., 250, 278, 404, 906
  Vol. 3: 55, 96, 1117
Mythology **Vol. 1:** 124, 126, 140, 229 f., 233, 508, 514, 522, 563
  Vol. 2: 158, 188 f., 200, 394, 430, 479, 688 f.
  Vol. 3: 617, 645, 733, 903

Naamah **Vol. 3:** 867
Naaman **Vol. 1:** 144, 246
  Vol. 2: 396, 464
  Vol. 3: 156, 986, 991
Naasene hymn **Vol. 3:** 936
Nabal **Vol. 2:** 649
Naboth **Vol. 1:** 165, 640
  Vol. 3: 1091
Nablus **Vol. 3:** 457
Nachman ben Isaac, Rabbi **Vol. 3:** 367
Nacre **Vol. 3:** 395
Nadab **Vol. 2:** 638
Nag Hammadi **Vol. 1:** 616, 646
  Vol. 2: 219, 751, 925
Nahal Mishmar **Vol. 2:** 97
Nahum **Vol. 1:** 66
  Vol. 2: 432, 679
  Vol. 3: 78
Nail **Vol. 1:** 330, 393, 402
  Vol. 2: 98, 348
Nain **Vol. 2:** 600, 630
  Vol. 3: 280, 303, 558, 1059, 1071
Naked **Vol. 1: 312–317**
  Vol. 2: 207, 212, 854, 926
  Vol. 3: 310, 359, 547, 563
Namara **Vol. 3:** 453
Name **Vol. 1:** 101, 146, 152, 167, 174, 179, 192, 200, 205, 209, 211, 244, 247, 271–274, 276, 290, 293, 309, 321, 338, 340, 345 f., 382, 415, 455, 466, 471, 489, 499, 550, 555 f., 566, 570 f., 581, 600, 607, 616, 618 f., 700, 715
  Vol. 2: 32, 68, 71, 74 f., 86, 110, 117, 120, 122, 134, 148, 157, 160, 190 f., 193, 200, 203, 217, 226, 228–231, 247, 254, 262, 281, 305–308, 317–320, 324–327, 330–335, 338, 340, 342 f., 358 f., 376, 381, 387, 425, 427, 450, 458, 512–514, 556, 560, 572, 574, 602, 624, 627, **648–656,** 666, 676, 695, 722, 777, 791, 800, 803, 810, 837, 858, 865, 868, 871, 928 f.
  Vol. 3: 178, 181, 191, 202, 206, 209, 212 f., 224, 231, 233, 237, 257, 271 f., 316, 320 f., **324 f.,** 341–344, 395, 434, 475 f., 479, 484, 487, 490, 500, 576, 608, 611, 621, 645, 647 f., 658, 660, 670, 725, 729, 741, 746, 763, 784, 786, 819, 871 f., 913, 924, 969, 1041, 1043, 1053, 1056, 1157, 1162, 1210
Name changes **Vol. 2:** 649
Namelessness **Vol. 2:** 649
Names of God (→ God, names of)
Naomi **Vol. 3:** 191

Naphtali **Vol. 2:** 317
  Vol. 3: 873
Naramsin **Vol. 1:** 140
Narcotic **Vol. 1:** 443
  Vol. 2: 28
Narrative **Vol. 1:** 57 f., 62, 66, **573–584**
  Vol. 2: 113
  Vol. 3: 234
Narrow **Vol. 2:** 812, 888
Narrow door **Vol. 1:** 646
  Vol. 2: 29, 31
Nathan **Vol. 1:** 108, 177 f., 210, 426
  Vol. 2: 374, 612, 614, 691
  Vol. 3: 78, 636, 648, 654 f., 659, 787, 1090, 1092
Nathanael **Vol. 1:** 724
  Vol. 2: 339
  Vol. 3: 115, 517, 893
Nation **Vol. 1:** 612, 625, 641, 677, 685, 687 f., 734, 740
  Vol. 2: 105, 128, 179, 310, 319 f., 349, 363 f., 415, 435, 437, 786, **788–805**
  Vol. 3: 36, 39, 65, 79, 206, 227, 356 f., 407, 522, 807, 826, **870–873**, 1079, 1096
National **Vol. 1:** 269, 409, 426, 539, 545, 626, 654, 724
  Vol. 2: 305, 309, 337, 373, 376, 795
  Vol. 3: 355
National differences **Vol. 2:** 83
National guardians **Vol. 1:** 102
National unity **Vol. 1:** 332
Nationalistic **Vol. 2:** 377, 385, 389
Nationalists **Vol. 3:** 377, 980
Nationality **Vol. 1:** 258
Nations **Vol. 1:** 58, 97, 101, 109, 111, 115, 142, 164, 186, 214, 224, 374, 380, 390, 407, 477, 508, 519, 523, 541, 550, 574, 640, 685 f., 688, 692, 699, 735
  Vol. 2: 32, 45, 70, 74, 83, 190, 226, 237 f., 240, 242, 308–310, 316, 359, 364, 374–378, 396, 432 f., 460 f., 492, 615, 627, 650, 654, 690, 697, 701 f., 724, **788–805**, 863, 888, 890, 893
  Vol. 3: 79 f., 159, 192, 202, 207, 250 f., 268, 357, 363, 567, 633, 638, 648, 791, 866, 871, 913
Nativity **Vol. 1:** 623
Natorp, P. **Vol. 3:** 899
Natural **Vol. 1:** 441, 469, 551, 616 f., 631, 647, 654, 679 f., 690, 702, 722 f., 725, 742
  Vol. 2: 138, 182, 267, 271, 414, 419, 548, **656–661**, 712, 806
  Vol. 3: 231, 281, 301, 706
Natural law **Vol. 2:** 165, 236
Natural man **Vol. 1:** 422 f.
  Vol. 2: 75, 101, 182, 184, 605, 609
  Vol. 3: 684
Natural order **Vol. 2:** 77, 162, 631
Natural phenomena **Vol. 1:** 102
  Vol. 2: 602, 607
Natural products **Vol. 3:** 415
Natural science **Vol. 3:** 1029
Natural theology **Vol. 1: 70**
  Vol. 2: 287
  Vol. 3: 327, 885

Naturalism **Vol. 1:** 669
Naturalistic **Vol. 3:** 1106
Nature **Vol. 1:** 68, 70, 101, 107, 167, 179, 182, 186, 288, 315, 380, 384, 437, 470, 481, 483 f., 488, 492, 535, 538, 542 f., 548, 555, 561, 564, 620, 625–627, 636, 643 f., 653, 670, 677, 679, 692, 694, 699, 703, 705 f., 710, 712, 714–716, 725 f., 734
  Vol. 2: 47, 75, 86, 105, 162, 179 f., 245, 279, 287–289, 303, 340, 356, 375, 393 f., 396, 432, 439, 441, 446, 476, 500–508, 514, 552, 564, 601 f., 617, 628 f., 633, 651, **656–662**, 672, 675 f., 863
  Vol. 3: 23, 118, 174, 204, 260, 325, 327, 330 f., 528, 560, 595, 764, 835, 845 f., 867, 993, 1105, 1157
Nature miracles **Vol. 2:** 630
Nature of God **Vol. 1:** 108
  Vol. 2: 68 f.
  Vol. 3: 514 f.
Nature of Jesus **Vol. 3:** 516
Nature of language **Vol. 3: 1123–1126**, 1140
Nature religions **Vol. 3:** 246
Nature-idolatry **Vol. 3:** 837
Navigation **Vol. 3:** 731, 735
Nazara **Vol. 2:** 333
Nazarene **Vol. 1:** 535, 600
  Vol. 2: 312, **330, 332–334, 346**, 867
Nazareth **Vol. 1:** 123, 170, 279, 384, 600, 669, 693, 738
  Vol. 2: 101, 165, 194, **330–335**, 338, 341–343, **346**, 624, 728, 730, 825
  Vol. 3: 56, 213, 472, 507, 1030
Nazirite **Vol. 1:** 645
  Vol. 2: 224 f., 227 f., 440, 450, 638
  Vol. 3: 101, 206, 420, 422, 431, 793, 919, 921
Neapolis **Vol. 3:** 453, 458
Near **Vol. 2: 52–66**, 73, 113, 237, 382
Nearest **Vol. 1:** 665
Nearness **Vol. 2:** 30, 168, 366, 384, 388, 479, 491, 518
  Vol. 3: 762 f., 997
Nebo **Vol. 3:** 453, 806
Nebuchadnezzar **Vol. 1:** 140 f., 340, 686
  Vol. 2: 96, 98, 320, 431, 555
  Vol. 3: 50, 110, 147, 193, 202, 269, 392, 557, 608, 782, 788, 851, 866, 914, 918, 1161
Necessary **Vol. 2:** 130, 244, 310, 350, **663–666**, 845
  Vol. 3: 48, 728, 758, **956–958**
Necessity **Vol. 1:** 173, 278, 310, 318, 326, 384, 561, 611, 623, 679, 692
  Vol. 2: 139, 480, 505, 588, **662–669**, 808, 912
  Vol. 3: 39, 56, 261, 324, 444, 504, 573, 723, 779, 835, **956–958**, 1054
Neck **Vol. 1:** 241, 609
  Vol. 3: 1164
Necromancy **Vol. 1:** 450
  Vol. 2: 206, 553 f.
Necropolis **Vol. 1:** 431
Nectas **Vol. 1:** 513
Nedebaeus **Vol. 3:** 949
Need **Vol. 1:** 143, 165, 191, 257 f., 272, 278, 285, 314, 318 f., 409, 426, 436, 473, 500, 525, 544,

507

548, 578, 597, 600, 604, 614, 622, 642, 673, 679 f., 702, 741
Vol. 2: 71, 100, 116, 190, 197, 201 f., 211, 230, 243, 254, 257, 263, 265–267, 272, 313, 320, 355, 412 f., 600, 631, 737, **820–829**, 855, **860 f.,** 864, 871, 874, 877
Vol. 3: 149, 173, 216, 377 f., 402, 408, 454, 536 f., 547, 553, 686, 727–729, 746, 771, 783, 804, 810, 854, **952–958**
Needle **Vol. 1:** 116
Needy **Vol. 1:** 115, 218, 410, 570, 642
Vol. 2: 71, 194, 397, **820–829**
Vol. 3: 98, 206, 357, 980
Negation **Vol. 1:** 66
Vol. 2: 394
Vol. 3: 741
Negative **Vol. 1:** 352, 553, 561, 583
Vol. 2: 312
Negeb **Vol. 1:** 76
Vol. 2: 98, 319
Vol. 3: 606
Neglect **Vol. 1:** 460, 698, 713
Vol. 2: 43, 92, 150, 211
Vol. 3: 251, 583
Neglect duty **Vol. 3:** 574
Negligible **Vol. 1:** 561
Negotiate **Vol. 1:** 193
Vol. 3: 50, 820
Negotiator **Vol. 1:** 194, 373 f.
Nehemiah **Vol. 1:** 52 f., 98, 108, 196, 377
Vol. 2: 307, 439, 467
Vol. 3: 35, 250, 407, 451, 560, 853
Nehunya ben Kanah, Rabbi **Vol. 3:** 1162
Nehushtan **Vol. 1:** 509
Neighbour **Vol. 1:** 232, **254–260**, 334 f., 337, 386, 439, 455, 554, 556, 560, 667, 690 f., 720, 726, 730, 738
Vol. 2: 49, 63 f., 141, 143, 163, 177, 184, 203, 275, 287, 297, 418, 427, 435, 442, 449, 503, 540–545, 600, 611, 668, 739, 749, 779, 803, 813, 815, 857
Vol. 3: 136, 173, 183, 201, 346, 378, 529, 545, 547, 576, 593, 597 f., 810, 944, 979, 1057, 1079, 1155
Neo-Kantianism **Vol. 3:** 899 f.
Neo-Platonism **Vol. 1:** **66**, 432, 522, 595
Vol. 2: 67
Vol. 3: 146, 501, 1084
Neo-Pythagoreans **Vol. 1:** 484, 494, 741
Neo-scholasticism **Vol. 1:** 65
Nephele **Vol. 3:** 1000
Nephew **Vol. 1:** 254
Neptune **Vol. 2:** 85
Neri **Vol. 3:** 654 f.
Nero **Vol. 1:** 113, 119, 126, 235, 606
Vol. 2: 511, 684, 898
Vol. 3: 203, 446, 571
Nero *redivivus* **Vol. 1:** 119, 126
Vol. 2: 288, 684
Vol. 3: 715
Nerva **Vol. 3:** 753
Nest **Vol. 2:** 586
Vol. 3: 734, 813
Nestorian Christ **Vol. 3:** 663

Net **Vol. 2:** 104, 714, 834
Vol. 3: 119, 350, 469, 543, 952
Neugebauer, F. **Vol. 3:** 85
Neutral **Vol. 1:** 373, 482, 739
Vol. 2: 325
Vol. 3: 1155
Never **Vol. 3:** 829
Never-failing **Vol. 3:** 987
New **Vol. 1:** 613, 620, 628, 634, 642 f., 661, 666, 678, 681, 686 f., 689, 699, 708, 713, 717, 721
Vol. 2: 120, 138, 156, 226, 328, 426, 641, **669–676,** 714–716, 754, 789
Vol. 3: 47, 493, 543, 906, 1154
New age **Vol. 1:** 86, 124, 219, 251, 317, 421, 513, 601
Vol. 2: 53, 131, 169, 228, 605, 698, 701, 714, 754, 892, 920
Vol. 3: 47, 56 f., 62, 82, 696, 698, 701, 779, 829–831, 922, 956, 1020
New birth **Vol. 1:** 178, 359
Vol. 2: 242, 625, 929
New commandment **Vol. 1:** 526
Vol. 2: 43, 671, 673, 779
New community **Vol. 3:** 868
New covenant **Vol. 1:** 185, 224, 304, 368, 374, 386, 408–411, 448, 593, 601, 666, 690, 700
Vol. 2: 71, 73, 77, 83, 155, 213, 240, 276, 306, 312, 320, 328, 356, 444, 446–448, 516, 524, 533, 591–593, 595, 661, 670 f., 673 f., 694, 716, 786, 797, 854, 867, 872
Vol. 3: 59, 69, 73 f., 107, 136, 143, 160, 183, 200, 227, 233, 243, 257, 327, 366, 433, 486, 546, 548, 576, 578, 729, 1014, 1074
New creation (→ Creation, New)
New creature **Vol. 1:** 702
Vol. 3: 529, 1154
New day **Vol. 2:** 364
New dispensation **Vol. 3:** 584
New earth **Vol. 1:** 56, 65, 185, 380, 518, 525
Vol. 2: 240, 245, 340, 420, 483, 670 f., 674, 692, 702, 779, 804, 836, 867
Vol. 3: 71, 180, 224, 371, 558, 829, 832, 1013
New era **Vol. 2:** 108 f., 374, 383, 676, 698
New existence **Vol. 1:** 272, 470, 643
New heart **Vol. 1:** 151, 354
Vol. 2: 155, 184, 867
New heaven **Vol. 1:** 56, 65, 185, 380, 518, 525
Vol. 2: 245, 340, 420, 482 f., 670 f., 674, 692, 702, 779, 836, 867
Vol. 3: 71, 180, 224, 371, 832, 1013
New hermeneutic **Vol. 3:** 1138 f.
New humanity **Vol. 3:** 363
New to the incense **Vol. 2: 294**
New Israel **Vol. 3:** 363, 393, 868, 871, 1007
New Jerusalem (→ Jerusalem, new)
New law **Vol. 1:** 586, 602, 689
Vol. 2: 123, 281, 451
Vol. 3: 221, 1163
New life **Vol. 1:** 359, 437, 439, 443, 469, 474, 486, 489, 675, 701 f.
Vol. 2: 102, 113, 217, 262, 349, 420, 453, 617–619, 671, 676, 716, 925
Vol. 3: 581, 886, 928, 931, 934, 1143, 1061
New man **Vol. 1:** 185, 311, 316, 359, 386, 402

New man (cont'd)
  Vol. 2: 121, 163, 237, 251, 473, 566, 670 f.,
    674 f., 715
  Vol. 3: 172, 186
New moon Vol. 1: 245, 626
  Vol. 2: 128, 226
  Vol. 3: 410, 426 f., 556, 733
New name Vol. 2: 649, 652 f., 671, 673 f., 754
New nature Vol. 1: 315, 654
New order Vol. 1: 73, 643
  Vol. 2: 399
  Vol. 3: 121, 180, 351 f., 524, 616, 913, 1093 f.
New people Vol. 1: 76, 380
  Vol. 2: 83, 127, 242, 349, 573, 652, 722, 788,
    800, 918
  Vol. 3: 251 f., 363, 435, 568, 920
New relationship Vol. 3: 168
New sanctuary Vol. 3: 366
New song Vol. 2: 380, 670 f., 674
  Vol. 3: 673
New spirit Vol. 1: 151, 354
  Vol. 2: 155
New teaching Vol. 3: 769
New temple Vol. 2: 252, 326, 410, 612, 893
  Vol. 3: 404, 787, 813
New wine Vol. 3: 921 f.
New world Vol. 1: 327, 630, 723
  Vol. 2: 267
  Vol. 3: 871
New year Vol. 1: 626, 628
  Vol. 3: 233, 487
New year festival Vol. 2: 613, 644
  Vol. 3: 269, 274
New year litany Vol. 1: 618
Newborn Vol. 1: 283 f., 360
  Vol. 2: 270
  Vol. 3: 346, 1118
Newly planted Vol. 2: 674–676
Newness Vol. 2: 670–674, 718, 781
News Vol. 1: 167, 298, 322, 529, 612, 741
  Vol. 2: 107 f., 173, 175, 179
  Vol. 3: 45, 48
Next Vol. 1: 665 f.
Next of Kin Vol. 2: 53
Nicea Vol. 2: 497, 506
Nicene creed Vol. 1: 178
  Vol. 2: 84, 497
Niche Vol. 1: 264
Nickname Vol. 1: 271, 273
  Vol. 2: 648
Nicodemus Vol. 1: 147, 179, 265 f., 284, 290,
    420
  Vol. 2: 295, 448, 625, 812
  Vol. 3: 115, 767, 791, 1132
Nicolaitans Vol. 1: 407
  Vol. 2: 676–678, 763
Nicolas (Nicolaus) Vol. 2: 676–678
Nicole, Roger R. Vol. 3: 153
Nicopolis Vol. 3: 453
Nida, E.A. Vol. 3: 1126 f., 1141
Niddah Vol. 3: 989
Nietzsche, Friedrich W. Vol. 1: 57
  Vol. 3: 899
Night Vol. 1: 272, 323, 366, 420–425, 450, 512 f.,
    559, 630, 634, 652, 731

  Vol. 2: 232, 332, 368, 490 f., 493, 495 f., 528,
    658, 887, 922
  Vol. 3: 111, 200, 731, 733, 846, 849
Nightmare Vol. 3: 557
Nihilism Vol. 1: 381, 550 f.,
Nike Vol. 2: 849
Nile Vol. 1: 531
  Vol. 2: 636 f.
  Vol. 3: 985
Nilus Vol. 1: 318
Nimrod Vol. 1: 140
Nimrûd Vol. 1: 140
Nine Vol. 2: 697
Nineham, D.E. Vol. 3: 63
Nineveh Vol. 1: 140, 358
  Vol. 2: 351, 365, 423, 678–681, 831
  Vol. 3: 52 f.
Ninevites Vol. 2: 350, 678–681
Ninth hour Vol. 2: 685
Ninurta Vol. 1: 140
Niobe Vol. 1: 287
Nisan Vol. 1: 628 f., 632
No Vol. 3: 741
Noachian decrees (commandments) Vol. 1: 360,
    691
  Vol. 2: 309, 682
  Vol. 3: 106, 158, 931
Noah Vol. 1: 72, 182, 366, 452, 691, 713
  Vol. 2: 91, 300 f., 309, 382, 591, 681–683, 692,
    880
  Vol. 3: 52 f., 106, 158, 203, 211, 215, 248, 264,
    325, 365, 370, 418, 425, 468, 522, 578, 605,
    626 f., 633, 642, 683, 841, 851, 906, 918 f.,
    991
Nob Vol. 3: 33 f., 426, 812
Nobility Vol. 1: 117, 717
  Vol. 2: 788, 800
Noble Vol. 1: 187, 438, 665, 683, 715 f.
  Vol. 2: 57, 98, 102, 290, 652
  Vol. 3: 912
Noble-minded Vol. 2: 256
Nobleman Vol. 1: 165
Noetic Vol. 2: 493
Noise Vol. 3: 111–114
Nomads Vol. 1: 519
  Vol. 2: 305
  Vol. 3: 564, 811
Nominate Vol. 1: 475
Nomism Vol. 1: 309
Non-believer Vol. 3: 1114
Non-Christian Vol. 1: 282, 506 f., 593, 601, 630
  Vol. 2: 94, 127, 230, 250, 258, 271, 333 f., 349
Non-citizen Vol. 2: 690
Non-cultic Vol. 1: 292
  Vol. 2: 233
  Vol. 3: 154 f.
Non-elect Vol. 2: 156
Non-Israelite Vol. 1: 360, 690
  Vol. 2: 49, 51, 53, 154, 790
Non-Jew Vol. 1: 360, 382, 385, 581, 623, 689
  Vol. 2: 90, 381, 641, 660 f.
Non-Jewish Vol. 1: 360
  Vol. 2: 285
Non-objective Vol. 1: 71
Non-reality Vol. 2: 402

Non-Semitic **Vol. 2:** 331
Non-violence **Vol. 3:** 971, 980
Nonentity **Vol. 1:** 551 f.
  Vol. 2: 285
Noon **Vol. 3:** 731
Norm **Vol. 1:** 546, 602, 604
  Vol. 2: 438–451
  Vol. 3: 135, **399–404**, 583, 726, 833
Normal **Vol. 1:** 527, 664, 679
  Vol. 3: 349
Normative **Vol. 1:** 333
  Vol. 2: 442
Normative ethics (→ Ethics, Normative)
Northern kingdom **Vol. 1:** 543, 716 f.
  Vol. 2: 38, **305** f., 325, 635, 916
  Vol. 3: 33 f., 79, 94, 104, 426, 449–451
Nose **Vol. 1:** 108
Nostrils **Vol. 3:** 476, 691
Not standing test **Vol. 3: 808–810**
Not-my-people **Vol. 3:** 1103
Notch **Vol. 2:** 288
Note **Vol. 1:** 694
Nothing **Vol. 1:** 639, 678
  Vol. 2: 41, 128, 239
  Vol. 3: 1153
Nothingness **Vol. 1:** 446, 523, 546 f., 550 f.
  Vol. 2: 286, 471
  Vol. 3: 555, 690, 842
Notice **Vol. 1:** 484, 506, 693, 695
  Vol. 2: 267, 392, 395, 398
  Vol. 3: 122–130, 512 f., 516
Notification **Vol. 3: 68–74**
Notify **Vol. 3:** 45, **316 f.**
Notorious **Vol. 1:** 701
Nourish **Vol. 2:** 372, 837
  Vol. 3: 423
Nourishment **Vol. 2:** 264, 462
  Vol. 3: 678, 986
Novel **Vol. 2:** 670
  Vol. 3: 903
Novice **Vol. 1:** 611
  Vol. 2: 299, 676
Now **Vol. 2:** 242 f., 907, 930
  Vol. 3: 826, **833–839**, 841, 844, 848
Null **Vol. 1:** 550
  Vol. 2: 453
Nullify **Vol. 1: 73,** 462
  Vol. 3: 1057
Number **Vol. 1:** 119, 126, 136, 165, 508, 625, 711, 728, 731–734, 739
  Vol. 2: 37, 53, 63, 159, 207, 288, 299, 313, 352, 389, 428, 497, 653, **683–704**, 725, 734, 739, 763, 795, 809, 887, 892, 931
  Vol. 3: 88, 179 f., 277, 349, 404, 417, 470 f., 500, 557, 680, 706, 715, 729 f., 734, 736, 841, 843, 846, 851, 855, 1085
Number of the beast **Vol. 1:** 126
  Vol. 2: 574, **684**
Number of a man **Vol. 2: 684**
Numbers, book of **Vol. 1:** 65 f.
Numbers, problem of large **Vol. 2: 698**
Numerical structure of Matthew **Vol. 3:** 657
Numerical value **Vol. 2:** 683
Numerous **Vol. 1:** 729

  Vol. 2: 130, 683
Numinous **Vol. 1:** 498
  Vol. 2: 91
  Vol. 3: 381
Numismatic emblem **Vol. 1:** 406
Nun **Vol. 2:** 331
Nunc Dimittis **Vol. 3:** 118, 674, 790
Nurse **Vol. 1:** 239 f., 282
Nursery **Vol. 1:** 285
Nuzi **Vol. 2:** 316 f.

Oak **Vol. 2:** 318
  Vol. 3: 782, 866 f.
Oarsman **Vol. 1:** 408
Oasis **Vol. 1:** 252
  Vol. 2: 266
Oath **Vol. 1:** 98, 344, 346, 356, 372, 374 f., 415, 494, 658 f., 731
  Vol. 2: 134, 142, 149, 159, 190, 224, 226, 301, 307, 447, 472, 648, 650, 652, 797, **861–864, 867–875**
  Vol. 3: 41, 74, 429, 560, 583, 650, **737–743**, 792, 882, 1018, **1038–1050**, 1052 f.
Oath of initiation **Vol. 3:** 740
Oath of innocence **Vol. 2:** 583
Oath of purification **Vol. 3:** 740
Oath of testimony **Vol. 3:** 740
Oath under pledge **Vol. 3:** 740
Obadiah **Vol. 1:** 66
  Vol. 3: 250, 608
Obdurate **Vol. 2:** 153
  Vol. 3: 1020
Obedience **Vol. 1:** 58, 67, 77, 79–81, 109, 123, 138, 166, 210, 211, 223, 236, 238, 244, 265, 286, 293 f., 296, 304, 332, 337, 347, 349 f., 358, 367 f., 372, 375, 389, 398 f., 401, 408, 456, 461, 463, 472, 480, 482, 484, 487 f., 491–493, 501 f., 506, 525, 537 f., 540, 542 f., 548 f., 552, 556, 571, 593, 598, 601 f., 604, 615 f., 618 f., 622, 626, 638 f., 655, 659, 679 f., 681, 703, 713, 722, 730
  Vol. 2: 30 f., 42, 56, 70, 80, 91–95, 118, 122, 130, 132, 137, 156, 165, **172–180**, 182 f., 186, 199, 202–204, 228, 230, 241, 258, 267, 272, 278, 289, 301, 312, 336, 343, 361, 378, 386, 391, 395, 399, 401, 403 f., 426, 441–443, 445 f., 473, 479, 492, 500, 540 f., 566, 605, 608, 620, 636, 670, 682, 716, 724, 748, 775, 797, 810, 812, 816, 868, 892
  Vol. 3: 73, 107, 139, 141, 165, 183, 194, 232, 235, 243, 352, 357 f., 363, 394, 427, 432, 434 f., 470, 486, 531 f., 550, 595–597, 613, 646 f., 724, 742, 750, 760 f., 766, 769, 776, 783, 785, 806, 824, 835–837, 869, 905, 927, 930 f., 934, 938, 954, 1022 f., 1025, 1028, 1067, 1148, 1150 f., 1155
Obedient **Vol. 2:** 184, 227, 259, 262, 478, 504, 509, 706, 721, 816, 856
  Vol. 3: 54, 120, 136, 349, 529, 804, 810, 888, 1020
Obeisance **Vol. 2: 875–879**
Obey **Vol. 1:** 106, 219, 234, 339, 381, 481, 484, 588 f., 591–594, 674
  Vol. 2: 132, 134 f., 156, 158, **172–180**, 259,

Obey (*cont'd*)
313, 394, 399, 439, 444, 449, 462, 514, 650, 817
Vol. 3: 113, 138, 233, 572, 685, 777, 800, 885, 1134
Object **Vol. 1:** 492, 525, 538, 567, 658, 687, 705, 709, 711
Vol. 3: 778
Objection **Vol. 1:** 596, 659, 701
Objective **Vol. 1:** 71, 436, 697
Vol. 2: 357
Vol. 3: 299
Obligation **Vol. 1:** 98, 120, 210, 270, 275, 310, 340, 401, 439, 471, 481, 499, 509, 536, 556, 595, 618–621, 639, 647, 687, 690 f., 698, 716, 734
Vol. 2: 43, 76, 92, 134, 174, 177, 223, 236 f., 265, 271, 286, 418, 549, 606, **662–669**, 842, 856, 858
Vol. 3: 134 f., 138, 142, 190, 353, 358, 536, 573, 583, 593, 800, 853, 930 f., 934, 1044, 1053
Obligatory **Vol. 1:** 601
Oblige **Vol. 2:** 115 f.
Vol. 3: 140
Obliterate **Vol. 1:** 471
Vol. 2: 287, 308
Obscenity **Vol. 1:** 501
Obscure **Vol. 2:** 214, 218, 316, 781
Obscurity **Vol. 1:** 420 f., 577, 581
Vol. 2: 313
Observable **Vol. 3:** 862
Observance **Vol. 1:** 592, 626
Vol. 2: 132, 135, 150, 268, 327, 442, 449
Vol. 3: 253, 410, 440, 584, 944, 1053
Observation **Vol. 2:** 132, 385
Vol. 3: 677, 693, 1087
Observe **Vol. 1:** 189, 333, 627, 632, 693
Vol. 2: 132, 135, 237, 270, 354, 363, 393, 395, 440
Vol. 3: 122–130, 511–518, 520
Observer **Vol. 1:** 585
Obsolete **Vol. 1:** 371
Vol. 2: 231, 669, 675, **713–716**
Vol. 3: 106, 183
Obstacle **Vol. 1:** 370
Vol. 2: 220, 223, 394, **705–708**
Vol. 3: 534
Obstinacy **Vol. 1:** 506
Vol. 2: 154
Obstinate **Vol. 2:** 106, 153
Obtain **Vol. 1:** 713
Vol. 2: 116, 298, 317, 361, 367, **838–840**
Obtain justice **Vol. 2:** 363
Obvious **Vol. 1:** 711
Occasion **Vol. 1:** 52
Vol. 2: 137
Occult **Vol. 1:** 420
Vol. 2: 557 f.
Occupation **Vol. 1:** 275, 625, 629, 633
Vol. 2: 254, 303, 331
Vol. 3: 545, 566, 673, 758, 799, 910, 965, 1147, **1155–1158**
Occupy **Vol. 1:** 728

Vol. 2: 247, 438
Ocean **Vol. 1:** 422, 522
Vol. 2: 188–190, 205
Vol. 3: 983
O'Collins, G. **Vol. 3: 298**
Octavian **Vol. 2:** 849
Vol. 3: 731
Ode **Vol. 3: 668–670, 672–675**
Odes of Solomon **Vol. 2:** 159
Vol. 3: 85, 674, 936
Odour **Vol. 3:** 238, 424 f.
Odysseus **Vol. 2:** 372, 552
Vol. 3: 839
Oedipus **Vol. 2:** 457
Vol. 3: 577, 720
Oehler, G.F. **Vol. 3:** 151
Oetinger, F.C. **Vol. 3:** 148
Offence **Vol. 1:** 345, 399, 414, 448, 473, 547, 555, 608, 684, 699, 733
Vol. 2: 93, 159, 161, 358, 364, 406, 429, 450, 625, **705–710**
Vol. 3: 98, 157, 363, 389, 394, 573 f., 577, 697, 810, 996, 1000, 1031
Offend **Vol. 1:** 514
Vol. 2: 63, 127, 363
Vol. 3: 420
Offended **Vol. 1:** 217
Vol. 2: 705–707
Vol. 3: 151
Offender **Vol. 1:** 415, 466, 471
Vol. 3: 97
Offensive **Vol. 1:** 386
Vol. 2: 268
Offer **Vol. 1:** 96, 115, 172, 224, 351 f., 405, 414, 455, 478, 482, 546, 628, 655, 702, 731
Vol. 2: 41, 78, 107, 147, 184, 233, 273, 286, 327 f., 350, 367, 386, 402, 440, 447
Vol. 3: 50, 57, 68, 173, 220, 838
Offer money **Vol. 2:** 28
Offer sacrifice **Vol. 2:** 235, 293, 718
Vol. 3: 33
Offering **Vol. 1:** 175, 234, 250, 294, 413, 479, 648, 654, 677, 731 f.
Vol. 2: 29, 39–43, 166, 230, 235, 238, 294, 297, 410–412, 447 f., 461, 815, 860, 862
Vol. 3: 159, 164, 196, 239, **415–436**, 600, 744 f., 790, 794, 852, 919
Offering brought **Vol. 3: 417–436**
Offering of sheaves **Vol. 1:** 628
Office **Vol. 1:** 95, 122, 128 f., 131 f., 134 f., 163, 178, 188, 190–193, 195, 197–200, 275, 300, 302, 315, 329, 371, 375, 405, 407, 461, 471 f., 474, 478, 514, 533, 536, 540, 560, 574, 666 f., 698
Vol. 2: 48–51, 114, 122 f., 149, 151 f., 164, 195, 233, **253–256**, 294, 334 f., 342, 373 f., 376, 380 f., 406, 415, 456, 500, 505, 607, 730
Vol. 3: 53, 84, 88, 97, 101, 147, 259, 322, 342, 478, 534, 548, 721, 747, 763 f., 768, 771, 924, 1075, 1152
Office-bearer **Vol. 2:** 362, 607
Officer **Vol. 1:** 190, 407, 462
Vol. 2: 368
Vol. 3: 115, 120, 355, 547, 966

Official **Vol. 1:** 189, 196, 255, 259, 274, 302, 330, 363, 373, 393, 402, 536 f., 560, 573 f., 579 f., 687
Vol. 2: 234, 254, 335, 363, 369, 376, 777
Vol. 3: 115, 134, 144, 160, 480, 738, 755, 905, 930, 957, 1028
Officious **Vol. 1:** 266
Offscouring **Vol. 1:** 479
Vol. 3: 102–108
Offspring **Vol. 1:** 239 f., 280, 287, 427, 721 f., 729
Vol. 2: 77, 85, 311, 571
Vol. 3: 521–524
Og **Vol. 3:** 960
Ogden, C.K. **Vol. 3:** 1129 f.
Oil **Vol. 1:** 118–121, 471, 498, 627, 648
Vol. 2: 226, 294, 334 f., **710–713**, 794, 875
Vol. 3: 159, 238, 422, 727, 852, 870, 917, 921 f., 989, 1053, 1060, 1162
Oil of gladness **Vol. 2:** 294, 354
Oil press **Vol. 2:** 710
Ointment **Vol. 1:** 119–121, 319
Vol. 2: 294 f., 710
Vol. 3: 243, 600
Old **Vol. 1:** 164, 167, 192 f., 197 f., 277, 339, 363, 386, 433, 448, 470, 512, 601, 613, 631, 634, 666, 701
Vol. 2: 49, 75, 669–676, **713–716**, 834
Vol. 3: 493, 543, 906, 921
Old aeon **Vol. 1:** 421
Old age **Vol. 1:** 86, 93, 124, 219, 227, 562
Vol. 2: 272
Old Latin **Vol. 1:** 71
Old man **Vol. 1:** 311, 386, 401, 616, 657, 702, 718
Vol. 2: 127, 250, 473, 675, 715
Old nature **Vol. 1:** 106, 168, 315, 402, 457, 469
Old-fashioned **Vol. 1:** 192
Oleaster **Vol. 2:** 712
Vol. 3: 869
Olive **Vol. 1:** 644, 648
Vol. 2: 660, **710–713**, 737, 794
Vol. 3: 227, 416, 866–870, 921
Olivet (→ Mount of Olives)
Olympia **Vol. 3:** 782
Olympus **Vol. 2:** 185, 232
Vol. 3: 845, 959, 1009
Omega **Vol. 2:** 59
Omens **Vol. 1:** 172
Vol. 2: 148, 233, 554, 626, 633
Vol. 3: 76
Ominous **Vol. 1:** 420 f.
Omit **Vol. 2:** 351
Omnipotence **Vol. 2:** 149, 509, 689, 877 f.
Vol. 3: 645
Omnipotent **Vol. 1:** 180, 548 f.
Omnipresence **Vol. 1:** 102, 548 f.
Vol. 2: 73, 146, 613, 862
Omniscience **Vol. 1:** 102, 106, 548 f., 565, 694
Vol. 2: 183
Omri **Vol. 1:** 543
Vol. 3: 449
Onan **Vol. 2:** 577
Once **Vol. 2:** 703, **716–725**

Once-for-all **Vol. 1:** 355
Vol. 2: 447, **716–725**
One **Vol. 1:** 94 f., 616, 636, 664 f., 667, 678 f., 738
Vol. 2: 70, 73, 79, 84, 124, 278, 288, 309, 377, 396, 408, 450, 564, 618, 703, **716–725**
Vol. 3: 82, 231, 314, 535, 539, 723, **908 f.**, 1062, 1082
One mind **Vol. 3: 908 f.**
One-sided **Vol. 1:** 365
One's own **Vol. 2: 838–840**
Oneness **Vol. 1:** 240
Vol. 2: 80, 204, 445, 926
Vol. 3: 572
Onesimus **Vol. 1:** 675
Vol. 2: 434, 550
Vol. 3: 596, 930
Onesiphorus **Vol. 3:** 686
Onkelos **Vol. 3:** 485
Onlooker **Vol. 1:** 530
Only **Vol. 1:** 664 f.
Vol. 2: 76, 81, 408, 703, **716–725**
Vol. 3: 54, 646
Only-begotten **Vol. 1:** 256, 575
Vol. 2: 75, **723–725**
Onomatopoeia **Vol. 3:** 1124
Onomatopoeic **Vol. 3:** 1051
Ontic **Vol. 1: 64**
Ontological **Vol. 1: 64**
Vol. 2: 396
Ontology **Vol. 1: 64 f.**, 491
Onyx **Vol. 3:** 236, 396
Open **Vol. 1:** 253, 486, 581, 667, 681, 687, 690, 692, 717, 719
Vol. 2: 31, 179, 194, 302, 401, 411, 560, 673, **726–734**, 795, 813, 897
Vol. 3: 97, 177, 188, 192, **317–324**, 384, 387 f., 394, 568, 623, 652, 693, 717, 763, 860, 916
Open air **Vol. 3:** 761
Open the ear **Vol. 3:** 311
Open space **Vol. 1:** 741
Opening **Vol. 2:** 29 f., **726–729**
Openly **Vol. 3:** 75, **317–324**
Openness **Vol. 1:** 328 f., 611, 660, 702, 715, 720
Vol. 2: 308 f., 311, **734–737**
Vol. 3: 74, 143, 886
Operate **Vol. 1:** 540 f., 720
Operation **Vol. 1:** 647, 694
Vol. 3: 1147–1152
Operative **Vol. 2:** 287
Ophites **Vol. 1:** 510
Vol. 2: 645
Ophrah **Vol. 3:** 425
Opinion **Vol. 1:** 130, 330, 350, 357, 481, 485, 594, 602
Vol. 2: 44 f., 169, 311, 362, 392 f., 398, 430, 719, 767
Vol. 3: 130, 543, **747–751**, 759, 761, **820 f.**, 822, 1042
Opponent **Vol. 1:** 125, 138, 199, 261, 281, 331, 335, 365, 413, 445, 468, 496, 515, 529, 553, 554, 598, 604, 623, 638, 644, 647, 671, 678, 710, 727, 731, 742
Vol. 2: 112, 140 f., 183, 263, 311 f., 315 f., 327,

Opponent (cont'd)
340, 378, 401, 431, 434, 437, 448, 460, 469, 473
Vol. 3: 439, 495, 801 f., 804, 868, 935, 963, 1018, 1031
Opportune **Vol. 3: 833–839**
Opportunist **Vol. 2:** 899
Opportunity **Vol. 1:** 268, 274, 335 f., 364 385, 432, 438, 473, 533, 536
Vol. 2: 30, 101, 132, 137, 156, 351, 417, 728, 730, 770 f., 892
Vol. 3: 410, 596, 603, 818, 826, **833–839**, 842, 912, 1043
Oppose **Vol. 1:** 687, 693, 709, 740
Vol. 2: 314, 380, 385
Opposite **Vol. 1:** 424
Vol. 2: 198
Opposition **Vol. 1:** 102, 241, 244, 302, 328, 339, 364, 396, 399, 404, 424, 455, 501, 514, 525, 532, 535, 562 f., 565, 593, 597 f., 600, 609, 631, 638, 641, 647, 651, 675 f., 681, 699
Vol. 2: 129, 144, 202, 314, 372, 383, 435, 631, 676, 734, 764, 794
Vol. 3: 111, 136, 392, 504
Oppress **Vol. 2:** 260, 363, **807–809**, 822
Vol. 3: 192, 379, 574, 856
Oppressed **Vol. 2:** 257 f., 821
Vol. 3: 95, 206
Oppression **Vol. 1:** 408, 411, 612, 640, 644, 651, 679
Vol. 2: 100, 201, 206, 368, 424, 680, **807–809**
Vol. 3: 193, 357, 818, 1103
Oppressive **Vol. 1:** 482
Oppressor **Vol. 2:** 363
Vol. 3: 343, 366
Optimism **Vol. 2:** 430
Optimum **Vol. 1:** 679
Optional **Vol. 1:** 722
Oracle **Vol. 1:** 58, 62, 245 f., 426, 444, 519, 527, 574 f., 577, 594, 611, 730, 734
Vol. 2: 107 f., 296, 367, 879, 881, 890, 914
Vol. 3: 75, 78 f., 113, 124, 324, 403, 531, 720, 782, 1090, 1106, 1118, 1120
Oracle of God **Vol. 3:** 1098
Oracular spirit **Vol. 3:** 75
Oral instruction **Vol. 1:** 485
Vol. 2: 440
Oral tradition (→ Tradition, oral)
Oral transmission **Vol. 1:** 70
Oration **Vol. 2:** 369
Orator **Vol. 2:** 150
Vol. 3: 138, 346, 561, 1086
Oratory **Vol. 1:** 248
Vol. 3: 1083
Orchard **Vol. 3:** 918
Orcus **Vol. 2:** 85
Ordain **Vol. 1:** 259, 330, 445, 473, 612, 626, 695 f.
Vol. 2: 235, **438–451**
Vol. 3: 39, 481
Ordained theologian **Vol. 3:** 480
Ordeal **Vol. 1:** 646
Vol. 3: 110, 243
Order **Vol. 1:** 107, 109, 116, 197, 243, 269,

271 f., **330–343**, 369, 408, 476, 521 f., 524, 572, 595, 600, 625, 641, 654, 662, 664–667, 692, 696, 715, 718, 731
Vol. 2: 50, 57, 67, 101–103, 134, 142, 160–163, 189, 213, 254, 266, 300, 390, 392, 436, 439 f., 452, 459, 592, 603, 609, 633, 658–660, 698, 719, 776
Vol. 3: 49, 51, 56, 71, 84, 122, 210, 217, 483, 574, 577, 702, 807, 832, 1029, 1056, 1066, 1078, 1087
Order of widows **Vol. 3:** 1065
Orderliness **Vol. 2:** 95
Orderly **Vol. 2: 438–451**, 476
Vol. 3: 1082
Ordinal number **Vol. 1:** 665
Ordinance **Vol. 1:** 70, 109, 301, 308, 330–337, 370 f., 381, 386, 402, 496, 716, 734
Vol. 2: 92, 128, 132, 150, 160, 228, 236, **440**
Vol. 3: 41, 182, 186, 250, 354, 488, 584, 717, 760 f., 947
Ordinary **Vol. 1:** 62, 680
Ordination **Vol. 1:** 196 f., 478
Vol. 2: 151 f.
Vol. 3: 115, 424, 480, 767
Ordination of women **Vol. 3:** 1066
Organ **Vol. 1:** 230, 239, 350, 423, 451
Vol. 2: 180–182, **391**, 599
Vol. 3: 127
Organism **Vol. 1:** 232, 234, 237 f., 300, 302, 522
Vol. 2: 253
Vol. 3: 710
Organization **Vol. 1:** 300, 302–304, 521
Organized **Vol. 1:** 642
Orgiastic **Vol. 1:** 514
Vol. 2: 353
Orgy **Vol. 2:** 355
Oriental **Vol. 1:** 521 f.
Vol. 2: 336
Vol. 3: 827, 1055
Orientation **Vol. 1:** 583
Vol. 2: 404, 864
Origen **Vol. 1:** 49, 51, 104, 148, 251 f., 266, 315, 319, 535, 561, 636
Vol. 2: 81, 219, 506, 754 f., 869
Vol. 3: 148, 231, 291, 855
Origenists **Vol. 2:** 506 f.
Origin **Vol. 1:** 53, 56, 64, 95, **164–169**, 176, 179, 181, 426, 434, 440, 469, 498, 520 f., 561 f., 563, 576, 578, 616, 619, 624, 631, 654, 656, 669
Vol. 2: 35, 66, 76, 79, 124, 127, 129, 137 f., 157, 160, 217, 235, 305, 310 f., 334, 339 f., 394, 406, 656
Vol. 3: 646, 653, 657, 774, 803, 865, 868
Original **Vol. 1:** 664, 721, 737
Vol. 2: 287, 713
Original sin **Vol. 1:** 433, 721
Vol. 3: 581, 663
Original state **Vol. 1:** 654
Originate **Vol. 1:** 377
Originator **Vol. 1: 164–169**, 378, 736, 739
Vol. 2: 80, 128
Orion **Vol. 3:** 950
Ormazd **Vol. 3:** 693

Ornament Vol. 1: 241, 495, 521 f.
  Vol. 2: 92, 159
  Vol. 3: 483
Ornan Vol. 3: 426
Orphan Vol. 1: 191, 324, 477, 616, 691
  Vol. 2: 71, 359, 540, 737 f., 823
  Vol. 3: 357, 483, 852, 855, 1073–1075
Orpheans Vol. 3: 103
Orpheus Zeus Vol. 1: 665
Orphic Vol. 1: 182, 432, 528
  Vol. 2: 158, 188
  Vol. 3: 259, 929, 1085
Orphism Vol. 1: 616
  Vol. 2: 643
  Vol. 3: 231, 679
Orthodox Vol. 1: 549, 631, 669
  Vol. 2: 126, 316, 718
  Vol. 3: 180
Orthodoxy Vol. 1: 590
  Vol. 2: 505, 864
  Vol. 3: 770
Osiris Vol. 1: 184, 595
  Vol. 2: 274, 556
  Vol. 3: 388, 1085
Ossuary Vol. 1: 264, 393
  Vol. 2: 573
Ostentatious Vol. 1: 613
  Vol. 2: 136
  Vol. 3: 32, 389, 874
Ostraca Vol. 3: 483
Ostracism Vol. 2: 772
  Vol. 3: 361, 910
Ostracize Vol. 3: 913
Other Vol. 1: 666
  Vol. 2: 404, 739–742, 785 f.
  Vol. 3: 166, 247–253, 1080
Other-worldly Vol. 2: 357
Otherness Vol. 1: 679
Othniel Vol. 3: 557
Out of date Vol. 2: 443
Out of tune Vol. 2: 434
Outburst Vol. 2: 653
Outcast Vol. 1: 616, 685
  Vol. 2: 57, 170
  Vol. 3: 200, 560, 758, 1062
Outcome Vol. 1: 590, 741
  Vol. 2: 55, 63, 364
Outcry Vol. 1: 410
Outflank Vol. 1: 728
Outgoing Vol. 1: 547
Outlaw Vol. 1: 616, 686
  Vol. 3: 92, 183
Outline Vol. 2: 284, 291
Outlook Vol. 1: 534, 540, 598, 602, 605, 643,
  680 f., 686, 709
  Vol. 2: 49, 313, 452, 723
Outpost Vol. 1: 710 f.
Outpouring Vol. 1: 549
  Vol. 2: 230, 328
Outrage Vol. 2: 92
  Vol. 3: 28
Outside Vol. 1: 300, 303, 534, 685
  Vol. 2: 49, 445, 812
Outsider Vol. 1: 488, 581, 626

Vol. 2: 216, 343, 379, 402, 456 f., 748, 752
Outstanding Vol. 1: 729
Outward Vol. 1: 469, 552, 703–705, 708 f.
  Vol. 2: 150, 217
  Vol. 3: 244, 320, 903
Outward appearance Vol. 2: 288 f.
Outweigh Vol. 2: 357
Outwit Vol. 1: 137
Outworking Vol. 1: 723
Oven Vol. 1: 249
Over-shepherd Vol. 3: 564–568
Overcome Vol. 1: 85, 205, 328, 391, 424, 431 f.,
  437, 441, 443, 597, 623 f., 645, 650 f., 674,
  700, 723
  Vol. 2: 42, 136, 157 f., 221, 240, 243, 260, 282,
  359, 419 f., 438, 446, 453, 763 f.
  Vol. 3: 780, 810, 1012
Overcomer Vol. 3: 795
Overflow Vol. 1: 728 f., 731
  Vol. 2: 121, 128, 130 f.
  Vol. 3: 810
Overjoyed Vol. 2: 352–354, 436
Overlook Vol. 2: 266
Overlord Vol. 2: 158, 308
Overpassionate Vol. 2: 587–589
Overreaching Vol. 2: 201
Overripe Vol. 2: 587–589
Overrule Vol. 2: 299
Overseer Vol. 1: 188–190, 477
  Vol. 2: 318, 777
  Vol. 3: 478, 700, 930
Overshadow Vol. 3: 553–556
Oversight Vol. 1: 191
  Vol. 2: 411, 777
  Vol. 3: 585, 1065
Overstamp coins Vol. 2: 308
Overstep Vol. 3: 583–585
Overtake Vol. 1: 623
Overthrow Vol. 1: 599, 610
  Vol. 2: 146
Overtones Vol. 1: 483, 604
  Vol. 2: 315
  Vol. 3: 217
Overturn Vol. 3: 933–935
Overweening Vol. 2: 130
Overwhelmingly strong Vol. 2: 587–589
Ovid Vol. 3: 861
Owe Vol. 1: 498
  Vol. 2: 115, 666–668
Owl Vol. 3: 672
Own Vol. 1: 684
  Vol. 2: 413, 438, 456
Owner Vol. 2: 50, 297, 508–520, 581, 833
  Vol. 3: 416, 754, 920
Ownership Vol. 1: 299, 642
  Vol. 2: 438, 572–574, 858
  Vol. 3: 194, 594, 701, 853
Ox Vol. 1: 115
  Vol. 3: 1160

P source Vol. 1: 57, 61, 66
Pace Vol. 2: 369
Pacific Christ, concept of Vol. 3: 976 f.

Pacify **Vol. 2:** 777
　Vol. 3: 150, 152
Pack **Vol. 1:** 711
Paederast **Vol. 1:** 625
Paedophilia **Vol. 1:** 497 f.
Pagan **Vol. 1:** 109, 111 f., 139, 159, 208, 237,
　282, 320, 327 f., 341, 360 f., 405, 407, 449,
　453, 499, 501, 503 f., 551 f., 598, 628, 631 f.,
　639, 643, 717
　Vol. 2: 71, 102, 124, 126 f., 177, 199, 211, 221,
　235, 285 f., 309, 398, 516, 680, **790–795**, 885,
　923, 928
　Vol. 3: 81, 112, 162, 197 f., 426, 431, 498, 733,
　785, 793, 802, 839, 862, 913, 1118, 1165
Paganism **Vol. 1:** 452, 481, 547, 598, 611
　Vol. 2: 85, 173, 242, 309, 507, 576, 687, 720,
　742
　Vol. 3: 113, 346, 431
Pain **Vol. 1:** 187, 239 f., 260, 262, 288, 352 f.,
　392, 459, 461, 466, 471, 510, 564, 734
　Vol. 2: 28, 181, 414, 416, **419–421**, 674, 807
　Vol. 3: 111, 682, 829, 832, 848, 858, 1051
Pain of labour **Vol. 3: 857 f.**
Painful **Vol. 1:** 725
　Vol. 2: 243
Paint **Vol. 1:** 121
　Vol. 2: 334
　Vol. 3: 483
Painting **Vol. 2:** 287
Pair **Vol. 2:** 575, 686
　Vol. 3: 1160–1165
Palace **Vol. 2:** 190, 247, 254
　Vol. 3: 782 f., 786 f., 794
Palate **Vol. 3:** 449
Palestine **Vol. 1:** 55, 72, 81, 117, 121, 166, 249,
　363 f., 392, 394, 510, 544, 613, 615, 618, 620,
　633, 642, 684, 691, 743
　Vol. 2: 27, 125, 285, 327, 331, 791, 796, 823,
　836, 847, 849
　Vol. 3: 58, 84, 195, 269, 401, 407, 635, 756 f.,
　759, 785, 853 f., 991, 1001
Palestinian Christianity **Vol. 1:** 548, 601, 613
　Vol. 2: 785
Palisade **Vol. 3: 948–952**
Pallas **Vol. 2:** 224
Pallas Athene **Vol. 3:** 759
Palm **Vol. 1:** 648
Palm Sunday **Vol. 1:** 623, 724 f.
Pangs **Vol. 2:** 157
　Vol. 3: 858
Panic **Vol. 1:** 527, 621
Pannenberg, Wolfhart **Vol. 1:** 60
　Vol. 2: 908 f.
　Vol. 3: 301 f., 333, 900 f.
Panoply **Vol. 3: 959–967**
Pant **Vol. 3: 689–708**
Pantheism **Vol. 1:** 95, 636, 654, 692
Pantheistic **Vol. 1:** 734 f.
　Vol. '2: 77, 919
Pantheon **Vol. 1:** 140
　Vol. 2: 67, 85, 190, 375
Panticapaeum **Vol. 2:** 767
Papal infallibility **Vol. 3:** 386
Papal supremacy **Vol. 3: 384–388**

Papias **Vol. 1:** 51, 582
　Vol. 3: 64
Papyrus **Vol. 1:** 243, 247
　Vol. 3: 483
Parable **Vol. 1:** 57 f., 154, 430, 575, 577 f., 580,
　582 f., 652, 689, 724, 737
　Vol. 2: 217, 254, 279, 329, 382, 389, 401, 413,
　462, 501 f., 619, 643, 660, 667, 736, **743–760**,
　801, 803, 852, 889, 904 f., 916
　Vol. 3: 131, 161, 173, 336, 348, 503, 510, 522,
　532, 595, 762, 866, 868 f., 906, 916, 920 f.,
　951, 978, 1025, 1058 f., 1061, 1070, 1106,
　1109, 1121, 1137, 1140, 1155, 1157, 1161,
　1163
Parables of the Kingdom **Vol. 2:** 388
Parables in NT, List of **Vol. 2: 749–751**
Parabolic **Vol. 2:** 280 f., 529, 532, 630
Paraclete **Vol. 1: 88–92**, 324
　Vol. 2: 84, 231, 709, 787, 878, 883
　Vol. 3: 47, 242, 362, 704, 892 f., 1046
Paradigm **Vol. 3:** 336
Paradise **Vol. 1:** 103, 113 f., 389 f., 509
　Vol. 2: 45, 191, 205, 208, 688 f., **760–764**, 920
　Vol. 3: 36, 211, 241, 265, 271, 315, 602, 682,
　687, 694, 986–988
Paradigm **Vol. 3:** 1135
Paradox **Vol. 1:** 375, 427, 643
　Vol. 2: 327, 359, 433 f., 449, 884
Paraenesis **Vol. 1:** 65, 215, 502, 570, 604, 693
　Vol. 2: 129, 890
　Vol. 3: 30 f., 42, 59, 934, 988, 1026, 1150
Paraenetic **Vol. 3:** 930, 938, 1005, 1064
Parallelism **Vol. 1:** 117
　Vol. 2: 870, 893, 919
　Vol. 3: 170, 1132
Paralysis **Vol. 1:** 516
　Vol. 3: 993–1000
Paralytic **Vol. 1:** 701
　Vol. 2: 415
　Vol. 3: 999 f.
Paralyzed **Vol. 3:** 912
Paraphrase **Vol. 1:** 69
　Vol. 3: 487, 1181
Paraplegia **Vol. 3:** 1000
Parch **Vol. 3:** 422, 914
Parchment **Vol. 1:** 243
　Vol. 3: 484
Pardon **Vol. 1:** 219, 697–699, 702
　Vol. 2: 42, 115 f., 118–121, 131, 185, 865
　Vol. 3: 152, **177–189**, 836
Parentage **Vol. 1:** 619
　Vol. 2: 694
Parental power **Vol. 3:** 1070
Parenthood **Vol. 3:** 1068
Parents **Vol. 1:** 212, 219, 280, 285–289, 335,
　423, 490, 497, 619, 622, 687, 739
　Vol. 2: 43, 49 f., 92, 180, 224, 539, 739, 816,
　834, 871
　Vol. 3: 94 f., 775, 777, 779, 928–930, 1056
Parish **Vol. 1:** 690
Park **Vol. 2:** 760
Parmenides **Vol. 3:** 123, 875 f., **1082–1084**
Parody **Vol. 1:** 126
　Vol. 2: 430

515

Paronomasia **Vol. 2:** 655, 831
Parousia **Vol. 1:** 50, 53, 59, **65**, 73, 247, 298, 303, 313, 315 f., 342, 410, 425, 449, 469 f., 496, 514, 571, 657, 668, 693
Vol. 2: 33, 48, 63, 192, 194, 196, 230, 243, 245, 252, 272, 354, 382 f., 387 f., 447, 486, 503, 517, 531, 534, 630, 653, 738, 771, 789, 846, 875, **886–935**
Vol. 3: 59, 63, 188, 199, 215, 245, 252, 305, 365, 378, 394, 505, 569, 618, 626, 628, 633, 642, 644, 659, 826, 830, 832, 839, 844, 847, 849, 863, 930, 1003, 1158
Parseeism **Vol. 1:** 452
Vol. 3: 827, 829
Parsees **Vol. 1:** 451
Parsley **Vol. 1:** 406
Part **Vol. 1:** 300, 534, 537, 689, 706, 740
Vol. 2: 295, 302, **303 f.**, 445, 452
Vol. 3: 192
Partake **Vol. 1:** 414
Vol. 2: **269–271**, 661, 718
Vol. 3: 706
Parthenon **Vol. 3:** 1071
Parthenos **Vol. 3:** 1071
Partiality **Vol. 1:** 585, 587
Vol. 2: 449, 625
Participant **Vol. 1:** 639, 733
Participate **Vol. 1:** 95, 329, 414, 483, 595, **635–644**, 651, 685, 687, 715, 740
Vol. 2: 288, 355
Vol. 3: 245, 511
Participation **Vol. 1:** 709, 736
Vol. 2: 40, 162, 268, 270, 273, 360, 446
Vol. 3: 646 f., 747, 832
Particularist **Vol. 2:** 350
Particularity **Vol. 2:** 307
Parting **Vol. 1:** 241
Vol. 2: 352, 356, 416
Partisan **Vol. 2:** 622
Partition **Vol. 1:** 676
Vol. 2: 722
Vol. 3: 795
Partition-wall **Vol. 3:** **948–950**
Partner **Vol. 1:** 366 f., 507, 587, 635, 639, 642, 644, 660
Vol. 2: 111, 221, 230, 250, 349, 520, 581, 667
Vol. 3: 1055
Parnership **Vol. 1:** 291, 367, 678
Vol. 2: 307, 742
Parturition **Vol. 3:** 858
Party **Vol. 1:** 533, 535, 645
Vol. 2: 116, 298, 303, 311, 343
Vol. 3: 439, 441
Party division **Vol. 3:** 1032
Pashhur **Vol. 3:** 1097
Pass **Vol. 1:** 320–322, 698, 718
Vol. 2: 29
Pass away **Vol. 1:** 421, 458, 518, 525, 566, 673, 709
Vol. 2: 193, 304, 396, 419, 714, 910
Pass by **Vol. 1:** 699
Vol. 2: 281, 600
Vol. 3: 583
Pass judgment **Vol. 2:** 365, 370, 429

Pass night **Vol. 3:** 178
Pass on **Vol. 2:** 101
Vol. 3: **772–775**
Pass over **Vol. 1:** 697, 701
Vol. 2: **184–187**, 438, 766
Vol. 3: 255
Past test **Vol. 3:** 224
Pass through **Vol. 3:** 799
Passing **Vol. 1:** 304, 470
Vol. 2: 213
Vol. 3: 555, **833–839**
Passion **Vol. 1:** 58, 63, 105–108, 162, 186, 198 f., 231, 233 f., 396, 401, 435, 445, 456, 458 f., 469, 495, 501, 528, 572, 630, 633, 654 f., 674, 715, 725
Vol. 2: 112, 116, 123, 179 f., 182, 216, 257, 274, 299, 311, 314, 327–329, 341, 368, 411, 434, 526, 644, 661, 787, 795, 808, 880
Vol. 3: 28, 35, 47, 109, 132, 210, 212, 218, 221, 225, 294, 340, 517, 536, 624, 627, 682, **719–725**, 844, 922, 963 f., 1061
Passionate **Vol. 1:** 107
Vol. 2: 149, 265
Passionate love **Vol. 2:** **538–547**
Passionless **Vol. 1:** 432
Passive **Vol. 2:** 846
Passover **Vol. 1:** 157, 205, 223, 240 f., 265, 294 f., 308, 360, 364, 384, 437, **624–635**, 641, 691, 699, 713
Vol. 2: 54, 185, 277, 355, 410 f., 437, 441, 461–463, 478, 521 f., 569, 637, 644, 676, 716, 783, 892
Vol. 3: 47, 101, 117 f., 120, 159, 194, 200, 237, 244, 417, 424, 430, 472, 550, 669 f., 796, 846, 886, 911, 919, 953, 1017, 1053
Passover liturgy **Vol. 2:** **522**
Past **Vol. 1:** 164, 493, 496, 597, 681, 702
Vol. 2: 295, 314, 353 f., 393, 396, 407, 714, 891, 905
Vol. 3: 79, 238, 826, 834, 836, 840
Past the peak **Vol. 2:** **587–589**
Pastor **Vol. 1:** 103, 303
Vol. 2: 114, 187
Pastoral **Vol. 1:** 191, 475
Vol. 2: 303, 411
Pastoral Epistles **Vol. 1:** 55, **65**, 198, 200, 487, 647, 690
Vol. 2: 93, 133, 135, 152, 164, 170 f.
Pasture **Vol. 1:** 632, 743
Vol. 2: 211, 412, 438, 586
Vol. 3: 564
Patch **Vol. 1:** 613
Vol. 3: 543
Paternal **Vol. 1:** 572
Paternal estate **Vol. 2:** 317
Path **Vol. 1:** 481, 605
Vol. 2: 407
Vol. 3: 350–352
Patience **Vol. 1:** 80, 99, 215, 217, 257, 339, 364, 496 f., 593, 639, 644, 646, 679, 712
Vol. 2: 49, 63, 79, 105, 183, 240, 243–245, 261, 264, 361, 366, 385, 410 f., 682, **764–776**, 782, 806, 809, 834, 901
Vol. 3: 52, 73, 143, 229, 364, 366, 505, 725,

Patience (cont'd)
810
Patient **Vol. 2:** 168, 245, 291, 301, 712, **772–776**
  Vol. 3: 685, 691
Patina **Vol. 2:** 27
Patmos **Vol. 1:** 623
  Vol. 2: 775
  Vol. 3: 1049
Patriarchal **Vol. 1:** 56, 195, 539
Patriarchate **Vol. 3:** 1069
Patriarchs **Vol. 1: 65**, 66, 72, 76–78, 81, 165, 200, 327, 381, 541, 604, 615–617, 637, 675, 689–691, 713, 732
  Vol. 2: 104, 297, 314, 317–319, 442, 635, 791, 803
  Vol. 3: 70, 72, 263 f., 359, 416, 459, 465, 486, 564, 658 f., 734, 787, 811, 836, 851, 870, 1055
Patristic period **Vol. 1:** 61
Patroclus' ghost **Vol. 3:** 678
Patron **Vol. 3:** 598
Patronym **Vol. 3:** 653
Pattern **Vol. 1:** 71, 301, 304, 333, 366, 371, 380, 492, 512, 689 f., 716
  Vol. 2: 51, 191, 284, **290 f.**, 501, 619, 775, 889
  Vol. 3: 61, 120, 303, 332, 336, 513, 555, 569, 645, 724, 788, 909, 1135
Paul **Vol. 1:** 73, 78–81, 83 f., 86 f., 95 f., 98, 103, 106, 110–112, 114 f., 123, 129–136, 138, 144, 146 f., 150, 154, 157, 159 f., 163, 166, 168 f., 171, 173, 176, 179–183, 185, 191, 197, 205, 212–217, 220, 222, 228 f., 231 f., 234–238, 245, 247 f., 254, 256 f., 261–263, 266–269, 273–279, 281 f., 284, 286, 289, 298–301, 303, 305, 309–311, 313–318, 322, 324 f., 328–330, 334–337, 340 f., 343 f., 346, 350–352, 356, 359, 361, 365, 369–372, 374, 384–386, 389 f., 394, 397–403, 405–407, 410, 413–415, 417, 419–421, 424 f., 430 f., 435–442, 445 f., 448, 453, 455, 457 f., 460–462, 464–470, 472–483, 491 f., 495 f., 499–503, 507, 510–513, 519 f., 524, 528 f., 532, 539–541, 545, 547, 551 f., 554, 556, 558 f., 563 f., 567 f., 570 f., 582, 589–593, 599, 601 f., 604 f., 607, 610, 613, 615, 619 f., 623, 628, 630 f., 637–639, 641–643, 646–651, 657, 661–666, 674–676, 679–681, 684, 689–691, 693, 695, 697, 700–702, 704, 706–710, 712, 714, 717 f., 723, 727, 729–731, 737–742
  Vol. 2: 28, 32 f., 38, 40, 42, 45–47, 54, 57 f., 61 f., 65, 73 f., 76–78, 80 f., 83–85, 94 f., 100–102, 104–106, 110–113, 118–123, 126 f., 129, 131, 135–137, 139, 141, 144 f., 147 f., 152, 155–162, 169, 171, 175–177, 179, 188, 192, 202 f., 211–214, 216–219, 221–223, 229 f., 235 f., 241, 243, 245, 249, 252 f., 255, 262 f., 267, 273, 276 f., 279, 282 f., 286, 288, 300–302, 304, 310, 312, 314 f., 319 f., 326, 328 f., 338–340, 343, 349, 354–357, 359–361, 365 f., 368–370, 378, 380, 387 f., 391, 397–403, 405–407, 420, 422–425, 428 f., 434 f., 437 f., 442–448, 450–452, 456 f., 459, 462 f., 480, 503, 523, 550, 557, 573, 580 f., 587, 596 f., 600, 604 f., 618–620, 623, 632, 641, 660 f., 671–673, 678, 682, 691, 695, 699, 702,

707, 713, 722, 728 f., 736, 740–742, 755 f., 762 f., 765, 768, 770 f., 773–775, 786, 789, 793–795, 800 f., 804, 806 f., 809, 815–819, 826–828, 834 f., 844, 847, 861, 868, 880, 882–885, 895, 899, 902 f., 905, 907, 913, 919–927
  Vol. 3: 27 f., 31, 38, 40, 42, 46–48, 50, 52–55, 57 f., 60–66, 70–73, 81, 84–87, 96 f., 99, 101, 105–107, 112, 114, 117 f., 121 f., 125–132, 135, 137, 141 f., 144, 157, 163–165, 167–174, 180, 184 f., 188 f.,195, 197–199, 202 f., 211, 214 f., 220, 225–230, 243, 251 f., 257, 268, 274, 278, 280–286, 288, 290, 292 f., 296 f., 299, 301, 303–305, 312, 314 f., 318, 320–325, 332, 335 f., 346–349, 351, 359 f., 363, 365–370, 372 f., 377, 379 f., 383, 387, 389, 393, 397, 400 f., 403, 410, 412, 416 f., 428, 432 f., 436, 448, 456, 471, 475 f., 482, 489, 492–495, 499, 504 f., 518, 520 f., 523–525, 529, 531 f., 534–539, 541–544, 546–550 f., 552 f., 557, 560 f., 563, 568, 570–572, 575–577, 579–581, 584–586, 591 f., 595 f., 600–602, 604, 612 f., 632, 643–645, 651, 661 f., 671, 674, 683 f., 686 f., 694 f., 700–703, 705–707, 710 f., 714, 725, 727–729, 731 f., 742, 746, 749–752, 754 f., 759, 761, 764 f., 770 f., 773 f., 778–780, 784 f., 802, 808–810, 812–814, 818 f., 821 f., 824–826, 829–832, 837, 844, 847, 854, 857, 869, 872–874, 883–888, 903, 905 f., 909, 912, 914 f., 917, 921, 927, 932, 935, 940, 942, 944, 946–949, 951, 953–957, 962–967, 970, 994–996, 1008, 1018–1021, 1026, 1030–1032, 1036, 1042–1044, 1047, 1053 f., 1063–1067, 1070, 1072 f., 1075, 1079 f., 1110, 1112–1114, 1118 f., 1122 f., 1133, 1150–1152, 1158, 1164 f., 1167, 1176 f., 1179, 1181–1184, 1187 f., 1190–1195, 1196, 1199, 1201–1203, 1205–1208, 1211
Paul and James on justification **Vol. 3: 369 f.**
Paul of Samosata **Vol. 2:** 506
Paulus Fabius Maximus **Vol. 2:** 108
Paulus, H.E.G. **Vol. 3:** 292
Pauper **Vol. 1:** 479
Pausanias **Vol. 3:** 851
Pause **Vol. 1:** 594, 624
  Vol. 3: 405
Pawnbroker **Vol. 1:** 373
Pay **Vol. 1:** 226, 248, 250, 377, 684, 734
  Vol. 2: 62, 386
  Vol. 3: 138–144, 192, 566, **752–755**
Pay attention **Vol. 1:** 591
  Vol. 2: 132, 134, 175, 890
  Vol. 3: 129, 515
Pay back **Vol. 3: 134–136**
Pay court **Vol. 2:** 30
Pay damages **Vol. 3:** 134
Pay debt **Vol. 3:** 135, 379
Pay tax **Vol. 2:** 621, 850
Pay tithe **Vol. 2: 693 f.**
  Vol. 3: 851–855
Pay vow **Vol. 3:** 134, 424
Pay what is owed **Vol. 3: 755–759**
Payment **Vol. 1:** 484, 684, 687, 716
  Vol. 2: 41, 43, 118, 898

Vol. 3: 69, **144 f.**, 189, 1156
Pax Romana **Vol. 1:** 959
Peace **Vol. 1:** 114, 118, 123, 141, 208, 210 f., 222, 224, 237, 239, 269, 275, 301, 321 f., 341, 348, 366 f., 402, 459, 469, 489, 543, 555, 585, 638, 648, 653, 730, 732 f.
  Vol. 2: 72, 78, 83, 108 f., 113, 170, 183, 216, 230, 257, 268, 328, 357, 359, 363, 374, 388, 439, 482, 517, 521, 585, 590–593, 597, 617, 666, 720–723, **776–783**, 807, 817, 819, 866, 874, 899
  Vol. 3: 50 f., 70, 84, 97, 111, 118, 128, 169, 171 f., 185 f., 212, 217, 219, 221, 239, 250, 255–258, 369, 422, 447 f., 525, 528, 592, 605, 648, 682, 692, 710, 748, 778, 823, 825, 842, 866, 959, 966, 978, 981, 986 f., 1178
Peace-offering **Vol. 2:** 461
  Vol. 3: 422 f., 425 f., 873
Peaceable **Vol. 1:** 646
Peaceful **Vol. 2:** **776–783**
Peacemaker **Vol. 1:** 290
  Vol. 2: **776–783**
Pearl **Vol. 1:** 117, 647
  Vol. 2: 386, 502, 714, 833 f.
  Vol. 3: **381–399**, 532, 948
Peasant **Vol. 1:** 642
  Vol. 2: 820, 822
Peculiar **Vol. 1:** 305
  Vol. 2: 245, 310
Pedagogic **Vol. 3:** 1083
Pedantry **Vol. 2:** 448
Peddler **Vol. 1:** 138
Pederast **Vol. 2:** **569–571**
Pedersen, J. **Vol. 3:** 1125
Pedigree **Vol. 3:** 872
Peitho **Vol. 1:** 588
Pelc, J. **Vol. 3:** 1130
Peloponnesian war **Vol. 2:** 802
Penal **Vol. 1:** 393 f., 396, 398, 429
Penalty **Vol. 1:** 61, 309, 364, 391, 394, 430, 433, 468, 500, 505, 572
  Vol. 2: 48, 142, 449, 572, 858
  Vol. 3: 95 f., 151, 199, 575
Penance **Vol. 1:** 51
  Vol. 2: 208, 263 f., 666
Penetrate **Vol. 1:** 517
  Vol. 2: 349
Peniel **Vol. 2:** 317
Peninnah **Vol. 3:** 1057
Penitence **Vol. 1:** 109 f., 145 f., 148, 333, 349, **353–362**, 466, 520, 572
  Vol. 2: 157, 159, 183, 420, 864
  Vol. 3: 102, 421, 427, 542, 589, 691, 793, 859
Penitent **Vol. 2:** 152, 817
  Vol. 3: 241, 361, 588
Penitential prayers **Vol. 2:** 384
Penitential Psalms **Vol. 1:** 346
  Vol. 3: 997
Penitential ritual **Vol. 2:** 157
Pentateuch **Vol. 1:** 54, 56 f., 61 f., **65**, 66–68, 70, 72, 243 f., 293, 296, 331, 378, 442, 581, 622, 689, 698
  Vol. 2: 331, 357, 440, 442, 444, 638, 641
  Vol. 3: 440, 485

Pentateuchal criticism **Vol. 1:** 66
Pentecost **Vol. 1:** 129, 148, 153, 157 f., 323, 340, 395, 528, 532, 632, 634, 738 f.
  Vol. 2: 91, 176, 186, 252, 400, 426, 629, 699, 703, 732, 739 f., 768, **783–788**, 855, 916, 918
  Vol. 3: 71, 86, 109–111, 229, 344, 417, 422 f., 695, 697 f., 700, 707 f., 732, 813, 922, 1065, 1079 f., 1143
Pentecostalism **Vol. 2:** 785
People **Vol. 1:** 431, 433, 520, 541, 690, 715, 731 f.
  Vol. 2: 34 f., 38, 70, 92, 106, 124, 127, 131, 134, 151, 158, 185, 222, 224 f., 237, 241, 252, 254, 256, 306 f., 310, 312, 315, 319, 321, 326–328, 331 f., 334 f., 342 f., 349, 351, 363, 373, 399, 410, 412, 425, 438, 448, 457, 498, 539, 562, 642, **788–805**
  Vol. 3: 49, 69, 106, 219, 252, 353, 454, 574
People of the eye **Vol. 3:** 513
People of God **Vol. 1:** 76, 125, 129, 146, 159, 180, 191, 223, 243, 255 f., 297, 299 f., 302–304, 311, 332, 369–373, 385, 410 f., 433, 462, 465, 489, 499, 508 f., 532, 535, 540 f., 543, 553, 604, 619, 634, 637, 650 f., 661, 663, 684 f., 687–689, 713, 716 f., 720, 732 f.
  Vol. 2: 34, 38, 53, 56, 63 f., 69, 71, 73, 83, 86 f., 99 f., 105 f., 129, 134, 149, 154, 161–163, 175, 190, 194, 202, 215, 218, 226, 230, 236 f., 239 f., 242, 248 f., 255, 268, 275, 295, 297, 301, **306 f.**, 310, 315, 328–330, 337, 349 f., 353, 358, 363 f., 367 f., 374, 380, 385, 412 f., 425, 432, 442, 460, 512, 514, 541, 572 f., 577, 580 f., 583, 587, 628, 652, 670, 673, 680, 695 f., 698, 701, 712, 718, 722, 731 f., 738, 788–805, 810, 812, 835, 839–841, 873, 918, 927
  Vol. 3: 37, 74, 93, 104, 117–119, 150, 181, 193, 196, 198, 201, 208, 210, 224, 227, 232, 236, 243, 245, 249, 251 f., 256 f., 263, 266, 268 f., 279, 300, 318, 320, 325, 351, 355 f., 363, 387, 390, 397, 411, 435 f., 445, 463, 470 f., 495, 500, 505, 531, 552, 565, 567 f., 600, 625, 629, 637, 654, 692, 722, 740, 742, 748, 776 f., 787, 789–793, 799, 801, 809, 811, 813, 817, 824, 841, 853, 869–871, 879 f., 890, 905, 913, 920, 927, 937 f., 944 f., 962, 970, 1006 f., 1068 f., 1166
People of the land **Vol. 2:** 801
  Vol. 3: 105
People of Yahweh **Vol. 2:** 796
Peor **Vol. 2:** 638
Perceive **Vol. 1:** 106, 674, 692 f., 735
  Vol. 2: 132, 172, 269, **392–406**
  Vol. 3: **122–133**, 511
Perception **Vol. 2:** 172, 391, **392–406**
  Vol. 3: 125, 517, 677 f., 681, 1024
Perdiccas **Vol. 3:** 450
Perdition **Vol. 1:** 462–464, 467
  Vol. 3: 830
Perea **Vol. 2:** 849
  Vol. 3: 757
Perez **Vol. 3:** 950
Perfect **Vol. 1:** 163, 225, 231, 281, 304, 399, 467, 474, 521, 604, 623, 627, 668 f., 708, 720, 727, 740

Perfect (cont'd)
  Vol. 2: 59, 61 f., 65, 98, 101, 144, 162, 229, 304, 354, 359, 366, 402, 415, 447–449, 477, 531, 563, 566, 592 f., 669, 681, 717, 781 f., 789, 824, 832
  Vol. 3: 42, 215, 228, 315, 349 f., 502, 504, 645, 936, 1031
Perfecter Vol. 1: 168, 604
  Vol. 2: 59 f., 64, 185, 331
Perfection Vol. 1: 282, 371 f., 475, 521, 647, 649, 694, 729
  Vol. 2: 59–62, 64 f., 77, 96, 105, 143, 320, 411, 483, 546, 606, 690, 695, 741, 762, 908
  Vol. 3: 357, 725, 736, 766, 927, 1032, 1166
Perfectionist Vol. 3: 278
Perform Vol. 1: 484, 600, 610
  Vol. 2: 350
Perform oath Vol. 3: 135
Performance Vol. 1: 624
  Vol. 2: 327, 351
  Vol. 3: 1142
Performative theory of truth Vol. 3: 897
Perfume Vol. 1: 649 f., 683
  Vol. 2: 294 f.
Pergamum (Pergamon) Vol. 1: 407, 640
  Vol. 2: 233, 676, 678, 686
  Vol. 3: 432, 765, 915, 1047
Pericope Vol. 1: 65, 576
  Vol. 3: 62
Peridot Vol. 3: 395
Peril Vol. 1: 241, 419 f., 421, 510, 513
  Vol. 3: 205
Period Vol. 1: 473, 612, 628 f., 735
  Vol. 2: 61, 255, 887
  Vol. 3: 826, 839–845
Peripatetics Vol. 1: 711
Periphrasis Vol. 2: 426
  Vol. 3: 1120
Perish Vol. 1: 203, 397, 462–471, 500, 547, 603, 672, 725
  Vol. 2: 159, 214, 269 f., 284, 394, 459, 705, 831
  Vol. 3: 214, 323, 680, 826
Perishable Vol. 1: 390, 406, 468–470, 671
  Vol. 2: 657, 659
  Vol. 3: 267
Perizzites Vol. 2: 636
Perjured Vol. 3: 737–743
Perjurer Vol. 3: 737–743
Perjurious oath Vol. 3: 740
Perjury Vol. 2: 471
  Vol. 3: 75 f., 95, 737–743, 1049
Permanence Vol. 1: 207, 516, 609, 611, 661, 680, 711, 718
  Vol. 2: 189
Permanent Vol. 2: 220, 305, 349
  Vol. 3: 686, 730, 811, 1003
Permeate Vol. 1: 734
  Vol. 2: 461
Permissible Vol. 1: 351
  Vol. 2: 273
Permission Vol. 1: 657
  Vol. 2: 607 f.
Permit Vol. 1: 467, 478, 500, 698

  Vol. 2: 123, 732
  Vol. 3: 183
Permitted Vol. 2: 606–611, 811
Perpetual Vol. 1: 705
Perpetuate Vol. 3: 812
Perplexity Vol. 3: 559
Persecute Vol. 2: 805–809
  Vol. 3: 551
Persecution Vol. 1: 126, 166, 174, 183, 215, 233, 261, 263, 269, 278, 301, 303, 322, 347, 382, 394–396, 399, 403, 406, 455, 460, 462, 491, 493, 508, 540 f., 553, 559, 567, 571, 604, 607, 613, 639, 644, 651, 653
  Vol. 2: 34, 37, 136, 196, 231, 258, 270, 309–311, 316, 358–361, 363, 368, 373, 381, 383, 460, 663 f., 700, 730, 736, 766, 774, 776, 781, 804, 805–809, 840, 844, 904, 911–913, 915–918
  Vol. 3: 27 f., 96, 240, 257, 291, 357, 382, 452, 481, 501, 603, 626 f., 686, 697, 705, 711, 801, 818, 845, 849, 857, 859, 942, 951, 998, 1048, 1113, 1167
Persecutor Vol. 1: 694
  Vol. 2: 605, 806
  Vol. 3: 97, 201, 343, 712, 757
Persephone Vol. 2: 729
  Vol. 3: 739
Perseverance Vol. 1: 80, 494, 570, 712
  Vol. 2: 240, 245, 736, 767 f., 868
Persevere Vol. 2: 767 f., 772–776
  Vol. 3: 223–229
Persia Vol. 1: 141, 405
  Vol. 2: 95
  Vol. 3: 566, 788, 960
Persian Vol. 1: 64, 104, 124, 374, 393, 653, 656, 687
  Vol. 2: 207, 306 f., 335 f., 811, 847, 850
  Vol. 3: 270, 275, 829, 851, 1035
Persist Vol. 2: 154, 767 f.
Persistence Vol. 2: 131, 462, 767 f.
  Vol. 3: 1059
Person Vol. 1: 71, 233–236, 240 f., 272, 274, 276, 324, 329, 338, 347, 358, 375, 426, 491, 501, 526 f., 563, 565, 585–587, 595, 662, 665, 672, 688, 705, 707, 709, 716, 732 f.
  Vol. 2: 49, 146, 149, 157 f., 181 f., 217, 220, 233, 313, 341, 391 f., 534 f., 566–568, 648, 652, 864
  Vol. 3: 52, 54 f., 237, 303, 531, 679
Person of Christ (→ Christ, Person of)
Personal Vol. 1: 244, 269, 336, 357, 360, 368, 483, 491, 499, 546, 553, 562 f., 566, 579, 586 f., 590, 592, 597, 603, 618, 636, 644, 650, 692 f., 698, 702, 739
  Vol. 2: 67, 70, 99 f., 107, 121, 129, 148, 156, 158, 187, 215, 241–244, 288, 305, 332, 342, 377, 392, 395 f., 398 f., 403 f., 437, 444, 456, 511, 582, 863, 867
  Vol. 3: 246, 493, 581
Personal truth Vol. 3: 894
Personality Vol. 1: 229, 233, 432, 453, 457, 485, 492, 643, 707
  Vol. 2: 181 f., 568, 841
  Vol. 3: 226, 474, 545, 677, 680, 683, 823

Personalize **Vol. 1:** 695
Personification **Vol. 1:** 125, 410, 431, 463, 501, 508, 561, 563, 566, 655
   Vol. 2: 115, 190, 442, 444
   Vol. 3: 357, 731, 1029
Personify **Vol. 3:** 487, 492, 1056, 1069, 1083
Perspective **Vol. 2:** 240, 360
Persuade **Vol. 1: 587–606,** 733
   Vol. 2: 350 f., 398
   Vol. 3: 1123
Persuasion **Vol. 1:** 588 f.
   Vol. 3: 711, 951
Persuasive **Vol. 1:** 588
Pervade **Vol. 1:** 616, 723
Perverse **Vol. 2:** 36, 72, 469
Perversion **Vol. 1:** 460 f., 677
   Vol. 2: 51
   Vol. 3: 344, 1103
Perversity **Vol. 1:** 725
   Vol. 3: 574, 943
Pervert **Vol. 1:** 219, 397, 412 f.
   Vol. 2: 221, 370, 566, 822
   Vol. 3: 310
Pesher exegesis **Vol. 1: 65 f.,** 67
   Vol. 2: 187, 314, 754
   Vol. 3: 268
Pesikta **Vol. 1:** 628
Pessimism **Vol. 1:** 262, 434, 459
   Vol. 2: 241, 276
Pestilence **Vol. 1:** 109, 118, 716
   Vol. 2: 349, 911
   Vol. 3: 249, 268
Pet **Vol. 1:** 117
Peter **Vol. 1:** 52, 111, 130 f., 133, 135, 158, 160, 168, 171, 173, 175, 200–202, 302, 310, 313, 318, 321, 343 f., 359, 361, 390, 395, 404, 448, 455, 462, 473, 476–478, 493, 504, 512, 528, 572, 582, 623, 643, 690, 708, 739
   Vol. 2: 28, 111, 114, 119, 136, 152, 194, 231, 252, 302 f., 319, 341, 354, 368, 404, 433 f., 469, 542, 557, 596 f., 618, 624 f., 641, 652 f., 689, 691, 708, 728, 731–733, 736, 754, 769, 786, 794 f., 840, 851, 858, 877, 895, 916
   Vol. 3: 40, 64, 65 f., 71, 87, 98, 112 f., 115, 118, 121, 148, 160, 188, 213, 240 f., 282–284, 288, 294, 296, 317, 320, 325, 352, **381–388,** 394, 454, 481, 506, 509, 520, 529, 543, 555, 558 f., 568 f., 591, 699, 707, 711, 713, 717, 732, 742, 750 f., 753, 763, 793, 804, 807, 812, 822, 908, 985, 990, 1059, 1066, 1113, 1122, 1164, 1179
Peter's successor **Vol. 3:** 729
Petition **Vol. 1:** 410, 566 f.
   Vol. 2: 117, **860 f.,** 878, **882–885**
   Vol. 3: 97, 819
Petrify **Vol. 2:** 153
Petronius **Vol. 2:** 899
Phabi **Vol. 3:** 35
Phallus **Vol. 1:** 625
Phantom **Vol. 2:** 284
Phanuel **Vol. 3:** 81, 873
Pharaoh **Vol. 1:** 177, 195, 208, 330, 393, 452, 508, 560, 616
   Vol. 2: 116, 154 f., 200, 265, 378, 557, 569, 636 f., 640, 796, 835

   Vol. 3: 50, 279, 531, 550, 660, 866 f.
Pharisaic **Vol. 1:** 309, 630, 730
   Vol. 2: 43, 136, 261, 281, 309, 314, 579, 864, 866
   Vol. 3: 83
Pharisaism **Vol. 1:** 99
   Vol. 2: 309, **810–814**
   Vol. 3: 106
Pharisees **Vol. 1:** 72, 111, 116, 120, 153, 168, 174, 196, 199, 205, 220, 265, 267, 288 f., 337, 340, 346, 361, 363 f., 417, 427, 434, 487 f., 509, 516, 534 f., 539, 565, 567, 572, 612, 627, 630, 643, 680, 729 f.
   Vol. 2: 101, 133, 138, 144, 147, 170, 203, 207, 211, 222, 254, 262, 272, 281, 303, 311, 313, 316, 321, 350, 382, 385, 399, 419, 434, 442 f., 448, 460, 462, 467–469, 474, 570, 584, 596, 610, 623 f., 640, 693 f., 708 f., 712, 730, 732, 785, 801, **810–814,** 823, 842 f., 865, 880, 921
   Vol. 3: 39 f., 105, 108, 110, 115 f., 128, 141, 181, 183 f., 250, 253, 270, 313, 360 f., 378, 408 f., 428 f., 440–442, 445, 480–482, 486–488, 494 f., 507, 534, 538–540, 542, 566, 580, 584, 603 f., 649, 712, 741, 753, 757 f., 768 f., 785, 790, 792, 796, 804, 819, 854, 868, 883 f., 920, 942, 979, 1002, 1037, 1045, 1052 f., 1109, 1150, 1162 f., 1168
Pharnabazus **Vol. 2:** 848
Pharsalos **Vol. 2:** 124
Phases of moon **Vol. 3:** 733
Phenomenon **Vol. 1:** 680
   Vol. 2: 137 f.
Phenomenological approach **Vol. 3:** 330
Pherecydes of Syros **Vol. 3:** 259
Philadelphia **Vol. 1:** 254, 257
   Vol. 2: 399, 474, 550, 727, 775
Philemon **Vol. 1:** 247, 675, 690
   Vol. 2: 122, 550, 600
   Vol. 3: 596, 930
Philetus **Vol. 2:** 550
   Vol. 3: 915
Philip, apostle **Vol. 2:** 334
   Vol. 3: 728
Philip, evangelist **Vol. 2:** 114, 387, 550, 557, 728, 768
   Vol. 3: 56, 65 f., 81, 87, 456 f., 548, 602, 609, 1067
Philip (guardian of Antiochus V) **Vol. 3:** 498
Philip Herod I **Vol. 2:** 550
   Vol. 3: 540
Philip Herod II **Vol. 2:** 550
Philip of Macedon **Vol. 3:** 217
Philip II of Macedon **Vol. 2:** 550
   Vol. 3: 550
Philippi **Vol. 1:** 168, 267, 278, 340, 361, 407, 592
   Vol. 2: 136, 550, 707, 895, 899
   Vol. 3: 81, 557, 559, 592, 670, 794, 955, 964, 987, 1063, 1065, 1067, 1112, 1157
Philippians **Vol. 1:** 229, 570, 623, 739, 741
   Vol. 2: 131, 179, 218, 343, 354, 360, 550, 804, 816
   Vol. 3: 431, 552, 600, 674, 955
Philistines **Vol. 1:** 170, 195, 393, 433
   Vol. 2: 45, 98, 225, 260, 306, 308, 374, 637,

Philistines (*cont'd*)
742
Vol. 3: 250, 469, 782, 788
Phillips, J.B. **Vol. 3:** 1142
Philo **Vol. 1:** 49, 63, 77, 85, 87, 89, 92, 102, 108, 153, 175, 178, 184–186, 201–204, 216 f., 221, 227 f., 230, 243, 253, 259, 262, 277, 309, 313, 330, 334, 341 f., 349, 355, 360, 363, 368, 374, 377 f., 387, 409 f., 412, 428, 435, 442, 444, 450, 459 f., 465, 468 f., 495, 502 f., 509–514, 520, 523, 527, 533 f., 559, 563, 574 f., 577 f., 580 f., 598 f., 618, 627, 639, 641, 645 f., 648, 674, 683, 688, 691, 694 f., 700, 709, 720, 734, 742
Vol. 2: 33, 61, 72, 99, 109, 125, 128, 134, 137, 140, 150, 158, 169, 182, 187, 192, 222, 234 f., 241, 249, 266, 288–291, 310, 324, 332, 355, 357, 363, 373, 377, 462, 493, 512, 573, 579, 583, 590, 592 f., 607 f., 651, 658–660, 681, 690, 707, 738, 754, 756 f., 762, 779, 784 f., 798, 821, 878, 883
Vol. 3: 35–37, 41, 51, 98, 125 f., 129, 194, 210, 332, 377, 396, 407, 418, 451, 479, 486, 515, 522, 524, 526, 531, 545, 552, 554, 556, 570, 575, 595, 639, 669, 681, 684, 721, 740, 766, 769, 772, 789, 827, 842 f., 871, 875–877, 904, 938 f., 946, 989, 996, 1035, 1042, 1069, 1116, 1120, 1157, 1166
Philodemus of Gadara **Vol. 2:** 259
Philologus **Vol. 2:** 550
Philology **Vol. 1:** 57, 61, 68, 140
Philosopher **Vol. 1:** 443, 484, 616, 640
Vol. 2: 92, 265, 355, 372, 456, 550
Vol. 3: 103, 111, 217, 646, 748, 760, 766, 996, **1034–1036**, 1039, 1086, 1118
Philosopher king **Vol. 2:** 372
Philosophical **Vol. 1:** 230, 432, 481, 595, 598, 616, 660 f., 694, 711 f., 715
Vol. 2: 67, 124
Vol. 3: 123, 128, 778, 842, 865, 935, 938, 1081
Philosophical ethics (→ Ethics, Philosophical)
Philosophical schools **Vol. 1:** 68, 484, 488
Vol. 3: 1037 ·
Philosophy **Vol. 1:** 57, 59, 64, 70, 127, 164, 268, 330, 460, 483, 485, 501, 604, 636, 654, 664 f., 687
Vol. 2: 103, 125, 170, 257, 269, 284, 377, 392 f., 418 f., 430 f., 439, 442, 453, 460, 538, 550, 648
Vol. 3: 50, 122, 127, 399, 402, 486, 501, 678, 681, 689, 694, 824, 827, 875, 877, 939, 1027, 1031, **1034–1036**, 1069, 1084, 1087, 1136, 1169
Philosophy, moral (→ Moral philosophy)
Philosophy of religion **Vol. 1:** 59
Phinehas **Vol. 1:** 544
Vol. 3: 159
Phoebe **Vol. 3:** 546, 1063, 1065 f., 1158
Phoebus **Vol. 2:** 85
Phoenicia **Vol. 2:** 847
Vol. 3: 458
Phoenician **Vol. 2:** 126, 848
Vol. 3: 787
Phoenix **Vol. 2:** 725

Photinus **Vol. 2:** 507
Phrygia **Vol. 1:** 344
Vol. 3: 261
Phrygian stone **Vol. 3:** 518
Phylacteries **Vol. 1:** 254
Vol. 2: 136
Vol. 3: 105, 487, 490, 559
Physical **Vol. 1:** 71, 138, 230, 234–236, 240 f., 308 f., 365, 436, 440–443, 447, 461 f., 466 f., 494 f., 518, 539, 560–563, 565, 595, 600, 616 f., 650, 667 f., 674 f., 677–681, 710, 726 f., 735
Vol. 2: 59, 164, 172, 180–182, 184, 193, 220, 263, 265, 267, 271, 274, 350–352, 415, 419 f., 422–424, 478, 539, 719, 920
Vol. 3: 102, 105, 212, 215, 244, 260, 301, 305, 349, 504, 539, **676–687**, 694, 716, 946, 993, 1147
Physical sciences **Vol. 3:** 1034
Physician **Vol. 2:** 164, **166–170**, 386
Vol. 3: 428, 723
Physics **Vol. 3:** 900
Physiological **Vol. 1:** 742
Vol. 3: 689
Physique **Vol. 1:** 183
Vol. 2: 129, 659
Piaget, J. **Vol. 3:** 1125
Pick out **Vol. 1:** 536
Pick up **Vol. 3:** 1081
Picture **Vol. 2:** 279, 281, 746, 927
Vol. 3: 904
Piece **Vol. 1:** 729
Vol. 2: 296
Pierce **Vol. 1:** 444
Pierce, C.S. **Vol. 3:** 896
Pierced ear **Vol. 3:** 594
Pietists **Vol. 3:** 108
Piety **Vol. 1:** 58, 102, 399, 451, 481, 539, 594 f., 597, 599, 604, 622, 694, 708
Vol. 2: 47, 75, 85, **90–95**, 100, 106, 160, 201, 216, 225, **236–238**, 275, 353, 355, 426, 469, 473, 588, 605, 863 f.
Vol. 3: 141, 210
Pig **Vol. 1:** 117, 119, 125, 226
Vol. 3: 1121
Pigeon **Vol. 1:** 172
Pilate **Vol. 1:** 83, 162, 168, 179, 222, 270, 395 f., 427, 512, 554, 556, 696
Vol. 2: 139, 150, 331, 339, 368 f., 378 f., 449, 451, 526 f., 549, 623 f., 799, 801, 849 f.
Vol. 3: 63, 173, 430, 441, 452, 558, 589, 592, 723, 893, 990, 977 f., 1017, 1045, 1047, 1121
Pilfer **Vol. 3:** 379
Pilgrim **Vol. 1:** 100, 173, 205, 305, 628, 632, 691
Vol. 2: 194, 437, 873
Vol. 3: 965
Pilgrim festivals **Vol. 2:** 311
Pilgrimage **Vol. 1:** 626, 661
Vol. 2: 326, 329, 376, 920
Vol. 3: 814
Pillar **Vol. 1:** 131, 302, 420, 523, 626, 656, 712
Vol. 2: 188 f., 249, 493, 827
Vol. 3: 391, **795**, 822, 1154
Pillar of cloud **Vol. 3:** 257

Pilot **Vol. 1:** 194
Pindar **Vol. 2:** 140
Pine **Vol. 1:** 509, 648, 723
Pinnacle **Vol. 2:** 235
   Vol. 3: 805
Pioneer **Vol. 1:** 168, 604, 669
   Vol. 2: 331, 669
   Vol. 3: 215
Pious **Vol. 1:** 112, 218, 358, 416, 492, 527 f., 552, 562, 612, 614, 708
   Vol. 2: 49, 57, 71 f., 91, 105, 125, 134, 176, 178, 216, 232, 237, 257, 288, 309, 335, 394, 432, 450, 565, 810, 817, 867
   Vol. 3: 549–551, 745, 799, 829
Pirate **Vol. 3:** 377
Pisces **Vol. 2:** 558
Pisgah **Vol. 2:** 638
   Vol. 3: 806, 1009
Pishon **Vol. 3:** 986
Pisidian Antioch **Vol. 1:** 462
   Vol. 2: 33, 300, 451
   Vol. 3: 561
Pit **Vol. 1:** 470
   Vol. 2: 205, 351, 701
   Vol. 3: 262, 498 f., 732
Pitch **Vol. 3:** 153
Pitch-fork **Vol. 1:** 685
Pith **Vol. 2:** 180
Pithom **Vol. 2:** 635 f.
Pitiless **Vol. 2:** 267, 594–598
Pitiful **Vol. 2: 594–598**
Pity **Vol. 1:** 565, 569, 715
   Vol. 2: 543, 581, 593, **594–600**, 738
   Vol. 3: 1053
Pius IX **Vol. 3:** 663
Pivotal **Vol. 2:** 227
Placate **Vol. 1:** 479
   Vol. 2: 860
   Vol. 3: 152–154
Place **Vol. 1:** 275, 331, 413, 474 f., 477, 660 f., 666, 680, 684–686, 690, 696, 742
   Vol. 2: 161, 276, 303
   Vol. 3: 745, 932
Place of honour **Vol. 1:** 664
   Vol. 3: 587–589
Place of meeting **Vol. 1:** 69
Place of rest **Vol. 3: 254–258**
Place of sacrifice **Vol. 3:** 418
Place under **Vol. 1:** 710
   Vol. 2: 368
Plague **Vol. 1:** 114, 124, 162 f., 241, 380, 463, 465, 509, 568, 612, 651, 721, 743
   Vol. 2: 58, 586, 625, 628, 637, 654, 711, 720, 889
   Vol. 3: 192, 267, 590, 788, 846, 857, 984, 996
Plain **Vol. 1:** 577
   Vol. 3: 316 f., 1004 1014
Plan **Vol. 1:** 194, 244, 322, 329 f., 332, 346, 356, 380, 383, 430, 471–473, 476, 540 f., 552, 562, 662, 671, 692 f., 695–697, 730, 735–738
   Vol. 2: 72 f., 77, 149, 156, 195, 198, 216, 220, **253–256**, 290, 298, 302, 336, 376, 666, 819, 912
   Vol. 3: 69, 123, 125, 129, 189, 214, 220, 224, 279, 311, 502, 654, 691, 820, 823 f., 1017, 1033, 1149
Planet-gods **Vol. 1:** 631
Planets **Vol. 2:** 459, 509, 558
   Vol. 3: 717, 735 f., 840
Planned procedure **Vol. 3: 935–943**
Plant **Vol. 1:** 178, 187, 313, 380, 389, 406, 515 f., 560, 586, 625, 652, 721 f., 725 f., 743
   Vol. 2: 27, 59, 129, 180, 185, 198, **210 f.**, 252 f., 312, 474, 476, 520, 565, 601, 657 f., 889
   Vol. 3: 27, **521–527**, 554 f., 835, **865–870**, 986, 1002
Plantation **Vol. 2:** 248
Plaster **Vol. 1:** 471
Platform **Vol. 2:** 185, 369
Plato **Vol. 1:** 65 f., 232, 431 f., 483, 521, 533, 561 f., 573–575, 579, 616, 636, 640, 705
   Vol. 2: 98 f., 103, 188, 259, 284, 372, 430, 439, 457, 498, 643, 648, 719, 772, 776
   Vol. 3: 42, 75, 81, 98 f., 122–124, 138, 152 f., 217, 231, 259 f., 353, 402, 554, 593, 635, 679, 690, 775 f., 840 f., 875 f., 925–927, 1027, 1034, 1083, 1085 f., 1119, 1124, 1129, 1139
Platonic **Vol. 1:** 49, **66**, 491, 512, 595, 602, 636, 671, 734
   Vol. 2: 72
   Vol. 3: 210, 843, 889, 905, 926, 1117
Platonism **Vol. 2:** 919
   Vol. 3: 684, 877, 900, 1156
Plausible **Vol. 1:** 592
Play **Vol. 1:** 267, 590, 708, 710
   Vol. 2: 430, 436, 468
   Vol. 3: 474, 521
Play at funerals **Vol. 2:** 418
Play on words **Vol. 1:** 592 f.
   Vol. 2: 431 f., 434, 715, 766, 837
   Vol. 3: 796, 805, 867, 950, 1096, 1162
Playfulness **Vol. 2:** 431
Plea **Vol. 1:** 410
   Vol. 2: 215, 307, 383
Plead **Vol. 2: 882–885**
   Vol. 3: 677
Pleasant **Vol. 1:** 458
   Vol. 2: 98, 103, 105, 116, 211, 271, 297, 475
   Vol. 3: 744–746, 817, **845–849**
Please **Vol. 1:** 349, 534, 544, 680, 687
   Vol. 2: 116, 160, 241, 244, 357, 780, **814–820**, 858
   Vol. 3: 219, 264, 925
Pleasing **Vol. 2:** 103, 432, 774, 789, **814–817**
   Vol. 3: 264, 424, **744–746**
Pleasure **Vol. 1:** 431, **456–461**, 498, 530, 534, 537, 623, 630, 713
   Vol. 2: 118, 138, 271, 273–275, 352, 356, 419, 458, 550, **814–820**
   Vol. 3: 256, 270, 677, 902
Pleasure-loving **Vol. 2:** 475
Pledge **Vol. 1:** 369, 372, 375, 440, 594, 638, 663, 710, 713, 719
   Vol. 2: 39–44, 142, 667, 881
   Vol. 3: 355, 484, 740, 1074
Plenary inspiration **Vol. 3:** 329
Plentiful **Vol. 2:** 128, 130

Plenty **Vol. 2:** 690
Pliable **Vol. 3:** 915
Pliny **Vol. 2:** 553, 556 f.
  Vol. 3: 111
Plot **Vol. 1:** 363
  Vol. 2: 296, 318, 430, 748, 757
  Vol. 3: 125
Plotinus **Vol. 1:** 66, 522, 562, 636
  Vol. 3: 1084
Plough **Vol. 1:** 115
  Vol. 2: 385, 742
  Vol. 3: 407, 543, 1160
Ploughman **Vol. 1:** 493
Pluck **Vol. 1:** 721
  Vol. 2: 267
  Vol. 3: 671, 792, 1163
Pluck out **Vol. 1:** 561, 727
Pluck up **Vol. 2:** 252
Plumbline **Vol. 2:** 239
  Vol. 3: 392
Plunder **Vol. 1:** 508, 546
  Vol. 3: 137, 377, **379**, 470, 472, 533, **601–605**,
  943
Plunge **Vol. 1:** 611
  Vol. 2: 150, 198
Plurality **Vol. 1:** 94
Plutarch **Vol. 2:** 259, 289 f.
  Vol. 3: 81, 690, 739, 827
Pluto **Vol. 2:** 85, 729
Pneumatic **Vol. 1:** 133, 500, 502
  Vol. 3: 571, 1029, 1032
Pneumatological **Vol. 1: 66**
Pneumatology **Vol. 1: 66**
  Vol. 2: 388
  Vol. 3: 704
Pneumatopsychosomatic **Vol. 2:** 567
Pod **Vol. 1:** 117
Poet **Vol. 1:** 579
  Vol. 2: 85, 233, 326
  Vol. 3: 76, 81
Poetic truth **Vol. 3:** 894
Poetry **Vol. 1:** 59, 582, 640
  Vol. 3: 500, 564, 668, 672, 1081, 1086
Pogrom **Vol. 2:** 309
Poimandres **Vol. 1:** 60
Point **Vol. 1:** 574, 726, 731
  Vol. 2: 354, 717
  Vol. 3: 182
Point of time **Vol. 3: 833–839**, 841, **845–849**
Point out **Vol. 3:** 569
Pointless **Vol. 1:** 547
Poiseidon **Vol. 3:** 216
Poison **Vol. 1:** 108, 202, 459, 510, 563
  Vol. 2: 27–29, 295, 334, 349, **552–562**, 661
Poisoner **Vol. 2: 552–562**
Poisonous **Vol. 3:** 866
Pole **Vol. 1:** 389
Polemic **Vol. 1:** 248, 302, 383, 672, 676
  Vol. 2: 261, 263, 310–315, 403 f., 449
  Vol. 3: 36, 495, 621
Police **Vol. 1:** 337, 396
Policy **Vol. 2:** 802
  Vol. 3: 391
Polish **Vol. 1:** 471

Vol. 3: 395
Politarch **Vol. 2: 801–804**
Politeness **Vol. 2:** 513 f.
Political **Vol. 1:** 124, 267, 291,. 475–478, 492,
  501, 517–519, 532, 534–536, 539, 545, 596,
  606 f., 610, 624, 627, 640, 715–718, 720, 732
  Vol. 2: 107, 110 f., 147, 257, 259, 306, 310 f.,
  325, 341, 372, 374, 376, 385, 438 f., 475,
  497, 657, 777, 788, 802, 887, 903, 905, 921
  Vol. 3: 33, 45, 49 f., 79, 146, 148, 193, 259,
  346, 502, 551, 559, 598, 979
Political equality **Vol. 2:** 309
Political organization **Vol. 3:** 870
Politician **Vol. 3:** 389, 949
Politics **Vol. 1:** 645
  Vol. 2: 306, 509
  Vol. 3: 75, 111, 461, 574, 738, 886, 1069
Poll-tax **Vol. 1:** 269
  Vol. 2: 850
  Vol. 3: 752–755, 853, 979
Pollution **Vol. 1:** 265, 447, 449
  Vol. 2: 286
  Vol. 3: 102, 783
Polyandry **Vol. 2:** 575
Polybius **Vol. 2:** 290
Polycarp **Vol. 1:** 51, 154, 406
  Vol. 3: 279
Polycrates' ring **Vol. 3:** 753
Polygamy **Vol. 2:** 564, 575 f., 578 f.
  Vol. 3: 95, 1055, 1057, 1075
Polynesian tribes **Vol. 1:** 308
Polysemy (multiple meaning) **Vol. 3:** 878, 1124
  f.
Polytheism **Vol. 2:** 66, 71, 284 f., 396, 507
Polytheistic **Vol. 2:** 278
  Vol. 3: 662
Pommel **Vol. 1:** 647
Pomp **Vol. 2:** 44
Pompeii **Vol. 2:** 683
  Vol. 3: 394
Pompey **Vol. 2:** 308
  Vol. 3: 452, 598, 756, 788, 815
Pompous **Vol. 2:** 198
Pond **Vol. 3:** 982, 992
Ponder **Vol. 1:** 106
  Vol. 3: 231, **820 f.**
Pontus **Vol. 2:** 34
Pool **Vol. 1:** 581, 637
Pool of reeds **Vol. 3:** 992
Poor **Vol. 1:** 216 f., 219, 249, 334 f., 358, 489,
  542, 547, 555, 564 f., 642, 733
  Vol. 2: 49 f., 56, 63, 71, 110, 118, 141, 200,
  255, 257, 259–261, 263–267, 273, 275, 300
  f., 329, 358, 363, 379, 386, 388, 396, 400,
  429, 453, 499, 540, 543, 594, 596, **820–829**,
  834, 842–844, 846 f., 852
  Vol. 3: 70, 93, 95, 119, 145, 192 f., 202, 206,
  241–243, 253, 313, 351, 357, 369, 423, 499,
  525, 545 f., 548, 553, 572, 580, 696 f., 744,
  752, 790, 810, 853–855, 953, 969, 994, 1043,
  1059 f., 1074, 1103, 1105, 1110, 1158
Poor in spirit **Vol. 2: 824**
Pope **Vol. 3:** 385
Poplar **Vol. 3:** 866

Populace **Vol. 1:** 731, 733
  Vol. 2: 788–790
Popular **Vol. 2:** 437
Popular asembly **Vol. 2: 788–790**
Popularity **Vol. 1:** 681
Popularize **Vol. 1:** 671
Populate **Vol. 1:** 518
Population **Vol. 1:** 519, 728, 731 f.
  Vol. 2: 305, 788, 795, 801
Porch **Vol. 1:** 68
  Vol. 2: 30
  Vol. 3: 782, 787, 795
Porcupine **Vol. 1:** 725
Porphyry **Vol. 1:** 601
Portable **Vol. 3:** 782
Portent **Vol. 1:** 622
  Vol. 2: 192, 629, **633**, 911
  Vol. 3: 559
Porter **Vol. 2:** 254
Portico **Vol. 3:** 789
Portion **Vol. 1:** 640, 673
  Vol. 2: 295–304, 791
Portrayal **Vol. 2:** 431
Pose **Vol. 3:** 821
Poseidon **Vol. 1:** 189
  Vol. 2: 85, 233
  Vol. 3: 556
Posidonius **Vol. 2:** 639
Position **Vol. 1:** 129, 188, 299, 471, 533, 538, 540, 610, 651, 667, 739
  Vol. 2: 44, 48–50, 80, 102, 158, 198, 257, 259, 319, 325, 336, 373, 378, 446, 674, 862
  Vol. 3: 128, 251, 420, 440, 584, 586, 779, 1055
Positive **Vol. 1:** 98, 496, 553, 583, 654, 678–680, 686
  Vol. 2: 310, 312, 315, 451
Possess **Vol. 1:** 548, 557, 635 f., 659 f., 729, 739
  Vol. 2: 200, 295–304, 311, 316 f., 364, 397, 438, 538
  Vol. 3: 1064
Possessed **Vol. 1:** 428, 450, 453, 516, 528 f., 673, 734
  Vol. 2: 691
Possession **Vol. 1:** 539, 615, 636, 637, 639, 661, 664, 688
  Vol. 2: 49, 267, 297–303, 307, 310, 325, 335, 499, 649, 791, 794, 797, 800, 828
  Vol. 3: 473, **474–476**, 734, 1057, 1074, 1080, 1158
Possession, right of **Vol. 3:** 716
Possessions **Vol. 1:** 137–139, 143, 272, 277, 292, 381, 456 f., 482, 495, 508, 514, 641 f., 644, 684, 717, 729, 743
  Vol. 2: 51, 63, 99, 191, 255, 286, 302, 305, 308, 356, 428 f., 438, 501, 539, 549, 582, 596, 619, 800, 820, 824 f., **829–853**
  Vol. 3: 140 f., 143, 145, 151, 184, 190, 193, 213, 225, 251, 253, 324, 340, 372, 381, 484, 497, 545, 547, 553, 560, 576, 595, 604, 638, 748, 751, 812, 853–855, 953, 994
Possible **Vol. 1:** 714, 730, 742
  Vol. 2: 606–611
  Vol. 3: 213

Possibility **Vol. 1:** 493, 600, 678, 681, 705, 738
  Vol. 2: 399
Post **Vol. 1:** 314, 476
Post-apostolic **Vol. 1:** 602
Post-exilic **Vol. 2:** 309
Post-millenarianism **Vol. 2:** 389
Posterity **Vol. 1:** 209, 431, 721, 729
Postmillennialist **Vol. 1: 53**, 508
  Vol. 2: 702
Posture **Vol. 1:** 609, 635
  Vol. 2: 869
Pot **Vol. 1:** 252
  Vol. 2: 349
  Vol. 3: 910–917
Potency **Vol. 1:** 497, 625
Potentate **Vol. 1:** 406
  Vol. 2: 70
Potiphar **Vol. 1:** 560
  Vol. 2: 116
  Vol. 3: 591
Potsherd **Vol. 3:** 483, 912–914
Potter **Vol. 1:** 93, 380, 387, 520
  Vol. 2: 434, 609
  Vol. 3: 910–917
Potter's field **Vol. 1:** 93, 520, 689
  Vol. 3: 912
Potter's wheel **Vol. 3:** 916 f.
Pound **Vol. 2:** 838
  Vol. 3: 752
Pour **Vol. 1:** 369, 520, 548, 648, 651, 653, 683, 702
  Vol. 2: 785, 787, **853–855**
  Vol. 3: 422
Pour out **Vol. 3:** 432
Poverty **Vol. 1:** 142, 172, 277, 313 f., 489, 547, 564, 731
  Vol. 2: 197, 201, 267, **820–829**, 831, 882
  Vol. 3: 377, 430, 608, 790 f., **952–956**, 994, 1055, 1074
Power **Vol. 1:** 100, 106, 111, 119, 122 f., 130, 141 f., 149, 151 f., 163–167, 171, 175, 180, 186, 190, 205, 207–209, 214, 219, 221, 223–225, 236, 241, 244, 250, 269, 271, 276, 299, 311, 315, 323, 329, 335 f., 344, 347, 369, 371, 378, 380 f., 383, 386 f., 398–401, 413–417, 421–424, 427, 429 f., 432, 434, 436–440, 443, 445, 451–454, 457–460, 466, 469, 473, 476, 485, 494, 496–498, 500, 504, 507 f., 511, 514 f., 525–528, 530, 543–547, 551, 555, 562–567, 579, 594 f., 597, 599 f., 602 f., 609 f., 612, 623, 647, 650–652, 655, 657, 669, 676, 688, 692, 694, 701 f., 706–709, 712, 718, 722 f., 727, 730 f., 739
  Vol. 2: 30, 44, 46–48, 51, 61 f., 64, 68, 70–75, 78 f., 86, 94, 99, 111, 113, 119 f., 128, 142, 146–151, 159, 162, 165, 169, 177, 181–185, 191, 194 f., 198, 200, 204, 207, 210, 215, 223–225, 230, 232 f., 237, 243, 245, 271 f., 282, 287 f., 290, 303, 309, 318, 335 f., 358 f., 368, 372, 376, 380, 382, 384, 388, 398 f., 403, 411–413, 430, 433, 462, 508, 510–514, 516 f., **601–611**, 625, 648 f., 654, 660, 680, 693, 712, 716, 718, 783, 788, 834, 842 f., 868, 874, 877 f., 883, 916 f., 921, 918 f.

Power (cont'd)
  Vol. 3: 27, 36, 56 f., 88, 97 f., 101, 103, 110, 147, 149, 193 f., 205 f., 214 f., 218, 230, 263, 266, 270, 276 f., 279 f., 281, 310, 315, 317, 323, 345, 347, 350, 359, 367, 372 f., 457, 469, 484, 498, 504, 523, 559, 621, 627, 632, 643, 686, 691, 693, 701, 703, 705, **711–718**, 728 f., 805, 861, 864, 886, 913, 935, 982, 993, 995, 1012, 1026, 1033, 1083, 1147, 1189
Power of attorney **Vol. 1:** 331
  Vol. 2: 608
Power of darkness **Vol. 2:** 608
Power of language **Vol. 3:** 1123, 1142
Power of words **Vol. 3:** 1125
Powerful **Vol. 1:** 451, 610, 669
  Vol. 2: 109, 425, **601–616**
  Vol. 3: 317–324, 563, **712–714, 1147–1152**
Powerless **Vol. 1:** 209, 217, 277, 315, 336, 418, 420, 549, 552, 616
  Vol. 2: 147, 259, 393, **601–616**
  Vol. 3: 204, 363, 473, 585, 915, **993–996**
Powers **Vol. 1:** 95, 102 f., 113 f., 118, 120, 124, 127, 167, 169, 208 f., 222–224, 236, 238, 301–303, 315, 327, 343, 374, 389, 402, 413 f., 424, 438, 443, 449, 452, 454, 457, 459, 461 f., 467, 476, 509, 519, 525, 527, 564, 610, 631, 644, 647, 649–651, 657, 676, 701, 718 f.
  Vol. 2: 67, 69, 73–75, 101, 165–167, 179, 195 f., 198–200, 213, 251, 270 f., 274, 284–286, 364, 393, 430, 457 f., 460 f., 485, 514, 518, 559, 602–606, 631, 645, 736, 868
Powers that be **Vol. 2: 609**
Practical **Vol. 1:** 601
  Vol. 2: 390, 400
Practical virtues **Vol. 3:** 926
Practice **Vol. 1:** 70, 526, 613, 686–688
  Vol. 2: 61, 147, 391, 437, 659
  Vol. 3: 756, 891, 934, **1147–1152**, 1155
Practise **Vol. 1:** 481, 494 f., 733
Practise magic **Vol. 2: 552–562**
Praetor **Vol. 3: 958–967**
Praetorian guard **Vol. 3:** 320
Praetorium **Vol. 2:** 32, 378
Pragmatic theory of truth **Vol. 3: 896 f**.
Praise **Vol. 1:** 99–101, 103, 116, 200, 206, 208, 210, 212 f., 227, 257, 263, 281, 320, 344–346, 370 f., 379–382, 387, 409, 413, 444, 469, 508, 514, 521, 523, 597 f., 651, 689, 695, 703, 731 f.
  Vol. 2: 44, 46 f., 49, 58, 80, 83, 100, 105, 128, 159, 173, 176, 190 f., 194, 201 f., 206, 243, 260 f., 265, 272, 290, 294, 302, 305, 319, 328, 353 f., 418, 422, 425 f., 436, 478, 516 f., 528, 540, 596, 602, 604, 625, 650, 724, 738, 744, 784, 797, 823, 841, 844, 855, 862, 865, 868, 874, 883, 893, 925
  Vol. 3: 42, 48, 52, 113, 142, 199, 210, 224, 230, 237, 243, 245 f., 256, 262, 271, 428, 434, 558, 565, 592, 600, 671 f., 675, 728, 792, 810, **816–819**, 828, 842, 854, 879, 908 f., 923, 965, 1079 f., 1122, 1143. 1166
Praiseworthy **Vol. 1:** 456 f.

  Vol. 2: 98
  Vol. 3: 927, 933
Prattle **Vol. 1:** 550, 552
Prayer **Vol. 1:** 76, 98 f., 107, 109 f., 120 f., 128, 143, 151, 163, 207, 210 f., 223, 225, 227, 246 f., 251 f., 272, 274, 276, 278, 285, 320 f., 323, 332, 339, 345, 380–382, 409, 411, 420, 426, 433, 452, 459, 484, 487, 504, 509, 515, 528, 544, 562 f., 566 f., 569, 586, 592, 609 f., 612–620, 625, 627 f., 633, 637, 642, 646 f., 650, 704, 723, 727, 730, 732, 734, 740
  Vol. 2: 32, 64, 71, 73 f., 77, 83, 118, 122, 152, 160 f., 166 f., 174 f., 178, 185, 190, 194, 212, 216, 221, 227, 229, 231, 235, 237, 239, 244, 259 f., 291, 294, 297, 299, 311, 313, 320, 325–327, 351, 353, 359 f., 366, 396, 400, 416, 424, 428, 469, 509, 512, 518, 521, 530, 561, 596, 619, 626, 650, 653 f., 666, 669, 721, 726, 730, 735–737, 768, 771, 774, 793, 797, 803, 807, 816–819, **855–886**, 927
  Vol. 3: 30, 49, 70, 93, 105, 130, 149, 152, 160, 167, 169, 194, 197, 199, 203, 210 f., 219, 221, 230, 232, 235, 238, 242, 244–246, 268, 275, 319, 369, 378, 380, 389, 391, 402, 417, 427, 432, 436, 460, 470, 474, 476, 485, 487, 509, 528, 531, 533, 536, 550, 525 f., 565, 595, 608, 611, 614, 638–640, 649–651, 657, 669 f., 672, 675, 682, 687, 702, 705, 713, 722, 744, 783, 791, 802 f., 808, 817, 819, 847, 857, 861, 869, 873, 879, 908, 930, 967, 987, 990, 997, 1004, 1007, 1009–1012, 1022, 1032, 1065–1067, 1080, 1119 f., 1205
Prayer for the dead **Vol. 3:** 1206
Prayer of Azariah **Vol. 1:** 50
Prayer of Manasses **Vol. 1:** 50
Prayer of sanctification **Vol. 2:** 522
Prayer-bands **Vol. 2:** 136
Prayer-straps **Vol. 2:** 864
Praying in the Spirit **Vol. 2:** 873, 883
Preach **Vol. 2:** 107, 109, 126, 169, 367, 413, 447, 632, 816
  Vol. 3: 44–68, 242, 286, 313, 352, 410, 763 f., 774, 821, 1054, 1092, 1110
Preacher **Vol. 1:** 131 f., 199, 211, 298, 662
  Vol. 2: 113, 381
  Vol. 3: 77, 469, 525, 616, 1050, 1118
Preaching **Vol. 1:** 54 f., 62, 95, 111, 121, 123, 129, 131, 158, 160, 168, 213 f., 216, 235, 238 f., 246, 263, 266, 289, 322, 324, 358 f., 396 f., 400, 445 f., 475, 486, 489, 496, 508, 519, 540, 543, 545, 547, 551, 558, 572, 589, 599, 601, 613, 619, 644, 660, 665, 675, 677, 684, 686, 689, 701 f., 727, 735, 738
  Vol. 2: 73, 75 f., 85, 100 f., 111 f., 129, 152, 155, 169, 176, 179, 208, 221 f., 250, 255, 338–340, 342, 351 f., 358–360, 366, 377, 379, 382–388, 418, 443, 451, 543, 547, 603, 633, 654, 665, 676, 679 f., 709, 732, 740, 780, 782, 818, 844, 902, 904, 908, 916, 918
  Vol. 3: 42, **48–57**, 66, 107, 127, 141, 144, 168, 214 f., 245, 277, 314 f., 322 f., 326, 328, 361, 365, 417, 521, 532, 558, 570, 580, 600, 619, 639, 661, 729, 760–762, 771, 785, 809, 838, 906, 919, 941, 944, 954, 1018, 1026, 1031 f.,

1059, 1067, 1080, 1091, 1112, 1114, 1157
Precaution **Vol. 3:** 446
Precedence **Vol. 1:** 78, 134, 533, 556, 729
  Vol. 2: 57, 157, 427, 429
  Vol. 3: 1022
Precedent **Vol. 2:** 373, 443
Precept **Vol. 1:** 332, 340, 525
  Vol. 2: 261, 270
  Vol. 3: 542
Precious **Vol. 1:** 260, 478, 480, 537, 596, 634, 665
  Vol. 2: 49, 76, 541
Precious stones **Vol. 1:** 205, 380
  Vol. 2: 674
  Vol. 3: 381–399
Precious stones in the Apocalypse **Vol. 3: 395–398**
Preciousness **Vol. 3:** 989
Precipitation **Vol. 1:** 683
Preclude **Vol. 1:** 668, 730, 736
Preconceived **Vol. 2:** 363
  Vol. 3: 533
Precondition **Vol. 3:** 309, 482, 619, 702
  Vol. 2: 775
  Vol. 3: 171, 212, 419
Predestination **Vol. 1:** 244, 378, 382, 471, 473, 478, **692–697**, 707
  Vol. 2: 298, 397, 609
  Vol. 3: 439, 529, 1017, 1019
Predetermination **Vol. 1:** 692
  Vol. 3: 654
Predict **Vol. 1:** 692
  Vol. 2: 320, 351
  Vol. 3: 28, 74
Prediction **Vol. 1:** 198, 290, 381, 541, 545, 572, 737
  Vol. 2: 339, 880
  Vol. 3: 79, 82, 87, 241, 267, 276, 294, 624, 627, 1008, 1122
Pre-eminence **Vol. 1:** 135, 193, 666 f.
Pre-ethical **Vol. 2:** 230
Pre-existence **Vol. 1: 66**, 166, 178, 232, 522, 547, 549, 619, 668, 706
  Vol. 2: 46, 828
  Vol. 3: 463, 643, 724, 776, 1033
Pre-existent **Vol. 1:** 707
  Vol. 2: 189, 289, 326, 329, 500, 504, 546, 565, 645, 652
  Vol. 3: 82, 187, 516, 597, 1023
Preface **Vol. 1:** 247
Prefect **Vol. 1:** 270
Preference **Vol. 1:** 534, 536, 539, 587, 667
  Vol. 2: 364
Prefiguration **Vol. 3:** 41
Prefigure **Vol. 1:** 619
  Vol. 2: 191
Pregnancy **Vol. 1:** 176, 186, 288, 466, 506, 512
  Vol. 2: 423, 587
  Vol. 3: 1072
Pregnant with meaning **Vol. 3:** 816
Prehistory **Vol. 1:** 56
  Vol. 2: 889
Preincarnate **Vol. 1:** 677
Prejudgment **Vol. 1:** 584

Prejudice **Vol. 2:** 363 f.
Premature **Vol. 1:** 183
Premillenarianism **Vol. 2:** 389
Premillennialist **Vol. 1: 52**, 508
  Vol. 2: 701
Premises **Vol. 2:** 247
Premonition **Vol. 2:** 599, 624
Preoccupation **Vol. 1:** 400
  Vol. 3: 533
Preordain **Vol. 1:** 695
Preparation **Vol. 1:** 411, 612, 625, 630, 633
  Vol. 2: 54, 315, 334
  Vol. 3: 116–118, 349–351, 405–411, 548, 663, 804, 844, 915, 917
Preparation for the Passover **Vol. 2:** 527
Prepare **Vol. 1:** 423, 475, 541, 543, 561, 611, 633, 646, 662, 722
  Vol. 2: 229, 253, 382, 388
  Vol. 3: 116–122, 349–351, 503, 873, 915
Prepare beforehand **Vol. 3: 116–118**
Preparedness **Vol. 2:** 165
Prerequisite **Vol. 1:** 600
Prerogative **Vol. 1:** 697
  Vol. 2: 320
  Vol. 3: 97, 917
Presage **Vol. 1:** 737
Presbyter **Vol. 1:** 136, **188–201**, 477
  Vol. 2: 563
  Vol. 3: 700
Presbyterate **Vol. 1:** 197
Presbyterian **Vol. 1:** 199
Prescience **Vol. 1:** 383
Prescribe **Vol. 1:** 54, 573
  Vol. 3: 483, 759
Prescription **Vol. 2:** 813
Presence **Vol. 1:** 65, 90 f., 102–104, 175, 223, 232, 239, 250, 272, 276, 280, 299–301, 335, 346, 384, 409, 466, 474 f., 490, 525, 586, 607, 612, 629, 681, 723, 734
  Vol. 2: 45, 47, 68, 70, 82, 86 f., 100, 129, 150, 160 f., 163, 165, 186, 215, 282, 326, 354, 356, 387, 463, 484, 489, 491, 493, 517, 523, 535 f., 585, 627, 650, 656 f., 718, 777 f., 782, 869, 881, 884, **886–935**
  Vol. 3: 55, 98, 106, 227, 235, 266, 298, 310, 407, 449, 514, 543, 555 f., 602, 627, 640, 729, 784, 788–790, 794 f., 805, 812–814, 828, 844, 863, 1003, 1096, 1117, 1180
Present (gift) **Vol. 1:** 234, 406
  Vol. 2: 96, 437
  Vol. 3: 421, 744, 747
Present (time and place) **Vol. 1:** 234, 305, 319 f., 323, 327, 400, 425, 437, 466, 469, **471–478**, 491, 508, 525, 590, 603, 607, 638 f., 646, 671–673, 696, 701 f., 706 f., 713, 717, 719, 728, 736 f.
  Vol. 2: 40 f., 54, 65, 110, 112, 122, 130, 186, 190, 192, 242, 246, 252, 266 f., 277, 282, 287 f., 298, 313, 315, 329, 343, 350, 353, 357, 359 f., 363, 367, 370, 382–389, 393, 396, 417, 420 f., 426, 447, 461, 496, 503, 515, 517–519, 527, 530 f., 536, 543, 606, 613, 630, 633, 654, 674–676, 703, 714, 749, 789 f., 798, 809, 844, 846, **886–935**

Present (time and place) (*cont'd*)
 Vol. 3: 52, 55 f., 63, 79, 86, 99, 199, 214, 221,
 238, 244 f., 252, 277, 279, 282, 305, 310,
 315 f., 318 f., 320, 333, 349, 393, 412, 470,
 505 f., 511, 603, 605, 617, 626, 732, 737,
 793, 826, 831 f., 834, 838, 840, 842, 844,
 849, 924, 962, 965, 981, 1001, 1075
Present (verb) **Vol. 1:** 235, 572, 647 f., 655, 657
 Vol. 2: 354, 482
 Vol. 3: 220, 432, 745, 925
Present age **Vol. 1:** 326, 524, 566, 677
 Vol. 2: 245, 275, 383, 672, 843
Presentation **Vol. 1:** 474, 696
 Vol. 3: 159, 1071
Presentation formula **Vol. 2: 279**
Presenting **Vol. 3:** 417
Preservation **Vol. 1:** 266, 498
 Vol. 2: 123, 141, 364, 572, 781, 862, 868
 Vol. 3: 205–216, 250, 527, 818, 1088, 1148
Preservative **Vol. 3:** 443, 445
Preserve **Vol. 1:** 333, 463, 479, 597, 631, 640,
 657, 662, 685, 700, 715, 717
 Vol. 2: 95, 99, 132, 134, 159, 295, **838–840**
 Vol. 3: 177, **200–216**, 444, 686
Preserver **Vol. 3: 216–221**
Preside **Vol. 1:** 199
President **Vol. 1:** 190, 196, 666
 Vol. 2: 158, 234
Press **Vol. 1:** 649
Press into **Vol. 3:** 712
Press upon **Vol. 2: 807–809**
Pressure **Vol. 1:** 568, 607, 678 f., 729, 733
 Vol. 2: 306, 765, 808
 Vol. 3: 759, 916
Prestige **Vol. 2:** 334
 Vol. 3: 440
Prestigious **Vol. 3:** 589
Presume **Vol. 3:** 583, 687, 822
Presumption **Vol. 1:** 412, 551
 Vol. 2: 834
 Vol. 3: 799
Presumptuous **Vol. 2:** 130, 201
 Vol. 3: 29 f., 32
Presupposition **Vol. 1:** 583, 598
 Vol. 2: 340, 343, 393, 631
 Vol. 3: 104, 327, 372, 640
Pretence **Vol. 1:** 587
 Vol. 2: 49, **468–470**
Pretend **Vol. 2: 468–470**
Pretender **Vol. 1:** 629
 Vol. 2: 34, 314, 338, 379, 430, **468–470**
Pretension **Vol. 2:** 462
Pretext **Vol. 1:** 334, 719
Prevail **Vol. 1:** 303, 731
 Vol. 2: 305
 Vol. 3: 712–714
Prevarication **Vol. 2:** 400
Prevent **Vol. 1:** 457, 497, 499, 560, 608, 676,
 687, 715
 Vol. 2: 220–223, 326, 394
Previously **Vol. 1:** 666, 695
Prey **Vol. 1:** 114, 172, 484, 550, 611, 709
 Vol. 2: 421, 470
Price **Vol. 1:** 268, 432, 572

 Vol. 2: 43, 48 f., 711
 Vol. 3: 139, 142, 155, 166, 174, 180, 1057
Price of release **Vol. 3: 189–200**
Priceless **Vol. 2:** 480
Prick **Vol. 1:** 726
 Vol. 2: 572
Prickle **Vol. 1:** 725
Pride **Vol. 1:** 113, 140, 227, 229, 259, 311, 381,
 405 f., 458, 531, 644
 Vol. 2: 120, 148, 162, 198 f., 243, 249, 259–
 261, 264, 352, 358, 403, 436, 442, 617 f., 661
 Vol. 3: 27–32, 357, 544, 561, 734, 824, 1032,
 1052, 1054
Pride of life **Vol. 2:** 475
 Vol. 3: 32
Priest **Vol. 1:** 53, 80, 100, 122, 152, 190, 196,
 198, 204, 208, 210–212, 214, 216, 219, 221,
 255, 271 f., 294, 305, 322, 344, 360, 363,
 373–375, 405, 414, 416, 474, 485, 499, 511,
 537 f., 543, 574 f., 579, 586, 596, 617, 625,
 628, 633, 687, 690, 699, 731, 733
 Vol. 2: 53, 61, 63, 141, 154, 167, 223, 226–
 228, 231, **232–236**, 238, 240, 256, 287, 294,
 296 f., 307, 311, 320 f., 335, 367, 380, 411,
 415, 437, 440 f., 447, 456 f., 464–467, 569,
 577, 590–594, 631, 649, 652, 693 f., 701,
 711, 726, 795, 799, 811, 813, 823 f., 842, 863
 Vol. 3: 32–44, 50, 76, 78, 89, 95, 103–105,
 108, 149 f., 154 f., 164, 190, 207 f., 239, 250,
 342, 347, 408, 415, 419, 421, 423, 432 f.,
 435 f., 439, 478, 550–553, 561, 582, 585,
 588, 711, 715, 742, 745, 777, 781, 797, 815,
 852 f., 1060, 1074, 1154
Priest, chief **Vol. 1:** 83, 199, 281, 337, 395, 413,
 665
 Vol. 2: 32, 167, 234, 339, 469, 623, 641
 Vol. 3: 185, 211, 480, 792, 965
Priest, high **Vol. 1:** 122 f., 151, 168, 198, 205,
 221, 321 f., 324, 327, 340 f., 351, 356 f., 363,
 371, 375, 386, 405, 448, 472, 487, 544, 619,
 637, 665, 685, 689
 Vol. 2: 63, 80, 123, 178, 194 f., 199, 217, 226,
 230 f., **232–236**, 238, 244, 282, 289, 293, 296,
 327, 335–337, 368, 378 f., 447, 451, 577,
 590–593, 598, 614, 625, 642, 651 f., 664,
 669, 674, 717 f., 799
 Vol. 3: 32–44, 120 f., 129, 161 f., 189, 198 f.,
 244, 313, 317, 323, 366, 396 f., 420, 424,
 433, 441 f., 478, 483, 552, 582, 723, 742,
 788 f., 794, 812, 815, 822, 853, 925, 941,
 947, 966, 1074, 1113
Priest-king **Vol. 1:** 99, 619
 Vol. 2: 335, 378, 590–593, 694
Priest-Logos **Vol. 3:** 36
Priestess **Vol. 3:** 1055
Priesthood **Vol. 1:** 61, 66, 80, 120, 305, 333,
 405, 408, 619, 677, 731
 Vol. 2: 64, 125, 225, 228, 230, **232–236**, 249,
 320, 327, 380, 436, 448, 505, 574, 579, 590–
 593, 638, 693 f., 839, 899
 Vol. 3: 32–44, 228, 336, 366, 435, 654, 782
Priesthood of believers **Vol. 3:** 435
Priestly **Vol. 1:** 426, 630, 699
 Vol. 2: 53, 147, 149, 228, **232–236**

Priestly anointing **Vol. 1:** 123
Priestly code **Vol. 3:** 418
Priestly decision **Vol. 1:** 70
Priestly garment **Vol. 1:** 312
Priestly office **Vol. 2: 232–236**, 447
Priestly oracle **Vol. 1:** 58
  Vol. 2: 240
Priestly ordinances **Vol. 1:** 66
Priestly party **Vol. 3:** 440
Priestly people **Vol. 1:** 309
Priestly service **Vol. 2:** 195, **232–236**
  Vol. 3: 785
Priestly tradition **Vol. 1:** 53
Priestly writing **Vol. 1:** 53, 65, **66**
Priests' court **Vol. 3:** 789
Primacy of Peter **Vol. 3:** 384
Primal **Vol. 1:** 654, 697
  Vol. 2: 52, 205, 657
Primal man **Vol. 1:** 302
  Vol. 2: 158, 162, 195, 249, 645 f.
  Vol. 3: 617, 632
Primary **Vol. 1:** 664, 711
Prime numbers **Vol. 1:** 665
Primeval **Vol. 1:** 422, 507 f., 522, 640 f.
  Vol. 2: 197, 394, 452, 889
  Vol. 3: 35 f., 40
Primeval water **Vol. 3:** 983
Primitive **Vol. 1:** 99, 298, 303, 457, 473, 528, 545, 599, 613, 619, 634, 642, 645, 686
  Vol. 2: 250, 337–339
Prince **Vol. 1:** 102, 164, 168, 293 f., 464, 648
  Vol. 2: 70, 205, 307, 312, 372, 376, 562, 797
  Vol. 3: 49, 51, 588, 714
Prince of demons **Vol. 1:** 452
  Vol. 3: 472
Prince of evil **Vol. 1:** 452
Prince of gods **Vol. 2:** 71
Prince of light **Vol. 2:** 492
Prince of peace **Vol. 2:** 779
Prince of this world **Vol. 1:** 458, 525
  Vol. 2: 365, 609 f.
  Vol. 3: 469 f., 582, 705, 802
Principalities **Vol. 1:** 315, 424, 525, 647
  Vol. 2: 162, 195 f., 559, 645, 736
  Vol. 3: 172
Principle **Vol. 1:** 166, 230, 256, 271, 353, 483, 502, 542, 549, 561, 563, 565, 569, 578, 582 f., 619, 653 f., 675, 705, 715, 719
  Vol. 2: 66, 157, 188, 289, 309, 314, 327, 366 f., 427, 436 f., 446 f., 452, 663
  Vol. 3: 57, 524, 764, 1034
Principle of verification **Vol. 3:** 1135
Prior **Vol. 2:** 187
Priority **Vol. 1:** 334, 664, 666, 697
  Vol. 2: 160, 314, 800
Priscilla **Vol. 2:** 847
  Vol. 3: 89, 1063, 1065
Prison **Vol. 1:** 171, 229, 328, 340, 487, 522, 717
  Vol. 2: 29 f., 132, 134, 136, 205, 393, 434, 736, 818
  Vol. 3: 121, 227, 273, 359, 558 f., **591 f.**, 679, 794, 1157
Prison warder **Vol. 3: 591 f.**
Prisoner **Vol. 1:** 191, 505, 649

  Vol. 2: 121, 132, 168, 268, 295, 367, 517, 828
  Vol. 3: 170, 189, 379, **589–599**, 713
Prisoner of war **Vol. 1:** 716
  Vol. 3: 590 f., 601
Private **Vol. 1:** 535, 577–579, 582, 641–643, 647, 680
  Vol. 2: 107, 273, 325, 438, 456, 838, 869
Private profit **Vol. 2:** 235
Privilege **Vol. 1:** 385, 480, 538 f., 621, 666, 716, 739
  Vol. 2: 49, 81, 122, 247, 294, 307, 309, 317, 350
  Vol. 3: 137, 381, 561, 954
Prize **Vol. 1:** 406, 470, **644–652**
  Vol. 2: 62, 97, 807
  Vol. 3: 49, 142, 261, **601–605**, 682
Probability **Vol. 1:** 60, 326
Probation **Vol. 2:** 696, 838
  Vol. 3: 808
Problem **Vol. 1:** 500, 505, 532, 564, 577 f., 583 f., 592, 603, 716
  Vol. 2: 123, 160, 235, 286, 314, 374, 442, 453
  Vol. 3: 75
Procedure **Vol. 1:** 364, 535, 580
  Vol. 2: 440
  Vol. 3: 935–943
Proceed **Vol. 1:** 320, 322
  Vol. 2: 222
Proceedings **Vol. 1:** 364, 698
Proceeds **Vol. 2:** 847
Process **Vol. 1:** 432, 437, 484, 486, 541, 597, 600, 602, 625, 652, 654, 656, 666, 668 f., 711, 722, 736, 740–742
  Vol. 2: 52, 62, 65, 128 f., 131, 269, 334, 364, 370, 383–385, 391
  Vol. 3: 53, 574, 702, 1147
Procession **Vol. 1:** 492, 625 f., 629, 647
  Vol. 3: 45, 873, 913
Procksch, O. **Vol. 3:** 1124
Proclaim **Vol. 1:** 89, 222, 245, 277, 338–340, 371, 402, 409, 423, 431, 436–438, 485, 489, 532, 544, 590, 594, 640, 662, 689, 708, 717, 729
  Vol. 2: 68, 78, 83, 107, 114, 125, 154, 179, 212, 255, 263, 274, 328, 373, 382, 401, 404, 443, 622
  Vol. 3: 44–68, 68–74, 77, 169, 232, 237, 245, 504, 764, 914, 1042, 1092, 1097, 1152
Proclaimer **Vol. 3: 74–89**
Proclamation **Vol. 1:** 62 f., 95, 111, 127, 135, 146 f., 167, 179, 237, 248, 272, 297 f., 310, 340, 346, 355, 384, 397, 399, 409 f., 445, 454, 495, 523, 568, 572, 599, 647, 650, 662, 677, 688, 701 f., 716, 719
  Vol. 2: 36, 54, 75, 77 f., 108 f., 111, 113 f., 121, 147, 175, 206, 221 f., 261 f., 269, 338 f., 343, 351, 357, 360, 375, 380 382, 384–387, 395, 536, 630–632, 654, 682, 740, 915, 928
  Vol. 3: 44–68, 85, 166, 170, 216, 232, 242–244, 247, 277, 285, 314 f., 322 f., 326, 330, 401, 430, 456, 462, 495, 504, 546, 548, 626, 696 f., 718, 766, 770, 774, 780, 837 f., 927, 942, 969, 1042, 1044, 1047, 1050, 1080, 1088, 1091, 1093, 1098, 1101, 1106, 1108–

Proclamation (cont'd)
1112, 1121, 1123
Proconsul **Vol. 1:** 270
Vol. 2: 369
Procreate **Vol. 2: 476–484**
Procreation **Vol. 1:** 79, 177, 497
Vol. 3: 678
Procurator **Vol. 1:** 166, 270
Vol. 2: 258, 308, 334
Vol. 3: 456
Procure **Vol. 1:** 374, 680
Vol. 3: 529
Prodigal **Vol. 1:** 110, 436, 446, 729
Vol. 2: 32, 170, 349, 386, 475, 600, 790
Vol. 3: 28, 278, 348, 674, 751, 954, 1061
Prodigy **Vol. 2: 633**
Produce **Vol. 1:** 176, 186, 378, 380, 383, 714, 722 f., 725
Vol. 2: 271
Produce of land **Vol. 3:** 852
Product **Vol. 1:** 165
Production **Vol. 1:** 642
Productivity **Vol. 3:** 444
Profane **Vol. 1:** 344, 379, 447 f., 467, 639, 641
Vol. 2: 223 f., 226 f., 230, 236, 650, 653
Vol. 3: 28, 104, 415
Profane language **Vol. 3:** 341
Profess **Vol. 2:** 669
Vol. 3: 68–74
Profession **Vol. 1:** 201
Vol. 3: 61, 70, 965
Professional **Vol. 1:** 512, 575
Professional mourners **Vol. 2:** 418
Profit **Vol. 1:** 546, 678
Vol. 2: 254
Vol. 3: 29, 134, **136–138**, 174, 1054
Profit-motive **Vol. 3:** 137
Profitable **Vol. 3:** 760
Profound **Vol. 1:** 707
Profuse **Vol. 1:** 728
Profusion **Vol. 1:** 729
Progenitor **Vol. 2:** 319
Programme **Vol. 2:** 308, 341
Progress **Vol. 1:** 164 f., 584, 742
Vol. 2: 128, 130, 221
Progression **Vol. 1:** 548
Vol. 3: 229
Progressive **Vol. 1:** 432
Prohibition **Vol. 1:** 226, 231, 340, 384, 426, 499 f., 625, 670, 688
Vol. 2: 268, 272, 281, 284, 286 f., 415, 554, 580, 732
Vol. 3: 105, 343, 740 f., 1066, 1153, 1160
Projections of altar **Vol. 3:** 715
Proletariat **Vol. 1:** 500
Prologue **Vol. 1:** 576, 628
Vol. 2: 927
Prometheus **Vol. 1:** 654
Vol. 2: 457, 490
Prominence **Vol. 1:** 680
Vol. 3: 481, 1059
Promiscuity **Vol. 1:** 497
Vol. 3: 1072
Promise **Vol. 1:** 53, 72–74, 76 f., 80 f., 98 f.,
112, 123, 128, 141, 146, 148, 159, 173, 185, 208–211, 214 f, 217–219, 224, 237 f., 262, 271, 276, 286, 296, 305, 308, 311, 317, 324, 327 f., 339, 344, 346 f., 350, 358 f., 367–372, 374 f., 385, 407, 410, 412, 422, 426 f., 439, 445 f., 458, 460 f., 466, 483 f., 489 f., 504 f., 518, 531 f., 537, 541, 545, 551, 556 f., 571, 581, 587–589, 595 f., 598, 600, 603 f., 609, 615, 617, 633, 637 f., 640, 644, 651, 658–660, 663, 678, 681, 685, 688–691, 697, 701, 713 f., 717, 719, 731 f., 733, 737, 744
Vol. 2: 39, 54, 65, 68, 70, 73, 76 f., 86, 100, 102, 107 f., 111, 120, 122, 129 f., 142, 152, 155 f., 159, 170, 176, 202 f., 238–240, 242 f., 244 f., 250, 252, 258, 260–263, 265–267, 271, 276, 278, 282, 295, 297, 300–302, 310, 314, 317–319, 328, 330, 332, 342, 358 f., 380, 386, 388, 395 f., 399, 402, 415, 417, 419–421, 429, 435, 444 f., 447–449, 453, 472, 474, 478, 543, 570, 605, 617, 626, 631, 636, 641, 648 f., 653, 661, 695, 709, 716, 727 f., 763, 775, 778 f., 786 f., 797, 823, 825, 835, 854, 856 f., 863, 881, 897, 909, 916, 923
Vol. 3: 42, 48, 55, **68–74**, 101, 117, 129, 143, 145, 171 f., 198, 202, 211, 228 f., 235, 257, 264, 268, 314, 350, 366, 371, 382, 389, 404, 456, 485 f., 495, 516, 523 f., 560, 582, 590, 606, 620, 637 f., 648–651, 686, 692 f., 697, 699, 733, 740, 742 f., 749, 762, 783 f., 786, 795, 805–807, 816, 828, 839, 844, 847, 849, 852, 865, 905, 911, 928, 944 f., 954, 960, 987, 1012, 1014, 1018, 1074, 1087 f., 1100 f., 1103, 1105 f., 1112, 1113, 1120, 1143, 1150, 1154
Promise-breaking **Vol. 1:** 74
Promised land **Vol. 1:** 321, 682, 684, 691, 723
Vol. 2: 258, **295–304**, 331, 638
Vol. 3: 69, 95, 135, 256, 434, 740, 777, 806 f., 814, 872, 954, 970, 988, 1009
Promissory **Vol. 1:** 319
Promissory history **Vol. 3:** 968
Promissory oath **Vol. 3:** 738 f.
Promote **Vol. 1:** 499
Prompt **Vol. 1:** 719
Vol. 3: 846
Promulgate **Vol. 3:** 1113
Pronounce **Vol. 1:** 208, 216 f., 414, 447, 466, 581, 603, 699, 702
Vol. 2: 69, 147, 362, 370
Pronounce as righteous **Vol. 3: 352–377**
Pronouncement **Vol. 2:** 370, 395
Proof **Vol. 1:** 65, 398, 417, 547, 588, 594, 714, 736 f.
Vol. 2: 77, 140, 165, 282, 284, **290 f.**, 338, 359, 379, 546, 631, 653, 743, 858
Vol. 3: 249, 326, 331, 334, 485, 488, 494, **569–571**, 763 f., 769, 841, **1038–1050**
Proof-texts **Vol. 3:** 82, 487
Propaganda **Vol. 1:** 688, 708
Vol. 2: 438
Vol. 3: 900
Propagate **Vol. 1:** 451
Proper **Vol. 2:** 105, **606–611**, 668
Property **Vol. 1:** 360, 373, 398, 505, 639–641,

643, 688, 710, 716
Vol. 2: 134, 235, 247, 257, 296–298, 436, 438, 462, 552, 582, 820 f., 824, 829–835, **836–847**, 898
Vol. 3: 193 f., 200, 227, 256, **324 f.**, 372, 498, 594, 641, 701, 756, 913, 978
Property law **Vol. 2:** 511
Prophecy **Vol. 1:** 73, 117, 124, 135, 170, 185, 199, 290, 320, 329, 339, 411, 429, 512, 519, 527, 529, 545, 554, 578 f., 623, 657, 735, 737, 739
Vol. 2: 37, 86, 121, 165, 168, 228, 250, 252, 258, 314, 329, 367, 374, 379, 389, 410, 443, 487, 490, 545, 677, 680, 741, 797, 909 f., 915
Vol. 3: 33, 39, **74–89**, 110, 147 f., 198, 234, 269, 362, 454, 495, 500, 557, 629, 696, 699, 703, 791, 826, 1013, 1073, 1080, 1121 f., 1161, 1183
Prophesy **Vol. 2:** 161, 212, 470, 599
Vol. 3: 492, 533, 691, 700, 1066
Prophet **Vol. 1:** 58, **66**, 67, 76, 116, 121, 125, 128 f., 131 f., 135, 146, 163, 167, 174, 191 f., 198, 200, 208, 210, 222, 248, 265, 273, 328, 335, 358, 373–375, 394 f., 403, 423, 474, 482, 485, 492, 512, 527, 530, 543, 548, 556, 569 f., 574, 578 f., 581 f., 590, 595–597, 612, 617, 626, 641, 643, 662, 686, 717, 720, 729 f., 735 f., 738, 740
Vol. 2: 114, 129, 152, 154, 167, 174, 176, 187, 216 f., 226, 228, 240, 252 f., 257, 306 f., 312 f., 320, 326, 328, 337, 341, 352, 358, 367, 380, 432, 440, 442–444, 448, 453, 461, 472, 542, 559, 573, 626 f., 629, 633, 636, 638, 641, 665, 686, 711, 715, 724, 730, 737, 744, 786, 791, 803, 806, 827, 863, 913–915
Vol. 3: 42, 45, 50 f., 53, 55, 60, 69 f., 73, **74–89**, 99, 103, 110 f., 140, 147, 163, 181, 183, 195, 215, 221, 311, 313, 317, 329 f., 357, 360, 387, 390, 393, 407, 460, 479, 481, 485, 487, 502, 505, 513, 532, 548, 554, 565, 608, 610, 659, 691, 711, 721, 724, 762, 768, 780 f., 797, 806, 836, 875, 920, 960, 1042 f., 1053, 1058, **1088–1105**, 1118
Prophetess **Vol. 3: 74–89**, 1057, 1067
Prophetic **Vol. 1:** 202, 208, 246, 326, 328, 332, 334 f., 358, 371, 409 f., 414, 429, 445, 527–529, 574, 597, 619, 638, 659, 693, 699
Vol. 2: 174, 228, 276, 311 f., 432, 441
Vol. 3: 347, 462, 750, 967, 1007, 1091
Prophetic perspective **Vol. 2:** 910
Propitiate **Vol. 3: 145–176**
Propitiation **Vol. 1:** 89, 349, 39ʌ, 438, 694, 697, 700
Vol. 2: 766
Vol. 3: 145–176, 198, 364
Propitiation and expiation **Vol. 3: 151–160**
Propitiatory **Vol. 1:** 437, 700
Vol. 3: 199, 239, 366
Propitiatory sacrifice **Vol. 3: 148–166**
Propitious **Vol. 1:** 516
Vol. 2: 318
Proportion **Vol. 3:** 404, 752
Proposal **Vol. 1:** 61, 325
Propose **Vol. 1:** 692, 696

Proposition **Vol. 1:** 664
Vol. 3: 876, 1086
Propositional revelation **Vol. 3:** 336
Propriety **Vol. 1:** 501, 628, 684
Vol. 2: 160 f., 235
Vol. 3: 100–102
Prorogative **Vol. 1:** 557
Proscribe **Vol. 3:** 183
Prosecute **Vol. 1:** 415
Vol. 2: 805
Prosecution **Vol. 2:** 450
Prosecutor **Vol. 1:** 349, 475, 558
Proselyte **Vol. 1:** 77 f., 145, 149 f., 154–159, 180, 255, 258, **353–362**, 555, 560, 688 f.
Vol. 2: 54, 85, 126, 311, 377, 438, 442, 457, 652, 732, 740, 792, 866
Vol. 3: 82, 228, 869, 872, 931, 1052
Proselyte baptism **Vol. 1: 145**, 154 f.
Proselyte catechism **Vol. 3:** 928 f., 931
Proselytizing **Vol. 1:** 228, 516
Vol. 2: 792
Vol. 3: 480, 951
Prospect **Vol. 1:** 623, 643
Vol. 2: 267, 319
Prospective **Vol. 1:** 601
Prosper **Vol. 2:** 128, 452, 817
Vol. 3: 854, 943
Prosperity **Vol. 1:** 210, 216, 354, 682, 724
Vol. 2: 49, 478 f., 711, 776 f.
Vol. 3: 217, 262, 523, 672, 807, 866, 986
Prostitute **Vol. 1:** 117, 231 f., **494–503**, 507
Vol. 2: 212, 325, 517, 541, **582–584**
Vol. 3: 475, 535, 1059, 1062
Prostitution **Vol. 1:** 497, 499 f., 560, 625
Vol. 2: 576
Vol. 3: 1055
Prostrate **Vol. 2:** 862, **875–879**
Protagoras **Vol. 3:** 876
Protect **Vol. 1:** 212, 221, 277, 332, 340, 451, 468, 510, 542, 617, 632, 662, 688, 716, 740
Vol. 2: 133–135, 244, 254, 265, 314, 438, 653, 822
Vol. 3: 120 f., 200, 205, 212, 263, 497 f., 500, 949
Protection **Vol. 1:** 96, 101, 122, 151, 211, 218, 269, 272, 280 f., 316, 360, 367, 411, 541, 562, 595 f., 607, 625, 653, 686–691, 717
Vol. 2: 70, 83, 135 f., 149, 194, 213, 224, 247, 368, 412 f., 429, 460, 521, 572–574, 626, 649, 660, 713, 821–823, 844, 860
Vol. 3: 57, 95, 200, 469, 501, 554, 608, 692, 727, 729, 733, 797, 805, 807, 868 f., 948, 950, 952, 978
Protector **Vol. 1:** 654
Vol. 2: 821–823
Vol. 3: 193, 216, 263
Protector of Israel **Vol. 1:** 104
Protest **Vol. 1:** 284, 410
Prototype **Vol. 1:** 81, 266
Vol. 2: 58
Vol. 3: 303, 568, 592, **903–906**, 990
Proud **Vol. 1:** 709, 742
Vol. 2: 34, **198–200**, 201, 262, 468, 617 f.
Vol. 3: 27–32, 127, 691 f., 718

Prove **Vol. 1:** 303, 542, 571, 598, 604, 622, 656, 659, 708, 713, 731
 Vol. 2: 245, 252, 318, 355, 361, 883
 Vol. 3: 492, **569–571**
Provender **Vol. 1:** 743
Proverb **Vol. 1:** 139, 580
 Vol. 2: 433, 462, **743–760**, 881, 890
 Vol. 3: 78, 606, 777, 816, 888, 948
Proverbial **Vol. 1:** 218
Proverbs, Book of **Vol. 1:** 58, 412
 Vol. 2: 261, 745
Provide **Vol. 1:** 683, 693 f., 731
 Vol. 2: 201, 411, 846
 Vol. 3: 728
Providence **Vol. 1:** 173, 203, 278, 377, 383, 450, 467, 471, 478 f., 562, **692–697**
 Vol. 2: 117 f., 223, 236, 663 f., 828
 Vol. 3: 117 f., 157, 317, 720, 762, 865
Providential **Vol. 1:** 462, 523, 670
 Vol. 2: 628
Province **Vol. 1:** 392, 466
 Vol. 2: 320, 324, 788
Provincial **Vol. 2:** 234
Provision **Vol. 1:** 143, 252, 276–278, 425, 512, 531, 670, 693–695, 716
 Vol. 2: 265, 318, 587, 737, 825, 832
 Vol. 3: 121, 145, 1074
Provisional **Vol. 2:** 580
Provocation **Vol. 1:** 107
 Vol. 2: 259
Provoke **Vol. 1:** 107, 202
 Vol. 2: 131, 308, 447, 450, 516
 Vol. 3: 1123
Proximity **Vol. 2:** 53, 382, 384
Proxy **Vol. 1:** 128
Prudence **Vol. 1:** 412, **494–503**, 536
 Vol. 3: 354, 925, 1025
Prudent **Vol. 2:** 216, **616–620**
Prune **Vol. 3:** 227
Prytaneis **Vol. 1:** 291
Psalm titles **Vol. 3:** 669, 673
Psalms **Vol. 1:** 58, 244, 409, 538, 736, 744
 Vol. 2: 240, 297, 375, 444, 530, 864, 874
 Vol. 3: 233, 236, 407, 479, 494, **668–676**
Psalms of lament **Vol. 3:** 720
Psalms of Solomon **Vol. 1:** 66
 Vol. 2: 241, 823, 867
 Vol. 3: 650, 669
Pseudepigrapha **Vol. 1:** 50, **66**, 67, 452, 618
 Vol. 2: 191, 222
 Vol. 3: 492
Pseudo-apostle **Vol. 1:** 710
Pseudo-Hippocrates **Vol. 2:** 690
Pseudo-king **Vol. 2:** 339
Pseudo-messiah **Vol. 2:** 339, 633
Pseudo-pregnancy **Vol. 3:** 474
Pseudo-spirituality **Vol. 3:** 963
Pseudonym **Vol. 2:** 86
Pseudonymity **Vol. 1:** 247
 Vol. 2: 37
 Vol. 3: 80
Pseudonymous **Vol. 1:** 66
Psoriasia **Vol. 2:** 464
Psyche **Vol. 3:** 1017

Psychic **Vol. 2:** 359, 556
Psychological **Vol. 1:** 507, 583, 678 f.
 Vol. 2: 169, 182, 204, 220, 288, 422, 437
Psychological illness **Vol. 2:** 166
Psychological pressure **Vol. 3:** 886
Psychological schools **Vol. 2:** 567–569
Psychology **Vol. 3:** 900, 1081
Psychology of memory **Vol. 3:** 234
Psychology and NT **Vol. 2: 567–569**
Psychosomatic **Vol. 2:** 567
Ptah **Vol. 1:** 616
 Vol. 3: 1088
Ptolemaic period **Vol. 1:** 665
 Vol. 2: 898
Ptolemy **Vol. 2:** 849
 Vol. 3: 634
Ptolemy Epiphanes **Vol. 3:** 635
Ptolemy II Philadelphus **Vol. 3:** 756
Ptolemy Philometor **Vol. 3:** 766
Puberty **Vol. 1:** 308
 Vol. 2: 437
 Vol. 3: 1071
Public **Vol. 1:** 330, 346 f., 390–392, 402, 407, 410, 501, 535 f., 582, 590, 613, 639, 649, 689, 696, 715, 738
 Vol. 2: 150, 159 f., 212, 352 f., 493, 736, **788–790**, 800
Public crier **Vol. 3:** 51
Public figure **Vol. 3:** 479
Public life **Vol. 3:** 738
Public opinion **Vol. 2:** 308
 Vol. 3: 481, 757
Public speaker **Vol. 2:** 369
Publican **Vol. 3:** 253, 361
Publication **Vol. 3:** 311
Publicly **Vol. 3:** 75
Publish **Vol. 1:** 71, 572
 Vol. 2: 108
Publius **Vol. 1:** 690
Puffed up **Vol. 1:** 107
 Vol. 2: 253, 422
 Vol. 3: 1119
Pun **Vol. 2: 432**
 Vol. 3: 1096
Punctilious **Vol. 3:** 1053
Punish **Vol. 1:** 189, 332, 381, 509, 568, 688, 735
 Vol. 2: 101, 140 f., 155, 189, 226, 266, 363, 510
 Vol. 3: 76, **92–100**, 165, 342, 354, 358, 740, 839, 847, 1151, 1054
Punishment **Vol. 1:** 85, 107, 109, 113, 125, 141, 162 f., 190 f., 195, 219, 241, 264, 288, 308, 329, 333, 345, 354, 380, 391 f., 394, 396, 398, 403, 414–416, 418, 432–434, 436, 438, 444, 448, 450 f., 465 f., 529, 537, 555, 562, 564, 568 f., 572, 586, 607, 623, 655–657, 686–688, 698–700, 721, 734
 Vol. 2: 29, 117, 136, 138, 141–143, 149, 157, 192, 206–209, 212, 265 f., 272, 275, 285, **362–367**, 370, 415, 428, 439, 458 f., 478, 481, 570, 572, 630, 667, 775, 779, 792 f., 807, 823
 Vol. 3: 92–100, 110, 134–136, 138–140, 145, 149 f., 156, 190, 214, 257, 260, 273, 305, 353, 357, 377, 381, 394, 439, 448, 502, 527,

573 f., 578, 583, 590 f., 594, 714, 719, 721, 751, 809, 836, 842, 856 f., 905, 932, 936, 1008, 1149
Punitive **Vol. 1:** 414
  Vol. 2: 167, 201
  Vol. 3: 999
Puny **Vol. 1:** 673
Pupil **Vol. 1:** 69, 280, 282, 285, 287, 480–487, 492, 617
  Vol. 2: 151, 291, 428, 445
  Vol. 3: 759–765, 771 f.
Purchase **Vol. 1:** 93, 606
Purchaser **Vol. 1:** 120
Pure **Vol. 1:** 143, 205, 220, 223–225, 284, 351, 368, 447, 469, 495, 502, 512, 521, 542, 544 f., 552, 604, 640
  Vol. 2: 102, 144, 178, 183, 224 f., 227, 237 f., 249, 270, 357, 810
  Vol. 3: 100–108, 125, 167, 207, 220, 261, 348, 470, 932, 989 f., 992, 997, 1053
Purgatory **Vol. 1:** 656
  Vol. 2: 208
Purge **Vol. 1:** 151, 537
  Vol. 3: 97, 104, 419
Purge away **Vol. 3:** 152
Purification **Vol. 1:** 119, 143, 145, 149–151, 153 f., 221, 223, 225, 371, 432, 612, 654 f., 677
  Vol. 2: 149, 225, 228, 307, 336, 472, 485, 623, 690
  Vol. 3: 100–102, 695, 740, 784, 793, 823, 842, 982, 986, 1053, 1058, 1085, 1154
Purificatory **Vol. 2:** 811, 854
  Vol. 3: 149, 579
Purify **Vol. 1:** 116, 154, 204, 221, 224, 543, 654, 657
  Vol. 2: 230, 235, 266, 289, 307, 326, 360, 423, 675, 717
  Vol. 3: 100–108, 149, 152, 167, 315, 419, 572, 809, 912
Purim **Vol. 1:** 626
  Vol. 3: 237
Puritanical **Vol. 1:** 687
Purity **Vol. 1:** 152, 204, 284, 294, 360, 413, 448, 499, 653
  Vol. 2: 51, 95, 143 f., 183, 244, 311, 503, 596, 742
  Vol. 3: 35, **100–108**, 431, 886, 926, 988, 1055
Purple **Vol. 1:** 205, 317, 361
Purpose **Vol. 1:** 69, 74, 80 f., 87, 99, 127, 219, 243, 275, 278, 355, 357, 383, 392, 426, 459, 474 f., 483, 506, 510, 536–538, 540 f., 543, 550, 562, 569, 577, 597, 612, 625, 632, 638, 654 f., 668 f., 696 f., 737
  Vol. 2: 52, 79, 92, 94, 106, 121 f., 139, 145, 154, 218, 231, 251, 287, 294, 299, 362, 384, 396, 403, 420, 434, 477, 487, 546, 610, 668, 718, 721, 818 f., 926
  Vol. 3: 168, 172, 181, 212, 214, 228, 236, 251 f., 293, 316, 323, 332, 389, 468, 502–504, 542, 645, 656, 728, 779, 820, 824 f., 911, 916, 925, 1000 f., 1016 f., 1183
Purposeful **Vol. 1:** 533, 692, 694
Purposelessness **Vol. 2:** 569

Purse **Vol. 1:** 142
  Vol. 3: 120, 498 f., 954
Pursue **Vol. 1:** 481, 648 f., 681
  Vol. 2: 317, **805–807**
Put asunder **Vol. 3:** 542
Put away **Vol. 1:** 202, 479, 505 f., 606, 662, 731
Put forward **Vol. 1:** 696
Put in charge **Vol. 1:** 471
Put in motion **Vol. 1:** 697
Put in order **Vol. 1:** 521, 524
  Vol. 3: 349–351
Put in prison **Vol. 3: 590 f.**
Put off **Vol. 1:** 311, 314 f., 469, 676
  Vol. 2: 318
  Vol. 3: 815, 839, 1158
Put on **Vol. 1:** 158, 311, 314–316, 386, 470, 674
  Vol. 2: 127, 264, 587, 925
  Vol. 3: 120
Put on oath **Vol. 3:** 737–743
Put on trial **Vol. 3: 798–808**
Put out **Vol. 3:** 109
Put to death **Vol. 2:** 441
  Vol. 3: 1158
Put to shame **Vol. 3:** 98, **562–564**
Put to silence **Vol. 3:** 1026
Put to the test **Vol. 3: 798–808**
Putrefaction **Vol. 3:** 444 f.
Pyrrhus **Vol. 1:** 205, 656
Pythagoras **Vol. 3:** 635
Pythagorean **Vol. 1:** 432, 484, 640, 642
  Vol. 3: 103, 259, 678, 739, 843, 929, 1085
Pythia **Vol. 3:** 75 f.
Pythian priestess **Vol. 1:** 734
Python **Vol. 1:** 508
  Vol. 2: 552–562

Q source **Vol. 1:** 62 f., 67, 402
  Vol. 2: 341, 872
Qerioth **Vol. 2:** 321
Qoheleth **Vol. 1:** 512
Quack **Vol. 3:** 32
Quadratus **Vol. 3:** 40
Quail **Vol. 1:** 173, 195, 252, 460, 672
  Vol. 2: 32, 628, 637
  Vol. 3: 427, 508, 804, 1001
Qualification **Vol. 1:** 198, 297, 500, 538 f., 597
  Vol. 2: 299, 424, 440
  Vol. 3: 49, 393, 750, 765, 924, 1044
Qualificatory formula **Vol. 2: 279**
Qualified **Vol. 3: 728–730**
Qualifier **Vol. 3:** 99, 1133
Qualify **Vol. 1:** 648, 715
  Vol. 2: 228
  Vol. 3: 728–730
Qualitative **Vol. 2:** 424, 670, 739, 891
Quality **Vol. 1:** 272, 284, 314 f., 459, 485, 491, 525, 538, 557, 596, 603, 617, 658, 711, 722, 739
  Vol. 2: 101, 120, 128, 151 f., 197, 200, 235, 237, 256, 398, 657, 661, 683, 685, 774
  Vol. 3: 351, 354, 444 f., 572, 681, 832, 925
Quantitative **Vol. 2:** 424, 891
Quantity **Vol. 1:** 728
  Vol. 2: 128, 130 f., 683, 685, 801

Quarantine **Vol. 2:** 465
Quarrel **Vol. 1:** 106, 108, 377, 503 f., 535, 644–646, 654
  Vol. 2: 140, 363, 429, 447, 587, 645
  Vol. 3: 346, 448, 532
Quarrelsome **Vol. 2:** 550
  Vol. 3: 821
Quart **Vol. 2:** 711
Quarter **Vol. 2:** 689
Quarterly **Vol. 1:** 627
Quartodecimans **Vol. 1:** 634
Quartz **Vol. 3:** 396
Quasi-egalitarian **Vol. 1:** 641
Quasi-divine claim **Vol. 2:** 380
Quasi-personal **Vol. 1:** 437
Queen **Vol. 2:** 372–389, 511
Queen of heaven **Vol. 3:** 1070
Queen of the South **Vol. 2:** 381, 680
  Vol. 3: 1030
Quell **Vol. 3: 109–111**
Quench **Vol. 2:** 275
  Vol. 3: 109–111, 966, 988
Question **Vol. 1:** 413, 540, 577, 583 f., 725
  Vol. 2: 101, 141, 144, 235, 266, 270, 334, 342, 362, 364, 374, 379, 382, 384, 387, 393 f., 396 f., 399, 426, 430, 434, 469, 707, 857, **879–881**
  Vol. 3: 75, 97, 531, 556, 657, 777, 821, 1066
Questionable **Vol. 2:** 266
Questioner **Vol. 3:** 275
Quick at apprehending **Vol. 3: 130–133**
Quicken **Vol. 3:** 163
Quiet **Vol. 1:** 210, 420, 469, 529, 630, 681
  Vol. 2: 218
  Vol. 3: 111–114, 254 f., 1078
Quieten **Vol. 2:** 260
Quintessence **Vol. 3:** 690
Quirinius **Vol. 2:** 320
Quiver **Vol. 2:** 422
  Vol. 3: 379, 557
Qumran **Vol. 1:** 50, 54, 65, **67**, 89, 96, 98, 102 f., 109, 144 f., 152, 178, 190, 197, 212, 219, 225, 233, 255, 258 f., 273, 280, 288, 296, 305, 309, 321 f., 333 f., 345, 355, 357, 360, 367 f., 374, 382, 394, 407, 412, 416, 423, 444, 450, 452, 463, 465, 481, 499, 523, 539, 544, 554, 556, 563, 578, 598 f., 607, 618 f., 627, 629 f., 641, 646, 656, 661, 673, 676, 700, 732, 735
  Vol. 2: 45, 53 f., 56, 58, 61, 71 f., 100, 105, 117 f., 134, 141 f., 158, 161, 174, 194, 197, 199, 216, 227 f., 237, 241, 248 f., 257 f., 261, 263, 279, 285, 298 f., 302, 312–314, 335, 337, 353, 357, 364, 397, 459, 471 f., 480 f., 492, 512, 522, 542, 558, 565, 591, 595, 602, 609, 614, 640, 651, 667, 672, 696, 699, 707, 738, 779, 792 f., 798, 818, 824, 836, 851, 893, 897, 899
  Vol. 3: 28, 30 f., 34, 39, 52, 80, 82, 88, 96, 105, 160 f., 169, 187, 193–195, 197, 210, 218, 233, 250, 265, 268, 272 f., 359, 367, 382, 384, 392, 398, 428, 465, 469–472, 479, 484–486, 489 f., 492, 495, 499, 503, 508, 510, 531, 533, 545, 566, 610, 614–616, 637, 647, 650, 652, 669, 671, 680, 692 f., 695, 722, 735, 761, 766, 783 f., 801 f., 823, 828, 831, 836, 842, 871 f., 874, 882–885, 926, 928 f., 933, 939, 941–943, 949, 961, 963, 1006, 1016, 1020, 1029, 1068, 1107, 1120, 1149, 1165, 1167
Qumran calendar **Vol. 1:** 627
Qumran canon **Vol. 3: 486 f.**
Quotation **Vol. 1:** 736 f.
  Vol. 2: 186, 444
  Vol. 3: 48, 52, 82, 188, 202, 393, 488, 563, 611, 650 f., 718, 732, 764, 790, 805, 826, 887, 1011, **1038–1050**, 1090

Ra'amses **Vol. 2: 635 f.**
Rabbi **Vol. 1:** 67, 69, 213, 259, 360, 368, 370, 409, 442, 451, 486, 488, 491, 527, 560, 581, 656, 688 f., 691
  Vol. 2: 47, 125, 159, 174, 191, 208, 241, 261, 266, 327, 337, 358, 399, 432, 448, 514, 544, 549, 580, 629, 640, 652, 665, 721, 757, 818
  Vol. 3: 51, 59, 80, 87, 113, **115 f.**, 188, 194, 358, 377, 408, 480–482, 657, 696, 748, 761 f., 765–767, 774, 780, 805, 853, 867, 872 f., 949, 997, 1042, 1058, 1063, 1116, 1121, 1152, 1163
Rabbinic **Vol. 1:** 371, 599
  Vol. 2: 100, 192 f., 204, 227, 250, 261, 287, 353, 355, 357, 893
  Vol. 3: 45, 194, 218, 429, 740, 779, 1066
Rabbinic formula **Vol. 3:** 429
Rabbinic parables **Vol. 2:** 433
Rabbinic schools **Vol. 3:** 777
Rabbinic theology **Vol. 1:** 67, 321, 619
  Vol. 2: 426, 791, 824, 864
Rabbinical oath **Vol. 3:** 740
Rabbinism **Vol. 1:** 64, **67**, 69
  Vol. 2: 671
Rabble-rouser **Vol. 1:** 267
Rabshakeh **Vol. 3:** 202
Race **Vol. 1:** 176, 541, 548, 637, 647, 649, 662, 684 f.
  Vol. 2: 35, 195, 221, 247, 411
  Vol. 3: 142, 635, 865, **945–947**
Rachel **Vol. 1:** 170
  Vol. 2: 317 f., 578
  Vol. 3: 113, 233, 872, 1057
Racial **Vol. 2:** 309
Racial differences **Vol. 2:** 83
Radiance **Vol. 2:** 44, 46, 213, 284, **289 f.**
  Vol. 3: 398, 862, 864
Radiant **Vol. 2: 484–486**
Radiate **Vol. 2:** 44, 355, 484
Radiate heat **Vol. 3:** 689
Radical **Vol. 1:** 598, 730
  Vol. 2: 427
Rag-picker **Vol. 3:** 525
Rage **Vol. 1:** 105 f., 108, 528, 543, 608
  Vol. 2: 421, 652
  Vol. 3: 76, 908
Rahab **Vol. 1:** 523, 593, 713
  Vol. 2: 142
  Vol. 3: 30, 369 f., 656 f., 1062, 1067
Rahner, K. **Vol. 3:** 900 f.

Raider **Vol. 3:** 377
Rail at **Vol. 3: 345 f.**
Railer **Vol. 3: 345 f.**
Railing **Vol. 3: 345 f.**
Raiment **Vol. 1:** 204, 319, 708
Rain **Vol. 1:** 187, 209, 416, 498, 513, 517, 543, 597, 614, 653, 743
   Vol. 2: 154, 188 f., 191, 193, 211, 265, 274, 866
   Vol. 3: 117, 267, 269, 360, 692, 835, 846, 982, **1000–1004**
Rainbow **Vol. 2:** 626
   Vol. 3: 398, **1000–1004**
Raise **Vol. 1:** 103, 125, 234, 236, 261, 265, 346, 384, 399–401, 430, 437, 439, 443, 445, 470, 592, 643, 653, 668, 673, 718
   Vol. 2: 78, 80, 91, 190, 192, **200–204**, 206, 217, 252, 312, 358, 363, 388, 399, 446, 481, 631, 641, 718, 865
   Vol. 3: 113, **259–281**, 715
Raise hand **Vol. 3:** 738
Raise voice **Vol. 2:** 201
Ram **Vol. 1:** 677
   Vol. 3: 155 f., 191, 421, 425
Ramah **Vol. 3:** 426
Ramoth-gilead **Vol. 2:** 754
Ramp **Vol. 2:** 185
Rampart **Vol. 3: 951 f.**
Ram's horn **Vol. 3:** 873
Ramsey, F.P. **Vol. 3:** 897
Ramsey, I.T. **Vol. 3:** 99, 336, 1133 f.
Rank **Vol. 1:** 123, 165, 192 f., 197, 200, 272 f., 532, 664–669, 687
   Vol. 2: 55, 57, 59, 158, 234, 298, 424, 436, 451, 720, 800
   Vol. 3: 120, 630, 653, 717
Ransom **Vol. 1:** 96 f., 223, 308, 322, 438, 479
   Vol. 2: 42, 367, 795
   Vol. 3: 153, 157, 174, **177–221**, 267, 429, 435, 547, 612, 623, 673, 682, 935, 1180
Ransom money **Vol. 3:** 167, 752
Ransom price **Vol. 3:** 166
Rapacious **Vol. 3: 601–605**
Rapacity **Vol. 1:** 495
   Vol. 3: 601–605
Rape **Vol. 1:** 505
   Vol. 2: 260, 577
   Vol. 3: 95, 601, 711, 872
Raphael **Vol. 1:** 102
Rapid **Vol. 1:** 610
Rapt **Vol. 1:** 529
Rapture **Vol. 1:** 545, 673
   Vol. 2: 352, 359, 482, 862
   Vol. 3: 601–605
Ras Shamra **Vol. 3:** 267, 269, 427
Rash **Vol. 1:** 364
Ratification **Vol. 2:** 59, 374
Ratify **Vol. 1:** 664
   Vol. 2: 659, 673
   Vol. 3: 739
Ration money **Vol. 3:** 379
Rational **Vol. 1:** 353, 481, 521, 582, 676, 680, 692
   Vol. 2: 181, 230, 287, 339, 390 f., 659

   Vol. 3: 434, 681, 1081–1119
Rationalism **Vol. 1:** 694
   Vol. 3: 898
Rationalist **Vol. 3:** 305
Rationality **Vol. 3:** 1034
Rationalize **Vol. 2:** 67
Rations **Vol. 3:** 134
Rave **Vol. 1:** 528
   Vol. 3: 230
Raven **Vol. 1:** 173, 408 f.
Ravenous **Vol. 3: 601–605**
Ravish **Vol. 3:** 601
Razis **Vol. 3:** 271
Re **Vol. 2:** 200, 279
Reach **Vol. 1:** 730
   Vol. 3: 727
Reach decisions **Vol. 3:** 880
Reaction **Vol. 1:** 528, 530, 561, 585, 603, 688
   Vol. 2: 125, 373, 416, 422, 434 f., 568, 621
   Vol. 3: 479
Read **Vol. 1:** 245, 247, 536, 628
   Vol. 2: 213, 218, 309, 357, 369
   Vol. 3: 489, 492, 761, 1058
Reader **Vol. 1:** 685
   Vol. 3: 766
Readily **Vol. 3: 116–118**
Readiness **Vol. 1:** 514, 634, 646, 699, 702
   Vol. 2: 105, 122, 307, 386, 433, 448, 654, 668, 717, 880
Readmission **Vol. 2:** 152
Ready **Vol. 1:** 358, 475, 482 f., 489, 516, 546, 612, 690, 700, 712
   Vol. 2: 244, 366
   Vol. 3: 116–122, 352, 605, 628, 1059
Ready-made **Vol. 2:** 442
Reaffirm **Vol. 1:** 664
Real **Vol. 1:** 80, 711 f.
   Vol. 2: 135, 194 f., 280, 286, 393
   Vol. 3: 874–901
Real presence **Vol. 3:** 244, 245
Reality **Vol. 1:** 436, 461, 551, 563, 601, 620, 629, 640, 662, 673, 679, 703 f., 707–709, 711, 714, 719
   Vol. 2: 120 f., 166, 186, 281 f., 284, 287, 291, 308, 311, 314 f., 366, 375, 382, 395, 404 f., 430, 448, 663
   Vol. 3: 234, 461, 631, 693, 726, 776, 839, 841, 846, **874–901**, 1034, 1139 f.
Realization **Vol. 1:** 597, 697, 699, 703, 711, 713, 740
   Vol. 2: 59, 65, 240, 300, 313, 382 f., 385, 389, 406, 446
Realized eschatology (→ Eschatology, realized)
Realm **Vol. 1:** 707, 718, 738
   Vol. 2: 74
Reanimation **Vol. 1:** 184
   Vol. 3: 303
Reap **Vol. 1:** 469, 681, 719
   Vol. 2: 34
   Vol. 3: 189, **525–527**
Reaper **Vol. 1:** 204, 453
   Vol. 2: 32
   Vol. 3: 143, **525–527**
Rear **Vol. 1:** 287, 492

Re-arrange **Vol. 1:** 576
Reason **Vol. 1:** 63, 68, 107, 232, 281, 355 f., 413, 432, 450, 460, 481, 507, 521, 527, 529, 547, 562, 595, 636, 650, 654, 671, 674, 693, 708
　Vol. 2: 67, 130, 137–139, 141, 143 f., 157, 179 f., 182, 259, 356, 374, 408, 476, 493, 565, 567, 590, 657, 722
　Vol. 3: 35, 76, 98, **122–133**, 337, 572, 677 f., 681, 684, 687, 776, **820 f.**, 823 f., 826, 899, 1026, 1034, 1036
Reasonable **Vol. 1:** 501 f.
　Vol. 2: 476
　Vol. 3: **1081–1119**
Reasoning **Vol. 3: 820 f.**
Reassurance **Vol. 1:** 104, 590
Rebekah **Vol. 1:** 81
　Vol. 2: 316 f., 587
　Vol. 3: 879, 1057, 1069
Rebel **Vol. 1:** 202, 294, 438, 537, 606
　Vol. 2: 174
　Vol. 3: 357, 916
Rebellion **Vol. 1:** 51, 142, 203, 270, 436, 468, 535, 606 f., 680, 741
　Vol. 2: 227, 311, 396, 432, 435, 566, 617, 638, 702, 722
　Vol. 3: 218, 275, 363, 577, 585, 642, 954, 1025
Rebellious **Vol. 1:** 372, 385
　Vol. 2: 448
Rebirth **Vol. 1:** 176, 178, 181, 184 f., 187, 284, 290, 521
　Vol. 2: 113, 202, 242, 244, 394, 604
　Vol. 3: 703, 722, 791
Rebuild **Vol. 1:** 734
　Vol. 2: 252
　Vol. 3: 469
Rebuke **Vol. 1:** 340, 425, **567–573**
　Vol. 2: 140 f.
　Vol. 3: 344
Recalcitrant **Vol. 3:** 916
Recall **Vol. 1:** 683
　Vol. 2: 32
　Vol. 3: 230–247, 515
Recapitulate **Vol. 2:** 156, 163
Receipt **Vol. 2:** 433
Receive **Vol. 1:** 123, 185, 285, 300, 487, 597, 601, 605, 607, 620, 639, 668, 673, 675, 677, 689 f., 702, 722, 730 f., 742
　Vol. 2: 83, 116, 123, 131, 146, 156, 186, 194, 221, 231, 238, **244–246,** 255, 268, 300, 302, 329, 358, 369, 381 f., 385, 388, 403, 406 f., 440, 447, 775, 843, 868, 929
　Vol. 3: 61, 326, 541, **744–751,** 759, 806
Receive share **Vol. 3: 747–751**
Received text **Vol. 1:** 70
Receiver **Vol. 3:** 417
Receiving **Vol. 3: 747–751**
Receptacle **Vol. 3:** 744
Reception **Vol. 1:** 534, 599 f., 737
　Vol. 3: 744–751
Receptive **Vol. 3:** 758
Receptivity **Vol. 2:** 178, 269
Rechabites **Vol. 3:** 565, 811, 919, 1005

Recipient **Vol. 1:** 739
　Vol. 2: 435
Reciprocal **Vol. 2:** 51
Reciprocity **Vol. 3:** 829
Recitation **Vol. 2:** 174
Recite **Vol. 3:** 668
Reckless **Vol. 1:** 715
Recklessness **Vol. 1:** 710
　Vol. 3: 776
Reckon **Vol. 1:** 311, 472, 596, 600, 627, 630, 675
　Vol. 2: 427, 445, 458
　Vol. 3: 136, 369, **820–826**
Reclaim **Vol. 2:** 858
Recline **Vol. 1:** 471, 633
　Vol. 3: 588 f.
Recognition **Vol. 1:** 245, 347, 486–488, 516, 522, 529, 541, 543, 568, 588, 594 f., 603, 607, 616, 620, 631, 643, 731, 742
　Vol. 2: 44, 48, 118, 147, 244, 335, **392–406,** 407, 815–817, 859
　Vol. 3: 401, 675, 817, 911, 1043
Recognition formula **Vol. 2: 279**
Recognize **Vol. 1:** 708, 722, 728
　Vol. 2: 127, 155, 160 f., 282, 289, 300, 314, 328, 352, 363, 365, 378, **392–407,** 438, 443, 448, 739
　Vol. 3: 118, 232, 511, 582, 717, 749, 822, 844
Recoil **Vol. 1:** 606
Recollection **Vol. 1:** 483
　Vol. 3: 1038, 1043
Recommend **Vol. 1:** 65, 246, 248, 690
　Vol. 2: 263, 743
Recommendation **Vol. 3:** 499
Recompense **Vol. 1:** 217, 240, 648
　Vol. 2: 41, 115
　Vol. 3: 92–97, 134–145, 190, 1149
Reconcile **Vol. 3: 145–176,** 227
Reconciliation **Vol. 1:** 89, 97, 107, 113, 167, 197, 222–224, 237, 275, 279, 298, 304, 385, 398, 401 f., 415, 430, 437, 477, 521, 525, 544, 666, 694, 697, 699–703, 740
　Vol. 2: 42, 83, 137, 195, 318, 366, 370, 545, 585, 604, 614, 781 f., 827, 875
　Vol. 3: 145–176, 180, 186, 188, 190, 192 f., 195 f., 198 f., 221, 228, 320, 363 f., 372, 374, 419, 423, 425, 428, 431, 435 f., 535, 547, 575, 579, 581, 586, 611, 680, 720, 723, 725, 751, 781, 788, 797, 812, 815, 824 f., 956
Reconnoitre **Vol. 1:** 481
Reconsecration **Vol. 1:** 626
Reconstitute **Vol. 1:** 698
Reconstitution **Vol. 3:** 275
Record **Vol. 1:** 242, 544, 582
　Vol. 3: 236, **482–495,** 757
Recording angel **Vol. 1:** 104
Recount **Vol. 1:** 574
　Vol. 3: 1081
Recover **Vol. 1:** 446
　Vol. 3: 254
Recovery **Vol. 1:** 611
　Vol. 2: 163
　Vol. 3: 279, 357, 997
Recreate **Vol. 2:** 193

Recreation **Vol. 1:** 147, 175
  Vol. 3: 254
Red **Vol. 1:** 84, **203–206**, 224, 653, 656 f.
  Vol. 2: 496
  Vol. 3: 40, 143, 347, 349, 360, 362, 396
Red heifer **Vol. 2:** 32
  Vol. 3: 104, 989
Red Sea **Vol. 1:** 149, 373, 381, 516
  Vol. 2: 134, 637
  Vol. 3: 77, 238, 674, 983 f., 986, 990
Redaction **Vol. 1:** 57, **67**, 68
Redaction criticism **Vol. 1:** 57, **67**
  Vol. 3: 58, 63
Redaktionsgeschichte **Vol. 1: 67**
Rededication **Vol. 3:** 165
Redeem **Vol. 1:** 267, 282, 317, 413, 438, 468, 518, 525, 617, 634, 668, 678, 694, 697, 738
  Vol. 2: 60, 79, 226, 274, 358, 394, 405, 411, 441, 675, 865
  Vol. 3: 158, **177–221**, 625, 407, 784, 939
Redeemer **Vol. 1:** 54, 133, 148, 152, 187, 214, 227, 230, 253, 320, 434, 438, 455, 526, 547, 669, 672
  Vol. 2: 60, 111 f., 158, 195, 202, 209. 242, 249, 280, 330, 453, 640 f., 645 f., 655, 865, 867, 877
  Vol. 3: 178, **189–200**, 202, 231 f., 582, 598, 642, 936, 940, 1116
Redeemer-myth **Vol. 2:** 645 f.
  Vol. 3: 643
Redemption **Vol. 1:** 53, 57 f., 64, 123, 125, 142, 145–148, 150, 158, 191, 210, 214, 219, 223 f., 230, 233, 238, 268, 301, 313 f., 320, 371 f., 380 f., 385, 397 f., 409, 417, 436, 438, 440, 464, 470, 518, 525, 538 f., 541, 545, 552, 596, 611, 617 f., 629, 631, 633 f., 638, 669, 697, 701, 703, 716, 722, 730
  Vol. 2: 37, 39, 42 f., 54, 78 f., 101, 111, 120, 122, 145, 158, 195, 202, 204, 229 f., 243, 302, 307, 343, 388, 425, 435, 509, 521, 565, 601, 611, 631, 777, 780, 798, 819, 866, 877, 883 f., 912
  Vol. 3: 163, 174, **177–221**, 228, 235, 253, 261, 277, 320, 329, 355, 372, 374, 412, 417, 420, 429, 435 f., 462, 484, 491 f., 502, 529, 537, 544, 546, 575, 586, 588, 596, 611, 682, 723, 725, 781, 795, 797, 836, 956, 1006, 1135
Redemptive **Vol. 1:** 496, 651
  Vol. 2: 355, 445, 672, 713
  Vol. 3: 105, 232, 235–238, 318, 721, 724
Redirect **Vol. 1:** 480, 485, 568
Reduce **Vol. 2:** 308
Redundancy theory of truth **Vol. 3: 897**
Reed **Vol. 3:** 110, 399, 559
Re-establish **Vol. 1:** 627, 664
  Vol. 2: 313
  Vol. 3: 146–148
Refashion **Vol. 3:** 912
Referee **Vol. 2:** 362
Reference **Vol. 1:** 680
Refine **Vol. 1:** 146
  Vol. 2: 96, 419, 490
Reflect **Vol. 1:** 105 f., 712
  Vol. 2: 75, 284, 390

  Vol. 3: 231, 398, 512
Reflection **Vol. 1:** 105 f., 353, 540, 583 f., 612, 699, 707, 719
  Vol. 2: 103, 284, **289 f.**, 392, 923
  Vol. 3: 122, 126, 508, 531, 554, 1083
Reflective **Vol. 1:** 502
Reflex **Vol. 2:** 568
Reform **Vol. 1:** 427, 632, 687
  Vol. 3: 1096
Reformation **Vol. 1:** 200, 603
  Vol. 2: 823
  Vol. 3: 351 f., 371
Reformed faith **Vol. 3:** 783
Reforms of Hezekiah **Vol. 3:** 853
Refrain **Vol. 1:** 587, 727, 734
  Vol. 2: 286, 312
Refresh **Vol. 3:** 254 f., 686
Refreshment **Vol. 1:** 420, 441, 513, 729
  Vol. 2: 274, 281, 355, 590, 600
  Vol. 3: 682
Refuge **Vol. 1:** 174, 327, 531 f., 559, 589, 653, 687
  Vol. 2: 91, 215, 240, 307, 471, 602, 779, 801
  Vol. 3: 380 f., 389, 1009, 1011
Refusal **Vol. 2:** 155, 223
  Vol. 3: 57
Refuse **Vol. 1:** 272, 308, 324, 400, 414, 419, 424, 454 f., **479 f.,** 545, 600, 629, 684, 688 f., 696
  Vol. 2: 86, 126, 175, 179, 222, 296, 314, 340, 351, 358, 400, 405 f., 781, **855–859**
  Vol. 3: 102–108, 325, 758, 1014, 1019
Refuse to listen **Vol. 3:** 950
Refute **Vol. 1:** 199, 504, 545, 688
  Vol. 2: 140, 152
Regain **Vol. 2:** 123
Regard **Vol. 1:** 675, 710
  Vol. 2: 261, 286, 310, 364, 438
  Vol. 3: 126, **561 f**.
Regard favourably **Vol. 2: 817–820**
Regeneration **Vol. 1:** 147, 153 f., 158, 160, **176–188**, 290, 616
  Vol. 2: 836
  Vol. 3: 220, 705, 1178
Region **Vol. 1:** 472, 742
Register **Vol. 1:** 243, 544
Registrar **Vol. 3:** 477
Regret **Vol. 1:** 356, 357, 467, 741
  Vol. 2: 420, 598
Regularity **Vol. 3:** 1086
Regularize **Vol. 2:** 439
Regulate **Vol. 1:** 365
  Vol. 2: 254, 366, 436, 442, 447, 447, 452
Regulation **Vol. 1:** 327, 330, 367, 370, 401, 439, 457, 521, 525, 677, 687, 689
  Vol. 2: 123, 134, 259, 270, 298, 447 f., 453, 461, 659, 666
  Vol. 3: 106, **352–377**
Rehabilitation **Vol. 3:** 51
Rehoboam **Vol. 1:** 170, 195, 510
  Vol. 3: 788
Rehoboth-lr **Vol. 1:** 140
Reign **Vol. 1:** 234, 440, 467, 640, 643, 653
  Vol. 2: 64, 109, 147, 240, 248, 308, 326,

Reign (cont'd)
372–389, 701, 775, 832
Vol. 3: 45, 143, 259
Reign of Christ **Vol. 1:** 52, 649
Vol. 2: 62, 98
Vol. 3: 204
Reign of God **Vol. 1:** 121, 185, 489
Vol. 2: 54, 326, 871
Reign of sin **Vol. 1:** 457
Reimarus, H.S. **Vol. 2:** 902 f.
Vol. 3: 291, 977
Reincarnation **Vol. 3:** 146
Reinstate **Vol. 3:** 147
Reinterpretation **Vol. 2:** 276, 339
Reisenfeld, H. **Vol. 3:** 59
Reiterate **Vol. 2:** 317
Reject **Vol. 1:** 73 f., 239, 336, 356, 359, 370,
372, 375, 386, 399, 424 f., 453–455, 462,
464, 486, 499, 504, 532, 538–542, 544, 554–
557, 569, 590, 610, 625, 631, 638, 643 f.,
646, 666, 678, 681, 693, 715, 730, 733
Vol. 2: 82 f., 147, 229, 272, 309, ·327, 368,
377, 400, 407, 417, 438, 449, 585, 622 f.,
629, 709, 712, 794, 917
Vol. 3: 136, 202, 252, 344, 388, 390, 393,
430, 468, 533, 560, 624, 642, 723, 751, 807,
808–810, 821, 1043–1045, 1096
Rejection **Vol. 2:** 135, 155, 159, 270, 291, 315,
374, 385, 407, 600, 680, 843 f., 916
Vol. 3: 168, 251, 580, 586, 628, 745, 790,
908, 920
Rejoice **Vol. 1:** 741
Vol. 2: 243, **352–361**, 420, 436, 517
Vol. 3: 128, 257, 955
Rejoicing **Vol. 1:** 99, 227, 625
Rejuvenate **Vol. 3:** 869
Relate **Vol. 1:** 573, 576
Vol. 2: 280
Vol. 3: 45
Relationship **Vol. 1:** 84 f., 192, 236, 240, 254–
259, 269–271, 280, 282, 285–287, 289, 300–
302, 316, 332, 343 f., 349, 357 f., 365–369,
371, 373 f., 384 f., 409, 420, 433 f., 442, 455,
459, 469, 472, 480–482, 484–486, 488, 491,
496, 498 f., 501, 522 f., 525, 528, 535, 547,
549, 551, 553, 583, 585, 587 f., 595–597,
601, 604, 606 f., 615–618, 620, 622, 624,
636–640, 643, 662, 667, 672 f., 675, 678,
680 f., 686, 690, 693, 698, 701, 704, 707,
709, 711, 714 f., 730
Vol. 2: 44, 50 f., 71, 75 f., 80, 84, 94, 99 f.,
117, 121, 131, 133, 135, 160, 162, 178,
184 f., 200, 206, 217, 222 f., 230, 237,
242, 256, 260, 268, 272, 275 f., 287, 289,
295 f., 298, 301, 307, 317 f., 334, 336, 340,
349, 366, 391–393, 395 f., 398, 400, 404,
413, 430, 432, 438 f., 458, 479, 481, 503,
510 f., 516–518, 534 f., 539–543, 545 f., 548,
569 f., 579–590, 593, 605, 612, 619, 626,
648, 667, 707, 735, 738, 742, 772, 777, 779,
781 f., 786, 794, 798, 806, 812, 832, 834,
843, 858, 862, 871, 873, 877, 919 f., 928
Vol. 3: 27, 31, 33, 42, 72, 79, 98, 118, 136,
138, 140, 144 f., 153, 157, 162, 166, 168,
187, 191, 199, 212–214, 219, 224–226, 235,
237, 253, 268, 300, 335 f., 340, 348, 351,
268, 300, 335 f., 340, 348, 351, 355–357,
372 f., 377, 400, 407, 411, 415, 417, 430,
444 f., 454, 459, 468, 472, 505, 512, 517,
524, 527, 531, **535–543**, 550, 552, 562 f., 567,
572, 574 f., 578, 584, 586, **589–599**, 607–664,
678, 680, 684 f., 695, 701, 759, 761, 767,
777, 783, 793, 803, 824, 828, 836, 838, 847,
859, 861, 864, 870, 873, 887, **903–906**, 913,
917, 928, 944, 980, 1056 f., 1062–1065,
1067 f., 1070 f., 1078 f., 1081 f., 1085, 1158,
1161, 1167, 1185, 1204 f.
Relative **Vol. 2:** 43, 53, 225, 418, 538, **547–550**,
737
Relativism **Vol. 1:** 60, 550
Vol. 3: 895, 899, 901, 1143
Relativization **Vol. 2:** 439
Relax **Vol. 1:** 513, 527, 698
Vol. 3: 111, 178, 183, 254
Relearn **Vol. 1:** 708
Release **Vol. 1:** 173, 429, 431, 438, 505, 508,
576–578, 613, 697 f., 701
Vol. 2: 121, 149, 378, 457, 858
Vol. 3: 158, **166–174, 177–221,** 227, 256, 424,
592, 677
Release life **Vol. 3:** 424
Relevant **Vol. 1:** 681
Reliable **Vol. 1:** 99, 595, 658–660
Vol. 2: 626
Vol. 3: 862, 880
Reliance **Vol. 1:** 372, 461, 546, 680, 713
Vol. 2: 340
Relief **Vol. 1:** 473
Vol. 2: 107, 600, 681
Vol. 3: 111, 206, 255, 874, 904
Relieve **Vol. 3:** 119
Religion **Vol. 1:** 450, 453, 552, 686
Vol. 2: 85, 91, 103, 124, 453, 669
Vol. 3: 50, 75, 113, **549–551**
Religiosity **Vol. 2:** 340
Religious **Vol. 1:** 69, 643, 688
Vol. 2: 85, 90–92, 234, 237–239, 259, 287,
315, 325, 349 f., 353, 438 f., 659, 738, 887
Vol. 3: 349
Religious formula **Vol. 2:** 278
Relinquish **Vol. 1:** 505
Reluctance **Vol. 2:** 156, 829, 856
Reluctant **Vol. 1:** 459
Vol. 2: 435
Rely **Vol. 1:** 588 f., 596 f., 730
Vol. 2: 226, 240
Rely on **Vol. 3:** **254–258**
Remain **Vol. 1:** 676, 686, 713, 738
Vol. 2: 297, 328, 546, 764, 772
Vol. 3: **223–230**, 258, 537, 543, 588
Remain in **Vol. 3:** **223–230**
Remain longer **Vol. 3:** **224–229**
Remainder **Vol. 3:** 248
Remaining **Vol. 3:** **247–253**
Remarkable **Vol. 2:** **621–626**
Remarriage **Vol. 1:** 500, 506 f.
Vol. 2: 563 f., 583
Vol. 3: 95, 173, **535–543,** 1074 f.

537

(*also* → Second marriage)
Remedy **Vol. 2: 552–562**
Remember **Vol. 1:** 582, 679
   Vol. 2: 206, 318, 533, 649, 871
   Vol. 3: 173, 221, **230–247,** 405, 423, 780, 800
Remembrance **Vol. 1:** 247, 333, 370, 612
   Vol. 2: 149, 177, 892
   Vol. 3: 230–247, 866
Remind **Vol. 1:** 487, 542, 567 f., 578, 633
   Vol. 2: 359, 361, 431, 863
   Vol. 3: 47, **230–247,** 489
Reminder **Vol. 3:** 107, 407, 484
Reminiscence **Vol. 3:** 64
Remission **Vol. 1:** 154, 156, 698, 702
   Vol. 2: 118, 351, 386, 667
   Vol. 3: 1184
Remit **Vol. 1:** 697, 700
   Vol. 2: 116
Remnant **Vol. 1:** 296, 302, 305, 368, 370, 452, 541, 545
   Vol. 2: 100, 228, 301, 306, 308, 312 f., 315, 471, 572, 691, 699, 798
   Vol. 3: 247–253, 325, 436, 608, 616, 651, 792, 867
Remonstrate **Vol. 1:** 626
Remorse **Vol. 1:** 357
   Vol. 2: 416 f., 421 f.
   Vol. 3: 340
Remote **Vol. 3:** 838
Remould **Vol. 1:** 491
Removal **Vol. 1:** 314 f., 699
   Vol. 2: 151, 404
Remove **Vol. 1:** 466, 526, 587, 602, 606, 667, 700, 719, 722 f., 738
   Vol. 2: 213, 244, 309, 315, 360, 363, 460
   Vol. 3: 153, 166, 243, 825, 1012
Remuneration **Vol. 2:** 50
   Vol. 3: 140, 144
Renaissance **Vol. 1:** 59
Rend **Vol. 1:** 672
   Vol. 2: 190
   Vol. 3: 543
Render **Vol. 1:** 477
   Vol. 3: 134
Render service **Vol. 3: 544–549**
Renew **Vol. 1:** 106, 185, 221, 223, 509, 518, 626, 703, 716
   Vol. 2: 122, 129 f., 307, 313 f., 326, **670–676**
   Vol. 3: 267
Renewal **Vol. 1:** 143, 147 f., 153, 176, 184 f., 290, 332, 367, 371, 416, 452, 708, 724
   Vol. 2: 163, 183, **670–674,** 737, 786, 885, 892
   Vol. 3: 146, 148, 686, 705
Renounce **Vol. 1:** 414, 454 f., 561, 641
   Vol. 2: 244, 309, 340
   Vol. 3: 323
Renovation **Vol. 3:** 146
Renown **Vol. 1:** 296
Rent **Vol. 3: 138–144**
Renunciation **Vol. 1:** 186, 309, 358, 398, 400, 403, 455, 488 f., 495, 599, 604, 647, 675
   Vol. 2: 117, 244, 307, 332, 429, 534, 824, 846
   Vol. 3: 603, 679
Repair **Vol. 1:** 663

Vol. 3: 259, 350
Reparation **Vol. 3:** 151, 856, 1053
Repay **Vol. 2:** 157 f., 230, 254, 667, 825
   Vol. 3: 134–136, 141, 420
Repayment **Vol. 3: 134–136**
Repeat **Vol. 1:** 58, 64
   Vol. 2: 447, 717
Repentance **Vol. 1:** 77, 110, 144, 146 f., 150, 152, 154, 156 f., 159, 163, 167, 189, 308, 316, 319, 322, 339 f., 345 f., **353–362,** 356–359, 422 f., 464 f., 467, 476, 509, 545, 559, 564, 599 f., 607, 700, 702 f., 716, 722, 725, 742
   Vol. 2: 61, 70, 101, 106, 157, 270, 276, 285 f., 290, 307, 312, 318, 326, 350–352, 358 f., 366, 383 f., 408, 418–420, 422, 487, 566, 584, 680, 700, 717 f., 720, 737, 749, 770 f., 843, 859, 865, 867
   Vol. 3: 50, 52 f., 55, 79, 82, 135, 155, 167, 173 f., 207, 211, 240, 251, 361, 419, 428, 529, 567, 580, 616, 634, 638, 644, 686, 695, 721 f., 779, 809, 836, 842, 869, 938, 940, 1167
Repercussion **Vol. 1:** 680
Repetition **Vol. 1:** 64, 632
Rephidim **Vol. 2:** 637
Replace **Vol. 1:** 741
   Vol. 3: 192
Replacement **Vol. 2:** 273
Replica **Vol. 2:** 284
Report **Vol. 1:** 57, 574, 585
   Vol. 2: 172
   Vol. 3: 44–48, 54, **112–114,** 483, 894, 1106
Repose **Vol. 2:** 200
   Vol. 3: 254 f.
Reprehensible **Vol. 1:** 565
   Vol. 2: 349
   Vol. 3: 808–810, 1149
Represent **Vol. 1:** 680
   Vol. 2: 80, 158, 287, 313 f., 316, 320, 341, 376
Representation **Vol. 1:** 360, 489, 491, 654, 670, 712, 724
   Vol. 2: 284, 287, **288 f.**
   Vol. 3: 232, 899, 1196
Representative **Vol. 1:** 85, 102, 121, 127 f., 134, 177, 193, 195 f., 198 f., 285, 294, 296, 372–374, 385, 398, 423, 472, 478, 538, 628, 633, 666, 741
   Vol. 2: 57, 127, 200, 313, 327, 336
   Vol. 3: 41, 150, 171, 194–196, 239, 278, 619 f., 631, 637, 643, 670, 1044, 1112
Repress **Vol. 1:** 572
Repression **Vol. 2:** 568
Reproach **Vol. 1:** 215, 341, 453, 637, 704
   Vol. 2: 140, 143, 835
   Vol. 3: 340, 346, **923–928,** 1074
Reprobation **Vol. 1:** 378
   Vol. 3: 265
Reproduction **Vol. 1:** 492
   Vol. 2: 288 f.
Reproof **Vol. 2:** 140 f.
Reprove **Vol. 1:** 349
Reptile **Vol. 1:** 175

Reptile (*cont'd*)
Vol. 2: 661
Repudiation **Vol. 1:** 529, 604
    Vol. 2: 813, 819
    Vol. 3: 809, 1094
Repugnant **Vol. 1:** 694
Repulse **Vol. 3:** 903
Repulsive **Vol. 1:** 480
Reputation **Vol. 1:** 546, 558, 565, 590
    Vol. 2: 652, 683
    Vol. 3: 137, 141, 261, 1081
Repute **Vol. 1:** 546
    Vol. 2: 44, 46, 367
Request **Vol. 1:** 278, 425, 511, 569 f., 609
    Vol. 2: 116, 175, 179, 388, **855–864, 867–875, 879–881**
    Vol. 3: 114, 348
Require **Vol. 1:** 730
    Vol. 2: 236, 244, 307, 318, 446
Requirement **Vol. 1:** 714, 729, 738
    Vol. 2: 211, 440, 443, 447
    Vol. 3: 204, **352–377**
Requisition **Vol. 1:** 536
Requital **Vol. 1:** 598
Requite **Vol. 1:** 324
    Vol. 2: 735
    Vol. 3: 134–136, 342, 621
Rescue **Vol. 1:** 464, 544, 547, 713
    Vol. 2: 82, 126, 260, 630
    Vol. 3: 177, **205–216,** 318, 370, 379, 407, 528, 532, 802
Research **Vol. 1:** 504
Resemblance **Vol. 2:** 343, **500–508**
    Vol. 3: 1056
Resent **Vol. 1:** 547, 553
Reservation **Vol. 1:** 482
Reserve **Vol. 2: 829–836**
Reserved **Vol. 1:** 721
    Vol. 2: 332
Resident **Vol. 1:** 687, 689 f.
Resident alien **Vol. 1:** 690 f.
    Vol. 2: 804
Residue **Vol. 1:** 711
    Vol. 3: 247
Resignation **Vol. 1:** 262, 551
    Vol. 2: 360, 769, 772
Resin **Vol. 1:** 723
Resist **Vol. 1:** 354, 446, 458, 515, 550, 559, 710
    Vol. 2: 80
    Vol. 3: 755, 778
Resistance **Vol. 1:** 392, 539, 568, 686, 710
    Vol. 2: 764
    Vol. 3: 978
Resistance movement **Vol. 2:** 307
Resolution **Vol. 1:** 293, 475, 534, 692
    Vol. 3: 116, 799, 1016
Resolve **Vol. 1:** 363, 533, 540, 696 f., 737
    Vol. 2: 364, 818
    Vol. 3: 122, **1015–1018**
Resources **Vol. 1:** 319
    Vol. 2: 34, **601–616**
Respect **Vol. 1:** 192, 206, 288, 301, 462, 491 f., 498, 512, 542, 572, 586, 614, 617 f., 621, 686
    Vol. 2: 48, 90, 92, 124, 128, 134, 203, 225,

328, 336, 438, 446, 549, 810
    Vol. 3: 115, 219, **561–564,** 755, 779, 823, 930
Respectable **Vol. 1:** 520, 524
    Vol. 2: 447
    Vol. 3: 923
Respectful **Vol. 1:** 585, 615 f.
    Vol. 2: 90, 103, 310
Respond **Vol. 2:** 156, 270, 740
Response **Vol. 1:** 319, 324, 335, 460, 476, 482, 508, 525, 538, 540, 578, 595, 603, 699, 726
    Vol. 2: 196, 224, 350 f., 395, 568, 718, 826 f., 904
    Vol. 3: 60, 236, 246, 336, 522, 758, 769, 791, 793, 1046, 1052
Responsibility **Vol. 1:** 54, 104, 131, 191, 261, 276, 285, 288, 302, 317, 353, 373, 395, 415, 452, 525, 529, 536, 552, 614, 619, 660, 679
    Vol. 2: 137–139, 145, 150, 156, 159, 163, 181 f., 275, 295, 313, 335, 337, 562 f., 663, 667 f., 790, 819
    Vol. 3: 134, 260, 474, 481, 523, 525, 529, 545, 560, 568, 579, 582, 595, 677, 720, 741, 838, 853, 930, 1020, 1052 f., 1074, 1169
Responsibility in using language **Vol. 3:** 1142 f.
Responsible **Vol. 1:** 562, 610, 617
    Vol. 2: 137 f., 327, 336, 372, 737
    Vol. 3: 135, 185, 439, 802, 854, 933
Responsive **Vol. 2:** 680, 825
    Vol. 3: 693, 912, 916
Rest **Vol. 1:** 95, 115, 239, 263, 280, 321, 327, 335, 372, 521, 595, 600, 626, 675, 688, 727
    Vol. 2: 156, 262, 281, 363, 586 f., 681, 729, 777, 794, 809, 889 f.
    Vol. 3: 73, **111–114,** 120, 405 f., 433, 530, 639, 742, 835, 954, 1113, 1148, 1162
Rest of heart **Vol. 3:** 411
Restate **Vol. 2:** 315
Resting **Vol. 3: 254–258**
Resting place **Vol. 2:** 207
    Vol. 3: 254–258
Restitution **Vol. 1:** 545
    Vol. 3: 95, 155 f., 997
Restive **Vol. 3:** 27
Restless **Vol** 1: 239
    Vol. 2: 661, 724
    Vol. 3: 559
Restoration **Vol. 1:** 109, 113, 184–186, 225, 385, 467, 486, 508, 521, 531, 544, 545, 701 f.
    Vol. 2: 163, 252, 298, 307, 628, 687, 692, 893, 920
    Vol. 3: 145–176, 240, 269, 349, 351, 657, 692, 812
Restore **Vol. 2:** 161, **166–169,** 270, 363, 433, 480, 717 f., 921
    Vol. 3: 145–176, 209, **349–351,** 420, 950
Restrain **Vol. 2: 221–223**
Restraint **Vol. 1:** 422, 494, 501, 574, 679
    Vol. 2: 135, 161, 459, 462, **765–767**
    Vol. 3: 1080
Restriction **Vol. 1:** 331, 365, 495, 651, 681, 688, 742
    Vol. 2: 257
    Vol. 3: 551
Result **Vol. 1:** 165, 436, 437, 542, 546, 562,

580, 590, 592, 607, 609, 611, 697, 721, 723
Vol. 2: 132, 139, 155, 230, 310, 352, 400, 415, 420, 460
Vol. 3: 728
Resurrection **Vol. 1:** 53 f., 56 f., 65, 73, 78, 86 f., 131 f., 134, 136, 142, 144, 147 f., 150, 158, 167, 179–185, 224, 233, 236, 239, 242, 265 f., 290, 298, 303, 310, 313 f., 323–325, 351, 365, 375, 393, 399 f., 419, 427, 433–435, 437, 440, 442–446, 469 f., 473, 478, 511, 544, 551, 560, 564, 601 f., 630 f., 634, 638, 643, 649, 651, 668 f., 672, 695, 702, 707, 719, 740
Vol. 2: 48, 58, 79, 111, 159, 178, 187, 203, 208, 216, 218, 230, 238, 241–243, 245, 252, 271, 280, 282, 295, 299, 304, 319, 327 f., 340 f., 343, 351, 354, 356, 370, 380, 386–388, 402 f., 419, 429, 444, 479–481, 483, 489, 504, 514, 526, 545, 550, 559, 568, 580, 603–606, 625, 632 f., 640, 645, 655, 665, 672, 675, 680, 687, 691 f., 696, 701 f., 718, 728, 738 f., 746, 762, 764, 785–787, 799, 811, 866 f., 882, 893 f., 900 f., 903, 905, 908 f., 911, 918–920, 924–926, 928 f.
Vol. 3: 48, 55–57, 62, 65, 99, 168, 178 f., 185, 198, 200, 202, 211, 215, 225, 231, 243, 247, **259–309,** 290, 296, 312, 314, 328, 333, 361, 365, 372, 390, 412, 417, 433, 439 f., 453, 482, 489, 501, 505 f., 510, 515, 517 f., 524 f., 557 f., 567, 579 f., 584, 602, 628, 631 f., 643, 651, 677 f., 682–684, 686 f., 692, 698, 703 f., 706, 722, 724 f., 763, 772, 774, 785, 793, 812 f., 825, 830–832, 858, 861, 874, 936, 942, 970, 1035, 1044, 1047, 1060, 1067, 1073, 1100, 1110 f.
Resurrection body **Vol. 1:** 87, 114, 236, 241, 313, 316
Vol. 2: 245, 597, 739
Vol. 3: 298, 301, 305, 417, 449, 504, 684, 706, 731, 734, 814
Resurrection in contemporary theology **Vol. 3:** **281–305**
Resurrection, general **Vol. 2:** 387 f.
Resurrection and immortality **Vol. 3:** 302
Resuscitation **Vol. 1:** 470
Vol. 3: 281, 297, 684
Retain **Vol. 1:** 467, 703
Vol. 2: 286
Retention of sins **Vol. 2:** 787
Rethink **Vol. 1:** 699
Reticence **Vol. 1:** 375, 528
Retract **Vol. 2:** 159
Retreat **Vol. 2:** 220
Retribution **Vol. 1:** 392, 410, 659, 683
Vol. 2: 169, 276, 364, 366
Vol. 3: 94, 98, 140, 209, 260, 526, 720
Return **Vol. 1:** 184, 262, 354 f., 359, 410, 523, 543 f., 607, 611 f., 667, 671, 673, 678, 685 f., 720, 737, 741
Vol. 2: 54, 115, 154, 244, 250, 266, 308, 316 f., 321, 351, 356, 358, 360, 394, 447, 517, 546, 584, 604, 675, 713, 787, 887, 889, 909, 930
Vol. 3: 69, **134–136,** 146, 250, 255, 364, 474,

823, 848, 1104
Return of Christ **Vol. 1:** 229, 244, 315, 386, 607, 634, 649, 651
Vol. 2: 46, 83, 95, 187, 245, 353 f., 488
Vol. 3: 71, 277, 830, 838
Return of exiles **Vol. 2:** 307
Return property **Vol. 3:** 379
Reuben **Vol. 2:** 317
Vol. 3: 872
Reubenites **Vol. 2:** 638
Reunion **Vol. 2:** 309
Revaluation **Vol. 2:** 427
Reveal **Vol. 1:** 103, 106, 112, 305, 313, 324, 327, 338, 400, 472, 474, 484, 487, 541, 543, 575, 598, 620, 629, 638, 649, 680, 719, 726, 730, 735 f., 738
Vol. 2: 56, 73, 75, 141, 177 f., 183, 198, 212, 216–218, 296, 299, 328, 335, 350, 354, 359, 366 f., 369, 379, 382, 396 f., 404, 407, 447 f., **488–490,** 517, 819, 863
Vol. 3: **310–324,** 462, 848, 1006
Revealer **Vol. 1:** 85, 250, 253, 303, 337, 423, 556, 678
Vol. 2: 79, 119, 133, 135, 185, 204, 472 f., 494, 636, 640, 642, 646, 722, 724
Vol. 3: 782, 838, 1022, 1045, 1150
Revealing word **Vol. 3:** 892
Revel **Vol. 1:** 458, 460, 628
Vol. 2: 636
Revelation **Vol. 1:** 50, 52, 62, 70, 78, 90, 101, 103, 111 f., 127, 146 f., 180, 222, 244, 250, 272, 282, 294, 304, 336, 373 f., 385, 387, 412, 427 f., 441, 483, 486 f., 504, 511, 528, 530, 535, 550 f., 559, 566, 575 f., 587, 594 f., 598, 605, 610, 619, 627, 666, 727, 737, 740
Vol. 2: 45, 48, 67, 70–72, 74 f., 83, 94, 106, 122 f., 127, 141, 162, 173 f., 176, 178, 191, 193, 198, 201 f., 212, 215–220, 229, 240, 244, 250, 273, 278 f., 289 f., 308, 315, 340, 350, 359, 367, 383, 393 f., 396–398, 400, 403–408, 448 f., 461, 482, 494, 503, 518, 548 f., 637, 650, 653, 762, 806, 834 f., 900, 908 f.
Vol. 3: 54, 55, 72, **74–89,** 117, 131, 205, 216, 220, 246, 264, 286, 301, **309–340,** 381, 384, 404, 482, 492, 495, 500, 502, 504–506, 513, 515 f., 521, 528, 569, 571, 610, 630 f., 639 f., 645, 705 f., 710, 728, 733, 749, 751, 773, 777, 783, 790 f., 793, 806, 831, 844, 881, 885, 887, 890–893, 898, 906, 1004 f., 1017, 1020, 1029, 1045, 1085, 1087, 1091, 1118, 1121, 1143
Revelation, book of **Vol. 3:** 312
Revelation in contemporary theology **Vol. 3:** **325–337**
Revelation, structure of book of **Vol. 2:** **691, 702**
Revelry **Vol. 2:** **274–277,** 356, 586
Revenge **Vol. 1:** 555
Vol. 2: 157 f.
Vol. 3: 680
Revenue **Vol. 3:** 183, 417, 753 f., **755–759**
Revere **Vol. 1:** 653
Vol. 2: 232, 352
Reverence **Vol. 1:** 71, 239, 450, 609, 621–623,

Reverence (*cont'd*)
687
Vol. 2: 85, 90–93, 229, 331, 439, **875–879**
Vol. 3: 424, **561 f.,** 583, 1064
Reversal **Vol. 2:** 843 f.
Reversed values **Vol. 2:** 420
Review **Vol. 1:** 189
Revile **Vol. 1:** 415
Vol. 2: 143, 406, 661, 775
Vol. 3: 340–347, 364, 696, 743
Reviler **Vol. 3: 346 f.**
Revival **Vol. 1:** 185
Vol. 3: 692
Revive **Vol. 1:** 437
Vol. 2: 181
Revoke **Vol. 1:** 207, 367
Revolt **Vol. 1:** 459, 535, 606, 688
Vol. 2: 34, 291
Vol. 3: 259, 279, 756
Revolution **Vol. 1:** 275, 543, 640
Vol. 2: 343
Revolutionary **Vol. 1:** 643
Vol. 2: 308 f.
Vol. 3: 377–379
Revolutionize **Vol. 2:** 386
Reward **Vol. 1:** 98, 111, 367, 406, 432, 450,
489, 537, 598, 648, 651, 688, 716, 734
Vol. 2: 47, 57, 104, 107 f., 117–120, 157 f.,
165, 192 f., 203, 206 f., 216, 261, 297 f., 302,
319, 353, 358, 366, 370, 426, 428 f., 433,
449, 498 f., 738, 772, 792 f., 813, 825, 830,
834 f., 844 f., 866 f., 929
Vol. 3: 134–145, 167, 348, 357, 360, 389, 439,
525 f., 544, 751, 802, 832, 839, 871, 980,
1054, 1149, 1151, 1158
Rewarding **Vol. 1:** 647
Rework **Vol. 3:** 916
Rezon **Vol. 3:** 468
Rhadamanthys **Vol. 3:** 739
Rhetoric **Vol. 1:** 574
Vol. 2: 93, 743
Vol. 3: 65, 1031, 1081, **1085–1087**
Rhetorical **Vol. 2:** 334, 685
Rhodes **Vol. 1:** 189
Vol. 2: 291
Vol. 3: 149
Rhyme **Vol. 2:** 870
Rhythm **Vol. 1:** 628
Vol. 2: 870
Rhythm of life **Vol. 1:** 624
Rib **Vol. 1:** 672
Vol. 3: 1056
Rich **Vol. 1:** 109, 116, 319, 341, 466, 515, 547,
571, 587, 596, 688, 722, 730, 732 f., 735
Vol. 2: 28, 57, 79, 130, 133, 263, 267, 273,
285, 301, 416, 499, 660, 811, 820–822, 824,
826, 828, 833, 838, **840–845**
Vol. 3: 99, 143, 253, 369, 682 f., 749, 758,
791, 856, 1017, 1053, 1061
Richards, I.A. **Vol. 3:** 1129 f.
Richardson, Alan **Vol. 3: 289 f.**
Riches **Vol. 1:** 142, 457, 684, 726, 730
Vol. 2: 78 f., 243, 245, 255, 349, 388, 460,
597, 794, 828 f., 837, **840–845**

Vol. 3: 324, 469, 978
Rickets **Vol. 2:** 414
Riddle **Vol. 1:** 657
Vol. 2: 743–760
Ride **Vol. 2:** 190
Rider **Vol. 1:** 118, 203, 205, 317, 430, 657
Vol. 3: 266
Ridicule **Vol. 1:** 455
Vol. 2: 343, 429, 431–433, 436
Vol. 3: 340 f., 521, 563
Rigaux, B. **Vol. 3:** 300
Right **Vol. 1:** 56, 193, 200, 219, 295, 299, 329,
336, 352, 360, 368, 375, 392, 400, 413, 460,
475, 484 f., 500, 555, 571 f., 639–641, 648,
668 f., 679, 684, 686 f., 690 f., 700, 715, 717,
720
Vol. 2: 49 f., 99, 120, 183, 201, 221, 247, 250,
256–258, 285, 302, 316 f., 336, 363, 370,
378, 440, 446, 497, 540, 582, **606–611,** 716,
737 f., 815, 857
Vol. 3: 142, 145, **347–352,** 577, 730, 765, 887,
938, 964, 1028, 1073
Right hand **Vol. 1:** 167, 384, 643, 663
Vol. 2: 80, **146–153,** 188, 194, 196, 199, 204,
245, 380, 385, 475, 614, 883
Vol. 3: 62, 219, 244, 303, 500, 588, 614, 627,
633, 735, 749
Right moment **Vol. 3: 833–839**
Right time **Vol. 3: 845–849**
Righteous **Vol. 1:** 110, 115, 174, 216, 222, 274,
278, 288, 356, 358, 371, 381–383, 390, 395,
398, 408, 410 f., 422, 434, 444, 472, 554,
556, 564, 586, 597 f., 605, 627, 650, 706 f.,
713, 721, 738
Vol. 2: 47, 51, 56, 66, 72, 82, 91 f., 94 f., 144,
149, 155, 179, 191, 201–204, 206 f., 215,
228, 237, 259, 272, 276, 298, 313, 326, 370,
431, 434, 479, 481, 486, 659, 681, 707, 724,
735 f., 761, 798, 808, 824, 832, 837, 861,
866 f., 899
Vol. 3: 144, 157, 162, 195, 199, 204, 224,
226, 242, 265, 272, 313, 350, **352–377,** 428,
469, 498, 527, 610, 616, 624, 626, 638, 680,
684, 713, 722, 732, 832, 847, 856, 866, 946,
997, 1050
Righteous deed **Vol. 3: 352–377**
Righteousness **Vol. 1:** 78 f., 86, 89, 96, 107 f.,
110, 112, 115, 118, 147, 181, 185, 217, 231,
234, 273, 278, 311, 314, 317, 321, 332, 339,
346, 358, 370 f., 382, 386, 390, 397 f., 438,
446, 475, 495, 501, 515, 519, 559, 581, 591,
598, 601, 607, 639, 649, 673, 675, 680 f.,
700–702, 710, 714, 720, 723, 729 f., 738 f.
Vol. 2: 42, 48, 53, 72 f., 78, 93, 101, 111, 119,
121, 128, 133, 136 f., 141, 148, 179, 229,
236, 242, 245, 258, 267 f., 275, 287, 299 f.,
307, 363, 366, 370, 374, 387 f., 396, 442,
444, 453, 469, 482 f., 492, 494, 497, 499,
539 f., 543 f., 546, 590–593, 595, 600, 641,
669, 676, 682, 723, 742, 777, 779, 781 f.,
794, 806, 817 f., 835, 842 f., 864, 884, 899
Vol. 3: 30, 45, 52, 70, 72, 82, 92 f., 98 f., 117,
121, 130, 136–138, 140–142, 145, 160 f.,
163, 165–170, 181, 184, 188, 207 f., 211,

224 f., 233, 268, 278, 311, 315, 321, 352, 383, 388 f., 427, 436, 471, 525, 532, 546 f., 549, 551, 569, 573, 575 f., 581, 583, 585 f., 597, 637, 647–650, 657, 682, 692 f., 725, 730, 734, 748 f., 763, 766, 783, 790, 823–826, 831, 836, 879, 919, 932 f., 939, 942, 966, 986, 1041, 1043, 1095, 1148–1152, 1155, 1158, 1181
Rightly **Vol. 3: 351 f.**
Rightly handle **Vol. 3: 351 f.**
Rights **Vol. 3:** 93, 381, 576, 583, 645
Rights of a citizen **Vol. 2: 801–804**
Rigid **Vol. 2:** 153, 812
Rigidity **Vol. 1:** 516
Rigour **Vol. 2:** 270
Rimmon **Vol. 3:** 156
Ring **Vol. 1:** 683
 Vol. 3: 497
Ringgren, H. **Vol. 3:** 1125
Ringleader **Vol. 1:** 535
Rinse **Vol. 1:** 144, 152 f., 224
Riot **Vol. 1:** 419
 Vol. 2: 623
 Vol. 3: 203
Ripe **Vol. 1:** 204, 516, 682
 Vol. 3: 845–849
Ripen **Vol. 1:** 722
 Vol. 2: 675
Rise **Vol. 1:** 495, 497, 591, 625, 692
 Vol. 2: 63, 242, 327
 Vol. 3: 200, 259, 731
Risen **Vol. 1:** 86 f., 130, 168, 174, 178, 183, 204, 213, 266, 300, 303, 328, 399, 437, 476, 517, 551, 592, 601, 643, 668, 677, 708
 Vol. 2: 58, 81, 83, 113 f., 176, 186, 194, 196, 207, 242, 282, 302, 332, 340, 342, 354, 358–361, 388, 399, 488, 624, 785, 787, 902, 915
 Vol. 3: 48, 55 f., 58, 60, 71, 114, 132, 244, 314, 516, 571, 1060
Rising **Vol. 1:** 145, 147, 225, 359
 Vol. 2: 367, 644
 Vol. 3: 205, 227
Risk **Vol. 1:** 364 f., **419–420,** 592, 658, 710
 Vol. 2: 104, 159, 350, 368
 Vol. 3: 158, 799
Rite **Vol. 1:** 115 f., 123, 158 f., 237, 288 f., 309, 426, 432, 497 f., 611 f., 625 f., 630, 654, 699 f., 702, 705, 716
 Vol. 2: 59, 152, 228, 233, 236, 252
 Vol. 3: 103, 149–151, 157, 205
Ritschl, A.B. **Vol. 1:** 65
Ritual **Vol. 1:** 53, 70, 121 f., 177, 308, 316, 448, 525, 611, 625 f., 701
 Vol. 2: 86, 151, 157, 199, 223, 236, 268, 272, 326 f., 336, 415, 556
 Vol. 3: 38, 94 f., 100 f., 103–107, 119, 162, 198, 243, 323, 356, 366, 407, 409, 415, 421, 426–428, 434, 996, 1053, 1149
Ritual anointing **Vol. 1:** 122
 Vol. 2: 711
Ritual bath **Vol. 1:** 144 f., 152 f.
 Vol. 2: 652
 Vol. 3: 1168
Ritual cleansing **Vol. 1:** 149, 447, 654

 Vol. 2: 285
Ritual institutions **Vol. 1:** 66
Ritual law **Vol. 1:** 61
Ritual purification **Vol. 1:** 225
Ritual washing **Vol. 1:** 152–154
 Vol. 2: 150
Ritualistic **Vol. 2:** 225
Rival **Vol. 1:** 269, 486, 558
 Vol. 2: 372, 374
Rivalry **Vol. 1:** 650
 Vol. 2: 818
River **Vol. 1:** 165, 654, 682 f.
 Vol. 2: 130, 157, 232, 274
 Vol. 3: 117, 21 , 695, 813, 902, **982–992**
River of life **Vol. 1:** 390
River-bed **Vol. 3:** 985
Road **Vol. 1:** 254, 520
 Vol. 2: 220
 Vol. 3: 146, 229, 352, 747, 902, **935–943,** 1006
Roam **Vol. 1:** 519
 Vol. 2: 457
Roar **Vol. 2:** 421, 423
 Vol. 3: 112, 324
Roast **Vol. 1:** 249
Rob **Vol. 1:** 439, 705
 Vol. 2: 361
 Vol. 3: 377–381, 788, 853
Rob temples **Vol. 2: 232–236**
Robber **Vol. 1:** 419
 Vol. 2: 236
 Vol. 3: 377–379, 430, **601–605,** 756
Robbery **Vol. 3:** 95, 137, 448, **601–605,** 1053
Robe **Vol. 1:** 122, 315, 317
 Vol. 2: 412
 Vol. 3: 120 f., 470, 789
Robins, R.H. **Vol. 3:** 1129
Robust **Vol. 1:** 727
Rock **Vol. 1:** 80, 240, 382, 610, 636, 662, 673, 683
 Vol. 2: 30, 129, 159, 177, 218, 220, 249, 253, 277, 313, 433, 619, 623, 652, 705 f., 709 f., 731–734, 754 f.
 Vol. 3: 84, 363, **381–399,** 435, 446, 504, 508, 543, 554, 558 f., 568, 623, 706 f., 782, 784, 795, 797, 809, 986, 1001, 1013, 1108
Rock of stumbling **Vol. 2:** 706
 Vol. 3: 382, 389–391
Rod **Vol. 1:** 51, 111, 161 f., 164, **405–408**
 Vol. 2: 378
 Vol. 3: 870, 913
Rod of iron **Vol. 2:** 570, 795
Rod of Jesse **Vol. 1:** 407
Role **Vol. 1:** 134, 302, 373, 549, 641, 687, 708, 717, 727, 737
 Vol. 2: 147 f., 158, 160 f., 231, 447
 Vol. 3: 49, 78, 80, 85, 88
Role valuations **Vol. 3:** 1063
Roll **Vol. 1:** 53
 Vol. 2: 157, 418
 Vol. 3: 497
Roll up **Vol. 3:** 399, 735–737
Roll of widows **Vol. 3:** 1075
Rolling **Vol. 3:** 558–560

Roman **Vol. 1:** 72, 75, 119, 125, 140, 142, 162, 175, 199, 205, 220, 299, 309, 363, 392, 394–396, 403, 407, 431, 506, 518 f., 574, 591, 606, 624, 633
Vol. 2: 32, 85, 125, 222, 233, 324, 373, 378–381, 383, 430, 438, 451, 461, 572, 608, 802, 849–851, 899, 922
Vol. 3: 138, 203, 217, 230, 441, 480, 558, 635, 715, 731, 736, 739, 756, 758, 788, 791, 868, 915, 952, 960 f., 964–967, 976 f., 1147, 1168
Roman citizen **Vol. 2:** 331, 804
Roman colony **Vol. 2:** 308
Roman empire **Vol. 1:** 55, 59, 519
Vol. 2: 125
Roman procurator **Vol. 2:** 334
Vol. 3: 456
Romans **Vol. 1:** 61 f., 264, 348, 364, 392, 395 f., 403, 407 f., 435, 627, 687 f.
Vol. 2: 139, 234, 308
Vol. 3: 39 f., 97, 109, 142, 361, 440, 452, 538, 603, 706, 752 f., 840, 949, 979
Romanticism **Vol. 1:** 694
Rome **Vol. 1:** 108, 127, 141 f., 264, 79, 395, 476, 501, 532, 559, 569, 616, 631, 687
Vol. 2: 130, 221 f., 311, 316, 451, 640, 792, 804, 816, 847, 850, 884, 918
Vol. 3: 65, 132, 164, 180, 203, 211, 226, 240, 261, 296, 385 f., 388, 446, 452 f., 598, 789, 851, 976 f., 995, 1008, 1013, 1114
Roof **Vol. 1:** 632
Vol. 3: 796
Roof tile **Vol. 3: 910–913**
Rook **Vol. 3:** 525
Room **Vol. 1:** 718, 741 f.
Vol. 2: 224–229
Root **Vol. 1:** 118, 138, 202, 427, 459, 516, 563, 652, 660, 680, 730
Vol. 2: 253, 312, 315, 406
Vol. 3: 416, 736, **865–870**
Root of bitterness **Vol. 2:** 782
Vol. 3: 869
Root and branch **Vol. 3:** 866
Root of David **Vol. 3:** 180
Root and fruit **Vol. 3:** 866
Root up **Vol. 3:** 523
Rope **Vol. 3:** 120
Rosetta Stone **Vol. 3:** 635
Rostrum **Vol. 2:** 369
Rot **Vol. 1:** 463, 683
Rotten **Vol. 1:** 722
Rough **Vol. 2:** 153, 155, 464
Vol. 3: 709
Rouse **Vol. 2:** 136
Vol. 3: 279–281
Route **Vol. 2:** 266
Row **Vol. 2:** 451
Rower **Vol. 1:** 408, 521
Vol. 3: 546
Royal **Vol. 2: 372–389**
Royal anointing **Vol. 1:** 123
Royal cult **Vol. 1:** 426
Royal family **Vol. 2:** 437
Royal household **Vol. 2:** 249

Royal priesthood **Vol. 1:** 305
Vol. 2: 228, 380, 839
Royal Psalms **Vol. 1:** 288
Vol. 2: 374
Vol. 3: 649
Royal rite **Vol. 1:** 640
Royal road **Vol. 3:** 939
Royal sanctuaries **Vol. 2: 225**
Royal way **Vol. 3:** 946
Royalty **Vol. 1:** 405 f., 469
Vol. 2: 96
Rub **Vol. 1:** 479
Vol. 2: 334
Vol. 3: 840
Rubbish **Vol. 1:** 479 f.
Ruby **Vol. 3:** 396
Rudder **Vol. 1:** 118
Vol. 2: 435
Rude **Vol. 3:** 439
Rudiments **Vol. 2: 451–453**
Rue **Vol. 2: 210 f.**
Ruin **Vol. 1:** 106, 451, **462–471**, 561, 562, 608, 610 f., 693
Vol. 2: 149, 308, 328, 367, 583, 609, 629
Vol. 3: 573, 996, 1005
Rule **Vol. 1:** 51, 59, 95, 99, 121, 135, 142, 163, **164–169**, 192, 235, 243, 300 f., 330, 333, 358, 387, 395 f., 408, 423, 426, 435, 449, 457, 459, 509, 518 f., 524 f., 533, 543, 580, 582, 607, 614, 619, 648, 651, 707, 715, 729
Vol. 2: 73, 76, 83, 95, 120, 123, 129, 183, 189, 213, 240, 242, 257 f., 261 f., 305, 308, 311, 326 f., 335, 337, 360, 363, 365, **372–389**, 394, 396, 436, **438–452**, 499, **510–520**, 548, 603, 631, 781, 877
Vol. 3: 57, 107, 204, **399–404**, 430, 436, 439, 485, 493, 495, 518, 555, 677, 692, **716–718**, 730, 734, 774, 780, 981, 985 f., 998, 1064
Rule the household **Vol. 2: 508–510**
Rule out **Vol. 1:** 639
Ruler **Vol. 1:** 95, 109, 111, 123, **164–169**, 170, 194, 198, 246, 269 f., 273 f., 325, 335, 365, 378, 407, 422, 450, 482, 495, 508, 512, 593, 610, 622, 647–649, 651, 665, 686, 718
Vol. 2: 57, 70 f., 105, 133, 135, 158, 160, 202, 257, 265, 288, 301, 337, **372–389**, 412, 456, 512, 514, 519, 539, 568, **601–616**, 637, 641, 674, 693, 777, 792, 796, 832, 840, 844, 898
Vol. 3: 45, 148, 217, 220, 243, 310, 318, 377, 379, 391, 549, 566, 633, 635, 649, 735, 739, 746, 866, 871, 1063, 1152
Ruler of the world **Vol. 3: 716–718**
Ruling **Vol. 3:** 188, 384
Ruling class **Vol. 2:** 315
Ruling power **Vol. 2: 606–611**
Ruling principle **Vol. 3:** 122
Rumbling **Vol. 3:** 557
Rumour **Vol. 2:** 172, 457
Vol. 3: 112, 1106
Rumours of wars **Vol. 3:** 962
Run **Vol. 1:** 262, 648, 682
Vol. 3: 933–947
Run after **Vol. 2: 805–807**
Runner **Vol. 1:** 493

Vol. 2: 807
Running before **Vol. 3: 945–947**
Rupture **Vol. 1:** 640
Russell, Bertrand **Vol. 3:** 1124, 1129, 1135 f.
Rust **Vol. 1:** 463
   Vol. 2: 27 f., 831, 836
Rustling **Vol. 3:** 678
Ruth **Vol. 1:** 53, 58 f., 170
   Vol. 2: 116, 577, 888
   Vol. 3: 191, 555, 656 f., 867, 1055, 1057, 1062, 1069

Sabaoth **Vol. 2:** 556
Sabarin **Vol. 3:** 453
Sabbath **Vol. 1:** 83, 115, 245, 310, 335, 360, 384, 625–628, 630 f., 634, 654, 688, 691, 699
   Vol. 2: 133, 165, 174, 226, 267, 396, 426, 499, 514, 518 f., 625 f., 665, 692, 697, 754, 800, 811, 871, 880, 887, 889, 931
   Vol. 3: 37, 74, 94, 120, 128, 180, 186 f., 235, 239, 258, **405–415,** 423, 427, 429, 441 f., 488, 508, 542, 556, 608, 623, 717, 792, 814, 849, 996, 1149, 1163, 1168
Sabbath-breaker **Vol. 1:** 294
   Vol. 2: 499
Sabbath-day's journey **Vol. 3:** 940
Sabbath-observance **Vol. 3:** 255, 440
Sabbath-offering **Vol. 2:** 410
Sabbath-rest **Vol. 3:** 255 f., 594
Sabbatical year **Vol. 1:** 691
   Vol. 2: 298, 822
   Vol. 3: 191, 194
Sabellianism **Vol. 2:** 507
Sabellius **Vol. 2:** 507
Sack **Vol. 3:** 498
Sackcloth **Vol. 1:** 203, 672
   Vol. 2: 418
   Vol. 3: 589, 732
Sacral **Vol. 1:** 211, 267, 374
   Vol. 2: 189, 206, 274, 306, 326, 334, 336
   Vol. 3: 33
Sacral kingship **Vol. 2:** 644
Sacral manumission **Vol. 3:** 597
Sacrament **Vol. 1:** 58, 149, 285, 358, 466, 629
   Vol. 2: 534 f.
   Vol. 3: 82, 675, 1137
Sacramental **Vol. 1:** 123, 145, 282, 288, 344, 445 f.
   Vol. 2: 271, 273
   Vol. 3: 232, 489, 647
Sacramentalism **Vol. 1:** 54
   Vol. 2: 393, 535, 906
Sacred **Vol. 1:** 61, 172, 414, 498, 560, 573 f., 588, 625
   Vol. 2: 224–232, 233–235, 270, 309, 373
   Vol. 3: 45, 415, 424, 860
Sacred marriage **Vol. 2: 576,** 584
Sacred number **Vol. 3:** 851
Sacred poles **Vol. 3:** 865
Sacred scribe **Vol. 3:** 480
Sacred song **Vol. 3: 670–672**
Sacred time **Vol. 2:** 891
Sacrifice **Vol. 1:** 57, 61, 74 f., 107, 113–116, 122, 125, 145, 151 f., 166, 172, 211, 219–

226, 230, 234 f., 239, 250, 252, 261, 292–294, 308, 320, 325, 350–352, 360, 371 f., 375, 398 f., 402, 405, 414, 426, 437, 451, 475, 479, 488, 497, 538, 546, 625–627, 629, 639, 642 f., 649, 655, 666, 669, 673, 685, 699 f., 702 f., 713, 732
   Vol. 2: 39–43, 49, 59, 63 f., 74, 78, 94, 97, 102, 107 f., 116, 118 f., 132, 147, 151, 199, 208, 211, 223, 225, 228, 230, **232–236,** 237 f., 244, 249, 259, 272 f., 285 f., 293, 327 f., 386, 410–414, 447, 449, 461, 463, 521, 525, 535 f., 555 f., 559, 569, 593, 610, 618, 638, 650, 652, 664, 676, 689, 692 f., 711, 713, 717 f., 720, 803, 816–818, 854 f., 860, 885
   Vol. 3: 35, 38, 41 f., 45, 49, 78, 84, 89, 103, 106–108, 110, 117, 120, 138, **148–166,** 171, 173 f., 181, 190, 194 f., 198, 200, 215, 221, 238 f., 243 f., 246, 258, 261, 277, 303, 323, 356, 366, 407, **415–436,** 443, 445–447, 495, 543, 547, 552 f., 575, 579, 582, 586, 600 f., 608, 624, 676, 686, 701, 715, 722 f., 728, 739, 744–746, 756 f., 781–783, 787, 791, 797, 812, 814 f., 817, 847, 852, 855 f., 919, 941, 953, 965, 996, 1010, 1023, 1118f., 1143, 1148, 1165
Sacrifice of Isaac (→ Isaac, Sacrifice of)
Sacrifice of praise **Vol. 3:** 817
Sacrificed to idols **Vol. 3: 417–436**
Sacrificer **Vol. 2:** 151, 234
Sacrificial **Vol. 1:** 398, 468, 474 f., 552, 630, 634, 648, 653, 655, 691
   Vol. 2: 74, 164, 174, 225, 234, 286, 288, 326 f., 355, 440 f., 447, 533, 549, 599, 604, 674, 854
   Vol. 3: 94, 102, 242, 349, 364, 372
Sacrilege **Vol. 1:** 125, 212
   Vol. 2: 233, 235
Sacrosanct **Vol. 1:** 122
Sad **Vol. 1:** 565
   Vol. 2: 386, **419–423**
Saddle **Vol. 1:** 317
   Vol. 2: 317
Sadducees **Vol. 1:** 101, 196, 364, 434, 487, 534 f., 627
   Vol. 2: 207, 303, 311, 321, 462, 578, 580, 584, 640, 691, 785, 810–813, 880
   Vol. 3: 40, 184, 263 f., 270, 273 f., 277, **439–443,** 480, 488, 753, 769, 1002, 1035
Sadness **Vol. 2:** 180, 357, 359
Safe **Vol. 1:** 660, 663
   Vol. 2: 134, 240, 244
   Vol. 3: 565, 713
Safe return **Vol. 3:** 205
Safeguard **Vol. 1:** 663
   Vol. 2: 136, 738
Safety **Vol. 1:** 483, 501
   Vol. 2: 297, 364, 777
   Vol. 3: 217, 419
Sagacious **Vol. 3:** 445
Sage **Vol. 1:** 574
   Vol. 2: 377
   Vol. 3: 480
Sail **Vol. 1:** 698
   Vol. 3: 913

Sailor **Vol. 1:** 559
Saints **Vol. 1:** 78, 204, 222, 266, 275, 300, 302, 305, 321, 514, 642, 689, 691, 731
  Vol. 2: 83, 217, **223–238**, 243, 294, 298, 302, 380, 389, 401, 429, 489, 600, 604, 613, 625, 642, 669, 702, 718, 731, 776, 798, 826, 868, 882
  Vol. 3: 84, 350, 436, 558, 614, 819, 854, 962, 1047, 1161
Saints of the Most High **Vol. 2:** 376, 607, 610
Sake **Vol. 2:** 115, 387
Salamis **Vol. 1:** 624
Salary **Vol. 2:** 433
  Vol. 3: 134, 144, 444
Sale **Vol. 1:** 505
  Vol. 2: 273
Salem **Vol. 2:** 324, 378, **590–593,** 694
  Vol. 3: 36
Salim **Vol. 2:** 592
Sallustius **Vol. 1:** 176
Salome **Vol. 3:** 1060
Salt **Vol. 1:** 657, 670
  Vol. 2: 746
  Vol. 3: 422, 436, **443–449,** 713, 1012, 1025
Salt pits **Vol. 3:** 444
Salt Sea **Vol. 3:** 444
Salt springs **Vol. 3:** 988
Salt water **Vol. 3:** 992
Saltless **Vol. 3: 443–449**
Salty **Vol. 3: 443–449**
Salutary **Vol. 2:** 419
Salutation **Vol. 2:** 780 f.
Salute **Vol. 2:** 358, 795
Salvation **Vol. 1:** 54, 68, 73, 77 f., 80, 87, 100, 112 f., 123, 141, 148–150, 157 f., 168, 184, 186, 190 f., 208–210, 214, 217 f., 239, 246, 248, 251 f., 257, 284, 289, 297, 299 f., 310, 314, 316 f., 322, 330 f., 346 f., 356 f., 359, 367 f., 370, 373–375, 379, 382–384, 397, 399–401, 410, 414 f., 420–422, 424, 436 f., 440 f., 455, 461, 464 f., 467, 469, 472 f., 477, 484, 489, 492, 499, 510, 519, 523, 525, 534, 541, 544, 554, 557, 560, 564, 572, 585, 594–597, 600 f., 603 f., 607, 609–613, 620, 623, 626, 629, 632, 636–638, 641, 647, 660, 669, 696, 719, 723, 732, 735–738, 740
  Vol. 2: 31, 37, 40, 45, 47, 50, 53–56, 58, 61, 63, 72–75, 77 f., 80, 83, 99–101, 106, 108 f., 111–114, 116, 119, 122, 134 f., 138, 141, 147, 149, 156, 160, 168, 170, 174, 176, 178 f., 189, 193–195, 198, 200, 203, 213, 216, 226, 239–243, 245, 255 f., 258, 265–268, 270f., 275, 277 f., 280, 300–303, 306–309, 313–315, 331 f., 335, 337, 342 f., 353–355, 357 f., 363 f., 388, 393–397, 400, 402–407, 411, 420, 431, 433, 441, 444–446, 451, 458, 470, 480, 484, 490–493, 498 f., 532, 535 f., 545, 548, 566, 581, 585, 597 f., 603–605, 627, 629–633, 649, 664–666, 668–671, 675 f., 690, 699, 705 f., 708 f., 714 f., 717 f., 722 f., 737, 741, 746, 770 f., 773, 777–781, 791–794, 808 f., 819, 825, 830, 838 f., 844, 859, 863 f., 873, 878 f., 881, 887–891, 900, 908, 918, 925, 928

  Vol. 3: 34, 38, 42, 46, 50 f., 53, 56, 70, 72–74, 78 f., 82 f., 117 f., 123, 127–129, 132, 135, 140, 142–144, 147 f., 162, 168, 171 f., **177–221,** 224, 226, 228 f., 239, 250 f., 264, 270, 277, 287, 311, 315 f., 342, 349 f., 355, 357, 366 f., 371, 388, 391, 393, 400, 402, 409, 460–462, 470, 475, 492, 501, 515, 529, 547 f., 550, 567, 584 f., 592, 630–633, 637, 640, 644 f., 649, 651 f., 659, 671, 685 f., 692, 702, 714 f., 723, 732, 746, 749, 751, 762 f., 779, 785, 818, 824, 829, 831 f., 837 f., 844, 860, 886, 905, 938, 940, 942, 949, 954, 965, 974, 988, 997, 1005 f., 1011, 1018 f., 1022, 1031, 1035 f., 1043, 1052, 1058, 1079, 1093, 1095, 1102, 1104–1106, 1112, 1114, 1117 f., 1135, 1142, 1148, 1151
Salvation history **Vol. 1:** 59, 186, 286, 289, 296, 303, 367, 375, 438, 604
  Vol. 2: 45, 47, 75, 80, 84, 111, 119, 123, 130, 135, 255, 298, 300, 303, 314, 364, 396, 408, 443, 527, 570, 663–665, 691, 695, 787, 807, **907 f.,** 917, 920
  Vol. 3: 66, 291, 333, 633, 836, 843, 906, 986
Salvation of Israel **Vol. 2: 308,** 899
Salvation of Zion **Vol. 2:** 308
Samareitikon **Vol. 3:** 453
Samaria **Vol. 1:** 52, **67,** 116, 166, 269, 303, 629
  Vol. 2: 74, 86, 306, 387, 557, 849, 878, 918, 921
  Vol. 3: 56, 94, 427, **449–466,** 483, 890, 980, 1059, 1114, 1132
Samaritan **Vol. 1:** 52, **67,** 114, 148, 257 f., 335, 599, 657, 685
  Vol. 2: 104, 177, 301, 306, 321, 339, 427, 467, 544, 550, 591, 596, 600, 698, 742, 749, 784 f., 793, 805, 878, 927
  Vol. 3: 37, 106, 143, 147, 173, 216, 219, 378, 439, **449–466,** 539, 633, 635, 699, 752, 781, 789, 891, 980, 987, 1046
Samaritan Pentateuch **Vol. 1:** 67
  Vol. 3: 464–466
Samaritanisms **Vol. 3:** 465
Same **Vol. 3:** 839
Sammael **Vol. 1:** 125
Sample **Vol. 1:** 577
  Vol. 2: 290
Samson **Vol. 2:** 225, 228, 458
  Vol. 3: 235, 591 f.
Samuel **Vol. 1:** 50, 53, 66, 68, 195, 273, 425 f., 511, 538
  Vol. 2: 374, 432, 554
  Vol. 3: 73, 218, 263, 270, 311, 427, 827, 841, 1041, 1057, 1090 f., 1120
Sanballat **Vol. 3:** 451
Sanctification **Vol. 1:** 122, 152, 222, 223, 231, 371 f., 475, 564, 722, 730, 739
  Vol. 2: 64, 78, 144, **223–238,** 781, 819
  Vol. 3: 107, 163, 199, 215, 226, 701, 779, 892, 1023, 1064 f.
Sanctifier **Vol. 1:** 669
Sanctify **Vol. 1:** 211, 221, 275, 305, 462, 542, 552, 669
  Vol. 2: 63, 75, **223–238,** 302, 326, 800
  Vol. 3: 72, 105, 152–154, 214, 434, 1165

Sanction **Vol. 2:** 161, 236
  Vol. 3: 816
Sanctuary **Vol. 1:** 55, 115, 122, 151, 174, 224,
  250, 272, 280, 294, 308, 320, 351, 372, 408,
  497 f., 500, 511, 523, 586 f., 627, 648, 668
  Vol. 2: 45, 53, 64, 91, 184 f., 194, 199, 228,
  232–236, 244, 247 f., 250, 306, 324 f., 374 f.,
  410, 415, 466, 478, 614, 642, 673, 675, 706,
  817, 864
  Vol. 3: 33 f., 42, 78, 101, 159, 163, 192, 317,
  366, 415, 423, 430, 552, 560, 634, 650, 752,
  781–785, 805, 814 f., 852 f., 905, 941, 947 f.,
  965, 1060
Sand **Vol. 3:** 559, 707, 1001
Sandal **Vol. 1:** 674
  Vol. 3: 560
Sanhedrin **Vol. 1:** 51, 83, 168, 195–199, 341,
  362–364, 394 f.
  Vol. 2: 50, 176, 194, 282, 341, 379, 448, 526,
  850, 880
  Vol. 3: 35, 39 f., 401, 407, 480 f., 544, 742,
  822, 1157
Sap **Vol. 1:** 252, 743
Sapir **Vol. 3:** 1127
Sapphira **Vol. 1:** 446, 466 f., 642
  Vol. 2: 846
  Vol. 3: 387
Sapphire **Vol. 3:** 396, 398
Sarah **Vol. 1:** 78, **80,** 189, 284, 378, 411, 444 f.,
  452, 531 f., 650
  Vol. 2: 431, 627 f., 847
  Vol. 3: 73, 1057, 1067, 1069, 1072
Sarai **Vol. 1:** 80
Sarapis **Vol. 2:** 520
Sarcasm **Vol. 2:** 432
Sardis **Vol. 2:** 830
Sardius **Vol. 3:** 396
Sardonyx **Vol. 3:** 396
Sarepta **Vol. 3:** 558
Sargon **Vol. 1:** 140
Sariel **Vol. 1:** 102
Sarkic **Vol. 1:** 500
Satan **Vol. 1:** 53, 83–85, 89, 103 f., 124 f., 163,
  168 f., 205, 254, 297, 355, 424, 436, 449–
  454, 458, 466 f., 496, 508–510, 524, 554,
  563, 566 f., 572, 610, 637, 645, 657, 710,
  718, 727, 739
  Vol. 2: 74, 136, 191, 193, 196, 198, 205,
  208–210, 214, 221, 229, 314, 368, 370, 381–
  383, 401, 432, 458, 460, 471, 473 f., 495,
  510, 560 f., 574 f., 609 f., 618, 631, 633, 642,
  665, 674, 677, 692, 701 f., 706, 708, 733,
  781, 795, 809, 811, 858, 877, 901
  Vol. 3: 128, 179 f., 197, 203, 232, 342, 344,
  389, 409, **468–476,** 507, 509, 522 f., 536, 579,
  586, 603, 628, 693–696, 713, 725, 738, 779,
  797, 800–807, 809 f., 831, 839, 856, 864,
  872, 903, 943, 961 f., 1001, 1152, 1163
Satan-Sammael **Vol. 3:** 469
Satanic powers **Vol. 1:** 111, 423, 519
  Vol. 2: 74, 165
  Vol. 3: 985
Satanic trinity **Vol. 1:** 114
Sate **Vol. 1:** 743

Satire **Vol. 2:** 430, 432
Satisfaction **Vol. 1:** 741, 743
  Vol. 2: 48, 115, 264, 272, 351, 817
  Vol. 3: 154, 179, 532
Satisfactory **Vol. 1:** 610
Satisfy **Vol. 1:** 217, 459 f., 673, 731, 733–735,
  743 f.
  Vol. 2: 123, 237, 266 f., 274
  Vol. 3: 726–730
Satrap **Vol. 3:** 851
Satrapy **Vol. 2:** 234
Saturn **Vol. 2:** 558
  Vol. 3: 735
Satyr **Vol. 1:** 451
Sauce **Vol. 1:** 633
Saul **Vol. 1:** 53, 61, 195, 264, 393, 433, 478,
  538, 574, 709, 716
  Vol. 2: 116, 296, 306, 374, 554
  Vol. 3: 77, 117, 154, 159, 195, 270, 426 f.,
  474, 531, 560, 608, 812, 872, 994, 1057,
  1091
Saul of Tarsus **Vol. 2:** 91, 136, 320
  Vol. 3: 519, 708, 912, 948
Saussure, F. de **Vol. 3:** 1123, 1126, 1131,
  1140–1142
Savage **Vol. 1:** 261, 520
  Vol. 3: 709
Save **Vol. 1:** 100, 185 f., 223, 228, 322 f., 345,
  359, 371, 380, 390, 395, 414, 464, 466, 483,
  509 f., 525, 531, 547, 571, 593–595, 599,
  601, 604, 713, 730 f., 740
  Vol. 2: 60, 86, 122, 194, 228, 278, 280, 312 f.,
  315, 329, 331 f., 354, 387, 446, 510, 610,
  799, 818, **838–840**
  Vol. 3: 46, **177–221,** 228, 250, 369, 646, 682,
  1177
Save up **Vol. 2: 829–836**
Saving **Vol. 3:** 65, 107, **216–221,** 336, 344
Saving act **Vol. 1:** 77, 181, 185, 224, 239, 319,
  346 f., 422, 484, 524, 598, 600, 605, 640,
  713, 717
  Vol. 2: 56, 78, 87, 119, 129, 149, 202, 241,
  300, 388, 396, 509, 627, 665 f., 671, 717
  Vol. 3: 120, 161, 772, 846, 940, 1151
Saving event **Vol. 1:** 62, 345, 401, 601, 603
  Vol. 2: 112, 276
  Vol. 3: 151, 648
Saving grace **Vol. 2:** 78
Saving plan **Vol. 1:** 697
Saving power **Vol. 1:** 336, 532
  Vol. 2: 78, 492, 627, 806
Saving presence **Vol. 1:** 324
  Vol. 2: 86
Saving proclamation **Vol. 1:** 397
Saving purpose **Vol. 2:** 79, 119, 353, 408
  Vol. 3: 790, 801
Saving truth **Vol. 1:** 86
Saving work **Vol. 1:** 68, 221, 224, 326, 331, 600,
  669, 730
  Vol. 2: 42, 78 f., 141, 158, 193, 196, 208, 354,
  357, 367, 413, 419, 516, 544, 653, 655, 665,
  670, 717
  Vol. 3: 999
Saviour **Vol. 1:** 77, 127, 168, 320, 323, 396, 509,

Saviour (*cont'd*)
519, 567, 636
Vol. 2: 78, 82, 108, 167, 215, 243, 245, 262, 265, 307, 332, 335, 337, 343, 349, 358, 363, 366 f., 404, 518, 584, 645, 804, 922
Vol. 3: 71, **177–221**, 232, 279, 318 f., 363, 462, 1022
Saviour-king **Vol. 2:** 111, 330, 341
Sawyer, J.F.A. **Vol. 3:** 1141
Say **Vol. 2:** 281, 443, 488
Vol. 3: 54, 74, 345, 348, 821, **1081–1119**
Saying **Vol. 1:** 62, 68, 70, 575, 582
Vol. 2: 109, 155, 385, 751, 757, 929
Vol. 3: 74 → 89, 236, **1081**–1119
Sayings of Jesus **Vol. 1:** 57 f., 68, 600, 619
Vol. 2: 449 (*also* → Word of Jesus)
Scabby **Vol. 2:** 464
Scaffold **Vol. 1:** 393
Scale of values **Vol. 3:** 400
Scales of Kronos **Vol. 2:** 23
Scaly **Vol. 2:** 464
Scandal **Vol. 1:** 439
Vol. 2: **705–710**
Scandal-monger **Vol. 3:** 903
Scandalous **Vol. 1:** 397, 546
Scanty **Vol. 2:** 821
Scapegoat **Vol. 1:** 479
Vol. 2: 151
Vol. 3: 150, 159, 1005
Scar **Vol. 1:** 235
Vol. 2: 288, 573
Vol. 3: 904
Scaraboid **Vol. 3:** 497
Scarcity **Vol. 3:** 1162
Scarlet **Vol. 1:** 205
Scarlet beast **Vol. 3:** 396
Scatter **Vol. 1:** 55, 109, 629, 686
Vol. 2: **31–35**, 38, 226, 412 f.
Vol. 3: 718
Scattered **Vol. 1:** 685
Vol. 2: 380, 854
Scavenger **Vol. 1:** 117
Scent **Vol. 3:** **599–601**
Sceptic **Vol. 1:** 70
Sceptical **Vol. 2:** 101
Scepticism **Vol. 1:** 59, 211, 512, 550 f., 595
Vol. 2: 100, 341, 384, 431
Vol. 3: 83, 506, 899, 901
Sceptre **Vol. 1:** 162 f., **405–408**, 648 f.
Vol. 2: 98
Vol. 3: 49, 650, 867, 870
Sceva **Vol. 2:** 519
Vol. 3: 476
Schaeffer, F. **Vol. 3:** 899
Schematization in Luke **Vol. 3:** 698
Scheming **Vol. 3:** **935–943**
Schism **Vol. 1:** 238
Vol. 2: 618
Schizophrenic **Vol. 3:** 474
Schleiermacher, Friedrich **Vol. 1:** 59, 582 f.
Vol. 3: 148, 1138
Schmidt, K.L. **Vol. 3:** 62
Schmithals, W. **Vol. 3:** 58
Scholar **Vol. 1:** 69, 486

Vol. 3: 477
Scholarly **Vol. 3:** 1106
Schonfield, H. **Vol. 3:** 292
School **Vol. 1:** 486–488, 533, 535, 627, 631, 671
Vol. 2: 311, 445
Vol. 3: 488, 777 f.
School of Hillel **Vol. 1:** 67, 69, 155, 506
Vol. 2: 43, 811
Vol. 3: 534, 538, 980
School of philosophy **Vol. 1:** 533 f.
School of Shammai **Vol. 1:** 67, 69, 155, 500, 506
Vol. 2: 43, 811
Vol. 3: 534, 538
Schoolmaster **Vol. 1:** 568
Schopenhauer, A. **Vol. 3:** 899
Schulz, S. **Vol. 3:** 58
Schweitzer, Albert **Vol. 2:** 902 f.
Vol. 3: 506
Schweizer, E. **Vol. 3:** 618
Science **Vol. 3:** 1081
Scientific criticism (→ Criticism, scientific)
Scoff **Vol. 1:** 296
Vol. 2: 432, 843
Vol. 3: 29, 235
Scoffer **Vol. 2:** 58, 479
Vol. 3: 844, 868
Scold **Vol. 1:** 626
Vol. 2: 144
Scorching **Vol. 1:** 515, 652 f.
Scorn **Vol. 1:** 418, 607, 642
Vol. 2: 49, 356, 394, 399, 429, 431–433, 448
Vol. 3: 29
Scornful **Vol. 2:** 149, 417, 433
Scorpio **Vol. 2:** 688
Scorpion **Vol. 1:** 464, **507–511**
Vol. 2: 29
Vol. 3: 944
Scourge **Vol. 1:** **161–164**, 364, 393, 395, 657
Vol. 3: 96, 109, 778, 996
Scratch **Vol. 2:** 288
Scratch letters **Vol. 3:** 478
Scratch on **Vol. 3:** 483
Scream **Vol. 1:** 94
Scribes **Vol. 1:** 64, 174, 196, 199 f., 205, 248, 265, 281, 311, 363 f., 395, 413, 427, 451, 487 f., 509, 544 f., 567, 574, 617, 631, 729
Vol. 2: 32, 43, 101, 147, 170, 174, 177, 222, 227, 262, 281, 327 f., 368, 399, 467, 469, 584, 610, 640 f., 714 f., 730, 799, 801, 811, 830, 834
Vol. 3: 39, 115 f., 181–185, 211, 313, 342, 344, 360, 378, 429, 445–447, **477–482**, 485, 622, 628, 741, 757, 763, 769, 780, 792, 796, 804, 854, 861, 911, 953, 1020, 1052, 1096, 1109, 1121, 1162
Script **Vol. 2:** 308 f.
Vol. 3: 483
Scripture **Vol. 1:** 167, 245 f., 248, 437, 485, 544, 577–579, 584, 641, 662, 680, 695, 735–738
Vol. 2: 62 f., 114, 126, 186, 219, 227 f., 235, 291, 307, 312–315, 327, 342, 380, 432, 443 f., 448, 505, 624, 641, 665 f., 681, 714 f., 774, 811, 834, 927
Vol. 3: 34, 48, 62, 70, 82, 87–89, 112, 127–

547

129, 132, 185 f., 188, 196, 215, 252, 275, 310 f., **325–337,** 365, 401, 404, 429, 465, 478, 480, **482–495,** 533, 690, 702, 705, 708, 761, 763, 771, 780, 892, 943, 1023, 1033, 1045, 1048, 1050, 1052, 1106, 1143
Scroll **Vol. 1:** 53, 58, 118, 202, 243 f.
  Vol. 2: 189, 727
  Vol. 3: 180, 478, 500, 673, 735 f., 1097–1099
Scruples **Vol. 1:** 449
  Vol. 2: 223, 402
Scrupulosity **Vol. 1:** 265
  Vol. 2: 150, 385
  Vol. 3: 432, 1053
Scrutinize **Vol. 1:** 189, 241
Scrutiny **Vol. 2:** 370
  Vol. 3: 810
Scum **Vol. 1:** 479
Scutum **Vol. 3:** 109, 966
Scythians **Vol. 2:** 127, 679
  Vol. 3: 915
Scythopolis **Vol. 2:** 592
  Vol. 3: 453, 818
Sea **Vol. 1:** 144, 240, 382 f., 387, 419, 508, 515, 517, 617, 698, 734 f.
  Vol. 2: 130, 187, 197, 281, 421, 615, 623, 625, 642, 657, 661, 691, 840
  Vol. 3: 112, 398, 443, 558–560, 735, 950, **982–992**
Sea of glass **Vol. 3:** 984
Sea-captain **Vol. 3:** 115
Sea-creature **Vol. 1:** 670
Sea-dragon **Vol. 2:** 200
Sea-monster **Vol. 1:** 670 f.
  Vol. 3: 983
Sea-snake **Vol. 1:** 507
Seal **Vol. 1:** 79, 118, 123, 225, 244, 308 f., 311, 393, 403, 658, 660
  Vol. 2: 40, 146, 158, 269, 411, 691, 695, 700, 727
  Vol. 3: 73, 82, 180, 199, 344, 362, 368, **497–501,** 557, 673, 701, 732, 734, 736, 740, 904, 1001
Sealed book **Vol. 2:** 194
Sear **Vol. 1:** 350, 352
Search **Vol. 1:** 737
  Vol. 2: 182 f., 386, 424, 834
  Vol. 3: 532 f., 1034
Search for **Vol. 2: 805–807**
  Vol. 3: 530–532
Search out **Vol. 1:** 64, 503
  Vol. 3: 532 f.
Season with salt **Vol. 3: 443–449**
Seasonable **Vol. 3: 845–849**
Seasoning **Vol. 2:** 211
  Vol. 3: 1025
Seasons **Vol. 1:** 624, 724, 737
  Vol. 2: 193, 270, 375, 688, 921
  Vol. 3: 349, 445, 833, 835, 841 f., 845
Seat **Vol. 1:** 521, 661, 666, 710
  Vol. 2: 245, 325, 369, 388, **611–615**
  Vol. 3: 587–589
Seat of government **Vol. 2:** 601
Seat of honour **Vol. 1:** 664, 666
  Vol. 2: 612

Seba **Vol. 2:** 367
Sebaste **Vol. 3:** 450, 456 f.
Sebastos **Vol. 3:** 457
Seclusion **Vol. 1:** 421, 641
Second **Vol. 1:** 54 f., 666
  Vol. 3: 952
Second Adam **Vol. 3:** 659
Second coming **Vol. 1:** 52, 56, 235, 315, 319 f., 323 f., 425, 508, 514
  Vol. 2: 38, 461, 713, **886–935**
  Vol. 3: 118, 121, 323, 367, 505 (*also* → Parousia)
Second death **Vol. 1:** 441, 501
  Vol. 2: 304, 701
Second man (→ Man, second)
Second marriage **Vol. 3:** 1075 (*also* → Remarriage)
Second sight **Vol. 2:** 559
Second Temple (→ Temple, second)
Secondary **Vol. 1:** 664
Secondary authority **Vol. 2:** 446
Secrecy **Vol. 1:** 421
  Vol. 3: 377, 748
Secret **Vol. 1:** 50, 129, 167, 175, 244, 370, 375, 452, 466, 529, 539 f., 574, 578, 613, 625, 628, 722, 729, 737
  Vol. 2: 71, 75, 182, 211 f., **214–220,** 255, 279, 317, 353, 365, 379, 397, 401, 408, 469, 488, 493, 560, 652, 727, 753, 758, 762, 794, 835, 899, 903
  Vol. 3: 45, 54, 77, 80, 129, 131–133, 141, 310 f., 314, 316, 476, 497–500, **501–510,** 523, 527, 717, 844, 950, 955, 1036, 1109, 1113
Secret royal line **Vol. 3:** 655
Secretary **Vol. 1:** 248, 582
  Vol. 3: 477–482
Secretly **Vol. 1:** 120, 424
Secrets of Enoch **Vol. 3:** 265
Sect **Vol. 1:** 510, 533–535, 554
  Vol. 2: 676
  Vol. 3: 108, 439
Sectarian **Vol. 1:** 294, 644
  Vol. 2: 438
Section **Vol. 1:** 65
Secular **Vol. 1:** 209, 211, 497, 574, 583, 588, 614, 618, 643, 675, 717
  Vol. 2: 230, 239 f., 273, 334, 373, 376, 670
Secular time **Vol. 2:** 891
Secularists **Vol. 3:** 440
Secularization **Vol. 1:** 367, 500
Secure **Vol. 1:** 464, 651, 658, 660–663, 680 f.
  Vol. 2: 203, 244, 295
Security **Vol. 1:** 95, 97, 208, 277, 392, 426, 440, 466, 483, 596, 599, 623, 663, 713
  Vol. 2: 149, 239, 297, 777, 843 f., 846
  Vol. 3: 252, 555, 559, 692, 807, 822, 865, 948 (*also* → False security)
Sedar **Vol. 1:** 64
Sedative **Vol. 2:** 28
Sedentary **Vol. 1:** 661
Sediment **Vol. 1:** 711
Sedition **Vol. 3:** 448
Seduce **Vol. 1:** 468, 555
  Vol. 2: 458, 582, 629

Seduce (*cont'd*)
  Vol. **3**: 1054
Seduction Vol. **3**: 95, 770
Seductive Vol. **1**: 526
  Vol. **2**: 460
See Vol. **1**: 230, 261, 421, 444, 603 f., 613, 667, 672, 677, 692, 694, 708, 712 f., 727, 735, 740, 743
  Vol. **2**: 45, 77, 110, 134, 154, 173, 176, 180, 183, 211 f., 214 f., 230, 243 f., 270, 279, 282, 285, 289, 358, 379, 387, 393, 395, 403 f., 488, 494, 496, 633, 710, 857
  Vol. **3**: 106, 126, 129, 179, 285, 310 f., 313 f., **511–521,** 572, 806
See again Vol. **3**: **519**
See God Vol. **3**: 890
Seed Vol. **1**: 159, 173 f., 186, 226, 236, 377 f., 469 f., 517, 560, 653, 686, 722
  Vol. **2**: 35, 104, 131 f., 177, 180, 211, 364, 514, 586, 662, 843, 861
  Vol. **3**: 73, 143, 251, 278, 304, 382, **521–527,** 684, 701, 704, 870, 922
Seed of Abraham Vol. **1**: 159
  Vol. **2**: 899
Seed of David Vol. **1**: 177
  Vol. **3**: 650 f., 653, 661, 1073
Seed-time Vol. **1**: 624
Seedling Vol. **1**: 281
Seek Vol. **1**: 266, 322, 397, 430, 464, 473, 603, 630, 666, 681, 687, 735
  Vol. **2**: 116, 127, 164, 257, 271, 275, 327, 351, 355, 361, 381, 386 f., 806, 832, 857
  Vol. **3**: 54, 93, 360, **527–533,** 116 –1169
Seek help Vol. **2**: 201
Seem Vol. **1**: **55**
  Vol. **2**: 286
  Vol. **3**: **821 f.**
Seemly Vol. **2**: **668 f.**
Seer Vol. **1**: 208, 582
  Vol. **2**: 193, 625, 633
  Vol. **3**: 33, 77, 513
Segregation Vol. **1**: 688
  Vol. **3**: 1058
Sehetepibre Vol. **3**: 259
Seir Vol. **3**: 1013
Seize Vol. **1**: 343, 533
  Vol. **3**: **601–605,** 641, **716–718, 747–751**
Select Vol. **2**: 362
  Vol. **3**: 513
Selection Vol. **1**: 191, 536 f., 540, 629
  Vol. **2**: 362
Selene Vol. **3**: 733
Seleucids Vol. **1**: 62, 196, 627
  Vol. **2**: 234, 810, 849
  Vol. **3**: 35, 217, 452 f., 479, 756, 788, 961
Seleucus IV Vol. **1**: 694
Self Vol. **1**: 235, 236, 240, 335 f., 386, 401, 455, 460, 466 f., 475, 680, 716
  Vol. **2**: 49, 394, 566, 818, 919
  Vol. **3**: 127, 680, 710
Self-abandonment Vol. **3**: 174
Self-abasement Vol. **1**: 609
  Vol. **2**: 202, 263, 270, 618
  Vol. **3**: 597, 608

Self-adjustment Vol. **1**: 602
Self-assertion Vol. **1**: 531, 676
  Vol. **2**: 202
  Vol. **3**: 532
Self-assurance Vol. **1**: 386
  Vol. **2**: 416
Self-attesting Vol. **3**: 326
Self-authenticating Vol. **3**: 625
Self-awareness Vol. **1**: 604
  Vol. **3**: 772
Self-castration Vol. **1**: 560 f.
Self-centred Vol. **3**: 137, 1053 f.
Self-chosen Vol. **2**: 825
  Vol. **3**: 938
Self-communication Vol. **3**: 1078
Self-conceit Vol. **3**: 707
Self-condemnation Vol. **3**: 249
Self-condemned Vol. **2**: 363, 365
Self-confidence Vol. **1**: 228, 499, 592, 736
  Vol. **2**: 430, 844
  Vol. **3**: 82, 240, 581, 673, 1092
Self-consciousness Vol. **1**: 322, 349, 427, 529
  Vol. **2**: 308 f., 312, 341 f., 567
  Vol. **3**: 618
Self-consecration Vol. **2**: 225
Self-contained Vol. **1**: 355
Self-contradictory Vol. **1**: 473
  Vol. **3**: 891
Self-contrived Vol. **2**: 843
Self-control Vol. **1**: 398, 459, 494–496, 501 f., 515, 623, 645, 647, 675, 681
  Vol. **3**: 184, 225, 253, 815 f.,
Self-correction Vol. **1**: 491
Self-critical Vol. **1**: 602
Self-deception Vol. **1**: 400, 587
  Vol. **2**: 470
  Vol. **3**: 283, 822, 881
Self-denial Vol. **1**: 470, 475, 483
  Vol. **2**: 117, 386
Self-deprecating Vol. **2**: 305
Self-description Vol. **3**: 914
Self-designation Vol. **2**: 109, 228, 237, 310, 312, 378
  Vol. **3**: 619, 623, 648
Self-destruction Vol. **1**: 460
Self-determination Vol. **2**: 121
Self-determined Vol. **1**: 722
Self-direction Vol. **1**: 601
Self-discipline Vol. **1**: 163, 459
  Vol. **2**: 102 f.
Self-disclosure Vol. **2**: 79
  Vol. **3**: 330, 337, 1102
Self-effacing Vol. **2**: 259, 428 f.
Self-emptying Vol. **1**: 548
  Vol. **2**: 262, 828, 844
  Vol. **3**: 645
Self-esteem Vol. **1**: 112, 540
  Vol. **3**: 561
Self-evident Vol. **2**: 447, 709
  Vol. **3**: 334, 967, 1108
Self-exaltation Vol. **2**: 201, **202**
  Vol. **3**: 1031
Self-examination Vol. **1**: 415
  Vol. **2**: 392

Self-explanatory **Vol. 1:** 577
Self-expression **Vol. 1:** 460
  Vol. 2: 256
  Vol. 3: 691
Self-fulfilment **Vol. 3:** 225
Self-giving **Vol. 1:** 338, 492
  Vol. 3: 198, 931, 1064
Self-glorification **Vol. 1:** 228
  Vol. 3: 771, 848, 1032, 1045
Self-governing **Vol. 2:** 788
Self-gratification **Vol. 1:** 496
  Vol. 2: 202
Self-humbling **Vol. 2:** 262
Self-humiliation **Vol. 1:** 399
  Vol. 2: 262 f.
Self-identification **Vol. 2:** 83, 823
Self-immolation **Vol. 1:** 235
  Vol. 2: 307
Self-important **Vol. 2:** 399
Self-indulgence **Vol. 1:** 448, 495
  Vol. 2: 275, 712
Self-interest **Vol. 1:** 420
  Vol. 2: 568
Self-involving language **Vol. 3:** 1139
Self-irony **Vol. 2:** 432
Self-justification **Vol. 1:** 675 f.
  Vol. 2: 448
  Vol. 3: 140
Self-knowledge **Vol. 1:** 590
  Vol. 2: 402, 404
  Vol. 3: 640
Self-love **Vol. 1:** 228
  Vol. 2: 659
Self-manifestation **Vol. 2:** 491
  Vol. 3: 334
Self-offering **Vol. 2:** 230, 535 f.
Self-perfection **Vol. 2:** 103
  Vol. 3: 778, 1169
Self-perpetuating **Vol. 1:** 364
Self-pity **Vol. 3:** 1054
Self-possession **Vol. 2:** 539
Self-praise **Vol. 1:** 227 f.
  Vol. 2: 844
  Vol. 3: 817
Self-preparation **Vol. 3:** 117 f.
Self-presentation **Vol. 2:** 278
Self-preservation **Vol. 3:** 137, 530
Self-projection **Vol. 3:** 236
Self-realization **Vol. 1:** 497
  Vol. 3: 589
Self-reformation **Vol. 2:** 407
  Vol. 3: 256
Self-reliance **Vol. 1:** 681
Self-renunciation **Vol. 1:** 403
Self-reproachful **Vol. 2:** 431
Self-respect **Vol. 1:** 679
Self-restraint **Vol. 1:** 494
Self-revealing **Vol. 2:** 197
Self-revelation **Vol. 1:** 222, 384
  Vol. 2: 45, 80, 229, 281, 343, 395, 442, 633
  Vol. 3: 314, 776
Self-righteous **Vol. 2:** 106, 416, 434, 443
  Vol. 3: 370, 580 f., 603
Self-righteousness **Vol. 1:** 439, 680

  Vol. 2: 155, 170, 267, 584
Self-sacrifice **Vol. 1:** 474, 539, 731
  Vol. 2: 339, 546, 563, 615, 673, 833
  Vol. 3: 41 f., 905, 954, 1019, 1064, 1168
Self-salvation **Vol. 2:** 394
  Vol. 3: 168
Self-satisfaction **Vol. 2:** 404, 443
  Vol. 3: 819
Self-security **Vol. 1:** 730
  Vol. 2: 435
Self-seeking **Vol. 1:** 398, 400, 638
  Vol. 3: 568, 945
Self-sufficiency **Vol. 1:** 319, 661, 680
  Vol. 2: 295, 657, 820
  Vol. 3: 391, **727 f.,** 1052–1054
Self-supporting **Vol. 3:** 727
Self-surrender **Vol. 1:** 397, 548
  Vol. 2: 532 f., 864
  Vol. 3: 55
Self-trust **Vol. 2:** 815
Self-understanding **Vol. 1:** 59, 488
  Vol. 2: 342
  Vol. 3: 328, 561, 697, 928, 1139
Self-will **Vol. 1:** 365, 532, 608
  Vol. 3: 1066
Selfish **Vol. 1:** 106, 381, 384, 547, 681
  Vol. 2: 32, 221, 518, 550, 844
  Vol. 3: 137, 804, 1054
Selfless **Vol. 2:** 563
Sell **Vol. 1:** 118, **267 f.,** 288, 352, 497, 688, 691
  Vol. 2: 32, 63, 832, 846
  Vol. 3: 190, 243, 253, 590, 954
Seller **Vol. 1:** 120
Semantic **Vol. 3:** 206
Semantic theory of truth **Vol. 3: 897**
Semantic triangle **Vol. 3:** 1129
Semantics **Vol. 1: 68**
Semblance **Vol. 1:** 709
  Vol. 2: 287
Semi-political **Vol. 2:** 307
Semite **Vol. 1: 68,** 308
  Vol. 2: 898
Semitic **Vol. 1: 68,** 603
  Vol. 2: 920
  Vol. 3: 185, 640
Semitisms **Vol. 1:** 272
  Vol. 2: 149, 403, 427, 526, 530, 680, 727, 880
  Vol. 3: 65, 509
Send **Vol. 1:** 126–129, 131, 133 f., 136, 246, 332, 453, 510, 526, 581, 603, 637, 689, 698, 704 f., 738
  Vol. 2: 79, 152, 351, 404 f., 426, 610, 632, 819
Send away **Vol. 3:** 177
Seneca **Vol. 1:** 51, 68, 349, 679
  Vol. 2: 77, 239, 542, 792
Seniority **Vol. 1:** 193
Sennacherib **Vol. 1:** 104, 673
  Vol. 2: 679
  Vol. 3: 484
Sensation **Vol. 3:** 684, 899
Sensationalism **Vol. 2:** 168
Sense **Vol. 1:** 546, 681, 700
  Vol. 2: 172 f., 175 f., 327, 390–392, 395, 416,

Sense (*cont'd*)
434, 568, 591
Sense perception **Vol. 3:** 899
Senseless **Vol. 1:** 424, 546
  Vol. 3: 124, 126, 130, **1023–1026**
Senses **Vol. 1:** 56, 432, 443 f., 458 f., 523, 527, 530, 652
  Vol. 3: 689, 694
Sensible **Vol. 1:** 501
  Vol. 2: 169, **616–620**
Sensitive **Vol. 1:** 352
  Vol. 3: 694, 916
Sensory **Vol. 3:** 123
Sensual **Vol. 2:** 138, 265, 539
  Vol. 3: 231
Sensuality **Vol. 1:** 494, 498, 680
  Vol. 3: 1054, 1075
Sensuous **Vol. 1:** 676
Sent **Vol. 3:** 313
Sentence **Vol. 1:** 86, 364, 393, 395, 415, 479, 597, 630, 677
  Vol. 2: 139, 143, 178, 309, 368, 370, 419, 434, 505
  Vol. 3: 354, 484, 617, 1049, 1119
Sentence analysis **Vol. 3:** 1085
Sentence of death **Vol. 3:** 156, 342
Sentiment **Vol. 2:** 435
Sentinel **Vol. 2:** 136
Sentry **Vol. 1:** 314
Separate **Vol. 1:** 413, 419, 422, 441, 444, 455, 459, 472 f., 503 f., 506 f., 525, 533, 539, 545, 556, 564, 566, 606–608, 625, 653, 677f., 707, 718 f., 741
  Vol. 2: 83, 199 f., 267, 273, 282, 307, 359, **362–367**, 413, 442, 720, 809 f.
  Vol. 3: 98, 172 f., 188 f., 468, **534–544**, 565, 567, 680, 941, 1057, 1064, 1070, 1072, 1075, 1164
Separated **Vol. 3:** **534–543**
Separation **Vol. 1:** 60, 115, 145, 155, 239 f., 289, 360, 405, 433, 488, 500, 503 f., 522, 537, 565, 607, 674
  Vol. 2: 54, 197, 224, 226, 307, 309–312, 316 f., 362, 393, 517, 629, 707, 709, 715, 742, 813, 825
  Vol. 3: 173, 277, 360, 362, 392, 404, 444, 470, 526 f., **535–543**, 597, 621, 647, 949, 1005, 1149, 1165
Sepphoris **Vol. 3:** 441 f.
Septimius Severus **Vol. 3:** 635
Septuagint **Vol. 1:** 50, 53–55, 57, 62, 65, **68,** 71
  Vol. 2: 125, 219, 338, 690, 697
  Vol. 3: 486
Sepulchre **Vol. 1:** 264 f.
Sequence **Vol. 1:** 473
  Vol. 2: 387
Seraph **Vol. 1:** 101, 239, 279 f., 509
  Vol. 2: 173, 212
Serapis **Vol. 1:** 64
  Vol. 2: 224
  Vol. 3: 138, 160, 216, 859
Serene **Vol. 3:** 673
Serfdom **Vol. 1:** 707
Sergius Paulus **Vol. 1:** 530

Vol. 2: 557
Seriousness **Vol. 1:** 627
  Vol. 2: 95, 276
  Vol. 3: 1065, 1169
Sermon **Vol. 1:** 58, 245
Sermon on the mount **Vol. 1:** 110, 120, 217, 231, 277 f., 335, 339, 384, 702, 738
  Vol. 2: 43, 118, 133, 177, **281,** 443, 449, 469, 543 f., 580, 825, 831 f., 871 f., 893
  Vol. 3: 181, 382, 402, 428 f., 445, 540, 580, 584, 742, 763, 770, 805, 940, 1009, 1011 f., 1107, 1109, 1110
Sermon on the plain **Vol. 1:** 217, 277
  Vol. 2: 598
Serpent **Vol. 1:** 86 f., 168, 175, 413, 465, 468, **507–511,** 523, 562, 565, 568, 653, 705
  Vol. 2: 29, 132, 458, 619, 638, 642, 701
  Vol. 3: 472, 944
Serpent-charming **Vol. 2:** 554
Servant **Vol. 1:** 177, 219, 226, 272, **280–291,** 311, 404, 426, 474, 477, 479, 481, 485, 492, 513, 538 f., 547, 549, 565, 569, 598, 617, 646, 655, 667, 702 f., 706, 709 f., 720, 729, 741
  Vol. 2: 129, 136, 152, 164, 167, 192, 249, 262, 301, 305, 307, 313, 328, 336, 364, 382, 411, 413, 467, 508 f., 511, 596, 600, 610, 642, 667, 833, 838, 866, 888, 917
  Vol. 3: 34, 62, 110, 118, 121, 134, 173, 195 f., 319, **544–549, 551–553, 589–599, 607–664,** 732, 748, 758, 856, 864, 951, 998 f., 1064, 1157, 1163
Servant of God **Vol. 1:** 96 f., 102, 111, 281, 290, 385, 587, 597, 699
  Vol. 2: 165, 336, 411, 540, 731, 768, 816, 854
  Vol. 3: 578, **607–664,** 765, 867
Servant of the Lord **Vol. 1:** 262, 283, 409, 544, 707
  Vol. 2: 49, 165, 410, 492
  Vol. 3: 692, 825
Servant of Yahweh **Vol. 1:** 373–375
  Vol. 2: 309, 368
  Vol. 3: 218, 258, 420
Servant Songs **Vol. 1:** 273, 651
  Vol. 2: 279, 337
  Vol. 3: 69, 269, **609, 611,** 1041
Serve **Vol. 1:** 101 f., 116, 129, 136, 173, 191 f., 198, 200, 212, 231, 305, 307, 335, 351, 381, 469, 474, 481, 486, 551 f., 676, 718–720, 741
  Vol. 2: 63, 77, 83, 94, 147, 152, 160, 164, 238, 253, 256, 262, 266, 282, 284, 286, 319, 349, 427, 429, 447, 466, 518, 671, 675, 715, 809, 816, 823, 840, 847, 876, 885
  Vol. 3: 27, 69, 171, 195, 233, 269, 420, 432, 435 f., **544–553,** 590, **592–598,** 625, 673, 724, 755, 806, 1001, 1065 f., 1152
Serve as deacon **Vol. 3:** **544–549**
Serve as soldier **Vol. 3:** **958–967**
Service **Vol. 1:** 96, 99, 115 f., 127, 129, 135, 143, 190 f., 235, 238 f., 245–248, 259, 273, 275, 283, 285, 293, 304, 319, 336, 382, 384, 386, 421, 474–476, 482, 489 f., 493, 505, 513, 536–538, 542, 600, 619, 625, 630 f., 646, 659, 674, 720, 731, 740

Vol. 2: 50 f., 68, 92, 121, 152, 164, 174, 203, 211, 222, 229, 233, 242, 255, 263, 269–271, 285, 291, 293, 305, 327–329, 339, 399, 403, 429, 451, 475, 517, 547, 559, 566, 611, 615, 650, 652, 655, 736, 765, 774
Vol. 3: 32–44, 51, 101, 117, 121, 134, 140 f., 145, 162, 197, 215, 225, 227, 373, 489, **544–549, 551–553,** 584, 590, 613, 752, 789, 793, 804, 810, 827, 854, 1075
Service of God **Vol. 3: 549–551**
Serviceable **Vol. 2:** 98
Servile **Vol. 1:** 485
   Vol. 2: 259
Servility **Vol. 2:** 859
Serving **Vol. 3: 551–553**
Servitude **Vol. 1:** 209, 531, 674, 707, 719
   Vol. 3: 1162
Session **Vol. 2:** 147, 369
Set **Vol. 1:** 314, 413, 471, 477, 494, 518, 523, 604, 609, 696
Set about **Vol. 3:** 860
Set apart **Vol. 1:** 336, 472–474, 537
   Vol. 2: 232
Set aside **Vol. 1:** 74, 337, 719
Set at naught **Vol. 1:** 74
Set at variance **Vol. 3:** 468
Set forth **Vol. 3:** 316
Set forth publicly **Vol. 3: 482–495**
Set free **Vol. 1:** 437, 505, 698, 715 f.
   Vol. 2: 91, 116, 150
   Vol. 3: 166–174, 177–189, 196, 201, **352–377,** 537, 713, 1164
Set mind on **Vol. 2: 616–620**
Set prayers **Vol. 2:** 869
Set up **Vol. 1:** 474, 476
   Vol. 3: 117
Set up again **Vol. 3: 351 f.**
Set upon **Vol. 2:** 150
Seth **Vol. 2:** 556
   Vol. 3: 388
Setting **Vol. 2:** 327
   Vol. 3: 234
Settle **Vol. 1:** 576, 578
   Vol. 2: 247–251, 305, 365
   Vol. 3: 167
Settle down **Vol. 3:** 255
Settled **Vol. 1:** 518 f., 543
   Vol. 2: 711
Settlement **Vol. 1:** 685
   Vol. 2: 131, 296, 333, 373
   Vol. 3: 1106
Seven **Vol. 1:** 129, 361
   Vol. 2: 114, 152, 550, 625, 651, 667, 685, 687 f., **690–692,** 693, 697 f., 700, 756, 769, 784, 827, 931
   Vol. 3: 88, 490, 500, 548, 657, 715, 731, 736, 739, 851, 958, 1066 f., 1075
Seven churches **Vol. 1:** 304
   Vol. 2: 487, 685, 691
   Vol. 3: 85, 88, 490, 505 f., 706, 736
Seven lampstands **Vol. 1:** 304
   Vol. 2: 487
   Vol. 3: 736
Seven rules of Hillel **Vol. 1:** 580

Seven sages **Vol. 3:** 1027
Seven seals **Vol. 3:** 490
Seven stars **Vol. 3:** 735 f.
Seven thousand **Vol. 3:** 248
Seven years **Vol. 2:** 317
Seven-branched lampstand **Vol. 2:** 485, 487
Sevenfold **Vol. 2:** 690
Seventh day **Vol. 1:** 211
   Vol. 3: 257, **405–415**
Seventy **Vol. 1:** 142, 195, 282, 489
   Vol. 2: 358, 638, 641, 690, **696 f.,** 754, 769, 784, 920
   Vol. 3: 470, 569, 944
Sever **Vol. 1:** 74, 515
   Vol. 2: 120
Severance **Vol. 1:** 713
Severe **Vol. 2:** 360 f.
Severity **Vol. 1:** 568, 611, 727, 731
   Vol. 2: 270
Sex **Vol. 1:** 85 f., 233, 235, 285, 459, 497
Sex cell **Vol. 3:** 663
Sexes **Vol. 1:** 87
   Vol. 2: 160, 660
Sexual **Vol. 1:** 137, 169, 420, 441, 448 f., 457, 461, 494–502, 509, 612, 625, 656
   Vol. 2: 161, 260, 350, 540 f., 599
   Vol. 3: 100, 102–104, 310, 534–543, 563 f., 925, 989, 997, 1024, 1157, 1165
Sexual deviations **Vol. 2:** 660
Sexual ethics **Vol. 3:** 1064
Sexual needs **Vol. 3:** 1065
Sexual offences **Vol. 2:** 579
   Vol. 3: 96, 535
Sexual relations **Vol. 1:** 138, 151, 232, 322, 448, 451, 498–502, 637, 678
   Vol. 2: 224, 349 f., 392, 395, 398, 570, 575–580, 638, 659 f., 668, 722, 923
   Vol. 3: 534–543, 859–861, 1072, 1121
Shaalbin **Vol. 3:** 453
Shade **Vol. 1:** 431, 433, 653, 705
   Vol. 2: 284
   Vol. 3: 553–556
Shades **Vol. 2:** 206, 555
   Vol. 3: 268
Shadow **Vol. 1:** 327, 371, 435, 559
   Vol. 2: 194, 275, 288, 291, 447, 451, 475, 717, 804
   Vol. 3: 42, **553–556,** 660, 840, 1158
Shadowy existence **Vol. 2:** 206
Shadrach **Vol. 2:** 628
   Vol. 3: 110
Shaft **Vol. 2:** 97
Shake **Vol. 1:** 540
   Vol. 3: 317, **556–561,** 736
Shake down **Vol. 3: 556–558**
Shake head **Vol. 2:** 159
Shake off **Vol. 3: 560 f.**
Shake off dust **Vol. 3:** 1043
Shake out **Vol. 3: 560 f.**
Shake together **Vol. 3: 709 f.**
Shaking **Vol. 3: 556–558**
Shaliah **Vol. 3:** 746
Shallow **Vol. 1:** 546
Shalmaneser I **Vol. 2:** 679

Sham **Vol. 1:** 709
  Vol. 2: 632
Shamash **Vol. 3:** 730
Shame **Vol. 1:** 85, 113, 314, 349, 390, 399–401,
  461, 559, 608, 649, 723
  Vol. 2: 48 f., 51, 91, 157, 159, 217, 262, 359,
  361, 385, 417, 442, 478, 709, 737
  Vol. 3: 96, **561–564**, 601, 714, 731, 856, 918
Shameful **Vol. 2:** 50, 182, 260, 291, 368
  Vol. 3: **562–564**
Shameless **Vol. 2:** 356
  Vol. 3: 1024
Shammai **Vol. 1:** 67, 69, 153, 155, 485, 500, 506
  Vol. 2: 311, 579, 811
  Vol. 3: 184, 534, 538
Shammaites **Vol. 1:** 627
  Vol. 2: 309
Shamshi-Adad I **Vol. 2:** 679
Shape **Vol. 1:** 383, 705, 708
  Vol. 2: 95, 159, 290, 424, 501
  Vol. 3: 119, 352, 915, 1153
Shaphan **Vol. 3:** 478
Share **Vol. 1:** 123, 158, 316, 359 f., 375, 468,
  478, 489, 492 f., 526, 534, 558, 571, 615,
  618, **635–644**, 669, 671, 676, 691, 696, 702,
  707, 712, 723
  Vol. 2: 40, 42, 46, 64, 83, 101, 120, 151, 163,
  165, 230, 262, 271 f., 276 f., 287, 295–298,
  300, 302, **303 f.**, 311, 314 f., 328, 350, 358,
  360, 380, 405 f., 475, 498, 520, 532, 534,
  777, 787, 841, 846, 888
  Vol. 3: 258, 278, 316, 356, 422, 433, 504,
  588, 648, 702, 705, 724, 756, 778, 819, 855,
  908, 913, 990
Share rule **Vol. 2:** **372–389**
Shared life **Vol. 2:** 579
Sharing **Vol. 3:** **747–751**
Sharp **Vol. 1:** 726
Sharpen **Vol. 2:** 288, 573
  Vol. 3: 951
Shatter **Vol. 1:** 610
  Vol. 3: 166, 913
Shave **Vol. 2:** 417
Shaven **Vol. 2:** 157, 160
Shealtiel **Vol. 2:** 691
  Vol. 3: 654 f., 659
Shear-jashub **Vol. 3:** 249
Shearer **Vol. 2:** 410
Sheaves **Vol. 2:** 737
  Vol. 3: 591
Sheba **Vol. 1:** 577
  Vol. 2: 381, 680
  Vol. 3: 606
Shechem **Vol. 1:** 195, 367
  Vol. 2: 67, 318, 591, 796
  Vol. 3: 450, 452, 458 f., 464, 786 f.
Shechemites **Vol. 2:** 521
  Vol. 3: 450, 455 f.
Shed **Vol. 1:** 97, 152, 220–223, 369, 654
  Vol. 2: 525
Shed blood **Vol. 2:** **853–855**
  Vol. 3: 103, 158, 160, 164, 582
Sheep **Vol. 1:** 114–116, 118 f., 190, 299, 319,
  453, 463 f., 503, 559, 684

  Vol. 2: 31, 34, 148, 177, 280, 314, 358, 386,
  410–414, 458 f., 461, 543, 599, 695, 728, 839
  Vol. 3: 98, 170, 454, **564–568**, 628, 683, 717,
  920
Sheep's clothing **Vol. 1:** 118 f.
Sheep-shearing **Vol. 1:** 626
Sheepfold **Vol. 2:** 586
Sheet **Vol. 2:** 95, 689
Shekel **Vol. 3:** 192, **752–755**
Shekel (Tyrian) **Vol. 2:** 851
Shekel of Israel **Vol. 2:** 308, 852
Shekalim **Vol. 3:** 752
Shekinah **Vol. 2:** 628, 899
  Vol. 3: 555, 634, 697, 788, 792
Shell **Vol. 1:** 704, 706, 709
Shell-fish **Vol. 1:** 205
Shell-shock **Vol. 3:** 474
Shelter **Vol. 1:** 653
  Vol. 3: 109, 381, 547, 554 f., 813, 867, 948
Shem **Vol. 1:** 68, 182
  Vol. 2: 591
  Vol. 3: 36
Shema **Vol. 2:** 73, 173 f., 177, 313, 721, 864,
  867
  Vol. 3: 105, 559, 806, 1120, 1161
Sheol **Vol. 1:** 433
  Vol. 2: 29, 32, 351 f., 432, 491, 924
  Vol. 3: 178, 180, 201, 237, 262 f., 267 f., 270,
  272, 274, 602, 880, 946
Shepherd **Vol. 1:** 65, 163, 190–192, 303, 305,
  407, 453, 464, 483, 559, 625, 684
  Vol. 2: 31, 34, 101, 104, 136, 176, 279 f., 305,
  332, 386, 412 f., 458–461, 599, 624, 652,
  696, 721, 723, 728, 757, 928
  Vol. 3: 88, 219, 323, 335, 378, 446, 529, 531,
  564–568, 628, 649, 683, 685, 811, 873, 913,
  1007, 1071
Shepherd of Hermas **Vol. 1:** 52, 577
  Vol. 2: 219
  Vol. 3: 312, 402
Shepherd of Israel **Vol. 1:** 598
  Vol. 3: 565
Shepherd-gods **Vol. 2:** 104
Shepherdless **Vol. 3:** 567
Sherlock, Thomas **Vol. 3:** 291
Shield **Vol. 1:** 103, 648, 656, 689
  Vol. 2: 237, 297, 865
  Vol. 3: 109, 112, 731, **959–967**
Shield of faith **Vol. 3:** 966
Shift **Vol. 1:** 504, 680
Shiloh **Vol. 1:** 511, 543
  Vol. 3: 33 f., 426, 782, 786 f., 812
Shimei **Vol. 3:** 78
Shine **Vol. 1:** 211, 424, 585–587
  Vol. 2: 46, 289 f., **484–496**
  Vol. 3: 270, 318, 731 f., 734, 867
Shining **Vol. 2:** 96, **484–486, 490–496**
Ship **Vol. 1:** 118, 476, 537, 645, 694, 698, 734,
  743
  Vol. 2: 212, 244
  Vol. 3: 119, 180, 558, 711, 757, 935
Ship's cabin **Vol. 3:** 811
Shipwreck **Vol. 1:** 608
  Vol. 3: 211, 1002

553

Shishak **Vol. 3:** 788
Shock **Vol. 1:** 530
  Vol. 3: 681, 709 f.
Shoe **Vol. 1:** 241
Shoot **Vol. 1:** 426
  Vol. 2: 333, 340
Shoot of David **Vol. 3:** 637, 651
Shoot forth **Vol. 3: 865–870**
Short **Vol. 2:** 692
Short-lived **Vol. 2:** 211
Shortcoming **Vol. 3:** 952
Shorthand **Vol. 3:** 757
Shortness of life **Vol. 1:** 433, 609, 743 f.
Shortsighted **Vol. 2:** 153
Shoulder **Vol. 1:** 241, 391, 403
Shout **Vol. 1:** 94, 271, 342, 408–411
  Vol. 2: 144, 352, 433, 855, 862, 924
  Vol. 3: 816
Show **Vol. 1:** 574, 649 f., 720, 722, 724
  Vol. 3: 316, **317–324**, 569–671
Show kindness **Vol. 3: 1147–1152**
Show mercy **Vol. 2: 594–598**
  Vol. 3: 164
Show pity **Vol. 2: 594–598**
Showbread **Vol. 1:** 586, 696 f.
  Vol. 2: 293
  Vol. 3: 117, 423, 787–789, 812, 814
Shrewd **Vol. 2:** 169, 254
  Vol. 3: 1029
Shrine **Vol. 2:** 67, 74, 85, 199, 224, 235, 635
  Vol. 3: 781–785
Shrink **Vol. 2:** 91, 775, 818
Shrivel **Vol. 3:** 999
Shroud **Vol. 3:** 296
Shun **Vol. 1:** 558, 564
Shunammite **Vol. 2:** 225
  Vol. 3: 261, 558
Shut **Vol. 1:** 545, 694
  Vol. 2: 31, 154, 193, 727, **729–734**
  Vol. 3: 501
Sibyl **Vol. 1:** 529
  Vol. 2: 744
Sibylline oracles **Vol. 1:** 155 f.
Sicarii **Vol. 3:** 1167
Sicily **Vol. 1:** 322
Sick **Vol. 1:** 118, 120, 356, 411, 446, 450, 564 f.,
  599 f., 674
  Vol. 2: 259, 386, 543, 813
  Vol. 3: 123, 146 f., 211, 216, 359, 547, 555,
  713, 748, 750, 758, 856, 859–861, 980, **993–
1000**
Sick bed **Vol. 2:** 586
Sickle **Vol. 1:** 204
Sickness **Vol. 1:** 84, 108, 151, 163, 346, 348, 433,
  443, 452 f., 463, 635, 673 f., 679, 727
  Vol. 2: 163–172, 206, 221, 320, 362, 419, 478,
  663, 855, 875, 893, 924
  Vol. 3: 202, 205, 224, 279, 470, 474 f., 558,
  579, 778 f., 860, **993–1000**, 1005
Siddim **Vol. 3:** 444
Side of boat **Vol. 2:** 303
Sidereal hour **Vol. 1:** 710
Sidon **Vol. 2:** 226, 767, 789, 848
  Vol. 3: 446, 908, 1052, 1062

Sidon, Mount **Vol. 3:** 444
Sidonians **Vol. 3:** 450
Siege **Vol. 3:** 756, 959
Siege-engine **Vol. 3:** 963
Siege-mound **Vol. 3:** 951
Siegeworks **Vol. 3:** 952
Sieve **Vol. 1:** 480
Sift **Vol. 2:** 362, 364
  Vol. 3: 804
Sigh **Vol. 1:** 385, 552
  Vol. 2: 215, 420, **423 f.**, 862, 865, 884
Sight **Vol. 1:** 219, 424, 703 f.
  Vol. 2: 211, 218, 392
  Vol. 3: 511–518, 602, 945
Sign **Vol. 1:** 119, 124 f., 129, 219 f., 275, 309,
  311, 347, 358, 386, 391, 397, 399, 403, 415,
  454, 474, 492, 503, 508, 525, 527, 603, 622,
  626, 641, 648, 652, 655–657, 659, 686, 692,
  702, 723, 733
  Vol. 2: 116, 133, 149–151, 157, 194, 259, 261,
  272, 286, 307, 310 f., 315, 338, 350–352, 381,
  385, 396, 422, 435, 546, 569, 572, 574, 584,
  620–635, 708 f., 741, 858, 892, 901, 912, 921
  Vol. 3: 52, 56, 189, 216, 246, 257, 277, 310,
  406 f., 430, 481, 483, 497 f., 559 f., 569 f., 633
  f., 649, 663, 732, 735 f., 763, 777, 793, 844,
  848, 1002, 1057, 1079 f., 1088, 1098
Signal **Vol. 1:** 341 f., 408, 410
  Vol. 3: 873, 911, 1009
Signature **Vol. 3:** 497
Signet **Vol. 3: 497–501**
Significance **Vol. 1:** 219, 302, 399, 605, 624, 628,
  631, 651, 675, 694, 723
  Vol. 2: 87, 109, 147, 149, 161, 268, 276, 281,
  327, 330, 333, 337, 353, 379, 443 f., 462, 621,
  683–702, 749, 910, 916
  Vol. 3: 182, 235, 630, 701, 704 f., 783, 807,
  1045 f.
Significant **Vol. 1:** 68, 290, 727, 737
  Vol. 2: 307, 332, 340
  Vol. 3: 1057
Signs of the times **Vol. 3:** 844, 848, 867, 1002
Signs and wonders **Vol. 2:** 626 f.
Sihon **Vol. 3:** 960
Silas **Vol. 1:** 130, 160, 168, 330, 340, 570 f.
  Vol. 2: 136, 302, 321, 550
  Vol. 3: 87 f., 475, 557, 670, 794, 908
Silence **Vol. 1:** 340, 543, 609, 619
  Vol. 2: 312, 393, 446, 867, 878, 880
  Vol. 3: 84, **111–114**, 270, 506, 583, 721, 951,
  1058, 1063
Silly **Vol. 3:** 572
Silly women **Vol. 3: 1055–1068**
Siloam **Vol. 1:** 581
  Vol. 3: 173, 483, 814, 976
Silvanus (→ Silas)
Silver **Vol. 1:** 93, 498, 537, 648
  Vol. 2: 28, 44, **95–98**, 225, 235, 836, 844
  Vol. 3: 200, 391 f., 752, 784, 793, 873, 912–
915
Silver age **Vol. 2:** 96
Silversmith **Vol. 2:** 74, 623
Simein **Vol. 3:** 658
Simeon **Vol. 2:** 91, 245, 317, 624

Simeon (cont'd)
 Vol. 3: 84, 118, 276, 313, 324, 361, 455 f., 658, 674, 790, 873, 1059, 1122
Simeon, Rabbi Vol. 3: 1056
Simeon ben Kosebah Vol. 3: 510
Similar Vol. 2: 286, **500–508**, 744
Simile Vol. 1: 577
 Vol. 2: 211, 279, 287, 435, 743–760
 Vol. 3: 734
Similitude Vol. 2: 743–760
Similitudes of Enoch Vol. 3: 265, 272, 614–616
Simlai, Rabbi Vol. 3: 367
Simon Vol. 2: 321, 817
Simon the Cananean Vol. 3: 1167
Simon of Cyrene Vol. 2: 740
Simon bar Giora Vol. 3: 1168
Simon the Just Vol. 2: 652
Simon the leper Vol. 2: 464
 Vol. 3: 1060 f.
Simon Magus Vol. 1: 202
 Vol. 2: 28, 152, 302, 557f., 768, 847
 Vol. 3: 457, 463, 635
Simon (Peter) Vol. 1: 344
 Vol. 3: 383
Simon the Pharisee Vol. 3: 1059, 1061
Simon, Rabbi Vol. 2: 672
Simonians Vol. 2: 557
Simonides Vol. 3: 1119
Simple Vol. 2: 458
 Vol. 3: 571 f., 1024
Simple one of God Vol. 3: 640
Simple-minded Vol. 1: 563
Simpleton Vol. 2: 412
Simplicity Vol. 1: 280–282, 504
 Vol. 2: 868
 Vol. 3: 571 f., 811
Simultaneous Vol. 3: 819
Sin Vol. 1: 57, 77, 78, 85–87, 89, 96 f., 108, 111–113, 115, 125 f., 138, 144, 146–148, 150–152, 154, 156, 163, 166, 181, 187, 202, 204, 216, 221–225, 228 f., 231, 234–236, 268, 277, 294, 301, 303, 320, 324 f., 328, 336, 343, 345 f., 349, 355, 357, 359, 370–372, 374, 390 f., 398 f., 401 f., 417 f., 420, 423 f., 430, 433 f., 436–441, 446, 451, 459, 461, 465 f., 469–471, 474 f., 496, 499, 501, 504, 524 f., 532, 551, 554, 556, 562–565, 567, 569, 606–609, 611, 639, 641, 643 f., 651, 653, 673–677, 685, 698–703, 717–719, 721, 723, 725, 730, 733–735, 738, 740, 742
 Vol. 2: 28, 42, 51, 71 f., 78, 80, 83, 86, 92–94, 101–103, 105 f., 117–120, 131, 137, 141, 143, 145, 151, 155 f., 166, 168–170, 182, 197, 204, 212, 214 f., 225, 237 f., 251, 258, 261, 263, 269 f., 282, 285–289, 302 f., 332, 349 f., 366, 368, 380, 385 f., 398, 400 f., 403 f., 406 f., 415, 422, 445–449, 457, 459 f., 470, 478, 483, 488–490, 494, 504 f., 519, 523, 533, 536, 565 f., 579, 588, 605 f., 617f., 653, 655, 667 f., 675, 677, 699, 705, 707–710, 714, 716–718, 723, 737, 761, 767, 769 f., 787, 791, 799 f., 860, 865, 867 f., 875, 879
 Vol. 3: 27, 35, 41, 48, 52, 55 f., 62, 71, 73, 79, 93, 101 f., 105, 107 f., 127, 135–138, 143,

145 f., 150–152, 160–165, 167, 169 f., 172, 174, 177, 180 f., 188, 193, 196, 199–201, 204, 209, 212 f., 221, 227, 234, 236, 241, 243, 269, 277 f., 315, 320, 323, 332, 343, 347, 362 f., 366, 374, 377, 394, 419, 421, 425, 436, 444, 448, 472 f., 498, 518, 524, 535, 544, 546, 549, 560, 564, **573–586**, 596 f., 624, 628, 641, 701, 705, 721–725, 750, 778 f., 783, 802, 809 f., 824 f., 829, 832, 856, 882, 905, 929, 956, 964, 974, 997 f., 1019, 1021, 1025, 1053 f., 1079, 1109, 1117, 1149 f., 1155
Sin (*moon-god*) Vol. 1: 616
Sin-bearing Vol. 1: 266
Sin-offering Vol. 1: 114, 172, 225, 294
 Vol. 2: 293, 339
 Vol. 3: 156, 170 f., 423, 428, 582, 723, 815
Sinai Vol. 1: 78, 81, 103 f., 159, 195, 222, 224 f., 252, 293, 308, 367 f., 370, 373, 411, 585, 626, 659
 Vol. 2: 48, 98, 145, 186, 190, 212, 215, 281, 313, 315 f., 452, 485, 521, 533, 635, 637, 640, 642, 670 f., 755, 784 f., 854, 871 f.
 Vol. 3: 33, 117, 143, 186, 246, 324, 433, 557, 631, 763, 772, 788, 860 f., 949, 1005, 1009, 1011, **1013 f.**, 1070, 1113, 1120 f.
Sinaiticus Vol. 1: 53
Sincere Vol. 3: 127, **571 f.**, **874–901**
Sincerity Vol. 1: 351, 469, 552, 604, 631, 695, 710
 Vol. 2: 463, 676, 716
 Vol. 3: **100–102**, **571 f.**, 886, 891
Sinew Vol. 1: 671 f.
Sinful Vol. 1: 168, 401 f., 416 f., 466, 468, 488, 518, 562, 585, 677, 696, 701, 718, 723
 Vol. 2: 78, 145, 179, 187, 215, 226, 859, 893, 918
 Vol. 3: **577–583**, 1149
Sinfulness Vol. 2: 36, 565
 Vol. 3: 41, 403
Sing Vol. 1: 344, 411, 574, 633, 651
 Vol. 2: 353 f., 416 f., 436, 862, 874
 Vol. 3: 268, **668–676**, 816, 865
Singer Vol. 1: 53, 200, 665
 Vol. 2: 578
Single Vol. 1: 705
 Vol. 2: 87, 487
 Vol. 3: 172 f., 537, **571 f.**, 1055
Sinister Vol. 1: 203, 550, 686, 699
Sink Vol. 3: 750
Sinless Vol. 3: 194, 645
Sinless perfection Vol. 1: 186
Sinlessness Vol. 1: 284, 434, 544
 Vol. 2: 411, 449, 504, 892
 Vol. 3: 170, 534, 579, 663
Sinner Vol. 1: 109, 141, 147, 171, 239, 274, 322, 333, 343, 349, 358 f., 379, 381, 399, 417, 436, 439, 451, 465, 472, 501, 680 f., 699, 701 f., 706, 733 f.
 Vol. 2: 94, 101, 106, 120, 141, 152, 209, 214, 271 f., 276, 282, 332, 358, 386, 388, 411, 422, 432, 470, 499, 523, 543, 545 f., 549, 566, 584, 604, 630, 660, 669, 790, 798, 813, 882, 884, 888
 Vol. 3: 106, 145, 160, 169, 214, 265, 314, 346,

349, 358, 361, 428, 529, 566, **577–583,** 603, 656, 757, 883, 938, 969, 980, 994, 1100
Sion (→ Zion)
Sip **Vol. 2:** 270
Sippar **Vol. 3:** 264
Sirach (→ Ecclesiasticus)
Siricius **Vol. 3:** 453
Sisera **Vol. 3:** 1057
Sister **Vol. 1:** 254–256, 556
   Vol. 2: 250, 549
   Vol. 3: 1062, 1070, 1163
Sit **Vol. 1:** 363, 474, 482, 658, 661
   Vol. 2: 123, 147, 276, 363, 370, 380, 612, 917
   Vol. 3: 254, **587–589,** 629, 633, 761
Site **Vol. 2:** 317
Situation **Vol. 1:** 271, 603, 625, 686, 702 f.
   Vol. 2: 367, 392, 659
   Vol. 3: 76
Situational theology **Vol. 3:** 974
Sitz im Leben **Vol. 1:** 57 f., **68**
   Vol. 2: 905
   Vol. 3: 60
Six **Vol. 2:** 692
Sixth hour **Vol. 2:** 685
Size **Vol. 1:** 93, 522, 671
   Vol. 2: 800
Skeleton **Vol. 1:** 431, 444
Sketch out **Vol. 3:** 483
Skilful **Vol. 2:** 146
Skilful in teaching **Vol. 3: 759–765**
Skill **Vol. 1:** 239, 412, 512
   Vol. 2: 40
   Vol. 3: 31, 760, 766, 911
Skilled **Vol. 1:** 735
Skin **Vol. 1:** 114, 162, 671 f.
   Vol. 2: 464–466
   Vol. 3: 269, 483
Skinflint **Vol. 2:** 211
Skotos **Vol. 1:** 421
Skull **Vol. 1:** 581
Sky **Vol. 1:** 517, 545, 587
   Vol. 2: 184, 187 f.
   Vol. 3: 112, 730, 736 f.
Slacken **Vol. 1:** 698
Slain **Vol. 1:** 118, 164, 264, 438, 444, 532
   Vol. 2: 32, 147, 411
Slander **Vol. 1:** 110, 413, 561, 654
   Vol. 2: 270, 449, 469, 653
   Vol. 3: 340–347, 532, 1025, 1119
Slanderer **Vol. 3: 345 f., 468–476,** 935, 1065
Slanderous **Vol. 3: 341–345, 468–476**
Slaughter **Vol. 1:** 205, 482, 629, 737
   Vol. 2: 234 f., 410, 674, 893
   Vol. 3: 417–436
Slave **Vol. 1:** 120, 234, 256, 261, 268, 275, 280, 283 f., 299, 308, 360, 366, 371, 392, 457–459, 462, 498 f., 513, 587, 609 f., 637 f., 650, 667, 675, 680, 684, 698, 703, 715–718, 720
   Vol. 2: 49–51, 57, 143, 183, 250, 254, 258, 262, 298, 393, 412, 434, 445, 453, 467, 499, 508–511, 513, 517, 534, 562, 564, 572 f., 652 f., 735, 775, 816 f., 828, 841, 859
   Vol. 3: 94–96, 121, 190 f., 193 f., 211, 225, 256, 364, 406 f., 497, 544 f., 548, 550, 553,

572, 582 f., **589–599,** 608 f., 634, 685, 756, 771, 775, 779, 827, 854, 928–930, 932, 1058, 1062, 1152, 1165, 1168
Slave-dealer **Vol. 3: 380**
Slave-girl **Vol. 2:** 581
Slave-market **Vol. 1:** 268
Slave-owner **Vol. 1:** 366
   Vol. 2: 438
Slave-wife **Vol. 1:** 453
Slavery **Vol. 1:** 222, 412, 438, 498, 629, 633, 647, 716
   Vol. 2: 188, 226, 394, 424, 452, 521, 772
   Vol. 3: 235, 311, 379, **592–598,** 1162
Slavish outlook **Vol. 2:** 259
Slavonic Enoch **Vol. 3:** 265
Slay **Vol. 1:** 509
   Vol. 2: 234
Sleep **Vol. 1:** 93, 261, 382, 420, 425, **429–447,** 672
   Vol. 2: 55, 486, 777, 922, 924 f., 927
   Vol. 3: 259, 270 f., 275, 279, 845, 860
Sleeper **Vol. 1:** 421
Sleepless **Vol. 2:** 134, 137
Slide **Vol. 3:** 559
Slip away **Vol. 3:** 206, 209
Slip through **Vol. 3:** 209
Slogan **Vol. 2:** 611, 620
   Vol. 3: 57
Sluggish **Vol. 3:** 1024
Sly **Vol. 1:** 412, 509
Sly calculation **Vol. 3:** 820
Small **Vol. 1:** 118, 597, 600, 670, 732
   Vol. 2: 259, **424–429,** 443, 675, 709
Smaller **Vol. 2: 427–429,** 675
Smash **Vol. 3:** 914
Smear **Vol. 1:** 121
   Vol. 2: 334, 410
Smell **Vol. 2:** 211
   Vol. 3: 599–601
Smelting **Vol. 1:** 711
   Vol. 2: 97, 628
Smelting crucible **Vol. 2:** 98
Smile **Vol. 2:** 431
Smite **Vol. 1:** 163 f.
   Vol. 2: 159
Smith **Vol. 1:** 279
   Vol. 2: 689
Smitten **Vol. 1:** 683
   Vol. 2: 414
Smoke **Vol. 1:** 449, 657
   Vol. 2: 293 f., 484
   Vol. 3: 75, 417, 601, 676, 732
Smother **Vol. 3:** 109
Smuggle **Vol. 1:** 453
Smyrna **Vol. 1:** 406
   Vol. 2: 136, 692 f., 826, 844
Snake **Vol. 1:** 507–510
   Vol. 2: 27, 586
   Vol. 3: 96, 561, 1079
Snare **Vol. 1:** 343, 433, 531 f., 609
   Vol. 2: 705, 707
   Vol. 3: 201
Snatch **Vol. 2:** 34
   Vol. 3: 201, 377, 381, 567, **601–605,** 712

Snatch away **Vol. 3:** 192
Sneer **Vol. 2:** 430
Sniff out **Vol. 3:** 532
Snow **Vol. 1:** 204, 682, 708
  Vol. 2: 189, 830
  Vol. 3: 1000–1004, 1105
Soak **Vol. 2:** 274
Sober **Vol. 1:** 425, 501, **513–515,** 528 f.
  Vol. 2: 137, 169, 458, 925
Social **Vol. 1:** 289, 312, 496, 566, 640, 716
  Vol. 2: 93, 259, 263, 777, 822
  Vol. 3: 346, **993–1000,** 1055, 1066, 1123
Social class **Vol. 2:** 303
  Vol. 3: 756
Social duties **Vol. 3:** 931
Social egalitarianism **Vol. 3:** 932
Social habit **Vol. 3:** 1124
Social implications **Vol. 3:** 929, 979
Social life **Vol. 2:** 310, 364, 436, 820–829
Social order **Vol. 3:** 353, 1162
Social pleasantries **Vol. 3:** 1143
Social standing **Vol. 2:** 305
Socialist society **Vol. 3:** 971
Society **Vol. 1:** 138, 209, 255, 269, 280, 287, 479, 506, 521, 536, 640, 642, 686, 715, 717
  Vol. 2: 50, 90, 160–162, 263, 383, 415, 430, 462 f., 466, 497, 569, 700, 810, 820–829, 840
  Vol. 3: 49 f., 353, 562, **589–599,** 654, 756, 758, 852, 979, 981, 1057
Sociological **Vol. 2:** 310
Socrates **Vol. 1:** 483, 561 f., 705
  Vol. 2: 92, 103, 430, 439, 666, 719
  Vol. 3: 138, 260, 678, 727, 766, 775, 1027, 1034, 1039, 1083
Socrates (*church historian*) **Vol. 2:** 507
Socratic dialogue **Vol. 3:** 1086
Sodom **Vol. 1:** 394, 532, 657, 677
  Vol. 2: 216, 329, 366, 682, 767
  Vol. 3: 93, 96, 203, 240, 344, 444, 455, 560, 628, 856, 1002
Sodomite **Vol. 1:** 255
  Vol. 2: 569–571
Sodomy **Vol. 2:** 142
  Vol. 3: 95
Soft **Vol. 2:** 98
  Vol. 3: 915
Softness **Vol. 3:** 996, **999**
Soil **Vol. 1:** 381, 517, 520, 691, 722 f.
  Vol. 2: 197, 297
  Vol. 3: 444 f., 522, 809, 866, 868
Sojourn **Vol. 1:** 360, 531, 685
Sojourner **Vol. 1:** 683 f., 686, 690 f., 713 f.
  Vol. 2: 636, 737, **788–790,** 803
  Vol. 3: 406, 852, 855, 1074
Sol Invictus **Vol. 3:** 730
Solar year **Vol. 1:** 627
  Vol. 3: 264
Soldier **Vol. 1:** 259, 359, 396, 406, 650, 652
  Vol. 2: 222, 290, 295, 299, 378 f., 572, 689, 737, 816
  Vol. 3: 49, 134, 138, 144, 377, 558, 608
Soldier's pay **Vol. 3:** 379
Solemn **Vol. 2:** 149, 234
Solemnity **Vol. 1:** 622

Solemnize **Vol. 3:** 232
Solicit **Vol. 2:** 587
Solicitude **Vol. 1:** 695
Solid **Vol. 1:** 660, 682
Solidarity **Vol. 1:** 146, 641
  Vol. 2: 243, 827, 920
  Vol. 3: 597
Solitary **Vol. 3: 1004–1008,** 1056
Solitude **Vol. 2:** 724
  Vol. 3: 111
Solomon **Vol. 1:** 50, 52 f., 61, 122, 153, 195, 209 f., 280, 332, 426, 451, 511, 531, 577, 688
  Vol. 2: 97, 215, 248, 306, 329, 336, 349, 381, 428, 556, 576, 680, 745, 848
  Vol. 3: 86, 157, 207, 418, 426, 439, 465, 476, **605–607,** 649, 651, 653 f., 752, 782 f., 787–789, 812, 873, 879, 950, 1010, 1028 f., 1030, 1055, 1120, 1163
Solomon's portico **Vol. 2:** 236
  Vol. 3: 789, 795 f.
Solomon's temple **Vol. 3: 787 f.,** 795, 815, 836
Solon **Vol. 1:** 529
  Vol. 2: 657, 690, 820
Solstice **Vol. 1:** 631
Solution **Vol. 1:** 65, 531
  Vol. 2: 314
Solve **Vol. 1:** 532, 576–578
  Vol. 3: 177
Somalia **Vol. 2:** 293 f.
Son **Vol. 1:** 123, 177, 209, 255 f., 273, **280–291,** 337 f., 374 f., 408, 410, 430, 440, 473, 487, 500, 509, 511, 525 f., 532, 549, 556, 595, 603, 614 f., 619–621, 637, 643, 655, 667–669, 676, 684, 693, 703, 707, 719, 729, 737 f.
  Vol. 2: 42, 58, 81, 84, 119, 147, 170, 179, 183, 185 f., 194, 200, 202, 216, 231, 249, 289, 301–303, 305, 307, 313, 318, 326, 336, 341, 343, 354, 356, 358, 363, 374, 403–405, 411, 428, 437, 447 f., 450, 500, 506 f., 543, 546, 548 f., 566, 571, 588, 595, 604, 609 f., 625, 630, 635, 642, 653 f., 656, 717, 720, 781, 824, 828, 856, 884, 904, 917, 928 f.
  Vol. 3: 41, 55, 204 f., 281, 300, 403, 510, 580, 590, 593, 597, **607–664,** 753, 776, 810, 843, 863, 869, 920, 1003, 1017, 1058, 1075, 1085, 1113, 1118, 1133, 1154, 1178, 1186
Son of Abraham **Vol. 1:** 182, 286, 288 f.
  Vol. 3: 656, 970
Son of Belial **Vol. 1:** 288
Son of consolation **Vol. 1:** 571
Son of corruption **Vol. 1:** 288
Son of the covenant **Vol. 1:** 288
Son of darkness **Vol. 1:** 102, 287 f., 554, 556, 646
  Vol. 2: 71, 261, 298, 312, 314, 492, 565, 696, 779, 893
  Vol. 3: 233, 272, 469, 503, 647, 961
Son of David **Vol. 1:** 63, 100, 122, 182, 288, 290, 427 f., 675
  Vol. 2: 147, 341, 376, 378, 515, 595, 614
  Vol. 3: 244, 508, **607–664,** 792, 1105, 1163
Son of the day **Vol. 1:** 425
Son of destruction **Vol. 1:** 289
Son of the devil **Vol. 1:** 289
Son of disobedience **Vol. 1:** 110, 289, 593

Son of encouragement **Vol. 1:** 289
Son of evil **Vol. 3:** 503
Son of the evil one **Vol. 1:** 289
Son of favour **Vol. 3:** 637
Son of God **Vol. 1:** 63, 85, 93, 96, 101 f., 117, 177, 240, 256, 272, 274, 276, 281, 283, 287–290, 323, 325, 373, 385, 397, 448, 473, 522 f., 531, 538, 597, 616, 619, 638, 669, 684, 740
Vol. 2: 79 f., 82, 87, 111 f., 178, 203, 213, 228 f., 231, 267, 270, 289, 313, 337, 343, 368, 370, 374, 376, 378, 380, 403, 449, 458, 503, 505, 514, 519, 544, 598, 607, 694, 706, 718, 724, 800, 835, 873, 877, 900, 928 f.
Vol. 3: 28, 42, 56, 62, 114, 132, 147, 186 f., 216, 225, 313, 315 f., 321, 403, 503, 508, **607–664,** 698, 721, 742, 754, 791, 800, 807, 965, 1046, 1048, 1110
Son of God's good pleasure **Vol. 1:** 288
Vol. 2: 818
Son of grace **Vol. 1:** 288
Vol. 3: 637
Son of heaven **Vol. 1:** 102, 225, 288
Son of hell **Vol. 1:** 289
Son of light **Vol. 3:** 161, 233, 272, 503, 637, 647, 839, 961
Son of iniquity **Vol. 1:** 288
Son of Israel **Vol. 1:** 294
Vol. 2: 49, **305,** 314, 791
Son of Jerusalem **Vol. 2:** 324
Son of Joseph **Vol. 2:** 333
Son of the kingdom **Vol. 1:** 77, 289
Vol. 2: 382, 385
Son of lies **Vol. 2:** 339
Son of light **Vol. 1:** 102–104, 287–290, 423, 452, 554, 556, 593, 646
Vol. 2: 71 f., 298, 353, 364, 492–494, 565, 619, 696, 708, 779, 793, 837, 893, 925
Son of his love **Vol. 1:** 424
Son of man **Vol. 1:** 62 f., 84, 96, 113, 118, 185, 204, 290, 321–323, 326 f., 410, 489, 510, 725
Vol. 2: 32, 37 f., 54, 80, 112, 146 f., 185, 190, 194 f., 202, 204, 216, 252, 269, 271, 276, 282, 313, 337, 339, 351, 364, 369, 376, 380, 382, 387, 433, 482, 503, 514, 527, 535, 604, 607, 610, 614, 630, 652, 680, 682, 709, 731, 739, 782, 808, 835, 888, 894, 901, 905, 910–912, 916 f., 928 f.
Vol. 3: 37, 113, 135, 147, 195–197, 213, 265, 272, 293, 343 f., 455, 489 f., 499, 506, 509 f., 527, 530, 532, 547, 559 f., 563, 604 f., **607–664,** 699, 792, 809, 831, 847, 868, 1001, 1109
Son of Mary **Vol. 2:** 333
Son of mischief **Vol. 1:** 288
Son of the Most High **Vol. 1:** 274
Vol. 3: 187
Son of Noah **Vol. 2:** 309
Son of peace **Vol. 3:** 258
Son of perdition **Vol. 1:** 125, 463 f.
Son of perversity **Vol. 3:** 944
Son of prophecy **Vol. 3:** 87
Son of the prophets **Vol. 1:** 288
Son of the resurrection **Vol. 1:** 288, 290
Vol. 2: 920
Son of righteousness **Vol. 1:** 288

Vol. 3: 359, 503, 944
Son of a star **Vol. 2:** 308, 339, 495
Vol. 3: 735
Son of thunder **Vol. 1:** 289, 572
Son of truth **Vol. 1:** 288
Vol. 2: 71, 471
Son of unrighteousness **Vol. 1:** 288
Son of wickedness **Vol. 2:** 100, 105
Vol. 3: 944
Son of the world **Vol. 1:** 288
Son of this world **Vol. 2:** 619, 837
Song **Vol. 1:** 58, 103, 213, 344, 381, 440, 469, 580, 625
Vol. 2: 58, 191, 233, 260 f., 353, 380, 418, 724, 819, 864, 874, 885
Vol. 3: 245, 321, **668–676,** 706, 835
Song of Deborah **Vol. 2:** 796
Song of faith **Vol. 1:** 598
Song of the Lamb **Vol. 2:** 625
Vol. 3: 674
Song of Moses **Vol. 2:** 36, 625, 638
Vol. 3: 77, 263, 674, 1041
Song of praise **Vol. 3:** **668–670,** 816
Song of Solomon **Vol. 1:** 59
Vol. 3: 385, 606, 673
Song of Songs (→ Song of Solomon)
Song of the Three Children **Vol. 1:** 50
Song of triumph **Vol. 3:** 984
Sonship **Vol. 1:** 188, 286, 385, 417, 619, 623, 637, 639, 675, 696
Vol. 2: 245, 445, 653, 775
Vol. 3: 72, 189, 314, 698, 701, 704, 778 f., 864, 1019, 1059, 1073
Soothe **Vol. 1:** 328
Soothsayer **Vol. 1:** 208, 575
Vol. 2: 234, 554
Vol. 3: 33, 76, 79
Soothsayer priest **Vol. 3:** 1028
Soothsaying **Vol. 2:** 142
Vol. 3: 81
Sophism **Vol. 1:** 477
Vol. 2: 439, 648, 656, 719
Sophists **Vol. 1:** 484
Vol. 3: 28, 593, 775 f., 875 f., 1027, 1034, 1082 f., 1086
Sophocles **Vol. 2:** 239
Vol. 3: 739
Sorcerer **Vol. 2:** **552–562**
Sorceress **Vol. 2:** 555
Sorcery **Vol. 1:** 420, 452, 499
Vol. 2: 286, **552–562,** 795
Sore **Vol. 1:** 117
Vol. 2: 466
Sorrow **Vol. 1:** 162, 217, 240 f., 316 f., 356 f., 456, 467, 569, 741
Vol. 2: 149, 236, 360 f., **416–424,** 475, 522, 594, 632, 865
Vol. 3: 236, 683, 731, 1052
Sorrowful **Vol. 3:** 980
Sorry **Vol. 3:** 149
Sort **Vol. 2:** 501
Sosthenes **Vol. 2:** 369
Soteriological **Vol. 1:** 68, 386, 396, 402, 523, 617, 668

Soteriological (cont'd)
   Vol. 2: 192, 202, 300, 380, 504, 827, 844, 889, 903
   Vol. 3: 39, 167, 211 f., 256, 630, 645, 723
Soteriology **Vol. 1:** 53, **68,** 220, 401, 620
   Vol. 2: 388, 397
   Vol. 3: 319, 432, 1105, 1151
Soul **Vol. 1:** 66, 79, 103, 106, 191, 221, 229 f., 232, 233, 235 f., 250, 312, 422, 431–436, 442–444, 446, 450, 459 f., 463 f, 480, 483, 495, 501, 512, 522, 544, 555, 562, 611 f., 621, 623, 636, 653, 665, 671–674, 677, 682, 687, 705, 711, 713, 724, 731
   Vol. 2: 40, 99, 103, 125, 137, 157, 181 f., 191, 197, 202, 207 f., 225, 241, 249, 261, 266, 288, 391, 393 f., 406, 458, 476 f., 480, 483 f., 525, 564 f., 567–569, 571, 584, 590, 648, 658, 830, 838 f., 854, 919, 926
   Vol. 3: 35 f., 99, 122, 124, 146, 151, 158, 174, 205, 210, 218, 231, 234, 245, 260 f., 263, 272 f., 277, 279, 303 f., 471, 522, 534, 568, 572, 602, 675, **676–687,** 689, 692, 694, 706, 710, 719, 789, 811, 827, 865, 876, 927, 936, 989
Sound **Vol. 1:** 501
   Vol. 2: 60, 102, 169–172, 361, 487
   Vol. 3: 111–114, 349–351, 422, 671, 770, 1078
Sound mind **Vol. 1:** 501 f.
   Vol. 2: 169
Sound a trumpet **Vol. 3:** 873 f.
Soundness **Vol. 1:** 604
   Vol. 2: 102
Sour **Vol. 2:** 461
Source **Vol. 1:** 55 f., 62 f., 66–68, 70, 433, 435, 441, 561, 563, 566, 598, 710, 723, 736
   Vol. 2: 138, 147, 157 f., 160, 287, 290, 341, 357, 359, 656
   Vol. 3: 58, 60, 65, 215, 868, **985–988,** 1063, 1178
Source criticism **Vol. 1:** 68
South **Vol. 3:** 1003
South wind **Vol. 3:** 1000–1004
Southern kingdom **Vol. 1:** 716 f.
   Vol. 2: 305 f., 319, 325
   Vol. 3: 34, 79, 249, 426, 451, 1104
Souvenir **Vol. 2:** 85
Sovereign **Vol. 1:** 614 f., 734
   Vol. 2: 70, 74, 77, 185, 203, 240, 262, 335, 366, 372, 411, 413, **601–616,** 624, 650, 819, 877
   Vol. 3: 140 f., 143, 167, 578, 912, 920, 1017
Sovereignty **Vol. 1:** 80, 95, 243, 358, 413, 477, 538, 543, 562, 594, 715
   Vol. 2: 145, 160, 199 f., 233, 274, 319, 327, 368, 426, 587, 819, 859
   Vol. 3: 392, 523, 565, 736, 831, 917, 960
Sow **Vol. 1:** 299, 313, 377, 468–470, 612, 627, 681, 686
   Vol. 2: 34, 129, 177, 359, 826
   Vol. 3: 134, 382, **521–525,** 684, 868
Sower **Vol. 1:** 173, 278, 459, 516 f., 578
   Vol. 2: 129, 714, 773, 834
   Vol. 3: 143, 382, 470, 522, 526, 868
Space **Vol. 1:** 102, 236, 521, 728

   Vol. 2: 70, 198, 397, 404, 424, 497, 658
   Vol. 3: 301, 830, 899
Spacious **Vol. 3:** 255
Spain **Vol. 2:** 826
Span **Vol. 3:** 1161
Span of life **Vol. 2:** 428
Spare **Vol. 1:** 390, 414, 632 f., 725, 727, 729, 734
   Vol. 2: 411, 660
   Vol. 3: 136
Spark **Vol. 1:** 422, 616
Sparkle **Vol. 3:** 395 f.
Sparrow **Vol. 1:** 173
Sparta **Vol. 1:** 193, 287, 498, 687
   Vol. 2: 500
   Vol. 3: 775, 1055
Spartan **Vol. 3:** 1119
Spatial **Vol. 1:** 692
   Vol. 2: 184 f., 195, 197–199, 210, 459
Speak **Vol. 1:** 206, 271, 332, 340, 429, 579, 598, 729, 739 f.
   Vol. 2: 72, 74, 109, 129, 154, 363
   Vol. 3: 45, 275, 324, 341, 345, **1081–1119,** 1157
Speak against **Vol. 2:** 450
Speak allegorically **Vol. 2:** 743–756
Speak boldly **Vol. 2:** 734–737
Speak evil **Vol. 1:** 415
   Vol. 3: 345 f.
Speak ill **Vol. 2:** 364, 450
Speak openly **Vol. 2:** 734–737
Speak to **Vol. 3:** 1059
Speak in tongues (→ Tongues, speaking in)
Speak the truth **Vol. 3:** 874–901
Speak out **Vol. 2:** 734–737
Speak well **Vol. 2:** 416
Speaker **Vol. 2:** 85, 369, 434
   Vol. 3: 75
Speaking a foreign language **Vol. 3:** 1078–1081
Spear **Vol. 3:** 556, 590
Spear-point **Vol. 1:** 656
Special **Vol. 1:** 540, 620, 666–668
Species **Vol. 1:** 670, 722
   Vol. 2: 158, 501, 657
Specific **Vol. 2:** 863, 867
Specify **Vol. 1:** 581
   Vol. 2: 648
Speck **Vol. 3:** 129
Spectacle **Vol. 1:** 649
   Vol. 2: 291, 434
   Vol. 3: 512, 520 f.
Spectators **Vol. 1:** 646
Speculation **Vol. 1:** 71, 641, 707, 740
   Vol. 2: 191, 314, 393, 397, 402, 405, 644 f., 921
   Vol. 3: 35, 40, 532, 632, 646, 654 f., 678, 804, 1005 f., 1032, 1121
Speculative **Vol. 1:** 601–603, 607, 694
   Vol. 2: 392, 396
   Vol. 3: 42, 639 f., 1035
Speculative thought **Vol. 3:** 1081
Speech **Vol. 1:** 66, 69 f., 206, 212, 421, 428, 528, 571, 574 f., 578 f., 582, 587–589, 715
   Vol. 2: 49, 78, 108 f., 157, 260, 290, 591, 643, 659, 899

Vol. 3: 64, 111, 113, 311, 316, 351, 448 f., 689, 699, 703, 741 f., 886, 914, **1078–1081**
Speech for the defence **Vol. 2:** 594
Speeches in Acts **Vol. 3:** 62–67
Spell **Vol. 1:** 450, 477
  Vol. 2: 115, 552, 560
  Vol. 3: 476, 1087, 1100
Spend **Vol. 1:** 551
Spend the night **Vol. 3:** 255, 449
Spend time **Vol. 3: 839–845**
Sperm **Vol. 1:** 498
Sphere **Vol. 2:** 303
Spherical **Vol. 1:** 521
Spices **Vol. 1:** 121, 264–266, 743
  Vol. 2: 295
Spider **Vol. 1:** 490, 510
Spike **Vol. 3:** 865
Spill **Vol. 2:** 854
Spin **Vol. 1:** 490
Spinoza, B. de **Vol. 3:** 896
Spirit **Vol. 1:** 55, 58, 66, 91, 105, 108, 138, 144, 146–148, 152 f., 160, 171, 179, 200, 217, 225, 230, 232, 234–237, 246, 248, 279, 286, 289 f., 300, 303–305, 311, 318, 322, 324, 327, 329, 335 f., 340, 349, 368 f., 379, 410, 414, 424, 428, 430, 440, 443, 446, 449, 452, 458, 466 f., 470, 473, 490, 496, 498, 500 f., 504, 514 f., 557 f., 562–565, 570, 578 f., 595, 601 f., 605, 609, 615, 623, 625, 631, 637, 642, 649, 654, 657, 662, 665–667, 672 f., 675–679, 682 f., 700, 705, 711, 717, 719, 722 f., 729, 734 f., 737–739
  Vol. 2: 42, 58, 66, 71, 75 f., 78, 83, 100, 106, 117, 121, 123, 129, 136, 147, 150 f., 155 f., 162, 169, 178, 182 f., 185 f., 189, 199, 213 f., 218, 260 f., 265, 275, 277, 282 f., 311 f., 314, 343, 350, 353, 364, 368, 382, 398, 402 f., 418, 424, 439, 446 f., 452, 481, 491, 499, 513, 519, 545 f., 558, 561, 565 f., 571, 602, 611, 615, 617, 619, 625, 641, 670–672, 675, 712, 715, 719, 721, 728, 738, 762, 771, 775, 778, 781, 784–787, 806, 816, 828, 831, 839, 854 f., 873, 878, 882–884, 898 f., 916, 919, 921, 927–929
  Vol. 3: 28, 47, 77 f., 82, 85–88, 102, 109–113, 125, 129 f., 138, 147, 172, 174, 199, 204, 244, 256–258, 263, 266, 269, 280, 300, 313, 317, 322 f., 336, 344, 401, 403, 417, 432, 435, 440, 444, 458 f., 471, 473–475, 493, 504, 513, 523–525, 533, 547 f., 551, 571, 581, 594, 597, 602, 604, 628, 637, 639 f., 647–649, 651, 671 f., 674, 680 f., 683, 687, **689–708,** 718, 734, 742, 748, 789, 804, 808, 849, 854, 922, 927, 939, 944, 967, 987–990, 994 f., 1020 f., 1023, 1030, 1032, 1036, 1046, 1061, 1067, 1080, 1089, 1100, 1122, 1143, 1163, 1167, 1178, **1199 f.**
Spirit, Holy **Vol. 1:** 52, 66, 90 f., 95, 106, 116, 122, 128 f., 146, 148, 155, 158, 160, 168 f., 175 f., 185 f, 202, 232, 235, 248, 355, 372, 375, 414, 417, 491, 511, 526–528, 530, 535, 584, 592, 598, 623, 628 f., 643, 656, 660, 679–681, 704, 719, 723, 730, 735, 738 f.
  Vol. 2: 28, 39 f., 48, 79, 84, 86 f., 122, 127, 143, 152, 193 f., 227–231, 242 f., 245, 249, 251, 259, 268, 270, 300, 328, 359 f., 388, 424, 445, 448, 473, 507, 516, 557, 596 f., 603–605, 632 f., 645, 653 f., 718, 722 f., 736, 739 f., 768, 774, 783, 794, 817, 838, 842, 847, 855, 857, 868, 874, 881, 893, 911, 918, 921
  Vol. 3: 38, 63, 71–73, 80, 83 f., 171, 198, 214–216, 220, 225, 228, 242, 257, 314, 317, 324, 327, 329, 343, 380, 412, 431, 456, 461, 472–474, 488, 493, 499, 570, 660, 663 f., **689–708,** 713 f., 732, 742, 749, 763 f., 790, 807, 810, 813 f., 855, 891, 921, 991, 1018, 1048, 1079, 1152, 1178
Spirit of darkness **Vol. 3:** 469
Spirit of divination **Vol. 1:** 340
  Vol. 2: 552–562
Spirit of glory **Vol. 3:** 257
Spirit of God **Vol. 2:** 122, 150, 168, 218, 223, 250
Spirit of holiness **Vol. 2:** 79
  Vol. 3: 651
Spirit of light **Vol. 1:** 452
  Vol. 2: 105
  Vol. 3: 469
Spirit of prophecy **Vol. 3: 699 f.,** 705 f.
Spirit and truth **Vol. 3:** 891
Spirit of truth **Vol. 1:** 89 f., 123
  Vol. 3: 892
Spirit–baptism **Vol. 3:** 55
Spirits **Vol. 1:** 102, 118, 123, 166, 167, 347, 382, 401, 411, 450–453, 463, 504, 556, 563, 621, 674
  Vol. 2: 69, 121, 184, 207, 209, 298, 391, 417, 458, 553 f., 691, 707, 828
Spirits in prison **Vol. 2:** 136, 208
  Vol. 3: 947
Spiritual **Vol. 1:** 71, 75, 183, 290, 311, 336, 338, 398 f., 406, 416, 435, 444, 449, 455, 482, 484, 492, 528, 531, 539, 563, 566, 569, 595, 616 f., 619, 628, 638 f., 642, 647, 650, 662, 665, 674, 678–681, 725–727, 742
  Vol. 2: 121, 180–182, 187, 189, 193, 196, 230, **249,** 264–267, 276, 316, 325, 327 f., 339, 351, 355, 364, 398, 438, 539, 619, 842, 861
  Vol. 3: 106, 208, 231, 281, 301, 305, 410, 434, 504, 551, **689–708,** 946, 963 f., **993–1000,** **1081–1119**
Spiritual anointing **Vol. 1:** 123
Spiritual armour **Vol. 1:** 316, 647, 656
  Vol. 3: 802
Spiritual body **Vol. 1:** 236
  Vol. 2: 567, 924
  Vol. 3: 303
Spiritual building **Vol. 2: 250 f.**
  Vol. 3: 391
Spiritual death **Vol. 1:** 406, 431, 436, 440
Spiritual drink **Vol. 3:** 383
Spiritual evil **Vol. 1:** 429
Spiritual fire **Vol. 3:** 689
Spiritual food **Vol. 3:** 383
Spiritual fornication **Vol. 2:** 587
Spiritual gifts **Vol. 1:** 129, 535
  Vol. 2: 44, 79, **115–124,** 169, 255, 360, 391, 828, 868
  Vol. 3: 707
Spiritual house **Vol. 1:** 305

Spiritual house (*cont'd*)
  Vol. 2: 230, 249
  Vol. 3: 383, 387, 393
Spiritual inheritance **Vol. 2:** 295
Spiritual Israel **Vol. 2: 316**
Spiritual life **Vol. 1:** 70, 138, 249
  Vol. 2: 446
Spiritual man **Vol. 1:** 85, 127, 133
  Vol. 2: 75
  Vol. 3: 684, 707
Spiritual marriage **Vol. 2:** 581, 588
Spiritual milk **Vol. 1:** 284
  Vol. 2: 270
  Vol. 3: 1118
Spiritual party **Vol. 3:** 1030
Spiritual poverty **Vol. 1:** 313, 358
Spiritual power **Vol. 1:** 424
Spiritual priesthood **Vol. 2:** 249
Spiritual reality **Vol. 2:** 249
Spiritual riches **Vol. 2:** 299
Spiritual rock **Vol. 3:** 383
Spiritual sacrifices **Vol. 2:** 249
  Vol. 3: 35, 37, 383, 435, 706
Spiritual songs **Vol. 3:** 674 f., 706
Spiritual stones **Vol. 2:** 249
  Vol. 3: 706
Spiritual understanding **Vol. 3:** 706
Spiritual worship **Vol. 3:** 1119
Spiritualist **Vol. 2:** 559
Spirituality **Vol. 1:** 352
  Vol. 2: 884
  Vol. 3: 705
Spiritualization **Vol. 1:** 625, 650
  Vol. 2: 67, 339
  Vol. 3: 57, 104, 380
Spittle **Vol. 2:** 167 f.
  Vol. 3: 916
Splendid **Vol. 3: 317–324**
Splendour **Vol. 1:** 474, 552, 650, 730
  Vol. 2: 46, 289, 339, 425 f., **484–486,** 779
  Vol. 3: 514
Splinter **Vol. 1:** 116, 453, 667, 726
Split **Vol. 1:** 535
  Vol. 2: 306
  Vol. 3: 543 f.
Spoil **Vol. 1:** 467, 565
  Vol. 2: 99, 182, 590, 693 f.,
  Vol. 3: 713, 851 f.
Spoken word **Vol. 1:** 416, 679, 736
Spokesman **Vol. 1:** 194, 373, 579 f.
  Vol. 3: 49
Spontaneous **Vol. 1:** 500
  Vol. 2: 607, 694
Sport **Vol. 1:** 470, 625, 644 f., 648
  Vol. 2: 710
Spot **Vol. 1:** 634
  Vol. 2: 411
  Vol. 3: 200
Spotless **Vol. 2:** 290
  Vol. 3: 923–928
Spotted **Vol. 1:** 556
Spouse **Vol. 2:** 59, 798
Spread **Vol. 1:** 457, 647–649, 653, 733, 741 f.
  Vol. 2: 34, **334–343,** 360

Spring **Vol. 1:** 195, 201, 319, 441, 513, 632, 743
  Vol. 3: 449, 459, 709, 845, 982, **985–988**
Sprinkle **Vol. 1:** 114, 144, 151, **220–226,** 304, 351, 369, 633
  Vol. 2: 853–855
  Vol. 3: 164, 435
Sprout **Vol. 2:** 211
  Vol. 3: 865–870
Spur on **Vol. 2:** 244
Spurious **Vol. 1:** 187, 590
  Vol. 2: 338
Spurn **Vol. 1:** 448
  Vol. 2: 817
  Vol. 3: 341
Spy **Vol. 1:** 294
  Vol. 2: 142, 318, 469
  Vol. 3: 126, 875
Squander **Vol. 1:** 464
  Vol. 2: 34
Square number **Vol. 2:** 700
Stability **Vol. 1:** 661, 675, 711
  Vol. 2: 374
Stable **Vol. 1:** 661
  Vol. 3: 228, 911
Stadium **Vol. 1:** 645 f.
  Vol. 3: 946
Staff **Vol. 1:** 161 f., 407
  Vol. 2: 642
  Vol. 3: 49, 404, 737, 870
Stage **Vol. 1:** 282, 540, 549
  Vol. 2: 748
  Vol. 3: 811
Stage of life **Vol. 3:** 845
Stagger **Vol. 1:** 514, 673
  Vol. 2: 458
  Vol. 3: 994
Stain **Vol. 1:** 447, 641
Stake **Vol. 1:** 389, 391–394, 726
  Vol. 3: 713, 951
Stalk of grain **Vol. 3:** 399
Stamp **Vol. 1:** 712
  Vol. 2: 75, 284, **288 f., 573 f.,** 657
  Vol. 3: 904
Stand **Vol. 1:** 51, 411, 474, 543, 651, 658, 660, 672, 685, 719
  Vol. 2: 156, 369, 773, 861, 869
  Vol. 3: 224, 228, 259, 635, 761, 825
Stand in awe **Vol. 2:** 224
  Vol. 3: 100
Stand before **Vol. 1:** 474, 622
Stand between **Vol. 1:** 739
Stand by **Vol. 1:** 474
  Vol. 2: 310
  Vol. 3: 203
Stand firm **Vol. 2:** 517, 764
Stand in line **Vol. 2: 451–453**
Stand on rights **Vol. 3:** 576
Stand still **Vol. 3:** 731
Stand test **Vol. 3:** 319
Stand under **Vol. 1:** 710
Stand up **Vol. 3:** 279
Standard **Vol. 1:** 51, 175, 220, 273, 396, 443, 460, 542, 546, 604, 675, 729
  Vol. 2: 267, 361, 366, 374, 390, 399, 415, 427,

561

452, 499
Vol. 3: 353, 355 f., 358, **399–404,** 562, 586, 726, 728 f., **903–906,** 949, 1050
Standing **Vol. 1:** 351, 430, 472, 536, 544, 610, 659
    Vol. 2: 123, 144, 148, 182, 259, 426, 497, 821, 839
    Vol. 3: 563
Stanton, G.N. **Vol. 3:** 60
Star **Vol. 1:** 102, 124, 272, 380, 407, 451, 508, 522 f., 610, 621, 627, 657, 740
    Vol. 2: 27–29, 46, 69, 188 f., 192, 196, 198, 270, 313, 337, 459, 488, 490 f., 495 f., 555, 557 f., 622, 649, 691, 695, 916
    Vol. 3: 224, 397, 498, 557, 583, 650, 718, **730–737,** 950, 1102
Star of Jacob **Vol. 3:** 649
Start **Vol. 1:** 600, 741
    Vol. 2: 327
    Vol. 3: 259
Starting point **Vol. 1:** 710
    Vol. 3: 522
Startle **Vol. 2:** 358
Starvation **Vol. 1:** 328, 611
Starve **Vol. 3:** 1025
State **Vol. 1:** 168, 189, 232, 275, 392, 468, 501, 508, 519, 549, 565, 611, 617, 639 f., 678, 687, 715, 723–725
    Vol. 2: 49, 234, 253, 306, 309, 373, 375, 420, 439, 456, 511, 657, 737, 775, 791, 796, **801–804,** 922
    Vol. 3: 79, 96 f., 217, 353, 553, 756, 775 f., 783, 930, 1156
Stateless **Vol. 2:** 306
Statement **Vol. 1:** 573 f., 588
    Vol. 2: 407
    Vol. 3: 69
Stater **Vol. 2:** 851
    Vol. 3: **752–755,** 985
Statesman **Vol. 1:** 193
    Vol. 3: 217
Statesmanship **Vol. 3:** 606
Station **Vol. 1:** 275, 476
    Vol. 3: 1055
Station code **Vol. 3:** 929
Statue **Vol. 2:** 27, 158, 287
    Vol. 3: 259
Stature **Vol. 1:** **92 f.,** 183, 277, 740
    Vol. 2: 428 f., 588
    Vol. 3: 350, 403
Status **Vol. 1:** 131, 268, 275, 324, 364, 385, 398, 432, 439, 538 f., 549, 615, 618–620, 664, 694
    Vol. 2: 160 f., 170, 218, 262, 334, 338, 342, 351 f., 373, 386, 427, 439, 442, 563, 619
    Vol. 3: 32, 49, 593, 654, 888, 1055, 1058, 1066 f., 1073
Statute **Vol. 1:** 330, 332, 335, 350, 677
    Vol. 2: 363, 441
    Vol. 3: 354, 550
Statutory **Vol. 1:** 578
Stave **Vol. 1:** 390
Stay **Vol. 1:** 690
    Vol. 2: 772
    Vol. 3: **223–229**

Stay on **Vol. 3:** **223–229**
Stay with **Vol. 3:** **224–229,** 449
Staying **Vol. 3:** **224–229**
Steadfast **Vol. 1:** 217, 494, 602, 607, 660, 662 f., 674, 710
    Vol. 2: 117, 611, **764–776**
    Vol. 3: 228, 691
Steadfast love **Vol. 2:** 227
    Vol. 3: 879
Steadfastness **Vol. 2:** **764–776,** 858
    Vol. 3: 73, 818
Steady **Vol. 1:** 658
    Vol. 3: 878
Steal **Vol. 1:** 208
    Vol. 2: 871
    Vol. 3: 54, **377–381,** 602
Stealth **Vol. 3:** 377
Steam **Vol. 3:** 689
Steamed **Vol. 1:** 226
Steep **Vol. 2:** 349
Steer **Vol. 1:** 694
Step **Vol. 1:** 600
    Vol. 2: 369
    Vol. 3: 350
Step-mother **Vol. 1:** 500
Stephanas **Vol. 1:** 741
    Vol. 2: 899
    Vol. 3: 416, 574
Stephen **Vol. 1:** 174, 297, 440, 739
    Vol. 2: 91, 119, 135, 148, 155, 178, 248, 318, 418, 421, 437, 450, 636, 641, 729
    Vol. 3: 65 f., 199, 257 f., 320, 431, 464 f., 481, 548, 607, 633, 700, 714, 736, 773, 785, 793, 815, 964, 1014, 1030, 1043 f., 1067, 1122
Stephen, Pope **Vol. 3:** 385
Steppes **Vol. 2:** 305
    Vol. 3: 1004
Stereotype **Vol. 3:** 1063
Stern, G. **Vol. 3:** 1129
Steward **Vol. 1:** 684
    Vol. 2: 123, **247–256,** 619, 714
    Vol. 3: 49, 468, 489, 504, 529, 576, 701, 854
Stewardship **Vol. 2:** 832
Stewed **Vol. 1:** 226
Stick **Vol. 1:** 161 f., 657, 726
Stick to **Vol. 2:** **348–350**
Stiffnecked **Vol. 2:** 153
Stigma **Vol. 2:** 835
Stigmata **Vol. 2:** **572 f.**
Still **Vol. 1:** 384, 419
    Vol. 2: 240, 396, 630 f.
    Vol. 3: 111, 211, 1002
Still birth **Vol. 1:** 183
Stimulate **Vol. 3:** 489, 1123
Stimulating **Vol. 3:** 445
Sting **Vol. 1:** 436, **507–511,** 719, 738
    Vol. 2: 29
    Vol. 3: 267 f., 865
Stinginess **Vol. 1:** 214
Stipulation **Vol. 2:** 320
Stir **Vol. 1:** 563
    Vol. 2: 136, 366
Stir up **Vol. 3:** **556–558, 709 f.**
Stoa **Vol. 1:** 68, 277, 349, 643

Stoa (cont'd)
  Vol. 3: 577, 635, 1084
Stock **Vol. 1:** 427, 710, 721
  Vol. 3: 865
Stock of Jesse **Vol. 3:** 649
Stoic **Vol. 1:** 63, 108, 137, 164, 178, 184 f., 232, 255, 271, 334, 432, 444, 446, 450, 459 f., 481, 493, 498, 501, 512, 521, 537, 616, 640, 645, 654, 656, 692, 694, 715, 718, 734
  Vol. 2: 49–51, 72, 128, 130, 141, 188, 265, 289, 396, 406 f., 419, 439, 449, 459, 476 f., 481, 497, 565, 648, 651, 657 f., 660 f., 719, 723, 765, 769, 776, 783, 807, 836, 841, 919
  Vol. 3: 31–33, 35, 50 f., 54, 205, 257, 525, 562, 571, 593, 635, 678 f., 690, 719, 727, 739 f., 764, 776, 778, 827, 835, 924, 926 f., 930 f., 1027, 1034, 1036, 1039, 1084–1086, 1116 f., 1129, 1157, 1169
Stoicism **Vol. 1:** 59, **68 f.,** 127, 253, 351, 432, 502, 595
  Vol. 2: 140
  Vol. 3: 123, 146, 149, 331, 689, 727, 928
Stolen **Vol. 2:** 858
Stomach **Vol. 1: 169,** 202, 500, 611, 742
  Vol. 2: 266
Stone **Vol. 1:** 74, 77, 140, 205, 240, 248, 294, 308, 332, 377, 390, 393 f., 409, 463, 477, 496, 610, 660, 662, 682, 724
  Vol. 2: 29, 129, 217, 231, 249, 288, 296, 418, 450, 582, 622 f., 705 f., 708 f., 711, 800
  Vol. 3: 146, 227, 281, **381–399,** 418, 483, 490, 493, 497, 499, 557, 714, 739, 796, 805, 1062
Stone of offence **Vol. 2:** 705
  Vol. 3: 382, 389–391, 393
Stones crying out **Vol. 3:** 393
Stoning **Vol. 3:** 94 f., 538
Stop **Vol. 3: 254–258,** 950 f.
Store **Vol. 2:** 134, 318
Store up **Vol. 2: 829–836**
Storehouse **Vol. 2:** 189, 191, **829–836**
Storeroom **Vol. 2: 829–836**
Stores **Vol. 2:** 32
Storm **Vol. 1:** 384, 419, 572
  Vol. 2: 623, 630 f.
  Vol. 3: 211, 266, 514, 557, 559, 707, **1000–1004,** 1091
Storm-tossed **Vol. 3:** 560
Story **Vol. 1:** 575
  Vol. 2: 643–647
  Vol. 3: 816
Strabo **Vol. 1:** 319, 497
  Vol. 2: 324, 679
Straight **Vol. 2:** 144
  Vol. 3: 351 f., 834, 903, 942, 1028
Straightforward **Vol. 3: 351 f.**
Strain **Vol. 3:** 858
Strain out **Vol. 1:** 116
Straits **Vol. 2:** 29, **807–809**
Strange **Vol. 1:** 509, 671, 683 f., 686, 688–690, 728
  Vol. 2: 367, **739–742**
Stranger **Vol. 1:** 180, 203, 221, 255, 258, 265, 305, 346, 360, 528, **683–692,** 717
  Vol. 2: 34, 251, 326, 404, 541, **788–790,** 803

  Vol. 3: 545, 567, 815, 1073
Strangled **Vol. 1: 220–226,** 261
Strangulation **Vol. 1:** 391 f.
Strata **Vol. 1:** 68
Strategy **Vol. 2:** 329
Strauss, D.F. **Vol. 1:** 54
  Vol. 3: 1138
Straw **Vol. 1:** 390
Strawson, P.F. **Vol. 3: 895–897**
Stray **Vol. 1:** 115, 239
  Vol. 2: 413, 710
Straying cattle **Vol. 3:** 95
Stream **Vol. 1:** 652 f., 655, 682 f.
  Vol. 2: 232
  Vol. 3: 985–988
Street crossing **Vol. 3:** 940
Strength **Vol. 1:** 106, 119, 122, 173, 229, 239, 314, 329, 343, 436, 445, 467, 531, 551, 564, 607, 636, 650, 667, 680, 686, 710, 732, 736
  Vol. 2: 78, 98 f., 148, 177, 180, 202, 215, 240, 244 f., 263, 273, 360, 540, **601–616,** 767, 806, 817
  Vol. 3: 31, 121, 381, 544, 557, 677, **711–718,** 730, 925
Strengthen **Vol. 1:** 99, 463, 492, 570, 604, 639, 658
  Vol. 2: 183, 357, **601–616**
  Vol. 3: 88, 226, **716–718**
Strenuous work **Vol. 3: 858 f.**
Stress **Vol. 1:** 420, 597, 638, 720, 739
  Vol. 2: 663, 748
Stretch **Vol. 1:** 478, 649
  Vol. 3: 399
Stretch out **Vol. 1:** 127, 460
  Vol. 2: 150, 200 f., 239
  Vol. 3: 870
Stretch out hand **Vol. 3:** 750, 860
Strew **Vol. 2:** 157
Strict **Vol. 1:** 500, 568, 688
Strictness **Vol. 2:** 351
Stride **Vol. 2:** 369
Strife **Vol. 1:** 380, 535, 555, 558, 638, 681
  Vol. 2: 263, 282 f., 808, 911
  Vol. 3: 532, **958–967**
Strike **Vol. 1:** 161–163, 376, 585, 653
  Vol. 2: 157, 220, 413, 416, **417–419,** 451, **705–707**
  Vol. 3: 903
Strike down **Vol. 3:** 396
Strike fire **Vol. 3:** 396
Strike with fist **Vol. 3: 857**
Strike out **Vol. 1:** 529
Strip **Vol. 1:** 313 f., 393, 564
  Vol. 3: 310, 867
Strip off **Vol. 3:** 379
Stripes **Vol. 2:** 696
Strive **Vol. 1:** 80, 456, 460 f., 469, 637, 645 f., 673, 723, 731
  Vol. 2: 103, 230, 244 f., 266, 305, 426, 617, 806, 814–817
  Vol. 3: 346, 775, 799, 820, 1168
Strive after **Vol. 3:** 231
Strive for **Vol. 3: 530–532**
Stroke **Vol. 1:** 161, 241, 260

563

Stroll **Vol. 3:** 943
Strong **Vol. 1:** 103, 352, 366, 475, 504, 508, 650 f., 727, 731
Vol. 2: 102, 155, 169 f., 244, 269, 517, **601–616,** 657, 764, **767 f.,** 815
Vol. 3: 432, **712–714, 716–718, 993–996,** 998
Strong ones **Vol. 1:** 101
Strong-box **Vol. 2:** 830
Stronger **Vol. 2:** 382
Stronger One **Vol. 3:** 55, 473
Strongest **Vol. 2:** 435
Stronghold **Vol. 2:** 324
Structuralism **Vol. 3:** 1142
Structure **Vol. 1:** 390
Vol. 2: 249, 288, 427
Struggle **Vol. 1:** 336, 503, 539, 564, 595, 602, 604, 626, 644–647, 649, 651, 687, 716–718
Vol. 2: 65, 165, 273, 307 f., 311
Vol. 3: 838
Stubborn **Vol. 1:** 152, 241, 308, 424, 426, 554
Vol. 2: 97, 153, 312
Vol. 3: 94, 715
Student **Vol. 1:** 484, 486
Vol. 3: 115
Study **Vol. 1:** 219, 459, 485 f., 580, 641, 656, 662, 735
Vol. 2: 381, 442
Vol. 3: 478, 480 f., 1162
Stumble **Vol. 1:** 610, 663
Vol. 2: 429, **705–707**
Vol. 3: 382, 433, 446, 573, 922, 994
Stumbling-block **Vol. 1:** 535
Vol. 2: 705–710
Vol. 3: 994, 996, 1020
Stump **Vol. 2:** 333
Vol. 3: 866
Stunt **Vol. 2:** 222
Stupid **Vol. 2:** 412
Vol. 3: 130, 577, **1023–1026**
Stupify **Vol. 2:** 154
Style **Vol. 2:** 288
Vol. 3: 65, 904
Stylistic variation **Vol. 3:** 1176
Stylus **Vol. 3:** 865
Subdue **Vol. 1:** 336, 647, 671
Vol. 2: 260, 777
Vol. 3: 109
Subject **Vol. 1:** 235, 360, 366, 385, 436 f., 444, 446, 457 f., 470, 492, 538, 542 f., 548, 552, 583, 595, 603, 610, 660, 685, 687, 692, 707, 716, 720
Vol. 2: 110, 139, 142, 162, 244, 263, 265, 286, 298, 377, 399, 418, 609, 790
Vol. 3: 204, 268, 470, **592–598,** 695, 756, 1064
Subject to suffering **Vol. 3: 719–725**
Subjection **Vol. 1:** 439, 509, 524 f., 586, 591, 609, 676, 718
Vol. 2: 51, 374
Vol. 3: 545, 548, 581, 589, 595, 1161
Subjective **Vol. 1:** 284
Vol. 2: 239–241, 243, 352, 355, 357
Vol. 3: 283, 285
Subjectivity **Vol. 1:** 583 f.
Subjugate **510–520**
Sublimation **Vol. 2:** 336

Sublime **Vol. 2:** 92–94
Submerge **Vol. 1:** 144
Submission **Vol. 1:** 81, 239, 281, 330, 347, 401, 415, 439, 475, 600, 647
Vol. 2: 179, 218, 240, 244, 343, 615, 764, 859, 864, 888
Vol. 3: 84, 250, 745, 929
Submissive **Vol. 1:** 364, 593
Vol. 2: 262
Vol. 3: 243, 691, 930 f., 1067
Submit **Vol. 1:** 602
Vol. 2: 180, 203, 261, 270, 363, 378
Vol. 3: 360
Subordinate **Vol. 1:** 283, 452, 481, 485, 501, 508, 523, 599, 605, 712
Vol. 2: 160, 372, 404
Vol. 3: 758, 1066
Subordination **Vol. 1:** 190, 386, 492
Vol. 2: 80, 84, 162
Vol. 3: 593, 636, 929, 1063
Subordinationism **Vol. 3:** 1064
Suborn **Vol. 2:** 686
Subservience **Vol. 1:** 670
Subservient **Vol. 1:** 492
Subsistence **Vol. 2:** 845–847
Substance **Vol. 1:** 327, 605, 679, **703–714**
Vol. 2: 243, 284, 289, 452, 497, **845–847**
Substantial **Vol. 1:** 710 f.
Vol. 2: 291
Substantiate **Vol. 2:** 321
Vol. 3: 1041
Substitute **Vol. 1:** 319, 504, 629, 681
Vol. 2: 42, 199
Vol. 3: 159, 171, 194, 427, 750, 1150
Substitution **Vol. 1:** 398, 417, 426, 437 f.
Vol. 3: 1179, 1196
Substitutionary **Vol. 3:** 103, 196, 723
Substitutionary death **Vol. 2:** 123, 530, 532 f., 535 f.
Subterfuge **Vol. 2:** 317, 630
Subterranean **Vol. 1:** 509
Vol. 2: 205
Subversive **Vol. 2:** 645
Subvert **Vol. 2:** 370
Succeed **Vol. 2:** 452
Vol. 3: 943
Success **Vol. 1:** 412, 557, 611 f., 688, 741
Vol. 2: 119, 146, 237, 478, 778
Vol. 3: 322
Succession **Vol. 1:** 200, 301, 426, 664 f.
Vol. 2: 152, 389, 428, 433
Vol. 3: 481
Successor **Vol. 2:** 151, 331, 374
Vol. 3: 648
Succoth **Vol. 1:** 195
Succumb **Vol. 1:** 467
Vol. 2: 285, 307
Suck **Vol. 3:** 1062
Suckling **Vol. 1:** 281
Sudden **Vol. 1:** 609
Vol. 2: 382, 384, 894, 900, 910
Vol. 3: 379, 394, 1001
Sue **Vol. 3:** 576
Suffer **Vol. 1:** 55, 191, 239 f., 260, 395, 483, 489, 553, 612

Suffer (*cont'd*)
  Vol. 2: 29, 122, 139, 258, 267, 289, 307, 327, 339, 358, 370, 806, 809, 835
  Vol. 3: 128, 142 f., 147, 194, 243, 371, 513, 643, **719–725**
Suffer damage **Vol. 3: 136–138**
Suffer evil **Vol. 3: 719–725**
Suffer loss **Vol. 3: 136–138**
Suffer together **Vol. 3: 719–725**
Sufferer **Vol. 3:** 588
Suffering **Vol. 1:** 68, 108, 123, 129, 163, 165, 173, 211, 214, 219, 223, 227, 261, 273, 276, 301, 305, 326–328, 374 f., 385 f., 389, 391, 395 f., 400 f., 404, 406, 411, 432, 440 f., 444 f., 455, 460, 462, 482 f., 487, 489, 491, 493, 510, 519, 539, 541, 545, 561 f., 564 f., 571, 598, 623, 625, 628, 632, 638 f., 643–649, 651–653, 656 f., 669, 675, 677, 679, 689, 700, 707, 720, 726 f., 731, 741
  Vol. 2: 48, 51, 63, 75, 104, 112, 123, 149, 179, 199, 203 f., 228, 231, 245, 276, 291, 303, 310, 313 f., 340, 354, 359–361, 363, 368, 403, 410 f., 413, 416 f., 419–421, 423, 434, 498, 501, 510, 540, 544, 619, 622, 631, 640–642, 654, 665, 669, 674 f., 688, 708, 713, 765, 771, 774, 776, 782, 808, 825, 840, 844, 883, 888, 911, 924
  Vol. 3: 28, 132, 140, 157, 186, 194–197, 202, 215, 218, 239, 257 f., 271, 278, 293, 316 f., 322, 349, 446, 470, 489, 494, 503, 528, 552, 571, 576 f., 579, 582, 592, 602, 610–612, 617 f., 622, 624, 644, 670, 672, 697, 705, **719–725**, 735, 778, 825, 837 f., 848, **858 f.,** 864, 905, 955 f., 980, 995, 997, 1023, 1042, 1044, 1054, 1095–1097, 1099, 1102, 1109, 1113, 1122
Suffice **Vol. 2:** 342, 820
  Vol. 3: 726–730
Sufficiency **Vol. 2:** 429
  Vol. 3: 727 f.
Sufficient **Vol. 1:** 163, 248, 727 f.
  Vol. 2: 162, 238, 341
  Vol. 3: 315, **726–730**, 857
Suffocation **Vol. 1:** 393, 395
Suggestion **Vol. 1:** 61, 510, 544
  Vol. 2: 166
Suicide **Vol. 1:** 93, 432 f.
  Vol. 2: 659
Suit **Vol. 1:** 478, 536
Suitability **Vol. 1:** 536 f.
Suitable **Vol. 2:** 102, 105, **668 f.**
  Vol. 3: 349–351
Suitably **Vol. 3: 348 f.**
Sukkah **Vol. 3:** 812
Sully **Vol. 1:** 447
Sulphur **Vol. 1:** 657
Sum **Vol. 1:** 521, 598
  Vol. 2: 157
Sum up **Vol. 2:** 156 f., 163
Sumerian **Vol. 1:** 140
  Vol. 3: 782, 786
Sumerian king-lists **Vol. 3:** 564
Sumerian law **Vol. 3:** 95
Summer **Vol. 1:** 627, 724
  Vol. 2: 382

  Vol. 3: 269, 845
Summit **Vol. 1:** 165
Summon **Vol. 1:** 88, 270 f., 292 f., 295, 308, 331, 340, 342, 489, 492, 569, 570, 600, 638, 689, 719
  Vol. 2: 354, 358, 405
  Vol. 3: 68, **113 f.,** 1029
Sumptuous **Vol. 2: 484–486**
Sun **Vol. 1:** 124, 203, 252, 314, 420, 425, 449, 451, 515 f., 586 f., 627, 652 f., 728
  Vol. 2: 128, 191 f., 265, 289 f., 484, 487 f., 491, 493, 495 f., 622, 628, 690 f., 695, 889, 916
  Vol. 3: 443, **730–737**, 862, 1067 f.
Sun of righteousness **Vol. 3:** 731
Sun-cult **Vol. 1:** 631
Sun-god **Vol. 2:** 200
  Vol. 3: 264, 617
Sun-myth **Vol. 3:** 266
Sun-worship **Vol. 3:** 397
Sun-worshippers **Vol. 1:** 631
Sunburn **Vol. 1:** 652
Sunday **Vol. 1:** 631, 634
  Vol. 3: 412, 855
Sundial **Vol. 2:** 451, 628
  Vol. 3: 553, 846
Sunlight **Vol. 2:** 490
Sunrise **Vol. 1:** 665
  Vol. 3: 514
Sunset **Vol. 1:** 633
Superabundance **Vol. 1:** 729
  Vol. 2: 119
  Vol. 3: 918
Supererogation **Vol. 3:** 1053
Superficial **Vol. 3:** 105, 820
Superfluous **Vol. 1:** 266, 371, 728 f., 731
  Vol. 2: 487
  Vol. 3: 728
Superhuman **Vol. 1:** 450
  Vol. 3: 636
Superintend **Vol. 1:** 189
Superior **Vol. 1:** 588, 644, 659
  Vol. 2: 157, 160, 164, 166, 196, 267, 401, 433, 442, 510, 513, 533, 856, 859 f., 862, 877
  Vol. 3: 712, 714, 1063
Superiority **Vol. 1:** 301, 337, 356, 371, 386, 408 f., 427, 539, 650 f.
  Vol. 2: 158, 394, 431, 435, 447, 612, 694, 824
  Vol. 3: 474
Supernatural **Vol. 1:** 60, 104, 113, 122, 167, 413, 424, 504, 511, 607, 609, 647, 718
  Vol. 2: 166, 189, 268, 274, 326, 335, 364, 386, 477, 491, 556, 601, 603, 607
  Vol. 3: 103, 149, 328, 512–514, 516, 602, 640, 647, 691, 698, 706, 862, 965, 1073
Supernova **Vol. 2:** 558
  Vol. 3: 735
Superscription **Vol. 1:** 132, 392, 396
  Vol. 2: 289
  Vol. 3: 482–495
Supersede **Vol. 1:** 601, 631, 666
  Vol. 2: 447
  Vol. 3: 815
Superstition **Vol. 1:** 450, 453
  Vol. 2: 85, 560
Superstitious **Vol. 2:** 85

Supervise **Vol. 1:** 450
  Vol. 2: 327, 445
Supervisor **Vol. 2:** 191
Supper **Vol. 2: 520–538**
  Vol. 3: 732
Supper, great **Vol. 1:** 324
  Vol. 2: 358
Supper of God **Vol. 2:** 33
Supplant **Vol. 2:** 431
Supplement **Vol. 1:** 70
Suppliant **Vol. 1:** 612, 687
  Vol. 2: 74, 856–860, 863
  Vol. 3: 588
Supplication **Vol. 1:** 239, 320, 600
  Vol. 2: 91, 117, 149, 768, 855 f., **860–863,** 868
  Vol. 3: 211
Supply **Vol. 1:** 318, 731
  Vol. 2: 117
  Vol. 3: 771
Support **Vol. 1:** 115, 261, 288, 328, 474, 554, 614, 636, 658
  Vol. 2: 99, 146, 237, 263, 272, 311, 446, 448, 460, 834, 837
  Vol. 3: 144, 255, **544–549, 795,** 853, 964, 1053
Suppose **Vol. 1:** 61, 330, 475, 670
  Vol. 2: 44, 239
  Vol. 3: 821 f.
Suppress **Vol. 1:** 494, 502, 718
  Vol. 3: 1161
Suppress truth **Vol. 3:** 885
Supratemporal **Vol. 3:** 827
Supreme **Vol. 1:** 616, 668
  Vol. 2: 426
  Vol. 3: 716
Sure **Vol. 1:** 365, 591, 594, 596, 658–660, 663, 729
  Vol. 2: 243
Surety **Vol. 1:** 372, 374, 669
  Vol. 2: 40
Surface **Vol. 1:** 585, 587
Surmount **Vol. 1:** 71
Surname **Vol. 2: 648–656**
Surpass **Vol. 1:** 137, 650, 730, 740
Surplus **Vol. 1:** 728, 731
  Vol. 2: 130
  Vol. 3: 137
Surprise **Vol. 1:** 425, 466, 540
  Vol. 2: 382, 432, **621–626**
  Vol. 3: 624, 750
Surrender **Vol. 1:** 70, 223, 309, 335, 355, 417, 435, 455, 486, 499, 525, 561, 709, 715
  Vol. 2: 146, 198, 394, 405
  Vol. 3: 106, 164, 183, 196, 551, 572, 705
Surround **Vol. 1:** 405
  Vol. 3: 948, 950, 952
Surround with light **Vol. 2: 484–486**
Survival **Vol. 1:** 540, 592, 596, 687
  Vol. 3: 231, 274, 302
Survive **Vol. 2:** 83, 274, 309, 383, 412, 772
  Vol. 3: 247, 251, 253, 263
Survivor **Vol. 3:** 248–250
Susanna **Vol. 3:** 1059
Susceptibility **Vol. 2:** 675
Suspect **Vol. 1:** 414
Suspend **Vol. 1:** 523

Suspicion **Vol. 1:** 563
  Vol. 3: 820, 1119
Sustain **Vol. 1:** 549, 616
  Vol. 2: 101, 162, 866
  Vol. 3: 172, 1102
Sustainer **Vol. 2:** 74, 76
Sustenance **Vol. 1:** 84, 173, 249 f., 711
  Vol. 2: 264
  Vol. 3: 807
Swallow **Vol. 1:** 116, 173, 440, 470, 490, 651
  Vol. 2: 274
  Vol. 3: 267, 1112
Swamp **Vol. 1:** 688
  Vol. 3: 992
Swear **Vol. 1:** 203, 344, 346, 554, 659
  Vol. 2: 159, 301, 614, 650
  Vol. 3: 70, 183, 347, 429, 474, **737–743,** 785, 792, 840, 1018, 1038, 1053, 1113, 1163
Swear falsely **Vol. 3: 737–743**
Sweep **Vol. 3:** 102
Sweet **Vol. 1:** 202, 458, 480, 513
  Vol. 2: 211, 273, 293
Swell **Vol. 1:** 94, 107, 240
  Vol. 2: 462
Swift **Vol. 1:** 280
Swim **Vol. 2:** 412
Swindler **Vol. 3: 601–605**
Swine **Vol. 1:** 117, 672
  Vol. 3: 475, 985, 1011
Swineherd **Vol. 1:** 559
Swollen **Vol. 2:** 465
Swoon theory **Vol. 3:** 292
Sword **Vol. 1:** 109, 118, 272, 322, 377, 380, 407, 464, 513, 559, 655, 716
  Vol. 2: 98, 189, 367, 686, 795
  Vol. 3: 96, 590, 729, 747, **958–967,** 978, 1079, 1102, 1113
Sword of the Spirit **Vol. 3:** 966
Sycamine **Vol. 3:** 1012
Sychar **Vol. 3:** 457 f.
Syllable **Vol. 2:** 452
Syllogism **Vol. 3:** 1086
Symbol **Vol. 1:** 87, 115 f., 119–122, 126, 146, 148 f., 152, 156, 158 f., 171, 175, 185, 201, 203–205, 209, 225, 238 f., 241, 252, 254, 266, 280, 284, 294, 297, 316 f., 321, 351, 377, 389, 391, 420, 422, 448, 470, 489, 497, 507, 509 f., 512, 514, 516, 531 f., 577, 625, 629 f., 650, 652, 655, 724–726
  Vol. 2: 37, 96–98, 148 f., 151, 214, 270, 276, 294, 372, 376, 426, 482, 485, 495, 504, 539, 573 f., 580, 582, 585, 597, 607, 612, 626, 630, 632, 637, 648 f., 655, 679, 685–703, 711 f., 714, 738, 745 f., 804, 909, 916–918
  Vol. 3: 35, 47, 80, 104, 149, 159, 164, 211, 226, 237, 260, 266, 269, 334–336, 392, 397, 430, 433, 436, 444 f., 448, 459, 484, 486, 499, 501 f., 505, 522, 557, 559, 561, 581, 600, 620, 630, 634 f., 695, 706, 715, 718, 733, 736, 783, 788, 793, 795, 807, 851, 868, 918 f., 947, 961, 963, 965, 967, 987, 990, 1002 f., 1008 f., 1011, 1013 f., 1054, 1067 f., 1093, 1099, 1130, 1137, 1161 f.
Symbolic **Vol. 3:** 79, 87, 203, 922
Symbolize **Vol. 2:** 272 f., 275, 415

Symbolize (cont'd)
 Vol. 3: 948
Symmachus Vol. 1: 379, 382, 387
 Vol. 2: 141, 707
 Vol. 3: 453, 486
Symmetry Vol. 1: 206
 Vol. 2: 102
Sympathize Vol. 2: 123, 361, 594
 Vol. 3: 719–725
Sympathy Vol. 1: 220, 329
 Vol. 2: 117, 424, 598–600
 Vol. 3: 235, 758
Symptom Vol. 1: 445
Synagogue Vol. 1: 59, 67, 69, 128, 163, 166, 168,
 181, 194, 196, 199, 219, 245, 257, 291–307,
 321, 334, 347, 360 f., 395, 414, 453, 589 f.,
 607, 623 f., 628, 666, 738
 Vol. 2: 90, 118, 126, 155, 158–161, 174, 229,
 308, 311, 316, 333, 368, 437, 451, 590, 641,
 740, 799, 823, 825, 864 f.
 Vol. 3: 51, 56, 83, 87, 115, 179, 188, 220, 228,
 250, 348, 389, 396, 407, 409 f., 428, 441 f.,
 452, 458, 520, 545, 552, 589, 598 f., 671, 756,
 761, 785, 821, 867, 1020, 1058, 1168
Synagogue of the Olive Tree Vol. 3: 868
Synagogue of Satan Vol. 2: 314, 474
Synchronic linguistics Vol. 3: 1140
Synchrony Vol. 3: 1142
Syncretism Vol. 1: 58–61, 69, 487, 500, 595, 640
 Vol. 2: 201, 269, 306, 393 f., 453, 515, 895
 Vol. 3: 123, 827, 928, 1091
Synecdoche Vol. 1: 239 f.
Synergism Vol. 2: 119
Synod Vol. 1: 52
Synonym Vol. 2: 388
Synoptic criticism Vol. 1: 62
Synoptic Gospels Vol. 1: 67 f., 69
Syntyche Vol. 1: 344
 Vol. 3: 1164
Syracuse Vol. 1: 640
Syria Vol. 1: 121, 125, 133, 143, 189, 243, 634
 Vol. 2: 86, 125 f., 308, 372
 Vol. 3: 40, 84, 266, 635, 756
Syrian Antioch (→ Antioch)
Syrian church Vol. 2: 333
Syrians Vol. 3: 756
Syro-Canaanite Vol. 2: 375
Syro-Palestine Vol. 2: 320
Syrophoenician Vol. 1: 117
 Vol. 2: 126
 Vol. 3: 475, 980, 1059
System Vol. 1: 660, 700
 Vol. 2: 436
Systematization Vol. 3: 1078
Systematized doctrine Vol. 1: 702

Taber, C.R. Vol. 3: 1141
Taberah Vol. 2: 638
Tabernacle Vol. 1: 66, 114, 122, 252, 280, 380,
 735
 Vol. 2: 96 f., 189, 290, 294, 487, 637 f., 711,
 746, 889
 Vol. 3: 120, 156, 164 f., 317, 323, 397, 402,
 407, 418, 433 f., 436, 465, 550, 556, 593, 691,

781, 786 f., 792, 794 f., 811–815, 851, 888,
 1011, 1040
Tabitha Vol. 2: 596
 Vol. 3: 1065 f.
Table Vol. 1: 252, 586, 641
 Vol. 2: 272 f., 275 f., 516, 520–538, 556
 Vol. 3: 399, 424, 488, 588
Table of demons Vol. 2: 520
 Vol. 3: 1165
Table of the Lord Vol. 2: 522
Table of the presence Vol. 3: 812
Table of showbread Vol. 3: 814
Table-fellowship Vol. 2: 521 f.
Tables of stone Vol. 3: 815
Tablet Vol. 1: 243, 248
 Vol. 2: 192
 Vol. 3: 493, 702, 811, 1013, 1040, 1094
Tablets of destiny Vol. 2: 553
Taboo Vol. 2: 223 f., 236, 268, 270, 461, 552
 Vol. 3: 100
Tabor Vol. 3: 1010, 1012
Taheb Vol. 3: 147, 462
Tail Vol. 1: 508, 510
 Vol. 2: 158
Taint Vol. 1: 265, 641
 Vol. 2: 28
 Vol. 3: 756, 758
Take Vol. 1: 343, 533, 587
 Vol. 3: 253, 605, 744–751
Take advantage Vol. 3: 377
Take along Vol. 3: 747–751
Take apart Vol. 1: 533
Take aside Vol. 3: 747
Take away Vol. 1: 115, 225, 701 f.
 Vol. 2: 225, 359, 411, 606
 Vol. 3: 151, 489, 601–605
Take breath Vol. 3: 255
Take captive Vol. 3: 590 f.
Take care Vol. 1: 189
 Vol. 2: 90
Take counsel Vol. 2: 744
Take dimensions Vol. 3: 402–404
Take heart Vol. 1: 327
 Vol. 2: 360
Take heed Vol. 2: 178
Take hold Vol. 3: 859
Take in Vol. 3: 744–746
Take in vain Vol. 3: 342, 344
Take issue Vol. 1: 504
Take a long journey Vol. 2: 788–790
Take offence Vol. 1: 653
 Vol. 3: 516
Take on board Vol. 3: 749
Take out Vol. 1: 453
Take over Vol. 3: 747–751
Take pleasure in Vol. 3: 1018–1023
Take possession Vol. 1: 534, 635
 Vol. 2: 352
 Vol. 3: 633, 726–718, 747–751
Take prisoner Vol. 3: 824, 960
Take rest Vol. 3: 254–258
Take root Vol. 3: 865–870
Take seriously Vol. 3: 824
Take sides Vol. 1: 585
 Vol. 2: 617

567

Take time **Vol. 3: 839–845**
Take up **Vol. 2:** 238
   Vol. 3: 266, **744–751**
Take up cross **Vol. 1:** 455, 482
   Vol. 2: 420
   Vol. 3: 349
Take a wife **Vol. 2:** 578
Take with **Vol. 3: 747–751**
Taken up **Vol. 1:** 677
   Vol. 2: 203
Taking an oath **Vol. 3: 737–743**
Tale-bearer **Vol. 3:** 346
Tale-bearing **Vol. 3:** 346
Talent **Vol. 2:** 155, 216, 790, 838
   Vol. 3: 138, 141, 526, 703, 756
Talk **Vol. 1:** 550, 574
   Vol. 3: 1081–1119
Talmud **Vol. 1:** 58 f., 64, 67, **69,** 414
   Vol. 2: 125 f., 174, 309, 312, 583
   Vol. 3: 439
Talmud, Babylonian **Vol. 1:** 64, **69**
   Vol. 2: 43, 350
Talmud, Jerusalem (Palestinian) **Vol. 1:** 64, **69**
   Vol. 2: 308
Talmudic Judaism (→ Judaism, Talmudic)
Tamar **Vol. 2:** 212, 577
   Vol. 3: 356, 656, 1062
Tamarisk **Vol. 1:** 252
Tame **Vol. 1:** 495
   Vol. 2: 256, 412, 661, 899
Tammuz **Vol. 2:** 166
   Vol. 3: 104, 274 f.
Tamper **Vol. 3:** 886
Tangible **Vol. 1:** 679
Tannaim **Vol. 1:** 49, 67, **69**
Tannaitic **Vol. 1:** 51
Tares **Vol. 2:** 33, 488, 714, 834
   Vol. 3: 470, 523, 527, 627, 831
Targum **Vol. 1:** 51, 63, **69**
   Vol. 2: 309
   Vol. 3: 485–487, 494, 524, 610
Tarnish **Vol. 2:** 28
Tarquin **Vol. 1:** 314
Tarry **Vol. 2:** 773
Tarrying **Vol. 3: 224–229**
Tarshish **Vol. 3:** 1001
Tarski, A. **Vol. 3:** 897
Tarsus **Vol. 2:** 320, 328, 804, 848, 895
Tartarus **Vol. 2:** 682
   Vol. 3: 260
Task **Vol. 1:** 273, 331, 412, 476, 522, 533, 536, 544, 568 f., 583, 602, 610, 617, 624, 626, 650
   Vol. 2: 101, 121, 254, 263, 366, 668
   Vol. 3: 799, **1155–1158**
Taskmaster **Vol. 3:** 779
Taste **Vol. 1:** 201 f., 439, 458 f.
   Vol. 2: 27, 29, 194, **264–277,** 293, 718
   Vol. 3: 445, 809, 1078
Taste death **Vol. 2: 271,** 382
Tat son of Hermes **Vol. 3:** 1085
Tattoo **Vol. 2:** 572
   Vol. 3: 594
Tau **Vol. 2:** 572
Taught **Vol. 3: 759–765**

Taunt **Vol. 2:** 82, 263, 434
   Vol. 3: 202
Taurus **Vol. 2:** 688
Tawny **Vol. 1:** 205
Tax **Vol. 1:** 269 f., 537, 684, 687
   Vol. 2: 40, 62, 311, 326, 329, 624, 667, 728, 737, 813, 830, 850–852, 898
   Vol. 3: 192, 415, 444, 446, **751–759,** 851, 853, 855, 943, 979, 985, 1156, 1168, 1179
Tax census **Vol. 2:** 320
Tax-collector **Vol. 1:** 356, 488, 499
   Vol. 2: 272, 386, 417, 523, 549, 790, 795, 851
   Vol. 3: 106, 160 f., 361, 428, 558, 580, 603, 657, **751–759,** 790, 883, 920, 969, 980, 1062, 1157
Tax evasion **Vol. 2:** 222
Tax farmer **Vol. 3: 755–759**
Tax office **Vol. 3: 755–759**
Tax official **Vol. 3:** 756
Taxation **Vol. 3:** 606
Teach **Vol. 1:** 87, 164, 191, 197, 248, 340 f., 485 f., 488, 494, 502, 535, 568, 598 f., 620, 628
   Vol. 2: 113 f., 137, 140, 362, 367 f., 445, 453, 461, 472, 485, 608, 669, 719, 758
   Vol. 3: 54–56, 67, 79, 86, 112, 163, 228, 310, 493, 495, 501, 580, 675, 729, **759–780,** 791, 914, 935, **1026–1034,** 1058, 1063
Teach different (heretical) doctrine **Vol. 3: 766–768**
Teacher **Vol. 1:** 69, 90, 123, 132, 191 f., 198–200, 259, 280, 282, 287, 333, 480–482, 484–486, 490, 492, 515, 530, 533, 548, 572, 581, 598, 614, 617, 684, 708
   Vol. 2: 113 f., 151 f., 187, 262, 281, 309, 313 f., 358, 406, 430, 432, 440, 444, 535, 595, 669, 715, 721, 731
   Vol. 3: 44, 57, 59, 84, 88, 112, 115 f., 188, 447, 531, 588, 616, 629, **759–768, 771 f., 775–780,** 903, 1029, 1118 f., 1152
Teacher of the law **Vol. 2:** 49, **438–451**
   Vol. 3: 477–482, 765–768
Teacher of righteousness **Vol. 1:** 96, 598
   Vol. 3: 34, 80, 359, 367, 494, 503, 510, 610, 1120
Teaching **Vol. 1:** 55, 62, 69, 166, 171, 192, 220, 261, 263, 292, 305, 331, 335, 339, 347, 386, 400, 483, 486–488, 490 f., 495, 506, 530, 533 f., 539, 548, 558, 563, 566–568, 572, 577, 579, 589 f., 595, 599–604, 607, 623, 640, 642, 662, 669, 689, 702, 708 f., 720, 722, 730 f., 742
   Vol. 2: 36, 112, 118, 121, 123, 125, 132, 135, 147, 152, 155, 158 f., 164 f., 172, 177, 185, 235, 258, 280, 296, 315 f., 319, 327, 383, 406, 413, 432, 435, 437, 443 f., 462, 467, 550, 610, 623, 629, 640 f., 652, 671, 677, 708, 713, 718 f., 736, 743–760, 766, 768, 801, 833 f., 836, 843, 870–873, 879, 883, 889 f., 903–905, 908, 910 f., 914–917, 921, 930
   Vol. 3: 31, 56–61, 65, 85, 107, 123, 131, 181, 183, 185, 215, 224, 481, 509, 540–542, 632, 700, 704, 740, 748, **759–780,** 785, 791, 813, 820 f., 854, 867 f., 905, 930, 942, 987, 1020,

Teaching (cont'd)
1052, 1063, 1065–1067, 1081, 1106, 1109,
1162 f.
Teaching office **Vol. 3:** 768
Teaching in parables **Vol. 3:** 507
Teaching what is good **Vol. 3: 765–768**
Team **Vol. 1:** 648
Tear **Vol. 1:** 533
  Vol. 2: 189, 328
  Vol. 3: 543 f., 795
Tear clothes **Vol. 1:** 317
Tears **Vol. 1:** 471, 683
  Vol. 2: 178, 263, 416, 418, 631, 674
  Vol. 3: 268, 680, 1002
Tease **Vol. 2:** 432
Technical **Vol. 1:** 495, 722
Technical term **Vol. 2:** 363, 368, 457, 727, 743,
  764, 766, 783, 854, 862
  Vol. 3: 77, 102, 115, 146, 218, 317, 342, 366,
  373, 378, 501, 530 f., 534, 583, 603, 668, 717,
  746, 771, 794, 808, 854, 869, 871, 999, 1081,
  1087
Technique **Vol. 1:** 723
Tegea **Vol. 2:** 898
Tekel **Vol. 3:** 1160
Tekoa **Vol. 3:** 1092
Telchines **Vol. 2:** 552
Telemachus **Vol. 2:** 233
Teleological **Vol. 2:** 780
  Vol. 3: 331
Teleology **Vol. 1: 69**
Tell **Vol. 1:** 57, **573–584**
  Vol. 2: 108, 488, 648
  Vol. 3: 56
Tell el-Yehudieh **Vol. 2:** 331
Tell Nebi Yunus **Vol. 2:** 680
Tell Quyunjiq **Vol. 2:** 679
Telmessian oracle **Vol. 1:** 573
Temper **Vol. 1:** 107, 202
Temperament **Vol. 1:** 107, 540
  Vol. 2: 259
Temperance **Vol. 1:** 501
  Vol. 3: 354, 926
Temperate **Vol. 1:** 513 f., 671
  Vol. 3: 1065
Temperature **Vol. 1:** 318
Tempest **Vol. 1:** 653
  Vol. 3: 266
Tempestuous wind **Vol. 3:** 1000–1004
Temple **Vol. 1:** 53, 73, 75, 125, 174, 195, 210,
  221, 234 f., 245, 256, 269, 272, 274, 280, 293,
  295, 314, 321, 344, 360, 395 f., 413 f., 429,
  448, 467 f., 478, 497, 500, 530, 537, 555,
  586 f., 607, 626 f., 629, 632 f., 652, 661, 684,
  687 f., 700, 725, 735
  Vol. 2: 29 f., 38, 43, 77, 83, 96 f., 126, 173 f.,
  185, 190, 194, 199, 215, 217, 225 f., 228,
  230 f., **232–236,** 238, 247–249, 251, 253, 256,
  284–286, 290, 294, 296, 311 f., 321, 325–329,
  373, 379, 426, 437, 450, 467, 485, 487, 527,
  610, 624, 650 f., 698, 711, 713, 727, 730, 732,
  742, 754, 763, 768, 793, 795, 799 f., 830, 851,
  864, 866, 880, 885, 887, 904, 914–918, 920,
  927
  Vol. 3: 34–37, 39, 42, 78, 82, 101–104, 106 f.,
  116 f., 156 f., 160, 165, 173, 185 f., 189, 194,
  198, 207 f., 210 f., 213, 250, 258, 266, 269,
  317, 323, 343, 350, 366, 378, 380 f., 387,
  389–393, 402, 404 407–409, 424, 426–430,
  432 f., 435, 440, 451, 465, 469, 471, 478,
  483–485, 490, 494 f., 498, 509, 531, 543,
  550 f., 553, 557, 566, 589, 593, 605–607, 649,
  668 f., 674, 715, 735, 741, 752 f., 761 f., 764,
  781–797, 805–807, 810, 812, 814 f., 827 f.,
  853, 874, 908, 921, 941, 944 f., 947–949, 955,
  977, 986, 988, 1006, 1010, 1052, 1058,
  1070 f., 1096 f., 1122, 1148, 1154, 1162,
  1165, 1168
Temple of idol **Vol. 2: 284–286**
Temple robber **Vol. 2: 235**
Temple scribes **Vol. 3:** 478
Temple, second **Vol. 2:** 313
  Vol. 3: 788
Temple slaves **Vol. 2:** 311
Temple tax **Vol. 2:** 311, 326, 329, 823, 827, 851
  Vol. 3: 753 f., 792
Temple-keeper **Vol. 3: 796**
Temple-sweeper **Vol. 3:** 796
Temple, William **Vol. 3: 328,** 421
Temporal **Vol. 1:** 542, 667, 692, 734, 737
  Vol. 2: 36, 52, 54, 670, 674, 903
  Vol. 3: 827, 832, 848
Temporality **Vol. 1:** 500
Temporary **Vol. 1:** 408, 675 f., 687, 734, 739
  Vol. 2: 205, 207, 213, 220, 717
  Vol. 3: 228, 380, **833–839**
Tempt **Vol. 1:** 452, 466, 496, 563
  Vol. 2: 461, 776, 808
  Vol. 3: 476, 586, 725, **798–810,** 1014
Temptation **Vol. 1:** 244, 290, 304, 335, 384 f.,
  433, 457, 519, 540, 567, 597, 607, 625, 644,
  660, 727
  Vol. 2: 42, 95, 196, 240, 267, 269, 285, 289,
  307, 357, 361, 505, 664, 673, 706, 708, 721,
  779, 808, 863, 868, 871, 883 f., 893
  Vol. 3: 109, 470 f., 517, 536, 565, 569, 643,
  657–659, 693, 790, **798–810,** 838, 842, 845 f.,
  857, 945, 1007, 1010 f., 1017, 1052, 1096,
  1157
Temptation of Jesus **Vol. 1:** 125
  Vol. 2: 80, 82
Tempter **Vol. 1:** 599, 718
Tempting **Vol. 3: 798–808**
Ten **Vol. 1:** 54
  Vol. 2: 685, **692–694**
  Vol. 3: 851
Ten Commandments (→ Decalogue)
Ten lost tribes **Vol. 3:** 873
Ten virgins **Vol. 3:** 1072
Tenant **Vol. 1:** 640
  Vol. 2: 50, 301, 607
  Vol. 3: 641 f., 868, 920
Tend **Vol. 2:** 543
  Vol. 3: 564–568, 919
Tendency **Vol. 1:** 613, 619
  Vol. 2: 401
Tender **Vol. 1:** 240
Tenderhearted **Vol. 2: 599 f.**

Tenderly loving **Vol. 2: 538–547**
Tenet **Vol. 2:** 313
Tension **Vol. 1:** 423, 496, 502, 595, 599, 602–604, 624, 628, 738
   Vol. 2: 102, 239 f., 243, 245, 271, 306, 309, 312, 316, 367, 429, 448
   Vol. 3: 69, 596, 909
Tent **Vol. 1:** 294, 585, 684, 691
   Vol. 2: 40, 189, 226, 248, 253, 256, 467, 637, 727, 885
   Vol. 3: 120, 156, 163, 189, 198, 317, 323, 418, 424, 465, 550, 553, 569, 715, 781, 787, 797, **811–815,** 851, 888, 905, 941, 947, 1005
Tent of meeting **Vol. 1:** 294
   Vol. 2: 419, 423, 786, 811
Tent of testimony **Vol. 3:** 811, 1040
Tent-maker **Vol. 1:** 279
   Vol. 3: 811–815
Tenth **Vol. 2:** 590–592, **692–694**
   Vol. 3: 851–855
Teraphim **Vol. 2:** 555
Terminology **Vol. 2:** 403, 405
Terms **Vol. 1:** 366
Terracotta **Vol. 3:** 913
Terrain **Vol. 1:** 520
   Vol. 2: 324
Terrible **Vol. 1:** 611, 621 f.
   Vol. 2: 197, 225, 622, 648
   Vol. 3: 317–324
Terrify **Vol. 1:** 527 f.
   Vol. 2: 287, 621, 642
   Vol. 3: 873
Territory **Vol. 1:** 519
   Vol. 2: 303, 319
Terror **Vol. 1:** 224, 430, 422, 431 f., 527, 529, 610, 621 f., 685
   Vol. 2: 53, 91, 202, 205, 266, 426, 621
   Vol. 3: 563, 848
Terrorize **Vol. 1:** 610
Tertullian **Vol. 1:** 51, 117, 251, 256, 467, 648
   Vol. 2: 506, 869
Tertullus **Vol. 1:** 695
   Vol. 2: 258, 707
Test **Vol. 1:** 188, 347, 390, 414, 516, 562, 567, 653, 656 f., 679, 731
   Vol. 2: 140, 182 f., 237, 272, 289, 299, 370, 583, 629, 825, 858
   Vol. 3: 124, 724, **798–810,** 818, 849, 937, 1052
Testament **Vol. 1:** 332, 365
   Vol. 3: 487
Testament of Levi **Vol. 1:** 155
Testaments of the Twelve Patriarchs **Vol. 1:** 66, 124, 155, 233, 468
   Vol. 3: 272, 871
Testator **Vol. 1:** 371
Tested **Vol. 1:** 596
   Vol. 3: 808–810
Testify **Vol. 1:** 684
   Vol. 2: 114, 297, 353
   Vol. 3: 326, 489, **1038–1050**
Testify against **Vol. 3: 1038–1050**
Testify in support **Vol. 3:** 1038
Testifying **Vol. 3: 1038–1050**
Testimonia **Vol. 3:** 65 f., 368

Testimony **Vol. 1:** 122, 151, 200, 248, 266, 346, 350, 402, 406, 445, 597 f., 603, 639, 680, 731
   Vol. 2: 64, 73 f., 77, 239, 332, 396, 443, 448, 461, 559, 630, 686, 701, 736, 775
   Vol. 3: 53, 71, 82, 187, 198, 246, 253, 276 f., 290, 347, 356, 454, 456, 474, 493, 630, 651, 700, 706, 740, 769, 773, 824, 880, 938, 954, 967, **1038–1050**
Testing **Vol. 3: 808–810**
Tests of life **Vol. 3:** 703
Tether **Vol. 3: 591 f.**
Tetradrachma **Vol. 2:** 851
Tetragrammaton **Vol. 1:** 71 f.
   Vol. 2: 512 f., 652
   Vol. 3: 1181
Tetrarch **Vol. 2:** 550
Text **Vol. 1:** 63, 68–71, 254
   Vol. 2: 309, 869
   Vol. 3: 488
Textual criticism (→ Criticism, textual)
Textual variants **Vol. 3:** 488, 494
Textus receptus **Vol. 1: 70**
Thais **Vol. 1:** 469
Thanatos **Vol. 3:** 984
Thank **Vol. 1:** 206, 213, 278, 344 f., 381, 384, 413, 492
   Vol. 2: 855, 862, 868, 885
   Vol. 3: 233, **816–819**
Thank-offering **Vol. 3:** 208, **422 f.**
Thankful **Vol. 1:** 433, 685
   Vol. 2: 353, 874
   Vol. 3: 816–819
Thankfulness **Vol. 2:** 115, 121, 268, 360
Thanks **Vol. 2:** 115, 121, 261, 353, 421, 654, 666, 806, 866
   Vol. 3: 105, 243, 391, 422, 425, 519, **816–819,** 853
Thanksgiving **Vol. 1:** 99, 213, 227, 247, 278, 385, 597, 609, 650, 730 f.
   Vol. 2: 131, 166 f., 260, 275, 447, 456, 517, 521, 631, 823, 855 f., 862 f., 868, 873–875, 877 f.
   Vol. 3: 244, 424, 436, 640, 670, 673–675, 750, **816–819,** 828, 997, 1080
Theatre **Vol. 2:** 233, 458, 467 f.
   Vol. 3: 520 f.
Theatrical **Vol. 1:** 590
Thebes **Vol. 2:** 233
Thebez **Vol. 3:** 394
Theft **Vol. 2:** 317, 572
   Vol. 3: 377, 448, 574
Theism **Vol. 1: 70,** 71
Theistic **Vol. 1: 70**
Theme of Scripture **Vol. 1:** 59
Theocentric **Vol. 2:** 260
Theocracy **Vol. 1:** 426
   Vol. 2: 327
Theocratic **Vol. 1:** 425
   Vol. 2: 325, 374
Theocritus **Vol. 3:** 564
Theodation **Vol. 1:** 83, 379, 539
   Vol. 2: 707
   Vol. 3: 486, 494
Theognis **Vol. 2:** 239

Theologian **Vol. 3:** 83
Theological **Vol. 3:** 53
Theological reflection **Vol. 1:** 65
Theological thought **Vol. 1:** 70
Theologoumenon **Vol. 1: 70**
Theology **Vol. 2:** 309
  Vol. 3: 1081
Theology, comparative **Vol. 1:** 60
Theology in Greek NT **Vol. 3: 1171–1215**
Theology of hope **Vol. 3: 968–970**
Theology of liberation **Vol. 3: 972–974**
Theology, natural (→ Natural theology)
Theology of Scripture **Vol. 3:** 494 f.
Theology, systematic **Vol. 2:** 908 f.
Theomorphic **Vol. 3:** 514
Theophany **Vol. 1:** 655, 661
  Vol. 2: 68, 225, 281, 430, 485, 636, 735
  Vol. 3: 266, 318, 330, 398, 514, 517, 874,
  1001, 1005
Theophilus **Vol. 1:** 663
  Vol. 2: 86
Theophrastus **Vol. 1:** 654
Theoretical **Vol. 1:** 595
  Vol. 2: 261, 390, 399, 401
Theory **Vol. 2:** 342
Theory of reference **Vol. 3:** 1128
Therapeutae **Vol. 2:** 785
Therapy **Vol. 2:** 164
Thereafter **Vol. 3: 952–956**
Thermopylae **Vol. 3:** 840, 1119
Thespiae **Vol. 1:** 476
Thessalonians **Vol. 1:** 55, 229, 282, 298 f., 406,
  731
  Vol. 2: 131, 144, 179, 774 f., 901
  Vol. 3: 112, 230, 214, 888, 940, 955, 1064
Thessalonica **Vol. 1:** 261, 269, 298, 329
  Vol. 2: 221, 243, 302, 380, 623, 729, 789, 804,
  809, 818
  Vol. 3: 453, 955, 1063, 1065, 1112
Theudas **Vol. 1:** 591
  Vol. 2: 34
  Vol. 3: 378
Thick **Vol. 2:** 154
Thicken **Vol. 2:** 153
Thief **Vol. 1:** 323, 420 f., 425, 572
  Vol. 2: 59, 415, 433, 510, 831, 920, 926
  Vol. 3: 118, 201, **377–379**, 567, 750, 756, 848
Thin **Vol. 2:** 822
Thing **Vol. 3: 1119–1123, 1147–1152, 1155–1158**
Think **Vol. 1:** 106, 276, 330, 461, 472, 528 f.,
  552, 589, 693, 727, 730
  Vol. 2: 44, 72, 181 f., 239, 259, 393, 399,
  616–620
  Vol. 3: 133, 230, 681, **747–751, 820–826**, 1036
Think highly **Vol. 2:** 198
Think ill **Vol. 2:** 364
Think out **Vol. 3:** 759
Think worthy **Vol. 3:** 348 f.
Thinker **Vol. 1:** 484
Third **Vol. 1:** 666
  Vol. 2: 687 f., 739
Third day **Vol. 2:** 63, **687,** 893
  Vol. 3: 267, 287
Third heaven **Vol. 2:** 688, 762

Third hour **Vol. 2:** 685
Thirst **Vol. 1:** 217, 546, 653, 671 f., 683
  Vol. 2: 28, **264–277,** 349, 478
  Vol. 3: 360, 677, 680, 986, 988
Thirsty **Vol. 2:** 157, **264–277**
  Vol. 3: 359
Thistles **Vol. 1:** 416, **721–728**
  Vol. 3: 809
Thomas **Vol. 1:** 141
  Vol. 2: 81, 515
  Vol. 3: 289
Thomasius, Gottfried **Vol. 1:** 548 f.
Thomism **Vol. 1:** 65
Thorn **Vol. 1:** 163, 226, 406, 416, 457, 460, 674,
  721–728, 743
  Vol. 3: 182, 257, 268, 809, 950
Thorn in the flesh **Vol. 1:** 467, 726 f.
  Vol. 2: 762
  Vol. 3: 40, 471, 714, 728, 802, 814, 857, 995,
  998
Thoth **Vol. 1:** 60
  Vol. 2: 554, 556, 635
  Vol. 3: 1088
Thought **Vol. 1:** 105 f., 230, 322, 350, 357, 448,
  456, 457, 469, 509, 528, 551 f., 561, 567,
  579–581, 587, 679 f., 693, 695, 711
  Vol. 2: 94, 158, 179 f., 182, 216, 260, 392 f.,
  442, 591
  Vol. 3: **122–133,** 360, 534, 677 f., 680, 682,
  689, **820–826,** 894, 1027
Thought-patterns **Vol. 3:** 334
Thought-word **Vol. 3:** 335
Thoughtful **Vol. 1:** 502
  Vol. 2: 103, 256, **616–620**
Thoughtlessness **Vol. 3:** 439
Thousand **Vol. 1:** 52
  Vol. 2: 697–703
Thousand years **Vol. 1:** 508, 649
  Vol. 2: 64, 136, 205, 207, 389, 697, 887
  Vol. 3: 260, 277
Thrace **Vol. 2:** 849
Thracian **Vol. 3:** 28
Thrash **Vol. 3:** 778
Threat **Vol. 1:** 416, 422, 426, 430, 433, 451,
  459 f., 499, 501, 508 f., 512, 519, 524, 544,
  562, 594, 611, 626, 675, 678, 688, 731
  Vol. 2: 63, 86, 160, 209, 262, 267, 307, 320,
  351, 357, 413, 440, 530, 706
  Vol. 3: 53, 149, 205, 209, 212, 469, 711, 928,
  987, 1051, 1103
Threaten **Vol. 3:** 103, 204, 391, 442, 556, 566,
  693, 982 f., 986, 1008
Three **Vol. 2: 686 f.,** 748, 769
  Vol. 3: 657, 851
Three days **Vol. 1:** 395
  Vol. 2: 252, 351, 680, 687 f., 893
  Vol. 3: 211, 343
Three and a half **Vol. 2:** 686, **688**
Three years and six months **Vol. 2: 688**
Three-decker universe **Vol. 2:** 645
Threefold **Vol. 2:** 687
Threshing **Vol. 3:** 526 f.
Threshing-floor **Vol. 2:** 233, 411
  Vol. 3: 787, 853

571

Threshold **Vol. 1:** 613
Throat **Vol. 1:** 241
  Vol. 2: 28
  Vol. 3: 679
Throne **Vol. 1:** 102, 116, 122, 185, 198, 200, 386, 426 f., 482, 508, 656
  Vol. 2: 92, 96, 109, 123, 146 f., 186, 191, 201, 369, 376 f., 379, 428, **601–616,** 701
  Vol. 3: 180, 258, 271, 588 f., 716, 988, 1003, 1098
Throne of David **Vol. 3:** 652
Throne of glory **Vol. 2:** 612, 614
Throne of God **Vol. 1:** 101, 103, 204, 279 f., 304, 510, 654
  Vol. 2: 45, 74, 193–195, 207, 225, 326, 570, **612–614,** 763, 801
  Vol. 3: 117, 156, 277, 429, 988, 1003
Throne of grace **Vol. 1:** 322
  Vol. 2: 123, 614
Throne-chariot **Vol. 1:** 280
Throng **Vol. 1:** 731
  Vol. 2: 653, 801 f.
Throw **Vol. 1:** 70, 376, 508, 520, 608
  Vol. 2: 382
  Vol. 3: 468
Throw alongside **Vol. 2: 743–756**
Throw away **Vol. 1:** 479
Throw into disorder **Vol. 2: 621–626**
  Vol. 3: 709 f.
Throw up palisade **Vol. 3: 959–967**
Thucydidean model **Vol. 3:** 64
Thucydides **Vol. 2:** 643
Thunder **Vol. 1:** 108
  Vol. 2: 215, 652 f., 691
  Vol. 3: 113, 500, **1000–1004,** 1013
Thunderbolt **Vol. 2:** 628
Thunderstorm **Vol. 2:** 628
  Vol. 3: 984
Thursday lections **Vol. 1:** 245
Thut-mose III **Vol. 2:** 200
Thutmosis **Vol. 2:** 635
Thwart **Vol. 1:** 552
  Vol. 2: 220
Thyatira **Vol. 1:** 407
  Vol. 2: 582, 677 f., 775
  Vol. 3: 432, 765, 913, 1067
Tiamat **Vol. 1:** 523
  Vol. 2: 200, 553
Tiberias **Vol. 3:** 441 f.
Tiberius **Vol. 2:** 511, 850
Tide **Vol. 3:** 733
Tidings **Vol. 1:** 239, 576
  Vol. 2: 107–115
  Vol. 3: 45
Tie **Vol. 1:** 171, 289, 482, 493, 538, 619, 626, 636, 690
  Vol. 2: 402
Tie around **Vol. 3: 120 f.**
Tigris **Vol. 2:** 678
  Vol. 3: 986
Till **Vol. 1:** 381
  Vol. 3: 119
Tillich, Paul **Vol. 3:** 335, 1137
Timber **Vol. 3:** 952

Time **Vol. 1:** 86, 93, 102, 124, 164–167, 203, 236, 268; 294, 321 f., 325 f., 390, 397, 420 f., 423, 476 f., 521, 523 f., 526, 601, 624, 626 f., 629, 632, 638, 697, 711, 718 f., 724, 728, 732, 734 f., 737 f.
  Vol. 2: 37, 52, 56, 61 f., 64 f., 69 f., 106, 108, 132, 136, 158, 187, 205, 255 f., 270, 272, 316, 366, 397, 404, 429, 442, 483, 497, 568, 609, 658, 698, 703, 749, 809, 886, 899, 906 f., 919, 927 f., 931
  Vol. 3: 99, 123, 206, 236, 252, 276, 279 f., 292, 301, 312, 317, 321, 412, 504, 729, 733 f., 737, **826–849,** 1041
Time-lag **Vol. 3:** 774
Time-limit **Vol. 1:** 477
Time-scale **Vol. 2:** 910, 915
Timeless **Vol. 1:** 703
  Vol. 2: 590
  Vol. 3: 827, 830, 875
Timely occurrence **Vol. 3:** 845
Times of the Gentiles **Vol. 1:** 737
  Vol. 2: 37
  Vol. 3: 837
Times of ignorance **Vol. 3:** 844
Times of refreshing **Vol. 3:** 148, 686
Times and seasons **Vol. 2:** 75
Timetable **Vol. 2:** 384, 892
Timidity **Vol. 1:** 622 f.
  Vol. 3: 993–996
Timnah **Vol. 2:** 97
Timothy **Vol. 1:** 65, 83, 160, 200, 286, 310, 337, 341, 559, 570, 684
  Vol. 2: 114, 135, 138, 152, 451, 499, 644, 770, 809
  Vol. 3: 31, 230, 241, 320, 431, 491, 765, 768, 809, 903, 915, 922, 934, 955, 963, 1047, 1067, 1070
Tin **Vol. 2:** 96
  Vol. 3: 392
Tip the scales **Vol. 3:** 348
Tired **Vol. 1:** 262, 548, 561, 563
Tiro, Marcus Tullius **Vol. 3:** 757
Tishbe **Vol. 1:** 543
Tishri **Vol. 1:** 626
  Vol. 3: 813
Tithe **Vol. 1:** 80, 116
  Vol. 2: 211, 466, 590–592, **692–694,** 737, 811, 813, 823, 851
  Vol. 3: 41, 416, 424, 748, **851–855,** 1053, 1074
Titius Justus **Vol. 1:** 361
Title **Vol. 1:** 66, 188 f., 191, 193, 197, 199 f., 220, 255 f., 273, 281, 297, 304, 375, 469, 560, 616 f., 619, 647, 665–669, 708
  Vol. 2: 105, 126, 147, 231, 233 f., 254, 257, 305, 330, 332, 338, 340 f., 343, 372, 375 f., 378, 510 f., 514, 651, 687, 797, 878
  Vol. 3: 40, 83, 115, 177, 187, 217, 220 f., 233, 318 f., 462, 477, 485, 509, 564–566, 568, 594 f., 604, 607, 611, 619–622, 625, 631 f., 636, 643 f., 648, 651 f., 656, 659, 673, 704, 716 f., 767 f., 796, 940, 953, 960, 1057, 1060, 1147, 1152, 1167
Titles of the Psalms **Vol. 3:** 239
Tittle **Vol. 3:** 182

Titus **Vol. 1:** 65, 130, 286, 310, 571
  Vol. 2: 360, 600, 826, 899
  Vol. 3: 203, 253, 952
Titus, emperor **Vol. 1:** 72
  Vol. 3: 789
Tobias **Vol. 1:** 218, 479, 734
Tobit **Vol. 1:** 50, 212, 345, 626
  Vol. 3: 873
Today **Vol. 1:** 179, 251, 738
  Vol. 2: 63, 155, 242, 892
  Vol. 3: 826, **833–839,** 841, 844
Together **Vol. 2:** 500
  Vol. 3: 908
Tohoroth **Vol. 3:** 989
Toil **Vol. 1:** 115, 173, 209, 260–263, 546, 564 f.,
  647, 728
  Vol. 2: 478, 890
  Vol. 3: 953
Token **Vol. 1:** 655
  Vol. 2: 159, 626, 674
Tolerable **Vol. 1:** 431
  Vol. 2: **765–767**
Toleration **Vol. 1:** 499
Toll **Vol. 3:** **751–759**
Toll on fish **Vol. 3:** 757
Tomb **Vol. 1:** 174, 204 f., **263–266,** 623
  Vol. 2: 30, 146, 351, 526, 573
  Vol. 3: 239, 246, 268, **282 f.,** 286–288, 290–
  293, 296, 301, 360, 378, 380, 382, 557, 663,
  947, 1053, 1060
Tomorrow **Vol. 1:** 251, 597
  Vol. 2: 63, 832
  Vol. 3: 838
Tone **Vol. 3:** 113
Tongue **Vol. 1:** 118, 175, 182, 201, 231, 382,
  418, 530, 532, 564, 579, 656, 735
  Vol. 2: 28, 125, 349, 426, 505, 661, 727, 785,
  928
  Vol. 3: 109, 449, 576, 860, 866, **1078–1123**
Tongues, gift of **Vol. 1:** 103, 198, 300, 723, 739
  Vol. 2: 121, 222, 456, 883
  Vol. 3: 113
Tongues, interpretation of **Vol. 2:** 121
Tongues, speaking in **Vol. 1:** 300, 528 f., 581 f.
  Vol. 2: 97, 121, 222, 253, 446, 457, **739–742,**
  785 f.
  Vol. 3: 75, 110, 112, 119, 129 f., 505, 672,
  699 f., 770 f., 819, 962, **1078–1081,** 1113
Toothache **Vol. 3:** 444
Top **Vol. 2:** 157
Topaz **Vol. 3:** 395 f.
Torah **Vol. 1:** 62, 64–67, 69, **70,** 83, 180, 230,
  243–245, 316, 374, 405, 416, 433, 459, 481,
  484–486, 539, 597, 617, 619, 656, 665, 668
  Vol. 2: 174, 187, 209, 226–228, 234, 281, 397,
  432, 442, 446, 452, 462, 493, 540, 542, 544,
  592, 603, 608, 660, 665, 677, 730, 76:, 791,
  798, 811–813, 824, 848, 865
  Vol. 3: 33 f., 105 f., 115, 157, 169, 184, 201,
  210, 251, 264, 277, 311, 428, 442, 444, 453,
  461, 479 f., 485, 487 f., 502, 531, 616, 748,
  753, 761, 763, 767, 777, 783, 914, 987, 1029,
  1040, 1058, 1095, 1103, 1107 f., 1116, 1118,
  1121 f., 1154, 1161 f.

Torch **Vol. 1:** 656
  Vol. 2: **484–486,** 490
  Vol. 3: 736, 739
Torch-bearer **Vol. 2:** 578
Torch races **Vol. 2:** 490
Torment **Vol. 1:** 161, 163 f., 461, 612, 655, 710
  Vol. 2: 421
  Vol. 3: 99, 474, 682, 725, **855–859,** 996
Torrance, T.F. **Vol. 3:** 900 f.
Torso **Vol. 1:** 232
Torts **Vol. 3:** 95
Torture **Vol. 1:** 163, 389–391, 393, 395, 466,
  511, 646, 656
  Vol. 2: 157
  Vol. 3: 200, 260, **855 f.,** 1039
Torturer **Vol. 3:** 758, **855 f.**
Torturing **Vol. 3:** **855 f.**
Tosefta **Vol. 1:** **70**
Tossing **Vol. 3:** **558–560**
Total **Vol. 2:** 683
Totality **Vol. 1:** 95–97, 301, 303, 501, 702, 740
  Vol. 2: 53, 59 f., 181, 313, 688, 690
  Vol. 3: 234, 866, 1079
Totality transfer **Vol. 3:** 1141
Totter **Vol. 3:** **558–560**
Touch **Vol. 1:** 121, 207, 241
  Vol. 2: 167, 212, 270, 282, 560
  Vol. 3: 211, 313, 717, 749, **859–861,** 1071,
  1162
Touchstone **Vol. 2:** 314
  Vol. 3: 855
Toughness **Vol. 1:** 658
Toulmin, S. **Vol. 3:** 1136
Tower **Vol. 1:** 272
  Vol. 2: 157, 189, 369
  Vol. 3: 341, 782, 787
Town **Vol. 1:** 520, 665, 689
  Vol. 2: 363
  Vol. 3: 1006
Town clerk **Vol. 1:** 578
  Vol. 2: 235
  Vol. 3: 480
Townsmen **Vol. 2:** 822
Trace **Vol. 1:** 71
  Vol. 2: 291
  Vol. 3: 532, 904
Trace descent **Vol. 2:** 35
Track down **Vol. 3:** 532
Tractate **Vol. 1:** 64, 70
Trade **Vol. 1:** 267 f., **279,** 319, 419, 484, 558, 688
  Vol. 2: 39, 125, 235 f., 294, 303, 475, 841
  Vol. 3: 139, 606, 758, 910, 919, **1155–1158**
Trade-guild **Vol. 2:** 678
  Vol. 3: 910
Trader **Vol. 3:** 1054
Tradition **Vol. 1:** 57, 59 f., 63, 69, **70 f.,** 99, 102,
  116, 129, 131, 134 f., 153, 171, 194–196, 199,
  209, 216 f., 247, 250, 252, 278, 289, 297,
  304 f., 309, 332, 335, 346, 359, 394–396, 403,
  425, 473, 482, 484–487, 489 f., 499 f., 502,
  506, 509, 531, 539, 543–545, 580 f., 585,
  595–600, 602–604, 620, 625, 628, 630–632,
  641, 657, 707, 730, 739
  Vol. 2: 37, 43, 80, 85, 125, 132 f., 135, 144,

171, 191, 219, 234, 237, 269, 277, 313, 315, 327, 331, 333, 337 f., 340–342, 367 f., 372, 375, 379, 385 f., 405, 436 f., 439, 453, 526, 530 f., 544, 560, 635, 640, 652 f., 674, 677, 684, 688, 692, 697, 714–716, 718, 748, 780, 784–786, 811–813, 824, 888, 894, 904, 913 f., 921, 926 f.
Vol. 3: 40, 44, 55, 58 f., 61 f., 65, 80, 85, 97, 184 f., 221, 235–238, 241, 261, 270, 283, 285–287, 301, 321, 333, 360, 369, 372, 384, 401, 408, 458 f., 462, 465, 479–481, 484–490, 493, 502 f., 522, 584, 590, 604, 610, 614–618, 621 f., 624–629, 633 f., 637–640, 642, 647–650, 652, 654–657, 695, 697, 702, 706, 717, 748, 751, **759–780**, 784, 836, 872, 909, 921, 930 f., 942, 944 f., 1053, 1073, 1091–1093, 1110, 1135, 1162, 1167
Tradition criticism **Vol. 3:** 58
Tradition history **Vol. 1:** 70, **71**
Tradition, oral **Vol. 1:** 57 f., 71
Tragedy **Vol. 1:** 687
Vol. 2: 318, 430 f., 594
Tragic **Vol. 1:** 551
Train **Vol. 1:** 312 f.
Vol. 2: 122, 391
Vol. 3: 759–780
Training **Vol. 1:** 462, 481
Vol. 2: 141
Vol. 3: 365, **759–780**
Trait **Vol. 2:** 233, 407
Traitor **Vol. 2:** 531
Trajan **Vol. 2:** 308 f., 316
Vol. 3: 789
Trample **Vol. 1:** 109, 117
Vol. 2: 329
Vol. 3: 404, 943
Trance **Vol. 1:** 527 f.
Vol. 2: 176
Vol. 3: 77
Tranquility **Vol. 2:** 181
Vol. 3: 111
Transaction **Vol. 1:** 664, 721
Vol. 3: 1039
Transcend **Vol. 1:** 602, 625, 716
Vol. 2: 337, 873
Transcendence **Vol. 1: 71,** 101, 495, 679
Vol. 2: 195, 214, 436, 539, 613 f.
Vol. 3: 1116 f.
Transcendent **Vol. 1:** 70, 204, 360, 363, 380, 383, 422, 502, 521, 734
Vol. 2: 56, 66, 70–72, 74, 78, 376 f., 386, 403, 602, 621, 726, 834
Vol. 3: 328, 514
Transfer **Vol. 1:** 208 f., 699, 701
Vol. 2: 151, 226, 311, 316–318, 325, 335 f., 376, 553
Vol. 3: 151, 498, **601–605**
Transfiguration **Vol. 1:** 204, 290, 335, 406, 527, 541, 545, 587, 623, 659, 668, 708
Vol. 2: 48, 176, 271, 486, 493, 559, 640, 686, 819
Vol. 3: 48, 114, 298, 506, 555, 611, 731, 812, 848, **861–864**, 1003, 1010, 1012
Transfigure **Vol. 2:** 46, 606

Vol. 3: 272, **861–864**
Transform **Vol. 1:** 223, 375, 397, 600 f., 647, 705, 708
Vol. 2: 48, 207, 245, 263, 266, 288, 312, 316, 673
Vol. 3: 130, 729, **861–864**, 970
Transformation **Vol. 1:** 355, 470, 492, 539, 602, 643, 654, 705 f., 708–710
Vol. 2: 201, 263, 337, 398, 482, 606, 741, 831, 924
Vol. 3: 271, 278, 293, 304 f., 699, 701, **861–864,** 886, 1023, 1142
Transgress **Vol. 1:** 606, 729
Vol. 2: 123, 141, 144
Vol. 3: 583–585
Transgression **Vol. 1:** 83, 85 f., 97, 112, 322, 345, 353, 355, 357, 385, 434, 446 f., 452, 659, 699
Vol. 2: 71, 168, 368, 449, 463, 586, 867, 893
Vol. 3: 49, 93, 156, 169, 173, 200, 202, 269, 342, 359, 573 f., **577–586**
Transgressor **Vol. 1:** 85, 97, 463
Vol. 2: 445, 463, 479, 660
Vol. 3: 195, **583–585**
Transience **Vol. 1:** 406, 433
Vol. 2: 714
Vol. 3: 840, 845, 1101, 1117
Transient **Vol. 1:** 73, 316, 379, 444, 458, 515, 524, 526, 587
Vol. 2: 211, 253, 393, 480, 489, 844
Vol. 3: 260, 277, 827
Transition **Vol. 1:** 711
Transitional **Vol. 2:** 187
Vol. 3: 548
Transitoriness **Vol. 1:** 119, 222, 277, 337, 411, 552, 671, 673
Vol. 2: 304, 357, 420, 498, 564 f., 715
Vol. 3: 359, 555, 811
Transitory **Vol. 3:** 224 f., 229, 571, **833–839**
Transjordan **Vol. 1:** 543
Translation **Vol. 1:** 57, 69, 71, 433, 484, 578–582
Vol. 2: 125, 202, 219, 357, 627
Vol. 3: 75, 259, 264, 266, 494, 602, 615, 747, 761, 1137, 1141 f.
Translator **Vol. 1:** 580, 582
Vol. 2: 335
Transmigration of souls **Vol. 1:** 432, 594
Vol. 3: 259–261, 677, 679
Transmission **Vol. 2:** 338, 367 f., 748
Transmit **Vol. 1:** 735
Vol. 2: 161, 362
Vol. 3: 398, **772–775**
Transmute **Vol. 3:** 273
Transparency **Vol. 3:** 398
Transplant **Vol. 3:** 867, 918
Transubstantiation **Vol. 3:** 244, 337
Trap **Vol. 2:** 705, 707 f.
Vol. 3: 119, 747
Travail **Vol. 1:** 186 f., 411, 708
Vol. 2: 243, 423
Vol. 3: 180, 204, 260, 722, **857 f.**
Travel **Vol. 1:** 209, 268, 682, 727
Vol. 2: 788
Vol. 3: 945–947, 1155
Traveller **Vol. 1:** 117, 407, 520

Traveller (cont'd)
  Vol. 3: 352, 560, 1169
Travelling preachers Vol. 2: 401
Traverse Vol. 3: 402
Treachery Vol. 1: 241, 461, 725
Tread Vol. 1: 109, 510, 658
  Vol. 2: 358
  Vol. 3: 943-945
Treason Vol. 1: 270, 331, 392
Treasure Vol. 1: 566, 638, 647, 710
  Vol. 2: 28, 193, 215-217, 381, 386, 714 f., 795,
  829-853
  Vol. 3: 141, 184, 253, 262, 378, 380, 528, 912,
  914, 1032
Treasure-box Vol. 2: 829-836
Treasure-house Vol. 2: 191, 829
Treasured Vol. 1: 536
Treasurer Vol. 1: 560
  Vol. 2: 254, 730
  Vol. 3: 35
Treasures of darkness Vol. 2: 830
Treasury Vol. 2: 43, 475, 821
  Vol. 3: 498, 755, 757, 795 f., 955
Treasury room Vol. 3: 795 f.
Treat as just Vol. 3: 352-377
Treat as righteous Vol. 3: 352-377
Treatment Vol. 1: 119, 637, 670, 686
  Vol. 2: 99, 164, 312, 450
Treaty Vol. 1: 74, 189, 344, 594
  Vol. 2: 521, 879
  Vol. 3: 739
Tree Vol. 1: 120, 181, 234, 265, 389-405, 443,
  515, 520, 565, 652, 656, 722-725, 743
  Vol. 2: 199, 285, 293, 429, 708, 763
  Vol. 3: 248, 553-555, 557, 599, 865-870, 922
Tree of knowledge Vol. 1: 85
  Vol. 2: 271, 761, 889
  Vol. 3: 860
Tree of life Vol. 1: 279, 389 f., 722 f.
  Vol. 2: 280, 304, 482, 761, 763
  Vol. 3: 866, 868, 921, 986
Tremble Vol. 1: 622, 661
  Vol. 2: 876
  Vol. 3: 324, 557
Trembling Vol. 1: 622 f., 685
  Vol. 2: 91, 434, 819
Trent, council of Vol. 1: 71
  Vol. 2: 219
Trepidation Vol. 2: 92
Trespass Vol. 1: 333, 402, 437, 701, 730
  Vol. 2: 120, 445
  Vol. 3: 168 f., 171, 199, 204, 585 f., 824
Trial Vol. 1: 267, 346, 460, 467, 558, 629 f., 633,
  651
  Vol. 2: 42, 92, 136, 138 f., 143, 147, 217 f.,
  263, 360, 365, 369, 378 f., 450, 478, 498, 526,
  773, 916
  Vol. 3: 39, 118, 203, 219, 370, 446, 529, 627,
  629, 697, 729, 798-808, 849, 873, 1047
Tribal Vol. 1: 624
  Vol. 2: 247, 305
  Vol. 3: 33
Tribe Vol. 1: 195, 208, 255, 294, 366 f., 407, 463,
  489, 498, 518, 543 f., 619, 625, 640, 684

  Vol. 2: 187, 195, 234, 298, 306, 319 f., 325,
  331, 363, 373, 441, 466, 638, 695 f., 698, 700,
  789, 796, 802, 805
  Vol. 3: 454, 500, 870-873, 960, 1057, 1079
Tribulation Vol. 1: 125, 328, 381, 571, 607, 610,
  653
  Vol. 2: 37, 136, 353, 360, 478, 692, 709, 771,
  773, 781, 805-809, 892, 894 f., 911, 916, 920,
  924
  Vol. 3: 201, 211, 226, 270, 436, 592, 629, 803
Tribunal Vol. 3: 1043
Tribune Vol. 1: 340 f.
  Vol. 2: 363, 489
Tribute Vol. 1: 406, 537, 671, 684, 734
  Vol. 2: 40 f., 320
  Vol. 3: 421, 441 f., 752-755, 792, 978 f., 1168
Trick Vol. 2: 436, 457-461
  Vol. 3: 935-943
Trickery Vol. 1: 413
  Vol. 2: 166, 557
Trickle Vol. 1: 683
Trier, J. Vol. 3: 1128, 1141
Trim Vol. 1: 524
Trinitarian Vol. 2: 653
  Vol. 3: 648
Trinity Vol. 1: 535
  Vol. 2: 84, 508, 516, 687
  Vol. 3: 327, 661, 1056
Trip Vol. 2: 705, 708
Tripartite division of man Vol. 1: 235
  Vol. 3: 684
Tripartite pattern Vol. 2: 687
Tripartite world Vol. 3: 984, 523
Trito-Isaiah Vol. 1: 54
Triumph Vol. 1: 227, 239, 244, 261, 317, 410,
  440, 452, 469, 644-652, 727, 740
  Vol. 2: 136, 341, 400, 431, 433, 490
  Vol. 3: 277, 600 f.
Triumphal procession Vol. 1: 647, 649 f.
  Vol. 2: 453
Trivial Vol. 1: 727
Trivialization Vol. 1: 703
Troas Vol. 3: 410, 412
Troeltsch, Ernst Vol. 1: 49, 60
Troops Vol. 1: 292-297, 476, 537, 732
  Vol. 2: 601, 800 f., 898
  Vol. 3: 377, 958-967
Trophimus Vol. 3: 949
Trouble Vol. 1: 260, 262, 277, 433, 459, 519,
  550, 563, 568, 600, 612, 651 f., 675, 687, 698,
  726
  Vol. 2: 221, 395, 621-626, 791, 807, 820
  Vol. 3: 207 f., 216, 227, 239, 537, 545, 558,
  571, 691, 709 f., 869, 998, 1148
True Vol. 1: 56, 97, 99 f., 118, 178, 219, 225,
  250, 253, 255, 296 f., 299, 302 f., 305, 311,
  315, 338, 346 f., 386, 400, 406, 424, 446, 455,
  458, 460, 481, 483, 489, 498, 522, 527, 539,
  542, 590, 595, 598, 603, 628, 634, 637, 639,
  656, 659, 669, 676, 678, 684, 686 f., 690, 704,
  718 f., 722, 736
  Vol. 2: 59 f., 72-78, 82, 94, 103 f., 123, 135,
  194 f., 218, 221, 227, 229, 235 f., 248, 255,
  269, 273, 280 f., 285, 287-289, 307 f., 310,

314–317, 328, 335, 339, 360, 380, 384, 391, 402 f., 406, 408, 413, 426, 442, 450, 460, 469, 475, 477, 481, 488, 503, 607, 642, 645 f., 648 f., 659, 676, 686, 724, 810, 837
   Vol. 3: 42, 136, 160, 209, 351, 362, 499, 630, 871, 874–901, 1016, 1047
Truly Vol. 1: 98, 720
   Vol. 3: 874–901
Trumpet Vol. 1: 202, 273, 342, 410
   Vol. 2: 173, 691, 711, 784, 866, 922, 924 f.
   Vol. 3: 112, 119, 191, 237, 239, 732, 736, 856, 873 f., 1001, 1013, 1054
Trumpet-call Vol. 3: 873 f.
Trust Vol. 1: 142 f., 177, 203, 216, 223, 227, 278, 289, 351, 381, 411, 504, 510, 531, 542, 587–589, 591–596, 598–602, 604, 615 f., 622, 652, 658, 660, 673, 679–681, 683, 713, 729, 732
   Vol. 2: 71, 76, 82, 91, 94, 149, 237, 239 f., 307, 314, 342 f., 353, 392, 412, 453, 471, 650, 777, 822, 837, 858, 867
   Vol. 3: 55, 70, 79, 209, 249, 358 f., 366, 370, 391, 514, 625, 728, 839, 1073 f.
Trustee Vol. 1: 373
   Vol. 2: 254
   Vol. 3: 482
Trustworthiness Vol. 1: 311, 587 f., 594, 659
   Vol. 3: 358, 825
Trustworthy Vol. 3: 874–901
Truth Vol. 1: 70, 86 f., 89 f., 98, 102, 106, 114, 130, 166, 173, 188, 200, 219 f., 222, 225, 232, 238, 241, 266, 270 f., 304, 323 f., 336, 347, 359, 374, 382, 386, 413, 424, 461, 464, 470, 473, 483, 512, 525, 529, 540, 546, 563, 575, 577 f., 590–593, 598, 603, 631, 645, 653, 659, 662, 670 f., 678, 680, 708, 717, 740, 743
   Vol. 2: 56, 71, 78, 80, 119, 122, 129, 140, 162, 176, 179, 216, 231 f., 235, 249, 251, 261, 280, 312, 350, 357, 359, 364, 393, 399, 403, 405, 408, 448, 460 f., 463, 467, 469 f., 472–474, 492, 494, 559, 565, 568, 611, 643, 645, 676, 718, 721, 736, 745 f., 752 f., 757, 765, 793, 811, 817, 858, 873, 878, 927 f.
   Vol. 3: 61, 72, 122, 133, 163, 214, 224, 242, 280 f., 310, 314, 316, 320, 323 f., 326, 328 f., 336 f., 348, 352, 354, 379 f., 384, 460–462, 472, 489, 495, 503, 528, 571, 575 f., 586, 631, 637, 646, 693, 704, 738, 746, 749 f., 764, 795, 820, 837, 840, 874–901, 906, 936, 938 f., 942 f., 945 f., 966, 1024, 1036, 1039, 1050, 1052, 1079, 1081–1083, 1106, 1114, 1123, 1143, 1152
Truth, kinds of Vol. 3: 894
Truth in modern philosophy Vol. 3: 894–901
Truthful Vol. 2: 470–474
   Vol. 3: 741–743, 1041, 1049
Try Vol. 1: 364, 395
   Vol. 3: 798–808
Tubal-cain Vol. 2: 97
Tuition Vol. 3: 769
Tumult Vol. 1: 292
   Vol. 3: 112 f., 559, 709
Tunic Vol. 3: 543
Turks in Palestine Vol. 2: 308
Turmoil Vol. 2: 621–626

Turn Vol. 1: 353, 355, 358 f., 473, 585, 587, 601, 608, 688, 696, 700, 722
   Vol. 2: 154, 326, 357, 839
Turn about Vol. 3: 233
Turn aside Vol. 3: 583–585
Turn away Vol. 1: 585
   Vol. 2: 285 f.
   Vol. 3: 601–605, 902 f., 947
Turn back Vol. 3: 146, 255, 933–935, 1058
Turn round Vol. 3: 933–935
Turn tables Vol. 2: 34
Turn to Vol. 2: 882–885
Turning point Vol. 2: 59, 398
Turquoise Vol. 3: 396
Turret Vol. 3: 796
Turtledove Vol. 1: 172
Tutor Vol. 1: 370
   Vol. 3: 775–780
Twang Vol. 3: 671
Twelve Vol. 1: 489
   Vol. 2: 685, 687, 694–696, 697, 787
Twelve apostles Vol. 1: 50, 129–136, 142 f., 213, 274, 298, 407, 489, 540, 733
   Vol. 2: 313, 320 f., 365, 385, 563, 599, 614 f., 652, 695, 732, 754, 773, 780, 787, 902
   Vol. 3: 88, 283, 288, 297, 395, 397, 447, 454, 503, 560, 871 f., 948, 954, 1043, 1059, 1109
Twelve gates Vol. 3: 871 f., 948
Twelve stars Vol. 3: 736
Twelve thrones Vol. 1: 182
   Vol. 3: 871, 920
Twelve tribes Vol. 1: 134, 185, 324, 489
   Vol. 2: 34, 187, 306, 365, 615, 639, 652, 695, 700 f., 732, 754
   Vol. 3: 395–397, 418, 454, 490, 550, 736, 871 f., 920, 948, 1059
Twig Vol. 3: 870
Twilight Vol. 2: 324
Twin Vol. 2: 653
Twist Vol. 3: 492
Two Vol. 1: 55
   Vol. 2: 686, 748
Two ages Vol. 1: 524
   Vol. 2: 928
   Vol. 3: 827
Two-edged sword Vol. 3: 945
Two-natures doctrine Vol. 1: 548
Two powers Vol. 2: 608
Two ways Vol. 2: 479, 481
   Vol. 3: 929, 936, 939 f., 946
Two witnesses Vol. 1: 430
   Vol. 2: 487, 686, 712, 795
   Vol. 3: 1002, 1123
Type Vol. 1: 85 f., 88, 141, 149, 222, 273, 411, 487, 491, 508, 510, 524, 619, 679, 725
   Vol. 2: 277, 284, 291, 378, 462, 475, 504, 508, 598, 743–756, 700, 825, 835
   Vol. 3: 72, 265, 383, 560, 607, 903–906
Typical Vol. 1: 664, 666
   Vol. 2: 276, 312
Typological Vol. 2: 269, 316, 332
   Vol. 3: 863, 903–906
Typology Vol. 1: 49, 71, 86, 223, 436
   Vol. 2: 277, 447, 570, 692, 756

Typology (cont'd)
  Vol. 3: 82, 121, 495, **903–906,** 1006
Tyrannize Vol. 2: **606–611**
Tyranny Vol. 1: 124, 141
  Vol. 2: 772
  Vol. 3: 1161
Tyrant Vol. 1: 125, 269, 645
  Vol. 2: 291, 372
Tyre Vol. 1: 293, 324, 379
  Vol. 2: 97, 176, 767, 789, 848, 851
  Vol. 3: 605, 785, 908, 1052
Tyrian games Vol. 1: 645
Tyrian shekel Vol. 3: 754

Ugarit Vol. 1: 616
  Vol. 2: 67, 305, 324, 375, 644
Ugaritic Vol. 1: 68, 511
  Vol. 2: 190, 305, 495
Ugliness Vol. 1: 743
  Vol. 3: **562–564**
Ulcer Vol. 1: 520
Ullmann, Stephen Vol. 3: 1129
Ultimate Vol. 1: 651, 661, 713, 734
  Vol. 2: 357, 361
Umpire Vol. 1: 373, 648
Unable Vol. 2: 154, 405
Unacceptable Vol. 2: 155
Unambiguous Vol. 3: 572
Unanimity Vol. 1: 642
  Vol. 3: **908 f.**
Unanimous Vol. 3: **908 f.**
Unapproachable Vol. 2: 77, 214, 250, 648
Unassuming Vol. 2: 259
Unauthorized Vol. 1: 535
  Vol. 2: 362, 365
Unaware Vol. 1: 663, 690
Unbaptized Vol. 1: 117
  Vol. 3: 395
Unbegotten Vol. 1: 616
  Vol. 2: 506
Unbelief Vol. 1: 74, 76, 120, 159 f., 303, 473, 505, 529, 554, 559, **587–606,** 608, 678
  Vol. 2: 167, 177, 214, 303, 407, 419, 431, 433, 460, 469, 603, 624, 627, 631 f., 708 f., 717, 794, 868, 880
  Vol. 3: 73, 117, 136, 140, 202, 281, 320, 328, 582, 631, 692, 799, 805, 954
Unbeliever Vol. 1: 315, 350, 415, 439, 464, 473, 505, 507, 529, 566
  Vol. 2: 58, 217, 283, 304, 329, 366, 402, 457, 581, 654, 741 f., 828, 922
  Vol. 3: 97, 173, 226, 372, 380, 470, 535, 1080, 1150, 1164 f.
Unbelieving Vol. 3: 66, 470 f.
Unbiased Vol. 1: 485, 585
Unbind Vol. 1: 394
Unblemished Vol. 2: 59, 102
  Vol. 3: **923–928**
Unborn Vol. 1: 283, 285
  Vol. 2: 83
Unbridled Vol. 1: 494, 501
  Vol. 2: 256
  Vol. 3: 934

Unbrotherly Vol. 3: 750
Unburied Vol. 1: 264 f., 450
Uncanny Vol. 3: 1024
Unceasing Vol. 3: 54, **229 f.**
Uncertainty Vol. 1: 421, 505, 512
  Vol. 2: 100, 239, 241, 245
  Vol. 3: 910
Unchangeable Vol. 1: 357, 521, 660, 731
  Vol. 2: 340, 472
  Vol. 3: **583–585,** 828
Unchanged Vol. 1: 720, 726
Unchastity Vol. 1: 235, 261, 497, 500
  Vol. 2: 368, 581
  Vol. 3: 95 f., 469, 538, 540, 579, 799, 1069, 1157
Uncircumcised Vol. 1: 307–309, 311, 361, 675
  Vol. 2: 126, 178, 721
  Vol. 3: 363
Uncircumcision Vol. 1: 145, 155, 307, 310 f., 336, 385, 602, 676
  Vol. 2: 660
  Vol. 3: 714
Uncivilized Vol. 3: 353
Unclean Vol. 1: 62, 117, 122, 152 f., 155, 169, 172, 340, 444, 448, 452, 479, 488, 557, 637, 642, 685
  Vol. 2: 136, 206, 225, 268, 275, 434, 465, 631, 792
  Vol. 3: **102–108,** 113, 360, 459, 530, 695, 757, 860 f., 996, 1011, 1059
Unclean spirit Vol. 3: 256, 444, 472
Uncleanness Vol. 1: 151, 155, 205, 398, 448, 479 f., 641
  Vol. 2: 205, 225–227
  Vol. 3: 95, 101, **102–108,** 155
Uncommitted Vol. 1: 530, 731
Uncommon Vol. 2: 332
Unconcerned Vol. 2: 325
Unconditional Vol. 1: 207, 210, 483, 488, 611
  Vol. 2: 105 f., 243, 444
Unconditioned Vol. 1: 71, 538
Unconscious Vol. 1: 549
  Vol. 2: 568
  Vol. 3: 279, 677
Uncontrollable Vol. 3: 27
Uncontrolled Vol. 1: 494
Unconverted Vol. 2: 566
Uncover Vol. 1: 50, 313, 444
  Vol. 2: **212–214**
  Vol. 3: **310–316,** 1066
Uncreated Vol. 1: 653
Uncritical Vol. 1: 512
  Vol. 3: 64
Unction Vol. 1: 121, 123
Under Vol. 2: 209
Undefiled Vol. 1: 233, 447, 469
  Vol. 2: 300
  Vol. 3: **923–928**
Under law Vol. 2: **438–451**
Underground Vol. 2: 97
Underprivileged Vol. 2: 415
Understanding Vol. 1: 92, 103, 123, 212, 220, 253, 261, 282, 480 f., 485, 487, 489, 533, 537, 541, 556, 568, 578, 583 f., 597, 601 f., 671,

676, 680, 692, 694, 699, 714, 732, 735 f., 738, 742
Vol. 2: 61, 97, 116, 123, 154–156, 160–162, 169, 171, 173 f., 177–179, 183, 197, 279, 339 f., **390–406,** 419 f., 427, 434, 463, 476, 493, 567, 616, 621, 729, 777, 813, 923
Vol. 3: 75, 114, **122–133,** 166, 209, 236, 258, 313, 336, 351, 511–513, 516, 526, 649, 678, 680 f., 706, 744, 859, 916, 987, 1014, 1020, 1022, 1027 f., 1032, 1083, 1140
Undertake **Vol. 2:** 451
    Vol. 3: 799
Undertaking **Vol. 3: 1155–1158**
Undertone **Vol. 2:** 334
Undervalue **Vol. 2:** 429
Underworld **Vol. 1:** 101, 431, 449, 463 f., 523, 654
    Vol. 2: 30, 85, 136, 185, 187 f., 197, **205–208,** 644, 727, 729, 734
    Vol. 3: 678 f., 682, 936, 983, 1006
Underwrite **Vol. 3:** 755
Undeserved **Vol. 2:** 40, 117, 123, 291
    Vol. 3: 349
Undesired **Vol. 2:** 407
Undisciplined **Vol. 3:** 1026
Undisturbed **Vol. 3:** 255
Undress **Vol. 1:** 314
Undrinkable **Vol. 2:** 274
Uneducated **Vol. 1:** 498
    Vol. 2: 456 f., 625, 813
Unending **Vol. 1:** 716
Unenlightened **Vol. 1:** 561
Unequal **Vol. 3:** 1165
Unequally yoked **Vol. 2: 739–742**
    Vol. 3: 1160
Unequivocal **Vol. 2:** 351
Unethical **Vol. 3:** 160
Unexpected **Vol. 2:** 382
Unfading **Vol. 1:** 469
    Vol. 2: 300
Unfailing **Vol. 1:** 663
Unfairness **Vol. 3:** 757
Unfaithfulness **Vol. 1:** 109, 370, 449, 455, 461, 532, 594, 606
    Vol. 2: 797 f.
    Vol. 3: 79, 135, 585 f.
Unfamiliar **Vol. 2:** 670
Unfathomable **Vol. 1:** 594
    Vol. 2: 197, 205
    Vol. 3: 533
Unfavourable **Vol. 1:** 561
Unfeigned **Vol. 2: 468–470**
Unfettered **Vol. 1:** 718
    Vol. 3: 121
Unfit **Vol. 1:** 163, 274, 560, 565
    Vol. 3: 808–810
Unforgivable **Vol. 1:** 499, 700
    Vol. 3: 28, 343, 579
Unforgiving **Vol. 1:** 111, 226
    Vol. 2: 136, 301, 596, 600, 769 f., 868
    Vol. 3: 173
Unfounded **Vol. 1:** 546, 550
Unfree **Vol. 1:** 718
Unfruitful **Vol. 1:** 607, 721, 723

Vol. 3: 129, 672
Unfulfilled **Vol. 1:** 178
Ungodliness **Vol. 1:** 227, 352, 559, 622, 641
    Vol. 2: 94, 141, 193, 198, 329, 363, 682
Ungodly **Vol. 1:** 381 f., 409, 423, 444, 463, 466, 539, 597, 609, 656
    Vol. 2: 95, 139, 141, 155, 181, 202, 207, 251, 388, 431, 491–493, 570, 867
    Vol. 3: 161, 195, 201, 210, 363, 714, 799, 868, 961, 992, 994
Ungrateful **Vol. 1:** 552
Ungrudging **Vol. 1:** 214
Unhappy **Vol. 3:** 859
Unharness **Vol. 3:** 189
Unheeded **Vol. 1:** 410
    Vol. 2: 175
Unhewn stone **Vol. 3:** 789
Unhistorical **Vol. 1:** 208
    Vol. 2: 340
    Vol. 3: 507
Unholiness **Vol. 2:** 71
Unholy **Vol. 1:** 507
    Vol. 2: 236–238, 638
Unhonoured **Vol. 2:** 50
Unify **Vol. 2:** 144, 308
Unilateral **Vol. 1:** 641
Unimaginable **Vol. 3:** 124
Unimportant **Vol. 1:** 561
    Vol. 2: 259, 822
Unimpressive **Vol. 2:** 434
Uninformed **Vol. 2:** 406
Uninhabitable **Vol. 3:** 444
Uninhabited **Vol. 3:** 1004
Uninitiated **Vol. 2:** 457, 752
Uninjured **Vol. 2:** 133
Unintelligent **Vol. 3: 122–130**
Unintelligible **Vol. 1:** 582
    Vol. 2: 741
    Vol. 3: 124, 130, 1026
Unintentional **Vol. 1:** 609
    Vol. 2: 406 f.
    Vol. 3: 579, 586
Union **Vol. 1:** 148, 507, 513, 640, 643, 669, 678
    Vol. 2: 39, 94, 217, 251, 281, 314, 349 f., 357, 374, 585 f., 858
    Vol. 3: 422, 425, 703, 724, 886
Unique **Vol. 1:** 95, 474, 538, 540, 604, 615, 619 f., 665, 667, 713
    Vol. 2: 70, 73, 76, 79, 87, 169, 280, 289, 313, 332, 338, 340, 396, 426, 444, 632, 664, 716, 721 f., 724 f., 741, 808, 873
    Vol. 3: 238, 244, 323, 490, 630 f., 640 f., 696 f., 723, 827, 863 f., 947, 1041
Unit **Vol. 2:** 683, 698
Unit of meaning **Vol. 3:** 1128
Unite **Vol. 1:** 636, 639, 641, 730
    Vol. 2: 32, 243, 263, 306, 349 f., 355, 520, 653, 828
    Vol. 3: 1160
United in spirit **Vol. 3:** 687
Uniting factor **Vol. 3:** 680
Unity **Vol. 1:** 93, 209, 230, 237 f., 294, 296, 300, 302, 304, 325, 335, 370, 375, 399, 501, 522, 602, 630, 640, 642 f., 647, 669, 740

Unity (*cont'd*)
Vol. 2: 64, 135, 158, 163, 186, 192, 253, 261, 308, 313, 325, 328, 350, 404, 426, 439, 539, 598, 618–620, 633, **719–723,** 748, 776, 875, 921
Vol. 3: 463, 572, 635, 685, 724, 773, 819, 950, 1032, 1107, 1122, 1139, 1169
Universal **Vol. 1:** 52, 95, 99, 255, 375, 426, 432 f., 436, 512, 516, 535, 541, 616, 618, 621, 629, 641, 654, 739
Vol. 2: 56, 65, 78, 111, 167, 242, 303, 309, 330, 335, 375, 385, 389, 442, 444, 450, 511, 532, 536, 542, 631, 719, 888
Vol. 3: 220, 276, 406 f., 578 f., 585 f., 650, 656, 719, 1063
Universal law **Vol. 2:** 439
Vol. 3: 1081, 1084
Universal One **Vol. 2:** 67
Universalism **Vol. 3:** 148
Universality **Vol. 3:** 894, 1002
Universe **Vol. 1:** 53, 69 f., 94, 102, 238, 272, 317, 387, 439, 521–524, 616, 639, 654, 661, 712, 734
Vol. 2: 78, 158, 163, 189 f., 192, 203, 232, 270, 289, 353, 364, 393 f., 402, 404 f., 430, 452, 476, 514, 645, 648, 656, 660, 663, 688, 836
Vol. 3: 162, 345, 522, 681, 717, 775, 1035
Unjust **Vol. 1:** 563
Vol. 2: 93, 139, 236, 370, 659, 771
Vol. 3: 137, 187, **573–576,** 1002, 1025, 1041, 1074
Unjust judge **Vol. 3:** 1059
Unjust steward **Vol. 2:** 254, 668, 832, 837, 846
Vol. 3: 468, 489, 576
Unjustified **Vol. 1:** 228
Unkempt **Vol. 2:** 162
Unknowable **Vol. 2:** 406
Unknown **Vol. 1:** 686
Vol. 2: 109, 338, **406–408,** 669, 746 f.
Vol. 3: 45
Unknown god **Vol. 2:** 77, 85, 394, 407, 503
Vol. 3: 431
Unlawful **Vol. 1:** 155
Vol. 2: 282, **438–451,** 586
Vol. 3: 584
Unleash **Vol. 1:** 610
Unleavened **Vol. 1:** 249 f., 631, 633
Vol. 2: **461–463,** 522, 529, 676
Vol. 3: 422 f.
Unlettered **Vol. 2:** **456 f.**
Unlimited **Vol. 1:** 600
Unmarried **Vol. 1:** 217, 278, 561
Vol. 2: 816
Vol. 3: 224 f., 535–537, 542, 1055
Unmask **Vol. 1:** 439, 739
Vol. 2: 474
Unmerciful **Vol. 2:** 366, 594–598, 667
Vol. 3: 758
Unmerited **Vol. 2:** 42
Unmistakable **Vol. 2:** 106
Unmitigated **Vol. 2:** 360
Unmoved **Vol. 1:** 521
Unmutilated **Vol. 1:** 307
Unnatural **Vol. 1:** 499, 477

Vol. 2: 570, 660
Unnecessary **Vol. 1:** 728
Unobtrusive **Vol. 3:** 112
Unorganized **Vol. 2:** 801
Unpalatable **Vol. 1:** 202
Unpleasant **Vol. 2:** 856
Unprecedented **Vol. 2:** 443, 669
Unpredictable **Vol. 1:** 653, 666
Unprepared **Vol. 3:** 394
Unproductive **Vol. 1:** 73, 723
Vol. 3: 869
Unprofitable **Vol. 3:** 1026
Unprovable **Vol. 1:** 664
Vol. 2: 243
Unpunished **Vol. 1:** 698, 701
Unquenchable **Vol. 3:** 111, 447
Unreality **Vol. 1:** 550
Vol. 3: 724
Unreceptive **Vol. 2:** 174
Unrecognized **Vol. 2:** 281, 781
Unredeemed **Vol. 1:** 313, 398, 557
Vol. 3: 204, 347, 1021
Unregenerate **Vol. 1:** 319, 726
Vol. 2: 675
Unreliable **Vol. 1:** 594
Unrelieved **Vol. 3:** 593
Unrepeatable **Vol. 1:** 667
Vol. 2: 718
Vol. 3: 323
Unrepentant **Vol. 2:** 383, 630, 795
Unresponsive **Vol. 3:** 522, 911
Unrest **Vol. 1:** 642
Vol. 3: 1054
Unrestrained **Vol. 1:** 459, 552, 715
Unrestricted **Vol. 1:** 459
Unrighteous **Vol. 1:** 110, 115, 182, 202, 434, 554 f., 684, 721
Vol. 2: 93, 237, 544, 838, 844
Vol. 3: 99, 361, 722
Unrighteousness **Vol. 1:** 112, 591, 609, 662
Vol. 2: 193, 709, 818, 820, 892
Vol. 3: 163, **352–377, 573–576,** 580, 829
Unruly **Vol. 2:** 800
Unsalted **Vol. 3:** 443
Unsearchable **Vol. 2:** 365 f.
Vol. 3: **532 f.**
Unseemly **Vol. 3:** 574
Unseen **Vol. 1:** 80, 713
Vol. 3: 211
Unselfish **Vol. 1:** 547
Vol. 2: 413
Unserviceable **Vol. 2:** 669
Vol. 3: 143
Unsettle **Vol. 3:** **709 f.**
Unsettled **Vol. 1:** 518
Unshakeable **Vol. 1:** 658, 661
Vol. 2: 353
Vol. 3: **558–560**
Unshaken **Vol. 1:** 660, 663
Unskilled **Vol. 2:** **456 f.**
Unspeakable **Vol. 3:** 574
Unspiritual **Vol. 1:** 248
Vol. 3: 345, **676–687,** 705
Unstable **Vol. 2:** 657

579

Vol. 3: 558
Unstained Vol. 1: 337, 341
    Vol. 3: 534
Unsteady Vol. 2: 457
Unsubstantial Vol. 2: 284
Unsuitable Vol. 1: 561, 684
    Vol. 3: 111
Unsuspecting Vol. 1: 343
Untempted Vol. 3: 798–808
Untie Vol. 1: 577
    Vol. 3: 177–189
Untilled Vol. 1: 520
Untimely Vol. 1: 182, 184, 434
    Vol. 3: 833–839
Untouched Vol. 1: 563
    Vol. 3: 1071
Unusable Vol. 1: 565, 610, 722
    Vol. 2: 713
Unused Vol. 1: 73
Unutterable Vol. 1: 603
    Vol. 2: 763
Unveil Vol. 1: 312 f.
    Vol. 2: 160, 212–214
    Vol. 3: 309 f., 980
Unverifiable Vol. 3: 1136
Unwashed hands Vol. 2: 144
Unwavering Vol. 1: 503, 505, 597
Unwilling Vol. 1: 509
    Vol. 2: 106, 174
    Vol. 3: 132
Unwise Vol. 1: 108, 282, 288
    Vol. 2: 320
Unwitting Vol. 2: 358, 406
Unworthy Vol. 1: 183, 414 f.
    Vol. 2: 96, 530
    Vol. 3: 111, 141, 750
Unwritten Vol. 2: 436
Unwritten laws Vol. 3: 930 f.
Upbringing Vol. 1: 288, 569
    Vol. 2: 451
    Vol. 3: 775, 935
Upheaval Vol. 1: 610
Uphold Vol. 1: 658, 663, 697, 712
    Vol. 2: 287, 289, 366 f.
Upkeep Vol. 3: 433
Uplifted Vol. 2: 869
Upper room Vol. 2: 320
Upright Vol. 1: 479, 608
    Vol. 2: 94, 98, 144, 261, 395, 475
    Vol. 3: 101, 351–377, 1153–1155
Uprightness Vol. 3: 352–377, 571 f., 693
Uprising Vol. 1: 292
Uproar Vol. 1: 410
    Vol. 2: 621–626
Uproot Vol. 1: 600
    Vol. 3: 865–870
Upset Vol. 3: 557, 933–935
Upset salt Vol. 3: 448
Upstairs Vol. 2: 185
Upwards Vol. 1: 674
    Vol. 2: 187, 198, 617
Ur Vol. 3: 241
Uranus Vol. 2: 188
Urge Vol. 1: 65, 271, 456 f., 609, 689, 693, 731

Vol. 2: 181, 361
    Vol. 3: 556
Urgency Vol. 1: 239, 501, 611
    Vol. 2: 855, 859
Uriah Vol. 3: 656, 1062
Urim and Thummim Vol. 2: 296
Urn Vol. 1: 263, 674
Usage Vol. 1: 70
    Vol. 2: 436
Use Vol. 1: 548, 550, 619, 653, 687, 731, 742
    Vol. 2: 149, 270, 296, 364, 400, 447
Use force Vol. 3: 711 f.
Useful Vol. 2: 98, 102, 281, 412, 434
Usefulness Vol. 2: 105
    Vol. 3: 349, 912
Useless Vol. 1: 73, 337, 480, 546, 549 f., 565, 679, 722, 729
    Vol. 2: 434
    Vol. 3: 913, 1024
Usurp Vol. 2: 80, 877
    Vol. 3: 363
Utanapishtim Vol. 3: 259
Utensils Vol. 2: 233, 235
Utilize Vol. 2: 438
Utopia Vol. 1: 640
Utter oracles Vol. 3: 74–89
Utterance Vol. 1: 58, 582, 602, 734, 736 f.
    Vol. 2: 884
    Vol. 3: 760, 1078–1123
Utterly Vol. 2: 60
Uzziah Vol. 1: 54
    Vol. 2: 320
    Vol. 3: 609

Vacillation Vol. 2: 458
Vain Vol. 1: 209, 437, 459, 546–553, 571, 705
    Vol. 2: 41, 285, 517
    Vol. 3: 563
Vainglory Vol. 1: 228, 546
    Vol. 3: 143
Valentinian gnosticism Vol. 1: 301, 740
    Vol. 2: 645
Valentinus Vol. 1: 55
    Vol. 2: 401
Valerius Gratus Vol. 2: 849
    Vol. 3: 39
Valid Vol. 1: 98, 187, 286, 385, 402 f., 658, 660, 664, 666, 691
    Vol. 2: 40, 77, 216, 239, 241, 327, 336, 400, 442, 445, 719
    Vol. 3: 50, 165, 188, 224, 498, 712 f., 808, 828, 874–901, 1113
Validated Vol. 1: 398
Validation Vol. 3: 334
Validity Vol. 1: 439, 473, 486, 538, 594, 601, 609, 619, 659, 702
    Vol. 2: 62, 317, 394, 436, 439, 626
    Vol. 3: 363, 556, 741, 1112, 1137
Valley Vol. 1: 240, 422
Valley of dry bones Vol. 3: 269, 1100
Valley floor Vol. 2: 197
Valley of Shaveh Vol. 2: 590

Valuable **Vol. 1:** 665
  Vol. 2: 132, 547
  Vol. 3: 686
Valuation **Vol. 2:** 44
Value **Vol. 1:** 173, 311, 327, 349, 353, 457, 480, 496, 512 f., 565, 572, 613, 628, 654, 666, 670, 679, 710
  Vol. 2: 48–50, 96, 100, 104, 131 f., 149, 189, 270, 361 f., 394, 398 f., 420, 428 f., 435, 497–500, 566, 820 f., 831, 841 f., 844, 862
  Vol. 3: 137, 140, 142, 157, 444, 563, 627, 712, 848, 920, 933, 1024, 1148
Value-judgment **Vol. 1:** 681
  Vol. 2: 362, 424, 438, 719
  Vol. 3: 1143
Van Til, C. **Vol. 3:** 899
Vanishing **Vol. 1:** 681
Vanity **Vol. 1:** 262, 296, 546
  Vol. 2: 44, 100, 475, 565
Vanquished **Vol. 1:** 676, 686
Vapour **Vol. 1:** 449
  Vol. 3: 678
Variant reading **Vol. 1:** 69, **71**
Variety **Vol. 1:** 670
  Vol. 3: 1067
Varus **Vol. 3:** 441
Vassal **Vol. 3:** 268, 608, 828, 867
Vatican I **Vol. 3:** 386
Vaticanus **Vol. 1:** 53
Vault **Vol. 1:** 523
  Vol. 2: 188, 214
Vaunt **Vol. 1:** 727
Vegetables **Vol. 2: 210 f.**
  Vol. 3: 444
Vegetarian **Vol. 2:** 272
Vegetation **Vol. 2:** 274, 644, 691
  Vol. 3: 988, 1004
Vegetation gods **Vol. 2:** 265
Vehemence **Vol. 2:** 418
Veil **Vol. 1:** 73, 221, 245, 280, 587
  Vol. 2: 61, 159–162, **212–214,** 293, 328, 379, 522, 637, 641, 669
  Vol. 3: 153, 323, 520, 793, **794 f.,** 812, 886, 1066
Venerable **Vol. 1:** 616
  Vol. 2: 91, 128, 713
Veneration **Vol. 1:** 103, 384, 525
  Vol. 2: 94, 164, 498, 859
Vengeance **Vol. 1:** 107, 111, 225, 240, 375, 410, 539, 556, 735
  Vol. 2: 56, 58, 157, 230, 690, 770, 893
  Vol. 3: 92–100, 136, 242, 344, 874, 1054
Venom **Vol. 1:** 108
  Vol. 2: 27
Ventriloquist **Vol. 2:** 558
Venture **Vol. 1:** 710, 712
  Vol. 2: 349, 743
  Vol. 3: 799
Venus **Vol. 1:** 497
  Vol. 2: 85, 495
  Vol. 3: 736, 1068
Ver sacrum **Vol. 3:** 149
Veracious **Vol. 3: 874–901**
Verdict **Vol. 1:** 351, 386, 397, 545, 566, 604, 609,

679 f., 702
  Vol. 2: 214, **362–367,** 383, 392
  Vol. 3: 50 f., 128, 370, 372, 747, 817, 838, 892
Verdigris **Vol. 2:** 27
Verifiability **Vol. 3:** 1136
Verse **Vol. 3:** 1086
Versions **Vol. 1:** 69, **71**
Very small **Vol. 2: 427–429**
Vespasian **Vol. 2:** 167
  Vol. 3: 457, 752
Vessel **Vol. 1:** 149, 540, 546, 636, 638, 673, 733, 741 f.
  Vol. 2: 50 f., 96, 212, 274, 434, 726, 834
  Vol. 3: 104, 117, 459, 552, 788, **910–917,** 957, 990, 1053, 1064 f., 1067
Vessels of mercy **Vol. 1:** 112
  Vol. 3: 118
Vessels of the sanctuary **Vol. 1:** 122
Vessels of wrath **Vol. 1:** 112
  Vol. 3: 1020
Vesta **Vol. 1:** 653
Vestments **Vol. 2:** 233
  Vol. 3: 120
Vesuvius **Vol. 3:** 1013
Vetus Latina **Vol. 1:** 71
Vex **Vol. 2:** 260, 807
Via, D.O. **Vol. 3:** 1127
Vibration **Vol. 2:** 653
  Vol. 3: 558
Vicarious **Vol. 1:** 372
  Vol. 2: 413, 445, 532
  Vol. 3: 151, 164, 171, 195, 550, 721–724, 956, 999
Vice **Vol. 1:** 108, 110, 138, 202, 412, 452, 459, 496, 499, 513 f., 559, 593, 676, 687, 689, 739
  Vol. 2: 271, 791, 845 f.
  Vol. 3: 28, 30 f., 526, 563, 576, 839, 926–929
Viciousness **Vol. 1:** 511
Vicissitudes **Vol. 2:** 265, 357, 439
Victim **Vol. 1:** 239, 392 f., 410, 438, 459–461, 479, 498
  Vol. 2: 257, 412
  Vol. 3: 93, 95 f., 159 f., 164 f., 178, 190, 418
Victor **Vol. 1:** 303, 382, 467, 470, 526, 644, 648–650, 716
  Vol. 2: 62, 296, 653 f.
  Vol. 3: 49
Victorious **Vol. 1:** 663, 730
  Vol. 2: 359
Victory **Vol. 1:** 100, 114, 125, 239, 241, 244, 339, 359, 372, 405 f., 423, 432, 436–438, 440, 469 f., 508, 564, 624–627, **644–652**
  Vol. 2: 107, 109, 146, 205, 260, 270, 273, 315, 326, 357, 419, 435, 665, 889, 898, 907, 918
  Vol. 3: 45, 51, 172, 267 f., 357, 388, 686, 716, 736, 818, 990, 1006, 1046
Victory cry **Vol. 3:** 669
Vielhauer, P. **Vol. 3:** 58, **619**
Vienna circle **Vol. 3:** 1136
View **Vol. 1:** 70, 188, 599, 711
  Vol. 2: 44
  Vol. 3: 512
Vigil **Vol. 1:** 495
Vile **Vol. 1:** 564

Village **Vol. 1:** 520, 689
  Vol. 2: 29, 363, 803
  Vol. 3: 56, 153
Vindicate **Vol. 2:** 363 f., 771
  Vol. 3: 352–377, 790
Vindication **Vol. 1:** 175, 411, 434, 470, 529, 672, 677
  Vol. 2: 165, 203, 228, 340, 679, 905, 917
  Vol. 3: 97, 318, **352–377,** 611, 617, 629, 722, 913, 1059
Vindicator **Vol. 3:** 178 f.
Vine **Vol. 1:** 303, 722, 724
  Vol. 2: 33, 247, 278, 280 f., 307, 313, 382, 632
  Vol. 3: 227, 256, 335, 567, 613, 865–869, 893, **918–922,** 950 f.
Vine-dresser **Vol. 1:** 725
  Vol. 3: 918–922
Vinegar **Vol. 1:** 726
  Vol. 2: 28
Vineyard **Vol. 1:** 356, 430
  Vol. 2: 50, 154, 248, 301, 307, 313, 499, 681, 790
  Vol. 3: 95, 141, 525, 641 f., 867–869, **918–922,** 948, 950 f.
Vintage **Vol. 1:** 724
Violate **Vol. 2:** 130, 320, 440, 451, 582
  Vol. 3: 711
Violence **Vol. 1:** 288, 430, 532
  Vol. 2: 51, 63, 202, 363, 383, 821, 841
  Vol. 3: 353 f., 377, 379, 475, 578, 603, **711–718,** 971, 975, 980, 1054
Violent **Vol. 3: 27 f.,** 158, **711 f.**
Viper **Vol. 1:** 510
Virgin **Vol. 1:** 325, 414, 468, 505
  Vol. 2: 87, 212, 577, 584 f., 588, 619
  Vol. 3: 95, 118, 252, 536, 1055
Virgin birth **Vol. 1:** 179
  Vol. 2: 86 f.
  Vol. 3: 660–664, 1070, 1073
Virginity **Vol. 1:** 256, 449, 668
  Vol. 3: 1071
Virgo intacta **Vol. 3:** 660
Virtuality **Vol. 3:** 1142
Virtue **Vol. 1:** 175, 217, 314, 316, 431 f., 459, 461, 494, 496, 501 f., 559, 598, 603, 627, 645, 690, 700, 734
  Vol. 2: 49, 51, 61, 92, 94, 192, 259, 261, 290, 355, 437, 484, 497, 658 f., 772, 806, 820, 841
  Vol. 3: 32, 50, 102, 138, 261, 347, 351–353, 365, 522, 526, 562 f., 575, 678, 681 f., 719, 727, 766, **923–928,** 936, 939, 946–948, 1034, 1075, 1148, 1157, 1163
Virtuous **Vol. 1:** 435, 524
  Vol. 2: 261, 477
  Vol. 3: 355
Visible **Vol. 1:** 95, 219, 299, 490 f., 523, 595, 602, 650, 679, 703 f.
  Vol. 2: 46, 72, 82, 106, 147, 190, 192, 379, 394, 398 f., 421, 484, **488–490**
  Vol. 3: 128, 310, 312, 316, **317–324, 511–518,** 839
Vision **Vol. 1:** 103, 116, 175, 202, 204, 216, 274, 319, 420 f., 426, 429, 448, 469, 512, 527 f., 574, 576, 593, 597, 609, 623, 640, 675, 704,
727
  Vol. 2: 37, 45, 97, 173, 176, 181, 193, 240, 294, 320, 375, 477, 559, 604, 607, 610, 612 f., 622, 624, 673, 691 f., 701 f., 711 f., 728, 762, 785, 888 f., 931
  Vol. 3: 36, 77, 80, 87 f., 128, 241, 269, 283, 285 f., 288, 297, 310 f., 315 f., 362, 366, 502, **511–521,** 569, 606, 614, 616, 691 f., 706 f., 735, 847, 862, 871, 950, 1008, 1010, 1067 f., 1089, 1092–1094, 1096, 1100
Visionary **Vol. 1:** 527, 638
  Vol. 2: 56
  Vol. 3: 276, 690, 699
Visit **Vol. 1:** 188 f., 191, 207, 333, 420, 697
  Vol. 2: 358, 875
  Vol. 3: 134, 198, 359, 516, 547, 1074
Visitation **Vol. 1:** 188, 190 f., 562
  Vol. 2: 56, 167, 779, 893, 905
  Vol. 3: 503, 793, 836 f., 842, 943
Visitor **Vol. 1:** 529, 688
Visual **Vol. 1:** 735
  Vol. 2: 284
Vital **Vol. 1:** 671
  Vol. 3: 680
Vitality **Vol. 1:** 240
  Vol. 2: 311
  Vol. 3: 691, 867, 1071
Vitellius **Vol. 3:** 39, 756
Viticulture **Vol. 3:** 918
Vivid **Vol. 1:** 670
Vizier **Vol. 2:** 376
  Vol. 3: 594
Vocation **Vol. 1:** 271, 275, 522, 690
  Vol. 2: 298, 566
  Vol. 3: 173, 621, 790, 920, 1088, 1095
Voice **Vol. 1:** 280, 292, 372, 410 f., 476, 541, 543, 684, 704 f.
  Vol. 2: 48, 114, 177 f., 193, 206, 316, 354, 413, 426, 444, 784, 819, 863, 924, 929
  Vol. 3: 48 f., 51, 54, 80, **111–114,** 639–641, 705–714, 807, 863, 874, 909, 990, 1001–1003, 1078
Void **Vol. 1:** 334, 546 f., 638
  Vol. 2: 301, 453
  Vol. 3: 258
Volcano **Vol. 1:** 655, 657
  Vol. 3: 1013
Volition **Vol. 1:** 686
  Vol. 2: 567, 817
  Vol. 3: 1015–1023
Voluntary **Vol. 1:** 355, 482, 613, 626, 642, 697
Voluntary contributions **Vol. 3:** 752, 854 f.
von Campenhausen, Hans **Vol. 3:** 290
von Rad, G. **Vol. 3:** 151, 333, 1124
von Soden, H. **Vol. 3:** 85
Vote **Vol. 1:** 478
  Vol. 2: 497
  Vol. 3: 49, 913
Voter **Vol. 1:** 732
Votive offering **Vol. 1:** 413 f.
  Vol. 3: 422 f.
Vouch **Vol. 1:** 659
Vow **Vol. 1:** 107, 203, 344, 352, 472, 734
  Vol. 2: 43, 157, 162, **861–864, 867–875**

Vow (*cont'd*)
  Vol. 3: 68, 101, 425, 431, 539, 816, 919, 921, 1057
Voyage **Vol. 3:** 935
Vulgate **Vol. 1:** 50, **71**
  Vol. 2: 219
Vulnerable **Vol. 1:** 678
Vulture **Vol. 1:** 172 f., 175, 610
  Vol. 2: 32 f., 115
  Vol. 3: 1054

Wady **Vol. 3:** 985
Waft **Vol. 1:** 683
Wag **Vol. 3:** 556
Wages **Vol. 1:** 117, 436, 723
  Vol. 2: 711, 770, 851
  Vol. 3: **134–145,** 379, 549, 727
Wages of sin **Vol. 2:** 120, 715
Wagon **Vol. 3:** 811
Wail **Vol. 1:** 420
  Vol. 2: 416–424
  Vol. 3: 113
Wait **Vol. 1:** 482, 552, 596, 646, 650
  Vol. 2: 118, 239 f., **244–246,** 385, 585, 682, 772
  Vol. 3: 97, 224, 365, 371, 628, 953
Wait at table **Vol. 3:** 545
Wait for **Vol. 2:** 132, 194, 238 f., **244–246,** 328
  Vol. 3: 744–746
Waiting **Vol. 2:** 243 f., 360
Wake **Vol. 2:** 55, 925
  Vol. 3: 279–281
Wakefulness **Vol. 2:** 137
Walk **Vol. 1:** 59, 110, 257, 262, 354, 384, 420, 422, 424, 458, 483, 571, 623, 644, 675, 704, 713, 723, 741
  Vol. 2: 61, 184, 302, 358, 369, 414 f., 440, 452, 461, 473, 492, 494 f., 517, 668, 706, 718, 771, 777, 795, 804, 815, 817
  Vol. 3: 118, 266, 324, 336, 361, 400, 432, 528, 550, 572, 633, 702, 800, 860, 891, **933–947,** 985, 990, 1002, 1006, 1014, 1167
Walk beside **Vol. 3:** 583
Walk uprightly **Vol. 3: 351 f.**
Walking on water **Vol. 2:** 281, 559, 630
Wall **Vol. 1:** 205, 377, 676
  Vol. 2: 111, 157, 199, 465, 646, 722, 760, 801, 831
  Vol. 3: 200, 350, 378, 382, 397, 557, **948–952**
Wander **Vol. 1:** 320, 322
  Vol. 2: 412, **457–461**
  Vol. 3: 29, 560, 736, 888
Wander from truth **Vol. 3:** 888
Wandering **Vol. 1:** 209, 304, 424, 488, 568
  Vol. 2: 138, 265
  Vol. 3: 560
Wandering stars **Vol. 3:** 736
Waning **Vol. 3:** 733
Want **Vol. 1:** 456, 556, 565, 623, 687, 717, 731
  Vol. 2: 92, 263, 265, 351, 822, 855
  Vol. 3: 230 f., 251, **530–532, 952–958, 1015–1023**
Wanton **Vol. 3:** 27, 29
War **Vol. 1:** 67, 102, 118, 124, 151, 224, 293 f., 340 f., 392, 409, 429, 452, 484, 492, 529, 553,

558, 612, 645 f., 650, 652–654, 656 f., 674, 677, 683, 686 f., 720, 741 f.
  Vol. 2: 146, 167, 226 f., 238, 258, 265, 343, 367, 497, 602, 665, 776 f., 780, 809, 844, 893, 904, 907, 911, 930
  Vol. 3: 45, 49, 79, 111, 121, 147, 179, 205, 233, 249, 253, 266, 356, 593, 702, 715, 730, 749, 873, **958–967,** 1169
War Scroll of Qumran **Vol. 3:** 961
Ward **Vol. 2:** 581
Ward off **Vol. 1:** 646
  Vol. 3: 102, 727
Wares **Vol. 3:** 139
Warfield, B.B. **Vol. 3: 329**
Warm **Vol. 1:** 614 f.
  Vol. 2: 435
  Vol. 3: 678
Warn **Vol. 1:** 156, 163, 247, 329, 341, 372, 403, 419, 463, 469, 496, 526, 559, **567–573,** 587, 607, 679 f., 683 f., 689, 709, 725, 729, 731
  Vol. 2: 127, 178 f., 263
  Vol. 3: 79, 211, 325
Warning **Vol. 1:** 109, 205, 235, 244, 247, 286, 352, 404, 410, 417, 462, 501, 512 f., 538, **567–573,** 578, 591, 593, 604, 608, 610 f., 623, 690 f., 734, 742
  Vol. 2: 37, 136, 174, 180, 230, 244, 260, 262, 277, 286, 290 f., 307, 310, 318, 320, 357 f., 366, 397, 401, 417, 426, 429, 460, 462, 587, 706, 718 f., 721, 823, 832, 901, 917, 921
  Vol. 3: 79, 99, 143, 204, 214, 221, 227, 249, **324 f.,** 343, 370, 430, 522, 721, 759, 806, 949, 1025, 1043, 1054
Warnock, G.J. **Vol. 3:** 897
Warrior **Vol. 1:** 102, 732
  Vol. 2: 562
  Vol. 3: 583, 953
Warrior God **Vol. 2:** 69
Wash **Vol. 1:** 117, **143–154,** 185 f., 224 f., 239, 351, 395, 471, 625, 630, 698, 701
  Vol. 2: 75, 159, 228, 230, 303
  Vol. 3: 107, 366, 990
Wash fee (→ Feet-washing)
Wash garments **Vol. 3:** 101
Wash hands **Vol. 2:** 149 f.
  Vol. 3: 105, 481
Wash out **Vol. 3:** 109
Waste **Vol. 1:** 464, 467, 470
  Vol. 2: 33, 266
Waste time **Vol. 3: 839–845**
Watch **Vol. 1:** 217, 294, 420, 474, 655
  Vol. 2: 132–137, 244, 689, 717, 917
  Vol. 3: 114, 126, 378, **511–518,** 626, 685, 713, 1096
Watch over **Vol. 1:** 189, 543
  Vol. 2: 438, 441
Watcher **Vol. 1:** 101 f.
  Vol. 3: 468
Watchfulness **Vol. 1:** 425, 442, 460, 693
  Vol. 2: 37, 910, 916
  Vol. 3: 529, 627
Watchman **Vol. 2:** 111
  Vol. 3: 1100
Water **Vol. 1:** 113, 143, 151–153, 158, 160, 164,

175, 179 f., 185, 201 f., 224 f., 319, 351, 379, 384, 389, 420, 433, 508 f., 513, 515, 517 f., 522 f., 526, 610, 612, 617, 623, 629, 652, 670, 683, 710 f., 735, 742
Vol. 2: 28 f., 80, 150, 153, 157, 188 f., 205, 222, 226, 267, **274–277,** 278, 281, 284, 349, 452, 497, 583, 630, 658, 691, 854, 881
Vol. 3: 102, 104, 109, 112, 141, 147, 208, 211, 220, 324, 335, 382 f., 449, 459, 543, 599, 647, 703 f., 707, 709, 713, 737, 814, 866, 910, 913, 915, 917, 919, 922, 980, **982–992,** 1003–1007, 1177 f.
Water of bitterness **Vol. 2:** 140
Water of conviction **Vol. 2:** 140
Water of life **Vol. 2:** 267, 275, 277, 482, 486, 615, 761, 763, 928
Vol. 3: 988, 991
Water-jar **Vol. 3:** 911
Waterless **Vol. 3:** 988
Wave **Vol. 3:** 983
Wave hand as signal **Vol. 3: 556–558**
Wave-loaf **Vol. 3:** 424
Wave-offering **Vol. 2:** 461
Vol. 3: 416, 424
Waver **Vol. 1:** 503, 505
Vol. 2: 244
Vol. 3: 558–560
Waves **Vol. 1:** 520
Vol. 2: 212
Vol. 3: 112, 559 f., 711
Wax **Vol. 1:** 471
Vol. 2: 128
Vol. 3: 483
Waxing **Vol. 3:** 733
Way **Vol. 1:** 168, 191, 225, 272, 292, 339, 375, 403, 411, 415, 423, 426, 464, 491–493, 499, 541, 543, 547, 564, 568, 571, 594, 596, 630, 668, 695, 719, 726, 731, 733
Vol. 2: 75, 80, 123 f., 132, 134, 202, 215, 221, 225, 256, 258, 262, 280, 310, 400, 436–438, 444, 458–460, 493, 806
Vol. 3: 50, 163, 207, 316, 366, 380, 503, 530, 584, 629, 764, 888, 891, 916, **933–947**
Way of Balaam **Vol. 3:** 942
Way of Cain **Vol. 3:** 942
Way of God **Vol. 3:** 937
Way of life **Vol. 1:** 269, 513, 551 f., 717
Vol. 2: 436–438
Vol. 3: 933–943
Way of thinking **Vol. 2: 616–620**
Way of truth **Vol. 3:** 888
Way, truth, life **Vol. 3:** 891
Waylay **Vol. 2:** 132
Wayside **Vol. 1:** 608
Wayward **Vol. 1:** 556
Vol. 2: 407
Weak **Vol. 1:** 334, 366, 449, 475, 542, 561, 602, 676 f., 716
Vol. 2: 117 f., 123, 259, 273, 306, 402, 422, 446, 453, 706, 822, 899
Vol. 3: 106, 410, 559, 563, 751, 802, 914, 955, **993–1000,** 1026
Weaken **Vol. 1:** 680
Vol. 2: 461

Weaker **Vol. 3:** 1067
Weaker brother **Vol. 1:** 352
Vol. 2: 611, 815
Vol. 3: 107
Weakness **Vol. 1:** 163, 192, 218, 222, 229, 281, 337, 399, 467, 551, 679, 727, 731
Vol. 2: 62 f., 116, 121, 136, 166, 171, 206, 414, 428, 432, 434 f., 446 f., 460, 564, 606, 710, 772, 809, 818, 882–884
Vol. 3: 41, 281, 315, 475, 560, 571, 586, 601, 702, 714, 724 f., 814, 857, **993–1000,** 1017, 1190
Weal **Vol. 1:** 379
Wealth **Vol. 1:** 119, 138 f., 205, 319, 322, 381, 515, 536, 683, 731, 735
Vol. 2: 48 f., 51, 255, 265, 317, 422, 475, 549, **829–853**
Vol. 3: 209, 224, **324 f.,** 379, 598, 678, 727, 812, 953
Wealthy **Vol. 1:** 188
Vol. 2: 820, 838
Wean **Vol. 1:** 614
Weapon **Vol. 1:** 120, 314, 379, 390, 392, 468, 652 f., 656, 675, 726
Vol. 2: 97, 495, 815, 830
Vol. 3: 268, 364, **958–967,** 1001
Weapons of righteousness **Vol. 2:** 148
Vol. 3: 886, 963
Wear **Vol. 1:** 241, 648
Vol. 2: 160, 296
Wear away **Vol. 3:** 840
Weary **Vol. 1:** 262 f., 426, 496 f., 729
Vol. 2: 215, 221, 265, 281
Vol. 3: 859, 1102
Weather **Vol. 3:** 737, 835, **1000–1004**
Weave **Vol. 1:** 490
Vol. 3: 950
Wedding **Vol. 1:** 120, 122, 274, 317, 506, 612
Vol. 2: 339, **575–582**
Vol. 3: 403
Wedding feast **Vol. 1:** 110
Vol. 2: 502, 575, 676
Vol. 3: 252
Wedding guests **Vol. 2:** 32, 358, 585
Wedding hall **Vol. 2: 584 f.**
Wedlock **Vol. 1:** 187 f., 616
Weeds **Vol. 1:** 289, 299
Vol. 2: 211, 708
Vol. 3: 868
Week **Vol. 1:** 627–631
Vol. 2: 692, 696 f.
Weekday work **Vol. 1:** 631
Weep **Vol. 1:** 201, 329, 395
Vol. 2: 267, 328, 357, **416–424,** 433, 824 f., 862
Vol. 3: 680, 1062
Weigh **Vol. 1:** 106, 591
Vol. 3: 136, 230, 752, 1160 f.
Weigh facts **Vol. 2:** 392
Weight **Vol. 1:** 260 f.
Vol. 2: 370
Vol. 3: 27, 348, 514, 752, 1097
Weightier **Vol. 2:** 281
Weights and measures **Vol. 3:** 356, 752

Welcome **Vol. 1:** 206, 211, 213, 325
  Vol. 2: 244–246, 328, 358, 450, 538 f.
  Vol. 3: 744–746, 751, 920
Welfare **Vol. 1:** 562
  Vol. 2: 320, 564
  Vol. 3: 167, 568, 593, 1167
Well **Vol. 1:** 116
  Vol. 2: 92, **169–171,** 318, 367, 386
  Vol. 3: 146, 158, 208, 351, 717, 950, 980, **982–992**
Well-behaved **Vol. 3:** 817
Well-being **Vol. 1:** 208, 210–216, 232, 400, 553, 671
  Vol. 2: 99, 115, 163, 170, 266, 352, 478, 777, 781
  Vol. 3: 357, 422, 528, 566, 755, 918, 1157
Well-born **Vol. 1: 176–188**
Well-disposed **Vol. 2:** 550, 818
Well-doing **Vol. 3:** 1147–1155
Well-favoured **Vol. 1:** 188
Well-mannered **Vol. 3:** 818
Well-ordered **Vol. 1:** 666
Well-pleasing **Vol. 2:** 857
  Vol. 3: 266, 810
Wellhausen, Julius **Vol. 1:** 66
Wenham, J.W. **Vol. 3:** 329
Werner, Martin **Vol. 2:** 903
West **Vol. 3:** 1055
West-Semitic peoples **Vol. 1:** 308
Westcott, B.F. **Vol. 1:** 70
Whale **Vol. 1:** 670
Wheat **Vol. 1:** 118, 249, 289, 625
  Vol. 2: 32, 488, 711, 783, 834
  Vol. 3: 470, 523, 527, 804, 831
Wheel **Vol. 1:** 182
  Vol. 3: 557
While **Vol. 2:** 304
Whip **Vol. 1:** 161 f.
  Vol. 3: 778
Whirlwind **Vol. 3:** 266
Whisper **Vol. 1:** 510
  Vol. 2: 554
Whisperer **Vol. 3:** 346
White **Vol. 1:** 115, **203–206,** 265, 317, 319, 656 f., 708
  Vol. 2: 96, 293, 464, 470, 484, 493, 496
  Vol. 3: 40, 143, 347, 349, 360, 362, 862, 1004, 1053
White stone **Vol. 2:** 673 f.
Whitewash **Vol. 1:** 205, 471
  Vol. 2: 334
  Vol. 3: 360, 948, 1053
Whitsun **Vol. 1:** 631
Whole **Vol. 1: 94 f.,** 294 f., 302, 518, 672, 674 f., 677, 706, 708 f., 732, 738
  Vol. 2: 60, 62 f., 779
  Vol. 3: 422, 860, 925
Whole burnt-offering **Vol. 3: 417–436**
Whole-offering **Vol. 2:** 60
Wholehearted **Vol. 3:** 572, 687
Wholeness **Vol. 2:** 64 f., 102, 130, 593, 780–782
  Vol. 3: 572
Wholesome **Vol. 3:** 449
Wholly other **Vol. 3:** 326

Whore **Vol. 1:** 481, 497, 501
  Vol. 3: 1008, 1093
Whoredom **Vol. 1:** 514
Whorf, Benjamin Lee **Vol. 3:** 1126 f.
Wick **Vol. 3:** 110
Wicked **Vol. 1:** 103, 109, 146, 194, 343, 479, 646, 673, 702, 726
  Vol. 2: 29, 104, 106, 138, 329, 351, 370, 421, 737
  Vol. 3: 134, 201, 203, 357, 360, 641, 919
Wicked husbandmen **Vol. 2:** 790
  Vol. 3: 641, 869
Wicked tenants **Vol. 3:** 951
Wickedness **Vol. 1:** 96, 112, 231, 296, 332, 349, 382, 420, 550, 555, **561–567,** 645, 647, 654, 673, 731, 733, 742 f.
  Vol. 2: 56, 94, 106, 364, 677, 679
  Vol. 3: 125, 209, **562–564,** 574, 681, 837, 926, 983, 996, 1024
Wide **Vol. 1: 253 f.**
  Vol. 3: 255
Widespread **Vol. 1:** 733
Widow **Vol. 1:** 187, 191, 266, 322, 341, 499, 690 f., 729 f.
  Vol. 2: 43, 50, 71, 475, 564, 599, 730, 737 f., 771, 821, 823, 850, 858
  Vol. 3: 97, 178, 191, 225, 357, 482, 537, 548 f., 790, 852, 855, 903, 930, **1055–1075**
Widower **Vol. 3:** 537
Wife **Vol. 1:** 80, 84, 87, 232, 235, 302, 395, 498, 505–507, 537, 555 f., 637
  Vol. 2: 50 f., 139, 213, 221, 307, 317 f., 349, 400, 511, 513, 539, 541, 563 f., 575, 584, 684, 880, 922
  Vol. 3: 138, 172, 188 f., 219, **534–543,** 747, 928–930, 1055, **1160–1165**
Wilckens, Ulrich **Vol. 3: 286 f.**
Wild **Vol. 1: 520,** 726
Wild beast **Vol. 3:** 203
Wild olive **Vol. 2:** 660, **710–713**
Wild vine **Vol. 3:** 918
Wilderness **Vol. 1:** 99, 114, 249, 253, 294, 303, 380, 411, 453, 460, 465, 473, 510, 519, 527, 531, 568, 593, 626, 629
  Vol. 2: 206, 218, 228, 412, 458, 460, 541, 636 f., 640, 642, 696, 819, 835, 871 f., 893, 928
  Vol. 3: 56, 73, 118, 121, 427, 431, 459, 559, 602, 697, 706, 724, 752, 800, 804, 810 f., 905, 919, 937, 953 f., **1004–1014,** 1094
Wilderness of Sin **Vol. 2:** 637
Wiles **Vol. 1:** 282
  Vol. 3: 965
Wilful **Vol. 1:** 607
  Vol. 3: 1018
Will **Vol. 1:** 74, 177, 231, 234, 244, 355, 365, 368–371, 376, 378, 416, 437, 447, 457, 460 f., 477, 495, 497, 533–535, 564, 567 f., 575, 594, 623, 643, 647, 655, 664, 670 f., 681, 696, 699, 708, 719, 742
  Vol. 2: 83, 102, 166, 181–183, 211, 258, 289, 296, 368, 377, 392, 400, 434, 472, 588, 617, 664, 811, 818 f., 876
  Vol. 3: 72, 76, 110, 118, 122, 124, 127, 177,

585

224, 234, 293, 314, 532, 593, 677, 681, 684, 713, **1015–1023,** 1156
Will, Free **Vol. 1:** 54
  Vol. 2: 663, 811
  Vol. 3: 69, 1020
Will, Human **Vol. 1:** 54, 355, 594, 608, 722
  Vol. 2: 811
Will of God **Vol. 1:** 70, 95, 103, 121, 145, 166, 173, 187, 203, 243, 268, 273, 275, 282, 289, 311, 326, 350, 370, 384, 386, 456–459, 473, 476, 484–488, 494, 496, 506, 540, 549, 565, 575, 593 f., 597, 602 f., 641, 647, 659, 669, 674, 677, 696 f., 699, 708, 717, 719, 728, 738
  Vol. 2: 42, 62, 72–75, 77, 94, 103, 128, 174, 177 f., 194, 216, 229–232, 275, 281, 296, 300, 326 f., 336, 343, 359, 397, 399 f., 413, 425, 446, 448, 481, 540 f., 561, 581, 604, 610, 618, 653 f., 660, 664–667, 673, 675, 721, 775, 811, 815–819, 832, 857 f., 863 f., 867 f., 871, 875, 882 f., 885, 929
  Vol. 3: 31, 46, 72, 79, 93 f., 128 f., 157, 195, 198, 329, 360, 363, 377, 420, 433 f., 504, 509, 532 f., 566, 578, 609, 692, 702, 725, 760–763, 765, 769, 774, 777, 779, 787, 810, 825, 828, 835 f., 848, 885, 912, 931, 938, 940, 942, 944, 946, 1003, **1015–1023,** 1026, 1028, 1030, 1044, 1062, 1102 f., 1154
Willing **Vol. 3:** 821, 994
Willingness **Vol. 1:** 546, 604, 606
  Vol. 2: 262 f., 350, 600, 826, 847
  Vol. 3: 1169
Wilt **Vol. 2:** 211
Win **Vol. 1:** 423, 651
Wind **Vol. 1:** 66, 280, 379 f., 517, 673, 678, 683, 740
  Vol. 2: 34, 155, 189, 222, 688 f., 785, 830, 865
  Vol. 3: 76, 112 f., 389, 559, 672, **689–708,** 718, 990, **1000–1004,** 1005, 1095
Window **Vol. 2:** 726
  Vol. 3: 787
Window of heaven **Vol. 2:** 189, 726
Wine **Vol. 1:** 106, 116, 118, 224, 237, 250, 381, 498, 513–515, 613, 625 f., 633, 641, 672
  Vol. 2: 28 f., 105, 143, 272, 277, 295, 458, 497, 522, 529, 532, 590 f., 630, 632 f., 671, 675 f., 711, 714, 795, 836, 854
  Vol. 3: 27, 47, 144, 208, 244, 415, 423, 435, 600, 819, 852, 910, 913 f., **918–922,** 957, 990, 996, 1053
Wine-drinker **Vol. 3: 918–922**
Wine-skin **Vol. 3:** 911, 921
Winepress **Vol. 1:** 106, 109, 111
  Vol. 2: 33
Wing **Vol. 1:** 173 f., 262, 280, 451
  Vol. 2: 212
  Vol. 3: 554, 797, 805
Winged **Vol. 1:** 172, 279, 509
Wink, W. **Vol. 3:** 899
Winnow **Vol. 2:** 34
  Vol. 3: 526 f., 560, 804
Winter **Vol. 1:** 743
  Vol. 3: 845
Wipe **Vol. 1:** 479
Wipe away **Vol. 1:** 471

Vol. 3: 154, 268, 359
Wipe out **Vol. 2:** 411
Wisdom **Vol. 1:** 74, 92, 103, 109, 165, 169, 173–175, 192 f., 225, 228, 268, 277, 281, 285 f., 302, 322, 363, 380–382, 397–400, 418, 439, 452, 463, 485, 501 f., 505, 510, 537, 547, 551, 555, 589, 592 f., 597, 602, 604, 648, 653, 675, 692, 695 f., 728 f., 739
  Vol. 2: 49, 51, 61, 71, 75, 78, 99, 119 f., 126 f., 132, 143, 149, 151, 167, 171, 179, 196 f., 216 f., 228, 258, 261, 266, 269 f., 275, 279, 290, 298, 318, 349, 355, 357, 372, 377, 381, 391, 397, 400, 406, 408, 430, 440, 442, 470, 479, 492 f., 538 f. 569, 603, 616, 619 f., 680 f., 708, 735, 744 f., 758, 782, 834 f., 840 f., 845, 878, 890, 892
  Vol. 3: 30 f., 57, 76, 86, 89, 125, 130–133, 139, 163, 168, 199, 209, 256, 258, 261, 265, 271, 311, 348, 446 f., 449, 459, 462, 479, 482, 492, 502, 504, 522, 525, 528, 532 f., 570, 590, 601, 606, 614, 616, 623, 637, 641, 643, 647, 649, 651, 678, 721, 727, 745, 748, 763, 776 f., 827, 842, 866, 880, 898, 911, 914, 919, 925 f., 937–939, 957, 987, 1016, **1023–1036,** 1056, 1069, 1111 f., 1115 f., 1124, 1161 f.
Wisdom of Amenemope **Vol. 3:** 1028
Wisdom literature **Vol. 1:** 568, 698
  Vol. 2: 51, 93, 100, 117, 132, 141, 261, 745
  Vol. 3: 777, 880, 1028
Wisdom of Solomon **Vol. 1:** 50
  Vol. 2: 370
  Vol. 3: 1029
Wisdom schools **Vol. 3:** 606
Wise **Vol. 1:** 68, 107, 175, 188, 216, 282, 321, 395, 413, 432, 463, 468, 481, 512 f., 574, 650, 675, 680, 728
  Vol. 2: 72, 77, 94, 216, 255 f., 320, 354, 357, 377, 431, 557, 764, 798, 832
  Vol. 3: 33, 75, 132, 154, 270, 313, 445 f., 563, 572, 719, 1017, **1026–1034,** 1059, 1092, 1096
Wise men **Vol. 2:** 151
Wise saying **Vol. 2: 756–758**
Wish **Vol. 1:** 227, 344, 416, 456 f., 534, 734
  Vol. 2: 119, 244, 283, 319, 352, 556, **817–820**
  Vol. 3: 1015–1023
Wish-prayer **Vol. 2:** 874 f.
Wit **Vol. 3:** 445, 817, 898
Withdraw **Vol. 1:** 211, 431, 585, 606 f.
  Vol. 2: 53, 309, 477, 783
  Vol. 3: 255, 1092
Wither **Vol. 1:** 406, 411, 417, **515 f.,** 673, 678, 743
  Vol. 2: 274
  Vol. 3: 409, 869, 999
Withhold **Vol. 1:** 648
  Vol. 2: 222 f., 266, 318
Without beginning or end **Vol. 3: 826–833**
Without measure **Vol. 3: 402–404**
Without pity **Vol. 2: 594–598**
Without speech **Vol. 3: 1081–1119**
Without strength **Vol. 3: 993–996**
Without temptation **Vol. 3: 798–808**
Withstand **Vol. 1:** 660, 678, 710
Witness **Vol. 1:** 83, 91, 95, 98 f., 131 f., 135 f.,

Witness (cont'd)
183, 189, 195, 222, 228, 243, 246, 248, 265, 271, 275 f., 285, 294, 298, 301, 303, 305, 308, 311, 322–324, 349 f., 366 f., 369, 373 f., 383 f., 410, 430, 476, 478, 490, 511 f., 517, 522, 540, 554, 576, 587, 559, 600, 602 f., 620, 625 f., 638, 640, 657, 659, 669, 693, 704, 723
  Vol. 2: 48, 64, 75, 84, 110 f., 129 f., 141, 148, 152, 156, 174, 176, 237, 240, 299, 303, 307, 314, 317, 334, 338, 353, 403, 471 f., 487, 489, 494, 497, 499, 625, 627, 630, 632, 641, 653, 665, 685–688, 700, 712, 736, 799, 809, 868, 903, 911, 921
  Vol. 3: 44, 46, 49, 52 f., 54, 73, 89, 95, 178, 250, 280, 284, 293, 296, 310, 314, 326, 484, 498–500, 551, 568, 596, 617, 626, 633, 662, 706, 724, 738–742, 748 f., 756, 773, 792, 825, 890, 892–894, 954, 1004, **1038–1050,** 1060, 1094, 1097, 1122, 1150, 1152
Wittgenstein, L. Vol. 3: 894 f., 1123, 1127–1132, 1134–1135, 1143
Wizard Vol. 2: 554
Woe Vol. 1: 216, 282, 321, 358, 379, 473, 571
  Vol. 2: 267, 366, 418, 433, 443, 470, 812 f., 824
  Vol. 3: 429, 482, 657, 725, 741, 838, 911, **1051–1055**
Wolf Vol. 1: 118 f., 261
  Vol. 2: 34, 104, 411, 413
Wolff, Christian Vol. 1: 65
Woman Vol. 1: 84 f., 87 f., 109, 155 f., 266, 293, 361, 385, 466, 497, 517, 521, 594, 612, 621, 672, 678, 704 f., 709, 720, 738
  Vol. 2: 116, 159–162, 213, 217, 235, 287, 302, 307, 309, 329, 339, 349, 431, 444, 446, 562–564, 569–571, 575–590, 649, 661, 669, 695, 787, 846, 880
  Vol. 3: 81, 112, 215, 228, 549, 562, 590, 664, 732, 734, 765, 913, 932, 980, 994, 1007, 1047, **1055–1075**
Woman taken in adultery Vol. 2: 580
Womb Vol. 1: 169, 254, 667, 673, 739
  Vol. 2: 226, 229, 353, 358, 599, 726, 729
  Vol. 3: 660, 1062, 1071
Wonder Vol. 1: 119, 129, 220, 381, 531, 659, 692
  Vol. 2: 91 f., 194, 350, **620–635,** 901
  Vol. 3: 216, 503, 570
Wonder-worker Vol. 1: 415
Wonder-working Vol. 2: 149
Wonderful Vol. 1: 424, 574
  Vol. 2: 380, **621–626**
Wonders of the world Vol. 2: 85
Woo Vol. 2: 541
  Vol. 3: 799
Wood Vol. 1: 389–405, 463, 516, 537
  Vol. 2: 180, 288, 296
  Vol. 3: 391, 483, 543, **865–870,** 915
Wool Vol. 1: 204, 319
  Vol. 3: 519, 566, 794
Woolston, Thomas Vol. 3: 291
Word Vol. 1: 54, 56, 70, 79, 96–99, 102 f., 107, 123, 147, 153, 158, 166–168, 173, 178, 180, 188, 206 f., 214, 216, 234, 245, 248, 273 f., 333, 337 f., 340–342, 369, 374, 379–382, 384,

386, 397–400, 413, 418, 421, 424, 436–439, 453 f., 456 f., 462, 466, 468, 476 f., 485 f., 490 f., 499, 510, 512, 526, 530, 533, 536, 540, 546 f., 549 f., 566, 575, 578–580, 591–594, 596 f., 600, 633, 637 f., 658–660, 662, 671, 678 f., 682, 708, 711 f., 722, 731, 733 f., 736, 738 f., 741 f.
  Vol. 2: 30, 42, 49, 59, 63 f., 71 f., 75, 78 f., 81, 83 f., 104, 109 f., 113 f., 118 f., 129, 148, 152, 154–156, 158, 170 f., 175–178, 180, 185 f., 217, 231, 239 f., 245, 250–252, 256, 267, 269, 281, 287, 302, 317 f., 338, 357 f., 366 f., 383, 399, 404, 426, 434, 436, 447, 449, 452, 470, 480–482, 492 f., 505, 507, 513, 535, 546, 552, 590, 604, 626, 632, 643, 651, 654, 659, 661, 683, 686, 699, 763, 768, 786, 842, 863, 898, 907 f., 915, 918, 926–928
  Vol. 3: 48, 51, 61, 67, 69, **74–89,** 111 f., 122 f., 127, 138, 169, 187, 214, 235, 245, 280, 310, 313, 326, 335–337, 346, 348, 351, 357, 462, 470, 474, 482, 489, 495, 500, 502, 505, 516, 533, 546, 570 f., 576, 584, 674, 738, 740 f., 744 f., 748 f., 763, 765, 770, 777, 780, 800, 824 f., 838, 868, 880, 882 f., 887, 892, 905 f., 914, 967, 989, 1026, 1036, 1044, **1078–1123,** 1163, 1204
Word of God Vol. 1: 49, 79, 96 f., 166, 171, 180, 222, 241, 250, 273, 313, 322, 325, 329, 350 f., 353, 380 f., 411, 413, 451, 469, 499, 504, 516, 531, 550, 578, 594, 596 f., 604 f., 609, 638, 653, 655, 658–660, 702, 726, 733 f., 742
  Vol. 2: 33, 43, 71, 100, 113, 134, 150, 173 f., 177 f., 181, 183, 186, 240, 252, 266 f., 270, 275, 301, 407, 474, 480, 488, 492, 630, 701, 718, 740, 920, 922, 926
  Vol. 3: 36, 71, 73, 128, 184, 186, 225, 230, 314 f., 323 f., **325–337,** 342 f., 377, 381 f., 485, 493, 513, 522, 578, 583, 609, 633, 707, 765, 773, 779, 807, 809, 819, 846, 892 f., 954, 966 f., 974, 1030, 1046, 1062, **1087–1106**
Word of Jesus Vol. 1: 63, 99, 299, 439, 476, 515, 583, 620, 623, 719, 738, 741
  Vol. 2: 135, 165, 168, 176 f., 250, 366, 386, 624, 758, 858, 867
  Vol. 3: 136, 185, 212, 216, 226, 241, 382, 411, 459, 675, 941, 1048
Word of reconciliation Vol. 3: 1111
Word of truth Vol. 3: 352, 416, 809, 880
Word of Yahweh Vol. 1: 499, 655
  Vol. 2: 190
  Vol. 3: 202, 311, 1087, 1098
Word studies Vol. 1: 57
Word-history Vol. 3: 1140
Word-magic Vol. 3: 1125, 1140
Wordless prayer Vol. 2: 883
Words of institution Vol. 2: 368, **522–536,** 896
  Vol. 3: 239, 245, 704, 751, 773, 819 (also→ Lord's supper)
Work Vol. 1: 89, 95, 115, 131, 168, 198, 219, 228, 250, 260, 262 f., 266, 271, 275, 279, 287, 300, 304, 313, 319, 324, 341, 358, 372, 378, 382, 387, 401, 414, 429, 467, 471, 476 f., 489, 495, 497, 517, 527 f., 541–543, 547, 549, 551, 562, 564, 566, 584, 591 f., 600, 602, 607, 610,

618, 623–625, 639, 644, 647, 650, 654, 657,
659, 684, 688, 689, 701, 708, 723, 730 f.,
733 f., 741
Vol. 2: 30, 44, 63, 74, 112, 114, 148, 152, 158,
171, 263, 269, 272, 301, 317, 340, 359, 370,
395 f., 434, 447, 453, 499, 517, 626, 659, 716,
816, 820, 845
Vol. 3: 111, 123, 138, 141, 144 f., 167, 186,
256, 379, 405 f., 408 f., 412, 548 f., 595, 702,
719, 911, 920, **1147–1158**
Work of Christ (→ Christ, work of)
Work of God **Vol. 2:** 35, 200
Work out **Vol. 1:** 623
   Vol. 2: 135
Work together **Vol. 1:** 700
Worker **Vol. 1:** 115, 643
   Vol. 2: 775
   Vol. 3: 134, 809, 964
Working **Vol. 3: 1147–1152**
Working together **Vol. 3: 1147–1152**
Workman **Vol. 1: 279**
   Vol. 2: 833
   Vol. 3: 352, **1147–1152**
Workmanship **Vol. 1:** 228, 386, 657
   Vol. 2: 83
   Vol. 3: 118
Works **Vol. 1:** 73, 78 f., 81, 116, 157, 197, 228,
329, 385 f., 408, 424, 436, 446, 462, 532, 535,
555–557, 594, 599 f., 603–605, 612, 620, 622,
668, 671, 676, 681, 702, 714, 723, 739, 743
Vol. 2: 42, 64, 78 f., 95, 101 f., 104, 118–120,
122, 134, 177, 214, 217, 267, 279, 319, 365 f.,
384, 426, 444, 450, 699, 866
Vol. 3: 52, 72, 136, 142, 187, 220, 224, 310,
320 f., 363 f., 366, 369, 370, 373, 383, 436,
551, 730
World **Vol. 1:** 49, 53, **58,** 59 f., 66, 68, **69,** 71, 73,
77, 79, 95, 97, 164, 166, 168, 178, 185, 214,
217, 237 f., 243 f., 250, 254, 257, 281, 300,
303, 319, 323, 325, 328, 337, 377–379, 383,
385, 387, 397, 399–401, 421–424, 432, 438,
457 f., 460 f., 463 f., 466, 468 f., 473, 481–483,
490 f., 495, 500, 502, 507–509, 513 f., **517–
526,** 530, 532, 537, 539, 542, 544, 551 f.,
556 f., 559, 562, 566, 583, 586, 595, 598,
602 f., 610, 614 f., 623–625, 627 f., 640,
646 f., 649, 651, 654–656, 659, 661, 665, 667,
672, 676–679, 681, 684, 687–689, 691–695,
700, 702, 704, 706–709, 711, 714, 716, 720,
723, 726, 735, 740, 742
Vol. 2: 28, 46, 48, 50, 52, 62, 64, 66 f., 70–80,
83, 95, 106, 108 f., 111, 118, 122, 125, 130,
142, 147, 164, 167, 187 f., 190, 199 f., 203–
205, 217 f., 226, 229, 263, 266–268, 270 f.,
279 f., 287, 290, 301 f., 304, 308, 310, 316,
320, 326–329, 334, 339, 342, 355, 358–360,
364–366, 375–378, 381, 384 f., 387 f., 390–
395, 398, 403–405, 407, 411 f., 420, 434 f.,
438, 446, 448, 452 f., 457, 477, 493 f., 514,
523, 535, 548 f., 567, 582, 607, 609–611, 613,
615, 619, 625, 629, 641, 645, 650, 656 f.,
659–661, 665, 674, 681 f., 691 f., 698, 709 f.,
712, 720 f., 723, 736, 771, 773, 779, 781, 783,
786, 789, 792, 798, 806, 808, 836, 840, 843,

885, 909, 911, 918, 923, 928 f.
Vol. 3: 45, 52, 56, 118, 121 f., 128, 146, 148,
168 f., 171, 174, 204, 211, 214, 217, 219, 224,
234, 242, 250, 313, 321–323, 347, 353, 361 f.,
365, 372 f., 402, 445, 469, 500, 503, 512 f.,
522, 548, 563, 574, 582, 637, 646, 661, 675,
691, 704, 710, 747, 761, 780, 806 f., 827,
829–833, 837, 840, 843, 853, 864, 945, 950,
970, 1017, 1025 f., 1029 f., 1034, 1045, 1054,
1060, 1069, 1082 f., 1085–1087, 1102, 1111,
1112, 1117, 1152, 1165
World kingdom **Vol. 2:** 693
World to come **Vol. 1:** 77, 97, 586, 604, 700
   Vol. 2: 311, 632, 643, 789, 791, 798, 830, 834
World-cycles **Vol. 3:** 653
World-power **Vol. 1:** 610
   Vol. 2: 56, 227, 607
World-reason **Vol. 2:** 67
   Vol. 3: 126
World-rulers **Vol. 1:** 73
   Vol. 2: 514
World-soul **Vol. 1:** 626, 711
   Vol. 2: 719
   Vol. 3: 679, 681, 1117
World-systems **Vol. 3:** 833
World-view **Vol. 1:** 524
   Vol. 3: 281, 335, 595
World-weeks **Vol. 3:** 658
Worldly **Vol. 1:** 397, 467, 521, 532, 547
   Vol. 2: 119, 832
   Vol. 3: 31, 200, 684, 963
Worldly sorrow **Vol. 2:** 420
Worldly wisdom **Vol. 3:** 209
Worldwide **Vol. 1:** 686
Worm **Vol. 1:** 116
   Vol. 3: 110, 178, 448
Wormwood **Vol. 1:** 202
   Vol. 2: 27–29, 295
   Vol. 3: 737
Worn out **Vol. 2:** 713
Worry **Vol. 1:** 92, 276–278, 384, 420
   Vol. 2: 272
Worse **Vol. 1:** 731
Worship **Vol. 1:** 53, 55, 69 f., 75, 98 f., 111, 114,
119, 125, 145, 198, 210 f., 213, 244, 271 f.,
280, 291, 293, 295 f., 304, 311, 320, 324,
339–341, 344, 360 f., 367, 384–387, 409 f.,
452, 488, 495, 508, 538, 551 f., 582, 586, 607,
622, 626 f., 632, 637, 642, 650, 655, 667, 672,
698, 733
Vol. 2: 47 f., 53, 68, 73, 77, 85, 90 f., 93 f., 126,
147, 158–162, 164, 174, 181 f., 189, 191, 194,
202, 206, 218, 223 f., 230, 237 f., 247 f., 263,
267, 284–286, 288, 293 f., 296, 306, 309 f.,
325, 329, 336, 352–354, 356 f., 368, 373, 376,
381, 396, 410–412, 437–439, 441, 450, 453,
457, 472, 478, 487, 503, 511, 514, 547, 555,
559, 604, 615, 637, 650, 675, 701, 705, 724,
796, 798, **855–886,** 927
Vol. 3: 50 f., 59, 84, 94, 104, 106, 113, 132,
143, 150, 208, 216, 219, 224, 232, 237, 246,
256, 310, 321, 333, 356, 404, 407, 409, 412,
427–429, 431, 434, 460, 462, 485, 531 f.,
544–553, 556, 565, 568, 593–595, 606, 668,

Worship (*cont'd*)
671, 675, 702, 705, 714, 731, 733, 735 f., 753, 782 f., 785, 789–791, 793, 800 f., 806, 815, 817, 834, 838, 854–856, 891, 908, 913, 959 f., 964, 1001, 1014, 1034, 1063, 1066, 1073 f., 1080 f., 1119
Worship of idols **Vol. 2: 284–286**
Worshipper **Vol. 1:** 618, 625, 627, 687
Vol. 2: 201, 240, **284–286, 875–879**
Vol. 3: 237, 239, 424, 589, 608, 729, 893
Worth **Vol. 1:** 598, 664 f.
Vol. 2: 48, 96, 306
Vol. 3: 165, 348 f., 563, 593, 840, 886, 1055
Worthily **Vol. 3: 348 f.**
Worthless **Vol. 1:** 436, 480, 520, 546, 549–551, 565, 700
Vol. 2: 669, 683, 713
Vol. 3: 388, **808–810**
Worthy **Vol. 1:** 275, 329, 384, 386, 475, 571
Vol. 2: 91, 93, 230, 294, 355, 548, 615, 878
Vol. 3: 55, **347–352,** 529, 627, 673, 726, **728–730,** 863, 933
Wound **Vol. 1:** 114, 119, 161, 163, 182, 235, 241
Vol. 2: 349, 423, 573, 712
Vol. 3: 448, 857
Woven **Vol. 1:** 712
Wrangling **Vol. 1:** 106, 108, 645 f.
Vol. 2: 363
Vol. 3: 887, 1119
Wrap **Vol. 2:** 295
Wrath **Vol. 1: 105–113,** 163, 211, 286, 320, 327, 354, 413, 415, 417, 449, 464 f., 467, 529, 559, 651, 653, 657, 673, 685, 687, 734, 739, 741, 743
Vol. 2: 28, 33, 58, 64, 72, 76, 94, 139, 155, 168, 193, 209, 215 f., 218, 265, 275, 284, 366 f., 400, 412, 421, 540, 544, 565, 570, 625, 633, 663, 715, 764, 767–700, 791, 830, 834, 836, 844, 855, 924
Vol. 3: 28, 49, 132, 149, 151, 154–157, 164, 169 f., 207 f., 214, 224, 242, 315, 372, 436, 469, 471, 549, 576, 685, 691, 731 f., 755, 762, 779, 822, 842, 865, 868, 885, 913, 917, 922, 949, 986, 996, 1001, 1020, 1053 f., 1073, 1157, 1166
Wreath **Vol. 1:** 405 f., 648
Vol. 2: 556
Wrede, William **Vol. 3:** 506–510
Wrestle **Vol. 1:** 600, 645 f., 679
Vol. 2: 305, 317, 710
Wretched **Vol. 2:** 283, 353, 423, 433, 475
Vol. 3: 858 f., 994
Wright, G.E. **Vol. 3:** 332
Wrinkled **Vol. 2:** 588
Wrist **Vol. 2:** 150, 415
Write **Vol. 1:** 582
Vol. 2: 288
Vol. 3: 477 f., **482–495,** 1094
Writing **Vol. 1:** 53, 70, 243, 246 f., 332
Vol. 2: 113, 227, 288, 291, 469, 556
Vol. 3: 482–495, 904, 1091
Writing on wall **Vol. 3:** 846
Writing prophets **Vol. 3:** 77, 311, 1092
Writing-tablet **Vol. 1:** 471

Writings **Vol. 1: 58**
Vol. 2: 442, 448
Vol. 3: 485, 671
Written **Vol. 1:** 485, 604
Vol. 2: 358, 440, 444, 446, 653, 671, 675
Vol. 3: 329
Wrong **Vol. 1:** 56, 138, 352, 414, 423, 468, 506, 561, 564, 568, 680, 727
Vol. 2: 137, 320 f.
Vol. 3: 193, 357, **573–576**
Wrongdoer **Vol. 2:** 138
Wrongdoing **Vol. 3:** 102, 134, **573–576,** 859
Wrongfully **Vol. 2:** 257
Wycliffe **Vol. 1:** 299

Xenophanes **Vol. 2:** 476
Xenophon **Vol. 1:** 405, 579 f.
Vol. 2: 678
Vol. 3: 685, 877

Yah **Vol. 2:** 67, 70
Vol. 3: 208
Yahweh **Vol. 1:** 55 f., 58, 63, 67, **71,** 72, 76, 100–102, 108 f., 121 f., 141, 151, 173, 195, 208–211, 216, 243, 245, 250, 276, 280 f., 293–296, 308, 324, 331–333, 345, 355, 360, 366–369, 379–381, 409, 425–427, 433 f., 444, 451, 463, 481, 484, 498 f., 508–510, 512 f., 523, 529, 537, 543, 546 f., 551, 555, 562, 572, 585 f., 596, 636, 640 f., 655, 661, 668, 672 f., 688, 691, 699, 716 f., 735
Vol. 2: 32, 53, 56, 67–70, 72, 86, 100, 103–105, 109, 117, 137, 141, 146, 151, 167, 190 f., 201 f., 206, 224–227, 237, 239 f., 248, 257, 260, 278 f., 281, 285, 287, 291, 296–298, 301, 305, 325–327, 331 f., 336 f., 367, 373–376, 395 f., 412, 416, 428, 441, 485, 491, 501 f., 511 f., 521, 541 f., 555 f., 572 f., 576 f., 583–585, 613, 626–629, 633, 635–638, 644, 649–654, 663, 670, 689, 698, 720 f., 737 f., 740, 769, 777 f., 781, 791, 796–798, 803, 817, 822 f., 830, 841, 854, 856, 862 f., 876, 880 f., 890, 892, 899, 925
Vol. 3: 33–36, 38, 46, 51 f., 69 f., 77, 79, 93–95, 97, 104 f., 110, 121, 124, 140, 149–151, 153 f., 156, 159 f., 190–194, 201–203, 206–208, 212 f., 218, 224, 235–239, 242, 248–250, 252, 256, 258, 262 f., 266–269, 274, 311, 319, 333, 341 f., 345, 350 f., 356 f., 388 f., 391, 402, 415, 419–426, 450 f., 468, 474, 498, 514, 522, 531, 550, 555, 562 f., 565, 569, 578, 590, 595, 605, 608, 612, 632, 636, 649, 673 f., 691, 715, 721 f., 729, 733, 739 f., 745, 756, 777, 782 f., 786 f., 790, 799 f., 804–806, 813, 819, 828, 835 f., 841 f., 847, 866 f., 877, 918 f., 926, 937, 941, 950, 960, 962, 966, 983, 986–989, 997, 1005 f., 1009 f., 1013, 1028 f., 1040 f., 1057, 1063, 1069, 1074, 1087–1106, 1116, 1148, 1153 f., 1160–1162
Yahweh of hosts **Vol. 3:** 959 f.
Yahweh Sabaoth **Vol. 2:** 602
Yahwist **Vol. 1:** 61, 65, **72**
Vol. 2: 138
Yahwistic narrative **Vol. 3:** 484

589

Yardstick **Vol. 2:** 460
  Vol. 3: 578
Yawar **Vol. 1:** 89
Year **Vol. 1:** 624, 626, 629, 734, 737
  Vol. 2: 308, 317, 696, 866, 887, 892
  Vol. 3: 396, 826, 841, 847
Year of jubilee **Vol. 1:** 698
  Vol. 2: 226, 298
  Vol. 3: 191, 194
Year of release **Vol. 1:** 272, 698
  Vol. 2: 168
  Vol. 3: 193
Yearn **Vol. 1:** 456, 558
  Vol. 2: 123, **538–547**
  Vol. 3: 229
Yeast **Vol. 2:** 461
Yellow **Vol. 1:** 204 f.
Yes **Vol. 3:** 741 f., 750, 1112
YHWH **Vol. 1:** 72
Yield **Vol. 1:** 454, 475, 591, 709, 723
  Vol. 2: 256
  Vol. 3: 364
Yielding **Vol. 2: 256–259**
Yigdal **Vol. 2:** 313
Yohane **Vol. 2:** 557
Yoke **Vol. 1:** 262, 284
  Vol. 2: 106, 119, 281, 377
  Vol. 3: 192, 257 f., 590, 592, 599, 1098, **1160–1165**
Yoke together **Vol. 3: 1160–1165**
Yoke-fellow **Vol. 3:** 1160
Young **Vol. 1:** 193, 198, 283 f.
  Vol. 2: 428, 584, **674–676**
Young woman **Vol. 2:** 87, 584
Younger **Vol. 2:** 319, **427–429, 674–676**
Youngest **Vol. 2:** 675
Youth **Vol. 1:** 203, 281, 283, 462, 559
  Vol. 2: 674–676
  Vol. 3: 845

Zacchaeus **Vol. 1:** 77
  Vol. 2: 434, 825, 844, 846
  Vol. 3: 213, 758, 980
Zadok the Pharisee **Vol. 3:** 1168
Zadok the priest **Vol. 3:** 34, 36, 439
Zadokite **Vol. 2:** 327
  Vol. 3: 34 f., 487
Zaparwa **Vol. 3:** 469
Zaphon **Vol. 3:** 1009
Zarephath **Vol. 1:** 328
  Vol. 2: 730
  Vol. 3: 261, 1062
Zaw **Vol. 1:** 383
Zeal **Vol. 1:** 197, 278, 361, 543, 568, 637, 655, 675, 688, 733
  Vol. 2: 400, 641, 806
  Vol. 3: 79, 322, 430, 961, 981, **1166–1169**
Zealots **Vol. 1: 72**, 269, 403, 488, 599, 627, 717

  Vol. 2: 308, 311, 313, 331, 383, 385, 752, 812
  Vol. 3: 377 f., 603, 641, 949, 967, 976–980, **1166–1168**
Zealous **Vol. 1:** 318, 730
  Vol. 2: 246, 448, 450
  Vol. 3: 1166–1169
Zebaba **Vol. 3:** 469
Zebedee **Vol. 1:** 321, 657
  Vol. 2: 276, 652
  Vol. 3: 662, 1002, 1071
Zebulun **Vol. 1:** 170
  Vol. 3: 956
Zechariah **Vol. 1:** 52, 66, 93, 174, 212, 429, 478, 512, 623, 683
  Vol. 2: 178, 294, 337, 353, 358, 624, 712, 728
  Vol. 3: 37, 78, 80, 82, 84, 198, 202, 212, 241, 250, 361, 391 f., 430, 436, 489, 552, 674, 715, 785, 790, 881, 931, 962
Zedekiah **Vol. 2:** 336, 754
  Vol. 3: 78, 249, 715, 918, 1097
Zenas **Vol. 3:** 480
Zenith **Vol. 2:** 198
Zeno **Vol. 1:** 68, 417
  Vol. 2: 32, 840
Zenobius **Vol. 2:** 757
Zephaniah **Vol. 1:** 66
  Vol. 2: 679 f.
Zerubbabel **Vol. 2:** 336, 466, 691, 712
  Vol. 3: 391 f., 609, 654 f., 659, 867
Zeus **Vol. 1:** 75, 125, 127, 189, 232, 450, 552, 588, 616, 687
  Vol. 2: 85, 124, 151, 167, 188, 224, 232 f., 372 f., 503, 553, 612, 648, 849
  Vol. 3: 27, 200, 205, 216 f., 259, 331, 353, 457, 461, 634 f., 738, 782, 851, 959, 1071, 1085
Zeus Hellenios **Vol. 3:** 452
Zeus Olympios **Vol. 3:** 1006
Ziesler, J.A. **Vol. 3:** 373
Ziggurat **Vol. 1:** 140
Zilpah **Vol. 2:** 317
Zimri **Vol. 3:** 159
Zion **Vol. 1:** 55, 96, 122, 239, 304, 538, 570, 596, 661
  Vol. 2: 190, 306, **324–330**, 376, 433, 585, 695, 791, 803, 830, 866
  Vol. 3: 143, 203, 250, 389, 391, 433, 460 f., 732, 782 f., 836, 842, 914, 1010, 1014, 1068 f., 1071, 1094
Zionism **Vol. 2:** 306
Zipporah **Vol. 2:** 636 f.
Zodiac **Vol. 2:** 509, 688 f.
  Vol. 3: 396 f.
Zoology **Vol. 1:** 670
Zoroaster **Vol. 2:** 556
Zoroastrianism **Vol. 1:** 563, 653
  Vol. 2: 71
  Vol. 3: 275, 827
Zu, myth of **Vol. 2:** 553
Zwingli **Vol. 3:** 244

Errata

(Line numbers in parentheses are counted from the bottom of the page)

Page	Line	Instead of	Read
Volume 1			
86	(8)	1 Cor. 14:45 ff.	1 Cor. 15:45 ff.
109	18	Wis. 11:90	Wis. 11:9
115	(6)	2 Tim. 5:18	1 Tim. 5:18
116	9	Jud. 6:25a, 28a	Jdg. 6:25a, 28a
165	32	Ezek 9:27	Ezek. 7:27
175	(4)	Rev. 8:17	Rev. 8:13
184	(5)	Isa. 60:31	Isa. 60:21
280	13	Ki. 19:15	2 Ki. 19:15
339	(9)	Hermas, *Sim.* 10, 3, 9	Hermas, *Sim.* 10, 4, 1
341	23	*Leg. All.* 2; 28	*Leg. All.* 2, 28
367	(11)	Jos. 23:24	Jos. 24:24
396	19	*War* 2,2,261 ff.	*War* 2,261 ff.
409	12	54:16	55:16
415	20	Deut. 20:27	Deut. 20:17
415	21	Deut. 20:27	Deut. 20:17
451	1	1 Sam. 28:36	1 Sam. 28:9
490	9	Jn. 61:66	Jn. 6:66
503	(14)	Joel 4:2	Joel 3:2
513	(25)	Ezek. 22:33	Ezek. 23:33
520	14	Jer. 14:51	Jer. 14:5
559	2	3 Ki. 2:29	1 Ki. 2:29
626	(10)	Lev. 23:32–32	Lev. 23:26–32
634	11	Lk. 22–19 f.	Lk. 22:19 f.
648	3	Tim. 4:6	2 Tim. 4:6
666	20	Rom. 29:9, 10	Rom. 2:9, 10
683	3	Ps. 104:41	Ps. 105:41
685	(10)	Test. Ass. 7:2	Test. Ash. 7:2
710	(16)	4 Esd. 8:36	4 Ezra 8:36
733	17	Acts 6:17	Acts 7:17
Volume 2			
63	11	Lk. 16:36	Lk. 6:36
69	12	Gen. 20:28	Gen. 20:18
69	27	Amos 3:18	Amos 3:13
80	2	cf. 31:5 f.	cf. 3:15 f.
113	22	1 Pet. 23–25	1 Pet. 1:23–25
150	37	Acts 7:78	Acts 7:48
211	16	4 Ki. 19:26	2 Ki. 19:26
248	18	Matt. 7:27–7	Matt. 7:24–27
253	(9)	1 Cor. 3:10–4	1 Cor.3:10–14
268	(8)	1 God. 8:8	1 Cor. 8:8
268	(15)	66:27, 55	6:27, 55

Page	Line	Instead of	Read
295	14	Lk. 28:56	Lk. 23:56
303	(13)	Pos. 50[49]:18	Pss. 50[49]:18
306	19	Gen. 40:50 ff.	Gen. 41:50 ff.
314	(1)	Acts 41:1	Acts 14:1
316	26	4:15	4:14
363	(5)	Joel 4:2	Joel 3:2
381	(5)	19:34	19:24
403	7	Rom. 6:3–3	Rom. 6:3–13
403	9	Phil. 3;10	Phil. 3:10
404	(5)	Jn. 5:69	Jn. 6:69
417	(4)	1 Ki. 25:1; 28:3	1 Sam. 25:1; 28:3
431	5	Ezr. 23:32	Ezek. 23:32
433	(5)	Lk. 16:23–37	Lk. 16:23–31
448	11	Deut. 19:15; 10:34	Deut. 19:15; Jn. 10:34
458	(18)	Job 12:33	Job 12:16
459	7	1 Jn. 2:66	1 Jn. 2:26
498	26	Wis. 7:3 6	Wis. 7:3, 6
535	(8)	Jn. 13; 14, 20	Jn. 13:14, 20
555	23	Mal. 5:5	Mal. 3:5
565	15	1QS 3:13–4:26	1QS 3:13–4:26
577	15	Lev. 12:12–18	Lev. 18:6–18
580	16	Mk. 10:2–2	Mk. 10:2–12
581	(17)	Lk. 20:20:34 f.	Lk. 20:34 f.
602	17	Sam. 22:32 ff.	2 Sam. 22:32 ff.
605	18	1 Cor. 12:10; 28;	1 Cor. 12:10, 28;
629	12	Jn. 2:11; 18, 23	Jn. 2:11, 18, 23
630	11	15:1 ff., 19:7	15:1 ff.; Lk. 19:7
630	(1)	26:51 ff.; 27:39 ff.	Matt. 26:51 ff.; 27:39 ff.
636	(5)	Exod. 2:27–31	Exod. 4:27–31
641	25	2 Cor. 2:9	2 Cor. 3:9
650	2	Ezek. 34:50	Ezek. 34:30
660	5	*Ap.* 273, 275	*Ap.* 2, 273; 275
675	5	Gen. 19:31, 34 f., 39	Gen. 19:31, 34 f., 38
679	3	*Ant.* 9, 10, 21	*Ant.* 9, 10, 2
688	18	*War* 1, 7, 19	*War* 1, 19
691	(19)	8:2–40:1	8:2 ff.
695	9	2 Chron. 6:60–80	1 Chr. 6:61–81
696	(8)	4, 8 23 (248)	4, 8, 23 (248)
709	16	1 Pet. 2:66	1 Pet. 2:6
711	3	18:4, 51	18:4; 28:51
714	20	Lk. 5:56 f.	Lk. 5:36 f.
722	15	Gal. 2:28	Gal. 3:28

Page	Line	Instead of	Read	Page	Line	Instead of	Read
739	16	except 16:12	except 19:37	444	14	Zeph. 2:19	Zeph. 2:9
767	23	Ezek. 26:28	Ezek. 26:2 f.	448	12	Deut. 25:22	Deut. 25:12
771	26	Pss. 10:38	Pss. 10:18	455	9	Lk. 10:51, 53	Lk. 9:51, 53
778	(4)	Pss. 4:8 29[28]:10	Pss. 4:8; 29[28]:10	470	23	Mk. 8:53	Mk. 8:33
793	7	1Qflor 1:4	4Qflor 1:4	487	4	Deut. 35:10	Deut. 25:10
793	(19)	Isa. 8:23	Isa. 9:1	509	(12)	Mk. 15:61	Mk. 14:61
803	10	Isa. 32:28	Isa. 32:18	515	10	*Spec. Leg.* 1 20,	*Spec. Leg.* 1, 20,
842	10	Est. 10:10	Est. 10:3	515	17	Matt. 28:27	Matt. 28:7
854	9	1 Sam. 59:7	1 Sam. 25:3	517	8	1 Jn. 1:11	1 Jn. 1:1
863	6	2 Macc. 20:10	2 Macc. 2:10	532	34	2 Tim. 2:33	2 Tim. 2:23
863	(11)	Gen. 28:22–23	Gen. 18:22–23	589	22	Matt. 10:46	Mk. 10:46
874	8	1 Cor. 15, 26	1 Cor. 15:26	595	4	Ps. 119[118],17	Ps. 119[118]:17
874	(1)	2 Tim. 16, 18	2 Tim. 1:16, 18	613	10	Acts 15:47	Acts 13:47
875	9	Cor. 1:3, 9–14	Col. 1:3, 9–14	614	(16)	Dan. 18:26 f.	Dan. 8:26 f.
890	12	Eccl. 11:19	Eccl. 11:9	629	17	Matt. 19:38	Matt. 19:28
890	19	Joel 4:14	Joel 3:14	651	(19)	Ps. 16:20	Ps. 16:10
893	17	1Q 14:7 ff.	1QM 14:7 ff.	669	(13)	Matt. 16:30	Matt. 26:30
893	(13)	Exod. 34:38	Exod. 34:28	686	(4)	Ps. 39[38]:14	Ps. 39[38]:13
896	8	Did. 10, 6	Did. 10:6	691	(8)	1 Sam. 11:16	1 Sam. 11:6
				703	6	Rom. 1:11, 1;	Rom. 1:11; 1 Cor.
Volume 3						Cor. 12:8–11	12:8–11
28	3	Mk. 11:45	Lk. 11:45	711	(16)	4 Macc. 8; 24;	4 Macc. 8:24;
33	(5)	1 Sam. 21:27	1 Sam. 21:1	714	30	2 Thess. 1:19	2 Thess. 1:9
35	15	Neh. 13:4–9:28	Neh. 13:4–9, 28	722	16	1QH3:5–18	1QH 3:5–18
45	(5)	Ps. 71:[70]:17	Ps. 71[70]:17	732	(10)	Acts 2:38, 40; 3;	Acts 2:38, 40;
46	17	3:18);	3:18;			19, 23	3:19, 23
69	(3)	Exod. 3:24 f.	Exod. 2:24 f.	733	(4)	Isa. 60; 19	Isa. 60:19
110	15	Matt. 12:18:21	Matt. 12:18, 21	760	(6)	Ezr. 44:23	Ezek. 44:23
110	(13)	Jdt. 16:17	Jdg. 16:17	760	(11)	Ps. 94(93); 10, 12;	Ps. 94(93):10, 12;
137	24	Tit. 1:17	Tit. 1:7	760	(12)	Ps. 34(33) 11;	Ps. 34(33):11;
161	(10)	Isa. 55:15	Isa. 54:14	786	15	1 Ki. 17:7, 50	1 Ki. 7:50; 17:7
165	25	Rom. 3:35	Rom. 3:25	786	17	Hos. 8:16	Hos. 8:14
181	(10)	Mk. 10:1–12:	Mk. 10:1–12;	786	(9)	Ezek. 9:6, 23, 38	Ezek. 9:6; 23:38
192	25	Ps. 49(48)7	Ps. 49(48):7	799	(1)	Exod. 29:49 f.	Exod. 29:45 f.
193	(13)	Ps. 130(129);7	Ps. 130(129):7	817	1	2 Chr. 16:27	1 Chr. 16:27
207	12	Ps. 74(73);12	Ps. 74(73):12	823	(18)	4 Macc. 2:2–34	4 Macc. 2:2–24
207	29	2 Sam. 11:13	1 Sam. 11:13	871	17	(*Life* 1, 1)	(*Life* 1)
225	11	1 Cor. 13:15	1 Cor. 13:13	924	7	Ps. 37(36), 18	Ps. 37(36):18
238	(10)	Ezek. 21:37[32]:	Ezek. 21:37[32];	939	29	Test. Ash. 8:9	Test. Ash. 1:9
		25:10	25:10	964	(16)	Amos 5:27 ff.	Amos 5:27 ff.
257	10	Ps. 95,11	Ps. 95:11	983	23	Job 7:82	Job 7:12
272	(19)	cf. 95:33 ff.	cf. 95:3 ff.	989	21	Ezek. 26:25 ff.	Ezek. 36:25 ff.
287	24	Heb. 13:20;ff.	Heb. 13:20 ff.	1006	21	Isa. 35:15 f.	Isa. 35:5 f.
310	(1)	Ezek. 16:36 f., 57:	Ezek. 16:36 f., 57;	1010	3	1 Sam. 19:25	1 Sam. 9:25
331	16	Matt. 6:16 ff., 45	Matt. 6:16 ff.; 5:45	1024	(13)	Ps. 94(93:8;	Ps. 94(93):8;
342	27	2 Macc. 9:4, 12,	2 Macc. 9:4, 12,	1024	(21)	Prov. 9:6 (4, 16)	Prov. 9:6 (4:16)
		38	28	1024	(23)	2 Sam. 25:25	1 Sam. 25:25
342	(9)	2 Pet:10 ff.	2 Pet. 2:10 ff.	1024	(24)	Eccl. 4:17, 25	Eccl. 4:17; 7:25
346	(5)	Prov. 20:31	Prov. 20:3	1041	2	1 Sam. 8:24	1 Sam. 9:24
354	(25)	Num. 30:17	Num. 30:16	1065	(5)	1 Tim. 5:39	1 Tim. 5:9
355	3	Joel 4:19	Joel 3:19	1074	3	Zech. 7:20	Zech. 7:10
365	2	Heb. 8:38	Heb. 10:38	1095	(5)	Jer. 2:4:5	Jer. 2:1–4:5
402	20	2 Chr. 23:29	1 Chr. 23:29	1099	(8)	Ezek. 26:28	Ezek. 26:2 f.
433	7	1 Cor. 19:19	1 Cor. 10:19	1157	(10)	Gal. 5:69 ff.	Gal. 5:19 ff.